SOCIAL SECURITY LEGISLATION 2024/25

VOLUME IV: HMRC-ADMINISTERED SOCIAL SECURITY BENEFITS AND SCOTLAND

SOCIAL SECURITY LEGISLATION 2024/25

General Editor
Nick Wikeley, MA (Cantab)

VOLUME IV: HMRC-ADMINISTERED SOCIAL SECURITY BENEFITS AND SCOTLAND

Commentary By

Nick Wikeley, MA (Cantab)
Judge of the Upper Tribunal,
Emeritus Professor of Law, University of Southampton

Edward Mitchell, LLB
Judge of the Upper Tribunal

Ian Hooker, LLB
Formerly Lecturer in Law, University of Nottingham,
Formerly Chairman, Social Security Tribunals

Consultant Editor
Child Poverty Action Group

Sweet & Maxwell

Published in 2024 by Thomson Reuters, trading as Sweet & Maxwell.
Registered in England and Wales, Company Number 1679046,
Registered office and address for service: 5 Canada Square,
Canary Wharf, London E14 5AQ.

For further information on our products and services, visit
www.sweetandmaxwell.co.uk

Typeset by Servis Filmsetting Ltd, Stockport, Cheshire
Printed and bound by CPI Group (UK) Ltd, Croydon, CR0 4YY

Thomson Reuters, the Thomson Reuters Logo and
Sweet & Maxwell® are trademarks of Thomson Reuters.

A CIP catalogue record for this book is available from the British Library

ISBN (print): 978-0-414-12158-4
ISBN (e-book): 978-0-414-12171-3
ISBN (print and e-book): 978-0-414-12159-1

Crown copyright material is reproduced with the permission of the Controller of HMSO and the King's Printer for Scotland.

All rights reserved. No part of this publication may be reproduced or transmitted in any form or by any means, or stored in any retrieval system of any nature without prior written permission, except for permitted fair dealing under the Copyright, Designs and Patents Act 1988, or in accordance with the terms of a licence issued by the Copyright Licensing Agency in respect of photocopying and/or reprographic reproduction. Application for permission for other use of copyright material including permission to reproduce extracts in other published works shall be made to the publishers. Full acknowledgement of author, publisher and source must be given.

The essential elements are the symbol © plus the name of the copyright owner and the date. Wherever new material in which copyright is required has been added, then the copyright notice should be updated. Copyright can belong to the publisher(s), the author(s) or can be held jointly.

Commentators have asserted their moral rights under the Copyright, Designs and Patents Act 1988 to be identified as the authors of the commentary in this Volume.

© 2024 Thomson Reuters

CHILD POVERTY ACTION GROUP

The Child Poverty Action Group (CPAG) is a charity, founded in 1965, which campaigns for the relief of poverty in the United Kingdom. It has a particular reputation in the field of welfare benefits law derived from its legal work, publications, training and parliamentary and policy work, and is widely recognised as the leading organisation for taking test cases on social security law.

CPAG is therefore ideally placed to act as Consultant Editor to this five-volume work—**Social Security Legislation**. CPAG is not responsible for the detail of what is contained in each volume, and the authors' views are not necessarily those of CPAG. The Consultant Editor's role is to act in an advisory capacity on the overall structure, focus and direction of the work.

For more information about CPAG, its rights and policy publications or training courses, its address is 30 Micawber Street, London, N1 7TB (telephone: 020 7837 7979—website: *http://www.cpag.org.uk*).

FOREWORD

These volumes of Social Security Legislation are an indispensable resource for the judiciary of the First-tier Tribunal (Social Entitlement Chamber) and all those involved in social security proceedings. Along with expert commentaries, they provide comprehensive, up-to-date and learned coverage of this vast and complex field of law. Given the scale and complexity of the legislation and the continuing development of the jurisprudence by the Upper Tribunal and appellate courts, the subject matter would be practically inaccessible without these books. As ever, I am grateful to the authors and to Sweet and Maxwell for their continued commitment to producing them each year.

Judge Kate Markus KC
Chamber President of the First-tier Tribunal, Social Entitlement Chamber

PREFACE

HMRC-administered Social Security Benefits and Scotland is Volume IV of the series *Social Security Legislation 2024/25*. The companion volumes are Hooker, Mesher, Mitchell, Ward and Wikeley, *Volume I: Non-Means Tested Benefits*; Mesher, Royston and Wikeley, *Volume II: Universal Credit, State Pension Credit and the Social Fund*; and Rolt and Ward, *Volume III: Administration, Adjudication and the European Dimension*, plus Mesher, Poynter and Wikeley, Volume V: *Income Support and the Legacy Benefits 2021/22*, as up-dated in the Cumulative Supplement located at the end of Volume II. The "year" in the title of the works relates to the tax/contribution year and conveys the period the books (and the Supplement) are designed to cover.

This volume has a chequered history. The Tax Credits Act 2002, introducing Child Tax Credit (CTC) and Working Tax Credit (WTC) from April 2003, represented a radical shift for the benefits system and provided the initial impetus for this fourth volume in the series. This volume, designed in the same format as its companion volumes, covers CTC and WTC along with social security benefits administered and paid by His Majesty's Revenue and Customs (HMRC), namely Child Benefit and Guardian's Allowance, as well as those administered by HMRC but paid by employers: statutory sick pay (SSP), statutory maternity pay (SMP), ordinary and additional statutory paternity pay (SPP), statutory adoption pay (SAP), statutory shared parental pay (ShPP) and now statutory shared parental bereavement pay. This volume also includes the statutory provisions relating to both tax-free childcare payments and free childcare for working parents as well as those for child trust funds.

A decade or so ago, we noted the start of the "roll out" of the measures embodied in the Welfare Reform Act 2012, presaged in the 2010 Budget. Under these reforms, CTC and WTC will be phased out of the legislation and merged into Universal Credit by stages. However, progress in introducing Universal Credit has been slower than originally planned. As a result, the tax credits regime remains very much alive for a significant number of claimants on low incomes. Universal Credit is now dealt with by the second volume in the series (following the recent reorganization of material between volumes).

The UK Government estimates that the transfer to Universal Credit of those currently in receipt of tax credits will not be completed until the end of 2025. The transfer legislation is complex and takes account not only of tax credits but all "legacy benefits". Since advisers may find themselves frequently called upon to give transfer advice to tax credits clients, this volume includes the most significant pieces of secondary legislation that underpin transfer from tax credits to Universal Credit. Provisions that relate to other legacy benefits are not included in this volume, but the full legislation may be consulted in Volumes II and V of this series.

Preface

Each of the volumes in the series provides a legislative text, clearly showing the form and date of amendments, reflecting the multifarious changes made by regulations to the scope of WTC and CTC, as well as commentary, up to date to April 11, 2024. The volume includes commentary on significant Upper Tribunal decisions on evidential, procedural and substantive issues arising in tax credits appeals as well as, where possible, references to some later case law. As previously, given that there continues to be considerable public interest in the issue of overpayments of tax credits, we have included the text of leaflet WTC7 on Tax Credits penalties and HMRC's Code of Practice 26 (COP 26) on the recovery of overpayments. We have also included the HMRC Charter to assist readers.

Readers are also reminded that the legislation and the authoritative commentary on the decision-making and appeals statutory provisions, and on the tribunal procedural rules, are to be found in Volume III of this series (as are human rights aspects and European law issues, most notably those arising out of Brexit).

As always, revising and updating the legislative text and commentary has required considerable flexibility on the part of the publisher and a great deal of help from several sources, including CPAG as advisory editor to the series. We remain grateful for this assistance in our task of providing an authoritative reflection on the current state of the law. Users of these volumes in this series, and their predecessors, have also over the years provided valuable comments which have invariably been helpful to the editors in ensuring that the selection of legislative material for inclusion and the commentary upon it reflect the sorts of difficulties encountered in practice. In doing so, readers have thus helped to shape the content of each of the volumes in the current series. We also hope that users of the work will continue to provide such helpful input and feedback. This is all the more important given the major restructuring of the series that has taken place. Please write to the General Editor of the series, Emeritus Professor Nick Wikeley, c/o School of Law, University of Southampton, Highfield, Southampton SO17 1BJ (njw@soton.ac.uk), and he will pass on any comments received to the appropriate commentator.

Our gratitude also goes to the Chamber President of the Social Entitlement Chamber of the First-tier Tribunal and her staff for continuing the tradition of help and encouragement.

Last, but by no means least, we wish to recognise that the 2023/24 main edition of Vol.III in this series was the last for which Mark Rowland had a direct responsibility (although much of what he has written will undoubtedly continue to feature in the book for many editions to come). The current editors of all the volumes would like to take this opportunity to pay tribute to Mark's tremendous contribution to the series as a whole since 1993, when he first produced the volume on *Medical and Disability Appeal Tribunals* that went into three editions before the restructuring of the series in 2000. In that restructuring, he took on joint responsibility with Robin White for Vol.III, *Administration, Adjudication and the European Dimension*. Thus, for more than 20 years Mark has brought his formidable knowledge and experience of social security law and adjudication, from his work as an advocate, as a part-time chair of appeal tribunals and then as a Social Security Commissioner and later Upper Tribunal Judge to bear on the often opaque legislative material on administration, decision-making and appeals. Latterly he made a major contribution to Vol.IV with his expert

Preface

commentary on the new legislative provisions relating to social security in Scotland. As readers will know, his gift for clarity of exposition enabled his commentary both to bring out matters of principle and to provide practical guidance to tribunals and users with an appreciation of the way problems actually arise. More behind the scenes, Mark's contribution to the way in which the series as a whole has developed, from wise advice about the needs of readers to knowledge of why choices were or were not made over the years, cannot be overstated. The current editors will greatly miss having that wisdom and experience on tap.

August 2024

Nick Wikeley
Edward Mitchell
Ian Hooker

CONTENTS

	Page
Foreword	vii
Preface	ix
Using this Book: an Introduction to Legislation and Case Law	xxi
Major Changes to Credits and Benefits	xxxiii
Change of Name from Department of Social Security to Department for Work and Pensions	xxxv
Changes in Terminology Consequent upon the Entry into Force of the Treaty of Lisbon	xxxvii
The Marriage (Same Sex Couples) Act 2013	xxxix
Table of Cases	xli
Table of Social Security Commissioners' Decisions 1948–2009	li
Table of Abbreviations used in this Series	liii

PART I
UNITED KINGDOM AND GREAT BRITAIN STATUTES

	Paras
Taxes Management Act 1970	1.1
Social Security Contributions and Benefits Act 1992	1.36
Social Security Administration Act 1992	1.209
Social Security Act 1998	1.225
Social Security Contributions (Transfer of Functions, etc.) Act 1999	1.228
Tax Credits Act 2002	1.254
Employment Act 2002	1.465
Income Tax (Earnings and Pensions) Act 2003	1.495
Child Trust Funds Act 2004	1.617
Income Tax (Trading and Other Income) Act 2005	1.715
Commissioners for Revenue and Customs Act 2005	1.843
Income Tax Act 2007	1.875
Welfare Reform Act 2012	1.898
Welfare Benefits Up-rating Act 2013	1.906
Childcare Payments Act 2014	1.910
Childcare Act 2016	1.1056
Welfare Reform and Work Act 2016	1.1065
Parental Bereavement (Leave and Pay) Act 2018	1.1070
Coronavirus Act 2020	1.1074

Contents

PART II
TAX CREDITS
PART A
TAX CREDITS COMMENCEMENT ORDERS AND TRANSITIONAL PROVISIONS

	Paras
The Welfare Reform Act 2012 (Commencement No.9 and Transitional and Transitory Provisions and Commencement No.8 and Savings and Transitional Provisions (Amendment)) Order 2013	2.1
The Welfare Reform Act 2012 (Commencement No.23 and Transitional and Transitory Provisions) Order 2015	2.11
The Welfare Reform Act 2012 (Commencement No.29 and Commencement No.17, 19, 22, 23 and 24 and Transitional and Transitory Provisions (Modification)) Order 2017	2.18
The Welfare Reform Act 2012 (Commencement No.32 and Savings and Transitional Provisions) Order 2019	2.23
The Universal Credit (Transitional Provisions) Regulations 2014	2.33

PART B
TAX CREDITS REGULATIONS

The Working Tax Credit (Entitlement and Maximum Rate) Regulations 2002	2.120
The Tax Credits (Definition and Calculation of Income) Regulations 2002	2.200
The Child Tax Credit Regulations 2002	2.268
The Tax Credits (Income Thresholds and Determination of Rates) Regulations 2002	2.309
The Tax Credits (Claims and Notifications) Regulations 2002	2.336
The Tax Credits (Payment by the Commissioners) Regulations 2002	2.410
The Tax Credits (Administrative Arrangements) Regulations 2002	2.438
The Tax Credits (Appeals) (No.2) Regulations 2002	2.445
The Tax Credits (Interest Rate) Regulations 2003	2.458
The Tax Credits (Immigration) Regulations 2003	2.464
The Tax Credits (Residence) Regulations 2003	2.476
The Tax Credits (Official Error) Regulations 2003	2.494
The Tax Credits (Provision of Information) (Functions Relating to Health) Regulations 2003	2.500
The Tax Credits (Polygamous Marriages) Regulations 2003	2.505
The Tax Credits (Provision of Information) (Functions Relating to Health) (No.2) Regulations 2003	2.518
The Tax Credits (Provision of Information) (Function Relating to Employment and Training) Regulations 2003	2.522
The Tax Credits Act 2002 (Child Tax Credit) (Transitional Provisions) Order 2003	2.525
The Tax Credits (Provision of Information) (Evaluation and Statistical Studies) Regulations 2003	2.529

Contents

The Tax Credits (Provision of Information) (Evaluation and Statistical Studies) (Northern Ireland) Regulations 2004	2.531
The Tax Credits (Provision of Information) (Functions Relating to Health) (Scotland) Regulations 2004	2.533
The Tax Credits (Provision of Information) (Function Relating to Employment and Training) Regulations 2005	2.535
The Tax Credits (Child Care Providers) Miscellaneous Revocation and Transitional Provisions) (England) Scheme 2007	2.537
The Loss of Tax Credits (Specified Day) Order 2013	2.543
The Loss of Tax Credits Regulations 2013	2.546
The Tax Credits (Late Appeals) Order 2014	2.550
The Tax Credits, Child Benefit and Guardian's Allowance Reviews and Appeals Order 2014	2.553
The Tax Credits (Settlement of Appeals) Regulations 2014	2.558
The Tax Credits (Exercise of Functions) Order 2014	2.562
The Tax Credits Act 2002 (Additional Payments Modification and Disapplication) Regulations 2022	2.568

PART III
CHILDREN AND GUARDIANS

	Paras
The Child Benefit (General) Regulations 2006	3.1
The Child Benefit (Residence and Persons Abroad) Regulations 1976	3.59
The Child Benefit (Rates) Regulations 2006	3.60
The Guardian's Allowance (General) Regulations 2003	3.66
The Tax Credits, Child Benefit and Guardian's Allowance Up-rating Regulations 2024	3.82
The Guardian's Allowance Up-rating Regulations 2024	3.84

PART IV
STATUTORY SICK PAY

	Paras
The Statutory Sick Pay (General) Regulations 1982	4.1
The Statutory Sick Pay (Mariners, Airmen and Persons Abroad) Regulations 1982	4.47
The Statutory Sick Pay (Medical Evidence) Regulations 1985	4.68
The Statutory Sick Pay (National Health Service Employees) Regulations 1991	4.76
The Statutory Sick Pay and Statutory Maternity Pay (Decisions) Regulations 1999	4.83
The Statutory Sick Pay Percentage Threshold (Revocations, Transitional and Saving Provisions) (Great Britain and Northern Ireland) Order 2014	4.88
The Statutory Sick Pay (Coronavirus) (Suspension of Waiting Days and General Amendment) Regulations 2020	4.93
The Statutory Sick Pay (Coronavirus) (Funding of Employers' Liabilities) Regulations 2020	4.100
The Statutory Sick Pay (Medical Evidence) Regulations 2021	4.115

	Paras
The Statutory Sick Pay (Coronavirus) (Funding of Employers' Liabilities) Regulations 2022	4.118
The Statutory Sick Pay (General) (Coronavirus Amendment) Regulations 2022	4.132
The Statutory Sick Pay (Coronavirus) (Suspension of Waiting Days) (Saving Provision) Regulations 2022	4.135

PART V
STATUTORY MATERNITY PAY

	Paras
The Statutory Maternity Pay (General) Regulations 1986	5.1
The Statutory Maternity Pay (Medical Evidence) Regulations 1987	5.58
The Statutory Maternity Pay (Persons Abroad and Mariners) Regulations 1987	5.63
The Statutory Maternity Pay (National Health Service Employees) Regulations 1991	5.75
The Statutory Maternity Pay (Compensation of Employers) and Miscellaneous Amendment Regulations 1994	5.82
The Statutory Maternity Pay (General) (Modification and Amendment) Regulations 2000	5.94
The Statutory Maternity Pay and Statutory Adoption Pay (Curtailment) Regulations 2014	5.101
The Maternity Allowance, Statutory Maternity Pay, Statutory Paternity Pay, Statutory Adoption Pay, Statutory Shared Parental Pay and Statutory Parental Bereavement Pay (Normal Weekly Earnings etc.) (Coronavirus) (Amendment) Regulations 2020	5.116

PART VI
STATUTORY PATERNITY PAY
AND STATUTORY ADOPTION PAY

	Paras
The Statutory Paternity Pay and Statutory Adoption Pay (Weekly Rates) Regulations 2002	6.1
The Statutory Paternity Pay and Statutory Adoption Pay (National Health Service Employees) Regulations 2002	6.8
The Statutory Paternity Pay and Statutory Adoption Pay (Administration) Regulations 2002	6.16
The Statutory Paternity Pay and Statutory Adoption Pay (Persons Abroad and Mariners) Regulations 2002	6.33
The Statutory Paternity Pay and Statutory Adoption Pay (General) Regulations 2002	6.46
The Social Security Contributions and Benefits Act 1992 (Application of Parts 12ZA, 12ZB and 12ZC to Adoptions from Overseas) Regulations 2003	6.102
The Statutory Paternity Pay (Adoption) and Statutory Adoption Pay (Adoptions from Overseas) (Administration) Regulations 2003	6.111

Contents

The Statutory Paternity Pay (Adoption) and Statutory Adoption Pay (Adoptions from Overseas) (No.2) Regulations 2003	6.116
The Ordinary Statutory Paternity Pay (Adoption), Additional Statutory Paternity Pay (Adoption) and Statutory Adoption Pay (Adoptions from Overseas) (Persons Abroad and Mariners) Regulations 2010	6.139
The Additional Statutory Paternity Pay (National Health Service Employees) Regulations 2010	6.144
The Additional Statutory Paternity Pay (General) Regulations 2010	6.145
The Additional Statutory Paternity Pay (Adoptions from Overseas) Regulations 2010	6.146
The Additional Statutory Paternity Pay (Weekly Rates) Regulations 2010	6.147
The Social Security Contributions and Benefits Act 1992 (Application of Parts 12ZA, 12ZB and 12ZC to Parental Order Cases) Regulations 2014	6.148
The Statutory Paternity Pay and Statutory Adoption Pay (Parental Orders and Prospective Adopters) Regulations 2014	6.158
The Statutory Maternity Pay and Statutory Adoption Pay (Curtailment) Regulations 2014	6.188

PART VII
STATUTORY SHARED PARENTAL PAY

	Paras
The Statutory Shared Parental Pay (Administration) Regulations 2014	7.1
The Statutory Shared Parental Pay (General) Regulations 2014	7.17
The Statutory Shared Parental Pay (Adoption From Overseas) Regulations 2014	7.92
The Statutory Shared Parental Pay (Parental Order Cases) Regulations 2014	7.109
The Statutory Shared Parental Pay (Persons Abroad and Mariners) Regulations 2014	7.127

PART VIII
STATUTORY PARENTAL BEREAVEMENT PAY

	Paras
The Statutory Parental Bereavement Pay (General) Regulations 2020	8.1
The Statutory Parental Bereavement Pay (Administration) Regulations 2020	8.31
The Statutory Parental Bereavement Pay (Persons Abroad and Mariners) Regulations 2020	8.46

PART IX
CHILD TRUST FUNDS

	Paras
The Child Trust Funds Act 2004 (Commencement No.1) Order 2004	9.1

Contents

	Paras
The Child Trust Funds Act 2004 (Commencement No.2) Order 2004	9.4
The Child Trust Funds Regulations 2004	9.7
The Child Trust Funds (Insurance Companies) Regulations 2004	9.62
The Child Trust Funds (Non-tax Appeals) Regulations 2005	9.84
The Child Trust Funds (Appeals) Regulations 2005	9.90

PART X
TAX-FREE CHILDCARE

	Paras
The Childcare Payments (Eligibility) Regulations 2015	10.1
The Childcare Payments Regulations 2015	10.20
The Childcare Payments (Appeals) Regulations 2016	10.43

PART XI
FREE CHILDCARE FOR WORKING PARENTS

	Paras
The Childcare Act 2016 (Consequential Amendments) Regulations 2016	11.1
Childcare (Free of Charge for Working Parents) (England) Regulations 2022	11.5

PART XII
HMRC CHARTER, CODES OF PRACTICE AND GUIDANCE

	Paras
The HMRC Charter ("Your Charter")	12.1
WTC7—Tax Credits Penalties	12.16
COP 26—What happens if we've paid you too much tax credits	12.29

PART XIII
SCOTTISH SOCIAL SECURITY LEGISLATION

	Paras
Social Security (Scotland) Act 2018	13.1
The Early Years Assistance (Best Start Grants) (Scotland) Regulations 2018 (SSI 2018/370)	13.128
The Funeral Expense Assistance (Scotland) Regulations 2019 (SSI 2019/292)	13.165
The Carer's Assistance (Young Carer Grants) (Scotland) Regulations 2019 (SSI 2019/324)	13.180
The Carer's Allowance (Coronavirus) (Breaks in Care) (Scotland) Regulations 2020 (SSI 2020/117)	13.194
The Scottish Child Payment Regulations 2020 (SSI 2020/351)	13.198
The Winter Heating Assistance for Children and Young People (Scotland) Regulations 2020 (SSI 2020/352)	13.251
The Social Security Co-ordination (EU Exit) (Scotland) (Amendments etc.) Regulations 2020 (SSI 2020/399)	13.263

Contents

The Carer's Allowance Supplement and Young Carer Grants (Residence Requirements and Procedural Provisions) (EU Exit) (Scotland) Regulations 2020 (SSI 2020/475)	13.272
The Disability Assistance for Children and Young People (Consequential Amendment and Transitional Provision) (Scotland) Regulations 2021 (SSI 2021/73)	13.289
The Disability Assistance for Children and Young People (Scotland) Regulations 2021 (SSI 2021/174)	13.292
The Social Security Information-sharing (Scotland) Regulations 2021 (SSI 2021/178)	13.351
The Disability Assistance for Working Age People (Consequential and Miscellaneous Amendment and Transitional Provision) (Scotland)Regulations 2022 (SSI 2022/31)	13.359
The Disability Assistance for Working Age People (Scotland) Regulations 2022 (SSI 2022/54)	13.362
The Disability Assistance for Working Age People (Transitional Provisions and Miscellaneous Amendment) (Scotland) Regulations 2022 (SSI 2022/517)	13.438
The Winter Heating Assistance (Low Income) (Scotland) Regulations 2023 (SSI 2023/16)	13.455
The Carer's Assistance (Carer Support Payment) (Scotland) Regulations 2023 (SSI 2023/302)	13.465

PART XIV
SCOTTISH TRIBUNALS LEGISLATION

	Paras
Tribunals (Scotland) Act 2014	14.1
The Scottish Tribunals (Time Limits) Regulations 2016 (SSI 2016/231)	14.49
The First-tier Tribunal for Scotland Social Security Chamber (Procedure) Regulations 2018 (SSI 2018/273)	14.55
The Upper Tribunal for Scotland (Social Security Rules of Procedure)Regulations 2018 (SSI 2018/274)	14.115
The Social Security Appeals (Expenses and Allowances) (Scotland) Regulations 2018 (SSI 2018/275)	14.154
The First-tier Tribunal for Scotland (Allocation of Functions to the Social Security Chamber) Regulations 2018 (SSI 2018/350)	14.157

	Page
Index	1851

USING THIS BOOK: AN INTRODUCTION TO LEGISLATION AND CASE LAW

Introduction

This book is not a general introduction to, or general textbook on, the law relating to social security but it is nonetheless concerned with both of the principal sources of social security law—*legislation* (both primary and secondary) and *case law*. It sets out the text of the most important legislation, as currently in force, and then there is added commentary that refers to the relevant case law. Lawyers will be familiar with this style of publication, which inevitably follows the structure of the legislation.

This note is designed primarily to assist readers who are not lawyers to find their way around the legislation and to understand the references to case law, but information it contains about how to find social security case law is intended to be of assistance to lawyers too.

Primary legislation

Primary legislation of the United Kingdom Parliament consists of *Acts of Parliament* (also known as *Statutes*). They will have been introduced to Parliament as *Bills*. There are opportunities for Members of Parliament and peers to debate individual clauses and to vote on amendments before a Bill is passed and becomes an Act (at which point the clauses become sections). No tribunal or court has the power to disapply, or hold to be invalid, an Act of Parliament, although, until December 31, 2020, that could be done if it was inconsistent with European Union law.

An Act is known by its "short title", which incorporates the year in which it was passed (e.g. the Social Security Contributions and Benefits Act 1992), and is given a chapter number (abbreviated as, for instance, "c.4" indicating that the Act was the fourth passed in that year). It is seldom necessary to refer to the chapter number but it appears in the running headers in this book.

Each *section* (abbreviated as "s." or, in the plural, "ss.") of an Act is numbered and may be divided into *subsections* (abbreviated as "subs." and represented by a number in brackets), which in turn may be divided into *paragraphs* (abbreviated as "para." and represented by a lower case letter in brackets) and *subparagraphs* (abbreviated as "subpara." and represented by a small roman numeral in brackets). Subparagraph (ii) of para.(a) of subs.(1) of s.72 will usually be referred to simply as "s.72(1)(a)(ii)". Upper case letters may be used where additional sections or subsections are inserted by amendment and additional lower case letters may be used where new paragraphs and subparagraphs are inserted. This accounts for the rather ungainly s.109B(2A)(aa) of the Social Security Administration Act 1992.

Sections of a large Act may be grouped into a numbered *Part*, which may even be divided into *Chapters*. It is not usual to refer to a Part or a Chapter unless referring to the whole Part or Chapter.

Using this Book

Where a section would otherwise become unwieldy because it is necessary to include a list or complicated technical provisions, the section may simply refer to a *Schedule* at the end of the Act. A Schedule (abbreviated as "Sch.") may be divided into paragraphs and subparagraphs and further divided into heads and subheads. Again, it is usual to refer simply to, say, "para.23(3)(b)(ii) of Sch.3". Whereas it is conventional to speak of a section *of* an Act, it is usual to speak of a Schedule *to* an Act.

Secondary legislation

Secondary legislation (also known as *subordinate legislation* or *delegated legislation*) is made by *statutory instrument* in the form of a set of *Regulations* or a set of *Rules* or an *Order*. The power to make such legislation is conferred on ministers and other persons or bodies by Acts of Parliament. To the extent that a statutory instrument is made beyond the powers (in Latin, *ultra vires*) conferred by primary legislation, it may be held by a tribunal or court to be invalid and ineffective. Secondary legislation must be laid before Parliament. However, most secondary legislation is not debated in Parliament and, even when it is, it cannot be amended although an entire statutory instrument may be rejected.

A set of Regulations or Rules or an Order has a name indicating its scope and the year it was made and also a number, as in the Social Security (Disability Living Allowance) Regulations 1991 (SI 1991/2890) (the 2890th statutory instrument issued in 1991). Because there are over a thousand statutory instruments each year, the number of a particular statutory instrument is important as a means of identification and it should usually be cited the first time reference is made to that statutory instrument.

Sets of Regulations or Rules are made up of individual *regulations* (abbreviated as "reg.") or *rules* (abbreviated as "r." or, in the plural, "rr."). An Order is made up of *articles* (abbreviated as "art."). Regulations, rules and articles may be divided into paragraphs, subparagraphs and heads. As in Acts, a set of Regulations or Rules or an Order may have one or more Schedules attached to it. The style of numbering used in statutory instruments is the same as in sections of, and Schedules to, Acts of Parliament. As in Acts, a large statutory instrument may have regulations or rules grouped into Parts and, occasionally, Chapters. Statutory instruments may be amended in the same sort of way as Acts.

Scottish legislation

Most of the social security legislation passed by the United Kingdom Parliament applies throughout Great Britain, i.e. in England, Wales and Scotland, but a separate Scottish social security system is gradually being developed and relevant legislation is included in this volume of this series. Acts of the Scottish Parliament are similar to Acts of the United Kingdom Parliament and Scottish Statutory Instruments are also similar to their United Kingdom counterparts. One minor difference is that "schedule" usually has a lower case "s" and references are to a schedule *of* an Act, rather than *to* an Act.

Northern Ireland legislation

Most of the legislation set out in this series applies only in Great Britain, social security not generally being an excepted or reserved matter in relation to Northern Ireland. However, Northern Irish legislation—both primary legislation, most relevantly in the form of *Orders in Council* (which, although statutory instruments, had the effect of primary legislation in Northern Ireland while there was direct rule from Westminster and still do when made under the Northern Ireland (Welfare Reform) Act 2015) and *Acts of the Northern Ireland Assembly,* and subordinate legislation, in the form of *statutory rules*—largely replicates legislation in Great Britain so that much of the commentary in this book will be applicable to equivalent provisions in Northern Ireland legislation. Although there has latterly been a greater reluctance in Northern Ireland to maintain parity with Great Britain, one example of which led to some delay in enacting legislation equivalent to the Welfare Reform Act 2012, this is usually resolved politically by, for instance, the allocation of funds to allow the effects of some of the changes to be mitigated in Northern Ireland while the broad legislative structure remains similar.

European Union legislation

European Union primary legislation is in the form of the *Treaties* agreed by the Member States. Relevant subordinate legislation is in the form of *Regulations,* adopted to give effect to the provisions of the Treaties, and *Directives,* addressed to Member States and requiring them to incorporate certain provisions into their domestic laws. Directives are relevant because, where a person brings proceedings against an organ of the State, as is invariably the case where social security is concerned, that person may rely on the Directive as having direct effect if the Member State has failed to comply with it. Treaties, Regulations and Directives are divided into *Articles* (abbreviated as "Art.").

While the United Kingdom was a Member State of the European Union, United Kingdom legislation that was inconsistent with European Union legislation had to be disapplied. The United Kingdom ceased to be a Member State on January 31, 2020, but the effect of the European Union (Withdrawal Act) 2018, as amended in 2020, is that, with very limited exceptions, European Union law continued to apply in the United Kingdom during the implementation period ending on December 31, 2020. After that date, European Union law remains relevant only to the extent that United Kingdom legislation so provides. For instance, the 2018 Act, as amended, provides for the enforcement of the Withdrawal Agreement, under which rights acquired by individuals before the end of the implementation period may be retained.

Finding legislation in this book

If you know the name of the piece of legislation for which you are looking, use the list of contents at the beginning of each volume of this series which lists the pieces of legislation contained in the volume. That will give you the paragraph reference to enable you to find the beginning of the piece of legislation. Then, it is easy to find the relevant section, regulation, rule, article or Schedule by using the running headers on the right hand pages. If you do not know the name of the piece of legislation, you will probably need to use the index at the end of the volume in order to find the relevant paragraph number but will then be taken straight to a particular provision.

The legislation is set out as amended, the amendments being indicated by numbered sets of square brackets. The numbers refer to the numbered

Using this Book

entries under the heading "AMENDMENTS" at the end of the relevant section, regulation, rule, article or Schedule, which identify the amending statute or statutory instrument. Where an Act has been consolidated, there is a list of "DERIVATIONS" identifying the provisions of earlier legislation from which the section or Schedule has been derived.

As regards the European Union, United Kingdom legislation concerned with the consequences of the United Kingdom's withdrawal is set out in Part V of Volume III in this series, together with relevant extracts from the Withdrawal Agreement and the Social Security Protocol to the Trade and Cooperation Agreement. Following the extracts from the Withdrawal Agreement is up-dating commentary on the European Union legislation that is set out in Part III of the 2020–21 edition of Volume III. Readers are encouraged to retain that volume so as to be able to find the main text of relevant European Union legislation there.

Finding other legislation

United Kingdom legislation and legislation made by the legislatures in Scotland, Wales and Northern Ireland may now be found on *http://www. legislation.gov.uk* in both its original form and (usually) its amended form. Northern Ireland social security legislation may also be found at *https://www. communities-ni.gov.uk/services/law-relating-social-security-northern-ireland-blue-volumes*. European Union legislation may be found at *https://eur-lex.europa. eu/homepage.html*.

Interpreting legislation

Legislation is written in English (or, at least, there is an official English version) and generally means what it says. However, languages being complicated, more than one interpretation is often possible. Most legislation itself contains definitions. Sometimes these are in the particular provision in which a word occurs but, where a word is used in more than one place, any definition will appear with others. In an Act, an interpretation section is usually to be found towards the end of the Act or of the relevant Part of the Act. In a statutory instrument, an interpretation provision usually appears near the beginning of the statutory instrument or the relevant Part of it. In the more important pieces of legislation in this series, there is included after every section, regulation, rule, article or Schedule a list of "DEFINITIONS", showing where definitions of words used in the provision are to be found.

However, not all words are statutorily defined and there is in any event more to interpreting legislation than merely defining its terms (see the note to s.3(1) of the Tribunals, Courts and Enforcement Act 2007 in Part III of Volume III of this series). Decision-makers and tribunals need to know how to apply the law in different types of situations. That is where case law comes in.

Case law and the commentary in this book

In deciding individual cases, courts and tribunals interpret the relevant law and incidentally establish legal principles. Decisions on questions of legal principle of the superior courts and appellate tribunals are said to be binding on decision-makers and the First-tier Tribunal, which means that decision-makers and the First-tier Tribunal must apply those principles. Thus the judicial decisions of the superior courts and appellate tribunals form part of the law. The commentary to the legislation in this series, under the heading "GENERAL NOTE" after a section, regulation, rule, article or Schedule, refers to this *case law*.

Most case law regarding social security benefits is in the form of decisions of the Upper Tribunal (Administrative Appeals Chamber), to which the functions of the former Social Security Commissioners and Child Support Commissioners in Great Britain were transferred on November 3, 2008. However, decisions of those Commissioners remain relevant, as are decisions of the Commissioners who still sit in Northern Ireland.

The commentary in this series is not itself binding on any decision-maker or tribunal because it is merely the opinion of the author. It is what is actually said in the legislation or in the judicial decision that is important. The legislation is set out in this series, but it will generally be necessary to look elsewhere for the precise words used in judicial decisions. The way that decisions are cited in the commentary enables that to be done.

The reporting of decisions of the Upper Tribunal and Commissioners

A few of the most important decisions of the Administrative Appeals Chamber of the Upper Tribunal are selected to be "reported" each year in the Administrative Appeals Chamber Reports (AACR), using the same criteria as were formerly used for reporting Commissioners' decisions in Great Britain. The selection is made by an editorial board of judges and decisions are selected for reporting only if they are of general importance and command the assent of at least a majority of the relevant judges. The term "reported" simply means that they are published in printed form as well as on the Internet (see *Finding case law*, below) with headnotes (i.e. summaries) and indexes, but reported decisions also have a greater precedential status than ordinary decisions (see *Judicial precedent* below).

A handful of Northern Ireland Commissioners' decisions are also selected for reporting in the Administrative Appeals Chamber Reports each year, the selection being made by the Chief Social Security Commissioner in Northern Ireland.

Citing case law

As has been mentioned, much social security case law is still to be found in decisions of Social Security Commissioners and Child Support Commissioners, even though the Commissioners have now effectively been abolished in Great Britain.

Reported decisions of Commissioners were known merely by a number or, more accurately, a series of letters and numbers beginning with an "R". The type of benefit in issue was indicated by letters in brackets (e.g. "IS" was income support, "P" was retirement pension, and so on) and the year in which the decision was selected for reporting or, from 2000, the year in which it was published as a reported decision, was indicated by the last two digits, as in *R(IS) 2/08*. In Northern Ireland there was a similar system until 2009, save that the type of benefit was identified by letters in brackets after the number, as in *R 1/07 (DLA)*.

Unreported decisions of the Commissioners in Great Britain were known simply by their file numbers, which began with a "C", as in *CIS/2287/2008*.

Using this Book

The letters following the "C" indicated the type of benefit in issue in the case. Scottish and, at one time, Welsh cases were indicated by a "S" or "W" immediately after the "C", as in *CSIS/467/2007*. The last four digits indicated the calendar year in which the case was registered, rather than the year it was decided. A similar system operated in Northern Ireland until 2009, save that the letters indicating the type of benefit appeared in brackets after the numbers and, from April 1999, the financial year rather than the calendar year was identified, as in *C 10/06-07 (IS)*.

Decisions of the Upper Tribunal, of courts and, since 2010, of the Northern Ireland Commissioners are generally known by the names of the parties (or just two of them in multi-party cases). In social security and some other types of cases, individuals are anonymised through the use of initials in the names of decisions of the Upper Tribunal and the Northern Ireland Commissioners. Anonymity is much rarer in the names of decisions of courts. In this series, the names of official bodies are also abbreviated in the names of decisions of the Upper Tribunal and the Northern Ireland Commissioners (e.g. "SSWP" for the Secretary of State for Work and Pensions, "HMRC" for Her/His Majesty's Revenue and Customs, "CMEC" for the Child Maintenance and Enforcement Commission, "DSD" for the Department for Social Development in Northern Ireland and "DC" for the Department for Communities in Northern Ireland). Since 2010, such decisions have also been given a "flag" in brackets to indicate the subject matter of the decision, which in social security cases indicates the principal benefit in issue in the case. Thus, the name of one universal credit case is *SSWP v AJ (UC)*.

Any decision of the Upper Tribunal, of a court since 2001 or of a Northern Ireland Commissioner since 2010 that has been intended for publication has also given a neutral citation number which enables the decision to be more precisely identified. This indicates, in square brackets, the year the decision was made (although in relation to decisions of the courts it sometimes merely indicates the year the number was issued) and also indicates the court or tribunal that made the decision (e.g. "UKUT" for the Upper Tribunal (which sits in Great Britain for social security purposes but throughout the United Kingdom for some others), "UT" for the separate Upper Tribunal for Scotland, "NICom" for a Northern Ireland Commissioner, "EWCA Civ" for the Civil Division of the Court of Appeal in England and Wales, "NICA" for the Court of Appeal in Northern Ireland, "CSIH" for the Inner House of the Court of Session (in Scotland), "UKSC" for the Supreme Court and so on). A number is added so that the reference is unique and finally, in the case of the Upper Tribunal or the High Court in England and Wales, the relevant chamber of the Upper Tribunal or the relevant division or other part of the High Court is identified (e.g. "(AAC)" for the Administrative Appeals Chamber, "(Admin)" for the Administrative Court and so on). Examples of decisions of the Upper Tribunal and a Northern Ireland Commissioner with their neutral citation numbers are *SSWP v AJ (UC)* [2020] UKUT 48 (AAC) and *AR v DSD (IB)* [2010] NICom 6.

If the case is reported in the Administrative Appeals Chamber Reports or another series of law reports, a reference to the report usually follows the neutral citation number. Conventionally, this includes either the year the case was decided (in round brackets) or the year in which it was reported (in square brackets), followed by the volume number (if any), the name of the series of reports (in abbreviated form, so see the Table of Abbreviations at the beginning of each volume of this series) and either the page number or the case number. However, before 2010, cases reported in the Administrative Appeals Chamber Reports or with Commissioners' decisions were numbered in the same way as reported Commissioners' decisions. *Abdirahman v Secretary of State for Work and Pensions* [2007] EWCA Civ 657; [2008] 1 W.L.R. 254 (also reported as *R(IS) 8/07)* is a Court of Appeal decision, decided in 2007 but reported in 2008 in volume 1 of the Weekly Law Reports at page 254 and also in the 2007 volume of reported Commissioners' decisions. *NT v SSWP* [2009] UKUT 37 (AAC); *R(DLA) 1/09* is an Upper Tribunal case decided in 2009 and reported in the Administrative Appeals Chamber Reports in the same year. *Martin v Secretary of State for Work and Pensions* [2009] EWCA Civ 1289; [2010] AACR 9 is a decision of the Court of Appeal that was decided in 2009 and was the ninth decision reported in the Administrative Appeals Chamber Reports in 2010.

It is usually necessary to include the neutral citation number or a reference to a series of reports only the first time a decision is cited in any document. After that, the name of the case is usually sufficient.

All decisions of the Upper Tribunal that are on their website have neutral citation numbers. If you wish to refer a tribunal or decision-maker to a decision of the Upper Tribunal that does not have a neutral citation number, contact the office of the Administrative Appeals Chamber (*adminappeals@ justice.gov.uk*) who will provide a number and add the decision to the website.

Decision-makers and claimants are entitled to assume that judges of both the First-tier Tribunal and the Upper Tribunal have immediate access to reported decisions of Commissioners or the Upper Tribunal and they need not provide copies, although it may sometimes be helpful to do so. However, where either a decision-maker or a claimant intends to rely on an unreported decision, it will be necessary to provide a copy of the decision to the judge and other members of the tribunal. A copy of the decision should also be provided to the other party before the hearing because otherwise it may be necessary for there to be an adjournment to enable that party to take advice on the significance of the decision.

Finding case law

The extensive references described above are used so as to enable people easily to find the full text of a decision. Most decisions of any significance since the late 1990s can be found on the Internet.

Decisions of the Upper Tribunal may be found at *https://www.gov.uk/ administrative-appeals-tribunal-decisions*. The link from that page to "decisions made in 2015 or earlier" leads also to decisions of the Commissioners in Great Britain. This includes reported decisions since 1991 and other decisions considered likely to be of interest to tribunals and tribunal users since about 2000, together with a few older decisions. Decisions of Commissioners in Northern Ireland may be found on *https://iaccess.communities-ni.gov.uk/NIDOC*.

The Administrative Appeals Chamber Reports are also published by the Stationery Office in bound volumes which follow on from the bound volumes of Commissioners' decisions published from 1948.

Using this Book

Copies of decisions of the Administrative Appeals Chamber of the Upper Tribunal or of Commissioners that are otherwise unavailable may be obtained from the offices of the Upper Tribunal (Administrative Appeals Chamber) or, in Northern Ireland, from the Office of the Social Security and Child Support Commissioners.

Decisions of a wide variety of courts and tribunals in the United Kingdom may be found on the free website of the British and Irish Legal Information Institute, *http://www.bailii.org*. It includes all decisions of the Supreme Court and provides fairly comprehensive coverage of decisions given since about 1996 by the House of Lords and Privy Council and most of the higher courts in England and Wales, decisions given since 1998 by the Court of Session and decisions given since 2000 by the Court of Appeal and High Court in Northern Ireland. Some earlier decisions have been included, so it is always worth looking and, indeed, those decisions dating from 1873 or earlier and reported in the English Reports may be found through a link to *http://www.commonlii.org/uk/cases/EngR/*. Since 2022, decisions of the Upper Tribunal, the Employment Appeal Tribunal and most courts that sit in England and Wales are also to be found on The National Archives' website at *https://caselaw.nationalarchives.gov.uk/structured_search*. However, courts and tribunals that sit only in Wales, Scotland or Northern Ireland are not included there. Decisions of the Upper Tribunal for Scotland and of Scottish courts can be found at *https://www.scotcourts.gov.uk*.

Decisions of the Court of Justice of the European Union are all to be found at *https://curia.europa.eu*.

Decisions of the European Court of Human Rights are available at *https://www.echr.coe.int*.

Most decisions of the courts in social security cases, including decisions of the Court of Justice of the European Union on cases referred by United Kingdom courts and tribunals, are reported in the Administrative Appeals Chamber Reports or with the reported decisions of Commissioners and may therefore be found on the same websites and in the same printed series of reported decisions. So, for example, *R(I) 1/00* contains Commissioner's decision *CSI/12/1998*, the decision of the Court of Session upholding the Commissioner's decision and the decision of the House of Lords in *Chief Adjudication Officer v Faulds*, reversing the decision of the Court of Session. The most important decisions of the courts can also be found in the various series of law reports familiar to lawyers (in particular, in the *Law Reports*, the *Weekly Law Reports*, the *All England Law Reports*, the *Public and Third Sector Law Reports*, the *Industrial Cases Reports* and the *Family Law Reports*) but these are not widely available outside academic or other law libraries, or subscription-based websites. See the Table of Cases at the beginning of each volume of this series for all the places where a decision mentioned in that volume is reported.

If you know the name or number of a decision and wish to know where in a volume of this series there is a reference to it, use the Table of Cases or the Table of Commissioners' Decisions 1948–2009 in the relevant volume to find the paragraph(s) where the decision is mentioned.

Judicial precedent

As already mentioned, decisions of the Upper Tribunal, the Commissioners and the higher courts in Great Britain become case law because they set

Using this Book

binding precedents which must be followed by decision-makers and the First-tier Tribunal in Great Britain. This means that, where the Upper Tribunal, Commissioner or court has decided a point of legal principle, decision-makers and appeal tribunals must make their decisions in conformity with the decision of the Upper Tribunal, Commissioner or court, applying the same principle and accepting the interpretation of the law contained in the decision. So a decision of the Upper Tribunal, a Commissioner or a superior court explaining what a term in a particular regulation means, lays down the definition of that term in much the same way as if the term had been defined in the regulations themselves. The decision may also help in deciding what the same term means when it is used in a different set of regulations, provided that the term appears to have been used in a similar context.

Only decisions on points of law set precedents that are binding and, strictly speaking, only decisions on points of law that were necessary to the overall conclusion reached by the Upper Tribunal, Commissioner or court are binding. Other parts of a decision (which used to be known as obiter dicta) may be regarded as helpful guidance but need not be followed if a decision-maker or the First-tier Tribunal is persuaded that there is a better approach. It is particularly important to bear this in mind in relation to older decisions of Social Security Commissioners because, until 1987, most rights of appeal to a Commissioner were not confined to points of law.

Where there is a conflict between precedents, a decision-maker or the First-tier Tribunal is generally free to choose between decisions of equal status. For these purposes, most decisions of the Upper Tribunal and decisions of Commissioners are of equal status. However, a decision-maker or First-tier Tribunal should generally prefer a reported decision to an unreported one unless the unreported decision was the later decision and the Commissioner or Upper Tribunal expressly decided not to follow the earlier reported decision. This is simply because the fact that a decision has been reported shows that at least half of the relevant judges of the Upper Tribunal or the Commissioners agreed with it at the time. A decision of a Tribunal of Commissioners (i.e. three Commissioners sitting together) or a decision of a three-judge panel of the Upper Tribunal must be preferred to a decision of a single Commissioner or a single judge of the Upper Tribunal.

A single judge of the Upper Tribunal will normally follow a decision of a single Commissioner or another judge of the Upper Tribunal, but is not bound to do so. A three-judge panel of the Upper Tribunal will generally follow a decision of another such panel or of a Tribunal of Commissioners, but similarly is not bound to do so, whereas a single judge of the Upper Tribunal will always follow such a decision.

Strictly speaking, the Northern Ireland Commissioners do not set binding precedent that must be followed in Great Britain but their decisions are relevant, due to the similarity of the legislation in Northern Ireland, and are usually regarded as highly persuasive with the result that, in practice, they are generally given as much weight as decisions of the Great Britain Commissioners. The same approach is taken in Northern Ireland to decisions of the Upper Tribunal on social security matters and to decisions of the Great Britain Commissioners. Similarly, the Upper Tribunal and the Upper Tribunal for Scotland are likely to find each other's decisions persuasive where the issues are the same, or similar.

Using this Book

Decisions of the superior courts in Great Britain and Northern Ireland on questions of legal principle are almost invariably followed by decision-makers, tribunals and the Upper Tribunal, even when they are not strictly binding because the relevant court was in a different part of the United Kingdom or exercised a parallel–but not superior–jurisdiction.

Decisions of the Court of Justice of the European Union come in two parts: the Opinion of the Advocate General and the decision of the Court. It is the decision of the Court which is binding. The Court is assisted by hearing the Opinion of the Advocate General before itself coming to a conclusion on the issue before it. The Court does not always follow its Advocate General. Where it does, the Opinion of the Advocate General often elaborates the arguments in greater detail than the single collegiate judgment of the Court. Within the European Union, courts and tribunals must apply decisions of the Court of Justice of the European Union, where relevant to cases before them, in preference to other authorities binding on them. This is no longer so in the United Kingdom, but it will still be necessary for courts and tribunals in the United Kingdom to take account of such decisions when issues of European Union law are relevant, and they are arguably bound by a decision of the Court of Justice on the interpretation of the Citizens' Rights provisions of the Withdrawal Agreement.

The European Court of Human Rights in Strasbourg is quite separate from the Court of Justice of the European Union in Luxembourg and serves a different purpose: interpreting and applying the European Convention on Human Rights, which is incorporated into United Kingdom law by the Human Rights Act 1998. Since October 2, 2000, public authorities in the United Kingdom, including courts, Commissioners, tribunals and decision-makers have been required to act in accordance with the incorporated provisions of the Convention, unless statute prevents this. They must take into account the Strasbourg case law and are required to interpret domestic legislation, so far as it is possible to do so, to give effect to the incorporated Convention rights. Any court or tribunal may declare secondary legislation incompatible with those rights and, in certain circumstances, invalidate it. Only the higher courts can declare a provision of primary legislation to be incompatible with those rights, but no court, tribunal or Upper Tribunal can invalidate primary legislation. The work of the Strasbourg Court and the impact of the Human Rights Act 1998 on social security are discussed in the commentary in Part IV of Volume III of this series.

See the note to s.3(2) of the Tribunals, Courts and Enforcement Act 2007 in Part III of Volume III of this series for a more detailed and technical consideration of the rules of precedent.

Other sources of information and commentary on social security law

For a comprehensive overview of the social security system in Great Britain, CPAG's *Welfare Benefits and Tax Credits Handbook*, published annually each spring, is unrivalled as a practical introduction from the claimant's viewpoint.

From a different perspective, the Department for Work and Pensions publishes the 14-volume *Decision Makers' Guide* and the newer *Advice for Decision Making*, which covers personal independence payment, universal credit and the "new" versions of Jobseeker's Allowance and Employment

Using this Book

and Support Allowance (search for the relevant guide by name at *https:// www.gov.uk* under the topic "Welfare"). Similarly, His Majesty's Revenue and Customs publish manuals relating to tax credits, child benefit and guardian's allowance, which they administer, see *https://www.gov.uk/govern ment/collections/hmrc-manuals*. (Note that the *Child Benefit Technical Manual* also covers guardian's allowance.) These guides and manuals are extremely useful but their interpretation of the law is not binding on tribunals and the courts, being merely internal guidance for the use of decision-makers.

There are a number of other sources of valuable information or commentary on social security case law: see in particular publications such as the *Journal of Social Security Law*, CPAG's *Welfare Rights Bulletin*, *Legal Action* and the *Adviser*. As far as online resources go there is little to beat *Rightsnet* (*https://www.rightsnet.org.uk*). This site contains a wealth of resources for people working in the welfare benefits field but of special relevance in this context are Commissioners'/Upper Tribunal Decisions section of the "Toolkit" area and also the "Briefcase" area which contains summaries of the decisions (with links to the full decisions). Sweet and Maxwell's online subscription service *Westlaw* is another valuable source (*https://legalsolutions. thomsonreuters.co.uk/en/products-services/westlaw-uk.html*), as is LexisNexis Lexis (*https://www.lexisnexis.co.uk*).

Conclusion

The internet provides a vast resource but a search needs to be focused. Social security schemes are essentially statutory and so in Great Britain the legislation which is set out in this series forms the basic structure of social security law. However, the case law shows how the legislation should be interpreted and applied. The commentary in this series should point the way to the case law relevant to each provision and the Internet can then be used to find it where that is necessary.

MAJOR CHANGES TO CREDITS AND BENEFITS

On the face of the statute book, child tax credit and working tax credit were abolished on February 1, 2019 (the date on which s.33(1)(f) of the Welfare Reform Act 2012, which repeals most of the Tax Credits Act 2002, came into force). In that case, why does Volume IV of this work remain in publication? This is because the abolition of tax credits was subject to savings provisions under which the majority of existing awards remain in place for the time being (Welfare Reform Act 2012 (Commencement No.32 and Savings and Transitional Provisions) Order 2019 (SI 2019/167)).

The abolition of tax credits is part of the project for implementing Universal Credit (UC). The main transfer to UC of recipients of what are termed 'legacy benefits', including both child tax credit and working tax credit, has been named 'managed migration' by the UK Government. However, before it had even begun, managed migration faced legal difficulties. For example, parts of the draft Universal Credit (Managed Migration Pilot and Miscellaneous Amendments) Regulations 2019 were declared unlawful in a decision given by the High Court in May 2019 (*R (TP, AR & SXC) v Secretary of State for Work & Pensions* [2019] EWHC 1127 (QB), subsequently upheld by the Court of Appeal in January 2020 in *R (TP, AR and SXC) v Secretary of State for Work and Pensions* [2020] EWCA Civ 37 (for more detail on the Government's response to the High Court's decision, see further the account in last year's edition of this Volume).

The legislation governing the UC managed migration pilot is contained in the new Part 4 of the Universal Credit (Transitional Provisions) Regulations 2014 (SI 2014/1230), inserted by reg.3(7) of the Universal Credit (Managed Migration Pilot and Miscellaneous Amendments) Regulations 2019 (SI 2019/1152) as from July 24, 2019 (which were formally laid before Parliament under the negative resolution procedure). During the 12-month test period, up to 10,000 existing 'legacy benefit' claimants (including tax credit claimants) were expected to be transferred to UC. However, due to the impact of the coronavirus crisis (from March 2020) the Harrogate pilot was suspended. Managed migration has since restarted in restricted areas under the Universal Credit (Transitional Provisions) (Amendment) Regulations 2022. The intention is to complete the whole process by the end of 2024. Past experience suggests that this target date may yet be pushed back further. For further details, see Vol.II in this series.

CHANGE OF NAME FROM DEPARTMENT OF SOCIAL SECURITY TO DEPARTMENT FOR WORK AND PENSIONS

The Secretaries of State for Education and Skills and for Work and Pensions Order 2002 (SI 2002/1397) makes provision for the change of name from the Department of Social Security to Department for Work and Pensions. Article 9(5) provides:

"(5) Subject to article 12 [which makes specific amendments], any enactment or instrument passed or made before the coming into force of this Order shall have effect, so far as may be necessary for the purposes of or in consequence of the entrusting to the Secretary of State for Work and Pensions of the social security functions, as if any reference to the Secretary of State for Social Security, to the Department of Social Security or to an officer of the Secretary of State for Social Security (including any reference which is to be construed as such as reference) were a reference to the Secretary of State for Work and Pensions, to the Department for Work and Pensions or, as the case may be, to an officer of the Secretary of State for Work and Pensions."

CHANGES IN TERMINOLOGY CONSEQUENT UPON THE ENTRY INTO FORCE OF THE TREATY OF LISBON

Note that The Treaty of Lisbon (Changes in Terminology) Order 2011 (SI 2011/1043) (which came into force on April 22, 2011) makes a number of changes to terminology used in primary and secondary legislation as a consequence of the entry into force of the Treaty of Lisbon. The Order accomplishes this by requiring certain terms in primary and secondary legislation to be read in accordance with the requirements of the Order. No substantive changes to the law are involved.

The changes are somewhat complex because of the different ways in which the term "Community" is used, and the abbreviations "EC" or "EEC" are used. References to the "European Community", "European Communities", "European Coal and Steel Communities", "the Community", "the EC" and "the EEC" are generally to be read as references to the "European Union."

The following table shows the more common usages involving the word "Community" in the first column which are now to be read in the form set out in the second column:

Original term	To be read as
Community treaties	EU treaties
Community institution	EU institution
Community instrument	EU instrument
Community obligation	EU obligation
Enforceable Community right	Enforceable EU right
Community law, or European Community law	EU law
Community legislation, or European Community legislation	EU legislation
Community provision, or European Community provision	EU provision

Provision is also made for changes to certain legislation relating to Wales in the Welsh language.

Relevant extracts from the Order can be found in *Volume III: Administration, Adjudication and the European Dimension*.

THE MARRIAGE (SAME SEX COUPLES) ACT 2013

The Marriage (Same Sex Couples) Act 2013 (c.30) provides in s.3 and Schedules 3 and 4 that the terms "marriage", "married couple" and being "married" in existing and future legislation in England and Wales are to be read as references to a marriage between persons of the same sex. The same approach is taken to any legislation about couples living together as if married. This is subject to certain specified exclusions contained in Schedule 4, and in any Order providing for a contrary approach to be taken.

Schedule 2 to The Marriage (Same Sex Couples) Act 2013 (Consequential and Contrary Provisions and Scotland) Order 2014 (SI 2014/560) contains a substantial list of contrary provisions to s.11(1) and (2) and paras 1–3 of Sch.3 to the 2013 Act. Most of these relate to specific enactments, but note that Pt 2 of the Schedule provides that s.11(1) and (2) do not apply to "EU instruments". This term is defined in Sch.1 to the European Communities Act 1972 (as amended) as "any instrument issued by an EU institution". It refers mainly to regulations, directives, decisions, recommendations and opinions issued by the institutions.

TABLE OF CASES

AA v HMRC (TC) [2012] UKUT 121 (AAC) **2.353**, **2.471**
AB v HMRC (TC) [2019] UKUT 410 (AAC) 2.275
AB v HMRC (TC) [2021] UKUT 328 (AAC) **1.353**, **1.403**
Abdirahman v Secretary of State for Work and Pensions; Ullusow v Secretary of State for Work and Pensions; Abdirahman v Leicester City Council [2007] EWCA Civ 657; [2008] 1 W.L.R. 254; [2007] 4 All E.R. 882; [2007] 7 WLUK 105; [2007] 3 C.M.L.R. 37; [2007] Eu. L.R. 814 .... 2.486
Aberdeen City Council v LS. *See* Aberdeen City Council v Nisbet
Aberdeen City Council v Nisbet [2020] 12 WLUK 547; 2021 G.W.D. 7-98; [2021] UT 1 .... 14.6, 14.64, 14.112
Aberdeenshire Council v SS [2020] 3 WLUK 516; 2020 G.W.D. 16-224; [2020] UT 25 .... 14.11
ABM v HMRC [2018] UKUT 317 (AAC) 2.155
AC v HMRC (CTC) [2018] UKUT 233 (AAC) 1.324
AD v Secretary of State for Work and Pensions [2009] UKUT 46 (AAC) 3.5
AG v HMRC (TC) [2013] UKUT 530 (AAC) **1.405**, 2.497
AG v HMRC (TC) [2017] UKUT 67 (AAC) **2.136**
AG v HMRC & AG (TC) [2018] UKUT 318 (AAC) 2.275
AH v HMRC (TC) [2019] UKUT 5 (AAC) 2.209, 2.220
AH (Sudan) v Secretary of State for the Home Department; sub nom. Secretary of State for the Home Department v AH (Sudan) [2007] UKHL 49; [2008] 1 A.C. 678; [2007] 3 W.L.R. 832; [2008] 4 All E.R. 190; [2007] 11 WLUK 328; [2008] Imm. A.R. 289; [2008] I.N.L.R. 100; (2007) 151 S.J.L.B. 1500 .... 14.102
Ahmed v Russell [2023] UT 7; 2023 S.L.T. (Tr) 33; [2023] 2 WLUK 371; 2023 G.W.D. 8-90 .... 14.11
AK v Social Security Scotland [2024] UT 5; [2024] 2 WLUK 218; 2024 G.W.D. 13-105 .... 14.61
Alabaster v Barclays Bank Plc and Secretary of State for Social Security. *See* Alabaster v Woolwich Plc (CA)
Alabaster v Woolwich Plc (C-147/02) EU:C:2004:192; [2004] E.C.R. I-3101; [2004] 3 WLUK 831; [2004] 2 C.M.L.R. 9; [2005] All E.R. (EC) 490; [2004] C.E.C. 261; [2005] I.C.R. 695; [2004] I.R.L.R. 486 .... 1.104, 5.38
Alabaster v Woolwich Plc (Reference to ECJ) [2002] EWCA Civ 211; [2002] 2 WLUK 667; [2002] 1 C.M.L.R. 56; [2002] I.R.L.R. 420 .... **1.104**
Alabaster v Woolwich Plc; sub nom. Alabaster v Barclays Bank Plc (formerly Woolwich Plc) [2005] EWCA Civ 508; [2005] 5 WLUK 2; [2005] 2 C.M.L.R. 19; [2005] Eu. L.R. 824; [2005] I.C.R. 1246; [2005] I.R.L.R. 576 .... 1.104, 5.38
Alase v Iveson [2022] UT 29; [2022] 12 WLUK 250; 2023 G.W.D. 5-53 .... 14.11
Ali v Birmingham City Council; Tomlinson v Birmingham City Council; Ibrahim v Birmingham City Council; Moran v Manchester City Council; R. (on the application of Aweys) v Birmingham City Council; sub nom. Birmingham City Council v Ali [2010] UKSC 8; [2010] 2 A.C. 39; [2010] 2 W.L.R. 471; [2010] 2 All E.R. 175; [2010] P.T.S.R. 524; [2010] 2 WLUK 494; [2010] H.R.L.R. 18; [2010] U.K.H.R.R. 417; [2010] H.L.R. 22; [2010] B.L.G.R. 401; (2010) 154(7) S.J.L.B. 37 .... **1.326**
AP v HMRC (TC) [2015] UKUT 580 (AAC) **1.381**
AR-L v HMRC (TC) [2015] UKUT 303 (AAC) **1.404**
Arshad v Khawaja [2021] UT 33; [2021] 8 WLUK 349; 2022 Hous. L.R. 2; 2022 G.W.D. 9-140 .... 14.93
Arthur v Revenue and Customs Commissioners [2017] EWCA Civ 1756; [2018] S.T.C. 1; [2017] 11 WLUK 55; [2017] B.T.C. 33; [2017] S.T.I. 2271; [2018] AACR 10 .... 1.277, 2.482
AS v HMRC (CB) [2013] NI Comm. 15 .... 3.34, 3.40

xli

Table of Cases

AS v HMRC (TC) [2017] UKUT 361 (AAC); [2018] AACR 14 ....2.168
AT v HMRC (TC) [2009] UKUT 78 (AAC)..1.361
Awodiya v Revenue and Customs Commissioners [2019] EWHC 251 (Admin); [2019] 2 WLUK 177 ....1.364
Bank Mellat v HM Treasury [2013] UKSC 39; [2014] A.C. 700; [2013] 3 W.L.R. 179; [2013] 4 All E.R. 533; [2013] 6 WLUK 527; [2013] H.R.L.R. 30; [2013] Lloyd's Rep. F.C. 580..2.297
Barber v Secretary of State for Social Security. See R. (on the application of Barber) v Secretary of State for Work and Pensions
Barr Environmental Ltd v Revenue Scotland [2022] UT 11; [2022] 5 WLUK 361; 2022 G.W.D. 18-270 ....14.3, 14.95, **14.99**
Belgian Linguistic Case (A/6) [1968] 7 WLUK 102; (1979-80) 1 E.H.R.R. 252 ECtHR..2.294
Boyle v Ford [2023] UT 4; [2023] 1 WLUK 394; 2023 Hous. L.R. 21; 2023 G.W.D. 6-70 ....**14.11**
Bressol v Gouvernement de la Communauté Française [2010] 3 C.M.L.R. 559 ....3.40
Brown v Chief Adjudication Officer [1996] 10 WLUK 141; [1997] I.C.R. 266; [1997] I.R.L.R. 110; (1996) 93(42) L.S.G. 28; (1996) 140 S.J.L.B. 221; CA (Civ Div) **1.77**
C v HMRC (TC) [2019] UKUT 69 (AAC)..1.324
Campus Living Villages UK Ltd v HMRC and Sexton [2016] UKFTT 738 (TC) **1.100, 5.36, 5.38**
CB v HMRC and AE (CHB) [2016] UKUT 506 (AAC)................. 1.59, 1.194, 2.448, 3.59
CD v Social Security Scotland [2024] UT 12; 2024 S.L.T. (Tr) 53; [2024] 3 WLUK 114; 2024 G.W.D. 10-87 ....13.2, 13.48, 13.170
Cenlon Finance Co Ltd v Ellwood (Inspector of Taxes); sub nom. Tableau Holdings v Williams [1962] A.C. 782; [1962] 2 W.L.R. 871; [1962] 1 All E.R. 854; [1962] 3 WLUK 9; 40 T.C. 176; (1962) 41 A.T.C. 11; [1962] T.R. 1; (1962) 106 S.J. 280 HL..1.23
Centre Public d'Aide Sociale, Courcelles v Lebon (316/85) EU:C:1987:302; [1987] E.C.R. 2811; [1987] 6 WLUK 218; [1989] 1 C.M.L.R. 337..1.632
Chester v Secretary of State for Social Security. See R. (on the application of Chester) v Secretary of State for Social Security
Chief Adjudication Officer v Ellis. See R(IS) 22/95
CI v HMRC (TC) [2014] UKUT 158 (AAC)..**1.326**
Clixby v Pountney [1968] Ch. 719; [1968] 2 W.L.R. 865; [1968] 1 All E.R. 802; [1967] 12 WLUK 34; 44 T.C. 575; (1967) 46 A.T.C. 398; [1967] T.R. 383; 117 N.L.J. 1343; (1968) 112 S.J. 16 Ch D 1.379
CM v HMRC (TC) [2010] UKUT 400 (AAC)..2.274
CM v HMRC (TC) [2014] UKUT 272 (AAC)..2.448
Colraine v Bridges [2023] UT 9; [2023] 1 WLUK 493; 2023 G.W.D. 9-96 ....14.11
Cowan v Somasundaram [2021] UT 4; [2020] 12 WLUK 610; 2021 G.W.D. 13-195......14.11
Customs and Excise Commissioners v Medway Draughting and Technical Services Ltd; Customs and Excise Commissioners v Adplates Offset Ltd [1989] S.T.C. 346; [1989] 2 WLUK 140; [1989] B.T.C. 5070; [1989] C.O.D. 497 QBD 1.380
Denham v HMRC and HT Personnel Ltd [2016] UKFTT 668 (TC); [2016] 9 WLUK 405 ....1.231
Devine v Bailo [2022] UT 14; [2022] 5 WLUK 439; 2022 G.W.D. 20-280 ....**14.97**
DF v HMRC (TC) [2016] UKUT 47 (AAC) 1.337
DG v HMRC (TC) [2013] UKUT 631 (AAC)..**1.279**
DG v HMRC and EG (TC) [2016] UKUT 505 (AAC) 1.324, 1.342, 1.361
Doherty v City of Edinburgh Council [2021] UT 10; [2021] 1 WLUK 524; 2021 G.W.D. 13-200 ....**14.109**
Dymoke v Best [2020] UT 18; [2020] 3 WLUK 473; 2020 Hous. L.R. 56; 2020 G.W.D. 18-254 ....14.66
Eba v Advocate General for Scotland [2011] UKSC 29; [2012] 1 A.C. 710; [2011] 3 W.L.R. 149; [2011] P.T.S.R. 1095; [2011] S.T.C. 1705; 2012 S.C. (U.K.S.C.) 1; 2011 S.L.T. 768; [2011] 6 WLUK 522; [2011] Imm. A.R. 745; [2011] S.T.I. 1941; (2011) 108(27) L.S.G. 24; (2011) 161 N.L.J. 917..14.22
Edenred (UK Group) Ltd v HM Treasury [2015] UKSC 45; [2016] 1 All E.R. 763; [2015] P.T.S.R. 1088; [2015] 7 WLUK 2; [2015] 3 C.M.L.R. 47........................1.914
Edwards (Inspector of Taxes) v Clinch [1982] A.C. 845; [1981] 3 W.L.R. 707; [1981] 3 All E.R. 543; [1981] S.T.C. 617; [1981] 10 WLUK 235; 56 T.C. 367; [1981] T.R. 393; (1981) 125 S.J. 762 HL..2.215

Table of Cases

EG v HMRC (TC) [2011] UKUT 467 (AAC) **1.277**, 2.471
EM v HMRC (TC) [2010] UKUT 323 (AAC) 1.276
Ensign Tankers (Leasing) Ltd v Stokes (Inspector of Taxes) [1992] 1 A.C. 655; [1992] 2 W.L.R. 469; [1992] 2 All E.R. 275; [1992] S.T.C. 226; [1992] 3 WLUK 169; 64 T.C. 617; [1992] S.T.I. 364; (1992) 89(17) L.S.G. 49; (1992) 136 S.J.L.B. 89 HL 2.230
FK v HMRC [2009] UKUT 134 (AAC) **2.471**
Flemington Care Home v Revenue and Customs [2017] UKFTT 300 (TC) 1.233
Flemming v Secretary of State for Work and Pensions. *See* R(G) 2/02
FZ (Democratic Republic of Congo) v Secretary of State for the Home Department; sub nom. Zoumbas v Secretary of State for the Home Department [2013] UKSC 74; [2013] 1 W.L.R. 3690; [2014] 1 All E.R. 638; 2014 S.C. (U.K.S.C.) 75; [2013] 11 WLUK 715; [2014] 1 F.C.R. 141; [2014] Imm. A.R. 479; [2014] I.N.L.R. 262 .... 2.297
Garrett v Your Place Property Management Ltd [2020] 1 WLUK 604; 2020 G.W.D. 35-462; [2020] UT 32 .... 14.11
Garrett v Your Place Property Management Ltd [2020] 6 WLUK 619; 2020 G.W.D. 35-457; [2020] UT 34 .... 14.11
GC v HMRC (TC) [2014] UKUT 251 (AAC) 2.129, **2.488**
GG v HMRC and DC (CHB) [2018] UKUT 223 (AAC) 2.448
Gillespie v Northern Health and Social Services Board (No.2); Todd v Eastern Health and Social Services Board [1997] N.I. 190; [1997] 4 WLUK 410; [1997] Eu. L.R. 566; [1997] I.R.L.R. 410 CA (NI) 1.104
GJ v HMRC (TC) [2013] UKUT 561 (AAC) 2.273
GL v Revenue and Customs Commissioners [2023] UKUT 100 (AAC); [2023] 1 W.L.R. 4481; [2023] 4 WLUK 509; [2023] B.T.C. 524 .... **1.270**, 2.488
Gladders v Prior (Inspector of Taxes) [2003] 2 WLUK 895; [2003] S.T.C. (S.C.D.) 245; [2003] S.T.I. 946 Sp Commrs 1.380
Goodyear v Highland Council [2022] UT 4; [2022] 2 WLUK 524; 2022 G.W.D. 14-221 .... 14.11, 14.87
Gray (Inspector of Taxes) v Matheson [1993] 1 W.L.R. 1130; [1993] S.T.C. 178; [1993] 1 WLUK 838; 65 T.C. 577; [1993] S.T.I. 214; (1993) 90(10) L.S.G. 36; (1993) 137 S.J.L.B. 46 Ch D 1.23
Great Western Rly Co v Bater (Surveyor of Taxes) [1920] 3 K.B. 266; [1920] 6 WLUK 8 KBD 2.215
Grzelczyk v Centre Public d'Aide Sociale d'Ottignies Louvain la Neuve (C-184/99) EU:C:2001:458; [2001] E.C.R. I-6193; [2001] 9 WLUK 285; [2002] 1 C.M.L.R. 19; [2003] All E.R. (EC) 385; [2002] I.C.R. 566 .... 1.632
Gusa v Minister for Social Protection (C-442/16) EU:C:2017:1004; [2018] P.T.S.R. 1699; [2017] 12 WLUK 541; [2018] 2 C.M.L.R. 23; [2018] C.E.C. 971 .... 3.34
HA v HMRC (TC) [2015] UKUT 708 (AAC) 1.277, 2.482
Hamilton v Glasgow Housing Association Ltd [2020] 9 WLUK 432; 2021 Hous. L.R. 22; 2020 G.W.D. 38-483; [2020] UT 37 .... 14.95
Hillenbrand v Inland Revenue Commissioners, 1966 S.L.T. 213; [1966] 2 WLUK 58; 42 T.C. 617; (1966) 45 A.T.C. 224; [1966] T.R. 201 IH (1 Div) 1.379
Hinchy v Secretary of State for Work and Pensions [2005] UKHL 16; [2005] 1 W.L.R. 967; [2005] 2 All E.R. 129; (2005) 102(17) L.S.G. 32; (2005) 149 S.J.L.B. 299 .... 1.293, 1.325
HMRC v AB [2021] UKUT 209 (AAC) **2.48**, 2.49
HMRC v Adnan [2022] CSIH 2; 2022 S.L.T. 97; [2022] 1 WLUK 164; 2022 G.W.D. 2-32 .... 2.471
HMRC v AS (TC) [2023] UKUT 67 (AAC); [2023] 3 WLUK 657; [2023] B.T.C. 511 .... 2.119
HMRC v CB (TC) [2013] UKUT 484 (AAC) 2.175
HMRC v DH [2009] UKUT 24 (AAC) 1.310, 2.272, 2.274
HMRC v ED (TC) [2021] UKUT 195 (AAC); [2021] 7 WLUK 666 .... 1.342, 2.347
HMRC v HD and GP (CHB) [2017] UKUT 11 (AAC) 3.34
HMRC v JS, EL and LG [2021] UKUT 264 (AAC) 11.2
HMRC v PD (TC) [2012] UKUT 230 (AAC) 1.276, 1.279
HMRC v PS (TC) [2012] UKUT 492 (AAC) 2.396
HMRC v RS [2022] UKUT 246 (AAC); [2022] 9 WLUK 308 .... **2.43**, 2.348
HMRC v Ruas. *See* Revenue and Customs Commissioners v Ruas
HMRC v Secretary of State for Work and Pensions (TC) [2022] UKUT 350 (AAC); [2022] 12 WLUK 590 .... **2.47**

Table of Cases

HMRC v Secretary of State for Work and Pensions [2023] UKUT 9 (AAC); [2023] 1 WLUK 366 ....**2.49**
HMRC v SJ (TC) [2018] UKUT 83 (AAC) 1.371
HMRC v TK (TC) [2016] UKUT 45 (AAC) **2.140**
HO v HMRC (TC) [2018] UKUT 105 (AAC) 1.333, 1.342, 1.403, 1.407
Hockenjos v Secretary of State for Social Security [2004] EWCA Civ 1749; [2004] 12 WLUK 618; [2005] Eu. L.R. 385; [2005] I.R.L.R. 471; [2005] 1 F.L.R. 1009; [2005] 1 F.C.R. 286; [2005] Fam. Law 464; (2005) 102(7) L.S.G. 27 ....1.310
Hudson v Hathway [2022] EWCA Civ 1648; [2023] 2 W.L.R. 1227; [2022] 12 WLUK 175; [2023] 1 F.L.R. 1252; [2023] H.L.R. 13; [2023] W.T.L.R. 207; 25 I.T.E.L.R. 787; [2023] 2 P. & C.R. DG2 ....14.52
Hudson v Humbles [1965] 1 WLUK 1; 42 T.C. 380; (1965) 44 A.T.C. 124; [1965] T.R. 135; (1965) 109 S.J. 315 ....1.379
Hughes v Glasgow City Council [2021] UT 12; [2021] 2 WLUK 579; 2021 Hous. L.R. 41; 2021 G.W.D. 30-395 ....**14.11**
Humphreys v Revenue and Customs Commissioners [2012] UKSC 18; [2012] AACR 46; [2012] 1 W.L.R. 1545; [2012] 4 All E.R. 27; [2012] P.T.S.R. 1024; [2012] 5 WLUK 496; [2012] 3 F.C.R. 403; [2012] H.R.L.R. 21; [2012] Eq. L.R. 714; [2012] S.T.I. 1664; (2012) 162 N.L.J. 712; (2012) 156(20) S.J.L.B. 31 ....**1.310**
IRC v Lysaght; sub nom. Lysaght v Inland Revenue Commissioners [1928] A.C. 234; [1928] All E.R. Rep. 575; [1928] 3 WLUK 25; 13 T.C. 511 HL..............................**2.482**
JF v HMRC (TC) [2017] UKUT 334 (AAC) 2.124
JH v HMRC (CHB) [2015] UKUT 479 (AAC); [2016] AACR 15 .... **3.5**
JH v HMRC (TC) [2015] UKUT 397 (AAC)...1.279
JI v HMRC (TC) [2013] UKUT 199 (AAC).......**1.22**, **1.276**, 1.414, 1.415, 2.274, 2.347, 2.456
JL v Calderdale MBC [2022] UKUT 9 (AAC); [2022] P.T.S.R. 808; [2022] 1 WLUK 361 .... **2.48**, 2.49
JL v HMRC (TC) [2013] UKUT 325 (AAC) 1.278, **2.384**
JL v HMRC (TC) [2019] UKUT 94 (AAC) 2.284
JN v HMRC (TC) [2010] UKUT 288 (AAC) **2.284**
Jones v Leeming; sub nom. Leeming v Jones; Leeming v Jones (Inspector of Taxes) [1930] A.C. 415; [1930] 3 WLUK 40 HL...2.230
JP v HMRC (TC) [2013] UKUT 519 (AAC) **1.406, 2.499**
JQ v HMRC (TC) [2020] UKUT 340 (AAC) 2.211
JR v HMRC (TC) [2009] UKUT 18 (AAC)...3.31
JR v HMRC (TC) [2015] UKUT 192 (AAC) 1.335, 1.406
JW v HMRC (TC) [2015] UKUT 369 (AAC) 1.345, 1.406, 1.407
JW v HMRC [2019] UKUT 114 (AAC)..2.124
JY v HMRC (TC) [2016] UKUT 407 (AAC) **1.337**
Kerr v Department for Social Development [2004] UKHL 23; [2004] 1 W.L.R. 1372; [2004] 4 All E.R. 385; [2004] N.I. 397; [2004] 5 WLUK 98 ....14.61
KI v Revenue and Customs Commissioners (TC) [2023] UKUT 212 (AAC); [2023] 8 WLUK 335 .... 2.382, **2.497**
Kindreich v Countrywide Residential Lettings Ltd (t/a Slater Hogg & Howison) [2022] UT 16; [2022] 6 WLUK 489; 2022 G.W.D. 25-348 ....**14.61**
King v United Kingdom (No.2) (13881/02) [2005] S.T.C. 438; [2004] 11 WLUK 420; (2005) 41 E.H.R.R. 2; 76 T.C. 699; [2007] B.T.C. 85; 7 I.T.L. Rep. 339; [2004] S.T.I. 2396 ECtHR 1.380
KN v HMRC [2009] UKUT 79 (AAC) **2.275**
Ladiverova v Commissioners for HMRC and Chokdee Ltd [2016] UKFTT 244 (TC).....1.208
Leeves v Chief Adjudication Officer [1998] 11 WLUK 101; [1999] E.L.R. 90 CA (Civ Div) 2.240
Levene v IRC [1928] A.C. 217; [1928] All E.R. Rep. 746; [1928] 3 WLUK 26; 13 T.C. 486 HL..2.482
LS & RS v HMRC (TC) [2017] UKUT 257 (AAC); [2018] AACR 2 .... 1.324, 1.331, **1.337**
Lune Metal Products Ltd (In Administration), Re [2006] EWCA Civ 1720; [2007] Bus. L.R. 589; [2006] 12 WLUK 377; [2007] B.C.C. 217; [2007] 2 B.C.L.C. 746 ....**2.49**
LV v HMRC (TC) [2010] UKUT 483 (AAC) **2.382, 2.387**
Mahmood v Glasgow West Enterprises Ltd [2021] UT 29; [2021] 1 WLUK 644; 2022 G.W.D. 3-35 .... **14.110**
Malloch v Bernisdale Homes Ltd [2021] UT 34; [2021] 9 WLUK 557; 2022 G.W.D. 8-133 .... **14.123**
Mansfield v Thomson [2019] 8 WLUK 306; 2020 G.W.D. 12-167; [2020] UT 14 ....14.11

Table of Cases

Martínez Sala v Freistaat Bayern (C-85/96) EU:C:1998:217; [1998] E.C.R. I-2691 ..... 1.632
McLaughlin's Application for Judicial Review, Re [2018] UKSC 48; [2018] 1 W.L.R. 4250; [2019] 1 All E.R. 471; [2018] 8 WLUK 268; [2018] H.R.L.R. 21; 46 B.H.R.C. 268 .... 2.295
MD v HMRC (TC) [2017] UKUT 106 (AAC) **1.403**, 1.407
ME v HMRC (TC) [2017] UKUT 227 (AAC) 1.333, 1.335, 1.336
Meyers v Adjudication Officer (C-116/94) EU:C:1995:247; [1995] E.C.R. I-2131; [1995] 7 WLUK 174; [1996] 1 C.M.L.R. 461; [1995] All E.R. (E.C.) 705; [1995] I.R.L.R. 498 .... 1.320
MH v HMRC (TC) [2016] UKUT 79 (AAC) 2.132
MI v HMRC [2009] UKUT 73 (AAC) 2.471
Midlothian Council v PD [2019] UT 52; [2019] 8 WLUK 249; 2019 G.W.D. 34-539 .... **14.103**
Midlothian Council v PD [2021] UT 17; 2021 S.L.T. (Tr) 1; [2019] 11 WLUK 830; 2021 G.W.D. 14-204 .... **14.101**
MK v HMRC (TC) [2018] UKUT 238 (ACC) 2.347, 2.348, 2.471
Morrell v Secretary of State for Work and Pensions [2003] EWCA Civ 526; [2003] 4 WLUK 400 .... 2.240
Moxon v IPSOS RSL Ltd Ltd [2002] 9 WLUK 61; [2002] All E.R. (D) 109 EAT 4.13
Mucelli v Albania; Moulai v France [2009] UKHL 2; [2009] 1 W.L.R. 276; [2009] 3 All E.R. 1035; [2009] 1 WLUK 306; [2009] Extradition L.R. 122; (2009) 153(4) S.J.L.B. 28 .... 1.415
Mulvey v Secretary of State for Social Security, 1997 S.C. (H.L.) 105; 1997 S.L.T. 753; 1997 S.C.L.R. 348; [1997] 3 WLUK 269; [1997] B.P.I.R. 696; 1997 G.W.D. 11-488 HL 1.648
Murphy's Application for Judicial Review, Re [2023] NIKB 119; [2023] 12 WLUK 552 .... **1.195**
Murray Group Holdings Ltd v Revenue and Customs Commissioners; sub nom. RFC 2012 Plc (In Liquidation) (formerly Rangers Football Club Plc) v Advocate General for Scotland, Revenue and Customs Commissioners v Murray Group Holdings Ltd, Advocate General for Scotland v Murray Group Holdings Ltd [2015] CSIH 77; [2016] S.T.C. 468; 2016 S.C. 201; 2015 S.L.T. 765; 2016 S.C.L.R. 485; [2015] 11 WLUK 80; [2015] B.T.C. 36; 2015 G.W.D. 36-583 .... 14.11, 14.123
NA v HMRC (TC) [2016] UKUT 404 (AAC) 1.337, **2.170**
Natwest Markets Plc v Bilta (UK) Ltd (In Liquidation) [2021] EWCA Civ 680; [2021] 5 WLUK 66 .... **14.99**
NB v HMRC (TC) [2016] NI Com 47; [2018] AACR 26 .... 1.320, 2.171
NB v Social Security Scotland [2023] UT 35 .... 13.2, 13.364, 14.61
Nethermere (St Neots) Ltd v Gardiner; sub nom. Nethermere (St Neots) Ltd v Taverna [1984] 5 WLUK 26; [1984] I.C.R. 612; [1984] I.R.L.R. 240; (1984) 81 L.S.G. 2147; (1984) 134 N.L.J. 544 CA (Civ Div) 2.131
New Lanark Hotels Ltd v Office of the Scottish Charity Regulator [2020] UT 9; [2020] 2 WLUK 271; 2020 G.W.D. 9-130 .... 14.12
New Lanark Trading Ltd v Office of the Scottish Charity Regulator [2020] UT 10; [2020] 2 WLUK 266; 2020 G.W.D. 9-129 .... 14.12
NN v HMRC (TC) [2019] UKUT 386 (AAC) 2.130
North Yorkshire Police Authority v Revenue and Customs Commissioners; sub nom. Wade v North Yorkshire Police Authority [2011] 1 WLUK 40; [2011] I.R.L.R. 393 .... 1.102, **5.6**
Nu-Swift International Ltd v Mallinson [1978] 10 WLUK 85; [1979] I.C.R. 157; [1978] I.R.L.R. 537 EAT 1.100
OFCOM v Morrissey and Information Commissioner [2011] UKUT 116 (AAC); [2012] AACR 1 .... 1.405
Office of the Scottish Charity Regulator v New Lanark Hotels Ltd [2021] CSIH 7; 2021 S.L.T. 490; [2021] 1 WLUK 340; 2021 G.W.D. 5-60 .... 14.12
OM v HMRC (CTC) [2019] UKUT 263 (AAC) 2.124
Ostendorf v Rollos Solicitors & Estate Agents [2021] UT 11; [2021] 2 WLUK 588; 2021 Hous. L.R. 49; 2021 G.W.D. 30-403 .... 14.11
Oxfam v Revenue and Customs Commissioners [2009] EWHC 3078 (Ch); [2010] S.T.C. 686; [2009] 11 WLUK 709; [2010] B.V.C. 108; [2010] A.C.D. 50; [2010] S.T.I. 556 .... 1.405
Pandey v Revenue and Customs (Income Tax/Corporation Tax: Penalty) [2017] UKFTT 216 (TC) 1.407

xlv

Table of Cases

Patmalniece v Secretary of State for Work and Pensions [2011] UKSC 11; [2011] 1 W.L.R. 783; [2011] 3 All E.R. 1; [2011] P.T.S.R. 680; [2011] 3 WLUK 509; [2011] 2 C.M.L.R. 45; [2011] Eq. L.R. 508; (2011) 108(13) L.S.G. 23; (2011) 155(11) S.J.L.B. 31 ....3.40
PD v HMRC and CD (TC) [2010] UKUT 159 (AAC).................................... 1.300, 2.448
PD v Midlothian Council [2021] UT 19; [2020] 10 WLUK 619; 2021 G.W.D. 14-206 ....14.123
Petrovic v Austria (20458/92) [1998] 3 WLUK 568; (2001) 33 E.H.R.R. 14; 4 B.H.R.C. 232; [1998] H.R.C.D. 366 ECtHR.. 2.295, 2.297
PG v HMRC and NG (TC) [2016] UKUT 216 (AAC); [2016] AACR 45..................**2.274, 2.275, 2.448**
PM v United Kingdom (6638/03); sub nom. M v United Kingdom (6638/03) [2005] S.T.C. 1566; [2005] 7 WLUK 565; [2005] 3 F.C.R. 101; (2006) 42 E.H.R.R. 45; 18 B.H.R.C. 668; 7 I.T.L. Rep. 970 ECtHR **1.380**
Point West GR Ltd v Bassi [2020] EWCA Civ 795; [2020] 1 W.L.R. 4102; [2020] 6 WLUK 307; [2020] H.L.R. 45...14.6
PW v HMRC (TC) [2018] UKUT 12 (AAC) 2.155
R. (on the application of Barber) v Secretary of State for Work and Pensions; sub nom. Barber v Secretary of State for Work and Pensions [§ (Admin); [2002] 7 WLUK 468; [2002] 2 F.L.R. 1181; [2002] Fam. Law 888; (2002) 99(36) L.S.G. 40.........1.195
R. (on the application of Bidar) v Ealing LBC (C-209/03) EU:C:2005:169; [2005] Q.B. 812; [2005] 2 W.L.R. 1078; [2005] E.C.R. I-2119; [2005] 3 WLUK 503; [2005] 2 C.M.L.R. 3; [2005] All E.R. (EC) 687; [2005] C.E.C. 607; [2005] E.L.R. 404 .... 1.632, 1.633
R. (on the application of Chester) v Secretary of State for Social Security [2001] EWHC Admin 1119; [2001] 12 WLUK 189..1.195
R. (on the application of D) v Secretary of State for Work and Pensions [2004] EWCA Civ 1468 ....3.40
R. (on the application of DA) v Secretary of State for Work and Pensions; R. (on the application of DS) v Secretary of State for Work and Pensions [2019] UKSC 21; [2019] 1 W.L.R. 3289; [2020] 1 All E.R. 573; [2019] P.T.S.R. 1072; [2019] 5 WLUK 194; [2019] H.R.L.R. 12; [2019] H.L.R. 31...1.900
R. (on the application of Ford) v Revenue and Customs Commissioners; sub nom. R. (on the application of Ford) v Board of Inland Revenue [2005] EWHC 1109 (Admin); [2005] 5 WLUK 452 ....1.195
R. (on the application of JS) v Secretary of State for Work and Pensions; sub nom. R. (on the application of SG) v Secretary of State for Work and Pensions [2015] UKSC 16; [2015] 1 W.L.R. 1449; [2015] 4 All E.R. 939; [2015] P.T.S.R. 471; [2015] 3 WLUK 507; [2015] H.R.L.R. 5; [2015] H.L.R. 21; (2015) 18 C.C.L. Rep. 215.................. 2.297
R. (on the application of Public Law Project) v Secretary of State for Justice; sub nom. R. (on the application of Public Law Project) v Lord Chancellor; Public Law Project v Lord Chancellor [2016] UKSC 39; [2016] A.C. 1531; [2016] 3 W.L.R. 387; [2017] 2 All E.R. 423; [2016] 7 WLUK 266; [2016] H.R.L.R. 17 ....1.403
R. (on the application of RB) v First-tier Tribunal (Review) [2010] UKUT 160 (AAC); [2010] 5 WLUK 801; [2010] M.H.L.R. 192; [2010] AACR 41..............................14.6
R. (on the application of Saleem) v Secretary of State for the Home Department. See R. v Secretary of State for the Home Department Ex p. Saleem
R. (on the application of SC) v Secretary of State for Work and Pensions [2019] EWCA Civ 615; [2019] 1 W.L.R. 5687; [2019] 4 All E.R. 787; [2019] 4 WLUK 252 ....2.288, 2.294, 2.304
R. (on the application of SG and JS) v Secretary of State for Work and Pensions. See R. (on the application of JS) v Secretary of State for Work and Pensions
R. (on the application of Sier) v Cambridge City Council Housing Benefit Review Board [2001] EWCA Civ 1523; [2001] 10 WLUK 174..2.499
R. (on the application of TD) v Secretary of State for Work And Pensions [2020] EWCA Civ 618; [2020] 5 WLUK 91 ....2.35
R. v Allen (Brian Roger) [2001] UKHL 45; [2002] 1 A.C. 509; [2001] 3 W.L.R. 843; [2001] 4 All E.R. 768; [2001] S.T.C. 1537; [2001] 10 WLUK 348; [2002] 1 Cr. App. R. 18; [2002] H.R.L.R. 4; 74 T.C. 263; [2001] B.T.C. 421; 4 I.T.L. Rep. 140; [2001] S.T.I. 1348 ....1.380
R. v Barnet LBC Ex p. Shah; Akbarali v Brent LBC; Abdullah v Shropshire CC; Shabpar v Barnet LBC; Shah (Jitendra) v Barnet LBC; Ablack v Inner London Education Authority; R. v Shropshire CC Ex p. Abdullah [1983] 2 A.C. 309;

Table of Cases

[1983] 2 W.L.R. 16; [1983] 1 All E.R. 226; [1982] 12 WLUK 164; 81 L.G.R. 305; (1983) 133 N.L.J. 61; (1983) 127 S.J. 36 HL 2.482
R. v Emmett (Brian); R. v Emmett (Michael) [1998] A.C. 773; [1997] 3 W.L.R. 1119; [1997] 4 All E.R. 737; [1997] 11 WLUK 229; [1998] 1 Cr. App. R. 247; [1998] Crim. L.R. 413; (1997) 94(46) L.S.G. 29; (1997) 147 N.L.J. 1690; (1997) 141 S.J.L.B. 247 HL 1.403
R. v Secretary of State for the Home Department Ex p. Saleem; sub nom. R. v Immigration Appeal Tribunal Ex p. Saleem; Saleem v Secretary of State for the Home Department [2001] 1 W.L.R. 443; [2000] 4 All E.R. 814; [2000] 6 WLUK 231; [2000] Imm. A.R. 529; [2000] I.N.L.R. 413 CA (Civ Div) 2.450
R(CJ) v Secretary of State for Work and Pensions [2017] UKUT 324 (AAC); [2018] AACR 5 ....1.403
Ramanathan v Patel [2023] UT 8; 2023 S.L.T. (Tr) 1; [2023] 1 WLUK 491; 2023 G.W.D. 9-93 ....**14.52**
Ransom (Inspector of Taxes) v Higgs; Restorick v Godber, Parry; Motley v Higgs Trustees; Kilmorie (Aldridge) Ltd v Dickinson (Inspector of Taxes); Grant (Inspector of Taxes) v Downes Settlement Trustees; Dickinson (Inspector of Taxes) v Downes; Motley (Inspector of Taxes) v Higgs Settlement Trustees; sub nom. Dickinson v Kilmorie (Aldridge) Downes [1974] 1 W.L.R. 1594; [1974] 3 All E.R. 949; [1974] S.T.C. 539; [1974] 11 WLUK 66; [1974] T.R. 281; (1974) 118 S.J. 849 HL 2.230
Rasmussen v Denmark (A/87); sub nom. Rasmussen v Denmark (8777/79) [1984] 11 WLUK 246; (1985) 7 E.H.R.R. 371 ECtHR...2.297
Reddy v General Medical Council [2012] EWCA Civ 310; [2012] 3 WLUK 413; [2012] C.P. Rep. 27...1.415
Reina v Landeskreditbank Baden-Württemberg (C-65/81) EU:C:1982:6; [1982] E.C.R. 33; [1982] 1 WLUK 665; [1982] 1 C.M.L.R. 744...1.632
Revenue and Customs Commissioners v Arrbab; sub nom. Arrbab v Revenue and Customs Commissioners [2024] EWCA Civ 16; [2024] 3 W.L.R. 295; [2024] 1 WLUK 198; [2024] B.T.C. 4; [2024] 3 C.L. 176 .... 1.353, **1.403**
Revenue and Customs Commissioners v Ruas; sub nom. Ruas v Revenue and Customs Commissioners [2010] EWCA Civ 291; [2010] AACR 31; [2010] P.T.S.R. 1757; [2010] 3 WLUK 641; [2010] 2 F.L.R. 634; [2010] Fam. Law 695................. 1.63, 3.31
Revenue and Customs Commissioners v Spiridonova [2014] NICA 63; [2014] 9 WLUK 199; [2015] 1 C.M.L.R. 26..3.34, 3.40
Revenue and Customs Commissioners v Thorn Baker Ltd [2007] EWCA Civ 626; [2007] 6 WLUK 633; [2008] I.C.R. 46; 79 T.C. 1; (2007) 104(28) L.S.G. 29; (2007) 151 S.J.L.B. 890..**1.198**
RF v HMRC (TC) [2016] UKUT 399 (AAC) **1.337**
RJ v Revenue and Customs Commissioners [2021] UKUT 40 (AAC); [2021] 2 WLUK 597 .... 1.278, 2.374
RK v HMRC (CHB) [2015] UKUT 357 (AAC); [2016] AACR 4...................................**1.53**
Roberts v Hacking and Paterson [2020] 7 WLUK 669; 2020 G.W.D. 34-442; [2020] UT 30 ....14.71
SA v HMRC (TC) [2016] UKUT 63 (AAC) 1.336
SA v HMRC (TC) [2017] UKUT 90 (AAC) 1.279
Saint Prix v Secretary of State for Work and Pensions (C-507/12); sub nom. St Prix v Secretary of State for Work and Pensions (C-507/12) EU:C:2014:2007; [2014] P.T.S.R. 1448; [2014] 6 WLUK 566; [2015] 1 C.M.L.R. 5; [2014] All E.R. (EC) 987; [2014] Imm. A.R. 1076; [2015] I.N.L.R. 240 ....3.34
SB v HMRC (CHB) [2013] UKUT 24 (AAC)..**1.52**
SC v Secretary of State for Work and Pensions. *See* R. (on the application of SC) v Secretary of State for Work and Pensions
Scorer (Inspector of Taxes) v Olin Energy Systems Ltd; sub nom. Olin Energy Systems Ltd v Scorer (Inspector of Taxes) [1985] A.C. 645; [1985] 2 W.L.R. 668; [1985] 2 All E.R. 375; [1985] S.T.C. 218; [1985] 3 WLUK 195; (1985) 82 L.S.G. 1943; (1985) 129 S.J. 248 HL 1.23
Seaton v Revenue and Customs Commissioners [2011] UKUT 297 (TCC) **1.77**, **1.98**, **1.198**
Secretary of State for Social Services v Smith [1983] 1 W.L.R. 1110; [1983] 3 All E.R. 173; [1983] 5 WLUK 48; (1983) 80 L.S.G. 2684; (1983) 127 S.J. 663 CA (Civ Div) 1.66, 1.195
Secretary of State for Work and Pensions v Deane; sub nom. Deane v Secretary of State for Work and Pensions [2010] EWCA Civ 699; [2010] AACR 42; [2011]

Table of Cases

1 W.L.R. 743; [2011] P.T.S.R. 289; [2010] 6 WLUK 537; [2010] E.L.R. 662; (2010) 107(27) L.S.G. 17 .... 3.5
Secretary of State for Work and Pensions v HMRC (TC) [2014] UKUT 383 (AAC) ... 1.280
Secretary of State for Work and Pensions v MN (BB) [2018] UKUT 68 (AAC) 3.51
Secretary of State for Work and Pensions v TB and HMRC (RP) [2010] UKUT 88 (AAC); [2010] AACR 38 .... 1.231
SG v HMRC (TC) [2011] UKUT 199 (AAC) 1.326, 1.340, 1.405
SH v HMRC and SC (TC) [2013] UKUT 297 (AAC) **1.404, 1.406**
Shah v Barnet LBC. *See* R. v Barnet LBC Ex p. Shah (Nilish)
Sharfudeen v TJ Morris Ltd (t/a Home Bargains) (Appeal No. UKEAT/0272/16/LA) 3 March 2017 EAT 1.122
Sharkey v Revenue and Customs Commissioner; sub nom. Sharkey v De Croos (Inspector of Taxes); Sharkey v De Cross (Inspector of Taxes) [2005] 1 WLUK 428; [2005] S.T.C. (S.C.D.) 336; [2005] S.T.I. 223 Sp Commrs 1.380
Sharma v Renfrewshire Council [2023] CSOH 40; [2023] 6 WLUK 349; 2023 G.W.D. 25-219 .... 14.128
Shilton v Wilmshurst (Inspector of Taxes) [1991] 1 A.C. 684; [1991] 2 W.L.R. 530; [1991] 3 All E.R. 148; [1991] S.T.C. 88; [1991] 2 WLUK 77; 64 T.C. 78; (1991) 135 S.J. 250 HL 2.132
Singh v Secretary of State for the Home Department [2016] EWCA Civ 492; [2016] 4 W.L.R. 183; [2016] 5 WLUK 639; [2016] I.N.L.R. 679 .... 14.109
SK v Revenue and Customs Commissioners (TC) [2016] UKUT 441 (AAC) ... **1.407**, 2.170
SK v Revenue and Customs Commissioners [2022] UKUT 10 (AAC); [2022] P.T.S.R. 818; [2022] 1 WLUK 369 .... **2.48**, 2.49
Skoll v Humanes [2020] 8 WLUK 322; 2020 G.W.D. 35-454; [2020] UT 36 .... 14.8
Snook v London and West Riding Investments Ltd [1967] 2 Q.B. 786; [1967] 2 W.L.R. 1020; [1967] 1 All E.R. 518; [1967] 1 WLUK 724; (1967) 111 S.J. 71 CA (Civ Div) 2.220
Social Security Scotland v FK 2024 UT 23; [2024] 4 WLUK 280; 2024 G.W.D. 19-179 .... 13.373, 13.375, 13.377
South Lanarkshire Council v Boyd [2021] UT 24; [2021] 5 WLUK 641 .... **14.102**
South Lanarkshire Council v Boyd [2021] UT 31; [2021] 8 WLUK 347; 2022 Hous. L.R. 8; 2022 G.W.D. 8-126 .... 14.6, 14.16
South Lanarkshire Council v Boyd [2022] CSIH 41; [2022] 9 WLUK 42; 2022 Hous. L.R. 91; 2022 G.W.D. 29-425 .... 14.11, 14.16, 14.103
SP v HMRC (TC) (No.2) [2017] UKUT 329 (AAC) 1.383
SP v HMRC (TC) [2009] UKUT 42 (AAC) **2.361**
SP v HMRC (TC) [2016] UKUT 238 (AAC); [2016] AACR 46 .... **1.378, 1.381**
Spence v HMRC Commissioners [2012] UKFTT 213 .... 1.98, 4.38
ST v Secretary of State for Work and Pensions (ESA) [2012] UKUT 469 (AAC) 1.407
Stec v United Kingdom (Admissibility) (65731/01) [2005] 7 WLUK 127; (2005) 41 E.H.R.R. SE18 ECtHR 2.295
Taylor Gordon & Co Ltd (t/a Plan Personnel) v Timmons [2003] 9 WLUK 324; [2004] I.R.L.R. 180; (2003) 100(44) L.S.G. 32 EAT 1.68, **1.231**
TM v HMRC (TC) [2013] UKUT 444 (AAC) **1.406**
TM v HMRC (TC) [2016] UKUT 512 (AAC) 1.361
Tomlinson v Birmingham City Council. *See* Ali v Birmingham City Council
TS v HMRC (TC) [2015] UKUT 507 (AAC) 1.279, **1.345**
UA v HMRC (TC) [2019] UKUT 113 (ACC) 1.279, 1.281
VH v HMRC (TC) [2017] UKUT 128 (AAC) **1.368**
VK v HMRC (TC) [2016] UKUT 331 (AAC); [2017] AACR 3 .... 1.415, 2.456
VO v HMRC (TC) [2017] UKUT 343 (AAC) 1.407, 2.124, 2.134
W v HMRC (TC) [2020] UKUT 239 (AAC) 2.22, **2.42**
W v L [1974] Q.B. 711; [1973] 3 W.L.R. 859; [1973] 3 All E.R. 884; [1973] 5 WLUK 113; 72 L.G.R. 36; (1973) 4 Fam. Law 134; (1973) 117 S.J. 775 CA (Civ Div) 2.194
Wade v North Yorkshire Police Authority. *See* North Yorkshire Police Authority v Revenue and Customs Commissioners
Whelan v Chief Adjudication Officer, Independent, 14 November 1994 .... 2.274
Wilson v Fife Properties Ltd [2021] UT 27; [2021] 7 WLUK 764; 2022 G.W.D. 13-201 .... 14.109
Wordie Property Co Ltd v Secretary of State for Scotland, 1984 S.L.T. 345; [1983] 2 WLUK 40 IH (1 Div) **14.101**

Table of Cases

Woro v Brown, 2022 S.L.T. (Tr) 97; [2022] 10 WLUK 520; 2022 G.W.D. 37-537 Upper Tribunal (Scotland) **14.61**
WW v HM Revenue and Customs [2011] UKUT 11 (AAC) **1.293**
X v Austria (19010/07) [2013] 2 WLUK 501; [2013] 1 F.C.R. 387; (2013) 57 E.H.R.R. 14; 35 B.H.R.C. 85; [2013] Eq. L.R. 396 ECtHR 2.297
X v Latvia (27853/09) [2013] 11 WLUK 710; [2014] 1 F.L.R. 1135; (2014) 59 E.H.R.R. 3; [2014] Fam. Law 269 ECtHR 2.297
YK v HMRC (TC) [2016] UKUT 118 (AAC) 1.353
Zahorowicz v Pawlowska [2020] 2 WLUK 586; 2020 G.W.D. 13-182; [2020] UT 19 .... 14.123
Zalewska v Department for Social Development [2008] UKHL 67; [2008] 1 W.L.R. 2602; [2009] 2 All E.R. 319; [2009] N.I. 116; [2008] 11 WLUK 255; [2009] 1 C.M.L.R. 24; [2009] Eu. L.R. 344; (2008) 158 N.L.J. 1643; (2008) 152(45) S.J.L.B. 27 .... **2.486, 3.40**
ZB v HMRC (TC) [2015] UKUT 198 (AAC) **1.335**, 1.336, 1.406, 1.407
ZM and AB v HMRC (TC) [2013] UKUT 547 (AAC); [2014] AACR 17 .... **1.325, 1.405, 2.347**
Zoumbas v Secretary of State for the Home Department. *See* FZ (Democratic Republic of Congo) v Secretary of State for the Home Department
Zukowski v Charles White Ltd [2020] UT 26; [2020] 2 WLUK 697; 2020 G.W.D. 30-386 .... 14.112

TABLE OF SOCIAL SECURITY COMMISSIONERS' DECISIONS 1948–2009

C6/05–06(IS) 2.486	CTC/3611/2008 .... 1.299
CCS/6302/1999 .... 2.450	CTC/3692/2008 .... 1.325, 1.421, 2.471
CCS/2288/2005 .... 2.450	CTC/1853/2009 .... 1.276
CDWA/3123/1997 .... 2.187, 2.188	CTC/0838/2011 .... 2.471
CF/3348/2002 .... 1.53, 1.195	CTC/3443/2012 .... 2.134
CF/1968/2007 .... 3.44	CTC/135/2013 .... 2.273
CF/2826/2007 .... 1.59, 1.194, 3.56	CTC/2409/2013 .... 2.275
CFC/1537/1995 .... 2.273, 2.274	CTC/923/2018 .... **2.47**
CG/60/92 .... 1.41, 1.42	R1/04 (SF) 14.61
CG/2973/2004 .... 2.450	R3/74 (P) 1.41
CIB/303/1999 .... 2.450	R3/75 (P) 1.41
CIS/49/1991 .... 2.274	R(A) 2/92 .... 2.194, 2.195
CIS/995/2004 .... 1.273, 1.327, 2.341, 2.344	R(A) 2/06 .... 2.448
CIS/2559/2005 .... 2.486	R(DLA) 3/05 .... 2.450
CIS/2680/2005 .... 2.486	R(F) 3/60 .... 3.9
CIS/3573/2005 .... 2.486	R(F) 2/79 .... 1.52, 2.273
CIS/1813/2007 .... 2.384	R(F) 2/81 .... 1.52, 2275
CIS/3101/2007 .... 2.49	R(F) 3/81 .... 1.195, 3.49
CIS/2457/2008 .... 1.195	R(F) 1/82(S) 1.66
CPC/2920/2005 .... 2.486	R(F) 4/85 .... 1.195, 3.49
CSG/8/92 .... 1.42	R(F) 1/93 .... 3.5
CSIS/48/1992 .... 1.272	R(F) 1/08 .... 1.66, 1.195
CSTC/326/2003 .... 1.266	R(FC) 2/90 .... 1.313
CSTC/76/2006 .... 2.155, 2.177	R(FC) 1/92 .... 2.134
CSTC/724/2006 .... 1.276	R(FIS) 6/85 .... 2.124
CSTC/840/2014 .... 1.337	R(FIS) 1/86 .... 2.132
CTC/2090/2004 .... 1.281, 2.448	R(G) 3/68 .... 1.41, 1.42
CTC/2576/2004 .... 1.334	R(G) 2/83 .... 1.41, 1.42
CTC/3059/2004 .... 1.280	R(G) 4/83(T) 1.46
CTC/3543/2004 .... 1.282	R(G) 2/02 .... 3.5
CTC/3864/2004 .... 1.276	R(IB) 2/04 .... 1.325
CTC/4390/2004 .... 1.333, 2.274, 2.448	R(IS) 12/92 .... 1.313
CTC/262/2005 .... 2.499	R(IS) 22/95 .... 2.132, 2.134
CTC/643/2005 .... 2.155	R(IS) 9/98 .... 2.471
CTC/2612/2005 .... 2.448	R(IS) 13/01 .... 2.49
CTC/2662/2005 .... 1.337, 1.342, 1.371	R(IS) 8/07 .... 2.486
CTC/3981/2005 .... 1.334, 1.337	R(M) 1/85 .... 2.482
CTC/31/2006 .... 1.326, 1.405, 2.347, 2.471	R(M) 2/89 .... 2.186
CTC/1594/2006 .... 1.340, 1.408	R(S) 11/51 .... 2.185
CTC/2103/2006 .... 2.134	R(S) 24/54 .... 4.5
CTC/2113/2006. 1.297, 1.342, 2.218, 2.314	R(S) 2/63 .... 2.367
CTC/3981/2006 .... 1.371	R(S) 1/72 .... 4.5
CTC/1586/2007 .... 2.448	R(S) 4/93 .... 4.5
CTC/1686/2007 .... 2.274, 2.275	R(SB) 19/83 .... 2.450
CTC/1907/2007 .... 1.371	R(SB) 55/83 .... 2.450
CTC/2270/2007 .... 1.300, 1.371, 2.327	R(SSP) 1/85 .... 4.13
CTC/3096/2007 .... 2.275	R(SSP) 1/86 .... 1.199
CTC/3646/2007 .... 2.171	R(SSP) 1/89 .... 4.38
CTC/244/2008 .... 1.325	R(TC) 2/06 .... 1.279

TABLE OF ABBREVIATIONS USED IN THIS SERIES

1975 Act	Social Security Act 1975
1977 Act	Marriage (Scotland) Act 1977
1979 Act	Pneumoconiosis (Workers' Compensation) Act 1979
1986 Act	Social Security Act 1986
1996 Act	Employment Rights Act 1996
1998 Act	Social Security Act 1998
2002 Act	Tax Credits Act 2002
2004 Act	Gender Recognition Act 2004
2006 Act	Armed Forces Act 2006
2008 Act	Child Maintenance and Other Payments Act 2008
2013 Act	Marriage (Same Sex Couples) Act 2013
2014 Act	Marriage and Civil Partnership (Scotland) Act 2014
A1P1	Art.1 of Protocol 1 to the European Convention on Human Rights
AA	Attendance Allowance
AA 1992	Attendance Allowance Act 1992
AAC	Administrative Appeals Chamber
AACR	Administrative Appeals Chamber Reports
A.C.	Law Reports, Appeal Cases
A.C.D.	Administrative Court Digest
Admin	Administrative Court
Admin L.R.	Administrative Law Reports
Administration Act	Social Security Administration Act 1992
Administration Regulations	Statutory Paternity Pay and Statutory Adoption Pay (Administration) Regulations 2002
AIP	assessed income period
All E.R.	All England Reports
All E.R. (E.C.)	All England Reports (European Cases)
AMA	Adjudicating Medical Authorities
AO	Adjudication Officer
AOG	*Adjudication Officers Guide*
art.	article
Art.	Article
ASD	Autistic Spectrum Disorder
ASPP	Additional Statutory Paternity Pay

liii

Table of Abbreviations used in this Series

ASVG	Allgemeines Sozialversicherungsgesetz (General Social Security Act)
A.T.C.	Annotated Tax Cases
Attendance Allowance Regulations	Social Security (Attendance Allowance) Regulations 1991
AWT	All Work Test
BA	Benefits Agency
Benefits Act	Social Security Contributions and Benefits Act 1992
B.H.R.C.	Butterworths Human Rights Cases
B.L.G.R.	Butterworths Local Government Reports
Blue Books	*The Law Relating to Social Security*, Vols 1–11
B.P.I.R.	Bankruptcy and Personal Insolvency Reports
BSVG	Bauern-Sozialversicherungsgesetz (Social Security Act for Farmers)
B.T.C.	British Tax Cases
BTEC	Business and Technology Education Council
B.V.C.	British Value Added Tax Reporter
B.W.C.C.	Butterworths Workmen's Compensation Cases
c.	chapter
C	Commissioner's decision
C&BA 1992	Social Security Contributions and Benefits Act 1992
CAA 2001	Capital Allowances Act 2001
CAB	Citizens Advice Bureau
CAO	Chief Adjudication Officer
CB	Child Benefit
CBA 1975	Child Benefit Act 1975
CBJSA	Contribution-Based Jobseeker's Allowance
C.C.L. Rep.	Community Care Law Reports
CCM	HMRC *New Tax Credits Claimant Compliance Manual*
C.E.C.	European Community Cases
CERA	cortical evoked response audiogram
CESA	Contribution-based Employment and Support Allowance
CFS	chronic fatigue syndrome
Ch.	Chancery Division Law Reports; Chapter
Citizenship Directive	Directive 2004/38/EC of the European Parliament and of the Council of April 29, 2004
CJEC	Court of Justice of the European Communities
CJEU	Court of Justice of the European Union
Claims and Payments Regulations	Social Security (Claims and Payments) Regulations 1987
Claims and Payments Regulations 1979	Social Security (Claims and Payments) Regulations 1979

Table of Abbreviations used in this Series

Claims and Payments Regulations 2013	Universal Credit, Personal Independence Payment, Jobseeker's Allowance and Employment and Support Allowance (Claims and Payments) Regulations 2013
CM	Case Manager
CMA	Chief Medical Adviser
CMEC	Child Maintenance and Enforcement Commission
C.M.L.R.	Common Market Law Reports
C.O.D.	Crown Office Digest
COLL	*Collective Investment Schemes Sourcebook*
Community, The	European Community
Computation of Earnings Regulations	Social Security Benefit (Computation of Earnings) Regulations 1978
Computation of Earnings Regulations 1996	Social Security Benefit (Computation of Earnings) Regulations 1996
Consequential Provisions Act	Social Security (Consequential Provisions) Act 1992
Contributions and Benefits Act	Social Security Contributions and Benefits Act 1992
Contributions Regulations	Social Security (Contributions) Regulations 2001
COPD	chronic obstructive pulmonary disease
CP	Carer Premium; Chamber President
CPAG	Child Poverty Action Group
CPR	Civil Procedure Rules
Cr. App. R.	Criminal Appeal Reports
CRCA 2005	Commissioners for Revenue and Customs Act 2005
Credits Regulations 1974	Social Security (Credits) Regulations 1974
Credits Regulations 1975	Social Security (Credits) Regulations 1975
Crim. L.R.	Criminal Law Review
CRU	Compensation Recovery Unit
CSA 1995	Children (Scotland) Act 1995
CSIH	Inner House of the Court of Session (Scotland)
CSM	Child Support Maintenance
CS(NI)O 1995	Child Support (Northern Ireland) Order 1995
CSOH	Outer House of the Court of Session (Scotland)
CSPSSA 2000	Child Support, Pensions and Social Security Act 2000
CTA	Common Travel Area
CTA 2009	Corporation Tax Act 2009
CTA 2010	Corporation Tax Act 2010
CTB	Council Tax Benefit
CTC	Child Tax Credit
CTC Regulations	Child Tax Credit Regulations 2002
CTF	child trust fund

Table of Abbreviations used in this Series

CTS	Carpal Tunnel Syndrome
DAC	Directive 2011/16/ EU (Directive on administrative co-operation in the field of taxation)
DAT	Disability Appeal Tribunal
dB	decibels
DCA	Department for Constitutional Affairs
DCP	Disabled Child Premium
Decisions and Appeals Regulations 1999	Social Security Contributions (Decisions and Appeals) Regulations 1999
Dependency Regulations	Social Security Benefit (Dependency) Regulations 1977
DfEE	Department for Education and Employment
DHSS	Department of Health and Social Security
Disability Living Allowance Regulations	Social Security (Disability Living Allowance) Regulations
DIY	do it yourself
DLA	Disability Living Allowance
DLA Regs 1991	Social Security (Disability Living Allowance) Regulations 1991
DLAAB	Disability Living Allowance Advisory Board
DLADWAA 1991	Disability Living Allowance and Disability Working Allowance Act 1991
DM	Decision Maker
DMA	Decision-making and Appeals
DMG	*Decision Makers' Guide*
DMP	Delegated Medical Practitioner
DP	Disability Premium
DPP	Director of Public Prosecutions
DPT	diffuse pleural thickening
DPTC	Disabled Person's Tax Credit
DRO	Debt Relief Order
DSD	Department for Social Development (Northern Ireland)
DSM IV; DSM-5	Diagnostic and Statistical Manual of Mental Disorders of the American Psychiatric Association
DSS	Department of Social Security
DTI	Department of Trade and Industry
DWA	Disability Working Allowance
DWP	Department for Work and Pensions
DWPMS	Department for Work and Pensions Medical Service
EAA	Extrinsic Allergic Alveolitis
EAT	Employment Appeal Tribunal
EC	European Community
ECHR	European Convention on Human Rights

Table of Abbreviations used in this Series

ECJ	European Court of Justice
E.C.R.	European Court Reports
ECSC	European Coal and Steel Community
ECSMA	European Convention on Social and Medical Assistance
EEA	European Economic Area
EEC	European Economic Community
EESSI	Electronic Exchange of Social Security Information
E.G.	Estates Gazette
E.G.L.R.	Estates Gazette Law Reports
EHC plan	education, health and care plan
EHIC	European Health Insurance Card
EHRC	European Human Rights Commission
E.H.R.R.	European Human Rights Reports
EL	employers' liability
E.L.R	Education Law Reports
EMA	Education Maintenance Allowance
EMP	Examining Medical Practitioner
Employment and Support Allowance Regulations	Employment and Support Allowance Regulations 2008
EPS	extended period of sickness
Eq. L.R.	Equality Law Reports
ERA	evoked response audiometry
ERA scheme	Employment, Retention and Advancement scheme
ES	Employment Service
ESA	Employment and Support Allowance
ESA Regs 2013	Employment and Support Allowance Regulations 2013
ESA Regulations	Employment and Support Allowance Regulations 2008
ESA WCAt	Employment and Support Allowance Work Capability Assessment
ESC	employer supported childcare
ESE Scheme	Employment, Skills and Enterprise Scheme
ESE Regulations	Jobseeker's Allowance (Employment, Skills and Enterprise Scheme) Regulations 2011
ESES Regulations	Jobseeker's Allowance (Employment, Skills and Enterprise Scheme) Regulations 2011
ETA 1973	Employment and Training Act 1973
ETA(NI) 1950	Employment and Training Act (Northern Ireland) 1950
ETS	European Treaty Series
EU	European Union
Eu.L.R.	European Law Reports

Table of Abbreviations used in this Series

EUWA 2018	European Union (Withdrawal) Act 2018
EWCA Civ	Civil Division of the Court of Appeal (England and Wales)
EWHC Admin	Administrative Court, part of the High Court (England and Wales)
FA 1993	Finance Act 1993
FA 1996	Finance Act 1996
FA 2004	Finance Act 2004
Fam. Law	Family Law
FCDO	Foreign, Commonwealth and Development Office
FAS	Financial Assistance Scheme
F.C.R.	Family Court Reporter
FEV	forced expiratory volume
FIS	Family Income Supplement
FISMA 2000	Financial Services and Markets Act 2000
F.L.R.	Family Law Reports
FME	further medical evidence
F(No.2)A 2005	Finance (No.2) Act 2005
FOTRA	Free of Tax to Residents Abroad
FRAA	flat rate accrual amount
FRS Act 2004	Fire and Rescue Services Act 2004
FSCS	Financial Services Compensation Scheme
FTT	First-tier Tribunal
General Benefit Regulations 1982	Social Security (General Benefit) Regulations 1982
General Regulations	Statutory Shared Parental Pay (General) Regulations 2014
GMC	Group Medical Coverage
GMCA	Greater Manchester Combined Authority
GMFRA	Greater Manchester Fire and Rescue Authority
GMP	Guaranteed Minimum Pension
GMWDA	Greater Manchester Waste Disposal Authority
GNVQ	General National Vocational Qualification
GP	General Practitioner
GRA	Gender Recognition Act 2004
GRB	Graduated Retirement Benefit
GRP	Graduated Retirement Pension
GSVG	Gewerbliches Sozialversicherungsgesetz (Federal Act on Social Insurance for Persons engaged in Trade and Commerce)
HB	Housing Benefit
HB (WSP) R (NI) 2017	Housing Benefit (Welfare Social Payment) Regulations (Northern Ireland) 2017
HBRB	Housing Benefit Review Board
HCA	Homes and Communities Agency

Table of Abbreviations used in this Series

HCD	House of Commons Debates
HCP	healthcare professional
HCV	Hepatitis C virus
Health Service Act	National Health Service Act 2006
Health Service (Wales) Act	National Health Service (Wales) Act 2006
HIV	Human Immunodeficiency Virus
HL	House of Lords
H.L.R.	Housing Law Reports
HMIT	His Majesty's Inspector of Taxes
HMRC	His Majesty's Revenue and Customs
HMSO	His Majesty's Stationery Office
Hospital In-Patients Regulations 1975	Social Security (Hospital In-Patients) Regulations 1975
HP	Health Professional
HPP	Higher Pensioner Premium
HRA 1998	Human Rights Act 1998
H.R.L.R.	Human Rights Law Reports
HRP	Home Responsibilities Protection
HSE	Health and Safety Executive
IAC	Immigration and Asylum Chamber
IAP	Intensive Activity Period
IB	Incapacity Benefit
IB PCA	Incapacity Benefit Personal Capability Assessment
IB Regs	Social Security (Incapacity Benefit) Regulations 1994
IB Regulations	Social Security (Incapacity Benefit) Regulations 1994
IB/IS/SDA	Incapacity Benefits Regime
IBJSA	Income-Based Jobseeker's Allowance
IBS	Irritable Bowel Syndrome
ICA	Invalid Care Allowance
I.C.R.	Industrial Cases Reports
ICTA 1988	Income and Corporation Taxes Act 1988
IFW Regulations	Incapacity for Work (General) Regulations 1995
IH	Inner House of the Court of Session
I.I.	Industrial Injuries
IIAC	Industrial Injuries Advisory Council
IIDB	Industrial Injuries Disablement Benefit
ILO	International Labour Organization
Imm. A.R.	Immigration Appeal Reports
Incapacity for Work Regulations	Social Security (Incapacity for Work) (General) Regulations 1995
Income Support General Regulations	Income Support (General) Regulations 1987

Table of Abbreviations used in this Series

IND	Immigration and Nationality Directorate of the Home Office
I.N.L.R.	Immigration and Nationality Law Reports
I.O.	Insurance Officer
IPPR	Institute of Public Policy Research
IRESA	Income-Related Employment and Support Allowance
I.R.L.R.	Industrial Relations Law Reports
IS	Income Support
IS Regs	Income Support Regulations
IS Regulations	Income Support (General) Regulations 1987
ISA	Individual Savings Account
ISBN	International Standard Book Number
ITA 2007	Income Tax Act 2007
ITEPA 2003	Income Tax, Earnings and Pensions Act 2003
I.T.L. Rep.	International Tax Law Reports
I.T.R.	Industrial Tribunals Reports
ITS	Independent Tribunal Service
ITTOIA 2005	Income Tax (Trading and Other Income) Act 2005
IVB	Invalidity Benefit
IW (General) Regs	Social Security (Incapacity for Work) (General) Regulations 1995
IW (Transitional) Regs	Incapacity for Work (Transitional) Regulations
Jobseeker's Allowance Regulations	Jobseeker's Allowance Regulations 1996
Jobseeker's Regulations 1996	Jobseeker's Allowance Regulations 1996
JSA	Jobseeker's Allowance
JSA 1995	Jobseekers Act 1995
JSA (NI) Regulations	Jobseeker's Allowance (Northern Ireland) Regulations 1996
JSA (Transitional) Regulations	Jobseeker's Allowance (Transitional) Regulations 1996
JSA Regs 1996	Jobseeker's Allowance Regulations 1996
JSA Regs 2013	Jobseeker's Allowance Regulations 2013
JS(NI)O 1995	Jobseekers (Northern Ireland) Order 1995
J.S.S.L.	Journal of Social Security Law
J.S.W.L.	Journal of Social Welfare Law
K.B.	Law Reports, King's Bench
L.& T.R.	Landlord and Tenant Reports
LCW	limited capability for work
LCWA	Limited Capability for Work Assessment
LCWRA	limited capability for work-related activity
LDEDC Act 2009	Local Democracy, Economic Development and Construction Act 2009
LEA	local education authority
LEL	Lower Earnings Limit

Table of Abbreviations used in this Series

LET	low earnings threshold
L.G. Rev.	Local Government Review
L.G.L.R.	Local Government Reports
L.J.R.	Law Journal Reports
LRP	liable relative payment
L.S.G.	Law Society Gazette
Luxembourg Court	Court of Justice of the European Union (also referred to as CJEC and ECJ)
MA	Maternity Allowance
MAF	Medical Assessment Framework
Maternity Allowance Regulations	Social Security (Maternity Allowance) Regulations 1987
MDC	Mayoral development corporation
ME	myalgic encephalomyelitis
Medical Evidence Regulations	Social Security (Medical Evidence) Regulations 1976
MEN	Mandatory Employment Notification
Mesher and Wood	*Income Support, the Social Fund and Family Credit: the Legislation* (1996)
M.H.L.R.	Mental Health Law Reports
MHP	mental health problems
MIF	minimum income floor
MIG	minimum income guarantee
Migration Regulations	Employment and Support Allowance (Transitional Provisions, Housing Benefit and Council Tax Benefit (Existing Awards) (No.2) Regulations 2010
MP	Member of Parliament
MRSA	methicillin-resistant Staphylococcus aureus
MS	Medical Services
MWA Regulations	Jobseeker's Allowance (Mandatory Work Activity Scheme) Regulations 2011
MWAS Regulations	Jobseeker's Allowance (Mandatory Work Activity Scheme) Regulations 2011
NCB	National Coal Board
NDPD	Notes on the Diagnosis of Prescribed Diseases
NHS	National Health Service
NI	National Insurance
N.I..	Northern Ireland Law Reports
NICA	Northern Ireland Court of Appeal
NICom	Northern Ireland Commissioner
NICs	National Insurance Contributions
NINO	National Insurance Number
NIRS 2	National Insurance Recording System
N.L.J.	New Law Journal
NMC	Nursing and Midwifery Council
Northern Ireland Contributions and	Social Security Contributions and Benefits

Table of Abbreviations used in this Series

Benefits Act	(Northern Ireland) Act 1992
N.P.C.	New Property Cases
NRCGT	non-resident capital gains tax
NTC Manual	Clerical procedures manual on tax credits
NUM	National Union of Mineworkers
NUS	National Union of Students
OCD	obsessive compulsive disorder
Ogus, Barendt and Wikeley	A. Ogus, E. Barendt and N. Wikeley, *The Law of Social Security* (1995)
Old Cases Act	Industrial Injuries and Diseases (Old Cases) Act 1975
OPB	One Parent Benefit
O.P.L.R.	Occupational Pensions Law Reports
OPSSAT	Office of the President of Social Security Appeal Tribunals
Overlapping Benefits Regulations	Social Security (Overlapping Benefits) Regulations 1975
P	retirement pension case
P. & C.R.	Property and Compensation Reports
para.	paragraph
Pay Regulations	Statutory Paternity Pay and Statutory Adoption Pay (General) Regulations 2002; Statutory Shared Parental Pay (General) Regulations 2014
PAYE	Pay As You Earn
PC	Privy Council
PCA	Personal Capability Assessment
PCC	Police and Crime Commissioner
PD	Practice Direction; prescribed disease
Pens. L.R.	Pensions Law Reports
Pensions Act	Pension Schemes Act 1993
PEP	Personal Equity Plan
Persons Abroad Regulations	Social Security Benefit (Persons Abroad) Regulations 1975
Persons Residing Together Regulations	Social Security Benefit (Persons Residing Together) Regulations 1977
PIE	Period of Interruption of Employment
PILON	pay in lieu of notice
Pilot Scheme Regulations	Universal Credit (Work-Related Requirements) In Work Pilot Scheme and Amendment Regulations 2015
PIP	Personal Independence Payment
P.I.Q.R.	Personal Injuries and Quantum Reports
Polygamous Marriages Regulations	Social Security and Family Allowances (Polygamous Marriages) Regulations 1975
PPF	Pension Protection Fund
Prescribed Diseases Regulations	Social Security (Industrial Injuries) (Prescribed Diseases) Regulations 1985

Table of Abbreviations used in this Series

PSCS	Pension Service Computer System
Pt	Part
PTA	pure tone audiometry
P.T.S.R.	Public and Third Sector Law Reports
PTWR 2000	Part-time Workers (Prevention of Less Favourable Treatment) Regulations 2000
PVS	private and voluntary sectors
Q.B.	Queen's Bench Law Reports
QBD	Queen's Bench Division
QCS Board	Quality Contract Scheme Board
QEF	qualifying earnings factor
QYP	qualifying young person
r.	rule
R	Reported Decision
R.C.	Rules of the Court of Session
REA	Reduced Earnings Allowance
reg.	regulation
REULRRA	Retained EU Law (Revocation and Reform) Act 2023
RIPA	Regulation of Investigatory Powers Act 2000
RMO	Responsible Medical Officer
rr.	rules
RR	reference rate
RSI	repetitive strain injury
RTI	Real Time Information
R.V.R.	Rating & Valuation Reporter
s.	section
S	Scottish Decision
SAP	Statutory Adoption Pay
SAPOE Regulations	Jobseeker's Allowance (Schemes for Assisting Persons to Obtain Employment) Regulations 2013
SAWS	Seasonal Agricultural Work Scheme
SAYE	Save As You Earn
SB	Supplementary Benefit
SBAT	Supplementary Benefit Appeal Tribunal
SBC	Supplementary Benefits Commission
S.C.	Session Cases
S.C. (H.L.)	Session Cases (House of Lords)
S.C. (P.C.)	Session Cases (Privy Council)
S.C.C.R.	Scottish Criminal Case Reports
S.C.L.R.	Scottish Civil Law Reports
Sch.	Schedule
SDA	Severe Disablement Allowance

Table of Abbreviations used in this Series

SDP	Severe Disability Premium
SEC	Social Entitlement Chamber
SEN	special educational needs
SERPS	State Earnings Related Pension Scheme
ShPP	statutory shared parental pay
ShPP Regulations	Statutory Shared Parental Pay (General) Regulations 2014
SI	Statutory Instrument
SIP	Share Incentive Plan
S.J.	Solicitors Journal
S.J.L.B.	Solicitors Journal Law Brief
SLAN	statement like an award notice
S.L.T.	Scots Law Times
SMP	Statutory Maternity Pay
SMP (General) Regulations 1986	Statutory Maternity Pay (General) Regulations 1986
SPC	State Pension Credit
SPC Regulations	State Pension Credit Regulations 2002
SPCA 2002	State Pension Credit Act 2002
SPL Regulations	Shared Parental Leave Regulations 2014
SPP	Statutory Paternity Pay
ss.	sections
SS (No.2) A 1980	Social Security (No.2) Act 1980
SSA 1975	Social Security Act 1975
SSA 1977	Social Security Act 1977
SSA 1978	Social Security Act 1978
SSA 1979	Social Security Act 1979
SSA 1981	Social Security Act 1981
SSA 1986	Social Security Act 1986
SSA 1988	Social Security Act 1988
SSA 1989	Social Security Act 1989
SSA 1990	Social Security Act 1990
SSA 1998	Social Security Act 1998
SSAA 1992	Social Security Administration Act 1992
SSAC	Social Security Advisory Committee
SSAT	Social Security Appeal Tribunal
SSCBA 1992	Social Security Contributions and Benefits Act 1992
SSCB(NI)A 1992	Social Security Contributions and Benefits (Northern Ireland) Act 1992
SSCPA 1992	Social Security (Consequential Provisions) Act 1992
SSD	Secretary of State for Defence
SSHBA 1982	Social Security and Housing Benefits Act 1982
SSHD	Secretary of State for the Home Department

Table of Abbreviations used in this Series

SSI	Scottish Statutory Instrument
SS(MP)A 1977	Social Security (Miscellaneous Provisions) Act 1977
SSP	Statutory Sick Pay
SSP (General) Regulations	Statutory Sick Pay (General) Regulations 1982
SSPA 1975	Social Security Pensions Act 1975
SSPP	statutory shared parental pay
SSWP	Secretary of State for Work and Pensions
State Pension Credit Regulations	State Pension Credit Regulations 2002
S.T.C.	Simon's Tax Cases
S.T.C. (S.C.D.)	Simon's Tax Cases: Special Commissioners' Decisions
S.T.I.	Simon's Tax Intelligence
STIB	Short-Term Incapacity Benefit
subpara.	subparagraph
subs.	subsection
T	Tribunal of Commissioners' Decision
T.C.	Tax Cases
TCA 1999	Tax Credits Act 1999
TCA 2002	Tax Credits Act 2002
TCC	Technology and Construction Court
TCEA 2007	Tribunals, Courts and Enforcement Act 2007
TCGA 1992	Taxation of Chargeable Gains Act 2002
TCTM	*Tax Credits Technical Manual*
TEC	Treaty Establishing the European Community
TENS	transcutaneous electrical nerve stimulation
TEU	Treaty on European Union
TFC	tax-free childcare
TFEU	Treaty on the Functioning of the European Union
TIOPA 2010	Taxation (International and Other Provisions) Act 2010
TMA 1970	Taxes Management Act 1970
T.R.	Taxation Reports
Transfer of Functions Act	Social Security Contributions (Transfer of Functions etc.) Act 1999
Tribunal Procedure Rules	Tribunal Procedure (First-tier Tribunal)(Social Entitlement Chamber) Rules 2008
UB	Unemployment Benefit
UC	Universal Credit
UC Regs 2013	Universal Credit Regulations 2013
UCITS	Undertakings for Collective Investments in Transferable Securities
UKAIT	UK Asylum and Immigration Tribunal
UKBA	UK Border Agency of the Home Office

Table of Abbreviations used in this Series

UKCC	United Kingdom Central Council for Nursing, Midwifery and Health Visiting
UKFTT	United Kingdom First-tier Tribunal Tax Chamber
UKHL	United Kingdom House of Lords
U.K.H.R.R.	United Kingdom Human Rights Reports
UKSC	United Kingdom Supreme Court
UKUT	United Kingdom Upper Tribunal
UN	United Nations
Universal Credit Regulations	Universal Credit Regulations 2013
URL	uniform resource locator
USI Regs	Social Security (Unemployment, Sickness and Invalidity Benefit) Regulations 1983
USI Regulations	Social Security (Unemployment, Sickness and Invalidity Benefit) Regulations 1983
UT	Upper Tribunal
VAT	Value Added Tax
VCM	vinyl chloride monomer
Vol.	Volume
VWF	Vibration White Finger
W	Welsh Decision
WCA	Work Capability Assessment
WCAt	limited capability for work assessment
WFHRAt	Work-Focused Health-Related Assessment
WFI	work-focused interview
WFTC	Working Families Tax Credit
Wikeley, Annotations	N. Wikeley, "Annotations to Jobseekers Act 1995 (c.18)" in *Current Law Statutes Annotated* (1995)
Wikeley, Ogus and Barendt	Wikeley, Ogus and Barendt, *The Law of Social Security* (2002)
W.L.R.	Weekly Law Reports
WLUK	Westlaw UK
Workmen's Compensation Acts	Workmen's Compensation Acts 1925 to 1945
WP	Widow's Pension
WPS	War Pensions Scheme
WRA 2007	Welfare Reform Act 2007
WRA 2009	Welfare Reform Act 2009
WRA 2012	Welfare Reform Act 2012
W-RA Regulations	Employment and Support Allowance (Work-Related Activity) Regulations 2011
WRAAt	Work-Related Activity Assessment
WRPA 1999	Welfare Reform and Pensions Act 1999
WRP(NI)O 1999	Welfare Reform and Pensions (Northern Ireland) Order 1999
WRWA 2016	Welfare Reform and Work Act 2016

Table of Abbreviations used in this Series

WSP (LCP) R (NI) 2016	Welfare Supplementary Payment (Loss of Carer Payments) Regulations (Northern Ireland) 2016
WSP (LDRP) R (NI) 2016	Welfare Supplementary Payment (Loss of Disability-Related Premiums) Regulations (Northern Ireland) 2016
WSPR (NI) 2016	Welfare Supplementary Payment Regulations (Northern Ireland) 2016
WTC	Working Tax Credit
WTC Regulations	Working Tax Credit (Entitlement and Maximum Rate) Regulations 2002

PART I

HM REVENUE AND CUSTOMS
TAX CREDITS AND SOCIAL SECURITY

Taxes Management Act 1970

(1970 c.9)

ARRANGEMENT OF SELECTED SECTIONS

PART I

ADMINISTRATION

1.	Responsibility for certain taxes	1.1

PART II

RETURNS OF INCOME AND GAINS

Income tax

8.	Personal return
8ZA.	Interpretation of section 8(4A)
9.	Returns to include self-assessment
9ZA.	Amendment of personal or trustee return by taxpayer
9ZB.	Correction of personal or trustee return by Revenue
9A.	Notice of enquiry
9B.	Amendment of return by taxpayer during enquiry
9C.	Amendment of self-assessment during enquiry to prevent loss of tax

Records

12B.	Records to be kept for purposes of returns

PART IV

ASSESSMENTS AND CLAIMS

28A.	Completion of enquiry into personal or trustee return
29.	Assessment where loss of tax discovered

Relief for excessive assessments

32.	Double assessment
33.	Error or mistake

Taxes Management Act 1970

Time-limits

34. Ordinary time-limit of four years
34A. Ordinary time-limit for self-assessments
35. Time-limit: income received after year for which it is assessable
36. Loss of tax brought about carelessly or deliberately, etc.

PART V

APPEALS AND OTHER PROCEEDINGS

Proceedings before Commissioners

54. Settling of appeals by agreement
54A. No questioning in appeal of amounts of certain social security income
54B. Notifications of taxable amounts of certain social security income
54C. Interpretation of sections 54A and 54B: "appropriate officer" etc

PART X

PENALTIES, ETC.

105. Evidence in cases of fraud and wilful default

PART XI

MISCELLANEOUS AND SUPPLEMENTAL

Documents

112. Loss, destruction or damage to assessments, returns, etc.
114. Want of form or errors not to invalidate assessments, etc.

Interpretation

118. Interpretation

INTRODUCTION AND GENERAL NOTE

1.2   The TMA 1970 was a consolidation measure, but it has been extensively and repeatedly amended since 1970. Only two sections apply directly to tax credits: s.1 (read to include tax credits) and s.54. For the express application of s.54, see Tax Credits (Appeals) Regulations 2002 reg.3. But TCA 2002 refers to several other sections. Set out below are the key sections of the TMA 1970 that apply for the purposes of the income tax assessments, alongside which tax credit calculations will be made in most cases.

(1970 c.9)

In addition, the selection includes other provisions setting out the power of HMRC to investigate and deal with income tax assessments, the scope for a taxpayer to amend a self-assessment or request an amendment of an assessment, and formal sections dealing with evidence and documentation.

As s.1 indicates, this Act also deals with assessments and administration of capital gains tax and corporation tax, but all provisions relating only to those taxes have been excluded from this selection, as have provisions dealing with other taxes or past taxes.

Part I

Administration

Responsibility for certain taxes

1.—The Commissioners for Her Majesty's Revenue and Customs shall be responsible for the collection and management of—
 (a) income tax,
 (b) corporation tax, and
 (c) capital gains tax.

Part II

Returns of Income and Gains

Income tax

Personal return

8.—(1) For the purpose of establishing the amounts in which a person is chargeable to income tax and capital gains tax for a year of assessment, and the amount payable by him by way of income tax for that year, ... he may be required by a notice given to him by an officer of the Board—
 (a) to make and deliver to the officer, a return containing such information as may reasonably be required in pursuance of the notice, and
 (b) to deliver with the return such accounts, statements and documents, relating to information contained in the return, as may reasonably be so required.

(1A) *(repealed)*

(1AA) For the purposes of subsection (1) above—
 (a) the amounts in which a person is chargeable to income tax and capital gains tax are net amounts, that is to say, amounts which take into account any relief or allowance a claim for which is included in the return; and
 (b) the amount payable by a person by way of income tax is the difference between the amount in which he is chargeable to income tax and the aggregate amount of any income tax deducted at source.

(1B) In the case of a person who carries on a trade, profession, or business in partnership with one or more other persons, a return under this section shall include each amount which, in any relevant statement, is stated to be equal to his share of any income, loss, tax, credit or charge for the period in respect of which the statement is made.

(1C) In subsection (1B) above "relevant statement" means a statement which, as respects the partnership, falls to be made under section 12AB of this Act for a period which includes, or includes any part of, the year of assessment.

(1D) A return under this section for a year of assessment (Year 1) must be delivered—
- (a) in the case of a non-electronic return, on or before 31st October in Year 2, and
- (b) in the case of an electronic return, on or before 31st January in Year 2.

(1E) But subsection (1D) is subject to the following two exceptions.

(1F) Exception 1 is that if a notice in respect of Year 1 is given after 31st July in Year 2 (but on or before 31st October), a return must be delivered—
- (a) during the period of 3 months beginning with the date of the notice (for a non-electronic return), or
- (b) on or before 31st January (for an electronic return).

(1G) Exception 2 is that if a notice in respect of Year 1 is given after 31st October in Year 2, a return (whether electronic or not) must be delivered during the period of 3 months beginning with the date of the notice.

(1H) The Commissioners—
- (a) shall prescribe what constitutes an electronic return, and
- (b) may make different provision for different cases or circumstances.

(2) Every return under this section shall include a declaration by the person making the return to the effect that the return is to the best of his knowledge correct and complete.

(3) A notice under this section may require different information, accounts and statements for different periods or in relation to different descriptions of source of income.

(4) Notices under this section may require different information, accounts and statements in relation to different descriptions of person.

(4A) Subsection (4B) applies if a notice under this section is given to a person within section 8ZA of this Act (certain persons employed etc by person not resident in United Kingdom who perform their duties for UK clients).

(4B) The notice may require a return of the person's income to include particulars of any general earnings (see section 7(3) of ITEPA 2003) paid to the person.

(5) In this section and sections 8A, 9 and 12AA of this Act, any reference to income tax deducted at source is a reference to income tax deducted or treated as deducted from any income or treated as paid on any income.

Interpretation of section 8(4A)

1.5   8ZA.—(1) For the purposes of section 8(4A) of this Act, a person ("F") is within this section if each of conditions A to C is met.

(2) Condition A is that F performs in the United Kingdom, for a continuous period of 30 days or more, duties of an office or employment.

(3) Condition B is that the office or employment is under or with a person who—

(a) is not resident in the United Kingdom, but
(b) is resident outside the United Kingdom.

(4) Condition C is that the duties are performed for the benefit of a person who—
(a) is resident in the United Kingdom, or
(b) carries on a trade, profession or vocation in the United Kingdom.

Returns to include self-assessment

9.—(1) Subject to subsections (1A) and (2) below, every return under section 8 or 8A of this Act shall include a self-assessment, that is to say—
(a) an assessment of the amounts in which, on the basis of the information contained in the return and taking into account any relief or allowance a claim for which is included in the return, the person making the return is chargeable to income tax and capital gains tax for the year of assessment; and
(b) an assessment of the amount payable by him by way of income tax, that is to say, the difference between the amount in which he is assessed to income tax under paragraph (a) above and the aggregate amount of any income tax deducted at source

but nothing in this subsection shall enable a self-assessment to show as repayable any income tax treated as deducted or paid by virtue of section 246D(1) of the principal Act, section 626 of ITEPA or section 399(2) or 530(1) of ITTOIA 2005.

(1A) The tax to be assessed on a person by a self-assessment shall not include any tax which—
(a) is chargeable on the scheme administrator of a registered pension scheme under Part 4 of the Finance Act 2004,
(aa) is chargeable, on the scheme manager of a qualifying recognised overseas pension scheme or a former such scheme, under Part 4 of the Finance Act 2004,
(ab) is chargeable on the sub-scheme administrator of a sub-scheme under Part 4 of the Finance Act 2004 as modified by the Registered Pensions (Splitting of Schemes) Regulations 2006, or
(b) is chargeable on the person who is (or persons who are) the responsible person in relation to an employer financed retirement benefits scheme under section 394(2) of ITEPA 2003.

(2) A person shall not be required to comply with subsection (1) above if he makes and delivers his return for a year of assessment—
(a) on or before the 31st October next following the year; or
(b) where the notice under section 8 or 8A of this Act is given after the 31st August next following the year, within the period of two months beginning with the day on which the notice is given.

(3) Where, in making and delivering a return, a person does not comply with subsection (1) above, an officer of the Board shall, if subsection (2) above applies, and may in any other case—
(a) make the assessment on his behalf on the basis of the information contained in the return; and
(b) send him a copy of the assessment so made.

(3A) An assessment under subsection (3) above is treated for the purposes of this Act as a self-assessment and as included in the return.

Amendment of personal or trustee return by taxpayer

9ZA.—(1) A person may amend his return under section 8 or 8A of this Act by notice to an officer of the Board.

(2) An amendment may not be made more than 12 months after the filing date.

(3) In this section "the filing date", in respect of a return for a year of assessment (Year 1), means—
   (a) 31st January of Year 2, or
   (b) if the notice under section 8 or 8A is given after 31st October of Year 2, the last day of the period of three months beginning with the date of the notice.

Correction of personal or trustee return by Revenue

9ZB.—(1) An officer of the Board may amend a return under section 8 or 8A of this Act so as to correct—
   (a) obvious errors or omissions in the return (whether errors of principle, arithmetical mistakes or otherwise), and
   (b) anything else in the return that the officer has reason to believe is incorrect in the light of information available to the officer.

(2) A correction under this section is made by notice to the person whose return it is.

(3) No such correction may be made more than nine months after—
   (a) the day on which the return was delivered, or
   (b) if the correction is required in consequence of an amendment of the return under section 9ZA of this Act, the day on which that amendment was made.

(4) A correction under this section is of no effect if the person whose return it is gives notice rejecting the correction.

(5) Notice of rejection under subsection (4) above must be given—
   (a) to the officer of the Board by whom the notice of correction was given,
   (b) before the end of the period of 30 days beginning with the date of issue of the notice of correction.

Notice of enquiry

9A.—(1) An officer of the Board may enquire into a return under section 8 or 8A of this Act if he gives notice of his intention to do so ("notice of enquiry")—
   (a) to the person whose return it is ("the taxpayer"),
   (b) within the time allowed.

(2) The time allowed is—
   (a) if the return was delivered on or before the filing date, up to the end of the period of twelve months after the day on which the return was delivered;
   (b) if the return was delivered after the filing date, up to and including the quarter day next following the first anniversary of the day on which the return was delivered;
   (c) if the return is amended under section 9ZA of this Act, up to and including the quarter day next following the first anniversary of the day on which the amendment was made.

For this purpose, the quarter days are 31st January, 30th April, 31st July and 31st October.

(3) A return which has been the subject of one notice of enquiry may not be the subject of another, except one given in consequence of an amendment (or another amendment) of the return under section 9ZA of this Act.

(4) An enquiry extends to—
(a) anything contained in the return, or required to be contained in the return, including any claim or election included in the return,
(b) consideration of whether to give the taxpayer a transfer pricing notice under section 168(1) of TIOPA 2010 (provision not at arm's length: medium-sized enterprise),
(c) consideration of whether to give the taxpayer a notice under section 81(2) of TIOPA 2010 (notice to counteract scheme or arrangement designed to increase double taxation relief),
but this is subject to the following limitation.

(5) If the notice of enquiry is given as a result of an amendment of the return under section 9ZA of this Act—
(a) at a time when it is no longer possible to give notice of enquiry under subsection (2)(a) or (b) above,
(b) after a final closure notice has been issued in relation to an enquiry into the return, or
(c) after a partial closure notice has been issued in such an enquiry in relation to the matters to which the amendment relates or which are affected by the amendment,
the enquiry into the return is limited to matters to which the amendment relates or which are affected by the amendment.

(6) In this section "the filing date" means, in relation to a return, the last day for delivering it in accordance with section 8 or section 8A.

Amendment of return by taxpayer during enquiry

9B.—(1) This section applies if a return is amended under section 9ZA of this Act (amendment of personal or trustee return by taxpayer) or in accordance with Chapter 2 of Part 4 of the Finance Act 2014 (amendment of return after follower notice) at a time when an enquiry into the return is in progress in relation to any matter to which the amendment relates or which is affected by the amendment.

(2) The amendment does not restrict the scope of the enquiry but may be taken into account (together with any matters arising) in the enquiry.

(3) So far as the amendment affects the amount stated in the self-assessment included in the return as the amount of tax payable, it does not take effect while the enquiry is in progress in relation to any matter to which the amendment relates or which is affected by the amendment and—
(a) if the officer states in a partial or final closure notice that he has taken the amendment into account and that—
(i) the amendment has been taken into account in formulating the amendments contained in the notice, or
(ii) his conclusion is that the amendment is incorrect,
the amendment shall not take effect;
(b) otherwise, the amendment takes effect when a partial closure notice is issued in relation to the matters to which the amendment relates or

which are affected by the amendment or, if no such notice is issued, a final closure notice is issued.

(4) For the purposes of this section the period during which an enquiry is in progress in relation to any matter is the whole of the period—
  (a) beginning with the day on which notice of enquiry is given, and
  (b) ending with the day on which a partial closure notice is issued in relation to the matter or, if no such notice is issued, a final closure notice is issued.

Amendment of self-assessment during enquiry to prevent loss of tax

1.11 9C.—(1) This section applies where an enquiry into a return is in progress in relation to any matter as a result of notice of enquiry by an officer of the Board under section 9A(1) of this Act.

(2) If the officer forms the opinion—
  (a) that the amount stated in the self-assessment contained in the return as the amount of tax payable is insufficient; and
  (b) that unless the assessment is immediately amended there is likely to be a loss of tax to the Crown,
he may by notice to the taxpayer amend the assessment to make good the deficiency so far as it relates to the matter.

(3) In the case of an enquiry which under section 9A(5) of this Act is limited to matters arising from an amendment of the return, subsection (2) above only applies so far as the deficiency is attributable to the amendment.

(4) For the purposes of this section the period during which an enquiry is in progress in relation to any matter is the whole of the period—
  (a) beginning with the day on which notice of enquiry is given, and
  (b) ending with the day on which a partial closure notice is issued in relation to the matter or, if no such notice is issued, a final closure notice is issued.

Records

Records to be kept for purposes of returns

1.12 12B.—(1) Any person who may be required by a notice under section 8, 8A, or 12AA of this Act to make and deliver a return for a year of assessment or other period shall—
  (a) keep all such records as may be requisite for the purpose of enabling him to make and deliver a correct and complete return for the year or period; and
  (b) preserve those records until the end of the relevant day, that is to say, the day mentioned in subsection (2) below or, where a return is required by a notice given on or before that day, whichever of that day and the following is the latest, namely—
    (i) where enquiries into the return are made by an officer of the Board, the day on which, by virtue of 28A(1B) or 28B(1B) of this Act, those enquiries are completed; and
    (ii) where no enquiries into the return are so made, the day on which such an officer no longer has power to make such enquiries.

(2) The day referred to in subsection (1) above is—

(1970 c.9 s.12B)

    (a) in the case of a person carrying on a trade, profession or business alone or in partnership or a company, the fifth anniversary of the 31st January next following the year of assessment or (as the case may be) the sixth anniversary of the end of the period;

    (b) otherwise, the first anniversary of the 31st January next following the year of assessment . . .

or (in either case) such earlier day as may be specified in writing by the Commissioners for Her Majesty's Revenue and Customs (and different days may be specified for different cases).

(2A) Any person who—

    (a) is required, by such a notice as is mentioned in subsection (1) above given at any time after the end of the day mentioned in subsection (2) above, to make and deliver a return for a year of assessment or other period; and

    (b) has in his possession at that time any records which may be requisite for the purpose of enabling him to make and deliver a correct and complete return for the year or period,

shall preserve those records until the end of the relevant day, that is to say, the day which, if the notice had been given on or before the day mentioned in subsection (2) above, would have been the relevant day for the purposes of subsection (1) above.

(3) In the case of a person carrying on a trade, profession or business alone or in partnership—

    (a) the records required to be kept and preserved under subsection (1) or (2A) above shall include records of the following, namely—

        (i) all amounts received and expended in the course of the trade, profession or business and the matters in respect of which the receipts and expenditure take place, and

        (ii) in the case of a trade involving dealing in goods, all sales and purchases of goods made in the course of the trade . . .

(3A) The Commissioners for Her Majesty's Revenue and Customs may by regulations—

    (a) provide that the records required to be kept and preserved under this section include, or do not include, records specified in the regulations, and

    (b) provide that those records include supporting documents so specified.

(4) The duty under subsection (1) or (2A) to preserve records may be discharged—

    (a) by preserving them in any form and by any means, or

    (b) by preserving the information contained in them in any form and by any means,

subject to subsection (4A) and any conditions or further exceptions specified in writing by the Commissioners for Her Majesty's Revenue and Customs.

(4A) Subsection (4)(b) does not apply in the case of the following kinds of records—

    (a) any statement in writing such as is mentioned in—

        (i) subsection (1) of section 1100 of CTA 2010 (amount of distribution, formerly amount of qualifying distribution and tax credit); or

        (ii) section 495(1) or 975(2) or (4) of ITA 2007 (statements about deduction of income tax),

which is furnished by the company or person there mentioned, whether after the making of a request or otherwise;
  (b) any record (however described) which is required by regulations under section 70(1)(c) of the Finance Act 2004 to be given to a sub-contractor (within the meaning of section 58 of that Act) on the making of a payment to which section 61 of that Act (deductions on account of tax) applies;
  (c) any such record as may be requisite for making a correct and complete claim in respect of, or otherwise requisite for making a correct and complete return so far as relating to, an amount of tax—
    (i) which has been paid under the laws of a territory outside the United Kingdom, or
    (ii) which would have been payable under the law of a territory outside the United Kingdom ("territory F") but for a development relief.
(4B) In subsection (4A)(c) "development relief" means a relief—
(a) given under the law of territory F with a view to promoting industrial, commercial, scientific, educational or other development in a territory outside the United Kingdom, and
(b) about which provision is made in arrangements that have effect under section 2(1) of TIOPA 2010 (double taxation relief by agreement with territories outside the United Kingdom).
(5) Subject to subsections (5A) and (5B) below any person who fails to comply with subsection (1) or (2A) above in relation to a year of assessment or accounting period shall be liable to a penalty not exceeding £3,000.
(5A) Subsection (5) above does not apply where the records which the person fails to keep or preserve are records which might have been requisite only for the purposes of claims, elections or notices which are not included in the return.
(5B) Subsection (5) above also does not apply where—
(a) the records which the person fails to keep or preserve are records falling within paragraph (a) of subsection (4A) above; and
(b) an officer of the Board is satisfied that any facts which he reasonably requires to be proved, and which would have been proved by the records, are proved by other documentary evidence furnished to him.
(5BA) Regulations under this section may make provision, in relation to relevant transfer pricing records specified, or of a description specified, in the regulations—
(a) as to the form or manner in which those records are to be kept and preserved;
(b) by reference to things specified in the transfer pricing guidelines (within the meaning of section 164 of TIOPA 2010 (interpretation in accordance with OECD principles)).
(5C) Regulations under this section may—
(a) make different provision for different cases, and
(b) make provision by reference to things specified in a notice published by the Commissioners for Her Majesty's Revenue and Customs in accordance with the regulations (and not withdrawn by a subsequent notice).
(6) For the purposes of this section—
(a) a person engaged in the letting of property shall be treated as carrying on a trade;

(aa) records are "relevant transfer pricing records" if the Commissioners for His Majesty's Revenue and Customs reasonably consider that the records may relate to the calculation of profits or losses in accordance with Part 4 of TIOPA 2010 (transfer pricing);
(b) "supporting documents" includes accounts, books, deeds, contracts, vouchers and receipts.

Part IV

Assessment and Claims

Completion of enquiry into personal or trustee return

28A.—(1) This section applies in relation to an enquiry under section 9A(1) of this Act.

(1A) Any matter to which the enquiry relates is completed when an officer of Revenue and Customs informs the taxpayer by notice (a "partial closure notice") that the officer has completed his enquiries into that matter.

(1B) The enquiry is completed when an officer of Revenue and Customs informs the taxpayer by notice (a "final closure notice")—
(a) in a case where no partial closure notice has been given, that the officer has completed his enquiries, or
(b) in a case where one or more partial closure notices have been given, that the officer has completed his remaining enquiries.

(2) A partial or final closure notice must state the officer's conclusions and—
(a) state that in the officer's opinion no amendment of the return is required, or
(b) make the amendments of the return required to give effect to his conclusions.

(3) A partial or final closure notice takes effect when it is issued.

(4) The taxpayer may apply to the tribunal for a direction requiring an officer of the Board to issue a partial or final closure notice within a specified period.

(5) Any such application is to be subject to the relevant provisions of Part 5 of this Act (see, in particular, section 48(2)(b)).

(6) The tribunal shall give the direction applied for unless satisfied that there are reasonable grounds for not issuing the partial or final closure notice within a specified period.

(7) In this section "the taxpayer" means the person to whom notice of enquiry was given.

(8) In the Taxes Acts, references to a closure notice under this section are to a partial or final closure notice under this section.

Assessment where loss of tax discovered

29.—(1) If an officer of the Board or the Board discover, as regards any person (the taxpayer) and a year of assessment—
(a) that an amount of income tax or capital gains tax ought to have been assessed but has not been assessed,

(b) that an assessment to tax is or has become insufficient, or

(c) that any relief which has been given is or has become excessive,

the officer or, as the case may be, the Board may, subject to subsections (2) and (3) below, make an assessment in the amount, or the further amount, which ought in his or their opinion to be charged in order to make good to the Crown the loss of tax.

(2) Where—

(a) the taxpayer has made and delivered a return under section 8 or 8A of this Act in respect of the relevant year of assessment, and

(b) the situation mentioned in subsection (1) above is attributable to an error or mistake in the return as to the basis on which his liability ought to have been computed,

the taxpayer shall not be assessed under that subsection in respect of the year of assessment there mentioned if the return was in fact made on the basis or in accordance with the practice generally prevailing at the time when it was made.

(3) Where the taxpayer has made and delivered a return under section 8 or 8A of this Act in respect of the relevant year of assessment, he shall not be assessed under subsection (1) above—

(a) in respect of the year of assessment mentioned in that subsection; and

(b) in the same capacity as that in which he made and delivered the return,

unless one of the two conditions mentioned below is fulfilled.

(4) The first condition is that the situation mentioned in subsection (1) above was brought about carelessly or deliberately by the taxpayer or a person acting on his behalf.

(5) The second condition is that at the time when an officer of the Board—

(a) ceased to be entitled to give notice of his intention to enquire into the taxpayer's return under section 8 or 8A of this Act in respect of the relevant year of assessment; or

(b) in a case where a notice of enquiry into the return was given—

(i) issued a partial closure notice as regards a matter to which the situation mentioned in subsection (1) above relates, or

(ii) if no such partial closure notice was issued, issued a final closure notice,

the officer could not have been reasonably expected, on the basis of the information made available to him before that time, to be aware of the situation mentioned in subsection (1) above.

(6) For the purposes of subsection (5) above, information is made available to an officer of the Board if—

(a) it is contained in the taxpayer's return under section 8 or 8A of this Act in respect of the relevant year of assessment (the return), or in any accounts, statements or documents accompanying the return;

(b) it is contained in any claim made as regards the relevant year of assessment by the taxpayer acting in the same capacity as that in which he made the return, or in any accounts, statements or documents accompanying any such claim;

(c) it is contained in any documents, accounts or particulars which, for the purposes of any enquiries into the return or any such claim by an officer of the Board, are produced or furnished by the taxpayer to the officer; or

(d) it is information the existence of which, and the relevance of which as regards the situation mentioned in subsection (1) above—

(i) could reasonably be expected to be inferred by an officer of the Board from information falling within paragraphs (a)–(c) above; or

(ii) are notified in writing by the taxpayer to an officer of the Board.

(7) In subsection (6) above—

(a) any reference to the taxpayer's return under section 8 or 8A of this Act in respect of the relevant year of assessment includes—

(i) a reference to any return of his under that section for either of the two immediately preceding chargeable periods; and

(ii) where the return is under section 8 and the taxpayer carries on a trade, profession or business in partnership, a reference to any partnership return with respect to the partnership for the relevant year of assessment or either of those periods; and

(b) any reference in paragraphs (b) to (d) to the taxpayer includes a reference to a person acting on his behalf.

(7A) The requirement to fulfil one of the two conditions mentioned above does not apply so far as regards any income or chargeable gains of the taxpayer in relation to which the taxpayer has been given, after any enquiries have been completed into the taxpayer's return, a notice under section 81(2) of TIOPA 2010 (notice to counteract scheme or arrangement designed to increase double taxation relief).

(8) An objection to the making of an assessment under this section on the ground that neither of the two conditions mentioned above is fulfilled shall not be made otherwise than on an appeal against the assessment.

(9) Any reference in this section to the relevant year of assessment is a reference to—

(a) in the case of the situation mentioned in paragraph (a) or (b) of subsection (1) above, the year of assessment mentioned in that subsection; and

(b) in the case of the situation mentioned in paragraph (c) of that subsection, the year of assessment in respect of which the claim was made.

Relief for excessive assessments

Double assessment

32.—(1) If on a claim made to the Board it appears to their satisfaction that a person has been assessed to tax more than once for the same cause and for the same chargeable period, they shall direct the whole, or such part of any assessment as appears to be an overcharge, to be vacated, and thereupon the same shall be vacated accordingly.

(2) An appeal may be brought against the refusal of a claim under this section.

(3) Notice of appeal under subsection (2) must be given—
(a) in writing;
(b) within 30 days after the day on which notice of the refusal is given;
(c) to the officer of Revenue and Customs by whom that notice was given.

Recovery of overpaid tax etc

33.—Schedule 1AB contains provision for and in connection with claims for the recovery of overpaid income tax and capital gains tax.

Time limits

Ordinary time-limit of four years

1.17 **34.**—(1) Subject to the following provisions of this Act, and to any other provisions of the Taxes Acts allowing a longer period in any particular class of case, an assessment to income tax or capital gains tax may be made at any time not more than 4 years after the end of the year of assessment to which it relates.

(2) An objection to the making of any assessment on the ground that the time-limit for making it has expired shall only be made on an appeal against the assessment.

(3) In this section "assessment" does not include a self-assessment.

Ordinary time-limit for self-assessments

1.18 **34A.**—(1) Subject to subsections (2) and (3), a self assessment contained in a return under section 8 or 8A may be made and delivered at any time not more than 4 years after the end of the year of assessment to which it relates.

(2) Nothing in subsection (1) prevents–
 (a) a person who has received a notice under section 8 or 8A within that period of 4 years from delivering a return including a self-assessment within the period of 3 months beginning with the date of the notice,
 (b) [*omitted*].

(3) Subsection (1) has effect subject to the following provisions of this Act and to any other provisions of the Taxes Acts allowing a longer period in any particular class of case.

(4) [*omitted*].

Time limit: income received after year for which it is assessable

1.19 **35.**—Where income to which this section applies is received in a year of assessment subsequent to that for which it is assessable, an assessment to income tax as respects that income may be made at any time not more than 4 years after the end of the year of assessment in which it was received.

(2) This section applies to—
 (a) employment income,
 (b) pension income, and
 (c) social security income.

Loss of tax brought about carelessly or deliberately etc.

1.20 **36.**—(1) An assessment on a person in a case involving a loss of income tax or capital gains tax brought about carelessly by the person may be made at any time not more than 6 years after the end of the year of assessment to which it relates (subject to subsection (1A) and any other provision of the Taxes Acts allowing a longer period).

(1A) An assessment on a person in a case involving a loss of income tax or capital gains tax—
 (a) brought about deliberately by the person,
 (b) attributable to a failure by the person to comply with an obligation under section 7,

(c) attributable to arrangements in respect of which the person has failed to comply with an obligation under section 309, 310 or 313 of the Finance Act 2004 (obligation of parties to tax avoidance schemes to provide information to Her Majesty's Revenue and Customs), or

(d) attributable to arrangements that were expected to give rise to a tax advantage in respect of which the person was under an obligation to notify the Commissioners for Her Majesty's Revenue and Customs under section 253 of the Finance Act 2014 (duty to notify Commissioners of promoter reference number) but failed to do so,

may be made at any time not more than 20 years after the end of the year of assessment to which it relates (subject to any provision of the Taxes Acts allowing a longer period).

(1B) In subsections (1) and (1A) references to a loss brought about by the person who is the subject of the assessment include a loss brought about by another person acting on behalf of that person.

(2) Where the person mentioned in subsection (1) or (1A) ("the person in default") carried on a trade, profession or business with one or more other persons at any time in the period for which the assessment is made, an assessment in respect of the profits or gains of the trade, profession or business in a case mentioned in subsection (1A) or (1B) may be made not only on the person in default but also on his partner or any of his partners.

(3) If the person on whom the assessment is made so requires, in determining the amount of the tax to be charged for any chargeable period in any assessment made in a case mentioned in subsection (1) or (1A) above, effect shall be given to any relief or allowance to which he would have been entitled for that chargeable period on a claim or application made within the time allowed by the Taxes Acts.

(3A) In subsection (3) above, "claim or application" does not include an election under any of sections 47 to 49 of ITA 2007 (tax reductions for married couples and civil partners: elections to transfer relief).

(4) Any act or omission such as is mentioned in section 98B below on the part of a grouping (as defined in that section) or member of a grouping shall be deemed for the purposes of subsections (1) and (1A) to be the act or omission of each member of the grouping.

PART V

APPEALS AND OTHER PROCEEDINGS

Proceedings before the Commissioners

Settling of appeals by agreement

54.—(1) Subject to the provisions of this section, where a person gives notice of appeal and, before the appeal is determined by the [^{1} [^{2} [^{3} [^{4} First-tier Tribunal]]]], [^{1} [^{4} an officer of Revenue and Customs]] and the appellant come to an agreement, whether in writing or otherwise, that the

1.21

[⁴ determination] or decision under appeal should be treated as upheld without variation, or as varied in a particular manner or as discharged or cancelled, the like consequences shall ensue for all purposes as would have ensued if, at the time when the agreement was come to, the tribunal had determined the appeal and had upheld the [⁴ determination] or decision without variation, had varied it in that manner or had discharged or cancelled it, as the case may be.

(2) Subsection (1) of this section shall not apply where, within thirty days from the date when the agreement was come to, the appellant gives notice in writing to [¹ [⁴ an officer of Revenue and Customs]] that he desires to repudiate or resile from the agreement.

[¹ [⁴ (3) Where an agreement is not in writing—
  (a) the preceding provisions of this section shall not apply unless the Board give notice, in such form and manner as they consider appropriate, to the appellant of the terms agreed between the officer of Revenue and Customs and the appellant; and
  (b) the references in those preceding provisions to the time when the agreement was come to shall be construed as references to the date of that notice.]]

(4) Where—
  (a) a person who has given a notice of appeal notifies [¹ [⁴ an officer of Revenue and Customs]], whether orally or in writing, that he desires not to proceed with the appeal; and
  (b) thirty days have elapsed since the giving of the notification without [¹ [⁴ an officer of Revenue and Customs]] giving to the appellant notice in writing indicating that he is unwilling that the appeal should be treated as withdrawn,

the preceding provisions of this section shall have effect as if, at the date of the appellant's notification, the appellant and [¹ [⁴ an officer of Revenue and Customs]] had come to an agreement, orally or in writing, as the case may be, that the [⁴ determination] or decision under appeal should be upheld without variation.

(5) The references in this section to an agreement being come to with an appellant and the giving of notice or notification to or by an appellant include references to an agreement being come to with, and the giving of notice or notification to or by, a person acting on behalf of the appellant in relation to the appeal.

[¹(6) In subsection (1) "appeal tribunal" means an appeal tribunal [² . . .] constituted in Northern Ireland under Chapter 1 of Part 2 of the Social Security (Northern Ireland) Order 1998 (social security appeals: Northern Ireland).]

AMENDMENTS AND MODIFICATIONS

1. Modifications made to tax credit cases by the Tax Credits (Appeals) Regulations 2002 (SI 2002/2926) reg.3 (December 17, 2002).

2. Amendments made by the Tribunals, Courts and Enforcement Act 2007 (Transitional and Consequential Provisions) Order 2008 (SI 2008/2683) art.6 and Sch.1 para.193 (November 3, 2008).

3. Amendments made by the Transfer of Tribunal Functions and Revenue and Customs Appeals Order 2009 (SI 2009/56) art.3 and Sch.1 para.33 (April 1, 2009).

4. Modifications made to tax credits cases by the Tax Credits (Settlement of Appeals) Regulations 2014 (SI 2014/1933) reg.3 (August 12, 2014).

(1970 c.9 s.54)

Definitions

"appeal tribunal"—see subs.(6).
"the Board"—see s.67 of the Tax Credits Act 2002 but note that the functions of the Board have now been transferred to the Commissioners for Her Majesty's Revenue and Customs (Commissioners for Revenue and Customs Act 2005 s.5(2)).

General Note

The major modifications made to s.54 by the Tax Credits (Settlement of Appeals) Regulations 2014 (SI 2014/1933) should be read with the close and careful decision of Upper Tribunal Judge Rowland in *JI v HMRC* [2013] UKUT 199 (AAC). As that decision makes clear, the previous state of s.54 as applied (if it was applied) to tax credits was a mess. The 2014 amendments update, clarify and tidy up the previously messy and incomplete provisions. In particular they confirm that the general settlement powers used by HMRC to deal with income tax and similar disputes apply to the settlement of tax credits appeals. Section 54 is also subject to modifications for child trust funds appeals made by the Child Trust Funds (Non-tax Appeals) Regulations 2005 (SI 2005/191), along parallel lines to those in the Tax Credits (Appeals) Regulations 2002, subject to some very minor consequential adjustments (however, the modifications exclusive to child trust fund appeals are not captured in the text of s.54 as set out above). Similar modifications are also made in the case of childcare payments appeals by reg.7 of the Childcare Payments (Appeals) Regulations 2016 (SI 2016/1078).

1.22

Subsection (1)

This allows the parties to compromise an appeal and reach an agreement that is as final as a decision of a tribunal. Indeed, it is more final because, not actually being a decision of a tribunal, there can be no appeal to the Upper Tribunal. Note that the agreement must be reached before the appeal tribunal determines the appeal. Therefore, this sort of agreement cannot put an end to an appeal to the Upper Tribunal, notwithstanding the definition of "tax credit appeal" in reg.2 of the Tax Credits (Appeals) Regulations 2002, although a judge or registrar would no doubt have regard to any agreement when deciding whether or not to allow an appeal to be withdrawn under r.17 of the Tribunal Procedure (Upper Tribunal) Rules 2008. If a judge sets aside a decision of an appeal tribunal and refers the case to another tribunal, it again becomes possible for an agreement to be made.

1.23

The effect of an agreement is to prevent an officer of Revenue and Customs from making any further decision in respect of the same issue and the same period (*Cenlon Finance Co Ltd v Ellwood* [1961] Ch.50). However, an officer is not barred from making a new decision if it is discovered that the agreement was based on incorrect information supplied by the appellant (*Gray v Matheson* [1993] 1 W.L.R. 1130). It is suggested that an officer is also not barred from making a decision under s.18 of the Tax Credits Act 2000 if the agreement related to a s.14 decision and it may also not be inappropriate to revise, under, says s.15 or s.16, an agreed award, depending on what exactly had been the scope of the agreement. In the context of tax credit cases there will not often be any doubt as to the scope of the agreement but where there was more than one issue between the parties—perhaps where the amount of earnings from self-employment is in dispute—the test is whether, looking objectively at all the relevant circumstances (including, in particular, the issues raised by the appellant and all the material known to have been in the possession of Her Majesty's Revenue and Customs), a reasonable person would conclude that the officer had accepted all the appellant's contentions (*Scorer v Olin Energy Systems Ltd* [1984] 1 W.L.R. 675). If the agreement is not in writing, see subs.(3).

Subsection (2)

1.24 This provides a 30-day cooling-off period for an appellant (but not an officer of Revenue and Customs) and may be particularly relevant in the light of subs.(5). It could give rise to delay if a hearing date is cancelled in the light of an agreement from which an appellant later resiles. On the other hand, the delay is no greater than can arise in a social security case where the Secretary of State makes a new decision, causing an appeal to lapse under s.9(6) of the Social Security Act 1998 but generating a new right of appeal.

Subsection (3)

1.25 If an agreement is not in writing, Her Majesty's Revenue and Customs must set out in writing their understanding of the agreement and give the appellant 30 days to object. This ensures a reasonable degree of certainty as to the terms of the agreement. The appellant is not required expressly to accept the written version.

Subsection (4)

1.26 There is no provision in the Tax Credits (Appeals) (No.2) Regulations 2002 allowing an appellant to withdraw an appeal by giving notice to the clerk to the tribunal (compare r.17 of the Tribunal Procedure (First-tier Tribunal)(Social Entitlement Chamber) Rules 2008. Instead, an appellant may give notice of his desire to abandon the appeal to the officer of Revenue and Customs and the officer has 30 days in which to object. If the officer signifies agreement within the 30 days, subss.(1)–(3) will be brought into operation, as will be the case if the officer does nothing for 30 days. If the officer objects within the 30 days, the appeal proceeds. Presumably that means that any attempt to withdraw an appeal is ineffective for 30 days unless the officer consents. This provision applies only to appeals. The 2008 Rules permit the unilateral withdrawal of an application for a direction or penalty proceedings where a tribunal has a first instance jurisdiction.

Subsection (5)

1.27 By virtue of this subsection, an agreement under subs.(1) may be entered into by an appellant's representative. However, such an agreement may be repudiated by the appellant under subs.(2).

No questioning in appeal of amounts of certain social security income

1.28 **54A.**—(1) Subsection (2) applies if an amount is notified under section 54B(1) and—
 (a) no objection is made to the notification within 60 days after its date of issue, or such further period as may be allowed under section 54B(4) and (5), or
 (b) an objection is made but is withdrawn by the objector by notice.
 (2) The amount is not to be questioned in any appeal against any assessment in respect of income including the amount.
 (3) Subsection (4) applies if an amount is notified under section 54B(1) and—
 (a) an objection is made to the notification within 60 days after its date of issue, or such further period as may be allowed under section 54B(4) and (5),
 (b) the appropriate officer and the objector come to an agreement that the amount notified should be varied in a particular manner, and

(c) the officer confirms that agreement in writing.

(4) The amount, as varied, is not to be questioned in any appeal against any assessment in respect of income including that amount.

(5) Subsection (4) does not apply if, within 60 days from the date when the agreement was come to, the objector gives to the appropriate officer notice that the objector wishes to repudiate or resile from the agreement.

Notifications of taxable amounts of certain social security income

54B.—(1) The appropriate officer may by notice notify a person who is liable to pay any income tax charged on any unemployment benefit, jobseeker's allowance or income support—
  (a) of the amount on which the tax is charged, or
  (b) of an alteration in an amount previously notified under paragraph (a) or this paragraph.

(2) A notification under subsection (1) must—
  (a) state its date of issue, and
  (b) state that the person notified may object to the notification by notice given within 60 days after that date.

(3) A notification under subsection (1)(b) cancels the previous notification concerned.

(4) An objection to a notification under subsection (1) may be made later than 60 days after its date of issue if, on an application for the purpose—
  (a) the appropriate officer is satisfied—
    (i) that there was a reasonable excuse for not objecting before the end of the 60 days, and
    (ii) that the application was made without unreasonable delay after the end of the 60 days, and
  (b) the officer gives consent in writing.

(5) If the officer is not so satisfied, the officer is to refer the application for determination by the tribunal.

GENERAL NOTE

The tribunal for the purposes of s.54B(5) is the First-tier Tribunal (s.47C defines "the tribunal" as such). It seems that applications referred under subs.(5) are to be determined by the Tax Chamber of the First-tier Tribunal rather than the Social Entitlement Chamber. The Social Entitlement Chamber's jurisdiction is limited to appeals relating to entitlement to and payment of social security benefits (see arts 6 and 7 of the First-tier Tribunal and Upper Tribunal (Chambers) Order 2010 (SI 2010/2655)). It is suggested that a reference under subs.(5) is not an appeal relating to entitlement or payment of social security benefits. This is reinforced by s.54C(2)'s exclusion of ss.54A and 54B from the definition of appeal in s.48(1)(a) ("appeal" means "any appeal under the Taxes Acts").

Interpretation of sections 54A and 54B: "appropriate officer" etc

54C.– (1) In section 54A and 54B "the appropriate officer" means the appropriate officer—
  (a) in Great Britain, of the Department for Work and Pensions, and
  (b) in Northern Ireland, of the Department for Social Development.

(2) Section 48(1)(a) (meaning of "appeal" in the following provisions of Part 5) does not apply for the purposes of section 54A and 54B.

Taxes Management Act 1970

Part X

Penalties, etc.

Admissibility of evidence not affected by offer of settlement etc

1.32   **105.**—(1) Statements made or documents produced by or on behalf of a person shall not be inadmissible in any such proceedings as are mentioned in subsection (2) below by reason only that it has been drawn to his attention—
  (a) that where serious tax fraud has been committed the Board may accept a money settlement and that the Board will accept such a settlement, and will not pursue a criminal prosecution, if he makes a full confession of all tax irregularities, or
  (b) that the extent to which he is helpful and volunteers information is a factor that will be taken into account in determining the amount of any penalty,
and that he was or may have been induced thereby to make the statements or produce the documents.
    (2) The proceedings mentioned in subsection (1) above are—
  (a) any criminal proceedings against the person in question for any form of fraudulent conduct in connection with or in relation to tax; and
  (b) any proceedings against him for the recovery of any tax due from him and
  (c) any proceedings for a penalty or on appeal against the determination of a penalty.

Part XI

Miscellaneous and Supplemental

Documents

Loss, destruction or damage to assessments, returns, etc.

1.33   **112.**—(1) Where any assessment to tax, or any duplicate of assessment to tax, or any return or other document relating to tax, has been lost or destroyed, or been so defaced or damaged as to be illegible or otherwise useless, HMRC may, notwithstanding anything in any enactment to the contrary, do all such acts and things as they might have done, and all acts and things done under or in pursuance of this section shall be as valid and effectual for all purposes as they would have been, if the assessment or duplicate of assessment had not been made, or the return or other document had not been made or furnished or required to be made or furnished.
    Provided that, where any person who is charged with tax in consequence or by virtue of any act or thing done under or in pursuance of this section proves to the satisfaction of the tribunal that he has already paid any tax for the same chargeable period in respect of the subject matter and on the account in respect of and on which he is so charged, relief shall be given to the extent

to which the liability of that person has been discharged by the payment so made either by abatement from the charge or by repayment, as the case may require.

...

(3) The references in subsection (1) above to assessments to tax include references to determinations of penalties; and in its application to such determinations the proviso to that subsection shall have effect with the appropriate modifications.

Want of form or errors not to invalidate assessments, etc.

114.—(1) An assessment or determination, warrant or other proceeding which purports to be made in pursuance of any provision of the Taxes Acts shall not be quashed, or deemed to be void or voidable, for want of form, or be affected by reason of a mistake, defect or omission therein, if the same is in substance and effect in conformity with or according to the intent and meaning of the Taxes Acts, and if the person or property charged or intended to be charged or affected thereby is designated therein according to common intent and understanding.

(2) An assessment or determination shall not be impeached or affected—
(a) by reason of a mistake therein as to—
   (i) the name or surname of a person liable, or
   (ii) the description of any profits or property, or
   (iii) the amount of the tax charged, or
(b) by reason of any variance between the notice and the assessment or determination.

Interpretation

Interpretation

118.—(1) In this Act, unless the context otherwise requires—
"Act" includes an Act of the Parliament of Northern Ireland and "enactment" shall be construed accordingly;
"the Board" means the Commissioners of Inland Revenue;
"body of persons" means any body politic, corporate or collegiate, and any company, fraternity, fellowship and society of persons, whether corporate or not corporate;
"chargeable gain" has the same meaning as in the 1992 Act;
"chargeable period" means a year of assessment or a company's accounting period;
"collector" means any collector of taxes;
"company" has the meaning given by section 1121(1) of CTA 2010 (with section 617 of that Act);
"CTA 2009" means the Corporation Tax Act 2009,
"CTA 2010" means the Corporation Tax Act 2010,
...
"HMRC" means Her Majesty's Revenue and Customs;
...
"inspector" means any inspector of taxes;
"ITEPA 2003" means the Income Tax (Earnings and Pensions) Act 2003;

"ITTOIA 2005" means the Income Tax (Trading and Other Income) Act 2005;
"ITA 2007" means the Income Tax Act 2007;
"partner" is to be construed in accordance with section 12AA(10B) of this Act;
"partnership return" has the meaning given by section 12AA(10A) of this Act;
"the principal Act" means the Income and Corporation Taxes Act 1988;
"the relevant trustees", in relation to a settlement, shall be construed in accordance with section 7(9) of this Act;
"return" includes any statement or declaration under the Taxes Acts;
. . .
"successor", in relation to a person who is required to make and deliver, or has made and delivered, a partnership return, and "predecessor" and "successor", in relation to the successor of such a person, shall be construed in accordance with section 12AA(11) of this Act;
"tax", where neither income tax nor capital gains tax nor corporation tax nor development land tax is specified, means any of those taxes;
"the Taxes Acts" means this Act and—
(a) the Tax Acts; and
(b) the Taxation of Chargeable Gains Act 1992 and all other enactments relating to capital gains tax;
"the 1992 Act" means the Taxation of Chargeable Gains Act 1992;
"the TCEA 2007" means the Tribunals, Courts and Enforcement Act 2007;
"TIOPA 2010" means the Taxation (International and other Provisions) Act 2010;
"trade" includes every trade, manufacture, adventure or concern in the nature of trade.
"the tribunal" is to be read in accordance with section 47C;

(2) For the purposes of this Act, a person shall be deemed not to have failed to do anything required to be done within a limited time if he did it within such further time, if any, as the Board or the tribunal or officer concerned may have allowed; and where a person had a reasonable excuse for not doing anything required to be done he shall be deemed not to have failed to do it unless the excuse ceased and, after the excuse ceased, he shall be deemed not to have failed to do it if he did it without unreasonable delay after the excuse had ceased.

. . .

(4) For the purposes of this Act, the amount of tax covered by any assessment shall not be deemed to be finally determined until that assessment can no longer be varied, whether by the tribunal on an appeal notified to it or by the order of any court.

(5) For the purposes of this Act a loss of tax or a situation is brought about carelessly by a person if the person fails to take reasonable care to avoid bringing about that loss or situation.

(6) Where—
(a) information is provided to Her Majesty's Revenue and Customs,
(b) the person who provided the information, or the person on whose behalf the information was provided, discovers some time later that the information was inaccurate, and
(c) that person fails to take reasonable steps to inform Her Majesty's Revenue and Customs,

(1970 c.9 s.118)

any loss of tax or situation brought about by the inaccuracy shall be treated for the purposes of this Act as having been brought about carelessly by that person.

(7) In this Act references to a loss of tax or a situation brought about deliberately by a person include a loss of tax or a situation that arises as a result of a deliberate inaccuracy in a document given to Her Majesty's Revenue and Customs by or on behalf of that person.

Social Security Contributions and Benefits Act 1992

(1992 c.4)

SECTIONS REPRODUCED

PART III

NON-CONTRIBUTORY BENEFITS

77. Guardian's allowance   1.36

PART IX

CHILD BENEFIT

141. Child benefit
142. "Child" and "qualifying young person"
143. Meaning of person responsible for child or qualifying young person
144. Exclusions and priority
145. Rate of child benefit
145A. Entitlement after death of child or qualifying young person
146. Presence in Great Britain
146A. Persons subject to immigration control
147. Interpretation of Part IX and supplementary provisions

PART XI

STATUTORY SICK PAY

Employer's liability

151. Employer's liability

The qualifying conditions

152. Period of incapacity for work

153. Period of entitlement
154. Qualifying days

Limitations on entitlement, etc.

155. Limitations on entitlement
156. Notification of incapacity for work

Rates of payment, etc.

157. Rates of payment
158. Recovery by employers of amounts paid by way of statutory sick pay (*repealed*)
159. Power to substitute provisions for section 158(2) (*repealed*)
159A. Power to provide for recovery by employers of sums paid by way of statutory sick pay
159B. Funding of employers' statutory sick pay liabilities in relation to coronavirus

Miscellaneous

160. Relationship with benefits and other payments, etc.
161. Crown employment—Part XI
162. Special classes of persons
163. Interpretation of Part XI and supplementary provisions

Part XII

Statutory Maternity Pay

164. Statutory maternity pay—entitlement and liability to pay
165. The maternity pay period
166. Rate of statutory maternity pay
167. Funding of employers' liabilities in respect of statutory maternity pay
168. Relationship with benefits and other payments, etc.
169. Crown employment—Part XII
170. Special classes of persons
171. Interpretation of Part XII and supplementary provisions

Part XIIZA

Statutory Paternity Pay

171ZA. Entitlement: birth
171ZB. Entitlement: adoption
171ZC. Entitlement: general
171ZD. Liability to make payments
171ZE. Rate and period of pay
s.171ZEA. *Repealed*
s.171ZEB. *Repealed*
s.171ZEC. *Repealed*
s.171ZED. *Repealed*
s.171ZEE. *Repealed*
171ZF. Restrictions on contracting out

(1992 c.4)

171ZG.	Relationship with contractual remuneration
171ZH.	Crown employment—Part XIIZA
171ZI.	Special classes of person
171ZJ.	Part XIIZA: supplementary
171ZK.	Power to apply Part XIIZA to adoption cases not involving placement

PART XIIZB

STATUTORY ADOPTION PAY

171ZL.	Entitlement
171ZM.	Liability to make payments
171ZN.	Rate and period of pay
171ZO.	Restrictions on contracting out
171ZP.	Relationship with benefits and other payments, etc.
171ZQ.	Crown employment—Part XIIZB
171ZR.	Special classes of person
171ZS.	Part XIIZB: supplementary
171ZT.	Power to apply Part XIIZB to adoption cases not involving placement

PART XIIZC

STATUTORY SHARED PARENTAL PAY

171ZU.	Entitlement: birth
171ZV.	Entitlement: adoption
171ZW.	Entitlement: general
171ZX.	Liability to make payments
171ZY.	Rate and period of pay
171ZZ.	Restrictions on contracting out
171ZZ1.	Relationship with contractual remuneration
171ZZ2.	Crown employment
171ZZ3.	Special classes of person
171ZZ4.	Part XIIZC: supplementary
171ZZ5.	Power to apply Part XIIZC

PART 12ZD

STATUTORY PARENTAL BEREAVEMENT PAY

171ZZ6.	Entitlement
171ZZ7.	Entitlement: supplementary
171ZZ8.	Liability to make payments
171ZZ9.	Rate and period of pay
171ZZ10.	Restrictions on contracting out
171ZZ11.	Relationship with contractual remuneration
171ZZ12.	Crown employment
171ZZ13.	Special classes of person
171ZZ14.	Supplementary
171ZZ15.	Application in relation to stillbirths

Social Security Contributions and Benefits Act 1992

Part XIII

General

Interpretation

172. Application of Act in relation to territorial waters
173. Age
174. References to Acts

Schedules

Schedule 9—Exclusions from entitlement to child benefit
Schedule 10—Priority between persons entitled to child benefit
Schedule 11—Circumstances in which periods of entitlement to statutory sick pay do not arise
Schedule 12—Relationship of statutory sick pay with benefits and other payments, etc.
Schedule 13—Relationship of statutory maternity pay with benefits and other payments, etc.

Guardian's allowance

Guardian's allowance

1.37

77.—(1) A person shall be entitled to a guardian's allowance in respect of a child [³ or qualifying young person] if—
  (a) he is entitled to child benefit in respect of that child [³ or qualifying young person], and
  (b) the circumstances are any of those specified in subsection (2) below; [¹...]

(2) The circumstances referred to in subsection (1)(b) above are—
  (a) that both of the [³ parents of the child or qualifying young person] are dead; or
  (b) that one of the [³ parents of the child or qualifying young person] is dead and the person claiming a guardian's allowance shows that he was at the date of the death unaware of, and has failed after all reasonable efforts to discover, the whereabouts of the other parent; or
  (c) that one of the [³ parents of the child or qualifying young person] is dead and the other is in prison.

(3) There shall be no entitlement to a guardian's allowance in respect of a child [³ or qualifying young person] unless at least one of the [³ parents of the child or qualifying young person] satisfies, or immediately before his death satisfied, such conditions as may be prescribed as to nationality, residence, place of birth or other matters.

(4) Where, apart from this subsection, a person is entitled to receive, in respect of a particular child [³ or qualifying young person], payment of an amount by way of a guardian's allowance, that amount shall not be payable unless one of the conditions specified in subsection (5) below is satisfied.

(5) Those conditions are—
  (a) that the beneficiary would be treated for the purposes of Part IX of this Act as having the child [³ or qualifying young person] living with him; or

(b) that the requisite contributions are being made to the cost of providing for the child [³ or qualifying young person].

(6) The condition specified in subsection (5)(b) above is to be treated as satisfied if, but only if—
(a) such contributions are being made at a weekly rate not less than the amount referred to in subsection (4) above—
  (i) by the beneficiary; or
  (ii) where the beneficiary is one of two spouses [² or civil partners] residing together, by them together; and
(b) except in prescribed cases, the contributions are over and above those required for the purpose of satisfying section 143(1)(b) below.

(7) A guardian's allowance in respect of a child [³ or qualifying young person] shall be payable at the weekly rate specified in Schedule 4, Part III, paragraph 5.

(8) Regulations—
(a) may modify subsection (2) or (3) above in relation to cases in which a child [³ or qualifying young person] has been adopted or is illegitimate, or the marriage of [³ the parents of a child or qualifying young person] has been terminated by divorce [² or the civil partnership of the child's parents has been dissolved];
(b) shall prescribe the circumstances in which a person is to be treated for the purposes of this section as being in prison (by reference to his undergoing a sentence of imprisonment for life or of a prescribed minimum duration, or to his being in legal custody in prescribed circumstances); and
(c) may, for cases where entitlement to a guardian's allowance is established by reference to a person being in prison, provide—
  (i) for requiring him to pay to the National Insurance Fund sums paid by way of a guardian's allowance;
  (ii) for suspending payment of an allowance where a conviction, sentence or order of a court is subject to appeal, and for matters arising from the decision of an appeal;
  (iii) for reducing the rate of an allowance in cases where the person in prison contributes to the cost of providing for the child [³ or qualifying young person].

(9) Where [⁴ a man and woman are married to, or civil partners of, each other and are residing together] and, apart from this subsection, they would each be entitled to a guardian's allowance in respect of the same child [³ or qualifying young person], only [⁴ the woman] shall be entitled, but payment may be made either to her or to him unless she elects in the prescribed manner that payment is not to be made to him.

(10) Subject to subsection (11) below, no person shall be entitled to a guardian's allowance in respect of a child [³ or qualifying young person] of which he or she is the parent.

(11) Where a person—
(a) has adopted a child [³ or qualifying young person]; and
(b) was entitled to guardian's allowance in respect of the child [³ or qualifying young person] immediately before the adoption,
subsection (10) above shall not terminate his entitlement.

Amendments

1. Tax Credits Act 2002 s.60 and Sch.6 (April 6, 2003).
2. Civil Partnership Act 2004 s.254 and Sch.24 para.34 (December 5, 2005).
3. Child Benefit Act 2005 s.1 and Sch.1 para.4 (April 10, 2006).
4. Civil Partnership (Opposite-sex Couples) Regulations 2019 (SI 2019/1458) reg.41(a) and Sch.3 Pt 1 para.14(3)(a) and (b) (December 2, 2019).

Definitions

"child"—s.122.
"entitled"—s.122.
"Great Britain"—by art.1 of the Union with Scotland Act 1706, this means England, Scotland and Wales.
"United Kingdom"—by Sch.1 of the Interpretation Act 1978, this means Great Britain and Northern Ireland.
"week"—s.122.

General Note

1.38 Since April 2003 responsibility for the administration of Guardian's Allowance has lain with HMRC. Arrangements for claims, payments, decisions and appeals are now to be found in the Child Benefit and Guardian's Allowance (Administration) Regulations (SI 2003/492), the Child Benefit and Guardian's Allowance (Administrative Arrangements) Regulations (SI 2003/494), and the Child Benefit and Guardian's Allowance (Decisions and Appeals) Regulations (SI 2003/916). These regulations may be found in Vol.III of this work.

Subsection (1)

1.39 Guardian's Allowance is a benefit paid to those caring for children who are, or are in effect, orphans. The claimant does not have to be in any legal sense the guardian of the child (e.g. under the Children Act 1989), but they must be entitled to child benefit in respect of the child (whether or not they actually receive it) or be treated as if they are entitled.

Subsection (2)

1.40 A claim for Guardian's Allowance can only succeed if it is shown that either:

(a) both of the child's parents are dead,

(b) that one of them is dead and the whereabouts of the other is and has been unknown since the date of that death, or

(c) that one of them is dead and the other is in prison.

Proof of death will normally be supplied by production of a death certificate though death might be presumed in circumstances similar to those for bereavement benefits.

In showing that the whereabouts of a surviving parent are unknown it is necessary for the claimant to show that this has always been the situation since the death of the other, and remains the situation despite having made all reasonable efforts of discovery.

1.41 In considering whether the whereabouts of a surviving parent can reasonably be discovered under (b) above, a tribunal may take into account information which came to light after the claim had been made but before the decision maker had come to a decision, even where the whereabouts of the surviving parent became known otherwise than through the efforts of the claimant. The operative date is the date of decision by the DM. The tribunal must consider the case on the basis of the facts known as at the date of the decision (*R(G) 3/68*). Once the whereabouts of the parent have become known, the claim to the allowance cannot be resurrected on the subsequent disappearance of that parent (*R(G)2/83*). This was a case where the surviving parent attended the funeral of the dead parent but then disappeared and his whereabouts could not be ascertained. The claim to the allowance failed. In the same case the Commissioner said that "all reasonable efforts" means the efforts someone could reasonably be expected to make if they wished to find the person for whom they were searching. "Whereabouts" is not the same as residence, so knowing the town but not the address where the missing parent lives may be enough to defeat the claim to benefit. It should be noted that Commissioners in Northern Ireland have taken a different view, saying that in an urban environment "whereabouts" must mean a place identifiable with "some particularity" (*R3/74(P)*). Indeed, Commissioners in Northern Ireland have taken an altogether more generous view of the conditions to be satisfied, holding that knowledge that a parent is alive does not defeat a claim if the whereabouts of the living parent cannot be ascertained after reasonable efforts (*R3/74/(P)* and *R3/75/(P)*, a decision of a Tribunal of Commissioners). In *R3/75/(P)*, the Tribunal of Commissioners suggested that the Commissioners in Great Britain appeared to be regarding the inquiries as being directed to whether the other parent was alive rather than where that parent was living. In an obiter statement in *R(G) 2/83* the Commissioner appears to share this view, suggesting that mere evidence that the second parent is alive will not amount to knowledge of whereabouts so as to defeat a claim, but this does not, of course, overrule the earlier decisions noted above. It seems that the Northern Ireland Commissioners have viewed the benefit as one payable in the absence of a parent able to assume financial responsibility for the child, whereas the British Commissioners see it as concerned primarily with those rendered orphans.

Two unreported Commissoners' decisions demonstrate just how difficult it has become to interpret this subsection where the underlying philosophy of the provisions is unclear.

In the first of them (*CG/60/92*), the claimant grandmother had custody of a child whose mother had died. The father was known and had visited the child at the grandmother's house on four occassions since the death of the mother. As well, he had been served notice of custody proceedings either at, or through, his parents' address, though subsequently they denied knowledge of his whereabouts. The Commissioner held that the claimant must be taken to have known of the father's whereabouts when she had him in her house and could talk to him. An argument was pressed that knowing the whereabouts of someone must mean knowing an address of residence, or of employment, or at any rate of regular attendance, at which something like service of process could be accomplished. If the reason behind GA has indeed shifted to the idea of a resource for maintenance of the child then there would be something to be said for this argument, but the Commissioner thought that the essence of knowing the whereabouts of a person meant no more than being able in some way to communicate with him, and that was clearly achieved here on the four occasions of his visits. The Commissioner relied in this case on the view expressed in *R(G) 2/83* (where the claimant was visited once, and knew of an address that was valid for a week) which also seems to accept that an ability to communicate with the parent is the touchstone.

In the other case (*CSG/8/92*), the claimant, again a grandmother with the custody of her deceased daughter's child, had had no contact with the child's father, but she had provided an address for service in custody proceedings, she had said that she knew where the other parent was living at the time of her daughter's death, and that she had been told that he was at the funeral, though she had not seen him herself. There was no suggestion that the custody address had been effective and it would appear that at a subsequent SSAT appeal the claimant must have given evidence suggesting that the other matters were based only on rumour. The Commissioner allowed an appeal by the adjudication officer on the ground that the SSAT had failed to explain adequately why they were rejecting the original statements and preferring her later accounts, and he sent the matter back for consideration by another tribunal.

1.42

In doing so he gave further attention to the meaning of reasonable steps to discover the whereabouts of a parent. First, he seems to accept that actual contact with the other parent, or even a chance to communicate, is a conclusive block to the claimant; she cannot in those circumstances say that at all times since the death she has been unaware of the whereabouts of the other parent. Seeing the other parent at the funeral is probably enough to preclude her claim because she could have taken the opportunity to establish contact. It is not enough for the claimant to say that she had no wish to speak to the other (probably estranged) parent, because the test suggested in *R(G) 2/83*, and adopted in these cases, is that reasonable efforts to discover the whereabouts of another person mean the steps that would be reasonable for a person who *wanted* to find that other person. (Though, quaere, it might be possible to argue that one could want to find another person and yet reasonably refrain from making inquiries upon an occasion of particular emotion and distress such as the funeral.)

Both cases (and *R(G) 2/83*), therefore, agree that where actual contact has been made, even though transitory, the claimant knows (or rather has known) the whereabouts of the other parent and the claim must fail. The Commissioner goes on to consider, however, the question of how much knowledge of the other parent's location will suffice if no contact is made. Put another way, the question is what is meant by "whereabouts" when someone is being sought, and how much do you have to know in order to say you have found him? Knowing that the parent is somewhere in the world cannot be sufficient because, as has been pointed out, this equates to knowing that he is alive, whereas the statute requires knowledge of his whereabouts. There seems much good sense in the observation of the Northern Ireland Commissioner that while the name of a village may suffice to locate someone living there, something more must be known of someone in an urban environment. *R(G) 3/68* held that knowing an address (in Russia) from which letters had purported to have been sent, but from which no reply was obtained, did amount to knowing the whereabouts of that person. *CG/60/92* rejects the argument that "whereabouts" should be equated with address for service, but only in the context of a claimant who had actual, if transitory, contact. In *CSG/8/92*, the Commissioner seemed ready to accept that "whereabouts" should now be taken to mean knowledge of the person's residence, of employment, or place of attendance by habit (such as a public house) by which he could be located without undue further difficulty. An unresponsive address in Russia would fail this test. This seems a workable and common sense approach and is one step towards rationalising GA, at least in part, as a benefit for the replacement of parental maintenance.

The circumstances in which a child is regarded as "orphaned" by the surviving parent being in prison are defined in reg.7 of the Guardian's Allowance (General) Regulations 2003.

Where a child has been adopted the adopted parents are put for all purposes in the place of the child's parents. Where a child has been adopted by only one parent a claim may be made in respect of that child when only that parent has died (see reg.4 of the Guardian's Allowance (General) Regulations 2003).

Where a child's parents are not married to each other a claim may be made following the death of the mother if paternity of the child has not been established by a court and is not regarded as having been established by the determining authority (reg.4 of the Guardian's Allowance (General) Regulations 2003).

Where a child's parents have been divorced a claim may be made following the death of the parent with whom the child was living if there is no residence order in favour of the surviving parent and no liability for that parent to maintain the child either under a court order or a decision in force under the Child Support Act 1991 (reg.6 of the Guardian's Allowance (General) Regulations 2003).

Subsections (3)

1.43 Conditions as to residence of the child's parents are to be found in reg.9 of the Guardian's Allowance (General) Regulations 2003.

Subsections (4), (5) and (6)
A claim for GA can only succeed if the claimant is either:

(a) treated as having the child living with them for the purpose of a claim for Child Benefit, or

(b) is contributing (or if living with their spouse, the spouse is contributing) to the cost of maintaining the child to an extent equal to the amount of GA that is payable. This contribution must be in addition to any contribution necessary to qualify for the payment of child benefit.

Subsection (9)
This is a curiously worded provision. Where husband and wife are living together and, but for this provision, they would each be entitled to claim GA, only the wife is to be entitled. Nevertheless HMRC could make payment to the husband unless his wife has elected in the proper way to deny payment to her husband.

Subsection (10)
This prevents a claim for GA by a parent of the child. But for this purpose a step-parent is not regarded as a parent and such a claim could also succeed if it is made by the natural parent of a child whose adoptive parents have died—the effect of the adoption is to substitute the adoptive parents as the child's "parents" for this purpose. (*R(G)4/83(T)*—and see reg.4 of the Guardian's Allowance (General) Regulations 2003.)

Part IX

Child Benefit

Child benefit

141.—A person who is responsible for one or more children [1 or qualifying young persons] in any week shall be entitled, subject to the provisions of this Part of this Act, to a benefit (to be known as "child benefit") for that week in respect of the [1 child or qualifying young person, or each of the children or qualifying young persons] for whom he is responsible.

Amendment

1. Child Benefit Act 2005 s.1 (April 10, 2006).

General Note

Since April 2003 administration of Child Benefit has lain with HMRC, but the structure of the benefit remains substantially unchanged.

The administrative arrangements for claims, payments, decisions and appeals are now to be found in Child Benefit and Guardian's Allowance (Administration) Regulations (SI 2003/492), the Child Benefit and Guardian's Allowance (Administrative Arrangements) Regulations (SI 2003/494) and the Child Benefit and Guardian's Allowance (Decisions and Appeals) Regulations 2003 (SI 2003/916). All of these are to be found in Vol.III of this work.

Child Benefit is a benefit paid to those responsible for a child or qualifying young person. Under the new definitions adopted from 2006 a "child" is a person under the age of 16 (whether or not they are in education) and a "qualifying young person" will be defined by regulation generally as a young person who remains in non-advanced education or in certain forms of training up to the age of 20 (see s.142

below). Those responsible for a child include not only those with whom the child is living, but also those contributing sufficiently to the cost of maintaining that child.

Child Benefit is paid at a higher rate in respect of the first or only child and at a lower rate for all other children in the family.

Claimants for Child Benefit are also subject to conditions as to residence and presence (including the presence of the child) and are disqualified while they are subject to immigration control—see Immigration and Asylum Act 1999, s.115(1)(i).

Some of those responsible for children who receive child benefit also receive or are entitled to child tax credit. See s.8 of the Tax Credits Act 2002 para.1.250.

Section 8 of, and Sch.1 to, the Finance Act 2012 introduce a new High Income Child Benefit Charge. This took initial effect from January 7, 2013 and full effect for the tax year 2013/14 under Sch.1 para.7 of that Act. The charge is detailed in what are now ss.681B–681H of the Income Tax (Earnings and Pensions) Act 2003. The detail of those provisions is beyond the scope of this work. The effect is to impose an income tax charge equal to all child benefit received on any taxpayer whose income exceeds £60,000 with a 50 per cent charge imposed on a taxpayer where income exceeds £50,000 to the extent that that taxpayer's income exceeds £50,000. In other words, a taxpayer over the higher limit receives no long-term advantage from child benefit while there is a tapered removal of advantage where income is below £60,000.

With effect from the tax year 2024–25 these figures are increased to £60,000 and £80,000 respectively—see Finance (No,2) Act 2025 s.5.

Amendments to s.7 of the Taxes Management Act 1970 (not contained in this work) and the addition of s.13A of the Social Security Administration Act 1992 (see para.1.178 below) allow individuals who would lose all advantage from child benefit under these provisions to elect not to receive child benefit.

[¹ "Child" and "qualifying young person"

1.49   **142.**—(1) For the purposes of this Part of this Act a person is a child if he has not attained the age of 16.

(2) In this Part of the Act "qualifying young person" means a person, other than a child, who—
   (a) Has not attained such age (greater than 16) as is prescribed by regulations made by the Treasury, and
   (b) satisfies conditions so prescribed.]

AMENDMENT

1. Child Benefit Act 2005 s.1 (April 10, 2006).

Meaning of "person responsible for [³ child or qualifying young person]"

1.50   **143.**—(1) For the purposes of this Part of this Act a person shall be treated as responsible for a child [³ or qualifying young person] in any week if—
   (a) he has the child [³ or qualifying young person] living with him in that week; or
   (b) he is contributing to the cost of providing for the child [³ or qualifying young person] at a weekly rate which is not less than the weekly rate of child benefit payable in respect of the child [³ or qualifying young person] for that week.

(2) Where a person has had a child [⁴ or qualifying young person] living with him at some time before a particular week he shall be treated for the purposes of this section as having the child [⁴ or qualifying young person] living with him in that week notwithstanding their absence from one another unless, in the 16 weeks preceding that week, they were absent from

one another for more than 56 days not counting any day which is to be disregarded under subsection (3) below.

(3) Subject to subsection (4) below, a day of absence shall be disregarded for the purposes of subsection (2) above if it is due solely to the [⁴ the fact that the child or qualifying young person is]—
- (a) receiving [⁴ education or training of a description prescribed by regulations made by the Treasury];
- (b) undergoing medical or other treatment as an in-patient in a hospital or similar institution; or
- (c) [⁴ ...], in such circumstances as may be prescribed, in residential accommodation pursuant to arrangements made under—
  [¹ [⁵ (i)   [⁶ ...]   [⁷ ...]
  - (ii) the Children Act 1989;]
  [² (iii) the Social Work (Scotland) Act 1968;
  - (iv) the National Health Service (Scotland) Act 1978;
  - (v) the Education (Scotland) Act 1980;
  - (vi) the Mental Health (Scotland) Act 1984; [⁷ ...];
  - (vii) the Children (Scotland) Act 1995;]
  [⁷ (vii) the Children (Scotland) Act 1995; [⁸ ...]
  - (viii) the Children's Hearings (Scotland) Act 2011;] [⁸ or]
  [⁸ (ix) Part 4 of the Social Services and Well-being (Wales) Act 2014.]

(4) The number of days that may be disregarded by virtue of subsection (3)(b) or (c) above in the case of any child [⁴ or qualifying young person] shall not exceed such number as may be prescribed unless the person claiming to be responsible for the child [⁴ or qualifying young person] regularly incurs expenditure in respect [⁴ of him].

(5) Regulations may prescribe the circumstances in which a person is or is not to be treated—
- (a) as contributing to the cost of providing for a child [⁴ or qualifying young person] as required by subsection (1)(b) above; or
- (b) as regularly incurring expenditure in respect of a child [⁴ or qualifying young person] as required by subsection (4) above;

and such regulations may in particular make provision whereby a contribution made or expenditure incurred by two or more persons is to be treated as made or incurred by one of them or whereby a contribution made or expenditure incurred by one of two spouses [³ or civil partners] residing together is to be treated as made or incurred by the other.

AMENDMENTS

1. Social Security (Consequential Provisions) Act 1992 s.6 and Sch.4 para.5 (April 1, 1993).
2. Child Support Pensions and Social Security Act 2000 s.72 (October 9, 2000).
3. Civil Partnership Act 2004 s.254 and Sch.24 para.47 (December 5, 2005).
4. Child Benefit Act 2005 s.1 and Sch.1 para.9 (April 10, 2006).
5. National Health Service (Consequential Provisions) Act 2006 Sch.1 para.146 (March 1, 2007).
6. Care Act 2014 and Children and Families Act 2014 (Consequential Amendments) Order 2015 (SI 2015/914) Sch. art.54 (April 1, 2015).
7. Children's Hearings (Scotland) Act 2011 (Consequential and Transitional Provisions and Savings) Order 2013 (SI 2013/1465) art.17 Sch.1 para.4(2) (June 24, 2013).
8. Social Services and Well-being (Wales) Act 2014 (Consequential Amendments) Regulations 2016 (SI 2016/413) (W.131) reg.131 (April 6, 2016).

Social Security Contributions and Benefits Act 1992

GENERAL NOTE

1.51   The provisions in this section are to be compared with the equivalent (but different) rules for child tax credit. See Child Tax Credit Regulations 2002 reg.3 (para.2.194 below).

Subsection (1)

1.52   A person is regarded as being "responsible for a child or qualifying young person" if they either have the child living with them, or if they are contributing to the upkeep of that child a weekly sum not less that the amount of Child Benefit payable for that week. See reg.11 of the Child Benefit (General) Regulations 2006. To be "living with" the claimant in this context requires that the child resides in the same house in a "settled course of daily living". In *R(F) 2/81* the claimant failed because his daughter spent only the day time hours each weekend in his home. Mere residence on its own may be insufficient if the child is normally living elsewhere (as for example where a child spends its holidays living away from home). But where the child is living with a parent who has rights of care and control it may be regarded as living with that parent even though at other times it may be living with the other parent *(R(F) 2/79)*.

The importance of focusing on the right question in deciding whether a child is living with the claimant is demonstrated by *SB v HMRC* [2013] UKUT 24 (AAC). The claimant, who was a Polish national, had come to this country together with her four-year-old daughter. Shortly after arrival, and when she was in employment, she claimed both Child Benefit and Child Tax Credit ("CTC"). The claimant was asked to provide documentary evidence of the fact that the child was attending school and was registered at a GP surgery. At first both benefits were refused because the claimant had not provided that documentation. However, after appealing, the documents were received by the section dealing with CTC and that claim was allowed. An electronic file dealing with that claim was stored on the HMRC computer system. But the Child Benefit appeal was rejected and an appeal to the FTT was also dismissed. At the tribunal hearing the claimant produced a letter from the school confirming attendance, but no GP documentation. The FTT regarded the school letter as deficient and the absence of the other as significant.

In the Upper Tribunal, Judge Wikeley was critical of the approach adopted both within HMRC and the FTT. As he pointed out, the sole relevant question was whether the child was "living with" her mother. No questions were asked by the FTT that addressed that issue. The documents requested could be evidence of the child's existence, but, unless they recorded the child's address as being the same as that of the claimant, they really said nothing about the living arrangements. It does appear, however, that in practice such evidence is all that is required by HMRC, because on the basis of the documents that had been received, the claim to CTC had been accepted. Judge Wikeley also pointed out that the existence of the CTC appeal was revealed on the papers relating to the claim for Child Benefit and he had been assured by HMRC's representative that it would be easy for each section to access the information used by the other—as he put it, a lamentable failure by the left hand to know of what was done by the right. This is a prime example of what an FTT should have done in exercising its inquisitorial function. The appeal was allowed.

1.53   Where the claimant does not have the child living with them it must be shown that they are providing for the child "at a weekly rate which is not less than the weekly rate of child benefit". The meaning of this phrase has been examined in a decision of Judge Knowles QC, *RK v HMRC* [2015] UKUT 357 (AAC). The claimant, living and working in the UK but whose wife and children remained in Poland, had initially taken sums of money back to his family himself or sent them with friends who were returning there; subsequently he made payments periodically through a money transfer system. The claim for Child Benefit was refused and an appeal to the FTT rejected on the ground that he had not contributed at the required rate. In the UT Judge Knowles found, on the evidence, that he had done so; the FTT were in error, she held, because they had assumed that what the claimant had shown on his claim form as "living expenses" related only to himself (thereby leaving too little to have sent home to his family) whereas the claimant had included there the living expenses that he was providing for both himself and his wife. But although the representative of HMRC accepted that this did allow for contributions to have been made at the necessary rate they argued further, that the payments needed to have been made as weekly payments. The judge rejected that argument. She found nothing in this section or in the Child Benefit (General) Regulations to compel her to reach that conclusion and observed that, on the contrary, it would be inconvenient for persons who were paid at intervals greater than a week, or who were self-employed, if they had to budget for those amounts and then pay them each week.

The interaction of subss.(1) and (2) together with s.144(3) and Sch.10 referred to there is applied in *CF/3348/2002*. There the child remained with the wife when her husband, who had been in receipt of Child Benefit, left her. In accordance with s.144(3) and Sch.10, he nevertheless remained entitled to receive the benefit for the next three weeks.

Subsection (2)
A child may continue to live with the claimant even though one or other of them may be absent provided that the absence is not more than 56 days in a period of 16 weeks. Where the absence is continuous, therefore, entitlement will cease after 8 weeks.

1.54

Subsection (3)
In counting days of absence certain days are disregarded. These include days away at boarding school, days in hospital or otherwise undergoing medical treatment, or days in local authority care on disability or health grounds—reg.9 of the Child Benefit (General) Regulations 2006.

1.55

Subsection (4)
Where the child is absent for medical treatment or in care on grounds of disability or health the period of permitted absence is extended to 12 weeks—reg.10 of the Child Benefit (General) Regulations 2006.

However, entitlement may be continued further provided that the claimant can show that they are regularly incurring expenditure in respect of the child.

1.56

Subsection (5)
Regulation 11 of the Child Benefit (General) Regulations 2006 provides for the aggregation of amounts where two or more persons are contributing to the cost of maintaining a child and for either agreement between them or, failing that, a determination by the Board as to which of them will be treated as entitled to benefit. Where spouses are residing together a contribution made by one of them may be treated as having been made by the other.

1.57

Exclusions and priority

144.—(1) [1 . . .]

(2) Schedule 9 to this Act shall have effect for excluding entitlement to child benefit [1 . . .].

(3) Where, apart from this subsection, two or more persons would be entitled to child benefit in respect of the same child [1 or qualifying young person] for the same week, one of them only shall be entitled; and the question which of them is entitled shall be determined in accordance with Schedule 10 to this Act.

1.58

AMENDMENT

1. Child Benefit Act 2005 s.1 and Sch.1 para.10 (April 10, 2006).

GENERAL NOTE

1.59 Note that recourse to Sch.10 is appropriate only where two or more people are entitled to Child Benefit in respect of the same child for the same week. If, therefore, only one of them remains entitled under s.143 there is no recourse to Sch.10. But where, for example, a child has ceased to reside with one parent (s.143(1)) that parent may remain entitled for a period by the application of the other provisions of s.143 and by the effect of s.13(2) of the SSAA 1992. See *CF/2826/2007* and the notes following Sch.10; see also *CB v HMRC and AE (CHB)* [2016] UKUT 506 (AAC). Compare the different approach taken for child tax credit in Child Tax Credit Regulations 2002 reg.3 (see para.2.273 below) to that in Sch.10.

Rate of child benefit

1.60 145.—(1) Child benefit shall be payable at such weekly rate as may be prescribed.

(2) Different rates may be prescribed in relation to different cases, whether by reference to the age of the child [² or qualifying young person] in respect of whom the benefit is payable or otherwise.

(3) The power to prescribe different rates under subsection (2) above shall be exercised so as to bring different rates into force on such day as the Secretary of State may by order specify.

(4) No rate prescribed in place of a rate previously in force shall be lower than the rate that it replaces.

(5) [¹ . . .]

(6) An order under subsection (3) above may be varied or revoked at any time before the date specified thereby.

(7) An order under that subsection shall be laid before Parliament after being made.

AMENDMENTS

1. Tax Credits Act 2002 s.60 and Sch.6 (April 1, 2003).
2. Child Benefit Act 2005 s.1 and Sch.1 para.11 (April 10, 2006).

[¹ Entitlement after death of child [³ or qualifying young person]

1.61 145A.—(1) If a child [³ or qualifying young person] dies and a person is entitled to child benefit in respect of him for the week in which his death occurs, that person shall be entitled to child benefit in respect of the child [³ or qualifying young person] for a prescribed period following that week.

(2) If the person entitled to child benefit under subsection (1) dies before the end of that prescribed period and, at the time of his death, was—
(a) a member of a married couple [² or civil partnership] and living with the person to whom he was married [² or who was his civil partner], or
(b) a member of [⁴a cohabiting couple],

that other member of the [² couple or partnership] shall be entitled to child benefit for the period for which the dead person would have been entitled to child benefit under subsection (1) above but for his death.

(3) If a child [³ or qualifying young person] dies before the end of the week in which he is born, subsections (1) and (2) apply in his case as if

(1992 c.4 s.145A)

references to the person entitled to child benefit in respect of a child [³ or qualifying young person] for the week in which his death occurs were to the person who would have been so entitled if the child had been alive at the beginning of that week (and if any conditions which were satisfied, and any facts which existed, at the time of his death were satisifed or existed then).

(4) Where a person is entitled to child benefit in respect of a child under this section, section 77 applies with the omission of subsections (4) to (6).

(5) In this section—

[² "civil partnership" means two people [⁴ ...] who are civil partners of each other and are neither—
  (a) separated under a court order, nor
  (b) separated in circumstances in which the separation is likely to be permanent,

[⁴ "cohabiting couple" means two people who are not married to, or civil partners, of each other but are living together as if they were a married couple or civil partners;]

"married couple" means a man and a woman who are married to each other and are neither—
  (a) separated under a court order, nor
  (b) separated in circumstances in which the separation is likely to be permanent, and

[⁴ ...]
[⁴ ...[² ...]]

AMENDMENTS

1. Tax Credits Act 2002 s.56 (April 1, 2003).
2. Civil Partnership Act 2004 s.254 and Sch.24 para.48 (December 5, 2005).
3. Child Benefit Act 2005 s.1 and Sch.1 para.12 (April 10, 2006).
4. Civil Partnership (Opposite-sex Couples) Regulations 2019 (SI 2019/1458) reg.41(a) and Sch.3 Pt 1 para.14(4)(a)–(c) (December 2, 2019).

[¹Presence in Great Britain

146.—(1) No child benefit shall be payable in respect of a child [² or qualifying young person] for a week unless he is in Great Britain in that week.

(2) No person shall be entitled to child benefit for a week unless he is in Great Britain in that week.

(3) Circumstances may be prescribed in which [² any] person is to be treated for the purposes of [² subsection (1) or (2) above] as being, or as not being, in Great Britain.]

AMENDMENTS

1. Tax Credits Act 2002 s.56 (April 1, 2003).
2. Child Benefit Act 2005 s.1 and Sch.1 para.13 (April 10, 2006).

GENERAL NOTE

This section was inserted with effect from April 2003. It replaces an earlier version, but the effect of this section when combined with the Child Benefit (General) Regulations is largely the same. See the notes to those Regulations. While the UK was a member of the European Union it was possible for a claim to be made by a person resident in this country in respect of children resident in another EU country—see *Commissioners for HMRC v Ruas* [2010] EWCA Civ 291; [2010] AACR 31. Since the withdrawal of the UK from the EU, continuing entitlement will depend upon the claimant's status as a settled, or even possibly a pre-settled person in accordance with the terms of the European Union (Withdrawal) Act 2018 and the Retained EU Law (Revocation and Reform) Act 2023, as to which see Vol.III of this work.

Persons subject to immigration control

1.64 [¹ 146A.—[² . . .]]

AMENDMENTS

1. Asylum and Immigration Act 1996 s.10 (August 19, 1996).
2. Immigration and Asylum Act 1999 s.169(3) and Sch.16 (April 3, 2000).

Interpretation of Part IX and supplementary provisions

1.65 147.—(1) In this Part of this Act—
"prescribed" means prescribed by regulations;
"recognised educational establishment" [² omitted]
"voluntary organisation" means a body, other than a public or local authority, the activities of which are carried on otherwise than for profit; and
"week" means a period of 7 days beginning with a Monday.

(2) Subject to any provision made by regulations, references in this Part of this Act to any condition being satisfied or any facts existing in a week shall be construed as references to the condition being satisfied or the facts existing at the beginning of that week.

(3) References in this Part of this Act to a parent, father or mother of a child [² or qualifying young person] shall be construed as including references to a step-parent, step-father or step-mother.

(4) Regulations may prescribe the circumstances in which persons are or are not to be treated for the purposes of this Part of this Act as residing together.

(5) Regulations may make provision as to the circumstances in which [¹ a marriage during the subsistence of which a party to it is at any time married to more than one person is to be treated for the purposes of this Part of this Act as having, or not having, the same consequences as any other marriage.]

(6) Nothing in this Part of this Act shall be construed as conferring a right to child benefit on any body corporate; but regulations may confer such a right on voluntary organisations and for that purpose may make such modifications as the Secretary of State thinks fit—
   (a) of any provision of this Part of this Act; or
   (b) of any provision of the Administration Act relating to child benefit.

AMENDMENTS

1. Private International Law (Miscellaneous Provisions) Act 1995 the Schedule para.4(3) (January 8, 1996).
2. Child Benefit Act 2005 s.1 and Sch.1 para.14 (April 10, 2006).

GENERAL NOTE

"week"

1.66 A week is defined as a period of seven days beginning on a Monday. Falling short of a full week by a few hours can be ignored: *R(F) 1/82(S)*. The provision in subs.(2) is a trap for the unwary. It means that, subject to provisions in regulations imposing a different rule, a condition to be satisfied or circumstances existing on a Monday (which, of course, begins at midnight on Sunday) are taken as subsisting for the whole week.

The meaning of parent is also extended by the effect of the Children Act 1989, to include any person in whose favour a residence order has been made. This is because the "parental responsibility" conferred by the order made under that Act is defined to include all the rights which, by law, a parent has in relation to that child. For the purposes of the Contributions and Benefits Act, the word parent is to be construed as the "legal parent" of the child. (See *Secretary of State for Social Services v Smith* [1983] 1 W.L.R. 1110, where the effect of an order made under equivalent legislation then in force, was to include an adoptive parent of the child and at the same time to exclude the natural parent.) The same reasoning was applied by Commissioner Howell in *R(F) 1/08* where a lesbian couple had two children with the assistance of artificial insemination and after they had separated a residence order had been made in favour of both of them. The Commissioner held that both must be regarded as parents, not just the biological mother, and consequently it became necessary for HMRC to exercise the discretion provided for at [5].

Part XI

Statutory Sick Pay

General Note

Statutory Sick Pay ("SSP") was originally introduced in April 1983 by the Social Security and Housing Benefits Act 1982. The main primary legislation is now to be found in Pt XI, annotated here; there are also various sets of regulations, principally the SSP (General) Regulations 1982 (SI 1982/894), which are contained in Pt III of this volume. Section 151(1) of the SSCBA 1992 provides that an employer is liable to pay to an employee for any day of incapacity for work in relation to the employee's contract of service with that employer, where the day in question is a qualifying day (see s.154) which forms part of a period of incapacity to work (see s.152) and falls within a period of entitlement as between that employer and that employee (s.153 and Sch.11). Incapacity must be duly notified to the employer, and SSP may be withheld in the event of non-existent or late notification (see s.156). Those who are self-employed (who by definition lack an employer) and those who are unemployed are excluded from entitlement to SSP. Some employees are also excluded from SSP. Section 153(3) and Sch.11 prevent the requisite period of entitlement arising as between employer and employees in various types of case (e.g. low earners, women at a certain stage of pregnancy, some persons affected by trade disputes).

Statutory Sick Pay is payable at a weekly rate. The daily rate will depend on the number of qualifying days in the week (see s.157). Statutory Sick Pay is not payable in respect of the first three qualifying days (or "waiting days") in any period of entitlement (see s.155(1)). Statutory Sick Pay cannot be paid in kind or by the provision of board and lodging or other services or facilities (SSP (General) Regulations 1982 (SI 1982/894) reg.8). Any day of incapacity for work in relation to a contract of service which falls within a period of entitlement to SSP precludes concurrent entitlement to incapacity benefit (Sch.12 para.1). Employees reach their maximum entitlement to SSP as against any one employer in any one period of entitlement when they have been entitled in that period to 28 times the appropriate weekly rate of SSP (see s.155(4)). This is typically after 28 weeks of continuous incapacity. If the person remains incapacitated after that, he or she must look to incapacity benefit or, failing that, a means-tested benefit.

At the start of the SSP scheme in 1983, employers were able to recoup the entire amount paid from the National Insurance contributions and the PAYE tax that they were required to collect and account for to the Inland Revenue. The initial effect of SSP was thus to transfer the cost of administration from the State to the employer. The Statutory Sick Pay Act 1991 limited employers to recouping 80 per cent of the cost of SSP payments, but "small employers" were still able to claim full

1.67

reimbursement. This was followed by the Statutory Sick Pay Act 1994, which abolished employers' general right to recover (some of) the costs of SSP. The special rules for reimbursing small employers were then repealed. Instead, any employer could recover the costs of SSP under the Percentage Threshold Scheme ("PTS"), but only if the employer's expenditure on SPP exceeded 13 per cent of their gross National Insurance contributions liability (Statutory Sick Pay Threshold Order 1995 (SI 1995/512)). The PTS was then abolished from April 6, 2014 by the Statutory Sick Pay Percentage Threshold (Revocations, Transitional and Saving Provisions) (Great Britain and Northern Ireland) Order 2014 (SI 2014/897). Abolition was justified by the Government on the basis that the PTS acted as a disincentive to employers by providing compensation for sickness absence rather than supporting them to actively manage sickness absence in the workplace.

However, an employer refund scheme (at least for small and medium sized employers) was reintroduced in the wake of the coronavirus crisis (see s.159B of the Contributions and Benefits Act (inserted by s.39 of the Coronavirus Act 2020) and the Statutory Sick Pay (Coronavirus) (Funding of Employers' Liabilities) Regulations 2020 (SI 2020/512)). These regulations provide for small and medium-size employers (those with fewer than 250 employees enrolled on their PAYE scheme as at February 28, 2020) to apply to HMRC for a refund of the cost of paying SSP to their employees. The scheme refunds eligible employers the costs of SSP for 2 weeks per affected employee where an employee's incapacity for work is related to coronavirus.

1.68 In certain circumstances, where an employer does not, or because of insolvency, cannot, discharge their statutory liability to pay SSP, that liability became that of the Board of Inland Revenue (s.151(6) of the SSP (General) Regulations 1982 (SI 1982/894) regs 9A–9C). This liability was transferred from the Secretary of State to the Board of the Inland Revenue with effect from April 1, 1999, under the Social Security Contributions (Transfer of Functions, etc.) Act 1999 s.1(2) and Sch.2, along with those functions under SSP (General) Regulations 1982 regs 10 and 14.

The arrangements for resolving disputes about entitlement to SSP were changed with effect from April 1, 1999. Before that date, certain questions could be referred to an AO, thus opening up the usual channels of appeal to SSATs, Commissioners and ultimately the courts. Since that date the Social Security Contributions (Transfer of Functions, etc.) Act 1999 and the Statutory Sick Pay and Statutory Maternity Pay (Decisions) Regulations 1999 (SI 1999/776) have replaced the AO with an officer of Revenue and Customs. Consequently, decision-making and appeals are now governed by Pt II of the 1999 Act, with the right of appeal lying to the tax chamber of the First-tier Tribunal. An employment tribunal has no jurisdiction under the Employment Rights Act 1996 to entertain an employee's complaint that SSP has not been paid: (per Mr Recorder Luba QC in *Taylor Gordon & Co Ltd v Timmons* ([2004] I.R.L.R. 180 at [43])).

Employer's liability

Employer's liability

1.69 **151.**—(1) Where an employee has a day of incapacity for work in relation to his contract of service with an employer, that employer shall, if the conditions set out in sections 152 to 154 below are satisfied, be liable to make him, in accordance with the following provisions of this Part of this Act, a payment (to be known as "statutory sick pay") in respect of that day.

(2) Any agreement shall be void to the extent that it purports—
  (a) to exclude, limit or otherwise modify any provision of this Part of this Act; or
  (b) to require an employee to contribute (whether directly or indirectly) towards any costs incurred by his employer under this Part of this Act.

(1992 c.4 s.151)

(3) For the avoidance of doubt, any agreement between an employer and an employee authorising any deductions from statutory sick pay which the employer is liable to pay to the employee in respect of any period shall not be void by virtue of subsection (2)(a) above if the employer—
  (a) is authorised by that or another agreement to make the same deductions from any contractual remuneration which he is liable to pay in respect of the same period, or
  (b) would be so authorised if he were liable to pay contractual remuneration in respect of that period.

(4) For the purposes of this Part of this Act [¹a day of incapacity for work in relation to a contract of service means a day on which] the employee concerned is, or is deemed in accordance with regulations to be, incapable by reason of some specific disease or bodily or mental disablement of doing work which he can reasonably be expected to do under that contract.

[³ (4A) Regulations under subsection (4) may make provision about whether an employee is deemed to be incapable (as referred to in that subsection) in relation to severe acute respiratory syndrome coronavirus 2 by reference to guidance or any other document published by Public Health England, NHS National Services Scotland, the Public Health Wales National Health Service Trust or any other person specified in the regulations as that guidance or other document is amended from time to time.]

(5) In any case where an employee has more than one contract of service with the same employer the provisions of this Part of this Act shall, except in such cases as may be prescribed and subject to the following provisions of this Part of this Act, have effect as if the employer were a different employer in relation to each contract of service.

(6) Circumstances may be prescribed in which, notwithstanding the provisions of subsections (1) to (5) above, the liability to make payments of statutory sick pay is to be a liability of the [²Commissioners of Inland Revenue].

[²(7) Regulations under subsection (6) above must be made with the concurrence of the Commissioners of Inland Revenue.]

AMENDMENTS

1. Social Security (Incapacity for Work) Act 1994 s.11(1) and Sch.1 para.34 (April 13, 1995).
2. Social Security Contributions (Transfer of Functions, etc.) Act 1999 s.1(1) and Sch.1 para.9 (April 1, 1999).
3. Coronavirus Act 2020 s.41(1) (March 25, 2020).

DEFINITIONS

"contract of service"—see s.163(1).
"employee"—see s.163(1). and SSP (General) Regulations 1982 reg.16.
"employer"—see s.163(1).
"prescribed"—see s.163(1).

GENERAL NOTE

Subsections (1)–(3)
  The general liability on employers to pay SSP—where the qualifying conditions are fulfilled by the employee—is set out in subs.(1). Employers cannot contract out of this liability (subs.(2), but note the qualification in subs.(3)).

1.70

Social Security Contributions and Benefits Act 1992

Subsection (4)

1.71   For the purposes of SSP, a day of incapacity for work in relation to any contract of service may arise in either of two ways. The first is where the employee is actually incapable by reason of some specific disease or bodily or mental disablement of doing work which he or she can reasonably be expected to do under that contract. On "incapable of work" and "by reason of some specific disease or bodily or mental disablement", see the annotations to SSCBA 1992 s.171B(2) in Vol.I to this series. The second, and alternative, possibility is where the employee, although not actually incapable, falls within the protection of regulations which deem a day to be one of incapacity for work. On deemed incapacity, see SSP (General) Regulations 1982 (SI 1982/894) reg.2.

Note that regulations made under subs.(4) in relation to severe acute respiratory syndrome coronavirus 2 may provide for a person to exercise a discretion in dealing with any matter under those regulations: see s.175(5A) of the Contributions and Benefits Act as amended by s.41(2) of the Coronavirus Act 2020.

Subsection (5)

1.72   This contemplates that an employee who has more than one contract of service with the same employer could get SSP in respect of each contract of service, where the eligibility conditions were satisfied with respect to each contract. This provision is modified by SSP (General) Regulations 1982 (SI 1982/894) reg.21.

Subsection (6)

1.73   See SSP (General) Regulations 1982 (SI 1982/894) regs 9A–9C and see also General Note to Pt XI of this Act, above.

The qualifying conditions

Period of incapacity for work

1.74   **152.**—(1) The first condition is that the day in question forms part of a period of incapacity for work.

(2) In this Part of this Act "period of incapacity for work" means any period of four or more consecutive days, each of which is a day of incapacity for work in relation to the contract of service in question.

(3) Any two periods of incapacity for work which are separated by a period of not more than 8 weeks shall be treated as a single period of incapacity for work.

(4) The Secretary of State may by regulations direct that a larger number of weeks specified in the regulations shall be substituted for the number of weeks for the time being specified in subsection (3) above.

(5) No day of the week shall be disregarded in calculating any period of consecutive days for the purposes of this section.

(6) A day may be a day of incapacity for work in relation to a contract of service, and so form part of a period of incapacity for work, notwithstanding that—
  (a) it falls before the making of the contract or after the contract expires or is brought to an end; or
  (b) it is not a day on which the employee concerned would be required by that contract to be available for work.

Definitions

"contract of service"—see s.163(1).
"employee"—see s.163(1). and SSP (General) Regulations 1982 reg.16.
"period of incapacity for work"—see subs.(2).
"week"—see s.163(1).

General Note

Liability to pay SSP can only arise if the qualifying day which is one of incapacity for work also forms part of a period of incapacity for work (subs.(1)). A period of incapacity for work is formed by any period of four or more consecutive days of incapacity for work in relation to the contract of service in question (subs.(2)). Every day of the week counts for determining periods of consecutive days (subs.(4)). Any two periods of incapacity "link" to form a single period where they are not separated by more than eight weeks, counting the separation period from the end of the "first" period. Note that under subs.(5), a day can still be one of incapacity for work in relation to the contract of service and thus be part of a period of incapacity for work where it is not one on which the contract would require the employee to be available for work, or where it falls before the contract was made or after it expires or is otherwise brought to an end.

1.75

Period of entitlement

153.—(1) The second condition is that the day in question falls within a period which is, as between the employee and his employer, a period of entitlement.

1.76

(2) For the purposes of this Part of this Act a period of entitlement, as between an employee and his employer, is a period beginning with the commencement of a period of incapacity for work and ending with whichever of the following first occurs—
  (a) the termination of that period of incapacity for work;
  (b) the day on which the employee reaches, as against the employer concerned, his maximum entitlement to statutory sick pay (determined in accordance with section 155 below);
  (c) the day on which the employee's contract of service with the employer concerned expires or is brought to an end;
  (d) in the case of an employee who is, or has been, pregnant, the day immediately preceding the beginning of the disqualifying period.

(3) Schedule 11 to this Act has effect for the purpose of specifying circumstances in which a period of entitlement does not arise in relation to a particular period of incapacity for work.

(4) A period of entitlement as between an employee and an employer of his may also be, or form part of, a period of entitlement as between him and another employer of his.

(5) The Secretary of State may by regulations—
  (a) specify circumstances in which, for the purpose of determining whether an employee's maximum entitlement to statutory sick pay has been reached in a period of entitlement as between him and an employer of his, days falling within a previous period of entitlement as between the employee and any person who is or has in the past been an employer of his are to be counted; and
  (b) direct that in prescribed circumstances an employer shall provide a person who is about to leave his employment, or who has been employed by him in the past, with a statement in the prescribed form containing such information as may be prescribed in relation to any entitlement of the employee to statutory sick pay.

(6) Regulations may provide, in relation to prescribed cases, for a period of entitlement to end otherwise than in accordance with subsection (2) above.

(7) In a case where the employee's contract of service first takes effect on a day which falls within a period of incapacity for work, the period of entitlement begins with that day.

(8) In a case where the employee's contract of service first takes effect between two periods of incapacity for work which by virtue of section 152(3) above are treated as one, the period of entitlement begins with the first day of the second of those periods.

(9) In any case where, otherwise than by virtue of section 6(1)(b) above, an employee's earnings under a contract of service in respect of the day on which the contract takes effect do not attract a liability to pay secondary Class 1 contributions, subsections (7) and (8) above shall have effect as if for any reference to the contract first taking effect there were substituted a reference to the first day in respect of which the employee's earnings attract such a liability.

(10) Regulations shall make provision as to an employer's liability under this Part of this Act to pay statutory sick pay to an employee in any case where the employer's contract of service with that employee has been brought to an end by the employer solely, or mainly, for the purpose of avoiding liability for statutory sick pay.

(11) Subsection (2)(d) above does not apply in relation to an employee who has been pregnant if her pregnancy terminated, before the beginning of the disqualifying period, otherwise than by confinement.

(12) In this section—

"confinement" is to be construed in accordance with section 171(1) below;

"disqualifying period" means—
  (a) in relation to a woman entitled to statutory maternity pay, the maternity pay period; and
  (b) in relation to a woman entitled to maternity allowance, the maternity allowance period;

"maternity allowance period" has the meaning assigned to it by section 35(2) above; and

"maternity pay period" has the meaning assigned to it by section 165(1) below.

DEFINITIONS

"confinement"—see subs.(12).
"contract of service"—see s.163(1).
"disqualifying period"—see subs.(12).
"employee"—see s.163(1) and SSP (General) Regulations 1982 reg.16.
"employer"—see s.163(1).
"maternity allowance"—see s.163(1).
"maternity allowance period"—subs.(12).
"maternity pay period"—subs.(12).
"period of incapacity for work"—see s.163(1).
"prescribed"—see s.163(1).
"week"—see s.163(1).

GENERAL NOTE

Subsections (1) and (2)

1.77　　There can be no liability to pay SSP unless the qualifying day, being one of incapacity for work forming part of a period of incapacity for work, also falls within a period of entitlement as between the employee and his employer (subs.(1)). Such a period of entitlement generally begins on the first day of a period of incapacity for work (subs.(2)), but note the modifications effected by subss.(7), (8), and (9). A period of entitlement ends with whichever of the circumstances set out in subs.(2)(a)–(d) first occurs. Note that subs.2(d) does not apply in the circumstances set out in subs.(11).

The position of "regular casual" workers was dealt with by the Court of Appeal in *Brown v Chief Adjudication Officer* [1997] I.R.L.R. 110. So long as such workers have worked continuously for a period of three months, or for a series of periods totalling three months in aggregate and not separated by more than eight weeks, they become entitled to the minimum periods of notice provided for by s.86 of Employment Rights Act 1996, and their contract of employment will not terminate unless it is frustrated or is terminated by their employer. See further the commentary to Sch.11 para.2 below.

The First-tier Tribunal (Tax Chamber) has held that where a person has no weekly earnings for a period, owing to the default of her employer, then a "period of entitlement" does not arise within subs.(2) and so there is no entitlement to SSP. This was because the words "the average weekly earnings which in the relevant period have been paid to him" in s.163(2) referred to actual payments of wages and did not cover subsequent payments made in respect of the relevant period, e.g. as a result of a claim in the employment tribunal for unlawful deduction of wages: *Seaton v Revenue and Customs Commissioners* [2010] UKFTT 270 (TC).

Subsection (3)
In the circumstances set out in Sch.11 below, no period of entitlement arises with respect to the particular period of incapacity for work there referred to, thus excluding certain employees from SSP in respect of that period of incapacity for work.   1.78

Subsection (4)
An employee may have a period of entitlement with more than one employer at the same time, albeit that the length of the period with each is not coterminous.   1.79

Subsection (5)
See SSP (General) Regulations 1982 (SI 1982/894) reg.3A.   1.80

Subsection (6)
See SSP (General) Regulations 1982 (SI 1982/894) reg.3 dealing with prisoners, pregnant women entitled neither to SMP nor to maternity allowance, and setting a maximum three-year limit on any one period of entitlement.   1.81

Subsection (10)
See SSP (General) Regulations 1982 (SI 1982/894) reg.4.   1.82

Qualifying days

154.—(1) The third condition is that the day in question is a qualifying day.   1.83
(2) The days which are for the purposes of this Part of this Act to be qualifying days as between an employee and an employer of his (that is to say, those days of the week on which he is required by his contract of service with that employer to be available for work or which are chosen to reflect the terms of that contract) shall be such day or days as may, subject to regulations, be agreed between the employee and his employer or, failing such agreement, determined in accordance with regulations.

(3) In any case where qualifying days are determined by agreement between an employee and his employer there shall, in each week (beginning with Sunday), be at least one qualifying day.

(4) A day which is a qualifying day as between an employee and an employer of his may also be a qualifying day as between him and another employer of his.

DEFINITIONS

"contract of service"—see s.163(1).
"employee"—see s.163(1). and SSP (General) Regulations 1982 reg.16.
"employer"—see s.163(1).
"week"—see s.163(1).

GENERAL NOTE

1.84 In order to attract SSP liability, the day of incapacity which forms part of a period of incapacity for work and falls within a period of entitlement must also be a qualifying day (subs.(1)). Under subs.(2) an employer and employee are permitted a degree of freedom to determine by agreement which days of the week will for them rank as such, although subs.(3) stipulates that such agreements must specify at least one qualifying day per week. Furthermore SSP (General) Regulations 1982 (SI 1982/894) reg.5(3) renders ineffective an agreement treating as qualifying days any day identified expressly or otherwise by reference to it being a day of incapacity for work in relation to the employee's contract of service with an employer, or by reference to a period of incapacity for work or to a period of entitlement. Where there is no agreement on qualifying days or the only agreement is one rendered ineffective by reg.5(3), qualifying days are determined in accordance with SSP (General) Regulations 1982 reg.5(2).

Limitations on entitlement, etc.

Limitations on entitlement

1.85 **155.**—(1) Statutory sick pay shall not be payable for the first three qualifying days in any period of entitlement.

(2) An employee shall not be entitled, as against any one employer, to an aggregate amount of statutory sick pay in respect of any one period of entitlement which exceeds his maximum entitlement.

(3) The maximum entitlement as against any one employer is reached on the day on which the amount to which the employee has become entitled by way of statutory sick pay during the period of entitlement in question first reaches or passes the entitlement limit.

(4) The entitlement limit is an amount equal to 28 times [¹the weekly rate applicable in accordance with] section 157 below.

(5) Regulations may make provision for calculating the entitlement limit in any case where an employee's entitlement to statutory sick pay is calculated by reference to different weekly rates in the same period of entitlement.

AMENDMENT

1. Social Security (Incapacity for Work) Act 1994 s.8 (April 6, 1995).

DEFINITIONS

"employee"—see s.163(1) and SSP (General) Regulations 1982 reg.16.
"employer"—see s.163(1).
"period of entitlement"—see s.163(1).
"qualifying day"—see s.163(1).

(1992 c.4 s.155)

GENERAL NOTE

Subsection (1)
This provides for the general rule that there are three "waiting days" before SSP can be paid. However, during the 2020 Coronavirus crisis the rule that SSP is not paid for the first three qualifying days of incapacity for work was suspended by the Statutory Sick Pay (Coronavirus) (Suspension of Waiting Days and General Amendment) Regulations 2020 (SI 2020/374). Accordingly, SSP was payable from day one of an employee's absence from work, rather than day four, where that absence was related to coronavirus. The suspension applied in relation to an employee where (a) that employee's period of incapacity for work was related to coronavirus; and (b) the first day of incapacity for work in that period arose on or after March 13, 2020 (see reg.2(1) of SI 2020/374). For these purposes "a period of incapacity for work is related to coronavirus if the employee is (i) incapable by reason of infection or contamination with coronavirus, or (ii) deemed, in accordance with regulation 2(1)(c) of the Statutory Sick Pay (General) Regulations 1982, to be incapable by reason of coronavirus, of doing work which the employee can reasonably be expected to do under the employee's contract of service" (reg.2(3)(b) of SI 2020/374). The 2020 instrument also inserted a Schedule into these Regulations, which specifies when a person is deemed to be incapable of work because the person is staying home. This includes people with symptoms of coronavirus staying at home for 7 days and people in the household of someone with symptoms of coronavirus staying at home for 14 days. It has also been amended to include those individuals classed as extremely vulnerable and at very high risk of severe illness from coronavirus and who were advised to remain at home for at least 12 weeks (i.e. the practice known as shielding). For discussion of further amendments see the commentary to Sch.1 to SI 1982/894.

1.86

Notification of incapacity for work

156.—(1) Regulations shall prescribe the manner in which, and the time within which, notice of any day of incapacity for work is to be given by or on behalf of an employee to his employer.

1.87

(2) An employer who would, apart from this section, be liable to pay an amount of statutory sick pay to an employee in respect of a qualifying day (the "day in question") shall be entitled to withhold payment of that amount if—
- (a) the day in question is one in respect of which he has not been duly notified in accordance with regulations under subsection (1) above; or
- (b) he has not been so notified in respect of any of the first three qualifying days in a period of entitlement (a "waiting day") and the day in question is the first qualifying day in that period of entitlement in respect of which the employer is not entitled to withhold payment—
    - (i) by virtue of paragraph (a) above; or
    - (ii) in respect of an earlier waiting day by virtue of this paragraph.

(3) Where an employer withholds any amount of statutory sick pay under this section—
- (a) the period of entitlement in question shall not be affected; and
- (b) for the purposes of calculating his maximum entitlement in accordance with section 155 above the employee shall not be taken to have become entitled to the amount so withheld.

Social Security Contributions and Benefits Act 1992

Rates of payment, etc.

Rates of payment

1.88   **157.**—(1) Statutory sick pay shall be payable by an employer at the weekly rate of [²£116.75].

(2) The Secretary of State may by order—

[¹(a) amend subsection (1) above so as to substitute different provision as to the weekly rate or rates of statutory sick pay; and]

(b) make such consequential amendments as appear to him to be required of any provision contained in this Part of this Act.

(3) The amount of statutory sick pay payable by any one employer in respect of any day shall be the weekly rate applicable on that day divided by the number of days which are, in the week (beginning with Sunday) in which that day falls, qualifying days as between that employer and the employee concerned.

AMENDMENTS

1. Social Security (Incapacity for Work) Act 1994 s.8 (April 6, 1995).
2. Social Security Benefits Up-rating Order 2024 (SI 2024/242) art.8 (April 7, 2024).

Recovery by employers of amounts paid by way of statutory sick pay

1.89   **158.**—[¹ . . .]

AMENDMENT

1. Statutory Sick Pay Percentage Threshold Order 1995 (SI 1995/512) reg.5(a) (April 6, 1995).

Power to substitute provisions for section 158(2)

1.90   **159.**—[¹ . . .]

AMENDMENT

1. Statutory Sick Pay Percentage Threshold Order 1995 (SI 1995/512) reg.5(a) (April 6, 1995).

[¹Power to provide for recovery by employers of sums paid by way of statutory sick pay

1.91   **159A.**—(1) The Secretary of State may by order provide for the recovery by employers, in accordance with the order, of the amount (if any) by which their payments of, or liability incurred for, statutory sick pay in any period exceeds the specified percentage of the amount of their liability for contributions payments in respect of the corresponding period.

(2) An order under subsection (1) above may include provision—

(a) as to the periods by reference to which the calculation referred to above is to be made;

(b) for amounts which would otherwise be recoverable but which do not exceed the specified minimum for recovery not to be recoverable;

(c) for the rounding up or down of any fraction of a pound which would otherwise result from a calculation made in accordance with the order; and

(d) for any deduction from contributions payments made in accordance with the order to be disregarded for such purposes as may be specified,

and may repeal sections 158 and 159 above and make any amendments of other enactments which are consequential on the repeal of those sections.

(3) In this section—

"contributions payments" means payments which a person is required by or under any enactment to make in discharge of any liability of his as an employer in respect of primary or secondary Class 1 contributions; and

"specified" means specified in or determined in accordance with an order under subsection (1).

(4) The Secretary of State may by regulations make such transitional and consequential provision, and such savings, as he considers necessary or expedient for or in connection with the coming into force of any order under subsection (1) above.]

AMENDMENT

1. Statutory Sick Pay Act 1994 s.3 (February 10, 1994).

[1 Funding of employers' statutory sick pay liabilities in relation to coronavirus

159B.—(1) The Commissioners for Her Majesty's Revenue and Customs may by regulations make provision for the payment by employers of statutory sick pay in respect of incapacity for work related to coronavirus to be funded by Her Majesty's Revenue and Customs to such extent and in such manner as may be prescribed.

(2) Regulations under subsection (1) may—
(a) make provision for a person who has made a payment of statutory sick pay in respect of an employee whose incapacity for work is related to coronavirus to be entitled, except in prescribed circumstances, to recover some or all of that payment;
(b) include provision for a person who has made a payment of statutory sick pay in respect of an employee whose incapacity for work is related to coronavirus to be entitled, except in prescribed circumstances, to recover an additional amount, determined in such manner as may be prescribed.

(3) Regulations under subsection (1) may make provision about when an employee's incapacity for work is related to coronavirus.

(4) Regulations under subsection (1) may, in particular, make provision—
(a) for funding in advance as well as in arrear;
(b) for funding, or the recovery of amounts due under provision made by virtue of subsection (2)(b), by means of deductions from such amounts for which employers are accountable to Her Majesty's Revenue and Customs as may be prescribed, or otherwise;
(c) for the recovery by Her Majesty's Revenue and Customs of any sums overpaid to employers under the regulations.

(5) Where in accordance with any provision of regulations under subsection (1) an amount has been deducted from an employer's contributions payments, the amount so deducted is (except in such cases as may be prescribed) to be treated for the purposes of any provision made by or under any enactment in relation to primary or secondary Class 1 contributions—

1.92

(a) as having been paid (on such date as may be determined in accordance with the regulations), and
(b) as having been received by Her Majesty's Revenue and Customs,
towards discharging the employer's liability in respect of such contributions.
(6) Regulations under subsection (1) may make provision—
(a) about the procedure for an employer to make a claim under those regulations;
(b) about the determination of claims by Her Majesty's Revenue and Customs;
(c) requiring an employer to keep records in relation to payments of statutory sick pay in respect of incapacity for work related to coronavirus.
(7) Regulations under subsection (1) may have retrospective effect in relation to a day of incapacity for work that falls on or after 13 March 2020.
(8) In this section—
"contributions payments", in relation to an employer, means any payments which the employer is required, by or under any enactment, to make in discharge of any liability in respect of primary or secondary Class 1 contributions;
"coronavirus" means severe acute respiratory syndrome coronavirus 2.
(9) Regulations under subsection (1) must be made with the concurrence of the Secretary of State.]

AMENDMENT

1. Coronavirus Act 2020 s.39(1) (March 25, 2020).

GENERAL NOTE

1.93 See the Statutory Sick Pay (Coronavirus) (Funding of Employers' Liabilities) Regulations 2020 (SI 2020/512).
Regulations made under this section may provide for a person to exercise a discretion in dealing with any matter under those regulations: see s.175(5A) of the Contributions and Benefits Act as amended by s.41(2) of the Coronavirus Act 2020.

Miscellaneous

Relationship with benefits and other payments, etc.

1.94 **160.**—Schedule 12 to this Act has effect with respect to the relationship between statutory sick pay and certain benefits and payments.

Crown employment—Part XI

1.95 **161.**—(1) Subject to subsection (2) below, the provisions of this Part of this Act apply in relation to persons employed by or under the Crown as they apply in relation to persons employed otherwise than by or under the Crown.
(2) The provisions of this Part of this Act do not apply in relation to persons serving as members of Her Majesty's forces, in their capacity as such.
(3) For the purposes of this section Her Majesty's forces shall be taken to consist of such establishments and organisations as may be prescribed [¹by regulations made by the Secretary of State with the concurrence of the

Treasury], being establishments and organisations in which persons serve under the control of the Defence Council.

AMENDMENT

1. Social Security Contributions (Transfer of Functions, etc.) Act 1999 s.1(1) and Sch.1 para.10 (April 1, 1999).

Special classes of persons

162.—(1) The Secretary of State [¹may with the concurrence of the Treasury] make regulations modifying this Part of this Act in such manner as he thinks proper in their application to any person who is, has been or is to be—

(a) employed on board any ship, vessel, hovercraft or aircraft;
(b) outside Great Britain at any prescribed time or in any prescribed circumstances; or
(c) in prescribed employment in connection with continental shelf opeations, as defined in section 120(2) above.

(2) Regulations under subsection (1) above may in particular provide—

(a) for any provision of this Part of this Act to apply to any such person, notwithstanding that it would not otherwise apply;
(b) for any such provision not to apply to any such person, notwithstanding that it would otherwise apply;
(c) for excepting any such person from the application of any such provision where he neither is domiciled nor has a place of residence in any part of Great Britain;
(d) for the taking of evidence, for the purposes of the determination of any question arising under any such provision, in a country or territory outside Great Britain, by a British consular official or such other person as may be determined in accordance with the regulations.

1.96

AMENDMENT

1. Social Security Contributions (Transfer of Functions, etc.) Act 1999 s.1(1) and Sch.1 para.11 (April 1, 1999).

Interpretation of Part XI and supplementary provisions

163.—(1) In this Part of this Act—

"contract of service" (except in paragraph (a) of the definition below of "employee") includes any arrangement providing for the terms of appointment of an employee;

"employee" means a person who is—

(a) gainfully employed in Great Britain either under a contract of service or in an office (including elective office) with [⁴ [⁷ earnings (within the meaning of Parts 1 to 5 above)]];

[⁵...]

but subject to regulations, which may provide for cases where any such person is not to be treated as an employee for the purposes of this Part of this Act and for cases where any person who would not otherwise be an employee for those purposes is to be treated as an employee for those purposes;

1.97

[⁵"employer", in relation to an employee and a contract of service of his, means a person who—
(a) under section 6 above is liable to pay secondary Class 1 contributions in relation to any earnings of the employee under the contract, or
(b) would be liable to pay such contributions but for—
   (i) the condition in section 6(1)(b), or
   (ii) the employee being under the age of 16:]
"period of entitlement" has the meaning given by section 153 above;
"period of incapacity for work" has the meaning given by section 152 above;
[¹. . .]
"prescribed" means prescribed by regulations;
"qualifying day" has the meaning given by section 154 above;
"week" means any period of seven days.

(2) For the purposes of this Part of this Act an employee's normal weekly earnings shall, subject to subsection (4) below, be taken to be the average weekly earnings which in the relevant period have been paid to him or paid for his benefit under his contract of service with the employer in question.

(3) For the purposes of subsection (2) above, the expressions "earnings" and "relevant period" shall have the meaning given to them by regulations.

(4) In such cases as may be prescribed an employee's normal weekly earnings shall be calculated in accordance with regulations.

(5) Without prejudice to any other power to make regulations under this Part of this Act, regulations may specify cases in which, for the purposes of this Part of this Act or such of its provisions as may be prescribed—
(a) two or more employers are to be treated as one;
(b) two or more contracts of service in respect of which the same person is an employee are to be treated as one.

(6) Where, in consequence of the establishment of one or more National Health Service trusts under [⁶the National Health Service Act 2006, the National Health Service (Wales) Act 2006] or the National Health Service (Scotland) Act 1978, a person's contract of employment is treated by a scheme under [⁶any of those Acts] as divided so as to constitute two or more contracts, [³or where an order [⁶paragraph 26(1) of Schedule 3 to the National Health Service Act 2006] provides that a person's contract of employment is so divided,] regulations may make provision enabling him to elect for all of those contracts to be treated as one contract for the purposes of this Part of this Act or of such provisions of this Part of this Act as may be prescribed; and any such regulations may prescribe—
(a) the conditions that must be satisfied if a person is to be entitled to make such an election;
(b) the manner in which, and the time within which, such an election is to be made;
(c) the persons to whom, and the manner in which, notice of such an election is to be given;
(d) the information which a person who makes such an election is to provide, and the persons to whom, and the time within which, he is to provide it;
(e) the time for which such an election is to have effect;
(f) which one of the person's employers under the two or more contracts is to be regarded for the purposes of statutory sick pay as his employer under the one contract;

and the powers conferred by this subsection are without prejudice to any other power to make regulations under this Part of this Act.

(7) Regulations may provide for periods of work which begin on one day and finish on the following day to be treated, for the purposes of this Part of this Act, as falling solely within one or other of those days.

AMENDMENTS

1. Jobseekers Act 1995 s.41(5) and Sch.3 (April 1, 1996).
2. Social Security Act 1998 s.86 and Sch.7 para.74 (April 6, 1999).
3. Health Act 1999 (Supplementary, Consequential etc. Provisions) Order 2000 (SI 2000/90) art.3(1) and Sch.1 para.27 (February 8, 2000).
4. Income Tax (Earnings and Pensions) Act 2003 s.722 and Sch.6 para.181 (April 6, 2003).
5. Employment Equality (Age) Regulations 2006 (SI 2006/1031) reg.49(1) and Sch.8 para.9 (October 1, 2006).
6. National Health Service (Consequential Provisions) Act 2006 s.2 and Sch.1 para.147 (March 1, 2007).
7. National Insurance Contributions Act 2014 s.15 and Sch.2 para.3 (May 13, 2014).

GENERAL NOTE

Normal weekly earnings: see subs.(2)–(4) and also *Seaton v Commissioners for HMRC* [2011] UKUT 297 (TCC) and *Spence v Commissioners for HMRC* [2012] UKFTT 213 (TC).

1.98

PART XII

STATUTORY MATERNITY PAY

Statutory maternity pay—entitlement and liability to pay

164.—(1) Where a woman who is or has been an employee satisfies the conditions set out in this section, she shall be entitled, in accordance with the following provisions of this Part of this Act, to payments to be known as "statutory maternity pay".

1.99

(2) The conditions mentioned in subsection (1) above are—
(a) that she has been in employed earner's employment with an employer for a continuous period of at least 26 weeks ending with the week immediately preceding the 14th week before the expected-week of confinement but has ceased to work for him, [³ . . .];
(b) that her normal weekly earnings for the period of eight weeks ending with the week immediately preceding the 14th week before the expected week of confinement are not less than the lower earnings limit in force under section 5(1)(a) above immediately before the commencement of the 14th week before the expected week of confinement; and
(c) that she has become pregnant and has reached, or been confined before reaching, the commencement of the 11th week before the expected week of confinement.

(3) The liability to make payments of statutory maternity pay to a woman is a liability of any person of whom she has been an employee as mentioned in subsection (2)(a) above.

[³(4) A woman shall be entitled to payments of statutory maternity pay only if—
  (a) she gives the person who will be liable to pay it notice of the date from which she expects his liability to pay her statutory maternity pay to begin; and
  (b) the notice is given at least 28 days before that date or, if that is not reasonably practicable, as soon as is reasonably practicable.]

(5) The notice shall be in writing if the person who is liable to pay the woman statutory maternity pay so requests.

(6) Any agreement shall be void to the extent that it purports—
  (a) to exclude, limit or otherwise modify any provision of this Part of this Act; or
  (b) to require an employee or former employee to contribute (whether directly or indirectly) towards any costs incurred by her employer or former employer under this Part of this Act.

(7) For the avoidance of doubt, any agreement between an employer and an employee authorising any deductions from statutory maternity pay which the employer is liable to pay to the employee in respect of any period shall not be void by virtue of subsection (6)(a) above if the employer—
  (a) is authorised by that or another agreement to make the same deductions from any contractual remuneration which he is liable to pay in respect of the same period; or
  (b) would be so authorised if he were liable to pay contractual remuneration in respect of that period.

(8) Regulations shall make provision as to a former employer's liability to pay statutory maternity pay to a woman in any case where the former employer's contract of service with her has been brought to an end by the former employer solely, or mainly, for the purpose of avoiding liability for statutory maternity pay.

(9) The Secretary of State may by regulations—
  (a) specify circumstances in which, notwithstanding subsections (1) to (8) above, there is to be no liability to pay statutory maternity pay in respect of a week;
  (b) specify circumstances in which, notwithstanding subsections (1) to (8) above, the liability to make payments of statutory maternity pay is to be a liability [²of the Commissioners of Inland Revenue];
  (c) specify in what circumstances employment is to be treated as continuous for the purposes of this Part of this Act;
  (d) provide that a woman is to be treated as being employed for a continuous period of at least 26 weeks where—
    (i) she has been employed by the same employer for at least 26 weeks under two or more separate contracts of service; and
    (ii) those contracts were not continuous;
  (e) provide that any of the provisions specified in subsection (10) below shall have effect subject to prescribed modifications [³in such cases as may be prescribed]
[³(ea) provide that subsection (4) above shall not have effect, or shall have effect subject to prescribed modifications, in such cases as may be prescribed;]
  (f) provide for amounts earned by a woman under separate contracts of service with the same employer to be aggregated for the purposes of this Part of this Act; and

(g) provide that—
  (i) the amount of a woman's earnings for any period; or
  (ii) the amount of her earnings to be treated as comprised in any payment made to her or for her benefit,
shall be calculated or estimated in such manner and on such basis as may be prescribed and that for that purpose payments of a particular class or description made or falling to be made to or by a woman shall, to such extent as may be prescribed, be disregarded or, as the case may be, be deducted from the amount of her earnings.

(10) The provisions mentioned in subsection (9)(e) above are—
(a) subsection (2)(a) and (b) above; and
(b) [4 section 166(1) and (2)], [1 . . .] below.

[2(11) Any regulations under subsection (9) above which are made by virtue of paragraph (b) of that subsection must be made with the concurence of the Commissioners of Inland Revenue.]

AMENDMENTS

1. Maternity Allowance and Statutory Maternity Pay Regulations 1994 (SI 1994/1230) reg.6 (October 16, 1994).
2. Social Security Contributions (Transfer of Functions, etc.) Act 1999 s.1(1) and Sch.1 para.12 (April 1, 1999).
3. Employment Act 2002 s.20 (April 6, 2003).
4. Employment Act 2002 s.53 and Sch.7 para.6 (April 6, 2003).

DEFINITIONS

"confined"—see s.171(1).
"confinement"—see s.171(1).
"earnings"—see s.171(1) and reg.20 of the Statutory Maternity Pay (General) Regulations 1986.
"employee"—see s.171 and reg.17 of the Statutory Maternity Pay (General) Regulations 1986.
"employed earner"—see s.2.
"employer"—see s.171(1).
"modifications"—see s.171(1).
"normal weekly earnings"—see s.171(4).
"prescribed"—see s.171(1).
"week"—see s.171(1).

GENERAL NOTE

Statutory Maternity Pay (SMP) provides an income for employees and former employees during a period of maternity leave. In order to qualify for SMP a woman must have worked for an employer for 26 weeks continuously into the week (known as the qualifying week) preceding the 14th week before the expected date of her confinement (subs.(2)(a)). Part III of the SMP (General) Regulations 1986 (SI 1986/1960) defines the concept of continuous employment. The woman must also have been earning during the last eight weeks of her employment an amount at least equal to the lower earnings limit for contribution purposes (subs.(2)(b)). She must, moreover, have become pregnant and have reached (or given birth before reaching) the start of the 11th week before the expected week of confinement (subs.(2)(c)). The further requirement that she must actually have left that employment because of her pregnancy or confinement was repealed by the Employment Act 2002. This repeal itself effectively supersedes reg.2 of the Statutory Maternity Pay (General) (Modification and Amendment) Regulations 2000 (SI 2000/2883), which modified the original version of subs.(2)(a) of the Act in relation to pregnant

1.100

women who were dismissed or whose employment was otherwise terminated without consent.

Where a woman leaves her employment earlier than 11 weeks before the expected week of confinement she loses her entitlement to SMP (unless she has given birth), but if her employer has dismissed her solely or mainly for the purpose of avoiding the liability to pay SMP she will remain entitled. This applies even if she has been working for that employer for only a short period, so long as it is at least eight continuous weeks (see reg.3 of the SMP General Regulation 1986 (SI 1986/1960)). If a woman qualifies for SMP from more than one employer she is entitled to receive it from each of them (SI 1986/1960 reg.18).

It is a precondition of entitlement to SMP that the woman has given notice of her intention to leave by reason of pregnancy or confinement at least 28 days (21 days before the Employment Act 2002) before leaving, unless it is not reasonably practicable to do so and she gives it thereafter as soon as it is reasonably practicable to do so (subs.(4); see further SMP (General) Regulations 1986 (SI 1986/1960) reg.23). This would be so if the baby arrives unexpectedly early, but may also extend to a woman who did not know of the notice requirement and had not been put on inquiry about it. (That was the position taken by the Employment Appeal Tribunal in *Nu-Swift International Ltd v Mallinson* [1979] I.C.R. 157 in relation to maternity pay.) The notice must be in writing if the employer so requests (subs.(5)).

For an illustration of the principle set out in subs.(6), see the decision by the First-tier Tribunal in the Finance and Tax Chamber in *Campus Living Villages UK Ltd v HMRC and Sexton* [2016] UKFTT 738 (TC). The employee, a Head of Finance, was dismissed for redundancy while pregnant. She subsequently settled an employment tribunal case for £60,000 in full and final settlement of all and any claims relating to her contract of employment. The Tribunal held that although the compromise agreement purported to be in full and final settlement of all her claims in relation to her former employment "such a provision cannot exclude her entitlement to SMP and is void to the extent it purports to do so under section 164(6) of the 1992 Act."

A woman is not entitled to SMP if at any time during the maternity pay period (on which see s.165) she is imprisoned or sentenced to imprisonment (other than suspended). Statutory Maternity Pay is lost for the remainder of the period whether or not she is imprisoned for the whole period (see reg.9 of the SMP (General) Regulations 1986 (SI 1986/1960)).

The liability to pay SMP rests with the employer (subs.(3)). In certain circumstances, where an employer does not, or because of insolvency, cannot discharge his liability to pay SMP, that liability is discharged by the Board, now HMRC (at least since April 1, 1999; see subs.(9)(b), SMP (General) Regulations 1986 (SI 1986/1960) reg.7 and Social Security Contributions (Transfer of Functions, etc.) Act 1999 s.1(2) and Sch.2.; the same applies to the Secretary of State's functions under SMP (General) Regulations regs 25, 30 and 31).

Statutory Maternity Pay, therefore, like Statutory Sick Pay, is administered by the employer whilst HMRC is responsible for the resolution of certain disputes about entitlement. Until April 1, 1999, this was achieved by enabling the reference of certain questions to an AO, thereby opening up the usual channels of appeal to SSATs, Commissioners and the courts. With effect from April 1, 1999, the Social Security Contributions (Transfer of Functions, etc.) Act 1999, and the Statutory Sick Pay and Statutory Maternity Pay (Decisions) Regulations 1999 (SI 1999/776) replaced the role of AO with that of an officer of the Board of Inland Revenue (now HMRC). Consequently decision-making and appeals relating to SMP are governed by Pt II of the 1999 Act, with the right of appeal lying to the Tax Chamber of the First-tier Tribunal.

The maternity pay period

1.101

165.—(1) Statutory maternity pay shall be payable, subject to the provisions of this Part of this Act, in respect of each week during a prescribed period ("the maternity pay period") of a duration not exceeding [²52 weeks].

[³(2) Subject to subsections (3) and (7), the maternity pay period shall begin with the 11th week before the expected week of confinement.

(3) Cases may be prescribed in which the first day of the period is to be a prescribed day after the beginning of the 11th week before the expected week of confinement, but not later than the day immediately following the day on which she is confined.]

[⁵ (3A) Regulations may provide for the duration of the maternity pay period as it applies to a woman to be reduced, subject to prescribed restrictions and conditions.

(3B) Regulations under subsection (3A) are to secure that the reduced period ends at a time—
 (a) after a prescribed period beginning with the day on which the woman is confined, and
 (b) when at least a prescribed part of the maternity pay period remains unexpired.

(3C) Regulations under subsection (3A) may, in particular, prescribe restrictions and conditions relating to—
 (a) the end of the woman's entitlement to maternity leave;
 (b) the doing of work by the woman;
 (c) the taking of prescribed steps by the woman or another person as regards leave under section 75E of the Employment Rights Act 1996 in respect of the child;
 (d) the taking of prescribed steps by the woman or another person as regards statutory shared parental pay in respect of the child.

(3D) Regulations may provide for a reduction in the duration of the maternity pay period as it applies to a woman to be revoked, or to be treated as revoked, subject to prescribed restrictions and conditions.]

(4) [³Except in such cases as may be prescribed,] statutory maternity pay shall not be payable to a woman by a person in respect of any week during any part of which she works under a contract of service with him.

(5) It is immaterial for the purposes of subsection (4) above whether the work referred to in that subsection is work under a contract of service which existed immediately before the maternity pay period or a contract of service which did not so exist.

(6) Except in such cases as may be prescribed, statutory maternity pay shall not be payable to a woman in respect of any week after she has been confined and during any part of which she works for any employer who is not liable to pay her statutory maternity pay.

(7) Regulations may provide that this section shall have effect subject to prescribed modifications in relation—
 (a) to cases in which a woman has been confined before the 11th week before the expected week of confinement; and
 (b) to cases in which—
  (i) a woman is confined [¹ at any time after the end of the week immediately preceding the 11th week] before the expected week of confinement; and
  (ii) the maternity pay period has not then commenced for her.

[³(8) In subsections (1), (4) and (6) "week" means a period of seven days beginning with the day of the week on which the maternity pay period begins.]

Social Security Contributions and Benefits Act 1992

AMENDMENTS

1. Maternity Allowance and Statutory Maternity Pay Regulations 1994 (SI 1994/1230) reg.3 (October 16, 1994).
2. Employment Act 2002 s.18 (April 6, 2003).
3. Work and Families Act 2006 s.1 (October 1, 2006).
4. Work and Families Act 2006 s.11 and Sch.1 para.7 (October 1, 2006).
5. Children and Families Act 2014 s.120(4) (June 30, 2014).

DEFINITIONS

"confined"—see s.171(1).
"confinement"—s.171(1).
"employer"—s.171(1).
"maternity pay period"—s.171(1).
"modifications"—s.171(1).
"prescribed"—s.171(1).
"week"—s.171(1).

GENERAL NOTE

1.102   Statutory Maternity Pay is now payable for a period of 39 weeks (previously 26 weeks as a result of the Employment Act 2002, in force in April 2003, before which the maximum period was 18 weeks). As a general rule, the maternity pay period begins with the 11th week before the expected week of confinement (subs.(2)). Regulations provide for this period to be varied when the woman gives birth early (see SMP (General) Regulations 1986 (SI 1986/1960) reg.2).

The normal rule under subs.(4) that a woman is not entitled to receive SMP for any week in which she works for the employer who is liable to pay her SMP has now been relaxed. A woman may now work for her employer for a maximum of 10 days without losing entitlement to SMP (see reg.9A of the SMP (General) Regulations 1986 (SI 1986/1960)). A woman is not entitled to SMP if she works for another employer after her confinement (subs.(6)) unless she had worked for two or more employers up to her qualifying week, one of whom was not liable to pay her SMP, and it is now that employer for whom she is working after confinement (see reg.8 of the SMP (General) Regulations 1986 (SI 1986/1960)). But where she works for a new employer after her confinement, even if she works only briefly, she loses her entitlement for the remainder of the maternity pay period. Apparently there is no restriction on working for another employer before confinement.

On some of the difficulties in establishing the start of the maternity pay period, see *Wade and North Yorkshire Police Authority v HMRC* (FTC/35/2009, FTC/42/2009 and FTC/43/2009) [2011] I.R.L.R. 393.

[¹**Rate of statutory maternity pay**

1.103   **166.**—(1) Statutory maternity pay shall be payable to a woman—
(a) at the earnings-related rate, in respect of the first six weeks in respect of which it is payable; and
(b) at whichever is the lower of the earnings-related rate and such weekly rate as may be prescribed, in respect of the remaining portion of the maternity pay period.

[²(1A) In subsection (1) "week" means any period of seven days.]

(2) The earnings-related rate is a weekly rate equivalent to 90 per cent of a woman's normal weekly earnings for the period of eight weeks immediately preceding the 14th week before the expected week of confinement.

(3) The weekly rate prescribed under subsection (1)(b) above must not be less than the weekly rate of statutory sick pay for the time being specified in

(1992 c.4 s.166)

section 157(1) above or, if two or more such rates are for the time being so specified, the higher or highest of those rates.]

[²(4) Where for any purpose of this Part of this Act or of regulations it is necessary to calculate the daily rate of statutory maternity pay, the amount payable by way of statutory maternity pay for any day shall be taken as one seventh of the weekly rate.]

AMENDMENTS

1. Employment Act 2002 s.19 (April 6, 2003).
2. Work and Families Act 2006 s.11 and Sch.1 para.8 (October 1, 2006).

DEFINITIONS

"confinement"—see s.171(1).
"maternity pay period"—s.171(1).
"normal weekly earnings"—s.171(1).
"prescribed"—s.171(1).
"week—s.171(1).

GENERAL NOTE

A new s.166 was substituted by s.19 of the Employment Act 2002. This preserved the pre-existing position so far as the rate of payment for the first six weeks of the maternity pay period is concerned. During this initial period SMP is paid at the earnings-related rate of 90 per cent of the woman's average weekly earnings in the eight weeks preceding the qualifying week (subss.(1)(a) and (2)). Thereafter, SMP is paid at either the standard prescribed rate (£184.03 in 2024/25) or the earnings-related rate, whichever is the lower (subs.(1)(b)), for the balance of 20 weeks. Previously the balance of the maternity pay period was just 12 weeks, but the then lower rate was always payable, irrespective of whether the earnings-related rate was lower.

1.104

There remains an important issue relating to the SMP earnings calculation and the extent to which this takes into account pay rises. As a result of the decision of the European Court of Justice in *Gillespie v Northern Health and Social Services Board* [1996] I.R.L.R. 214, the earnings calculation for SMP purposes must take into account any pay rise which is backdated into the "relevant period" (on the meaning of which see SSCBA 1992 s.171(4) and (5) and SMP (General) Regulations 1986 (SI 1986/1960 reg.21)). The *Gillespie* decision led to a limited amendment to the relevant regulations (SMP (General) Regulations 1986 reg.21(7), inserted by the SMP (General) Amendment Regulations 1996 (SI 1996/1335)). The question remains whether a woman on maternity leave should receive the benefit of any pay rise which has been implemented after the qualifying week and before the end of paid maternity leave. The original reg.21(7), it was argued, failed to give full effect to the ruling in *Gillespie* by limiting it to cases in which the pay increase is backdated into the relevant period. The Court of Appeal referred a series of questions on this point to the European Court of Justice in *Alabaster v Woolwich Plc* [2002] EWCA Civ. 211; [2002] 1 C.M.L.R. 56; [2002] I.R.L.R. 420. On the request for a preliminary ruling, the ECJ ruled as follows:

> "Article 119 of the Treaty must be interpreted as requiring that, in so far as the pay received by the worker during her maternity leave is determined, at least in part, on the basis of the pay she earned before her maternity leave began, any pay rise awarded between the beginning of the period covered by the reference pay and the end of the maternity leave must be included in the elements of pay taken into account in calculating the amount of such pay. This requirement is not limited to cases where the pay rise is back-dated to the period covered by the reference pay."

Alabaster v Woolwich Plc and Secretary of State for Social Security (C-147/02) [2004] I.R.L.R. 486 at [50].

A new reg.21(7) was subsequently inserted with effect from April 6, 2005, to ensure that a woman's entitlement (or potential entitlement) to statutory maternity pay reflects any pay rise that the woman would have received, but for her maternity leave, and which is effective at any time between the start of the period used to calculate her entitlement and the end of her maternity leave. See further Statutory Maternity Pay (General) (Amendment) Regulations 2005 (SI 2005/729) reg.3. A month later (May 3, 2005), the Court of Appeal delivered its judgment following the decision of the ECJ: see *Alabaster v Barclays Bank Plc and the Secretary of State for Social Security* [2005] EWCA Civ 508. The Court of Appeal held that in order to give effect to the appellant's rights under EU law it was necessary to disapply those parts of Equal Pay Act 1970 s.1 which imposed the requirement for a male comparator.

[¹Funding of employers' liabilities in respect of statutory maternity pay

1.105   **167.**—(1) Regulations shall make provision for the payment by employers of statutory maternity pay to be funded by the Commissioners of Inland Revenue to such extent as may be prescribed.

(2) Regulations under subsection (1) shall—
 (a) make provision for a person who has made a payment of statutory maternity pay to be entitled, except in prescribed circumstances, to recover an amount equal to the sum of—
  (i) the aggregate of such of those payments as qualify for small employers' relief; and
  (ii) an amount equal to 92 per cent of the aggregate of such of those payments as do not so qualify; and
 (b) include provision for a person who has made a payment of statutory maternity pay qualifying for small employers' relief to be entitled, except in prescribed circumstances, to recover an additional amount, determined in such manner as may be prescribed—
  (i) by reference to secondary Class 1 contributions paid in respect of statutory maternity pay;
  (ii) by reference to secondary Class 1 contributions paid in respect of statutory sick pay; or
  (iii) by reference to the aggregate of secondary Class 1 contributions paid in respect of statutory maternity pay and secondary Class 1 contributions paid in respect of statutory sick pay.

(3) For the purposes of this section a payment of statutory maternity pay which a person is liable to make to a woman qualifies for small employers' relief if, in relation to that woman's maternity pay period, the person liable to make the payment is a small employer.

(4) For the purposes of this section "small employer", in relation to a woman's maternity pay period, shall have the meaning assigned to it by regulations, and, without prejudice to the generality of the foregoing, any such regulations—
 (a) may define that expression by reference to the amount of a person's contributions payments for any prescribed period; and
 (b) if they do so, may in that connection make provision for the amount of those payments for that prescribed period—
  (i) to be determined without regard to any deductions that may be made from them under this section or under any other enactment or instrument; and

(ii) in prescribed circumstances, to be adjusted, estimated or otherwise attributed to him by reference to their amount in any other prescribed period.

(5) Regulations under subsection (1) may, in particular, make provision—
(a) for funding in advance as well as in arrear;
(b) for funding, or the recovery of amounts due under provision made by virtue of subsection (2)(b), by means of deductions from such amounts for which employers are accountable to the Commissioners of Inland Revenue as may be prescribed, or otherwise;
(c) for the recovery by the Commissioners of Inland Revenue of any sums overpaid to employers under the regulations.

(6) Where in accordance with any provision of regulations under subsection (1) an amount has been deducted from an employer's contributions payments, the amount so deducted shall (except in such cases as may be prescribed) be treated for the purposes of any provision made by or under any enactment in relation to primary or secondary Class 1 contributions—
(a) as having been paid (on such date as may be determined in accordance with the regulations); and
(b) as having been received by the Commissioners of Inland Revenue, towards discharging the employer's liability in respect of such contributions.

(7) Regulations under this section must be made with the concurrence of the Commissioners of Inland Revenue.

(8) In this section, "contributions payments", in relation to an employer, means any payments which the employer is required, by or under any enactment, to make in discharge of any liability in respect of primary or secondary Class 1 contributions.]

AMENDMENT

1. Employment Act 2002 s.21 (April 6, 2003).

DEFINITIONS

"contributions payments"—see subs.(8).
"employer"—see s.171(1).
"maternity pay period"—see s.171(1).
"prescribed"—see s.171(1).

GENERAL NOTE

The new s.167, substituted by s.21 of the Employment Act 2002, is different from its predecessor in two main respects. First, it allows regulations to be made which enable employers to recover SMP from tax and other payments due to HMRC (see subs.(5)(b) and now Statutory Maternity Pay (Compensation of Employers) and Miscellaneous Amendment Regulations 1994 (SI 1994/1882) reg.6), and not just from payments of national insurance contributions, as was previously the case. Secondly, as with the tax credits regime, it provides for regulations to be made enabling employers to apply to HMRC for advance funding (SI 1994/1882 reg.5). Formerly employers could only deduct, in arrears, the amount of SMP payments from contributions payments due to the Revenue.

1.106

Relationship with benefits and other payments, etc.

168.—Schedule 13 to this Act has effect with respect to the relationship between statutory maternity pay and certain benefits and payments.

1.107

GENERAL NOTE

1.108 As a general rule, entitlement to SMP precludes any entitlement to maternity allowance, SSP or incapacity benefit for the same period. Where SMP is paid, it is treated as going towards the employer's contractual obligation (if any) to pay maternity pay for the same period. If a woman receives maternity allowance because she does not earn enough to qualify for SMP, but then receives a backdated pay increase, making her then entitled to SMP, the employer is required to meet the difference between the maternity allowance paid and the SMP due (SMP (General) Regulations 1986 (SI 1986/1960) reg.21B).

Crown employment—Part XII

1.109 **169.**—The provisions of this Part of this Act apply in relation to women employed by or under the Crown as they apply in relation to women employed otherwise than by or under the Crown.

Special classes of persons

1.110 **170.**—(1) The Secretary of State may [¹with the concurrence of the Treasury] make regulations modifying this Part of this Act in such manner as he thinks proper in their application to any person who is, has been or is to be—
  (a) employed on board any ship, vessel, hovercraft or aircraft;
  (b) outside Great Britain at any prescribed time or in any prescribed circumstances; or
  (c) in prescribed employment in connection with continental shelf operations, as defined in section 120(2) above.
(2) Regulations under subsection (1) above may in particular provide—
  (a) for any provision of this Part of this Act to apply to any such person, notwithstanding that it would not otherwise apply;
  (b) for any such provision not to apply to any such person, notwithstanding that it would otherwise apply;
  (c) for excepting any such person from the application of any such provision where he neither is domiciled nor has a place of residence in any part of Great Britain;
  (d) for the taking of evidence, for the purposes of the determination of any question arising under any such provision, in a country or territory outside Great Britain, by a British consular official or such other person as may be determined in accordance with the regulations.

AMENDMENT

1. Social Security Contributions (Transfer of Functions, etc.) Act 1999 s.1(1) and Sch.1 para.14 (February 25, 1999).

DEFINITIONS

"Great Britain"—see s.172(a).
"prescribed"—see s.171(1).

Interpretation of Part XII and supplementary provisions

1.111 **171.**—(1) In this Part of this Act—
"confinement" means—
  (a) labour resulting in the issue of a living child; or

(b) labour after [¹24 weeks] of pregnancy resulting in the issue of a child whether alive or dead;

and "confined" shall be construed accordingly; and where a woman's labour begun on one day results in the issue of a child on another day she shall be taken to be confined on the day of the issue of the child or, if labour results in the issue of twins or a greater number of children, she shall be taken to be confined on the day of the issue of the last of them;

"dismissed" is to be construed in accordance with [³Part X of the Employment Rights Act 1996];

"employee" means a woman who is—
  (a) gainfully employed in Great Britain either under a contract of service or in an office (including elective office) with [⁵ [¹⁰ earnings (within the meaning of Parts 1 to 5 above)]]

[⁷. . .]

but subject to regulations [⁴made with the concurrence of [⁵Her Majesty's Revenue and Customs] which may provide for cases where any such woman is not to be treated as an employee for the purposes of this Part of this Act and for cases where a woman who would not otherwise be an employee for those purposes is to be treated as an employee for those purposes;

[⁷"employer", in relation to a woman who is an employee, means a person who—
  (a) under section 6 above is liable to pay secondary Class 1 contributions in relation to any of her earnings; or
  (b) would be liable to pay such contributions but for—
    (i) the condition in section 6(1)(b), or
    (ii) the employee being under the age of 16;]

"maternity pay period" has the meaning assigned to it by section 165(1) above;

"modifications" includes additions, omissions and amendments, and related expressions shall be construed accordingly;

"prescribed" means specified in or determined in accordance with regulations;

[⁸. . .]

[⁸(1A) In this Part, except section 165(1), (4) and (6), section 166(1) and paragraph 3(2) of Schedule 13, "week" means a period of 7 days beginning with Sunday or such other period as may be prescribed in relation to any particular case or class of case.]

(2) Without prejudice to any other power to make regulations under this Part of this Act, regulations may specify cases in which, for the purposes of this Part of this Act or of such provisions of this Part of this Act as may be prescribed—
  (a) two or more employers are to be treated as one;
  (b) two or more contracts of service in respect of which the same woman is an employee are to be treated as one.

(3) Where, in consequence of the establishment of one or more National Health Service trusts [⁹the National Health Service Act 2006, the National Health Service (Wales) Act 2006] or the National Health Service (Scotland) Act 1978, a woman's contract of employment is treated by a scheme under [⁹any of those Acts] as divided so as to constitute two or more contracts, [²or where an order under [⁹paragraph 26(1)

of Schedule 3 to the National Health Service Act 2006] provides that a woman's contract of employment is so divided,] regulations may make provision enabling her to elect for all of those contracts to be treated as one contract for the purposes of this Part of this Act or of such provisions of this Part of this Act as may be prescribed; and any such regulations may prescribe—
  (a) the conditions that must be satisfied if a woman is to be entitled to make such an election;
  (b) the manner in which, and the time within which, such an election is to be made;
  (c) the persons to whom, and the manner in which, notice of such an election is to be given;
  (d) the information which a woman who makes such an election is to provide, and the persons to whom, and the time within which, she is to provide it;
  (e) the time for which such an election is to have effect;
  (f) which one of the woman's employers under the two or more contracts is to be regarded for the purposes of statutory maternity pay as her employer under the one contract;
and the powers conferred by this subsection are without prejudice to any other power to make regulations under this Part of this Act.

(4) For the purposes of this Part of this Act a woman's normal weekly earnings shall, subject to subsection (6) below, be taken to be the average weekly earnings which in the relevant period have been paid to her or paid for her benefit under the contract of service with the employer in question.

(5) For the purposes of subsection (4) above "earnings" and "relevant period" shall have the meanings given to them by regulations.

(6) In such cases as may be prescribed a woman's normal weekly earnings shall be calculated in accordance with regulations.

[4(7) Regulations under any of subsections (2) to (6) above must be made with the concurrence of the Commissioners of Inland Revenue.]

AMENDMENTS

  1. Still-Birth (Definition) Act 1992 s.2 (October 1, 1992).
  2. Health Act 1999 (Supplementary, Consequential etc. Provisions) Order 2000 art.3 Sch.1 para.27 (SI 2000/90) (February 8, 2000).
  3. Employment Rights Act 1996 s.240 and Sch.1 para.51(5) (August 23, 1996).
  4. Social Security Contributions (Transfer of Functions, etc.) Act 1999 s.1(1) and Sch.1 para.15 (April 1, 1999).
  5. Income Tax (Earnings and Pensions) Act 2003 s.722 and Sch.6 para.182 (April 6, 2003).
  6. Commissioners for Revenue and Customs Act 2005 s.50 and Sch.4 para.43 (April 18, 2005).
  7. Employment Equality (Age) Regulations 2006 (SI 2006/1031) reg.49(1) and Sch.8 para.10 (October 1, 2006).
  8. Work and Families Act 2006 s.11 and Sch.1 para.9 (October 1, 2006).
  9. National Health Service (Consequential Provisions) Act 2006 s.2 and Sch.1 para.148 (March 1, 2007).
  10. National Insurance Contributions Act 2014 s.15 and Sch.2 para.4 (May 13, 2014).

(1992 c.4 s.171)

[¹Part XIIZA]

[² [³ . . .] Statutory Paternity Pay]

Amendments

1. Part XIIZA was inserted by the Employment Act 2002 s.2 (December 8, 2002).
2. Work and Families Act 2006 s.11(1) Sch.1 para.10 (April 6, 2010).
3. Children and Families Act 2014 s.126 and Sch.7 para.10 (April 5, 2015).

General Note

Part XIIZA of the SSCBA 1992 was inserted by the Employment Act 2002. The 2002 Act followed the Employment Relations Act 1999, which itself included a number of "family friendly" employment measures (e.g. new rights to 13 weeks' unpaid parental leave and to unpaid time off to deal with family crises). The ordinary period of maternity leave was also increased in 1999 from 14 to 18 weeks (this period was extended to 26 weeks in April 2003 by other provisions in the Employment Act 2002), along with several other reforms designed to simplify the notoriously complex rules governing maternity leave and pay. A further review was announced in the 2000 Budget statement, which led to the publication of a Green Paper, *Work and Parents: Competitiveness and Choice* (DTI, December 2000). The Government's decisions on that review were announced at or around the time of the 2001 Budget statement, and were followed by the issue of three further consultation documents on the frameworks for maternity, paternity and adoption leave and pay. In November 2001 the DTI published a summary of responses to these various papers in the *Government's Response on Simplification of Maternity Leave, Paternity Leave and Adoption Leave.*

1.112

The Government's proposals were then brought forward in the Bill which became the Employment Act 2002. Part I of the 2002 Act dealt with statutory leave and pay. Thus, s.1 introduced a right to paternity leave in the Employment Rights Act 1996 (inserting ss.80A–80E), while s.2 inserted this Pt XIIZA into the SSCBA 1992 to make provision for statutory paternity pay (SPP). Sections 3 and 4 dealt with adoption leave and statutory adoption pay (SAP) respectively (on the latter see SSCBA 1992 Pt XIIZB). The procedural provisions relating to SPP and SAP were contained in ss.5–16 of the 2002 Act. (The 2002 Act also included measures to establish statutory minimum dismissal, disciplinary and grievance procedures and changes to employment tribunal procedures.)

The amendments made by c.1 of Pt I of the Employment Act 2002 relating to paternity and adoption, including the insertion of Pt XIIZA into the SSCBA 1992, came into force on December 8, 2002 (Employment Act 2002 (Commencement No.3 and Transitional and Saving Provisions) Order 2002 art.2(2) and Sch.1, Pt II). However, art.3 and Sch.3, para.1 of the same Order provide that Pt XIIZA shall have effect only in relation to a person who satisfies the prescribed conditions of entitlement in respect of a child who is either: (a) born on or after April 6, 2003 (or whose expected week of birth begins on or after that date); or (b) matched for the purposes of adoption with a person who is notified of having been matched on or after April 6, 2003 (or placed for adoption on or after that date).

Statutory Paternity Pay is payable for a two-week period only (SSCBA 1992 s.171ZE(2)). Such paid paternity leave must be taken in a single block within the first eight weeks after the child's birth (SSCBA 1992 s.171ZE(3)). There are, in fact, two forms of SPP, known in the regulations (the Statutory Paternity Pay and Statutory Adoption Pay (General) Regulations 2002 (SI 2002/2822)) as SPP (birth) and SPP (adoption), although these terms do not appear in the primary legislation. The principal eligibility criteria for SPP (birth) are set out in SSCBA 1992 s.171ZA and for SPP (adoption) in s.171ZB. Entitlement to SPP (birth) arises in respect of children born on or after April 6, 2003, or whose expected week of birth begins on or after that date (SPP and SAP (General) Regulations 2002 reg.3(1)(a); see also (Employment Act 2002 (Commencement No.3 and Transitional and Saving Provisions) Order 2002 art.3 and Sch.3). Similarly, entitlement to SPP (adoption) arises where the adoptive parent is notified of having been matched on or after April 6, 2003 or the child is placed for adoption on or after that date (SPP and SAP (General) Regulations 2002 reg.3(1)(b)). Section 171ZC contains general conditions of entitlement (e.g. as to giving the requisite notice to the employer). Section 171ZD places the liability to make payments of SPP on employers (the recovery mechanisms are the same as for SMP), while s.171ZE, with the associated regulations, deals with matters such as the rate and period of pay. Although paid for a shorter period than SMP, SPP is paid at the same rate as SMP. Sections 171ZF–171ZK make provision for various types of special cases and matters of interpretation, etc.

[²[³ . . .]]

[¹**Entitlement: birth**

1.113   **171ZA.**—(1) Where a person satisfies the conditions in subsection (2) below, he shall be entitled in accordance with the following provisions of this Part to payments to be known as [² [³ statutory paternity pay]].

(2) The conditions are—
  (a) that he satisfies prescribed conditions—
      (i) as to relationship with a newborn child; and
      (ii) as to relationship with the child's mother;
  (b) that he has been in employed earner's employment with an employer for a continuous period of at least 26 weeks ending with the relevant week;
  (c) that his normal weekly earnings for the period of eight weeks ending with the relevant week are not less than the lower earnings limit in force under section 5(1)(a) above at the end of the relevant week; and
  (d) that he has been in employed earner's employment with the employer by reference to whom the condition in para.(b) above is satisfied for a continuous period beginning with the end of the relevant week and ending with the day on which the child is born.

(3) The references in subsection (2) above to the relevant week are to the week immediately preceding the 14th week before the expected week of the child's birth.

(4) A person's entitlement to [² [³ . . . statutory paternity pay] under this section shall not be affected by the birth, or expected birth, of more than one child as a result of the same pregnancy.

(5) In this section, "newborn child" includes a child stillborn after 24 weeks of pregnancy.]

AMENDMENTS

1. Employment Act 2002 s.2 (December 8, 2002).
2. Work and Families Act 2006 s.11(1) Sch.1 paras 11 and 12 (April 6, 2010).
3. Children and Families Act 2014 s.126 and Sch.7 paras 11 and 12 (April 5, 2015).

(1992 c.4 s.171ZA)

DEFINITIONS

"employer"—see s.171ZJ(1).
"newborn child"—see subs.(5).
"prescribed"—see s.171ZJ(1).
"the relevant week"—see subs.(3).
"week"—see s.171ZJ(5).

GENERAL NOTE

Subsection (2)(a)
The entitlement conditions referred to in subs.(2)(a) are those prescribed in regs 4(2)(b) and (c) of the Paternity and Adoption Leave Regulations 2002 (SI 2002/2788), which are incorporated by the cross-reference in reg.4 of the SPP and SAP (General) Regulations 2002 (SI 2002/2822). These requirements are that the employee is, first, either: (i) the father of the child, or (ii) married to or the partner of the child's mother, but not the child's father (reg.4(2)(b)); and, secondly, has, or expects to have: (i) responsibility for the upbringing of the child (if he is the child's father); or (ii) the main responsibility (apart from any responsibility of the mother) for the upbringing of the child (if he is the mother's husband or partner but not the child's father) (reg.4(2)(c)).

1.114

Subsection (2)(b)
On the extended meaning of continuous employment, see SPP and SAP (General) Regulations 2002 regs 33–37.

1.115

Subsection (2)(c)
The minimum threshold requirement that the claimant's earnings are not less than the National Insurance lower earnings limit necessarily excludes those fathers on very low incomes, and typically in part-time work, from SPP. Arguably this is the group of men whose families are most at risk of social exclusion and thus most in need of support such as SPP. The problem is exacerbated by the fact that the National Insurance scheme, unlike the income tax system, does not aggregate earnings from, e.g. two part-time jobs with different employers. (But note the special case of associated employers: see SPP and SAP (General) Regulations 2002 reg.38.) Women who do not meet the lower earnings limit requirement do not qualify for SMP (SSCBA 1992 s.164(2)(b)) but may qualify for maternity allowance (SSCBA 1992 s.35—see Vol.I of this series). There is, at present, no such alternative form of income maintenance for fathers in a similar position. This was the one aspect in relation to this part of the Employment Act 2002 which caused considerable disquiet amongst Government back-benchers during the Standing Committee debates on the Bill (Standing Committee F, January 10, 2002, cols 333–360). The minister promised members that the DWP and Department of Health were actively considering how to provide support for low-wage adoptive parents with some form of support equivalent to maternity allowance.

1.116

Subsection (2)(b)–(d)
The entitlement conditions are modified if a person fails to meet the conditions set out in subs.(2)(b)–(d) because the child's birth occurred earlier than the 14th week before the expected week of the birth: see SPP and SAP (General) Regulations 2002 reg.5. This modification is in exercise of the regulation-making powers under s.171ZC(3)(a).

1.117

Subsection (4)
Thus, SPP is not paid for twice as long in the case of a father of twins.

1.118

[¹**Entitlement: adoption**

171ZB.—(1) Where a person satisfies the conditions in subsection (2) below, he shall be entitled in accordance with the following provisions of this Part to payments to be known as [² [⁴ . . . statutory paternity pay]].
(2) The conditions are—
   (a) that he satisfies prescribed conditions—
       (i) as to relationship with a child who is placed for adoption under the law of any part of the United Kingdom, and
       (ii) as to relationship with a person with whom the child is so placed for adoption;
   (b) that he has been in employed earner's employment with an employer for a continuous period of at least 26 weeks ending with the relevant week;
   (c) that his normal weekly earnings for the period of 8 weeks ending with the relevant week are not less than the lower earnings limit in force under section 5(1)(a) at the end of the relevant week;
   (d) that he has been in employed earner's employment with the employer by reference to whom the condition in paragraph (b) above is satisfied for a continuous period beginning with the end of the relevant week and ending with the day on which the child is placed for adoption; and
   (e) where he is a person with whom the child is placed for adoption, that he has elected to receive statutory paternity pay.
(3) The references in subsection (2) to the relevant week are to the week in which the adopter is notified of being matched with the child for the purposes of adoption.
(4) A person may not elect to receive [² [⁴ . . .] statutory paternity pay] if he has elected in accordance with section 171ZL below to receive statutory adoption pay.
(5) Regulations may make provision about elections for the purposes of subsection (2)(e) above.
(6) A person's entitlement to [² [⁴ . . .] statutory paternity pay] under this section shall not be affected by the placement for adoption of more than one child as part of the same arrangement.
(7) In this section, "adopter", in relation to a person who satisfies the condition under subsection (2)(a)(ii) above, means the person by reference to whom he satisfies that condition.
[³ (8) This section has effect in a case involving a child placed under section 22C of the Children Act 1989 by a local authority in England with a local authority foster parent who has been approved as a prospective adopter with the following modifications—
   (a) the references in subsection (2) to a child being placed for adoption under the law of any part of the United Kingdom are to be treated as references to a child being placed under section 22C in that manner;
   (b) the reference in subsection (3) to the week in which the adopter is notified of being matched with the child for the purposes of adoption is to be treated as a reference to the week in which the prospective adopter is notified that the child is to be, or is expected to be, placed with the prospective adopter under section 22C;
   (c) the reference in subsection (6) to placement for adoption is to be treated as a reference to placement under section 22C;

(d) the definition in subsection (7) is to be treated as if it were a definition of "prospective adopter".

(9) Where, by virtue of subsection (8), a person becomes entitled to statutory paternity pay in connection with the placement of a child under section 22C of the Children Act 1989, the person may not become entitled to payments of statutory paternity pay in connection with the placement of the child for adoption.]

[5 (10) This section has effect in a case involving a child placed under section 81 of the Social Services and Well-being (Wales) Act 2014 by a local authority in Wales with a local authority foster parent who has been approved as a prospective adopter with the following modifications—

(a) the references in subsection (2) to a child being placed for adoption under the law of any part of the United Kingdom are to be treated as references to a child being placed under section 81 in that manner;
(b) the reference in subsection (3) to the week in which the adopter is notified of being matched with the child for the purposes of adoption is to be treated as a reference to the week in which the prospective adopter is notified that the child is to be, or is expected to be, placed with the prospective adopter under section 81;
(c) the reference in subsection (6) to placement for adoption is to be treated as a reference to placement under section 81;
(d) the definition in subsection (7) is to be treated as if it were a definition of "prospective adopter".

(11) Where, by virtue of subsection (10), a person becomes entitled to statutory paternity pay in connection with the placement of a child under section 81 of the Social Services and Well-being (Wales) Act 2014, the person may not become entitled to payments of statutory paternity pay in connection with the placement of the child for adoption.]]

AMENDMENTS

1. Employment Act 2002 s.2 (December 8, 2002).
2. Work and Families Act 2006 s.11(1) Sch.1 para.13 (April 6, 2010).
3. Children and Families Act 2014 s.121(3) (June 30, 2014).
4. Children and Families Act 2014 s.126 and Sch.7 para.13 (April 5, 2015).
5. Social Services and Well-being (Wales) Act 2014 (Consequential Amendments) Regulations 2016 (SI 2016/413) (W.131) reg.132 (April 6, 2016).

DEFINITIONS

"adopter"—see subs.(7).
"employer"—see s.171ZJ(1).
"normal weekly earnings"—see s.171ZJ(6).
"prescribed"—see s.171ZJ(1).
"the relevant week"—see subs.(3).
"week"—see s.171ZJ(5).

GENERAL NOTE

The conditions prescribed under subs.(2)(a) are, first, that the claimant is married to or the partner of a child's adopter (or in a case where there are two adopters, married to or the partner of the other adopter) and, secondly, has, or expects to have, the main responsibility for the upbringing of the child (apart from the responsibility of the child's adopter, or in a case where there two adopters, together

1.120

with the other adopter): SPP and SAP (General) Regulations 2002 (SI 2002/2822) reg.11. Note that, unusually, reg.11 specifically includes same-sex partners. "Partner" is defined by reg.11(2) as meaning a person (excluding certain defined relatives) "who lives with the adopter and the child in an enduring family relationship", irrespective of whether the relationship between the adults is heterosexual or same-sex in nature.

[¹Entitlement: general

1.121   **171ZC.**—(1) A person shall be entitled to payments of [² [⁴...] statutory paternity pay] in respect of any period [³ only if he gives the person who will be liable to pay it notice of the week or weeks in respect of which he expects there to be liability to pay him statutory paternity pay.]

[³ (1A) Regulations may provide for the time by which notice under subsection (1) is to be given.]

(2) The notice shall be in writing if the person who is liable to pay the [² [⁴...] statutory paternity pay] so requests.

(3) The Secretary of State may by regulations—
  (a) provide that subsection (2)(b), (c) or (d) of section 171ZA or 171ZB above shall have effect subject to prescribed modifications in such cases as may be prescribed;
  (b) provide that subsection (1) above shall not have effect, or shall have effect subject to prescribed modifications, in such cases as may be prescribed;
  (c) impose requirements about evidence of entitlement;
  (d) specify in what circumstances employment is to be treated as continuous for the purposes of section 171ZA or 171ZB above;
  (e) provide that a person is to be treated for the purposes of section 171ZA or 171ZB above as being employed for a continuous period of at least 26 weeks where—
    (i) he has been employed by the same employer for at least 26 weeks under two or more separate contracts of service; and
    (ii) those contracts were not continuous;
  (f) provide for amounts earned by a person under separate contracts of service with the same employer to be aggregated for the purposes of section 171ZA or 171ZB above;
  (g) provide that—
    (i) the amount of a person's earnings for any period; or
    (ii) the amount of his earnings to be treated as comprised in any payment made to him or for his benefit,
shall be calculated or estimated for the purposes of section 171ZA or 171ZB above in such manner and on such basis as may be prescribed and that for that purpose payments of a particular class or description made or falling to be made to or by a person shall, to such extent as may be prescribed, be disregarded or, as the case may be, be deducted from the amount of his earnings.]

AMENDMENTS

1. Employment Act 2002 s.2 (December 8, 2002).
2. Work and Families Act 2006 s.11(1) Sch.1 para.14 (April 6, 2010).
3. Children and Families Act 2014 s.123(2) (June 30, 2014).
4. Children and Families Act 2014 s.126 and Sch.7 para.14 (April 5, 2015).

(1992 c.4 s.171ZC)

DEFINITIONS

"employer"—see s.171ZJ(1).
"modifications"—see s.171ZJ(1).
"prescribed"—see s.171ZJ(1).
"week"—see s.171ZJ(5).

GENERAL NOTE

Note that the claimant's notice to the employer must be in writing if so requested: see subs.(2) and *Sharfudeen v T.J. Morris Ltd t/a Home Bargains* [2017] UKEAT 272, where the notice to the employer was out of time in any event. See further regs 6 and 7 of the SPP and SAP (General) Regulations 2002 (SI 2002/2822) on the period of payment and notice requirements for SPP (birth). The requirements relating to evidence of entitlement are in reg.9. The equivalent provisions for SPP (adoption) are in regs 12, 13 and 15.

1.122

[¹**Liability to make payments**

171ZD.—(1) The liability to make payments of [² [³...]] statutory paternity pay under section 171ZA or 171ZB above is a liability of any person of whom the person entitled to the payments has been an employee as mentioned in subsection (2)(b) and (d) of that section.

(2) Regulations shall make provision as to a former employer's liability to pay [² [³...] statutory paternity pay] to a person in any case where the former employee's contract of service with him has been brought to an end by the former employer solely, or mainly, for the purpose of avoiding [² liability for [³...] statutory paternity pay [³...]].

(3) The Secretary of State may, with the concurrence of the Board, by regulations specify circumstances in which, notwithstanding this section, liability to make payments of statutory paternity pay is to be a liability of the Board.]

1.123

AMENDMENTS

1. Employment Act 2002 s.2 (December 8, 2002).
2. Work and Families Act 2006 s.11(1) Sch.1 para.15 (April 6, 2010).
3. Children and Families Act 2014 s.126 and Sch.7 para.15 (April 5, 2015).

DEFINITIONS

"the Board"—see s.171ZJ(1).
"employer"—see s.171ZJ(1).

GENERAL NOTE

This section, placing the liability to make payments of SPP on employers, follows the same approach as the provisions governing SMP (ss.164(3) and (8)). Note that there is no liability to pay SPP in respect of any week during which the claimant either is entitled to SSP or is detained in custody (or sentenced to imprisonment): SPP and SAP (General) Regulations 2002 (SI 2002/2822) reg.18. Similarly, there is no liability to pay SPP in the week that the person entitled dies.

The rules governing the funding of SPP and employers' responsibilities in connection with SPP payments are contained in the SPP and SAP (Administration) Regulations 2002 (SI 2002/2820). The special circumstances in which the Board is liable to pay SPP under subs.(3) are set out in SPP and SAP (General) Regulations 2002 reg.43.

1.124

Social Security Contributions and Benefits Act 1992

[¹**Rate and period of pay**

171ZE.—(1) [³ [⁵ . . .] Statutory paternity pay] shall be payable at such fixed or earnings-related weekly rate as may be prescribed by regulations, which may prescribe different kinds of rate for different cases.

(2) [³ [⁵ . . .] statutory paternity pay] shall be payable in respect of—
  (a) a period of two consecutive weeks within the qualifying period beginning on such date within that period as the person entitled may choose in accordance with regulations; or
  (b) if regulations permit the person entitled to choose to receive [³ [⁵ . . .] statutory paternity pay] in respect of—
    (i) a period of a week, or
    (ii) two non-consecutive periods of a week,
  such week or weeks within the qualifying period as he may choose in accordance with regulations.

(3) For the purposes of subsection (2) above, the qualifying period shall be determined in accordance with regulations, which shall secure that it is a period of at least 56 days beginning—
  (a) in the case of a person to whom the conditions in section 171ZA(2) above apply, with the date of the child's birth, and
  (b) in the case of a person to whom the conditions in section 171ZB(2) above apply, with the date of the child's placement for adoption.

[⁴ (3A) Statutory paternity pay is not payable to a person in respect of a statutory pay week if—
  (a) statutory shared parental pay is payable to that person in respect of any part of that week or that person takes shared parental leave in any part of that week, or
  (b) statutory shared parental pay was payable to that person or that person has taken shared parental leave in respect of the child before that week.]

(4) [³ [⁵ . . .] Statutory paternity pay] shall not be payable to a person in respect of a statutory pay week if it is not his purpose at the beginning of the week—
  (a) to care for the child by reference to whom he satisfies the condition in sub-paragraph (i) of section 171ZA(2)(a) or 171ZB(2)(a) above; or
  (b) to support the person by reference to whom he satisfies the condition in sub-paragraph (ii) of that provision.

(5) A person shall not be liable to pay [³ [⁵ . . .] statutory paternity pay] to another in respect of a statutory pay week during any part of which the other works under a contract of service with him.

(6) It is immaterial for the purposes of subsection (5) above whether the work referred to in that subsection is work under a contract of service which existed immediately before the statutory pay week or a contract of service which did not so exist.

(7) Except in such cases as may be prescribed, [³ [⁵ . . .] statutory paternity pay] shall not be payable to a person in respect of a statutory pay week during any part of which he works for any employer who is not liable to pay him [³ [⁵ . . .] statutory paternity pay].

(8) The Secretary of State may by regulations specify circumstances in which there is to be no liability to pay [³ [⁵ . . .] statutory paternity pay] in respect of a statutory pay week.

(1992 c.4 s.171ZE)

(9) Where more than one child is born as a result of the same pregnancy, the reference in subsection (3)(a) to the date of the child's birth shall be read as a reference to the date of birth of the first child born as a result of the pregnancy.

(10) Where more than one child is placed for adoption as part of the same arrangement, the reference in subsection (3)(b) to the date of the child's placement shall be read as a reference to the date of placement of the first child to be placed as part of the arrangement.

[²(10A) Where for any purpose of this Part of this Act or of regulations it is necessary to calculate the daily rate of [⁵...] statutory paternity pay, the amount payable by way of [⁵...] statutory paternity pay for any day shall be taken as one seventh of the weekly rate.]

(11) In this section—

"statutory pay week", in relation to a person entitled to [⁵...] statutory paternity pay, means a week chosen by him as a week in respect of which [⁵...] statutory paternity pay shall be payable;

"week" means any period of seven days.

[⁴ (12) Where statutory paternity pay is payable to a person by virtue of section 171ZB(8), this section has effect as if—
(a) the references in subsections (3)(b) and (10) to placement for adoption were references to placement under section 22C of the Children Act 1989;
(b) the references in subsection (10) to being placed for adoption were references to being placed under section 22C.]

[⁶ (13) Where statutory paternity pay is payable to a person by virtue of section 171ZB(10), this section has effect as if—
(a) the references in subsections (3)(b) and (10) to placement for adoption were references to placement under section 81 of the Social Services and Well-being (Wales) Act 2014;
(b) the references in subsection (10) to being placed for adoption were references to being placed under section 81.]]

AMENDMENTS

1. Employment Act 2002 s.2 (December 8, 2002).
2. Work and Families Act 2006 s.11 and Sch.1 para.16(1) and (3) (October 1, 2006).
3. Work and Families Act 2006 s.11(1) Sch.1 para.16(1) and (2) (April 6, 2010).
4. Children and Families Act 2014 ss.120(5) and 121(4) (June 30, 2014).
5. Children and Families Act 2014 s.126 and Sch.7 para.16 (April 5, 2015).
6. Social Services and Well-being (Wales) Act 2014 (Consequential Amendments) Regulations 2016 (SI 2016/413) (W.131) reg.133 (April 6, 2016).

DEFINITIONS

"employer"—see s.171ZJ(1).
"statutory pay week"—see subs.(11).
"week"—see subs.(11).

GENERAL NOTE

The weekly rate of SPP for 2024/25 is the lesser of £184.03 and 90 per cent of normal weekly earnings (on which see SPP and SAP (General) Regulations 2002 (SI 2002/2822) reg.40): SPP and SAP (Weekly Rates) Regulations 2002 (SI 2002/2818) reg.2.

1.126

Social Security Contributions and Benefits Act 1992

The qualifying period for SPP (birth), i.e. the period within which the SPP period must occur, is the period of 56 days from the date of the child's birth (SPP and SAP (General) Regulations 2002 reg.8). For SPP (adoption), the 56 days runs from the date of the child's placement for adoption: see reg.14.

Regulation 18 of the SPP and SAP (General) Regulations 2002, made under para.(8), sets out the circumstances in which there is no liability to pay SPP (where SSP is payable, or the person has died or is in legal custody).

The rules governing the time for paying SPP are set out in reg.42 of the SPP and SAP (General) Regulations 2002. SPP may be paid in the same way as ordinary remuneration but must not include payment in kind or by way of board and lodging: reg.41.

[¹ [²**Entitlement to additional statutory paternity pay: birth**

1.127   **171ZEA.**—[³ . . .]]

AMENDMENTS

1. Employment Act 2002 s.2 (December 8, 2002).
2. Work and Families Act 2006 s.6 (March 3, 2010).
3. Children and Families Act 2014 s.125(2) (April 5, 2015).

[¹ [²**Entitlement to additional statutory paternity pay: adoption**

1.128   **171ZEB.**—[³ . . .]]

AMENDMENTS

1. Employment Act 2002 s.2 (December 8, 2002).
2. Work and Families Act 2006 s.7 (March 3, 2010).
3. Children and Families Act 2014 s.125(2) (April 5, 2015).

[¹ [²**Entitlement to additional statutory paternity pay: general**

1.129   **171ZEC.**—[³ . . .]]

AMENDMENTS

1. Employment Act 2002 s.2 (December 8, 2002).
2. Work and Families Act 2006 s.8 (March 3, 2010).
3. Children and Families Act 2014 s.125(2) (April 5, 2015).

[¹ [²**Liability to make payments of additional statutory paternity pay**

1.130   **171ZED.**—[³ . . .]]

AMENDMENTS

1. Employment Act 2002 s.2 (December 8, 2002).
2. Work and Families Act 2006 s.9 (March 3, 2010).
3. Children and Families Act 2014 s.125(2) (April 5, 2015).

[¹ [²**Rate and period of pay: additional statutory paternity pay**

1.131   **171ZEE.**—[³ . . .]]

AMENDMENTS

1. Employment Act 2002 s.2 (December 8, 2002).
2. Work and Families Act 2006 s.10 (March 3, 2010).
3. Children and Families Act 2014 s.125(2) (April 5, 2015).

(1992 c.4 s.171ZF)

[² [³ ...]]

[¹Restrictions on contracting out

171ZF.—(1) Any agreement shall be void to the extent that it purports—
(a) to exclude, limit or otherwise modify any provision of this Part of this Act; or
(b) to require an employee or former employee to contribute (whether directly or indirectly) towards any costs incurred by his employer or former employer under this Part of this Act.

(2) For the avoidance of doubt, any agreement between an employer and an employee authorising any deductions from [² [³ statutory paternity pay]] which the employer is liable to pay to the employee in respect of any period shall not be void by virtue of subsection (1)(a) above if the employer—
(a) is authorised by that or another agreement to make the same deductions from any contractual remuneration which he is liable to pay in respect of the same period; or
(b) would be so authorised if he were liable to pay contractual remuneration in respect of that period.]

AMENDMENTS

1. Employment Act 2002 s.2 (December 8, 2002).
2. Work and Families Act 2006 s.11(1) Sch.1 paras 17 and 18 (April 6, 2010).
3. Children and Families Act 2014 s.126 and Sch.7 paras 18 and 19 (April 5, 2015).

DEFINITION

"employer"—see s.171ZJ(1).

GENERAL NOTE

These restrictions on contracting out follow the equivalent provisions for SSP (s.151(2)–(3)) and SMP (s.164(6)–(7)).

[¹Relationship with contractual remuneration

171ZG.—(1) Subject to subsections (2) and (3) below, any entitlement to statutory paternity pay shall not affect any right of a person in relation to remuneration under any contract of service ("contractual remuneration").

(2) Subject to subsection (3) below—
(a) any contractual remuneration paid to a person by an employer of his in respect of any period shall go towards discharging any liability of that employer to pay statutory paternity pay to him in respect of that period; and
(b) any statutory paternity pay paid by an employer to a person who is an employee of his in respect of any period shall go towards discharging any liability of that employer to pay contractual remuneration to him in respect of that period.

(3) Regulations may make provision as to payments which are, and those which are not, to be treated as contractual remuneration for the purposes of subsections (1) and (2) above.

[²(4) [³ ...]]

AMENDMENTS

1. Employment Act 2002 s.2 (December 8, 2002).
2. Work and Families Act 2006 s.11(1) Sch.1 para.19 (April 6, 2010).
3. Children and Families Act 2014 s.126 and Sch.7 para.20 (April 5, 2015).

DEFINITIONS

"contractual remuneration"—see subs.(1).
"employer"—see s.171ZJ(1).

GENERAL NOTE

1.135   This section mirrors Sch.12, para.2 the equivalent provision in relation to SSP, and Sch.13 para.3, which governs SMP to the same effect. The basic principle is that entitlement to SPP does not affect a claimant's rights to any contractual remuneration (subs.(1)), subject to the significant exception that any payment of contractual remuneration can be regarded as the discharge of SPP liability and vice versa (subs.(2)). Regulations made under subs.(3) provide that the payments to be treated as contractual remuneration are sums payable under a contract of service: (a) by way of remuneration, (b) for incapacity for work due to sickness or injury, or (c) by reason of the birth or adoption of a child (SPP and SAP (General) Regulations 2002 (SI 2002/2822) reg.19).

[¹Crown employment—Part XIIZA

1.136   **171ZH.**—The provisions of this Part of this Act apply in relation to persons employed by or under the Crown as they apply in relation to persons employed otherwise than by or under the Crown.]

AMENDMENT

1. Employment Act 2002 s.2 (December 8, 2002).

GENERAL NOTE

1.137   This mirrors s.169, the equivalent provision for SMP.

[¹Special classes of person

1.138   **171ZI.**—(1) The Secretary of State may with the concurrence of the Treasury make regulations modifying any provision of this Part of this Act in such manner as he thinks proper in its application to any person who is, has been or is to be—
(a) employed on board any ship, vessel, hovercraft or aircraft;
(b) outside Great Britain at any prescribed time or in any prescribed circumstances; or
(c) in prescribed employment in connection with continental shelf operations, as defined in section 120(2) above.
(2) Regulations under subsection (1) above may, in particular, provide—
(a) for any provision of this Part of this Act to apply to any such person, notwithstanding that it would not otherwise apply;
(b) for any such provision not to apply to any such person, notwithstanding that it would otherwise apply;
(c) for excepting any such person from the application of any such provision where he neither is domiciled nor has a place of residence in any part of Great Britain;

(d) for the taking of evidence, for the purposes of the determination of any question arising under any such provision, in a country or territory outside Great Britain, by a British consular official or such other person as may be determined in accordance with the regulations.]

AMENDMENT

1. Employment Act 2002 s.2 (December 8, 2002).

DEFINITIONS

"Great Britain"—see s.172(a).
"prescribed"—see s.171ZJ(1).

GENERAL NOTE

This enabling provision is in the same terms as s.162, which applies to SSP. See further the Statutory Paternity Pay and Statutory Adoption Pay (Persons Abroad and Mariners) Regulations 2002 (SI 2002/2821).

[¹Part XIIZA: supplementary

171ZJ.—(1) In this Part of this Act—
"the Board" means the Commissioners of Inland Revenue;
[³"employer", in relation to a person who is an employee, means a person who—
(a) under section 6 above is, liable to pay secondary Class 1 contributions in relation to any of the earnings of the person who is an employee; or
(b) would be liable to pay such contributions but for—
   (i) the condition in section 6(1)(b), or
   (ii) the employee being under the age of 16;]
[⁶ "local authority" has the same meaning as in the Children Act 1989 (see section 105(1) of that Act);
"local authority foster parent" has the same meaning as in the Children Act 1989 (see [⁹ section 105(1)] of that Act);]
"modifications" includes additions, omissions and amendments, and related expressions are to be read accordingly;
"prescribed" means prescribed by regulations.
(2) In this Part of this Act, "employee" means a person who is—
(a) gainfully employed in Great Britain either under a contract of service or in an office (including elective office) with [² [⁷ earnings (within the meaning of Parts 1 to 5 above)]]
[³. . .]
(3) Regulations may provide—
(a) for cases where a person who falls within the definition in subsection (2) above is not to be treated as an employee for the purposes of this Part of this Act; and
(b) for cases where a person who would not otherwise be an employee for the purposes of this Part of this Act is to be treated as an employee for those purposes.
(4) Without prejudice to any other power to make regulations under this Part of this Act, regulations may specify cases in which, for the purposes of this Part of this Act or of such provisions of this Part of this Act as may be prescribed—

1.139

1.140

(a) two or more employers are to be treated as one;
(b) two or more contracts of service in respect of which the same person is an employee are to be treated as one.

(5) In this Part, except [5 [8 section 171ZE]], "week" means a period of seven days beginning with Sunday or such other period as may be prescribed in relation to any particular case or class of cases.

(6) For the purposes of this Part of this Act, a person's normal weekly earnings shall, subject to subsection (8) below, be taken to be the average weekly earnings which in the relevant period have been paid to him or paid for his benefit under the contract of service with the employer in question.

(7) For the purposes of subsection (6) above, "earnings" and "relevant period" shall have the meanings given to them by regulations.

(8) In such cases as may be prescribed, a person's normal weekly earnings shall be calculated in accordance with regulations.

(9) Where—
(a) in consequence of the establishment of one or more National Health Service trusts under [4the National Health Service Act 2006, the National Health Service (Wales) Act 2006], or the National Health Service (Scotland) Act 1978 a person's contract of employment is treated by a scheme under [4any of those Acts] as divided so as to constitute two or more contracts; or
(b) an order under [4paragraph 26(1) of Schedule 3 to the National Health Service Act 2006] provides that a person's contract of employment is so divided;

regulations may make provision enabling the person to elect for all of those contracts to be treated as one contract for the purposes of this Part of this Act or such provisions of this Part of this Act as may be prescribed.

(10) Regulations under subsection (9) above may prescribe—
(a) the conditions that must be satisfied if a person is to be entitled to make such an election;
(b) the manner in which, and the time within which, such an election is to be made;
(c) the persons to whom, and the manner in which, notice of such an election is to be given;
(d) the information which a person who makes such an election is to provide, and the persons to whom, and the time within which, he is to provide it;
(e) the time for which such an election is to have effect;
(f) which one of the person's employers under two or more contracts is to be regarded for the purposes of [5 [8 statutory paternity pay]] as his employer under the contract.

(11) The powers under subsections (9) and (10) are without prejudice to any other power to make regulations under this Part of this Act.

(12) Regulations under any of subsections (4) to (10) above must be made with the concurrence of the Board.

AMENDMENTS

1. Employment Act 2002 s.2 (December 8, 2002).
2. Income Tax (Earnings and Pensions) Act 2003 s.722 and Sch.6 para.183 (April 6, 2003).
3. Employment Equality (Age) Regulations 2006 (SI 2006/1031) reg.49(1) and Sch.8 Pt 1 para.11(2) (October 1, 2006).

4. National Health Service (Consequential Provisions) Act 2006 s.2 and Sch.1 para.149 (March 1, 2007).
5. Work and Families Act 2006 s.11(1) Sch.1 para.20 (April 6, 2010).
6. Children and Families Act 2014 s.121(7)(a) (June 30, 2014).
7. National Insurance Contributions Act 2014 s.15 and Sch.2 para.5 (May 13, 2014).
8. Children and Families Act 2014 s.126 and Sch.7 para.21 (April 5, 2015).
9. Social Services and Well-being (Wales) Act 2014 (Consequential Amendments) Regulations 2016 (SI 2016/413) (W.131) reg.134 (April 6, 2016).

GENERAL NOTE

"*Earnings*": The definition and enabling power under subss.(6) and (7) should be read with reg.39 of the SPP and SAP (General) Regulations 2002 (SI 2002/2822), which defines this term.

"*Employee*": The definition under subs.(2) is modified by regulations made under subs.(3). Thus those who are treated as employed earners under the Social Security (Categorisation of Earners) Regulations 1978 (SI 1978/1689) are also treated as employees for the purpose of SPP: SPP and SAP (General) Regulations 2002 reg.32(1). Apprentices are also covered (reg.32(2)). Employed earners who do not meet the residence or presence requirements under the rules governing National Insurance contributions are excluded from the definition of employee for these purposes (reg.32(3)). Continuous employment is dealt with by regs 33–37. Employment with more than one employer (subs.(4)) is covered by reg.38.

"*National Health Service trusts*": The special position of NHS employees with more than one contract of employment (e.g. with different NHS trusts) is dealt with by the SPP and SAP (National Health Service Employees) Regulations 2002 (SI 2002/2819). These regulations enable such employees to elect to treat two or more such contracts as one contract of employment.

"*Normal weekly earnings*": The definition and enabling power under subss.(6) and (7) should be read with reg.40 of the SPP and SAP (General) Regulations 2002, which defines this term.

1.141

[¹Power to apply Part 12ZA [². . .]

171ZK.—[²(1)] The Secretary of State may by regulations provide for this Part to have effect in relation to cases which involve adoption, but not the placement of a child for adoption under the law of any part of the United Kingdom, with such modifications as the regulations may prescribe.

[²(2) The Secretary of State may by regulations provide for this Part to have effect in relation to cases which involve a person who has applied, or intends to apply, with another person for a parental order under section 54 of the Human Fertilisation and Embryology Act 2008 and a child who is, or will be, the subject of the order, with such modifications as the regulations may prescribe.]]

1.142

AMENDMENTS

1. Employment Act 2002 s.2 (December 8, 2002).
2. Children and Families Act 2014 s.122(5) (April 5, 2015).

DEFINITIONS

"modifications"—see s.171ZJ(1).
"United Kingdom"—see s.172(b).

GENERAL NOTE

1.143 See further the Social Security Contributions and Benefits Act 1992 (Application of Pts 12ZA and 12ZB to Adoptions from Overseas) Regulations 2003 (SI 2003/499) and the Statutory Paternity Pay (Adoption) and Statutory Adoption Pay (Adoptions from Overseas) (No.2) Regulations 2003 (SI 2003/1194).

[¹PART XIIZB

STATUTORY ADOPTION PAY]

AMENDMENT

1. Part XIIZB was inserted by the Employment Act 2002 s.4 (December 8, 2002).

GENERAL NOTE

1.144 Part XIIZB of the SSCBA 1992 was inserted by the Employment Act 2002. On the background to the introduction of statutory adoption pay (SAP), see the General Note to Pt XIIZA on statutory paternity pay (SPP), introduced at the same time. The amendments made by c.1 of Pt I of the Employment Act 2002 relating to paternity and adoption, including the insertion of Pt XIIZB into the SSCBA 1992, came into force on December 8, 2002 (Employment Act 2002 (Commencement No.3 and Transitional and Saving Provisions) Order 2002 art.2(2) and Sch.1 Pt 2). However, art.3 and Sch.3 para.2 of the same Order provide that Pt XIIZB shall have effect only in relation to a person with whom a child is, or is expected to be placed for adoption on or after April 6, 2003.

Adoptive parents have a right under employment legislation to 26 weeks' ordinary adoption leave with the option of 26 weeks' additional adoption leave, mirroring the arrangements now in place for maternity leave. Statutory Adoption Pay is payable for 26 weeks (SSCBA 1992 s.171ZN(2)), as with SMP (but unlike the mere two weeks for SPP). The rules governing entitlement to SAP are set out in SSCBA 1992 s.171ZL: employees must have completed 26 weeks' service with their employer by the time they are matched with the child to be adopted and their earnings, on average, must be at least equal to the lower earnings limit for the purpose of National Insurance contributions. The liability to make payments of SAP is placed on employers (SSCBA 1992 s.171ZM), with the recovery arrangements being as for SMP. Provision for various types of special cases and for matters of interpretation is to be found in SSCBA 1992 ss.171ZO–171ZT.

[¹**Entitlement**

1.145 **171ZL.**—(1) Where a person who is, or has been, an employee satisfies the conditions in subsection (2) below, he shall be entitled in accordance with the following provisions of this Part to payments to be known as "statutory adoption pay".

(2) The conditions are—
(a) that he is a person with whom a child is, or is expected to be, placed for adoption under the law of any part of the United Kingdom;
(b) that he has been in employed earner's employment with an employer for a continuous period of at least 26 weeks ending with the relevant week;
(c) that he has ceased to work for the employer;

(d) that his normal weekly earnings for the period of 8 weeks ending with the relevant week are not less than the lower earnings limit in force under section 5(1)(a) at the end of the relevant week; and
(e) that he has elected to receive statutory adoption pay.

(3) The references in subsection (2)(b) and (d) above to the relevant week are to the week in which the person is notified that he has been matched with the child for the purposes of adoption.

(4) A person may not elect to receive statutory adoption pay if—
(a) he has elected in accordance with section 171ZB above to receive statutory paternity pay, or
[²(b) he falls within subsection (4A);
(4A) A person falls within this subsection if—
(a) the child is, or is expected to be, placed for adoption with him as a member of a couple;
(b) the other member of the couple is a person to whom the conditions in subsection (2) above apply; and
(c) the other member of the couple has elected to receive statutory adoption pay.

(4B) For the purposes of subsection (4A), a person is a member of a couple if—
(a) in the case of an adoption or expected adoption under the law of England and Wales, he is a member of a couple within the meaning of section 144(4) of the Adoption and Children Act 2002;
(b) in the case of an adoption or an expected adoption under the law [³ . . .] of Northern Ireland, he is a member of a married couple;]
[³ (c) in the case of an adoption or expected adoption under the law of Scotland he is a member of a relevant couple within the meaning of section 29(3) of the Adoption and Children (Scotland) Act 2007.]

(5) A person's entitlement to statutory adoption pay shall not be affectedby the placement, or expected placement, for adoption of more than one childas part of the same arrangement.

(6) A person shall be entitled to payments of statutory adoption pay only if—
(a) he gives the person who will be liable to pay it notice of the date from which he expects the liability to pay him statutory adoption pay to begin; and
(b) the notice is given at least 28 days before that date or, if that is not reasonably practicable, as soon as is reasonably practicable.

(7) The notice shall be in writing if the person who is liable to pay the statutory adoption pay so requests.

(8) The Secretary of State may by regulations—
(a) provide that subsection (2)(b), (c) or (d) above shall have effect subject to prescribed modifications in such cases as may be prescribed;
(b) provide that subsection (6) above shall not have effect, or shall have effect subject to prescribed modifications, in such cases as may be prescribed;
(c) impose requirements about evidence of entitlement;
(d) specify in what circumstances employment is to be treated as continuous for the purposes of this section;
(e) provide that a person is to be treated for the purposes of this section as being employed for a continuous period of at least 26 weeks where—
(i) he has been employed by the same employer for at least 26 weeks under two or more separate contracts of service; and

(ii) those contracts were not continuous;
(f) provide for amounts earned by a person under separate contracts of service with the same employer to be aggregated for the purposes of this section;
(g) provide that—
(i) the amount of a person's earnings for any period; or
(ii) the amount of his earnings to be treated as comprised in any payment made to him or for his benefit;
shall be calculated or estimated for the purposes of this section in such manner and on such basis as may be prescribed and that for that purpose payments of a particular class or description made or falling to be made to or by a person shall, to such extent as may be prescribed, be disregarded or, as the case may be, be deducted from the amount of his earnings;
(h) make provision about elections for statutory adoption pay.

[4 (9) This section has effect in a case involving a child who is, or is expected to be, placed under section 22C of the Children Act 1989 by a local authority in England with a local authority foster parent who has been approved as a prospective adopter with the following modifications—
(a) the references in subsections (2)(a) and (4A)(a) to a child being placed for adoption under the law of any part of the United Kingdom are to be treated as references to a child being placed under section 22C in that manner;
(b) the reference in subsection (3) to the week in which the person is notified that he has been matched with the child for the purposes of adoption is to be treated as a reference to the week in which the person is notified that the child is to be, or is expected to be, placed with him under section 22C;
(c) the references in subsection (4B)(a) to adoption are to be treated as references to placement under section 22C;
(d) the reference in subsection (5) to placement, or expected placement, for adoption is to be treated as a reference to placement, or expected placement, under section 22C.

(10) Where, by virtue of subsection (9), a person becomes entitled to statutory adoption pay in respect of a child who is, or is expected to be, placed under section 22C of the Children Act 1989, the person may not become entitled to payments of statutory adoption pay as a result of the child being, or being expected to be, placed for adoption.]

[5 (11) This section has effect in a case involving a child who is, or is expected to be, placed under section 81 of the Social Services and Well-being (Wales) Act 2014 by a local authority in Wales with a local authority foster parent who has been approved as a prospective adopter with the following modifications—
(a) the references in subsections (2)(a) and (4A)(a) to a child being placed for adoption under the law of any part of the United kingdom are to be treated as references to a child being placed under section 81 in that manner;
(b) the reference in subsection (3) to the week in which the person is notified that he has been matched with the child for the purposes of adoption is to be treated as a reference to the week in which the person is notified that the child is to be, or is expected to be placed with him under section 8;

(c) the references in subsection (4B)(a) to adoption are to be treated as references to placement under section 81;
(d) the reference in subsection (5) to placement, or expected placement, for adoption is to be treated as a reference to placement, or expected placement under section 81.

(12) Where, by virtue of subsection (11), a person becomes entitled to statutory adoption pay in respect of a child who is, or is expected to be, placed under section 81 of the Social Services and Well-being (Wales) Act 2014, the person may not become entitled to payments of statutory adoption pay as a result of the child being, or being expected to be, placed for adoption.]]

AMENDMENTS

1. Employment Act 2002 s.4 (December 8, 2002).
2. Adoption and Children Act 2002 (Consequential Amendment to Statutory Adoption Pay) Order 2006 (SI 2006/2012) art.3 (October 1, 2006).
3. Adoption and Children (Scotland) Act 2007 (Consequential Modifications) Order 2011 (SI 2011/1740) art.2 and Sch.1 para.4 and Pt 3 (July 15, 2011).
4. Children and Families Act 2014 s.121(5) (June 30, 2014).
5. Social Services and Well-being (Wales) Act 2014 (Consequential Amendments) Regulations 2016 (SI 2016/413) (W.131) reg.135 (April 6, 2016).

DEFINITIONS

"employee"—see s.171ZS(2).
"employer"—see s.171ZS(1).
"modifications"—see s.171ZS(1).
"normal weekly earnings"—see s.171ZS(6).
"prescribed"—see s.171ZS(1).
"relevant week"—see subs.(3).
"United Kingdom"—see s.172(b).
"week"—see s.171ZS(5).

GENERAL NOTE

This section sets out the qualifying conditions for receipt of SAP. A person is entitled to SAP if he or she meets each of five conditions (subs.(2)). First, the claimant must have an approved match with the child. Secondly, the person must be an employee who has satisfied the service qualification of continuous service with the same employer for at least 26 weeks by the week in which the approved match is made. Thirdly, the person must have actually stopped working for that employer (see also s.171ZN(3) (and (4)). Fourthly, the employee's average weekly earnings must be not less than the lower earnings limit for National Insurance contributions. Finally, the person must have elected to receive SAP, which requires that he or she provide the employer with an appropriate notification (see subss.(6) and (7); see also reg.23 of the SPP and SAP (General) Regulations 2002 (SI 2002/2822)) and evidence of entitlement (SPP and SAP (General) Regulations 2002 reg.24).

Statutory Adoption Pay is available to an adoptive parent of a child newly placed for adoption, whether the child is being adopted within the UK or from overseas. There are, however, some slight differences in the provisions for SAP for domestic and overseas adoptions respectively: see further SSCBA 1992 s.171ZT. It is also important to note that entitlement to SAP arises only for children who are newly placed for adoption. It is therefore not possible to receive SAP for a step-family adoption or where the child is adopted by his or her existing foster carers.

1.146

[¹Liability to make payments

1.147   **171ZM.**—(1) The liability to make payments of statutory adoption pay is a liability of any person of whom the person entitled to the payments has been an employee as mentioned in section 171ZL(2)(b) above.

(2) Regulations shall make provision as to a former employer's liability to pay statutory adoption pay to a person in any case where the former employee's contract of service with him has been brought to an end by the former employer solely, or mainly, for the purpose of avoiding liability for statutory adoption pay.

(3) The Secretary of State may, with the concurrence of the Board, by regulations specify circumstances in which, notwithstanding this section, liability to make payments of statutory adoption pay is to be a liability of the Board.]

AMENDMENT

1. Employment Act 2002 s.4 (December 8, 2002).

DEFINITIONS

"the Board"—see s.171ZS(1).
"employee"—see s.171ZS(2).
"employer"—see s.171ZS(1).

GENERAL NOTE

1.148   This section, placing the liability to make payments of SAP on employers, follows the same approach as the provisions governing SMP (ss.164(3) and (8)) and SPP (s.171ZD). Note that there is no liability to pay SAP in respect of any week during which the claimant either is entitled to SSP or is detained in custody (or sentenced to imprisonment): SPP and SAP (General) Regulations 2002 (SI 2002/2822) reg.27 (but note that, unlike with SPP, there are exceptions to the latter preclusionary rule: reg.27(2)). As with SPP, however, there is no liability to pay SAP in the week that the person entitled dies.

The rules governing the funding of SAP and employers' responsibilities in connection with SAP payments are contained in the SPP and SAP (Administration) Regulations 2002 (SI 2002/2820). The special circumstances in which HMRC is liable to pay SAP under subs.(3) are set out in SPP and SAP (General) Regulations 2002 regs 43 and 44 (the latter applying solely to SAP and not SPP).

[¹Rate and period of pay

1.149   **171ZN.**—(1) [⁵...].

(2) Statutory adoption pay shall be payable, subject to the provisions of this Part of this Act, in respect of each week during a prescribed period ("the adoption pay period") of a duration not exceeding [²52 weeks].

[⁴ (2A) Regulations may provide for the duration of the adoption pay period as it applies to a person ("A") to be reduced, subject to prescribed restrictions and conditions.

(2B) Regulations under subsection (2A) are to secure that the reduced period ends at a time—

(a) after a prescribed part of the adoption pay period has expired, and
(b) when at least a prescribed part of the adoption pay period remains unexpired.

(2C) Regulations under subsection (2A) may, in particular, prescribe restrictions and conditions relating to—
(a) the end of A's entitlement to adoption leave;
(b) the doing of work by A;
(c) the taking of prescribed steps by A or another person as regards leave under section 75G of the Employment Rights Act 1996 in respect of the child;
(d) the taking of prescribed steps by A or another person as regards statutory shared parental pay in respect of the child.

(2D) Regulations may provide for a reduction in the duration of the adoption pay period as it applies to a person to be revoked, or to be treated as revoked, subject to prescribed restrictions and conditions.]

[[5] (2E) Statutory adoption pay shall be payable to a person—
(a) at the earnings-related rate, in respect of the first 6 weeks in respect of which it is payable; and
(b) at whichever is the lower of the earnings-related rate and such weekly rate as may be prescribed, in respect of the remaining portion of the adoption pay period.

(2F) The earnings-related rate is a weekly rate equivalent to 90 per cent of a person's normal weekly earnings for the period of 8 weeks ending with the week in which the person is notified that the person has been matched with a child for the purposes of adoption.

(2G) The weekly rate prescribed under subsection (2E)(b) must not be less than the weekly rate of statutory sick pay for the time being specified in section 157(1) or, if two or more such rates are for the time being so specified, the higher or highest of those rates.]

(3) [[2]Except in such cases as may be prescribed,] a person shall not be liable to pay statutory adoption pay to another in respect of any week during any part of which the other works under a contract of service with him.

(4) It is immaterial for the purposes of subsection (3) above whether the work referred to in that subsection is work under a contract of service which existed immediately before the adoption pay period or a contract of service which did not so exist.

(5) Except in such cases as may be prescribed, statutory adoption pay shall not be payable to a person in respect of any week during any part of which he works for any employer who is not liable to pay him statutiory adoption pay.

(6) The Secretary of State may by regulations specify circumstances in which there is to be no liability to pay statutory adoption pay in respect of a week.

[[3](6A) Where for any purpose of this Part of this Act or of regulations it is necessary to calculate the daily rate of statutory adoption pay, the amount payable by way of statutory adoption pay for any day shall be taken as one seventh of the weekly rate.]

(7) In [[5] subsections (2) and (2E)] above, "week" means any period of seven days.

(8) In subsection (3), (5) and (6) above, "week" means a period of seven days beginning with the day of the week on which the adoption pay period begins.

[[4] (9) Where statutory adoption pay is payable to a person by virtue of section 171ZL(9), this section has effect as if the reference in subsection (2F) to the week in which the person is notified that he has been matched with a child for the purposes of adoption were a reference to the week in which the person is notified that a child is to be, or is expected to be, placed with him under section 22C of the Children Act 1989.]

[6 (10) Where statutory adoption pay is payable to a person by virtue of section 171ZL(11), this section has effect as if the reference in subsection (2F) to the week in which the person is notified that he has been matched with a child for the purposes of adoption were a reference to the week in which the person is notified that a child is to be, or is expected to be, placed with him under section 81 of the Social Services and Well-being (Wales) Act 2014.]]

AMENDMENTS

1. Employment Act 2002 s.4 (December 8, 2002).
2. Work and Families Act 2006 s.2 (October 1, 2006).
3. Work and Families Act 2006 s.11 and Sch.1 para.21 (October 1, 2006).
4. Children and Families Act 2014 ss.120(6) and 121(6) (June 30, 2014).
5. Children and Families Act 2014 s.124(1) (April 5, 2015).
6. Social Services and Well-being (Wales) Act 2014 (Consequential Amendments) Regulations 2016 (SI 2016/413) (W.131) reg.136 (April 6, 2016).

DEFINITIONS

"adoption pay period"—see subs.(2).
"employer"—see s.171ZS(1).
"prescribed"—see s.171ZS(1).
"week"—see subss.(7) and (8).

GENERAL NOTE

1.150 This section provides that SAP is payable for a period of up to 52 weeks (the "adoption pay period" under subs.(2)). The rate of SAP is the same as that for SMP, namely (from April 2024) the lesser of £184.03 a week or 90 per cent of the employee's average weekly earnings: SPP and SAP (Weekly Rates) Regulations 2002 (SI 2002/2818) reg.3. More detailed rules relating to the adoption pay period are set out in regs 21 and 22 of the SPP and SAP (General) Regulations 2002 (SI 2002/2822).

[1**Restrictions on contracting out**

1.151   171ZO.—(1) Any agreement shall be void to the extent that it purports—
(a) to exclude, limit or otherwise modify any provision of this Part of this Act; or
(b) to require an employee or former employee to contribute (whether directly or indirectly) towards any costs incurred by his employer or former employer under this Part of this Act.

(2) For the avoidance of doubt, any agreement between an employer and an employee authorising any deductions from statutory adoption pay which the employer is liable to pay to the employee in respect of any period shall not be void by virtue of subsection (1)(a) above if the employer—
(a) is authorised by that or another agreement to make the same deductions from any contractual remuneration which he is liable to pay in respect of the same period; or
(b) would be so authorised if he were liable to pay contractual remuneration in respect of that period.]

(1992 c.4 s.171ZO)

AMENDMENT

1. Employment Act 2002 s.4 (December 8, 2002).

DEFINITIONS

"employee"—see s.171ZS(2).
"employer"—see s.171ZS(1).

GENERAL NOTE

These restrictions on contracting out are in the same terms as the equivalent provisions for SSP (s.151(2)–(3)), SMP (s.164(6)–(7)) and SPP (s.171ZF). See also SPP and SAP (General) Regulations 2002 (SI 2002/2822) reg.30.

1.152

[1Relationship with benefits and other payments etc.

171ZP.—(1) Except as may be prescribed, a day which falls within the adoption pay period shall not be treated as a day of incapacity for work for the purposes of determining, for this Act, whether it forms part of a period of incapacity for work for the purposes of incapacity benefit.

(2) Regulations may provide that in prescribed circumstances a day which falls within the adoption pay period shall be treated as a day of incapacity for work for the purposes of determining entitlement to the higher rate of short-term incapacity benefit or to long-term incapacity benefit.

(3) Regulations may provide that an amount equal to a person's statutory adoption pay for a period shall be deducted from any such benefit in respect of the same period and a person shall be entitled to such benefit only if there is a balance after the deduction and, if there is such a balance, at a weekly rate equal to it.

(4) Subject to subsections (5) and (6) below, any entitlement to statutory adoption pay shall not affect any right of a person in relation to remuneration under any contract of service ("contractual remuneration").

(5) Subject to subsection (6) below—
(a) any contractual remuneration paid to a person by an employer of his in respect of a week in the adoption pay period shall go towards discharging any liability of that employer to pay statutory adoption pay to him in respect of that week; and
(b) any statutory adoption pay paid by an employer to a person who is an employee of his in respect of a week in the adoption pay period shall go towards discharging any liability of that employer to pay contractual remuneration to him in respect of that week.

(6) Regulations may make provision as to payments which are, and those which are not, to be treated as contractual remuneration for the purposes of subsections (4) and (5) above.

(7) In subsection (5) above, "week" means a period of seven days beginning with the day of the week on which the adoption pay period begins.]

1.153

AMENDMENT

1. Employment Act 2002 s.4 (December 8, 2002).

DEFINITIONS

"adoption pay period"—see s.171ZN(2).
"contractual remuneration"—see subs.(4).

"employee"—see s.171ZS(2).
"employer"—see s.171ZS(1).
"prescribed"—see s.171ZS(1).
"week"—see subs.(7).

GENERAL NOTE

1.154   The basic principle is that entitlement to SAP does not affect a claimant's rights to any contractual remuneration (subs.(4)), subject to the significant exception that any payment of contractual remuneration can be regarded as the discharge of SAP liability and vice versa (subs.(5)). Regulations made under subs.(6) provide that the payments to be treated as contractual remuneration are sums payable under a contract of service: (a) by way of remuneration, (b) for incapacity for work due to sickness or injury, or (c) by reason of the adoption of a child (SPP and SAP (General) Regulations 2002 (SI 2002/2822) reg.28).

[¹Crown employment—Part XIIZB

1.155   **171ZQ.**—The provisions of this Part of this Act apply in relation to persons employed by or under the Crown as they apply in relation to persons employed otherwise than by or under the Crown.]

AMENDMENT

1. Employment Act 2002 s.4 (December 8, 2002).

GENERAL NOTE

1.156   This mirrors s.169, the equivalent provision for SMP, and s.171ZH, which deals with SPP.

[¹Special classes of person

1.157   **171ZR.**—(1) The Secretary of State may with the concurrence of the Treasury make regulations modifying any provision of this Part of this Act in such manner as he thinks proper in its application to any person who is, has been or is to be—
   (a) employed on board any ship, vessel, hovercraft or aircraft;
   (b) outside Great Britain at any prescribed time or in any prescribed circumstances; or
   (c) in prescribed employment in connection with continental shelf operations, as defined in section 120(2) above.
(2) Regulations under subsection (1) above may, in particular, provide—
   (a) for any provision of this Part of this Act to apply to any such person, notwithstanding that it would not otherwise apply;
   (b) for any such provision not to apply to any such person, notwithstanding that it would otherwise apply;
   (c) for excepting any such person from the application of any such provision where he neither is domiciled nor has a place of residence in any part of Great Britain;
   (d) for the taking of evidence, for the purposes of the determination of any question arising under any such provision, in a country or territory outside Great Britain, by a British consular official or such other person as may be determined in accordance with the regulations.]

(1992 c.4 s.171ZR)

AMENDMENT

1. Employment Act 2002 s.4 (December 8, 2002).

DEFINITIONS

"Great Britain"—see s.172(a).
"prescribed"—see s.171ZS(1).

GENERAL NOTE

This enabling provision is in the same terms as s.162, which applies to SSP, and s.171ZI, which deals with SPP. See further the Statutory Paternity Pay and Statutory Adoption Pay (Persons Abroad and Mariners) Regulations 2002 (SI 2002/2821).

1.158

[¹Part XIIZB: supplementary

171ZS.—(1) In this Part of this Act—
"adoption pay period" has the meaning given by section 171ZN(2) above;
"the Board" means the Commissioners of Inland Revenue;
[³"employer", in relation to a person who is an employee, means a person who—
(a) under section 6 above is liable to pay secondary Class 1 contributions in relation to any of the earnings of the person who is an employee; or
(b) would be liable to pay such contributions but for—
    (i) the condition in section 6(1)(b), or
    (ii) the employee being under the age of 16;]
[⁵ "local authority" has the same meaning as in the Children Act 1989 (see section 105(1) of that Act);
"local authority foster parent" has the same meaning as in the Children Act 1989 (see [⁷ section 105(1)] of that Act);]
"modifications" includes additions, omissions and amendments, and related expressions are to be read accordingly;
"prescribed" means prescribed by regulations.
(2) In this Part of this Act, "employee" means a person who is—
(a) gainfully employed in Great Britain either under a contract of service or in an office (including elective office) with [² [⁶ earnings (within the meaning of Parts 1 to 5 above)]]
[³...]
(3) Regulations may provide—
(a) for cases where a person who falls within the definition in subsection (2) above is not to be treated as an employee for the purposes of this Part of this Act; and
(b) for cases where a person who would not otherwise be an employee for the purposes of this Part of this Act is to be treated as an employee for those purposes.
(4) Without prejudice to any other power to make regulations under this Part of this Act, regulations may specify cases in which, for the purposes of this Part of this Act or of such provisions of this Part of this Act as may be prescribed—
(a) two or more employers are to be treated as one;
(b) two or more contracts of service in respect of which the same person is an employee are to be treated as one.

1.159

(5) In this Part, except sections 171ZN and 171ZP, "week" means a period of seven days beginning with Sunday or such other period as may be prescribed in relation to any particular case or class of cases.

(6) For the purposes of this Part of this Act, a person's normal weekly earnings shall, subject to subsection (8) below, be taken to be the average weekly earnings which in the relevant period have been paid to him or paid for his benefit under the contract of service with the employer in question.

(7) For the purposes of subsection (6) above, "earnings" and "relevant period" shall have the meanings given to them by regulations.

(8) In such cases as may be prescribed, a person's normal weekly earnings shall be calculated in accordance with regulations.

(9) Where—
   (a) in consequence of the establishment of one or more National Health Service trusts under [4the National Health Service Act 2006, the National Health Service (Wales) Act 2006] or the National Health Service (Scotland) Act 1978, a person's contract of employment is treated by a scheme under [4any of those Acts] as divided so as to constitute two or more contracts; or
   (b) an order under [4paragraph 26(1) of Schedule 3 to the National Health Service Act 2006] provides that a person's contract of employment is so divided;
regulations may make provision enabling the person to elect for all of those contracts to be treated as one contract for the purposes of this Part of this Act or such provisions of this Part of this Act as may be prescribed.

(10) Regulations under subsection (9) above may prescribe—
   (a) the conditions that must be satisfied if a person is to be entitled to make such an election;
   (b) the manner in which, and the time within which, such an election is to be made;
   (c) the persons to whom, and the manner in which, notice of such an election is to be given;
   (d) the information which a person who makes such an election is to provide, and the persons to whom, and the time within which, he is to provide it;
   (e) the time for which such an election is to have effect;
   (f) which one of the person's employers under two or more contracts is to be regarded for the purposes of statutory adoption pay as his employer under the contract.

(11) The powers under subsections (9) and (10) are without prejudice to any other power to make regulations under this Part of this Act.

(12) Regulations under any of subsections (4) to (10) above must be made with the concurrence of the Board.]

AMENDMENTS

1. Employment Act 2002 s.4 (December 8, 2002).

2. Income Tax (Earnings and Pensions) Act 2003 s.722 and Sch.6 para.184 (April 6, 2003).

3. Employment Equality (Age) Regulations 2006 (SI 2006/1031) reg.49(1) and Sch.8 Pt 1 para.12 (October 1, 2006).

4. National Health Service (Consequential Provisions) Act 2006 s.2 and Sch.1 para.150 (March 1, 2007).

5. Children and Families Act 2014 s.121(7)(b) (June 30, 2014).

(1992 c.4 s.171ZS)

6. National Insurance Contributions Act 2014 s.15 and Sch.2 para.6 (May 13, 2014).
7. Social Services and Well-being (Wales) Act 2014 (Consequential Amendments) Regulations 2016 (SI 2016/413) (W.131) reg.137 (April 6, 2016).

DEFINITIONS

"Earnings"—see General Note to s.171ZJ.
"Employee"—see General Note to s.171ZJ.
"National Health Service trusts"—see General Note to s.171ZJ.
"Normal weekly earnings"—see General Note to s.171ZJ.

[¹ Power to apply Part 12ZB [. . .]

171ZT.—[²(1)] The Secretary of State may by regulations provide for this Part to have effect in relation to cases which involve adoption, but not the placement of a child for adoption under the law of any part of the United Kingdom, with such modifications as the regulations may prescribe.

[² [³ (2) The Secretary of State may by regulations provide for this Part to have effect, with such modifications as the regulations may prescribe, in relation to—
  (a) cases which involve a person who has applied, or intends to apply, with another person for a parental order under section 54 of the Human Fertilisation and Embryology Act 2008 and a child who is, or will be, the subject of the order,
  (b) cases which involve a person who has applied, or intends to apply, for a parental order under section 54A of that Act and a child who is, or will be, the subject of the order.]

(3) Regulations under subsection (2) may modify section 171ZL(8)(c) so as to enable regulations to impose requirements to make statutory declarations as to—
  (a) eligibility to apply for a parental order [³ under section 54 or 54A of the Human Fertilisation and Embryology Act 2008];
  (b) intention to apply for such an order.]]

1.160

AMENDMENTS

1. Employment Act 2002 s.2 (December 8, 2002).
2. Children and Families Act 2014 s.122(6) (April 5, 2015).
3. Human Fertilisation and Embryology Act 2008 (Remedial) Order 2018 (SI 2018/1413) art.7 (January 3, 2019).

GENERAL NOTE

See further the Social Security Contributions and Benefits Act 1992 (Application of Pts 12ZA and 12ZB to Adoptions from Overseas) Regulations 2003 (SI 2003/499) and the Statutory Paternity Pay (Adoption) and Statutory Adoption Pay (Adoptions from Overseas) (No.2) Regulations 2003 (SI 2003/1194).

1.161

[¹ PART 12ZC

STATUTORY SHARED PARENTAL PAY

Entitlement: birth

171ZU.—(1) Regulations may provide that, where all the conditions in subsection (2) are satisfied in relation to a person who is the mother of

1.162

a child ("the claimant mother"), the claimant mother is to be entitled in accordance with the following provisions of this Part to payments to be known as "statutory shared parental pay".

(2) The conditions are—
(a) that the claimant mother and another person ("P") satisfy prescribed conditions as to caring or intending to care for the child;
(b) that P satisfies prescribed conditions—
  (i) as to employment or self-employment,
  (ii) as to having earnings of a prescribed amount for a prescribed period, and
  (iii) as to relationship either with the child or with the claimant mother;
(c) that the claimant mother has been in employed earner's employment with an employer for a continuous period of at least the prescribed length ending with a prescribed week;
(d) that at the end of that prescribed week the claimant mother was entitled to be in that employment;
(e) that the claimant mother's normal weekly earnings for a prescribed period ending with a prescribed week are not less than the lower earnings limit in force under section 5(1)(a) at the end of that week;
(f) if regulations so provide, that the claimant mother continues in employed earner's employment (whether or not with the employer by reference to whom the condition in paragraph (c) is satisfied) until a prescribed time;
(g) that the claimant mother became entitled to statutory maternity pay by reference to the birth of the child;
(h) that the claimant mother satisfies prescribed conditions as to the reduction of the duration of the maternity pay period;
(i) that the claimant mother has given the person who will be liable to pay statutory shared parental pay to her notice of—
  (i) the number of weeks in respect of which she would be entitled to claim statutory shared parental pay in respect of the child if the entitlement were fully exercised (disregarding for these purposes any intention of P to claim statutory shared parental pay in respect of the child),
  (ii) the number of weeks in respect of which she intends to claim statutory shared parental pay, and
  (iii) the number of weeks in respect of which P intends to claim statutory shared parental pay;
(j) that the claimant mother has given the person who will be liable to pay statutory shared parental pay to her notice of the period or periods during which she intends to claim statutory shared parental pay in respect of the child;
(k) that a notice under paragraph (i) or (j)—
  (i) is given by such time as may be prescribed, and
  (ii) satisfies prescribed conditions as to form and content;
(l) that P consents to the extent of the claimant mother's intended claim for statutory shared parental pay;
(m) that it is the claimant mother's intention to care for the child during each week in respect of which statutory shared parental pay is paid to her;

(1992 c.4 s.171ZU)

(n) that the claimant mother is absent from work during each week in respect of which statutory shared parental pay is paid to her;

(o) that, where she is an employee within the meaning of the Employment Rights Act 1996, the claimant mother's absence from work during each such week is absence on shared parental leave.

(3) Regulations may provide that, where all the conditions in subsection (4) are satisfied in relation to a person ("the claimant"), the claimant is to be entitled in accordance with the following provisions of this Part to payments to be known as "statutory shared parental pay".

(4) The conditions are—

(a) that the claimant and another person ("M") who is the mother of a child satisfy prescribed conditions as to caring or intending to care for the child;

(b) that the claimant satisfies—
   (i) prescribed conditions as to relationship with the child, or
   (ii) prescribed conditions as to relationship with M;

(c) that M satisfies prescribed conditions—
   (i) as to employment or self-employment, and
   (ii) as to having earnings of a prescribed amount for a prescribed period;

(d) that the claimant has been in employed earner's employment with an employer for a continuous period of at least the prescribed length ending with a prescribed week;

(e) that at the end of that prescribed week the claimant was entitled to be in that employment;

(f) that the claimant's normal weekly earnings for a prescribed period ending with a prescribed week are not less than the lower earnings limit in force under section 5(1)(a) at the end of that week;

(g) if regulations so provide, that the claimant continues in employed earner's employment (whether or not with the employer by reference to whom the condition in paragraph (d) is satisfied) until a prescribed time;

(h) that M became entitled, by reference to the birth of the child, to—
   (i) a maternity allowance, or
   (ii) statutory maternity pay;

(i) that M satisfies prescribed conditions as to—
   (i) the reduction of the duration of the maternity allowance period, or
   (ii) the reduction of the duration of the maternity pay period, as the case may be;

(j) that the claimant has given the person who will be liable to pay statutory shared parental pay to the claimant notice of—
   (i) the number of weeks in respect of which the claimant would be entitled to claim statutory shared parental pay in respect of the child if the entitlement were fully exercised (disregarding for these purposes any intention of M to claim statutory shared parental pay in respect of the child),
   (ii) the number of weeks in respect of which the claimant intends to claim statutory shared parental pay, and
   (iii) the number of weeks in respect of which M intends to claim statutory shared parental pay;

(k) that the claimant has given the person who will be liable to pay statutory shared parental pay to the claimant notice of the period or periods during which the claimant intends to claim statutory shared parental pay in respect of the child;
(l) that a notice under paragraph (j) or (k)—
  (i) is given by such time as may be prescribed, and
  (ii) satisfies prescribed conditions as to form and content;
(m) that M consents to the extent of the claimant's intended claim for statutory shared parental pay;
(n) that it is the claimant's intention to care for the child during each week in respect of which statutory shared parental pay is paid to the claimant;
(o) that the claimant is absent from work during each week in respect of which statutory shared parental pay is paid to the claimant;
(p) that, where the claimant is an employee within the meaning of the Employment Rights Act 1996, the claimant's absence from work during each such week is absence on shared parental leave.

(5) Regulations may provide for—
(a) the determination of the extent of a person's entitlement to statutory shared parental pay in respect of a child;
(b) when statutory shared parental pay is to be payable.

(6) Provision under subsection (5)(a) is to secure that the number of weeks in respect of which a person is entitled to payments of statutory shared parental pay in respect of a child does not exceed the number of weeks of the maternity pay period reduced by—
(a) where the mother of the child takes action that is treated by regulations as constituting for the purposes of this section her return to work without satisfying conditions prescribed under subsection (2)(h) or, as the case may be, subsection (4)(i)—
  (i) the number of relevant weeks in respect of which maternity allowance or statutory maternity pay is payable to the mother, or
  (ii) if that number of relevant weeks is less than a number prescribed by regulations, that prescribed number of weeks, or
(b) except where paragraph (a) applies, the number of weeks to which the maternity allowance period is reduced by virtue of section 35(3A) or, as the case may be, the maternity pay period is reduced by virtue of section 165(3A).

(7) In subsection (6)(a) "relevant week" means—
(a) where maternity allowance is payable to a mother, a week or part of a week falling before the time at which the mother takes action that is treated by regulations as constituting for the purposes of this section her return to work;
(b) where statutory maternity pay is payable to a mother, a week falling before the week in which the mother takes action that is so treated.

For these purposes "week" has the meaning given by section 122(1), in relation to maternity allowance, or the meaning given by section 165(8), in relation to statutory maternity pay.

(8) In determining the number of weeks for the purposes of subsection (6)(b)—
(a) "week" has the same meaning as in subsection (7), and
(b) a part of a week is to be treated as a week.

(9) Provision under subsection (5)(a) is to secure that, where two persons are entitled to payments of statutory shared parental pay in respect of a child, the extent of one's entitlement and the extent of the other's entitlement do not, taken together, exceed what would be available to one person (see subsection (6)).

(10) Provision under subsection (5)(b) is to secure that no payment of statutory shared parental pay may be made to a person in respect of a child after the end of such period as may be prescribed.

(11) Provision under subsection (5)(b) is to secure that no payment of statutory shared parental pay in respect of a child may be made to a person who is the mother of the child before the end of the mother's maternity pay period.

(12) Regulations may provide that, where the conditions in subsection (13) are satisfied in relation to a person who is entitled to statutory shared parental pay under subsection (1) or (3) ("V"), V may vary the period or periods during which V intends to claim statutory shared parental pay in respect of the child in question, subject to complying with provision under subsection (14) where that is relevant.

(13) The conditions are—
(a) that V has given the person who will be liable to pay statutory shared parental pay to V notice of an intention to vary the period or periods during which V intends to claim statutory shared parental pay;
(b) that a notice under paragraph (a)—
 (i) is given by such time as may be prescribed, and
 (ii) satisfies prescribed conditions as to form and content.

(14) Regulations may provide that, where the conditions in subsection (15) are satisfied in relation to a person who is entitled to statutory shared parental pay under subsection (1) or (3) ("V"), V may vary the number of weeks in respect of which V intends to claim statutory shared parental pay.

(15) The conditions are—
(a) that V has given the person who will be liable to pay statutory shared parental pay to V notice of—
 (i) the extent to which V has exercised an entitlement to statutory shared parental pay in respect of the child,
 (ii) the extent to which V intends to claim statutory shared parental pay in respect of the child,
 (iii) the extent to which another person has exercised an entitlement to statutory shared parental pay in respect of the child, and
 (iv) the extent to which another person intends to claim statutory shared parental pay in respect of the child;
(b) that a notice under paragraph (a)—
 (i) is given by such time as may be prescribed, and
 (ii) satisfies prescribed conditions as to form and content;
(c) that the person who is P or, as the case may be, M in relation to V consents to that variation.

(16) A person's entitlement to statutory shared parental pay under this section is not affected by the birth of more than one child as a result of the same pregnancy.]

AMENDMENT

1. Children and Families Act 2014 s.119 (June 30, 2014).

[¹ Entitlement: adoption

171ZV.—(1) Regulations may provide that, where all the conditions in subsection (2) are satisfied in relation to a person with whom a child is, or is expected to be, placed for adoption under the law of any part of the United Kingdom ("claimant A"), claimant A is to be entitled in accordance with the following provisions of this Part to payments to be known as "statutory shared parental pay".

(2) The conditions are—
- (a) that claimant A and another person ("X") satisfy prescribed conditions as to caring or intending to care for the child;
- (b) that X satisfies prescribed conditions—
  - (i) as to employment or self-employment,
  - (ii) as to having earnings of a prescribed amount for a prescribed period, and
  - (iii) as to relationship either with the child or with claimant A;
- (c) that claimant A has been in employed earner's employment with an employer for a continuous period of at least the prescribed length ending with a prescribed week;
- (d) that at the end of that prescribed week claimant A was entitled to be in that employment;
- (e) that claimant A's normal weekly earnings for a prescribed period ending with a prescribed week are not less than the lower earnings limit in force under section 5(1)(a) at the end of that week;
- (f) if regulations so provide, that claimant A continues in employed earner's employment (whether or not with the employer by reference to whom the condition in paragraph (c) is satisfied) until a prescribed time;
- (g) that claimant A became entitled to statutory adoption pay by reference to the placement for adoption of the child;
- (h) that claimant A satisfies prescribed conditions as to the reduction of the duration of the adoption pay period;
- (i) that claimant A has given the person who will be liable to pay statutory shared parental pay to claimant A notice of—
  - (i) the number of weeks in respect of which claimant A would be entitled to claim statutory shared parental pay in respect of the child if the entitlement were fully exercised (disregarding for these purposes any intention of X to claim statutory shared parental pay in respect of the child),
  - (ii) the number of weeks in respect of which claimant A intends to claim statutory shared parental pay, and
  - (iii) the number of weeks in respect of which X intends to claim statutory shared parental pay;
- (j) that claimant A has given the person who will be liable to pay statutory shared parental pay to claimant A notice of the period or periods during which claimant A intends to claim statutory shared parental pay in respect of the child;
- (k) that a notice under paragraph (i) or (j)—
  - (i) is given by such time as may be prescribed, and
  - (ii) satisfies prescribed conditions as to form and content;
- (l) that X consents to the extent of claimant A's intended claim for statutory shared parental pay;

(m) that it is claimant A's intention to care for the child during each week in respect of which statutory shared parental pay is paid to claimant A;

(n) that claimant A is absent from work during each week in respect of which statutory shared parental pay is paid to claimant A;

(o) that, where claimant A is an employee within the meaning of the Employment Rights Act 1996, claimant A's absence from work during each such week is absence on shared parental leave.

(3) Regulations may provide that, where all the conditions in subsection (4) are satisfied in relation to a person ("claimant B"), claimant B is to be entitled in accordance with the following provisions of this Part to payments to be known as "statutory shared parental pay".

(4) The conditions are—

(a) that claimant B and another person ("Y") who is a person with whom a child is, or is expected to be, placed for adoption under the law of any part of the United Kingdom satisfy prescribed conditions as to caring or intending to care for the child;

(b) that claimant B satisfies—
  (i) prescribed conditions as to relationship with the child, or
  (ii) prescribed conditions as to relationship with Y;

(c) that Y satisfies prescribed conditions—
  (i) as to employment or self-employment, and
  (ii) as to having earnings of a prescribed amount for a prescribed period;

(d) that claimant B has been in employed earner's employment with an employer for a continuous period of at least the prescribed length ending with a prescribed week;

(e) that at the end of that prescribed week claimant B was entitled to be in that employment;

(f) that claimant B's normal weekly earnings for a prescribed period ending with a prescribed week are not less than the lower earnings limit in force under section 5(1)(a) at the end of that week;

(g) if regulations so provide, that claimant B continues in employed earner's employment (whether or not with the employer by reference to whom the condition in paragraph (d) is satisfied) until a prescribed time;

(h) that Y became entitled to statutory adoption pay by reference to the placement for adoption of the child;

(i) that Y satisfies prescribed conditions as to the reduction of the duration of the adoption pay period;

(j) that claimant B has given the person who will be liable to pay statutory shared parental pay to claimant B notice of—
  (i) the number of weeks in respect of which claimant B would be entitled to claim statutory shared parental pay in respect of the child if the entitlement were fully exercised (disregarding for these purposes any intention of Y to claim statutory shared parental pay in respect of the child),
  (ii) the number of weeks in respect of which claimant B intends to claim statutory shared parental pay, and
  (iii) the number of weeks in respect of which Y intends to claim statutory shared parental pay;

(k) that claimant B has given the person who will be liable to pay statutory shared parental pay to claimant B notice of the period or periods

during which claimant B intends to claim statutory shared parental pay in respect of the child;
(l) that a notice under paragraph (j) or (k)—
  (i) is given by such time as may be prescribed, and
  (ii) satisfies prescribed conditions as to form and content;
(m) that Y consents to the extent of claimant B's intended claim for statutory shared parental pay;
(n) that it is claimant B's intention to care for the child during each week in respect of which statutory shared parental pay is paid to claimant B;
(o) that claimant B is absent from work during each week in respect of which statutory shared parental pay is paid to claimant B;
(p) that, where claimant B is an employee within the meaning of the Employment Rights Act 1996, claimant B's absence from work during each such week is absence on shared parental leave.

(5) Regulations may provide for—
(a) the determination of the extent of a person's entitlement to statutory shared parental pay in respect of a child;
(b) when statutory shared parental pay is to be payable.

(6) Provision under subsection (5)(a) is to secure that the number of weeks in respect of which a person is entitled to payments of statutory shared parental pay in respect of a child does not exceed the number of weeks of the adoption pay period reduced by—
(a) where the person who became entitled to receive statutory adoption pay takes action that is treated by regulations as constituting for the purposes of this section the person's return to work without satisfying conditions prescribed under subsection (2)(h) or, as the case may be, subsection (4)(i)—
  (i) the number of relevant weeks in respect of which statutory adoption pay is payable to the person, or
  (ii) if that number of relevant weeks is less than a number prescribed by regulations, that prescribed number of weeks, or
(b) except where paragraph (a) applies, the number of weeks to which the adoption pay period has been reduced by virtue of section 171ZN(2A).

(7) In subsection (6)(a) "relevant week" means a week falling before the week in which a person takes action that is treated by regulations as constituting for the purposes of this section the person's return to work, and for these purposes "week" has the meaning given by section 171ZN(8).

(8) In determining the number of weeks for the purposes of subsection (6)(b)—
(a) "week" has the same meaning as in subsection (7), and
(b) a part of a week is to be treated as a week.

(9) Provision under subsection (5)(a) is to secure that, where two persons are entitled to payments of statutory shared parental pay in respect of a child, the extent of one's entitlement and the extent of the other's entitlement do not, taken together, exceed what would be available to one person (see subsection (6)).

(10) Provision under subsection (5)(b) is to secure that no payment of statutory shared parental pay may be made to a person in respect of a child after the end of such period as may be prescribed.

(11) Provision under subsection (5)(b) is to secure that no payment of statutory shared parental pay in respect of a child may be made to a person who became entitled to receive statutory adoption pay in respect of the child before the end of the person's adoption pay period.

(12) Regulations may provide that, where the conditions in subsection (13) are satisfied in relation to a person who is entitled to statutory shared parental pay under subsection (1) or (3) ("V"), V may vary the period or periods during which V intends to claim statutory shared parental pay in respect of the child in question, subject to complying with provision under subsection (14) where that is relevant.

(13) The conditions are—
(a) that V has given the person who will be liable to pay statutory shared parental pay to V notice of an intention to vary the period or periods during which V intends to claim statutory shared parental pay;
(b) that a notice under paragraph (a)—
   (i) is given by such time as may be prescribed, and
   (ii) satisfies prescribed conditions as to form and content.

(14) Regulations may provide that, where the conditions in subsection (15) are satisfied in relation to a person who is entitled to statutory shared parental pay under subsection (1) or (3) ("V"), V may vary the number of weeks in respect of which V intends to claim statutory shared parental pay.

(15) The conditions are—
(a) that V has given the person who will be liable to pay statutory shared parental pay to V notice of—
   (i) the extent to which V has exercised an entitlement to statutory shared parental pay in respect of the child,
   (ii) the extent to which V intends to claim statutory shared parental pay in respect of the child,
   (iii) the extent to which another person has exercised an entitlement to statutory shared parental pay in respect of the child, and
   (iv) the extent to which another person intends to claim statutory shared parental pay in respect of the child;
(b) that a notice under paragraph (a)—
   (i) is given by such time as may be prescribed, and
   (ii) satisfies prescribed conditions as to form and content;
(c) that the person who is X or, as the case may be, Y in relation to V consents to that variation.

(16) A person's entitlement to statutory shared parental pay under this section is not affected by the placement for adoption of more than one child as part of the same arrangement.

[2 (17) Regulations are to provide for entitlement to statutory shared parental pay in respect of a child placed, or expected to be placed—
(a) under section 22C of the Children Act 1989 by a local authority in England, or
(b) under section 81 of the Social Services and Well-being (Wales) Act 2014 by a local authority in Wales,
with a local authority foster parent who has been approved as a prospective adopter.

(18) This section has effect in relation to regulations made by virtue of subsection (17) as if—

Social Security Contributions and Benefits Act 1992

(a) references to a child being placed for adoption under the law of any part of the United Kingdom were references to being placed under section 22C of the Children Act 1989 or section 81 of the Social Services and Well-being (Wales) Act 2014 with a local authority foster parent who has been approved as a prospective adopter;

(b) references to a placement for adoption were references to placement under section 22C of the Children Act 1989 or section 81 of the Social Services and Well-being (Wales) Act 2014 with such a person.]

AMENDMENTS

1. Children and Families Act 2014 s.119 (June 30, 2014).
2. Social Services and Well-being (Wales) Act 2014 (Consequential Amendments) Regulations 2016 (SI 2016/413) (W.131) reg.138 (April 6, 2016).

[¹ **Entitlement: general**

1.164

171ZW.—(1) Regulations may—
(a) provide that the following do not have effect, or have effect subject to prescribed modifications, in such cases as may be prescribed—
  (i) section 171ZU(2)(a) to (o),
  (ii) section 171ZU(4)(a) to (p),
  (iii) section 171ZU(13)(a) and (b),
  (iv) section 171ZU(15)(a) to (c),
  (v) section 171ZV(2)(a) to (o),
  (vi) section 171ZV(4)(a) to (p),
  (vii) section 171ZV(13)(a) and (b), and
  (viii) section 171ZV(15)(a) to (c);
(b) impose requirements about evidence of entitlement and procedures to be followed;
(c) specify in what circumstances employment is to be treated as continuous for the purposes of section 171ZU or 171ZV;
(d) provide that a person is to be treated for the purposes of section 171ZU or 171ZV as being employed for a continuous period of at least the prescribed period where—
  (i) the person has been employed by the same employer for at least the prescribed period under two or more separate contracts of service, and
  (ii) those contracts were not continuous;
(e) provide for amounts earned by a person under separate contracts of service with the same employer to be aggregated for the purposes of section 171ZU or 171ZV;
(f) provide that—
  (i) the amount of a person's earnings for any period, or
  (ii) the amount of the person's earnings to be treated as comprised in any payment made to the person or for the person's benefit,
are to be calculated or estimated for the purposes of section 171ZU or 171ZV in such manner and on such basis as may be prescribed and that for that purpose payments of a particular class or description made or falling to be made to or by a person are, to such extent as may be prescribed, to be disregarded or, as the case may be, to be deducted from the amount of the person's earnings.

(2) The persons upon whom requirements may be imposed by virtue of subsection (1)(b) include—
(a) a person who, in connection with another person's claim to be paid statutory shared parental pay, is required to satisfy conditions prescribed under section 171ZU(2)(b) or (4)(c) or 171ZV(2)(b) or (4)(c);
(b) an employer or former employer of such a person.
(3) In subsection (1)(d) "the prescribed period" means the period of the length prescribed by regulations under section 171ZU(2)(c) or (4)(d) or 171ZV(2)(c) or (4)(d), as the case may be.]

AMENDMENT

1. Children and Families Act 2014 s.119 (June 30, 2014).

[1 Liability to make payments

171ZX.—(1) The liability to make payments of statutory shared parental pay under section 171ZU or 171ZV is a liability of any person of whom the person entitled to the payments has been an employee as mentioned in section 171ZU(2)(c) or (4)(d) or 171ZV(2)(c) or (4)(d), as the case may be.
(2) Regulations must make provision as to a former employer's liability to pay statutory shared parental pay to a person in any case where the former employee's contract of service with the person has been brought to an end by the former employer solely, or mainly, for the purpose of avoiding liability for statutory shared parental pay.
(3) The Secretary of State may, with the concurrence of the Commissioners for Her Majesty's Revenue and Customs, by regulations specify circumstances in which, notwithstanding this section, liability to make payments of statutory shared parental pay is to be a liability of the Commissioners.]

AMENDMENT

1. Children and Families Act 2014 s.119 (June 30, 2014).

[1 Rate and period of pay

171ZY.—(1) Statutory shared parental pay is payable at such fixed or earnings-related weekly rate as may be prescribed by regulations, which may prescribe different kinds of rate for different cases.
(2) Subject to the following provisions of this section, statutory shared parental pay is payable to a person in respect of each week falling within a relevant period, up to the number of weeks determined in the case of that person in accordance with regulations under section 171ZU(5) or 171ZV(5).
(3) Except in such cases as may be prescribed, statutory shared parental pay is not payable to a person in respect of a week falling within a relevant period if it is not the person's intention at the beginning of the week to care for the child by reference to whom the person satisfies—
(a) the condition in section 171ZU(2)(a) or (4)(a), or
(b) the condition in section 171ZV(2)(a) or (4)(a).
(4) Except in such cases as may be prescribed, statutory shared parental pay is not payable to a person in respect of a week falling within a relevant period during any part of which week the person works for any employer.

(5) The Secretary of State may by regulations specify circumstances in which there is to be no liability to pay statutory shared parental pay in respect of a week falling within a relevant period.

(6) Where for any purpose of this Part or of regulations it is necessary to calculate the daily rate of statutory shared parental pay, the amount payable by way of statutory shared parental pay for any day shall be taken as one seventh of the weekly rate.

(7) For the purposes of this section a week falls within a relevant period if it falls within a period specified in a notice under—
   (a) section 171ZU(2)(j), (4)(k) or (13)(a), or
   (b) section 171ZV(2)(j), (4)(k) or (13)(a),

and is not afterwards excluded from such a period by a variation of the period or periods during which the person in question intends to claim statutory shared parental pay.

(8) In this section "week", in relation to a relevant period, means a period of seven days beginning with the day of the week on which the relevant period starts.]

AMENDMENT

1. Children and Families Act 2014 s.119 (June 30, 2014).

[¹ Restrictions on contracting out

171ZZ.—(1) An agreement is void to the extent that it purports—
   (a) to exclude, limit or otherwise modify any provision of this Part, or
   (b) to require a person to contribute (whether directly or indirectly) towards any costs incurred by that person's employer or former employer under this Part.

(2) For the avoidance of doubt, an agreement between an employer and an employee, authorising deductions from statutory shared parental pay which the employer is liable to pay to the employee in respect of any period, is not void by virtue of subsection (1)(a) if the employer—
   (a) is authorised by that or another agreement to make the same deductions from any contractual remuneration which the employer is liable to pay in respect of the same period, or
   (b) would be so authorised if the employer were liable to pay contractual remuneration in respect of that period.]

AMENDMENT

1. Children and Families Act 2014 s.119 (June 30, 2014).

[¹ Relationship with contractual remuneration

171ZZ1.—(1) Subject to subsections (2) and (3), any entitlement to statutory shared parental pay is not to affect any right of a person in relation to remuneration under any contract of service ("contractual remuneration").

(2) Subject to subsection (3)—
   (a) any contractual remuneration paid to a person by an employer of that person in respect of any period is to go towards discharging any liability of that employer to pay statutory shared parental pay to that person in respect of that period; and

(b) any statutory shared parental pay paid by an employer to a person who is an employee of that employer in respect of any period is to go towards discharging any liability of that employer to pay contractual remuneration to that person in respect of that period.

(3) Regulations may make provision as to payments which are, and those which are not, to be treated as contractual remuneration for the purposes of subsections (1) and (2).]

AMENDMENT

1. Children and Families Act 2014 s.119 (June 30, 2014).

[¹ Crown employment

171ZZ2.—The provisions of this Part apply in relation to persons employed by or under the Crown as they apply in relation to persons employed otherwise than by or under the Crown.]

AMENDMENT

1. Children and Families Act 2014 s.119 (June 30, 2014).

[¹ Special classes of person

171ZZ3.—(1) The Secretary of State may with the concurrence of the Treasury make regulations modifying any provision of this Part in such manner as the Secretary of State thinks proper in its application to any person who is, has been or is to be—
  (a) employed on board any ship, vessel, hovercraft or aircraft;
  (b) outside Great Britain at any prescribed time or in any prescribed circumstances; or
  (c) in prescribed employment in connection with continental shelf operations, as defined in section 120(2).

(2) Regulations under subsection (1) may, in particular, provide—
  (a) for any provision of this Part to apply to any such person, notwithstanding that it would not otherwise apply;
  (b) for any such provision not to apply to any such person, notwithstanding that it would otherwise apply;
  (c) for excepting any such person from the application of any such provision where the person neither is domiciled nor has a place of residence in any part of Great Britain;
  (d) for the taking of evidence, for the purposes of the determination of any question arising under any such provision, in a country or territory outside Great Britain, by a British consular official or such other person as may be determined in accordance with the regulations.]

AMENDMENT

1. Children and Families Act 2014 s.119 (June 30, 2014).

[¹ Part 12ZC: supplementary

171ZZ4.—(1) In this Part—
"adoption pay period" has the meaning given in section 171ZN(2);
"employer", in relation to a person who is an employee, means a person who—

(a) under section 6 is liable to pay secondary Class 1 contributions in relation to any of the earnings of the person who is an employee, or
(b) would be liable to pay such contributions but for—
　(i) the condition in section 6(1)(b), or
　(ii) the employee being under the age of 16;
"local authority" has the same meaning as in the Children Act 1989 (see section 105(1) of that Act);
"local authority foster parent" has the same meaning as in the Children Act 1989 (see [³ section 105(1)] of that Act);
"maternity allowance period" has the meaning given in section 35(2);
"maternity pay period" has the meaning given in section 165(1);
"modifications" includes additions, omissions and amendments, and related expressions are to be read accordingly;
"prescribed" means prescribed by regulations.

(2) In this Part "employee" means a person who is gainfully employed in Great Britain either under a contract of service or in an office (including elective office) with general earnings (as defined by section 7 of the Income Tax (Earnings and Pensions) Act 2003).

(3) Regulations may provide—
(a) for cases where a person who falls within the definition in subsection (2) is not to be treated as an employee for the purposes of this Part, and
(b) for cases where a person who would not otherwise be an employee for the purposes of this Part is to be treated as an employee for those purposes.

(4) Without prejudice to any other power to make regulations under this Part, regulations may specify cases in which, for the purposes of this Part or of such provisions of this Part as may be prescribed—
(a) two or more employers are to be treated as one;
(b) two or more contracts of service in respect of which the same person is an employee are to be treated as one.

(5) In this Part, except where otherwise provided, "week" means a period of seven days beginning with Sunday or such other period as may be prescribed in relation to any particular case or class of cases.

(6) For the purposes of this Part, a person's normal weekly earnings are, subject to subsection (8), to be taken to be the average weekly earnings which in the relevant period have been paid to the person or paid for the person's benefit under the contract of service with the employer in question.

(7) For the purposes of subsection (6) "earnings" and "relevant period" have the meanings given to them by regulations.

(8) In such cases as may be prescribed, a person's normal weekly earnings are to be calculated in accordance with regulations.

(9) Where—
(a) in consequence of the establishment of one or more National Health Service trusts under the National Health Service Act 2006, the National Health Service (Wales) Act 2006 or the National Health Service (Scotland) Act 1978, a person's contract of employment is treated by a scheme under any of those Acts as divided so as to constitute two or more contracts, or
(b) an order under paragraph 26(1) of Schedule 3 to the National Health Service Act 2006 provides that a person's contract of employment is so divided,

regulations may make provision enabling the person to elect for all of those contracts to be treated as one contract for the purposes of this Part or such provisions of this Part as may be prescribed.

(10) Regulations under subsection (9) may prescribe—
(a) the conditions that must be satisfied if a person is to be entitled to make such an election;
(b) the manner in which, and the time within which, such an election is to be made;
(c) the persons to whom, and the manner in which, notice of such an election is to be given;
(d) the information which a person who makes such an election is to provide, and the persons to whom, and the time within which, the person is to provide it;
(e) the time for which such an election is to have effect;
(f) which one of the person's employers under two or more contracts is to be regarded for the purposes of statutory shared parental pay as the person's employer under the contract.

(11) The powers under subsections (9) and (10) are without prejudice to any other power to make regulations under this Part.

(12) Regulations under any of subsections (4) to (10) must be made with the concurrence of the Commissioners for Her Majesty's Revenue and Customs.]

AMENDMENTS

1. Children and Families Act 2014 s.119 (June 30, 2014).
2. Social Services and Well-being (Wales) Act 2014 (Consequential Amendments) Regulations 2016 (SI 2016/413) (W.131) reg.139 (April 6, 2016).

[¹ Power to apply Part 12ZC

171ZZ5.—(1) The Secretary of State may by regulations provide for this Part to have effect in relation to cases which involve adoption, but not the placement of a child for adoption under the law of any part of the United Kingdom, with such modifications as the regulations may prescribe.

(2) The Secretary of State may by regulations provide for this Part to have effect in relation to cases which involve a person who has applied, or intends to apply, with another person for a parental order under section 54 of the Human Fertilisation and Embryology Act 2008 and a child who is, or will be, the subject of the order, with such modifications as the regulations may prescribe.

(3) Where section 171ZW(1)(b) has effect in relation to such cases as are described in subsection (2), regulations under section 171ZW(1)(b) may impose requirements to make statutory declarations as to—
(a) eligibility to apply for a parental order;
(b) intention to apply for such an order."

(2) In section 176 of the Social Security Contributions and Benefits Act 1992 (Parliamentary control of subordinate legislation), in subsection (1) (affirmative procedure), in paragraph (a), at the appropriate place there is inserted— "any of sections 171ZU to 171ZY;".]

AMENDMENT

1. Children and Families Act 2014 s.119 (June 30, 2014).

Social Security Contributions and Benefits Act 1992

[¹PART 12ZD

Statutory parental bereavement pay

Entitlement

171ZZ6.—(1) A person who satisfies the conditions in subsection (2) is entitled in accordance with the following provisions of this Part to payments to be known as "statutory parental bereavement pay".

(2) The conditions are—
(a) that the person is a bereaved parent,
(b) that the person has been in employed earner's employment with an employer for a continuous period of at least 26 weeks ending with the relevant week,
(c) that at the end of the relevant week the person was entitled to be in that employment (but see subsection (7)),
(d) that the person's normal weekly earnings for the period of 8 weeks ending with the relevant week are not less than the lower earnings limit in force under section 5(1)(a) at the end of the relevant week, and
(e) that the person has been in employed earner's employment with the employer by reference to whom the condition in paragraph (b) is satisfied for a continuous period beginning with the end of the relevant week and ending with the day on which the child dies.

(3) For the purposes of subsection (2) an employee is a "bereaved parent" if the employee satisfies prescribed conditions as to relationship with a child who has died.

(4) The conditions prescribed under subsection (3) may be framed, in whole or in part, by reference to the employee's care of the child before the child's death.

(5) In subsection (2) "relevant week" means the week immediately before the one in which the child dies.

(6) Where a person satisfies the conditions in subsection (2) as a result of the death of more than one child, the person is entitled to statutory parental bereavement pay in respect of each child.

(7) In relation to a bereaved parent whose child dies before the day on which section 63(3) of the Welfare Reform Act 2012 comes fully into force, subsection (2) above is to be read as if paragraph (c) were omitted.]

AMENDMENT

1. Parental Bereavement (Leave and Pay) Act 2018 s.1(b) and Sch. para.5 (January 18, 2020).

[¹**Entitlement: supplementary**

171ZZ7.—(1) A person is entitled to payments of statutory parental bereavement pay in respect of any period only if the person gives notice to whoever is liable to make the payments stating the week or weeks in respect of which they are to be made.

(2) Regulations may provide for the time by which notice under subsection (1) must be given.

(3) The notice must be in writing if the person who is liable to pay the statutory parental bereavement pay so requests.

(4) The Secretary of State may by regulations—
(a) provide that section 171ZZ6(2)(b), (d) or (e) has effect subject to prescribed modifications in such cases as may be prescribed;
(b) provide for circumstances in which section 171ZZ6(2)(c) does not have effect;
(c) provide that subsection (1) of this section does not have effect, or has effect subject to prescribed modifications, in such cases as may be prescribed;
(d) impose requirements about evidence of entitlement;
(e) specify in what circumstances employment is to be treated as continuous for the purposes of section 171ZZ6;
(f) provide that a person is to be treated for the purposes of section 171ZZ6 as being employed for a continuous period of at least 26 weeks where—
   (i) the person has been employed by the same employer for at least 26 weeks under two or more separate contracts of service, and
   (ii) those contracts were not continuous;
(g) provide for amounts earned by a person under separate contracts of service with the same employer to be aggregated for the purposes of section 171ZZ6;
(h) provide that—
   (i) the amount of a person's earnings for any period, or
   (ii) the amount of the person's earnings to be treated as comprised in any payment made to the person or for the person's benefit,
   is to be calculated or estimated for the purposes of section 171ZZ6 in such manner and on such basis as may be prescribed and that for that purpose payments of a particular class or description made or falling to be made to or by a person shall, to such extent as may be prescribed, be disregarded or, as the case may be, be deducted from the amount of the person's earnings.]

AMENDMENT

1. Parental Bereavement (Leave and Pay) Act 2018 s.1(b) and Sch. para.5 (January 18, 2020).

[¹Liability to make payments

171ZZ8.—(1) The liability to make payments of statutory parental bereavement pay under section 171ZZ6 is a liability of any person of whom the person entitled to the payments has been an employee as mentioned in subsection (2)(b) and (e) of that section.

(2) The Secretary of State must by regulations make provision as to a former employer's liability to pay statutory parental bereavement pay to a former employee in any case where the employee's contract of service with the employer has been brought to an end by the employer solely, or mainly, for the purpose of avoiding liability for statutory parental bereavement pay.

(3) The Secretary of State may, with the concurrence of the Commissioners for Her Majesty's Revenue and Customs, by regulations specify circumstances in which, notwithstanding this section, liability to make payments of statutory parental bereavement pay is to be a liability of the Commissioners.]

AMENDMENT

1. Parental Bereavement (Leave and Pay) Act 2018 s.1(b) and Sch. para.5 (January 18, 2020).

[¹**Rate and period of pay**

1.176   **171ZZ9.**—(1) Statutory parental bereavement pay is payable at such fixed or earnings-related weekly rate as may be prescribed by regulations, which may prescribe different kinds of rate for different cases.

(2) Statutory parental bereavement pay is payable in respect of—
(a) such week within the qualifying period, or
(b) such number of weeks, not exceeding the prescribed number of weeks, within the qualifying period,
as the person entitled may choose in accordance with regulations.

(3) Provision under subsection (2)(b) must secure that the prescribed number of weeks is not less than two.

(4) Regulations under subsection (2)(b) may permit a person entitled to receive statutory parental bereavement pay to choose to receive such pay in respect of non-consecutive periods each of which is a week or a number of weeks.

(5) For the purposes of subsection (2), the qualifying period is to be determined in accordance with regulations, which must secure that it is a period of at least 56 days beginning with the date of the child's death.

(6) A person is not liable to pay statutory parental bereavement pay to another in respect of any statutory pay week during any part of which the other works under a contract of service with the person.

(7) It is immaterial for the purposes of subsection (6) whether the work referred to in that subsection is work under a contract of service which existed immediately before the statutory pay week or a contract of service which did not so exist.

(8) Except in such cases as may be prescribed, statutory parental bereavement pay is not payable to a person in respect of a statutory pay week during any part of which the person works for any employer who is not liable to pay the person statutory parental bereavement pay.

(9) The Secretary of State may by regulations specify circumstances in which there is to be no liability to pay statutory parental bereavement pay in respect of a statutory pay week.

(10) Where for any purpose of this Part or of regulations it is necessary to calculate the daily rate of statutory parental bereavement pay, the amount payable by way of statutory parental bereavement pay for any day is to be taken as one seventh of the weekly rate.

(11) In this section—
"statutory pay week", in relation to a person entitled to statutory parental bereavement pay, means a week chosen by the person as a week in respect of which statutory parental bereavement pay is to be payable;
"week" means any period of seven days.]

AMENDMENT

1. Parental Bereavement (Leave and Pay) Act 2018 s.1(b) and Sch. para.5 (January 18, 2020).

[¹**Restrictions on contracting out**

171ZZ10.—(1) An agreement is void to the extent that it purports—
(a) to exclude, limit or otherwise modify any provision of this Part, or
(b) to require a person to contribute (whether directly or indirectly) towards any costs incurred by that person's employer or former employer under this Part.

(2) An agreement between an employer and an employee, authorising any deductions from statutory parental bereavement pay which the employer is liable to pay to the employee in respect of any period, is not void by virtue of subsection (1)(a) if the employer—
(a) is authorised by that or another agreement to make the same deductions from any contractual remuneration which the employer is liable to pay in respect of the same period, or
(b) would be so authorised if the employer were liable to pay contractual remuneration in respect of that period.]

AMENDMENT

1. Parental Bereavement (Leave and Pay) Act 2018 s.1(b) and Sch. para.5 (January 18, 2020).

[¹**Relationship with contractual remuneration**

171ZZ11.—(1) Subject to subsections (2) and (3), any entitlement to statutory parental bereavement pay does not affect any right of a person in relation to remuneration under any contract of service ("contractual remuneration").

(2) Subject to subsection (3)—
(a) any contractual remuneration paid to a person by an employer of that person in respect of any period is to go towards discharging any liability of that employer to pay statutory parental bereavement pay to that person in respect of that period; and
(b) any statutory parental bereavement pay paid by an employer to a person who is an employee of that employer in respect of any period is to go towards discharging any liability of that employer to pay contractual remuneration to that person in respect of that period.

(3) Regulations may make provision as to payments which are, and those which are not, to be treated as contractual remuneration for the purposes of subsections (1) and (2).]

AMENDMENT

1. Parental Bereavement (Leave and Pay) Act 2018 s.1(b) and Sch. para.5 (January 18, 2020).

[¹**Crown employment**

171ZZ12.—The provisions of this Part apply in relation to persons employed by or under the Crown as they apply in relation to persons employed otherwise than by or under the Crown.]

AMENDMENT

1. Parental Bereavement (Leave and Pay) Act 2018 s.1(b) and Sch. para.5 (January 18, 2020).

[¹ Special classes of person

1.180   **171ZZ13.**—(1) The Secretary of State may with the concurrence of the Treasury make regulations modifying any provision of this Part in such manner as the Secretary of State thinks proper in its application to any person who is, has been or is to be—
  (a) employed on board any ship, vessel, hovercraft or aircraft;
  (b) outside Great Britain at any prescribed time or in any prescribed circumstances; or
  (c) in prescribed employment in connection with continental shelf operations, as defined in section 120(2).
(2) Regulations under subsection (1) may, in particular, provide—
  (a) for any provision of this Part to apply to any such person, notwithstanding that it would not otherwise apply;
  (b) for any such provision not to apply to any such person, notwithstanding that it would otherwise apply;
  (c) for excepting any such person from the application of any such provision where the person neither is domiciled nor has a place of residence in any part of Great Britain;
  (d) for the taking of evidence, for the purposes of the determination of any question arising under any such provision, in a country or territory outside Great Britain, by a British consular official or such other person as may be determined in accordance with the regulations.]

AMENDMENT

1. Parental Bereavement (Leave and Pay) Act 2018 s.1(b) and Sch. para.5 (January 18, 2020).

Supplementary

1.181   [¹ **171ZZ14.**—(1) In this Part—
"child" means a person under the age of 18 (see also section 171ZZ15 for the application of this Part in relation to stillbirths);
"employer", in relation to a person who is an employee, means a person who—
  (a) under section 6 is liable to pay secondary Class 1 contributions in relation to any of the earnings of the person who is an employee, or
  (b) would be liable to pay such contributions but for—
    (i) the condition in section 6(1)(b), or
    (ii) the employee being under the age of 16;
"modifications" includes additions, omissions and amendments, and related expressions are to be read accordingly;
"prescribed" means prescribed by regulations.
(2) In this Part, "employee" means a person who is gainfully employed in Great Britain either under a contract of service or in an office (including elective office) with earnings (within the meaning of Parts 1 to 5).
(3) Regulations may provide—
  (a) for cases where a person who falls within the definition in subsection (2) is not to be treated as an employee for the purposes of this Part, and
  (b) for cases where a person who would not otherwise be an employee for the purposes of this Part is to be treated as an employee for those purposes.

(4) Without prejudice to any other power to make regulations under this Part, regulations may specify cases in which, for the purposes of this Part or of such provisions of this Part as may be prescribed—
  (a) two or more employers are to be treated as one;
  (b) two or more contracts of service in respect of which the same person is an employee are to be treated as one.

(5) In this Part, except section 171ZZ9, "week" means a period of 7 days beginning with Sunday or such other period as may be prescribed in relation to any particular case or class of cases.

(6) For the purposes of this Part, a person's normal weekly earnings are, subject to subsection (8), to be taken to be the average weekly earnings which in the relevant period have been paid to the person or paid for the person's benefit under the contract of service with the employer in question.

(7) For the purposes of subsection (6), "earnings" and "relevant period" have the meanings given to them by regulations.

(8) In such cases as may be prescribed, a person's normal weekly earnings are to be calculated in accordance with regulations.

(9) Where in consequence of the establishment of one or more National Health Service trusts under the National Health Service (Wales) Act 2006, a person's contract of employment is treated by a scheme under that Act as divided so as to constitute two or more contracts, regulations may make provision enabling the person to elect for all of those contracts to be treated as one contract for the purposes of this Part or such provisions of this Part as may be prescribed.

(10) Regulations under subsection (9) may prescribe—
  (a) the conditions that must be satisfied if a person is to be entitled to make such an election;
  (b) the manner in which, and the time within which, such an election is to be made;
  (c) the persons to whom, and the manner in which, notice of such an election is to be given;
  (d) the information which a person who makes such an election is to provide, and the persons to whom, and the time within which, the person is to provide it;
  (e) the time for which such an election is to have effect;
  (f) which one of the person's employers under two or more contracts is to be regarded for the purposes of statutory parental bereavement pay as the person's employer under the contract.

(11) The powers under subsections (9) and (10) are without prejudice to any other power to make regulations under this Part.

(12) Regulations under any of subsections (4) to (10) must be made with the concurrence of the Commissioners for Her Majesty's Revenue and Customs.]

AMENDMENT

1. Parental Bereavement (Leave and Pay) Act 2018 s.1(b) and Sch. para.5 (January 18, 2020).

[¹Application in relation to stillbirths

171ZZ15.—In this Part—
  (a) references to a child include a child stillborn after twenty-four weeks of pregnancy, and

(b) references to the death of a child are to be read, in relation to a still-born child, as references to the birth of the child.]

AMENDMENT

1. Parental Bereavement (Leave and Pay) Act 2018 s.1(b) and Sch. para.5 (January 18, 2020).

PART XIII

GENERAL

Interpretation

Application of Act in relation to territorial waters

1.183   **172.**—In this Act—
(a) any reference to Great Britain includes a reference to the territorial waters of the United Kingdom adjacent to Great Britain;
(b) any reference to the United Kingdom includes a reference to the territorial waters of the United Kingdom.

Age

1.184   **173.**—For the purposes of this Act a person—
(a) is over or under a particular age if he has or, as the case may be, has not attained that age; and
(b) is between two particular ages if he has attained the first but not the second;
and in Scotland (as in England and Wales) the time at which a person attains a particular age expressed in years is the commencement of the relevant anniversary of the date of his birth.

References to Acts

1.185   **174.**—In this Act—
"the 1975 Act" means the Social Security Act 1975;
"the 1986 Act" means the Social Security Act 1986;
"the Administration Act" means the Social Security Administration Act 1992;
"the Consequential Provisions Act" means the Social Security (Consequential Provisions) Act 1992;
"the Northern Ireland Contributions and Benefits Act" means the Social Security Contributions and Benefits (Northern Ireland) Act 1992;
"the Old Cases Act" means the Industrial Injuries and Diseases (Old Cases) Act 1975; and
"the Pensions Act" means the [1 Pensions Schemes Act 1993].

AMENDMENT

1. Pension Schemes Act 1993 s.190 and Sch.8 para.41 (February 7, 1994).

(1992 c.4 Sch.9)

SCHEDULE 9

EXCLUSIONS FROM ENTITLEMENT TO CHILD BENEFIT

Children [⁴ and qualifying young persons] in detention, care, etc.

1.—Except where regulations otherwise provide, no person shall be entitled to child benefit in respect of a child [⁴ or qualifying young person] for any week if in that week the child [⁴ or qualifying young person]—

(a) is undergoing imprisonment or detention in legal custody;

[⁵ (b) is subject to a compulsory supervision order (within the meaning of section 83 of the Children's Hearings (Scotland) Act 2011) and is residing in a residential establishment (within the meaning of section 202(1) of that Act);]

(c) is in the care of a local authority in such circumstances as may be prescribed.

1.186

Employed trainees, etc.

2.—[⁴ . . .]

1.187

Married children [⁴ and qualifying young persons]

3.—Except where regulations otherwise provide, no person shall be entitled to child benefit in respect of a child [⁴ or qualifying young person] who is married [³ or is a civil partner].

1.188

Persons exempt from tax

4.—[² . . .].

1.189

Children entitled to severe disablement allowance

5.—[¹ . . .].

1.190

DEFINITIONS

"child"—s.142.
"week"—s.147.

AMENDMENTS

1. Welfare Reform and Pensions Act 1999 Sch.13 part IV (April 6, 2001)
2. Tax Credits Act 2002 s.57 Sch.6 (April 7, 2003).
3. Civil Partnership Act 2004 s.254 and Sch.24 para.54 (December 5, 2004).
4. Child Benefit Act 2005 s.1 and Sch.1 para.17 (April 10, 2006).
5. Children's Hearings (Scotland) Act 2011 (Consequential and Transitional Provisions and Savings) Order 2013 (SI 2013/1465) art.17 Sch.1 para.4(3) (June 24, 2013).

SCHEDULE 10

PRIORITY BETWEEN PERSONS ENTITLED TO CHILD BENEFIT

Person with prior award

1.—(1) Subject to sub-paragraph (2) below, as between a person claiming child benefit in respect of a child [¹ or qualifying young person] for any week and a person to whom child benefit in respect of that child [¹ or qualifying young person] for that week has already been awarded when the claim is made, the latter shall be entitled.

(2) Sub-paragraph (1) above shall not confer any priority where the week to which the claim relates is later than the third week following that in which the claim is made.

1.191

Person having child [¹ and qualifying young person] living with him

2.—Subject to paragraph 1 above, as between a person entitled for any week by virtue of paragraph (a) of subsection (1) of section 143 above and a person entitled by virtue of paragraph (b) of that subsection the former shall be entitled.

[² Opposite-sex spouses or civil partners

1.192 3. Subject to paragraphs 1 and 2 above, as between a man and woman who are married to, or civil partners of, each other and are residing together, the woman shall be entitled.]

Parents

4.—(1) Subject to paragraphs 1 to 3 above, as between a person who is and one who is not a parent of the child [¹ or qualifying young person] the parent shall be entitled.

(2) Subject as aforesaid, as between two persons residing together who are parents of the child [¹ or qualifying young person] but [² do not fall within paragraph 3], the mother shall be entitled.

Other cases

1.193 **5.**—As between persons not falling within paragraphs 1 to 4 above, such one of them shall be entitled as they may jointly elect or, in default of election, as the Secretary of State may in his discretion determine.

Supplementary

6.—(1) Any election under this Schedule shall be made in the prescribed manner.

(2) Regulations may provide for exceptions from the modifications of the provisions of paragraphs 1 to 5 above in relation to such cases as may be prescribed.

AMENDMENTS

1. Child Benefit Act 2005 s.1 and Sch.7 para.18 (April 10, 2006).
2. Civil Partnership (Opposite-sex Couples) Regulations 2019 (SI 2019/1458) reg.41(b) and Sch.3 para.14(5) (December 2, 2019).

DEFINITIONS

"child"—s.142.
"parent, father or mother"—s.147(3).
"week"—s.147.

GENERAL NOTE

1.194 Under s.143 it is possible for more than one person to be entitled to claim Child Benefit. For example, the child may live with one parent while being maintained to the requisite extent by the other; or the child may live with a parent in the home of a grandparent. In such cases only one award of Child Benefit can be made and Sch.10 determines the order of priority between multiple claimants. Note that s.144 and Sch.10 apply only where more than one person is entitled to benefit for the same child in respect of that week. Where the child has ceased to live with one parent as provided for in s.143, and a claim is not precluded by the effect of s.13(2) of SSAA 1992 (which prevents a claim being made where payment of benefit has been made already to another claimant, and the decision to make such payment has not been revised, nor has the payment been repaid voluntarily) then Sch.10 does not apply. In that case the DM should decide the case on the basis of s.143 alone. For an explanation of these provisions and their interaction see *CF/2826/2007*.

CF/2826/2007 was applied and further instructions given to a tribunal dealing with these matters in *CB v HMRC and AE (CHB)* [2016] UKUT 506 (AAC). The claim was in respect of a child whose parents were separated. The child was said to be living in the home of her father, but the mother made a claim for benefit on the ground that the child had moved from there and had been living at her boyfriend's place.

The mother claimed to have been providing for her to the requisite extent. In the UT, Judge Wikeley allowed an appeal against the refusal of that claim because the FTT had failed to deal at all with the factual question of where the child was living. but note that the tribunal will have jurisdiction only in respect of the period for which she has claimed if the exception to s.13(2) of SSAA 1992 that is provided for in reg.38 of the Child Benefit (General) Regulations can be applied—see *CF/2826/2007*.

In the first place no payment will be made unless there has been a claim, so that if only one claim is made, even by a person of lower priority, that claim will be met. Where, however, there are multiple claims priority will be given in the following order:

(1) The person with whom the child is living.

(2) The wife, as between a husband and wife who are residing together.

(3) A parent, as between a person who is a parent and one who is not.

(4) The mother, as between parents who are residing together but are not married.

(5) The person agreed by them, as between any other persons.

(6) The person determined by a decision maker of HMRC, where such other persons cannot agree.

Where there is an existing award of Child Benefit in payment at the time a rival claim is made, the existing award will continue to be paid for a period of three weeks (provided the claimant continues to satisfy the other conditions of entitlement), even though the new claimant may be entitled thereafter by priority. The reservation of entitlement to the current claimant for a period of three weeks was applied in *CF/3348/2002*.

1.195

The meaning of "residing together" for the purposes of Child Benefit is dealt with largely by reg.34 of the Child Benefit (General) Regulations, and is not the same as in other benefit contexts. Spouses and parents who are not married to each other are treated as residing together if their separation is not likely to be permanent and, in the case of spouses only, if it is for the purposes of medical treatment. In *R(F) 4/85* it was held that a couple who married while the husband was in prison, and who had never lived together, had to be treated under this regulation as if they were residing together because their separation was not likely to be permanent—they could be expected to commence cohabitation when the husband was released from prison. (The effect in this case was to deprive the claimant of the increase for one parent benefit.) It has also been accepted in this context that parties may not be residing together if they maintain separate households under the same roof (*R(F) 3/81*).

Where the parents of a child are residing together (whether married or not) and the mother of the child obtains a certificate of gender recognition as a man he will continue to be regarded as the mother of their child for this purpose because s.12 of the Gender Recognition Act 2004, provides that the acquired status does not affect the status of a person as the mother or father of a child.

A "parent" for the purposes of Child Benefit is given an extended meaning by s.147(3) to include a step parent. The meaning of parent is also extended by the effect of the Children Act 1989, to include any person in whose favour a residence order has been made. This is because the parental responsibility conferred by the order made under that Act is defined to include all the rights which, by law, a parent has in relation to that child. For the purposes of the Contributions & Benefits Act, the word parent is to be construed as the "legal parent" of the child. (See *Secretary of State v Smith* [1983] 1 W.L.R. 1110, where the effect of an order made under equivalent legislation then in force, was to include an adoptive parent of the child and at the same time to exclude the natural parent.) The same reasoning was applied by Commissioner Howell in *R(F) 1/08* where a lesbian couple had two children with the assistance of artificial insemmination and after they had separated a residence order had been made in favour of both of them. The Commissioner held that both must be regarded as parents, not just the biological mother and, consequently it became necessary for HMRC to exercise the discretion provided for at [5].

The particular problem that arises when the parents of a child have separated and the care of the child is then shared between them (e.g. in holidays and at weekends) is referred to by Judge Wikeley in *CIS/2457/2008*. The issue arose only indirectly in that case, which was a determination of the claimant's entitlement to Income Support, but that entitlement depended, in turn, on her right to receive Child Benefit, and the judge added an appendix to his decision that covers earlier cases (*Chester v Secretary of State for Social Security* [2001] EWHC Admin 1119; *Barber v Secretary of State for Social Security* [2002] EWHC 1915 (Admin) and *R. (on the relation of Ford) v Board of Inland Revenue* [2005] EWHC 1109 (Admin)) where decisions awarding all of the Child Benefit to one parent had been quashed on review.

A decision by HMRC in default of agreement is not appealable but an application for revision or review may be made. In *Chester v Secretary of State for Social Security* [2001] EWHC Admin 1119, (approved in *Barber* [2002] EWHC 1915) it was held that such a default decision engaged the right to private and family life in art.8 ECHR though in that case there was no need for the claimant to rely upon it. Note too, that it is now possible for an application for judicial review to be transferred to the Upper Tribunal.

See also *Re Murphy's application for judicial review* [2023] NIKB 119, a decision of the Northern Ireland High Court (Simpson J.) on entitlement to child benefit in the context of shared care. The applicant (the mother) was on the minimum wage and reliant on tax credits and child benefit. Her ex-husband earned more than £60,000 p.a. and so was liable to the high income child benefit charge. The couple had three children and shared care 50:50. HMRC awarded child benefit for two children to the applicant and for one child to the father. The applicant applied for judicial review. Simpson J., referring to the considerations set out in HMRC's *Child Benefit Procedural Guide 9520—Rival Claims Legislative: Discretionary Decisions*, held that HMRC, in breach of its own policy, had failed to consider "who stands to lose most": "Entirely conscious as I am that the legislation provides a very wide discretion, and that the guidance is not to be interpreted like a statute, it is my view that the decision-maker misdirected herself." She decided that the "responsibility of care is clear" but that was not the question which the guidance indicated she should ask. The question in the guidance, and the one which she should have asked herself, was "whether one parent or the other has the greater responsibility of care". If she had asked that question, the only answer would have been that neither had the greater responsibility of care, so while "responsibility of care" was clear, there was no such clarity as to which parent had the greater responsibility of care. Accordingly, in my view, it was incumbent on the decision-maker to go on to consider the impact of the decision and the further test, viz "who stands to lose most" ([45]–[46]). The case was remitted to HMRC for a fresh decision.

The procedure for making an election as to priority, and for waiving priority, is provided for in regs 14 and 15 of the Child Benefit (General) Regulations 2006.

Section 153(3) SCHEDULE 11

Circumstances in Which Periods of Entitlement to Statutory Sick Pay Do Not Arise

1.196

1.—A period of entitlement does not arise in relation to a particular period of incapacity for work in any of the circumstances set out in para.2 below or in such other circumstances as may be prescribed.

[⁴1A.—Regulations made under paragraph 1 must be made with the concurrence of the Treasury.]

2.—The circumstances are that—
  (a) [⁶...]
  (b) [⁵...];

(c) at the relevant date the employee's normal weekly earnings are less than the lower earnings limit then in force under section 5(1)(a) above;

[¹(d) in the period of 57 days ending immediately before the relevant date the employee had at least one day on which—
  (i) he was entitled to incapacity benefit (or would have been so entitled had he satisfied the contribution conditions mentioned in section 30A(2)(a) above); or
  (ii) [³...]
  (iii) he was entitled to a severe disablement allowance;]

[⁸(dd) in the period of 85 days ending immediately before the relevant date the employee had at least one day on which he was entitled to an employment and support allowance (or would have been so entitled had he satisfied the requirements in section 1(2) of the Welfare Reform Act 2007.]

(e) [¹...]

(f) the employee has done no work for his employer under his contract of service;

(g) on the relevant date there is [²...] a stoppage of work due to a trade dispute at the employee's place of employment;

(h) the employee is, or has been, pregnant and the relevant date falls within the disqualifying period (within the meaning of section 153(12) above).

3.—In this Schedule, "relevant date" means the date on which a period of entitlement would begin in accordance with section 153 above if this Schedule did not prevent it arising.

4.— [⁵...]

5.— [¹...]

[⁷**5A.** —(1) Paragraph 2(d)(i) above does not apply if, at the relevant date, the employee is over pensionable age and is not entitled to incapacity benefit.

(2) Paragraph 2(d)(i) above ceases to apply if, at any time after the relevant date, the employee is over pensionable age and is not entitled to incapacity benefit.

(3) In this paragraph "pensionable age" has the meaning given by the rules in paragraph 1 of Schedule 4 to the Pensions Act 1995.]

6.—For the purposes of paragraph 2(f) above, if an employee enters into a contract of service which is to take effect not more than eight weeks after the date on which a previous contract of service entered into by him with the same employer ceased to have effect, the two contracts shall be treated as one.

7.—Paragraph 2(g) above does not apply in the case of an employee who proves that at no time on or before the relevant date did he have a direct interest in the trade dispute in question.

8.—Paragraph 2(h) above does not apply in relation to an employee who has been pregnant if her pregnancy terminated, before the beginning of the disqualifying period, otherwise than by confinement (as defined for the purposes of statutory maternity pay in section 171(1) above).

AMENDMENTS

1. Social Security (Incapacity for Work) Act 1994 s.11(1) and Sch.1 para.43 (April 6, 1995).

2. Jobseekers Act 1995 s.41(5) and Sch.3 (October 7, 1996).

3. Social Security Act 1998 s.73 (April 6, 1999).

4. Social Security Contributions (Transfer of Functions, etc.) Act 1999 s.1(1) and Sch.1 para.20 (April 1, 1999).

5. Fixed-term Employees (Prevention of Less Favourable Treatment) Regulations 2002 (SI 2002/2034) reg.11 and Sch.2 para.1 (October 1, 2002).

6. Employment Equality (Age) Regulations 2006 (SI 2006/1031) reg.49(1) and Sch.8 Pt 1 para.13(1) (October 1, 2006).

7. Employment Equality (Age) (Consequential Amendments) Regulations 2007 (SI 2007/825) reg.2 (April 6, 2007).

8. Employment and Support Allowance (Consequential Provisions) (No.2) Regulations 2008 (SI 2008/1554) reg.44 (October 27, 2008).

DEFINITIONS

"contract of service"—see s.163(1).
"disqualifying period"—see s.153(12).
"employee"—see s.163(1) and SSP (General) Regulations 1982 reg.16.
"employer"—see s.163(1).

"period of entitlement"—see s.163(1).
"period of incapacity for work"—see s.163(1).
"prescribed"—see s.163(1).
"relevant date"—see para.(3).

GENERAL NOTE

Paragraph 1

1.197 The general rule, stated here, is that no period of entitlement to SSP can arise in any of the circumstances set out in para.2 or in such circumstances as are prescribed by regulations. The relevant regulation is reg.3 of the SSP (General) Regulations 1982 (SI 1982/894), which excludes prisoners and women entitled neither to SMP nor to maternity allowance who have reached a particular stage in their pregnancy or have been confined before reaching that stage.

Paragraph 2

1.198 This sets out the categories of persons for whom a period of entitlement does not arise for the purposes of para.1, and so who are excluded from the scope of SSP. The "relevant date" is the date on which a period of entitlement would otherwise begin were it not for the provisions of this Schedule (para.3). Thus the relevant date will usually be the first day of incapacity for work in the period of incapacity for work in question (s.153(2), but note the modifying provisions in (7), (8) and (9)). Those persons who are excluded from SSP by virtue of this paragraph may be able to claim incapacity benefit or, in the case of pregnant women, SMP or maternity allowance. The particular exclusions are:

(1) employees whose earnings are below the National Insurance lower earnings limit (sub-para.2(c)). Note that if, irrespective of contractual entitlement, the employer pays nothing during the relevant period, then the exclusion in sub-para.(2)(c) does not come into play at all: *Seaton v Commissioners for HMRC* [2011] UKUT 297 (TCC) at [29] and [31];

(2) claimants whose day of incapacity links back to a recent entitlement to incapacity benefit (sub-para.2(d)). But note also para.5A, which ensures that employees who cannot return to incapacity benefit as they are now over pensionable age, but who would have returned to IB rather than becoming entitled to SSP had they been under pensionable age, are now entitled to SSP;

(3) employees who have yet to start work under the contract of service (sub-para.2(f), but note the linking rule in para.6);

(4) employees who are subject to a stoppage of work due to a trade dispute at their place of employment (sub-para.2(g), but note the exception in para.7);

(5) employees who are or have been pregnant and where the relevant date falls within the disqualifying period for persons entitled to SMP or maternity allowance (sub-para.2(h), but note the exception in para.8); and

(6) employees who had entitlement to ESA in the previous 85 days (sub-para.(dd)).

In addition, under the original para.(2)(b), employees with a contract of service for a specified period of not more than three months were excluded from entitlement to SSP. This exclusion was repealed by the Fixed-term Employees (Prevention of Less Favourable Treatment) Regulations 2002 (SI 2002/2034) as from October 1, 2002. The effect of this amendment was considered by Lewison J in *Commissioners for HMRC v Thorn Baker Ltd* [2006] EWHC 2190 (Ch), who held that the 2002 Regulations had no impact on employees working under fixed-term contracts who were agency workers. The effect of that decision was that SSP was not payable to agency workers whose contract with the agency was for a specified period of three months or less. The Court of Appeal dismissed HMRC's appeal ([2007]

(1992 c.4 Sch.11)

EWCA Civ 626). However, the 2002 Regulations were then amended by the Fixed-term Employees (Prevention of Less Favourable Treatment) (Amendment) Regulations 2008 (SI 2008/2776) to enable agency workers with contracts of three months or less to have the same access to SSP as other workers.

Paragraph 7
The effect of the wording of this exception is that if the employee has at some time before the relevant date had a direct interest in the trade dispute, he or she cannot take advantage of this provision and so is caught by the exclusion in sub-para.2(g): see *R(SSP)1/86*.

1.199

Section 160   SCHEDULE 12

RELATIONSHIP OF STATUTORY SICK PAY WITH BENEFITS
AND OTHER PAYMENTS, ETC.

The general principle

1.—Any day which—
   (a) is a day of incapacity for work in relation to any contract of service; and
   (b) falls within a period of entitlement (whether or not it is also a qualifying day);
shall not be treated for the purposes of this Act as a day of incapacity for work for the purposes of determining whether a period is [² . . .] [¹ a period of incapacity for work for the purposes of incapacity benefit].

1.200

Contractual remuneration

2.—(1) Subject to sub-paragraphs (2) and (3) below, any entitlement to statutory sick pay shall not affect any right of an employee in relation to remuneration under any contract of service ("contractual remuneration").
   (2) Subject to sub-para.(3) below—
   (a) any contractual remuneration paid to an employee by an employer of his in respect of a day of incapacity for work shall go towards discharging any liability of that employer to pay statutory sick pay to that employee in respect of that day; and
   (b) any statutory sick pay paid by an employer to an employee of his in respect of a day of incapacity for work shall go towards discharging any liability of that employer to pay contractual remuneration to that employee in respect of that day.
   (3) Regulations may make provision as to payments which are, and those which are not, to be treated as contractual remuneration for the purposes of sub-paragraph (1) or (2) above.

1.201

[¹*Incapacity benefit*

3.—(1) This paragraph and paragraph 4 below have effect to exclude, where a period of entitlement as between an employee and an employer of his comes to an end, the provisions by virtue of which short-term incapacity benefit is not paid for the first three days.
   (2) If the first day immediately following the day on which the period of entitlement came to an end—
   (a) is a day of incapacity for work in relation to that employee; and
   (b) is not a day in relation to which paragraph 1 above applies by reason of any entitlement as between the employee and another employer,
that day shall, except in prescribed cases, be or form part of a period of incapacity for work notwithstanding section 30C(1)(b) above (by virtue of which a period of incapacity for work must be at least 4 days long).
   (3) Where each of the first two consecutive days, or the first three consecutive days, following the day on which the period of entitlement came to an end is a day to which paragraph (a) and (b) of sub-paragraph (2) above apply, that sub-paragraph has effect in relation to the second day or, as the case may be, in relation to the second and third days, as it has effect in relation to the first.
   4.—(1) Where a period of entitlement as between an employee and an employer of his comes to an end, section 30A(3) above (exclusion of benefit for first three days of period) does not apply in relation to any day which—
   (a) is or forms part of a period of incapacity for work (whether by virtue of paragraph 3 above or otherwise); and
   (b) falls within the period of 57 days immediately following the day on which the period of entitlement came to an end.

1.202

Social Security Contributions and Benefits Act 1992

(2) Where sub-paragraph (1) above applies in relation to a day, section 30A(3) above does not apply in relation to any later day in the same period of incapacity for work.]

[¹*Incapacity benefit for widows and widowers*]

1.203 5.—Paragraph 1 above does not apply for the purpose of determining whether the conditions specified in section 40(3) or (4) or section 41(2) or (3) above are satisfied.]

Unemployability supplement

6.—Paragraph 1 above does not apply in relation to paragraph 3 of Schedule 7 to this Act and accordingly the references in paragraph 3 of that Schedule to a period of interruption of employment shall be construed as if the provisions re-enacted in this Part of this Act had not been enacted.

AMENDMENTS

1. Social Security (Incapacity for Work) Act 1994 s.11(1) and Sch.1 para.44 (April 13, 1995).
2. Jobseekers Act 1995 s.41(5) and Sch.3 para.1 (October 7, 1996).

GENERAL NOTE

Paragraph 1

1.204 No day which falls within a period of entitlement for the purposes of SSP (whether or not it is a qualifying day) can count as a day of incapacity for the purposes of establishing entitlement to incapacity benefit.

Paragraphs 3 and 4

1.205 These paragraphs assist certain persons, not caught by para.1, who have days of incapacity subsequent to the end of a period of entitlement, to qualify for incapacity benefit by not applying the normal rules, e.g. on waiting days. See further, SSP (General) Regulations 1982 (SI 1982/894) reg.12.

Section 168 SCHEDULE 13

RELATIONSHIP OF STATUTORY MATERNITY PAY WITH BENEFITS AND OTHER PAYMENTS, ETC.

The general principle

1.206 [²1.—Except as may be prescribed, a day which falls within the maternity pay period shall not be treated as a day of incapacity for work for the purposes of determining, for this Act, whether it forms part of a period of incapacity for work for the purposes of incapacity benefit.]

[¹*Incapacity benefit*

2.—(1) Regulations may provide that in prescribed circumstances a day which falls within the maternity pay period shall be treated as a day of incapacity for work for the purpose of determining entitlement to the higher rate of short-term incapacity benefit or to long-term incapacity benefit.

(2) Regulations may provide that an amount equal to a woman's statutory maternity pay for a period shall be deducted from any such benefit in respect of the same period and a woman shall be entitled to such benefit only if there is a balance after the deduction and, if there is such a balance, at a weekly rate equal to it.]

Contractual remuneration

1.207 3.—(1) Subject to sub-paragraphs (2) and (3) below, any entitlement to statutory maternity pay shall not affect any right of a woman in relation to remuneration under any contract of service ("contractual remuneration").

(2) Subject to sub-paragraph (3) below—
  (a) any contractual remuneration paid to a woman by an employer of hers in respect of a week in the maternity pay period shall go towards discharging any liability of that employer to pay statutory maternity pay to her in respect of that week; and
  (b) any statutory maternity pay paid by an employer to a woman who is an employee of his in respect of a week in the maternity pay period shall go towards discharging any liability of that employer to pay contractual remuneration to her in respect of that week.
[³(2A) In sub-paragraph (2) "week" means a period of seven days beginning with the day of the week on which the maternity pay period begins.]
(3) Regulations may make provision as to payments which are, and those which are not, to be treated as contractual remuneration for the purposes of sub-paragraphs (1) and (2) above.

AMENDMENTS

1. Social Security (Incapacity for Work) Act 1994 s.11(1) and Sch.1 para.45(3) (April 6, 1995).
2. Jobseekers Act 1995 s.41(4) and Sch.2 para.37 (October 7, 1996).
3. Work and Families Act 2006 s.11 and Sch.1 para.23 (October 1, 2006).

GENERAL NOTE

For a FTT decision from the Tax Chamber ruling that contractual payments in lieu of notice (PILON) had to be set off against SMP due to the employee, see *Ladiverova v Commissioners for HMRC and Chokdee Ltd* [2016] UKFTT 0244 (TC). 1.208

Social Security Administration Act 1992

(1992 c.5)

SECTIONS REPRODUCED

PART I

CLAIMS FOR PAYMENTS AND GENERAL ADMINISTRATION OF BENEFIT

Child benefit

13A.   Election not to receive child benefit 1.209

Statutory sick pay

14.   Duties of employees, etc. in relation to statutory sick pay

Statutory maternity pay

15.   Duties of women etc. in relation to statutory maternity pay

PART III

OVERPAYMENTS AND ADJUSTMENTS OF BENEFIT

Misrepresentation etc

71. Overpayments—general

Social Security Administration Act 1992

PART VI

ENFORCEMENT

113A. Statutory sick pay and statutory maternity pay: breach of regulations
113B. Statutory sick pay and statutory maternity pay: fraud and negligence

PART VII

INFORMATION

Information held by tax authorities

122AA. Disclosure of contributions etc. information by [Her Majesty's Revenue and Customs]

Statutory sick pay and other benefits

129. Disclosure by Secretary of State for purpose of determination of period of entitlement to statutory sick pay
130. Duties of employers—statutory sick pay and claims for other benefits

Statutory maternity pay and other benefits

131. Disclosure by Secretary of State for purpose of determination of period of entitlement to statutory maternity pay
132. Duties of employers—statutory maternity pay and claims for other benefits

PART I

CLAIMS FOR AND PAYMENTS AND GENERAL ADMINISTRATION OF BENEFIT

Child benefit

[¹ **Election not to receive child benefit**

1.210   **13A.**—(1) A person ("P") who is entitled to child benefit in respect of one or more children may elect for all payments of the benefit to which P is entitled not to be made.

(2) An election may be made only if P reasonably expects that, in the absence of the election, P or another person would be liable to a high income child benefit charge in respect of the payments to which the election relates made for weeks in the first tax year.

(3) An election has effect in relation to payments made for weeks beginning after the election is made.

(4) But where entitlement to child benefit is backdated, an election may have effect in relation to payments for weeks beginning in the period of three months ending immediately before the claim for the benefit was made.

(5) An election may be revoked.

(6) A revocation has effect in relation to payments made for weeks beginning after the revocation is made.

(7) But if—
(a) P makes an election which results in all payments, in respect of child benefit, to which P is entitled for one or more weeks in a tax year not being paid, and
(b) had no election been made, neither P nor any other person would have been liable to a high income child benefit charge in relation to the payments,

P may, no later than two years after the end of the tax year, revoke the election so far as it relates to the payments.

(8) Subsections (2) to (7) are subject to directions under subsection (9).

(9) The Commissioners for Her Majesty's Revenue and Customs may give directions as to—
(a) the form of elections and revocations under this section, the manner in which they are to be made and the time at which they are to be treated as made, and
(b) the circumstances in which, if child benefit is not being paid to a person at the full rate or the Commissioners are satisfied that there are doubts as to a person's entitlement to child benefit for a child, an election or revocation is not to have effect or its effect is to be postponed.

(10) For the purposes of this section—

"child" includes a qualifying young person;

"first tax year", in relation to an election, means the tax year in which the first week beginning after the election is made falls;

"week" means a period of 7 days beginning with a Monday; and a week is in a tax year if (and only if) the Monday with which it begins is in the tax year.]

AMENDMENT

1. Finance Act 2012 Sch.1 para.3 (July 17, 2012).

GENERAL NOTE

See the note to SSCBA s.143 about the imposition from 2013/14 of the High Income Child Benefit Charge. This provision was introduced so that high earners who will no longer receive any economic benefit from receiving child benefit can elect not to receive the benefit. But note that this provision allows the election to be revoked if, with the benefit of hindsight, some economic benefit would have been received from a claim. The wording of the provision suggests that the election is not to receive payment. It is not clear whether it is therefore necessary for someone to claim the benefit and then exercise the election in order to protect this prospective right. 1.211

Statutory Sick Pay

Duties of employees, etc. in relation to statutory sick pay

14.—(1) Any employee who claims to be entitled to statutory sick pay from his employer shall, if so required by his employer, provide such information as may reasonably be required for the purpose of determining the duration of the period of entitlement in question or whether a period of entitlement exists as between them. 1.212

(2) The Secretary of State may by regulations [¹ made with the concurrence of the Inland Revenue] direct—

(a) that medical information required under subsection (1) above shall, in such cases as may be prescribed, be provided in a prescribed form;
(b) that an employee shall not be required under subsection (1) above to provide medical information in respect of such days as may be prescribed in a period of incapacity for work.

(3) Where an employee asks an employer of his to provide him with a written statement, in respect of a period before the request is made, of one or more of the following—
(a) the days within that period which the employer regards as days in respect of which he is liable to pay statutory sick pay to that employee;
(b) the reasons why the employer does not so regard the other days in that period;
(c) the employer's opinion as to the amount of statutory sick pay to which the employee is entitled in respect of each of those days,
the employer shall, to the extent to which the request was reasonable, comply with it within a reasonable time.

AMENDMENT

1. Social Security Contributions (Transfer of Functions, etc.) Act 1999 s.2 and Sch.3 para.42 (April 1, 1999).

Statutory maternity pay

Duties of women, etc. in relation to statutory maternity pay

15.—(1) A woman shall provide the person who is liable to pay her statutory maternity pay—
(a) with evidence as to her pregnancy and the expected date of confinement in such form and at such time as may be prescribed; and
(b) where she commences work after her confinement but within the maternity pay period, with such additional information as may be prescribed.

[¹(1A) Any regulations for the purposes of subsection (1) above must be made with the concurrence of the Inland Revenue.]

(2) Where a woman asks an employer or former employer of hers to provide her with a written statement, in respect of a period before the request is made, of one or more of the following—
(a) the weeks within that period which he regards as weeks in respect of which he is liable to pay statutory maternity pay to the woman;
(b) the reasons why he does not so regard the other weeks in that period; and
(c) his opinion as to the amount of statutory maternity pay to which the woman is entitled in respect of each of the weeks in respect of which he regards himself as liable to make a payment;
the employer or former employer shall, to the extent to which the request was reasonable, comply with it within a reasonable time.

AMENDMENT

1. Social Security Contributions (Transfer of Functions, etc.) Act 1999 s.2 and Sch.3 para.43 (April 1, 1999).

(1992 c.5 s.71)

Part III

Overpayments And Adjustments Of Benefit

Misrepresentation etc

Overpayments—general

71.—(1) Where it is determined that, whether fraudulently or otherwise, any person has misrepresented, or failed to disclose, any material fact and in consequence of the misrepresentation or failure–
  (a) a payment has been made in respect of a benefit to which this section applies; or
  (b) any sum recoverable by or on behalf of the Secretary of State in connection with any such payment has not been recovered,
the Secretary of State shall be entitled to recover the amount of any payment which he would not have made or any sum which he would have received but for the misrepresentation or failure to disclose.

(2) Where any such determination as is referred to in subsection (1) above is made, the person making the determination shall in the case of the Secretary of State or a First- tier Tribunal, and may in the case of the Upper Tribunal or court—
  (a) determine whether any, and if so what, amount is recoverable under that subsection by the Secretary of State, and
  (b) specify the period during which that amount was paid to the person concerned.

(3) An amount recoverable under subsection (1) above is in all cases recoverable from the person who misrepresented the fact or failed to disclose it.

(4) In relation to cases where payments of benefit to which this section applies have been credited to a bank account or other account under arrangements made with the agreement of the beneficiary or a person acting for him, circumstances may be prescribed in which the Secretary of State is to be entitled to recover any amount paid in excess of entitlement; but any such regulations shall not apply in relation to any payment unless before he agreed to the arrangements such notice of the effect of the regulations as may be prescribed was given in such manner as may be prescribed to the beneficiary or to a person acting for him.

(5) . . .

(5A) Except where regulations otherwise provide, an amount shall not be recoverable under subsection (1) or under regulations under subsection (4) above unless the determination in pursuance of which it was paid has been reversed or varied on an appeal or has been revised under section 9 or superseded under section 10 of the Social Security Act 1998.

(6) Regulations may provide—
  (a) that amounts recoverable under subsection (1) above or regulations under subsection (4) above shall be calculated or estimated in such manner and on such basis as may be prescribed;
  (b) for treating any amount paid to any person under an award which it is subsequently determined was not payable—
    (i) as properly paid; or

1.214

(ii) as paid on account of a payment which it is determined should be or should have been made,

and for reducing or withholding any arrears payable by virtue of the subsequent determination;

(c) for treating any amount paid to one person in respect of another as properly paid for any period for which it is not payable in cases where in consequence of a subsequent determination—

(i) the other person is himself entitled to a payment for that period; or

(ii) a third person is entitled in priority to the payee to a payment for that period in respect of the other person,

and for reducing or withholding any arrears payable for that period by virtue of the subsequent determination.

(7) [...]

(8) Where any amount paid other than an amount paid in respect of child benefit or guardian's allowance is recoverable under—

(a) subsection (1) above;
(b) regulations under subsection (4) above; or
(c) section 74 below,

it may, without prejudice to any other method of recovery, be recovered by deduction from prescribed benefits.

(9) [...]
(9A) [...]
(9B) [...]
(9C) [...]
(10) [...]
(10A) [...]
(11) This section applies to the following benefits—

(a) benefits as defined in section 122 of the Contributions and Benefits Act;

[...]

(f) child benefit.

(12) In this section, "couple" has the meaning given by section 137(1) of the Contributions and Benefits Act.

GENERAL NOTE

1.215   Section 71 of the Administration Act is a much amended and much litigated section. For a full commentary on the section, its amendments and the extensive case law see the detailed analysis in Vol.III of this work. The extracts included in this volume are of those parts of the section that apply specifically to the benefits administered by HMRC, namely child benefit and guardian's allowance. These benefits are included within the scope of the section by subs.(12). The regime for tax credit overpayments is entirely separate and is dealt with in the Tax Credits Act 2002. The extracts above do not refer to the many amendments to the section or the alternative wording operating for different benefits for different purposes, nor to provisions not relevant to the two benefits stated. Full details are in Vol. III. There were provisions amending this section in the Tax Credits Act 1999 and applying this section to those tax credits. However, the provisions were fully repealed by the 2002 Act and may now be regarded as entirely spent.

Note that subs.(8) expressly prevents overpayments of these benefits being collected by deduction from other benefits.

(1992 c.5 s.113A)

Part VI

Enforcement

[¹Statutory sick pay and statutory maternity pay: breach of regulations

113A.—(1) Where a person fails to produce any document or record, or provide any information, in accordance with—
(a) regulations under section 5(1)(i) and (5), so far as relating to statutory sick pay or statutory maternity pay,
(b) regulations under section 130 or 132, or
(c) regulations under section 153(5)(b) [² or 159B] of the Contributions and Benefits Act,
that person is liable to the penalties mentioned in subsection (2).

(2) The penalties are—
(a) a penalty not exceeding £300, and
(b) if the failure continues after a penalty is imposed under paragraph (a), a further penalty or penalties not exceeding £60 for each day on which the failure continues after the day on which the penalty under that paragraph was imposed (but excluding any day for which a penalty under this paragraph has already been imposed).

(3) Where a person fails to maintain a record in accordance with regulations under section 130 or 132 [² of this Act, or section 159B of the Contributions and Benefits Act], he is liable to a penalty not exceeding £3,000.

(4) No penalty may be imposed under subsection (1) at any time after the failure concerned has been remedied.

(5) But subsection (4) does not apply to the imposition of a penalty under subsection (2)(a) in respect of a failure to produce any document or record in accordance with regulations under section 130(5) or 132(4).

(6) Where, in the case of any employee, an employer refuses or repeatedly fails to make payments of statutory sick pay or statutory maternity pay in accordance with any regulations under section 5, the employer is liable to a penalty not exceeding £3,000.

(7) Section 118(2) of the Taxes Management Act 1970 (extra time for compliance etc) applies for the purposes of subsections (1), (3) and (6) as it applies for the purposes of that Act.

(8) Schedule 1 to the Employment Act 2002 (penalties relating to statutory paternity pay and statutory adoption pay: procedures and appeals) applies in relation to penalties imposed under this section (with the modifications set out in subsection (9)).

(9) That Schedule applies as if—
(a) references to a penalty under section 11 or 12 of that Act were to a penalty under this section,
(b) in paragraph 1(2), the reference to section 11(2)(a) of that Act were to subsection (2)(a) of this section, and
(c) the provisions of the Taxes Management Act 1970 having effect in relation to an appeal mentioned in paragraph 3(2) of that Schedule did not include section 50(9) of that Act.]

Amendments

1. National Insurance Contributions and Statutory Payments Act 2004 s.9(5) (April 6, 2005).
2. Coronavirus Act 2020 s.39(2) (March 25, 2020).

General Note

1.217 This provision brings in a compliance regime based on civil penalties, as with the administration of tax. Section 113A provides for civil penalties for failures to keep records, to produce records, to provide information or to pay either statutory sick pay or statutory maternity pay. The appeals procedures for such penalties are governed by Sch.1 to the Employment Act 2002 (see ss.113A(8) and (9)). Section 113B below is concerned with breaches by commission, and provides for penalties in cases of fraud or negligence which involve employers making incorrect statements or declarations, producing incorrect documents or records, making incorrect payments of statutory sick pay and statutory maternity pay and receiving incorrect advances of statutory maternity pay. HMRC has stated that penalties will be reserved for "serious situations such as where there has been a deliberate manipulation of the schemes, where a failure has continued after we have put the employer right and where the employer has failed to pay after the appeal period against a formal decision on liability" (*Regulatory Impact Assessment*, Annex E, para.7).

[¹Statutory sick pay and statutory maternity pay: fraud and negligence

1.218 **113B.**—(1) Where a person fraudulently or negligently—
   (a) makes any incorrect statement or declaration in connection with establishing entitlement to statutory sick pay or statutory maternity pay, or
   (b) produces any incorrect document or record or provides any incorrect information of a kind mentioned in—
      (i) regulations under section 5(1)(i) and (5), so far as relating to statutory sick pay or statutory maternity pay,
      (ii) regulations under section 130 or 132, or
      (iii) regulations under section 153(5)(b) [² or 159B] of the Contributions and Benefits Act,

he is liable to a penalty not exceeding £3,000.

(2) Where an employer fraudulently or negligently makes an incorrect payment of statutory sick pay or statutory maternity pay, he is liable to a penalty not exceeding £3,000.

[² (2A) Where an employer fraudulently or negligently receives a payment in pursuance of regulations under section 159B of the Contributions and Benefits Act (funding of employers' statutory sick pay liabilities in relation to coronavirus), the employer is liable to a penalty not exceeding £3,000.]

(3) Where an employer fraudulently or negligently receives an overpayment in pursuance of regulations under section 167 of the Contributions and Benefits Act (statutory maternity pay: advance payments to employers), he is liable to a penalty not exceeding £3,000.

(4) Schedule 1 to the Employment Act 2002 (penalties relating to statutory paternity pay and statutory adoption pay: procedures and appeals) applies in relation to penalties imposed under this section (with the modifications set out in subsection (5)).

(5) That Schedule applies as if—

(a) references to a penalty under section 11 or 12 of that Act were to a penalty under this section, and
(b) the provisions of the Taxes Management Act 1970 having effect in relation to an appeal mentioned in paragraph 3(2) of that Schedule did not include section 50(9) of that Act.]

AMENDMENTS

1. National Insurance Contributions and Statutory Payments Act 2004 s.9(5) (April 6, 2005).
2. Coronavirus Act 2020 s.39(3) (March 25, 2020).

PART VII

[¹INFORMATION

Information held by tax authorities

[¹Disclosure of contributions etc. information by [⁴ Her Majesty's Revenue and Customs]

122AA.—(1) No obligation as to secrecy imposed by statute or otherwise on [⁴ Revenue and Customs officials (within the meaning of section 18 of the Commissioners for Revenue and Customs Act 2005 (confidentiality)] shall prevent information held for the purposes of the functions of [⁴ Her Majesty's Revenue and Customs] in relation to contributions, statutory sick pay [², statutory maternity pay, [⁷ statutory paternity pay,] statutory adoption pay [⁶[⁸, statutory shared parental pay or statutory parental bereavement pay]] from being disclosed—
(a) to any of the authorities to which this paragraph applies, or any person authorised to exercise any function of that authority, for the purposes of the functions of that authority, or
(b) in a case where the disclosure is necessary for the purpose of giving effect to any agreement to which an order under section 179(1) below relates.
(2) The authorities to which subsection(1)(a) above applies are—
(a) the Health and Safety Executive,
(b) the Government Actuary's Department,
(c) the [⁵ Statistics Board], and
(d) the [³ Pensions Regulator.]

AMENDMENTS

1. Social Security Contributions (Transfer of Functions, etc.) Act 1999 s.6 and Sch.6 para.3 (April 1, 1999).
2. Employment Act 2002 s.53 and Sch.7 paras 8 and 13 (December 8, 2002).
3. Pensions Act 2004 s.319 and Sch.12 para.7 (April 6, 2005).
4. Commissioners for Revenue and Customs Act 2005 s.50(4) and Sch.4 para.46 (April 18, 2005).
5. Statistics and Registration Service Act 2007 s.46 and Sch.2 para.5 (April 1, 2008).
6. Children and Families Act 2014 s.126(1) and Sch.7 paras 23 and 25(b) (December 1, 2014).

7. Children and Families Act 2014 s.126(1) and Sch.7 paras 23 and 25(a) (April 5, 2015).
8. Parental Bereavement (Leave and Pay) Act 2018 s.1(c) and Sch. para.16 (January 18, 2020).

Statutory sick pay and other benefits

Disclosure by Secretary of State for purpose of determination of period of entitlement to statutory sick pay

1.221   **129.**—Where the Secretary of State considers that it is reasonable for information held by him to be disclosed to an employer, for the purpose of enabling that employer to determine the duration of a period of entitlement under Part XI of the Contributions and Benefits Act in respect of an employee, or whether such a period exists, he may disclose the information to that employer.

Duties of employers—statutory sick pay and claims for other benefits

1.222   **130.**—(1) Regulations may make provision requiring an employer, in a case falling within subsection (3) below to furnish information in connection with the making, by a person who is, or has been, an employee of that employer, of a claim for—
[⁶ (za) universal credit;]
  [¹(a) short-term incapacity benefit;]
  (b) a maternity allowance;
  [¹(c) long-term incapacity benefit;]
  (d) industrial injuries benefit; [³ . . .]
  (e) [³ . . .].
  [⁵(f) an employment and support allowance.]
  (2) Regulations under this section shall prescribe—
  (a) the kind of information to be furnished in accordance with the regulations;
  (b) the person to whom information of the prescribed kind is to be furnished; and
  (c) the manner in which, and period within which, it is to be furnished.
  (3) The cases are—
  (a) where, by virtue of paragraph 2 of Schedule 11 to the Contributions and Benefits Act or of regulations made under paragraph 1 of that Schedule, a period of entitlement does not arise in relation to a period of incapacity for work;
  (b) where a period of entitlement has come to an end but the period of incapacity for work which was running immediately before the period of entitlement came to an end continues; and
  (c) where a period of entitlement has not come to an end but, on the assumption that—
    (i) the period of incapacity for work in question continues to run for a prescribed period; and
    (ii) there is no material change in circumstances;
  the period of entitlement will have ended on or before the end of the prescribed period.

(4) Regulations [²made with the concurrence of the Inland Revenue]—
(a) may require employers to maintain such records in connection with statutory sick pay as may be prescribed;
(b) may provide for—
   (i) any person claiming to be entitled to statutory sick pay; or
   (ii) any other person who is a party to proceedings arising under Part XI of the Contributions and Benefits Act;
   to furnish to the Secretary of State [² or the Inland Revenue (as the regulations may require)], within a prescribed period, any information required for the determination of any question arising in connection there with; and
(c) may require employers who have made payments of statutory sick pay to furnish to the Secretary of State [² or the Inland Revenue (as the regulations may require)] such documents and information, at such times, as may be prescribed.

[⁴(5) Regulations made with the concurrence of the Inland Revenue may require employers to produce wages sheets and other documents and records to officers of the Inland Revenue, within a prescribed period, for the purpose of enabling them to satisfy themselves that statutory sick pay has been paid, and is being paid, in accordance with regulations under section 5 above, to employees or former employees who are entitled to it.]

AMENDMENTS

1. Social Security (Incapacity for Work) Act 1994 s.11(1) and Sch.1 para.49 (April 6, 1995).
2. Social Security Contributions (Transfer of Functions, etc.) Act 1999 s.6 and Sch.6 para.3 (April 1, 1999).
3. Welfare Reform and Pensions Act 1999 s.88 and Sch.13 Pt IV (April 6, 2001).
4. National Insurance Contributions and Statutory Payments Act 2004 s.9(2) (January 1, 2005).
5. Welfare Reform Act 2007 s.28(1) and Sch.3 para.10(1) and (19) (October 27, 2008).
6. Welfare Reform Act 2012 s.31 and Sch.2 paras 3 and 20 (April 29, 2013).

Statutory maternity pay and other benefits

Disclosure by Secretary of State for purpose of determination of period of entitlement to statutory maternity pay

131.—Where the Secretary of State considers that it is reasonable for information held by him to be disclosed to a person liable to make payments of statutory maternity pay for the purpose of enabling that person to determine—
(a) whether a maternity pay period exists in relation to a woman who is or has been an employee of his; and
(b) if it does, the date of its commencement and the weeks in it in respect of which he may be liable to pay statutory maternity pay,
he may disclose the information to that person.

Social Security Administration Act 1992

Duties of employers—statutory maternity pay and claims for other benefits

132.—(1) Regulations may make provision requiring an employer in prescribed circumstances to furnish information in connection with the making of a claim by a woman who is or has been his employee for—
[6 (za) universal credit;]
    (a) a maternity allowance;
[5(aa) an employment and support allowance.]
    (b) [1short-term incapacity benefit;]
    (c) [1long-term incapacity benefit under section 30A], 40 or 41 of the Contributions and Benefits Act; [3...]
    (d) [3...].
(2) Regulations under this section shall prescribe—
    (a) the kind of information to be furnished in accordance with the regulations;
    (b) the person to whom information of the prescribed kind is to be furnished; and
    (c) the manner in which, and period within which, it is to be furnished.
(3) Regulations [2made with the concurrence of the Inland Revenue]—
    (a) may require employers to maintain such records in connection with statutory maternity pay as may be prescribed;
    (b) may provide for—
        (i) any woman claiming to be entitled to statutory maternity pay; or
        (ii) any other person who is a party to proceedings arising under Part XII of the Contributions and Benefits Act,
    to furnish to the Secretary of State [2or the Inland Revenue (as the regulations may require)], within a prescribed period, any information required for the determination of any question arising in connection there with; and
    (c) may require persons who have made payments of statutory maternity pay to furnish to the Secretary of State [2or the Inland Revenue (as the regulations may require)] such documents and information, at such time, as may be prescribed.
[4(4) Regulations made with the concurrence of the Inland Revenue may require employers to produce wages sheets and other documents and records to officers of the Inland Revenue, within a prescribed period, for the purpose of enabling them to satisfy themselves that statutory maternity pay has been paid, and is being paid, in accordance with regulations under section 5 above, to employees or former employees who are entitled to it.]

AMENDMENTS

1. Social Security (Incapacity for Work) Act 1994 s.11(1) and Sch.1 para.50 (April 6, 1995).
2. Social Security Contributions (Transfer of Functions, etc.) Act 1999 s.6 and Sch.1 para.27 (April 1, 1999).
3. Welfare Reform and Pensions Act 1999 s.88 and Sch.13 Pt IV (April 6, 2001).
4. National Insurance Contributions and Statutory Payments Act 2004 s.9(3) (January 1, 2005).
5. Welfare Reform Act 2007 s.28(1) and Sch.3 para.10(1) and (20) (October 27, 2008).
6. Welfare Reform Act 2012 s.31 and Sch.2 paras 3 and 21 (April 29, 2013).

(1998 c.14)

Social Security Act 1998

(1998 c.14)

An Act to make provision as to the making of decisions and the determination of appeals under enactments relating to social security, child support, vaccine damage payments and war pensions; to make further provision with respect to social security; and for connected purposes.

1.225

Appeal to [2First-tier Tribunal]

12.—(1) [¹ . . .]
(2) [¹ . . .]
(3) [¹ . . .]
(4) [¹ . . .]
(5) [¹ . . .]
(6) [¹ . . .]
(7) Regulations may [³ . . .]
[³ (a) make provision as to the manner in which, and the time within which, appeals are to be brought;
(b provide that, where in accordance with regulations under subsection (3A) there is no right of appeal against a decision, any purported appeal may be treated as an application for revision under section 9.]
(8) In deciding [¹ a child trust fund appeal], [² the First-tier Tribunal]—
(a) [¹ . . .]
(b) shall not take into account any circumstances not obtaining at the time when the decision appealed against was made.
(9) [¹ . . .].

1.226

AMENDMENTS

1. Child Trust Funds (Non-tax Appeals) Regulations 2005 (SI 2005/191) reg.6 (February 25, 2005).
2. Transfer of Tribunal Functions Order 2008 (SI 2008/2833) art.9(1) and Sch.3 para.149 (November 3, 2008).
3. Welfare Reform Act 2012 s.102(4) (February 25, 2013).

GENERAL NOTE

This is the version of s.12 of the 1998 Act as modified for the purposes of child trust fund appeals.

1.227

Social Security Contributions (Transfer of Functions, etc.) Act 1999

(1999 c.2)

An Act to transfer from the Secretary of State to the Commissioners of Inland Revenue or the Treasury certain functions relating to national insurance contributions, the National Insurance Fund, statutory sick pay, statutory maternity

1.228

Social Security Contributions (Transfer of Functions, etc.) Act 1999

pay or pension schemes and certain associated functions relating to benefits; to enable functions relating to any of those matters in respect of Northern Ireland to be transferred to the Secretary of State, the Commissioners of Inland Revenue or the Treasury; to make further provision, in connection with the functions transferred, as to the powers of the Commissioners of Inland Revenue, the making of decisions and appeals; to provide that rebates payable in respect of members of money purchase contracted-out pension schemes are to be payable out of the National Insurance Fund; and for connected purposes.

ARRANGEMENT OF SECTIONS

PART II

DECISIONS AND APPEALS

1.229
8. Decisions by officers of Board
9. Regulations with respect to decisions
10. Decisions varying or superseding earlier decisions
11. Appeals against decisions of Board
12. Exercise of right of appeal
13. Regulations with respect to appeals
14. Matters arising as respects decisions
15. (*Omitted*)
16. (*Omitted*)
17. Arrangements for discharge of decision-making functions
18. Amendments relating to decisions and appeals
19. Interpretation of Part II

PART III

MISCELLANEOUS AND SUPPLEMENTAL

27. Interpretation

PART II

DECISIONS AND APPEALS

Decisions by officers of Board

1.230
8.—(1) Subject to the provisions of this Part, it shall be for an officer of the Board—
  (a) to decide whether for the purposes of Parts I to V of the Social Security Contributions and Benefits Act 1992 a person is or was an earner and, if so, the category of earners in which he is or was to be included;

136

(b) to decide whether a person is or was employed in employed earner's employment for the purposes of Part V of the Social Security Contributions and Benefits Act 1992 (industrial injuries);
(c) to decide whether a person is or was liable to pay contributions of any particular class and, if so, the amount that he is or was liable to pay,
(d) to decide whether a person is or was entitled to pay contributions of any particular class that he is or was not liable to pay and, if so, the amount that he is or was entitled to pay,
(e) to decide whether contributions of a particular class have been paid in respect of any period,
[5 (ea) to decide whether a person is or was entitled to make a deduction under section 4 of the National Insurance Contributions Act 2014 (deductions etc of employment allowance) and, if so, the amount the person is or was entitled to deduct,
(eb) to decide whether a person is or was entitled to a repayment under that section and, if so, the amount of the repayment,]
(f) subject to and in accordance with regulations made for the purposes of this paragraph by the Secretary of State with the concurrence of the Board, to decide any issue arising as to, or in connection with, entitlement to statutory sick pay, [4, statutory maternity pay, [7 statutory paternity pay,] statutory adoption pay]] [6 [9, statutory shared parental pay or statutory parental bereavement pay]],
(g) to make any other decision that falls to be made [4under Parts XI to [9 12ZD]] of the Social Security Contributions and Benefits Act 1992 (statutory sick pay, statutory maternity pay, [7 statutory paternity pay,] statutory adoption pay]] [6 [9, statutory shared parental pay and statutory parental bereavement pay]],
[4(ga) to make any decision that falls to be made under regulations under section 7 of the Employment Act 2002 (funding of employers' liabilities to make payments of [7 statutory paternity pay,] statutory adoption pay]] [6 [9, statutory shared parental pay or statutory parental bereavement pay];];
(h) to decide any question as to the issue and content of a notice under subsection (2) of section 121C of the Social Security Administration Act 1992 (liability of directors etc. for company's contributions);
(i) to decide any issue arising under section 27 of the Jobseekers Act 1995 (employment of long-term unemployed: deductions by employers), or under any provision of regulations under that section, as to—
  (i) whether a person is or was an employee or employer of another;
  (ii) whether an employer is or was entitled to make any deduction from his contributions payments in accordance with regulations under section 27 of that Act;
  (iii) whether a payment falls to be made to an employer in accordance with those regulations;
  (iv) the amount that falls to be so deducted or paid; or
  (v) whether two or more employers are, by virtue of regulations under section 27 of that Act, to be treated as one,
[3(ia) to decide whether to give or withdraw an approval for the purposes of para.3B(1)(b) of Sch.1 to the Social Security Contributions and Benefits Act 1992,];
(j) [2 . . .];

(k) to decide whether a person is liable to a penalty under—
  (i) paragraph 7A(2) or 7B(2)(h) of Schedule 1 to the Social Security Contributions and Benefits Act 1992; or
  (ii) section 113(1)(a) of the Social Security Administration Act 1992;
(l) to decide the [2 ...] penalty payable under any of the provisions mentioned in [2paragraph (k)] above; and
(m) to decide such issues relating to contributions, other than the issues specified in paragraphs (a) to (l) above or in paragraphs 16 and 17 of Schedule 3 to the Social Security Act 1998, as may be prescribed by regulations made by the Board.

[8 (1A) No decision in respect of Class 2 contributions under section 11(2) of the Social Security Contributions and Benefits Act 1992 may be made under subsection (1) in relation to an issue specified in paragraph (c) or (e) of that subsection if the person to whom the decision would relate—
  (a) has appealed under Part 5 of the Taxes Management Act 1970 in relation to that issue,
  (b) can appeal under that Part in relation to that issue, or
  (c) might in the future, without the agreement of Her Majesty's Revenue and Customs or permission of the tribunal, be able to appeal under that Part in relation to that issue.]

(2) Subsection (1)(c) and (e) above do not include any decision relating to Class 4 contributions other than a decision falling to be made—
  (a) under subsection (1) of section 17 of the Social Security Contributions and Benefits Act 1992 as to whether by regulations under that subsection a person is or was excepted from liability for Class 4 contributions, or his liability is or was deferred; or
  (b) under regulations made by virtue of subsection (3) or (4) of that section or section 18 of that Act.

(3) Subsection (1)(g) above does not include—
  (a) any decision as to the making of subordinate legislation; or
  (b) any decision as to whether the liability to pay statutory sick pay [4, statutory maternity pay, [7 statutory paternity pay,] statutory adoption pay]] [6 [9, statutory shared parental pay or statutory parental bereavement pay]] is a liability of the Board rather than the employer.

(4) [1 ...].

AMENDMENTS

1. Welfare Reform and Pensions Act 1999 s.88 and Sch.13 Pt VI (April 6, 2000).
2. Child Support, Pensions and Social Security Act 2000 ss.76(6) and 85 and Sch.9 Pt VIII (July 28, 2000).
3. Child Support, Pensions and Social Security Act 2000 ss.77(5) (July 28, 2000).
4. Employment Act 2002 ss.9(2) and (3) (December 8, 2002).
5. National Insurance Contributions Act 2014 s.6(1) (April 6, 2014).
6. Children and Families Act 2014 s.126(1) Sch.7 paras 44 and 45(1), (2)(b) (c) and (e) (December 1, 2014).
7. Children and Families Act 2014 s.126(1) Sch.7 paras 44 and 45(1)(2)(a) and (d) (April 5, 2015).
8. National Insurance Contributions Act 2015 s.2 and Sch.1 para.25 (April 6, 2015).
9. Parental Bereavement (Leave and Pay) Act 2018 s.1(c) and Sch. para.30 (January 18, 2020).

DEFINITIONS

"Board"—see s.27.
"contributions"—see s.27.
"employed earner"—see SSCBA 1992 s.2(1)(a).
"employment"—see SSCBA 1992 s.122.

GENERAL NOTE

This section provides for HMRC to take decisions on a range of specified questions in relation to SMP, SSP, NICs, employment status and related matters. The extensive list of such decisions, set out in subs.(1), covers much of the former jurisdiction of the Secretary of State for Social Security under SSAA 1992 s.17(1), with the addition of some further matters. For example, the function of making decisions as to entitlement to SMP or SSP (subs.(1)(f)) was traditionally a function of an adjudication officer (SSAA 1992 s.20(3)) but was then transferred to the Secretary of State (SSA 1998 s.8(1)(d)) before now moving to an officer of the Board (now HMRC). This is one of the areas in which the power to make regulations still rests with the Secretary of State (albeit with the agreement of HMRC), as the policy responsibility for these benefits is retained by the DWP (see General Note to s.2). However, in terms of decision-making on matters of entitlement to SSP (and, by analogy, to SMP, SPP and SAP), HMRC has an "exclusive and exhaustive jurisdiction" (per Mr Recorder Luba QC in *Taylor Gordon & Co Ltd v Timmons* ([2004] I.R.L.R. 180 at [43]). Thus an employment tribunal has no jurisdiction under the Employment Rights Act 1996 to entertain an employee's complaint that SSP has not been paid.

A First-tier Tribunal in the Tax Chamber has ruled that the power "to decide any issue arising as to, or in connection with, entitlement to ... statutory maternity pay" in s.8(1)(f) means that the Board's officers, and on appeal the FTT, have jurisdiction to determine the extent of the actual payment of SMP in addition to the amount of the entitlement: see *Denham v HMRC and HT Personnel Ltd* [2016] UKFTT 668 (TC) at [32]–[43].

For the relevant regulation-making powers, see s.9 and for provision for variation and supersession of decisions made under s.8, see s.10. From April 6, 2009 appeals go to the First-tier Tribunal Tax Chamber. One result of the tribunal reforms introduced then is that a number of judges now sit both to hear tax appeals and appeals under this section as well as appeals on social security matters in the Social Entitlement Chamber.

For the procedure to be adopted where a national insurance contributions issue arises in relation to a benefit appeal, see *Secretary of State for Work and Pensions v TB and HMRC (RP)* [2010] UKUT 88 (AAC), [2010] AACR 38.

Section 126 of the Welfare Reform Act 2012 provides legislative powers to transfer any tax credit function exercised by the Treasury or HMRC to the Secretary of State, or for any such function to be exercised jointly. The policy is to provide that during the staged transfer of claimants from tax credits to universal credits the administration is transferred across from HMRC to the DWP. This is being done in part by transferring (and in some cases transferring back) the relevant staff from HMRC to DWP.

Regulations with respect to decisions

9.—(1) Subject to the provisions of this Part and of the Social Security Administration Act 1992, provision may be made by the Board by regulations as to the making by their officer of any decision under or in connection with the Social Security Contributions and Benefits Act 1992, the Social Security Administration Act 1992 or the Jobseekers Act 1995 which falls to be made by such an officer.

Social Security Contributions (Transfer of Functions, etc.) Act 1999

(2) Where it appears to an officer of the Board that a matter before him involves a question of fact requiring special expertise, he may direct that in dealing with that matter he shall have the assistance of one or more experts.

(3) In subsection (2) above "expert" means a person appearing to the officer of the Board to have knowledge or experience which would be relevant in determining the question of fact requiring special expertise.

DEFINITIONS

"Board"—see s.27.
"expert"—see subs.(3).

GENERAL NOTE

1.233 Subsection (1), modelled on SSA 1998 s.11, provides for HMRC to make regulations governing procedural matters relating to decisions made by HMRC staff under s.8.

Subsections (2) and (3) enable HMRC to seek specialist advice before making a decision (e.g. as to medical evidence relevant to a claim for SSP). In the first instance SMP or SSP decisions are made by the employer, and only referred for a formal decision where the parties are unable to reach agreement. There are only about 500 referrals each year concerning SMP or SSP; most of these cases concern the linking or employment rules, with perhaps no more than 50 involving a medical issue (per Baroness Hollis of Heigham, Parliamentary Under-Secretary of State for Social Security, *Hansard*, H.L. Debs. Vol.596, col.322 (January 14, 1999)) For one such (rare) case that went to appeal, see for example *Flemington Care Home v Revenue and Customs* [2017] UKFTT 300 (TC), in which the FTT (Tax) dismissed the employer's appeal against the HMRC decision, taken after referral to doctors under s.9, that the appellant (who had a foot injury but had allegedly been seen dancing at a concert) was entitled to SSP.

Decisions varying or superseding earlier decisions

1.234 **10.**—(1) [¹ Subject to subsection (2A) below,] the Board may by regulations make provision—

(a) for any decision of an officer of the Board under section 8 of this Act (including a decision superseding an earlier decision) to be varied either within the prescribed period or in prescribed cases or circumstances;

(b) for any such decision to be superseded, in prescribed circumstances, by a subsequent decision made by an officer of the Board; and

(c) for any such decision as confirmed or varied by the [² First-tier Tribunal or Upper Tribunal] on appeal to be superseded, in the event of a material change of circumstances since the decision was made, by a subsequent decision made by an officer of the Board.

(2) The date as from which—

(a) any variation of a decision, or

(b) any decision superseding an earlier decision,

is to take effect shall be determined in accordance with the regulations.

[¹(2A) The decisions in relation to which provision may be made by regulations under this section shall not include decisions falling within section 8(1)(ia) above.]

(3) In this section "prescribed" means prescribed by regulations under this section.

(1999 c.2 s.10)

AMENDMENTS

1. Child Support, Pensions and Social Security Act 2000 s.77(6) (July 28, 2000).
2. Transfer of Tribunal Functions and Revenue and Customs Appeals Order 2009 (SI 2009/56) art.3 and Sch.1 (April 1, 2009).

DEFINITIONS

"Board"—s.27.
"prescribed"—subs.(3).

GENERAL NOTE

This enabling provision reflects similar powers, governing Secretary of State decisions, contained in SSA 1998 ss.9 (revision) and 10 (supersession). 1.235

Appeals against decisions of Board

11.—(1) This section applies to any decision of an officer of the Board under section 8 of this Act or under regulations made by virtue of section 10(1)(b) or (c) of this Act (whether as originally made or as varied under regulations made by virtue of section 10(1)(a) of this Act). 1.236

(2) In the case of a decision to which this section applies—
  (a) if it relates to a person's entitlement to statutory sick pay [¹, statutory maternity pay, [⁴ statutory paternity pay,] statutory adoption pay]] [³ [⁵, statutory shared parental pay or statutory parental bereavement pay]] the employee and employer concerned shall each have a right to appeal to the [² tribunal], and
  (b) in any other case, the person in respect of whom the decision is made and such other person as may be prescribed shall have a right to appeal to the [² tribunal].

(3) In subsection (2)(b) above "prescribed" means prescribed by the Board by regulations.

(4) This section has effect subject to section 121D of the Social Security Administration Act 1992 (appeals in relation to personal liability notices).

AMENDMENTS

1. Employment Act 2002 s.9(4) (December 8, 2002).
2. Transfer of Tribunal Functions and Revenue and Customs Appeals Order 2009 (SI 2009/56) art.3 and Sch.1 (April 1, 2009).
3. Children and Families Act 2014 s.126(1) Sch.7 paras 44, 46(b) (December 1, 2014).
4. Children and Families Act 2014 s.126(1) Sch.7 paras 44, 46(a) (April 5, 2015).
5. Parental Bereavement (Leave and Pay) Act 2018 s.1(c) and Sch. para.31 (January 18, 2020).

DEFINITIONS

"Board"—see s.27.
"prescribed"—see subs.(3)
"tribunal"—see s.19

GENERAL NOTE

This provides a right of appeal to the First-tier Tribunal. It will normally go to the Tax Chamber (but see First-tier Tribunal and Upper Tribunal (Chambers) 1.237

Social Security Contributions (Transfer of Functions, etc.) Act 1999

(Amendment No.3) Order 2009 (SI 2009/1590) with effect from September 1, 2009). Tribunal reforms allow this to be dealt with by a judge familiar with both tax law and social security law, so allowing consideration to be given to the problem that a s.8 appeal may be considered while removed from its social security context. Both employees and employers have a right of appeal in relation to decisions on SMP and SSP entitlement (subs.(2)(a)). Note also that subs.(2)(b) contains a broader regulation-making power to give interested parties in other decisions a right of appeal. This provision only provides for additional rights of appeal; unlike SSA 1998 s.12(2), there is no power to prescribe in regulations for cases in which there is to be no right of appeal.

Exercise of right of appeal

1.238   **12.**—(1) Any appeal against a decision must be brought by a notice of appeal in writing given within 30 days after the date on which notice of the decision was issued.

(2) The notice of appeal shall be given to the officer of the Board by whom notice of the decision was given.

[¹ (3) The notice of appeal shall specify the grounds of appeal.]

(4) [¹. . .]

(5) [¹. . .]

AMENDMENT

1. Transfer of Tribunal Functions and Revenue and Customs Appeals Order 2009 (SI 2009/56) art.3 and Sch.1 (April 1, 2009).

DEFINITIONS

"Board"—see s.27.

GENERAL NOTE

1.239   This section, governing rights of appeal, is modelled on the provisions governing tax appeals (Taxes Management Act 1970 s.31) rather than those for social security matters (SSA 1998 s.12).

Subsection (1)

1.240   This provision adopts the standard 30-day appeal deadline in s.31(1) of the Taxes Management Act 1970.

Subsection (2)

1.241   This requirement mirrors s.31(2) of the Taxes Management Act 1970.

Regulations with respect to appeals

1.242   **13.**—(1) The Board may, by regulations made with the concurrence of the Lord Chancellor and the [Secretary of State], make provision with respect to appeals to the [¹tribunal] under this Part.

(2) Regulations under subsection (1) above may, in particular—
 (a) make provision with respect to any of the matters dealt with in the following provisions of the Taxes Management Act 1970—
  (i) [². . .]
  (ii) sections 48 to 54 (appeals to the [²tribunal] under the Taxes Acts); and
  (iii) [² section 56 (payment of tax where there is a further appeal)] or

(b) provide for any of those provisions of that Act to apply, with such modifications as may be specified in the regulations, in relation to an appeal to the [²tribunal] under this Part.

[³ (2A) Regulations under subsection (1) above may provide for sections 11(2) and 13(2) of the Tribunals, Courts and Enforcement Act 2007 to apply with such modifications as may be specified in the regulations in relation to an appeal to the tribunal under this Part.]

[²...]

AMENDMENTS

1. Transfer of Functions (Lord Advocate and Secretary of State) Order 1999 (SI 1999/678) art.2(1).
2. Transfer of Tribunal Functions and Revenue and Customs Appeals Order 2009 (SI 2009/56) art.3 and Sch.1 (April 1, 2009).
3. Revenue and Customs Appeals Order 2009 (SI 2009/777) art.3 (April 1, 2009).

DEFINITION

"Board"—see s.27.

GENERAL NOTE

This section enables HMRC to make regulations about the procedures to apply for appeals to the tax appeal Commissioners against decisions under s.8. Such regulations can only be made with the concurrence of the Lord Chancellor and the Lord Advocate, who are responsible for funding the tax appeal Commissioners. In general terms, most of the provisions about appeals in Pt V of the Taxes Management Act 1970 are adopted for the purposes of such appeals. However, given that there are material differences between tax and matters such as SSP and SMP, subs.(2)(b) provides for appropriate modifications to be made to these appellate procedures. This reflects the existing arrangements for appeals to the Tax Chamber of the First-tier Tribunal in relation to Class 4 NICs, under SSCBA 1992 Sch.2 para.8.

1.243

Matters arising as respects decisions

14.—(1) The Board may by regulations make provision as respects matters arising—
   (a) pending any decision of an officer of the Board under section 8 of this Act which relates to—
      (i) statutory sick pay [¹, statutory maternity pay, [⁴ statutory paternity pay,] statutory adoption pay]] [³ [⁵, statutory shared parental pay or statutory parental bereavement pay]], or
      (ii) any person's liability for contributions;
   (b) pending the determination by the [²tribunal] of an appeal against any such decision,
   (c) out of the variation, under regulations made under section 10 of this Act or on appeal, of any such decision, or
   (d) out of the making of a decision which, under regulations made under that section, supersedes an earlier decision.
(2) Regulations under this section may, in particular—
   (a) make provision making a person liable to pay contributions pending the determination by the [²tribunal] of an appeal against a decision of an officer of the Board; and

1.244

(b) make provision as to the repayment in prescribed circumstances of contributions paid by virtue of the regulations.

(3) Regulations under this section must be made with the concurrence of the Secretary of State in so far as they relate to statutory sick pay [¹, statutory maternity pay, [⁴ statutory paternity pay,] statutory adoption pay]] [³ [⁵, statutory shared parental pay or statutory parental bereavement pay].

AMENDMENTS

1. Employment Act 2002 s.9(5) (December 8, 2002).
2. Transfer of Tribunal Functions and Revenue and Customs Appeals Order 2009 (SI 2009/56) art.3 and Sch.1 (April 1, 2009).
3. Children and Families Act 2014 s.126(1) Sch.7 paras 44, 47(1) and (2)(b) (June 30, 2014).
4. Children and Families Act 2014 s.126(1) Sch.7 paras 44, 47(1) and (2)(a) (April 5, 2015).
5. Parental Bereavement (Leave and Pay) Act 2018 s.1(c) and Sch. para.32 (January 18, 2020).

DEFINITIONS

"Board"—see s.27.
"contributions"—s.27.

GENERAL NOTE

1.245   This section is modelled on SSA 1998 s.18. It vests HMRC with a parallel regulation-making power to deal with matters arising before a decision is made or an appeal is heard (subss.(1)(a) and (b)), or concerning the consequences of varying or superseding a previous decision (including a variation following an appeal) (subss.(1)(c) and (d)). As such regulations may have implications for benefit rights in relation to SMP and SSP, in those instances the power can only be exercised with the agreement of the Secretary of State for Work and Pensions (subs.(3)).

Arrangements for discharge of decision-making functions

1.246   **17.**—(1) The Secretary of State may make arrangements with the Board for any of his functions under Chapter II of Part I of the Social Security Act 1998 in relation to—
  (a) a decision whether a person was (within the meaning of regulations) precluded from regular employment by responsibilities at home; or
  (b) a decision whether a person is entitled to be credited with earnings or contributions in accordance with regulations made under section 22(5) [¹ or (5ZA)] of the Social Security Contributions and Benefits Act 1992;
to be discharged by the Board or by officers of the Board.

(2) No such arrangements shall affect the responsibility of the Secretary of State or the application of Chapter II of Part I of the Social Security Act 1998 in relation to any decision.

(3) Until the commencement of Chapter II of Part I of the Social Security Act 1998, the references to that chapter in subsections (1) and (2) above shall have effect as references to Part II of the Social Security Administration Act 1992.

(1999 c.2 s.17)

AMENDMENT

1. Pensions Act 2014 (Consequential and Supplementary Amendments) Order 2016/224 art. 5 (April 6, 2016).

DEFINITION

"Board"—see s.27.

GENERAL NOTE

This section enables decisions on home responsibilities protection or credits to be performed by HMRC as agents for the Secretary of State for Work and Pensions. This arrangement is appropriate as such decisions primarily impact upon entitlement to social security benefits.

1.247

Amendments relating to decisions and appeals

18.—Schedule 7 to this Act (which contains amendments relating to decisions and appeals) shall have effect.

1.248

GENERAL NOTE

Schedule 7 provides for the detailed responsibilities of existing legislation relating to decision-making and appeals (Taxes Management Act 1970, SSCBA 1992, SSAA 1992, Pensions Schemes Act 1993, Employment Rights Act 1996 and SSA 1998).

1.249

[¹ Interpretation of Part II

19.—In this Part—
"tribunal" means the First-tier Tribunal or, where determined by or under Tribunal Procedure Rules, the Upper Tribunal.]

1.250

AMENDMENT

1. Transfer of Tribunal Functions and Revenue and Customs Appeals Order 2009 (SI 2009/56) art.3 and Sch.1 (April 1, 2009).

PART III

MISCELLANEOUS AND SUPPLEMENTAL

20.–26.—[*Omitted.*]

1.251

Interpretation

27.—In this Act, unless a contrary intention appears—
"the Board" means the Commissioners of Inland Revenue;
"contributions" means contributions under Part I of the Social Security Contributions and Benefits Act 1992.

1.252

GENERAL NOTE

The provisions in Pt III (with the exception of s.27) fall outside the scope of this volume and so are omitted. Section 20 provides that rebates in respect of money purchase contracted-out pension schemes should be funded from the National Insurance Fund. Sections 21 and 22 deal with the transfer of contracts and

1.253

Social Security Contributions (Transfer of Functions, etc.) Act 1999

property from the former DSS to the Inland Revenue. Section 23 provides for the transfer of functions by Order in Council. Section 24 enables provision to be made for Northern Ireland by Order in Council while s.25 concerns regulation and Order making powers generally; s.26 introduces Schs 8 (savings and transitional provisions), 9 (consequential amendments) and 10 (repeals and revocations). Section 28 governs the short title, commencement and extent of the Act.

Tax Credits Act 2002

(2002 c.21)

ARRANGEMENT OF SECTIONS

PART I

TAX CREDITS

General

1.254
1. Introductory
2. Functions of Commissioners
3. Claims
4. Claims: supplementary
5. Period of awards
6. Notifications of changes of circumstances
7. Income test

Child tax credit

8. Entitlement
9. Maximum rate

Working tax credit

10. Entitlement
11. Maximum rate
12. Child care element

Rate

13. Rate

Decisions

14. Initial decisions
15. Revised decisions after notifications
16. Other revised decisions

17.	Final notice
18.	Decisions after final notice
19.	Power to enquire
20.	Decisions on discovery
21.	Decisions subject to official error
21A.	Reviews of decisions
21B.	Late application for a review
21C.	Late review: award of relevant disability benefits
22.	Information, etc. requirements: supplementary
23.	Notice of decisions

Payment

24.	Payments
25.	Payments of working tax credit by employers (*omitted*)
26.	Liability of officers for sums paid to employers (*omitted*)
27.	Rights of employees
28.	Overpayments
29.	Recovery of overpayments
30.	Underpayments

Penalties

31.	Incorrect statements, etc.
32.	Failure to comply with requirements
33.	Failure by employers to make correct payments (*omitted*)
34.	Supplementary

Fraud

35.	Offence of fraud
36.	Powers in relation to documents
36A.	Loss of working tax credit in case of conviction etc. for benefit offence
36B.	Section 36A: supplementary
36C.	Loss of working tax credit for repeated benefit fraud
36D.	Section 36C: supplementary

Interest

37.	Interest

Appeals

38.	Appeals
39.	Exercise of right of appeal
39A.	Late appeals

Supplementary

40.	Annual reports
41.	Annual review
42.	Persons subject to immigration control
43.	Polygamous marriages
44.	Crown employment

45. Inalienability
46. Giving of notices by Board
47. Consequential amendments
48. Interpretation

Part II

Child Benefit and Guardian's Allowance

49.–57. (*Omitted*)

Part III

Supplementary

Information etc.

58. Administrative arrangements
59. Use and disclosure of information

Other supplementary provisions

60. Repeals
61. Commencement
62. Transitional provisions and savings
63. Tax credits appeals etc.: temporary modifications
64. Northern Ireland
65. Regulations, orders and schemes
66. Parliamentary etc. control of instruments
67. Interpretation
68. Financial provision (*omitted*)
69. Extent (*omitted*)
70. Short title (*omitted*)

Schedule 1—Rights of employees (*omitted*)
Schedule 2—Penalties: supplementary
Schedule 3—Tax credits: consequential amendments (*omitted*)
Schedule 4—Transfer of functions: consequential amendments (*omitted*)
Schedule 5—Use and disclosure of information (*omitted*)
Schedule 6—Repeals and revocations (*omitted*)

General Note

Repeal of Part 1 of the Act

1.255   Section 33(1)(f) of the Welfare Reform Act 2012 provides for the abolition of tax credits and the repeal of Part 1 of the Act. Section 33(1)(f) was brought into force on February 1, 2019 by the Welfare Reform Act 2012 (Commencement No.32 and Savings and Transitional Provisions) Order 2019 (SI 2019/167). However, savings provisions in art.3 of the Order provide that, for the time being, in many cases Part 1 of the Act is treated as if it were still in force. For a discussion of the savings provisions, see the general note to the 2019 Order below in this volume.

(2002 c.21)

Scope and scheme of the Act

The Tax Credits Bill 2001 was introduced to the House of Commons as a Treasury measure. It was subject to minimal amendment as it went through its parliamentary proceedings in the House of Commons. The Speaker ruled that it was not a Money Bill (possibly because of Pt II of the Act). It was subject to rigorous challenge in the House of Lords. The criticisms ranged from normal political confrontations about tax and social security measures to a challenge to the fundamental approach, even the title, of the Bill itself. It was at that stage also (after strong protests from the opposition parties and an apology from the minister piloting the Bill through the House) that important government technical and drafting amendments were tabled. The main focus of opposition criticism was on the issue whether tax credits counted as public expenditure or as tax uncollected. In fact, that issue did not feature in the Bill at all as it does not require legislation. The answer (after a disagreement about the right approach, recorded in the note) was published in the Red Book (the Financial Statement) published by the Treasury to accompany the Chancellor 2002 Budget (See *2002 Financial Statement*, Box C2, p.216). It is that tax credits count as public expenditure in so far as they exceed the income tax due from the claimant, and as negative taxation in so far as they do not. Tax credits under the Tax Credits Act 1999 are classified as public expenditure. During Parliamentary debates, it was said that as a ball-park figure, 90 per cent of the amount was public expenditure and 10 per cent tax foregone.

1.256

The Tax Credits Act 2002 ("this Act") repeals and replaces the Tax Credits Act 1999 ("TCA 1999") in its entirety and carries further the reforms started by that Act. The Act is structured in three Parts. Part I (Tax credits) provides the necessary primary legislative framework to introduce the child tax credit and working tax credit. It also provides a common procedure for those tax credits. Schedules 1–3 to the Act are associated with this Part. Part II (Child benefit and guardian's allowance) makes provision for the transfer of functions concerning child benefit and guardian's allowance to the Treasury and HMRC, and the associated minor amendments to entitlement. Schedule 4 is associated with this Part. Part III (Supplementary) makes additional provision for both other Parts. Schedules 5 and 6 are associated with this Part.

Repeal of the 2002 Act

Schedule 14 Pt 1 to the Welfare Reform Act 2012 contains the legislation necessary to repeal the whole of the Tax Credits Act 2002, with the exception of Schs 1 and 3 to the 2002 Act. Paragraphs 1 and 6 of Sch.6 to the 2012 Act contain wide powers to allow the staged transfer of claimants from tax credits to universal credit. Government policy was to introduce the transfer by initial pilots and then by stages. As at October 2015 a major roll-out of universal credit started, with a focus in particular on single claimants and therefore on those who could claim working tax credit rather than child tax credit. As an area was brought within universal credit, so entitlement to tax credits was abated. The roll-out gathered pace and moved into a further series of phases with effect from April 2016, under which a 'full service' universal credit became operative by the local Jobcentres in specified local authority areas. In those areas it was generally no longer possible for someone to make a new claim for tax credits. Where a current claimant was required to report a change of circumstances affecting an existing award of tax credits, the effect might only be to alter the ongoing award. However, if the effect of the change resulted in a loss of entitlement to tax credits, then the claimant might feel obliged to make an application for universal credit. This had the double effect of moving the claimant from entitlement determined by reference to the tax credits rules to those determined by the universal credit rules and also from administration of the benefit by HMRC to administration by DWP through the Jobcentre (see further e.g. *W v HMRC* [2020] UKUT 239 (AAC) and *RJ v HMRC; HMRC v RJ* [2021] UKUT 40 (AAC)). Universal credit was finally rolled out to (virtually) all new claimants in December 2018. The roll-out of universal credit and the difficulties around 'managed' and 'natural' migration are covered in more detail by Vol.V of this work.

1.257

Tax credits under the Tax Credits Act 2002

1.258 The introduction of the current reforms was announced by the Chancellor of the Exchequer, Gordon Brown, in his 1999 Budget and confirmed in his 2000 Budget. The detailed shape of the proposals was first announced in an HMRC consultation paper published in July 2001: *New Tax Credits: Supporting families, making work pay and tackling poverty*. This received significant comment from many sources and the HMRC published its *Response* in November 2001.

For details of the transitional legislation and relevant case law, see the notes to the Welfare Reform Act 2012 Commencement Orders and the Universal Credit (Transitional Provisions) Regulations 2014 (SI 2014/1230) in Part A of Part II of this volume.

Child tax credit

1.259 CTC is a means-tested social security benefit for all those responsible for children and qualifying young persons, although it is presented as a tax credit.

Support for children through the tax and social security systems was previously provided in several ways. The first and most important provision was child benefit. The second line of support for children in poorer families was by way of an addition or increase to individual means-tested benefits (or tax credits). Thirdly, and separately from the income-related benefits, contributory and other social security benefits also made provision for dependent children (e.g. the child dependency increases under SSCBA 1992 ss.80 and 85 and the child increase for carer's allowance under SSCBA 1992 s.90). There were further provisions in the Social Security (Dependency) Regulations 1977 (SI 1977/343). Moreover, a few individuals looking after children as their guardians can claim guardian's allowance, under SSCBA 1992 s.77. Finally, and separately again from these sources of assistance for those bringing up children, the Finance Act 2000 introduced the children's tax credit as s.257AA of the ICTA 1988, supported by Sch.13B to that Act. Despite its name, this was not a tax credit, but an income tax reduction. It only overlapped with the social security benefits in so far as the claimants of those benefits were also income tax payers. This Act sweeps away all mention of SSCBA 1992 ss.80 and 90 (but *not* s.85, which allows for increases for retirement pensioners for an adult caring for children for whom the pensioner is receiving child credit). With them go the relevant regulations. Section 257AA of ICTA 1988 also goes. So also, by regulation, does the overlap between child benefit and CTC. Any overlap with WTC is also avoided by regulation. Further regulations under s.1 were intended to transfer all child elements from all income-related benefits to CTC. That proved far harder than was anticipated. The provisions originally intended to be in place in 2004 were repeatedly postponed, and are now being phased in for new claims from 2009 as detailed in the note to s.1.

Working tax credit

1.260 Until 2012, WTC was not strictly a social security benefit. This is because, from the introduction of WTC, one element of the tax credit replaced an employment-related payment known as New Deal 50 Plus. This was an employment credit under the Employment and Training Act 1973. As its name suggests, this was a cash incentive designed to encourage those over 50 to go back to work. Further, it was paid not by the DWP but by the former Department for Education and Employment. The 50 Plus element of WTC was abolished from April 6, 2012 and the relevant legislation has been repealed or revoked from then. There is, however, a partial replacement of a credit entitlement for some individuals over 60. Arguably, what is left is now a social security payment.

WTC is stated to be a general provision for all in "qualifying remunerative work", though tantalisingly the Act does not define that central term. Rather, regulations specify what work will qualify. That specification was tightened in 2012. The definition is by reference to hours worked in a week. The requirement is:

(1) 16 hours in total from one person if the claimant is a lone parent responsible for a child or young person; or a couple responsible for a child where one partner is over 60 or qualifies for the disability element of WTC; or a couple responsible for a child where one partner is working and the other partner is incapacitated or unable to work for other specified reasons.
(2) 24 hours in total from both joint claimants if the claim is by a couple responsible for a child and one of the partners is working 16 hours a week. (This was increased from 16 hours in 2012.)
(3) 30 hours in total if the claimant (or joint claimants) have no responsibility for children and is (or are) aged 25 or over.

How CTC and WTC developed

The tax credit system was designed as a redistributive system, with lower paid families as particular beneficiaries but also with other lower paid workers and families more generally put within its original scope. Over the decade that followed the elements of the system that helped lower paid families were increased, while those helping better paid families were allowed to reduce in level by inflation-based erosion. They have now been reduced deliberately following the emergency budget in 2010. But Chancellors gave undertakings that the main elements of CTC would be increased in line with earnings rather than inflation in the cost of living, and this has occurred. The child care element of the system is part of WTC, not CTC, and so was not within this undertaking. At first the maximum amount payable towards child care expenses was increased, but this was later put into reverse. The effect is a reduction in the potential value of the system to lower paid working families, while those who are not required to work and can claim income support, or who are claiming jobseeker's allowance, are still assisted to the original levels set within the system.

1.261

Commencement

Section 61 (Commencement) and subsequent sections came into effect on Royal Assent (8 July 2002). Pt I (ss.1–48) is brought into effect under the Tax Credits Act 2002 (Commencement No.1) Order 2002 (SI 2002/1727) made that day. The balance of the Act was brought in by the Tax Credits Act 2002 (Commencement No.2) Order 2003 (SI 2003/392) (Pt II), the Tax Credits Act 2002 (Commencement No.3 and Transitional Provisions and Savings) Order 2003 (SI 2003/938) (the abolition of the child additions and benefits under s.1(3) of the Act) and Tax Credits Act 2002 (Commencement No.4, Transitional Provisions and Savings) Order 2003 (SI 2003/962) (the remainder).

1.262

The pattern of introduction of tax credits is as follows:

General:
July 9, 2002   regulation-making powers.

For all claimants except those on income support and jobseeker's allowance:
August 1, 2002   making claims and relevant provisions
January 1, 2003   making decisions on claims
April 6, 2003   entitlements to payment of awards and abolition of child additions from all benefits save as below.

For claimants over 60 transferring to or qualifying for state pension credit:
October 1, 2003   making claims and awards.

For other claimants of income support or jobseeker's allowance:
December 31, 2008   phased introduction of CTC to all claimants.

However, tax credits are being phased out before the full introduction has been completed. See the note on *Repeal of the 2002 Act* above.

Tax Credits Act 2002

General problems with the 2002 Act

1.263 The first two years of the operation of the Tax Credits Act 2002 cannot, by any stretch of imagination, be called an outstanding success. Overall, it proved far harder to start the system than anticipated. However, the Government was proved right on one aspect of the new tax credits. Some claimed that the take-up rates for the credits would be low. This was a longstanding problem with family credit. But the estimated take-up for child tax credit in its first year was 80 per cent, compared to 65 per cent and 57 per cent in the first years of working families' tax credit and family credit respectively. In addition, no less than 480,000 claimants claimed nil credits (i.e. they put in protective claims in 2004/5 but did not receive anything).

General administration of tax credits proved far more complex than planned. Indeed, the government was forced to abandon its intentions of having the credits paid through people's pay packets. This was an aim of government as long ago as 1973 when family income supplement was turned into family credit. It was a firm aim of government in 2002, following the approach of s.6 of the Tax Credits Act 1999. But the 2002 Act contained a more limited measure than the original proposals. Section 25 provides for payment of working tax credit, or prescribed elements, by employers. This was never used to pay the full credit, as the child care element was paid direct to the family. In 2004 the Chancellor announced that even the partial payment was to cease. Also, by April 2006 all payments by employers ceased. From then, payment is made only by HMRC.

Changes since enactment

1.264 Four aspects of the original scheme have been delayed, watered-down or abandoned: (1) all payments are made direct by HMRC and none through the pay packet; (2) CTC is yet to be made payable to all claimants of income related benefits under s.1 of the 2002 Act; (3) the power to make shared awards of CTC where there is shared responsibility for a child has not been used; and (4) despite the terms of s.7, awards are based almost entirely on income of the previous year.

In the tax year 2020–21 there were some 2 million families benefiting from tax credits, down from a high of 6.31 million families in April 2011. The reduction over the past decade was primarily because of policy changes enacted by the 2010–15 coalition government and particularly the reduction and eventual removal of the second threshold (in 2012–13) along with the rollout of Universal Credit (from April 2013). The trend in the numbers of in-work families without children – those receiving WTC only—had shown a steady increase from around 164,000 in 2003–04 to 540,000 in 2011–12 but has since fallen to 217,000 in 2020–21.

Problems with error and fraud have abated but still remain significant. The HMRC *Child and Working Tax Credits error and fraud statistics, tax year 2020–21* (June 2022) estimate tax credit error and fraud in favour of the claimant as amounting to 5.3 per cent, representing £940 million. Some 0.9 per cent of finalised decisions are thought to involve underpayments of tax credits (a total of £170 million).

Two sets of further major changes to the tax credits system were announced in 2015. The first was a major extension of the introduction of universal credit to replace tax credits, with the first additional stage of the extension taking place in October 2015. See the comment at para.1.255 above and the separate commentary on this in Vol.II of this series.

1.265 The second set of changes was announced by the Chancellor of the Exchequer in the Summer Budget 2015 that followed the General Election. Together they amounted to a significant trimming of the levels of entitlement of many tax credit claimants, with smaller groups obtaining an increased benefit. The main intended changes were published in 2015 as a draft statutory instrument, the draft *Tax Credits (Income Thresholds and Determination of Rates) (Amendment) Regulations*. However, following a series of defeats of Government policy for tax credit changes in the House of Lords in October 2015, in the following month the Chancellor announced in the Autumn Statement 2015 that the Government was not proceeding with proposals to introduce those changes. The draft regulations were therefore

(2002 c.21)

not confirmed. Instead, the Chancellor announced that the planned reductions in entitlement would occur when tax credit claimants were to be transferred to universal credit. He also announced that any new claimant for tax credits from 2018 would instead be required to claim universal credit. As a result, for new claimants, the abolition of the tax credits scheme took place in December 2018. Existing claimants will transfer to universal credit either by 'natural' migration (e.g. a change in circumstances leading to a claim for universal credit) or, following a pilot, by 'managed' migration (on DWP instructions). The latest target date (in 2020) for the completion of this process is now 2024.

Welfare Reform Act 2012 and anti-fraud measures
The Welfare Reform Act 2012 amends the Secretary of State's powers as regards investigating benefit fraud. Previously tax credits were not classed as relevant social security benefits, and so the definition of "benefit offence" did not apply to them under the SSAA 1992.

1.266

Section 122 of WRA 2012 extends the Secretary of State's powers of investigation to cover investigations in respect of the commission, or suspected commission, of tax credit fraud by inserting a new s.109A(9) into SSAA 1992 (authorisations for investigators).

Section 123 of WRA 2012 amends s.122B of SSAA 1992 (supply of government information for fraud prevention, etc.), enabling the DWP to receive information for use in the prevention, detection, investigation or prosecution of offences relating to tax credits.

Section 125 of WRA 2012 amends Sch.4 to the SSAA 1992 (persons employed in social security administration or adjudication) so as to provide further safeguards against inappropriate disclosure of information that DWP staff receive during the course of their employment.

These amendments were brought into force with effect from June 6, 2012 (art.2 of the Welfare Reform Act 2012 (Commencement No.2) (Amendment) Order 2012 (SI 2012/1440), amending art.2(2) of the Welfare Reform Act 2012 (Commencement No.2) Order 2012 (SI 2012/1246). Section 124 of the WRA 2012 amends s.35 of the Tax Credits Act 2002 (tax credit fraud: prosecution and penalties), but to date these amendments have not been brought into force.

PART I

TAX CREDITS

General

Introductory

1.—(1) This Act makes provision for—
(a) a tax credit to be known as child tax credit, and
(b) a tax credit to be known as working tax credit.
(2) In this Act references to a tax credit are to either of those tax credits and references to tax credits are to both of them.
(3) The following (which are superseded by tax credits) are abolished—
(a) children's tax credit under section 257AA of the Income and Corporation Taxes Act 1988 (Chapter 1),
(b) working families' tax credit,
(c) disabled person's tax credit,

1.267

(d) the amounts which, in relation to income support and income-based jobseeker's allowance, are prescribed as part of the applicable amount in respect of a child or young person, the family premium, the enhanced disability premium in respect of a child or young person and the disabled child premium,

(e) increases in benefits in respect of children under sections 80 and 90 of the Social Security Contributions and Benefits Act 1992 (Chapter 4) and sections 80 and 90 of the Social Security Contributions and Benefits (Northern Ireland) Act 1992 (Chapter 7), and

(f) the employment credit under the schemes under section 2(2) of the Employment and Training Act 1973 (Chapter 50) and section 1 of the Employment and Training Act (Northern Ireland) 1950 (Chapter 29 (NI)) known as "New Deal 50 Plus".

DEFINITIONS

"child tax credit"—see s.8.
"tax credit"—see subs.2.
"working tax credit"—see s.10.

GENERAL NOTE

1.268   Section 1 is, as its title states, purely an introductory section. Strictly it adds nothing to the enacting provisions of Pt I, but it flags up the two kinds of tax credit payable under the Act and also the benefits repealed (by s.60 and Sch.6). Subsection (1) lists the two tax credits introduced by the Act, but (as with the rest of Pt I) is drafted so that other tax credits could be added to the list in the sub, and the machinery sections of the Act (which apply to "tax credits" as defined in subs. (2)) would then apply to the new tax credits also. At the date of writing, no specific further tax credits have been suggested. The abolition of the child premiums to income support and JSA were deferred to December 31, 2008, and deferred again to December 31, 2011, and then to December 2014 and finally indefinitely.

Indeed, it has proved harder than anticipated to introduce child tax credits for those on income support and jobseeker's allowance. It is understood that there are many cases where one parent of a child is claiming one of these benefits with child addition while the other parent is claiming child tax credit for the same child or children. In *CSTC/326/2003* Commissioner Parker considered an argument that the measures taken to postpone the introduction of s.1(3)(d) discriminated against those receiving income support as against those who received the tax credits direct. The appellant's wife received income support. Entitlement to child tax credit was higher than to income support. But under the transitional legislation the appellant could claim CTC only from the date of his claim. No backdating was allowed. The appellant argued that either this was ultra vires the TCA 2002 or it was discriminatory under the European Convention on Human Rights. The Commissioner rejected both arguments. In dealing with somewhat unfocussed arguments about the European Convention on Human Rights, the Commissioner took the view that CTC is a means-tested social security benefit but assumed for the purposes of argument that both art.8 of, and art.1, Protocol 1 to, the Convention were engaged. She then considered if there was discrimination within the meaning of art.14 but found none. Her decision reveals that the process of suspending s.1(3)(d) while benefit claimants are "migrated" to it as being in some confusion. Of the relevant subordinate legislation (in particular SI 2005/773, SI 2005/776 and SI 2005/1106), she comments (at [16]):

"the last minute nature of the amendment order, the curiosity of two substantially overlapping measures produced on the same day (the transitional provisions order 2005 and the second transitional provisions order), a draft order which was never laid, and the failure to enact a consistent statutory scheme of backdating to prevent double recovery, indicate a history of some haste and confusion by the legislators. There has been a complex web of measures, note always successful, necessitated because the prospects for the completion of intended migration seem ever to recede."

[¹Function of Commissioners

2.—The Commissioners for Her Majesty's Revenue and Customs shall be responsible for the payment and management of tax credits.]

1.269

AMENDMENT

1. Commissioners for Revenue and Customs Act 2005 Sch.4 para.88 (April 6, 2005).

DEFINITIONS

"tax credits"—see s.1(2).
"the Commissioners for Revenue and Customs"—see CRCA 2005 s.4.

GENERAL NOTE

This short section replaced its lengthy predecessor as CRCA 2005 came into effect. That Act repealed and replaced the Inland Revenue Regulation Act 1890 to which this section previously referred. All necessary provisions for both the payment of tax credits (and repayment) and management and administration are now either in the CRCA 2005 or this Act. The wording of this section reflects the similar wording in CRCA 2005 applying also to taxes, duties and benefits. See the general note to CRCA 2005 about the powers to transfer these functions back to the Treasury and HMRC as part of the staged abolition of tax credits.

1.270

The Tax Credits (Exercise of Functions) Order 2014 (SI 2014/3280), made on December 10, 2014, empowers the Secretary of State to exercise some tax credit functions concurrently with HMRC. From April 1, 2015 those functions are the recovery of overpayments and of any penalty imposed.

In *GL v HMRC* [2023] UKUT 100 (AAC); [2023] 1 W.L.R. 4481, Deputy Upper Tribunal Judge Buley KC doubted the correctness of HMRC's argument that, in principle, they had discretion, in an exceptional case, to continue to pay tax credits to a person who, falling outside the Tax Credits (Residence) Regulations 2003 reg.4, was not in the UK (Tax Credits Act 2002 s.3(3) provides that a claim for a tax credit may be made by a person "in the United Kingdom"). The judge suspected that HMRC may have mistakenly assumed that a recognised extra-statutory discretion, applicable in connection with HMRC's tax collection functions, was also applicable in connection with their tax credits functions. HMRC's case seemed to have overlooked the "fundamental problem" that their statutory powers to pay tax credits do not permit payment of a tax credit to a person who fails to satisfy the statutory conditions, and that s.2's authority to make payment of tax credits is to be read as an authority to make payment in accordance with, rather than outwith, the statutory scheme.

Claims

3.—(1) Entitlement to a tax credit for the whole or part of a tax year is dependent on the making of a claim for it.

1.271

(2) Where the Board—
(a) decide under section 14 not to make an award of a tax credit on a claim, or
(b) decide under section 16 to terminate an award of a tax credit made on a claim,

(subject to any appeal) any entitlement, or subsequent entitlement, to the tax credit for any part of the same tax year is dependent on the making of a new claim.

(3) A claim for a tax credit may be made—
- (a) jointly by the members of a [²couple] both of whom are aged at least sixteen and are in the United Kingdom [(and neither of whom are members of a polygamous unit)]¹; or
- [(aa) jointly by the members of a polygamous unit all of whom are aged at least sixteen and are in the United Kingdom, or]¹;
- (b) by a person who is aged at least sixteen and is in the United Kingdom but is not entitled to make a claim under paragraph (a) (jointly with another).

(4) Entitlement to a tax credit pursuant to a claim ceases—
- (a) in the case of a joint claim, if the persons by whom it was made could no longer jointly make a joint claim; and
- [(aa) in the case of a joint claim under subsection (3)(a), if a member of the [²couple] becomes a member of a polygamous unit, and
- (ab) in the case of a joint claim under subsection (3)(aa), if there is any change in the persons who comprise the polygamous unit, and]¹
- (b) in the case of a single claim, if the person by whom it was made could no longer make a single claim.

(5) [² . . .

(5A) In this Part "couple" means]—

[³(a) two people who are married to, or civil partners of, each other and are neither—
- (i) separated under a court order, nor
- (ii) separated in circumstances in which the separation is likely to be permanent, or
- (b) two people who are not married to, or civil partners of, each other but are living together as if they were a married couple or civil partners.]

(6) [² . . .]

[(6A) In this Part, "polygamous unit" has the meaning given by regulation 2 of the Tax Credits (Polygamous Marriages) Regulations 2003.]¹

(7) Circumstances may be prescribed in which a person is to be treated for the purposes of this Part as being, or as not being, in the United Kingdom.

(8) In this Part—

"joint claim" means a claim under paragraph (a) [or (aa)]¹ of subsection (3), and

"single claim" means a claim under paragraph (b) of that subsection.

AMENDMENTS

1. Modifications for the purposes of application to polygamous units by Tax Credits (Polygamous Marriages) Regulations 2003 (SI 2003/742) reg.4 (April 6, 2003).
2. Civil Partnership Act 2004 s.254 and Sch.24 para.144 (December 5, 2005).
3. Civil Partnership (Opposite-sex Couples) Regulations 2019 (SI 2019/1458) reg.41(a) and Sch.3 Pt 1 para.23(2) (December 2, 2019).

DEFINITIONS

"award"—see s.14(1).
"the Board"—see s.67.
"claim"—see subs.(1), s.4.

"couple"—see subs.(5A).
"entitlement"—see s.18(1).
"joint claim"—see subs.(8).
"prescribed"—see s.67.
"single claim"—see subs.(8).
"tax credit"—see s.1(2).
"tax year"—see s.47.

GENERAL NOTE

This is the first of the sections in the Act that create the necessary compromise for tax credits between the general approach of income tax administration and the general approach of social security administration. Subsection (1) adopts and adapts the requirement from SSAA 1992 s.1(1), that there can be no entitlement to a tax credit without a claim. Subsection (2) reinforces this. Subsections (3) and following set out both the main conditions for making a claim and the requirement that both (or all) those who are partners to a marriage (or equivalent) join in making the claim. Subsection (8) adopts appropriate definitions for joint and single claims. There is also a definition of "claimant" in s.9(8), which would be better placed here in subs.(8).

Determining when a claim is made is important because of the operation of the "three-month" rule for a new claim following some changes of circumstances. The ability to make claims by telephone or email in addition to the traditional posted claim means that this may be a matter to be determined on appeal in the light of conflicting evidence from the claimants and HMRC. See *CSIS/48/1992* for the presumption that a document that can be served by post is delivered in ordinary course of post. HMRC treat the rule with a little generosity because it directs staff to assume that for these purposes three months is always 91 days and a single month always has 31 days.

Subsection (1)

This requires a claim before any award can be made under s.14. If no valid claim is made, then HMRC cannot make an award. HMRC take the view that it is for HMRC to decide if a claim is valid in accordance with reg.5(1) of the Tax Credits (Claims and Notifications) Regulations 2002 (see below), and that the decision is not appealable. On the latter argument, see note to s.38 (Appeals) below.

The standard claim form is TC600 for new claims. In practice claims can be made over the telephone. See TC(Claims and Notifications) Regs 2002 reg.5 and *CIS/995/2004* discussed at para.2.347 below. Further, although renewal claims are needed each year, a renewal claim may be treated as being made as the procedure for checking a past claim takes place at the end of that year of claim.

HMRC have accepted that it is appropriate in some cases to make protective claims where a claim will lead to a nil award on the then current information about income, but where a claimant may later in the tax year be entitled to tax credits. In such cases, nil awards will be made. See *Tax Adviser*, June 2003, p.13. HMRC statistics show that in December 2006 there were about 0.8 million claimants with zero awards. This suggests that these claims have become standard practice for many advisers, as the total number of recipients of credit had not risen in the previous two years while the number of zero awards doubled. Another explanation is that 0.6 million lower paid individuals (perhaps self-employed) without children now receive zero awards, and the number of such claimants also doubled in that period. Another reason is that HMRC may revise an award to zero rather than cancel it when a claimant is no longer entitled to receive a positive award. However, the abolition of the family element from 2012 will now have affected these figures.

Subsection (2)

This adopts in part a policy of SSA 1998 s.8, that a claim ceases to have effect when a decision has been made on it. A new claim is required if the Board refuses or ends a tax credit award for a tax year and for any reason the claimant wants that decision revisited. In practice, however, the Board may choose to make a "nil" award, so leaving the matter open to review if circumstances change, rather than a reclaim.

Subsection (3)

1.275 This is the primary provision entitling a claim to be made. It imposes a series of conditions on all claimants:
  (a) if a claimant is one of a married or unmarried couple (or of a polygamous unit) then the claim can only be made in the names of both (or all) of them;
  (b) the claimant or claimants must be over 16; and
  (c) the claimant or claimants (and if more than one, all) must be "in the UK".

The following subsections make provisions for those conditions. But s.42 excludes those subject to immigration control from entitlement except in specified cases. The approach of requiring joint claims is also reinforced by s.4(1)(g), which enables regulations to treat a single claim as a joint claim. This has been extended by regulations under s.43 to cover polygamous units, the policy again being that all the members of a polygamous unit must be linked to the claim.

Following the enactment of the Gender Recognition Act 2004, HMRC have issued guidance that if an individual has gender recognition certificate issues under the Act, then this will or affect the status of the individual as a single or joint claimant: see TCTM 06100. However, there will be a potential interaction with the new definition of "couple" following the enactment of the Civil Partnership Act 2004. See below.

1.276 In *CSTC/724/2006* the Commissioner considered the application of subs.(3)(a) and (b) to an entitlement decision under s.19. The Commissioner followed the comments of the deputy Commissioner in *CTC/3864/2004* (an appeal about a s.16 decision) in confirming that the paragraphs are mutually exclusive. An individual cannot acquire entitlement to a tax credit if he or she did not claim it. The Commissioner rejected a decision of a tribunal that took the view that HMRC had the power to amend an award to take into account that the claimant became one of a couple. The appropriate single and joint claims must remain exclusive. Therefore a member of a couple who made a claim as a single claimant could have no entitlement to tax credits in either capacity. The other member of the couple could not be made liable for any overpayment in respect of any such decision if he or she was not a claimant.

For discussion of the importance of proper fact-finding in cases of separating spouses, see *HMRC v PD (TC)* [2012] UKUT 230 (AAC). Judge Lane held on the facts that although a separating married couple were living in the same house, they were no longer living in the same household at the material time. And see also the comments of Judge Rowland in *JI v HMRC* [2013] UKUT 199 (AAC) about the scope for treating notification of a breakup of a relationship as a new claim for child tax credits for children of the household.

In *CTC/1853/2009* it was held that claimants resident not in the UK but elsewhere in the EU could not claim child tax credit under art.77 of Council Regulation (EEC) 1408/71. This was agreed in *EM v HMRC (TC)* [2010] UKUT 323 (AAC), although it was commented that in some circumstances there might be a claim under other European legislation. However, both judges noted that the Regulation was replaced by Council Regulation (EC) 883/2004 from May 2010. HMRC will now pay child tax credit to claimants such as those in these appeals (payment having been stopped in both cases).

1.277 HMRC is reminding all claimants by letter of the need to report a change of circumstances, including in particular whether a claim should be a joint claim or single claim. This followed recognition that in 2008/9 150,000 claims (2.5 per cent of the total) were incorrect single claims.

One situation not expressly covered by this provision is that of a married couple who are not formally separated but only one of whom is "in the United Kingdom" as defined in the Tax Credits (Residence) Regulations 2003 (see para.2.476 below). If one of a married couple is ordinarily resident in the UK but the other is not, then the resident spouse should make a single claim. For that purpose, the non-resident spouse's income is not relevant to the claim. See *HA v HMRC (TC)* [2015] UKUT

708 (AAC) where the claimant's husband had resided in the UK for several extended periods, had moved address with her, had worked until he had been made redundant (when he claimed JSA), had obtained indefinite leave to remain and was on the electoral roll in the UK. However, at the same time he had also retained strong links in Ghana, where he had both an apartment and employment. In the Upper Tribunal, Judge Hemingway dismissed the claimant's appeal against the FTT decision that she was not entitled to claim tax credits as a single person for the 2011/12 tax year. In dismissing the claimant's further appeal, the Court of Appeal in *Arthur v HMRC* [2017] EWCA Civ 1756; [2018] AACR 10 held that the claimant's husband was a person who was "ordinarily resident" in the UK as at April 6, 2011 for the purposes of a joint tax credit claim under s.3(3). Accordingly, the claimant herself was not able to make claim tax credits as a single person. Newey LJ helpfully set out the relevant legal principles on ordinary residence at [16] of his judgment (see further the note to reg.3 of the Tax Credits (Residence) Regulations 2003 (SI 2003/654) below).

For cases with an EU dimension, see *EG v HMRC (TC)* [2011] UKUT 467 (AAC). The two joint claimants, who were both UK nationals, were a married couple, and neither legally separated or estranged. However, they maintained separate residences: the husband throughout being both resident and ordinarily resident in the UK, but the wife, who received UK incapacity benefit, being resident in Spain and not ordinarily resident in the UK. The claim was in respect of their children, who at all times lived with their mother in Spain. Judge Howell QC held that she was within the provision in art.73 of Council Regulation 1408/71/EEC, namely that an "employed person subject to the legislation of a member state" is to be entitled to family benefits (which include child tax credits) in respect of members of his or her family residing in another Member State. The UK was the competent member state in relation to her social insurance for the relevant year as she was neither employed or self-employed in Spain at that time. It followed that she was entitled to participate in the joint claim by virtue of art.73 of EU Regulation 1408/71, disapplying the national condition about her own residence, and a decision was accordingly given confirming their entitlement to the child tax credits for that year. For discussion of art.73 and its replacement by arts 67 and following of Regulation 883/2004 of Vol.III of this work.

Subsection (4)

This is designed to stop the claim under subs.(3) continuing if the identity of the claimant(s) changes because an individual gains a partner, a couple breaks up, or a polygamous unit changes membership. Subsection (4) also brings entitlement under a joint claim to an end if one member of a couple dies (*RJ v HMRC; HMRC v RJ* [2021] UKUT 40 (AAC); [2021] 1 W.L.R. 3350). In *RJ*, Upper Tribunal Judge West also rejected the argument that a widower's inability to re-claim tax credits, following the death of his partner, because he lived in in a Universal Credit Full Service Area amounted to discrimination contrary to Article 14 of the European Convention on Human Rights. Subsection (4) deals with *entitlement* not *award*, and its inclusion at this point in this section is a little obscure. It links with the provisions on joint claims (or deemed joint claims) to withdraw *entitlement* where joint claimants are no longer *entitled to make* a joint claim, thus stopping both joint claims and claims deemed to be joint. Nonetheless its interaction with ss.17 and 18 and with a continuing *award* is not clear. It appears to suggest that an award can continue without underlying entitlement. However, under the Tax Credits (Claims and Notifications) Regulations 2002 (SI 2002/2014) reg.21, notification must be given whenever a joint claim should become a single claim, or the reverse. In practice, this applies to awards as much as to entitlement. See further *JL v HMRC (TC)* [2013] UKUT 325, discussed in the commentary to reg.21 of the Claims and Notifications Regulations.

1.278

Subsections (5A)—separation issues (spouses and civil partners)

In the case of spouses and civil partners, the issue is whether they are separated under a court order or in circumstances in which the separation is likely to be permanent. Identifying separation under a court order is straightforward. More difficult

1.279

is the task of identifying whether separation is likely to be permanent in those majority of cases where there is no relevant court order. This is ultimately an objective rather than subjective test; the views of the parties or other family members are not determinative (*UA v HMRC* (TC) [2019] UKUT 113). Case law contains the following rulings on the law and connected guidance about how tribunals should approach the question whether a separation is likely to be permanent:

- According to the Social Security Commissioner decision in *R(TC) 2/06*, before deciding that a separation is likely to be permanent, a tribunal must consider why it occurred and any indications that the couple may be "reconciled". *R(TC) 2/06* also suggests that a tribunal "must conclude that there is at least a 50 per cent chance of a reconciliation" before it may properly find that a separation is unlikely to be permanent although this is simply a re-statement of the applicable standard of proof rather than a call for fact-finding at mathematical levels of precision;
- Whether the parties share a household is a potentially important consideration. However, sharing living accommodation does not necessarily indicate a common household (*HMRC v PD* [2012] UKUT 230 (AAC));
- While a common household may be indicative of a non-permanent separation, it is not determinative. In *DG v HMRC* (TC) [2013] UKUT 631 (AAC), Judge Wikeley declined to follow *PD* insofar as it suggested otherwise. The Judge held that the main focus of enquiry should instead be the nature of the relationship in particular whether there is an emotional, rather than simply physical, separation or estrangement. It is suggested that Judge Wikeley's approach is to be preferred—the exigencies of life may compel former couples to maintain a common household or, at least, some of the links they developed before becoming estranged despite the loss of the emotional bond they once enjoyed. As Judge Jacobs said in *SA v HMRC* [2017] UKUT 90 (AAC), "it is inherent in such a situation that the couple may continue to have some involvement with each other, over family and financial matters if nothing else";
- Generally, the longer two separated spouses or civil partners continue to live under the same roof and/or maintain a common household without a legal termination of their relationship, the weaker is the argument that their separation is likely to be permanent. But, again, it should be borne in mind that there are no hard and fast rules: context is everything. As Judge Jacobs put it in *SA*, "it would be wrong to reason that because they remain married, their separation cannot be permanent. There may, after all, be good reasons—reasons that make sense to the parties—not to divorce. It may be that they cannot afford it. It might, realistically, make no practical difference to their situation. They may be happy as they are and not wish relations to be soured by legal proceedings. They may just find the idea of legal proceedings intimidating. My point is that the length of the separation must be considered in the context of all the circumstances";
- The degree to which the parties continue to be involved with each other and in each other's lives may indicate that they have not truly separated (*SA*). Nevertheless, continued involvement is capable of being consistent with permanent separation. Factors such as joint responsibility for children, financial dependence and ongoing mutual support may explain why, despite a permanent separation, parties continue to be involved in each other's lives (*SA*);
- The fact that divorce proceedings have been put on hold does not necessarily indicate a non-permanent separation (*R(TC) 2/06*);
- Tribunals should not routinely place too much weight on the evidence of a "financial footprint" as compared with other evidence (*TS v HMRC* [2015] UKUT 507 (AAC)), a point which also applies in considering whether an unmarried couple are living together as husband and wife;
- Tribunals should avoid assessing the nature of a relationship by asking what a reasonable person should or would have done. One risk of doing so is that culturally relevant considerations may be overlooked. More generally, it cannot

properly be assumed that all relationships operate, or fall apart, according to some common template. These points were made by Judge Wikeley in *UA* (drawing on Upper Tribunal Judge Markus QC's analysis in *JH v HMRC* (TC) [2015] UKUT 397 (AAC)), a case in which the Appellant wife gave evidence that, in her community, divorce was likely to result in ostracisation and loss of family support and so she had tried to keep her separation 'very private and discreet'. If accepted, the wife's explanation of her actions would have influenced the inferences that could properly have been drawn from her evidence about how she dealt with her marital difficulties. The First-tier Tribunal, however, did not address this aspect of the wife's case.

Subsection (5A)—unmarried couples

Decisions by HMRC that two individuals are a couple, and must therefore make a joint claim, are frequently disputed. Such disputes also arise in relation to many other welfare benefits. In *CTC/3059/2004*, Deputy Social Security Commissioner White said it was helpful in tax credits cases to use the wider body of case about the term 'living together as husband and wife' (see volume II of this work). The Commissioner went on to hold "that framework [of case law indicates] a number of factors should be considered as a whole in deciding whether, on the balance of probabilities, a man and a woman are living together as husband and wife" including where the parties live; financial support; sexual relationship; stability of relationship; care of any children; and public acknowledgement of the relationship. Note, however, that the Commissioner accepted that there were difficulties in using the latter three factors with regard to an engaged couple.

1.280

HMRC issues extensive guidance about identifying couples and related questions. See *Tax Credits Claims Compliance Manual* paragraphs CCM 15000–CCM 15350. This guidance is of course not binding on tribunals. CCM 15040 follows the standard DWP approach to identifying who are a couple, save that the reference to sexual relationships is omitted. CCM 15120 confirms the policy and gives officials the following guidance:

"Appeal tribunals sometimes ask claimants about their sexual relationships, however, it remains our policy that you must not ask such questions. If a tribunal asks you why you have not established the position you should say that our internal policy, in common with that in DWP, is not to ask about this side of the relationship."

CCM 15045 stresses the nature of "modern-day relationships":

"By 2004, 70% of first domestic partnerships involved unmarried couples and it is now common for each party in a couple to work full-time, keep their own incomes and bank accounts and perhaps only pay money into a joint account for items of joint responsibility. Often because of demands on time both parties share childcare and domestic tasks."

In *SS v HMRC (TC)* [2014] UKUT 383 (AAC) Judge Rowley gives a close and critical analysis of the conduct of decision-making by HMRC officers and a First-tier Tribunal about whether two adults were a couple. The decision is critical of both HMRC and the tribunal but in discussion the judge examines the evidence that both parties put and should have put before the tribunal and the approach the tribunal should have taken.

Subsection (5A)—evidential and procedural issues

In *CTC/2090/2004* Social Security Commissioner Bano dealt with some of the consequences of competing claims for child tax credit. He resisted HMRC's argument that the tribunal in that case should have summonsed the mother to give evidence before finding for the father on a claim made by him. Nevertheless, where resolution of a subsection (5A) dispute turns on issues of credibility, a tribunal

1.281

should proceed carefully before making an adverse credibility finding against a party who has not been given the opportunity to participate in the proceedings.

In *UA v HMRC* (TC) [2019] UKUT 113, involving the issue whether a spousal separation was likely to be permanent, the First-tier Tribunal directed the Appellant wife that she should ensure her husband's attendance at the hearing of the appeal and, should she fail to do so, an adverse factual inference might be drawn. The Upper Tribunal doubted the wisdom of directing the wife to secure her husband's attendance, who was in the circumstances of this case a potentially hostile witness, rather than simply directing the husband to attend. The First-tier Tribunal placed the wife in a Catch-22 situation. If she secured her husband's attendance, she risked a finding that her relationship had not broken down to the extent claim. If she failed to secure his attendance, she risked a finding that he did not support her appeal (e.g. he did not accept their separation was likely to be permanent). Furthermore, as a matter of general principle an adverse factual inference may only fairly be drawn if a party fails to produce evidence that the party could reasonably be expected to produce. The First-tier Tribunal did not address the question whether the wife could reasonably have been expected to procure the attendance of her estranged husband. In fact, it seems that the husband's non-attendance may have been relied on by the First-tier Tribunal to justify it not making findings of fact on the detailed factual case put forward by the wife.

1.282   In *CTC/3543/2004* Commissioner Jacobs considered who are the parties to proceedings in cases where there are joint claims. In his view where there is a joint claim both the claimants must be parties to any proceedings against one of them. Conversely it would follow that where a claim should be a joint claim but is not, the non-claimant is not automatically subject to a decision against the claimant.

See the note to s.6 for the effect of the introduction of the potential change of status of couples who become civil partners after December 5, 2005 while one or both of them is receiving tax credits, or who are to be treated as if they are living together as civil partners from that date while one or both is claiming tax credits. Anyone making a new claim after that date must disclose if she or he has a civil partner or is living together with another person as civil partners.

Subsection (7)

1.283   This allows jurisdictional limits to be placed on entitlement to tax credit. Again, this breaks away from social security practice (which deals with Great Britain and Northern Ireland separately) to adopt income tax practice. It is supplemented by s.42 (persons subject to immigration control) and regulations made under that section. The main regulations under this subsection are the Tax Credits (Residence) Regulations 2003 (SI 2003/642). These impose a test of "ordinary residence" on most claimants.

Claims: supplementary

1.284   **4.**—(1) Regulations may—
(a) require a claim for a tax credit to be made in a prescribed manner and within a prescribed time,
(b) provide for a claim for a tax credit made in prescribed circumstances to be treated as having been made on a prescribed date earlier or later than that on which it is made,
(c) provide that, in prescribed circumstances, a claim for a tax credit may be made for a period wholly or partly after the date on which it is made,
(d) provide that, in prescribed circumstances, an award on a claim for a tax credit may be made subject to the condition that the requirements for entitlement are satisfied at a prescribed time,
(e) provide for a claim for a tax credit to be made or proceeded with in the name of a person who has died,

(f) provide that, in prescribed circumstances, one person may act for another in making a claim for a tax credit,
(g) provide that, in prescribed circumstances, a claim for a tax credit made by one member of a [2...] couple is to be treated as also made by the other member of [2 the couple]1, and
(h) provide that a claim for a tax credit is to be treated as made by a person or persons in such other circumstances as may be prescribed.

(2) The Board may supply to a person who has made a claim for a tax credit (whether or not jointly with another)—
(a) any information relating to the claim, to an award made on the claim or to any change of circumstances relevant to the claim or such an award,
(b) any communication made or received relating to such an award or any such change of circumstances, and
(c) any other information which is relevant to any entitlement to tax credits pursuant to the claim or any such change of circumstances or which appeared to be so relevant at the time the information was supplied.

AMENDMENTS

1. Tax Credits (Polygamous Marriages) Regulations 2003 (SI 2003/742) amends s.4(1)(g) as follows for the purposes of polygamous marriages:
"In section 4(1)(g)—
(a) for 'member of a married couple or an unmarried couple' substitute 'or more members of a polygamous unit';
(b) for 'of the married couple or unmarried couple' substitute 'or members'."
2. Civil Partnership Act 2004 s.254 and Sch.24 para.145 (December 5, 2005).

DEFINITIONS

"award"—see s.14(1).
"the Board"—see s.67.
"claim"—see s.3(1).
"couple"—see s.3(5A).
"entitlement"—see s.18(1).
"joint claim"—see s.3(8).
"prescribed"—see s.67.
"single claim"—see s.3(8).
"tax credit"—see s.1(2).
"tax year"—see s.47.

GENERAL NOTE

Regulations for the purposes of subs.(1) are made by HMRC by negative procedure: ss.65(2) and 66(3). The main regulations made are the Tax Credits (Claims and Notifications) Regulations 2002 (SI 2002/2014). References to "the Board" are now references to the Commissioners for Revenue and Customs: CRCA 2005 s.4.

The most important point relevant to this section is that, from 2012/13, a claim must be made not later than 31 days after the date on which it can operate. For a claim to be effective from the beginning of a tax year, it must therefore be made not later than May 6 in that year. If made later, it will operate back only 31 days from the date of claim. There is no discretion to extent this back-dating rule, although it was previously 93 days, and the only exception applies to claims where there is a disability element. See regs 7 and 8 of those regulations.

1.285

Subsection (2) gives HMRC power that it would otherwise not have to inform a claimant of information of which it knows that is relevant to a claim, or to an award or entitlement continuing. This will ensure that either member of a joint claiming couple can be informed of anything that the other member of the couple tells HMRC. This cuts across the privacy as between members of a couple that was respected by HMRC following the introduction of individual self-assessment for income tax.

Period of awards

1.286   **5.**—(1) Where a tax credit is claimed for a tax year by making a claim before the tax year begins, any award of the tax credit on the claim is for the whole of the tax year.

(2) An award on any other claim for a tax credit is for the period beginning with the date on which the claim is made and ending at the end of the tax year in which that date falls.

(3) Subsections (1) and (2) are subject to any decision by the Board under section 16 to terminate an award.

DEFINITIONS

"award"—see s.14(1).
"the Board"—see s.67.
"claim"—see s.3(1).
"tax credit"—see s.1(2).
"tax year"—see s.47.

GENERAL NOTE

1.287   This section applies to both CTC and WTC. It confirms the importance of s.3(1), namely that a claim is for one tax year at a time, and provides that any award is for that tax year (or, if made during the year, for what is left of it). This is subject to the power in s.16 to end an award, after which a new claim must be made (s.3(2)). Effect is given to these provisions by the Tax Credits (Claims and Notifications) Regulations 2002 (SI 2002/2014) regs 4–11. Regulations 11 and 12 of those regulations provide a mechanism whereby a reply to a notice relating to one year of claim under s.17 of this Act can be treated as a claim for the following year.

Subsection (2), on its face, prevents retrospective claims, but it must be read with reg.4 and following of the Tax Credits (Claims and Notifications) Regulations 2002. These make provision for the "date on which a claim is made". Under reg.7, the general rule is that a claim is treated as made for the purposes of this subsection up to three months before the date on which the claim is received by an appropriate office, if *entitlement* extends that far back. This, like other issues about *award* and *entitlement*, seems to conflate the making of an award with entitlement (see the note to s.6). It will only be known that a person is entitled once a final decision is made under s.17 of this Act after the end of the year, while the award operates on the basis that the person is probably entitled.

See also Tax Credits Act 2002 (Transitional Provisions) Order 2005 (SI 2005/773) art.6.

Notifications of changes of circumstances

1.288   **6.**—(1) Regulations may provide that any change of circumstances of a prescribed description which may increase the maximum rate at which a person or persons may be entitled to a tax credit is to do so only if notification of it has been given.

(2) Regulations under subsection (1) may—

(a) provide for notification of a change of circumstances given in prescribed circumstances to be treated as having been given on a prescribed date earlier or later than that on which it is given,
(b) provide that, in prescribed circumstances, a notification of a change of circumstances may be given for a period wholly or partly after the date on which it is given, and
(c) provide that, in prescribed circumstances, an amendment of an award of a tax credit in consequence of a notification of a change of circumstances may be made subject to the condition that the requirements for entitlement to the amended amount of the tax credit are satisfied at a prescribed time.

(3) Regulations may require that, where a person has or persons have claimed a tax credit, notification is to be given if there is a change of circumstances of a prescribed description which may decrease the rate at which he is or they are entitled to the tax credit or mean that he ceases or they cease to be entitled to the tax credit.

[[1](3A) For the purposes of this section, a change of circumstances shall be treated as having occurred where by virtue of the coming into force of Part 14 of Schedule 24 to the Civil Partnership Act 2004 (amendments of the Tax Credits Act 2002) two people of the same sex are treated as a couple.

(3B) In subsection (3A), "couple" has the meaning given in paragraph 144(3) of Part 14 of Schedule 24 to the Civil Partnership Act 2004.]

(4) Regulations under this section may—
(a) require a notification to be given in a prescribed manner and within a prescribed time,
(b) specify the person or persons by whom a notification may be, or is to be, given, and
(c) provide that, in prescribed circumstances, one person may act for another in giving a notification.

AMENDMENT

1. Tax Credits Notification of Changes of Circumstances (Civil Partnership) (Transitional Provisions) Order 2005 (SI 2005/828) art.2 (April 8, 2005). Note that these provisions have effect only for the tax year 2005/06.

DEFINITIONS

"award"—see s.14(1).
"claim"—see s.3(1).
"entitlement"—see s.18(1).
"maximum rate"—see ss.9 and 11.
"prescribed"—see s.67.
"tax credit"—see s.1(2).

GENERAL NOTE

The Bill on which this Act was based was tabled in, and passed through, the House of Commons without a clear distinction being drawn between the measures relating to *award* of a tax credit on a claim and the later issue of *entitlement* to that credit. As a result, there is no clear progression in the sections of the Act from claims to award to entitlement. This section might from context appear to be about awards, but subs.(1) is drafted to cover only entitlement issues. The link is provided partly under subs.(2) and partly by s.15, which links changes in awards to the rate at which someone *may be* entitled to a tax credit.

Tax Credits Act 2002

"Change of circumstances" is, of course, a familiar social security concept on which the SSA 1998 relies heavily for powers to change decisions after they are made but where they have continuing effect. There is also a general duty on claimants to report changes of circumstances of relevance to benefit awards. This section allows a similar duty to be imposed on tax credit claimants. The section is purely empowering. Regulations may be made by the Revenue by negative procedure: ss.65(2) and 66(3). The relevant regulations are the Tax Credits (Claims and Notifications) Regulations 2002 (SI 2002/2014) regs 19–29. Those regulations, however, take a substantially different approach to changes of circumstances to those operated for social security benefits.

The nature of a "change of circumstances" and the treatment adopted for making and dealing with changes of circumstance requires some further explanation because of the differences in the ways in which the rules operate compared with those for income support or jobseeker's allowance. The main differences are:
 (a) not all changes of circumstances during a year will result in a change of circumstances affecting the award or entitlement;
 (b) the duty to notify changes of circumstances is limited in scope and applies only to some changes; and
 (c) failure to notify when there is a duty to do so may make the person failing to notify liable to penalties and penalty proceedings under ss.31(1) and 32(3).

Relevant changes of circumstances

1.290   Because the income test under s.7 is applied to the tax year (or period of award) as a whole, a change in income levels during a year may be irrelevant to award or entitlement levels, and so not constitute a change of circumstances. This will be particularly so towards the end of a tax year. Further, because of the "buffer" built into the income test by s.7(3), any increase of income over the year as a whole of less than £10,000 is irrelevant in any event. Changes in capital are also immaterial, as it is only the (taxable) income from capital that affects the level of award and entitlement. For similar reasons, a change of job (with a gap of under seven days between jobs) will also not affect an award or entitlement unless either it changes the income level significantly over the year as a whole or it decreases the hours worked below 16, or—for WTC only—it increases or decreases the hours above or below 30.

The changes that are relevant are significant income changes, as noted above, and other changes that will stop entitlement or cause its overall level to be changed. This may apply differently to CTC and WTC. But not all those changes must be reported. Nonetheless, this remains a very wide provision, and notification may affect the start date for an award even if it does not affect the weekly amount. For example, take the case of disablement leading to a claim for disability living allowance and for a disability element to a tax credit claim. Regulation 26A of the Tax Credits (Claims and Notifications) Regulations 2002 (see below in this volume) assumes that the date of claim for DLA and the date on which it is first payable both represent changes of circumstances, as will the date of award or of any increase or decrease in award, and the date on which an individual becomes disabled or more or less disabled.

Changes that must be reported

1.291   There is no general duty to report all changes of circumstances, although it may be in a claimant's interest to do so. See Code of Practice 26 at the end of this volume.

HMRC handle the issue of changes by requiring some changes to be reported within one month of the change. The list of items that must be reported within one month is in reg.21 of the Tax Credits (Claims and Notifications) Regulations 2002. See below in this volume.

It is important to note that since April 2016 beneficiaries in certain areas will find that notification of a change of circumstances activates a transfer of entitlement from tax credits to universal credit, if the effect of the change of circumstances is to bring the existing claim for tax credits to an end. This will occur, for example, where a couple break up so that only single claims may thereafter be made. The areas will expand as the Government phases in full service or digital provision of universal credit by local authority areas. This will involve a transfer of the claim to the local Jobcentre and the need to make a new application. The relevant provisions (including the details of the areas involved) are set out in Vol.V of this work. The list of authorities is also available on the GOV.UK website. Where HMRC considers that someone should be making a claim for universal credit instead of tax credits, a form TC601U should be issued to inform the claimant that this is so. That constitutes a s.14 decision and so is subject to review and appeal.

Changes that may be reported

Under regs 20 and 25 of the Tax Credits (Claims and Notifications) Regulations 2002, a change of circumstances that may increase an award or entitlement to either WTC or CTC will only do so if notification of the change has been given to HMRC within one month of the date when the change occurred. Later notice will be backdated not more than one month. This time limit is, however, extended under reg.26 for those claiming the disability or severe disability elements of WTC. In all other cases, notification of any change of circumstances that will or may benefit the claimant should be made within the three months' limit to prevent both loss of award and loss of entitlement.

1.292

Current HMRC guidance on voluntary reporting is:

"You do not have to tell us about the following changes, but it is in your interest to do so because they may increase the amount of tax credits you are due.
Please tell us if:

- A young person over 16 continues in full time education, registers with a careers service, Connexions, or equivalent, or joins an approved Government training scheme. If you do not tell us, their Child Tax Credit will stop on 1st September after their 16th birthday.
- Your income goes down.
- Your income goes up. This may not affect your current tax credits, but it will affect how much we should pay you for next year. If we pay you too much because you delay telling us about any changes, you will be asked to pay back any tax credits overpaid.
- Your child care costs go up by £10 a week or more.
- Your usual working hours change from less than 16 hours a week to 16 or more.
- Your usual working hours change from less than 30 hours a week to 30 or more. For couples with children, it is your joint working hours that count towards the 30 hours.
- To report a change please call the tax credits Helpline on 0845 300 3900. The lines are open from 8.00am–8.00pm seven days a week."

Where changes are reported, HMRC practice is to issue a new award notice based on the details reported. Claimants are asked to check the award notice and report any errors. They are also asked to enquire if they do not receive a new award notice within one month of notifying the changes. See s.15 and COP 26 below.

Automatic notification?

Part II of this Act transfers responsibility for child benefit to HMRC. The decision of the House of Lords in *Hinchy v Secretary of State for Work and Pensions* [2005] UKHL 16 confirms the traditional view that a claimant must tell the relevant office about changes of circumstances. It is therefore not enough that, for example, a claimant tells the HMRC Child Benefit Office but not the tax credits office or the local social security office or housing benefit authority of the changed position of one of the claimant's children. However, the growth of public computer-based records and the interlinking of records between departments under the Generalised Matching Service increasingly notifies one department of information known to another. That is no defence under the tax credit scheme to liability to repay any

1.293

overpaid tax credit. It will be for consideration whether this is relevant to any penalty proceedings under ss.31 or 32. It is understood that HMRC is notified automatically about decisions of the termination of disability living allowance awards.

See also *WW v HM Revenue and Customs* [2011] UKUT 11 (AAC), where an Upper Tribunal judge held that a DWP officer had ostensible authority to make oral representations to a claimant about onward transmission to HMRC of changes of circumstances about child benefit entitlement. However, as the judge pointed out, there is also a continuing duty to disclose where a change of circumstances continues.

Failure to report

1.294 Leaving aside fraudulent or other cases of deliberate non-disclosure, if a change of circumstances is not reported when it happens it will be picked up directly or indirectly when the claimant replies to HMRC's final notice issued under s.17. This is because of the declaration necessary under s.17. If it is a relevant change, then the entitlement to WTC and/or CTC will be confirmed at a different rate to that of the award. This will result in an overpayment (see s.28) if the level of award is, as a result, higher than the level of entitlement. It could also result in an underpayment (see s.30), but only to the extent that the notification is regarded as in time for any part of the relevant tax year. In most cases, if the notification is more than three months after the end of the tax year then the right to an increased entitlement will have been lost.

HMRC has announced that it will not seek penalties from a taxpayer who has a nil award following a claim and who then fails to make a mandatory notification of a change of circumstances. See *Tax Adviser*, June 2003, p.13.

Both the Parliamentary Ombudsman and the Citizens Advice Bureaux published further reports about tax credits in October 2007. *Tax Credits: Getting it wrong?* was published as the 5th Report of the Parliamentary Ombudsman (HC 1010, Session 2006–07). The report contains detailed case studies about, in particular, overpayments and their recovery, and notes that complaints about tax credits continue to form a growing part of the workload of the Ombudsman. In the year starting on April 1, 2007 to the end of August, tax credits complaints formed 26 per cent of the Ombudsman's workload, and three quarters of those complaints were upheld either in whole or in part. It also comments on the complaints and appeals procedures. Nearly all current complaints are about overpayments.

The National Association of Citizens Advice Bureaux published a report at the same time entitled *Tax Credits: the current picture*. This summarises the comments of 1,500 respondents to a survey on their experiences of tax credits—drawn from 186,000 people helped by CABs in handling their tax credits in the last year. The report notes as worrying the number of respondents who stopped claiming tax credits because of the problems involved.

Income test

1.295 7.—(1) The entitlement of a person or persons of any description to a tax credit is dependent on the relevant income—
  (a) not exceeding the amount determined in the manner prescribed for the purposes of this paragraph in relation to the tax credit and a person or persons of that description (referred to in this Part as the income threshold), or
  (b) exceeding the income threshold by only so much that a determination in accordance with regulations under section 13(2) provides a rate of the tax credit in his or their case.

(2) Subsection (1) does not apply in relation to the entitlement of a person or persons to a tax credit for so long as the person, or either of the persons, is entitled to any social security benefit prescribed for the purposes of this subsection in relation to the tax credit.

(3) In this Part "the relevant income" means—
(a) if an amount is prescribed for the purposes of this paragraph and the current year income exceeds the previous year income by not more than that amount, the previous year income,
(b) if an amount is prescribed for the purposes of this paragraph and the current year income exceeds the previous year income by more than that amount, the current year income reduced by that amount,
(c) if an amount is prescribed for the purposes of this paragraph and the previous year income exceeds the current year income by not more than that amount, the previous year income,
(d) if an amount is prescribed for the purposes of this paragraph and the previous year income exceeds the current year income by more than that amount, the current year income increased by that amount, and
(e) otherwise, the current year income.
(4) In this Part "the current year income" means—
(a) in relation to persons by whom a joint claim for a tax credit is made, the aggregate income of the persons for the tax year to which the claim relates, and
(b) in relation to a person by whom a single claim for a tax credit is made, the income of the person for that tax year.
(5) In this Part "the previous year income" means—
(a) in relation to persons by whom a joint claim for a tax credit is made, the aggregate income of the persons for the tax year preceding that to which the claim relates, and
(b) in relation to a person by whom a single claim for a tax credit is made, the income of the person for that preceding tax year.
(6) Regulations may provide that, for the purposes of this Part, income of a prescribed description is to be treated as being, or as not being, income for a particular tax year.
(7) In particular, regulations may provide that income of a prescribed description of a person for the tax year immediately before the preceding tax year referred to in subsection (5) is to be treated as being income of that preceding tax year (instead of any actual income of that description of the person for that preceding tax year).
(8) Regulations may for the purposes of this Part make provision—
(a) as to what is, or is not, income, and
(b) as to the calculation of income.
(9) Regulations may provide that, for the purposes of this Part, a person is to be treated—
(a) as having income which he does not in fact have, or
(b) as not having income which he does in fact have.
(10) The Board may estimate the amount of the income of a person, or the aggregate income of persons, for any tax year for the purpose of making, amending or terminating an award of a tax credit; but such an estimate does not affect the rate at which he is, or they are, entitled to the tax credit for that or any other tax year.

AMENDMENTS

1. Subsection (2) is amended as it applies to polygamous units by Tax Credits (Polygamous Marriages) Regulations 2003 (SI 2003/742) reg.6.
2. References to "the Board" are now references to the Commissioners for Revenue and Customs: CRCA 2005 s.4.

Tax Credits Act 2002

DEFINITIONS

"award"—see s.14(1).
"the Board"—see s.67.
"claim"—see s.3(1).
"couple"—see s.3(5A).
"entitlement"—see s.18(1).
"joint claim"—see s.3(8).
"prescribed"—see s.67.
"single claim"—see s.3(8).
"tax credit"—see s.1(2).
"tax year"—see s.47.

GENERAL NOTE

1.296 This is a framework and empowering section making provision for the imposition of an income test on all claimants for both CTC and WTC. The relevant regulations are the Tax Credits (Definition and Calculation of Income) Regulations 2002 (SI 2002/2006) and the Tax Credits (Income Thresholds and Determination of Rates) Regulations 2002 (SI 2002/2008). The powers to make regulations are Treasury powers requiring affirmative procedures. Further, the regulations link the income test closely to income tax rules, thus breaking away from the separate social security means tests.

For modifications of this section where a claimant claims universal credit during a tax year in which he or she was entitled to a tax credit, see para.2 of the Schedule to the Universal Credit (Transitional Provisions) Regulations 2014 (SI 2014/1230).

Subsection (1)

1.297 Although this section defines the amounts of income above which tax credits are reduced by reference to income as "income threshold", HMRC literature, including formal papers, refers to them instead as "taper start points". A Commissioner criticised this change of language, without any accompanying explanation, in *CTC/2113/2006*. In that case, which concerned the operation of these start points or threshold, the Commissioner criticised the failure of HMRC to explain how its language fitted in with the statutory language. This left a claimant unable to understand the HMRC submissions and the appeal tribunal's decision agreeing with the submission (but using the statutory language also without explanation).

Subsection (2)

1.298 This disapplies the income test, so allowing payment of a tax credit without reference to separate means-testing, where the prescribed benefits are in payment. The benefits are prescribed by Tax Credits (Income Thresholds and Determination of Rates) Regulations 2002 reg.4 as covering only some claimants for income support, employment and support allowance, state pension credit and jobseeker's allowance.

Subsections (3)–(5)

1.299 These provisions are intended to enable a practical way of moving between the current year assessment rules that apply to all income tax assessments and a previous year assessment that would allow an award to be made ahead of the year in question. However, implementing the rules proved more problematic than anticipated and the rules were only fully implemented from 2012/13. Until that year no figures were set under s.7(3)(c) and (d) so stopping that aspect of the rule working. From 2012/13 the figure has been set at £2,500 (see the Tax Credits (Income Thresholds and Determination of Rates) Regulations 2002 reg.5. That regulation sets the figure for s.7(3)(a) and (b) at £10,000. This was reduced from £10,000 to £5,000 for 2013/14. The limit was returned to £2,500 for 2016/17. This was officially

(2002 c.21 s.7)

estimated (in reply on February 3, 2016 to a Parliamentary question (WA 22572)) to apply to 800,000 claimants, and was brought forward as part of the transfer to universal credit. However, as was emphasised in *CTC/3611/2008* these apply to entitlement decisions rather than awards. See further the comment on that regulation.

Subsection (4)

CTC/2270/2007 confirmed HMRC's interpretation on an important aspect of subs.(7)(a). Where two individuals become a couple during a year and make a joint claim, this requires that the aggregate income for the year is the income for the entire year of both of the couple. The Deputy Commissioner rejected the argument of a man whose partner, and later wife, moved in with him during the year that her income before she moved in was irrelevant to the joint claim made after she moved in. The plain language of Parliament required that the full income for the year of both of them was to be calculated, and then apportioned to the part of the year during which they made the joint claim. It followed that part of the wife's income was to be taken into account in respect of the joint income even though she had earned nothing since she moved in with her husband. The Deputy Commissioner reasoned that:

1.300

"... the position is that Parliament in passing the Act and the Treasury in making the Regulations have chosen a method of determining income that may be criticised as somewhat rough and ready and as such producing anomalous outcomes in cases like the present, but is nevertheless relatively simple to operate compared with the alternative of enquiring into the actual income of each single and joint claimant in respect of claim periods of less than a year."

The result of this interpretation is that in every case the full year income of any individual must be taken into account under subs.(4)(b), with the amount relevant to any claim being apportioned. The subsection as a whole is anomalous. The result where A and B became partners during a year and then split up again during that year is that the incomes of both A and B are to be taken into account from the beginning of the year to the time they split up, but then apportioned to the period of the joint claim. But after the couple split up their incomes must be disaggregated and any claim by either A or B is then to be based only on her or his income for that year. *CTC/2270/2007* was followed by an Upper Tribunal judge in *PD v HMRC and CD (TC)* [2010] UKUT 159 (AAC).

Subsections (6)–(9)

See the Tax Credits (Definition and Calculation of Income) Regulations 2002, as amended.

1.301

Subsection (10)

This is a wide power to deal with awards. It allows HMRC to make, change or stop an award during the tax year on the basis of an estimate only. That estimate will be the decision made under ss.14(1), 15(1) or 16(1). Any of these decisions are subject to appeal and, on appeal, it will be for the appeal tribunal to make the estimate (subject to any settlement of the appeal under s.54 of the TMA 1970). See further the note to s.39 below. It is understood that the standard practice of HMRC is to make all initial decisions on the basis of the previous year's income using this power. Where a claim form indicates that the current year's income should be used, HMRC then makes an immediate revision under s.15.

1.302

Modifications where claim made for universal credit

For the modifications to s.7 where a person's entitlement to a tax credit was interrupted by the making of a claim for universal credit, see reg.12A of, and Sch.1 to, the Universal Credit (Transitional Provisions) Regulations 2014 (SI 2014/1230), below in this volume.

Tax Credits Act 2002

Child tax credit

Entitlement

8.—(1) The entitlement of the person or persons by whom a claim for child tax credit has been made is dependent on him, or either of them, being responsible for one or more children or qualifying young persons.

(2) Regulations may make provision for the purposes of child tax credit as to the circumstances in which a person is or is not responsible for a child or qualifying young person.

(3) For the purposes of this Part a person is a child if he has not attained the age of sixteen; but regulations may make provision for a person who has attained that age to remain a child for the purposes of this Part after attaining that age for a prescribed period or until a prescribed date.

(4) In this Part "qualifying young person" means a person, other than a child, who—

(a) has not attained such age (greater than 16) as is prescribed, and
(b) satisfies prescribed conditions.

(5) Circumstances may be prescribed in which a person is to be entitled to child tax credit for a prescribed period in respect of a child or qualifying young person who has died.

AMENDMENT

1. Subsection (1) is amended as it applies to polygamous units by Tax Credits (Polygamous Marriages) Regulations 2003 (SI 2003/742) reg.7.

DEFINITIONS

"child"—see subs.(3).
"prescribed"—see s.67.
"qualifying young person"—see subs.(4).

GENERAL NOTE

This section sets the central tests for claiming child tax credits, namely that there be a child or young person for whom the claimant is, or joint claimants are, responsible. Subsection (1) provides that entitlement to child tax credit is dependent on these tests. It is deliberately parallel to SSCBA 1992 s.141, the section entitling claimants to child benefit for each of the children for whom a claimant is responsible. Subsection (2) makes provision for regulations defining responsibility for a child. This is covered by SSCBA 1992 s.143 and supporting regulations. The regulations also deal with competing claims for child tax credit for the same child. See paras 2.194–2.198. Subsection (3) defines a child as someone who has not reached the age of 16, but also allows the age to be extended by regulation. Child benefit is payable for all children who have not reached 16 (SSCBA 1992 s.142(1)). Child benefit is also payable for certain children over 16, but for child tax credit purposes they are known as "qualifying young persons". Subsection (4) allows regulations to define that category. The intention is, as with child benefit, to include certain young persons over 16 but not over 19, depending on ongoing education (but not covering students undergoing higher education). The effect confirms a general policy to exclude those over 16 from being "children" for state benefit purposes, but to include them, along with students, in a separate category. This is because those over 16 can claim some benefits in their own right. See further the Child Tax Credit Regulations 2002 (SI 2002/2007).

(2002 c.21 s.8)

The question whether claimants caring for children elsewhere in the European Union were entitled to child tax credit has been considered by the Upper Tribunal in two appeals. See note to s.3(3) above.

Note that the various amendments made to s.9 by s.13 of the Welfare Reform and Work Act 2016 came into force on March 16, 2016, but only for the purpose of making regulations; in all other respects they come into force on April 6, 2017 (see further s.36(4) of the Welfare Reform and Work Act 2016). See also the DWP consultation document *Exceptions to the limiting of the individual Child Element of Child Tax Credit and the Child Element of Universal Credit to a maximum of two children* (October 2016).

Subsection (5)

This makes identical provision as that in s.54 of this Act, ensuring that both child benefit and child tax credit remain payable for a period (set by regulations at eight weeks) after the death of a child or, in the case of child tax credit, qualifying young person.

Maximum rate

9.—(1) The maximum rate at which a person or persons may be entitled to child tax credit is to be determined in the prescribed manner.

(2) The prescribed manner of determination must involve the inclusion of—

(a) an element which is to be included in the case of [² every person or persons entitled to child tax credit who is, or either or both of whom is or are, responsible for a child or qualifying young person who was born before 6 April 2017,]

(b) an element in respect of each child or qualifying young person for whom the person is, or either of them is or are, responsible [² , and

(c) an element which is to be included in the case of a child or qualifying young person who is disabled or severely disabled.]

(3) The element specified in paragraph (a) of subsection (2) is to be known as the family element of child tax credit and that specified in paragraph (b) of that subsection is to be known as the individual element of child tax credit [² and that specified in paragraph (c) of that subsection is to be known as the disability element of child tax credit].

[² (3A) Subsection (3B) applies in the case of a person or persons entitled to child tax credit where the person is, or either or both of them is or are, responsible for a child or qualifying young person born on or after 6 April 2017.

(3B) The prescribed manner of determination in relation to the person or persons must not include an individual element of child tax credit in respect of the child or qualifying young person unless—

(a) he is (or they are) claiming the individual element of child tax credit for no more than one other child or qualifying young person, or

(b) a prescribed exception applies.]

(4) The prescribed manner of determination may involve the inclusion of such other elements as may be prescribed.

(5) The prescribed manner of determination—

(a) may include provision for the amount of the family element of child tax credit to vary according to the age of any of the children or qualifying young persons or according to any such other factors as may be prescribed,

(b) may include provision for the amount of the individual element of child tax credit to vary according to the age of the child or qualifying young person or according to any such other factors as may be prescribed, and

[² (c) may include provision for the amount of the disability element of child tax credit to vary according to whether the child or qualifying young person is disabled or severely disabled.]

(6) A child or qualifying young person is disabled, or severely disabled, for the purposes of this section only if—
   (a) he satisfies prescribed conditions, or
   (b) prescribed conditions exist in relation to him.

(7) If, in accordance with regulations under section 8(2), more than one claimant may be entitled to child tax credit in respect of the same child or qualifying young person, the prescribed manner of determination may include provision for the amount of any element of child tax credit included in the case of any one or more of them to be less than it would be if only one claimant were so entitled.

(8) "Claimant" means—
   (a) in the case of a single claim, the person who makes the claim; and
   (b) in the case of a joint claim, the persons who make the claim.

AMENDMENTS

1. Subsection (2) is amended as it applies to polygamous units by Tax Credits (Polygamous Marriages) Regulations 2003 (SI 2003/742) reg.8.
2. Welfare Reform and Work Act 2016 s.13 (April 6, 2017).

DEFINITIONS

"child"—see s.8(3).
"child tax credit"—see s.8.
"claimant"—see subs.(8).
"disabled"—see subs.(6).
"prescribed"—see s.67.
"qualifying young person"—see s.8(4).
"severely disabled"—see subs.(6).

GENERAL NOTE

1.308 This section is again a mixture of defining provisions and empowering provisions. Subsection (1) provides that the way in which entitlement to CTC is to be calculated is to be set out in regulations. The regulations for this purpose are the Child Tax Credit Regulations 2002 (SI 2002/2007). Subsections (2) and (3) provide that in every case an award of CTC must involve both a "family element" for the claimant and an "individual element" for each child or young person. The amount of the individual element must be higher for children or young persons who are disabled, and higher again if they are seriously disabled, but definition of those conditions is left to regulations: subss.(5)(c) and (6). The other provisions in the section are permissive.

The two child policy

1.309 The amendments to this section made by the Welfare Reform and Work Act 2016 give effect to the policy of not paying child benefit or child tax credit to more than two children in the same household (with prescribed exceptions) where a child is born on or after April 6, 2017. That has an obvious prospective effect from July 2016. The prescribed exceptions are contained in regs 9–14 of the Child Tax Credit Regulations 2002, as inserted by the Child Tax Credit (Amendment) Regulations 2017 (SI 2017/387). See the general notes to the 2002 Regulations.

(2002 c.21 s.9)

On 9 July 2011, the Supreme Court held that the child tax credit two child limit, as provided for by and under subsections (3A) and (3B), was not incompatible with certain rights under the European Convention on Human Rights protected by the Human Rights Act 1998 (*R. (SC, CB and 8 children) v Secretary of State for Work & Pensions and others* [2021] UKSC 26). The case was brought by both adults and children who claimed to have been disadvantaged by the two child limit. The Court held that the two child limit involved no direct breach of article 8 of the Convention (right to respect for private and family life) because the legislative intention was not to discourage women in receipt of child benefit from having more than two children nor would the limit hamper the integration of third and subsequent children into their families. Regarding article 14 of the Convention (prohibition of discrimination in enjoyment of Convention rights), the Appellants' case was brought in conjunction with article 8 and article 1 of the First Protocol (rights in relation to possessions), and it was on this aspect of the case that the Court focussed.

In relation to the female adult appellants, the Supreme Court held that the two child limit affects more women than men giving rise to a presumption of discrimination on the ground of sex in relation to articles 8 and 1. In relation to the child appellants, the Court held that the complaints of discrimination fell within the ambit of article 8 (it was accepted that the children's complaint was not within the ambit article 1 of Protocol 1 since they could not themselves claim child tax credit). For children living in households with three or more children as compared to households with one or two children, the Court held that there was, on the face of it, a relevant difference of treatment contrary to article 14 taken with article 8.

The two child limit did not give rise to direct discrimination between children and adults, held the Supreme Court, because children have no entitlement to child tax credit and, when it is paid to their parent/s by HMRC, is not earmarked for any particular child. Indirect discrimination did not arise from the fact that households affected by the two child limit inevitably contain more children than adults. Children and adults are not affected by the two child limit in comparable ways because child tax credit is not paid to adults for their own benefit but to assist then in meeting the needs of their children.

The key issue, therefore, concerned two potentially discriminatory situations as between, firstly, men and women and, secondly, children in larger and smaller households. The question was whether, in these cases, the differences in treatment arising from the two child limit were justified. In determining that question, the Supreme Court was guided by three principles. First, it was inappropriate for a domestic court to decide whether the UK was in violation of its obligations under international treaties such as the UN Convention on the Rights of the Child. Second, a "low intensity of review" was generally appropriate where social and economic policy judgements informed a particular legislative measure, and the court should generally accept the legislature's view that a difference in treatment is appropriate unless it is "manifestly unreasonable" but always bearing in mind that "very weighty reasons" are required to justify a difference of treatment on certain suspect grounds such as sex, gender or race. Third, legislative / Parliamentary intention is not to be identified by reference to Ministerial statements. The touchstone is the legislative wording itself although material placed before Parliament and debate on draft legislation may be relevant background information in ascertaining the objective of legislation and its probable impact.

The Supreme Court, applying the above principles, held that, as between men and women, the two child limit had an objective and reasonable justification. It pursued a legitimate aim namely protecting the economic well-being of the country and it was inevitable that, in order to achieve that aim, the two child limit would have a disproportionate impact on women because they are more likely than men to be responsible for raising children. In the Court's view, the importance of this legislative aim outweighed its disproportionate impact on women. As between children in larger and smaller households, the Court found that Parliament pursued the legitimate objective of seeking to make the child tax credit scheme fair and reasonable by limiting the extent to which recipients' income rose as the number of children in their household grew. The Court was satisfied that Parliament took account of the impact of the two child limit on the interests of affected children but nevertheless determined that this impact was outweighed by the reasons for the limit. Asking whether the measure chosen by Parliament was proportionate really involved asking if Parliament made the right choice. On a matter of such intense political controversy, the question whether Parliament made the right choice was not capable of being answered by any process of legal reasoning. Were the Court to seek to do so, it would breach the constraints placed upon the judicial branch under a constitution that enshrined a separation of powers between legislature, executive and judiciary. In short, the claims failed and the Supreme Court rejected the argument that the two child limit was incompatible with the rights protected by the Human Rights Act 1998.

Subsection (7)

1.310   As with child benefit, both HMRC and the appeal tribunals are regularly faced with disputes between two estranged parents or others both claiming child tax credit for the same child or children. The rules giving HMRC a discretion to decide to whom to pay child benefit do not apply to child tax credits. And the power to divide a single award in this subsection has not been used. In some cases the optimal approach where there is more than one child is for the parents (or other carers) to agree to split the award, or to have it paid to the claimant who can claim most. For the rules that apply where they cannot agree see Child Tax Credit Regulations reg.3.

In *HMRC v DH* [2009] UKUT 24 (AAC) Judge Jacobs found that any breach of the human rights of a claimant for CTC who had a substantial minority responsibility for the shared care of a child because HMRC declined to share an award was justified by HMRC's evidence. This is set out at length in the decision. A further appeal against that decision was dismissed by the Court of Appeal in *Humphreys v HM Revenue and Customs* [2010] EWCA Civ 56, where the Court ruled at [66] that:

> "taking into account everything we have said about the similarities and differences between this case and *Hockenjos*, and allowing for the broad margin of appreciation, we have come to the conclusion that the Commissioners have established a sufficient justification for drawing the line where they have and adhering to a system of single payment of CTC. There may well be a better or fairer way of distributing CTC, but a particular policy choice has been made and it cannot in our judgment be characterised as unreasonable or as being manifestly without reasonable foundation."

The Supreme Court has endorsed the decisions of Judge Jacobs and the Court of Appeal in a single judgment that looks closely at the Government's approach to the policy of paying tax credit to one parent only both by reference to Parliamentary record and to the post-*Hockenjos* review. This was in *Humphreys v Revenue and Customs Commissioners* [2012] UKSC 18; [2012] 1 W.L.R. 1545; [2012] AACR 46:

> "9. Although the Act allows for sharing, the decision not to provide for it in the regulations was deliberate. The Paymaster General, Mrs Dawn Primarolo, explained to Parliament (*Hansard House of Commons Debates*, 26 June 2002, vol 387, col 926–927):
>
> > 'Together [the Act and the regulations] create a system that ensures that the family with main responsibility for a child will be provided with a suitable level of support, depending on their needs. That is similar to many current systems of support for children, and we believe that–currently–it provides the most suitable means to ensure that we can focus support on raising children out of poverty. Our present aim is to enable one family to claim support for any particular child at any one time. That is the principle on which the Bill, the draft regulations and the business systems being developed are based. There are several sound reasons for that approach. Usually, the person or couple who have the main responsibility for care of a child bear more of the everyday responsibilities for the child, and meet the everyday expenditure for him or her. It is vital, especially for families

Working tax credit

Entitlement

10.—(1) The entitlement of the person or persons by whom a claim for working tax credit has been made is dependent on him, or either of them, being engaged in qualifying remunerative work.

(2) Regulations may for the purposes of this Part make provision—
 (a) as to what is, or is not, qualifying remunerative work, and
 (b) as to the circumstances in which a person is, or is not, engaged in it.

(3) The circumstances prescribed under subsection (2)(b) may differ by reference to—
 (a) the age of the person or either of the persons,
 (b) whether the person, or either of the persons, is disabled,
 (c) whether the person, or either of the persons, is responsible for one or more children or qualifying young persons, or
 (d) any other factors.

(4) Regulations may make provision for the purposes of working tax credit as to the circumstances in which a person is or is not responsible for a child or qualifying young person.

AMENDMENT

1. Subsections (1) and (3) are amended as they apply to polygamous units by Tax Credits (Polygamous Marriages) Regulations 2003 (SI 2003/742) reg.9.

DEFINITIONS

 "child"—see s.8(3).
 "disabled"—see s.11(7).
 "engaged"—see subs.(2).
 "qualifying remunerative work"—see subs.(2).
 "qualifying young person"—see s.8(4).
 "responsible for a child"—see subs.(4).

GENERAL NOTE

This section is the parallel to s.8, laying down the central test for claiming WTC by single or joint claimants, and defining or providing for definition of the key terms.

Subsection (1)

This makes the central test for WTC "being engaged in qualifying remunerative work". It is used in the regulations defining entitlement to income support and jobseeker's allowance. See the notes to Income Support (General) Regulations 1987 reg.4, and Jobseeker's Allowance Regulations 1996 reg.51, in Vol.II of this work. The test of "work" has been held by Commissioners to be wider than "employment" (*R(FC) 2/90*), although the requirement that it be "remunerative"—defined as work done for payment or in expectation of payment—excludes volunteers (*R(IS) 12/92*).

Although the test is the same both for tax credits and for income support and JSA, experience has shown that gaps can occur between one award ending and the other starting, particularly where work ends near the end of a tax year for example because of ill health or disablement. HMRC has no powers to assist someone who stops being a credit claimant in these circumstances and is under no duty to forward a claim to the Department for Work and Pensions. Nor can an appeal assist such a claimant.

Subsection (2)

1.314   This provides for further definition of what is "qualifying" work, and also when someone is "engaged" in work. This is used to set the number of hours that must be worked in order to count for WTC purposes, but it also allows the start and finish of a period of work to be defined and intermittent work patterns to be subject to regulation.

See the WTC (Entitlement and Maximum Rate) Regulations 2002 (SI 2002/2005) reg.4.

Subsection (3)

1.315   This permits the qualifying conditions for WTC to be varied between different claimants. Regulation 4 of the Working Tax Credit (Entitlement and Maximum Rate) Regulations 2002 provides that the minimum work level is 16 hours a week for single claimants with children and those suffering from disabilities, 24 hours for couples with children, and 30 hours for other claimants over 25. No WTC is payable to those under 25 unless they can claim on another basis.

Subsection (4)

1.316   This provides that responsibility for a child or qualifying young person may be defined differently for WTC purposes to the definition under s.8 for CTC purposes. This links with s.12, the child care element of WTC. However, the regulations have not to date adopted any distinction.

Maximum rate

1.317   **11.**—(1) The maximum rate at which a person or persons may be entitled to working tax credit is to be determined in the prescribed manner.

(2) The prescribed manner of determination must involve the inclusion of an element which is to be included in the case of all persons entitled to working tax credit.

(3) The prescribed manner of determination must also involve the inclusion of an element in respect of the person, or either or both of the persons, engaged in qualifying remunerative work—

(a) having a physical or mental disability which puts him at a disadvantage in getting a job, and

(b) satisfying such other conditions as may be prescribed.

(4) The element specified in subsection (2) is to be known as the basic element of working tax credit and the element specified in subsection (3) is to be known as the disability element of working tax credit.

(5) The prescribed manner of determination may involve the inclusion of such other elements as may be prescribed.

(6) The other elements may (in particular) include—

(a) an element in respect of the person, or either of the persons or the two taken together, being engaged in qualifying remunerative work to an extent prescribed for the purposes of this paragraph;

(b) an element in respect of the persons being the members of [¹ a couple],

(c) an element in respect of the person not being a member of [¹ a couple] but being responsible for a child or qualifying young person;

(d) an element in respect of the person, or either or both of the persons, being severely disabled; and

(e) an element in respect of the person, or either or both of the persons, being over a prescribed age, satisfying prescribed conditions and having been engaged in qualifying remunerative work for not longer than a prescribed period.

(2002 c.21 s.11)

(7) A person has a physical or mental disability which puts him at a disadvantage in getting a job, or is severely disabled, for the purposes of this section only if—
(a) he satisfies prescribed conditions, or
(b) prescribed conditions exist in relation to him.

AMENDMENTS

1. For the purposes of applying this section to polygamous units, Tax Credits (Polygamous Marriages) Regulations 2003 (SI 2003/742) reg.10 omits subs.(6)(c) and introduces alternative wording to subss.(3) and (6).
2. Civil Partnership Act 2004 s.254 and Sch.24 para.145 (December 5, 2005).

DEFINITIONS

"child"—see s.8(3).
"couple"—see s.3(5A).
"physical or mental disability"—see subs.(7).
"prescribed"—see s.67.
"qualifying young person"—see s.8(4).
"severely disabled"—see subs.(7).

GENERAL NOTE

This parallels s.9 for WTC. Subsection (1) allows the determination of WTC rates to be set by regulations, but subss.(2) and (4) require that anyone entitled to WTC must receive a basic element of credit. There must also be an additional disability element in appropriate cases (carrying forward the policy of DPTC): subss.(3) and (4). Subsection (7) sets the test for the disability element. There may also be a child care element, but this is provided for in s.12. Subsections (5) and (6) are purely permissive. Effect is given to these provisions by the WTC (Entitlement and Maximum Rate) Regulations 2002 (SI 2002/2005).

1.318

Child care element

12.—(1) The prescribed manner of determination of the maximum rate at which a person or persons may be entitled to working tax credit may involve the inclusion, in prescribed circumstances, of a child care element.

1.319

(2) A child care element is an element in respect of a prescribed proportion of so much of any relevant child care charges as does not exceed a prescribed amount.

(3) "Child care charges" are charges of a prescribed description incurred in respect of child care by the person, or either or both of the persons, by whom a claim for working tax credit is made.

(4) "Child care", in relation to a person or persons, means care provided—
(a) for a child of a prescribed description for whom the person is responsible, or for whom either or both of the persons is or are responsible, and
(b) by a person of a prescribed description.

(5) The descriptions of persons prescribed under subsection (4)(b) may include descriptions of persons approved in accordance with a scheme made by the appropriate national authority under this subsection.

(6) "The appropriate national authority" means—
(a) in relation to care provided in England, the Secretary of State,
(b) in relation to care provided in Scotland, the Scottish Ministers,
(c) in relation to care provided in Wales, the [²Welsh Ministers], and

Tax Credits Act 2002

(d) in relation to care provided in Northern Ireland, the Department of Health, Social Services and Public Safety.

(7) The provision made by a scheme under subsection (5) must involve the giving of approvals, in accordance with criteria determined by or under the scheme, by such of the following as the scheme specifies—
  (a) the appropriate national authority making the scheme;
  (b) one or more specified persons or bodies or persons or bodies of a specified description, and
  (c) persons or bodies accredited under the scheme in accordance with criteria determined by or under it.

(8) A scheme under subsection (5) may authorise—
  (a) the making of grants or loans to, and
  (b) the charging of reasonable fees by, persons and bodies giving approvals.

AMENDMENTS

1. Subsections (3) and (4) are modified, as they apply to polygamous units, by Tax Credits (Polygamous Marriages) Regulations 2003 (SI 2003/742) reg.11.
2. Child Minding and Day Care (Wales) Regulations 2010 (SI 2010/2574) Sch.1 (April 1, 2011).

DEFINITIONS

"appropriate national authority"—see subs.(6).
"child"—see s.8(3).
"child care"—see subs.(4).
"child care charges"—see subs.(3).
"maximum rate"—see s.11(1).
"prescribed"—see s.67.
"tax credit"—see s.1(2).

GENERAL NOTE

1.320 The child care element was introduced to family credit in response to a successful discrimination challenge to the previous law before the European Court of Justice in *Meyers v Adjudication Officer* (C-116/94) [1995] All E.R. (EC) 705. Successive governments have made it more generous, and it is now given further prominence by its own section in this Act. However, the section is in form entirely permissive, even if the failure to implement it at all might invite a further challenge to the European Court. Subsections (2)–(4) provide that the element is a credit for a part of the charges incurred by a claimant for "child care" provided for prescribed children by prescribed persons. Regulation 7 of the Tax Credits (Income Thresholds and Determination of Rates) Regulations 2002 (SI 2002/2008) specifies the proportion as 80 per cent from April 2006. The important issue here is the identity of those who may provide the child care. Government policy is that child care providers should be licensed or supervised. But the way in which that is to be done is a devolved matter for the separate governments of England, Scotland, Wales and Northern Ireland. This reflects the fact that both education and social welfare functions are now functions of the separate national authorities. Subsections (5)–(8) give effect to this. Responsibility for both policy and operation of the child care registration rules is therefore outside the responsibilities of HMRC and outside the jurisdiction of the appeal tribunals.

Parents are often able to secure free or subsidised child care through their employers or from national or local schemes. In these cases, the child care element is only paid for costs not met by the other scheme. For example if a nursery place is free for the child but the parent has to meet costs such as food, then those costs alone may be claimed.

(2002 c.21 s.12)

Employers can provide employees with free child care places or vouchers for child care, often in exchange for a salary sacrifice. See ss.318–318C of ITEPA (set out below). Where there are such schemes, parents may be able to choose between receiving employer vouchers or the child care element of working tax credit, but they cannot receive both. It is a matter for individual calculation as to which is better.

A Tribunal of Commissioners in Northern Ireland considered the scope of s.12 in *NB v HMRC (TC)* [2016] NI Com 47; [2018] AACR 26. The Tribunal of Commissioners concluded that s.12 does not provide for schemes enabling "a person of a prescribed description" (see subs.(4)(b)) to provide child care otherwise than in Great Britain or Northern Ireland. Section 12 was narrower in scope than its immediate predecessor, s.15 of the Tax Credits Act 1999. It followed that the Tax Credits (New Category of Child Care Providers) Regulations 2002 (SI 2002/1417) (not included in the main Vol.IV), which had been intra vires the 1999 Act, were now ultra vires the 2002 Act.

Rate

Rate

13.—(1) Where, in the case of a person or persons entitled to a tax credit, the relevant income does not exceed the income threshold (or his or their entitlement arises by virtue of section 7(2)), the rate at which he is or they are entitled to the tax credit is the maximum rate for his or their case.

(2) Regulations shall make provision as to the manner of determining the rate (if any) at which a person is, or persons are, entitled to a tax credit in any other case.

(3) The manner of determination prescribed under subsection (2)—
(a) may involve the making of adjustments so as to avoid fractional amounts, and
(b) may include provision for securing that, where the rate at which a person or persons would be entitled to a tax credit would be less than a prescribed rate, there is no rate in his or their case.

DEFINITIONS

"the income threshold"—see s.7(1)(a).
"maximum rate"—see ss.9(1) and 11(1).
"prescribed"—see s.67.
"relevant income"—see s.7(3).
"tax credit"—see s.1(2).

GENERAL NOTE

This short section supplements s.7 in defining the maximum rate of WTC for a claimant, and a minimum level of payment, and provides for regulations to determine these. See the Tax Credits (Income Thresholds and Determination of Rates) Regulations 2002 (SI 2002/2008), which set out a multi-stage formula.

Decisions

Initial decisions

14.—(1) On a claim for a tax credit the Board must decide—
(a) whether to make an award of the tax credit, and

Tax Credits Act 2002

(b) if so, the rate at which to award it.

(2) Before making their decision the Board may by notice—

(a) require the person, or [either or both][any or all]¹ of the persons, by whom the claim is made to provide any information or evidence which the Board consider they may need for making their decision, or

(b) require any person of a prescribed description to provide any information or evidence of a prescribed description which the Board consider they may need for that purpose, by the date specified in the notice.

(3) The Board's power to decide the rate at which to award a tax credit includes power to decide to award it at a nil rate.

AMENDMENTS

1. Subsection (2) is modified in its application to polygamous units by Tax Credits (Polygamous Marriages) Regulations 2003 (SI 2003/742) reg.12.

2. References to "the Board" are now references to the Commissioners for Revenue and Customs: CRCA 2005 s.4.

3. The section is disapplied for claimants subject to immigration control. See Tax Credits (Immigration) Regulations 2003 (SI 2003/623) regs 3 and 4.

DEFINITIONS

"claim"—see s.3(8).
"the Board"—see s.67.
"tax credit"—see s.1(2).

GENERAL NOTE

1.324 This section imposes a duty on HMRC to decide a claim properly made under s.3 by making an award (or not), but it sets no time limit on that decision. An award is a decision to pay the tax credit. It is not a decision on entitlement. That is made later, under s.18. As Upper Tribunal Judge Wright noted in *DG v HMRC and EG (TC)* [2016] UKUT 505 (AAC) the distinction between "awards" and "entitlement" made by the Act creates a "conceptual problem". An individual may be receiving payments of tax credit throughout a tax year but does not become "entitled" until some later date, normally after the end of the tax year. This explains the section title "initial decisions" (in the first draft of the Bill it was "provisional decisions"). Section 7(10) provides that HMRC may make this decision on the basis of an estimate. A decision under subs.(1) can be appealed (s.38). HMRC terms these notices "award notices".

In *LS & RS v HMRC* [2017] UKUT 257 (AAC); [2018] AACR 2 a three-judge panel of the Upper Tribunal arguably expressed the view that a s.18 decision (fixing entitlement for a tax year) would cause an appeal to the First-tier Tribunal against a s.14 decision to lapse. In *C v HMRC* (TC) [2019] UKUT 69 (AAC) Upper Tribunal Judge Mitchell held that, insofar *LS & RS* panel's *obiter dicta* suggested that an appeal against a s.14 decision **not** to make an award would lapse in the event of a subsequent s.18 decision, it should not be followed. If HMRC decide not to make an award of tax credit, there will be no subsequent s.18 decision (i.e. no lapsing event). A s.18 decision can only be given where a tax credit has been awarded for the whole or part of a tax year (since the preceding s.17 notice may only be issued in such circumstances). It follows that s.18 decisions may not be given, and no lapsing event occurs, in cases where the s.14 decision was not to make an award. Upper Tribunal Judge Poynter arrived at a similar conclusion to Judge Mitchell in *AC v HMRC (CTC)* [2018] UKUT 233 (AAC).

C v HMRC (TC) also addresses HMRC's practice of seemingly awarding a single day's tax credit even in cases where they say that, under s.14, they refuse to make an award. HMRC's written submission to the Upper Tribunal explains why:

"Due to the computer system's limitations, it has not been possible to update so as to show the claimant was not due an award at all. The workaround in this case does not reflect the actual decision made and for this H.M.R.C. apologise."

Judge Mitchell commented that "presumably ... the apparent payment of a single day's working tax credit was made on some extra-statutory basis". Whatever the basis for the payment of a single day's working tax credit, the Judge was satisfied that it did not indicate that, under s.14, HMRC decided to make an award of tax credit. Had an award been made, a s.17 notice could subsequently have been given, and a s.18 decision taken, which would, in accordance with *LS & RS*, have caused an appeal to the First-tier Tribunal against the section 14 decision to lapse. As it was, no s.14 award decision was taken and no lapsing event of the type identified in *LS & RS* was capable of occurring.

This section imposes the formal duty to deal with a claim by making or refusing an award. HMRC may use the power to estimate the income of claimants under s.7(10) rather than wait for information from an examination of the claim. Or it may make an award and examine the claim more thoroughly afterwards. A decision to award or refuse under this subsection is subject to appeal: s.38(1). However, HMRC practice is to attempt to deal with any such appeal by a settlement under the terms of s.54 of the Taxes Managements Act 1970. See the note to s.39 below. If HMRC take the view that a valid claim has not been made then no decision will be made under this section. For discussion about whether that is an appealable decision, see commentary to s.38 below.

HMRC has now automated most of the process. There is no "ownership" of a tax credits decision. One team run the computers that make the initial award decisions, then other teams take over to deal with other aspects of the case. There is also no "local office" culture in HMRC tax credit administration. That being so, it would appear to be arguable that the recognition of that aspect of DWP administration by the House of Lords in *Hinchy* would have no application to HMRC.

1.325

For judicial criticism of the practice of HMRC issuing informal decisions and then, sometimes after several months, later issuing formal decisions see *CTC/244/2008*, at [3]. In *CTC/3692/2008* a social security commissioner applied *R(IB) 2/04*, a decision of a Tribunal of three Commissioners, to HMRC tax credit decisions in the same way as to social security decisions. He decided that an HMRC decision was so faulty that the only proper course was to allow the appeal and send the issue back to HMRC to take the decision properly.

ZM and AB v HMRC (TC) [2013] UKUT 547 (AAC); [2014] AACR 17 is the decision of the Upper Tribunal in a test case brought by the Child Poverty Action Group about the meaning of s.14. The case concerned a joint claim refused by HMRC because of a query about the identity of one of the couple. This turned in part on reg.5 of the Tax Credits (Claims and Notifications) Regulations 2002. HMRC argued that a decision whether a claim was properly made under that regulation was not subject to any statutory procedure.

Judge Ward accepted that argument with regard to UK domestic legislation but then turned to an argument based by CPAG on the Human Rights Act 1988, ss.3 and 6, and art.6 of the European Convention on Human Rights. It was not in dispute before him that determination of a claim for tax credits was a determination of the claimant's civil rights. That must follow from the decision of the Supreme Court in *Tomlinson v Birmingham CC* [2010] UKSC 8. Judge Ward considered in detail whether the availability of judicial review was an art.6-compliant remedy for this kind of case. He decided that it was not, drawing support from the reasoning about the scope of judicial review of a First-tier Tribunal in the decision of Judge Turnbull in *SG v HMRC (TC)* [2011] UKUT 199 (AAC) and the decision of (then) Commissioner Levenson in *CTC/31/2006* (unreported) which he cited at some length. He concluded that he was required by the Human Rights Act 1998 to read s.14(1):

1.326

"as if it said 'On a claim for a tax credit or on what would constitute such a claim but for the Board's view that the person or one of the persons making the claim could not avail themselves of regulation 5(8) of the Tax Credits (Claims and Notifications) Regulations 2002 where that provision is in issue . . .'"

Judge Ward noted that reg.5(8) had been introduced by amending regulations without any certificate of compliance with the 1998 Act and that it was not in contemplation when the 2002 Act was passed. He concluded that his approach was a proper approach to be taken as a matter of rights-compliant interpretation and was not in effect judicial legislation.

While the judge carefully kept his focus on the specific issue in dispute, the strength of the arguments suggest that they might be applied to any other "decision" that is not regarded by HMRC as appealable save where (as with overpayments) there is clear legislative authority that the determination is not appealable.

The decision in that case, but not the full reasoning, was followed by Judge Mark in *CI v HMRC (TC)* [2014] UKUT 158 (AAC). Judge Mark agreed that judicial review was not an adequate remedy in dealing with rejection of a claim. But he emphasised that the fact that a claim was bound to fail did not prevent it being justiciable. So in that case the failure to provide a NINO for the claimant's wife would probably mean that the claim would fail but did not prevent the claimant appealing against a refusal by HMRC. There may have been questions about immigration control that should have been investigated but were not.

Subsection (2)

1.327 This empowers HMRC to require further information before making the decision by notice (see s.45 as to the notice). Penalties attach to failure to reply to a notice or to wrong replies (ss.31 and 32). The subsection also permits information to be required from others. This has been applied by the Tax Credits (Claims and Notifications) Regulations 2002 (SI 2002/2014) regs 30–32 to employers and those providing child care.

HMRC practice appears not to be using this section and those that follow as drafted. Subsection (2) gives the Revenue powers to seek information "before making their decision". There are separate powers once an award is made. HMRC practice is to examine claims both before and during the award in the same way. In other words, the award is often made and then examined. This is possible for tax credits, as they are based on a full year's claim at a time, in a way that is not possible for most social security benefits, to which individuals have entitlements on a daily or weekly basis. Rather, it follows the approach long used by HMRC under the PAYE system for taxing employment income.

In decision *CIS/995/2004* Commissioner Mesher confirmed the view stated above that the power in this section is available to deal with enquiries only *before* a decision is made. The Commissioner also criticises the standard letter TC602 used by HMRC in connection with these enquiries. It follows that HMRC have no power to impose a penalty under s.32 for failure to answer an enquiry that is purportedly made under this section but not in accordance with its terms. However, the power cited by HMRC in its notices to claimants about both enquiries and examinations cite s.19 powers, not s.14 powers (see WTC/FS1 and WTC/FS2 issued in 2013). But the power under s.19 is available only after a s.18 decision has been taken. If *CIS/995/2004* is correct, it would seem there is no power to impose a penalty for a failure to respond to a check made between the issue of the initial award under this section and the final decision under s.18 save where HMRC can show reasonable grounds for using its s.16 powers. This provides a limit on HMRC checking powers that may not have been intended but nonetheless removes liability to penalties.

Subsection (3)

1.328 This allows the award of a nil rate, so awarding a tax credit without payment. This "has the effect of keeping an entitlement going even though no money is in payment or in process. It makes it easier for the claimant and it makes it easier for us" (Baroness Hollis, House of Lords Grand Committee, May 23, 2002, CWH 146). This again reflects the fact that at this stage the decision is an initial decision only. It also means that a claimant with a nil award can ask for a review to deal with a change of circumstances rather than having to make a new claim. This gives a practical solution to a recurring problem under the SSAA 1992 and the SSA 1998 of reviews, revisions and supersessions. The adoption of this practice will, in particular, avoid some of the more awkward aspects of supersession.

Additional payments under the Social Security (Additional Payments) Act 2022

Sections 14 to 19 are disapplied in respect of an additional payment under ss.1(2) or 4(1) or (2) of the Social Security (Additional Payments) Act 2022 (see Vol.II of this work) made to a person or persons not entitled to the payment (reg.3 of the Tax Credits Act 2002 (Additional Payments Modification and Disapplication) Regulations 2002 (SI 2002/1208)). This prevents a person from making a request for mandatory reconsideration of, or appealing against, a decision to recover an overpaid additional payment. 1.329

Revised decisions after notifications

15.—(1) Where notification of a change of circumstances increasing the maximum rate at which a person or persons may be entitled to a tax credit is given in accordance with regulations under section 6(1), the Board must decide whether (and, if so, how) to amend the award of the tax credit made to him or them. 1.330

(2) Before making their decision the Board may by notice—
(a) require the person by whom the notification is given to provide any information or evidence which the Board consider they may need for making their decision; or
(b) require any person of a prescribed description to provide any information or evidence of a prescribed description which the Board consider they may need for that purpose,

by the date specified in the notice.

AMENDMENT

1. The section is disapplied for claimants subject to immigration control. See Tax Credits (Immigration) Regulations 2003 (SI 2003/623) regs 3 and 4.

DEFINITIONS

"the Board"—see s.67.
"maximum rate"—see ss.9(1) and 11(1).
"prescribed"—see s.67.
"tax credit"—see s.1(2).

GENERAL NOTE

Section 6 makes provision for a claimant to tell HMRC of a change of circumstances that should or may increase the tax credit to be awarded. This section imposes a duty on HMRC to consider if the award made under s.14 should be amended if such a notification is given (subs.(1)). The decision, including a decision not to amend, is appealable (s.38). Subsection (2) gives HMRC the same powers to enquire as s.14(2). The same provisions about notice (s.45) and penalties (ss.31 and 32) apply. Following the comment in s.14, it may be noted that although the heading of the section refers to revision, the text of the section does not. The power in this section is to "amend". That is the term used in the TMA 1970 when either the taxpayer or HMRC changes a tax return (see ss.9ZA and 9ZB of the TMA 1.331

1970). In *LS & RS v HMRC* [2017] UKUT 257 (AAC); [2018] AACR 2 a three-judge panel of the Upper Tribunal expressed the view that a s.18 decision (fixing entitlement for a tax year) would cause an appeal to the First-tier Tribunal against a s.15 decision to lapse.

Other revised decisions

1.332

16.—(1) Where, at any time during the period for which an award of a tax credit is made to a person or persons, the Board have reasonable grounds for believing—
 (a) that the rate at which the tax credit has been awarded to him or them for the period differs from the rate at which he is, or they are, entitled to the tax credit for the period; or
 (b) that he has, or they have, ceased to be, or never been, entitled to the tax credit for the period,
the Board may decide to amend or terminate the award.

(2) Where, at any time during the period for which an award of a tax credit is made to a person or persons, the Board believe—
 (a) that the rate at which a tax credit has been awarded to him or them for the period may differ from the rate at which he is, or they are, entitled to it for the period, or
 (b) that he or they may have ceased to be, or never been, entitled to the tax credit for the period,
the Board may give a notice under subsection (3).

(3) A notice under this subsection may—
 (a) require the person, or either or both of the persons, to whom the tax credit was awarded to provide any information or evidence which the Board consider they may need for considering whether to amend or terminate the award under subsection (1); or
 (b) require any person of a prescribed description to provide any information or evidence of a prescribed description which the Board consider they may need for that purpose,
by the date specified in the notice.

AMENDMENTS

1. Subsection (3) is modified as it appplies to polygamous units by Tax Credits (Polygamous Marriages) Regulations 2003 (SI 2003/742) reg.13.
2. The section is disapplied for claimants subject to immigration control. See Tax Credits (Immigration) Regulations 2003 (SI 2003/623) regs 3 and 4.

DEFINITIONS

 "the Board"—see s.67.
 "tax credit"—see s.1(2).

GENERAL NOTE

1.333

Subsection (1) gives HMRC power to "at any time during the period for which an award of a tax credit is made" to amend or terminate the award where they have reasonable grounds for believing that either of the grounds in subs.(1)(a) or (b) is made out. As Judge Wright pointed out in *HO v HMRC* (TC) [2018] UKUT 105 (AAC), "'during' makes it clear that s.16 may only apply *before* the end of 5 April in the tax year for which the award has been made" and "it cannot be used after the end of the tax year to change the award for that year". After the end of the tax year, s.18 requires HMRC to fix entitlement for the tax year and that may result in a decision that entitlement is more than, less than or equivalent to the award made for the tax year. These general terms reflect the flexibility given to the Secretary of State under the SSA 1998, and transferred to the Board by the TCA 1999. But it is clear that, unlike that under the TCA 1999, the procedure is not a mirror of the 1998 Act procedure. As noted in s.15, the drafter has deliberately avoided the revision and supersession language of both the SSAA 1992 and the SSA 1998. Despite the heading of the section, the operative power is to "amend" or "terminate" an award. Both this section and s.15 also avoid introducing the troublesome distinction between revisions and supersessions under the SSA 1998.

Again in contrast to the 1998 procedures, this section provides a power, not a duty. In *CTC/4390/2004* the Commissioner noted that on an appeal against a s.16 decision the tribunal also had a power, not a duty, to act. The express right to appeal a s.16 decision is granted in s.38(1). In such cases it is for the tribunal to decide for itself if there are reasonable grounds to make the decision, and if so it whether a decision is to be made.

The Board has power to give notice if it "believes" that the award of a tax credit may be wrong (subs.(2)). As might be expected, this is wider than the power to amend or terminate. Accordingly, the giving of a subs.(2) notice is not a necessary precondition to the exercise of subs.(1) powers: *ME v HMRC* (TC) [2017] UKUT 227 (AAC). The notice may require information or evidence from claimants and others, as defined in regulations (subs.(3)). Since a subs.(2) notice may only be given during the tax year under investigation, a HMRC letter dated after the end of the tax year, which informs a claimant that their award has been "selected for review", cannot be a subs.(2) notice (*HO v HMRC* (TC) [2018] UKUT 105 (AAC)). Current regulations empower HMRC to seek information from employers and child care providers (see note to s.14). Penalties attach to the failure to respond or to a false response (ss.31 and 32).

A standard HMRC use of the section is, somewhat obscurely, announced as a footnote to the regular series of official statistics on tax credits. They explain by way of a note to the table of total awards why, every year, there has been a reduction in the total number of awards made for both forms of tax credit in December as compared with the previous April as follows: 1.334

> "Note: between each April and December families' awards are stopped at (a) 31 August if their only qualifying child falls out of entitlement at that date, or (b) in the autumn if they fail to return their Annual Declaration for the previous year. This introduces some seasonality into the figures."

In *CTC/2576/2004* the Commissioner set aside a decision of a tribunal confirming a decision of HMRC under s.16. The Commissioner also set aside the s.16 decision and referred the matter back to HMRC. HMRC could not produce the actual decision made, and had contradicted itself in letters to the claimant. The tribunal considered this in the same way as a revision or supersession under the SSA 1998. The Commissioner found that the tribunal erred in this approach and should have relied on the TCA 2002 procedures. In addition, HMRC had erred in both its versions of its original decision. The Commissioner commented that "the decision of the Board was not properly articulated in that the intimations of it to the claimant were contradictory". It is not clear from the decision whether s.23 of this Act was also considered, as HMRC conceded that its decisions were in error.

In *CTC/3981/2005* the Commissioner analysed both the s.16 procedure and the effectiveness of appeals against s.16 decisions.

Recent decisions of the Upper Tribunal highlight a lack of focus both by HMRC and by the First-tier Tribunal on the requirements of this section. Indeed, some decisions reflect a failure both by HMRC and by the tribunal to identify specifically which provisions are used in decisions changing an initial award of tax credits to a claimant. For example, in *JR v HMRC* [2015] UKUT 192 (AAC) the Upper Tribunal judge commented in a decision setting aside both the decision of the First-tier Tribunal and of HMRC (with the agreement of the latter): 1.335

"[4] The HMRC submission to the FTT is, to put it mildly, light if not slight. There is no reference or citation of any legislation relied on by HMRC. Presumably (but this is supposition on my part) HMRC was relying on section 16 of the Tax Credits Act 2002. HMRC plainly has the power to terminate a tax credits awards under s.16(1) where it has reasonable grounds for believing certain matters to be the case. Alternatively, if it thinks that such matters in s.16(1) "may" be the case, then by s.16(2) and (3)(a) HMRC may issue the claimant with a notice requiring information or evidence. However, as I understand it, there is no power to disallow tax credits for a simple failure to provide information—rather, the HMRC decision maker must actually decide the issue arising under s.16(1)."

See also *ZB v HMRC* [2015] UKUT 198 (AAC), a decision made by the same judge the following day.

In that context, it is to be emphasised that it is not sufficient for the exercise of the powers in s.16(1) that HMRC has some reason to doubt the accuracy of an award it has made. The first issue must be the basis of the underlying award decision under s.14. Did this merely accept the claim made by the claimant or was it on some other basis? The second issue is whether there has been any notification giving rise to the power to revise upon changes of circumstance under s.15. The powers under s.16 only arise if those two powers have not triggered the necessary power to decide or revise. Also, they arise only if HMRC has some reasonable ground other than notification of a change of circumstances to call into question the award decision. The power in s.16(2) arises if there is a "belief" that the decision may be wrong for unnotified reasons. While the wording of the subsection does not require that belief to have "reasonable grounds", there must be some basis. HMRC cannot therefore engage in a "fishing expedition" or random investigation (see *ME v HMRC (TC)* [2017] UKUT 227 (AAC)). It can only act on that investigation if, after receiving any response from the request for information, there are then reasonable grounds for making the s.16 decision. That must be decided expressly even if there is no reply from the claimant.

1.336
As was emphasised in the decisions noted above, that decision is then appealable and if appealed must be expressly decided by the tribunal. Further, the tribunal must decide the appeal on the evidence before it and on the balance of probabilities. That will of course include any evidence before it that relates to the circumstances at the date of the original decision. There is a further source of confusion here because of the process of mandatory reconsideration. If the request for evidence is only made *after* HMRC has taken the s.16 decision and the claimant has asked for reconsideration, then it is not a request made under s.16—that power has already become spent by the decision. Further, that will mean that HMRC has to establish its reasonable grounds before the tribunal without reference to any further evidence. That must be done, in the ordinary course of events, by a submission to the tribunal that gives the factual basis on which HMRC has established those reasonable grounds. Otherwise the decision cannot without more be confirmed. The burden of proof under s.16 is on HMRC and therefore HMRC must offer evidence and submissions to show that it is probably right in making the decision. To confirm such a decision otherwise may also be a breach of the principles of natural justice, in that it does not allow the claimant to challenge the evidential basis for the decision and may inadvertently reverse the burden of proof. In the worst case, as Judge Wikeley commented in *ZB v HMRC* [2015] UKUT 198 (AAC), a claimant is faced with an unidentified decision made on unidentified evidence and that "is the stuff of Kafka (para.[8])."

The decision in *ZB* was followed in *SA v HMRC (TC)* [2016] UKUT 63 (AAC), although it was emphasised that that case was not another Kafka case!

The role of the First-tier Tribunal on a s.16(1) appeal was examined by Judge Wright in *ME v HMRC (TC)* [2017] UKUT 227 (AAC). HMRC's power to amend or terminate an award under s.16(1) arises where it has "reasonable grounds for believing" the rate of tax credit awarded is not the rate to which an individual is entitled or an individual is not entitled to any award. Does the First-tier Tribunal simply address whether, in its determination, those "reasonable grounds" exist or does it squarely address actual entitlement? Judge Wright decided that the Tribunal is to "stand in the shoes of the HMRC decision maker" and decide for itself whether there were reasonable grounds for believing any of the matters referred to in s.16(1). If the answer is yes, the Tribunal is to go on to decide whether to terminate or amend the award, as from the date of the HMRC decision under appeal. Note, the Tribunal is not required to amend or terminate, it simply has the power to do so.

A practical problem arises when there is a s.16 decision under appeal but HMRC makes a s.18 decision before the s.16 appeal is decided. This is because the s.18 decision will replace the s.16 decision, so may remove the basis for that appeal. In such cases the Upper Tribunal in *DF v HMRC* [2016] UKUT 47 (AAC) made it clear that HMRC was under a duty to inform the tribunal of the s.18 decision.

1.337

The inter-relationship between s.16 and s.18 decisions has been considered in a series of decisions of the Upper Tribunal. In his joint decision in *CTC/2662/2005* and *CTC/3981/2005* Commissioner Jacobs identified two possible analyses. One was that the existence of a subsequent s.18 decision meant that an appeal against a previous s.16 decision necessarily lapsed. The alternative view was that in such circumstances the tribunal had a discretion to hear the s.16 appeal but should not do so if it had been rendered academic in the light of a s.18 decision. In *CSTC/840/2014* Judge May QC held that a s.16 appeal lapses once a relevant s.18 decision is made (this was also accepted without argument and with the agreement of the parties in *NA v HMRC (TC)* [2016] UKUT 404 (AAC) at [10], notwithstanding Judge Rowland's observation that "this system of adjudication seems bizarre"). This has the potential to cause practical difficulties for certain claimants, namely those who appeal against a s.16 decision but not the subsequent s.18 decision in the belief, perhaps, that the s.16 appeal has served to bring the matters in dispute before a tribunal. If the time for appealing the s.18 decision expires, under the "lapsing" approach the claimant is left without recourse to the First-tier Tribunal. The difficulties are heightened if HMRC pursue recovery of any overpayment generated by the s.18 decision since the recovery decision is not subject to a right of appeal (see the note to s.28). In *RF v HMRC (TC)* [2016] UKUT 399 (AAC) Judge Gray disagreed with the "automatic lapsing" view. The judge considered implied automatic lapsing to be inappropriate and there could be cases in which it was of benefit to an appellant to continue to pursue the s.16 appeal. The authorities were analysed by Judge Brunner QC in *JY v HMRC (TC)* [2016] UKUT 407 (AAC). While she accepted Judge Gray's conclusion that a s.18 decision did not automatically lapse a s.16 appeal, she held that the discretion to hear an outstanding s.16 appeal should only "be exercised in very limited circumstances", and narrower than those envisaged by Judge Gray. Thus "it should be a very rare event for either the FTT or this tribunal to hear an appeal against a s.16 decision when a s.18 decision has been made" (at [39]). The Chamber President of the Administrative Appeals Chamber of the Upper Tribunal then directed that a three-judge panel be convened to address the relationship between s.16 and s.18 decisions and appeals.

The three-judge panel's decision is *LS and RS v HMRC* [2017] UKUT 257 (AAC); [2018] AACR 2. In summary, the Upper Tribunal's decision was that where HMRC "have made a decision under section 18 of the Tax Credits Act 2002 for a tax year, any decision made under section 16 for that tax year ceases retrospectively to have any operative effect, any appeal that has been brought against that section 16 decision therefore lapses, the First-tier Tribunal ceases to have jurisdiction in relation to that appeal and that tribunal must strike out the proceedings" (at [1]). The Upper Tribunal gave the following further guidance:

"52. If the First-tier Tribunal lacks jurisdiction to hear an appeal, the proper disposal before that tribunal is to strike out the proceedings. It is unlikely that the Upper Tribunal would give permission to appeal if the tribunal took a different course, such as refusing to admit the appeal, dismissing it or recording that it has lapsed. But the strike out procedure contains an important safeguard in that the claimant has a chance to make representations, which the duty of fairness would require the tribunal to respect if it did take another course. That is not a mere formality; it may save a tribunal from using its powers inappropriately or without first ensuring that the conditions for a strike out are met."

1.338 However, the three-judge panel also decided that the Upper Tribunal, unlike the First-tier Tribunal, had jurisdiction to hear an appeal against a "decision" of the First-tier Tribunal in a lapsed s.16 case. In the exercise of that jurisdiction, the Upper Tribunal has power to hear and decide an issue that has become academic as between the parties. The three-judge panel also decided that, following the introduction of the requirement for an appellant to seek "Mandatory Reconsideration" before exercising the right of appeal (s.38), it is no longer possible for the First-tier Tribunal to treat an extant s.16 appeal as continuing against the s.18 decision that has replaced the s.16 decision.

Another practical issue of importance in the operation of s.16 is the practice of stopping payment of tax credits while a s.16 enquiry is pursued. The power to do this is in reg.11 of the Tax Credits (Payment by the Commissioners) Regulations 2002 (see para.2.361 below) and arises not when the notice is issued but only when an individual has failed to supply requested information or evidence by a specified date. It is open to question whether that power is operative where the claimant or someone on the claimant's behalf has responded within the time limit until a view has been taken by HMRC (or more usually their contractual agent such as Concentrix) that there has been a failure. Further, there appears to be no administrative procedure in place to notify a claimant why a postponement has been authorised. Postponement clearly requires a decision to be taken by someone, although such a decision is not appealable (as not within s.38 of the 2002 Act), so leaving administrative remedies or judicial review as ways of challenging it.

In replies by the Treasury (David Gauke MP) to written Parliamentary questions asked by Frank Field MP (and answered on February 3, 2016) it was stated that the average time then being taken by Concentrix to deal with s.16 decisions was 24 days. It appears from the information provided in the written answers (WA 22572 and other grouped questions) that by that date Concentrix has conducted some 350,000 reviews since its contract with HMRC commenced in April 2014. As regards the contractual arrangements entered into by HMRC with Concentrix, see para.1.841 below.

Final notice

1.339 17.—(1) Where a tax credit has been awarded for the whole or part of a tax year—
 (a) for awards made on single claims, the Board must give a notice relating to the tax year to the person to whom the tax credit was awarded, and
 (b) for awards made on joint claims, the Board must give such a notice to the persons to whom the tax credit was awarded (with separate copies of the notice for each of them if the Board consider appropriate).
(2) The notice must either—
 (a) require that the person or persons must, by the date specified for the purposes of this subsection, declare that the relevant circumstances were as specified or state any respects in which they were not, or
 (b) inform the person or persons that he or they will be treated as having declared in response to the notice that the relevant circumstances were as specified unless, by that date, he states or they state any respects in which they were not.
(3) "Relevant circumstances" means circumstances (other than income) affecting—
 (a) the entitlement of the person, or joint entitlement of the persons, to the tax credit, or
 (b) the amount of the tax credit to which he was entitled, or they were jointly entitled, for the tax year.

(4) The notice must either—
(a) require that the person or persons must, by the date specified for the purposes of this subsection, declare that the amount of the current year income or estimated current year income (depending on which is specified) was the amount, or fell within the range, specified or comply with subsection (5), or
(b) inform the person or persons that he or they will be treated as having declared in response to the notice that the amount of the current year income or estimated current year income (depending on which is specified) was the amount, or fell within the range, specified unless, by that date, he complies or they comply with subsection (5).
(5) To comply with this subsection the person or persons must either—
(a) state the current year income or his or their estimate of the current year income (making clear which); or
(b) declare that, throughout the period to which the award related, subsection (1) of section 7 did not apply to him or them by virtue of subsection (2) of that section.
(6) The notice may—
(a) require that the person or persons must, by the date specified for the purposes of subsection (4), declare that the amount of the previous year income was the amount, or fell within the range, specified or comply with subsection (7), or
(b) inform the person or persons that he or they will be treated as having declared in response to the notice that the amount of the previous year income was the amount, or fell within the range, specified unless, by that date, he complies or they comply with subsection (7).
(7) To comply with this subsection the person or persons must either—
(a) state the previous year income, or
(b) make the declaration specified in subsection (5)(b).
(8) The notice must inform the person or persons that if he or they—
(a) makes or make a declaration under paragraph (a) of subsection (4), or is or are treated as making a declaration under paragraph (b) of that subsection, in relation to estimated current year income (or the range within which estimated current year income fell); or
(b) states or state under subsection (5)(a) his or their estimate of the current year income;

he or they will be treated as having declared in response to the notice that the amount of the (actual) current year income was as estimated unless, by the date specified for the purposes of this subsection, he states or they state the current year income.

(9) "Specified", in relation to a notice, means specified in the notice.
(10) Regulations may—
(a) provide that, in prescribed circumstances, one person may act for another in response to a notice under this section, and
(b) provide that, in prescribed circumstances, anything done by one member of a [²couple] in response to a notice given under this section is to be treated as also done by the other member of [²the couple].

AMENDMENTS

1. Subsection (10) is modified as it applies to polygamous units by Tax Credits (Polygamous Marriages) Regulations 2003 (SI 2003/742) reg.14.
2. Civil Partnership Act 2004 s.254 and Sch.24 para.145 (December 5, 2005).

3. The section is disapplied for claimants subject to immigration control. See Tax Credits (Immigration) Regulations 2003 (SI 2003/623) regs 3 and 4.

DEFINITIONS

"the Board"—see s.67.
"couple"—see s.3(5A).
"current year income"—see s.7(4).
"joint claims"—see s.3(8).
"prescribed"—see s.67.
"previous year income"—see s.7(5).
"relevant circumstances"—see subs.(3).
"specified"—see subs.(9).
"tax credit"—see s.1(2).
"tax year"—see s.47.

GENERAL NOTE

1.340 What are now ss.17 and 18 were originally drafted as one clause. It was divided by amendments in the House of Lords into the notice provisions (s.17) and the decision provisions (s.18), to avoid it being overlong. Together the two sections provide the regime for checking the s.14 initial decision on an award before turning it into an entitlement, and then for making the entitlement decision. The underlying pattern is that the award decision must be made in response to a claim. Payment is then made under the award decision for a tax year. At the end of the tax year, HMRC uses the s.17 powers to check whether the claimant is, or remains, entitled to the tax credit awarded, or to some higher or lower rate of tax credit. After checking, a "final decision" is made on entitlement.

The effect of subs.(1) is that all awards of tax credit must be checked. In every case a notice must be sent to a claimant (or joint claimants). Notices must take one of two forms. One is a demand for a declaration that there has been no change of relevant circumstances (subs.(2)(a)). It can also demand details (or an estimate) of the current year's income (subs.(4)(a)). The other is a notice telling people that it will be assumed that there is no change of circumstances unless any changes are reported by a given date (subs.(2)(b)). It can also tell people that it is assumed that their income is of an assumed level or range unless a declaration is made stating otherwise (subs.(4)(b)). The notice may also take either of those approaches about the previous year's income (subs.(6)). Further provisions are laid down in the Tax Credits (Claims and Notifications) Regulations 2002 (SI 2002/2014). The section also states the ways in which people must comply with these notices. Penalties may be imposed on failures to reply and wrong replies (ss.31 and 32).

HMRC calls the notices issued under this section "Annual Declarations". The annual declarations may also constitute claims under s.3. The point may arise as to which years the declaration and claim relate to. In *CTC/1594/2006* the Commissioner accepted HMRC's argument that it was for HMRC to decide this, subject to judicial review rather than appeal, but also suggested it might depend on the wording used. And see *SG v HM Revenue and Customs (TC)* [2011] UKUT 199 (AAC) about the effects of failing to respond to a final notice. For modifications of this section where a claimant claims universal credit during a tax year in which he or she was entitled to a tax credit, see para.3 of the Schedule to the Universal Credit (Transitional Provisions) Regulations 2014 (SI 2014/1230).

Modifications where claim made for universal credit

For the modifications to s.17 where a person's entitlement to a tax credit was interrupted by the making of a claim for universal credit, see reg.12A of, and Schedule 1 to, the Universal Credit (Transitional Provisions) Regulations 2014 (SI 2014/1230), below in this volume.

Decisions after final notice

18.—(1) After giving a notice under section 17, the Board must decide—
   (a) whether the person was entitled, or the persons were jointly entitled, to the tax credit, and
   (b) if so, the amount of the tax credit to which he was entitled, or they were jointly entitled,
for the tax year.

(2) But, subject to subsection (3), that decision must not be made before a declaration or statement has been made in response to the relevant provisions of the notice.

(3) If a declaration or statement has not been made in response to the relevant provisions of the notice on or before the date specified for the purposes of section 17(4), that decision may be made after that date.

(4) In subsections (2) and (3) "the relevant provisions of the notice" means—
   (a) the provision included in the notice by virtue of subsection (2) of section 17,
   (b) the provision included in the notice by virtue of subsection (4) of that section, and
   (c) any provision included in the notice by virtue of subsection (6) of that section.

(5) Where the Board make a decision under subsection (1) on or before the date referred to in subsection (3), they may revise it if a new declaration or statement is made on or before that date.

(6) If the person or persons to whom a notice under section 17 is given is or are within paragraph (a) or (b) of subsection (8) of that section, the Board must decide again—
   (a) whether the person was entitled, or the persons were jointly entitled, to the tax credit, and
   (b) if so, the amount of the tax credit to which he was entitled, or they were jointly entitled,
for the tax year.

(7) But, subject to subsection (8), that decision must not be made before a statement has been made in response to the provision included in the notice by virtue of subsection (8) of section 17.

(8) If a statement has not been made in response to the provision included in the notice by virtue of that subsection on or before the date specified for the purposes of that subsection, that decision may be made after that date.

(9) Where the Board make a decision under subsection (6) on or before the date referred to in subsection (8), they may revise it if a new statement is made on or before that date.

(10) Before exercising a function imposed or conferred on them by subsection (1), (5), (6) or (9), the Board may by notice require the person, or either or both of the persons, to whom the notice under section 17 was given to provide any further information or evidence which the Board consider they may need for exercising the function by the date specified in the notice.

(11) Subject to sections [319, 20, [421A, 21B and 21C]] and regulations under section 21 (and to any revision under subsection (5) or (9) and any appeal)—
   (a) in a case in which a decision is made under subsection (6) in relation to a person or persons and a tax credit for a tax year, that decision, and

(b) in any other case, the decision under subsection (1) in relation to a person or persons and a tax credit for a tax year,

is conclusive as to the entitlement of the person, or the joint entitlement of the persons, to the tax credit for the tax year and the amount of the tax credit to which he was entitled, or they were jointly entitled, for the tax year.

AMENDMENTS

1. Subsection (10) is modified as it applies to polygamous units by Tax Credits (Polygamous Marriages) Regulations 2003 (SI 2003/742) reg.15.
2. The section is modified for claimants subject to immigration control. See Tax Credits (Immigration) Regulations 2003 (SI 2003/623) regs 3 and 4.
3. Tax Credits, Child Benefit and Guardian's Allowance Reviews and Appeals Order 2014 (SI 2014/886) art.2(2) (April 6, 2014).
4. Tax Credits Reviews and Appeals (Amendment) Order 2021 art.2(2) (January 15, 2021).

DEFINITIONS

"the Board"—see s.67.
"prescribed"—see s.67.
"relevant provisions of the notice"—see subs.(4).
"tax credit"—see s.1(2).
"tax year"—see s.47.

GENERAL NOTE

1.342   HMRC calls these notices "finalised awards". In *CTC/2113/2006* a Commissioner criticised this use of language, and a more general failure to distinguish between awards and entitlements, in HMRC notices and literature in the case papers.

In *HMRC v ED* (TC) [2021] UKUT 195 (AAC), Upper Tribunal Judge Rowland expressed doubt as to whether HMRC had power to make a section 18 decision that would effectively negate a live appeal made against an earlier tax credits decision:

"14 ... It seems to me to be arguable that it is improper for HMRC to make a section 18 decision in circumstances where a properly-made challenge to an earlier decision is under active consideration and the effect of making a section 18 decision is to force the claimant to go back to square one. If everything that had been done in relation to the earlier decision, including any application for mandatory reconsideration or any decision on mandatory reconsideration, were to be treated as having been done in relation to the section 18 decision, that would be one thing, but for the process to have be repeated in its entirety is likely to be unfair to the claimant and a waste of HMRC's resources in any case where the section 18 decision is to the same effect as the decision that is being challenged."

Even where HMRC decide a person is not entitled to a tax credit for a tax year, their decisions often record a single day's entitlement. In *HO v HMRC (TC)* [2018] UKUT 105 (AAC), HMRC informed the Upper Tribunal that the award for one day "is as close as HMRC's computer systems come to implementing a decision that there was no entitlement for the entire tax year where an award has previously been made".

See the note to s.17 for the general scheme of which this is part. Subsection (1) of this section imposes the duty on HMRC to make a decision on entitlement in every case, but only after the s.17 notice procedure has been followed (subs.(2)) or the full time to comply has been allowed (subs.(3)). The wording of subs.(1)—in that the duty to decide entitlement only arises "after giving a notice under section 17"—means a valid s.18(1) decision may not be made unless a s.17 notice has been given. As Upper Tribunal Judge Wright put it in *DG v HMRC and EG (TC)* [2016] UKUT 505 (AAC), a s.18(1) decision is "parasitic" on a s.17 notice. Subsection (4) links the procedures under this section with the relevant notice provisions in s.17. Subsection (5) allows an entitlement decision under subs.(1) to be revised if there is a reply or further reply from a claimant after a decision has been made. The use of "revise" was avoided in earlier sections in favour of "amend" (despite their headings: see ss.15 and 16), but is here applied to changes to a final decision. Such revisions can be of the whole or only part of the decision. The language avoids attaching formalities or threshold conditions to the process. Subsections (6)–(9) repeat the substance of subss. (1)–(5) for claimants who estimated their current year income in their claims or initial responses to the s.17 notice. In either case, HMRC may require further information (subs.(10)). The standard penalty regime applies to subs.(10). Subsection (11) makes a subs.(1) or subs.(6) decision conclusive unless it is revised under subss.(5) or (9), or it is appealed under s.38, or it is altered under any of the powers in ss.19–21C. In *HO v HMRC (TC)* [2018] UKUT 105 (AAC), Judge Wright said that "the recognition in the statutory language that the final nature of a section 18 decision is subject to an appeal against that decision under section 38 in itself provides a strong implication that the decision on the appeal will overset or replace the HMRC decision under section 18". The Claimant Compliance Manual ("CCM") (on the CCM, see note to TCA 2002 s.31 below) emphasises that a decision under subs.(6) should be taken by an officer as a "best judgment" decision, not just a guess. "You can use some guesswork but it must be honest guess-work" (at [10270]). HMRC literature emphasises that the procedure under ss.17 and 18 does not provide a mechanism to take into account a change of circumstances that would lead to an increase in tax credits for the year. Such changes must be notified through the change of circumstances procedure. It is understood that this view is thought by some to be open to challenge, and that the procedure should operate in both ways. However, that would cut across the provisions for notification in s.15 and linked regulations.

For an analysis of the procedure under s.18, see *CTC/2662/2005*.

The addition of the references to ss.21A to 21C in para.(11) ensures that this regulation is compatible with the provisions about reviews added by those sections.

On the inter-relationship between s.16 and s.18 decisions, see further the note to s.16 above.

For modifications of this section where a claimant claims universal credit during a tax year in which he or she was entitled to a tax credit, see para.4 of the Schedule to the Universal Credit (Transitional Provisions) Regulations 2014 (SI 2014/1230).

Modifications where claim made for universal credit
For the modifications to s.18 where a person's entitlement to a tax credit was interrupted by the making of a claim for universal credit, see reg.12A of, and Schedule 1 to, the Universal Credit (Transitional Provisions) Regulations 2014 (SI 2014/1230), below in this volume.

1.343

Power to enquire

19.—(1) The Board may enquire into—
(a) the entitlement of a person, or the joint entitlement of persons, to a tax credit for a tax year, and
(b) the amount of the tax credit to which he was entitled, or they were jointly entitled, for the tax year,
if they give notice to the person, or each of the persons, during the period allowed for the initiation of an enquiry.

(2) As part of the enquiry the Board may by notice—
(a) require the person, or either or both of the persons, to provide any information or evidence which the Board consider they may need for the purposes of the enquiry, or
(b) require any person of a prescribed description to provide any information or evidence of a prescribed description which the Board consider they may need for those purposes, by the date specified in the notice.

1.344

(3) On an enquiry the Board must decide—
(a) whether the person was entitled, or the persons were jointly entitled, to the tax credit, and
(b) if so, the amount of the tax credit to which he was entitled, or they were jointly entitled,
for the tax year.

(4) The period allowed for the initiation of an enquiry is the period beginning immediately after the relevant section 18 decision and ending—
(a) if the person, or either of the persons, to whom the enquiry relates is required by section 8 of the Taxes Management Act 1970 (c.9) to make a return, with the day on which the return becomes final (or, if both of the persons are so required and their returns become final on different days, with the later of those days), or
(b) in any other case, one year after the beginning of the relevant section 17 date.

(5) "The relevant section 18 decision" means—
(a) in a case in which a decision must be made under subsection (6) of section 18 in relation to the person or persons and the tax year to which the enquiry relates, that decision; and
(b) in any other case, the decision under subsection (1) of that section in relation to the person or persons and that tax year.

(6) "The relevant section 17 date" means—
(a) in a case in which a statement may be made by the person or persons in response to provision included by virtue of subsection (8) of section 17 in the notice given to him or them under that section in relation to the tax year, the date specified in the notice for the purposes of that subsection, and
(b) in any other case, the date specified for the purposes of subsection (4) of that section in the notice given to him or them under that section in relation to the tax year.

(7) A return becomes final—
(a) if it is enquired into under section 9A of the Taxes Management Act 1970 (c.9), when the enquiries are completed (within the meaning of section 28A of that Act), or
(b) otherwise, at the end of the period specified in subsection (2) of that section in relation to the return.

(8) An enquiry is completed at the time when the Board give notice to the person or persons of their decision under subsection (3); but if the Board give notice to the persons at different times the enquiry is completed at the later of those times.

(9) The person, or either of the persons, to whom the enquiry relates may at any time before such notice is given apply for a direction that the Board must give such a notice.

[4 (10) Any such application is to be subject to the relevant provisions of Part 5 of the Taxes Management Act 1970 (see, in particular, section 48(2)(b) of that Act), and the tribunal must give the direction applied for unless satisfied that the Board have reasonable grounds for not making the decision or giving the notice.]

(11) Where the entitlement of a person, or the joint entitlement of persons, to a tax credit for a tax year has been enquired into under this section, it is not to be the subject of a further notice under subsection (1).

(12) Subject to sections [⁵19, 20, [⁶21A, 21B and 21C]] and regulations under section 21 (and to any appeal), a decision under subsection (3) in relation to a person or persons and a tax credit for a tax year is conclusive as to the entitlement of the person, or the joint entitlement of the persons, to the tax credit for the tax year and the amount of the tax credit to which he was entitled, or they were jointly entitled, for the tax year.

AMENDMENTS

1. Subsections (2), (4) and (9) are modified for polygamous units by Tax Credits (Polygamous Marriages) Regulations 2003 (SI 2003/742) reg.16.
2. Subsection (10) is modified by TCA 2002 s.63(5)(a), the modification being indicated by square brackets.
3. The section is modified for claimants subject to immigration control. See Tax Credits (Immigration) Regulations 2003 (SI 2003/623) regs 3 and 4.
4. Transfer of Tribunal Functions and Revenue and Customs Appeals Order 2009 (SI 2009/56) art.3(1) and Sch.1 para.313 (April 1, 2009).
5. Tax Credits, Child Benefit and Guardian's Allowance Reviews and Appeals Order 2014 (SI 2014/886) art.2(3) (April 6, 2014).
6. Tax Credits Reviews and Appeals (Amendment) Order 2021 art.2(3) (January 15, 2021).

DEFINITIONS

"the Board"—see s.67.
"General Commissioners"—see s.47.
"prescribed"—see s.67.
"Special Commissioners"—see s.47.
"the relevant section 17 date"—see subs.(6).
"the relevant section 18 decision"—see subs.(5).
"tax credit"—see s.1(2).

GENERAL NOTE

This provision gives HMRC a broad general power similar to that in s.9A of the TMA 1970 (power to enquire into self-assessment returns) to enquire into the correctness of a s.18 entitlement decision. An enquiry under this section can be opened at any time after the s.18 decision is made until a year after the final date for replying to a s.17 notice, unless HMRC uses its power to issue a demand for a personal tax return under s.8 of the TMA 1970 on the claimant. A return for a year must be made by January 31 next after the tax year ends (each April) or, if demanded later, three months after it is required. Section 9A (which entitles HMRC to issue a notice of enquiry into a return under s.8) allows about a year (the period is defined precisely) for a HMRC enquiry to follow a personal return.

In *TS v HMRC* [2015] UKUT 507 (AAC) the Upper Tribunal judge ruled that the burden of proof in an appeal against a decision of HMRC made under s.19 is on HMRC not the claimant. It is particularly important therefore in such cases that a tribunal considering an appeal ensures that it has all the relevant evidence before it, and in particular all evidence that a claimant has submitted to HMRC in response to its power to enquire. A s.19 enquiry must commence with notice to the person or persons making the claim under enquiry, so putting the claimant on notice to provide evidence. The section also empowers the requirement that evidence be produced. Any evidence so produced must be put before the tribunal on an appeal and it is the duty of the tribunal to ensure that this is done. This was emphasised by Judge Wright in *JW v HMRC* [2015] UKUT 369 (AAC). A failure to do this will be both a failure to comply with the Tribunal Procedural Rules and a breach of natural justice.

1.345

An individual who is the subject of an enquiry has the same power to apply to a tribunal to stop the enquiry as exists for the equivalent income tax provisions, save that the application goes to the appeal tribunal (see s.63), not a tax tribunal.

Subsections (9) and (10) allow an individual to ask a tribunal to close an HMRC enquiry. This power has been created because there is otherwise no time limit to end an enquiry provided that it is started by HMRC within the correct time limits. The practice of tax tribunals, approved by the courts, is to deal with many applications by setting a time limit on HMRC rather than closing the enquiry immediately. It is also clear that rejection by a tribunal of one application to close an enquiry does not prevent an individual later making another application if the enquiry continues. The amended version of subs.(10) aligns the procedure with the new procedure for reviewing all tax decisions introduced by the Finance Act 2008 by way of amendments now in the Taxes Management Act 1970 from s.48. HMRC is given the right to review any decision before it goes forward to a tribunal, unless the appellant directly notifies the tribunal of the decision that is subject to appeal.

The addition of the references to ss.21A to 21C in para.(12) ensures that this regulation is compatible with the provisions about reviews added by those sections.

The power to look into a decision about entitlement to tax credits is referred to both in this section and in practice as an enquiry. This is to be distinguished from an investigation into a claim for, or award of, a tax credit, which is referred to by HMRC as an examination. The key difference is that an award is provisional, while an enquiry relates to an award that has been or is being finalised to give rise to entitlement.

HMRC have issued a short series of factsheets about its powers and practices for claimants: WTC/FS1 on enquiries; WTC/FS2 on examinations; WTC/FS3 on formal requests for information; and WTC/FS4 on meetings with an officer of Revenue and Customs.

For modifications of this section where a claimant claims universal credit during a tax year in which he or she was entitled to a tax credit, see para.5 of the Schedule to the Universal Credit (Transitional Provisions) Regulations 2014 (SI 2014/1230).

Modifications where claim made for universal credit

1.346
For the modifications to s.19 where a person's entitlement to a tax credit was interrupted by the making of a claim for universal credit, see reg.12A of, and Schedule 1 to, the Universal Credit (Transitional Provisions) Regulations 2014 (SI 2014/1230), below in this volume.

Decisions on discovery

1.347
20.—(1) Where in consequence of a person's income tax liability being revised the Board have reasonable grounds for believing that a conclusive decision relating to his entitlement to a tax credit for a tax year (whether or not jointly with another person) is not correct, the Board may decide to revise that decision.

(2) A person's income tax liability is revised—
  (a) on the taking effect of an amendment of a return of his under section 9ZA(1) of the Taxes Management Act 1970,
  (b) on the issue of a notice of correction under section 9ZB of that Act amending a return of his (provided that he does not give a notice of rejection before the end of the period of thirty days beginning with the date of issue of the notice of correction),
  (c) on the amendment of an assessment of his by notice under section 9C of that Act,
  (d) on the amendment of a return of his under section 12ABA(3)(a) of that Act,

(e) on the amendment of a return of his under subsection (6)(a) of section 12ABB of that Act after the correction of a partnership return under that section (provided that the amendment does not cease to have effect by reason of the rejection of the correction under subsection (4) of that section),
(f) on the issue of [³ a partial or final closure notice] under section 28A of that Act making amendments of a return of his;
(g) on the amendment of a return of his under section 28B(4)(a) of that Act,
(h) on the making of an assessment as regards him under section 29(1) of that Act,
(i) on the vacation of the whole or part of an assessment of his under section 32 of that Act,
(j) on giving him relief under section 33 of that Act, or
(k) on the determination (or settlement) of an appeal against the making, amendment or vacation of an assessment or return, or a decision on a claim for relief, under any of the provisions mentioned in paragraphs (c), (f) and (h) to (j).

(3) But no decision may be made under subsection (1)—
(a) unless it is too late to enquire into the person's entitlement under section 19, or
(b) after the period of one year beginning when the person's income tax liability is revised [³ as specified in subsection (1)].

(4) Where the Board have reasonable grounds for believing that—
(a) a conclusive decision relating to the entitlement of a person, or the joint entitlement of persons, to a tax credit for a tax year is not correct, and
(b) that is attributable to fraud or neglect on the part of the person, or of either of the persons, or on the part of any person acting for him, or either of them,

the Board may decide to revise that decision.

(5) But no decision may be made under subsection (4)—
(a) unless it is too late to enquire into the entitlement, or joint entitlement, under section 19, or
(b) after the period of five years beginning with the end of the tax year to which the conclusive decision relates.

(6) "Conclusive decision", in relation to the entitlement of a person, or joint entitlement of persons, to a tax credit for a tax year, means—
(a) a decision in relation to it under section 18(1), (5), (6) or (9) or 19(3) or a previous decision under this section, or
(b) a decision under regulations under section 21 relating to a decision within paragraph (a),[² . . .]
[²(c) a decision within paragraph (a) or (b) as varied under section [⁴21A(4)(b) or 21C(4)(b)], or
(d) a decision on an appeal against a decision within paragraph (a), (b) or (c).]

(7) Subject to any subsequent decision under this section and to regulations under section 21 [²and to any review under section 21A [⁴ or 21C]] (and to any appeal), a decision under subsection (1) or (4) in relation to a person or persons and a tax credit for a tax year is conclusive as to the entitlement of the person, or the joint entitlement of the persons, to the tax credit for the tax year and the amount of the tax credit to which he was entitled, or they were jointly entitled, for the tax year.

Amendments

1. Subsection (4) is modified as it applies to polygamous units by Tax Credits (Polygamous Marriages) Regulations 2003 (SI 2003/742) reg.17.
2. Tax Credits, Child Benefit and Guardian's Allowance Reviews and Appeals Order 2014 (SI 2014/886) art.2(4) and (5) (April 6, 2014).
3. Finance (No.2) Act 2017 s.63 and Sch.15 para.35 (these amendments have effect in relation to an enquiry under ss.9A, 12ZM or 12AC of the Taxes Management Act 1970, or under Sch.18 to the Finance Act 1998, where notice of the enquiry is given on or after November 16, 2017 or the enquiry is in progress immediately before November 16, 2017: Finance (No.2) Act 2017 s.63 and Sch.15 para.44).
4. Tax Credits Reviews and Appeals (Amendment) Order 2021 art.2(4) (January 15, 2021).

Cross-References

TMA 1970:

s.9ZA	Amendment of personal or trustee return by taxpayer
s.9ZB	Correction of personal return by taxpayer
s.9C	Amendment of self-assessment during enquiry to prevent loss of tax
s.12ABA	Amendment of partnership return by taxpayer
s.12ABB	Correction of partnership return by Revenue
s.28A	Completion of enquiry into personal or trustee return
s.28B	Completion of enquiry into partnership return
s.29	Assessment where loss of tax discovered
s.32	Double assessment
s.33	Error or mistake

Definitions

"conclusive decision"—see subs.(6).
"income tax"—see ICTA 1988 s.1.
"prescribed"—see s.67.
"tax credit"—see s.1(2).

General Note

1.348   Discovery is the traditional term used for finding out or taking informed guesses about undisclosed income for income tax purposes. The power to make assessments where loss of tax is discovered is in s.29 of the TMA 1970. This section is wider than that, although in part it flows from it. Section 29 allows an officer who discovers unassessed tax or excessive relief to make an assessment of the amount which, in the officer's opinion, ought to be charged to tax, and also imposes other conditions before the power can be used. This section, by contrast, allows action by HMRC in two sets of circumstances.

The first is if HMRC has reasonable grounds for believing an otherwise conclusive decision about tax credit (defined in subs.(6)) is not correct because of a revision of income tax liability (subs.(1)). HMRC may act if one of the TMA 1970 powers listed in subs.(2) has been used for a revision. These include s.29 and also the powers to revisit personal and partnership tax returns and decisions made by settlement or on appeal. Revisions under this power can be made only if it is too late to use s.19. And they cannot be made unless the revision is made within a year of the income tax revision (subs.(3)).

The second power (in subs.(4)) arises where HMRC has reasonable grounds to believe that an otherwise conclusive decision is wrong because of "fraud or neglect". "Fraud or neglect" are not defined in the Act. They are based on the version of s.29(4) of the Taxes Management Act 1970 in force when this Act was enacted. From April 6, 2009 s.29(4) is amended to refer to "carelessly or deliberately" and those terms are given definitions. The new terms apply to all tax penalties but have not been applied to tax credits.

A decision made under this section is itself conclusive, subject only to further decisions, under this section, on review, or on appeal or because of official error (subs.(7)).

For modifications of this section where a claimant claims universal credit during a tax year in which he or she was entitled to a tax credit, see para.6 of the Schedule to the Universal Credit (Transitional Provisions) Regulations 2014 (SI 2014/1230).

Subsection (5A) permits the HMRC to decide that an additional payment made by HMRC under the Social Security (Additional Payments) Act 2022 was paid incorrectly where a person had no entitlement to such a payment. Linked modifications to s.28 of the Act define the incorrect payment as an overpayment so that it may be recovered in the same way as an overpayment of a tax credit.

Modifications where claim made for universal credit
For the modifications to s.20 where a person's entitlement to a tax credit was interrupted by the making of a claim for universal credit, see reg.12A of, and Schedule 1 to, the Universal Credit (Transitional Provisions) Regulations 2014 (SI 2014/1230), below in this volume.

Decisions subject to official error

21.—Regulations may make provision for a decision under section 14(1), 15(1), 16(1), 18(1), (5), (6) or (9), 19(3) or 20(1) or (4) to be revised in favour of the person or persons to whom it relates if it is incorrect by reason of official error (as defined by the regulations).

GENERAL NOTE

"Official error" is defined by the Tax Credits (Official Error) Regulations 2003 (SI 2003/692). See the note on those regulations. The provision is significantly narrower than the equivalent provision for income tax in s.33 of the TMA 1970 (error or mistake), which applies to any error or mistake.

For modifications of this section where a claimant claims universal credit during a tax year in which he or she was entitled to a tax credit, see para.7 of the Schedule to the Universal Credit (Transitional Provisions) Regulations 2014 (SI 2014/1230).

[1 Review of decisions

21A.—(1) The Commissioners for Her Majesty's Revenue and Customs must review any decision within section 38(1) if they receive a written application to do so that identifies the applicant and decision in question, and—
  (a) that application is received within 30 days of the date of the notification of the original decision or of the date the original decision was made if not notified because of section 23(3), or
  (b) it is received within such longer period as may be allowed under section 21B.

(2) The Commissioners must carry out the review as soon as is reasonably practicable.

(3) When the review has been carried out, the Commissioners must give the applicant notice of their conclusion containing sufficient information to enable the applicant to know—
  (a) the conclusion on the review,
  (b) if the conclusion is that the decision is varied, details of the variation, and
  (c) the reasons for the conclusion.

(4) The conclusion on the review must be one of the following—
(a) that the decision is upheld;
(b) that the decision is varied;
(c) that the decision is cancelled.
(5) Where—
(a) the Commissioners notify the applicant of further information or evidence that they may need for carrying out the review, and
(b) the information or evidence is not provided to them by the date specified in the notice,
the review may proceed without that information or evidence.]

AMENDMENT

1. Section added by Tax Credits, Child Benefit and Guardian's Allowance Reviews and Appeals Order 2014 (SI 2014/886) art.2(6) (April 6, 2014).

GENERAL NOTE

This new section and s.21B give effect from April 6, 2014 to the Government's announced policy of requiring any potential appellant to apply for mandatory reconsideration by HMRC of any decision made about tax credits before an appeal may be made to a tribunal. A footnote to the Order introducing this review power specifically notes that "in practice, this review will be known as a 'mandatory reconsideration'". That makes the language actually used consistent with that used by the Secretary of State for Work and Pensions since October 2013 when considering revision of decisions made about social security benefits. The social security changes were implemented by statutory instruments made under Social Security Act 1998 s.12(3A) and (3B) (see Vol.III of this series). An equivalent set of legislative provisions for revision applying to income tax decisions are optional. A taxpayer may apply for reconsideration of a decision before going to a tribunal, but is not required to do so.

Subsection (1) requires HMRC to review any appealable decision (as listed in s.38(1)) once a written application to do so is received. There is a 30-day time limit of the date of the notification of the decision. That period may be extended under limited circumstances as defined by s.21B below, subject to an absolute time limit of 13 months.

It is not clear why the language of this section does not echo the language of the original Act in referring to "the date on which notice of the decision was given" and so tying the timing of the service of the notice in with s.23 of the Act (notice of decisions). Is the date on which a decision is notified the same as the date on which notice is given? In any event, it is arguable that if notice is not given then the time limit for applying for a review cannot start.

HMRC itself is not subject to any specific time limit in conducting the mandatory reconsideration. It has powers to seek further information while doing so but is not required to await a reply when information is requested. It is required to give reasons for the conclusion it reaches on the reconsideration.

Some of the practical problems about s.21A are reviewed by the Upper Tribunal in *YK v HMRC* [2016] UKUT 118 (AAC). The First-tier Tribunal is reminded that the appeal period only starts when HMRC has issued a decision on the reconsideration not when the procedure was started. If HMRC has not issued a notice then either the tribunal should not accept the appeal (leaving it to the claimant to chase the decision and then appeal) or it should enquire into what has happened to the decision. It was also held that HMRC must establish its grounds of decision before the tribunal and produce all relevant evidence considered in doing so.

In *HMRC v Arrbab* [2024] EWCA Civ 16, the Court of Appeal held that the Upper Tribunal's decision in *AB v HMRC (TC)* [2021] UKUT 328 (AAC) was wrongly decided. In *AB*, the Upper Tribunal held that there was a right of appeal to the First-tier Tribunal against HMRC's refusal to extend time for making an application for review. As a matter of statutory construction, s.38(1A) excluded such a right of appeal. However, the Court of Appeal went on to hold that s.38(1A), which prohibits an appeal against a tax credits decision in the absence of a review under s.21A, was itself invalid. This is further explained in the note to s.38.

[¹ Late application for a review

21B.—(1) The Commissioners for Her Majesty's Revenue and Customs may in a particular case extend the time limit specified in section 21A(1)(a) for making an application for a review if all of the following conditions are met.

(2) The first condition is that the person seeking a review has applied to the Commissioners for an extension of time.

(3) The second condition is that the application for the extension—
(a) explains why the extension is sought, and
(b) is made within 13 months of the notification of the original decision or of the date the original decision was made if not notified because of section 23(3).

(4) The third condition is that the Commissioners are satisfied that due to special circumstances it was not practicable for the application for a review to have been made within the time limit specified in section 21A(1)(a).

(5) The fourth condition is that the Commissioners are satisfied that it is reasonable in all the circumstances to grant the extension.

(6) In determining whether it is reasonable to grant an extension, the Commissioners must have regard to the principle that the greater the amount of time that has elapsed between the end of the time limit specified in section 21A(1)(a) and the date of the application, the more compelling should be the special circumstances on which the application is based.

(7) An application to extend the time limit specified in section 21A(1)(a) which has been refused may not be renewed.]

AMENDMENT

1. Section added by Tax Credits, Child Benefit and Guardian's Allowance Reviews and Appeals Order 2014 (SI 2014/886) art.2(6) (April 6, 2014).

GENERAL NOTE

See the note to s.21A above.

[¹Late review: award of relevant disability benefits

21C.—(1) The Commissioners for Her Majesty's Revenue and Customs must review a relevant decision if they are notified (whether in writing or otherwise) within the period mentioned in subsection (3)—
(a) of the identity of the person seeking a review;
(b) of the decision in question; and
(c) that the condition in subsection (2) is met.

(2) The condition is that it has been determined that the person is entitled, whether in respect of themselves or a child for whom they are responsible, to a relevant disability benefit in respect of a tax year to which the relevant decision related.

(3) The period is the period of one month beginning with the day on which the person's claim for the benefit is determined in that person's favour.

(4) The sole purpose of a review under this section is to consider whether, as a result of the condition in subsection (2) being met, the relevant decision should—

(a) be upheld;
(b) be varied;
(c) be cancelled.

(5) The Commissioners must carry out the review as soon as is reasonably practicable.

(6) When the review has been carried out, the Commissioners must give the person notice of the conclusion containing sufficient information to enable that person to know—

(a) the conclusion on the review;
(b) if the conclusion is that the relevant decision is varied, details of the variation, and
(c) the reasons for the conclusion.

(7) Where—

(a) the Commissioners notify the person of further information or evidence that they may need for carrying out the review, and
(b) that information or evidence is not provided to them by the date specified in the notice,

the review may proceed without that information or evidence.

(8) In this section—

"relevant decision" means a decision within section 38(1) or any variation of such a decision resulting from an appeal brought against it;

"relevant disability benefit", in relation to any part of the United Kingdom, means—

(a) armed forces independence payment;
(b) attendance allowance;
(c) disability assistance;
(d) disability living allowance;
(e) employment and support allowance;
(f) housing benefit, where a pensioner or a disability premium is included;
(g) incapacity benefit (whether short term or long term);
(h) income support where a pensioner or a disability premium is included;
(i) jobseeker's allowance where a pensioner or a disability premium is included;
(j) limited capability for work credit;
(k) a mobility supplement or a constant attendance allowance where the supplement or benefit is paid in conjunction with a war pension or industrial injuries disablement benefit;
(l) personal independence payment;
(m) severe disablement allowance;
(n) statutory sick pay.]

AMENDMENT

1. Tax Credits Reviews and Appeals (Amendment) Order 2021 art.2(5) (January 15, 2021).

(2002 c.21 s.21C)

GENERAL NOTE

This section requires HMRC to review a tax credits decision where they are notified that a claimant, or a child for whom a claimant is responsible, is entitled to a disability benefit specified in subs.(8) for a year in which a tax credit was awarded. Its purpose is to allow a tax credit disability element, entitlement to which is established by award of a disability benefit, to be backdated to the start of the relevant tax credits year. For example, if a person successfully appealed to the First-tier Tribunal against a refusal to award a disability benefit, a process which may take some time, section 21C would allow the person to obtain a linked tax credit disability element backdated to the start date of the disability benefit award. Previously, regulation 25 of the Tax Credits (Claims and Notifications) Regulations 2002 (see below in this volume) would often have prevented backdating of a tax credit disability element for more than one month from the date of notification of the award of a disability benefit.

Notification is to be given to HMRC within one month of the date on which a disability benefit was awarded failing which HMRC are not required to review the decision (subs.(3)). Note that notification may be given verbally as well as in writing (subs.(1)). A review under this section is not a fresh consideration of all aspects of entitlement to a tax credit. The review is limited to considering the tax credits consequences of the award of the disability benefit (subs.(4)).

It should be noted that HMRC have undertaken to replicate the effect of section 21C in certain cases where a disability benefit was awarded before it came into force. The Explanatory Memorandum to the statutory instrument that added section 21C to this Act states:

"7.5... As a temporary measure, the Commissioners for Revenue and Customs have agreed to use their discretionary powers of payment and management1 to pay any cases where a claimant notifies HMRC within the statutory period between the start of the 2020–21 tax year and the coming into force of the legislation."

1.357

Information, etc. requirements: supplementary

22.—(1) Regulations may make provision as to the manner and form in which—
  (a) information or evidence is to be provided in compliance with a requirement imposed by a notice under section 14(2), 15(2), 16(3), 18(10) or 19(2), or
  (b) a declaration or statement is to be made in response to a notice under section 17.
(2) Regulations may make provision as to the dates which may be specified in a notice under section 14(2), 15(2), 16(3), 17, 18(10) or 19(2).

1.358

GENERAL NOTE

These regulation-making powers are necessary because the standard regulations applying to social security decision-making (the Social Security and Child Support (Decisions and Appeals) Regulations 1999 (SI 1999/991)) do not apply and there are no equivalents in the TMA 1970. The regulations made under these powers are the Tax Credits (Claims and Notifications) Regulations 2002 (SI 2002/2014).

1.359

Notice of decisions

23.—(1) When a decision is made under section 14(1), 15(1), 16(1), 18(1), (5), (6) or (9), 19(3) or 20(1) or (4) or regulations under section 21, the Board must give notice of the decision to the person, or each of the persons, to whom it relates.

1.360

Tax Credits Act 2002

(2) Notice of a decision must state the date on which it is given and include details of any right [¹to a review under section 21A and of any subsequent right] to appeal against the decision under section 38.

(3) Notice need not be given of a decision made under section 14(1) or 18(1) or (6) on the basis of declarations made or treated as made by the person or persons in response to the notice given to him or them under section 17 if—

(a) that notice, or

(b) in the case of a decision under subsection (6) of section 18, that notice or the notice of the decision under subsection (1) of that section,

stated what the decision would be and the date on which it would be made.

AMENDMENT

1. Tax Credits, Child Benefit and Guardian's Allowance Reviews and Appeals Order 2014 (SI 2014/886) art.2(7) (April 6, 2014).

DEFINITION

"the Board"—see s.67.

GENERAL NOTE

1.361 This section requires HMRC to adopt the same approach as for social security decisions of giving formal notice of every decision (save in limited cases where notice has already been given). The notice must set out any appeal rights. Section 46 makes provision for the form of a notice. Further details are laid down in the Tax Credits (Claims and Notifications) Regulations 2002 (SI 2002/2014). However, it may be viewed as significant that this provision is in primary legislation, while the equivalent for social security purposes (Social Security and Child Support (Decisions and Appeals) Regulations 1999 (SI 1999/991) reg.28) is made by regulation only. It is suggested therefore that the mandatory terms of subs.(1) (the Board *must* give notice) and subs.(2) (the notice *must* state) are not amenable to the somewhat relaxed approach to formalities applied to the social security equivalent (see the note to reg.28 of those Regulations). In particular, if no notice is given, it is arguable that no effective decision has been made, or alternatively that the decision is not final and the appeal period cannot start running.

The resulting effect on appeal rights is compounded by HMRC practice to give informal decisions before giving decisions to which this provision applies. See for example the criticism in *AT v HMRC (TC)* [2009] UKUT 78 (AAC) at [3].

This practice sows the seeds for utter confusion. A case in which those seeds bore a most unhappy fruit was *TM v HMRC* [2016] UKUT 512 (AAC) in which Upper Tribunal Judge Wikeley deprecated HMRC's practice of issue a "Statement Like an Award Notice" (or SLAN) without any reference to appeal rights. HMRC informed the Upper Tribunal that a SLAN was "not a decision carrying appeal rights. Instead it is a notice issued in the period after the tax credits year has ended and showing the change has been applied to the tax credits computer system pending the final decision for the year being made". However, since a SLAN looks like an award (or decision) notice, it is not unreasonable for a claimant to respond to it as if it is a decision notice. That was what the appellant did in *TM*. On his appeal to the First-tier Tribunal, HMRC's stance was that his appeal was both out-of-time (not having been made within the required period after the "real" decision was taken) and, in any event, was an attempt to appeal against a non-existent decision. In solving the problems raised in this case, Judge Wikeley left the realm of "Kafkaesque officialdom" for the real world. He held that, in the circumstances, the "SLAN" did in fact amount to a real decision so that the appellant's appeal was in time:

(2002 c.21 s.23)

"44. . . . a SLAN should only be treated as a 'real' decision (e.g. under section 18) if that reading is sustainable on the facts and assists the claimant in achieving a just resolution to the appeal, as here. In any event if the claimant does not appeal the SLAN in time, then time cannot start to run as the SLAN will not comply with the legal requirement to give notice of appeal rights (see section 23(2) of the 2002 Act). So more often than not a SLAN will not amount to a lawful decision as it omits that statutory notification. However, *this* Appellant should not be disadvantaged simply because he took the decision letter at face value and immediately lodged an appeal."

The lawfulness of HMRC's professed inability to supply First-tier Tribunals with copies of decision notices was doubted by Upper Tribunal Judge Wright in *DG v HMRC and EG (TC)* [2016] UKUT 505 (AAC):

"26. . . . On an appeal where an appealable decision has been made, given the duty under section 23 of the Tax Credits Act 2002 it seems to me plain that HMRC are under a duty to provide the First-tier Tribunal with a copy of the decision under appeal. By not doing so, HMRC stands in breach of its legal duty under rule 24(4)(a) of the [Tribunal Procedure (First-tier Tribunal) (Social Entitlement Chamber) Rules 2008 (S.I. 2008/2685)]. In my judgment it is no answer to this to say, as HMRC's appeal responses to the First-tier Tribunal habitually say, that the decision was issued automatically by HMRC's computer to the claimant only and a copy of the decision cannot thereafter be obtained by HMRC. HMRC must be able to obtain it in order to meet its statutory duty of disclosure in any case where an appeal is made against the decision."

For modifications of this section where a claimant claims universal credit during a tax year in which he or she was entitled to a tax credit, see para.8 of the Schedule to the Universal Credit (Transitional Provisions) Regulations 2014 (SI 2014/1230).

Modifications where claim made for universal credit
For the modifications to s.23 where a person's entitlement to a tax credit was interrupted by the making of a claim for universal credit, see reg.12A of, and Schedule 1 to, the Universal Credit (Transitional Provisions) Regulations 2014 (SI 2014/1230), below in this volume.

1.362

Payment

Payments

24.—(1) Where the Board have made an award of a tax credit, the amount of the tax credit awarded must be paid to the person to whom the award is made, subject to subsections (2) and (3).

1.363

(2) Where an award of a tax credit is made to the members of [²a couple], payments of the tax credit, or of any element of the tax credit, are to be made to whichever of them is prescribed.

(3) Where an award of a tax credit is made on a claim which was made by one person on behalf of another, payments of the tax credit, or of any element of the tax credit, are to be made to whichever of those persons is prescribed.

(4) Where an award of a tax credit has been made to a person or persons for the whole or part of a tax year, payments may, in prescribed circumstances, continue to be made for any period, after the tax year, within which he is or they are entitled to make a claim for the tax credit for the next tax year.

(5) Payments made under subsection (4) are to be treated for the purposes of this section and the following provisions of this Part as if they were payments of the tax credit for the next tax year.

(6) Subject to section 25, payments of a tax credit must be made by the Board.

(7) Regulations may make provision about the time when and the manner in which a tax credit, or any element of a tax credit, is to be paid by the Board.

(8) If the regulations make provision for payments of a tax credit, or any element of a tax credit, to be made by the Board by way of a credit to a bank account or other account notified to the Board, the regulations may provide that entitlement to the tax credit or element is dependent on an account having been notified to the Board in accordance with the regulations.

AMENDMENTS

1. Subsection (2) is modified as it applies to polygamous units by Tax Credits (Polygamous Marriages) Regulations 2003 (SI 2003/742) reg.18.
2. Civil Partnership Act 2004 s.254 and Sch.24 para.145 (December 5, 2005).

DEFINITIONS

"claim"—see s.3(8).
"couple"—see s.3(5A).
"the Board"—see s.67.
"prescribed"—see s.67.
"tax credit"—see s.1(2).
"tax year"—see s.47.

GENERAL NOTE

1.364   The principal purpose of s.24(4) is to enable HMRC to maintain tax credits payments, following the end of a tax year, pending their decision whether to award a tax credit for the next tax year. This prevents an interruption in payments while HMRC decide whether to continue to pay tax credits and is necessary because tax credits awards, rather than being ongoing, are made for specific tax years (see s.5).

Section 38 provides for no right of appeal against a refusal by HMRC to make, or continue making, payments under s.24(4). In *Awodiya v HMRC* [2019] EWHC 251 (Admin) the High Court refused permission to claim judicial review of HMRC's refusal to make s.24(4) payments because the child tax credit claimants had refused to supply relevant information. In refusing permission to appeal, Turner J said:

"It was thus entirely rational for the defendants to refuse to exercise their discretion to make provisional CTC payments to the claimants whilst the latter maintained their refusal to provide the requisite information in support of their assertion that the children continued to live with them."

Moreover, the claimants had an effective alternative remedy namely a right of appeal to the First-tier Tribunal against HMRC's subsequent decision whether, under s.14, to award tax credits for a tax year. Turner J said "it would be inappropriate to permit them to circumvent, through the mechanism of judicial review, the statutory procedures now open to them".

From April 2006 HMRC makes all WTC and CTC payments. Payment by employers has been discontinued. Sections 25 (Payment by employers), 26 (liability of officers for sums paid to employers) and 33 (failure by employers to make correct payments) and the related regulations therefore have no current relevance and are not set out in this volume. For the texts see the volume for previous years.

(2002 c.21 s.27)

Rights of employees

27.—Schedule 1 (rights of employees not to suffer unfair dismissal or other detriment) has effect.

DEFINITION

"employee"—see s.25(5).

GENERAL NOTE

This section introduces Sch.1. Both this section and the Schedule are based on s.7 of, and Sch.3 to, the TCA 1999. The aim is to provide employees with direct rights to ensure that employers do not discriminate against them because of WTC. The underlying fear is that employers would rather get rid of employees than implement the WTC process. Schedule 1 makes the necessary amendments to the Employment Rights Act (GB) and Order (NI) to give employees a right not to suffer detriment and a right not to be unfairly dismissed because of tax credits. The text of Sch.1 is not included here as it is a matter of employment law.

Overpayments

28.—(1) Where the amount of a tax credit paid for a tax year to a person or persons exceeds the amount of the tax credit to which he is entitled, or they are jointly entitled, for the tax year (as determined in accordance with the provision made by and by virtue of sections 18 to [[^{3}21C]]), the [^{2} Commissioners may] decide that the excess, or any part of it, is to be [^{2} —
 (a) repaid to the Commissioners; or
 (b) treated as if it were an amount recoverable by the Secretary of State under section 71ZB of the Administration Act(1) or (as the case may be) by the relevant Northern Ireland Department under section 69ZB of the Administration (Northern Ireland) Act.]

(2) In this Part such an excess is referred to as an overpayment.

(3) For overpayments made under awards on single claims, the person to whom the tax credit was awarded is liable to repay [^{2} to the Commissioners, the Secretary of State or (as the case may be) the relevant Northern Ireland Department, the amount which the Commissioners decide is to be repaid or treated as recoverable under subsection (1)(b).]

(4) For overpayments made under awards on joint claims, the persons to whom the tax credit was awarded are jointly and severally liable to repay [^{2} to the Commissioners, the Secretary of State or (as the case may be) the relevant Northern Ireland Department, the amount mentioned in subsection (3) unless the Commissioners decide that each is liable for] a specified part of that amount.

(5) Where it appears to the Commissioners that there is likely to be an overpayment of a tax credit for a tax year under an award made to a person or persons, the Commissioners may, with a view to reducing or eliminating the overpayment, amend the award or any other award of any tax credit made to the person or persons; but this subsection does not apply once a decision is taken in relation to the person or persons for the tax year under section 18(1).

(6) Where the Commissioners decide under section 16 to terminate an award of a tax credit made to a person or persons on the ground that at

Tax Credits Act 2002

no time during the period to which the award related did the person or persons satisfy—
  (a) section 8(1) (if the award related to child tax credit), or
  (b) section 10(1) (if it related to working tax credit),
the Commissioners may decide that the amount paid under the award, or any part of it, is to be treated for the purposes of this Part (apart from subsection (5)) as an overpayment.

[² (7) In this section and in section 29—
"the Administration Act" means the Social Security Administration Act 1992;
"the Administration (Northern Ireland) Act" means the Social Security Administration (Northern Ireland) Act 1992;
"the relevant Northern Ireland Department" means the Department for Communities.

(8) In this section, "the Commissioners" means the Commissioners for Her Majesty's Revenue and Customs.]

AMENDMENTS

1. Tax Credits, Child Benefit and Guardian's Allowance Reviews and Appeals Order 2014 (SI 2014/886) art.2(8) (April 6, 2014).
2. Tax Credits (Exercise of Functions in relation to Northern Ireland and Notices for Recovery of Tax Credit Overpayments) Order 2017 (SI 2017/781) art.6(2) (September 25, 2017).
3. Tax Credits Reviews and Appeals (Amendment) Order 2021 art.2(6) (January 15, 2021).

DEFINITIONS

"the Board"—see s.67.
"joint claim"—see s.3(8).
"overpayment"—see subs.(2).
"single claim"—see s.3(8).
"tax credit"—see s.1(2).
"tax year"—see s.47.

GENERAL NOTE

1.368   An overpayment is an excess of a tax credit awarded and paid as against the amount of tax credit to which a claimant is entitled under a final decision about entitlement (subs.(2)). This will usually arise where the final decision on entitlement is for a lesser amount than the amount awarded. It may also arise under a later revision under ss.19 or 20, or when an award was made that should not have been made (subs. (6)). Subsection (1) gives a power to (but does not impose a duty on) HMRC to require overpayments to be repaid to HMRC or, following the amendment made by SI 2017/781 treated as an amount recoverable by the Secretary of State for Work & Pensions under s.71ZB of the Social Security Administration Act 1992. Section 71ZB is the DWP's relatively new power to recover certain overpaid benefits, a power which is not conditional on a finding of misrepresentation or failure to disclose a material fact.. As Upper Tribunal Judge Wikeley explained in *VH v HMRC* [2017] UKUT 128 (AAC), HMRC's decision whether or not to require an overpayment to be repaid is not subject to appeal, and is not subject to the fulfilment of any test by the claimant:

"15. . . .under the tax credits regime issues of fault do not come into play when considering legal liability for overpayments. In other words, arguments that the claimant did not misrepresent anything or did not fail to disclose a change in circumstances because she was unaware of such a change have no purchase.

Those types of arguments may have some traction in relation to most DWP social security benefits other than universal credit (see Social Security Administration Act 1992, section 71), but they are irrelevant in the HMRC tax credits context (see Tax Credits Act 2002, sections 28 and 29). In short, if tax credits have been paid but it later transpires there is no entitlement to tax credits, there is an overpayment, and in principle any overpayment is recoverable. That explains the logic behind the absence of appeal rights...If there are mitigating circumstances, they can at best go to the (non-appealable) discretionary issue of whether HMRC should recover the overpayment (on which see HMRC Code of Practice 26), and not the prior question of legal liability for the overpayment."

The government has consistently failed to act on the recommendations of the Parliamentary Ombudsman and others that there be a right of appeal against overpayment decisions. Dispute about the underlying entitlement to tax credits are appealable, though such disputes do not often reach tribunals. Disputes about the amount of overpayments are dealt with as recovery questions. See further s.29.

This section applies with modifications where a person, as a result of making a claim for universal credit, is paid tax credits for a "part tax year" as defined in the modified version of s.48 of this Act (interpretation): see reg.12 of the Universal Credit (Transitional Provisions) Regulations 2014 (SI 2014/1230) (below in this volume).

Section 20(5) permits HMRC to decide that an additional payment under the Social Security (Additional Payments) Act 2022 was paid incorrectly. Modifications made to s.28 treat the incorrect payment as an overpayment, which means that the payment, or part of it, may be recovered from the person to whom it was paid in the same way as an overpayment of tax credit.

Recovery of overpayments

29.—(1) Where an amount is liable to be repaid [³ or paid] by a person or persons under section 28, the Board must give him, or each of them, a notice specifying the amount.

(2) The notice must state which of subsections (3) to (5) is to apply in relation to the amount or any specified part of the amount; and a notice may at any time be replaced by another notice containing a different statement.

(3) Where a notice states that this subsection applies in relation to an amount (or part of an amount), it is to be treated for the purposes of Part 6 of the Taxes Management Act 1970 (c.9) (collection and recovery) as if it were tax charged in an assessment and due and payable by the person or persons to whom the notice was given at the end of the period of 30 days beginning with the day on which the notice is given.

[³ (4) Where a notice states that this subsection applies in relation to an amount (or part of an amount), it may be recovered—
  (a) subject to provision made by regulations, by deduction from payments of any tax credit under an award made for any period to the person, or either or both of the persons, to whom the notice was given;
  (b) by the Secretary of State—
     (i) by deductions under section 71ZC of the Administration Act (deduction from benefit);
     (ii) by deductions under section 71ZD of that Act (deduction from earnings); or
     (iii) as set out in section 71ZE of that Act (court action etc); or
  (c) by the relevant Northern Ireland Department—
     (i) by deductions under section 69ZC of the Administration (Northern Ireland) Act (deduction from benefit);

(ii) by deductions under section 69ZD of that Act (deduction from earnings); or

(iii) as set out in section 69ZE of that Act (court action etc).]

(5) Where a notice states that this subsection applies in relation to an amount (or part of an amount), [¹ PAYE regulations] apply to it as if it were an under payment of [² income tax] for a previous year of assessment by the person or persons to whom the notice was given [² that is not a relevant debt (within the meaning of section 684 of the Income Tax (Earnings and Pensions) Act 2003))].

AMENDMENTS

1. Words amended by ITEPA 2003 Sch.6 para.266 (April 6, 2003). Subsection (4) is modified by the Tax Credits (Polygamous Marriages) Regulations 2003 (SI 2003/742) reg.12 as it applies to polygamous units.
2. Finance Act 2009 s.110 and Sch.58 para.8 (July 21, 2009).
3. Tax Credits (Exercise of Functions in relation to Northern Ireland and Notices for Recovery of Tax Credit Overpayments) Order 2017 (SI 2017/781) art.6(3) (September 25, 2017).

DEFINITIONS

"the Board"—see s.67.
"overpayment"—see s.28(2).

GENERAL NOTE

1.371 There is no appeal against a decision about either recovery or recoverability under this Act. The absence of a right of appeal has been consistently confirmed by Commissioners. See *CTC/2662/2005*, *CTC/3981/2006* and *CTC/2270/2007*. As that last decision emphasises, the approach is not the same as that applied to the former WFTC (as illustrated by *CTC/1907/2007*). The decision that can be appealed is the entitlement decision under which the overpayment arises. That decision must be notified to the claimant under s.23, save where one of the exceptions in s.23(3) applies. It may be anticipated that, following equivalent experience in social security cases, some recipients will only object, and attempt to appeal, when they receive notice of an overpayment under this section rather than notice of the decision that gives rise to the overpayment. Whether this can amount to an effective and timely appeal against the entitlement decision will depend on part on how and when the required notices are given, and is for decision under s.39. In the absence of a duly made appeal against the underlying entitlement decision, the First-tier Tribunal can be of no assistance for a claimant who seeks to avoid an overpayment or overpayment recovery, decision (*HMRC v SJ* [2018] UKUT 83 (AAC)).

This section is the equivalent of s.30 of the TMA 1970. HMRC may give a formal notice to someone whom it has decided has been overpaid tax credit. The notice may activate all or any of three alternative methods of recovering the overpaid tax credit. The first, under subs.(3), is by using ss.60–70A of the TMA 1970. These empower HMRC's collection and recovery powers for unpaid income tax demands. These allow distraint and action in both civil courts and magistrates' courts. Subsection (4) entitles HMRC to collect the overpayment by deducting it from other payments of tax credit or, where the overpayment is treated as recoverable under s.71ZB of the Social Security Administration Act 1992 (see s.28), for the Secretary of State to use the recovery mechanisms in ss.71ZC–71ZD of the 1992 Act (deduction from benefit or earnings or court action): see further Tax Credits (Payments by the Board) Regulations 2002 (SI 2002/2173) reg.12A, inserted by the Tax Credits (Miscellaneous Amendments) Regulations 2004 (SI 2004/762) reg.18. Subsection (5) allows overpayments of tax credits to be collected with income tax and NI contributions but this power is not used.

The way in which HMRC decides on the recovery of overpayments and then collects them continues to be a matter of controversy as there is no direct appeal to the First-tier Tribunal against an overpayment or recovery decision. HMRC however publicises this as an appeal against the overpayment (see form TC846). Only the underlying entitlement decision may be appealed. The way in which overpayments are collected is set out in Code of Practice 26, now updated annually, the most recent version of which is set out in full at the end of this volume.

The Income Tax (Pay as You Earn) (Amendment No 4) Regulations 2014 (SI 2014/2689) empower Her Majesty's Revenue and Customs to start recovering tax credit debts by using the PAYE coding and tax deduction machinery to collect such debts. Separate legislation increases the HMRC power to use tax coding in this way to a total debt of £17,000. These regulations allow that maximum to be used for tax credit debts. This starts with codings for the tax year 2015/16.

1.372

Someone wishing to dispute recovery of an overpayment should send a copy of form TC846 (available on the HMRC website) to the Overpayments Dispute Team, Tax Credits Office, Preston PR1 0SB (or Belfast BT2 7WF).

Note also that s.684(7A) of ITEPA was amended by Finance Act 2009 s.110 and Sch.58 para.7 to permit HMRC to agree with a payer of PAYE income to collect amounts other than tax. Section 684(7AA) of ITEPA defines a relevant debt as a sum payable by the payee to the Commissioners either under or by virtue of an enactment (other than an excluded debt) or under a contract settlement. Subsection (7AB)(a) provides that for the purposes of subs.(7AA) child tax credit or working tax credit that the payee is liable to repay is an excluded debt. These amendments allow HMRC to recover overpaid tax credits through the PAYE system with the consent of the individual.

HMRC has published detailed guidance for intermediaries and advisers in a new leaflet *How HMRC handle tax credit overpayments*.

HMRC also has power to collect debts such as these directly using the courts. It is required by the Finance (No 2) Act 2015 to do this in accordance with a published policy to reflect difficulties in payment. That policy is published as *Direct Recovery of Debt and Vulnerable Claimants* available on the GOV.UK website. The policy recognises as relevant difficulties to be taken into account: disabilities and long-term health problems; certain temporary illnesses or conditions; major personal issues such as redundancy or a family death; and lower levels of literacy and numeracy.

Underpayments

30.—(1) Where it has been determined in accordance with the provision made by and by virtue of sections 18 to [[²21C]] that a person was entitled, or persons were jointly entitled, to a tax credit for a tax year and either—

1.373

(a) the amount of the tax credit paid to him or them for that tax year was less than the amount of the tax credit to which it was so determined that he is entitled or they are jointly entitled, or

(b) no payment of the tax credit was made to him or them for that tax year,

the amount of the difference, or of his entitlement or their joint entitlement, must be paid to him or to whichever of them is prescribed.

(2) Where the claim for the tax credit was made by one person on behalf of another, the payment is to be made to whichever of those persons is prescribed.

AMENDMENTS

1. Tax Credits, Child Benefit and Guardian's Allowance Reviews and Appeals Order 2014 (SI 2014/886) art.2(8) (April 6, 2014).

2. Tax Credits Reviews and Appeals (Amendment) Order 2021 art.2(7) (January 15, 2021).

DEFINITIONS
"prescribed"—see s.67.
"tax credit"—see s.1(2).
"tax year"—see s.47.

GENERAL NOTE

1.374 This provision is the converse of s.28. However, the procedure that triggers it is not a mirror of the provisions giving rise to an overpayment. In particular, see the note to s.6 on notifications of changes of circumstances. If there is an underpayment, this section requires HMRC to make it good. However underpayments, unlike repayments of income tax, or overpayments of tax credit, do not carry interest. Nor does the section impose any time-limit on the payment. For modifications of this section where a claimant claims universal credit during a tax year in which he or she was entitled to a tax credit, see para.9 of the Schedule to the Universal Credit (Transitional Provisions) Regulations 2014 (SI 2014/1230).

Modifications where claim made for universal credit

1.375 For the modifications to s.30 where a person's entitlement to a tax credit was interrupted by the making of a claim for universal credit, see reg.12A of, and Schedule 1 to, the Universal Credit (Transitional Provisions) Regulations 2014 (SI 2014/1230), below in this volume.

Penalties

Incorrect statements, etc.

1.376 **31.**—(1) Where a person fraudulently or negligently—
(a) makes an incorrect statement or declaration in or in connection with a claim for a tax credit or a notification of a change of circumstances given in accordance with regulations under section 6 or in response to a notice under section 17, or
(b) gives incorrect information or evidence in response to a requirement imposed on him by virtue of section 14(2), 15(2), 16(3), 18(10) or 19(2) or regulations under section 25 [²or in response to a notification under section 21A(5)],
a penalty not exceeding £3,000 may be imposed on him.

(2) Where a person liable to a penalty under subsection (1) is a person making, or who has made, a claim for a tax credit for a period jointly with another and the penalty is imposed—
(a) under paragraph (a) of that subsection in respect of the claim, a notification relating to the tax credit claimed or a notice relating to the tax credit awarded on the claim, or
(b) under paragraph (b) of that subsection in respect of a requirement imposed on him with respect to the tax credit for the period,
a penalty of an amount not exceeding £3,000 may be imposed on the other person unless subsection (3) applies.

(3) This subsection applies if the other person was not, and could not reasonably have been expected to have been, aware that the person liable to the penalty under subsection (1) had fraudulently or negligently made the incorrect statement or declaration or given the incorrect information or evidence.

(4) Where penalties are imposed under subsections (1) and (2) in respect of the same statement, declaration, information or evidence, their aggregate amount must not exceed £3,000.

(2002 c.21 s.31)

(5) Where a person acts for another—
(a) in or in connection with a claim or notification referred to in subsection (1), or
(b) in response to a notice so referred to,

subsection (1) applies to him (as well as to any person to whom it applies apart from this subsection).

AMENDMENTS

1. Subsection (2) is modified as it applies to polygamous units by Tax Credits (Polygamous Marriages) Regulations 2003 (SI 2003/742) reg.20.
2. Tax Credits, Child Benefit and Guardian's Allowance Reviews and Appeals Order 2014 (SI 2014/886) art.2(9) (April 6, 2014).

DEFINITIONS

"change of circumstances"—see s.6(1).
"claim"—see s.3(8).
"joint claim"—see s.3(8).
"tax credit"—see s.1(2).

GENERAL NOTE

This Act reflects a concern about potential fraud with regard to claims and payments. There were originally several sources of concern. One—abuse by employers in payments through the wage packet—no longer applies. All payments are made by HMRC. Concern about the payment process itself is dealt with in part by ensuring that most payments are made direct to bank accounts. The remaining original concern was fraud by claimants. Events showed that another, unanticipated, source of fraud proved a big problem. This was the fraudulent use by third parties of the facility to make claims online. This resulted in the online facility being closed down some years ago. It has yet to be reinstated. The focus of ss.31–34 and Sch.2 is now mainly claimants. The powers are wide enough to catch anyone else involved, such as someone providing child care on the basis of false information. 1.377

Sections 31–34 draw on the then regime applying for income tax. This was in Pt X of the TMA 1970. After full consultation, HMRC secured a complete rewrite of tax penalty powers in the Finance Act 2008. This came into effect on April 1, 2009. It applies to all direct and indirect taxes. It does not apply to tax credits. There have been no changes to these sections equivalent to the changes for tax purposes, so the "old" law continues to apply here.

This section deals with the problem where anyone required to make a declaration, statement or notification or to give information or evidence does so "incorrectly" and where the person does so "fraudulently or negligently". It applies both to the person making the declaration, etc. and to anyone acting for that person (subs.(5)), and both could be subject to penalty proceedings in connection with the same matter.

HMRC have published two leaflets of guidance about the exercise of their penalty powers: WTC3, *Tax Credit Penalties, How tax credit examinations are settled*, and WTC4, *Tax Credit penalties, How tax credit enquiries are settled*. They apply to penalties under both this section and s.32. These reflect the differences between examinations (taking place about current claims or awards) and enquiries (taking place when an award is finalised or after entitlement has been established). They are now combined with WTC7, which is set out at the end of this volume. The leaflets set out the procedure for dealing with the imposition of penalties and the basis on which HMRC decide at what level a penalty will be set. HMRC's practice follows that applying for similar income tax examinations and enquiries. Discounts to the maximum penalty will be applied to reflect: the extent to which the error was disclosed voluntarily by the claimant; the extent to which the claimant has co-operated with HMRC in the 1.378

examination or enquiry; the seriousness of the errors or omissions; and whether this is a first or subsequent occasion on which there has been an error or omission.

In *SP v HMRC* [2016] UKUT 238 (AAC); [2016] AACR 46 Upper Tribunal Judge Levenson gave guidance to the First-tier Tribunal on both the relevance to its proceedings of HMRC guidance about tax credit penalties and, more generally, the determination of penalty appeals:

> "25. In summary the following propositions represent what, in my view, is the correct approach to tax credit penalties. This is not intended to be an exhaustive list and, of course, much will depend on the circumstances of the particular case. However, by following this kind of approach tribunals are less likely to fall into error of law.
>
> (a) The imposition of any penalty involves the exercise of a discretion whether or not to impose any penalty at all or a penalty of a particular amount.
> (b) It is proper for HMRC to adopt guidance even though there is no statutory requirement to do so.
> (c) It is proper for the First-tier Tribunal to take that guidance as a starting point for the calculation of any penalty.
> (d) In applying the guidance, the First-tier Tribunal must be satisfied as to the underlying facts on which the calculation of the penalty is based, including the amount of any overpayment said to have been made. It must also be satisfied that any incorrect statement can in fact be attributed to the period in respect of which the penalty is being considered. A distinction will usually need to be made between past reports and future predictions—the design of HMRC forms is not always very helpful on this matter.
> (e) In most cases it will be relevant for the First-tier Tribunal to find whether the claimant acted innocently and/or reasonably, or negligently (that is, with a lack of due care), or fraudulently.
> (f) Having identified the amount of penalty that the guidance would produce, the First-tier Tribunal must consider whether there are any aggravating or mitigating factors and must take into account the principle that the maximum penalty is reserved for the worst offences.
> (g) At each stage the First-tier Tribunal must give reasons for its conclusions."

All penalty decisions are open to appeal. Appeals go to the First-tier Tribunal and then the Upper Tribunal. Since the introduction of the new appeal system an appellant must obtain leave to appeal to take the appeal to the Upper Tribunal. Under the original system no leave was needed to appeal against a penalty to the social security commssioners. No such appeal was considered by them, and few were considered by the social security tribunals. This is in part because HMRC were reluctant at first to use the penalty provisions. It is also because HMRC usually offer to settle a penalty with the individual under the terms of s.54 of the TMA 1970.

Fraudulently or negligently

1.379 The former penalty provisions in TMA 1970 had been subject to consideration in the courts on a number of occasions, and it is to be expected that the common phraseology of those sections and these (such as "fraudulently or negligently") will receive a similar interpretation. On this basis, the fraud or neglect of an agent will be regarded as the fraud or neglect of the claimant: *Clixby v Pountney* (1968) 44 T.C. 575. It is clearly established in income tax law that the onus of proving fraud or neglect is on HMRC. *Hillenbrand v IRC* (1966) 42 T.C. 617 established that there is no presumption of fraud or neglect because of an omission, although the omission might give a factual basis for a decision on this point. However, if HMRC establish the fraud or neglect, then the burden shifts to the taxpayer to show that any assessment made by HMRC as a result is incorrect. It is also established that HMRC does not have to show the precise nature of discovered income: *Hudson v Humbles* (1965) 42 T.C. 380. That is part of the process of making and appealing an assessment. It is suggested that the same approaches would be appropriate here, save that in addition HMRC and appeal tribunal will be able to take account of evidence gathered for income tax purposes in deciding the outcome of a s.20 review.

Additionally, since the Human Rights Act 1998 came into effect, it is arguable that this section imposes a "criminal" liability under art.6(3) of the European Convention on Human Rights. (For the text, see Vol.III of this work). Courts have applied the criminal standard to equivalent provisions in income tax and VAT legislation. If art.6(3) applies then close consideration needs to be given to the burden of proof under this section, the evidence available for establishing or resisting the application of the section and the availability of legal aid.

A penalty under this section bears interest under s.37. It is treated as unpaid tax for the purposes of recovery and collection (Sch.2 para.7). Appeals against penalty decisions are dealt with in Sch.2 (see s.34).

Subsections (2) and (3) deal with a problem that is no longer relevant to income tax, namely the case where one of a couple making a joint claim has failed fully to co-operate with the other, so that the declaration is wrong but one of the joint claimants is not aware that this is so. In such cases responsibility remains joint and several unless one of the claimants can show that the defence in subs. (3) applies. This imposes a double test of both fact and reasonableness.

The conduct of penalty cases

Appeals under s.31 are "criminal" in the sense that arts 6(2) and (3) of the European Convention on Human Rights apply in addition to art.6(1). This is clear from the decision of the European Court of Human Rights in *King v United Kingdom (No.2)*, Application 13881/02, of February 17, 2004, [2004] S.T.C. 911. See Vol.III of this work for the text of the article and commentary. That approach will be strengthened by the decision of that court in *PM v United Kingdom*, Application 6638/03, [2005] S.T.C. 1566. In that case a taxpayer was held entitled to invoke the scope of art.1, Protocol 1 (rights of property) in alleging discrimination about the terms of entitlement to a deduction for maintenance payments under s.347 of the Income and Corporation Taxes Act 1988. As there was no internal remedy for discrimination caused by primary legislation, the European Court awarded damages to the appellant.

The HMRC Claimant Compliance Manual (CCM) refers to s.31 as being a power to punish. But this does not apply to s.32. See the detailed analysis of the equivalent income tax provisions in *Gladders v Prior* [2003] S.T.C. (S.C.D.) 245 (decision of Special Commissioner of Income Tax, not appealed). A notice requiring information does not breach the rule on self-incrimination. See *Sharkey v De Croos* [2005] S.T.C. (S.C.D.) 336 citing *R. v Allen* [2002] A.C. 509 on a similar income tax provision.

There is authority that receipt of a relevant notice is crucial to the activation of the sections, and that the Interpretation Act presumptions do not apply: Macpherson J in *CEC v Medway Draughting and Technical Services Ltd* [1989] S.T.C. 346 dealing with a similar VAT provision.

The burden of proof rests with HMRC, who should open any appeal. The degree of proof remains the civil burden, namely that something is "more likely than not".

In *SP v HMRC* [2016] UKUT 238 (AAC); [2016] AACR 46 HMRC argued that, on an appeal to the First-tier Tribunal against the imposition of a penalty under this section, the tribunal could only address whether the conditions for imposing a penalty were made out and not the amount of the penalty. Upper Tribunal Judge Levenson disagreed (as had Judge Mark in *AP v HMRC* [2015] UKUT 580 (AAC)). Judge Levenson said:

"19. On the issue of the assessment of the appropriate penalty, HMRC argued before me that the appeal to the First-tier Tribunal was not about that but about whether the claimant had indeed been negligent. This is wrong. The appeal to

1.380

1.381

Tax Credits Act 2002

the First-tier Tribunal was against the outcome decision to impose a penalty. In its very nature the appeal encompassed both an appeal against there being any penalty and an appeal against the calculation of the penalty. This is consistent with the powers specifically conferred on the First-tier Tribunal in such an appeal, with the inquisitorial function of the First-tier Tribunal, with the fact that on an appeal the First-tier Tribunal stands in the shoes of the decision-maker (here HMRC) and with the absence of any statutory indication as to what the penalty should be (other than the prescribed £3,000 maximum)."

The level of penalties: HMRC's Claimant Compliance Manual

1.382 The procedure to be followed by HMRC officers when imposing or applying for tax credits penalties are set out in the *New Tax Credits Claimant Compliance Manual* (abbreviated as CCM). This is available on the HMRC website at: *http://www.hmrc.gov.uk/manuals/ccmmanual/Index.htm*. However, some parts of CCM have been withheld from publication under the Freedom of Information Act 2000. See, for example, CCM 10070 (even the number of that paragraph is withheld, but it is referred to in cross-references not withheld as covering "Penalties: calculation of penalties in incorrect claims"). The main issue withheld in that paragraph is the calculation of the amount of a penalty to be imposed under subs.(4) of this section. CCM 10080 on the calculation of a percentage of an overpaid claim is not withheld, although it makes little sense in the absence of CCM 10070. This is in contrast to the approach adopted by HMRC with regard to penalties under the income tax penalty regime, and in which percentages play a major role. See now the recently published *Code of Practice 9 (2005)* on civil investigation into cases of suspected serious fraud. This specifically details reductions of maximum penalties by the following percentages:

— up to 20 per cent for voluntary disclosure (or 30 per cent for full disclosure with no risk of discovery);

— up to 40 per cent for cooperation with an investigation, including full disclosures of information requested; and

— up to 40 per cent for seriousness of errors and omissions.

Withholding information under the 2000 Act does not apply when HMRC must explain to an appeal tribunal how it reaches the level of penalty it has selected. As a result, various parts of the withheld information have come to the attention of individual appeal tribunals. That is not a satisfactory situation.

It would seem that the approach broadly follows the income tax penalty approach save that in the case of tax penalties the maximum amount of the penalty is a set figure and not a percentage of the income tax under-declared. For example, CCM 10080 shows that an officer should look at the percentage of the overclaimed credits as compared with total credits originally claimed. CCM 10090 refers to "the relatively small amount of penalties for first offences". CCM 10100 refers to an abatement of a maximum of 50 per cent for full and prompt co-operation with an enquiry or examination. These statements, and the examples at CCM 10110, all point to the same broad approach as that used for income tax. CCM also emphasises that penalties for second and subsequent incorrect statements are likely to be significantly higher than initial penalties. Officers are required to notify claimants of this when imposing an initial penalty.

1.383 That aside, CCM sets out in considerable detail the procedures to be used by individual HMRC officers in the process of imposing or requesting penalties.

CCM 10040 emphasises that the penalty power related to s.17 notifications applies only once although the information applies to two years. However, if there are incorrect s.17 notices at both ends of a year, HMRC may levy two penalties. In addition, there may be separate penalties up to the maximum where there is an incorrect s.17 notification and some other "offence" as the CCM terms it.

(2002 c.21 s.31)

In *SP v HMRC (No.2)* [2017] UKUT 329 (AAC) Judge Levenson decided that, in fixing the amount of a penalty, it is "necessary to mark the seriousness of the issue" but, for a first-time penalty involving only negligence, it is not necessary to create "additional hardship". The judge allowed the appellant's appeal and replaced a £500 penalty with a £100 penalty which was "more than a nominal penalty but not so great as to be disproportionate or create inappropriate additional hardship". In that case, the appellant had "guessed" that her annual income was £11,000 when in fact it was some £22,000.

Failure to comply with requirements

32.—(1) Where a person fails—
(a) to provide any information or evidence which he is required to provide by virtue of section 14(2), 15(2), 16(3), 18(10) or 19(2) or regulations under section 25, or
(b) to comply with a requirement imposed on him by a notice under section 17 by virtue of subsection (2)(a), (4)(a) or (6)(a) of that section,
the penalties specified in subsection (2) may be imposed on him.

(2) The penalties are—
(a) a penalty not exceeding £300, and
(b) if the failure continues after a penalty is imposed under paragraph (a), a further penalty or penalties not exceeding £60 for each day on which the failure continues after the day on which the penalty under that paragraph was imposed (but excluding any day for which a penalty under this paragraph has already been imposed).

(3) Where a person fails to give a notification required by regulations under section 6(3), a penalty not exceeding £300 may be imposed on him.

(4) No penalty under subsection (2) may be imposed on a person in respect of a failure after the failure has been remedied.

(5) For the purposes of this section a person is to be taken not to have failed to provide information or evidence, comply with a requirement or give a notification which must be provided, complied with or given by a particular time—
(a) if he provided, complied with or gave it within such further time (if any) as the Board may have allowed,
(b) if he had a reasonable excuse for not providing, complying with or giving it by that time, or
(c) if, after having had such an excuse, he provided, complied with or gave it without unreasonable delay.

(6) Where the members of [¹ a couple] both fail as mentioned in subsection (1)(b), the aggregate amount of any penalties under subsection (2) imposed on them in relation to their failures must not exceed the amounts specified in that subsection; and where the members of [¹ a couple] both fail as mentioned in subsection (3), the aggregate amount of any penalties imposed on them in relation to their failures must not exceed £300.

AMENDMENT

1. Civil Partnership Act 2004 s.254 and Sch.24 para.145 (December 5, 2005).

DEFINITIONS

"the Board"—see s.67.
"couple"—see s.3(5A).

GENERAL NOTE

1.385 See the note to s.31 on the penalty regime as a whole. This section imposes penalties on those who fail to comply with any notices under s.17, who fail to provide information or evidence under any of the powers to require this, or who fail to give notification of a change of circumstances under s.6. It imposes a potential penalty on all failures, regardless of the reason for the failure. There is no test of fraud or negligence. The policy of all these measures is to impose a relatively low initial maximum penalty (£300 in all cases), but then to provide a cumulatively daily penalty as a strong deterrent to those who choose to ignore not only the notices and requirements but also the initial penalty. In each case, the maximum daily rate is £60. But the daily rate stops when the failure is remedied.

A penalty under this section bears interest under s.37. It is treated as unpaid tax for the purposes of recovery and collection (Sch.2 para.7). Appeals against penalty decisions are dealt with in Sch.2 (see s.34). By contrast with s.31, this section does not demand proof of fraud or negligence, and may therefore impose a civil penalty rather than a criminal penalty for the purposes of the European Convention on Human Rights.

For details of HMRC's practice in setting and dealing with penalties, see the note to s.31 and HMRC. The full text of WTC7 is set out at the end of the volume. HMRC has announced that it will, on a concessionary basis, not seek penalties from those who fail to comply with the mandatory provisions in this section when the award made to the individual is a nil award.

1.386 Subsection (1) lists the powers under which HMRC can demand information within the penalty regime. It is important to note that those powers are not all-embracing but are subject to clear time limits laid down in primary legislation. See further the notes to ss.14 and 19 above.

The CCM (Claimant Compliance Manual—see note to p.161 above) states that:

"Penalties under s.32(1) are not intended to punish a person who will not provide information. The penalties are intended to encourage the person to comply with the notice and if you do not think the penalties will achieve this result you should not normally begin penalty action." (CCM 10230).

The guidance also states that s.32 penalties will not normally be needed for s.14(2) or s.15(2) failures. In-year challenges will normally only be those under s.16 (CCM 10235, 10240). Similarly, CCM discourages s.32 penalties for s.17 notices.

See also the note to s.31 with regard to the duty of tribunals in appeals about penalties.

Supplementary

1.387 **34.**—Schedule 2 (penalties: supplementary) has effect.

Fraud

Offence of fraud

1.388 **35.**—(1) A person commits an offence if he is knowingly concerned in any fraudulent activity undertaken with a view to obtaining payments of a tax credit by him or any other person.

(2) A person who commits an offence under subsection (1) is liable—

(a) on summary conviction, to imprisonment for a term not exceeding six months, or a fine not exceeding the statutory maximum, or both, or
(b) on conviction on indictment, to imprisonment for a term not exceeding seven years, or a fine, or both.

DEFINITION

"tax credit"—see s.1(2).

GENERAL NOTE

Like the penalties provisions, this section reflects the fear of fraud by claimants and others abusing the tax credits system. There is still no equivalent of this section in the TCA 1999. The new offence is briefly stated and is clearly intended to have a wide reach. It is not confined to claimants or employers and could be applied, for example, to a child care provider.

Section 124 of the Welfare Reform Act 2012 contains detailed provisions to amend this section to increase the penalties. That is still not yet in effect. That Act contains related measures, some of which are in effect since June 2012 but are beyond the scope of this work, to increase DWP and HMRC powers to investigate tax credit frauds. In particular, a series of amendments to other legislation treat tax credits as social security benefits for the purposes of benefit offences and their investigation.

1.389

Powers in relation to documents

36.—(1) Section 20BA of the Taxes Management Act 1970 (c.9) (orders for delivery of documents) applies (with Schedule 1AA and section 20BB) in relation to offences involving fraud in connection with, or in relation to, tax credits as in relation to offences involving serious fraud in connection with, or in relation to, tax.

(2) [¹ . . .]

(3) [¹ . . .]

(4) Any regulations under Schedule 1AA to the Taxes Management Act 1970 which are in force immediately before the commencement of subsection (1) apply, subject to any necessary modifications, for the purposes of that Schedule as they apply by virtue of that subsection (until amended or revoked).

1.390

AMENDMENT

1. Finance Act 2007 s.84(4) and Sch.22 para.14 (December 1, 2007).

DEFINITION

"tax credit"—see s.1(2).

GENERAL NOTE

This applies specific powers available to HMRC for dealing with tax fraud to tax credit fraud. Sections 20BA and 20BB of the TMA 1970 deal with orders for delivery of documents and offences of fraud respectively. The statutory instrument currently made under Sch.1AA is the Orders for the Delivery of Documents (Procedure) Regulations 2000 (SI 2000/2875).

1.391

Tax Credits Act 2002

Loss of tax credit provisions

[¹ **Loss of working tax credit in case of conviction etc for benefit offence**

36A.—(1) Subsection (4) applies where a person ("the offender")—
  (a) is convicted of one or more benefit offences in any proceedings, or
  (b) after being given a notice under subsection (2) of the appropriate penalty provision by an appropriate authority, agrees in the manner specified by the appropriate authority to pay a penalty under the appropriate penalty provision to the appropriate authority, in a case where the offence to which the notice relates is a benefit offence, or
  (c) is cautioned in respect of one or more benefit offences.
(2) In subsection (1)(b)—
  (a) "the appropriate penalty provision" means section 115A of the Social Security Administration Act 1992 (penalty as alternative to prosecution) or section 109A of the Social Security Administration (Northern Ireland) Act 1992 (the corresponding provision for Northern Ireland);
  (b) "appropriate authority" means—
    (i) in relation to section 115A of the Social Security Administration Act 1992, the Secretary of State or an authority which administers housing benefit or council tax benefit, and
    (ii) in relation to section 109A of the Social Security Administration (Northern Ireland) Act 1992, the Department (within the meaning of that Act) or the Northern Ireland Housing Executive.
(3) Subsection (4) does not apply by virtue of subsection (1)(a) if, because the proceedings in which the offender was convicted constitute the current set of proceedings for the purposes of section 36C, the restriction in subsection (3) of that section applies in the offender's case.
(4) If this subsection applies and the offender is a person who would, apart from this section, be entitled (whether pursuant to a single or joint claim) to working tax credit at any time within the disqualification period, then, despite that entitlement, working tax credit shall not be payable for any period comprised in the disqualification period—
  (a) in the case of a single claim, to the offender, or
  (b) in the case of a joint claim, to the offender or the other member of the couple.
(5) Regulations may provide in relation to cases to which subsection (4)(b) would otherwise apply that working tax credit shall be payable, for any period comprised in the disqualification period, as if the amount payable were reduced in such manner as may be prescribed.
(6) For the purposes of this section, the disqualification period, in relation to any disqualifying event, means the relevant period beginning with such date, falling after the date of the disqualifying event, as may be determined by or in accordance with regulations.
(7) For the purposes of subsection (6) the relevant period is—
  (a) in a case falling within subsection (1)(a) where the benefit offence, or one of them, is a relevant offence, the period of three years,
  (b) in a case falling within subsection (1)(a) (but not within paragraph (a) above), the period of 13 weeks, or
  (c) in a case falling within subsection (1)(b) or (c), the period of 4 weeks.

(8) The Treasury may by order amend subsection (7)(a), (b) or (c) to substitute a different period for that for the time being specified there.

(9) This section has effect subject to section 36B.

(10) In this section and section 36B—

"benefit offence" means any of the following offences committed on or after the day specified by order made by the Treasury—
  (a) an offence in connection with a claim for a disqualifying benefit;
  (b) an offence in connection with the receipt or payment of any amount by way of such a benefit;
  (c) an offence committed for the purpose of facilitating the commission (whether or not by the same person) of a benefit offence;
  (d) an offence consisting in an attempt or conspiracy to commit a benefit offence;

"disqualifying benefit" has the meaning given in section 6A(1) of the Social Security Fraud Act 2001;

"disqualifying event" means—
  (a) the conviction falling within subsection (1)(a);
  (b) the agreement falling within subsection (1)(b);
  (c) the caution falling within subsection (1)(c);

"relevant offence" has the meaning given in section 6B of the Social Security Fraud Act 2001.]

AMENDMENT

1. Welfare Reform Act 2012 s.120 (April 6, 2013) (see Welfare Reform Act 2012 (Commencement No.7) Order 2013 (SI 2013/178) art.2).

DEFINITIONS

"caution"—see s.67.
"disqualifying benefit—see Social Security Fraud Act 2001 s.6A(1) as amended by the Welfare Reform Act 2012 s.117.
"joint claim"—see s.3(3).
"working tax credit"—see s.8.

GENERAL NOTE

The Welfare Reform Act 2012 introduced this section and ss.36B–36D in parallel with equivalent provisions for social security benefits. They provide the legislation necessary to carry forward the Government's policy of penalising by loss of benefit those who commit benefit frauds. This is separate from any criminal penalty imposed and any recovery of wrongly paid benefit. The provisions apply to working tax credit, but not to child tax credit. Where the working tax credit is paid on a joint claim, these sections apply to both joint claimants save as specified by or under this section. The effect of the section is to stop the tax credit being payable for a stated period despite any continuing entitlement to the credit. That is normally a complete stop to payment for a "disqualification period", but a reduced level of payment applies in some cases, as noted below.

As subs.(1) makes clear, these sections apply not only to cases where a claimant has been convicted of a benefit offence, but also where a claimant has agreed to pay a penalty to the Secretary of State or any other relevant authority or has accepted a caution. And they apply regardless of the specific benefit for which the conviction, penalty or caution is imposed. So, for example, the loss of tax credits could apply because of an accepted fraud with regard to housing benefit.

Where the offender is one of a couple and the other member of the couple is not subject to a disqualification period at the same time, provision is made by regulation

1.393

that payment of the working tax is to continue at a 50 per cent rate. See Loss of Tax Credit Regulations 2013 (SI 2013/715) reg.3 (para.2.491, below).

For the date from which subs.(6) operates see the Loss of Tax Credit Regulations 2013 (SI 2013/715) reg.2 (para.2.490, below).

[¹ **Supplementary**

1.394

36B.—(1) Where—
  (a) the conviction of any person of any offence is taken in account for the purposes of the application of section 36A in relation to that person, and
  (b) that conviction is subsequently quashed,
all such payments and other adjustments shall be made as would be necessary if no restriction had been imposed by or under section 36A that could not have been imposed if the conviction had not taken place.

(2) Where, after the agreement of any person ("P") to pay a penalty under the appropriate penalty provision is taken into account for the purposes of the application of section 36A in relation to that person—
  (a) P's agreement to pay the penalty is withdrawn under subsection (5) of the appropriate penalty provision, or
  (b) it is decided on an appeal or in accordance with regulations under the Social Security Act 1992 or the Social Security (Northern Ireland) Order 1998 (S.I. 1998/1506 (N.I. 10)) that the overpayment to which the agreement relates is not recoverable or due,
all such payments and other adjustments shall be made as would be necessary if no restriction had been imposed by or under section 36A that could not have been imposed if P had not agreed to pay the penalty.

(3) Where, after the agreement ("the old agreement") of any person ("P") to pay a penalty under the appropriate penalty provision is taken into account for the purposes of the application of section 36A in relation to P, the amount of any overpayment made to which the penalty relates is revised on an appeal or in accordance with regulations under the Social Security Act 1998 or the Social Security (Northern Ireland) Order 1998—
  (a) section 36A shall cease to apply by virtue of the old agreement, and
  (b) subsection (4) shall apply.

(4) Where this subsection applies—
  (a) if there is a new disqualifying event consisting of—
      (i) P's agreement to pay a penalty under the appropriate penalty regime in relation to the revised overpayment, or
      (ii) P being cautioned in relation to the offence to which the old agreement relates,
    the disqualification period relating to the new disqualifying event shall be reduced by the number of days in so much of the disqualification period relating to the old agreement as had expired when subsection 36A ceased to apply by virtue of the old agreement, and
  (b) in any other case, all such payments and other adjustments shall be made as would be necessary if no restriction had been imposed by or under section 36A that could not have been imposed if P had not agreed to pay the penalty.

(5) For the purposes of section 36A—
  (a) the date of a person's conviction in any proceedings of a benefit offence shall be taken to be the date on which the person was found guilty of that offence in those proceedings (whenever the person was

sentenced) or in the case mentioned in paragraph (b)(ii) the date of the order for absolute discharge, and
(b) references to a conviction include references to—
   (i) a conviction in relation to which the court makes an order for absolute or conditional discharge,
   (ii) an order for absolute discharge made by a court of summary jurisdiction in Scotland under section 246(3) of the Criminal Procedure (Scotland) Act 1995 without proceeding to a conviction, and
   (iii) a conviction in Northern Ireland.
(6) In this section "the appropriate penalty provision" has the meaning given by section 36A(2)(a).]

AMENDMENT

1. Welfare Reform Act 2012 s.120 (April 6, 2013) (see Welfare Reform Act 2012 (Commencement No.7) Order 2013 (SI 2013/178) art.2).

DEFINITIONS

"benefit offence"—see s.36A(10).
"caution"—see s.67.

GENERAL NOTE

See the note to s.36A above. This section makes provision where either the imposition of a disqualifying period becomes inappropriate either because an event ceases to be a disqualifying event or because of a new disqualifying event.

[¹ Loss of working tax credit for repeated benefit fraud

36C.—(1) If—
(a) a person ("the offender") is convicted of one or more benefit offences in a set of proceedings ("the current set of proceedings"),
(b) within the period of five years ending on the date on which the benefit offence was, or any of them were, committed, one or more disqualifying events occurred in relation to the offender (the event, or the most recent of them, being referred to in this section as "the earlier disqualifying event"),
(c) the current set of proceedings has not been taken into account for the purposes of any previous application of this section in relation to the offender,
(d) the earlier disqualifying event has not been taken into account as an earlier disqualifying event for the purposes of any previous application of this section in relation to the offender, and
(e) the offender is a person who would, apart from this section, be entitled (whether pursuant to a single or joint claim) to working tax credit at any time within the disqualification period, then, despite that entitlement, the restriction in subsection (3) shall apply in relation to the payment of that benefit in the offender's case.

(2) The restriction in subsection (3) does not apply if the benefit offence referred to in subsection (1)(a), or any of them, is a relevant offence.

(3) Working tax credit shall not be payable for any period comprised in the disqualification period—
(a) in the case of a single claim, to the offender, or

(b) in the case of a joint claim, to the offender or the other member of the couple.

(4) Regulations may provide in relation to cases to which subsection (3)(b) would otherwise apply that working tax credit shall be payable, for any period comprised in the disqualification period, as if the amount payable were reduced in such manner as may be prescribed.

(5) For the purposes of this section the disqualification period, in an offender's case, means the relevant period beginning with a prescribed date falling after the date of the conviction in the current set of proceedings.

(6) For the purposes of subsection (5) the relevant period is—
  (a) in a case where, within the period of five years ending on the date on which the earlier disqualifying event occurred, a previous disqualifying event occurred in relation to the offender, the period of three years;
  (b) in any other case, 26 weeks.

(7) In this section and section 36D—

"appropriate penalty provision" has the meaning given in section 36A(2)(a);

"benefit offence" means any of the following offences committed on or after the day specified by order made by the Treasury—
  (a) an offence in connection with a claim for a disqualifying benefit;
  (b) an offence in connection with the receipt or payment of any amount by way of such a benefit;
  (c) an offence committed for the purpose of facilitating the commission (whether or not by the same person) of a benefit offence;
  (d) an offence consisting in an attempt or conspiracy to commit a benefit offence;

"disqualifying benefit" has the meaning given in section 6A(1) of the Social Security Fraud Act 2001;

"disqualifying event" has the meaning given in section 36A(10);

"relevant offence" has the meaning given in section 6B of the Social Security Fraud Act 2001.

(8) Where a person is convicted of more than one benefit offence in the same set of proceedings, there is to be only one disqualifying event in respect of that set of proceedings for the purposes of this section and—
  (a) subsection (1)(b) is satisfied if any of the convictions take place in the five year period there;
  (b) the event is taken into account for the purposes of subsection (1)(d) if any of the convictions have been taken into account as mentioned there;
  (c) in the case of the earlier disqualifying event mentioned in subsection (6)(a), the reference there to the date on which the earlier disqualifying event occurred is a reference to the date on which any of the convictions take place;
  (d) in the case of the previous disqualifying event mentioned in subsection (6)(a), that provision is satisfied if any of the convictions take place in the five year period mentioned there.

(9) The Treasury may by order amend subsection (6) to substitute different periods for those for the time being specified there.

(10) An order under subsection (9) may provide for different periods to apply according to the type of earlier disqualifying event or events occurring in any case.

(11) This section has effect subject to section 36D.]

(2002 c.21 s.36C)

AMENDMENT

1. Welfare Reform Act 2012 s.120 (April 6, 2013) (Welfare Reform Act 2012 (Commencement No.7) Order 2013 (SI 2013/178) art.2).

DEFINITIONS

"benefit offence"—see s.36A(10).
"caution"—see s.67.
"disqualifying benefit—see Social Security Fraud Act 2001 s.6A(1) as amended by the Welfare Reform Act 2012 s.117.
"joint claim"—see s.3(3).
"working tax credit—see s.8.

GENERAL NOTE

See the note to s.36A above. As the title to this section indicates, this deals with repeat cases that result or may result or could have resulted in loss of tax credit, including past events.

For regulations under subss.(3) and (4) see the Loss of Tax Credit Regulations 2013 (SI 2013/715) reg.3 (see para.2.491, below). This provides for a 50 per cent reduction rather than a total loss of tax credit where these provisions are triggered by actions or failures of one of a couple making a joint claim but not by the other member of the couple.

[¹ **Section 36C: supplementary**

36D.—(1) Where—
(a) the conviction of any person of any offence is taken into account for the purposes of the application of section 36C in relation to that person, and
(b) that conviction is subsequently quashed,

all such payments and other adjustments shall be made as would be necessary if no restriction had been imposed by or under section 36C that could not have been imposed if the conviction had not taken place.

(2) Subsection (3) applies where, after the agreement of any person ("P") to pay a penalty under the appropriate penalty provision is taken into account for the purposes of the application of section 36C in relation to that person—
(a) P's agreement to pay the penalty is withdrawn under subsection (5) of the appropriate penalty provision,
(b) it is decided on an appeal or in accordance with regulations under the Social Security Act 1998 or the Social Security (Northern Ireland) Order 1998 (S.I. 1998/1506 (N.I. 10)) that any overpayment made to which the agreement relates is not recoverable or due, or
(c) the amount of any over payment to which the penalty relates is revised on an appeal or in accordance with regulations under the Social Security Act 1998 or the Social Security (Northern Ireland) Order 1998 and there is no new agreement by P to pay a penalty under the appropriate penalty provision in relation to the revised overpayment.

(3) In those circumstances, all such payments and other adjustments shall be made as would be necessary if no restriction had been imposed by or under section 36C that could not have been imposed if P had not agreed to pay the penalty.

(4) For the purposes of section 36C—

(a) the date of a person's conviction in any proceedings of a benefit offence shall be taken to be the date on which the person was found guilty of that offence in those proceedings (whenever the person was sentenced) or in the case mentioned in paragraph (b)(ii) the date of the order for absolute discharge, and
(b) references to a conviction include references to—
  (i) a conviction in relation to which the court makes an order for absolute or conditional discharge,
  (ii) an order for absolute discharge made by a court of summary jurisdiction in Scotland under section 246(3) of the Criminal Procedure (Scotland) Act 1995 without proceeding to a conviction, and
  (iii) a conviction in Northern Ireland.
(5) In section 36C references to any previous application of that section—
(a) include references to any previous application of a provision having an effect in Northern Ireland corresponding to provision made by that section, but
(b) do not include references to any previous application of that section the effect of which was to impose a restriction for a period comprised in the same disqualification period.]

AMENDMENT

1. Welfare Reform Act 2012 s.120 (April 6, 2013) (Welfare Reform Act 2012 (Commencement No.7) Order 2013 (SI 2013/178) art.2).

DEFINITIONS

"appropriate penalty provision"—see s.36A(2).
"benefit offence"—see s.36A(10).
"caution"—see s.67.
"disqualifying benefit—see Social Security Fraud Act 2001 s.6A(1) as amended by the Welfare Reform Act 2012 s.117.
"joint claim"—see s.3(3).
"working tax credit—see s.8.

GENERAL NOTE

1.399   See the note to s.36A above.

Interest

Interest

1.400   **37.**—(1) If an overpayment of a tax credit for a period is attributable to fraud or neglect on the part of the person, or either or both of the persons, to whom the award of the tax credit was made (or a person acting for him, or for either or both of them, in making the claim for the tax credit), the Board may decide that the whole or any part of the overpayment is to carry interest.
(2) Where the Board so decide the overpayment (or part of the overpayment) carries interest at a prescribed rate from the date 30 days after the appropriate date.
(3) "The appropriate date" is—

(a) in the case of an amount treated as an overpayment by virtue of section 28(6), the date of the decision under section 16 to terminate the award; and
(b) in any other case, the date specified for the purposes of subsection (4) of section 17 in the notice given to the person or persons under that section in relation to the tax credit.

(4) The Board must give notice of a decision under subsection (1) to the person, or each of the persons, to whom it relates; and the notice must state the date on which it is given and include details of the right to appeal against the decision under section 38.

(5) A penalty under any of sections 31 to 33 carries interest at the prescribed rate from the date on which it becomes due and payable; but the Board may in their discretion mitigate any interest or entirely remit any interest which would otherwise be carried by a penalty.

(6) Any interest carried under this section by an overpayment or penalty is to be regarded for the purposes of section 29(3) to (5) or paragraph 7 of Schedule 2 as if it were part of the overpayment or penalty.

AMENDMENT

Subsection (1) is modified as it applies to polygamous units by the Tax Credits (Polygamous Marriages) Regulations 2003 (SI 2003/742) reg.21.

DEFINITIONS

"the Board"—see s.67.
"prescribed"—see s.67.
"overpayment"—see s.28.
"tax credit"—see s.1(2).

GENERAL NOTE

Interest has long been imposed on taxpayers who do not make timely payments of income tax. This includes an underpayment (or repayment) of tax reliefs and deductions (see TMA 1970 s.86). By contrast, interest is not imposed on those required to repay an overpayment of social security benefits. Interest was not imposed on overpayments under the TCA 1999, although penalties under s.9 of that Act carried interest (Sch.4 para.8 to that Act).

This section adopts a compromise in imposing interest payments on overpayments caused by fraud or neglect, but not generally. It also imposes again an interest charge on payments of penalties. Interest does not run unless a decision is made to impose it, and that cannot start until either the date on which the award of tax credit was terminated under s.16 or the closing date of a notice issued under s.17.

The "prescribed rate" is set out in the Tax Credits (Interest Rate) Regulations 2003 (SI 2003/123).

1.401

Appeals

Appeals

38.—(1) An appeal may [2 , subject to subsection (1A),] be brought against—
(a) a decision under section 14(1), 15(1), 16(1), 19(3) or 20(1) or (4) or regulations under section 21,

1.402

Tax Credits Act 2002

  (b) the relevant section 18 decision in relation to a person or persons and a tax credit for a tax year and any revision of that decision under that section,
  (c) a determination of a penalty under paragraph 1 of Schedule 2, [¹. . .]
[¹ (ca) a decision under section 36A or 36C that working tax credit is not payable (or is not payable for a particular period), and]
  (d) a decision under section 37(1).
[²(1A) An appeal may not be brought by virtue of subsection (1) against a decision unless a review of the decision has been carried out under section 21A [³ or section 21C] and notice of the conclusion on the review has been given under section 21A(3) [³or 21C(6) (as the case may be)].
  (1B) If in any case the conclusion of a review under section 21A [³or 21C] is to uphold the decision reviewed, an appeal by virtue of subsection (1) in that case may be brought only against the original decision.
  (1C) If in any case the conclusion of a review under section 21A [³or 21C] is to vary the decision reviewed, an appeal by virtue of subsection (1) in that case may be brought only against the decision as varied.]
  (2) "The relevant section 18 decision" means—
  (a) in a case in which a decision must be made under subsection (6) of section 18 in relation to the person or persons and the tax credit for the tax year, that decision, and
  (b) in any other case, the decision under subsection (1) of that section in relation to the person or persons and the tax credit for the tax year.

AMENDMENTS

1. Welfare Reform Act 2012 s.120 (April 6, 2013).
2. Tax Credits, Child Benefit and Guardian's Allowance Reviews and Appeals Order 2014 (SI 2014/886) art.2(10) and (11) (April 6, 2014).
3. Tax Credits Reviews and Appeals (Amendment) Order 2021 art.2(8) (January 15, 2021).

DEFINITIONS

"tax credit"—see s.1(2).
"tax year"—see s.47.

GENERAL NOTE

1.403   This section concerns appeal rights. Although using the language of "review", subsections (1A)–(1C) in effect impose a requirement for a mandatory reconsideration before exercising the right of appeal.

In *HMRC v Arrbab* [2024] EWCA Civ 16, the Court of Appeal held that the Upper Tribunal's decision in *AB v HMRC (TC)* [2021] UKUT 328 (AAC) was wrongly decided. In *AB*, the Upper Tribunal held that there was a right of appeal to the First-tier Tribunal against HMRC's refusal to extend time for making an application for review. As a matter of statutory construction, s.38(1A) excluded such a right of appeal. However, the Court of Appeal went on to hold that s.38(1A), which prohibits an appeal against a tax credits decision in the absence of a review under s.21A, was itself invalid.

The wording of s.38(1A) was clear, held the Court of Appeal, and did not admit of any other construction than that a right of appeal is excluded where a late request for a review under s.21A is made but HMRC refuse under s.21B to extend time. The Upper Tribunal mistakenly adopted the approach taken in *R(CJ) v SSWP* [2017] UKUT 324 (AAC); [2018] [AACR] 5 without appreciating that *CJ* turned on the interpretation of social security appeal legislation that is not reflected in the appeal provisions of the Tax Credits Act 2002. However, the Court of Appeal went on to consider whether the secondary legislation that inserted s.38(1A), so as to purportedly restrict rights of appeal to the First-tier Tribunal, and hence s.38(1A) itself, was ultra vires. That secondary legislation—the Tax Credits, Child Benefit and Guardian's Allowance Reviews and Appeals Order 2014 (SI 2014/886)—was made under enabling powers provided for by the Finance Act 2008 s.124. Such powers, being powers that authorise secondary legislation to amend an Act of Parliament, are known as Henry VIII powers and, in the case of doubt as to their extent, must be interpreted restrictively (*R. (on the application of Public Law Project) v Secretary of State for Justice* [2016] UKSC 39; [2016] A.C. 1531). This includes a presumption that Henry VIII powers are assumed not to extend to authorising provision that restricts rights of appeal (*R. v Emmett* [1998] A.C. 773; [1997] 3 W.L.R. 1119). The Court of Appeal held that "there is nothing in s.124 FA 2008 that makes clear that it authorises a provision which has the effect of making the decision maker the effective gatekeeper of appeals to the FTT in the event of a late challenge, subject only to the possibility of judicial review". The Tax Credits Act 2002 s.38(1A) was struck out and, accordingly, to be treated as of no effect.

This section creates a series of specific rights of appeal. In *HO v HMRC (TC)* [2018] UKUT 105 (AAC), Judge Wright held that "where the First-tier Tribunal decides an appeal under section 38—be it under section 14(1), 15(1), 16(1), the entitlement decision for the tax year under section 18, section 19(3), 20(1) or (4), or regulations made under section 21—HMRC are prevented (i.e. estopped) from remaking that decision under the same section for the same period". Note that Judge Wright emphasised that his conclusion was not to be read as preventing HMRC from altering a decision taken under one section of the Act in the exercise of powers under another section. For example, a decision of the First-tier Tribunal on a s.18 appeal might in principle be revised by HMRC under s.20 or "a First-tier Tribunal's decision on a section 16(1) appeal cannot preclude HMRC from making the end-of-year section 18 decision the statute calls to be made."

In *MD v HMRC* [2017] UKUT 106 (AAC) Upper Tribunal Judge Hemingway reminded the First-tier Tribunal that "the right of appeal afforded under section 38 of the Tax Credits Act 2002 is a full right of appeal in the sense that the tribunal, on appeal, is required to make its own findings of fact and make its own decision on the appeal based upon the facts as found. It is not exercising some form of supervisory jurisdiction similar to that to be found in Judicial Review proceedings". In *HO v HMRC (TC)* [2018] UKUT 105 (AAC), Judge Wright arrived at effectively the same conclusion. In *MD*, Judge Hemingway held that the First-tier Tribunal erred in law "because it seemed to direct itself exclusively to the making of an enquiry as to whether or not the decision taken by HMRC was or was not a 'reasonable one'".

The following decisions or actions of HMRC are subject to the appeal process:

(a) an initial decision to award or refuse tax credits under s.14(1);

(b) a decision whether (and if so, how) to amend a s.14 decision under s.15(1);

(c) a decision amending or terminating a s.14 decision under s.16(1);

(d) a decision on entitlement made under s.18(1) or (6);

(e) a decision after an enquiry under s.19(3);

(f) a decision revising a previous decision on entitlement under s.20(1);

(g) a decision revising a previous decision on entitlement on the grounds of fraud or neglect under s.20(4);

(h) a decision to revise a decision on entitlement because of official error under s.21;

(i) a determination of a penalty under Sch.2 para.1; and

(j) a decision to impose interest under s.37(1).

1.404 As is emphasised above in the note to s.16, HMRC must in all cases identify under which provision any final decision is made. In practice, the only decision that will fall out with the jurisdiction of the First-tier Tribunal will be an overpayment decision. The underlying decision causing the overpayment will be appealable and must have been identified to the claimant.

Upper Tribunal Judge Jacobs has recently issued the following guidance to any First-tier Tribunal faced with a submission from HMRC that failed to make clear the decision under appeal:

> "The proper course ... to have taken was not to struggle on to make the best sense ... of what was presented ..., it was to remit the case back to the Commissioners with directions on how to remedy the deficiencies in their submission" (*AR-L v HMRC (TC)* [2015] UKUT 303 (AAC) at [8]).

In *SH v HMRC and SC (TC)* [2013] UKUT 297 (AAC) Judge Wikeley drew attention to the sensitivity of appeals involving the relationships of two separated parents to a child or children, particularly where there was a dispute between them about a child. Allowing an appeal, he gave careful directions to the First-tier Tribunal requiring anonymity for all aspects of the further hearing of the appeal by that tribunal.

1.405 In *CTC/31/2006* the Commissioner rejected as outside his jurisdiction an attempt to appeal a decision of HMRC that a claim was not properly made. The claim had been made on an income tax return, and HMRC had refused to accept it. The Commissioner held that this was not within the terms of s.38. He also held that it could not be read into the section by reference to the European Convention on Human Rights. In the view of the Commissioner judicial review was an adequate means of challenging a decision to refuse a claim that was alleged to be unlawful. However, this decision predated the creation of the new tribunal system and the broader powers now given to tribunals to deal with issues that are in effect judicial review. The Upper Tribunal, if not the First-tier Tribunal, now has express power to deal with judicial review. And, in the light of that, a broad approach to jurisdiction such as that taken on a tax issue by Sales J in *Oxfam v HMRC* [2009] EWHC 3078, Ch D., may suggest that the matter should be within s.38. But see also *OFCOM v Morrissey and Information Commissioner* [2011] UKUT 116 (AAC); [2012] AACR 1.

However, *CTC/31/2006* must also now be treated with some caution given developments in the case law. For example, Upper Tribunal Judge Turnbull in *SG v HMRC (TC)* [2011] UKUT 199 (AAC) expressed the view that "the correct analysis is probably that the words 'an appeal may be brought against (a) a decision under section 14' in s.38 must be read as including a decision as to whether a claim has been made or must be treated under reg. 11 [of the Tax Credits (Claims and Notifications) Regulations 2002] as having been made". This approach was taken a step further by Upper Tribunal Judge Ward in *ZM and AB v HMRC (TC)* [2013] UKUT 547 (AAC); [2014] AACR 17, where HMRC had argued that a decision as to whether a claim had been properly made (in the light of an identity query involving reg.5(8) of the Tax Credits (Claims and Notifications) Regulations 2002) was not subject to any statutory appeals procedure. Judge Ward held that in such circumstances the availability of judicial review was not an adequate remedy and so the necessary words were read into s.14(1) to ensure that the legislation was human rights compliant. See further the General Note to s.14 above.

In a robust decision criticising both HMRC's submissions to a First-tier Tribunal and the failure of that tribunal to note their deficiencies, Judge Ward sets out in some detail in his decision in *AG v HMRC (TC)* [2013] UKUT 530 (AAC) the extent to which HMRC is required to provide a First-tier Tribunal with evidence about a tax credit appeal. The case concerned a claim by an appellant that he had provided information to HMRC about a change of circumstances. A First-tier Tribunal had directed HMRC to produce further details about the case. HMRC had produced nothing relevant and had failed to respond to part of the direction, but a second First-tier Tribunal ignored the failure and found against the appellant. In the Upper Tribunal, Judge Ward directed full disclosure. In response he was given details of the telephone conversations recorded by HMRC from its helpline. He rules that this should have been provided to the First-tier Tribunal, noting that the failure to do so was a breach of r.24(3) of the First-tier Tribunal's procedural rules. It followed that the decision of that tribunal was in error of law for failure to consider the full case. The judge helpfully scheduled to his decision part of an affidavit of evidence from HMRC about the evidence it records and how it is recorded.

The change of practice by HMRC with regard to the provision of full evidence and submissions to the First-tier Tribunal is noted and discussed by Upper Tribunal Judge Wright in *JW v HMRC* [2015] UKUT 369 (AAC). As he notes there, it is accepted by HMRC that templates used in the Tax Credit Office before May 2014 did not comply with the relevant requirements. HMRC has now stopped the use of those templates and, more generally, revised its guidance to officials preparing submissions for tribunals. See HMRC *Tax Credits Manual* at TCM0014000. It follows that any submission made by the Tax Credits Office before then is likely to be non-compliant and should be questioned on any appeal.

1.406

See also the criticisms about the failure of HMRC to provide First-tier Tribunal hearings with full papers in the decisions of Judge Wikeley in *SH v HMRC (TC)* [2013] UKUT 297 (AAC) and Judge Turnbull in *JP v HMRC (TC)* [2013] UKUT 519 (AAC), where he commented that this was not the first time on which he had noted a reluctance of HMRC to put all potentially relevant documents before a First-tier Tribunal. In *TM v HMRC (TC)* [2013] UKUT 444 (AAC) Judge Wright set aside a First-tier Tribunal decision in a case where HMRC produced its submission only at the last minute to the tribunal. The appellant had not been given an adequate time to consider it as HMRC had not issued it to the appellant. The failure to issue to the appellant was a breach of the duty on HMRC under the tribunal procedure rules, unless a tribunal had expressly waived the requirement.

See also the decisions of Upper Tribunal Judge Wikeley in *JR v HMRC* [2015] UKUT 192 (AAC) and *ZB v HMRC* [2015] UKUT 198 (AAC) endorsing these decisions but adding a comment from HMRC (recorded at [17] of the decision) that:

> "HMRC's approach in the present case, and others like it, does not reflect the current approach which is that full details of the case are always included in the written response, and the response itself is accompanied by all relevant documents, in compliance with Tribunal Procedure Rules. The current and compliant approach has been in place since May 2014."

If HMRC fail to supply the First-tier Tribunal with all documentation in their possession relevant to a tax credits appeal, that will amount to an error of law in the proceedings before the First-tier Tribunal, albeit not one of the tribunal's own making. *SK v HMRC* [2016] UKUT 441 (AAC) is an example of such a case. In *SK* Upper Tribunal Judge Wikeley said:

1.407

> "14. ...[HMRC is] subject to the duty under rule 24(4)(b) of the Tribunal Procedure (First-tier Tribunal) (Social Entitlement Chamber) Rules 2008 (SI 2008/2685), which provides that 'The decision maker must provide with the response...copies of *all documents relevant* to the case in the decision maker's possession, unless a practice direction or direction states otherwise' (emphasis added; see further *ST v Secretary of State for Work and Pensions (ESA)* [2012] UKUT 469 (AAC)). On the face of it, the HMRC submission on this appeal appeared to set out both the history of the case and the issues arising for decision. However, once one digs down a bit further, the gaps in that account become evident. As this decision will show, the HMRC submission lamentably failed to comply with rule 24(4)(b)."

Despite the assurances given by HMRC in proceedings before the Upper Tribunal, as described above, doubts persist as to whether, in all cases, HMRC appeal responses comply with the requirements of the Tribunal Procedure (First-tier Tribunal) (Social Entitlement Chamber) Rules 2008. The decision in *SK*, for example, arose from an appeal to the First-tier Tribunal made in February 2015 against a HMRC decision about entitlement in tax year 2013/14. HMRC supplied the First-tier Tribunal with their appeal response in March 2015. In granting the appellant permission to appeal to the Upper Tribunal against the First-tier Tribunal's decision, Upper Tribunal Judge Wikeley remarked "I am not at all confident that all relevant evidence was presented to the FTT by HMRC". The judge was proved right. It transpired that HMRC had not supplied the First-tier Tribunal with a quantity of documentation relevant to tax year 2013/14. Judge Wikeley ended his decision with these words:

"38. The Upper Tribunal has previously been assured that HMRC's former unsatisfactory approach to FTT submissions, which was not compliant with rule 24(4)(b), had been corrected with effect from May 2014 (see *ZB v HMRC* [2015] UKUT 198 (AAC) and *JW v HMRC (TC)* [2015] UKUT 369 (AAC)). The HMRC submission in the present appeal for the FTT was dated 3 March 2015. Plainly HMRC's best intentions have yet to be fully realised, but tax credit claimants and their advisers up and down the country probably do not need me to tell them that."

Worryingly, more recent cases suggest that HMRC's "formerly unsatisfactory approach to FTT submissions" has not been wholly remedied. Recent examples include the decisions of Judge Hemingway in *MD v HMRC* [2017] UKUT 106 (AAC) and Judge Wright in *HO v HMRC (TC)* [2018] UKUT 105 (AAC). Another led to scathing criticisms by Judge Wikeley in *VO v HMRC* [2017] UKUT 343 (AAC), a decision which began by stating "well, here we go yet again" before going on:

"2. I used the phrase 'Well, here we go again' with a sense of frustration, bordering on despair, to open my decision in *NI v HMRC* [2015] UKUT 160 (AAC), a case in which I criticised Her Majesty Revenue and Customs (HMRC) for both its decision making processes and its conduct of appeals in relation to tax credits claims. That phrase has been echoed in other tribunal jurisdictions where HMRC's conduct has come under similar critical scrutiny: see, e.g. *Pandey v Revenue and Customs (Income Tax/Corporation Tax: Penalty)* [2017] UKFTT 216 (TC).
3. So, yes, in short this is yet another sorry tale of HMRC institutional incompetence and inefficiency which could well have led to injustice, were it not for the persistence of the Appellant."

In *VO*, HMRC's written response to the appellant's appeal failed to mention or include all relevant documentary evidence. The possible existence of undisclosed material was clearly suggested by the material that was disclosed. For example, the appellant's statement that she had sent further information to HMRC and the HMRC's calculation of hours worked indicated that some raw data applied by HMRC was absent from the appeal response. The First-tier Tribunal erred in law by failing to recognise these clear "alarm bells".

1.408 *CTC/1594/2006* illustrates the importance of checking for which year or years an appeal is made. This is potentially more of a problem for tax credits than most benefits because of the effect of having an award decision during the same year as the entitlement decision for the previous year. The Commissioner accepted the arguments for HMRC in that case that a claimant could not use an appeal to challenge more than the specific decisions challenged. As Commissioners have observed on more than one occasion, this means that challenges against award decisions may be of limited value. HMRC is no more debarred from altering a tribunal decision about an award at the end of the year than any other award decision. This issue is not always easy to clarify as HMRC uses terminology in its literature that conflates awards and entitlement decisions. See para.1.324.

It is to be emphasised that this section gives the right of appeal, and s.39 as amended by s.63 is concerned only with how the appeal is made. It is often said that the appeal is to HMRC and not an appeal tribunal. That is not correct. The appeal is to the tribunal, while notification is to HMRC. The importance of this used to be that it was for HMRC to deal with passing a tribunal a case for listing. There was a major change of approach adopted for all tax cases when the Special and General Commissioners were abolished and replaced by the Tax Chamber of the First-tier Tribunal. It was agreed that listing was no longer for HMRC but is now a function of the Tribunals Service, operating through its Tax Chamber offices. The trigger in direct tax cases is notification of the appeal directly to the Tribunals Service by the appellant. The same should therefore apply to all tax credit appeals. These should therefore be listed by the Tribunals Service for hearing or decision as it considers appropriate when an appellant notifies the tribunal of the appeal. This change may deal with some of the recurring complaints that appeals about tax credits entitlement (as against unappealable decisions about overpayments) do not reach the tribunals.

The absence of appeals undoubtedly reflects the power of the Inland Revenue and now the HMRC to settle cases under s.54 of the TMA 1970. This is a power not possessed by the Department for Work and Pensions or local authorities (or the former Customs and Excise Commissioners). That power is particularly useful in dealing with questions of disputed income and with penalty cases, although it is of limited use in cases such as whether two individuals should be making a joint claim. But on one view HMRC is making too wide a use of that power. In *Tax Credits Agenda for Improvement*, published in September 2004 jointly by the Chartered Institute of Taxation, Citizens Advice, CPAG, The Institute of Chartered Accountants of England and Wales, the Low Income Tax Reform Group, and One Parent Families, the approach of HMRC to settlement was criticised. The bodies jointly asked for:

"adherence to proper procedures when the IR decide to settle an appeal, rather than 'cancelling' the appeal and issuing revised decisions outside the appeal process."

While HMRC have, as noted, a power to settle under s.54 of the TMA it is a process with its own safeguards (see para.1.21, above). Similarly, once an appeal has been made it cannot be "cancelled" otherwise than by a properly reached settlement or as part of the appeal process. Any attempt to interfere with the appeal process outside those protective limits is an interference by one party in the appeal process and as such is likely to be in breach of the "equality of arms" principle laid down by the European Court of Human Rights. That principle demands that all parties have equal access to a court or tribunal as part of the fundamental principle of fair hearings laid down in art.6 of the European Convention on Human Rights. (See Vol.III of this series for that provision and the Human Rights Act 1998 that introduces it into UK law.)

1.409

This section clearly gives separate appeal rights against s.14 decisions as against s.18 decisions. The automated process, followed by checks, that is used for awards (see the notes to s.14) would suggest that the administrative approach adopted by HMRC, while undoubtedly efficient in many cases, may be the reason why the joint protest has arisen.

Separately from these, the appellate authorities can be invoked in two other situations. HMRC cannot itself make a determination of daily penalties under s.32(2) and must instead start proceedings for such penalties before the appellate authorities. This is not technically an appeal (see Sch.2 para.3). An individual subject to an enquiry under s.19 can, under s.19(8), apply to the appellate authorities to direct the enquiry to end. Such an application is to be treated as if it was an appeal (s.19(10)).

The 2007 special report of the Parliamentary Ombudsman noted above continues to recommend that appeal rights should be given to an independent tribunal in connection with overpayments. It also sets out the government response to that recommendation, which is an enhanced complaints procedure. This procedure is now applied by both HMRC and the Ombudsman to all tax credits complaints, including appeals. In effect, a complaint only gets to the Ombudsman or an appeal to a tribunal as a fourth level of review.

Tax credits appeals and transition to universal credit

1.410 Where a person entitled to universal credit brings a successful appeal to the First-tier Tribunal against a tax credits decision, the effect of reg.13(3) of the Universal Credit (Transitional Provisions) Regulations 2014 (SI 2014/1230), see below in this volume, is that any tax credit award made by the tribunal terminates on the day before the person became entitled to universal credit. Where a person brings a successful appeal against a universal credit decision, reg.14 of the 2014 Regulations terminates a tax credit to which the person has become entitled under the tribunal's decision as from the day on which the person is entitled to universal credit.

For the modifications to s.38 where a person's entitlement to a tax credit was interrupted by the making of a claim for universal credit, see reg.12A of, and Schedule 1 to, the Universal Credit (Transitional Provisions) Regulations 2014 (SI 2014/1230), below in this volume.

Exercise of right of appeal

1.411 **39.**—(1) [¹...]

(2) [¹...]

(6) Part 5 of the Taxes Management Act 1970 (appeals and other proceedings) applies in relation to appeals under section 38 (as in relation to appeals under the Taxes Acts, within the meaning of that Act), but subject to such modifications as are prescribed.

AMENDMENT

1. Tax Credits, Child Benefit and Guardian's Allowance Reviews and Appeals Order 2014 (SI 2014/886) art.2(12) (April 6, 2014).

GENERAL NOTE

1.412 This section, as amended, has to be read subject to two very large health warnings. The first is that the version as set out above, with the repeal of paras (1) and (2), applies in relation to HMRC decisions made on or after April 6, 2014. See further s.39A below and the General Note to that new provision. For the version of s.39 which applied to HMRC decisions before that date, please see previous editions of this Volume. The second health warning is that the first health warning applies only to England, Wales and Scotland. However, with regard to the second health warning, the Tax Credits, Child Benefit and Guardian's Allowance Appeals (Appointed Day) (Northern Ireland) Order 2014 (SI 2014/2881) apply the provisions in SI 2014/886 to Northern Ireland from March 2, 2015.

[² Late appeals

1.413 **39A.**—(1) The Commissioners for Her Majesty's Revenue and Customs may treat a late appeal under section 38 as made in time where the conditions specified in subsections (2) to (6) are satisfied, except that the Commissioners may not do so in the case of an appeal made more than one year after the expiration of the time (original or extended) for appealing.

(2) An appeal may be treated as made in time if the Commissioners are satisfied that it is in the interests of justice to do so.

(3) For the purposes of subsection (2) it is not in the interests of justice to treat an appeal as made in time unless—
 (a) the special circumstances specified in subsection (4) are relevant; or
 (b) some other special circumstances exist which are wholly exceptional and relevant, and as a result of those special circumstances it was not practicable for the appeal to be made in time.

(4) The special circumstances mentioned in subsection (3)(a) are—

(a) the appellant or a partner or dependant of the appellant has died or suffered serious illness;
(b) the appellant is not resident in the United Kingdom; or
(c) normal postal services were disrupted.

(5) In determining whether it is in the interests of justice to treat an appeal as made in time, regard shall be had to the principle that the greater the amount of time that has elapsed between the expiration of the time for appealing and the submission of the notice of appeal, the more compelling should be the special circumstances.

(6) In determining whether it is in the interests of justice to treat an appeal as made in time, no account shall be taken of the following—
(a) that the appellant or any other person acting for the appellant was unaware of or misunderstood the law applicable to the appellant's case (including ignorance or misunderstanding of any time limit); or
(b) that the Upper Tribunal or a court has taken a different view of the law from that previously understood and applied.

(7) If in accordance with the preceding provisions of this section the Commissioners for Her Majesty's Revenue and Customs treat a late appeal under section 38 as made in time, it is to be treated as having been brought within any applicable time limit.]

AMENDMENT

1. Text of section added by Tax Credits (Late Appeals) Order 2014 (SI 2014/885) art.2 (April 1, 2014).

GENERAL NOTE

HMRC offered the following explanation for the new section in its explanatory note for the draft Order to the Joint Committee on Statutory Instruments:

1.414

"Article 2 makes provision which mirrors that provided by regulation 5 (late appeals) of the Tax Credits (Appeals) (No.2) Regulations 2002 (S.I. 2002/3196). Regulation 5 of S.I. 2002/3196 was made under powers contained in section 12(7) (appeal to First-tier Tribunal) of the Social Security Act 1998 (c. 14) which applied (as modified) to tax credit appeals by virtue of regulation 4 of the Tax Credits (Appeals) Regulations 2002 (S.I. 2002/2926). S.I. 2002/2926, made under the power in section 63(8) of the 2002 Act (tax credits appeals etc: temporary modifications), lapsed in respect of its application in Great Britain, as a result of amendments to section 63 by the Transfer of Tribunal Functions and Revenue and Customs Appeals Order 2009 (S.I. 2009/56) ("the 2009 Order") following the transfer of the functions of the tax tribunals to the new tribunals established under the Tribunals, Courts and Enforcement Act 2007 (c. 15). Tax credits appeals in Great Britain were transferred from the Social Security and Child Support Appeals Tribunal to the Social Entitlement Chamber of the First-tier Tribunal and amendments were made to section 63 by S.I. 2009/56 to reflect these changes. Article 3 of, and paragraph 316 of Schedule 1 to, the 2009 Order amended section 63 by substituting references to the "appeal tribunal", defined by reference to Northern Ireland legislation, which did not include the First-tier Tribunal in Great Britain. As a result of those amendments to the regulation-making power in section 63 was that S.I. 2002/2926, and therefore S.I. 2002/3196 (which applied only in respect of appeals in Great Britain), no longer applied in respect of appeals in Great Britain (but continued to apply in respect of appeals in Northern Ireland). The Revenue and Customs Appeals Order 2012 (S.I. 2012/533) amended sections 63(5) and (8) by inserting a reference to the First-tier Tribunal to correct this defect."

That explanation fails to note that Judge Rowland held that the provision dealing with late appeals in the No.2 Regulations to be invalid in *JI v HMRC* [2013] UKUT 199 (AAC). See para.2.389.

There has clearly been both confusion and inconsistency in dealing with late appeals notwithstanding the introduction of the new provisions of s.39A from April 1, 2014. This is in part because the general view appears now to be that s.39A only achieved part of its purpose, notwithstanding the views expressed to Parliament in the explanatory note to the statutory instrument introducing it. Historically, it is clear that both HMRC (and its predecessor) and tribunals had power to deal with late appeals before November 4, 2008. A minor result—presumably unintended—of the major reforms in 2008 is now accepted to be that from that date while HMRC continued to have power to deal with late appeals, the relevant tribunal (the First-tier Tribunal) did not have that power. Then on April 1, 2009—again presumably without any specific intention so to do—other legislative changes took away the power of HMRC to deal with late appeals. While it has been argued that the decision of Judge Rowland is open to criticism for failure to deal with human rights issues and is limited in its binding effect to the position before the introduction of s.39A and supporting provisions, those are arguably arguments that must be set against the plainly binding authority of the central elements of the decision and the close reasoning of the whole decision. The position for any period before April 1, 2014 must therefore be that set out in that decision.

1.415 Unfortunately, and notwithstanding the careful rehearsal of the legislative history of this topic in Judge Rowland's decision, a third set of errors appear to have been made—yet again it is assumed unintentionally—when the new provisions incorporated in s.39A took effect on April 1, 2014. Here the result appeared to be that HMRC again had power to deal with late appeals both before and after the new provisions take effect. However, there was no provision giving the power back to tribunals retrospectively and the effect of the one-year absolute time limit in s.39A(1) appeared to bar consideration of any late appeal made before April 1, 2013. So it appeared that old late appeals may still be caught by the unintended bar against late appeals and more recent appeals made before the new rules came in may enter a limbo where a tribunal had no jurisdiction to consider the matter.

There is often an additional kind of confusion in these cases. Bearing in mind that there are at least two separate operative decisions for each tax year (and often more), it is always necessary to check against which decision or decisions a claimant is seeking to appeal. It may be that the result is that some decisions can be admitted late and considered while others remain late and outside the jurisdiction of a tribunal. A final point is that the time limit only starts when the notice provisions in s.23(2) of the Act are met. See paras 1.359–1.360 above. If there has been no proper notice of decision, then time cannot start running.

The explanation for the draft Order also noted that:

> "Article 2(3) [of the 2014 Order] deals with cases that are in the pipeline, and sometimes have been pending and in uncertainty for a very long time. HMRC have not opposed late appeals of late, relying on their management function in section 2 of the Tax Credits Act 2002 to forward them to the tribunal. So article 2(3) simply validates, going forward, HMRC decisions to allow such late appeals."

In July 2016 a three-judge panel of the Administrative Appeals Chamber decided a test case appeal on the validity of the new rules: *VK v HMRC* [2016] UKUT 331(AAC); [2017] AACR 3. The three-judge panel disagreed with Judge Rowland's decision in *JI v HMRC* that the First-tier Tribunal had, by April 2009, lost power to extend time for appealing against a tax credits decision. Rather, the Upper Tribunal accepted CPAG's primary argument for the claimant that the Tribunals, Courts and Enforcement Act (TCEA) 2007 allowed tribunal procedure rules to empower the tribunal to extend the statutory time limit for appealing. Paragraph 4 of Sch.5 to the TCEA 2007 authorises rules to "make provision for time limits as respects initiating... proceedings" in the First-tier Tribunal. The three-judge panel decided this permits rules to provide for extension of statutory time limits, given the broad words of Sch.5(4) and the fact that such an outcome is consistent with the purposes of the TCEA 2007 and its careful distribution of responsibilities for making procedure rules ([78]–[91]).

JI, in contrast, had applied the House of Lords' decision in *Mucelli v Government of Albania* [2009] UKHL 2; [2009] 1 W.L.R. 287 to hold that procedural rules cannot confer power to extend time unless a specific enabling provision in primary legislation permits this and there was no such provision in the TCEA 2007. The three-judge panel concluded Mucelli did not as such impose a prohibition on procedural rules providing for extensions of time. Rather, reading the decision as a whole, the ratio was correctly described in *Reddy v GMC* [2012] EWCA Civ 310 as requiring some statutory authority for extending a time limit; it did not depart from existing authorities that rules are capable of providing for extensions of time ([65]–[69]). The Upper Tribunal also analysed the provision made in other Chambers' rules (paras 33–58), observing that many rules assume they can provide for extensions of time and indeed the Tax Chamber's own rules clearly provide for the extension of statutory time limits. The three-judge panel also considered whether, properly construed, the tribunal's rule 5(3)(a) power to extend time for complying with a rule extends to a time limit adopted in rules by reference. It decided the power does so extend (paras 93–103).

Supplementary

Annual reports

40.—(1) The Board must make to the Treasury an annual report about—
(a) [¹...]
(b) the number of awards of child tax credit and of working tax credit,
(c) the number of enquiries conducted under section 19,
(d) the number of penalties imposed under this Part, and
(e) the number of prosecutions and convictions for offences connected with tax credits.

(2) The Treasury must publish each annual report made to it under subsection (1) and lay a copy before each House of Parliament.

AMENDMENTS

1. Commissioners for Revenue and Customs Act 2005 s.50 and Sch.4 para.89 (April 18, 2005).
2. References to "the Board" are now references to the Commissioners for Revenue and Customs: CRCA 2005 s.4.

DEFINITIONS

"the Board"—see s.67.
"child tax credit"—see s.8.
"tax credits"—see s.1(2).
"working tax credit"—see s.10.

GENERAL NOTE

This section derives from a clause adopted by the House of Lords against the wishes of government, and represents the one major amendment in the Act not moved by the Government itself. The aim is to ensure a specific report that would be put before Parliament each year about both the scale of the tax credits system and the extent of fraud within it. The wording of the section comes from a government amendment moved to replace the Lords clause in the House of Commons. It was recognised that to some extent it duplicates figures already published by HMRC in its more general reports.

Annual review

1.418
41.—(1) The Treasury must, in each tax year, review the amounts specified in subsection (2) in order to determine whether they have retained their value in relation to the general level of prices in the United Kingdom as estimated by the Treasury in such manner as it considers appropriate.

(2) The amounts are monetary amounts prescribed—
(a) under subsection (1)(a) of section 7;
(b) for the purposes of any of paragraphs (a) to (d) of subsection (3) of that section;
(c) under section 9;
(d) under section 11, otherwise than by virtue of section 12, or
(e) under subsection (2) of section 13, otherwise than by virtue of subsection (3) of that section.

(3) The Treasury must prepare a report of each review.

(4) The report must include a statement of what each amount would be if it had fully retained its value.

(5) The Treasury must publish the report and lay a copy of it before each House of Parliament.

DEFINITION

"prescribed"—see s.67.

GENERAL NOTE

1.419
This provides for the annual uprating review of the monetary amounts used in awarding tax credits. Section 12 of the Welfare Reform and Work Act 2016 modifies s.41 so that, until the end of tax year 2018/19, a review need not address, in relation to working tax credit, the basic element, the 30 hour element, the second adult element and the lone parent element and, in relation to child tax credit, the individual amount for a child or qualifying young person.

Persons subject to immigration control

1.420
42.—(1) Regulations may make provision in relation to persons subject to immigration control or in relation to prescribed descriptions of such persons—
(a) for excluding entitlement to, or to a prescribed element of, child tax credit or working tax credit (or both), or
(b) for this Part to apply subject to other prescribed modifications.

(2) "Person subject to immigration control" has the same meaning as in section 115 of the Immigration and Asylum Act 1999 (c.33).

DEFINITIONS

"child tax credit"—see s.8.
"modifications"—see s.67.
"persons subject to immigration control"—see Immigration and Asylum Act 1999 s.115.
"prescribed"—see s.67.
"working tax credit"—see s.10.

General Note

Although listed in the "supplementary" part of Pt I of the Act, this makes provision for excluding anyone from entitlement to tax credits if they are "subject to immigration control", a phrase derived from the Immigration and Asylum Act 1999. The definition covers those who are not nationals of an EEA state and who require leave to enter the UK or have certain forms of conditional leave. For the detailed application of this section, see the Tax Credits (Immigration) Regulations 2003 (SI 2003/653). An attempt to challenge the regulations made under this section as discriminatory by reference to the Human Rights Act 1999 failed in *CTC/3692/2008*.

Polygamous marriages

43.—(1) Regulations may make provision for this Part to apply in relation to persons who are parties to polygamous marriages subject to prescribed modifications.
(2) A person is a party to a polygamous marriage if—
(a) he is a party to a marriage entered into under a law which permits polygamy, and
(b) either party to the marriage has a spouse additional to the other party.

Definition

"modifications"—see s.67.

General Note

This is another of the necessary compromises between the general approach to income tax and the general approach to social security. Social security benefits have long contained special provisions dealing with polygamous marriages, if only to prevent more than two of the marriage partners benefiting for a particular benefit as a married couple. In contrast, the point is not so significant in the context of income tax as there is now individual assessment. The standard treatment of monogamous marriages is set out in s.3.

Effect is given to this section by the Tax Credits (Polygamous Marriages) Regulations 2003 (SI 2003/742). Where those regulations provide for a modification of the sections of this Act, that is noted in this volume as an amendment to the section.

Crown employment

44.—This Part applies in relation to persons employed by or under the Crown (as in relation to other employees).

Definitions

"Crown"—see Interpretation Act 1978 Sch.1.
"employed"—see s.25(5).

General Note

This section avoids any unintended exclusion of civil and other public servants by reason of the Crown Proceedings Act 1947 or otherwise. The Tax Credits (Residence) Regulations 2003 (SI 2003/642) extend this further by applying the Act to Crown Servants working overseas and their partners. The main concern of both this section and those regulations is that Crown servants receive full entitlement to CTC.

Inalienability

1.426 **45.**—(1) Every assignment of or charge on a tax credit, and every agreement to assign or charge a tax credit, is void; and, on the bankruptcy of a person entitled to a tax credit, the entitlement to the tax credit does not pass to any trustee or other person acting on behalf of his creditors.

(2) In the application of subsection (1) to Scotland—
  (a) the reference to assignment is to assignation ("assign" being construed accordingly), and
  (b) the reference to the bankruptcy of a person is to the sequestration of his estate or the appointment on his estate of a judicial factor under section 41 of the Solicitors (Scotland) Act 1980 (c.46).

DEFINITION

"tax credit"—see s.1(2).

GENERAL NOTE

1.427 This mirrors (and repeats much of the wording of) SSAA 1992 s.187. While informal pledges of both benefit and benefit books occur, that section renders any such arrangement unenforceable in the courts or as against government departments. This section ensures that this also applies to tax credits.

Giving of notices by Board

1.428 **46.**—The Board may give any notice which they are required or permitted to give under this Part in any manner and form which the Board consider appropriate in the circumstances.

DEFINITION

"the Board"—see s.67.

GENERAL NOTE

1.429 No provision is made in this section for regulations or for deemed notice. There is no equivalent of TMA 1970 s.114 (want of form not to invalidate assessments) or s. 115 (delivery and service of documents) provided for in the Act. However, it is suggested that this does not discharge HMRC from the duty of complying with specific provisions as to content in this Act, in the Tax Credits (Claims and Notifications) Regulations 2002 (SI 2002/2014), or elsewhere. HMRC is also required, by reason of the art.6 of the European Convention on Human Rights and the Human Rights Act 1998 (see Vol.III in this series), to ensure that proper notice is given of any appeal to the appeal tribunals or the appellant as the case may be.

Consequential amendments

1.430 **47.**—Schedule 3 (consequential amendments) has effect.

GENERAL NOTE

1.431 This section gives effect to Sch.3 (not included in this volume). Section 68(1) ensures that those provisions are co-extensive with the provisions they affect. Most of the provisions are concerned to replace WFTC with WTC and to substitute a reference to CTC in place of references to the various previous child benefits and credits. Paragraph 25 amends s.30C of the SSCBA 1992, and para.30 amends s.42 of that Act. Both deal with transfers between benefit and tax credit.

(2002 c.21 s.48)

Interpretation

48.—[¹(1)] In this Part—
"child" has the meaning given by section 8(3),
[¹"couple" has the meaning given by section 3(5A)],
"the current year income" has the meaning given by section 7(4),
"employee" and "employer" have the meaning given by section 25(5),
[² . . .]
"the income threshold" has the meaning given by section 7(1)(a),
"joint claim" has the meaning given by section 3(8),
[¹ . . .],
"overpayment" has the meaning given by section 28(2) and (6),
"the previous year income" has the meaning given by section 7(5),
"qualifying remunerative work", and being engaged in it, have the meaning given by regulations under section 10(2),
"qualifying young person" has the meaning given by section 8(4),
"the relevant income" has the meaning given by section 7(3),
"responsible", in relation to a child or qualifying young person, has the meaning given by regulations under section 8(2) (for the purposes of child tax credit) or by regulations under section 10(4) (for the purposes of working tax credit),
"single claim" has the meaning given by section 3(8),
[² . . .]
"tax year" means a period beginning with 6th April in one year and ending with 5th April in the next, and
[¹ . . .].
[¹(2) [³ . . .]]

1.432

AMENDMENTS

1. Civil Partnership Act 2004 ss.254 and 261(4) and Sch.24 para.147 and Sch.30 (December 5, 2005).
2. Transfer of Tribunal Functions and Revenue and Customs Appeals Order 2009 (SI 2009/56) art.3(1) and Sch.1 para.315 (April 1, 2009).
3. Civil Partnership (Opposite-sex Couples) Regulations 2019 (SI 2019/1458) reg.41(a) and Sch.3 Part 1 para.23(3) (December 2, 2019).

GENERAL NOTE

See also s.67 for further definitions.

1.433

This section applies to a person whose tax credit payments were terminated, as a result of a claim for universal credit, as if it included a definition of "part tax year" which is "a period of less than a year beginning with 6th April and ending with the date on which the award of a tax credit terminated": see reg.12 of the Universal Credit (Transitional Provisions) Regulations 2014 (SI 2014/1230) (below in this volume). The term "part tax year" is used in s.28 as modified by reg.12.

PART II

CHILD BENEFIT AND GUARDIAN'S ALLOWANCE

49.–57.—*(Omitted)*

1.434

Tax Credits Act 2002

Part III

Supplementary

Information etc.

Administrative arrangements

1.435   **58.**—(1) This section applies where regulations under—
(a) section 4 or 6 of this Act,
(b) section 5 of the Social Security Administration Act 1992 (c.5), or
(c) section 5 of the Social Security Administration (Northern Ireland) Act 1992 (c.8),
permit or require a claim or notification relating to a tax credit, child benefit or guardian's allowance to be made or given to a relevant authority.
(2) Where this section applies, regulations may make provision—
(a) for information or evidence relating to tax credits, child benefit or guardian's allowance to be provided to the relevant authority (whether by persons by whom such claims and notifications are or have been made or given, by the Board or by other persons),
(b) for the giving of information or advice by a relevant authority to persons by whom such claims or notifications are or have been made or given, and
(c) for the recording, verification and holding, and the forwarding to the Board or a person providing services to the Board, of claims and notifications received by virtue of the regulations referred to in subsection (1) and information or evidence received by virtue of paragraph (a).
(3) "Relevant authority" means—
(a) the Secretary of State,
(b) the Northern Ireland Department, or
(c) a person providing services to the Secretary of State or the Northern Ireland Department.

Definitions

"child benefit"—see SSCBA 1992 s.141.
"claim"—see s.3(8).
"guardian's allowance"—see SSCBA 1992 s.77.
"relevant authority"—see subs.(3).
"tax credit"—see s.1(2).

General Note

1.436   Section 5 of the SSAA 1992 and its Northern Ireland equivalent provide the authority for the Social Security (Claims and Payments) Regulations 1987 (SI 1987/1968) under which regulations for all aspects of claiming benefits are detailed. This section enables claims and notifications for tax credits and child benefit being validly given to both HMRC and the social security authorities, and to anyone acting under contract to the social security authorities. It will, for example, allow claims for child benefit and CTC to be made together to one authority. See also the Tax Credits (Administrative Arrangements) Regulations 2002 (SI 2002/3036).

CRCA 2005 contains a wide general power for HMRC to use for all its statutory purposes all the information that comes into its possession for any purpose. This is subject to limits in Sch.2 of that Act. There are no limits in the Schedule relevant to the management and payment of tax credits.

Use and disclosure of information

59.—Schedule 5 (use and disclosure of information) has effect.

GENERAL NOTE

This section incorporates Sch.5 into the Act. The Schedule adds further provisions to the statutory authority already available so that tax authorities, social security authorities, other government departments, and local authorities can exchange information. The widest power is the power to give information to anyone for the purposes of the Learning and Skills Act 2000 (para.10). This wide power is linked to a new criminal offence if it is misused (para.10(4)). Paragraph 11 includes disclosures about tax credits in the general offence of disclosing information held by a person in connection with tax, tax credit and social security functions unless the information is disclosed with lawful authority or certain other conditions are met. This replaces the inclusion of tax credits within that section under s.12 of the TCA 1999. Paragraph 9 of the Schedule has given effect by the Tax Credits (Provision of Information) (Functions Relating to Health) Regulations 2003 (SI 2003/731) and the Tax Credits (Provision of Information) (Functions Relating to Health) (No.2) Regulations 2003 (SI 2003/1650) and a series of other short specific provisions.

Other supplementary provisions

Repeals

60.—Schedule 6 (repeals) has effect.

GENERAL NOTE

This section incorporates the standard repeals Schedule into the Act. It provides the authority for the abolitions flagged up in s.1(3). It confirms that this Act replaces the whole of the TCA 1999.

Commencement

61.—Apart from section 54(1) and (2), the preceding provisions of this Act come into force in accordance with orders made by the Treasury.

GENERAL NOTE

See end of the introductory General Note to the Act as a whole.

Transitional provisions and savings

62.—(1) The Secretary of State may by order make as respects England and Wales and Scotland, and the Northern Ireland Department may by order make as respects Northern Ireland, any transitional provisions or savings which appear appropriate in connection with the commencement of the abolition of the increases referred to in section 1(3)(e).

(2) Subject to any provision made by virtue of subsection (1), the Treasury may by order make any transitional provisions or savings which appear

appropriate in connection with the commencement of any provision of this Act.

GENERAL NOTE

1.444   See the note to the previous section.

Tax credits appeals etc.: temporary modifications

1.445   **63.**—(1) Until such day as the Treasury may by order appoint, Part I of this Act has effect subject to the modifications specified in this section; and an order under this subsection may include any transitional provisions or savings which appear appropriate.

[² (2) Except in the case of an appeal against an employer penalty, an appeal under section 38 is to—
(a) in Great Britain, the First-tier Tribunal; or
(b) in Northern Ireland, the appeal tribunal;
and in either case section 39(6) shall not apply.]

[² (3) The function of giving a direction under section 19(10) is a function of—
(a) in Great Britain, the First-tier Tribunal; or
(b) in Northern Ireland, the appeal tribunal;
and in either case the relevant provisions of Part 5 of the Taxes Management Act 1970 shall not apply.]

[² (4) In Northern Ireland, except in the case of an employer information penalty, proceedings under paragraph 3 of Schedule 2 are by way of information in writing, made to the appeal tribunal (rather than to the tribunal), and upon summons issued by them to the defendant to appear before them at a time and place stated in the summons; and they must hear and decide each case in a summary way.]

(5) So far as is appropriate in consequence of subsections (2) to (4)—
(a) the references to the [² tribunal in section 19(10)] and paragraphs 2 and 3(2) of Schedule 2 are to the [³ the First-tier Tribunal or] [² appeal tribunal], [² . . .]
(b) [² . . .]

[² (6) In Northern Ireland, an appeal under paragraph 2(2) or 4(1) of Schedule 2 from a decision of, or against the determination of a penalty by, the appeal tribunal lies to the Northern Ireland Social Security Commissioner (rather than to the Upper Tribunal).]

(7) So far as is appropriate in consequence of subsection (6), the references in paragraphs 2(2) and 4 of Schedule 2 [² to the Upper Tribunal are to the Northern Ireland Social Security Commissioner].

(8) Regulations may apply any provision contained in—
(a) Chapter 2 of Part I of the Social Security Act 1998 (c.14) (social security appeals: Great Britain),
(b) Chapter 2 of Part II of the Social Security (Northern Ireland) Order 1998 (SI 1998/1506 (N.I. 10)) (social security appeals: Northern Ireland), or
(c) section 54 of the Taxes Management Act 1970 (c.9) (settling of appeals by agreement),
in relation to appeals which, by virtue of this section, are to [³ the First-tier Tribunal or] [¹ the appeal tribunal or lie to] [[¹a]Northern Ireland Social Security Commissioner], but subject to such modifications as are prescribed.

(2002 c.21 s.63)

[² ...]

([¹ (10) "Appeal tribunal" means an appeal tribunal constituted under Chapter 1 of Part 2 of the Social Security (Northern Ireland) Order 1998.]

(11) "Employer penalty" means—
(a) a penalty under section 31 or 32 relating to a requirement imposed by virtue of regulations under section 25, or
(b) a penalty under section 33.

(12) "Employer information penalty" means a penalty under section 32(2)(a) relating to a requirement imposed by virtue of regulations under section 25.

(13) ["Northern Ireland Social Security Commissioner" means] the Chief Social Security Commissioner or any other Social Security Commissioner appointed under the Social Security Administration (Northern Ireland) Act 1992 (c.8) or a tribunal of two or more Commissioners constituted under Article 16(7) of the Social Security (Northern Ireland) Order 1998 (SI 1998/1506 (N.I. 10)).

[¹ (14) "tribunal" (other than in the expression "appeal tribunal") shall have the meaning in section 47C of the Taxes Management Act 1970.]

AMENDMENTS

1. Transfer of Tribunals Functions Order 2008 (SI 2008/2833) art.9(1) Sch.3 para.191 (November 3, 2008).
2. Transfer of Tribunal Functions and Revenue and Customs Appeals Order 2009 (SI 2009/56) art.3(1) Sch.1 para.316 (April 1, 2009).
3. Revenue and Customs Appeals Order 2012 (SI 2012/533) art.2 (March 1, 2012).

DEFINITIONS

"appeal tribunal"—see subs.(10).
"employer information penalty"—see subs.(12).
"employer penalty"—see subs.(11).
"General Commissioners"—see s.47.
"modifications"—see s.67.
"Social Security Commissioner"—see subs.(13).
"Special Commissioners"—see s.47.

GENERAL NOTE

The original aim of this section was to introduce what was said to be a temporary transfer of tax credits from the General and Special Commissioners to the social security tribunals. No such transfer took place, and events have been overtaken by the more general reforms of both tribunals. The choice is now between the Social Entitlement Chamber of the First-tier Tribunal, where appeals are now heard, and the Tax Chamber of the same tribunal, where it is still the policy intention to have the appeals heard. In practice, the distinction matters little as the rules and practices are now substantially the same and there are, in any event, few tax credits appeals. A major focus of difficulty in the appeals now heard are on the issue of whether a claim should have been a joint claim (that is, the claimant is living with a partner). That is a kind of appeal in which the social entitlement tribunals have considerable experience and the tax tribunals have none.

The "temporary modifications" to s.63 are unlikely to be modified before the whole Act is itself repealed when tax credits are replaced, as provided for the Welfare Reform Act 2012 by the universal credit. Under that Act power is given to transfer tax credits functions in whole or in part from Her Majesty's Revenue and Customs to the relevant Secretary of State.

As part of those reforms, the procedure on appeals is now the standard First-tier Tribunal procedure. See Vol.III of this work. Again as part of those reforms,

1.446

appeals from the tax tribunals no longer go to the High Court or Court of Session, but now go to the Upper Tribunal, as do all social entitlement appeals.

There was no equivalent reform of the Northern Ireland system. The section therefore provides that appeals go to the "old" tribunals and Commissioners there.

Northern Ireland

1.447

64.—(1) The Northern Ireland Act 1998 (c.47) has effect subject to the amendments in subsections (2) and (3).

(2) In Schedule 2 (excepted matters), after paragraph 10 insert—

"10A. Tax credits under Part 1 of the Tax Credits Act 2002.
10B. Child benefit and guardian's allowance."

(3) In section 87 (consultation and co-ordination on social security matters), after subsection (6) insert—

"(6A) But this section does not apply to the legislation referred to in subsection (6) to the extent that it relates to child benefit or guardian's allowance."

(4) For the purposes of that Act, a provision of—
(a) an Act of the Northern Ireland Assembly; or
(b) a Bill for such an Act,
which amends or repeals any of the provisions of the Employment Rights (Northern Ireland) Order 1996 (SI 1996/1919 (N.I. 16)) dealt with in Schedule 1 shall not be treated as dealing with tax credits if the Act or Bill deals with employment rights conferred otherwise than by that Schedule in the same way.

DEFINITION

"tax credits"—see s.1(2).

GENERAL NOTE

1.448

The provisions on Northern Ireland are necessary because of the transfer of the administration of child benefit and guardian's allowance from the Northern Ireland authorities to the Home Civil Service. The amendments also confirm the effect of s.16 of the Tax Credits Act 1999 in reserving tax credits as excepted matters.

Regulations, orders and schemes

1.449

65.—(1) Any power to make regulations under sections 3, 7 to 13, 42 and 43, and any power to make regulations under this Act prescribing a rate of interest, is exercisable by the Treasury.

(2) Any other power to make regulations under this Act is exercisable by the Board.

(3) Subject to subsection (4), any power to make regulations, orders or schemes under this Act is exercisable by statutory instrument.

(4) The power—
(a) of the Department of Health, Social Services and Public Safety to make schemes under section 12(5), and
(b) of the Northern Ireland Department to make orders under section 62(1),
is exercisable by statutory rule for the purposes of the Statutory Rules (Northern Ireland) Order 1979 (S.I. 1979/1573 (N.I. 12)).

(5) Regulations may not be made under section 25 or 26 in relation to appeals in Scotland without the consent of the Scottish Ministers.

(6) Regulations may not be made under section 39(6) or 63(8) without the consent of the Lord Chancellor [1, the Department of Justice in Northern Ireland] and the Scottish Ministers.

(7) Any power to make regulations under this Act may be exercised—
  (a) in relation to all cases to which it extends, to all those cases with prescribed exceptions or to prescribed cases or classes of case,
  (b) so as to make as respects the cases in relation to which it is exercised the full provision to which it extends or any less provision (whether by way of exception or otherwise),
  (c) so as to make the same provision for all cases in relation to which it is exercised or different provision for different cases or classes of case or different provision as respects the same case or class of case for different purposes,
  (d) so as to make provision unconditionally or subject to any prescribed condition,
  (e) so as to provide for a person to exercise a discretion in dealing with any matter.

(8) Any regulations made under a power under this Act to prescribe a rate of interest may—
  (a) either themselves specify a rate of interest or make provision for any such rate to be determined by reference to such rate or the average of such rates as may be referred to in the regulations,
  (b) provide for rates to be reduced below, or increased above, what they otherwise would be by specified amounts or by reference to specified formulae,
  (c) provide for rates arrived at by reference to averages to be rounded up or down,
  (d) provide for circumstances in which alteration of a rate of interest is or is not to take place, and
  (e) provide that alterations of rates are to have effect for periods beginning on or after a day determined in accordance with the regulations in relation to interest running from before that day as well as from or from after that day.

(9) Any power to make regulations or a scheme under this Act includes power to make any incidental, supplementary, consequential or transitional provision which appears appropriate for the purposes of, or in connection with, the regulations or scheme.

AMENDMENT

1. Northern Ireland Act 1998 (Devolution of Policing and Justice Functions) Order 2010 (SI 2010/ 976) art.15(5) and Sch.18 para.60 (April 12, 2010).

DEFINITIONS

"the Board"—see s.67, but note that the functions of the Board have been transferred to Her Majesty's Revenue and Customs by the Commissioners for Revenue and Customs Act 2005.

"prescribe"—see s.67.

Tax Credits Act 2002

Parliamentary etc. control of instruments

1.450   **66.**—(1) No [¹ order or] regulations to which this subsection applies may be made unless a draft of the instrument containing [¹ the order or regulations] (whether or not together with other provisions) has been laid before, and approved by a resolution of, each House of Parliament.

(2) Subsection (1) applies to—

[¹(za) an order made by the Treasury under section 36A(8) or 36C(9),

(zb) regulations made under section 36A(5) or 36C(4),]

(a) regulations prescribing monetary amounts that are required to be reviewed under section 41,

(b) regulations made by virtue of subsection (2) of section 12 prescribing the amount in excess of which charges are not taken into account for the purposes of that subsection, and

(c) the first regulations made under sections 7(8) and (9), 9, 11, 12 and 13(2).

(3) [¹ An order or] a statutory instrument containing—

(a) regulations under this Act,

(b) a scheme made by the Secretary of State under section 12(5), or

(c) an Order in Council under section 52(7),

is (unless a draft of the instrument has been laid before, and approved by a resolution of, each House of Parliament) subject to annulment in pursuance of a resolution of either House of Parliament.

(4) A statutory instrument containing a scheme made by the Scottish Ministers under section 12(5) is subject to annulment in pursuance of a resolution of the Scottish Parliament.

(5) A statutory rule containing a scheme made by the Department of Health, Social Services and Public Safety under section 12(5) is subject to negative resolution within the meaning of section 41(6) of the Interpretation Act (Northern Ireland) 1954 (c. 33 (N.I.)).

AMENDMENT

1. Welfare Reform Act 2012 s.120(4) (April 6, 2013).

Interpretation

1.451   **67.**—In this Act—

"the Board" means the Commissioners of Inland Revenue,

[¹ "cautioned", in relation to any person and any offence, means cautioned after the person concerned has admitted the offence; and "caution" is to be interpreted accordingly;]

"modifications" includes alterations, additions and omissions, and "modifies" is to be construed accordingly,

"the Northern Ireland Department" means the Department for Social Development in Northern Ireland,

"prescribed" means prescribed by regulations, and

"tax credit" and "tax credits" have the meanings given by section 1(2).

AMENDMENT

1. Welfare Reform Act 2012 s.120(3) (April 6, 2013).

GENERAL NOTE

1.453   For references to "the Board" see now s.2 above and CRCA 2005 s.1.

(2002 c.21 Sch.2)

68.–70.—*Omitted.*

Sch.1.—*Omitted.*

SCHEDULE 2
PENALTIES: SUPPLEMENTARY

Determination of penalties by Board

1.—(1) The Board may make a determination—
  (a) imposing a penalty under section 31, 32(2)(b) or (3) or 33; and
  (b) setting it at such amount as, in their opinion, is appropriate.
(2) The Board must give notice of a determination of a penalty under this paragraph to the person on whom the penalty is imposed.
(3) The notice must state the date on which it is given and give details of the right to appeal against the determination under section 38.
(4) After the notice of a determination under this paragraph has been given the determination must not be altered except on appeal.
(5) A penalty determined under this paragraph becomes payable at the end of the period of 30 days beginning with the date on which the notice of determination is given.

2.—(1) On an appeal [· . . .] under section 38 against the determination of a penalty under [¹ paragraph 1 that is notified to the First-tier Tribunal, the tribunal] may—
  (a) if it appears that no penalty has been incurred, set the determination aside,
  (b) if the amount determined appears to be appropriate, confirm the determination,
  (c) if the amount determined appears to be excessive, reduce it to such other amount (including nil) as [¹ the First-tier Tribunal considers] appropriate, or
  (d) if the amount determined appears to be insufficient, increase it to such amount not exceeding the permitted maximum [¹ the First-tier Tribunal considers] consider appropriate.

[¹ (2) In addition to any right of appeal on a point of law under section 11(2) of the Tribunals, Courts and Enforcement Act 2007, the person liable to the penalty may appeal to the Upper Tribunal against the amount of the penalty which has been determined under sub-paragraph (1), but not against any decision which falls under section 11(5)(d) or (e) of that Act and was made in connection with the determination of the amount of the penalty.

(2A) Section 11(3) and (4) of the Tribunals, Courts and Enforcement Act 2007 applies to the right of appeal under sub-paragraph (2) as it applies to the right of appeal under section 11(2) of that Act.

(2B) On an appeal under this paragraph the Upper Tribunal has the same powers as are conferred on the First-tier Tribunal by virtue of this paragraph.]

Penalty proceedings before [¹ tribunal]

3.—(1) The Board may commence proceedings for a penalty under section 32(2)(a) [¹ before the tribunal].

[¹ (2) The person liable to the penalty shall be a party to the proceedings.

(3) "tribunal" is to be read in accordance with section 47C of the Taxes Management Act 1970.]

4.—[¹ (1) In addition to any right of appeal on a point of law under section 11(2) of the Tribunals, Courts and Enforcement Act 2007, the person liable to the penalty may appeal to the Upper Tribunal against the determination of a penalty in proceedings under paragraph 2(1), but not against any decision which falls under section 11(5)(d) or (e) of that Act and was made in connection with the determination of the amount of the penalty.

(1A) Section 11(3) and (4) of the Tribunals, Courts and Enforcement Act 2007 applies to the right of appeal under sub-paragraph (1) as it applies to the right of appeal under section 11(2) of that Act.]

(2) On any such appeal the [¹Upper Tribunal] may—
  (a) if it appears that no penalty has been incurred, set the determination aside,
  (b) if the amount determined appears to be appropriate, confirm the determination,
  (c) if the amount determined appears to be excessive, reduce it to such other amount (including nil) as the [¹Upper Tribunal] considers appropriate, or
  (d) if the amount determined appears to be insufficient, increase it to such amount not exceeding the permitted maximum as the [¹Upper Tribunal] considers appropriate.

Mitigation of penalties

1.457   **5.**—The Board may in their discretion mitigate any penalty under this Part or stay or compound any proceedings for any such penalty and may also, after judgment, further mitigate or entirely remit any such penalty.

Time limits for penalties

1.458   **6.**—(1) In the case of a penalty under s.31 relating to a tax credit for a person or persons for the whole or part of a tax year (other than a penalty to which sub-paragraph (3) applies), the Board may determine the penalty at any time before the latest of—
  (a) the end of the period of one year beginning with the expiry of the period for initiating an enquiry under section 19 into the entitlement of the person, or the joint entitlement of the persons, for the tax year,
  (b) if such an enquiry is made, the end of the period of one year beginning with the day on which the enquiry is completed, and
  (c) if a decision relating to the entitlement of the person, or the joint entitlement of the persons, for the tax year is made under section 20(1) or (4), the end of the period of one year beginning with the day on which the decision is made.
(2) In the case of a penalty under section 32 relating to a tax credit for a person or persons for the whole or part of a tax year (other than a penalty to which sub-paragraph (3) applies), the Board may determine the penalty, or commence proceedings for it, at any time before—
  (a) if an enquiry into the entitlement of the person, or the joint entitlement of the persons, for the tax year is made under section 19, the end of the period of one year beginning with the day on which the enquiry is completed, and
  (b) otherwise, the end of the period of one year beginning with the expiry of the period for initiating such an enquiry.
(3) In the case of—
  (a) a penalty under section 31 or 32 relating to a requirement imposed by virtue of regulations under section 25; or
  (b) a penalty under section 33,
the Board may determine the penalty, or commence proceedings for it, at any time before the end of the period of six years after the date on which the penalty was incurred or began to be incurred.

Recovery of penalties

1.459   **7.**—(1) A penalty payable under this Part is to be treated for the purposes of Part VI of the Taxes Management Act 1970 (c.9) (collection and recovery) as if it were tax charged in an assessment and due and payable.
(2) Regulations under section 203(2)(a) of the Income and Corporation Taxes Act 1988 (c.1) (PAYE) apply to a penalty payable under this Part as if it were an underpayment of tax for a previous year of assessment.

AMENDMENT

1. Transfer of Tribunal Functions and Revenue and Customs Order 2009 (SI 2009/56) Sch.1 paras 312, 317 and 318 (April 1, 2009).

DEFINITIONS

"appeal tribunal"—s.63(10).
"the Board"—s.57 but note that the functions of the Board have been transferred to HMRC by CRCA 2005.
"Social Security Commissioner"—s.63(13).
"tax credit"—by virtue of s.67, see s.1(2).
"tax year"—s.47.

GENERAL NOTE

1.460   This Schedule is set out as modified by s.63, which has the effect that, except in cases involving employer penalties or employer information penalties (neither of which can arise since payment by employers was abolished from April 6, 2006), the jurisdiction of the General Commissioners and Special Commissioners was exercised by appeal tribunals and the jurisdiction of the High Court and the Court of Session as the Court of Exchequer in Scotland was exercised by Social Security Commissioners. Since April 2009 all appeals now go to the First-tier Tribunal and then the Upper Tribunal. For more general information, see the note to s.39.

Paragraph 2

Initial penalty determinations are by HMRC under para.1 except where the penalty is an initial penalty for failing to provide information to be imposed under s.32(2)(a). Section 38 provides a right of appeal against determinations under para.1 and s.39 provides for its exercise. Paragraph 2 makes provision for the powers of the tribunal and, as modified by ss.63(6) and (7) for an appeal to the Upper Tribunal on issues of quantum. In other words, the appeal is not confined to points of law. But the power to appeal without first obtaining permission to appeal has been removed.

1.461

Paragraphs 3 and 4

Paragraph 3 provides for HMRC to bring proceedings before a tribunal for an initial information penalty under s.32(2)(a). See para.6(2) for the time limit for bringing such proceedings. Paragraph 4 provides a right of appeal to the Upper Tribunal. It is similar to that provided in para.2 but see the note to s.63(8).

1.462

Paragraph 5

Section 54 of the Taxes Management Act 1970 would enable an appeal to a tribunal under para.2 to be compromised but this provision also allows proceedings under para.3 to be abandoned and for an appeal to the Upper Tribunal to be compromised. Note that HMRC may reduce a penalty imposed by a tribunal but may not increase it. There is no provision for an appeal by HMRC against the amount of any reduction in a penalty.

1.463

Sch.3–Sch.6—*Omitted.*

1.464

Employment Act 2002

Employment Act 2002

(2002 c.22)

ARRANGEMENT OF SECTIONS

PART I

STATUTORY LEAVE AND PAY

CHAPTER 1

PATERNITY AND ADOPTION

Rights to leave and pay

1.465

1. Paternity leave [*omitted*]
2. Statutory paternity pay [*omitted*]*
3. Adoption leave [*omitted*]
4. Statutory adoption pay [*omitted*]*

Administration and enforcement: pay

5. [*repealed*]
6. Financial arrangements [*omitted*]
7. Funding of employers' liabilities
8. Regulations about payment
9. Decisions and appeals [*omitted*]
10. Powers to require information
11. Penalties: failures to comply
12. Penalties: fraud, etc.
13. Supply of information held by the Board
14. Supply of information held by the Secretary of State
15. Use of information by the Board
16. Interpretation

CHAPTER 2

MATERNITY

17. Rights during and after maternity leave [*omitted*]
18. Maternity pay period [*omitted*]*
19. Rate of statutory maternity pay [*omitted*]*
20. Entitlement to statutory maternity pay [*omitted*]*
21. Funding of employers' liabilities: statutory maternity pay [*omitted*]*

(2002 c.22)

Part II

Tribunal Reform

22–28. [*Omitted*]

Part III

Dispute Resolution, etc.

29–40. [*Omitted*]

Part IV

Miscellaneous and General

41–55. [*Omitted*]

Schedule 1—Penalties: procedure and appeals
Schedules 2–8 [*Omitted*]

*These sections make amendments to SSCBA 1992 which are incorporated in the text of that legislation elsewhere in this volume.

General Note

On the background to the Employment Act 2002, see the General Note to SSCBA 2002 Pt 12ZA.

1.466

Part I

Statutory Leave and Pay

Chapter 1

Paternity and Adoption

Administration and enforcement: pay

Financial arrangements

6.—[*Omitted.*]

1.467

Employment Act 2002

GENERAL NOTE

1.468 This section amends SSAA 1992 and SSCBA 1992 to ensure that SPP and SAP are treated in the same was as SPP and SMP in terms of their administration.

Funding of employers' liabilities

1.469 7.—(1) The Secretary of State shall by regulations make provision for the payment by employers of [3 statutory paternity pay,] statutory adoption pay [4, statutory shared parental pay and statutory parental bereavement pay] to be funded by the Board to such extent as the regulations may specify.

(2) Regulations under subsection (1) shall—
 (a) make provision for a person who has made a payment of [3 statutory paternity pay,] statutory adoption pay [4, statutory shared parental pay or statutory parental bereavement pay] to be entitled, except in such circumstances as the regulations may provide, to recover an amount equal to the sum of—
  (i) the aggregate of such of those payments as qualify for small employers' relief; and
  (ii) an amount equal to 92 per cent of the aggregate of such of those payments as do not so qualify; and
 (b) include provision for a person who has made a payment of [3 statutory paternity pay,] statutory adoption pay [4, statutory shared parental pay or statutory parental bereavement pay] qualifying for small employers' relief to be entitled, except in such circumstances as the regulations may provide, to recover an additional amount equal to the amount to which the person would have been entitled under section 167(2)(b) of the Social Security Contributions and Benefits Act 1992 (corresponding provision for statutory maternity pay) had the payment been a payment of statutory maternity pay.

(3) For the purposes of subsection (2), [1 a payment of] [3 statutory paternity pay,] statutory adoption pay [4, statutory shared parental pay or statutory parental bereavement pay] qualifies for small employers' relief if it would have so qualified were it a payment of statutory maternity pay, [2 treating—
 (a) the period for which the payment of statutory paternity pay is made,
 (b) the payee's adoption pay period, [4 . . .]
 (c) the period for which the payment of statutory shared parental pay is made, [4 or
 (d) the period for which the payment of statutory parental bereavement pay is made,]
as the maternity pay period.]

(4) Regulations under subsection (1) may, in particular—
 (a) make provision for funding in advance as well as in arrear;
 (b) make provision for funding, or the recovery of amounts due under provision made by virtue of subsection (2)(b), by means of deductions from such amounts for which employers are accountable to the Board as the regulations may provide, or otherwise;
 (c) make provision for the recovery by the Board of any sums overpaid to employers under the regulations.

(5) Where in accordance with any provision of regulations under subsection (1) an amount has been deducted from an employer's contributions payments, the amount so deducted shall (except in such cases as the Secretary of State may by regulations provide) be treated for the purposes

of any provision made by or under any enactment in relation to primary or secondary Class 1 contributions—
  (a) as having been paid (on such date as may be determined in accordance with the regulations), and
  (b) as having been received by the Board, towards discharging the employer's liability in respect of such contributions.

(6) Regulations under this section must be made with the concurrence of the Board.

(7) In this section, "contributions payments", in relation to an employer, means any payments which the employer is required, by or under any enactment, to make in discharge of any liability in respect of primary or secondary Class 1 contributions.

AMENDMENTS

1. Work and Families Act 2006 s.11(1) Sch.1 para.50 (April 6, 2010).
2. Children and Families Act 2014 Sch.7 paras 51(2)(b), 51(3)(a)(ii), 51(3)(b)(ii), 51(4)(b) and 51(4)(c) (June 30, 2014).
3. Children and Families Act 2014 Sch.7 paras 51(2)(a), 51(3)(a)(i), 51(3)(b)(i) and 51(4)(a) (April 5, 2015).
4. Parental Bereavement (Leave and Pay) Act 2018, s.2(2), Sch. para.36(2)–(4) (January 18, 2020).

DEFINITIONS

"the Board"—see s.16.
"contributions payments"—see subs.(7).
"employer"—see subs.(7).

GENERAL NOTE

See further the SPP and SAP (Administration) Regulations 2002, especially regs 3–8.

Regulations about payment

8.—(1) The Secretary of State may make regulations with respect to the payment by employers of [1 statutory paternity pay,] statutory adoption pay [2, statutory shared parental pay and statutory parental bereavement pay].

(2) Regulations under subsection (1) may, in particular, include provision—
  (a) about the records to be kept by employers in relation to payments of [1 statutory paternity pay,] statutory adoption pay [2, statutory shared parental pay and statutory parental bereavement pay], including the length of time for which they are to be retained;
  (b) for the production of wages sheets and other documents and records to officers of the Board for the purpose of enabling them to satisfy themselves that [1 statutory paternity pay,] statutory adoption pay [2, statutory shared parental pay and statutory parental bereavement pay] have been paid and are being paid, in accordance with the regulations, to employees who are entitled to them;
  (c) for requiring employers to provide information to employees (in their itemised pay statements or otherwise);
  (d) for requiring employers to make returns to the Board containing such particulars with respect to payments of [1 statutory paternity pay,] statutory adoption pay [2, statutory shared parental pay and statutory parental bereavement pay] as the regulations may provide.

(3) Regulations under subsection (1) must be made with the concurrence of the Board.

AMENDMENTS

1. Children and Families Act 2014 Sch.7 paras 52(2)(a), 52(3)(a)(i), 52(3)(b)(i) and 52(3)(c)(i) (April 5, 2015).
2. Parental Bereavement (Leave and Pay) Act 2018, s.2(2), Sch. para.37 (January 18, 2020).

DEFINITIONS

"the Board"—see s.16.
"employer"—see s.16.

GENERAL NOTE

1.472 See further the SPP and SAP (Administration) Regulations 2002 regs 9 and 10.

Decisions and appeals

9.—[*Omitted.*]

GENERAL NOTE

1.473 This section amends ss.8, 11 and 14 of the Social Security Contributions (Transfer of Functions, etc.) Act 1999; the relevant amendments are incorporated elsewhere in this volume.

Powers to require information

1.474 10.—(1) The Secretary of State may by regulations make provision enabling an officer of the Board authorised by the Board for the purposes of this section to require persons of a description specified in the regulations to provide, or produce for inspection, within such period as the regulations may require, such information or documents as the officer may reasonably require for the purpose of ascertaining whether [¹ statutory paternity pay,] statutory adoption pay [², statutory shared parental pay or statutory parental bereavement pay] is or was payable to or in respect of any person.

(2) The descriptions of person which may be specified by regulations under subsection (1) include, in particular—
  (a) any person claiming to be entitled to [¹ statutory paternity pay,] statutory adoption pay [², statutory shared parental pay or statutory parental bereavement pay],
  (b) any person who is, or has been, the spouse or partner of such a person as is mentioned in paragraph (a),
  (c) any person who is, or has been, an employer of such a person as is mentioned in paragraph (a),
  (d) any person carrying on an agency or other business for the introduction or supply to persons requiring them of persons available to do work or to perform services, and
  (e) any person who is a servant or agent of any such person as is specified in paragraphs (a) to (d).

(3) Regulations under subsection (1) must be made with the concurrence of the Board.

(2002 c.22 s.10)

AMENDMENTS

1. Children and Families Act 2014 Sch.7 paras 53(2)(a) and 53(3)(a) (April 5, 2015).
2. Parental Bereavement (Leave and Pay) Act 2018, s.2(2), Sch. para.38 (January 18, 2020).

DEFINITIONS

"the Board"—see s.16.
"employer"—see s.16.

GENERAL NOTE

See further the SPP and SAP (Administration) Regulations 2002, especially regs 11–14.

Penalties: failures to comply

11.—(1) Where a person—
(a) fails to produce any document or record, provide any information or make any return, in accordance with regulations under section 8, or
(b) fails to provide any information or document in accordance with regulations under section 10,

he shall be liable to the penalties mentioned in subsection (2) below (subject to subsection (4)).

(2) The penalties are—
(a) a penalty not exceeding £300, and
(b) if the failure continues after a penalty is imposed under paragraph (a), a further penalty or penalties not exceeding £60 for each day on which the failure continues after the day on which the penalty under that paragraph was imposed (but excluding any day for which a penalty under this paragraph has already been imposed).

(3) Where a person fails to keep records in accordance with regulations under section 8, he shall be liable to a penalty not exceeding £3,000.

(4) Subject to subsection (5), no penalty shall be imposed under subsection (2) or (3) at any time after the failure concerned has been remedied.

(5) Subsection (4) does not apply to the imposition of a penalty under subsection (2)(a) in respect of a failure within subsection (1)(a).

(6) Where, in the case of any employee, an employer refuses or repeatedly fails to make payments of [¹ statutory paternity pay,] statutory adoption pay [², statutory shared parental pay or statutory parental bereavement pay] in accordance with any regulations under section 8, the employer shall be liable to a penalty not exceeding £3,000.

(7) Section 118(2) of the Taxes Management Act 1970 (c.9) (extra time for compliance, etc.) shall apply for the purposes of subsections (1), (3) and (6) as it applies for the purposes of that Act.

(8) Schedule 1 to this Act (penalties: procedure and appeals) has effect in relation to penalties under this section.

AMENDMENTS

1. Children and Families Act 2014 Sch.7 para.54(a) (April 5, 2015).
2. Parental Bereavement (Leave and Pay) Act 2018, s.2(2), Sch. para.39 (January 18, 2020).

DEFINITIONS

"the Board"—see s.16.
"employer"—see s.16.

GENERAL NOTE

1.477 This provision, imposing penalties on employers who fail to comply with the requirements of the SPP and SAP schemes, is modelled on the equivalent provision for tax credits: TCA 2002 s.32.

Penalties: fraud, etc.

1.478 **12.**—(1) Where a person fraudulently or negligently—
(a) makes any incorrect statement or declaration in connection with establishing entitlement to [¹ [³ ...] statutory paternity pay] [⁴or statutory parental bereavement pay], or
(b) provides any incorrect information or document of a kind mentioned in regulations under section 10(1) so far as relating to [¹ [³ ...] statutory paternity pay] [⁴or statutory parental bereavement pay],
he shall be liable to a penalty not exceeding £300.

(2) Where a person fraudulently or negligently—
(a) makes any incorrect statement or declaration in connection with establishing entitlement to statutory adoption pay [¹ or [² statutory shared parental pay]], or
(b) provides any incorrect information or document of a kind mentioned in regulations under section 10(1) so far as relating to statutory adoption pay [¹ or [² statutory shared parental pay]],
he shall be liable to a penalty not exceeding £3,000.

(3) Where an employer fraudulently or negligently makes incorrect payments of [¹ [³ ...] statutory paternity pay] [⁴or statutory parental bereavement pay], he shall be liable to a penalty not exceeding £300.

(4) Where an employer fraudulently or negligently makes incorrect payments of statutory adoption pay [² statutory shared parental pay], he shall be liable to a penalty not exceeding £3,000.

(5) Where an employer fraudulently or negligently—
(a) produces any incorrect document or record, provides any incorrect information or makes any incorrect return, of a kind mentioned in regulations under section 8; or
(b) receives incorrect payments in pursuance of regulations under section 7;
he shall be liable to a penalty not exceeding £3,000 or, if the offence relates only to [¹ [³ ...] statutory paternity pay] [⁴or statutory parental bereavement pay], £300.

(6) Schedule 1 (penalties: procedure and appeals) has effect in relation to penalties under this section.

AMENDMENTS

1. Work and Families Act 2006 s.11(1) and Sch.1 para.54 (April 6, 2010).
2. Children and Families Act 2014 Sch.7 para.55(3) and (5) (December 1, 2014).
3. Children and Families Act 2014 Sch.7 para.55(2),(4) and (6) (April 5, 2015).
4. Parental Bereavement (Leave and Pay) Act 2018, s.2(2), Sch. para.40 (January 18, 2020).

(2002 c.22 s.12)

DEFINITIONS

"the Board"—see s.16.
"employer"—see s.16.

GENERAL NOTE

This provision, imposing penalties on employers who act fraudulently in connection with the SPP and SAP schemes, is modelled on the equivalent provision for tax credits: TCA 2002 s.31.

1.479

Supply of information held by the Board

13.—(1) This section applies to information which is held for the purposes of functions relating to [⁴, statutory paternity pay,] statutory adoption pay [⁵, statutory shared parental pay or statutory parental bereavement pay]—

(a) by the Board, or
(b) by a person providing services to the Board, in connection with the provision of those services.

(2) Information to which this section applies may be supplied—

(a) to the Secretary of State [¹ [² . . .]] or the Department; or
(b) to a person providing services to the Secretary of State or the Department;

for use for the purposes of functions relating to social security, child support or war pensions [¹ [³ . . .]].

1.480

AMENDMENTS

1. Child Support (Consequential Provisions) (No.2) Regulations 2008 (SI 2008/2656) reg.2 (November 1, 2008).
2. Public Bodies (Child Maintenance and Enforcement Commission: Abolition and Transfer of Functions) Order 2012 (SI 2012/2007) Sch.1 para.66 (August 1, 2012).
3. Children and Families Act 2014 Sch.7 para.56(b) (December 1, 2014).
4. Children and Families Act 2014 Sch.7 para.56(a) (April 5, 2015).
5. Parental Bereavement (Leave and Pay) Act 2018, s.2(2), Sch. para.41 (January 18, 2020).

DEFINITIONS

"the Board"—see s.16.
"the Department"—see s.16.

Supply of information held by the Secretary of State

14.—(1) This section applies to information which is held for the purposes of functions relating to [¹ statutory paternity pay,] statutory adoption pay [², statutory shared parental pay or statutory parental bereavement pay]—

(a) by the Secretary of State or the Department, or
(b) by a person providing services to the Secretary of State or the Department, in connection with the provision of those services.

(2) Information to which this section applies may be supplied—

(a) to the Board, or
(b) to a person providing services to the Board,

for use for the purposes of functions relating to [¹ statutory paternity pay,] statutory adoption pay [¹ or statutory shared parental pay].

1.481

Employment Act 2002

AMENDMENTS

1. Children and Families Act 2014 Sch.7 paras 57(2)(a) and 57(3)(a) (April 5, 2015).
2. Parental Bereavement (Leave and Pay) Act 2018, s.2(2), Sch. para.42 (January 18, 2020).

DEFINITIONS

"the Board"—see s.16.
"the Department"—see s.16.

Use of information by the Board

1.482 **15.**—(1) Information which is held—
(a) by the Board, or
(b) by a person providing services to the Board, in connection with the provision of those services,
for the purposes of any functions specified in any paragraph of subsection (2) below may be used for the purposes of, or for any purposes connected with, the exercise of any functions specified in any other paragraph of that subsection, and may be supplied to any person providing services to the Board for those purposes.
(2) The functions referred to in subsection (1) above are—
(a) the functions of the Board in relation to [^{1} [^{3} . . .]] statutory paternity pay;
[^{1}(aa) [^{3} . . .]
(b) their functions in relation to statutory adoption pay, [^{2} . . .]
[^{2} (ba) their functions in relation to statutory shared parental pay; [^{5} . . .]]
[^{5} (bb) their functions in relation to statutory parental bereavement pay; and]
(c) their functions in relation to tax, contributions, statutory sick pay, statutory maternity pay or tax credits, or functions under Part III of the Pension Schemes Act 1993 (c.48) [^{4} (schemes that were contracted-out etc)] or Part III of the Pension Schemes (Northern Ireland) Act 1993 (c.49) (corresponding provisions for Northern Ireland).
(3) In subsection (2)(c) above, "contributions" means contributions under Part I of the Social Security Contributions and Benefits Act 1992 (c.4) or Part I of the Social Security Contributions and Benefits (Northern Ireland) Act 1992 (c.7).

AMENDMENTS

1. Work and Families Act 2006 s.11(1) and Sch.1 para.57 (April 6, 2010).
2. Children and Families Act 2014 Sch.7 para.58(c) and (d) (December 1, 2014).
3. Children and Families Act 2014 Sch.7 para.58(a) and (b) (April 5, 2015).
4. Pensions Act 2014 Sch.13 para.72 (April 6, 2016).
5. Parental Bereavement (Leave and Pay) Act 2018, s.2(2), Sch. para.43 (January 18, 2020).

DEFINITION

"the Board"—see s.16.

Interpretation

1.483 **16.**—In sections 5 to 15—
"the Board" means the Commissioners of Inland Revenue;

(2002 c.22 s.16)

"the Department" means the Department for Social Development or the Department for Employment and Learning;
"employer" and "employee" have the same meanings as in Parts 12ZA and 12ZB of the Social Security Contributions and Benefits Act 1992.

CHAPTER 2

MATERNITY

17.–21—[*Omitted.*]

GENERAL NOTE

Section 17 amends the provisions governing the right to maternity leave under the Employment Rights Act 1996. Sections 18–20 amend ss.164 and 165 of the SSCBA 1992, and substitutes a new s.166 of that Act, while s.21 substitutes a new s.167 of the same Act. These amendments are incorporated elsewhere in this volume.

SCHEDULE 1

PENALTIES: PROCEDURE AND APPEALS

Determination of penalties by officer of Board

1.—(1) Subject to sub-paragraph (2) and except where proceedings have been instituted under paragraph 5, an officer of the Board authorised by the Board for the purposes of this paragraph may make a determination—
  (a) imposing a penalty under section 11 or 12, and
  (b) setting it at such amount as, in his opinion, is correct or appropriate.
(2) Sub-paragraph (1) does not apply to the imposition of such a penalty as is mentioned in section 11(2)(a).
(3) Notice of a determination of a penalty under this paragraph shall be served on the person liable to the penalty and shall state the date on which it is issued and the time within which an appeal against the determination may be made.
(4) After the notice of a determination under this paragraph has been served the determination shall not be altered except in accordance with this paragraph or on appeal.
(5) If it is discovered by an officer of the Board authorised by the Board for the purposes of this paragraph that the amount of a penalty determined under this paragraph is or has become insufficient, the officer may make a determination in a further amount so that the penalty is set at the amount which, in his opinion, is correct or appropriate.

Provisions supplementary to paragraph 1

2.—(1) A penalty determined under paragraph 1 above shall be due and payable at the end of the period of thirty days beginning with the date of the issue of the notice of determination.
(2) Part 6 of the Taxes Management Act 1970 (c.9) shall apply in relation to a penalty determined under para.1 as if it were tax charged in an assessment and due and payable.

Appeals against penalty determinations

3.—(1) An appeal may be brought against the determination of a penalty under paragraph 1.
(2) The provisions of the Taxes Management Act 1970 relating to appeals, except section 50(6) to (8), shall have effect in relation to an appeal against such a determination as they have effect in relation to an appeal against an assessment to tax [¹ except that references to the tribunal shall be taken to be references to the First-tier Tribunal].
(3) On an appeal by virtue of sub-paragraph (2) against the determination of a penalty under paragraph 1, the [¹ First-tier Tribunal] may—
  (a) if it appears [¹ . . .] that no penalty has been incurred, set the determination aside,
  (b) if the amount determined appears [¹. . .] to be appropriate, confirm the determination,

Employment Act 2002

(c) if the amount determined appears [¹ ...] to be excessive, reduce it to such other amount (including nil) as [¹ the tribunal considers] appropriate,

(d) if the amount determined appears [¹ ...] to be insufficient, increase it to such amount not exceeding the permitted maximum as [¹ the tribunal considers] appropriate.

[¹(4) In addition to any right of appeal on a point of law under section 11(2) of the Tribunals, Courts and Enforcement Act 2007, the person liable to the penalty may appeal to the Upper Tribunal against the amount of the penalty which had been determined under sub-paragraph (3), but not against any decision which falls under section 11(5)(d) or (e) of that Act and was made in connection with the determination of the amount of the penalty.

(4A) Section 11(3) and (4) of the Tribunals, Courts and Enforcement Act 2007 applies to the right of appeal under sub-paragraph (4) as it applies to the right of appeal under section 11(2) of that Act.

(4B) On an appeal under this paragraph the Upper Tribunal has the like jurisdiction as is conferred on the First-tier Tribunal by virtue of this paragraph.]

Penalty proceedings before [¹ First-tier Tribunal]

1.489   **4.**—(1) An officer of the Board authorised by the Board for the purposes of this paragraph may commence proceedings for any penalty to which sub-paragraph (1) of paragraph 1 does not apply by virtue of sub-paragraph (2) of that paragraph.

[¹ (2) The person liable to the penalty shall be a party to the proceedings.]

(3) Part 6 of the Taxes Management Act 1970 (c.9) shall apply in relation to a penalty determined in proceedings under this paragraph as if it were tax charged in an assessment and due and payable.

[¹ (4) In addition to any right of appeal on a point of law under section 11(2) of the Tribunals, Courts and Enforcement Act 2007, the person liable to the penalty may appeal to the Upper Tribunal against the determination of a penalty in proceedings under sub-paragraph (1), but not against any decision which falls under section 11(5)(d) or (e) of that Act and was made in connection with the determination of the amount of the penalty.

(4A) Section 11(3) and (4) of the Tribunals, Courts and Enforcement Act 2007 applies to the right of appeal under sub-paragraph (4) as it applies to the right of appeal under section 11(2) of that Act.]

(5) On any such appeal the [¹Upper Tribunal] may—

(a) if it appears that no penalty has been incurred, set the determination aside;

(b) if the amount determined appears to be appropriate, confirm the determination;

(c) if the amount determined appears to be excessive, reduce it to such other amount (including nil) as the [¹Upper Tribunal] considers appropriate;

(d) if the amount determined appears to be insufficient, increase it to such amount not exceeding the permitted maximum as the [¹Upper Tribunal] considers appropriate.

Penalty proceedings before court

1.490   **5.**—(1) Where in the opinion of the Board the liability of any person for a penalty under section 11 or 12 arises by reason of the fraud of that or any other person, proceedings for the penalty may be instituted before the High Court or, in Scotland, the Court of Session as the Court of Exchequer in Scotland.

(2) Subject to sub-paragraph (3), proceedings under this paragraph shall be instituted—

(a) in England and Wales, in the name of the Attorney General; and

(b) in Scotland, in the name of the Advocate General for Scotland.

(3) Sub-paragraph (2) shall not prevent proceedings under this paragraph being instituted in England and Wales under the Crown Proceedings Act 1947 (c.44) by and in the name of the Board as an authorised department for the purposes of that Act.

(4) Any proceedings under this paragraph instituted in England and Wales shall be deemed to be civil proceedings by the Crown within the meaning of Part II of the Crown Proceedings Act 1947.

(5) If in proceedings under this paragraph the court does not find that fraud is proved but considers that the person concerned is nevertheless liable to a penalty, the court may determine a penalty notwithstanding that, but for the opinion of the Board as to fraud, the penalty would not have been a matter for the court.

Mitigation of penalties

1.491   **6.**—The Board may in their discretion mitigate any penalty under section 11 or 12, or stay or compound any proceedings for a penalty, and may also, after judgment, further mitigate or entirely remit the penalty.

(2002 c.22 Sch.1)

Time-limits for penalties

7.—A penalty under section 11 or 12 may be determined by an officer of the Board, or proceedings for the penalty may be commenced before the [¹Tribunal] or the court, at any time within six years after the date on which the penalty was incurred or began to be incurred.

1.492

Interest on penalties

8.—(1) After paragraph (p) of section 178(2) of the Finance Act 1989 (c.26) (setting rates of interest) there shall be inserted—

"(q) paragraph 8 of Schedule 1 to the Employment Act 2002."

(2) A penalty under section 11 or 12 shall carry interest at the rate applicable under section 178 of the Finance Act 1989 from the date on which it becomes due and payable until payment.

1.493

Interpretation

9.—In this Schedule—
"the Board" means the Commissioners of Inland Revenue;
[¹...]

1.494

AMENDMENT

1. Transfer of Tribunal Functions and Revenue and Customs Order 2009 (SI 2009/56) Sch.1 paras 322–325 (April 1, 2009).

Income Tax (Earnings and Pensions) Act 2003

(2003 c.1)

ARRANGEMENT OF SELECTED SECTIONS

PART 1

OVERVIEW

1.	Overview of contents of this Act	**1.495**
2.	Abbreviations and general index in Schedule 1	

PART 2

EMPLOYMENT INCOME: CHARGE TO TAX

CHAPTER 1

INTRODUCTION

3. Structure of employment income Parts
4. "Employment" for the purposes of the employment income Parts
5. Application to offices and officeholders

Income Tax (Earnings and Pensions) Act 2003

Chapter 2

Tax on Employment Income

6. Nature of charge to tax on employment income
7. Meaning of "employment income", "general earnings" and "specific employment income"
8. Meaning of "exempt income"

Chapter 3

Operation of Tax Charge

9. Amount of employment income charged to tax
10. Meaning of "taxable earnings" and "taxable specific income"
11. Calculation of "net taxable earnings"
12. Calculation of "net taxable specific income"
13. Person liable for tax

Chapter 7

Application of Provisions to Agency Workers

Agency workers

44. Treatment of workers supplied by agencies

Part 3

Employment Income: Earnings and Benefits, etc. Treated as Earnings

Chapter 1

Earnings

62. Earnings

Chapter 2

Taxable Benefits: The Benefits Code

The benefits code

63. The benefits code
64. Relationship between earnings and benefits code

(2003 c.1)

General definitions for benefits code

66. Meaning of "employment" and related expressions

CHAPTER 3

TAXABLE BENEFITS: EXPENSES PAYMENTS

70. Sums in respect of expenses
71. Meaning of paid or put at disposal by reason of the employment
72. Sums in respect of expenses treated as earnings

CHAPTER 4

TAXABLE BENEFITS: VOUCHERS AND CREDIT-TOKENS

Cash vouchers: introduction

73. Cash vouchers to which this chapter applies
74. Provision for, or receipt by, member of employee's family

Meaning of "cash voucher"

75. Meaning of "cash voucher"
76. Sickness benefits-related voucher

Benefit of cash voucher treated as earnings

81. Benefit of cash voucher treated as earnings

Non-cash vouchers: introduction

82. Non-cash vouchers to which this chapter applies

Meaning of "non-cash voucher"

84. Meaning of "non-cash voucher"

Benefit of non-cash voucher treated as earnings

87. Benefit of non-cash voucher treated as earnings

Credit-tokens: introduction

90. Credit-tokens to which this chapter applies

Meaning of "credit-token"

92. Meaning of "credit-token"

Income Tax (Earnings and Pensions) Act 2003

Benefit of credit-token treated as earnings

94. Benefit of credit-token treated as earnings

General supplementary provisions

95. Disregard for money, goods or services obtained

CHAPTER 10

TAXABLE BENEFITS: RESIDUAL LIABILITY TO CHARGE

Introduction

201. Employment-related benefits
202. Excluded benefits

Cash equivalent of benefit treated as earnings

203. Cash equivalent of benefit treated as earnings

Determination of the cost of the benefit

204. Cost of the benefit: basic rule
210. Exemption of minor benefits

PART 4

EMPLOYMENT INCOME: EXEMPTIONS

CHAPTER 11

MISCELLANEOUS EXEMPTIONS

318. Childcare: exemption for employer-provided care
318A. Childcare: exemption for other care
318AZA. Meaning of "eligible employee"
318AA. Meaning of "relevant earnings amount" and "required time"
318B. Childcare: meaning of "care", "child" and "parental responsibility"
318C. Childcare: meaning of "qualifying child care"

(2003 c.1)

PART 5

EMPLOYMENT INCOME: DEDUCTIONS ALLOWED FROM EARNINGS

CHAPTER 1

DEDUCTIONS ALLOWED FROM EARNINGS: GENERAL RULES

Introduction

327. Deductions from earnings: general

General rules

328. The income from which deductions may be made
329. Deductions from earnings not to exceed earnings
330. Prevention of double deductions
331. Order for making deductions
332. Meaning of "the deductibility provisions"

CHAPTER 2

DEDUCTIONS FOR EMPLOYEE'S EXPENSES

Introduction

333. Scope of this chapter: expenses paid by the employee
334. Effect of reimbursement, etc.

General rule for deduction of employee's expenses

336. Deductions for expenses: the general rule

Travel expenses

337. Travel in performance of duties
338. Travel for necessary attendance
339. Meaning of "workplace" and "permanent workplace"

Income Tax (Earnings and Pensions) Act 2003

PART 9

PENSION INCOME

CHAPTER 1

INTRODUCTION

565. Structure of Part 9

CHAPTER 2

TAX ON PENSION INCOME

566. Nature of charge to tax on pension income and relevant definitions
567. Amount charged to tax
568. Person liable for tax

CHAPTER 3

UNITED KINGDOM PENSIONS: GENERAL RULES

569. United Kingdom pensions
570. "Pension": interpretation
571. Taxable pension income
572. Person liable for tax

CHAPTER 5

UNITED KINGDOM SOCIAL SECURITY PENSIONS

577. United Kingdom social security pensions
578. Taxable pension income
579. Person liable for tax

(2003 c.1)

PART 10

SOCIAL SECURITY INCOME

CHAPTER 1

INTRODUCTION

655. Structure of Part 10

CHAPTER 2

TAX ON SOCIAL SECURITY INCOME

656. Nature of charge to tax on social security income
657. Meaning of "social security income", "taxable benefits", etc.
658. Amount charged to tax
659. Person liable for tax

CHAPTER 3

TAXABLE UK SOCIAL SECURITY BENEFITS

660. Taxable benefits: UK benefits—Table A
661. Taxable social security income
662. Person liable for tax

CHAPTER 4

TAXABLE UK SOCIAL SECURITY BENEFITS: EXEMPTIONS

Incapacity benefit

663. Long-term incapacity benefit: previous entitlement to invalidity benefit
664. Short-term incapacity benefit not payable at the higher rate

Income support

665. Exempt unless payable to member of couple involved in trade dispute
666. Child maintenance bonus
667. Amounts in excess of taxable maximum
668. Taxable maximum
669. Interpretation

Jobseeker's allowance

670. Child maintenance bonus
671. Amounts in excess of taxable maximum
672. Taxable maximum: general
673. Taxable maximum: income-based jobseeker's allowance
674. Taxable maximum: contribution-based jobseeker's allowance
675. Interpretation

Increases in respect of children

676. Increases in respect of children

CHAPTER 5

UK SOCIAL SECURITY BENEFITS WHOLLY EXEMPT FROM INCOME TAX

677. UK social security benefits wholly exempt from tax: Table B

CHAPTER 6

TAXABLE FOREIGN BENEFITS

678. Taxable benefits: foreign benefits
679. Taxable social security income
680. Person liable for tax

PART 13

SUPPLEMENTARY PROVISIONS

Interpretation

720. [*repealed*]
721. Other definitions

INTRODUCTION AND GENERAL NOTE

1.496 This Act (destined to be known as ITEPA or ITEPA 2003) is the second of the major income tax Acts produced by the Tax Law Rewrite Project. (The first was the Capital Allowances Act 2001.) It took effect from and including the start of the 2003/04 income tax year, April 6, 2003, the same day that the TCA 2002 came fully into effect. It is of considerable importance to tax credits because it entirely rewrites the income tax rules dealing with earnings from employments and offices, pension income, and social security income. The time-hallowed "Schedule E" and its charge to tax on "offices and employments on emoluments therefrom" has at last been relegated to history and a codified set of provisions taxing employment income, pension income and social security income put in its place. The approach of TCA 2002 is to rely on income tax rules for the calculation of income for tax credits purposes. The provisions of ITEPA are therefore the rules that will apply to the great majority of claimants for tax credits.

ITEPA is of considerable length and detail, running to 725 sections and eight Schedules on enactment. It has been drafted in the form of a code, and therefore

(2003 c.1)

includes signposting provisions and a far stronger internal structure than the previous legislation.

ITEPA also uses, where possible, plain English. Its language is therefore updated from the "old" language of "Sch.E" and "emoluments".

The Tax Credits (Definition and Calculation of Income) Regulations 2002, as amended to take into account ITEPA, refer to a considerable number of provisions of ITEPA. This selection of sections from ITEPA includes the more important of those sections, together with the sections that set out the internal signposting of ITEPA and its definitions. It is not a complete reproduction of all ITEPA sections, as some of the anti-avoidance provisions that are applied to tax credits are highly technical and, in practice, sometimes quite controversial in application, while others will, it is anticipated, rarely be directly relevant to tax credits claims. In particular, the following parts are entirely omitted:

Part 4: Employment income: Exemptions
Part 6: Employment Income: Income which is not earnings or share-related
Part 7: Employment income: Share-related income and exemptions
Part 8: Former employees: Deductions for liabilities
Part 9: Pay As You Earn
Schs 2–8

Part 2, Chapter 8 of ITEPA (ss.48–61) deal with the so-called IR35 provisions, namely the provisions under which income of a "pocket book" company could be treated as the employment income of the individual who owned the company so that income was not diverted so as to be excluded from income tax. It was understood that these sections would apply to tax credits and they were therefore included in the 2003/04 edition of this volume. However, amendments to the Working Tax Credit (Entitlement and Maximum Rate) Regulations 2002 were made by the Tax Credits (Miscellaneous Amendments No.2) Regulations 2003 (SI 2003/2815) to clarify the intended policy that these provisions do not apply to tax credits. They are therefore no longer of relevance to this volume.

Part 7 of ITEPA was repealed completely and replaced by new provisions by the Finance Act 2003 s.140 and Sch.22 with effect from April 15, 2003. The original Pt 7 was outside the scope of tax credits income calculations. The new Pt 7 is not, by reason of amendment of the Tax Credits (Definition and Calculation of Income) Regulations 2002 (SI 2002/2006) reg.4. See the note to that regulation. The text of the new Pt 7 is not reproduced in this volume.

However, particular attention has been paid to sections making special provision for those who are sick or disabled, and to the taxation of state pensions and social security benefits.

ITEPA and the Commissioners for Revenue and Customs Act 2005

The merger of the Inland Revenue and HM Customs and Excise, and the creation of the new joint HMRC (the new Commissioners and its officers under the new title "officer of Revenue and Customs"), requires textual amendment to most sections in ITEPA. The approach taken by the Rewrite team was to replace previous references—in many forms to "the Commissioners", "the Board", or "an inspector" or "an officer" with either "the Board" (if the function was unlikely to be delegated) or "an officer of the Board" in all other cases. CRCA 2005 adopts a different approach not entirely consistent with this. This is of limited importance in ITEPA. But, for example, the reference to the Board of Inland Revenue in s.343 should now be read as a reference to "the Commissioners", but probably "the Inland Revenue" in s.344 should now be "an officer of Revenue and Customs"—although that is not clear. This lack of clarity is emphasised by the repeal of the definition of those terms as part of the repeal of the definitions in s.720 (which formerly defined "the Inland Revenue" as meaning any officer of the Board. The old text—save for s.720—has not been amended by CRCA 2005 expressly and has been left in this edition.

1.497

1.498

Income Tax (Earnings and Pensions) Act 2003

Part 1

Overview

Overview of contents of this Act

1.499   **1.**—(1) This Act imposes charges to income tax on—
(a) employment income (see Parts 2 to 7A),
(b) pension income (see Part 9), and
(c) social security income (see chapters 1 to 7 of Part 10)
(2) *Repealed*
(3) This Act also—
(a) confers certain reliefs in respect of liabilities of former employees (see Part 8);
(aa) makes provision for the high income child benefit charge (see chapter 8 of Part 10);
(b) provides for the assessment, collection and recovery of income tax in respect of employment, pension or social security income that is PAYE income (see Part 2);
(ba) allows deductions to be made from such income in respect of certain debts payable to the Commissioners for Her Majesty's Revenue and Customs (see Part 11), and
(c) allows deductions to be made from such income in respect of payroll giving (see Part 12).

Abbreviations and general index in Schedule [1]

1.500   **2.**—(1) Schedule 1 (abbreviations and defined expressions) applies for the purposes of this Act.
(2) In Schedule 1—
(a) Part 1 gives the meaning of the abbreviated references to Acts and instruments used in this Act; and
(b) Part 2 lists the places where expressions used in this Act are defined or otherwise explained.
(3) *Omitted.*

Part 2

Employment Income: Charge to Tax

Chapter 1

Introduction

Structure of employment income Parts

1.501   **3.**—(1) The structure of the employment income Parts is as follows—
This Part imposes the charge to tax on employment income, and sets out—
(a) how the amount charged to tax for a tax year is to be calculated;

and

(b) who is liable for the tax charged;

Part 3 sets out what are earnings and provides for amounts to be treated as earnings;

Part 4 deals with exemptions from the charge to tax under this Part (and, in some cases, from other charges to tax);

Part 5 deals with deductions from taxable earnings;

Part 6 deals with employment income other than earnings or share-related income;

Part 7 deals with share-related income and exemptions; and

Part 7A deals with employment income provided through third parties.

(2) In this Act "the employment income Parts" means this Part and Parts 3 to 7A.

GENERAL NOTE

Part 4 (Employment income: Exemptions)—ss.227–326—is entirely omitted from this work. It comprises a codified list of all exemptions from the charge to income tax otherwise imposed by ITEPA on various earnings and benefits, under the following chapter heads: mileage allowances and passenger payments; transport travel and subsistence; education and training; recreational benefits; non-cash vouchers and credit-tokens; removal benefits and expenses; special kinds of employee; pension provision; termination of employment; and miscellaneous. The general rule of income tax law is that it is for a claimant to claim for, and show that he or she is entitled to, the benefit of an exemption.

Part 6 is also entirely omitted. It comprises ss.386–416, and deals with payments to, and benefits from, non-approved pension schemes, and payments on termination of employment.

Part 7 is also entirely omitted. It is a lengthy part—ss.417–564 and Schs 2–5. They deal with the detail of the various kinds of tax charge on, and exemption of, share-related income including all forms of benefits obtained by shares or interests in shares.

1.502

"Employment" for the purposes of the employment income Parts

4.—(1) In the employment income Parts "employment" includes in particular—

(a) any employment under a contract of service,

(b) any employment under a contract of apprenticeship, and

(c) any employment in the service of the Crown.

(2) In those Parts, "employed", "employee" and "employer" have corresponding meanings.

1.503

GENERAL NOTE

There are no general income tax (or, more generally, tax) rules defining whether an individual is an employee or self-employed, or whether a relationship is an employment relationship. That is a matter to be decided by general law. There is considerable case law on the subject, some of it deriving from income tax and some from social security cases. Under the Social Security Contributions (Transfer of Functions) Act 1999 s.8, decisions about the same question for the purposes of the Social Security Contributions and Benefits Act 1992 were transferred to the Inland Revenue and, on appeal, to the tax appeal tribunals. There is, however, no equivalent provision in the TCA 2002. It would seem, therefore, that appeals about Revenue decisions about employment for tax credit purposes go to appeal tribunals, not tax appeal tribunals.

1.504

Application to offices and office-holders

1.505 **5.**—(1) The provisions of the employment income Parts that are expressed to apply to employments apply equally to offices, unless otherwise indicated.

(2) In those provisions as they apply to an office—
(a) references to being employed are to being the holder of the office;
(b) "employee" means the office-holder;
(c) "employer" means the person under whom the office-holder holds office.

(3) In the employment income Parts "office" includes in particular any position which has an existence independent of the person who holds it and may be filled by successive holders.

CHAPTER 2

TAX ON EMPLOYMENT INCOME

Nature of charge to tax on employment income

1.506 **6.**—(1) The charge to tax on employment income under this Part is a charge to tax on—
(a) general earnings; and
(b) specific employment income.

The meaning of "employment income", "general earnings" and "specific employment income" is given in section 7.

(2) The amount of general earnings or specific employment income which is charged to tax in a particular tax year is set out in section 9.

(3) The rules in Chapters 4 and 5 of this Part, which are concerned with—
(a) the residence and domicile of an employee in a tax year;
(aa) whether section 809B, 809D or 809E of ITA 2007 (remittance basis) applies to an employee for a tax year, and
(b) the tax year in which amounts are received or remitted to the United Kingdom; apply for the purposes of the charge to tax on general earnings but not that on specific employment income.

(3A) The rules in Chapter 5B, which are concerned with the matters mentioned in subsection (3)(a) to (b), apply for the purposes of the charge to tax on certain specific employment income arising under Part 7 (securities etc).

(4) The person who is liable for any tax charged on employment income is set out in section 13.

(5) Employment income is not charged to tax under this Part if it is within the charge to tax under Part 2 of ITTOIA by virtue of section 15 of that Act (divers and diving supervisors).

Meaning of "employment income", "general earnings" and "specific employment income"

1.507 **7.**—(1) This section gives the meaning for the purposes of the Tax Acts of "employment income", "general earnings" and "specific employment income".

(2) "Employment income" means—
(a) earnings within Chapter 1 of Part 3;
(b) any amount treated as earnings (see subsection (5)); or
(c) any amount which counts as employment income (see subsection (6)).

(3) "General earnings" means—
(a) earnings within Chapter 1 of Part 3; or
(b) any amount treated as earnings (see subsection (5));
excluding in each case any exempt income.

(4) "Specific employment income" means any amount which counts as employment income (see subsection (6)), excluding any exempt income.

(5) Subsection (2)(b) or (3)(b) refers to any amount treated as earnings under—
(a) Chapters 7 to 10 of this Part (agency workers, workers under arrangements made by intermediaries, and workers providing services through managed service companies),
(b) Chapters 2 to 10 of Part 3 (the benefits code),
(c) Chapters 12 of Part 3 (payments treated as earnings), or
(d) section 262 of CAA 2001 (balancing charges to be given effect by treating them as earnings).

(6) Subsection (2)(c) or (4) refers to any amount which counts as employment income by virtue of—
(a) Part 6 (income which is not earnings or share-related),
(b) Part 7 (income and exemptions relating to securities and securities options),
(ba) Part 7A (employment income provided through third parties), or
(c) any other enactment.

Meaning of "exempt income"

8.—For the purposes of the employment income Parts, an amount of employment income within paragraph (a), (b) or (c) of section 7(2) is "exempt income" if, as a result of any exemption in Part 4 or elsewhere, no liability to income tax arises in respect of it as such an amount.

1.508

CHAPTER 3

OPERATION OF TAX CHARGE

Amount of employment income charged to tax

9.—(1) The amount of employment income which is charged to tax under this Part for a particular tax year is as follows.

(2) In the case of general earnings, the amount charged is the net taxable earnings from an employment in the year.

(3) That amount is calculated under section 11 by reference to any taxable earnings from the employment in the year (see section 10(2)).

1.509

(4) In the case of specific employment income, the amount charged is the net taxable specific income from an employment for the year.

(5) That amount is calculated under section 12 by reference to any taxable specific income from the employment for the year (see section 10(3)).

(6) Accordingly, no amount of employment income is charged to tax under this Part for a particular tax year unless—
- (a) in the case of general earnings, they are taxable earnings from an employment in that year; or
- (b) in the case of specific employment income, it is taxable specific income from an employment for that year.

Meaning of "taxable earnings" and "taxable specific income"

1.510   **10.**—(1) This section explains what is meant by "taxable earnings" and "taxable specific income" in the employment income Parts.

(2) "Taxable earnings" from an employment in a tax year are to be determined in accordance with Chapters 4 and 5 of this Part.

(3) "Taxable specific income" from an employment for a tax year means the full amount of any specific employment income which, by virtue of Part 6, 7 or 7A or any other enactment, counts as employment income for that year in respect of the employment.

(4) Subsection (3) is subject to Chapter 5B (taxable specific income from employment-related securities etc: internationally mobile employees).

(5) Subsection (3) is also subject to sections 554Z9 to 554Z11 (employment income under Part 7A: remittance basis).

Calculation of "net taxable earnings"

1.511   **11.**—(1) For the purposes of this Part, the "net taxable earnings" from an employment in a tax year are given by the formula—

$$TE - DE,$$

where—
TE means the total amount of any taxable earnings from the employment in the tax year; and
DE means the total amount of any deductions allowed from those earnings under provisions listed in sections 327(3) to (5) (deductions from earnings: general).

(2) If the amount calculated under subsection (1) is negative, the net taxable earnings from the employment in the year are to be taken to be nil instead.

(3) Relief may be available under section 128 of ITA 2007 (set-off against general income)—
- (a) where TE is negative; or
- (b) in certain exceptional cases where the amount calculated under subsection (1) is negative.

(4) If a person has more than one employment in a tax year, the calculation under subsection (1) must be carried out in relation to each of the employments.

Calculation of "net taxable specific income"

12.—(1) For the purposes of this Part the "net taxable specific income" from an employment for a tax year is given by the formula—

$$TSI - DSI,$$

where—

TSI means the amount of any taxable specific income from the employment for the tax year; and

DSI means the total amount of any deductions allowed from that income under provisions of the Tax Acts not included in the lists in section 327(3) and (4) (deductions from earnings: general).

(2) If the amount calculated under subsection (1) is negative, the net taxable specific income from the employment for the year is to be taken to be nil instead.

(3) If a person has more than one kind of specific employment income from an employment for a tax year, the calculation under subsection (1) must be carried out in relation to each of those kinds of specific employment income; and in such a case the "net taxable specific income" from the employment for that year is the total of all the amounts so calculated.

Person liable for tax

13.—(1) The person liable for any tax on employment income under this Part is the taxable person mentioned in subsection (2) or (3). This is subject to subsection (4).

(2) If the tax is on general earnings, "the taxable person" is the person to whose employment the earnings relate.

(3) If the tax is on specific employment income, "the taxable person" is the person in relation to whom the income is, by virtue of Part 6, 7 or 7A or any other enactment, to count as employment income.

(4) If the tax is on general earnings received, or remitted to the United Kingdom, after the death of the person to whose employment the earnings relate, the person's personal representatives are liable for the tax.

(4B) Subject to section 554Z12, if—
(a) the tax is on specific employment income under Chapter 2 of Part 7A, and
(b) the relevant step is taken, or (if relevant) the income is remitted to the United Kingdom, after the death of A, A's personal representatives are liable for the tax.

(4C) Terms used in subsection (4B) have the same meaning as in Part 7A.

(5) If subsection (4), (4A) or (4B) or section 554Z12(3) applies, the tax is accordingly to be assessed on the personal representatives and is a debt due from and payable out of the estate.

Income Tax (Earnings and Pensions) Act 2003

CHAPTER 7

APPLICATION OF PROVISIONS TO AGENCY WORKERS

Agency workers

Treatment of workers supplied by agencies

44.—(1) This section applies if—
(a) an individual ("the worker") personally provides services (which are not excluded services) to another person ("the client"),
(b) there is a contract between—
   (i) the client or a person connected with the client, and
   (ii) a person other than the worker, the client or a person connected with the client ("the agency"), and
(c) under or in consequence of that contract—
   (i) the services are provided, or
   (ii) the client or any person connected with the client pays, or otherwise provides consideration, for the services.
(2) But this section does not apply if—
(a) it is shown that the manner in which the worker provides the services is not subject to (or to the right of) supervision, direction or control by any person, or
(b) remuneration receivable by the worker in consequence of providing the services constitutes employment income of the worker apart from this Chapter.
(3) If this section applies—
(a) the worker is to be treated for income tax purposes as holding an employment with the agency, the duties of which consist of the services the worker provides to the client, and
(b) all remuneration receivable by the worker (from any person) in consequence of providing the services is to be treated for income tax purposes as earnings from that employment, but this is subject to subsections (4) to (6).
(4) Subsection (5) applies if (whether before or after the worker begins to provide the services)—
(a) the client provides the agency with a fraudulent document which is intended to constitute evidence that, by virtue of subsection (2)(a), this section does not or will not apply, or
(b) a relevant person provides the agency with a fraudulent document which is intended to constitute evidence that, by virtue of subsection (2)(b), this section does not or will not apply.
(5) In relation to services the worker provides to the client after the fraudulent document is provided—
(a) subsection (3) does not apply,
(b) the worker is to be treated for income tax purposes as holding an employment with the client or (as the case may be) with the relevant person, the duties of which consist of the services, and

(c) all remuneration receivable by the worker (from any person) in consequence of providing the services is to be treated for income tax purposes as earnings from that employment.

(6) In subsections (4) and (5) "relevant person" means a person, other than the client, the worker or a person connected with the client or with the agency, who—
  (a) is resident, or has a place of business, in the United Kingdom, and
  (b) is party to a contract with the agency or a person connected with the agency, under or in consequence of which—
    (i) the services are provided, or
    (ii) the agency, or a person connected with the agency, makes payments in respect of the services.

PART 3

EMPLOYMENT INCOME: EARNINGS AND BENEFITS, ETC. TREATED AS EARNINGS

CHAPTER 1

EARNINGS

Earnings

62.—(1) This section explains what is meant by "earnings" in the employment income Parts.

(2) In those Parts, "earnings", in relation to an employment, means—
(a) any salary, wages or fee;
(b) any gratuity or other profit or incidental benefit of any kind obtained by the employee if it is money or money's worth; or
(c) anything else that constitutes an emolument of the employment.

(3) For the purposes of subsection (2), "money's worth" means something that is—
(a) of direct monetary value to the employee; or
(b) capable of being converted into money or something of direct monetary value to the employee.

(4) Subsection (1) does not affect the operation of statutory provisions that provide for amounts to be treated as earnings (and see section 721(7)).

1.515

Income Tax (Earnings and Pensions) Act 2003

Chapter 2

Taxable Benefits: The Benefits Code

The benefits code

The benefits code

1.516   **63.**—(1) In the employment income Parts "the benefits code" means—this chapter,
Chapter 3 (expenses payments),
Chapter 4 (vouchers and credit-tokens),
Chapter 5 (living accommodation),
Chapter 6 (cars, vans and related benefits),
Chapter 7 (loans), and
Chapter 10 (residual liability to charge).
(2)–(4) [*Repealed*]
(5) The benefits code has effect subject to section 554Z2(2).

Relationship between earnings and benefits code

1.517   **64.**—(1) This section applies if, apart from this section, the same benefit would give rise to two amounts ("A" and "B")—
(a) A being an amount of earnings as defined in Chapter 1 of this Part; and
(b) B being an amount to be treated as earnings under the benefits code.
(2) In such a case—
(a) A constitutes earnings as defined in Chapter 1 of this Part; and
(b) the amount (if any) by which B exceeds A is to be treated as earnings under the benefits code.
(3) This section does not apply in connection with living accommodation to which Chapter 5 of this Part applies.
(4) In that case section 109 applies to determine the relationship between that chapter and Chapter 1 of this Part.

General definitions for benefits code

Meaning of "employment" and related expressions

1.518   **66.**—(1) In the benefits code—
(a) "employment" means a taxable employment under Part 2; and
(b) "employed", "employee" and "employer" have corresponding meanings.
(2) Where a chapter of the benefits code applies in relation to an employee—
(a) references in that chapter to "the employment" are to the employment of that employee; and
(b) references in that chapter to "the employer" are to the employer in respect of that employment.

(3) For the purposes of the benefits code an employment is a "taxable employment under Part 2" in a tax year if the earnings from the employment for that year are (or would be if there were any) general earnings to which the charging provisions of Chapter 4 or 5 of Part 2 apply.

(4) In subsection (3)—
(a) the reference to an employment includes employment as a director of a company; and
(b) "earnings" means earnings as defined in Chapter of this Part.

(5) In the benefits code "lower-paid employment as a minister of religion" has the same meaning as in Part 4 (see section 290D).

CHAPTER 3

TAXABLE BENEFITS: EXPENSES PAYMENTS

Sums in respect of expenses

70.—(1) This chapter applies to a sum paid to an employee in a tax year if the sum—
(a) is paid to the employee in respect of expenses; and
(b) is so paid by reason of the employment.

(2) This chapter applies to a sum paid away by an employee in a tax year if the sum—
(a) was put at the employee's disposal in respect of expenses;
(b) was so put by reason of the employment; and
(c) is paid away by the employee in respect of expenses.

(3) For the purposes of this chapter it does not matter whether the employment is held at the time when the sum is paid or paidaway so long as it is held at some point in the tax year in which the sum is paid or paidaway.

(4) References in this chapter to an employee accordingly include a prospective or former employee.

(5) This chapter does not apply to the extent that the sum constitutes earnings from the employment by virtue of any other provision.

Meaning of paid or put at disposal by reason of the employment

71.—(1) If an employer pays a sum in respect of expenses to an employee it is to be treated as paid by reason of the employment unless—
(a) the employer is an individual, and
(b) the payment is made in the normal course of the employer's domestic, family or personal relationships.

(2) If an employer puts a sum at an employee's disposal in respect of expenses it is to be treated as put at the employee's disposal by reason of the employment unless—
(a) the employer is an individual, and
(b) the sum is put at the employee's disposal in the normal course of the employer's domestic, family or personal relationships.

Sums in respect of expenses treated as earnings

72.—(1) If this chapter applies to a sum, the sum is to be treated as earnings from the employment for the tax year in which it is paid or paidaway.

(2) Subsection (1) does not prevent the making of a deduction allowed under any of the provisions listed in subsection (3).
(3) The provisions are—
  section 336 (deductions for expenses: the general rule);
  section 337 (travel in performance of duties);
  section 338 (travel for necessary attendance);
  section 340 (travel between group employments);
  section 340A (travel between linked employments);
  section 341 (travel at start or finish of overseas employment);
  section 342 (travel between employments where duties performed abroad);
  section 343 (deduction for professional membership fees);
  section 344 (deduction for annual subscriptions);
  section 346 (deduction for employee liabilities);
  section 353 (deductions from earnings charged on remittance).

CHAPTER 4

TAXABLE BENEFITS: VOUCHERS AND CREDIT-TOKENS

Cash vouchers: introduction

Cash vouchers to which this chapter applies

1.522   **73.**—(1) This chapter applies to a cash voucher provided for an employee by reason of the employment which is received by the employee.
(2) A cash voucher provided for an employee by the employer is to be regarded as provided by reason of the employment unless—
  (a) the employer is an individual; and
  (b) the provision is made in the normal course of the employer's domestic, family or personal relationships.
(3) A cash voucher provided for an employee and appropriated to the employee—
  (a) by attaching it to a card held for the employee; or
  (b) in any other way;
is to be treated for the purposes of this chapter as having been received by the employee at the time when it is appropriated.

Provision for, or receipt by, member of employee's family

1.523   **74.**—For the purposes of this chapter any reference to a cash voucher being provided for or received by an employee includes a reference to it being provided for or received by a member of the employee's family.

Meaning of "cash voucher"

Meaning of "cash voucher"

1.524   **75.**—(1) In this chapter "cash voucher" means a voucher, stamp or similar document capable of being exchanged for a sum of money which is—
  (a) greater than;

(b) equal to; or
(c) not substantially less than,

the expense incurred by the person at whose cost the voucher, stamp or similar document is provided.

(2) For the purposes of subsection (1) it does not matter whether the document—
(a) is also capable of being exchanged for goods or services;
(b) is capable of being exchanged singly or together with other vouchers, stamps, or documents;
(c) is capable of being exchanged immediately or only after a time.

(3) Subsection (1) is subject to section 76 (sickness benefits-related voucher).

Sickness benefits-related voucher

76.—(1) This section applies where—
(a) the expense incurred by the person at whose cost a voucher, stamp or similar document is provided ("the provision expense") includes costs to that person of providing sickness benefits ("sickness benefits costs"),
(b) the voucher, stamp or document would be a cash voucher (apart from this section) but for the fact that the sum of money for which it is capable of being exchanged ("the exchange sum") is substantially less than the provision expense, and
(c) the whole or part of the difference between the exchange sum and the provision expense represents the sickness benefits costs.

(2) The voucher, stamp or document is a cash voucher within the meaning of this chapter if—

$$E = \frac{PE}{D}$$

or

$$E \text{ is not substantially less than } \frac{PE}{D},$$

where—
  E is the exchange sum;
  PE is the provision expense; and
  D is the amount of the difference between E and PE which represents the sickness benefits costs.

(3) In this section "sickness benefits" mean benefits in connection with sickness, personal injury or death.

Benefit of cash voucher treated as earnings

Benefit of cash voucher treated as earnings

81.—(1) The cash equivalent of the benefit of a cash voucher to which this chapter applies is to be treated as earnings from the employment for the tax year in which the voucher is received by the employee.

(1A) Where a cash voucher to which this Chapter applies is provided pursuant to optional remuneration arrangements—
(a) subsection (1) does not apply, and

Income Tax (Earnings and Pensions) Act 2003

　　(b) the relevant amount is to be treated as earnings from the employment for the tax year in which the voucher is received by the employee.

(1B) In this section "the relevant amount" means—
　　(a) the cash equivalent, or
　　(b) if greater, the amount foregone with respect to the benefit of the voucher (see section 69B).

(2) The cash equivalent is the sum of money for which the voucher is capable of being exchanged.

(3) For the purposes of subsection (1B), assume that the cash equivalent is zero if the condition in subsection (4) is met.

(4) The condition is that the benefit of the voucher would be exempt from income tax but for section 228A (exclusion of certain exemptions).

Non-cash vouchers: introduction

Non-cash vouchers to which this chapter applies

1.527　　**82.**—(1) This chapter applies to a non-cash voucher provided for an employee by reason of the employment which is received by the employee.

(2) A non-cash voucher provided for an employee by the employer is to be regarded as provided by reason of the employment unless—
　　(a) the employer is an individual; and
　　(b) the provision is made in the normal course of the employer's domestic, family or personal relationships.

(3) A non-cash voucher provided for an employee and appropriated to the employee—
　　(a) by attaching it to a card held for the employee; or
　　(b) in any other way,
is to be treated for the purposes of this chapter as having been received by the employee at the time when it is appropriated.

Meaning of "non-cash voucher"

Meaning of "non-cash voucher"

1.528　　**84.**—(1) In this chapter "non-cash voucher" means—
　　(a) a voucher, stamp or similar document or token which is capable of being exchanged for money, goods or services;
　　(ab) a childcare voucher
　　(b) a transport voucher, or
　　(c) a cheque voucher,
but does not include a cash voucher.

(2) For the purposes of subsection (1)(a) it does not matter whether the document or token is capable of being exchanged—
　　(a) singly or together with other vouchers, stamps, documents or tokens;
　　(b) immediately or only after a time.

(2A) In this chapter "childcare voucher" means a voucher, stamp or similar document or token intended to enable a person to obtain the provision of case for a child (whether or not in exchange for it).

(3) In this chapter "transport voucher" means a ticket, pass or other document or token intended to enable a person to obtain passenger transport services (whether or not in exchange for it).

(4) In this chapter "cheque voucher" means a cheque—
(a) provided for an employee; and
(b) intended for use by the employee wholly or mainly for payment for—
   (i) particular goods or services; or
   (ii) goods or services of one or more particular classes;

and, in relation to a cheque voucher, references to a voucher being exchanged for goods or services are to be read accordingly.

Benefit of non-cash voucher treated as earnings

Benefit of non-cash voucher treated as earnings

87.—(1) The cash equivalent of the benefit of a non-cash voucher to which this chapter applies is to be treated as earnings from the employment for the tax year in which the voucher is received by the employee.

(2) The cash equivalent is the difference between—
(a) the cost of provision; and
(b) any part of that cost made good by the employee, to the person incurring it, on or before 6 July following the relevant tax year.

(2A) If the voucher is a non-cash voucher other than a cheque voucher, the relevant tax year is—
(a) the tax year in which the cost of provision is incurred, or
(b) if later, the tax year in which the employee receives the voucher.

(2B) If the voucher is a cheque voucher, the relevant tax year is the tax year in which the voucher is handed over in exchange for money, goods or services.

(3) In this chapter the "cost of provision" means, in relation to a non-cash voucher, the expense incurred in or in connection with the provision of—
(a) the voucher, and
(b) the money, goods or services for which it is capable of being exchanged,

by the person at whose cost they are provided.

(3A) In the case of a childcare voucher, the reference in subsection (3)(b) to the services for which the voucher is capable of being exchanged is to the provision of care for a child which may be obtained by using it.

(4) In the case of a transport voucher, the reference in subsection (3)(b) to the services for which the voucher is capable of being exchanged is to the passenger transport services which may be obtained by using it.

(5) If a person incurs expense in or in connection with the provision of non-cash vouchers for two or more employees as members of a group or class, the expense incurred in respect of one of them is to be such part of that expense as is just and reasonable.

1.529

Income Tax (Earnings and Pensions) Act 2003

Credit-tokens: introduction

Credit-tokens to which this chapter applies

1.530 **90.**—(1) This chapter applies to a credit-token provided for an employee by reason of the employment which is used by the employee to obtain money, goods or services.

(2) A credit-token provided for an employee by the employer is to be regarded as provided by reason of the employment unless—
  (a) the employer is an individual; and
  (b) the provision is made in the normal course of the employer's domestic, family or personal relationships.

Meaning of "credit-token"

Meaning of "credit-token"

1.531 **92.**—(1) In this chapter "credit-token" means a credit card, debit card or other card, a token, a document or other object given to a person by another person ("X") who undertakes—
  (a) on the production of it, to supply money, goods or services on credit; or
  (b) if a third party ("Y") supplies money, goods or services on its production, to pay Y for what is supplied.

(2) A card, token, document or other object can be a credit-token even if—
  (a) some other action is required in addition to its production in order for the money, goods or services to be supplied;
  (b) X in paying Y may take a discount or commission.

(3) For the purposes of this section—
  (a) the use of an object given by X to operate a machine provided by X is to be treated as its production to X, and
  (b) the use of an object given by X to operate a machine provided by Y is to be treated as its production to Y.

(4) A "credit-token" does not include a cash voucher or a non-cash voucher.

Benefit of credit-token treated as earnings

Benefit of credit-token treated as earnings

1.532 **94.**—(1) On each occasion on which a credit-token to which this chapter applies is used by the employee in a tax year to obtain money, goods or services, the cash equivalent of the benefit of the token is to be treated as earnings from the employment for that year.

(2) The cash equivalent is the difference between—
  (a) the cost of provision; and
  (b) any part of that cost made good by the employee—
    (i) to the person incurring it, and
    (ii) on or before 6 July following the tax year which contains the occasion in question.

(3) In this section the "cost of provision" means the expense incurred—
(a) in or in connection with the provision of the money, goods or services obtained on the occasion in question; and
(b) by the person at whose cost they are provided.

(4) If a person incurs expense in or in connection with the provision of credit-tokens for two or more employees as members of a group or class, the expense incurred in respect of one of them is to be such part of that expense as is just and reasonable.

General supplementary provisions

Disregard for money, goods or services obtained

95.—(1) This section applies if the cash equivalent of the benefit of a cash voucher, a non-cash voucher or a credit-token or the relevant amount in respect of a cash voucher, a non-cash voucher or a credit-token—
(a) is to be treated as earnings from an employee's employment under this chapter;
(b) [*repealed*].

(2) Money, goods or services obtained—
(a) by the employee or another person in exchange for the cash voucher or non-cash voucher; or
(b) by the employee or a member of the employee's family by use of the credit-token,

are to be disregarded for the purposes of the Income Tax Acts.

(3) But the goods or services are not to be disregarded for the purposes of applying sections 362 and 363 (deductions where non-cash voucher or credit-token provided).

(3A) In the case of a childcare voucher, the reference in subsection (2)(a) to the services obtained in exchange for the voucher is to the provision of care for a child which may be obtained by using it.

(4) In the case of a transport voucher, the reference in subsection (2)(a) to the services obtained in exchange for the voucher is to the passenger transport services obtained by using it.

Chapter 10

Taxable Benefits: Residual Liability to Charge

Introduction

Employment-related benefits

201.—(1) This chapter applies to employment-related benefits.
(2) In this chapter—
"benefit" means a benefit or facility of any kind;

"employment-related benefit" means a benefit, other than an excluded benefit, which is provided in a tax year—
  (a) for an employee; or
  (b) for a member of an employee's family or household;
    by reason of the employment.
For the definition of "excluded benefit" see section 202.

(3) A benefit provided by an employer is to be regarded as provided by reason of the employment unless—
  (a) the employer is an individual; and
  (b) the provision is made in the normal course of the employer's domestic, family or personal relationships.

(4) For the purposes of this chapter it does not matter whether the employment is held at the time when the benefit is provided so long as it is held at some point in the tax year in which the benefit is provided.

(5) References in this chapter to an employee accordingly include a prospective or former employee.

Excluded benefits

202.—(1) A benefit is an "excluded benefit" for the purposes of this chapter if—
  (a) any of Chapters 3 to 9 of the benefits code applies to the benefit;
  (b) any of those chapters would apply to the benefit but for an exception; or
  (c) the benefit consists in the right to receive, or the prospect of receiving, sums treated as earnings under section 221 (payments where employee absent because of sickness or disability).

(1A) But a benefit provided to an employee or member of an employee's family or household is to be taken not to be an excluded benefit by virtue of subsection (1)(c) so far as it is provided under optional remuneration arrangements.

(2) In this section, "exception", in relation to the application of a chapter of the benefits code to a benefit, means any enactment in the chapter which provides that the chapter does not apply to the benefit. But for this purpose section 86 (transport vouchers under pre-26th March 1982 arrangements) is not an exception.

Cash equivalent of benefit treated as earnings

Cash equivalent of benefit treated as earnings

203.—(1) The cash equivalent of an employment-related benefit is to be treated as earnings from the employment for the tax year in which it is provided.

(2) The cash equivalent of an employment-related benefit is the cost of the benefit less any part of that cost made good by the employee, to the persons providing the benefit, on or before 6 July following the tax year in which it is provided.

(3) The cost of an employment-related benefit is determined in accordance with section 204 unless—

(a) section 205 provides that the cost is to be determined in accordance with that section; or
(b) section 206 provides that the cost is to be determined in accordance with that section.

Determination of the cost of the benefit

Cost of the benefit: basic rule

204.—The cost of an employment-related benefit is the expense incurred in or in connection with provision of the benefit (including a proper proportion of any expense relating partly to provision of the benefit and partly to other matters).

Exemption of minor benefits

210.—(1) The Treasury may make provision by regulations for exempting from the application of this Chapter such minor benefits as may be specified by regulation.

(2) An exemption conferred by such regulations is conditional on the benefit being made available to the employer's employees generally on similar terms.

GENERAL NOTE

For Regulations made under this section see the Income Tax (Exemption of Minor Benefits) Regulations 2002 (SI 2002/205). The 2002 Regulations are not included in this volume. They remove from taxation minor benefits, such as free meals, provided by employers that would otherwise be liable to taxation.

The 2002 Regulations have been amended by the Income Tax (Exemption of Minor Benefits) (Amendment) Regulations 2003 (SI 2003/1434), the Income Tax (Exemption of Minor Benefits) (Amendment) Regulations 2004 (SI 2004/3087), the Income Tax (Exemption of Minor Benefits) (Amendment) Regulations 2007 (SI 2007/2090), the Income Tax (Exemption of Minor Benefits) (Revocation) Regulations 2009 (SI 2009/695), the Income Tax (Exemption of Minor Benefits) (Amendment) Regulations 2012 (SI 2012/1808), section 3(3) of the Finance (No 2) Act 2017 and the Income Tax (Benefits in Kind) (Exemption for Welfare Counselling) (Amendment) Regulations 2020 (SI 2020/291)). Further exemptions are provided for by the Income Tax (Exemption of Minor Benefits) (Coronavirus) Regulations 2020 (SI 2020/1293), the Income Tax (Exemption for Coronavirus Related Home Office Expenses) Regulations 2020 (SI 2020/524), as amended by SI 2021/225, and the Income Tax (Exemption of Minor Benefits) (Coronavirus) Regulations 2020 (SI 2020/1293).

Income Tax (Earnings and Pensions) Act 2003

Part 4

Employment Income: Exemptions

Chapter 11

Miscellaneous Exemptions

Childcare: exemption for employer-provided care

1.540   **318.**—(1) No liability to income tax arises in respect of the provision for an employee of care for a child if conditions A to D are met. For the meaning of "care" and "child", see section 318B.

(2) If those conditions are met only as respects part of the provision, no such liability arises in respect of that part.

(3) Condition A is that the child—
   (a) is a child or stepchild of the employee and is maintained (wholly or partly) at the employee's expense,
   (b) is resident with the employee, or
   (c) is a person in respect of whom the employee has parental responsibility.
For the meaning of "parental responsibility", see section 318B.

(4) Condition B is that—
   (a) the premises on which the care is provided are not used wholly or mainly as a private dwelling, and
   (b) any applicable registration requirement is met.

(5) The registration requirements are—
   (za) in England, that under . . . Part 3 of the Childcare Act 2006;
   (a) in . . . Wales, that under Part 2 of the Children and Families (Wales) Measure 2010;
   (b) in Scotland, that under Part 5 of the Public Services Reform (Scotland) Act 2010;
   (c) in Northern Ireland, that under Part XI of the Children (Northern Ireland) Order 1995.

(6) Condition C is that—
   (a) the premises on which the care is provided are made available by the scheme employer alone, or
   (b) the partnership requirements are met.
In this section "scheme employer" means the employer operating the scheme under which the care is provided (who need not be the employer of the employee).

(7) The partnership requirements are—
   (a) that the care is provided under arrangements made by persons who include the scheme employer,
   (b) that the premises on which it is provided are made available by one or more of those persons, and
   (c) that under the arrangements the scheme employer is wholly or partly responsible for financing and managing the provision of the care.

(8) Condition D is that the care is provided under a scheme that is open—
   (a) to the scheme employer's employees generally, or
   (b) generally to those of the scheme employer's employees at a particular location,

and that the employee to whom it is provided is either an employee of the scheme employer or is an employee working at the same location as employees of the scheme employer to whom the scheme is open.

General Note

This and the following sections are inserted into ITEPA by Finance Act 2004 s.78 and Sch.13 from April 6, 2005. They are set out here as they are seen by some as alternatives to the provision of childcare in return for payment by an individual using the childcare element of WTC.

Section 318C was amended from April 6, 2007 for England by the Income Tax (Qualifying Child Care) Regulations 2007 (SI 2007/849). The formal introduction to the regulations makes clear that these changes were made in co-ordination with changes to the equivalent regulations for the childcare element of tax credits.

Childcare: limited exemption for other care

318A.—(1) If conditions A to D are met in relation to the provision for an eligible employee of care for a child—
(a) no liability to income tax arises by virtue of section 62 (general definition of earnings), and
(b) liability to income tax by virtue of Chapter 10 of Part 3 (taxable benefits: residual liability to charge) arises only in respect of so much of the amount treated as earnings in respect of the benefit by virtue of section 203(1) or 203A(1) (as the case may be) as exceeds the exempt amount.

For the meaning of "eligible employee", see section 318AZA, and for the meaning of "care" and "child", see section 318B.

(2) If those conditions are met only as respects part of the provision, subsection (1) applies in respect of that part.

(3) Condition A is that the child—
(a) is a child or stepchild of the employee and is maintained (wholly or partly) at the employee's expense, or
(b) is resident with the employee and is a person in respect of whom the employee has parental responsibility.

For the meaning of "parental responsibility", see section 318B.

(4) Condition B is that the care is qualifying child care.

For the meaning of "qualifying child care", see section 318C.

(5) Condition C is that the care is provided under a scheme that is open—
(a) to the employer's eligible employees generally, or
(b) generally to those at a particular location.

(5A) Where the scheme under which the care is provided involves—
(a) relevant salary sacrifice arrangements, or
(b) relevant flexible remuneration arrangements,
Condition C is not prevented from being met by reason only that the scheme is not open to relevant low-paid employees.

(5B) In subsection (5A)—
"relevant salary sacrifice arrangements" means arrangements (whenever made) under which the employees for whom the care is provided give up the right to receive an amount of general earnings or specific employment income in return for the provision of the care;
"relevant flexible remuneration arrangements" means arrangements (whenever made) under which the employees for whom the care is

provided agree with the employer that they are to be provided with the care rather than receive some other description of employment income; "relevant low-paid employees" means any of the employer's employees who are remunerated by the employer at a rate such that, if the relevant salary sacrifice arrangements or relevant flexible remuneration arrangements applied to them, the rate at which they would then be so remunerated would be likely to be lower than the national minimum wage.

(5C) Condition D is that the employer has, at the required time, made an estimate of the employee's relevant earnings amount for the tax year in respect of which the care is provided (see section 318AA).

(6) For the purposes of this section the "exempt amount", in any tax year, is the appropriate amount for each qualifying week in that year.

(6A) In subsection (6) "the appropriate amount", in the case of an employee, means—
  (a) if the relevant earnings amount in the case of the employee for the tax year, as estimated in accordance with subsection (5C), exceeds the higher rate limit for the tax year, £25,
  (b) if the relevant earnings amount in the case of the employee for the tax year, as so estimated, exceeds the basic rate limit for the tax year but does not exceed the higher rate limit for the tax year, £28, and
  (c) otherwise, £55.

(7) A "qualifying week" means a tax week in which care is provided for a child in circumstances in which conditions A to C are met. "tax week" means one of the successive periods in a tax year beginning with the first day of that year and every seventh day after that (so that the last day of a tax year or, in the case of a tax year ending in a leap year, the last two days is treated as a separate week).

(8) An employee is only entitled to one exempt amount even if care is provided for more than one child. It does not matter that another person may also be entitled to an exempt amount in respect of the same child.

(9) An employee is not entitled to an exempt amount under this section and under section 270A (limited exemption for childcare vouchers) in respect of the same tax week.

GENERAL NOTE

1.543   The amendments made to s.318A have effect for the tax year 2011/12, save for those made by inserting subss.(5A) and (5B), which have effect for the tax year 2005/06 and subsequent tax years.

Meaning of "eligible employee"

1.544   318AZA.—(1) An employee is an eligible employee for the purposes of section 318A if conditions A to C are met in relation to the employee.

(2) Condition A is that the employee—
  (a) was employed by the employer immediately before the relevant day, and
  (b) has not ceased to be employed by the employer on or after that day.

(3) "The relevant day" means the day specified by the Treasury in regulations for the purposes of this section.

(4) Condition B is that there has not been a period of 52 tax weeks ending on or after the relevant day which has not included at least one qualifying week.

(5) In subsection (4)—

"qualifying week" means a tax week in which care for a child has been provided for the employee under the scheme by the employer in circumstances in which conditions A to D in section 318A are met, and "tax week" has the meaning given by section 318A(7).

(6) Condition C is that the employee has not given the employer a childcare account notice.

(7) A "childcare account notice" is a written notice informing the employer that the employee wishes to leave the scheme in order to be able to open a childcare account under section 17 of the Childcare Payments Act 2014 or enable the employee's partner to do so.

(8) In subsection (7) "partner" is to be read in accordance with regulations made under section 3(5) of that Act.

(9) For the meaning of "care" and "child", see section 318B.

Meaning of "relevant earnings amount" and "required time"

318AA.—(1) For the purposes of section 318A, "relevant earnings amount", in the case of an employee provided with care by an employer for any qualifying week in a tax year, means—
 (a) the aggregate of—
  (i) the amount of any relevant earnings for the tax year from employment by the employer, and
  (ii) any amounts treated under Chapters 2 to 12 of Part 3 as earnings from such employment, less
 (b) the aggregate of any excluded amounts.

(2) But if the employee becomes employed by the employer during the tax year, what would otherwise be the amount of the aggregate mentioned in subsection (1)(a) is the relevant multiple of that amount; and the relevant multiple is—

$$\frac{365}{RD}$$

where RD is the number of days in the period beginning with the day on which the employee becomes employed by the employer and ending with the tax year.

(3) In subsection (1)—

"relevant earnings" has the same meaning as in subsection (1)(a) of section 270B (see subsection (3) of that section), and

"excluded amounts" has the same meaning as in subsection (1)(b) of section 270B (see subsection (4) of that section).

(4) In section 318A "the required time", in the case of an employee, means—
 (a) if the employee joins the scheme under which the care is provided at a time during the tax year, that time, and
 (b) otherwise, the beginning of the tax year.

(5) For the purposes of subsection (5)(a) the employee is taken to join the scheme as soon as—
 (a) the employer has agreed that care will be provided under the scheme for the employee, and
 (b) there is a child falling within section 318A(3)(a) or (b) in relation to the employee.

(6) The Treasury may by order amend this section.

Childcare: meaning of "care", "child" and "parental responsibility"

1.546   **318B.**—(1) For the purposes of sections 318 to 318AZA (exemptions for employer-provided or employer-contracted childcare) "care" means any form of care or supervised activity that is not provided in the course of the child's compulsory education.

(2) For the purposes of those sections a person is a "child" until the last day of the week in which falls the 1st September following the child's fifteenth birthday (or sixteenth birthday if the child is disabled).

(3) For the purposes of subsection (2) a child is disabled if—
- (a) a disability living allowance or personal independence payment is payable in respect of him, has ceased to be payable solely because he is a patient,
- (aa) disability assistance is given in respect of the child in accordance with regulations made under section 31 of the Social Security (Scotland) Act 2018,
- (b) he is certified as severely sight impaired or blind by a consultant ophthalmologist, or
- (c) he ceased to be certified as severely sight impaired or blind by a consultant ophthalmologist within the previous 28 weeks.

(4) In subsection (3)(a) "patient" means a person (other than a person who is serving a sentence imposed by a court in a prison or custody institution or, in Scotland, a young offenders' institution) who is regarded as receiving free in-patient treatment within the meaning of the Social Security (Hospital In-Patients) Regulations 1975 or the Social Security (Hospital In-Patients) Regulations (Northern Ireland) 1975.

(5) For the purposes of sections 318 and 318A "parental responsibility" means all the rights, duties, powers, and authority which by law a parent of a child has in relation to the child and the child's property.

(6) In this section and section 318C "local authority" means—
- (a) in relation to England, the council of a county or district, a metropolitan district, a London Borough, the Common Council of the City of London or the Council of the Isles of Scilly;
- (b) in relation to Wales, the council of a county or county borough;
- (c) in relation to Scotland, a council constituted under section 2 of the Local Government etc. (Scotland) Act 1994.

Childcare: meaning of "qualifying child care"

1.547   **318C.**—(1) For the purposes of section 318A "qualifying child care" means registered or approved care within any of subsections (2) to (6) below that is not excluded by subsection (7) below.

(2) Care provided for a child in England is registered or approved care if it is provided—
- (a) ...
- (b) ...
- (ba) by a person registered under Part 3 of the Childcare Act 2006,
- (c) by or under the direction of the proprietor of a school on the school premises (subject to subsection (2B)), or
- (d) ...
- (e) ...

(2003 c.1 s.318C)

(ea) ...
(eb) ...
(f) by a carer supplied by a person registered under Chapter 2 of Part 1 of the Health and Social Care Act 2008 in respect of the activity within paragraph 1 of Schedule 1 (regulated activities: personal care) to the Health and Social Care Act 2008 (Regulated Activities) Regulations 2014.

(2A) In subsection (2)(c)—
"proprietor", in relation to a school, means—
(a) the governing body incorporated under section 19 of the Education Act 2002, or
(b) if there is no such body, the person or body of persons responsible for the management of the school;
"school" means a school that Her Majesty's Chief Inspector of Education, Children's Services and Skills (the "Chief Inspector") is or may be required to inspect;
"school premises" means premises that may be inspected as part of an inspection of the school by the Chief Inspector.

(2B) Care provided for a child in England is not registered or approved care under subsection (2)(c) if—
(a) it is provided during school hours for a child who has reached compulsory school age, or
(b) it is provided in breach of a requirement to register under Part 3 of the Childcare Act 2006.

(3) Care provided for a child in Wales is registered or approved care if it is provided—
(a) by a person registered under Part 2 of the Children and Families (Wales) Measure 2010,
(b) by a person in circumstances where, but for article 11, 12 or 14 of the Child Minding and Day Care Exceptions (Wales) Order 2010, the care would be day care for the purposes of Part 2 of the Children and Families (Wales) Measure 2010,
(c) in the case of care provided for a child out of school hours, by a school on school premises or by a local authority,
(d) by a child care provider approved by an organisation accredited under the Tax Credit (New Category of Child Care Provider) Regulations 1999,
(e) by a domiciliary care worker under the Domiciliary Care Agencies (Wales) Regulations 2004,
(f) by a child care provider approved under the Tax Credits (Approval of Child Care Providers) (Wales) Scheme 2007 or the Approval of Home Childcare Providers (Wales) Scheme 2021, or
(g) by a foster parent in relation to a child (other than one whom the foster parent is fostering) in circumstances where, but for the fact that the child is too old, the care would be–
  (i) child minding, or day care, for the purposes of Part 2 of the Children and Families (Wales) Measure 2010, or
  (ii) qualifying child care for the purposes of the Tax Credits (Approval of Child Care Providers) (Wales) Scheme 2007 or the Approval of Home Childcare Providers (Wales) Scheme 2021.

(4) Care provided for a child in Scotland is registered or approved care if it is provided—

(a) by a person in circumstances where the care service provided by him—
  (i) consists of child minding or of day care of children as defined by paragraphs 12 and 13 respectively of Schedule 12 to the Public Services Reform (Scotland) Act 2010, and
  (ii) is registered under Chapter 3 of Part 5 of that Act, or
(b) by a local authority in circumstances where the care service provided by the local authority—
  (i) consists of child minding or of day care of children as defined by paragraphs 12 and 13 respectively of Schedule 12 to the Public Services Reform (Scotland) Act 2010, and
  (ii) is registered under Chapter 4 of Part 5 of that Act.

(5) Care provided for a child in Northern Ireland is registered approved care if it is provided—
(a) by a person registered under Part XI of the Children (Northern Ireland) Order 1995, or
(b) by an institution or establishment that does not need to be registered under that Part to provide the care because of an exemption under Article 121 of that Order, or
(c) in the case of care provided for a child out of school hours, by a school on school premises or by an education and library board or an HSS trust, or
(d) ...
(e) by a home child care provider approved in accordance with the Tax Credits (Approval of Home Child Care Providers) Scheme (Northern Ireland) 2006, or
(f) by a foster parent in relation to a child (other than one whom the foster parent is fostering) in circumstances where, but for the fact that the child is too old, the care would be—
  (i) child minding, or day care, for the purposes of Part XI of the Children (Northern Ireland) Order 1995, or
  (ii) qualifying child care for the purposes of the Tax Credits (Approval of Home Child Care Providers) Scheme (Northern Ireland) 2006.

(6) Care provided for a child outside the United Kingdom is registered or approved child care if it is provided by a child care provider within regulation 14(2)(d)(i) of the Working Tax Credit (Entitlement and Maximum Rate) Regulations 2002.

(7) Child care is excluded from section 318A—
(a) if it is provided by the partner of the employee in question,
(b) if it is provided by a relative of the child wholly or mainly in the child's home or (if different) the home of a person having parental responsibility for the child, or
(c) in the case of care falling within subsection (3)(f) if—
  (i) it is provided wholly or mainly in the home of a relative of the child, and
  (ii) the provider usually provides care there solely in respect of one or more children to whom the provider is a relative, or
(d) if it is provided by a foster parent, in respect of a child whom that person is fostering.

(8) In subsection (7)—

(2003 c.1 s.318C)

"partner" means one of a couple (within the meaning given by section 137(1) of Social Security Contributions and Benefits Act 1992 or section 133(1) of SSCB(NI)A 1992); and

"relative" means parent, grandparent, aunt, uncle, brother or sister, whether by blood, half blood or marriage or civil partnership.

(9) In subsection (7)(c), "relative in relation to a child, also includes—
(a) a local authority foster parent in relation to the child,
(b) a foster parent with whom the child has been placed by a voluntary organisation,
(c) a person who fosters the child privately (within the meaning of section 66 of the Children Act 1989, or
(d) a step-parent of the child.

PART 5

EMPLOYMENT INCOME: DEDUCTIONS ALLOWED FROM EARNINGS

CHAPTER 1

DEDUCTIONS ALLOWED FROM EARNINGS: GENERAL RULES

Introduction

Deductions from earnings: general

327.—(1) This Part provides for deductions that are allowed from the taxable earnings from an employment in a tax year in calculating the net taxable earnings from the employment in the tax year for the purposes of Part II (see section 11(1)).

(2) In this Part, unless otherwise indicated by the context—
(a) references to the earnings from which deductions are allowed are references to the taxable earnings mentioned in subsection (1); and
(b) references to the tax year are references to the tax year mentioned there.

(3) The deductions for which this Part provides are those allowed under—
Chapter 2 (deductions for employee's expenses);
Chapter 3 (deductions from benefits code earnings);
Chapter 4 (fixed allowances for employee's expenses);
Chapter 5 (deductions for earnings representing benefits or reimbursed expenses); and
Chapter 6 (deductions from seafarers' earnings).

(4) Further provision about deductions from earnings is made in—
section 232 (giving effect to mileage allowance relief);
section 262 of CAA 2001 (capital allowances to be given effect by treating them as deductions from earnings).

(5) Further provision about deductions from income including earnings is made in—
Part 12 (payroll giving); and
sections 188 to 194 of FA 2004 (contributions to registered pension schemes).

1.548

General rules

The income from which deductions may be made

1.549

328.—(1) The general rule is that deductions under this Part are allowed—
  (a) from any earnings from the employment in question; and
  (b) not from earnings from any other employment. This is subject to subsections (2) to (4).

(2) Deductions under section 351 (expenses of ministers of religion) are allowed from earnings from any employment as a minister of a religious denomination.

(3) Deductions under section 368 (fixed sum deductions from earnings payable out of public revenue) are allowed only from earnings payable out of the public revenue.

(4) Deductions limited to specified earnings (see subsection (5)) are allowed—
  (a) only from earnings from the employment that are taxable earnings under certain of the charging provisions of Chapters 4 and 5 of Part 2; and
  (b) not from other earnings from it.

(5) "Deductions limited to specified earnings" are deductions under—
sections 336 to 342 (deductions from earnings charged on receipt: see sections 335(2) and 354);
section 353 (deductions from earnings charged on remittance);
sections 370 to 374 (travel deductions from earnings charged on receipt).

Deductions from earnings not to exceed earnings

1.550

329.—(1) The amount of a deduction allowed under this Part may not exceed the earnings from which it is deductible.

(1A) If the earnings from which a deduction allowed under this Part is deductible include earnings that are "excluded" within the meaning of section 15(1A)—
  (a) the amount of the deduction allowed is a proportion of the amount that would be allowed under this Part if the tax year were not a split year, and
  (b) that proportion is equal to the proportion that the part of the earnings that is not "excluded" bears to the total earnings.

(2) If two or more deductions allowed under this Part are deductible from the same earnings, the amounts deductible may not in aggregate exceed those earnings (or, in a case within subsection (1A), the part of those earnings that is not "excluded").

(3) If deductions allowed otherwise than under this Part fall to be allowed from the same earnings as amounts deductible under this Part, the amounts deductible under this Part may not exceed the earnings (or, in a case within subsection (1A), the part of the earnings that is not "excluded") remaining after the other deductions.

(4) Subsections (1) and (2) do not apply to a deduction under section 351 (expenses of ministers of religion), and subsection (3) applies as if such a deduction were allowed otherwise than under this Part.

(5) This section is to be disregarded for the purposes of the deductibility provisions (see section 332).

(6) See also section 128 of ITA 2007 (which provides that where a loss in an employment is sustained, relief may be given against other income).

Prevention of double deductions

330.—(1) A deduction from earnings under this Part is not allowed more than once in respect of the same costs or expenses.

(2) If apart from this subsection—
(a) a deduction would be allowed under Chapter 4 of this Part (fixed allowances for employee's expenses) for a sum fixed by reference to any kind of expenses; and
(b) the employee would be entitled under another provision to a deduction for an amount paid in respect of the same kind of expenses;

only one of those deductions is allowed.

Order for making deductions

331.—(1) This Part needs to be read with section 25(1) to (3) of ITA 2007 (general rule that deductions are to be allowed in the order resulting in the greatest reduction of liability to income tax).

In the case of deductions under this Part, the general rule in that section is subject to—
(a) section 23(3) (which requires certain deductions to be made in order to establish "chargeable overseas earnings"); and
(b) section 381 (which requires deductions under other provisions to be taken into account before deductions under Chapter 6 of this Part (seafarers)).

Meaning of "the deductibility provisions"

332.—For the purposes of this Part, "the deductibility provisions" means the following provisions (which refer to amounts or expenses that would be deductible if they were incurred and paid by an employee)—

the definition of "business travel" in section 171(1) (definitions for Chapter 6 of Part 3),

section 179(6) (exception for certain advances for necessary expenses),
the definition of "business travel" in section 236(1) (definitions for Chapter 2 of Part 4),

section 240(1)(c) and (5) (exemption of incidental overnight expenses and benefits),

section 252(3) (exception from exemption of work-related training provision for non-deductible travel expenses),

section 257(3) (exception from exemption for individual learning account training provision for non-deductible travel expenses),

section 305(5) (offshore oil and gas workers: mainland transfers),

section 310(6)(b) (counselling and other outplacement services),

section 311(5)(b) (retraining courses),

section 361(b) (scope of Chapter 3 of this Part: cost of benefits deductible as if paid by employee),

section 362(1)(c) and (2)(b) (deductions where non-cash voucher provided),

section 363(1)(b) and (2)(b) (deductions where credit-token provided), section 364(1)(b) and (2) (deductions where living accommodation provided),

section 365(1)(b) and (2) (deductions where employment-related benefit provided).

Chapter 2

Deductions for Employee's Expenses

Introduction

Scope of this chapter: expenses paid by the employee

1.554   **333.**—(1) A deduction from a person's earnings for an amount is allowed under the following provisions of this chapter only if the amount—
(a) is paid by the person; or
(b) is paid on the person's behalf by someone else and is included in the earnings.

(2) In the following provisions of this chapter, in relation to a deduction from a person's earnings, references to the person paying an amount include references to the amount being paid on the person's behalf by someone else if or to the extent that the amount is included in the earnings.

(3) Subsection (1)(b) does not apply to the deductions under—
(a) section 351(2) and (3) (expenses of ministers of religion); and
(b) section 355 (deductions for corresponding payments by non-domiciled employees with foreign employers),
and subsection (2) does not apply in the case of those deductions.

(4) Chapter 3 of this Part provides for deductions where—
(a) a person's earnings include an amount treated as earnings under Chapter 4, 5 or 10 of Part 3 (taxable benefits: vouchers, etc., living accommodation and residual liability to charge); and
(b) an amount in respect of the benefit in question would be deductible under this chapter if the person had incurred and paid it.

Effect of reimbursement, etc.

1.555   **334.**—(1) For the purposes of this chapter, a person may be regarded as paying an amount despite—
(a) its reimbursement; or
(b) any other payment from another person in respect of the amount.

(2) But where a reimbursement or such other payment is made in respect of an amount, a deduction for the amount is allowed under the following provisions of this chapter only if or to the extent that—
(a) the reimbursement; or
(b) so much of the other payment as relates to the amount; is included in the person's earnings.

(3) *Omitted*.

(2003 c.1 s.336)

General rule for deduction of employee's expenses

Deductions for expenses: the general rule

336.—(1) The general rule is that a deduction from earnings is allowed for an amount if—   **1.556**
- (a) the employee is obliged to incur and pay it as holder of the employment; and
- (b) the amount is incurred wholly, exclusively and necessarily in the performance of the duties of the employment.

(2) The following provisions of this chapter contain additional rules allowing deductions for particular kinds of expenses and rules preventing particular kinds of deductions.

(3) No deduction is allowed under this section for an amount that is deductible under sections 337 to 342 (travel expenses).

Travel expenses

Travel in performance of duties

337.—(1) A deduction from earnings is allowed for travel expenses if—   **1.557**
- (a) the employee is obliged to incur and pay them as holder of the employment; and
- (b) the expenses are necessarily incurred on travelling in the performance of the duties of the employment.

(2) This section needs to be read with section 359 (disallowance of travel expenses: mileage allowances and reliefs).

Travel for necessary attendance

338.—(1) A deduction from earnings is allowed for travel expenses if—   **1.558**
- (a) the employee is obliged to incur and pay them as holder of the employment; and
- (b) the expenses are attributable to the employee's necessary attendance at any place in the performance of the duties of the employment.

(2) Subsection (1) does not apply to the expenses of ordinary commuting or travel between any two places that is for practical purposes substantially ordinary commuting.

(3) In this section, "ordinary commuting" means travel between—
- (a) the employee's home and a permanent workplace; or
- (b) a place that is not a workplace and a permanent workplace.

(4) Subsection (1) does not apply to the expenses of private travel or travel between any two places that is for practical purposes substantially private travel.

(5) In subsection (4), "private travel" means travel between—
- (a) the employee's home and a place that is not a workplace; or
- (b) two places neither of which is a workplace.

(6) This section needs to be read with section 359 (disallowance of travel expenses: mileage allowances and reliefs).

Meaning of "workplace" and "permanent workplace"

1.559 339.—(1) In this Part, "workplace", in relation to an employment, means a place at which the employee's attendance is necessary in the performance of the duties of the employment.

(2) In this Part "permanent workplace", in relation to an employment, means a place which—
 (a) the employee regularly attends in the performance of the duties of the employment; and
 (b) is not a temporary workplace.
This is subject to subsections (4) and (8).

(3) In subsection (2), "temporary workplace", in relation to an employment, means a place which the employee attends in the performance of the duties of the employment—
 (a) for the purpose of performing a task of limited duration; or
 (b) for some other temporary purpose.
This is subject to subsections (4) and (5).

(4) A place which the employee regularly attends in the performance of the duties of the employment is treated as a permanent workplace and not a temporary workplace if—
 (a) it forms the base from which those duties are performed; or
 (b) the tasks to be carried out in the performance of those duties are allocated there.

(5) A place is not regarded as a temporary workplace if the employee's attendance is—
 (a) in the course of a period of continuous work at that place—
  (i) lasting more than 24 months, or
  (ii) comprising all or almost all of the period for which the employee is likely to hold the employment; or
 (b) at a time when it is reasonable to assume that it will be in the course of such a period.

(6) For the purposes of subsection (5), a period is a period of continuous work at a place if over the period the duties of the employment are performed to a significant extent at the place.

(7) An actual or contemplated modification of the place at which duties are performed is to be disregarded for the purposes of subsections (5) and (6) if it does not, or would not, have any substantial effect on the employee's journey, or expenses of travelling, to and from the place where they are performed.

(8) An employee is treated as having a permanent workplace consisting of an area if—
 (a) the duties of the employment are defined by reference to an area (whether or not they also require attendance at places outside it);
 (b) in the performance of those duties the employee attends different places within the area;
 (c) none of the places the employee attends in the performance of those duties is a permanent workplace; and
 (d) the area would be a permanent workplace if subsections (2), (3), (5), (6) and (7) referred to the area where they refer to a place.

(2003 c.1 s.565)

PART 9

PENSION INCOME

CHAPTER 1

INTRODUCTION

Structure of Part 9

565.—The structure of this Part is as follows—
Chapter 2—
(a) imposes the charge to tax on pension income; and
(b) provides for deductions to be made from the amount of income chargeable;
Chapters 3 to 15 set out the types of income which are charged to tax under this Part and, for each type of income, identify—
(a) the amount of income chargeable to tax for a tax year; and
(b) the person liable to pay any tax charged;
Chapter 15A—
(a) provides for certain amounts paid under registered pension schemes in the form of lump sums to be subject to the charge to tax on pension income, and
(b) deals with exemptions from the charge to tax (whether under this Part or any other provision) in relation to certain other amounts paid under registered pension schemes in the form of lump sums;
Chapters 17 and 18 deal with other exemptions from the charge to tax (whether under this Part or any other provision).

1.560

GENERAL NOTE

In the ICTA, most forms of pension income were taxed in the same way as emoluments under Schedule E. One of the main changes undertaken as part of the Tax Law Rewrite Project was to extract all the various provisions relating to the taxation of pensions of employees and office holders (both in the UK and overseas) and put them together in a single code. That code now forms Pt 9 of ITEPA 2003. It contains all the primary legislation from the ICTA 1988 and successive Finance Acts on the taxation of state pensions (including social security pensions), occupational pensions payable to officeholders and employees, and personal pensions. It recognises the division between earnings and pensions, but prevails over the separate provisions in Pt 10, dealing with social security income. It includes provisions in separate chapters dealing with foreign pension income.

The Tax Credits (Definition and Calculation of Income) Regulations 2002 rely on that code for defining pension income for the purposes of the tax credits income test. This selection of sections sets out the key provisions from that code. Foreign pensions, are not, however, included as pension income for tax credits purposes, so no reference is made to those chapters of Pt 9 of ITEPA. Foreign pensions should therefore be considered as foreign income, not pension income, for tax credits purposes. The Finance Act 2004 Pt 4 and associated Schedules, completely replaced the taxation rules applying to pensions and pension funds (though not the taxation of ordinary social security pension income) with a fundamentally new regime.

1.561

Income Tax (Earnings and Pensions) Act 2003

As part of that, much of Pt 9 of this Act was repealed and replaced. But the new provisions are beyond the scope of this volume and are omitted. Only the general rules and social security pension rules are included.

CHAPTER 2

TAX ON PENSION INCOME

Nature of charge to tax on pension income and relevant definitions

1.562 **566.**—(1) The charge to tax on pension income under this Part is a charge to tax on that income excluding any exempt income.

(2) "Pension income" means the pensions, annuities and income of other types to which the provisions listed in subsection (4) apply.

This definition applies for the purposes of the Tax Acts.

(3) "Exempt income" means pension income on which no liability to income tax arises as a result of any provision of Chapters 15A to 18 of this Part.

This definition applies for the purposes of this Part.

(4) These are the provisions referred to in subsection (2)—

Provision	*Income*	*Chapter (of this Part)*
Section 569	United Kingdom pensions	Chapter 3
Section 573	Foreign pensions	Chapter 4
Section 577	United Kingdom social security pensions	Chapter 5
Section 579A	Pensions under registered pension schemes	Chapter 5A
Section 609	Annuities for the benefit of dependants	Chapter 10
Section 610	Annuities under sponsored superannuation schemes	Chapter 10
Section 611	Annuities in recognition of another's services	Chapter 10
Section 615	Certain overseas government pensions paid in the United Kingdom	Chapter 11
Section 619	The House of Commons Members' Fund	Chapter 12
Section 629	Pre-1973 pensions paid under OPA 1973	Chapter 14
Section 633	Voluntary annual payments	Chapter 15
Section 637B	Pensions treated as arising from payment of pension commencement excess lump sums under registered pension schemes	Chapter 15A
Section 637G	Pensions treated as arising from payment of trivial commutation lump sums and winding-up lump sums under registered pension schemes	Chapter 15A

| Section 637N | Pensions treated as arising from payment of trivial commutation lump sum death benefits under registered pension schemes | Chapter 15A |

Amount charged to tax

567.—(1) The amount of pension income which is charged to tax under this Part for a particular tax year is as follows.

(2) In relation to each pension, annuity or other item of pension income, the amount charged to tax is the "net taxable pension income" for the tax year.

(3) The net taxable pension income for a pension, annuity or other item of pension income for a tax year is given by the formula—

$$\frac{TPI}{DPI}$$

where—
TPI means the amount of taxable pension income for that pension, annuity or item of pension income for that year (see subsection (4)); and
DPI means the total amount of any deductions allowed from the pension, annuity or item of pension income (see subsection (5)).

(4) For the purposes of this Act—
(a) the amount of taxable pension income for a pension, annuity or other item of pension income for a tax year is determined in accordance with Chapters 3 to 15A of this Part (which contain provisions relating to this amount for each type of pension income); and
(b) in determining the amount of taxable pension income for a pension, annuity or other item of pension income, any exempt income is to be excluded.

(5) The deductions allowed from a pension, annuity or other item of pension income are those under—
section 567A (deduction to avoid double taxation where Part 7A has applied to the source of the pension income);
section 617 (10% deduction from an overseas government pension to which section 615 applies);
Part 22 (payroll giving).

Person liable for tax

568.—For the provision identifying which person is liable for any tax charged under this Part on a pension, annuity or other item of pension income, see Chapters 3 to 15A.

Chapter 3

United Kingdom Pensions: General Rules

United Kingdom pensions

569.—(1) This section applies to any pension paid by or on behalf of a person who is in the United Kingdom.

(2) But this section does not apply to a pension if any provision of Chapters 5 to 14 of this Part applies to it.

(3) For pensions paid by or on behalf of a person who is outside the United Kingdom, see Chapter 4 of this Part.

GENERAL NOTE

1.566 Most UK pensions will be caught under the new Chapter 5A ss.579A–D, taxing pensions under registered pension schemes on the same basis as ss.571 and 572 below, subject to the exceptions for some lump sums and other payments detailed in the FA 2004 provisions. The detailed new provisions are omitted as they will be of limited importance to most tax credit claimants.

"Pension": interpretation

1.567 570.—In this chapter, "pension" includes a pension which is paid voluntarily or is capable of being discontinued.

Taxable pension income

1.568 571.—If section 569 applies, the taxable pension income for a tax year is the full amount of the pension accruing in that year, irrespective of when any amount is actually paid.

Person liable for tax

1.569 572.—If section 569 applies, the person liable for any tax charged under this Part is the person receiving or entitled to the pension.

CHAPTER 5

UNITED KINGDOM SOCIAL SECURITY PENSIONS

United Kingdom social security pensions

1.570 577.—(1) This section applies to—
the state pension;
graduated retirement benefit;
industrial death benefit;
widowed mother's allowance;
widowed parent's allowance; and
widow's pension.

(1A) But this section does not apply to any social security pension lump sum (within the meaning of section 7 of F(No.2)A 2005).

(2) In this section—
"state pension" means any pension payable under—
  (za) any provision of Part 1 of the Pensions Act 2014 or any corresponding provision under the law of Northern Ireland,
  (a) section 44, 48A, 48AA, 48B, 48BB, 51 or 78 of SSCBA 1992; or
  (b) section 44, 48, 48A, 48B, 48BB, 51 or 78 of SSCB(NI)A 1992 or any provision under the law of Northern Ireland that corresponds to section 48AA of SSCBA 1992;

"graduated retirement benefit" means any benefit payable under—
  (a) section 36 or 37 of the National Insurance Act 1965 (Chapter 51); or

(b) section 35 or 36 of the National Insurance Act (Northern Ireland) 1966 (Chapter 6 (NI));

"industrial death benefit" means any benefit payable under—
(a) section 94 of, and Part 6 of Schedule 7 to SSCBA 1992; or
(b) section 94 of, and Part 6 of Schedule 7 to SSCB(NI)A 1992;

"widowed mother's allowance" means any allowance payable under—
(a) section 37 of SSCBA 1992; or
(b) section 37 of SSCB(NI)A 1992;

"widowed parent's allowance" means any allowance payable under—
(a) section 39A of SSCBA 1992; or
(b) section 39A of SSCB(NI)A 1992;

"widow's pension" means any pension payable under—
(a) section 38 of SSCBA 1992; or
(b) section 38 of SSCB(NI)A 1992.

(3) ...

(4) Chapter 17 of this Part provides a partial exemption for a pension to which this section applies in respect of any part of the pension which is attributable to an increase in respect of a child (see section 645).

GENERAL NOTE

This section lists forms of state pension to be brought within the charge to tax in s.578. The exclusion of social security lump sums is because separate provision is made to tax those sums in ss.7 and 8 of F(No.2)A 2005. Lump sums are treated as income for income tax purposes but are given special treatment to prevent the recipients losing their age-related personal allowances. They are also to be taxed regardless of the residence or domicile of the recipients. Section 8 sets the date on which the tax charge is to apply. It is usually in the tax year in which the right to the pension starts.

Taxable pension income

578.—If section 577 applies, the taxable pension income for a tax year is the full amount of the pension, benefit or allowance accruing in that year, irrespective of when any amount is actually paid.

Person liable for tax

579.—If section 577 applies, the person liable for any tax charged under this Part is the person receiving or entitled to the pension, benefit or allowance.

PART 10

SOCIAL SECURITY INCOME

CHAPTER 1

INTRODUCTION

Structure of Part 10

655.—(1) The structure of this Part is as follows—
Chapter 2—
(a) imposes the charge to tax on social security income; and

(b) provides for deductions to be made from the amount of income chargeable;

Chapter 3 sets out the United Kingdom social security benefits which are charged to tax under this Part and identifies—

(a) the amount of income chargeable to tax for a tax year; and
(b) the person liable to pay any tax charged;

Chapters 4 and 5 deal with exemptions from the charge to tax on United Kingdom social security benefits (whether under this Part or any other provision);

Chapters 6 and 7 make provisions about foreign benefits.

Chapter 8 makes provision for the high income child benefit charge.

(2) For other provisions about the taxation of social security benefits see—

section 151 of FA 1996 (power for the Treasury to make orders about the taxation of benefits payable under Government pilot schemes);

section 781 of ITA 2007 (exemption of payments under New Deal 50plus);

section 782 of ITA 2007 (exemption of payments under Employment Zones programme)

section 44 of FA 2016 (tax treatment of supplementary welfare payments: Northern Ireland);

section 13 of FA 2020 (power to exempt social security benefits from income tax);

section 27 of F(No.2)A 2023 (power to clarify tax treatment of devolved social security benefits).

(3) For the charge to tax on social security pensions see Part 9.

GENERAL NOTE

1.575 "Social security income" is another head of charge created from the Tax Law Rewrite Project. Previously, all forms of social security income were fitted, sometimes somewhat uncomfortably, in Sch.E. Part 10 of ITEPA is now used to codify the charge to income tax on all forms of social security benefit and allowance other than pensions. As this section records, Pt 9 deals with pensions. The opportunity has also been taken to set out the various provisions in a systematic way, and dealing with both UK and other benefits.

Because of the general importance of these provisions for social security purposes, the Part has been included more extensively than other Parts of ITEPA for social security purposes, and not restricted to those relevant only for tax credits purposes.

Subsection (1) is a signposting provision.

1.576 Subsection (2) lists the provisions (not included in this volume) under which limited exemptions from income tax may be made for social security benefits. The power under s.151 of FA 1996 is used to exempt payments made to claimants under pilot schemes. For current exemptions under this provision, see: the Taxation of Benefits under Government Pilot Schemes (Return to Work Credit and Employment Retention and Advancements Schemes) Order 2003 (SI 2003/2339) (not reproduced in this volume), in effect from October 1, 2003; and the Taxation of Benefits under government Pilot Schemes (Working Neighbourhoods Pilot and In Work Credit) Order 2004 (SI 2004/575), in effect from April 6, 2004. Both orders fully exempt payments under those schemes form income tax. The reference to s.84 of FA 2000 is superseded from the start of working tax credit as New Deal payments have now been incorporated into the credit.

Subsection (3) is a signpost to s.577 (UK social security pensions).

Chapter 2

Tax on Social Security Income

Nature of charge to tax on social security income

656.—(1) The charge to tax on social security income is a charge to tax on that income excluding any exempt income.

(2) "Exempt income" is social security income on which no liability to income tax arises as a result of any provision of Chapters 4, 5 or 7 of this Part.

This definition applies for the purposes of this Part.

Definitions

"social security income"—see s.657(2).
"tax"—see ICTA s.832(3).

General Note

This section is extremely important because it emphasises that the exemption provisions in the Part override the charges to tax. In practice, very few forms of UK social security income are chargeable to tax under this Part. Remember that pensions are chargeable under Pt 9. In most cases statutory sick pay and the other statutory payments are chargeable to tax under Pt 2. Any such payments that are not caught by Pt 3 are caught by a "safety net" provision in this Part.

Provisions in this part exempt child benefit, guardian's allowance and child tax credit and so exclude all child-related benefit. Other provisions exempt all disablement related benefits payable to the disabled or incapacitated individual.

Tax credits under the TCA 2002 are themselves exempted from tax under this Part. So are the local government benefits of housing benefit and council tax benefit. Benefits received from the national health service, in kind or in cash, are not income for any income tax purpose, and are not affected by this Part. Welfare benefits in kind, such as welfare foods and publicly provided accommodation, are not within the definition of "social security income" in s.657 and so are excluded from the charge to tax under this Part. They do not fall to be charged under any other part of ITEPA 2003.

This leaves income tax payable only on some parts of some payments of income support, jobseeker's allowance and incapacity benefit, and also on bereavement allowance (in practice linked with pension entitlements but not a form of pension income) and carer's allowance (formerly known as invalid care allowance).

The equivalent approach is adopted for foreign social security payments.

Meaning of "social security income", "taxable benefits", etc.

657.—(1) This section defines—
"social security income" for the purposes of the Tax Acts; and
"taxable benefits", "Table A" and "Table B" for the purposes of this Part.
(2) "Social security income" means—
(a) the United Kingdom social security benefits listed in Table A;
(b) the United Kingdom social security benefits listed in Table B;
(c) the foreign benefits to which section 678 applies; and
(d) the foreign benefits to which section 681(2) applies.
(3) "Taxable benefits" means—
(a) the United Kingdom social security benefits listed in Table A; and
(b) the foreign benefits to which section 678 applies.
(4) Subsections (2) and (3) are subject to section 660(2).

(5) "Table A" means Table A in section 660.
(6) "Table B" means Table B in section 677.

General Note

1.581   This section defines the term "social security income" used in s.656, which is the charging section. Unless a form of income is within the scope of the definition in subs.(2), it is not liable to income tax under this Part. Nor will it be liable to income tax under any other general provision in the Taxes Act. However, the interpretation of the scope of this section must take into account the very wide provisions dealing with benefits provided by employers in Pt 2, which in practice covers some forms of payments that are in principle social security payments (such as statutory maternity pay). Further, anything that is a "pension" is taxable under Pt 9 and is removed from this Part by s.655(3).

Amount charged to tax

1.582   **658.**—(1) The amount of social security income which is charged to tax under this Part for a particular tax year is as follows.

(2) In relation to a taxable benefit, the amount charged to tax is the net taxable social security income for the tax year.

(3) The net taxable social security income for a taxable benefit for a tax year is given by the formula—

$$TSSI - PGD$$

where—
  TSSI means the amount of taxable social security income for that benefit for that year (see subsections (4) to (7)); and
  PGD means the amount of the deduction (if any) allowed from the benefit under Part 12 (payroll giving).

(4) In relation to bereavement allowance, carer's allowance, carer's allowance supplement, carer support payment, contributory employment and support allowance, incapacity benefit, income support, welfare supplementary payments payable pursuant to the loss of contributory employment and support allowance and welfare supplementary payments payable pursuant to the loss of, or a reduction in the amount payable of, income support (which are listed in Table A), the amount of taxable social security income is determined in accordance with section 661.

(5) In relation to any other benefit listed in Table A, the amount of taxable social security income is the amount of the benefit that falls to be charged to tax.

(6) In relation to foreign benefits to which section 678 applies, the amount of taxable social security income is determined in accordance with section 679.

(7) In determining for the purposes of this Act the amount of taxable social security income, any exempt income is to be excluded.

Definitions

"exempt income"—see s.656(2).
"social security income"—see s.657(2).
"tax year"—see s.721(1).
"taxable benefit"—see s.657(3).

Person liable for tax

659.—The person liable for any tax charged under this Part is identified in—
(a) section 662 (United Kingdom benefits); or
(b) section 680 (foreign benefits).

1.583

CHAPTER 3

TAXABLE UNITED KINGDOM SOCIAL SECURITY BENEFITS

Taxable benefits: United Kingdom benefits—Table A

660.—(1) This is Table A:

1.584

TABLE A

1.585

TAXABLE UK BENEFITS

Social security benefit	Payable under	
Carer's allowance	SSCBA 1992	Section 70
	SSCB(NI)A 1992	Section 70
Carer's allowance supplement	SS(S)A 2018	Sections 24 and 28
Carer support payment	CA(CSP)(S)R 2023	Regulation 3
Employment and support allowance	WRA 2007	Section 1(2) (a)
	Any provision made for Northern Ireland which corresponds to section 1(2)(a) of WRA 2007	
Incapacity benefit	SSCBA 1992	Section 30A(1) or (5), 40 or 41
	SSCB(NI)A 1992	Section 30A(1) or (5), 40 or 41
Income support	SSCBA 1992	Section 123
	SSCB(NI)A 1992	Section 124
Jobseeker's allowance	JSA 1995	Section 1
	JS(NI)O 1995	Article 3
Statutory sick pay	SSCBA 1992	Section 151
	SSCB(NI)A 1992	Section 147
Statutory adoption pay	SSCBA 1992	Section 171ZL
	Any provision made for Northern Ireland which corresponds to section 171ZL of SSCBA 1992	
Statutory maternity pay	SSCBA 1992	Section 164
	SSCB(NI)A 1992	Section 160
Statutory paternity pay	SSCBA 1992	Section 171ZL
Statutory shared parental pay	SSCBA 1992	Section 171ZU or 171ZV

Statutory parental bereavement pay	Any provision made for Northern Ireland which corresponds to section 171ZU or 171ZV of SSCBA 1992 SSCBA 1992 Any provision made for Northern Ireland which corresponds to section 171ZZ6 of SSCBA 1992	Section 171ZZ6

Welfare supplementary payment payable pursuant to the loss of carer's allowance	WSP(LCP) R(NI) 2016	Regulation 7
Welfare supplementary payment payable pursuant to the loss of contributory employment and support allowance	WSPR(NI) 2016	Regulation 8 (when the recipient is entitled to the payment by meeting the condition in regulation 8(2)(c)) or regulation 12
Welfare supplementary payment payable pursuant to the loss of, or a reduction of the amount payable of, income support	WSP(LCP) R(NI) 2016	
Welfare supplementary payment payable pursuant to a reduction of the amount payable of jobseekers allowance	WSP(LDRP) R(NI) 2016 WSP(LCP) R(NI) 2016 WSP(LDRP) R(NI) 2016	Regulation 4, 5 or 6 Regulation 8 (when the recipient is entitled to the payment by meeting the condition in regulation 8(2)(a)) Regulation 11, 12, 13, 14 or 15.

(2) A benefit listed below is not "social security income" or a "taxable benefit" if it is charged to tax under another Part of this Act—
   statutory adoption pay;
   statutory maternity pay;
   statutory parental bereavement pay;
   statutory paternity pay;
   statutory shared parental pay;
   statutory sick pay.

DEFINITIONS

   "social security income"—see s.657(2).
   "taxable benefit"—see s.657(3).

GENERAL NOTE

This section and those that follow need updating to take account of the changes made to social security benefits by the Welfare Reform Act 2012. See the note on that Act below. For the full forms of the abbreviations in Table A see Sch.1 Pt 1 to the Act. Subsection (2) provides that a charge to tax under Pt 2 of the Act takes priority over this Part, but the section ensures that all statutory payments are taxable.

Taxable social security income

661.—(1) This section applies in relation to each of the following taxable benefits listed in Table A—
bereavement allowance;
carer's allowance;
carer's allowance supplement;
carer support payment;
contributory employment and support allowance;
incapacity benefit;
income support;
welfare supplementary payments payable pursuant to the loss of contributory employment and support allowance, and
welfare supplementary payments payable pursuant to the loss of, or a reduction of the amount payable of, income support.

(2) The amount of taxable social security income for a taxable benefit for a tax year is the full amount of the benefit accruing in the tax year irrespective of when any amount is actually paid.

DEFINITIONS
"tax year"—see s.721(1).
"taxable benefit"—see s.675(3).

GENERAL NOTE

This is a new rule under ITEPA introduced to replace both inconsistent previous legislation and a lack of legislation, the rules apparently varying from one benefit to another for no good reason. "Accrued" is standard income tax language not normally used for social security purposes. In social security terms, as the section makes clear, it means payable not paid.

Person liable for tax

662.—The person liable for any tax charged under this Part on a taxable benefit listed in Table A is the person receiving or entitled to the benefit.

GENERAL NOTE

"Received or entitled" is familiar income tax language applied to social security income by ITEPA in place of a lack of any clear previous rule. As the wording indicates it covers both the person for whom the benefit is payable and the person who actually receives it. The wording will make joint claimants for jobseeker's allowance both liable for any income tax on the allowance. It is, however, not clear how this is applied to appointees appointed to receive income support for a claimant.

Income Tax (Earnings and Pensions) Act 2003

CHAPTER 4

TAXABLE UK SOCIAL SECURITY BENEFITS: EXEMPTIONS

Incapacity benefit

Long-term incapacity benefit: previous entitlement to invalidity benefit

1.591   **663.**—(1) No liability to income tax arises on long-term incapacity benefit if—
   (a) a person is entitled to the benefit for a day of incapacity for work which falls in a period of incapacity for work which is treated for the purposes of that benefit as having begun before April 13, 1995; and
   (b) the part of that period which is treated as having fallen before that date includes a day for which that person was entitled to invalidity benefit.
(2) In this section—
"invalidity benefit" means invalidity benefit under—
   (a) Part 2 of SSCBA 1992; or
   (b) Part 2 of SSCB(NI)A 1992;
"long-term incapacity benefit" means incapacity benefit payable under—
   (a) section 30A(5), 40 or 41 of SSCBA 1992; or
   (b) section 30A(5), 40 or 41 of SSCB(NI)A 1992.

Short-term incapacity benefit not payable at the higher rate

1.592   **664.**—(1) No liability to income tax arises on short-term incapacity benefit unless it is payable at the higher rate.
(2) In this section—
   (a) "short-term incapacity benefit" means incapacity benefit payable under—
      (i) section 30A(1) of SSCBA 1992; or
      (ii) section 30A(1) of SSCB(NI)A 1992;
   (b) the reference to short-term incapacity benefit payable at the higher rate is to be construed in accordance with—
      (i) section 30B of SSCBA 1992; or
      (ii) section 30B of SSCB(NI)A 1992.

Income support

Exempt unless payable to a person involved in trade dispute

1.593   **665.**—(1) No liability to income tax arises on income support unless—
   (a) the income support is payable to one member of a couple ("the claimant"); and
   (b) section 126 of SSCBA 1992 or section 125 of SSCB(NI)A 1992 (trade disputes) applies to the claimant but not to the other member of the couple.
(2) In this section, couple has the same meaning as in section 137(1) of SSCBA 1992 or section 133(1) of SSCB(NI)A 1992.

(3) No liability to income tax arises on a relevant welfare supplementary payment unless the whole or part of the payment relates to a period in which the claimant was prevented from being entitled to jobseeker's allowance by—
  (a) section 14 of the Jobseekers Act 1995 (trade disputes), or
  (b) Article 16 of the Jobseekers (Northern Ireland) Order 1995 (trade disputes) or would have been so prevented if otherwise entitled to that benefit.

(4) Where part of a relevant welfare supplementary payment relates to such a period no liability to income tax arises on the part that does not relate to such a period.

Child maintenance bonus

666.—No liability to income tax arises on a part of income support which is attributable to a child maintenance bonus (within the meaning of section 10 of CSA 1995 or Article 4 of CS(NI)O 1995).

Amounts in excess of taxable maximum

667.—(1) If the amount of income support and relevant welfare supplementary payments paid to a person ("the claimant") for a week or a part of a week exceeds the claimant's taxable maximum for that period, no liability to income tax arises on the excess.

(2) The claimant's taxable maximum for a period is determined—
  (a) under section 668(1), (2) and (3) where the claimant is a member of a couple, and
  (b) under section 668(2A) and (3) where the claimant is not a member of a couple.

Taxable maximum

668.—(1) A claimant's taxable maximum for a week is determined under this subsection if the applicable amount for the purpose of calculating the income support consists only of an amount in respect of the relevant couple.

The taxable maximum is equal to one half of the applicable amount.

(2) A claimant's taxable maximum for a week is determined under this subsection if the applicable amount includes amounts that are not in respect of the relevant couple.

The taxable maximum is equal to one half of the amount which is included in the applicable amount in respect of the relevant couple.

(2A) A claimant's taxable maximum for a week is determined under this subsection if the claimant is not a member of a couple.

The taxable maximum is equal to the applicable amount.

(3) A claimant's taxable maximum for a part of a week is determined as follows—

Step 1

Assume that the income support is paid to the claimant for the whole of, rather than part of, the week.

Step 2

Determine under subsection (1) or (2) what the claimant's taxable maximum for that week would be on that assumption.

Step 3

Determine the claimant's taxable maximum for the part of the week using this formula—

$$\frac{N}{7} \times TMW$$

where—
N is the number of days in the part of the week for which the claimant is actually paid the income support; and
TMW is the taxable maximum for the whole week determined under step 2.

Interpretation

669.—(A1) In sections 665 and 667 "relevant welfare supplementary payment" means a payment to which a person is entitled under—
(a) regulation 8 (when the recipient is entitled to the payment by meeting the condition in regulation 8(2)(c)) or regulation 12 of WSP(LCP)R(NI) 2016, or
(b) regulation 4, 5 or 6 of WSP(LDRP)R(NI) 2016.
(1) In section 668, except in relation to Northern Ireland—
"applicable amount" means the amount prescribed in relation to income support in regulations made under section 135 of SSCBA 1992;
"couple" has the same meaning as in section 137(1) of Social Security Contributions and Benefits Act 1992;
(2) In section 668, in relation to Northern Ireland—
"applicable amount" means the amount prescribed in relation to income support in regulations made under section 131 of SSCB(NI)A 1992;
"couple" has the same meaning as in section 133(1) of Social Security Contributions and Benefits (Northern Ireland) Act 1992;
(3) In section 668, "relevant couple", in relation to a claimant, means the couple of which the claimant is a member.

GENERAL NOTE

This section applies the definition of "couple" adopted for social security purposes following the replacement by the Civil Partnership Act 2004 of all references to "married couples" and "unmarried couples" for the purposes of ITEPA. The effect is to impose the social security meaning of "couple" on the income tax treatment of social security income, and not the income tax definition.

Jobseeker's allowance and relevant welfare supplementary payments

Child maintenance bonus

670.—No liability to income tax arises on a part of a jobseeker's allowance which is attributable to a child maintenance bonus (within the meaning of section 10 of CSA 1995 or Article 4 of CS(NI)O 1995).

(2003 c.1 s.671)

Amounts in excess of taxable maximum

671.—(1) If the amount of jobseeker's allowance and relevant welfare supplementary payments paid to a person ("the claimant") for a week or a part of a week exceeds the claimant's taxable maximum for that period, no liability to income tax arises on the excess.

(2) The claimant's taxable maximum for a period is determined under sections 672 to 674.

1.600

Taxable maximum: general

672.—(1) A claimant's taxable maximum for a week is determined—
(a) under section 673, if the claimant is paid an income-based jobseeker's allowance for that week; or
(b) under section 674, if the claimant is paid a contribution-based jobseeker's allowance for that week.

(2) A claimant's taxable maximum for a part of a week is determined as follows—

1.601

Step 1

Assume that the jobseeker's allowance is paid to the claimant for the whole of, rather than part of, the week.

Step 2

Determine under section 673 or 674 what the claimant's taxable maximum for that week would be on that assumption.

Step 3

Determine the claimant's taxable maximum for the part of the week using this formula—

$$\frac{N}{7} \times TMW$$

where—
N is the number of days in the part of the week for which the claimant is actually paid the jobseeker's allowance; and
TMW is the taxable maximum for the whole week determined under step 2.

Taxable maximum: income-based jobseeker's allowance

673.—(1) A claimant's taxable maximum for a week is determined under this section if—
(a) the claimant is paid an income-based jobseeker's allowance for that week, or
(b) the claimant is assumed under section 672(2) to be paid an income-based jobseeker's allowance for that week.

(2) If the claimant is not a member of a couple, the claimant's taxable maximum for the week is equal to the age-related amount which would be applicable to the claimant if a contribution based jobseeker's allowance were payable to the claimant for that week.

(3) If the claimant is a member of a couple, the claimant's taxable maximum for the week is equal to the portion of the applicable amount which is included in the jobseeker's allowance in respect of the couple for that week.

1.602

(4) But if—
(a) the claimant is a member of a couple; and
(b) the other member of that couple is prevented by section 14 of JSA 1995 or Article 16 of JS(NI)O 1995 (trade disputes) from being entitled to a jobseeker's allowance;
the claimant's taxable maximum for that week is equal to half the portion of the applicable amount which is included in the jobseeker's allowance in respect of the couple for that week.

Taxable maximum: contribution-based jobseeker's allowance

1.603   **674.**—(1) A claimant's taxable maximum for a week is determined under this section if—
(a) the claimant is paid a contribution-based jobseeker's allowance for that week; or
(b) the claimant is assumed under section 672(2) to be paid a contribution-based jobseeker's allowance for that week.
(2) If the claimant is not a member of a couple, the claimant's taxable maximum for the week is equal to the age-related amount which is applicable to the claimant for that week.
(3) If the claimant is a member of a couple, the claimant's taxable maximum for the week is equal to the portion of the applicable amount which would be included in the jobseeker's allowance in respect of the couple if an income-based jobseeker's allowance were payable to the claimant for that week.

Interpretation

1.604   **675.**—(A1) In section 671 "relevant welfare supplementary payments" means payments to which a person is entitled under—
(a) regulation 8 (when the recipient is entitled to the payment by meeting the condition in regulation 8(2)(a)) of WSP(LCP)R(NI) 2016, or
(b) regulation 11, 12, 13, 14 or 15 of WSP(LDRP)R(NI) 2016.
(1) In sections 671 to 674, except in relation to Northern Ireland—
"age-related amount" and "applicable amount" mean the amounts determined as such in accordance with regulations made under section 4 of JSA 1995;
"contribution-based jobseeker's allowance" means a jobseeker's allowance entitlement to which is based on the claimant's satisfying conditions which include those set out in section 2 of JSA 1995;
"income-based jobseeker's allowance" means a jobseeker's allowance entitlement to which is based on the claimant's satisfying conditions which include those set out in section 3 of JSA 1995 or a joint-claim jobseeker's allowance (which means a jobseeker's allowance entitlement to which arises by virtue of section 1(2B) of JSA 1995);
"couple" has the same meaning as in section 35(1) of JSA 1995.
(2) In sections 671 to 674, in relation to Northern Ireland—
"age-related amount" and "applicable amount" mean the amounts determined as such in accordance with regulations made under Article 6 of JS(NI)O 1995;
"contribution-based jobseeker's allowance" and "income-based jobseeker's allowance" have the same meaning as in Article 3(4) of JS(NI)O 1995;
"couple" has the same meaning as in Article 2(2) of JS(NI)O 1995.

(2003 c.1 s.676)

Increases in respect of children

Increases in respect of children

676.—No liability to income tax arises on a part of a taxable benefit listed in Table A which is attributable to an increase in respect of a child.

GENERAL NOTE

This was superseded from 2003/04 for incapacity benefit and carer's allowance, by the introduction of child tax credit, which is exempt from tax.

CHAPTER 5

UK SOCIAL SECURITY BENEFITS WHOLLY EXEMPT FROM INCOME TAX

UK social security benefits wholly exempt from tax: Table B

677.—(1) No liability to income tax arises on the United Kingdom social security benefits listed in Table B.

TABLE B—PART I

BENEFITS PAYABLE UNDER PRIMARY LEGISLATION AND NORTHERN IRELAND WELFARE SUPPLEMENTARY PAYMENTS

Social security benefit	Payable under	
Attendance allowance	SSCBA 1992	Section 64
	SSCB(NI)A 1992	Section 64
Adult Disability Payment	SS(S)A 2018	Sections 24 and 31
Back to work bonus	JSA 1995	Section 26
	JS(NI)O 1995	Article 28
Bereavement payment		
Best start grant	SS(S)A 2018	Sections 24 and 32
Child benefit	SSCBA 1992	Section 141
	SSCB(NI)A 1992	Section 137
Child's special allowance	SSCBA 1992	Section 56
	SSCB(NI)A 1992	Section 56
Child tax credit	TCA 2002	Part 1
Council tax benefit	SSCBA 1992	Section 131
Disability assistance for children and young people	SS(S)A 2018	Sections 24 and 31
Disability living allowance	SSCBA 1992	Section 71
	SSCB(NI)A 1992	Section 71
Discretionary housing payment	SS(S)A 2018	Section 88
Discretionary support award	DSR(NI) 2016	Regulation 2
Funeral expense assistance	SS(S)A 2018	Section 24 and 34
Flexible support fund payment	ETA 1973	Section 2
Guardian's allowance	SSCBA 1992	Section 77

	SSCB(NI)A 1992	Section 77
Health in Pregnancy Grant	SSCBA 1992	Section 140A
	SSCB(NI)A 1992	Section 136A
Housing benefit	SSCBA 1992	Section 130
	SSCB(NI)A 1992	Section 129
Income-related employment and support allowance	WRA 2007	Section 1(2)(b)
	Any provision made for Northern Ireland which corresponds to section 1(2)(b) of WRA 2007	
In-work credit	ETA 1973	Section 2
	ETA(NI) 1950	Section 1
In-work emergency discretion fund payment	ETA 1973	Section 2
In-work emergency fund payment	ETA(NI) 1950	Section 1
Industrial injuries benefit (apart from industrial death benefit)	SSCBA 1992	Section 94
	SSCB(NI)A 1992	Section 94
Job start	ETA 1973	Section 2
Pensioner's Christmas bonus	SSCBA 1992	Section 148
	SSCB(NI)A 1992	Section 144
Payments out of the social fund	SSCBA 1992	Section 138
Payments under a council tax reduction scheme: England	LGFA 1992	Section 13A(2)
Payments made under the Parental Transitions Support scheme	LGSA 2003	Section 20
Personal independence payment	WRA 2012	Section 77
	Any provision made for Northern Ireland which corresponds to section 77 of WRA 2012	
	SSCB(NI)A 1992	Section 134
Return to work credit	ETA 1973	Section 2
	ETA(NI) 1950	Section 1
Severe disablement allowance	SSCBA 1992	Section 68
	SSCB(NI)A 1992	Section 68
Short-term assistance	SS(S)A 2018	Section 36
State maternity allowance	SSCBA 1992	Section 35 or 35B
	Any provision made for Northern Ireland which corresponds to s.35 or 35B of SSCBA 1992	
State pension credit	SPCA 2000	Section 1
	SPCA(NI) 2002	Section 1
Universal Credit	WRA 2012	Part 1
	Any provision made for Northern Ireland which corresponds to Part 1 of WRA 2012	
Welfare supplementary payment payable pursuant a reduction of the amount payable of housing benefit	HB(WSP)R(NI) 2017	Regulation 2
	WSPR(NI) 2016	Regulation 4

Welfare supplementary payment payable pursuant to a reduction of the amount payable of employment and support allowance	WSP(LCP)R(NI) 2016 regulation 8 (when the recipient is entitled to the payment by meeting the condition in regulation 8(2)(b)) WSP(LDRP)R(NI) 2016 Regulation 20, 21 or 22	
Welfare supplementary payment payable pursuant to the loss of disability living allowance	WSP(LDLA)R(NI) 2016 Regulation 4, 8, 13 or 14	
Welfare supplementary payment payable pursuant to a reduction in the amount payable of state pension credit	WSP(LCP)R(NI) 2016 Regulation 16	
Welfare supplementary payment payable pursuant to a reduction in the amount payable of working tax credit	WSP(LDRP)R(NI) 2016 Regulation 27 or 28	
Welfare supplementary payment payable pursuant to a reduction in the amount payable of state pension tax credit	WSP(LDRP)R(NI) 2016 Regulation 33 or 34	
Winter heating assistance	SS(S)A 2018	Section 30
Working tax credit	TCA 2002	Part 1
Young carer grant	SS(S)A 2018	Section 24 and 28

(1A) In this section—
(a) "the Covid Winter Grant Scheme" means the scheme that was the subject of guidance published by the Department for Work and Pensions on 23 November 2020; and
(b) "the Covid Local Support Grant" means the grant that was the subject of guidance published by that Department on 17 April 2021 and further guidance published by that Department on 21 June 2021.
(1B) References in this section to payments made pursuant to—
(a) the Covid Winter Grant Scheme or the Covid Local Support Grant; or
(b) any scheme or grant in Scotland, Wales or Northern Ireland corresponding to the scheme or grant in sub-paragraph (a),
are references only to payments made pursuant to such a scheme or grant for the tax year 2020–21 and subsequent tax years.

Income Tax (Earnings and Pensions) Act 2003

Table B—Part 2

1.609 Benefits Payable Under Regulations

Social security benefit		Payable under regulations made under
Discretionary housing payment	CSPSSA 2000	Section 69
Payments made under the Best Start Foods scheme	SSA 1998	Section 13
Payments made under the Healthy Start scheme	SSA 1998	Section 13
Payments to reduce under-occupation by housing benefit claimants	WRPA 1999 WRP(NI)O 1999	Section 79 Article 70
Payment under a council tax reduction scheme: Wales	LGFA 1992	Section 13A(4)
Scottish child payment	SS(S)A 2018	Section 79

(2) Industrial death benefit is charged to tax under Part 9 (see section 577).

(3) In this section "industrial death benefit" means any benefit payable under—
  (a) section 94 of, and Part 6 of Schedule 7 to, SSCBA 1992; or
  (b) section 94 of, and Part 6 of Schedule 7 to, SSCB(NI)A 1992.

(4) In this section—
  (a) "the Council Tax Rebate Discretionary Fund" means the grant that was the subject of guidance published by the Department for Levelling up, Housing and Communities on 23 February 2022 (and as updated from time to time);
  (b) "the Household Support Fund Grant" means any grant paid under the Household Support Fund Grant Determination No 31/5787 and subsequent determinations made under section 31 of LGA 2003 to provide support of a similar nature.

(5) References in this section to payments made pursuant to any scheme or grant in Scotland, Wales or Northern Ireland corresponding to any scheme or grant defined in subparagraphs (a) and (b) of section 4 are references only to payments made pursuant to such a scheme or grant for the tax year 2021–22 and subsequent tax years.

General Note

1.610 The provisions in both tables need amending to deal with the changes to social security benefits and the replacement of council tax benefit with council tax reduction under the Welfare Reform Act 2012. It may, however, be argued that council tax reductions are no longer in a form that can be regarded as a social security benefit and therefore as income and do not need any exempting provision.

A revised definition of "state maternity allowance" was inserted by reg.3 of the Social Security (Maternity Allowance) (Participating Wife or Civil Partner of Self-employed Earner) Regulations 2014 (SI 2014/606).

Chapter 6

Taxable Foreign Benefits

Taxable benefits: foreign benefits

678.—(1) This section applies to any benefit which is payable under the law of a country or territory outside the United Kingdom if—
  (a) it is substantially similar in character to a benefit listed in Table A, and
  (b) it is payable to a person resident in the United Kingdom.
(2) But this section does not apply to a benefit which is charged to tax under Pt 9 (pension income).

General Note

This is a new statutory provision in ITEPA. Until its enactment, the Revenue and Customs refrained from taxing foreign social security benefits on the basis of an extra-statutory concession. The only real problem area is the divide between social security income, exempt under this provision, and pension income, taxed under Pt 9.

Taxable social security income

679.—(1) If section 678 applies, the taxable social security income for a taxable benefit for a tax year is the full amount of the social security income arising in the tax year, but subject to subsection (2).
(2) That income is treated as relevant foreign income for the purposes of Chapters 2 and 3 of Part 8 of ITTOIA 2005 (relevant foreign income: remittance basis and deductions and reliefs).
(3) See also Chapter 4 of that Part (unremittable income).

Person liable for tax

680.—The person liable for any tax charged under this Part on a benefit to which section 678 applies is the person receiving or entitled to the benefit.

Part 13

Supplementary Provisions

Interpretation

Other definitions

721.—(1) In this Act—
  "cash voucher" has the same meaning as in Chapter 4 of Part 3 (see section 75);
  "the Contributions and Benefits Act" means SSCBA 1992 or SSCB(NI) A 1992;

"credit-token" has the same meaning as in Chapter 4 of Part 3 (see section 92);

"foreign employer" means an individual, partnership or body of persons resident outside, and not resident in, the United Kingdom;

"non-cash voucher" has the same meaning as in Chapter 4 of Part 3 (see section 84);

(3) Any reference in this Act to being domiciled in the United Kingdom is to be read as a reference to being domiciled in any part of the United Kingdom.

(4) For the purposes of this Act the following are members of a person's family—
   (a) the person's spouse or civil partner,
   (b) the person's children and their spouses or civil partners,
   (c) the person's parents, and
   (d) the person's dependants.

(5) For the purposes of this Act the following are members of a person's family or household—
   (a) members of the person's family,
   (b) the person's domestic staff, and
   (c) the person's guests.

(6) The following provisions (which relate to the legal equality of illegitimate children) are to be disregarded in interpreting references in this Act to a child or children—
   (a) section 1 of the Family Law Reform Act 1987 (Chapter 42),
   (b) the paragraph inserted in Schedule 1 to the Interpretation Act 1978 (Chapter 30) by paragraph 73 of Schedule 2 to the 1987 Act,
   (c) section 1(2) of the Law Reform (Parent and Child) (Scotland) Act 1986 (Chapter 9),
   (d) Article 155 of the Children (Northern Ireland) Order 1995 (SI 1995 No.755 (NI 2)).

(7) In the employment income Parts any reference to earnings which is not limited by the context—
   (a) to earnings within Chapter 1 of Part 3, or
   (b) to any other particular description of earnings; includes a reference to any amount treated as earnings by any of the provisions mentioned in section 7(5) (meaning of "employment income" etc.).

GENERAL NOTE

1.616 See further for definitions ITA 2007 Sch.4 of which (not included in this work) includes an index of terms defined for the Income Tax Acts.

Child Trust Funds Act 2004

(2004 c.6)

ARRANGEMENT OF SECTIONS

Introductory

1.617 1. Child trust funds
2. Eligible children

3. Requirements to be satisfied
4. Inalienability

Opening and transfers

5. Opening by responsible person or child
6. Opening by Inland Revenue
7. Transfers
7A. Transfers to other accounts for children
7B. Transfers on child reaching 18
7C. Powers to safeguard interests of children

Contributions and subscriptions

8. Initial contribution by Inland Revenue
9. Supplementary contribution by Inland Revenue
10. Further contributions by Inland Revenue
11. Recouping Inland Revenue contributions
12. Subscription limits

Tax

13. Relief from income tax and capital gains tax
14. Insurance companies and friendly societies

Information etc.

15. Information from account providers, etc.
16. Information about children in care of authority
17. Use of information
18. Disclosure of information

Payments after death

19. Payments after death of child

Penalties

20. Penalties
21. Decisions, appeals, mitigation and recovery

Appeals

22. Rights of appeal
23. Exercise of rights of appeal
24. Temporary modifications

Child Trust Funds Act 2004

Supplementary

25. Northern Ireland
26. Money
27. Commencement
28. Regulations and orders
29. Interpretation
30. Extent
31. Short title

An Act to make provision about child trust funds and for connected purposes.

INTRODUCTION AND GENERAL NOTE

1.618 The basic scheme of the Child Trust Fund Act 2004 is that all children in the UK born after August 31, 2002 will have a "child trust fund account", which will in effect be a universal savings policy. Building societies and other financial institutions will have to seek HMRC approval to be an "account provider" under this Act. It is a condition of approval that account providers offer equity-based stakeholder accounts (although cash accounts may also be offered). The Treasury provides an initial endowment of £250 for each child at the point when the account is opened, or £500 in the case of children in low income families or those who are being looked after by a local authority. The Government subsequently approved a further endowment (of £250, or £500 for children in low income families) when every child reaches the age of seven. Parents, relatives and family friends are able to make further contributions to the child trust fund account at any time. The minimum such investment is £10 (unless the account provider permits smaller deposits) and the maximum annual aggregate contribution by family and friends is £1,200. Subject to some very narrow exceptions, no withdrawals will be permitted until the child is 18, so that the child reaches adulthood with a "nest-egg" which can then be re-invested, spent on education or setting up in business, etc. The cost of the scheme is estimated to be in the order of £4 billion over 18 years.

The Government has set out four objectives for child trust fund accounts. These are "to help people understand the benefits of saving and investing; to encourage parents and children to develop the savings habit; to ensure that all children have a financial asset at the start of their adult life; and to build on financial education and help people make better financial choices throughout their lives" (Lord McIntosh of Haringey, Parliamentary Under-Secretary of State, *Hansard* HL Debates Vol.658, col.351, February 26, 2004). The Child Trust Fund Act may thus be seen as an example of the Government's commitment to the principles of "asset-based welfare" and "progressive universalism". It will, of course, take some time to assess whether the scheme fulfils its goals.

The idea of child trust funds emerged through the work of the Institute of Public Policy Research (IPPR) in 2000 and was canvassed by the Treasury in its consultation paper *Savings and Assets for All*, The Modernisation of Britain's Tax and Benefit System, Number 8 (April 2001). The proposal also appeared in the Labour Party's 2001 general election manifesto. The Government set out its proposals more fully in the Treasury papers *Delivering Saving and Assets* (November 2001) and especially in *Detailed proposals for the Child Trust Fund* (October 2003). The House of Commons Treasury Committee has issued a report supporting the initiative, although making some further recommendations: *Child Trusts Funds* (Second Report of Session 2003–04, HC 86), and see further *Government Response to the Committee's Second Report on Child Trust Funds* (HC 86) (First Special Report of Session 2003–04, HC 387). In the 2003 Budget the Chancellor of the Exchequer announced the Government's intention that the scheme should commence operations in April 2005 (but confirming that it would also apply to all children born after August 31, 2002). For a full analysis of the scheme, see N. Wikeley, "Child Trust Funds—asset-based welfare or a recipe for increased inequality?" (2004) 11 *Journal of Social Security Law* 189.

(2004 c.6)

Section 1 of the Act explains what is meant by a child trust fund, whilst s.2 defines the crucial qualifying category of "eligible children". The nature and management of child trust fund accounts is governed by s.3. Funds in such accounts are inalienable (s.4). The expectation is that accounts will be opened by a "responsible person", typically a parent, or by the child (in the case of a child aged 16 or over, who, for example, has just arrived in the country); see s.5, which makes the award of child benefit the trigger for entitlement to a child trust fund account. The fallback position is that HMRC will open an account (s.6) for any child lacking a child trust fund. Accounts may be transferred to another financial institution (s.7). The initial and supplementary Treasury contributions to be made at the opening of the account are governed by ss.8 and 9. All children receive the initial contribution under s.8 (children being looked after by local authorities receive a higher rate) and children in low income families qualify for the supplementary contribution under s.9. Section 10 makes provision for further Treasury contributions to be made at some late date (or dates). Where Treasury contributions have been credited in error, they can be recovered by virtue of s.11. Section 12 deals with contributions by parents and others to child trust fund accounts. The tax position is covered by ss.13 and 14 while ss.15–18 make provision for the disclosure and exchange of information relating to accounts. Section 19 makes special provision for the situation where a payment is due after a child beneficiary has died. Sections 20 and 21 concern penalties and ss.22–24 set out appeal rights. The remaining sections of the Act are supplementary in nature (ss.25–31). The first regulations under the Act are the Child Trust Funds Regulations 2004 (SI 2004/1450).

1.619

A child trust fund is not a "reportable account" for the purpose of the International Tax Compliance Regulations 2015 (SI 2015/878), which were introduced to give effect to Council Directive 2011/16/EU ("the DAC") and other international agreements designed to improve international tax compliance (see reg.2(2)(a) and Sch.2 para.5 of the 2015 Regulations).

The future of child trust funds
On May 24, 2010, the coalition Government announced that as part of its package of saving £6.2 billion in 2010/11, it would save £320 million from reducing and then stopping government contributions to the Child Trust Fund. The Government proposed to scale back payments from August 2010 and then to stop payments from January 1, 2011. Section 1 of the Savings Accounts and Health in Pregnancy Grant Act 2010 subsequently implemented the second phase of the cancellation of the scheme by stopping all government payments altogether. It did this by amending s.2 of the 2004 Act to remove eligibility from children born after January 2, 2011 and from certain children who would otherwise become eligible on or after that date.

1.620

See further S. McKay, L. Tian and A. Lymer, "What happened to the Child Trust Fund? The abandonment of universal savings for UK children" (2024) 58 *Social Policy and Administration* 18–38.

Commencement and extent
The supplementary provisions in this Act (ss.25–31) came into force on Royal Assent (May 13, 2004): see s.27. Various procedural provisions came into force on January 1, 2005: Child Trust Funds Act 2004 (Commencement No.1) Order 2004 (SI 2004/2422 (C.103). The remainder of the Act was brought into force by the Child Trust Funds Act 2004 (Commencement No.2) Order 200 (SI 2004/3369 (C.158). The Child Trust Funds Regulations 2004 (SI 2004/1450) came into force for various purposes on January 1, 2005 and for remaining purposes on "the appointed day", namely April 6, 2005. The Act extends to the whole of the UK (see further ss.25 and 30).

1.621

Child Trust Funds Act 2004

Introductory

Child trust funds

1.622 **1.**—(1) This Act makes provision about child trust funds and related matters.

(2) In this Act "child trust fund" means an account which—
(a) is held by a child who is or has been an eligible child (see section 2),
(b) satisfies the requirements imposed by and by virtue of this Act (see section 3), and
(c) has been opened in accordance with this Act (see sections 5 and 6).

(3) The matters dealt with by and under this Act are to be under the care and management of the Inland Revenue.

DEFINITIONS

"child"—s.29.
"child trust fund"—subs.(2) and s.29.
"eligible child"—ss.2 and 29.
"Inland Revenue"—s.29.

GENERAL NOTE

1.623 This is a genuinely introductory section.

Subsection (1)

1.624 This provision is no more illuminating than the long title to the Act.

Subsection (2)

1.625 This is more helpful than subs.(1) in that it stipulates the three defining characteristics of a child trust fund—that it be held by an "eligible child" (see s.2), that it meet the statutory requirements (see s.3) and that it has been opened in the appropriate manner (either by a "responsible person" (typically a parent) under s.5 or by HMRC under s.6).

Subsection (3)

1.626 This reflects a standard principle of revenue law (see, e.g. Taxes Management Act 1970 s.1(1)), namely that such matters are "under the care and management of the Inland Revenue". The only difference is one of nomenclature in the reference to "the Inland Revenue", rather than the more usual statutory formula of "the Board". This principle enables the Revenue to apply the law with a degree of administrative flexibility in appropriate cases. For example, in the context of taxation, this is the basis upon which the Revenue has traditionally promulgated extra-statutory concessions and reached settlements in disputes with taxpayers.

Eligible children

1.627 **2.**—(1) For the purposes of this Act a child is an "eligible child" if the child was born after 31st August 2002 [² and before 3rd January 2011] and either—
(a) a person is entitled to child benefit in respect of the child, or
(b) entitlement to child benefit in respect of the child is excluded by the provisions specified in subsection (2)(a) or (b) (children in care of authority),
but subject as follows.

(2) The provisions referred to in subsection (1)(b) are—
  (a) paragraph 1(c) of Schedule 9 to the Social Security Contributions and Benefits Act 1992 (c. 4) and regulations made under it, and
  (b) paragraph 1(1)(f) of Schedule 9 to the Social Security Contributions and Benefits (Northern Ireland) Act 1992 (c. 7) and regulations made under it.

(3) Where entitlement to child benefit in respect of a child is excluded because of a directly applicable Community provision or an international agreement, subsection (1) applies as if that exclusion did not apply.

(4) Where a person is entitled to child benefit in respect of a child only because of a directly applicable Community provision or an international agreement, subsection (1) applies as if the person were not so entitled.

(5) A child who—
  (a) does not have the right of abode in the United Kingdom within the meaning given by section 2 of the Immigration Act 1971 (c.77),
  [¹(b) is not entitled to enter or remain in the United Kingdom by virtue of an enforceable Community right or any provision made under section 2(2) of the European Communities Act 1972, and]
  (c) is not settled in the United Kingdom within the meaning given by section 33(2A) of the Immigration Act 1971,
is not an eligible child.

[² (5A) A child born before 3rd January 2011 who would otherwise have become an eligible child on or after that date is not an eligible child unless subsection (5B) or (5C) applies to the child.

(5B) This subsection applies to a child (who accordingly is an eligible child by virtue of subsection (1)(a)) if—
  (a) a person is entitled to child benefit in respect of the child,
  (b) the first day for which child benefit is paid falls on or before 3rd January 2011, and
  (c) either subsection (5) does not apply to the child at the beginning of 3rd January 2011, or that subsection applies to the child at that time but ceases to apply to the child before 3rd April 2011.

(5C) This subsection applies to a child (who accordingly is an eligible child by virtue of subsection (1)(b)) if—
  (a) the child is in the United Kingdom at the beginning of 3rd January 2011,
  (b) the provisions specified in subsection (2)(a) or (b) apply in relation to the child before 3rd April 2011, and
  (c) either subsection (5) does not apply to the child at the beginning of 3rd January 2011, or that subsection applies to the child at that time but ceases to apply to the child before 3rd April 2011.]

(6) A person is not to be regarded for the purposes of subsection (1)(a) [or 5B(a)] as entitled to child benefit in respect of a child (otherwise than by virtue of subsection (3)) unless it has been decided in accordance with—
  (a) Chapter 2 of Part 1 of the Social Security Act 1998 (c.14), or
  (b) Chapter 2 of Part 2 of the Social Security (Northern Ireland) Order 1998 (SI 1998/1506 (N.I. 10)),
that the person is so entitled (and that decision has not been overturned).

(7) Regulations may amend subsection (1) by substituting for the reference to 31st August 2002 a reference to an earlier date.

Amendments

1. Immigration (European Economic Area) (Amendment) Regulations 2009 (SI 2009/1117) reg.3 and Sch.2 para.1 (June 1, 2009).
2. Savings Accounts and Health in Pregnancy Grant Act 2010 s.1 (December 16, 2010).

Definitions

"child"—s.29.
"eligible child"—subs.(1) and s.29.

General Note

1.628 This section defines the concept of an "eligible child", the first of the three fundamental features of a child trust fund. The basic definition is to be found in subs.(1), as expanded by subs.(2) to deal with the special case of children being looked after by a local authority. Cases that have an international dimension are covered by subss.(3)–(5). Subsection (6) acts as a definition provision for subs.(1). Subsection (7) provides the potential for the scope of the child trust fund scheme to be expanded to include children born before the cut-off date for eligibility for a child trust fund.

Subsection (1)

1.629 This is the core definition of who is an "eligible child". There are two basic rules. First, the child must have been born *after* August 31, 2002. This date was chosen to align entitlement with the school year (at least in England and Wales), so that all pupils in any given school year (after that date) would be equally entitled. There will, however, be cases involving siblings born either side of the eligibility date: for the position of children who were born *before* September 1, 2002, see further the annotation to subs.(7) below. Secondly, the child must have been born *before* January 3, 2011. This reflects the coalition Government's decision to close down access to the child trust fund scheme. Thirdly, *either* someone must be entitled to child benefit for that child (subs.(1)(a); see further subs.(6)) *or* that person's entitlement is excluded because the child is being looked after by a local authority (subss.(1)(b) and (2)). Thus in general terms, and subject to that special case, entitlement to child benefit is employed as a gateway to eligibility for a child trust fund. Subsections (3)–(5) make special provision for cases with an international dimension.

Subsection (2)

1.630 The case of a child being looked after by a local authority is the only situation in which the rule requiring that a person be entitled to child benefit in respect of the child is waived. It must follow that in the other situations set out in SSCBA 1992 Sch.9 in which there is no entitlement to child benefit, there is also no entitlement to a child trust fund. These situations include children in detention (but see s.10(4)) and married children. These exclusions, and particularly the latter, may eventually affect a handful of children who are recent immigrants to the country.

Subsection (3)

1.631 There will be some children who live in the UK but in respect of whom child benefit is not payable because of EU law or an international agreement. This provision ensures that such children remain eligible for a child trust fund, notwithstanding that there is no child benefit entitlement. In practice this will apply most commonly to some children who live in Northern Ireland but whose parent works in the Republic of Ireland. In such circumstances, under the EU rules governing the benefit entitlement of migrant workers in Regulation 1408/71, child benefit is payable by the benefit authorities in the Republic. As a result of subs.(3) such children are eligible for a child trust fund account.

(2004 c.6 s.2)

Subsection (4)

This deals with the converse position to that in subs.(3). In some cases there is entitlement to child benefit in the UK solely because of provisions in EU law or under an international agreement. This would apply where a citizen and resident of the Republic of Ireland (or any other EU country) works in the UK but his or her child lives in the Republic (or other Member State). Again, EU Regulation 1408/71 provides that child benefit is payable by the UK authorities. This subsection provides, in effect, that children in this type of case will not be eligible for a child trust fund, unless and until they come to live in the UK. This will affect fewer than 500 children, according to official estimates. The Government's view is that "there is no case for the UK Government to pay endowments to encourage saving for and by children whose ties are not within the UK" (Ruth Kelly, Financial Secretary to the Treasury, Standing Committee A, col.37, January 6, 2004). This exclusion will not affect the special position of the children of Crown servants, such as army personnel, who are entitled to child benefit when stationed overseas by virtue of a provision in purely domestic law (Child Benefit (General) Regulations 2003 (SI 2003/493) reg.30).

1.632

However, it is by no means certain that the exclusion of EU workers (and their children) who reside outside but work in the UK from eligibility for child trust funds will necessarily survive legal scrutiny. There are a number of different avenues that might be used to challenge the validity of this provision under EU law. First, art.7(2) of EU Regulation 1612/68 requires migrant workers to "enjoy the same social and tax advantages as national workers". Of course, one of the fundamental purposes of the child trust fund scheme is to benefit the child, rather than the worker. Indeed, case law demonstrates that the social or tax advantage must be of some direct or indirect benefit to the worker, and not just to a family member (*Centre Public d'Aide Sociale de Courcelles v Lebon* (316/85) [1987] E.C.R. 2811). But a broad view of the child trust fund scheme might meet this requirement. See also *Reina v Landeskredit Bank Baden-Württemberg* (65/81) [1982] E.C.R. 33, in which it was held that an interest-free childbirth loan granted only to German nationals was a social advantage within art.7(2), and so could not be denied to an Italian couple. Although one of the fundamental objectives of the child trust fund scheme is to benefit *children* by providing them with a valuable asset on attaining their majority, it does not require too much imagination to see that the scheme might be construed as being of indirect benefit to the parent-worker. Yet the other purposes of the 2004 Act are framed in terms of domestic policy imperatives, such as encouraging savings, which have no obvious linkage with the free movement of labour. Moreover, the ECJ jurisprudence on art.7(2) has typically concerned the migrant worker who goes both to work and *live* in another Member State, and not merely to work there; the problem identified in this note is strictly more to do with "frontier workers" than "migrant workers". On that basis, therefore, it may be that s.2(4) is not inconsistent with art.7(2) of Regulation 1612/68.

Even if this is the case, it does not necessarily follow that s.2(4) is EU-compliant. A second or parallel type of challenge might be made on the basis that the child trust fund scheme confers a "family benefit" within the scope of Regulation 1408/71, so bringing into play Ch.7 of that Regulation. Given the linkage between entitlement to child benefit and eligibility for a child trust fund payment, this point is at least arguable. Finally, there remains the broader argument that this provision in the 2004 Act is in breach of art.12 of the Treaty itself, which prohibits "within the scope of the application" of the Treaty "any discrimination on grounds of nationality". Section 2(4) makes no express reference to parents' nationality, but may be viewed as indirectly discriminatory in that its operation in practice is more likely to affect (for example) Irish nationals than British nationals. In recent years the ECJ has demonstrated greater willingness to invoke art.12 for the benefit of citizens of other Member States (see, e.g. *Martinez Sala* [1998] E.C.R. I-2691 and *Grzelczyk* (C-184/99) [2001] E.C.R. I-6193; *R. (Bidar) v Ealing London BC* (C-209/03) [2005] 2 W.L.R. 1078; and see further, R.C.A. White, "Residence, Benefit Entitlement and Community Law" [2005] 12 *Journal of Social Security Law* 10).

Subsection (5)

1.633 A child who lacks a proper immigration status cannot be an "eligible child". This covers children who, under the Immigration Act 1971, have no right of abode or are not settled in the UK. However, subs.(5)(c) may give rise to problems in the context of citizenship of the Union: see further the Advocate General's Opinion of November 11, 2004 in *Bidar* (C-209/03). Children who have no entitlement to reside in the UK under EEA law are likewise excluded from access to the child trust fund scheme.

Subsections (5A)–(5C)

1.634 Subsection (5A) provides that a child born *before* January 3, 2011 who would otherwise become eligible *on or after* that date may not be an eligible child unless either subs.(5B) or (5C) applies.

Subsection (5B)(a) and (b) reflect the processes involved in claiming child benefit and the fact that entitlement can only commence on a Monday and can only be backdated for up to three months. Subsection (5B)(c) reflects the fact that a child who is subject to immigration control is not an eligible child under subs.(5), even though child benefit may be being received in respect of that child. To provide parity with the possibility of backdating for three months under the child benefit regime, the same window of three months will apply to such children born before January 3, 2011.

Subsection (5C) provides that a looked-after child born before January 3, 2011 will still be an eligible looked-after child if the conditions set out there are met. The requirement that the child becomes a looked-after child before April 3, 2011 provides parity with the child qualifying under the usual child benefit route.

Subsection (6)

1.635 This provides that a person is not entitled to child benefit until a decision has been taken to that effect (and has not been overturned) in accordance with the SSA Act 1998 (or its Northern Ireland equivalent). Thus HMRC decision to award child benefit acts as the trigger for eligibility for a child trust fund account.

Subsection (7)

1.636 For the purposes of this Act a child is only an "eligible child" if born after August 31, 2002 (subs.(1)). This provision allows the Government to use secondary legislation to substitute an earlier date for the purpose of this definition, thus bringing older children into the scope of eligibility for a child trust fund account. Given the effect of the 2010 amendments, requiring that an eligible child must have been born *before* January 3, 2011, and thereafter closing the child trust funds scheme, there is clearly no prospect of this power being exercised.

Requirements to be satisfied

1.637 **3.**—(1) A child trust fund may be held only with a person (referred to in this Act as an "account provider") who has been approved by the Inland Revenue in accordance with regulations.

(2) An account is not a child trust fund unless it is an account of one of the descriptions prescribed by regulations.

(3) The provision which may be made by regulations under subsection (1) includes making approval of an account provider dependent on the person undertaking to provide accounts of such of the descriptions for which provision is made by regulations under subsection (2) as is prescribed by the regulations.

(4) The terms of a child trust fund must—
   (a) secure that it is held in the name of a child,
   (b) secure that the child is beneficially entitled to the investments under it,

(c) secure that all income and gains arising on investments under it constitute investments under it,
(d) prevent withdrawals from it except as permitted by regulations [¹ under this section or any other provision of this Act], and
(e) provide that instructions may be given to the account provider with respect to its management only by the person who has the authority to manage it.

(5) Regulations may impose other requirements which must be satisfied in relation to child trust funds.

(6) The person who has the authority to manage a child trust fund held by a child—
[² (a) if the child is 16 or over and has elected to manage the child trust fund, is the child;
(b) in any other case, is the person who has that authority by virtue of subsection (7) (but subject to subsection (10)).]

(7) If there is one person who is a responsible person in relation to the child, that person has that authority; and if there is more than one person who is such a person, which of them has that authority is to be determined in accordance with regulations.

(8) For the purposes of this Act a person is a responsible person in relation to a child [² ...] if the person has parental responsibility in relation to the child and is not—
(a) a local authority or, in Northern Ireland, an authority within the meaning of the Children (Northern Ireland) Order 1995 (S.I. 1995/755 (N.I. 2)), or
(b) a person under 16.

(9) "Parental responsibility" means—
(a) parental responsibility within the meaning of the Children Act 1989 (c.41) or the Children (Northern Ireland) Order 1995, or
(b) parental responsibilities within the meaning of the Children (Scotland) Act 1995 (c.36).

(10) Regulations may provide that, in circumstances prescribed by the regulations, the person who has the authority to manage a child trust fund held by a child [² ...][² is to be a person appointed by the Treasury or by the Secretary of State]

(11) A person who has the authority to manage a child trust fund by virtue of subsection (10) is entitled to give any instructions to the account provider with respect to its management which appear to the person who has that authority to be for the benefit of the child.

[² (11A) Regulations under subsection (10) may provide that, where the terms on which a person is appointed by the Treasury or by the Secretary of State include provision for payment to the person, the payment must be made by a government department specified in the regulations (instead of by the person making the appointment).

(11B) Regulations may provide that, where a person authorised to manage a child trust fund by virtue of subsection (10) ceases to be so authorised, the person must provide any information held by that person in connection with the management of the fund to the person (if any) who becomes authorised by virtue of that subsection to manage the trust fund instead.]

(12) Where a contract is entered into by or on behalf of a child who is 16 or over in connection with a child trust fund—
(a) held by the child, or

(b) held by another child in relation to whom the child has parental responsibility,

the contract has effect as if the child had been 18 or over when it was entered into.

AMENDMENTS

1. Deregulation Act 2015 s.62(4) (March 26, 2015 for purposes of making regulations, April 6, 2015 for other purposes).
2. Deregulation Act 2015 ss.60 and 61 (May 26, 2015).

DEFINITIONS

"account provider"—subs.(1) and s.29.
"child"—s.29.
"child trust fund"—s.29.
"Inland Revenue"—s.29.
"parental responsibility"—subs.(9).
"responsible person"—subs.(8).

GENERAL NOTE

1.638 This section sets out various administrative and procedural requirements which must be satisfied in order for a child trust fund account to come into existence. Only authorised financial institutions may offer child trust fund accounts (subs.(1)) and such accounts must meet a number of criteria (subss.(2)–(5)). This section also defines who has the authority to manage the child's account. This will usually be a person with parental responsibility or, in the case of a child aged at least 16, the child him or herself (subss.(6)–(12)).

Subsection (1)

1.639 Financial institutions, known as "account providers" in this Act, must be approved by HMRC before they can offer child trust fund accounts. The details of the approval process, which are set out in regulations, are modelled on those that apply to Individual Savings Accounts (ISAs) (see Child Trust Funds Regulations 2004 regs 14–17 and 19–20). Institutions denied approval have a right of appeal (see s.22(1)).

Subsection (2)

1.640 Approval operates at two levels. First, the account provider itself must be approved by HMRC under subs.(1). Secondly, by virtue of this subsection, only certain types of accounts may qualify as child trust fund accounts. In order to qualify an account must meet the criteria which are set out in regulations and are based on the arrangements governing ISAs (see Child Trust Funds Regulations 2004 reg.8).

Subsection (3)

1.641 This provision means that the regulations governing the approval of financial institutions may require account providers to provide particular types of account as a condition of such approval. The general rule is that, in order to be authorised as an account provider for the purposes of the child trust fund scheme, institutions must offer stakeholder accounts to the general public (see Child Trust Funds Regulations 2004 reg.14(2)(b)(i)). The characteristics of a stakeholder account are defined in the Schedule to the Regulations. The policy justification for this requirement is that it will enable beneficiaries to gain from the potentially higher returns from equities as a long-term investment. Further, the risk of a fall in the value of equities is reduced by the requirement to spread the investment over a number of companies (*ibid.*, para.2(2)(c)) and to transfer the investment to other assets (e.g. cash or gilts) as the maturity date nears.

Subsection (4)

This provision sets out the core requirements which must be met in order for an account to qualify for the purposes of the child trust fund scheme. For further details, see Child Trust Funds Regulations 2004 reg.8.

1.642

The general rule is that no withdrawals are permitted from a child trust fund account before the child attains 18 (subs.(4)(d)). The Government's argument is that this restriction is essential if such accounts are to achieve their long-term goals. The only exceptions to this principle in the regulations as originally drafted related to withdrawals on closure in the event of the child's death and to deductions for management charges due (Child Trust Funds Regulations 2004 reg.18; there is a cap of 1.5 per cent on administration fees: *ibid.*, Sch. para.3(2)). However, following sustained pressure in Parliament, the Government conceded that a further exception should be made in the case of children suffering from a terminal illness. See now Child Trust Funds Regulations 2004 reg.18A. In contrast to the tight restrictions on withdrawals before the age of 18, there are no controls whatsoever on how young adults apply their child trust fund account holdings on reaching that age.

Subsection (5)

For further details, see Child Trust Funds Regulations 2004 reg.8.

1.643

Subsection (6)

The effect of this provision, taken together with the definitions and qualifications in the following subsections, is that the child trust fund account is managed by the child, if they are 16 or over, and otherwise by the person with parental responsibility in respect of that child. This provision was inserted as a government amendment to the original Bill, which had given 16 and 17-year-olds in Scotland the right to manage their accounts, but not their peers south of the border (reflecting the special rules in Scots law relating to the age of majority). Following debate, the Government accepted that it was difficult to sustain this distinction in the context of the child trust fund, and so brought forward this provision to ensure that all 16 and 17-year-olds in the UK have the right to manage their child trust fund account. Such individuals are deemed to have full contractual authority to manage their accounts by virtue of subs.(12). They will not be able to withdraw funds until they reach the age of 18 (see subs.(4)(d)).

1.644

Subsections (7)–(9)

In the case of children under the age of 16, the "responsible person" is designated as the individual with the authority to manage the child trust fund account (subs.(7)). The basic rule is that the "responsible person" in respect of a child under 16 is the person with parental responsibility for that child under the Children Act 1989 (or the relevant legislation for other parts of the UK: see subs.(9)). There are two exceptions to this rule (subs.(8))—first, a local authority (which may have parental responsibility by virtue of a care order) cannot be a "responsible person"; secondly, a young parent under the age of 16 cannot assume that role. It follows, for example, that the child trust fund accounts of both a 15-year-old mother and her baby will have to be managed by a third party.

1.645

It is common, of course, for two individuals to share parental responsibility for a child, as in the case of a married couple (Children Act 1989 s.2(1)). In such cases voucher will be sent to the holder of the child benefit award (see s.5 and Child Trust Funds Regulations 2004 reg.3(2)). Moreover, there can be only one person with authority to manage the child trust fund account, known as the "registered contact" (Child Trust Funds Regulations 2004 reg.8(1)(d)). Typically this will be a "single responsible person", i.e. a person with parental responsibility (see further *ibid.*, reg.13).

Subsection (10)

This was another government amendment to the original Bill. It is designed to deal with the problem created by the lack of a "responsible person" for some children in local authority care. A local authority cannot be a responsible person (subs.

1.646

(8)(a)). In the case of most children being looked after by a local authority, this will not matter, as the child's parent will retain parental responsibility and so be a responsible person. However, there will be a minority of cases in which no individual person holds parental responsibility (e.g. some orphans in care). The Government has announced that the Official Solicitor (in England, Wales and Northern Ireland) or the Accountant of Court (in Scotland) will undertake the function of managing the accounts of children in care for whom there is no one with parental responsibility. See now Child Trust Funds Regulations 2004 reg.33A.

Inalienability

1.647

4.—(1) Any assignment of, or agreement to assign, investments under a child trust fund, and any charge on or agreement to charge any such investments, is void.

(2) On the bankruptcy of a child by whom a child trust fund is held, the entitlement to investments under it does not pass to any trustee or other person acting on behalf of the child's creditors.

(3) "Assignment" includes assignation; and "assign" is to be construed accordingly.

(4) "Charge on or agreement to charge" includes a right in security over or an agreement to create a right in security over.

(5) "Bankruptcy", in relation to a child, includes the sequestration of the child's estate.

DEFINITIONS

"assign"—subs.(3).
"assignment"—subs.(3).
"bankruptcy"—subs.(5)
"charge on or agreement to charge"—subs.(4).
"child trust fund"—s.29.

GENERAL NOTE

1.648

The principle of the inalienability of social security benefits is enshrined in SSAA 1992 s.187 (see also Tax Credits Act 2002 s.45). This section provides, in similar fashion, for the inalienability of investments held under a child trust fund. The parallel provision in SSAA 1992 s.187 was applied (in the Scottish context) in *Mulvey v Secretary of State for Social Security* 1997 S.C. (HL) 105, where the House of Lords held that the bankrupt's right to income support could not be owed to the permanent trustee (the Scottish equivalent of a trustee in bankruptcy). However, the House of Lords held that deductions could lawfully be made from income support to pay a social fund debt incurred prior to sequestration.

Opening and transfers

Opening by responsible person or child

1.649

5.—(1) In the case of each child who is first an eligible child by virtue of section 2(1)(a) the Inland Revenue must issue, in a manner prescribed by regulations, a voucher in such form as is so prescribed.

(2) The voucher must be issued to the person who is entitled to child benefit in respect of the child (or, in the case of a child who is such an eligible child because of section 2(3), to a responsible person).

(3) An application may be made—
(a) if the child is 16 or over, by the child, or
(b) otherwise, by a responsible person,
to open for the child with an account provider a child trust fund of any description provided by the account provider.

(4) The application is to be made—
(a) within such period beginning with the day on which the voucher is issued as is prescribed by regulations, and
(b) in accordance with regulations.

(5) When the application has been made the account provider must—
(a) open, in accordance with regulations, a child trust fund of that description for the child, and
(b) inform the Inland Revenue in accordance with regulations.

DEFINITIONS

"account provider"—s.29.
"child"—s.29.
"child trust fund"—s.29.
"eligible child"—s.2(1) and s.29.
"Inland Revenue"—s.29.
"responsible person"—ss.3(8) and 29.

GENERAL NOTE

This section sets out the framework within which child trust fund accounts are to be opened, typically by the "responsible person" (as defined by s.3(8)) and in exceptional cases by the child (assuming he or she is 16 or over). The default position is that an account must be opened by HMRC (see further s.6). 1.650

Subsection (1)
This places a duty on HMRC to issue a voucher in respect of any eligible child (within the normal definition in s.2(1)(a)). The issue of the voucher will be triggered by the award of child benefit (which, as a result of the Tax Credits Act 2002, is now administered by HMRC rather than the Department for Work and Pensions). See further Child Trust Funds Regulations 2004 reg.3. 1.651

Subsection (2)
The voucher must be issued to the individual who is entitled to child benefit. The voucher is in the amount of the initial Treasury contribution to be paid to all eligible children (£250). It should be noted that the process of issuing vouchers is designed to be an automatic process—there is no requirement in the legislation for the parent or other responsible person to make an independent claim for a child trust fund account voucher. In the special cross-border situation where the child lives in the UK but the parent works in an EU Member State (e.g. the Republic of Ireland) there will be no child benefit recipient in this jurisdiction (see annotation to s.2(3)). Accordingly in such cases the voucher must be issued to a responsible person for that child. 1.652

Subsection (3)
This enables the "responsible person" to apply to open a child trust fund account with an approved account provider (see further subs.(4)). As originally drafted, the Bill would have required the responsible person physically to present the voucher to the account provider. As a result of a government amendment, the details of this procedure are now left to regulations. The Child Trust Funds Regulations 2004 still envisage a physical transfer of the voucher (reg.5(1), condition 1), but may in the future make provision for an entirely on-line application process. The "responsible 1.653

person" is not, as such, under a statutory duty to make such an application. If he or she fails to do so, the default position is that ultimately HMRC will step in (see further s.6). In exceptional cases a child aged 16 or 17 may make an application to open a child trust fund account in his or her own name. The most likely circumstance in which this will arise is in the future where a child (born after August 31, 2002) moves to the UK at the age of 16 having never previously had an entitlement to a child trust fund account.

Subsection (4)

1.654 The application procedure is set out in regulations (see Child Trust Funds Regulations 2004 regs 5 and 13). The responsible person can select both the account provider and the type of account for the child trust fund. The voucher issued by HMRC will be valid for one year from the date of issue (*ibid.*, reg.3(2)), so applicants have a year in which to make the application. If they fail to do so, HMRC's default duty under s.6 arises.

Subsection (5)

1.655 Once a valid application has been made, an account provider is required to open a child trust fund account for the child in question and to inform the Revenue that it has done so. The Child Trust Funds Regulations 2004 require institutions to make both fortnightly and annual returns of such information to the Revenue (regs 30 and 32).

Opening by Inland Revenue

1.656 **6.**—(1) In the case of each child to whom this section applies, the Inland Revenue must apply to open for the child with an account provider selected in accordance with regulations a child trust fund of a description so selected.

(2) The application is to be made in accordance with regulations.

(3) The account provider must—
  (a) open, in accordance with regulations, a child trust fund of that description for the child, and
  (b) inform the Inland Revenue in accordance with regulations.

(4) This section applies—
  (a) to a child in respect of whom a voucher is issued under section 5(1) but in whose case subsection (5) is satisfied, and
  (b) to a child who is first an eligible child by virtue of section 2(1)(b).

(5) This subsection is satisfied in the case of a child if—
  (a) the period prescribed under section 5(4) expires without a child trust fund having been opened for the child, or
  (b) the child is under 16 and it appears to the Inland Revenue that there is no-one who is a responsible person in relation to the child.

(6) No liability is to arise in respect of the selection of an account provider, or a description of child trust fund, in accordance with regulations under this section.

DEFINITIONS

"account provider"—s.29.
"child"—s.29.
"child trust fund"—s.29.
"eligible child"—s.2(1) and s.29.
"Inland Revenue"—s.29.
"responsible person"—ss.3(8) and 29.

General Note

Normally a child's parent (or other adult who is the child benefit recipient), as a "responsible person", will make an application for a child trust fund account in accordance with s.5. There will inevitably be cases where no such application is made. This section therefore performs a "mop-up" function, placing the onus on HMRC to ensure that accounts are opened for such children who would otherwise miss out. HMRC's obligation under subs.(1) to open a child trust fund account arises in two types of case. The first is where either, following an award of child benefit, a voucher has been issued to the "responsible person" but no application has been made to open a child trust fund account for that child within the required period (12 months) or there appears to be no "responsible person" for that child (subss.(4)(a) and (5)). The second is where the child is being looked after by a local authority and so there is no individual entitled to child benefit (subs.(4)(b)).

Subsection (1)

In cases to which this section applies (see subss.(4) and (5) and the General Note), HMRC *must* take the initiative and apply to open a child trust fund account for the child in question. The details of the procedure to be adopted are set out in the Child Trust Funds Regulations 2004 reg.6. Account providers are not required to offer these default HMRC-allocated accounts under this arrangement. However, *if* institutions do agree to offer such accounts, they must then accept any HMRC application to open such an account (see subs.(3) and Child Trust Funds Regulations 2004 reg.6(2)). HMRC will maintain a list of account providers willing to offer such accounts, and select account holders in rotation to ensure parity of treatment (*ibid.*, reg.6(3)). If account holders offer more than one type of stakeholder account, the account will likewise be chosen in rotation (*ibid.*, reg.6(4)). The legislation expressly exempts HMRC from any liability in respect of such decisions (subs.(6)). In these cases HMRC's role is furthermore limited to *opening* the account; it will have no role in *managing* the account in such a case. It will always be open to parents to transfer the account to another provider (s.7).

Subsection (2)

See further Child Trust Funds Regulations 2004 reg.6.

Subsection (3)

This is in parallel terms to the obligation imposed on account providers by s.5(5).

Subsections (4) and (5)

See the General Note to this section.

Subsection (6)

See the annotation to subs.(1).

Transfers

7.—Regulations may make provision about the circumstances in which—
(a) a child trust fund which is an account of one of the descriptions prescribed by regulations may become an account of another of those descriptions, and
(b) a child trust fund held with one account provider may be transferred to another.

Definitions

"account provider"—s.29.
"child trust fund"—s.29.

GENERAL NOTE

1.664　This allows regulations to be made which permit the responsible person to change the type of child trust fund account (e.g. from a cash to a stakeholder account) and to move from one provider to another. The procedural rules for transfers are similar to those relating to transfers of ISA accounts, but require transfers to be free of charge (save for share dealing costs); see further Child Trust Funds Regulations 2004 reg.21.

[¹ 7A.—Transfers to other accounts for children

1.665　(1) Regulations may make provision requiring an account provider, at the request of a person who has the authority to manage a child trust fund, to—
  (a) transfer all the investments under the fund, or an amount representing their value in cash, to a protected child account that is provided by a person chosen by the person making the request, and
  (b) when all the investments have been transferred, close the child trust fund.
(2) An account is a protected child account if—
  (a) there is relief from income tax and capital gains tax in respect of investments under it,
  (b) it may be held only by a child, and
  (c) it satisfies any other conditions prescribed in regulations under this section.]

AMENDMENT

1. Deregulation Act 2015 s.62(2) (March 26, 2015 for purposes of making regulations, April 6, 2015 for other purposes).

DEFINITIONS

"account provider"—s.29.
"child trust fund"—s.29.

[¹ 7B.—Transfers on child reaching 18

1.666　(1) Regulations may make provision requiring an account provider to transfer all the investments under a child trust fund held by a person immediately before his or her 18th birthday to a protected account of a description prescribed in the regulations.
(2) Regulations under subsection (1) must include provision that the requirement does not apply if the person gives instructions, in accordance with the regulations, to the account provider as to what is to be done with the investments.
(3) An account is a protected account if—
  (a) there is relief from income tax and capital gains tax in respect of investments under it, and
  (b) it satisfies any other conditions prescribed in regulations under this section.]

AMENDMENT

1. Deregulation Act 2015 s.62(3) (March 26, 2015 for purposes of making regulations, April 6, 2015 for other purposes).

(2004 c. 6 s. 7B)

DEFINITIONS

"account provider"—s.29.
"child trust fund"—s.29.
"protected account"—subs.(3).

[¹ Powers to safeguard interests of children

7C.—Powers to safeguard interests of children

(1) The Treasury may make regulations under this section if the Treasury think it appropriate to do so for the purpose of safeguarding the financial interests of children, or any group of children, who hold child trust funds.

(2) The regulations may authorise the Treasury to permit withdrawals from—
(a) any child trust funds;
(b) any child trust funds held with an account provider that is prescribed, or of a description prescribed, in the regulations.

(3) The regulations may authorise the Treasury to require any account provider or any account provider that is prescribed, or of a description prescribed, in the regulations to take one or more of the following steps in relation to every child trust fund held with it—
(a) to seek to transfer the fund to another account provider;
(b) to seek to transfer all the investments under the fund to a protected child account that can be used for investments of that kind and is provided by a person chosen by the account provider;
(c) to seek to transfer an amount in cash representing the value of all the investments under the fund (whether consisting of cash or stocks and shares) to a protected child account that can be used for investments in cash and is provided by a person chosen by the account provider;
(d) to transfer an amount in cash representing the value of all the investments under the fund (whether consisting of cash or stocks and shares) to a protected child account that can be used for investments in cash and is provided by a person specified by the Treasury.

(4) The regulations may provide—
(a) that child trust funds held with an account provider that is prescribed, or of a description prescribed, in the regulations are to be treated for all purposes as if they were protected child accounts of a description so prescribed;
(b) that, where child trust funds are (under the regulations) to be treated as protected child accounts of a particular description, the account provider is to be treated, for such purposes as may be prescribed in the regulations, as a person who lawfully provides protected child accounts of that description.

(5) If the regulations authorise the Treasury to require that one or more of the steps mentioned in subsection (3)(b) to (d) be taken, the regulations may also authorise the Treasury to require an account provider who, in pursuance of such a requirement, transfers all the investments under a child trust fund, or an amount representing the value of all the investments, to close the child trust fund.

(6) If the regulations authorise the Treasury to require an account provider to take more than one of the steps mentioned in subsection (3), the regulations must also—

1.667

Child Trust Funds Act 2004

(a) authorise the Treasury to specify the order in which the steps are to be taken, and

(b) provide that if (as a result of complying with a requirement to take a particular step) an account holder no longer holds investments under any child trust fund, any requirement imposed on that provider to take another step lapses.

(7) The Treasury is not liable in respect of—

(a) the selection by an account provider of a person to whom to make a transfer in response to a requirement of a kind mentioned in subsection (3)(a) to (c), or

(b) a decision made by it as to the person to be specified in a requirement of a kind mentioned in subsection (3)(d).

(8) In this section, "protected child account" means an account which is a protected child account for the purposes of section 7A.]

AMENDMENT

1. Deregulation Act 2015 s.63 (March 26, 2015 for purposes of making regulations, April 6, 2015 for other purposes).

Contributions and subscriptions

Initial contribution by Inland Revenue

1.668

8.—(1) The Inland Revenue must pay to an account provider such amount as is prescribed by regulations if the account provider has—
(a) informed the Inland Revenue under section 5(5) or 6(3) that a child trust fund has been opened, and
(b) made a claim to the Inland Revenue in accordance with regulations.

(2) On receipt of the payment the account provider must credit the child trust fund with the amount of the payment.

DEFINITIONS

"account provider"—s.29.
"child trust fund"—s.29.
"Inland Revenue"—s.29.

GENERAL NOTE

1.669

This section explains how the initial Treasury contribution of £250 stated on the voucher issued to the child benefit recipient is actually converted, albeit indirectly, into cash (the voucher itself cannot be exchanged for money: see Child Trust Funds Regulations 2004 reg.3(1)). Once a child trust fund account has been opened, either in the normal way (s.5) or through the process of HMRC allocation (s.6), the account provider is required to notify HMRC. Account providers then make a claim to HMRC (these are to be made on a fortnightly basis—see Child Trust Funds Regulations 2004 reg.30. HMRC must in turn pay the account holder "such amount as is prescribed by regulations" by way of an initial contribution (subs.(1)), which the account holder must credit to the relevant account (subs.(2)). Children born into the poorest families may also qualify for a "supplementary contribution" under s.9. There is, moreover, a further Treasury contribution for all eligible children when they reach the age of seven (see s.10).

The regulations describe the "initial" and "supplementary" contributions as "Government contributions" (Child Trust Funds Regulations 2004 reg.7). The basic rule for children born on or after the appointed day (April 6, 2005) is that the initial contribution will be £250, or £500 for those in local authority care (Child Trust Funds Regulations 2004 reg.7(4)). Slightly higher amounts have been prescribed for those born on or after September 1, 2002 (the first date on which a child could qualify as an eligible child under s.2(1)) but before the appointed day. These higher amounts are designed to reflect the fact that these children have not had the benefit of interest on their investments to date. The rates are £277 for children born after August 31, 2002 but before the end of the 2002/03 tax year, £268 for those born in the 2003/04 tax year, and £256 for those born between April 6, 2004 and the appointed day (*ibid.*, reg.7(2)). For children in care, the equivalent figures are £554, £536 and £512.

Supplementary contribution by Inland Revenue

9.—(1) If this section applies to a child the Inland Revenue must inform the account provider with whom a child trust fund is held by the child that this section applies to the child.

(2) If the account provider makes a claim to the Inland Revenue in accordance with regulations, the Inland Revenue must pay to the account provider such amount as is prescribed by regulations.

(3) On receipt of the payment the account provider must credit the child trust fund with the amount of the payment.

(4) This section applies to a child if—
(a) a child trust fund is held by the child,
(b) the child was first an eligible child by virtue of section 2(1)(a), and
(c) the condition in subsection (5) is satisfied in relation to the child.

(5) That condition is that it has been determined in accordance with the provision made by and by virtue of sections 18 to 21 of the Tax Credits Act 2002 (c. 21)—
(a) that a person was, or persons were, entitled to child tax credit in respect of the child for the child benefit commencement date, and
(b) that either the relevant income of the person or persons for the tax year in which that date fell does not exceed the income threshold or the person, or either of the persons, was entitled to a relevant social security benefit for that date,

and that determination has not been overturned.

(6) In subsection (5)(b)—
"the income threshold" has the meaning given by section 7(1)(a) of the Tax Credits Act 2002,
"the relevant income", in relation to a person or persons and a tax year, has the meaning given by section 7(3) of that Act in relation to a claim by the person or persons for a tax credit for the tax year,
"relevant social security benefit" means any social security benefit prescribed for the purposes of section 7(2) of that Act, and
"tax year" means a period beginning with 6th April in one year and ending with 5th April in the next.

(7) If the child benefit commencement date is earlier than 6th April 2005, this section applies in relation to the child even if the condition in subsection (5) is not satisfied in relation to the child provided that the condition in subsection (8) is so satisfied.

(8) That condition is that—
(a) income support, or income-based jobseeker's allowance, was paid for the child benefit commencement date to a person whose applicable amount included an amount in respect of the child, or

1.670

(b) working families' tax credit, or disabled person's tax credit, was paid for that date to a person whose appropriate maximum working families' tax credit, or appropriate maximum disabled person's tax credit, included a credit in respect of the child.

(9) If the child benefit commencement date is earlier than 6th April 2003, subsection (5) has effect as if—
(a) the reference in paragraph (a) to the child benefit commencement date were to any date in the tax year beginning with 6th April 2003,
(b) the reference in paragraph (b) to the tax year in which the child benefit commencement date fell were to the tax year beginning with 6th April 2003, and
(c) the reference in paragraph (b) to being entitled to a relevant social security benefit for the child benefit commencement date were to being so entitled for any date in that tax year for which the person was, or the persons were, entitled to child tax credit in respect of the child.

(10) "Child benefit commencement date", in relation to a child, means—
(a) the first day for which child benefit was paid in respect of the child (otherwise than because of a directly applicable Community provision or an international agreement), or
(b) in the case of a child to whom section 2(3) applies or section 2(5) has applied, such day as is prescribed by regulations.

DEFINITIONS

"account provider"—s.29.
"child"—s.29.
"child benefit commencement date"—subs.(10).
"child trust fund"—s.29.
"eligible child"—ss.2(1) and 29.
"income threshold"—subs.(6).
"Inland Revenue"—s.29.
"relevant income"—subs.(6).
"relevant social security benefit"—subs.(6).
"tax year"—subs.(6).

GENERAL NOTE

1.671   In addition to the initial contribution under s.8, children born into families on low incomes will be eligible for a "supplementary contribution" to boost their child trust fund account investment at the outset. This section sets out the rules governing the award of the supplementary contribution. Subsections (1)–(3) specify the procedure to be followed. Subsection (4) spells out the criteria for receipt of the supplementary condition. Children being looked after in local authority care will *not* qualify for this extra amount (see subs.(4)(b)), but they will in any event qualify for an equivalent amount under s.8 by virtue of their status. The means-test is explained in subs.(5), with various terms defined by subss.(6) and (10). Subsections (7)–(9) deal with various awkward transitional cases.

Subsection (1)

1.672   There is no need for parents on low incomes to claim the supplementary contribution; indeed, there is no facility for them to do so. Instead, the legislation requires HMRC to inform the account provider if a child is eligible for the supplementary contribution. HMRC will have this information as it is responsible for administering child tax credit under the Tax Credits Act 2002, which acts as the trigger for entitlement to the extra Treasury contribution (see subss.(4)(c) and (5)).

Subsections (2) and (3)
Having been informed that the child in question is eligible for the supplementary contribution, the account provider may then make a claim for that extra amount (subs.(2); see Child Trust Funds Regulations 2004 reg.30(6)(b)). This section then requires HMRC to pay the account provider the appropriate amount by way of a supplementary contribution. In the case of children born after the appointed day, this is a further £250 (Child Trust Funds Regulations 2004 reg.7(7)), making £500 in total. The amounts are increased for those born on or after September 1, 2002 but before the appointed day (Child Trust Funds Regulations 2004 reg.7(6)). The account provider must then credit the extra amount to the child's account (subs.(3)). Subsequent regulations amending the amount of the supplementary contribution under subs.(2) will be subject to the affirmative procedure (see ss.28(5) and (6)(b)).

1.673

Subsection (4)
This sets out the criteria for the award of the supplementary contribution. The child must have a child trust fund account, have qualified on the basis of an award of child benefit and meet the child tax credit means-test set out in subs.(5). The second of these requirements has the effect of excluding children who initially qualified for an account because they were in care (see s.2(1)(b)), as they will, in any event, receive the higher initial contribution (see annotation to s.8).

1.674

Subsection (5)
This provision sets out the means-test which determines whether a child is eligible to receive the supplementary as well as the initial Treasury contribution. Two separate conditions must each be satisfied. In the case of both these requirements, the determination of entitlement must have been a final one in accordance with ss.18–21 of the Tax Credits Act 2002 and must not have been overturned.

1.675

The first condition is that someone was entitled to child tax credit for the child in question at the date when child benefit was first paid (known as the "child benefit commencement date": see subs.(10)). The second requirement is that *either* their income does not exceed the child tax credit income threshold for the tax year in issue *or* that person is entitled to a "relevant social security benefit". The statutory authority for the child tax credit income threshold is Tax Credits Act 2002 s.7(1)(a) (see subs.(6)). The annual amount of this threshold is prescribed in regulations, and for the 2020/21 tax year is £16,385 (Tax Credits (Income Threshold and Determination of Rates) Regulations 2002 (SI 2002/2008 reg.3(3)). The expression "relevant social security benefit" is defined by reference to Tax Credits Act 2002 s.7(2)) (see subs.(6)), and so includes only income support, income-based jobseeker's allowance, income-related employment and support allowance and pension credit (Tax Credits (Income Threshold and Determination of Rates) Regulations 2002 (SI 2002/2008) reg.4).

These tests require some modification so that they operate in the desired fashion for eligible children born in the transitional period between August 31, 2002 and April 6, 2005. There are two sets of special transitional rules contained in subss. (7)–(9).

Subsections (7) and (8)
The first transitional problem relates to the phasing in of child tax credit for families in receipt of income support or income-based jobseeker's allowance. Child tax credit, payable under the Tax Credits Act 2002, came into force on April 6, 2003, at least so far as new claimants and those claiming working tax credit (the successor to working families' tax credit) were concerned. Originally it was anticipated that families already in receipt of income support or income-based jobseeker's allowance would move over to child tax credit a year later on April 6, 2004. In fact, only new

1.676

claimants of these benefits have received child tax credit from that date. The revised plan was that the process of "migration" for existing benefits cases would then start in October 2004, with a view to such transfers being completed by the end of the 2004–05 tax year. (In the meantime all such families have received the cash equivalent of child tax credit through their existing benefits). Some families have therefore not met the strict terms of subs.(5) because, although they were getting income support or income-based jobseeker's allowance at the material time, they were not yet, as a result of this phasing process, receiving child tax credit. Subsections (7) and (8) deal with this by disapplying the means-test based on entitlement to child tax credit in subs.(5). Instead, they provide alternatively that it is sufficient that a child born before April 6, 2005 was in a household which received one of the means-tested benefits or tax credits listed in subs.(8) in respect of that child.

As matters have transpired, this process of migration has been further delayed and had not been commenced, let alone completed, by the end of the 2004–05 tax year. The plan was to have this process completed by December 31, 2014: see Tax Credits Act 2002 (Commencement No.4, Transitional Provisions and Savings) Order 2003 (SI 2003/962 (c.51)) as amended. As the commentary to that provision notes, this target has now been abandoned.

Subsection (9)

1.677   This deals with a separate transitional problem relating to children born between September 1, 2002 and April 5, 2003. The first condition in the means-test (subs.(5)(a)) is that a person was entitled to child tax credit in respect of the child when child benefit was first paid. However, child tax credit did not come into operation until April 6, 2003, and so subs.(5)(a) cannot be satisfied if child benefit was payable *before* that date. There are also knock-on problems in terms of complying with subs.(5)(b) in such cases. This subsection resolves these problems by deeming the child benefit commencement date (and hence the entitlement to child tax credit) as having been in the 2003/04 tax year.

Further contributions by Inland Revenue

1.678   **10.**—(1) Regulations may make provision for the making by the Inland Revenue in the circumstances mentioned in subsection (2) of payments to account providers of child trust funds held by—
  (a) eligible children, or
  (b) any description of eligible children,
of amounts prescribed by, or determined in accordance with, regulations.
  (2) The circumstances referred to in subsection (1) are—
  (a) the children attaining such age as may be prescribed by the regulations, or
  (b) such other circumstances as may be so prescribed.
  (3) The regulations must include provision—
  (a) for making account providers aware that such amounts are payable,
  (b) about the claiming of such payments by account providers, and
  (c) about the crediting of child trust funds by account providers with the amount of such payments.
  (4) For the purposes of this section, a child is to be treated as being an eligible child if entitlement to child benefit in respect of the child is excluded by—
  (a) paragraph 1(a) of Schedule 9 to the Social Security Contributions and Benefits Act 1992 (c. 4) (children in custody), or
  (b) paragraph 1(1)(a) to (d) of Schedule 9 to the Social Security Contributions and Benefits (Northern Ireland) Act 1992 (c. 7) (corresponding provision for Northern Ireland).

Definitions

"account provider"—s.29.
"child"—s.29.
"child trust fund"—s.29.
"eligible child"—ss.2(1) and 29.
"Inland Revenue"—s.29.

General Note

This is an enabling measure, allowing regulations to be made which may provide for a further Treasury contribution to be credited to the child's account at a later date. Any regulations made under subs.(1) or (2) will be subject to the affirmative procedure (see s.28(5) and (6)(a)).

Subsections (1) and (2)

The powers enshrined in the section are expressed in broad terms—thus regulations may provide that further contributions are made to all eligible children, or just to a subset of them (subs.(1)). The trigger for a further contribution may be when the child attains a particular age, as set out in regulations, or some other factor (subs.(2)). The Government's stated intention is that there will be one further contribution which will be payable to all eligible children at the age of seven (rather than three payments at ages 5, 11 and 16, as suggested in *Savings and Assets for All*). It follows that the first such payments will not become due until 2009 (see now Child Trust Funds Regulations 2004 reg.7A). In its 2004 Pre-Budget Report the Government announced a consultation process on the appropriate levels for such further contributions. The consultation paper suggested that there be a further universal payment of £250 at age seven, with an extra £250 for children in low-income families (Treasury Press Notice 5, December 2, 2004). A further consultation was initiated by the 2005 Budget, with a view to seeing whether there is support for a further contribution to children of secondary school age and, if so, at what age and in what amounts. In both consultations the Government has invited views on the appropriate ratio of progressivity (currently 1:2, i.e. £250 universal and £500 means-tested). The rationale for further contributions is that they will enable additional endowment funds to be targeted on those most in need. It will also help to keep the accounts "live" by reminding both children and their parents of the existence and growth of such funds. Note also that account providers will have to issue annual account statements (Child Trust Funds Regulations 2004 reg.10).

Subsection (3)

As well as specifying matters such as the amount of the further contribution and the age at which it becomes payable, the regulations which are to be made nearer the time must also address the various procedural matters referred to in this subsection.

Subsection (4)

A child will remain an eligible child for these purposes even if there is no child benefit entitlement at the date when the further contribution becomes payable because he or she is detained in custody. Clearly children aged seven are not going to be in custody. However, a future government might decide to make further Treasury contributions to children at the age of 12 or over, when this could become an issue. The Government's view, as a matter of principle, was that it was not justifiable "to disadvantage such children on the grounds that they were in custody on a particular birthday". Such an exclusion from the further contribution might also result in anomalies depending on the length of time the child was in custody and when their birthday fell.

Recouping Inland Revenue contributions

1.683 **11.**—(1) Regulations may make provision requiring that, in circumstances prescribed by the regulations, a person of a description so prescribed is to account to the Inland Revenue for amounts credited to a child trust fund in respect of Inland Revenue contributions (together with any income and gains arising in consequence of the crediting of those amounts).

(2) "Inland Revenue contributions" means payments made by the Inland Revenue which were required to be made under or by virtue of sections 8 to 10 or which the Inland Revenue considered were required to be so made.

DEFINITIONS

"child trust fund"—s.29.
"Inland Revenue"—s.29.
"Inland Revenue contributions"—subs.(2).

GENERAL NOTE

1.684 In some cases payments will be made under ss.8, 9 or 10 which should not have been so credited; in social security parlance these would be described as overpayments. This section allows the Treasury to make regulations governing the recovery of such payments, e.g. where more than one account has been opened or where the child in question was never an eligible child within s.2. The intention is that recovery will be possible from the account provider, the child, the registered contact (typically the parent) and anyone into whose hands the funds have come.

Subscription limits

1.685 **12.**—(1) No subscription may be made to a child trust fund otherwise than by way of a monetary payment.

(2) Regulations may prescribe the maximum amount that may be subscribed to a child trust fund in each year (otherwise than by way of credits made under or by virtue of this Act or income or gains arising on investments under the child trust fund).

(3) "Year", in relation to a child trust fund held by a child, means—
   (a) the period beginning with the day on which the child trust fund is opened and ending immediately before the child's next birthday, and
   (b) each succeeding period of twelve months.

DEFINITIONS

"child trust fund"—s.29.
"year"—subs.(3).

GENERAL NOTE

1.686 Whereas ss.8–11 are all concerned with Treasury contributions to a child trust fund account, this section deals with contributions to such accounts by others, for example a child's family and friends. Such non-governmental contributions may only be in money terms (subs.(1)), and so shares cannot be transferred to a child trust fund account. There will also be an annual aggregate limit on such non-governmental contributions, prescribed by regulations made under subs.

(2). This cap is to be £1,200 a year at the outset (Child Trust Fund Regulations 2004 reg.9(2); there is no facility to carry over any unused allowance to a following year (*ibid.*, reg.9(3)). A year, in this context, means each year from the date of the individual child's birthday (subs.(3)), not each calendar year or each tax year. The minimum contribution on any one transaction is £10, unless the account provider permits a smaller amount (Child Trust Fund Regulations 2004 Sch. para.2(4)).

There is no provision in the Act for automatic indexation of the annual aggregate limit; the Government intends to treat the cap in the same way as the ISA limit, so any uprating will be announced in the Budget or simply through regulations.

Tax

Relief from income tax and capital gains tax

13.—(1) Regulations may make provision for and in connection with giving relief from—
(a) income tax, and
(b) capital gains tax,
in respect of investments under child trust funds.

(2) The regulations may, in particular, include—
(a) provision for securing that losses are disregarded for the purposes of capital gains tax where they accrue on the disposal of investments under child trust funds, and
(b) provision dealing with anything which, apart from the regulations, would have been regarded for those purposes as an indistinguishable part of the same asset.

(3) The regulations may specify how tax relief is to be claimed by persons entitled to it or by account providers on their behalf.

(4) The regulations may include provision requiring that, in circumstances prescribed by the regulations, the person prescribed by the regulations is to account to the Inland Revenue for—
(a) tax from which relief has been given under the regulations, and
(b) income or gains arising in consequence of the giving of relief under the regulations,
or for an amount determined in accordance with the regulations in respect of such tax.

(5) Provision made by virtue of this section may disapply, or modify the effect of, any enactment relating to income tax or capital gains tax.

DEFINITIONS

"account provider"—s.29.
"child trust fund"—s.29.
"Inland Revenue"—s.29.

GENERAL NOTE

This section is concerned with the tax treatment of investments held in child trust funds. It allows regulations to make provision for relief in respect of income tax and capital gains tax (subs.(1)), and how such tax relief should be claimed (subs.(3)). Such regulations may effectively ring-fence child trust fund investments from any other investments held by the child concerned; this will mean that any capital losses arising on the disposal of child trust fund investments will not be deductible from any capital gains outside the child trust fund (subs.(2)(a)). Regulations will also provide for the separate identification of disposals of shares within and outside a child trust fund (subs.(2)(b)). Regulations may provide for the repayment of tax relief that is given in circumstances where it should not have been (subs.(4)). Subsection (5) is a general power that enables regulations to modify income tax and capital gains tax legislation for child trust fund accounts (see generally Child Trust Funds Regulations 2004 Pt 3 and especially regs 24 and 36).

Insurance companies and friendly societies

14.—[¹ . . .]

AMENDMENT

1. Finance Act 2007 s.114 and Sch.27 pt 2 (July 19, 2007).

Information, etc.

Information from account providers, etc.

15.—(1) Regulations may require [¹ . . .] any [¹person who is or has been the account provider in relation to a child trust fund]—
  (a) to make documents available for inspection on behalf of the Inland Revenue, or
  (b) to provide to the Inland Revenue any information,
relating to, or to investments which are or have been held under, [¹the child trust fund].
  (2) [¹ . . .]
  (3) The regulations may include provision requiring documents to be made available or information to be provided—
  (a) in the manner and form, and
  (b) by the time and at the place,
prescribed by or under the regulations.

AMENDMENT

1. Finance Act 2009 s.96 and Sch.48 (Appointed Day, Savings and Consequential Amendments) Order 2009 (SI 2009/3054) art.3 and Sch. para.12 (April 1, 2010).

DEFINITIONS

"account provider"—s.29.
"child"—s.29.
"child trust fund"—s.29.
"Inland Revenue"—s.29.
"relevant person"—subs.(2).

GENERAL NOTE

This section enables the Treasury to make regulations requiring account providers and other "relevant persons" (as defined by subs.(2)) to supply information or make documents available for inspection (and subject to requirements stipulated under subs.(3)). The Child Trust Funds Regulations 2004 require account holders to supply HMRC with both fortnightly and annual returns (regs 30 and 32). The fortnightly returns will both act as a claim for payment of the government contributions and enable HMRC to identify children for whom accounts have not been opened.

Information about children in care of authority

16.—(1) Regulations may require, or authorise officers of the Inland Revenue to require, an authority—

(a) to make documents available for inspection on behalf of the Inland Revenue [¹ or by a person appointed under regulations under section 3(10)], or

(b) to provide to the Inland Revenue [¹ or to such a person] any information,

which the Inland Revenue [¹ or (as the case may be) the person] may require for the discharge of any function relating to child trust funds and which is information to which subsection (2) applies.

(2) This subsection applies to information relating to a child who falls or has fallen within—

(a) paragraph 1(c) of Schedule 9 to the Social Security Contributions and Benefits Act 1992 (c. 4), or

(b) paragraph 1(1)(f) of Schedule 9 to the Social Security Contributions and Benefits (Northern Ireland) Act 1992 (c. 7),

by reason of being, or having been, in the care of the authority in circumstances prescribed by regulations under that provision.

(3) The regulations may include provision requiring documents to be made available or information to be provided—

(a) in the manner and form, and

(b) by the time and at the place,

prescribed by or under the regulations.

1.692

AMENDMENT

1. Deregulation Act 2015 s.60(4) (May 26, 2015).

DEFINITIONS

"child"—s.29.
"child trust fund"—s.29.
"Inland Revenue"—s.29.

GENERAL NOTE

The normal rule is that a child is an "eligible child" if child benefit is payable in respect of him or her (s.2(1)(a)). Receipt of child benefit thus acts as a passport to entitlement to the child trust fund. HMRC is also responsible for administering child benefit and accordingly has access to all the relevant information in such cases. However, child benefit cannot be claimed for children in local authority care, for whom special provision has to be made to make them "eligible children" (ss.2(1)(b) and 2(2)). As these children will not appear in the records of current child benefit payments, HMRC will have to obtain the necessary information direct from local authorities. This section accordingly enables the Treasury to make regulations requiring local authorities to provide the information necessary to arrange for a child trust fund account to be opened or for further contributions to be made. Local authorities are required to make monthly returns (Child Trust Funds Regulations 2004 reg.33).

1.693

Use of information

1.694 **17.**—(1) Information held for the purposes of any function relating to child trust funds—
  (a) by the Inland Revenue, or
  (b) by a person providing services to the Inland Revenue, in connection with the provision of those services,
may be used, or supplied to any person providing services to the Inland Revenue, for the purposes of, or for any purposes connected with, the exercise of any such function.

(2) Information held for the purposes of any function relating to child trust funds—
  (a) by the Inland Revenue, or
  (b) by a person providing services to the Inland Revenue, in connection with the provision of those services,
may be used, or supplied to any person providing services to the Inland Revenue, for the purposes of, or for any purposes connected with, the exercise of any other function of the Inland Revenue.

(3) Information held for the purposes of any function other than those relating to child trust funds—
  (a) by the Inland Revenue, or
  (b) by a person providing services to the Inland Revenue, in connection with the provision of those services,
may be used, or supplied to any person providing services to the Inland Revenue, for the purposes of, or for any purposes connected with, the exercise of any function of the Inland Revenue relating to child trust funds.

(4) Information held by the Secretary of State or the Department for Social Development in Northern Ireland, or any person providing services to the Secretary of State or that Department, may be supplied to—
  (a) the Inland Revenue, or
  (b) a person providing services to the Inland Revenue, in connection with the provision of those services,
for use for the purposes of, or for any purposes connected with, the exercise of any function of the Inland Revenue relating to child trust funds.

DEFINITIONS

"child trust fund"—s.29.
"Inland Revenue"—s.29.

GENERAL NOTE

1.695 This section allows information relating to child trust funds to be shared both within government and between government departments and their contractors (typically their IT providers). Subsection (1) allows information relating to child trust funds to be used for purposes relating to such funds. Subsection (2), on the other hand, enables such information to be used for other (non-child trust fund) purposes by HMRC (e.g. official evaluations of savings policies). Subsection (3) permits information held by HMRC in connection with other purposes to be used for child trust fund purposes. This allows HMRC to access information about a person's child tax credit status in order to determine eligibility for the supplementary contribution (see s.9(5)). Finally, subs.(4) allows other government departments to provide information to HMRC (or its contractors) for reasons connected with child trust funds. In particular, this will enable HMRC to obtain information from the Department for Work and Pensions about a person's benefit status. This will be relevant to determining entitlement to the supplementary condition in respect of children born on or after September 1, 2002 but before child tax credit became payable to the household in question.

Disclosure of information

18.—[*Section omitted.*]

GENERAL NOTE

This section amends the Finance Act 1989 s.182 and so brings the child trust fund scheme within the existing statutory provisions which deal with the confidentiality of personal information held by HMRC, and the exceptions to that principle.

Payments after death

Payments after death of child

19.—(1) Where a relevant child dies, the Inland Revenue may make a payment to the personal representatives of the child if any one or more of the conditions specified in subsection (3) is satisfied.

(2) "Relevant child" means a child who is or has been an eligible child (or would have been had this Act come into force on the date referred to in section 2(1)).

(3) The conditions are—
(a) that either no payment had been made under section 8 by the Inland Revenue or, if one had, the amount of the payment had not been credited to the child trust fund held by the child,
(b) that section 9 applied to the child (or would have had this Act come into force on the date referred to in section 2(1)) but either no payment had been made under that section by the Inland Revenue or, if one had, the amount of the payment had not been credited to the child trust fund held by the child, and
(c) that the Inland Revenue was required by regulations under section 10 to make a payment in respect of the child but either the payment had not been made or, if it had, the amount of the payment had not been credited to the child trust fund held by the child.

(4) The amount of the payment is to be equal to the amount of the payment or payments which had not been made or credited.

DEFINITIONS

"child"—s.29.
"child trust fund"—s.29.
"eligible child"—s.29.
"Inland Revenue"—s.29.
"relevant child"—subs.(2).

GENERAL NOTE

This section gives HMRC the power to make child trust fund payments in respect of children born after August 31, 2002 but who have died before such payments have been credited to an account. Any one (or more) of three requirements must be satisfied. These are: (1) that no initial contribution has been paid under s.8 (or it has not been credited to the account); (2) that the child was entitled to a supplementary contribution under s.9 but this had not been paid or credited to the account; or (3) that a further contribution was due under s.10 but again had not been paid or credited (subs.(3)). The amount payable is a sum equal to the amount of the outstanding payment(s) (subs.(4)) and is payable to the child's personal representatives (subs.(1)). Note that there is no absolute right to such a payment; HMRC *may* make such a payment. The element of discretion has been inserted to allow HMRC to refuse to make payments in cases where the child has been unlawfully killed by the parent. The personal representatives have a right of appeal in the event of a dispute about payment (s.22(5)).

Penalties

Penalties

1.700
20.—(1) A penalty of £300 may be imposed on any person who fraudulently—
  (a) applies to open a child trust fund,
  (b) makes a withdrawal from a child trust fund otherwise than as permitted by regulations under section 3(4)(d), or
  (c) secures the opening of a child trust fund by the Inland Revenue.
(2) A penalty not exceeding £3,000 may be imposed on—
  (a) an account provider who fraudulently or negligently makes an incorrect statement or declaration in connection with a claim under section 8 or 9 or regulations under section 10 or 13, and
  (b) any person who fraudulently or negligently provides incorrect information in response to a requirement imposed by or under regulations under section 15.
(3) Penalties may be imposed on—
  (a) an account provider who fails to make a claim under section 8 or 9 or regulations under section 10 by the time required by regulations under the section concerned, and
  (b) any person who fails to make a document available, or provide information, in accordance with regulations under section 15.
(4) The penalties which may be imposed under subsection (3) are—
  (a) a penalty not exceeding £300, and
  (b) if the failure continues after a penalty under paragraph (a) is imposed, a further penalty or penalties not exceeding £60 for each day on which the failure continues after the day on which the penalty under that paragraph was imposed (but excluding any day for which a penalty under this paragraph has already been imposed).
(5) No penalty under subsection (3) may be imposed on a person in respect of a failure after the failure has been remedied.
(6) For the purposes of subsection (3) a person is to be taken not to have failed to make a claim, make available a document or provide information which must be made, made available or provided by a particular time—
  (a) if the person made it, made it available or provided it within such further time (if any) as the Inland Revenue may have allowed,
  (b) if the person had a reasonable excuse for not making it, making it available or providing it by that time, or

(c) if, after having had such an excuse, the person made it, made it available or provided it without unreasonable delay.

(7) A penalty may be imposed on an account provider in respect of—
 (a) the provision by the account provider, as a child trust fund, of an account which does not meet the condition in subsection (8),
 (b) a failure by the account provider to comply with section 8(2) or 9(3) or with a requirement imposed on the account provider by regulations under section 5(5), 6(3), 7 [1, 7A, 7B] or 10(3), or
 (c) a breach of section 12(1), or regulations under section 12(2), in relation to a child trust fund held with the account provider.

(8) An account meets the condition referred to in subsection (7)(a) if—
 (a) it is of one of the descriptions prescribed by regulations under section 3(2),
 (b) section 3(4) is complied with in relation to it, and
 (c) the requirements imposed by regulations under section 3(5) are satisfied in relation to it.

(9) The penalty which may be imposed under subsection (7) on the account provider is a penalty not exceeding—
 (a) £300, or
 (b) £1 in respect of each account affected by the matter, or any of the matters, in respect of which the penalty is imposed,
whichever is greater.

AMENDMENT

1. Deregulation Act 2015 s.62(5) (March 26, 2015 for purposes of making regulations, April 6, 2015 for other purposes).

DEFINITIONS

"account provider"—s.29.
"child trust fund"—s.29.
"Inland Revenue"—s.29.

GENERAL NOTE

This section makes provision for penalties to be imposed in connection with child trust fund applications and related matters. Individuals who fraudulently apply to open or secure the opening of an account, or make an account withdrawal, are subject to a penalty of £300 (subs.(1)). Account providers and others who make fraudulent or negligent statements or declarations are liable to a penalty not exceeding £3,000 (subs.(2)). Account providers and others are also liable to a £300 penalty (and £60 per day thereafter for continued non-compliance) for failing to make claims in respect of reimbursements or for failing to provide information or produce documentation (subss.(3) and (4); see further subss. (5) and (6)). Subsections (7)–(9) make further provision for penalties to be imposed on account providers in respect of non-compliance with various statutory requirements.

Any penalties under this section are imposed by HMRC (s.21(1)), subject to the various procedural requirements in s.21. There is a right of appeal against any decision to impose a penalty, or its amount (s.22(6)).

1.701

Decisions, appeals, mitigation and recovery

21.—(1) It is for the Inland Revenue to impose a penalty under section 20.

(2) If the Inland Revenue decide to impose such a penalty the decision must (subject to the permitted maximum) set it at such amount as, in their opinion, is appropriate.

(3) A decision to impose such a penalty may not be made after the end of the period of six years beginning with the date on which the penalty was incurred or began to be incurred.

(4) The Inland Revenue must give notice of such a decision to the person on whom the penalty is imposed.

(5) The notice must state the date on which it is given and give details of the right to appeal against the decision under section 22.

(6) After the notice has been given, the decision must not be altered except on appeal.

(7) But the Inland Revenue may, in their discretion, mitigate any penalty under section 20.

(8) A penalty under section 20 becomes payable at the end of the period of 30 days beginning with the date on which notice of the decision is given.

(9) On an appeal under section 22 against a decision under this section, the [¹ appropriate tribunal] may—
 (a) if it appears that no penalty has been incurred, set the decision aside,
 (b) if the amount set appears to be appropriate, confirm the decision,
 (c) if the amount set appears to be excessive, reduce it to such other amount (including nil) as [¹ the tribunal considers] appropriate, or
 (d) if the amount set appears to be insufficient, increase it to such amount not exceeding the permitted maximum as [¹ the tribunal considers] appropriate.

[¹(10) In addition to any right of appeal on a point of law under section 11(2) of the Tribunals, Courts and Enforcement Act 2007, the person liable to the penalty may appeal to the Upper Tribunal against the amount of a penalty which has been determined under subsection (9), but not against any decision which falls under section 11(5)(d) and (e) of that Act and was made in connection with the determination of the amount of the penalty.

(10A) Section 11(3) and (4) of the Tribunals, Courts and Enforcement Act 2007 applies to the right of appeal under subsection (10) as it applies to the right of appeal under section 11(2) of that Act.

(10B) On an appeal under this section the Upper Tribunal has a similar jurisdiction to that conferred on the First-tier Tribunal by virtue of this section.

(10C) In Northern Ireland, an appeal from a decision of the appropriate tribunal lies, at the instance of the person on whom the penalty was imposed to a Northern Ireland Social Security Commissioner, who shall have a similar jurisdiction on such an appeal to that conferred on the appeal tribunal by subsection (9).]

(11) A penalty is to be treated for the purposes of Part 6 of the Taxes Management Act 1970 (c. 9) (collection and recovery) as if it were tax charged in an assessment and due and payable.

AMENDMENT

1. Transfer of Tribunal Functions and Revenue and Customs Appeals Order 2009 (SI 2009/56) art.3(1) and Sch.1 para.415 (April 1, 2009).

DEFINITIONS

"appeal tribunal"—s.24(6).
"the Inland Revenue"—s.29 but note that the functions of the Inland Revenue have been transferred to HMRC by CRCA 2005.

Appeals

Rights of appeal

22.—(1) A person may appeal against—
 (a) a decision by the Inland Revenue not to approve the person as an account provider, or
 (b) a decision by the Inland Revenue to withdraw the person's approval as an account provider.

(2) A person who is a relevant person in relation to a child may appeal against a decision by the Inland Revenue—
 (a) not to issue a voucher under section 5 in relation to the child,
 (b) not to open a child trust fund for the child under section 6,
 (c) not to make a payment under section 8 or 9 in respect of the child, or
 (d) not to make a payment under regulations under section 10 in respect of the child.

(3) "Relevant person", in relation to a child, means—
 (a) the person (if any) entitled to child benefit in respect of the child,
 (b) anyone who applied to open a child trust fund for the child, and
 (c) anyone who has, at any time, given instructions with respect to the management of the child trust fund held by the child.

(4) A person who is required by the Inland Revenue to account for an amount under regulations under section 11 or 13 may appeal against the decision to impose the requirement.

(5) The personal representatives of a child who has died may appeal against a decision by the Inland Revenue not to make a payment to them under section 19.

(6) A person on whom a penalty under section 20 is imposed may appeal against the decision to impose the penalty or its amount.

DEFINITIONS

"account provider"—s.29.
"child"—s.29.
"child trust fund"—s.29.
"Inland Revenue"—s.29.
"relevant person"—subs.(3).

GENERAL NOTE

This section sets out the categories of person who can appeal against a decision relating to the child trust fund. In so far as there are any appeals, most appeals will presumably be brought by individuals and will concern the entitlement to child trust fund payments in individual cases (subs.(2)). However, companies who are refused permission by HMRC to act as account providers also have a right of appeal (subs.(1)). Subsections (4)–(6) ensure that various other persons have a right of appeal as appropriate. In particular, subs.(6) provides that any person on whom a penalty is imposed has a right of appeal against both the decision to levy the penalty and also the amount. The tribunal's powers on hearing appeals under this section are set out in s.21(9). In the short to medium term, child trust fund appeals will be heard by the First-tier Tribunal and, on further appeal, by the Upper Tribunal (s.24, temporarily modifying s.23: see General Note to s.21).

Exercise of rights of appeal

23.—(1) Notice of an appeal under section 22 against a decision must be given to the Inland Revenue in the manner prescribed by regulations within the period of thirty days after the date on which notice of the decision was given.

(2) Notice of such an appeal must specify the grounds of appeal.

[¹ (3) An appeal under section 22 is to the appropriate tribunal.]

(4) [¹. . .]

(5) On the hearing of an appeal under section 22 the [¹appeal tribunal] may allow the appellant to put forward grounds not specified in the notice, and take them into consideration if satisfied that the omission was not wilful or unreasonable.

[¹ (6) Regulations may apply (with or without modifications) any provision contained in—
(a) the Social Security Act 1998 (c. 14) (social security appeals: Great Britain),
(b) the Social Security (Northern Ireland) Order 1998 (SI 1998/1506 (NI 10)) (social security appeals: Northern Ireland), or
(c) section 54 of the Taxes Management Act 1970 (settling of appeals by agreement),
in relation to appeals which by virtue of this section are to the appropriate tribunal or in relation to appeals under this Act which lie to a Social Security Commissioner.]

(7) [¹. . .]

AMENDMENT

1. Transfer of Tribunal Functions and Revenue and Customs Appeals Order 2009 (SI 2009/56) art.3(1) and Sch.1 para.416 (April 1, 2009).

DEFINITION

"the Inland Revenue"—s.29 but note that the functions of the Inland Revenue have been transferred to HMRC by CRCA 2005.

Temporary modifications

24.—[¹. . .]

AMENDMENT

1. Transfer of Tribunal Functions and Revenue and Customs Appeals Order 2009 (SI 2009/56) art.3(1) and Sch.1 para.417 (April 1, 2009).

Supplementary

Northern Ireland

25.—In Schedule 2 to the Northern Ireland Act 1998 (c. 47) (excepted matters), after paragraph 9 insert—
"9A Child Trust Funds."

(2004 c.6 s.25)

GENERAL NOTE

The child trust fund scheme is added to the Schedule of excepted matters in the Northern Ireland Act 1998, so ensuring that the Fund is governed by legislation common to the whole of the UK (see also s.30). 1.708

26.—[*Omitted.*] 1.709

27.—[*Omitted.*] 1.710

28.—[*Omitted.*] 1.711

Interpretation

29.—In this Act— 1.712
"account provider" is to be construed in accordance with section 3(1),
[¹ "appropriate tribunal" means
(a) the First-tier Tribunal, or
(b) in Northern Ireland, an appeal tribunal constituted under Chapter 1 of Part 2 of the Social Security (Northern Ireland) Order 1998,]
"child" means a person under the age of 18,
"child trust fund" has the meaning given by section 1(2),
"eligible child" is to be construed in accordance with section 2,
[¹ . . .]
"the Inland Revenue" means the Commissioners of Inland Revenue,
[¹ "Northern Ireland Social Security Commissioner" means the Chief Social Security Commissioner or any other Social Security Commissioner appointed under the Social Security Administration (Northern Ireland) Act 1992 (c. 8) or a tribunal of three or more Commissioners constituted under article 16(7) of the Social Security (Northern Ireland) Order 1998,]
"responsible person" has the meaning given by section 3(8), and
[¹ . . .]

AMENDMENT

1. Transfer of Tribunal Functions and Revenue and Customs Appeals Order 2009 (SI 2009/56) art.3(1) and Sch.1 para.418 (April 1, 2009).

30.—[*Omitted.*] 1.713

31.—[*Omitted.*] 1.714

Income Tax (Trading and Other Income) Act 2005

(2005 c.5)

CONTENTS

PART 1

OVERVIEW

1. Overview of Act 1.715
2. Overview of priority rules

Income Tax (Trading and Other Income) Act 2005

PART 2

TRADING INCOME

CHAPTER 1

INTRODUCTION

3. Overview of Part 2
4. Provisions which must be given priority over Part 2

CHAPTER 2

INCOME TAXED AS TRADE PROFITS

Charge to tax on trade profits

5. Charge to tax on trade profits
6. Territorial scope of charge to tax
6A. Arrangements for avoiding tax
7. Income charged
8. Person liable

Trades and trade profits

9. Farming and market gardening

Starting and ceasing to trade

17. Effect of becoming or ceasing to be a UK resident

Rent-a-room and qualifying care relief

23. Rent-a-room and foster-care relief

CHAPTER 3

TRADE PROFITS: BASIC RULES

24. Professions and vocations
24A. Cash basis to apply by default
25. Generally accepted accounting practice
26. Losses calculated on same basis as profits
27. Receipts and expenses
28. Items treated under CAA 2001 as receipts and expenses
28A. Money's worth
29. Interest
31. Relationship between rules prohibiting and allowing deductions

(2005 c.5)

Chapter 3A

Trade Profits: Cash Basis

31D. Effect of election under section 25A

Calculation of profits on cash basis

31E. Calculation of profits on cash basis

Overview of rest of Part 2

31F. Overview of rest of Part 2 as it applies to cash basis

Chapter 4

Trade Profits: Rules Restricting Deductions

Introduction

32. Professions and vocations

Cash basis accounting

32A. Application of Chapter to the cash basis

Capital expenditure

33. Capital expenditure
33A. Cash basis: capital expenditure

Wholly and exclusively and losses rules

34. Expenses not wholly and exclusively for trade and unconnected losses

Bad and doubtful debts

35. Bad and doubtful debts

Unpaid remuneration

36. Unpaid remuneration

Business entertainment and gifts

45. Business entertainment and gifts: general rule

Social security contributions

53. Social security contributions

CHAPTER 6

TRADE PROFITS: RECEIPTS

Introduction

95. Professions and vocations

Cash basis accounting

95A. Application of Chapter to the cash basis

Capital receipts

96. Capital receipts
96A. Capital receipts under, or after leaving, cash basis
96B. Section 96A: supplementary provision

Debts released

97. Debts incurred and later released

PART 3

PROPERTY INCOME

CHAPTER I

INTRODUCTION

260. Overview of Part 3
261. Provisions which must be given priority over Part 3
262. Priority between Chapters within Part 3

(2005 c.5)

Chapter 2

Property Businesses

Introduction

263. Introduction

Basic meaning of UK and overseas property business

264. UK property business
265. Overseas property business

Generating income from land

266. Meaning of "generating income from land"

Chapter 3

Profits of Property Businesses: Basic Rules

Charge to tax on profits of a property business

268. Charge to tax on profits of a property business
269. Territorial scope of charge to tax
270. Income charged
271. Person liable

Calculation of profits

272ZA. Application of trading income rules: cash basis

Part 4

Savings and Investment Income

Chapter 1

Introduction

365. Overview of Part 4
366. Provisions which must be given priority over Part 4
367. Priority between Chapters within Part 4
368. Territorial scope of Part 4 charges

Income Tax (Trading and Other Income) Act 2005

CHAPTER 2

INTEREST

Charge to tax on interest

369. Charge to tax on interest
370. Income charged
370A. Valuation of interest not paid in cash
371. Person liable

Other income taxed as interest

372. Building society dividends

CHAPTER 3

DIVIDENDS ETC. FROM UK RESIDENT COMPANIES AND TAX TREATED AS PAID IN RESPECT OF CERTAIN DISTRIBUTIONS

Introduction

382. Contents of Chapter

Charge to tax on dividends and other distributions

383. Charge to tax on dividends and other distributions
384. Income charged
385. Person liable

CHAPTER 4

DIVIDENDS FROM NON-UK RESIDENT COMPANIES

Charge to tax on dividends from non-UK resident companies

402. Charge to tax on dividends from non-UK resident companies
403. Income charged
404. Person liable

(2005 c.5)

CHAPTER 7

PURCHASED LIFE ANNUITY PAYMENTS

422. Charge to tax on purchased life annuity payments
423. Meaning of "purchased life annuity"
424. Income charged
425. Person liable

PART 5

MISCELLANEOUS INCOME

CHAPTER 1

INTRODUCTION

574. Overview of Part 5
575. Provisions which must be given priority over Part 5
576. Priority between Chapters within Part 5

CHAPTER 5

SETTLEMENTS: AMOUNTS TREATED AS INCOME OF SETTLOR

Charge to tax under Chapter 5

619. Charge to tax under Chapter 5
619A. Income treated as highest part of settlor's total income
620. Meaning of "settlement" and "settlor"

Income charged and person liable

621. Income charged
622. Person liable

CHAPTER 8

INCOME NOT OTHERWISE CHARGED

687. Charge to tax on income not otherwise charged
688. Income charged
689. Person liable

Income Tax (Trading and Other Income) Act 2005

PART 6

EXEMPT INCOME

CHAPTER 1

INTRODUCTION

690.   Overview of Part 6

CHAPTER 2

NATIONAL SAVINGS INCOME

691.   National Savings Bank ordinary account interest [*omitted*]
692.   Income from savings certificates [*omitted*]

CHAPTER 8

OTHER ANNUAL PAYMENTS

Certain annual payments by individuals

730.   Foreign maintenance payments

Periodical payments of personal injury damages etc.

731.   Periodical payments of personal injury damages
732.   Compensation awards
733.   Persons entitled to exemptions for personal injury payments etc.
734.   Payments from trusts for injured persons

Health and employment insurance payments

735.   Health and employment insurance payments
736.   Health and employment risks and benefits

Payments to adopters

744.   Payments to adopters etc.: England and Wales
745.   Payments to adopters, etc.: Scotland

CHAPTER 9

OTHER INCOME

751.   Interest on damages for personal injury
753.   Interest on repayment of student loan

776. Scholarship income
780. Disabled person's vehicle maintenance grant

CHAPTER 10

GENERAL

783. General disregard of exempt income for income tax purposes

PART 7

INCOME CHARGED UNDER THIS ACT: RENT-A-ROOM AND QUALIFYING CARE RELIEF

CHAPTER 1

RENT-A-ROOM RELIEF

Introduction

784. Overview of Chapter 1
785. Person who qualifies for relief

Basic definitions

786. Meaning of "rent-a-room receipts"
787. Meaning of "residence"
788. Meaning of "total rent-a-room amount"

Individual's limit

789. The individual's limit

CHAPTER 2

QUALIFYING-CARE RELIEF

Introduction

803. Overview of Chapter 2
804. Person who qualifies for relief
804A. Shared lives care: further condition for relief

Basic definitions

805. Meaning of "qualifying-care receipts"
805A. Meaning of providing qualifying care
806. Meaning of providing foster care
806A. Meaning of providing shared lives care
806B. Meaning of "residence"
807. Calculation of "total qualifying care receipts"

808. The individual's limit
809. Share of fixed amount: residence used by more than one carer
810. Share of fixed amount: income period not a year
811. The amount per adult or child
812. Full qualifying care relief: introduction
813. Full qualifying care relief: trading income
814. Full qualifying care relief: income chargeable under Chapter 8 of Part 5

PART 10

GENERAL PROVISIONS

CHAPTER 1

INTRODUCTION

864. Overview of Part 10

CHAPTER 2

GENERAL CALCULATON RULES ETC.

868. Social security contributions: non-trades, etc.

INTRODUCTION AND GENERAL NOTE

1.716 ITTOIA is the third of the series of Acts produced under the Tax Law Rewrite Project. It came into effect on April 6, 2005. Together with ITEPA it has rewritten all the main charging provisions of income tax as they apply to individuals, partnerships and trusts. Provisions applying to companies have not been rewritten, but they are not relevant to tax credits.

ITTOIA completes the abolition of all the former income tax schedules as its provisions replace the old Sch.A (taxation of income from land in the UK) and Sch.D, Cases I to VI (trading and professional income, investment income, and foreign source income). Following the approach adopted in ITEPA it also merges provisions about the taxation of UK-source income with the taxation of foreign source income. The relevance here is that assessment of income for tax credits purposes includes worldwide income. With effect from the tax year 2006/07 no reference therefore need be made to the old law for tax credits purposes.

The pattern adopted by ITTOIA is as follows. The charges to tax under the various Schedules and other separate charging sections have been converted into charges on different classes of income, and the rules relating to each kind of income are set out in separate Parts of the Act. These are then followed by general exemptions and other provisions. Each part has "signposts" in it, including an initial overview and provisions dealing with priorities between charging provisions.

1.717 The most important difference between kinds or classes of income is the one that lies between ITEPA and ITTOIA: is an individual employed or self-employed? ITTOIA operates if ITEPA does not, but the decision whether someone is employed or not in that narrower sense is left outside both Acts and for the ordinary law—and in the social security context is usually to be determined under the provisions of s.8 of the Social Security (Transfer of Functions) Act 1999.

The new charges to tax, exemptions and reliefs are:

Part 2 Trading income (including professions and vocations)

Part 3 Property income (including both UK and foreign land)

Part 4 Savings and investment income (including interest and dividends)

Part 5 Miscellaneous income (the "sweeper")

Part 6 Exempt income

Part 7 Rent-a-room and qualifying care reliefs

Trading income replaces the old Sch.D Cases I and II and part of Case VI. Property income replaces the old Sch.A and part of Sch.D Case V. Savings and investment income replaces the old Sch.D Case III and Case IV, part of Case V and part of Case VI. It also replaces Sch.F. (It also includes the former Sch.C, which was repealed and replaced by provisions included in Sch.D some years ago). As the former Sch.B was repealed many years ago, this completes the repeal for income tax (and therefore tax credits) purposes of all the old 1803 income tax schedules.

A consistent pattern within each part is to place the most important provisions at the start of the Part. For example, in the savings and investment income part the charge on interest comes first, then dividends, with less commonly used provisions following in decreasing order of importance. The Act also seeks to put all the important measures in the main text of the Act, rather than in schedules. This explains the need for a lengthy Pt 7, dealing with the important but inevitably detailed provisions that exempt small incomes from income tax if drawn from renting rooms in the individual's only or main residence or from foster care payments (or both).

The sections selected for inclusion

The sections set out in this work are selected for two reasons: first, they are the main sections of the Act and the ones to which reference is most likely to be made, directly or indirectly, in straightforward tax credits cases involving either the self-employed or forms of savings and investment income. Secondly, sections are included where they deal expressly with social security income or the kinds of income received in particular by those with disabilities. Provisions providing exemption from two specific kinds of income widely received by those with entitlement to tax credits are also included: tax relief under the rent-a-room scheme exempting income where a resident owner lets part of his or her house to a lodger; and the exemption of income paid to foster parents and other carers under qualifying care relief.

1.718

The law is as applied after any amendments in the Finance Acts. No history of amendments is set out. However, the full history of the original ITTOIA provisions (to which as yet little amendment has been made) are in the full explanatory notes to ITTOIA issued by the Tax Law Rewrite Project.

PART 1

OVERVIEW

Overview of Act

1.—(1) This Act imposes charges to income tax under—
(a) Part 2 (trading income),
(b) Part 3 (property income),
(c) Part 4 (savings and investment income), and
(d) Part 5 (certain miscellaneous income).
(2) *Repealed.*
(3) Exemptions from those charges are dealt with in Part 6 (exempt income) but any Part 6 exemptions which are most obviously relevant to

1.719

particular types of income are also mentioned in the provisions about those types of income.

(4) What is or is not mentioned in those provisions does not limit the effect of Part 6.

(5) This Act also contains—
- (za) provision about a trading allowance and property allowance (see Part 6A),
- (a) provision about rent-a-room relief and qualifying care relief (see Part 7),
- (b) special rules for foreign income (see Part 8),
- (c) special rules for partnerships (see Part 9), and
- (d) certain calculation rules and general provisions (see Part 10).

(6) For abbreviations and defined expressions used in this Act, see 885 and Sch.4.

Overview of priority rules

1.720   **2.**—(1) This Act contains some rules establishing an order of priority in respect of certain amounts which would otherwise—
- (a) fall within a charge to income tax under two or more Chapters or Parts of this Act, or
- (b) fall within a charge to income tax under a Chapter or Part of this Act and ITEPA 2003.

(2) See, in particular—
section 4 (provisions which must be given priority over Part 2),
section 261 (provisions which must be given priority over Part 3),
section 262 (priority between Chapters within Part 3),
section 366 (provisions which must be given priority over Part 4),
section 367 (priority between Chapters within Part 4),
section 575 (provisions which must be given priority over Part 5), and
section 576 (priority between Chapters within Part 5).

(3) But the rules in those sections need to be read with other rules law (whether in this Act or otherwise) about the scope of particular provisions or the order of priority to be given to them.

(4) Section 171(2) of FA 1993 (profits of Lloyd's underwriters charged only under Chapter 2 of Part 2 of this Act) is one example of another rule of law.

PART 2

TRADING INCOME

CHAPTER 1

Overview of Part 2

1.721   **3.**—(1) This Part imposes charges to income tax under—
- (a) Chapter 2 (the profits of a trade, profession or vocation which meet the territorial conditions mentioned in section 6),
- (b) Chapter 17 (amounts treated as adjustment income under section 228), and

(c) Chapter 18 (post-cessation receipts that are chargeable under this Part).

(2) Part 6 deals with exemptions from the charges under this Part.

(3) See, in particular, the exemptions under sections 777 (VAT repayment supplements) and 778 (incentives to use electronic communications).

(4) The charges under this Part apply to non-UK residents as well as UK residents but this is subject to sections 6(1A), (2) and (3) and 243(3) and (4) (charges on non-UK residents only on UK income).

(5) The rest of this Part contains rules relevant to the charges to tax under this Part.

(6) This section needs to be read with the relevant priority rules (see sections 2 and 4).

GENERAL NOTE

Part 2 rewrites (and to some extent also codifies) the previous provisions in Sch.D Case I (income from trade wholly or partly in the UK) and Case II (income from professions and vocations) and aspects of Case IV (other income) previously in ICTA 1988 and subsequent Finance Acts. But the definition of "trade" remains in ICTA 1988 s.832. The charges under this Part on non-UK residents are not covered in this work.

Provisions which must be given priority over Part 2

4.—(1) Any receipt or other credit item, so far as it falls within—
(a) Chapter 2 of this Part (receipts of trade, profession or vocation), and
(b) Chapter 3 of Part 3 so far as it relates to a UK property business,
is dealt with under Part 3.

(2) Any receipt or other credit item, so far as it falls within—
(a) this Part, and
(b) Part 2, 9 or 10 of ITEPA 2003 (employment income, pension income or social security income),
is dealt with under the relevant Part of ITEPA 2003.

CHAPTER 2

INCOME TAXED AS TRADE PROFITS

Charge to tax on trade profits

Charge to tax on trade profits

5.—Income tax is charged on the profits of a trade, profession or vocation.

Territorial scope of charge to tax

6.—(1) Profits of a trade arising to a UK resident are chargeable to tax under this Chapter wherever the trade is carried on.

(1A) Profits of a trade of dealing in or developing UK land arising to a non-UK resident are chargeable to tax under this Chapter wherever the trade is carried on.

(2) Profits of a trade other than a trade of dealing in or developing UK land arising to a non-UK resident are chargeable to tax under this Chapter only if they arise—

(a) from a trade carried on wholly in the United Kingdom, or
(b) in the case of a trade carried on partly in the United Kingdom and partly elsewhere, from the part of the trade carried on in the United Kingdom.

(2A) If the tax year is a split year as respects a UK resident individual, this section has effect as if, for the overseas part of that year, the individual were non-UK resident.

(3) This section applies to professions and vocations as it applies to trades.

1.726 **Arrangements for avoiding tax**

6A.—(1) Subsection (3) applies if a person has entered into an arrangement the main purpose or one of the main purposes of which is to obtain a relevant tax advantage for the person.

(2) In subsection (1) the reference to obtaining a relevant tax advantage includes obtaining a relevant tax advantage by virtue of any provisions of double taxation arrangements, but only in a case where the relevant tax advantage is contrary to the object and purpose of the provisions of the double taxation arrangements (and subsection (3) has effect accordingly, regardless of anything in section 6(1) of TIOPA 2010).

(3) The relevant tax advantage is to be counteracted by means of adjustments.

(4) For this purpose adjustments may be made (whether by an officer of Revenue and Customs or by the person) by way of an assessment, the modification of an assessment, amendment or disallowance of a claim, or otherwise.

(5) In this section "relevant tax advantage" means a tax advantage in relation to income tax to which the person is chargeable (or would without the tax advantage be chargeable) by virtue of section 6(1A).

(6) In this section "tax advantage" includes—
(a) a relief or increased relief from tax,
(b) repayment or increased repayment of tax,
(c) avoidance or reduction of a charge to tax or an assessment to tax,
(d) avoidance of a possible assessment to tax,
(e) deferral of a payment of tax or advancement of a repayment of tax, and
(f) avoidance of an obligation to deduct or account for tax.

(7) In this section—
"arrangement" (except in the phrase "double taxation arrangements") includes any agreement, understanding, scheme, transaction or series of transactions, whether or not legally enforceable;
"double taxation arrangements" means arrangements which have effect under section 2(1) of TIOPA 2010 (double taxation relief by agreement with territories outside the United Kingdom).

Income charged

1.727 **7.**—(1) Tax is charged under this Chapter on the full amount of the profits of the tax year (including amounts treated as profits of the tax year under section 23E(1)).
(2) [*repealed*]
(3) [*repealed*]
(4) This section is subject to Part 8 (foreign income: special rules).

(5) And, for the purposes of section 830 (meaning of "relevant foreign income"), the profits of a trade, profession or vocation arise from a source outside the United Kingdom only if the trade, profession or vocation is carried on wholly outside the United Kingdom.

Person liable

8.—The person liable for any tax charged under this Chapter is the person receiving or entitled to the profits.

1.728

Trades and trade profits

Farming and market gardening

9.—(1) Farming or market gardening in the United Kingdom is treated for income tax purposes as the carrying on of a trade or part of a trade (whether or not the land is managed on a commercial basis and with a view to the realisation of profits).

1.729

(2) All farming in the United Kingdom carried on by a person, other than farming carried on as part of another trade, is treated for income tax purposes as one trade.

(3) In the case of farming carried on by a firm, this rule is explained by section 859(1).

Starting and ceasing to trade

Effect of becoming or ceasing to be a UK resident

17.—(1) This section applies if—

1.730

(a) an individual carries on a trade (alone or in partnership), and
(b) there is a change of residence.

(1A) For the purposes of this section there is a "change of residence" if—
(a) the individual becomes or ceases to be UK resident, or
(b) a tax year is, as respects the individual, a split year.

(1B) The change of residence occurs—
(a) in a case falling within subsection (1A)(a), at the start of the tax year for which the individual becomes or ceases to be UK resident, and
(b) in a case falling within subsection (1A)(b), at the start of whichever of the UK part or the overseas part of the tax year is the later part.

(2) If this section applies and the individual does not actually cease permanently to carry on the trade immediately before the change of residence occurs, the individual is treated for income tax purposes—
(a) as permanently ceasing to carry on the trade at the time of the change of residence, and
(b) so far as the individual continues to carry on the trade, as starting to carry on a new trade immediately afterwards.

(3) But subsection (2) does not prevent a loss made before the change of residence from being deducted under section 83 of ITA 2007 from profits arising after the change.

(4) This section applies to professions and vocations as it applies to trades.

Rent-a-room and qualifying care relief

1.731   **23.**—(1) The rules for calculating the profits of a trade carried on by an individual are subject to Chapter 1 of Part 7 (rent-a-room relief).

(2) That Chapter provides relief on income from the use of furnished accommodation in the individual's only or main residence (see, in particular, sections 792 and 796).

(3) The rules for calculating the profits of a trade, profession or vocation carried on by an individual are subject to Chapter 2 of Part 7 (qualifying care relief).

(4) That Chapter provides relief on income from the provision by the individual of qualifying care (see, in particular, sections 813, 816, 822 and 823).

CHAPTER 3

TRADE PROFITS: BASIC RULES

Professions and vocations

1.732   **24.**—Apart from section 30 (animals kept for trade purposes), the provisions of this Chapter apply to professions and vocations as they apply to trades.

Cash basis to apply by default

1.733   **24A.**—(1) The profits of a trade for a tax year must be calculated on the cash basis, unless—
   (a) the trade is an excluded trade in relation to the tax year (see section 25B), or
   (b) an election under section 25C(1) has effect in relation to the trade for the tax year.

(2) In this Part—
   (a) references to calculating the profits of a trade on the cash basis are references to doing so in accordance with this section, and
   (b) references to a trade in relation to which the cash basis applies are to a trade the profits of which are required by virtue of subsection (1) to be calculated on the cash basis.

(3) Chapter 3A contains provision about the calculation of profits on the cash basis and the application of the rest of this Part in relation to the cash basis.

(4) Where the cash basis applies in relation to a trade, sections 27, 28 and 30 do not apply in relation to the calculation of the profits of the trade.

(5) This section does not affect provisions of the Income Tax Acts relating to the calculation of the profits of Lloyd's underwriters.

Generally accepted accounting practice

1.734   **25.**—(1) The profits of a trade to which the cash basis does not apply must be calculated in accordance with generally accepted accounting practice, subject to any adjustment required or authorised by law in calculating profits for income tax purposes.

(2) This does not—

(a) require a person to comply with the requirements of the Companies Act 2006 or subordinate legislation made under that Act except as to the basis of calculation, or
(b) impose any requirements as to audit or disclosure.
(3) [*repealed*]
(4) This section does not affect provisions of the Income Tax Acts relating to the calculation of the profits of Lloyd's underwriters.

Losses calculated on same basis as profits

26.—(1) The same rules apply for income tax purposes in calculating losses of a trade as apply in calculating profits.
(2) This is subject to any express provision to the contrary.

Receipts and expenses

27.—(1) In the Income Tax Acts, in the context of the calculation of the profits of a trade, references to receipts and expenses are to any items brought into account as credits or debits in calculating the profits.
(2) There is no implication that an amount has been actually received or paid.
(3) This section is subject to any express provision to the contrary.

Items treated under CAA 2001 as receipts and expenses

28.—The rules for calculating the profits of a trade need to be read with—
(a) the provisions of CAA 2001 which treat charges as receipts of a trade, and
(b) the provisions of CAA 2001 which treat allowances as expenses of a trade.

Money's worth

28A.—(1) Subsection (2) applies—
(a) for the purpose of bringing into account an amount arising in respect of a transaction involving money's worth entered into in the course of a trade, and
(b) if an amount at least equal to the amount that would be brought into account under that subsection is not otherwise brought into account as a receipt in calculating the profits of a trade under a provision of this Part other than a provision mentioned in subsection (3).
(2) For the purpose of calculating the profits of the trade, an amount equal to the value of the money's worth is brought into account as a receipt if, had the transaction involved money, an amount would have been brought into account as a receipt in respect of it.
(3) But where another provision of this Part makes express provision for the bringing into account of an amount in respect of money's worth as a receipt in calculating the profits of a trade (however expressed), that other provision applies instead of subsection (2).

Interest

29.—For the purpose of calculating the profits of a trade, interest is an item of a revenue nature, whatever the nature of the loan.

Relationship between rules prohibiting and allowing deductions

1.740

31.—(1) Any relevant permissive rule in this Part—
  (a) has priority over any relevant prohibitive rule in this Part, but
  (b) is subject to section 36 (unpaid remuneration), section 38 (employee benefit contributions), section 48 (car hire) and section 55 (crime-related payments).

(1A) But, if the relevant permissive rule would allow a deduction in calculating the profits of a trade in respect of an amount which arises directly or indirectly in consequence of, or otherwise in connection with, relevant tax avoidance arrangements, that rule—
  (a) does not have priority under subsection (1)(a), and
  (b) is subject to any relevant prohibitive rule in this Part (and to the provisions mentioned in subsection (1)(b)).

(2) In this section "any relevant permissive rule in this Part" means any provision of—
  (a) Chapter 5 (apart from sections 60 to 67),
  (aa) Chapter 5A,
  (b) Chapter 11,
  (c) Chapter 13, or
  (d) Chapter 17A,
which allows a deduction in calculating the profits of a trade.

(3) In this section "any relevant prohibitive rule in this Part", in relation to any deduction, means any provision of this Part (apart from sections 36, 38, 48 and 55) which might otherwise be read as—
  (a) prohibiting the deduction, or
  (b) restricting the amount of the deduction.

(4) In this section "relevant tax avoidance arrangements" means arrangements—
  (a) to which the person carrying on the trade is a party, and
  (b) the main purpose, or one of the main purposes, of which is the obtaining of a tax advantage (within the meaning of section 1139 of CTA 2010).

"Arrangements" includes any agreement, understanding, scheme, transaction or series of transactions (whether or not legally enforceable).

CHAPTER 3A

TRADE PROFITS: CASH BASIS

Calculation of profits on cash basis

Calculation of profits on cash basis

1.741

31E.—(1) This section applies to professions and vocations as it applies to trades.

(2) To determine the profits of a trade for a tax year on the cash basis—

Step 1

Calculate the total amount of receipts of the trade received during the tax year.

Step 2

Deduct from that amount the total amount of expenses of the trade paid during the tax year.

(3) Subsection (2) is subject to any adjustment required or authorised by law in calculating profits for income tax purposes.

(4) In determining the profits of a trade on the cash basis, section 7A(2) applies as if the profits or losses of a period of account were determined in accordance with subsection (2) of this section (and for these purposes, references in subsection (2) of this section to a tax year are to be read as references to a period of account).

Overview of rest of Part 2

Overview of rest of Part 2 as it applies to cash basis

31F.—(1) For provision about the application of Chapters 4 to 6 (rules about deductions and receipts) in relation to the cash basis, see sections 32A, 56A and 95A.

(2) For provision about the application of Chapter 11 (trade profits: other specific trades) in relation to the cash basis, see section 148K.

(3) The following Chapters apply only where profits are calculated on the cash basis—

Chapter 6A (trade profits: amounts not reflecting commercial transactions),

Chapter 17A (cash basis: adjustments for capital allowances).

(4) The following Chapters do not apply in relation to the cash basis—

Chapter 8 (trade profits: herd basis rules),

Chapter 9 (trade profits: sound recordings),

Chapter 10 (trade profits: certain telecommunication rights),

Chapter 10A (leases of plant or machinery: special rules for long funding leases),

Chapter 11A (trade profits: changes in trading stock),

Chapter 13 (deductions from profits: unremittable amounts),

Chapter 14 (disposal and acquisition of know-how),

Chapter 16 (averaging profits of farmers and creative artists),

Chapter 16ZA (compensation for compulsory slaughter of animal),

Chapter 16A (oil activities).

CHAPTER 4

TRADE PROFITS: RULES RESTRICTING DEDUCTIONS

Introduction

Professions and vocations

32.—The provisions of this Chapter apply to professions and vocations as they apply to trades.

Cash basis accounting

Application of Chapter to the cash basis

1.744   **32A.**—(1) The following sections do not apply in calculating the profits of a trade on the cash basis—

section 33 (capital expenditure),
section 35 (bad and doubtful debts),
sections 36 and 37 (unpaid remuneration),
section 43 (employee benefit contributions: profits calculated before end of 9 month period),
sections 48 to 50B (car hire).

(2) For rules restricting deductions that apply only where profits are calculated on the cash basis, see Section 33A (cash basis: capital expenditure).

Capital expenditure

Capital expenditure

1.745   **33.**—In calculating the profits of a trade, no deduction is allowed for items of a capital nature.

Cash basis: capital expenditure

1.746   **33A.**—(1) This section applies in relation to the calculation of the profits of a trade on the cash basis.

(2) No deduction is allowed for an item of a capital nature incurred on, or in connection with, the acquisition or disposal of a business or part of a business.

(3) No deduction is allowed for an item of a capital nature incurred on, or in connection with, education or training.

(4) No deduction is allowed for an item of a capital nature incurred on, or in connection with, the provision, alteration or disposal of—

   (a) any asset that is not a depreciating asset (see subsections (6) and (7)),
   (b) any asset not acquired or created for use on a continuing basis in the trade,
   (c) a car (see subsection (14)),
   (d) land,
   (e) a non-qualifying intangible asset (see subsections (8) to (11)), or
   (f) a financial asset (see subsection (12)).

(5) But subsection (4)(d) does not prevent a deduction being made for expenditure that—

   (a) is incurred on the provision of a depreciating asset which, in being provided, is installed or otherwise fixed to land so as to become, in law, part of the land, but
   (b) is not incurred on, or in connection with, the provision of—
      (i) a building,
      (ii) a wall, floor, ceiling, door, gate, shutter or window or stairs,
      (iii) a waste disposal system,
      (iv) a sewerage or drainage system, or

(v) a shaft or other structure in which a lift, hoist, escalator or moving walkway may be installed.

(6) An asset is a "depreciating" asset if, on the date the item of a capital nature is incurred, it is reasonable to expect that before the end of 20 years beginning with that date—
(a) the useful life of the asset will end, or
(b) the asset will decline in value by 90% or more.

(7) The useful life of an asset ends when it could no longer be of use to any person for any purpose as an asset of a business.

(8) "Intangible asset" means anything that is capable of being an intangible asset within the meaning of FRS 105 and, in particular, includes—
(a) an internally-generated intangible asset, and
(b) intellectual property.

(9) An intangible asset is "non-qualifying" unless, by virtue of having a fixed maximum duration, it must cease to exist before the end of 20 years beginning with the date on which the item of a capital nature is incurred.

(10) An intangible asset is "non-qualifying" if it consists of a right, whether conditional or not, to obtain an intangible asset without a fixed maximum duration by virtue of which that asset must, assuming the right is exercised at the last possible time, cease to exist before the end of 20 years beginning with the date on which the item of a capital nature is incurred.

(11) Where—
(a) the trader has an intangible asset, and
(b) the trader grants a licence or any other right in respect of that asset to another person,
any intangible asset that consists of a licence or other right granted to the trader in respect of the intangible asset mentioned in paragraph (a) is "non-qualifying".

(12) A "financial asset" means any right under or in connection with—
(a) a financial instrument, or
(b) an arrangement that is capable of producing a return that is economically equivalent to a return produced under any financial instrument.

(13) A reference to acquisition, provision, alteration or disposal includes potential acquisition, provision, alteration or (as the case may be) disposal.

(14) In this section—
"arrangement" includes any agreement, understanding, scheme, transaction or series of transactions (whether or not legally enforceable);
"building" includes any fixed structure;
"car" has the same meaning as in Part 2 of CAA 2001 (see section 268A of that Act);
"financial instrument" has the same meaning as in FRS 105;
"FRS 105" means Financial Reporting Standard 105 (the Financial Reporting Standard applicable to the Micro-entities Regime), issued by the Financial Reporting Council in July 2015;
"intellectual property" means—
(a) any patent, trade mark, registered design, copyright or design right, plant breeders' rights or rights under section 7 of the Plant Varieties Act 1997,
(b) any right under the law of a country or territory outside the United Kingdom corresponding or similar to a right within paragraph (a),

(c) any information or technique not protected by a right within paragraph (a) or (b) but having industrial, commercial or other economic value, or
(d) any licence or other right in respect of anything within paragraph (a), (b) or (c);

"provision" includes creation, construction or acquisition;

"the trader" means the person carrying on the trade.

Wholly and exclusively and losses rules

Expenses not wholly and exclusively for trade and unconnected losses

1.747   **34.**—(1) In calculating the profits of a trade, no deduction is allowed for—
(a) expenses not incurred wholly and exclusively for the purposes of the trade, or
(b) losses not connected with or arising out of the trade.

(2) If an expense is incurred for more than one purpose, this section does not prohibit a deduction for any identifiable part or identifiable proportion of the expense which is incurred wholly and exclusively for the purposes of the trade.

Bad and doubtful debts

Bad and doubtful debts

1.748   **35.**—(1) In calculating the profits of a trade, no deduction is allowed for a debt owed to the person carrying on the trade, except so far as—
(a) the debt is bad,
(b) the debt is estimated to be bad, or
(c) the debt is released wholly and exclusively for the purposes of the trade as part of a statutory insolvency arrangement.

(2) If the debtor is bankrupt or insolvent, the whole of the debt is estimated to be bad for the purposes of subsection (1)(b), except so far as any amount may reasonably be expected to be received on the debt.

Unpaid remuneration

Unpaid remuneration

1.749   **36.**—(1) This section applies if, in calculating the profits of a trade of a period of account—
(a) an amount is charged in the accounts for the period in respect of employees' remuneration, and
(b) a deduction for the remuneration would otherwise be allowable for the period.

(2) No deduction is allowed for the remuneration for the period of account unless it is paid before the end of the period of 9 months immediately following the end of the period of account.

(3) If the remuneration is paid after the end of that 9 month period, deduction for it is allowed for the period of account in which it is paid.

Business entertainment and gifts

Business entertainment and gifts: general rule

45.—(1) The general rule is that no deduction is allowed in calculating the profits of a trade for expenses incurred in providing entertainment or gifts in connection with the trade.

(2) A deduction for expenses which are incurred—
(a) in paying sums to or on behalf of an employee of the person carrying on the trade ("the trader"), or
(b) in putting sums at the disposal of an employee of the trader,

is prohibited by the general rule if (and only if) the sums are paid, or put at the employee's disposal, exclusively for meeting expenses incurred or to be incurred by the employee in providing the entertainment or gift.

(3) The general rule is subject to exceptions—
for entertainment (see section 46), and
for gifts (see section 47).

(4) For the purposes of this section and those two sections—
(a) "employee", in relation to a company, includes a director of the company and a person engaged in the management of the company,
(b) "entertainment" includes hospitality of any kind, and
(c) the expenses incurred in providing entertainment or a gift include expenses incurred in providing anything incidental to the provision of entertainment or a gift.

1.750

Social security contributions

Social security contributions

53.—(1) In calculating the profits of a trade, no deduction is allowed for any contribution paid by any person under—
(a) Part 1 of the Social Security Contributions and Benefits Act 1992 (c. 4), or
(b) Part 1 of the Social Security Contributions and Benefits (Northern Ireland) Act 1992 (c.7).

(2) But this prohibition does not apply to an employer's contribution.
(3) For this purpose "an employer's contribution" means—
(a) a secondary Class 1 contribution,
(b) a Class 1A contribution, or
(c) a Class 1B contribution,

within the meaning of Part 1 of the Social Security Contributions and Benefits Act 1992 or of the Social Security Contributions and Benefits (Northern Ireland) Act 1992.

1.751

Chapter 6

Trade Profits: Receipts

Introduction

Professions and vocations

1.752   **95.**—Apart from section 105 (industrial development grants), the provisions of this Chapter apply to professions and vocations as they apply to trades.

Cash basis accounting

Application of Chapter to the cash basis

1.753   **95A.**—(1) For rules about receipts that apply only for the purpose of calculating profits on the cash basis, see the following—
   section 97A (cash basis: value of trading stock on cessation of trade),
   section 97B (cash basis: value of work in progress on cessation of profession or vocation).
   (2) Section 96A makes provision about capital receipts in certain cases where the profits of a trade are calculated on the cash basis or have previously been calculated on the cash basis (and see also section 96B).

Capital receipts

Capital receipts

1.754   **96.**—(1) Items of a capital nature must not be brought into account as receipts in calculating the profits of a trade.
   (2) But this does not apply to items which, as a result of any provision of this Part, are brought into account as receipts in calculating the profits of the trade.

Capital receipts under, or after leaving, cash basis

1.755   **96A.**—(1) This section applies in relation to a trade carried on by a person in two cases—
   (a) Case 1 (see subsections (2) to (3A)), and
   (b) Case 2 (see subsections (3B) to (3E)).
   (2) Case 1 is a case in which conditions A and B are met.
   (3) Condition A is that the person receives disposal proceeds or a capital refund in relation to an asset at a time when the cash basis applies in relation to the trade.
      For the meaning of "disposal proceeds" and "capital refund" see subsections (3F) and (3G).
      (3A) Condition B is that—
      (a) an amount of capital expenditure (see subsection (3H)) relating to the asset has been brought into account in calculating the profits of the trade on the cash basis, or

(b) an amount of capital expenditure relating to the asset which—
  (i) has been incurred (or treated as incurred) by the person before the tax year for which the person last entered the cash basis, and
  (ii) is cash basis deductible in relation to that tax year (see section 96B(4)) except to the extent that it is expenditure in respect of which a capital allowance is made under Part 2A of that Act,

has been brought into account in calculating the profits of the trade for a tax year in which the cash basis did not apply in relation to the trade.

(3B) Case 2 is a case in which—
(a) condition C is met, and
(b) condition D or E is met.

(3C) Condition C is that disposal proceeds or a capital refund arise to the person in relation to an asset at a time—
(a) when the cash basis does not apply in relation to the trade, and
(b) which is after a time when the cash basis did apply in relation to the trade.

(3D) Condition D is that an amount of capital expenditure relating to the asset—
(a) has been paid at a time the cash basis applied in relation to the trade,
(b) has been brought into account in calculating the profits of the trade on the cash basis, and
(c) on the assumption that the cash basis had not applied at the time the expenditure was paid, would not have been qualifying expenditure.

(3E) Condition E is that an amount of capital expenditure relating to the asset has been brought into account in calculating the profits of the trade for a tax year—
(a) in which the cash basis did not apply in relation to the trade, and
(b) which is before the tax year for which the person last entered the cash basis.

The reference in this subsection to expenditure brought into account does not include a reference to expenditure brought into account under CAA 2001 (see section 96B(5)).

(3F) "Disposal proceeds" means—
(a) any proceeds arising from the disposal of an asset or any part of it,
(b) any proceeds arising from the grant of any right in respect of, or any interest in, the asset, or
(c) any amount of damages, proceeds of insurance or other compensation received in respect of the asset.

See also subsections (4) and (5) for circumstances in which a person is to be regarded as disposing of an asset.

(3G) "Capital refund" means an amount that is (in substance) a refund of capital expenditure relating to an asset.

(3H) "Capital expenditure" means expenditure of a capital nature incurred, or treated as incurred, on or in connection with—
(a) the provision, alteration or disposal of an asset, or
(b) the potential provision, alteration or disposal of an asset.

(3I) The disposal proceeds or capital refund mentioned in condition A or (as the case may be) condition C are to be brought into account as a receipt in calculating the profits of the trade.

(3J) In a case where only part of the total capital expenditure incurred, or treated as incurred, by the person in relation to the asset has been brought into account in calculating the profits of the trade (whether or not on the cash basis), the amount brought into account under subsection (3I) is proportionately reduced.

The reference in this subsection to expenditure brought into account includes a reference to expenditure brought into account under CAA 2001 (see section 96B(5)).

(3K) Subsection (3I) does not apply if the whole of the amount which would otherwise be brought into account under that subsection—
  (a) has already been brought into account as a receipt in calculating the profits of the trade under this section,
  (b) is brought into account as a receipt in calculating the profits of the trade under any other provision of this Part (except section 240D(3) (assets not fully paid for)), or
  (c) is brought into account under any Part of CAA 2001 as a disposal value.

(3L) If part of the amount which would otherwise be brought into account under subsection (3I) has already been or is brought into account as mentioned in subsection (3K), subsection (3I) applies in relation to the remainder of that amount.

(4) If—
  (a) at any time the person ceases to use the asset or any part of it for the purposes of the trade, but
  (b) the person does not dispose of the asset (or that part) at that time,
  the person is to be regarded for the purposes of this section as disposing of the asset (or that part) at that time for an amount equal to the market value amount.

(5) If at any time there is a material increase in the person's non-business use of the asset or any part of it, the person is to be regarded for the purposes of this section as disposing of the asset (or that part) at that time for an amount equal to the relevant proportion of the market value amount.

(6) For the purposes of subsection (5)—
  (a) there is an increase in a person's non-business use of an asset (or part of an asset) if—
    (i) the proportion of the person's use of the asset (or that part) that is for the purposes of the trade decreases, and
    (ii) the proportion of the person's use of the asset (or that part) that is for other purposes (the "non-business use") increases;
  (b) "the relevant proportion" is the difference between—
    (i) the proportion of the person's use of the asset (or part of the asset) that is non-business use, and
    (ii) the proportion of the person's use of the asset (or that part) that was non-business use before the increase mentioned in subsection (5).

Section 96A: supplementary provision

96B.—(1) This section has effect for the purposes of section 96A.

(2) Any question as to whether or to what extent expenditure is brought into account in calculating the profits of a trade is to be determined on such basis as is just and reasonable in all the circumstances.

(3) A person carrying on a trade "enters the cash basis" for a tax year if—
  (a) the cash basis applies in relation to the trade for the tax year, and
  (b) the cash basis did not apply in relation to the trade for the previous tax year.

(4) Expenditure is "cash basis deductible" in relation to a tax year if, on the assumption that the expenditure was paid in that tax year, a deduction would be allowed in respect of the expenditure in calculating the profits of the trade on the cash basis for that tax year.

(5) Expenditure is "brought into account under CAA 2001" in calculating the profits of a trade if and to the extent that—
  (a) a capital allowance made under Part 2, 2A, 5, 6, 7 or 8 of that Act in respect of the expenditure is treated as an expense in calculating those profits (see, for example, section 247 of that Act), or
  (b) qualifying expenditure (within the meaning of Part 2, 7 or 8 of CAA 2001) is allocated to a pool for the trade and is set-off against different disposal receipts.

(6) An amount of qualifying expenditure is "set-off against different disposal receipts" if—
  (a) the amount would have been unrelieved qualifying expenditure carried forward in the pool for the trade, but
  (b) the amount is not so carried forward because (and only because) one or more disposal values in respect of one or more assets, other than the asset in respect of which the qualifying expenditure was incurred (or treated as incurred), have at any time been brought into account in that pool.

(7) For the purposes of subsection (6), an amount of qualifying expenditure incurred (or treated as incurred) by a person is not to be regarded as not carried forward because the person enters the cash basis.

(8) In this section and in section 96A—
"disposal value" means—
(a) in section 96A(3K)(c)—
  (i) a disposal value for the purposes of Part 2, 4A, 5, 6, 7 8 or 10 of CAA 2001 (for example, in relation to Part 2 of that Act, see (in particular) section 61 of that Act), or
  (ii) proceeds from a balancing event for the purposes of Part 3 or 3A of that Act (see sections 316 and 360O of that Act), and
(b) in subsection (6), a disposal value for the purposes of—
  (i) Part 2 of that Act (see, in particular, section 61 of that Act),
  (ii) Part 7 of that Act (see section 462 of that Act), or
  (iii) Part 8 of that Act (see sections 476 and 477 of that Act);
"market value amount" means the amount that would be regarded as normal and reasonable—
(a) in the market conditions then prevailing, and
(b) between persons dealing with each other at arm's length in the open market;
"pool" means—
(a) the main pool or a class pool to which qualifying expenditure is allocated under Part 2 of CAA 2001 (see section 54 of that Act),
(b) a pool to which qualifying expenditure is allocated under Part 7 of that Act (see section 456 of that Act), or
(c) a pool to which qualifying expenditure is allocated under Part 8 of that Act (see section 470 of that Act);

"provision" includes creation, construction or acquisition;
"qualifying expenditure" means—
(a) qualifying expenditure within the meaning of Part 2 of CAA 2001 (see section 11(4) of that Act for the general rule),
(b) qualifying expenditure within the meaning of Part 5 of that Act (see section 395 of that Act),
(c) qualifying expenditure within the meaning of Part 6 of that Act (see section 439 of that Act),
(d) qualifying expenditure within the meaning of Part 7 of that Act (see section 454 of that Act), or
(e) qualifying trade expenditure within the meaning of Part 8 of that Act (see section 468 of that Act);
"unrelieved qualifying expenditure" means unrelieved qualifying expenditure for the purposes of—
(a) Part 2 of CAA 2001 (see section 59(1) and (2) of that Act),
(b) Part 7 of that Act (see section 461 of that Act), or
(c) Part 8 of that Act (see section 475 of that Act).

Debts released

Debts incurred and later released

1.757   **97.**—(1) This section applies if—
(a) in calculating the profits of a trade, a deduction is allowed for the expense giving rise to a debt owed by the person carrying on the trade,
(b) all or part of the debt is released, and
(c) the release is not part of a statutory insolvency arrangement.
(2) The amount released—
(a) is brought into account as a receipt in calculating the profits of the trade, and
(b) is treated as arising on the date of the release.

PART 3

PROPERTY INCOME

CHAPTER 1

INTRODUCTION

Overview of Part 3

1.758   **260.**—(1) This Part imposes charges to income tax under—
(a) Chapter 3 (the profits of a UK property business or an overseas property business),
(b) Chapter 7 (amounts treated as adjustment income under section 330),

(c) Chapter 8 (rent receivable in connection with a UK section 12(4) concern),
(d) Chapter 9 (rent receivable for UK electric-line wayleaves), and
(e) Chapter 10 (post-cessation receipts arising from a UK property business).

(2) Part 6 deals with exemptions from the charges under this Part.

(3) See, in particular, the exemptions under sections 769 (housing grants), 777 (VAT repayment supplements) and 778 (incentives to use electronic communications).

(4) The charges under Chapters 3, 7, 8, 9 and 10 apply to non-UK residents as well as UK residents but this is subject to section 269 (charges on non-UK residents only on UK source income).

(5) This section needs to be read with the relevant priority rules (see sections 2 and 261).

General Note

Part 3 brings together and rewrites the income tax rules formerly in Sch.A (applying to income from UK land) and Sch.D Case V (applying to income from overseas land) formerly in ICTA 1988 as amended. The way in which income from land has been taxed has varied over the years. The most recent approach, adopted here, is to align the income of landlords and others receiving income from the exploitation of land closely to the taxation of income from trade, and therefore to the rules now set out in Pt 2.

Provisions which must be given priority over Part 3

261.—Any receipt or other credit item, so far as it falls within—
(a) Chapter 3 of this Part so far as it relates to an overseas property business or Chapter 8 or 9 of this Part (rent receivable in connection with a UK section 12(4) concern or for UK electric-line wayleaves), and
(b) Chapter 2 of Part 2 (receipts of a trade, profession or vocation),
is dealt with under Part 2.

Priority between Chapters within Part 3

262.—(1) Any receipt, so far as it falls within—
(a) Chapter 3 so far as it relates to a UK property business, and
(b) Chapter 8 (rent receivable in connection with a UK section 12(4) concern),
is dealt with under Chapter 8.

(2) Any receipt, so far as it falls within—
(a) Chapter 3 so far as it relates to a UK property business, and
(b) Chapter 9 (rent receivable for UK electric-line wayleaves),
is dealt with under Chapter 9.

(3) Any receipt, so far as it falls within Chapter 8 (rent receivable in connection with a UK section 12(4) concern) and Chapter 9 (rent receivable for UK electric-line wayleaves), is dealt with under Chapter 9.

Income Tax (Trading and Other Income) Act 2005

CHAPTER 2

PROPERTY BUSINESSES

Introduction

Introduction

1.762   **263.**—(1) This Chapter explains for the purposes of this Act what is meant by—
(a) a person's UK property business (see section 264), and
(b) a person's overseas property business (see section 265).
(2) Both those sections need to be read with—
(a) section 266 (which explains what is meant by generating income from land), and
(b) section 267 (which provides that certain activities do not count as activities for generating income from land).
(3) In the case of the property business of a firm, the basic rules in sections 264 and 265 are explained in section 859(2) and (3).
(4) References in this Act to an overseas property business are to an overseas property business so far as any profits of the business are chargeable to tax under Chapter 3 (as to which see, in particular, section 269).
(5) Accordingly, nothing in Chapter 4 or 5 is to be read as treating an amount as a receipt of an overseas property business if the profits concerned would not be chargeable to tax under Chapter 3.
(6) In this Act "property business" means a UK property business or an overseas property business.

Basic meaning of UK and overseas property business

UK property business

1.763   **264.**—A person's UK property business consists of—
(a) every business which the person carries on for generating income from land in the United Kingdom, and
(b) every transaction which the person enters into for that purpose otherwise than in the course of such a business.

Overseas property business

1.764   **265.**—A person's overseas property business consists of—
(a) every business which the person carries on for generating income from land outside the United Kingdom, and
(b) every transaction which the person enters into for that purpose otherwise than in the course of such a business.

(2005 c.5 s.266)

Generating income from land

Meaning of "generating income from land"

266.—(1) In this Chapter "generating income from land" means exploiting an estate, interest or right in or over land as a source of rents or other receipts.

(2) "Rents" includes payments by a tenant for work to maintain or repair leased premises which the lease does not require the tenant to carry out.

(3) "Other receipts" includes—
  (a) payments in respect of a licence to occupy or otherwise use land,
  (b) payments in respect of the exercise of any other right over land, and
  (c) rentcharges and other annual payments reserved in respect of, or charged on or issuing out of, land.

(4) For the purposes of this section a right to use a caravan or houseboat at only one location is treated as a right deriving from an estate or interest in land.

CHAPTER 3

PROFITS OF PROPERTY BUSINESSES: BASIC RULES

Charge to tax on profits of a property business

Charge to tax on profits of a property business

268.—Income tax is charged on the profits of a property business.

Territorial scope of charge to tax

269.—(1) Profits of a UK property business are chargeable to tax under this Chapter whether the business is carried on by a UK resident or a non-UK resident.

(2) Profits of an overseas property business are chargeable to tax under this Chapter only if the business is carried on by a UK resident.

Income charged

270.—(1) Tax is charged under this Chapter on the full amount of the profits arising in the tax year.

(2) Subsection (1) is subject to Part 8 (foreign income: special rules).

(3) If, as respects an individual carrying on an overseas property business, the tax year is a split year—
  (a) tax is charged under this Chapter on so much of the profits referred to in subsection (1) as arise in the UK part of the tax year, and
  (b) the portion of the profits arising in the overseas part of the tax year is, accordingly, not chargeable to tax under this Chapter.

(4) In determining how much of the profits arise in the UK part of the tax year—
  (a) determine first how much of the non-CAA profits arise in the UK part by apportioning the non-CAA profits between the UK part and the overseas part on a just and reasonable basis, and

(b) then adjust the portion of the non-CAA profits arising in the UK part by deducting any CAA allowances for the year and adding any CAA charges for the year.

(5) In subsection (4)—

"CAA allowances" means allowances treated under section 250 or 250A of CAA 2001 (capital allowances for overseas property businesses) as an expense of the business;

"CAA charges" means charges treated under either of those sections as a receipt of the business;

"non-CAA profits" means profits before account is taken of any CAA allowances or CAA charges.

Person liable

271.—The person liable for any tax charged under this Chapter is the person receiving or entitled to the profits.

Calculation of profits

Application of trading income rules: cash basis

272ZA.—(1) In relation to a property business whose profits are calculated on the cash basis, the provisions of Part 2 (trading income) which apply as a result of section 271E(1) are limited to the following—

In Chapter 3 (basic rules) —	
section 26	losses calculated on same basis as profits
section 28A	money's worth
section 29	Interest
In Chapter 4 (rules restricting deductions) —	
section 34	expenses not wholly and exclusively for trade and unconnected losses
sections 38 to 42 and 44	employee benefit contributions
sections 45 to 47	business entertainment and gifts
section 52	exclusion of double relief for interest
section 53	social security contributions
section 54	penalties [and interest]2
section 55	crime-related payments
section 55A	expenditure on integral features
In Chapter 5 (rules allowing deductions) —	
section 57	pre-trading expenses
sections 58 and 59	incidental costs of obtaining finance
section 69	payments for restrictive undertakings
sections 70 and 71	seconded employees
section 72	payroll deduction schemes: contributions to agents' expenses

sections 73 to 75	counselling and retraining expenses
sections 76 to 80	redundancy payments etc
section 81	personal security expenses
sections 82 to 86	contributions to local enterprise organisations or urban regeneration companies
sections 86A and 86B	contributions to flood and coastal erosion risk management projects
sections 87 and 88	scientific research
sections 89 and 90	expenses connected with patents, designs and trade marks
section 91	payments to Export Credits Guarantee Department
In Chapter 5A *(deductions allowable at a fixed rate)*	
section 94C	exclusion of provisions of Chapter 5A for firms with partner who is not an individual
sections 94D to 94G	expenditure on vehicles
In Chapter 6 *(receipts)* —	
section 96	capital receipts
section 97	debts incurred and later released
section 104	distribution of assets of mutual concerns
section 105(1) and (2)(b) and (c)	industrial development grants
section 106	sums recovered under insurance policies etc.
In Chapter 6A *(amounts not reflecting commercial transactions)*—	
section 106C	amounts not reflecting commercial transactions
section 106D	capital receipts
section 106E	gifts to charities etc.
In Chapter 7 *(gifts to charities etc.)*—	
section 109	receipt by donor or connected person of benefit attributable to certain gifts

(2) In those provisions, the expression *"this Part"* is to be read as a reference to those provisions as applied by subsection (1) and to the other provisions of Part 3.

(3) In section 106D, the reference to subsection (4) or (5) of section 96A is to be read as a reference to subsection (2), (3) or (5) of section 307F (deemed capital receipts under, or after leaving, cash basis).

Part 4

Savings and Investment Income

Chapter 1

Introduction

Overview of Part 4

1.771　365.—(1) This Part imposes charges to income tax under—
(a) Chapter 2 (interest),
(aa) Chapter 2A (disguised interest),
(b) Chapter 3 (dividends etc. from UK resident companies etc.),
(c) Chapter 4 (dividends from non-UK resident companies),
(d) Chapter 5 (stock dividends from UK resident companies),
(e) Chapter 6 (release of loan to participator in close company),
(f) Chapter 7 (purchased life annuity payments),
(g) Chapter 8 (profits from deeply discounted securities),
(h) Chapter 9 (gains from contracts for life insurance etc.),
(i) ...
(j) Chapter 11 (transactions in deposits),
(k) ...
(l) Chapter 13 (sales of foreign dividend coupons).
(2) Part 6 deals with exemptions from the charges under this Part.
(3) See, in particular, any exemptions mentioned in the particular Chapters.
(4) The charges under this Part apply to non-UK residents as well as UK residents but this is subject to section 368(2) (charges on non-UK residents only on UK source income).
(5) This section needs to be read with the relevant priority rules (see sections 2 and 366).

General Note

1.772　Part 4 brings together a number of separate charges to income tax on what used to be termed unearned income: interest and similar income from the former Sch.D Cases III (UK source) and IV (foreign securities) and V (foreign possessions), with dividends from the former Sch.F (distributions from UK companies) and again Sch.D Case V (dividends from foreign companies), and other payments such as annuities and income gains from life assurance policies and other forms of investment. Originally to be called investment income, it was given a wider flavour by adding "savings" to the heading. However, it is not all-encompassing because other forms of unearned income are included in Pt 5. In practice, wide use is made of tax-exempt forms of saving and investment. The details of the exemptions are in Pt 6 of the Act, which—along with pension savings under Pt 9 of ITEPA and the treatment of capital gains under the separate regime under the Taxation of Chargeable Gains Act 1992—mean that many people pay only limited income tax on their savings income. Most of these exemptions also apply for tax credits. Tax credits also take no account of capital gains. As a result, claimants can protect their savings from tax credits as well as income tax.

Provisions which must be given priority over Part 4

366.—(1) Any income, so far as it falls within—
(a) any Chapter of this Part, and
(b) Chapter 2 of Part 2 (receipts of a trade, profession or vocation),
is dealt with under Part 2.
(2) Any income, so far as it falls within—
(a) any Chapter of this Part, and
(b) Chapter 3 of Part 3 so far as the Chapter relates to a UK property business,
is dealt with under Part 3.
(3) Any income, so far as it falls within—
(a) any Chapter of this Part other than Chapter 3 or 6, and
(b) Part 2, 9 or 10 of ITEPA 2003 (employment income, pension income or social security income),
is dealt with under the relevant Part of ITEPA 2003.
(4) Nothing in this section prevents amounts both—
(a) being counted as income for the purposes of Chapter 9 of this Part (gains from contracts for life insurance etc.), and
(b) being taken into account in calculating income, or counting as income, for the purposes of other Parts of this Act,
but see section 527 (reduction for sums taken into account otherwise than under Chapter 9).

Priority between Chapters within Part 4

367.—(1) Any income, so far as it falls within Chapter 2 (interest) and Chapter 8 (profits from deeply securities), is dealt with under Chapter 8.
(2) Any income, so far as it falls within Chapter 3 (dividends etc. UK resident companies etc.) and another Chapter, is dealt with under Chapter 3 (but this is subject to subsection (3)).
(3) Any income, so far as it falls within—
(a) Chapter 2 (interest) as a result of section 372 (building society dividends), 378A (offshore fund distributions) or 379 (payments by registered societies or certain co-operatives), and
(b) Chapter 3 or Chapter 4 (or both),
is dealt with under Chapter 2.

Territorial scope of Part 4 charges

368.—(1) Income arising to a UK resident is chargeable to tax under this Part whether or not it is from a source in the United Kingdom.
(2) Income arising to a non-UK resident is chargeable to tax under this Part only if it is from a source in the United Kingdom.
(2A) If income arising to an individual who is UK resident arises in the overseas part of a split year, it is to be treated for the purposes of this section as arising to a non-UK resident.
(3) References in this section to income which is from a source in the United Kingdom include, in the case of any income which does not have a source, references to income which has a comparable connection to the United Kingdom.
(4) This section is subject to any express or implied provision to the contrary in this Part (or elsewhere in the Income Tax Acts).

CHAPTER 2

INTEREST

Charge to tax on interest

Charge to tax on interest

1.776   **369.**—(1) Income tax is charged on interest.
(2) The following sections extend what is treated as interest for certain purposes—
   section 372 (building society dividends),
   section 373 (open-ended investment company interest distributions),
   section 376 (authorised unit trust interest distributions),
   section 378A (offshore fund distributions)
   section 379 (payments by registered societies or certain co-operatives),
   section 380 (funding bonds)
   section 380A (FSCS payments representing interest), and
   section 381 (discounts).
(3) For exemptions, see in particular—
   (a) Chapter 2 of Part 6 (national savings income),
   (b) Chapter 3 of Part 6 (income from individual investment plans),
   (c) Chapter 4 of Part 6 (SAYE interest),
   (d) Chapter 6 of Part 6 (income from FOTRA securities),
   (e) sections 749 to 756A (repayment interest, interest arising from repayment supplements, damages for personal injury, employees' share schemes, repayments of student loans, unpaid relevant contributions, the redemption of funding bonds, certain foreign currency securities and interest on certain deposits of victims of National-Socialist persecution), and
   [(f) *repealed*].
(4) Subsection (1) is also subject to Chapter 3 of Part 12 of ITA 2007 (exemptions for interest on securities to which Chapter 2 of that Part applies).
(5) See also Chapter 3A of Part 14 of ITA 2007 (which provides for the receipts of certain types of company being wound up to be charged to income tax under that Chapter instead of under any other provision that would otherwise apply).

Income charged

1.777   **370.**—(1) Tax is charged under this Chapter on the full amount of the interest arising in the tax year.
(2) Subsection (1) is subject to Part 8 (foreign income: special rules).

Valuation of interest not paid in cash

1.778   **370A.**—(1) This section applies to the payment of an amount of interest in the form of—
   (a) goods or services, or
   (b) a voucher.

(2) Where this section applies by virtue of subsection (1)(a), the amount of the payment is to be taken to be equal to the market value, at the time the payment is made, of the goods or services.

(3) Where this section applies by virtue of subsection (1)(b), the amount of the payment is to be taken to be equal to whichever is the higher of—
  (a) the face value of the voucher,
  (b) the amount of money for which the voucher is capable of being exchanged, or
  (c) the market value, at the time the payment is made, of any goods or services for which the voucher is capable of being exchanged.

(4) In this section references to a voucher are to a voucher, stamp or similar document or token which is capable of being exchanged for money, goods or services.

Person liable

371.—The person liable for any tax charged under this Chapter is the person receiving or entitled to the interest.

Other income taxed as interest

Building society dividends

372.—(1) Any dividend paid by a building society is treated as interest for the purposes of this Act.

(2) In this section "dividend" includes any distribution (whether or not described as a dividend).

CHAPTER 3

DIVIDENDS ETC. FROM UK RESIDENT COMPANIES AND TAX TREATED AS PAID IN RESPECT OF CERTAIN DISTRIBUTIONS

Introduction

Contents of Chapter

382.—(1) This Chapter—
  (a) imposes a charge to income tax on dividends and other distributions of UK resident companies (see section 383),
  (b) treats dividends as paid in some circumstances (see sections 386 to 391),
  (c) makes special provision where the charge is in respect of shares awarded under a Schedule 2 share incentive plan (see sections 392 to 396).
  (d) treats distributions as made in some circumstances (see section 396A).

(2) This Chapter also makes provision about tax being treated as paid and reliefs available in respect of certain distributions which applies whether or not the distributions are otherwise dealt with under this Chapter (see sections 399 to 401).

(3) For exemptions from the charge under this Chapter, see in particular—

Chapter 3 of Part 6 (income from individual investment plans),

Chapter 5 of that Part (venture capital trust dividends),

section 770 (amounts applied by SIP trustees acquiring dividend shares or retained for reinvestment), and

section 498 of ITEPA 2003 (no charge on shares ceasing to be subject to SIP in certain circumstances).

(4) In this Chapter "dividends" does not include income treated as arising under section 410 (stock dividends).

Charge to tax on dividends and other distributions

Charge to tax on dividends and other distributions

1.782   **383.**—(1) Income tax is charged on dividends and other distributions of a UK resident company.

(2) For income tax purposes such dividends and other distributions are to be treated as income.

(3) For the purposes of subsection (2), it does not matter that those dividends and other distributions are capital apart from that subsection.

Income charged

1.783   **384.**—(1) Tax is charged under this Chapter on the amount or value of the dividends paid and other distributions made in the tax year.

(2) Subsection (1) is subject to—

section 393(2) and (3) (later charge where cash dividends retained in SIPs are paid over), and

section 394(3) (distribution when dividend shares cease to be subject to SIP).

Person liable

1.784   **385.**—(1) The person liable for any tax charged under this Chapter is—

(a) the person to whom the distribution is made or is treated as made (see Part 6 of ICTA and sections 386(3), 389(3) and 389(3)), or

(b) the person receiving or entitled to the distribution.

(2) Subsection (1) is subject to—

section 393(4) (later charge where cash dividends retained in SIPs are paid over), and

section 394(4) (distribution when dividend shares cease to be subject to SIP).

(2005 c.5 s.402)

Chapter 4

Dividends From Non-UK Resident Companies

Charge to tax on dividends from non-UK resident companies

Charge to tax on dividends from non-UK resident companies

402.—(1) Income tax is charged on dividends of a non-UK resident company.

(2) For exemptions, see in particular section 770 (amounts applied by SIP trustees acquiring dividend shares or retained for reinvestment).

(3) Subsection (1) is also subject to section 498 of ITEPA 2003 (no charge on shares ceasing to be subject to SIP in certain circumstances).

(4) In this Chapter "dividends" does not include dividends of a capital nature.

Income charged

403.—(1) Tax is charged under this Chapter on the amount of the dividends arising in the tax year.

(2) Subsection (1) is subject to—

section 406(2) and (3) (later charge where cash dividends retained in SIPs are paid over),

section 407(3) (dividend payment when dividend shares cease to be subject to SIP), and

Part 8 (foreign income: special rules).

Person liable

404.—(1) The person liable for any tax charged under this Chapter is the person receiving or entitled to the dividends.

(2) Subsection (1) is subject to—

section 406(4) (later charge where cash dividends retained in SIPs are paid over), and

section 407(4) (dividend payment when dividend shares cease to be subject to SIP).

Chapter 7

Purchased Life Annuity Payments

Charge to tax on purchased life annuity payments

422.—(1) Income tax is charged on annuity payments made under a purchased life annuity.

(2) For exemptions, see in particular—

(a) section 717 (exemption for part of purchased life annuity payments),
(b) section 725 (annual payments under immediate needs annuities),
(c) section 731 (periodical payments of personal injury damages), and
(d) section 732 (compensation awards).

Meaning of "purchased life annuity"

1.789   **423.**—(1) In this Chapter "purchased life annuity" means an annuity—
(a) granted for consideration in money or money's worth in the ordinary course of a business of granting annuities on human life, and
(b) payable for a term ending at a time ascertainable only by reference to the end of a human life.
(2) For this purpose it does not matter that the annuity may in some circumstances end before or after the life.

Income charged

1.790   **424.**—(1) Tax is charged under this Chapter on the full amount of the annuity payments arising in the tax year.
(2) Subsection (1) is subject to Part 8 (foreign income: special rules).

Person liable

1.791   **425.**—The person liable for any tax charged under this Chapter is the person receiving or entitled to the annuity payments.

PART 5

MISCELLANEOUS INCOME

CHAPTER 1

INTRODUCTION

Overview of Part 5

1.792   **574.**—(1) This Part imposes charges to income tax under—
(a) Chapter 2 (receipts from intellectual property),
(aa) Chapter 2A (offshore receipts in respect of intangible property),
(b) Chapter 3 (films and sound recordings: non-trade businesses),
(c) Chapter 4 (certain telecommunication rights: non-trading income),
(d) Chapter 5 (settlements: amounts treated as income of settlor),
(e) Chapter 6 (beneficiaries' income from estates in administration),
(f) Chapter 7 (annual payments not otherwise charged), and
(g) Chapter 8 (income not otherwise charged).
(2) Part 6 deals with exemptions from the charges under this Part (but see section 608X).

(3) See, in particular, any exemptions mentioned in the Chapters of this Part.

(4) The charges under this Part apply to non-UK residents as well as UK residents but this is subject to section 577(2) (charges on non-UK residents only on UK source income).

(5) This section needs to be read with the relevant priority rules (see sections 2, 575 and 576).

Provisions which must be given priority over Part 5

575.—(1) Any income, so far as it falls within—
 (a) any Chapter of this Part, and
 (b) Chapter 2 of Part 2 (receipts of a trade, profession or vocation),
is dealt with under Part 2.

(2) Any income, so far as it falls within—
 (a) any Chapter of this Part, and
 (b) Chapter 3 of Part 3 so far as the Chapter relates to a UK property business,
is dealt with under Part 3.

(3) Any income, so far as it falls within—
 (a) any Chapter of this Part, and
 (b) Chapter 2 or 3 of Part 4 (interest and dividends etc. from UK resident companies etc.),
is dealt with under the relevant Chapter of Part 4.

(4) Any income, so far as it falls within—
 (a) any Chapter of this Part, and
 (b) Part 2, 9 or 10 of ITEPA 2003 (employment income, pension income or social security income),
is dealt with under the relevant Part of ITEPA 2003.

Priority between Chapters within Part 5

576.—(1) Any income, so far as it falls within Chapter 2 (receipts from intellectual property) and Chapter 2A (offshore receipts in respect of intangible property), is dealt with under Chapter 2.

(2) Any income, so far as it falls within Chapter 2 (receipts from intellectual property) and Chapter 3 (films and sound recordings: non-trade businesses), is dealt with under Chapter 3.

CHAPTER 5

SETTLEMENTS: AMOUNTS TREATED AS INCOME OF SETTLOR

Charge to tax under Chapter 5

Charge to tax under Chapter 5

619.—(1) Income tax is charged on—
 (a) income which is treated as income of a settlor as a result of section 624 (income where settlor retains an interest),

(b) income which is treated as income of a settlor as a result of section 629 (income paid to relevant children of settlor),
(c) capital sums which are treated as income of a settlor as a result of section 633 (capital sums paid to settlor by trustees of settlement), and
(d) capital sums which are treated as income of a settlor as a result of section 641 (capital sums paid to settlor by body connected with settlement),
(e) benefits whose amount or value is treated as income of the settlor or a close family member as a result of section 643A (benefits provided out of protected foreign-source income), and
(f) amounts treated as income of the settlor or a close family member by section 643J or 643L (gifts provided out of benefits).

(2) For the purposes of Chapter 2 of Part 2 of ITA 2007 (rates at which income tax is charged), where income of another person is treated as income of the settlor and is charged to tax under subsection (1)(a) or (b) above, it shall be charged in accordance with whichever provisions of the Income Tax Acts would have been applied in charging it if it had arisen directly to the settlor.

GENERAL NOTE

1.796 The provisions in this chapter are complex but important as they include very wide anti-avoidance provisions that can affect income earners at all levels. They are all applied to the calculation of income for tax credit purposes, and therefore now have a double effect on many middle range income earners who seek to use trusts to cut their incomes. Sections 624–628 contain provisions designed to stop tax avoidance by putting money into a form of trust where the settlor has an interest in the trust, unless it is a trust between spouses or partners, or it is to a charity. Section 629 is a very widely drawn provision that has the effect of transferring back to a settlor any income given by the settlor to an unmarried minor child of the settlor (for example, by putting money in a building society account in the name of the child, or buying National Savings Certificates in the child's name). But see now the tax provisions designed to assist child trust funds, which allow all these provisions to be sidestepped to a limited extent if a child trust fund is used.

Income treated as highest part of settlor's total income

1.797 **619A.**—(1) This section applies to income which is treated as income of a settlor as a result of section 624 (income where settlor retains an interest) or 629 (income paid to unmarried minor children of settlor).

(2) The income is treated as the highest part of the settlor's total income for the purposes of section 619 (so far as it relates to the income).

(3) See section 1012 of ITA 2007 (relationship between highest part rules) for the relationship between—
(a) the rule in subsection (2), and
(b) other rules requiring particular income to be treated as the highest part of a person's total income.

Meaning of "settlement" and "settlor"

1.798 **620.**—(1) In this Chapter—
"settlement" includes any disposition, trust, covenant, agreement, or transfer of assets (except that it does not include a charitable loan arrangement), and

(2005 c.5 s.620)

"settlor", in relation to a settlement, means any person by whom the settlement was made.

(2) A person is treated for the purposes of this Chapter as having made a settlement if the person has made or entered into the settlement directly or indirectly.

(3) A person is, in particular, treated as having made a settlement if the person—
  (a) has provided funds directly or indirectly for the purpose of the settlement,
  (b) has undertaken to provide funds directly or indirectly for the purpose of the settlement, or
  (c) has made a reciprocal arrangement with another person for the other person to make or enter into the settlement.

(4) This Chapter applies to settlements wherever made.

(5) In this section—

"charitable loan arrangement" means any arrangement so far as it consists of a loan of money made by an individual to a charity either—
  (a) for no consideration, or
  (b) for a consideration which consists only of interest, and

"charity" includes—
  (a) trustees of the National Heritage Memorial Fund, and
  (b) Historical Buildings and Monuments Commission for England.

Income charged and person liable

Income charged

621.—Tax is charged under this Chapter on all income, capital sums and benefits to which section 619(1) applies.

1.799

Person liable

622.—The person liable for any tax charged under this Chapter is the settlor, but this is subject to sections 643A and 643I to 643M.

1.800

CHAPTER 8

INCOME NOT OTHERWISE CHARGED

Charge to tax on income not otherwise charged

687.—(1) Income tax is charged under this Chapter on income from any source that is not charged to income tax under or as a result of any other provision of this Act or any other Act.

1.801

(2) Subsection (1) does not apply to annual payments or to income falling within Chapter 2A of Part 4.

(3) Subsection (1) does not apply to income that would be charged to income tax under or as a result of another provision but for an exemption.

(4) The definition of "income" in section 878(1) does not apply for the purposes of this section.

Income charged

1.802   **688.**—(1) Tax is charged under this Chapter on the amount of the income arising in the tax year.
(2) Subsection (1) is subject to—
(za) Chapter 1 of Part 6A (which gives relief on relevant income which may consist of or include income chargeable under this Chapter: see, in particular, sections 783AB, 783AC, 783AG and 783AJ),
(a) Chapter 1 of Part 7 (which provides relief on income from the use of furnished accommodation in an individual's only or main residence: see, in particular, sections 794 and 798),
(b) Chapter 2 of that Part (which provides relief on income from the provision by an individual of qualifying care: see, in particular, sections 814 and 817), and
(c) Part 8 (foreign income: special rules).

Person liable

1.803   **689.**—The person liable for any tax charged under this Chapter is the person receiving or entitled to the income.

PART 6

EXEMPT INCOME

CHAPTER 1

INTRODUCTION

Overview of Part 6

1.804   **690.**—(1) This Part provides for certain exemptions from charges to income tax under this Act.
(2) The exemptions are dealt with in—
(a) Chapter 2 (national savings income),
(b) Chapter 3 (income from individual investment plans),
(c) Chapter 4 (SAYE interest),
(d) Chapter 5 (venture capital trust dividends),
(e) Chapter 6 (income from FOTRA securities),
(f) Chapter 7 (purchased life annuity payments),
(g) Chapter 8 (other annual payments), and
(h) Chapter 9 (other income).
(3) Chapter 10 explains that, in general, the effect of the exemptions is that the exempt amounts are ignored for other income tax purposes.

(2005 c.5 s.690)

(4) Other exemptions, such as exemptions relating to particular categories of persons, may also be relevant to the charges to income tax under this Act.

(5) And the exemptions dealt with in this Part may themselves be relevant to charges to income tax outside this Act.

CHAPTER 8

OTHER ANNUAL PAYMENTS

Certain annual payments by individuals

Foreign maintenance payments

730.—(1) No liability to income tax arises under Part 5 in respect of an annual payment if—   1.805
  (a) it is a maintenance payment,
  (b) it arises outside the United Kingdom, and
  (c) had it arisen in the United Kingdom it would be exempt from income tax under section 727 (certain annual payments by individuals).

(2) In subsection (1) "maintenance payment" means a periodical payment which meets conditions A and B.

(3) Condition A is that the payment is made under a court order or a written or oral agreement.

(4) Condition B is that the payment is made by a person—
  (a) as one of the parties to a marriage or civil partnership to, or for the benefit of, and for the maintenance of, the other party,
  (b) to any person under 21 for that person's own benefit, maintenance or education, or
  (c) to any person for the benefit, maintenance or education of a person under 21.

(5) In subsection (4) "marriage" includes a marriage that has been dissolved or annulled, and "civil partnership" includes a civil partnership that has been dissolved or annulled.

(6) Subsection (1) also applies to a payment made by an individual's personal representatives if—
  (a) the individual would have been liable to make it, and
  (b) that subsection would have applied if the individual had made it.

Periodical payments of personal injury damages etc.

Periodical payments of personal injury damages

731.—(1) No liability to income tax arises for the persons specified in section 733 in respect of periodical payments to which subsection (2) or annuity payments to which subsection (3) applies.   1.806

(2) This subsection applies to periodical payments made pursuant to—

(a) an order of the court, so far as it is made in reliance on section 2 of the Damages Act 1996 (c. 48) (periodical payments) (including an order as varied),
(b) an order of a court outside the United Kingdom which is similar to an order made in reliance on that section (including an order as varied),
(c) an agreement, so far as it settles a claim or action for damages in respect of personal injury (including an agreement as varied),
(d) an agreement, so far as it relates to making payments on account of damages that may be awarded in such a claim or action (including an agreement as varied), or
(e) a Motor Insurers' Bureau undertaking in relation to a claim or action in respect of personal injury (including an undertaking as varied).

(3) This subsection applies to annuity payments made under an annuity purchased or provided—
(a) by the person by whom payments to which subsection (2) applies would otherwise fall to be made, and
(b) in accordance with such an order, agreement or undertaking as is mentioned in subsection (2) or a varying order, agreement or undertaking.

(4) In this section "damages in respect of personal injury" includes in respect of a person's death from personal injury.

(5) In this section "personal injury" includes disease and impairment of physical or mental condition.

(6) In this section "a Motor Insurers' Bureau undertaking" means an undertaking given by—
(a) the Motor Insurers' Bureau (being the company of that name incorporated on 14th June 1946 under the Companies Act 1929 (c. 23)), or
(b) an Article 75 insurer under the Bureau's Articles of Association.

Compensation awards

1.807   **732.**—(1) No liability to income tax arises for the persons specified in section 733 in respect of annuity payments if they are made under an annuity purchased or provided under an award of compensation made under the Criminal Injuries Compensation Scheme or the Victims of Overseas Terrorism Compensation Scheme.

(2) The Treasury may by order provide for sections 731, 733 and 734 to apply, with such modifications as they consider necessary, to periodical payments by way of compensation for personal injury for which provision is made under a scheme or arrangement other than the Criminal Injuries Compensation Scheme or the Victims of Overseas Terrorism Compensation Scheme.

(3) In this section—
"the Criminal Injuries Compensation Scheme" means—
(a) the schemes established by arrangements made under the Criminal Injuries Compensation Act 1995 (c. 53),
(b) arrangements made by the Secretary of State for compensation for criminal injuries in operation before the commencement of those schemes, or

(c) the scheme established under the Criminal Injuries (Northern Ireland) Order 2002 (S.I. 2002/796) (N.I.1), and

"personal injury" includes disease and impairment of physical or mental condition.

Persons entitled to exemptions for personal injury payments etc.

733.—The persons entitled to the exemptions given by sections 731(1) and 732(1) for payments are—
(a) the person entitled to the damages under the order, agreement, or to the compensation under the award in question ("A"),
(b) a person who receives the payment in question on behalf of A, and
(c) a trustee who receives the payment in question on trust for the benefit of A under a trust under which A is, while alive, the only person who may benefit.

Payments from trusts for injured persons

734.—(1) No liability to income tax arises for the persons specified in subsection (2) in respect of sums paid under a lifetime trust—
(a) to the person ("A") who is entitled to—
    (i) a payment under an order, agreement or undertaking within section 731(2) or an annuity purchased or provided as mentioned in section 731(3), or
    (ii) compensation under an award within section 732(1), or
(b) for the benefit of A.
(2) The persons are—
(a) A, and
(b) if subsection (1)(b) applies, a person who receives the sum on behalf of A.
(3) For the purposes of subsection (1), sums are paid under a lifetime trust if they are paid—
(a) by the trustees of a trust under which A is, while alive, the only person who may benefit, and
(b) out of payments within section 731(2) or (3) or 732(1) which are received by them on trust for A.

Health and employment insurance payments

Health and employment insurance payments

735.—(1) No liability to income tax arises under this Act in respect of an annual payment under an insurance policy if—
(a) the payment is a benefit provided under so much of the policy as insures against a health or employment risk (see section 736),
(b) no part of any premiums under the policy has been deductible in calculating the income of the insured for income tax purposes, and
(c) the conditions in sections 737 and 738 and, so far as applicable, in sections 739 and 740 are met in relation to the policy.
(2) Subsection (1)(b) is subject to section 743.
(3) For the meaning of "the insured", see sections 742 and 743(2).

Health and employment risks and benefits

1.811   **736.**—(1) For the purposes of sections 735 and 737 to 743, a policy insures against a health risk if it insures against the insured becoming, or becoming in any specified way, subject—
  (a) to any physical or mental illness, disability, infirmity or defect, or
  (b) to any deterioration in a condition resulting from any such illness, disability, infirmity or defect.

(2) For the purposes of sections 735 and 737 to 743, a policy insures against an employment risk if it insures against circumstances arising as a result of which the insured ceases—
  (a) to be employed or hold office, or
  (b) to carry on any trade, profession or vocation.

(3) For the purposes of section 735, this section and sections 737 to 743, references to insurance against a risk include insurance providing for benefits payable otherwise than by way of indemnity if the circumstances insured against occur.

Payments to adopters

Payments to adopters, etc.: England and Wales

1.812   **744.**—(1) No liability to income tax arises in respect of the following payments—
  (a) any payment or reward falling within section 57(3) of the Adoption Act 1976 (c. 36) (payments authorised by the court) which is made to a person who has adopted or intends to adopt a child,
  (b) payments under section 57(3A)(a) of that Act (payments by adoption agencies of legal or medical expenses of persons seeking to adopt),
  (c) payments of allowances under regulations under section 57A of that Act (permitted allowances to persons who have adopted or intend to adopt children),
  (d) payments of financial support made in the course of providing adoption support services within the meaning of the Adoption and Children Act 2002 (c. 38) (see section 2(6) and (7) of that Act),
  (e) payments made under regulations under paragraph 3(1) of Schedule 4 to that Act (transitional and transitory provisions: adoption support services),
  (f) payments made under regulations under section 14F of the Children Act 1989 (special guardianship support services) to a person appointed as a child's special guardian,
  (g) payments made to a person under section 17 of that Act (provision of services for children in need, their families and others) by reason of that person being a person named in a child arrangements order as a person with whom a child is to live,
  (h) payments made to a person, in respect of a child, under paragraph 15 of Schedule 1 to that Act (local authority contribution to child's maintenance to recipients with whom child is living, or is to live, as a result of a child arrangements order), and
  (i) payments made in accordance with—

(i) an order under that Schedule (orders for financial relief against parents etc), or
(ii) a maintenance agreement,
for the benefit of a child, to a person appointed as the child's special guardian or a person named in a child arrangements order as a person with whom the child is to live,
(j) payments made to a person under sections 37 to 39 of the Social Services and Well-being (Wales) Act 2014 (meeting care and support needs of children) by reason of that person being named in a child arrangements order as a person with whom a child is to live.

(2) But a payment is not within subsection (1)(f), (g), (h), (i) or (j) if—
(a) it is made to an excluded relative of the child,
(b) it is made to a person appointed as the child's special guardian and an excluded relative is also appointed as the child's special guardian, or
(c) it is made to a person ("P") named in a child arrangements order as a person with whom the child is to live and an excluded relative who lives in the same household as P is also named in that order as a person with whom the child is to live.

(3) In this section—
"child arrangements order" has the meaning given by section 8 of that Act;
"excluded relative", in relation to a child, means—
(a) a parent of the child, or
(b) a person who is, or has been, the husband or wife or civil partner of a parent of the child;
"maintenance agreement" has the meaning given by paragraph 10(1) of Schedule 1 to the Children Act 1989;
"residence order" has the meaning given by section 8 of that Act.

Payments to adopters, etc: Scotland

745.—(1) No liability to income tax arises in respect of the following payments—
(a) any payment which is an excepted payment by virtue of paragraph (a) or (c) of subsection (2) of section 73 of the Adoption and Children (Scotland) Act 2007 (asp 4), which is made to a person who has adopted or intends to adopt a child,
(b) payments which are excepted payments by virtue of paragraph (b) of that subsection,
(c) ...
(d) payments of allowances in accordance with an adoption allowances scheme under section 71 of that Act;
(e) payments made to a person under section 50 of the Children Act 1975, or section 22 of the Children (Scotland) Act 1995, by reason of that person being a person with whom a child is to live by virtue of a residence order, and
(f) payments of aliment made—
(i) in accordance with an award of aliment under the Family Law (Scotland) Act 1985, or
(ii) under an agreement (within the meaning of section 7(5) of that Act),

for the benefit of a child, to a person in whose favour a residence order with respect to the child is in force

(2) A payment is not within subsection (1)(e) or (f) if—
   (a) it is made to an excluded relative of the child, or
   (b) it is made to a person in whose favour a residence order is in force with respect to the child and that order is also in favour of an excluded relative.

(3) In this section—

"excluded relative", in relation to a child, means—
   (a) a parent of the child, or
   (b) a person who is, or has been, the husband or wife or civil partner of a parent of the child;

"residence order" has the meaning given by section 11(2)(c) of the Children (Scotland) Act 1995.

CHAPTER 9

OTHER INCOME

Interest on damages for personal injury

1.814　　751.—(1) No liability to income tax arises in respect of interest on damages for personal injury or death if—
   (a) it is included in a sum awarded by a court,
   (b) it does not relate to the period between the making and satisfaction of the award, and
   (c) in the case of an award by a court in a country outside the United Kingdom, it is exempt from any charge to tax in that place.

(2) No liability to income tax arises in respect of interest if—
   (a) it is included in a payment in satisfaction of a cause of action (including a payment into court), and
   (b) it would fall within subsection (1) if it were included in a sum awarded by a court in respect of a cause of action.

(3) In subsection (1)—

"damages" in Scotland includes solatium, and

"personal injury" includes disease and impairment of physical or mental condition.

Interest on repayment of student loan

1.815　　753.—(1) No liability to income tax arises in respect of interest if—
   (a) it is paid to a person to whom a student loan has been made, and
   (b) it relates to an amount repaid to the person after being recovered from the person in respect of the loan.

(2) In this section "student loan" means a loan made under—

section 22 of the Teaching and Higher Education Act 1998 (c. 30),

section 73(f) of the Education (Scotland) Act 1980 (c. 44), or

Article 3 of the Education (Student Support) (Northern Ireland) Order 1998 (S.I. 1998/1760 (N.I. 14)).

Scholarship income

776.—(1) No liability to income tax arises in respect of income from a scholarship held by an individual in full-time education at a university, college, school or other educational establishment.

(2) This exemption is subject to section 215 of ITEPA 2003 (under which only the scholarship holder is entitled to the exemption if the scholarship is provided by reason of another person's employment).

(2A) No liability to income tax arises in respect of income from a payment made under section 23C(5A) of the Children Act 1989 (duty to make payments to former relevant children who pursue higher education) or under sections 110(6) or 112(2) of the Social Services and Well-being (Wales) Act 2014 (duty to make payments to certain young people who pursue higher education).

(3) In this section "scholarship" includes a bursary, exhibition or other similar educational endowment.

Disabled person's vehicle maintenance grant

780.—(1) No liability to income tax arises in respect of a disabled person's vehicle maintenance grant.

(2) For this purpose a "disabled person's vehicle maintenance grant" means a grant to any person owning a vehicle that is made under—
  (a) paragraph 10 of Schedule 1 to the National Health Service Act 2006 or paragraph 10 of Schedule 1 to National Health Service (Wales) Act 2006,
  (b) section 46(3) of the National Health Service (Scotland) Act 1978 (c. 29), or
  (c) Article 30 of the Health and Personal Social Services (Northern Ireland) Order 1972 (S.I. 1972/1265 (N.I. 14)), and Training Act (Northern Ireland) 1950 (c. 29 (N.I.)).

CHAPTER 10

GENERAL

General disregard of exempt income for income tax purposes

783.—(1) Amounts of income which are exempt from income tax as a result of this Part (whether because the type of income concerned is exempt from every charge to income tax or because it is exempt from every charge that is relevant to those particular amounts) are accordingly to be ignored for all other income tax purposes.

(2) There are exceptions to this in the following cases.

(2A) Interest on deposits in ordinary accounts with the National Savings Bank which is exempt under this Part from every charge to income tax is not to be ignored for the purpose of providing information.

(2B) Interest paid to or in respect of victims of National-Socialist persecution which is so exempt is not to be ignored for the purposes of sections 17 and 18 of TMA 1970 (information provisions relating to interest).

(3) These express exceptions to subsection (1) are without prejudice to the existence of any other implied or express exception to that subsection (whether in connection with the provision of information or otherwise).

Income Tax (Trading and Other Income) Act 2005

PART 7

INCOME CHARGED UNDER THIS ACT: RENT-A-ROOM AND QUALIFYING CARE RELIEF

CHAPTER 1

RENT-A-ROOM RELIEF

Introduction

Overview of Chapter 1

1.819   **784.**—(1) This Chapter provides relief on income from the use of furnished accommodation in an individual's only or main residence. The relief is referred to in this Chapter as "rent-a-room relief".

(2) The form of relief depends on whether the individual's total rent-a-room amount exceeds the individual's limit (see sections 788 to 790).

(3) If it does not, the income is not charged to income tax unless the individual elects otherwise (see sections 791 to 794).

(4) If it does, the individual may elect for alternative methods of calculating the income (see sections 795 to 798).

Person who qualifies for relief

1.820   **785.**—(1) An individual qualifies for rent-a-room relief for a tax year if the individual—
   (a) has rent-a-room receipts for the tax year (see section 786), and
   (b) does not derive any taxable income other than rent-a-room receipts from a relevant trade, letting or agreement.

(2) "Taxable income" means receipts or other income in respect of which the individual is liable to income tax for the tax year.

(3) A relevant trade, letting or agreement is one from which the individual derives rent-a-room receipts for the tax year.

Basic definitions

Meaning of "rent-a-room receipts"

1.821   **786.**—(1) For the purposes of this Chapter an individual has rent-a-room receipts for a tax year if—
   (a) the receipts are in respect of the use of furnished accommodation in a residence in the United Kingdom or in respect of goods or services supplied in connection with that use,
   (b) they accrue to the individual during the income period for those receipts (see subsections (3) and (4)),
   (c) for some or all of that period the residence is the individual's only or main residence, and
   (d) the receipts would otherwise be brought into account in calculating the profits of a trade or UK property business or chargeable to income tax under Chapter 8 of Part 5 (income not otherwise charged).

(2) Meals, cleaning and laundry are examples of goods or services supplied in connection with the use of furnished accommodation in a residence.

(3) [*repealed*]

(4) The income period is the period which—
(a) begins at the beginning of the tax year or, if later, the beginning of the letting in respect of which the receipts arise, and
(b) ends at the end of the tax year or, if earlier, the end of that letting.

(5) Subsections (6) and (7) apply if—
(a) the receipts would otherwise be brought into account in calculating the profits of a trade, and
(b) the profits of the trade are required under section 24A to be calculated on the cash basis.

(6) Any amounts brought into account under section 96A (capital receipts under, or after leaving, cash basis) as a receipt in calculating the profits of the trade are to be treated as receipts within paragraph (a) of subsection (1) above.

(6A) Subsections (6B) and (7) apply if—
(a) the receipts would otherwise be brought into account in calculating the profits of a UK property business, and
(b) the profits are calculated on the cash basis (see section 271D).

(6B) Any amounts brought into account under section 307E (capital receipts under, or after leaving, cash basis) as a receipt in calculating the profits of the property business are to be treated as receipts within paragraph (a) of subsection (1) above.

(7) The reference in subsection (1)(b) to receipts that accrue to an individual during the income period for those receipts is to be read as a reference to receipts that are received by the individual during that period.

Meaning of "residence"

787.—(1) In this Chapter "residence" means—
(a) a building, or part of a building, occupied or intended to be occupied as a separate residence, or
(b) a caravan or houseboat.

(2) If a building, or part of a building, designed for permanent use as a single residence is temporarily divided into two or more separate residences, it is still treated as a single residence.

Meaning of "total rent-a-room amount"

788.—(1) For the purposes of this Chapter an individual's "total rent-a-room amount" for a tax year is the total of—
(a) the individual's rent-a-room receipts for the tax year, and
(b) any relevant balancing charges for the tax year (see section 802).

(2) In calculating the total rent-a-room amount, no deduction is allowed for expenses or any other matter.

Individual's limit

The individual's limit

1.824   **789.**—(1) For the purposes of this Chapter an individual's limit for a tax year depends on whether the individual meets the exclusive receipts condition for the tax year (see section 790).

(2) If the individual does, the individual's limit for the tax year is the basic amount for the tax year.

(3) If the individual does not, the individual's limit for the tax year is half that amount.

(4) The basic amount for a tax year is £7500.

(5) The Treasury may by order amend the sum for the time being specified in subsection (4).

CHAPTER 2

QUALIFYING CARE RELIEF

Introduction

Overview of Chapter 2

1.825   **803.**—(1) This Chapter provides relief on income from the provision by an individual of qualifying care.

The relief is referred to in this Chapter as "qualifying care relief".

(2) The form of relief depends on whether the individual's total qualifying care receipts exceed the individual's limit (see sections 807 to 811).

(3) If they do not, the income is not charged to income tax (see sections 812 to 814).

(4) If they do, the individual may elect for an alternative method of calculating the income (see sections 815 to 819).

(5) If the qualifying care receipts are the receipts of a trade, special rules apply—
 (a) if the period of account of the trade does not end on 5th April (see sections 820 to 823), and
 (b) in relation to capital allowances (see sections 824 to 827).

(6) The provisions of this Chapter which are expressed to apply in relation to trades also apply in relation to professions and vocations.

Person who qualifies for relief

1.826   **804.**—(1) An individual qualifies for qualifying care relief for a tax year if the individual—
 (a) has qualifying care receipts for the tax year (see section 805), and
 (b) does not derive any taxable income, other than qualifying care receipts, from a relevant trade or arrangement.

(2) "Taxable income" means receipts or other income in respect of which the individual is liable to income tax for the tax year.

(3) A relevant trade or arrangement is one from which the individual derives qualifying care receipts for the tax year.

(4) Subsection (1) is subject to section 804A.

Shared lives care: further condition for relief

804A.—(1) This section applies if an individual ("N") has qualifying care receipts for a tax year in respect of the provision of shared lives care.

(2) N does not qualify for qualifying care relief in respect of those receipts if the placement cap is exceeded for the residence (or any of the residences) used by N to provide the care from which those receipts are derived.

(3) The placement cap is exceeded for a residence if, at any given time during the relevant period, shared lives care is being provided there (whether by N or anyone else) for more than 3 people in total.

(4) The relevant period, in relation to a residence, is the period for which the residence is N's only or main residence during the income period for the receipts (see section 805).

(5) If the placement cap is so exceeded but N also has qualifying care receipts for the tax year in respect of the provision of foster care, this Chapter is to apply to N for the tax year as if—
 (a) references to qualifying care were to foster care, and
 (b) accordingly, references (other than in this section) to qualifying care receipts did not include receipts in respect of the provision of shared lives care.

(6) In determining the number of people for whom shared lives care is being provided at any given time, brothers and sisters (including half-brothers and half-sisters) count as one person.

Basic definitions

Meaning of "qualifying care receipts"

805.—(1) For the purposes of this Chapter an individual has qualifying care receipts for a tax year if—
 (a) the receipts are in respect of the provision of qualifying care,
 (b) they accrue to the individual during the income period for those receipts (see subsection (3)), and
 (c) the receipts would otherwise be brought into account in calculating the profits of a trade or chargeable to income tax under Chapter 8 of Part 5 (income not otherwise charged).

(2) [*repealed*]

(3) The income period is the tax year.

(4) Subsections (5) and (6) apply if—
 (a) the receipts would otherwise be brought into account in calculating the profits of a trade, and
 (b) the profits of the trade are required under section 24A to be calculated on the cash basis.

(5) Any amounts brought into account under section 96A (capital receipts under, or after leaving, cash basis) as a receipt in calculating the profits of the trade are to be treated as receipts within paragraph (a) of subsection (1) above.

Income Tax (Trading and Other Income) Act 2005

(6) The reference in subsection (1)(b) to receipts that accrue to an individual during the income period for those receipts is to be read as a reference to receipts that are received by the individual during that period.

Meaning of providing qualifying care

1.829 **805A.**—For the purposes of this Chapter qualifying care is provided if an individual (alone or in partnership) provides—
   (a) foster care but not shared lives care,
   (b) shared lives care but not foster care, or
   (c) both foster care and shared lives care.

Meaning of providing foster care

1.830 **806.**—(1) For the purposes of this Chapter foster care is provided if an individual—
   (a) provides accommodation and maintenance for a child, and
   (b) does so as a foster carer.

(2) An individual is a foster carer if the child is placed with the individual by virtue of a compulsory supervision order or interim compulsory supervision order, or under any of the following enactments, unless the individual is excluded by subsection (5).

(3) The enactments are—
   (a) section 22C or 59(1)(a) of the Children Act 1989 (c. 41) (provision of accommodation for children by local authorities or voluntary organisations),
   (aa) section 81 of the Social Services and Well-being (Wales) Act 2014 (provision of accommodation for children by local authorities),
   (b) regulations under section 5 of the Social Work (Scotland) Act 1968 (c. 49),
   (c) ..., and
   (d) Article 27(2)(a) or 75(1)(a) of the Children (Northern Ireland) 1995 (S.I. 1995/755 (N.I. 2)) (provision of accommodation for children by authorities or voluntary organisations).

(4) An individual is also a foster carer if the individual is approved as a foster carer by a local authority or a voluntary organisation in accordance with regulations under section 5 of the Social Work (Scotland) Act 1968, and the child in respect of whom the accommodation is provided—
   (a) is being looked after by a local authority within the meaning of section 17(6) of the Children (Scotland) Act 1995, or
   (b) is subject to an order or warrant made by the children's hearing or sheriff under the Children's Hearings (Scotland) Act 2011,
unless the individual is excluded by subsection (5).

(5) The following are excluded individuals—
   (a) a parent of the child,
   (b) an individual who is not a parent of the child but who has parental responsibility (or, in Scotland, parental responsibilities) in relation to the child,
   (ba) where the child is in care and there was a child arrangements order in force with respect to the child immediately before the care order was made, a person named in the child arrangements order as a person with whom the child was to live,

(bb) (in Scotland) where the child is in care and there was a child arrangements order in force with respect to the child immediately before the child was placed in care, a person named in the child arrangements order as a person with whom the child was to live, spend time or otherwise have contact,
(c) if the child is in care and there was a residence order in force with respect to the child immediately before the care order was made, an individual in whose favour the residence order was made, and
(d) (in Scotland) if the child is in care and there was a residence order or contact order in force with respect to the child immediately before the child was placed in care, an individual in whose favour the residence order or contact order was made, and
(e) an individual with whom the child is placed under a placement falling within section 22C(6)(d) of the Children Act 1989,
(f) an individual with whom the child is placed under a placement falling within section 81(6)(d) of the Social Services and Well-being (Wales) Act 2014.

(6) In this section—

"compulsory supervision order" has the meaning given by section 83 of the Children's Hearings (Scotland) Act 2011; and

"interim compulsory supervision order" has the meaning given by section 86 of that Act.

Meaning of providing shared lives care

806A.—(1) For the purposes of this Chapter shared lives care is provided by an individual if—
(a) the individual provides accommodation and care for an adult or child ("X") who has been placed with the individual, and
(b) the conditions in subsection (2) are met.

(2) The conditions are—
(a) the accommodation is in the individual's own home,
(b) the accommodation and care are provided on the basis that X will share the individual's home and daily family life during the placement,
(c) the placement is made under a specified social care scheme,
(d) the individual does not provide the accommodation and care as a foster carer, and
(e) the individual is not excluded within the meaning of section 806(5).

(3) Section 806(5) has effect for the purposes of subsection (2)(e) as if references to the child were to X (whatever X's age).

(4) "Specified social care scheme" means a social care scheme of a kind specified or described in an order made by the Treasury.

(5) An order under subsection (4) may make provision having effect in relation to the tax year current on the day on which the order is made.

(6) In this section—
"care" means personal care, including assistance and support;
"home" means an individual's only or main residence;

"social care scheme" means a scheme, service or arrangement for those who, by reason of age, illness, disability or other vulnerability, are in need of care.

Meaning of "residence"

1.832

806B.—(1) In this Chapter "residence" means—
   (a) a building, or part of a building, occupied or intended to be occupied as a separate residence, or
   (b) a caravan or houseboat.

(2) If a building, or part of a building, designed for permanent use as a single residence is temporarily divided into two or more separate residences, it is still treated as a single residence.

Calculation of "total qualifying care receipts"

1.833

807.—For the purposes of this Chapter, in calculating an individual's "total qualifying care receipts" for a tax year, no deduction is allowed for expenses or any other matter.

The individual's limit

1.834

808.—(1) For the purposes of this Chapter an individual's limit for a tax year is the total of—
   (a) the fixed amount for the tax year or, if section 809 or 810 applies, the individual's share of that amount, and
   (b) each amount per adult or child for the individual for the tax year (see section 811).

(2) For the purposes of this Chapter the fixed amount for a tax year is £19,360.

(3) [repealed]

Share of fixed amount: residence used by more than one carer

1.835

809.—(1) This section applies if in a tax year—
   (a) the residence used to provide the qualifying care from which an individual's qualifying care receipts for the tax year are derived is also used by another individual to provide qualifying care, and
   (b) the other individual also has qualifying care receipts for the tax year.

(2) Each individual's share of the fixed amount for the tax year is the fixed amount divided by the total number of individuals who—
   (a) use the residence in the tax year to provide qualifying care, and
   (b) have qualifying care receipts for the tax year.

Share of fixed amount: income period not a year

1.836

810.—(1) This section applies if in a tax year an individual's income period for the individual's qualifying care receipts is a period other than a year.

(2) The individual's share of the fixed amount for the tax year is—

$$(AS \times D) / 365$$

where—
AS is the fixed amount or (if section 809 applies) the individual's share of the fixed amount, and
D is the number of days in the individual's income period.

The amount per adult or child

811.—(1) An individual's amount per adult or child for a tax year is found by multiplying—
(a) the number of weeks during the income period for the tax year in which the individual provides qualifying care for the adult or child, by
(b) the weekly amount for the adult or child.

(1A) The weekly amount for an adult is £485.

(2) The weekly amount for a child is—
(a) £405 for a week throughout which the child is under 11 years old, and
(b) £485 for other weeks.

(3) [*repealed*]

(4) If an individual provides qualifying care for an adult or child during an income period for only part of a week, the part is treated as a whole week.

(5) If an income period begins or ends during a week, the week is treated as falling within the income period ending during the week.

But if there is no such income period, the week is treated as falling within the income period beginning during the week.

(6) A week is a period of 7 days beginning with a Monday.

1.837

Full qualifying care relief: introduction

812. Sections 813 and 814 (which give the full form of qualifying care relief) apply if—
(a) an individual qualifies for qualifying care relief for a tax year,
(b) the individual's total qualifying care receipts for the tax year do not exceed the individual's limit for the tax year, and
(c) sections 822 and 823 do not apply (accounting date for trade not 5 April).

1.838

Full qualifying care relief: trading income

813.—(1) This section applies if the individual's qualifying care receipts for the tax year would otherwise be brought into account in calculating the profits of a trade.

(2) The profits or losses of the trade for the tax year are treated as nil.

1.839

Full qualifying care relief: income chargeable under Chapter 8 of Part 5

814.—(1) This section applies if the individual's qualifying care receipts for the tax year would otherwise be chargeable to income tax under Chapter 8 of Part 5 (income not otherwise charged).

(2) For each arrangement from which those receipts arise, the amount of—
(a) those receipts arising in the tax year from the arrangement, less

1.840

(b) any expenses associated with them,
is treated as nil.

Part 10

General Provisions

Chapter 1

Introduction

Overview of Part 10

1.841   **864.**—This Part—
(a) contains general rules which are of wider application than to a particular Part of this Act including certain calculation rules (see Chapter 2), and
(b) deals with supplementary matters including general definitions (see Chapter 3).

Social security contributions

Social security contributions: non-trades etc.

1.842   **868.**—(1) This section applies for the purpose of calculating profits or other income charged to income tax.
(2) For this purpose "profits or other income" does not include—
(a) the profits of a trade, profession, or vocation,
(b) the profits of a property business, or
(c) employment income,
but see subsection (6).
(3) No deduction is allowed for any contribution paid by any person under—
(a) Part 1 of the Social Security Contributions and Benefits Act 1992 (c.4), or
(b) Part 1 of the Social Security Contributions and Benefits (Northern Ireland) Act 1992 (c.7).
(4) But this prohibition does not apply to an employer's contribution.
(5) For this purpose "an employer's contribution" means—
(a) a secondary Class 1 contribution,
(b) a Class 1A contribution, or
(c) a Class 1B contribution,
within the meaning of Part 1 of the Social Security Contributions and Benefits Act 1992 (c.4) or of the Social Security Contributions and Benefits (Northern Ireland) Act 1992 (c.7).
(6) Provision corresponding to that made by this section is made by—
(a) section 53 (in relation to trades, professions and vocations),
(b) sections 272 and 272ZA (in relation to property businesses), and
(c) section 360A of ITEPA 2003 (in relation to employment income).

(2005 c.11)

Commissioners for Revenue and Customs Act 2005

(2005 c.11)

ARRANGEMENT OF SECTIONS

Commissioners and officers

1. The Commissioners
2. Officers of Revenue and Customs
3. Declaration of confidentiality
4. Her Majesty's Revenue and Customs

Functions

5. Commissioners' initial functions
7. Former Inland Revenue matters
9. Ancillary powers

Exercise of functions

12. Commissioners' arrangements
13. Exercise of Commissioners' functions by officers
14. Delegation
16A. Charter of Standards and Values

Information

17. Use of information
18. Confidentiality
19. Wrongful disclosure
20. Public interest disclosure
21. Disclosure to prosecuting authority
22. Data protection, etc
23. Freedom of information

Proceedings

24. Evidence

Inspection and complaints

28. Complaints and misconduct: England and Wales

Offences

31. Obstruction
32. Assault
33. Power of arrest

General

50. Consequential amendments, &c.
51. Interpretation

Schedule 1 Former Inland Revenue Matters

1.843

Commissioners for Revenue and Customs Act 2005

INTRODUCTION AND GENERAL NOTE

1.844 This Act provides the necessary statutory machinery to bring about a major restructuring of the policy formation and administration of all UK taxes and of the tax credits, benefits and other matters formerly administered by the Commissioners (or Board) of Inland Revenue and the Commissioners of HM Customs and Excise. Although this may seem a major reform in the British context as it abolishes the oldest British government department, it is perhaps a catching-up exercise with others. The UK is the last of the EU states to bring together the collection of its direct and indirect taxes. The process was not simply a merger. The central policy teams of both the Inland Revenue and Customs and Excise were transferred to the Treasury, uniting the previously divided fiscal policy teams. Law enforcement has also been transferred elsewhere. The Act creates a separate Revenue and Customs Prosecution Office (under provisions not set out in this book), while some enforcement officers were transferred to the new Serious Crimes agency.

The opportunity was also taken to start the process of rationalising the powers of the previous two Departments, reflecting a process of integration that started some time before the formal merger took place in April 2005. The Inland Revenue Regulation Act 1890, set out in previous editions of this volume, has been repealed in entirety as have other administrative provisions dealing with the two Departments. Like its predecessors, the new Department, formally known as Her Majesty's Revenue and Customs (or HMRC), is headed by a body of Commissioners and not Ministers of the Crown. But for legal purposes the Commissioners for Revenue and Customs (as they are known) together are deemed to be a Minister of the Crown. As part of the merger, the hallowed (if not revered) status of Her Majesty's Inspector of Taxes has gone, as have other separate roles for individual officers of the two Departments. Instead, they now become "officers of Revenue and Customs"—though we doubt that the old practice of using initials (HMIT) will be used for the new name! One result is that the past custom of having the names of individual inspectors of tax on the names of court and tribunal cases has ended. All new tax, duty, tax credit and benefit cases will be taken in the name of HM Revenue and Customs.

The Act provides the relevant authority for HMRC to take over all existing responsibilities from the previous Boards and officers and for all necessary changes to be read into Acts of Parliament and subordinate legislation. We have adopted those revisions in this volume. References to "the Board" (meaning the Board of Inland Revenue) are therefore replaced by references to "the Commissioners", and references to "an officer of the Board" or similar by references to "an officer of Revenue and Customs". This will have the incidental effect of standardising widely variant language in past Acts. Further, wide powers of delegation are contained in this Act. In practice powers will be given to "the Commissioners" or "an officer of Revenue and Customs". But the former has authority to delegate almost all its functions to officers. An example of this delegation being standard practice is the delegation under the Tax Credits Act 2002. This Act replaces s.2 of that Act and, in effect, reads this Act into the administrative provisions relevant to that Act.

The Act was intended to come into effect on April 1, 2005, the beginning of the financial and tax year. The start was delayed a few days by the process leading up to the general election in May, but in effect HMRC may be regarded as being established with effect from the beginning of the 2005 tax year.

Commissioners and officers

The Commissioners

1.845 1.—(1) Her Majesty may by Letters Patent appoint Commissioners for Her Majesty's Revenue and Customs.

(2) The Welsh title of the Commissioners shall be Comisynwyr Cyllid a Thollau Ei Mawrhydi.

(3) A Commissioner—
(a) may resign by notice in writing to the Treasury, and
(b) otherwise, shall hold office in accordance with the terms and conditions of his appointment (which may include provision for dismissal).

(4) In exercising their functions, the Commissioners act on behalf of the Crown.

(5) Service as a Commissioner is service in the civil service of the State.

Officers of Revenue and Customs

2.—(1) The Commissioners may appoint staff, to be known as officers of Revenue and Customs.

(2) A person shall hold and vacate office as an officer of Revenue and Customs in accordance with the terms of his appointment (which may include provision for dismissal).

(3) An officer of Revenue and Customs shall comply with directions of the Commissioners (whether he is exercising a function conferred on officers of Revenue and Customs or exercising a function on behalf of the Commissioners).

(4) Anything (including anything in relation to legal proceedings) by or in relation to one officer of Revenue and Customs may be continued by or in relation to another.

(5) Appointments under subsection (1) may be made only with the approval of the Minister for the Civil Service as to terms and conditions of service.

(6) Service in the employment of the Commissioners is service in the civil service of the State.

(7) In Schedule 1 to the Interpretation Act 1978 (c. 30) (defined expressions) at the appropriate place insert—
"'Officer of Revenue and Customs' has the meaning given by section 2(1) of the Commissioners for Revenue and Customs Act 2005."

Declaration of confidentiality

3.—(1) Each person who is appointed under this Act as a Commissioner or officer of Revenue and Customs shall make a declaration acknowledging his obligation of confidentiality under section 18.

(2) A declaration under subsection (1) shall be made—
(a) as soon as is reasonably practicable following the person's appointment, and
(b) in such form, and before such a person, as the Commissioners may direct.

(3) For the purposes of this section, the renewal of a fixed term appointment shall not be treated as an appointment.

"Her Majesty's Revenue and Customs"

4.—(1) The Commissioners and the officers of Revenue and Customs may together be referred to as Her Majesty's Revenue and Customs.

(2) The Welsh title of the Commissioners and the officers of Revenue and Customs together shall be Cyllid a Thollau Ei Mawrhydi.

(3) In Schedule 1 to the Interpretation Act 1978 (defined expressions) at the appropriate place insert—

" 'Her Majesty's Revenue and Customs' has the meaning given by section 4 of the Commissioners for Revenue and Customs Act 2005."

Functions

Commissioners' initial functions

1.849

5.—(1) The Commissioners shall be responsible for—
(a) the collection and management of revenue for which the Commissioners of Inland Revenue were responsible before the commencement of this section, and
(b) the collection and management of revenue for which the Commissioners of Customs and Excise were responsible before the commencement of this section, and
(c) the payment and management of tax credits for which the Commissioners of Inland Revenue were responsible before the commencement of this section.

(2) The Commissioners shall also have all the other functions which before the commencement of this section vested in—
(a) the Commissioners of Inland Revenue (or in a Commissioner), or
(b) the Commissioners of Customs and Excise (or in a Commissioner).

(3) This section is subject to section 35.

(4) In this Act "revenue" includes taxes, duties and national insurance contributions.

Former Inland Revenue matters

1.850

7.—(1) This section applies to the matters listed in Schedule 1.

(2) A function conferred by an enactment (in whatever terms) on any of the persons specified in subsection (3) shall by virtue of this subsection vest in an officer of Revenue and Customs—
(a) if or in so far as it relates to a matter to which this section applies, and
(b) in so far as the officer is exercising a function (whether or not by virtue of paragraph (a)) which relates to a matter to which this section applies.

(3) Those persons are—
(a) an officer of the Commissioners of Inland Revenue,
(b) an officer of the Board of Inland Revenue,
(c) an officer of inland revenue,
(d) a collector of Inland Revenue,
(e) an inspector of taxes,
(f) a collector of taxes,
(g) a person authorised to act as an inspector of taxes or collector of taxes for specific purposes,
(h) an officer having powers in relation to tax,
(i) a revenue official,
(j) a person employed in relation to Inland Revenue (or "the Inland Revenue"), and
(k) an Inland Revenue official.

(2005 c.11 s.7)

(4) In so far as an officer of Revenue and Customs is exercising a function which relates to a matter to which this section applies, section 6(1) shall not apply.

(5) This section is subject to section 35.

Ancillary powers

9.—(1) The Commissioners may do anything which they think—   **1.851**
(a) necessary or expedient in connection with the exercise of their functions, or
(b) incidental or conducive to the exercise of their functions.

(2) This section is subject to section 35.

Commissioners' arrangements

12.—(1) The Commissioners shall make arrangements for—   **1.852**
(a) the conduct of their proceedings, and
(b) the conduct of the proceedings of any committee established by them.

(2) Arrangements under subsection (1) may, in particular—
(a) make provision for a quorum at meetings;
(b) provide that a function of the Commissioners—
   (i) may be exercised by two Commissioners, or
   (ii) may be exercised by a specified number of Commissioners (greater than two).

(3) A decision to make arrangements under subsection (1) must be taken with the agreement of more than half of the Commissioners holding office at the time.

Exercise of Commissioners' functions by officers

13.—(1) An officer of Revenue and Customs may exercise any function   **1.853**
of the Commissioners.

(2) But subsection (1)—
(a) does not apply to the functions specified in subsection (3), and
(b) is subject to directions under section 2(3) and arrangements under section 12.

(3) The non-delegable functions mentioned in subsection (2)(a) are—
(a) making, by statutory instrument, regulations, rules or an order,
(b) ...
(c) ...
(d) giving instructions for the disclosure of information under section 20(1)(a), except that an officer of Revenue and Customs may give an instruction under section 20(1)(a) authorising disclosure of specified information relating to—
   (i) one or more specified persons,
   (ii) one or more specified transactions, or
   (iii) specified goods.

Delegation

14.—(1) Arrangements under section 12 may, in particular, enable the   **1.854**
Commissioners,

or a number of Commissioners acting in accordance with arrangements by virtue of section 12(2)(b), to delegate a function of the Commissioners, other than a function specified in subsection (2) below—
  (a) to a single Commissioner,
  (b) to a committee established by the Commissioners (which may include persons who are neither Commissioners nor staff of the Commissioners nor officers of Revenue and Customs), or
  (c) to any other person.
(2) The non-delegable functions mentioned in subsection (1) are—
  (a) making, by statutory instrument, regulations, rules or an order, Commissioners for Revenue and Customs Act 2005
  (b) ...
  (c) ...
(3) The Commissioners may not delegate the function under section 20(1)(a) except to a single Commissioner.
(4) The delegation of a function by virtue of subsection (1) by the Commissioners or a number of Commissioners—
  (a) shall not prevent the exercise of the function by the Commissioners or those Commissioners, and
  (b) shall not, subject to express provision to the contrary in directions under section 2(3) or arrangements under section 12, prevent the exercise of the function by an officer of Revenue and Customs.
(5) Where the Commissioners or a number of Commissioners delegate a function
to a person by virtue of subsection (1)(c)—
  (a) the Commissioners or those Commissioners shall monitor the exercise of the function by that person, and
  (b) in the exercise of the function the delegate shall comply with any directions of the Commissioners or of those Commissioners.

GENERAL NOTE

1.855   This section has been added to this edition of the volume because of the use made by HMRC of s.14(1)(c). With effect from 2014, HMRC appointed SYNNEX-Concentrix UK Ltd, a wholly owned subsidiary of the US listed corporation SYNNEX Corporation, to act on its behalf in checking individual tax credits claims and awards. Concentrix is stated to have been authorised to make tax credit checks with claimants, employers and others on behalf of HMRC. According to the statement on the GOV.UK contract finder, the contract is for three years from May 6, 2014. The purpose of the contract is to provide HMRC with additional capacity and capability "to correct working tax credit claims that are potentially running with incorrect information ... The price paid for the services will be based on commission on the losses prevented; which are estimated to be between £55 million to £75 million." The website sets out some further details of the contract. It is not clear how far that amounts to directions for the purpose of subs.(5).

As widely reported in the press, MPs, welfare rights groups and others voiced serious concerns about the impact of certain of the activities of Concentrix on tax credit claimants, particularly in relation to "undisclosed partner interventions". Complaints made include stopping tax credit awards using incorrect information, forcing some into debt, and claimants being accused of living together with individuals unconnected to them, including, notoriously, people already deceased. For further details, see the House of Commons Work & Pensions Committee's Fourth Report of Session 2016–17 (*Concentrix* (HC 720) December 1, 2016) and the House of Commons Public Accounts Committee's 29th Report of 2016/17 (*HM*

Revenue & Customs Performance in 2015–16, p.6). In a statement to the House of Commons, the Financial Secretary to the Treasury, Jane Ellison, announced that in the light of evidence that the contractor's performance in recent weeks "had not been acceptable", HMRC had decided not to renew Concentrix's contract beyond May 2017 (HC Debs Vol.614, col.904, September 14, 2016). She also announced that HMRC would no longer be passing new cases to Concentrix and had redeployed Departmental staff with immediate effect to help resolve outstanding issues with tax credits claims.

Charter of standards and values

16A.—(1) The Commissioners must prepare a Charter.

(2) The Charter must include standards of behaviour and values to which Her Majesty's Revenue and Customs will aspire when dealing with people in the exercise of their functions.

(3) The Commissioners must—
(a) regularly review the Charter, and
(b) publish revisions, or revised versions, of it when they consider it appropriate to do so.

(4) The Commissioners must, at least once every year, make a report reviewing the extent to which Her Majesty's Revenue and Customs have demonstrated the standards of behaviour and values included in the Charter.]

General Note

The Charter prepared by HMRC under this section was last revised in November 2020; it is reproduced in Part XII of this volume.

Information

Use of information

17.—(1) Information acquired by the Revenue and Customs in connection with a function may be used by them in connection with any other function.

(2) Subsection (1) is subject to any provision which restricts or prohibits the use of information and which is contained in—
(a) this Act,
(b) any other enactment, or
(c) an international or other agreement to which the United Kingdom or Her Majesty's Government is party.

(3) In subsection (1) "the Revenue and Customs" means—
(a) the Commissioners,
(b) an officer of Revenue and Customs,
(c) a person acting on behalf of the Commissioners or an officer of Revenue and Customs,
(d) a committee established by the Commissioners,
(e) a member of a committee established by the Commissioners,
(f) the Commissioners of Inland Revenue (or any committee or staff of theirs or anyone acting on their behalf),
(g) the Commissioners of Customs and Excise (or any committee or staff of theirs or anyone acting on their behalf), and
(h) a person specified in section 6(2) or 7(3).

Commissioners for Revenue and Customs Act 2005

(4) In subsection (1) "function" means a function of any of the persons listed in subsection (3).

(5) In subsection (2) the reference to an enactment does not include—
  (a) an Act of the Scottish Parliament or an instrument made under such an Act,
  (aa) an Act of the National Assembly for Wales or an instrument made under such an Act, or
  (b) an Act of the Northern Ireland Assembly or an instrument made under such an Act.

(6) Part 2 of Schedule 2 (which makes provision about the supply and other use of information in specified circumstances) shall have effect.

Confidentiality

1.859   **18.**—(1) Revenue and Customs officials may not disclose information which is held by the Revenue and Customs in connection with a function of the Revenue and Customs.

(2) But subsection (1) does not apply to a disclosure—
  (a) which—
    (i) is made for the purposes of a function of the Revenue and Customs, and
    (ii) does not contravene any restriction imposed by the Commissioners,
  (b) which is made in accordance with section 20 or 21,
  (c) which is made for the purposes of civil proceedings (whether or not within the United Kingdom) relating to a matter in respect of which the Revenue and Customs have functions,
  (d) which is made for the purposes of a criminal investigation or criminal proceedings (whether or not within the United Kingdom) relating to a matter in respect of which the Revenue and Customs have functions,
  (e) which is made in pursuance of an order of a court,
  (f) which is made to Her Majesty's Inspectors of Constabulary, the Scottish inspectors or the Northern Ireland inspectors for the purpose of an inspection by virtue of section 27,
  (g) which is made to the Independent Police Complaints Commission, or a person acting on its behalf, for the purpose of the exercise of a function by virtue of section 28, or
  (h) which is made with the consent of each person to whom the information relates,
  (i) which is made to Revenue Scotland in connection with the collection and management of a devolved tax within the meaning of the Scotland Act 1998,
  (j) which is made to the Welsh Revenue Authority in connection with the collection and management of a devolved tax within the meaning of the Government of Wales Act 2006, or
  (k) which is made in connection with (or with anything done with a view to) the making or implementation of an agreement referred to in section 64A(1) or (2) of the Scotland Act 1998 (assignment of VAT).

(2A) Information disclosed in reliance on subsection (2)(k) may not be further disclosed without the consent of the Commissioners (which may be general or specific).

(3) Subsection (1) is subject to any other enactment permitting disclosure.

(4) In this section—
(a) a reference to Revenue and Customs officials is a reference to any person who is or was—
   (i) a Commissioner,
   (ii) an officer of Revenue and Customs,
   (iii) a person acting on behalf of the Commissioners or an officer of Revenue and Customs, or
   (iv) a member of a committee established by the Commissioners,
(b) a reference to the Revenue and Customs has the same meaning as in section 17,
(c) a reference to a function of the Revenue and Customs is a reference to a function of—
   (i) the Commissioners, or
   (ii) an officer of Revenue and Customs,
(d) a reference to the Scottish inspectors or the Northern Ireland inspectors has the same meaning as in section 27, and
(e) a reference to an enactment does not include—
   (i) an Act of the Scottish Parliament or an instrument made under such an Act,
   (ia) an Act of the National Assembly for Wales or an instrument made under such an Act, or
   (ii) an Act of the Northern Ireland Assembly or an instrument made under such an Act.

Wrongful disclosure

19.—(1) A person commits an offence if he contravenes section 18(1) or (2A) or 20(9) by disclosing revenue and customs information relating to a person whose identity—

(a) is specified in the disclosure, or
(b) can be deduced from it.

(2) In subsection (1) "revenue and customs information relating to a person" means information about, acquired as a result of, or held in connection with the exercise of a function of the Revenue and Customs (within the meaning given by section 18(4)(c)) in respect of the person; but it does not include information about internal administrative arrangements of Her Majesty's Revenue and Customs (whether relating to Commissioners, officers or others).

(3) It is a defence for a person charged with an offence under this section of disclosing information to prove that he reasonably believed—
(a) that the disclosure was lawful, or
(b) that the information had already and lawfully been made available to the public.

(4) A person guilty of an offence under this section shall be liable—
(a) on conviction on indictment, to imprisonment for a term not exceeding two years, to a fine or to both, or
(b) on summary conviction, to imprisonment for a term not exceeding the general limit in a magistrates' court, to a fine not exceeding the statutory maximum or to both.

(5) A prosecution for an offence under this section may be instituted in England and Wales only by or with the consent of the Director of Public Prosecutions.

(6) A prosecution for an offence under this section may be instituted in Northern Ireland only—
  (a) by the Commissioners, or
  (b) with the consent of the Director of Public Prosecutions for Northern Ireland.
(7) In the application of this section to Scotland or Northern Ireland the reference in subsection (4)(b) to 12 months shall be taken as a reference to six months.
(8) This section is without prejudice to the pursuit of any remedy or the taking of any action in relation to a contravention of section 18(1) or (2A) or 20(9) (whether or not this section applies to the contravention).

Public interest disclosure

1.861   **20.**—(1) Disclosure is in accordance with this section (as mentioned in section 18(2)(b)) if—
  (a) it is made on the instructions of the Commissioners (which may be general or specific),
  (b) it is of a kind—
    (i) to which any of subsections (2) to (7) applies, or
    (ii) specified in regulations made by the Treasury, and
  (c) the Commissioners are satisfied that it is in the public interest.
(2) This subsection applies to a disclosure made—
  (a) to a person exercising public functions (whether or not within the United Kingdom),
  (b) for the purposes of the prevention or detection of crime, and
  (c) in order to comply with an obligation of the United Kingdom, or Her Majesty's Government, under an international or other agreement relating to the movement of persons, goods or services.
(3) This subsection applies to a disclosure if
  (a) it is made to a body which has responsibility for the regulation of a profession,
  (b) it relates to misconduct on the part of a member of the profession, and
  (c) the misconduct relates to a function of the Revenue and Customs.
(4) This subsection applies to a disclosure if—
  (a) it is made to a constable, and
  (b) either—
    (i) the constable is exercising functions which relate to the movement of persons or goods into or out of the United Kingdom, or
    (ii) the disclosure is made for the purposes of the prevention or detection of crime.
(5) This subsection applies to a disclosure if it is made—
  (a) to the National Criminal Intelligence Service, and
  (b) for a purpose connected with its functions under section 2(2) of the Police Act 1997 (criminal intelligence).
(6) This subsection applies to a disclosure if it is made—
  (a) to a person exercising public functions in relation to public safety or public health, and
  (b) for the purposes of those functions.
(7) This subsection applies to a disclosure if it—

(a) is made to the Secretary of State for the purpose of enabling information to be entered in a computerised database, and
(b) relates to—
   (i) a person suspected of an offence,
   (ii) a person arrested for an offence,
   (iii) the results of an investigation, or
   (iv) anything seized.
(8) Regulations under subsection (1)(b)(ii)—
(a) may specify a kind of disclosure only if the Treasury are satisfied that it relates to—
   (i) national security,
   (ii) public safety,
   (iii) public health, or
   (iv) the prevention or detection of crime;
(b) may make provision limiting or restricting the disclosures that may be made in reliance on the regulations; and that provision may, in particular, operate by reference to—
   (i) the nature of information,
   (ii) the person or class of person to whom the disclosure is made,
   (iii) the person or class of person by whom the disclosure is made,
   (iv) any other factor, or
   (v) a combination of factors;
(c) shall be made by statutory instrument;
(d) may not be made unless a draft has been laid before and approved by resolution of each House of Parliament.
(9) Information disclosed in reliance on this section may not be further disclosed without the consent of the Commissioners (which may be general or specific); (but the Commissioners shall be taken to have consented to further disclosure by use of the computerised database of information disclosed by virtue of subsection (7)).

Disclosure to prosecuting authority

21.—(1) Disclosure is in accordance with this section (as mentioned in section 18(2)(b)) if made—
(a) to a prosecuting authority, and
(b) for the purpose of enabling the authority—
   (i) to consider whether to institute criminal proceedings in respect of a matter considered in the course of an investigation conducted by or on behalf of Her Majesty's Revenue and Customs,
   (ii) to give advice in connection with a criminal investigation or criminal proceedings, or
   (iii) in the case of the Director of Public Prosecutions, to exercise his functions under, or in relation to, Part 5 or 8 of the Proceeds of Crime Act 2002.
(2) In subsection (1) "prosecuting authority" means—
(a) the Director of Public Prosecutions,
(b) in Scotland, the Lord Advocate or a procurator fiscal, and
(c) in Northern Ireland, the Director of Public Prosecutions for Northern Ireland.
(2A) In subsection (1) "criminal investigation" means any process—
   (i) for considering whether an offence has been committed,

(ii) for discovering by whom an offence has been committed, or
(iii) as a result of which an offence is alleged to have been committed.
(3) Information disclosed to a prosecuting authority in accordance with this section may not be further disclosed except—
   (a) for a purpose connected with the exercise of the prosecuting authority's functions, or
   (b) with the consent of the Commissioners (which may be general or specific).
(4) A person commits an offence if he contravenes subsection (3).
(5) It is a defence for a person charged with an offence under this section to prove that he reasonably believed—
   (a) that the disclosure was lawful, or
   (b) that the information had already and lawfully been made available to the public.
(6) A person guilty of an offence under this section shall be liable—
   (a) on conviction on indictment, to imprisonment for a term not exceeding two years, to a fine or to both, or
   (b) on summary conviction, to imprisonment for a term not exceeding the general limit in a magistrates' court, to a fine not exceeding the statutory maximum or to both.
(7) A prosecution for an offence under this section may be instituted in England and Wales only by or with the consent of the Director of Public Prosecutions.
(8) A prosecution for an offence under this section may be instituted in Northern Ireland only—
   (a) by the Commissioners, or
   (b) with the consent of the Director of Public Prosecutions for Northern Ireland.
(9) In the application of this section to Scotland or Northern Ireland the reference in subsection (6)(b) to 12 months shall be taken as a reference to six months.

Data protection, etc

1.863   **22.**—(1) Nothing in sections 17 to 21 authorises the making of a disclosure which—
   (a) contravenes the data protection legislation, or
   (b) is prohibited by any of Parts 1 to 7 or Chapter 1 of Part 9 of the Investigatory Powers Act 2016.
(2) In this section, "the data protection legislation" has the same meaning as in the Data Protection Act 2018 (see section 3 of that Act).

Freedom of information

1.864   **23.**—(1) Revenue and customs information relating to a person, the disclosure of which is prohibited by section 18(1), is exempt information by virtue of section 44(1)(a) of the Freedom of Information Act 2000 (c. 36) (prohibitions on disclosure) if its disclosure—
   (a) would specify the identity of the person to whom the information relates, or
   (b) would enable the identity of such a person to be deduced.
(1A) Subsections (2) and (3) of section 18 are to be disregarded in determining for the purposes of subsection (1) of this section whether the

disclosure of revenue and customs information relating to a person is prohibited by subsection (1) of that section.

(2) Except as specified in subsection (1), information the disclosure of which is prohibited by section 18(1) is not exempt information for the purposes of section 44(1)(a) of the Freedom of Information Act 2000.

(3) In subsection (1) "revenue and customs information relating to a person" has the same meaning as in section 19.

Proceedings

Evidence

24.—(1) A document that purports to have been issued or signed by or with the authority of the Commissioners—
  (a) shall be treated as having been so issued or signed unless the contrary is proved, and
  (b) shall be admissible in any legal proceedings.

(2) A document that purports to have been issued by the Commissioners and which certifies any of the matters specified in subsection (3) shall (in addition to the matters provided for by subsection (1)(a) and (b)) be treated as accurate unless the contrary is proved.

(3) The matters mentioned in subsection (2) are—
  (a) that a specified person was appointed as a commissioner on a specified date,
  (b) that a specified person was appointed as an officer of Revenue and Customs on a specified date,
  (c) that at a specified time or for a specified purpose (or both) a function was delegated to a specified Commissioner,
  (d) that at a specified time or for a specified purpose (or both) a function was delegated to a specified committee, and
  (e) that at a specified time or for a specified purpose (or both) a function was delegated to another specified person.

(4) A photographic or other copy of a document acquired by the Commissioners shall, if certified by them to be an accurate copy, be admissible in any legal proceedings to the same extent as the document itself.

(5) Section 2 of the Documentary Evidence Act 1868 (c 37) (proof of documents) shall apply to a Revenue and Customs document as it applies in relation to the documents mentioned in that section.

(6) In the application of that section to a Revenue and Customs document the Schedule to that Act shall be treated as if—
  (a) the first column contained a reference to the Commissioners, and
  (b) the second column contained a reference to a Commissioner or a person acting on his authority.

(7) In this section—
  (a) "Revenue and Customs document" means a document issued by or on behalf of the Commissioners, and
  (b) a reference to the Commissioners includes a reference to the Commissioners of Inland Revenue and to the Commissioners of Customs and Excise.

GENERAL NOTE

1.866   Subsection (1)'s presumption of authenticity applies to tax credits documentation.

Inspection and complaints

Complaints and misconduct: England and Wales

1.867   **28.**—(1) The Treasury may make regulations conferring functions on the Director General of the Independent Office for Police Conduct in relation to—
(a) the Commissioners for Her Majesty's Revenue and Customs, and
(b) officers of Revenue and Customs.
(2) Regulations under subsection (1)—
(a) may apply (with or without modification) or make provision similar to any provision of or made under Part 2 of the Police Reform Act 2002 (c 30) (complaints);
(b) may confer on the Director General, or on a person acting on the Director General's behalf, a power of a kind conferred by this Act or another enactment on an officer of Revenue and Customs;
(c) may make provision for payment by the Commissioners to or in respect of the [Director General.
(3) The Director General and the Parliamentary Commissioner for Administration may disclose information to each other for the purposes of the exercise of a function—
(a) by virtue of this section, or
(b) under the Parliamentary Commissioner Act 1967 (c 13).
(4) The Director General and the Parliamentary Commissioner for Administration may jointly investigate a matter in relation to which—
(a) the Director General has functions by virtue of this section, and
(b) the Parliamentary Commissioner for Administration has functions by virtue of the Parliamentary Commissioner Act 1967.
(5) Regulations under subsection (1)—
(a) shall be made by statutory instrument, and
(b) shall be subject to annulment in pursuance of a resolution of either House of Parliament.
(6) Regulations under subsection (1) shall relate to the Commissioners or officers of Revenue and Customs only in so far as their functions are exercised in or in relation to England and Wales, including the sea and other waters within the seaward limits of the territorial sea adjacent to England and Wales.

GENERAL NOTE

1.868   If tax credit claimants or recipients are aggrieved at HMRC's administration of tax credits claims or awards, it is open to them to make a complaint. Despite this section's title, it does not provide for a comprehensive HMRC complaints procedure. Regulations made under this section are concerned with particularly serious complaints.

Complaints of maladministration, such as excessive delay in determining a claim or an incompetent or inadequate 'living together' investigations should be made to

HMRC in the first instance. Complaints may be made in writing or by telephone but, according to the gov.uk website, an on-line complaint may only be made if a complainant has a Government Gateway user ID and password.

If a complainant is dissatisfied with HMRC's response to a complaint, they may take their case to The Adjudicator. Complaints are unlikely to proceed rapidly to this stage. The Adjudicator will not consider a complaint unless a complainant has already asked for a first and second review by HMRC, referred to as Tier 1 and Tier 2 reviews by HMRC (see The Adjudicator's guide to making a complaint at *http://www.gov.uk/guidance/how-to-complain-to-the-adjudicators-office-about-hmrc-or-the-voa*). A Service Level Agreement between HMRC and The Adjudicator identifies the types of complaint that may be considered by The Adjudicator:

- if policy and guidance were applied fairly and consistently,
- administrative errors including unreasonable delays, mistakes and poor or misleading advice,
- how discretion was applied,
- staff conduct which led to poor customer service.

If a complainant is dissatisfied with The Adjudicator's decision, a complaint of maladministration against HMRC may be then be brought to the Parliamentary Commissioner for Administration (commonly referred to as the Parliamentary and Health Service Ombudsman). However, the Commissioner may only receive complaints referred by MPs. Complainants need, therefore, to persuade their local MP to refer a case to the Commissioner. Both The Adjudicator and The Ombudsman have power to recommend that HMRC pay compensation to a complainant.

The Adjudicator's 2020 Annual Report identified the following themes within complaints made to it about HMRC's tax credits performance:

- "Evidence of a lack of focus on the customer and ownership of their issues where they span tax credits and Universal Credit. This can result in customers being unable to resolve issues where one or other department are at fault because resolution of their complaint falls between the two departments. This can happen where each department narrowly considers the part of the process that they are responsible for and fails to take ownership for resolving issues that arise from the customer's overall experience. This also relates to the use of the HMRC/DWP complaint handling protocol and the impact for customers following HMRC and DWP appeals";

- "Evidence that the department does not always recognise the impact, for the customer, of misadvice or error. They do not always recognise that process, intended to apply where no error occurred, may not be appropriate following an official error. This includes the application of processes which would apply where new tax credits are no longer available which, in some cases, leads to ongoing financial loss";

- "Evidence that the department does not always follow guidance, where an official error or misadvice led to tax credits overpayments";

- "The requirement to transfer responsibility for collection of outstanding debts from HMRC's tax credits to DWP's Universal Credit has been a planned business activity for several years, which allowed time for HMRC to put policies and processes in place. However, we continue to see complaints because of gaps in guidance that should provide protection for vulnerable customers."

The Revenue and Customs (Complaints and Misconduct) Regulations 2010 (SI 2010/1813), made under s.28 but not reproduced in this volume, deal with a narrow category of more serious complaints. These include a complaint of behaviour which is liable to lead to a disciplinary sanction where (a) it was aggravated by discriminatory behaviour on the grounds of a person's race, sex, religion, or other status identified in guidance issued by the Director General of the Independent Office for Police Conduct, and (b) it appears to HMRC that the complaint contains an indication that a person behaved in a manner likely to lead to the termination of the person's employment. In such cases, HMRC are required to refer the complaint to the Director General (reg.28(1)). HMRC also have power to refer other complaints to the Director General if they consider it appropriate to do so in the light of the gravity of the subject-matter or any exceptional circumstances (reg.28(4)).

Obstruction

1.869   **31.**—(1) A person commits an offence if without reasonable excuse he obstructs—
  (a) an officer of Revenue and Customs,
  (b) a person acting on behalf of the Commissioners or an officer of Revenue and Customs, or
  (c) a person assisting an officer of Revenue and Customs.
(2) A person guilty of an offence under this section shall be liable on summary conviction to—
  (a) imprisonment for a period not exceeding 51 weeks,
  (b) a fine not exceeding level 3 on the standard scale, or
  (c) both.
(3) In the application of this section to Scotland or Northern Ireland the reference in subsection (2)(a) to 51 weeks shall be taken as a reference to six months.

Assault

1.870   **32.**—(1) A person commits an offence if he assaults an officer of Revenue and Customs.
(2) A person guilty of an offence under this section shall be liable on summary conviction to—
  (a) imprisonment for a period not exceeding 51 weeks,
  (b) a fine not exceeding level 5 on the standard scale, or
  (c) both.
(3) In the application of this section to Scotland or Northern Ireland the reference in subsection (2)(a) to 51 weeks shall be taken as a reference to six months.

Power of arrest

1.871   **33.**—(1) An authorised officer of Revenue and Customs may arrest a person without warrant if the officer reasonably suspects that the person—
  (a) has committed an offence under section 30, 31 or 32,
  (b) is committing an offence under any of those sections, or
  (c) is about to commit an offence under any of those sections.
(2) In subsection (1) "authorised" means authorised by the Commissioners.
(3) Authorisation for the purposes of this section may be specific or general.
(4) In Scotland or Northern Ireland, a constable may arrest a person without warrant if the constable reasonably suspects that the person—
  (a) has committed an offence under this Act,
  (b) is committing an offence under this Act, or
  (c) is about to commit an offence under this Act.

General

Consequential amendments, &c.

50.—(1) In so far as is appropriate in consequence of section 5 a reference in an enactment, instrument or other document to the Commissioners of Customs and Excise, to customs and excise or to the Commissioners of Inland Revenue (however expressed) shall be taken as a reference to the Commissioners for Her Majesty's Revenue and Customs.

(2) In so far as is appropriate in consequence of sections 6 and 7 a reference in an enactment, instrument or other document to any of the persons specified in section 6(2) or 7(3) (however expressed) shall be taken as a reference to an officer of Revenue and Customs.

Interpretation

51.– (1) In this Act—

...

"officer of Revenue and Customs" means a person appointed under section 2, and

"revenue" has the meaning given by section 5(4).

(2) In this Act—
(a) "function" means any power or duty (including a power or duty that is ancillary to another power or duty), and
(b) a reference to the functions of the Commissioners or of officers of Revenue and Customs is a reference to the functions conferred—
   (i) by or by virtue of this Act, or
   (ii) by or by virtue of any enactment passed or made after the commencement of this Act.

...

(4) In this Act a reference to information acquired in connection with a matter includes a reference to information held in connection with that matter.

SCHEDULE 1

FORMER INLAND REVENUE MATTERS

1 Capital gains tax.
2 Charities.
3 Child benefit.
4 Child tax credit.
5 Child trust funds.
6 Corporation tax (and amounts assessable or chargeable as if they were corporation tax).
7 Guardian's allowance.
8 Income tax.
9 Inheritance tax.
10 The issue of bank notes.
11 National insurance contributions.
12 The National Insurance Fund.

13   The national minimum wage.
14   Oil and gas royalties.
15   Payment of or in lieu of rates.
16   Payment in lieu of tax reliefs, in so far as the Commissioners of Inland Revenue were responsible before the commencement of section 5.
17   Pension schemes.
18   Petroleum revenue tax.
19   Rating lists.
20   Recovery of taxes due in other member States, in relation to matters corresponding to those for which the Commissioners of Inland Revenue were responsible before the commencement of section 5.
21   Stamp duty.
22   Stamp duty land tax.
23   Stamp duty reserve tax.
24   Statutory adoption pay.
25   Statutory maternity pay.
26   Statutory paternity pay.
26A   . . .
26B   Statutory shared parental pay.
26C   Statutory parental bereavement pay.
27   Statutory sick pay.
28   Student loans.
29   Valuation lists in relation to council tax.
30   Valuation of property.
31   Working tax credit.

Income Tax Act 2007

(2007 c.3)

ARRANGEMENT OF SELECTED SECTIONS

PART 1

OVERVIEW

1.   Overview of Income Tax Acts
2.   Overview of Act

(2007 c.3)

PART 2

BASIC PROVISIONS

CHAPTER 1

CHARGES TO INCOME TAX

3. Overview of charges to income tax
4. Income tax an annual tax

PART 14

INCOME TAX LIABILITY: MISCELLANEOUS RULES

CHAPTER 3

JOINTLY HELD PROPERTY

836. Jointly held property
837. Jointly held property: declarations of unequal beneficial interests

PART 16

INCOME TAX ACT DEFINITIONS, ETC

CHAPTER 1

DEFINITIONS

988. Overview of Chapter
989. The definitions
992. Meaning of "company"

CHAPTER 2

OTHER INCOME TAX ACTS PROVISIONS

1011. References to married persons, or civil partners, living together

(SCHEDULES OMITTED)

INTRODUCTION AND GENERAL NOTE

1.875

This Act came into effect on April 6, 2007. It is the fourth of the Acts produced as part of the Tax Law Rewrite Project. It brings to a close the complete rewrite of all primary legislation dealing with income tax save only for the areas (not relevant to this work) listed in s.1 below. As s.1 signposts, it is to be read with ITEPA and ITTOIA. Save as mentioned in that section, all the parts of the Income and Corporation Taxes Act 1988 that referred to income tax have now been repealed and replaced. The extracts from that Act previously in this volume have therefore been deleted. Only a few sections from this Act are relevant to this work, but s.2 is included to show the full and extensive contents of the Act. As with the other Tax Law Rewrite Acts, an extensive explanatory note (running for this Act to three volumes) was published with the Act. Anyone wishing to consider any reference to the Act further should look at that note as a starting point.

PART 1

OVERVIEW

Overview of Income Tax Acts

1.876

1.—(1) The following Acts make provision about income tax—
(a) ITEPA 2003 (which is about charges to tax on employment income, pension income and social security income and makes provision for the high income child benefit charge),
(b) ITTOIA 2005 (which is about charges to tax on trading income, property income, savings and investment income and some other miscellaneous income), and
(c) this Act (which contains the other main provisions about income tax).

(2) There are also provisions about income tax elsewhere: see in particular—
(a) Part 2 of TIOPA 2010 (double taxation relief),
(b) CAA 2001 (allowances for capital expenditure), and
(c) Part 4 of FA 2004 (pension schemes etc).

(3) Schedule 1 to the Interpretation Act 1978 (c.30) defines "the Income Tax Acts" (as all enactments relating to income tax).

Overview of Act

1.877

2.—(1) This Act has 17 Parts.
(2) Part 2 contains basic provisions about income tax including-
(a) provision about the annual nature of income tax (Chapter 1),
(b) the rates at which income tax is charged (Chapter 2), and
(c) the calculation of income tax liability (Chapter 3).
(3) Part 3 is about taxpayers' personal reliefs including—
(a) personal allowances (Chapter 2),
(b) blind persons' allowances (Chapter 2), and
(c) tax reductions for married couples and civil partners (Chapter 3).
(4) Part 4 is about loss relief including relief for—
(a) trade losses (Chapters 2 and 3),
(b) losses from property businesses (Chapter 4),
(c) losses in an cmployment or office (Chapter 5),
(d) losses on disposal of shares (Chapter 6), and
(e) losses from miscellaneous transactions (Chapter 7).

(5) Part 5 is about relief under the enterprise investment scheme.
(5A) Part 5A is about relief under the seed enterprise investment scheme.
(5B) Part 5B is about relief for social investments.
(6) Part 6 is about—
(a) relief for investment in venture capital trusts, and
(b) other matters relating to venture capital trusts.
(7) Part 7 is about community investment tax relief.
(8) Part 8 is about a variety of reliefs including relief for—
(a) interest payments (Chapter 1),
(b) gifts to charity including gift aid (Chapters 2 and 3),
(c) annual payments (Chapter 4), and
(d) maintenance payments (Chapter 5).
(9) Part 9 contains special rules about settlements and trustees including—
(a) general provision about settlements and trustees (Chapter 2),
(b) special income tax rates for trusts (Chapters 3, 4 and 5),
(c) rules about trustees' expenses (Chapters 4 and 8),
(d) rules about trustees' discretionary payments (Chapter 7),
(e) ..., and
(f) rules about heritage maintenance settlements (Chapter 10).
(9A) Part 9A is about the treatment of certain transactions in UK land.
(10) Part 10 contains special rules about charitable trusts etc.
(10A) Part 10A is about alternative finance arrangements.
(11) ...
(11ZA) Part 11ZA is about manufactured payments.
(11A) Part 11A is about leasing arrangements involving finance leases or loans.
(12) Part 12 is about accrued income profits.
(12A) Part 12A is about sale and lease-back etc.
(13) Part 13 is about tax avoidance in relation to—
(a) transactions in securities (Chapter 1),
(b) transfers of assets abroad (Chapter 2),
(c) ...,
(d) sales of occupation income (Chapter 4),
(e) trade losses (Chapter 5),
(g) finance arrangements (Chapter 5B),
(h) loan or credit transactions (Chapter 5C)],
(ha) disposals of assets through partnerships (Chapter 5D),
(hb) disguised investment management fees (Chapter 5E),
(hc) income-based carried interest (Chapter 5F),
(i) leases of plant and machinery (Chapter 6), and
(j) tax relief for interest (Chapter 7).
(14) Part 14 deals with some miscellaneous rules about income tax liability, including—
(za) an alternative basis for charge (the remittance basis) for certain income and gains of certain individuals (Chapter A1),
(a) limits on liability to income tax for non-UK residents (Chapter 1),
(aa) exemption for persons not domiciled in United Kingdom (Chapter 1A),
(b) special rules about residence (Chapter 2),
(ba) rules about UK representatives of non-UK residents (Chapters 2B and 2C),

(c) rules about jointly held property (Chapter 3),
(d) imposition of the charge to income tax on the receipts of certain types of company being wound up (Chapter 3A).

(15) Part 15 is about the deduction of income tax at source.

(16) Part 16 contains definitions which apply for the purposes of the Income Tax Acts and other general provisions which apply for the purposes of those Acts.

(17) Part 17—
(a) contains provisions to be used in interpreting this Act,
(b) introduces Schedule 1 (minor and consequential amendments),
(c) introduces Schedule 2 (transitional provisions and savings),
(d) introduces Schedule 3 (repeals and revocations, including of spent enactments),
(e) introduces Schedule 4 (index of defined expressions that apply for the purposes of this Act),
(f) confers powers on the Treasury to make orders, and
(g) makes provision about the coming into force of this Act.

PART 2

BASIC PROVISIONS

CHAPTER 1

CHARGES TO INCOME TAX

Overview of charges to income tax

1.878   3.—(1) Income tax is charged under—
(a) Part 2 of ITEPA 2003 (employment income),
(b) Part 9 of ITEPA 2003 (pension income),
(c) Part 10 of ITEPA 2003 (social security income),
(d) Part 2 of ITTOIA 2005 (trading income),
(e) Part 3 of ITTOIA 2005 (property income),
(f) Part 4 of ITTOIA 2005 (savings and investment income), and
(g) Part 5 of ITTOIA 2005 (miscellaneous income).

(2) Income tax is also charged under other provisions, including—
(a) Chapter 5 of Part 4 of FA 2004 (registered pension schemes: tax charges),
(b) section 7 of F(No.2)A 2005 (social security pension lump sums),
(c) Part 10 of this Act (special rules about charitable trusts etc),
(d) Chapter 2 of Part 12 of this Act (accrued income profits),
(e) Part 13 of this Act (tax avoidance), and
(f) Chapter 3A of Part 14 of this Act (banks etc in compulsory liquidation).

Income tax an annual tax

4.—(1) Income tax is charged for a year only if an Act so provides.

(2) A year for which income tax is charged is called a "tax year".

(3) A tax year begins on 6 April and ends on the following 5 April.

(4) "The tax year 2007–08" means the tax year beginning on 6 April 2007 (and any corresponding expression in which two years are similarly mentioned is to be read in the same way).

(5) Every assessment to income tax must be made for a tax year.

(6) Subsection (5) is subject to Chapter 15 of Part 15 (by virtue of which an assessment may relate to a return period).

GENERAL NOTE

The Rewrite Acts retain the long-standing approach of providing framework legislation for income tax. It is the relevant section in each year's Finance Act that actually imposes the tax for the year. That section triggers s.4 and thence the charging sections in s.3 and in ITEPA and ITTOIA. The list of charging sections here may be compared with the similar—but not identical—list of chapters to the Tax Credits (Definition and Calculation of Income) Regulations 2002 below.

PART 14

INCOME TAX LIABILITY: MISCELLANEOUS RULES

CHAPTER 3

JOINTLY HELD PROPERTY

Jointly held property

836.—(1) This section applies if income arises from property held in the names of individuals—

(a) who are married to, or are civil partners of, each other, and

(b) who live together.

(2) The individuals are treated for income tax purposes as beneficially entitled to the income in equal shares.

(3) But this treatment does not apply in relation to any income within any of the following exceptions.

Exception A

Income to which neither of the individuals is beneficially entitled.

Exception B

Income in relation to which a declaration by the individuals under section 837 has effect (unequal beneficial interests).

Exception C

Income to which Part 9 of ITTOIA 2005 applies (partnerships).

Exception DA

Income arising from an overseas property business which consists of, or so far as it includes, the commercial letting of furnished holiday accommodation (within the meaning of Chapter 6 of Part 3 of ITTOIA 2005) in one or more EEA states.

Exception D

Income arising from a UK property business which consists of, or so far as it includes, the commercial letting of furnished holiday accommodation (within the meaning of Chapter 6 of Part 3 of ITTOIA 2005).

Exception E

Income consisting of a distribution arising from property consisting of—

    (a) shares in or securities of a close company to which one of the individuals is beneficially entitled to the exclusion of the other, or

    (b) such shares or securities to which the individuals are beneficially entitled in equal or unequal shares.

"Shares" and "securities" have the same meaning as in section 1117 of CTA 2010.

Exception F

Income to which one of the individuals is beneficially entitled so far as it is treated as a result of any other provision of the Income Tax Acts as—

    (a) the income of the other individual, or

    (b) the income of a third party.

GENERAL NOTE

1.882   This section and the machinery section that follows should be read with s.1011 below. It sets out the general rule that couples living together are assumed to own any property, and therefore to receive any income from that property, in equal shares. Section 837 allows the couple to alter that position. However, that will make little difference to tax credits claims as entitlement is assessed on the total incomes of both members of the couple. Note that this rule does not apply to unmarried or unregistered couples, but again that does not affect tax credit entitlement. It does however affect income tax liability where the two members of the couple are liable to income tax at different rates at the margin.

Jointly held property: declarations of unequal beneficial interests

1.883   **837.**—(1) The individuals may make a joint declaration under this section if—

    (a) one of them is beneficially entitled to the income to the exclusion of the other, or

    (b) they are beneficially entitled to the income in unequal shares, and their beneficial interests in the income correspond to their beneficial interests in the property from which it arises.

(2) The declaration must state the beneficial interests of the individuals in—

    (a) the income to which the declaration relates, and

    (b) the property from which that income arises.

(3) The declaration has effect only if notice of it is given to an officer of Revenue and Customs—

    (a) in such form and manner as the Commissioners for Her Majesty's Revenue and Customs may prescribe, and

    (b) within the period of 60 days beginning with the date of the declaration.

(4) The declaration has effect in relation to income arising on or after the date of the declaration.

(5) The declaration continues to have effect until such time (if any) as there is a change in the beneficial interests of the individuals in either—
(a) the income to which the declaration relates, or
(b) the property from which that income arises.

PART 16

INCOME TAX ACTS DEFINITIONS, ETC

CHAPTER 1

DEFINITIONS

Overview of Chapter

988.—(1) This Chapter contains definitions which apply for the purposes of the Income Tax Acts, except where, in those Acts, the context otherwise requires.

(2) To find a definition go first to section 989, which sets out some of the definitions in full.

(3) If a definition is not set out in full in section 989, the section indicates where it is set out in full.

(4) In some cases it is stated that a definition does not apply for the purposes of specified provisions of the Income Tax Acts (see, for example, sections 990(2), 992(3) and 1007(4)).

(5) And in some cases it is stated that a definition has effect only for the purposes of specific provisions of the Income Tax Acts (see, for example, sections 991, 993, 995 and 1006).

1.884

The definitions

989.—The following definitions apply for the purposes of the Income Tax Acts—
"Act" has the meaning given by section 990,
"additional rate" means the rate of income tax determined in pursuance of section 6(2),
"authorised unit trust" is to be read in accordance with sections 616 and 619 of CTA 2010,
. . .
"bank" is to be read in accordance with section 991,
"basic rate" means the rate of income tax determined in pursuance of section 6(2),
"basic rate limit" has the meaning given by section 10,
. . .
"body of persons" means any body politic, corporate or collegiate and any company, fraternity, fellowship or society of persons whether corporate or not corporate,
. . .
"capital allowance" means any allowance under CAA 2001,
"the Capital Allowances Act" means CAA 2001,

1.885

"chargeable gain" has the same meaning as in TCGA 1992,
"chargeable period" means an accounting period of a company or a tax year,
...
"company" has the meaning given by section 992,
...
"dividend additional rate" means the rate of income tax specified in section 8(3),
"dividend income" has the meaning given by section 19
...
"farming" has the meaning given by section 996,
"for accounting purposes" has the meaning given by section 997(4),
...
"generally accepted accounting practice" has the meaning given by section 997(1) and (3),
"grossing up" is to be read in accordance with section 998,
...
"international accounting standards" has the meaning given by section 997(5),
...
"non-UK resident" means not resident in the United Kingdom (and references to a non-UK resident or a non-UK resident person are to a person who is not resident there),
"normal self-assessment filing date", in relation to a tax year, means the 31 January following the tax year,
"notice" means notice in writing or in a form authorised (in relation to the case in question) by directions under section 43E (1) of TMA 1970,
...
"overseas property business" has the meaning given by Chapter 2 of Part 3 of ITTOIA 2005,
"period of account"—
(a) in relation to a person, means any period for which the person draws up accounts, and
(b) in relation to a trade, profession, vocation or other business, means any period for which the accounts of the business are drawn up,
...
"personal representatives" in relation to a person who has died, means—
(a) in the United Kingdom, persons responsible for administering the estate of the deceased, and
(b) in a territory outside the United Kingdom, those persons having functions under its law equivalent to those of administering the estate of the deceased,
"profits or gains" does not include chargeable gains,
...
"relevant foreign income" has the meaning given by section 830(1) to (3) of ITTOIA 2005 but also includes, for any purpose mentioned in any provision listed in section 830(4) of that Act, income treated as relevant foreign income for that purpose by that provision,
"research and development" is to be read in accordance with section 1006,

"retail prices index" means—
(a) the general index of retail prices (for all items) published by the Statistics Board, or
(b) if that index is not published for a relevant month, any substituted index or index figures published by the Board,

. . .
. . .

"settled property" (together with references to property comprised in a settlement) is to be read in accordance with section 466,
"settlor" is to be read in accordance with sections 467 to 473,

. . .

"stepchild", in relation to a civil partner, is to be read in accordance with section 246 of the Civil Partnership Act 2004 (c.33),

. . .

"tax", if neither income tax nor corporation tax is specified, means either of those taxes,
"tax year" has the meaning given by section 4(2),
"the tax year 2007–08" (and any corresponding expression in which two years are similarly mentioned) has the meaning given by section 4(4),
"total income" has the meaning given by section 23 (see Step 1 in that section and also section 31),
"trade" includes any venture in the nature of trade,
"tribunal" means the First-tier Tribunal or, where determined by or under Tribunal Procedure Rules, the Upper Tribunal,

. . .

"UK generally accepted accounting practice" has the meaning given by section 997(2),
"UK property business" has the meaning given by Chapter 2 of Part 3 of ITTOIA 2005,
"UK resident" means resident in the United Kingdom (and references to a UK resident or a UK resident person are to a person who is resident there),

. . .

"year of assessment" means a tax year, and
"the year 1988–1989" means the tax year 1988–1989 (and any corresponding expression in which two years are similarly mentioned is to be read in the same way).

Meaning of "company"

992.—(1) In the Income Tax Acts "company" means any body corporate or unincorporated association, but does not include a partnership, a local authority or a local authority association.

(2) Subsection (1) needs to be with read with section 617 of CTA 2010 (authorised unit trust treated as UK resident company).

. . .

References to married persons, or civil partners, living together

1011.—Individuals who are married to, or are civil partners of, each other are treated for the purposes of the Income Tax Acts as living together unless—

(a) they are separated under an order of a court of competent jurisdiction,
(b) they are separated by deed of separation, or
(c) they are in fact separated in circumstances in which the separation is likely to be permanent.

Welfare Reform Act 2012

(2012 c.5)

Arrangement of Selected Sections

Part 1

Universal Credit

1.888
33. Abolition of benefits
36. Migration to universal credit

Part 3

Other Benefit Changes

76. Calculation of working tax credit

Part 5

Social Security: General

96. Benefit cap

Schedule 6

Migration To Universal Credit

1. General
2. Claims before the appointed day
3. Claims after the appointed day
4. Awards
6. Tax credits

Introduction and General Note

1.889 This Act started to come into force so as to affect tax credits in February 2013 (when regulatory powers came into effect) and started replacing tax credits with the new universal credit as from April 6, 2013. As from that date universal credit was introduced for a small subset of new claimants in certain areas of the North West of England. Those new claimants who lived in the relevant postcode districts and fell into the "Pathfinder Group" (later the gateway conditions) qualified for universal credit in place of other benefits including any child tax credit or working tax credit to which they were previously entitled. The position has now been reached where, for virtually all practical purposes, it is impossible to make a new claim for any of the legacy (means-tested) benefits replaced by universal credit, the last remaining theoretical obstacle having been removed in July 2022. Someone of working age, not already in receipt of a legacy benefit, whose income is insufficient now has only universal credit as a choice for a means-tested benefit to claim. The pilot for "managed migration", the transfer of existing recipients of legacy benefits at the Department's direction, was postponed on the onset of the Covid-19 pandemic, but has now restarted in restricted areas under the Universal Credit (Transitional Provisions) (Amendment) Regulations 2022. The intention is to complete the whole process by the end of 2024. The relevant provisions are in Pt 1 of the Act. For further details, see Vol.II in this series.

Most of the rest of this lengthy Act is not relevant to the benefits in this volume. Only s.76 is relevant to tax credits of the material in Pts 2, 3, and 4. A number of provisions of Pt 5 are relevant as these deal with social security general administrative provisions.

PART 1

UNIVERSAL CREDIT

Universal credit and other benefits

Abolition of benefits

33.—(1) The following benefits are abolished—   1.890
[. . .]
  (f) child tax credit and working tax credit under the Tax Credits Act 2002.

GENERAL NOTE

Subsection (1)(f) was brought into force on February 1, 2019 by art.2 of the Welfare Reform Act 2012 (Commencement No.32 and Savings and Transitional Provisions) Order 2019 (SI 2019/167) (see below in this volume). However, the abolition of child tax credit and working tax credit, and the transfer from those benefits to universal credit, is subject to extensive transitional saving provisions: see the note to Schedule 6 to this Act.   1.891

Tax credits are being replaced by Universal Credit. A Parliamentary Written Answer given on May 1, 2019 by Alok Sharma MP, Minister of State for Employment, set out the UK Government's estimated timescale for the implementation of Universal Credit, including the transfer of claimants in receipt of those benefits replaced by Universal Credit. The majority of the monthly transfers arising due to a change of circumstances are likely to be tax credit recipients. Alok Sharma stated:

"The Department has forecasted flows onto Universal Credit to 2024.

The below table shows a breakdown of the average monthly volumes per calendar year from 2019 (rounded to the nearest 10,000 where appropriate).

	2019	2020	2021	2022	2023	2024
Rapid Reclaims	40,000	40,000	40,000	50,000	50,000	50,000
Pure new awards	100,000	100,000	100,000	90,000	90,000	90,000
Movement due to a change in circumstance	50,000	40,000	30,000	20,000	10,000	-
Being moved without a change in circumstance	Less than 500	Less than 1000	10,000	40,000	90,000	-
Total	190,000	180,000	190,000	200,000	230,000	140,000"

Migration to universal credit

1.892 **36.**—Schedule 6 contains provision about the replacement of benefits by universal credit.

GENERAL NOTE

1.893 Insofar as they were not already in force, s.36 and Sch.6 were brought fully into force by the Welfare Reform Act 2012 (Commencement No.33) Order 2019 (SI 2019/1135) with effect from July 18, 2019.

OTHER BENEFIT CHANGES

Working tax credit

Calculation of working tax credit

1.894 **76.**—(1) Step 5 in regulation 7(3) of the 2002 Regulations has effect in relation to awards of working tax credit for the whole or part of the relevant year as if from the beginning of the day on 6 April 2011 the percentage to be applied under step 5 in finding the amount of the reduction were 41% (instead of 39%).

(2) Anything done by the Commissioners before the coming into force of this section in relation to awards of working tax credit for the whole or part of the relevant year is to be treated as having been duly done, if it would have been duly done but for being done on the basis that from the beginning of the day on 6 April 2011 the percentage to be applied under step 5 was 41%.

(3) In this section—

"the 2002 Regulations" means the Tax Credits (Income Thresholds and Determination of Rates) Regulations 2002 (S.I. 2002/2008);

"the Commissioners" means the Commissioners for Her Majesty's

Revenue and Customs;
"the relevant year" means the year beginning with 6 April 2011.

GENERAL NOTE

This is a deeming provision designed to validate retrospectively the failure to provide proper legislative authority at the correct time for the reduction rate of tax credits being increased under the emergency budget of 2010 from 39 per cent to 41 per cent.

Benefit cap

96.—(1) Regulations may provide for a benefit cap to be applied to the welfare benefits to which a single person or couple is entitled.

(2) For the purposes of this section, applying a benefit cap to welfare benefits means securing that, where a single person's or couple's total entitlement to welfare benefits in respect of the reference period exceeds the relevant amount, their entitlement to welfare benefits in respect of any period of the same duration as the reference period is reduced by an amount up to or equalling the excess.

(3) In subsection (2) the "reference period" means a period of a prescribed duration.

(4) Regulations under this section may in particular—
(a) make provision as to the manner in which total entitlement to welfare benefits for any period, or the amount of any reduction, is to be determined;
(b) make provision as to the welfare benefit or benefits from which a reduction is to be made;
(c) provide for exceptions to the application of the benefit cap;
(d) make provision as to the intervals at which the benefit cap is to be applied;
(e) make provision as to the relationship between application of the benefit cap and any other reduction in respect of a welfare benefit;
(f) provide that where in consequence of a change in the relevant amount, entitlement to a welfare benefit increases or decreases, that increase or decrease has effect without any further decision of the Secretary of State;
(g) make supplementary and consequential provision.

[¹(5) Regulations under this section may make provision for determining the "relevant amount" for the reference period applicable in the case of a single person or couple by reference to the annual limit applicable in the case of that single person or couple.

(5A) For the purposes of this section the "annual limit" is—
(a) [³ £25,323 or £16,967], for persons resident in Greater London;
(a) [³ £22,020 or £14,753], for other persons.

(5B) Regulations under subsection (5) may—
(a) specify which annual limit applies in the case of—
 (i) different prescribed descriptions of single person;
 (ii) different prescribed descriptions of couple;
(b) define "resident" for the purposes of this section;
(c) provide for the rounding up or down of an amount produced by dividing the amount of the annual limit by the number of periods of a duration equal to the reference period in a year.]
 [¹...]

1.895

1.896

(9) Regulations under this section may not provide for any reduction to be made from a welfare benefit—
- (a) provision for which is within the legislative competence of the Scottish Parliament;
- (b) provision for which is within the legislative competence of the National Assembly for Wales;
- (c) provision for which is made by the Welsh Ministers, the First Minister for Wales or the Counsel General to the [¹ Welsh Government].

(10) In this section—
"couple" means two persons of a prescribed description;
"prescribed" means prescribed in regulations;
"regulations" means regulations made by the Secretary of State;
"single person" means a person who is not a member of a couple;
"welfare benefit" [² means—
- (a) bereavement allowance (see section 39B of the Social Security Contributions and Benefits Act 1992),
- (b) child benefit (see section 141 of the Social Security Contributions and Benefits Act 1992),
- (c) child tax credit (see section 1(1)(a) of the Tax Credits Act 2002),
- (d) employment and support allowance (see section 1 of the Welfare Reform Act 2007), including income-related employment and support allowance (as defined in section 1(7) of the Welfare Reform Act 2007),
- (e) housing benefit (see section 130 of the Social Security Contributions and Benefits Act 1992),
- (f) incapacity benefit (see section 30A of the Social Security Contributions and Benefits Act 1992),
- (g) income support (see section 124 of the Social Security Contributions and Benefits Act 1992),
- (h) jobseeker's allowance (see section 1 of the Jobseekers Act 1995), including income-based jobseeker's allowance (as defined in section 1(4) of the Jobseekers Act 1995),
- (i) maternity allowance under section 35 or 35B of the Social Security Contributions and Benefits Act 1992,
- (j) severe disablement allowance (see section 68 of the Social Security Contributions and Benefits Act 1992),
- (k) universal credit,
- (l) widow's pension (see section 38 of the Social Security Contributions and Benefits Act 1992),
- (m) widowed mother's allowance (see section 37 of the Social Security Contributions and Benefits Act 1992), or
- (n) widowed parent's allowance (see section 39A of the Social Security Contributions and Benefits Act 1992).]

[²...]

AMENDMENTS

1. Wales Act 2014 s.4(4)(a) (February 17, 2015).

2. Welfare Reform and Work Act 2016 s.8 (March 16, 2018 for purpose of making regulations, November 7, 2016 otherwise).

3. Benefit Cap (Annual Limit) (Amendment) Regulations 2023 (SI 2023/335) reg.1(4) (April 1, 2023).

GENERAL NOTE

1.897
This section provides for the inclusion of child tax credit within the 'benefit cap' mechanism. While child tax credit is taken into account in determining whether a person is subject to capping, the cap is not achieved through a reduction in child tax credit. Instead, the cap operates by reducing the amount of housing benefit (or universal credit) to which a person is entitled.

The benefit cap applies to persons whose relevant welfare benefits income exceeds a specified amount. As originally enacted, this section provided for the amount to be specified in regulations and determined by reference to the estimated average net earnings of a working household in Britain. Regulations provided for an amount of £26,000 (or £18,200 in the case of single claimants). Amendments made by the Welfare Reform and Work Act 2016 mean that 'annual limits' are now specified in s.96 itself. The annual limits specified in subs.(5A) are lower than those previously provided for in regulations. For example, in the case of a couple resident outside Greater London the limit is now £22,020.

Subsection (10) provides that working tax credit is not to be taken into account in determining whether, for benefit cap purposes, a person's annual welfare benefits income exceeds the 'annual limit'. Moreover, persons in receipt of working tax credit are for the time being entirely excluded from the benefit capping provisions. This is provided for in regulations (reg.75F of the Housing Benefit Regulations 2006).

The appellants in the Supreme Court case of *R (DA and others) (DS and others) v Secretary of State for Work & Pensions* [2019] UKSC 21 argued that it was impracticable for them to claim working tax credit (and avoid the benefit cap) because they could not satisfy the requirement for a claimant to engage in work for at least 16 hours each week. They said this was due to a combination of their parental responsibilities and a lack of adequate care and support. The appellants could not mount a challenge under the Human Rights Act 1998 to the 'annual limit', since it is provided for in primary legislation (s.6(2) of the 1998 Act provides that a public authority that acts incompatibly with a Convention right does not act unlawfully if, as a result of primary legislation, the authority could not have acted any differently). For this reason, the appellants, which included children of the adult appellants, argued that the UK Government's failure to provide for an exception applicable to their circumstances involved unjustified discrimination contrary to art.14 of the European Convention on Human Rights. The appellants in *DA* succeeded before the High Court but its decision was reversed by the Court of Appeal. The Supreme Court dismissed the appellants' challenge to the Court of Appeal's decision. Briefly, the Court held that, if there was a relevant difference of treatment, it was not 'manifestly without reasonable foundation' and hence not discriminatory for the purposes of art.14.

SCHEDULE 6

MIGRATION TO UNIVERSAL CREDIT

General

1.898
1.—(1) Regulations may make provision for the purposes of, or in connection with, replacing existing benefits with universal credit.
(2) In this Schedule "existing benefit" means—
  (a) a benefit abolished under section 33(1);
  (b) any other prescribed benefit.
(3) In this Schedule "appointed day" means the day appointed for the coming into force of section 1.

Claims before the appointed day

1.899
2.—(1) The provision referred to in paragraph 1(1) includes—

(a) provision for a claim for universal credit to be made before the appointed day for a period beginning on or after that day;
(b) provision for a claim for universal credit made before the appointed day to be treated to any extent as a claim for an existing benefit;
(c) provision for a claim for an existing benefit made before the appointed day to be treated to any extent as a claim for universal credit.

(2) The provision referred to in paragraph 1(1) includes provision, where a claim for universal credit is made (or is treated as made) before the appointed day, for an award on the claim to be made in respect of a period before the appointed day (including provision as to the conditions of entitlement for, and amount of, such an award).

Claims after the appointed day

1.900 3.—(1) The provision referred to in paragraph 1(1) includes—
(a) provision permanently or temporarily excluding the making of a claim for universal credit after the appointed day by—
   (i) a person to whom an existing benefit is awarded, or
   (ii) a person who would be entitled to an existing benefit on making a claim for it;
(b) provision temporarily excluding the making of a claim for universal credit after the appointed day by any other person;
(c) provision excluding entitlement to universal credit temporarily or for a particular period;
(d) provision for a claim for universal credit made after the appointed day to be treated to any extent as a claim for an existing benefit;
(e) provision for a claim for an existing benefit made after the appointed day to be treated to any extent as a claim for universal credit.

(2) The provision referred to in paragraph 1(1) includes provision, where a claim for universal credit is made (or is treated as made) after the appointed day, for an award on the claim to be made in respect of a period before the appointed day (including provision as to the conditions of entitlement for, and amount of, such an award).

Awards

1.901 4.—(1) The provision referred to in paragraph 1(1) includes—
(a) provision for terminating an award of an existing benefit;
(b) provision for making an award of universal credit, with or without application, to a person whose award of existing benefit is terminated.

(2) The provision referred to in sub-paragraph (1)(b) includes—
(a) provision imposing requirements as to the procedure to be followed, information to be supplied or assessments to be undergone in relation to an award by virtue of that sub-paragraph or an application for such an award;
(b) provision as to the consequences of failure to comply with any such requirement;
(c) provision as to the terms on which, and conditions subject to which, such an award is made, including—
   (i) provision temporarily or permanently disapplying, or otherwise modifying, conditions of entitlement to universal credit in relation to the award;
   (ii) provision temporarily or permanently disapplying, or otherwise modifying, any requirement under this Part for a person to be assessed in respect of capability for work or work-related activity;
(d) provision as to the amount of such an award;
(e) provision that fulfilment of any condition relevant to entitlement to an award of an existing benefit, or relevant to the amount of such an award, is to be treated as fulfilment of an equivalent condition in relation to universal credit.

(3) Provision under sub-paragraph (2)(d) may secure that where an award of universal credit is made by virtue of sub-paragraph (1)(b)—
(a) the amount of the award is not less than the amount to which the person would have been entitled under the terminated award, or is not less than that amount by more than a prescribed amount;
(b) if the person to whom it is made ceases to be entitled to universal credit for not more than a prescribed period, the gap in entitlement is disregarded in calculating the amount of any new award of universal credit.

Work-related requirements and sanctions

5.—(1) The provision referred to in paragraph 1(1) includes—
[...]
  (b) provision relating to the application of sanctions.
(2) The provision referred to in sub-paragraph (1)(a) includes—
  (a) provision that a claimant commitment for a relevant benefit is to be treated as a claimant commitment for universal credit;
  (b) provision that a work-related requirement for a relevant benefit is treated as a work-related requirement for universal credit;
  (c) provision for anything done which is relevant to compliance with a work-related requirement for a relevant benefit to be treated as done for the purposes of compliance with a work-related requirement for universal credit;
  (d) provision temporarily disapplying any provision of this Part in relation to work-related requirements for universal credit.
[...]

Tax credits

6.—In relation to the replacement of working tax credit and child tax credit with universal credit, the provision referred to in paragraph 1(1) includes—
  (a) provision modifying the application of the Tax Credits Act 2002 (or of any provision made under it);
  (b) provision for the purposes of recovery of overpayments of working tax credit or child tax credit (including in particular provision for treating overpayments of working tax credit or child tax credit as if they were overpayments of universal credit).

Supplementary

7.—*Regulations under paragraph 1(1) may secure the result that any gap in entitlement to an existing benefit (or what would, but for the provisions of this Part, be a gap in entitlement to an existing benefit) is to be disregarded for the purposes of provision under such regulations.*

GENERAL NOTE

The replacement of tax credits by universal credit is governed by a complex set of transitional legislative provisions. While s.33(1)(f) of this Act, which abolishes tax credits, was brought into force on February 1, 2019, the relevant commencement order contains a number of savings provisions which mean that, currently, many existing recipients of tax credits have not had to claim universal credit. For details of the savings, see the note to the Welfare Reform Act 2012 (Commencement No.32 and Savings and Transitional Provisions) Order 2019 (SI 2019/167) below in this volume. However, the No.32 Commencement Order does not tell the whole transitional story.

Separate, but inter-linked legislation, prevents certain individuals from making a claim for a tax credit. The most important are the Welfare Reform Act 2012 Commencement Orders No.9 (SI 2013/983), 23 (SI 2015/634) and 29 (SI 2017/664), and the Universal Credit (Transitional Provisions) Regulations 2014 (SI 2014/1230). For an explanation of the combined operation of this legislation, see the note to art.14 of the Welfare Reform Act 2012 (Commencement No.29 and Commencement No.17, 19, 22, 23 and 24 and Transitional and Transitory Provisions (Modification)) Order 2017 (SI 2017/664), below in this volume.

There are also free-standing transitional regulations, the Universal Credit (Transitional Provisions) Regulations 2014 (SI 2014/1230), see below in this volume. The transitional regulations have two functions: (a) to set out the legal consequences that follow once a person who was entitled to tax credit claims universal credit; and (b) to provide the legal basis for the UK Government's scheme for 'managed migration' from existing benefits to universal credit. The UK Government describes other transfers to universal credit as 'natural migration' (i.e. cases where individuals have to claim universal credit because they either fall outside the exceptions to the commencement order provisions that restrict new claims for tax credits (Orders No.9, 23 and 29) or fall outside the savings provisions linked to the abolition of tax credits (Order No.32).

Welfare Benefits Up-rating Act 2013

(2013 c.16)

ARRANGEMENT OF SELECTED SECTIONS

1.906   2.   Up-rating of tax credits for tax years 2014–15 and 2015–16
Schedule: Meaning of the "relevant sums" and the "relevant amounts"

Up-rating of tax credits for tax years 2014–15 and 2015–16

1.907   **2.**—(1) The Treasury must, in each of the tax years ending with 5 April 2014 and 5 April 2015, make an order by statutory instrument increasing each of the relevant amounts by 1%. For the meaning of the "relevant amounts" see paragraph 2 of the Schedule.

(2) An order under this section must be framed so that it has effect in relation to awards of tax credits for the tax year following that in which the order is made.

(3) The Treasury may, in providing for an increase under subsection (1), adjust the amount of the increase so as to round any amount up or down to the extent the Treasury think appropriate.

(4) Subsection (1) does not apply in relation to a tax year if, on the review in that tax year under section 41 of the Tax Credits Act 2002, the Treasury determine that the general level of prices in the United Kingdom has not increased, or has increased by less than 1%, over the period under review.

(5) Where subsection (1) applies in relation to a tax year, the Treasury must not exercise any other power to vary any of the relevant amounts if that variation would take effect in relation to awards of tax credits for the tax year following that in which the order is made.

SCHEDULE

Sections 1 and 2

MEANING OF THE "RELEVANT SUMS" AND THE "RELEVANT AMOUNTS"

...

The "relevant amounts" for the purposes of section 2

1.908   2.—The "relevant amounts" for the purposes of section 2 are the monetary amounts—
   (a) specified in Schedule 2 to the Working Tax Credit (Entitlement and Maximum Rate) Regulations 2002 (S.I. 2002/2005) for the basic element, the 30-hour element, the second adult element and the lone parent element;
   (b) specified in regulation 7(4)(c) and (f) of the Child Tax Credit Regulations 2002 (S.I. 2002/2007).

General Note

1.909   With effect from April 6, 2014, s.2 of the Welfare Benefits Up-rating Act 2013 requires the Treasury to increase the non-disability elements of working and child tax credits in the annual up-rating exercise by no more than 1 per cent in 2014/15 and 2015/16. Schedule 2 to the Act details the specific elements affected.

(2014 c.28)

Childcare Payments Act 2014

(2014 c.28)

ARRANGEMENT OF SECTIONS

Introductory

1. Entitlement to receive money towards costs of childcare   1.910
2. Qualifying childcare

Eligibility

3. Eligible persons
4. Declarations of eligibility
5. Entitlement periods

Conditions of eligibility

6. The person must be 16 or over
7. The person must be responsible for the child
8. The person must be in the UK
9. The person and his or her partner must be in qualifying paid work
10. The income of the person and his or her partner must not exceed limit
11. Neither the person nor his or her partner may be claiming universal credit
12. The person and his or her partner must not be in a relevant childcare scheme
13. Neither the person nor his or her partner may be receiving other childcare support

Qualifying children

14. Qualifying child

Childcare accounts

15. Childcare accounts
16. Account providers
17. Opening a childcare account
18. Cases where there is more than one eligible person
19. Payments into childcare accounts
20. Payments that may be made from childcare accounts
21. Calculating the top-up element of payments etc
22. Withdrawals
23. Refunds of payments made from childcare accounts
24. Imposing restrictions on childcare accounts
25. Closure of childcare accounts

Childcare Payments Act 2014

Information

26. Power to obtain information or documents
27. Information sharing between HMRC and others
28. Wrongful disclosure of information received by others from HMRC
29. Supply of information to HMRC by childminder agencies

Special rules affecting tax credit and universal credit claimants

30. Termination of tax credit awards
31. Power to provide for automatic termination of universal credit
32. Power to disqualify tax credit claimants from obtaining top-up payments
33. Power to disqualify universal credit claimants from obtaining top-up payments
34. Disqualification notices

Recovery of top-up payments

35. Recovery of top-up payments where tax credits award made on a review
36. Recovery of top-up payments where tax credits award made on appeal
37. Recovery of top-up payments where universal credit award made on revision
38. Recovery of top-up payments where universal credit award made on appeal
39. Recovery of top-up payments where person fails to give childcare account notice
40. Recovery of top-up payments in other cases
41. Assessment and enforcement of recoverable amounts

Penalties

42. Penalties for inaccurate declarations of eligibility
43. Penalties for failure to comply with information notice
44. Penalties for providing inaccurate information or documents
45. Penalties for making prohibited payments
46. Penalties for dishonestly obtaining top-up payments, etc
47. Assessment and enforcement of penalties
48. Double jeopardy

Other enforcement powers

49. Disqualification orders
50. Power to exclude childcare from being qualifying childcare
51. Power to charge interest
52. Deduction of recoverable amounts from tax credit awards
53. Recovery of debts from childcare accounts
54. Set-off
55. Order in which payments are taken to discharge debts

Reviews and appeals

56. Appealable decisions
57. Review of decisions
58. Extension of time limit for applications for review
59. Exercise of right of appeal
60. Powers of tribunal
61. Cases where there is more than one eligible person

Compensatory payments

62. Compensatory payments

Withdrawal of existing tax exemptions

63. Restrictions on claiming tax exemption for childcare vouchers
64. Restrictions on claiming tax exemption for employer-contracted childcare

General

65. Functions of Commissioners for Revenue and Customs
66. Tax treatment of top-up payments
67. Set-off against tax liabilities etc
68. Northern Ireland

Final provisions

69. Regulations: general
70. Regulations: Parliamentary control
71. Interpretation
72. Power to make consequential amendments
73. Financial provisions
74. Extent
75. Commencement and short title

An Act to make provision for and in connection with the making of payments to persons towards the costs of childcare; and to restrict the availability of an exemption from income tax in respect of the provision for an employee of childcare, or vouchers for obtaining childcare, under a scheme operated by or on behalf of the employer.

GENERAL NOTE

The initiative enshrined in this Act has been some time in gestation. As long ago as March 2013 the then Prime Minister and Deputy Prime Minister in the Coalition Government outlined proposals for a new scheme for Tax-Free Childcare (TFC), originally scheduled to be available from autumn 2015. These proposals were enacted in the Childcare Payments Act 2014.

The existing scheme for supporting parents with the costs of childcare (outside provision in means-tested benefit schemes such as help with childcare costs under working tax credit) is known as ESC (Employer Supported Childcare). The Government concluded ESC was neither effective nor fair as many working families were unable to access it. For example, fewer than 5 per cent of employers offered ESC and ESC was by definition not available to the self-employed. The Government plans to phase out the employers' disregard under the national insurance contributions scheme as the new scheme is introduced.

The new scheme is not actually part of the tax system at all; rather, it is a new state-funded contribution towards childcare costs for families earning above a minimum threshold. In summary, TFC is thus a new system of support for working families with childcare costs for a child under 12 (or under 17 if disabled). Those eligible will pay money into a childcare account run by NS&I on behalf of HMRC and will receive a top-up payment from the government. The payment will be £2 for every £8 paid in, subject to an annual limit of £2,000 a child (equal to tax relief at 20 per cent on costs of £10,000) or £4,000 for a disabled child (the higher rate for disabled children in s.19 of the Act was effected by the amendment from June 1, 2015 in reg.2 of the Childcare Payments Act 2014 (Amendment) Regulations 2015 (SI 2015/537)).

The basic eligibility conditions are as follows:

(i) both parents (or a lone parent) must be in paid work;

(ii) children must be under the age of 12 (disabled children must be under 17);

(iii) the parent must be 16 or over and responsible for and normally living with the child;

(iv) both parents (or a lone parent) must not receive support via tax credits, Universal Credit, ESC or any other Government funded support with childcare costs;

(v) both parents (or a lone parent) must not be an additional rate taxpayer; and

(vi) all parents will need to meet a minimum income level set at £52 a week on average over the course of an entitlement period (but with special rules for self-employed parents).

Official estimates are that 1.9 million families will be eligible, of which 1.25 million are likely to have qualifying childcare costs.

In July 2014 HM Treasury took the decision that NS&I would deliver the new TFC policy by providing and administering the childcare accounts and supporting services. This led to a challenge by a company involved in providing services to employers under the existing tax-relief scheme for childcare costs, on the basis that HM Treasury's decision was contrary to EU public procurement rules, as implemented in domestic law by the Public Contract Regulations 2006. The Supreme Court dismissed that claim in *Edenred (UK Group) Ltd v HM Treasury* [2015] UKSC 45, at the same time setting aside an interim order made in October 2014 which had prevented implementation of TFC. However, on the same day that the Supreme Court delivered its judgment, the Government announced that implementation of TFC would be delayed until "early 2017".

The March 2016 Budget policy paper therefore announced as follows (at para.3.24):

"From early 2017, the government is introducing Tax-Free Childcare to help working parents with the cost of childcare, ensuring more parents who want to can go out to work or increase the number of hours they work. Tax-Free Childcare will be rolled out in such a way that allows the youngest children to enter the scheme first, with all eligible parents brought in by the end of 2017. The existing scheme Employer-Supported Childcare will remain open to new entrants until April 2018 to support the transition between the schemes. This will sit alongside doubling the free childcare entitlement from 15 hours to 30 hours a week for working families with three and four year olds from September 2017."

The full arrangement of the Act is set out above. The text of those provisions of the 2014 Act which have been brought into force (for the most part on a trial basis—see *Commencement* below) is reproduced below. The main regulations made under the Childcare Payments Act 2014 are the Childcare Payments (Eligibility) Regulations 2015 (SI 2015/448) and the Childcare Payments Regulations 2015 (SI 2015/522), both as amended.

Appealable decisions are set out in s.56(3) of the 2014 Act. For example, parents who disagree with the HMRC's decision to reject an individual's application to join the scheme will be able to appeal to the First-tier Tribunal. Such appeals are allocated to the Social Entitlement Chamber: see First-tier Tribunal and Upper Tribunal (Chambers) Order 2010 (SI 2010/2655) art.6(ea), as amended by the First-tier Tribunal and Upper Tribunal (Chambers) (Amendment) Order 2015 (SI 2015/1563) art.2(3). See further the Childcare Payments (Appeals) Regulations 2016 (SI 2016/1078).

COMMENCEMENT

Sections 65 and 68, 69–72, 73(1), 74 and 75 all came into force on Royal Assent (December 17, 2014), as did all the regulation-making powers in the Act: see s.75(1). Sections 26–29, 43 and (for certain purposes) 47 all came into force on July 20, 2016 (see Childcare Payments Act 2014 (Commencement No.1) Regulations 2016 (2016/763) reg.2). Almost all of the remainder of the Act was brought into force on November 14, 2016 for the purposes of a trial (see Childcare Payments Act 2014 (Commencement No.2) Regulations 2016 (SI 2016/1083) reg.2). Regulation 1(2) of those Regulations provides as follows:

"'the trial' means a test of all the systems required to deliver the childcare payments scheme, which the Treasury considers necessary and which will run for six months from 14th November 2016 to 15th May 2017 and will involve a range of parents and others responsible for children".

The following four sections have at the time of writing not been brought into force to any extent at all: ss.12 (the person and his or her partner must not be in a relevant childcare scheme), 39 (recovery of top-up payments where person fails to give childcare account notice), 63 (restrictions on claiming tax exemption for childcare vouchers) and 64 (restrictions on claiming tax exemption for employer-contracted childcare).

The Childcare Payments Act 2014 (Commencement No.3 and Transitional Provisions) Regulations 2017 (SI 2017/578) brought into force on April 21, 2017 and those sections of the Childcare Payments Act 2014 that were set out in regs 2 and 3. Regulation 2 commenced specified sections of the Act (ss.1, 3, 4, 6 to 15, 17–25, 62 and 73(2)–(4)) in relation to children under four years old on September 1, 2017, those who have their fourth birthday on that day, disabled children, and any sibling of those children (as defined in reg.2) on April 21, 2017. Regulation 3 commences the remaining sections of the Act that are not already in force (ss.2, 5, 16, 30–42, 44–61, 63, 64, 66 and 67) in relation to all persons. Regulation 4 appointed May 16, 2017 as the commencement day for all remaining sections of the Act that were not already in force in relation to those persons recruited to participate in the trial, which ended on May 15, 2017. Regulations 5–8 contained transitional provisions.

The Childcare Payments Act 2014 (Commencement No.4) Regulations 2017 (SI 2017/750) brought into force on July 14, 2017 and those sections of the Childcare Payments Act 2014 set out in reg.2. That regulation commenced specified sections of the Act on July 14, 2017 in relation to a relevant child (meaning a child born on or after April 1, 2013 and before September 1, 2013) and any sibling (as also defined in reg.2(3)). The sections concerned were ss.1, 3, 4, 6–15, 17–25, 62 and 73(2)–(4).

1.912

The Childcare Payments Act 2014 (Commencement No.5) Regulations 2017 (SI 2017/1116) brought into force on November 24, 2017 and the same sections of the Childcare Payments Act 2014 in relation to a relevant child (born on or after November 24, 2011 and before April 1, 2013) and any sibling (as defined in reg.2(3)).

Finally, the Childcare Payments Act 2014 (Commencement No.6) Regulations 2018 (SI 2018/27) brought into force on January 15, 2018 and the same sections of the Childcare Payments Act 2014 in relation to a relevant child (meaning a child born on or after January 15, 2009 and before November 24, 2011) and any sibling (as defined in reg.2(4)). Regulation 2(2) brought into force on February 14, 2018 those sections of the Act that were not yet in force; from that date the Act has been in force in its entirety.

Introductory

Entitlement to receive money towards costs of childcare

1.913

1.—(1) This Act contains provision for HMRC to make payments ("top-up payments") to be used towards the costs of qualifying childcare.

For the meaning of "qualifying childcare", see section 2.

(2) A person is entitled to receive a top-up payment for an entitlement period in respect of a child if—

(a) the person is an eligible person for the entitlement period (see section 3),

(b) the person has made a valid declaration of eligibility for the entitlement period (see section 4),

(c) the child is a qualifying child (see section 14),

(d) the person holds a childcare account in respect of the child (see section 15), and

(e) a qualifying payment is made into the childcare account during the entitlement period (see section 19).

(3) HMRC must pay the top-up payment into the childcare account.

(4) The amount of the top-up payment is 25% of the amount of the qualifying payment.

(For provision limiting the amount of qualifying payments that may be made into a childcare account in an entitlement period, see section 19(4).)

(5) Regulations may amend subsection (4) so as to substitute a different percentage for the percentage for the time being specified there.

(6) Sections 17 to 25 contain provision about childcare accounts, including restrictions on the kinds of payments that may be made from childcare accounts.

(7) Sections 26 to 29 contain provision about obtaining and sharing information.

(8) Sections 30 to 34 contain special rules about persons who are claiming tax credits or universal credit.

(9) Sections 35 to 55 contain provision about penalties and other enforcement powers, including powers to recover top-up payments in certain circumstances.

(10) Sections 56 to 61 contain provision about reviews and appeals.

(11) Section 62 contains provision enabling HMRC in certain circumstances to compensate persons who have been deprived of the opportunity to receive top-up payments.

(12) Sections 63 and 64 contain provision for the withdrawal of tax exemptions in respect of certain kinds of employer-provided childcare schemes.

DEFINITIONS

"declaration of eligibility"—see s.71(1).
"entitlement period"—see s.71(1).
"HMRC"—see s.71(1).
"qualifying child"—see ss.14 and 71(1).
"qualifying childcare"—see s.71(1).
"qualifying payment"—see ss.19 and 71(1).
"tax credit"—see s.71(1).
"top-up payments"—see subs.(1) and s.71(1).
"universal credit"—s.71(1).
"valid declaration of eligibility"—see s.71(2).

COMMENCEMENT

All regulation making powers under the Act were brought into force on Royal Assent (December 17, 2014); see s.75(1)(c). The rest of this section was brought into force for the purposes of the trial on November 14, 2016 (see Childcare Payments Act 2014 (Commencement No.2) Regulations 2016 (SI 2016/1083) reg.2(a)).

Qualifying childcare

2.—(1) In this Act "childcare" means any form of care or supervised activity for a child that is not provided in the course of the child's compulsory education.

(2) Childcare that is provided for a person is "qualifying childcare" for the purposes of this Act if—
  (a) it is registered or approved childcare, and
  (b) the main reason, or one of the main reasons, for incurring the costs of the childcare is—
    (i) to enable the person to work, or
    (ii) where the person has a partner, to enable both the person and the person's partner to work.

(3) Regulations may—
  (a) make provision about what is, or is not, to be regarded as registered or approved childcare for the purposes of this section;
  (b) define what is meant by "work" for the purposes of this section;
  (c) specify cases where the condition in subsection (2)(b) is to be treated as met;
  (d) specify cases where that condition does not need to be met.

(4) Regulations made under subsection (3)(a) may, in particular, provide that childcare provided outside the United Kingdom is registered or approved childcare if it is provided by a person approved by an organisation that is accredited by a person or body under an enactment.

(5) Subsection (2) is subject to any direction made under section 50 (which enables HMRC in certain circumstances to direct that childcare provided by a person is not qualifying childcare).

DEFINITIONS

"childcare"—see subs.(1) and s.71(1).
"enactment"—see s.71(1).

"HMRC"—see s.71(1).
"partner"—see s.71(1).

COMMENCEMENT

1.915 All regulation making powers under the Act were brought into force on Royal Assent (December 17, 2014); see s.75(1)(c). The rest of this section was brought into force for the purposes of the trial on November 14, 2016 (see Childcare Payments Act 2014 (Commencement No.2) Regulations 2016 (SI 2016/1083) reg.2(a)).

Eligibility

Eligible persons

1.916 **3.**—(1) A person is an eligible person for an entitlement period if—
(a) the person meets the conditions of eligibility in sections [¹ 6 to 11 and 13], and
(b) in a case where the person has a partner, the person's partner meets the conditions of eligibility in sections [¹ 9 to 11 and 13].

(2) In sections [¹ 6 to 11 and 13] "the date of the declaration" means the day on which the person makes a declaration of eligibility for the entitlement period (see section 4).

(3) Sections [¹ 6 to 11 and 13] need to be read with—
(a) regulations made under them, and
(b) regulations made under subsection (4).

(4) Regulations may provide for exceptions to the requirement for any of the conditions of eligibility in sections [¹ 6 to 11 and 13] to be met by a person.

(5) Regulations may make provision about when a person is, or is not, to be regarded as another person's partner for the purposes of this Act.

DEFINITIONS

"the date of the declaration"—see subs.(2).
"declaration of eligibility"—see s.71(1).
"entitlement period"—see s.71(1).
"partner"—see s.71(1).

AMENDMENT

1. Adapted for purposes of trial by Childcare Payments Act 2014 (Commencement No.2) Regulations 2016 (SI 2016/1083) reg.3 (November 14, 2016).

COMMENCEMENT

1.917 All regulation making powers under the Act were brought into force on Royal Assent (December 17, 2014); see s.75(1)(c). The rest of this section was brought into force for the purposes of the trial on November 14, 2016 (see Childcare Payments Act 2014 (Commencement No.2) Regulations 2016 (SI 2016/1083) reg.3).

Declarations of eligibility

4.—(1) For the purposes of this Act a "declaration of eligibility" is a statement made by a person for an entitlement period which states that the person is an eligible person for the entitlement period.

(2) A declaration of eligibility made by a person for an entitlement period is "valid" for the purposes of this Act if—
 (a) HMRC are satisfied that the person is an eligible person for the entitlement period,
 (b) on the day on which the declaration is made, there is no other person who—
   (i) holds an active childcare account in respect of the relevant child (see subsection (4)), or
   (ii) is seeking to hold an active childcare account in respect of that child (see subsection (5)), and
 (c) the declaration is made in accordance with regulations under this section.

(3) But subsection (2)(b) does not apply for the purpose of determining whether a declaration of eligibility made for the purposes of opening a childcare account is valid (see instead section 17(2)(c)).

(4) In subsection (2)(b) "the relevant child" means the child in respect of whom the person making the declaration holds a childcare account.

For what is meant by an "active" childcare account, see section 17(3).

(5) For the purposes of this section a person is "seeking to hold an active childcare account" if—
 (a) the person has applied to open a childcare account and the application has not yet been determined,
 (b) the person has made a valid declaration of eligibility for an entitlement period which has not yet begun, or
 (c) the person has made a declaration of eligibility for an entitlement period which, if valid, would result in the person holding an active childcare account for that period.

(6) Regulations may make further provision about declarations of eligibility, including, in particular—
 (a) provision specifying, or enabling HMRC to specify, information which a person making a declaration of eligibility is required to provide to HMRC;
 (b) provision specifying, or enabling HMRC to specify, the form and manner in which declarations of eligibility may be made;
 (c) provision specifying the times when declarations of eligibility may be made;
 (d) provision about the consequences of making a declaration of eligibility—
   (i) after the beginning of the entitlement period for which it is made, or
   (ii) at such other time as may be specified;
 (e) provision for any consequences specified by virtue of paragraph (d) not to apply in specified circumstances or if specified conditions are met;
 (f) provision specifying circumstances in which a person, or a person of a specified description, may make a declaration of eligibility on another person's behalf, including provision enabling HMRC to appoint a person for that purpose;

(g) provision treating things done, or omitted to be done, by a person who makes a declaration of eligibility on another person's behalf as having been done, or omitted, by that other person.

(7) In subsection (6) "specified" means specified in the regulations.

DEFINITIONS

"active child care account"—see s.71(2).
"declaration of eligibility"—see subs.(1).
"entitlement period"—see s.71(1).
"HMRC"—see s.71(1).
"the relevant child"—see subs.(4).
"seeking to hold an active childcare account"—see subs.(5).
"specified"—see subs.(7).
"valid"—see subs.(2).

COMMENCEMENT

1.919 All regulation making powers under the Act were brought into force on Royal Assent (December 17, 2014); see s.75(1)(c). The rest of this section was brought into force for the purposes of the trial on November 14, 2016 (see Childcare Payments Act 2014 (Commencement No.2) Regulations 2016 (SI 2016/1083) reg.2(b)).

Entitlement periods

1.920 **5.**—(1) The length of an entitlement period is 3 months.
This is subject to the following provision.

(2) Regulations may—
  (a) amend subsection (1) so as to alter the length of an entitlement period, and
  (b) in consequence of any provision made under paragraph (a), amend any reference in this Act to a period which begins on the day on which a declaration of eligibility is made and is the same length as an entitlement period.

(3) Regulations may make further provision about entitlement periods, including, in particular—
  (a) provision for determining when entitlement periods are to begin or end, and
  (b) provision enabling HMRC, in circumstances specified in the regulations, to vary the length of an entitlement period in particular cases.

(4) Provision made by virtue of subsection (3)(b) may not enable HMRC to vary the length of an entitlement period by more than [¹ 2 months].

AMENDMENT

1. Small Charitable Donations and Childcare Payments Act 2017 s.5(2) (March 16, 2017).

DEFINITIONS

"declaration of eligibility"—see s.71(1).
"entitlement period"—see s.71(1).
"HMRC"—see s.71(1).

(2014 c.28 s.5)

COMMENCEMENT

All regulation making powers under the Act were brought into force on Royal Assent (December 17, 2014); see s.75(1)(c). The rest of this section was brought into force for the purposes of the trial on November 14, 2016 (see Childcare Payments Act 2014 (Commencement No.2) Regulations 2016 (SI 2016/1083) reg.2(b)).

Conditions of eligibility

The person must be 16 or over

6.—A person meets the condition of eligibility in this section if the person is at least 16 years old on the date of the declaration.

COMMENCEMENT

This section was brought into force for the purposes of the trial on November 14, 2016 (see Childcare Payments Act 2014 (Commencement No.2) Regulations 2016 (SI 2016/1083) reg.2(b)).

The person must be responsible for the child

7.—(1) A person meets the condition of eligibility in this section if, at the date of the declaration, the person is responsible for the relevant child.

(2) In subsection (1) "the relevant child" means the child in respect of whom the person holds, or wishes to open, a childcare account.

(3) Regulations may make provision as to the circumstances in which a person is, or is not, to be regarded as responsible for a child for the purposes of this Act.

DEFINITION

"the relevant child"—see subs.(2).

COMMENCEMENT

All regulation making powers under the Act were brought into force on Royal Assent (December 17, 2014); see s.75(1)(c). The rest of this section was brought into force for the purposes of the trial on November 14, 2016 (see Childcare Payments Act 2014 (Commencement No.2) Regulations 2016 (SI 2016/1083) reg.2(b)).

The person must be in the UK

8.—(1) A person meets the condition of eligibility in this section if the person is in the United Kingdom on the date of the declaration.

(2) Regulations may—
 (a) specify circumstances in which a person is to be treated as being, or not being, in the United Kingdom;
 (b) specify circumstances in which temporary absence from the United Kingdom is disregarded;
 (c) modify the application of this Act in relation to persons of a specified description who are treated as being in the United Kingdom for the purposes of this Act.

(3) In subsection (2) "specified" means specified in the regulations.

DEFINITION

"specified"—see subs.(3).

COMMENCEMENT

1.927   All regulation making powers under the Act were brought into force on Royal Assent (December 17, 2014); see s.75(1)(c). The rest of this section was brought into force for the purposes of the trial on November 14, 2016 (see Childcare Payments Act 2014 (Commencement No.2) Regulations 2016 (SI 2016/1083) reg.2(b)).

The person and his or her partner must be in qualifying paid work

1.928   **9.**—(1) A person meets the condition of eligibility in this section if the person is in qualifying paid work on the date of the declaration.

(2) Regulations may—
(a) make provision as to what is, or is not, qualifying paid work, and
(b) specify circumstances in which a person is, or is not, to be regarded as in such work.

(3) Regulations under subsection (2) may, in particular—
(a) make provision for calculating a person's expected income from any work for a period specified in the regulations,
(b) provide that a person is in qualifying paid work only if the person's expected income from the work for the period, taken together with the person's expected income from any other work for the period, is greater than or equal to an amount specified in, or determined in accordance with, the regulations, and
(c) specify cases in which the condition mentioned in paragraph (b) does not need to be met.

DEFINITION

"partner"—see s.71(1).

COMMENCEMENT

1.929   All regulation making powers under the Act were brought into force on Royal Assent (December 17, 2014); see s.75(1)(c). The rest of this section was brought into force for the purposes of the trial on November 14, 2016 (see Childcare Payments Act 2014 (Commencement No.2) Regulations 2016 (SI 2016/1083) reg.2(b)).

The income of the person and his or her partner must not exceed limit

1.930   **10.**—(1) A person meets the condition of eligibility in this section if, at the date of the declaration, the person's expected income for the relevant tax year is not greater than an amount specified in, or determined in accordance with, regulations for the purposes of this section.

(2) Regulations may make provision for calculating a person's expected income for a tax year.

(3) Regulations may provide that a person is treated as meeting the condition of eligibility in this section (whether or not any provision has been made under subsection (1)) if the person does not expect to pay income tax at the additional rate or the dividend additional rate for the relevant tax year.

(4) Regulations may provide that a person is treated as not meeting the condition of eligibility in this section in any of the following cases—
 (a) if the person has made, or expects to make, a claim under section 809B of the Income Tax Act 2007 (claim for remittance basis to apply) for the relevant tax year;
 (b) if the person expects section 809E of that Act (application of remittance basis in certain cases without claim) to apply to the person for the relevant tax year;
 (c) if the person meets any other conditions specified in the regulations.

(5) In this section "the relevant tax year", in relation to a declaration of eligibility, means the tax year in which the date of the declaration falls.

DEFINITIONS

"declaration of eligibility"—see s.71(1).
"partner"—see s.71(1).
"the relevant tax year"—see subs.(3).

COMMENCEMENT

All regulation making powers under the Act were brought into force on Royal Assent (December 17, 2014); see s.75(1)(c). The rest of this section was brought into force for the purposes of the trial on November 14, 2016 (see Childcare Payments Act 2014 (Commencement No.2) Regulations 2016 (SI 2016/1083) reg.2(b)).

Neither the person nor his or her partner may be claiming universal credit

11.—(1) A person meets the condition of eligibility in this section if, at the date of the declaration—
 (a) universal credit is not payable to the person in respect of any relevant assessment period (see subsection (2)), and
 (b) there is no subsisting claim that would result in universal credit becoming payable to the person in respect of a relevant assessment period.

(2) In subsection (1) "relevant assessment period", in relation to a declaration of eligibility, means any assessment period (within the meaning of the relevant legislation) that includes—
 (a) the date of the declaration, or
 (b) the whole or any part of the entitlement period for which the declaration is made.

(3) For the purposes of subsection (1) universal credit is payable to a person in respect of a relevant assessment period if it would be so payable but for the reduction of the award of universal credit to nil under the relevant legislation.

(4) In the case of a declaration of eligibility made for the purposes of opening a childcare account, the reference in subsection (2) to the entitlement period for which the declaration is made is to be read as a reference to the period of 3 months beginning with the date of the declaration.

DEFINITIONS

"declaration of eligibility"—see s.71(1).
"entitlement period"—see s.71(1).
"partner"—see s.71(1).
"relevant assessment period"—see subs.(2).
"universal credit"—s.71(1).

COMMENCEMENT

1.933   This section was brought into force for the purposes of the trial on November 14, 2016 (see Childcare Payments Act 2014 (Commencement No.2) Regulations 2016 (SI 2016/1083) reg.2(b)).

The person and his or her partner must not be in a relevant childcare scheme

1.934   **12.**—(1) A person ("P") meets the condition of eligibility in this section if, at the date of the declaration—
(a) P is not an eligible employee in relation to a relevant childcare scheme (see subsections (2) and (3)),
(b) in a case where the declaration is made for the purposes of opening a childcare account, P intends to give P's employer a childcare account notice (see subsection (4)) before the end of the period of 3 months beginning with the date of the declaration, or
(c) in a case where—
  (i) the declaration is not made for the purposes of opening a childcare account, and
  (ii) P is a new partner of the person making the declaration (see subsection (5)),
P intends to give P's employer a childcare account notice before the end of the entitlement period for which the declaration is made.
(2) "Relevant childcare scheme" means—
(a) a scheme under which qualifying childcare vouchers (within the meaning of section 270A of ITEPA 2003) are provided for employees, or
(b) a scheme under which care for a child is provided for employees in circumstances in which conditions A to D in section 318A of ITEPA 2003 are met.
(3) "Eligible employee"—
(a) in relation to a scheme within subsection (2)(a), has the meaning given by section 270AA of ITEPA 2003, and
(b) in relation to a scheme within subsection (2)(b), has the meaning given by section 318AZA of that Act.
(4) "Childcare account notice", in relation to a person who is an eligible employee in relation to a relevant childcare scheme, means a written notice informing the employer that the employee wishes to leave the scheme in order to be able to open a childcare account or enable the employee's partner to do so.
(5) For the purposes of this section P is a person's new partner at the date of the declaration made by the person if P has not been the person's partner at any time when the person has previously made a valid declaration of eligibility.

(6) For provision enabling HMRC to recover top-up payments where P fails to give P's employer a childcare account notice as mentioned in subsection (1)(b) or (c), see section 39.

DEFINITIONS

"childcare account notice"—see subs.(4).
"declaration of eligibility"—see s.71(1).
"eligible employee"—see subs.(3).
"entitlement period"—see s.71(1).
"HMRC"—see s.71(1).
"P"—see subs.(1).
"partner"—see s.71(1).
"relevant childcare scheme"—see subs.(2).
"top-up payment"—see s.71(1).
"valid declaration of eligibility"—see s.71(2).

Neither the person nor his or her partner may be receiving other childcare support

13.—(1) A person meets the condition of eligibility in this section if, at the date of the declaration—
  (a) no other relevant childcare support is payable to the person in respect of any relevant period, and
  (b) the person has not made, and does not intend to make, a claim that would result in any other relevant childcare support becoming payable to the person in respect of any relevant period.
(2) "Other relevant childcare support" means any payments towards the costs of childcare which are made out of funds provided by a national authority, other than—
  (a) payments under this Act, or
  (b) payments of a description specified in regulations.
(3) In subsection (2) "national authority" means any of the following—
  (a) a Minister of the Crown (within the meaning of the Ministers of the Crown Act 1975);
  (b) the Scottish Ministers;
  (c) the Welsh Ministers;
  (d) a Northern Ireland department.
(4) "Relevant period", in relation to a declaration of eligibility, means a period which—
  (a) includes the date of the declaration,
  (b) includes the whole or any part of the entitlement period for which the declaration is made, or
  (c) falls within that entitlement period.
(5) In the case of a declaration of eligibility made for the purposes of opening a childcare account, any reference in subsection (4) to the entitlement period for which the declaration is made is to be read as a reference to the period of 3 months beginning with the date of the declaration.

1.935

DEFINITIONS

"declaration of eligibility"—see s.71(1).
"entitlement period"—see s.71(1).
"national authority"—see subs.(3).
"other relevant childcare support"—see subs.(2).

"partner"—see s.71(1).
"relevant period"—see subs.(4).

COMMENCEMENT

1.936 This section was brought into force for the purposes of the trial on November 14, 2016 (see Childcare Payments Act 2014 (Commencement No.2) Regulations 2016 (SI 2016/1083) reg.2(c)).

Qualifying children

Qualifying child

1.937 **14.**—(1) For the purposes of this Act "qualifying child" means a child of a description specified in regulations.
(2) Regulations under this section may, in particular, specify different descriptions for different periods.

DEFINITION

"qualifying child"—see subs.(1).

COMMENCEMENT

1.938 All regulation making powers under the Act were brought into force on Royal Assent (December 17, 2014); see s.75(1)(c). The rest of this section was brought into force for the purposes of the trial on November 14, 2016 (see Childcare Payments Act 2014 (Commencement No.2) Regulations 2016 (SI 2016/1083) reg.2(c)).

Childcare accounts

Childcare accounts

1.939 **15.**—(1) In this Act "childcare account" means an account which—
(a) is held by a person for the purpose of receiving top-up payments in respect of a qualifying child,
(b) is provided by a person or body within section 16(1),
(c) satisfies the requirements imposed by or under this Act, and
(d) has been opened in accordance with this Act.
(2) Each childcare account must be held in respect of one child only.
(3) Regulations may—
(a) impose other requirements which must be satisfied in relation to childcare accounts, and
(b) make provision about the way in which payments may be made into, or from, childcare accounts.
(4) Regulations may provide that a person of a specified description may, or may in specified circumstances, manage a childcare account on behalf of the account-holder.
(5) The provision that may be made by regulations under subsection (4) includes—

(a) provision enabling HMRC to appoint a person for the purpose of managing a childcare account on the account-holder's behalf, and
(b) provision specifying functions in relation to the management of a childcare account which persons, or persons of a specified description, may not perform on an account-holder's behalf.

(6) In subsections (4) and (5) "specified" means specified in the regulations.

(7) Where a contract is entered into by or on behalf of a person who is 16 or 17 years old in connection with a childcare account held by the person, the contract has effect as if the person had been 18 or over when it was entered into.

(8) If the Commissioners so consent, fees may be charged in connection with a childcare account by the account provider.

(9) But the account provider may not charge any fees merely for—
(a) providing a childcare account,
(b) enabling a qualifying payment to be made into a childcare account (see section 19), or
(c) enabling a payment to be made from a childcare account in respect of qualifying childcare for the child in respect of whom the account is held.

(10) In this Act—
(a) the "account-holder", in relation to a childcare account, means the person who holds the childcare account, and
(b) the "account provider", in relation to a childcare account, means the person or body who provides the childcare account.

DEFINITIONS

"account-holder"—see subs.(10)(a)
"account provider"—see subs.(10)(b).
"childcare account"—see subs.(1).
"the Commissioners"—see s.71(1).
"HMRC"—see s.71(1).
"qualifying child"—see s.71(1).
"qualifying childcare"—see s.71(1).
"qualifying payment"—see s.71(1).
"specified"—see subs.(6).
"top-up payment"—s.71(1).

COMMENCEMENT

All regulation making powers under the Act were brought into force on Royal Assent (December 17, 2014); see s.75(1)(c). The rest of this section was brought into force for the purposes of the trial on November 14, 2016 (see Childcare Payments Act 2014 (Commencement No.2) Regulations 2016 (SI 2016/1083) reg.2(c)).

1.940

Account providers

16.—(1) Childcare accounts may be provided by any of the following—
(a) the Commissioners for Her Majesty's Revenue and Customs,
(b) a person or body with whom the Commissioners have entered into arrangements for the provision of childcare accounts, and
(c) if the Treasury so determine, the Director of Savings ("the Director").

1.941

(2) If the Director provides childcare accounts, the Director must in doing so act in accordance with any arrangements made between the Director and the Commissioners with respect to the provision of childcare accounts.

(3) Arrangements made between the Commissioners and a person or body within paragraph (b) or (c) of subsection (1) may include provision for the making of payments by the Commissioners to the person or body in respect of the provision of childcare accounts (and accordingly nothing in section 15(8) or (9) affects the inclusion of such provision in the arrangements).

(4) If the Commissioners provide childcare accounts—
  (a) any reference to the account provider paying an amount to HMRC from a childcare account, or to HMRC directing the account provider to do so, is to be read as a reference to HMRC deducting the amount from the account,
  (b) any requirement for the account provider to notify HMRC of any matter, or for HMRC to notify the account provider of any matter, is to be disregarded, and
  (c) any requirement for the account provider to give anything to HMRC, or for HMRC to give anything to the account provider, is to be disregarded.

DEFINITIONS

"account provider"—see s.71(1).
"the Commissioners"—see s.71(1).
"the Director"—see subs.(1)(c).
"HMRC"—see s.71(1).

COMMENCEMENT

1.942 This section was brought into force for the purposes of the trial on November 14, 2016 (see Childcare Payments Act 2014 (Commencement No.2) Regulations 2016 (SI 2016/1083) reg.2(c)).

Opening a childcare account

1.943 **17.**—(1) A person who wishes to receive top-up payments (the "applicant") must make an application to HMRC to open a childcare account.

(2) HMRC may grant the application only if—
  (a) the applicant has made a valid declaration of eligibility,
  (b) the child in respect of whom the account is to be held ("the relevant child") is a qualifying child at the date of the application, and
  (c) on the day on which the application is granted, there is no other person who holds an active childcare account in respect of the relevant child (see subsection (3)).

(3) For the purposes of this Act a childcare account is "active" at any time if—
  (a) qualifying payments may be made into the account at that time (see section 19), or
  (b) such payments could, in the absence of section 19(4) (limit on amount of qualifying payments that may be made in entitlement period), be made into the account at that time.

(4) Regulations may make further provision about opening a childcare account, including, in particular—
(a) provision about the making of applications to open a childcare account, including provision enabling HMRC to specify the form and manner in which such applications may be made;
(b) provision specifying, or enabling HMRC to specify, information which applicants must provide to specified persons or to persons of a specified description;
(c) provision specifying circumstances in which a person, or a person of a specified description, may make an application to open a childcare account on behalf of an applicant, including provision enabling HMRC to appoint a person for that purpose;
(d) provision requiring HMRC to provide specified information to specified persons or to persons of a specified description.
(5) In subsection (4) "specified" means specified in the regulations.

DEFINITIONS

"active"—see subs.(3).
"active child care account"—see s.71(2).
"applicant"—see subs.(1).
"declaration of eligibility"—see s.71(1).
"entitlement period"—see s.71(1).
"HMRC"—see s.71(1).
"qualifying child"—see s.71(1).
"qualifying payment"—see s.71(1).
"the relevant child"—see subs.(2)(b).
"specified"—see subs.(5).
"top-up payment"—s.71(1).
"valid declaration of eligibility"—see s.71(2).

COMMENCEMENT

All regulation making powers under the Act were brought into force on Royal Assent (December 17, 2014); see s.75(1)(c). The rest of this section was brought into force for the purposes of the trial on November 14, 2016 (see Childcare Payments Act 2014 (Commencement No.2) Regulations 2016 (SI 2016/1083) reg.2(c)).

1.944

Cases where there is more than one eligible person

18.—(1) If two or more persons have applied to open a childcare account in respect of the same child, HMRC may determine which of them (if any) may open a childcare account in respect of the child.

1.945

(2) If—
(a) a person—
(i) has applied to open a childcare account in respect of a child, or
(ii) wishes to make a declaration of eligibility in relation to a childcare account held in respect of a child, and
(b) another person holds a childcare account in respect of the child,
HMRC may determine which of them (if any) may hold an active childcare account in respect of the child (see section 17(3)).

(3) For provision enabling HMRC to make an account restriction order to give effect to a determination under subsection (2), see section 24.

DEFINITIONS

"active childcare account"—see s.71(2).
"declaration of eligibility"—see s.71(1).
"HMRC"—see s.71(1).

COMMENCEMENT

1.946 This section was brought into force for the purposes of the trial on November 14, 2016 (see Childcare Payments Act 2014 (Commencement No.2) Regulations 2016 (SI 2016/1083) reg.2(c)).

Payments into childcare accounts

1.947 **19.**—(1) In this Act "qualifying payment" means any payment made into a childcare account, other than—
  (a) a top-up payment, or
  (b) a repayment of the whole or part of any payment made from the childcare account.
But for the purposes of paragraph (b) a withdrawal made by the account-holder is not to be regarded as a payment made from a childcare account.

(2) Any person (including the account-holder) may make a qualifying payment into a childcare account during an entitlement period, provided that—
  (a) the account-holder has made a valid declaration of eligibility for the entitlement period, and
  (b) the child in respect of whom the account is held is a qualifying child at the time of the payment.
This is subject to any provision made by or under this Act.

(3) More than one qualifying payment may be made into a childcare account during an entitlement period.

(4) But the sum of any qualifying payments made into a childcare account in an entitlement period must not exceed the relevant maximum for the entitlement period.

(5) The relevant maximum for an entitlement period [1 is—
  (a) in the case of a disabled child, £4,000, and
  (b) in the case of any other child, £2,000.]
This is subject to subsection (6).

(6) Regulations may provide, or enable HMRC to provide, that in circumstances specified in the regulations the relevant maximum for an entitlement period is an amount—
  (a) specified in, or determined in accordance with, the regulations, or
  (b) determined by HMRC in accordance with powers conferred by the regulations.

(7) Regulations may amend subsection (5) so as to substitute a different amount or amounts for any amount for the time being specified there.

(8) For the purposes of subsection (4), any amount paid into a childcare account at any time during an entitlement period is to be disregarded if at a later time during the entitlement period an equivalent amount is withdrawn from the account by the account-holder.

(9) The account provider must notify HMRC of any qualifying payments made into a childcare account.

[² (10) In subsection (5) "disabled child" is to be read in accordance with regulations made under section 14(1).]

AMENDMENT

1. Childcare Payments Act 2014 (Amendment) Regulations 2015 (SI 2015/537) reg.2 (June 1, 2015).

DEFINITIONS

"account provider"—see s.71(1).
"account provider"—see s.71(1).
"account-holder"—see s.71(1).
"declaration of eligibility"—see s.71(1).
"disabled child"—see subs.(10).
"entitlement period"—see s.71(1).
"HMRC"—see s.71(1).
"qualifying child"—see s.71(1).
"qualifying payment"—see subs.(1) and s.71(1).
"top-up payment"—s.71(1).
"valid declaration of eligibility"—see s.71(2).

COMMENCEMENT

All regulation making powers under the Act were brought into force on Royal Assent (December 17, 2014); see s.75(1)(c). The rest of this section was brought into force for the purposes of the trial on November 14, 2016 (see Childcare Payments Act 2014 (Commencement No.2) Regulations 2016 (SI 2016/1083) reg.2(c)).

Payments that may be made from childcare accounts

20.—(1) The only payments which the account-holder may authorise to be made from a childcare account are—
  (a) payments in respect of qualifying childcare for the relevant child, and
  (b) withdrawals made by the account-holder.
(2) In this section "the relevant child", in relation to a childcare account, means the child in respect of whom the account is held.
(3) A payment within subsection (1) is referred to in this Act as a permitted payment.
(4) A payment made from a childcare account which—
  (a) is not a permitted payment, and
  (b) is not made by the account provider to HMRC under this Act,
is referred to in this Act as a prohibited payment.
(5) Permitted payments may be made from a childcare account in an entitlement period whether or not the account-holder has made a valid declaration of eligibility for the entitlement period.
(6) Where—
  (a) a payment is made from a childcare account, and
  (b) only part of the payment is in respect of qualifying childcare for the relevant child,
so much of the payment as is properly attributable to the costs of qualifying childcare for the relevant child is to be treated as a permitted payment, and the remainder is to be treated as a prohibited payment.
(7) Regulations may make provision for determining, for the purposes of subsection (6), how much of a payment is properly attributable to the costs of qualifying childcare for the relevant child.

(8) For the meaning of "qualifying childcare", see section 2.

DEFINITIONS

"account-holder"—see s.71(1).
"account provider"—see s.71(1).
"declaration of eligibility"—see s.71(1).
"entitlement period"—see s.71(1).
"HMRC"—see s.71(1).
"permitted payment"—see subs.(3).
"qualifying childcare"—see s.71(1).
"the relevant child"—see subs.(2).
"valid declaration of eligibility"—see s.71(2).

COMMENCEMENT

1.950 All regulation making powers under the Act were brought into force on Royal Assent (December 17, 2014); see s.75(1)(c). The rest of this section was brought into force for the purposes of the trial on November 14, 2016 (see Childcare Payments Act 2014 (Commencement No.2) Regulations 2016 (SI 2016/1083) reg.2(c)).

Calculating the top-up element of payments etc

1.951 **21.**—(1) For the purposes of this Act the "top-up element" of any amount is an amount equal to the relevant percentage of that amount.

(2) The "relevant percentage" is the percentage given by—

$$\frac{R}{100 + R} \times 100$$

where R is the percentage for the time being specified in section 1(4).

DEFINITIONS

"relevant percentage"—subs.(2).
"top-up element"—subs.(1).

COMMENCEMENT

1.952 This section was brought into force for the purposes of the trial on November 14, 2016 (see Childcare Payments Act 2014 (Commencement No.2) Regulations 2016 (SI 2016/1083) reg.2(c)).

Withdrawals

1.953 **22.**—(1) Where the account-holder makes a withdrawal from a childcare account, the account provider must pay the corresponding top-up amount to HMRC from the childcare account.

(2) The "corresponding top-up amount", in relation to a withdrawal, is R% of the amount of the withdrawal, where R is the percentage for the time being specified in section 1(4).

(3) Accordingly, the maximum amount that may be withdrawn from a childcare account at any time is the relevant percentage of the total amount of funds held in the account at that time.

(4) The "relevant percentage" is the percentage given by—

$$\frac{100}{100 + R} \times 100$$

where R is the percentage for the time being specified in section 1(4).

(5) A withdrawal may not be made from a childcare account at any time when a top-up payment is payable into the account.

DEFINITIONS

"account-holder"—see s.71(1).
"account provider"—see s.71(1).
"corresponding top-up amount"—see subs.(2).
"HMRC"—see s.71(1).
"relevant percentage"—see subs.(4).
"top-up payment"—s.71(1).

COMMENCEMENT

This section was brought into force for the purposes of the trial on November 14, 2016 (see Childcare Payments Act 2014 (Commencement No.2) Regulations 2016 (SI 2016/1083) reg.2(c)).

Refunds of payments made from childcare accounts

23.—(1) Where—
(a) a payment is made to a person from a childcare account, and
(b) the whole or part of the payment is repayable by that person to the account-holder,

so much of the payment as is repayable must be repaid by that person into the childcare account.

(2) Where—
(a) a payment made to a person consists of an amount paid from a childcare account and an amount that is not paid from the childcare account, and
(b) the whole or part of the payment ("the repayable amount") is repayable by that person to the account-holder,

so much of the repayable amount as exceeds the amount not paid from the childcare account must be repaid by that person into the childcare account.

(3) In a case where—
(a) a person would (in the absence of this subsection) be required by subsection (1) or (2) to repay an amount ("the repayable amount") into a childcare account, but
(b) the childcare account has been closed,

the person must pay the repayable amount to the person or body who was the account provider in relation to the account ("the relevant account provider").

(4) The relevant account provider must—
(a) pay the top-up element of the repayable amount to HMRC, and
(b) pay the remainder of that amount to the person who held the childcare account.

(For provision about calculating the top-up element of an amount, see section 21.)

DEFINITIONS

"account-holder"—see s.71(1).
"account provider"—see s.71(1).

"HMRC"—see s.71(1).
"the relevant account provider"—subs.(3).
"the repayable amount"—subss.(2)(b) and (3)(a).
"top-up element"—s.71(1).

COMMENCEMENT

1.956 This section was brought into force for the purposes of the trial on November 14, 2016 (see Childcare Payments Act 2014 (Commencement No.2) Regulations 2016 (SI 2016/1083) reg.2(c)).

Imposing restrictions on childcare accounts

1.957 **24.**—(1) If such conditions as may be specified in regulations are met, HMRC may make an account restriction order.

(2) An "account restriction order" is an order imposing any of the following restrictions in relation to a childcare account specified in the order—
  (a) a restriction that prevents the making of any qualifying payments into the childcare account;
  (b) a restriction that prevents the making of any payments from the childcare account in respect of qualifying childcare.

(3) Regulations may, in particular, provide that HMRC may make an account restriction order where—
  (a) a person wishes—
    (i) to open a childcare account in respect of a child, or
    (ii) to make a declaration of eligibility in relation to a childcare account held in respect of a child, and
  (b) another person holds a childcare account in respect of the child.

(4) Regulations may make further provision about account restriction orders, including, in particular—
  (a) provision about the procedure for making an account restriction order;
  (b) provision enabling an account restriction order to impose a restriction for a period specified in the order (which may be unlimited);
  (c) provision enabling an account restriction order to provide that a restriction does not apply in such cases as may be specified in the order;
  (d) provision enabling a person who wishes to open a childcare account or make a declaration of eligibility to apply to HMRC for an account restriction order to be made in relation to another person who holds a childcare account;
  (e) provision enabling an account restriction order to be revoked, including provision for the account-holder to apply for its revocation;
  (f) provision specifying the circumstances in which such an application may be granted.

(5) If an account restriction order is made in relation to a childcare account—
  (a) HMRC must give a copy of the order to the account-holder and to the account provider, and
  (b) the account provider must comply with the order.

DEFINITIONS

"account-holder"—see s.71(1).

"account provider"—see s.71(1).
"account restriction order"—subs.(2).
"declaration of eligibility"—see s.71(1).
"HMRC"—see s.71(1).
"qualifying childcare"—see s.71(1).
"qualifying payment"—see s.71(1).

COMMENCEMENT

All regulation making powers under the Act were brought into force on Royal Assent (December 17, 2014); see s.75(1)(c). The rest of this section was brought into force for the purposes of the trial on November 14, 2016 (see Childcare Payments Act 2014 (Commencement No.2) Regulations 2016 (SI 2016/1083) reg.2(c)).

1.958

Closure of childcare accounts

25.—(1) Regulations may make provision about closing childcare accounts.

1.959

(2) The provision that may be made by regulations under this section includes, in particular—
   (a) provision requiring a childcare account to be closed in specified circumstances or if specified conditions are met;
   (b) provision about what is to happen to any funds held in a childcare account when it is closed;
   (c) provision for the repayment to HMRC of a proportion of any such funds, calculated in accordance with the regulations.

(3) In subsection (2) "specified" means specified in the regulations.

DEFINITION

"specified"—subs.(3).

COMMENCEMENT

All regulation making powers under the Act were brought into force on Royal Assent (December 17, 2014); see s.75(1)(c). The rest of this section was brought into force for the purposes of the trial on November 14, 2016 (see Childcare Payments Act 2014 (Commencement No.2) Regulations 2016 (SI 2016/1083) reg.2(c)).

1.960

Information

Power to obtain information or documents

26.—(1) HMRC may by notice in writing require a person of a description specified in regulations to provide information or documents which HMRC require in connection with their functions under this Act.

1.961

(2) HMRC may require a person to provide information or a document only if it is in the person's possession or power.

(3) Regulations may make provision about notices under subsection (1), including, in particular—

(a) provision requiring a notice to contain information specified in the regulations;
(b) provision requiring, or enabling a notice to require, information or documents to be provided in a form or manner specified in the regulations or the notice;
(c) provision requiring, or enabling a notice to require, information or documents to be provided at a time, or within a period, specified in the regulations or the notice;
(d) provision requiring, or enabling a notice to require, information or documents to be provided in respect of a period specified in the regulations or the notice;
(e) provision specifying descriptions of information or document which a notice may not require a person to provide;
(f) provision about determining in specified cases whether information or documents are of such a description, including provision for that determination to be made by a person or body specified in the regulations.

COMMENCEMENT

1.962 This section came into force on July 20, 2016 (see Childcare Payments Act 2014 (Commencement No.1) Regulations 2016 (SI 2016/763) reg.2(1)).

Information sharing between HMRC and others

1.963 **27.**—(1) Subsection (2) applies to information which is held as mentioned in section 18(1) of the Commissioners for Revenue and Customs Act 2005 (confidentiality).

(2) Information to which this subsection applies may be disclosed to any person for use for the purpose of enabling or assisting the exercise of any of the functions of HMRC under this Act.

(3) Information disclosed in reliance on subsection (2) may not be further disclosed to any other person without the authority of the Commissioners (which may be general or specific).

(4) A person who holds information may disclose that information to HMRC if the disclosure is made for the purposes of the exercise by HMRC of their functions under this Act.

(5) This section does not limit the circumstances in which information may be disclosed apart from this section.

(6) In section 127 of the Welfare Reform Act 2012 (information-sharing between Secretary of State and HMRC), in subsection (7), in the definition of "HMRC function"—
(a) at the end of paragraph (a), omit "or", and
(b) at the end of paragraph (b) insert ", or
(c) which is conferred by or under the Childcare Payments Act 2014;".

DEFINITIONS

"the Commissioners"—see s.71(1).
"HMRC"—see s.71(1).

COMMENCEMENT

1.964 This section came into force on July 20, 2016 (see Childcare Payments Act 2014 (Commencement No.1) Regulations 2016 (SI 2016/763) reg.2(1)).

Wrongful disclosure of information received by others from HMRC

28.—(1) If revenue and customs information relating to a person is disclosed in contravention of section 27(3) and the identity of the person—
(a) is specified in the disclosure, or
(b) can be deduced from it,
section 19 of the Commissioners for Revenue and Customs Act 2005 (wrongful disclosure) applies in relation to the disclosure as it applies in relation to a disclosure of such information in contravention of section 20(9) of that Act.

(2) "Revenue and customs information relating to a person" has the meaning given by section 19(2) of the Commissioners for Revenue and Customs Act 2005.

DEFINITIONS

"HMRC"—see s.71(1).
"Revenue and customs information relating to a person"—subs.(2).

COMMENCEMENT

This section came into force on July 20, 2016 (see Childcare Payments Act 2014 (Commencement No.1) Regulations 2016 (SI 2016/763) reg.2(1)).

Supply of information to HMRC by childminder agencies

29.—In section 83A of the Childcare Act 2006 (supply of information to HMRC etc by childminder agencies), in subsection (2), in paragraph (b), for the words from "for the purposes of" to the end of that paragraph substitute "for the purposes of—
  (i) their functions in relation to tax credits, or
  (ii) their functions under the Childcare Payments Act 2014;".

DEFINITION

"HMRC"—see s.71(1).

COMMENCEMENT

This section came into force on July 20, 2016 (see Childcare Payments Act 2014 (Commencement No.1) Regulations 2016 (SI 2016/763) reg.2(1)).

Special rules affecting tax credit and universal credit claimants

Termination of tax credit awards

30.—(1) In this section "the relevant day", in relation to a person who has made a declaration of eligibility for an entitlement period, means—
(a) the first day of the entitlement period, or
(b) if later, the day on which the declaration of eligibility for the entitlement period was made.
(2) This subsection applies where—
(a) a person ("P") has made a valid declaration of eligibility for an entitlement period,

(b) an award of a tax credit is or has been made—
(i) to P or to a person who is P's partner on the relevant day (whether on a single claim or a joint claim), or
(ii) to both of them on a joint claim, and
(c) the award is for a period that includes the relevant day.

(3) Where subsection (2) applies, the award of the tax credit terminates immediately before the relevant day, regardless of whether the decision on the claim was made before or after the relevant day.

This is subject to subsections (4) to (7).

(4) Where a person has made a valid declaration of eligibility for more than one entitlement period beginning during the determination period (see subsection (5)), the award of the tax credit is terminated immediately before the day which is the relevant day in relation to the first of those entitlement periods.

(5) In subsection (4) the "determination period", in relation to an award of a tax credit, means the period—
(a) beginning with the day on which the claim for the tax credit was made, and
(b) ending with the day on which the decision on the claim was made.

(6) Where—
(a) a person has applied for a review under section 21A of the Tax Credits Act 2002 of a decision not to make an award of a tax credit or to terminate such an award, and
(b) the conclusion on the review is that the decision is varied or cancelled,
subsection (3) does not apply in respect of the award in relation to any entitlement period beginning before the day on which the person is notified of the conclusion on the review.

(7) Where—
(a) a person has brought an appeal under section 38 of the Tax Credits Act 2002 against a decision not to make an award of a tax credit or to terminate such an award, and
(b) the appeal is upheld,
subsection (3) does not apply in respect of the award in relation to any entitlement period beginning before the day on which the person is notified of the decision on the appeal.

(8) Where an award of a tax credit made to a person is terminated by virtue of this section—
(a) HMRC must notify the person of that fact,
(b) the tax credits legislation applies in relation to the person with such modifications as may be made in regulations, and
(c) the amount of any tax credit to which the person is entitled is to be calculated in accordance with the tax credits legislation, subject to any such modifications of that legislation.

(9) Regulations may make further provision for the purpose of securing that, where a person makes a valid declaration of eligibility, any entitlement of the person, or a person who is the person's partner, to payments under the tax credits legislation ceases immediately before the relevant day.

(10) Regulations under subsection (9) may, in particular—
(a) provide that the tax credits legislation applies in relation to the person whose entitlement to such payments has ceased with such modifications as may be specified in the regulations, and

(b) apply any provision of this section with such modifications as may be so specified.

(11) If—

(a) a person makes a declaration of eligibility for an entitlement period, and

(b) at any time after the relevant day HMRC determine that the declaration was not valid,

that does not affect anything done by virtue of this section as a result of the making of the declaration.

(12) In this section—

"joint claim" and "single claim" have the same meaning as in the Tax Credits Act 2002;

"the tax credits legislation" means the Tax Credits Act 2002 and any provision made under that Act.

(13) This section ceases to have effect when the repeal of Part 1 of the Tax Credits Act 2002 made by Schedule 14 to the Welfare Reform Act 2012 has fully come into force.

DEFINITIONS

"declaration of eligibility"—see s.71(1).
"determination period"—see subs.(5).
"entitlement period"—see s.71(1).
"HMRC"—see s.71(1).
"joint claim"—see subs.(12).
"P"—see subs.(2)(a).
"partner"—see s.71(1).
"the relevant day"—see subs.(1).
"single claim"—see subs.(12).
"tax credit"—see s.71(1).
"the tax credit legislation"—see subs.(12).
"valid declaration of eligibility"—see s.71(2).

COMMENCEMENT

All regulation making powers under the Act were brought into force on Royal Assent (December 17, 2014); see s.75(1)(c). The rest of this section was brought into force for the purposes of the trial on November 14, 2016 (see Childcare Payments Act 2014 (Commencement No.2) Regulations 2016 (SI 2016/1083) reg.2(d)).

1.969

Power to provide for automatic termination of universal credit

31.—(1) Regulations may make provision for the purpose of securing that, where a person has made a valid declaration of eligibility—

(a) any award of universal credit made to the person, or to a person who is the person's partner, is terminated,

(b) any claim which the person, or a person who is the person's partner, has made for universal credit may not be proceeded with, and

(c) any entitlement of the person, or a person who is the person's partner, to payments under relevant social security legislation ceases.

(2) The provision that may be made by regulations under subsection (1) includes—

(a) provision amending this Act, including—

(i) provision amending or repealing section 11, and

1.970

(ii) provision made in consequence of any provision made by regulations under subsection (1);

(b) provision conferring power on the appropriate national authority to make regulations containing—

(i) provision about calculating, in a case falling within subsection (1)(a) to (c), the amount of any payment to which a person is entitled;

(ii) provision modifying the application of any relevant social security legislation, or any provision made under any such legislation, in such a case.

(3) In subsection (2)(b) "the appropriate national authority" means—

(a) in relation to universal credit payable under Part 1 of the Welfare Reform Act 2012, the Secretary of State;

(b) in relation to universal credit payable under any provision made for Northern Ireland which corresponds to that Part of that Act, a Northern Ireland department.

(4) The following is "relevant social security legislation" for the purposes of this section—

(a) the Social Security Administration Act 1992;
(b) the Social Security Administration (Northern Ireland) Act 1992;
(c) the Social Security Act 1998;
(d) the Social Security (Northern Ireland) Order 1998 (S.I. 1998/1506 (N.I. 10));
(e) Part 1 of the Welfare Reform Act 2012;
(f) any provision made for Northern Ireland which corresponds to that Part of that Act.

DEFINITIONS

"the appropriate national authority"—see subs.(3).
"partner"—see s.71(1).
"relevant social security legislation"—see subs.(4).
"universal credit"—see s.71(1).
"valid declaration of eligibility"—see s.71(2).

COMMENCEMENT

1.971   All regulation making powers under the Act were brought into force on Royal Assent (December 17, 2014); see s.75(1)(c).

Power to disqualify tax credit claimants from obtaining top-up payments

1.972   **32.**—(1) This section applies in relation to a person ("P") if—

(a) P, or a person who is P's partner, makes a claim (whether a single or a joint claim) that results in an award of a tax credit being made for a relevant period (see subsection (2)),

(b) the claim is made during an entitlement period for which P or P's partner has made a valid declaration of eligibility,

(c) there has not been a change of circumstances in relation to P or P's partner since the beginning of the entitlement period, and

(d) P, or a person who is P's partner, makes a declaration of eligibility within the period of 12 months beginning with the day on which the claim was made.

(2) In subsection (1)(a) "relevant period", in relation to an entitlement period, means a period that includes the whole or any part of the entitlement period.

(3) If this section applies in relation to a person, HMRC may give the person a warning notice.

(4) A warning notice is a notice stating that, if this section or section 33 (power to disqualify universal credit claimants from obtaining top-up payments) applies in relation to the person at any time during the period of 4 years beginning with the day on which the notice is given, HMRC may give the person a disqualification notice (see section 34).

(5) Regulations may make provision—
(a) about what is, or is not, to be regarded as a change of circumstances in relation to a person for the purposes of this section;
(b) specifying cases in which something which would otherwise be a change of circumstances is not to be treated as such for the purposes of this section.

(6) Regulations may amend subsection (1)(d) so as to substitute a different period for the period for the time being specified there.

(7) In this section "joint claim" and "single claim" have the same meaning as in the Tax Credits Act 2002.

DEFINITIONS

"declaration of eligibility"—see s.71(1).
"entitlement period"—see s.71(1).
"HMRC"—see s.71(1).
"joint claim"—see subs.(7).
"P"—see subs.(1).
"partner"—see s.71(1).
"relevant period"—see subs.(2).
"single claim"—see subs.(7).
"tax credit"—see s.71(1).
"top-up payment"—s.71(1).
"universal credit"—s.71(1).
"valid declaration of eligibility"—see s.71(2).

COMMENCEMENT

All regulation making powers under the Act were brought into force on Royal Assent (December 17, 2014); see s.75(1)(c). The rest of this section was brought into force for the purposes of the trial on November 14, 2016 (see Childcare Payments Act 2014 (Commencement No.2) Regulations 2016 (SI 2016/1083) reg.2(e)).

1.973

Power to disqualify universal credit claimants from obtaining top-up payments

33.—(1) This section applies in relation to a person ("P") if—
(a) P, or a person who is P's partner, makes a claim (whether jointly or otherwise) that results in universal credit becoming payable for a relevant assessment period (see subsection (2)),
(b) the claim is made during an entitlement period for which P or P's partner has made a valid declaration of eligibility,
(c) there has not been a change of circumstances in relation to P or P's partner since the beginning of the entitlement period, and

1.974

(d) P, or a person who is P's partner, makes a declaration of eligibility within the period of 12 months beginning with the day on which the claim was made.

(2) In subsection (1)(a) "relevant assessment period", in relation to an entitlement period, means any assessment period (within the meaning of the relevant legislation) that includes the whole or any part of the entitlement period.

(3) If this section applies in relation to a person, HMRC may give the person a warning notice.

(4) A warning notice is a notice stating that, if this section or section 32 (power to disqualify tax credit claimants from obtaining top-up payments) applies in relation to the person at any time during the period of 4 years beginning with the day on which the notice is given, HMRC may give the person a disqualification notice (see section 34).

(5) Regulations may make provision—
  (a) about what is, or is not, to be regarded as a change of circumstances in relation to a person for the purposes of this section;
  (b) specifying cases in which something which would otherwise be a change of circumstances is not to be treated as such for the purposes of this section.

(6) Regulations may amend subsection (1)(d) so as to substitute a different period for the period for the time being specified there.

(7) In this section "the relevant legislation" means—
  (a) Part 1 of the Welfare Reform Act 2012, or
  (b) any provision made for Northern Ireland which corresponds to that Part of that Act.

DEFINITIONS

"declaration of eligibility"—see s.71(1).
"entitlement period"—see s.71(1).
"HMRC"—see s.71(1).
"P"—see subs.(2).
"partner"—see s.71(1).
"relevant assessment period"—see subs.(2).
"the relevant legislation"—see subs.(7).
"tax credit"—see s.71(1).
"top-up payment"—s.71(1).
"universal credit"—s.71(1).
"valid declaration of eligibility"—see s.71(2).

COMMENCEMENT

1.975 All regulation making powers under the Act were brought into force on Royal Assent (December 17, 2014); see s.75(1)(c). The rest of this section was brought into force for the purposes of the trial on November 14, 2016 (see Childcare Payments Act 2014 (Commencement No.2) Regulations 2016 (SI 2016/1083) reg.2(e)).

Disqualification notices

1.976 34.—(1) If—
  (a) a person has been given a warning notice under section 32(3) or 33(3), and

(b) section 32 or 33 applies in relation to the person at any time during the period of 4 years beginning with the day on which the notice is given,

HMRC may give the person a disqualification notice under this section.

(2) Where a person has been given a disqualification notice—
(a) the person may not open a childcare account,
(b) no qualifying payments may be made into any childcare account held by the person, and
(c) any declaration of eligibility made by the person for an entitlement period for which the notice has effect is not valid.

(3) A disqualification notice has effect for the period specified in the notice.

(4) But a disqualification notice may not have effect for a period longer than 3 years.

(5) The period specified in a disqualification notice—
(a) may begin before the day on which the notice is given, but
(b) may not begin before the start of the entitlement period for which the declaration of eligibility that resulted in the giving of the notice was made.

(6) If HMRC give a person a disqualification notice, HMRC must give a copy of the notice to any person or body which provides childcare accounts.

(7) HMRC may revoke a disqualification notice.

DEFINITIONS

"declaration of eligibility"—see s.71(1).
"entitlement period"—see s.71(1).
"HMRC"—see s.71(1).
"qualifying payment"—see s.71(1).

COMMENCEMENT

This section was brought into force for the purposes of the trial on November 14, 2016 (see Childcare Payments Act 2014 (Commencement No.2) Regulations 2016 (SI 2016/1083) reg.2(e)).

Recovery of top-up payments

Recovery of top-up payments where tax credits award made on a review

35.—(1) This section applies where—
(a) a person ("P"), or (in the case of a joint claim) P or P's partner at the time of the claim, applies for a review under section 21A of the Tax Credits Act 2002 of a decision not to make an award of a tax credit or to terminate such an award, and
(b) the conclusion on the review is that the decision is varied or cancelled.

(2) P is liable to pay HMRC an amount equal to the sum of—
(a) any top-up payments made to P for an entitlement period falling wholly within the relevant period, and

(b) the relevant proportion of the sum of any top-up payments made to P for an entitlement period falling partly within the relevant period.

(3) The "relevant period" means the period in relation to which the following conditions are met—
(a) it falls within the review period (see subsection (4)),
(b) it is a period for which an award of a tax credit is made, or continues, as a result of the variation or cancellation of the decision, and
(c) where the award has been made to P and P's partner on a joint claim, the person who was P's partner at the time of the claim has been P's partner throughout the period.

(4) The "review period" means the period which—
(a) begins with the day on which the decision was made, and
(b) ends with—
  (i) the day on which the person who applied for the review is notified of its conclusions, or
  (ii) if that day falls within an entitlement period for which P has made a valid declaration of eligibility, the last day of the entitlement period.

(5) In subsection (2)(b) the "relevant proportion", in relation to top-up payments made for an entitlement period, means a proportion equal to the proportion of the entitlement period which falls within the relevant period.

(6) In this section "joint claim" has the same meaning as in the Tax Credits Act 2002.

(7) For provision about terminating an award of a tax credit when a declaration of eligibility is made for a subsequent entitlement period, see section 30.

DEFINITIONS

"declaration of eligibility"—see s.71(1).
"entitlement period"—see s.71(1).
"HMRC"—see s.71(1).
"joint claim"—see subs.(6)
"P"—see subs.(1).
"partner"—see s.71(1).
"review period"—see subs.(4).
"relevant proportion"—see subs.(5).
"tax credit"—see s.71(1).
"top-up payment"—s.71(1).
"valid declaration of eligibility"—see s.71(2).

COMMENCEMENT

1.979 This section was brought into force for the purposes of the trial on November 14, 2016 (see Childcare Payments Act 2014 (Commencement No.2) Regulations 2016 (SI 2016/1083) reg.2(e)).

Recovery of top-up payments where tax credits award made on appeal

1.980 **36.**—(1) This section applies where—
(a) a person ("P"), or (in the case of a joint claim) P or P's partner at the time of the claim, has brought an appeal under section 38 of the Tax Credits Act 2002 against a decision not to make an award of a tax credit or to terminate such an award, and

(b) the appeal is upheld.

(2) P is liable to pay HMRC an amount equal to the sum of—
(a) any top-up payments made to P for an entitlement period falling wholly within the relevant period, and
(b) the relevant proportion of the sum of any top-up payments made to P for an entitlement period falling partly within the relevant period.

(3) The "relevant period" means the period in relation to which the following conditions are met—
(a) it falls within the appeal period (see subsection (4)),
(b) it is a period for which an award of a tax credit is made, or continues, as a result of the appeal being upheld, and
(c) where the award has been made to P and P's partner on a joint claim, the person who was P's partner at the time of the claim has been P's partner throughout the period.

(4) The "appeal period" means the period which—
(a) begins with the day on which the decision was made, and
(b) ends with—
   (i) the day on which the person who brought the appeal is notified of the decision on the appeal, or
   (ii) if that day falls within an entitlement period for which P has made a valid declaration of eligibility, the last day of the entitlement period.

(5) In subsection (2)(b) the "relevant proportion", in relation to top-up payments made for an entitlement period, means a proportion equal to the proportion of the entitlement period which falls within the relevant period.

(6) In this section "joint claim" has the same meaning as in the Tax Credits Act 2002.

(7) For provision about terminating an award of a tax credit when a declaration of eligibility is made for a subsequent entitlement period, see section 30.

Definitions

"appeal period"—see subs.(4).
"declaration of eligibility"—see s.71(1).
"entitlement period"—see s.71(1).
"HMRC"—see s.71(1).
"joint claim"—see subs.(6).
"P"—see subs.(1)(a).
"partner"—see s.71(1).
"relevant period"—see subs.(4).
"relevant proportion"—see subs.(5).
"tax credit"—see s.71(1).
"top-up payment"—s.71(1).

Commencement

This section was brought into force for the purposes of the trial on November 14, 2016 (see Childcare Payments Act 2014 (Commencement No.2) Regulations 2016 (SI 2016/1083) reg.2(e)).

Recovery of top-up payments where universal credit award made on revision

1.982 37.—(1) This section applies where any of the following decisions has been revised under section 9 of the Social Security Act 1998 or Article 10 of the Social Security (Northern Ireland) Order 1998 (S.I. 1998/1506 (N.I. 10))—
  (a) a decision not to make an award of universal credit to a person ("P") or to P and P's partner jointly;
  (b) a decision to terminate such an award.
(2) P is liable to pay HMRC an amount equal to the sum of—
  (a) any top-up payments made to P for an entitlement period falling wholly within the relevant period, and
  (b) the relevant proportion of the sum of any top-up payments made to P for an entitlement period falling partly within the relevant period.
(3) The "relevant period" means the period in relation to which the following conditions are met—
  (a) it falls within the revision period (see subsection (4)),
  (b) it is a period for which an award of universal credit is made, or continues, as a result of the revision of the decision, and
  (c) where the award has been made to P and P's partner jointly, the person who was P's partner at the time of the decision has been P's partner throughout the period.
(4) The "revision period" means the period which—
  (a) begins with the day on which the decision was made, and
  (b) ends with—
    (i) the day on which the person in relation to whom the decision was made is notified that the decision has been revised, or
    (ii) if that day falls within an entitlement period for which P has made a valid declaration of eligibility, the last day of the entitlement period.
(5) In subsection (2)(b) the "relevant proportion", in relation to top-up payments made for an entitlement period, means a proportion equal to the proportion of the entitlement period which falls within the relevant period.

DEFINITIONS

"declaration of eligibility"—see s.71(1).
"entitlement period"—see s.71(1).
"HMRC"—see s.71(1).
"P"—see subs.(1)(a).
"partner"—see s.71(1).
"relevant period"—see subs.(3).
"revision period"—see subs.(4).
"relevant proportion"—see subs.(5).
"top-up payment"—s.71(1).
"universal credit"—s.71(1).
"valid declaration of eligibility"—see s.71(2).

COMMENCEMENT

1.983 This section was brought into force for the purposes of the trial on November 14, 2016 (see Childcare Payments Act 2014 (Commencement No.2) Regulations 2016 (SI 2016/1083) reg.2(e)).

(2014 c.28 s.38)

Recovery of top-up payments where universal credit award made on appeal

38.—(1) This section applies where—
(a) a person ("P"), or (in the case of a claim made jointly) P or P's partner at the time of the claim, has brought an appeal under the appropriate legislation against a decision not to make an award of universal credit or to terminate such an award, and
(b) the appeal is upheld.

(2) In subsection (1) "the appropriate legislation" means any of the following—
(a) the Social Security Act 1998;
(b) the Social Security (Northern Ireland) Order 1998 (S.I. 1998/1506 (N.I. 10));
(c) Part 1 of the Welfare Reform Act 2012;
(d) any provision made for Northern Ireland which corresponds to that Part of that Act.

(3) P is liable to pay HMRC an amount equal to the sum of—
(a) any top-up payments made to P for an entitlement period falling wholly within the relevant period, and
(b) the relevant proportion of the sum of any top-up payments made to P for an entitlement period falling partly within the relevant period.

(4) The "relevant period" means the period in relation to which the following conditions are met—
(a) it falls within the appeal period (see subsection (5)),
(b) it is a period for which an award of universal credit is made, or continues, as a result of the appeal being upheld, and
(c) where the award has been made to P and P's partner jointly, the person who was P's partner at the time of the claim has been P's partner throughout the period.

(5) The "appeal period" means the period which—
(a) begins with the day on which the decision was made, and
(b) ends with—
   (i) the day on which the person who brought the appeal is notified of the decision on the appeal, or
   (ii) if that day falls within an entitlement period for which P has made a valid declaration of eligibility, the last day of the entitlement period.

(6) In subsection (3)(b) the "relevant proportion", in relation to top-up payments made for an entitlement period, means a proportion equal to the proportion of the entitlement period which falls within the relevant period.

1.984

DEFINITIONS

"appeal period"—see subs.(5).
"the appropriate legislation"—see subs.(2).
"declaration of eligibility"—see s.71(1).
"entitlement period"—see s.71(1).
"HMRC"—see s.71(1).
"P"—see subs.(1)(a).
"partner"—see s.71(1).
"relevant period"—see subs.(4).
"relevant proportion"—see subs.(6).
"top-up payment"—s.71(1).

"universal credit"—s.71(1).
"valid declaration of eligibility"—see s.71(2).

COMMENCEMENT

1.985 This section was brought into force for the purposes of the trial on November 14, 2016 (see Childcare Payments Act 2014 (Commencement No.2) Regulations 2016 (SI 2016/1083) reg.2(e)).

Recovery of top-up payments where person fails to give childcare account notice

1.986 **39.**—(1) This section applies where—
(a) a person has made a declaration of eligibility for an entitlement period,
(b) on the day on which the person made the declaration, the person, or a person who was the person's partner at that time, ("E") was an eligible employee in relation to a relevant childcare scheme, and
(c) E has failed to give E's employer a childcare account notice before the end of the relevant period (see subsection (2)).
(2) In subsection (1)(c) "the relevant period" means—
(a) the entitlement period for which the declaration was made, or
(b) where the declaration was made for the purposes of opening a childcare account, the period of 3 months beginning with the day on which it was made.
(3) The person who made the declaration is liable to pay HMRC an amount equal to the sum of any top-up payments made to the person for the entitlement period.
(4) Expressions used in this section and in section 12 have the same meaning in this section as they have in that section.

DEFINITIONS

"childcare account"—see s.71(1).
"childcare account notice"—see s.12(4).
"declaration of eligibility"—see s.71(1).
"E"—see subs.(1)(b).
"eligible employee"—see s.12(3).
"entitlement period"—see s.71(1).
"HMRC—see s.71(1).
"relevant childcare scheme"—see s.12(2).
"the relevant period"—see subs.(2).
"top-up payment"—see s.71(1).
"valid declaration of eligibility"—see s.71(2).

Recovery of top-up payments in other cases

1.987 **40.**—(1) If—
(a) a top-up payment is made into a childcare account, and
(b) the account-holder is not entitled to the top-up payment,
the account-holder is liable to pay HMRC an amount equal to the amount of the top-up payment.
(2) If—
(a) a person who holds a childcare account causes or permits a prohibited payment to be made from the account, and

(b) at the time of the payment the person knew, or ought to have known, that the payment was a prohibited payment,

the person is liable to pay HMRC an amount not exceeding the top-up element of the prohibited payment.

(3) If a person fails to make a payment in accordance with a requirement imposed by subsections (1) to (3) of section 23 (refunds of payments made from childcare accounts), the person is liable to pay HMRC the top-up element of the payment.

(4) If a prohibited payment is made to a person from a childcare account as a result of the dishonesty of that or some other person, each of those persons is liable to pay HMRC the top-up element of the prohibited payment.

(5) Where—
(a) a body corporate is liable under subsection (3) or (4) to pay an amount to HMRC, and
(b) the liability is attributable (wholly or partly) to the dishonesty of a person falling within subsection (6),

that person (as well as the body corporate) is liable to pay that amount to HMRC.

(6) The persons are—
(a) a director, manager, secretary or similar officer of the body corporate;
(b) any person who was purporting to act in such a capacity.

(7) Where the affairs of a body corporate are managed by its members, subsection (5) applies in relation to the acts and defaults of a member, in connection with that management, as if the member were a director of the body corporate.

(8) Where—
(a) a Scottish firm is liable under subsection (3) or (4) to pay an amount to HMRC, and
(b) the liability is attributable (wholly or partly) to the dishonesty of a partner of the firm or a person purporting to act as such a partner,

that person (as well as the firm) is liable to pay that amount to HMRC.

(9) For provision about calculating the top-up element of a payment, see section 21.

DEFINITIONS

"account-holder"—see s.71(1).
"HMRC"—see s.71(1).
"prohibited payment"—see s.71(1).
"top-up element"—s.71(1).
"top-up payment"—s.71(1).

COMMENCEMENT

This section was brought into force for the purposes of the trial on November 14, 2016 (see Childcare Payments Act 2014 (Commencement No.2) Regulations 2016 (SI 2016/1083) reg.2(f)).

Assessment and enforcement of recoverable amounts

41.—(1) Where a person is liable under any of sections 35 to 40 ("the relevant section") to pay an amount to HMRC—

(a) HMRC may assess the amount, and
(b) if they do so, they must notify the person.
(2) No assessment may be made under this section after—
(a) the end of the period specified in subsection (3), or
(b) if earlier, the end of the period of 12 months beginning with the day on which HMRC first believed, or had reasonable grounds for believing, that the person was liable under the relevant section to pay an amount to HMRC.
(3) The period referred to in subsection (2)(a) is—
(a) the period of 4 years beginning with the day on which the person became liable under the relevant section to pay an amount to HMRC, or
(b) in a case where the person became liable under the relevant section to pay an amount to HMRC as a result of the person's dishonesty, the period of 20 years beginning with that day.
(4) Where two or more persons—
(a) are liable under section 40(3) or (4) to pay an amount to HMRC, and
(b) have each been notified of an assessment under this section in respect of the amount,
each of those persons is jointly and severally liable to pay the amount assessed under this section.
(5) Where a person is notified of an assessment under this section, the amount payable as a result of the assessment must be paid—
(a) in a case where the person does not apply for a review of the assessment within the period specified in section 57(2)(a), before the end of that period,
(b) in a case where the person applies for a review of the assessment but does not give notice of an appeal against the assessment, before the end of the period in which notice of such an appeal could have been given, or
(c) in a case where notice of such an appeal has been given, on the day on which the appeal is determined or withdrawn.
(6) A requirement to pay an amount to HMRC under any of sections 35 to 40 may be enforced as if the amount were income tax charged in an assessment and due and payable.
See also sections 52 to 54 (which contain further powers to recover amounts owed to HMRC).

DEFINITIONS

"HMRC"—see s.71(1).
"the relevant section"—see subs.(1).

COMMENCEMENT

1.990   This section was brought into force for the purposes of the trial on November 14, 2016 (see Childcare Payments Act 2014 (Commencement No.2) Regulations 2016 (SI 2016/1083) reg.2(f)).

(2014 c.28 s.42)

Penalties

Penalties for inaccurate declarations of eligibility

42.—(1) A person is liable to a penalty under this section if the person meets condition A or B.

(2) Condition A is that—
(a) the person makes a declaration of eligibility that contains an inaccuracy, and
(b) the inaccuracy is careless or deliberate.

An inaccuracy is careless if it is due to a failure by the person to take reasonable care.

(3) Condition B is that—
(a) a declaration of eligibility containing an inaccuracy is made by or on behalf of a person,
(b) the person discovers the inaccuracy after the declaration of eligibility has been made, and
(c) the person fails to take reasonable steps to inform HMRC.

(4) In a case where the inaccuracy is deliberate, the amount of the penalty is 50% of the maximum available top-up payment for the entitlement period for which the declaration of eligibility was made.

(5) In any other case, the amount of the penalty is 25% of the maximum available top-up payment for the entitlement period for which the declaration of eligibility was made.

(6) "The maximum available top-up payment" for an entitlement period is the amount that would be payable by HMRC if qualifying payments equal to the relevant maximum for the entitlement period were made into the childcare account in respect of which the declaration was made.

(For the relevant maximum for an entitlement period, see section 19(5) and (6).)

(7) If—
(a) in the absence of this subsection, the relevant maximum for the entitlement period for which the declaration of eligibility was made would be the amount specified in section 19(5), but
(b) the person made representations to HMRC that the relevant maximum for the entitlement period should be a greater amount determined by or under regulations under section 19(6),
then for the purposes of subsection (6) above the relevant maximum for the entitlement period is to be taken to be that greater amount.

DEFINITIONS

"declaration of eligibility"—see s.71(1).
"entitlement period"—see s.71(1).
"HMRC"—see s.71(1).
"the maximum available top-up payment"—see subs.(6).
"qualifying payment"—see s.71(1).
"top-up payment"—s.71(1).

COMMENCEMENT

This section was brought into force for the purposes of the trial on November 14, 2016 (see Childcare Payments Act 2014 (Commencement No.2) Regulations 2016 (SI 2016/1083) reg.2(f)).

Penalties for failure to comply with information notice

1.993   **43.**—(1) If—
(a) a person fails to comply with a notice under section 26 (an "information notice") before the end of the period within which the person was required to comply with it, and
(b) the information notice has become final (see subsection (6)),
HMRC may give the person a warning notice.

(2) A "warning notice" is a notice requiring the person to comply with the information notice before the end of the period of 30 days beginning with the day on which the warning notice is given.

(3) If a person fails to comply with a warning notice given under this section, the person is liable to a penalty under this section.

(4) The amount of the penalty may not exceed £300.

(5) Regulations may amend subsection (4) so as to substitute a different amount for the amount for the time being specified there.

(6) An information notice becomes final—
(a) in a case where the person does not apply for a review of the decision to give the information notice within the period specified in section 57(2)(a), at the end of that period,
(b) in a case where—
  (i) the person applies for a review of the decision but does not give notice of an appeal against the decision, and
  (ii) the decision has not been cancelled,
at the end of the period in which notice of an appeal against the decision could have been given, or
(c) in a case where—
  (i) notice of such an appeal has been given, and
  (ii) the decision has not been quashed on appeal,
on the day on which the appeal is determined or withdrawn.

(7) Accordingly—
(a) if a person is granted an extension of the period for making an application for a review of a decision to give an information notice, any warning notice given to the person in respect of the information notice before the application for the review is made is of no effect, and
(b) if a person is permitted to give notice of an appeal against an information notice after the end of the period mentioned in subsection (6)(b), any warning notice given to the person in respect of the information notice before the notice of appeal is given is of no effect.

DEFINITIONS

"HMRC"—see s.71(1).
"information notice"—subs.(1)(a).
"warning notice"—subs.(2).

COMMENCEMENT

1.994   All regulation making powers under the Act were brought into force on Royal Assent (December 17, 2014); see s.75(1)(c). The rest of this section came into force on July 20, 2016 (see Childcare Payments Act 2014 (Commencement No.1) Regulations 2016 (2016/763) reg.2(1)).

Penalties for providing inaccurate information or documents

44.—(1) A person is liable to a penalty under this section if—
(a) in complying with a notice under section 26, the person provides inaccurate information or provides a document that contains an inaccuracy, and
(b) condition A, B or C is met.

(2) Condition A is that the inaccuracy is careless or deliberate.

An inaccuracy is careless if it is due to a failure by the person to take reasonable care.

(3) Condition B is that the person knows of the inaccuracy at the time the information or document is provided but does not inform HMRC at that time.

(4) Condition C is that the person—
(a) discovers the inaccuracy some time later, and
(b) fails to take reasonable steps to inform HMRC.

(5) The amount of a penalty under this section may not exceed £3,000.

(6) Regulations may amend subsection (5) so as to substitute a different amount for the amount for the time being specified there.

DEFINITION

"HMRC"—see s.71(1).

COMMENCEMENT

All regulation making powers under the Act were brought into force on Royal Assent (December 17, 2014); see s.75(1)(c). The rest of this section was brought into force for the purposes of the trial on November 14, 2016 (see Childcare Payments Act 2014 (Commencement No.2) Regulations 2016 (SI 2016/1083) reg.2(g)).

Penalties for making prohibited payments

45.—(1) A person is liable to a penalty under this section if—
(a) HMRC has given the person a warning notice under this section,
(b) at any time when the warning notice has effect, the person causes or permits a prohibited payment to be made from a childcare account held by the person, and
(c) the person is notified of an assessment under section 41 in respect of the prohibited payment.

(2) HMRC may give a person a warning notice under this section if—
(a) the person causes or permits a prohibited payment to be made from a childcare account held by the person,
(b) the person is notified of an assessment under section 41 in respect of the prohibited payment, and
(c) the assessment has become final (see subsection (7)).

(3) A warning notice is a notice which—
(a) subject to subsection (4), has effect for a period of 4 years beginning with the day on which the notice is given ("the relevant 4-year period"), and
(b) states that the person will be liable to a penalty under this section if at any time during the relevant 4-year period the person causes or permits a prohibited payment to be made from a childcare account held by the person.

(4) If a person is notified of a penalty under this section, the warning notice given to the person under this section ceases to have effect.

(5) But subsection (4) does not prevent HMRC from giving the person a fresh warning notice as a result of the prohibited payment in respect of which the person was notified of the penalty.

(6) Where a person is liable to a penalty under this section for causing or permitting a prohibited payment to be made, the amount of the penalty is 25% of the amount assessed under section 41 in respect of the prohibited payment.

(7) For the purposes of this section an assessment under section 41 becomes final—
- (a) in a case where the person does not apply for a review of the assessment within the period specified in section 57(2)(a), at the end of that period,
- (b) in a case where—
  - (i) the person applies for a review of the assessment but does not give notice of an appeal against the assessment, and
  - (ii) the assessment has not been cancelled,

at the end of the period in which notice of an appeal against the assessment could have been given, or
- (c) in a case where—
  - (i) notice of such an appeal has been given, and
  - (ii) the assessment has not been quashed on appeal,

on the day on which the appeal is determined or withdrawn.

(8) Accordingly—
- (a) if a person is granted an extension of the period for making an application for a review of an assessment, any warning notice given to the person in respect of the assessment before the application for the review is made is of no effect, and
- (b) if a person is permitted to give notice of an appeal against an assessment after the end of the period mentioned in subsection (7)(b), any warning notice given to the person in respect of the assessment before the notice of appeal is given is of no effect.

DEFINITIONS

"HMRC"—see s.71(1).
"prohibited payment"—see s.71(1).
"the relevant 4-year period"—subs.(3)(a).

COMMENCEMENT

This section was brought into force for the purposes of the trial on November 14, 2016 (see Childcare Payments Act 2014 (Commencement No.2) Regulations 2016 (SI 2016/1083) reg.2(g)).

Penalties for dishonestly obtaining top-up payments, etc

46.—(1) A person ("P") is liable to a penalty under this section if—
- (a) for the purpose of obtaining a relevant payment for P or another (see subsection (2)), P does, or omits to do, any act, and
- (b) P's conduct involves dishonesty.

(2) The following payments are "relevant payments"—
- (a) a top-up payment;

(b) a payment from a childcare account.

(3) The amount of the penalty may not exceed—
(a) £3,000, or
(b) the sum of any relevant amounts obtained as mentioned in subsection (1),

whichever is greater.

(4) In subsection (3) "relevant amount" means—
(a) in the case of a top-up payment, the amount of the payment, and
(b) in the case of a payment from a childcare account, an amount equal to the top-up element of the payment.

(For provision about calculating the top-up element of a payment, see section 21.)

(5) Regulations may amend subsection (3)(a) so as to substitute a different amount for the amount for the time being specified there.

(6) Where—
(a) a body corporate is liable to a penalty under this section, and
(b) the liability is attributable (wholly or partly) to the dishonesty of a person falling within subsection (7),

that person (as well as the body corporate) is liable to a penalty under this section.

(7) The persons are—
(a) a director, manager, secretary or similar officer of the body corporate;
(b) any person who was purporting to act in such a capacity.

(8) Where the affairs of a body corporate are managed by its members, subsection (6) applies in relation to the acts and defaults of a member, in connection with that management, as if the member were a director of the body corporate.

(9) Where—
(a) a Scottish firm is liable to a penalty under this section, and
(b) the liability is attributable (wholly or partly) to the dishonesty of a partner of the firm or a person purporting to act as such a partner,

that person (as well as the firm) is liable to a penalty under this section.

DEFINITIONS

"P"—subs.(1).
"relevant amount"—subs.(4).
"relevant payments"—subs.(2).
"top-up element"—s.71(1).
"top-up payment"—s.71(1).

COMMENCEMENT

All regulation making powers under the Act were brought into force on Royal Assent (December 17, 2014); see s.75(1)(c). The rest of this section was brought into force for the purposes of the trial on November 14, 2016 (see Childcare Payments Act 2014 (Commencement No.2) Regulations 2016 (SI 2016/1083) reg.2(g)).

Assessment and enforcement of penalties

47.—(1) Where a person becomes liable to a penalty under this Act—
(a) HMRC may assess the penalty, and
(b) if they do so, they must notify the person.

(2) No assessment of a penalty may be made under this section after—
(a) the end of the period specified in subsection (3), or
(b) if earlier, the end of the period of 12 months beginning with the day on which HMRC first believed, or had reasonable grounds for believing, that the person was liable to the penalty.
(3) The period referred to in subsection (2)(a) is—
(a) the period of 4 years beginning with the day on which the person became liable to the penalty, or
(b) in a case where the person became liable to the penalty as a result of the person's dishonesty, the period of 20 years beginning with that day.
(4) Where a person is notified of an assessment under this section, the penalty payable as a result of the assessment must be paid—
(a) in a case where the person does not apply for a review of the penalty within the period specified in section 57(2)(a), before the end of that period,
(b) in a case where the person applies for a review of the penalty but does not give notice of an appeal against the penalty, before the end of the period in which notice of such an appeal could have been given, or
(c) in a case where notice of such an appeal has been given, on the day on which the appeal is determined or withdrawn.
(5) A penalty under this Act may be enforced as if it were income tax charged in an assessment and due and payable.

See also section 53 (recovery of debts from childcare accounts).

DEFINITION

"HMRC"—see s.71(1).

COMMENCEMENT

1.1002   This section came into force on July 20, 2016 in respect of penalties under section 43 (see Childcare Payments Act 2014 (Commencement No.1) Regulations 2016 (2016/763) reg.2(2)).

Double jeopardy

1.1003   **48.**—A person is not liable to a penalty under this Act in respect of anything in respect of which the person has been convicted of an offence.

COMMENCEMENT

1.1004   This section was brought into force for the purposes of the trial on November 14, 2016 (see Childcare Payments Act 2014 (Commencement No.2) Regulations 2016 (SI 2016/1083) reg.2(g)).

Other enforcement powers

Disqualification orders

1.1005   **49.**—(1) HMRC may make a disqualification order in relation to a person if condition A, B or C is met.
(2) Condition A is that, on more than one occasion in the period of 4 years ending with the day on which the disqualification order is made, the person—

(a) has become liable to a penalty under this Act, and
(b) has been notified of the penalty.

(3) Condition B is that—
(a) the person ("P") has done, or omitted to do, any act for the purpose of obtaining a relevant payment for P or another (see subsection (4)),
(b) P's conduct involved dishonesty, and
(c) as a result P has been convicted of an offence or has been notified of a penalty under section 46.

(4) The following payments are "relevant payments"—
(a) a top-up payment;
(b) a payment from a childcare account.

(5) Condition C is that—
(a) the person ("P") has done, or omitted to do, any act for the purpose of obtaining a relevant benefit for P or another (see subsection (6)),
(b) P's conduct involved dishonesty, and
(c) as a result P has been convicted of an offence.

(6) "Relevant benefit" means any benefit or other payment of a description specified in regulations.

(7) Where a disqualification order has effect in relation to a person—
(a) the person may not open a childcare account,
(b) no qualifying payments may be made into any childcare account held by the person, and
(c) any declaration of eligibility made by the person for an entitlement period for which the order has effect is not valid.

(8) A disqualification order has effect for the period specified in the order.

(9) But a disqualification order may not have effect for a period longer than 3 years.

(10) If HMRC make a disqualification order under this section, HMRC must give a copy of the order to—
(a) the person in relation to whom the order is made, and
(b) any person or body which provides childcare accounts.

(11) HMRC may revoke a disqualification order made under this section.

DEFINITIONS

"declaration of eligibility"—see s.71(1).
"entitlement period"—see s.71(1).
"HMRC"—see s.71(1).
"P"—subss.(3)(a) and (5)(a).
"qualifying payment"—see s.71(1).
"relevant benefit"—subs.(6).
"relevant payments"—subs.(4).
"top-up payment"—s.71(1).

COMMENCEMENT

This section was brought into force for the purposes of the trial on November 14, 2016 (see Childcare Payments Act 2014 (Commencement No.2) Regulations 2016 (SI 2016/1083) reg.2(g)).

Power to exclude childcare from being qualifying childcare

50.—(1) This section applies if—
(a) a person has done, or omitted to do, any act for the purpose of obtaining a payment from a childcare account,

Childcare Payments Act 2014

(b) the person's conduct involved dishonesty, and
(c) as a result the person has been convicted of an offence or has been notified of a penalty under section 46.

(2) HMRC may direct that any childcare provided by the person is not qualifying childcare for the purposes of this Act.

(3) A direction under this section has effect for 12 months beginning with the day on which it is made.

(4) Regulations may amend subsection (3) so as to substitute a different period for the period for the time being specified there.

(5) Where a direction under this section is made in relation to a person, the direction also applies in relation to—
(a) any body corporate of which the person is a director or other officer,
(b) any body corporate of which the person is a member, if the affairs of the body corporate are managed by its members, and
(c) any Scottish firm of which the person is a partner.

(6) HMRC must—
(a) give a copy of a direction under this section to—
(i) the person or persons in relation to whom it applies, and
(ii) any person or body which provides childcare accounts, and
(b) publish the direction in the way appearing to HMRC to be best calculated to bring it to the attention of those who may be affected by it.

(7) HMRC may revoke a direction made under this section.

DEFINITIONS

"HMRC"—see s.71(1).
"qualifying childcare"—see s.71(1).

COMMENCEMENT

1.1008   All regulation making powers under the Act were brought into force on Royal Assent (December 17, 2014); see s.75(1)(c). The rest of this section was brought into force for the purposes of the trial on November 14, 2016 (see Childcare Payments Act 2014 (Commencement No.2) Regulations 2016 (SI 2016/1083) reg.2(g)).

Power to charge interest

1.1009   **51.**—(1) Where—
(a) an amount has been assessed under section 41 or 47 as payable to HMRC by a person under this Act, and
(b) some or all of the amount has not been paid to HMRC by the time specified in section 41(5) or 47(4) (as the case may be),

HMRC may give the person a notice in writing requiring the person to pay interest on the amount that has not been paid ("the relevant debt").

(2) If a notice is given to a person under this section, the relevant debt carries interest for a period which—
(a) begins with the late payment interest start date (which may be earlier than the day on which the notice is given), and
(b) ends with the specified day or, if earlier, the day on which the relevant debt is paid.

(3) "The late payment interest start date" means—

(a) in the case of an amount assessed under section 41, the day on which the person became liable to pay it;

(b) in the case of a penalty, the day after the last day of the period within which the penalty is required to be paid in accordance with section 47(4).

(4) "The specified day", in relation to a notice given to a person under this section, means—

(a) the day specified in the notice, or

(b) where on that day the relevant debt has not been paid, the day specified in a further notice given to the person by HMRC.

(5) The specified day must fall within the period of 6 months beginning with the day on which the notice is given.

(6) Interest under this section is payable at the late payment interest rate.

(7) The "late payment interest rate" is—

(a) the rate provided for in regulations made by the Treasury under section 103(1) of the Finance Act 2009, or

(b) if there is more than one such rate, the lowest such rate.

(8) Where two or more persons—

(a) have been notified of an assessment under section 41 in respect of the same amount, and

(b) have been given a notice under this section,

each of those persons is jointly and severally liable to pay interest on the relevant debt.

DEFINITIONS

"HMRC"—see s.71(1).
"late payment interest rate"—subs.(7).
"the late payment interest start date"—subs.(3).
"the relevant debt"—subs.(1).
"the specified day"—subs.(4).

COMMENCEMENT

This section was brought into force for the purposes of the trial on November 14, 2016 (see Childcare Payments Act 2014 (Commencement No.2) Regulations 2016 (SI 2016/1083) reg.2(g)).

Deduction of recoverable amounts from tax credit awards

52.—(1) This section applies where, as a result of a review of, or an appeal against, a tax credits decision—

(a) a person is required to pay an amount ("the relevant debt") to HMRC under section 35 or 36, and

(b) an amount of tax credit ("the award") is payable to the person or to the person and the person's partner jointly.

(2) The relevant debt may be deducted from the award before it is paid.

(3) The requirement to pay the relevant debt is discharged to the extent that it is deducted from the award under this section.

(4) In this section "tax credits decision" means a decision not to make an award of a tax credit or to terminate such an award.

(5) This section ceases to have effect when the repeal of Part 1 of the Tax Credits Act 2002 made by Schedule 14 to the Welfare Reform Act 2012 has fully come into force.

DEFINITIONS
"the award"—subs.(1)(b).
"HMRC"—see s.71(1).
"partner"—see s.71(1).
"the relevant debt"—subs.(1)(a).
"tax credit"—see s.71(1).
"tax credits decision"—subs.(4).

COMMENCEMENT

1.1012 This section was brought into force for the purposes of the trial on November 14, 2016 (see Childcare Payments Act 2014 (Commencement No.2) Regulations 2016 (SI 2016/1083) reg.2(g)).

Recovery of debts from childcare accounts

1.1013 53.—(1) This section applies where—
(a) an amount has been assessed under section 41 or 47 as payable to HMRC under this Act by a person who holds a childcare account in respect of a child,
(b) the assessment was made as a result of something done, or omitted to be done, in connection with that account or any other childcare account which the person has held in respect of the child, and
(c) some or all of the amount assessed ("the relevant debt") has not been paid to HMRC by the time specified in section 41(5) or 47(4) (as the case may be).

(2) HMRC may direct the account provider to pay a specified amount from the account to HMRC in order to discharge the whole or part of the relevant debt.

"Specified" means specified in the direction.

(3) The account provider must comply with a direction given under this section.

(4) Subsections (5) to (8) apply in a case where the relevant debt consists of an amount of recoverable top-up payments.

In this section an "amount of recoverable top-up payments" means an amount which a person is liable to pay HMRC under any of sections 35 to 39 or section 40(1) (recovery of top-up payments).

(5) HMRC may make a direction under this section only if the childcare account is not active at the time of the direction (see section 17(3)).

(6) Where the account provider makes a payment to HMRC in accordance with the direction, the account provider must make a payment from the childcare account to the account-holder of the appropriate qualifying amount.

(7) "The appropriate qualifying amount", in relation to a direction under this section, is the amount which, if paid into a childcare account, would entitle the account-holder to a top-up payment equal to—
(a) the amount specified in the direction, or
(b) if that amount is greater than the top-up element of the funds held in the account, the top-up element of those funds.

(For provision about calculating the top-up element of funds held in an account, see section 21.)

(8) If the amount specified in the direction is greater than the top-up element of the funds, the difference is to be deducted from the appropriate

qualifying amount by the account provider and paid to HMRC in accordance with the direction.

(9) Subsections (10) to (13) apply in a case where the relevant debt consists of any amount other than an amount of recoverable top-up payments.

(10) HMRC may not specify in the direction an amount which is greater than the relevant percentage of the funds held in the account.

(11) The "relevant percentage" is the percentage given by—

$$\frac{100}{100 + R} \times 100$$

where R is the percentage for the time being specified in section 1(4).

(12) Where the account provider makes a payment to HMRC in accordance with the direction, the account provider must make a payment from the childcare account to HMRC of the corresponding top-up amount.

(13) "The corresponding top-up amount", in relation to a payment made in accordance with a direction under this section, is R% of the amount of the payment, where R is the percentage for the time being specified in section 1(4).

(14) If a direction is made under this section both in respect of an amount of recoverable top-up payments and in respect of any other amount—
  (a) any amount payable to HMRC in accordance with the direction made in respect of that other amount is to be set off against the amount payable to the account-holder by virtue of subsection (6), and
  (b) any amount payable to HMRC by virtue of subsection (12) is to be set off against the amount payable to HMRC in accordance with the direction made in respect of the amount of recoverable top-up payments.

(15) If the Commissioners provide childcare accounts, a direction under this section may not be made in respect of any fees charged in connection with a childcare account in accordance with section 15(8).

(16) This section does not affect any other power of HMRC to recover amounts that are due and payable to HMRC.

DEFINITIONS

"account-holder"—see s.71(1).
"account provider"—see s.71(1).
"amount of recoverable top-up payments"—subs.(4).
"the appropriate qualifying amount"—subs.(7).
"the Commissioners"—see s.71(1).
"the corresponding top-up amount"—subs.(13).
"HMRC"—see s.71(1).
"the relevant debt"—subs.(1)(c).
"relevant percentage"—subs.(11).
"specified"—subs.(3).
"top-up element"—s.71(1).
"top-up payment"—s.71(1).

COMMENCEMENT

This section was brought into force for the purposes of the trial on November 14, 2016 (see Childcare Payments Act 2014 (Commencement No.2) Regulations 2016 (SI 2016/1083) reg.2(g)).

Set-off

1.1015   **54.**—(1) This section applies where—
(a) an amount ("the relevant debt") is due and payable to HMRC under this Act by a person who holds a childcare account in respect of a child,
(b) the childcare account is not active (see section 17(3)), and
(c) the relevant debt consists of an amount which the person is liable to pay HMRC under any of sections 35 to 39 or section 40(1) (recovery of top-up payments) as a result of something done, or omitted to be done, in connection with that account or any other childcare account which the person has held in respect of the child.

(2) If the account-holder makes a withdrawal from the childcare account, the amount payable to HMRC under section 22 (the "corresponding top-up amount" of the withdrawal) is to be set off against the relevant debt.

(3) In a case where the whole or part of the corresponding top-up amount of a withdrawal ("the set-off amount") is set off against the relevant debt, so much of the withdrawal as generated the set-off amount is to be ignored for the purposes of section 19(8).

DEFINITIONS

"account-holder"—see s.71(1).
"corresponding top-up amount"—subs.(2).
"HMRC"—see s.71(1).
"the relevant debt"—subs.(1)(a).
"the set-off amount"—subs.(3).

COMMENCEMENT

1.1016   This section was brought into force for the purposes of the trial on November 14, 2016 (see Childcare Payments Act 2014 (Commencement No.2) Regulations 2016 (SI 2016/1083) reg.2(g)).

Order in which payments are taken to discharge debts

1.1017   **55.**—(1) This section applies where an amount (a "relevant debt") is due and payable to HMRC under this Act by a person.

(2) For the purposes of this section—
(a) a relevant debt is within this paragraph if it consists of a penalty or other amount not falling with paragraph (b) or (c),
(b) a relevant debt is within this paragraph if it consists of an amount of recoverable top-up payments, and
(c) a relevant debt is within this paragraph if it consists of an amount of interest payable under section 51.

(3) In determining whether a relevant debt is an amount of recoverable top-up payments for the purposes of section 53 or 54, any amount paid to HMRC by the person in the discharge of a relevant debt is to be taken to have discharged a relevant debt within paragraph (b) of subsection (2) only if any relevant debt within paragraph (a) of that subsection has been discharged.

(4) Any amount paid to HMRC by the person in the discharge of a relevant debt is to be taken to have discharged any relevant debt within

paragraph (c) of subsection (2) only if any relevant debt within paragraph (a) or (b) of that subsection has been discharged.

(5) Any amount paid to HMRC in accordance with a direction under section 53 made in respect of a relevant debt within paragraph (b) or (c) of subsection (2) is to be taken to have discharged any relevant debt within paragraph (c) only if any relevant debt within paragraph (b) has been discharged.

(6) In this section an "amount of recoverable top-up payments" means an amount which a person is liable to pay HMRC under any of sections 35 to 39 or section 40(1) (recovery of top-up payments).

DEFINITIONS

"amount of recoverable top-up payments"—subs.(6).
"HMRC"—see s.71(1).
"relevant debt"—subs.(1).
"top-up payment"—s.71(1).

COMMENCEMENT

This section was brought into force for the purposes of the trial on November 14, 2016 (see Childcare Payments Act 2014 (Commencement No.2) Regulations 2016 (SI 2016/1083) reg.2(g)).

Reviews and appeals

Appealable decisions

56.—(1) A person who is affected by an appealable decision (see subsection (3)) may appeal against the decision.

(2) But a person may not appeal against any decision unless—
(a) the person has applied under section 57 for a review of the decision, and
(b) either—
 (i) the person has been notified of the conclusion on the review, or
 (ii) the person has not been notified of the conclusion on the review and the period for notifying the person of that conclusion has ended.

(3) The following decisions are "appealable decisions"—
(a) a decision not to open a childcare account;
(b) a decision that a declaration of eligibility is not valid;
(c) a decision as to whether or not to make or revoke an account restriction order under section 24;
(d) a decision to give a person a notice under section 26;
(e) a decision to give a person a disqualification notice under section 34;
(f) a decision to make an assessment, or to make an assessment of a particular amount, under section 41;
(g) a decision to assess a penalty, or to assess a penalty of a particular amount, under section 47;
(h) a decision to make a disqualification order under section 49;
(i) a decision to make a direction under section 50;
(j) a decision to give a person a notice under section 51;
(k) a decision to give a direction under section 53.

(4) Where a person is notified of an appealable decision under this Act, the notification must include details of the person's right to apply for a review of the decision and to appeal against the decision.

(5) The effect of an appealable decision falling within paragraph (d), (f), (g), (j) or (k) of subsection (3) is suspended by—
  (a) the making of an application for a review of the decision, or
  (b) the making of an appeal against the decision.

(6) The effect of any other appealable decision is not suspended by the making of such an application or appeal.

DEFINITIONS

"appealable decisions"—subs.(3).
"declaration of eligibility"—see s.71(1).

COMMENCEMENT

1.1020   This section was brought into force for the purposes of the trial on November 14, 2016 (see Childcare Payments Act 2014 (Commencement No.2) Regulations 2016 (SI 2016/1083) reg.2(g)).

Review of decisions

1.1021   **57.**—(1) A person who is affected by an appealable decision ("the applicant") may apply to the Commissioners for Her Majesty's Revenue and Customs for a review of the decision.

(2) The application must be made—
  (a) within the period of 30 days beginning with the day on which the applicant was notified of the decision, or
  (b) if the period for making the application has been extended under section 58, within the extended period.

(3) The application must—
  (a) be made in writing,
  (b) contain sufficient information to identify the applicant and the decision, and
  (c) set out the reasons for seeking a review of the decision.

[¹ (3A) Regulations may make provision specifying, or enabling HMRC to specify, the form and manner in which the application may be made (subject to subsection (3)(a)).]

(4) If an application for a review of a decision is made to the Commissioners in accordance with this section [¹ (and any provision made under subsection (3A))], the Commissioners must review the decision.

(5) On a review under this section, the Commissioners may—
  (a) uphold the decision,
  (b) vary the decision, or
  (c) cancel the decision.

(6) If the applicant makes any representations to the Commissioners at a stage which gives the Commissioners a reasonable opportunity to consider them, the Commissioners must take account of them when carrying out the review.

(7) Where—
  (a) the Commissioners notify the applicant of further information or evidence which they may need for carrying out the review, and

(b) the information or evidence is not provided to them within the period of 15 days beginning with the day on which the notice is given,

the review may proceed without that information or evidence.

(8) The Commissioners must notify the applicant of the matters set out in subsection (9) within—
   (a) the period of 30 days beginning with the day on which the Commissioners received the application for the review,
   (b) if the applicant has been given a notice under subsection (7), the period of 45 days beginning with that day, or
   (c) such other period as the applicant and the Commissioners may agree.

(9) The matters referred to in subsection (8) are—
   (a) the conclusion on the review,
   (b) if the conclusion is that the decision is varied, details of the variation, and
   (c) the reasons for the conclusion.

(10) If the Commissioners do not comply with subsection (8), the review is to be treated as having concluded that the decision is upheld.

In such a case, the Commissioners must notify the applicant of that conclusion.

AMENDMENT

1. Small Charitable Donations and Childcare Payments Act 2017 s.5(3) (March 16, 2017).

DEFINITIONS

"appealable decision"—see s.71(1).
"the applicant"—subs.(1).
"the Commissioners"—see s.71(1).

COMMENCEMENT

This section was brought into force for the purposes of the trial on November 14, 2016 (see Childcare Payments Act 2014 (Commencement No.2) Regulations 2016 (SI 2016/1083) reg.2(g)).

Extension of time limit for applications for review

58.—(1) A person who wishes to make an application for a review under section 57 may apply to the Commissioners for an extension of the period for making the application.

(2) An application under this section—
   (a) must be made before the end of the period of 6 months beginning with the day after the last day of the period mentioned in section 57(2)(a) ("the standard period"), and
   (b) must set out the reasons for seeking the extension.

[¹ (2A) Regulations may make provision specifying, or enabling HMRC to specify, the form and manner in which an application under this section may be made.]

(3) The Commissioners may grant an extension under this section if they are satisfied that—
   (a) due to special circumstances, it was not practicable for the person to make the application under section 57 within the standard period, and

(b) it is reasonable in all the circumstances to grant the extension.

(4) If an application under this section is refused, it may not be renewed.

DEFINITIONS

"the Commissioners"—see s.71(1).
"the standard period"—subs.(2)(a).

AMENDMENT

1. Small Charitable Donations and Childcare Payments Act 2017 s.5(4) (March 16, 2017).

COMMENCEMENT

1.1024 This section was brought into force for the purposes of the trial on November 14, 2016 (see Childcare Payments Act 2014 (Commencement No.2) Regulations 2016 (SI 2016/1083) reg.2(g)).

Exercise of right of appeal

1.1025 **59.**—(1) An appeal under section 56 is to the appropriate tribunal.

(2) "The appropriate tribunal" means—
   (a) the First-tier Tribunal, or
   (b) in Northern Ireland, the appeal tribunal.

(3) "Appeal tribunal" means an appeal tribunal constituted under Chapter 1 of Part 2 of the Social Security (Northern Ireland) Order 1998 (S.I. 1998/1506 (N.I. 10)).

(4) Regulations may provide for any provision contained in or made under the following legislation to apply in relation to appeals under section 56, with such modifications as may be specified in regulations—
   (a) Chapter 2 of Part 1 of the Social Security Act 1998 (social security appeals: Great Britain);
   (b) Chapter 2 of Part 2 of the Social Security (Northern Ireland) Order 1998 (social security appeals: Northern Ireland);
   (c) section 54 of the Taxes Management Act 1970 (settling of appeals by agreement).

DEFINITIONS

"appeal tribunal"—subs.(3).
"the appropriate tribunal"—subs.(2).

COMMENCEMENT

1.1026 All regulation making powers under the Act were brought into force on Royal Assent (December 17, 2014); see s.75(1)(c). The rest of this section was brought into force for the purposes of the trial on November 14, 2016 (see Childcare Payments Act 2014 (Commencement No.2) Regulations 2016 (SI 2016/1083) reg.2(g)).

Powers of tribunal

1.1027 **60.**—(1) This section applies where a person is appealing to the Tribunal under section 56 against an appealable decision.

(2) In a case where the appealable decision is a decision under section 47 to assess a penalty, or to assess a penalty of a particular amount, the Tribunal may do any of the following—

(a) uphold the penalty;
(b) set aside the penalty;
(c) substitute for the penalty a penalty of an amount decided by the Tribunal.

(3) In any other case, the Tribunal must either—
(a) dismiss the appeal, or
(b) quash the whole or part of the decision to which the appeal relates.

(4) The Tribunal may act as mentioned in subsection (3)(b) only to the extent that it is satisfied that the decision was wrong on one or more of the following grounds—
(a) that the decision was based, wholly or partly, on an error of fact;
(b) that the decision was wrong in law.

(5) If the Tribunal quashes the whole or part of a decision, it may either—
(a) refer the matter back to HMRC with a direction to reconsider and make a new decision in accordance with its ruling, or
(b) substitute its own decision for that of HMRC.

This is subject to section 61(8).

(6) The Tribunal may not direct HMRC to take any action which they would not otherwise have the power to take in relation to the decision.

(7) A decision of the Tribunal made by virtue of this section has the same effect as, and may be enforced in the same manner as, a decision of HMRC.

(8) In this section "the Tribunal" means—
(a) the First-tier Tribunal, or
(b) in Northern Ireland, the appeal tribunal (within the meaning of section 59(3)).

DEFINITIONS

"appealable decision"—see s.71(1).
"HMRC"—see s.71(1).
"the Tribunal"—subs.(8).

COMMENCEMENT

This section was brought into force for the purposes of the trial on November 14, 2016 (see Childcare Payments Act 2014 (Commencement No.2) Regulations 2016 (SI 2016/1083) reg.2(g)).

Cases where there is more than one eligible person

61.—(1) This section applies in the following cases.

(2) The first case is where—
(a) two or more persons ("the applicants") have applied to open a childcare account in respect of the same child, and
(b) any of the applicants is appealing against a decision not to allow the applicant to open a childcare account in respect of the child.

(3) The second case is where—
(a) one or more persons ("the applicants") have applied to open a childcare account in respect of a child,
(b) another person ("the existing account-holder") holds a childcare account in respect of the child, and
(c) any of the applicants is appealing against a decision not to allow the applicant to open a childcare account in respect of the child.

(4) The third case is where—

(a) a person is appealing against a decision not to make an account restriction order in relation to another person, or
(b) a person is appealing against a decision to make an account restriction order in relation to the person so as to enable another person to open a childcare account or make a declaration of eligibility in relation to such an account.

(5) In this section "the affected parties" means—
(a) in the case described in subsection (2), the applicants;
(b) in the case described in subsection (3), the applicants and the existing account-holder;
(c) in the case described in subsection (4), each of the persons mentioned in paragraph (a) or (b) of that subsection (as the case may be).

(6) Notice of the appeal must be given to each of the affected parties (other than the person bringing the appeal).

(7) Each of the affected parties is to be treated as a party to the appeal.

(8) If the Tribunal quashes the whole or part of the decision, it must substitute its own decision for that of HMRC.

(9) A decision of the Tribunal made by virtue of this section has the same effect as, and may be enforced in the same manner as, a decision of HMRC.

(10) In this section "the Tribunal" has the same meaning as in section 60.

DEFINITIONS

"account-holder"—see s.71(1).
"the affected parties"—subs.(3)(b).
"the applicants"—subss.(2)(a) and (3)(a).
"declaration of eligibility"—see s.71(1).
"the existing account holder""—subs.(3)(b).
"HMRC"—see s.71(1).
"the Tribunal"—subs.(10).

COMMENCEMENT

This section was brought into force for the purposes of the trial on November 14, 2016 (see Childcare Payments Act 2014 (Commencement No.2) Regulations 2016 (SI 2016/1083) reg.2(g)).

Compensatory payments

Compensatory payments

62.—(1) Where a person has in circumstances specified in regulations been deprived of the opportunity to receive top-up payments in respect of a child for a period, HMRC must pay the person an amount equal to 20% of the costs incurred on qualifying childcare in respect of the child during the period.

(2) But the amount paid to a person by HMRC under this section for a period may not exceed a maximum amount specified in, or determined in accordance with, regulations.

(3) The circumstances that may be specified in regulations under this section include, in particular—
(a) where an appealable decision is varied or cancelled on a review under section 57, and

(b) where an appealable decision is quashed (whether wholly or partly) under section 60.

(4) Payments may be made to a person under this section regardless of whether the person—
(a) has opened a childcare account, or
(b) has made a valid declaration of eligibility.

(5) Regulations may make further provision about making payments under this section.

(6) Regulations may substitute a different percentage for the percentage for the time being specified in subsection (1).

DEFINITIONS

"appealable decision"—see s.71(1).
"declaration of eligibility"—see s.71(1).
"qualifying childcare"—see s.71(1).
"top-up payment"—s.71(1).
"valid declaration of eligibility"—see s.71(2).

COMMENCEMENT

All regulation making powers under the Act were brought into force on Royal Assent (December 17, 2014); see s.75(1)(c). The rest of this section was brought into force for the purposes of the trial on November 14, 2016 (see Childcare Payments Act 2014 (Commencement No.2) Regulations 2016 (SI 2016/1083) reg.2(g)).

Withdrawal of existing tax exemptions

Restrictions on claiming tax exemption for childcare vouchers

63.—(1) Section 270A of ITEPA 2003 (limited exemption from income tax for qualifying childcare vouchers) is amended as follows.
(2) In subsection (1)—
(a) before "employee" insert "eligible", and
(b) at the end insert—
"For the meaning of "eligible employee", see section 270AA."
(3) In subsection (5)(a), before "employees" insert "eligible".
(4) After section 270A of ITEPA 2003 insert—

"270AA Meaning of 'eligible employee'
(1) An employee is an eligible employee for the purposes of section 270A if conditions A to C are met in relation to the employee.
(2) Condition A is that the employee—
   (a) was employed by the employer immediately before the relevant day, and
   (b) has not ceased to be employed by the employer on or after that day.
(3) "The relevant day" means the day specified by the Treasury in regulations for the purposes of this section.
(4) Condition B is that there has not been a period of 52 tax weeks ending on or after the relevant day which has not included at least one qualifying week.
(5) In subsection (4)—
   "qualifying week" means a tax week in respect of which a qualifying childcare voucher has been provided for the employee under the scheme by the employer in respect of a child, and
   "tax week" has the meaning given by section 270A(7).

(6) Condition C is that the employee has not given the employer a childcare account notice.

(7) A "childcare account notice" is a written notice informing the employer that the employee wishes to leave the scheme in order to be able to open a childcare account under section 17 of the Childcare Payments Act 2014 or enable the employee's partner to do so.

(8) In subsection (7) "partner" is to be read in accordance with regulations made under section 3(5) of that Act."

(5) In section 717 of ITEPA 2003 (orders and regulations), in subsection (4), after "employments)," insert "section 270AA(3) (exemption from income tax for qualifying childcare vouchers: meaning of "eligible employee")".

Restrictions on claiming tax exemption for employer-contracted childcare

64.—(1) Section 318A of ITEPA 2003 (childcare: limited exemption from income tax for other care) is amended as follows.

(2) In subsection (1)—
  (a) before "employee" insert "eligible", and
  (b) after "For" insert "the meaning of "eligible employee", see section 318AZA, and for".

(3) In subsection (5)(a), before "employees" insert "eligible".

(4) After section 318A of ITEPA 2003 insert—

"318AZA Meaning of "eligible employee"
(1) An employee is an eligible employee for the purposes of section 318A if conditions A to C are met in relation to the employee.
(2) Condition A is that the employee—
  (a) was employed by the employer immediately before the relevant day, and
  (b) has not ceased to be employed by the employer on or after that day.
(3) "The relevant day" means the day specified by the Treasury in regulations for the purposes of this section.
(4) Condition B is that there has not been a period of 52 tax weeks ending on or after the relevant day which has not included at least one qualifying week.
(5) In subsection (4)—
  "qualifying week" means a tax week in which care for a child has been provided for the employee under the scheme by the employer in circumstances in which conditions A to D in section 318A are met, and
  "tax week" has the meaning given by section 318A(7).
(6) Condition C is that the employee has not given the employer a childcare account notice.
(7) A "childcare account notice" is a written notice informing the employer that the employee wishes to leave the scheme in order to be able to open a childcare account under section 17 of the Childcare Payments Act 2014 or enable the employee's partner to do so.
(8) In subsection (7) "partner" is to be read in accordance with regulations made under section 3(5) of that Act.
(9) For the meaning of "care" and "child", see section 318B."

(5) In section 318B of ITEPA 2003 (childcare: meaning of "care", "child" etc), in subsection (1), for "318 and 318A" substitute "318 to 318AZA".

(6) In section 717 of ITEPA 2003 (orders and regulations), in subsection (4), before "section 343(3)" insert "section 318AZA(3) (exemption from income tax for other care: meaning of "eligible employee"),".

(2014 c.28 s.65)

General

Functions of Commissioners for Revenue and Customs

65.—The matters dealt with by and under this Act are to be under the management of the Commissioners for Her Majesty's Revenue and Customs.

COMMENCEMENT

This section came into force on Royal Assent (December 17, 2014); see s.75(1)(a).

Tax treatment of top-up payments

66.—A top-up payment made into a childcare account is not to be regarded as income of the account-holder for the purposes of the Income Tax Acts.

DEFINITIONS

"account-holder"—see s.71(1).
"top-up payment"—s.71(1).

COMMENCEMENT

This section was brought into force for the purposes of the trial on November 14, 2016 (see Childcare Payments Act 2014 (Commencement No.2) Regulations 2016 (SI 2016/1083) reg.2(gh)).

Set-off against tax liabilities etc

67.—The following payments are not to be regarded as a credit for the purposes of section 130 of the Finance Act 2008 (set-off)—
  (a) top-up payments;
  (b) payments under section 62 (compensatory payments);
  (c) where the Commissioners provide childcare accounts, any funds held in a childcare account.

DEFINITIONS

"the Commissioners"—see s.71(1).
"top-up payment"—s.71(1).

COMMENCEMENT

This section was brought into force for the purposes of the trial on November 14, 2016 (see Childcare Payments Act 2014 (Commencement No.2) Regulations 2016 (SI 2016/1083) reg.2(h)).

Northern Ireland

68.—In Schedule 2 to the Northern Ireland Act 1998 (excepted matters), after paragraph 10B insert—
  "10C The operation of the Childcare Payments Act 2014."

COMMENCEMENT

This section came into force on Royal Assent (December 17, 2014); see s.75(1)(a).

Childcare Payments Act 2014

Final provisions

Regulations: general

69.—(1) Any power to make regulations under this Act is exercisable by statutory instrument.

(2) Any power to make regulations under the following provisions of this Act is exercisable by the Treasury—
  (a) section 1(5) (power to amend rate of top-up payment);
  (b) section 2(3)(b) to (d) (qualifying childcare);
  (c) sections 3, 7 to 11 and 13 (eligibility);
  (d) section 5(2) (power to alter length of entitlement period);
  (e) section 14 (qualifying child);
  (f) section 19(7) (power to amend the relevant maximum);
  (g) section 30 (termination of tax credit awards);
  (h) section 31 (power to provide for automatic termination of universal credit);
  (i) sections 32 and 33 (disqualification of tax credit or universal credit claimants from obtaining top-up payments);
  (j) sections 43(5), 44(6) and 46(5) (powers to vary certain penalties);
  (k) section 50(4) (power to alter period for which directions under section 50 have effect);
  (l) section 62(6) (power to amend rate of compensatory payments);
  (m) section 72 (power to make consequential amendments);
  (n) section 75 (commencement).

(3) Any power to make regulations under a provision of this Act that is not mentioned in subsection (2) is exercisable by the Commissioners for Her Majesty's Revenue and Customs.

(4) Regulations under this Act may—
  (a) make different provision for different purposes or in relation to different areas,
  (b) contain incidental, supplemental, consequential or transitional provision or savings, and
  (c) provide for a person to exercise a discretion in dealing with any matter.

(5) Subsection (4) does not apply to regulations under section 75 (see instead subsection (3) of that section).

COMMENCEMENT

This section came into force on Royal Assent (December 17, 2014); see s.75(1)(b).

Regulations: Parliamentary control

70.—(1) A statutory instrument containing regulations under this Act is subject to annulment in pursuance of a resolution of either House of Parliament, unless the instrument—
  (a) is required by subsection (3) or any other enactment to be laid in draft before, and approved by a resolution of, each House, or
  (b) contains only regulations under section 75.

(2) Subsection (3) applies to a statutory instrument that contains (with or without other provisions)—

(a) regulations under section 1(5);
(b) regulations under section 2(3)(b), (c) or (d);
(c) the first regulations under each of sections 3 and 7 to 10;
(d) regulations under section 5(2);
(e) the first regulations under section 14;
(f) regulations under section 19(7) which substitute a lower amount for any amount for the time being specified in section 19(5);
(g) regulations under section 31;
(h) the first regulations under each of sections 32(5) and 33(5);
(i) regulations under section 32(6) or 33(6);
(j) regulations under section 43(5), 44(6) or 46(5);
(k) regulations under section 50(4);
(l) regulations under section 62(6);
(m) regulations under section 72.

(3) A statutory instrument to which this subsection applies may not be made unless a draft of the instrument has been laid before, and approved by a resolution of, each House of Parliament.

DEFINITION

"enactment"—see s.71(1).

COMMENCEMENT

This section came into force on Royal Assent (December 17, 2014); see s.75(1)(b).

Interpretation

71.—(1) In this Act—
"account-holder" has the meaning given by section 15(10);
"account provider" has the meaning given by section 15(10);
"appealable decision" has the meaning given by section 56(3);
"childcare" has the meaning given by section 2(1);
"childcare account" has the meaning given by section 15;
"the Commissioners" means the Commissioners for Her Majesty's Revenue and
Customs;
"declaration of eligibility" has the meaning given by section 4;
"enactment" includes—
(a) an enactment contained in subordinate legislation,
(b) an enactment contained in, or in an instrument made under, an Act of the Scottish Parliament,
(c) an enactment contained in, or in an instrument made under, a Measure or Act of the National Assembly for Wales, and
(d) an enactment contained in, or in an instrument made under, Northern Ireland legislation;
"entitlement period" means a period determined in accordance with section 5;
"HMRC" means Her Majesty's Revenue and Customs;
"ITEPA 2003" means the Income Tax (Earnings and Pensions) Act 2003;
"partner" is to be read in accordance with regulations made under section 3(5);
"permitted payment" has the meaning given by section 20(3);
"prohibited payment" has the meaning given by section 20(4);

"qualifying child" has the meaning given by section 14;
"qualifying childcare" has the meaning given by section 2(2);
"qualifying payment" has the meaning given by section 19;
"tax credit" has the same meaning as in the Tax Credits Act 2002;
"top-up element", in relation to an amount, has the meaning given by section 21;
"top-up payment" is to be read in accordance with section 1;
"universal credit" means universal credit payable under—
(a) Part 1 of the Welfare Reform Act 2012, or
(b) any provision made for Northern Ireland which corresponds to that Part of that Act.
(2) In this Act—
(a) references to a valid declaration of eligibility are to be read in accordance with section 4(2), and
(b) references to an active childcare account are to be read in accordance with section 17(3).

COMMENCEMENT

1.1048   This section came into force on Royal Assent (December 17, 2014); see s.75(1)(b).

Power to make consequential amendments

1.1049   72.—(1) Regulations may make such provision amending, repealing, revoking or applying with modifications any enactment to which this section applies as the Treasury consider necessary or expedient in consequence of any provision made by or under this Act.
(2) This section applies to—
(a) any enactment passed or made before the passing of this Act, and
(b any enactment passed or made on or before the last day of the Session in which this Act is passed.

DEFINITION

"enactment"—see s.71(1).

COMMENCEMENT

1.1050   This section came into force on Royal Assent (December 17, 2014); see s.75(1)(b).

Financial provisions

1.1051   73.—(1) There is to be paid out of money provided by Parliament any increase attributable to this Act in the sums payable under any other Act out of money so provided.
(2) Subsections (3) and (4) apply if childcare accounts are provided by the Commissioners or the Director of Savings ("the relevant account provider").
(3) Sums paid into childcare accounts are not to be paid into the Consolidated Fund.
(4) Sums payable from childcare accounts are not to be regarded as expenditure of the relevant account provider.

(2014 c.28 s.73)

DEFINITIONS

"the Commissioners"—see s.71(1).
"the relevant account provider"—subs.(2).

COMMENCEMENT

Subsection (1) came into force on Royal Assent (December 17, 2014); see s.75(1)(b). The rest of this section was brought into force for the purposes of the trial on November 14, 2016 (see Childcare Payments Act 2014 (Commencement No.2) Regulations 2016 (SI 2016/1083) reg.2(i)).

Extent

74.—(1) Except as provided by subsection (2), this Act extends to England and Wales, Scotland and Northern Ireland.
(2) Any amendment or repeal made by this Act has the same extent as the provision amended or repealed.

COMMENCEMENT

This section came into force on Royal Assent (December 17, 2014); see s.75(1)(b).

Commencement and short title

75.—(1) The following provisions of this Act come into force on the day on which this Act is passed—
(a) sections 65 and 68;
(b) sections 69 to 72, 73(1), 74 and this section;
(c) any power to make regulations under this Act.
(2) The remaining provisions of this Act come into force in accordance with provision contained in regulations.
(3) Regulations under subsection (2) may—
(a) make different provision for different purposes or in relation to different areas;
(b) make such transitory or transitional provision, or savings, as the Treasury consider necessary or expedient, including (in particular) such adaptations of provisions of this Act brought into force as appear to be necessary or expedient in consequence of other provisions of this Act not yet having come into force.

COMMENCEMENT

This section came into force on Royal Assent (December 17, 2014); see s.75(1)(b).

Childcare Act 2016

(2016 CH 5)

An Act to make provision about free childcare for young children of working parents and about the publication of information about childcare and related matters by local authorities in England.

Childcare Act 2016

[16TH MARCH 2016]

ARRANGEMENT OF SECTIONS

Availability of free childcare

1. Duty to secure 30 hours free childcare available for working parents
2. Discharging the section 1(1) duty
3. Sections 1 and 2: consequential amendments
4. Supplementary provision about regulations under sections 1 and 2

Publication of information

5. Duty to publish information about childcare and related matters

General

6. Extent
7. Commencement
8. Short title

GENERAL NOTE

1.1056 There is a confusing patchwork of Government support for childcare. In part, this support takes the form of the longstanding arrangements for the childcare element in working tax credit (and now universal credit) as well as childcare vouchers for employer-supported childcare. In addition, two more ambitious schemes have been launched which have a wider reach.

The first is Tax-Free Childcare (TFC), established by the Childcare Payments Act 2014, a scheme assisting towards the costs of childcare for working families. Roll-out of the TFC scheme was completed in February 2018. Typically, the scheme operates through an online account which claimants can pay into to cover the cost of childcare for qualifying children with a registered provider. TFC is a UK wide scheme covering England, Scotland, Wales and Northern Ireland.

The second is a separate Government scheme providing for free childcare, as extended by the Childcare Act 2016. Notably, the Childcare Act 2016 s.1 places a duty on the Secretary of State to secure the availability of 30 hours of free childcare for qualifying children of working parents. These free childcare arrangements are different for each of the four nations of the UK. For example, in England, all three and four year olds can have 570 hours of free early education or childcare per year (around 15 hours a week over 38 weeks). In addition, families in paid work may be able to claim an additional 15 hours a week free childcare; hence, the scheme became known as the 30 Hours Free Childcare scheme. The details were originally governed by the Childcare (Early Years Provisions Free of Charge) (Extended Entitlement) Regulations 2016 (SI 2016/1257) (as amended). However, with effect from December 1, 2022, those Regulations were (for the most part) replaced by the Childcare (Free of Charge for Working Parents) (England) Regulations 2022 (SI 2022/1134). Furthermore, and following the extension of the scheme to include 15 hours free childcare for children aged from nine months to two years old (see the Childcare (Free of Charge for Working Parents) (England) (Amendment and Transitional Provision) Regulations 2023 (SI 2023/1330)), the 30 hour scheme is now known as the Free Childcare for Working Parents (or FCWP).

Although claims for the TFC scheme under the 2014 Act and for free childcare under the 2016 Act are made through the same online process, the appellate arrangements differed at the outset. The First-tier Tribunal (Social Entitlement Chamber) has had jurisdiction to decide appeals relating to appealable decisions within the meaning of s.56(3) of the Childcare Payments Act 2014 since October 1, 2015 (see art.6(ea) of the First-tier Tribunal and Upper Tribunal (Chambers) Order 2010 (SI 2010/2655) as inserted by art.2(3) of the First-tier Tribunal and Upper Tribunal (Chambers) (Amendment) Order 2015 (SI 2015/1563)). However, appeals under the 2016 Act initially went to the Tax Chamber (see art.7 of the 2010 Order). They were only brought within the jurisdiction of the Social Entitlement Chamber with effect from March 6, 2020 – see art.6(eb) of the 2010 Order as amended by art.2(2) of the First-tier Tribunal and Upper Tribunal (Chambers) (Amendment) Order 2020 (SI 2020/137).

AVAILABILITY OF FREE CHILDCARE

Duty to secure 30 hours free childcare available for working parents

1.—(1) The Secretary of State must secure that childcare is available free of charge for qualifying children of working parents for, or for a period equivalent to, 30 hours in each of 38 weeks in any year.

(2) "Qualifying child of working parents" means a young child—
(a) who is under compulsory school age,
(b) who is in England,
(c) who is of a description specified in regulations made by the Secretary of State,
(d) in respect of whom any conditions relating to a parent of the child, or a partner of a parent of the child, which are specified in such regulations, are met, and
(e) in respect of whom a declaration has been made, in accordance with such regulations, to the effect that the requirements of paragraphs (a) to (d) are satisfied.

(3) The conditions mentioned in subsection (2)(d) may, in particular, relate to the paid work undertaken by a parent or partner.

(4) For the purposes of subsections (2) and (3), the Secretary of State may by regulations—
(a) make provision about when a person is, or is not, to be regarded as another person's partner;
(b) make provision as to what is, or is not, paid work;
(c) specify circumstances in which a person is, or is not, to be regarded as in such work;
(d) make provision about—
  (i) the form of a declaration and the manner in which it is to be made;
  (ii) the conditions to be met by the person making a declaration;
  (iii) the period for which a declaration has effect.

(5) For the purposes of assisting the Secretary of State in the discharge of the duty imposed by subsection (1), the Commissioners for Her Majesty's Revenue and Customs may carry out functions in connection with the making of determinations as to whether a child is a qualifying child of working parents.

Childcare Act 2016

(6) In determining, for the purposes of subsection (1), the amount of childcare that is available—
(a) account is to be taken of any childcare available under the duty imposed by section 7(1) of the Childcare Act 2006 (duty of English local authorities to secure early years provision free of charge in accordance with regulations), but
(b) no account is to be taken of childcare available otherwise than by virtue of that duty or the duty imposed by subsection (1).

(7) The Secretary of State must set out in regulations when a year begins for the purposes of determining in relation to a child whether the duty in subsection (1) has been discharged.

(8) The Secretary of State may by regulations make provision about the circumstances in which a child is, or is not, in England for the purposes of this section.

(9) In this section—
"childcare" has the meaning given by section 18 of the Childcare Act 2006;
"parent", in relation to a child, includes any individual who—
(a) has parental responsibility for the child, or
(b) has care of the child;
"parental responsibility" has the same meaning as in the Children Act 1989;
"young child": a child is a "young child" during the period—
(a) beginning with the child's birth, and
(b) ending immediately before the 1 September next following the date on which the child attains the age of 5.

Discharging the section 1(1) duty

1.1058   2.—The Secretary of State may make regulations for the purpose of discharging the duty imposed by section 1(1) ("extended entitlement regulations").

(2) Extended entitlement regulations may (amongst other things)—
(a) require an English local authority to secure that childcare of such a description as may be specified is made available free of charge for children in their area who are qualifying children of working parents;
(b) make provision about how much childcare is to be so made available for each child, and about the times at which, and periods over which, that childcare is to be made available;
(c) make provision about the terms of any arrangements made between English local authorities and providers or arrangers of childcare for the purposes of meeting any requirement imposed under paragraph (a) or (b);
(d) impose obligations or confer powers on the Commissioners for Her Majesty's Revenue and Customs;
(e) make provision requiring information or documents to be provided by a person to the Secretary of State, the Commissioners for Her Majesty's Revenue and Customs or an English local authority;
(f) make provision for the purpose of enabling any person to check whether a child is a qualifying child of working parents;
(g) for that purpose, make provision about the disclosure of information held by a Minister of the Crown, the Commissioners for Her Majesty's Revenue and Customs or an English local authority;

(h) create criminal offences in connection with the onward disclosure of information obtained under paragraph (g) where that information relates to a particular person and is not disclosed in a way authorised by or specified in the regulations;
(i) make provision for reviews of, or appeals to the First-tier Tribunal against, determinations relating to a child's eligibility for childcare under section 1;
(j) make provision for a person specified in the regulations to impose financial penalties on persons in connection with—
(i) false or misleading information provided, or statements made or provided, in connection with a determination of a child's eligibility for childcare under section 1, or
(ii) dishonest conduct in connection with the process of making such a determination;
(k) require English local authorities, when discharging their duties under the regulations, to have regard to any guidance given from time to time by the Secretary of State.

(3) Extended entitlement regulations which impose a duty, or confer a power, on the Commissioners for Her Majesty's Revenue and Customs, or authorise disclosure of information held by the Commissioners, may only be made with the consent of the Treasury.

(4) In relation to a criminal offence created by virtue of subsection (2)(h), extended entitlement regulations may not provide for a penalty of imprisonment on conviction on indictment greater than imprisonment for a term not exceeding two years (whether or not accompanied by a fine).

(5) If provision is made by virtue of subsection (2)(j)—
(a) the maximum amount of any penalty that may be specified in, or determined in accordance with, the regulations is £3,000;
(b) the regulations must include provision enabling a person on whom a financial penalty is imposed—
(i) to require a review of the imposition of the penalty or its amount by the person who imposed the penalty;
(ii) to appeal against the imposition of the penalty or its amount to the First-tier Tribunal.

(6) The Secretary of State may by regulations substitute a different amount for the amount for the time being specified in subsection (5)(a).

(7) In section 15 of the Childcare Act 2006 (powers of Secretary of State to secure proper performance of English local authorities' powers and duties under Part 1 of that Act) references to Part 1 of that Act are to be read as including a reference to section 1 and this section.

(8) In this section—
"childcare" has the meaning given by section 18 of the Childcare Act 2006;
"English local authority" means—
(a) a county council in England;
(b) a metropolitan district council;
(c) a non-metropolitan district council for an area for which there is no county council;
(d) a London borough council;
(e) the Common Council of the City of London (in their capacity as a local authority);
(f) the Council of the Isles of Scilly;

"parent" has the same meaning as in section 1;
"qualifying child of working parents" has the meaning given by section 1(2).

Sections 1 and 2: consequential amendments

1.1059 3.—(1) In section 99 of the Childcare Act 2006 (provision of information about young children: England), in subsection (1), omit the "and" at the end of paragraph (aa) and after paragraph (b) insert ", and
  (c) any other person who provides early years provision for the purposes of section 1(1) of the Childcare Act 2016 (Secretary of State's duty to secure 30 hours free childcare available for working parents),".
(2) In Chapter 4 of Part 2 of the School Standards and Framework Act 1998 (financing of maintained schools)—
  (a) in section 45A (determination of specified budgets of local authority), after subsection (4B) insert—
"(4C) For the purposes of this Part, a duty imposed on a local authority in England under section 2 of the Childcare Act 2016 (duties in connection with Secretary of State's duty to secure 30 hours free childcare for working parents) is also to be treated as an education function of the authority.";
  (b) in section 47ZA (free of charge early years provision outside a maintained school: budgetary framework: England), in subsection (3), for paragraph (a) (but not the "and" after it) substitute—
"(a) for the purpose of the discharge of—
    (i) the authority's duty under section 7 of the Childcare Act 2006, or
    (ii) a duty imposed on the authority under section 2 of the Childcare Act 2016,".

Supplementary provision about regulations under sections 1 and 2

1.1060 4.—(1) In this section "regulations" means regulations under section 1 or 2.
(2) Regulations may—
  (a) confer a discretion on any person;
  (b) make different provision for different purposes;
  (c) make consequential, incidental, supplemental, transitional or saving provision;
  (d) amend, repeal or revoke any provision made by or under an Act (whenever passed or made).
(3) Regulations are to be made by statutory instrument.
(4) A statutory instrument containing (whether alone or with other provision) regulations mentioned in subsection (5) may not be made unless a draft of the instrument has been laid before and approved by a resolution of each House of Parliament.
(5) The regulations referred to in subsection (4) are—
  (a) the first regulations made under section 1;
  (b) the first regulations made under section 2(1);
  (c) any regulations under section 2(6);
  (d) any other regulations that amend or repeal provision made by an Act.

(6) Any other statutory instrument containing regulations is subject to annulment in pursuance of a resolution of either House of Parliament.

Publication of information

Duty to publish information about childcare and related matters

5. In section 12 of the Childcare Act 2006 (duty to provide information, advice and assistance), after subsection (6) insert—
"(6A) Regulations may require each English local authority to publish information which is of a prescribed description and relates to any of the matters mentioned in paragraphs (a) to (c) of subsection (2).
(6B) Regulations under subsection (6A) may require information to be published—
(a) at prescribed intervals;
(b) in a prescribed manner.
(6C) Subsection (3) applies in relation to information prescribed under subsection (6A) as it applies in relation to information prescribed under subsection (2)."

General

Extent

6. This Act extends to England and Wales only.

Commencement

7.—(1) The following provisions come into force on the day on which this Act is passed—
(a) section 1(5);
(b) section 6;
(c) this section;
(d) section 8.
(2) The remaining provisions of this Act come into force on such day or days as may be appointed by regulations made by the Secretary of State.
(3) Regulations under subsection (2) may appoint different days for different purposes or different areas.
(4) The Secretary of State may by regulations make transitional or saving provision in connection with the coming into force of any provision of this Act.
(5) Regulations under this section are to be made by statutory instrument.

Short title

8. This Act may be cited as the Childcare Act 2016.

Welfare Reform and Work Act 2016

(2016 c.7)

ARRANGEMENT OF SELECTED SECTIONS

1.1065
11. Freeze of certain social security benefits for four years
12. Freeze of certain tax credit amounts for four years
13. Changes to child tax credit
    Schedule 1: Meaning of "the relevant sums" and "the relevant amounts"

Freeze of certain social security benefits for four tax years

1.1066   **11.**—(1) For each of the tax years ending with 5 April 2017, 5 April 2018, 5 April 2019 and 5 April 2020, the amount of each of the relevant sums is to remain the same as it was in the tax year ending with 5 April 2016.

(2) For each of the tax years ending with 5 April 2017, 5 April 2018, 5 April 2019 and 5 April 2020, the rates of child benefit are to remain the same as they were in the tax year ending with 5 April 2016.

(3) A review under section 150(1) of the Social Security Administration Act 1992 (review of whether certain benefits have retained their value) in the tax years ending with 5 April 2016, 5 April 2017, 5 April 2018 and 5 April 2019 need not cover any of the relevant sums or the rates of child benefit.

(4) A draft up-rating order which is laid before Parliament under section 150(2) of that Act in the tax years ending with 5 April 2016, 5 April 2017, 5 April 2018 and 5 April 2019 need not cover any of the relevant sums or the rates of child benefit.

(5) In each of the tax years ending with 5 April 2016, 5 April 2017, 5 April 2018 and 5 April 2019, the Secretary of State must lay before Parliament a copy of a report by the Government Actuary or the Deputy Government Actuary giving that Actuary's opinion on the likely effect of the provision in subsection (1) on the National Insurance Fund in the following tax year, so far as that provision relates to any sums payable out of the Fund.

(6) In this section—
"child benefit"—
  (a) in relation to England and Wales and Scotland, has the same meaning as in Part 9 of the Social Security Contributions and Benefits Act 1992;
  (b) in relation to Northern Ireland, has the same meaning as in Part 9 of the Social Security Contributions and Benefits (Northern Ireland) Act 1992;
"the relevant sums" means the sums described in paragraph 1 of Schedule 1;
"tax year" means a period beginning with 6 April in one year and ending with 5 April in the next.

Freeze of certain tax credit amounts for four tax years

1.1067   **12.**—(1) For each of the tax years ending with 5 April 2017, 5 April 2018, 5 April 2019 and 5 April 2020, each of the relevant amounts is to remain the same as it was in the tax year ending with 5 April 2016.

(2016 c.7 s.12)

(2) A review under section 41 of the Tax Credits Act 2002 (review of whether certain tax credit amounts have retained their value) in the tax years ending with 5 April 2016, 5 April 2017, 5 April 2018 and 5 April 2019 need not cover any of the relevant amounts.

(3) In this section—

"the relevant amounts" means the amounts described in paragraph 2 of Schedule 1;

"tax year" means a period beginning with 6 April in one year and ending with 5 April in the next.

Changes to child tax credit

Section 13 amends s.9 of the Tax Credits Act 2002 (maximum rate of child tax credit) and the amendments are included there.

SCHEDULES

Sections 11 and 12 **SCHEDULE 1**

MEANING OF "THE RELEVANT SUMS" AND "THE RELEVANT AMOUNTS"

1.—*None of "the relevant sums" are relevant to this volume and the paragraph is therefore omitted.*
2.—"The relevant amounts" for the purposes of section 12 are the amounts—
   (a) specified in Schedule 2 to the Working Tax Credit (Entitlement and Maximum Rate) Regulations 2002 for the basic element, the 30 hour element, the second adult element and the lone parent element;
   (b) specified in regulation 7(4)(c) and (f) of the Child Tax Credit Regulations 2002.

Parental Bereavement (Leave and Pay) Act 2018

(2018 c.24)

ARRANGEMENT OF SECTIONS

1. Parental bereavement leave and pay.
2. Extent, commencement and short title

Parental bereavement leave and pay

1.—In the Schedule—
   (a) Part 1 creates a statutory entitlement to parental bereavement leave,
   (b) Part 2 creates a statutory entitlement to parental bereavement pay, and
   (c) Part 3 contains related amendments.

Extent, commencement and short title

2.—(1) An amendment or repeal made by the Schedule has the same extent as the provision to which it relates.

(2) Section 1 and the Schedule come into force on such day as the Secretary of State may by regulations made by statutory instrument appoint; and different days may be appointed for different purposes.

(3) This section comes into force on the day on which this Act is passed.

(4) This Act may be cited as the Parental Bereavement (Leave and Pay) Act 2018.

GENERAL NOTE

1.1073   The Parental Bereavement (Leave and Pay) Act 2018, originally introduced in Parliament as a private member's bill, provides parents with 2 weeks' paid leave if they lose a child under the age of 18 (to be taken within 8 weeks of the date of death of the child) or suffer a stillbirth after 24 weeks of pregnancy. To be eligible for statutory parental bereavement pay, the employee must have a minimum of 26 weeks' service with the employer with average earnings that meet or exceed the national insurance lower earnings limit. Section 2 of the Act has been in force as of the date of Royal Assent (September 13, 2018), while s.1 and the Schedule to the Act were brought into force on January 18, 2020 (see Parental Bereavement (Leave and Pay) Act 2018 (Commencement) Regulations 2020, reg.2). Schedule 1 made extensive amendments to existing legislation, including to the Contributions and Benefits Act.

Coronavirus Act 2020

(2020 C.7)

ARRANGEMENT OF SECTIONS

1.1074
1	Meaning of "coronavirus" and related terminology
40	Statutory sick pay: power to disapply waiting period limitation
76	HMRC functions
77	Up-rating of working tax credit etc

Meaning of "coronavirus" and related terminology

1.1075   **1.**—(1) In this Act—
"coronavirus" means severe acute respiratory syndrome coronavirus 2 (SARS-CoV-2);
"coronavirus disease" means COVID-19 (the official designation of the disease which can be caused by coronavirus).

(2) A reference in this Act to infection or contamination, however expressed, is a reference to infection or contamination with coronavirus.

(3) But a reference in this Act to persons infected by coronavirus, however expressed, does not (unless a contrary intention appears) include persons who have been infected but are clear of coronavirus (unless re-infected).

Statutory sick pay: power to disapply waiting period limitation

1.1076   **40.**—(1) The Secretary of State may by regulations make provision disapplying section 155(1) of the Social Security Contributions and Benefits

Act 1992 in relation to an employee whose incapacity for work is related to coronavirus.

(2) Regulations under subsection (1) may make provision about when an employee's incapacity for work is related to coronavirus.

(3) Section 175(3) to (5) of the Social Security Contributions and Benefits Act 1992 applies to regulations made under subsection (1) as if that subsection were contained in that Act.

(4) Regulations under subsection (1) may have retrospective effect in relation to a day of incapacity for work that falls on or after 13 March 2020.

(5) In this section "employee" and "incapacity for work" have the same meaning as in Part 11 of the Social Security Contributions and Benefits Act 1992.

(6) Regulations under subsection (1) are to be made by statutory instrument.

(7) A statutory instrument containing regulations under subsection (1) is subject to annulment in pursuance of a resolution of either House of Parliament.

HMRC functions

76. Her Majesty's Revenue and Customs are to have such functions as the Treasury may direct in relation to coronavirus or coronavirus disease.

Up-rating of working tax credit etc

77.—(1) In the Working Tax Credit (Entitlement and Maximum Rate) Regulations 2002 (S.I. 2002/2005), in the table in Schedule 2 (maximum rates of the elements of a working tax credit), item 1 (basic element) has effect in relation to the tax year 2020-21 as if the amount specified in the second column (maximum annual rate) were £3,040.

(2) The modification made by subsection (1) does not apply for the purposes of any annual review carried out in accordance with section 41 of the Tax Credits Act 2002.

(3) Where a sum mentioned in section 150(1) of the Social Security Administration Act 1992 (annual review in relation to up-rating of benefits) is modified in relation to the tax year 2020-21 for purposes connected with coronavirus or coronavirus disease, the modification does not apply for the purposes of any annual review carried out in accordance with that section.

GENERAL NOTE

Section 77 expired with effect from 9 December 2021: see regulations 2 and 3 of the Coronavirus Act 2020 (Early Expiry) (No.2) Regulations 2021 (SI 2021/1399).

PART II

TAX CREDITS

PART A

Tax Credits Commencement Orders and Transitional Provisions

The Welfare Reform Act 2012 (Commencement No.9 and Transitional and Transitory Provisions and Commencement No.8 and Savings and Transitional Provisions (Amendment)) Order 2013

(SI 2013/983) (AS AMENDED)

The Secretary of State, in exercise of the powers conferred by section 150(3) and (4)(a), (b)(i) and (c) of the Welfare Reform Act 2012, makes the following Order:

Arrangement of Articles

1. Citation.
2. Interpretation.
3. Day appointed for commencement of the universal credit provisions in Part 1 of the Act.
3A. Incorrect information regarding residence in a relevant district.

Schedule 1. Postcode Districts.
Schedule 2. Universal Credit Provisions Coming into Force in Relation to Certain Claims and Awards.

General Note

This volume reproduces only those provisions of the Order that are relevant to tax credit claimants. For the full text of the Order, see Vol.V in this series.

The Order itself is of limited effect since all it does is authorise the making of universal credit claims in six postcode districts. It is included in this volume because it is part of a set of inter-linked commencement orders that, taken together, prevent many people from making a new claim for a tax credit, as is further explained in the note to the Welfare Reform Act 2012 (Commencement No.29 and Commencement No.17, 19, 22, 23 and 24 and Transitional and Transitory Provisions (Modification)) Order 2017 (below in this volume).

Citation

1. This Order may be cited as the Welfare Reform Act 2012 (Commencement No.9 and Transitional and Transitory Provisions and Commencement No.8 and Savings and Transitional Provisions (Amendment)) Order 2013.

Interpretation

2.—(1) In this Order—
"the Act" means the Welfare Reform Act 2012 (apart from in Schedule 4);
"the amending provisions" means the provisions referred to in article 4(1)(a) to (c);

535

...[¹ "claimant"—
...(c) in relation to universal credit, has the same meaning as in Part 1 of the Act;]
"appointed day" means the day appointed for the coming into force of the amending provisions in accordance with article 4(3);
..."the Claims and Payments Regulations 2013" means the Universal Credit, Personal Independence Payment, Jobseeker's Allowance and Employment and Support Allowance (Claims and Payments) Regulations 2013;
..."the Decisions and Appeals Regulations 2013" means the Universal Credit, Personal Independence Payment, Jobseeker's Allowance and Employment and Support Allowance (Decisions and Appeals) Regulations 2013;
..."First-tier Tribunal" has the same meaning as in the Social Security Act 1998;
...[² "joint claimants", in relation to universal credit, has the same meaning as in Part 1 of the Act;]
..."relevant districts" means the postcode districts specified in Schedule 1;
[³ "single claimant", in relation to universal credit, has the same meaning as in Part 1 of the Act;]
..."tax credit" (including "child tax credit" and "working tax credit") has the same meaning as in the Tax Credits Act 2002;]
...[³ "the 2014 Transitional Regulations" means the Universal Credit (Transitional Provisions) Regulations 2014;
"the Universal Credit Regulations" means the Universal Credit Regulations 2013;
"Upper Tribunal" has the same meaning as in the Social Security Act 1998.]
[³ (2) For the purposes of this Order—
(a) the Claims and Payments Regulations 2013 apply for the purpose of deciding—
   (i) whether a claim for universal credit is made or is to be treated as made; and
   (ii) the date on which such a claim is made; and
(b) where a couple is treated, in accordance with regulation 9(8) of the Claims and Payments Regulations 2013, as making a claim for universal credit, references to the date on which the claim is treated as made are to the date of formation of the couple.]

AMENDMENTS

1. The Welfare Reform Act 2012 (Commencement No.9, 11, 13, 14, 16, 17 and 19 and Transitional and Transitory Provisions (Amendment)) Order 2014 (SI 2014/3067) art.6 (November 24, 2014).

2. The Welfare Reform Act 2012 (Commencement No.9, 11, 13, 14, 16 and 17 and Transitional and Transitory Provisions (Amendment)) Order 2014 (SI 2014/1661) art.4 (June 30, 2014).

3. The Welfare Reform Act 2012 (Commencement No.9, 11, 13, 14 and 16 and Transitional and Transitory Provisions (Amendment)) Order 2014 (SI 2014/1452) art.4 (June 4, 2014).

(SI 2013/983 reg.2) (as amended)

GENERAL NOTE

The Claims and Payments Regulations 2013, the Decisions and Appeals Regulations 2013 and the Universal Credit Regulations 2013 are reproduced in Vol.V in this series. The universal credit provisions of the Welfare Reform Act 2012 are also found in Vol.V. For the 2014 Transitional Regulations, see below in this volume.

Day appointed for commencement of the universal credit provisions in Part 1 of the Act

3.—(1) 29th April 2013 is the day appointed for the coming into force of—
  (a) sections 29 (delegation and contracting out), 37(1), (2), (8) and (9) (capability for work or work-related activity), 38 (information) and 39(1), (2), (3)(b) and (c) (couples) of the Act;
  (b) the following paragraphs of Schedule 2 to the Act (universal credit: amendments) and section 31 of the Act (supplementary and consequential amendments) in so far as it relates to those paragraphs, in so far as they are not already in force—
    (i) paragraphs 1, 2, 32 to 35, 37 to 42, 52 to 55 and 65;
    (ii) paragraphs 4, 8, 10 to 23, 25 and 27 to 31 and paragraph 3 in so far as it relates to those paragraphs; and
    (iii) paragraphs 44, 45, 47, 49, 50(2) and 50(1) in so far as it relates to 50(2), and paragraph 43 in so far as it relates to those paragraphs and sub-paragraphs; and
  (c) paragraph 1 of Schedule 5 to the Act (universal credit and other working-age benefits) and section 35 of the Act in so far as it relates to that paragraph.

(2) The day appointed for the coming into force of the provisions of the Act listed in Schedule 2, in so far as they are not already in force, in relation to the case of a claim referred to in paragraph (3)(a) to (d) and any award that is made in respect of such a claim, and in relation to the case of an award referred to in paragraph (3)(e) or (f), is the day appointed in accordance with paragraph (4).

[¹ [² (3) The claims and awards referred to are—
  (a) a claim for universal credit where, on the date on which the claim is made, the claimant resides in one of the relevant districts [³ . . .];
  [(b) a claim for universal credit where—
    (i) in the case of a single claimant, the claimant gives incorrect information regarding the claimant residing in a relevant district [³. . .] and the claimant does not reside in such a district [³. . .] on the date on which the claim is made;
    (ii) in the case of joint claimants, either or both of the joint claimants gives or give incorrect information regarding his or her (or their) residing in such a district [³. . .] and one or both of them does not or do not reside in such a district [³. . .] on the date on which the claim is made; and
    (iii) after a decision is made that the single claimant is, or the joint claimants are, entitled to universal credit and one or more payments have been made in respect of the single claimant or the joint claimants, the Secretary of State discovers that incorrect information has been given regarding residence [³. . .];

(c) a claim for universal credit that is treated as made by a couple in the circumstances referred to in regulation 9(8) of the Claims and Payments Regulations 2013 (claims for universal credit by members of a couple) where the claim complies with paragraph (7);

[² (d) a claim for universal credit by a former member of a couple who were joint claimants of universal credit, whether or not the claim is made jointly with another person, where the former member is not exempt from the requirement to make a claim by virtue of regulation 9(6) of the Claims and Payments Regulations 2013 (claims for universal credit by members of a couple), where the claim is made during the period of one month starting with the date on which notification is given to the Secretary of State that the former joint claimants have ceased to be a couple, and where the claim complies with paragraph (8);]

(e) an award of universal credit that is made without a claim in the circumstances referred to in regulation 6(1) or (2) of the Claims and Payments Regulations 2013 (claims not required for entitlement to universal credit in some cases) where the circumstances referred to in paragraph (9) apply; and

(f) an award of universal credit that is made without a claim in the circumstances referred to in regulation 9(6), (7) or (10) of the Claims and Payments Regulations 2013 (claims for universal credit by members of a couple) where the circumstances referred to in paragraph (9) apply.]]

(4) The day appointed in relation to the cases of the claims and awards referred to in paragraph (2) is—

(a) in the case of a claim referred to in paragraph (3)(a) to (d), the first day of the period in respect of which the claim is made or treated as made;

(b) in the case of an award referred to in paragraph (3)(e) or (f), the first day on which a person is entitled to universal credit under that award.

(5) [¹ . . .]

(6) For the purposes of paragraph (4)(a), where the time for making a claim for universal credit is extended under regulation 26(2) of the Claims and Payments Regulations 2013, the reference to the first day of the period in respect of which the claim is made or treated as made is a reference to the first day of the period in respect of which the claim is, by reason of the operation of that provision, timeously made or treated as made.

[¹ (7) A claim that is treated as made by a couple in the circumstances referred to in regulation 9(8) of the Claims and Payments Regulations 2013 complies with this paragraph where, on the date on which the claim is treated as made, the member of the couple who did not previously have an award of universal credit [⁴ . . .] is not entitled to state pension credit.

(8) A claim by a former member of a couple that is made in the circumstances referred to in paragraph (3)(d) complies with this paragraph where, on the date on which the claim is made, [⁴ neither the former member nor his or her partner (if any) is entitled to state pension credit].

(9) The circumstances referred to are where the relevant person is not entitled to state pension credit and, save where an award of universal credit is made in the circumstances referred to in regulation 9(7) of the Claims

and Payments Regulations 2013, his or her partner (if any) is not entitled to [⁴ state pension credit].

(10) For the purposes of paragraph (9), "relevant person" means—
(a) where an award of universal credit is made in the circumstances referred to in regulation 6(1) or (2) of the Claims and Payments Regulations 2013, the former claimant referred to in that regulation 6(1);
(b) where an award of universal credit is made in the circumstances referred to in paragraph (6) of regulation 9 of the Claims and Payments Regulations 2013, [4 as that paragraph has effect apart from the amendments made by the Digital Service Regulations 2014,] the member of the former couple referred to in that paragraph;

[⁴ (ba) where an award of universal credit is made in the circumstances referred to in paragraph (6) of regulation 9 of the Claims and Payments Regulations 2013, as that paragraph has effect as amended by the Digital Service Regulations 2014, the former joint claimant of universal credit to whom a new award of universal credit is made as referred to in sub-paragraph (a) or (b) of that paragraph;]

(c) where an award of universal credit is made in the circumstances referred to in paragraph (7) of regulation 9 of the Claims and Payments Regulations 2013, each of the joint claimants referred to in that paragraph;
(d) where an award of universal credit is made in the circumstances referred to in paragraph (10) of regulation 9 of the Claims and Payments Regulations 2013, the surviving partner referred to in that paragraph.

[⁴ (10A) In paragraph (3)—
(a) in sub-paragraph (c), the reference to regulation 9(8) of the Claims and Payments Regulations 2013 is a reference to that provision both as it has effect as amended by the Digital Service Regulations 2014 and as it has effect apart from that amendment;
(b) in sub-paragraph (d), the reference to regulation 9(6) of the Claims and Payments Regulations 2013 is a reference to that provision as it has effect apart from the amendment made by the Digital Service Regulations 2014;
(c) in sub-paragraph (f), the reference to regulation 9(6) of the Claims and Payments Regulations 2013 is a reference to that provision both as it has effect as amended by the Digital Service Regulations 2014 and as it has effect apart from that amendment.]

(11) For the purposes of paragraphs (8) and (9), "partner" means a person who forms part of a couple with the person in question, where "couple" has the same meaning as it has in section 39 of the Act.]

AMENDMENTS

1. The Welfare Reform Act 2012 (Commencement No.9, 11, 13, 14 and 16 and Transitional and Transitory Provisions (Amendment)) Order 2014 (SI 2014/1452) art.5 (June 4, 2014).

2. The Welfare Reform Act 2012 (Commencement No.9, 11, 13, 14, 16 and 17 and Transitional and Transitory Provisions (Amendment) (No.2)) Order 2014 (SI 2014/1923) art.4 (July 28, 2014).

3. The Welfare Reform Act 2012 (Commencement No.9, 21 and 23 (Amendment), Commencement No.11, 13, 17, 19, 22, 23 and 24 (Modification), Transitional and Transitory Provisions) Order 2018 (SI 2018/138) art.3 (March 7, 2018).
4. The Welfare Reform Act 2012 (Commencement No.20 and Transitional and Transitory Provisions and Commencement No.9 and Transitional and Transitory Provisions (Amendment)) Order 2014 (SI 2014/3094) art.7 (November 26, 2014).

DEFINITIONS

"the Act"—see art.2(1).
"Claims and Payments Regulations 2013"—see art.2(1).
"joint claimants"—see art.2(1).
"relevant districts"—see art.2(1).
"single claimant"—see art.2(1).

[¹ Incorrect information regarding residence in a relevant district [² . . .]

2.7   **3A.**—(1) This article applies where a claim for universal credit is made and it is subsequently discovered that the single claimant or either or both of two joint claimants gave incorrect information regarding his or her (or their) residing in one of the relevant districts [² and the condition referred to in paragraph (2) is met].

[² (2) The condition referred to is that, on the date on which the claim was made, the claimant did not reside in one of the relevant districts (unless paragraph (3) applies).]

(3) This paragraph applies where the claimant resided in an area apart from the relevant districts with respect to which the provisions of the Act referred to in Schedule 2 were in force in relation to a claim for universal credit and the conditions (if any) that applied to such a claim, for those provisions to come into force, were met [³ (and a determination had not been made under regulation 4 of the Universal Credit (Transitional Provisions) Regulations 2014, preventing a claim for universal credit being made with respect to the area in question or the category of case in question)].

(4) Where the discovery is made before the claim for universal credit has been decided—
   (a) the claimant is to be informed that the claimant is not entitled to claim universal credit;
. . .(d) if the claimant (or, in the case of joint claimants, either of them) makes a claim for a tax credit and that claim is received by a relevant authority at an appropriate office (within the meaning of the Tax Credits (Claims and Notifications) Regulations 2002 ("the 2002 Regulations")) during the period of one month beginning with the date on which the information required by sub-paragraph (a) was given—
      (i) the claim for a tax credit is to be treated as having been received by a relevant authority at an appropriate office on the date on which the claim for universal credit was made or the first date on which the claimant would have been entitled to a tax credit if a claim had been so received on that date, if later; and
      (ii) any provision of the 2002 Regulations under which the claim is treated as having been made on a later date does not apply.

(5) Where the discovery is made after a decision has been made that the claimant is entitled to universal credit, but before any payment has been made—
(a) that decision is to cease to have effect immediately, by virtue of this article;
(b) the claimant is to be informed that they are not entitled to claim universal credit; and
(c) sub-paragraphs (b) to (d) of paragraph (4) apply.

(6) Where the discovery is made after a decision has been made that the claimant is entitled to universal credit and one or more payments have been made in respect of the claimant, the decision is to be treated as a decision under section 8 of the Social Security Act 1998.

. . ..]

AMENDMENTS

1. The Welfare Reform Act 2012 (Commencement No.9, 11, 13, 14, 16 and 17 and Transitional and Transitory Provisions (Amendment) (No.2)) Order 2014 (SI 2014/1923) art.4 (July 28, 2014).
2. The Welfare Reform Act 2012 (Commencement No.9, 21 and 23 (Amendment), Commencement No.11, 13, 17, 19, 22, 23 and 24 (Modification), Transitional and Transitory Provisions) Order 2018 (SI 2018/138) art.3 (March 7, 2018).
3. The Welfare Reform Act 2012 (Commencement No.23 and Transitional and Transitory Provisions) Order 2015 (SI 2015/634) art.8 (March 18, 2015).

DEFINITIONS

"the Act"—see art.2(1).
"joint claimants"—see art.2(1).
"relevant districts"—see art.2(1).

GENERAL NOTE

Social Security Act 1998–see volume 1 in this series.
Tax Credits (Claims and Notifications) Regulations 2002–see below in this volume.
Universal Credit (Transitional Provisions) Regulations 2014–see below in this volume.

SCHEDULE 1

POSTCODE DISTRICTS (ARTICLE 2(1))

1. M43
2. OL6
3. OL7
4. SK16

SCHEDULE 2

UNIVERSAL CREDIT PROVISIONS COMING INTO FORCE IN RELATION TO CERTAIN CLAIMS AND AWARDS

(ARTICLE 3(2)).

GENERAL NOTE

The list of commenced provisions is not reproduced in this volume. In summary, the list refers to the provisions of the Welfare Reform Act 2012 that deal with entitlement to universal credit, claims for universal credit and regulation of an ongoing award of universal credit. The list may be consulted in the entry in respect of this Order in Vol.V in this series.

The Welfare Reform Act 2012 (Commencement No.23 and Transitional and Transitory Provisions) Order 2015

(SI 2015/634)

The Secretary of State for Work and Pensions makes the following Order in exercise of the powers conferred by section 150(3) and (4)(a), (b)(i) and (c) of the Welfare Reform Act 2012:

ARRANGEMENT OF ARTICLES

1. Citation.
2. Interpretation.
3. Day appointed for the coming into force of the universal credit provisions.
7. Transitional provision: claims for...a tax credit

Citation

1. This Order may be cited as the Welfare Reform Act 2012 (Commencement No.23 and Transitional and Transitory Provisions) Order 2015.

Interpretation

2.—(1) In this Order–
"the Act" means the Welfare Reform Act 2012;
..."claimant"–
...(c) in relation to universal credit, has the same meaning as in Part 1 of the Act;
... "joint claimants", in relation to universal credit, has the same meaning as in Part 1 of the Act;
"the No 9 Order" means the Welfare Reform Act 2012 (Commencement No.9 and Transitional and Transitory Provisions and Commencement No.8 and Savings and Transitional Provisions (Amendment)) Order 2013;
... "the No 50 relevant districts" means the postcode part-districts SM6 7 and SM6 8;
"the No 51 relevant districts" means the postcode part-districts CR0 4 and SM6 9;
"the No 52 relevant districts" means the postcode part-districts CR0 2 and SE1 5;
"single claimant", in relation to universal credit, has the same meaning as in Part 1 of the Act.
(2) For the purposes of this Order, the Universal Credit, Personal Independence Payment, Jobseeker's Allowance and Employment and

Support Allowance (Claims and Payments) Regulations 2013 apply for the purpose of deciding—
(a) whether a claim for universal credit is made; and
(b) the date on which such a claim is made.

GENERAL NOTE

2.14 See Vol.V of this work for the Universal Credit, Personal Independence Payment, Jobseeker's Allowance and Employment and Support Allowance (Claims and Payments) Regulations 2013 (SI 2013/380).
See above in this volume for the No.9 Order.

Day appointed for the coming into force of the universal credit provisions

2.15 **3.**—(1) The day appointed for the coming into force of the provisions of the Act listed in Schedule 2 to the No 9 Order, in so far as they are not already in force, in relation to the case of a claim referred to in paragraph (2), and any award that is made in respect of the claim, is the day appointed in accordance with paragraph (3).

(2) The claims referred to are—
(a) a claim for universal credit that is made on or after 18th March 2015 in respect of a period that begins on or after 18th March 2015 where, on the date on which the claim is made, the claimant resides in one of the No 50 relevant districts;
(b) a claim for universal credit that is made on or after 10th June 2015 in respect of a period that begins on or after 10th June 2015 where, on the date on which the claim is made, the claimant resides in one of the No 51 relevant districts;
(c) a claim for universal credit that is made on or after 4th November 2015 in respect of a period that begins on or after 4th November 2015 where, on the date on which the claim is made, the claimant resides in one of the No 52 relevant districts;
(d) a claim for universal credit that is made on or after the date referred to in any of sub-paragraphs (a) to (c), in respect of a period that begins on or after that date where—
  (i) in the case of a single claimant, the claimant gives incorrect information regarding the claimant residing in a district as referred to in the sub-paragraph in question and the claimant does not reside in such a district on the date on which the claim is made;
  (ii) in the case of joint claimants, either or both of the joint claimants gives or give incorrect information regarding his or her (or their) residing in such a district and one or both of them does not or do not reside in such a district on the date on which the claim is made,
and after a decision is made that the single claimant is, or the joint claimants are, entitled to universal credit and one or more payments have been made in respect of the single claimant or the joint claimants, the Secretary of State discovers that incorrect information has been given regarding residence.

(3) The day appointed in relation to the case of a claim referred to in paragraph (2), and any award that is made in respect of the claim, is the first day of the period in respect of which the claim is made.

(4) article 3(6) of the No 9 Order applies for the purposes of paragraph (3) as it applies for the purposes of article 3(4)(a) of the No 9 Order.

DEFINITIONS

"joint claimants"—see art.2(1).
Relevant districts, no's 50-52—see art.2(1).
"claimant"—see art.2(1)
"the No 9 Order"—see art.2(1)

Transitional provision: claims for. . .a tax credit

2.16   7.—(1) Except as provided by paragraphs (2) to (6), a person may not make a claim for. . .a tax credit (in the latter case, whether or not as part of a Tax Credits Act couple) on any date where, if that person made a claim for universal credit on that date (in the capacity, whether as a single person or as part of a couple, in which he or she is permitted to claim universal credit under the Universal Credit Regulations 2013), the provisions of the Act listed in Schedule 2 to the No 9 Order would come into force under article 3(1) and [1 (2)(a) to (c) of this Order in relation to that claim] for universal credit.

(2) Paragraph (1) does not apply to a claim for. . .a tax credit where, . . .[2. . .by virtue of regulation [3 4A]] of the Universal Credit (Transitional Provisions) Regulations 2014, [4 or by virtue of article 4(11) of the Welfare Reform Act 2012 (Commencement No.32 and Savings and Transitional Provisions) Order 2019] the person in question would be prevented from making a claim for universal credit as referred to in that paragraph.

. . .(5) Paragraph (1) does not apply to a claim for a tax credit where a person or persons makes or make a claim for child tax credit or working tax credit and on the date on which he or she (or they) makes or make the claim he or she (or they) [4 has or have an award of working tax credit or child tax credit respectively].

(6) Paragraph (1) does not apply to a claim for a tax credit where a person [4 has or had, or persons have or had, an award of] child tax credit or working tax credit in respect of a tax year and that person or those persons makes or make (or is or are treated as making) a claim for that tax credit for the next tax year.

[4 (7) In paragraph (5), the reference to a person having an award of a tax credit includes where the person is "treated as being entitled to a tax credit" in the circumstances referred to in regulation 11(1) and (2)(a) to (ca) of the Universal Credit (Transitional Provisions) Regulations 2014 but as if, in regulation 11(1), for "For the purposes of regulations 7(7) and 8(4)" there were substituted "For the purposes of article 7(5) of the Welfare Reform Act 2012 (Commencement No.23 and Transitional and Transitory Provisions) Order 2015".]

(8) Subject to paragraph (9), for the purposes of this article—
   (a) a claim for . . . a tax credit is made by a person on the date on which he or she takes any action which results in a decision on a claim being required under the relevant Regulations; and
   (b) it is irrelevant that the effect of any provision of the relevant Regulations is that, for the purpose of those Regulations, the claim is made or treated as made on a date that is earlier than the date on which that action is taken.

. . .

(11) For the purposes of this article—
  (a) "couple" (apart from in the expressions "State Pension Credit Act couple" and "Tax Credit Act couple"), has the meaning given in section 39 of the Act;
  ...
  (g) "the relevant Regulations" means—
  ...
    (iii) in the case of a claim for a tax credit, the Tax Credits (Claims and Notifications) Regulations 2002;
  ...
  (j) "tax credit" (including "child tax credit" and "working tax credit") and "tax year" have the same meanings as in the Tax Credits Act 2002;
  (k) "Tax Credits Act couple" means a couple as defined in section 3(5A) of the Tax Credits Act 2002...

AMENDMENTS

1. The Welfare Reform Act 2012 (Commencement No.23 and Transitional and Transitory Provisions) (Amendment) Order 2015 (SI 2015/740) art.2 (March 17, 2015).
2. The Social Security (Restrictions on Amounts for Children and Qualifying Young Persons) Amendment Regulations 2017 (SI 2017/376) reg.4 (April 6, 2017).
3. The Universal Credit (Transitional Provisions) (SDP Gateway) Amendment Regulations 2019 (SI 2019/10) reg.3 (January 16, 2019).
4. The Welfare Reform Act 2012 (Commencement No.32 and Savings and Transitional Provisions) Order 2019 (SI 2019/167), art.5 (February 1, 2019).

DEFINITIONS

"the Act"—see art.2(1).
"the No.9 Order"—see art.2(1).

GENERAL NOTE

The provisions originally enacted in art.7 have been re-enacted in the main Universal Credit transitional regulations: see the Universal Credit (Transitional Provisions) Regulations 2014 (SI 2014/1230) reg.6A below in this volume and the annotation thereto.

The Welfare Reform Act 2012 (Commencement No.29 and Commencement No.17, 19, 22, 23 and 24 and Transitional and Transitory Provisions (Modification)) Order 2017

(SI 2017/664)

The Secretary of State for Work and Pensions makes the following Order in exercise of the powers conferred by section 150(3) and (4)(a), (b)(i) and (c) of the Welfare Reform Act 2012:

Citation

1. This Order may be cited as the Welfare Reform Act 2012 (Commencement No.29 and Commencement No.17, 19, 22, 23 and 24 and Transitional and Transitory Provisions (Modification)) Order 2017.

Welfare Reform Act 2012 (Commencement No. 29) Order 2017

Interpretation

2.19 2.—(1) In this Order—
"claimant"–

...

(c) in relation to universal credit, has the same meaning as in Part 1 of the Welfare Reform Act 2012;

...

"the No 23 Order" means the Welfare Reform Act 2012 (Commencement No.23 and Transitional and Transitory Provisions) Order 2015; ...

(2) In this Order, references to "designated postcodes", by numbered "Part", are to any postcode district or part-district in the corresponding numbered Part of the Schedule to this Order.

(3) For the purposes of this Order, the Universal Credit, Personal Independence Payment, Jobseeker's Allowance and Employment and Support Allowance (Claims and Payments) Regulations 2013 apply for the purpose of deciding—
  (a) whether a claim for universal credit is made; and
  (b) the date on which the claim is made.

...

GENERAL NOTE

2.20 See Vol. III of this work for the Universal Credit, Personal Independence Payment, Jobseeker's Allowance and Employment and Support Allowance (Claims and Payments) Regulations 2013 (SI 2013/380).
See above in this volume for the No.23 Order.

Modification of the No 23 Order: claims for housing benefit, income support or a tax credit

2.21 14. Article 7 of the No 23 Order (prevention of claims for. . .a tax credit) applies as though the reference in paragraph (1) of that article to article 3(1) and (2)(a) to (c) of that Order included—
  (a) a reference to paragraph (1) and sub-paragraphs (a), (i) and (k) of paragraph (2) of article 3 of the No 17 Order, in respect of claims in relation to which those sub-paragraphs are modified respectively by article 5(2)(a), 5(2)(b) and 5(2)(c) of this Order;
  (b) a reference to paragraph (1) and sub-paragraph (b) of paragraph (2) of article 3 of the No 19 Order, in respect of claims in relation to which that sub-paragraph is modified by article 5(2)(d) of this Order;
  (c) a reference to paragraph (1) and sub-paragraphs (e), (j), (n), (s) and (t) of paragraph (2) of article 3 of the No 22 Order, in respect of claims in relation to which those sub-paragraphs are modified respectively by articles 4(2)(b), 4(2)(e), 4(2)(f), 4(2)(g) and 3(2)(f) of this Order;
  (d) a reference to paragraph (1) and sub-paragraphs (a), (c), (f), (g), (h) and (l) of paragraph (2) of article 3 of the No 22 Order, in respect of claims in relation to which those sub-paragraphs are modified respectively by articles 3(2)(a), 4(2)(a) and 7(2)(a), articles 3(2)(b) and 7(2)(b), articles 3(2)(c) and 9(2)(a), articles 3(2)(d), 4(2)(c) and 5(2)(e), articles 4(2)(d) and 5(2)(f), and articles 3(2)(e), 8(2)(a) and 9(2)(b) of this Order;

(e) a reference to paragraph (1) and sub-paragraphs (c), (f), (i), (o), (r) and (bb) of paragraph (2) of article 3 of the No 24 Order, in respect of claims in relation to which those sub-paragraphs are modified respectively by articles 9(2)(c), 3(2)(h), 3(2)(i), 7(2)(d), 9(2)(e) and 3(2)(l) of this Order; and

(f) a reference to paragraph (1) and sub-paragraphs (a), (d), (h), (l), (p), (q) and (aa) of paragraph (2) of article 3 of the No 24 Order, in respect of claims in relation to which those sub-paragraphs are modified respectively by articles 3(2)(g), 4(2)(h) and 8(2)(b), articles 5(2)(g) and 6(2)(a), articles 5(2)(h) and 7(2)(c), articles 3(2)(j), 4(2)(i) and 9(2)(d), articles 5(2)(i) and 6(2)(b), articles 5(2)(j) and 8(2)(c), and articles 3(2)(k) and 7(2)(e) of this Order.

DEFINITION

"No.23 Order"—see art.2(1).

GENERAL NOTE

As Upper Tribunal Judge Mitchell observed in *W v HMRC* (TC) [2020] UKUT 239 (AAC), "the complex UC/tax credits transitional legislation is hardly accessible to a specialist legal representative let alone a lay person".

This article is important because its effect is to expand significantly the number of individuals who are prevented from making a claim for a tax credit. In order to determine whether a tax credit recipient is caught by the restriction on making a claim, it is necessary to track through the various commencement orders referred to in art.14 of this Order and the modifications made to them by earlier articles of this Order. These orders and articles are not reproduced in this volume but may be consulted in Vol.5 of this series.

The modifications to earlier commencement orders made by prior articles of this Order removed the requirement for the "gateway conditions" to be met in order for a person living in a designated postcode area to be able to make a claim for universal credit. The result was a significant expansion of the numbers of tax credit recipients to whom the universal credit provisions applied. The next stop in the paper chase is reg.6A of the Universal Credit (Transitional Provisions) Regulations 2014 (SI 2014/1230) (which makes provision previously contained in art.7 of the No.23 Order (SI 2015/634)). This prevents a person to whom the universal credit provisions apply from making a claim for a tax credit. It is by this route that art.14 of this Order rendered large numbers of tax credits recipients, subject to exceptions, unable to make a new claim for a tax credit.

The transitional picture is further complicated by savings provisions in the Welfare Reform Act 2012 (Commencement No.32 and Savings and Transitional Provisions) Order 2019 (SI 2019/167) (below in this volume). This order commences s.33(1)(f) of the Welfare Reform Act 2012, which abolishes tax credits, with effect from February 1, 2019. However, it also includes a number of savings provisions, especially for those with existing awards of tax credits. For those falling within the savings provisions, tax credits are not abolished so that existing awards may be maintained and, provided that a person is not prevented from claiming a tax credit by reg.6A of the Universal Credit (Transitional Provisions) Regulations 2014, new claims may be also made (since tax credits are awarded annually, a new claim, actual or deemed, is required each year).

2.22

Welfare Reform Act 2012 (Commencement No.32 and Savings and Transitional Provisions) Order 2019

(SI 2019/167)

2.23   The Secretary of State for Work and Pensions makes the following Order in exercise of the powers conferred by section 150(3) and (4)(a), (b)(i) and (c) of the Welfare Reform Act 2012.

Arrangement of Articles

1. Citation and Interpretation
2. Commencement of provisions on abolition of tax credits
3. Savings
4. Appointed day – coming into force of universal credit provisions and abolition of income-related employment and support allowance and income-based jobseeker's allowance: persons resident outside Great Britain
5. Amendment of the No.9, No.21 and No.23 Orders

Citation and Interpretation

2.24   **1.**—(1) This Order may be cited as the Welfare Reform Act 2012 (Commencement No.32 and Savings and Transitional Provisions) Order 2019.

(2) In this Order—
"the Act" means the Welfare Reform Act 2012;
"the 2002 Act" means the Tax Credits Act 2002;
"the 2015 Order (N.I.)" means the Welfare Reform (Northern Ireland) Order 2015;
"the No.8 Order (N.I.)" means the Welfare Reform (Northern Ireland) Order 2015 (Commencement No.8 and Transitional and Transitory Provisions) Order 2017;
"the No.9 Order" means the Welfare Reform Act 2012 (Commencement No.9 and Transitional and Transitory Provisions and Commencement No.8 and Savings and Transitional Provisions (Amendment)) Order 2013;
"the No.21 Order" means the Welfare Reform Act 2012 (Commencement No.21 and Transitional and Transitory Provisions) Order 2015;
"the No.23 Order" means the Welfare Reform Act 2012 (Commencement No.23 and Transitional and Transitory Provisions) Order 2015;
"the Claims and Payments Regulations 1987" means the Social Security (Claims and Payments) Regulations 1987;
"couple" means a couple as defined in section 3(5A) of the 2002 Act;
"employment and support allowance" means an employment and support allowance under Part 1 of the Welfare Reform Act 2007;
"jobseeker's allowance" means a jobseeker's allowance under the Jobseekers Act 1995;
"joint-claim couple" has the same meanings as in the Jobseeker's Act 1995;
"Her Majesty's forces" has the same meaning as in the Armed Forces Act 2006;

"mixed-age couple" means a couple, one member of which has attained the qualifying age and the other of which has not;

"polygamous unit" means a polygamous unit within the meaning of the Tax Credits (Polygamous Marriages) Regulations 2003;

"qualifying age" means the qualifying age for state pension credit as defined in section 1(6) of the State Pension Credit Act 2002;

"single claimant" means a person who makes a single claim for a tax credit as referred to in section 3(3)(b) of the 2002 Act;

"tax credit" (including "child tax credit" and "working tax credit") have the same meanings as in the 2002 Act and "tax year" has the same meaning as in Part 1 of that Act;

"UC age condition" means the condition in section 4(1)(b) of the Act for Great Britain or Article 9(1)(b) of the 2015 Order (N.I.) for Northern Ireland, subject to any exceptions in any instrument made under the Act or 2015 Order (N.I.);

"UC couple" means a couple as defined in section 39 of the Act for Great Britain or Article 45 of the 2015 Order (N.I.) for Northern Ireland (in article 4, as defined in that section 39);

"UC joint claimants" means joint claimants as defined in section 40 of the Act for Great Britain or Article 46 of the 2015 Order (N.I.) for Northern Ireland (in article 4, as defined in that section 40);

"UC provisions" means the provisions listed in Schedule 2 to the No.9 Order;

"UC single claimant" means a single claimant as defined in section 40 of the Act for Great Britain or Article 46 of the 2015 Order (N.I.) for Northern Ireland (in article 4, as defined in that section 40);

"UC transitional provisions" means the orders made under section 150(3) of the Act or Article 2(2) of the 2015 Order (N.I.) that commence the UC provisions, or the provisions listed in Schedule 1 to the No.8 Order (N.I.), respectively, and the regulations made under Schedule 6 to the Act or Schedule 6 to the 2015 Order (N.I.).

(3) In this Order—

(a) "frontier worker" means a person, other than a person referred to in sub-paragraph (b), who is in Great Britain for the purposes of section 4(1)(c) of the Act but who does not reside in Great Britain or Northern Ireland;

(b) the person referred to is a crown servant or member of Her Majesty's forces posted overseas (where "crown servant" and "posted overseas" have the same meanings as in regulation 10 of the Universal Credit Regulations 2013).

Commencement of provisions on abolition of tax credits

2. The day appointed for the coming into force of section 33(1)(f) of the Act (abolition of tax credits) and the repeal of Part 1 of the 2002 Act (but not Schedule 1 or 3), by Part 1 of Schedule 14 to the Act, is 1st February 2019.

Savings

3.—(1) Section 33(1)(f) of the Act, and the repeal of Part 1 of the 2002 Act (but not Schedule 1 or 3) by Part 1 of Schedule 14 to the Act, shall be treated as though they had not come into force, in relation to a case as referred to in paragraph (2), (3), (4), (5) or (9).

(2) The case referred to is the case of an award of a tax credit that has effect for a period that includes 31st January 2019.

(3) The case referred to is the case of an award of a tax credit where the period for which it has effect begins on or after 1st February 2019 and where the claim for the award is made by—
- (a) a single claimant who is, or a couple both members of which are, aged under the qualifying age on the day that the claim is made;
- (b) a mixed-age couple which is also a UC couple on that day; or
- (c) a polygamous unit which on that day consists wholly of persons who, ignoring any restrictions on claiming universal credit in the UC transitional provisions, could claim universal credit, and meet the UC age condition, as—
  - (i) UC joint claimants and one or more UC single claimants; or
  - (ii) a number of UC single claimants.

(4) The case referred to is the case of an award of a tax credit where the period for which it has effect begins on or after 1st February 2019 and where the claim for the award is made by—
- (a) a mixed-age couple apart from one referred to in paragraph (3)(b); or
- (b) a polygamous unit apart from one referred to in paragraph (3)(c),

where, on the day on which the claim is made, a member of the couple, or a member or members of the polygamous unit, would be able to claim universal credit were it not for restrictions on claiming universal credit in the UC transitional provisions.

(5) The case referred to is a case, not falling within paragraph (3) or (4), of—
- (a) an award of child tax credit where the period for which it has effect begins on or after 1st February 2019 and where, on the day on which the claimant or claimants of the award makes or make the claim for it, he or she (or they) has or have an award of working tax credit;
- (b) an award of working tax credit where the period for which it has effect begins on or after 1st February 2019 and where, on the day on which the claimant or claimants of the award makes or make the claim for it, he or she (or they) has or have an award of child tax credit;
- (c) an award of child tax credit or working tax credit where the period for which it has effect begins on or after 1st February 2019 and where the claimant or claimants who makes or make the claim for the award had an award of the same type of tax credit for the previous tax year to the tax year for which the award is made.

(6) For the purposes of paragraph (5)(a) and (b)—
- (a) a person is to be treated as having an award of working tax credit with effect from the start of a tax year ("current tax year") even though a decision has not been made under section 14 of the 2002 Act in respect of a claim for that tax credit for that tax year, if the person had an award of working tax credit for the previous tax year and any of the cases specified in paragraph (7) applies; and
- (b) a person is to be treated as having an award of child tax credit with effect from the start of a tax year ("current tax year") even though a decision has not been made under section 14 of the 2002 Act in

respect of a claim for that tax credit for that tax year, if the person had an award of child tax credit for the previous tax year and any of the cases specified in paragraph (7) applies.

(7) The cases are—

(a) a final notice has not been given to the person under section 17 of the 2002 Act in respect of that previous tax year;

(b) a final notice has been given, which includes provision by virtue of subsections (2) and (4) of section 17, or a combination of those subsections and subsection (6) of that section and—
  (i) the date specified in the notice for the purposes of section 17(2) and (4) or, where different dates are specified, the later of them, has not yet passed and no claim for a tax credit for the current tax year has been made, or treated as made; or
  (ii) a claim for a tax credit has been made, or treated as made, on or before the date mentioned in paragraph (i), but no decision has been made in relation to that claim under section 14(1) of the 2002 Act;

(c) a final notice has been given, no claim for a tax credit for the current tax year has been made, or treated as made, and no decision has been made under section 18(1) of the 2002 Act in respect of entitlement to a tax credit for the previous tax year;

(d) a final notice has been given and the person made a declaration in response to a requirement included in that notice by virtue of section 17(2)(a), (4)(a) or (6)(a), or any combination of those provisions—
  (i) by the date specified on the final notice;
  (ii) if not in accordance with paragraph (i), within 30 days following the date on the notice to the person that payments of a tax credit under section 24(4) of the 2002 Act have ceased due to the person's failure to make the declaration by the date specified in the final notice; or
  (iii) if not in accordance with paragraph (i) or (ii), before 31st January in the tax year following the period to which the final notice relates and, in the opinion of Her Majesty's Revenue and Customs, the person had good reason for not making the declaration in accordance with paragraph (i) or (ii).

(8) In this article, a reference to the date on which a claim for a tax credit is made is a reference to the date on which such a claim is made or treated as made as provided for in the Tax Credits (Claims and Notifications) Regulations 2002.

(9) The case referred to is the case of an award of a tax credit that had effect for a period that ended on or before 30th January 2019.

Appointed day – coming into force of universal credit provisions and abolition of income-related employment and support allowance and income-based jobseeker's allowance: persons resident outside Great Britain

4.—(1) The day appointed for the coming into force of the UC provisions, in so far as they are not already in force, in relation to the case of a claim referred to in paragraph (2), and any award that is made in respect of the claim, is the day appointed in accordance with paragraph (3).

(2) The claim referred to is a claim for universal credit that is made on or after 1st February 2019 in respect of a period that begins on or after 1st February 2019 where, on the date that the claim is made, the claimant (in the case of UC joint claimants, either claimant) resides outside Great Britain.

(3) The day appointed in relation to the case of a claim referred to in paragraph (2), and any award that is made in respect of the claim, is the first day of the period in respect of which the claim is made.

(4) Article 3(6) of the No.9 Order applies for the purposes of paragraph (3) as it applies for the purposes of article 3(4)(a) of the No.9 Order.

(5) The day appointed for the coming into force of the provisions referred to in article 4(1)(a) to (c) of the No.9 Order, in so far as they are not already in force, in relation to the case of a claim referred to in paragraph (6), and any award that is made in respect of the claim, is the day appointed in accordance with paragraph (7).

(6) The claims referred to are—
(a) a claim for universal credit that is made on or after 1st February 2019 in respect of a period that begins on or after 1st February 2019 where, on the date that the claim is made, the claimant (in the case of UC joint claimants, either claimant) resides outside Great Britain;
(b) a claim for an employment and support allowance or a jobseeker's allowance that is made on or after 1st February 2019 in respect of a period that begins on or after 1st February 2019 where, on the date that the claim is made, the claimant (in the case of a claim for a jobseeker's allowance by a joint-claim couple, or a claim for either allowance by a person who would form part of a UC couple for the purposes of universal credit, either member of the couple) resides outside Great Britain;
(c) a claim for an employment and support allowance or a jobseeker's allowance other than one referred to in sub-paragraph (b) that is made or treated as made during the relevant period by a UC single claimant or by either of two UC joint claimants who has or have made a claim for universal credit under sub-paragraph (a).

(7) The day appointed in relation to the case of a claim referred to in paragraph (6), and any award that is made in respect of the claim, is the first day of the period in respect of which the claim is made.

(8) Paragraphs (6), (7), (9) and (10) of article 4 of the No.9 Order apply in relation to a claim for universal credit referred to in paragraph (6)(a) (and any award that is made in respect of the claim) as they apply to a claim for universal credit referred to in sub-paragraph (a) or (b) of article 4(2) of the No.9 Order (and any award that is made in respect of the claim).

(9) Article 5(8) of the No.9 Order applies for the purposes of paragraph (7) as it applies for the purposes of article 4(3)(a) of the No.9 Order.

(10) Article 7 of the No.23 Order applies as though the reference in paragraph (1) of that article to article 3(1) and (2)(a) to (c) of that Order included a reference to paragraphs (1) and (2).

(11) No claim may be made for universal credit on or after 1st February 2019 by a UC single claimant who is, or UC joint claimants each of whom is, a frontier worker.

(12) Articles 9 to 22 of the No.9 Order apply in connection with the coming into force of the provisions referred to in article 4(1)(a) to (c) of the No.9 Order, in relation to the case of a claim referred to in paragraph (6), and any award made in respect of the claim, as they apply in connection

with the coming into force of those provisions in relation to the case of a claim referred to in sub-paragraph (a) or (g) of article 4(2) of the No.9 Order and any award that is made in respect of the claim.

(13) In this article—
- (a) "claimant"—
    - (i) in relation to an employment and support allowance, has the same meaning as in Part 1 of the Welfare Reform Act 2007;
    - (ii) in relation to a jobseeker's allowance, has the same meaning as in the Jobseeker's Act 1995 (as it applies apart from the amendments made by Part 1 of Schedule 14 to the Act that remove references to an income-based jobseeker's allowance), save as mentioned in paragraph (6)(b);
    - (iii) in relation to universal credit, has the same meaning as in Part 1 of the Act, save as mentioned in paragraph (2) and (6)(a);
- (b) "relevant period" means, in relation to a claim for universal credit within paragraph (6)(a), any UC claim period, and any period subsequent to any UC claim period in respect of which the claimant is entitled to an award of universal credit in respect of the claim;
- (c) "UC claim period" means a period when—
    - (i) a claim for universal credit within paragraph (6)(a) has been made but a decision has not yet been made on the claim; or
    - (ii) a decision has been made that the claimant is not entitled to universal credit and—
- (aa) the Secretary of State is considering whether to revise that decision under section 9 of the Social Security Act 1998, whether on an application made for that purpose or on the Secretary of State's own initiative; or
- (bb) the claimant has appealed against that decision to the First-tier Tribunal and that appeal, or any subsequent appeal to the Upper Tribunal or a court, has not yet been finally determined;
- (d) the Universal Credit, Personal Independence Payment, Jobseeker's Allowance and Employment and Support Allowance (Claims and Payments) Regulations 2013 apply for the purpose of deciding—
    - (i) whether a claim for universal credit is made;
    - (ii) the date on which such a claim is made;
- (e) the Claims and Payments Regulations 1987 apply, subject to sub-paragraphs (f) and (g), for the purpose of deciding—
    - (i) whether a claim for an employment and support allowance or a jobseeker's allowance is made; and
    - (ii) the date on which the claim is made or treated as made;
- (f) subject to sub-paragraph (g)—
    - (i) a person makes a claim for an employment and support allowance or a jobseeker's allowance if he or she takes any action which results in a decision on a claim being required under the Claims and Payments Regulations 1987; and
    - (ii) it is irrelevant that the effect of any provision of those Regulations is that, for the purposes of those Regulations, the claim is made or treated as made at a date that is earlier than the date on which that action is taken;
- (g) where, by virtue of—
    - (i) regulation 6(1F)(b) or (c) of the Claims and Payments Regulations 1987, in the case of a claim for an employment and support allowance; or

(ii) regulation 6(4ZA) to (4ZD) and (4A)(a)(i) and (b) of those Regulations, in the case of a claim for a jobseeker's allowance,

a claim for an employment and support allowance or a jobseeker's allowance is treated as made at a date that is earlier than the date on which the action referred to in sub-paragraph (f)(i) is taken, the claim is treated as made on that earlier date.

Amendment of the No.9, No.21 and No.23 Orders

2.28   5.—(1) With effect from 1st February 2019, the No.9, No.21 and No.23 Orders are amended as follows.

(2) In the No.9 Order—

(a) in article 5A(1), after "disability premium)" insert "or article 4(11) of the Welfare Reform Act 2012 (Commencement No.32 and Savings and Transitional Provisions) Order 2019 (no claims for universal credit by frontier workers)";

(b) in article 6(1)(e)(ii), for the words after "made)" substitute "or the claim is or would be one to which regulation 4A of those Regulations (restriction on claims for universal credit by persons entitled to a severe disability premium) or article 4(11) of the Welfare Reform Act 2012 (Commencement No.32 and Savings and Transitional Provisions) Order 2019 (no claims for universal credit by frontier workers) applies".

(3) In article 6 of the No.21 Order—

(a) in paragraph (3), omit "or a tax credit" in the words before sub-paragraph (a), and omit sub-paragraph (b);

(b) in paragraph (4), for the words "is or are entitled" to the end substitute "has or have an award of working tax credit or child tax credit respectively";

(c) in paragraph (5), for the words "is or was, or persons are or were, entitled to" substitute "has or had, or persons have or had, an award of";

(d) for paragraph (6) substitute—

"(6) In paragraph (4), the reference to a person having an award of a tax credit includes where the person is "treated as being entitled to a tax credit" in the circumstances referred to in regulation 11(1) and (2)(a) to (ca) of the Universal Credit (Transitional Provisions) Regulations 2014 but as if, in regulation 11(1), for "For the purposes of regulations 7(7) and 8(4)" there were substituted "For the purposes of article 6(4) of the Welfare Reform Act 2012 (Commencement No.21 and Transitional and Transitory Provisions) Order 2015".";

(e) in paragraph (11), after "2014," insert "or by virtue of article 4(11) of the Welfare Reform Act 2012 (Commencement No.32 and Savings and Transitional Provisions) Order 2019".

(4) In article 7 of the No.23 Order(5)—

(a) in paragraph (2), after "2014," insert "or by virtue of article 4(11) of the Welfare Reform Act 2012 (Commencement No.32 and Savings and Transitional Provisions) Order 2019";

(b) in paragraph (4), omit "or a tax credit" in the words before sub-paragraph (a), and omit sub-paragraph (b);

(c) in paragraph (5), for the words "is or are entitled" to the end substitute "has or have an award of working tax credit or child tax credit respectively";
(d) in paragraph (6), for the words "is or was, or persons are or were, entitled to" substitute "has or had, or persons have or had, an award of";
(e) for paragraph (7) substitute—
"(7) In paragraph (5), the reference to a person having an award of a tax credit includes where the person is "treated as being entitled to a tax credit" in the circumstances referred to in regulation 11(1) and (2)(a) to (ca) of the Universal Credit (Transitional Provisions) Regulations 2014 but as if, in regulation 11(1), for "For the purposes of regulations 7(7) and 8(4)" there were substituted "For the purposes of article 7(5) of the Welfare Reform Act 2012 (Commencement No.23 and Transitional and Transitory Provisions) Order 2015".".

GENERAL NOTE

Section 33(1)(f) of the Welfare Reform Act 2012 provides for the abolition of both child tax credit and working tax credit, together with Part 1 of the Tax Credits Act 2002. Article 2 of the Order brings section 33(1)(f) into force on 1 February 2019. Article 2 is subject to the savings provisions in Art.3, which specifies five cases to which s.33(1)(f) does not apply. In these cases, s.33(1)(f) is treated as if it had not come into force.

For the UK Government's estimates of the rate at which claimants of existing benefits will transfer (or migrate) to universal credit, see the note to s.33 of the Welfare Reform Act 2012, above in this volume.

It should be noted that, generally, the legal consequences of a universal credit claim, made by a person entitled to a tax credit, are not dealt with in the Order. The consequences are provided for by the Universal Credit (Transitional Provisions) Regulations 2014 (SI 2014/1230): see below in this volume.

Case 1–article 3(2)

Case 1 applies to an award of a tax credit that has effect for a period that includes January 31, 2019. Since most tax credits awards are made for the entire tax year, the majority of tax credits recipients for tax year 2018/19 will be unaffected by the commencement of s.33(1)(f).

Case 2–article 3(3)

Case 2 applies to an award of a tax credit for a period beginning on or after February 1, 2019 where:
(a) the claim for the tax credit was made by a single claimant, couple or polygamous unit; and
(b) the single claimant, both members of the couple or all members of the polygamous unit could claim universal credit (UC) and meet the UC age condition (in s.4 of the Welfare Reform Act 2012).

Case 3–article 3(4)

Case 3 applies to an award of child tax credit or working tax credit that has effect for a period beginning on or after February 1, 2019 where:
(a) the claim is made by a couple or a polygamous unit where only one member of the couple, or only some members of the polygamous unit, could claim UC and meet the UC age condition, and

Welfare Reform Act 2012 (Commencement No.32) Order 2019

(b) where the member or members who could claim UC, and meet the age condition, cannot claim UC by virtue of restrictions in a transitional provisions order made under section 150(3) of the 2012 Act or regulations made under Sch.6 to that Act.

Cases 2 and 3–persons who may claim Universal Credit
Cases 2 and 3 refer to a person who may claim UC. The Universal Credit (Transitional Provisions) Regulations 2014 (SI 2014/1230) set out the categories of person who are capable of claiming UC. The general rule is that a person who is able to make a claim for UC is unable to claim a tax credit (reg.6A of the 2014 Regulations).

Case 4–article 3(5)

2.32   Case 4 applies to an award, not falling with Case 2 or Case 3, for a period beginning on or after February 1, 2019, of:
(a) child tax credit where, on the date of claim, the person/s have an award of working tax credit; and
(b) working tax credit where, on the date of claim, the person/s have an award of child tax credit;
(c) either tax credit where the claimant/s had an award of the same type of tax credit for the previous tax year.
For these purposes, a person is treated as having an award of tax credit even if a decision on a claim for tax credit under s.14 of the Tax Credits Act 2002 is awaited, in the cases described in art.3(7).

Case 5–article 3(9)
Case 5 applies to an award of a tax credit that had effect for a period that ended on or before January 30, 2019.

The Universal Credit (Transitional Provisions) Regulations 2014

(SI 2014/1230) (As Amended)

The Secretary of State for Work and Pensions makes the following Regulations in exercise of the powers conferred by section 42(2) and (3) of and paragraphs 1(1) and (2)(b), 3(1)(a) to (c), 4(1)(a), 5(1), (2)(c) and (d) and (3)(a) and 6 of Schedule 6 to the Welfare Reform Act 2012.

In accordance with section 172(1) of the Social Security Administration Act 1992 ("the 1992 Act"), the Secretary of State has referred proposals in respect of these Regulations to the Social Security Advisory Committee.

In accordance with section 176(1) of the 1992 Act and, in so far as these Regulations relate to housing benefit, the Secretary of State has consulted with organisations appearing to him to be representative of the authorities concerned in respect of proposals for these Regulations.

Arrangement of Regulations

Part 1

Introductory

2.33   1.   Citation and commencement.
       2.   Interpretation.

(SI 2014/1230) as amended

PART 2

TRANSITION TO UNIVERSAL CREDIT

Chapter 2–Entitlement to Other Benefits

5. Exclusion of entitlement to certain benefits.
6A. Restriction on claims for housing benefit, income support or a tax credit.
7. Termination of awards of certain existing benefits: new claimant partners.
8. Termination of awards of certain existing benefits: other claimants.
9. Treatment of ongoing entitlement to certain benefits: benefit cap.
11. Ongoing awards of tax credits.
12. Modification of tax credits legislation: overpayments and penalties.
12A. Modification of tax credits legislation: finalisation of tax credits.
13. Appeals etc relating to certain existing benefits.
14. Appeals etc relating to universal credit.

Chapter 3–Effect of Transition to Universal Credit

15. Modification of Claims and Payments Regulations in relation to universal credit claimants.
16. Persons unable to act.
17. Advance payments of universal credit.
28. Meaning of "qualifying young person".
37. Loss of benefit penalties: transition from working tax credit.

PART 3

ARRANGEMENTS REGARDING CHANGES TO THE CHILD ELEMENT FROM APRIL 2017

41. Availability of the child element where maximum exceeded—continuation of exception from a previous award of child tax credit. . .
42. Evidence for non-consensual conception where claimant previously had an award of child tax credit.
43. Abolition of higher amount of the child element for first child or qualifying young person—saving where claimant responsible for a child or qualifying young person born before 6th April 2017.

PART 4

MANAGED MIGRATION TO UNIVERSAL CREDIT

The Migration Process

44. Migration notice.
45. Extension of the deadline day.
46. Termination of existing benefits if no claim before the deadline.

The Universal Credit (Transitional Provisions) Regulations 2014

Transitional Protection

47. Meaning of "qualifying claim".
48. Meaning of "migration day".
49. Secretary of State to determine whether transitional protection applies.
50. The transitional capital disregard.
51. The transitional element.
52. The transitional element–total legacy amount.
53. The transitional element–indicative UC amount.
54. The transitional element–initial amount and adjustment where other elements increase.

Ending of transitional protection

55. Circumstances in which transitional protection ceases.
56. Application of transitional protection to a subsequent award.

Miscellaneous

57. Qualifying claim–Secretary of State may set later commencement day.
58. Minimum income floor not to apply for first 12 months.
59. Protection for full-time students until course completed.
60. Rounding
61. Effect of revision, appeal etc of an award of an existing benefit.

SCHEDULES

SCHEDULE 1–MODIFICATION OF TAX CREDITS LEGISLATION (FINALISATION OF TAX CREDITS)

GENERAL NOTE

2.34   This volume reproduces those provisions of the Universal Credit (Transitional Provisions) Regulations 2014 that apply to the transition (or migration) from tax credits to universal credit. For the full text of the 2014 Regulations, see Vol.II in this series.

'Managed migration' and 'natural migration' to universal credit

2.35   These Regulations do not specify types of claimant who are required to claim universal credit. This function is now performed by commencement orders made under the Welfare Reform Act 2012. Of most significance in this respect is the Welfare Reform Act 2012 (Commencement No.29 and Commencement No.17, 19, 22, 23 and 24 and Transitional and Transitory Provisions (Modification)) Order 2017 (see above in this volume).

Claimants who transfer to universal credit because of commencement order provisions are referred to by the DWP as having been 'naturally migrated'. Part 4 of these Regulations, added by amendment with effect from July 24, 2019, confer 'managed migration' powers on the Secretary of State, that is powers to require claimants, on a case-by-case basis, to claim universal credit. Whether a claim is made under managed migration or through natural migration, certain legal consequences of a universal claim for entitlement to tax credits are provided for by these Regulations.

An important difference between 'managed migration' and 'natural migration' is that, at the time of writing, natural migration does not presently attract transitional protection (although there are specific transitional protection rules for naturally migrating claimants whose existing benefits include a severe disability premium). This difference in treatment has already attracted legal challenges.

(SI 2014/1230) as amended

In *TD & Others v Secretary of State for Work & Pensions* [2019] EWHC 462 (Admin), the High Court rejected a judicial review challenge linked to the UK Government's failure to confer transitional protection on all claimants migrating from existing benefits, including tax credits, to universal credit. However, the High Court's decision was overturned by the Court of Appeal in *R (TD & Ors) v Secretary of State for Work And Pensions* [2020] EWCA Civ 618. The Appellants in *TD* had made universal credit claims even though the transitional legislation did not effectively require them to do so. It seems that the Appellants claimed universal credit because they were wrongly advised by benefits officials that they had to. Once the Appellants had claimed universal credit, reg.8 of the 2014 Regulations (see below) caused their existing awards to terminate. The Appellants' universal credit awards were of lower value than their previous awards. The Court of Appeal accepted the Appellants' argument that, in their cases, the absence of transitional protection constituted discrimination contrary to art.14 of the European Convention on Human Rights. For art.14 purposes, the comparator group was, according to the Court of Appeal, "people who were entitled to legacy benefits and in whose cases no error was made by the Respondent". The High Court's analysis was flawed because, in considering whether the difference of treatment to which the Appellants had been subjected was justified, the judge failed to decide that matter for herself. Instead, the judge rejected the Appellants' case because she was persuaded that justification had been adequately considered by the Secretary of State. The Court of Appeal went on to decide that the difference of treatment was not justified and its effect was manifestly disproportionate for the Appellants so that their rights under art.14 had been breached. The key consideration was identified in para.83 of the Court's judgment:

> "83...these Appellants were treated as they were despite their successful reviews, for reasons to do with administrative cost and complexity, which have nothing to do with the merits of their cases; and that the only reason in reality why they moved from legacy benefits to UC was as a result of errors of law by the state itself."

The Court of Appeal gave a declaration that the Appellants' art.14 rights had been breached but added "it will be a matter for the Secretary of State to decide how to respond to a declaration". Whether or not the response will be to introduce transitional protection for all claimants, rather than limiting it to those undergoing 'managed migration', remains to be seen. The Court's decision was not based on a finding that the absence of transitional protection was, in general, discrimination contrary to art.14. However, nor did the Court rule that its absence was, in general, justified. As explained above, the Court decided the case by reference to the, hopefully, infrequent circumstance of a misadvised claimant. Whether, in the absence of such circumstances, the UK Government's policy of granting transitional protection to universal credit 'managed migrants', but not 'natural migrants. falls foul of art.14 remains to be determined.

PART 1

INTRODUCTORY

Citation and commencement

1.—(1) These Regulations may be cited as the Universal Credit (Transitional Provisions) Regulations 2014.
(2) These Regulations come into force on 16th June 2014.

2.36

Interpretation

2.—(1) In these Regulations—
"the 2002 Act" means the Tax Credits Act 2002;
...
"the Act" means the Welfare Reform Act 2012;

2.37

The Universal Credit (Transitional Provisions) Regulations 2014

"assessment period" has the same meaning as in the Universal Credit Regulations;
[¹ "childcare costs element" has the meaning in the Universal Credit Regulations;]
"the Claims and Payments Regulations" means the Universal Credit, Personal Independence Payment, Jobseeker's Allowance and Employment and Support Allowance (Claims and Payments) Regulations 2013;
. . .
[¹ "deadline day" has the meaning in regulation 44;]
[¹ "earned income" has the meaning in Chapter 2 of Part 6 of the Universal Credit Regulations;]
"existing benefit" means income-based jobseeker's allowance, income-related employment and support allowance, income support, housing benefit and child tax credit and working tax credit under the 2002 Act, but see also [¹ paragraph (3) and] regulation 25(2);
[¹ "final deadline" has the meaning in regulation 46;]
"First-tier Tribunal" has the same meaning as in the Social Security Act 1998;
[¹ "HMRC" means Her Majesty's Revenue and Customs;]
"housing benefit" means housing benefit under section 130 of the Social Security Contributions and Benefits Act 1992;
"income-based jobseeker's allowance" has the same meaning as in the Jobseekers Act 1995;
"income-related employment and support allowance" means an income-related allowance under Part 1 of the 2007 Act;
"income support" means income support under section 124 of the Social Security Contributions and Benefits Act 1992;
[¹ "indicative UC amount" has the meaning in regulation 54;]
"joint-claim jobseeker's allowance" means old style JSA, entitlement to which arises by virtue of section 1(2B) of the Jobseekers Act 1995;
[¹ "migration day" has the meaning in regulation 49;]
[¹ "migration notice" has the meaning in regulation 44;]
"new claimant partner" has the meaning given in regulation 7;
"new style ESA" means an allowance under Part 1 of the 2007 Act as amended by the amendments made by Schedule 3, and Part 1 of Schedule 14, to the Act that remove references to an income-related allowance;
"new style JSA" means an allowance under the Jobseekers Act 1995 as amended by the amendments made by Part 1 of Schedule 14 to the Act that remove references to an income-based allowance;
[₁ "notified person" has the meaning in regulation 44;]
"old style ESA" means an employment and support allowance under Part 1 of the 2007 Act as that Part has effect apart from the amendments made by Schedule 3, and Part 1 of Schedule 14, to the Act that remove references to an income-related allowance;
"old style JSA" means a jobseeker's allowance under the Jobseekers Act 1995 as that Act has effect apart from the amendments made by Part 1 of Schedule 14 to the Act that remove references to an income-based allowance;
"partner" in relation to a person ("A") means a person who forms part of a couple with A;
[¹ "qualifying claim" has the meaning in regulation 48;]
[² "qualifying young person" has the same meaning as in the Universal Credit Regulations, but see also regulation 28;]
. . .

(SI 2014/1230 reg.2) as amended

[¹ "total legacy amount" has the meaning in regulation 53;]
[¹ "transitional capital disregard" has the meaning in regulation 51;]
[¹ "transitional element" has the meaning in regulation 52;]
"tax credit" (including "child tax credit" and "working tax credit"), "tax credits" and "tax year" have the same meanings as in the 2002 Act;
"the Universal Credit Regulations" means the Universal Credit Regulations 2013;
"Upper Tribunal" has the same meaning as in the Social Security Act 1998.
(2) For the purposes of these Regulations—
(a) the date on which a claim for universal credit is made is to be determined in accordance with the Claims and Payments Regulations;
(b) where a couple is treated, in accordance with regulation 9(8) of the Claims and Payments Regulations, as having made a claim for universal credit, references to the date on which the claim is treated as made are to the date of formation of the couple;
(c) where a regulation refers to entitlement to an existing benefit on the date on which a claim for universal credit is made or treated as made, such entitlement is to be taken into account notwithstanding the effect of regulations 5, 7 and 8 or termination of an award of the benefit before that date by virtue of an order made under section 150(3) of the Act.
...]

AMENDMENTS

1. The Universal Credit (Managed Migration Pilot and Miscellaneous Amendments) Regulations 2019 (SI 2019/1152) reg.3 (July 24, 2019).
2. The Social Security (Restrictions on Amounts for Children and Qualifying Young Persons) Amendment Regulations 2017 (SI 2017/376) reg.3 (July 24, 2019).

GENERAL NOTE

Certain provisions of these Regulations operate by reference to the main Universal Credit regulations. The following regulations are reproduced in Vol.V in this series: 2.38

- the Universal Credit Regulations 2013 (SI 2013/376);
- the Universal Credit, Personal Independence Payment, Jobseeker's Allowance and Employment and Support Allowance (Claims and Payments) Regulations 2013 (SI 2013/380).

PART 2

TRANSITION TO UNIVERSAL CREDIT

Chapter 2–Entitlement to Other Benefits

Exclusion of entitlement to certain benefits

5.—(1) Except as provided in paragraph (2), a claimant is not entitled to— 2.39
...(c) a tax credit...
in respect of any period when the claimant is entitled to universal credit.

(2) Entitlement to universal credit does not preclude the claimant from entitlement—

...(b) during the first assessment period for universal credit, where the claimant is a new claimant partner, to—

...(iii) a tax credit, where an award to which the new claimant partner is entitled terminates, in accordance with the 2002 Act, after the first date of entitlement to universal credit.

DEFINITIONS

"new claimant partner"—see reg.7.
"first assessment period" –under reg.21(1) of the Universal Credit Regulations 2013 (SI 2013/376), an assessment period is "a period of one month beginning with the first date of entitlement".

GENERAL NOTE

2.40 Regulation 5(2) protects a claimant who becomes entitled to a joint award of universal credit upon forming a couple with an existing universal credit claimant. Separately from reg.5(1), the claimant's existing tax credit award as a single claimant terminates upon the claimant becoming a member of a couple. This may result in an overlap period during which the claimant is in principle entitled to a single person's tax credit award and a joint award of universal credit. If so, reg.5(2) maintains that joint entitlement during the first universal credit assessment period.

[¹**Restriction on claims for housing benefit, income support or a tax credit**

2.41 **6A.**—(1) Except as provided by paragraphs (2) to (7) a person may not make a claim for housing benefit, income support, or a tax credit.

...

(6) Paragraph (1) does not apply to a claim for a tax credit where a person makes or persons make a claim for child tax credit or working tax credit and on the date on which he or she (or they) makes or make the claim he or she (or they) has or have an award of working tax credit or child tax credit respectively.

(7) Paragraph (1) does not apply to a claim for a tax credit where a person has or had, or persons have or had, an award of child tax credit or working tax credit in respect of a tax year and that person or those persons makes or make (or is or are treated as making) a claim for that tax credit for the next tax year.

(8) For the purposes of this regulation—
(a) "polygamous marriage" has the same meaning as in regulation 3(5) of the Universal Credit Regulations;
(b) "State Pension Credit Act couple" means a couple as defined in section 17(1) of the State Pension Credit Act 2002,

and a reference to the date on which a claim for a tax credit is made is a reference to the date on which such claim is made or treated as made as provided for in the Tax Credits (Claims and Notifications) Regulations 2002.]

AMENDMENT

1. Universal Credit (Transitional Provisions) Amendment Regulations 2022 (SI 2022/752) reg.4 (July 25, 2022).

(SI 2014/1230 reg.6A) as amended

GENERAL NOTE

Paragraph (1) enacts the general rule that no one may make a claim for a tax credit. The general rule is subject to two exceptions. First, where, at the date of claim, the person (or couple) has an award of a tax credit (reg.6A(6)). According to the Explanatory Memorandum to the amending instrument, SI 2022/752, this is intended to allow tax credit awards to continue to be renewed annually pending a claimant's transfer to Universal Credit. Secondly, where a person (or couple) has or had an award of a tax credit for a particular tax year and makes (or is treated as making) a claim for the same type of tax credit for the next tax year (reg.6A(7)).

Regulation 6A is a re-enactment of much of art.7 of the Welfare Reform Act 2012 (Commencement No.23 and Transitional and Transitory Provisions) Order 2015 (SI 2015/634). The provisions were relocated to the main transitional regulations in order to "simplify and improve the legislative position so it can be read in conjunction with the other provisions relating to the transition to UC" (Explanatory Memorandum to SI 2022/752).

Regulation 6A(7) re-enacts without alteration art.7(6) of the 2015 Order. Accordingly, Upper Tribunal Judge Mitchell's construction of the art.7(6) in *W v HMRC (TC)* [2020] UKUT 239 (AAC) remains applicable. Judge Mitchell held that the exception in art.7(6) (now reg.6A(7)) was not satisfied where a person whose original award was as a member of a couple subsequently claimed a tax credit as a single person:

"11...After the introductory injunction ('paragraph (1) does not apply to a claim for a tax credit', Article 7(6) contains two components whose purpose is to identify the class of individuals that benefit from that injunction:

(a) the first component identifies a wide class comprised of two groups: (i) a person who has or had an award of a tax credit; and (ii) persons who have or had an award of tax credit;
(b) the second component narrows down that wide class. In doing so, it maintains, and operates on, the distinction drawn by the first component between sole and joint claimants, as is shown by it use of the referential pronouns 'that' and 'those'.

For a person within group (i) under what I have described as the first component, 'that person' must make a claim for tax credit for the next tax year to avoid being filtered out of article 7(6) [now regulation 6A(7)]. For persons within group (ii), 'those persons' must make a claim.

12.. A person in Mr W's position, that is a person residing in a UC 'Full Service Area' who jointly claimed a tax credit in the previous tax year, will only benefit from article 7(6) [now regulation 6A(7)] if he re-claims together with the previous year's partner."

The issue in *Revenue and Customs Commissioners v RS* [2022] UKUT 246 (AAC) was the meaning of "for the next tax year", a component of the exception provided for by reg.6A(7) (the issue arose under art.7 of the No.23 commencement order but, as mentioned above, that provision is re-enacted in reg.6A(7)). In particular, whether a claim made part-way through a tax year was made "for the next tax year". The claimant had a tax credit award for 2018/19, which terminated with effect from June 26, 2019, and he made a new claim on August 1, 2019; the question was whether that claim was made for 2019/20, which was the "next tax year". Upper Tribunal Judge Wikeley held not, so that the claimant did not satisfy the exception. A tax year runs from April 6 in one calendar year to April 5 in the next year (Tax Credits Act 2002 s.48). The legislative intention, therefore, must have been that the phrase "for the next tax year" meant the whole of the next tax year. Since the claimant had not made a claim for the (whole of) the next tax year, he fell outside the exception and was therefore caught by the general legislative prohibition on new claims being made for tax credits.

2.42

2.43

The Universal Credit (Transitional Provisions) Regulations 2014

Termination of awards of certain existing benefits: new claimant partners

2.44

7.—(1) This regulation applies where—
  (a) a person ("A") who was previously entitled to universal credit [¹...] ceases to be so entitled on becoming a member of a couple;
  (b) the other member of the couple ("the new claimant partner") was not entitled to universal credit [¹...] immediately before formation of the couple; [²and]
  (c) the couple is treated, in accordance with regulation 9(8) of the Claims and Payments Regulations, as having made a claim for universal credit [²...]
  [...]
  (6) Where an award terminates by virtue of this regulation, any legislative provision under which the award terminates on a later date does not apply.
  (7) Where the new claimant partner was, immediately before forming a couple with A, treated by regulation 11 as being entitled to a tax credit, the new claimant partner is to be treated, for the purposes of the 2002 Act, as having made a claim for the tax credit in question for the current tax year.

AMENDMENTS

1. The Universal Credit (Digital Service) Amendment Regulations 2014 (SI 2014/2887) reg.3 (November 26, 2014).
2. Universal Credit (Transitional Provisions) Amendment Regulations 2022 (SI 2022/752) reg.5(2) (July 25, 2022).

Termination of awards of certain existing benefits: other claimants

2.45

8.—(1) This regulation applies where—
  (a) a claim for universal credit (other than a claim which is treated, in accordance with regulation 9(8) of the Claims and Payments Regulations, as having been made) is made [², whether or not subsequently withdrawn].
  [²...]
  (2) [¹Where] this regulation applies, all awards of...a tax credit to which the claimant (or, in the case of joint claimants, either of them) is entitled on the date on which the claim is made are to terminate, by virtue of this regulation—
  (a) on the day before the first date on which the claimant is entitled to universal credit in connection with the claim; or
  (b) if the claimant is not entitled to universal credit, on the day before the first date on which he or she would have been so entitled, if all of the basic and financial conditions applicable to the claimant had been met.
  ...
  [² (2B) This regulation does not apply in the case of a single claimant who has reached the qualifying age for state pension credit or in the case of joint claimants who have both reached the qualifying age for state pension credit.]
  (4) Where this regulation applies and the claimant (or, in the case of joint claimants, either of them) is treated by regulation 11 as being entitled to a tax credit—

(SI 2014/1230 reg.8) as amended

(a) the claimant (or, as the case may be, the relevant claimant) is to be treated, for the purposes of the 2002 Act and this regulation, as having made a claim for the tax credit in question for the current tax year; and

(b) if the claimant (or the relevant claimant) is entitled on the date on which the claim for universal credit was made to an award of a tax credit which is made in respect of a claim which is treated as having been made by virtue of sub-paragraph (a), that award is to terminate, by virtue of this regulation—
 (i) on the day before the first date on which the claimant is entitled to universal credit; or
 (ii) if the claimant is not entitled to universal credit, on the day before the first date on which he or she would have been so entitled, if all of the basic and financial conditions applicable to the claimant had been met.

(5) Where an award terminates by virtue of this regulation, any legislative provision under which the award terminates on a later date does not apply.

AMENDMENTS

1. The Universal Credit (Miscellaneous Amendments, Saving and Transitional Provision) Regulations 2018 (SI 2018/65) reg.6 (April 11, 2018).
2. Universal Credit (Transitional Provisions) Amendment Regulations 2022 (SI 2022/752) reg.5(3) (July 25, 2022).

DEFINITIONS

"the Act"—see reg.2(1).
"basic conditions specified in section 4(1)(a) to (d)" refers to a person (a) being at least 18 years old; (b) not having reached the qualifying age for state pension credit; (c) being in Great Britain; and (d) not receiving education.
"new claimant partner"—see reg.7.
"Claims and Payments Regulations"—see reg.2(1).

2.46

GENERAL NOTE

As originally enacted, reg. 8 made its termination of entitlement to a tax credit, consequent on the making of a Universal Credit (UC) claim, conditional on a Secretary of State determination that an individual satisfied the UC basic conditions specified in reg. 8(1)(b). Since July 25, 2022, at which date reg.8(1)(b) was revoked, no such determination has been required.

In *HMRC v Secretary of State for Work and Pensions & SA* (TC) [2022] UKUT 350 (AAC), a three-judge panel of the Upper Tribunal considered the pre-July 25, 2022 requirement for the Secretary of State to be satisfied that a claimant met the UC basic conditions specified in reg. 8(1)(b). The basic condition in question required a person to be "in Great Britain" (s.4(1)(c), Welfare Reform Act 2012). Whether a person is "in Great Britain" is determined in accordance with reg.9 of the Universal Credit Regulations 2013 which requires a person to have a qualifying right to reside in the UK (or certain islands). The issue was whether the First-tier Tribunal, on an appeal consequent on a reg.8 termination of benefit, would consider whether the Secretary of State had been entitled to determine that a claimant met the UC basic conditions or if it was restricted to considering whether, in fact, the Secretary of State had been satisfied that the conditions were met. Given the complexities of right to reside law, it would often not be obvious whether the Secretary of State had been entitled to determine that a claimant was "in Great Britain". The Upper Tribunal held that the First-tier Tribunal could not decide if the Secretary

2.47

of State had been entitled to make a particular UC basic conditions determination. That would involve reading words into reg.8(1)(b) for which there was no justification. The only issue for the tribunal is a simple question of fact—did the Secretary of State make a UC basic conditions determination. Typically, this will be evidence by the 'stop notice' used by the DWP to inform HMRC of a reg.8(1) determination.

The three-judge panel in *SA* also disapproved Upper Tribunal Judge Poynter's observation in *MR v HMRC* (TC) (CTC/923/2018) that if, following termination of benefit under reg.8, the Secretary of State decided that a claimant was not, after all, entitled to UC, that would tend to show that the Secretary of State had not been satisfied, for reg.8(1)(b) purposes, that the basic conditions were satisfied. Under the three-judge panel's decision, the only issue is one of pure fact namely whether the Secretary of State determined that the UC basic conditions were met, and no qualitative considerations arise.

2.48 As originally enacted, reg.8(1)(a) said nothing about withdrawal of a UC claim. As subsequently amended, reg.8(1)(a) expressly provides that withdrawal of a UC claim makes no difference to its application. Therefore, the Upper Tribunal decisions considered below, about the legal consequences for reg.8 of withdrawal, or purported withdrawal, of UC claims, are only relevant to the operation of reg.8 before July 25, 2022.

In *HMRC v AB* [2021] UKUT 209 (AAC), HMRC accepted that a claimant withdrew her UC claim before the Secretary of State had determined whether the UC basic conditions were met. HMRC went on to argue that withdrawal of the claim made no difference to the operation of reg.8 so that, despite withdrawal, the subsequent determination that the UC basic conditions were met triggered reg.8(2) and terminated entitlement to tax credits. Upper Tribunal Judge Mitchell rejected HMRC's argument and held that, if a UC claim were withdrawn before the Secretary of State had made a UC basic conditions determination under reg.8(1)(b), reg.8(2) did not operate to terminate entitlement to a tax credit.

In *JL v Calderdale MBC* [2022] UKUT 9 (AAC); [2022] P.T.S.R. 808, the claimant attempted to withdraw his UC claim about three hours after it was made online. By that time, the DWP's computer systems had already accepted that the claimant met the UC basic conditions and notified the local authority responsible for the claimant's housing benefit award. The local authority decided that, under reg.8(2), the claimant's housing benefit award had been terminated. Upper Tribunal Judge Jacobs held that a DWP computer made a valid computerised determination that the UC basic conditions were met (s.2 of the Social Security Act 1998 provides authority, in certain circumstances, for decisions and determinations to be made by a computer). In other words, the claimant was too late. When he attempted to withdraw his UC claim, a determination had already been made that the UC basic conditions were met, and the UC claim could not be withdrawn because a determination had been made on it (reg.31(1) of the Universal Credit [etc.] (Claims and Payments) Regulations 2013). Judge Jacobs' related decision in *SK v Revenue and Customs Commissioners* [2022] UKUT 10 (AAC); [2022] P.T.S.R. 818 describes the DWP's evidence about their computerised decision/determination-making processes. If that evidence is accepted, as it was in *SK*, it follows, in Judge Jacobs' words, that "the making of the claim and the determination under regulation 8(1)(b) take effect simultaneously through the universal credit system". On this approach, a claimant has no opportunity to withdraw a UC claim before a UC basic conditions determination is made and there was no need for reg.8(1) to have been amended to provide that withdrawal of a UC claim has no effect on the operation of reg.8.

2.49 In *Revenue and Custom Commissioners v Secretary of State for Work and Pensions* [2023] UKUT 9 (AAC), Upper Tribunal Judge West approached the decisions in *AB* and *SK/JL* on the basis that they were in conflict, and it was necessary to choose which one to follow. However, that was not strictly accurate. The difference between the decisions was evidential or factual rather than principled. *AB* proceeded on the agreed factual basis that a UC claim was in fact withdrawn *before* a UC basic conditions determination had been made. By contrast, *SK* involved an attempt to withdraw a UC claim *after* a basic conditions determination had been made. *SK* did not address the legal consequences of withdrawal of a UC claim in advance of a UC basic conditions determination because the Judge accepted evidence that this was impossible under the DWP's computerised decision-making arrangements. Be that as it may, Judge West said that *SK* and *AB* were inconsistent decisions and that he would follow *SK* because it was a more recent decision and a cogent reason for not following *SK* was absent. The Judge said that this approach was mandated by the Court of Appeal in *Lune Metal Products Ltd (In Administration), Re* [2006] EWCA Civ 1720; [2007] B.C.C. 217, although that decision dealt with the case "where a first instance judge is faced with a point on which there are two previous inconsistent decisions from judges of co-ordinate jurisdiction" (the Upper Tribunal's jurisdiction, as a second-tier appellate body, is not analogous to the jurisdiction of a first instance judge). In fact, there are conflicting decisions as to whether this approach to choosing between inconsistent decisions applies in the jurisdiction now exercised by the Upper Tribunal (in *CIS/3101/2007* Social Security Commissioner Jacobs thought not; in *R(IS) 13/01* Social Security Commissioner Rowland thought it did apply). Arguably, the Upper Tribunal's responsibility for overseeing the orderly and principled development of social security law militates against following the *Re Lune* approach when deciding which of two conflicting Upper Tribunal decisions should be followed.

Regulation 8 does not apply to single claimants who have reached the qualifying age for state pension credit or joint claimants both of whom have reached that age (reg.8(2B)).

Treatment of ongoing entitlement to certain benefits: benefit cap

9.—(1) This regulation applies where a claimant who is a new claimant partner, or who has (in accordance with regulation 26 of [² the Claims and Payments Regulations]) been awarded universal credit in respect of a period preceding the date on which the claim for universal credit was made or treated as made—

(a) is entitled, in respect of the whole or part of the first assessment period for universal credit, to a welfare benefit (other than universal credit) mentioned in [¹ section 96(10) of the Act (benefit cap)]; and

(b) is entitled to housing benefit at any time during the first assessment period for universal credit, or would be so entitled were it not for the effect of these Regulations.

(2) Where this regulation applies, regulation 79 of the Universal Credit Regulations applies, in relation to the claimant, as if the benefit in question was not included in the list of welfare benefits in [¹ section 96(10) of the Act].

2.50

AMENDMENTS

1. The Benefit Cap (Housing Benefit and Universal Credit) (Amendment) Regulations 2016 (SI 2016/909) reg.5 (November 7, 2016).
2. Social Security and Universal Credit (Miscellaneous Amendments) Regulations 2023 (SI 2023/543) reg.6(2) (June 29, 2023).

DEFINITIONS

"first assessment period"–under regulation 21(1) of the Universal Credit Regulations 2013 (SI 2013/376), an assessment period is "a period of one month beginning with the first date of entitlement".

"new claimant partner"—see reg.7.

2.51

The Universal Credit (Transitional Provisions) Regulations 2014

GENERAL NOTE

2.52   In relation to the claimants described in reg.9(1), reg.9(2) ensures that, for the purposes of the benefit cap within universal credit, entitlement to an existing benefit is ignored. This is because it should already have been taken into account under the existing benefit cap (which relates to housing benefit, a benefit that is also replaced by universal credit).

Ongoing awards of tax credits

2.53   **11.**—(1) For the purposes of [¹ these Regulations]—
(a) a person is to be treated as being entitled to working tax credit with effect from the start of the current tax year even though a decision has not been made under section 14 of the 2002 Act in respect of a claim for that tax credit for that tax year, if the person was entitled to working tax credit for the previous tax year and any of the cases specified in paragraph (2) applies; and
(b) a person is to be treated as being entitled to child tax credit with effect from the start of the current tax year even though a decision has not been made under section 14 of the 2002 Act in respect of a claim for that tax credit for that tax year, if the person was entitled to child tax credit for the previous tax year and any of the cases specified in paragraph (2) applies [1 and references to an award of a tax credit are to be read accordingly].
(2) The cases are—
(a) a final notice has not been given to the person under section 17 of the 2002 Act in respect of the previous tax year;
(b) a final notice has been given, which includes provision by virtue of subsection (2) or (4) of section 17, or a combination of those subsections and subsection (6) and—
   (i) the date specified in the notice for the purposes of section 17(2) and (4) or, where different dates are specified, the later of them, has not yet passed and no claim for a tax credit for the current tax year has been made, or treated as made; or
   (ii) a claim for a tax credit has been made, or treated as made, on or before the date mentioned in paragraph (i), but no decision has been made in relation to that claim under section 14(1) of the 2002 Act;
(c) a final notice has been given, no claim for a tax credit for the current year has been made, or treated as made, and no decision has been made under section 18(1) of the 2002 Act in respect of entitlement to a tax credit for the previous tax year;
[² (ca) a final notice has been given and the person made a declaration in response to a requirement included in that notice by virtue of section 17(2)(a), (4)(a) or (6)(a), or any combination of those provisions—
   (i) by the date specified on the final notice;
   (ii) if not in accordance with paragraph (i), within 30 days following the date on the notice to the person that payments of tax credit under section 24(4) of the 2002 Act have ceased due to the person's failure to make the declaration by the date specified in the final notice; or
   (iii) if not in accordance with paragraph (i) or (ii), before 31 January in the tax year following the period to which the final notice

(SI 2014/1230 reg.11) as amended

relates and, in the opinion of Her Majesty's Revenue and Customs, the person had good reason for not making the declaration in accordance with paragraph (i) or (ii); or]
(d) a final notice has been given and—
   (i) the person did not make a declaration in response to provision included in that notice by virtue of section 17(2)(a), (4)(a) or (6)(a), or any combination of those provisions, by the date specified in the notice;
   (ii) the person was given due notice that payments of tax credit under section 24(4) of the 2002 Act had ceased due to his or her failure to make the declaration; and
   (iii) the person's claim for universal credit is made during the period of 30 days starting with the date on the notice referred to in paragraph (ii) or, where the person is a new claimant partner, notification of formation of a couple with a person entitled to universal credit is given to the Secretary of State during that period.

AMENDMENTS

1. The Universal Credit (Managed Migration Pilot and Miscellaneous Amendments) Regulations 2019 (SI 2019/1152) reg.3 (July 24, 2019).
2. The Universal Credit (Miscellaneous Amendments, Saving and Transitional Provision) Regulations 2018 (SI 2018/65) reg.6 (February 14, 2018).

DEFINITIONS

"2002 Act"—see reg.2(1).
"current tax year"—see the definition of "tax year" in section 48(1) of the Tax Credits Act 2002 (below in this volume).

GENERAL NOTE

2.54
This section takes account of the fact that, under the Tax Credits Act 2002, ongoing payments of tax credits tend to precede formal decisions awarding tax credits for a tax year. Under the 2002 Act, (a) awards of a tax credit are made before a formal decision is taken as to a person's entitlement to that tax credit; and (b) in the case of on-going awards, payments are maintained in advance of a formal decision to award tax credits for the current tax year under s.14 of the 2002 Act. The entitlement decision is normally taken in the tax year following that to which an award of a tax credit relates and involves HMRC first issuing a notice under s.17 of the 2002 Act, setting out presumed income for that previous tax year and inviting a claimant to make a declaration as to the accuracy of the figures set out in the notice, after which a final entitlement decision is taken under the 2002 Act. While this process is underway (often referred to as the renewal period), tax credits normally remain in payment in advance of a formal award for the current tax year under s.14 of the 2002 Act. A consequence of this feature of the 2002 Act is that, year-on-year, ongoing tax credits payments tend to be made in advance of formal decisions to award tax credits for a tax year.

Where this regulation applies, it ensures that reg.8 operates to end tax credits payments even though a formal tax credits award decision for a tax year has not been made. In other words, it accommodates tax credits claimants transferring to universal credit during the annual renewal period.

Modification of tax credits legislation: overpayments and penalties

2.55   **12.**—(1) This regulation applies where—
(a) a claim for universal credit is made, or is treated as having been made; [³ and]
(b) the claimant is, or was at any time during the tax year in which the claim is made or treated as made, entitled to a tax credit [³ . . .]
(c) [³ . . .].
(2) Where this regulation applies, the 2002 Act applies in relation to the claimant with the following modifications.
(3) In section 28—
(a) in subsection (1)—
(i) after "tax year" in both places where it occurs, insert "or part tax year";
[¹(ii) in paragraph (b), for the words from "as if it were" to the end substitute "as an overpayment of universal credit";]
[¹ (b). . .];
(c) omit subsection (5);
(d) in subsection (6) omit "(apart from subsection (5))".
[² [¹ (4). . .]]
(5) In section 48 after the definition of "overpayment" insert—
""part tax year" means a period of less than a year beginning with 6th April and ending with the date on which the award of a tax credit terminated,".
(6) In Schedule 2, in paragraph 6(1)(a) and (c) and (2)(a), after "for the tax year" insert "or part tax year".

AMENDMENTS

1. The Tax Credits (Exercise of Functions in relation to Northern Ireland and Notices for Recovery of Tax Credit Overpayments) Order 2017 (SI 2017/781) art.7 (September 25, 2017).
2. The Universal Credit (Transitional Provisions) (Amendment) Regulations 2016 (SI 2016/232) reg.2 (April 1, 2016).
3. Universal Credit (Transitional Provisions) Amendment Regulations 2022 (SI 2022/752) reg.5(4) (July 25, 2022).

DEFINITIONS

"basic conditions specified in section 4(1)(a) to (d) of the Act" refers to a person (a) being at least 18 years old; (b) not having reached the qualifying age for state pension credit; (c) being in Great Britain; and (d) not receiving education.
"the Act"—see reg.2(1).

GENERAL NOTE

2.56   This regulation modifies the overpayment provisions of the Tax Credits Act 2002 so that they apply to a person who, as a result of claim for universal credit, was paid tax credits for a "part tax year".

[¹ Modification of tax credits legislation: finalisation of tax credits

2.57   **12A.**—(1) This regulation applies where—
(a) a claim for universal credit is made, or is treated as having been made [³, or a migration notice is issued and the notified person fails to make a claim on or before the deadline day];

(b) the claimant is, or was at any time during the tax year in which the claim is made or treated as made [³ or in which the deadline day falls], entitled to a tax credit [² . . .]

(c) [² . . .].

(2) Subject to paragraph (3), where this regulation applies, the amount of the tax credit to which the person is entitled is to be calculated in accordance with the 2002 Act and regulations made under that Act, as modified by the Schedule to these Regulations ("the modified legislation").

(3) Where, in the opinion of the Commissioners for Her Majesty's Revenue and Customs, it is not reasonably practicable to apply the modified legislation in relation to any case or category of cases, the 2002 Act and regulations made under that Act are to apply without modification in that case or category of cases.]

AMENDMENTS

1. The Universal Credit (Transitional Provisions) (Amendment) Regulations 2014 (SI 2014/1626) reg.4 (October 13, 2014).
2. Universal Credit (Transitional Provisions) Amendment Regulations 2022 (SI 2022/752) reg.5(5) (July 25, 2022).
3. Social Security and Universal Credit (Migration of Tax Credit Claimants and Miscellaneous Amendments) Regulations 2024 (SI 2024/341) reg.8(3) (April 6, 2024).

DEFINITIONS

"basic conditions specified in section 4(1)(a) to (d) of the Act" refers to a person (a) being at least 18 years old; (b) not having reached the qualifying age for state pension credit; (c) being in Great Britain; and (d) not receiving education.

"the Act"—see reg.2(1).

GENERAL NOTE

Where a person's tax credits entitlement to a tax credit for a tax year is interrupted by the making of a claim for universal credit, the amount of the person's entitlement for the tax tear is to be calculated in accordance with the tax credits legislation as modified by Schedule 1 to these Regulations.

As a result of amendments to reg.12A, the same now applies where a claimant is issued with a migration notice under reg.44 but fails to make a claim on or before the deadline day specified in the notice (if the claimant was entitled to a tax credit for the tax year in which the deadline day falls). According to the Explanatory Memorandum which accompanied the amending instrument, this "will avoid the need for complex, confusing and potentially delayed interactions with HMRC that claimants would otherwise face". But this does not apply in the circumstances described in reg.12A(3).

2.58

Appeals etc relating to certain existing benefits

13.—(1) This regulation applies where, after an award of universal credit has been made to a claimant—

(a) an appeal against a decision relating to the entitlement of the claimant to. . . a tax credit (a "relevant benefit") is finally determined;

. . .

(d) a decision relating to the claimant's entitlement to a tax credit is revised under section 19 or 20 of the 2002 Act, or regulations made under section 21 of that Act, or is varied or cancelled under section 21A of that Act.

2.59

...

(3) Where the claimant is not a new claimant partner and, as a result of determination of the appeal or, as the case may be, revision, supersession, variation or cancellation of the decision, the claimant would (were it not for the effect of these Regulations) be entitled to a relevant benefit on the date on which the claim for universal credit was made, awards of relevant benefits are to terminate in accordance with regulation 8 [1 [2 or 46]].

(4) The Secretary of State is to consider whether it is appropriate to revise under section 9 of the 1998 Act the decision in relation to entitlement to universal credit or, if that decision has been superseded under section 10 of that Act, the decision as so superseded (in either case, "the UC decision").

(5) Where it appears to the Secretary of State to be appropriate to revise the UC decision, it is to be revised in such manner as appears to the Secretary of State to be necessary to take account of—
   (a) the decision of the First-tier Tribunal, Upper Tribunal or court, or, as the case may be, the decision relating to entitlement to a relevant benefit, as revised, superseded, varied or cancelled; and
   (b) any finding of fact by the First-tier Tribunal, Upper Tribunal or court.

AMENDMENTS

1. Universal Credit (Managed Migration Pilot and Miscellaneous Amendments) Regulations 2019 (SI 2019/1152) reg.4(7) (July 22, 2020).
2. Universal Credit (Transitional Provisions) Amendment Regulations 2022 (SI 2022/752) reg.11 and Sch. para.1(6) (July 25, 2022).

DEFINITIONS

"First-tier Tribunal"—see reg.2(1).
"Upper Tribunal"—see reg.2(1).

GENERAL NOTE

2.60   Where a person entitled to universal credit brings a successful appeal to the First-tier Tribunal against a tax credits decision, the effect of reg.13(3) is that any tax credit award made by the tribunal terminates on the day before the person became entitled to universal credit.

Appeals etc relating to universal credit

2.61   **14.**—(1) This regulation applies where—
   (a) a decision is made that a claimant is not entitled to universal credit ("the UC decision");
   (b) the claimant becomes entitled to. . .a tax credit (a "relevant benefit");
   (c) an appeal against the UC decision is finally determined, or the decision is revised under section 9 of the Social Security Act 1998;
   (d) an award of universal credit is made to the claimant in consequence of entitlement arising from the appeal, or from the decision as revised; and
   (e) the claimant would (were it not for the effect of regulation 5 and this regulation) be entitled to both universal credit and a relevant benefit in respect of the same period.

(SI 2014/1230 reg.14) as amended

(2) Subject to paragraph (3), where this regulation applies—
(a) all awards of a relevant benefit to which the claimant would (were it not for the effect of these Regulations) be entitled are to terminate, by virtue of this regulation, at the beginning of the first day of entitlement to that award; and
(b) any legislative provision . . . under which an award would otherwise terminate on a later date does not apply.
(3) *[omitted]*

Chapter 3–Effect of Transition to Universal Credit

Modification of Claims and Payments Regulations in relation to universal credit claimants

15.—(1) Where a claim for universal credit is made by a person who was previously entitled to an existing benefit, regulation 26 of the Claims and Payments Regulations (time within which a claim for universal credit is to be made) applies in relation to that claim with the modification specified in paragraph (2).
(2) In paragraph (3) of regulation 26, after sub-paragraph (a) insert—

"(aa) the claimant was previously in receipt of an existing benefit (as defined in the Universal Credit (Transitional Provisions) Regulations 2014) and notification of expiry of entitlement to that benefit was not sent to the claimant before the date that the claimant's entitlement expired;".

DEFINITIONS

"Claims and Payments Regulations"—see reg.2(1).

GENERAL NOTE

The effect of this regulation is to allow a universal credit claim to be backdated for up to one month where a tax credits claimant was not sent a notice of expiry of entitlement before the date of expiry. The claimant must also show that, as a result of that failure to send a notice of expiry, s/he could not reasonably have been expected to make an earlier claim (see reg.26(2) of the Universal Credit, Personal Independence Payment, Jobseeker's Allowance and Employment and Support Allowance (Claims and Payments) Regulations 2013 (SI 2013/380) in Vol.V of this series).

Persons unable to act

16.—(1) Paragraph (2) applies where—
. . .
(b) a person ("P2") has been appointed under regulation 18(3) of the Tax Credits (Claims and Notifications) Regulations 2002 ("the 2002 Regulations") (circumstances where one person may act for another in making a claim—other appointed persons) to act for a person who is unable to act ("P1") in making a claim for a tax credit.
(2) Where this paragraph applies and P1 is, or may be, entitled to universal credit, the Secretary of State may, if P2 agrees, treat the appointment of P2 as if it were made under regulation 57(1) of the Claims and Payments

The Universal Credit (Transitional Provisions) Regulations 2014

Regulations (persons unable to act) and P2 may carry out the functions set out in regulation 57(4) of those Regulations in relation to P1.

(3) Paragraph (4) applies where a person ("P2") was appointed, or treated as appointed, under regulation 57(1) of the Claims and Payments Regulations to carry out functions in relation to a person who is unable to act ("P1") and who was, or might have been, entitled to universal credit, but who has ceased to be so entitled, or was not in fact so entitled.

(4) Where this paragraph applies—

...

(b) the Board (within the meaning of the 2002 Regulations) may, if P2 agrees, treat the appointment of P2 as if it were made under regulation 18(3) of the 2002 Regulations and P2 may act for P1 in making a claim for a tax credit.

DEFINITIONS

"Claims and Payments Regulations"—see reg.2(1).

GENERAL NOTE

2.65 This regulation provides for an appointment to act made for tax credits purposes to have effect for the purposes of universal credit. The appointee must agree and, if so, the Secretary of State has a power, not a duty, to treat the appointment as having effect for universal credit purposes.

Advance payments of universal credit

2.66 **17.**—(1) This regulation applies where—
(a) the Secretary of State is deciding a claim for universal credit, other than a claim which is treated as having been made, in accordance with regulation 9(8) of the Claims and Payments Regulations;
(b) the claimant is, or was previously, entitled to an existing benefit ("the earlier award"); and
(c) if the earlier award terminated before the date on which the claim for universal credit was made, the claim for universal credit was made during the period of one month starting with the date of termination.

(2) Where this regulation applies—
(a) a single claimant may request an advance payment of universal credit;
(b) joint claimants may jointly request such a payment,
at any time during the first assessment period for universal credit.

(3) Where a request has been made in accordance with this regulation, the Secretary of State may make an advance payment to the claimant, or joint claimants, of such amount in respect of universal credit as the Secretary of State considers appropriate.

(4) After an advance payment has been made under this regulation, payments of any award of universal credit to the claimant or, in the case of joint claimants, to either or both of them, may be reduced until the amount of the advance payment is repaid.

DEFINITIONS

2.67 "Claims and Payments Regulations"—see reg.2(1).

(SI 2014/1230 reg.17) as amended

"first assessment period"—under regulation 21(1) of the Universal Credit Regulations 2013 (SI 2013/376), an assessment period is "a period of one month beginning with the first date of entitlement".

GENERAL NOTE

This regulation is intended to benefit claimants who are transferring to universal credit, with its monthly payment cycle, from a benefit that was paid more frequently than monthly.

2.68

Meaning of "qualifying young person"

28. Where a person who would (apart from the provision made by this regulation) be a "qualifying young person" within the meaning of regulation 5 of the Universal Credit Regulations is entitled to an existing benefit—

2.69

(a) that person is not a qualifying young person for the purposes of the Universal Credit Regulations; and
(b) regulation 5(5) of those Regulations applies as if, after "a person who is receiving" there were inserted "an existing benefit (within the meaning of the Universal Credit (Transitional Provisions) Regulations 2014),".

DEFINITIONS

"Universal Credit Regulations"—see reg.2(1).

GENERAL NOTE

This regulation prevents a young person who is entitled to a tax credit from being a 'qualifying young person' for universal credit purposes. This means, for instance, that a universal credit claimant cannot receive the child element for the young person under reg.24 of the Universal Credit Regulations 2013 (SI 2013/376), and is intended to avoid double provision for such young people.

2.70

[¹ Loss of benefit penalties: transition from working tax credit

37.—(1) This regulation applies where an award of universal credit is made to a claimant who—

2.71

(a) was previously entitled to working tax credit; and
(b) is an offender, within the meaning of the 2002 Act.

(2) Where this regulation applies, the Social Security (Loss of Benefit) Regulations 2001 apply as if in regulation 3ZB of those Regulations—

(a) in paragraph (1) at the beginning there were inserted "Subject to regulation 38 of the Universal Credit (Transitional Provisions) Regulations 2014,";
(b) "disqualification period" includes a disqualification period within the meaning of the 2002 Act;
(c) "offender" includes an offender within the meaning of the 2002 Act; and
(d) "offender's family member" includes a person who is a member of the family (within the meaning of section 137(1) of the Social Security Contributions and Benefits Act 1992) of a person who is an offender within the meaning of the 2002 Act.]

AMENDMENT

1. The Universal Credit (Transitional Provisions) (Amendment) Regulations 2014 (SI 2014/1626) reg.6 (October 13, 2014).

DEFINITIONS

"the 2002 Act"—see reg.2(1).
"offender"—see section 36A(1) of the Tax Credits Act 2002.

GENERAL NOTE

2.72 This regulation provides for disqualification penalty periods applied to offenders, when entitled to working tax credit, under s.36A of the Tax Credits Act 2002, to have effect for the purposes of the reduction of universal credit provisions in reg.3ZB of the Social Security (Loss of Benefit) Regulations 2001 (SI 2001/4022).

PART 3

ARRANGEMENTS REGARDING CHANGES TO THE CHILD ELEMENT FROM APRIL 2017

[¹ **Availability of the child element where maximum exceeded—continuation of exception from a previous award of child tax credit...**

2.73 41.—(1) Where—
(a) the claimant ("C") is the step-parent of a child or qualifying young person ("A"); and
(b) within the 6 months immediately preceding the first day on which C became entitled to an award of universal credit, C had an award of child tax credit...in which an exception corresponding with an exception under paragraph 2, 3, 5 or 6 of Schedule 12 to the Universal Credit Regulations applied in respect of A,
paragraph 6 of that Schedule is to apply as if sub-paragraph (c) of that paragraph were satisfied, despite the fact that the previous award was not an award of universal credit.
(2) In this regulation, "step-parent" has the same meaning as in the Universal Credit Regulations.]

AMENDMENT

1. The Social Security (Restrictions on Amounts for Children and Qualifying Young Persons) Amendment Regulations 2017 (SI 2017/376) reg.3 (April 6, 2017).

DEFINITIONS

"qualifying young person"–reg.5 of the Universal Credit Regulations 2013 (SI 2013/376) (see Vol.V in this series).

GENERAL NOTE

2.74 This regulation concerns the 'two-child limit' in universal credit, which reflects the limit introduced into child tax credit by amendments made to reg.7 of the Child Tax Credit Regulations 2002 (SI 2002/2007). Generally, reg.7(2A) of the 2002 Regulations prevents an individual child element from being included within an award of child tax credit for third or subsequent children born on or after April 6, 2017. The child tax credit limit does not apply in certain cases. This regulation maintains certain of these exceptions in the case of step-parents who transfer from child tax credit to universal credit, in particular those relating to multiple births, adoption, non-consensual adoption, where a child tax credit exception applied within the previous six months. The reason why step-parents are the subject of specific transitional provision is that, under the Universal Credit Regulations 2013 (SI 2013/376), the multiple birth, adoption and non-consensual adoption exceptions to the two-child limit can be claimed by parents but not step-parents. Regulation 41 therefore prevents step-parents from losing the benefit of an exception that they had enjoyed under child tax credit.

[¹ Evidence for non-consensual conception where claimant previously had an award of child tax credit

42.—(1) This regulation applies for the purposes of paragraph 5 of Schedule 12 to the Universal Credit Regulations (exception for non-consensual conception).

(2) The Secretary of State may treat the condition in sub-paragraph (3)(a) of that paragraph 5 as met if the Secretary of State is satisfied that the claimant has previously provided the evidence referred to in that sub-paragraph to the Commissioners for her Majesty's Revenue and Customs for the purposes of the corresponding exception in relation to child tax credit.]

2.75

AMENDMENT

1. The Social Security (Restrictions on Amounts for Children and Qualifying Young Persons) Amendment Regulations 2017 (SI 2017/376) reg.3 (April 6, 2017).

DEFINITIONS

"Universal Credit Regulations"—see reg.2(1).

GENERAL NOTE

This regulation concerns a child tax credit claimant to whom the non-consensual conception exception to the two-child limit in reg.2(7A) of the Child Tax Credit Regulations 2002 (SI 2002/2007) applied. On a transfer to universal credit, the Secretary of State may treat the evidential requirements for the non-consensual conception exception, within universal credit, as being satisfied on the basis that a claimant, for child tax credit purposes, supplied to HMRC the evidence specified in reg.13(6) of the 2002 Regulations.

2.76

[¹ Abolition of higher amount of the child element for first child or qualifying young person—saving where claimant responsible for a child or qualifying young person born before 6th April 2017

43.—Section 14(5)(b) of the Welfare Reform and Work Act 2016 (which amends the Universal Credit Regulations by omitting the amount of the child element payable for the first child or qualifying young person) does not apply where the claimant is responsible for a child or qualifying young person born before 6th April 2017.]

2.77

AMENDMENT

1. The Social Security (Restrictions on Amounts for Children and Qualifying Young Persons) Amendment Regulations 2017 (SI 2017/376) reg.3 (April 6, 2017).

GENERAL NOTE

2.78 This regulation has the effect of continuing the savings provisions that accompanied the general abolition, as from April 6, 2017, of the inclusion of a family element within an award of Child Tax Credit.

[¹ PART 4

MANAGED MIGRATION TO UNIVERSAL CREDIT

The Migration Process

[¹ **Migration notice**

2.79 **44.**—(1) The Secretary of State may, at any time, issue a notice ("a migration notice") to a person who is entitled to an award of an existing benefit—
  (a) informing the person that all awards of any existing benefits to which they are entitled are to terminate and that they will need to make a claim for universal credit; and
  (b) specifying a day ("the deadline day") by which a claim for universal credit must be made.

(2) The migration notice may contain such other information as the Secretary of State considers appropriate.

(3) The deadline day must not be within the period of three months beginning with the day on which the migration notice is issued.

(4) If the person who is entitled to an award of an existing benefit is, for the purposes of that award, a member of a couple or a member of a polygamous marriage, the Secretary of State must also issue the migration notice to the other member (or members).

(5) The Secretary of State may cancel a migration notice issued to any person—
  (a) if it has been issued in error; [² or]
  (b) [² ...]
  (c) in any other circumstances where the Secretary State considers it necessary to do so in the interests of the person, or any class of person, or to safeguard the efficient administration of universal credit.

(6) A "notified person" is a person to whom a migration notice has been issued.]

AMENDMENTS

1. The Universal Credit (Managed Migration Pilot and Miscellaneous Amendments) Regulations 2019 (SI 2019/1152) reg.3 (July 24, 2019).
2. Universal Credit (Transitional Provisions) Amendment Regulations 2022 (SI 2022/752) reg.11 and Sch. para.1(7) (July 25, 2022).

GENERAL NOTE

Part 4 of the Regulations provides for transfer to universal credit of those tax credits claimants who are not required, under other legislation, to make a claim for universal credit or face termination of existing benefits. The Regulations term this process 'managed migration'. It begins with the issue of a 'migration notice' informing a person that an existing award will terminate and specifying a date by which a universal credit claim must be made. Regulation 44(3) means that claimants will have at least three months to claim universal credit from the date of issue of the migration notice.

[1 Extension of the deadline day

45.—(1) The Secretary of State may determine that the deadline day should be changed to a later day either—
(a) on the Secretary of State's own initiative; or
(b) if a notified person requests such a change before the deadline day, where there is a good reason to do so.
(2) The Secretary of State must inform the notified person or persons of the new deadline day.]

AMENDMENT

1. The Universal Credit (Managed Migration Pilot and Miscellaneous Amendments) Regulations 2019 (SI 2019/1152) reg.3 (July 24, 2019).

DEFINITION

"deadline day"—see reg.44(1)(b).

GENERAL NOTE

A decision of the Secretary of State under this regulation cannot be appealed to the First-tier Tribunal.

[1 Termination of existing benefits if no claim before the deadline

46.—(1) Where a notified person has not made a claim for universal credit on or before the deadline day, all awards of any existing benefits to which the person is entitled terminate—
(a) in the case of housing benefit, on the last day of the period of two weeks beginning with the deadline day; and
(b) in the case of any other existing benefit, on the day before the deadline day.
[...]
(3) Where paragraph (1) applies and the notified person makes a claim for universal credit—
(a) after the deadline day; and
(b) on or before the final deadline specified in paragraph (4),
then, notwithstanding anything in regulation 26 of the Claims and Payments Regulations (time within which a claim for universal credit is to be made) as modified by regulation 15 of these Regulations, the award is to commence on the deadline day.
(4) The final deadline is the day that would be the last day of the first assessment period in relation to an award commencing on the deadline day.
(5) [2 ...]]

AMENDMENTS

1. The Universal Credit (Managed Migration Pilot and Miscellaneous Amendments) Regulations 2019 (SI 2019/1152) reg.3 (July 24, 2019).
2. Universal Credit (Transitional Provisions) Amendment Regulations 2022 (SI 2022/752) reg.11 and Sch. para.1(8) (July 25, 2022).

DEFINITIONS

"deadline day"—see reg.44(1)(b).
"first assessment period"–under regulation 21(1) of the Universal Credit Regulations 2013 (SI 2013/376), an assessment period is "a period of one month beginning with the first date of entitlement".
"notified person"—see reg.44(6).

GENERAL NOTE

2.84 A claim made after the 'deadline day' is not ineffective provided it is made on or before the final deadline specified in reg.46(4). However, in such cases, a claimant will be making a claim after the previous award of tax credits has already terminated: see the rule in regulation 46(1). If a claim is made after the final deadline, the claimant will not be a 'managed migration' case and, as such, will not qualify for transitional protection under regulation 51 or 52.

[¹ Notified persons who claim as a different benefit unit

2.85   47.—[². . .]]

AMENDMENTS

1. The Universal Credit (Managed Migration Pilot and Miscellaneous Amendments) Regulations 2019 (SI 2019/1152) reg.3 (July 24, 2019).
2. The Universal Credit (Transitional Provisions) Amendment Regulations 2022 (SI 2022/752) reg.6(1) (July 25, 2022).

GENERAL NOTE

2.86 As originally enacted, reg.47 dealt with claimants who were part of a couple upon receipt of a managed migration notice, but who had become single claimants, or members of a different couple, by the time that Universal Credit (UC) was claimed. For instance, where the couple had separated by the time of the UC claim or where claimants had been treated as a couple for tax credits purposes but single for UC purposes. In such cases, existing entitlements of both members of the original couple ceased upon either one of them claiming UC.

With effect from July 25, 2022, reg.47 was revoked. The reason for its revocation was described as follows by the Explanatory Memorandum that accompanied the amendment regulations:

"The [original provision] does not align with the current treatment of cases of natural migration following couple separation. In these situations, where one of the separated couple makes a single claim for UC, their ex-partner (provided they were the lead claimant for their legacy benefit) will remain entitled to their existing benefits which will be reassessed for them as single awards. The removal of regulation 47... means that there will be consistency between when couples separate and naturally claim UC due to the change of circumstance and the position for couples who separate after being issued with a migration notice. In both cases, the claimant who is receiving the benefit payments can remain on that benefit until they make a new Universal Credit (UC) claim."

(SI 2014/1230 reg.48) as amended

[¹ Transitional Protection

Meaning of "qualifying claim"

48. A "qualifying claim" is a claim for universal credit by a single claimant who is a notified person or by joint claimants, both of whom are notified persons, where the claim is made on or before the final deadline (see regulation 46(4)).]

AMENDMENT

1. The Universal Credit (Managed Migration Pilot and Miscellaneous Amendments) Regulations 2019 (SI 2019/1152) reg.3 (July 24, 2019).

DEFINITIONS

"notified person"—see reg.44(6).

GENERAL NOTE

Newly-formed or separated couples will not qualify for transitional protection. In such cases, the definition of 'qualifying claim' will not be met since the migration notice issued will not match the benefit unit in respect of which universal credit is claimed.

[¹ Meaning of "migration day"

49. "Migration day", in relation to a qualifying claim, means the day before the first day on which the claimant is entitled to universal credit in connection with that claim.]

AMENDMENT

1. The Universal Credit (Managed Migration Pilot and Miscellaneous Amendments) Regulations 2019 (SI 2019/1152) reg.3 (July 24, 2019).

DEFINITION

"qualifying claim"—see reg.48.

[¹ Secretary of State to determine whether transitional protection applies

50.– (1) Before making a decision on a qualifying claim the Secretary of State must first determine whether—
 (a) a transitional capital disregard is to apply; or
 (b) a transitional element is to be included,
 (or both) in the calculation of the award.
(2) But the Secretary of State is not to determine whether a transitional element is to be included in a case] [² where—
 (a) notified persons who were a couple for the purposes of an award of an existing benefit when the migration notice was issued are single persons or members of a different couple for the purposes of a claim for universal credit; or
 (b) notified persons who were single for the purposes of an award of an existing benefit when the migration notice was issued are a couple for the purposes of a claim for universal credit; or

(c) notified persons who were members of a polygamous marriage for the purposes of an award of an existing benefit when the migration notice was issued are a couple or single persons for the purposes of a claim for universal credit.]

AMENDMENTS

1. The Universal Credit (Managed Migration Pilot and Miscellaneous Amendments) Regulations 2019 (SI 2019/1152) reg.3 (July 24, 2019).
2. Universal Credit (Transitional Provisions) Amendment Regulations 2022 (SI 2022/752) reg.6(2) (July 25, 2022).

DEFINITIONS

"transitional capital disregard"—see reg.51.
"transitional element"—see reg.52.

[¹ The transitional capital disregard

2.91
51.—(1) A transitional capital disregard is to apply where, on the migration day, the claimant—
(a) is entitled to an award of a tax credit; and
(b) has capital exceeding £16,000.
(2) Where a transitional capital disregard applies, any capital exceeding £16,000 is to be disregarded for the purposes of—
(a) determining whether the financial condition in section 5(1)(a) or 5(2)(a) of the Act (capital limit) is met; and
(b) calculating the amount of an award of universal credit (including the indicative UC amount).
(3) Where a transitional capital disregard has been applied in the calculation of an award of universal credit but, in any assessment period, the claimant no longer has (or joint claimants no longer have) capital exceeding £16,000, the transitional capital disregard is not to apply in any subsequent assessment period.
(4) A transitional capital disregard is not to apply for more than 12 assessment periods.]

AMENDMENT

1. The Universal Credit (Managed Migration Pilot and Miscellaneous Amendments) Regulations 2019 (SI 2019/1152) reg.3 (July 24, 2019).

DEFINITION

"assessment period" –under regulation 21(1) of the Universal Credit Regulations 2013 (SI 2013/376), an assessment period is "a period of one month beginning with the first date of entitlement".

GENERAL NOTE

2.92
The transitional capital disregard reflects the fact that there is no capital limit within tax credits. Under universal credit, by contrast, a person is not entitled if s/he has capital in excess of £16,000. This regulation ensures that migrating tax credits claimants with capital in excess of £16,000 may nevertheless be entitled to universal credit. However, such claimants will, in accordance with normal universal credit rules, be treated as generating income on capital in excess of £6,000 up to £16,000.

(SI 2014/1230 reg.51) as amended

The Universal Credit Regulations 2013 assume an income of £4.35 per month for each complete £250 over £6,000. The monthly capital deduction for migrating tax credits claimants with the transitional capital disregard will therefore be £174 (£10,000 ÷ £250 x £4.35 = £174).

By virtue of reg.51(4), a transitional capital disregard cannot apply for more than 12 months.

The Explanatory Memorandum that accompanied SI 2019/1152 estimates that 35,000 migrating working tax credit claimants will have capital in excess of £16,000 and, as such, receive a transitional capital disregard.

[¹ The transitional element

52.—(1) A transitional element is to be included in the calculation of an award if the total amount of any awards of existing benefits determined in accordance with regulation 53 ("the total legacy amount") is greater than the amount of an award of universal credit determined in accordance with regulation 54 ("the indicative UC amount").

(2) Where a transitional element is to be included in the calculation of an award, the amount of that element is to be treated, for the purposes of section 8 of the Act (calculation of awards), as if it were an additional amount to be included in the maximum amount under section 8(2) before the deduction of income under section 8(3).]

AMENDMENT

1. The Universal Credit (Managed Migration Pilot and Miscellaneous Amendments) Regulations 2019 (SI 2019/1152) reg.3 (July 24, 2019).

DEFINITIONS

"the Act"—see reg.2(1).

GENERAL NOTE

The Explanatory Memorandum that accompanied SI 2019/1152 estimates that 900,000 'households' will receive a transitional element upon migration to universal credit.

[¹ The transitional element—total legacy amount

53.—(1) The total legacy amount is the sum of the representative monthly rates of all awards of any existing benefits to which a claimant is, or joint claimants are, entitled on the migration day.

Tax credits

(2) To calculate the representative monthly rate of an award of working tax credit or child tax credit—
 (a) take the figure for the daily rate of the award on the migration day provided by HMRC and calculated on the basis of the information as to the claimant's circumstances held by HMRC on that day; and
 (b) convert to a monthly figure by multiplying by 365 and dividing by 12.

(3) For the purposes of paragraph (2)(a) "the daily rate" is—
 (a) in a case where section 13(1) of the 2002 Act applies (relevant income does not exceed the income threshold or the claimant is entitled to a prescribed social security benefit), the maximum rate of each element to which the claimant is entitled on the migration day divided by 365; and

(b) in any other case, the rate that would be produced by applying regulations 6 to 9 of the Tax Credits (Income Thresholds and Determination of Rates) Regulations 2002 as if the migration day were a relevant period of one day.

...

The benefit cap

(11) Where—
(a) the existing benefits do not include an award of housing benefit, or they include an award of housing benefit that has been reduced to the minimum amount by virtue of Part 8A of the Housing Benefit Regulations 2006 (the benefit cap);
(b) Part 7 of the Universal Credit Regulations (the benefit cap) applies in the calculation of the indicative UC amount; and
(c) the claimant's total entitlement to welfare benefits (as defined in section 96(10) of the Act) on the migration day is greater than the relevant amount,

the total legacy amount is reduced by the excess (minus the amount for childcare costs referred to regulation 54(2)(b) where applicable) over the relevant amount.

(12) For the purposes of paragraph (11)—
(a) the amount of each welfare benefit is the monthly equivalent calculated in the manner set out in regulation 73 (unearned income calculated monthly) of the Universal Credit Regulations; and
(b) the "relevant amount" is the amount referred to in regulation 80A of those Regulations which is applicable to the claimant.]

AMENDMENT

1. The Universal Credit (Managed Migration Pilot and Miscellaneous Amendments) Regulations 2019 (SI 2019/1152) reg.3 (July 24, 2019).

DEFINITIONS

"indicative UC amount"—see reg.54.
"migration day"—see reg.49.
"Universal Credit Regulations"—see reg.2(1).

GENERAL NOTE

2.96   Regulation 53(2) is necessary because tax credits are paid at a daily rate whereas universal credit is paid monthly. Regulation 53(11) incorporates the benefit cap into the calculation of the total legacy amount.

[¹ The transitional element—indicative UC amount

2.97   **54.**—(1) The indicative UC amount is the amount to which a claimant would be entitled if an award of universal credit were calculated in accordance with section 8 of the Act by reference to the claimant's circumstances on the migration day, applying the assumptions in paragraph (2).

(2) The assumptions are—
(a) if the claimant is entitled to an award of child tax credit, the claimant is responsible for any child or qualifying young person in respect of whom the individual element of child tax credit is payable;

(b) if the claimant is entitled to an award of working tax credit that includes the childcare element, the indicative UC amount includes the childcare costs element and, for the purposes of calculating the amount of that element, the amount of the childcare costs is equal to the relevant weekly childcare charges included in the calculation of the daily rate referred to in regulation 53(2), converted to a monthly amount by multiplying by 52 and dividing by 12;

(c) the amount of the claimant's earned income is—
   (i) if the claimant is entitled to an award of a tax credit, the annual amount of any employment income or trading income, as defined by regulation 4 or 6 respectively of the Tax Credits (Definition and Calculation of Income) Regulations 2002, by reference to which the representative monthly rate of that tax credit is calculated for the purposes of regulation 53(2) converted to a net monthly amount by—

(aa) dividing by 12, and

(bb) deducting such amount for income tax and national insurance contributions as the Secretary of State considers appropriate,...

(3) If the claimant would not meet the financial condition in section 5(1)(b) of the Act (or, in the case of joint claimants, they would not meet the condition in section 5(2)(b) of the Act) the claimant is to be treated, for the purposes of calculating the indicative UC amount, as if they were entitled to an award of universal credit of a nil amount.

(4) If a transitional capital disregard is to apply, the claimant is to be treated as having met the financial condition in section 5(1)(a) or 5(2)(a) of the Act (capital limit).

(5) The indicative UC amount is to be calculated after any reduction under Part 7 of the Universal Credit Regulations (the benefit cap) but before any reduction under section 26 (higher-level sanctions) or 27 (other sanctions) of the Act.

(6) But there is to be no reduction for the benefit cap under that Part where the amount of the claimant's earned income (or, in the case of a couple their combined earned income) on the migration day, calculated in accordance with paragraph (2)(c), is equal to or exceeds the amount specified in paragraph (1)(a) of regulation 82 (exceptions—earnings) of the Universal Credit Regulations.

(7) The calculation of the indicative UC amount is to be based on the information that is used for the purposes of calculating the total legacy amount, supplemented as necessary by such further information or evidence as the Secretary of State requires.]

AMENDMENT

1. The Universal Credit (Managed Migration Pilot and Miscellaneous Amendments) Regulations 2019 (SI 2019/1152) reg.3 (July 24, 2019).

DEFINITIONS

"migration day"—see reg.49.
"the Act"—see reg.2(1).
"total legacy amount"—see reg.53.
"transitional capital disregard"—see reg.51.
"Universal Credit Regulations"—see reg.2(1).

GENERAL NOTE

2.98 Since capital is not taken into account in determining entitlement to tax credits, but is relevant under universal credit, the power in reg.54(7) might be exercised to require a migrating tax credits claimant to disclose information about capital.

[¹ The transitional element—initial amount and adjustment where other elements increase

2.99 **55.**—(1) The initial amount of the transitional element is—
(a) if the indicative UC amount is greater than nil, the amount by which the total legacy amount exceeds the indicative UC amount; or
(b) if the indicative UC amount is nil, the total legacy amount plus any amount by which the income which fell to be deducted in accordance with section 8(3) of the Act exceeded the maximum amount.

(2) The amount of the transitional element to be included in the calculation of an award is—
(a) for the first assessment period, the initial amount;
(b) for the second assessment period, the initial amount reduced by the sum of any relevant increases in that assessment period;
(c) for the third and each subsequent assessment period, the amount that was included for the previous assessment period reduced by the sum of any relevant increases (as in sub-paragraph (b)).

(3) If the amount of the transitional element is reduced to nil in any assessment period, a transitional element is not to apply in the calculation of the award for any subsequent assessment period.

(4) A "relevant increase" is [², subject to paragraph (5),] an increase in any of the amounts that are included in the maximum amount under sections 9 to 12 of the Act (including any of those amounts that is included for the first time), apart from the childcare costs element.]

[²(5) In cases where the LCW element is replaced by the LCWRA element, the "relevant increase" is to be treated as the difference between the amounts of those elements.

(6) In this regulation, "LCW element" and "LCWRA element" have the same meaning as in regulation 2 of the Universal Credit Regulations.]

AMENDMENTS

1. The Universal Credit (Managed Migration Pilot and Miscellaneous Amendments) Regulations 2019 (SI 2019/1152) reg.3 (July 24, 2019).

2. Universal Credit (Transitional Provisions) Amendment Regulations 2022 (SI 2022/752) reg.7 (July 25, 2022).

DEFINITIONS

"the Act"—see reg.2(1).
"assessment period" –under regulation 21(1) of the Universal Credit Regulations 2013 (SI 2013/376)—see Vol.5 in this series–an assessment period is "a period of one month beginning with the first date of entitlement".
"indicative UC amount"—see reg.54.
"total legacy amount"—see reg.53.

GENERAL NOTE

2.100 In cases where the total of existing benefits (the total legacy amount) exceeds the indicative UC amount, calculation of the transitional element should be straightforward. Under reg.55(1)(a), it is the difference between the two amounts.

(SI 2014/1230 reg.55) as amended

Regulation 55(1)(b) is designed to protect migrating tax credits claimants whose level of earnings is such as to (a) produce an indicative UC amount of nil, and (b) reduce further the amount of universal credit paid as the transitional element. The provision prevents erosion of the transitional element.

The Explanatory Memorandum that accompanied SI 2019/1152 provides the following worked example of the application of reg.55:

> "A claimant who is a lone parent with one child and who is in receipt of IS, CTC and HB, will be entitled to the following benefits on the day before the UC claim is made:
>
> CTC daily rate of £9.11
>
> IS weekly amount of £73.10
>
> HB weekly rate of £225.00
>
> These amounts are then turned into monthly amounts as follows:
>
> CTC daily rate £9.11 x 365 ÷ 12 = £277.09
> IS weekly amount £73.10 x 52 ÷ 12 = £316.77
> HB weekly rate £225 x 52 ÷ 12 = £975.00

Total monthly legacy amount £1,568.86

> The UC indicative amount is also calculated:
> Standard Allowance £317.82
> Child Element £277.08
> Housing Element £975.00

Total monthly UC indicative amount £1,569.90

> These two amounts are then compared to see whether the transitional element needs to be applied to the UC award. In this case, no transitional element would be awarded
> because the claimant would not receive a lower UC entitlement, i.e., an award that is less that £1,568.86.
>
> The transitional element will be included as part of the overall UC award. Any future deductions for earnings, other income or capital will be made from that overall UC award and not directly from any specific element. This means the transitional element
> itself will not reduce if a claimant's earnings have temporarily increased."

The Explanatory Memorandum also includes a worked example of the erosion of the transitional element under reg.55(2):

> "The regulations also allow for the transitional element to be eroded by an increase in the second or subsequent assessment period if another element included in the UC award increases, or when a new UC element is added to the UC award. An illustrative example of how this would work is below.
>
> A claimant is in receipt of £1,901.57 UC, which is made up as follows:
>
> Child Element for 2 children £277.08 + £231.67
>
> Standard Allowance £317.82
>
> Housing Element £975.00
>
> Transitional Element £100.00

Total monthly UC indicative amount £1,901.57

However, if the claimant reports an increase in rent by £25 to £1,000 in an assessment period after the transitional element has been awarded, the UC award would be adjusted as follows:

Child Element £277.08 + £231.67

Standard Allowance £317.82

Housing Element £1000.00

Transitional Element £75.00

Total monthly UC indicative amount £1,901.57."

Regulation 55(4) prevents new or increased childcare costs from eroding the transitional element, presumably as a work incentive.

[¹ Ending of transitional protection

Circumstances in which transitional protection ceases

56.—(1) A transitional capital disregard or a transitional element does not apply in any assessment period to which paragraph (2) or (4) applies, or in any subsequent assessment period.

Cessation of employment or sustained drop in earnings
(2) This paragraph applies to an assessment period if the following condition is met—
(a) in the case of a single claimant—
  (i) it is the assessment period after the third consecutive assessment period in which the claimant's earned income is less than the amount specified in regulation 99(6)(a) of the Universal Credit Regulations ("the single administrative threshold"), and
  (ii) in the first assessment period of the award, the claimant's earned income was equal to or more than that threshold; or
(b) in the case of joint claimants—
  (i) it is the assessment period after the third consecutive assessment period in which their combined earned income is less than the amount specified in regulation 99(6)(b) of the Universal Credit Regulations ("the couple administrative threshold"), and
  (ii) in the first assessment period of the award, their combined earned income was equal to or more than that threshold.
[²(3) For the purposes of paragraph (2)—
  (a) references to the amount specified in regulation 99(6)(a) and 99(6)(b) respectively of the Universal Credit Regulations are to the amount that was applicable on the first day of the award; and
  (b) a claimant is to be treated as having earned income that is equal to or more than the single administrative threshold and the couple administrative threshold

respectively in any assessment period in respect of which regulation 62 (minimum income floor) of the Universal Credit Regulations applies to that claimant or would apply but for regulation 62(5) of those Regulations (minimum income floor not to apply in a start-up period).]

Couple separating or forming
(4) This paragraph applies to an assessment period in which—
(a) joint claimants cease to be a couple or become members of a different couple; or
(b) a single claimant becomes a member of a couple, unless it is a case where the person may, by virtue of regulation 3(3) of the Universal Credit Regulations (claimant with an ineligible partner), claim as a single person.]

AMENDMENTS

1. The Universal Credit (Managed Migration Pilot and Miscellaneous Amendments) Regulations 2019 (SI 2019/1152) reg.3 (July 24, 2019).
2. Universal Credit (Administrative Earnings Threshold) (Amendment) Regulations 2023 (SI 2023/7) reg.3 (January 30, 2023).

DEFINITIONS

"assessment period" – under regulation 21(1) of the Universal Credit Regulations 2013 (SI 2013/376)—see Vol.5 in this series–an assessment period is "a period of one month beginning with the first date of entitlement".
"transitional capital disregard"—see reg.51.
"transitional element"—see reg.52.
"Universal Credit Regulations"—see reg.2(1).

[¹ Application of transitional protection to a subsequent award

57.—(1) Where—
(a) a transitional capital disregard is applied, or a transitional element is included, in the calculation of an award, and that award terminates; or
(b) the Secretary State determines (in accordance with regulation 50) that a transitional capital disregard is to apply, or a transitional element is to be included in the calculation of an award, but the decision on the qualifying claim is that there is no entitlement to an award,

no transitional capital disregard is to apply and no transitional element is to be included in the calculation of any subsequent award unless paragraph (2) applies.

(2) This paragraph applies if—
(a) the reason for the previous award terminating or, as the case may be, there being no entitlement to an award, was that the claimant (or joint claimants) had earned income on account of which the financial condition in section 5(1)(b) or 5(2)(b) of the Act (income is such that the amount payable is at least 1p) was not met; and
(b) the claimant becomes entitled to an award within the period of three months beginning with—
(i) where paragraph (1)(a) applies, the last day of the month that would have been the final assessment period of the previous award (had it not terminated), or

(ii) where paragraph (1)(b) applies, the day that would have been the last day of the first assessment period had there been entitlement to an award.

(3) Where paragraph (2) applies in a case where a previous award has terminated, the new award is to be treated for the purposes of regulation 51 (transitional capital disregard), 55 (transitional element—initial amount and adjustment where other elements increase) and 56 (circumstances in which transitional protection ceases) as if it were a continuation of that award.]

AMENDMENT

1. The Universal Credit (Managed Migration Pilot and Miscellaneous Amendments) Regulations 2019 (SI 2019/1152) reg.3 (July 24, 2019).

DEFINITIONS

"the Act"—see reg.2(1).
"assessment period" – under regulation 21(1) of the Universal Credit Regulations 2013 (SI 2013/376)—see Vol.5 in this series–an assessment period is "a period of one month beginning with the first date of entitlement".
"qualifying claim"—see reg.48.
"transitional capital disregard"—see reg.51.
"transitional element"—see reg.52.

GENERAL NOTE

2.103   Regulation 57(2) provides a type of linking-rule under which transitional protection may be re-applied to an award of universal credit that ended because of an increase in earnings.

[¹ Miscellaneous

Qualifying claim—Secretary of State may set later commencement day

2.104   **58.** Where the Secretary of State decides a qualifying claim, and it is not a case where the award is to commence before the date of claim by virtue of regulation 46(3) [² . . .] (claim made by the final deadline) or regulation 26 of the Claims and Payments Regulations (time within which a claim for universal credit is to be made) as modified by regulation 15 of these Regulations, the Secretary of State may determine a day on which the award of universal credit is to commence that is after, but no more than one month after, the date of claim.]

AMENDMENTS

1. The Universal Credit (Managed Migration Pilot and Miscellaneous Amendments) Regulations 2019 (SI 2019/1152) reg.3 (July 24, 2019).
2. Universal Credit (Transitional Provisions) Amendment Regulations 2022 (SI 2022/752) reg.11 and Sch. para.1(9) (July 25, 2022).

DEFINITIONS

"qualifying claim"—see reg.48.
"Claims and Payments Regulations"—see reg.2(1).

(SI 2014/1230 reg.58) as amended

[²[¹ Minimum income floor not to apply for first 12 months]

59. [*repealed*]

AMENDMENTS

1. The Universal Credit (Managed Migration Pilot and Miscellaneous Amendments) Regulations 2019 (SI 2019/1152) reg.3 (July 24, 2019).
2. The Universal Credit (Managed Migration Pilot and Miscellaneous Amendments) Regulations 2019 (SI 2019/1152) reg.6(2) (September 23, 2020).

[¹ Protection for full-time students until course completed

60. [² (1)] Where a notified person does not meet the basic condition in section 4(1)(d) of the Act (not receiving education) on the day on which all awards of any existing benefit are to terminate as a consequence of a claim for universal credit because the person is undertaking a full-time course (see regulation 12(2) and 13 of the Universal Credit Regulations), that condition is not to apply in relation to the notified person while they are continuing to undertake that course.]

[²(2) Paragraph (1) does not apply to any assessment period in respect of which a transitional element or transitional capital disregard would (if the claimant had been entitled to that element or that disregard) have ceased to apply by virtue of regulation 56 (circumstances in which transitional protection ceases) or regulation 57 (application of transitional protection to a subsequent award).]

AMENDMENTS

1. The Universal Credit (Managed Migration Pilot and Miscellaneous Amendments) Regulations 2019 (SI 2019/1152) reg.3 (July 24, 2019).
2. Universal Credit (Transitional Provisions) Amendment Regulations 2022 (SI 2022/752) reg.8 (July 25, 2022).

DEFINITIONS

"notified person"—see reg.44(6).
"Universal Credit Regulations"—see reg.2(1).

GENERAL NOTE

Section 4(1)(d) of the Welfare Reform Act 2012 provides that a person who is receiving education does not meet the basic conditions for universal credit. This regulation ensures that full-time students who undergo managed migration are nevertheless entitled to universal credit for so long as they continue to undertake the course of education being undertaken on migration.

Regulation 60(2), effective from July 25, 2022, prevents the student exemption under reg.60(1) from being reapplied if a student's Universal Credit award ends, unless the claimant would continue to qualify for transitional protection. It also has the effect of removing the student exemption in circumstances which would, in other migration cases, bring to an end the Transitional Element and Transitional Capital Disregard provided for elsewhere in these Regulations.

[¹ Rounding

61. Regulation 6 of the Universal Credit Regulations (rounding) applies for the purposes of calculating any amount under this Part.]

The Universal Credit (Transitional Provisions) Regulations 2014

AMENDMENT

1. The Universal Credit (Managed Migration Pilot and Miscellaneous Amendments) Regulations 2019 (SI 2019/1152) reg.3 (July 24, 2019).

DEFINITIONS

2.110   "Universal Credit Regulations"—see reg.2(1).

[¹ Effect of revision, appeal etc of an award of an existing benefit

2.111   **62.**—(1) Nothing in regulation 53 (total legacy amount) or 54 (indicative UC amount) requiring a calculation in relation to the transitional element to be made on the basis of information held on the migration day prevents the Secretary of State from revising or superseding a decision in relation to a claim for, or an award of, universal credit where—
   (a) in the opinion of the Secretary of State, the information held on that day was inaccurate or incomplete in some material respect because of—
      (i) a misrepresentation by a claimant,
      (ii) a failure to report information that a claimant was required to report where that failure was advantageous to the claimant, or
      (iii) an official error; or
   (b) a decision has been made on or after the migration day on—
      (i) an application made before migration day to revise or supersede a decision in relation to an award of an existing benefit (including the report of a change of circumstances), or
      (ii) an appeal in relation to such an application.
(2) In this regulation "official error" means an error that—
   (a) was made by an officer of, or an employee of a body acting on behalf of, the Department for Work and Pensions, HMRC or a local authority that administers housing benefit; and
   (b) was not caused, or materially contributed to, by any person outside that body or outside the Department, HMRC or local authority,
but excludes any error of law which is shown to have been such by a subsequent decision of the Upper Tribunal or of a court as defined in section 27(7) of the Social Security Act 1998.]

AMENDMENT

1. The Universal Credit (Managed Migration Pilot and Miscellaneous Amendments) Regulations 2019 (SI 2019/1152) reg.3 (July 24, 2019).

DEFINITIONS

"migration day"—see reg.49.
"transitional element"—see reg.52.
"Upper Tribunal"—see reg.2(1).

GENERAL NOTE

2.112   This regulation provides the Secretary of State with power to revise or supersede her decision as to the amount of a claimant's transitional element.

(SI 2014/1230 Sch.1) as amended

[¹[² SCHEDULE 1–MODIFICATION OF TAX CREDITS LEGISLATION (FINALISATION OF TAX CREDITS (REGULATION 12A))]]

2.113

[¹ **Modifications to the Tax Credits Act 2002**

1. Paragraphs 2 to 10 prescribe modifications to the application of the 2002 Act where regulation 12A of these Regulations applies.
2. In section 7 (income test)—
   (a) in subsection (3), before "current year income" in each place where it occurs, insert "notional";
   (b) [³ . . .]
   (c) after subsection (4), insert—
   "(4A) In this section "the notional current year income" means—
   (a) in relation to persons by whom a joint claim for a tax credit is made, the aggregate income of the persons for the part tax year to which the claim relates, divided by the number of days in that part tax year, multiplied by the number of days in the tax year in which the part tax year is included and rounded down to the next whole number of pence; and
   (b) in relation to a person by whom a single claim for a tax credit is made, the income of the person for that part tax year, divided by the number of days in that part tax year, multiplied by the number of days in the tax year in which the part tax year is included and rounded down to the next whole number of pence.".
3. In section 17 (final notice)—
   (a) in subsection (1)—
      (i) omit "the whole or"; and
      (ii) in sub-paragraph (a), before "tax year" insert "part";
   (b) in subsection (3), before "tax year" insert "part";
   (c) in subsections (4)(a) and (4)(b), for "current year" in both places where it occurs, substitute "current part year";
   (d) in subsection (5)(a) for "current year" in both places where it occurs, substitute "current part year";
   (e) omit subsection (8).
4. In section 18 (decisions after final notice)—
   (a) in subsection (1), before "tax year" insert "part";
   (b) omit subsections (6) to (9);
   (c) in subsection (10), for "subsection (1), (5), (6) or (9)" substitute "subsection (1) or (5)";
   (d) in subsection (11)—
      (i) after "subsection (5)" omit "or (9)";
      (ii) omit paragraph (a);
      (iii) in paragraph (b) omit "in any other case,";
      (iv) before "tax year" in each place where it occurs, insert "part".
5. In section 19 (power to enquire)—
   (a) in subsection (1)(a) and (b), before "tax year" insert "part";
   (b) in subsection (3), before "tax year" insert "part";
   (c) for subsection (5) substitute—
   "(5) "The relevant section 18 decision" means the decision under subsection (1) of section 18 in relation to the person or persons and the part tax year.";
   (d) for subsection (6) substitute—
   "(6) "The relevant section 17 date" means the date specified for the purposes of subsection (4) of section 17 in the notice given to a person or persons under that section in relation to the part tax year.";
   (e) in subsection (11), before "tax year" insert "part";
   (f) in subsection (12), before "tax year" in each place where it occurs, insert "part".
6. In section 20 (decisions on discovery)—
   (a) in subsection (1), before "tax year" insert "part";
   (b) in subsection (4)(a), before "tax year" insert "part";
   (c) in subsection (5)(b), before "tax year" insert "part";
   (d) in subsection (6)—
      (i) before "tax year" insert "part";
      (ii) in paragraph (a), for "section 18(1), (5), (6) or (9)" substitute "section 18(1) or (5)";

(e) in subsection (7), before "tax year" in each place where it occurs, insert "part".
7. In section 21 (decisions subject to official error), for "18(1), (5), (6) or (9)" substitute "18(1) or (5)".
8. In section 23 (notice of decisions)—
   (a) in subsection (1), for "18(1), (5), (6) or (9)" substitute "18(1) or (5)";
   (b) in subsection (3)—
      (i) after "18(1)" omit "or (6)";
      (ii) for paragraph (b) substitute—
"(b) the notice of the decision under subsection (1) of section 18,".
9. In section 30(1) (underpayments), before "tax year" in each place where it occurs, insert "part".
10. In section 38 (appeals)—
   (a) in subsection (1)(b), before "tax year" insert "part";
   (b) for subsection (2), substitute—
"(2) "The relevant section 18 decision" means the decision under subsection (1) of section 18 in relation to the person or persons and the tax credit for the part tax year.".

Modifications to the Tax Credits (Definition and Calculation of Income) Regulations 2002

11. Paragraphs 12 to 23 prescribe modifications to the application of the Tax Credits (Definition and Calculation of Income) Regulations 2002 where regulation 12A of these Regulations applies.
12. In regulation 2(2) (interpretation), after the definition of "the Macfarlane Trusts" insert—
""part tax year" means a period of less than a year beginning with 6th April and ending with the date on which the award of a tax credit terminated;".
13. In regulation 3 (calculation of income of claimant)—
   (a) in paragraph (1)—
      (i) before "tax year" insert "part";
      (ii) in Steps 1 and 2, after "of the claimant, or, in the case of a joint claim, of the claimants" insert "received in or relating to the part tax year";
      (iii) in the second and third sentences of Step 4, before "year" insert "part";
   (b) in paragraph (6A), for the words from "ending on 31st March" to the end, substitute "ending on the last day of the month in which the claimant's award of a tax credit terminated";
   (c) in paragraph (8)(b), before "year" insert "part".
14. In regulation 4 (employment income)—
   (a) in paragraph (1)(a), before "tax year" insert "part";
   (b) in paragraph (1)(b), (c), (d), (e), (g) and (k), before "year" insert "part";
   (c) in paragraph (1)(f), after "ITEPA" insert "which is treated as received in the part tax year and in respect of which the charge arises in the part tax year";
   (d) in paragraph (1)(h), after "week" insert "in the part tax year";
   (e) in paragraph (1)(i), for "that year" substitute "the tax year" and after "ITEPA" insert "which is treated as received in the part tax year";
   (f) in paragraph (1)(j), after "applies" insert "which is received in the part tax year";
   (g) in paragraph (1)(l), for "that year" substitute "the tax year" and after "ITEPA" insert "in respect of which the charge arises in the part tax year";
   (h) in paragraph (1)(m), after "paid" insert "in the part tax year";
   (i) in paragraph (4), in the first sentence and in the title of Table 1, after "employment income" insert "received in the part tax year";
   (j) in paragraph (5), after "calculating earnings" insert "received in the part tax year".
15. In regulation 5 (pension income)—
   (a) in paragraph (1), after ""pension income" means" insert "any of the following received in or relating to the part tax year";
   (b) in paragraph (2), in the first sentence and in the title of Table 2, after "pension income" insert "received in or relating to the part tax year";
   (c) in paragraph (3), after "income tax purposes", insert "in relation to the part tax year".
16. In regulation 6 (trading income)—
   (a) re-number the existing regulation as paragraph (1);
   (b) in paragraph (1) (as so re-numbered)—
      (i) in sub-paragraph (a), for "taxable profits for the tax year" substitute "actual or estimated taxable profits attributable to the part tax year";

(ii) in sub-paragraph (b), for "taxable profit for the" substitute "actual or estimated taxable profit attributable to the part tax";

[⁴(c) after paragraph (1) insert—

"(2) Actual or estimated taxable profits attributable to the part tax year ('the relevant trading income') is to be calculated by reference to the basis period (determined by reference to paragraph 63 or paragraph 65 of Schedule 1 to the Finance Act 2022, whichever applies) ending with 5th April 2024.

(3) The relevant trading income is to be calculated by—
   (a) taking the figure for the actual or estimated taxable income earned in the basis period referred to in paragraph (2);
   (b) dividing that figure by the number of days in that period to give the daily figure; and
   (c) multiplying the daily figure by the number of days in the part tax year on which the trade, profession or vocation was carried on."]

17. In regulation 7 (social security income)—
   (a) in paragraph (1), after "social security income" insert "received in the part tax year";
   (b) in paragraph (3), in the opening words and in the title of Table 3, after "social security income" insert "received in the part tax year".

18. In regulation 8 (student income), after "in relation to a student" insert ", any of the following which is received in the part tax year".

19. In regulation 10 (investment income)—
   (a) in paragraph (1), after "gross amount" insert "received in the part tax year";
   (b) in paragraph (1)(e), before "year" insert "part tax";
   (c) in paragraph (2), in the opening words and in the title of Table 4, after "investment income" insert "received in the part tax year".

20. In regulation 11(1) (property income)—
   (a) omit "annual";
   (b) after "taxable profits" insert "for the part tax year".

21. In regulation 12(1) (foreign income), before "year" insert "part tax".

22. In regulation 13 (notional income), after "means income" insert "received in the part tax year".

23. In regulation 18 (miscellaneous income), after "means income" insert "received in the part tax year".

Modifications to the Tax Credits (Income Thresholds and Determination of Rates) Regulations 2002

24. Paragraphs 25 to 27 prescribe modifications to the application of the Tax Credits (Income Thresholds and Determination of Rates) Regulations 2002 where regulation 12A of these Regulations applies.

25. In regulation 2 (interpretation)—
   (a) [³ . . .]
   (b) in the definition of "the relevant income" insert "as modified by the Universal Credit (Transitional Provisions) Regulations 2014" at the end.

26. In regulation 7(3) (determination of rate of working tax credit)—
   (a) in Step 1, in the definition of "MR", after "maximum rate" insert "(determined in the manner prescribed at the date on which the award of the tax credit terminated)";
   (b) [³ . . .]

27. In regulation 8(3) (determination of rate of child tax credit)—
   (a) in Step 1, in the definition of "MR", after "maximum rate" insert "(determined in the manner prescribed at the date on which the award of the tax credit terminated)";
   (b) [³ . . .]

Modifications to the Tax Credits (Claims and Notifications) Regulations 2002

28. Paragraphs 29 to 34 prescribe modifications to the application of the Tax Credits (Claims and Notifications) Regulations 2002 where regulation 12A of these Regulations applies.

29. In regulation 4 (interpretation), omit paragraph (b).

30. Omit regulation 11 (circumstances in which claims to be treated as made).

31. Omit regulation 12 (further circumstances in which claims to be treated as made).

32. In regulation 13 (circumstances in which claims made by one member of a couple to be treated as also made by the other)—

(a) in paragraph (1), after "prescribed by paragraph" omit "(2) or";
(b) omit paragraph (2).
33. In regulation 15(1)(c) (persons who die after making a claim)—
(a) omit "the whole or" and "after the end of that tax year but"; and
(b) for "section 18(1), (5), (6) or (9)" substitute "section 18(1) or (5)".
34. In regulation 33 (dates to be specified in notices)—
(a) in paragraph (a), for the words from "not later than 31st July" to "if later", substitute "not less than 30 days after the date on which the notice is given";
(b) omit paragraph (b) and the "and" which precedes it.

Modification to the Tax Credits (Payment by the Commissioners) Regulations 2002

2.117   35. Paragraph 36 prescribes a modification to the application of the Tax Credits (Payment by the Commissioners) Regulations 2002 where regulation 12A of these Regulations applies.
36. Omit regulation 7 (prescribed circumstances for certain purposes).

Modification to the Tax Credits (Residence) Regulations 2003

2.118   37. Paragraph 38 prescribes a modification to the application of the Tax Credits (Residence) Regulations 2003 where regulation 12A of these Regulations applies.
38. In regulation 3(5)(a) (circumstances in which a person is treated as not being in the United Kingdom), omit "under regulation 11 or 12 of the Tax Credits (Claims and Notifications) Regulations 2002 or otherwise".]

AMENDMENTS

1. Universal Credit (Transitional Provisions) (Amendment) Regulations 2014 (SI 2014/1626) reg.4 (October 13, 2014).
2. Universal Credit (Managed Migration Pilot and Miscellaneous Amendments) Regulations 2019 (SI 2019/1152) reg.3 (July 24, 2019).
3. Social Security and Universal Credit (Miscellaneous Amendments) Regulations 2023 (SI 2023/543) reg.6(5) (June 29, 2023).
4. Social Security and Universal Credit (Migration of Tax Credit Claimants and Miscellaneous Amendments) Regulations 2024 (SI 2024/341) reg.8(4) (April 6, 2024).

GENERAL NOTE

2.119   Upper Tribunal Judge Wikeley's decision in *HMRC v AS* (TC) [2023] UKUT 67 (AAC) illustrates the potential pitfalls if it assumed that in-year finalisation of tax credits entitlement, where tax credits entitlement ceases upon transfer to Universal Credit, is determined according to the usual rules for calculating income for tax credits purposes. In other words, if entitlement is determined without taking into account the modifications to tax credits legislation provided for in Schedule 1. The modified legislation calls for calculation of a person's notional current year income (section 7 of the Tax Credits Act 2002, as modified by para. 2(c) of the Schedule. In *AS* the First-tier Tribunal failed to appreciate that, for the purposes of this calculation, reg. 4(1)(a) of the Tax Credits (Determination and Calculation of Income) Regulations 2002 is modified so that, rather than earnings from an employment attributable to the relevant part tax year, the calculation takes into account earnings from an employment received in the part tax year.

(SI 2002/2005) as amended

PART B

TAX CREDITS REGULATIONS

The Working Tax Credit (Entitlement and Maximum Rate) Regulations 2002

(SI 2002/2005) (AS AMENDED)

Whereas a draft of this instrument, which prescribes the amount in excess of which, by virtue of subsection (2) of section 12 of the Tax Credits Act 2002, charges are not to be taken into account for the purposes of that subsection, and which also contains the first regulations made under sections 11 and 12 of that Act, has been laid before, and approved by resolution of, each House of Parliament:

Now, therefore, the Treasury, in exercise of the powers conferred upon them by sections 10, 11, 12, 65(1) and (7) and 67 of the Tax Credits Act 2002, hereby make the following Regulations:

REGULATIONS

PART 1

GENERAL

1. Citation, commencement and effect.
2. Interpretation.
3. Other elements of working tax credit.

PART II

CONDITIONS OF ENTITLEMENT

BASIC ELEMENT

4. Entitlement to basic element of working tax credit: qualifying remunerative work.
5. Time off in connection with childbirth and adoption.
5A. Time off in connection with childbirth and placement for adoption: further provisions.
6. Periods of illness or incapacity for work.
7. Term-time and other seasonal workers.
7A. Strike periods.
7B. Persons suspended from work.
7C. Pay in lieu of notice.

7D. Ceasing to undertake work or working for less than 16 hours per week.
7E. *Alteration in hours worked due to coronavirus (revoked)*
8. Gaps between jobs.

Disability element

9. Disability element and workers who are to be treated as at a disadvantage in getting a job.
9A. Initial claims.
9B. Training for work, etc.

30-hour element

10. 30-hour element.

Second-adult element

11. Second-adult element.

Lone-parent element

12. Lone-parent element.

Child care element

13. Entitlement to child care element of working tax credit.
14. Entitlement to child care element of working tax credit.
15. Calculation of relevant child care charges.
16. Change of circumstances.

Severe disability element

17. Severe disability element.

50 Plus element

18. 50 Plus element *(repealed)*

Death of a child or qualifying young person for whom the claimant is responsible

19. Entitlement after death of a child or qualifying young person for whom the claimant is responsible.

Part III

Maximum Rate

20. Maximum rates of elements of working tax credit.

Schedule 1—Disability which puts a person at a disadvantage in getting a job.
Schedule 2—Maximum rates of the elements of a working tax credit.

(SI 2002/2005 reg.1) as amended

PART I

GENERAL

Citation, commencement and effect

1.—These Regulations may be cited as the Working Tax Credit (Entitlement and Maximum Rate) Regulations 2002 and shall come into force—
(a) for the purpose of enabling claims to be made, on 1st August 2002;
(b) for the purpose of enabling decisions on claims to be made, on 1st January 2003; and
(c) for all other purposes, on April 6, 2003;
and shall have effect for the tax year beginning on 6th April 2003 and subsequent tax years.

DEFINITIONS

"claim"—see TCA 2002 s.3(8).
"tax year"—see TCA 2002 s.47.

GENERAL NOTE

These regulations give substance to ss.10 (entitlement) and 11 (maximum rate) of the TCA 2002. These are the only sections in the Act that apply specifically to the award and entitlement to working tax credit. Most of the provisions in those sections are enabling only. These are the regulations giving substance to working tax credit.

Interpretation

2.—(1) In these Regulations, except where the context otherwise requires—
"the Act" means the Tax Credits Act 2002, and a reference without more to a numbered section is a reference to the section of the Act bearing that number;
[[10] "armed forces independence payment" means armed forces independence payment under the Armed Forces and Reserve Forces (Compensation Scheme) Order 2011;]
"the Board" means the Commissioners of Inland Revenue;
"the Contributions and Benefits Act" means the Social Security Contributions and Benefits Act 1992;
"child" has the same meaning as it has in the Child Tax Credit Regulations 2002;
"claim" means a claim for working tax credit and "joint claim" and "single claim" have the meanings respectively assigned in [[1]section 3(8)];
"claimant" means the person making a claim and, in the case of a joint claim, means either of the claimants;
[[6] "contributory employment and support allowance" means a contributory allowance under Part 1 of the Welfare Reform Act [[11] ("the 2007 Act") as amended by the provisions of Schedule 3, and Part 1 of Schedule 14, to the Welfare Reform Act 2012 that remove references to an income-related allowance, and a contributory allowance under Part 1 of the 2007 Act as that Part has effect apart from those provisions];]
[[14]"coronavirus" means severe acute respiratory syndrome coronavirus 2;
"Coronavirus Job Retention Scheme" means the scheme of that name established under the direction given by the Chancellor of the Exchequer

2.121

2.122

2.123

under section 76 of the Coronavirus Act 2020 on 15th April 2020 (as that Scheme has effect from time to time);
"coronavirus-impacted worker" has the meaning given by regulation 7E(3);]
[³"couple" has the meaning given by section 3(5A) of the Act;]
"the determination of the maximum rate" means the determination of the maximum rate of working tax credit;
[¹"employed", except in the expression "self-employed" means employed under a contract of service or apprenticeship where the earnings under the contract are chargeable to income tax as employment income under Parts II–VII of the Income Tax (Earnings and Pensions) Act 2003 [² otherwise than by reason of Chapter 8 of Part 2 of that Act (deemed employment in respect of arrangements made by intermediaries)];]
[⁴"employment zone" means an area within Great Britain—
(a) subject to a designation for the purposes of the Employment Zones Regulations 2003 by the Secretary of State, or
[⁵(b) listed in the Schedule to the Employment Zones (Allocation to Contractors) Pilot Regulations 2006],
pursuant to section 60 of the Welfare Reform and Pensions Act 1999.]
"employment zone programme" means a programme which is—
(a) established for one or more employment zones; and
(b) designed to assist claimants for a jobseeker's allowance to obtain sustainable employment;
[¹⁴ "furloughed employee under the Coronavirus Job Retention Scheme" means a person who is within paragraph 6.1 of the Schedule to the direction given by the Chancellor of the Exchequer under section 76 of the Coronavirus Act 2020 [¹⁵or a person who is within paragraph 10.1 of the Schedule to the further direction given by the Chancellor under section 76 of that Act on 25th June 2020];]
[¹"initial claim" shall be construed in accordance with regulation 9A;]
[⁸ "limited capability for work credit" refers to a credit under regulation 8B(1) of the Social Security (Credits) Regulations 1975 where paragraph (2)(a)(iv) or (2)(a)(v) of that regulation applies, and which follows the cessation of the entitlement period of contributory employment and support allowance;]
"local authority" means—
(a) in relation to England, the council of a county or district, a metropolitan district, a London Borough, the Common Council of the City of London or the Council of the Isles of Scilly;
(b) in relation to Wales, the council of a county or county borough; or;
(c) in relation to Scotland, a council constituted under section 2 of the Local Government, etc. (Scotland) Act 1994;
[¹"partner" means a member of a [³. . .] couple making a joint claim;]
"patient" means a person (other than a person who is serving a sentence, imposed by a court, in a prison or youth custody institution or, in Scotland, a young offenders' institution) who is regarded as receiving free in-patient treatment within the meaning of the Social Security (Hospital In-Patients) Regulations [⁸2005];
"period of award" shall be construed in accordance with [¹section 5];
[⁹ "personal independence payment" means personal independence payment under Part 4 of the Welfare Reform Act 2012;]

"qualifying young person" means a person who satisfies regulation 5 of the Child Tax Credit Regulations 2002;

"relevant child care charges" has the meaning given by regulation 14;

[^{16}"Scottish disability assistance" means a payment made by the Scottish ministers under section 31 of the Social Security (Scotland) Act 2018;]

[^{1}...]

[^{12} "self-employed" means engaged in carrying on a trade, profession or vocation on a commercial basis and with a view to the realisation of profits, either on one's own account or as a member of a business partnership and the trade, profession or vocation is organised and regular;]

"sports award" means an award made by one of the Sports Councils named in section 23(2) of the National Lottery etc. Act 1993 out of sums allocated to it for distribution under that section;

"surrogate child" means a child in respect of whom an order has been made under section 30 of the Human Fertilisation and Embryology Act 1990 [^{7} (parental orders) or section 54 of the Human Fertilisation and Embryology Act 2008 (parental orders)];

[^{1}...]

"training allowance" means an allowance (whether by way of periodical grants or otherwise) payable—

(a) out of public funds by a Government department or by or on behalf of the Secretary of State, Scottish Enterprise or Highlands and Islands Enterprise or the Department for [^{13} Communities or the Department for the Economy] ("the relevant paying authority");

(b) to a person in respect of his maintenance or in respect of a member of his family; and

(c) for the period, or part of the period, during which he is following a course of training or instruction—

(i) provided by, or in pursuance of arrangements made with, the relevant paying authority; or

(ii) approved by the relevant paying authority in relation to him,

but does not include an allowance, paid by a Government department, Northern Ireland department or the Scottish Executive to or in respect of a person by reason of the fact that he is training as a teacher, or is following a course of full-time education, other than under arrangements made under section 2 of the Employment and Training Act 1973, section 2 or 3 of the Disabled Persons (Employment) Act (Northern Ireland) 1945, or section 1(1) of the Employment and Training Act (Northern Ireland) 1950;

[^{1}"training for work" shall be construed in accordance with regulation 9B;]

"week" means a period of seven days beginning with midnight between Saturday and Sunday.

[^{6} "the Welfare Reform Act" means the Welfare Reform Act 2007.]

(2) For the purposes of these Regulations a person is responsible for a child or qualifying young person if he is treated as being responsible for that child or qualifying young person in accordance with the rules contained in regulation 3 of the Child Tax Credit Regulations 2002.

(3) A reference in these Regulations to an enactment applying to Great Britain but not to Northern Ireland shall, unless the context otherwise requires, include a reference to the corresponding enactment applying in Northern Ireland.

[¹(4) In these Regulations as they apply to an office a reference to being employed includes a reference to being the holder of an office.]

[⁶ (5) For the purpose of these Regulations—
(a) two or more periods of entitlement to employment and support allowance are linked together if they satisfy the conditions in regulation 145 of the Employment and Support Allowance Regulations 2008 [¹¹or regulation 86 of the Employment and Support Allowance Regulations 2013]; and
(b) a period of entitlement to employment and support allowance is linked together with a period of entitlement to statutory sick pay if it follows that period within 12 weeks.]

AMENDMENTS

1. Working Tax Credit (Entitlement and Maximum Rate) (Amendment) Regulations 2003 (SI 2003/701) reg.3 (April 6, 2003).
2. Tax Credits (Miscellaneous Amendments No.2) Regulations 2003 (SI 2003/2815) reg.13 (November 26, 2003).
3. Civil Partnership Act 2004 (Tax Credits, etc.) (Consequential Amendments) Order 2005 (SI 2005/2919) art.2(2) (December 5, 2005).
4. Tax Credits (Miscellaneous Amendments) Regulations 2006 (SI 2006/766) reg.20(2) (April 6, 2006).
5. Tax Credits (Miscellaneous Amendments) Regulations 2007 (SI 2007/824) reg.3 (April 6, 2007).
6. Employment and Support Allowance (Consequential Provisions) (No.3) Regulations 2008 (SI 2009/1879) reg.20(2) (October 27, 2008).
7. Human Fertilisation and Embryology (Parental Orders) (Consequential, Transitional and Saving Provisions) Order 2010 (SI 2010/986) art.2 and Sch. para.7 (April 6, 2010).
8. Tax Credits (Miscellaneous Amendments) Regulations 2012 (SI 2012/848) reg.2(2) (April 6, 2012).
9. Personal Independence Payment (Supplementary Provisions and Consequential Amendments) Regulations 2013 (SI 2013/388) reg.8 and Sch. para.28(2) (April 8, 2013).
10. Armed Forces and Reserve Forces Compensation Scheme (Consequential Provisions: Subordinate Legislation) Order 2013 (SI 2013/591) art.7 and Sch. para.24(2) (April 8, 2013).
11. Universal Credit (Consequential, Supplementary, Incidental and Miscellaneous Provisions) Regulations 2013 (SI 2013/630) reg.77(2) (April 29, 2013).
12. Working Tax Credit (Entitlement and Maximum Rate) (Amendment) Regulations 2015 (SI 2015/605) reg.3 (April 6, 2015).
13. Tax Credits, Child Benefit and Childcare Payments (Miscellaneous Amendments) Regulations 2019 (SI 2019/364) reg.2(2) (March 21, 2019).
14. Tax Credits (Coronavirus, Miscellaneous Amendments) Regulations 2020 (SI 2020/534) reg.2(2) (May 23, 2020).
15. Tax Credits (Coronavirus, Miscellaneous Amendments) (No.2) Regulations 2020 (SI 2020/941) reg.3(2) (September 25, 2020).
16. Tax Credits and Child Benefit (Miscellaneous Amendments) Regulations 2021 (SI 2021/1286) reg.2(2) (December 9, 2021).

DEFINITIONS

See also TCA 2002 s.47. For definitions of terms used in income tax legislation see ITEPA 2003 Sch.1 and the index of definitions in ITA 2007 Sch.4 (not included in this work). The direction given by the Chancellor of the Exchequer on April 25, 2020, as referred to in the definition of "Coronavirus Job Retention Scheme", and the Chancellor's direction of June 25, 2020, as referred to in the definition of

(SI 2002/2005 reg.2) as amended

"furloughed employee under the Coronavirus Job Creation Scheme", are available at http://www.gov.uk/government/publications/treasury-direction-made-under-sec tions-71-and-76-of-the-coronavirus-act-2020

GENERAL NOTE

The definition of "self-employed" effective from April 6, 2015 replaces an earlier wider definition: "engaged in the carrying on of a trade profession or vocation". The new definition is deliberately narrower. HMRC's *Revenue and Customs Brief 7 (2015)* indicated their intention to take a proactive approach to the new test for self-employment:

2.124

> "Self-employed WTC claimants with earnings below a threshold (this will be based on working hours and the National Minimum Wage) will be asked by HMRC to provide evidence that they are in a regular and organised trade, profession or vocation on a commercial basis and with a view to achieving profit.
> The information we ask for should be available as part of normal business activity, for example receipts and expenses, records of sales and purchases. We may also ask for supporting documents such as a business plan, planned work, cash flow and profit projections."

The Chancellor added in the 2015 Budget:

> "Autumn Statement 2014 announced measures to close down vulnerable gateways in the tax credit system to self-employed claimants. From 6 April 2015 a new test will require those Working Tax Credits (WTC) claimants relying on self-employment to meet the entitlement conditions to be undertaking an activity which is commercial and profitable, or working towards profitability. This test will apply to the working hours required to qualify for WTC as a self-employed claimant. The new requirement for the same claimants to register their self-employment for self-assessment purposes and provide a Unique Tax Reference number will begin from the following April. Throughout the 2015-16 tax year HMRC will be encouraging claimants to take the necessary action to meet this new requirement from 6 April 2016."

In *JF v HMRC (TC)* [2017] UKUT 334 (AAC) Judge Wikeley decided that the new definition did not displace the long-standing principle that that, in the context of self-employment, remunerative work means work carried out with the desire, hope and intention of claiming a reward or profit (*R(FIS) 6/85*), nor did it require un-costed activities or non-remunerated hours to be discounted, "without due consideration". Judge Wikeley also noted that claimants seeking to establish self-employed status should not be expected to provide business plans of too exacting a standard:

> "31. ....Empirical evidence demonstrates the heterogeneity of the many different forms of self-employment...Self-employed working tax credit claimants (typically) are not putting together business proposals of sufficient rigour to pass muster on a Masters of Business Administration course or to withstand scrutiny in an episode of Dragons' Den. Usually they are much more modest enterprises, as in the present case, and expectations about the documentary paper trail should be adjusted accordingly."

In *JF* Judge Wikeley also rejected the argument that, under the new definition of "self-employed", time spent setting up a business and handing out leaflets door-to-door could not count. In *VO v HMRC (TC)* [2017] UKUT 343 (AAC) Judge Wikeley also decided that time spent on networking and promoting a business was not categorically excluded. These activities are potentially relevant in deciding whether a person is "self-employed" and in quantifying hours of work done in expectation of payment for the purposes of reg.4.

The term 'on a commercial basis' is not statutorily defined. In *JW v HMRC* [2019] UKUT 114 (AAC); [2019] AACR 23 Upper Tribunal Judge Poole QC gave a valuable analysis of the meaning of 'on a commercial basis' as used in the definition of self-employment. Judge Poole held that the meaning of the term "must be ascertained by considering the context in which it appears" before going on to identify the purpose of the term within the working tax credit scheme–the general context–as well as the interpretative implications of the wider statutory definition of "self-employment" of which 'on a commercial basis' is but one component. Care should be taken before applying tax case law about the link between profitability and commerciality in interpreting 'on a commercial basis'. Tax case law is unlikely to be transferable to a statutory scheme that uses the concept of commerciality for a different purpose than does tax legislation.

Judge Poole identified the wider contextual considerations as: working tax credit was introduced "with a stated purpose of making work pay" being one part of a range of initiatives to tackle poverty; given the relevant income thresholds and award tapers, working tax credit "was predicated on a low level of earnings"; a more restrictive definition of self-employment was introduced for the purpose of tackling abuse of the system by bogus self-employment yet the opportunity was not taken to impose a minimum income condition for self-employed claimants. Drawing these considerations together, Judge Poole rightly concludes that the original purpose of working tax credit, that of 'making work pay', was unaffected by the introduction of a new definition of self-employment. The new definition was intended to tackle bogus self-employment, not to alter fundamental purpose of working tax credit.

Judge Poole went on to analyse the function of 'on a commercial basis' within the definition of self-employment taking into account the relationship between the various components of the definition. Profits are mentioned separately—'on a commercial basis with a view to the realisation of profits'—which indicates that actual profitability is not required. An activity that generates no or little profits is capable of being carried out on a commercial basis with a view to the realisation of profits. Other components of the definition require the trade, profession or vocation in question to be 'organised' and 'regular'. 'Organised' directs consideration of matters of business organisation such as accounts, sales returns and tax records. 'Regular' looks to the conduct of business, matters such as regularity of business and opening hours, and, of itself, is capable of identifying cases of bogus self-employment.

In *OM v HMRC (CTC)* [2019] UKUT 263 (AAC) Judge Hemingway made the point that a limited number of financial transactions within a tax year does not necessarily prevent an activity from meeting the 'organised and regular' requirement.

The overall scheme of the Regulations also sheds light on the purpose of 'on a commercial basis' within the definition of self-employment in particular the meaning of qualifying remunerative work as prescribed by reg.4. The minimum hours of work requirements in condition 2 of reg.4 help to ensure that entitlement is limited to those who are genuinely working. The condition 4 requirement for work to be done for payment or in the expectation of payment allows HMRC, in Judge Poole's words, to "look at the economics of the business".

In the light of the above considerations, Judge Poole held that it is an error of law to conclude that self-employment is not on a commercial basis simply because it is unprofitable for the following reasons: to equate 'commercial' with 'profitable' would undermine the fundamental purpose of working tax credit; the definition of self-employment was re-drawn in order to tackle bogus self-employment rather than disqualify those pursuing genuine self-employment; the legislative scheme contains a number of other features capable of excluding bogus self-employment so that it is unnecessary to equate 'commercial' with 'profitable' in order to tackle abuse of the scheme by cases of bogus self-employment; other components of the definition of self-employment take into account profitability issues, in particular the requirement for the trade etc. to be carried on with a view to the realisation of profits. Judge Poole added that focussing on profitability in determining whether self-employment is 'on a commercial basis' is contrary to the essence of commerciality:

(SI 2002/2005 reg.2) as amended

"25.4 Using profitability as the touchstone of commerciality ignores the core meaning of "commercial". "Commercial" is essentially about commerce, or buying and selling, and in my opinion that should be the focus of the "commercial" part of the definition of "self-employed". Consideration has to be given to whether a business is truly engaged in buying and selling exchanges, or if there is bogus self-employment abusing the WTC system. Relevant factors are whether the business: generates goods or services by enterprise and effort; makes available and exposes goods or services for sale, for example by advertising, supplying to shops, or listing for sale online; actually makes sales, and the terms on which those sales are made. Also potentially relevant are: the age of the business; business plans for future commerce; and steps being taken to increase income from the work, all bearing in mind the dicta in *JR v HMRC* [2017] UKUT 334 about the extent of documentary support required of modest businesses."

Linking commerciality with profitability would also "fail adequately to make provision for businesses which are growing but not yet profitable, or situations of volatile markets, and potentially disincentivise people to take the risks associated with setting up self-employment to get off welfare into work".

Judge Poole's reasoning regarding the relevance of profitability was followed by Upper Tribunal Judge Hemingway in *OM v HMRC (CTC)* [2019] UKUT 263 (AAC).

Importantly, Judge Poole further decided that HMRC's threshold for investigating self-employed claimants, as set out in paragraph 2.92 of the Autumn Statement 2014, cannot be used as a test for determining whether self-employment is on a commercial basis. Paragraph 2.92 stated "those declaring income less than the equivalent of working 24 hours a week at the National Minimum Wage will also be required to provide evidence to HMRC that the work they are undertaking is genuine and effective". At the date of Judge Poole's decision, the income limit for the maximum rate of working tax credit was £6,420. Working 24 hours per week for the current minimum wage for those aged 25 or above would generate an annual income - £10,246.08 - well in excess of the income limit. Yet the legislative scheme anticipates those with an annual income of less than £6,420 receiving the maximum rate (after which a taper reduces the amount of the award). Otherwise, what would be the point of the income limit? Judge Poole also makes the point that the Regulations do not require self-employment to be 'genuine and effective'. While HMRC seem to have adopted this as a test for gauging self-employment, it has no statutory basis. A tribunal that applies a test of genuineness and effectiveness is likely to err in law. Other express features of the working tax credit legislation are more than capable of dealing with bogus self-employment. The 'genuine and effective' so-called test is best ignored in determining whether a person is self-employed for the purposes of the working tax credit definition.

Other elements of working tax credit

3.—(1) For the purposes of determining the maximum rate of working tax credit, in addition to the basic element and the disability element, the following elements are prescribed—

(a) a 30 hour element;
(b) a second adult element;
(c) a lone parent element;
(d) a child care element; [¹ and]
(e) a severe disability element; [¹ . . .]
(f) [¹ . . .].

(2) It is a condition of entitlement to the other elements of working tax credit that the person making the claim for working tax credit is entitled to the basic element.

2.125

(3) If the claim for working tax credit is a joint claim, and both members of the couple satisfy the conditions of entitlement for—
  (a) the disability element; [¹ or]
  (b) the severe disability element; [¹ . . .]
  (c) [¹ . . .]
the award must include two such elements.

AMENDMENT

1. Tax Credits (Miscellaneous Amendments) Regulations 2012 (SI 2012/848) reg.2(3) (April 6, 2012).

DEFINITIONS

"basic element"—see TCA 2002 s.11(4).
"claim"—see reg.2.
"joint claim"—see reg.2.

GENERAL NOTE

2.126
Section 11(2) of the TCA 2002 requires that all awards of working tax credit must contain a common element (known as the basic element—see s.11(4)). Section 11(3) requires that there be an element related to those with disabilities putting them at a disadvantage in getting a job. The list of other elements in s.11(6) is, however, permissive only. This regulation sets out the other elements to which claimants may for the time being be entitled as part of their working tax credit award, save one: the child care element is not included because it is dealt with separately under s.12 of the TCA 2002.

The structure adopted is to require all claimants to show that they are entitled to the basic element in accordance with reg.4. Unless a claimant establishes that entitlement, he or she does not qualify for working tax credit at all. Once entitlement to the basic element is shown, a claimant may claim any or all of the other elements—subject, of course, to showing additional separate entitlement to each of them.

PART II

CONDITIONS OF ENTITLEMENT

Basic element

Entitlement to basic element of working tax credit: qualifying remunerative work

2.127
4.—(1) Subject to the qualification in paragraph (2), a person shall be treated as engaged in qualifying remunerative work if, and only if, he satisfies all of the following conditions [⁷ (and in the case of the Second condition, one of the variations in that condition)].

First condition

The person [⁹ is employed or self-employed and]—
  (a) is working at the date of the claim; or
  (b) has an offer of work which he has accepted at the date of the claim and the work is expected to commence within 7 days of the making of the claim.

In relation to a case falling within sub-paragraph (b) of this condition, references in the second third and fourth conditions below to work which the person undertakes are to be construed as references to the work which the person will undertake when it commences.

In such a case the person is only to be treated as being in qualifying remunerative work when he begins the work referred to in that subparagraph.

Second condition

[⁷ First variation: In the case of a single claim, the person—]
[¹(a) is aged at least 16 and—
- (i) undertakes work for not less than 16 hours per week,
- (ii) [⁷ ...] is responsible for a child or qualifying young person, or he has a physical or mental disability which puts him at a disadvantage in getting a job and satisfies regulation 9(1)(c),]
(b) [⁷ ...] [⁶ ...]
(c) is aged at least 25 and undertakes not less than 30 hours work per week [⁶ ...] [⁶; or
(d) is aged at least 60 and undertakes not less than 16 hours work per week]

[⁵[⁷ Second variation: In the case of a joint claim where neither person is responsible for a child or qualifying young person, the person—
- (a) is aged at least 16 and undertakes work for not less than 16 hours per week and has a physical or mental disability which puts that person at a disadvantage in getting a job and satisfies regulation 9(1)(c);
- (b) is aged at least 25 and undertakes work for not less than 30 hours per week; or
- (c) is aged at least 60 and undertakes work for not less than 16 hours per week.

Third variation: In the case of a joint claim where a person or that person's partner is responsible for a child or qualifying young person, the person—
- (a) is aged at least 16 and is a member of a couple where at least one partner undertakes work for not less than 16 hours per week and the aggregate number of hours for which the couple undertake work is not less than 24 hours per week;
- (b) is aged at least 16 and undertakes work for not less than 16 hours per week and has a physical or mental disability which puts that person at a disadvantage in getting a job and satisfies regulation 9(1)(c);
- (c) is aged at least 16 and undertakes work for not less than 16 hours per week and that person's partner is—
  - (i) incapacitated and satisfies any of the circumstances in [⁸regulation 13(4) to (12)]; or
  - (ii) an in-patient in hospital; or
  - (iii) in prison (whether serving a custodial sentence or remanded in custody awaiting trial or sentence); or
  - (iv) entitled to carer's allowance under section 70 of the Social Security Contributions and Benefits Act 1992; [¹⁵ or]
  - [¹⁵(v) entitled to carer's assistance given in accordance with regulations made under section 28 of the Social Security (Scotland) Act 2018;]

(d) is aged at least 60 and undertakes work for not less than 16 hours per week.]]

Third condition

The work which the person undertakes is expected to continue for at least 4 weeks after the making of the claim or, in a case falling within sub-paragraph (b) of the first condition, after the work starts.

Fourth condition

The work is done for payment or in expectation of payment. [⁷ . . .]
[⁵ A social security benefit is not payment for the purposes of satisfying this condition.]
[⁷ (1A) For the purposes of interpretation of paragraph (1)—
(a) paragraphs (3) and (4) provide the method of determining the number of hours of qualifying remunerative work that a person undertakes;
(b) regulations 5, 5A, 6 and 7A and 7B apply in relation to periods of absence from work connected with childbirth or adoption, sickness, strike periods or suspension from work;
(c) [¹⁴ . . .]
(d) regulation 7D applies where a person or, in the case of a joint claim, one or both persons cease to work or reduce their hours to the extent that they no longer satisfy the Second condition in paragraph (1);
[¹²(da) [¹⁴ . . .]
(e) regulation 8 applies where there is a gap between jobs;
(f) regulation 9 prescribes the conditions which must be satisfied by, or exist in relation to, a person so that he is to be treated as having a physical or mental disability which puts him at a disadvantage in getting a job.],
(2) A person who would otherwise satisfy the conditions in paragraph (1) shall not be regarded as engaged in qualifying remunerative work to the extent that he is—
(a) engaged by a charitable or voluntary organisation, or is a volunteer, if the only payment received by him or due to be paid to him is a payment by way of expenses which falls to be disregarded under item 1 in Table 7 in regulation 19 of the Tax Credits (Definition and Calculation of Income) Regulations 2002;
(b) engaged in caring for a person who is not a member of his household but is temporarily residing with him if the only payment made to him for providing that care is disregarded income by virtue of item 3 or 4 in Table 8 in regulation 19 of the Tax Credits (Definition and Calculation of Income) Regulations 2002;
(c) engaged on a scheme for which a training allowance is being paid;
(d) participating in the Intensive Activity Period specified in regulation 75(1)(a)(iv) of the Jobseeker's Allowance Regulations 1996 or the Preparation for Employment Programme specified in regulation 75(1)(a)(v) of the Jobseeker's Allowance Regulations (Northern Ireland) 1996;
(e) engaged in an activity in respect of which—
(i) a sports award has been made, or is to be made, to him, and
(ii) no other payment is made, or is expected to be made, to him; or

(SI 2002/2005 reg.4) as amended

    (f) participating in an employment zone programme, that is to say a programme established for one or more areas designated pursuant to section 60 of the Welfare Reform and Pensions Act 1999, and subject to the [³ Employment Zones 2003 and the Employment Zones (Allocation to Contractors) Pilot Regulations 2005] if he receives no payments under that programme other than—
        (i) discretionary payments disregarded in the calculation of a claimant's income under item 6(b) in [¹Table 6] in regulation 19 of the Tax Credits (Definition and Calculation of Income) Regulations 2002; or
        (ii) training premiums.
  [⁴(g) a person who—
        (i) is serving a custodial sentence or has been remanded in custody awaiting trial or sentence, and
        (ii) is engaged in work (whether inside or outside a prison) while he is serving the sentence or remanded in custody.]
  [²This is subject to the following qualification.
  (2A) Neither sub-paragraph (c) nor sub-paragraph (d) of paragraph (2) applies if—
    (a) in a case falling within sub-paragraph (c), the training allowance, or
    (b) in a case falling within sub-paragraph (d), any payment made by the Secretary of State, or, in Northern Ireland, by the Department for [¹¹ Communities], in connection with the Intensive Activity Period,
is chargeable to income tax as the profits of a trade, profession or vocation.]
  (3) The number of hours for which a person undertakes qualifying remunerative work is—
    (a) in the case of an apprentice, employee or officeholder, the number of hours of such work which he normally performs—
        (i) under the contract of service or of apprenticeship under which he is employed, or
        (ii) in the office in which he is employed;
    (b) in the case of an agency worker, the number of hours in respect of which remuneration is normally paid to him by an employment agency with whom he has a contract of employment; or
    (c) in the case of a person who is self-employed, the number of hours he normally performs for payment or in expectation of payment.
This is subject to the following qualification.
  (4) In reckoning the number of hours of qualifying remunerative work which a person normally undertakes—
    (a) any period of customary or paid holiday, [¹² ...]
    (b) any time allowed for meals or refreshment, unless the person is, or expects to be paid earnings in respect of that time, [¹³ ...[¹²]]]
  [¹² (c) any period of absence from work due to taking emergency volunteering leave under Schedule 7 to the Coronavirus Act 2020,] [¹³ [¹⁶...]]
  [¹³(d) any period of absence from work resulting from that person—
        (i) having been instructed by NHS Test and Trace, to self-isolate due to coronavirus; or
        (ii) having been instructed not to attend work as a direct consequence of restrictions imposed under any enactment as a consequence of coronavirus][¹⁶, and]

[^16(e) any period of absence from work due to taking carer's leave under section 80J of the Employment Rights Act 1996]
shall be disregarded.

[^1(5) In reckoning the number of hours of qualifying remunerative work which a person normally undertakes, any time allowed for visits to a hospital, clinic or other establishment for the purpose only of treating or monitoring the person's disability shall be included; but only if the person is, or expects to be, paid in respect of that time.]

[^10 (6) In this regulation "work" shall be construed as a reference to any work that the person undertakes whether as a person who is employed or self-employed or both.]

[^13(7) In this regulation "NHS Test and Trace" means the service introduced by the National Health Service in England to trace the spread of coronavirus or any service established in Scotland, Wales or Northern Ireland for a similar purpose.]

AMENDMENTS

1. Working Tax Credit (Entitlement and Maximum Rate) (Amendment) Regulations 2003 (SI 2003/701) reg.4 (April 6, 2003).
2. Tax Credits (Miscellaneous Amendments) Regulations 2004 (SI 2004/762) reg.5 (April 6, 2004).
3. Tax Credits (Miscellaneous Amendments) Regulations 2006 (SI 2006/766) reg.20(3) (April 6, 2006).
4. Tax Credits (Miscellaneous Amendments) Regulations 2007 (SI 2007/824) reg.4 (April 6, 2007).
5. Tax Credits (Miscellaneous Amendments) Regulations 2009 (SI 2009/697) reg.3 (April 6, 2009).
6. Tax Credits (Miscellaneous Amendments) (No.3) Regulations 2010 (SI 2010/2914) reg.11 (April 6, 2011).
7. Tax Credits (Miscellaneous Amendments) Regulations 2012 (SI 2012/848) reg.2(4) and (5) (April 6, 2012).
8. Working Tax Credit (Entitlement and Maximum Rate) (Amendment) Regulations 2013 (SI 2013/1736) reg.2 (August 5, 2013).
9. Working Tax Credit (Entitlement and Maximum Rate) (Amendment) Regulations 2015 (SI 2015/695) reg.4 (April 6, 2015).
10. Working Tax Credit (Entitlement and Maximum Rate) (Amendment) Regulations 2015 (SI 2015/605) reg.5 (April 6, 2015).
11. Tax Credits, Child Benefit and Childcare Payments (Miscellaneous Amendments) Regulations 2019 (SI 2019/364) reg.2(3) (March 21, 2019).
12. Tax Credits (Coronavirus, Miscellaneous Amendments) Regulations 2020 (SI 2020/534) reg.2(3) (May 23, 2020).
13. Tax Credits, Childcare Payments and Childcare (Extended Entitlement) (Coronavirus and Miscellaneous Amendments) Regulations 2020 (SI 2020/1515) reg.2(2) (January 14, 2021).
14. Tax Credits and Child Benefit (Miscellaneous Amendments) Regulations 2022 (SI 2022/555) reg.5(2) (June 9, 2022).
15. Tax Credits and Child Benefit (Miscellaneous Amendments) Regulations 2023 (SI 2023/179) reg.3(2) (March 15, 2023).
16. Carer's Leave (Consequential Amendments to Subordinate Legislation) Regulations 2024 (SI 2024/266) reg.3 (April 6, 2024).

DEFINITIONS

"agency worker"—see ITEPA 2003 s.44.
"child"—see reg.2.

(SI 2002/2005 reg.4) as amended

"claim"—see reg.2.
"employed"—see reg.2.
"Employment Zone programme"—see reg.2.
"office-holder"—see ITEPA 2003 s.5.
"partner"—see reg.2.
"qualifying young person"—see reg.2.
"responsible for a child"—see TCA 2002 s.48.
"self-employed"—see reg.2.
"sports award"—see reg.2.
"training allowance"—see reg.2.
"week"—see reg.2.

GENERAL NOTE

The structure of this key regulation is somewhat misleading. It suggests that there are four conditions for qualifying for entitlement to the basic element of working tax credit. This somewhat disguises the fact that there are four different and alternative bases for claiming working tax credit, all of which are wrapped up together in the "second condition", while the other three conditions are common to all groups of claimant. A fifth condition was added by amendment to the "second condition" in 2011.

2.128

First condition

Section 10(1) requires that all claimants for working tax credit must be in "qualifying remunerative work". This condition defines the scope of being "in" work. It does this by identifying individuals who are to be "treated as" being in qualifying remunerative work. Whether or not they are in work, in an everyday sense, does not matter. A claimant cannot receive working tax credit until he or she has started work (or, in the case of joint claimants or members of a polygamous unit, one of them has started work), or the work is to start within seven days. The addition of a specific mention of the self-employed to the first condition in April 2015 emphasises that self-employment must be shown to be current and ongoing. See the general note to reg.2 above.

2.129

As to whether the work concerned has to be in the UK, see the comments of Judge Rowland in *GC v HMRC (TC)* [2014] UKUT 251 (AAC) noted at para.2.488.

Second condition

This creates alternative conditions for, or routes to, entitlement. These routes have been modified in several ways with effect from April 6, 2012. The routes now are:

2.130

- **Route 1** is for a single claimant working 16 or more hours a week who is responsible for a child or qualifying young person. The requirement of responsibility for a child or qualifying young person is the same test as for child tax credit purposes, and the regulations adopt the same definitions. In practical terms, they are also the same tests as those for claiming child benefit. However, this does not apply to a person who is claiming child benefit only because he or she is contributing to the child's maintenance costs at the specified rate.
- **Route 2** is for a disabled claimant suffering prejudice in the job market. The test for work is again a 16-hour test.
- **Route 3** is for a couple making a joint claim where one is responsible for a child or qualifying young person. Here there are alternative requirements. The main rule is that the couple between them work 24 hours a week, with one of the couple working at least 16 hours. However, the test remains a 16-hour test if a claimant is entitled to the disability premium or the partner is incapacitated in one of the ways relevant for the childcare premium or is in hospital or in prison. The total of 24 hours for the couple together is new, although the minimum requirement remains that one of them must be working for 16 hours.

- **Route 4** is for single or joint claimants over 60 working 16 hours a week. There will be an interaction in some cases with state pension credit, as working tax credit counts as income for that purpose.
- **Route 5** is the safety net route. It applies to single or joint claimants who are over 25 and working 30 hours a week. In practice, this will be of benefit to those who are not working a full working week but are earning at the minimal level. This could also include the self-employed with low levels of profit despite continuing a work pattern of the required level.

The previous route for those over 50 has been repealed.

Disputes as to whether an individual in fact works the necessary hours each week (at least 16 or 30, depending on the applicable route) often turn on matters of credibility. For a summary of the case law concerning the limited circumstances in which the Upper Tribunal may interfere with the First-tier Tribunal's credibility findings, since its jurisdiction is limited to errors on points of law, see Upper Tribunal Judge Wikeley's decision in *NN v HMRC (TC)* [2019] UKUT 386 (AAC). That case was an unsuccessful appeal against the First-tier Tribunal's finding that the Appellant's evidence that she did at least 16 hours paid work each week was not credible.

Third condition

2.131 This imposes a minimum level of continuity before working tax credit can be claimed. It is separate from, but to be read with, the 16- and 30-hour requirements of the second condition. In other words, it would seem that it has in cases of doubt to be shown that the work will be at a level of 16 or 30 hours a week for those four weeks. That will be a question of fact in all cases. The self-employed may have to show that they are, in that sense, "ordinarily self employed", which is the test for payment of Class 2 NI contributions. In the modern context of flexible employment and allegedly zero-hours contracts, close attention may have to be paid not only to the terms of agreement between the two parties to the work relationship but also to whether there is "an irreducible minimum of obligation on each side to create a contract of service": Stephenson LJ in *Nethermere (St Neots) Ltd v Gardiner* [1984] I.C.R. 612, CA. If there is, the question is then whether on the facts it is shown that it will (or, at the end of the year, did) last for four weeks at the required level. But there is a possible practical problem of timing for a claimant in this sort of work because of the interaction of this requirement with the terms of the first condition—requiring that the work start within seven days of the offer of work—and the backdating rule that prevents a claim being made more than three months after entitlement starts.

Fourth condition

2.132 This echoes the well known test from income support (reg.5 of the Income Support (General) Regulations 1987 (SI 1987/1967)). The test is that the work is done either for payment or in the expectation of it. There is considerable case law from the Courts and Commissioners on whether work is, in this sense, remunerative. The same test will apply to tax credits also. For the question whether work is remunerative, see in particular *R(IS) 22/95* and the decision of the Court of Appeal in *Chief Adjudication Officer v Ellis* (reported as the appendix to that decision). In *R(FIS) 1/86* it was established that the remuneration did not come from the work. That may cause other problems for tax credits, as it may not be clear whether money received in this way from work is "employment income". However, the courts have found, for example, that tips paid to a taxi driver are earnings from the driver's employment even though paid by third parties: see *Shilton v Wilmshurst* [1991] S.T.C. 88 HL. But the question whether the work is remunerative, and the question of the level of earnings from the work, are for separate determination.

The fourth condition was considered further by Judge Rowland in *MH v HMRC (TC)* [2016] UKUT 79 (AAC), where the appellant and his wife were employed by a company which they owned, working from home, marketing and maintaining IT for independent travel agents. However, the business had declined significantly.

The tribunal dismissed their appeal on the basis that neither satisfied the fourth condition, finding that the business had made a loss over a number of years and that by the first tax year in question, the claimant had accepted that he would derive no personal income from the business. He had continued to work because it enabled him to cover some of his household expenses, which were treated for tax purposes as having been incurred wholly and exclusively by the company. Judge Rowland held that "in order for a person to be entitled to working tax credit, work must be in expectation that he or she personally will be paid; an expectation that the company for whom the work is done will be paid is not enough" (at 9). In this case, it was clear that payments to meet the claimant's household expenses were not made directly to him and that he received no income directly from the company. However, the appeal was allowed and remitted for rehearing as the tribunal had failed to make sufficient findings as to whether the work was done in expectation of payment:

"... work may be done in expectation of payment notwithstanding that no profit is in fact made. Moreover, work may be done in expectation of payment even if it is known that no profit will be made for some time but it is expected that the relevant business will become profitable in the future" (at 12).

Paragraph (2)
This paragraph lists seven specific activities that are excepted from "work" for working tax credit purposes. The addition of condition (g) in 2007 avoids claims that arose in individual cases from prisoners working in the community on day release.

2.133

The number of hours worked
Paragraphs (3)–(5), together with regs 5–8, help define the number of hours worked by a claimant or partner. Subject to the specific provisions, it is essentially a question of fact to be determined over the claim period which will (unlike for the previous benefits replaced by working tax credit) normally be a full year. The practical approach of *R(FC) 1/92* was to look at the hours actually worked, rather than the contractual requirements. The wording of this form of the rule would suggest that this is the proper approach to be taken.

2.134

Paragraph (3) provides the starting point for deciding the number of hours, but each category of work is tested against what is "normal". The main previous test was by reference to the hours worked in the week of claim, or either of the two previous weeks, or the following week, or the week next following any current holiday. Anyone meeting those tests was then assumed to be "normally" employed at the relevant level. This makes it clearer that the issue is one of fact, and is for most claimants a significant simplification of the rules. Paragraph (4) repeats the previous disregard of paid holidays and unpaid breaks as well as new disregards for certain absences from work connected to coronavirus measures and statutory carer's leave (provided for by the Carer's Leave Act 2023), and para.(5) extends this to allow the inclusion of paid medical visits.

In *CTC/2103/2006* (a decision followed by Judge Wikeley in *VO v HMRC (TC)* [2017] UKUT 343 (AAC)), a Deputy Commissioner decided that it was not correct to calculate the number of hours worked in a fluctuating situation by averaging hours across a month from a monthly pay slip. There was also no requirement in the legislation that 16 hours be worked every week. There was no set, or hard and fast, rule for deciding the number of hours worked. It is a question of fact in each case. However, it is one that causes repeated problems in administering tax credits. For this reason claimants are now required to notify HMRC within one month if their work hours change so that they stop working for 30, or 16, hours a week, as the case may be. See para.2.314. It will not always be easy to establish when that duty arises in cases of uncertainty such as that in *CTC/2103/2006*. But reg.7D below will provide a one-month period that deals with most cases.

The Working Tax Credit (Entitlement and Maximum Rate) Regulations 2002

In *CTC/3443/2012* the Upper Tribunal applied the decision of the Court of Appeal in *R(IS) 22/95* to the appeal of a claimant arguing that he was undertaking work for 30 hours a week. The judge emphasised that this is a question of fact taking into account work necessary for a particular employment and that the work must be undertaken in expectation of payment for that work.

[¹Time off in connection with [² childbirth][¹⁰, parental bereavement] [¹⁰or] adoption

2.135   5.—(1) This regulation applies for any period during which a person—
(a) is paid maternity allowance,
(b) is paid statutory maternity pay,
(c) is absent from work during an ordinary maternity leave period under section 71 of the Employment Rights Act 1996 or Article 103 of the Employment Rights (Northern Ireland) Order 1996;
[³(ca) is absent from work during the first 13 weeks of an additional maternity leave period under section 73 of the Employment Rights Act 1996 or article 105 of the Employment Rights (Northern Ireland) Order 1996,]
(d) is paid [⁵ statutory paternity pay [⁸. . .]]
[⁵ (da) [⁸. . .]
(e) is absent from work during [⁸ a] paternity leave period under sections 80A or 80B of the Employment Rights Act 1996 or Articles 112A or 112B of the Employment Rights (Northern Ireland) Order 1996,
(ea) [⁹. . .]
(f) is paid statutory adoption pay, [³. . .]
(g) is absent from work during an ordinary adoption leave period under section 75A of the Employment Rights Act 1996 or Article 107A of the Employment Rights (Northern Ireland) Order 1996. [³,or
(ga) is absent from work during the first 13 weeks of an additional adoption leave period under section 75B of the Employment Rights Act 1996 or article 107B of the Employment Rights (Northern Ireland) Order 1996]
[⁷ (h) is paid statutory shared parental pay,
(i) is absent from work during a period of shared parental leave under section 75E or 75G of the Employment Rights Act 1996][¹⁰,
(j) is paid statutory parental bereavement pay,
(k) is absent from work during a period of parental bereavement leave under section 80EA of the Employment Rights Act 1996].
(2) For the purposes of the [⁴ conditions of entitlement in this Part], the person is treated as being engaged in qualifying remunerative work during the period.
This is subject to [⁶ paragraphs (3), (3A) [¹⁰, (3C)] and regulation 7D].
(3) The person must have been engaged in qualifying remunerative work [¹¹, or treated under regulation 7E as being engaged in such work,] immediately before the beginning of the period.
[⁵ (3A) A person shall only be treated as being engaged in qualifying remunerative work by virtue of paragraph (1)(ea) for such period as that person would have been paid additional statutory paternity pay had the conditions of entitlement in [⁸. . .] Parts 2 or 3 of the Additional Statutory Paternity Pay (General) Regulations (Northern Ireland) 2010 been satisfied.]

(SI 2002/2005 reg.5) as amended

[⁷ (3B) A person shall only be treated as being engaged in qualifying remunerative work by virtue of paragraph (1)(i) for such period as that person would have been paid statutory shared parental pay had the conditions of entitlement in Parts 2 or 3 of the Statutory Shared Parental Pay (General) Regulations 2014 been satisfied.]

[¹⁰ (3C) A person shall only be treated as being engaged in qualifying remunerative work by virtue of paragraph (1)(k) for such period as that person would have been paid statutory parental bereavement pay had the conditions of entitlement in Part 2 of the Statutory Parental Bereavement Pay (General) Regulations 2020 been satisfied.]

(4) A person who is self-employed is treated as engaged in qualifying remunerative work for the requisite number of hours during any period for which paragraph (1) would have applied in his case but for the fact that the work he performed in the week immediately before the period began, although done for payment or in the expectation of payment, was not performed under a contract of service or apprenticeship.]

AMENDMENTS

1. Working Tax Credit (Entitlement and Maximum Rate) (Amendment) Regulations 2003 (SI 2003/701) reg.5 (April 6, 2003).
2. Tax Credits (Miscellaneous Amendments) Regulations 2004 (SI 2004/762) reg.6 (April 6, 2004).
3. Tax Credits (Miscellaneous Amendments) Regulations 2007 (SI 2007/824) reg.5 (April 6, 2007).
4. Tax Credits (Entitlement and Maximum Rate) (Amendment) Regulations 2009 (SI 2009/1829) regs 2 and 3 (July 31, 2009).
5. Tax Credits (Miscellaneous Amendments) (No.2) Regulations 2010 (SI 2010/2494) reg.3 (November 14, 2010).
6. Tax Credits (Miscellaneous Amendments) Regulations 2012 (SI 2012/848) reg.2(6) (April 6, 2012).
7. Shared Parental Leave and Statutory Shared Parental Pay (Consequential Amendments to Subordinate Legislation) Order 2014 (SI 2014/3255) art.11(2)(e) and (4) (December 31, 2014).
8. Shared Parental Leave and Statutory Shared Parental Pay (Consequential Amendments to Subordinate Legislation) Order 2014 (SI 2014/3255) art.11(2)(a)–(d) and (3) (April 5, 2015).
9. Tax Credits and Child Benefit (Miscellaneous Amendments) Regulations 2016 (SI 2016/360) reg.2(2) (April 6, 2016).
10. Parental Bereavement Leave and Pay (Consequential Amendments to Subordinate Legislation) Regulations 2020 (SI 2020/354) reg.11 (April 6, 2020).
11. Tax Credits, Childcare Payments and Childcare (Extended Entitlement) (Coronavirus and Miscellaneous Amendments) Regulations 2020 (SI 2020/1515) reg.2(3) (January 14, 2021).

DEFINITIONS

"qualifying remunerative employment"—see reg.4.
"self-employed"—see reg.2.
"week"—see reg.2.

GENERAL NOTE

2.136 This regulation was rewritten to take account of the extended rights of mothers and fathers, including adoptive parents, to parental leave as from 2003 and further amended in 2020 to take account of statutory parental bereavement pay and leave. It is designed to stop an award of working tax credit being terminated by such leave. See also reg.5A.

In *AG v HMRC* [2017] UKUT 67 (AAC) Upper Tribunal Judge Ward considered the relationship between this regulation and reg.7D (the four-week "run-on" of entitlement—qualifying remunerative work status—where a person ceases to be in qualifying remunerative employment). Regulations 5(1) and (2) deem a person to be in qualifying remunerative work during periods when the person is in receipt of certain statutory payments or exercising certain statutory rights connected to childbirth or adoption. For example, a woman is treated as being in qualifying remunerative work during any period in which she is paid maternity allowance. This was the case for the Appellant in *AG*. However, regs 5(1) and (2) are subject to reg.5(3) which requires a person to have been engaged in qualifying remunerative work "immediately before the beginning of the period". It appears that AG qualified for the four-week run-on under reg.7D when she reduced her weekly working hours to 11. Then, 26 days into the run-on period, AG began to be paid maternity allowance. AG argued that she was in qualifying remunerative work, by virtue of reg.7D, immediately before she started being paid maternity allowance. If AG was right, she would have continued to be treated as in qualifying remunerative work under this regulation, and entitled to working tax credit, while being paid maternity allowance.

Judge Ward noted the puzzle posed by the fact that reg.5(2) is made "subject to" reg.7D. It is also made subject to regs 5(3) and 5(3A) but that is readily understandable since those provisions "impose extra conditions which limit a person's rights under regulation 5". Regulation 7D, however, does not: "where [reg.7D] applies it confers an additional period of entitlement to WTC on a claimant". Judge Ward concluded that, in making reg.5(2) subject to reg.7D, "the sole legislative intention was to preserve the ability to rely on the additional four week period of which a claimant would not otherwise have the benefit and that it did not form part of that intention as expressed in the Regulations (as amended) to allow reliance on reg. 7D to subvert the otherwise clear intention of reg 5(3)". Accordingly, AG could not rely on her deemed qualifying remunerative work status under reg.7D for the purposes of reg.5. Regulation 5(3) meant she needed to have been in actual qualifying remunerative work immediately before she started to receive maternity allowance. She was not and, accordingly, could not be treated as in qualifying remunerative work for the purposes of reg.5.

[¹ Time off in connection with childbirth and placement for adoption: further provisions

2.137

5A.—(1) This regulation applies to a person for any period—
(a) which falls within a period to which regulation 5 applies; and
(b) which follows the birth or the placement for adoption of the child in connection with whose birth or placement entitlement to the allowance, pay or leave mentioned in regulation 5(1) arises.

(2) [³ A person who would have been treated as being engaged in qualifying remunerative work if they or, in the case of a joint claim, they or their partner had been responsible for a child or "qualifying young person"] immediately before the beginning of a period to which regulation 5 applies, shall be treated as [² being engaged in qualifying remunerative work for purposes of the conditions of entitlement in this Part] during the period mentioned in paragraph (1) above.

(3) Paragraph (4) of regulation 5 applies for the purpose of this regulation as it applies for the purpose of that regulation.]

[³ (4) This regulation is subject to regulation 7D.]

(SI 2002/2005 reg.5A) as amended

AMENDMENTS

1. Tax Credits (Miscellaneous Amendments) Regulations 2004 (SI 2004/762) reg.7 (April 6, 2004).
2. Working Tax Credit (Entitlement and Maximum Rate) (Amendment) Regulations 2009 (SI 2009/1829) regs 2 and 4 (July 31, 2009).
3. Tax Credits (Miscellaneous Amendments) Regulations 2012 (SI 2012/848) reg.2(7) (April 6, 2012).

GENERAL NOTE

This regulation reduces the number of hours, for which a person must have been engaged in qualifying remunerative work immediately before beginning a period of statutory leave in connection with the birth or placement for adoption of a child, in order to qualify for tax credit for so much of that period as follows the birth or placement for adoption of the relevant child.

2.138

[¹Periods of illness [², incapacity for work or limited capability for work]

6.—(1) This regulation applies for any period during which a person—
(a) is paid statutory sick pay;
(b) is paid short-term incapacity benefit at the lower rate under sections 30A–30E of the Contributions and Benefits Act;
(c) is paid income support on the grounds of incapacity for work under paragraphs 7 and 14 of Schedule 1B to the Income Support (General) Regulations 1987,
[²(cc) is paid an employment and support allowance under Part 1 of the Welfare Reform Act, or]
(d) receives national insurance credits on the grounds of incapacity for work [² or limited capability for work] under reg.8B of the Social Security (Credits) Regulations 1975.

(2) For the purposes of the [³ conditions of entitlement in this Part], the person is treated as being engaged in qualifying remunerative work during the period.
This is subject to [⁴ paragraphs (3), (4) and regulation 7D].

(3) The person must have been engaged in qualifying remunerative work[⁵, or treated under regulation 7E as being engaged in such work,] immediately before the beginning of the period.

(4) If the person is paid income support as specified in paragraph (1) (c) [² or employment and support allowance as specified in paragraph (1) (cc)] or receives national insurance credits as specified in paragraph (1) (d) he is treated as being engaged in qualifying remunerative work for a period of 28 weeks only, beginning with the day on which he is first paid income support [² or employment and support allowance] or receives national insurance credits (as the case may be).

(5) A person who is self-employed is treated as engaged in qualifying remunerative work for the requisite number of hours during any period for which paragraph (1) would have applied in his case but for the fact that the work he performed in the week immediately before the period began, although done for payment or in the expectation of payment, was not performed under a contract of service or apprenticeship.]

2.139

The Working Tax Credit (Entitlement and Maximum Rate) Regulations 2002

AMENDMENTS

1. Working Tax Credit (Entitlement and Maximum Rate) (Amendment) Regulations 2003 (SI 2003/701) reg.6 (April 6, 2003).
2. Employment and Support Allowance (Consequential Provisions) (No.3) Regulations 2008 (SI 2009/1879) reg.20(3) (October 27, 2008).
3. Working Tax Credit (Entitlement and Maximum Rate) (Amendment) Regulations 2009 (SI 2009/1829) regs 2 and 5 (July 31, 2009).
4. Tax Credits (Miscellaneous Amendments) Regulations 2012 (SI 2012/848) reg.2(8) (April 6, 2012).
5. Tax Credits, Childcare Payments and Childcare (Extended Entitlement) (Coronavirus and Miscellaneous Amendments) Regulations 2020 (SI 2020/1515) reg.2(4) (January 14, 2021).

DEFINITIONS

"incapacity for work"—see SSCBA 1992 s.171A.
"qualifying remunerative employment"—see reg.4.
"self-employed"—see reg.2.
"week"—see reg.2.

GENERAL NOTE

2.140 This paragraph allows continuity of a claim for working tax credit into a period of sickness or disability, provided that one of the alternative forms of benefit is received for the period. Paragraph 7 of Sch.1B to the Income Support (General) Regulations 1987 (SI 1987/1967) deal with those treated as incapable of work under the SSCBA 1992 and those entitled to statutory sick pay. Paragraph 14 deals with pregnant women who are incapable of work by reason of the pregnancy or are within 11 weeks before the expected date of confinement or seven weeks after the pregnancy ends. There is a 28-week limit on the overlap between working tax credit and either income support or contribution credits.

The interpretation of this regulation was considered in the Upper Tribunal in *HMRC v TK* [2016] UKUT 45 (AAC). The question at issue was the period to be taken into account where a claimant was receiving statutory sick pay. The judge agreed with the HMRC argument that the maximum award under the regulation was a period of 28 weeks from the start of the statutory sick pay and not a later period for which the claimant had argued.

Term time and other seasonal workers

2.141 **7.**—(1) For the purposes of the [¹ conditions of entitlement in this Part], paragraph (2) applies if a person—
   (a) works at a school, other educational establishment or other place of employment;
   (b) there is a recognisable cycle to his employment there; and
   (c) the length of that recognisable cycle is one year and includes periods of school holidays or similar vacations during which he does not work.

(2) If this paragraph applies, the periods mentioned in paragraph (1)(c) are disregarded in determining whether the [¹ conditions of entitlement in this Part] are satisfied.

AMENDMENT

1. Working Tax Credit (Entitlement and Maximum Rate) (Amendment) Regulations 2009 (SI 2009/1829) regs 2 and 6 (July 31, 2009).

(SI 2002/2005 reg.7) as amended

GENERAL NOTE

This regulation deals with cyclical and "term time only" employment. To claim working tax credit the claimant must establish normal work of 16 hours a week. The income test is by reference to actual earnings over the entire year. As a consequence, this rule will operate to the advantage of those such as supply teachers, school learning support assistants and seasonal staff. They will continue to get their working tax credit throughout the year if the conditions of this regulation are met, while their earnings will be established without reference to assumed earnings during assumed hours of work. For example, someone working 20 hours a week for 40 weeks a year at, say, £125 a week, will meet the hours test for every week of the year if the conditions of this regulation are met, but will earn from that source only £5,000 so will be below the minimum figure of earnings for claiming working tax credit in full. This means also a continuing entitlement to claim child care charges when appropriate. In addition, because child tax credit is now separated from working tax credit and will be separated from all other benefits, there will be no adverse effect on any child tax credit entitlement from fluctuating work patterns.

[¹Strike periods

7A.—(1) This regulation applies for any period during which a person is on strike.

(2) For the purposes of the [² conditions of entitlement in this Part], the person is treated as being engaged in qualifying remunerative work during the period.

This is subject to [³ paragraph (3) and regulation 7D].

(3) The person—
(a) must have been engaged in qualifying remunerative work immediately before the beginning of the period, and
(b) must not be on strike for longer than a period of 10 consecutive days on which he should have been working.]

AMENDMENTS

1. Working Tax Credit (Entitlement and Maximum Rate) (Amendment) Regulations 2003 (SI 2003/701) reg.7 (April 6, 2003).
2. Working Tax Credit (Entitlement and Maximum Rate) (Amendment) Regulations 2009 (SI 2009/1829) regs 2 and 7 (July 31, 2009).
3. Tax Credits (Miscellaneous Amendments) Regulations 2012 (SI 2012/848) reg.2(9) (April 6, 2012).

DEFINITION

"qualifying remunerative employment"—see reg.4.

GENERAL NOTE

This rule is a relaxation from the strict set of rules preventing workers benefitting during a strike. The effect of this regulation is to stop a break in entitlement occurring for a strike of 10 consecutive days or fewer.

[¹Persons suspended from work

7B.—(1) This regulation applies for any period during which a person is suspended from work while complaints or allegations against him are investigated.

The Working Tax Credit (Entitlement and Maximum Rate) Regulations 2002

(2) For the purposes of the [² conditions of entitlement in this Part], the person is treated as being engaged in qualifying remunerative work during the period.

This is subject to [³ paragraph (3) and regulation 7D].

(3) The person must have been engaged in qualifying remunerative work immediately before the beginning of the period.]

AMENDMENTS

1. Working Tax Credit (Entitlement and Maximum Rate) (Amendment) Regulations 2003 (SI 2003/701) reg.7 (April 6, 2003).
2. Working Tax Credit (Entitlement and Maximum Rate) (Amendment) Regulations 2009 (SI 2009/1829) regs 2 and 7 (July 31, 2009).
3. Tax Credits (Miscellaneous Amendments) Regulations 2012 (SI 2012/848) reg.2(9) (April 6, 2012).

DEFINITION

"qualifying remunerative employment"—see reg.4.

GENERAL NOTE

2.146   This deals with a practical problem similar in part to that behind reg.7A. However, in the case of someone is suspended from work, for example while a complaint is investigated, the period of suspension will often not be known.

[¹Pay in lieu of notice

2.147   **7C.**—(1) This regulation applies if a person stops work and receives pay in lieu of notice.

(2) For the purposes of the [³ conditions of entitlement in this Part], the person shall not be treated as being engaged in qualifying remunerative work during the period for which he receives the pay.]

[² (3) This regulation is subject to regulation 7D.]

AMENDMENTS

1. Working Tax Credit (Entitlement and Maximum Rate) (Amendment) Regulations 2003 (SI 2003/701) reg.7 (April 6, 2003).
2. Working Tax Credit (Entitlement and Maximum Rate) (Amendment) Regulations 2007 (SI 2007/968) reg.2 (April 6, 2007).
3. Working Tax Credit (Entitlement and Maximum Rate) (Amendment) Regulations 2009 (SI 2009/1829) regs 2 and 7 (July 31, 2009)

DEFINITION

"qualifying remunerative employment"—see reg.4.

GENERAL NOTE

2.148   This deals in a pragmatic way with the problem caused when someone stops work before a period of notice has ended, but who receives pay in lieu of notice (often abbreviated to PILON). This regulation excludes the claimant from entitlement to working tax credit. But a problem may arise if the employee does not find other work during that period (and he or she may be prevented from doing so). The provisions about calculating earnings from employment for jobseeker's allowance purposes allow sums to be spread over the period for which they are paid, unless they are excluded from earnings for that purpose, and so may exclude entitlement to JSA. See regs 94 and 98 of the Jobseeker's Allowance Regulations 1996 (SI 1996/207) and the notes to them in Vol.II of this work. So the individual may be excluded from both working tax credit and jobseeker's allowance.

(SI 2002/2005 reg. 7D) as amended

[¹Ceasing to undertake work or working for less than 16 [², 24] or 30 hours per week

7D.—(1) This regulation applies for the four-week period immediately after—
  (a) a person, not being a member of a couple, who is engaged in qualifying remunerative work for not less than 16 hours per week, ceases to work or starts to work less than 16 hours per week,
  (b) a person, being a member of a couple only one of whom is engaged in qualifying remunerative work for not less than 16 hours per week, ceases to work or starts to work less than 16 hours per week,
  (c) both members of a couple, each of whom is engaged in qualifying remunerative work for not less than 16 hours per week, cease to work or start to work less than 16 hours per week,
  (d) a person, being a member of a couple who is entitled to the childcare element of working tax credit each of whom is engaged in qualifying remunerative work for not less than 16 hours per week, ceases to work or start to work less than 16 hours per week, or
  (e) a person who satisfies paragraph (c) [² of the first variation or paragraph (b) of the second variation] of the second condition in regulation 4(1) and who is engaged in qualifying remunerative work for not less than 30 hours per week, ceases to work or starts to work less than 30 hours per week.
[² (f) one or both members of a couple who satisfy paragraph (a) of the third variation of the Second condition in regulation 4(1) and are engaged in qualifying remunerative work cease to work or reduce their hours to the extent that they cease to meet the condition that one member of the couple works not less than 16 hours per week and the aggregate number of hours for which the couple are engaged in qualifying remunerative work is not less than 24 hours per week.]

(2) For the purposes of the conditions of entitlement in this Part, the person is treated as being engaged in qualifying remunerative work during that period.]
[³(3) [¹⁴ . . .]]

AMENDMENTS

1. Working Tax Credit (Entitlement and Maximum Rate) (Amendment) Regulations 2009 (SI 2009/1829) reg.8 (July 31, 2009).
2. Tax Credits (Miscellaneous Amendments) Regulations 2012 (SI 2012/848) reg.2(10) (April 6, 2012).
3. Tax Credits (Coronavirus, Miscellaneous Amendments) Regulations 2020 (SI 2020/534) reg.2(4) (May 23, 2020).
4. Tax Credits and Child Benefit (Miscellaneous Amendments) Regulations 2022 (SI 2022/555) reg.5(3) (June 9, 2022).

GENERAL NOTE

This regulation provides for a four week run-on of WTC to those claimants whose hours fall below 16 hours a week. Where entitled, claimants will be eligible to claim income support or JSA whilst in receipt of WTC for the four week period (although the WTC will be treated as income for assessing entitlement to those benefits). The purpose of this rule is to reduce overpayments of tax credits and to ease the transition from tax credits to benefits. It is consistent with the shift from April 2007 of a mandatory reporting requirement on tax credits claimants to inform HMRC within a month of ceasing work.

The Working Tax Credit (Entitlement and Maximum Rate) Regulations 2002

Note that where the four week run-on applies, the claimant's child remains entitled to free school lunches by virtue of s.512ZB of the Education Act 1996 (see Education (Free School Lunches) (Working Tax Credit) (England) Order 2009 (SI 2009/830) art.2).

The new version of reg.7D, and the associated amendments to other regulations, introduce a more detailed test of hours worked, to include the hours worked by joint claimant couples as well as individual claimants.

See the note to reg.16 below about the relationship between this regulation and reg.16.

[¹Alteration in hours worked due to coronavirus

2.151   **7E.**—[²...]]

AMENDMENTS

1. Tax Credits (Coronavirus, Miscellaneous Amendments) Regulations 2020 (SI 2020/534) reg.2(5) (May 23, 2020).
2. Tax Credits and Child Benefit (Miscellaneous Amendments) Regulations 2022 (SI 2022/555) reg.5(4) (June 9, 2022).

Gaps between jobs

2.152   **8.**—For the purposes of the [¹ conditions of entitlement in this Part], a person shall be treated as being engaged in qualifying remunerative work for the requisite number of hours if he has been so engaged within the past seven days.

AMENDMENT

1. Working Tax Credit (Entitlement and Maximum Rate) (Amendment) Regulations 2009 regs 2 and 9 (July 31, 2009).

DEFINITION

"qualifying remunerative employment"—see reg.4.

GENERAL NOTE

2.153   Regulation 4 allows someone to make a claim for working tax credit if he or she has an offer of a job starting within seven days of the claim (see the first condition in reg.4). However, if there is a gap of not more than that period between jobs, this regulation allows the gap to be bridged so as to avoid the need to make a new claim. This is also consistent with the provisions of the Tax Credits (Claims and Notifications) Regulations 2002 (SI 2002/2014) reg.10, allowing claims for working tax credit seven days in advance.

Disability element

[¹Disability element and workers who are to be treated as at a disadvantage in getting a job

2.154   **9.**—(1) The determination of the maximum rate must include the disability element if the claimant, or, in the case of a joint claim, one of the claimants—

(SI 2002/2005 reg.9) as amended

(a) undertakes qualifying remunerative work for at least 16 hours per week;
(b) has any of the disabilities listed in Part I of Schedule 1, or in the case of an initial claim, satisfies the conditions in Part II of Schedule 1; and
(c) is a person who satisfies any of Cases A to G on a day for which the maximum rate is determined in accordance with these Regulations.

[⁴ (2) Case A is where the person has, for at least one day in the preceding 182 days ("the qualifying day"), been in receipt of—
(a) higher rate short-term incapacity benefit;
(b) long-term incapacity benefit;
(c) severe disablement allowance; or
(d) employment and support allowance [⁶ or a limited capability for work credit,] where entitlement to employment and support allowance [⁶ or that credit] or statutory sick pay [⁵ or a benefit or allowance mentioned in sub-paragraphs (a) to (c) or the income support payable under paragraph (3)(a)] has existed for a period of 28 weeks immediately preceding the qualifying day comprising one continuous period or two or more periods which are linked together.]

(3) Case B is where, for at least one day in the preceding 182 days, the person has been a person [² for whom at least one of the following benefits has been payable and for whom the applicable amount] included a higher pensioner or disability premium [²in respect of him] determined—
(a) in the case of income support, in accordance with [² paragraphs 10(1)(b) or (2)(b) or 11, and where applicable 12,] of Part III of Schedule 2 to the Income Support (General) Regulations 1987;
(b) in the case of income-based jobseeker's allowance, in accordance with [² paragraphs 12(1)(a), or (b)(ii), or (c), or 13, and where applicable 14 of Part 3 of] Schedule 1 to the Jobseeker's Allowance Regulations 1996;
(c) in the case of housing benefit, in accordance with [² [³paragraphs 11(1)(b) or 11(2)(b) or 12, and where applicable, 13 of Part 3 Schedule 3 of the Housing Benefit Regulations 2006];
(d) [¹⁰ ...]

For the purposes of this Case "the applicable amount" has the meaning given by section 135 of the Contributions and Benefits Act.

(4) Case C is where the person is a person to whom at least one of the following is payable—
(a) a disability living allowance;
(b) an attendance allowance;
(c) a mobility supplement or a constant attendance allowance which is paid, in either case, in conjunction with a war pension or industrial injuries disablement benefit;

[⁷ (d) personal independence payment;]
[⁸ (e) armed forces independence payment;
[¹¹(f) Scottish disability assistance.]

(5) Case D is where the person has an invalid carriage or other vehicle provided under—
(a) section 5(2)(a) of, and Schedule 2 to, the National Health Service Act 1977,
(b) section 46 of the National Health Service (Scotland) Act 1978; or
(c) Article 30(1) of the Health and Personal Social Services (Northern Ireland) Order 1972.

(6) Case E is where the person—
[⁴ (a) has received—
  (i) on account of his incapacity for work, statutory sick pay, occupational sick pay, short-term incapacity benefit payable at the lower rate or income support, for a period of 140 qualifying days, or has been credited with Class 1 or Class 2 contributions under the Contributions and Benefits Act for a period of 20 weeks on account of incapacity for work, and where the last of those days or weeks (as the case may be) fell within the preceding 56 days; or
  (ii) on account of his [⁵ incapacity for work or] having limited capability for work, an employment and support allowance [⁵, or the pay or benefit mentioned in paragraph (i),] for a period of 140 qualifying days, or has been credited with Class 1 or Class 2 contributions under the Contributions and Benefits Act for a period of 20 weeks on account of [⁵ incapacity for work or] having limited capability for work, and where the last of those days or weeks (as the case may be) fell within the preceding 56 days;]
(b) has a disability which is likely to last for at least six months, or for the rest of his life if his death is expected within that time; and
(c) has gross earnings which are less than they were before the disability began by at least the greater of 20 per cent and £15 per week.

For the purpose of this Case "qualifying days" are days which form part of a single period of incapacity for work within the meaning of Part XI of the Contributions and Benefits Act [⁴ or a period of limited capability for work within the meaning of regulation 2(1) of the Employment and Support Allowance Regulations 2008].

(7) Case F is where the person—
(a) has undertaken training for work for at least one day in the preceding 56 days; and
[⁴ (b) has, within 56 days before the first day of that period of training for work, received—
  (i) higher rate short-term incapacity benefit;
  (ii) long-term incapacity benefit;
  (iii) severe disablement allowance; or
  (iv) contributory employment and support allowance [⁶ or a limited capability for work credit,] where entitlement to that allowance [⁶ or credit] or statutory sick pay [⁵ or a benefit or allowance mentioned in paragraphs (i) to (iii),] has existed for a period of 28 weeks comprising one continuous period or two or more periods which are linked together provided that, if the person received statutory sick pay, the person satisfied the first and second contribution conditions set out in paragraphs 1 and 2 of Schedule 1 to the Welfare Reform Act.]

[⁴ Regulation 9B explains the meaning of "training for work" and of a period of training for work.]

[⁹(7A) In paragraph (7)(b)(iv), the reference to contributory employment and support allowance is a reference to an allowance under Part 1 of the Welfare Reform Act 2007 ("the 2007 Act") as amended by the provisions of Schedule 3, and Part 1 of Schedule 14, to the Welfare Reform Act 2012 that remove references to an income-based allowance, and a contributory allowance under Part 1 of the 2007 Act as that Part has effect apart from those provisions.]

(8) Case G is where the person was entitled, [² for at least one day in the preceding 56 days], to the disability element of working tax credit or to disabled person's tax credit by virtue of his having satisfied the requirements of Case A, B, E or F at some earlier time.

For the purposes of this Case a person is treated as having an entitlement to the disability element of working tax credit if that element is taken into account in determining the rate at which the person is entitled to a tax credit.

(9) For the purposes of the Act, a person who satisfies paragraph (1)(b) is to be treated as having a physical or mental disability which puts him at a disadvantage in getting a job.]

AMENDMENTS

1. Working Tax Credit (Entitlement and Maximum Rate) (Amendment) Regulations 2003 (SI 2003/701) reg.8 (April 6, 2003).
2. Tax Credits (Miscellaneous Amendments No.2) Regulations 2003 (SI 2003/2815) reg.14 (November 26, 2003).
3. Housing Benefit and Council Tax Benefit (Consequential Provisions) Regulations 2006 (SI 2006/217) reg.22(2) (March 6, 2006).
4. Employment and Support Allowance (Consequential Provisions) (No.3) Regulations 2008 (SI 2008/1879) reg.20(4) (October 27, 2008).
5. Tax Credits (Miscellaneous Amendments) Regulations 2012 (SI 2012/848) reg.2(11)(c), (12) and (13)(c) (April 6, 2012).
6. Tax Credits (Miscellaneous Amendments) Regulations 2012 (SI 2012/848) regs 2(11)(a) and (b) and 2(13)(a) and (b) (May 1, 2012).
7. Personal Independence Payment (Supplementary Provisions and Consequential Amendments) Regulations 2013 (SI 2013/388) reg.8 and Sch. para.28(3) (April 8, 2013).
8. Armed Forces and Reserve Forces Compensation Scheme (Consequential Provisions: Subordinate Legislation) Order 2013 (SI 2013/591) art.7 and Sch. para.24(3) (April 8, 2013).
9. Universal Credit (Consequential, Supplementary, Incidental and Miscellaneous Provisions) Regulations 2013 (SI 2013/630) reg.77(3) (April 29, 2013).
10. Tax Credits (Miscellaneous Amendments) Regulations 2014 (SI 2014/658) reg.2 (April 6, 2014).
11. Tax Credits and Child Benefit (Miscellaneous Amendments) Regulations 2021 (SI 2021/1286) reg.2(3) (December 9, 2021).

DEFINITIONS

"claim"—see reg.2.
"initial claim"—see reg.9A.
"joint claim"—see reg.2.
"qualifying remunerative employment"—see reg.4.
"training for work"—see reg.9B.
"week"—see reg.2.

GENERAL NOTE

This regulation, read with Sch.1, provides the tests for claiming working tax credit by Route 2, the route for those with disabilities. It imposes three separate sets of conditions, all of which must be met to meet the second condition in reg.4 of these Regulations. The first of the three conditions is the requirement that the claimant work 16 or more hours a week in qualifying remunerative work. This restates one of

2.155

the requirements of the second condition, but with the specific addition of the reference to "qualifying remunerative" work. The other two conditions may be termed the "disability conditions".

In *CTC/643/2005* a Commissioner decided that entitlement under reg.9(1) arises only during the period when a claimant is also entitled under one of the cases A to G. This follows from the reference in reg.9(1)(c) to the claimant satisfying any of Cases A to G "on a day for which the maximum rate is determined . . .". A claimant could not claim the disability element throughout a year unless he or she met the requirements of one of the cases throughout the year.

In *CSTC/76/2006* the Commissioner considered how the conditions are to be applied to joint claimants. She confirmed the view of HMRC that all the disablement conditions are to be met by the same individual and that individual must also undertake work for at least 16 hours a week. She rejected an attempt to argue a claim under this regulation where one of the joint claimants worked to the required extent and the other was disabled. This reflects the origin of this provision in the former disabled person's tax credit and disability working allowance. It is also consistent with the entitlement of a working partner to claim carer's allowance if caring for a disabled partner to the required level.

The revocation of reg.9(3)(d) removed a reference to council tax benefit following the abolition of that benefit.

First disability condition

To come within this condition, the claimant must have one or more of the disabilities listed in Pt 1 of Sch.1 to these Regulations (see below). Paragraph (9) emphasises that a person meeting this condition is to be treated as being put at a disadvantage by reason of the disability.

Second disability condition

To come within this condition, the claimant must meet the conditions of one or more of seven separate "cases" labelled Case A to Case G. If HMRC propose to amend an award so as to remove the disability element on the ground that a claimant no longer satisfies a particular Case, they must first consider whether any other Case applies (*PW v HMRC (TC)* [2018] UKUT 12 (AAC)). Briefly these link with other benefits or activities as follows:

Case A: entitlement to long-term incapacity benefit, the higher rate of short-term incapacity benefit, severe disablement allowance or employment and support allowance and/or a limited capability for work credit when a benefit is no longer payable. In *PW v HMRC (TC)* [2018] UKUT 12 (AAC) Judge Poynter decided that "once the disability element has been awarded under Case A, it continues in payment on an indefinite basis until the claimant either ceases to be entitled to WTC or ceases to have a disability which puts her or him at a disadvantage in getting a job" because "as soon as such a claimant ceases to be in Case A, she or he instead immediately falls within Case G". This is because Case G applies where a person was entitled to the disability element of WTC at "some earlier time".

Case B: entitlement to a higher pension or disability premium of income support, income-based jobseeker's allowance, housing benefit;

Case C: entitlement to disability living allowance, attendance allowance, mobility supplement or constant attendance, personal independence payment or armed forces independence payment or Scottish disability assistance under section 31 of the Social Security (Scotland) Act 2018;

Case D: membership of the Motability scheme;

Case E: entitlement to occupational or statutory sick pay, short-term incapacity benefit, income support, employment and support allowance or "disability credits"; a continuing disability; and earnings that have reduced since the disability started by 20 per cent or £15 a week;

Case F: training for work linked with payment of the benefits in Case A;

Case G: entitlement to the disability element of WTC or DPTC under Cases A, B, E or F at "some earlier time". In *PW v HMRC (TC)* [2018] UKUT 12 (AAC) Judge Poynter held that "some earlier time" must refer back to the words "a day for which the maximum rate is determined in accordance with these Regulations". A single day will suffice. In *ABM v HMRC* [2018] UKUT 317 (AAC) Upper Tribunal Judge West held that the amendment of Case G in 2003 so as to substitute "entitled" for "qualified" did not remove "the link between what a recipient's entitlement should have been, if determined correctly, in tax year one and his entitlement in tax year two" and the definition of "entitled" in the second paragraph of Case G was intended to clarify, rather than alter, meaning. In simple terms, "entitled" means "correctly entitled" and the purpose of that second paragraph is to:

"provide certainty in those cases where the entitlement conditions have been found to have been satisfied for a particular year, but no disability element has actually been paid, or was due in that year as a result of the level of the claimant's income…[and] Case G was intended to support recipients with the continuation of an entitlement, but for one year alone, following a decision, particularly since the decision on entitlement was made after the end of the tax year to which it related and in which the tax credits were received [given the distinction drawn by the Tax Credits Act 2002 between the award of tax credit for a tax year and entitlement for that year, which is fixed by a decision under section 18 typically following the end of the tax year in question]".

In *ABM v HMRC* [2018] UKUT 317 (AAC) Judge West held that the First-tier Tribunal erred in law by failing to consider whether an appellant satisfied any of the Cases. Instead, the tribunal's consideration was limited solely to Case C, which had been the focus of HMRC's appeal submission.

There are special rules that apply to initial claims, noted under reg.9A below.

Where a passporting disability benefit is awarded after a person was awarded working tax credit without the disability element, it is now possible in certain circumstances for the tax credit award to be reviewed so as to fully backdate entitlement to the disability element: see section 21C of the Tax Credits Act 2002 (above in this volume).

[¹Initial claims

9A.—(1) In regulation 9(1)(b) an "initial claim" means a claim which—   2.156
(a) is made for the disability element of working tax credit, and
(b) relates to a person who has not had an entitlement to that element or to disabled person's tax credit during the two years immediately preceding the making of the claim.

(2) In paragraph (1) any reference to the making of a claim includes the giving of notification, in accordance with regulation 20 of the Tax Credits (Claims and Notifications) Regulations 2002, of a change of circumstances falling within that regulation.

(3) For the purposes of paragraph (1)(b), a person is treated as having an entitlement to the disability element of working tax credit if, by virtue of

The Working Tax Credit (Entitlement and Maximum Rate) Regulations 2002

the person being a person who satisfies regulation 9, that element is taken into account in determining the rate at which the person is entitled to a tax credit.]

AMENDMENT

1. Working Tax Credit (Entitlement and Maximum Rate) (Amendment) Regulations 2003 (SI 2003/701) reg.8 (April 6, 2003).

DEFINITIONS

"claim"—see reg.2.
"claimant"—see reg.2.
"disability element"—see reg.9.

GENERAL NOTE

2.157   This regulation makes clear that an "initial claim" for the purposes of reg.9 is a first claim involving disability, or a notification that may involve the addition of a disability element to an award already made on other grounds. This clarifies the scope of reg.9(1), which extends the test of disability under the second disability condition for a first claim. An initial claim will have an extended relevance for working tax credit as compared with its predecessors as the claim will, in normal course of events, last for the balance of the tax year from the effective date of claim.

[¹**Training for work, etc.**

2.158   **9B.**—(1) In [²regulation 9], "training for work" means training for work received—
   (a) in pursuance of arrangements made under—
      (i) section 2(1) of the Employment and Training Act 1973,
      (ii) section 2(3) of the Enterprise and New Towns (Scotland) Act 1990, or
      (iii) section 1(1) of the Employment and Training Act 1950, or
   (b) on a course whose primary purpose is the teaching of occupational or vocational skills, and which the person attends for 16 hours or more a week.

(2) For the purposes of regulation 9(7), a period of training for work means a series of consecutive days of training for work, there being disregarded any day specified in paragraph (3).

(3) Those days are any day on which the claimant was—
   (a) on holiday;
   (b) attending court as a justice of the peace, a party to any proceedings, a witness or a juror;
   (c) suffering from some disease or bodily or mental disablement as a result of which he was unable to attend training for work, or his attendance would have put at risk the health of other persons;
   (d) unable to participate in training for work because—
      (i) he was looking after a child because the person who usually looked after that child was unable to do so;
      (ii) he was looking after a member of his family who was ill;
      (iii) he was required to deal with some domestic emergency; or
      (iv) he was arranging or attending the funeral of his partner or a relative; or
   (e) authorised by the training provider to be absent from training for work.

(SI 2002/2005 reg.9B) as amended

(4) For the purposes of paragraph (3)(d)(iv) "relative" means close relative, grandparent, grandchild, uncle, aunt, nephew or niece; and in this paragraph "close relative" means parent, parent-in-law, son, son-in-law, daughter, daughter-in-law, step-parent, step-son, step-daughter, brother, sister, or the spouse of any of the preceding persons or, if that person is one of an unmarried couple, the other member of that couple.]

AMENDMENTS

1. Working Tax Credit (Entitlement and Maximum Rate) (Amendment) Regulations 2003 (SI 2003/701) reg.8 (April 6, 2003).
2. Tax Credits (Miscellaneous Amendments) Regulations 2004 (SI 2004/762) reg.8 (April 6, 2004).

DEFINITIONS

"claim"—see reg.2.
"claimant"—see reg.2.
"week"—see reg.2.

GENERAL NOTE

This definition is necessary to clarify the scope of Case F in reg.9(7).

30 hour element

30 hour element

10.—(1) The determination of the maximum rate must include a 30 hour element if the claimant, or in the case of a joint claim, at least one of the claimants, is engaged in qualifying remunerative work for at least 30 hours per week [^{3}[^{4}...]].

(2) The determination of the maximum rate must also include the 30-hour element if—
 (a) the claim is a joint claim,
 (b) at least one of the claimants is responsible for one or more children or qualifying young people,
 (c) the aggregate number of hours for which the couple engage in qualifying remunerative work is at least 30 hours per week, and
 (d) at least one member of the couple engages in qualifying remunerative work for at least 16 hours per week.

[^{1}(3) [^{2}...].]
[^{3}(4) [^{4}...]
(5) [^{4}...]]

AMENDMENTS

1. Working Tax Credit (Entitlement and Maximum Rate) (Amendment) Regulations 2003 (SI 2003/701) reg.9 (April 6, 2003).
2. Tax Credits (Miscellaneous Amendments) Regulations 2012 (SI 2012/848) reg.2(14) (April 6, 2012).
3. Tax Credits (Coronavirus, Miscellaneous Amendments) Regulations 2020 (SI 2020/534) reg.2(6) (May 23, 2020).
4. Tax Credits and Child Benefit (Miscellaneous Amendments) Regulations 2022 (SI 2022/555) reg.5(5) (June 9, 2022).

DEFINITIONS

"child"—see reg.2.
"claim"—see reg.2.
"claimant"—see reg.2.
"couple"—see reg.2.
"joint claim"—see TCA 2002 s.3.
"qualifying remunerative work"—see reg.4.
"qualifying young person"—see reg.2.
"responsible"—see TCA 2002 s.48.
"week"—see reg.2.

GENERAL NOTE

2.161 An additional element of £1,015 a year is payable if the claimant or couple work 30 hours a week. Paragraphs (1) and (2) together ensure that the total of 30 hours can be worked by either of the couple or by both together if one or both of them are responsible for a child or qualifying young person.

Second adult element

[¹**Second adult element**

2.162 **11.**—(1) The determination of the maximum rate must include the second adult element if the claim is a joint claim.
This is subject to the following provisions of this regulation.
(2) [⁴ . . .]
(3) [⁴ . . .]
[² (4) The determination of the maximum rate shall [⁴ . . .] not include the second adult element if neither claimant has responsibility for a child or qualifying young person, and
    (a) one claimant is serving a custodial sentence of more than twelve months, or
    (b) one claimant is subject to immigration control within the meaning of [³ section 115(9)] of the Immigration and Asylum Act 1999.]
[³ (5) Paragraph (4)(b) does not apply where the claimant subject to immigration control is a person to whom Case 4 of regulations 3(1) of the Tax Credits (Immigration) Regulations 2003 applies.]

AMENDMENTS

1. Working Tax Credit (Entitlement and Maximum Rate) (Amendment) Regulations 2003 (SI 2003/701) reg.10 (April 6, 2003).
2. Tax Credits (Miscellaneous Amendments) Regulations 2009 (SI 2009/697) reg.4 (April 6, 2009).
3. Tax Credits (Miscellaneous Amendments) (No.2) Regulations 2009 (SI 2009/2887) reg.3 (October 30, 2009).
4. Tax Credits (Miscellaneous Amendments) Regulations 2012 (SI 2012/848) reg.2(15) (April 6, 2012).

DEFINITIONS

"50 Plus element"—see reg.18.
"child"—see reg.2.

(SI 2002/2005 reg.11) as amended

"claimant"—see reg.2.
"joint claim"—see reg.2.
"qualifying remunerative work"—see reg.4.
"qualifying young person"—see reg.2.
"responsible"—see TCA 2002 s.48.
"week"—see reg.2.

GENERAL NOTE

The value of the second adult element is a little above the value of the basic element. The deleted provisions related to the former 50 Plus credit.

Lone parent element

Lone parent element

12.—The determination of the maximum rate must include the lone parent element if—
(a) the claim is a single claim; and
(b) the claimant is responsible for [¹a child or qualifying young person].

AMENDMENT

1. Working Tax Credit (Entitlement and Maximum Rate) (Amendment) Regulations 2003 (SI 2003/701) reg.11 (April 6, 2003).

DEFINITIONS

"child"—see reg.2.
"claim"—see reg.2.
"qualifying young person"—see reg.2.
"responsible"—see TCA 2002 s.48.

GENERAL NOTE

The value of the lone parent element is the same as that of the second adult element.

Childcare element

Entitlement to child care element of working tax credit

13.—(1) The determination of the maximum rate must include a child care element where that person, or in the case of a joint claim at least one of those persons, is incurring relevant childcare charges and—
(a) is a person, not being a member of a [³. . .] couple, engaged in [¹qualifying remunerative work];
[¹(b) is a member or are members of a [³. . .] couple where both are engaged in qualifying remunerative work [⁵ for not less than 16 hours per week]; or
(c) is a member or are members of a [³. . .] couple where one is engaged in qualifying remunerative work [⁵ for not less than 16 hours per week] and the other—
  (i) is incapacitated;
  (ii) is an in-patient in hospital; or

(iii) is in prison (whether serving a custodial sentence or remanded in custody awaiting trial or sentence) [⁷; or]]
[⁷ (iv) is entitled to carer's allowance under section 70 of the Social Security Contributions and Benefits Act 1992 [¹³; or]
[¹³(v) entitled to carer's assistance given in accordance with regulations made under section 28 of the Social Security (Scotland) Act 2018.]

(2) For the purposes of paragraph (1), a person is not treated as incurring relevant child care charges where the average weekly charge calculated in accordance with regulation 15 is nil or where an agreement within regulation 15(4) has not yet commenced.

[¹(3) [². . .]

(4) For the purposes of para.(1)(c)(i), the other member of a couple is incapacitated in any of the circumstances specified in [⁹paragraphs (5) to (12)].]

[¹⁰ (5) The circumstances specified in this paragraph are where housing benefit is payable under Part 7 of the Contributions and Benefits Act to the other member or the other member's partner and the applicable amount of the person entitled to the benefit includes a disability premium on account of the other member's incapacity or regulation 28(1)(c) of the Housing Benefit Regulations 2006 (treatment of child care charges) applies in that person's case.]

(6) The circumstances specified in this paragraph are where there is payable [⁶ or – in the case of a credit–an entitlement] in respect of him one or more of the following [⁶ . . .]—

(a) short-term incapacity benefit [¹payable at the higher rate] under section 30A of the Contributions and Benefits Act;
(b) long-term incapacity benefit under section 40 or 41 of the Contributions and Benefits Act;
(c) attendance allowance under section 64 of that Act;
(d) severe disablement allowance under section 68 of that Act;
(e) disability living allowance under section 71 of that Act;
(f) increase of disablement pension under section 104 of that Act;
(g) a pension increase under a war pension scheme or an industrial injuries scheme which is analogous to an allowance or increase of disablement pension under sub-paragraph (b), (d) or (e) above;
[⁴ (h) contributory employment and support allowance [⁶ or a limited capability for work credit] where entitlement to that allowance [⁶ or credit] or statutory sick pay [⁵ or a benefit or allowance mentioned in sub-paragraph (a) or (b) or (d),] has existed for a period of 28 weeks comprising one continuous period or two or more periods which are linked together provided that, if the person received statutory sick pay, the person satisfied the first and second contribution conditions set out in paragraphs 1 and 2 of Schedule 1 to the Welfare Reform Act;]
[⁷ (i) personal independence payment;]
[⁸ (j) armed forces independence payment;]
[¹¹ (k) any benefit, allowance or credit of another EEA state or Switzerland which is substantially similar in character to the benefits, allowances and credits in sub-paragraphs (a) to (j).]
[¹²(l) Scottish disability assistance.]

[⁹ (6A) In paragraph (6)(h), the reference to contributory employment and support allowance is a reference to an allowance under Part 1 of the

Welfare Reform Act 2007 ("the 2007 Act") as amended by the provisions of Schedule 3, and Part 1 of Schedule 14, to the Welfare Reform Act 2012 that remove references to an income-related allowance, and a contributory allowance under Part 1 of the 2007 Act as that Part has effect apart from those provisions.]

(7) The circumstances specified in this paragraph are where a pension or allowance to which sub-paragraph [^{1} (c)], (d), (e) or (f) of paragraph (6) refers, was payable on account of his incapacity but has ceased to be payable only in consequence of his becoming a patient.

(8) The circumstances specified in this paragraph are where he has an invalid carriage or other vehicle provided to him under section 5(2)(a) of and Schedule 2 to the National Health Service Act 1977, section 46 of the National Health Service (Scotland) Act 1978; or Article 30(1) of the Health and Personal Social Services (Northern Ireland) Order 1972.

[^{10} (9) The circumstances specified in this paragraph are where, on 31st March 2013, council tax benefit was payable under Part 7 of the Contributions and Benefits Act (as then in force) to the other member or the other member's partner and the applicable amount of the person entitled to the benefit included a disability premium on account of the other member's incapacity.

(10) Paragraph (9) is subject to paragraphs (11) and (12).

(11) Paragraph (9) does not apply unless the other member of the couple was incapacitated (for the purposes of paragraph (1)(c)(i) and regulation 4(1) Second condition, Third variation (c)(i)) solely by virtue of that person or their partner having been in receipt, on 31st March 2013, of council tax benefit which included a disability premium on account of the other member's incapacity, and none of the other circumstances specified in paragraphs (5) to (8) applied on that date.

(12) If—
(a) the other member of the couple is incapacitated in the circumstances specified in paragraph (9), and
(b) the couple ceases to be entitled to working tax credit (for any reason) on or after 1st April 2013,

that member of the couple shall not be treated as incapacitated in the circumstances specified in paragraph (9) in relation to any subsequent claim.]

AMENDMENTS

1. Working Tax Credit (Entitlement and Maximum Rate) (Amendment) Regulations 2003 (SI 2003/701) reg.12 (April 6, 2003).

2. Tax Credits (Miscellaneous Amendments) Regulations 2004 (SI 2004/762) reg.9 (April 6, 2004).

3. Civil Partnership Act 2004 (Tax Credits, etc.) (Consequential Amendments) Order 2005 (SI 2005/2919) art.2(3) (December 5, 2005).

4. Employment and Support Allowance (Consequential Provisions) (No.3) Regulations 2008 (SI 2008/1879) reg.20(5) (October 27, 2008).

5. Tax Credits (Miscellaneous Amendments) Regulations 2012 (SI 2012/848) reg.2(16) and (17)(c)(iii) (April 6, 2012).

6. Tax Credits (Miscellaneous Amendments) Regulations 2012 (SI 2012/848) regs 2(17)(a) and (b) and 2(17)(c)(i) and (ii) (May 1, 2012).

7. Personal Independence Payment (Supplementary Provisions and Consequential Amendments) Regulations 2013 (SI 2013/388) reg.8 and Sch. para.28(4) (April 8, 2013).

8. Armed Forces and Reserve Forces Compensation Scheme (Consequential Provisions: Subordinate Legislation) Order 2013 (SI 2013/591) art.7 and Sch. para.24(4) (April 8, 2013).

9. Universal Credit (Consequential, Supplementary, Incidental and Miscellaneous Provisions) Regulations 2013 (SI 2013/630) reg.77(4) (April 29, 2013).

10. Working Tax Credit (Entitlement and Maximum Rate) (Amendment) Regulations 2013 (SI 2013/1736) reg.3 (August 5, 2013).

11. Tax Credits and Childcare (Miscellaneous Amendments) Regulations 2018 (SI 2018/365) reg.4(2) (April 6, 2018).

12. Tax Credits and Child Benefit (Miscellaneous Amendments) Regulations 2021 (SI 2021/1286) reg.2(4) (December 9, 2021).

13. Tax Credits and Child Benefit (Miscellaneous Amendments) Regulations 2023 (SI 2023/179) reg.3(3) (March 15, 2023).

DEFINITIONS

"child"—see reg.2.
"childcare"—see reg.14.
"couple"—see TCA 2002 s.3.
"claimant"—see reg.2.
"joint claim"—see reg.2.
"partner"—see reg.2.
"patient"—see reg.2.
"qualifying remunerative work"—see reg.4.
"relevant child care charges"—see reg.14.

GENERAL NOTE

2.167 Specific provision is made for the child care element in TCA 2002 s.12. The element may be claimed by those entitled to working tax credit and incurring relevant childcare charges for a child for whom a claimant is responsible in three circumstances:
(a) a lone parent working 16 hours a week;
(b) a couple both of whom are working 16 hours a week; or
(c) a couple, one of whom is working 16 hours a week and the other of whom is incapacitated, in hospital or in prison.

Incapacitated

2.168 The definition of "incapacitated" is set out in paras (5)–(12). The definition is referential in that it operates by reference to the award of some disability or incapacity-related benefit or a disability or incapacity-related adjustment to a benefit or war pension, or the provision of the NHS service referred to in para.(8). Save for the EU law point described below, this definition is exhaustive. Whether or not a person might in everyday language be considered incapacitated is irrelevant (*AS v HMRC* [2017] UKUT 361 (AAC).

AS v HMRC [2017] UKUT 361 (AAC) involved a Dutch invalidity benefit whose British equivalent would fall within reg.13(6)(b). Judge Jacobs held that the regulation needed to be read as including the Dutch invalidity benefit. Otherwise, the appellant would be deprived of a social advantage contrary to art.7(2) of Regulation (EU) 492/2011.

Entitlement to child care element of working tax credit

2.169 **14.**—(1) [¹Subject to paragraph (1A),] for the purposes of section 12 of the Act charges incurred for child care are charges paid by the person, or in the case of a joint claim, by either or both of the persons, for child care provided for any child for whom the person, or at least one of the persons, is responsible [² within the meaning of regulation 3 of the Child Tax Credit Regulations 2002].

(SI 2002/2005 reg.14) as amended

In these Regulations, such charges are called "relevant child care charges".

[¹(1A) Child care charges do not include charges in respect of care provided by [⁴—
  (a) a relative of the child, wholly or mainly in the child's home, or
  (b) [¹² ...]
[⁷(c) a provider mentioned in regulation 14(2)(c), in circumstances where the care is excluded from being qualifying child care by article 4(2)(c) of the Tax Credits (Approval of Home Child Care Providers) Scheme (Northern Ireland) 2006.]
[⁸(d) a provider mentioned in [¹³ regulation 14(2)(f)(vii)], in circumstances where the care is excluded from being qualifying child care by [²⁴Article 5(2)(d) of The Approval of Home Childcare Providers (Wales) Scheme 2021].]
[¹² [(e) a foster parent [¹³, a foster carer or a kinship carer] in respect of a child whom [¹³ that person is fostering or is looking after as the child's kinship carer]].

(1B) For the purposes of this regulation—
  (a) "relative" means parent, grandparent, aunt, uncle, brother or sister whether by blood, half blood, marriage [⁵, civil patnership] or affinity;
  (b) "the child's home" means the home of the person, or in the case of a joint claim of either or both of the persons, responsible for the child.]
[¹³ (c) "foster parent" in relation to a child—
    (i) in relation to England, means a person with whom the child is placed under [²⁴ the Care Planning, Placement and Case Review (England) Regulations 2010];
    (ii) in relation to Wales, means a person with whom the child is placed under [²⁴ the Care Planning, Placement and Case Review (Wales) Regulations 2015];
    (iii) in relation to Northern Ireland, means a person with whom the child is placed under the Foster Placement (Children) Regulations (Northern Ireland) 1996; [²¹ ...]
  (d) "foster carer" and "kinship carer" have the meanings given in regulation 2 of the Looked After Children (Scotland) Regulations 2009 [²¹; and
  (e) "Ministry of Defence personnel" means Her Majesty's forces, which has the same meaning as in the Armed Forces Act 2006, and their families, and civil servants employed by the Ministry of Defence and their families.]
(2) "Child care" means care provided for a child—
  (a) in England [¹⁰ ...]—
    (i) [¹² ...]
    (ii) [¹¹ ...]
  [¹¹ (iia) by a person registered under Part 3 of the Childcare Act 2006;]
  [¹¹ (iii) in respect of any period on or before the last day the child is treated as a child for the purpose of this regulation by or under the direction of the proprietor of a school on the school premises [¹² (subject to paragraph 2(B))]]
    (iv) [⁹ ...] [¹⁰ ...]
    [³(v) [¹² ...;]
    [¹⁰(vi) [¹² ...;]

[¹⁹ (vii) by a carer provided by a person who is a service provider within the meaning of the Health and Social Care Act 2008 (Regulated Activities) Regulations 2014 in relation to the regulated activity of personal care within paragraph 1 of Schedule 1 to those Regulations;] or
   (viii) [¹¹ . . .;]
(b) in Scotland—
   (i) by a person in circumstances where the care service provided by him consists of child minding or of day care of children within the meaning of [¹⁵ schedule 12 to the Public Services Reform (Scotland) Act 2010 and is registered under Part 5 of that Act;]; [² . . .]
   [⁷(ia) by a child care agency where the service consists of or includes supplying, or introducing to persons who use the service, child carers within the meaning of [¹⁵ paragraph 5 of schedule 12 to the Public Services Reform (Scotland) Act 2010; or]]
   (ii) by a local authority in circumstances where the care service provided by the local authority consists of child minding or of day care of children within the meaning of [¹⁵ schedule 12 to the Public Services Reform (Scotland) Act 2010 and is registered under Part 5 of that Act; or] [²[¹⁴ . . .]]
[³[¹³ (iii) [¹⁴ . . .]]]
(c) in Northern Ireland—
   (i) by persons registered under Part XI of the Children (Northern Ireland) Order 1995; [² . . .]
   (ii) by institutions and establishments exempt from registration under that Part by virtue of Article 121 of that Order; or
   [³(iii) in respect of any period ending on or before the day on which he ceases to be a child for the purposes of this regulation, where the care is provided out of school hours by a school on school premises or by [²¹ the Education Authority] or a Health and Social Services Trust; or
   (iv) [¹⁴ . . .]
   [⁷(v) by a child care provider approved in accordance with the Tax Credits (approval of Home Child Care Providers) Scheme (Northern Ireland) 2006; [¹⁴ or
   (vi) by a foster parent in relation to a child (other than one whom the foster parent is fostering) in circumstances where, but for the fact that the child is too old, the care would fall within one of the descriptions in paragraph (2C);]
[²¹ (d) anywhere outside the United Kingdom—
   (i) by a child care provider, which is inspected by a person whose functions include regulating the provision of child care in accordance with the statutory requirements of the Department for Education, where a claim is made by Ministry of Defence personnel; or
   (ii) in any other case, where care is provided within an EEA state or Switzerland, by a child care provider which is approved, regulated or accredited under the legislation of the relevant state, by a person whose functions include regulating the provision of education or child care;] or
   (ii) [¹ . . .]

(SI 2002/2005 reg.14) as amended

[¹⁰ . . .]
[¹⁰ (f) in Wales—
    (i) by persons registered under [¹⁴ Part 2 of the Children and Families (Wales) Measure 2010;]
    [¹⁴ (ii) by a person in circumstances where, but for article 11, 12 or 14 of the Child Minding and Day Care Exceptions (Wales) Order 2010(5), the care would be day care for the purposes of Part 2 of the Children and Families (Wales) Measure 2010;]
    (iii) in respect of any period on or before the last day he is treated as a child for the purposes of this regulation, where the care is provided out of school hours, by a school on school premises or by a local authority;
    (iv) by a child care provider approved by an accredited organisation within the meaning given by regulation 4 of the Tax Credit (New Category of Child Care Provider) Regulations 1999;
    (v) [¹⁴ . . .]
    [²⁰ (vi) by a person who is employed or engaged under a contract for services to provide care and support by the provider of a domiciliary support service within the meaning of Part 1 of the Regulation and Inspection of Social Care (Wales) Act 2016;] [¹⁴ . . .]
    (vii) by a child care provider approved under [²⁴. . .] [²³ The Approval of Home Childcare Providers (Wales) Scheme 2021]; [¹⁴ or
    (viii) by a foster parent in relation to a child (other than one whom the foster parent is fostering) in circumstances where, but for the fact that the child is too old, the care would fall within one of the descriptions in paragraph (2D).]

[¹¹ (2A) In paragraph (2)(a)(iii)—
"proprietor", in relation to a school, means –
(a) the governing body incorporated under section 19 of the Education Act 2002, or
(b) if there is no such body, the person or body of persons responsible for the management of the school;
"school" means a school that Her Majesty's Chief Inspector of Education, Children's Services and Skills (the "Chief Inspector") is or may be required to inspect;
"school premises" means premises that may be inspected as part of an inspection of the school by the Chief Inspector.

(2B) Care provided for a child in England is not [¹² child care] under paragraph (2)(a)(iii) if—
(a) it is provided during school hours for a child who has reached compulsory school age, or
(b) it is provided in breach of a requirement to register under Part 3 of the Childcare Act 2006.]

[¹⁴ (2C) The descriptions referred to in paragraph (2)(c)(vi) are—
(a) child minding or day care for the purposes of Part 11 of the Children (Northern Ireland) Order 1995(7); and
(b) qualifying child care for the purposes of the Tax Credits (Approval of Home Child Care Providers) Scheme (Northern Ireland) 2006(8).

(2D) The descriptions referred to in paragraph (2)(f)(viii) are—
(a) child minding, or day care, for the purposes of Part 2 of the Children and Families (Wales) Measure 2010; and

(b) qualifying child care for the purposes of [24...] [23 The Approval of Home Childcare Providers (Wales) Scheme 2021].]

(3) For the purposes of this regulation a person is a child until the last day of the week in which falls 1st September following that child's 15th birthday (or 16th birthday if the child is disabled).

(4) For the purposes of paragraph (3), a child is disabled where—
  (a) a disability living allowance is payable [22 under section 71 of the Contributions and Benefits Act or section 31 of the Social Security (Scotland) Act 2018] in respect of that child, or has ceased to be payable solely because he is a patient;
[19 (b) the child is certified as severely sight impaired or blind by a consultant ophthalmologist;]
  (c) the child ceased to be [19 certified as severely sight impaired or blind by a consultant ophthalmologist] within the 28 weeks immediately preceding the date of claim; [16 [17...]
  (d) personal independence payment is payable in respect of that child, or would be payable but for regulations under section 86(1) (hospital in-patients) of the Welfare Reform Act 2012;] [17 or
  (e) armed forces independence payment is payable in respect of that child.]

(5) Charges paid in respect of the child's compulsory education or charges paid by a person to a partner or by a partner to the person in respect of any child for whom either or any of them is responsible are not relevant child care charges.

(6) Where regulation 15(4) (agreement for the provision of future child care) applies—
  (a) the words "charges paid" in paragraph (1) include charges which will be incurred; and
  (b) the words "child care provided" in paragraph (1) include care which will be provided.

(7) [2...]

(8) Relevant child care charges are calculated on a weekly basis in accordance with regulation 15.

AMENDMENTS

1. Working Tax Credit (Entitlement and Maximum Rate) (Amendment) Regulations 2003 (SI 2003/701) reg.13 (April 6, 2003).
2. Tax Credits (Miscellaneous Amendments) Regulations 2004 (SI 2004/762) reg.10 (April 6, 2004).
3. Working Tax Credit (Entitlement and Maximum Rate) (Amendment) Regulations 2004 (SI 2004/1276) reg.2 (June 1, 2004).
4. Working Tax Credit (Entitlement and Maximum Rate) (Amendment) Regulations 2005 (SI 2005/769) reg.4(b) (April 6, 2005).
5. Civil Partnership Act 2004 (Tax Credits, etc.) (Consequential Amendments) Order 2005 (SI 2005/2919) art.2(4) (December 5, 2005).
6. Working Tax Credit (Entitlement and Maximum Rate) (Amendment) Regulations 2005 (SI 2005/769) reg.4(a) (January 1, 2006).
7. Tax Credits (Miscellaneous Amendments) Regulations 2006 (SI 2006/766) reg.20(4) (April 6, 2006).
8. Tax Credits (Miscellaneous Amendments) Regulations 2007 (SI 2007/824) reg.6 (April 6, 2007).
9. Working Tax Credit (Entitlement and Maximum Rate) (Amendment No.2) Regulations 2007 (SI 2007/2479) reg.2 (October 1, 2007).

(SI 2002/2005 reg.14) as amended

10. Tax Credits (Miscellaneous Amendments) Regulations 2008 (SI 2008/604) reg.3 (April 6, 2008).
11. Tax Credits (Miscellaneous Amendments) (No.2) Regulations 2008 (SI 2008/2169) reg.2 (September 1, 2008).
12. Tax Credits (Miscellaneous Amendments) Regulations 2009 (SI 2009/697) reg.5 (April 6, 2009).
13. Tax Credits (Miscellaneous Amendments) (No.2) Regulations 2009 (SI 2009/2887) reg.4 (April 6, 2010)
14. Tax Credits (Miscellaneous Amendments) Regulations 2011 (SI 2011/721) reg.3 (April 6, 2011).
15. Public Services Reform (Scotland) Act 2010 (Consequential Modifications of Enactments) Order 2011 (SI 2011/2581) art.2 and Sch.2 para.36 (October 28, 2011).
16. Personal Independence Payment (Supplementary Provisions and Consequential Amendments) Regulations 2013 (SI 2013/388) reg.8 and Sch. para.28(5) (April 8, 2013).
17. Armed Forces and Reserve Forces Compensation Scheme (Consequential Provisions: Subordinate Legislation) Order 2013 (SI 2013/591) art.7 and Sch. para.24(5) (April 8, 2013).
18. Child Benefit (General) and Tax Credits (Miscellaneous Amendments) Regulations 2014 (SI 2014/2924) reg.4(2) (November 28, 2014).
19. Tax Credits and Child Benefit (Miscellaneous Amendments) Regulations 2016 (SI 2016/360) reg.2(3) (April 6, 2016).
20. Tax Credits and Childcare (Miscellaneous Amendments) Regulations 2018 (SI 2018/365) reg.4(3) (April 6, 2018).
21. Tax Credits, Child Benefit and Childcare Payments (Miscellaneous Amendments) Regulations 2019 (SI 2019/364) reg.2(4) (March 21, 2019).
22. Tax Credits, Child Benefit, Guardian's Allowance and Childcare Payments (Miscellaneous Amendments) Regulations 2020 (SI 2020/297) reg.2 (April 6, 2020).
23. Tax Credits and Child Benefit (Miscellaneous Amendments) Regulations 2021 (SI 2021/1286) reg.2(5) (December 9, 2021).
24. Tax Credits and Child Benefit (Miscellaneous Amendments) Regulations 2022 (SI 2022/555) reg.5(6) (June 9, 2022).

DEFINITIONS

"child"—see reg.2.
"claim"—see reg.2.
"partner"—see reg.2.
"patient"—see reg.2.

GENERAL NOTE

The main content of this regulation is the definition of the main phrases on which reg.13 relies. "Child" receives a slightly limited definition compared with the standard approach for child tax credit and working tax credit, as para.(3) puts an upper limit on the relevant age of a child. The provision does not apply at all to those over 16, who are known as "qualifying young persons" for working tax credit and child tax credit purposes. There is an upwards extension of the age limit for disabled children in paras (3) and (4). This is by reference to payment of any level of disability living allowance or by blindness. There is also a limit applying to the youngest children. Paragraph (7) links with reg.13(3) to exclude a claim by someone on maternity, paternity or adoption leave by reference only to the child in respect of whom the leave is granted.

"Child care" is given an extensive definition. This is necessary because responsibility for childcare legislation is part of the devolved responsibilities of the Scottish and Northern Irish parliaments and the Welsh assembly. In addition, the definition has been extended to childcare outside the UK. This links with the provisions in the Tax Credits (Residence) Regulations 2003 (SI 2003/642) under which Crown servants outside the UK, and their partners, are regarded as being in the UK for tax credits purposes.

2.170

Accordingly, staff provided with approved childcare facilities by, for example, defence establishments, can qualify for the childcare element of working tax credit. Any dispute about whether someone is providing "childcare" is for the authorities responsible for that particular set of registration rules.

"Relevant childcare charges" is defined by reference to charges for "childcare", with the important exception in para.(1A) of childcare provided by a (registered) relative in the child's home. It can, however, be provided in the carer's home even though the carer is, say, a grandparent. The condition ensures that both the carer, and the carer's premises, are open to inspection. Paragraph (5) excludes charges for education as against care, and payments made by one of a married or unmarried couple to the other (although the one to whom the payments are made may not be responsible for the child).

Cases arise in which HMRC argue collusion between claimants and childcare providers, involving, for example, alleged inflated childcare charges. In *NA v HMRC (TC)* [2016] UKUT 404 (AAC) Upper Tribunal Judge Rowland warned of the potential for unfairness if HMRC rely on the undisclosed tax returns of childcare providers in support of such arguments. In that case HMRC argued the £39,000 per annum in childcare fees said to have been made to the provider by the claimant was "far in excess of the total income declared by the care provider to HMRC" yet did not supply the First-tier Tribunal with copies of the tax returns. Apparent "discrepancies" between tax data and charges said to have been paid by a claimant should not be relied on unless the relevant tax returns are disclosed. It should also be noted that there is no limit to the number of hours of childcare utilised for the purposes of reg.14 nor is there any requirement for childcare costs to be proportionate to household income (see *SK v HMRC* (TC) [2016] UKUT 441 (AAC) at [33] and also *NA v HMRC* (TC) [2016] UKUT 404 (AAC) at [6], reminding tribunals that a claimant may have other benefit income).

Regulation 14(2)(c) and (d)

2.171
Regulation 14(2)(c) concerns eligible childcare provision in Northern Ireland while reg.14(2)(d) applies (a) in the case of claims by Ministry of Defence personnel, to childcare subject to inspection against regulatory requirements imposed by the Department for Education and, (b) in other cases, to childcare provided in an EEA State or Switzerland if the provider is approved, regulated or accredited by a person whose functions include regulation of education or childcare against the requirements of the relevant state's legislation. The latter types of childcare were probably brought within eligible childcare in response to the decision of a Tribunal of Northern Ireland Social Security Commissioners in *NB v HMRC* (TC) [2016] NI Com 47. In *NB* the claimant, a UK national, lived and worked in Northern Ireland but used childcare just over the border in the Republic of Ireland. Initially she was paid working tax credit including the childcare element. On review, the childcare element was withdrawn as the provider was situated outside Northern Ireland. The case plainly fell outside reg.14(2)(c). The claimant relied on art.56 of the TFEU, i.e. the right to provide and receive services under EU law. HMRC argued that the 2002 Child Care Regulations were not, under reg.14(2)(d), confined to Crown servants and military establishments, and that the Irish child care provider in question should have registered for authorisation under the 2002 Child Care Regulations.

A Tribunal of Commissioners in Northern Ireland examined changes made to the enabling powers conferred by the 1999 and 2002 Tax Credits Acts. They concluded that the 2002 Child Care Regulations were authorised by the 1999 Act but not the 2002 Act. Hence the regulations were invalid and could not be relied on by HMRC. The Tribunal further held that, even if the accreditation scheme was valid under domestic law, it was not transparent and accessible as required by EU law and so could not be relied on to justify any restriction on the art.56 right to provide and receive services. Accordingly, the claimant was not disentitled from the childcare element of working tax credit simply because her childcare provider was based outside the UK.

The scope of reg.14(5) was discussed by the deputy Commissioner in *CTC/3646/2007*, where the deputy Commissioner upheld a tribunal's decision to refuse to take account of apportioned fees for a "waiting class". Regulation 15(3) could not therefore be applied on the facts. The issue is further clarified by the addition of a definition of "full time education" to the Child Tax Credit Regulations by SI 2008/2169 reg.7(3) with effect from September 1, 2008.

Calculation of relevant child care charges

15.—(1) Relevant child care charges are calculated by aggregating the average weekly charge paid for child care for each child in respect of whom charges are incurred [¹and rounding up the total to the nearest whole pound]. This is subject to [¹paragraphs (1A) and (2)].

[¹(1A) In any case in which the charges in respect of child care are paid weekly, the average weekly charge for the purposes of paragraph (1) is established—
- (a) where the charges are for a fixed weekly amount, by aggregating the average weekly charge paid for child care for each child in respect of whom charges are incurred in the most recent four complete weeks; or
- (b) where the charges are for variable weekly amounts, by aggregating the charges for the previous 52 weeks and dividing the total by 52.]

(2) In any case in which the charges in respect of child care are paid monthly, the average weekly charge for the purposes of paragraph (1) is established—
- (a) where the charges are for a fixed monthly amount, by multiplying that amount by 12 and dividing the product by 52; or
- (b) where the charges are for variable monthly amounts, by aggregating the charges for the previous 12 months and dividing the total by 52.

(3) In a case where there is insufficient information for establishing the average weekly charge paid for child care in accordance with paragraphs (1) and (2), an officer of the Board shall estimate the charge—
- (a) in accordance with information provided by the person or persons incurring the charges; and
- (b) by any method which in the officer's opinion is reasonable.

(4) If a person—
- (a) has entered into an agreement for the provision of child care; and
- (b) will incur under that agreement relevant child care charges in respect of child care during the period of the award, the average weekly charge for child care is based upon a written estimate of the future weekly charges provided by that person.

AMENDMENT

1. Working Tax Credit (Entitlement and Maximum Rate) (Amendment) Regulations 2003 (SI 2003/701) reg.14 (April 6, 2003).

DEFINITIONS

"child"—see reg.14(3).
"childcare"—see reg.14(2).
"relevant child care charges"—see reg.14(1).

GENERAL NOTE

This regulation sets out the methods to be used in calculating the amount of child care charges on which the child care element is to be based. The regulation was amended just before it came into effect because the previous form of the regulation was accepted as being seriously flawed. This created potential unfairness as between those who pay monthly for their child care on an annualised basis and those who pay weekly on an actual basis. While the monthly payers usually have a steady pattern of payments, the weekly payers often pay more during school terms than during school holidays.

The rules deal with monthly payments by either using the fixed monthly charge, or the average of the last 12 monthly charges, to determine the weekly figure. Varying weekly charges are calculated by reference to the last 52 weeks, while fixed weekly charges are calculated by reference to the last four weeks. Presumably, however, regard must be had to more than four past weeks in applying this rule to avoid the problem of assessing the charges for the wrong four weeks.

There are two important provisos to these rules. The first is that HMRC may rely on estimates based on "any method . . . which is reasonable". This should allow a solution to the problem of increases in the charges that should be reflected in increases in the child care element. The second proviso, in para.(4), allows an estimate of the future charges to be taken into account provided that the claimant has entered into a written agreement for the provision of child care.

Change of circumstances

2.174

16.—(1) There is a relevant change in circumstances if—
 (a) [¹. . .]
 (b) [¹during the period of an award, the weekly relevant child care charges, rounded up to the nearest whole pound]—
  (i) exceed the average weekly charge calculated in accordance with regulation 15 by £10 a week or more;
  (ii) are less than the average weekly charge calculated in accordance with regulation 15 by £10 a week or more; or
  (iii) are nil.
 If there is a relevant change in circumstances, the amount of the child care element of working tax credit shall be recalculated with effect from the specified date.

[¹(2) For the purposes of paragraph (1), the weekly relevant child care charge—
 (a) where the child care charges are for a fixed weekly amount, is the aggregate of the weekly charge paid for child care for each child in respect of whom charges are incurred in each of the four consecutive weeks in which the change occurred; or
 (b) where the child care charges are for variable weekly amounts, is established by aggregating the anticipated weekly charge paid for child care for each child in respect of whom charges will be incurred for the following 52 weeks and dividing the total by 52.]

(3) If in any case the charges in respect of child care are paid monthly, the weekly relevant child care charge for the purposes of paragraph (1) is established—
 (a) where the charges are for a fixed monthly amount, by multiplying that amount by 12 and dividing the product by 52; or
 (b) where the charges are for variable monthly amounts, by aggregating the [¹anticipated] charges for the [¹next] 12 months and dividing the total by 52.

(4) In a case where there is insufficient information for establishing the weekly relevant child care charge paid for child care in accordance with paragraphs (2) and (3), an officer of the Board shall estimate the charge—
 (a) in accordance with information provided by the person or persons incurring the charges; and
 (b) by any method which in the officer's opinion is reasonable.

(SI 2002/2005 reg.16) as amended

(5) For the purpose of paragraph (1) the specified date is—
(a) where the child care charges are increased, the later of—
  (i) the first day of the week in which the change occurred, and
  (ii) the first day of the week in which falls the day which is [³ one month] prior to the date notification of the change is given,
[² (b) where the child care charges are decreased—
  (i) in a case where an award of child care charges is a fixed period, the length of which is known when the award is first made, the first day of the week following the end of that fixed period, and
  (ii) in all other cases, the first day of the week following the four consecutive weeks in which the change occurred.]

AMENDMENTS

1. Working Tax Credit (Entitlement and Maximum Rate) (Amendment) Regulations 2003 (SI 2003/701) reg.15 (April 6, 2003).
2. Working Tax Credit (Entitlement and Maximum Rate) (Amendment) Regulations 2010 (SI 2010/918) reg.3 (April 15, 2010).
3. Tax Credits (Miscellaneous Amendments) Regulations 2012 (SI 2012/848) reg.2(18) (April 6, 2012).

DEFINITIONS

"award"—see TCA 2002 s.14.
"change of circumstances"—see TCA 2002 s.6.

GENERAL NOTE

This regulation brings into play the mechanisms for amending or terminating an award of working tax credit. Section 6(3) of the TCA 2002 makes provision for regulations to impose a duty on a claimant to report a change of circumstances that may decrease the rate of entitlement to a tax credit. Regulation 21 of the Tax Credits (Claims and Notifications) Regulations 2002 (SI 2002/2014) imposes the requirement that notification of a change of circumstances as defined in this regulation must be given within one month of the change occurring. Regulations 22–24 of those Regulations set out how and by whom this is to be done.

Failure to notify may make the claimant liable to a penalty of £300 under s.32(3) of the TCA 2002.

In *HMRC v CB (TC)* [2013] UKUT 484 (AAC) the Upper Tribunal considered the interaction of reg.16 with reg.7D. The question in issue was the length of time for which entitlement to tax credits continued after a claimant who had been working 40 hours a week stopped working. The specific issue was the period for which the childcare element remained payable. There had been a timely notification of changes of circumstances. HMRC argued that the "run on" periods in reg.7D and reg.16 ran concurrently, while the appellant argued that they should be applied consecutively. Judge Ovey agreed with the appellant's arguments in part, noting that reg.13 determined the questions of entitlement to the childcare element and that reg.16 is concerned with actual changes only and with the date of any required recalculation. However, on the facts, this did not assist the appellant.

2.175

Severe disability element

Severe disability element

17.—(1) The determination of the maximum rate must include the severe disability element if the claimant, or, in the case of a joint claim, one of the claimants satisfies paragraph [⁴(2), (3), (4), (5) or (6)]

2.176

(2) A person satisfies this paragraph if a disability living allowance, attributable to the care component payable at the highest rate prescribed under section 72(3) of the Contributions and Benefits Act or an attendance allowance at the higher rate prescribed under section 65(3) of that Act—
  (a) is payable in respect of him; or
  (b) would be so payable but for a suspension of benefit by virtue of regulations under section 113(2) of the Contributions and Benefits Act (suspension during hospitalisation), or an abatement as a consequence of hospitalisation.

[¹ (3) A person satisfies this paragraph if the enhanced rate of the daily living component of personal independence payment under section 78(2) of the Welfare Reform Act 2012—
  (a) is payable in respect of that person; or
  (b) would be so payable but for regulations made under section 86(1) (hospital in-patients) of that Act.]

[² (4) A person satisfies this paragraph if an armed forces independence payment is payable in respect of him.]

[³[⁴(5) A person satisfies this paragraph if the enhanced rate of the daily living component of the Adult Disability Payment under regulation 5(3) of the Disability Assistance for Working Age People (Scotland) Regulations 2022—
  (a) is payable in respect of that person; or
  (b) would be so payable but for regulation 28 (effect of admission to hospital on ongoing entitlement to Adult Disability Payment) of those Regulations.]]

[⁴(6) A person satisfies this paragraph if they—
  (a) have reached pensionable age (within the meaning given by the rules in Part 1 of Schedule 4 to the Pensions Act 1995),
  (b) and the higher rate of Scottish disability assistance—
    (i) is payable in respect of that person; or
    (ii) would be so payable but for a reduction because that person is undergoing medical or other treatment as an in-patient at a hospital or similar institution.]

AMENDMENTS

1. Personal Independence Payment (Supplementary Provisions and Consequential Amendments) Regulations 2013 (SI 2013/388) reg.8 and Sch. para.28(6) (April 8, 2013).

2. Armed Forces and Reserve Forces Compensation Scheme (Consequential Provisions: Subordinate Legislation) Order 2013 (SI 2013/591) art.7 and Sch. para.24(6) (April 8, 2013).

3. Tax Credits and Child Benefit (Miscellaneous Amendments) Regulations 2021 (SI 2021/1286) reg.2(6) (December 9, 2021).

4. Tax Credits (Miscellaneous Amendments) Regulations 2024 (SI 2024/176) reg.4 (March 13, 2024).

DEFINITIONS

"claimant"—see reg.2.
"joint claim"—see reg.2.

(SI 2002/2005 reg.17) as amended

General Note

This provision is amended to deal with the replacement of disability living allowance with the new personal independence payment provided for in the Welfare Reform Act 2012. This is being introduced in stages. For the initial stages see: the Welfare Reform Act 2012 (Commencement No.8 and Savings and Transitional Provisions) Order 2013 (SI 2013/358).

This is separate from the disability element provided for in reg.9. It adds a further £1,705 to the entitlement of the claimant or claimants. But it is restricted to the case where the disabled individual is receiving the highest rate of the care component of disability living allowance (or the attendance allowance equivalent), which means that both day and night attention or supervision are needed.

There is no express provision dealing with interaction with the disability element. *CSTC/76/2006* makes it clear that the language of reg.9 requires that, in the case of a joint claim, the person who is disabled must also be the same person who is working 16 hours a week: see para.2.154, above. But this regulation does not repeat that language. Nor is this element dependent on the receipt of the disability element under reg.9. The mandatory language of reg.17 suggests that all joint claimants are entitled to the severe disability element if either of them meets the general conditions to claim WTC and either is in receipt of the highest rate of the care component of disability living allowance (or the higher rate of attendance allowance). It would follow that this element may be claimed by claimants following any of the four Routes noted at para.2.128, above, and not merely Route 2.

Where a passporting disability benefit is awarded after a person was awarded working tax credit without the disability element, it is now possible in certain circumstances for the tax credit award to be reviewed so as to fully backdate entitlement to the disability element: see section 21C of the Tax Credits Act 2002 (above in this volume).

50 Plus element

50 Plus element

18.—[¹ . . .]

Amendment

1. Tax Credits (Miscellaneous Amendments) Regulations 2012 (SI 2012/848) reg.2(19) (April 6, 2012).

Death of a child or qualifying young person for whom the claimant is responsible

Entitlement after death of a child or qualifying young person for whom the claimant is responsible

19.—(1) Paragraph (2) applies if—
(a) the death occurs of a child or qualifying young person;
(b) working tax credit is payable to a person who was, or to a couple at least one of whom was, immediately before the death responsible for that child or qualifying young person;
(c) the prescribed conditions for an element of working tax credit were satisfied because the claimant, or at least one of the claimants, was responsible for that child or qualifying person, but would not have been satisfied but for that responsibility; and
(d) the prescribed conditions would have continued to be satisfied but for the death.

(2) If this paragraph applies, working tax credit shall continue to be payable, as if the child or qualifying young person had not died, for the period for which child tax credit continues to be payable in accordance with regulation 6 of the Child Tax Credit Regulations 2002.

DEFINITIONS

"child"—see reg.2.
"qualifying young person"—see reg.2.

GENERAL NOTE

2.180 Section 55 of the TCA 2002 provides an extension of the payment of child benefit for a period of eight weeks after the death of a child for whom the benefit is paid. Section 5(5) makes similar provision for child tax credit, and effect is given to this by reg.6 of the Child Tax Credit Regulations 2002 (SI 2002/2007). This regulation matches those extensions for working tax credit also, s.10(3)(d) of the TCA 2002 providing authority for this.

Claimants are required, from November 2006, to report the death of a child or qualifying young person for whom they are receiving additional credit within one month of the death. See para.2.384 below.

PART III

MAXIMUM RATE

Maximum rates of elements of Working Tax Credit

2.181 **20.**—(1) The maximum annual rate of working tax credit (excluding the child care element) payable to a single claimant or to a couple making a joint claim is the sum of whichever of the following elements are applicable—
  (a) the basic element specified in column.(2) of the table in Schedule 2 at paragraph 1;
  (b) in respect of a claimant who satisfies regulation 9(1), the disability element specified in column (2) of the table in Schedule 2 at paragraph 2;
  (c) the 30-hour element specified in column (2) of the table in Schedule 2 at paragraph 3 in respect of—
    (i) a single claimant who works for not less than 30 hours per week;
    (ii) a couple either or both of whom work for not less than 30 hours per week; or
    (iii) a couple, at least one of whom is responsible for a child or a qualifying young person and at least one of whom works for 16 hours per week if their hours of work when aggregated amount to at least 30 hours per week;
  (d) the second-adult element specified in column (2) of the table in Schedule 2 at paragraph 4 where regulation 11 so provides;
  (e) the lone-parent element specified in column (2) of the table in Schedule 2 at paragraph 5 where regulation 12 applies; [⁴ and]
  (f) the severe disability element specified in column (2) of the table in Schedule 2 at paragraph 6—
    (i) in respect of a single claimant who satisfies regulation 17; or
    (ii) in respect of a member of a couple making a joint claim who satisfies regulation 17 [⁴ . . .]

(SI 2002/2005 reg.20) as amended

(g) [⁴...].

(2) The maximum rate of the child care element of a working tax credit is [³70 per cent] of the maxima specified in paragraph (3).

(3) The maxima are—

(a) [²£175] per week, where the [¹claimant or, in the case of a joint claim, at least one of the claimants, is responsible for] only one child in respect of whom relevant child care charges are paid; and

(b) [²£300] per week where the [¹claimant or, in the case of a joint claim, at least one of the claimants, is responsible for] more than one child in respect of whom relevant child care charges are paid.

AMENDMENTS

1. Working Tax Credit (Entitlement and Maximum Rate) (Amendment) Regulations 2003 (SI 2003/701) reg.16 (April 6, 2003).
2. Tax Credits Up-rating Regulations 2005 (SI 2005/681) reg.3(1) (April 6, 2005).
3. Tax Credits Up-rating Regulations 2011 (SI 2011/1035) reg.3(2) (April 6, 2011).
4. Tax Credits (Miscellaneous Amendments) Regulations 2012 (SI 2012/848) reg.2(20) (April 6, 2012).

DEFINITIONS

"claimant"—see reg.2.
"joint claim"—see reg.2.

GENERAL NOTE

This regulation emphasises that the entitlement of a claimant or claimants to working tax credit is made up of each of the elements to which there is entitlement. It is "the sum of whichever of the ... elements are applicable". However, as noted above, there must be entitlement under reg.4. to the basic element in all cases. Paragraph (1) provides the necessary drafting provision to tie each of the other elements (save for the child care element), the conditions for which have been defined above, into the rate of award and entitlement to working tax credit to the claimant or claimants under s.11 of the TCA 2002.

Paragraphs (2) and (3) then provide the effective rate of the child care element. They set the maximum weekly child care element at £300 for care for two or more children, and £175 for care for a single child.

The current figures for the maximum rates of all elements other than the child care element are in Sch.2.

The varying levels of working tax credit by reference to these differing elements and the different routes by which, under reg.4, claims can be made for working tax credit can be illustrated by some short examples. The examples show the maximum entitlement to working tax credit in each case. They do not take into account the income or benefit entitlements of the claimant(s) nor the temporary increase of the basic element to £3,040 for tax year 2020/21 made by section 77(1) of the Coronavirus Act 2020.

2.182

Route 1: Lone parent with three children, working 32 hours a week, and incurring childcare costs of £300 a week.

Basic element	£2,435
30-hour element	£1,015
Lone-parent element	£2,500
Childcare element	£10,920 (limited to 70 per cent of £300 p.w.)
Maximum entitlement	£16,870

The Working Tax Credit (Entitlement and Maximum Rate) Regulations 2002

The parent will also be entitled to child benefit.

Route 2: Single claimant suffering prejudice in the job market, receiving disability living allowance, and working 20 hours a week.

Basic element	£2,435
Disability element	£3,935
Maximum entitlement	£6,370

Route 3: Couple with one child making joint claim, with one of the couple working 20 hours a week, and the other working 8 hours a week.

Basic element	£2,435
Second adult element	£2,500
Childcare element	
Childcare element	£6,370 (limited to 70 per cent of £175 p.w.)
Maximum entitlement	£11,305

The couple will also be entitled to child benefit.

Route 4: Single claimant over 60 working 16 hours a week.

Basic element	£2,435
Maximum entitlement	£2,435

The claimant may also be entitled to state pension credit.

Route 5: Single claimant over 25 working 30 hours a week.

Basic element	£2,435
Maximum entitlement	£2,435

SCHEDULE 1   **Regulation 9(1)**

DISABILITY WHICH PUTS A PERSON AT A DISADVANTAGE IN GETTING A JOB

PART I

1.—When standing he cannot keep his balance unless he continually holds onto something.

2.—Using any crutches, walking frame, walking stick, prosthesis or similar walking aid which he habitually uses, he cannot walk a continuous distance of 100 metres along level ground without stopping or without suffering severe pain.

3.—He can use neither of his hands behind his back as in the process of putting on a jacket or of tucking a shirt into trousers.

4.—He can extend neither of his arms in front of him so as to shake hands with another person without difficulty.

5.—He can put neither of his hands up to his head without difficulty so as to put on a hat.

6.—Due to lack of manual dexterity he cannot, with one hand, pick up a coin which is not more than $2^{1}/_{2}$ centimetres in diameter.

7.—He is not able to use his hands or arms to pick up a full jug of 1 litre capacity and pour from it into a cup, without difficulty.

8.—He can turn neither of his hands sideways through 180 degrees.

[¹ **9.**—He is certified as severely sight impaired or blind by a consultant ophthalmologist.]

10.—He cannot see to read 16 point print at a distance greater than 20 centimetres, if appropriate, wearing the glasses he normally uses.

11.—He cannot hear a telephone ring when he is in the same room as the telephone, if appropriate, using a hearing aid he normally uses.

12.—In a quiet room he has difficulty in hearing what someone talking in a loud voice at a distance of 2 metres says, if appropriate, using a hearing aid he normally uses.

13.—People who know him well have difficulty in understanding what he says.

14.—When a person he knows well speaks to him, he has difficulty in understanding what that person says.

15.—At least once a year during waking hours he is in a coma or has a fit in which he loses consciousness.

16.—He has a mental illness for which he receives regular treatment under the supervision of a medically qualified person.

17.—Due to mental disability he is often confused or forgetful.

18.—He cannot do the simplest addition and subtraction.

19.—Due to mental disability he strikes people or damages property or is unable to form normal social relationships.

20.—He cannot normally sustain an 8-hour working day or a 5-day working week due to a medical condition or intermittent or continuous severe pain.

PART II

21.—As a result of an illness or accident he is undergoing a period of habilitation or rehabilitation.

2.184

AMENDMENT

1. Child Benefit (General) and Tax Credits (Miscellaneous Amendments) Regulations 2014 (SI 2014/2924) reg.4(3) (November 28, 2014).

GENERAL NOTE

Under reg.9 of these Regulations, a person is treated as having a disability which puts him or her at a disadvantage in getting a job only if one of the paragraphs of this Schedule applies to him or her. If a paragraph does apply, reg.9 deems the claimant to be at a disadvantage in getting a job, whether or not the disability actually has that effect. See the notes to regs 9 and 9A for the application of these tests to initial and repeat claims.

2.185

The Schedule requires the exercise of a considerable amount of judgement. For instance, the words "without difficulty" frequently appear. The difficulty need not be severe and plainly a person may have difficulty with an action without necessarily suffering pain when performing it. Slowness may well be sufficient.

Attention is drawn to the final condition in para.20 before detailed comment is made on the specific disabilities. This is the overarching condition that a person cannot sustain a full working day or a full working week due either to a medical condition (of any nature, physical or mental) or intermittent or continuous severe pain. *R(S) 11/51* emphasised that this has to be determined by what a claimant can reasonably be expected to do with regard to his or her age, education, training and other personal factors. It is suggested that this should be the starting point for consideration of the application of this Schedule, with reference being made to the specific disabilities in that context.

Paragraph 2

Note that this test is not the same as the test prescribed in reg.12(1)(a)(ii) of the Social Security (Disability Living Allowance) Regulations 1991 (SI 1991/2890) in respect of the mobility component of disability living allowance. Not only is the

2.186

distance of 100 metres prescribed, but the question is whether that distance can be walked "without stopping" or without "severe pain" (rather than "severe discomfort"). It should also be noted that only artificial aids which are habitually used are to be taken into account, so there is no need to consider whether an aid which is not used might be suitable. In *R(M) 2/89*, the Commissioner held that a person walks only when putting one foot in front of the other, so that a person who has to swing through crutches, rather than using them to help him or her move both legs separately, cannot walk.

Paragraph 6

2.187   Two-and-a-half centimetres (1 inch) is the diameter of a 50 pence coin. Since their reduction in size, other coins, apart from the £2 coin, are smaller. Note that the claimant satisfies the test (and so may qualify for benefit) if he or she can pick up a large coin in one hand but not the other. In *CDWA 3123/1997* the claimant had no thumb on his left hand and the terminal joint of his right thumb was missing. He maintained that he was only able to pick up a coin of 2.5 centimetres in diameter by pushing it across a surface and catching it in his hand. The Commissioner holds that the tests in Sch.1 were to be performed in the normal way and not by employing some unusual or awkward manoeuvre. The normal way of picking up coins with one hand was to use the pinch grip between the thumb and fingers. An ability to pick up with the fingers alone was irrelevant because that ability did not demonstrate the presence or absence of the pinch grip. The Commissioner also confirmed that para.6 would be satisfied if the claimant could not pick up a coin of the prescribed size with one hand even if he could with the other.

Paragraph 7

2.188   This is a test of both steadiness and strength, using both hands or arms at once if necessary. The Commissioner in *CDWA 3123/1997* confirmed that the position was different under para.7 (as compared with para.6) since, here, the question was whether the claimant could perform the pouring task using both hands and arms together. An inability to do so with either hand alone is immaterial if he or she can manage the task with both hands. But any realistic difficulty, however slight, in carrying out that task would satisfy the test in para.7. Arguably, an ability to pick up and pour with one hand alone, where the claimant has no use of the other arm at all, would mean that the claimant would not qualify under this paragraph, although that question did not arise in that case.

Paragraph 8

2.189   Presumably, this is a test of wrist movements and is intended to be performed with the elbows kept still.

Paragraph 9

2.190   This paragraph replaces from November 2014 the previous tests that relied on entries in registers maintained by local or health authorities. That process was becoming complicated with increasing divergences of approach in national and local governments as the issue is a devolved issue.

Paragraph 10

2.191   16 point print is 4 mm high. It is this size.

Paragraphs 12–14

2.192   If hearing or understanding is possible, but only with difficulty (perhaps after repetition), the claimant still qualifies. The precise relationship between paras 12 and 14

(SI 2002/2005 Sch.1) as amended

is unclear. Difficulty in understanding may arise for reasons other than loss of hearing and, indeed, a person without hearing may be able to understand through lip-reading. Can a person who can hear a loud voice, but not an ordinary conversational voice, at a distance of two metres qualify under para.14 if he or she cannot lip-read? In principle, the answer would seem to be "yes". That would not mean that para.12 had no effect because the person would only be able to qualify under para.14 if he or she was further disadvantaged by an inability to make use of other methods of comprehending speech.

Paragraph 16
Medication taken on prescription will be enough, provided that it is regular. Mental illness is not defined, but, if a person is receiving treatment there is likely to be a diagnosis of an illness and if it is an illness of the mind it will be mental illness.

2.193

Paragraph 17
Mental disability is not defined and neither is the extent of confusion or forgetfulness required. On one view, any confusion or forgetfulness suggests some disability of the mind and the question is whether the degree of confusion or forgetfulness is sufficient to warrant the view that the legislator intended such a claimant to qualify (see the approach of the Court Appeal in *W v L* [1974] Q B.711). On the other hand, in *R(A) 2/92*, a Commissioner considered that a specific diagnosis was required and that suggests that the first question is whether there is such a diagnosis. Only after that has been answered does one go on to consider whether there is any resulting confusion or forgetfulness.

2.194

Paragraph 19
See the note to para.17. The approach taken in *R(A) 2/92* would create real difficulties here given the view expressed there that "personality disorder" can be distinguished from "mental disability".

2.195

Paragraph 21
This applies only on an initial claim.

2.196

SCHEDULE 2   **Regulation 20(1)**

MAXIMUM RATES OF THE ELEMENTS OF A WORKING TAX CREDIT

[¹*Relevant element of working tax credit*	*Maximum annual rate*
1. Basic element	[¹£2,435]
2. Disability element	[¹£3,935]
3. 30-hour element	[¹£1,015]
4. Second adult element	[¹£2,500]
5. Lone-parent element	[¹£2,500]
6. Severe disability element	[¹£1,705]

2.197

AMENDMENT

1. Tax Credits, Child Benefit and Guardian's Allowance Up-rating Regulations 2024 (SI 2024/247) reg.2 (April 6, 2024).

The Working Tax Credit (Entitlement and Maximum Rate) Regulations 2002

GENERAL NOTE

2.198 Having been frozen for four years, from April 6, 2016, in accordance with s.12 of the Welfare Reform and Work Act 2016, the rates for the basic element, the 30-hour element, the second adult element and the lone parent element began to be subject to annual up-rating once again, from April 6, 2020. For tax year 2020/21, item 1 (basic element) is to be read as if the amount specified were £3,040 rather than £1,995. This temporary modification to item 1 was made by section 77 of the Coronavirus Act 2020.

The Tax Credits (Definition and Calculation of Income) Regulations 2002

(SI 2002/2006) (AS AMENDED)

Whereas a draft of this instrument, which contains the first regulations made under section 7(8) and (9) of the Tax Credits Act 2002, has been laid before, and approved by resolution of, each House of Parliament:

Now, therefore, the Treasury, in exercise of the powers conferred upon them by sections 7(8) and (9), 65(1), (7) and (9) and 67 of the Tax Credits Act 2002, hereby make the following Regulations:

PART I

General provisions

2.199 1. Citation, commencement and effect.
2. Interpretation.

PART II

INCOME FOR THE PURPOSES OF TAX CREDITS

General

3. Calculation of income of claimant.

CHAPTER 2

Employment income

4. Employment income.

(SI 2002/2006) (as amended)

CHAPTER 3

Pension income

5. Pension income.

CHAPTER 4

Trading income

6. Trading income.

CHAPTER 5

Social security income

7. Social security income.

CHAPTER 6

Student income

8. Student income.
9. Payments of income in connection with students to be disregarded for the purposes of regulation 3.

CHAPTER 7

Investment income

10. Investment income.

CHAPTER 8

Property income

11. Property income.

The Tax Credits (Definition and Calculation of Income) Regulations 2002

CHAPTER 9

Foreign income

12. Foreign income.

CHAPTER 10

Notional income

13. Introduction.
14. Claimants treated for any purpose as having income by virtue of the Income Tax Acts.
15. Claimants depriving themselves of income in order to secure entitlement.
16. Claimants to whom income becomes available upon the making of a claim.
17. Claimants providing services to other persons for less than full earnings.

CHAPTER 11

Miscellaneous income

18. Miscellaneous income.

PART III

Sums disregarded in the calculation of income

General disregards in the calculation of income

19. General disregards in the calculation of income.

INTRODUCTION AND GENERAL NOTE

2.200   Section 7 of TCA 2002 provides that entitlement to a tax credit is subject to an income test. These regulations provide the detail of that test. They do so by adopting, with some important modifications, the rules for deciding on the income of an individual in the rewritten income tax legislation adopted over the last few years by Parliament from the draft bills produced by the Tax Law Rewrite Project. The Acts produced by the Rewrite Project have modernised the language and presentation of income tax law, and parallel changes in annual Finance Acts have also rationalised parts of it. This has made it easier to abandon the previous approach of having a different set of defining rules of income for benefit purposes and to adopt the income tax rules into the benefit system.

(SI 2002/2006) (as amended)

The rewritten income tax law
With effect from April 6, 2007 all the former primary legislation dating back to the 1840s under which income tax was imposed and collected has been repealed and replaced by the new rewritten legislation. This is contained in three major Acts, the Income Tax (Earnings and Pensions) Act 2003, the Income Tax (Trading and Other Income) Act 2005 and the Income Tax Act 2007. In practice these contain all the income rules necessary for any tax credits calculation save for the rules about capital allowances in the Capital Allowances Act 2000, another rewrite measure.

2.201

A fundamental change in approach
The income test used for tax credits is fundamentally different to that used for the income-related benefits such as income support, jobseeker's allowance and housing benefit. The main differences are as follows:

2.202

(1) *There is no capital rule.* There has never been a wealth tax in the UK, save for that, in effect, imposed on those claiming means-tested benefits. The approach is to tax income from capital as (and if) it arises. This is the approach now adopted for tax credits.

(2) *Capital gains are irrelevant.* Income tax is supplemented for individuals by a separate capital gains tax, e.g. on the capital gain made on selling an asset. Capital gains are also ignored for tax credits purposes.

(3) *There are no rules deeming income from capital held.* The rules treating capital as income, and attributing tariff income to capital, have been abolished and not replaced.

(4) *There is no all-inclusive definition of income.* The previous approach was to base the calculation of non-earned income on "gross income and any capital treated as income". The income tax based approach is to calculate income from each named source and to then aggregate the totals to establish the relevant income. If income arises from a source that is not one of the named sources, it is excluded from the calculation.

(5) *Claimants may choose forms of income that avoid the calculation.* The rules generally follow the approach of income tax in looking at actual income from capital, if any. They no longer follow the approach of the rules for the income-related benefits (perhaps more correctly the income and capital related benefits) of assuming income from capital at set rates while ignoring actual income from capital. They also leave any capital gains out of account. However, there remain some important anti-avoidance provisions based on the former family credit rules that take some account of capital and notional income. See regs 13–17 below.

Differences between tax credits income calculations and income tax assessments
The calculation of income for tax credits is based closely on the income tax approach. This allows HMRC to base its tax credits calculations on its income tax assessments or, in most cases, on the self-assessments of those individuals to income tax or the assessment and collection of income tax from employees by employers and agencies through the PAYE (Pay As You Earn) system. There are, however, some important differences from income tax assessments and these should also be noted:

2.203

(1) *Couples are assessed jointly, not separately.* The income tax system was transferred from a system in which married couples were assessed on their joint incomes in the name of the husband to a system of separate assessment of each partner in 1990. One reason for this was the growing concern about

The Tax Credits (Definition and Calculation of Income) Regulations 2002

discrimination against couples who were married, and assessed jointly, as against those who were unmarried and separately assessed. The new rules require both married and unmarried couples to make joint applications for working tax credit and child tax credit. This is the first time that HMRC has been concerned to calculate the joint income of unmarried couples, and it will bring sharply into focus the need to look carefully at when two individuals are required to make a joint claim. The starting point in any calculation of income for tax credits purposes is therefore to establish who the claimant is or claimants are. If two people become a couple, or a couple breaks up, then that fact must be reported to HMRC and a new claim made.

(2) *The income tax personal allowances do not apply to tax credits.* Instead, claimants are entitled to the appropriate "elements". One important effect of this, combined with the first point, is that the widespread practice of transferring income from the working partner of a couple to the non-working partner, so as to claim the maximum value from personal allowances and to minimise higher-rate tax, and so to reduce income tax, will not work to reduce income for tax credits purposes.

(3) *The taxable forms of income are not identical to those used for income tax.* They are similar, but include some additional items, including rules dealing with income foregone and income of which a person has deprived himself or herself.

(4) *Claimants are taxed on worldwide income.* This is linked to (3). Tax credits may only be claimed by those who are ordinarily resident in the UK, but they are subject to the obligation to declare their full incomes, regardless of any reliefs by way of double taxation or exemption that they might receive under the Income Tax Acts or double taxation agreements.

(5) *Claimants are usually assessed on last year's income.* The income tax rules now use the current year's income from any source for almost all current year income tax assessments. From 2007, calculations of income for both awards of, and entitlement to, tax credit purposes were based usually on the previous year's income. They were changed to a current year basis when s.7(3) applied. However, from 2013/14 that subsection has been given greater importance because rises in total income from the previous year are now taken into account if they exceed £5,000 and falls in total income are taken into account if over £2,500.

(6) *The thresholds for income tax and each tax credit are different.* There is now a single personal allowance for income tax and NI contributions for all those under 65, with a higher figure for those over 65. But there are separate thresholds for working tax credit and child tax credit, and these are not linked to income tax.

(7) *Deductions and exclusions are not identical.* Nor are specific inclusions, so the assessment of income from employment for income tax purposes will not be identical, and nor will the total income.

The drafting techniques used in these Regulations are also those of the Rewrite Project, for example in the use of signposting provisions and the use of the "command" tense of verbs in taking the user step by step through a calculation. Following this approach, reg.3 lays down in clear terms how income is to be calculated. But it is, in practice, the fifth of five questions that need to be answered to establish the relevant income of a claimant or claimants.

The questions to be decided:

2.204 (1) Who is claiming?

(SI 2002/2006) as amended

(2) IS or JSA ... or SPC?

(3) Which tax year?

(4) Are there any income changes during the tax year?

(5) What income?

The questions are as follows:

(1) Who is claiming?
Is the claim a single claim, a joint claim or a claim by a polygamous unit? The income of each claimant must be calculated.

(2) IS, JSA, SPC?
Automatic entitlement to child tax credit has yet to be introduced for those on income support and jobseeker's allowance, although it now exists for those of pensionable age receiving state pension credit instead. The 16-hour rule effectively prevents those on these benefits claiming working tax credit as well.

(3) Which tax year?
As noted above, in most cases the relevant income for tax credits is the income of the previous year not the current year income used for most income tax purposes. But attention must be paid to current income where there is a sharp increase in income between one year and the next. (This does not apply to capital gains, so will most often catch employees, as sums received from employment are seldom regarded as capital.)

(4) Are there any changes during the year?
The award of tax credit under ss.5 and 14 of the Act are by reference initially to the income of the previous year. But there may be relevant changes of circumstances that lead to a revision of the award if there is a notified change of circumstances under reg.6. The decision on entitlement is made only after the end of the tax year under s.19.

(5) What kinds of income?
This is determined by the current regulations.

CROSS-REFERENCES

The notes to each paragraph set out in full the Parts, Chapters and Section titles to all Chapters and Sections of the Taxes Act, ITEPA and Finance Acts referred to in these regulations. The regulations include cross references to a considerable number of income tax provisions, only some of which will be of more than occasional importance to tax credits assessments. In addition, as explained below, major parts of both Acts are of no relevance to tax credits. The volume contains a selection of the more important provisions from both Acts, and the cross references supplement that by noting the full title of each Chapter and Section referred to in these Regulations. 2.205

Modifications where claim made for universal credit
For the modifications to the Regulations where a person's entitlement to a tax credit was interrupted by the making of a claim for universal credit, see reg.12A of, and Schedule 1 to, the Universal Credit (Transitional Provisions) Regulations 2014 (SI 2014/1230), below in this volume. 2.206

The Tax Credits (Definition and Calculation of Income) Regulations 2002

PART I

General provisions

Citation, commencement and effect

2.207   **1.**—These Regulations may be cited as the Tax Credits (Definition and Calculation of Income) Regulations 2002 and shall come into force—
    (a) for the purpose of enabling claims to be made, on 1st August 2002;
    (b) for the purpose of enabling awards to be made, on 1st January 2003; and
    (c) for all other purposes, on 6th April 2003;
and shall have effect for the tax year beginning on 6th April 2003 and subsequent tax years.

DEFINITIONS
    "award"—see TCA 2002 s.5.
    "claim"—see TCA 2002 s.3.
    "tax year"—see reg.2.

Interpretation

2.208   **2.**—(1) In these Regulations, unless the context otherwise requires—
"the Act" means the Tax Credits Act 2002;
"the Contributions and Benefits Act" means the Social Security Contributions and Benefits Act 1992; [³...]
"the Employment Act" means the Employment and Training Act 1973 [³; and
"the Northern Ireland Contributions and Benefits Act" means the Social Security Contributions and Benefits (Northern Ireland) Act 1992.]
(2) In these Regulations except where the context otherwise requires—
"the 1992 Fund" means moneys made available from time to time by the Secretary of State for Social Security for the benefit of persons eligible for payment in accordance with the provisions of a scheme established by him on 24th April 1992 as respects England and Wales and Northern Ireland and on 10th April 1992 as respects Scotland;
[⁶"the Board" means the Commissioners for Her Majesty's Revenue and Customs";]
"child" has the meaning given in the Child Tax Credit Regulations 2002;
"claim" means a claim for child tax credit or working tax credit and "joint claim" and "single claim" shall be construed in accordance with [²section 3(8)] of the Act and "claimant" shall be construed accordingly;
[¹⁴"coronavirus" means severe acute respiratory syndrome coronavirus 2;
""coronavirus support scheme" means—
    (a) any scheme in relation to which HMRC have functions by virtue of a direction made under section 76 of the Coronavirus Act 2020 (HMRC functions);
    (b) the scheme known as the Small Business Grant Fund established in response to coronavirus;
    (c) any scheme established in the tax year 2020-2021 in response to coronavirus to support the fishing industry;

(SI 2002/2006 reg.2) as amended

   (d) the scheme known as the Retail, Hospitality and Leisure Grant Fund established in response to coronavirus;
   (e) the scheme known as the Newly Self-Employed Hardship Fund established by the Scottish Ministers in the tax year 2020-2021 in response to coronavirus; and
   (f) any other support scheme established in the tax year 2020-2021 [^{15}or 2021-2022] in response to coronavirus;]
[^{4}"couple" has the meaning given by section 3(5A) of the Act;]
[^{1}"earnings" shall be construed in accordance with section 62 of the ITEPA;]
"the Eileen Trust" means the charitable trust of that name established on 29th March 1993 out of funds provided by the Secretary of State for Social Security for the benefit of persons eligible in accordance with its provisions;
[^{1}...];
[^{5}"employment zone" means an area within Great Britain—
   (i) subject to a designation for the purposes of the Employment Zones Regulations 2003 by the Secretary of State, or
[^{7}(ii) listed in the Schedule to the Employment Zones (Allocation to Contractors) Pilot Regulations 2006,]
pursuant to section 60 of the Welfare Reform and Pensions Act 1999;]
"employment zone programme" means a programme which is—
   (a) established for one or more employment zones; and
   (b) designed to assist claimants for a Jobseeker's Allowance to obtain sustainable employment;
"family" means—
   (a) in the case of a joint claim, the [^{4}...] couple by whom the claim is made and any child or qualifying young person for whom at least one of them is responsible, in accordance with regulation 3 of the Child Tax Credit Regulations 2002; and
   (b) in the case of a single claim, the claimant and any child or qualifying young person for whom he is responsible in accordance with regulation 3 of the Child Tax Credit Regulations 2002;
"the Independent Living Fund" means the charitable trust of that name established out of funds provided by the Secretary of State for Social Services for the purpose of providing financial assistance to those persons incapacitated by or otherwise suffering from very severe disablement who are in need of such assistance to enable them to live independently;
[^{9} "the Independent Living Fund (2006)" means the Trust of that name established by a deed dated 10th April 2006 and made between the Secretary of State for Work and Pensions of the one part and Margaret Rosemary Cooper, Michael Beresford Boyall and Marie Theresa Martin of the other part;]
"the Independent Living Funds" means the Independent Living Fund, [^{9} the Independent Living (Extension) Fund, the Independent Living (1993) Fund and the Independent Living Fund (2006)]
"the Independent Living (Extension) Fund" means the trust of that name established on 25th February 1993 by the Secretary of State for Social Security and Robin Glover Wendt and John Fletcher Shepherd;
"the Independent Living (1993) Fund" means the trust of that name established on 25th February 1993 by the Secretary of State for Social Security and Robin Glover Wendt and John Fletcher Shepherd;

The Tax Credits (Definition and Calculation of Income) Regulations 2002

[⁸ "ITA" means the Income Tax Act 2007]
[¹"ITEPA" means the Income Tax (Earnings and Pensions) Act 2003;]
[⁶"ITTOIA" means the Income Tax (Trading and Other Income) Act 2005;]
"the Macfarlane (Special Payments) Trust" means the trust of that name established on 29th January 1990 partly out of funds provided by the Secretary of State for Health for the benefit of certain persons suffering from haemophilia;
"the Macfarlane (Special Payments) (No.2) Trust" means the trust of that name established on 3rd May 1991 partly out of funds provided by the Secretary of State for Health for the benefit of certain persons suffering from haemophilia and other beneficiaries;
"the Macfarlane Trust" means the charitable trust established partly out of funds provided by the Secretary of State for Health to the Haemophilia Society for the relief of poverty or distress among those suffering from haemophilia;
"the Macfarlane Trusts" means the Macfarlane Trust, the Macfarlane (Special Payments) Trust and the Macfarlane (Special Payments) (No.2) Trust;
"pensionable age" has the meaning given by the rules in paragraph 1 of Schedule 4 to the Pensions Act 1995;
"pension fund holder", in relation to a [⁵registered pension scheme], means the trustees, managers or scheme administrators of the scheme [⁵...];
[¹² "qualifying care receipts" has the meaning given to that expression by section 805 of the Income Tax (Trading and Other Income) Act 2005;]
"qualifying young person" has the meaning given in the Child Tax Credit Regulations 2002;
[⁵"registered pension scheme" has the meaning given by section 150(2) of the Finance Act 2004;]
[¹⁰ [¹³ ...]]
[⁵...]
[⁵...]
[⁶...];
[¹...];
[¹¹...]
[¹⁴"Scottish Ministers" has the meaning given by section 44(2) of the Scotland Act 1998].
"tax year" means a period beginning with the 6th April in one year and ending with 5th April in the next;
"the Taxes Act" means the Income and Corporation Taxes Act 1988;
"voluntary organisation" means a body, other than a public or local authority, the activities of which are carried on otherwise than for profit;
"war pension" has the meaning given in section 25(4) of the Social Security Act 1989.

(3) For the purposes of these Regulations, whether a person is responsible for a child or a qualifying young person is determined in accordance with regulaton 3 of the Child Tax Credit Regulations 2002.

(4) In these Regulations—
(a) a reference to a claimant's partner is a reference to a claimant's spouse [⁴or civil partner] or a person with whom the claimant lives as a spouse [⁴or civil partner]; and

(SI 2002/2006 reg.2) as amended

(b) a reference to a claimant's former partner is a reference to a claimant's former spouse [⁴or civil partner] or a person with whom the claimant has lived as a spouse [⁴or civil partner]; and
(c) a reference in these Regulations to an Extra Statutory Concession is a reference to that Concession as published by the Inland Revenue on 1st July 2002.

AMENDMENTS

1. Tax Credits (Definition and Calculation of Income) (Amendment) Regulations 2003 (SI 2003 No.732) reg.4 (April 6, 2003).
2. Tax Credits (Miscellaneous Amendments No.2) Regulations 2003 (SI 2003/2815) reg.3 (November 26, 2003).
3. Tax Credits (Miscellaneous Amendments) Regulations 2004 (SI 2004/762) reg.13 (April 6, 2004).
4. Civil Partnership Act 2004 (Tax Credits, etc.) (Consequential Amendments) Order 2005 (SI 2005/2919) art.3(2) (December 5, 2005).
5. Taxation of Pension Schemes (Consequential Amendments) Order 2006 (SI 2006/745) art.26(2) (April 6, 2006).
6. Tax Credits (Miscellaneous Amendments) Regulations 2006 (SI 2006/766) reg.7 (April 6, 2006).
7. Tax Credits (Miscellaneous Amendments) Regulations 2007 (SI 2007/824) reg.8 (April 6, 2007).
8. Tax Credits (Definition and Calculation of Income) (Amendment) Regulations 2007 (SI 2007/1305) reg.3 (May 16, 2007).
9. Independent Living Fund (2006) Order 2007 (SI 2007/2538) art.7 (October 1, 2007).
10. Tax Credits (Miscellaneous Amendments) Regulations 2010 (SI 2010/751) reg.3 (April 6, 2010).
11. Tax Credits (Miscellaneous Amendments) (No.3) Regulations 2010 (SI 2010/2914) reg.3 (December 31, 2010).
12. Tax Credits (Miscellaneous Amendments) Regulations 2011 (SI 2011/721) reg.2(2) (April 6, 2011).
13. Tax Credits and Childcare (Miscellaneous Amendments) Regulations 2018 (SI 2018/365) reg.2(2) (April 6, 2018).
14. Tax Credits (Coronavirus, Miscellaneous Amendments) Regulations 2020 (SI 2020/534) reg.3(2) (May 23, 2020).
15. Tax Credits, Childcare Payments and Childcare (Extended Entitlement) (Coronavirus and Miscellaneous Amendments) Regulations 2020 (SI 2020/1515) reg.3(2) (January 14, 2021).

GENERAL NOTE

See also the definitions in TCA 2002 ss.48 and 65 (above) and ITA 2007 Sch.4 (not included in this work).

For the definition of "earnings", see s.62(2) of ITEPA 2003 in this work (above). In *AH v HMRC (TC)* [2019] UKUT 5 (AAC), Upper Tribunal Judge Wikeley pointed out that, under s.62(2), 'earnings' is not simply a synonym for salary or wages. It also includes "any gratuity or other profit or incidental benefit of any kind obtained by the employee if it is money or money's worth" and "anything else that constitutes an emolument of the employment". Judge Wikeley's decision also contains an analysis of the key tax case law about the meaning of 'earnings'. Since the Regulations adopt the tax legislation definition of earnings, this case law is directly relevant to disputes about whether or not a particular financial item forms part of a person's earnings for tax credits purposes.

2.209

The Tax Credits (Definition and Calculation of Income) Regulations 2002

PART II

INCOME FOR THE PURPOSES OF TAX CREDITS

CHAPTER 1

General

Calculation of income of claimant

2.210   **3.**—(1) The manner in which income of a claimant, or, in the case of a joint claim, the aggregate income of the claimants, is to be calculated for a tax year for the purposes of Part I of the Act is as follows.

Step 1

Calculate and then add together—
  (a) the pension income (as defined in regulation 5(1));
  (b) the investment income (as defined in regulation 10);
  (c) the property income (as defined in regulation 11);
  (d) the foreign income (as defined in regulation 12); and
  (e) the notional income (as defined in regulation 13),
of the claimant, or, in the case of a joint claim, of the claimants.
  If the result of this step is £300 or less, it is treated as nil.
  If the result of this step is more than £300, only the excess is taken into account in the following steps.

Step 2

Calculate and then add together—
  (a) the employment income (as defined in regulation 4);
  (b) the social security income (as defined in regulation 7);
  (c) the student income (as defined in regulation 8); and
  (d) the miscellaneous income (as defined in regulation 18), of the claimant, or in the case of a joint claim, of the claimants.

Step 3

Add together the results of steps 1 and 2.

Step 4

Calculate the trading income (as defined in regulation 6) of the claimant, or in the case of a joint claim, of the claimants.
  Add the result of this step to that produced by step 3 [¹ . . .] in the year.
  If there has been a trading loss in the year, [¹ subtract] the amount of that loss from the result of step 3.
  [⁴A loss shall not be available for tax credit purposes, unless the trade was being carried on upon a commercial basis and with a view to the realisation of profits in the trade or, where the carrying on of the trade formed part of a larger undertaking, in the undertaking as a whole.]
  [²Any trading loss in the year not set off as a result of the calculations in Steps One to Four above due to an insufficiency of income may be carried

(SI 2002/2006 reg.3) as amended

forward and set off against trading income (if any) of the same trade, profession or vocation in subsequent years (taking earlier years first) for the purposes of calculation of income under this regulation.]

(2) Subject to the qualifications in the following paragraphs of this regulation, and the provisions of Part III, the result of step 4 in paragraph (1) is the income of the claimant, or, in the case of a joint claim, of the claimants, for the purposes of the Act.

(3) Income which—
  (a) arises in a territory outside the United Kingdom; and
  (b) is, for the time being, unremittable for the purposes of [⁴Chapter 4 of Part 8 of ITTOIA],
is disregarded in calculating the income of the claimant or, in the case of a joint claim, of the claimants.

(4) Paragraph (5) applies in the case of a claimant who is [¹, for income tax purposes]
  (a) resident [¹and domiciled [⁷...] in the United Kingdom; [²...]
  (b) resident [⁷...] but not domiciled in the United Kingdom; [⁷...]

(5) In the case of a person to whom this paragraph applies—
  [¹(a) any income arising outside the United Kingdom is to be taken into account, subject to any specific provision of these Regulations, regardless of the domicile or residence of the claimant; and;]
  (b) references to a sum being [¹taken into account] are to be construed as including a sum which would be taxable if he were resident [⁷...] and domiciled in the United Kingdom.

[¹(5A) Any income is to be taken into account, subject to any specific provision of these Regulations, notwithstanding the provision of any Order in Council under section 788 of the Taxes Act (double taxation agreements).]

(6) In the case of a claimant who would be chargeable to income tax but for some special exemption or immunity from income tax, income shall be calculated on the basis of the amounts which would be so chargeable but for that exemption or immunity.

[¹(6A) Income paid to a claimant in a currency other than sterling shall be converted into sterling at the average of the exchange rates applicable for the conversion of that currency into sterling in the period of 12 months [⁵ending on 31st March] in the tax year in which the income arises.]

(7) In calculating income under this Part there shall be deducted [¹...]—
  (a) [¹the amount of] any banking charge or commission payable in converting to sterling a payment of income which is made in a currency other than sterling;
  (b) [¹the grossed up amount of] any qualifying donation (within the meaning of [⁶ Chapter 2 of Part 8 of ITA (gift aid)]), made by the claimant or, in the case of a joint claim, by either or both of the claimants; [²...] [⁴...]
  [³(c) the amount of any contribution made by the claimant, or in the case of a joint claim, by either or both of the claimants to a registered pension scheme together with the amount of any tax relief due on those contributions.]
[³...]
[²(8) If—

The Tax Credits (Definition and Calculation of Income) Regulations 2002

(a) a claimant has sustained a loss in relation to a [⁴ UK property business] or an overseas property business; and
(b) the relief to which he is entitled in accordance with [⁶ section 120 of ITA (deduction of property losses from general income)] exceeds the amount of his property income or foreign income for tax credits purposes, for the year in question;

the amount of his total income for tax credit purposes, computed in accordance with the preceding provisions of this regulation, shall be reduced by the amount of the excess.

[⁴In this paragraph "UK property business" and "overseas property business" have the same meaning as they have in Chapter 2 of Part 3 of ITTOIA.]

AMENDMENTS

1. Tax Credits (Definition and Calculation of Income) (Amendment) Regulations 2003 (SI 2003/732) reg.5 (April 6, 2003).
2. Tax Credits (Miscellaneous Amendments No.2) Regulations 2003 (SI 2003/2815) reg.4 (November 26, 2003).
3. Taxation of Pension Schemes (Consequential Amendments) Order 2006 (SI 2006/745) art.26(3) (April 6, 2006).
4. Tax Credits (Miscellaneous Amendments) Regulations 2006 (SI 2006/766) reg.8 (April 6, 2006).
5. Tax Credits (Miscellaneous Amendments) Regulations 2007 (SI 2007/824) reg.9 (April 6, 2007).
6. Tax Credits (Definition and Calculation of Income) (Amendment) Regulations 2007 (SI 2007/1305) reg.4 (May 16, 2007).
7. Tax Credits (Miscellaneous Amendments) Regulations 2014 (SI 2014/658) reg.4(2)–(4) (April 6, 2014).

GENERAL NOTE

2.211 Regulation 3(1) and (2) states that there are four steps to calculating the aggregate income of a claimant or joint claimants for a tax year, but it is suggested that this would be better presented as five steps. The four steps are:
(1) Add the totals of income from sources subject to the £300 discount and deduct that discount.
(2) Add the totals from all other sources, apart from trading income.
(3) Add the totals of (1) and (2).
(4) Add to, or subtract from, the total from (3) the net income (or net loss) from trading income.

The "fifth step" is then to deduct from that sum the various general deductions, exclusions, exemptions and disregards in these regulations. These are set out in reg.3(3) (unremittable income), reg.3(7) (other general deductions), reg.9 (exempt scholarship income) and the Tables 6, 7 and 8 in reg.19 (general disregards).

Paragraph (7) is part of the "fifth step", along with para.(3). It provides for two important deductions commonly made against income for income tax purposes. The first is to allow the deduction from income for tax credits purposes of any sums given to charities within the terms of the FA 1990 s.25. That is the provision authorising the tax deduction for "gift aid" payments for all non-refundable gifts of money to charities made otherwise than by covenant, the charity being treated as receiving the sum under deduction of tax at the basic rate. The other allows deductions from total income for contributions to registered pension schemes under the FA 2004 and related provisions.

(SI 2002/2006 reg.3) as amended

Paragraphs (3)–(6) are a motley of provisions dealing with foreign elements. The combined effect of paras (4), (5), and (5A) includes all foreign income in the income to be used to calculate tax credits notwithstanding that for income tax purposes the income is excluded from a charge to income tax in the UK either because of the domicile of the taxpayer or because of a double tax agreement. It seems that para.(6) has, in part, the same aim, but it is not clear how it can override the tax exemptions applicable to diplomats and consuls under general international law and, in the UK, the Diplomatic Privileges Act 1964 and the Consular Relations Act 1968.

The amendments to paragraphs in 2014 reflect the abolition of the concept of "ordinary residence" for income tax purposes and other, minor, income tax changes.

In *JQ v HMRC (TC)* [2020] UKUT 340 (AAC) Upper Tribunal Judge Jones dismissed the claimant's appeal against a decision of the First-tier Tribunal that he was not entitled to offset against his tax credits income an asserted property loss relief under section 120(1) of the Income Tax 2007. Section 120(1) provides that a person may make a claim for property loss relief against general income where a loss "has a capital allowances connection". In deciding that the First-tier Tribunal's decision involved no error on a point of law, Judge Jones relied on the apparently undisputed evidence before the First-tier Tribunal that the claimant had not, as section 120(1) anticipates and section 3 of the Capital Allowances Act 2001 requires, made any claim in a tax return for property loss relief to be offset against an income tax liability for the relevant tax year. In any event, on that evidence, the First-tier Tribunal was bound to find that the claimant was not in fact carrying on an overseas property business during the relevant tax year. The evidence was that, during the tax year, the claimant received no income from his overseas property. The claimant's overseas property was in the nature of an investment rather than a business. Moreover, there was no evidence that the claimant incurred expenditure on plant or machinery. Section 123 of the 2007 Act defines a loss "with a capital connection" and, in doing so, expressly excludes structures and buildings allowances under Part 2A of the Capital Allowances Act 2001, so that this claimant would have needed to establish that his claimed loss involved expenditure on plant or machinery. There was no evidence that the claimant incurred expenditure on plant and machinery for his overseas property business during the relevant tax year.

CHAPTER 2

Employment income

Employment income

4.—(1) In these Regulations, "employment income" means—

(a) any [1earnings] from an office or employment received in the tax year;

(b) so much of any payment made to a claimant in that year in respect of expenses as is chargeable to income tax [1by virtue of section 62 or section 72 of ITEPA];

(c) [1the cash equivalent of] any non-cash voucher received by the claimant in that year and chargeable to income tax under [1section 87 of ITEPA] [14 or, where there is an optional remuneration arrangement, the relevant amount];

2.212

(d) [¹the cash equivalent of] any credit-token received by the claimant in that year and chargeable to income tax under [¹section 94 of ITEPA] [¹⁴ or, where such a credit-token is provided pursuant to an optional remuneration arrangement, the relevant amount;]

(e) [¹the cash equivalent of] any cash voucher received by the claimant in that year and chargeable to income tax under [¹section 81 of ITEPA] [¹⁴ or, where there is an optional remuneration arrangement, the relevant amount,];

[¹(f) any amount chargeable to tax under Chapter 3 of Part VI of ITEPA;]

(g) so much of a payment of statutory sick pay, received by the claimant during the year, as is subject to income tax [¹by virtue of section 660 of ITEPA;]

[¹³ (h) the amount (if any) by which a payment of statutory maternity pay, statutory paternity pay, statutory shared parental pay [¹⁷, statutory parental bereavement pay or statutory adoption pay] exceeds £100 per week;]

(i) any amount charged to income tax for that year [¹under section 120 or section 149 of ITEPA;]

[¹⁴ (ia) the relevant amount in cases where a car is made available to the claimant or a member of the claimant's family pursuant to an optional remuneration arrangement where the car's CO2 emissions figure exceeds 75 grams per kilometre;]

[¹(j) any sum to which section 225 of ITEPA applies;]

(k) any amount paid in that year by way of strike pay to the claimant as a member of a trade union;

[²(l) any amount charged to income tax for that year under Part 7 of ITEPA.]

[⁶(m) any amount paid to a person serving a custodial sentence or remanded in custody awaiting trial or sentence, for work done while serving the sentence or remanded in custody.]

For the purposes of this paragraph, references to the receipt of a payment of any description are references to its receipt by or on behalf of the claimant, or in the case of a joint claim of either of the claimants, in any part of the world.

This paragraph is subject to the following qualifications.

(2) Employment income does not include pension income.

[³(2A) [⁵ . . .]

(2B) [⁵ . . .]

[²(3) This paragraph applies if (apart from section 64 of ITEPA) the same benefit would give rise to two amounts ("A" and "B")—

(a) "A" being an amount of earnings from a claimant's employment as defined in section 62 of ITEPA, and

(b) "B" being an amount to be treated as earnings under any provision of Chapter 10 of Part 3 of ITEPA.

In such a case, the amount to be taken into account in computing the claimant's employment income is the greater of A and B, and the lesser amount shall be disregarded.]

(4) In calculating employment income, the payments and benefits listed in Table 1 shall be disregarded [¹⁴ except where the payment or benefit is provided pursuant to optional remuneration arrangements and is neither a special case benefit nor an excluded benefit].

(SI 2002/2006 reg. 4) as amended

Table 1. Payments [¹and benefits] disregarded in the calculation of employment income

1. Any payment in respect of qualifying removal expenses, or the provision of any qualifying removal benefit, within the meaning of [¹Chapter 7 of Part 4 of ITEPA].

[¹2A. The payment or reimbursement of expenses incurred in the provision of transport to a disabled employee (as defined in section 246(4) of ITEPA) by his employer, if no liability to income tax arises in respect of that payment or reimbursement (as the case may be) by virtue of section 246 of ITEPA.

2B. The provision to a disabled employee (as defined in section 246(4) of ITEPA) by his employer of a car, the provision of fuel for the car, or the reimbursement of expenses incurred in connection with the car, if no liability to income tax arises in respect of that provision or reimbursement (as the case may be) by virtue of section 247 of ITEPA.

2C. The payment or reimbursement of expenses incurred on transport, if no liability to income tax arises in respect of that payment or reimbursement (as the case may be) by virtue of section 248 of ITEPA.]

3. Travel facilities provided for the claimant as a member of the naval, military or air forces of the Crown for the purpose of going on, or returning from, leave.

[⁶3A. The payment [¹²under a Royal Warrant made under section 333 of the Armed Forces Act 2006] of an operational allowance to a member of Her Majesty's forces in respect of service in an operational area specified by the Secretary of State for Defence.]

[⁷3B. A payment designated [¹²under a Royal Warrant made under section 333 of the Armed Forces Act 2006] as Council Tax Relief and made by the Secretary of State for Defence to a member of Her Majesty's forces.]

[¹¹3C. The payment under a Royal Warrant made under section 333 of the Armed Forces Act 2006, of the Continuity of Education Allowance to or in respect of members of the armed forces of the Crown during their employment under the Crown or after their deaths.]

[¹⁵3D. Any accommodation allowance which is payable out of public revenue for, or towards, the costs of accommodation to, or in respect of, a member of the armed forces of the Crown, providing that the payment meets any conditions which have been specified in regulations made by the Treasury.]

4. Payment or reimbursement of expenses in connection with the provision for, or use by, the claimant as a person holding an office or employment of a car-parking space at or near his place of work.

5. Any benefit or non-cash voucher provided to the claimant, or to any member of his family or household, [¹in respect of which no liability to income tax arises by virtue of Chapter 5 of Part 4 of ITEPA.]

6. Any payment of incidental overnight expenses [¹in respect of which no liability to income tax arises by virtue of section 240 of ITEPA.]

[¹7. Food, drink and mess allowances for the armed forces and training allowances payable to members of the reserve forces in respect of which no liability to income tax arises by virtue of section 297 or 298 of ITEPA.]

8. The value of meal vouchers issued to the claimant as an employee [¹if section 89 of ITEPA applies to the vouchers.]

9. Any cash payment received by the claimant as a miner in lieu of free coal, or the provision of the coal itself, [¹in respect of which no liability to income tax arises by virtue of section 306 of ITEPA.]

10. An award made to the claimant as a director or employee by way of a testimonial to mark long service [¹if, or to the extent that, no liability to income tax arises in respect of it by virtue of section 323 of ITEPA.]

11. Payment of a daily subsistence allowance [¹in respect of which no liability to income tax arises by virtue of section 304 of ITEPA.].

[¹**11A.** The payment or reimbursement of reasonable expenses incurred by an employee who has a permanent workplace at an offshore installation, on transfer transport, related accommodation and subsistence or local transport, if no liability to income tax arises in respect of that payment or reimbursement (as the case may be) by virtue of section 305 of ITEPA.

For the purposes of this item, expressions which are defined in section 305 of ITEPA have the same meaning here as they do there.

11B. Payment of an allowance to a person in employment under the Crown in respect of which no liability to income tax arises by virtue of section 299 of ITEPA.

11C. The payment or reimbursement to an employee of any sum in connection with work-related training, or individual learning account training (as respectively defined in sections 251 and 256 of ITEPA) if no liability to income tax arises in respect of that payment or reimbursement (as the case may be) by virtue of any provision of Chapter 4 of Part 4 of ITEPA.

11D. The provision for an employee of a non-cash voucher or a credit-token, to the extent that liability to income tax does not arise in respect of that voucher or credit-token (as the case may be), under Chapter 4 of [²Part 3 of ITEPA, by virtue of any provision of Chapter 6 of Part 4 of ITEPA.]

11E. The provision for an employee of free or subsidised meal vouchers or tokens (within the meaning of section 317(5) of ITEPA), if no liability to income tax arises in respect of that provision by virtue of section 317 of ITEPA.]

[⁶**11F.** The provision of one mobile telephone for an employee in respect of which no liability to income tax arises by virtue of section 319 of ITEPA.]

12. An award made to the claimant under a Staff Suggestion Scheme, if the conditions specified in [¹sections 321 and 322 of ITEPA [³are satisfied].]

13. Travelling and subsistence allowances paid to or on behalf of the claimant by his employer [¹in respect of which no liability to income tax arises by virtue of section 245 of ITEPA.]

14. Any gift consisting of goods, or a voucher or token to obtain goods, [¹in respect of which no liability to income tax arises by virtue of section 270 or 324 of ITEPA.]

[¹**14A.** Any payment or reimbursement of expenses incurred in connection with an employment-related asset transfer (as defined in section 326(2) of ITEPA), if no liability to income tax arises in respect of that

(SI 2002/2006 reg.4) as amended

payment or reimbursement (as the case may be) by virtue of section 326 of ITEPA.

14B. Any payment of expenses incurred by an employee in connection with a taxable car if no liability to income tax arises in respect of the payment by virtue of section 239(2) of ITEPA.]

[²**14C.** The discharge of any liability of an employee in connection with a taxable car if no liability to income tax arises by virtue of section 239(1) of ITEPA.

14D. A benefit connected with a taxable car if no liability to income tax arises by virtue of section 239(4) of ITEPA.]

15. A cash voucher, non-cash voucher or credit-token to the extent that it is used by the recipient for the provision of childcare, the costs of which if borne by the recipient would be relevant childcare charges within the meaning of regulation 14 of the Working Tax Credit (Entitlement and Maximum Rate) Regulations 2002.

[³**16.** A payment made by the Department for Work and Pensions under section 2 of the Employment Act—
  (a) by way of In-Work Credit [⁸, Better Off In-Work Credit], Job Grant or Return to Work Credit, [⁸ . . .]
  (b) under the Employment Retention and Advancement Scheme or the Working Neighbourhoods Pilot.]
[⁸ (c) under the City Strategy Pathfinder Pilots,
  (d) by way of an In-Work Emergency Discretion Fund payment pursuant to arrangements made by the Secretary of State, [⁹ . . .]
  (e) by way of an Up-front Childcare Fund payment pursuant to arrangements made by the Secretary of State [⁹, or
  (f) under the Future Capital pilot scheme.].]

[⁵**16A.** [¹⁶ . . .]]
[⁸**16B.** [¹⁶ . . .]]

[²**17.** The payment or reimbursement of reasonable additional household expenses incurred by an employee who works from home, within the meaning of section 316A of ITEPA.

18. The payment or reimbursement of retraining course expenses within the meaning of the section 311 of ITEPA.]

[⁴**19.** Provision of computer equipment in respect of which no liability to income tax arises by virtue of section 320 of ITEPA.]

[⁸**20.** Pay As You Earn (PAYE) settlement agreements made under Part 6 of the Income Tax (PAYE) Regulations ("the PAYE Regulations") 2003.

For the purposes of this item the special arrangements under regulation 141 of the PAYE Regulations also apply.]

[¹¹**21.** The payment or reimbursement of a fee within section 326A(1) of ITEPA(3) (fees relating to vulnerable persons' monitoring schemes).]

[¹² **22.** The payment of a qualifying bonus within section 312A of ITEPA (limited exemption for qualifying bonus payments).]

(5) From the amount of employment income, calculated in accordance with the preceding provisions of this regulation, there shall be deducted the amount of any deduction permitted in calculating [¹calculating earnings by virtue of any provision of sections [²231 to 232,] 336–344, or s.346, 347, 351, 352, 362, 363, 367, 368, 370, 371, 373, 374, 376, 377 or 713 of ITEPA].

[¹⁴ (6) For the purposes of this regulation, a benefit is provided pursuant to optional remuneration arrangements if it is provided under either—
(a) arrangements under which, in return for the benefit, the claimant gives up the right (or a future right) to receive an amount of earnings within Chapter 1 of Part 3 of ITEPA ("Type A arrangements"), or
(b) arrangements (other than Type A arrangements) under which the claimant agrees to be provided with the benefit rather than an amount of earnings within Chapter 1 of Part 3 of ITEPA.

(7) The relevant amount, in relation to a benefit provided pursuant to an optional remuneration arrangement, means the amount treated for income tax purposes as earnings from employment for the tax year by reason of the benefit being provided pursuant to optional remuneration arrangements.

(8) A benefit is a special case benefit if it is exempted from a charge to income tax by any of the following provisions in ITEPA—
(a) section 289A (exemption for paid or reimbursed expenses),
(b) section 289D (exemption for other benefits),
(c) section 308B (independent advice in respect of conversions and transfers of pension scheme benefits),
(d) section 312A (limited exemption for qualifying bonus payments),
(e) section 317 (subsidised meals),
(f) section 320C (recommended medical treatment), and
(g) section 323A (trivial benefits provided by employers).

(9) A benefit is an excluded benefit if—
(a) it is exempted from a charge to income tax by any of the following provisions in ITEPA—
  (i) section 239 (payments and benefits connected with taxable cars and vans and exempt heavy goods vehicles),
  (ii) section 244 (cycles and cyclist's safety equipment),
  (iii) section 266(2)(c) (non-cash voucher regarding entitlement to exemption under section 244),
  (iv) section 270A (limited exemption for qualifying childcare vouchers),
  (v) section 308 (exemption of contribution to registered pension scheme),
  (vi) section 308A (exemption of contribution to overseas pension scheme),
  (vii) section 309 (limited exemptions for statutory redundancy payments),
  (viii) section 310 (counselling and other outplacement services),
  (ix) section 311 (retraining courses),
  (x) section 318 (childcare: exemption for employer-provided care), or
  (xi) section 318A (childcare: limited exemption for other care), or
(b) it is a payment, or reimbursement of costs incurred by the claimant, in respect of pension advice and that payment or reimbursement is exempt from a charge to income tax under Chapter 9 of Part 4 of ITEPA.

(10) A car's CO2 emissions figure is to be determined in accordance with sections 133 to 138 of ITEPA (cars: the appropriate percentage).]

(SI 2002/2006 reg.4) as amended

AMENDMENTS

1. Tax Credits (Definition and Calculation of Income) (Amendment) Regulations 2003 (SI 2003/732) reg.6 (April 6, 2003).
2. Tax Credits (Miscellaneous Amendments No.2) Regulations 2003 (SI 2003/2815) reg.5 (November 26, 2003).
3. Tax Credits (Miscellaneous Amendments) Regulations 2004 (SI 2004/762) reg.14 (April 6, 2004).
4. Tax Credits (Miscellaneous Amendments No.3) Regulations 2004 (SI 2004/2663) reg.2 (November 3, 2004).
5. Tax Credits (Miscellaneous Amendments) Regulations 2006 (SI 2006/766) reg.9 (April 6, 2006).
6. Tax Credits (Miscellaneous Amendments) Regulations 2007 (SI 2007/824) reg.10 (April 6, 2007).
7. Tax Credits (Miscellaneous Amendments) Regulations 2008 (SI 2008/604) reg.2(2) (April 1, 2008).
8. Tax Credits (Miscellaneous Amendments) (No.2) Regulations 2008 (SI 2008/2169) reg.4 (September 1, 2008).
9. Tax Credits (Miscellaneous Amendments)(No.2) Regulations 2009 (SI 2009/2887) regs 5 and 6 (November 21, 2009).
10. Tax Credits (Miscellaneous Amendments) Regulations 2012 (SI 2012/848) reg.3(1) and (2) (April 6, 2012).
11. Tax Credits (Miscellaneous Amendments) Regulations 2014 (SI 2014/658) reg.4(5) (April 6, 2014).
12. Child Benefit (General) and Tax Credits (Miscellaneous Amendments) Regulations 2014 (SI 2014/2924) reg.5 (November 28, 2014).
13. Social Security and Tax Credits (Miscellaneous Amendments) Regulations 2015 (SI 2015/175) reg.7 (April 5, 2015).
14. Tax Credits (Definition and Calculation of Income) (Amendment) Regulations 2017 (SI 2017/ 396) reg.3 (April 6, 2017).
15. Tax Credits and Childcare (Miscellaneous Amendments) Regulations 2018 (SI 2018/365) reg.2(3) (April 6, 2018).
16. Tax Credits, Child Benefit and Childcare Payments (Miscellaneous Amendments) Regulations 2019 (SI 2019/364) reg.3(2) (March 21, 2019).
17. Parental Bereavement Leave and Pay (Consequential Amendments to Subordinate Legislation) Regulations 2020 (SI 2020/354) reg.12(2) (April 6, 2020).

CROSS-REFERENCES

The regulation adopts for tax credits purposes the following chapters and sections of ITEPA, all relating to employment income:

Pt 3: Employment income: Earnings and benefits, etc. treated as earnings
    s.62   Earnings
Pt 3: Ch.4: Taxable benefit: vouchers and credit-tokens
    s.72   Sums in respect of expenses treated as earnings
    s.81   Benefit of cash voucher treated as earnings
    s.87   Benefit of non-cash voucher treated as earnings
    s.89   Reduction for meal vouchers
    s.94   Benefit of credit-token treated as earnings
Pt 3: Ch.6: Taxable benefits: cars, vans and related vehicles
    s.120   Benefit of car treated as earnings
    s.149   Benefit of car fuel treated as earnings
Pt 3: Ch.10: Taxable benefits: residual liability to charge
    s.201   Employment-related benefits
    s.211   Special rules for scholarships: introduction
Pt 3: Ch.11: Taxable benefits: exclusion of lower-paid employments
Pt 3: Ch.12: Payments treated as earnings

The Tax Credits (Definition and Calculation of Income) Regulations 2002

	s.225	Payments for restrictive covenants

Pt 4: Employment income: exemptions

	s.239	Payments and benefits connected with taxable cars and vans and exempt heavy goods vehicles
	s.240	Incidental overnight expenses and benefits
	s.245	Travelling and subsistence during public transport strikes
	s.246	Transport between work and home for disabled employees
	s.247	Provision of cars for disabled employees
	s.248	Transport home: late-night working and failure of car-sharing arrangements

Pt 4: Ch.4: Exemptions: education and training

	s.251	Meaning of "work-related training"
	s.256	Meaning of "individual learning account training"

Pt 4: Ch.5: Exemptions; recreational benefits
Pt 4: Ch.6: Exemptions: non-cash vouchers and credit-tokens

	s.270	Exemptions of small gifts of vouchers and tokens from third parties

Pt 4: Ch.7: Exemptions: removal benefits and expenses

	s.297	Armed forces' food, drink and mess allowances
	s.298	Reserve and auxiliary forces' training allowances
	s.299	Crown employees' foreign service allowances
	s.304	Experts seconded to the European Commission
	s.305	Offshore oil and gas workers: mainland transfers
	s.306	Miners, etc.: coal and allowances in lieu of coal
	s.317	Subsidised meals
	s.321	Suggestion awards
	s.322	Suggestion awards: "the permitted maximum"
	s.323	Long service awards
	s.324	Small gifts from third parties
	s.326	Expenses incidental to transfer of a kind not normally met by transferor

Pt 5: Employment income: deductions allowed from earnings

	s.336	Deductions for expenses: the general rule
	s.337	Travel in performance of duties
	s.338	Travel for necessary attendance
	s.339	Meaning of "workplace" and "permanent workplace"
	s.340	Travel between group employments
	s.341	Travel at start and finish of overseas employment
	s.342	Travel between employments where duties performed abroad
	s.343	Deduction for professional membership fees
	s.344	Deduction for annual subscriptions
	s.346	Deduction for employee liabilities
	s.347	Payments made after leaving employment
	s.351	Expenses of ministers of religion
	s.352	Limited deduction for agency fees paid by entertainers
	s.362	Deductions where non-cash voucher provided
	s.363	Deductions where credit-token provided
	s.367	Fixed sum deductions for repairing and maintaining work equipment
	s.368	Fixed sum deductions from earnings payable out of public revenue
	s.370	Travel costs and expenses where duties performed abroad: employee's travel
	s.371	Travel costs and expenses where duties performed abroad: visiting spouse's or child's travel
	s.373	non-domiciled employee's travel costs and expenses where duties performed in United Kingdom

s.374	Non-domiciled employee's spouse's or child's travel costs and expenses where duties performed in United Kingdom
s.376	Foreign accommodation and subsistence costs and expenses (overseas employments)
s.377	Costs and expenses in respect of personal security assets and sevices

Pt 6: Ch.3: Payments and benefits on termination of employment
    s.660   Taxable benefits; United Kingdom benefits: Table A

Pt 12: Payroll giving
    s.713   Donations to charity: payroll deduction scheme

General Note

This regulation defines "employment income" for the purposes of reg.3. Although the result may be obvious in most cases, four questions have to be asked to set the context of a tax credits calculation of employment income when regard is had to a particular source of income:

What income is relevant?
What exemptions and deductions apply?
Whose income is it?
When is the income brought into calculation?

These are discussed in turn. The same pattern is followed in the notes on other regulations.

What income is relevant? The scope of ITEPA and reg.4

In marginal cases it is always necessary to ask both if an income-generating activity is employment, self-employment or something else, and what earnings come from any employment, as against any other source.

Employment and self-employment

The common context of a dispute about whether an activity is or is not an employment is the contention by the individual concerned that he or she is self-employed. This issue is discussed in the general note to reg.6 below. "Office" used to be a separate provision in the old Sch.E, reflecting the antiquity of the phraseology used. ITEPA s.5 now relegates the status of office-holders (rightly in terms of relative importance) to a secondary status in the legislation. It also codifies the common law definition of "office". For all tax credits purposes, as for all ITEPA purposes, "employee" is to be read as including office holders, and "being employed" includes holding an office. "Office" is now defined (in words adopted from the income tax case of *GWR v Bater* [1920] 3 K.B. 266) as including "any position which has an existence independent of the person who holds it and may be filled by successive holders". For a discussion of that in the context of the borderline between holding an office and being self-employed see *Edwards v Clinch* [1982] A.C. 845.

Employment income

ITEPA deals with the income taxation of employment income in Pts 1–8 of the Act. For the structure of those Parts, see s.3 of ITEPA, and for the main charge to tax, see s.6. As can be seen from the list of cross-references, the policy and drafting approaches taken for the purposes of calculating employment income for tax credits purposes are to select from the provisions of those parts (ss.1–564), rather than simply to adopt the whole code, or those parts of the code felt appropriate. TCTM04101 directs HMRC officers to "Note that, although based on income tax law, not all of the additional rules for income chargeable to tax as employment income have been included in the tax credit employment income rules", and "not all of the general exemptions and reliefs from inclusion as income chargeable as employment income have been included …". This will also apply to ITEPA. The only major part of the code omitted as a whole is Pt 7 (Employment income:

2.213

2.214

2.215

2.216

share-related income and exemptions—ss.417–554), although Pt 8 (relating to former employees) is also excluded. Elsewhere, close attention has to be paid to those charges and exemptions that are included (as listed in the cross-reference list derived from reg.3) and those that are excluded.

So, for example, while most sections in Pt 3 (Employment Income: earnings and benefits etc treated as earnings) are adopted, Ch.5 (taxable benefits: living accommodation) is not, nor is Ch.7 (taxable benefits: loans). Similarly, while most of the sections in Pt 4 (Employment income: exemptions) are allowed also as exemptions for tax credits purposes, again the approach has been to select those that are applied and those that are not. The same is true of Pt 5 (Employment income: deductions allowed from earnings). This reflects in part an assessment of the provisions that are not relevant (e.g. Pt 4, Ch.10 (exemptions on termination of employment)) are excluded as not relevant either to working tax credit or to child tax credit, but that does not always appear to explain the omission. For example, the exemption for subsidised meals in s.317 is applied, but not the exemption for care for children in s.318.

The resulting picture is one of some complexity, because one cannot simply adopt the income tax assessment of all employees for tax credits without looking through at least some of them to see on which sections of ITEPA the charge to tax is based or the exemption or deduction is claimed. In any case, other than the most straightforward, it may therefore be necessary to look at the breakdown of any charge to tax not based simply on earnings and the usual expenses and deductions. That also means that the approach of adopting a figure from the P45 or P60 supplied to an employee at the end of an employment or the end of a tax year may not be enough in those cases. While this might sound an over-exact approach to the calculation of income, it has to be borne in mind that the effective value of any charge or exemption for tax credit purposes is, at the margin, 41 per cent of the amount charged or claimed. So, a failure to allow a deduction for a £150 expense (which, if deductible at the basic rate of income tax, will have in effect cost the employee not £150 but £117) will "cost" the employee £61 in lost tax credits, or half the actual cost to the employee of the amount for which the deduction is claimed.

To follow that point with a relevant example, it would seem from the exclusion of s.317 that a claimant for WTC may claim for child care charges if paid by the employee, but is liable to have the value of the advantage of employer-provided child care taken into account as income for tax credits purposes although, of course, the employee will not be paying for, and therefore not able to claim for, that provision. However, this depends how the employer provides the advantage. If the employer provides child care through the mechanism of providing the employee with a cash voucher, non-cash voucher or credit-token, the exclusion from calculation of that value by Table 1, Item 15, is broader than the income tax exclusion. As the working tax credit child care element is not itself taxable to income tax (Taxes Act s.617A), the justification for this mismatch is not clear.

Differences between income tax assessments and tax credit calculations of employment income

2.217 The only full way of noting the differences between total net (i.e. after deductions) employment income for income tax purposes and for tax credits purposes is by precise reference to individual provisions in ITEPA. This must cover the ITEPA sections included in, and excluded from, reg.4 together with those provisions that are included in reg.4 but not by reference to specific provisions in ITEPA. Cross-references from reg.4 are not assisted by the reenactment of the employment income provisions since the regulation was drafted, as the previous drafting order of the regulation has been lost. As ITEPA is an immediately contemporary codification of employment income taxation, no reference for 2003–04 need be made to any other provision. In future years, it may be assumed that changes will, where appropriate, be made in parallel.

(SI 2002/2006 reg.4) as amended

The full list of sections of ITEPA included by cross reference is set out above, and from that the obvious gaps can be identified. There are no differences with regard to cash earnings or equivalent (see ss.62 and 72 of ITEPA). But only some parts of the Pt 3 provisions on taxable benefits apply. Chapter 3 (expense payments), Ch.4 (vouchers and credit-tokens), Ch.6 (cars, vans and related benefits) and Ch.10 (residual liability) apply, but no part of Ch.5 (living accommodation), Ch.7 (loans), Ch.8 (notional loans in respect of acquisition of shares), or Ch.9 (disposals of shares for more than market value) apply. And of the six specific payments treated as earnings by Ch.12, only one (restrictive covenants under s.225) is expressly brought into the calculation.

Three kinds of income only are mentioned in reg.4 that are not related directly to specific provisions in ITEPA. Regulation 4(1)(h) requires inclusion of only the excess of statutory maternity pay over £100. For income tax purposes the sum is fully taxable. Regulation 4(1)(k) requires the inclusion of strike pay, whether or not that is otherwise taxable under this or any other head of income. These both reflect social security rules rather than income tax rules. Regulation 4(1)(m) adds prisoners' earnings.

What exemptions and deductions apply?
The exclusions from para.(4) are far harder to summarise. Part 4 deals with exemptions. Chapter 1 deals with general exemptions rules. Of the specific rules, Ch.2 (mileage allowances and passenger payments) is not within the scope of tax credits, and nor are many of the specific exemptions related to transport, travel and subsistence in Ch.3. Of ss.237–248 in that Chapter, only ss.239, 240 and 245–8 are permitted exclusions for tax credits calculations. Chapter 4 (education and training) exemptions are allowed, as are Ch.5 (recreational benefits) and Ch.7 (removal expenses). However, the exemptions in Ch.8 (special kinds of employees) and Ch.11 (miscellaneous exemptions) are included on a selected basis only. In part, this selection excludes exemptions related to foreign elements, and to living accommodation (the benefit of which is excluded from the calculation of income), and so reflects the broader policy of the definition of relevant income. But there is no substitute in this Part of the Act for a detailed comparison of individual provisions.

2.218

There are only four groups of exemptions mentioned in reg.4 without express reference to ITEPA provisions. In the Table, Items 3, 3A and 3B (forces' payments) are defined broadly rather than in terms of s.296 of ITEPA, which is to the same effect. Item 4 (parking) is also broader than the equivalent s.237. Likewise, Item 15 (cash vouchers, etc.) is broader than ss.266–267. Items 16, 16A and 16B are tax-free public–funded payments.

By comparison, the deductions rules incorporated in para.(5) by section number follow closely the equivalent rules in Pt 5 of ITEPA, with only minor omissions. The differences are restricted largely to foreign issues or irrelevant categories of deduction, such as those related to (non-included) living accommodation.

TCTM confirms the HMRC view that most of the provisions in this regulation "mirror" or "are identical with" the equivalent ITEPA provisions. The guidance is to apply the same considerations for tax credits calculations in those cases as for income tax on employment income (and there are specific cross-references to the Inspectors Manual on employment income). It may in general be thought that the tax credits appeal authorities and tax appeal authorities would also strive to a common approach, as it may be predicted that that is the approach that superior courts would take if asked to consider the same rules in the different contexts.

In practice, HMRC relies on the information given by claimants to decide on any exemptions or deductions. If a claimant does not claim any expenses, then they will not usually be considered. And it will usually be too late to ask for them to be taken into account on an appeal, as the three-month rule applies to these changes as it does to all other aspects of a claim. See *CTC/2113/2006*.

The Tax Credits (Definition and Calculation of Income) Regulations 2002

Whose income is it?

2.219   This is rarely in issue in a tax credits context. One of the few practical problems arises where income is shared between husband and wife, but the joint claimant rules render that irrelevant here. The identity of the income tax payer, applying here also, is set out in ITEPA s.13. The taxable person, and therefore the person whose income it is for tax credits purposes, is the person to whose employment the earnings relate.

When is the income brought into calculation?

2.220   The employment income to be calculated for tax credits is the income "received by the claimant . . . in" or "paid to" the claimant in the tax year in question: para.(1). That tax year will either be the current year or the previous year, as determined under s.7(3) of the TCA 2002. The income for a tax year is therefore the income, in that sense, of the year. This is consistent with the general income tax rules for assessment on a current year basis. ITEPA s.19 provides for taxation to be based on the "net taxable earnings from an employment in the year". It is calculated when received, not when earned. That is a question of fact. This may be important for bonuses and other non-regular payments. In practice, that is also how the PAYE system operates.

AH v HMRC (TC) [2019] UKUT 5 (AAC) concerned sums paid to a claimant in settlement of an employment claim. The issue was whether the sums were earnings in the form of employment income or capital. A draft settlement agreement provided for the NHS employer to pay the appellant £16,000 within 14 days. However, neither party signed the draft agreement and it was not put into effect. A subsequent agreement provided for the employer to both make payments relating to salary deductions during the period July 2014 to July 2015 and employ the appellant on a fixed term contract. Under the agreement, two payments of £3,000 were to be made in August 2016 and March 2017. The fixed term contract was to run from August 1, 2016 to March 31, 2018. The agreement also provided for the employer to pay the appellant £500 per month for the duration of the fixed term contract. Before the fixed term had expired, in July 2017 the employer offered to pay the appellant £4,500 (the remaining sums due under the fixed term contract) and proposed that the fixed term contract be terminated by mutual consent. All that came to pass; the appellant's fixed term employment contract was terminated.

Subsequently, the appellant explained that the original draft settlement agreement could not proceed due to HM Treasury Rules that generally prevent NHS bodies from entering into settlements that provide for compensation exceeding £10,000. The subsequent agreement was designed, according to the appellant, as a means of compensating him the £16,000 due but in a manner that would not breach HM Treasury Rules.

The appellant made a tax credits claim for 2016/17. HMRC included within the appellant's earnings the two lump sum compensation payments of £3,000 and the monthly payments of £500 provided for under the appellant's fixed term contract. The appellant argued that none of these payments should be included within his earnings. The First-tier Tribunal dismissed the appellant's appeal against HMRC's decision holding that the payments constituted employment income for 2016/17.

Before the Upper Tribunal, the appellant argued that the payments in question were not earnings from an employment. Deciding the issue on the merits, the Upper Tribunal disagreed. Both the two lump sum payments and the monthly payments were undoubtedly earnings from an employment. That meant the appellant's only possible means of success was by showing that the agreement with the NHS employer was a sham, applying the test in *Snook v London & West Riding Investments Ltd* [1967] 2 QB 786, namely whether this was a case in which "acts done or documents executed by the parties to the 'sham' . . . are intended by them to give to third parties or to the court the appearance of creating between the parties legal rights and obligations different from the actual legal rights and obligations (if any) which the parties intend to create".

(SI 2002/2006 reg.4) as amended

In relation to the two lump sum payments, it was clear that the agreement reflected what both parties had objectively agreed. To this extent, the agreement was clearly not a sham. The monthly payments were less clear-cut. The appellant's case was that he did no real work for the NHS body and the purpose of the monthly payments was simply to get around HM Treasury settlement limits. However, Judge Wikeley disagreed. The fact that the post to which the fixed term contract related was unadvertised was neither here nor there. Similarly, the fact that the appellant, as a clinician, was commissioned to provide IT services did not show that the agreement failed to reflect the parties' objective agreement. The appellant argued that he did no actual work, although he conceded that he attended a single meeting. But, even if the meeting was left out of account, the appellant's argument did not work: "the position in law is that a contract of employment does not require actual service by an employee; rather, it presupposes that the employee is ready and willing to serve, as shown by *Cresswell v Inland Revenue Board* [1984] ICR 508". And, finally, had the agreement failed to reflect the parties' objective agreement, in relation to the monthly payments, there would have been no need to terminate it early. The appellant failed to establish that the agreement failed to reflect that which the parties had objectively agreed. He could not therefore show it was a sham. The Upper Tribunal dismissed the appellant's appeal against HMRC's decision.

CHAPTER 3

Pension income

Pension income

5.—[¹(1) In these Regulations, except where the context otherwise require, "pension income" means— 2.221
   (a) any pension to which section 577 or 629 of ITEPA applies;
   (b) any pension to which section 569 of ITEPA applies;
   (c) any voluntary annual payment to which section 633 of ITEPA applies;
[²(d) any pension, annuity or income withdrawal to which section 579A of ITEPA applies;
   (e) any unauthorised member payments to which section 208(2)(a) or (b) of the Finance Act 2004 applies;]
   (f) any periodical payment to which section 619 of ITEPA applies;
[². . .]
[². . .]
[². . .]
[². . .]
[²(k) any annuity paid under a retirement annuity contract to which Chapter 9 of Part 9 of ITEPA applies;]
   (l) any annuity to which section 609, 610 or 611 of ITEPA applies;
[⁴ . . .]
[³(n) any social security lump sum to which section 7 of the Finance Act 2005 applies; and
   (o) any lump sum to which section 636B or 636C of ITEPA applies.]
   (2) In calculating the amount of a person's pension income there shall be disregarded any [¹payment or benefit mentioned] in Column 1 of Table 2 to the extent specified in the corresponding entry in Column 2.

The Tax Credits (Definition and Calculation of Income) Regulations 2002

Table 2. [¹Pensions, other payments and benefits] disregarded in the calculation of pension income

1. Payment	2. Extent of disregard
1. A wounds pension or disability pension to which [¹section 641 of ITEPA] applies.	So much of the payment as is disregarded by virtue of [¹section 641 of ITEPA].
2. An annuity or additional pension payable to a holder of the Victoria Cross, George Cross or any other decoration mentioned in [¹section 638 of ITEPA].	The whole of the annuity or additional pension and, if both are payable, the whole of both such annuity and additional pension.
3. A pension or allowance to which [¹section 639 of ITEPA] applies.	[¹The amount of the pension or allowance.]
4. A pension or allowance by reason of payment of which a pension or allowance specified in [¹section 639 of ITEPA] is withheld or abated.	[¹The amount treated as falling within section 639 of ITEPA by virtue of section 640(2) of that Act.]
5. [⁵. . .]	
6. A mobility supplement, or a payment in respect of attendance, paid in conjunction with a war pension.	The amount of the supplement or payment.
7. [⁵. . .]	
8. A pension awarded at the supplementary rate under article 27(3) of the Personal Injuries (Civiliansw) Scheme 1983.	The amount for the time being specified in paragraph 1(c) of Schedule 4 to the Scheme.
9. A pension awarded on retirement through disability caused by injury on duty or by a work-related illness.	[¹The exempt amount of the pension calculated in accordance with section 644(3) of ITEPA.]
[¹**10.** A lump sum on which no liability to income tax arises by virtue of [² section 636A of ITEPA].	The amount of the lump sum.
11. Coal or smokeless fuel provided as mentioned in section 646(1) of ITEPA, or an allowance in lieu of such provision.	The amount on which no liability to income tax arises by virtue of that section.]

[¹(3) From the amount of pension income, calculated in accordance with the preceding provisions of this regulation, there shall be deducted any amount deductible for income tax purposes in computing pension income (as defined in ITEPA) under section 713 of that Act.]

(SI 2002/2006 reg.4) as amended

AMENDMENTS

1. Tax Credits (Definition and Calculation of Income) (Amendment) Regulations 2003 (SI 2003/732) reg.7 (April 6, 2003).
2. Taxation of Pension Schemes (Consequential Amendments) Order 2006 (SI 2006/745) art.26(4) (April 6, 2006).
3. Tax Credits (Miscellaneous Amendments) Regulations 2006 (SI 2006/766) reg.10 (April 6, 2006).
4. Tax Credits (Miscellaneous Amendments) Regulations 2008 (SI 2008/604) reg.2(2) (April 6, 2008).
5. Tax Credits (Miscellaneous Amendments) (No.3) Regulations 2010 (SI 2010/2914) reg.4 (December 31, 2010).

GENERAL NOTE

This regulation defines "pension income" for the purposes of reg.3. "Pension income" is a new concept evolved by the Tax Law Rewrite Project and launched in ITEPA. Previously, taxation of pensions has mainly been as if pensions were emoluments, and therefore subject to Sch.E, with other rules bringing certain kinds of pension into various cases of Sch.D. The pension income provisions in ITEPA bring together most of the various charges to tax on different kinds of pensions, including some pensions payable to the former self-employed, and also pensions payable without reference to work of any kind. It also includes social security provisions by way of pension.

2.222

What income is relevant?

ITEPA Pt 9 rewrote the whole of the relevant provisions of the then income tax legislation dealing with income tax on pensions. However, no sooner had it been rewritten than much of it was rewritten again—by the Finance Act 2004. The provisions of FA 2004 came into effect on April 6, 2006. The amended Pt 9 applies to all pension income (including social security pensions from the UK and abroad, voluntary pensions, and pensions payable for ill-health retirements). The aim behind reg.5 is to include all pensions as income under this regulation for tax credits purposes.

2.223

What exemptions and deductions apply?

Again, the pattern is to adopt all relevant provisions in ITEPA Pt 9. Of the three chapters dealing with exemptions, Ch.16 (exemption for certain lump sums) applies fully. Chapter 17 (exemptions: any taxpayer) applies in large part. The sections not applied relate for the most part to foreign pensions, and are dealt with under the foreign income provision in reg.12. This also applies to Ch.18 (exemptions: non-UK resident taxpayers). The only other section not applied is ITEPA s.645 (social security pensions: increases for children), which does not apply by reason of the repeal of those provisions and their replacement by child tax credit by TCA 2002 (save for the oversight of the rare payments under s.85 of the SSCBA 1992 not being repealed by the Act).

2.224

Whose income is it?

ITEPA s.572 provides that the person liable for any tax charged is the person receiving or entitled to the pension. This is therefore the operative rule for inclusion of pension income for the calculation of tax credits income. It is the alternative to deal with those who are not entitled to a pension being received (as with voluntary pensions), but will rarely present problems. There is no significance for tax credits purposes in most cases about pensions to couples. If it is significant then, of course, entitlement is a question of law and receipt a question of fact.

2.225

The Tax Credits (Definition and Calculation of Income) Regulations 2002

When is the income brought into the calculation?

2.226 This also follows from s.572. As a result, pension income is to be included when entitlement arises. If there is no entitlement, as with voluntary pensions, then it is when the pension is received. That should follow the income tax treatment.

CHAPTER 4

Trading income

[¹[²Trading income

2.227 **6.** —The claimant's ("C") trading income is—
(a) the amount of C's taxable profits for the tax year arising from—
(i) any trade carried on in the United Kingdom or elsewhere;
(ii) any profession or vocation the income from which does not fall under any other provision of these Regulations; or
(b) the amount of C's taxable profits for the year arising from C's share of the partnership trading or professional income where C is a partner in a trade, profession or vocation.
In this regulation "taxable profits" has the same meaning as it has in Part 2 of ITTOIA, but disregarding the relevant benefit amount in section 23E (tax treatment of relevant benefits) and Chapter 16 of that Part (averaging profits of farmers and creative artists) [³, and any amount of transition profits for the tax year 2023-24 under Step 5 of paragraph 70(2) and paragraphs 72 and 73 of Schedule 1 (abolition of basis periods) to the Finance Act 2022].]]

AMENDMENTS

1. Tax Credits (Coronavirus, Miscellaneous Amendments) Regulations 2020 (SI 2020/534) reg.3(3) (May 23, 2020).
2. Tax Credits (Coronavirus, Miscellaneous Amendments) (No.2) Regulations 2020 (SI 2020/941) reg.2(2) (September 25, 2020).
3. Tax Credits and Child Benefit (Miscellaneous Amendments) Regulations 2023 (SI 2023/179) reg.2(2) (March 15, 2023).

GENERAL NOTE

2.228 This regulation defines "trading income" for the purposes of reg.3. It does so, since 2006, by reference to the newly codified rules for taxing trading income set out in ITTOIA 2005. This now includes all income from trades, professions and vocations and some related forms of income. It covers income both sourced in the UK and sourced abroad. While the current text of regulation 6 was substituted by SI 2020/941, it is now in materially the same form as its pre-May 23, 2020, version. Between 23 May 2020 and 24 September 2020, regulation 6 was amended by SI 2020/534 to take account of certain coronavirus support scheme payments. Those amendments were removed by SI 2020/941 so that regulation 6 reverted, in material respects, to its earlier form.

Employment and self-employment

2.229 The critical distinction in the case of many of those with smaller incomes who claim to be traders or self-employed is whether that is a true description in both law and fact of the individual's status. This is directly relevant for the calculation of tax credits because it must be decided if regs 4 or 6 applies. Following from that decision are subsidiary questions about the exemptions and deductions that must be calculated in finding the net income; the question of which period of income is to be taken into account; and the provision in Step 4 of reg.3 allowing trading losses to be deducted from other income. The rules assume that there cannot be a net loss by way of employment income, and do not allow for it. But this is an important overall change in the tax credit rules because previously no income losses were allowed.

The status of employee or self-employed is important for several reasons besides the current context:
　Income tax: employment income or trading income?
　NI contributions: Class 1 or Class 2 contributions?
　VAT: is the person carrying on registerable activities?
　Benefits: is the individual entitled to benefits available only to employees?

In addition, there are other issues that arise from the employment status, such as the minimum wage, holiday entitlements, and employer liability, that are again to be decided separately.

Drawing a line between employment and self-employment has always been difficult. It is also wide open to abuse, for example to reduce NI contributions but to increase benefit entitlement. This has led to people claiming to be an employee for some purposes and self-employed for others, and to different government agencies in the past adopting different answers to an individual's status in different contexts.

One result has been a series of initiatives to concentrate the decision-making on this issue so as to avoid inconsistent official decisions. Another is a series of legislative initiatives to define more clearly where the borderline is and to deal with abusive situations.

As a result of various initiatives, HMRC are now the effective deciders, subject to appeal, of employment status. The Social Security (Transfer of Functions, etc.) Act 1999 transferred NI contribution administration to the Inland Revenue. In addition, s.8 of that Act transferred to the Inland Revenue the decision whether someone is employed or self-employed for most social security benefit purposes. Appeals from a HMRC decision under s.8, about contributions, and about income tax liability, all go to the tax appeal commissioners. In the case of the s.8 decisions, most of these were previously dealt with on appeal by social security appeal tribunals, so this was a transfer of appeal jurisdiction. HMRC has also inherited responsibility for the national minimum wage legislation.

There are several provisions that now provide that someone is, or is to be treated as, an employee rather than self-employed. Two of these deserve emphasis. The first is the category of workers who in practical terms are somewhere between the two main groups—agency workers. ITEPA Pt 1, Ch.7 deals with agency workers. Section 44 provides that in most such cases the worker is regarded as the employee of the agency even if that is not the formal status adopted. The second concerns Ch.8 of that Part, which codifies the controversial "IR35" rules for what are sometimes known as "pocket book companies". These rules provide that in stated situations an individual who is under an obligation to provide services to a third party via an intermediary in circumstances where the worker is not paid as an employee by the intermediary can be treated as being an employee of the intermediary with a deemed employment income from that intermediary. This is used, for example, where someone works for a genuine third party, but where the contractual relationship with the third party is, typically, through a company of which the individual is the only shareholder. The company then pays the individual in some indirect way—benefits, loans, dividends—which the individual claims (if asked) to be either not income at all or not employment income.

What income is relevant? What exemptions and deductions apply?
"Trade" is defined in the Taxes Act s.832 as "every trade, manufacture, adventure or concern in the nature of trade". There is considerable case law on this meaning, of which reference might be made in the marginal case to the decisions of the House of Lords in *Ransom v Higgs* [1974] 1 W.L.R. 1594 and *Ensign Tankers v Stokes* [1992] 1 A.C. 655. In *Ransom*, the House of Lords made clear the wide factual scope of "trade", in the light of the extending definition. The fact, for example, that no particular name could be given to the activity did not stop it being a trading activity

2.230

if it was an economic or commercial activity aimed at generating profit (even if it did not do so). The converse of this is that activities that appear to be commercial but are not aimed at making a profit may be regarded in some cases as tax avoidance manoeuvres and not as trading (*Ensign Tankers*). Reference in marginal cases is usually made to the so-called "badges of trade". The badges were first identified by the Royal Commission on the Taxation of Income in 1952 as:
- (a) the subject-matter of the sale or realisation;
- (b) the length of the period of ownership of assets realised;
- (c) the frequency or number of similar transactions by that person;
- (d) whether there was supplementary work on or in connection with the assets realised or the realisation;
- (e) the reasons for the realisation of the assets; and
- (f) motive.

Two other points should be emphasised. First, there is a need to distinguish activities generating capital from those generating income. For the calculation of tax credits income, all activities generating capital should be ignored. (This introduces into the tax credits context a much fought-over income tax borderline removed in part for income tax purposes by the introduction of capital gains tax.) Secondly, and seemingly by contrast to the first, a "one off" activity generating profit may be a trading activity. The statutory definition indicates that a single activity may be caught as an "adventure" or a "concern in the nature of trade". From these follow a third point: a payment is either a trading payment or it is capital. There is no middle ground. If a receipt is not a trading receipt, it cannot be brought into charge to income tax (and it is therefore suggested to tax credits either) under other income charging provisions. See *Jones v Leeming* [1930] A.C. 415.

As reg.6 reflects, the charge to income tax on the self-employed is based on the accounts of the business. Increasingly, both the legislative provision for, and the HMRC practice relating to, the taxation of commercial activity is accounts-based. The concern in calculating income for tax credits is therefore with the claimant's business accounts for any trade.

In practice, in simple cases, the accounts can be brief. HMRC will accept these for income tax purposes and presumably also for tax credits purposes.

A simplified form of self-assessment tax return (SA103S) is available for those whose annual business turnover is under £85,000 (similar to the VAT registration level). This requires only total figures for:
- (a) annual turnover;
- (b) total allowable expenses;
- (c) net profits or losses; and
- (d) capital allowances.

If turnover is over that limit, then full accounts itemising income and expenditure will need to be provided, or at least the individual will have to provide all the details required in the standard self-employment pages to the self-assessment form for income tax. In the more complex cases, there should be two sets of accounts: the ordinary working accounts produced for the business (be it company, partnership or individual) and the tax computations or adjustments necessary to change the accounts from the approach adopted for the business to the approach necessary for income tax purposes. For example, the standard item "depreciation" on capital assets held for the business must be removed and replaced by a claim for any specific capital allowances to which the taxpayer is entitled. A second and further set of such computations may be necessary for tax credits purposes—or at least points may need following up. It is common for a business run by a husband to make a payment to an otherwise-non-earning wife. That is a deduction for trading purposes, but must be added back in for the joint claim they should be making for tax credits purposes as earnings of the wife. The business may be paying rent for the accommodation to the owners of the premises used. If that is the jointly owned (or owned in common) home of the joint claimants, again the rental income needs to go back into the tax credits calculation as property income.

(SI 2002/2006 reg.6) as amended

Whose income is it?
It is the income of the individual or partner running the business. The tax credits rules are silent as to partners' shares, so it will be the same share of the trading income as for income tax. That is based on the proposition that for English law purposes (but not Scottish law) a partnership is not a separate entity, so the trading income of the partnership is directly the trading income of the partners, divided as they decide or, by default, under the general rules of the Partnership Act 1890.

2.231

When is the income to be brought into the calculation?
The standard rule for income tax, and therefore tax credits, is that the tax payable in any one tax year (April 6 to April 5) is the income of that year. But for ongoing trades the tax is charged instead on the income of the "basis period" for that year. The basis period for a year is defined as the 12 months immediately following the basis period of the previous year. This is designed to prevent gaps occurring between tax years. In practice, this will be the 12 months accounts period for the business ending in that tax year. Many businesses end their accounting years on April 30. This creates the maximum convenient (for the business) gap between the accounts year and the tax year. Where a business using this practice ends its accounts, for example, on April 30, 2019, that will be the basis period for the tax year 2019–20.

2.232

There are special rules for the opening and closing years of a business, and anti-avoidance rules where a business changes its accounting year.

CHAPTER 5

Social security income

Social security income

7.—(1) The claimant's social security income is the total amount payable—
(a) under any provision of the Social Security Act 1988, the Contributions and Benefits Act [³, the Jobseekers Act 1995 or Part 1 of the Welfare Reform Act 2007] or under section 69 of the Child Support, Pensions and Social Security Act 2000;
[¹² (aa) under Part 3 of the Welfare Supplementary Payments Regulations (Northern Ireland) 2016 or Part 2 of the Welfare Supplementary Payment (Loss of Carer Payments) Regulations (Northern Ireland) 2016;]
[¹⁵ (ab) under regulations made under section 28 of the Social Security (Scotland) Act 2018;]
(b) [¹. . .];
(c) by the Secretary of State in respect of the non-payment of a payment which ought to have been made under a provision mentioned in sub-paragraph (a); [¹⁵. . .]
[¹⁵(ca) by the Scottish Ministers in respect of the non-payment of a payment which ought to have been made under the regulations mentioned in sub-paragraph (ab); and]
(d) by way of an ex-gratia payment made by the Secretary of State, or in Northern Ireland by the [¹² Department for Communities], in connection with a benefit, pension or allowance under the Contributions and Benefits Act.

2.233

The Tax Credits (Definition and Calculation of Income) Regulations 2002

This is subject to the following provisions of this regulation.

(2) Pensions under the Contributions and Benefits Act which are pension income by virtue of regulation 5(1)(a) are not social security income.

(3) In calculating the claimant's social security income the payments in Table 3 shall be disregarded.

Table 3. Payments under, or in connection with, the Act, the Social Security Act 1988, the Contributions and Benefits Act [³ the Jobseekers Act 1995 or Part 1 of the Welfare Reform Act 2007] disregarded in calculation of social security income

1. An attendance allowance under section 64 of the Contributions and Benefits Act.
2. A back to work bonus under section 26 of the Jobseekers Act 1995.
[¹³**3.** A bereavement support payment under section 30 of the Pensions Act 2014.]
4. Child benefit under Part II of the Act.
5. A Christmas bonus under section 148 of the Contributions and Benefits Act.
6. Council tax benefit under section 131 of the Contributions and Benefits Act.
7. A disability living allowance under section 71 of the Contributions and Benefits Act.
8. Disabled person's tax credit under section 129 of the Contributions and Benefits Act.
9. Any discretionary housing payment pursuant to regulation 2(1) of the Discretionary Financial Assistance Regulations 2001.
10. An ex-gratia payment by the Secretary of State or, in Northern Ireland, the [¹² Department for Communities], to a person over pensionable age by way of supplement to incapacity benefit.
11. A guardian's allowance under section 77 of the Contributions and Benefits Act.
12. Housing benefit under section 130 of the Contributions and Benefits Act.
13. Income support under section 124 of the Contributions and Benefits Act, unless it is chargeable to tax under [¹section 665 of ITEPA.].
14. Incapacity benefit which is— (a) short term incapacity benefit payable at the lower rate; or (b) payable to a person who had received invalidity benefit before 13th April 1995 if the period of incapacity for work is treated, by virtue of regulation 2 of the Social Security (Incapacity Benefit) (Transitional) Regulations 1995 (days to be treated as days of incapacity for work) as having begun before that date.

(SI 2002/2006 reg. 7) as amended

15. Industrial injuries benefit [¹(except industrial death benefit)] under section 94 of the Contributions and Benefits Act.
16. A contribution-based jobseeker's allowance under the Jobseekers Act 1995 [⁷as amended by the provisions of Part 1 of Schedule 14 to the Welfare Reform Act 2012 that remove references to an income-based allowance, and a contribution-based allowance under the Jobseekers Act 1995 as that Act has effect apart from those provisions], to the extent that it exceeds the maximum contained in [¹section 674 of ITEPA.].
17. An income-based jobseeker's allowance under the Jobseekers Act 1995.
18. A maternity allowance under section 35 [⁸or section 35B(3)] of the Contributions and Benefits Act.
19. A severe disablement allowance under section 68 or 69 of the Contributions and Benefits Act
20. A social fund payment under Part VIII of the Contributions and Benefits Act.
[¹20A. Statutory adoption pay under Part XIIZB of the Contributions and Benefits Act.
21. Statutory maternity pay under Part XII of the Contributions and Benefits Act.
21A. [⁵[¹⁰. . .] Statutory paternity pay [¹¹. . .] [¹⁰. . .] under Part XIIZA of the Contributions and Benefits Act.]
[⁹ 21B. Statutory shared parental pay under Part 12ZC of the Contributions and Benefits Act.] [¹⁴ 21C Statutory parental bereavement pay under Part 12ZD of the Contributions and Benefits Act.]
[¹⁴ 21C. Statutory parental bereavement pay under Part 12ZD of the Contributions and Benefits Act.]
22. Statutory sick pay under Part IX of the Contributions and Benefits Act.
23. Working families' tax credit under section 128 of the Contributions and Benefits Act.
24. A payment by way of compensation for the non-payment of, or in respect of loss of entitlement (whether wholly or partly) of, income support, jobseeker's allowance, [²or housing benefit].
25. A payment in lieu of milk tokens or the supply of vitamins under the Welfare Food Regulations 1996.
[³ 26. An income-related employment and support allowance payable under Part 1 of the Welfare Reform Act 2007.]
[⁴ 27. A payment by way of health in pregnancy grant made pursuant to Part 8A of the Contributions and Benefits Act.]
[⁶ 28. Personal independence payment under Part 4 of the Welfare Reform Act 2012.]

The Tax Credits (Definition and Calculation of Income) Regulations 2002

(4) If an increase in respect of a child dependant is payable with an allowance, benefit, pension or other payment ("the main payment") listed in Table 3, the increase shall also be wholly disregarded in calculating the income of the recipient of the main payment.

(5) [¹...]

[¹(5A) From the amount of social security income, calculated in accordance with the preceding provisions of this regulation, there shall be deducted any amount deductible for income tax purposes in computing social security income (as defined in ITEPA) under section 713 of ITEPA.]

(6) A reference in this regulation to an enactment applying only in Great Britain includes a reference to a corresponding enactment applying in Northern Ireland.

AMENDMENTS

1. Tax Credits (Definition and Calculation of Income) (Amendment) Regulations 2003 (SI 2003/732) reg.8 (April 6, 2003).
2. Tax Credits (Miscellaneous Amendments No.2) Regulations 2003 (SI 2003/2815) reg.6 (November 26, 2003).
3. Employment and Support Allowance (Consequential Provisions) (No.3) Regulations 2008 (SI 2009/1879) reg.21 (October 27, 2008).
4. Tax Credits (Miscellaneous Amendments) Regulations 2009 (SI 2009/697) reg.7 (April 6, 2009).
5. Tax Credits (Miscellaneous Amendments) (No.2) Regulations 2010 (SI 2010/2494) reg.6 (November 14, 2010).
6. Personal Independence Payment (Supplementary Provisions and Consequential Amendments) Regulations 2013 (SI 2013/388) reg.8 and Sch. para.29 (April 8, 2013).
7. Universal Credit (Consequential, Supplementary, Incidental and Miscellaneous Provisions) Regulations 2013 (SI 2013/630) reg.78(2) (April 29, 2013).
8. Tax Credits (Miscellaneous Amendments) Regulations 2014 (SI 2014/658) reg.4(6) (April 6, 2014).
9. Shared Parental Leave and Statutory Shared Parental Pay (Consequential Amendments to Subordinate Legislation) Order 2014 (SI 2014/3255) art.12(3)(b) (December 31, 2014).
10. Shared Parental Leave and Statutory Shared Parental Pay (Consequential Amendments to Subordinate Legislation) Order 2014 (SI 2014/3255) art.12(3)(a) (April 6, 2015).
11. Tax Credits and Child Benefit (Miscellaneous Amendments) Regulations 2016 (SI 2016/360) reg.3(2) (April 6, 2016).
12. Tax Credits (Definition and Calculation of Income) (Amendment) Regulations 2016 (SI 2016/978) reg.2(2) (October 31, 2016).
13. Pensions Act 2014 (Consequential, Supplementary and Incidental Amendments) Order 2017 (SI 2017/422) art.22 (April 6, 2017).
14. Parental Bereavement Leave and Pay (Consequential Amendments to Subordinate Legislation) Regulations 2020 (SI 2020/354) reg.12(3) (April 6, 2020).
15. Tax Credits and Child Benefit (Miscellaneous Amendments) Regulations 2023 (SI 2023/179) reg.2(3) (March 15, 2023).

CROSS-REFERENCE

ITEPA s.713   Donations to charity: payroll giving scheme

GENERAL NOTE

2.234   This regulation defines "social security income" for the purposes of reg.3. "Social security income" is another creation of the Tax Law Rewrite Project. Like pension

(SI 2002/2006 reg.7) as amended

income, it forms a separate code in Pt 10 of ITEPA (ss.655–681). But, unlike the employment income and pensions income regulations, this regulation adopts the approach of parallel legislation to Pt 10 of ITEPA rather than adopting ITEPA provisions themselves. Nonetheless, the relevant ITEPA provisions are included in this volume both for cross-reference and for more general reference in handling social security benefits.

Part 10 of ITEPA is in the following pattern. Chapter 1 sets out the structure of the Part. Chapter 2 deals with general points on tax on social security income, including a definition of the terms used. Chapter 3 lists the taxable UK social security benefits. This is in the form of Table A to s.660. Chapter 4 lists exemptions from the Ch.3 charge to specific benefits. Chapter 5 lists benefits wholly exempt from tax, in the form of Table B to s.677. Chapter 6 lists taxable foreign benefits, and Ch.7 lists exemptions from the benefits brought in under Ch.6. Of those chapters, Chs 6 and 7 are irrelevant to the head of the tax credits income calculation as it is limited to UK benefits only.

What income is relevant?

As just noted, reg.7 is expressly limited to benefits to which a claimant is entitled under UK legislation only. Foreign social security benefits are to be included under foreign income. There are two other limitations on social security income. The first, deriving from a parallel with ITEPA, is that state retirement benefits are treated as pension income not as social security income. The second, not deriving from that source, is the treatment of the statutory payments (sick, maternity, adoption, paternal) as employment income. ITEPA treats these as social security income (although this is a default rule—if they are taxed as employment income then they are excluded here: ITEPA s.660(2)).

2.235

With those exclusions, the other benefits that are taxable under Table A in ITEPA, and also relevant for calculating tax credit income, are:

Widowed mother's/parent's allowance
Carer's allowance
Incapacity benefit (some)
Income support (some)
Jobseeker's allowance (some)

In each case there are provisions about how much of the income is taxed. In practice, much of that tax is collected under the PAYE scheme.

What exclusions and deductions apply?

The list in Table 3 parallels the list in Table B to s.677 of ITEPA (payments wholly exempt), along with the provisions, in particular, for jobseeker's allowance and incapacity benefit, save for the statutory payments (noted above) and the treatment of present and past tax credits. CTC and WTC are not taxable. The list is very extensive, and it leaves relevant to tax credits only the short list of benefits noted in the previous paragraph.

2.236

There is no specific provision in the regulations dealing with overpayments of benefit. In practice, this may not be a major problem because of the limited extent to which account is taken of benefits. But the position might arise where, say, a widowed parent's allowance was overpaid (perhaps because of the living together rule) so that income previously paid was required to be repaid. For income tax purposes, late account can be taken of this for up to five years after the event. For tax credits purposes, the reduction in income for the relevant period will be relevant only in so far as there can be a recalculation of the income for tax credits, and there is a timely claim made. As the main time-limit is three months, there will only be a limited extent to which such adjustments can be requested, even with the benefit of a rapid notification of the change of circumstances. The two benefits administered by HMRC, child benefit and guardian's allowance, are exempt in any event.

Social security beneficiaries may also set charitable giving against their income.

The Tax Credits (Definition and Calculation of Income) Regulations 2002

Whose income is it?

2.237   The regulation is silent on this point, which therefore falls to be decided by reference to the social security rules. ITEPA s.662 imposes the income tax on the person receiving or entitled to the benefit, so covering appointees as well as claimants.

When is the income brought into the calculation?

2.238   The calculation is based on the amount actually received in the year, regardless of the period for which it is received.

CHAPTER 6

Student income

[¹Student Income

2.239   8.—"Student income" means, in relation to a student—
[³ (a) in England, any adult dependant's grant payable [⁴ pursuant to regulations under section 22 of the Teaching and Higher Education Act 1998;]]
   (b) in Scotland, any dependant's grant payable under regulation 4(1)(c) of the Students' Allowances (Scotland) Regulations [⁴ 2007]; [²...]
   (c) in Northern Ireland, any grant which corresponds to income treated as student income in England [⁴ ...] by virtue of paragraph (a);] [² and
[³ (d) in Wales, any adult dependant's grant payable [⁴ pursuant to regulations under section 22 of the Teaching and Higher Education Act 1998.]]

AMENDMENTS

1. Tax Credits (Miscellaneous Amendments No.2) Regulations 2003 (SI 2003/2815) reg.7 (November 26, 2003).
2. Tax Credits (Miscellaneous Amendments) Regulations 2006 (SI 2006/766) reg.12 (April 6, 2006).
3. Tax Credits (Miscellaneous Amendments) (No.2) Regulations 2008 (SI 2008/2169) reg.5 (September 1, 2008).
4. Tax Credits (Miscellaneous Amendments) Regulations 2012 (SI 2012/848) reg.3(3) (April 6, 2012).

GENERAL NOTE

2.240   This regulation defines "student income" for the purposes of reg.3. "Student income" is not a head of taxation under the Taxes Act or under the scheme used by the Tax Law Rewrite Project. Instead, this is taken from social security law. It must be read with the exemptions in regs 9 and 19, and the general principles of income tax.

The effect of the narrow point in reg.8 with the various exemptions is to exclude most forms of income that students receive (other than earnings).

The award of student grants is now a devolved function, and differing rules now apply in the four countries of the UK. Only parts of the various forms of grant are included as student income, and most students' grants will be excluded. The equivalent income tax rules (in s.776 of ITTOIA) exempt most forms of scholarship income, subject to anti-avoidance provisions, on the principle that such income is a gift or grant, not taxable income. Interest on the reimbursement of student loan income is also exempt (s.753 of ITTOIA). (HMRC monitor this as it is the authority responsible for collecting repayments of student grants through earnings.) Regulation 9 applies these provisions to tax credit calculations.

(SI 2002/2006 reg.8) as amended

Two other sources of student "income", in the widest sense, are or may be exempt from inclusion under general principles: loans and gifts. The extent to which this is so illustrates the difference between the means-tested benefits approach to assessing a claimant's income, and the rules for calculating tax credits income.

The question of the status of loans was discussed by the Court of Appeal at some length in *Morrell v Secretary of State for Work and Pensions* [2003] EWCA Civ 526. A claimant for income support had been receiving regular monthly sums from her mother by way of loan. Some of the money was paid by the mother to the claimant's landlord. The question was whether the sums were income for the purposes of income support. The Court of Appeal followed the recent decision of that Court in *Leeves v Chief Adjudication Officer* [1999] 1 E.L.R. 90. In that case the question was whether a student grant was to be treated as income for income support purposes. Potter LJ adopted the submission for the claimant that "income" should be given its ordinary and natural meaning, and that money accruing in respect of which there was an obligation of immediate and equivalent repayment was not income. On the facts, the student grant for maintenance was income but immediately repayable debts were not. The grant was income until the demand for repayment was made, when it ceased to be income.

But a further question arises for tax credits purposes. The payments must not only have the quality of income, but must fall under one of the kinds of income being taken into account. The definition of "student income" in reg.8 does not cover these loans, nor gifts, even if they are recurring. The question is whether such loans or gifts are income within any of the other kinds of income in the regulations. We shall return to that at para.2.186, below.

Further sources of income linked to education and training are exempt under the specific provisions listed in Table 6 of reg.19—items 4, 5, 6 and 7 are all relevant.

[¹Payments of income in connection with students to be disregarded for the purposes of regulation 3

9.—Income which is exempt from income tax by virtue of section 753 or 776 of ITTOIA (which deal respectively with interest on the repayment of student loans and scholarship income) is disregarded in calculating a claimant's income under regulation 3.]

2.241

AMENDMENT

1. Tax Credits (Miscellaneous Amendments) Regulations 2006 (SI 2006/766) reg.13 (April 6, 2006).

GENERAL NOTE

This regulation is an exempting regulation only. See note to reg.8.

2.242

CHAPTER 7

Investment income

Investment income

10.—(1) In these Regulations, "investment income" means the gross amount of—
  (a) any interest of money whether yearly or otherwise, or any annuity or other annual payment, whether such payment is payable within or out of the United Kingdom, either as a charge on any property of

2.243

the person paying it by virtue of any deed or will or otherwise, or as a reservation out of it, or as a personal debt or obligation by virtue of any contract, or whether the payment is received and payable half-yearly or at any shorter or longer periods, but not including property income;
(b) any discounts on securities;
(c) any income from securities payable out of the public revenues of the United Kingdom or Northern Ireland;
(d) dividends and other distributions of a company resident in the United Kingdom and any tax credit associated with that payment; and
(e) any amount treated as forming part of the individual's income for the year for income tax purposes by virtue of [³Chapter 9 of Part 4 of ITTOIA disregarding section 535 (top slicing relief)].

This is subject to the following qualification.

(2) In calculating investment income, there shall be disregarded—
(a) any amount listed in column 1 of Table 4 to the extent shown in the corresponding entry in column 2;
(b) any amount listed in column 1 of Table 5 during the period shown in the corresponding entry in column 2;
(c) any income arising from savings certificates, and interest on tax reserve certificates, exempted from tax by [³section 692, 693 or 750 of ITTOIA] (savings certificates and tax reserve certificates);
(d) the first £70 in any tax year of interest on deposits with National Savings and Investments, exempted from income tax by [³section 691 of ITTOIA (National Savings Bank ordinary account interest)];
(e) any payment to a claimant which does not form part of his income for the purposes of income tax by virtue of [³section 727 of ITTOIA (certain annual payments by individuals)] [⁸; and
(f) any interest on a payment made under, or in connection with, the Windrush Compensation Scheme administered by the Home Office, for the period beginning on the date on which the payment is made and ending 52 weeks after that date]

Table 4. Payments disregarded in the calculation of investment income

1. Description of income to be disregarded	2. Extent of disregard

1. Any interest, dividends, distributions, profits or gains in respect of investments under—
    (a) a Personal Equity Plan; or
    (b) an Individual Savings Account;
in respect of which the claimant is entitled to relief from income tax under [³Chapter 3 of Part 6 of ITTOIA] or which is taxed only in accordance with regulation 23 of the Individual Savings Account Regulations 1998.
	The whole amount, unless it is interest under a personal equity plan to which regulation 17A(2) of the Personal Equity Plan Regulations 1989 applies. Interest to which that paragraph applies is disregarded only to the extent that it does not exceed the annual limit of £180 mentioned in that regulation.

(SI 2002/2006 reg.8) as amended

1. Description of income to be disregarded	2. Extent of disregard
2. [³...]	[³...]
[³3. Any interest payable under a certified SAYE savings arrangement for the purposes of Chapter 4 of Part 6 of ITTOIA.]	The whole amount.
4. Any winnings from betting, including pool betting, or lotteries or games with prizes.	The whole amount.
5. Any interest on a payment of £10,000 made by the Secretary of State to a person who was held prisoner by the Japanese during the Second World War or to the spouse of such a person, if the payment is held in a distinct account and no payment (other than interest) has been added to the account.	The whole amount of the interest.
6. Any interest on a payment made to the claimant by, or on behalf, of a government of a country outside the United Kingdom, either from its own resources or with contributions from any other organisation, by way of compensation for a victim of National Socialism if the payment is held in a distinct account and no payment (other than interest) has been added to the account. Here a reference to a victim of National Socialism is a reference to a person who was required to work as a slave or a forced labourer for National Socialists or their sympathisers during the Second World War, or suffered property loss, or suffered injury or is the parent of a child who died, at the hands of National Socialists or their sympathisers during the Second World War.	The whole amount of the interest.
7. Any monies paid to the claimant by a bank or building society as compensation in respect of an unclaimed account	The amount [⁴of interest exempted from income tax under section 756A of ITTOIA.]

1. Description of income to be disregarded	2. Extent of disregard
held by a Holocaust victim and which vested in the Custodian of Enemy Property under section 7 of the Trading with the Enemy Act 1939 and treated as exempt from income tax by [⁴section 756A of ITTOIA].	
8. Any interest, or payment [³. . .], which is disregarded for income tax purposes by virtue of— 　[³(a)　section 751 of ITTOIA (interest on damages for personal injury),or] 　(b)　[³section 731 of ITTOIA (periodical payments of personal injury damages)].	The amount so disregarded.
[¹9]. Annuity payments under an award of compensation made under the Criminal Injuries Compensation Scheme (within the meaning of [³section 732(3) of ITTOIA] [⁹ or under the Victims of Overseas Terrorism Compensation Scheme 2012 or any corresponding scheme established under section 47 of the Crime and Security Act 2010].	[⁹ The amount to which no liability to income tax arises under section 732 of ITTOIA.]
[¹10]. A payment under a life annuity.	The amount of interest eligible for relief under section 353 of the Taxes Act by virtue of section 365 of that Act.
[¹11]. Any interest, or payment in respect of interest, which is compensation to a person who is under the age of 18 years for the death of one or both of his parents.	The whole of the interest or payment.
12. A purchased life annuity to which [³Chapter 7 of Part 4 of ITTOIA] applies.	[³The amount exempted under section 717 of ITTOIA as calculated under section 719 of that Act.]

(SI 2002/2006 reg.10) as amended

1. Description of income to be disregarded	2. Extent of disregard
[³ **13.** Any payments which are exempt from Income tax by virtue of— (a) section 725 of ITTOIA (annual payments under immediate needs annuities), or	The whole amount.
(b) section 735 of ITTOIA (health and employment insurance payments).]	
[⁵ **14.** [⁷ . . .]]	
[⁶ **15.** Any payment of, or in respect of, a government bonus under section 1 [⁷ or 2] of the Savings (Government Contributions) Act 2017.	The whole amount.]

Table 5. Payments in connection with very severe disablement, Creutzfeldt–Jakob disease and haemophilia

1. Description of income to be disregarded	2. Applicable period
1. A trust payment made to — (a) a diagnosed person; (b) the diagnosed person's partner; or (c) the person who was his partner at the date of his death.	The period beginning on the date on which the trust payment is made and ending with the death of the person to whom the payment is made.
2. A trust payment made to a parent of a deceased diagnosed person, or a person acting in the place of his parent.	The period beginning on the date on which the trust payment is made and ending two years after that date.
3. The amount of any payment out of the estate of a person to whom a trust payment has been made, which is made to the person who was the diagnosed person's partner at the date of his death.	The period beginning on the date on which the payment is made and ending on the date on which that person dies.
4. The amount of any payment out of the estate of a person to whom a trust payment has been made, which is made to a parent of a deceased diagnosed person, or a person acting in the place of his parent.	The period beginning on the date on which the payment is made and ending two years after that date.

The Tax Credits (Definition and Calculation of Income) Regulations 2002

(3) The amounts disregarded under Items 3 and 4 in Table 5 shall not exceed the total amount of any trust payments made to the person to whom the trust payment had been made.

(4) In this regulation, "diagnosed person" means—
   (a) a person who has been diagnosed as suffering from, or who after his death has been diagnosed has having suffered from, variant Creutzfeldt–Jakob disease;
   (b) a person who is suffering or has suffered from haemophilia; or
   (c) a person in respect of whom a payment has been made from the 1992 Fund, the Eileen Trust or the Independent Living Funds; and a reference to a person being a member of the diagnosed person's household at the date of the diagnosed person's death includes a person who would have been a member of his household but for the diagnosed person being in residential accommodation, a residential care home or a nursing home on that date.

(5) In this regulation—
"relevant trust" means—
   (a) a trust established out of funds provided by the Secretary of State in respect of persons who suffered, or who are suffering, from variant Creutzfeldt–Jakob disease for the benefit of persons eligible for payments in accordance with its provisions;
   (b) the Macfarlane Trusts; or
   (c) the 1992 Fund, the Eileen Trust or the Independent Living Funds.
"residential accommodation", "residential care home" and "nursing home" have the meanings given by regulation 2(1) of the Income Support (General) Regulations 1987; and
"trust payment" means a payment under a relevant trust.

AMENDMENTS

1. Tax Credits (Definition and Calculation of Income) (Amendment) Regulations 2003 (SI 2003/732) reg.9 (April 6, 2003).
2. Tax Credits (Miscellaneous Amendments No.2) Regulations 2003 (SI 2003/2815) reg.8 (November 26, 2003).
3. Tax Credits (Miscellaneous Amendments) Regulations 2006 (SI 2006/766) reg.14 (April 6, 2006).
4. Tax Credits (Miscellaneous Amendments) Regulations 2007 (SI 2007/824) reg.12 (April 6, 2007).
5. Tax Credits (Miscellaneous Amendments) Regulations 2010 (SI 2010/751) reg.4 (April 6, 2010).
6. Tax Credits (Definition and Calculation of Income) (Amendment) Regulations 2017 (SI 2017/ 396) reg.4 (April 6, 2017).
7. Tax Credits and Childcare (Miscellaneous Amendments) Regulations 2018 (SI 2018/365) reg.2(4) (April 6, 2018).
8. Tax Credits, Child Benefit and Childcare Payments (Miscellaneous Amendments) Regulations 2019 (SI 2019/364) reg.3(4) (March 21, 2019).
9. Child Benefit and Tax Credits (Miscellaneous Amendments) Regulations 2023 (SI 2023/1139) reg.3(2) (October 27, 2023).

GENERAL NOTE

2.244 This regulation was drafted ahead of, and anticipated, the relevant provisions of ITTOIA. But there were some changes to the Rewrite Bill after this regulation was brought into force, including the retitling of the relevant part of ITTOIA to cover "Savings and investment income". That accurately reflects the scope of this

(SI 2002/2006 reg.10) as amended

regulation. It completely reshapes the relevant provisions in the previous income tax legislation and, more than any other part of the Rewrite Acts, should be considered in the new form and not as a continuation of old history.

The relevant provisions in ITTOIA are in Pt 4, which has the following structure:

Chapter 1	Introduction
Chapter 2	Interest
Chapter 3	Dividends from UK resident companies
Chapter 4	Dividends from non-UK resident companies
Chapter 5	Stock dividends from UK resident companies
Chapter 6	Release of loan to participator in close company
Chapter 7	Purchased life annuity payments
Chapter 8	Profits from deeply discounted securities
Chapter 9	Gains from contracts for life assurance
Chapter 10	Distributions from unauthorised unit trusts
Chapter 11	Transactions in deposits
Chapter 12	Disposals of futures and options involving guaranteed Returns
Chapter 13	Sales of foreign dividend coupons

Most of these chapters contain provisions designed to prevent avoidance, in particular by turning income into capital by one means or another. However, by bringing them all together the overall picture is now far clearer than it was before ITTOIA in that the full pattern of the scope of the income tax charges on forms of income from savings and investments can be seen from this list.

But reg.10 retains, at least for the time being, much of the flavour of the previous law, its wording still coming from the former s.18 of the Income and Corporation Taxes Act 1988.

Income from savings and investments is included in the calculation of income for tax credits purposes although no account is taken of capital when someone claims a tax credit under the 2002 Act. In practice, however, some of the most popular forms of savings are shielded from an income tax charge, and assessment to tax credits, by the very important disregards listed out in Table 4. Interest and dividends received from saving held within an ISA (individual savings account) are protected not only from income tax but also tax credits assessment by item 1. Interest and bonuses paid under SAYE schemes (save as you earn) are protected by item 3. But interest on ordinary deposits with banks or building societies is taxable (subject to deduction of income tax at source).

Regulation 10 was amended to take account of interest on payments made under the Windrush compensation scheme. Note, however, that the relevant provision in reg.10(2)(f) excludes interest on Windrush compensation payments for a period of only 52 weeks, beginning with the date of the compensation payment. The payments themselves are disregarded in the calculation of a claimant's income through an amendment adding these payments to Table 6 of reg.19.

Because reg.10 follows the former law, and not the present income tax law, express provision has been made to remove winnings from betting and lotteries. This is not an exemption but rather a limitation set by case law on the previous legislation. (Winnings were excluded to stop losses being claimed.)

CHAPTER 8

Property income

Property income

11.—(1) In these Regulations, "property income" means the annual taxable profits arising from a business carried on for the exploitation, as a

2.245

The Tax Credits (Definition and Calculation of Income) Regulations 2002

source of rents or other receipts, of any estate, interest or rights in or over land in the United Kingdom.

Expressions which are used in this paragraph which are defined in [² Part 3 of ITTOIA] for the purposes of [² that Part] bear the same meaning here as they bear in [² that Part].

This paragraph is subject to the following [¹qualifications].

[² (2) In calculating property income there shall be disregarded any profits—
 (a) treated as nil by section 791 to 794 of ITTOIA (full rent-a-room relief); or
 (b) excluded from profits by section 795 to 798 of ITTOIA (alternative calculation of profits if amount exceeds limit).]

[⁴ (2A) In calculating property income, the restrictions in section 272A of ITTOIA (restricting deductions for finance costs related to residential property) and section 399A of ITA (property partnerships: restriction of relief for investment loan interest) shall be disregarded.]

[¹(3) [² Where a property business (as defined in Part 3 of ITTOIA] makes a loss to which the relief provisions [³ contained in sections 118 (carry forward against subsequent property business profits) and 119 (how relief works) of ITA] apply, then such relief as may arise under [³ those sections] shall be applied in calculating property income for the purposes of this regulation.]

AMENDMENTS

1. Tax Credits (Miscellaneous Amendments No.2) Regulations 2003 (SI 2003/2815) reg.9 (November 26, 2003).
2. Tax Credits (Miscellaneous Amendments) Regulations 2006 (SI 2006/766) reg.15 (April 6, 2006).
3. Tax Credits (Definition and Calculation of Income) (Amendment) Regulations 2007 (SI 2007/1305) reg.6 (May 16, 2007).
4. Tax Credits (Definition and Calculation of Income) (Amendment) Regulations 2017 (SI 2017/ 396) reg.5 (April 6, 2017).

GENERAL NOTE

2.246   This regulation reflects Pt 3 of ITTOIA under the same heading. However, the label is perhaps the least helpful of the new titles created by the Tax Law Rewrite Project. Part 3 and this regulation are limited to real property, and do not apply to any other kind of property. But it was thought better to avoid referring to income from land because the drafters wished to use popular terms and avoid legal complications.

The rules in Pt 3 remove another distinction in the former income tax law. Because taxation of income from land is usually sourced-based—that is, taxed where the land is—different rules used to apply to income from land in the UK and income received in the UK from land elsewhere. That distinction has now largely been removed in ITTOIA. But it has not been removed for tax credits purposes. Following the pattern of the old law, income from foreign land is foreign income within reg.12. In income tax practice, double taxation agreements normally reserve the taxation of income from land to the state where the land is, exempting it—or providing relief—elsewhere. But that does not apply for tax credits purposes. So someone who has, say, an apartment in Spain which is let for part of the year may not pay any UK income tax on the rent, but should have it taken into account for tax credits purposes under reg.12 alongside any income from UK land brought within reg.11.

(SI 2002/2006 reg.12) as amended

CHAPTER 9

Foreign income

12.—(1) In these Regulations, "foreign income" means income arising, in the year in question, from [³a source outside the United Kingdom or from foreign holdings] which are not—
(a) employment income;
(b) trading income; or
(c) investment income falling within regulation 10(1)(e).
This is subject to the following provisions of this regulation.

[³(2) The reference in paragraph (1) to "foreign holdings" shall be construed in accordance with section 571 of ITTOIA.]

(3) In calculating the claimant's foreign income there shall be disregarded—
(a) any payment by way of an annuity or pension payable under any special provision for victims of National Socialist persecution which is made by the law of the Federal Republic of Germany, or any part of it, or of Austria;
[⁴(aa) any monies paid by a bank or building society which are exempted from income tax under section 756A of ITTOIA (interest on certain deposits of victims of National-Socialist persecution);]
[⁶(bb) any pension, annuity, allowance or other payment provided in accordance with the provisions of the scheme established under the law of the Netherlands and known as *Wet uitkeringen vervolgingsslachtoffers 1940–1945* (Netherlands Benefit Act for Victims of Persecution 1940–1945);]
[³(b) the amount authorised to be deducted by the relevant provision if the claimant's foreign income comprises or includes a pension to which the following provisions of ITEPA apply—
  (i) sections 567(5) and 617 (deduction allowed for taxable pension income);
  (ii) section 575(2) (taxable pension income: foreign pensions);
  (iii) section 613(3) (taxable pension income: foreign annuities); and
  (iv) section 635(3) (taxable pension income: foreign voluntary annual payments); and]
(c) any amount which would be disregarded for the purposes of income tax by virtue of—
  (i) Extra Statutory Concession A10 (lumps sums paid by overseas pension schemes);
  (ii) [¹s.681 of ITEPA];
  (iii) [³section 751(1)(c) of ITTOIA] (interest on damages for personal injuries awarded by a foreign court); or
  (iv) Extra Statutory Concession A44 (education allowances payable to public officials of overseas territories); [³or
  (v) section 730 of ITTOIA (foreign maintenance payments)].

[²(4) Where an overseas property business; [³(within the meaning of Part 3 of ITTOIA)] makes a loss to which the relief provisions [⁵ contained in sections 118 (carry forward against subsequent property business profits) and 119 (how relief works) of ITA apply], then such relief as may arise under [⁵ those sections] shall be applied in calculating foreign income for the purposes of this regulation.]

The Tax Credits (Definition and Calculation of Income) Regulations 2002

AMENDMENTS

1. Tax Credits (Definition and Calculation of Income) (Amendment) Regulations 2003 (SI 2003/732) reg.10 (April 6, 2003).
2. Tax Credits (Miscellaneous Amendments No.2) Regulations 2003 (SI 2003/2815) reg.10 (November 26, 2003).
3. Tax Credits (Miscellaneous Amendments) Regulations 2006 (SI 2006/766) reg.16 (April 6, 2006).
4. Tax Credits (Miscellaneous Amendments) Regulations 2007 (SI 2007/824) reg.13 (April 6, 2007).
5. Tax Credits (Definition and Calculation of Income) (Amendment) Regulations 2007 (SI 2007/1305) reg.7 (May 16, 2007).
6. Tax Credits and Child Benefit (Miscellaneous Amendments) Regulations 2016 (SI 2016/360) reg.3(3) (April 6, 2016).

GENERAL NOTE

2.248
The provisions in reg.3 above ensure that all forms of the foreign income of a tax credits claimant are potentially relevant to the calculation of income for tax credits purposes even if they would be exempt from income tax in the UK. "Foreign income" is not a specific head of charge for income tax purposes. And in practice most problems are dealt with not under the UK legislation but under the terms of the relevant double tax agreements. That approach and those agreements do not apply for tax credits purposes, so there is need to make express provision instead.

This regulation, as amended from 2006, provides for all foreign income charged to income tax to be relevant for tax credits save for specific exemptions. It also provides for the priorities between competing charges that arise, for example, where income is both foreign income and employment income, to prevent a double charge. The combination of exemptions and rules giving priority to other heads of assessment result in this head of charge still being of limited importance. But note that this provision will apply to some kinds of foreign pension and foreign savings or investment income.

"Foreign holdings" is defined in s.571 of ITTOIA as meaning shares and other securities outside the UK that are issued by a government or public authority of another country or by or on behalf of a body of persons not resident in the UK.

CHAPTER 10

Notional Income

Introduction

2.249
13.—In these Regulations, "notional income" means income which, by virtue of regulations 14 to 17 a claimant is treated as having, but which he does not in fact have.

GENERAL NOTE

2.250
This regulation emphasises that the provisions of regs 14–17 are not parallels to income tax in the ordinary sense, in that the income is not in fact income of the claimant (or any of the joint claimants). It may, as the notes to the following regulations show, be the income of someone else.

(SI 2002/2006 reg.14) as amended

Claimants treated for any purpose as having income by virtue of the Income Tax Acts

14.—(1) If an amount is treated for any purpose as the claimant's income under any provision mentioned in paragraph (2), he is to be treated as having that amount of income [³, but this is subject to paragraph (1A)].

[³(1A) Where paragraph (2)(b)(x) or (2)(b)(xi) applies, the amount of income that the claimant is to be treated as having is:

$$x - y$$

where
"x" is the amount of income under section 652, 654 or 655 of ITTOIA, and
"y" is the amount that would, but for section 272A of that Act, be deductible in calculating the profits for income tax purposes of a property business for the profits year.

(1B) In paragraph (1A) "profits year" has the meaning given by section 274A of ITTOIA (reduction for individuals).]

(2) The provisions mentioned in paragraph (1) are—
(a) the following provisions of the Taxes Act—
  [¹...];
  (ix) section 714 (transfers of securities: treatment of deemed sums and reliefs) or 716 (transfer of unrealised interest);
  (x) section 730 (transfer of income arising from securities);
  [²...]
  (xiv) section 761 (charge to income tax of offshore income gain); and
  [²...]
[¹(b) the following provisions of ITTOIA—
  (i) sections 277 to 283 (amounts treated as receipts: leases);
  (ii) Chapter 5 of Part 4 (stock dividends from UK resident companies);
  (iii) Chapter 6 of Part 4 (release of loan to participator in close company);
  (iv) section 427 (charge to tax on profits from deeply discounted securities);
  (v) Chapter 11 of Part 4 (transactions in securities);
  (vi) sections 624 to 628 (income treated as income of settlor: retained interests);
  (vii) sections 629 to 632 (income treated as income of settlor: unmarried children);
  (viii) section 633 (capital sums paid to settlor by trustees of settlement);
  (ix) section 641 (capital sums paid to settlor by body connected with settlement);
  (x) section 652 (estate income: absolute interests in residue); and
  (xi) sections 654 to 655 (estate income: interests in residue);
[² (ba) the following provisions of ITA—
  (i) Chapter 5 of Part 11 (price differences under repos);
  (ii) Chapter 2 of Part 13 (transfer of assets abroad); and
  (iii) Chapter 3 of Part 13 (transactions in land).]
(c) section 84 and Schedule 15 to the Finance Act 2004 (charge to income tax by reference to enjoyment of property previously owned).]

The Tax Credits (Definition and Calculation of Income) Regulations 2002

AMENDMENTS

1. Tax Credits (Miscellaneous Amendments) Regulations 2006 (SI 2006/766) reg.17 (April 6, 2006).
2. Tax Credits (Definition and Calculation of Income) (Amendment) Regulations 2007 (SI 2007/1305) reg.8 (May 16, 2007).
3. Tax Credits and Childcare (Miscellaneous Amendments) Regulations 2018 (SI 2018/365) reg.2(5) (April 6, 2018).

GENERAL NOTE

2.252

This regulation has been rewritten substantially with effect from the 2006–07 income tax year, but its contents remains broadly the same. It collects together a series of important income tax anti-avoidance provisions and includes them together as providing "notional income" for step 1 of the calculation of income for tax credits purposes under reg.3(1).

Before April 6, 2018, this regulation was worded so that, in all cases, the assessment for tax credit purposes would depend on self-assessment or an assessment for income tax purposes. A claimant who was treated as having an amount of any of these kinds of income for income tax purposes would be treated as having that amount of income for the purposes of this regulation. While this approach continues to apply in most cases, since April 6, 2018 an exception applies where a claimant receives property income through an estate rather than directly (the cases referred to in reg.14(2)(b)(x) and (xi)). In such cases, a person's estate income is calculated for tax credits purposes in accordance with reg.14(1A). The intended effect is to ensure consistency of treatment with claimants who receive property income directly.

The regulation collects together both well-known and less well-known anti-avoidance provisions. The newest, in para.(2)(c), attracted considerable attention when enacted. It is the provision that deems someone who has given her or his property away (usually for inheritance tax purposes) but who continues to have a right to reside in the property to be in receipt of income and so liable to income tax on (broadly) the rent that could have been received from the property. That also applies for a tax credit assessment.

Claimants depriving themselves of income in order to secure entitlement

2.253

15.—If a claimant has deprived himself of income for the purpose of securing entitlement to, or increasing the amount of, a tax credit, he is treated as having that income.

GENERAL NOTE

2.254

This is equivalent to Income Support (General) Regulations 1987 (SI 1987/1967) reg.42(1), and the note on that in Vol.II in this series should be consulted. Note, however, that this provision is defined by reference to deprivation for the purposes of securing or increasing entitlement to tax credits (and not, for example, income support). TCTM04920 gives the example of someone who transfers entitlement to an occupational pension to someone else by deed of gift. Without reference to authority, it emphasises that securing or increasing entitlement to tax credit may not be a claimant's main motive but it must be a significant one. That is a question of fact.

Claimants to whom income becomes available upon the making of a claim

2.255

16.—(1) If income would become available to a claimant upon the making of an application for that income, he is treated as having that income.

This is subject to the following qualification.

(SI 2002/2006 reg.16) as amended

(2) Paragraph (1) does not apply in relation to income—
  (a) under a trust derived from a payment made in consequence of a personal injury;
  (b) under a personal pension scheme or retirement annuity contract;
  (c) consisting in a sum to which Item 8 of Table 4 in regulation 10 refers (compensation for personal injuries which is administered by the Court); or
  (d) consisting in a rehabilitation allowance made under section 2 of the Employment Act.

[1(3) Paragraph (1) also does not apply to income by way of—
  (a) a Category A or Category B retirement pension,
[2(aa) a state pension under Part 1 of the Pensions Act 2014 or Part 1 of the Pensions Act (Northern Ireland) 2015,]
  (b) a graduated retirement benefit, or
  (c) a shared additional pension,
payment of which has been deferred.

Here—
"Category A retirement pension" means a pension to which a person is entitled by virtue of section 44 of the Contributions and Benefits Act or the Northern Ireland Contributions and Benefits Act;
"Category B retirement pension" means a pension to which a person is entitled by virtue of any of sections 48A to 48C of the Contributions and Benefits Act or sections 48A to 48C of the Northern Ireland Contributions and Benefits Act;
"graduated retirement benefit" means a pension payable under—
  (a) sections 36 and 37 of the National Insurance Act 1965; or
  (b) sections 35 and 36 of the National Insurance Act (Northern Ireland) 1966; and
"shared additional pension" means a pension to which a person is entitled by virtue of section 55A [2 or 55AA] of the Contributions and Benefits Act or section 55A [2 or 55AA] of the Northern Ireland Contributions and Benefits Act.]

AMENDMENTS

1. Tax Credits (Miscellaneous Amendments) Regulations 2004 (SI 2004/762) reg.15 (April 6, 2004).
2. Pensions Act 2014 (Consequential, Supplementary and Incidental Amendments) Order 2015 (SI 2015/1985) art.25 (April 6, 2016).

DEFINITIONS

"Category A retirement pension"—see para.(3).
"Category B retirement pension"—see para.(3).
"graduated retirement benefit"—see para.(3).
"shared additional pension"—see para.(3).

GENERAL NOTE

See the note to the similar provision in Income Support (General) Regulations 1987 (SI 1987/1967) reg.42(2)–(4). The precise operative scope of this provision is not clear. For income support, sums not received may not count as earnings or other income. But most of the charges to income tax, as noted above, are on those "receiving or entitled to". So entitlement is enough to bring the sums in both for income tax purposes and tax credit purposes, even if they are not received. This regulation could, however, extend that to cover sums to which entitlement had not arisen, for example because no demand had been made for the sum under a contractual entitlement operative on such demand.

The Tax Credits (Definition and Calculation of Income) Regulations 2002

Claimants providing services to other persons for less than full earnings

2.257   **17.**—(1) If a claimant provides a service for another person and—
(a) the other person makes no payment of earnings or pays less than those paid for a comparable employment (including self-employment) in the area; and
(b) the Board are satisfied that the means of the other person are sufficient for him to pay for, or to pay more for, the service,
the claimant is to be treated as having such an amount of employment income, or in the case of a service provided in the course of a trade or business, such an amount of trading income as is reasonable for the employment of the claimant to provide the service.
This is subject to the following qualification.
(2) Paragraph (1) does not apply where—
(a) the claimant is a volunteer or is engaged to provide the service by a charitable or voluntary organisation and the Board are satisfied that it is reasonable for the claimant to provide the service free of charge; or
(b) the service is provided in connection with the claimant's participation in an employment or training programme—
   (i) [¹(i) in Great Britain, which is approved by the Secretary of State;]; or
   (ii) in Northern Ireland in accordance with regulation 19(1)(p) of the Jobseeker's Allowance Regulations (Northern Ireland) 1996 other than where it is provided in connection with the claimant's participation in the Preparation for Employment Programme specified in regulation 75(1)(a)(v) of those Regulations.

AMENDMENT

1. Universal Credit (Consequential, Supplementary, Incidental and Miscellaneous Provisions) Regulations 2013 (SI 2013/630) reg.78(3) (April 29, 2013).

GENERAL NOTE

2.258   See the note in Vol.II in this series to the similar (though differently drafted) provision in Income Support (General) Regulations 1987 (SI 1987/1967) reg.42(6).

CHAPTER 11

Miscellaneous income

[¹Miscellaneous income

2.259   **18.**— In these Regulations "miscellaneous income" means income which does not fall within any other provision of these Regulations, and which is either —
(a) subject to income tax under Part 5 of ITTOIA; or
(b) a payment under, or in connection with, a coronavirus support scheme.]

AMENDMENT

1. Tax Credits (Coronavirus, Miscellaneous Amendments) Regulations 2020 (SI 2020/534) reg.3(4) (May 23, 2020).

(SI 2002/2006 reg.18) as amended

GENERAL NOTE

Part 5 of ITTOIA contains the "sweeper" provisions to bring within liability to income tax any forms of income that fall outside the specific charges to income tax. If, therefore, something can properly be regarded as employment income, trading income, savings and investment income, pension income, social security income or some other more specific form of income, then this provision does not apply. But it is not a "catch-all", and there is no global definition of "income" in UK income tax legislation.

Part 5 applies to "annual profits or gains" not otherwise charged to tax. It does not catch gifts or loans, nor does it catch single "one-off" payments unless they are of a trading or business nature. Nor does it catch receipts of capital sums, which in tax terms fall to be taxed under the Taxation of Chargeable Gains Act 2001, if at all. See the note to reg.6.

2.260

PART III

Sums disregarded in the calculation of income

General disregards in the calculation of income

19.—(1) For the purposes of regulation 3—
(a) the sums specified in Table 6 are disregarded in the calculation of income;
(b) the sums specified in column 1 of Table 7 are disregarded in the calculation of income if the condition in the corresponding entry in column 2 of that Table is satisfied; and
(c) the sums specified in column 1 of Table 8 are disregarded in the calculation of income to the extent specified in the corresponding entry in column 2 of that Table.

(2) In this regulation—
"the JSA Regulations" means the Jobseeker's Allowance Regulations 1996; [[31]...]
"the JSA (NI) Regulations" means the Jobseeker's Allowance (Northern Ireland) Regulations 1996 [[31]; and
"Scottish local authority" means a council constituted under section 2 of the Local Government etc. (Scotland) Act 1994.]
[[21] [[20]...]]

2.261

Table 6. Sums disregarded in the calculation of income

1. Any payment of an employment credit under a scheme under section 2(2) of the Employment Act known as "New Deal 50 Plus" or the corresponding scheme under section 1 of the Employment and Training Act (Northern Ireland) 1950.
2. Any payment made— (a) under section 15 of the Disabled Persons (Employment Act) 1944 or section 15 of the Disabled Persons (Employment) Act (Northern Ireland) 1945; or (b) in accordance with arrangements made under section 2 of the Employment Act or section 1 of the Employment and Training Act (Northern Ireland) 1950 to assist disabled persons to obtain or retain employment despite their disability.

3. Any mandatory top-up payment made pursuant to—
  (a) section 2 of the Employment Act [³ or section 1 of the Employment and Training Act (Northern Ireland) 1950] in respect of the claimant's participation in—
     (i) an employment programme specified in regulation 75(1)(a)(ii)(bb) of the JSA Regulations or regulation 75(1)(a)(ii) of the JSA (NI) Regulations (Voluntary Sector Option of the New Deal);
     (ii) an employment programme specified in regulation 75(1)(a)(ii)(cc) of the JSA Regulations (Environmental Task Force Option of the New Deal) or regulation 75(1)(a)(iii) of the JSA (NI) Regulations; [⁸ . . .]
     [⁸ (iia) an employment programme specified in regulation 75(1)(a)(ii)(dd) of the JSA Regulations (Community Task Force);]
     (iii) the Intensive Activity Period of the New Deal Pilots for 25 Plus specified in regulation 75(1)(a)(iv) of the JSA Regulations or, in Northern Ireland, the Preparation for Employment Programme specified in regulation 75(1)(a)(v) of the JSA (NI) Regulations; [⁸ or
     (iv) the Backing Young Britain programme pursuant to arrangements made under section 2 of the Employment Act);]
     [⁷ . . .]
  (b) a written arrangement entered into between—
     (i) the Secretary of State and the person who has arranged for the claimant's participation in the Intensive Activity Period of the New Deal for 25 Plus and which is made in respect of his participation in that Period; or
     (ii) the Department for Employment and Learning and the person who has arranged for the claimant's participation in the Preparation for Employment Programme and which is made in respect of the claimant's participation in the Programme [⁷; or]
  [⁷ (c) the Steps to Work Programme specified in regulation 75(1)(a)(vi) of the Jobseeker's Allowance Regulations (Northern Ireland) 1996.]
[³This item applies only to the extent that the payment is not taxable as a profit of a trade, profession or vocation.]

4. Any discretionary payment pursuant to section 2 of the Employment Act, or, in Northern Ireland, section 1(1) of the Employment and Training Act (Northern Ireland) 1950 to meet, or help to meet, special needs in respect of the claimant's participation in the Full-Time Education and Training Option of the New Deal as specified in regulation 75(1)(b)(ii) of the JSA Regulations or of the JSA (NI) Regulations.

5. Any—
  (a) education maintenance allowance in accordance with regulations made under section 518 of the Education Act 1996 (payment of school expenses; grant of scholarships, etc.); or
  (b) payment (not within sub-paragraph (a)) in respect of a course of study attended by a child or qualifying young person payable—

(SI 2002/2006 reg.19) as amended

   (i) in accordance with regulations made under section 518 of the Education (Scotland) Act 1980 (power to assist persons to take advantage of educational facilities) or section 12(2)(c) of the Further and Higher Education (Scotland) Act 1992 (provision of financial assistance to students); or
   (ii) by virtue of regulations made in Article 50, 51 or 55(1) of the Education and Libraries (Northern Ireland) Order 1986 (provisions to assist persons to take advantage of educational facilities).

6. Any payment made by an employment zone contractor payable in respect of the claimant's participation in the employment zone programme by way of—
  (a) a training premium;
  (b) a discretionary payment, being a fee, grant, loan or otherwise; or
  (c) any arrears of subsistence allowance paid as a lump sum.

7. [³...]

8. An amount of income equal to any qualifying maintenance payment within section 347B of the Taxes Act.

[¹⁰ **9.** Any payment by way of qualifying care receipts to the extent that those receipts qualify for relief under Chapter 2 of Part 7 of the Income Tax (Trading and Other Income) Act 2005(4).]

10. Any payment of maintenance, whether under a court order or not, which is made or due to be made by—
  (a) the claimant's former partner, or the claimant's partner's former partner; or
  (b) the parent of a child or qualifying young person where that child or qualifying young person is a member of the claimant's household except where that parent is the claimant or the claimant's partner.

11. Any payment in respect of a child or qualifying young person who is a member of the claimant's household made—
  [²(a) to adopters which is exempt from income tax by virtue of [⁵ sections 744 to 746 of ITTOIA];]
  (b) by a local authority in pursuance of paragraph 15(1) of Schedule 1 to the Children Act 1989 (local authority contribution to child's maintenance);
  [³(bb) by a local authority by way of special guardianship support services pursuant to regulations under section 14F(1)(b) of the Children Act 1989; or]
  (c) by an authority, as defined in Article 2 of the Children (Northern Ireland) Order 1995, in pursuance of Article 15 of, and paragraph 17 of Schedule 1 to, that Order (contribution by an authority to child's maintenance).

[⁹ **12.** Any payment in respect of travelling expenses—
  (a) in relation to England under regulation 5, 6 or 12 of the National Health Service (Travel Expenses and Remission of Charges) Regulations 2003;

(b) in relation to Wales under regulation 5, 6 or 11 of the National Health Service (Travelling Expenses and Remission of Charges) (Wales) Regulations 2007;
(c) in relation to Scotland, under regulation 3, 5, or 11 of the National Health Service (Travelling Expenses and Remission of Charges) (Scotland) (No.2) Regulations 2003;
(d) in relation to Northern Ireland, under regulation 5, 6 or 11 of the Travelling Expenses and Remission of Charges Regulations (Northern Ireland) 2004; or
(e) made by the Secretary of State for Health, the Scottish Ministers, the Welsh Ministers or the Department of Health [[18] and Social Care], Social Services and Public Safety and which is analogous to a payment specified in paragraph (a), (b), (c) or (d).]

13. Any payment made by the Secretary of State or the Scottish Ministers under a scheme established to assist relatives and other persons to visit persons in custody.

[[2]**14.** Any payment under the Community Care (Direct Payments) Act 1996, section 57 of the Health and Social Care Act 2001, [[13] . . .]Article 15A of the Health and Personal Social Services (Direct Payments) (Northern Ireland) Order 1996 [[4] or regulations made under section 57 of the Health and Social Care Act 2001 (direct payments)] [[15], sections 50 to 53 of the Social Services and Well-being (Wales) Act 2014] or section 8 of the Carers and Direct Payments Act (Northern Ireland) 2002 [[13] or as a direct payment as defined in section 4(2) of the Social Care (Self-directed Support) (Scotland) Act 2013].]

[[1]**14A.** Any payment made under the "Supporting People" programme—
(a) in England and Wales, under section 93 of the Local Government Act 2000;
(b) in Scotland, under section 91 of the Housing (Scotland) Act 2001; or
(c) in Northern Ireland, under Article 4 of the Housing Support Services (Northern Ireland) Order 2002.]

15. [[1]Any payment or a voucher] provided under section 95 or 98 of the Immigration and Asylum Act 1999 for any former asylum-seeker or his dependants.

16. Any payment of a provident benefit by a trade union.
Here—
"provident benefit" has the meaning given in section 467(2) of the Taxes Act; and
"trade union" has the meaning given in section 467(4) of the Taxes Act.

[[12] **17.** Armed forces independence payment under the Armed Forces and Reserve Forces (Compensation Scheme) Order 2011.]

[[16] **18.** Any payment made under the Welfare Supplementary Payment (Loss of Disability Living Allowance) Regulations (Northern Ireland) 2016, the Welfare Supplementary Payment (Loss of Disability-Related Premiums) Regulations (Northern Ireland) 2016, Part 2 of the Welfare

(SI 2002/2006 reg.19) as amended

Supplementary Payments Regulations (Northern Ireland) 2016, or Parts 3 to 5 of the Welfare Supplementary Payment (Loss of Carer Payments) Regulations (Northern Ireland) 2016 .]
[¹⁷ **19.** Any payment made by the Scottish Ministers to a claimant who is, or who has been, in receipt of carer's allowance under section 70 of the Contributions and Benefits Act (carer's allowance) during the relevant tax year to supplement that allowance. [²⁰. . .]
[¹⁷ **20.** Any payment in respect of funeral expense assistance which is made by the Scottish Ministers to a claimant who has accepted responsibility for the expenses of a funeral to meet, or help towards meeting, those expenses.]
[¹⁷ **21.** Any payment made by the Scottish Ministers in respect of early years assistance, which is made for the purposes of meeting some of the costs associated with having, or expecting to have, a baby or child in the family.]
[¹⁷ **22.** Any discretionary financial assistance payment which is made by a Scottish local authority to a claimant who is in receipt of housing benefit provided by virtue of a scheme under section 123 of the Contributions and Benefits Act (income-related benefits) to meet, or help towards meeting, a claimant's housing costs. [³¹. . .]
[¹⁹ **23.** Any discretionary payment made pursuant to the Discretionary Support Regulations (Northern Ireland) 2016.]
[¹⁹ **24.** Any payment made under, or in connection with, the Windrush Compensation Scheme administered by the Home Office.]

[²⁰**25.** Any payment made, in accordance with arrangements made by the Scottish Ministers, to a person to whom an offer of employment has been made, in order to assist that person to retain employment, if—
(a) that person—
  (i) was, at the date on which the offer of employment was made, at least 16 years of age but had not reached 25 years of age;
  (ii) had not been in employment at any time in the period of 6 months before the date on which that offer was made; and
  (iii) applies to the Scottish Ministers for assistance under arrangements made under section 2 of the Employment and Training Act 1973, within the period of one year beginning with the date on which that offer was made; or
(b) that person—
  (i) was, at the date on which the offer of employment was made, aged at least 16 years of age but had not reached 26 years of age;
  (ii) had been looked after by a local authority on or after that person's 16th birthday but was at the date that the offer of employment was made no longer looked after by a local authority; and

The Tax Credits (Definition and Calculation of Income) Regulations 2002

(iii) applies to the Scottish Ministers for assistance under arrangements made under section 2 of the Employment and Training Act 1973 within the period of one year beginning with the date on which that offer was made.
In this item "looked after by a local authority" has the same meaning as in regulation 2 (interpretation) of the Child Tax Credit Regulations 2002.]
[^{20}**26.** Any payment of disability assistance under section 31 of the Social Security (Scotland) Act 2018.]
[^{20}**27.** Any payment made in accordance with arrangements made by the Scottish Ministers for, or in connection with, the abuse or neglect of a person whilst that person was a child who was under the care or responsibility of a body, society or organisation in Scotland.]
[^{20}**28.** Any payment made by the Scottish Ministers in accordance with regulations made under section 79 of the Social Security (Scotland) Act 2018 to a person in respect of a child for whom that person is responsible.]
[^{20}**29.** Any payment of young carer grant made under the Carer's Assistance (Young Carers Grant) (Scotland) Regulations 2019.]
[^{20}**30.** Any payment in respect of short-term assistance given in accordance with section 36 of the Social Security (Scotland) Act 2018.]
[^{20}**31.** Any payment of winter heating assistance given in accordance with section 30 of the Social Security (Scotland) Act 2018.]
[^{20}**32.** Any payment made by the National Emergencies Trust (a registered charity established on 28th March 2019 with registered charity number: 1182809).]
[^{20}**33.** Any payment made under a scheme established by the Secretary of State in accordance with section 10 of the Northern Ireland (Executive Formation etc) Act 2019.]
[^{21}**34.** A payment, whether in cash or by way of a voucher, in lieu of free school meals.
35. A payment in connection with emergency volunteering leave under Schedule 7 to the Coronavirus Act 2020.
36. [^{22} . . .]]
[^{22} **37.** Any payment made under the scheme known as the NHS Test and Trace Self-Isolation Payment Scheme established on 1st September 2020 [^{23} . . .] [^{23}or the scheme known as the Test and Trace Support Payment scheme established on 28th September 2020 in respect of England or any other scheme established in any part of the United Kingdom for the purpose of providing financial support to people who are required to self-isolate due to coronavirus and cannot work from home].]
[^{23}**38.** Any payment, made by or on behalf of the Scottish Ministers under Part 5 of the Welfare Food (Best Start Foods) (Scotland) Regulations 2019.]
[^{23}**39.** Any payment, funded by the Scottish Government, for the purpose of supporting women affected by complications after mesh implant surgery.]

(SI 2002/2006 reg.19) as amended

[²³[²⁵**40.** Any payment made under the scheme known as the Covid Winter Grant Scheme, or the Covid Local Support Grant established under section 31 of the Local Government Act 2003 in respect of England or any corresponding schemes established by the Northern Ireland Executive, the Scottish Government or the Welsh Government for the purpose of providing financial support to families and vulnerable individuals to assist with the cost of food and utilities.]]

[²⁴**41.** A payment made under the Covid-19 support scheme: working households receiving tax credits.]

[²⁶**42.** Any payment made under the scheme known as the "Household Support Fund" in respect of England or any corresponding schemes established by the Northern Ireland Executive, the Scottish Government or the Welsh Government.]

[²⁷**43.** Any payment made in accordance with the terms of the Homes for Ukraine Scheme to a person who has been approved under that scheme to provide accommodation to persons who are eligible under that scheme.

In this item, "Homes for Ukraine Scheme" means the scheme established by the Department for Levelling Up, Housing and Communities on 18th March 2022.]

[²⁹**44.** An award of compensation made under the Victims of Overseas Terrorism Compensation Scheme 2012 or any corresponding scheme established under section 47 of the Crime and Security Act 2010.]

[³¹**45.** Any payment made by the Post Office or the Secretary of State for the purpose of providing compensation which is—
(a) in connection with the failings of the Horizon System, or
(b) otherwise payable following the judgment of *Bates and Others v Post Office Limited* ((No.3) "Common Issues").

In this item—
(a) "the Horizon System" means a version of the computer system used by the Post Office known as Horizon, Horizon Legacy, Horizon Online or HNG-X;
(b) "the Post Office" means Post Office Limited (registered number 02154540).]

[³¹**46.** Any payment made by a Scottish local authority to parents, under section 20 of the Local Government in Scotland Act 2003, as part of the scheme entitled Parental Transitions Support, to ease progression into work, the eligibility for which is dependent on—
(a) the receipt of certain social security benefits, as specified by that scheme, and
(b) the receipt of a formal offer to start work.]

[³¹**47.** Any payment made by a housing association or local authority in England, from funding granted by the Department for Work and Pensions under section 2 of the Employment Act, to a person residing in social housing, as an incentive to enter employment.]

The Tax Credits (Definition and Calculation of Income) Regulations 2002

Table 7. Sums disregarded in calculating income if conditions are satisfied

2.262

1. Description of payment	2. [³Conditions] that must be satisfied
1. Any payment in respect of any expenses incurred by a claimant who is engaged by a charitable or voluntary organisation or is a volunteer.	The claimant does not receive remuneration or profit from the engagement and is not treated as possessing any employment income under regulation 17 in respect of that engagement.
2. A payment by way of— (a) travelling expenses reimbursed to the claimant; (b) a living away from home allowance under section 2(2)(d) of the Employment Act, section 2(4)(c) of the Enterprise and New Towns (Scotland) Act 1990 or section 1 of the Employment and Training Act (Northern Ireland) 1950; (c) training grant; [⁷ . . .] (d) childcare expenses reimbursed to the claimant in respect of his participation in— (i) a New Deal option; (ii) the Intensive Activity Period of the New Deal Pilots for 25 Plus; [⁶ . . .] (iii) the Preparation for Employment Programme [⁶ [⁸ . . .]] [⁶ (iv) the Flexible New Deal specified in regulation 75(1)(a)(v) of the [⁸ JSA Regulations 1996]]; [⁸ (v) the Community Task Force specified in regulation 75(1) (a)(ii)(dd) of the JSA Regulations;] [⁷ or	The claimant— (a) participates in arrangements for training made under— (i) section 2 of the Employment Act; (ii) section 2 of the Enterprise and New Towns (Scotland) Act 1990; or (iii) section 1 of the Employment and Training Act (Northern Ireland) 1950; or (b) attends a course at an employment rehabilitation centre established under section 2 of the Employment Act. [³The payment is not taxable as a profit of a trade, profession or vocation.]

(SI 2002/2006 reg.19) as amended

1. Description of payment	2. [³*Conditions*] that must be satisfied
(e) child care expenses under the Steps to Work Programme specified in regulation 75(1)(a)(vi) of the [⁸ JSA (NI) Regulations]].	

Table 8. Sums partly disregarded in the calculation of income

Type of payment to be disregarded	Limit on, or exception to, the extent of disregard
1. Any discretionary payment made pursuant to section 2 of the Employment Act, or, in Northern Ireland, section 1(1) of the Employment and Training Act (Northern Ireland) 1950 to meet, or help meet, the claimant's special needs in undertaking a qualifying course within the meaning of regulation 17A(7) of the JSA Regulations or regulation 17A(7) of the JSA (NI) Regulations.	A payment is not within this item to the extent that it relates to travel expenses incurred as a result of the claimant's attendance on the course if an amount in respect of those expenses has already been disregarded pursuant to regulation 8.
2. Any payment made in respect of a career development loan paid pursuant to section 2 of the Employment Act.	A payment is not within this item to the extent that the loan has been applied for or paid in respect of living expenses for the period of education and training supported by the loan.
3. Any payment made to the claimant or his partner in respect of a person who is not normally a member of the claimant's household but is temporarily in his care, by— (a) a health authority; (b) a local authority; (c) a voluntary (c) organisation; (d) that person pursuant to section 26(3A) of the National Assistance Act 1948;	A payment is only to be disregarded by virtue of this item if [¹(a)] any profits[⁵...] arising from the payment mentioned in col.1 are treated as nil by [⁵ section 791 to 794 of ITTOIA (full rent-a-room relief)]; or[¹(b)] excluded from profits [⁵by section 795 to 798 of ITTOIA (alternative calculation of profits if amount exceeds limit).]

2.263

Type of payment to be disregarded	Limit on, or exception to, the extent of disregard
[¹⁴(dza) that person where the payment is for the provision of accommodation in respect of the meeting of that person's needs under section 18 or 19 of the Care Act 2014 (duty and power to meet needs for care and support) [¹⁵ or section 35 or 36 of the Social Services and Well-being (Wales) Act 2014 (duty and power to meet care and support needs of an adult)];] [¹¹(da) [²⁸ an integrated care board established under Chapter A3 of Part 2 of the National Health Service Act 2006]; (db) [³⁰NHS England]	
4. Any payment made in Northern Ireland to the claimant or his partner in respect of a person who is not normally a member of the claimant's household but is temporarily in his care— (a) pursuant to Article 36(7) of the Health and Personal Social Services (Northern Ireland) Order 1972 by an authority; a voluntary organisation; or the person concerned; or (b) by a training school within the meaning of section 137 of the Children and Young Persons Act (Northern Ireland) 1968.	A payment is only to be disregarded by virtue of this item if— [¹(a)] any profits [⁴...] arising from the payment mentioned in column 1 are treated as nil by [⁴ section 791 to 794 of ITTOIA (full rent-a-room relief)]; or [¹(b)] excluded from profits [⁴by section 795 to 798 of ITTOIA (alternative calculation of profits if amount exceeds limit).]

(SI 2002/2006 reg.19) as amended

Type of payment to be disregarded	Limit on, or exception to, the extent of disregard
In this item "an authority" has the meaning given by Article 2 of the Children (Northern Ireland) Order 1995.	
5. Any payment under an insurance policy taken out to insure against the risk of being unable to maintain the repayments— (a) on a loan which is secured on the dwelling house which the claimant occupies as his home; or (b) under a regulated agreement or under a hire-purchase agreement or a conditional sale agreement. For the purposes of paragraph (b)— "regulated agreement" has the meaning given in the Consumer Credit Act 1974; and "hire-purchase agreement" and "conditional sale agreement" have the meanings given in Part 3 of the Hire-Purchase Act 1964.	A payment is only to be disregarded by virtue of this item to the extent that it is used to— (a) maintain the repayments referred to in col.(1); and (b) meet any amount due by way of premiums on— (i) that policy; or (ii) in a case to which paragraph (a) of this item applies, an insurance policy taken out to insure against loss or damage to any building or part of a building which is occupied by the claimant as his home and which is required as a condition of the loan referred to in column (1).
[¹6]. Any payment in respect of the claimant's attendance at court as a juror or witness.	This item applies only to the extent that the payment is not compensation for loss of earnings or for the loss of payment of social security income.

The Tax Credits (Definition and Calculation of Income) Regulations 2002

Type of payment to be disregarded	Limit on, or exception to, the extent of disregard
[1 7]. Any payment of a sports award except to the extent that it has been made in respect of living expenses.	For the purposes of this item "living expenses" does not include— (a) the cost of vitamins, minerals or other special dietary supplements intended to enhance the performance of the claimant in the sport in respect of which the award was made; or (b) accommodation costs incurred as a consequence of living away from home whilst training for, or competing in, the sport in respect of which the award was made.

AMENDMENTS

1. Tax Credits (Definition and Calculation of Income) (Amendment) Regulations 2003 (SI 2003/732) reg.11 (April 6, 2003).
2. Tax Credits (Miscellaneous Amendments No.2) Regulations 2003 (SI 2003/2815) reg.11 (November 26, 2003).
3. Tax Credits (Miscellaneous Amendments) Regulations 2004 (SI 2004/762) reg.16 (April 6, 2004).
4. Community Care, Services for Carers and Children's Services (Direct Payments) (Wales) Regulations 2004 reg.12 and Sch.2 para.3 (November 1, 2004).
5. Tax Credits (Miscellaneous Amendments) Regulations 2006 (SI 2006/766) reg.19 (April 6, 2006).
6. Tax Credits (Miscellaneous Amendments) Regulations 2009 (SI 2009/697) reg.8 (October 5, 2009).
7. Tax Credits (Miscellaneous Amendments) (No.2) Regulations 2009 (SI 2009/2887) reg.7(2) and (3) (November 21, 2009).
8. Tax Credits (Miscellaneous Amendments) Regulations 2010 (SI 2010/751) reg.5(8) (April 6, 2010).
9. Tax Credits (Miscellaneous Amendments) (No.3) Regulations 2010 (SI 2010/2914) reg.5 (December 31, 2010).
10. Tax Credits (Miscellaneous Amendments) Regulations 2011 (SI 2011/721) reg.2(3) (April 6, 2011).
11. National Treatment Agency (Abolition) and the Health and Social Care Act 2012 (Consequential, Transitional and Saving Provisions) Order 2013 (SI 2013/235) art.11 and Sch.2 para.55 (April 1, 2013).
12. Armed Forces and Reserve Forces Compensation Scheme (Consequential Provisions: Subordinate Legislation) Order 2013 (SI 2013/591) art.7 and Sch. para.25 (April 8, 2013).
13. Social Care (Self-directed Support) (Scotland) Act 2013 (Consequential Modifications and Savings) Order 2014 (SI 2014/513) art.2 Sch. para.8 (April 1, 2014).
14. Care Act 2014 (Consequential Amendments) (Secondary Legislation) Order 2015 (SI 2015/643) art.20 (April 1, 2015).

(SI 2002/2006 reg.19) as amended

15. Tax Credits and Child Benefit (Miscellaneous Amendments) Regulations 2016 (SI 2016/360) reg.3(4) (April 6, 2016).
16. Tax Credits (Definition and Calculation of Income) (Amendment) Regulations 2016 (SI 2016/978) reg.2(3) (October 31, 2016).
17. Tax Credits and Childcare (Miscellaneous Amendments) Regulations 2018 (SI 2018/365) reg.2(6) (April 6, 2018).
18. Secretaries of State for Health and Social Care and for Housing, Communities and Local Government and Transfer of Functions (Commonhold Land) Order 2018 (SI 2018/378) art.15 and Sch. para.21(g) (April 11, 2018).
19. Tax Credits, Child Benefit and Childcare Payments (Miscellaneous Amendments) Regulations 2019 (SI 2019/364) reg.3(5) (March 21, 2019).
20. Tax Credits, Child Benefit, Guardian's Allowance and Childcare Payments (Miscellaneous Amendments) Regulations 2020 (SI 2020/297) reg.3 (April 6, 2020).
21. Tax Credits (Coronavirus, Miscellaneous Amendments) Regulations 2020 (SI 2020/534) reg.3(5) (May 23, 2020).
22. Tax Credits (Coronavirus, Miscellaneous Amendments) (No.2) Regulations 2020 (SI 2020/941) reg.2(3) (September 25, 2020).
23. Tax Credits, Childcare Payments and Childcare (Extended Entitlement) (Coronavirus and Miscellaneous Amendments) Regulations 2020 (SI 2020/1515) reg.3(3) (January 14, 2021).
24. Social Security and Tax Credits (Miscellaneous and Coronavirus Amendments) Regulations 2021 (SI 2021/495) reg.4 (May 13, 2021).
25. Tax Credits and Child Benefit (Miscellaneous and Coronavirus Amendments) Regulations 2021 (SI 2021/810) reg.2 (July 29, 2021).
26. Tax Credits and Child Benefit (Miscellaneous Amendments) Regulations 2021 (SI 2021/1286) reg.3 (December 9, 2021).
27. Child Benefit and Tax Credits (Amendment) Regulations 2022 (SI 2022/346) reg.3(2) (March 22, 2022).
28. Health and Care Act 2022 (Consequential and Related Amendments and Transitional Provisions) Regulations 2022 (SI 2022/634) reg.99 and Sch. (July 1, 2022).
29. Child Benefit and Tax Credits (Miscellaneous Amendments) Regulations 2023 (SI 2023/1139) reg.3(3) (October 27, 2023).
30. Health and Care Act 2022 (Further Consequential Amendments) (No.2) Regulations 2023 (SI 2023/1071) reg.6 (November 6, 2023).
31. Tax Credits (Miscellaneous Amendments) Regulations 2024 (SI 2024/176) reg.3 (March 13, 2024).

CROSS-REFERENCES

Taxes Act s.347B	Qualifying maintenance payments
F(2)A 1992 Sch.10	Furnished Accommodation

GENERAL NOTE

This regulation adds to the exemptions and exceptions in regs 3 and 9 that apply generally to income. Exceptions, exemptions and deductions that are specific to one or more kinds of income, but not all kinds of income, are detailed under the specific regulations.

2.264

Table 6

This sets out the sums to be disregarded in total. For fuller notes, see the similar items in Income Support (General) Regulations 1987 (SI 1987/1967) Sch.9 (in Vol.II in this series). Several of the provisions are wider than the equivalent provision in the Income Support (General) Regulations 1987 because these provisions also apply to Northern Ireland, while the Income Support (General) Regulations 1987 apply to Great Britain only.

2.265

Paragraph 1—see Sch.9 para.63.
Paragraph 2—see Sch.9 para.51.
Paragraph 3—see Sch.9 para.62.
Paragraph 4—see Sch.9 para.13.
Paragraph 5—see Sch.9 para.11.
Paragraph 6—see Sch.9 para.72.
Paragraph 8—this excludes all sums within the scope of ITA 2007 ss.453–456 (certain periodic payments made by one party to a marriage or former marriage to the other party for the maintenance of the other party or their children under a court order or agreement).
Paragraph 9—Under Ch.2 of P.7 to ITTOIA, foster-care receipts are only taxable if they are more than the fixed amount for the tax year (£10,000) plus the amounts for children: £200 a week for a child under 11 and £250 for a child over 11.
Paragraph 10—this widens out the scope of para.8.
Paragraph 11—see Sch.9 para.25.
Paragraph 12—see Sch.9 para.48.
Paragraph 13—see Sch.9 para.50.
Paragraph 14—see Sch.9 para.58.
Paragraph 14A—this is a new provision.
Paragraph 15—this is specifically focussed on former asylum-seekers or dependants.
Paragraph 16—s.467 of the Taxes Act provides exemption from tax to trade unions that provide provident benefits to their members not exceeding £4,000 as a capital sum or £825 a year as an annuity during sickness, incapacity or old age, or after an accident, theft or death. The excludes the annuities from counting as income of claimants.
Paragraph 17—armed forces independence payments.
Paragraph 18—payments under Northern Ireland legislation designed to offset loss of certain disability-related and carers' benefits.
Paragraphs 19–22—various social security-type payments made by the Scottish Ministers and discretionary housing assistance payments made by Scottish local authorities to Scottish housing benefit recipients.
Paragraph 23–discretionary payments under the Discretionary Support Regulations (Northern Ireland) 2016.
Paragraph 24–Windrush compensation scheme payments.
Paragraph 25–Payments by Scottish Ministers to assist a person to retain employment.
Paragraph 26–Disability assistance payment (Scotland).
Paragraph 27–Payments by Scottish Ministers related to institutional abuse or neglect.
Paragraph 28–Payments by Scottish Ministers to a person responsible for a child.
Paragraph 29–Young Carer Grant (Scotland).
Paragraph 30–Short-term Assistance Payment (Scotland).
Paragraph 31–Winter Heating Assistance Payment (Scotland).
Paragraph 32–Payments by National Emergencies Trust.
Paragraph 33–Payments in accordance with section 10 of the Northern Ireland (Executive Formation etc) Act 2019.
Paragraph 34–free school meal payments.
Paragraph 35–payments for Coronavirus-related emergency volunteering leave.
Paragraph 36–[*revoked*]
Paragraph 37–payments under the Coronavirus-related Self-Isolation Payment Scheme.
Paragraph 38–welfare food payments (Scotland).
Paragraph 39–mesh implant surgery support payments (Scotland).
Paragraph 40–Covid Winter Grant Scheme payments.
Paragraph 41–Payments made under the Covid-19 support scheme for recipients of working tax credit. The scheme provides for a single payment of £500 to be made to persons awarded working tax credit for 2020/21 whose employment income

may have been adversely affected by the pandemic. The direction establishing the scheme is available at *http://www.gov.uk/government/publications/treasury-direction-made-under-section-76-of-the-coronavirus-act-2020.*

Paragraph 42–Payments under the Household Support Fund or any corresponding fund established by the Northern Ireland Executive, the Scottish Government or the Welsh Government.

Paragraph 43–Payments under the Homes for Ukraine Scheme.

Paragraph 44–compensation payments under the Victims of Overseas Terrorism Compensation Scheme 2012 or a corresponding scheme under the Crime and Security Act 2010 s.47.

Paragraph 45–compensation payments related to the *Horizon* postmasters scandal.

Paragraph 46–payments under the Scottish Parental Transitions Support scheme.

Paragraph 47–DWP-funded payments to a person residing in social housing, as an incentive to enter employment.

However, there are some differences between the tax credit provisions and the income support provisions listed. For example, the disregard in para.11 in Table 6 omits to mention local authority payments in Scotland under ss.34(6) or 50 of the Children Act 1975, whereas these payments are included in the equivalent income support rule: see Income Support (General) Regulations 1987 (SI 1987/1967) Sch.9 para.25(1)(b)). This would suggest that such payments in Scotland are disregarded for income support purposes but not for tax credits assessments. Note that, so far as England and Wales is concerned, the Children Act 1975 was repealed by the Children Act 1989, but this did not extend to Scotland: Children Act 1989 s.108(11).

Table 7

For item 1 see also the Income Support (General) Regulations 1987 (SI 1987/1967) Sch.9 para.2. For Item 2, see Sch.9 para.13.

2.266

Table 8

The final table lists those disregards that apply to part only of a payment. Item 1 is to the same effect as Income Support (General) Regulations 1987 (SI 1987/1967) Sch.9 para.65. Item 2 is based on Sch.9 para.59. Item 3 is similar to Sch.9 para.27, but excepts from it any payments that are or would be protected from income tax under the rent-a-room provisions (see reg.11). Item 4 is the equivalent provision for Northern Ireland. Item 5 parallels Sch.9 paras 29 and 30ZA. Item 6 is the same as Sch.9 para.43. Item 7 is based on Sch.9 para.69.

2.267

The Child Tax Credit Regulations 2002

(SI 2002/2007) (AS AMENDED)

Whereas a draft of this instrument, which contains the first regulations made under section 9 of the Tax Credits Act 2002 has been laid before, and approved by resolution of, each House of Parliament:

Now, therefore, the Treasury, in exercise of the powers conferred on them by sections 8, 9, 65 and 67 of the Tax Credits Act 2002, hereby make the following Regulations:

ARRANGEMENT OF REGULATIONS

1. Citation, commencement and effect.
2. Interpretation.
3. Circumstances in which a person is or is not responsible for a child or qualifying young person.
4. Period for which a person who attains the age of 16 remains a child.

2.268

The Child Tax Credit Regulations 2002

5. Maximum age and prescribed conditions for a qualifying young person.
6. Entitlement to child tax credit after death of child or qualifying young person.
7. Determination of the maximum rate at which a person or persons may be entitled to child tax credit.
8. Prescribed conditions for a disabled or severely disabled child or qualifying young person.
9. Exceptions for the purposes of regulation 7(2A)(b)
10. Multiple births
11. Adoption
12. Non-parental caring arrangements
13. Non-consensual conception
14. Continuation of certain exceptions

Citation, commencement and effect

2.269   **1.**—These Regulations may be cited as the Child Tax Credit Regulations 2002 and shall come into force—
   (a) for the purpose of enabling claims to be made, on 1st August 2002;
   (b) for the purpose of enabling awards to be made, on 1st January 2003; and
   (c) for all other purposes on 6th April 2003; and shall have effect for the tax year beginning on 6th April 2003 and subsequent tax years.

Interpretation

2.270   **2.**—(1) In these Regulations, unless the context otherwise requires—
[¹⁴ "A", as a noun, has the meaning given by regulation 7(2A);]
"the Act" means the Tax Credits Act 2002;
"advanced education" means [¹²...]—
   (a) a course in preparation for a degree, a diploma of higher education, a higher national diploma, a higher national diploma or higher national certificate of Edexcel or the Scottish Qualifications Authority, or a teaching qualification; or
   (b) any other course which is of a standard above ordinary national diploma, a national diploma or national certificate of Edexcel [²...], a general certificate of education (advanced level), [²or Scottish national qualifications at higher or advanced higher level];
[⁴"approved training" has the meaning given by regulation 1(3) of the Child Benefit (General) Regulations 2006;]
[¹⁰"armed forces independence payment" means armed forces independence payment under the Armed Forces and Reserve Forces (Compensation Scheme) Order 2011;]
[¹"the Board" means the Commissioners [⁴for Her Majesty's Revenue and Customs];]
"the Careers Service" means—
   (a) in England and Wales, a person with whom the Secretary of State or the National Assembly of Wales has made arrangements under s.10(1) of the Employment Act, and a [⁶local authority] to whom the Secretary of State or the National Assembly of Wales has given a direction under section 10(2) of that Act;
   (b) in Scotland, a person with whom the Scottish Ministers have made arrangements under section 10(1) of the Employment Act and any education authority to which a direction has been given by the Scottish Ministers under section 10(2) of that Act; and

(SI 2002/2007 reg.1)

(c) [¹...];
"child" means a person who has not attained the age of sixteen [⁵...];
"claimant" has the meaning in section 9(8) of the Act, [¹⁴ except in regulations 7 and 9 to 14 (for which see regulations 7(1) and 13(13) to (15))];
"the Connexions Service" means a person of any description with whom the Secretary of State has made an arrangement under section 114(2)(a) of the Learning and Skills Act 2000 and section 10(1) of the Employment Act, and any person to whom he has given a direction under section 114(2)(b) of the former Act and section 10(2) of the latter Act;
"the Contributions and Benefits Act" means the Social Security Contributions and Benefits Act 1992;
[³"couple" has the meaning given by section 3(5A) of the Act];
"custodial sentence"—
   (a) in England and Wales, has the meaning in section 76 of the Powers of Criminal Courts (Sentencing) Act 2000 [¹⁶ or section 222 of the Sentencing Code];
   (b) in Scotland, means detention under a sentence imposed by a court under section 44, 205, 207 or 208 of the Criminal Procedure (Scotland) Act 1995; and
   (c) in Northern Ireland, means a custodial sentence under the Criminal Justice (Children) (Northern Ireland) Order 1998;
"disability living allowance" means a disability living allowance under section 71 of the Contributions and Benefits Act;
"the Employment Act" means the Employment and Training Act 1973;
"the family element of child tax credit" and "the individual element of child tax credit" shall be construed in accordance with section 9(3) of the Act;
[¹²...]
[¹⁴ "income support" means income support under section 124 of the Contributions and Benefits Act;]
"joint claim" and "single claim" shall be construed in accordance with section 3(8) of the Act;
"looked after by a local authority" has the meaning in section 22 of the Children Act 1989, [¹ section 74 of the Social Services and Well-being (Wales) Act 2014,] section 17(6) of the Children (Scotland) Act 1995 or (in Northern Ireland) Article 25 of the Children (Northern Ireland) Order 1995 (with the modification that for the reference to a local authority there is substituted a reference to an authority within the meaning in Article 2 of that Order) [¹, and (in Scotland) includes a child in respect of which a child assessment order within the meaning of section 35 of the Children's Hearings (Scotland) Act 2011 has been made or a child protection order within the meaning of section 37 of that Act has been made.];
the "main responsibility test" has the meaning given in rule 2.2. of regulation 3;
the "normally living with test" has the meaning given in rule 1.1. of regulation 3;
[¹⁴ "old style JSA" means a jobseeker's allowance under the Jobseekers Act 1995 as that Act has effect apart from the amendments made by Part 1 of Schedule 14 to the Welfare Reform Act 2012 that remove references to an income-based allowance;]

"Part I" means Part I of the Act;

"patient" means a person (other than a person who is serving a custodial sentence) who is regarded as receiving free in-patient treatment within the meaning of the Social Security (Hospital In-patients) Regulations 1975, or the Social Security (Hospital In-patients) Regulations (Northern Ireland) 1975;

[9"personal independence payment" means personal independence payment under Part 4 of the Welfare Reform Act 2012]

[8 "placing for adoption" means placing for adoption in accordance with—
(a) the Adoption Agencies Regulations 2005,
(b) the Adoption Agencies (Wales) Regulations 2005,
(c) the Adoption Agencies (Scotland) Regulations 2009, or
(d) the Adoption Agencies Regulations (Northern Ireland) 1989;]

[5 "qualifying body" means–
(a) the Careers Service or Connexions Service;
(b) the Ministry of Defence;
(c) in Northern Ireland, the Department for [15 Communities, the Department for the Economy or the Education Authority]; or
(d) for the purposes of applying Council Regulation (EEC) No.1408/71 [7 and Regulation (EC) No.883/2004 of the European Parliament and of the Council], any corresponding body in another member state;]

"qualifying young person" means a person, other than a child, who—
(a) has not attained the age of [4twenty]; and
(b) satisfies the conditions in regulation 5(3) and (4);

[5 . . .]

"remunerative work" means work which is—
(a) done for payment or in expectation of payment;
(b) undertaken for not less than 24 hours a week, calculated in accordance with regulation 4(3) of the Working Tax Credit (Entitlement and Maximum Rate) Regulations 2002; and
(c) not excluded from the meaning of engagement in remunerative work by regulation 4(2) of those Regulations;

[14 "step-parent", in relation to A, means a person who is not A's parent but—
(a) is a member of a couple, the other member of which is a parent of A, where both are responsible for A; or
(b) was previously a member of—
(i) a couple, the other member of which was a parent of A, or
(ii) a polygamous unit (within the meaning of the Tax Credits (Polygamous Marriages) Regulations 2003), another member of which was a parent of A,
if immediately prior to ceasing to be a member of that couple or that polygamous unit the person was, and has since remained, responsible for A;]

and other expressions have the same meanings as defined in the Act.

(2) In the application of these Regulations to Northern Ireland, a reference to a provision of an enactment which applies only to Great Britain or England and Wales, shall be construed, so far as necessary, as including a reference to the corresponding enactment applying to Northern Ireland.

(SI 2002/2007 reg.2) (as amended)

AMENDMENTS

1. Child Tax Credit (Amendment) Regulations 2003 (SI 2003/738) reg.3 (April 6, 2003).
2. Tax Credits (Miscellaneous Amendments No.2) Regulations 2003 (SI 2003/2815) reg.17 (November 26, 2003).
3. Civil Partnership Act 2004 (Tax Credits, etc.) (Consequential Amendments) Order 2005 (SI 2005/2919) art.4(2) (December 5, 2005).
4. Child Tax Credit (Amendment) Regulations 2006 (SI 2006/222) reg.3 (April 6, 2006).
5. Tax Credits (Miscellaneous Amendments) (No.2) Regulations 2008 (SI 2008/2169) reg.7 (September 1, 2008).
6. Local Education Authorities and Children's Services Authorities (Integration of Functions) (Local and Subordinate Legislation) Order 2010 (SI 2010/1172) art.4 and Sch.3 para.46 (May 5, 2010).
7. Tax Credits (Miscellaneous Amendments) (No.3) Regulations 2010 (SI 2010/2914) reg.9 (December 31, 2010).
8. Tax Credits (Miscellaneous Amendments) Regulations 2012 (SI 2012/848) reg.4(2) (April 6, 2012).
9. Personal Independence Payment (Supplementary Provisions and Consequential Amendments) Regulations 2013 (SI 2013/388) reg.8 and Sch. para.30(2) (April 8, 2013).
10. Armed Forces and Reserve Forces Compensation Scheme (Consequential Provisions: Subordinate Legislation) Order 2013 (SI 2013/591) art.7 and Sch. para.26(2) (April 8, 2013).
11. Children's Hearings (Scotland) Act 2011 (Consequential and Transitional Provisions and Savings) Order 2013 (SI 2013/1465) art.17 and Sch.1 para.19(2) (June 24, 2013).
12. Child Benefit (General) and Child Tax Credit (Amendment) Regulations 2014 (SI 2014/1231) reg.3 (June 4, 2014).
13. Tax Credits and Child Benefit (Miscellaneous Amendments) Regulations 2016 (SI 2016/360) reg.4(2) (April 6, 2016).
14. Child Tax Credit (Amendment) Regulations 2017 (SI 2017/387) reg.3 (April 6, 2017).
15. Tax Credits, Child Benefit and Childcare Payments (Miscellaneous Amendments) Regulations 2019 (SI 2019/364) reg.4(2) (March 21, 2019).
16. Sentencing Act 2020 Sch.24 para.331 (December 1, 2020).

Circumstances in which a person is or is not responsible for a child or qualifying young person

3.—(1) For the purposes of child tax credit the circumstances in which a person is or is not responsible for a child or qualifying young person shall be determined in accordance with the following Rules.

Rule 1

1.1. A person shall be treated as responsible for a child or qualifying young person who is normally living with him (the "normally living with test").

1.2. This Rule is subject to rules 2 to 4.

Rule 2 (Competing claims)

2.1. This Rule applies where—
(a) a child or qualifying young person normally lives with two or more persons in—

(i) different households; or
(ii) the same household, where those persons are not limited to the members of a [² . . .] couple; or
(iii) a combination of (i) and (ii); and
(b) two or more of those persons make separate claims (that is, not a single joint claim made by a [² . . .] couple) for child tax credit in respect of the child or qualifying young person.

2.2. The child or qualifying young person shall be treated as the responsibility of—
(a) only one of those persons making such claims; and
(b) whichever of them has (comparing between them) the main responsibility for him (the "main responsibility test");
subject to rules 3 and 4.

Rule 3

3.1. The persons mentioned in rule 2.2. (other than the child or qualifying young person) may jointly elect as to which of them satisfies the main responsibility test for the child or qualifying young person, and in default of agreement the Board may determine that question on the information available to them at the time of their determination.

Rule 4

4.1. A child or qualifying young person shall be treated as not being the responsibility of any person during any period in which any of the following Cases applies.

Case A	The child or qualifying young person is provided with, or placed in, accommodation under Part III of the Children Act 1989, [¹¹ Parts 4 or 6 of the Social Services and Well-being (Wales) Act 2014,] Part II of the Children (Scotland) Act 1995 [¹⁰ by virtue of a requirement in a child assessment order within the meaning of section 35 of the Children's Hearings (Scotland) Act 2011, a child protection order within the meaning of section 37 of that Act, a compulsory supervision order within the meaning of section 83 of that Act or an interim compulsory supervision order within the meaning of section 86 of that Act,] or Part IV of the Children (Northern Ireland) Order 1995, and the cost of that child's or qualifying young person's accommodation or maintenance is borne wholly or partly— (i) out of local authority funds under [⁹ section 22C(10)] [¹¹ . . .] of the Children Act 1989 [¹¹ or section 81(13) of the Social Services and Well-being (Wales) Act 2014] or [⁸ regulation 33 of the Looked After Children (Scotland) Regulations 2009]; (ii) in Northern Ireland, by an authority, within the meaning in Article 2, and under Article 27, of that Order; or (iii) out of other public funds. [⁴ . . .]

(SI 2002/2007 reg.3) (as amended)

Case B	The child or qualifying young person— (i) is being looked after by a local authority; and (ii) has been placed for adoption by that authority in the home of a person proposing to adopt him, and a local authority is making a payment in respect of the child's or qualifying young person's accommodation or maintenance, or both, under [⁹ section 22C(10)] [¹¹ . . .] of the Children Act 1989, [¹¹ section 81(13) of the Social Services and Well-being (Wales) Act 2014,] [⁸ regulation 33 of the Looked After Children (Scotland) Regulations 2009] or Article 27 of the Children (Northern Ireland) Order 1995. This Case applies in Northern Ireland with the modification that for references to a local authority there are substituted references to an authority (within the meaning in Article 2 of that Order).
Case C	A custodial sentence— (a) for life; (b) without limit of time; (c) of detention during Her Majesty's pleasure; (d) in Northern Ireland, of detention during the pleasure of the Secretary of State; or (e) for a term or period of more than four months, has been passed on the child or qualifying young person.
Case D	The [⁵ . . .] qualifying young person claims and is awarded child tax credit in his or her own right, in respect of a child for whom he or she is responsible, for that period.
[¹Case E	[⁵ . . .] The qualifying young person, claims incapacity benefit [⁶ or contributory employment and support allowance payable under Part 1 of the Welfare Reform Act 2007] in his or her own right and that benefit is paid to or in respect of him or her for that period. This Case does not apply at any time ("the later time") during a period of incapacity for work which began before 6th April 2004 in the case of a person in respect of whom, at a time— (a) during that period of incapacity, and (b) before that date, both incapacity benefit and child tax credit were payable, if child tax credit has been payable in respect of him or her continuously since 5th April 2004 until that later time. For the purposes of this Case "period of incapacity" shall be construed in accordance with section 30C of the 1992 Act (incapacity benefit: days and periods of incapacity for work) but disregarding subsections (5) and (5A) of that section.]

The Child Tax Credit Regulations 2002

[³Case F	[⁵ . . .] The qualifying young person claims and receives working tax credit in his or her own right (whether alone or on a joint claim). [⁵ . . .]
[⁵ Case G	The qualifying young person has a spouse, civil partner or partner with whom they are living and the spouse, civil partner or partner is not in full-time education or approved training as provided for under regulation 5(3).
Case H	The responsible person is the spouse, civil partner or partner of a qualifying young person with whom they are living. [⁷ Cases G and H do] not apply to persons in receipt of child tax credit for a qualifying young person who is living with a partner on the day before 1st September 2008.]

[⁴ **4.2.** Where a child or qualifying young person is in residential accommodation referred to in regulation 9 of the Child Benefit (General) Regulations 2006 and in the circumstances prescribed in paragraphs (a) or (b) of that regulation, he shall be treated as being the responsibility of any person who was treated as being responsible for him immediately before he entered that accommodation.]

(2) Where—
  (a) a claimant is treated as responsible for a child or qualifying young person by virtue of the preceding Rules, and
  (b) the child or qualifying young person has a child of his or her own, normally living with him or her,
the claimant shall also be treated as responsible for, and as having made a claim for child tax credit in respect of, the child of the child or qualifying young person (but without prejudice to the facts as to which of them is mainly responsible for that child).

AMENDMENTS

1. Tax Credits (Miscellaneous Amendments) Regulations 2004 (SI 2004/762) reg.2 (April 6, 2004).
2. Civil Partnership Act 2004 (Tax Credits, etc.) (Consequential Amendments) Order 2005 (SI 2005/2919) art.4(3) (December 5, 2005).
3. Child Tax Credit (Amendment No.2) Regulations 2006 (SI 2006/1163) reg.2 (May 24, 2006).
4. Child Tax Credit (Amendment) Regulations 2007 (SI 2007/2151) reg.3 (August 16, 2007).
5. Tax Credits (Miscellaneous Amendments) (No.2) Regulations 2008 (SI 2008/2169) reg.8 (September 1, 2008).
6. Employment and Support Allowance (Consequential Provisions) (No.3) Regulations 2008 (SI 2009/1879) reg.22(2) (October 27, 2008).
7. Tax Credits (Miscellaneous Amendments) Regulations 2009 (SI 2009/697) reg.10 (April 6, 2009).
8. Adoption and Children (Scotland) Act 2007 (Consequential Modifications) Order 2011 (SI 2011/1740) art.2 and Sch.1 para.29(3) (July 15, 2011).
9. Tax Credits (Miscellaneous Amendments) Regulations 2012 (SI 2012/848) reg.4(3) (April 6, 2012).
10. Children's Hearings (Scotland) Act 2011 (Consequential and Transitional Provisions and Savings) Order 2013 (SI 2013/1465) art.17 and Sch.1 para.19(3) (June 24, 2013).

(SI 2002/2007 reg.3) (as amended)

11. Tax Credits and Child Benefit (Miscellaneous Amendments) Regulations 2016 (SI 2016/360) reg.4(2) (April 6, 2016).

DEFINITIONS

"child"—see reg.2(1).
"claimant"—see reg.2(1).
"custodial sentence"—see reg.2(1).
"joint claim"—see reg.2(1).
"looked after by a local authority"—see reg.2(1).
"main responsibility test"—see reg.2(1).
"normally living with test"—see reg.2(1).
"placing for adoption"—see reg.2(1).
"qualifying young person"—see reg.2(1).

GENERAL NOTE

Section 8(1) of the TCA 2002 provides that entitlement to child tax credit is dependent upon the claimant (and/or his or her partner in the case of a joint claim) "being responsible for one or more children or qualifying young persons". The 2002 Act then provides that this expression may be defined further by regulations (s.8(2)). This regulation accordingly sets out a number of rules for determining whether a person is or is not responsible for a child or young person. The starting point is in r.1, namely that as a general rule, a person is responsible for a child or young person normally living with him or her. This presumption is then subject to r.2, which deals with competing claims, as well as r.3 (election by the parties or determination by HMRC in default of such agreement) and r.4 (special cases, principally involving children or young persons being accommodated at public expense and so not to be the subject of a child tax credit award). The Upper Tribunal rejected an attempt to challenge these rules as discriminatory against men in *HMRC v DH* [2009] UKUT 24 (AAC).

2.272

Paragraph (1)

Rule 1: The presumption is that a person is responsible for a child or qualifying young person "who is normally living with him" (r.1 para.1.1). This "normally living with test" has been inherited from WFTC (and, before that, family credit: see Family Credit (General) Regulations 1987 (SI 1987/1973) reg.7(1). The "normally living with test" was new to family credit, although the phrase "living with" the claimant was (and still is) used in the child benefit legislation (SSCBA 1992 s.143 and see, in particular *R(F) 2/79* and *R(F) 2/81*).

2.273

In the context of family credit (and later WFTC), *CFC 1537/1995* decided that a child "normally lives with" a person for the purposes of reg.7(1) if he or she spent more time with that person than anyone else. This was the construction that made sense of reg.7(2) of the 1987 Regulations, which made provision for cases where a child either spent equal amounts of time in different households or there was doubt as to which household a child was living in. But reg.7(2) only applied in cases of real doubt; if there was simply a factual dispute this was not enough to bring it into play. Where reg.7(2) applied, there was then a series of tests. The first was receipt of child benefit, the rules for which include methods of establishing priorities between claimants. If no one was receiving child benefit then if only one person had claimed child benefit, that person had priority. If there had been no claims (or more than one claim), the final test was who had "primary responsibility".

In *GJ v HMRC (TC)* [2013] UKUT 561 (AAC), Judge Wikeley emphasised that the "normally living with" test bears its ordinary meaning and that the relevant facts take priority over the terms of a residence order stating what ought to be the case. Such cases are therefore essentially to be determined on the evidence before a tribunal about the actual arrangements within which a child normally lives at relevant times. This was followed by Judge McKenna in *CTC/135/2013* where it was again emphasised that the test was a question of fact, and not to be determined by legal concepts such as parental responsibility.

2.274 *Rule 2:* Rule 2, which applies to competing claims for child tax credit, adopts a slightly different approach to the old reg.7(2). Accordingly, it does not necessarily follow that *CFC 1537/1995* applies in precisely the same way. Rule 2 applies where two or more people (not being a couple) make child tax credit claims and the relevant child or qualifying young person "normally lives with two or more persons" *either* in different households *or* in the same household (other than in the case of a couple with a child in the same household) *or* in an arrangement that is a combination of these two first possibilities (r.2 para.2.1). Thus, r.2 only comes into play when the child or young person may, as a matter of fact, already be regarded as "normally" (but separately) living with at least two persons. For example, a child might spend weekdays living with one parent and weekends with the other parent in a different household. Although the child will spend more time living with the weekday parent, it is perfectly proper to say that he or she *also* normally lives with the weekend parent, at least for part of the week. This being so, the definition of "normally living with" applied in *CFC 1537/1995* (i.e. spending more time with one person than anyone else) cannot apply for the purposes of the meaning of "normally lives" in r.2 para.2.1, as that is specifically designed to deal with the situation where a child or young person by definition "normally" lives in more than one place. However, where r.2 does so apply, the general rule is that, as between the competing claimants, the child or young person is treated as the responsibility of the person with "main responsibility" for him or her (r.2 para.2.2). Thus, although *CFC 1537/1995* should be applied with care in this context, ultimately it may be a distinction without a difference.

Further factual complexity can arise where a couple who were previously living together in the same household with children start to maintain separate households but in the same dwelling with the children still present. See for example *JI v HMRC* [2013] UKUT 199 (AAC). And see the strong criticisms by the judge in that decision about unfairness that may arise if proper claims are not made to deal with a breakup of a couple's marriage or partnership.

As we have seen, the former reg.7(2) of the 1987 Regulations resolved problematic cases by reference first to the person in receipt of child benefit and then, in the absence of a child benefit claim, to the person with "primary responsibility" for the child or young person. Rule 2 makes no reference to the child benefit position. Instead, cases of shared care—as these will inevitably be—are to be determined by reference to who has "main responsibility" for the child or young person. This is presumably likely to be determined on a time basis, and so the weekdays parent in the example above is likely to be regarded as the one with such responsibility. As with the former reg.7(2), "responsibility" has no special meaning in the legislation and so must be determined according to the ordinary everyday meaning of the word. It would not seem that there is any material difference between "primary responsibility" (reg.7) and "main responsibility" (r.2). It would also appear that under r.2, as under the former reg.7, responsibility or the normality of living may be judged on an overall basis over a period. This is different from the income support provision, where the test of responsibility still has to be applied week by week (*CIS 49/1991* and *Whelan v Chief Adjudication Officer, The Independent*, November 14, 1994).

It will be evident from the analysis above that there is, under these Rules, no provision for the division of child tax credit between competing parents. The Rules are premised on establishing which claimant (or which couple of joint claimants) is entitled to child tax credit for a given child or young person, not on apportioning child tax credit entitlement between separated individual claimants (e.g. 5/7 to the weekdays parent and 2/7 to the weekend parent). Although the practical and administrative difficulties with such an arrangement are obvious, it did appear from the primary legislation that this might be a possibility (see, e.g. TCA 2002 ss.8(2) and 9(7)). There remains, therefore, the prospect of human rights challenges in this area, as with social security benefits which have elements related to a child or children's presence in a particular household for part-weeks in cases of shared care: see the General Note to Income Support (General) Regulations 1987 (SI 1987/1967) reg.15, in Vol.II in this series). See now *HMRC v DH* [2009] UKUT 24 (AAC) discussed in the commentary to s.9(7) of the Tax Credits Act 2002.

The Commissioners considered competing claims in joint care cases both for child benefit and child tax credit. *CTC/4390/2004* decided that a tribunal must decide between two seemingly equally placed claimants, perhaps by looking at the one who would benefit more from the claim. *CTC/4390/2004* was not followed, and was criticised, by an Upper Tribunal judge in *CM v HMRC (TC)* [2010] UKUT 400 (AAC) on the issue of whether one party would benefit more than the other party from the relative amounts that may be claimed by the parties. In the reported decision *PG v HMRC and NG (TC)* [2016] AACR 45; [2016] UKUT 216 (AAC) Upper Tribunal Judge Jacobs agreed with those criticisms. *CTC/1686/2007* emphasises that the discretion available to the Secretary of State in child benefit cases is not available for child tax credit. On an appeal the tribunal must decide on the facts, and has no discretion. However, the Commissioner endorsed the view of the tribunal that it is better if the two competing claimants can agree between themselves. HMRC has indicated that it will respect such agreements, including where the result is that the competing claimants "divide" the children between them for claim purposes.

The attribution of responsibility for a child or young person to a particular person under r.2 is itself subject to rr.3 and 4.

In *CTC/3096/2007* the Commissioner emphasised the need to apply the "main responsibility" test; as Upper Tribunal Judge Wikeley said in *AG v HMRC & AG (TC)* [2018] UKUT 318 (AAC), "the language of Rule 2.2 is mandatory" and "not making a decision as to the issue of main responsibility is not an option". See also *CTC/1686/2007* where the Commissioner compares these rules with those for child benefit and child support. See also *KN v HMRC* [2009] UKUT 79 (AAC), in which Judge Gamble emphasised that the test is "responsibility" not "care". He put weight on the person responsible when the child was at school. These decisions were followed by Judge Humphrey in the unreported case of *CTC/2409/2013*.

In *PG v HMRC and NG* [2016] AACR 45; [2016] UKUT 216 (AAC) Judge Jacobs revisited the "main responsibility" test in Rule 2.2 with a useful review of previous decisions. Judge Jacobs agreed with Judge Gamble's view in *KN* that undue reliance should not be placed on "care", since that may divert attention from the statutory test of main responsibility, although he recognised, of course, the importance of caring arrangements in identifying who has main responsibility. The judge then set out useful guidance for determining where main responsibility may lie:

2.275

"29. Caring for a child is a major component of responsibility on any test. Although I agree with Judge Gamble's reasoning in *KN*, I warn against taking his remark at [5], that the test relates to responsibility rather than care, out of its context. The argument in that case was that neither parent should be treated as responsible for the time the child was at school. Judge Gamble rejected that argument and his remark was made in that context. He was making the point that there is more to responsibility than actual care, not that responsibility does not involve care as one of its components.

30. What are the components of taking practical responsibility for a child? Actually providing care is one of them, as I have just said. It also involves:

- making decisions from the mundane (what brand of trainers to buy for them) to the most significant (which school should they attend);
- providing for their needs by feeding and clothing them;
- nurturing them and protecting them in their physical, mental, educational and social development;
- being available in case of need.

Naturally, the extent to which there is a need for decisions and actions will vary according to the age of the child. I do not intend this list to be exhaustive.

31. Many of these actions and decisions will involve expenditure. That expenditure might be considerable; private education for example. The cost itself is not decisive. The issue depends on the exercise of responsibility, not the financial contribution. Main responsibility cannot be bought. It is not a prize for the parent with the deeper pocket or the more generous spirit.

32. The parents' arrangements may involve them in expenditure on themselves, most likely for the costs of their own travel and accommodation costs associated with contact. Those costs are not factors that can be taken into consideration. They are a consequence of the exercise of responsibility, not a part of it.

33. It is exceptional for parents to be able to devote themselves to their children 24 hours a day. Almost inevitably, they will leave some aspects of the most immediate care to others when the child is at school or they are working or otherwise busy. The others involved may be professionals, like teachers, or others, like baby sitters or grandparents. It may be a matter of choice or convenience to involve others. It may also be a matter of necessity if the parent is disabled, physically or mentally. Such parents may require a great deal of help with the practical aspects of caring and even with the decision-making. None of this means that parents are not responsible at times when others are also involved. They are nonetheless the person to go to in case of problems and the person who must ultimately take responsibility for making decisions and taking actions, whether this is done directly or with the assistance of others.

34. Parents vary in the quality of the decisions they make and the actions they take. Responsibility comes in many forms, as I have shown. In deciding who has the main responsibility, it is relevant to ask whether a parent is discharging particular aspects of responsibility. But it is not relevant to ask how well they are doing so, except in an extreme case where the discharge is so poor as not to amount to discharge at all. One person may be a good parent, another a bad parent, and a third an indifferent one. They all have responsibility for their children. And that is the test in rule 2.2. It is not a test of conscientiousness of effort or quality of attainment. The issue is who *has* the main responsibility, not the manner of its discharge."

In some cases, a parent argues that he or she must have main responsibility for a child or young person because the terms of a child arrangements order (previously residence order) which deals with a child's living arrangements require a child to spend the majority of his or her time with that parent. In *PG v HMRC and NG (TC)* [2016] AACR 45; [2016] UKUT 216 (AAC) (followed by Upper Tribunal Judge Wikeley in *AG v HMRC & AG (TC)* [2018] UKUT 318 (AAC)) Upper Tribunal Judge Jacobs held that such orders are not determinative of the main responsibility question. The judge set aside the decision of a tribunal that had taken the terms of a court order to be conclusive evidence that one parent had main responsibility:

"41. ....the tribunal's analysis of the time spent with each parent was based on the terms of the court order. The reasons record that there was no corroborative evidence of an agreement to vary the order, as envisaged by the order itself. That was wrong. The issue for the tribunal was which parent, comparatively speaking, had the main responsibility, not which parent should have had it under the strict terms of the court order. It should have made findings on the actual responsibility being exercised by each parent."

Judge Jacobs's decision in *PG* was followed by Deputy Upper Tribunal Judge May QC in *AB v HMRC (TC)* [2019] UKUT 410 (AAC). Having noted with approval Judge Jacobs's ruling in para.42 of PG that treating time spent with respective parents as determinative is a flawed approached because it "fails to take into account the lack of relationship between time spent and the nature of some of the decisions that are taken in the exercise of responsibility", Judge May held that it is also an

(SI 2002/2007 reg.3) (as amended)

error of law to treat as determinative a child's address as registered with professionals such as doctors, dentists and schools.

It is not permissible to determine the main responsibility test according to which of the competing claimants made the first claim (*AG v HMRC & AG (TC)* [2018] UKUT 318 (AAC)).

Rule 3: Where there are competing claims under r.2, the parties may by agreement notify HMRC as to which of them satisfies the main responsibility test for the child or young person in question. If the adults in question fail to agree, HMRC may determine that question on the information then available.

Rule 4: Rule 4 sets out a number of specific circumstances (or Cases) in which a child or young person is not to be treated as the responsibility of a tax credit claimant, even though any of rr.1–3 above might otherwise apply. Cases A–C all deal with situations in which a child or young person is being accommodated at public expense in one way or another and so payment of child tax credit is inappropriate. These are similar to the exclusions under the child benefit scheme. Case D covers the special case of a child (aged at least 16) or young person who has herself been awarded child tax credit in respect of her own child (see also para.(2) where child tax credit has not been awarded in such circumstances to the young parent).

Case A: This exclusion covers children or young persons who are provided with or placed in accommodation under Pt III of the Children Act 1989 or associated legislation. The exception in reg.3 of the Child Benefit (General) Regulations 1976 (now Child Benefit (General) Regulations 2006 (SI 2006/223) reg.9) deals with children or young persons who are provided with residential accommodation on account of their disability.

Case B: This exclusion applies where: (i) a child or young person is being looked after by a local authority (in the sense that term is used under the Children Act 1989); (ii) he or she has been placed for adoption; and (iii) a fostering allowance is in payment.

Case C: CTC will continue to be paid unless the child or young person has been sentenced to detention for a period of four months or longer. This is more generous than the equivalent rules for income support and income-based jobseeker's allowance, under which benefit for the child or young person ceases immediately he or she is taken into custody (Income Support (General) Regulations 1987 (SI 1987/1967) reg.16(5)(f) and (6); see also reg.15(3) regarding home leave). It is also more generous than the former WFTC and DPTC rules, under which there was no entitlement to the elements of those tax credits relating to children where a custodial sentence had been passed (Family Credit (General) Regulations 1987 (SI 1987/1973) reg.8(2)(e)). The justifications for the change given by ministers are the extra costs associated with contact and the need to enable families to maintain contact with the child or young person for whom they are responsible, and to assist with that person's re-integration in the community. It is difficult to see how these arguments do not apply equally forcefully in the context of income support and income-based jobseeker's allowance.

Case D: See also para.(2) below.

Case E: The effect of this provision is that a person is not to be treated as responsible for a child or a qualifying young person in respect of whom incapacity benefit is payable. There is transitional protection during a period of incapacity which began before April 6, 2004 for cases where both incapacity benefit and child tax credit were in payment in respect of the child or qualifying young person before that date.

Case F: This exclusion means that a person is not to be treated as responsible for a child or qualifying young person who is receiving WTC in his or her own right, whether alone or as part of a joint claim, with a spouse or partner. It also provides for a period of transitional protection for some CTC recipients.

Cases G and H: These exclusions ensure alignment between the rules for CTC and those for child benefit.

Paragraph (2): This deals with the special case where a person (the claimant) is found to be responsible for a child or young person under rr.1–4 above (and so the exception in Case D of r.4 does not apply) and that child or young person herself has a child. In such circumstances, the claimant is treated as responsible for child tax credit purposes for both his or her child (or young person) and that child's own child.

[¹ Period for which a person who attains the age of sixteen is a qualifying young person

2.281 **4.**—(1) [² Subject to paragraph (1A), a] person who attains the age of sixteen is a qualifying young person from the date on which that person attained that age until 31st August which next follows that date.

[² (1A) A person who attains the age of sixteen on 31st August is a qualifying young person from the date on which that person attained that age.]

(2) Paragraph (1) is subject to regulation 5 but as if there were no requirement to satisfy the first condition specified in paragraph (3) of that regulation.]

[² (2A) Paragraph (1A) is subject to regulation 5.]

AMENDMENTS

1. Tax Credits (Miscellaneous Amendments) (No.2) Regulations 2008 (SI 2008/2169) reg.9 (September 1, 2008).
2. Tax Credits (Miscellaneous Amendments) Regulations 2012 (SI 2012/848) reg.4(4) (April 6, 2012).

GENERAL NOTE

2.282 Section 8(3) of the TCA 2002 defines a child as a person who "has not attained the age of sixteen", but the same provision enables regulations to be made allowing a person to remain a "child" for tax credit purposes "for a prescribed period or until a prescribed date". This regulation provides that a child remains a child for both child tax credit and working tax credit purposes until August 31 following his or her 16th birthday.

Maximum age and prescribed conditions for a qualifying young person

2.283 **5.**—(1) For the purposes of Part I, a person ceases to be a qualifying young person (unless disqualified earlier under the following paragraphs) on the date on which he attains the age of [³twenty].

(2) A person who is not a child, but has not attained the age of [³twenty] years, is a qualifying young person for any period during which the following conditions are satisfied with regard to him [¹(and once a person falls within the terms of paragraph (3)(b), he shall be treated as having satisfied the first condition from the [⁴relevant leaving date] mentioned in that paragraph)].

(3) The first condition is that he is [³. . .]—
(a) receiving full-time education, not being—
 (i) advanced education, or
 (ii) education received by that person by virtue of his employment or of any office held by him; [³. . .]

(SI 2002/2007 reg.3) (as amended)

[³(ab) undertaking approved training [⁵, is enrolled or has been accepted to undertake such training,] which is not provided [⁷ by means of a contract of employment]; or]
(b) under the age of eighteen years and—
  [²[³(i) he ceased to receive full-time education or to undertake approved training (the date of that event being referred to as "the relevant leaving date");]
  (ii) within three months of the [³relevant leaving date], he has notified the Board (in the manner prescribed by regulation 22 of the Tax Credits (Claims and Notifications) Regulations 2002) that he is registered for work or training with [⁷ a qualifying body]; and
  (iii) not more than 20 weeks has elapsed since the [³relevant leaving date.]

[³(3A) A person who has attained the age of nineteen years satisfies paragraph (3)(a) or (ab) only where the course of education or training began before he attained that age [⁵, or he enrolled or was accepted to undertake that course before he attained that age].]

(4) The second condition is that the period in question is not (and does not include)—
(a) a week in which he (having ceased to receive full-time education [³or approved training]) becomes engaged in remunerative work; [³or]
(b) [³...]
(c) a period in respect of which that person receives income support [⁸income-related employment and support allowance payable under Part 1 of the Welfare Reform Act 2007] [⁸,]income-based jobseeker's allowance within the meaning of section 1(4) of the Jobseekers Act 1995 [⁸or universal credit under Part 1 of the Welfare Reform Act 2012].

[⁷ (5) For the purposes of paragraphs (3) and (4) a person shall be treated as being in full-time education if full-time education is received by that person by undertaking a course—
(a) at a school or college, or
(b) where that person has been receiving that education prior to attaining the age of sixteen, elsewhere, if approved by the Board,] [¹¹or,
(c) where that person begins to receive that education after attaining the age of 16, elsewhere, if approved by the Board, provided that—
  (i) that person has received a statement of special educational needs, and
  (ii) that programme of education has been assessed by a local authority as being suitable for that person's special needs,]
where in pursuit of that course, the time spent receiving instruction or tuition, undertaking supervised study, examination or practical work or taking part in any exercise, experiment or project for which provision is made in the curriculum of the course, exceeds or exceeds on average 12 hours a week in normal term-time [⁵ . . .] [¹⁰ and shall include gaps between the ending of one course and the commencement of another, where the person enrols on and commences the latter course].

[⁹ (5A) If paragraph (5) does not apply, then for the purposes of paragraphs (3) and (4) a person shall be treated as being in full-time education if that person is being provided with "appropriate full-time education" in England within section 4 (appropriate full-time education or training) of the Education and Skills Act 2008.]

(6) In calculating the time spent in pursuit of the course, no account shall be taken of time occupied by meal breaks or spent on unsupervised study.

[³(7) In determining whether a person is undertaking a course of fulltime education or approved training, there shall be disregarded any interruption—
  (a) for a period of up to 6 months, whether beginning before or after the person concerned attains age 16, to the extent that it is reasonable in the opinion of the Board to do so; and
  (b) for any period due to illness or disability of the mind or body of the person concerned provided that it is reasonable in the opinion of the Board to do so.]

[¹¹ (8) In this regulation "a statement of special educational needs" means a statement, plan or assessment made by a local authority, which identifies and assesses the special educational needs of a person and specifies the special educational provision required by that person.]

AMENDMENTS

1. Child Tax Credit (Amendment) Regulations 2003 (SI 2003/738) reg.4 (April 6, 2003).
2. Child Tax Credit (Amendment) Regulations 2003 (SI 2003/738) reg.5 (April 6, 2003).
3. Child Tax Credit (Amendment) Regulations 2006 (SI 2006/222) reg.4 (April 6, 2006).
4. Tax Credits (Miscellaneous Amendments) Regulations 2006 (SI 2006/766) reg.3 (April 6, 2006).
5. Child Tax Credit (Amendment) Regulations 2007 (SI 2007/2151) reg.4 (August 16, 2007).
6. Tax Credits (Miscellaneous Amendments) (No.2) Regulations 2008 (SI 2008/2169) reg.10 (September 1, 2008).
7. Employment and Support Allowance (Consequential Provisions) (No.3) Regulations 2008 (SI 2009/1879) reg.22(3) (October 27, 2008).
8. Universal Credit (Consequential, Supplementary, Incidental and Miscellaneous Provisions) Regulations 2013 (SI 2013/630) reg.79 (April 29, 2013).
9. Child Benefit (General) and Child Tax Credit (Amendment) Regulations 2014 (SI 2014/1231) reg.3 (June 4, 2014).
10. Child Benefit (General) and Tax Credits (Miscellaneous Amendments) Regulations 2014 (SI 2014/2924) reg.3(2) (November 28, 2014).
11. Tax Credits, Child Benefit, Guardian's Allowance and Childcare Payments (Miscellaneous Amendments) Regulations 2020 (SI 2020/297) reg.4(2) (April 6, 2020).

DEFINITIONS

"advanced education"—see reg.2(1).
"Careers Service"—see reg.2(1).
"Connexions Service"—see reg.2(1).
"child"—see reg.2(1).
"full-time education"—see para.(5).
"Pt I"—see reg.2(1).
"qualifying young person"—see reg.2(1).
"recognised educational establishment"—see reg.2(1).
"relevant training programme"—see reg.2(1).
"remunerative work"—see reg.2(1).
"a statement of special educational needs"—see para.(8).

(SI 2002/2007 reg.5) (as amended)

GENERAL NOTE

Section 8(4) of the TCA 2002 enables regulations to be made prescribing conditions to be met by a person in order to count as a "qualifying young person" (CTC being payable in respect of children and qualifying young persons (TCA 2002 s.8(1)). This regulation provides that the maximum age for a "qualifying young person" is the date on which he or she reaches the age of 20 (para.(1)). It also spells out the conditions which must be met by a person who is no longer a child (on which note the extended meaning of "child" in reg.4) in order to rank as a "qualifying young person" (paras (2)–(6)). Two conditions must be satisfied in this regard (they are cumulative and not alternative). First, the young person must *either* be receiving full-time education, as defined by para.(3)(a) (and see also paras (5) and (6)) *or* be aged under 18, have ceased to receive full-time education, be registered for work or training with one of the relevant official agencies, and have met the latter two criteria for no more than 20 consecutive weeks (para.(3)(b)). Secondly, the period in question must not be or include a week in which the young person becomes engaged in remunerative work (having ceased full-time education), or a period in which he or she received a training allowance under a training programme or received income support or income-based jobseeker's allowance (para.(4)).

2.284

These conditions are modelled on those that apply to child benefit, on which see SSCBA 1992 s.142 (and the commentary above). The definition of full-time education likewise is in identical terms to the relevant provision for child benefit purposes (Child Benefit (General) Regulations 2003 (SI 2003/493) reg.5.

In *JN v HMRC (TC)* [2010] UKUT 288 (AAC) the Upper Tribunal considered the meaning of "qualifying young person" before the 2008 amendments in a case where there was a gap in the education of the young person. The case concerned a young person who had left education in Kenya to come to Britain to continue studying here. The judge noted difficulties in treating the education in Kenya as taking place at a recognised establishment but accepted that the education itself could be recognised. On the facts tax credit was payable during the gap between leaving Kenya and starting a course in Britain.

An amendment to the definition of "approved training" in reg.1(3) of the Child Benefit (General) Regulations 2006 means that approved training no longer exists in England, only in Scotland and Wales, which is reflected in the amended paragraph (5)(b)'s reference to persons with a statement of special educational needs (such statements having been replaced in England, but not Wales, by Education, Health and Care Plans under the Children & Families Act 2014). The amending instrument, SI 2015/1512, omitted the definition of "approved training" in relation to England with effect from August 31, 2015.

HMRC's internal *Tax Credits Manual* states that it may be difficult to determine whether a young person is receiving full-time non-advanced education where "they are undertaking 'religious studies' and there is no recognisable course of education or an accredited qualification" (TCM0320300). The Manual sets out HMRC's guidelines for cases where religious studies have to be considered:

" - *Islamic studies* - where a young person is studying Islamic education the year of the study determines the level of the course. For example, year one of study equates to Level one, year two relates to Level two and so on. Years one to three are accepted as non-advanced education. Year four / level four may be advanced. However, unless there is evidence to show otherwise, level four should be accepted as non advanced education. Year five / level five is advanced.
Note: Islamic colleges may be referred to as Madrissa or Darul-Uloom.
Note: Alim and Fiqh are generic terms for a course of study.
Jewish studies - where the young person is studying at a Yeshiva in the UK this should be accepted as non advanced education."

In *JL v HMRC (TC)* [2019] UKUT 94 (AAC) Upper Tribunal Judge Levenson set aside the First-tier Tribunal's decision that a young person studying at a Yeshiva was not receiving full-time non-advanced education. Judge Levenson, having referred to TCM0320300, re-made the decision holding that the young person was receiving full-time non-advanced education.

Entitlement to child tax credit after death of child or qualifying young person

2.285

6.—If—
(a) a child or qualifying young person dies; and
(b) a person is (or would, if a claim had been made, have been) entitled to child tax credit in respect of the child or qualifying young person immediately before the death,

that person shall be entitled to child tax credit in respect of the child or qualifying young person for the period of eight weeks immediately following the death or, in the case of a qualifying young person, until the date on which he or she would have attained the age of [¹twenty] if earlier.

AMENDMENT

1. Child Tax Credit (Amendment) Regulations 2006 (SI 2006/222) reg.5 (April 6, 2006).

DEFINITIONS

"child"—see reg.2(1).
"qualifying young person"—see reg.2(1).

GENERAL NOTE

2.286
Section 8(5) of the TCA 2002 enables regulations to be made allowing entitlement to child tax credit to continue for a prescribed period notwithstanding the death of the relevant child or qualifying young person. This regulation makes provision for the continued payment of child tax credit for a further eight weeks in such a situation. The same concession has been made in relation to child benefit (SSCBA 1992 s.145A, inserted by TCA 2002 s.55).

Determination of the maximum rate at which a person or persons may be entitled to child tax credit

2.287

7.—(1) In the following paragraphs [³ and in regulations 9 to 12 and 14]
(a) in the case of a single claim (but not a joint claim), the person making the claim is referred to as the "claimant"; and
(b) in the case of a joint claim, the members of the [¹. . .] couple making the claim are referred to as the "joint claimants".

(2) The maximum rate at which a claimant or joint claimants may be entitled to child tax credit shall be the aggregate of—
(a) the family element of child tax credit [³ if the claimant is, or either or both the joint claimants are, responsible for a child or qualifying young person who was born before 6th April 2017]; and
(b) an individual element of child tax credit, in respect of each child or qualifying young person for whom—
(i) the claimant; or
(ii) either or both of the joint claimants;
as the case may be, is or are [³ responsible, but subject to paragraph (2A); and]

(SI 2002/2007 reg.7) (as amended)

[³ (c) a disability element of child tax credit in the case of each child or qualifying young person who is disabled or severely disabled.]

[³(2A) Where the claimant, or either or both of the joint claimants, is or are responsible for a child or qualifying young person born on or after 6th April 2017 ("A"), the maximum rate referred to in paragraph (2) shall not include an individual element of child tax credit in respect of A unless—
  (a) the claimant is, or the joint claimants are, claiming the individual element of child tax credit for no more than one other child or qualifying young person; or
  (b) an exception applies in relation to A in accordance with regulation 9.]

[² (3) The family element of child tax credit is £545.]

(4) The individual element of child tax credit for any child or qualifying young person referred to in paragraph (2)(b) above—
  (a) [³ . . .];
  (b) [³ . . .];
  (c) in the case of [³ a] child, is [⁵£3,455]
  (d) [³ . . .];
  (e) [³ . . .];
  and
  (f) in the case of [³ a] qualifying young person, is [⁵£3,455].

[⁴ (5) The disability element of child tax credit—
  (a) where the child or qualifying young person is disabled, is [⁵£4,170]
  (b) where the child or qualifying young person is severely disabled, is [⁵£5,850]].

AMENDMENTS

1. Civil Partnership Act 2004 (Tax Credits, etc.) (Consequential Amendments) Order 2005 (SI 2005/2919) art.4(4) (December 5, 2005).
2. Tax Credits Up-rating Regulations 2011 (SI 2011/1035) reg.2 (April 6, 2011).
3. Child Tax Credit (Amendment) Regulations 2017 (SI 2017/387) reg.4 (April 6, 2017).
4. Tax Credits and Guardian's Allowance Up-rating etc. Regulations 2017 (SI 2017/406) reg.3 (April 6, 2017).
5. Tax Credits, Child Benefit and Guardian's Allowance Up-rating Regulations 2024 (SI 2024/247) reg.3 (April 6, 2024).

DEFINITIONS

"child"—see reg.2(1).
"claimant"—see reg.2(1). and para.(1)(a).
"the family element of child tax credit"—see reg.2(1).
"the individual element of child tax credit"—see reg.2(1).
"joint claim"—see reg.2(1).
"qualifying young person"—see reg.2(1).
"single claim"—see reg.2(1).

GENERAL NOTE

Section 9 of the TCA 2002 makes provision for the maximum rate of child tax credit. This regulation provides the detail on how this rate is to be arrived at (para. (2)). It also sets out the actual annual rates for the component elements (paras (3) and (4)). Claimants who are entitled to income support or income-based jobseeker's allowance are automatically entitled to the maximum child tax credit applicable in their circumstances (TCA 2002 s.7(2) and Tax Credits (Income Thresholds and

2.288

Determination of Rates) Regulations 2002 (SI 2002/ 2008) reg.4). The entitlement of other claimants is dependent upon the operation of the thresholds and withdrawal rates specified in the Income Thresholds and Determination of Rates Regulations.

The amendment of subs.(3) removes, from April 6, 2011, previous entitlement for a double family element of £1,090 where the child or youngest child was under the age of one year and otherwise leaves the element at the same level as the previous year. Entitlement remains for those aged under one until April 5, 2011. All other elements have been increased above inflation, which is reflected in the amended paragraph (5)(b)'s reference to persons with a statement of special educational needs (such statements having been replaced in England, but not Wales, by Education, Health and Care Plans under the Children & Families Act 2014).

However, reversing this policy in part, s.12 of the Welfare Reform and Work Act 2016 froze the amounts set by reg.7(4)(c) and (f) at £2,780 until April 5, 2020. The other rates were also frozen at the 2015/16 rates for 2016/17 as part of the general Government policy of freezing benefit rates that year.

The amendments made to these regulations by the Child Tax Credit (Amendment) Regulations 2017 (SI 2017/387) implement, with effect from April 6, 2017, the UK Government's "two-child" tax credits policy. New para.(2A) qualifies the requirement in (2)(b) for an individual element for "each qualifying child or young person" to be included in the aggregate child tax credit award. As required by ss.9(3A) and (3B) of the Tax Credits Act 2002, the aggregate award must not include an element of child tax credit for qualifying children or young persons born on or after April 6, 2017 unless the claimant is claiming the individual element for no more than one other child or young person. In other words, the general rule is that third and subsequent children born on or after April 6, 2017 do not attract any individual element in the child tax credit award. However, this is subject to the exceptions provided for by regs.9–14.

SI 2017/387 also amended reg.7(2) to restrict entitlement to the family element of child tax credit to claimants who are responsible for a child or qualifying young person born before April 6, 2017.

SI 2017/387 omitted the prescribed amounts of the element for disabled and severely disabled children and young persons from reg.7(4). They were replaced by the Tax Credits and Guardian's Allowance Up-rating etc Order 2017 (SI 2017/406) which inserted reg.7(5) for this purpose. Note the two-child rule does not apply to the disability element of a child tax credit award.

In *SC v SSWP* [2018] EWHC 864 (Admin) Ouseley J dismissed the main element of CPAG's challenge to the "two-child" limit, but did find unlawful irrationality in the rules about the ordering of children in the rules about exceptions for non-parental caring arrangements (i.e. as regards foster children). Accordingly, Ouseley J held that the "two-child" provision was compatible with the ECHR, except for the ordering of the cared-for children exception. For further analysis of the decision of Ouseley J, and on appeal the Court of Appeal (*R (SC & Others) v Secretary of State for Work & Pensions and Others (Equality and Human Rights Commission intervening)* [2019] EWCA Civ 615) see the commentary to regulation 9 below.

Prescribed conditions for a disabled or severely disabled child or qualifying young person

2.289

8.—(1) For the purposes of section 9 of the Act a child or qualifying young person—
  (a) is disabled if he satisfies the requirements of paragraph (2); and
  (b) is severely disabled if he satisfies the requirements of paragraph [4 paragraph (3), (4), (5) or (6)].
(2) A person satisfies the requirements of this paragraph if—
  (a) disability living allowance is payable in respect of him, or has ceased to be so payable solely because he is a patient; or

(SI 2002/2007 reg.8) (as amended)

[³ (b) he is certified as severely sight impaired or blind by a consultant ophthalmologist;]
   (c) he ceased to be so [³. . .] certified as [³ severely sight impaired or] blind within the 28 weeks immediately preceding the date of claim [¹; or
   (d) personal independence payment is payable in respect of that person, or would be so payable but for regulations made under section 86(1) (hospital in-patients) of the Welfare Reform Act 2012 [⁴, or]
[⁴ (e) a payment of disability assistance is payable by the Scottish Ministers under section 31 of the Social Security (Scotland) Act 2018 [⁶, or would be so payable but for a reduction because that person is undergoing medical or other treatment as an in-patient at a hospital or similar institution].]

(3) A person satisfies the requirements of this paragraph if the care component of disability living allowance—
   (a) is payable in respect of him; or
   (b) would be so payable but for either a suspension of benefit in accordance with regulations under section 113(2) of the Contributions and Benefits Act or an abatement as a consequence of hospitalisation,
at the highest rate prescribed under section 72(3) of that Act.

[¹ (4) A person satisfies the requirements of this paragraph if the daily living component of personal independence payment—
   (a) is payable in respect of that person, or
   (b) would be so payable but for regulations made under section 86(1) (hospital in-patients) of the Welfare Reform Act 2012,
at the enhanced rate under section 78(2) of that Act.]

[² (5) A person satisfies the requirements of this paragraph if an armed forces independence payment is payable in respect of him.]

[⁴(6) A person satisfies the requirements of this paragraph if [⁵the care component of] disability assistance under section 31 of the Social Security (Scotland) Act 2018 is payable at the higher rate in respect of that person [⁶, or would be so payable but for a reduction because that person is undergoing medical or other treatment as an in-patient at a hospital or similar institution].

(7) In this regulation "Scottish Ministers" has the meaning given by section 44(2) of the Scotland Act 1998.]

AMENDMENTS

1. Personal Independence Payment (Supplementary Provisions and Consequential Amendments) Regulations 2013 (SI 2013/388) reg.8 and Sch. para.30(3) (April 8, 2013).
2. Armed Forces and Reserve Forces Compensation Scheme (Consequential Provisions: Subordinate Legislation) Order 2013 (SI 2013/591) art.7 and Sch. para.26(3) (April 8, 2013).
3. Child Benefit (General) and Tax Credits (Miscellaneous Amendments) Regulations 2014 (SI 2014/2924) reg.3(3) (November 28, 2014).
4. Tax Credits, Child Benefit, Guardian's Allowance and Childcare Payments (Miscellaneous Amendments) Regulations 2020 (SI 2020/297) reg.4(3) (April 6, 2020).
5. Tax Credits and Child Benefit (Miscellaneous Amendments) Regulations 2021 (SI 2021/1286) reg.4 (December 9, 2021).
6. Tax Credits (Miscellaneous Amendments) Regulations 2024 (SI 2024/176) (March 13, 2024).

The Child Tax Credit Regulations 2002

DEFINITIONS

"the Act"—see reg.2(1).
"child"—see reg.2(1).
"the Contributions and Benefits Act"—see reg.2(1).
"disability living allowance"—see reg.2(1).
"patient"—see reg.2(1).
"qualifying young person"—see reg.2(1).

GENERAL NOTE

2.290 This provision is amended to adjust it to deal with the replacement of disability living allowance with the new personal independence payment provided for in the Welfare Reform Act 2012. This is being introduced in stages. For the initial stages see the Welfare Reform Act 2012 (Commencement No.8 and Savings and Transitional Provisions) Order 2013 (SI 2013/358).

Sections 9(5)(d) and (6) of the TCA 2002 make provision for a disabled child element and a severely disabled child element to be component parts of child tax credit. This regulation defines those terms. Thus, a child or qualifying young person is disabled if disability living allowance (DLA) is payable for them (or has ceased to be payable but only because he or she is now a patient) or if he or she is a registered blind person (or has ceased to be so registered in the immediately preceding 28 weeks) (para.(2)). A child or qualifying young person is severely disabled if they are entitled to the highest rate of the DLA care component (i.e. they satisfy both the "day" and "night" conditions in terms of their need for personal care or supervision): para.(3). The rates for these elements are set out in regs 8(4)(a) and (b).

The amendment to para.(2)(b) replaces from November 2014 the previous tests that relied on entries in registers maintained by local or health authorities. That was a process being made more difficult to operate in parallel with the approach adopted centrally for social security benefits as devolved governments adopt different approaches.

The UK Government's 2016 Autumn Statement revealed that due to a "data feed" error, between 2011 and 2014, errors were made in processing claims of claimants whose children qualified for Disability Living Allowance (*HM Government, Autumn Statement 2016: policy costings*, p.33 (November 2016)). Some 28,000 families with disabled children were not in 2016/17 receiving the higher rate of CTC to reflect their children's DLA entitlement. £360 million has been set aside to meet these families future CTC entitlement. However, the UK Government announced there will be no back-dating beyond April 2016. It is understood that CPAG are applying for permission to appeal to the Upper Tribunal against First-tier Tribunal decisions that have refused backdated payments before this date. Examples of the arguments CPAG might run in these cases can be found in an article on the CPAG website (*http://www.cpag.org.uk/content/tax-credits-child-disability-element-fiasco*).

[¹*Individual element: exceptions to the restriction on numbers*

Exceptions for the purposes of regulation 7(2A)(b)

2.291 **9.**—[² (1) For the purposes of regulation 7(2A)(b), an exception applies in relation to A if—
    (a) A is (in accordance with paragraphs (5) and (6)) the third or subsequent child or qualifying young person for whom the claimant, or either or both of the joint claimants, is or are responsible and either—
        (i) any of regulations 10 to 14 applies in relation to A; or

(ii) all, or all but one, of the other children or qualifying young persons ("AA") for whom the claimant, or either or both of the joint claimants, is or are responsible are adopted within the meaning given by regulation 11 or cared for under a non-parental caring arrangement within the meaning given by regulation 12 (reading references to "A" in those regulations as if they were references to "AA"); or

(b) A is (in accordance with paragraphs (5) and (6)) the first or second child or qualifying young person for whom the claimant, or either or both of the joint claimants, is or are responsible.]

(2) [². . .]

(3) Where an exception applies in relation to A by virtue of paragraph (1), an exception applies also in relation to any other child or qualifying young person who was born on or after 6th April 2017 and for whom the claimant, or either or both of the joint claimants, is or are responsible, if—

(a) regulation 7(2A) would (apart from this paragraph) prevent the inclusion of an individual element of child tax credit in respect of that other child or qualifying young person, but would not do so if A were disregarded; and

(b) the claimant, or either or both of the joint claimants, was or were already responsible for that other child or qualifying young person before the date on which the claimant, or either or both of the joint claimants, became responsible for A.

(4) [². . .]

(5) For the purposes of [² this regulation], whether A is the first, second, third or subsequent child or qualifying young person is determined by treating children and qualifying persons as forming a single class and, subject to paragraph (6), the order of the members within that class is determined by the following date in relation to each member, taking the earliest date first:—

(a) where the claimant, or at least one of the joint claimants, is the member's parent or step-parent (in either case, other than by adoption), the member's date of birth; or

(b) in any other case, the date on which the claimant, or either or both of the joint claimants, became responsible for the member.

[² (6) In a case where the date determined under paragraph (5) is the same in respect of two or more members, their order (as between themselves only) is to be such as the Board determines to be appropriate to ensure that the individual element of child tax credit is included in respect of the greatest number of members.]

(7) Where joint claimants became responsible for a child or qualifying young person on different dates, any reference in this regulation to the date on which either or both of the joint claimants became responsible for that child or qualifying young person is a reference to the earliest of those dates.

(8) [². . .]].

AMENDMENTS

1. Child Tax Credit (Amendment) Regulations 2017 (SI 2017/387) reg.5 (April 6, 2017).

2. Child Tax Credit (Amendment) Regulations 2018 (SI 2018/1130) reg.3(a) (November 28, 2018).

GENERAL NOTE

2.292 Regulation 9 contains exceptions to the general rule in reg.7(2A) that child tax credit must not include an element for third or subsequent children born on or after April 6, 2017. According to the Explanatory Memorandum to SI 2017/387, which added reg.9 to the Child Tax Regulations 2002, these exceptions are designed for cases where claimants are "not fully able to make choices" about the numbers of children in their families. Below, references to child should be read as including a qualifying young person and a reference to claimant being responsible for a child as a reference, in the case of joint claimants, to either or both of the claimants being responsible for the child.

The four classes of exception

2.293 In seeking to understand this complex regulation, the legal mechanism by which reg.7(2) excludes a child from attracting a child element should be borne in mind. The general rule is that a child (referred to by the Regulations as 'A') born on or after April 6, 2017 is excluded unless a claimant is claiming the child element for only one other child. Regulation 9 sets out when 'A' attracts a child element even though s/he was born on or after April 6, 2017 and the claimant is already claiming the child element for at least two children.

The first exception, in reg.9(1)(a)(i) applies where A is the third or subsequent child for whom a claimant is responsible and any of regs 10 to 14 apply to A (those regulations are concerned with multiple births, adoption, non-parental caring arrangements (sometimes referred to as kinship care) and non-consensual conception). Accordingly, a child born on or after April 6, 2017 to whom any of regs 10 to 14 apply will always attract a child element in a tax credit award.

The second exception, in reg.9(1)(a)(ii), works in a different way. While its purpose is to identify when A (i.e. a child born on or after April 6, 2017 who is the third or subsequent child for whom a claimant is responsible) attracts a child element, it does so not by reference to A's circumstances but by reference to the circumstances of the other children for whom a claimant is responsible. Where all, or all but one, of these other children are adopted or cared for under a non-parental caring arrangement, A attracts a child element even though the claimant is already receiving a child element for at least two children. This exception was added by SI 2018/1130 in response, at least in part, to the High Court's decision in *SC & Others v Secretary of State for Work & Pensions* [2018] EWHC (864) (see below) and is intended to ensure that adoptive parents and non-parental carers are not prejudiced by the order in which adopted children, or children cared for under non-parental arrangement, join a claimant's household, as could happen under the original version of reg.9.

The third exception, in reg.9(1)(b) applies where A is, in accordance with reg.9(5) and (6), the first or second child for whom the claimant is responsible. Its purpose is not immediately obvious since the general rule in reg.7(2A) only operates to exclude a child born on or after April 6, 2017 if the claimant is already claiming the child element for two or more children. However, it does make sense if one considers the various ways in which a claimant might become responsible for children. Take for example, the case of a claimant who is claiming the child tax element for two natural children, one of whom was born after April 6, 2017. If the claimant then adopted a child born before April 6, 2017 then, without reg.9(1)(b), the claimant would lose the child element for the second natural child if the child element were claimed for the adopted child. Regulation 7(2A) would apply to the second natural child since s/he would be a child born on or after 2017 and the person responsible for the child would be claiming the child element for two other children. Regulation 9(1)(b) prevents this from happening since, under the sequence of responsibility rules in reg.9(5), the second natural child would be the second child for whom the claimant was responsible.

The fourth exception, in reg.9(3), only comes into play where an exception has already been established for A. It creates a further exception for a (different) child born on or after April 6, 2017 where (a) the general two-child rule in reg.7(2A) would ordinarily require the child to be ignored, and (b) the claimant was already responsible for the child before the date on which the claimant became responsible for A. For example, it would apply to a claimant whose natural child was born on or after April 6, 2017 and who subsequently adopted a child born on or after that date. The adoption would not displace entitlement to the child element for the claimant's natural child.

Regulations 9(5) and (6) contains rules for determining whether a child is the first, second, third etc. child for whom a claimant is responsible. In the case of children cared for by natural or step-parents, the sequence of responsibility is determined by the child's date of birth. In other cases, the sequence of responsibility order is determined by the date on which a claimant became responsible for a child. For example, take a claimant with two natural children born in April 2015 and September 2017 who in 2018 adopts a child born in July 2017. The sequence of responsibility is: (1) natural child born in April 2015; (2) natural child born in September 2017; (3) child adopted in 2018.

Where the rules operate so that a claimant became responsible for two or more children on the same date, reg.9(6) provides that the order of responsibility is to be such as HMRC determines appropriate to ensure that the individual element of child tax credit is included in respect of the greatest number of members. Such a determination might need to be made where a claimant adopts two or more children on the same date.

R (SC & Others) v Secretary of State for Work & Pensions

In *SC & Others v Secretary of State for Work & Pensions* [2018] EWHC (864) Mr Justice Ouseley held that the general two-child limit was not, in its entirety, contrary to the rights protected by the European Convention on Human Rights. Ouseley J appeared to accept that it is "inevitable that, if child–related benefits, paid to a parent and used by the household, are reduced or not made available for a third or further child, that that will affect more women, because of the higher proportion of single-parent households which they make up". On that basis, the introduction of the general two-child indirectly discriminated against women for the purposes of Art.14 of the European Convention on Human Rights (the Convention's anti-discrimination provision) when taken with Art.8 (right to respect for private and family life). However, Ouseley J went on to hold that the general two-child limit was justified and not therefore discriminatory. While it was likely to create a "perverse incentive not to form households", the general two-child limit was not manifestly without reasonable foundation taking into account the aim of limiting government spending and the other sources of support available to single-parent households. Ouseley J's decision, insofar as he refused to declare that the primary legislation under which the two-child provisions were made (s.9(2)(a) of the Tax Credits Act 2002, as amended by s.13 of the Welfare Reform and Work Act 2016) was incompatible with the rights protected by the Human Rights Act 1998, was challenged in the Court of Appeal (*R (SC & Others) v Secretary of State for Work & Pensions and Others (Equality and Human Rights Commission intervening)* [2019] EWCA Civ 615.

2.294

The Court of Appeal in *SC* agreed with Ouseley J that the purpose of the two-child provisions was not to discourage people with low incomes from having larger families, rather its aims included "encouraging people in receipt of tax credits to consider, before having additional children, whether they can afford to support them".

The Court of Appeal first considered whether the two-child provisions were incompatible with Art.8 of the European Convention on Human Rights, the right to respect for, amongst other things, a person's private and family life. Ouseley J correctly held that the provisions were not incompatible with Art.8 since they did not interfere with the exercise of Art.8 rights. The Convention is not aimed at securing social and economic rights and, more particularly, the essential object of Art.8 is to protect the individual from arbitrary interference by the state (*Belgian Linguistic* case (1979-80) 1 EHRR 252). While it is well established that there may be positive obligations inherent in respect for private and family life, the European Court of Human Rights has never interpreted Article 8 as obliging the state to "have in place any positive programme of financial support for private or family life". For similar reasons, the two-child provisions are not incompatible with Art.12 of the Convention (right to marry and found a family).

Before the Court of Appeal, it was further argued that the two-child provisions were incompatible with the Convention's anti-discrimination provision, Art.14, taken with Art.8 or, alternatively, art.1 of protocol 1 to the Convention (concerned with peaceful enjoyment of possession and protecting everyone from being deprived of their possession unless certain conditions are satisfied). Article 14 prohibits discrimination in the enjoyment of other Convention rights. Determining this, as with any Art.14 argument involved answering four questions:

(1) did the alleged discrimination concern the enjoyment of a right set forth in the Convention that is did the facts of the case fall within the 'ambit' of a Convention right?

(2) was the alleged ground of discrimination a 'status' for the purposes of Article 14?

(3) was the claimant treated less favourably than a class of persons whose situation is relevantly similar?

(4) if so, was there an objective and reasonable justification for the difference in treatment?

2.295   *Question 1 (A1, P1)–ambit*. Ouseley J wrongly held that the two-child provisions did not fall within the ambit of art.1 of protocol 1 since no existing benefit entitlement had been removed. The judge's reasoning disclosed a misunderstanding of the case put to him. The claimants did not argue the two-child provisions denied them a right they would have had if the law had stayed the same. Their arguments were not influenced by the fact that the law had changed; they would have put the same argument had the two-child provisions always been a part of the child tax credit legislative scheme. The argument was simply that, under the two-child provisions, persons were denied a benefit on the discriminatory ground that they are responsible for two or more children. It was clear that, but for the two-child provisions, the claimants would have had an enforceable domestic right to receive a child element for each qualifying child. The Court of Appeal held that, in this case, the ambit test in relation to welfare benefits in *Stec v United Kingdom* (2005) 41 EHRR SE 295 was met: "the relevant test is whether, but for the condition of entitlement about which the applicant complains, he or she would have had a right, enforceable under domestic law, to receive the benefit in question". This was because the claimants were denied a discrete individual element of benefit that would otherwise have been payable.

Question 1 (article 8)–ambit. Ouseley J proceeded on the basis that, in order for an alleged discriminatory measure to fall within the ambit of art.8, it had to have a 'direct and real' effect on family life. The general test formulated by the European Court of Human Rights in *Petrovic v Austria* (1998) 33 EHRR 33 was whether "the subject-matter of the disadvantage constitutes one of the modalities of the exercise of a right guaranteed" or the measures complained of are "linked to the exercise of a right guaranteed". More specifically in relation to article 8 and welfare benefits, the case law of the European Court of Human Rights reveals "the requisite link with the exercise of the right to respect for family life was established by the nature and purpose of the benefit in question, which was in each case specifically aimed at providing financial assistance for the care of children and could therefore be seen as a means by which the state expressed its support for family life". The European Court's reasoning was reflected in the Supreme Court's decision in *In re McLaughlin* [2018] UKSC 48; [2018] 1 WLR 4250. The Court of Appeal held that child tax credit "represents a measure by which the state shows respect for children and for family life" and so falls within the ambit of Art.8 for the purposes of Art.14.

Question 2–status. The Court of Appeal noted that the Supreme Court has taken an "increasingly generous view" of what is capable of amounting to a relevant status. Clearly, insofar as discrimination was alleged in relation to women and children, the necessary status was made out. Less straightforward was the question whether 'being a child with multiple siblings/multiple children in the same household' was a relevant status but "once it is accepted that a status need not be innate or an inherent aspect of an individual's personality but may be a feature of a person's circumstances or living situation on which a legal consequence depends, then being a member of a household or family unit which contains more than two children, or being a child member of such a household, can without difficulty be regarded as an "other status" for the purpose of article 14" taken with both article 8 and article 1 of protocol 1.

2.296

Question 3–less favourable treatment. The test here was whether the claimants are in an analogous or relevantly similar situation to the class of persons who are said to receive more favourable treatment than them. The test was clearly met in so far as discrimination on the ground of (female) sex was concerned because "women are more likely than men to be lone parents who rely on child tax credit to support their children". The test was also met in so far as the claimants complained that families which include more than two children are treated less favourably than families with one or two children. The test was not, however, met in so far as the child claimants argued they were discriminated against on the ground of their status as children. Here, the only comparator could be adults in general but "the two child limit on child tax credit does not disadvantage children in comparison with adults since child tax credit is a benefit that is payable solely in respect of children" and there is no equivalent benefit in respect of adults.

Question 4–justification. Given the Court of Appeal's answers to question 3, the question of justification only arose in so far as discrimination was alleged against women (as compared with men) and families with more than two children (as compared with families with one or two children). To answer the claim that these differences in treatment were justified the UK Government needed to show an objective and reasonable justification for the difference in treatment, which is to be judged by whether it pursues a "legitimate aim" and there is a "reasonable relationship of proportionality" between the aim and the means employed to realise (*Rasmussen v Denmark* (1985) 7 EHRR 37; *Petrovic v Austria* (2001) 33 EHRR 14; *X v Austria* (2013) 57 EHRR 14). Case law of the UK courts identifies four aspects to this proportionality test: (1) whether the objective of the measure is sufficiently important to justify the limitation of a protected right, (2) whether the measure is rationally connected to the objective, (3) whether a less intrusive measure could have been used without unacceptably compromising the achievement of the objective, and (4) whether, balancing the severity of the measure's effects on the rights of the persons to whom it applies against the importance of the objective, to the extent that the measure will contribute to its achievement, the former outweighs the latter (*Bank Mellat v HM Treasury (No 2)* [2013] UKSC 39; [2014] AC 700). However, in a sphere such as the present the courts should respect the proper role of different branches of the state in formulating and implementing policy:

2.297

"62...Within the UK's constitutional arrangements, the democratically elected branches of government are in principle better placed than the courts to decide what is in the public interest in such matters. Those branches of government are in a position to rank and decide among competing claims to public money, which a court adjudicating on a particular claim has neither the information nor the authority to do. In making such decisions, the legislature and the executive are also able and institutionally designed to take account of and respond to the views, interests and experiences of all citizens and sections of society in a way that courts are not. Above all, precisely because decisions made by Parliament and the executive on what is in the public interest on social or economic grounds are the product of a political process in which all are able to participate, those decisions carry a democratic legitimacy which the judgment of a court on such an issue does not have. For such reasons, in judging whether a difference in treatment is justified, it is now firmly established that the courts of this country will likewise respect a choice made by the legislature or executive in a matter of social or economic policy unless it is manifestly without reasonable foundation [*Humphreys v Revenue and Customs Commissioners* [2012] UKSC 18; [2012] 1 WLR 1545]".

In assessing proportionality, "the intensity with which a court will scrutinise a policy justification for a difference in treatment will depend on the circumstances". Three factors, in particular, are important in this respect: (1) the nature of the ground on which the difference in treatment is based is significant. Some grounds, such as race, nationality, gender, religion, sexual orientation require particularly convincing and weighty reasons to justify a difference of treatment. The status of 'member of family unit containing two or more children' is not a status "which requires particularly convincing or weighty reasons to justify making it a ground for treating people differently"; whether the measure in question has been approved by Parliament and, if so, with what degree of scrutiny; (3) whether or to what extent the values and interests relevant to the assessment of proportionality were actually considered when the policy choice was made: "where a public authority has addressed the particular issue before the court and has taken account of the relevant human rights considerations in making its decision, a court will be slower to upset the balance which was struck".

At this point in the Court of Appeal's analysis, it also considered the relevance of the UN Convention on the Rights of the Child. As the Court put it, "the issue is whether, in assessing whether the differences in treatment complained of are a proportionate means of pursuing a legitimate aim, it is relevant to take account of provisions of the United Nations Convention on the Rights of the Child (the "UNCRC")–and, if so, in what way". Not only should the UN Convention be used as an aid to interpreting the European Convention, it should also be taken into account in considering how the balance should be struck between the competing interests at stake, for the purpose of deciding whether interference with the applicants' article 8 rights to respect for their family life was justified under article 8(2) on the basis that it was a proportionate means of pursuing a legitimate aim (*X v Latvia* (2014) 59 EHRR 3). In this respect, the principle embodied in article 3(1) of the UN Convention—in all actions concerning children, the best interests of the child shall be a primary consideration—must be recognised as an integral part of the Article 8 proportionality assessment (*Zoumbas v Secretary of State for the Home Department* [2013] UKSC 74; [2013] 1 WLR 3690) although "a question to which, as yet, however, no definitive answer has been given is in what circumstances the child's best interests principle, or other provisions of the UNCRC, should be taken into account in assessing whether a difference in treatment is justified for the purpose of deciding whether there has been a breach of article 14". However, Leggatt LJ offered the opinion that "there is no basis in either legal principle or precedent for treating a state's compliance or lack of compliance with its obligations under other international treaties as relevant to whether it has acted compatibly with article 14 (or any other provision of the Convention)". Nevertheless, the judge went on to say "it seems to me that the child's best interests principle embodied in article 3(1) of the UNCRC is relevant to the issue of justification. Its relevance arises, as I see it, from the nature of the rationale relied on by the government to justify treating households with more than two children differently from households with one or two children". The judge then proceeded to consider that rationale in determining whether the differences of treatment under analysis were justified.

The Court of Appeal had no doubt that the measure in question pursued legitimate aims namely: reducing public expenditure on welfare benefits; ensuring a fair benefits system for taxpayers; equating those on benefits with those in work when it comes to considering the financial choices involved in deciding how many children to have; incentivising people to support themselves and their families through work.

The next issue addressed by the Court of Appeal was whether, in pursuing these legitimate aims, the disparate impact on women was justified. The claimants argued unjustified indirect discrimination against women: "where the discrimination alleged is indirect – that is, where a measure, though neutral on its face, has disproportionately prejudicial effects on one group as opposed to another—the relevant question is whether the measure is independently justified as a proportionate means of pursuing a legitimate aim" (*R (SG and JS) v Secretary of State for Work and Pensions* [2015] UKSC 16; [2015] 1 W.L.R. 1449). Any reduction in a child-related benefit would have a disparate effect on women. There was no basis for a court to conclude that there was an alternative means of meeting the UK Government's aims without affecting more women than men, nor for concluding that the disproportionately prejudicial effect was too high a price for women to have to pay. Further, the UK Government was well aware of the effect on women at the policy development stage; it was specifically referred to in the preceding impact assessment yet the Government decided the aims of the two-child provisions were sufficiently important to justify its adoption. In those circumstances, "the court is not in a position to say that this view was wrong, let alone that the disparate impact of the measure made it a manifestly disproportionate means of realising the government's legitimate aims". The Court of Appeal dismissed the challenge to Ouseley J's decision that the disparate impact of the two-child provisions on women was justified and not, therefore, discriminatory for the purposes of Art.14.

The remaining issue was whether the differential treatment of families with more than two children, in particular the children within those families, was justified. The argument advanced here was of direct discrimination. The Court held that not all of the aims relied on by the UK Government were "rationally capable of providing a justification for limiting entitlement to child tax credit on the ground of the number of children in the family". The aim of reducing public expenditure might supply a partial justification, but it does not supply a complete justification for treating certain families differently. Reducing spending on a welfare benefit does not supply a reason for placing the burden of the reduction on one category of person rather than another – some further rationale is needed – and so "the objective of saving money cannot be a sufficient reason to draw a distinction between larger families and smaller ones and to make entitlement to a child-related benefit depend on the number of children for whom a person or couple is responsible". Similarly, the aim of incentivising work could not provide a rational justification:

"97...We have been shown no evidence to suggest that a couple or lone parent with more than two children is more likely to respond or to be able to respond to incentives to find work or to earn more money from working than a couple or lone parent with one or two children. In the absence of any such evidence, it seems reasonable to expect that, at least in the case of a lone parent, the opposite is more likely to be true."

In the light of those findings, the burden of justifying the two-child provisions rests on the second and third aims–ensuring a benefit system that is fair to taxpayers and presenting those on benefits and those in work with the same financial

2.298

choices in respect of family size. The Court of Appeal accepted the obvious point that wealthier families have more options available to them than a family reliant on state benefits. But this did not fully answer the UK Government's argument, which concerned relative rather than absolute levels of income and nor did the evidence that most recipients of child tax credit are also in receipt of working tax credit and therefore in work. These points did not deal with the question how much additional financial support child tax credit recipients should receive from other taxpayers an area in which the Government must be given a "wide area of judgement". The Court of Appeal held that the two-child provisions were not a manifestly disproportionate means of achieving the second and third aims:

"102... given the wide area of judgment afforded to the executive and the legislature under the Convention in matters of social and economic policy, I consider that the aims relied on by the government – in the context of a perceived need to reduce spending on welfare benefits – of fairness to taxpayers and making people face similar choices are sufficient to justify treating parents differently in their entitlement to receive child tax credit for each child on the ground of how many children they have. Applying the relevant legal test, treating recipients of child tax credit differently on this ground is not a manifestly disproportionate means of pursuing those legitimate aims."

The fact that some of the UK Government's aims could be justified, but not others, did not necessarily lead to the conclusion that the measure in question – the two child provisions – was discriminatory contrary to Article 14:

"101. A policy measure is not shown to be flawed, however, just because the rationale for it does not apply to all cases covered by the rule adopted to implement the measure. Sometimes the importance attached to the general objective considered with the costs or practical difficulties involved in formulating a more flexible or nuanced rule outweigh the potential advantages of achieving more precise fairness in all individual cases...".

Up until this point, the Court of Appeal's analysis considered the position of parents/carers for children. The Court's final task was to consider justification from the standpoint of children within families affected by the two-child provisions. At this point, art.1 of protocol 1 fell out of consideration since, under article 1, the protected right is conferred on the owner of a possession which, in this context, means the claimant of child tax credit. Only Art.8, taken with Art.14, remained for analysis and, in this respect, the interests of all the children in an affected family were to be taken into account, not only those who do not attract a child element within their parent/s child tax credit award. Ouseley J decided that the best interests of children were at the forefront of the policy debate that preceded enactment of the two child provisions. The Court of Appeal could not agree with this conclusion in so far as it concerned policy development within government. The best interests of children were simply not mentioned in any relevant policy papers. The closest that anyone came to acknowledging the best interests of children were ministerial statements referring to the interests of children generally but not the interests of those children who would be affected by the enactment of the two-child provisions. The detrimental effect on such children is obvious and was raised in Parliamentary debate by those who opposed the measure. That the government did not confront the detriment "mandates greater scrutiny than would otherwise be appropriate". The Court went on:

"103... the point that children are not responsible for their parents' conduct and have no control over the size of the family into which they are born seems to me to be a complete answer to the justifications based on fairness and parental choice. It is not, however, conclusive of the issue of justification because there is in this context, as on many social issues, a conflict between the value attached to a child's own interests and the value attached to parental choice and responsibility... That means that the welfare of children inevitably depends on choices made by their parents – including choices about whether to have children and how many children to have. As parents differ widely in their financial means, the fortunes of children depend in great part on the lottery of birth. The child of a rich family may benefit from expensive holidays, private schooling and inherited wealth, while the child of a poor family will have none of those advantages. It is a matter of intense political controversy to what extent the state should seek to reduce or compensate for these inequalities, and to what extent it is fair to impose the costs of supporting or assisting children whose parents lack the means to do so on other members of society.

The government's justification for the two child limit on child tax credit directly engages this controversy. The arguments that children are not responsible for their parents' conduct and that fairness to children demands that the state should provide financial support for each individual child whose parents are not in work or have low incomes from work are pitted against arguments that it is fair to taxpayers to set a limit to the number of children in a household whom the state will support and to require parents to take full financial responsibility for supporting their children beyond that limit. The arguments based on the interests of children are not a trump card that render arguments based on what is fair to other taxpayers irrelevant. They are a primary consideration but one which has to be weighed against the interests of the community as a whole in placing responsibility, including financial responsibility, for the care of children on their parents.

... a court is not a suitable institution to decide between these competing views. There is no process of legal reasoning which can justify one view in preference to the other. Nor are courts attuned in the way that democratically elected institutions are attuned to reflect a collective sense of what is fair or where the balance of fairness lies on questions of distributive justice. In circumstances where the measure was scrutinised and debated by Parliament during the passage of the Bill, where the interests of the children affected – although given scant consideration by the executive – were considered by the legislature as part of that process of scrutiny, and where at the end of the process Parliament enacted the measure in primary legislation, a court should be very slow to displace the balance struck by Parliament on a contentious question of social and economic policy of this kind. Applying the relevant legal test, I do not consider that a court can properly conclude that the difference in treatment imposed by the two child limit is manifestly disproportionate to the legitimate aims pursued.".

The ultimate outcome, therefore, was that the Court of Appeal dismissed the challenge to the two-child provisions compatibility with the rights protected by the Human Rights Act 1998.

Not mentioned by the Court of Appeal in *SC* was that, before Ouseley J, the claimants were partially successful. Ouseley J went on to hold that one feature of the original two-child limit legislative scheme, as provided for in the amended Child Tax Regulations 2002, was irrational on traditional domestic judicial review principles and therefore not authorised by primary legislation (Tax Credits Act 2002). The scheme's defect concerned the original amended version of regulation 9 about the order in which a claimant is treated as becoming responsible for a child. The Judge held:

"215. The issue here relates to the ... Regulations and not to the primary legislation: Mr Drabble [for the applicants] contends that the exception in relation to a child cared for by the family is perverse because the availability of CTC for a third child depends on whether the third child was born before or after the family began to care for the second child. Mr Higlett [for the Secretary of State] suggests the justification that, because the cared for child is not to be treated as of any less value than a natural child of the family, and the family, caring for a child, should face the same choice about a third child as would a family not in receipt of CTC, the sequencing provision is rational and justifiable in domestic public law terms.

216. I do not accept that. I do not think that in so far as it was seriously considered, there is any rational justification for a parent's decision, about whether to have a child of their own, to be affected by whether that decision was made before or after another decision, as to whether they should care for someone else's child, which could need to be made quite independently of a decision about having their own children. The purpose of the exception is to encourage, or at least to avoid discouraging, a family from looking after a child who would otherwise be in local authority care, with the disadvantages to the child over family care which that can entail, and the public expenditure it can require. The choice which the family is being asked to make has a very different and indeed opposite purpose in relation to public expenditure, from that which is part of the principal thinking behind the two child provision. It is not rationally connected to the purposes of the legislation, and indeed it is in conflict with them. The perversity of the provision is well-illustrated by CC's evidence that HMRC advised her that a device was at hand whereby the two child provision could be circumvented, and in a way which CC and CD rejected, in the best interests of the cared for child. HMRC disputes giving any such advice, though seemingly not that the device would work.

217. It is not the exception itself which is unlawful but the sequencing or ordering part of it . . ."

[¹Multiple births

2.299

10.—This regulation applies in relation to A if—
(a) the claimant, or at least one of the joint claimants, is a parent (other than an adoptive parent) of A;
(b) A was one of two or more children born as a result of the same pregnancy;
(c) the claimant, or either or both of the joint claimants, is or are responsible for at least two of the children or qualifying young persons born as a result of that pregnancy; and
(d) A is not the first in the order of those children or qualifying young persons as determined in accordance with regulation 9.]

AMENDMENT

1. Child Tax Credit (Amendment) Regulations 2017 (SI 2017/387) reg.5 (April 6, 2017).

GENERAL NOTE

2.300

This regulation needs to be read with reg.9 (exceptions to the two-child rule). It sets out when, in multiple birth cases, the child element is to be included in an award of child tax credit where the element is sought for the third or subsequent child (referred to as "A" by reg.10) for whom a claimant is responsible (the meaning of responsibility being dealt with for this purpose by reg.9).

[¹Adoption

2.301

11.—(1) This regulation applies in relation to A if A has been—
(a) placed for adoption with the claimant or either or both of the joint claimants; or

(b) adopted by the claimant, or either or both of the joint claimants, in accordance with—
   (i) the Adoption and Children Act 2002 ("the 2002 Act");
   (ii) the Adoption and Children (Scotland) Act 2007 ("the 2007 Act"); or
   (iii) the Adoption (Northern Ireland) Order 1987 ("the 1987 Order").
(2) But this regulation does not apply in relation to A if—
   (a) the claimant or at least one of the joint claimants—
      (i) was a step-parent of A immediately prior to the adoption; or
      (ii) has been a parent of A (other than by adoption) at any time;
   (b) the adoption order was made as a Convention adoption order within the meaning of—
      (i) section 144 of the 2002 Act;
      (ii) section 119(1) of the 2007 Act; or
      (iii) article 2(2) of the 1987 Order; or
   (c) prior to the adoption, A was adopted by the claimant, or either or both of the joint claimants, under the law of any country or territory outside the British Islands.]

AMENDMENT

1. Child Tax Credit (Amendment) Regulations 2017 (SI 2017/387) reg.5 (April 6, 2017).

GENERAL NOTE

This regulation should be read with reg.9 (exceptions to the two-child rule). It sets out when, in adoption cases, the child element is to be included in an award of child tax credit where the element is sought for the first, second, third or subsequent child (referred to as "A" by reg.11) for whom a claimant is responsible (the meaning of responsibility being dealt with for this purpose by reg.9).

This regulation extends beyond adoption cases. It also applies where a child has been placed for adoption with a claimant. In England and Wales, a child is placed for adoption when he is or she is placed with prospective adopter/s by an adoption agency (usually a local authority) acting under the Adoption and Children Act 2002. Placing for adoption is a formal process which will always be accompanied by documentary evidence of the placement decision. The exceptions in reg.11(2)(a) concern types of adoption that are rarely encountered in practice, where the adoption order normally formalises a pre-existing family unit. According to the Explanatory Memorandum to the Child Tax Credit (Amendment) Regulations 2017, the rationale for the exceptions in reg.11(2)(b) (inter-country adoptions) is that "the exception is intended to help relieve pressure on children's services within the UK only".

[¹ **Non-parental caring arrangements**

12.—(1) This regulation applies in relation to A if the claimant or at least one of the joint claimants—
   (a) is a friend or family carer in relation to A; or
   (b) is responsible for a child or qualifying young person who is a parent of A.
(2) But this regulation does not apply in relation to A if the claimant, or at least one of the joint claimants, is—
   (a) a parent of A; or

(b) a step-parent of A.

(3) In this regulation, "friend or family carer" means a person who is responsible for A and—
  (a) is named, in—
    (i) a child arrangements order under section 8 of the Children Act 1989, or
    (ii) a residence order under article 8 of the Children (Northern Ireland) Order 1995,
  as a person with whom A is to live;
  (b) is a guardian of A appointed under—
    (i) section 5 of the Children Act 1989;
    (ii) section 7 of the Children (Scotland) Act 1995; or
    (iii) article 159 or 160 of the Children (Northern Ireland) Order 1995;
  (c) is a special guardian of A appointed under section 14A of the Children Act 1989;
  (d) is entitled to a guardian's allowance under section 77 of the Contributions and Benefits Act or section 77 of the Contributions and Benefits (Northern Ireland) Act 1992 in respect of A;
  (e) is a person in whose favour a kinship care order, as defined in section 72(1) of the Children and Young People (Scotland) Act 2014, subsists in relation to A;
  (f) is a person in whom one or more of the parental responsibilities or parental rights described in section 1 or 2 of [²the Children (Scotland) Act 1995] are vested by a permanence order made in respect of A under section 80 of the Adoption and Children (Scotland) Act 2007;
  (g) fell within any of paragraphs (a) to (f) immediately prior to A's 16th birthday and has since continued to be responsible for A; or
  (h) has undertaken the care of A in circumstances in which it is likely that A would otherwise be looked after by a local authority.]

AMENDMENTS

1. Child Tax Credit (Amendment) Regulations 2017 (SI 2017/387) reg.5 (April 6, 2017).
2. Child Tax Credit (Amendment) Regulations 2018 (SI 2018/1130) reg.4 (November 28, 2018).

GENERAL NOTE

2.304 This regulation should be read with reg.9 (exceptions to the two-child rule). It sets out when, in non-parental care cases, the child element is to be included in an award of child tax credit where the element is sought for the first, second, third or subsequent child (referred to as "A" by reg.12) for whom a claimant is responsible (the meaning of responsibility being dealt with for this purpose by reg.9).

This regulation deals with two types of case. The first is where a claimant is a "friend or family carer" in relation to A. The second is where a claimant is responsible for a child or qualifying young person who is a parent of A (i.e. particularly young mothers).

In most cases, it will be simple enough to identify whether a claimant is a friend or family carer. This is due to the way in which that status is linked to the orders and appointments specified in reg.12(3). The more difficult case is reg.12(3)(h). This poses a difficult factual question—but for the claimant's care, is it likely that A would have been looked after by a local authority? In some cases, a local authority care plan will provide clear evidence that the claimant's care was intended to avoid the need for the local authority to look after the child. However, the regulation does not in terms require any local authority involvement and there may well be cases in which reg.12(3)(h) is satisfied even without any evidence of local authority involvement with the child.

See further *SC v SSWP* [2018] EWHC 864 (Admin), discussed in the note to reg.7 above.

[¹ Non-consensual conception

13.—(1) This regulation applies in relation to A if—
(a) the claimant is A's parent; and
(b) the Board determines that—
   (i) A is likely to have been conceived as a result of sexual intercourse to which the claimant did not agree by choice, or did not have the freedom and capacity to agree by choice; and
   (ii) the claimant is not living at the same address as the other party to that intercourse ("B").

Control or coercion

(2) For the purposes of paragraph (1)(b)(i), the circumstances in which the claimant is to be treated as not having the freedom or capacity to agree by choice are to include (but are not limited to) circumstances in which, at or around the time A was conceived—
(a) B was—
   (i) personally connected to the claimant; and
   (ii) repeatedly and continuously engaging in behaviour towards the claimant that was controlling or coercive; and
(b) that behaviour had a serious effect on the claimant.

(3) For the purposes of paragraph (2)(a)(i), B is personally connected to the claimant if—
(a) B is in an intimate personal relationship with the claimant; or
(b) B and the claimant live together and—
   (i) are members of the same family; or
   (ii) have previously been in an intimate personal relationship with each other.

(4) For the purposes of paragraph (2)(b), behaviour has a serious effect on the claimant if—
(a) it causes the claimant to fear, on at least two occasions, that violence will be used against the claimant; or
(b) it causes the claimant serious alarm or distress which has a substantial adverse effect on the complainant's day-to-day activities.

(5) For the purposes of paragraph (3)(b)(i), B and the claimant are members of the same family if—
(a) they are, or have been, married to each other;
(b) they are, or have been, civil partners of each other;
(c) they are relatives (within the meaning of section 63(1) of the Family Law Act 1996);
(d) they have agreed to marry each other (whether or not the agreement has been terminated);
(e) they have entered into a civil partnership agreement (within the meaning of section 73 or 197 of the Civil Partnership Act 2004), whether or not the agreement has been terminated;

2.305

(f) they are both parents of the same child;
(g) they have, or have had, parental responsibility (within the meaning of section 3 of the Children Act 1989 or article 6 of the Children (Northern Ireland) Order 1995) for the same child; or
(h) they have, or have had, in respect of the same child, one or more of the parental responsibilities or parental rights described in section 1 or 2 of the Children (Scotland) Act 2007.

Determinations
(6) The Board may make a determination under paragraph (1)(b)(i) if, and only if—
  (a) the claimant provides evidence from an approved person which demonstrates that—
    (i) the claimant has had contact with that person or another approved person; and
    (ii) the claimant's circumstances are consistent with those of a person to whom paragraph (1)(a) and (b)(i) apply; or
  (b) there has been—
    (i) a conviction for—
(aa) an offence of rape under section 1 of the Sexual Offences Act 2003, section 1 of the Sexual Offences (Scotland) Act 2009 or article 5 of the Sexual Offences (Northern Ireland) Order 2008,
(bb) an offence of controlling or coercive behaviour in an intimate or family relationship under section 76 of the Serious Crime Act 2015, or
(cc) any offence under the law of any jurisdiction outside the United Kingdom that the Board considers to be analogous to an offence mentioned in paragraph (aa) or (bb), or
    (ii) an award under the Criminal Injuries Compensation Scheme in respect of a relevant criminal injury sustained by the claimant,
and it appears to the Board to be likely (disregarding the matters mentioned in paragraph (7)) that the offence was committed, or the relevant criminal injury was caused, by B and either resulted in the conception of A or diminished the claimant's freedom or capacity to agree by choice to the sexual intercourse which resulted in that conception.

(7) In considering, for the purposes of paragraph (6)(b), the likelihood that the offence or injury resulted in the conception of A the matters to be disregarded are any possibilities that the conception of A may have resulted from another such offence or injury, regardless of whether any conviction or award has occurred in respect of that other offence or injury.

(8) In paragraph (6)(a), "approved person" means a person of a description specified on a list approved by the Board for the purposes of this regulation and acting in the capacity referred to in the description.

(9) In paragraph (6)(b)(ii), "relevant criminal injury" means—
  (a) a sexual offence (including a pregnancy sustained as a direct result of being the victim of a sexual offence),
  (b) physical abuse of an adult, including domestic abuse, or
  (c) mental injury,
as described in the tariff of injuries in the Criminal Injuries Compensation Scheme.

(10) In paragraphs (6)(b)(ii) and (9), "Criminal Injuries Compensation Scheme" means the Criminal Injuries Compensation Scheme or the

(SI 2002/2007 reg.13) (as amended)

Northern Ireland Criminal Injuries Compensation Scheme as established from time to time under the Criminal Injuries Compensation Act 1995 or the Criminal Injuries Compensation (Northern Ireland) Order 2002 respectively.

(11) The Board may treat the condition in paragraph (6)(a) as met if the Board are satisfied that the claimant has provided the evidence to the Secretary of State for corresponding purposes in relation to universal credit, income support or old style JSA.(12) The Board may make a determination under paragraph (1)(b)(ii) if the claimant confirms that the criterion in paragraph (1)(b)(ii) is met.

Application to single and joint claims

(13) In this regulation, "claimant", in relation to a single claim, means the person who makes the claim.

(14) In relation to a joint claim—
(a) paragraph (1)(b)(i) applies if it applies to either of the joint claimants; and
(b) references in the other provisions of this regulation to "the claimant" mean the joint claimant to whom paragraph (1)(b)(i) applies (and, in paragraphs (6) and (11) include a joint claimant who purports to meet that criterion).

(15) In paragraph (14), "joint claimant" means a member of the couple making the claim.]

AMENDMENT

1. Child Tax Credit (Amendment) Regulations 2017 (SI 2017/387) reg.5 (April 6, 2017).

GENERAL NOTE

This regulation should be read with reg.9 (exceptions to the two-child rule). It sets out when, in non-consensual conception cases, the child element is to be included in an award of child tax credit where the element is sought for the third or subsequent child (referred to as "A" by reg.13) for whom a claimant is responsible (the meaning of responsibility being dealt with for this purpose by reg.9).

Regulation 13 raises matters of extreme sensitivity. However, those matters do not necessarily have to be investigated by HMRC since reg.13(12) permits them to determine that the criterion in reg.13(1)(b)(ii) is met if a claimant confirms it is met.

When the Social Security Advisory Committee (SSAC) were consulted on a draft of the "two child policy" amendments, reg.13 caused them particular concern. In response, Damian Green MP Minister for Employment, informed the SSAC by letter dated March 1, 2017 that, while HMRC will formally decide whether the reg.13 exception applies in any particular case, the decision will be based on information provided by "the third party". By this, the Minister must have meant the "approved person" referred to in reg.13(6). The Minister went on to state that "the third party will not be required to attest to the credibility of the claimant, just the consistency of the claimant's account with their circumstances" and HMRC envisaged supplying approved persons with a "tick-box" form to indicate if the reported circumstances were consistent with statements recorded on the form. If the "yes" box were ticked, the Minister said HMRC would accept that reg.13 applied and make a determination accordingly. Subsequently, HMRC and the DWP published a form entitled "Support for a Child Conceived without Your Consent" which includes a section for approved persons to provide evidence in support of a claim that reg.13 applies. The form

2.306

also lists the approved persons from whom claimants need to obtain supporting evidence for the purposes of reg.13(6)(a). They are: a healthcare professional in a Sexual Assault Referral Centre, other healthcare professionals "such as a doctor, nurse, midwife or health visitor", a registered social worker or a specialist support worker from an approved organisation listed at: *www.gov.uk/government/publi cations/support-for-a-child-conceived-without-your-consent*. Guidance notes are also available at that web page.

[¹ Continuation of certain exceptions

2.307

14.—(1) This regulation applies in relation to A if—
(a) no other exception applies in relation to A under these Regulations;
(b) the claimant, or at least one of the joint claimants, is A's step-parent (and, in this Regulation, "C" means the claimant or a joint claimant who is A's step-parent); and
(c) paragraph (2), (4) or (5) applies.
(2) This paragraph applies if—
(a) C has previously been entitled to child tax credit jointly with a parent of A;
(b) immediately before that joint entitlement ceased, an exception applied under regulation 9(1) [³. . .] in relation to A;
(c) since that joint entitlement ceased, C has continuously been entitled to child tax credit (whether or not jointly with another person); and
(d) where the criterion in sub-paragraph (b) is met by virtue of [³. . .] regulation 10, the condition in paragraph (3) is met.
(3) The condition in this paragraph is that—
(a) the claimant, or either or both of the joint claimants, is or are responsible for one or more other children or qualifying young persons born as a result of the same pregnancy as A; and
(b) A is not the first in the order of those children as determined in accordance with regulation 9.

Where a corresponding exception previously applied for the purposes of another benefit
(4) This paragraph applies if—
(a) within the 6 months immediately preceding the day on which a relevant CTC entitlement began—
  (i) C was entitled to an award of universal credit as a member of a couple jointly with a parent of A; or
  (ii) C and a parent of A were a couple and either of them was entitled to an award of income support or old style JSA;
(b) immediately before the entitlement mentioned in sub-paragraph (a)(i) or (ii) ceased, the amount of that entitlement included an amount in respect of A by virtue of any exception corresponding, for the purposes of that entitlement, to an exception under regulation 9(1) [³. . .] in relation to A;
(c) C has continuously been entitled to child tax credit (whether or not jointly with another person) since the relevant CTC entitlement mentioned in sub-paragraph (a); and
(d) where the criterion in sub-paragraph (b) is met by virtue of [³. . .] regulation 10, the condition in paragraph (3) is met.
(5) This paragraph applies if—

(SI 2002/2007 reg.14) (as amended)

(a) within the 6 months immediately preceding the day on which a relevant CTC entitlement began—
   (i) C was entitled to an award of universal credit (whether or not as a member of a couple jointly with another person); or
   (ii) C was entitled to an award of income support or old style JSA (whether or not C was in a couple with another person);
(b) immediately before the entitlement mentioned in sub-paragraph (a) (i) or (ii) ceased, the amount of that entitlement included an amount in respect of A by virtue of any exception corresponding, for the purposes of that entitlement, to the exception that, under regulation 9(1), applies where this regulation applies;
(c) C has continuously been entitled to child tax credit (whether or not jointly with another person) since the relevant CTC entitlement mentioned in sub-paragraph (a); and
(d) where the criterion in sub-paragraph (b) is met by virtue of [³ regulation 10], the condition in paragraph (3) is met.

Interpretation
(6) In this regulation—
"couple" has the same meaning as in Part 1 of the Welfare Reform Act 2012; and
"relevant CTC entitlement" means an entitlement of C (whether or not jointly with another person) to child tax credit.
(7) For the purposes of this regulation, an entitlement of C to child tax credit is to be regarded as continuous despite any interruption of less than 6 months in such an entitlement.]

AMENDMENTS

1. Child Tax Credit (Amendment) Regulations 2017 (SI 2017/387) reg.5 (April 6, 2017).
2. Child Tax Credit (Amendment) Regulations 2018 (SI 2018/1130) reg.5 (November 28, 2018).
3. Tax Credits, Child Benefit and Childcare Payments (Miscellaneous Amendments) Regulations 2019 (SI 2019/364) reg.4(3) (March 21, 2019).

GENERAL NOTE

This regulation sets out when the exceptions for multiple births, adoption and non-consensual adoption are to continue following the death of a claimant who originally qualified under regs 10, 11 and 13.

2.308

The Tax Credits (Income Thresholds and Determination of Rates) Regulations 2002

(SI 2002/2008) (AS AMENDED)

Whereas a draft of this instrument, which contains the first regulations made under section 13(2) of the Tax Credits Act 2002, has been laid before, and approved by resolution of, each House of Parliament:
Now, therefore, the Treasury, in exercise of the powers conferred upon them by sections 8(1) to (3), 13(2) and (3), 65(1) and (7) and 67 of the Tax Credits Act 2002, hereby make the following Regulations:

2.309

Made by the Treasury under ss.8(1)–(3), 13(2) and (3), 65(1) and (7) and 67 of the Tax Credits Act 2002.

Tax Credits (Income Thresholds and Determination of Rates) Regulations 2002

1. Citation, commencement and effect.
2. Interpretation.
3. Manner in which amounts to be determined for the purposes of section 7(1)(a) of the Act.
4. Social security benefits prescribed for the purposes of section 7(2) of the Act.
5. Amounts prescribed for the purposes of section 7(3) of the Act.
6. Manner of determining the rate at which a person is, or persons are, entitled to a tax credit.
7. Determination of rate of working tax credit.
8. Determination of rate of child tax credit.
8A. Cases where there is a reciprocal agreement
9. Cases in which there is no rate of tax credit.

Modifications where claim made for universal credit

2.310 For the modifications to these Regulations where a person's entitlement to a tax credit was interrupted by the making of a claim for universal credit, see reg.12A of, and Sch.1 to, the Universal Credit (Transitional Provisions) Regulations 2014 (SI 2014/1230), below in this volume.

Citation, commencement and effect

2.311 **1.**—(1) These Regulations may be cited as the Tax Credits (Income Thresholds and Determination of Rates) Regulations 2002 and shall come into force—

(a) for the purpose of enabling claims to be made, on August 1, 2002;
(b) for the purpose of enabling decisions on claims to be made, on 1st January 2003; and
(c) for all other purposes, on 6th April 2003.

(2) These Regulations shall have effect for the tax year beginning with 6th April 2003 and subsequent tax years.

DEFINITIONS

"claim"—see TCA 2002 s.3.
"decision on claim"—see TCA 2002 s.14.
"tax year"—see reg.2.

Interpretation

2.312 **2.**—In these Regulations—
"the Act" means the Tax Credits Act 2002;
"the income threshold" has the meaning given by section 7(1)(a) of the Act;
"period of award" shall be construed in accordance with section 5 of the Act;
"the relevant income" has the meaning given by section 7(3) of the Act;
"tax year" means a period beginning with 6th April in one year and ending with 5th April in the next.

Manner in which amounts to be determined for the purposes of section 7(1)(a) of the Act

2.313 **3.**—(1) This regulation prescribes the manner in which amounts are to be determined for the purposes of section 7(1)(a) of the Act.

(SI 2002/2008 reg.3) (as amended)

(2) In the case of a person or persons entitled to working tax credit, the amount in relation to that tax credit is [¹£7,955].

(3) In the case of a person or persons entitled to child tax credit, the amount in relation to that tax credit is [¹£19,995].

AMENDMENT

1. Tax Credits, Child Benefit and Guardian's Allowance Up-rating Regulations 2024 (SI 2024/247) reg.4(2) (April 6, 2024)

DEFINITION

"the Act"—see reg.2.

GENERAL NOTE

This regulation makes the necessary provision to give full operative effect to s.7(1) of the Act (income test).

HMRC does not use the term "income threshold". Instead it describes it in its literature as "taper start point". However, as the Commissioner noted in *CTC/2113/2006*, a failure to explain that this is how HMRC refers to the income thresholds can cause confusion.

2.314

Paragraph (1)

Section 7(1) of TCA 2002 imposes an income test on all claimants for tax credits, the test being whether the relevant income of the claimant (or claimants) for the tax year exceeds "the amount" for that tax credit. If the relevant income does exceed the amount, then it must be calculated by how much it does so. This applies to all claimants apart from those within s.7(2) and reg.4 below. In other words, "the amount" is the income threshold for claiming that tax credit. Only those with no incomes or incomes below the threshold can claim the full tax credit for the year. The section allows, and this regulation provides, different thresholds for different tax credits.

The thresholds are reconsidered annually, and have been set at:

2.315

Year	CTC (£ pa)	WTC (£ pa)
2003–04	13,230	5,060
2004–05	13,480	5,060
2005–06	13,910	5,220
2006–07	14,155	5,220
2007–08	14,495	5,220
2008–09	15,575	6,420
2009–10	16,040	6,420
2010–11	16,190	6,420
2011–12	15,860	6,420
2012–13	15,860	6,420
2013–14	15,910	6,420
2014–15	16,010	6,420
2015–16	16,105	6,420
2016–17	16,105	6,420
2017–18	16,105	6,420
2018–19	16,105	6,420
2019–20	16,105	6,420
2020–21	16,385	6,530
2021–22	16,480	6,565
2022–23	17,005	6,770
2023–24	18,725	7,455
2024–25	19,995	7,995

Tax Credits (Income Thresholds and Determination of Rates) Regulations 2002

The existence of separate thresholds means that in many cases separate calculations have to be made under s.7(1) about entitlement to each tax credit. The current thresholds have the effect that many more people are entitled to the child tax credit than to the working tax credit. Regulations 7 and 8 of these Regulations make provision for dealing with this. There was no change of rates from 2015–16 to 2019–20 despite the general policy of review following the government's general policy of freezing benefit increases. It also reflects the steady transfer of entitlement to universal credit and the rates of that benefit.

Social security benefits prescribed for the purposes of section 7(2) of the Act

2.316   **4.**—[4 (1) Subject to paragraph (2),] The following are social security benefits prescribed for the purposes of section 7(2) of the Act in relation to child tax credit and working tax credit—
(a) income support under Part VII of the Social Security Contributions and Benefit Act 1992 other than income support to which a person is entitled only by virtue of regulation 6(2) and (3) of the Income Support (General) Regulations 1987;
(b) income support under Part VII of the Social Security Contributions and Benefit (Northern Ireland) Act 1992 other than income support to which a person is entitled only by virtue of regulation 6(2) and (3) of the Income Support (General) Regulations (Northern Ireland) 1987;
(c) an income-based jobseeker's allowance within the meaning of the Jobseekers Act 1995 or the Jobseekers (Northern Ireland) Order 1995.
[1 (d) state pension credit within the meaning of the State Pension Credit Act 2002 or the State Pension Credit Act (Northern Ireland) 2002.]
[2 (e) an income-related employment and support allowance payable under Part 1 of the Welfare Reform Act 2007 [3 or Part 1 of the Welfare Reform Act (Northern Ireland) 2007].]
[4 (2) Paragraph (1) shall not apply in relation to working tax credit during the four-week period described in regulation 7D of the Working Tax Credit (Entitlement and Maximum Rate) Regulations 2002 (ceasing to undertake work or working for less than 16 or 30 hours per week).]

AMENDMENTS

1. Tax Credits (Miscellaneous Amendments No.2) Regulations 2003 (SI 2003/2815) reg.18 (November 26, 2003).
2. Employment and Support Allowance (Consequential Provisions) (No.3) Regulations 2008 (SI 2009/1879) reg.23 (October 27, 2008).
3. Employment and Support Allowance (Consequential Provisions No.2) Regulations (Northern Ireland) 2008 (SI 2008/412 (NI) reg.10 (October 27, 2008)).
4. Tax Credits (Miscellaneous Amendments) Regulations 2010 (SI 2010/751) reg.17(1) and (2) (April 6, 2010).

DEFINITION

"the Act"—see reg.2.

GENERAL NOTE

2.317   Section 7(2) of the TCA 2002 provides that those entitled to any of the social security benefits prescribed for the purposes of that subsection are not to be subject to the income test in s.7(1). This does not apply to exclude the claimant from any other requirements for an award.

(SI 2002/2008 reg.4) (as amended)

Four benefits only have been prescribed by this regulation. They are:
(1) income support payable to any claimant. The exception applies to anyone who is a lone parent treated by regs 6(2) or (3) of the Income Support (General) Regulations 1987 (and its Northern Ireland equivalent) as being entitled to income support for the first 14 days of a period of remunerative work because he or she was a lone parent who was, for at least 26 weeks before the work started, receiving income support or income-based jobseeker's allowance;
(2) income-based jobseeker's allowance;
(3) state pension credit; and
(4) income-related employment and support allowance.

[¹ Amounts prescribed for the purposes of section 7(3) of the Act

5.—The amount prescribed—   2.318
   (a) for the purposes of section 7(3)(a) and (b) of the Act is [² [³£2,500]]; and
   (b) for the purposes of section 7(3)(c) and (d) of the Act is £2,500.]

AMENDMENTS

1. Tax Credits Up-rating Regulations 2012 (SI 2012/849) reg.4(2) and (3) (April 6, 2012).
2. Tax Credits Up-rating, etc. Regulations 2013 (SI 2013/750) reg.4(2) (April 6, 2013).
3. Tax Credits (Income Thresholds and Determination of Rates) (Amendment) Regulations 2016 (SI 2016/393) reg.2 (April 6, 2016).

GENERAL NOTE

The figures in this regulation have been altered on a number of occasions since tax credits were introduced, in part in response to practical difficulties with the way such changes were handled in earlier years. From 2016–17 the limits for both increases and decreases of income are set at £2,500. Before 2016 increases were ignored unless equalling £5,000 or more. The new lower standard will affect many more claimants but in practice often does not do so until entitlement is reviewed at the end of a year when the effect will apply in the following year.   2.319

Manner of determining the rate at which a person is, or persons are, entitled to a tax credit

6.—Regulations 7, 8 and 9 make provision as to the manner of determining the rate (if any) at which a person is, or persons are, entitled to a tax credit in any case where—   2.320
   (a) the relevant income exceeds the income threshold; and
   (b) his or their entitlement does not arise by virtue of section 7(2) of the Act.

DEFINITIONS

"entitlement"—see TCA 2002 ss.8 and 10.
"income threshold"—see reg.2.
"relevant income"—see reg.2.
"the Act"—see reg.2.

GENERAL NOTE

This is, on its face, purely a signposting regulation. It serves to remind the reader of the exception from the income test in s.7 of the TCA 2002, and also to tie in the £26 rule in reg.9 with the two main regulations: reg.7 dealing with working tax   2.321

credit, and reg.8 dealing with child tax credit. As will be seen from those regulations, that order is intentional as entitlement to working tax credit, if any, must be calculated before entitlement to child tax credit.

There is, however, a drafting mismatch between the wording of this regulation and the approach of regs 7 and 8, which appears to deflect its intention. Regulation 6 states that the other regulations make provision for determining the rate of *entitlement* to tax credits. By contrast, regs 7 and 8 talk about periods of *award*. "Period of award" is defined in reg.2 of these Regulations by reference to s.5 of the TCA 2002 (entitled "periods of award"). And regs 7 and 8 of these Regulations refer to the elements of the credits to which a claimant "may be entitled" (regs 7(2)(a) and 8(2)).

The purpose of s.5 of TCA 2002 is to determine the period for which an award of tax credit is made. Awards are made under s.14 of the Act, and are made in advance of, or at the start of, the year of claim, using s.7(10) of the Act to estimate the income. At that point, the "period of award" can in most cases only be the whole tax year, or the balance of that year from the effective starting date of the award. Awards must ignore uncertain future changes as they are not then known. Regulations 7 and 8 set out in considerable detail how to deal with part-years. But, save for the case of claims made only part-way through a year, the "relevant period" for an award will always be the whole year, and the complexities of regs 7 and 8 are not needed.

The full calculations under regs 7 and 8 of these Regulations cannot be made until the end of the tax year, when the task of HMRC is to make entitlement decisions under s.18 of the Act. So why refer to periods of award rather than periods of entitlement? It would appear that this mismatch between *award* and *entitlement* is a leftover of the changes made to the Tax Credits Bill during its passage through Parliament (as discussed in the notes to those sections). It is suggested that, to make practical sense of this regulation, the definition of "period of award" as applied to both regs 7 and 8 has to take in periods of entitlement as well.

Determination of rate of working tax credit

7.—(1) In relation to a person or persons entitled to working tax credit, the rate shall be determined by finding the rate for each relevant period and, where necessary, adding together those rates.

(2) "Relevant period" means any part of the period of award throughout which—
  (a) the elements of working tax credit (other than the child care element) to which the person or persons may be entitled, remain the same; and
  (b) there is no relevant change of circumstances for the purposes of the child care element of working tax credit, within the meaning of regulation 16(1) of the Working Tax Credit (Entitlement and Maximum Rate) Regulations 2002 (change of circumstances for the purposes of child care element).

(3) The rate for each relevant period shall be found in accordance with the following steps—

Step 1—Finding the daily maximum rate for each element other than the child care element

For each element of the tax credit (other than the child care element) to be included in the case of the person or persons entitled to the tax credit, find the daily maximum rate using the following formula:

$$\frac{MR}{N1}$$

(SI 2002/2008 reg. 7) (as amended)

where:

"MR" is the maximum rate in relation to that element for the tax year to which the claim for the tax credit relates;

"N1" is the number of days in that tax year.

Step 2—Finding the maximum rate for the relevant period for each element other than the child care element

For each element of the tax credit to be so included, find the amount produced by multiplying the daily maximum rate (found under Step 1 and rounded up to the nearest penny) by the number of days in the relevant period.

Step 3—finding the income for the relevant period

Find the income for the relevant period by using the following formula:

$$\frac{I}{N1} \times N2$$

where:

"I" is the relevant income for the tax year to which the claim for the tax credit relates;

"N1" is the number of days in that tax year;

"N2" is the number of days in the relevant period.

Step 4—Finding the threshold for the relevant period

Find the threshold for the relevant period using the following formula:

$$\frac{[^3 £7,995]}{N1} \times N2$$

where:

"N1" is the number of days in that tax year;

"N2" is the number of days in the relevant period.

Step 5—Finding the amount of the reduction

Find the amount which is [¹ 41] per cent of the amount by which the income for the relevant period (found under Step 3 and rounded down to the nearest penny) exceeds the threshold for the relevant period (found under Step 4 and rounded up to the nearest penny).

Step 6—Reducing the elements of the tax credit (other than any child care element)

If the amount found under Step 5 (rounded down to the nearest penny) is less than or equal to the total of the amounts found under Step 2 for the elements of the tax credit, deduct the amount found under Step 5 (rounded down to the nearest penny) from the total of those amounts found under Step 2.

Step 7—Finding the actual weekly child care costs for the relevant period

Find the relevant child care charges for the relevant period in accordance with regulation 15 of the Working Tax Credit (Entitlement and Maximum Rate) Regulations 2002.

Tax Credits (Income Thresholds and Determination of Rates) Regulations 2002

Step 8—Finding the actual child care costs for the relevant period

Multiply the result of Step 7 by

$$\frac{52}{N1} \times N2$$

Here, N1 and N2 have the same meanings as in Step 3.

The result of this step is the amount of actual child care costs for the relevant period.

Step 9—Finding the prescribed maximum child care costs for the relevant period

Divide whichever of the maxima in regulation 20(3) of the Working Tax Credit (Entitlement and Maximum Rate) Regulations 2002 is applicable by seven, round the result up to the nearest penny and multiply the resulting figure by the number of days in the relevant period.

The result of this is the prescribed maximum child care costs for the relevant period.

Step 10—Finding the child care element for the period

Take the lesser of the results of Steps 8 and 9.
Multiply that figure by [²70 per cent] and round the result up to the nearest penny.
The result of this step is the maximum rate of the child care element for the relevant period.

Step 11—Reducing the elements of the tax credit (including any child care element)

If the amount found under Step 5 (rounded down to the nearest penny) exceeds the total of the amounts found under Step 2 for the elements of the tax credit—
  (a) deduct the excess from the amount found under Step 10 for any child care element; and
  (b) reduce the total of the amounts found under Step 2 for the other elements of the tax credit to nil.

Step 12—Finding the rate for the relevant period

Add together—
  (a) the total of the amounts found under Step 2 for the elements of the tax credit (other than any child care element) after reduction in accordance with Step 6 or Step 11; and
  (b) the amount found under Step 10 for any child care element after any reduction in accordance with Step 11.
This is the rate for the relevant period.
  (4) "Child care element" has the meaning given by section 12(2) of the Act.

AMENDMENTS

1. Tax Credits Up-rating Regulations 2008 (SI 2008/796) reg.4(4) (April 6, 2008).
2. Tax Credits Up-rating Regulations 2011 (SI 2011/1035) reg.4(4) (April 6, 2011).
3. Tax Credits, Child Benefit and Guardian's Allowance Up-rating Regulations 2024 (SI 2024/247) reg.4(3) (April 6, 2024).

(SI 2002/2008 reg.7) (as amended)

DEFINITIONS
"child care element"—see TCA 2002 s.12.
"period of award"—see reg.2.
"rate"—see TCA 2002 s.13.

GENERAL NOTE

See the general note to reg.6 above. The effect of this regulation and reg.8—both together and separately—is to limit the amount of tax credit that a claimant can have to the relevant daily (or in the case of child care element of working tax credit only, weekly) amount of the credit, if circumstances of a claimant change during a tax year. This approach is, as a result, less generous than the personal allowances for income tax, including children's tax credit. For example, the main personal allowance of an individual is the same amount for that individual throughout the year as is, for example, a bereaved person's allowance or a blind person's allowance. By contrast, the basis of calculation imposed by this regulation and reg.8 is that the elements of both working tax credit and child tax credit are payable only for the precise periods of the year for which the claimant can meet the requirement for that credit and element.

2.323

Paragraphs (1) and (2)
As noted above, "period of award" must be read as including also "period of entitlement" to make sense of this regulation. Likewise, the reference to "may be entitled" in para.(2) should include "is entitled".

2.324

Paragraph (3)
This paragraph is written in the "step-by-step" style, using the command tense of relevant verbs, that has been adopted as part of the Tax Law Rewrite approach to tax regulations. It is also written so that the rules in the paragraph can be operated in full by a computer.

2.325

Relevant periods of a full year
In most cases, as noted above, the complexities of this rule can be sidestepped because the question of an award of, or entitlement to, a tax credit can be judged by the full tax year. If the decision relates to a full year, then the steps can be telescoped as follows:

2.326

Step 1 with Step 2: Identify the annual amount of each element of working tax credit to which the claimant is entitled, apart from the child care element, for that tax year.

Step 3: Identify the relevant income for the tax year (current year income or previous year income).

Step 4 with Step 5 and Step 6: If the income from Step 3 exceeds the annual amount from Steps 1 and 2, reduce the amounts from Steps 1 and 2 by 41 per cent. The result is the excess income for that year. The rate of reduction, originally 37 per cent, was increased to 39 per cent in 2006 when the income tax rate was lowered. Section 75 of the Welfare Reform Act 2012 provides power retrospectively to amend Step 5 in reg.7(3) of the Tax Credits (Income Thresholds and Determination of Rates) Regulations 2002 to provide for a reduction of 41 per cent from April 6, 2011 for all purposes. This gives effect to the announcement in the Emergency Budget of 2011. However, it was questionable whether there was authority in primary legislation to amend the figure in the way it was amended. Section 76 of the Welfare Reform Act 2012 now provides retrospective authority for the change.

Step 7 with Step 8: Find the relevant child care charges for the tax year.

Tax Credits (Income Thresholds and Determination of Rates) Regulations 2002

Step 9 with Step 10: The maximum annual rate of the child care element (prescribed by regulation 20 of the Working Tax Credit (Entitlement and Maximum Rate Regulations 2002: see above in this volume) is now 70 per cent of £15,695 (£10,986.50) or of £9,125 for one child (£6,387.50)) or, if less, 70 per cent of the actual charges paid.

Steps 11 and 12: If there is excess income for the tax year from Steps 4–6, reduce the annual amount from Steps 1 and 2 by the amount of that excess, if necessary to nil. If the excess is greater than that amount, next reduce the amount from Steps 9 and 10 by the amount by which that excess income exceeds the annual amount from Steps 1 and 2. If the excess income is greater than both amounts, then the amount of working tax credit for the tax year is nil.

Note from this that the child care element of working tax credit is to be calculated on a weekly, not daily, basis in the event of any problem, and also is to be left in payment after the other elements have stopped being payable under these rules.

Relevant periods of less than a year

2.327　　These periods arise only where there is a change of circumstances during a year that brings a relevant period to an end and/or starts a new one. Until 2006 this could cause problems where this happened in circumstances where claimants were not under a duty to report changes. The extension of the duty to report under reg.21 of the Tax Credits (Claims and Notifications) Regulations 2002, together with the reduction of the period in which the changes must be reported to one month, and the extension of award or entitlement by reg.7D of the Working Tax Credit (Entitlement and Maximum Rate) Regulations 2002 for four weeks after someone ceases work or works for less than 16 hours a week, have removed many of these problems.

CTC/2270/2007 confirms that the relevant income of a couple is their income for the year even if they only become a couple during the year. See the note to TCA 2002 s.7(4) above.

Determination of rate of child tax credit

2.328　　**8.**—(1) In relation to a person or persons entitled to child tax credit, the rate shall be determined by finding the rate for each relevant period and, where necessary, adding together those rates.

(2) "Relevant period" means—
(a) in the case of a person or persons entitled to child tax credit only, any part of the period of award throughout which the maximum rate at which he or they may be entitled to the tax credit remains the same;
(b) in the case of a person or persons entitled to both child tax credit and working tax credit, any part of the period of award throughout which the maximum rate of child tax credit to which he or they may be entitled remains the same and both sub-paras (a) and (b) of regulation 7(2) are met.

(3) The rate for each relevant period shall be found in accordance with the following steps—

Step 1—Finding the daily maximum rate for each element

For each element of the tax credit to be included in the case of the person or persons entitled to the tax credit, find the daily maximum rate using the following formula:

$$\frac{MR}{NI}$$

(SI 2002/2008 reg. 7) (as amended)

where:

"MR" is the maximum rate in relation to that element for the tax year to which the claim for the tax credit relates;

"NI" is the number of days in that tax year.

Step 2—Finding the maximum rate for the relevant period for each element

For each element of the tax credit to be so included, find the amount produced by multiplying the maximum rate (found under Step 1 and rounded up to the nearest penny) by the number of days in the relevant period.

Step 3—Finding income for the relevant period

Find the income for the relevant period by using the following formula:

$$\frac{I}{NI} \times N2$$

where:

"I" is the relevant income for the tax year to which the claim for the tax credit relates;

"NI" is the number of days in that tax year;

"N2" is the number of days in the relevant period.

Step 4—Finding the threshold for the relevant period

Find the amount produced by the following formula:

$$\frac{[^3 £19,995]}{NI} \times N2$$

where:

"NI" is the number of days in that tax year;

"N2" is the number of days in the relevant period.

The threshold for the relevant period is—
   (a) in the case of a person or persons entitled to child tax credit only, that amount;
   (b) in the case of a person or persons entitled to both child tax credit and working tax credit—
      (i) that amount; or
      (ii) if greater, the lowest amount of income for the relevant period (found under Step 3) which, disregarding regulation 9, would result in a determination in accordance with regulation 7 providing for no rate of working tax credit in his or their case for that period.

Step 5—Finding the amount of the reduction of the elements of the tax credit [² ...]

Find the amount (if any) which is [¹ 41 per cent] of the amount by which the income for the relevant period (found under Step 3 and rounded down

Tax Credits (Income Thresholds and Determination of Rates) Regulations 2002

to the nearest penny) exceeds the threshold for the relevant period (found under Step 4 and rounded up to the nearest penny).

Step 6—Reducing the elements of the tax credit [² ...]

If the amount found under Step 5 (rounded down to the nearest penny) is less than the total of the amounts found under Step 2 for the elements of the tax credit [² ...], deduct the amount found under Step 5 (rounded down to the nearest penny) from the total of those amounts.

Step 7—Reducing the elements of the tax credit [² ...] to nil

If the amount found under Step 5 (rounded down to the nearest penny) is equal to or exceeds the total of the amounts found under Step 2 for the elements of the tax credit [² ...], reduce the total of those amounts to nil.
[² ...]

[² Step 8]—Finding the rate for the relevant period

[²The rate for the relevant period is the total of the amounts found under Step 2 for the elements of the tax credit after any reduction in accordance with Step 6 or Step 7.]

(4) "The family element" means the family element of child tax credit within the meaning given by section 9(3) of the Act.

AMENDMENTS

1. Tax Credits Up-rating Regulations 2011 (SI 2011/1035) reg.4(5) (April 6, 2011).
2. Tax Credits Up-rating Regulations 2012 (SI 2012/849) reg.4(5) (April 6, 2012).
3. Tax Credits, Child Benefit and Guardian's Allowance Up-rating Regulations 2024 (SI 2024/247) reg.4(4) (April 6, 2024).

DEFINITIONS

"period of award"—see reg.2.
"the Act"—see reg.2.

GENERAL NOTE

2.329 See the general note to reg.6 above and the opening note to reg.7.

Paragraphs (1) and (2)
The same comments apply as those to paras (1) and (2) of reg.7.

Paragraph (3)
2.330 This appears to be the equivalent for child tax credit of reg.7, but it has two additional elements. First, the effect of the steps is to remove an award of or entitlement to working tax credit before that of child tax credit. This may be important where one of a couple is receiving one of the credits while the other is receiving the other tax credit. The effect is to take the credit from the earner (and the duty to pay from the employer) before it is taken from the carer.

Secondly, the family element is reduced, then removed, only after a second, higher income threshold. Before April 6, 2011 this was £50,000 and the withdrawal rate was gradual: 6.67 per cent. From April 6, 2011 the threshold was reduced to £40,000 and the same withdrawal rate is applied as to the lower threshold—now 41 per cent. This reduces the maximum income permitting a claim for child tax credit substantially—from around £66,000 to below £50,000, depending on the number of children.

Relevant periods of a full year
In parallel with reg.7, reg.8 is straightforward as applied to a period of award of a full year. Steps 1–6 require that the annual amount of all elements (including the family element) be found, that the income for the year also be found, and that the excess of the income over the £19,995 threshold, if any, be calculated. The maximum amount of child tax credit is found by reducing the annual amount of all elements *excluding* the family element by 41 per cent of the excess of the income over the threshold.

Relevant periods of less than a year
The changes noted in para.2.329, above, for the equivalent rule for WTC apply equally to CTC and have also removed most of the potential problems for this provision also.

[¹ Cases where there is a reciprocal agreement

8A.-(1) This regulation applies where the United Kingdom is competent to pay family benefits in accordance with Article 39 of the Reciprocal Agreement with Ireland but where Ireland has primary competence for payment of those benefits.

(2) Where this regulation applies, child tax credit shall be paid at the rate according to the calculation set out in paragraph (4) of Article 39 of the Reciprocal Agreement with Ireland.

(3) Child tax credit shall be paid on a provisional basis where—
(a) Article 39(5) of the Reciprocal Agreement with Ireland applies;
(b) the United Kingdom is Party B in the circumstances set out under Article 40(1)(b) of the Reciprocal Agreement with Ireland; or
(c) the United Kingdom does not agree that it has primary competence for payment of family benefits where the child resides or the children reside in the United Kingdom and Article 63(2) of the Reciprocal Agreement with Ireland applies.

(4) In this regulation—
(a) "family benefits" has the meaning as set out in Article 3(1)(x) of the Reciprocal Agreement with Ireland; and
(b) "the Reciprocal Agreement with Ireland" means the Convention on Social Security between the Government of the United Kingdom of Great Britain and Northern Ireland and the Government of Ireland signed at Dublin on 1st February 2019.]

AMENDMENT

1. Tax Credits and Child Trust Funds (Amendment) (EU Exit) Regulations 2019 (SI 2019/713) reg.5 (31 December 2020, at 11 p.m.: see the definition of 'IP completion day' in s.39(1) of the European Union (Withdrawal Agreement) Act 2020).

DEFINITIONS

The Convention on Social Security between the Government of the United Kingdom and Northern Ireland and the Government of Ireland, as referred to in the definition of "the Reciprocal Agreement with Ireland" is scheduled to, and given effect in UK law by Article 2(1) of, the Social Security (Ireland) Order 2019 (SI 2019/622)).

Tax Credits (Income Thresholds and Determination of Rates) Regulations 2002

General Note

2.333 The relevant provisions of the Reciprocal Agreement with Ireland, reference to which is necessary to understand regulation 8A, are set out below:

"*Article 1*

Definitions

(1) For the purposes of this Convention the following definitions apply, except where the context otherwise requires:
…"competence", in relation to a Party, means responsibility for payment of a particular benefit under the legislation it applies to a person who:
  (i) is insured in that Party in relation to a benefit of that type, at the time of their claim for it; or …
  (ii) would be entitled to such benefit if they (or a member of their family or survivor, where relevant) resided in that Party,
and the word "competent" shall be construed accordingly;
…"insured" means, in relation to a person,
  (i) under the legislation of the United Kingdom, that they have the right to a type of benefit set out in Article 3(1), taking into account the provisions of this Convention …

Article 3

Scope of legislation

(1) This Convention shall apply:
(a) in relation to the United Kingdom, to … the Tax Credits Act 2002 …and the subordinate legislation made under those Acts … as they relate … to:
(x) the following family benefits:
… Child Tax Credit …

Article 7

Waiving of residence rules

Unless otherwise provided by this Convention, benefits payable to a person or a member of their family under the legislation of a Party, or by a Party under this Convention, shall not be subject to any reduction, amendment, suspension, withdrawal or confiscation on account of the fact that such a person or a member of their family resides in the other Party.

(SI 2002/2008 reg. 8A) (as amended)

Article 9

General provisions

(1) A person shall be subject to the legislation of a single Party which shall be determined in accordance with this Part.

(2) A person receiving a benefit from one Party because or as a consequence of their activity as an employed or self-employed person shall be considered to be pursuing that activity in that Party.

...(4) Subject to Articles 10 to 13:
  (a) a person pursuing an activity as an employed or self-employed person in one Party shall be subject to the legislation of that Party;
...(d) any other person to whom sub-paragraphs (a) to (d) do not apply shall be subject to the legislation of the Party in which they reside, without prejudice to other provisions of this Convention guaranteeing them benefits under the legislation of the other Party.

Article 38

Responsibility for payment of family benefits

(1) A person, other than a pensioner, shall be entitled to family benefits in accordance with the legislation applied by a Party where it is competent for the payment of such benefits, including for any members of the family residing in the other Party, as if they were residing in the former Party...

Article 39

Priority rules where both Parties' legislation applies

(1) Priority rules in this Article apply to determine which Party pays family benefits where during the same period and for the same family members a person (including a pensioner) is entitled to such benefits under the legislation of both Parties.

(2) Where such benefits are payable by both Parties on a different basis, the order of priority shall be decided on the basis of rights:
  (a) available on the basis of an activity as an employed or self-employed person;
  (b) available on the basis of receipt of a pension; and
  (c) obtained on the basis of residence.

(3) Where such benefits arc payable by both Parties on the same basis, the order of priority shall be decided by reference to the following criteria:
  (a) in the case of rights available on the basis of an activity as an employed or self-employed person, the Party of residence of the child or children in respect of whom benefits are paid;
  (b) in the case of rights available on the basis of receipt of pensions, the Party of residence of the child or children in respect of whom benefits are paid;
  (c) in the case of rights available on the basis of residence, the Party of residence of the child or children in respect of whom benefits are paid.

(4) Where such benefits are payable by both Parties, they shall be paid by the Party having priority in accordance with paragraphs (I) to (3) (the Party with priority), and the following rules shall apply:
  (a) entitlement to family benefits under the legislation applying to the other Party shall be suspended up to the amount provided by the Party with priority and a differential supplement shall, if necessary, be provided by the other Party for the sum which exceeds this amount;
  (b) but where entitlement to family benefits is based on residence only, and whichever Party has priority, no differential supplement is payable for a child or children residing in the other Party.

(5) Where the order of priority cannot be established on the basis of the child or children's place of residence in accordance with paragraphs (3)(a) and (b), the Party whose legislation provides for the higher level of benefits (Party A) shall pay the full amount of such benefits on a provisional basis. The payment shall be made taking into account any children not residing in Party A. Party A shall then be reimbursed by the other Party (Party B) half the sum it has paid up to the limit of the amount provided for in the legislation of Party B.

(6) Where a claim is made to the Party whose legislation is applicable but not by priority right in accordance with paragraphs (1) to (3) (Party A):
  (a) the relevant authority of Party A shall send the claim, without delay, to the relevant authority of the other Party (Party B), inform the person concerned and, without prejudice to Article 63(1), provide, if necessary, the differential supplement mentioned in paragraph (4);
  (b) the relevant authority of Party B will deal with this claim as though it had been submitted to it in the first instance, and the date on which the claim was submitted to the relevant authority of Party A shall be treated as the date on which it was received by Party B.

Article 40

Provisional award of family benefits

(1) Where family benefits are payable by both Parties, but no decision has been made on how the priority rules in Articles 39(1) to (3) apply to a particular claim, the following rules shall apply:
...(b) if Party A decides that the other Party (Party B) is competent to pay such benefits, it will forward the application without delay to the relevant authority of Party B and inform the person concerned;...

Article 63

Provisional application of legislation and provisional granting of benefits

...(2) Where there is a difference of views between the Parties as to which is competent for payment of a benefit to a person who has made a claim, they shall he entitled, on a provisional basis, to such benefits under the legislation of their Party of residence."

Cases in which there is no rate of tax credit

9.—(1) In the case of a person or persons entitled to working tax credit only or child tax credit only, where the rate at which the person or persons would be entitled to the tax credit (as determined in accordance with reg.7 or 8) would be less than £26, there is no rate in his or their case.

(2) In the case of a person or persons entitled to both working tax credit and child tax credit, where the total of the rates at which the person or persons would be entitled to the tax credits (as determined in accordance with regulations 7 and 8) would be less than £26, there are no rates in his or their case.

GENERAL NOTE

This cut-off provision is authorised by s.13(3)(b) of the Act.

The Tax Credits (Claims and Notifications) Regulations 2002

(SI 2002/2014) (AS AMENDED)

The Commissioners of Inland Revenue, in exercise of the powers conferred upon them by ss.4(1), 6, 14(2), 15(2), 16(3), 17(10), 19(2), 22(1)(b) and (2), 65(1), (2) and (7) and 67 of the Tax Credits Act 2002, hereby make the following Regulations:

ARRANGEMENT OF REGULATIONS

PART I

GENERAL

1. Citation, commencement and effect.
2. Interpretation.
3. Use of electronic communications to make claims or to give notices or notifications.

PART II

CLAIMS

4. Interpretation of this Part.
5. Manner in which claims to be made.
6. Amended claims.
7. Time-limit for claims (if otherwise entitled to tax credit up to 31 days earlier).
7A. Time limit for claims—the Childcare Payments Act 2014.
8. Date of claims—disability element of working tax credit.
9. Advance claims before the year begins.
10. Advance claims—working tax credit.
11. Circumstances in which claims to be treated as made—notices containing provision under section 17(2)(a), (4)(a) or (6)(a) of the Act.

12. Circumstances in which claims to be treated as made—notices containing provision under section 17(2)(b), (4)(b) and (6)(b) of the Act.
13. Circumstances in which claims made by one member of a couple to be treated as also made by the other member of the couple.
14. Circumstances in which awards to be conditional and claims treated as made—decisions under section 14(1) of the Act made before 6th April 2003.
15. Persons who die after making a claim.
16. Persons who die before making joint claims.
17. Circumstances where one person may act for another in making a claim—receivers, etc.
18. Circumstances where one person may act for another in making a claim—other appointed persons.

Part III

Notifications of Changes of Circumstances

19. Interpretation of this Part.
20. Increases of maximum rate of entitlement to a tax credit as a result of changes of circumstances to be dependent on notification.
21. Requirement to notify changes of circumstances which may decrease the rate at which a person or persons is or are entitled to tax credit or mean that entitlement ceases.
22. Manner in which notifications to be given.
21A. Coronavirus—date of notification—cases where change of circumstances which may decrease the rate at which a person is, or persons are, entitled to a tax credit or mean that entitlement to that tax credit ceases (revoked).
23. Person by whom notification may be, or is to be, given.
24. Amended notifications.
25. Date of notification—cases where change of circumstances which may increase the maximum rate.
25A. Coronavirus—date of notification—cases where change of circumstances may increase the maximum rate (revoked).
26. Date of notification—disability element and severe disability element for working tax credit.
26A. Date of notification—disability element and severe disability element for child tax credit.
26B. Coronavirus—date of notification of disability (revoked).
27. Advance notification.
28. Circumstances where one person may act for another in giving a notification—receivers, etc.
29. Circumstances where one person may act for another in giving a notification—other appointed persons.
29A. Form in which evidence of birth or adoption to be provided.

Part IV

Notices to Provide Information or Evidence

30. Employers.
31. Persons by whom child care is provided.
32. Dates to be specified in notices under section 14(2), 15(2), 16(3), 18(10) or 19(2) of the Act.

(SI 2002/2014) (as amended)

PART V

FINAL DECISIONS

33. Dates to be specified in notices under section 17 of the Act.
34. Manner in which declaration or statement in response to a notice under section 17 of the Act to be made.
35. Circumstances where one person may act for another in response to a notice under section 17 of the Act—receivers, etc.
36. Circumstances where one person may act for another in response to a notice under section 17 of the Act.

PART I

GENERAL

Citation, commencement and effect

1.—(1) These Regulations may be cited as the Tax Credits (Claims and Notifications) Regulations 2002 and shall come into force on 12th August 2002.

(2) These Regulations have effect in relation to claims for a tax credit for periods of award beginning on or after 6th April 2003.

Modifications where claim made for universal credit
For the modifications to these Regulations where a person's entitlement to a tax credit was interrupted by the making of a claim for universal credit, see reg.12A of, and Sch.1 to, the Universal Credit (Transitional Provisions) Regulations 2014 (SI 2014/1230), above in this volume.

Interpretation

2.—In these Regulations—
"the Act" means the Tax Credits Act 2002;
[^{3}"appropriate office" means [^{7} any] office specified in writing by the Board;]
[^{4} armed forces independence payment" means armed forces independence payment under the Armed Forces and Reserve Forces (Compensation Scheme) Order 2011;]
"the Board" means the Commissioners [^{9} for Her Majesty's Revenue and Customs];
[^{9} [^{11}...]]
[^{2}"couple" has the meaning given by section 3(5A) of the Act;]
[^{9} [^{11}...]]
"disability element" shall be construed in accordance with section 11(4) of the Act;
"joint claim" has the meaning given by section 3(8) of the Act;
[^{2}...]
[^{5}"personal independence payment" means personal independence payment under Part 4 of the Welfare Reform Act 2012 [^{6} or Part 5 of the Welfare Reform (Northern Ireland) Order 2015];]
[^{1}"relevant authority" means—

2.337

2.338

2.339

The Tax Credits (Claims and Notifications) Regulations 2002

    (a) the Board;
    (b) the Secretary of State or the Department for [⁸ Communities] in Northern Ireland; [¹⁰...]
    (c) a person providing services to the Board, the Secretary of State or that Department in connection with tax credits;] [¹⁰ or]
[¹⁰(d) the Department of Employment Affairs and Social Protection in Ireland, in connection with a claim to a child tax credit made pursuant to Part IV Section 4 of the Convention on Social Security between the Government of the United Kingdom of Great Britain and Northern Ireland and the Government of Ireland signed at Dublin on 1st February 2019;]
"severe disability element" has the meaning in regulation 17 of the Working Tax Credit Regulations;
"single claim" has the meaning given by section 3(8) of the Act;
"tax year" means a period beginning on 6th April in one year and ending with 5th April in the next;
[²...]
"the Working Tax Credit Regulations" means the Working Tax Credit (Entitlement and Maximum Rate) Regulations 2002.

AMENDMENTS

1. Tax Credits (Claims and Notifications and Payments by the Board) (Amendment) Regulations 2003 (SI 2003/723) reg.3(1) (April 6, 2003).
2. Civil Partnership Act 2004 (Tax Credits, etc.) (Consequential Amendments) Order 2005 (SI 2005/2919) art.4(2) (December 5, 2005).
3. Tax Credits (Miscellaneous Amendments) Regulations 2009 (SI 2009/697) reg.12 (April 6, 2009).
4. Armed Forces and Reserve Forces Compensation Scheme (Consequential Provisions: Subordinate Legislation) Order 2013 (SI 2013/591) art.17 and Sch.1 para.27(2) (April 8, 2013).
5. Personal Independence Payment (Supplementary Provisions and Consequential Amendments) Regulations 2013 (SI 2013/388) reg.8 and Sch. para.31(2) (April 8, 2013).
6. Personal Independence Payment (Supplementary Provisions and Consequential Amendments) Regulations (Northern Ireland) 2016 (SR 2016/228) reg.24 (June 20, 2016).
7. Tax Credits and Childcare (Miscellaneous Amendments) Regulations 2018 (SI 2018/365) reg.3 (April 6, 2018).
8. Tax Credits, Child Benefit and Childcare Payments (Miscellaneous Amendments) Regulations 2019 (SI 2019/364) reg.5(2) (March 21, 2019).
9. Tax Credits (Coronavirus, Miscellaneous Amendments) Regulations 2020 (SI 2020/534) reg.4(2) (May 23, 2020).
10. Tax Credits and Child Trust Funds (Amendment) (EU Exit) Regulations 2019 (SI 2019/713) reg.3(a) (December 31, 2020, at 11 p.m.).
11. Tax Credits and Child Benefit (Miscellaneous Amendments) Regulations 2022 (SI 2022/555) reg.6(2) (June 9, 2022).

Use of electronic communications to make claims or to give notices or notifications

2.340   **3.**—(1) In these Regulations "writing" includes writing produced by electronic communications that are approved by directions issued by or on behalf of the Board.

(2) If a claim which is required by these Regulations to be made to [¹a relevant authority at an appropriate office] is made in writing produced by electronic communications, it shall be treated for the purposes of these Regulations as having been made to, and received by, [¹a relevant authority at an appropriate office] on the date on which it is recorded on an official computer system.

(3) If a notice or notification which is required by these Regulations to be given to [¹a relevant authority at an appropriate office] is given in writing produced by electronic communications, it shall be treated for the purposes of these Regulations as having been given to, and received by, [¹a relevant authority at an appropriate office] on the date on which it is recorded on an official computer system.

(4) In this regulation—
   (a) "electronic communications" has the meaning given by section 132(10) of the Finance Act 1999;
   (b) "official computer system" means a computer system maintained by or on behalf of the Board to—
      (i) send or receive information, or
      (ii) process or store information.

AMENDMENT

1. Tax Credits (Claims and Notifications and Payments by the Board) (Amendment) Regulations 2003 (SI 2003/723) reg.3(2) (April 6, 2003).

DEFINITIONS

"appropriate office"—see reg.2.
"the Board"—see reg.2.
"electronic communications"—see para.(4)(a).
"official computer system"—see para.(4)(b).
"relevant authority"—see reg.2.
"writing"—see para.(1).

GENERAL NOTE

See further the decision of Mr Commissioner Mesher in *CIS/995/2004*, discussed in the annotations to reg.4 below and Tax Credits Act 2002 s.14(2) above.

This regulation enables use of the internet and an official website for claims. The HMRC website claim facility was closed down after severe problems with fraud. The House of Commons Public Accounts Committee has since disclosed that the website was established outside recommended security procedures. It remains closed at the time of writing.

2.341

2.342

PART II

CLAIMS

Interpretation of this Part

4.—In this Part (and Part III) "the relevant date", in relation to a claim for a tax credit, means—
   (a) in cases where regulation 6 applies, the date on which the claim would be treated as being made by that regulation disregarding [³ regulations 7, 7A and 8];

2.343

(b) in cases where sub-paragraph [²(d)] of regulation 11(3) applies, the date on which the claim would be treated as being made by that sub-paragraph disregarding [³ regulations 7, 7A and 8];

(c) in any other case, the date on which the claim is received by [¹ a relevant authority at an appropriate office].

AMENDMENTS

1. Tax Credits (Claims and Notifications and Payments by the Board) (Amendment) Regulations 2003 (SI 2003/723) reg.3(2) (April 6, 2003).
2. Tax Credits (Miscellaneous Amendments) Regulations 2009 (SI 2009/697) reg.13 (April 6, 2009).
3. Tax Credits (Claims and Notifications) (Amendment) Regulations 2015 (SI 2015/669) reg.3 (April 6, 2015).

DEFINITIONS

"appropriate office"—see reg.2.
"relevant authority"—see reg.2.
"the relevant date"—see reg.4.

GENERAL NOTE

2.344   The general rule is that the "relevant date" (or date of claim in social security terms) is the date on which the claim for tax credits is received by "a relevant authority at an appropriate office" (para.(c)). On the basis of the definition of these latter terms in reg.2, this will normally, but not always, be an HMRC office. For the date of receipt of electronic communications, e.g. online claims for tax credits, see reg.3. There are two modifications to the general rule in para.(c). First, amended claims are treated as made on the date on which the amended claim is received (see para.(a) and reg.6(3)). Secondly, where a claimant responds to a final notice under TCA 2002 s.17 within the specified time, the date of claim is the previous April 6 (reg.11(3)(a)). If the claimant's declaration is submitted beyond that time limit, then the date of claim is the latest date on which such declaration is received (see para.(b) and reg.11(3)(b)). Note that there are special rules governing the effective date of claim by refugees who have made a successful application for asylum and who subsequently make a retrospective claim for tax credits (see Tax Credits (Immigration) Regulations 2003 (SI 2003/653) regs 3 and 4).

Mr Commissioner Mesher's decision in *CIS/995/2004* deals with the complex interaction between tax credits and income support and what constitutes a claim for the former. Early in 2003 the claimant in *CIS/995/2004* claimed income support. On January 10, 2003, he also completed an online application form for child tax credit (CTC) and transmitted it to the Inland Revenue. In March 2003 the claimant received a TC602 letter from the Inland Revenue notifying him of his family's CTC entitlement for the 2003–04 tax year and asking him to sign and return the accompanying declaration. Having made further enquiries, the claimant discovered that he would be better off retaining entitlement to income support. He accordingly did not sign and return the TC602 declaration. However, the Revenue started making CTC payments in April 2003 and notified the DWP of this fact. This led the Secretary of State to decide that the claimant was no longer entitled to income support as his income exceeded his applicable amount.

The claimant appealed to a tribunal which disallowed his appeal, holding that reg.7 of the Social Security (Working Tax Credit and Child Tax Credit) Consequential Amendments Regulations 2003 (SI 2003/455) required the DWP to treat the claimant's income as including an amount equivalent to his CTC entitlement. Although finding error in the tribunal's reasoning in other respects, the Commissioner held that the tribunal had come to the only conclusion open to it as a matter of law and on

(SI 2002/2014 reg.4) (as amended)

the evidence before it. In particular, the Commissioner rejected the claimant's argument that he had only made a preliminary application for CTC which could not be completed until he had signed and returned the TC602 declaration. On the contrary, the online completion and transmission of the application form, notwithstanding the absence of any written confirmation at the time or later, amounted to a claim. Mr Commissioner Mesher thus held that the claimant had made a valid claim on January 10, 2003, whether in an approved electronic format (and so under regs 3 and 5(2)(a)—a point which did not have to be resolved) or alternatively under the wide power in reg.5(2)(b). A valid award of CTC had then followed. The Commissioner expressly left open the question whether an appeal tribunal or Commissioner has jurisdiction to go behind the Board's determination that a claim had been made.

The informality with which HMRC will accept renewals claims was emphasised in a public letter to the Institute of Chartered Accountants in England and Wales published on October 1, 2004. Speaking of renewal claims, the Deputy Chairman of the then Inland Revenue said:

"Claimants simply have to confirm or correct the information we hold about their circumstances and report their income for the year just finished. For those not in a position to provide actual income figures at the time they reply, an estimate will be accepted. The information necessary to renew can be accepted by telephone or through our e-portal or by filling in a short paper form."

He added:

"I should also make clear, in answer to a concern you raise, that renewals information is logged on receipt, even if it has not yet been processed, to make sure the payments continue."

Manner in which claims to be made

5.—(1) This regulation prescribes the manner in which a claim for a tax credit is to be made.

2.345

(2) A claim must be made to [¹a relevant authority at an appropriate office]—
   (a) in writing on a form approved or authorised by the Board for the purpose of the claim; or
[² (b) in such other manner as the Board may decide having regard to all the circumstances.]

(3) A claim must contain the information requested on the form (or such of that information as the Board may accept as sufficient in the circumstances of the particular case).

(4) In particular, a claim must include in respect of every person by whom the claim is made—
   (a) a statement of the person's national insurance number and information or evidence establishing that that number has been allocated to the person; or
   (b) information or evidence enabling the national insurance number that has been allocated to the person to be ascertained; or
   (c) an application for a national insurance number to be allocated to the person which is accompanied by information or evidence enabling such a number to be so allocated.

This paragraph is subject to [³ paragraphs (6) and (8)].

(5) "National insurance number" means the national insurance number allocated within the meaning of regulation 9 of the Social Security (Crediting and Treatment of Contributions, and National Insurance Numbers) Regulations 2001.

(6) Paragraph (4) does not apply if the Board are satisfied that the person or persons by whom the claim was made had a reasonable excuse for making a claim which did not comply with the requirements of that paragraph.

(7) At any time after a claim has been made but before the Board have given notice of their decision under section 14(1) of the Act in relation to the claim, the person or persons by whom the claim was made may amend the claim by giving notice orally or in writing to [¹a relevant authority at an appropriate office].

[³ (8) Paragraph (4) does not apply to any person who is subject to immigration control within the meaning set out in section 115(9)(a) of the Immigration and Asylum Act 1999 and to whom a national insurance number has not been allocated.]

AMENDMENTS

1. Tax Credits (Claims and Notifications and Payments by the Board) (Amendment) Regulations 2003 (SI 2003/723) reg.3(2) (April 6, 2003).
2. Tax Credits (Miscellaneous Amendments) (No.2) Regulations 2008 (SI 2008/2169) reg.12 (September 1, 2008).
3. Tax Credits (Miscellaneous Amendments) Regulations 2009 (SI 2009/697) reg.14 (April 6, 2009).

DEFINITIONS

"the Act"—see reg.2.
"appropriate office"—see reg.2.
"the Board"—see reg.2.
"National insurance number"—see para.(5).
"relevant authority"—see reg.2.
"writing"—see reg.3(1).

GENERAL NOTE

2.346   See the note to s.14 of the 2002 Act, above against p.141, for a decision on appeals against decisions under this regulation.

Paragraph (2)

2.347   This rule is similar to, but not identical to, the standard social security provision in reg.4(1) of the Social Security (Claims and Payments) Regulations 1987 (SI 1987/1968). The fundamental difference is that it is not possible to make an oral claim for a social security benefit under reg.4(1) of the 1987 Regulations. This appears to be possible in the case of tax credits as the requirement that the claim be in writing appears only in para.(a), which will cover the great majority of cases, and not in the residual category envisaged by para.(b). And see the comments of Judge Rowland in *JI v HMRC* [2013] UKUT 199 (AAC) about the scope for treating a notification of a change of circumstances as a new claim (for example, when one member of a couple orally reports the breakdown of their relationship to HMRC).

The issue in *MK v HMRC (TC)* [2018] UKUT 238 was whether a claimant's telephone call to HMRC about tax credits amounted to a claim for tax credits for the purposes of reg.2(5). Regulation 5(2)(a) enacts the general rule that a claim for tax credit is to be made in writing on a form approved or authorised by HMRC for the purposes of the claim. Regulation 5(2)(b), however, permits a claim to be made in such other manner as HMRC may decide "having regard to all the circumstances". Upper Tribunal Judge Wikeley noted that, in principle, reg.5(2)(b) could permit a claim to be made orally. However, the question whether HMRC should have allowed an oral claim was not within the First-tier Tribunal's jurisdiction (*CTC/31/2006*). Moreover, the telephone call made by the appellant of could not reasonably be construed as a claim. It was a request for a claim form.

In *HMRC v ED (TC)* [2021] UKUT 195 (AAC), Upper Tribunal Judge Rowland followed the finding in *MK v HMRC (TC)* [2018] UKUT 238 (AAC) that there is no right of appeal against decisions made by HMRC under reg.5(2)(b). However, the judge went on to express the view *obiter* that arguably a distinction ought to be drawn between the question whether, if information was provided, it should be treated as a claim and whether the information was in fact provided. Judge Rowland considered it at least arguable that the First-tier Tribunal has jurisdiction to determine an appeal on the question whether information has been provided. Judge Rowland considered that the First-tier Tribunal might have jurisdiction because such questions raise matter of pure fact rather than the exercise by HMRC of their discretion under reg.5(2)(b) whether to permit a claim to be made other than in writing on a form authorised or approved for the purposes of claiming a tax credit. To deny a right of appeal in such circumstances would arguably breach of the European Convention on Human Rights (see *ZM and AB v HMRC* (TC) [2013] UKUT 547 (AAC); [2014] AACR 17).

In *HMRC v RS (No.2)* [2022] UKUT 246 (AAC), the Upper Tribunal was informed by HMRC that, in consequence of the migration of tax credit claimants to Universal Credit, HMRC have not produced an approved tax credits claim form since the 2018/19 tax year. In relation to that (dwindling) category of individuals who remain entitled to claim a tax credit, HMRC has exercised its discretion under regulation 5(2)(b) to permit claims to be made by telephone. Upper Tribunal Judge Wikeley observed that, given the altered claims landscape under which written claims no longer appear to be a feasible option, the issue determined in in *MK* might need to be revisited in the light of current circumstances.

2.348

Paragraphs (4)–(6)
The requirement to provide a national insurance number (or the information or evidence specified) mirrors the requirement for social security benefits set out in SSAA 1992 s.1(1B). Note however HMRC discretion not to apply this requirement if satisfied that the claimant had a reasonable excuse for making a claim which failed to comply with it (para.(6)). There is no equivalent discretion to disapply the requirement in the social security scheme.

2.349

Paragraph (7)
This provision is similar to the social security rule in reg.5(1) of the Social Security (Claims and Payments) Regulations 1987 (SI 1987/1968). However, a tax credits claim can be amended by giving oral notice, whereas the social security rule requires written notice. See further reg.6 on the determination of the date of claim for amended claims for tax credits.

2.350

Amended claims

6.—(1) In the circumstances prescribed by paragraph (2) a claim for a tax credit which has been amended shall be treated as having been made as amended and, subject to [² regulations 7, 7A and 8], as having been made on the date prescribed by paragraph (3).

2.351

(2) The circumstances prescribed by this paragraph are where a person has amended or persons have amended the claim in accordance with reg.5(7).

(3) The date prescribed by this paragraph is the date on which the claim being amended was received by [¹ a relevant authority at an appropriate office].

The Tax Credits (Claims and Notifications) Regulations 2002

AMENDMENTS

1. Tax Credits (Claims and Notifications and Payments by the Board) (Amendment) Regulations 2003 (SI 2003/723) reg.3(2) (April 6, 2003).
2. Tax Credits (Claims and Notifications) (Amendment) Regulations 2015 (SI 2015/669) reg.3 (April 6, 2015).

DEFINITIONS

"appropriate office"—see reg.2.
"relevant authority"—see reg.2.

Time-limit for claims (if otherwise entitled to tax credit up to [² [³ 31] days] earlier)

2.352
7.—(1) In the circumstances prescribed by paragraph (2), a claim for a tax credit received by [¹ a relevant authority at an appropriate office] shall be treated as having been made on the date prescribed by paragraph (3).

(2) The circumstances prescribed by this paragraph are those where the person or persons by whom the claim is made would (if a claim had been made) have been entitled to the tax credit either—

(a) on the date falling [² [³ 31] days] before the relevant date (or on 6th April 2003, if later); or
(b) at any later time in the period beginning on the date in subparagraph (a) and ending on the relevant date.

(3) The date prescribed by this paragraph is the earliest date falling within the terms of paragraph (2)(a) or (b) when the person or the persons by whom the claim is made would (if a claim had been made) have become entitled to the tax credit.

AMENDMENTS

1. Tax Credits (Claims and Notifications and Payments by the Board) (Amendment) Regulations 2003 (SI 2003/723) reg.3(2) (April 6, 2003).
2. Tax Credits (Miscellaneous Amendments)(No.2) Regulations 2009 (SI 2009/2887) reg.8 (November 21, 2009).
3. Tax Credits (Miscellaneous Amendments) Regulations 2012 (SI 2012/848) reg.5(2)(a) and (b) (April 6, 2012).

DEFINITIONS

"appropriate office"—see reg.2.
"relevant authority"—see reg.2.

GENERAL NOTE

2.353
The standard rule until 2012/13 allowed backdating of claims for up to three months. From 2012/13, the rule has been changed to reduce the time limit to 31 days. This has given rise to a number of appeals, but there are no exceptions or discretions in the rule save for that in reg.8. Regulation 25 imposes a similar time limit on notifying changes of circumstances that may increase awards. This contrasts with the relevant income tax rule that allows corrections to be made (for example because no claim has been made for an allowance or no deduction for an expense) for up to six years after the relevant time. It also contrasts with the powers for HMRC to amend tax credits awards and entitlements to deal with overpayments.

(SI 2002/2014 reg. 7) (as amended)

Once a claim has been made, there may be an amendment to deal with corrections when the annual declaration is made ahead of the entitlement decision.

It is therefore better to make a claim if there may be entitlement rather than waiting to see. This has led to the widespread practice, accepted by HMRC, of protective claims, and also to the practice of HMRC reducing awards to nil rather than terminating them during the year where circumstances change. Statistics show that at any one time in recent years there are about ½ million nil or protective claims in the system.

In *AA v HMRC (TC)* [2012] UKUT 121 (AAC), Judge Turnbull held that there was no provision for backdating entitlement to tax credit for more than three months (the then maximum period allowed) in a case where the claimant had been granted indefinite leave to remain in the UK with retrospective effect for a longer period. The provisions for greater backdating in the case of refugees did not apply, and could not be made to apply by way of analogy to the claimant's situation.

[¹Time limit for claims – the Childcare Payments Act 2014

7A.—(1) Subject to [³ paragraphs (2A) to (4)], regulation 7 does not apply where the claim for a tax credit made by a person or persons is received by a relevant authority at an appropriate office during an entitlement period where the person making the claim, or in the case of joint claimants either person, has for that entitlement period made a valid declaration of eligibility under section 4(2) of the Childcare Payments Act 2014 (declarations of eligibility).

(2) Subject to [³ paragraphs (2A) to (4)], where a claim for tax credits is received by a relevant authority at an appropriate office during the period of 31 days beginning with the last day of the entitlement period for which the person making the claim or, in the case of joint claimants either person, has made a valid declaration of eligibility under section 4(2) of the Childcare Payments Act 2014, regulation 7 shall apply but the date prescribed by paragraph (3) of regulation 7 may be no earlier than the day following the last day of that entitlement period

[³ (2A) Where—
(a) a claim for a tax credit is received by a relevant authority at an appropriate office and the person making the claim, or in the case of joint claimants either person, has made a valid declaration of eligibility under section 4(2) of the Childcare Payments Act 2014,
(b) no payments under section 20(1)(a) of the Childcare Payments Act 2014 have been made out of any childcare account held by the person making the claim, or in the case of joint claimants either person, and
(c) all the childcare accounts held by the person making the claim for tax credits, or in the case of joint claimants both persons, have been closed,

regulation 7 shall apply.]

(3) For the purposes of this regulation, the "appropriate date" is the date on which—
(a) Her Majesty's Revenue and Customs makes an account restriction order in accordance with section 24 of the Childcare Payments Act 2014 (imposing restrictions on childcare accounts) for the purposes of giving effect to a determination made under section 18(2) of that Act (cases where there is more than one eligible person) and regulations made thereunder,

2.354

(b) a childcare account is closed in accordance with regulations made under section 25 of the Childcare Payments Act 2014 (closure of childcare accounts), or

(c) a child ceases to be a "qualifying child" for the purposes of the Childcare Payments Act 2014 as defined in regulation 5 of the Childcare Payments (Eligibility) Regulations 2015 except in the case where they cease to be a "disabled child" as defined in regulation 5(5) of those Regulations.

(4) Where a claim for tax credits is received by a relevant authority at an appropriate office—

(a) during an entitlement period relating to a childcare account where the person making the claim, or in the case of joint claimants either person, has for that entitlement period made a valid declaration of eligibility under section 4(2) of the Childcare Payments Act 2014, or

(b) during the period of 31 days beginning with the day following the last day of that entitlement period,

regulation 7 shall apply but the date prescribed in paragraph (3) of regulation 7 may be no earlier than the appropriate date.

(5) For the purposes of this regulation, the terms "childcare account" and "entitlement period" have the same meanings as they have for the purposes of the Childcare Payments Act 2014 and regulations made thereunder.]

AMENDMENTS

1. Tax Credits (Claims and Notifications) (Amendment) Regulations 2015 (SI 2015/669) reg.2 (April 6, 2015).

2. Tax Credits (Claims and Notifications) (Amendment) Regulations 2017 (SI 2017/597) reg.2 (May 17, 2017).

DEFINITIONS

"appropriate date"—see para.(3).
"appropriate office"—see reg.2.
"childcare account"—see para.(5).
"entitlement period"—see para.(5).

GENERAL NOTE

2.355   The inserted reg.7A modifies the effect of the backdating provisions in reg.7 in circumstances where a claimant or, in the case of a joint claim, either or both of them, has made a declaration of eligibility under s.4(2) of the Childcare Payments Act 2014.

Paragraph (1)

2.356   This establishes the basic rule that where the claim for tax credits is made during an entitlement period under the Childcare Payments Act 2014, the backdating provisions in reg.7 do not apply. This is subject to specific provisions in paras (2A) to (4).

Paragraph (2)

2.357   This provides that where the claim for tax credits is made within 31 days beginning with the last day of the entitlement period, the backdating provisions can only apply to the extent that they do not allow the backdating period to overlap with any day falling within that entitlement period. Again, this is made subject to the specific provisions in paras (2A) to (4).

(SI 2002/2014 reg.7A) (as amended)

Paragraph (2A)
This applies the usual backdating rule in reg.7, rather than the rules in this regulation, where a claimant/s has/have made a valid declaration of eligibility under the Childcare Payments Act 2014 but the claimant/s childcare account has/have been closed and no payments have been made out of the account.

2.358

Paragraphs (3) and (4)
These paragraphs modify the backdating provisions in reg.7. They apply in three types of situation which may arise during an entitlement period for tax free childcare or during the period of 31 days beginning with the day following the last day of the entitlement period. The three circumstances are where: (1) HMRC makes an account restriction order under s.24 of the Childcare Payments Act 2014 (imposing restrictions on childcare accounts) in order to give effect to a determination made under s.18(2) of that Act (cases where there is more than one eligible person); (2) a tax free childcare account is closed in accordance with regulations made under s.25 of the 2014 Act (closure of childcare accounts); or (3) a child ceases to be a "qualifying child" for the purposes of the 2014 Act as defined by reg.5 of the Childcare Payments (Eligibility) Regulations 2015 (SI 2015/448) (unless the child ceases to be a qualifying child by no longer being a "disabled child" as defined in para.(5) of that regulation). In these exceptional cases the backdating rules in reg.7 do not allow the tax credits claim to be backdated any earlier than the date that the account restriction order is made, the childcare account is closed or the child ceases to be a "qualifying child" (as appropriate).

2.359

[¹ Date of claims – disability element of working tax credit

8.—(1) In the circumstances prescribed by paragraph (2), the claim referred to in paragraph (2)(a) shall be treated as having been made on the date prescribed by paragraph (3).

2.360

(2) The circumstances prescribed by this paragraph are where—
(a) a claim for working tax credit including the disability element ("the tax credits claim") is made by a person or persons ("the claimants") which results in the Board making an award of working tax credit including the disability element;
(b) the claim is made within [² [³ 31] days] of the date that a claim for any of the benefits referred to in regulation 9(2) to (8) of the Working Tax Credit Regulations ("the benefits claim") is determined in favour of the claimants (or one of them); and
(c) the claimants would (subject to making a claim) have been entitled to working tax credit if (and only if) they had satisfied the requirements of regulation 9(1)(c) of the Working Tax Credit Regulations, on any day in the period—
  (i) beginning on the date of the benefits claim, and
  (ii) ending on the date of the tax credits claim.

(3) The date prescribed by this paragraph is—
(a) the first date in respect of which the benefit claimed is payable; or
(b) if later, the date falling [² [³ 31] days] before the claim for the benefit is made; or
(c) if later, the first day identified under paragraph (2)(c).]

AMENDMENTS

1. Tax Credits (Miscellaneous Amendments) Regulations 2009 (SI 2009/697) reg.15 (April 6, 2009).

2. Tax Credits (Miscellaneous Amendments)(No.2) Regulations 2009 (SI 2009/2887) reg.8 (November 21, 2009).
3. Tax Credits (Miscellaneous Amendments) Regulations 2012 (SI 2012/848) reg.5(2)(c) and (d) (April 6, 2012).

GENERAL NOTE

2.361   The new version of this regulation provides two special rules for claims for the disability element of a tax credit from 2009. In *SP v HMRC* [2009] UKUT 42 (AAC) the Upper Tribunal upheld a ruling that under the previous rule a claimant for disability living allowance had to inform the Tax Credit Office separately of both the claim for the allowance and the award of the allowance if the claim to a disability element of a tax credit was to operate from the date of award of the allowance. In that case a claim was made, but refused and then awarded on appeal. Because the claimant had not notified the claim, the disability element of the tax credit could only be backdated for three months from notification of the award, not the full year back to the date when the allowance had first been awarded. The 2009 amending regulations recognised and changed the weak drafting of the original version, and so the decision no longer applies. A claimant need only notify an award to have the disability element backdated to start at the same time as the allowance, even if that is more than three months in the past. However, the 2012 amending regulations then reduced the three-month period to just one month.

Advance claims before the year begins

2.362   **9.**—(1) In the circumstances prescribed by paragraph (2) a claim for a tax credit may be made for a period after the relevant date.
(2) The circumstances prescribed by this paragraph are where a tax credit is claimed for a tax year by making a claim before the tax year begins.
(3) This regulation shall cease to have effect in relation to the tax year beginning on 6th April 2004 and subsequent tax years.

DEFINITIONS

"the relevant date"—see reg.4.
"tax year"—see reg.2.

GENERAL NOTE

2.363   This regulation provides, at least at the outset of the tax credits scheme, for claims for such credits to be made before the beginning of the tax year to which they relate (see also reg.14). There is further provision in reg.10 for advance claims for working tax credit where a person is about to start work.

Advance claims—working tax credit

2.364   **10.**—(1) In the circumstances prescribed by paragraph (2) a claim for a tax credit may be made for a period after the relevant date.
(2) The circumstances prescribed by this paragraph are where—
(a) the tax credit in question is working tax credit; and
(b) the case falls within sub-paragraph (b) of the First Condition in regulation 4(1) of the Working Tax Credit Regulations (person who has accepted an offer of work which is expected to commence within seven days).
(3) In the circumstances prescribed by paragraph (2)—
(a) an award on a claim for tax credit may be made subject to the condition that the requirements for entitlement are satisfied no later than the date prescribed by paragraph (4); and

(SI 2002/2014 reg.10) (as amended)

(b) if those requirements are satisfied no later than that date, the claim shall be treated as being made on the date on which they are satisfied.

(4) The date prescribed by this paragraph is the date falling 7 days after the relevant date.

DEFINITIONS

"the relevant date"—see reg.4.
"the Working Tax Credit Regulations"—see reg.2.

GENERAL NOTE

This rule allows for working tax credit claims to be made up to seven days in advance where a person has accepted an offer of employment and is expected to commence within that week.

2.365

Circumstances in which claims to be treated as made—notices containing provision under section 17(2)(a), (4)(a) or (6)(a) of the Act

11.—(1) In the circumstances prescribed by paragraph (2), a claim for a tax credit is to be treated as made.

2.366

(2) The circumstances prescribed by this paragraph are where (in the case where there has been a previous single claim) a person has or (in the case where there has been a previous joint claim) [⁴ either person or] both persons have made a declaration in response to provision included in a notice under section 17 of the Act by virtue of—
  (a) subsection (2)(a) of that section;
  (b) subsection (4)(a) of that section;
  (c) subsection (6)(a) of that section; or
  (d) any combination of those subsections.

The declaration made shall (subject to regulation 5(3)) be treated as a claim for tax credit by that person or persons for the tax year following that to which the notice relates.

[² (3) The claim shall be treated as made—
  (a) in a case where the declaration is made by [⁴ the date specified on the section 17 notice], on 6th April [⁴ following the period to which the section 17 notice relates];
[³(aa) [⁴...]]
  (b) in a case where the declaration, not having been made by [⁴ the date specified on the section 17 notice], is made within 30 days following the date on the notice to the claimant that payments of tax credit under section 24(4) of the Act have ceased due to the claimant's failure to make the declaration, [³ on 6th April [⁴...] following [⁴ the period to which the section 17 notice relates]]; [⁵ or]
  (c) in a case where the declaration, not having been made by [⁴ the date specified on the section 17 notice] or within the 30 days specified in sub-paragraph (b), is made before [⁴ 31st January in the tax year following the period to which the section 17 notice relates], and, in the opinion of the Board, the claimant had good cause for not making the declaration as mentioned in sub-paragraphs (a) or (b), [⁴ on 6th April following the period to which the section 17 notice relates]; [⁵.]
  (d) [⁵...]

[¹(4) Paragraph (3) does not apply—
(a) in the case where there has been a previous single claim (to which the notice referred to in paragraph (2) relates) if the person by whom it was made could no longer make a single claim; [⁴ . . .]
(b) in the case where there has been a previous joint claim (to which the notice referred to in paragraph (2) relates) if the persons by whom it was made could no longer make a joint claim [⁴ ; or
(c) in the case where the response to the notice referred to in paragraph (2) specifies that such response is not to be treated as a new claim for the tax year beginning 6th April following the period to which the section 17 notice relates].]

AMENDMENTS

1. Tax Credits (Miscellaneous Amendments) Regulations 2004 (SI 2004/762) reg.3(2) (April 6, 2004).
2. Tax Credits (Miscellaneous Amendments) Regulations 2008 (SI 2008/604) reg.4(2) (April 6, 2008).
3. Tax Credits (Miscellaneous Amendments) Regulations 2009 (SI 2009/697) reg.16 (April 6, 2009).
4. Tax Credits (Miscellaneous Amendments) Regulations 2010 (SI 2010/751) reg.7 (April 6, 2010).
5. Tax Credits and Child Benefit (Miscellaneous Amendments) Regulations 2022 (SI 2022/555) reg.6(3) (June 9, 2022).

DEFINITIONS

"the Act"—see reg.2.
"appropriate office"—see reg.2.
"the Board"—see reg.2.
"joint claim"—see reg.2.
"relevant authority"—see reg.2.
"single claim"—see reg.2.
"tax year"—see reg.2.

GENERAL NOTE

2.367   This allows the claimant's (or claimants') declaration in response to a HMRC final notice under various provisions of the TCA 2002 s.17, to be treated as a claim for tax credits. This effectively eases the process of making renewal claims for subsequent tax years. This assumes that the claimant(s) provide the necessary information as requested on the official form (para.(2) and reg.5(3)). The date of claim is the preceding April 6, i.e. the start of the tax year, assuming the declaration is returned within the designated time (para.(3)). There are further deeming rules under reg.12 in relation to s.17 final notices.

HMRC indicated at the Tax Credits Consultation Group meeting on January 15, 2008, in connection with late renewals after July 31, that: "claims could be renewed after July 31 if customers had good cause for the delay. Most cases are restored without difficulty but, for a small number, technical problems may prevent them being restored—where that happens, manual payments would be set up" (*http://www.hmrc.gov.uk/taxcredits/minutes150108.htm*). Legislative effect was given to this from April 6, 2008 by the replacement of para.(3). "Good cause" is the standard social security test derived from *R(S) 2/63*.

As originally enacted, para.(3)(d) contained a sweep-up provision which provided for a late declaration to a s.17 notice to be treated as a new claim. With effect from June 9, 2022, this provision was revoked since, generally, no new claims to tax credits have been permitted since March 30, 2022.

(SI 2002/2014 reg.12) (as amended)

Circumstances in which claims to be treated as made—notices containing provision under section 17(2)(b), (4)(b) and (6)(b) of the Act

12.—(1) In either of the circumstances prescribed by paragraphs (2) and (4) a claim for a tax credit is to be treated as made.

(2) The circumstances prescribed by this paragraph are where a person is or persons are treated as having made a declaration in response to provision included in a notice under section 17 of the Act by virtue of—
  (a) subsection (2)(b) of that section; and
  (b) subsection (4)(b) of that section,
    or a combination of those subsections and subsection (6)(b) of that section.

(3) The declaration referred to in paragraph (2) shall (subject to regulation 5(3)) be treated as a claim by that person or persons for tax credit for the tax year following that to which the notice relates.

(4) The circumstances prescribed by this paragraph are where a person or any of the persons has—
  (a) made a statement under paragraph (b) of subsection (2) of section 17 of the Act in response to such a notice by the date specified for the purposes of that subsection; or
  (b) made a statement under paragraph (b) of subsection (4) of that section in response to such a notice by the date specified for the purposes of that subsection,
or a combination of any of those subsections and subsection (6)(b) of that section.

(5) The notice referred to in paragraph (4), together with (and as corrected by) the statement or statements there referred to, shall (subject to regulation 5(3)) be treated as a claim for tax credit by that person or persons for the tax year following that to which the notice relates.

(6) The claim shall be treated as made on 6th April preceding the dates specified in the notice for the purposes of subsection (2) or (4) of section 17 of the Act.

(7) [² Paragraph (3) and (5) shall not apply]
  (a) in the case where there has been a previous single claim (to which the notice relates), the person by whom it was made could no longer make a single claim; [¹. . .]
  (b) in the case where there has been a previous joint claim (to which the notice relates), the persons by whom it was made could no longer jointly make a joint claim [¹ ; [². . .]
[² (c) in the case where, before the specified date, the person or persons to whom a notice under section 17 of the Act is given advise the Board that the person or persons do not wish to be treated as making a claim for tax credit for the tax year following that to which the notice relates; or]
  (d) in the case where there has been a previous single claim to which a notice under section 17 of the Act relates—
    (i) a relevant notification is given to the person by whom the claim was made; and
    (ii) the person fails to make a relevant request; and

2.368

The Tax Credits (Claims and Notifications) Regulations 2002

(e) in the case where there has been a previous joint claim to which a notice under section 17 of the Act relates—
   (i) a relevant notification is given to the persons by whom the claim was made; and
   (ii) they fail to make a relevant request.]

[³ (8) In this regulation—
(a) "relevant notification" means a written notification to a person or persons by whom a claim for tax credit was made which—
   (i) is given by the Board at least 35 days before the Board gives notice under section 17 of the Act to the person or persons;
   (ii) states the date on which it is given;
   (iii) advises that the Board intends to give such a notice to the person or persons; and
   (iv) advises that this regulation will not have effect to treat the person or persons as making a claim for tax credit for the tax year following that to which the notice relates unless a relevant request is made;
(b) "relevant request" means a request made to the Board by a person or persons to whom a relevant notification is given that—
   (i) is made in response to the relevant notification within 30 days of the date on which it is given; and
   (ii) requests that the person or persons will be treated by virtue of this regulation as making a claim for tax credit for the tax year following that to which the notice relates;
(c) "specified date" means the date specified for the purposes of section 17(2) and (4) of the Act or, where different dates are specified, the later of them.]

AMENDMENTS

1. Tax Credits (Miscellaneous Amendments) Regulations 2010 (SI 2010/751) reg.8 (April 6, 2010).
2. Tax Credits (Miscellaneous Amendments) (No.3) Regulations 2010 (SI 2010/2914) reg.14 (December 31, 2010).
3. Tax Credits (Miscellaneous Amendments) (No.3) Regulations 2010 (SI 2010/2914) reg.15 (December 31, 2010).

DEFINITIONS

"the Act"—see reg.2.
"joint claim"—see reg.2.
"single claim"—see reg.2.
"tax year"—see reg.2.

GENERAL NOTE

2.369   Regulation 11 makes provision for the claimant's declaration in response to an HMRC final notice to be treated as a claim for tax credits for the following tax year. This regulation makes similar provision for those cases in which the claimant is sent a final notice informing them that they will be treated as having declared that their circumstances as are specified in the notice. On the position of couples, see further reg.13.

The amendments from 2010 make express provision for the case where claimants notify HMRC that they do not wish to renew a tax credits claim, so as to prevent a deemed claim.

(SI 2002/2014 reg.13) (as amended)

Circumstances in which claims made by one member of a couple to be treated as also made by the other member of the couple

13.—(1) In the circumstances prescribed by paragraph (2) [² or (3)] a claim for a tax credit made by one member of a [¹. . .] couple is to be treated as also made by the other member of the [¹. . .] couple.

(2) The circumstances prescribed by this paragraph are those where one member of a [¹. . .] couple is treated by [³ regulation 11 or] regulation 12 as having made a claim for a tax credit in response to a notice under section 17 of the Act given to both members of the couple.

[² (3) A claim for a tax credit made by one member of a couple is to be treated as also made by the other member of the couple in such manner and in such circumstances as the Board may decide.]

AMENDMENTS

1. Civil Partnership Act 2004 (Tax Credits, etc.) (Consequential Amendments) Order 2005 (SI 2005/2919) art.5(3) (December 5, 2005).
2. Tax Credits (Miscellaneous Amendments) (No.2) Regulations 2008 (SI 2008/2169) reg.13 (September 1, 2008).
3. Tax Credits (Miscellaneous Amendments) Regulations 2010 (SI 2010/751) reg.9 (April 6, 2010).

DEFINITIONS

"the Act"—see reg.2.
"couple"—see reg.2.

GENERAL NOTE

HMRC has indicated that the new provision in para.(3) initially applies to telephone claims only. The effect is to require both partners to fill in the forms confirming the claims while validating the initial claim as a joint claim.

Circumstances in which awards to be conditional and claims treated as made—decisions under section 14(1) of the Act made before 6th April 2003

14.—*(transitional only—spent)*

Persons who die after making a claim

15.—(1) This regulation applies where any person who has made a claim for a tax credit dies—
   (a) before the Board have made a decision in relation to that claim under section 14(1) of the Act;
   (b) having given a notification of a change of circumstances increasing the maximum rate at which a person or persons may be entitled to the tax credit, before the Board have made a decision whether (and, if so, how) to amend the award of tax credit made to him or them; or
   (c) where the tax credit has been awarded for the whole or part of a tax year, after the end of that tax year but before the Board have made a decision in relation to the award under section 18(1), (5), (6) or (9) of the Act.

(2) In the case of a single claim, the personal representatives of the person who has died may proceed with the claim in the name of that person.

(3) In the case of a joint claim where only one of the persons by whom the claim was made has died, the other person with whom the claim was made may proceed with the claim in the name of the person who has died as well as in his own name.

(4) In the case of a joint claim where both the persons by whom the claim was made have died, the personal representatives of the last of them to die may proceed with the claim in the name of both persons who have died.

(5) For the purposes of paragraph (4), where persons have died in circumstances rendering it uncertain which of them survived the other—
   (a) their deaths shall be presumed to have occurred in order of seniority; and
   (b) the younger shall be treated as having survived the elder.

DEFINITIONS

"the Act"—see reg.2.
"the Board"—see reg.2.
"joint claim"—see reg.2.
"single claim"—see reg.2.
"tax year"—see reg.2.

GENERAL NOTE

2.374 This regulation makes provision as to how a claim is to proceed after the person or persons die after making it. Regulation 15 is not concerned with entitlement to tax credits and cannot therefore affect the operation of section 3(4) of the Tax Credits Act 2002 under which the death of a member of a couple who were jointly awarded a tax credit brings entitlement to that joint award to an end (*RJ v. HMRC; HMRC v. RJ* [2021] UKUT 40 (AAC); [2021] 1 W.L.R. 3350). In short, the personal representatives of the deceased person(s) may proceed with the claim (paras (2) and (4)), although in the case of a couple where only one partner has died the survivor may proceed with the claim in both their names (para.(3); see further reg.16). Paragraph (5) reflects the property law rule on contemporaneous deaths to be found in Law of Property Act 1925 s.184.

Persons who die before making joint claims

2.375 **16.**—(1) This regulation applies where one member of a [1. . .] couple dies and the other member of the [1. . .] couple wishes to make a joint claim for a tax credit.

(2) The member who wishes to make the claim may make and proceed with the claim in the name of the member who has died as well as in his own name.

(3) Any claim made in accordance with this regulation shall be for a tax credit for a period ending with—
   (a) the date of the death of the member of the [1. . .] couple who has died; or
   (b) if earlier, 5th April in the tax year to which the claim relates.

AMENDMENT

1. Civil Partnership Act 2004 (Tax Credits, etc.) (Consequential Amendments) Order 2005 (SI 2005/2919) art.5(4) (December 5, 2005).

DEFINITIONS

"couple"—see reg.2.
"joint claim"—see reg.2.

GENERAL NOTE

See note to reg.15.

Circumstances where one person may act for another in making a claim—receivers, etc.

17.—(1) In the circumstances prescribed by paragraph (2), any receiver or other person mentioned in sub-paragraph (b) of that paragraph may act for the person mentioned in sub-paragraph (a) of that paragraph in making a claim for a tax credit.

(2) The circumstances prescribed by this paragraph are where—
(a) a person is, or is alleged to be, entitled to a tax credit but is unable for the time being to make a claim for a tax credit; and
(b) there are any of the following—
　(i) a receiver appointed by the Court of Protection with power to make a claim for a tax credit on behalf of the person;
　(ii) in Scotland, a tutor, curator or other guardian acting or appointed in terms of law who is administering the estate of the person; and
　(iii) in Northern Ireland, a controller appointed by the High Court, with power to make a claim for a tax credit on behalf of the person.

Circumstances where one person may act for another in making a claim—other appointed persons

18.—(1) In the circumstances prescribed by paragraph (2), any person mentioned in sub-paragraph (b) of that paragraph may act for the person mentioned in sub-paragraph (a) of that paragraph in making a claim for a tax credit.

(2) The circumstances prescribed by this paragraph are where—
(a) a person is, or is alleged to be, entitled to a tax credit but is unable for the time being to make a claim for a tax credit; and
(b) in relation to that person, there is a person appointed under—
　(i) regulation 33(1) of the Social Security (Claims and Payments) Regulations 1987;
　(ii) regulation 33(1) of the Social Security (Claims and Payments) Regulations (Northern Ireland) 1987; or
　(iii) paragraph (3).

(3) Where there is no person mentioned in regulation 17(2)(b) in relation to the person who is unable to act, the Board may appoint under this paragraph a person who—
(a) has applied in writing to the Board to be appointed to act on behalf of the person who is unable to act; and
(b) if a natural person, is aged 18 years or more.

(4) An appointment under paragraph (3) shall end if—
(a) the Board terminate it;
(b) the person appointed has resigned from the appointment having given one month's notice in writing to the Board of his resignation; or
(c) the Board are notified that a receiver or other person mentioned in regulation 17(2)(b) has been appointed in relation to the person who is unable to make a claim.

The Tax Credits (Claims and Notifications) Regulations 2002

DEFINITIONS

"the Board"—see reg.2.
"writing"—see reg.3(1).

GENERAL NOTE

2.379   HMRC has recently revised its procedures for recognising representatives. A claimant can authorise a representative to make a claim by filling in Form 64-8 (authorising your agent) for this and for tax purposes.
In certain circumstances, an appointment under reg.18(3) may be treated as having effect for the purposes of universal credit, e.g. where the claimant is undergoing 'migration' from tax credits to universal credit. See the Universal Credit (Transitional Provisions) Regulations 2014, above in this volume.

PART III

NOTIFICATIONS OF CHANGES OF CIRCUMSTANCES

Interpretation of this Part

2.380   **19.**—In this Part "the notification date", in relation to a notification, means—
(a) the date on which the notification is given to [¹a relevant authority at an appropriate office]; or
(b) in cases where regulation 24 applies, the date on which the notification would be treated by that regulation as being given disregarding regulations 25 and 26.

AMENDMENT

1. Tax Credits (Claims and Notifications and Payments by the Board) (Amendment) Regulations 2003 (SI 2003 No.723) reg.3(2) (April 6, 2003).

DEFINITIONS

"appropriate office"—see reg.2.
"relevant authority"—see reg.2.

Increases of maximum rate of entitlement to a tax credit as a result of changes of circumstances to be dependent on notification

2.381   **20.**—(1) Any change of circumstances of a description prescribed by para.(2) which may increase the maximum rate at which a person or persons may be entitled to tax credit is to do so only if notification of it has been given in accordance with this Part.
(2) The description of changes of circumstances prescribed by this paragraph are changes of circumstances other than those in consequence of which the Board have given notice of a decision under section 16(1) of the Act in accordance with section 23 of the Act.

DEFINITIONS

"the Act"—see reg.2.
"the Board"—see reg.2.

(SI 2002/2014 reg.20) (as amended)

GENERAL NOTE

The effect of this provision is that increases in the maximum rate of entitlement to a tax credit, as a result of some relevant change of circumstances, are dependent upon notification. The normal rule is that changes which have the effect of increasing entitlement are backdated for a maximum of one month from the date of notification (reg.25).

The scope of this provision is potentially very wide. In *LV v HMRC (TC)* [2010] UKUT 483 (AAC) (see further para.2.317), the Judge commented that "it is clear that becoming disabled, receiving a diagnosis, claiming DLA and being awarded DLA can each be regarded as a change of circumstances...".

In *KI v HMRC (TC)* [2023] UKUT 212 (AAC), Upper Tribunal Judge Hemingway rejected the argument that the requirement in reg.20(1) to give notification in accordance with Pt III of the Regulations was restricted to the reporting of changes of circumstances in the tax year in which they occur. A failure duly to notify a change of circumstances, that would increase the maximum rate of a tax credit, prevents such an increase, as provided for by reg.20(1), regardless of the tax year in which the change of circumstances occurred.

2.382

Requirement to notify changes of circumstances which may decrease the rate at which a person or persons is or are entitled to tax credit or mean that entitlement ceases

21.—(1) [¹Subject to paragraph (1A),] where a person has or persons have claimed a tax credit, notification is to be given within the time prescribed by paragraph (3) if there is a change of circumstances of the description prescribed by paragraph (2) which may decrease the rate at which he is or they are entitled to the tax credit or mean that he ceases or they cease to be entitled to the tax credit.

2.383

[¹(1A) Paragraph (1) does not apply where advance notification has been given under regulation [² 27(2), (2A) or (3)].]

(2) The changes of circumstances described by this paragraph are those where—

(a) entitlement to the tax credit ceases by virtue of section 3(4), or regulations made under section 3(7), of the Act;
(b) there is a change in the relevant child care charges which falls within regulation 16(1)(b) (omitting paragraph (i)) of the Working Tax Credit Regulations;
(c) a person ceases to undertake work for at least 16 hours per week for the purposes of—
 (i) the Second Condition in regulation 4(1) (read with regulations 4(3) to (5) and 5 to 8) [⁴ except where that person falls within paragraph (a) of the third variation of the Second Condition], or
 (ii) regulation 13(1),
of the Working Tax Credit Regulations;
[⁴ (d) a person ceases to undertake work for at least 30 hours per week for the purposes of the first or second variation of the Second Condition in regulation 4(1) of the Working Tax Credit Regulations (read with regulations 4(3) to (5) and 5 to 8), except in a case where that person still falls within the terms of paragraph (a) or (d) of the first variation or paragraph (a) or (c) of the second variation of that Condition;]
(e) a person ceases to undertake, or engage in, qualifying remunerative work for at least 16 hours per week for the purposes of—
 (i) regulation 9(1)(a) (disability element), [⁴ or]

(ii) regulation 10(2)(d) (30 hour element) [⁴ . . .]
(iii) [⁴ . . .],
of the Working Tax Credit Regulations;
(f) a person ceases to engage in qualifying remunerative work for at least 30 hours per week, for the purposes of—
  (i) regulation 10(1) (30 hour element), or
  (ii) regulation 11(2)(c) (second adult element), in a case where the other claimant mentioned in that provision is not so engaged for at least 30 hours per week,
of the Working Tax Credit Regulations;
(g) a couple cease to engage in qualifying remunerative work for at least 30 hours per week, for the purposes of regulation 10(2)(c) (30 hour element) of the Working Tax Credit Regulations;
(h) a person ceases to be treated as responsible for a child or qualifying young person, for the purposes of child tax credit or of the Working Tax Credit Regulations;
(i) in a case where a person has given advance notification under regulation 27(2B) that a child is expected to become a qualifying young person, the child does not become a qualifying young person for the purposes of Part 1 of the Act;
(j) a person ceases to be a qualifying young person for the purposes of Part 1 of the Act, other than by attaining the age of twenty; or
(k) a child or qualifying young person dies.]
[⁴ (l) one or both members of a couple who satisfy paragraph (a) of the third variation of the Second Condition in regulation 4(1) of the Working Tax Credit Regulations (read with regulations 4(3) to (5) and 5 to 8) and are engaged in qualifying remunerative work cease to meet the condition that one member of the couple works not less than 16 hours per week and the aggregate number of hours for which the couple are engaged in qualifying remunerative work is not less than 24 hours per week, except in a case where the person or their partner still falls within the terms of paragraph (b), (c) or (d) of the third variation of that Condition]

(3) The time prescribed by this paragraph is the period of [³ one] months beginning on the date on which the change of circumstances occurs or [²(except in the case of paragraph (2)(j))], if later, the period of [³one] months beginning on [² the date on which the person first becomes aware of the change in circumstances].

[⁵(4) [⁶ . . .]]

AMENDMENTS

1. Tax Credits (Claims and Notifications and Payments by the Board) (Amendment) Regulations 2003 (SI 2003/723) reg.4 (April 6, 2003).
2. Tax Credits (Claims and Notifications) (Amendment) Regulations 2006 (SI 2006/2689) regs 4 and 5 (November 1, 2006).
3. Tax Credits (Claims and Notifications) (Amendment) Regulations 2006 (SI 2006/2689) reg.6 (April 6, 2007).
4. Tax Credits (Miscellaneous Amendments) Regulations 2012 (SI 2012/848) reg.5(3) (April 6, 2012).
5. Tax Credits (Coronavirus, Miscellaneous Amendments) Regulations 2020 (SI 2020/534) reg.4(3) (May 23, 2020).
6. Tax Credits and Child Benefit (Miscellaneous Amendments) Regulations 2022 (SI 2022/555) reg.6(4) (June 9, 2022).

(SI 2002/2014 reg.21) (as amended)

DEFINITIONS

"the Act"—see reg.2.
"Working Tax Credit Regulations"—see reg.2.

GENERAL NOTE

The amendments to this regulation in 2006 significantly harden the previously relaxed regime about reporting changes that may terminate or decrease an award of credits. First, many more changes of circumstances must now be reported. Secondly, the time limit for reporting is reduced from three months to one month. The duty to notify is imposed by s.6(3) of TCA 2002 read with this regulation. Failure to comply with s.6(3) may incur a penalty not exceeding £300: s.32(3) of the Act. Fraudulently or negligently making an incorrect statement under that section can incur a penalty of up to £3,000: s.31(1)(a) of the Act. HMRC literature draws attention to these penalties.

In broad terms (and as stated by HMRC in the literature) the changes of circumstances that must now be reported within a month are:

For both tax credits:
- Getting married or becoming a civil partner.
- Living together with someone else as husband and wife or civil partners.
- Stopping living together with a spouse or civil partner or other partner.
- Leaving the UK for more than eight weeks.
- Death of child or young person for whom claimant is responsible.
- Child leaves home to live with someone else.

For CTC:
- Child does not become or stops being qualifying young person when 16 (e.g. leaves college or training) or until 20.
- Young person starts to claim benefits or credits personally.
- Child or young person stops being entitled to support from claimant.

For WTC:
- Claimant or partner stops working for 16 hours a week.
- Claimant or partner stops working for 30 hours a week.
- Claimant or partner stops paying for childcare or bill goes down by £10 a week.
- Being on strike for over 10 days.

The duty to report under this regulation also covers any other circumstance in which entitlement to or an award of tax credits should end under s.3(4) or (7) of TCA 2002. This includes changes in a polygamous relationship, ceasing to be entitled by reason of ceasing to be a resident of the UK, or adverse changes in immigration status. It does not include changes in disablement as for instance where disability living allowance stops being paid. This may be because HMRC is informed of this automatically by DWP. There is also no general duty to report changes of income if hours of work are not affected.

COP26 (set out in Pt VII below) indicates that HMRC also has 30 days to deal with notifications of changes of circumstances. After reminding readers of the duty to report changes as set out above, COP26 adds: "We also recommend that you report any changes in income as soon as possible to reduce the chance of receiving an overpayment." It also advises readers to notify HMRC of any failure to issue a new award notice after a change of circumstances within a month of the notification, or of any error in a new notice. COP26 sets these out as "your responsibilities". If a claimant fails in these responsibilities then COP26 indicates that any overpayment will normally be collected in full. The practical effect is to extend the duty to report beyond those set out in this regulation if recovery of any overpayment is to be avoided or reduced.

CIS/1813/2007 adds an additional reason for claimants ensuring they report changes promptly. In that case Deputy Commissioner Mark decided that where a claimant for income support had acted promptly and informed HMRC of a change in circumstances relating to tax credits, she was not to be penalised in connection with her claim for income support by delays on the part of HMRC to act on the information given. In that case the claimant properly notified HMRC that she had stopped work and no longer wished to claim working tax credit. HMRC took many weeks to stop payment. The overpayments were repayable to HMRC. The Deputy Commissioner was satisfied that the overpayments were not part of the claimant's income or, if that was incorrect, then that they were voluntary payments. He commented:

> "For such payments to prevent the award of income support would mean that one branch of government could foist on a claimant money that the claimant does not want and that that branch could later reclaim, and so deprive the claimant of money that she could otherwise legitimately claim from another branch of government. Given that the payments are normally made directly into the claimant's bank account by standing order, it would be impossible for a claimant to prevent such payments being received except by closing the account. I do not consider that she is required to go to such an extreme."

In *JL v HMRC (TC)* [2013] UKUT 325 (AAC) the Upper Tribunal allowed an appeal concerning a job swap between a husband and wife. They were jointly claiming tax credits. At the start of the period the husband worked 16 hours a week. At the end of one week the husband stopped working at that work, and the wife took over, working the same hours and earning the same money. HMRC decided that this required the joint claim to stop and for a new claim to be made because there had been a change of circumstances within reg.21. The judge could identify no provision in reg.21(2) that applied to the couple as there was no change in the working pattern (one of the couple working 16 hours a week) and no change in entitlement. Consequently there was no relevant change of circumstances. The HMRC decisions, affirmed by the First-tier Tribunal, that the joint claim had ended with the change, and that no new award could be made until a new claim was made, were set aside and entitlement throughout the relevant period confirmed.

[¹Coronavirus – date of notification – cases where change of circumstances which may decrease the rate at which a person is, or persons are, entitled to a tax credit or mean that entitlement to that tax credit ceases

2.385   21A.—[² . . .]]

AMENDMENTS

1. Tax Credits (Coronavirus, Miscellaneous Amendments) Regulations 2020 (SI 2020/534) reg.4(4) (May 23, 2020).
2. Tax Credits and Child Benefit (Miscellaneous Amendments) Regulations 2022 (SI 2022/555) reg.6(5) (June 9, 2022).

Manner in which notifications to be given

2.386   22.—(1) This regulation prescribes the manner in which a notification is to be given.

(2) A notification must be given to [¹a relevant authority at an appropriate office].

(3) A notification may be given orally or in writing.

(4) At any time after a notification has been given but before the Board have made a decision under section 15(1) or 16(1) of the Act in consequence of the notification, the person or persons by whom the notification was given may amend the notification by giving notice orally or in writing to [¹a relevant authority at an appropriate office].

(SI 2002/2014 reg.22) (as amended)

AMENDMENT

1. Tax Credits (Claims and Notifications and Payments by the Board) (Amendment) Regulations 2003 (SI 2003 No.723) reg.3(2) (April 6, 2003).

DEFINITIONS

"the Act"—see reg.2.
"appropriate office"—see reg.2.
"the Board"—see reg.2.
"relevant authority"—see reg.2.
"writing"—reg.3(1).

GENERAL NOTE

Problems of proof may emerge from the combination of reg.22(2) and (3) when linked in particular to penalty cases under s.32(3). Adequate notification to an "appropriate office" of a "relevant authority" would appear, from reg.2, to include notification given at a Jobcentre Plus office. This can give rise to disputes where an individual maintains that he or she has informed the local social security office and regards that as notification also to HMRC, particularly if the local office does not keep records in the same way as HMRC best practice. It is not clear whether local housing benefit services are regarded as persons providing services to the Secretary of State under the current regime by which investigations for housing benefit also include other benefits. There is a duty on such authorities to pass on information received. See Tax Credits (Administrative Arrangements) Regulations 2002 regs 3 and 5.

In *LV v HMRC (TC)* [2010] UKUT 483 (AAC) an Upper Tribunal judge decided that a mother who had reported by telephone on February 14, 2007 to an office of the DWP that her son had now been diagnosed as disabled made a sufficient notification of the disablement for the purposes of regs 22 and 26A for payment of additional child tax credit to be made for the disabled child when, on October 15, 2007 a tribunal awarded disability living allowance to the child from February 14, 2007. HMRC had argued that the notification had to be to HMRC. The judge decided that this was not required by the definition of "appropriate office" in reg.2. The judge commented that an alternative and narrower interpretation would be unfair because it would penalise the child in connection with the claim for tax credits because of the mistake made by the Secretary of State in handling the DLA claim. However, note that the definition of "appropriate office" has since been amended with effect from April 6, 2009.

2.387

Person by whom notification may be, or is to be, given

23.—(1) In the case of a single claim, notification is to be given by the person by whom the claim for a tax credit was made.

(2) In the case of a joint claim, notification may be given by either member of the [¹. . .] couple by whom the claim for a tax credit was made.

2.388

AMENDMENT

1. Civil Partnership Act 2004 (Tax Credits, etc.) (Consequential Amendments) Order 2005 (SI 2005/2919) art.5(5) (December 5, 2005).

DEFINITIONS

"couple"—see reg.2.
"joint claim"—see reg.2.
"single claim"—see reg.2.

The Tax Credits (Claims and Notifications) Regulations 2002

Amended notifications

24.—(1) In the circumstances prescribed by paragraph (2) a notification which has been amended shall be treated as having been given as amended and, subject to regulations [²25, 26 and 26A], as having been given on the date prescribed by paragraph(3).

(2) The circumstances prescribed by this paragraph are where the person or persons by whom the notification is given amends or amend the notification in accordance with regulation 22(4).

(3) The date prescribed by this paragraph is the date on which the notification being amended was given to [¹a relevant authority at an appropriate office].

AMENDMENTS

1. Tax Credits (Claims and Notifications and Payments by the Board) (Amendment) Regulations 2003 (SI 2003 No.723) reg.3(2) (April 6, 2003).
2. Tax Credits (Miscellaneous Amendments) Regulations 2004 (SI 2004/762) reg.3(3) (April 6, 2004).

DEFINITIONS

"appropriate office"—see reg.2.
"relevant authority"—see reg.2.

Date of notification—cases where change of circumstances which may increase the maximum rate

25.—(1) Where a notification of a change of circumstances which may increase the maximum rate at which a person or persons may be entitled to tax credit is given in the circumstances prescribed by paragraph (2), that notification is to be treated as having been given on the date specified by paragraph (3).

(2) The circumstances prescribed by this paragraph are where notification is given to [¹a relevant authority at an appropriate office] of a change of circumstances which has occurred other than in the circumstances prescribed by [²regulations] 26(2) [² and 26A(2)].

(3) The date specified by this paragraph is—
   (a) the date falling [³ one month] before the notification date; or
   (b) if later, the date of the change of circumstances.
[⁴(4) [⁵ . . .]]

AMENDMENTS

1. Tax Credits (Claims and Notifications and Payments by the Board) (Amendment) Regulations 2003 (SI 2003/723) reg.3(2) (April 6, 2003).
2. Tax Credits (Miscellaneous Amendments) Regulations 2009 (SI 2009/697) reg.17 (April 6, 2009).
3. Tax Credits (Miscellaneous Amendments) Regulations 2012 (SI 2012/848) reg.5(4)(a) (April 6, 2012).
4. Tax Credits (Coronavirus, Miscellaneous Amendments) Regulations 2020 (SI 2020/534) reg.4(5) (May 23, 2020).
5. Tax Credits and Child Benefit (Miscellaneous Amendments) Regulations 2022 (SI 2022/555) reg.6(6) (June 9, 2022).

(SI 2002/2014 reg.25) (as amended)

DEFINITIONS

"appropriate office"—see reg.2.
"the notification date"—see reg.19.
"relevant authority"—see reg.2.

GENERAL NOTE

Where a change in circumstances leads to an increase in the claimant's entitlement to tax credits, the change can only be backdated for up to one month before the date of notification. The requirement for notification itself in such circumstances is contained in reg.20. See also notes on reg.7 (time limit for claims).

[¹ **Coronavirus – date of notification – cases where change of circumstances may increase the maximum rate**

25A.—[² . . .]]

AMENDMENTS

1. Tax Credits (Coronavirus, Miscellaneous Amendments) Regulations 2020 (SI 2020/534) reg.4(6) (May 23, 2020).
2. Tax Credits and Child Benefit (Miscellaneous Amendments) Regulations 2022 (SI 2022/555) reg.6(7) (June 9, 2022).

[¹ **Date of notification—disability element and severe disability element of working tax credit**

26.—(1) In the circumstances prescribed by paragraph (2), the notification of a change in circumstances is to be treated as having been given on the date prescribed by paragraph (3).

(2) The circumstances prescribed by this paragraph are where–
(a) a notification is given of a change of circumstances in respect of a claim to working tax credit, which results in the Board making an award of the disability element or the severe disability element of working tax credit (or both of them) in favour of a person or persons; and
(b) the notification date is within [² one month] of the date that a claim for any of the benefits referred to in regulation 9(2) to (8) or 17(2) of the Working Tax Credit Regulations is determined in favour of those persons (or one of them).

(3) The date prescribed by this paragraph is the latest of the following:
(a) the first date in respect of which the benefit claimed was payable;
(b) the date falling [² one month] before the claim for the benefit was made;
(c) the date the claim for working tax credit was made (or treated as made under [³ regulations 7 and 7A]);
(d) (for the purposes of the disability element only), the first date that the person or persons satisfied the conditions of entitlement for the disability element.]

[⁴(4) [⁵. . .]]

AMENDMENTS

1. Tax Credits (Miscellaneous Amendments) Regulations 2009 (SI 2009/697) reg.18 (April 6, 2009).

The Tax Credits (Claims and Notifications) Regulations 2002

2. Tax Credits (Miscellaneous Amendments) Regulations 2012 (SI 2012/848) reg.5(4)(b) and (c) (April 6, 2012).
3. Tax Credits (Claims and Notifications) (Amendment) Regulations 2015 (SI 2015/669) reg.4 (April 6, 2015).
4. Tax Credits (Coronavirus, Miscellaneous Amendments) Regulations 2020 (SI 2020/534) reg.4(7) (May 23, 2020).
5. Tax Credits and Child Benefit (Miscellaneous Amendments) Regulations 2022 (SI 2022/555) reg.6(8) (June 9, 2022).

General Note

2.394   This regulation was replaced in 2009 at the same time as reg.8. See the General Note to that regulation.

The requirement of para.(3) emphasises that both the date in respect of which DLA becomes payable and the date on which a claim for DLA is made constitute changes of circumstances. A claimant therefore needs to make multiple disclosures when claiming for disablement to ensure timely and accurate payment of tax credit.

This regulation should now be considered alongside section 21C of the Tax Credits Act 2002 (see below in this volume) which was added to the 2002 Act as a means of enabling tax credits claimants, on review, to obtain fully backdated disability element awards following award of a passporting disability benefit, provided certain conditions are met.

[6 Date of notification — disability element where child is disabled or severely disabled]

2.395   **26A.**—(1) In the circumstances prescribed by paragraph (2), the notification of a change in circumstances is to be treated as having been given on the date prescribed by paragraph (3).

(2) The circumstances prescribed by this paragraph are where–
(a) a notification is given of a change of circumstances in respect of a claim to child tax credit which results in the Board making an award of the disability element [6 of that tax credit in favour of a person or persons, in respect of a child where that child is disabled or severely disabled;] and
(b) the notification date is within [2 one month] of the date that a claim for a [6 disability benefit] [3 or personal independence payment] [4 or armed forces independence payment] in respect of the child is determined in favour of those persons (or one of them).

(3) The date prescribed by this paragraph is the latest of the following:
(a) the first date in respect of which the [6 disability benefit] [3 or personal independence payment] [4 or armed forces independence payment] was payable;
(b) the date falling [2 one month] before the claim for the [6 disability benefit] [3 or personal independence payment] [4 or armed forces independence payment] was made;
(c) the date the claim for child tax credit was made (or treated as made under [5 regulations 7 and 7A]).]

[6 (4) In this regulation "disability benefit" means a disability living allowance under section 71 of the Social Security Contributions and Benefits Act 1992 or disability assistance under section 31 of the Social Security (Scotland) Act 2018.]

[7(5) [8 . . .]]

(SI 2002/2014 reg.26A) (as amended)

AMENDMENTS

1. Tax Credits (Miscellaneous Amendments) Regulations 2009 (SI 2009/697) reg.19 (April 6, 2009).
2. Tax Credits (Miscellaneous Amendments) Regulations 2012 (SI 2012/848) reg.5(4)(d) and (e) (April 6, 2012).
3. Personal Independence Payment (Supplementary Provisions and Consequential Amendments) Regulations 2013 (SI 2013/388) reg.8 and Sch. para.31(3) (April 8, 2013).
4. Armed Forces and Reserve Forces Compensation Scheme (Consequential Provisions: Subordinate Legislation) Order 2013 (SI 2013/591) art.17 and Sch.1 para.27(3) (April 8, 2013).
5. Tax Credits (Claims and Notifications) (Amendment) Regulations 2015 (SI 2015/669) reg.4 (April 6, 2015).
6. Tax Credits, Child Benefit, Guardian's Allowance and Childcare Payments (Miscellaneous Amendments) Regulations 2020 (SI 2020/297) reg.5 (April 6, 2020).
7. Tax Credits (Coronavirus, Miscellaneous Amendments) Regulations 2020 (SI 2020/534) reg.4(8) (May 23, 2020).
8. Tax Credits and Child Benefit (Miscellaneous Amendments) Regulations 2022 (SI 2022/555) reg.6(9) (June 9, 2022).

GENERAL NOTE

2.396

This provision is amended to adjust it to deal with the replacement of disability living allowance with the new personal independence payment provided for in the Welfare Reform Act 2012. This is being introduced in stages. For the initial stages see the Welfare Reform Act 2012 (Commencement No.8 and Savings and Transitional Provisions) Order 2013 (SI 2013/358).

The replacement of this regulation in 2009 was part of a package with regs 8 and 26. See the General Note to reg.8.

The requirement of para.(3) emphasises that both the date in respect of which DLA becomes payable and the date on which a claim for DLA is made constitute changes of circumstances. A claimant therefore needs to make multiple disclosures when claiming for a disabled child to ensure timely and accurate payment of tax credit. In *HMRC v PS (TC)* [2012] UKUT 492 (AAC) an Upper Tribunal Judge commented on potential problems in applying this rule, but did not go beyond the particular facts of the decision in solving them.

[¹Coronavirus – date of notification of disability

2.396.1

26B.—[² ...]]

AMENDMENTS

1. Tax Credits (Coronavirus, Miscellaneous Amendments) Regulations 2020 (SI 2020/534) reg.4(9) (May 23, 2020).
2. Tax Credits and Child Benefit (Miscellaneous Amendments) Regulations 2022 (SI 2022/555) reg.6(10) (June 9, 2022).

Advance notification

27.—(1) In [¹any] of the circumstances prescribed by paragraphs (2) [¹, [² to]] and (3) a notification of a change of circumstances may be given for a period after the date on which it is given.

2.397

(2) The circumstances prescribed by this paragraph are those prescribed by regulation 10(2) (working tax credit: person who has accepted an offer

of work expected to commence within seven days), the reference to "the claim" being read as a reference to the notification.

[¹(2A) The circumstances prescribed by this paragraph are where either regulation 15(4) (agreement for the provision of future child care) or regulation 16(1) (relevant change in circumstances) of the Working Tax Credit Regulations applies.]

[² (2B) The circumstances prescribed by this paragraph are those where a child is expected to become a qualifying young person for the purposes of Part 1 of the Act.]

(3) The circumstances prescribed by this paragraph are where a tax credit has been claimed for the tax year beginning on 6th April 2003 by making a claim before that tax year begins, and the notification relates to that tax year and is given before that date.

(4) In the circumstances prescribed by paragraph (2), an amendment of an award of a tax credit in consequence of a notification of a change of circumstances may be made subject to the condition that the requirements for entitlement to the amended amount of the tax credit are satisfied at the time prescribed by paragraph (5).

(5) The time prescribed by this paragraph is the latest date which—
  (a) is not more than seven days after the date on which the notification is given; and
  (b) falls within the period of award in which the notification is given.

[¹(5A) In the circumstances prescribed by paragraph (2A), an amendment of an award of tax credit in consequence of a notification of a change of circumstances may be made subject to the condition that the requirements for entitlement to the amended amount of the tax credit are satisfied at the time prescribed by paragraph (5B).

(5B) The time prescribed by this paragraph is the first day of the week—
  (a) in which the agreement within regulation 15(4) of the Working Tax Credit Regulations commences or the relevant change of circumstances occurs; and
  (b) which is not more than seven days after the date on which notification is given and falls within the period of award in which the notification is given.

(5C) For the purposes of paragraph (5B), "week" means a period of 7 days beginning with midnight between Saturday and Sunday.]

(6) "Period of award" shall be construed in accordance with section 5 of the Act.

AMENDMENTS

1. Tax Credits (Claims and Notifications and Payments by the Board) (Amendment) Regulations 2003 (SI 2003/723) reg.5 (April 6, 2003).

2. Tax Credits (Claims and Notifications) (Amendment) Regulations 2006 (SI 2006/2689) reg.7 (November 1, 2006).

DEFINITIONS

"the Act"—see reg.2.
"the claim"—see para.(2).
"period of award"—see para.(6).
"tax year"—see reg.2.
"week"—see para.(5C).

(SI 2002/2014 reg.28) (as amended)

Circumstances where one person may act for another in giving a notification—receivers, etc.

28.—(1) In the circumstances prescribed by paragraph (2) any receiver or other person mentioned in sub-paragraph (b) of that paragraph may act for the person mentioned in sub-paragraph (a) of that paragraph in giving a notification.

(2) The circumstances prescribed by this paragraph are where—
(a) a person is unable for the time being to give a notification; and
(b) there are any of the following—
   (i) a receiver appointed by the Court of Protection with power to proceed with a claim for a tax credit on behalf of the person;
   (ii) in Scotland, a tutor, curator or other guardian acting or appointed in terms of law who is administering the estate of the person; and
   (iii) in Northern Ireland, a controller appointed by the High Court, with power to proceed with a claim for a tax credit on behalf of the person.

GENERAL NOTE

See also reg.35 in respect of receivers, etc. acting in response to final notices under TCA 2002 s.17.

Circumstances where one person may act for another in giving a notification—other appointed persons

29.—(1) In the circumstances prescribed by paragraph (2) any person mentioned in sub-paragraph (b) of that paragraph may act for the person mentioned in sub-paragraph (a) of that paragraph in giving a notification.

(2) The circumstances prescribed by this paragraph are where—
(a) a person is unable for the time being to give a notification; and
(b) in relation to that person, there is a person appointed under—
   (i) regulation 33(1) of the Social Security (Claims and Payments) Regulations 1987;
   (ii) regulation 33(1) of the Social Security (Claims and Payments) Regulations (Northern Ireland) 1987; or
   (iii) regulation 18(3);
and the provisions of regulation 18(3) shall apply to notifications and (under regulation 36) responses to notices under section 17 of the Act, as they apply to claims.

DEFINITION

"the Act"—see reg.2.

GENERAL NOTE

See also reg.36 in respect of appointees acting in response to final notices under TCA 2002 s.17.

[¹Form in which evidence of birth or adoption to be provided

29A.—If the Board require the person, or either or both of the persons, by whom a claim is made to provide a certificate of a child's birth or adoption, the certificate so produced must be either an original certificate or a copy authenticated in such manner as would render it admissible in proceedings in any court in the jurisdiction in which the copy was made.]

AMENDMENT

1. Tax Credits (Miscellaneous Amendments No.2) Regulations 2004 (SI 2004/1241) reg.4 (May 1, 2004).

PART IV

NOTICES TO PROVIDE INFORMATION OR EVIDENCE

Employers

2.403

30.—(1) For the purposes of sections 14(2)(b), 15(2)(b), 16(3)(b) and 19(2)(b) of the Act the persons specified in paragraph (2) are prescribed, and, in relation to those persons, the information or evidence specified in paragraph (4) is prescribed.

(2) The persons specified in this paragraph are—
  (a) any person named by a person or either of the persons by whom a claim for a tax credit is made as his employer or the employer of either of them; and
  (b) any person whom the Board have reasonable grounds for believing to be an employer of a person or either of the persons by whom such a claim is made.

(3) "Employer" has the meaning given by section 25(5) of the Act.

(4) The information or evidence specified in this paragraph is information or evidence, including any documents or certificates, which relates to—
  (a) the claim for the tax credit in question;
  (b) the award of the tax credit in question; or
  (c) any question arising out of, or under, that claim or award.

DEFINITIONS

"the Act"—see reg.2.
"the Board"—see reg.2.
"employer"—see para.(3).

Persons by whom child care is provided

2.404

31.—(1) For the purposes of sections 14(2)(b), 15(2)(b), 16(3)(b) and 19(2)(b) of the Act the persons specified in paragraph (2) are prescribed, and, in relation to those persons, the information or evidence specified in paragraph (3) is prescribed.

(2) The persons specified in this paragraph are—
  (a) any person named by a person or persons by whom a claim for the child care element of working tax credit is made as being, in relation to him or either of them, a person by whom child care is provided; and

(SI 2002/2014 reg.31) (as amended)

(b) any person whom the Board have reasonable grounds for believing to be, in relation to a person or persons by whom such a claim is made, a person by whom child care is provided.

(3) The information or evidence specified in this paragraph is information or evidence, including any documents or certificates, which relates to—

(a) the claim for the tax credit in question;
(b) the award of the tax credit in question; or
(c) any question arising out of, or under, that claim or award.

(4) "Child care" has the meaning given by regulation 14(2) of the Working Tax Credit Regulations.

DEFINITIONS

"the Act"—see reg.2.
"the Board"—see reg.2.
'child care"—see para.(4).

Dates to be specified in notices under section 14(2), 15(2), 16(3), 18(10) or 19(2) of the Act

32.—In a notice under section 14(2), 15(2), 16(3), 18(10) or 19(2) of the Act, the date which may be specified shall not be less than 30 days after the date of the notice.

DEFINITION

"the Act"—see reg.2.

PART V

FINAL DECISION

[¹Dates to be specified in notices under section 17 of the Act

33.—In a notice under section 17 of the Act—
(a) the date which may be specified for the purposes of subsection (2) or subsection (4) shall be not later than [²31st July] following the end of the tax year to which the notice relates, or 30 days after the date on which the notice is given, if later; and
(b) the date which may be specified for the purposes of subsection (8) shall be not later than 31st January following the end of the tax year to which the notice relates, or 30 days after the date on which the notice is given, if later.]

AMENDMENTS

1. Tax Credits (Miscellaneous Amendments) Regulations 2004 (SI 2004/762) reg.3(5) (April 6, 2004).
2. Tax Credits (Miscellaneous Amendments) Regulations 2007 (SI 2007/824) reg.14(3) (April 6, 2007).

DEFINITIONS

"the Act"—see reg.2.
"tax year"—see reg.2.

[¹Manner in which declaration or statement in response to a notice under section 17 of the Act to be made

34.—(1) This regulation prescribes the manner in which a declaration or statement in response to a notice under section 17 of the Act must be made.

(2) A declaration or statement must be made—
   (a) in writing in a form approved by the Board for that purpose;
   (b) orally to an officer of the Board; or
   (c) in such other manner as the Board may accept as sufficient in the circumstances of any particular case.

(3) In a case falling within paragraph (2)(b) one of two joint claimants may act for both of them in response to a notice under section 17 if, at the time the declaration or statement is made, a joint claim could be made by both of them.]

AMENDMENT

1. Tax Credits (Miscellaneous Amendments) Regulations 2004 (SI 2004/762) reg.3(5) (April 6, 2004).

DEFINITIONS

"the Act"—see reg.2.
"the Board"—see reg.2.
"joint claim"—see reg.2.

Circumstances where one person may act for another in response to a notice under section 17 of the Act—receivers, etc.

35.—(1) In the circumstances prescribed by paragraph (2) any receiver or other person mentioned in sub-paragraph (b) of that paragraph may act for the person mentioned in sub-paragraph (a) of that paragraph in response to a notice under section 17 of the Act.

(2) The circumstances prescribed by this paragraph are where—
   (a) a person is unable for the time being to act in response to a notice under section 17 of the Act; and
   (b) there are any of the following—
      (i) a receiver appointed by the Court of Protection with power to proceed with a claim for a tax credit on behalf of the person;
      (ii) in Scotland, a tutor, curator or other guardian acting or appointed in terms of law who is administering the estate of the person; and
      (iii) in Northern Ireland, a controller appointed by the High Court, with power to proceed with a claim for a tax credit and proceed with the claim on behalf of the person.

DEFINITION

"the Act"—see reg.2.

Circumstances where one person may act for another in response to a notice under section 17 of the Act

36.—(1) In the circumstances prescribed by paragraph (2) any person mentioned in sub-paragraph (b) of that paragraph may act for the person mentioned in sub-paragraph (a) of that paragraph in response to a notice under section 17 of the Act.

(SI 2002/2014 reg.36) (as amended)

(2) The circumstances prescribed by this paragraph are where—
(a) a person is unable for the time being to act in response to a notice under section 17 of the Act; and
(b) in relation to that person, there is a person appointed under—
   (i) regulation 33(1) of the Social Security (Claims and Payments) Regulations 1987;
   (ii) regulation 33(1) of the Social Security (Claims and Payments) Regulations (Northern Ireland) 1987; or
   (iii) regulation 18(3).

DEFINITION

"the Act"—see reg.2.

The Tax Credits [¹(Payment by the Commissioners)] Regulations 2002

(SI 2002/2173) (AS AMENDED)

The Commissioners of Inland Revenue, in exercise of the powers conferred upon them by sections 24(2), (3), (4), (7) and (8), 65(1), (2) and (7) and 67 of the Tax Credits Act 2002, hereby make the following Regulations:

1. Citation, commencement and effect.
2. Interpretation.
3. Child tax credit and child care element—member of a couple prescribed for the purposes of s.24(2) of the Act.
4. Working tax credit (excluding any child care element)—member of a couple prescribed for the purposes of s.24(2) of the Act.
5. Member of a couple prescribed for the purposes of s.24(2) of the Act where one of the members of the couple has died.
6. Person prescribed for the purposes of s.24(3) of the Act where an award of a tax credit is made on a claim which is made by one person on behalf of another.
7. Prescribed circumstances for the purposes of s.24(4) of the Act.
8. Time of payment by way of a credit to a bank account or other account.
9. Time of payment other than by way of a credit to a bank account or other account, etc.
10. Single payment of small sums of tax credit.
11. Postponement of payment.
12. Amounts of payments.
12A. Recovery of overpayments of tax credits from other payments of tax credit.
13. Manner of payment.
14. Entitlement to tax credit or element dependent on a bank account or other account having been notified to the Board.

AMENDMENT

1. Tax Credit (Payment by Employers, etc.) (Amendment) Regulations 2005 (SI 2005/2200) reg.7(2) (August 29, 2005).

The Tax Credits (Payment by the Commissioners) Regulations 2002

GENERAL NOTE

2.411   The original policy intention of making employers responsible for payments of WTC (other than the child care element) has now been abandoned. Since April 2006 HMRC has assumed responsibility for making all payments of both CTC and WTC. Accordingly the Working Tax Credit (Payment by Employers) Regulations 2002 (SI 2002/2172) have now been revoked: see Tax Credit (Payment by Employers, etc.) (Amendment) Regulations 2005 (SI 2005/2200) reg.9.

Citation, commencement and effect

2.412   **1.**—(1) These Regulations may be cited as the Tax Credits (Payments by [²the Commissioners]) Regulations 2002 and shall come into force on 6th April 2003.

(2) These Regulations have effect in relation to payments of a tax credit, or any element of a tax credit, which must be made [¹. . .] in relation to the tax year beginning with 6th April 2003 and subsequent tax years.

[¹(3) Regulations 8 to 14 have effect only in relation to such payments as must be made by the Board.]

AMENDMENTS

1. Tax Credits (Claims and Notifications and Payments by the Board) (Amendment) Regulations 2003 (SI 2003/723) reg.7 (April 6, 2003).
2. Tax Credit (Payment by Employers, etc.) (Amendment) Regulations 2005 (SI 2005/2200) reg.7(2) (August 29, 2005).

Interpretation

2.413   **2.**—In these Regulations—
"the Act" means the Tax Credits Act 2002;
[¹"the Commissioners" means Commissioners for Her Majesty's Revenue and Customs (see section 1 of the Commissioners for Revenue and Customs Act 2005);]
[²"couple" has the meaning given by section 3(5A) of the Act;]
"employee" and "employer" have the meaning given by section 25(5) of the Act;
[². . .];
"period of award" shall be construed in accordance with section 5 of the Act;
"the relevant tax year" means the whole or part of the tax year for which an award of a tax credit has been made to a person or persons (referred to in section 24(4) of the Act);
"tax year" means a period beginning with 6th April in one year and ending with 5th April in the next;
[². . .].

AMENDMENTS

1. Tax Credit (Payment by Employers, etc.) (Amendment) Regulations 2005 (SI 2005/2200) reg.7(3) (August 29, 2005).
2. Civil Partnership Act 2004 (Tax Credits, etc.) (Consequential Amendments) Order 2005 (SI 2005/2919) art.6(2) (December 5, 2005).

(SI 2002/2173 reg.3) (as amended)

Child tax credit and child care element—member of a couple prescribed for the purposes of section 24(2) of the Act

3.—(1) This regulation has effect in relation to payments of—
(a) child tax credit; and
(b) any child care element of working tax credit.

(2) Subject to regulation 5, the member of a [4couple] prescribed by paragraph (3) is prescribed for the purposes of section 24(2) of the Act.

(3) The member of a [4couple] [2prescribed by this paragraph is—
(a) where the [4couple] are for the time being resident at the same address—
  (i) the member who is identified by both members of the [4couple] as the main carer;
  (ii) in default of a member being so identified, the member who appears to [3 the Commissioner] to be the main carer; and
(b) where—
  (i) the members of the [4couple] are for the time being resident at different addresses, or
  (ii) one member of the [4couple] is temporarily absent from the address at which they live together,
  the member who appears to [3 the Commissioner] to be the main carer.
Here "main carer" means the member of the [4 couple] who is the main carer for the children and qualifying young persons for whom either or both of the members is or are responsible.]

(4) "Children" means persons who have not attained the age of 16 or who fall within the terms of regulation 4 of the Child Tax Credit Regulations 2002.

(5) "Qualifying young persons" means persons, other than children, who—
(a) have not attained the age of [5 twenty]; and
(b) satisfy the conditions in regulation 5(3) and (4) of the Child Tax Credit Regulations 2002.

(6) Where payments are being made to the member of a [4couple] prescribed by virtue of paragraph (3) and the members of the [4couple] jointly give notice to [3 the Commissioners] that, as a result of a change of circumstances, the payments should be made to the other member as the main carer, the other member shall [2, except where the notice appears to [3the Commissioners] to be unreasonable,] be treated as prescribed by virtue of paragraph (3).

[1(7) For the purposes of this regulation, a person is responsible for a child or qualifying young person if he is treated as being responsible for that child or qualifying young person in accordance with the rules contained in regulation 3 of the Child Tax Credit Regulations 2002.]

AMENDMENTS

1. Tax Credits (Claims and Notifications and Payments by the Board) (Amendment) Regulations 2003 (SI 2003/723) reg.8 (April 6, 2003).
2. Tax Credits (Miscellaneous Amendments No.2) Regulations 2004 (SI 2004/1241) reg.5 (May 1, 2004).
3. Tax Credit (Payment by Employers, etc.) (Amendment) Regulations 2005 (SI 2005/2200) reg.7(4) (August 29, 2005).

The Tax Credits (Payment by the Commissioners) Regulations 2002

4. Civil Partnership Act 2004 (Tax Credits, etc.) (Consequential Amendments) Order 2005 (SI 2005/2919) art.6(3) (December 5, 2005).

5. Tax Credits and Child Benefit (Miscellaneous Amendments) Regulations 2022 (SI 2022/555) reg.7 (June 9, 2022).

DEFINITIONS

"the Act"—see reg.2.
"children"—see para.(4).
"couple"—see reg.2.
"qualifying young persons"—see para.(5).

GENERAL NOTE

2.415   Section 24(2) of the TCA 2002 permits payments of tax credits, or elements within tax credits, in the case of a joint claim to whichever member of a married or unmarried couple is prescribed. This regulation deals with the payment of child tax credit and any child care element of working tax credit by HMRC. It provides that such tax credits are payable by HMRC to the partner identified by the couple as the main carer of the children concerned or, in default, the partner identified as such by HMRC (para.(3)). The couple can ask HMRC to change the method of payment to the other partner as the main carer (para.(6)).

Working tax credit (excluding any child care element)—member of a couple prescribed for the purposes of section 24(2) of the Act

2.416   **4.**—(1) This regulation has effect in relation to payments of working tax credit other than payments of any child care element.

(2) Subject to regulation 5, the member of a [²couple] prescribed by para. (3) is prescribed for the purposes of section 24(2) of the Act.

(3) The member of a [²couple] prescribed by this paragraph is—
 (a) if only one member of the [²couple] is engaged in remunerative work, that member;
 (b) if both members of the [²couple] are engaged in remunerative work—
  (i) the member elected jointly by them; or
  (ii) in default of any election, such of them as appears to the Board to be appropriate.

(4) Where payments are being made to the member of [²couple] prescribed by virtue of paragraph (3)(b) and the members of the [²couple] jointly give notice to [¹the Commissioners] that, as a result of a change of circumstances, they wish payments to be made to the other member, the other member shall be treated as prescribed by virtue of paragraph (3)(b).

(5) For the purposes of paragraph (3), a member of a [²couple] is engaged in remunerative work if—
 (a) he is engaged in qualifying remunerative work; or
 (b) he works not less than 16 hours per week and the other member of the [²couple] is engaged in qualifying remunerative work.

(6) "Qualifying remunerative work", and being engaged in it, have the meaning given by regulation 4 of the Working Tax Credit (Entitlement and Maximum Rate) Regulations 2002.

AMENDMENTS

1. Tax Credit (Payment by Employers, etc.) (Amendment) Regulations 2005 (SI 2005/2200) reg.7(4) (August 29, 2005).

(SI 2002/2173 reg.4) (as amended)

2. Civil Partnership Act 2004 (Tax Credits, etc.) (Consequential Amendments) Order 2005 (SI 2005/2919) art.6(3) (December 5, 2005).

DEFINITIONS

"the Act"—see reg.2.
"couple"—see reg.2.
"qualifying remunerative work"—see para.(6).

GENERAL NOTE

This deals with payment of working tax credit (excluding any child care element, on which see reg.3) by HMRC. In the case of a couple, such working tax credit should be paid by HMRC to the member of the couple who is in remunerative work for working tax credit purposes (see paras (5) and (6)) or, if they both are, to the partner nominated jointly by the couple or, in default, as HMRC sees appropriate (para.(3)). As with reg.3, the couple have the option of changing their election (para. (4)).

Member of a couple prescribed for the purposes of section 24(2) of the Act where one of the members of the couple has died

5.—(1) This regulation applies where one of the members of a [¹couple] has died.

(2) The member of the [¹couple] prescribed by paragraph (3) is prescribed for the purposes of section 24(2) of the Act.

(3) The member of the [¹couple] prescribed by this paragraph is the member who survives.

(4) For the purposes of this regulation, where persons have died in circumstances rendering it uncertain which of them survived the other—
 (a) their deaths shall be presumed to have occurred in order of seniority; and
 (b) the younger shall be treated as having survived the elder.

AMENDMENT

1. Civil Partnership Act 2004 (Tax Credits, etc.) (Consequential Amendments) Order 2005 (SI 2005/2919) art.6(3) (December 5, 2005).

DEFINITIONS

"the Act"—see reg.2.
"couple"—see reg.2.

GENERAL NOTE

This regulation is self-explanatory. Paragraph (4) follows the general property law rule on survivorship laid down by s.184 of the Law of Property Act 1925.

Person prescribed for the purposes of section 24(3) of the Act where an award of a tax credit is made on a claim which is made by one person on behalf of another

6.—For the purposes of section 24(3) of the Act, the person prescribed is—
 (a) the person by whom the claim on behalf of another was made; or

(b) if at any time [¹the Commissioners] do not consider it appropriate for payments of the tax credit to be made to that person, the person on behalf of whom the claim was made.

AMENDMENT

1. Tax Credit (Payment by Employers, etc.) (Amendment) Regulations 2005 (SI 2005/2200) reg.7(4) (August 29, 2005).

DEFINITION

"the Act"—see reg.2.

GENERAL NOTE

2.421   See also regs 17, 18, 28 and 29 of the Tax Credits (Claims and Notifications) Regulations 2002 (SI 2002/2014).

Prescribed circumstances for the purposes of section 24(4) of the Act

2.422   7.—(1) Either of the circumstances prescribed by paragraphs (2) and (3) are prescribed circumstances for the purposes of section 24(4) of the Act.

(2) The circumstances prescribed by this paragraph are where—
(a) a claim for a tax credit for the next tax year has been made or treated as made by the person or persons by the date specified for the purposes of subsection (4) of section 17 of the Act in the notice given to him or them under that section in relation to the relevant tax year; and
(b) [¹the Commissioners] have not made a decision under section 14(1) of the Act in relation to that claim.

(3) The circumstances prescribed by this paragraph are where—
(a) a claim for a tax credit for the next tax year has not been made or treated as made by the person or persons; and
(b) [¹the Commissioners] have not made a decision under section 18(1) of the Act in relation to the person and persons for the relevant tax year.

AMENDMENT

1. Tax Credit (Payment by Employers, etc.) (Amendment) Regulations 2005 (SI 2005/2200) reg.7(4) (August 29, 2005).

DEFINITIONS

"the Act"—see reg.2.
"the relevant tax year"—see reg.2.
"tax year"—see *ibid*.

GENERAL NOTE

2.423   Section 24(4) of the TCA 2002 enables payments of tax credits to continue to be paid in a following tax year in the absence of a claim and award in certain circumstances. This regulation thus allows payments to continue to be made, without interruption, at the start of each tax year while claims are being renewed in two types of circumstances. The first is where a renewal claim has been made or treated as made but has yet to be determined by HMRC (para.(2)). The second is a step further back, where no such renewal claim has been made but HMRC similarly has yet to make its final decision on the previous year (para.(3)).

(SI 2002/2173 reg.7) (as amended)

Regulation 7 does not apply where a person's entitlement to a tax credit was interrupted by the making of a claim for universal credit: see reg.12A of, and Sch.1 to, the Universal Credit (Transitional Provisions) Regulations 2014 (SI 2014/1230), below in this volume.

Time of payment by way of a credit to a bank account or other account

8.—(1) [³...] This regulation applies where the tax credit or element is to be paid by way of a credit to a bank account or other account notified to [²the Commissioners].

(2) [⁴Subject to paragraphs (2A) and (2B),] the tax credit or element shall be paid—
   (a) each week; or
   (b) every four weeks,
in accordance with any election given by the person to whom payment is to be made.

[¹(2A) If a person makes elections under paragraph (2) for child tax credit and any child care element of working tax credit to be paid at differing intervals, the elections shall have no effect and [²the Commissioners] pay the child tax credit and any child care element together either each week or every four weeks as appears to them to be appropriate.]

[⁴ (2B) Notwithstanding the terms of any election under paragraph (2), the Commissioners may pay the tax credit or element either each week or every four weeks as appears to them to be appropriate.]

(3) [³...]

(4) This regulation is subject to regulations 10 and 11.

AMENDMENTS

1. Tax Credits (Claims and Notifications and Payments by the Board) (Amendment) Regulations 2003 (SI 2003/723) reg.9 (April 6, 2003).
2. Tax Credit (Payment by Employers, etc.) (Amendment) Regulations 2005 (SI 2005/2200) reg.7(4) (August 29, 2005).
3. Tax Credit (Payment by Employers, etc.) (Amendment) Regulations 2005 (SI 2005/2200) reg.9(2) (April 1, 2006).
4. Tax Credits (Miscellaneous Amendments) (No.3) Regulations 2010 (SI 2010/2914) reg.7 (December 31, 2010).

GENERAL NOTE

Employees paid tax credits by HMRC direct to their bank accounts have the option of having such payments paid weekly or four-weekly (para.(2)). However, it is not possible to have child tax credit and the child care element of working tax credit paid at different intervals (para.(2A)). The intervals for payment via methods other than direct to a bank account are left to the discretion of HMRC (see reg.9). However, payment via bank accounts is clearly intended to be the standard method for HMRC to pay tax credits (see regs 13 and 14).

Time of payment other than by way of a credit to a bank account or other account, etc.

9.—(1) This regulation applies where—
   (a) the tax credit or element is to be paid other than by way of a credit to a bank account or other account notified to [¹the Commissioners]; or
   (b) [²...].

The Tax Credits (Payment by the Commissioners) Regulations 2002

(2) The tax credit or element shall be paid at such times as appear to [¹the Commissioners] to be appropriate.

AMENDMENTS

1. Tax Credit (Payment by Employers, etc.) (Amendment) Regulations 2005 (SI 2005/2200) reg.7(4) (August 29, 2005).
2. Tax Credit (Payment by Employers, etc.) (Amendment) Regulations 2005 (SI 2005/2200) reg.9(2) (April 1, 2006).

[¹**Single payment of small sums of tax credit**

10.—The tax credit or element may be paid by way of a single payment, and at such time, and in such manner, as appear to [²the Commissioners] to be appropriate, in any of the following cases—
  (a) where [²the Commissioners] are paying only child tax credit to a person and the weekly rate at which it is payable is less than £2;
  (b) where [²the Commissioners] are paying both any child care element (but no other element) of working tax credit and child tax credit to a person and the total weekly rate at which they are payable is less than £2;
  (c) where [²the Commissioners] are paying only working tax credit (apart from any child care element) to a person and the weekly rate at which it is payable (excluding any such child care element) is less than £2;
  (d) where [²the Commissioners] are paying both working tax credit (including elements other than, or in addition to, any child care element) and child tax credit to a person who has elected under regulation 8(2) to have them paid at the same intervals and the total weekly rate at which they are payable is less than £2;
  (e) where [²the Commissioners] are paying both working tax credit (apart from any child care element) and child tax credit to a person who has elected under regulation 8(2) to have them paid at differing intervals and—
    (i) the total weekly rate at which any such child care element and the child tax credit are payable is less than £2; or
    (ii) the weekly rate at which the working tax credit is payable (excluding any such child care element) is less than £2.]

AMENDMENTS

1. Tax Credits (Claims and Notifications and Payments by the Board) (Amendment) Regulations 2003 (SI 2003/723) reg.10 (April 6, 2003).
2. Tax Credit (Payment by Employers, etc.) (Amendment) Regulations 2005 (SI 2005/2200) reg.7(4) (August 29, 2005).

GENERAL NOTE

The original version of this regulation, which was substituted by the version above before it came into force, was just one sentence long: so much for simplicity. The basic principle, however, remains the same: if tax credits are payable at an aggregate level of less than £2 a week, then HMRC will pay them in such manner as it deems appropriate (typically by way of a lump sum).

(SI 2002/2173 reg.11) (as amended)

Postponement of payment

11.—(1) [¹The Commissioners] may postpone payment of the tax credit or element in any of the circumstances specified in [⁴ paragraphs (2), (2A), (3) and (3A)].

(2) The circumstances specified in this paragraph are where there is a pending determination of an appeal against a decision of [² [³ the First-tier Tribunal, the appeal tribunal, the] Upper Tribunal, the Northern Ireland] Social Security Commissioner or a court relating to—
  (a) the case in question; or
  (b) another case where it appears to [¹the Commissioners] that, if the appeal were to be determined in a particular way, an issue would arise as to whether the award in the case in question should be amended or terminated under section 16(1) of the Act.

[⁴ (2A) The circumstances specified in this paragraph are where—
  (a) a notice in writing has been given by the Commissioners to a person to notify a bank account or other account to which the Commissioners may make payment of a tax credit or element to which the person is entitled;
  (b) a period of [⁵ four] weeks has elapsed since the day on which the Commissioners gave their notice; and
  (c) no bank account or other account has been notified to the Commissioners pursuant to their notice.]

(3) The circumstances specified in this paragraph are where confirmation is pending of—
  (a) the details of a bank account or other account by way of a credit to which payment is to be made; or
  (b) the address of the person to whom payment is to be made, where it appears to [¹the Commissioners] that such details or address as were previously notified to them are incorrect.

[⁴ (3A) The circumstances specified in this paragraph are where—
  (a) a notice under section 16(3) of the Tax Credits Act 2002 has been issued to the person, or either or both of the persons, to whom the tax credit or element was awarded, and
  (b) such person or persons have not provided the information or evidence requested in that notice by the date specified in such notice.]

(4) For the purposes of paragraph (2), the circumstances where a determination of an appeal is pending include circumstances where a decision of [² [³ the First-tier Tribunal, the appeal tribunal, the] Upper Tribunal, the Northern Ireland] Social Security Commissioner or a court has been made and [¹the Commissioners]—
  (a) are awaiting receipt of the decision;
  (b) in the case of a decision by [² the [³ First-tier Tribunal or the appeal tribunal]], are considering whether to apply for a statement of reasons or have applied for, and are awaiting receipt of, a statement of reasons; or
  (c) have received the decision or statement of reasons and are considering—
    (i) whether to apply for permission to appeal; or
    (ii) where permission is not needed or has been given, whether to appeal.

(5) "[³ Appeal tribunal]" has the meaning given by section 63(10) of the Act.

(6) "[² Northern Ireland Social] Security Commissioner" has the meaning given by section 63(13) of the Act.

[⁴ (7) The postponement of payment pursuant to the circumstances specified in paragraph (2A) shall cease at the earlier of the time when—
    (a) a bank account or other account is notified to the Commissioners; or
    (b) the entitlement to the tax credit or element ceases in accordance with regulation 14.]

AMENDMENTS

1. Tax Credit (Payment by Employers, etc.) (Amendment) Regulations 2005 (SI 2005/2200) reg.7(4) (August 29, 2005).
2. Tribunals, Courts and Enforcement Act 2007 (Transitional and Consequential Provisions) Order 2008 (SI 2008/2683) art.6 and Sch.1 para.205 (November 3, 2008).
3. Transfer of Tribunal Functions and Revenue and Customs Appeals Order 2009 (SI 2009/56) art.3(2) Sch.2 para.78 (April 1, 2009).
4. Tax Credits (Miscellaneous Amendments) Regulations 2010 (SI 2010/751) reg.10(1)–(5) (April 6, 2010).
5. Tax Credits (Miscellaneous Amendments) Regulations 2012 (SI 2012/848) reg.6(2) (April 6, 2012).

DEFINITIONS

"the Act"—see reg.2.
"Appeal tribunal"—see para.(5).
"Social Security Commissioner"—see para.(6).

GENERAL NOTE

2.430   This regulation sets out the circumstances in which a payment of tax credits by HMRC may be postponed. Postponement is permitted where a person has not duly notified bank account details to HMRC (para.(2A)), HMRC are awaiting confirmation of a person's bank account or address details (para.(2B)) or a person has not duly provided information or evidence specified in a notice given under s.16(3) of the Tax Credits Act 2002. Postponement is also permitted where there is an appeal pending in relation either to the particular case or to another case in which the outcome might lead to the amendment or termination of the award in the instant case (para.(2)). This is, therefore, the tax credits equivalent of the anti-test case rule. (But note, however, that it is limited to the postponement of payment, and does not make provision for limiting the effect of test cases in terms of backdating entitlement to tax credits.) The "pending determination" must be one against a decision of an appeal tribunal, Social Security Commissioner or court (para.(2)). The notion of "pending" is defined by para.(4). There are no explicit time limits stated within this regulation on HMRC's consideration of whether or not to lodge an appeal, but there are, of course, fairly tight time constraints on the exercise of such a right in the first place.

Amounts of payments

2.431   **12.**—(1) The tax credit or element shall be paid in accordance with the most recent decision by [¹the Commissioners] under section 14(1), 15(1) or 16(1) of the Act.

(2) Where the tax credit or element is to be paid other than by way of a single payment, it shall be paid so far as possible in such amounts as will

(SI 2002/2173 reg.12) (as amended)

result in the person to whom payment is to be made receiving regular payments of similar amounts over the entire period of award.

(3) Where an award of tax credit is amended, the total amount paid prior to the award being amended [²may] be taken into account by [¹the Commissioners] in determining the amount of any further payments for the remainder of the period of award.

[³ (4) Where payments under section 24(4) of the Act are to be made the Commissioners may take any or both of the following factors into account in determining the amount of those payments—
   (a) the rate at which the person or persons were entitled to the tax credit for the relevant tax year;
   (b) the estimated amount of income the person or persons referred to above may receive in the current tax year.]

AMENDMENTS

1. Tax Credit (Payment by Employers, etc.) (Amendment) Regulations 2005 (SI 2005/2200) reg.7(4) (August 29, 2005).
2. Tax Credits (Miscellaneous Amendments) Regulations 2007 (SI 2007/824) reg.15 (April 6, 2007).
3. Tax Credits (Miscellaneous Amendments) Regulations 2008 (SI 2008/604) reg.5(2) (April 6, 2008).

DEFINITION

"the Act"—see reg.2.

GENERAL NOTE

This regulation provides for the amount of tax credits payable to be determined by HMRC's most recent relevant decision (para.(1)). Such payments should, so far as possible, be apportioned equally over regular payment intervals (para.(2)). The original formulation of para.(2) was mandatory in requiring HMRC to take prior payments into account in arriving at the appropriate amount due for payment following an amended award. Paragraph (2) now gives HMRC more flexibility in deciding the amount of any further tax credits where an award of tax credits is amended. Since April 2007, HMRC have been able to exercise a discretion in such cases. So, where claimants report a fall in income during the year, their tax credit payments will be adjusted for the rest of the year but will not include a one-off payment for the earlier part of the year. Their final award will be determined at the end of the year when their actual income is known, and any underpayment will be made good at that stage. Amounts of tax credits for subsequent years can be based on a preceding year's tax credit entitlement (para.(4); see further reg.7).

2.432

[¹Recovery of overpayments of tax credit from other payments of tax credit

12A.—(1) This regulation applies where notice is given to a person or persons under subsection (4) of section 29 of the Act (deduction of overpayments from payments of tax credit).

2.433

(2) The maximum rate at which an overpayment may be recovered from payments of tax credit is—
   (a) where the only amount of tax credit to which the person is, or, in the case of a joint claim, the persons are, entitled, is the family element of child tax credit, 100% of that tax credit;

(b) where the total amount of tax credit to which the person is, or, in the case of a joint claim, the persons are, entitled is not subject to reduction—
  (i) by virtue of section 7(2) of the Act; or
  (ii) because their income for the relevant year does not exceed the relevant income threshold prescribed in his or their case in regulation 3 of the Tax Credits (Income Thresholds and Determination of Rates) Regulations 2002;
10% of that tax credit; and
(c) in any other case, [² the income-related percentage] of the tax credit to which the person is, or in the case of a joint claim, the persons are, entitled.
[² (2A) In paragraph (2)(c), "the income-related percentage" means—
(a) 50% if annual income exceeds £20,000; and
(b) 25% in any other case.
(2B) For the purposes of paragraph (2A)(a), "annual income"—
(a) means the annual income of the person or, in the case of a joint claim, the aggregate annual income of the persons, mentioned in paragraph (2)(c); and
(b) is to be taken to be the amount that the Commissioners are for the time being treating that income to be for the purposes of Part 1 of the Act, regardless of whether that amount is also "the relevant income" (as defined by section 7(3) of the Act) on which the entitlement to the tax credit mentioned in paragraph (2)(c) is dependent.]
(3) In paragraph (2) a reference to the amount to which a person is, or persons are, entitled is a reference to the amount to which they would be entitled but for the operation of that paragraph.]

AMENDMENTS

1. Tax Credits (Miscellaneous Amendments) Regulations 2004 (SI 2004/762) reg.18 (April 6, 2004).
2. Tax Credits and Child Benefit (Miscellaneous Amendments) Regulations 2016 (SI 2016/360) reg.5(2) (April 6, 2016).

DEFINITION

"the Act"—see reg.2.

Manner of payment

13.—(1) Subject to paragraph (2), the tax credit or element shall be paid by way of a credit to a bank account or other account notified to [²the Commissioners] by the person to whom payment is to be made.
(2) Where [¹it does not appear to [²the Commissioners] to be appropriate] for the tax credit or element to be paid by way of a credit to a bank account or other account notified to [²the Commissioners] by the person to whom payment is to be made, the tax credit or element may be paid in such manner as appears to [²the Commissioners] to be appropriate.
(3) Subject to regulation 14, if no bank account or other account has been notified to [²the Commissioners], the tax credit or element shall be paid in such manner as appears to [²the Commissioners] to be appropriate.

AMENDMENTS

1. Tax Credits (Claims and Notifications and Payments by the Board) (Amendment) Regulations 2003 (SI 2003/723) reg.11 (April 6, 2003).
2. Tax Credit (Payment by Employers, etc.) (Amendment) Regulations 2005 (SI 2005/2200) reg.7(4) (August 29, 2005).

GENERAL NOTE

This regulation establishes the presumption in favour of payment by HMRC of tax credits to be direct to recipients' bank accounts.

Entitlement to tax credit or element dependent on a bank account or other account having been notified to the Board

14.—[² (1) Subject to paragraph (3), where—
(a) payment of a tax credit or element is postponed pursuant to the circumstances specified in regulation 11(2A), and
(b) before the relevant time determined in accordance with this regulation, no bank account or other account is notified to the Commissioners by the person to whom a tax credit or element would have been paid if payment of it had not been postponed,

that person shall cease to be entitled to the tax credit or element for the remainder of the period of the award beginning on the day from which the Commissioners decide to postpone payment.]

(2) [² . . .]

(3) Where there are exceptional circumstances which are expected to result in a person not being able to obtain a bank account or other account throughout the period of award, paragraph (1) shall not have effect in relation to that person's entitlement to a tax credit or element for the period of award.

(4) [² . . .]

[² (4A) Subject to paragraphs (4C) and (4E), the relevant time is the earlier of—
(a) three months after the time when the Commissioners decide to postpone payment of a tax credit or element; or
(b) immediately after the end of the relevant tax year.

(4B) This paragraph applies where, before the time determined in accordance with paragraph (4A), the person entitled to payment of the tax credit or element—
(a) requests from the Commissioners authority to open an account for which such authority is required; and
(b) provides sufficient information from which the Commissioners can give that authority.

(4C) Subject to paragraph (4E), where paragraph (4B) applies, the relevant time is the later of—
(a) the time determined in accordance with paragraph (4A); and
(b) the expiry of the period of 3 weeks from the day on which the Commissioners give their authority following a request described in paragraph (4B)(a).

(4D) This paragraph applies where a person to whom a notice described in regulation 11(2A)(a) has been given has a reasonable excuse—
(a) for not being able to take all necessary steps to obtain a bank account or other account before a time determined in accordance with paragraphs (4A) or (4C), or

(b) for not being able to notify to the Commissioners the bank account or other account before a time determined in accordance with paragraphs (4A) or (4C).

(4E) Where paragraph (4D) applies, the relevant time is the later of—
(a) the time determined in accordance with paragraph (4A);
(b) where paragraph (4B) applies, the time determined in accordance with paragraph (4C); and
(c) the date by which the account can reasonably be expected to be notified to the Commissioners.]

(5) "Writing" includes writing produced by electronic communications that are approved by [¹the Commissioners].

AMENDMENTS

1. Tax Credit (Payment by Employers, etc.) (Amendment) Regulations 2005 (SI 2005/2200) reg.7(4) (August 29, 2005).
2. Tax Credits (Miscellaneous Amendments) Regulations 2010 (SI 2010/751) reg.10(1) and (6)–(8) (April 6, 2010).

DEFINITIONS

"the relevant period"—see para.(4).
"writing"—see para.(5).

GENERAL NOTE

2.437 This regulation further demonstrates that entitlement to a tax credit is to be dependent on a bank account or other account having been notified to HMRC.

The Tax Credits (Administrative Arrangements) Regulations 2002

(SI 2002/3036)

The Commissioners of Inland Revenue, in exercise of the powers conferred upon them by ss.58 and 65(1), (2), (7) and (9) of the Tax Credits Act 2002, hereby make the following Regulations:

ARRANGEMENT OF ARTICLES

2.438
1. Citation and commencement.
2. Interpretation.
3. Provision of information or evidence to relevant authorities.
4. Giving of information or advice by relevant authorities.
5. Recording, verification and holding, and forwarding, of claims, etc. received by relevant authorities.

GENERAL NOTE

2.439 Section 58 of the TCA 2002 provides for regulations to make provision as to the administrative arrangements to apply between a relevant authority (i.e. the Secretary of State, the equivalent Northern Ireland Department or a person providing services to either of these authorities: TCA 2002 s.58(3)) and HMRC, who have the care and management of tax credits (see TCA 2002 s.2). Section 58 applies where regulations under TCA 2002 ss.4 or 6 permit or require a claim or notification relating to a tax credit to be made or given to such a relevant authority. These Regulations have therefore been made under s.58 in order to provide for administrative arrangements in relation to claims and notifications made or given to a relevant authority in accordance with the Tax Credits (Claims and Notifications) Regulations 2002 (SI 2002/2014). Regulation 5 of those Regulations requires claims to be made to "an appropriate office", which means an office of the Board, the DWP or its Northern Ireland equivalent (reg.2).

Citation and commencement

1.—These Regulations may be cited as the Tax Credits (Administrative Arrangements) Regulations 2002 and shall come into force on 1st January 2003.

Interpretation

2.—In these Regulations—
"the Board" means the Commissioners of Inland Revenue;
"the principal Regulations" means the Tax Credits (Claims and Notifications) Regulations 2002;
"relevant authority" means—
  (a) the Secretary of State;
  (b) the Department for [¹ Communities] in Northern Ireland; or
  (c) a person providing services to the Secretary of State or that Department.

AMENDMENT

1. Tax Credits, Child Benefit and Childcare Payments (Miscellaneous Amendments) Regulations 2019 (SI 2019/364) reg.6(2) (March 21, 2019).

Provision of information or evidence to relevant authorities

3.—(1) Information or evidence relating to tax credits which is held—
(a) by the Board; or
(b) by a person providing services to the Board, in connection with the provision of those services,
may be provided to a relevant authority for the purposes of, or for any purposes connected with, the exercise of that relevant authority's functions under the principal Regulations.

(2) Information or evidence relating to tax credits may be provided to a relevant authority by persons other than the Board (whether or not persons by whom claims or notifications relating to tax credits are or have been made or given).

DEFINITIONS
"the Board" —see reg.2.
"the principal Regulations"—see reg.2.
"relevant authority"—see reg.2.

Giving of information or advice by relevant authorities

2.443   **4.**—A relevant authority to which a claim or notification is or has been made or given by a person in accordance with the principal Regulations may give information or advice relating to tax credits to that person.

DEFINITIONS

"the principal Regulations"—see reg.2.
"relevant authority"—see reg.2.

Recording, verification and holding, and forwarding, of claims etc. received by relevant authorities

2.444   **5.**—(1) A relevant authority may record and hold claims and notifications received by virtue of the principal Regulations and information or evidence received by virtue of regulation 3(2).

(2) Subject to paragraphs (3) and (4), a relevant authority must forward to the Board or a person providing services to the Board such a claim or notification, or such information or evidence, as soon as reasonably practicable after being satisfied that it is complete.

(3) Before forwarding a claim in accordance with paragraph (2), a relevant authority must verify—
   (a) that any national insurance number provided in respect of the person by whom the claim is made exists and has been allocated to that person;
   (b) that the matters verified in accordance with sub-paragraph (a) accord with—
      (i) its own records; or
      (ii) in the case of a person providing services to the Secretary of State or the Department for [2 Communities] in Northern Ireland, records held by the Secretary of State or that Department; and
   (c) whether the details of any relevant claim for benefit that have been provided are consistent with those held by it.

(4) If a relevant authority cannot locate any national insurance number in respect of a person by whom such a claim is made, it must forward to the Board or a person providing services to the Board the claim (notwithstanding that it is not complete).

(5) "National insurance number" means the national insurance number allocated within the meaning of—
   (a) regulation 9 of the Social Security (Crediting and Treatment of Contributions, and National Insurance Numbers) Regulations 2001; or
   (b) regulation 9 of the Social Security (Crediting and Treatment of Contributions, and National Insurance Numbers) Regulations (Northern Ireland) 2001.

(6) "Claim for benefit" means a claim for—
   (a) a benefit in relation to which—
      (i) the Secretary of State has functions under the Social Security Contributions and Benefits Act 1992; or
      (ii) the Department for [2 Communities] in Northern Ireland has functions under the Social Security Contributions and Benefits (Northern Ireland) Act 1992: [1. . .]

(SI 2002/3036 reg.5)

(b) a jobseeker's allowance under—
  (i) the Jobseekers Act 1995; or
  (ii) the Jobseekers (Northern Ireland) Order 1995 [¹ . . .]; [¹; or
(c) universal credit under Part 1 of the Welfare Reform Act 2012]

AMENDMENTS

1. Universal Credit (Consequential, Supplementary, Incidental and Miscellaneous Provisions) Regulations 2013 (SI 2013/630) reg.80 (April 29, 2013).
2. Tax Credits, Child Benefit and Childcare Payments (Miscellaneous Amendments) Regulations 2019 (SI 2019/364) reg.6(3) (March 21, 2019).

DEFINITIONS

"the Board"—see reg.2.
"the principal Regulations"—see reg.2.
"relevant authority"—see reg.2.

The Tax Credits (Appeals) (No.2) Regulations 2002

(SI 2002/3196) (AS AMENDED)

Made   *18th December 2002*
Coming into force   *1st January 2003*

ARRANGEMENT OF REGULATIONS

PART I

General

1. Citation, commencement, duration and interpretation   2.445
2. Service of notices or documents

PART II

General Appeal Matters

3. Other persons with a right of appeal or a right to make an application for a direction
4. Time within which an appeal is to be brought
5. Late appeals
6. (repealed)
7. (repealed)
8. Death of a party to an appeal or an application for a direction

PART III

Appeal Tribunals for Tax Credits

9–27. repealed   2.446

Whereas a draft of this instrument was laid before Parliament in accordance with section 80(1) of the Social Security Act 1998 and approved by a resolution of each House of Parliament.

PART I

GENERAL

Citation, commencement, duration and interpretation

1.—(1) These Regulations may be cited as the Tax Credits (Appeals) (No.2) Regulations 2002 and shall come into force on 1st January 2003.

(2) These Regulations shall cease to have effect on such day as is appointed by order made under section 63(1) of the Tax Credits Act 2002 (tax credits appeals etc.: temporary modifications).

(3) In these Regulations, unless the context otherwise requires—

"the Act" means the Social Security Act 1998;

"the 2002 Act" means the Tax Credits Act 2002;

"the Appeals Regulations" means the Tax Credits (Appeals) Regulations 2002;

"the Decisions and Appeals Regulations" means the Social Security and Child Support (Decisions and Appeals) Regulations 1999;

"the Working Tax Credit Regulations" means the Working Tax Credit (Entitlement and Maximum Rate) Regulations 2002;

"appeal" means an appeal under section 38 of the 2002 Act;

"an application for a direction" means an application for a direction to close down an enquiry made under section 19(9) of the 2002 Act;

[^{2}...]

[^{2}...]

[^{1}[^{3} "couple" means—

(a) two people who are married to, or civil partners of, each other and are members of the same household; or

(b) two people who are not married to, or civil partners of, each other but are living together as if they were a married couple or civil partners;]]

"court" means the High Court, the Court of Appeal, the Court of Session, the High Court or Court of Appeal in Northern Ireland, the House of Lords or the Court of Justice of the European Community;

[^{2}...]

[^{2}...]

[^{2}...]

"joint claim" means a claim made under section 3(3)(a) of the 2002 Act and any reference in these Regulations to "joint claimant" shall be construed accordingly;

[^{2}...]

[^{2}...]

[^{2}...]

[^{2}...]

[^{2}...]

(SI 2002/3196 reg.1) (as amended)

"partner" means, [¹...], the other member of [¹a] couple;
"party to the proceedings" means the Board and any other person—
(a) who is an appellant in an appeal brought against a decision or determination set out in section 38 of the 2002 Act;
(b) who is an applicant for a direction to close down an enquiry under section 19(9) of the 2002 Act;
(c) who is a defendant (or defender) in penalty proceedings brought under paragraph 3 of Schedule 2 to the 2002 Act;
(d) who is a person with a right of appeal or a right to make an application for a direction under regulation 3;
[²...]
[²...]
[²...]
"single claim" means a claim made under section 3(3)(b) of the 2002 Act;
"tax credit" means child tax credit or working tax credit, construing those terms in accordance with section 1(1) and (2) of the 2002 Act, and any reference in these Regulations to "child tax credit" or "working tax credit" shall be construed accordingly.

AMENDMENTS

1. Civil Partnership (Pensions, Social Security and Child Support) (Consequential, etc. Provisions) Order 2005 (SI 2005/2877) para.36(2) of Sch.3 (December 5, 2005).

2. Tribunals, Courts and Enforcement Act 2007 (Transitional and Consequential Provisions) Order 2008 (SI 2008/2683) art.6 and Sch.1 para.205 (November 3, 2008).

3. Civil Partnership (Opposite-sex Couples) Regulations 2019 (SI 2019/1458) reg.41(b) and Sch.3 Part 2 (December 2, 2019).

GENERAL NOTE

"party to the proceedings"

In *CTC/2612/2005*, the Commissioner pointed out that where only one member of a couple who should have been joint claimants had appealed, the other was not a party to the proceedings, which was unfair as she was potentially liable to repay an overpayment. The real problem was that it was unclear whether the Inland Revenue had issued a decision addressed to both of them. If they had, it is suggested that an appeal by one of member of the couple could have been treated as an appeal by both of them unless it was clear that only one of them wished to appeal (see *R(A) 2/06*).

It was pointed out in *PD v HMRC and CD (TC)* [2010] UKUT 159 (AAC) that *CTC/2612/2005* was decided under former procedures now replaced by the First-tier Tribunal (Social Entitlement Chamber) Rules 2008. Under those rules where one of a joint claim couple appeals a decision, the other is a respondent. The second claimant is therefore a party to the proceedings and should be notified of the proceedings and any proposal to deal with the appeal on the papers. This also applies to the decision in *CTC/2612/2005*. See now Tribunal Procedure (First-tier Tribunal) (Social Entitlement Chamber) Rules 2008 r.1 (definitions), 5 (case management powers), and 9 (substitution and addition of parties) in Vol.III of this work.

A more complex problem arose in *CTC/4390/2004*, where two separated parents each claimed child tax credit. It was pointed out that the legislation made no provision for them to be parties to a single appeal even though a decision could be binding only on the parties to it (see *CTC/2090/2004*). However, by the time the case reached the Commissioner, there were appeals by both parents (because the award

2.448

to one parent had been terminated when the other parent won his appeal before the tribunal) and, with the agreement of the parties, the Commissioner, when allowing an appeal against the tribunal's decision, directed that the appeal be reheard at the same time as the other parent's appeal against the termination of her award.

In *CTC/1586/2007* an Upper Tribunal judge dealt with problems that can arise when a tribunal attempts to deal with split entitlement to child tax credits at a single hearing. The father was awarded child tax credit for one of his three children, the mother being awarded child tax credit for the other two. The father appealed against the award to the mother (that is, against the refusal to award him child tax credit for the other children), and the mother also appealed. But while the mother elected for an oral hearing, the father asked for a decision on the papers. At the hearing the tribunal took into account the mother's evidence to take away the award to the father. The Upper Tribunal Judge granted permission to appeal to the father on the grounds that this was unfair, as the father had not been put on notice that this might happen. At a hearing of the appeal, the parents agreed that the father should again be awarded child tax credit for the oldest child. This resulted in awards being made to both the mother and the father for the same child for a common period. Judge Lloyd-Davies offered the following more general guidance:

"... where competing claims for tax credit in respect of a child or children are made by each parent, and the dispute is not otherwise resolved but proceeds to an appeal by both parents, then directions should be given which indicate that both appeals will be heard together, that an oral hearing will be held unless both parents agree to a paper hearing, and that, if an oral hearing is held, non-attendance by one parent may result in the evidence of the attending parent being accepted as evidence in the non-attending parent's appeal ... HMRC ... took issue with the fact that the mother in the present case had been joined as a party to the father's appeal and called a respondent, thereby possibly indicating that the mother would be bound by the result of the father's appeal when her award could not be affected by the outcome of the father's appeal: I agree and accept that the better course would have been to have invited the mother to give evidence, rather than become a party."

However, *CTC/1586/2007* was an unusual case in that both parents had competing appeals on foot in parallel against their respective child tax credit decisions, which had been made by HMRC concurrently. The more typical situation is where HMRC makes a decision in respect of only one parent but that decision may directly or indirectly impact on the other parent (e.g. the first parent has an award; later the second parent applies unsuccessfully for child tax credit and seeks to appeal their adverse HMRC decision). The best practice in such cases would seem to be active case management to ensure that e.g. the first parent is joined at as early a stage as possible to the second parent's appeal (see e.g. *PG v HMRC and NG (TC)* [2016] UKUT 216 (AAC); [2016] AACR 45)). Where there are such competing claims for child tax credit, the Upper Tribunal has suggested that the other claimant could be added as a party to the appeal even if they were initially unwilling (see *CM v HMRC (TC)* [2014] UKUT 272 (AAC)), not least as they would have the right to apply for set aside of the joinder direction. The same approach should equally be applied in child benefit appeals where there are rival claimants (see *CB v HMRC and AE (CHB)* [2016] UKUT 506 (AAC) and *GG v HMRC and DC (CHB)* [2018] UKUT 223 (AAC)).

Service of notices or documents

2.449

2.—Where, by any provision of these Regulations—
(a) any notice or other document is required to be given or sent [^{1}...] to the Board, that notice or document shall be treated as having been so given or sent on the day that it is received [^{1}...] by the Board, and

(SI 2002/3196 reg.2) (as amended)

(b) any notice or other document is required to be given or sent to any person other than [1 ...] the Board, that notice or document shall, if sent to that person's last known address, be treated as having been given or sent on the day that it was posted.

AMENDMENT

1. Tribunals, Courts and Enforcement Act 2007 (Transitional and Consequential Provisions) Order 2008 (SI 2008/2683) art.6 and Sch.1 para.206 (November 3, 2008).

DEFINITIONS

"the Board"—see s.39(1) of the Social Security Act 1998 as modified by reg.12 of the Tax Credits (Appeals) Regulations 2002.
"clerk to the appeal tribunal"—see reg.1(3).

GENERAL NOTE

A fax is received for the purposes of reg.2(a) when it is successfully transmitted to, and received by, a fax machine, irrespective of when it is actually collected from the fax machine (*R(DLA) 3/05*). Furthermore, the faxed request for a statement of reasons in that case was received by the clerk to the appeal tribunal when received at the tribunal venue, even though the clerk did not visit that venue until some days later. The Commissioner said that it would have been different if the venue had been a casual venue, such as local authority premises. Here, it was a dedicated venue and the fax number had been given to representatives precisely to enable them to communicate with the clerk. There was nothing in any document issued with the decision notice to indicate that the request for a statement of reasons had to be addressed to a different place.

The "last known address" to which documents must be sent for para.(b) to apply need not be the person's last known *residence* because the concepts are different. Moreover, the sender must consider the address to be reliable and, if he does not, should take reasonable steps to see whether a more reliable one exists (*CCS/2288/2005*). This approach exists to aid the innocent claimant and not the one who has failed to take reasonable steps to keep HMRC or the clerk to the tribunal aware of his whereabouts. Generally they are entitled to rely on a claimant to inform them of any move.

Deemed receipt of a document cannot cure a breach of the rules of natural justice so that, if a tribunal does not receive medical evidence submitted by the claimant in support of an application for a postponement, the decision of the tribunal can be set aside as being erroneous in point of law (*CG/2973/2004*). Decisions can also be set aside under reg.25 where documents go astray. That does not preclude an appeal, although an application for setting aside under reg.25 remains the more appropriate procedure (*CIB/303/1999*, declining to follow *R(SB) 55/83* but agreeing with *R(SB) 19/83*).

A provision similar to reg.2(b) relating to immigration appeals was held to be invalid in *R. (On the application of Saleem) v Secretary of State for the Home Department* [2001] 1 W.L.R. 443, but there are sufficient remedies in these Regulations for the injustice that reg.2(b) might otherwise cause and Commissioners have distinguished *Saleem* and held the equivalent provision relating to social security and child support appeals to be valid (*CCS/6302/1999* and *CIB/303/1999*).

2.450

The Tax Credits (Appeals) (No.2) Regulations 2002

Part II

General Appeal Matters

Other persons with a right of appeal or a right to make an application for a direction

2.451   **3.**—For the purposes of section 12(2) of the Act (as applied and modified by the Appeals Regulations), where—
(a) a person has made a claim for a tax credit but is unable for the time being to make an appeal against a decision in respect of that tax credit; or
(b) a person is the person in respect of whom an enquiry has been initiated under section 19(1) of the 2002 Act, but is unable for the time being to make an application for a direction,
the following other persons have a right of appeal to [² the First-tier Tribunal] or a right to make an application for a direction—
(i) a receiver appointed by the Court of Protection with power to make a claim for a tax credit on behalf of the person;
(ii) in Scotland, a [¹judicial factor, or guardian acting or appointed under the Adults with incapacity (Scotland) Act 2000 who has power to claim, or as the case may be, receive a tax credit on his behalf] who is administering the estate of the person;
(iii) a person appointed under regulation 33(1) of the Social Security (Claims and Payments) Regulations 1987 (persons unable to act);
(iv) where there is no person mentioned in sub-paragraph (iii) in relation to the person who is unable to act, a person who has applied in writing to the Board to be appointed to act on behalf of the person who is unable to act and, if a natural person, is aged 18 years or more and who has been so appointed by the Board for the purposes of this subparagraph.

Amendments

1. Social Security, Child Support and Tax Credits (Miscellaneous Amendments) Regulations 2005 (SI 2005/337) reg.4(2) (March 18, 2005).
2. Tribunals, Courts and Enforcement Act 2007 (Transitional and Consequential Provisions) Order 2008 (SI 2008/2683) art.6 and Sch.1 para.207 (November 3, 2008).

Definitions

"the Act"—see reg.1(3).
"the Appeals Regulations"—reg.1(3).
"appeal"—reg.1(3).
"an application for a direction"—reg.1(3).
"the Board"—see s.39(1) of the Social Security Act 1998 as modified by reg.12 of the Tax Credits (Appeals) Regulations 2002.
"tax credit"—reg.1(3).

General Note

2.452   Section 12(2) of the Social Security Act 1998, mentioned in the opening words of this regulation, has actually been "modified" out of existence because it and subs. (1) have been replaced by a single subsection. This regulation is made under the substituted s.12(1)(d).

It is arguable that this regulation is at least partly unnecessary as those mentioned in it could submit appeals on the basis of their general authority to act on behalf of the real appellant.

Time within which an appeal is to be brought

4.—(1) Where a dispute arises as to whether an appeal was brought within the time limit specified in section 39(1) of the 2002 Act, the dispute shall be referred to, and be determined by, [¹ the First-tier Tribunal].

(2) The time limit specified in section 39(1) of the 2002 Act may be extended in accordance with regulation 5.

AMENDMENT

1. Tribunals, Courts and Enforcement Act 2007 (Transitional and Consequential Provisions) Order 2008 (SI 2008/2683) art.6 and Sch.1 para.208 (November 3, 2008).

DEFINITIONS

"the 2002 Act"—see reg.1(3).
"appeal"—reg.1(3).
"legally qualified panel member"—see reg.1(3).

GENERAL NOTE

The time limit specified in s.39(1) of the Tax Credits Act 2002 is the 30 days usual in tax cases rather than the month usual in social security cases. However, note that ss.39(1) and (2) have now been repealed in England, Wales and Scotland by SI 2014/886 (see General Note to s.39) with the result that appeal time limits are governed by tribunal procedural rules.

Late appeals

5.—(1) [¹ *The Board may treat a late appeal as made in time*] *where the conditions specified in paragraphs* [¹ *(4)*] *to (8) are satisfied, but no appeal shall in any event be brought more than one year after the expiration of the last day for appealing under section 39(1) of the 2002 Act.*

[¹ ...]

[¹ *(4) An appeal may be treated as made in time if the Board is satisfied that it is in the interests of justice.*]

(5) For the purposes of paragraph (4) it is not in the interests of justice to [¹ treat the appeal as made in time unless the Board are] satisfied that—
  (a) the special circumstances specified in paragraph (6) are relevant [¹ ...]; or
  (b) some other special circumstances exist which are wholly exceptional and relevant [¹ ...],
and as a result of those special circumstances, it was not practicable for the appeal to be made within the time limit specified in section 39(1) of the 2002 Act.

(6) For the purposes of paragraph (5)(a), the special circumstances are that—
  (a) the [¹ appellant] or a partner or dependant of the [¹ appellant] has died or suffered serious illness;
  (b) the [¹ appellant] is not resident in the United Kingdom; or
  (c) normal postal services were disrupted.

(7) In determining whether it is in the interests of justice to [¹ treat the appeal as made in time], regard shall be had to the principle that the greater the amount of time that has elapsed between the expiration of the time within which the appeal is to be brought under section 39(1) of the 2002 Act and the [¹ submission of the notice of appeal, the more compelling should be the special circumstances.]

(8) In determining whether it is in the interests of justice to [¹ treat the appeal as made in time], no account shall be taken of the following—
   (a) that the applicant or any person acting for him was unaware of or misunderstood the law applicable to his case (including ignorance or misunderstanding of the time limit imposed by section 39(1) of the 2002 Act); or
   (b) that [¹ the Upper Tribunal] or a court has taken a different view of the law from that previously understood and applied.

[¹ ...]

AMENDMENT

1. Tribunals, Courts and Enforcement Act 2007 (Transitional and Consequential Provisions) Order 2008 (SI 2008/2683) art.6 and Sch.1 para.209 (November 3, 2008).

DEFINITIONS

"the 2002 Act"—see reg.1(3).
"appeal"—reg.1(3).
"the Board"—see s.39(1) of the Social Security Act 1998 as modified by reg.12 of the Tax Credits (Appeals) Regulations 2002.
"court"—reg.1(3).
"legally qualified panel member"—reg.1(3).
"panel member"—reg.1(3).
"partner"—reg.1(3).
"President"—reg.1(3).

GENERAL NOTE

In an important and thorough decision, issued as *JI v HMRC* [2013] UKUT 199 (AAC), Upper Tribunal Judge Rowland decides that this regulation is invalid as there is no authority in primary legislation for it. In his view, after a careful analysis of the secondary legislation since 2002 including the provisions in these Regulations, he accepts a concession by HMRC that there is no power in legislation to allow any extension of the absolute time limit in s.39(1) either under these provisions or under the Tribunal Procedure Rules applying to the First-tier Tribunal and Upper Tribunal. He also recommends new legislation to deal with the issue. Section 39 is retained in italics in this edition for earlier appeals. It continues to apply in Northern Ireland.

See now the new s.39A of the 2002 Act added from April 1, 2014. See further the commentary to that section, above, for discussion of the decision of the three-judge panel of the Upper Tribunal in *VK v HMRC (TC)* [2016] UKUT 331 (AAC); [2017] AACR 3.

Death of a party to an appeal or an application for a direction

8.—(1) In any proceedings relating to an appeal or an application for a direction, on the death of a party to those proceedings (other than the Board) the following persons may proceed with the appeal or application for a direction in the place of such deceased party—

(a) where the proceedings are in relation to a single claim, the personal representatives of the person who has died;
(b) where the proceedings are in relation to a joint claim, where only one of the persons by whom the claim was made has died, the other person with whom the claim was made;
(c) where the proceedings are in relation to a joint claim where both the persons by whom the claim was made have died, the personal representatives of the last of them to die;
(d) for the purposes of paragraph (c), where persons have died in circumstances rendering it uncertain which of them survived the other—
  (i) their deaths shall be presumed to have occurred in order of seniority; and
  (ii) the younger shall be treated as having survived the elder.

(2) Where there is no person mentioned in paragraphs (1)(a) to (1)(c) to proceed with the appeal or application for a direction, the Board may appoint such person as they think fit to proceed with that appeal or that application in the place of such deceased party referred to in paragraph (1).

(3) A grant of probate, confirmation or letters of administration to the estate of the deceased party, whenever taken out, shall have no effect on an appointment made under paragraph (2).

(4) Where a person appointed under paragraph (2) has, prior to the date of such appointment, taken any action in relation to the appeal or application for a direction on behalf of the deceased party, the effective date of appointment by the Board shall be the day immediately prior to the first day on which such action was taken.

DEFINITIONS

"appeal"—see reg.1(3).
"an application for a direction"—reg.1(3).
"the Board"—see s.39(1) of the Social Security Act 1998 as modified by reg.12 of the Tax Credits (Appeals) Regulations 2002.
"joint claimant"—reg.1(3).
"party to the proceedings"—reg.1(3).
"single claimant"—reg.1(3).

The Tax Credits (Interest Rate) Regulations 2003

(SI 2003/123)

The Treasury, in exercise of the powers conferred upon them by ss.37(2) and (5), 65(1) and (8) and 67 of the Tax Credits Act 2002, hereby make the following Regulations:

ARRANGEMENT OF ARTICLES

1. Citation and commencement.
2. Interpretation.
3. Interest on overpayments of tax credit and penalties.
4. Prescribed rate of interest.

The Tax Credits (Interest Rate) Regulations 2003

Citation and commencement

2.459   **1.**—These Regulations may be cited as the Tax Credits (Interest Rate) Regulations 2003 and shall come into force on 18th February 2003.

GENERAL NOTE

2.460   The tax credits regime does not adopt quite the same approach to interest on overpayments as HMRC does for late payments of income tax. Whereas interest on late payments of income tax has long been a feature of revenue law, s.37 of the TCA 2002 adopts a compromise approach to tax credits. Thus, interest is charged on overpayments caused by fraud or neglect, but not otherwise. These regulations specify the rate of interest to be applied on such overpayments, and also on any penalty under ss.31–33 (penalties for incorrect statements, failure to comply with requirements, etc.).

Interpretation

2.461   **2.**—(1) In these Regulations—
"the Board" means the Commissioners of Inland Revenue;
"established rate" means—
  (a) on the coming into force of these Regulations, 6.5 per cent per annum;
  (b) in relation to any date after the first reference date after the coming into force of these Regulations, the reference rate found on the immediately preceding reference date;
"operative date" means the sixth day of each month;
"reference date" means the day of each month which is the 12th working day before the sixth day of the following month;
"tax credit" means child tax credit or, as the case may be, working tax credit, provision for which is made by the Tax Credits Act 2002;
"working day" means any day other than a non-business day within the meaning of section 92 of the Bills of Exchange Act 1882.

(2) For the purposes of regulation 4(2) the reference rate found on a reference date is the percentage per annum found by averaging the base lending rates at close of business on that date of—
  (a) Bank of Scotland;
  (b) Barclays Bank plc;
  (c) Lloyds Bank plc;
  (d) HSBC Bank plc;
  (e) National Westminster Bank plc;
  (f) The Royal Bank of Scotland plc,
and, if the result is not a whole number, rounding the result to the nearest such number, with any result midway between two whole numbers rounded down.

DEFINITION

"reference rate"—see reg.4(2).

Interest on overpayments of tax credit and penalties

2.462   **3.**—(1) Where the Board decide in accordance with section 37(1) of the Tax Credits Act 2002 that the whole or part of an overpayment of a tax credit which is attributable to fraud or neglect is to carry interest, the rate of interest for the purposes of section 37(2) of that Act is that prescribed by regulation 4.

(SI 2003/123 reg.3)

(2) The rate of interest for the purposes of section 37(5) of the Tax Credits Act 2002 (interest on a penalty under any of sections 31–33 of that Act) is that prescribed by regulation 4.

DEFINITION

"the Board"—see reg.2(1).

Prescribed rate of interest

4.—(1) The rate of interest which is prescribed is, subject to paragraph (2), 6.5 per cent per annum.

(2) Where, on a reference date after the coming into force of these Regulations, the reference rate found on that date ("RR") differs from the established rate, the rate of interest which is prescribed shall, on and after the next operative date, be the percentage per annum found by applying the formula:

$$RR + 2.5.$$

DEFINITION

"established rate"—see reg.2(1).

The Tax Credits (Immigration) Regulations 2003

(SI 2003/653)

The Treasury, in exercise of the powers conferred upon them by sections 42 and 65(1), (3), (7) and (9) of the Tax Credits Act 2002, hereby make the following Regulations:

ARRANGEMENT OF ARTICLES

1. Citation and commencement
2. Interpretation
3. Exclusion of persons subject to immigration control from entitlement to tax credits
4. Modifications of Part 1 of the Act for refugees whose asylum claims have been accepted
5. Transitional relief—claimants moving from income support and income based Jobseeker's Allowance to child tax credit

Citation and commencement

1.—These Regulations may be cited as the Tax Credits (Immigration) Regulations 2003 and shall come into force on 6th April 2003.

Interpretation

2.—In these Regulations—
"the Act" means the Tax Credits Act 2002;

"the Child Tax Credit Regulations" means the Child Tax Credit Regulations 2002;
[¹"couple" has the meaning given by section 3(5A) of the Act;]
"immigration rules" has the meaning given by section 33 of the Immigration Act 1971;
"joint claim" has the meaning given by section 3(8) of the Act;
"limited leave" has the meaning given by section 33 of the Immigration Act 1971;
[¹ . . .]
"person subject to immigration control" has the meaning in section 115(9) of the Immigration and Asylum Act 1999;
"refugee" means a person who has been recorded by the Secretary of State as a refugee within the definition in Article 1 of the Convention relating to the Status of Refugees done at Geneva on 28th July 1951 as extended by Article 1(2) of the Protocol relating to the Status of Refugees done at New York on 31st January 1967;
"tax credit" refers to either child tax credit or working tax credit and references to tax credits are to both of them;
"the Working Tax Credit Regulations" means the Working Tax Credit (Entitlement and Maximum Rate) Regulations 2002.

AMENDMENT

1. Civil Partnership Act 2004 (Tax Credits, etc.) (Consequential Amendments) Order 2005 (SI 2005/2919) art.7(2) (December 5, 2005).

Exclusion of persons subject to immigration control from entitlement to tax credits

3.—(1) No person is entitled to child tax credit or working tax credit while he is a person subject to immigration control, except in the following Cases, and subject to paragraphs (2) to (9).

Case 1

He is a person who—
(a) has been given leave to enter, or remain in, the United Kingdom by the Secretary of State upon the undertaking of another person or persons, pursuant to the immigration rules, to be responsible for his maintenance and accommodation; and
(b) has been resident in the United Kingdom for a period of at least five years commencing on or after the date of his entry into the United Kingdom, or the date on which the undertaking was given in respect of him, whichever is the later.

Case 2

He is a person who—
(a) falls within the terms of paragraph (a) of Case 1; and
(b) has been resident in the United Kingdom for less than the five years mentioned in para.(b) of Case 1,
but the person giving the undertaking has died or, where the undertaking was given by more than one person, they have all died.

(SI 2003/653 reg.3)

Case 3

[³...]

Case 4

Where the claim is for working tax credit, he is—
(a) a national of a state which has ratified the European Convention on Social and Medical Assistance (done in Paris on 11th December 1953) or of a state which has ratified the Council of Europe Social Charter (signed in Turin on 18th October 1961); and
(b) lawfully present in the United Kingdom.
The Case so described also applies where—
(a) the claim is for child tax credit;
(b) the award of child tax credit would be made on or after 6th April 2004; and
(c) immediately before the award is made (and as part of the transition of claimants entitled to elements of income support and income-based Jobseeker's Allowance, to child tax credit) the person is, or will on the making of a claim be, entitled to any of the amounts in relation to income support or income-based Jobseeker's Allowance which are described in section 1(3)(d) of the Act.

Case 5

Where the claim is for child tax credit, he is [⁶ᵃ person who is lawfully working in the United Kingdom and —
(a) who —
  (i) made a claim before 1st January 2021; and
  (ii) is a national of a State with which the European Union had, before 1st January 2021, concluded an agreement under Article 217 of the Treaty on the Functioning of the European Union providing in the field of social security for the equal treatment of workers who are nationals of the signatory State and their families; or
(b) who is a national of a State with which the United Kingdom has concluded an agreement which replaces, in whole or in part, an agreement under Article 217 of the Treaty on the Functioning of the European Union which either —
(i) makes provision in the field of social security for the equal treatment of workers who are nationals of the State with which the agreement has been concluded and their families, or
(ii) makes provision for receipt of family allowances by members of a worker's family who are legally resident in the United Kingdom.]
(2) Where one member of a [¹ ...] couple is a person subject to immigration control, and the other member is not or is within any of Cases 1 to 5 or regulation 5—
(a) the calculation of the amount of tax credit under the Act, the Child Tax Credit Regulations and the Working Tax Credit Regulations (including any second adult element or other element in respect of, or determined by reference to, that person);
(b) the method of making (or proceeding with) a joint claim by the couple; and

(c) the method of payment of the tax credit,

shall, subject to paragraph (3), be determined in the same way as if that person were not subject to such control.

(3) Where the other member is within Case 4 or 5 or regulation 5, para. (2) shall only apply to the tax credit to which he (in accordance with those provisions) is entitled.

(4) Where a person has submitted a claim for asylum as a refugee and in consequence is a person subject to immigration control, in the first instance he is not entitled to tax credits, subject to paragraphs (5) to (9).

(5) If that person—
   (a) is notified that he has been recorded by the Secretary of State as a refugee [⁵ or has been granted section 67 leave]; and
   (b) claims tax credit within [² one month] of receiving that notification,

paragraphs (6) to (9) and regulation 4 shall apply to him.

(6) He shall be treated as having claimed tax credits—
   (a) on the date when he submitted his claim for asylum; and
   (b) on every 6th April (if any) intervening between the date in subparagraph (a) and the date of the claim referred to in paragraph (5)(b),

rather than on the date on which he makes the claim referred to in paragraph (5)(b).

(7) [⁴ Regulations 7, 7A and 8] of the Tax Credits (Claims and Notifications) Regulations 2002 shall not apply to claims treated as made by virtue of paragraph (6).

(8) He shall have his claims for tax credits determined as if he had been recorded as a refugee on the date when he submitted his claim for asylum.

(9) The amount of support provided under—
   (a) section 95 or 98 of the Immigration and Asylum Act 1999;
   (b) regulations made under Schedule 9 to that Act, by the Secretary of State in respect of essential living needs of the claimant and his dependants (if any); or
   (c) regulations made under paragraph 3 of Schedule 8 to that Act,

(after allowing for any deduction for that amount under regulation 21ZB(3) of the Income Support (General) Regulations 1987) shall be deducted from any award of tax credits due to the claimant by virtue of paragraphs (6) and (8).

[⁵ (10) In this regulation "section 67 leave" means leave to remain in the United Kingdom granted by the Secretary of State to a person who has been relocated to the United Kingdom pursuant to arrangements made by the Secretary of State under section 67 of the Immigration Act 2016.]

AMENDMENTS

1. Civil Partnership Act 2004 (Tax Credits, etc.) (Consequential Amendments) Order 2005 (SI 2005/2919) art.7(3) (December 5, 2005).

2. Tax Credits (Miscellaneous Amendments) Regulations 2012 (SI 2012/848) reg.7 (April 6, 2012).

3. Tax Credits (Miscellaneous Amendments) Regulations 2014 (SI 2014/658) reg.3 (April 6, 2014).

4. Tax Credits (Claims and Notifications) (Amendment) Regulations 2015 (SI 2015/669) reg.5 (April 6, 2015).

5. Child Benefit, Tax Credits and Childcare Payments (Section 67 Immigration Act 2016 Leave) (Amendment) Regulations 2018 (SI 2018/788) reg.5(2) (July 20, 2018).

(SI 2003/653 reg.3)

6. Social Security, Child Benefit and Child Tax Credit (Amendment) (EU Exit) Regulations 2020 (SI 2020/1505) reg.4(2) (January 1, 2021).

DEFINITIONS

"the Act"—see reg.2.
"the Child Tax Credit Regulations"—see reg.2.
"couple"—see reg.2.
"immigration rules"—see reg.2.
"joint claim"—see reg.2.
"limited leave"—see reg.2.
"person subject to immigration control"—see reg.2.
"refugee"—see reg.2.
"tax credit"—see reg.2.
"the Working Tax Credit Regulations"—see reg.2.

GENERAL NOTE

These regulations are made under s.42(1) of the Tax Credits Act 2002, which enables regulations to make provision for the exclusion of "persons subject to immigration control" from entitlement to child tax credit or working tax credit (or both). For these purposes, a "person subject to immigration control" has the same meaning as in s.115 of the Immigration and Asylum Act 1999. Section 115(9) of the 1999 Act is the starting point for this definition, and defines a "person subject to immigration control" as a person who *either* requires leave to enter or remain in the UK but does not have it *or* has such leave but this is: (i) subject to a condition that he does not have recourse to public funds, (ii) as a result of a maintenance undertaking, or (iii) through the continuation of leave pending certain appeals. For detailed commentary on this definition, see the annotations to reg.21(3) of the Income Support (General) Regulations 1987 (SI 1987/1967) in Vol.II in this series. It should be noted that a person who is a national of an EEA state (i.e. a national of an EU Member State or of Iceland, Liechtenstein or Norway) can *never* be a person subject to immigration control for the purposes of social security or tax credits.

The structure of reg.3 itself falls into three parts. Paragraph (1) sets out the general rule, along with certain exceptions. The position of couples, where one partner is a person subject to immigration control but the other is not, is dealt with in paras (2) and (3). Paragraphs (4)–(9) are concerned with the particular status of asylum seekers. These rules can never apply to British citizens. An individual who becomes a British citizen by naturalisation ceases to be subject to any immigration control on becoming a British citizen.

2.468

Paragraph (1)

The general rule is that a person subject to immigration control is not entitled to either child tax credit or working tax credit (para.(1)). This general rule is then subject to the exceptions listed in Cases 1–5. These Cases have been adapted from the exceptions to the general rule precluding persons subject to immigration control from being entitled to the various means-tested benefits, as set out in the Schedule to the Social Security (Immigration and Asylum) Consequential Amendments Regulations 2000 (SI 2000/636) see Vol.II in this series. Thus, Case 1 in para.(1) mirrors para.3 in Pt I of the Schedule to the 2000 Regulations; Case 2 follows para.2 of Pt I of the Schedule. These first two Cases operate as exceptions to the preclusionary rule for both child tax credit and working tax credit. The exception in Case 4 is in the same terms as para.4 in Pt I of the Schedule to the 2000 Regulations and applies to all working tax credit claims. It also applies to child tax credit claims in respect of awards made on or after April 6, 2004 where, immediately before the award the claimant was (or would have been) entitled to a child allowance or family or disabled child premium as part of an award of income support or income-based jobseeker's allowance.

2.469

837

The Tax Credits (Immigration) Regulations 2003

There is also a special rule, applying to child tax credit only, which provides transitional relief for claimants moving from income support or income-based jobseeker's allowance to child tax credit (see reg.5).

Case 5 was amended in consequence of the United Kingdom's withdrawal from the European Union. Previously Case 5 referred to a person working lawfully in the United Kingdom who was a national of a State party to a Community Agreement for the equal treatment, in the field of social security, of workers and their families. The current Case 5 draws a distinction between those who claim before 1 January 2021 and those who claim subsequently.

Those who claim before 1 January 2021 must be lawfully working in the UK and a national of a State that was party to an equal treatment agreement made with the European Union under Article 217 of the Treaty on the Functioning of the European Union.

For those claiming on or after 1 January 2021, the claimant must be a national of State with which the UK has entered into an equal treatment agreement, meeting a condition in (b)(i) or (ii) of Case 5, in place of an agreement under Article 217. This may include the Convention on Social Security between the Government of the United Kingdom and Northern Ireland and the Government of Ireland, of 1 February 2019, given effect in UK law by article 2 of the Social Security (Ireland) Order 2019 (SI 2019/622), which the UK Government has stated will have come into force by or on 31 December 2020. For details of that Convention, which covers child tax credit, see the note to regulation 8A of the Child Tax Credit Regulations 2002 above in this volume.

Paragraphs (2) and (3)

2.470 Paragraph (2) provides that where only one member of a married or unmarried couple is a person subject to immigration control, and the other is not, entitlement to tax credits is determined in the same way as if neither of them were so subject. The same applies where the other member is either within one of the excepted cases in para.(1) or covered by the transitional provisions in reg.5 below. Note also the qualification in para.(3).

Paragraphs (4)–(9)

2.471 These provisions enable backdated claims to tax credits to be made where an asylum claim has been accepted. A claimant who has submitted a claim for asylum is a person subject to immigration control and so in the first instance is not entitled to tax credits (para.(4)). However, if such an application is accepted, the claimant may claim tax credits retrospectively (para.(5)). Any such retrospective claim must be made within one month of the notification from the IND (para.(5)). This contrasts favourably with the 28 days allowed for retrospective claims for income support in similar situations (Income Support (General) Regulations 1987 (SI 1987/1967) reg.21ZB). In the event of a successful application for asylum, the claim for tax credits is treated as having been made on the date of the submission of the claim for asylum, not the post-acceptance date of the actual claim for tax credits (para.(6)(a)). The claim is also regarded as having been renewed on every intervening April 6, demonstrating an awareness of the delays which are well known in the system for determining asylum applications (para.(6)(b)). Accordingly, the normal time-limits in regs 7 and 8 of the Tax Credits (Claims and Notifications) Regulations 2002 (SI 2002/2014) for claiming tax credits are disapplied (para.(7)) and the claim treated as if the applicant had been recorded as a refugee on the date when the asylum application was actually made (para.(8)). Any arrears of tax credits which are due, following the application of these provisions, are then subject to an offset in recognition of any sums provided by way of asylum support under various statutory provisions (para.(9)).

The issue in *MK v HMRC (TC)* [2018] UKUT 238 (AAC) was whether a claimant's telephone call to HMRC about tax credits, made within one month of the date on which he was granted refugee status, amounted to a claim for tax credits for the purposes of reg.2(5). The telephone call was made on December 1, 2016 but a written claim form was not received by HMRC until February 9, 2017. If the claim was not made until the later date, the claimant's entitlement would commence from January 9, 2017 (one month before the claim was made). If the telephone call amounted to a claim, entitlement would commence from November 25, 2016, being the date on which the claimant was notified that he had been granted refugee status. The appeal turned on the provisions of reg.5(2) of the Tax Credits (Claims and Notifications) Regulations 2002. Regulation 5(2)(a) enacts the general rule that a claim for tax credit is to be made in writing on a form approved or authorised by HMRC for the purposes of the claim. Regulation 5(2)(b), however, permits a claim to be made in such other manner as HMRC may decide "having regard to all the circumstances". Upper Tribunal Judge Wikeley noted that, in principle, reg.5(2)(b) could permit a claim to be made orally. However, the question whether HMRC should have allowed an oral claim was not within the First-tier Tribunal's jurisdiction (*CTC/31/2006*). Moreover, the telephone call of December 1, 2016 could not reasonably be construed as a claim. It was a request for a claim form. Judge Wikeley held that the First-tier Tribunal correctly dismissed the appellant's appeal against HMRC's decision that his tax credit entitlement commenced from January 9, 2017.

Note that, by virtue of reg.4, the provisions of Pt I of the TCA 2002 apply to the determination of claims for tax credits made by refugees whose asylum claims have been accepted, subject to the omission of ss.14–17 and various modifications to ss.18 and 19 of the 2002 Act.

In *AA v HMRC (TC)* [2012] UKUT 121 (AAC), Judge Turnbull held that subs.(5), requiring additional backdating to tax credits in the case of a person "recorded by the Secretary of State as a refugee", did not permit backdating of entitlement to tax credit for more than three months (the then maximum) in a case where the claimant had been granted indefinite leave to remain in the UK with retrospective effect for a longer period. For cases with an EU dimension, see also *EG v HMRC (TC)* [2011] UKUT 467 (AAC), discussed in the note to TCA 2002 s.3(5A) above.

In *CTC/3692/2008* an Upper Tribunal Judge rejected a challenge to subss.(7)–(9) as discriminatory and in breach of the Human Rights Act 1998. The Commissioner decided on the facts that while the rules were not discriminatory they also had not been applied properly. After outlining what should have happened, the appeal was sent back to HMRC for it to be redetermined.

In *FK v HMRC* [2009] UKUT 134 (AAC) Judge Jacobs considered the date from which a claim for child tax credit should start when a claimant has her status as a refugee confirmed. A mother claimed child tax credit on August 8, 2007, following confirmation of her status on July 3, 2007. She was awarded tax credits from 2005, when she was treated as making a new asylum claim, although she first claimed asylum unsuccessfully on arrival in 2000. Judge Jacobs agreed with a submission by HMRC supporting the mother's appeal against a First-tier Tribunal decision confirming the award only from the second claim. He cited art.24 of the Convention relating to the Status of Refugees 1951 as supporting the approach, previously adopted by a Social Security Commissioner in *R(IS) 9/98*, that the "grant" of asylum was recognition of the claimant's status, not the creation of that status. The status existed from the time the mother first arrived in the UK and her first, then unsuccessful, claim for asylum. Her claim was therefore operative from that time. The judge has examined this rule in two other decisions: *MI v HMRC* [2009] UKUT 73 (AAC) and *CTC/0838/2011* in the latter of which he noted that there had been no appeals against these decisions and that therefore a First-tier Tribunal was correct in applying them.

In *HMRC v Adnan and Adnan* [2022] CSIH 2, Mr and Mrs Adnan applied for asylum in the UK in 2013. They were finally granted refugee status in December 2019, when they made a successful claim for universal credit. In January 2020 they also made a claim for CTC, requesting that it was backdated to the date of their original application. HMRC refused to accept the claim on the grounds that (i) there was no longer any entitlement to tax credits (art.2 of the Welfare Reform Act 2012 (Commencement No.32 and Savings and Transitional Provisions) Order 2019);

and (ii) claims for tax credits were not permitted in areas where universal credit had been fully rolled out (art.7 of the Welfare Reform Act 2012 (Commencement No.23 and Transitional and Transitory Provisions) Order 2015). The Outer House of the Court of Session ([2021] CSOH 63) granted a declaration that HMRC's decision to refuse the claim was unlawful and irrational as art.7(1) of the 2015 Order did not bar the petitioners from claiming CTC by virtue of reg.3(5)(b) and 3(6) of the 2003 Regulations. The Inner House dismissed HMRC's further appeal ([2022] CSIH 2). The decision of the Court of Session was followed by the High Court in *R (DK) v HMRC* [2021] EWHC 1845 (Admin) and then on appeal by the Court of Appeal in *R (DK) v HMRC* [2022] EWCA Civ 120.

Modifications of Part I of the Act for refugees whose asylum claims have been accepted

2.472   **4.**—(1) For the purposes of claims falling within paragraph (2), Part I of the Act shall apply subject to the modifications set out in paras (3)–(5).

(2) A claim falls within this paragraph if it is a claim for tax credits which a person is treated as having made by virtue of regulation 3(6), other than a claim which he is treated as having made in the tax year in which he made his claim under regulation 3(5).

(3) Omit sections 14 to 17 (initial decisions, revised decisions and final notices).

(4) In section 18 (decisions after final notices)—
(a) in subsection (1) for "After giving a notice under section 17" substitute "In relation to each claim for a tax credit made by a person or persons for the whole or part of a tax year";
(b) omit subsections (2) to (9);
(c) for subsection (10) substitute—
"(10) Before making their decision the Board may by notice—
(a) require the person, or either or both of the persons, by whom the claim is made to provide any information or evidence which the Board consider they may need for making their decision; or
(b) require any person of a prescribed description to provide any information or evidence of a prescribed description which the Board consider they may need for that purpose,
by the date specified in the notice.";
(d) in subsection (11) omit—
(i) "any revision under subsection (5) or (9) and";
(ii) paragraph (a);
(iii) in paragraph (b), "in any other case,".

(5) In section 19 (enquiries)—
(a) in subsection (4), for paragraphs (a) and (b) substitute "one year after that decision or, if—
(a) the person, or either of the persons, to whom the enquiry relates is required by section 8 of the Taxes Management Act 1970 to make a return; and
(b) the return becomes final on a day more than one year after that decision,
with that day (or, if both of the persons are so required and their returns become final on different days, with the later of those days).;"
(b) in subsection (5) omit paragraph (a) and, in paragraph (b) "in any other case,";
(c) omit subsection (6).

(SI 2003/653 reg.4)

DEFINITIONS

"the Act"—see reg.2.
"tax credit"—see reg.2.

GENERAL NOTE

See note to reg.3.

Transitional relief—claimants moving from income support and income-based jobseeker's allowance to child tax credit

5.—In relation to child tax credit, a person is not treated for the purposes of these Regulations as subject to immigration control where—
(a) the award of child tax credit would be made on or after 6th April 2004;
(b) immediately before the award of child tax credit is made, he is, or will on the making of a claim be, entitled to any of the amounts in relation to income support or income-based jobseeker's allowance which are described in section 1(3)(d) of the Act; and
(c) he is a person who, immediately before the award of child tax credit is made—
 (i) was receiving or entitled to income support by virtue of regulation 12(1) of the Social Security (Persons From Abroad) Miscellaneous Amendments Regulations 1996, and his claim for asylum has not been recorded by the Secretary of State as having been decided (other than on appeal) or abandoned; or
 (ii) was receiving or entitled to income support or income-based jobseeker's allowance by virtue of regulation 12(3) of the Social Security (Immigration and Asylum) Consequential Amendments Regulations 2000, and his claim for asylum has not been so recorded as having been decided (other than on appeal) or abandoned.

DEFINITIONS

"the Act"—see reg.2.
"person subject to immigration control"—see reg.2.

GENERAL NOTE

This provides for transitional relief (on or after April 6, 2004) for claimants moving over from the specified elements of income support or income-based jobseeker's allowance to child tax credit.

The Tax Credits (Residence) Regulations 2003

(SI 2003/654) (AS AMENDED)

The Treasury, in exercise of the powers conferred upon them by sections 3(7) and 65(1), (7) and (9) of the Tax Credits Act 2002, hereby make the following Regulations:

The Tax Credits (Residence) Regulations 2003

REGULATIONS

1. Citation and commencement
2. Interpretation
3. Circumstances in which a person is treated as not being in the United Kingdom
4. Persons temporarily absent from the United Kingdom
5. Crown servants posted overseas
6. Partners of Crown servants posted overseas
7. Transitional provision—income support and income-based Jobseeker's Allowance

Citation and commencement

1.—These Regulations may be cited as the Tax Credits (Residence) Regulations 2003 and shall come into force on 6th April 2003.

Interpretation

2.—(1) In these Regulations—
"the Act" means the Tax Credits Act 2002;
"child" has the same meaning as it has in the Child Tax Credit Regulations 2002;
[¹"couple" has the meaning given by section 3(5A) of the Act];
"Crown servant posted overseas" has the meaning given in regulation 5(2);
"partner" means where a person is a member of a [¹ . . .] couple, the other member of that couple;
"qualifying young person" has the meaning given in regulation 2, read with regulation 5, of the Child Tax Credit Regulations 2002;
"relative" means brother, sister, ancestor or lineal descendant.

(2) In these Regulations, a person is responsible for a child or qualifying young person if he is treated as being responsible for that child or qualifying young person in accordance with the rules contained in regulation 3 of the Child Tax Credit Regulations 2002.

AMENDMENT

1. Civil Partnership Act 2004 (Tax Credits, etc.) (Consequential Amendments) Order 2005 (SI 2005/2919) art.8(2) (December 5, 2005).

GENERAL NOTE

This regulation follows the pattern of all tax credit provisions in adopting the definitions of "child" and "qualifying young person" from the Child Tax Credit Regulations 2002 (SI 2002/2007).

Circumstances in which a person is treated as not being in the United Kingdom

3.—(1) A person shall be treated as not being in the United Kingdom for the purposes of Part I of the Act if he is not ordinarily resident in the United Kingdom.

(2) [⁵ Paragraphs (1) and (6) do] not apply to a Crown servant posted overseas or his partner.

(3) A person who is in the United Kingdom as a result of his deportation, expulsion or other removal by compulsion of law from another country to

the United Kingdom shall be treated as being ordinarily resident in the United Kingdom [⁵ and paragraph (6) shall not apply].

(4) For the purposes of working tax credit, a person shall be treated as being ordinarily resident if he is exercising in the United Kingdom his rights as a worker pursuant to [³ Parliament and Council Regulation (EU) No 492/2011] or he is a person with a right to reside in the United Kingdom pursuant to [² [⁷ the Immigration (European Economic Area) Regulations 2016]].

[¹(5) A person [¹¹(P)] shall be treated as not being in the United Kingdom for the purposes of Part 1 of the Act where [¹¹ ...]—
- (a) [¹¹ P] makes a claim for child tax credit (other than being treated as making a claim under regulation 11 or 12 of the Tax Credits (Claims and Notifications) Regulations 2002 or otherwise), on or after 1st May 2004 [¹¹and one of sub-paragraphs (b), (c) or (d) applies;]

[¹¹(b) P does not have a right to reside in the United Kingdom;
- (c) P has a right to reside under paragraph (1) of regulation 16 of the Immigration (European Economic Area) Regulations 2016, but only in a case where the right exists under that regulation because P satisfies the criteria in paragraph (5) of that regulation; or
- (d) P would fall within sub-paragraph (b) or (c) but for the fact that P has limited leave to enter, or remain in, the United Kingdom under the Immigration Act 1971 by virtue of —
  - (i) Appendix EU to the immigration rules; or
  - (ii) having arrived in the United Kingdom with an entry clearance that was granted under Appendix EU (Family Permit) to the immigration rules made under section 3(2) of that Act.]

[¹³(5A) Paragraph (5)(c) does not apply to a person who is lawfully working in the United Kingdom —
- (a) who —
  - (i) made a claim for child tax credit before 1st January 2021, and
  - (ii) is a national of a State with which the European Union had, before 1st January 2021, concluded an agreement under Article 217 of the Treaty on the Functioning of the European Union providing in the field of social security for the equal treatment of workers who are nationals of the signatory State and their families; or
- (b) who is a national of a State with which the United Kingdom has concluded an agreement which replaces, in whole or in part, an EU Agreement which has ceased to apply in the United Kingdom.]

[⁹(5B) Paragraph [11(5)(d)(i)] does not apply to a person who—
- (a) has limited leave to enter, or remain in, the United Kingdom under the Immigration Act 1971 which has been granted by virtue of Appendix EU to the Immigration Rules;
- (b) has been granted such leave in reliance of being a family member of a relevant person of Northern Ireland in accordance with those Rules; and
- (c) would have a right to reside under the Immigration (European Economic Area) Regulations 2016 if the relevant person of Northern Ireland were an EEA national within the meaning of regulation 2 of those Regulations.] of workers who are nationals of the signatory State and their families.]

[⁵ (6) Subject to paragraph (7), a person is to be treated as being in the United Kingdom for the purposes of Part 1 of the Act where he makes a claim for child tax credit only if that person has been living in the United Kingdom for 3 months before that claim plus any time taken into account by regulation 7 of the Tax Credits (Claims and Notifications) Regulations 2002 for determining for the purpose of that regulation when the claim is treated as having been made.

(7) Paragraph (6) shall not apply where the person—
  (a) most recently entered the United Kingdom before 1st July 2014;
  (b) is a worker or a self-employed person in the United Kingdom for the purposes of [⁷ regulation 4(1)(a) or (b) of the Immigration (European Economic Area) Regulations 2016];
  (c) retains the status of a worker or self-employed person in the United Kingdom pursuant to [⁷ regulation 6(2) or (4) of the Immigration (European Economic Area) Regulations 2016];
  (d) is treated as a worker in the United Kingdom pursuant to regulation 5 of the Accession of Croatia (Immigration and Worker Authorisation) Regulations 2013 (right of residence of a Croatian who is an "accession State national subject to worker authorisation");
  (e) is a family member of a person referred to in sub-paragraphs (b), (c), (d) [¹⁰, (i) or (o)];
  (f) is a person to whom regulation 4 applies (persons temporarily absent from the United Kingdom) and who returns to the United Kingdom within 52 weeks starting from the first day of the temporary absence;
  (g) returns to the United Kingdom after a period abroad of less than 52 weeks where immediately before departing from the United Kingdom that person had been ordinarily resident in the United Kingdom for a continuous period of 3 months;
  (h) returns to the United Kingdom otherwise as a worker or self-employed person after a period abroad and where, otherwise than for a period of up to 3 months ending on the day of returning, that person has paid either Class 1 or Class 2 contributions pursuant to regulation 114, 118, 146 or 147 of the Social Security (Contributions) Regulations 2001 or pursuant to an Order in Council having effect under section 179 of the Social Security Administration Act 1992;
[¹⁰(i) is not a national of an EEA State and would be a worker or self-employed person in the United Kingdom for the purposes of the Immigration (European Economic Area) Regulations 2016 if that person —
    (i) were a national of an EEA State; and
    (ii) a "member of the post-transition period group" within the meaning of paragraph 1 of Schedule 4 to the Immigration and Social Security Co-ordination (EU Withdrawal) Act 2020 (Consequential, Saving, Transitional and Transitory Provisions (EU Exit) Regulations 2020;]
  (j) is a refugee as defined in Article 1 of the Convention relating to the Status of Refugees done at Geneva on 28th July 1951, as extended by Article 1(2) of the Protocol relating to the Status of Refugees done at New York on 31st January 1967;

(SI 2003/654 reg.3) (as amended)

- (k) has been granted leave, or is deemed to have been granted leave, outside the rules made under section 3(2) of the Immigration Act 1971 where that leave is—
  - (i) granted by the Secretary of State with recourse to public funds, or
  - (ii) deemed to have been granted by virtue of regulation 3 of the Displaced Persons (Temporary Protection) Regulations 2005;
- (l) has been granted leave to remain in the United Kingdom by the Secretary of State pending an application for indefinite leave to remain as a victim of domestic violence;
- (m) has been granted humanitarian protection by the Secretary of State under Rule 339C of Part 11 of the rules made under section 3(2) of the Immigration Act 1971;
- [6 (n) has been granted section 67 leave;]
- [10(o) is a national of an EEA State and would satisfy the criteria in sub-paragraph (b) or (c) if they were a "member of the post-transition period group" within the meaning of paragraph 1 of Schedule 4 to the Immigration and Social Security Co-ordination (EU Withdrawal) Act 2020 (Consequential, Saving, Transitional and Transitory Provisions (EU Exit) Regulations 2020].

[12(7A) A person ("P") who is within Part IV Section 4 of the Reciprocal Agreement with Ireland will be treated as being ordinarily resident in the United Kingdom where P makes a claim for child tax credit if—
- (a) P resides in Ireland; and
- (b) P is in a relevant situation.

(7B) Both members of a couple ("A and B") who are within Part IV Section 4 of the Reciprocal Agreement with Ireland will be treated as being ordinarily resident in the United Kingdom where they make a joint claim for child tax credit tax if—
- (a) either —
  - (i) A or B is resident in Ireland; or
  - (ii) both A and B are resident in Ireland; and
- (b) either—
  - (i) A or B is in a relevant situation; or
  - (ii) both A and B are in a relevant situation and it does not matter if A and B are not in the same relevant situation.

(7C) For the purposes of paragraphs (7A) and (7B), a person is in a "relevant situation" if that person is—
- (a) an employed person as defined in Article 1 of the Reciprocal Agreement with Ireland and subject to the legislation of the United Kingdom in accordance with Part II of that Agreement;
- (b) a self-employed person as defined in Article 1 of the Reciprocal Agreement with Ireland and subject to the legislation of the United Kingdom in accordance with Part II of that Agreement;
- (c) receiving a contributory benefit from the United Kingdom in accordance with Article 9(2) of the Reciprocal Agreement with Ireland;
- (d) receiving a state pension from the United Kingdom within the meaning of Article 3(1)(a)(v) of the Reciprocal Agreement with Ireland; or
- (e) receiving a survivor's benefit from the United Kingdom within the meaning of Article 3(1)(a)(vi) of the Reciprocal Agreement with Ireland.

(7D) For the purposes of paragraphs (7A) to (7C), "the Reciprocal Agreement with Ireland" means the Convention on Social Security between the Government of the United Kingdom of Great Britain and Northern Ireland and the Government of Ireland signed at Dublin on 1st February 2019.]

(8) [9 For the purposes of paragraph (7)(e)], a "family member" means a person who is defined as a family member of another person in [7 regulation 7 of the Immigration (European Economic Area) Regulations 2016].

(9) In this regulation, "EEA State", in relation to any time, means a state which at that time is a member State, or any other state which at that time is a party to the agreement on the European Economic Area signed at Oporto on 2nd May, together with the Protocol adjusting that Agreement signed at Brussels on 17th March 1993, as modified or supplemented from time to time.]

[6 (10) In this regulation "section 67 leave" means leave to remain in the United Kingdom granted by the Secretary of State to a person who has been relocated to the United Kingdom pursuant to arrangements made by the Secretary of State under section 67 of the Immigration Act 2016.]

[9(11) In this regulation, "relevant person of Northern Ireland" means a person who —
- (a) is —
   - (i) a British citizen; or
   - (ii) an Irish citizen; or
   - (iii) a British citizen and an Irish citizen; and
- (b) was born in Northern Ireland and, at the time of that person's birth, at least one of their parents was —
   - (i) a British citizen;
   - (ii) an Irish citizen; or
   - (iii) a British citizen and an Irish citizen; or
   - (iv) otherwise entitled to reside in Northern Ireland without any restriction on their period of residence.]

[10(12) In this regulation references to the Immigration (European Economic Area) Regulations 2016 are to be read with Schedule 4 to the Immigration and Social Security Co-ordination (EU Withdrawal) Act 2020(Consequential, Saving, Transitional and Transitory Provisions) Regulations 2020.]

[13(13) In this regulation "EU Agreement" means —
- (a) an Association Agreement concluded under Article 217 of the Treaty on the Functioning of the European Union which makes provision in the field of social security for equal treatment for workers who are nationals of the State with which the agreement has been concluded and their families, or
- (b) a Stabilisation and Association Agreement concluded under Article 217 of the Treaty on the Functioning of the European Union which makes provision for receipt of family allowances for members of a worker's family who are legally resident in the United Kingdom.]

AMENDMENTS

1. Tax Credits (Residence) (Amendment) Regulations 2004 (SI 2004/1243) reg.3 (May 1, 2004).

2. Tax Credits (Miscellaneous Amendments) Regulations 2006 (SI 2006/766) reg.4 (April 6, 2006).

(SI 2003/654 reg.3) (as amended)

3. Tax Credits (Miscellaneous Amendments) Regulations 2012 (SI 2012/848) reg.8 (April 6, 2012).
4. Child Benefit and Child Tax Credit (Miscellaneous Amendments) Regulations 2012 (SI 2012/2612) regs 5 and 6 (November 8, 2012).
5. Child Benefit (General) and the Tax Credits (Residence) (Amendment) Regulations 2014 (SI 2014/1511) regs 2 and 6 (July 1, 2014).
6. Child Benefit, Tax Credits and Childcare Payments (Section 67 Immigration Act 2016 Leave) (Amendment) Regulations 2018 (SI 2018/788) reg.4(2) (July 20, 2018).
7. Tax Credits, Child Benefit and Childcare Payments (Miscellaneous Amendments) Regulations 2019 (SI 2019/364) reg.7(2) (March 21, 2019).
8. Child Benefit and Child Tax Credit (Amendment) (EU Exit) Regulations 2019 (SI 2019/867) reg.3(2) (May 7, 2019).
9. Child Benefit and Child Tax Credit (Persons of Northern Ireland) (Amendment) Regulations 2020 (SI 2020/672) reg.3(2) (August 24, 2020).
10. Immigration and Social Security Co-ordination (EU Withdrawal) Act 2020 (Consequential, Saving, Transitional and Transitory Provisions) (EU Exit) Regulations 2020 (SI 2020/1309) reg.61(2) (December 31, 2020).
11. Immigration (Citizens' Rights etc.) (EU Exit) Regulations 2020 (SI 2020/1372) reg.14(2) (December 31, 2020).
12. Tax Credits and Child Trust Funds (Amendment) (EU Exit) Regulations 2019 (SI 2019/713) reg.9 (December 31, 2020, at 11 p.m.).
13. Social Security, Child Benefit and Child Tax Credit (Amendment) (EU Exit) Regulations 2020 (SI 2020/1505) reg.5(2) (December 31, 2020, at 11 p.m.).

DEFINITIONS

"Crown servant posted overseas"—see reg.2.
"partner"—see reg.2.

GENERAL NOTE

Section 3(3) of the TCA 2002 makes it a requirement for entitlement to tax credits that the claimant is "in the United Kingdom". This regulation, authorised by s.3(7), imposes the income test of "ordinary residence" as an additional requirement for entitlement. Read together with the section, the regulations require that a claimant must show:
(a) ordinary residence in the UK, and
(b) presence in the UK or, if he or she is not present in the UK, that the absence is temporary.

The approach taken here is consistent with the general jurisdictional approach to income tax in the UK. In common with some other parts of the common law world, income tax is residence-based, rather than nationality-based (as in the United States) or source-based (as in other parts of Europe). Income tax uses two main tests: residence and ordinary residence. The Tax Credits (Definition and Calculation of Income) Regulations 2002 (SI 2002/2006) reg.3 removes the significance of both those tests for the purposes of defining the relevant income of a claimant. These Regulations impose the test at another level. Those Regulations also disapply the definitions of "residence" in the various UK double tax agreements (which, for income tax purposes, override the national legislation).

For full discussion of the rights under European law of a citizen of the European Union see Pt III of Vol.III of this work.

The Finance Act 2013 introduced a completely new and detailed tax regime for determining the residence and ordinary residence of individuals for income tax purposes, commencing for the tax year 2013–14 subject to transitional provisions. They therefore apply to income tax returns due for that and later years. The main change is one of approach. The former general case law-led factual approach is replaced by two extremely detailed sets of rules applying two new sets of tests.

2.481

The Tax Credits (Residence) Regulations 2003

The first is a statutory residence test (or, rather, a set of parallel tests) applied by s.218 of, and Sch.45 to, the 2013 Act. The other is the abolition of the test of ordinary residence entirely by s.219 of, and Sch.46 to, the 2013 Act, the concept being replaced by specific statutory tests, such as a three-year non-residence test for employees. The legislation deals in considerable detail with the new tests for all relevant aspects of income tax, including split year rules. As these have no direct effect on tax credits legislation to date, none of the detailed amendments to the income tax legislation have been included in this volume. The guidance about the former income tax treatment remains fully relevant to tax credits. Booklet IR20 has been kept on the HMRC website for reference although it has no current relevance to income tax. (For current income tax purposes it has been replaced by Guidance Notes, in particular RDR1 on *Residence, Domicile and the Remittance Basis.*)

Ordinary residence

2.482 "Ordinary residence" was used as the test for WFTC (Family Credit (General) Regulations 1987 (SI 1987/1973) reg.3) where the test was worded as a requirement that the claimant be both present and ordinarily resident. In *R(M) 1/85*, the Commissioner followed *Shah* (below) for those purposes as defining the term. The new form of words appears to avoid the problem with the previous wording commented on in Vol.II of the 2002 edition of this work. One change, however, is that the test is now applied to the whole of the UK, as Northern Ireland no longer has a separate system for these purposes.

"Ordinary residence" is a question of fact, not law. For the only relevant provisions in income tax law, see the ITA 2007 ss.829–832. It is separate from the other test used for income tax, "residence". "Residence" is determined for income tax purposes by reference to each tax year. "Ordinary residence" is based on a longer view, though perhaps not so long a view as "habitual residence". It is clear from both case law and practice that a claimant can have two ordinary residences at the same time for income tax purposes, and that the status of ordinary residence can be acquired on arrival in the UK if the claimant arrives with the intention of staying. That may be compared with the approach often taken for social security purposes to "habitual residence". For the leading authorities on the approach to be taken to the test see *Levene v IRC* [1928] A.C. 217; *IRC v Lysaght* [1928] A.C. 234; and *Shah v Barnet LBC* [1983] 2 A.C. 309 HL.

In *HA v HMRC (TC)* [2015] UKUT 708 (AAC) the claimant's husband had resided in the UK for several extended periods, had moved address with her, had worked until he had been made redundant (when he claimed JSA), had obtained indefinite leave to remain and was on the electoral roll in the UK. However, at the same time he had also retained strong links in Ghana, where he had both an apartment and employment. Judge Hemingway dismissed the claimant's appeal against the FTT decision that she was not entitled to claim tax credits as a single person for the 2011/12 tax year. In dismissing the claimant's further appeal, the Court of Appeal in *Arthur v HMRC* [2017] EWCA Civ 1756 held that the claimant's husband was a person who was "ordinarily resident" in the UK as at April 6, 2011 for the purposes of a joint tax credit claim under s.3(3) of the 2002 Act. Accordingly, the claimant herself was not able to make claim tax credits as a single person. The Court of Appeal also concluded it was open to the FTT to consider events after April 6, 2011 in deciding whether the husband was ordinarily resident (applying *Levene v IRC* [1928] A.C. 217). Newey LJ helpfully set out the relevant legal principles as follows:

"16. Guidance on the meaning of 'ordinarily resident' can be found in three decisions of the House of Lords: *Levene v Inland Revenue Commissioners [1928] AC 217, Inland Revenue Commissioners v Lysaght [1928] AC 234* and *R (Shah) v Barnet LBC* [1983] 2 AC 309. Those cases provide authority for the following propositions:

i) The expression 'ordinary residence' 'connotes residence in a place with some degree of continuity and apart from accidental or temporary absences' (*Levene*, at 225, per Viscount Cave LC);

ii) '[T]he converse to "ordinarily" is "extraordinarily" and ... part of the regular order of a man's life, adopted voluntarily and for settled purposes, is not "extraordinary"' (*Lysaght*, at 243, per Viscount Sumner). Consistently with this, 'ordinarily resident' 'refers to a man's abode in a particular place or country which he has adopted voluntarily and for settled purposes as part of the regular order of his life for the time being, whether of short or long duration' (*Shah*, at 343, per Lord Scarman);

iii) 'Ordinary residence' differs little from 'residence' (*Levene*, at 222, per Viscount Cave LC). 'Ordinarily resident' means 'no more than that the residence is not casual and uncertain but that the person held to reside does so in the ordinary course of his life' (*Lysaght*, at 248, per Lord Buckmaster);

iv) A person can be resident in a place even though 'from time to time he leaves it for the purpose of business or pleasure' and, conversely, 'a person who has his home abroad and visits the United Kingdom from time to time for temporary purposes without setting up an establishment in this country is not considered to be resident here' (*Levene*, at 222–223, per Viscount Cave LC);

v) A person can also be resident in a place even though he would prefer to be elsewhere. In *Lysaght*, Lord Buckmaster said (at 248):

'A man might well be compelled to reside here completely against his will; the exigencies of business often forbid the choice of residence, and though a man may make his home elsewhere and stay in this country only because business compels him, yet none the less, if the periods for which and the conditions under which he stays are such that they may be regarded as constituting residence, as in my opinion they were in this case, it is open to the Commissioners to find that in fact he does so reside';

vi) A person may reside in more than one place (*Levene*, at 223, per Viscount Cave LC);

vii) 'Ordinary residence' is not synonymous with 'domicile' or 'permanent home' (*Shah*, at 342–343 and 345, per Lord Scarman);

viii) 'Immigration status' 'may or may not be a guide to a person's intention in establishing a residence in this country' (*Shah*, 348, per Lord Scarman); and

ix) 'There are two, and no more than two, respects in which the mind of the "propositus" is important in determining ordinary residence': '[t]he residence must be voluntarily adopted' and 'there must be a degree of settled purpose', which could potentially be 'a specific limited purpose' (*Shah*, at 344 and 348, per Lord Scarman). Lord Scarman explained in *Shah* (at 344):

'The purpose may be one; or there may be several. It may be specific or general. All that the law requires is that there is a settled purpose. This is not to say that the "propositus" intends to stay where he is indefinitely; indeed his purpose, while settled, may be for a limited period. Education, business or profession, employment, health, family, or merely love of the place spring to mind as common reasons for a choice of regular abode. and there may well be many others. All that is necessary is that the purpose of living where one does has a sufficient degree of continuity to be properly described as settled."'

The Tax Credits (Residence) Regulations 2003

2.483   HMRC guidance document *HMRC6* (which replaced the code of guidance *IR20*) sets out how HMRC deal with disputed issues of ordinary residence for tax purposes. HMRC treat the question as partly one of intention and partly one of actual presence. However, *HMRC6*, at 2.2, states that HMRC will take a person to be resident in the UK for tax purposes if present here for at least 183 days of a tax year. For a person present for fewer than 183 days, *HMRC6* says the question whether the person is resident in the UK for tax purposes will "depend on how often and how long you are here, the purpose and pattern of your presence and your connections to the UK". In determining whether a person is *ordinarily* resident in the UK for tax purposes, *HMRC6* at 3.2, states that the following requirements must be met: a person's presence in the UK must have a settled purpose; their presence must form "part of the regular and habitual mode of your life for the time being"; and the person must have come to the UK voluntarily. While *HMRC6* may well influence HMRC's ordinary residence determinations in tax credits cases, it should be noted that it is concerned with residency questions for the purposes of tax liability. In tax credits cases, HMRC's Tax Credits Manual provides that, in determining ordinary residence for tax credits purposes, officials should use the guidance in TCM0128100, which states that the issue is whether "residence here has been adopted voluntarily for settled purposes as part of the regular order of their life for the time being". In contrast to *HMRC6*, which expects a person to have `come to the UK' voluntarily, TCM0128100 states that "a customer who is in the UK as a result of their deportation, expulsion or other removal by compulsion of law from another country should automatically be treated as ordinarily residing in the UK".

In practice, problems will usually arise in the following situations:

(1) When someone who has been ordinarily resident in the UK goes overseas: the usual issue here will be that the claimant is no longer as a matter of fact "in" the UK to claim child tax credit for any children. Subject to the temporary absence rule in reg.4, and the rules for Crown servants in regs 5 and 6, the claimant will cease to qualify for tax credits. However, if the person (or one of two joint claimants leaving together) returns often enough to remain "present", then it will be a question of fact whether the claimant is ordinarily resident despite the overseas link. Where one of two joint claimants goes overseas and the other does not, the claim should become a single claim.

(2) When someone arrives in the UK: the first practical requirement for working tax credit purposes is that the claimant has a job. If he or she has come to the UK to work and that work is likely to last at least three years, then current Revenue practice is to treat the person as ordinarily resident here on arrival. The position of the worker whose work here may not last that period but who has rights under EU law as a worker is protected by reg.3(4). It is suggested that if the person is accepted as ordinarily resident under either rule for working tax credit purposes then he or she should also be accepted as able to claim child tax credit as well. There will also be a practical argument in other cases that if the claimant is treated as liable to UK income tax, then he or she will expect UK tax credits. However, the liability to income tax may arise on residence alone before the individual becomes ordinarily resident in the UK.

(3) When someone has strong links with the UK and another state: there may be ordinary residence in both states. This will be a question of fact. Unlike regs 5 and 6 below, this regulation does not deal expressly with partners making joint claims (with the limited exception of reg.3(7B)). The position is clear from s.3 of the Act. A couple must make a joint claim if both are "in" the UK. If one of the couple is not present or ordinarily resident here, then only the other partner can make the claim. But this will have the effect of excluding the non-resident partner's income from the income calculation. It may therefore be in the interests of some claimants for child tax credit to claim, say, that the mother is present and ordinarily resident, but that the father is not. This is not now a concern for income tax purposes as all married couples are assessed to income tax separately.

(SI 2003/654 reg.3) (as amended)

Paragraphs (2) and (3)
Paragraph (2) relates to regs 5 and 6 below. Paragraph (3) deals with the problem that some of these individuals might not otherwise be regarded as ordinarily resident and so would be deprived of claims to either working tax credit or child tax credit. But see also the Tax Credits (Immigration) Regulations 2003 (SI 2003/653).

2.484

Paragraphs (4) to (5B)
Paragraphs (4) to (4C) provide a test for working tax credit, while paragraphs (5) to (5B) provide a test for child tax credit. They are different tests and it is important that they be considered separately.

2.485

Paragraph (4) makes express reference to legislation establishing the rights of freedom of movement of citizens of the European Union and domestic legislation intended to give effect to those rights. For a full discussion of the relevant EU law see Pt 3 of Vol.III of this work.

Paragraphs (4A) to (4C) were added as from the date on which the UK ceased to be subject to the law of the European Union (30 December 2020). They deem certain Irish citizens and UK nationals, who reside in Ireland, to be ordinarily resident in the UK, for working tax credit purposes, without needing to demonstrate that they are exercising rights as a worker or have the right to reside in the UK. The most obvious cases falling within paragraphs (4A) to (4C) are those of Irish resident-citizens who work in Northern Ireland and British nationals who reside in the Republic of Ireland but work in Northern Ireland

The rights of citizens of the European Union to claim child tax credit arise separately (and also separately from those for child benefit). Again, for full discussion see Vol.III.

It was intended to make para.(5) lapse on May 1, 2006 (see SI 2004/1243 reg.1), but the lapsing provision was itself revoked by SI 2006/766 reg.4, so continuing this paragraph in force without a time limit. Where a claimant claims universal credit during a tax year in which he or she was entitled to a tax credit, reg.5(a) applies as if the words "under regulation 11 or 12 of the Tax Credits (Claims and Notifications) Regulations 2002 or otherwise" were omitted. See para.38 of the Schedule to the Universal Credit (Transitional Provisions) Regulations 2014 (SI 2014/1230).

Paragraphs (5) to (5B) operate as follows:

- para. (5) retains, in material respects, its pre-Brexit wording so that it disentitles a child tax credit claimant (through deeming him/her not to be in the UK) where s/he either has no right to reside in the UK (para. (5)(b)) or whose right to reside is, briefly, a derivative right to reside attained through the claimant being the primary carer of a British citizen (para. (5)(c));
- para. (5A) disapplies para. (5)(c) where a person lawfully working in the UK is a national of a State with which the European Union has concluded an equal treatment agreement under Article 217 of the Treaty on the Functioning of the European Union but only in the case of child tax credits claims made before 1 January 2021. Para. (5A) also disapplies para. (5)(c), but without limiting its application to claims for child tax credit made before 1 January 2021, in respect of nationals of States with whom the UK has entered into an agreement in place of an agreement under Article 217, which may include the February 2019 Social Security Convention entered into between the Government of the United Kingdom and Northern Ireland and the Government of Ireland (for details of that Convention see the notes to the Child Tax Credit Regulations 2002 above in this volume);
- para. (5B) contains a further disapplication of para. (5)(c) but is limited in its application to certain family members of a relevant person of Northern Ireland.

The test, including its application to child tax credit, was considered in a series of decisions taken by a Tribunal of Commissioners as decisions *CIS/3573/2005, CPC/2920/2005, CIS/2559/2005* and *CIS/2680/2005*. The Tribunal decided that the test of "right to reside" is a general test applying to all potentially within its scope.

Further, the test is not met by reference to the other tests of lawful residence or actual habitual residence. Rather, it reflects the provisions of EU Council Directive 90/364 that Member States:

> "shall grant the right of residence to nationals of member states who do not enjoy this right under other provisions of Community Law ... provided they ... have sufficient resources to avoid becoming a burden on the social assistance system of the host member state during the period of their residence".

The Court of Appeal has dismissed an appeal against the decision of the Tribunal of Commissioners in *Abdirahman v Secrtary of State for Work and Pensions* [2007] EWCA Civ 657 *(R(IS)8/07)*; see further the commentary in Vol.II.

In *Zalewska v Department for Social Development* [2008] UKHL 67 the House of Lords upheld a decision of the Northern Ireland Court of Appeal and Social Security Commissioner that the use of the derogation from European Union law under which the test of "right to reside" was adopted was itself compatible with European Union law. The House of Lords also affirmed the decision of the Commissioner that, notwithstanding that the appellant in that case, who was Polish, was a worker, the Commissioner was correct in law in holding that the law permitted refusal of income support to the appellant in the circumstances of the case. The worker registration scheme was not disproportionate to its legitimate aims. The Commissioner's decision is C6/05-06(*IS*).

HMRC guidance about the operation of the "right to reside" rule is included in its detailed *Child and Working Tax Credits and Child Benefit: residence rules guidance for intermediaries.* See *http://www.hmrc.gov.uk/taxcredits/residence-rules.htm.* Following the approach of the Tribunal of Commissioners, this states that groups subject to the "right to reside" must have "sufficient resources not to become a burden on the social assistance system of the UK". This may be expected to exclude most of those claiming or seeking to claim income support, jobseeker's allowance, or housing benefit. But it is suggested that it cannot exclude all claimants from elsewhere in the European Economic Area for child tax credit, given that the income text for child tax credit is such that it is payable to all but the highest earning parents responsible for children. Nor does it exclude those who do have direct rights under European law.

For the modifications to reg.3(5) where a person's entitlement to a tax credit was interrupted by the making of a claim for universal credit, see reg.12A of, and Sch.1 to, the Universal Credit (Transitional Provisions) Regulations 2014 (SI 2014/1230), below in this volume.

2.486 *Paragraphs (6) and (7)*
Paragraph (6) enacts the general rule that a person must have been living in the UK for 3 month before claiming child tax credit. A range of exceptions to the general rule are provided for by paragraph (7).

Paragraphs (7A) to (7D)
These paragraphs deem certain claimants residing in Ireland to be ordinarily resident in the UK, for child tax credit purposes, and its presumed purpose is to meet the UK Government's obligations under the February 2019 Social Security Convention agreed with the Government of Ireland.

Persons temporarily absent from the United Kingdom

2.487 **4.**—(1) A person who is ordinarily resident in the United Kingdom and is temporarily absent from the United Kingdom shall be treated as being in the United Kingdom during the first—
  (a) 8 weeks of any period of absence; or
  (b) 12 weeks of any period of absence where that period of absence, or any extension to that period of absence, is in connection with—
    (i) the treatment of his illness or physical or mental disability;

(SI 2003/654 reg.4) (as amended)

(ii) the treatment of his partner's illness or physical or mental disability;
(iii) the death of a person who, immediately prior to the date of death, was his partner;
(iv) the death, or the treatment of the illness or physical or mental disability, of a child or qualifying young person for whom either he or his partner is, or both of them are, responsible; or
(v) the death, or the treatment of the illness or physical or mental disability, of his or his partner's relative.

(2) A person is temporarily absent from the United Kingdom if at the beginning of the period of absence his absence is unlikely to exceed 52 weeks.

DEFINITIONS

"ordinarily resident"—see reg.3.
"partner"—see reg.2.

GENERAL NOTE

This regulation deals with the practical application of the requirement that a claimant be "in" the UK as well as ordinarily resident here. It adopts the approach long used in social security law of ignoring temporary absence. See, for comparison, Income Support (General) Regulations 1987 (SI 1987/1967) reg.4. The current rule appears reasonably generous as it ignores the first eight weeks of "any" period of absence. Presumably, a claimant could make a visit back to the UK before the end of eight (or 12) weeks to re-establish presence before starting a second period of absence, and so on. On the facts, this would also avoid the 52-week rule in para.(2). On the wording, it would seem that the 52-week rule reapplies at the beginning of each period of absence.

In *GC v HMRC (TC)* [2014] UKUT 251 (AAC) Judge Rowland allowed an appeal by an appellant who was refused working tax credit while working in Spain. The appellant had returned to the United Kingdom for periods during the year. In that context, no attention had been paid to the provisions of reg.4 of these Regulations allowing a person to continue to be regarded as being in the UK during the first eight weeks of a temporary absence. These should be considered to see if the appellant continued to be ordinarily resident in the United Kingdom. Further, there was nothing in the Working Tax Credit (Entitlement and Maximum Rate) Regulations 2002 (SI 2002/2005) requiring that the work had to be in the UK.

In *GL v HMRC* [2023] UKUT 100 (AAC); [2023] 1 W.L.R. 4481, Deputy Upper Tribunal Judge Buley KC held that it was irrelevant, for the purposes of reg.4, that a person had been prevented from returning to the UK by Coronavirus-related foreign travel restrictions. The residency rules for certain social security benefits were amended (relaxed) to take account of Coronavirus-related travel restrictions but no similar amendment was made to reg.4. Accordingly, a person whose absence from the UK exceeded eight weeks due to pandemic-related restrictions could not, upon returning to the UK, be considered temporarily absent from the UK under reg.4. However, HMRC accepted before the Upper Tribunal that child tax credit was a "family benefit" within EU Regulation 833/2004, so that, for the purposes of art.11 of that Regulation, the claimant remained subject to the legislation of the UK while absent in Spain. HMRC further conceded that Regulation 883/2004 required "the UK to treat a claimant's presence in another member state as though it were presence in the UK which prevents [application of] the domestic temporary absence conditions". Judge Buley accepted HMRC's concessions but emphasised that he was doing so without hearing argument on the point.

Judge Buley in *GL* also expressed doubt as to the correctness of HMRC's argument that, in principle, they had discretion, in an exceptional case, to continue to pay tax credit to a person who, falling outside reg.4, was not in the UK (the Tax Credits Act 2002 s.3(3) provides that a claim for a tax credit may be made by a

2.488

person "in the United Kingdom"). The judge suspected that HMRC may have mistakenly assumed that a recognised extra-statutory discretion, applicable in connection with HMRC's tax collection functions, was also applicable in connection with HMRC's tax credits functions. HMRC's case seemed to have overlooked the "fundamental problem" that their statutory powers to pay tax credits do not permit payment of a tax credit to a person who fails to satisfy the statutory conditions.

See reg.6 below for a modification of this regulation as it applies to the partners of Crown servants employed overseas. One problem with these provisions in practice is that they allow an individual to be treated as remaining in the UK, but they do not allow the individual to be treated as continuing to work here. One result is that although the main elements of tax credits remain payable, an individual going overseas for a short period can retain WTC but lose the childcare credit. This parallels reg.24 of the Child Benefit (General) Regulations 2006 (para.3.35, below) which makes similar provisions.

Crown servants posted overseas

2.489

5.—(1) A Crown servant posted overseas shall be treated as being in the United Kingdom.

(2) A Crown servant posted overseas is a person performing overseas the duties of any office or employment under the Crown in right of the United Kingdom—
  (a) who is, or was, immediately prior to his posting or his first of consecutive postings, ordinarily resident in the United Kingdom; or
  (b) who, immediately prior to his posting or his first of consecutive postings, was in the United Kingdom in connection with that posting.

GENERAL NOTE

2.490

This regulation and reg.6 protect the position of British public servants and their partners (and therefore also their children) when working outside the UK. Section 44 of the TCA 2002 removes any doubt about the application of the tax credits scheme to Crown employees. See further reg.30 of the Child Benefit (General) Regulations 2006 (para.3.43, below) which makes similar provisions.

Partners of Crown servants posted overseas

2.491

6.—(1) The partner of a Crown servant posted overseas who is accompanying the Crown servant posted overseas shall be treated as being in the United Kingdom when he is either—
  (a) in the country where the Crown servant is posted; or
  (b) absent from that country in accordance with regulation 4 as modified by paragraphs (3) and (4).

(2) Regulation 4 applies to the partner of a Crown servant posted overseas with the modifications set out in paragraphs (3) and (4).

(3) Omit the words "ordinarily resident in the United Kingdom and is".

(4) In relation to a partner who is accompanying the Crown servant posted overseas the references to "United Kingdom" in the phrase "temporarily absent from the United Kingdom", in both places where it occurs, shall be construed as references to the country where the Crown servant is posted.

DEFINITIONS

"Crown servant posted overseas"—see reg.5.
"partner"—see reg.2.

(SI 2003/654 reg. 7) (as amended)

Transitional provision—income support and income-based jobseeker's allowance

7.—A person is exempt from the requirement to be ordinarily resident in the United Kingdom (which is set out in regulation 3(1)) in respect of child tax credit on and for three years after the date on which the award of child tax credit is made where—
 (a) the award of child tax credit would be made on or after 6th April 2004;
 (b) immediately before the award of child tax credit is made, he is, or will be on the making of a claim, entitled to any of the amounts in relation to income support and income-based jobseeker's allowance which are described in section 1(3)(d) of the Act; and
 (c) he is a person to which one or more of the following provisions applies—
   (i) paragraph (b) or (c) in the definition of "person from abroad" in regulation 21(3) of the Income Support (General) Regulations 1987;
   (ii) paragraph (b) or (c) in the definition of "person from abroad" in regulation 85(4) of the Jobseeker's Allowance Regulations 1996;
   (iii) paragraph (b) or (c) in the definition of "person from abroad" in regulation 21(3) of the Income Support (General) (Northern Ireland) Regulations 1987;
   (iv) paragraph (b) or (c) in the definition of "person from abroad" in regulation 85(4) of the Jobseeker's Allowance Regulations (Northern Ireland) 1996.

2.492

GENERAL NOTE

This is a narrow three-year transitional provision for child tax credit only. It took effect from or after April 6, 2004—the date when CTC was planned to replace the child additions to income support and jobseeker's allowance. It is limited to:
 (a) claimants receiving either income support or income-based jobseeker's allowance including child additions immediately before the rule comes into effect; but only if
 (b) they are claiming those benefits as refugees or following a grant of exceptional leave to enter or remain in the UK under the Immigration Acts.
It should be read with the Tax Credits (Immigration) Regulations 2003 (SI 2003/653).

2.493

The Tax Credits (Official Error) Regulations 2003

(SI 2003/692)

The Commissioners of Inland Revenue, in exercise of the powers conferred upon them by sections 21 and 65(2), (3), (7) and (9) of the Tax Credits Act 2002 hereby make the following Regulations:

ARRANGEMENT OF REGULATIONS

1. Citation and commencement
2. Interpretation
3. (*Untitled*)

2.494

The Tax Credits (Official Error) Regulations 2003

Citation and commencement

2.495   **1.**—These Regulations may be cited as the Tax Credits (Official Error) Regulations 2003 and shall come into force on 6th April 2003.

Interpretation

2.496   **2.**—(1) In these Regulations—
"the Board" means the Commissioners of Inland Revenue;
"official error" means an error relating to a tax credit made by—
    (a) an officer of the Board;
    (b) an officer of the Department for Work and Pensions;
    (c) an officer of the Department for [² Communities] in Northern Ireland; or
    (d) a person providing services to the Board or to an authority mentioned in paragraph (b) or (c) of this definition, in connection with a tax credit or credits,
to which the claimant, or any of the claimants, or any person acting for him, or any of them, did not materially contribute, excluding any error of law which is shown to have been an error by virtue of a subsequent decision by a "Social Security Commissioner or by a court;"
"Social Security Commissioner" has the meaning given by section 63(13);
[¹ . . .]
(2) In these Regulations, references to a section are to that section of the Tax Credits Act 2002.

AMENDMENTS

1. Tax Credits (Miscellaneous Amendments) Regulations 2010 (SI 2010/751) regs 11 and 12(1) (April 6, 2010).
2. Tax Credits, Child Benefit and Childcare Payments (Miscellaneous Amendments) Regulations 2019 (SI 2019/364) reg.8(2) (March 21, 2019).

GENERAL NOTE

2.497   In *KI v HMRC (TC)* [2023] UKUT 212 (AAC), Upper Tribunal Judge Hemingway rejected the argument that "a failure of an automatic information sharing system between the DWP and HMRC" amounted to an official error for the purposes of the 2003 Regulations. The claimant sought to rely on a failure of the data feed between HMRC and the DWP to argue that his notification to the DWP of a change of circumstances relevant to tax credit entitlement sufficed as notification to HMRC. The claimant's argument was contrary to existing Upper Tribunal authority (*AG v HMRC* [2013] UKUT 530 (AAC)) and, in the absence of a specific legal duty requiring information sharing between the DWP and HMRC, could not succeed.

The double inverted commas at the end of the very last line of the definition of "official error" are a typographical error in the HMSO version of these regulations. Moreover, the definition of Social Security Commissioner has failed to keep up with the amendment to the primary legislation. As a result of para.191(8) of Sch.3 to the Transfer of Tribunal Functions Order 2008 (SI 2008/2833), the definition of that term in s.63(13) of the Tax Credits Act 2002 is confined to the Northern Ireland meaning of the term. The lack of a heading to reg.3 is also unfortunate.

2.498   **3.**—(1) A decision under section 14(1), 15(1), 16(1), 18(1), (5), (6) or (9), 19(3) or 20(1) or (4) may be revised in favour of the person or persons

(SI 2003/692 reg.3)

to whom it relates if it is incorrect by reason of official error, subject to the following paragraphs.

(2) In revising a decision, the officer or person in question need not consider any issue that is not raised by the application for revision by the claimant or claimants or, as the case may be, did not cause him to act on his own initiative.

(3) A decision mentioned in paragraph (1) may be revised at any time not later than five years after [¹ the date of the decision].

AMENDMENT

1. Tax Credits (Miscellaneous Amendments) Regulations 2010 (SI 2010/751) regs 11 and 12(2) (April 6, 2010).

DEFINITIONS

"official error"—see reg.2(1).
"tax year"—see reg.2(1).

GENERAL NOTE

These regulations, made under s.21 of the TCA 2002, provide for decisions under the various specified sections of the Act (see reg.3(1)) to be revised in favour of the claimant(s) if they are incorrect because of "official error". The definition of "official error" in reg.2(1) is identical in all material respects to that which applies in the social security scheme under the Social Security and Child Support (Decisions and Appeals) Regulations 1999 (SI 1999/991) (see reg.1(3) and the commentary in Vol. III of this series). However, whereas a social security decision may be revised on the basis of official error and arrears of benefit paid back to the date of the original claim (SSA 1998 s.9(3) and reg.3(5)(a) of the 1999 Regulations), a claim for tax credits is subject to a time limit of five years after the end of the tax year to which the decision relates (reg.3(3)).

2.499

In *JP v HMRC (TC)* [2013] UKUT 519 (AAC), the Upper Tribunal considered reg.3 of the Regulations in a case where a DWP official assisted a claimant in making a tax credits claim but in doing so omitted a claim for the disability of the claimant's child. Judge Turnbull accepted as correct an HMRC concession that the actions of the DWP official were official actions. However, the error had led to the award decision under s.14 of the 2002 Act. That had been replaced by an entitlement decision under s.18. Following the decision in *CTC/262/2005*, the decision to be considered in the appeal was the s.18 decision, and the relevant question was whether the official error was the cause of that decision. On the facts, and applying a common-sense approach to causation as indicated in *R (Sier) v Cambridge CC HBRB* [2001] EWCA Civ 1523, it was decided that the original official error no longer operated to cause the error in the s.18 decision. The claimant had twice been warned to check the decision and had not done so.

The Tax Credits (Provision of Information) (Functions Relating to Health) Regulations 2003

(SI 2003/731) (AS AMENDED)

The Commissioners of Inland Revenue, in exercise of the powers conferred upon them by sections 65(2) and 67 of, and paragraph 9(2) of Schedule 5 to, the Tax Credits Act 2002, hereby make the following Regulations:

The Tax Credits (Provision of Information) (Functions Relating to Health) Regulations 2003

ARRANGEMENT OF REGULATIONS

2.500
1. Citation and commencement
2. Interpretation
3. Prescribed functions relating to health

Citation and commencement

2.501   **1.**—These Regulations may be cited as the Tax Credits (Provision of Information) (Functions Relating to Health) Regulations 2003 and shall come into force on 6th April 2003.

GENERAL NOTE

2.502   Section 59 of and Sch.5 to the TCA 2002 make provision for the use and disclosure of information relating to claims by and between HMRC and government departments. These regulations prescribe functions for the purposes of para.9 of Sch.5 to the 2002 Act, which enables information relating to tax credits, child benefit or guardian's allowance to be provided by HMRC to the Department of Health, the National Assembly for Wales, the Scottish Ministers, or the Department of Health, Social Services and Public Safety in Northern Ireland for the purposes of such functions relating to health as may be prescribed. These functions are set out in reg.3. Information may also be provided to persons providing services to, or exercising functions on behalf of, those Departments or persons.

These regulations are supplemented by the Tax Credits (Provision of Information) (Functions Relating to Health) (No.2) Regulations 2003 (SI 2003/1650).

Interpretation

2.503   **2.**—In these Regulations—
"child tax credit" shall be construed in accordance with section 8 of the Tax Credits Act 2002;
[¹"couple" has the meaning given by section 3(5A) of the Act;]
"disability element" means the disability element of working tax credit as specified in section 11(3) of the Tax Credits Act 2002;
"family" means—
   (a) in the case of a joint claim for a tax credit under the Tax Credits Act 2002, the [¹. . .] couple by whom the claim is made and any child or qualifying young person for whom at least one of them is responsible, in accordance with regulation 3 of the Child Tax Credit Regulations 2002;
   (b) in the case of a single claim for a tax credit under the Tax Credits Act 2002, the claimant and any child or qualifying young person for whom he is responsible in accordance with regulation 3 of the Child Tax Credit Regulations 2002;
"qualifying family" means a family—
[² (a) that has a relevant income of £16,190 or less, and
   (b) one member of which is a person who—
      (i) is receiving child tax credit, and
      (ii) is not eligible for working tax credit;]
"qualifying young person" has the meaning given by regulation 2(1), read with regulation 5(3) and (4), of the Child Tax Credit Regulations 2002;

(SI 2003/731 reg.2) (as amended)

"relevant income" has the same meaning as in section 7(3) of the Tax Credits Act 2002;
"working tax credit" shall be construed in accordance with section 10 of the Tax Credits Act 2002.

AMENDMENTS

1. Civil Partnership Act 2004 (Tax Credits, etc.) (Consequential Amendments) Order 2005 (SI 2005/2919) art.9(2) (December 5, 2005).
2. Tax Credits (Miscellaneous Amendments) Regulations 2011 (SI 2011/721) reg.4 (April 6, 2011).

Prescribed functions relating to health

3.—The following functions are prescribed for the purposes of paragraph 9 of Schedule 5 to the Tax Credits Act 2002 (provision of information by the Board of Inland Revenue for health purposes)—
   (a) the issue by or on behalf of the Secretary of State, the National Assembly for Wales, the Scottish Ministers or the Department of Health, Social Services, and Public Safety in Northern Ireland of a certificate confirming that the family is a qualifying family;
   (b) verification by or on behalf of the Secretary of State, the National Assembly for Wales, the Scottish Ministers or that Department at any time that a family is a qualifying family at that time;
[¹ (ba) the provision of benefits by or on behalf of the Secretary of State or the Department of Health, Social Services and Public Safety under a scheme established pursuant to section 13 of the Social Security Act 1988(2) or article 13 of the Social Security (Northern Ireland) Order 1988 in so far as such a scheme relates to the health of pregnant women, mothers or children.]
   (c) [¹...]
   (d) [¹...]
   (e) [¹...]

2.504

DEFINITIONS

"family"—see reg.2.
"qualifying family"—see reg.2.

AMENDMENT

1. Tax Credits (Miscellaneous Amendments) Regulations 2011 (SI 2011/721) reg.4 (April 6, 2011).

The Tax Credits (Polygamous Marriages) Regulations 2003

(SI 2003/742) (AS AMENDED)

The Treasury, in exercise of the powers conferred upon them by sections 3(7), 7(8) and (9), 8, 10 to 12, 42, 43 and 65(1), (3), (7) and (9) of the Tax Credits Act 2002, and the Commissioners of Inland Revenue, in exercise of the powers conferred on them by sections 4(1), 6, 24 and 65(2), (3), (7) and (9) of that Act, and of all other powers enabling them in that behalf, hereby make the following Regulations:

The Tax Credits (Polygamous Marriages) Regulations 2003

ARRANGEMENT OF REGULATIONS

2.505
1. Citation, commencement and effect
2. Interpretation
3–21. Modifications to Pt I of the Act for members of polygamous units
22–25. Amendments to the Child Tax Credit Regulations 2002
26–34. Amendments to the Working Tax Credit (Entitlement and Maximum Rate) Regulations 2002
35–47. Amendments to the Tax Credits (Definition and Calculation of Income) Regulations 2002
39–47A. Amendments to the Tax Credits (Claims and Notifications) Regulations 2002
48–50. Amendments to the Tax Credits (Payment by the Board) Regulations 2002
51–52. Amendments to the Tax Credits (Residence) Regulations 2003
53–56. Amendments to the Tax Credits (Immigration) Regulations 2003

INTRODUCTION AND GENERAL NOTE

2.506 These regulations provide alternative language to that of single claims and joint claims, and the associated definitions for single and joint claims, in cases where the claimant is a party to a polygamous marriage. Part I of the TCA 2002 and all relevant regulations are altered to give consistent effect to the policy that all the members of a polygamous marriage, or "unit" as it is called, must jointly claim for and be responsible for any tax credits payable to any of them. This is a different approach from that usually taken for social security benefits purposes, under which polygamous marriages are usually ignored for benefit purposes unless they are in fact monogamous. See the Social Security and Family Allowances (Polygamous Marriages) Regulations 1975 (SI 1975/561) in Vol.I of this work.

Section 43(1) of the TCA 2002 empowers regulations to apply Pt I of that Act to persons who are parties to a polygamous marriage. "Party to a polygamous marriage" is defined by s.43(2) to include any marriage entered into under a law which permits polygamy and under which any party to the marriage has more than one spouse, that is, more than one husband or wife. The drafters have chosen to adopt different language in these Regulations and the amendments made by these Regulations to the TCA 2002 and other regulations. Instead of "polygamous marriage", the term used throughout is "polygamous unit". The significance of this is discussed in reg.2 below.

The remaining regulations give effect to those modifications as necessary within the other regulations implementing the TCA 2002. Any necessary commentary is added to the relevant amended regulation.

Citation, commencement and effect

2.507 **1.**—(1) These Regulations may be cited as the Tax Credits (Polygamous Marriages) Regulations 2003 and shall come into force on 6th April 2003, immediately after the coming into force of the Child Tax Credit (Amendment) Regulations 2003.

(2) Regulations 22 to 56 only have effect in relation to members of polygamous units (and in the case of regulations 35 to 38, former members of such units).

(SI 2003/742 reg.2) (as amended)

Interpretation

2.—In these Regulations—
"the Act" means the Tax Credits Act 2002;
"polygamous couple" means a man and a woman who are married under a law which permits polygamy where—
  (a) they are not separated under a court order or in circumstances in which the separation is likely to be permanent; and
  (b) either of them has an additional spouse;
"polygamous unit" means—
  (a) a polygamous couple; and
  (b) any person who is married to either member of the polygamous couple and who is not separated from that member under a court order or in circumstances in which the separation is likely to be permanent.

GENERAL NOTE

Section 43(2) of the TCA 2002 provides that a person is a party to a polygamous marriage if:
  (a) he or she is a party to a marriage entered into under a law which permits polygamy; and
  (b) he or she has a spouse additional to any other party to the marriage.
The effect of this definition is to limit the scope of the operation of the modifications made under these Regulations to take account also of the definition of "married couple" in s.3(5) of the TCA 2002.

Modifications to Part I of the Act for members of polygamous units

3.—Regulations 4 to 21 prescribe modifications to Part I of the Act so far as it applies to members of polygamous units.

4.—In section 3—
  (a) in subsection (3)(a) after "United Kingdom", insert "(and neither of whom are members of a polygamous unit)";
  (b) after subsection (3)(a) insert—
    "(aa) jointly by the members of a polygamous unit all of whom are aged at least 16 and are in the United Kingdom, or";
  (c) in subsection (3)(b) after "paragraphs (a)", insert "or (aa)";
  (d) after subsection (4)(a), insert—
    "(aa) in the case of a joint claim under subsection (3)(a), if a member of the married or unmarried couple becomes a member of a polygamous unit; and
    (ab) in the case of a joint claim under subsection (3)(aa), if there is any change in the persons who comprise the polygamous unit, and";
  (e) after subsection (6), insert—
    "(6A) In this Part 'polygamous unit' has the meaning given by regulation 2 of the Tax Credits (Polygamous Marriages) Regulations 2003.";
  (f) in subsection (8), in the definition of "joint claim", after "para.(a)" insert "or para.(aa)".

5.—In section 4(1)(g)—
  (a) for "member of a married couple or an unmarried couple", substitute "or more members of a polygamous unit";
  (b) for "of the married couple or unmarried couple", substitute "or members".

6.—In section 7(2), for "either" substitute "any";

7.—In section 8(1), for "either or both" substitute "any or all".

8.—In [³ both section 9(2)(b) and (3A)], for "either or both" substitute "any or all".

9.—In section 10—
(a) in subsection (1), for "either or both" substitute "any or all";
(b) in subsection (3), for "either" wherever it appears substitute "any".

10.—In section 11—
(a) in subsection (3), for "either or both" substitute "any or all";
(b) in subsection (6)(a), for "either of the persons or the two" substitute "any of the persons or all";
(c) in subsection (6)(b), for "married couple or unmarried couple" substitute "polygamous unit";
(d) omit subsection (6)(c);
(e) in both subsection (6)(d) and (e), for "either or both" substitute "any or all".

11.—In both section 12(3) and (4)(a), for "either or both" substitute "any or all".

12.—In section 14(2)(a), for "either or both" substitute "any or all".

13.—In section 16(3)(a), for "either or both" substitute "any or all".

14.—In section 17(10)(b)—
(a) for "member of a married couple or an unmarried couple", substitute "or more members of a polygamous unit";
(b) for "married couple or unmarried couple", substitute "or members".

15.—In section 18(10), for "either or both" substitute "any or all".

16.—In section 19—
(a) in subsection (2)(a), for "either or both" substitute "any or all";
(b) in subsection (4)(a), for "either" substitute "any" and for "both" substitute "more than one";
(c) in subsection (9), for "either" substitute "any".

17.—In section 20(4)(b), for "either" (wherever it appears) substitute "any".

18.—In section 24(2)—
(a) for "married couple or an unmarried couple", substitute "polygamous unit";
(b) for "whichever of them" substitute "one or more of those persons as".

19.—In section 29(4), for "either or both" substitute "any or all".

20.—In section 31(2)—
(a) after "another" insert "or others";
(b) for "unless subsection (3) applies" substitute "or each of them unless subsection (3) applies to the person in question".

21.—In section 37(1), for "either or both" (in each place they appear) substitute "any or all".

Amendments to the Child Tax Credit Regulations 2002

2.511 22.—Amend the Child Tax Credit Regulations 2002 (for members of polygamous units only) as follows.

23.—In regulation 2(1)—
(a) for the definition of "joint claim", substitute the following definition—
"'joint claim' means a claim under section 3(3)(aa) of the Act, as inserted by regulation 4(b) of the Tax Credits (Polygamous Marriages) Regulations 2003;";

(b) insert at the appropriate place the following definition—"'polygamous unit' has the meaning in the Tax Credits (Polygamous Marriages) Regulations 2003;";

[⁴ (c) in the definition of "step-parent", in paragraph (a) only, for "couple, the other" substitute "polygamous unit, another"].

24.—In regulation 3(1), in rule 2.1., for "married couple or unmarried couple" in each place it appears substitute "polygamous unit".

25.—In regulation 7—
(a) in paragraph (1)(b), for "married couple or unmarried couple" substitute "polygamous unit";
(b) in [⁵ both paragraph (2)(a) and (b)(ii)], for "either or both" substitute "any or all";
[⁵ (c) in paragraph (2A) for "either or both" substitute "any or all".]

[⁶ **25A.**—In regulation 9—
(a) [⁸ [⁹ in paragraphs (1), (3) and (5) for "either or both" (in each place they appear) substitute "any or all";]]
(b) [⁹ . . .];
(c) in paragraph (7) for "either or both" substitute "any or all".

25B.—In regulation 10(c) for "either or both" substitute "any or all".

25C.—In regulation 11 for "either or both" (in each place they appear) substitute "any or all";

25D.—In regulation 13—
(a) in paragraph (14)(a) for "either" substitute "any";
(b) in paragraph (15) for "couple" substitute "polygamous unit".

25E.—In regulation 14(3)(a) for "either or both" substitute "any or all"].

Amendments to the Working Tax Credit (Entitlement and Maximum Rate) Regulations 2002

26.—Amend the Working Tax Credit (Entitlement and Maximum Rate) Regulations 2002 (for members of polygamous units only) as follows.

27.—In regulation 2(1)—
(a) for the definition of "joint claim", substitute the following definition—" 'joint claim' means a claim under section 3(3)(aa) of the Act (as inserted by regulation 4(b) of the Tax Credits (Polygamous Marriages) Regulations 2003);";
(b) insert at the appropriate place the following definition—" 'polygamous unit' has the meaning in the Tax Credits (Polygamous Marriages) Regulations 2003;".

28.—In regulation 3(3)—
(a) for "both members of the couple satisfy", substitute "more than one member of the polygamous unit satisfies"; and
(b) for "two such elements", substitute "one such element for each of them that satisfies those conditions".

[² **29.**—In regulation 4(1) in the third variation of the Second Condition—
(a) in the introduction, for "that person's partner" substitute "any other member of the polygamous unit"; and
(b) in paragraph (a)—
   (i) for "couple" (in both places) substitute "polygamous unit"; and
   (ii) for "partner" substitute "member of the unit".]

The Tax Credits (Polygamous Marriages) Regulations 2003

30.—In regulation 10(2)—
(a) in sub-paragraph (c), for "couple" substitute "members of the polygamous unit";
(b) in sub-paragraph (d), for "couple" substitute "unit".

31.—In regulation 11—
(a) in paragraph (1), after "element" insert "(and an additional such element for each member of the polygamous unit exceeding two in number)";
(b) in paragraph (2)(c), for "neither of the claimants" substitute "no claimant";
(c) in paragraph (4), in the words preceding sub-paragraph (a), after "adult element" insert "for any claimant";
(d) in paragraph (4)(a), for "neither claimant" substitute "none of the claimants"; and
(e) in paragraph (4)(b), for "one claimant" substitute "the claimant in question".

32.—In regulation 13—
(a) omit paragraph (1)(a);
(b) in paragraph (1)(b), for "married or unmarried couple where both" substitute "polygamous unit where at least two of them";
(c) in paragraph (1)(c), for the words preceding paragraph (i) substitute "is a member or are members of a polygamous unit where at least one member is engaged in qualifying remunerative work and at least one other".
(d) in paragraph (4), for "the other member of a couple" substitute "another member of the polygamous unit";
(e) in paragraph (5), for "the other member or his partner" substitute "him or another member of the polygamous unit".

33.—In regulation 14—
(a) in paragraph (1), for "either or both" substitute "any or all";
(b) in paragraph (1B), for "either or both" substitute "any or all";
(c) in paragraph (5), for "a partner or by a partner" substitute "another member of the same polygamous unit or".

34.—In regulation 20—
(a) in paragraph (1), for "single claimant or to a couple" substitute "polygamous unit";
(b) omit paragraph (1)(c)(i);
(c) in paragraph (1)(c)(ii), for "a couple either or both" substitute "the members of a polygamous unit, any or all of whom";
(d) in paragraph (1)(c)(iii), for "a couple" substitute "the members of a polygamous unit";
(e) omit paragraph (1)(e);
(f) omit paragraph (1)(f)(i);
(g) in paragraph (1)(f)(ii), for "couple" substitute "polygamous unit".

Amendments to the Tax Credits (Definition and Calculation of Income) Regulations 2002

2.513   35.—Amend the Tax Credits (Definition and Calculation of Income) Regulations 2002 (for members or former members of polygamous units only) as follows.

36.—In regulation 2 (interpretation)—
(a) in paragraph (2), in the definition of "family" for "married or unmarried couple" substitute "members of the polygamous unit";
(b) in paragraph (2), insert at the appropriate places the following definitions—
"'joint claim' means a claim under section 3(3)(aa) of the Act, as inserted by regulation 4(b) of the Tax Credits (Polygamous Marriages) Regulations 2003; "polygamous unit" has the meaning in the Tax Credits (Polygamous Marriages) Regulations 2003;";
(c) in paragraph (4)(a), for the words from "a claimant's spouse" to the end substitute "another member of the same polygamous unit";
(d) in paragraph (4)(b), for the words from "claimant's former spouse" to the end substitute "person who was formerly a member with the claimant of the same polygamous unit".

37.—In regulation 3(7), (calculation of income of claimant)—
(a) in sub-paragraph (b), for "either or both" substitute "any or all";
(b) in sub-paragraph (c), for "either or both" substitute "any or all".

38.—In regulation 4(1) (employment income), in the words succeeding sub-para.(k), for "either" substitute "any".

Amendments to the Tax Credits (Claims and Notifications) Regulations 2002

39.—Amend the Tax Credits (Claims and Notifications) Regulations 2002 (for members of polygamous units only) as follows.

40.—In regulation 2 (interpretation)—
(a) for the definition of "joint claim" substitute the following definition—
" 'joint claim', means a claim under section 3(3)(aa) of the Act, as inserted by regulation 4(b) of the Tax Credits (Polygamous Marriages) Regulations 2003;";
(b) insert at the appropriate place the following definition—
"'polygamous unit' has the meaning in the Tax Credits (Polygamous Marriages) Regulations 2003;".

41.—In regulation 11(2), for "both" substitute "all of the".

42.—In regulation 13—
(a) in paragraph (1), for the words from "one member" to the end substitute "one or more members of a polygamous unit is to be treated as also made by the other member or members of that unit";
(b) in paragraph (2)—
   (i) for "member of a married couple or an unmarried couple", substitute "or more members of a polygamous unit";
   (ii) for "both members of the couple", substitute "all the members of the unit".

43.—In regulation 15—
(a) in paragraph (3) for the words from "only one" to the end, substitute "one or more members of a polygamous unit die, the other member or members of the unit may proceed with the claim in the name or names of the person or persons who have died, as well as in their own name or names";
(b) in paragraph (4), for "both" (in each place it appears) substitute "all of".

44.—In regulation 16—
(a) in paragraph (1), for the words from "member of a" to the end, substitute "or more members of a polygamous unit die and the other member or members of the unit wish to make a joint claim for a tax credit";
(b) for paragraph (2), substitute—
"(2) The survivor or survivors may make and proceed with the claim in the name of the member or members who have died as well as in his or their own names.;"
(c) in paragraph (3)(a)—
(i) for "married couple or unmarried couple", substitute "polygamous unit";
(ii) add at the end "(or the earliest such date if more than one)".

45.—In regulation 23(2), for "either member of the married couple or unmarried couple" substitute "any member of the polygamous unit".

46.—In regulation 30(2), for "either" (in each place it appears) substitute "any".

47.—In regulation 31(2)(a), for "either" substitute "any".

[¹**47A.**—In regulation 34(3)—
(a) for "one of two joint claimants" substitute "any member of a polygamous unit"; and
(b) for "both" (in each place where it occurs) substitute "all".]

Amendments to the Tax Credits (Payment by the Board) Regulations 2002

48.—Amend the Tax Credits (Payments by the Board) Regulations 2002 (for members of polygamous units only) as follows.

49.—In regulation 2 (interpretation)—
(a) omit the definitions of "married couple" and "unmarried couple";
(b) insert at the appropriate place the following definition—
" 'polygamous unit' has the meaning in the Tax Credits (Polygamous Marriages) Regulations 2003;".

50.—In regulation 3—
(a) in the heading, for "couple" substitute "polygamous unit";
(b) for paragraphs (2) to (6) substitute—
"(2) There shall be established, for each particular child or qualifying young person for whom any or all of the members of the polygamous unit is or are responsible—
(a) the member of that unit who is (for the time being) identified by all the members of the unit as the main carer for that child or qualifying young person; or
(b) in default of such a member, the member of that unit who appears to the Board to be the main carer for that child or qualifying young person.

(3) The individual element [⁷, and any disability element,] of child tax credit for any child or qualifying young person shall be paid to the main carer of that child or qualifying young person.

(4) The family element of child tax credit for any polygamous unit shall be divided (pro rata) by the number of children and qualifying young persons for whom any or all of the members of that unit is or are responsible, and the proportion so attributable to each such child or qualifying

young person shall be paid to the main carer of that child or qualifying young person.

(5) Any child care element of working tax credit shall be divided (pro rata) by the number of children referred to in paragraph (2) in respect of whom relevant child care charges are paid, and the proportion so attributable to each such child shall be paid to the main carer of that child.

(6) In this regulation—

"child" has the meaning given by the Child Tax Credit Regulations 2002;

"qualifying young person" has the meaning given by those Regulations; and

"relevant child care charges" has the meaning given by regulation 14(1) of the Working Tax Credit (Entitlement and Maximum Rate) Regulations 2002."

Amendments to the Tax Credits (Residence) Regulations 2003

51.—Amend the Tax Credits (Residence) Regulations 2003 (for members of polygamous units only) as follows.

52.—In regulation 2 (Interpretation)—
(a) in the definition of "partner", for the words from "married" to the end, substitute "polygamous unit, any other member of that unit";
(b) insert at the appropriate place the following definition—" 'polygamous unit' has the meaning in the Tax Credits (Polygamous Marriages) Regulations 2003;".

Amendments to the Tax Credits (Immigration) Regulations 2003

53.—Amend the Tax Credits (Immigration) Regulations 2003 (for members of polygamous units only) as follows.

54.—In regulation 2 (Interpretation)—
(a) for the definition of "joint claim", substitute the following definition—"joint claim" means a claim under section 3(3)(aa) of the Act, as inserted by regulation 4(b) of the "Tax Credits (Polygamous Marriages) Regulations 2003";
(b) insert at the appropriate place the following definition—"polygamous unit" has the meaning in the "Tax Credits (Polygamous Marriages) Regulations 2003;".

55.—In regulation 3(2)—
(a) for the words from "married couple" to "and the other", substitute "polygamous unit is a person subject to immigration control and any other";
(b) in sub-paragraph (b), for "couple" substitute "unit".

56.—In regulation 4(1) (modifications to the Tax Credits Act 2002), add at the end "(which, in the case of a claim by the members of a polygamous unit, are subject to the modifications made by regulations 4 to 21 of the Tax Credits (Polygamous Marriages) Regulations 2003)".

AMENDMENTS

1. Tax Credits (Miscellaneous Amendments) Regulations 2004 (SI 2004/762) reg.19 (April 6, 2004).
2. Tax Credits (Miscellaneous Amendments) Regulations 2012 (SI 2012/848) reg.9 (April 6, 2012).
3. Child Tax Credit (Amendment) Regulations 2017 (SI 2017/387) reg.7 (April 6, 2017).

4. Child Tax Credit (Amendment) Regulations 2017 (SI 2017/387) reg.8 (April 6, 2017).
5. Child Tax Credit (Amendment) Regulations 2017 (SI 2017/387) reg.9 (April 6, 2017).
6. Child Tax Credit (Amendment) Regulations 2017 (SI 2017/387) reg.10 (April 6, 2017).
7. Child Tax Credit (Amendment) Regulations 2017 (SI 2017/387) reg.11 (April 6, 2017).
8. Child Tax Credit (Amendment) Regulations 2018 (SI 2018/1130) reg.6 (November 28, 2018).
9. Tax Credits, Child Benefit and Childcare Payments (Miscellaneous Amendments) Regulations 2019 (SI 2019/364) reg.9(2) (March 21, 2019).

The Tax Credits (Provision of Information) (Functions Relating to Health) (No.2) Regulations 2003

(SI 2003/1650)

The Commissioners of Inland Revenue, in exercise of the powers conferred upon them by sections 65(2) and 67 of, and paragraph 9 of Schedule 5 to the Tax Credits Act 2002 hereby make the following Regulations:

ARRANGEMENT OF REGULATIONS

2.518
1. Citation, commencement and extent
2. Prescribed functions relating to health

GENERAL NOTE

2.519   These regulations supplement the Tax Credits (Provision of Information) (Functions Relating to Health) Regulations 2003 (SI 2003/731).

Citation, commencement and extent

2.520   **1.**—(1) These Regulations may be cited as the Tax Credits (Provision of Information) (Functions Relating to Health) (No.2) Regulations 2003 and shall come into force on 17th July 2003.

(2) These Regulations do not extend to Northern Ireland.

Prescribed functions relating to health

2.521   **2.**—(1) The function specified in paragraph (2) is prescribed for the purposes of paragraph 9 of Schedule 5 to the Tax Credits Act 2002 (provision of information by the Board of Inland Revenue for health purposes).

(2) The function specified in this paragraph is the conduct, by a person providing services to the Secretary of State and the Scottish Ministers, of a survey of the mental health of persons in Great Britain who are under the age of 17 on 1st September 2003.

(3) Nothing in these Regulations limits the operation of the Tax Credits (Provision of Information Relating to Health) Regulations 2003.

(SI 2003/2041)

The Tax Credits (Provision of Information) (Function Relating to Employment and Training) Regulations 2003

(SI 2003/2041)

The Commissioners of Inland Revenue, in exercise of the powers conferred upon them by sections 65(2) and 67 of, and paragraph 5(2) of Schedule 5 to, the Tax Credits Act 2002, hereby make the following Regulations:

ARRANGEMENT OF REGULATIONS

1. Citation, commencement and extent
2. Prescribed function relating to employment and training

GENERAL NOTE

These regulations, made under para.5 of Sch.5 to the Tax Credits Act 2002, enable information relating to tax credits, child benefit or guardian's allowance to be provided by HMRC to the Secretary of State for the purposes of the operation of the Employment Retention and Advancement Scheme established under s.2 of the Employment and Training Act 1973.

Citation, commencement and extent

1.—(1) These Regulations may be cited as the Tax Credits (Provision of Information) (Function Relating to Employment and Training) Regulations 2003 and shall come into force on 29th August 2003.

(2) These Regulations do not extend to Northern Ireland.

Prescribed function relating to employment and training

2.—(1) The function specified in paragraph (2) is prescribed for the purposes of paragraph 5 of Schedule 5 to the Tax Credits Act 2002 (provision of information by the Board of Inland Revenue for employment and training purposes).

(2) The function specified in this paragraph is the operation of the Employment Retention and Advancement Scheme, that is to say the scheme for assisting persons to improve their job retention or career advancement, established by the Secretary of State under section 2 of the Employment and Training Act 1973.

The Tax Credits Act 2002 (Child Tax Credit) (Transitional Provisions) Order 2003

(SI 2003/2170)

The Treasury, in exercise of the powers conferred upon them by section 62(2) of the Tax Credits Act 2002, make the following Order:

Tax Credits Act 2002 (Child Tax Credit) (Transitional Provisions) Order 2003

ARRANGEMENT OF ARTICLES

1. Citation and commencement
2. Transitional provision

GENERAL NOTE

Section 1(3)(d) of the Tax Credits Act 2002 provides for the abolition of various component elements of the applicable amount for the purposes of income support and income-based jobseeker's allowance (namely the child allowances, family premium, disabled child premium and enhanced disability premium for a child or young person). This Order makes transitional provision in connection with the introduction of child tax credit, but only for pensioners formerly in receipt of the minimum income guarantee in income support. The Order thus applies to persons who were in receipt of income support, were aged not less than 60 and were responsible for a child, throughout the period beginning on August 22, 2003 and ending on September 28, 2003 (art.2(1)). In such a case a person is deemed to have made a claim for child tax credit (a) on August 22, 2003 for the purpose of enabling a decision to be made by HMRC on the claim, and (b) on the first day of the first benefit week beginning on or after September 29, 2003 for all other purposes, e.g. as regards payment (art.2(2)). This Order is thus associated with the introduction of state pension credit as from October 2003.

Citation and commencement

1.—This Order may be cited as the Tax Credits Act 2002 (Child Tax Credit) (Transitional Provisions) Order 2003 and shall come into force on 22nd August 2003.

Transitional provision

2.—(1) This article applies in the case of a person who throughout the period beginning on 22nd August 2003 and ending on 28th September 2003 is—
  (a) in receipt of income support;
  (b) aged not less than 60; and
  (c) responsible for a child (within the meaning of regulation 3 of the Child Tax Credit Regulations 2002).

(2) Where this article applies to a person, he shall be treated as having made a claim for child tax credit in respect of the child for whom he is responsible as mentioned in paragraph (1)(c) of this article—
  (a) on 22nd August 2003 for the purposes of enabling the Board to make an initial decision on the claim; and
  (b) on the first day of the first benefit week in relation to income support beginning on or after 29th September 2003 for all other purposes.

(3) In paragraph (2) "benefit week" has the same meaning—
  (a) in relation to a person in Great Britain, as it bears in regulation 2(1) of the Income Support (General) Regulations 1987; and
  (b) in relation to a person in Northern Ireland, as it bears in regulation 2(1) of the Income Support (General) Regulations (Northern Ireland) 1987.

(SI 2003/3308)

The Tax Credits (Provision of Information) (Evaluation and Statistical Studies) Regulations 2003

(SI 2003/3308)

The Commissioners of Inland Revenue, in exercise of the powers conferred upon them by sections 65(2) and 67 of, and paragraph 4(2) of Schedule 5 to, the Tax Credits Act 2002 make the following Regulations:

Citation, commencement and extent

1.—(1) These Regulations may be cited as the Tax Credits (Provision of Information) (Evaluation and Statistical Studies) Regulations 2003 and shall come into force on 9th January 2004.

(2) These Regulations do not extend to Northern Ireland.

Purposes for which information may be provided

2.—The purposes of conducting evaluation and statistical studies in relation to—
(a) the education of children and young people under the age of 17; and
(b) the provision and use of child care,
are prescribed under paragraph 4 of Schedule 5 to the Tax Credits Act 2002 (provision of information by the Board of Inland Revenue for evaluation and statistical studies).

Here "child care" means any care provided for a child whether or not of a description prescribed for any purpose under the Act.

The Tax Credits (Provision of Information) (Evaluation and Statistical Studies) (Northern Ireland) Regulations 2004

(SI 2004/1414)

The Commissioners of Inland Revenue, in exercise of the powers conferred upon them by sections 65(2) and 67 of, and paragraph 4(2) of Schedule 5 to, the Tax Credits Act 2002 make the following Regulations:

Citation, commencement and extent

1.—These Regulations may be cited as the Tax Credits (Provision of Information) (Evaluation and Statistical Studies) (Northern Ireland) Regulations 2004, shall come into force on 14th June 2004 and extend only to Northern Ireland.

Purposes for which information may be provided

2.—The purposes of conducting evaluation and statistical studies about community relations, education and employment of persons in Northern Ireland under the age of 18, are prescribed under paragraph 4 of Schedule

5 to the Tax Credits Act 2002 (provision of information by the Board of Inland Revenue for evaluation and statistical studies).

The Tax Credits (Provision of Information) (Functions Relating to Health) (Scotland) Regulations 2004

(SI 2004/1895 (S.6))

The Commissioners of Inland Revenue, in exercise of the powers conferred upon them by sections 65(2) and 67 of, and paragraph 9 of Schedule 5 to, the Tax Credits Act 2002, make the following Regulations:

Citation, commencement and extent

2.533   1.—These Regulations may be cited as the Tax Credits (Provision of Information) (Functions Relating to Health) (Scotland) Regulations 2004, shall come into force on 11th August 2004 and extend only to Scotland.

Purpose for which information may be provided

2.534   2.—(1) The purpose of conducting surveys of the health of children and young people under the age of 17 and their families, by the Scottish Ministers or persons providing services to them, or exercising functions on behalf of them, is prescribed under paragraph 9 of Schedule 5 to the Tax Credits Act 2002 (provision of information by the Board of Inland Revenue for health purposes).

(2) Nothing in these Regulations affects the operation of the Tax Credits (Provision of Information) (Functions Relating to Health) Regulations 2003 or the Tax Credits (Provision of Information) (Functions Relating to Health) (No.2) Regulations 2003.

The Tax Credits (Provision of Information) (Function Relating to Employment and Training) Regulations 2005

(SI 2005/66)

The Commissioners of Inland Revenue, in exercise of the powers conferred upon them by sections 65(2) and 67 of, and paragraph 5(2) of Schedule 5 to, the Tax Credits Act 2002, make the following Regulations:

Citation and commencement

2.535   1.—These Regulations may be cited as the Tax Credits (Provision of Information) (Function Relating to Employment and Training) Regulations 2005 and shall come into force on 8th February 2005.

Prescribed function relating to employment and training

2.536   2.—(1) The function specified in paragraph (2) is prescribed for the purposes of paragraph 5 of Schedule 5 to the Tax Credits Act 2002 (provision of information by the Board of Inland Revenue for employment and training purposes).

(2) The function specified in this paragraph is evaluation of, and research in relation to, the employment and training programmes administered—
(a) in Great Britain, by the Department for Work and Pensions; or
(b) in Northern Ireland, the Department for Employment and Learning.

The Tax Credits (Child Care Providers) (Miscellaneous Revocation and Transitional Provisions) (England) Scheme 2007

(2007/2481)

ARRANGEMENT OF SCHEME

1. Citation, commencement and application
2. Interpretation
3. Partial revocation of the 1999 Regulations and transitional provision
4. Revocation of the 2005 Scheme and transitional provision

The Secretary of State for Children, Schools and Families, being the appropriate national authority under section 12(6) of the Tax Credits Act 2002, and in exercise of the powers conferred by sections 12(5), (7) and (8) and 65(9) of that Act, makes the following Scheme:

Citation, commencement and application

1.—(1) This Scheme may be cited as the Tax Credits (Child Care Providers) (Miscellaneous Revocation and Transitional Provisions) (England) Scheme 2007.

(2) This Scheme comes into force—
(a) to the extent that it revokes the 2005 Scheme and the provisions of the 1999 Regulations other than regulations 11(a) and (b) and 12, on 1st October 2007; and
(b) to the extent that it revokes regulations 11(a) and (b) and 12 of the 1999 Regulations, on 1st October 2009.

(3) This Scheme applies in relation to England only.

Interpretation

2.—In this Scheme—
"the 1999 Regulations" means the Tax Credit (New Category of Child Care Provider) Regulations 1999;
"the 2005 Scheme" means the Tax Credits (Approval of Child Care Providers) Scheme 2005;
"the inspection provisions" means regulations 11(a) and (b) and 12 of the 1999 Regulations (access to information and records by officers of the Secretary of State and Her Majesty's Revenue and Customs); and
"the transitional period" means the period beginning on 1st October 2007 and ending on 1st October 2009.

The Tax Credits (Child Care Providers) Scheme 2007

Partial revocation of the 1999 Regulations and transitional provision

2.540 3.—(1) The 1999 Regulations are revoked to the extent that they make a Scheme for determining the description of persons by whom child care is provided, and whose charges fall to be taken into account in computing the child care element of working tax credit, subject to paragraph (3) of this article.

(2) Any accreditation of an organisation by the Secretary of State pursuant to the Scheme provided for by the 1999 Regulations, and any approval granted by such an organisation, shall lapse on 1st October 2007, except for the purposes of the inspection provisions.

(3) During the transitional period the inspection provisions shall have effect as if—
  (a) the reference in regulation 11 to the period for which an organisation is accredited were a reference to the transitional period; and
  (b) the reference in regulation 12 to the period during which a child care provider is approved by an accredited organisation were a reference to the transitional period.

DEFINITIONS

"the 1999 Regulations"—see art.2.
"the inspection provisions"—see art.2.
"the transitional period"—see art.2.

Revocation of the 2005 Scheme and transitional provision

2.541 4.—(1) The 2005 Scheme is revoked, subject to paragraph (2).

(2) The provisions of the 2005 Scheme continue to have effect [¹, with the modifications in paragraph (3),] in relation to—
  (a) any approval granted to a child care provider under that Scheme which is valid immediately before 1st October 2007; and
  (b) any application for approval under that Scheme which has not been granted before 1st October 2007.

[¹ (3) For the purposes of paragraph (2) the 2005 Scheme is amended as follows—
  (a) in article 2 omit the definitions of "the Tribunal" and "the Tribunal Regulations";
  (b) in article 11—
    (i) in paragraphs (1) and (5) for "Tribunal" substitute "First-tier Tribunal";
    (ii) for paragraph (2) substitute—
"(2) Tribunal Procedure Rules shall apply to an appeal under paragraph (1) as they apply to an appeal under section 79M of the 1989 Act."; and
  (c) omit paragraphs (3) and (4).]

AMENDMENT

1. Tribunals, Courts and Enforcement Act 2007 (Transitional and Consequential Provisions) Order 2008 (SI 2008/2683) art.6 and Sch.1 para.329 (November 3, 2008).

DEFINITION

"the 2005 Scheme"—see art.2.

(2007/2481 reg.4)

GENERAL NOTE

This Scheme partially revokes the Tax Credit (New Category of Child Care Provider) Regulations 1999 (SI 1999/3110) and revokes the Tax Credits (Approval of Child Care Providers) Scheme 2005 (SI 2005/93), with transitional provisions (see 2007 main Vol.IV paras 2.578–2.590 for the 2005 Scheme). The new Scheme applies in relation to England only. For Wales, see the Tax Credits (Approval of Child Care Providers) (Wales) Scheme 2007 (SI 2007/226 (W.20), as amended by the Tax Credits (Approval of Child Care Providers) (Wales) (Amendment) Scheme 2007 SI 2008/2687 (W.237). The revocations provided for by the Scheme mostly came into force on October 1, 2007. Provision of a Scheme for Wales is now a devolved function with responsibility transferred to Welsh Ministers. Those powers were exercised with effect from November 1, 2011 to amend the 2007 Welsh Scheme. The principal amendment is the revocation of the power providing for decisions on claims to be made by a private contractor. All new claims from that date are to be decided by the Welsh Ministers: Tax Credits (Approval of Child Care Applications) (Wales) (Amendment) Scheme 2011 / Cynllun Credydau Treth (Cymeradwyau Darparwyr Gofal Plant) (Cymru) (Diwygio) 2011 (SI 2011/993).

Article 3(1) revokes the 1999 Regulations to the extent that they make a Scheme for determining the description of persons by whom child care is provided, and whose charges fall to be taken into account in computing the child care element of working tax credit. Article 3(2) makes various transitional provision concerning the access to information and records by HMRC officers and for allied matters.

Article 4(1) revokes the 2005 Scheme. Article 4(2) makes transitional provision to ensure that approvals granted under the 2005 Scheme that were valid immediately before October 1, 2007 continue to have effect until the end of their period of validity.

The 1999 Regulations and the 2005 Scheme have been revoked following the introduction of a system of voluntary registration for certain childcare providers under the Childcare Act 2006 (see the Childcare (Voluntary Registration) Regulations 2007 (SI 2007/730)).

2.542

The Loss of Tax Credits (Specified Day) Order 2013

(SI 2013/524)

The Treasury make the following Order in exercise of the powers conferred by sections 36A(10) and 36C(7) of the Tax Credits Act 2002:

Citation and commencement

1.—This Order may be cited as the Loss of Tax Credits (Specified Day) Order 2013 and shall come into force on 6th April 2013.

2.543

Specified day

2.—The day specified under sections 36A(10) and 36C(7) of the Tax Credits Act 2002 for the purposes of sections 36A to 36D that Act is 6th April 2013.

2.544

GENERAL NOTE

This Order specifies April 6, 2013 as the day for the purposes of ss.36A to 36D of the Tax Credits Act 2002. Where an offence within the scope of those sections is committed after this date, it is a "benefit offence" for the purposes of ss.36A to 36D of the Act.

2.545

The Loss of Tax Credits Regulations 2013

(SI 2013/715)

The Commissioners for Her Majesty's Revenue and Customs make these Regulations in the exercise of the powers conferred by sections 36A(5) and (6), 36C(4) and (5), 65(2) and 67 of the Tax Credits Act 2002. A draft of this instrument was laid before and approved by a resolution of each House of Parliament in accordance with section 66(1) and (2)(zb) of the Tax Credits Act 2002.

Citation, commencement and interpretation

1.—(1) These Regulations may be cited as the Loss of Tax Credits Regulations 2013 and come into force on 6th April 2013.

(2) In these Regulations, references to sections of the Act are to sections of the Tax Credits Act 2002.

Loss of working tax credit for benefit offence and repeated benefit fraud: beginning of disqualification periods

2.—(1) For the purposes of section 36A(6) of the Act, the date on which the relevant period begins is the thirtieth day after the day on which the Commissioners for Her Majesty's Revenue and Customs ("the Commissioners") are notified of the disqualifying event mentioned in section 36A(1)—
  (a) in relation to England and Wales and Scotland, by the Secretary of State or by an authority which administers housing benefit or council tax benefit,
  (b) in relation to Northern Ireland, by the Department for Social Development, the Department of Finance and Personnel or the Northern Ireland Housing Executive.

(2) For the purposes of section 36C(5) of the Act, the prescribed date is the thirtieth day after the day on which the Commissioners are notified of the offender's conviction mentioned in that section, by the prosecuting authority responsible for bringing the current set of proceedings in which the offender was convicted.

Loss of working tax credit for benefit offence and repeated benefit fraud

3.—For the duration of any period—
  (a) comprised in the offender's disqualification period for the purposes of section 36A(4)(b) or 36C(3)(b) of the Act, and
  (b) not comprising any such disqualification period of the other member of the couple mentioned in either section,
the working tax credit in question shall be payable, but as if the amount payable were reduced by 50%.

GENERAL NOTE

These regulations provide for the date from which the disqualification period provided for in ss.36A to 36D of the 2002 Act operate.

Regulation 3 allows one of a joint couple to continue receiving half the previous working tax credit entitlement where the other of the couple has been convicted or is subject to a penalty under those sections.

(SI 2014/885)

The Tax Credits (Late Appeals) Order 2014

(SI 2014/885)

The Treasury make the following Order in exercise of the powers conferred by section 124(1), (2), (6) and (7) of the Finance Act 2008. A draft of this Order was laid before Parliament and approved by a resolution of each House of Parliament in accordance with section 124(9) of the Finance Act 2008.

Citation, commencement and extent

1.—(1) This Order may be cited as the Tax Credits (Late Appeals) Order 2014 and comes into force on the day after it is made.

(2) This Order extends to England and Wales and Scotland only.

Amendment of the Tax Credits Act 2002

2.—(1) The Tax Credits Act 2002 is amended as follows.

(2) [*inserts section 39A of the Tax Credits Act 2002*]

(3) Where, in respect of a late appeal made on or after 1 April 2013 and before this Order comes into force, the Commissioners for Her Majesty's Revenue and Customs have before this Order comes into force notified the appellant that they consider the appeal should proceed even though it was not made within the period specified in section 39(1) of the Tax Credits Act 2002, that notification is to have effect after this Order comes into force as a decision under section 39A to treat the appeal as made in time.

GENERAL NOTE

The Order adds the new s.39A to the 2002 Act. See the general note to that section. Article 2(3) gives retrospective effect to any admission of a late appeal by HMRC where that appeal was made on or after April 1, 2013, but before April 2, 2014, the day on which this Order took effect under art.1(2).

The Tax Credits, Child Benefit and Guardian's Allowance Reviews and Appeals Order 2014

(SI 2014/886)

The Treasury make this Order in exercise of the powers conferred by section 124(1), (2), (6) and (7) of the Finance Act 2008. A draft of this instrument was laid before and approved by resolution of the House of Commons in accordance with section 124(8) of that Act.

Citation, commencement and effect

1.—(1) This Order may be cited as the Tax Credits, Child Benefit and Guardian's Allowance

Reviews and Appeals Order 2014 and comes into force on 6th April 2014.

(2) But articles 2(13), 3(2) to (6), 5(2), 5(7)(a), (c), (e), (g), (h), (j) and (l), and 5(9) only come

into force on a day appointed by an order of the Treasury made by statutory instrument, and the Treasury may so appoint different days for different purposes.

(3) Articles 2(12) and 3(1) extend to England and Wales and Scotland only.

(4) Articles 2(13) and 3(2) to (6) extend to Northern Ireland only.

(5) Any amendment made by this Order only has effect in relation to an HMRC decision made on or after the amendment comes into force.

Amendment of the Tax Credits Act 2002

2.554   **2.**—[*Amendments included in the Act above*]

Revocation (for Great Britain) and amendment (for Northern Ireland) of the Tax Credits (Notice of Appeal) Regulations 2002

2.555   **3.**—(1) The Tax Credits (Notice of Appeal) Regulations 2002 are revoked (for England and Wales and Scotland).

...

Child benefit and guardian's allowance: amendment of the Social Security Act 1998 and the Social Security (Northern Ireland) Order 1998

2.556   **4.**—[*Amendments included in the 1998 Act above.*]

Amendment of the Child Benefit and Guardian's Allowance (Decisions and Appeals) Regulations 2003

2.557   **5.**—[*Amendments, so far as in force, included in the regulations above.*]

The Tax Credits (Settlement of Appeals) Regulations 2014

(SI 2014/1933)

2.558   The Commissioners for Her Majesty's Revenue and Customs in exercise of the powers conferred by sections 63(8) and 65(2) and (6) of the Tax Credits Act 2002 and with the consent of the Lord Chancellor, the Department of Justice in Northern Ireland and the Scottish Ministers, make the following Regulations.

Citation, commencement and extent

2.559   **1.**—(1) These Regulations may be cited as the Tax Credits (Settlement of Appeals) Regulations 2014 and come into force on 12th August 2014

(2) These Regulations extend to England and Wales and Scotland only.

Interpretation

2.560   **2.**—In these Regulations—

"tax credits appeal" means an appeal which, by virtue of section 63 of the Tax Credits Act 2002 (tax credits appeals etc: temporary modifications), is to the First-tier Tribunal.

(SI 2014/1933 reg.3)

Application of section 54 of the Taxes Management Act 1970

3.—(1) Section 54 of the Taxes Management Act 1970 (settling of appeals by agreement) shall apply to a tax credits appeal, with the modifications prescribed by paragraphs (2) to (7).

(2) In subsection (1) for "tribunal" (in both places) substitute "First-tier Tribunal".

(3) In subsections (1) and (4) for "assessment" (in each place) substitute "determination".

(4) In subsections (1), (2) and (4)(a) for "the inspector or other proper officer of the Crown" substitute "an officer of Revenue and Customs".

(5) For subsection (3) substitute—
"(3) Where an agreement is not in writing—
(a) the preceding provisions of this section shall not apply unless the Board give notice, in such form and manner as they consider appropriate, to the appellant of the terms agreed between the officer of Revenue and Customs and the appellant; and
(b) the references in those preceding provisions to the time when the agreement was come to shall be construed as references to the date of that notice.".

(6) In subsection (4)(b) for "the inspector or other proper officer" substitute "an officer of Revenue and Customs".

(7) In subsection (4), in the words after paragraph (b), for "the inspector or other proper officer" substitute "an officer of Revenue and Customs".

The Tax Credits (Exercise of Functions) Order 2014

(SI 2014/3280)

This Order in Council is made in exercise of the powers conferred by section 126(1), (2), (3)(a) and (b)(i) and (9) of the Welfare Reform Act 2012. Accordingly, Her Majesty is pleased, by and with the advice of Her Privy Council to order as follows:

Citation and commencement

1.—This Order may be cited as the Tax Credits (Exercise of Functions) Order 2014 and comes into force on 1st April 2015.

Interpretation

2.—(1) In this Order—
"the 2002 Act" means the Tax Credits Act 2002;
"the Administration Act" means the Social Security Administration Act 1992;
"the 2013 Regulations" means the Social Security (Overpayments and Recovery) Regulations 2013;
"notice" means a notice given under section 29 of the 2002 Act (recovery of overpayments of tax credits);
"penalty" means a penalty imposed under section 31 (incorrect statements etc.) or 32 (failure to comply with requirements) of the 2002 Act.

(2) Any interest carried under section 37 of the 2002 Act on an amount specified in a notice or on a penalty is to be regarded for the purpose of this Order as if it were specified in the notice or formed part of the penalty respectively.

Functions exercisable by the Secretary of State

2.564

3.—(1) The functions of the Commissioners under section 2 of the 2002 Act specified in paragraph (2) are to be exercisable concurrently with the Secretary of State.
(2) The functions are those that relate to—
 (a) the recovery from a person to whom a notice has been given of the amount specified in a notice;
 (b) the recovery from a person on whom a penalty has been imposed of the amount of the penalty.

Application of the Administration Act

2.565

4.—(1) Subject to paragraph (2), the amount specified in a notice or, as the case may be, the amount of a penalty is, for the purposes of the Administration Act, to be treated as if it were an amount recoverable under section 71ZB of that Act.
(2) Section 71ZB of the Administration Act has effect in relation to the amount specified in a notice or, as the case may be, the amount of a penalty, as if subsection (3) were omitted.

Application of the 2013 Regulations

2.566

5.—(1) The amount specified in a notice is, for the purposes of the 2013 Regulations, to be treated as if it were an overpayment as defined in regulation 2 of those Regulations.
(2) The amount of a penalty is, for the purposes of the 2013 Regulations, to be treated as if it were an amount recoverable under a provision of the Administration Act specified in regulation 3(2) of those Regulations.

Amendment of the 2013 Regulations

2.567

6.—In the definition of "overpayment" in regulation 2 of the 2013 Regulations (interpretation) omit paragraph (b).

The Tax Credits Act 2002 (Additional Payments Modification and Disapplication) Regulations 2022

(SI 2022/1208)

The Commissioners for His Majesty's Revenue and Customs, in exercise of the powers conferred by sections 6(5) and (6) and 10(1) of the Social Security (Additional Payments) Act 2022, make the following Regulations.

Citation, commencement and interpretation

2.568

1.—(1) These Regulations may be cited as the Tax Credits Act 2002 (Additional Payments Modification and Disapplication) Regulations 2022 and come into force on 22nd December 2022 but regulations 2 to 6 have effect from 28th June 2022.

(2) In these Regulations "additional payment" means [¹a payment] made by His Majesty's Revenue Customs in accordance with section 1(2) or 4(1) or (2) of the Social Security (Additional Payments) Act 2022 [¹or section 1(2) of the Social Security (Additional Payments) Act 2023].

Modification and disapplication of the Tax Credits Act 2002

2. The Tax Credits Act 2002 is modified as follows.

3. In respect of an additional payment, made to a person who is, or persons who are, not entitled to the additional payment, sections 14 to 19 are disapplied.

4. Section 20 has effect as if after subsection (5), there were inserted—

"(5A) Where the Board have reasonable grounds for believing that an additional payment has been paid to a person, or two persons jointly, by reference to a child tax credit or working tax credit and that the person or persons had no entitlement to the payment, the Board may decide that the additional payment was paid incorrectly.

(5B) But no decision may be made under subsection (5A) after the period of five years beginning with the end of the tax year in which the additional payment is made."

5. Section 28 has effect as if—
   (a) in subsection (1)—
      (i) after "sections 18 to 21C)," there were inserted "or where the Commissioners have decided that an additional payment was paid incorrectly,",
      (ii) after "any part of it," there were inserted "or the incorrectly paid additional payment, or any part of it,",
   (b) in subsection (2), after "an excess" there were inserted "or incorrectly paid additional payment",
   (c) in subsections (3) and (4), after "awarded" there were inserted "or to whom the additional payment was made".

6. Section 67 has effect as if, at the appropriate place, there were inserted—

""additional payment" means a payment made under section 1(2) or 4(1) or (2) of the Social Security (Additional Payments) Act 2022 [¹, a payment made under section 1(2) of the Social Security (Additional Payments) Act 2023,] or a payment purporting to be a payment under any of those provisions."

AMENDMENT

1. Social Security (Additional Payments) Act 2023 s.9(4) and (5) (March 23, 2023).

PART III

CHILDREN AND GUARDIANS

The Child Benefit (General) Regulations 2006

(SI 2006/223)

ARRANGEMENT OF REGULATIONS

PART 1

INTRODUCTORY

1. Citation, commencement and interpretation.   3.1

PART 2

QUALIFYING YOUNG PERSONS: PRESCRIBED CONDITIONS

2. Introduction.
3. Education and training condition.
4. Continuation of entitlement until 31st August: 16 year olds.
5. Extension period: 16 and 17 year olds.
6. Interruptions.
7. Qualifying young person: terminal dates.
8. Child benefit not payable in respect of qualifying young person: other financial support.

PART 3

PERSON RESPONSIBLE FOR CHILD OR QUALIFYING YOUNG PERSON

9. Child or qualifying young person in residential accommodation in prescribed circumstances.
10. Days disregarded in determining whether child or qualifying young person living with someone.
11. Prescribed circumstances relating to contributions and expenditure in respect of child or qualifying young person.

PART 4

EXCLUSIONS AND PRIORITY

12. Child benefit not payable: qualifying young person living with another as member of couple.
13. Qualifying young person in a relevant relationship

14. Election under Schedule 10 to SSCBA and Schedule 10 to SSCB(NI)A
15. Modification of priority between persons entitled to child benefit
16. Child or qualifying young persons in detention, care etc.
17. Child or qualifying young person undergoing imprisonment or detention in legal custody
18. Child or qualifying young person in care
19. Interpretation of facts existing in a week

PART 5

ENTITLEMENT AFTER DEATH OF CHILD OR QUALIFYING YOUNG PERSON

20. Entitlement after death of child or qualifying young person

PART 6

RESIDENCE

21. Circumstances in which a child or qualifying young person treated as being in Great Britain
22. Application of regulation 24 where the person is in Northern Ireland
23. Circumstances in which person treated as not being in Great Britain
24. Persons temporarily absent from Great Britain
25. Circumstances in which a child or qualifying young person treated as being in Northern Ireland
26. Application of regulation 28 where person in Great Britain
27. Circumstances in which person treated as not being in Northern Ireland
28. Persons temporarily absent from Northern Ireland
29. Overlap of entitlement to child benefit under both the legislation of Northern Ireland and Great Britain
30. Crown servants posted overseas
31. Partners of Crown servants posted overseas
32. Child or qualifying young persons normally living with Crown servants posted overseas
33. Transitional provisions for Part 6

PART 7

GENERAL AND SUPPLEMENTARY PROVISIONS

34. Persons treated as residing together
35. Polygamous marriages
36. Right to child benefit of voluntary organisations
37. No requirement to state national insurance number
38. Exception to rules preventing duplicate payment
39. Use of electronic communications

(SI 2006/223 reg.1)

PART 1

INTRODUCTORY

Citation, commencement and interpretation

1.—(1) These Regulations may be cited as the Child Benefit (General) Regulations 2006 and shall come into force on 10th April 2006 immediately after the Child Benefit Act 2005.

(2) In these Regulations—

"the 1989 Act" means the Children Act 1989;

"the 1995 Act" means the Children (Scotland) Act 1995;

"the 1995 Order" means the Children (Northern Ireland) Order 1995;

"SSCBA" means the Social Security Contributions and Benefits Act 1992;

"SSCB(NI)A" means the Social Security Contributions and Benefits (Northern Ireland) Act 1992.

(3) In these Regulations—

"advanced education" means full-time education for the purposes of—
  (a) a course in preparation for a degree, a diploma of higher education, [³ a higher national certificate,] a higher national diploma, or a teaching qualification; or
  (b) any other course which is of a standard above ordinary national diploma, a national diploma or national certificate of Edexcel, a general certificate of education (advanced level), or Scottish national qualifications at higher or advanced higher level;

[¹ "an appropriate office" means—
  (a) Waterview Park, Washington, Tyne and Wear; or
  (b) any other office specified in writing by the Commissioners.]

"approved training" means arrangements made by the Government—

[³ (a) [⁵ ...]];
  (b) in relation to Wales, known as [⁶ ...] [³ "Traineeships" or "Foundation Apprenticeships" [¹⁶ or "Jobs Growth Wales+"]];
[³ [⁴ [¹⁵ (c) in relation to Scotland, known as [¹⁶ ...] "No One Left Behind"; or]]]
[² [⁴ [⁷ (d) in relation to Northern Ireland, known as "PEACE IV Children and Young People 2.1" or [¹⁴ "Training for Success" or "Skills for Life and Work"]]]]

"arrangements made by the Government" means arrangements—
  (a) in relation to England and Wales, made by the Secretary of State under section 2 of the Employment and Training Act 1973;
  (b) in relation to Scotland, made—
    (i) by the Scottish Ministers under section 2 of the Employment and Training Act 1973;
    (ii) by Scottish Enterprise or Highlands and Islands Enterprise under section 2 of the Enterprise and New Towns (Scotland) Act 1990; or
  (c) in relation to Northern Ireland, made by the Department for [⁹ Communities or the Department for the Economy] under [³ sections 1 and 3] of the Employment and Training Act (Northern Ireland) 1950;

"the Careers Service" means—
(a) in England and Wales, a person with whom the Secretary of State or the National Assembly of Wales has made arrangements under section 10(1) of the Employment and Training Act 1973, and a [²local authority] to whom the Secretary of State or the National Assembly of Wales has given a direction under section 10(2) of that Act;
(b) in Scotland, a person with whom the Scottish Ministers have made arrangements under section 10(1) of the Employment and Training Act 1973 and any education authority to which a direction has been given by the Scottish Ministers under section 10(2) of that Act; [³ . . .]
(c) [³ . . .]

"child benefit" has the meaning given in section 141 of SSCBA and section 137 of SSCB(NI)A (child benefit);

"civil partnership" means two people [¹⁰ . . .] who are civil partners of each other and are neither—
(a) separated under a court order; nor
(b) separated in circumstances where the separation is likely to be permanent;
[¹⁰ . . .]

"the Commissioners" means the Commissioners for Her Majesty's Revenue and Customs (see section 1 of the Commissioners for Revenue and Customs Act 2005);

"the Connexions Service" means a person of any description with whom the Secretary of State has made an arrangement under section 114(2)(a) of the Learning and Skills Act 2000 and section 10(1) of the Employment and Training Act 1973, and any person to whom he has given a direction under section 114(2)(b) of the former, or section 10(2) of the latter, Act;

"couple" means two people—
[¹⁰(a) who are spouses residing together, or civil partners in a civil partnership; or
(b) who are not married to, or civil partners of, each other but are living together as if they were a married couple or civil partners;]

"court" means any court in the United Kingdom, the Channel Islands or the Isle of Man;

"Crown servant posted overseas" has the meaning given in regulation 30(2);

"EEA State" means—
(a) a member State, other than the United Kingdom, or
(b) Norway, Iceland or Liechtenstein;

"full-time education" [⁴ except in regulation 3(2)(ab)]—
(a) is education undertaken in pursuit of a course, where the average time spent during term time in receiving tuition, engaging in practical work, or supervised study, or taking examinations exceeds 12 hours per week; and
(b) in calculating the time spent in pursuit of the course, no account shall be taken of time occupied by meal breaks or spent on unsupervised study.

"hospital or similar institution" means a place in which persons suffering from mental disorders are or may be received for care or treatment but does not include a prison, a young offenders institution, Secure

(SI 2006/223 reg. 1)

Training Centre, Local Authority Secure Unit, Juvenile Justice Centre, Young Offenders Centre or, if outside the United Kingdom, any comparable place;

"mental disorder" shall be construed as including references to any mental disorder within the meaning of the Mental Health Acts;

"the Mental Health Acts" means the Mental Health Act 1983, the Mental Health (Care and Treatment) (Scotland) Act 2003 or the Mental Health (Northern Ireland) Order 1986;

"partner" means, in relation to a person who is a member of a couple, the other member of that couple;

"penalty" means, in the case of any court in Great Britain or Northern Ireland—

(a) in England and Wales, a sentence of a detention and training order under section 100 of the Powers of Criminal Courts (Sentencing) Act 2000 [[12] or Chapter 2 of Part 10 of the Sentencing Code] or detention in a young offenders institution, and a sentence of detention under sections 90, 91, 92 and 93 of the Powers of Criminal Courts (Sentencing) Act 2000[[12] or sections 250, 259 and 260 of the Sentencing Code];

(b) in Scotland, a sentence of detention under sections 44, 205, 207, 208 or 216(7) of the Criminal Procedure (Scotland) Act 1995;

(c) in Northern Ireland, a sentence of imprisonment, or detention under Article 39, 41, 45 or 54 of, or paragraph 6 of Schedule 2 to, the Criminal Justice (Children) (Northern Ireland) Order 1998, or an order for detention in a juvenile justice centre or young offenders centre,

and in the case of any court outside the United Kingdom, any comparable sentence or order;

"relevant education" means education which is—

(a) full-time; and
(b) not advanced education;

[[11] "relevant person of Northern Ireland" means a person who —

(a) is —
   (i) a British citizen; or
   (ii) an Irish citizen; or
   (iii) a British citizen and an Irish citizen; and
(b) was born in Northern Ireland and, at the time of that person's birth, at least one of their parents was --
   (i) a British citizen; or
   (ii) an Irish citizen; or
   (iii) a British citizen and an Irish citizen; or
   (iv) otherwise entitled to reside in Northern Ireland without any restriction on their period of residence;]

"remunerative work" means work of not less than 24 hours a week—

(a) in respect of which payment is made; or
(b) which is done in expectation of payment;

[[8] "section 67 leave" means leave to remain in the United Kingdom granted by the Secretary of State to a person who has been relocated to the United Kingdom pursuant to arrangements made by the Secretary of State under section 67 of the Immigration Act 2016.]

"the Taxes Act" means the Income and Corporation Taxes Act 1988;

The Child Benefit (General) Regulations 2006

"writing" includes writing produced by electronic communications used in accordance with regulation 39.

[¹³ (3A) In these Regulations references to the Immigration (European Economic Area) Regulations 2016 are to be read with Schedule 4 to the Immigration and Social Security Co-ordination (EU Withdrawal) Act 2020 (Consequential, Saving, Transitional and Transitory Provisions) Regulations 2020.]

(4) [¹⁰ . . .]

AMENDMENTS

1. Child Benefit and Guardian's Allowance (Miscellaneous Amendments) Regulations (SI 2009/3268) reg.5 (January 1, 2010).
2. Local Education Authorities and Children's Services Authorities (Integration of Functions) (Local and Subordinate Legislation) Order 2010 (SI 2010/1172) art.4 and Sch.3 para.66 (May 5, 2010).
3. Child Benefit (General) (Amendment) Regulations 2012 (SI 2012/818) regs 3–6 (April 6, 2012).
4. Child Benefit (General) and Child Tax Credit (Amendment) Regulations 2014 (SI 2014/1231) reg.2(2) (June 4, 2014).
5. Child Benefit (General) (Amendment) Regulations 2015 (SI 2015/1512) reg.2 (August 31, 2015).
6. Tax Credits and Child Benefit (Miscellaneous Amendments) Regulations 2016 (SI 2016/360) reg.6(2) (April 6, 2016).
7. Child Benefit (General) (Amendment) Regulations 2017 (SI 2017/607) reg.2(2) (June 1, 2017).
8. Child Benefit, Tax Credits and Childcare Payments (Section 67 Immigration Act 2016 Leave) (Amendment) Regulations 2018 (SI 2018/788) reg.2(2) (July 20, 2018).
9. Tax Credits, Child Benefit and Childcare Payments (Miscellaneous Amendments) Regulations 2019 (SI 2019/364) reg.11(2) (March 21, 2019).
10. Civil Partnership (Opposite-sex Couples) Regulations 2019 (SI 2019/1458) reg.41(b) and Sch.3 Pt 2 para.84(2) (December 2, 2019).
11. Child Benefit and Child Tax Credit (Persons of Northern Ireland) (Amendment) Regulations 2020 (SI 2020/672) reg.2(2) (August 24, 2020).
12. Sentencing Act 2020 Sch.24 para 346 (December 1, 2020).
13. Immigration and Social Security Co-ordination (EU Withdrawal) Act 2020 (Consequential, Saving, Transitional and Transitory Provisions) (EU Exit) Regulations 2020 (SI 2020/1309) reg. 66(2) (December 31, 2020).
14. Tax Credits and Child Benefit (Miscellaneous Amendments) Regulations 2021 (SI 2021/1286) reg.5 (December 9, 2021).
15. Tax Credits and Child Benefit (Miscellaneous and Coronavirus Amendments) Regulations 2021 (SI 2021/810) reg.3(2) (July 21, 2021).
16. Tax Credits and Child Benefit (Miscellaneous Amendments) Regulations 2023 (SI 2023/179) reg.6 (March 15, 2023).

PART 2

QUALIFYING YOUNG PERSONS: PRESCRIBED CONDITIONS

Introduction

2.—(1) Regulations 3 to 7 prescribe—
(a) the age which a person must not have attained, and

(b) the conditions which are to be satisfied,
for a person to be a qualifying young person.
(2) Where more than one of those regulations apply to a person, he is a qualifying young person until the last of them ceases to be satisfied.
(3) Regulations 3 to 7 are subject to the following qualifications.
(4) Regulation 8 prescribes an additional condition which must be satisfied for a person to be a qualifying young person in respect of a week.
(5) No-one who had attained the age of 19 before 10th April 2006 is a qualifying young person.

DEFINITIONS

"week"—SSCBA 1992 s.147.
"qualifying young person"—SSCBA 1992 s.142.

Education and training condition

3.—(1) This regulation applies in the case of a person who has not attained the age of 20.
(2) The condition is that the person—
(a) is undertaking a course of full-time education, which is not advanced education and which is not provided by virtue of his employment or any office held by him—
  (i) which is provided at a school or college; or
  (ii) which is provided elsewhere but is approved by the Commissioners;
[² (ab) is being provided with "appropriate full-time education" in England within section 4 (appropriate full-time education or training) of the Education and Skills Act 2008, which is not—
  (i) a course in preparation for a degree, a diploma of higher education, a higher national certificate, a higher national diploma, a teaching qualification, any other course which is of a standard [³ above ordinary national diploma, a national diploma or national certificate] of Edexcel, a general certificate of education (advanced level), or Scottish national qualifications at higher or advanced higher level;
  (ii) provided by virtue of his employment or any office held by him;]
(b) having undertaken such a course as is mentioned in [² paragraph (a) or (ab)] [¹ has been accepted or is enrolled to undertake a further such course.]; or
(c) is undertaking approved training that is not provided by means of a contract of employment.
[¹ or
(d) having undertaken a course mentioned in paragraph (a) or approved training mentioned in paragraph (c), has been accepted or is enrolled to undertake such approved training]
[⁴(3) A person (P) is not a qualifying young person by virtue of paragraph (2)(a)(ii) unless either—
(a) P was receiving the education referred to in that paragraph as a child, or
(b) P begins to receive that education after attaining the age of sixteen where—
  (i) P has received a statement of special educational needs; and

(ii) the local authority has assessed the programme of home education as being suitable for P's special needs.]

(4) A person who is aged 19 is only a qualifying young person by virtue of [² paragraph (2)(a), (2)(ab)] or (2)(c) if he began the education or training (as the case may be) referred to in that sub-paragraph [¹ or was accepted or enrolled to undertake that education or training] before attaining that age.

[⁴(5) In this regulation "a statement of special educational needs" means a statement, plan or assessment made by a local authority, which identifies and assesses the special educational needs of a person and specifies the special educational provision required by that person.]

AMENDMENTS

1. Child Benefit (General) (Amendment) Regulations 2007 (SI 2007/2150) reg.4 (August 16, 2007).
2. Child Benefit (General) and Child Tax Credit (Amendment) Regulations 2014 (SI 2014/1231) reg.2(3) (June 4, 2014).
3. Child Benefit (General) and Tax Credits (Miscellaneous Amendments) Regulations 2014 (SI 2014/2924) reg.2 (November 28, 2014).
4. Tax Credits, Child Benefit, Guardian's Allowance and Childcare Payments (Miscellaneous Amendments) Regulations 2020 (SI 2020/297) reg.6 (April 6, 2020).

DEFINITIONS

"approved training"—see reg.1.
"full-time education"—see reg.1.

GENERAL NOTE

3.5 Full-time education is defined in reg.1. That definition includes time spent in "supervised study". The difference between supervised and unsupervised study was considered in *R(F) 1/93* where it was held that supervision required close attention to the pupil by a teacher, but a different conclusion, and a much wider interpretation has been held by the Court of Appeal to apply (in the context of university education), in relation to a claim for Carer's Allowance (see *Flemming v Secretary of State for Work and Pensions, R(G) 2/02*). The cautious approach that was adopted to this question by Judge Mesher in *AD v SSWP* [2009] UKUT 46 (AAC), a case also concerning Carer's Allowance, has been reversed in the Court of Appeal under the name of *Secretary of State v Deane* [2010] EWCA Civ 699.

In *JH v HMRC* [2015] UKUT 479 (AAC); [2016] AACR 15 Judge Levenson decided an unusual case affecting a young person, the subject of a special educational needs statement, who had been educated at a special school until the age of 18 and then at home under an arrangement made by his local authority. His mother's claim for Child Benefit to be continued under this regulation was, however, refused because under reg.3(3) such a course of training could only be approved if it had commenced whilst he was still a child (i.e. under the age of 16). Judge Levenson allowed an appeal on grounds that had been agreed between the parties; the limitation in reg.3(3) was found only in secondary legislation. This meant that it should be disapplied if it were found to be in breach of the claimant's rights under the Human Rights Act 1998. The judge found that the unequal treatment between claimants whose child began home education under the age of 16 and those whose child was older, was a breach of the claimant's Convention rights under art.14 and art.1 Protocol 1 and could not be justified.

(SI 2006/223 reg.4)

Continuation of entitlement until 31st August: 16 year olds

4.—(1) This regulation applies in the case of a person who has not attained the age of 17 and who has left relevant education or training.

(2) The condition is that the 31st August next following the person's 16th birthday has not passed.

[¹ (3) In the case of a person who attains the age of 16 on 31 August in any year, the condition is that the 1st September immediately following has not passed.]

AMENDMENT

1. Child Benefit and Guardian's Allowance (Miscellaneous Amendments) Regulations (SI 2009/3268) reg.5 (January 1, 2010).

DEFINITION

"relevant education"—see reg.1.

Extension period: 16 and 17 year olds

5.—(1) This regulation applies in the case of a person who has not attained the age of 18.

(2) The condition is that—
(a) the person has ceased to be in education or training;
(b) the person is registered for work, education or for training with a qualifying body;
(c) the person is not engaged in remunerative work;
(d) the extension period which applies in the case of that person has not expired;
(e) immediately before the extension period begins, the person who is responsible for him is entitled to child benefit in respect of him without regard to this regulation; and
[¹(f) the individual who is responsible for that person, within three months of that person's ceasing education or training, has made a request for the payment of child benefit during the extension period to the Commissioners, in writing, or by such other means as the Commissioners may accept.]

(3) For the purposes of paragraph (2) the extension period—
(a) begins on the first day of the week after that in which the person ceased to be in education or training; and
(b) ends 20 weeks after it started.

(4) In this regulation "qualifying body" means—
(a) the Careers Service or Connexions Service;
(b) the Ministry of Defence;
(c) in Northern Ireland, the Department for [³ Communities, the Department for the Economy or the Education Authority;] or
(d) for the purposes of applying Council Regulation (EEC) No.1408/71 [² or Regulation (EC) No 883/2004 of the European Parliament and of the Council], any corresponding body in another member State.

AMENDMENTS

1. Child Benefit and Guardian's Allowance (Miscellaneous Amendments) Regulations (SI 2009/3268) reg.5 (January 1, 2010).

2. Child Benefit (General) (Amendment) Regulations 2012 (SI 2012/818) reg.7 (April 6, 2012).
3. Tax Credits, Child Benefit and Childcare Payments (Miscellaneous Amendments) Regulations 2019 (SI 2019/364) reg.11(3) (March 21, 2019).

DEFINITION

"remunerative work"—see reg.1.

Interruptions

6.—(1) This regulation applies in the case of a person who has not attained the age of 20.

(2) If, immediately before the commencement of an interruption specified in paragraph (3)(a) or (b), a person was a qualifying young person by virtue of any other provision of these Regulations, he is such a person throughout a period of interruption during which he satisfies the condition specified in that sub-paragraph.

(3) The periods of interruption are—
  (a) one of up to six months (whether beginning before or after the person concerned became 16) but only to the extent to which, in the opinion of the Commissioners, that the interruption is reasonable; and
  (b) one attributable to the illness or disability of mind or body of the person concerned for such period as is reasonable in the opinion of the Commissioners.

This is subject to the following qualification.

(4) Paragraph (3) does not apply to an interruption which is, or is likely to be, followed immediately by a period during which—
  (a) provision is made for training of that person which is not approved training;
  (b) he is receiving advanced education;
  (c) he is receiving education by virtue of his employment or of any office held by him.

DEFINITION

"advanced education"—see reg.1.

GENERAL NOTE

Note that the overall test under this regulation is whether the interruption in education is, in the eyes of HMRC reasonable. Such reasonable interruptions are then disregarded for up to six months, or, if the reason for interruption is illness or disability for a longer period that is accepted as reasonable by HMRC. This provision is clearly appropriate to bridge any gap caused by school holidays and interval caused by a change of schools. In *R(F) 3/60* a gap of five months was accepted because there was difficulty in finding a suitable school for the child who suffered from a mental disability.

Qualifying young person: terminal dates

7.—(1) This regulation applies in the case of a person who has not attained the age of 20.

(2) The condition is that the period found [¹ in accordance with —
  (a) Cases 1 and 2, or,
  (b) for Summer Term 2021 where a person has been entered as a 2021 candidate for external examinations in connection with relevant education that person was receiving and those examinations have been

(SI 2006/223 reg.7)

cancelled due to coronavirus, Cases 1 and 3, has not expired in his case.]

Case 1

1.1 The period is from the date on which he ceases to receive relevant education or approved training, up to and including—
(a) the week including the terminal date, or
(b) if he attains the age of 20 on or before that date, the week including the last Monday before he attains that age.

1.2 For the purposes of this Case the "terminal date" means—
(a) the last day in February,
(b) the last day in May,
(c) the last day in August,
(d) the last day in November,

whichever first occurs after the date on which the person's relevant education or approved training ceased (but subject to paragraph 1.3 of this Case).

1.3 In the case of a person in Scotland who—
(a) undertakes the Higher Certificate or Advanced Higher Certificate immediately before ceasing relevant education, and
(b) ceases relevant education on a date earlier than he would have done had he undertaken the comparable examination in England and Wales,

the terminal date shall be reckoned by reference to the date on which the cessation would have occurred had he undertaken the comparable examination.

Case 2

2.1. Where a person's name is entered as a candidate for any external examination in connection with relevant education which he is receiving at that time, so long as his name continues to be so entered before ceasing to receive such education, the prescribed period is—
(a) from the later of—
  (i) date when that person ceased to receive relevant education, or
  (ii) the date on which he attained the age of 16,
(b) up to and including—
  (i) whichever of the dates in paragraph 1.2 (as modified by paragraph 1.3 where appropriate) first occurs after the conclusion of the examination (or the last of the examinations if the person is entered for more than one), or
  (ii) the expiry of the week which includes the last Monday before his 20th birthday,

whichever is the earlier.

[¹ *Case 3*

3.1. Where external examinations have been cancelled due to coronavirus, in the case of a person whose name had been entered as a 2021 candidate for any external examination in connection with relevant education which that person was receiving at that time, the period is from the date on which that person ceases to receive relevant education up to and including —
(a) whichever of the dates in paragraph 1.2 of Case 1 (as modified by paragraph 1.3 where appropriate) first occurs after the scheduled date of conclusion of the examination, or the last of those examinations where the person was entered for more than one, or

(b) if that person attains the age of 20 on or before that date, the week including the last Monday before that person attains that age.]
This paragraph is subject to the following qualification.

(3) Child benefit is not payable in respect of a qualifying young person by virtue of this regulation for any week in which he is engaged in remunerative work.

[¹ (4) In this regulation—

"coronavirus" means severe acute respiratory syndrome coronavirus 2,

"entered as a 2021 candidate" includes a person who would have been entered as a candidate for one or more external examinations in Summer Term 2021 if the external examinations had not been cancelled before that person was entered as a candidate for such examinations,

"scheduled date" means the date on which the examination board setting the relevant examination had scheduled that examination to take place, and

"Summer Term 2021" means the period beginning with 1st June 2021 and ending with 31st August 2021.]

AMENDMENTS

1. Child Benefit (General) (Coronavirus) (Amendment) Regulations 2021 (SI 2021/630) reg.2 (May 31, 2021).

DEFINITIONS

"approved training"—see reg.1.
"relevant education"—see reg.1.
"remunerative work"—see reg.1.
"week"—see SSCBA 1992 s.147.

GENERAL NOTE

3.11   Case 1 of this regulation extends entitlement to benefit in respect of a child who has left school for a period of up to three months ending on the quarterly dates prescribed. It is a corollary of the disentitlement to Income Support that applies to the same period. Case 2 similarly covers the period between the time a child leaves school and the time he sits external examinations for which he is entered. Note the extension continues only as long as he continues to be entered for an examination so that if he withdraws this route to qualification for child benefit ceases.

Child benefit not payable in respect of qualifying young person: other financial support

3.12   **8.**—(1) This regulation applies in the case of a person who has not attained the age of 20 years.

(2) The condition is that the person is not in receipt, in a week, of—
  (a) income support,
  (b) income-based jobseeker's allowance within the meaning of section 1(4) of the Jobseekers Act 1995 or Article 3(4) of the Jobseekers (Northern Ireland) Order 1995,
  (c) incapacity benefit by virtue of being a person to whom section 30A(1)(b) of SSCBA or section 30A(1)(b) of SSCB(NI)A applies, [¹...]
  (d) tax credit under the Tax Credits Act 2002;
  [¹ (e) employment and support allowance payable under Part 1 of the Welfare Reform Act 2007 [² or Part 1 of the Welfare Reform Act (Northern Ireland) 2007]] [³; or
  (f) universal credit under Part 1 of the Welfare Reform Act 2012.]

(SI 2006/223 reg. 8)

AMENDMENTS

1. Employment and Support Allowance (Consequential Provisions) (No.3) Regulations 2008 (SI 2008/1897) reg.24 (October 27, 2008).
2. Employment and Support Allowance (Consequential Provisions No.2) Regulations (Northern Ireland) 2008 (SI 2008/412) reg.11 (October 27, 2008).
3. Universal Credit (Consequential, Supplementary, Incidental and Miscellaneous Provisions) Regulations 2013 (SI 2013/630) reg.84 (April 29, 2013).

PART 3

PERSON RESPONSIBLE FOR CHILD OR QUALIFYING YOUNG PERSON

Child or qualifying young person in residential accommodation in prescribed circumstances

9.—For the purposes of section 143(3)(c) of SSCBA and section 139(3)(c) of SSCB(NI)A (absence of child or qualifying young person in residential accommodation), the prescribed circumstances are that the residential accommodation has been provided solely—
   (a) because of the disability of the child or qualifying young person, or
   (b) because the child or qualifying young person's health would be likely to be significantly impaired, or further impaired, unless such accommodation were provided.

Days disregarded in determining whether child or qualifying young person living with someone

10.—(1) For the purpose of section 143(4) of SSCBA and section 139(4) of SSCB(NI)A (number of days that may be disregarded), the prescribed number of days is 84 consecutive days, calculated in accordance with paragraph (2).

(2) Two or more distinct relevant periods separated by one or more intervals each not exceeding 28 days are treated as a continuous period equal in duration to the total of such distinct periods and ending on the last day of the latter or last of such periods.

(3) In paragraph (2) "relevant periods" means periods to which—
   (a) section 143(3)(b) of SSCBA or section 139(3)(b) of SSCB(NI)A (absence of a child or qualifying young person undergoing medical or other treatment) applies;
   (b) section 143(3)(c) of SSCBA or section 139(3)(c) of SSCB(NI)A (absence of a child or qualifying young person in residential accommodation) applies.

Prescribed circumstances relating to contributions and expenditure in respect of child or qualifying young person

11.—(1) For the purposes of section 143(5)(a) of SSCBA and section 139(5)(a) of SSCB(NI)A (contributing to the cost of providing for a child or qualifying young person) the prescribed circumstances are that—
   (a) two or more persons are contributing to the cost of providing for the same child or qualifying young person;

(b) the aggregate weekly amount of their contributions equals or exceeds, but the weekly amount of each of their individual contributions is less than, the weekly rate of child benefit which would be payable in respect of that child or qualifying young person had the aggregate weekly amount of their contributions been contributed by one only of them; and
(c) they by agreement nominate in writing or, in default of such agreement, the Commissioners in their discretion determine, that the aggregate weekly amount of their contributions is to be treated as having been made by the person so nominated or determined.

This paragraph is subject to paragraph (3).

(2) The contribution subject to the nomination or determination made under paragraph (1) shall be treated as made by the person nominated or determined.

(3) Where pursuant to a nomination or determination made under paragraph (1) a person is awarded child benefit, the nomination or determination ceases to have effect in the week following that in which child benefit is awarded to that person (and accordingly thereafter the person shall be required to contribute to the maintenance of the child or qualifying young person at a rate which equals or exceeds the rate of child benefit payable in respect of that child or qualifying young person).

(4) Where spouses or civil partners are residing together a contribution made or expenditure incurred by one of them in respect of a child or qualifying young person shall if they agree, or in default of such agreement if the Commissioners in their discretion so determine, be treated as made or incurred by the other.

DEFINITIONS

"child or qualifying young person"—see SSCBA 1992 s.142.
"The Commissioners"—see reg.1.
"week"—see SSCBA 1992 s.147.
"writing"—see reg.1.

PART 4

EXCLUSIONS AND PRIORITY

Child benefit not payable: qualifying young person living with another as member of couple

12.—(1) Child benefit is not payable to any person ("the claimant") in respect of a qualifying young person for any week in which the qualifying young person is living with another [¹as if they were a married couple or civil partners,] unless paragraph (2) applies.

(2) This paragraph applies if—
(a) the cohabitee is receiving relevant education or approved training; and
(b) the claimant is not the cohabitee.

AMENDMENT

1. Civil Partnership (Opposite-sex Couples) Regulations 2019 (SI 2019/1458) reg.41(b) and Sch.3 Pt 2 para.84(3) (December 2, 2019).

(SI 2006/223 reg.12)

DEFINITIONS

"approved training"—see reg.1.
"cohabiting same-sex couple"—see reg.1.
"relevant education"—see reg.1.

GENERAL NOTE

The circumstances in which a couple are to regarded as living together are defined, in part, in reg.1(4).

Qualifying young person in a relevant relationship

13.—(1) A person ("the claimant") shall be entitled to child benefit in respect of a qualifying young person in a relevant relationship by virtue of paragraph 3 of Schedule 9 to SSCBA or paragraph 3 of Schedule 9 to SSCB(NI)A (entitlement: children or qualifying young persons who are married or civil partners) only if—

(a) the claimant is not the spouse or civil partner of that qualifying young person; and
(b) the qualifying young person is not residing with his spouse or civil partner, or, if he is, the spouse or civil partner is receiving relevant education or approved training.

(2) In paragraph (1) "relevant relationship" means a marriage or a civil partnership.

DEFINITIONS

"approved training"—see reg.1.
"relevant education"—see reg.1.

Election under Schedule 10 to SSCBA and Schedule 10 to SSCB(NI) A

14.—(1) An election under Schedule 10 to SSCBA and Schedule 10 to SSCB(NI)A (any election under that Schedule to be made in the prescribed manner) shall be made by giving notice in writing to the Commissioners at an appropriate office on a form approved by the Commissioners [1 or by telephone to an officer of Revenue and Customs at an appropriate office] or in such other manner being in writing as the Commissioners may accept as sufficient in the circumstances of any particular case or class of cases.

(2) An election is not effective to confer entitlement to child benefit in respect of a child or qualifying young person for any week earlier than the week following that in which it is made if the earlier week is one in respect of which child benefit has been paid in respect of that child or qualifying young person and has not been required to be repaid or voluntarily repaid or recovered.

(3) An election may be superseded by a subsequent election made in accordance with this regulation.

AMENDMENT

1. Child Benefit (General) (Amendment) Regulations 2007 (SI 2007/2150) reg.5 (August 16, 2007).

DEFINITIONS

"child or qualifying young person"—see SSCBA 1992 s.142.
"The Commissioners"—see reg.1.
"week"—see SSCBA 1992 s.147.
"writing"—see reg.1.

Modification of priority between persons entitled to child benefit

15.—(1) If a person entitled to child benefit in respect of a child or qualifying young person in priority to another person gives the Commissioners notice in writing at an appropriate office [¹ or gives an officer of the Inland Revenue and Customs notice by telephone at such an office] that he does not wish to have such priority, the provisions of Schedule 10 to SSCBA and Schedule 10 to SSCB(NI)A (priority between persons entitled) have effect with the modification that that person does not have such priority.

(2) A notice under paragraph (1)—
(a) is not effective in relation to any week, before the date on which the election becomes effective, for which child benefit in respect of that child or qualifying young person is paid to the person who made the election or to another person on his behalf; and
(b) ceases to have effect if the person who gave it makes a further claim to child benefit in respect of that child or qualifying young person.

AMENDMENT

1. Child Benefit (General) (Amendment) Regulations 2007 (SI 2007/2150) reg.6 (August 16, 2007).

DEFINITIONS

"child or qualifying young person"—see SSCBA 1992 s.142.
"The Commissioners"—see reg.1.
"week"—see SSCBA 1992 s.147.
"writing"—see reg.1.

Child or qualifying young persons in detention, care etc.

16.—(1) Paragraph 1 of Schedule 9 to SSCBA and paragraph 1 of Schedule 9 to SSCB(NI)A do not apply to disentitle a person to child benefit in respect of a child or qualifying young person for any week—
(a) unless that week is the 9th or a subsequent week in a series of consecutive weeks in which either of those paragraphs has applied to that child or qualifying young person; or
(b) notwithstanding paragraph (a), if—
  (i) that week is one in which falls the first day in a period of seven consecutive days in which the child or qualifying young person lives with that person for at least a part of the first day and throughout the following six days;
  (ii) that week is one in which falls the first day in a period of seven consecutive days throughout which the child or qualifying young person lives with that person, being a period of seven consecutive days which immediately follows either a similar period of seven consecutive days or the period of seven consecutive days referred to in head (i) above;

(SI 2006/223 reg.16)

    (iii) that week is one in which falls the day, or the first day in a period of less than seven consecutive days, throughout which the child or qualifying young person lives with that person, being a day or days which immediately follow the period of seven consecutive days referred to in head (i) above or a period of seven consecutive days referred to in head (ii), or

    (iv) as at that week that person establishes that he is a person with whom the child or qualifying young person ordinarily lives throughout at least one day in each week.

This paragraph is subject to the following qualifications.

(2) For the purposes of paragraph (1), a person shall not be regarded as having a child or qualifying young person living with him throughout any day or week unless he actually has that child or qualifying young person living with him throughout that day or week.

(3) Paragraph (1) does not apply for any day in any week to a person ("the carer") with whom a child or qualifying young person—

[² (a) is placed by a local authority in Great Britain in the carer's home in accordance with the provisions of—
    (i) the Placement of Children (Wales) Regulations 2007,
    (ii) the Review of Children's Cases (Wales) Regulations 2007,
    (iii) the Care Planning, Placement and Case Review (England) Regulations 2010,
    (iv) the Looked After Children (Scotland) Regulations 2009,
    (v) the Fostering Services (England) Regulations 2011, [³ ...]
    (vi) the Fostering Services (Wales) Regulations 2003, [³ or
    (vii) Parts 4 and 6 of the Social Services and Well-being (Wales) Act 2014 and any regulations made under those parts,]
and that authority is making a payment, in respect of either the child or qualifying young person's accommodation or maintenance or both, under section 22C(10) [³ ...] of the 1989 Act or under regulation 33 of the Looked After Children (Scotland) Regulations 2009 [³ or under section 81(13) of the Social Services and Well-being (Wales) Act 2014];]

(b) is placed by an authority in Northern Ireland, in the carer's home in accordance with the provisions of the Foster Placement (Children) Regulations (Northern Ireland) 1996 where the authority has a duty to provide accommodation and maintenance for the child under the Arrangements for Placement of Children (General) Regulations (Northern Ireland) 1996.

(4) Paragraph (1) does not apply in respect of any child or qualifying young person who—
    (a) is being looked after by a local authority in Great Britain or by an authority in Northern Ireland, and
    (b) has been placed for adoption by that authority in the home of a person proposing to adopt him,
provided that the local authority or authority is making a payment in respect of either the child or qualifying young person's accommodation or maintenance or both, under [² section 22C(10) [³ ...] of the 1989 Act, under regulation 33 of the Looked After Children (Scotland) Regulations [³2009,]] or under Article 27 of the 1995 Order [³ or under section 81(13) of the Social Services and Well-being (Wales) Act 2014].

(5) For the purposes of paragraph (4), placing for adoption means placing for adoption in accordance with—

The Child Benefit (General) Regulations 2006

[² (a) the Adoption Agencies Regulations 2005,
(aa) the Adoption Agencies (Wales) Regulations 2005,]
[¹ (b) the Adoption Agencies (Scotland) Regulations 2009, or]
(c) the Adoption Agencies Regulations (Northern Ireland) 1989.

AMENDMENTS

1. Adoption and Children (Scotland) Act 2007 (Consequential Modifications) Order 2011 (SI 2011/1740) art.2 and Sch.1 para.43 (July 15, 2011).
2. Child Benefit (General) (Amendment) Regulations 2012 (SI 2012/818) regs 8–10 (April 6, 2012).
3. Tax Credits and Child Benefit (Miscellaneous Amendments) Regulations 2016 (SI 2016/360) reg.6(3) (April 6, 2016).

DEFINITIONS

"child or qualifying young person"—see SSCBA 1992 s.142.
"week"—see reg.19.

GENERAL NOTE

3.22   Schedule 9 para.(1) of the Act provides that no claim can be made in respect of a child who is in prison, detention, legal custody or in certain circumstances in local authority care. But this regulation relieves from that disqualification to some extent. Disqualification does not apply to the first eight weeks of the detention, etc. nor does it apply if the child actually lives with the claimant (as distinct from being maintained by the claimant) and does so for the whole week and, in effect, part weeks that commence or end a succession of whole weeks. Alternatively the claimant can retain benefit if the child ordinarily lives with him throughout at least one day each week. This means that the child must sleep at home two nights in the week. The relief outlined above does not apply if the child is placed by a local authority in a private home, is fostered, or is placed for adoption.

Child or qualifying young person undergoing imprisonment or detention in legal custody

3.23   **17.**—(1) For the purposes of paragraph 1(a) of Schedule 9 to SSCBA and paragraph 1(1)(a) of Schedule 9 to SSCB(NI)A, a child or qualifying young person is not regarded as undergoing imprisonment or detention in legal custody in any week unless—
   (a) in connection with a charge brought or intended to be brought against him in criminal proceedings at the conclusion of those proceedings, or
   (b) in the case of default of payment of a sum adjudged to be paid on conviction, in respect of such default,
a court imposes a penalty upon him.
   (2) Subject to paragraph (3), paragraph 1(a) of Schedule 9 to SSCBA and paragraph 1(1)(a) of Schedule 9 to SSCB(NI)A do not apply to a child or qualifying young person in respect of any week in which that child or qualifying young person is liable to be detained in a hospital or similar institution in Great Britain or Northern Ireland as a person suffering from a mental disorder.
   (3) Subject to paragraph (5), paragraph (2) does not apply where subsequent to the imposition of a penalty, the child or qualifying young person was removed to the hospital or similar institution while still liable to be detained as a result of that penalty and, in the case of a person who is liable to be detained in the hospital or similar institution by virtue of

any provisions of the Mental Health Acts, a direction restricting his discharge has been given under any of those Acts and is still in force.

(4) In paragraph (3) a person who is liable to be detained by virtue of any provision of the Mental Health Acts shall be treated as if a direction restricting his discharge had been given under those Acts if he is to be so treated for the purposes of any of them.

(5) Where a certificate given by or on behalf of the Secretary of State shows the earliest date on which the child or qualifying young person would have been expected to be discharged from detention pursuant to the penalty if he had not been transferred to a hospital or similar institution, paragraph (3) shall not apply from the day following that date.

DEFINITIONS

"child or qualifying young person"—see SSCBA 1992 s.142.
"Court"—see reg.1.
"hospital or similar institution"—see reg.1.
"mental disorder"—see reg.1.
"the Mental Health Acts"—see reg.1.
"penalty"—see reg.1.
"week"—see reg.19.

GENERAL NOTE

This regulation provides that the disqualification from benefit in respect of a child who is in prison, detention in legal custody applies only if the child is sentenced to be detained.

This means that if benefit has been suspended during a period that the child is in custody on remand or awaiting sentence it may become payable if the child is not sentenced to a period of detention.

The disqualification does not apply if the child is detained as a result of a mental disorder, unless the child has been transferred to a hospital or similar institution after being sentenced to a period of detention, in which case, the disqualification continues only so long as the order for detention would have continued.

Child or qualifying young person in care

18.—For the purposes of paragraph 1(c) of Schedule 9 to SSCBA and paragraph 1(c) of Schedule 9 to SSCB(NI)A (child or qualifying young person in care in such circumstances as may be prescribed), the prescribed circumstances are that—
  (a) the child or qualifying young person is provided with, or placed in, accommodation under Part 3 of the 1989 Act, [² under Part 4 or 6 of the Social Services and Well-being (Wales) Act 2014,] under Part 2 of the 1995 Act [¹, by virtue of a requirement in a child assessment order within the meaning of section 35 of the Children's Hearings (Scotland) Act 2011, a child protection order within the meaning of section 37 of that Act, a compulsory supervision order within the meaning of section 83 of that Act or an interim compulsory supervision order within the meaning of section 86 of that Act,] or under Part 4 of the 1995 Order and the cost of that child or qualifying young person's accommodation or maintenance is borne wholly or partly out of local authority funds, authority funds or any other public funds, and
  (b) the child or qualifying young person is not in residential accommodation in the circumstances prescribed in regulation 9.

AMENDMENTS

1. Children's Hearings (Scotland) Act 2011 (Consequential and Transitional Provisions and Savings) Order 2013 (SI 2013/1465) art.17 Sch.1 para.25 (June 24, 2013).
2. Tax Credits and Child Benefit (Miscellaneous Amendments) Regulations 2016 (SI 2016/360) reg.6(4) (April 6, 2016).

DEFINITIONS

"child or qualifying young person"—see SSCBA 1992 s.142.
"the 1989 Act"—see reg.1.
"the 1995 Act"—see reg.1.
"the 1995 Order"—see reg.1.

Interpretation of facts existing in a week

19.—Where paragraph 1 of Schedule 9 to SSCBA or paragraph 1 of Schedule 9 to SSCB(NI)A applies, section 147(2) of SSCBA and section 143(2) of SSCB(NI)A (references to any condition being satisfied or any facts existing in a week to be construed as references to the condition being satisfied or the facts existing at the beginning of that week) has effect as if the words "at the beginning of that week" were substituted by "throughout any day in that week".

PART 5

ENTITLEMENT AFTER DEATH OF CHILD OR QUALIFYING YOUNG PERSON

Entitlement after death of child or qualifying young person

20.—The prescribed period for the purposes of section 145A of SSCBA and section 141A of SSCB(NI)A (entitlement after death of child or qualifying young person) is—
  (a) in the case of a child, eight weeks, and
  (b) in the case of a qualifying young person the shorter of—
    (i) the period of eight weeks; and
    (ii) the period commencing the week in which his death occurred and finishing on the Monday in the week following the week in which the qualifying young person would have attained the age of 20.

PART 6

RESIDENCE

Circumstances in which a child or qualifying young person treated as being in Great Britain

21.—(1) For the purposes of section 146(1) of SSCBA, a child or qualifying young person who is temporarily absent from Great Britain shall be treated as being in Great Britain during—
  (a) the first 12 weeks of any period of absence;
  (b) any period during which that person is absent by reason only of—

(i) his receiving full-time education by attendance at a [¹ school or college] in an EEA State or in Switzerland; or
(ii) his being engaged in an educational exchange or visit made with the written approval of the [¹ school or college] which he normally attends;
(c) any period as is determined by the Commissioners during which the child or qualifying young person is absent for the specific purpose of being treated for an illness or physical or mental disability which commenced before his absence began; or
(d) any period when he is in Northern Ireland.

(2) For the purposes of section 146(1) of SSCBA, where a child is born while his mother is absent from Great Britain in accordance with regulation 24, he shall be treated as being in Great Britain during such period of absence after his birth as is within 12 weeks of the date on which his mother became absent from Great Britain.

AMENDMENT

1. Child Benefit (General) (Amendment) Regulations 2007 (SI 2007/2150) reg.7 (August 16, 2007).

DEFINITIONS

"child or qualifying young person"—see SSCBA 1992 s.142.
"The Commissioners"—see reg.1.
"EEA State"—see reg.1.
"full time education"—see reg.1.

Application of regulation 24 where the person is in Northern Ireland

22.—If a person who is in Northern Ireland is treated as being in Great Britain in accordance with regulation 24, he is treated as not being in Northern Ireland for the purposes of section 142 of SSCB(NI)A.

3.29

Circumstances in which person treated as not being in Great Britain

23.—(1) A person shall be treated as not being in Great Britain for the purposes of section 146(2) of SSCBA if he is not ordinarily resident in the United Kingdom.

3.30

(2) [³ [¹⁴ Paragraph 1 does]] not apply to a Crown servant posted overseas or his partner.

(3) A person who is in Great Britain as a result of his deportation, expulsion or other removal by compulsion of law from another country to Great Britain shall be treated as being ordinarily resident in the United Kingdom [³ [¹⁴ . . .]].

(4) A person shall be treated as not being in Great Britain for the purposes of section 146(2) of SSCBA where he [¹ makes a claim for child benefit on or after 1st May 2004] [² and
(a) does not have a right to reside in the United Kingdom; [⁶ . . .]
[⁵ (b) has a right to reside by virtue of paragraph (1) of regulation 16 of the Immigration (European Economic Area) Regulations 2016, but only in a case where a right exists under that regulation because that person satisfies the criteria in paragraph (5) of that regulation]] [⁶; or
(c) would fall within sub-paragraph (a) or (b) but for the fact that that person has limited leave to enter, or remain in, the United Kingdom

The Child Benefit (General) Regulations 2006

under the Immigration Act 1971 which has been granted by virtue of [¹⁰ (i) Appendix EU to the immigration rules; or
  (ii) having arrived in the United Kingdom with an entry clearance that was granted under Appendix EU (Family Permit) to the immigration rules.]

[⁷ (4A) Paragraph (4)(b) does not apply to a person who is lawfully working in Great Britain and is a national of a State with which—
  (a) the European Union has concluded an agreement under article 217 of the Treaty on the Functioning of the European Union (an "EU Agreement") providing, in the field of social security, for the equal treatment of workers who are nationals of the signatory State and their families; or
  (b) the United Kingdom has concluded an agreement which replaces in whole or in part an EU Agreement in sub-paragraph (a) which has ceased to apply to, and in, the United Kingdom, providing, in the field of social security, for the equal treatment of workers who are nationals of the signatory State and their families.]

[⁸ (4B) Paragraph (4)(c)[¹⁰ (i)] does not apply to a person who --
  (a) has limited leave to enter, or remain in, the United Kingdom under the Immigration Act 1971 which has been granted by virtue of Appendix EU to the Immigration Rules;
  (b) has been granted such leave in reliance of being a family member of a relevant person of Northern Ireland in accordance with those Rules; and
  (c) would have a right to reside under the Immigration (European Economic Area) Regulations 2016 if the relevant person of Northern Ireland were an EEA national within the meaning of regulation 2 of those Regulations;]

[³ (5) [¹⁴ . . .]]
(6) [¹⁴ . . .]
(7) [⁸ [¹⁴ . . .]]

AMENDMENTS

1. Child Benefit (General) (Amendment) Regulations 2007 (SI 2007/2150) reg.8 (August 16, 2007).
2. Child Benefit and Child Tax Credit (Miscellaneous Amendments) Regulations 2012 (SI 2012/2612) regs 2 and 3 (November 8, 2012).
3. Child Benefit (General) and the Tax Credits (Residence) (Amendment) Regulations 2014 (SI 2014/1511) regs 2 and 3 (July 1, 2014).
4. Child Benefit, Tax Credits and Childcare Payments (Section 67 Immigration Act 2016 Leave) (Amendment) Regulations 2018 (SI 2018/788) reg.2(3) (July 20, 2018).
5. Tax Credits, Child Benefit and Childcare Payments (Miscellaneous Amendments) Regulations 2019 (SI 2019/364) reg.11(4) (March 21, 2019).
6. Child Benefit and Child Tax Credit (Amendment) (EU Exit) Regulations 2019 (SI 2019/867) reg.2(2) (May 7, 2019).
7. Social Security, Child Benefit and Child Tax Credit (Amendment) (EU Exit) Regulations 2019 (SI 2019/1431) reg.6(2) (January 31, 2020).
8. Child Benefit and Child Tax Credit (Persons of Northern Ireland) (Amendment) Regulations 2020 (SI 2020/672) reg.2 (August 24, 2020).
9. Immigration and Social Security Co-ordination (EU Withdrawal) Act 2020 (Consequential, Saving, Transitional and Transitory Provisions) (EU Exit) Regulations 2020 (SI 2020/1309) reg. 66 (December 31, 2020). Note that there are

(SI 2006/223 reg.23)

saving provisions that apply to these amendments in Sch.4 para.3(o) of the amending regulations. The saving provisions apply to a "member of the post-transition period group" as that term is defined in para.1(b) of the Schedule.

10. Immigration (Citizens' Rights etc.) (EU Exit) Regulations 2020 (SI 2020/1372) reg.22 (December 31, 2020).

11. Child Benefit (General) (Amendment) Regulations 2021 (SI 2021/1039) reg.2 (September 15, 2021).

12. Child Benefit and Tax Credits (Amendment) Regulations 2022 (SI 2022/346) reg.2 (March 22, 2022).

13. Child Benefit (General) (Amendment) Regulations 2023 (SI 2023/533) reg.2(2) (May 15, 2023).

14. Child Benefit and Tax Credits (Miscellaneous Amendments) Regulations 2023 (SI 2023/1139) reg.2 (October 27, 2023).

DEFINITIONS

"Crown servant posted overseas"—see regs 1 and 30.
"partner"—see regs 1 and 31.

GENERAL NOTE

Paragraph (1) of s.146 requires that both the claimant and the child in respect of whom the claim is made should be present in the UK. This regulation extends the concept of presence into that of being "ordinarily resident". This concept is considered in the note to reg.4 of the Persons Abroad Regulations in Vol.I of this work. But in brief, it requires that a person has made this country his place of abode as a voluntary and settled purpose in his life. Thus mere presence in the country is not enough. It must be legal presence, and at least for the time being, it should be his home. On cases involving EU nationals and the potential application of reg.1408/71, see *JR v HMRC* [2009] UKUT 18 (AAC), confirmed by the Court of Appeal in *HMRC v Ruas* [2010] EWCA Civ 291; [2010] AACR 31 (see note to SSCBA 1992 s.146 at para.1.62, above).

3.31

Paragraph 2: disapplies this requirement in relation to a Crown servant who is posted overseas, his partner, and his child. These concepts are dealt with further in regs 30, 31 and 32.

3.32

Paragraph 3: affirms that a person who is in this country only because he has been deported from another country is, nevertheless, to be regarded as ordinarily resident here.

3.33

Paragraph 4: since 2004 a claimant must show, as well, that they have the right to reside in the UK. The right to reside is accorded automatically to all British citizens. While the UK was a member of the EU it applied, as well, to EU citizens who came to the country as jobseekers and afterwards as workers. Since the UK has left the EU, continuing entitlement will depend upon their status as settled persons or possibly as a pre-settled person. For details of this and for the effect of the European Union (Withdrawal) Act 2018 and the Retained EU Law (Revocation and Reform) Act 2023, see Vol.III of this work.

3.34

Where the right to reside depends upon the claimant maintaining their status as a worker, problems can arise during a period of enforced absence. Two cases have examined the position of a self-employed person during what might be regarded as a period of maternity leave. In the case of an employed person this problem is unlikely to arise so long as the contract of employment is subsisting, but a self-employed person must demonstrate that her self-employed status continues as "an activity that is genuine and effective"—see *HMRC v HD and GP (CHB)* [2017] UKUT 11 (AAC). These cases show the importance for First-tier Tribunals of making a detailed inquiry as to the facts and findings based on those facts. Judge Ward held, after receiving further evidence, in the first case that the claimant had not demonstrated a continuing involvement in pursuing her business (that of a beauty therapist) to a sufficient extent, and that the income she had from the few engagements that she did have in that period, was a marginal increment to the maternity allowance on which she was relying. By contrast, in the second case (that of a self-employed cleaner) where the claimant had done no work at all in the period of leave, he found that she had nevertheless shown a sufficient involvement with her business because she had arranged for friends to undertake some of the work for part of the time, and had otherwise maintained contact with other clients and arranged to return to them when she was able to do so. In this case then, the claim for child benefit succeeded on the basis that the claimant had shown that she was, in fact, still engaged in activity that was genuine and effective. In the first case, however, the question remained of whether the claimant might succeed on an alternative argument that her status should be protected under the principal in the *Saint Prix* case decided by the CJEU (*Saint Prix* (C-507/12)). Some of the issues arising from that case have been referred again to the CJEU in *Florea Gusa v Minister for Social Protection, Attorney General* (C-442/16) by the Irish Court of Appeal. Judge Ward invited submissions for a stay of proceedings pending the outcome of that reference. For more detailed discussion of these issues see Vol. III of this work.

The requirement for a right to reside has been found to be lawful by the Court of Appeal of Northern Ireland in *Revenue and Customs v Spiridonova* [2014] NICA 63, reversing a decision of the Chief Commissioner for Northern Ireland (*AS v HMRC (CB)* [2013] NI Comm. 15).

See note to para.(3) of reg.27 below.

Persons temporarily absent from Great Britain

3.35

24.—(1) A person who is ordinarily resident in the United Kingdom and is temporarily absent from Great Britain shall be treated as being in Great Britain during the first—
(a) 8 weeks of any period of absence; or
(b) 12 weeks of any period of absence where that period of absence, or any extension to that period of absence, is in connection with—
  (i) the treatment of his illness or physical or mental disability;
  (ii) the treatment of his partner's illness or physical or mental disability;
  (iii) the death of a person who, immediately prior to the date of death, was his partner;
  (iv) the death, or the treatment of the illness or physical or mental disability, of a child or qualifying young person for whom either he or his partner is, or both of them are, responsible; or
  (v) the death, or the treatment of the illness or physical or mental disability, of his or his partner's relative.

Here "relative" means brother, sister, forebear or lineal descendant.

(2) A person is temporarily absent from Great Britain if at the beginning of the period of absence his absence is unlikely to exceed 52 weeks.

DEFINITIONS

"child or qualifying young person"—see SSCBA 1992 s.142.
"Partner"—see reg.1.

(SI 2006/223 reg.24)

GENERAL NOTE

A person may remain ordinarily resident and so for the purposes of s.146 "present" even though he is temporarily absent from the country. The concept of "temporary" absence is considered in the notes to reg.2 of the Persons Abroad Regulations in Vol.I of this work. This regulation limits temporary absence to an absence which at its outset must be unlikely to exceed 52 weeks, and then provides that the absence is, in any case, only waived for a period of eight weeks, or, if the reason for absence (or extended absence) is illness or death of one of the parties then a maximum of 12 weeks.

3.36

Circumstances in which a child or qualifying young person treated as being in Northern Ireland

25.—(1) For the purposes of section 142(1) of SSCB(NI)A a child or qualifying young person who is temporarily absent from Northern Ireland shall be treated as being in Northern Ireland during—

(a) the first 12 weeks of any period of absence;
(b) any period during which the child or qualifying young person is absent by reason only of—
 (i) his receiving full-time education by attendance at a [¹ school or college] in an EEA State or in Switzerland; or
 (ii) his being engaged in an educational exchange or visit made with the written approval of the [¹ school or college] which he normally attends;
(c) any period as is determined by the Commissioners during which the child or qualifying young person is absent for the specific purpose of being treated for an illness or physical or mental disability which commenced before his absence began; or
(d) any period when he is in Great Britain.

(2) For the purposes of section 142(1) of SSCB(NI)A, where a child is born while his mother is absent from Northern Ireland in accordance with regulation 28, he shall be treated as being in Northern Ireland during such period of absence after his birth as is within 12 weeks of the date on which his mother became absent from Northern Ireland.

3.37

AMENDMENT

1. Child Benefit (General) (Amendment) Regulations 2007 (SI 2007/2150) reg.9 (August 16, 2007).

DEFINITIONS

"child or qualifying young person"—see SSCBA 1992 s.142.
"The Commissioners"—see reg.1.
"EEA State"—see reg.1.
"full time education"—see reg.1.

Application of regulation 28 where person in Great Britain

26.—Where a person who is in Great Britain is treated as being in Northern Ireland in accordance with regulation 28, he is treated as not being in Great Britain for the purposes of section 146 of SSCBA.

3.38

Circumstances in which person treated as not being in Northern Ireland

3.39   **27.**—(1) A person shall be treated as not being in Northern Ireland for the purposes of section 142(2) of SSCB(NI)A if he is not ordinarily resident in the United Kingdom.

(2) A person who is in Northern Ireland as a result of his deportation, expulsion or other removal by compulsion of law from another country to Northern Ireland shall be treated as being ordinarily resident in the United Kingdom [³[¹⁴...]].

(3) A person shall be treated as not being in Northern Ireland for the purposes of section 142(2) of SSCB(NI)A where he [¹ makes a claim for child benefit on or after 1st May 2004] [² and

(a) does not have a right to reside in the United Kingdom; [⁶...]

[⁵(b) has a right to reside in the United Kingdom by virtue of paragraph (1) of regulation 16 of the Immigration (European Economic Area) Regulations 2016, but only in a case where a right exists under that regulation because that person satisfies the criteria in paragraph (5) of that regulation.]] [⁶; or

(c) would fall within sub-paragraph (a) or (b) but for the fact that that person has limited leave to enter, or remain in, the United Kingdom under the Immigration Act 1971 which has been granted by virtue of [¹⁰ (i) Appendix EU to the immigration rules; or

(ii) having arrived in the United Kingdom with an entry clearance that was granted under Appendix EU (Family Permit) to the immigration rules.]

[⁷ (3A) Paragraph (3)(b) does not apply to a person who is lawfully working in Northern Ireland and is a national of a State with which:

(a) the European Union has concluded an agreement under article 217 of the Treaty on the Functioning of the European Union (an "EU Agreement") providing, in the field of social security, for the equal treatment of workers who are nationals of the signatory State and their families; or

(b) the United Kingdom has concluded an agreement which replaces in whole or in part an EU Agreement in sub-paragraph (a) which has ceased to apply to, and in, the United Kingdom, providing, in the field of social security, for the equal treatment of workers who are nationals of the signatory State and their families.]

[⁸ (3B) Paragraph (3)(c) [¹⁰ (i)] does not apply to a person who --

(a) has limited leave to enter, or remain in, the United Kingdom under the Immigration Act 1971 which has been granted by virtue of Appendix EU to the Immigration Rules;

(b) has been granted such leave in reliance of being a family member of a relevant person of Northern Ireland in accordance with those Rules; and

(c) would have a right to reside under the Immigration (European Economic Area) Regulations 2016 if the relevant person of Northern Ireland were an EEA national within the meaning of regulation 2 of those Regulations;]

[³ (4) [¹⁴ ...]

(5) [¹⁴ ...]

(6) [⁸ [¹⁴ ...]]

(SI 2006/223 reg.27)

AMENDMENTS

1. Child Benefit (General) Amendment Regulations 2007 (SI 2007/2150) reg.10 (August 16, 2007).
2. Child Benefit and Child Tax Credit (Miscellaneous Amendments) Regulations 2012 (SI 2012/2612) regs 2 and 4 (November 8, 2012).
3. Child Benefit (General) and the Tax Credits (Residence) (Amendment) Regulations 2014 (SI 2014/1511) regs 2 and 4 (July 1, 2014).
4. Child Benefit, Tax Credits and Childcare Payments (Section 67 Immigration Act 2016 Leave) (Amendment) Regulations 2018 (SI 2018/788) reg.2(4) (July 20, 2018).
5. Tax Credits, Child Benefit and Childcare Payments (Miscellaneous Amendments) Regulations 2019 (SI 2019/364) reg.11(5) (March 21, 2019).
6. Child Benefit and Child Tax Credit (Amendment) (EU Exit) Regulations 2019 (SI 2019/867) reg.2(3) (May 7, 2019).
7. Social Security, Child Benefit and Child Tax Credit (Amendment) (EU Exit) Regulations 2019 (SI 2019/1431) reg.6(3) (January 31, 2020).
8. Child Benefit and Child Tax Credit (Persons of Northern Ireland) (Amendment) Regulations 2020 (SI 2020/672) reg.2 (August 24, 2020).
9. Immigration and Social Security Co-ordination (EU Withdrawal) Act 2020 (Consequential, Saving, Transitional and Transitory Provisions) (EU Exit) Regulations 2020 (SI 2020/1309) reg. 66 (December 31, 2020). Note that there are saving provisions that apply to these amendments in Sch.4 para.3(o) of the amending regulations. The saving provisions apply to a "member of the post-transition period group" as that term is defined in para.1(b) of the Schedule.
10. Immigration (Citizens' Rights etc.) (EU Exit) Regulations 2020 (SI 2020/1372) reg.22 (December 31, 2020).
11. Child Benefit (General) (Amendment) Regulations 2021 (SI 2021/1039) reg.2 (September 15, 2021).
12. Child Benefit and Tax Credits (Amendment) Regulations 2022 (SI 2022/346) reg.2 (March 22, 2022).
13. Child Benefit (General) (Amendment) Regulations 2023 (SI 2023/533) reg.2 (May 15, 2023).
14. Child Benefit and Tax Credits (Miscellaneous Amendments) Regulations 2023 (SI 2023/1139) reg.2 (October 27, 2023).

GENERAL NOTE

Paragraph (3): Since 2004 a claimant must show, as well, that they have the right to reside in the UK. The right to reside is accorded automatically to all British citizens. While the UK was a member of the EU it applied, as well, to EU citizens who came to Northern Ireland as jobseekers and afterwards as workers. Since the UK has left the EU, continuing entitlement will depend upon their status as settled persons or possibly as a pre-settled person. For details of this and for the effect of the European Union (Withdrawal) Act 2018 and the Retained EU Law (Revocation and Reform) Act 2023, see Vol.III of this work.

3.40

The requirement for a right to reside for CB was found to be lawful by the Court of Appeal of Northern Ireland in *Revenue and Customs v Spiridonova* [2014] NICA 63, reversing a decision of the Chief Commissioner for Northern Ireland *(AS v HMRC (CB)* [2013] NI Comm. 15).

In this case the claimant, a Latvian, had been living and working for almost all of 23 months in the country where she claimed CB in respect of a daughter living with her. Her claim was refused on the ground of right to reside because, at the time, Latvia was an A8 country which limited her right to claim. The Chief Commissioner had allowed her appeal on the ground that the right to reside requirement was directly discriminatory (as it would be satisfied automatically by a British citizen) and was therefore unlawful under art.3(1) of EC Regulation 1408/71 (now replaced by EC Regulation 883/04). In doing so he had distinguished the decision in *Patmalniece v SSWP* [2011] UKSC 11. The Commissioner went on to observe also, that if he were wrong in reaching this conclusion, that he would have found that the claimant had an alternative route to success derived from the *Patmalniece* decision on the basis that she was sufficiently integrated, economically and socially, to qualify anyway. So in the event that his finding of direct discrimination was not correct, the Chief Commissioner found that if the right to reside test was indirectly discriminatory, it was not objectively justified.

The Northern Ireland Court of Appeal reversed the Chief Commissioner's decision in *Revenue and Customs v Spiridonova* [2014] NICA 63. On the direct discrimination point, the Court of Appeal held that it was bound to follow the clear decision of the CJEU in *Bressol v Gouvernement de la Communaute Française* [2010] 3 C.M.L.R. 559, whatever its doubts about the CJEU's reasoning. As a result the conditions contained in reg.27(3) had to be viewed cumulatively. In this light the requirement under reg.27(3) that an accession state national had to have a right to reside in the UK in order to be eligible for CB was not directly discriminatory on the ground of nationality. Moreover, the fact that an accession state worker had achieved a certain degree of social and/or economic integration in the UK could not, of itself, operate as an exception to the right to reside test. It was, accordingly, still necessary to consider the specific statutory requirement that, to establish a right of residence in the UK as a worker, an accession state national had to be in continuous registered employment with an authorised employer in accordance with the Workers Registration Scheme, as established by the Accession (Immigration and Worker Registration) Regulations 2004. Since those Regulations were devised to apply to accession state workers, the fact that an individual had worked more or less continually for a period in Northern Ireland could not constitute an exception (*R. (on the application of D) v Secretary of State For Work and Pensions* [2004] EWCA Civ 1468 and *Zalewska v Department for Social Development* [2008] UKHL 67, [2008] 1 W.L.R. 2602 considered). The Chief Commissioner's decision that a degree of economic and/or social integration could operate as an exception to the right to reside requirement had inhibited him from any consideration of the specific statutory requirement that, to establish a right of residence in the UK as a worker, an accession state national had to be in continuous registered employment with an authorised employer under the Scheme. It followed that the Chief Commissioner did not make any finding as to whether the 2006 Regulations constituted a lawful means of attaining a legitimate objective and, if so, whether the means adopted were proportionate. In those circumstances, his conclusions as to indirect discrimination could not stand either.

Persons temporarily absent from Northern Ireland

3.41

28.—(1) A person who is ordinarily resident in the United Kingdom and is temporarily absent from Northern Ireland shall be treated as being in Northern Ireland during the first—
   (a) 8 weeks of any period of absence; or
   (b) 12 weeks of any period of absence where that period of absence, or any extension to that period of absence, is in connection with—
      (i) the treatment of his illness or physical or mental disability;
      (ii) the treatment of his partner's illness or physical or mental disability;
      (iii) the death of a person who, immediately prior to the date of death, was his partner;
      (iv) the death, or the treatment of the illness or physical or mental disability, of a child for whom either he or his partner is, or both of them are, responsible; or
      (v) the death, or the treatment of the illness or physical or mental disability, of his or his partner's relative.

Here "relative" has the same meaning as in regulation 24.

(2) A person is temporarily absent from Northern Ireland if, at the beginning of the period of absence, his absence is unlikely to exceed 52 weeks.

DEFINITION

"partner"—see reg.1.

Overlap of entitlement to child benefit under both the legislation of Northern Ireland and Great Britain

29.—(1) Where by virtue of these Regulations two or more persons would be entitled to child benefit in respect of the same child or qualifying young person for the same week under both the legislation of Northern Ireland and Great Britain, one of them only shall be so entitled.

(2) Where the child is in Great Britain (except where regulation 25(1)(d) applies) or is treated as being in Great Britain, the question of which of the persons is entitled shall be determined in accordance with the legislation applying to Great Britain.

(3) Where the child is in Northern Ireland (except where regulation 21(1)(d) applies) or is treated as being in Northern Ireland, the question of which of the persons is entitled shall be determined in accordance with the legislation applying to Northern Ireland.

DEFINITIONS

"child or qualifying young person"—see SSCBA 1992 s.142.
"week"—see SSCBA 1992 s.147.

Crown servants posted overseas

30.—(1) For the purposes of section [^{2} 146 (2)] of the Social Security and Contributions and Benefits Act, a Crown servant posted overseas shall be treated as being in Great Britain.

(2) A Crown servant posted overseas is a person performing overseas (but not in Northern Ireland) the duties of any office or employment under the Crown in right of the United Kingdom—
   (a) who is, or was, immediately prior to his posting or his first of consecutive postings, ordinarily resident in the United Kingdom; or
   (b) who, immediately prior to his posting or his first of consecutive postings, was in the United Kingdom in connection with that posting.

AMENDMENT

1. Child Benefit (General) (Amendment) Regulations 2007 (SI 2007/2150) reg.11 (August 16, 2007).

GENERAL NOTE

In *CF/1968/2007* Commissioner Williams held that the expression "Crown servant posted overseas" should include a consular correspondent who was appointed subsequently as an honorary consul of the UK. At all times, he said, the claimant was fulfilling functions defined in the Vienna Convention on Consular Relations. (Adopted in the UK by the Consular Relations Act 1968.) In doing so he was performing the duties of an officer under the Crown required by reg.30.

It did not matter whether the duties performed were included in the Convention. Nor did it matter that the claimant had been recruited whilst he was living in the overseas country, because, in the view of the Commissioner, the words "posted overseas" were only descriptive of the place where the duties were performed and not the process by which the claimant came to be there. There remained the matter of whether the claimant could show that he was, immediately before his posting, an ordinary resident in the UK; and on that the Commissioner referred the case for rehearing. There was some evidence that he may indeed have been an ordinary resident because he was a retired army officer who was paying UK income tax on his pension. Note, too, that although it will usually be necessary for the child in respect of whom the claim is made, to be resident in the UK there is an exception provided in reg.32; the child will be treated as being in Great Britain where he normally lives with a parent who is a Crown servant posted overseas.

Partners of Crown servants posted overseas

3.45

31.—(1) For the purposes of section [² 146 (2)] of the Social Security and Contributions and Benefits Act the partner of a Crown servant posted overseas who is accompanying the Crown servant posted overseas shall be treated as being in Great Britain when the partner is either—
  (a) in the country where the Crown servant is posted, or
  (b) absent from that country in accordance with regulation 24 as modified by paragraphs (3) and (4).

(2) Regulations 22 and 24 apply to the partner of a Crown servant posted overseas with the modifications set out in paragraphs (3) and (4).

(3) References to "Great Britain" in the phrase "temporarily absent from Great Britain" in paragraphs (1) and (2) of regulation 24 shall be construed as references to the country where the Crown servant is posted and regulation 21(2) shall apply, where appropriate, accordingly.

(4) In regulation 24 omit the words "ordinarily resident in the United Kingdom and is".

AMENDMENT

1. Child Benefit (General) (Amendment) Regulations 2007 (SI 2007/2150) reg.11 (August 16, 2007).

Child or qualifying young persons normally living with Crown servants posted overseas

3.46

32.—(1) For the purposes of section [¹ 146(1)] of the Social Security and Contributions and Benefits Act a child or qualifying young person who normally lives with a Crown servant posted overseas shall be treated as being in Great Britain when he is either—
  (a) in the country where the Crown servant is posted, or
  (b) absent from that country in accordance with regulation 21 as modified by paragraph (2).

(2) The reference to "Great Britain" in paragraph (1) of that regulation shall be construed as a reference to the country where the Crown servant is posted.

AMENDMENT

1. Child Benefit (General) (Amendment) Regulations 2007 (SI 2007/2150) reg.11 (August 16, 2007).

(SI 2006/223 reg.32)

DEFINITIONS

"child or qualifying young person"—see SSCBA 1992 s.142.
"Crown servant posted overseas"—see reg.1.

Transitional provisions for Part 6

33.—(1) In relation to a period of temporary absence which commenced before 7th April 2003, and continues after the coming into force of these Regulations, regulations 24 and 28 shall have effect subject to the modifications in paragraphs (2) and (3) respectively.

(2) For regulation 24(2) substitute—

"(2) A person is temporarily absent from Great Britain if at the beginning of the period of absence his absence was intended to be temporary and has throughout continued to be so intended."

(3) For regulation 28(2) substitute—

"(2) A person is temporarily absent from Northern Ireland if at the beginning of the period of absence his absence was intended to be temporary and has throughout continued to be so intended."

3.47

PART 7

GENERAL AND SUPPLEMENTARY PROVISIONS

Persons treated as residing together

34.—For the purposes of Part 9 of SSCBA and Part 9 of SSCB(NI)A, the prescribed circumstances in which persons are treated as residing together are that spouses, two persons who are civil partners of each other, or two persons who are parents of a child [¹ or, qualifying young person] are absent from one another—
(a) where such absence is not likely to be permanent; or
(b) by reason only of the fact that either of them is, or they both are, undergoing medical or other treatment as an in-patient in a hospital or similar institution whether such absence is temporary or not.

3.48

AMENDMENT

1. Child Benefit (General) (Amendment) Regulations 2007 (SI 2007/2150) reg.12 (August 16, 2007).

DEFINITIONS

"civil partners"—see reg.1.
"hospital or similar institution"—see reg.1.

GENERAL NOTE

The question whether parties are residing together may be important in determining priorities, and was formerly important in relation to one parent benefit.

This regulation provides a partial definition of what is meant by "residing together" by stating two instances in which they are not to be regarded as being apart. In the first, spouses or parents of a child who are not married are to be regarded as not being absent from each other (i.e. are residing together) so long as their absence is not permanent. There is no limit on the period of absence as long as

3.49

it can still be regarded as temporary. In *R(F) 4/85* this rule was applied to a couple who had never lived together. They married while the husband was serving a term of imprisonment having met through the wife's involvement as a prison visitor. Nevertheless the Commissioner held that a similarly worded regulation meant that they must be regarded as residing together.

In the second instance they will be regarded as not absent (i.e. are residing together) if one or both of them is undergoing medical treatment. In this case they will be regarded as being together even if the separation is expected to be permanent. This will cover the case of a parent who is in a hospice receiving terminal care. But the concept of residing together still requires that the parties share a household rather than just a roof (*R(F)3/81*).

Polygamous marriages

3.50   **35.**—(1) For the purposes of Part 9 of SSCBA and Part 9 of SSCB(NI)A, a polygamous marriage is treated as having the same consequences as a monogamous marriage for any day, but only for any day, throughout which the polygamous marriage is in fact monogamous.

(2) In paragraph (1)—
  (a) "monogamous marriage" means a marriage celebrated under a law which does not permit polygamy;
  (b) "polygamous marriage" means a marriage celebrated under a law which, as it applies to the particular ceremony and to the parties in question, permits polygamy;
  (c) a polygamous marriage is referred to as being in fact monogamous when neither party to it has any spouse additional to the other; and
  (d) the day on which a polygamous marriage is contracted, or on which it terminates for any reason, shall be treated as a day throughout which that marriage was in fact monogamous if at all times on that day after the time at which it was contracted, or as the case may be, before it terminated, it was in fact monogamous.

DEFINITION

"a polygamous marriage"—see para.(2).

GENERAL NOTE

3.51   A polygamous marriage (celebrated after July 31, 1971) is void if either of the parties was at the time domiciled in the UK (Matrimonial Causes Act 1973); see *SSWP v MN (BB)* [2018] UKUT 68 (AAC). This regulation is therefore most likely to affect parties who have contracted a marriage in polygamous form before they settle in this country. The marriage will be recognised in relation to Child Benefit so long as it remains monogamous or, if it was once polygamous, once the extra spouse has died or been divorced.

Right to child benefit of voluntary organisations

3.52   **36.**—(1) Subject to paragraph (4) and (5), for the purposes of section 147(6) of SSCBA and section 143(6) of SSCB(NI)A (right to child benefit of voluntary organisations), a voluntary organisation is regarded as the only person with whom a child is living for any week in which that child is—
  (a) living in premises which are provided or managed by the voluntary organisation, being premises which are required to be registered with

(SI 2006/223 reg.36)

a Government Department or local authority or which are otherwise regulated under or by virtue of any enactment relating to England and Wales, Scotland, or Northern Ireland; or

(b) placed by the voluntary organisation in the home of any person in accordance with the provisions of the [1 Fostering Services (England) Regulations 2011, the Fostering Services (Wales) Regulations 2003, the Looked After Children (Scotland) Regulations 2009] or the Foster Placement (Children) Regulations (Northern Ireland) 1996.

(2) A voluntary organisation shall not be regarded as having ceased to have a child living with it by reason only of any temporary absence of that child—

(a) if the child is undergoing medical or other treatment as an in-patient in a hospital, until such absence has lasted for more than 84 days; or

(b) if the child is temporarily absent for any other reason, until such absence has lasted for more than 56 days.

(3) In calculating the period of 84 days for the purposes of paragraph (2)(a), two or more distinct periods of temporary absence separated by one or more intervals each not exceeding 28 days shall be treated as a continuous period equal in duration to the total of such distinct periods and ending on the last day of the latter or last of such periods.

(4) A voluntary organisation shall not be regarded as a person with whom a child or qualifying young person is living in any week if in that week—

(a) that individual is in residential accommodation in the circumstances prescribed in regulation 3; or

(b) paragraph 1 of Schedule 9 to SSCBA or paragraph 1 of Schedule 9 to SSCB(NI)A applies to that individual.

(5) Where immediately before the week in which paragraph (1) applies to a child or qualifying young person, that individual was living with a person who was then entitled to child benefit in respect of him, paragraph (1) shall have effect in relation to that person as if the words "the only person" were omitted for so long as the child or qualifying young person is treated as continuing to live with that person by virtue of section 143(2) of SSCBA or section 139(2) of SSCB(NI)A.

(6) Section 143(1)(b) of SSCBA and section 139(1)(b) of SSCB(NI)A (person to be treated as responsible for a child in any week if he is contributing to the cost of providing for the qualifying individual at a weekly rate not less than the weekly rate of child benefit payable in respect of the child or qualifying young person for that week) and regulation 16(1) (child or qualifying young person in detention) shall not apply to a voluntary organisation.

AMENDMENT

1. Child Benefit (General) (Amendment) Regulations 2012 (SI 2012/818) reg.11 (April 6, 2012).

DEFINITIONS

"child or qualifying young person"—see SSCBA 1992 s.142.
"voluntary organisation"—see SSCBA 1992 s.147.
"week"—see SSCBA 1992 s.147.

General Note

3.53 This regulation enables a voluntary organisation to claim benefit in respect of a child who is living in accommodation provided, managed or arranged by it. Living with a voluntary organisation will normally preclude a claim by any other person, except that a claim may continue to be made by a person who previously had the child living with him and subsequently has continued to maintain the child to the requisite extent. In such a case the original claimant will continue to be entitled but a claim made by the voluntary organisation would take priority under the usual rules as to priority.

No requirement to state national insurance number

3.54 **37.**—For the purposes of section 147(6) of SSCBA and section 143(6) of SSCB(NI)A, section 13(1A) of the Social Security Administration Act 1992 and section 11(1A) of the Social Security Administration (Northern Ireland) Act 1992 (requirement to state national insurance number) shall not apply to a claim for child benefit in respect of a child or qualifying young person who is treated as living with a voluntary organisation by virtue of regulation 36.

Exception to rules preventing duplicate payment

3.55 **38.**—(1) A person is not disentitled to child benefit in respect of a child or qualifying young person by virtue of section 13(2) of the Social Security Administration Act 1992 and section 11(2) of the Social Security Administration (Northern Ireland) Act 1992 (persons not entitled to benefit for any week if benefit already paid for that week to another person, whether or not that other person was entitled to it) if in respect of that week—
 (a) the determining authority has decided that the Commissioners are entitled to recover the child benefit paid in respect of that child or qualifying young person from a person in consequence of his misrepresentation of, or his failure to disclose, any material fact and, where that determining authority is one from whose decision an appeal lies, the time limit for appealing has expired and no appeal has been made; or
 (b) the child benefit paid to the other person has been voluntarily repaid to, or recovered by, the Commissioners in a case where the determining authority has decided under section 9 or 10 of the Social Security Act 1998 or under Article 10 or 11 of the Social Security (Northern Ireland) Order 1998 either—
  (i) that, while there was no entitlement to benefit, it is not recoverable, or
  (ii) that there was no entitlement to benefit but has made no decision as to its recoverability.

(2) In this regulation "determining authority" means, as the case may require—
 (a) the Commissioners;
 (b) an appeal tribunal constituted under [1 . . .] or Article 8 of the Social Security (Northern Ireland) Act 1998;
 (c) the Chief or any other Social Security Commissioner, or a tribunal consisting of any three or more such Commissioners constituted in accordance with [1 . . .] Article 16(7) of the Social Security (Northern Ireland) Act 1998;
[1 (d) the First-tier Tribunal;
 (e) the Upper Tribunal.]

(SI 2006/223 reg.38)

AMENDMENT

1. Tribunals, Courts and Enforcement Act 2007 (Transitional and Consequential Provisions) Order 2008 art.6(1) and Sch.1 para.308 (November 3, 2008).

DEFINITIONS

"child or qualifying young person"—see SSCBA 1992 s.142.
"the Commissioners"—see reg.1.
"week"—see SSCBA 1992 s.147.

GENERAL NOTE

Section 13(2) of the SSAA 1992 prevents a payment of child benefit being made where benefit has already been paid to another person, but that is a general rule only. The opening words of that section are "Except where regulations otherwise provide". This regulation does provide otherwise in two circumstances; first, where the HMRC has taken a decision that the payment already made is recoverable, and secondly where a voluntary repayment has been made. However, neither exception exists merely because a competing claim has been made in respect of that period. Unless the Commissioners have decided to recover (or a voluntary payment has been made) the tribunal that is hearing an appeal against refusal of a second claim has no jurisdiction in respect of that period. See *CF/2826/2007* and the observations made in *CB v HMRC and AE (CHB)* [2016] UKUT 506 (AAC).

Use of electronic communications

39.—Schedule 2 to the Child Benefit and Guardian's Allowance (Administration) Regulations 2003 (use of electronic communications) applies to the delivery of information to or by the Commissioners which is authorised or required by these Regulations in the same manner as it applies to the delivery of information to or by the Commissioners which is authorised or required by those Regulations.

References in this regulation to the delivery of information shall be construed in accordance with section 132(8) of the Finance Act 1999.

PART 8

REVOCATIONS

Omitted

The Child Benefit (Residence and Persons Abroad) Regulations 1976

(SI 1976/963) *(as amended)*

These regulations were revoked with effect from April 6, 2003 by the Tax Credits Act 2002. There was a saving in respect of regs 6 and 7 until April 2, 2006. Those provisions may be found in earlier editions of this book.

The Child Benefit (Rates) Regulations 2006

(SI 2006/965) *(as amended)*

ARRANGEMENT OF REGULATIONS

1. Citation, commencement and interpretation.
2. Rate of child benefit.
3. Saving
4. *Revocations omitted.*

Citation, commencement and interpretation

1.—(1) These Regulations may be cited as the Child Benefit (Rates) Regulations 2006 and shall come into force on 10th April 2006 immediately after the Child Benefit (General) Regulations 2006.

(2) In these Regulations—

"SSCBA" means the Social Security Contributions and Benefits Act 1992;

"SSCB(NI)A" means the Social Security Contributions and Benefits (Northern Ireland) Act 1992;

"qualifying young person" means a person—
 (a) in Great Britain, who is such a person for the purposes of Part 9 of SSCBA; and
 (b) in Northern Ireland, who is such a person for the purposes of Part 9 of SSCB(NI)A.

(3) References in these Regulations to any condition being satisfied or any facts existing shall be construed as references to the condition being satisfied or the facts existing at the beginning of that week.

Rate of child benefit

2.—(1) The weekly rate of child benefit payable in respect of a child or qualifying young person shall be—
 (a) subject to paragraphs (2) to (5), in a case where in any week a child or qualifying young person is the only person or, if not the only person, the elder or eldest person in respect of whom child benefit is payable to a person, [^{1}£25.60] ("the enhanced rate");
 (b) in any other case, [^{1}£16.95].

(2) If, in any week—
 (a) a person is—
  (i) living with his spouse or civil partner,
  (ii) living with another person as his spouse or civil partner, or
  (iii) a member of a polygamous marriage and is residing with other members of that marriage;
 (b) child benefit would, but for this paragraph, be payable to that person in respect of a child or qualifying young person at the enhanced rate; and
 (c) child benefit would, but for this paragraph, be payable at that rate to one of the other persons listed in paragraphs (i) to (iii) of sub-paragraph (a) in respect of another child or qualifying person,

the enhanced rate shall be payable in that week in respect of only the elder or eldest of the children and qualifying young persons referred to in sub-paragraphs (b) and (c).

(3) For the purposes of paragraph (2)(a) a person is a member of a polygamous marriage if—
- (a) during the subsistence of the marriage any party to it is married to more than one person; and
- (b) the ceremony of marriage took place under the law of a country which permits polygamy.

(4) Child benefit shall not be payable at the enhanced rate if the person to whom child benefit is payable is—
- (a) a voluntary organisation; or
- (b) a person residing (otherwise than as mentioned in paragraph (2)(a)) with a parent of the child or qualifying young person in respect of whom it is payable.

(5) If an allowance, or an increase of a benefit, pension or allowance, which is a specified benefit, is paid in respect of a week—
- (a) to a person, and
- (b) in respect of the only, elder or eldest child or qualifying young person in respect of whom that person is entitled to child benefit,

child benefit shall be payable at the enhanced rate for that week.

(6) The following are specified benefits—
- (a) any benefit under SSCBA receipt of which entitles the recipient to an increase specified in column 2 of the Table in Part 4 of Schedule 4 to that Act (increases for dependants);
- (b) any benefit under SSCB(NI)A receipt of which entitles the recipient to an increase specified in column 2 of the Table in Part IV of Schedule 4 to that Act (increases for dependants in Northern Ireland);
- (c) an allowance for a child or a qualifying young person granted in respect of the death of a person due to service or war injury—
  - (i) under the Armed Forces and Reserve Forces (Compensation Scheme) Order 2005;
  - (ii) under the Naval, Military and Air Forces Etc. (Disablement and Death) Service Pensions Order 1983;
  - (iii) under the Pensions (Polish Forces) Scheme 1964;
  - (iv) under the War Pensions (Mercantile Marine) Scheme 1964;
  - (v) under the Warrant of 21st December 1964 concerning pensions and grants in respect of disablement or death due to service in the Home Guard;
  - (vi) under the Order of 22nd December 1964 concerning pensions and grants in respect of disablement or death due to service in the Home Guard after 27th April 1952;
  - (vii) under the Order by Her Majesty dated 4th January 1971 in respect of service in the Ulster Defence Regiment; or
  - (viii) which the Commissioners for Her Majesty's Revenue and Customs accept as being analogous to an allowance for a child granted in respect of the death of a person due to service or war injury under any of the preceding provisions of this sub-paragraph.

The Child Benefit (General) Regulations 2006

AMENDMENT

1. Tax Credits, Child Benefit and Guardian's Allowance Up-rating Regulations 2024 (SI 2024/247) reg.5 (April 8, 2024).

Saving

3.63   **3.**—(1) Despite the revocation, by regulation 4 of these Regulations, of—
   (a) the Child Benefit and Social Security (Fixing and Adjustment of Rates) Regulations 1976, and
   (b) the Child Benefit and Social Security (Fixing and Adjustment of Rates) Regulations (Northern Ireland) 1976,
if the amount of child benefit which would have been payable under those Regulations would, by virtue of the relevant transitional provisions and savings (had they remained in force), be greater than the amount prescribed by these Regulations, the greater amount shall be payable.

(2) In paragraph (1) "the relevant transitional provisions and savings" means—
   (a) in the case of child benefit payable under SSCBA, regulations 3 and 4 of the Child Benefit and Social Security (Fixing and Adjustment of Rates) (Amendment) Regulations 1998; and
   (b) in the case of child benefit payable under SSCB(NI)A, regulations 3 and 4 of the Child Benefit and Social Security (Fixing and Adjustment of Rates) (Amendment) Regulations (Northern Ireland) 1998.

REVOCATIONS

3.64   **4.**—*Omitted.*

GENERAL NOTE

3.65   These regulations specify the rate of Child Benefit. Since April 8, 1991 it has been paid at a higher rate in respect of the first or only child of the family (though not if the claimant is a voluntary organisation). Where two families are living together so that there could be two eldest children, the higher rate will be paid only in respect of one (the older) of them.

Until July 6, 1998, reg.2 of the Fixing and Adjustment of Rates Regulations 1976 provided also for the payment of a supplement where the claimant was not living with a spouse. This benefit, generally known (though never labelled in the Regulations) as One Parent Benefit (OPB) was ended for new claimants from that date. Saving provisions for existing and continuing claims were contained in the Fixing and Adjustment of Rates (Amendment) Regulations 1998.

The Guardian's Allowance (General) Regulations 2003

(SI 2003/495) (AS AMENDED)

ARRANGEMENT OF REGULATIONS

3.66
1. Citation and commencement.
2. Interpretation.
3. Modification to section 77(2) of the Act.

4. Adopted children.
5. Illegitimate children.
6. Children of divorced parents.
7. Circumstances in which a person is to be treated as being in prison.
8. Rate of allowance and payment to the National Insurance Fund or the Northern Ireland National Insurance Fund.
9. Residence condition.
10. Prescribed manner of making an election under section 77(9) of the Act or section 77(9) of the Northern Ireland Act.
11. *Omitted.*

SCHEDULE

REVOCATIONS

Part 1—*Omitted.*
Part 2—*Omitted.*

The Treasury, in exercise of the powers conferred upon them by section 77(3), (8) and (9) of the Social Security Contributions and Benefits Act 1992, section 77(3), (8) and (9) of the Social Security Contributions and Benefits (Northern Ireland) Act 1992, and section 54(1) of the Tax Credits Act 2002 hereby make the following Regulations:

Citation and commencement

1.—These Regulations may be cited as the Guardian's Allowance (General) Regulations 2003 and shall come into force on 7th April 2003 immediately after the commencement of section 49 of the Tax Credits Act 2002.

Interpretation

2.—(1) In these Regulations—
"the Act" means the Social Security Contributions and Benefits Act 1992;
"adopted" means adopted pursuant to—
(a) an order made in the United Kingdom, the Channel Islands or the Isle of Man;
(b) an overseas adoption within the meaning of section 72(2) of the Adoption Act 1976;
(c) a Convention adoption order within the meaning of section 72(1) of the Adoption Act 1976; or
(d) a foreign adoption order within the meaning of section 4(3) of the Adoption (Hague Convention) Act (Northern Ireland) 1969.
"the Board" means the [¹ Commissioners for Her Majesty's Revenue and Customs];
"the Northern Ireland Act" means the Social Security Contributions and Benefits (Northern Ireland) Act 1992.

AMENDMENT

1. Guardian's Allowance (General) (Amendment) Regulations 2006 (SI 2006/204) (April 10, 2006).

The Child Benefit (Rates) Regulations 2006

Modification to section 77(2) of the Act

3.70   3.—Section 77(2) of the Act and section 77(2) of the Northern Ireland Act shall be treated as modified where regulations 4 to 6 apply.

Adopted children

3.71   4.—(1) Where a child [¹ or qualifying young person] has been adopted by two persons jointly, a reference in section 77(2) of the Act or section 77(2) of the Northern Ireland Act to [¹ the parents of the child or qualifying young person] shall be read as a reference to those two persons.

(2) Where a child [¹ or qualifying young person] has been adopted by one person only, the circumstances to be satisfied in section 77(2) of the Act or section 77(2) of the Northern Ireland Act are that that person is dead.

AMENDMENT

1. Guardian's Allowance (General) (Amendment) Regulations 2006 (SI 2006/204) (April 10, 2006).

DEFINITIONS

"adopted"—reg.2.
"child"—SSCBA 1992 s.122.

Illegitimate children

3.72   5.—Where—
(a) a child's parents are [² not married to, or civil partners of, each other at the date of the birth]; and
(b) paternity has not been established—
   (i) by a court of competent jurisdiction; or
   (ii) in the opinion of the determining authority,
   the circumstances to be satisfied in section 77(2) of the Act or section 77(2) of the Northern Ireland Act are that the mother of the child [¹ or qualifying young person] is dead.

AMENDMENT

1. Guardian's Allowance (General) (Amendment) Regulations 2006 (SI 2006/204) (April 10, 2006).
2. Civil Partnership (Opposite-sex Couples) Regulations 2019 (SI 2019/1458) reg.41(b) and Sch.3 Part 2 para.65 (December 2, 2019).

DEFINITION

"child"—SSCBA 1992 s.122.

Children of divorced parents

3.73   6.—(1) Where—
(a) [¹ the marriage or the civil partnership of a child's parents has been terminated by divorce or dissolved];
(b) at the death of one of the parents the child [² or qualifying young person] was not in the custody of or maintained by the other parent;
(c) there is no court order—
   [² (i) providing that child or qualifying young person is to reside with that other parent; or]

(ii) imposing any liability on him for [² the maintenance of the child or qualifying young person]; and
(d) there is no maintenance assessment or maintenance calculation, as defined by section 54 of the Child Support Act 1991, or, for Northern Ireland, Article 2(2) of the Child Support (Northern Ireland) Order 1991 in force in respect of that other parent and child [² or qualifying young person],

the circumstances to be satisfied in section 77(2) of the Act or section 77(2) of the Northern Ireland Act are that one of [² the parents of the child or qualifying young persons] is dead.

(2) Where a child [² or qualifying young person] has been adopted by two persons jointly, any reference in paragraph (1) above to [² the parents of the child or qualifying young person] shall be read as a reference to those two persons.

AMENDMENTS

1. Civil Partnership Act 2004 (Tax Credits, etc.) (Consequential Amendments) Order 2005 (SI 2005/2919) (December 5, 2005).
2. Guardian's Allowance (General) (Amendment) Regulations 2006 (SI 2006/204) (April 10, 2006).

DEFINITIONS

"adopted"—reg.2.
"child"—SSCBA 1992 s.122.

Circumstances in which a person is to be treated as being in prison

7.—(1) The circumstances in which a person is to be treated as being in prison for the purposes of section 77 of the Act or section 77 of the Northern Ireland Act are that he is—
(a) serving a custodial sentence within the meaning of section 76 of the Powers of Criminal Courts (Sentencing) Act 2000, [³section 222 of the Sentencing Code or], Article 2(2) of the Criminal Justice (Northern Ireland) Order 1996 or a sentence of detention or imprisonment within the meaning of section 307(1) of the Criminal Procedure (Scotland) Act 1995, [² of at least 2 years and the other parent is deceased] or
(b) detained in a hospital by order of the court under—
    (i) section 37(1), 38, or 45A of the Mental Health Act 1983;
    (ii) section 5 of the Criminal Procedure (Insanity) Act 1964;
    (iii) section 6 or 14 of the Criminal Appeal Act 1968;
    (iv) section 57, section [¹ 57A] or 59A of the Criminal Procedure (Scotland) Act 1995;
    (v) Article 44, 45, 50A, or 51(2) and (3) of the Mental Health (Northern Ireland) Order 1986; or
    (vi) section 11 or 13(5A) and (6) of the Criminal Appeal (Northern Ireland) Act 1980.

(2) In calculating the length of the sentence for the purposes of paragraphs (1)(a) above and (4) below—
(a) disregard any reduction made to the length of the sentence to take account of any period spent in custody prior to sentencing; and

3.74

(b) include any period spent in custody immediately prior to sentencing, save that where he is serving a custodial sentence or sentence of detention or imprisonment with the meaning of paragraph (1)(a) above immediately prior to sentencing, include only such period of that sentence as remains following sentencing for the later sentence,

but nothing in this paragraph shall permit the payment of guardian's allowance in respect of any period in custody prior to sentencing.

(3) Subject to paragraph (4) below, a person shall not cease to be treated as being in prison in accordance with paragraph (1) above by virtue of the fact that he is temporarily released, unlawfully at large, or, in the case of a person serving a sentence, transferred to a hospital.

(4) A person serving a sentence in accordance with paragraph (1)(a) above shall cease to be treated as being in prison in accordance with that paragraph where—
  (a) he is released on licence, the remainder of his sentence is remitted, his sentence is reduced on appeal to a term of less than 2 years, or his conviction is quashed on appeal; or
  (b) he is not in custody and has not been in custody for a period at least equal to the remaining period of his sentence,
  but that where a person to whom sub-paragraph (b) applies returns to prison to serve the remainder of the sentence, the length of the sentence for the purposes of paragraph (1)(a) above shall be the period of the remainder of the sentence.

(5) This regulation shall apply, subject to the necessary modifications, to a parent who is outside Great Britain or Northern Ireland and serving a custodial sentence with not less than 2 years remaining from the death of the other parent or detained in a hospital by a court order.

AMENDMENTS

1. Mental Health (Care and Treatment) (Scotland) Act 2003 (Consequential Provisions) Order 2005 (SI 2005/2078) Sch.2 para.24 (October 5, 2005).
2. Tax Credits, Child Benefit, Guardian's Allowance and Childcare Payments (Miscellaneous Amendments) Regulations 2020 (SI 2020/297) reg.7(2) (April 6, 2020).
3. Sentencing Act 2020 Sch.24 para.334 (December 1, 2020).

GENERAL NOTE

3.75   A claim for Guardian's Allowance can succeed where one parent is dead and the other is serving a sentence of imprisonment, or is in custody in a hospital or youth offenders institution, but only so long as the period of the sentence remaining at the time of the death is two years or more. Calculation of the period of sentence remaining is complicated.

Paragraph (2) provides for disregard of any reduction of the sentence to be made if the prisoner is on remand at the time of the death, but for the inclusion of that period as part of the two years remaining to be spent in prison. Where the prisoner is sentenced on separate occasions, to consecutive but overlapping sentences the period will include the earlier sentence only to the extent that it is not subsumed by the latter.

In any case no order for payment of benefit can be made in respect of the period spent in prison prior to the sentence being imposed. Benefit remains payable until the prisoner is released from prison. Payment is not stopped if the prisoner escapes or is transferred to a hospital for medical treatment, until the remaining period of the sentence has expired. If the prisoner is subsequently returned to prison the claim may be renewed in respect of the period then remaining to be served.

Where the child or young person has only one "parent" because he has been adopted by only one person or because he is illegitimate and paternity is not established, or because his parents are divorced and no custody or maintenance order is applicable, there is no entitlement to Guardian's Allowance if that one parent is imprisoned.

Rate of allowance and payment to the National Insurance Fund or the Northern Ireland National Insurance Fund

8.—(1) Where a person treated as being in prison for the purposes of section 77 of the Act or section 77 of the Northern Ireland Act contributes to the cost of providing for a child [¹ or qualifying young person], the weekly rate of any guardian's allowance payable shall be reduced by the amount of the contribution made in the week preceding the week for which any allowance is payable.

(2) In a case where entitlement to guardian's allowance is established by reference to a person being in prison, that person shall, on notice being given by the Board, pay to the National Insurance Fund or the Northern Ireland National Insurance Fund an amount equal to that paid by way of guardian's allowance.

3.76

AMENDMENT

1. Guardian's Allowance (General) (Amendment) Regulations 2006 (SI 2006/204) (April 10, 2006).

DEFINITIONS

"child"—SSCBA 1992 s.122.
"week"—SSCBA 1992 s.122.

GENERAL NOTE

This regulation ensures that where a child or young person is being supported by a payment of Guardian's Allowance as a result of a person being in prison that person should, where possible, contribute towards the child's up keep and that such contribution should then be used to offset the cost of Guardian's Allowance. The Regulation appears to allow for this to happen in either of two ways—Paragraph (1) allows for a reduction in the benefit paid to the claimant. Paragraph (2) provides for the payment of a sum equal to the benefit, to the NI.fund.

3.77

Residence condition

9.—(1) There shall be no entitlement to guardian's allowance in respect of a child [¹ or qualifying young person] unless at least one of [¹ the parents of that child or qualifying young person]—
  (a) was born in the United Kingdom [² an EEA state or Switzerland]; or
  (b) at the date of death of the parent whose death gives rise to the claim for guardian's allowance, has, in any two year period since the age of 16, spent at least 52 weeks of that period in Great Britain or Northern Ireland, as the case may require.

(2) For the purposes of paragraph (1)(b) above, a person shall be treated as being present in Great Britain or Northern Ireland (as the case may require) where—

3.78

(a) his absence is by virtue of his employment—
  (i) as a serving member of the forces within the meaning of regulation 140 of the Social Security (Contributions) Regulations 2001;
  (ii) as an airman within the meaning of regulation 111 of those Regulations; or
  (iii) as a mariner within the meaning of regulation 115 of those Regulations; or
(b) his absence is by virtue of his employment and that employment is prescribed employment within the meaning of regulation 114(1) of those Regulations (continental shelf operations).

[¹ (3) Where a child or qualifying young person has been adopted by two persons jointly references in paragraph (1) above to the parents of the child or qualifying young person are to be read as references to those two persons.

(3A) Where a child or qualifying young person has been adopted by one person only, that person must satisfy the requirements of paragraph (1) above].

(4) Where regulation 5 applies, [¹ the mother of the child or qualifying young person] must satisfy the requirement of paragraph (1) above.

AMENDMENTS

1. Guardian's Allowance (General) (Amendment) Regulations 2006 (SI 2006/204) (April 10, 2006).
2. Tax Credits, Child Benefit, Guardian's Allowance and Childcare Payments (Miscellaneous Amendments) Regulations 2020 (SI 2020/297) reg.7(3) (April 6, 2020).

DEFINITIONS

"adopted"—reg.2.
"child"—SSCBA 1992 s.122.
"employed"—SSCBA 1992 s.122.

Prescribed manner of making an election under section 77(9) of the Act or section 77(9) of the Northern Ireland Act

10.—(1) An election under section 77(9) of the Act or section 77(9) of the Northern Ireland Act (payment of guardian's allowance not to be made to a husband) must—
(a) be in writing, and
(b) be made either—
  (i) on a form approved by the Board, or
  (ii) in such other manner as the Board may accept as sufficient in the circumstances of the particular case.

[¹ (2) Notice of the election must be given at an appropriate office.
[² (3) In paragraph (2) "an appropriate office" means—
(a) Waterview Park, Washington, Tyne and Wear; or
(b) any other office specified in writing by the Board.]

(4) An election may be given by means of electronic communication in accordance with Schedule 2 to the Child Benefit and Guardian's Allowance (Administration) Regulations 2003.

(SI 2003/495 reg.10) (as amended)

AMENDMENTS

1. Guardian's Allowance (General) (Amendment) Regulations 2006 (SI 2006/204) (April 10, 2006).
2. Child Benefit and Guardian's Allowance (Miscellaneous Amendments) Regulations 2009 (SI 2009/3268) reg.6 (January 1, 2010).

DEFINITION

"the Board"—reg.2.

Revocations

11.—*Omitted.* 3.80

Schedules omitted. 3.81

The Tax Credits, Child Benefit and Guardian's Allowance Up-rating Regulations 2024

(SI 2024/247)

Citation, commencement and effect

1.—(1) These Regulations may be cited as the Tax Credits, Child Benefit and Guardian's Allowance Up-rating Regulations 2024. 3.82

(2) This regulation and regulations 2, 3 and 4 come into force on 6th April 2024.

(3) Regulations 5, 6 and 7 come into force on 8th April 2024.

Amendment of Schedule 4 to the Social Security Contributions and Benefits Act 1992

6. In paragraph 5 of Part 3 of Schedule 4 to the Social Security Contributions and Benefits Act 1992 (weekly rate of guardian's allowance) for "£20.40" substitute "£21.75". 3.83

The Guardian's Allowance Up-rating Regulations 2024

(SI 2024/309)

Citation, commencement and interpretation

1.—(1) These Regulations may be cited as the Guardian's Allowance Up-rating Regulations 2024 and come into force on 8th April 2024. 3.84

(2) In these Regulations "the Up-rating Regulations" means the Tax Credits, Child Benefit and Guardian's Allowance Up-rating Regulations 2024.

Exceptions relating to payments of additional guardian's allowance by virtue of the Up-rating Regulations

3.85   **2.** Neither section 155(3) of the Social Security Administration Act 1992 nor section 135(3) of the Social Security Administration (Northern Ireland) Act 1992 shall apply if a question arises as to either—
  (a) the weekly rate at which guardian's allowance is payable by virtue of the Up-rating Regulations, or
  (b) whether the conditions for receipt of guardian's allowance at the altered rate are satisfied,
until that question has been determined in accordance with the provisions of section 8 of the Social Security Act 1998 or Article 9 of the Social Security (Northern Ireland) Order 1998.

Persons not ordinarily resident in either Great Britain or Northern Ireland

3.86   **3.** Regulation 5 of the Social Security Benefit (Persons Abroad) Regulations 1975 and regulation 5 of the Social Security Benefit (Persons Abroad) Regulations (Northern Ireland) 1978 (application of disqualification in respect of up-rating of benefit) shall apply to any additional benefit payable by virtue of the Up-rating Regulations.

PART IV

STATUTORY SICK PAY

The Statutory Sick Pay (General) Regulations 1982

(SI 1982/894) (AS AMENDED)

The Secretary of State for Social Services, in exercise of the powers conferred upon him by sections 1(3) and (4), 3(5) and (7), 4(2), 5(5), 6(1), 8(1) to (3), 17(4), 18(1), 20 and 26(1) and (3) to (5) of, paragraph 1 of Schedule 1 to, and paragraphs 2(3) and 3(2) of Schedule 2 to, the Social Security and Housing Benefits Act 1982(a) and of all other powers enabling him in that behalf, hereby makes the following regulations.

ARRANGEMENT OF REGULATIONS

1. Citation, commencement and interpretation
2. Persons deemed incapable of work
2A. Linking periods of incapacity for work
3. Period of entitlement ending or not arising
3A. Maximum entitlement to Statutory Sick Pay in a period of entitlement (repealed)
4. Contract of service ended for the purpose of avoiding liability for statutory sick pay
5. Qualifying days
6. Calculation of entitlement limit
7. Time and manner of notification of incapacity for work
8. Manner in which statutory sick pay may not be paid
9. Time limits for paying statutory sick pay
9A. Liability of the Secretary of State for payments of statutory sick pay
9B. Insolvency of employer
9C. Payments by the Secretary of State
10. Persons unable to act
11. Rounding to avoid fractional amounts
12. Days not to be treated as, or as parts of, periods of interruption of employment
13. [*repealed*]
13A. Production of employer's records
14. Provision of information in connection with determination of questions
15. Provision of information by employers to employees
15A. Statements relating to the payment of statutory sick pay (repealed)
16. Meaning of "employee"
17. Meaning of "earnings"
18. Payments to be treated or not to be treated as contractual remuneration
19. Normal weekly earnings
20. Treatment of one or more employers as one
21. Treatment of more than one contract of service as one
21A. Election to be treated as different employers not to apply to recovery of statutory sick pay
22. [*repealed*]
Schedule 1—Isolation due to Coronavirus [*repealed*]
Schedule 2—Shielding due to Coronavirus [*repealed*]

Citation, commencement and interpretation

1.—(1) These regulations may be cited as the Statutory Sick Pay (General) Regulations 1982, and shall come into operation on 6th April 1983.

(2) In these regulations—
"the Act" means the Social Security and Housing Benefits Act 1982;
[¹"the Contributions and Benefits Act" means the Social Security Contributions and Benefits Act 1992;]
[²"income tax month" means the period beginning on the 6th day of any calendar month and ending on the 5th day of the following calendar month;]
(3) Unless the context otherwise requires, any reference—
(a) in these regulations to a numbered section or Schedule is a reference to the section or Schedule, as the case may be, of or to the Act bearing that number;
(b) in these regulations to a numbered regulation is a reference to the regulation bearing that number in these regulations; and
(c) in any of these regulations to a numbered paragraph is a reference to the paragraph bearing that number in that regulation.

AMENDMENTS

1. Social Security (Miscellaneous Provisions) Amendment (No.2) Regulations 1992 (SI 1992/2595) reg.14 (November 16, 1992).
2. Social Security Contributions, Statutory Maternity Pay and Statutory Sick Pay (Miscellaneous Amendments) Regulations 1996 (SI 1996/777) reg.2(2) (April 6, 1996).

GENERAL NOTE

The relevant provisions in Pt I of the Social Security and Housing Benefits Act 1982 have now been replaced by Pt XII of the SSCBA 1992.

Persons deemed incapable of work

2.—(1) A person who is not incapable of work of which he can reasonably be expected to do under a particular contract of service may be deemed to be incapable of work of such a kind by reason of some specific disease or bodily or mental disablement for any day on which [³ . . .]
(a) (i) he is under medical care in respect of a disease or disablement as aforesaid,
(ii) it is stated by a registered medical practitioner that for precautionary or convalescent reasons consequential on such disease or disablement he should abstain from work, or from work of such a kind; and
(iii) he does not work under that contract of service; [³ . . .] [⁷ or]
[¹(b) he is—
(i) excluded or abstains from work, or from work of such a kind, pursuant to a request or notice in writing lawfully made under an enactment; or
(ii) otherwise prevented from working pursuant to an enactment, [² by reason of it being known or reasonably suspected that he is infected or contaminated by, or has been in contact with a case of, a relevant infection or contamination]] [³; [⁶ . . .]
(c) [⁷ . . .]
(d) [⁷ . . .]
(2) A person who at the commencement of any day is, or thereafter on that day becomes, incapable of work of such a kind by reason of some specific disease or bodily or mental disablement, and

(SI 1982/894 reg.2) (as amended)

(a) on that day, under that contract of service, does no work, or no work except during a shift which ends on that day having begun on the previous day; and
(b) does no work under that contract of service during a shift which begins on that day and ends on the next,

shall be deemed to be incapable of work of such a kind by reason of that disease or bodily or mental disablement throughout that day.

[¹(3) For the purposes of paragraph (1)(b)—
"enactment" includes an enactment comprised in, or in an instrument made under—
(a) an Act; or
(b) an Act of the Scottish Parliament; and
[² "relevant infection or contamination" means—
(a) in England and Wales—
   (i) any incidence or spread of infection or contamination, within the meaning of section 45A(3) of the Public Health (Control of Disease) Act 1984 in respect of which regulations are made under Part 2A of that Act (public health protection) for the purpose of preventing, protecting against, controlling or providing a public health response to, such incidence or spread, or
   (ii) any disease, food poisoning, infection, infectious disease or notifiable disease to which regulation 9 (powers in respect of persons leaving aircraft) of the Public Health (Aircraft) Regulations 1979 applies or to which regulation 10 (powers in respect of certain persons on ships) of the Public Health (Ships) Regulations 1979 applies; and
(b) in Scotland, any—
   (i) infectious disease within the meaning of section 1(5) of the Public Health etc (Scotland) Act 2008, or exposure to an organism causing that disease, or
   (ii) contamination within the meaning of section 1(5) of that Act, or exposure to a contaminant, to which sections 56 to 58 of that Act (compensation) apply.]

[³(4) [⁷ . . .]]

AMENDMENTS

1. Statutory Sick Pay (General) Amendment Regulations 2006 (SI 2006/799) reg.2 (April 10, 2006).
2. Social Security (Miscellaneous Amendments) (No.3) Regulations 2011 (SI 2011/2425) reg.6 (April 6, 2012).
3. Statutory Sick Pay (General) (Coronavirus Amendment) Regulations 2020 (SI 2020/287) (March 13, 2020).
4. Statutory Sick Pay (General) (Coronavirus Amendment) (No.2) Regulations 2020 (SI 2020/304) (March 17, 2020).
5. Statutory Sick Pay (Coronavirus) (Suspension of Waiting Days and General Amendment) Regulations 2020 (SI 2020/374) reg.3 (March 28, 2020).
6. Statutory Sick Pay (Coronavirus) (Suspension of Waiting Days and General Amendment) (No.2) Regulations 2020 (SI 2020/681) reg.2(2) and 2(3) (July 6, 2020).
7. Statutory Sick Pay (General) (Coronavirus Amendment) Regulations 2022 (SI 2022/380) reg.2(2) and (3) (March 25, 2022).

The Statutory Sick Pay (General) Regulations 1982

DEFINITION

"contract of service"—see SSCBA 1992 s.163(1).

GENERAL NOTE

Paragraph (1)

4.5   Regulation 2 of the SSP (General) Regulations is in virtually identical terms to the former regs 3(1) and (2) of the old Unemployment, Sickness and Invalidity Benefit Regulations 1983 (SI 1983/1598), which covered deemed sickness for the purposes of sickness benefit (see the 1994 volume of *Bonner*, p.687). The relevant case law in that context revolved around the vexed question of whether the regulation covers a pregnant claimant who is herself fit for work but is recommended to refrain from work because of the danger of contracting a disease which would threaten the life of the foetus she is carrying. Earlier cases have involved school teachers who are pregnant when there is an outbreak of rubella in the school.

There are two reported decisions under the old law which are worthy of note. In *R(S)24/54* it was held that a precautionary absence from work was not within sub-para.(a) of the regulation because she was not under medical care in respect of the disease during a period in which she had been advised to refrain from work simply to avoid contact with the disease. That decision was rejected by the Commissioner in *R(S)1/72* where the facts were identical, except that the claimant was awaiting the outcome of tests to determine whether she was immune to rubella and could therefore return to work. In fact, the results of those tests were not available for about five weeks owing in part to a postal strike. The Commissioner found that during the whole of that time she was under medical care in respect of the disease and was, therefore, deemed to be incapable of work and entitled to benefit. Fortunately for her, the results showed that she was immune and she was able to return to work. No question arose as to whether she would have continued to qualify for benefit if she had not been immune and had been advised to remain off work. But, the line of the Commissioner's reasoning in that case and his rejection of *R(S)24/54* rather than any attempt to distinguish it suggest that he may well have held that the claimant would remain under medical care until the danger from the infection was past.

In *R(S)4/93* the claimant was an assistant in a veterinary practice, who was potentially in danger of infection by toxoplasmosis from handling cats. She was given certificates advising her to refrain from work over a period of about six weeks. Her claim for statutory sick pay was refused by her employer and she applied to an AO for a decision on her entitlement to statutory sick pay. The Commissioner adopted the reasoning in both of the earlier cases. Thus she found that the claimant was entitled to benefit for a period of five days while awaiting the outcome of tests, which were negative, but not entitled for a further period of five weeks for which a claim had been made. The Commissioner did not specifically address the point that there had been a change in wording to the regulation since the earlier cases. The regulation now specifically refers to absence which is recommended for "precautionary" reasons. But, given that such reasons must be "consequential on such disease", meaning one for which she is "under medical care", it is probable that the new words add nothing to the interpretation.

It is, on the face of it, a rather fine distinction to hold, as in *R(S)4/93*, that the claimant is under medical care while awaiting the outcome of the tests but not under medical care once they are known. Nor is it in point to observe, as does the Commissioner in *R(S)24/54*, that the claimant is not unfit for work, only unable to work in the particular place she was employed, because the whole point of this regulation is for a claimant to be *deemed* unfit even though she may be fit. No doubt some justice is done for a claimant whose contribution record qualifies her for contribution-based jobseeker's allowance (presumably she is not to be disqualified for voluntary leaving), but where the claimant does not have such an entitlement the loss of statutory sick pay will be hard felt.

A female claimant could also now potentially qualify for ESA because the regulations for that benefit specifically provide for a pregnant woman who has to refrain from work because of a danger to herself or her unborn child (see Employment and Support Allowance Regulations 2008 (SI 2008/794) reg.20(d)—see Vol.I in this series).

The amendments made in 2006, substituting a new subs.(1)(b) and inserting a new (3), do not change the original policy intention, but merely update these provisions to reflect modern public health legislation, as do the amendments effective from 2012.

Paragraph (1)(c)
The insertion of the new para.(1)(c) was part of the emergency regulations in relation to the Government's response to coronavirus. This change was intended to provide certainty to individuals that they would be entitled to receive SSP if they were self-isolating and therefore unable to work as a result of following government advice. These measures were judged to be required as a matter of urgency as part of the Government response to a developing outbreak. The relevant amending regulations therefore came into force the day after they were laid, meaning that the usual period of 21 days between laying and coming into force did not apply. See further the General Note to the Schedule to these Regulations.

[¹Linking periods of incapacity for work

2A.—In subsection (3) of section 2 of the 1982 Act (linking periods of incapacity for work), 8 weeks shall be substituted for 2 weeks.]

AMENDMENT

1. Statutory Sick Pay (General) Amendment Regulations 1986 (SI 1986/477) reg.2 (April 6, 1986).

GENERAL NOTE

Section 2 of the 1982 Act, along with the other original provisions relating to statutory sick pay, was repealed by the Social Security (Consequential Provisions) Act 1992 s.3 and Sch.1. The eight-week linking rule is now to be found in SSCBA 1992 s.152(3).

Period of entitlement ending or not arising

3.—(1) In a case where an employee is detained in legal custody or sentenced to a term of imprisonment (except where the sentence is suspended) on a day which in relation to him falls within a period of entitlement, that period shall end with that day.

(2) A period of entitlement shall not arise in relation to a period of incapacity for work if the employee in question is in legal custody or sentenced to or undergoing a term of imprisonment (except where the sentence is suspended).

[⁴(2A) A period of entitlement in respect of an employee who was entitled to incapacity benefit, maternity allowance or severe disablement allowance shall not arise in relation to any day within a period of incapacity for work beginning with the first day on which paragraph 2(d) of Schedule 11 to the Contributions and Benefits Act ceases to have effect where the employee in question is a person to whom regulation 13A of the Social Security

(Incapacity for Work) (General) Regulations 1995 (welfare to work beneficiary) applies.]

[⁶(2B) Paragraph (2A) shall not apply, in the case of an employee who was entitled to incapacity benefit, where paragraph 2(d)(i) of Schedule 11 to the Contributions and Benefits Act ceases to have effect by virtue of paragraph 5A of that Schedule.]

[⁷ (2C) A period of entitlement in respect of an employee who was entitled to employment and support allowance shall not arise in relation to any day within a period of limited capability for work beginning with the first day on which paragraph 2(dd) of Schedule 11 to the Contributions and Benefits Act ceases to have effect where the employee in question is a person to whom regulation 148 of the Employment and Support Allowance Regulations 2008 (work and training beneficiaries) applies.]

[¹(3) A period of entitlement as between an employee and his employer shall end after 3 years if it has not otherwise ended in accordance with [³section 153(2) of the Contributions and Benefits Act] or with regulations (other than this paragraph) made under [³section 153(6) of the Contributions and Benefits Act].]

[²[³(4) Where a period of entitlement is current as between an employee and her employer and the employee—
  (a) is pregnant or has been confined; and
  (b) is incapable of work wholly or partly because of pregnancy or confinement on any day which falls on or after the beginning of the [⁵4th week] before the expected week of confinement; and
  (c) is not by virtue of that pregnancy or confinement entitled to statutory maternity pay under Part XII of the Contributions and Benefits Act or to maternity allowance under section 35 of that Act;
the period of entitlement shall end on that day or, if earlier, on the day she was confined.]

[³(5) Where an employee—
  (a) is pregnant or has been confined; and
  (b) is incapable of work wholly or partly because of pregnancy or confinement on any day which falls on or after the beginning of the [⁵4th week] before the expected week of confinement; and
  (c) is not by virtue of that pregnancy or confinement entitled to statutory maternity pay under Part XII of the Contributions and Benefits Act or to maternity allowance under section 35 of that Act;
a period of entitlement as between her and her employer shall not arise in relation to a period of incapacity for work where the first day in that period falls within 18 weeks of the beginning of the week containing the day referred to at (b) above or, if earlier, of the week in which she was confined.]

(6) In paragraphs (4) and (5), "confinement" and "confined" have the same, meanings as in [³section 171 of the Contributions and Benefits Act].]

AMENDMENTS

1. Statutory Sick Pay (General) Amendment Regulations 1986 (SI 1986/477) reg.3 (April 6, 1986).
2. Statutory Sick Pay (General) Amendment (No.2) Regulations 1987 (SI 1987/868) reg.2 (June 7, 1987).
3. Social Security Maternity Benefits and Statutory Sick Pay (Amendment) Regulations 1994 (SI 1994/1367) reg.9 (June 11, 1994).

(SI 1982/894 reg.3) (as amended)

4. Social Security (Welfare to Work) Regulations 1998 (SI 1998/2231) reg.6 (October 5, 1998).

5. Social Security, Statutory Maternity Pay and Statutory Sick Pay (Miscellaneous Amendments) Regulations 2002 (SI 2002/2690) reg.13 (November 24, 2002).

6. Employment Equality (Age) (Consequential Amendments) Regulations 2007 (SI 2007/825) reg.5(2) (April 6, 2007).

7. Employment and Support Allowance (Consequential Provisions) (No.2) Regulations 2008 (SI 2008/1554) reg.45 (October 27, 2008).

DEFINITIONS

"confined"—see para.(6).
"confinement"—see para.(6).
"employee"—see SSCBA 1992 s.163(1) and reg.16.
"employer"—see SSCBA 1992 s.163(1).
"period of entitlement"—see s.163(1).
"period of incapacity for work"—see s.163(1).
"week"—see s.163(1).

[¹Maximum entitlement to statutory sick pay in a period of entitlement

3A.—[² . . .]

AMENDMENTS

1. Statutory Sick Pay (General) Amendment Regulations 1986 (SI 1986/477) reg.4 (April 6, 1986).

2. Statutory Sick Pay (General) (Amendment) Regulations 2008 (SI 2008/1735) reg.3 (October 27, 2008).

Contract of service ended for the purpose of avoiding liability for statutory sick pay

4.—(1) The provisions of this regulation apply in any case where an employer's contract of service with an employee is brought to an end by the employer solely or mainly for the purpose of avoiding liability for statutory sick pay.

(2) Where a period of entitlement is current on the day on which the contract is brought to an end, the employer shall be liable to pay statutory sick pay to the employee until the occurrence of an event which, if the contract would have caused the period of entitlement to come to an end under section 3(2)(a), (b) or (d) or regulation 3(1) [¹of these regulations or regulation 10(2) of the Statutory Sick Pay (Mariners, Airmen and Persons Abroad) Regulations 1982], or (if earlier) until the date on which the contract would have expired.

AMENDMENT

1. Statutory Sick Pay (Mariners, Airmen and Persons Abroad) Regulations 1982 (SI 1982/1349) reg.10(3) (April 6, 1983).

DEFINITIONS

"contract of service"—see SSCBA 1992 s.163(1).
"employee"—see SSCBA 1992 s.163(1). and reg.16.
"employer"—see SSCBA 1992 s.163(1).
"period of entitlement"—see SSCBA 1992 s.163(1).

Qualifying days

4.12 **5.**—(1) In this regulation, "week" means a period of 7 consecutive days, beginning with Sunday.

(2) Where an employee and an employer of his have not agreed which day or days in any week are or were qualifying days [¹or where in any day or days are or were such as are referred to in paragraph (3)], the qualifying day or days in that week shall be—

  (a) the day or days on which it is agreed between the employer and employee that the employee is or was required to work (if not incapable) for that employer or, if it is so agreed that there is or was no such day;
  (b) the Wednesday, or, if there is no such agreement between and employee as mentioned in sub-paragraph (a);
  (c) every day, except that or those (if any) on which it is agreed between the employer and the employee that none of that employer's employees are or were required to work (any agreement that all day such days being ignored).

[¹(3) No effect shall be given to any agreement between an employer to treat as qualifying days—

  (a) any day where the day is identified, whether expressly or reference to that or another day being a day of incapacity relation to the employee's contract of service with an employer;
  (b) any day identified, whether expressly or otherwise, by period of entitlement or to a period of incapacity for work.]

AMENDMENT

1. Statutory Sick Pay (General) Amendment Regulations 1985 (SI 1985/126) reg.2 (March 5, 1985).

DEFINITIONS

  "contract of service"—see SSCBA 1992 s.163(1).
  "employee"—see SSCBA 1992 s.163(1). and reg.16.
  "employer"—see SSCBA 1992 s.163(1).
  "period of entitlement"—see SSCBA 1992 s.163(1).
  "period of incapacity for work"—see SSCBA 1992 s.163(1).
  "qualifying day"—see SSCBA 1992 s.163(1).
  "week"—see SSCBA 1992 s.163(1).

GENERAL NOTE

4.13 This prescribes the manner in which qualifying days are to be determined in the absence of any effective agreement between employer on which days are to rank as such (see also SSCBA 1992 s.154). R(SSP)1/85 decides that "required to work" in sub-paras (a) and (c) means obliged to work under one's terms of employment, and does not embrace the situation in which the employee was merely asked to work. Thus, there the employee's normal practice of working voluntary overtime on Saturdays could not turn Saturday into a qualifying day where the contract of service merely provided for 39 hours' work on Mon–Fri. That decision (at para.10) explains how what is now SSCBA 1992 s.154 and this paragraph interrelate to set out a series of alternatives, to be applied in turn as necessary, to determine qualifying days in any particular case. See also the decision of the EAT in *Moxon v Ipsos-RSL Ltd* [2002] All E.R. D 109 (Aug) (EAT/634/01), following and applying *R(SSP) 1/85.*

(SI 1982/894 reg. 5) (as amended)

Paragraph (3)
This renders ineffective any agreement which, expressly or otherwise, identifies qualifying days by reference to it or another day being one of incapacity, or by reference to a period of entitlement or period of incapacity for work.

Calculation of entitlement limit

6.—(1) Where an employee's entitlement to statutory sick pay is calculated by reference to different weekly rates in the same period of entitlement [²...], the entitlement limit shall be calculated in the manner described in paragraphs (2) and (3), or, as the case may be, (4) and (5); and where a number referred to in paragraph (2)(b) or (d) or (4)(a)(ii) or (d)(ii) is not a whole number [¹of thousandths, it shall be rounded up to the next thousandth].

(2) For the purpose of determining whether an employee has reached his maximum entitlement to statutory sick pay in respect of a period of entitlement there shall be calculated—
  (a) the amount of statutory sick pay to which the employee became entitled during the part of the period of entitlement before the change in the weekly rate;
  (b) the number by which the weekly rate (before the change) must be multiplied in order to produce the amount mentioned in subparagraph (a);
  (c) the amount of statutory sick pay to which the employee has so far become entitled during the part of the period of entitlement after the change in the weekly rate; and
  (d) the number by which the weekly rate (after the change) must be multiplied in order to produce the amount mentioned in subparagraph (c);
  (e) the sum of the amounts mentioned in sub-paragraphs (a) and (c); and
  (f) the sum of the number mentioned in sub-paragraphs (b) and (d).

(3) When the sum mentioned in paragraph (2)(f) reaches [²28], the sum mentioned in paragraph (2)(e) reaches the entitlement limit.
(4) [²...]
(5) [²...]

AMENDMENTS

1. Statutory Sick Pay (General) Amendment Regulations 1984 (SI 1984/385) reg.2(a) (April 16, 1984).
2. Statutory Sick Pay (General) Amendment Regulations 1986 (SI 1986/477) reg.9 (April 6, 1986).

DEFINITIONS

"employee"—see SSCBA 1992 s.163(1) and reg.16.
"period of entitlement"—see SSCBA 1992 s.163(1).

Time and manner of notification of incapacity for work

7.—(1) Subject to paragraph (2), notice of any day of incapacity for work shall be given by or on behalf of an employee to his employer—

The Statutory Sick Pay (General) Regulations 1982

    (a) in a case where the employer has decided on a time limit (not being one which requires the notice to be given earlier than [1. . .] the first qualifying day in the period of incapacity for work which includes that day of incapacity for work [1or by a specified time during that qualifying day]) and taken reasonable steps to make it known to the employee, within that time limit; and

    (b) in any other case, on or before the seventh day after that day of incapacity for work.

(2) Notice of any day of incapacity for work may be given [2one month] later than as provided by paragraph (1) where there is good cause for giving it later [2, or if in the particular circumstances that is not practicable, as soon as it is reasonably practicable thereafter] so however that it shall in any event be given on or before the 91st day after that day.

(3) A notice contained in a letter which is properly addressed and sent by prepaid post shall be deemed to have been given on the day on which it was posted.

(4) Notice of any day of incapacity for work shall be given by or on behalf of an employee to his employer—

    (a) in a case where the employer has decided on a manner in which it is to be given (not being a manner which imposes a requirement such as is specified in paragraph (5)) and taken reasonable steps to make it known to the employee, in that manner; and

    (b) in any other case, in any manner, so however that unless otherwise agreed between the employer and employee it shall be given in writing.

(5) The requirements mentioned in paragraph (4)(a) are that notice shall be given—

    (a) personally;
    (b) in the form of medical evidence;
    (c) more than once in every 7 days during a period of entitlement;
    (d) on a document supplied by the employer; or
    (e) on a printed form.

AMENDMENTS

1. Statutory Sick Pay (General) Amendment Regulations 1984 (SI 1984/385) reg.2(b) (April 16, 1984).

2. Social Security Contributions, Statutory Maternity Pay and Statutory Sick Pay (Miscellaneous Amendments) Regulations 1996 (SI 1996/777) reg.2(3) (April 6, 1996).

DEFINITIONS

    "employee"—see SSCBA 1992 s.163(1) and reg.16.
    "employer"—see SSCBA 1992 s.163(1).
    "period of entitlement"—see SSCBA 1992 s.163(1).
    "period of incapacity for work"—see SSCBA 1992 s.163(1).
    "qualifying day"—see SSCBA 1992 s.163(1).

Manner in which statutory sick pay may not be paid

    8.—Statutory sick pay may not be paid in kind or by way of the provision of board or lodging or of services or other facilities.

(SI 1982/894 reg.9) (as amended)

Time limits for paying statutory sick pay

9.—(1) In this regulation, "payday" means a day on which it has been agreed, or it is the normal practice, between an employer and an employee of his, that payments by way of remuneration are to be made, or, where there is no such agreement or normal practice, the last day of a calendar month.

(2) In any case where—
  (a) a decision has been made by an insurance officer, local tribunal or Commissioner in proceedings under Part I that an employee is entitled to an amount of statutory sick pay; and
  (b) the time for bringing an appeal against the decision has expired and either—
    (i) no such appeal has been brought; or
    (ii) such an appeal has been brought and has been finally disposed of, that amount of statutory sick pay is to be paid within the time specified in paragraph (3).

(3) Subject to paragraphs (4) and (5), the employer is required to pay the amount not later than the first pay day after—
  (a) where an appeal has been brought, the day on which the employer receives notification that it has been finally disposed of;
  (b) where leave to appeal has been refused and there remains no further opportunity to apply for leave, the day on which the employer receives notification of the refusal; and
  (c) in any other case, the day on which the time for bringing an appeal expires.

(4) Subject to paragraph (5), where it is impracticable, in view of the employer's methods of accounting for and paying remuneration, for the requirement of payment referred to in paragraph (3) to be met by the pay day referred to in that paragraph, it shall be met not later than the next following pay day.

(5) Where the employer would not have remunerated the employee for his work on the day of incapacity for work in question (if it had not been a day of incapacity for work) as early as the pay day specified in paragraph (3) or (if it applies) paragraph (4), the requirement of payment shall be met on the first day on which the employee would have been remunerated for his work on that day.

DEFINITIONS

  "employee"—see SSCBA 1992 s.163(1) and reg.16.
  "employer"—see SSCBA 1992 s.163(1).

[¹Liability of the Secretary of State for payments of statutory sick pay

9A.—(1) Notwithstanding the provisions of section 1 of the Act and subject to paragraph (4), where—
  (a) an adjudicating authority has determined that an employer is liable to
  (b) the time for appealing against the determination has expired; and

(c) no appeal against the determination has been lodged or leave to appeal against the determination is required and has been refused,

then for any day of incapacity for work in respect of which it was determined the employer was liable to make those payments, and for any further days of incapacity for work which fall within the same spell of incapacity for work and in respect of which the employer was liable to make payments of statutory sick pay to that employee, the liability to make payments of statutory sick pay in respect of those days shall, to the extent that payment has not been made by the employer, be that of the Secretary of State and not the employer.

(2) For the purposes of this regulation a spell of incapacity for work consists of consecutive days of incapacity for work with no day of the week disregarded.

(3) In paragraph (1) above "adjudicating authority" means, as the case may be, the Chief or other adjudication officer, [² the First-tier Tribunal or the Upper Tribunal.]

(4) This regulation shall not apply to any liability of an employer to make a payment of statutory sick pay where the day of incapacity for work in respect of which the liability arose falls within a period of entitlement which commenced before 6th April 1987.]

AMENDMENTS

1. Statutory Sick Pay (General) Amendment Regulations 1987 (SI 1987/ 372) reg.2 (April 6, 1987).

2. Tribunals, Courts and Enforcement Act 2007 (Transitional and Consequential Provisions) Order 2008 (SI 2008/2683) art.6 and Sch.1 para.18 (November 3, 2008).

DEFINITIONS

"employee"—see SSCBA 1992 s.163(1) and reg.16.
"employer"—see SSCBA 1992 s.163(1).
"period of entitlement"—see SSCBA 1992 s.163(1).
"week"—see SSCBA 1992 s.163(1).

GENERAL NOTE

4.20 This regulation, together with regs 9B and 9C, prescribe the circumstances in which the liability to pay statutory sick pay is to be that of the Board of the Inland Revenue (now HMRC) and not the employer. (Although the regulation still refers to the Secretary of State, those functions were transferred—along with those under regs 9B and 9C—to the Board by s.1(2) of and Sch.2 to the Social Security Contributions (Transfer of Functions, etc.) Act 1999.) The relevant circumstances are where it is determined that statutory sick pay is payable but the employer neither pays the amount due nor appeals against the decision (reg.9A) and where the employer was insolvent at the time (reg.9B). Provision is also made (reg.9C) requiring HMRC to make the payments for which they are liable at weekly intervals.

(SI 1982/894 reg.9B) (as amended)

[¹**Insolvency of employer**

9B.—(1) Notwithstanding the provisions of section 1 of the Act and subject to paragraph (3), any liability arising under Part I of the Act to make a payment of statutory sick pay in respect of a day of incapacity for work in relation to an employee's contract of service with his employer shall be that of the Secretary of State and not that of the employer where the employer is insolvent on that day.

(2) For the purposes of paragraph (1) an employer shall be taken to be insolvent if, and only if—
- (a) in England and Wales—
    - (i) he has been adjudged bankrupt or has made a composition or arrangement with his creditors;
    - (ii) he had died and his estate falls to be administered in accordance with an order under section 421 of the Insolvency Act 1986; or
    - (iii) where an employer is a company, a winding-up order [²...] is made or a resolution for voluntary winding-up is passed with respect to it [²or it enters administration], or a receiver or manager of its undertaking is duly appointed, or possession is taken by or on behalf of the holders of any debentures secured by a floating charge, or any property of the company comprised in or subject to the charge or a voluntary arrangement proposed for the purposes of Part 1 of the Insolvency Act 1986 is approved under that Part;
- (b) in Scotland—
    - (i) an award of sequestration is made on his estate or he executes a trust deed for his creditors or enters into a composition contract;
    - (ii) he has died and a judicial factor appointed under section 11A of the Judicial Factors (Scotland) Act 1889 is required by that section to divide his insolvent estate among his creditors; or
    - (iii) where the employer is a company, a winding-up order [²...] is made or a resolution for voluntary winding-up is passed with respect to it [²or it enters administration] or a receiver of its undertaking is duly appointed or a voluntary arrangement proposed for the purposes of Part 1 of the Insolvency Act 1986 is approved under that Part.

shall not apply where the employer became insolvent before 6th April 1987.]

AMENDMENTS

1. Statutory Sick Pay (General) Amendment Regulations 1987 (SI 1987/372) reg.2 (April 6, 1987).
2. Enterprise Act 2002 (Insolvency) Order 2003 (SI 2003/2096) art.5 and Sch.2 para.42 (September 15, 2003).

DEFINITIONS

"contract of service"—see SSCBA 1992 s.163(1).
"employee"—see SSCBA 1992 s.163(1). and reg.16.
"employer"—see SSCBA 1992 s.163(1).

[¹Payments by the Secretary of State

4.22   9C.—Where the Secretary of State becomes liable in accordance with regulation 9A or 9B to make payments of statutory sick pay to a person, the first payment shall be made as soon as reasonably practicable after he becomes so liable, and payments thereafter shall be made at weekly intervals, by means of an instrument of payment [², instrument for benefit payment] or by such other means as appears to the Secretary of State to be appropriate in the circumstances of the particular case.]

AMENDMENTS

1. Statutory Sick Pay (General) Amendment Regulations 1987 (SI 1987/372) reg.2 (April 6, 1987).
2. Social Security (Claims and Payments etc.) Amendment Regulations 1996 (SI 1996/672) reg.3 (April 4, 1996).

Persons unable to act

4.23   10.—(1) Where in the case of any employer—
(a) statutory sick pay is payable to him or he is alleged to be entitled to it;
(b) he is unable for the time being to act, and either—
 (i) no receiver has been appointed by the Court of Protection with power to receive statutory sick pay on his behalf; or
 (ii) in Scotland, his estate is not being administered by any tutor, curator or other guardian acting or appointed in terms of law,
the Secretary of State may, upon written application to him by a person who, if a natural person, is over the age of 18, appoint that person to exercise, on behalf of the employee, any right to which he may be entitled under Part I and to deal on his behalf with any sums payable to him.

(2) Where the Secretary of State has made an appointment under paragraph (1)—
(a) he may at any time in his absolute discretion revoke it;
(b) the person appointed may resign his office after having given one month's notice in writing to the Secretary of State of his intention to do so; and
(c) the appointment shall terminate when the Secretary of State is notified that a receiver or other person to whom paragraph (1)(c) applies has been appointed.

(3) Anything required by Part I to be done by or to any employee who is unable to act may be done by or to the person appointed under this regulation to act on his behalf, and the receipt of the person so appointed shall be a good discharge to the employee's employer for any sum paid.

DEFINITIONS

"employee"—see SSCBA 1992 s.163(1) and reg.16.
"employer"—see SSCBA 1992 s.163(1).

GENERAL NOTE

4.24   The Secretary of State's functions under this regulation were transferred to the Board of the Inland Revenue (now HMRC) by s.1(2) of and Sch.2 to the Social Security Contributions (Transfer of Functions, etc.) Act 1999.

(SI 1982/894 reg.11) (as amended)

Rounding to avoid fractional amounts

11.—Where any payment of statutory sick pay is made and the statutory sick pay due for the period for which the payment purports to be made includes a fraction of a penny, the payment shall be rounded up to the next whole number of pence.

4.25

Days not to be treated as, or as parts of, periods of interruption of employment

12.—In a case to which paragraph 3 of Schedule 2 applies, the day of incapacity for work mentioned in sub-paragraph (1)(b) of that paragraph shall not be, or form part of, a period of interruption of employment where it is a day which, by virtue of section 17(1) or (2) of the Social Security Act 1975 or any regulations made thereunder, is not to be treated as a day of incapacity for work.

4.26

Records to be maintained by employers

13.—[¹ . . .]

4.27

AMENDMENT

1. Statutory Sick Pay (Maintenance of Records) (Revocation) Regulations 2014 (SI 2014/55) reg.2 (April 6, 2014).

[¹Production of employer's records

13A.—(1) An authorised officer of the Commissioners of Inland Revenue may by notice require an employer to produce to him at the place of keeping such records as are in the employer's possession or power and as (in the officer's reasonable opinion) contain, or may contain, information relevant to satisfy him that statutory sick pay has been paid and is being paid in accordance with these regulations to employees or former employees who are entitled to it.

4.28

(2) A notice referred to in paragraph (1) shall be in writing and the employer shall produce the records referred to in that paragraph within 30 days after the date of such a notice.

(3) The production of records in pursuance of this regulation shall be without prejudice to any lien which a third party may have in respect of those records.

(4) References in this regulation to "records" means—
  (a) any wage sheet or deductions working sheet; or
  (b) any other document which relates to the calculation or payment of statutory sick pay to his employees or former employees,
whether kept in written form, electronically, or otherwise.

(5) In paragraph (1), "place of keeping" means such place in Great Britain that an employer and an authorised officer may agree upon, or, in the absence of such agreement—
  (a) any place in Great Britain where records referred to in paragraph (1) are normally kept; or
  (b) if there is no such place, the employer's principal place of business in Great Britain.]

The Statutory Sick Pay (General) Regulations 1982

AMENDMENT

1. Statutory Maternity Pay (General) and Statutory Sick Pay (General) (Amendment) Regulations 2005 (SI 2005/989) reg.3(2) (April 6, 2005).

DEFINITIONS

"records"—see reg.13A(4).
"place of keeping"—see reg.13A(5).

Provision of information in connection with determination of questions

4.29   **14.**—Any person claiming to be entitled to statutory sick pay, or any other person who is a party to proceedings arising under Part I, shall, if he receives notification from the Secretary of State that any information is required from him for the determination of any question arising in connection therewith, furnish that information to the Secretary of State within 10 days of receiving that notification.

GENERAL NOTE

4.30   The Secretary of State's functions under this regulation were transferred to the Board of the Inland Revenue (now HMRC) by s.1(2) of and Sch.2 to the Social Security Contributions (Transfer of Functions, etc.) Act 1999.

Provision of information by employers to employees

4.31   **15.**—(1) [³Subject to paragraph (1A),] in a case which falls within paragraph (a), (b) or (c) of section 18(3) (provision of information by employers in connection with the making of claims for [²short term incapacity] and other benefits), the employer shall furnish to his employee, in writing on a form approved by the Secretary of State for the purpose [³, or in a form in which it can be processed by equipment operating automatically in response to instructions given for that purpose], the information specified in paragraphs (2), (3) or (4) below, respectively within the time specified in the appropriate one of those paragraphs.

[³(1A) For the purposes of paragraph (1), where, in the particular circumstances of a case, it is not practicable for the employer to furnish the information within the specified time mentioned in paragraph (2), (3), (4)(b)(ii) or (5), he shall, not later than the first pay day within the meaning of regulation 9(1) immediately following the relevant specified time, furnish the information to his employee.]

(2) In a case which falls within paragraph (a) (no period of entitlement arising in relation to a period of incapacity for work) of section 18(3)—
- (a) the information mentioned in paragraph (1) is a statement of all the reasons why, under the provisions of paragraph 1 of Schedule 1 and regulations made thereunder, a period of entitlement does not arise; and
- (b) it shall be furnished not more than 7 days after the day on which the employee's employer is notified by or on behalf of the employee of the incapacity for work on the fourth day of the period of incapacity for work.

(3) In a case which falls within paragraph (b) (period of entitlement ending but period of incapacity for work continuing) of section 18(3)—

(SI 1982/894 reg.15) (as amended)

[⁴(a) the information mentioned in paragraph (1) above is a statement informing the employee of—
  (i) the reason why the period of entitlement ended;
  (ii) the date of the last day in respect of which the employer is or was liable to make a payment of statutory sick pay to him.]
(b) the statement shall be furnished not more than 7 days after the day on which the period of entitlement ended, or, if earlier, on the day on which it is already required to be furnished under paragraph (4).]

(4) In a case which falls within paragraph (c) (period of entitlement expected to end before period of incapacity for work ends, on certain assumptions) of section 18(3)—
[¹[⁴(a) the information mentioned in paragraph (1) above is a statement informing the employee of—
  (i) the reason why the period of entitlement is expected to end;
  (ii) the date of the last day in respect of which the employer is or was expected to be liable to make a payment of statutory sick pay to him.]
(b) the statement shall be furnished—
  (i) in a case where the period of entitlement is expected to end in accordance with section 3(2)(b) of the Act (maximum entitled to statutory sick pay), on or before the 42nd day before the period of entitlement is expected to end; or
  (ii) in any other case, on or before the seventh day before the period of entitlement is expected to end
[³. . .].]

(5) For the purposes of section 18(3)(c)(i) (period for which the period of incapacity for work is to be assumed to continue to run) the prescribed period shall be 14 days.

AMENDMENTS

1. Statutory Sick Pay (General) Amendment Regulations 1986 (SI 1986/477) reg.6 (April 6, 1986).
2. Social Security (Incapacity Benefit) (Consequential and Transitional Amendments and Savings) Regulations 1995 (SI 1995/829) reg.15 (April 13, 1995).
3. Social Security Contributions, Statutory Maternity Pay and Statutory Sick Pay (Miscellaneous Amendments) Regulations 1996 (SI 1996/777) reg.2(5) (April 6, 1996).
4. Statutory Sick Pay (General) (Amendment) Regulations 2008 (SI 2008/1735) reg.2 (October 27, 2008).

DEFINITIONS

"employee"—see SSCBA 1992 s.163(1) and reg.16.
"employer"—see SSCBA 1992 s.163(1).
"period of entitlement"—see SSCBA 1992 s.163(1).
"period of incapacity for work"—see SSCBA 1992 s.163(1).
"prescribed"—see SSCBA 1992 s.163(1).
"qualifying day"—see SSCBA 1992 s.163(1).
"week"—see SSCBA 1992 s.163(1).

GENERAL NOTE

4.32   The references to ss.3(2)(b) and 18(3) of the 1982 Act should now be read as referring to SSCBA 1992 s.153(2)(b) and SSAA 1992 s.130(3), respectively.

The Statutory Sick Pay (General) Regulations 1982

[¹Statements relating to the payment of statutory sick pay

4.33   **15A.**—[² . . .]

AMENDMENTS

1. Statutory Sick Pay (General) Amendment Regulations 1986 (SI 1986/477) reg.7 (April 6, 1986).
2. Statutory Sick Pay (General) (Amendment) Regulations 2008 (SI 2008/1735) reg.3 (October 27, 2008).

Meaning of "employee"

4.34   **16.**—(1) [²Subject to paragraph (1ZA),] in a case where, and in so far as, a person [². . .] is treated as an employed earner by virtue of the Social Security (Categorisation of Earners) Regulations 1978, he shall be treated as an employee for the purposes of Part I and in a case where, and in so far as, such a person is treated otherwise than as an employed earner by virtue of those regulations, he shall not be treated as an employee for the purposes of Part I.

[³(1ZA) Paragraph (1) shall have effect in relation to a person who—
  (a) is under the age of 16; and
  (b) would or, as the case may be, would not have been treated as an employed earner by virtue of the Social Security (Categorisation of Earners) Regulations 1978 had he been over that age,
as it has effect in relation to a person who is or, as the case may be, is not so treated.]

[¹(1A) Any person who is in employed earner's employment within the meaning of the Act under a contract of apprenticeship shall be treated as an employee for the purposes of Part I.]

(2) A person who is in employed earner's employment within the meaning of the Act but whose employer—
  (a) does not fulfil the conditions prescribed in regulation 119(1)(b) of the Social Security (Contributions) Regulations 1979 as to residence or presence in Great Britain, or
  (b) is a person who, by reason of any international treaty to which the United Kingdom is a party or of any international convention binding the United Kingdom—
      (i) is exempt from the provisions of the Act, or
      (ii) is a person against whom the provisions of that Act are not enforceable,
shall not be treated as an employee for the purposes of Part I.

AMENDMENTS

1. Statutory Sick Pay (Compensation of Employers) and Miscellaneous Provisions Regulations 1983 (SI 1983/376) reg.5(2) (April 6, 1983).
2. Employment Equality (Age) Regulations 2006 (SI 2006/1031) reg.49(1) and Sch.8 Pt 2 para.50 (October 1, 2006).
3. Employment Equality (Age) (Consequential Amendments) Regulations 2007 (SI 2007/825) reg.5(3) (April 6, 2007).

DEFINITIONS

  "employee"—see SSCBA 1992 s.163(1) and reg.16.
  "employer"—see SSCBA 1992 s.163(1).
  "prescribed"—see SSCBA 1992 s.163(1).

(SI 1982/894 reg.17) (as amended)

Meaning of "earnings"

17.—(1) [³...]   4.35

[⁴(2) For the purposes of section 163(2) of the Contributions and Benefits Act, the expression "earnings" refers to gross earnings and includes any remuneration or profit derived from a person's employment except any payment or amount which is—

(a) excluded [⁸or disregarded in the calculation of a person's earnings under regulation 25, 27 or 123 of, or Schedule 3 to, the Social Security (Contributions) Regulations 2001] [⁷(or would have been so excluded had he not been under the age of 16)];

(b) a chargeable emolument under section 10A of the Social Security Contributions and Benefits Act 1992, except where, in consequence of such a chargeable emolument being excluded from earnings, a person would not be entitled to statutory sick pay [⁷(or where such a payment or amount would have been so excluded and in consequence he would not have been entitled to statutory sick pay had he not been under the age of 16)].]

[¹(2A) [³...]]

(3) For the purposes of [⁵section 163(2) of the Contributions and Benefits Act] the expression "earnings" includes also—

[⁸(za) any amount retrospectively treated as earnings by regulations made by virtue of section 4B(2) of the Contributions and Benefits Act;]

(a) any sum payable by way of maternity pay or payable by the Secretary of State in pursuance of section 40 of the Employment Protection (Consolidation) Act 1978 in respect of maternity pay;

(b) any sum which is payable by the Secretary of State by virtue of section 122(3)(a) of that Act in respect of arrears of pay and which by virtue of section 42(1) of that Act is to go towards discharging a liability to pay maternity pay;

(c) any sum payable in respect of arrears of pay in pursuance of an order for reinstatement or re-engagement under that Act;

(d) any sum payable by way of pay in pursuance of an order under that Act for the continuation of a contract of employment;

(e) any sum payable by way of remuneration in pursuance of a protective award under the Employment Protection Act 1975;

(f) any sum payable to any employee under the Temporary Short time Working Compensation Scheme administered under powers conferred by the Employment Subsidies Act 1978;

(g) any sum paid in satisfaction of any entitlement to statutory sick pay;

[²(h) any sum payable by way of statutory maternity pay under Part V of the Social Security Act 1986, including sums payable in accordance with regulations made under section 46(8)(b) of that Act.]

[⁶(i) any sum payable by way of statutory paternity pay, including any sums payable in accordance with regulations made under section 171ZD(3) of the Contributions and Benefits Act;

(j) any sum payable by way of statutory adoption pay, including any sums payable in accordance with regulations made under section 171ZM(3) of the Contributions and Benefits Act;]

[⁹(k) any sum payable by way of statutory shared parental pay, including any sums payable in accordance with regulations made under section 171ZX(3) of the Contributions and Benefits Act [¹⁰;

(l) any sum payable by way of statutory parental bereavement pay, including any sums payable in accordance with regulations made under section 171ZZ8(3) of the Contributions and Benefits Act].
(4) [³...]
(5) [³...]

AMENDMENTS

1. Statutory Sick Pay (Compensation of Employers) and Miscellaneous Provisions Regulations 1983 (SI 1983/376) reg.5(3) (April 6, 1983).
2. Statutory Sick Pay (General) Amendment (No.2) Regulations 1987 (SI 1987/868) reg.4 (June 7, 1987).
3. Social Security (Miscellaneous Provisions) Amendment (No.2) Regulations 1992 (SI 1992/2595) reg.15 (November 16, 1992).
4. Social Security Contributions, Statutory Maternity Pay and Statutory Sick Pay (Miscellaneous Amendments) Regulations 1999 (SI 1999/567) reg.13 (April 6, 1999).
5. Social Security, Statutory Maternity Pay and Statutory Sick Pay (Miscellaneous Amendments) Regulations 2002 (SI 2002/2690) reg.14(a) (November 24, 2002).
6. Social Security, Statutory Maternity Pay and Statutory Sick Pay (Miscellaneous Amendments) Regulations 2002 (SI 2002/2690) reg.14(b) (April 6, 2003).
7. Employment Equality (Age) Regulations 2006 (SI 2006/1031) reg.49(1) and Sch.8 Pt 2 para.51 (October 1, 2006).
8. Social Security, Occupational Pension Schemes and Statutory Payments (Consequential Provisions) Regulations 2007 (SI 2007/1154) reg.5(2) and (3) (April 6, 2007).
9. Shared Parental Leave and Statutory Shared Parental Pay (Consequential Amendments to Subordinate Legislation) Order 2014 (SI 2014/3255) art.3 (December 31, 2014).
10. Parental Bereavement Leave and Pay (Consequential Amendments to Subordinate Legislation) Regulations 2020 (SI 2020/354) reg.3 (April 6, 2020).

DEFINITION

"employee"—see SSCBA 1992 s.163(1) and reg.16.

Payments to be treated or not to be treated as contractual remuneration

4.36   18.—For the purposes of paragraph 2(1) and (2) of Schedule 2 to the Act, those things which are included within the expression "earnings" by regulation (except paragraph (3)(g) thereof) shall be, and those things which are excluded from that expression by that regulation shall not be, treated as contractual remuneration.

Normal weekly earnings

4.37   19.—(1) For the purposes of section 26, an employee's normal weekly earnings shall be determined in accordance with the provisions of this regulation.
(2) In this regulation—
"the critical date" means the first day of the period of entitlement in relation to which a person's normal weekly earnings fall to be determined, or, in a case to which paragraph 2(c) of Schedule 1 applies, the relevant date within the meaning of Schedule 1;

(SI 1982/894 reg.19) (as amended)

"normal pay day" means a day on which the terms of an employee's contract of service require him to be paid, or the practice in his employment is for him to be paid, if any payment is due to him; and

"day of payment" means a day on which the employee was paid.

(3) Subject to paragraph (4), the relevant period (referred to in section 26(2)) is the period between—
  (a) the last normal pay day to fall before the critical date; and
  (b) the last normal pay day to fall at least 8 weeks earlier than the normal pay day mentioned in sub-paragraph (a), including the normal pay day mentioned in sub-paragraph (a) but excluding that first mentioned in sub-paragraph (b).

(4) In a case where an employee has no identifiable normal pay day, paragraph (3) shall have effect as if the words "day of payment" were substituted for the words "normal pay day" in each place where they occur.

(5) In a case where an employee has normal pay days at intervals of, or approximating to one or more calendar months (including intervals of or approximating to a year) his normal weekly earnings shall be calculated by dividing his earnings in the relevant period by the number of calendar months in that period (or, if it is not a whole number, the nearest whole number), multiplying the result by 12 and dividing by 52.

(6) In a case to which paragraph (5) does not apply and the relevant period is not an exact number of weeks, the employee's normal weekly earnings shall be calculated by dividing his earnings in the relevant period by the number of days in the relevant period and multiplying the result by 7.

(7) In a case where the normal pay day mentioned in sub-paragraph (a) of paragraph (3) exists but that first mentioned in sub-paragraph (b) of that paragraph does not yet exist, the employee's normal weekly earnings shall be calculated as if the period for which all the earnings under his contract of service received by him before the critical date represented payment were the relevant period.

(8) In a case where neither of the normal pay days mentioned in paragraph (3) yet exists, the employee's normal weekly earnings shall be the remuneration to which he is entitled, in accordance with the terms of his contract of service for, as the case may be—
  (a) a week's work; or
  (b) a number of calendar month's work, divided by that number of months multiplied by 12 and divided by 52.

DEFINITIONS

"contract of service"—see SSCBA 1992 s.163(1).
"employee"—see SSCBA 1992 s.163(1) and reg.16.
"period of entitlement"—see SSCBA 1992 s.163(1) and reg.16.

GENERAL NOTE

4.38 For some of the difficulties in applying this regulation, see *R(SSP)1/89*. There, the relevant period for a school dinner lady extended from the end of one term until the last pay day before her period of incapacity began. This was 11 weeks, but as the relevant period began the day after the last pay day at the end of term it could not include the lump-sum payment that was made as a retainer throughout the vacation. Without that sum her average weekly earnings did not qualify her for statutory sick pay. See also *Spence v Commissioners for HMRC* [2012] UKFTT 213 (TC).

Treatment of one or more employers as one

20.—(1) In a case where the earnings paid to an employee in respect of 2 more employments are aggregated and treated as a single payment of earnings under regulation 12(1) of the Social Security (Contributions) Regulations 1979, the employers of the employee in respect of those employments shall be treated as one for all purposes of Part I.

(2) Where 2 or more employers are treated as one under the provisions of paragraph (1), liability for the statutory sick pay payable by them to the employee shall be apportioned between them in such proportions as they may agree or, in default of agreement, in the proportions which the employee's earnings from each employment bear to the amount of the aggregated earnings.

(3) [¹Subject to paragraphs (4) and (5)] where a contract of service ("the current contract") was preceded by a contract of service entered into between the same employer and employee ("the previous contract"), and the interval between the date on which the previous contract ceased to have effect and that on which the current contract came into force was not more than 8 weeks, then, for the purposes of establishing the employee's maximum entitlement within the meaning of section 5 (limitation on entitlement to statutory sick pay in any one period of entitlement or tax year), the provisions of Part I shall not have effect as if the employer were a different employer in relation to each of those contracts of service.

[¹(4) Where a contract of service ("the current contract") was preceded by two or more contracts of service entered into between the same employer and employee ("the previous contracts") and the previous contracts—
  (a) existed concurrently for at least part of their length; and
  (b) the intervals between the dates on which each of the previous contracts ceased to have effect and that on which the current contract came into force was not more than 8 weeks,
then, for the purposes of establishing the employee's maximum entitlement within the meaning of section 5 the provisions of Part I shall not have effect as if the employer were a different employer in relation to the current contract and whichever of the previous contracts was the contract by virtue of which the employer had become liable to pay the greatest proportion of statutory sick pay in respect of any tax year or period of entitlement.

(5) If, in any case to which paragraph (4) applies, the same proportion of the employer's liability for statutory sick pay becomes due under each of the previous contracts, then, for the purpose of establishing the employee's maximum entitlement within the meaning of section 5, the provisions of Part I shall have effect in relation to only one of the previous contracts.]

AMENDMENT

1. Statutory Sick Pay (Compensation of Employers) and Miscellaneous Provisions Regulations 1983 (SI 1983/376) reg.5(4) (April 6, 1983).

DEFINITIONS

"contract of service"—see SSCBA 1992 s.163(1).
"employee"—see SSCBA 1992 s.163(1) and reg.16.
"employer"—see SSCBA 1992 s.163(1).
"period of entitlement"—see SSCBA 1992 s.163(1).

(SI 1982/894 reg.20) (as amended)

GENERAL NOTE

Specific provision is made in Statutory Sick Pay (National Health Service Employees) Regulations 1991 (SI 1991/589) in the case of NHS workers with divided contracts.

Treatment of more than one contract of service as one

21.—Where 2 or more contracts of service exist concurrently between one employer and one employee, they shall be treated as one for all purposes of Part I except where, by virtue of regulation 11 of the Social Security (Contributions) Regulations 1979, the earnings from those contracts of service are not aggregated for the purposes of earnings-related contributions.

DEFINITIONS

"contract of service"—see SSCBA 1992 s.163(1).
"employee"—see SSCBA 1992 s.163(1) and reg.16.
"employer"—see SSCBA 1992 s.163(1).

[¹Election to be treated as different employers not to apply to recovery of statutory sick pay

21A.—(1) Paragraph (2) below applies for the purposes of section 159A of the Contributions and Benefits Act (power to provide for recovery by employers of sums paid by way of statutory sick pay) and of any order made under that section.

(2) Where an employer has made 2 or more elections under regulation 3 of the Income Tax (Employments) Regulations 1993 to be treated as a different employer in respect of each of the groups of employees specified in the election, the different employers covered by each of those elections shall be treated as one employer.]

AMENDMENT

1. Statutory Sick Pay Percentage Threshold Order 1995 (Consequential) Regulations 1995 (SI 1995/513) reg.3 (April 6, 1995).

DEFINITIONS

"employee"—see SSCBA 1992 s.163(1) and reg.16.
"employer"—see SSCBA 1992 s.163(1).

[¹Offences

22.—[². . .]

AMENDMENTS

1. Statutory Maternity Pay (General) and Statutory Sick Pay (General) (Amendment) Regulations 2001 (SI 2001/206) reg.2 (February 23, 2001).
2. Statutory Maternity Pay (General) and Statutory Sick Pay (General) (Amendment) Regulations 2005 (SI 2005/989) reg.3(3) (immediately before April 6, 2005).

General Note

4.44 The repeal of this provision was consequential upon the bringing into force of the National Insurance Contributions and Statutory Payments Act 2004.

4.45

[¹SCHEDULE [²¹]   Regulation 2(1)

ISOLATION DUE TO CORONAVIRUS

Amendments

1. Statutory Sick Pay (Coronavirus) (Suspension of Waiting Days and General Amendment) Regulations 2020 (SI 2020/374) reg.3(4) and Sch. (March 28, 2020).
2. Statutory Sick Pay (Coronavirus) (Suspension of Waiting Days and General Amendment) (No.2) Regulations 2020 (SI 2020/681) reg.2(4)–(9) (July 6, 2020).
3. Statutory Sick Pay (General) (Coronavirus Amendment) Regulations 2022 (SI 2022/380) reg.2(4) (March 25, 2022).

General Note

4.46 The default position under statute has long been that SSP is not paid for the first three days that an employee is unable to work because of sickness, or because they are deemed incapable of work (the so-called "waiting days": see Contributions and Benefits Act s.155(1)). As the coronavirus crisis escalated, there was concern that the waiting days rule might encourage some people to go into work even if they were sick, or if they were not sick but had been advised to self-isolate as a result of Government advice. Temporarily suspending the waiting days rule would accordingly support the Government's efforts to prevent the spread of coronavirus.

The Statutory Sick Pay (Coronavirus) (Suspension of Waiting Days and General Amendment) Regulations 2020 (SI 2020/374; see below) in effect suspended the waiting days rule for employees who were unable to work because they were unwell or self-isolating as a result of coronavirus. This meant that SSP became payable from day one, rather than day four, and so provide additional support to employees affected by coronavirus.

These were thus emergency Regulations in relation to the Government's response to coronavirus. Although the Regulations came into force on March 28, 2020 (reg.1), the suspension of the waiting days rule applied retrospectively to absences beginning on or after March 13, 2020 (reg.2). The Regulations came into force on the day after they were laid, meaning that the usual period of 21 days between laying and coming into force did not apply.

The enabling power for the retrospective effect is in s.40(4) of the Coronavirus Act 2020. The Regulations were drafted with this effect so that the disapplication of the waiting days restriction applied in relation to the same period as the earlier Statutory Sick Pay (General) (Coronavirus Amendment) Regulations 2020 (SI 2020/287), which came into force on March 13, 2020 and provided for employees isolating themselves in accordance with guidance on coronavirus to be treated as incapable of work, and therefore potentially entitled to SSP.

The Statutory Sick Pay (Coronavirus) (Suspension of Waiting Days and General Amendment) Regulations 2020 inserted this Schedule into the Statutory Sick Pay (General) Regulations 1982. The Schedule specifies when a person is deemed to be incapable of work because the person is staying at home. This includes people with symptoms of coronavirus staying at home for 7 days and people in the household of someone with symptoms of coronavirus staying at home for 14 days (paras. (2)-(5)). The Schedule as originally enacted has already been subject to further amendment.

(SI 1982/894 Sch.1) (as amended)

The first amendments were made by the Statutory Sick Pay (General) (Coronavirus Amendment) (No.3) Regulations 2020 (SI 2020/427). These amended the Schedule so as also include a person who is defined in public health guidance as extremely vulnerable and at very high risk of severe illness from coronavirus because of an underlying health condition; and has been advised, by notification sent to, or in respect of, that person in accordance with that guidance, to follow rigorously shielding measures for the period specified in the notification (para.(5A)). This relates to those persons classed as extremely vulnerable and at very high risk of severe illness from coronavirus who were advised to remain at home for at least 12 weeks (i.e. the practice known as shielding). The amendment was designed to ensure entitlement to SSP in cases where people were unable to work because they were shielding themselves in accordance with the guidance and where they meet the SSP eligibility criteria. This was intended as a safety net for individuals in cases where their employer chose not to furlough them under the Coronavirus Job Retention Scheme and did not have other suitable policies in place (e.g. the ability to work from home or the provision of special leave). However, it is anticipated that SSP for those shielding will have been withdrawn by August 1, 2020 (see Parliamentary Answer, 23 June 2020, Written Question 63397).

The second set of amendments was made by the Statutory Sick Pay (General) (Coronavirus Amendment) (No.4) Regulations 2020 (SI 2020/539). These provide that a person who has been advised, by a "relevant notification", that they have had contact with a person who has coronavirus, and that they should stay at home and self-isolate as a result, is deemed to be incapable of work, and so entitled to SSP. This is designed to support the UK Government's Contact Tracing strategy for containing and limiting the spread of the virus.

The third set of amendments were made by the Statutory Sick Pay (Coronavirus) (Suspension of Waiting Days and General Amendment) (No.2) Regulations 2020 (SI 2020/681) with effect from July 6, 2020. These amendments were intended to clarify eligibility of the shielding group for SSP. They provided that where a person self-isolates for less than 7 or 14 days because they or a member of their household (or extended household in Scotland, or linked household in England and Wales) receives a negative test result for coronavirus, they do not have to serve waiting days for the days in self-isolation. They also provided that a person who has formed an extended household or a linked household and is self-isolating because a member of that other household has symptoms of coronavirus may be eligible for SSP.

The fourth set of amendments were made by the Statutory Sick Pay (General) (Coronavirus Amendment) (No.5) Regulations 2020 (SI 2020/829) with effect from August 5, 2020. They extend eligibility for SSP to cover people where they are self-isolating for a minimum of 10 days (previously 7 days) in line with Public Health England guidance published on July 30, 2020.

The fifth set of amendments were made by the Statutory Sick Pay (General) (Coronavirus Amendment) (No.6) Regulations 2020 (SI 2020/892) with effect from August 26, 2020. They extended SSP eligibility to people self-isolating for up to 14 days prior to admittance to hospital for planned or elective surgery. Revised NICE guidelines published on July 27, 2020 set out guidance for healthcare professionals on Covid-19 and arranging planned care in hospitals. Clinicians may recommend that a patient self-isolate for a period prior to their surgery, based on a number of individual and clinical risk factors. Patients may be advised to self-isolate for 3 days prior to being admitted into hospital, while those patients who are deemed at higher risk may be advised to self-isolate for 14 days prior.

The seventh set of amendments were made by the Statutory Sick Pay (General) (Coronavirus Amendment) (No.6) Regulations 2020 (SI 2020/892) and came into force on August 26, 2020. They provide that a person is entitled to statutory sick pay if they (a) have been notified that they are to undergo a surgical or other hospital procedure; (b) have been advised to stay at home for a period of up to 14 days before admission to hospital for that procedure; and (c) stay at home following that advice.

The eighth set of amendments were made by the Statutory Sick Pay (General) (Coronavirus Amendment) (No.7) Regulations 2020 (SI 2020/1638) and were effective from December 24, 2020. These reflect changes to the self-isolation requirements where a person has symptoms of coronavirus, tests positive for coronavirus or is a household contact of a person who has coronavirus.

The net result is that reg.2 (as amended) provides that individuals may be eligible for SSP if they are unable to work because they are staying at home and self-isolating in accordance with guidance because:

    a. They have symptoms of coronavirus;
    b. They live with, or are in a linked or extended household with, someone who has symptoms;
    c. They have been informed that they have had contact with a person who was, at the time of the contact, infected with coronavirus;
    d. They are shielding in accordance with public health guidance;
    e. They have tested positive for coronavirus;
    f. They live with someone who has tested positive for coronavirus;
    g. They have been advised that they should self-isolate for up to 14 days prior to a planned or elective surgical or other hospital procedure.

4.46.1

[¹ SCHEDULE 2   Regulation 2(1)

SHIELDING DUE TO CORONAVIRUS

[² . . .]]

AMENDMENTS

1. Statutory Sick Pay (Coronavirus) (Suspension of Waiting Days and General Amendment) (No.2) Regulations 2020 (SI 2020/681) reg.2(4)–(9) (July 6, 2020).

2. Statutory Sick Pay (General) (Coronavirus Amendment) Regulations 2022 (SI 2022/380) reg.2(4) (March 25, 2022).

The Statutory Sick Pay (Mariners, Airmen and Persons Abroad) Regulations 1982

(SI 1982/1349) (AS AMENDED)

The Secretary of State for Social Services, in exercise of the powers conferred upon him by sections 3(5) and (7), 22(1) and 26(1) of and paragraph 1 of Schedule 1 to the Social Security and Housing Benefits Act 1982(a) and of all other powers enabling him in that behalf, hereby makes the following regulations.

ARRANGEMENT OF REGULATIONS

4.47

1. Citation, commencement and interpretation
2. Mariners—interpretation
3. Airmen—interpretation
4. Continental shelf—interpretation
5. Persons in other member States—meaning of "employee"
5A. Persons absent from Great Britain—meaning of "employee"
6. Mariners—meaning of "employee"
7. Airmen—meaning of "employee"
8. Continental shelf—meaning of "employee"

9. Meaning of "employee"—general
10. Persons abroad—general
11. (*repealed*)
12. (*repealed*)
13. (*repealed*)
14. Time for compliance with requirements of Part I and regulations

Citation, commencement and interpretation

1.—(1) These regulations may be cited as the Statutory Sick Pay (Mariners, Airmen and Persons Abroad) Regulations 1982, and shall come into operation on 6th April 1983.

(2) In these Regulations—

"the Act" means the Social Security and Housing Benefits Act 1982;

"Part I" means Part I of the Act;

[1"the Contributions and Benefits Act," means the Social Security Contributions and Benefits Act 1992;

"the Contributions Regulations" means the Social Security (Contributions) Regulations 1979;]

"the General Regulations" means the Statutory Sick Pay (General) Regulations 1982;

and other expressions, unless the context otherwise requires, have the same meanings as in Part I.

(3) Unless the context otherwise requires, any reference—

(a) in these regulations to a numbered regulation is a reference to the regulation bearing that number in these regulations; and

(b) in any of these regulations to a numbered paragraph is a reference to the paragraph bearing that number in that regulation.

AMENDMENT

1. Social Security Contributions, Statutory Maternity Pay and Statutory Sick Pay (Miscellaneous Amendments) Regulations 1996 (SI 1996/777) reg.3(2) (April 6, 1996).

GENERAL NOTE

These Regulations make special provision for statutory sick pay under what is now Pt XI of the SSCBA 1992 as it affects mariners, airmen, persons abroad and persons employed in operations on the Continental Shelf. Under s.163(1) of the SSCBA 1992, a person is not, as a rule, an "employee", and therefore not qualified to receive statutory sick pay, unless he or she is employed in Great Britain. Regulations 5–8 prescribe exceptions to this rule, so that certain persons who are employed in other Member States but who are subject to the legislation of the UK, certain mariners and airmen, and certain persons employed on the Continental Shelf, are "employees", though employed outside Great Britain; and so that certain limited classes of mariners and airmen are not "employees" though employed in Great Britain. Further general provision on the meaning of "employee" is made by reg.9, while reg.10 makes general provision regarding persons from abroad. Regulations 11–13, which provided for exceptions to reg.10, were repealed in 1996.

Some of the requirements of the Act and regulations made under it impose time-limits. Regulation 14 relaxes those requirements in their application to persons who are outside the UK and for that reason cannot comply with them.

It should be noted that these regulations have never been fully updated to include appropriate references to SSCBA 1992. Accordingly, all references to Pt I of the Social Security and Housing Benefits Act 1982 in these regulations should be read as references to Pt XI of SSCBA 1992.

Mariners—interpretation

4.50   **2.**—In regulations 6 and 11, the expressions "British ship," "foreign-going ship" "managing owner," "mariner," "owner" and "radio officer" have the same meanings as in Case C of Part VIII of the Social Security (Contributions) Regulations 1979, and the expressions "ship" and "ship or vessel," except in regulation 6(2), include hovercraft.

GENERAL NOTE

4.51   The provisions relating to Case C of Pt VIII of the Social Security (Contributions) Regulations 1979 have been re-enacted in Case C of Pt IX of the Social Security Contributions Regulations 2001 (SI 2001/1004).

Airmen—interpretation

4.52   **3.**—In regulations 7 and 12—
"airman" means a person who is, or has been, employed under a contract of service either as a pilot, commander, navigator or other member of the crew of any aircraft, or in any other capacity on board any aircraft where—
(a) the employment in that other capacity is for the purposes of the aircraft or its crew or of any passengers or cargo or mails carried thereby; and
(b) the contract is entered into in the United Kingdom with a view to its performance (in whole or in part) while the aircraft is in flight, but does not include a person in so far as his employment is as a serving member of the forces;
"British aircraft" means any aircraft belonging to Her Majesty and any aircraft registered in the United Kingdom of which the owner (or managing owner if there is more than one owner) resides or has his principal place of business in Great Britain, and references to the owner of an aircraft shall, in relation to an aircraft which has been hired, be taken as referring to the person for the time being entitled as hirer to possession and control of the aircraft by virtue of the hiring or any subordinate hiring.

DEFINITION

"contract of service"—see SSCBA 1992 s.163(1).

Continental shelf—interpretation

4.53   **4.**—In this regulation and regulations 8 and 13—
"designated area" means any area which may from time to time be designated by Order in Council under the Continental Shelf Act 1964 as an area within which the rights of the United Kingdom with respect to the sea-bed and subsoil and their natural resources may be exercised;
"prescribed area" means an area over which Norway or any member State (other than the United Kingdom) exercises sovereign rights for the purpose of exploring the seabed and subsoil and exploiting their natural resources, being an area outside the territorial seas of Norway or that member State [¹or any other area which is from time to time specified under section 22(5) of the Oil and Gas (Enterprise) Act 1982];

"prescribed employment" means employment in a designated area or prescribed area in connection with [¹any activity mentioned in section 23(2) of the Oil and Gas (Enterprise) Act 1982 in any designated area or in any prescribed area.]

AMENDMENT

1. Social Security and Statutory Sick Pay (Oil and Gas (Enterprise) Act 1982) (Consequential) Regulations 1982 (SI 1982/1738) reg.5 (April 6, 1983).

DEFINITION

"prescribed"—see SSCBA 1992 s.163(1).

Persons in other member States—meaning of "employee"

5.—Subject to regulations 6(2), 7(2) and 9, a person who is—
(a) gainfully employed in a member State other than the United Kingdom in such circumstances that if his employment were in Great Britain he would be an employee for the purposes of Part I or a person treated as such an employee under regulation 16 of the General Regulations; and
(b) subject to the legislation of the United Kingdom under Council Regulation (EEC) No.1408/71 [¹, as amended from time to time, or Regulation EC No.883/2004 of the European Parliament and of the Council of 29 April 2004, as amended from time to time, on the coordination of social security systems];
notwithstanding that he is not employed in Great Britain, shall be treated as an employee for the purposes of Part I.

AMENDMENT

1. Social Security (Updating of EU References) (Amendment) Regulations 2018 (SI 2018/1084) reg.4 and Sch. para.2 (November 15, 2018).

DEFINITIONS

"Pt I"—see reg.1(2).
"the General Regulations"—*ibid.*

[¹Persons absent from Great Britain—meaning of "employee"

5A.—Subject to regulations 5, 6(2) and 9, where a person, while absent from Great Britain for any purpose, is gainfully employed by an employer who is liable to pay in respect of him secondary Class 1 contributions under section 6 of the Contributions and Benefits Act 1992 or regulation 120 of the Contributions Regulations, he shall be treated as an employee for the purposes of Part XI of the Contributions and Benefits Act.]

AMENDMENT

1. Social Security Contributions, Statutory Maternity Pay and Statutory Sick Pay (Miscellaneous Amendments) Regulations 1996 (SI 1996/777) reg.3(3) (April 6, 1996).

The Statutory Sick Pay (Mariners, etc.) Regulations 1982

Definitions

"employer"—see SSCBA 1992 s.163(1).
"the Contributions and Benefits Act"—see reg.1(2).
"the Contributions Regulations"—reg.1(2).

General Note

4.56 The Social Security Contributions Regulations 2001 (SI 2001/1004) have nowrevoked and superseded the Social Security Contributions Regulations 1979 (SI 1979/591). Regulation 146 of the 2001 Regulations is the parallel provision to reg.120 of the 1979 Regulations.

Mariners—meaning of "employee"

4.57   **6.**—(1) Subject to regulation 9, where a mariner—
  (a) is employed as such and—
    (i) the employment is on board a British ship; or
    (ii) the employment is on board a ship and the contract in respect of the employment is entered into the United Kingdom with a view to its performance (in whole or in part) while the ship or vessel is on her voyage; and
    (iii) in a case to which head (ii) applies, the person by whom the mariner's earnings are paid, or, in the case of employment as a master or member of the crewof a ship or vessel, either that person or the owner of the ship or vessel (or the managing owner if there is more than one owner) has a place of business in Great Britain; or
  (b) is employed as a master, member of the crew or radio officer on board any ship or vessel, not being a mariner to whom the last preceding subparagraph applies; and
    (i) in the case of the employment being as a radio officer, if the contract under which the employment is performed is entered into in the United Kingdom, the employer or the person paying the radio officer his earnings for that employment has a place of business in Great Britain, or,
    (ii) in the case of the employment being as a master, member of the crew or radio officer, if the contract is not entered into in the United Kingdom, the employer or the person paying the earnings has his principal place of business in Great Britain,
then, unless he is a mariner to whom paragraph (2) applies, he shall, notwithstanding that he may not be employed in Great Britain, be treated as an employee for the purposes of Part I.

  (2) A mariner who—
  (a) is in employment (including any period of leave, other than leave for the purpose of study, accruing from the employment) as a master or member of the crew of a ship, where—
    (i) the employment is on a foreign-going ship; or
    (ii) the employment is partly on a foreign-going ship and partly otherwise than on such a ship, and it is a requirement of the contract of service which relates to that employment that any payment of earnings in respect of that employment is to be made during the employment on the foreign-going ship; or
  (b) has been in such employment as is mentioned in sub-paragraph (a), where—

(i) not more than thirteen weeks have elapsed since he was last in such employment;
(ii) he continues to be employed by the employer by whom he was employed when he was last in such employment; and
(iii) he is not employed (by that employer or any other) on terms which are inconsistent with his being able to resume such employment as is mentioned in sub-paragraph (a) after not more than thirteen weeks have elapsed since he was last in such employment;

shall, notwithstanding that he may be employed in Great Britain, not be treated as an employee for the purposes of Part I.

DEFINITIONS

"British ship"—see reg.2.
"contract of service"—see SSCBA 1992 s.163(1).
"employer"—see SSCBA 1992 s.163(1).
"foreign-going ship"—see reg.2.
"managing owner"—see reg.2.
"mariner"—see reg.2.
"owner"—see reg.2.
"Pt I"—see reg.1(2).
"radio officer"—see reg.2.
"ship"—see reg.2.
"ship or vessel"—see reg.2.
"week"—see SSCBA 1992 s.163(1).

Airmen—meaning of "employee"

7.—(1) Subject to regulation 9 and the following provisions of this regulation, where an airman is employed as such on board any aircraft, and the employer of that airman or the person paying the airman his earnings in respect of the employment (whether or not the person making the payment is acting as agent for the employer) or the person under whose directions the terms of the airman's employment and the amount of the earnings to be paid in respect thereof are determined has—

(a) in the case of the aircraft being a British aircraft, a place of business in Great Britain; or
(b) in any other case, his principal place of business in Great Britain, then, notwithstanding that he may not be employed in Great Britain, he shall be treated as an employee for the purposes of Part I.

(2) Subject to the provisions of paragraph (3), an airman shall not be treated as an employee for those purposes if he is not domiciled, and has no place of residence, in Great Britain.

(3) The provisions of paragraph (2) shall have effect subject to any Order in Council giving effect to any reciprocal agreement made under section 143 of the Social Security Act 1975 (reciprocity with other countries).

DEFINITIONS

"airman"—see reg.3.
"British aircraft"—see reg.3.
"employee"—see SSCBA 1992 s.163(1).

"employer"—SSCBA 1992 s.163(1).
"Pt I"—see reg.1(2).

GENERAL NOTE

Paragraph (3)
4.59 Section 143 of the Social Security Act 1975 has now been replaced in similar terms by s.179 of the SSAA 1992.

Continental shelf—meaning of "employee"

4.60 **8.**—Subject to regulation 9, a person in prescribed employment, notwithstanding that he may not be employed in Great Britain, shall be treated as an employee for the purposes of Part I.

DEFINITIONS

"employee"—see SSCBA 1992 s.163(1).
"Part I"—see reg.1(2).
"prescribed employment"—see reg.4.
"prescribed"—see SSCBA 1992 s.163(1).

Meaning of "employee"—general

4.61 **9.**—No person who, by virtue of regulation 16 of the General Regulations, would not be treated as an employee for the purposes of Part I if his employment were in Great Britain, shall be treated as an employee by virtue of any of regulations 5–8.

DEFINITIONS

"employee"—see SSCBA 1992 s.163(1).
"Part I"—see reg.1(2).
"the General Regulations"—reg.1(2).

[¹Persons abroad—general

4.62 **10.**—In a case where a mariner, an airman or a continental shelf employee, respectively, within the meaning of regulation 6(1), 7 or 8, or a person who, is an employee or, is treated as an employee under regulation 5 or 5A, is incapable of work during a period of entitlement to statutory sick pay while absent from Great Britain, his entitlement to statutory sick pay shall cease only if he fails to satisfy the conditions of entitlement under Part XI of the Contributions and Benefits Act notwithstanding that his employer ceases, during the period of entitlement, to be liable to pay, in respect of him, secondary Class 1 contributions under section 6 of the Contributions and Benefits Act or regulation 120 of the Contributions Regulations.]

AMENDMENT

1. Social Security Contributions, Statutory Maternity Pay and Statutory Sick Pay (Miscellaneous Amendments) Regulations 1996 (SI 1996/777) reg.3(4) (April 6, 1996).

DEFINITIONS

"employee"—see SSCBA 1992 s.163(1).
"employer"—SSCBA 1992 s.163(1).

(SI 1982/1349 reg.10) (as amended)

"period of entitlement"—SSCBA 1992 s.163(1).
"the Contributions and Benefits Act"—see reg.1(2).
"the Contributions Regulations"—reg.1(2).

General Note

See note to reg.5A. 4.63

Mariners—exception to regulation 10

11.—[¹. . .] 4.64

Amendment

1. Social Security Contributions, Statutory Maternity Pay and Statutory Sick Pay (Miscellaneous Amendments) Regulations 1996 (SI 1996/777) reg.3(5) (April 6, 1996).

Airmen—exception to regulation 10

12.—[¹. . .] 4.65

Amendment

1. Social Security Contributions, Statutory Maternity Pay and Statutory Sick Pay (Miscellaneous Amendments) Regulations 1996 (SI 1996/777) reg.3(6) (April 6, 1996).

Continental shelf—exception to regulation 10

13.—[¹. . .] 4.66

Amendment

1. Social Security Contributions, Statutory Maternity Pay and Statutory Sick Pay (Miscellaneous Amendments) Regulations 1996 (SI 1996/777) reg.3(7) (April 6, 1996).

Time for compliance with requirements of Part I and regulations

14.—Where— 4.67
 (a) an employee is outside the United Kingdom;
 (b) Part I or regulations made there under require any act to be done forthwith or on the happening of a certain event or within a specified time; and
 (c) because the employee is outside the United Kingdom he or his employer cannot comply with the requirement;
the employee or the employer, as the case may be, shall be deemed to have complied with it if he performs the act as soon as reasonably practicable.

Definitions

"employee"—see SSCBA 1992 s.163(1).
"employer"—SSCBA 1992 s.163(1).
"Pt I"—see reg.1(2).

The Statutory Sick Pay (Medical Evidence) Regulations 1985

The Statutory Sick Pay (Medical Evidence) Regulations 1985

(SI 1985/1604) (AS AMENDED)

The Secretary of State for Social Services, in exercise of the powers conferred upon him by section 17(2A) of the Social Security and Housing Benefits Act 1982, and of all other powers enabling him in that behalf, by this instrument, which contains only provisions consequential upon section 20 of the Social Security Act 1985 and regulations made under the aforesaid section 17(2A), makes the following regulations:

ARRANGEMENT OF ARTICLES

4.68
1. Citation, commencement and interpretation
2. Medical information

SCHEDULE 1—Part I—Rules
Part II—Form of Doctor's Statement
Part III—Notes
SCHEDULE 1A—Part I—Rules
Part II—Form of Special Statement

Citation, commencement and interpretation

4.69 **1.**—(1) These regulations may be cited as the Statutory Sick Pay (Medical Evidence) Regulations 1985 and shall come into operation on 6th April 1986.

(2) In these regulations, unless the context otherwise requires
[[2] "the 1992 Act" means the Social Security Administration Act 1992;]
[[4]"healthcare professional" means a person, not being the patient, who is—
(a) a registered medical practitioner;
(b) a registered nurse;
(c) a registered occupational therapist or registered physiotherapist;
(d) a registered pharmacist within the meaning of article 3 of the Pharmacy Order 2010;]
"signature" means, in relation to a statement given in accordance with these regulations, the name by which the person giving that statement is usually known (any name other than the surname being either in full or otherwise indicated) written by that person in his own handwriting [[3]. . .].

(3) [[1]. . .]

AMENDMENTS

1. Social Security (Miscellaneous Provisions) Amendment Regulations 1992 (SI 1992/247) reg.6(2) (March 9, 1992).

2. Social Security (Medical Evidence) and Statutory Sick Pay (Medical Evidence) (Amendment) Regulations 2010 (SI 2010/137) reg.3(1) and (2) (April 6, 2010).

3. Social Security (Medical Evidence) and Statutory Sick Pay (Medical Evidence) (Amendment) Regulations 2022 (SI 2022/298) reg.3(2) (April 6, 2022).

4. Social Security (Medical Evidence) and Statutory Sick Pay (Medical Evidence) (Amendment) (No.2) Regulations 2022 (SI 2022/630) reg.3(2) (July 1, 2022).

(SI 1985/1604 reg.1) (as amended)

GENERAL NOTE

These Regulations and the rules in Sch.1 prescribe the form of the statement to be issued by a healthcare professional advising an employee that he or she should refrain from work (or need not refrain from work) for a period up to six months, or longer in certain circumstances. Regulation 2(2) provides that medical information cannot be required in respect of an employee's first seven days in any spell of incapacity for work.

Medical information

2.—[¹ (1) Medical information required under section 14(1) of the 1992 Act relating to incapacity for work shall be provided either—
  (a) in the form of a statement given by a [² healthcare professional] in accordance with the rules set out in Part 1 of Schedule 1 to these Regulations; or
  (b) by such other means as may be sufficient in the circumstances of any particular case.]
(2) An employee shall not be required under [¹ section 14(1) of the 1992 Act] to provide medical information in respect of the first 7 days in any spell of incapacity for work; and for this purpose "spell of incapacity" means a continuous period of incapacity for work which is immediately preceded by a day on which the claimant either worked or was not incapable of work.

AMENDMENTS

1. Social Security (Medical Evidence) and Statutory Sick Pay (Medical Evidence) (Amendment) Regulations 2010 (SI 2010/137) reg.3(1) and (3) (April 6, 2010). SSP (Medical Evidence) Regulations 1985 (SI 1985/1604).
2. Social Security (Medical Evidence) and Statutory Sick Pay (Medical Evidence) (Amendment) (No.2) Regulations 2022 (SI 2022/630) reg.3(3) (July 1, 2022).

GENERAL NOTE

See further the Statutory Sick Pay (Medical Evidence) Regulations 2021 (SI 2021/1453) modifying reg.2(2) for a limited period only in December 2021 and January 2022 by extending "the first 7 days" to "the first 28 days".

[¹ SCHEDULE 1   **Regulation 2(1)(a)**

PART 1

RULES

1.—In these rules, unless the context otherwise requires—

"assessment" means either a consultation between a patient and a [³healthcare professional] which takes place in person or by telephone or a consideration by a [³healthcare professional] of a written report by another [³healthcare professional] or other health [³...] professional;
"condition" means a specific disease or bodily or mental disability;
[³...]
[³"other health professional"] means a person (other than a [³healthcare professional] and not being the patient) who is [³...] a registered midwife, [³...] or a member of any profession regulated by a body mentioned in section 25(3) of the National Health Service Reform and Health Care Professions Act 2002;

"patient" means the person in respect of whom a statement is given in accordance with these rules.

2.—Where a [³healthcare professional] issues a statement to a patient in accordance with an obligation arising under a contract, agreement or arrangement under Part 4 of the National Health Service Act 2006 or Part 4 of the National Health Service (Wales) Act 2006 or Part 1 of the National Health Service (Scotland) Act 1978 the [³healthcare professional's] statement shall be in a form set out at Part 2 [²or Part 2A] of this Schedule [². . .].

3.—Where a [³healthcare professional] issues a statement in any case other than in accordance with rule 2, the [³healthcare professional's] statement shall be in the form set out in Part 2 [²or Part 2A] of this Schedule or in a form to like effect [². . .].

4.—A [³healthcare professional's] statement must be based on an assessment made by that [³healthcare professional].

5.—A [³healthcare professional's] statement [². . .] shall contain the following particulars—

(a) the patient's name;
(b) the date of the assessment (whether by consultation or consideration of a report as the case may be) on which the [³healthcare professional's] statement is based;
(c) the condition in respect of which the [³healthcare professional] advises the patient they are not fit for work;
(d) a statement, where the [³healthcare professional] considers it appropriate, that the patient may be fit for work;
(e) a statement that the [³healthcare professional] will or, as the case may be will not, need to assess the patient's fitness for work again;
(f) the date on which the [³healthcare professional's] statement is given;
(g) the address of the [³healthcare professional] [²; and]

[² (h) the name of the [³healthcare professional] (whether in the form of a signature or [³otherwise); and]]

[³ (i) the profession of the healthcare professional.]

[². . .]

[³5A. Where the healthcare professional's statement is in the form set out in Part 2 of this Schedule—

(a) the healthcare professional's name shall, irrespective of their profession, be recorded next to the words "doctor's signature";
(b) the healthcare professional's address shall, irrespective of their profession, be recorded next to the words "doctor's address"; and
(c) the healthcare professional shall record their profession within the statement in such place as appears to them to be appropriate.]

6.—Subject to rule 8, the condition in respect of which the [³healthcare professional] is advising the patient is not fit for work or, as the case may be, which has caused the patient's absence from work shall be specified as precisely as the [³healthcare professional's] knowledge of the patient's condition at the time of the assessment permits.

7.—Where a [3healthcare professional] considers that a patient may be fit for work the [³healthcare professional] shall state the reasons for that advice and where this is considered appropriate, the arrangements which the patient might make, with their employer's agreement, to return to work.

8.—The condition may be specified less precisely where, in the [³healthcare professional's] opinion, disclosure of the precise condition would be prejudicial to the patient's wellbeing, or to the patient's position with their employer.

9.—A [³healthcare professional's] statement may be given on a date after the date of the assessment on which it is based, however no further statement shall be furnished in respect of that assessment other than a [³healthcare professional's] statement by way of replacement of an original which has been lost, in which case it shall be clearly marked "duplicate".

10.—Where, in the [³healthcare professional's] opinion, the patient will become fit for work on a day not later than 14 days after the date of the assessment on which the [³healthcare professional's] statement is based, the [³healthcare professional's] statement shall specify that day.

11.—Subject to rules 12 and 13, the [³healthcare professional's] statement shall specify the minimum period for which, in the [³healthcare professional's] opinion, the patient will not be fit for work or, as the case may be, for which they may be fit for work.

12.—The period specified shall begin on the date of the assessment on which the [³healthcare professional's] statement is based and shall not exceed 3 months unless the patient has, on the advice of a [³healthcare professional], refrained from work for at least 6 months immediately preceding that date.

13.—Where—

(SI 1985/1604 Sch.1) (as amended)

(a) the patient has been advised by a [³healthcare professional] that they are not fit for work and, in consequence, has refrained from work for at least 6 months immediately preceding the date of the assessment on which the [³healthcare professional's] statement is based; and
(b) in the [³healthcare professional's] opinion, the patient will not be fit for work for the foreseeable future,

instead of specifying a period, the [³healthcare professional] may, having regard to the circumstances of the particular case, enter, after the words "case for", the words "an indefinite period".

PART 2

FORM OF [³ HEALTHCARE PROFESSIONAL'S] STATEMENT 4.73

STATEMENT OF FITNESS FOR WORK
FOR SOCIAL SECURITY OR STATUTORY SICK PAY

Patient's name: Mr, Mrs, Miss, Ms

I assessed your case on: / /

and, because of the following condition(s):

I advise you that:
☐ you are not fit for work.
☐ you may be fit for work taking account of the following advice:

If available, and with your employer's agreement, you may benefit from:

☐ a phased return to work ☐ amended duties
☐ altered hours ☐ workplace adaptations

Comments, including functional effects of your condition(s):

This will be the case for

or from / / to / /

I will/will not need to assess your fitness for work again at the end of this period.
(Please delete as applicable)

Doctor's signature

Date of statement / /

Doctor's address
]

The Statutory Sick Pay (Medical Evidence) Regulations 1985

[² PART 2A

4.74 ALTERNATIVE FORM OF [³ HEALTHCARE PROFESSIONAL'S] STATEMENT

Statement of Fitness for Work
For social security or Statutory Sick Pay

Patient's name	Mr, Mrs, Miss, Ms
I assessed your case on:	/ /
and, because of the following condition(s):	
I advise you that:	☐ you are not fit for work.
	☐ you may be fit for work taking account of the following advice:

If available, and with your employer's agreement, you may benefit from:

☐ a phased return to work ☐ amended duties
☐ altered hours ☐ workplace adaptations

Comments, including functional effects of your condition(s):

This will be the case for	
or from	/ / to / /

I will/will not need to assess your fitness for work again at the end of this period.
(Please delete as applicable)

Issuer's name

Issuer's profession

Date of statement / /

Issuer's address

AMENDMENTS

1. Social Security (Medical Evidence) and Statutory Sick Pay (Medical Evidence) (Amendment) Regulations 2010 (SI 2010/137) reg.3(1) and (4) (April 6, 2010).
2. Social Security (Medical Evidence) and Statutory Sick Pay (Medical Evidence) (Amendment) Regulations 2022 (SI 2022/298) reg.3(3)–(5) (April 6, 2022).

(SI 1985/1604 Sch.1) (as amended)

3. Social Security (Medical Evidence) and Statutory Sick Pay (Medical Evidence) (Amendment) (No.2) Regulations 2022 (SI 2022/630) reg.3(4)–(17) (July 1, 2022).

GENERAL NOTE

The new medical certificate for statutory sick pay was introduced at the same time as changes were made to the arrangements for medical certificates in respect of benefit claims generally and Employment and Support Allowance in particular (see Social Security (Medical Evidence) Regulations 1976 (SI 1976/615) as amended). The previous different forms have been consolidated into a single medical certificate. In addition, the new form enables a doctor to state not only that the patient is unfit for work but also whether the patient may be able to work with appropriate support. As part of the same package of reforms the previous Sch.1A was also repealed.

4.75

The Statutory Sick Pay (National Health Service Employees) Regulations 1991

(SI 1991/589) (AS AMENDED)

The Secretary of State for Social Security in exercise of the powers conferred by sections 26(1) and (5A), 45(1) and 47 of the Social Security and Housing Benefits Act 1982 and of all other powers enabling him in that behalf, by this instrument, which contains only regulations consequential upon paragraph 16 of Schedule 6 to the Social Security Act 1990, hereby makes the following Regulations:

ARRANGEMENT OF REGULATIONS

1. Citation, commencement and interpretation
2. Treatment of more than one contract of employment as one contract
3. Notification of election
4. Provision of information by employees
5. Treatment of two or more employers as one
6. Time for which an election is to have effect

4.76

Citation, commencement and interpretation

1.—(1) These Regulations may be cited as the Statutory Sick Pay (National Health Service Employees) Regulations 1991 and shall come into force on 1st April 1991.

(2) In these Regulations, a "health authority" [²shall in relation to Wales have the same meaning it has in section 8] of the National Health Service Act 1977, and in relation to Scotland mean the health board within the meaning of section 2 of the National Health Service (Scotland) Act 1978.

[¹(3) [⁴ . . .]]
[²(4) [⁴ . . .]]
[³(5) In these Regulations, a reference to "NHS trust" shall be construed to include a reference to an NHS foundation trust within the meaning of section 1(1) of the Health and Social Care (Community Health and Standards) Act 2003 where the application for authorisation to become an NHS foundation trust was made by an NHS trust.]

4.77

AMENDMENTS

1. Health Act 1999 (Supplementary, Consequential etc. Provisions) (No.2) Order 2000 (SI 2000/694) art.3 and Sch. para.2(2) (April 1, 2000).
2. National Health Service Reform and Health Care Professions Act 2002 (Supplementary, Consequential etc. Provisions) Regulations 2002 (SI 2002/2469) reg.4 and Sch.1, Pt 2, para.50 (October 1, 2002).
3. Health and Social Care (Community Health and Standards) Act 2003 (Supplementary and Consequential Provision) (NHS Foundation Trusts) Order 2004 (SI 2004/696) art.3(17) and Sch.17 (April 1, 2004).
4. National Treatment Agency (Abolition) and the Health and Social Care Act 2012 (Consequential, Transitional and Saving Provisions) Order 2013 (SI 2013/235) art.11 and Sch.2 para.15(2) (April 1, 2013).

Treatment of more than one contract of employment as one contract

4.78   2.—Where, in consequence of the establishment of one or more National Health Service Trusts under Part I of the National Health Service and Community Care Act 1990 or the National Health Service (Scotland) Act 1978, a person's contract of employment is treated by a scheme under that Part or Act as divided so as to constitute two or more contracts [^{1}[^{2} ...]] he may elect for all those contracts to be treated as one contract for the purposes of Part I of the Social Security and Housing Benefits Act 1982.

AMENDMENTS

1. Health Act 1999 (Supplementary, Consequential etc. Provisions) (No.2) Order 2000 (SI 2000/694) art.3 and Sch. para.2(3) (April 1, 2000).
2. National Treatment Agency (Abolition) and the Health and Social Care Act 2012 (Consequential, Transitional and Saving Provisions) Order 2013 (SI 2013/235) art.11 and Sch.2 para.15(3) (April 1, 2013).

Notification of election

4.79   3.—A person who makes an election under regulation 2 above shall give written notification of that election to each of his employers under the two or more contracts of service mentioned in that regulation, before the end of the fourth day of incapacity for work in the period of incapacity for work in relation to a contract of service with the employer with whom this day first occurs.

Provision of information by employees

4.80   4.—A person who makes an election under regulation 2 above shall, as soon as is reasonably practicable after giving notice of that election, provide each of his employers under the two or more contracts of service mentioned in that regulation with the following information—
   (a) the name and address of each of his employers; and
   (b) the date his employment with each of those employers commenced; and
   (c) details of his earnings during the relevant period and for this purpose "earnings" and "relevant period" have the same meanings as they have for the purposes of section 26(2) of the Social Security and Housing Benefits Act 1982.

(SI 1991/589 reg.5) (as amended)

Treatment of two or more employers as one

5.—The employer to be regarded for the purposes of statutory sick pay as the employee's employer under the one contract where 2 or more contacts of service are treated as one in accordance with regulation 2 above, shall be—

[¹(a) in the case of a person whose contract of employment is treated by a scheme under Part I of the National Health Service and Community Care Act 1990 or the National Health Service (Scotland) Act 1978 as divided—
  (i) the Health Authority [² . . .] from which the employee was transferred, in a case where any one of the employee's contracts of service is with that Health Authority [² . . .]; or
  (ii) the first NHS trust to which a contract of service was transferred in a case where none of the employee's contracts of service are with the Health Authority [² . . .] from which he was transferred.
[² . . .]

AMENDMENTS

1. Health Act 1999 (Supplementary, Consequential etc. Provisions) (No.2) Order 2000 (SI 2000/694) art.3 and Sch. para.2(4) (April 1, 2000).
2. National Treatment Agency (Abolition) and the Health and Social Care Act 2012 (Consequential, Transitional and Saving Provisions) Order 2013 (SI 2013/235) art.11 and Sch.2 para.15(4) (April 1, 2013).

Time for which an election is to have effect

6.—An election made under regulation 2 shall lapse at the end of the period of incapacity for work in relation to the contract of service with the employer mentioned in regulation 5.

The Statutory Sick Pay and Statutory Maternity Pay (Decisions) Regulations 1999

(SI 1999/776)

The Secretary of State for Social Security, in exercise of powers conferred by section 20(3) of the Social Security Administration Act 1992, sections 8(1)(f) and 25(3) of the Social Security Contributions (Transfer of Functions, etc.) Act 1999 and of all other powers enabling him in that behalf, with the concurrence of the Commissioners of Inland Revenue, hereby makes the following Regulations:

ARRANGEMENT OF REGULATIONS

1. Citation, commencement and interpretation
2. Application for the determination of any issue arising as to, or in connection with, entitlement to statutory sick pay or statutory maternity pay
3. Applications in connection with statutory sick pay or statutory maternity pay
4. Revocation of regulation 20 of the Social Security (Adjudication) Regulations 1995

Citation, commencement and interpretation

4.84   **1.**—(1) These Regulations may be cited as the Statutory Sick Pay and Statutory Maternity Pay (Decisions) Regulations 1999 and shall come into force on 1st April 1999.

(2) In these Regulations—
  (a) "the Contributions and Benefits Act" means the Social Security Contributions and Benefits Act 1992;
  (b) "employee" and "employer" have, in relation to—
    (i) statutory sick pay, the meanings given by section 163(1) of the Contributions and Benefits Act;
    (ii) statutory maternity pay, the meanings given by section 171(1) of the Contributions and Benefits Act.

Application for the determination of any issue arising as to, or in connection with, entitlement to statutory sick pay or statutory maternity pay

4.85   **2.**—(1) An application for the determination of any issue arising as to, or in connection with, entitlement to statutory sick pay or statutory maternity pay may be submitted to an officer of the Board by—
  (a) the Secretary of State; or
  (b) the employee concerned.

(2) Such an issue shall be decided by an officer of the Board only on the basis of such an application or on his own initiative.

DEFINITION

"employee"—see reg.1(2).

Applications in connection with statutory sick pay or statutory maternity pay

4.86   **3.**—(1) An application for the determination of any issue referred to in regulation 2 above shall be made only in writing, in a form approved for the purpose by the Board, or in such other manner, being in writing, as an officer of the Board may accept as sufficient in the circumstances.

(2) Where such an application is made by an employee, it shall—
  (a) be delivered or sent to an office of the Board within 6 months of the earliest day in respect of which entitlement to statutory sick pay or statutory maternity pay is in issue;
  (b) state the period in respect of which entitlement to statutory sick pay or statutory maternity pay is in issue; and
  (c) state the grounds (if any) on which the applicant's employer has denied liability for statutory sick pay or statutory maternity pay in respect of the period specified in the application.

DEFINITION

"employer"—see reg.1(2).

Revocation of regulation 20 of the Social Security (Adjudication) Regulations 1995

4.87   **4.**—Regulation 20 of the Social Security (Adjudication) Regulations 1995 is hereby revoked.

(SI 2014/897)

The Statutory Sick Pay Percentage Threshold (Revocations, Transitional and Saving Provisions) (Great Britain and Northern Ireland) Order 2014

(SI 2014/897)

A draft of this Order was laid before Parliament under section 176(1)(c) of the Social Security Contributions and Benefits Act 1992 and section 172(11A) of the Social Security Contributions and Benefits (Northern Ireland) Act 1992 and approved by a resolution of each House of Parliament.

The Secretary of State for Work and Pensions makes the following Order in exercise of the powers conferred by section 159A of the Social Security Contributions and Benefits Act 1992 and section 155A of the Social Security Contributions and Benefits (Northern Ireland) Act 1992.

4.88

ARRANGEMENT OF ARTICLES

1. Citation and commencement
2. Revocation
3. Transitional and saving provisions

Citation and commencement

1.—This Order may be cited as the Statutory Sick Pay Percentage Threshold (Revocations, Transitional and Saving Provisions) (Great Britain and Northern Ireland) Order 2014 and comes into force on 6th April 2014.

4.89

Revocation

2.—The following are revoked—
(a) the Statutory Sick Pay Percentage Threshold Order 1995,
(b) the Statutory Sick Pay Percentage Threshold Order (Northern Ireland) 1995.

4.90

Transitional and saving provisions

3.—Notwithstanding the revocation of the Statutory Sick Pay Percentage Threshold Order 1995 and the Statutory Sick Pay Percentage Threshold Order (Northern Ireland) 1995, those Orders continue to have effect for the period of two years beginning with 6th April 2014 for the purposes of entitling an employer to recover an amount of statutory sick pay (whether paid before, on or after 6th April 2014) in respect of any day of incapacity for work falling before 6th April 2014.

4.91

GENERAL NOTE

See previous editions of this Volume for the Statutory Sick Pay Percentage Threshold Order 1995 (SI 1995/512), now revoked but subject to the transitional and saving provision in art.3.

4.92

The Statutory Sick Pay (Coronavirus) Regulations 2020

The Statutory Sick Pay (Coronavirus) (Suspension of Waiting Days and General Amendment) Regulations 2020

(SI 2020/374)

The Secretary of State, in exercise of the powers conferred by sections 151(4) and (4A) and 175(1) and (3) to (5A) of the Social Security Contributions and Benefits Act 1992(a) and section 40(1) to (4) of the Coronavirus Act 2020(b), makes the following Regulations.

In accordance with section 173(1)(a) of the Social Security Administration Act 1992(c), it appears to the Secretary of State that by reason of the urgency of this matter it is inexpedient to refer the proposals in respect of regulations 3 to 5 of these Regulations to the Social Security Advisory Committee.

GENERAL NOTE

4.93   These Regulations ceased to have effect on March 24, 2022. See further the General Note to the Statutory Sick Pay (Coronavirus) (Suspension of Waiting Days) (Saving Provision) Regulations 2022 (SI 2022/381).

Citation and commencement

4.94   1. These Regulations may be cited as the Statutory Sick Pay (Coronavirus) (Suspension of Waiting Days and General Amendment) Regulations 2020 and come into force on 28th March 2020.

Suspension of waiting days

4.95   2.—(1) Section 155(1) (limitations on entitlement) of the Social Security Contributions and Benefits Act 1992 ("the 1992 Act") does not apply in relation to an employee where — (a) that employee's period of incapacity for work is related to coronavirus; and (b) the first day of incapacity for work in that period arose on or after 13th March 2020.

(2) Paragraph (1) applies in relation to a day of incapacity for work that falls on or after 13th March 2020.

(3) In this regulation—
 (a) "period of incapacity for work" has the meaning given by section 152 of the 1992 Act; and
 (b) a period of incapacity for work is related to coronavirus if the employee is—
  (i) incapable by reason of infection or contamination with coronavirus, or
  (ii) deemed, in accordance with regulation 2(1)(c) [^{1}or (d)] of the Statutory Sick Pay (General) Regulations 1982, to be incapable by reason of coronavirus, of doing work which the employee can reasonably be expected to do under the employee's contract of service.

(4) The reference to regulation 2(1)(c) [^{1}or (d)] in paragraph (3)(b) above is a reference to the regulation which was in force on the first day of incapacity for work in question."

AMENDMENTS

1. Statutory Sick Pay (Coronavirus) (Suspension of Waiting Days and General Amendment) (No.2) Regulations 2020 (SI 2020/681) reg.3 (July 6, 2020).

(SI 2020/374 reg.3)

Amendment of the Statutory Sick Pay (General) Regulations 1982

3.—*(Amendment incorporated into text of the Statutory Sick Pay (General) Regulations 1982)*   4.96

Amendment of the Statutory Sick Pay (General) (Coronavirus Amendment) Regulations 2020

4. Omit regulation 3 (expiry) of the Statutory Sick Pay (General) (Coronavirus Amendment) Regulations 2020.   4.97

Amendment of the Statutory Sick Pay (General) (Coronavirus Amendment) (No.2) Regulations 2020

5. Omit regulation 3 (expiry) of the Statutory Sick Pay (General) (Coronavirus Amendment) (No.2) Regulations 2020.   4.98

SCHEDULE   Regulation 3(4)

(Amendments incorporated into text of the Statutory Sick Pay (General) Regulations 1982)   4.99

The Statutory Sick Pay (Coronavirus) (Funding of Employers' Liabilities) Regulations 2020

(SI 2020/512)

The Commissioners for Her Majesty's Revenue and Customs, with the concurrence of the Secretary of State, make the following Regulations in exercise of the powers conferred by sections 159B and 175(3), (4) and (5A) of the Social Security Contributions and Benefits Act 1992.

ARRANGEMENT OF REGULATIONS   4.100

1. Citation and commencement
2. Interpretation
3. Funding of eligible employers' liabilities by HMRC
4. Meaning of eligible employer
5. When an employee's incapacity for work is related to coronavirus
6. Making a claim
7. Time limit for making a claim
8. Payments
9. Correcting a claim when the amount has been mistakenly overstated
10. Correcting a claim when the amount has been mistakenly understated
11. Recovery of overpayments
12. Preservation of records
13. Provision of information and records

GENERAL NOTE

These regulations, made under s.159B of the Contributions and Benefits Act (inserted by s.39 of the Coronavirus Act 2020), provide for certain small and medium-size employers to apply to HMRC for a refund of the cost of paying SSP to   4.101

their employees and came into force on May 26, 2020. The scheme refunds eligible employers the costs of SSP up to a certain threshold where an employee's incapacity for work is related to coronavirus. Refunds are payable in respect of periods of incapacity for work where the first day of incapacity for work related to coronavirus arose on or after March 13, 2020. The retrospective effect is permitted by s.159B(7) of the Contributions and Benefits Act.

Refunds are available to employers who have fewer than 250 employees enrolled on the employer's PAYE scheme as at February 28, 2020 (reg.4). When considering how many employees were enrolled on the employer's PAYE scheme, an employer will have to consider all the schemes it operates, where this is more than one, and the total number of employees on schemes operated by connected companies or charities. An employee's incapacity for work is related to coronavirus when they are either unwell, having been infected or contaminated with coronavirus, or are self-isolating or shielding in line with government guidance (reg.5). The maximum amount which an eligible employer may receive as a refund in relation to a single employee is £191.70 (2 weeks' SSP) and the total amount is £191.70 multiplied by the number of employees enrolled in their PAYE schemes on February 28, 2020 (reg.3). There is a time limit to make a claim of one year from the end of the employee's period of incapacity for work, or from 26th May 2020, whichever is the later (reg.7). HMRC will operate the decision-making process under s.8 of the Transfer of Functions Act in the event of a dispute about claims or overpayments under these regulations.

The amendments made by the Statutory Sick Pay (Coronavirus) (Funding of Employers' Liabilities) (Amendment) Regulations (SI 2020/1030) with effect from October 15, 2020 fall into three categories. First, they reflect further changes made by the European Commission to the provision of State aid to small and medium-sized enterprises (SMEs) in difficulty (a SME is a business with fewer than 250 employees and either turnover below €50m or balance sheet total below €43m) (see reg.4). Second, they ensure that SSP can be reclaimed by employers in line with the changes made by the DWP to extend eligibility to receive coronavirus related SSP. In particular, they ensure that employers can claim for coronavirus related SSP for those employees who were required to shield and formed part of an extended or linked household and are therefore eligible for SSP in accordance with the amendments made by the Statutory Sick Pay (Coronavirus) (Suspension of Waiting Days and General Amendment) (No.2) Regulations 2020 (SI 2020/681) with effect from July 6, 2020 (see reg.5). Third, they change the notification mechanism for employers who realise they have mistakenly overstated the amount of a previous claim (see reg.9). Statutory Sick Pay (Coronavirus) (Funding of Employers' Liabilities) Regulations 2020 (SI 2020/512).

The scheme was closed to new claims on September 30, 2021, and subsequently replaced by the arrangements under the Statutory Sick Pay (Coronavirus) (Funding of Employers' Liabilities) Regulations 2022 (SI 2022/5).

PART 1

INTRODUCTION

Citation and commencement

1. These Regulations may be cited as the Statutory Sick Pay (Coronavirus) (Funding of Employers' Liabilities) Regulations 2020 and come into force on 26th May 2020.

(SI 2020/512 reg.2)

Interpretation

2. In these Regulations—
"eligible employer" has the meaning given in regulation 4;
"employer PAYE reference number" means the number identifying a PAYE scheme which was given to the employer by HMRC when the employer registered the PAYE scheme with HMRC;
"HMRC" means Her Majesty's Revenue and Customs;
"in difficulty" has the meaning given in regulation 4(2);
"maximum temporary aid amount" means the maximum amount of aid permitted to be received by an undertaking in accordance with section 3.1 of the Communication from the Commission of 19 March 2020 on the Temporary Framework for State aid measures to support the economy in the current COVID-19 outbreak;
"original claim" has the meaning given in regulation 9(1)(a);
"PAYE scheme" means a pay as you earn scheme registered on HMRC's real time information system;
"reimbursement amount" has the meaning given in regulation 3(1).

PART 2

ELIGIBILITY FOR FUNDING

Funding of eligible employers' liabilities by HMRC

3.—(1) An eligible employer who has made a payment of statutory sick pay to an employee where—
(a) that employee's period of incapacity for work is related to coronavirus; and
(b) the first day of incapacity for work in that period falls on or after 13th March 2020 [²and no later than 30th September 2021],
is, subject to paragraphs (2) [², (2A)] and (3), entitled to recover the amount paid to the employee (the "reimbursement amount") from HMRC.
(2) An eligible employer is not entitled to recover a reimbursement amount from HMRC—
(a) if, were the eligible employer to receive the reimbursement amount claimed, the amount of State aid received by the eligible employer would exceed the maximum temporary aid amount for that eligible employer; or
(b) in respect of an employee for a period for which the eligible employer is entitled to a grant in respect of that employee under the Coronavirus Job Retention Scheme.
[²(2A) A reimbursement amount does not include any amount paid to an employee in respect of a qualifying day which falls after 30th September 2021.]
(3) The amount which an eligible employer may recover from HMRC under these Regulations is limited to—
(a) in relation to a single employee, [¹£192.70]; and
(b) in total, [¹£192.70] multiplied by the number of employees enrolled in PAYE schemes of the eligible employer on 28th February 2020, determined in accordance with regulation 4.

4.103

4.104

(4) In this regulation—
(a) an employee includes an employee who—
  (i) was employed by the eligible employer during a period of incapacity for work related to coronavirus,
  (ii) has received a payment of statutory sick pay from the eligible employer in respect of that period of incapacity for work, and
  (iii) no longer works for the eligible employer;
(b) the reference to the reimbursement amount in paragraph (2)(a) is to that amount converted into euros using the European Commission's—
  (i) official monthly accounting rate for the euro; and
  (ii) conversion rate for April 2020; and
(c) the "Coronavirus Job Retention Scheme" is the scheme set out in the Schedule to the Coronavirus Act 2020 Functions of Her Majesty's Revenue and Customs (Coronavirus Job Retention Scheme) Direction.

AMENDMENTS

1. Statutory Sick Pay (Coronavirus) (Funding of Employers' Liabilities) (Amendment) Regulations and the Statutory Sick Pay (Coronavirus) (Funding of Employers' Liabilities) (Northern Ireland) (Amendment) Regulations 2021 (SI 2021/281) reg.2 (April 6, 2021).
2. Statutory Sick Pay (Coronavirus) (Funding of Employers' Liabilities) (Closure) Regulations and the Statutory Sick Pay (Coronavirus) (Funding of Employers' Liabilities) (Northern Ireland) (Closure) Regulations 2021 (SI 2021/1013) reg.3 (September 30, 2021).

DEFINITIONS

"Coronavirus Job Retention Scheme"—para.(4)(c).
"eligible employer"—reg.2.
"HMRC"—*ibid*.
"maximum temporary aid amount"—*ibid*.
"reimbursement amount"—para.(1).

Meaning of eligible employer

4.—(1) An eligible employer is an employer who—
(a) on 28th February 2020, had fewer than 250 employees enrolled in all PAYE schemes operated by the employer; and
(b) on 31st December 2019, was not already in difficulty.
[¹(2) An employer is "in difficulty" if—
(a) in the case of an employer who is not an SME, it is reasonable to assume that the employer would be regarded as an undertaking in difficulty under Article 2(18) of the General Block Exemption Regulation; or
(b) in the case of an employer who is an SME, it is reasonable to assume that the employer would be regarded as an undertaking in difficulty under Article 2(18)(c) of the General Block Exemption Regulation, as if the words after "collective insolvency proceedings", in the first place it appears, to the end were omitted, or under Article 2(18)(d) of the General Block Exemption Regulation.]
(3) Where, on 28th February 2020, the employer was one of—
(a) two or more companies which were not charities and which were connected with one another, or

(b) two or more charities which were connected with one another,

the number of employees referred to in paragraph (1) is the total number of employees enrolled in all PAYE schemes operated by the connected companies or charities, as applicable.

(4) For the purposes of paragraph (3)—
(a) Part 1 of Schedule 1 to the National Insurance Contributions Act 2014 sets out the rules for determining if two or more companies are connected with one another;
(b) Part 2 of Schedule 1 to that Act sets out the rules for determining if two or more charities are connected with each other.

(5) In this regulation—

"charity" has the same meaning as in section 18(1) of the Small Charitable Donations Act 2012, subject to paragraph 8(5) of Schedule 1 to the National Insurance Contributions Act 2014; and

"company" has the meaning given by section 1121(1) of the Corporation Tax Act 2010 and includes a limited liability partnership.

[1"General Block Exemption Regulation" means Commission Regulation (EU) No.651/2014 of 17 June 2014 declaring certain categories of aid compatible with the internal market in application of Articles 107 and 108 of the Treaty;

"SME" means an employer who is within the category of micro, small and medium-sized enterprises in paragraph 1 of Annex 1 of the General Block Exemption Regulation.]

AMENDMENT

1. Statutory Sick Pay (Coronavirus) (Funding of Employers' Liabilities) (Amendment) Regulations (SI 2020/1030) reg.3 (October 15, 2020, but the amendments have effect in relation to any day of incapacity for work which falls on or after June 29, 2020).

DEFINITIONS

"charity"—para.(5).
"company"—*ibid.*
"eligible employer"—reg.2.
"in difficulty"—para.(2).
"PAYE scheme"—*ibid.*

When an employee's incapacity for work is related to coronavirus

5.—(1) An employee's incapacity for work is related to coronavirus if the employee is—
(a) incapable by reason of infection or contamination with coronavirus, or
(b) deemed, in accordance with regulation 2(1)(c) [1or (d)] of the Statutory Sick Pay (General) Regulations 1982, to be incapable by reason of coronavirus,

of doing work which the employee can reasonably be expected to do under the employee's contract of service, and references in these Regulations to an employee's period of incapacity for work related to coronavirus shall be construed in accordance with this regulation.

(2) The reference to regulation 2(1)(c) of the Statutory Sick Pay (General) Regulations 1982 in paragraph (1)(b) is a reference to the regulation which was in force on the first day of incapacity for work in question.

4.106

The Statutory Sick Pay (Coronavirus) Regulations 2020

AMENDMENT

1. Statutory Sick Pay (Coronavirus) (Funding of Employers' Liabilities) (Amendment) Regulations (SI 2020/1030) reg.4 (October 15, 2020, but the amendment has effect in relation to any day of incapacity for work which falls on or after June 29, 2020).

PART 3

CLAIMS

Making a claim

4.107

6.—(1) An employer who makes a claim for the recovery of a reimbursement amount must do so in accordance with this regulation.

(2) A claim may include one or more reimbursement amounts paid by the employer—

(a) to employees enrolled in the same PAYE scheme; and
(b) during the period of time specified by the employer in accordance with paragraph (3)(d).

(3) The claim must contain the following—

(a) the employer PAYE reference number for the PAYE scheme to which the claim relates;
(b) the number of employees the claim relates to;
(c) the amount claimed;
(d) the beginning and end dates of the period of time to which the amount specified in accordance with sub-paragraph (c) relates;
(e) details of the bank account into which the amount specified in accordance with sub-paragraph (c) is to be paid; and
(f) if required by regulation 9(2), the amount by which the original claim was overstated.

(4) The claim must contain a declaration by the employer that—

(a) the employer was not already in difficulty on 31st December 2019;
(b) receipt of the amount claimed will not result in the amount of State aid received by the employer exceeding the maximum temporary aid amount for that employer; and
(c) the matters stated in the claim are true and accurate.

(5) The claim must be submitted to HMRC electronically using the Government Gateway unless paragraph (6) [¹or regulation 9(2)] applies.

(6) If the employer considers that the employer is digitally excluded—

(a) the employer may make a request to HMRC to submit a claim in an alternative manner, and
(b) if HMRC are satisfied that the employer is digitally excluded, the employer must submit the claim in a manner agreed with HMRC.

(7) An employer is digitally excluded where—

(a) it is not reasonably practicable for the employer to use the Government Gateway to submit a claim for any reason including age, disability or remoteness of location, or

(SI 2020/512 reg.6)

(b) the employer is a person who is a practising member of a religious society or order whose beliefs are incompatible with using the Government Gateway.

(8) In this regulation "Government Gateway" means the secure online facility for accessing government services.

AMENDMENT

1. Statutory Sick Pay (Coronavirus) (Funding of Employers' Liabilities) (Amendment) Regulations (SI 2020/1030) reg.5(1) (October 15, 2020, but the amendment has effect in relation to any day of incapacity for work which falls on or after June 29, 2020).

DEFINITIONS

"employer PAYE reference number"—reg.2.
"Government Gateway" —para.(8).
"HMRC" —reg.2.
"in difficulty"—*ibid.*
"maximum temporary aid amount"—*ibid.*
"PAYE scheme"—*ibid.*
"reimbursement amount"—*ibid.*

Time limit for making a claim

[¹7. A claim may not be made after the earlier of—   4.108
(a) 31st December 2021; or
(b) the end of the period of 1 year beginning with the last qualifying day in the period of incapacity for work to which the reimbursement amount claimed relates.]

AMENDMENT

1. Statutory Sick Pay (Coronavirus) (Funding of Employers' Liabilities) (Closure) Regulations and the Statutory Sick Pay (Coronavirus) (Funding of Employers' Liabilities) (Northern Ireland) (Closure) Regulations 2021 (SI 2021/1013) reg.4 (September 30, 2021).

DEFINITION

"reimbursement amount"—reg.2.

PART 4

PAYMENTS, CORRECTIONS AND OVERPAYMENTS

Payments

8. Where HMRC accept a claim, HMRC must pay the amount specified   4.109
in the claim by the employer in accordance with regulation 6(3)(c), less any amount repayable under regulation 9(3), to the account specified by the employer in accordance with regulation 6(3)(e) as soon as reasonably practicable.

[¹ Correcting a claim when the amount has been mistakenly overstated

9. —(1) Where an employer—
   (a) becomes aware that the employer mistakenly overstated the amount in a claim (the "original claim"); and
   (b) has received payment from HMRC in respect of the original claim,

the employer must correct the error in accordance with this regulation.

[¹(2) The next claim that the employer makes under regulation 6 (the "next claim") must be made in the manner provided for in paragraph (8) and in it the employer must specify the amount by which the original claim was overstated.]

(3) The amount by which the original claim was overstated must be repaid to HMRC by the employer by way of set-off against the amount stated in the next claim, up to a maximum of the amount stated in the next claim.

(4) Where the amount by which the original claim was overstated exceeds the maximum amount required to be set off in accordance with paragraph (3), the employer must repay the excess to HMRC within the period of 30 days beginning on the day on which the next claim is made.

(5) Where an employer does not make another claim under regulation 6 within the period of 60 days beginning with the day on which the original claim was made, the employer must notify HMRC of the overstatement in accordance with paragraphs (6) to (8) [¹ . . .].

(6) [¹The employer must provide the following information to HMRC] —
   (a) the employer PAYE reference number for the PAYE scheme to which the original claim related;
   (b) the amount by which the original claim was overstated; and
   (c) the beginning and end dates of the period of time to which the original claim related.

[¹(7) The employer must declare to HMRC that the information provided under paragraph (6) is true and accurate.]

[¹(8) An employer who makes a next claim referred to in paragraph (2), a declaration under paragraph (7) or who provides information under paragraph (6) must do so by telephone or in writing, as determined by HMRC in its discretion and notified to the employer.]

(9) The employer must repay to HMRC the amount [¹referred to in paragraph (6)(b)] within the period of 30 days beginning on the day on which [¹the employer provides the information under paragraph (6) and the declaration under paragraph (7)].

AMENDMENT

1. Statutory Sick Pay (Coronavirus) (Funding of Employers' Liabilities) (Amendment) Regulations (SI 2020/1030) reg.5(2)-(8) (October 15, 2020).

(SI 2020/512 reg.9)

DEFINTIONS

"adjustment notice"—para.(5).
"HMRC"—reg.2.
"original claim"—para.(1)(a).
"next claim"—para.(2).
"PAYE scheme"—reg.2.
"reimbursement amount"—*ibid.*

Correcting a claim when the amount has been mistakenly understated

10. Where an employer becomes aware that the employer mistakenly understated the amount in a claim (the "understated claim"), the employer may submit a claim in accordance with regulation 6 for the amount understated in respect of the same period, PAYE scheme and employees specified in the understated claim.

4.111

DEFINTION

"PAYE scheme"—reg.2.

Recovery of overpayments

11.—(1) Where any sum has been overpaid to an employer under these Regulations (an "overpayment"), HMRC may recover it in accordance with this regulation.

4.112

(2) An officer of Revenue and Customs must decide the amount of the overpayment and must give notice in writing of the decision to the employer.

(3) The employer must repay the overpayment to HMRC within the period of 30 days beginning with the day on which the employer receives the notice of decision referred to in paragraph (2).

(4) Part 6 of the Taxes Management Act 1970 (collection and recovery) applies to the recovery of overpayments as if—

(a) the amount of the overpayment were income tax charged on the employer named in the notice of decision referred to in paragraph (2);

(b) that notice of decision were an assessment; and

(c) that notice of decision were the matter complained of for the purposes of section 65(3) of that Act.

(5) In the application of section 101(4) of the Finance Act 2009 (late payment interest on sums due to HMRC) in relation to a repayment to HMRC of an overpayment under this regulation, the overpayment becomes due and payable on the date on which HMRC give the notice of decision referred to in paragraph (2).

DEFINTIONS

"HMRC"—reg.2.
"overpayment"—para.(1).

PART 5

RECORDS AND INFORMATION REQUESTS

Preservation of records

12.—(1) An employer who makes a claim for a reimbursement amount must keep a record of the following in respect of the employee, or former employee, in relation to whom the amount was claimed—
  (a) the start date and end date of the period of incapacity for work related to coronavirus to which the reimbursement amount relates;
  (b) national insurance number;
  (c) the reason for incapacity for work provided by the employee or former employee; and
  (d) the days which were qualifying days in that period of incapacity for work.

(2) An employer who corrects the amount of a claim in accordance with regulation 9 or 10 must keep a record of the amount of the correction and the reason for the correction.

(3) The employer must keep the records specified in paragraphs (1) and (2) until the end of the period of 3 years beginning with the date on which payment under regulation 8 is received.

(4) An employer who makes a claim for a reimbursement amount must keep the confirmation of State aid letter until the end of the period of 4 years beginning on IP completion day.

(5) In paragraph (4), "the confirmation of State aid letter" means the letter containing confirmation of receipt of State aid under these Regulations sent by HMRC to the employer once a claim is made.

DEFINITIONS

"the confirmation of State aid letter"—para.(5).
"HMRC"—reg.2.
"reimbursement amount"—*ibid.*

Provision of information and records

13.—(1) HMRC may by notice require an employer who has made a claim for a reimbursement amount—
  (a) to provide to HMRC in the manner specified in the notice, or
  (b) to make available for inspection at a place within the United Kingdom by an officer of Revenue and Customs,
within the period specified in the notice, all documents, records and other information in the employer's possession or under the employer's control as HMRC may reasonably require to ascertain whether the employer was entitled to receive a reimbursement amount under these Regulations, including whether it was unlawful State aid.

(2) Where records are maintained by computer the employer required to make them available for inspection must provide the officer of Revenue and Customs making the inspection with all the facilities necessary for obtaining information from them.

(SI 2020/512 reg.13)

DEFINITIONS

"HMRC"—reg.2.
"reimbursement amount"—*ibid.*

The Statutory Sick Pay (Medical Evidence) Regulations 2021

(SI 2021/1453)

The Secretary of State, with the concurrence of the Commissioners for Her Majesty's Revenue and Customs, makes the following Regulations in exercise of the powers conferred by sections 14(2)(b), 189(1), (4) and (5) and 191 of the Social Security Administration Act 1992.
In accordance with section 173(1)(a) of the Social Security Administration Act 1992, it appears to the Secretary of State that by reason of the urgency of this matter it is inexpedient to refer the proposals in respect of these Regulations to the Social Security Advisory Committee.

Citation, commencement, extent and interpretation

1.—(1) These Regulations may be cited as the Statutory Sick Pay (Medical Evidence) Regulations 2021.
(2) These Regulations come into force on 17th December 2021.
(3) These Regulations extend to England and Wales and Scotland.
(4) In these Regulations—
"the 1985 Regulations" means the Statutory Sick Pay (Medical Evidence) Regulations 1985;
"spell of incapacity for work" has the meaning given by regulation 2(2) of the 1985 Regulations.

Modification of the 1985 Regulations

2.—(1) Where this regulation applies, regulation 2(2) of the 1985 Regulations has effect as if for "7 days" there were substituted "28 days".
(2) Regulation 2(1) applies in relation to a person who has a spell of incapacity for work which—
  (a) has commenced prior to the date on which these Regulations come into force but which, on that date, has lasted for no longer than 7 days; or
  (b) commences on any day during the inclusive period which—
      (i) begins with the date on which these Regulations come into force; and
      (ii) ends at the end of 26th January 2022.

4.115

4.116

GENERAL NOTE

This statutory instrument, which came into force on December 17, 2021, amended the Statutory Sick Pay (Medical Evidence) Regulations 1985 (S.I.1985/1604) so as to increase the number of days for which an employee is not required to provide medical evidence of sickness absence to their employer from 7 days to 28 days. This change was designed to increase GP capacity to support the coronavirus vaccine booster programme by

4.117

reducing the need for employees to visit their GP for medical evidence for the SSP purposes. The change was strictly time-limited, as it only covered spells of incapacity for work which started after commencement but before January 26, 2022.

The Statutory Sick Pay (Coronavirus) (Funding of Employers' Liabilities) Regulations 2022

(SI 2022/5)

The Commissioners for Her Majesty's Revenue and Customs, with the concurrence of the Secretary of State, make the following Regulations in exercise of the powers conferred by sections 159B and 175(3), (4) and (5A) of the Social Security Contributions and Benefits Act 1992.

Arrangement of Regulations

1. Citation and commencement
2. Interpretation
3. Funding of eligible employers' liabilities by HMRC
4. Meaning of eligible employer
5. When an employee's incapacity for work is related to coronavirus
6. Making a claim
7. Time limit for making a claim
8. Payments
9. Correcting a claim when the amount has been mistakenly overstated
10. Correcting a claim when the amount has been mistakenly understated
11. Recovery of overpayments
12. Preservation of records
13. Provision of information and records

GENERAL NOTE

4.118   These Regulations provide for certain small and medium size employers to reclaim some or all of their SSP costs from HMRC. Refunds are payable in respect of days of incapacity for work occurring on or after December 21, 2021 (and before March 17, 2022). They replaced the Statutory Sick Pay (Coronavirus) (Funding of Employers' Liabilities) Regulations 2020 (SI 2020/512) closed to new claims on September 30, 2021, by virtue of the Statutory Sick Pay (Coronavirus) (Funding of Employers' Liabilities) (Closure) Regulations and the Statutory Sick Pay (Coronavirus) (Funding of Employers' Liabilities) (Northern Ireland) (Closure) Regulations 2021 (SI 2021/1013).

(SI 2020/5)

Part 1

Introduction

Citation and commencement

1. These Regulations may be cited as the Statutory Sick Pay (Coronavirus) (Funding of Employers' Liabilities) Regulations 2022 and come into force on 14th January 2022.

4.119

Interpretation

2. In these Regulations—
"eligible employer" has the meaning given in regulation 4;
"employer PAYE reference number" means the number identifying a PAYE scheme which was given to the employer by HMRC when the employer registered the PAYE scheme with HMRC;
"HMRC" means Her Majesty's Revenue and Customs;
"in difficulty" has the meaning given in regulation 4(2);
"maximum temporary aid amount" means the maximum amount of aid permitted to be received by an undertaking in accordance with section 3.1 of the Communication from the Commission of 19 March 2020 on the Temporary Framework for State aid measures to support the economy in the current COVID-19 outbreak;
"original claim" has the meaning given in regulation 9(1)(a);
"PAYE scheme" means a pay as you earn scheme registered on HMRC's real time information system;
"reimbursement amount" has the meaning given in regulation 3(1).

4.120

Part 2

Eligibility for funding

Funding of eligible employers' liabilities by HMRC

3.—(1) An eligible employer who has made a payment of statutory sick pay to an employee where—
  (a) that employee's period of incapacity for work is related to coronavirus; and
  (b) any day of incapacity for work in that period falls on or after 21st December 2021,
is, subject to paragraphs (2) and (3), entitled to recover the amount paid to the employee in respect of those days of incapacity for work which fall on or after 21st December 2021 [¹and on or before 17th March 2022] (the "reimbursement amount") from HMRC.

(2) An eligible employer is not entitled to recover a reimbursement amount from HMRC—
  (a) if, were the eligible employer to receive the reimbursement amount claimed, the amount of State aid received by the eligible employer

4.121

would exceed the maximum temporary aid amount for that eligible employer; or

(b) in respect of an employee for a period for which the eligible employer is entitled to a government grant in respect of that employee due to the employee being furloughed from the employment for reasons related to COVID-19.

(3) The amount which an eligible employer may recover from HMRC under these Regulations is limited to—
  (a) in relation to a single employee, £192.70; and
  (b) in total, £192.70 multiplied by the number of employees enrolled in PAYE schemes of the eligible employer on 30th November 2021, determined in accordance with regulation 4.

(4) In this regulation—
(a) an employee includes an employee who—
    (i) was employed by the eligible employer during a period of incapacity for work related to coronavirus,
    (ii) has received a payment of statutory sick pay from the eligible employer in respect of that period of incapacity for work, and
    (iii) no longer works for the eligible employer; and
(b) the reference to the reimbursement amount in paragraph (2)(a) is to that amount converted into euros using the European Commission's—
    (i) official monthly accounting rate for the euro; and
    (ii) conversion rate for December 2021.

AMENDMENT

1. Statutory Sick Pay (Coronavirus) (Miscellaneous Amendments) Regulations 2022 (SI 2022/176) reg 2(2) (March 17, 2022).

Meaning of eligible employer

4.—(1) An eligible employer is an employer who—
  (a) on 30th November 2021, had fewer than 250 employees enrolled in all PAYE schemes operated by the employer; and
  (b) on 31st December 2019, was not already in difficulty.

(2) An employer is "in difficulty" if—
(a) in the case of an employer who is not a micro or small enterprise, it is reasonable to assume that the employer would be regarded as an undertaking in difficulty under Article 2(18) of the General Block Exemption Regulation; or
(b) in the case of an employer who is a micro or small enterprise, it is reasonable to assume that the employer would be regarded as an undertaking in difficulty either under Article 2(18)(c) of the General Block Exemption Regulation, as if the words after "collective insolvency proceedings", in the first place it appears, to the end were omitted, or under Article 2(18)(d) of the General Block Exemption Regulation.

(3) Where, on 30th November 2021, the employer was one of—
(a) two or more companies which were not charities and which were connected with one another; or
(b) two or more charities which were connected with one another,
the limit in paragraph (1)(a) applies to the total number of employees enrolled in all PAYE schemes operated by the connected companies or charities, as applicable.

(SI 2020/5 reg. 4)

(4) For the purposes of paragraph (3)—
(a) Part 1 of Schedule 1 to the National Insurance Contributions Act 2014 sets out the rules for determining if two or more companies are connected with one another;
(b) Part 2 of Schedule 1 to that Act sets out the rules for determining if two or more charities are connected with each other.

(5) In this regulation—

"charity" has the same meaning as in section 18(1) of the Small Charitable Donations Act 2012, subject to paragraph 8(5) of Schedule 1 to the National Insurance Contributions Act 2014;

"company" has the meaning given by section 1121(1) of the Corporation Tax Act 2010 and includes a limited liability partnership;

"General Block Exemption Regulation" means Commission Regulation (EU) No.651/2014 of 17 June 2014 declaring certain categories of aid compatible with the internal market in application of Articles 107 and 108 of the Treaty;

"micro or small enterprise" means an employer who is a micro-enterprise or a small enterprise within the meaning of Article 2 of Annex 1 of the General Block Exemption Regulation.

When an employee's incapacity for work is related to coronavirus

5.—(1) An employee's incapacity for work is related to coronavirus if the employee is—
(a) incapable by reason of infection or contamination with coronavirus, or
(b) deemed, in accordance with regulation 2(1)(c) or (d) of the Statutory Sick Pay (General) Regulations 1982, to be incapable by reason of coronavirus, of doing work which the employee can reasonably be expected to do under the employee's contract of service, and references in these Regulations to an employee's period of incapacity for work related to coronavirus shall be construed in accordance with this regulation.

(2) The reference to regulation 2(1)(c) or (d) of the Statutory Sick Pay (General) Regulations 1982 in paragraph (1)(b) is a reference to the regulation which was in force on the first day of incapacity for work in question.

PART 3

CLAIMS

Making a claim

6.—(1) An employer who makes a claim for the recovery of a reimbursement amount must do so in accordance with this regulation.

(2) A claim may include one or more reimbursement amounts paid by the employer—
(a) to employees enrolled in the same PAYE scheme, and
(b) during the period of time specified by the employer in accordance with paragraph (3)(d).

(3) The claim must contain the following—
(a) the employer PAYE reference number for the PAYE scheme to which the claim relates;
(b) the number of employees the claim relates to;
(c) the amount claimed;
(d) the beginning and end dates of the period of time to which the amount specified in accordance with sub-paragraph (c) relates;
(e) details of the bank account into which the amount specified in accordance with sub-paragraph (c) is to be paid; and
(f) if required by regulation 9(2), the amount by which the original claim was overstated.
(4) The claim must contain a declaration by the employer that—
(a) the employer was not already in difficulty on 31st December 2019;
(b) receipt of the amount claimed will not result in the amount of State aid received by the employer exceeding the maximum temporary aid amount for that employer; and
(c) the matters stated in the claim are true and accurate.
(5) The claim must be submitted to HMRC electronically using the Government Gateway unless paragraph (6) or regulation 9(2) applies.
(6) If the employer considers that the employer is digitally excluded—
(a) the employer may make a request to HMRC to submit a claim in an alternative manner, and
(b) if HMRC are satisfied that the employer is digitally excluded, the employer must submit the claim in a manner agreed with HMRC.
(7) An employer is digitally excluded where—
(a) it is not reasonably practicable for the employer to use the Government Gateway to submit a claim for any reason including age, disability or remoteness of location, or
(b) the employer is a person who is a practising member of a religious society or order whose beliefs are incompatible with using the Government Gateway.
(8) In this regulation "Government Gateway" means the secure online facility for accessing government services.

Time limit for making a claim

4.125

7. A claim may not be made after the end of 24th March 2022.

PART 4

PAYMENTS, CORRECTIONS AND OVERPAYMENTS

Payments

4.126

8. Where HMRC accept a claim, HMRC must pay the amount specified in the claim by the employer in accordance with regulation 6(3)(c), less any amount repayable under regulation 9(3), to the account specified by the employer in accordance with regulation 6(3)(e) as soon as reasonably practicable.

Correcting a claim when the amount has been mistakenly overstated

9.—(1) Where an employer—
(a) becomes aware that the employer mistakenly overstated the amount in a claim (the "original claim"); and
(b) has received payment from HMRC in respect of the original claim,
the employer must correct the error in accordance with this regulation.

(2) The next claim that the employer makes under regulation 6 (the "next claim") must be made in the manner provided for in paragraph (8) and in it, the employer must specify the amount by which the original claim was overstated.

(3) The amount by which the original claim was overstated must be repaid to HMRC by the employer by way of set-off against the amount stated in the next claim, up to a maximum of the amount stated in the next claim.

(4) Where the amount by which the original claim was overstated exceeds the maximum amount required to be set off in accordance with paragraph (3), the employer must repay the excess to HMRC within the period of 30 days beginning on the day on which the next claim is made.

(5) Where an employer does not make a next claim within the period of 60 days beginning with the day on which the original claim was made, the employer must notify HMRC of the overstatement in accordance with paragraphs (6) to (8).

(6) The employer must provide the following information to HMRC—
(a) the employer PAYE reference number for the PAYE scheme to which the original claim related;
(b) the amount by which the original claim was overstated; and
(c) the beginning and end dates of the period of time to which the original claim related.

(7) The employer must declare to HMRC that the information provided under paragraph (6) is true and accurate.

(8) An employer who makes a next claim, a declaration under paragraph (7) or who provides information under paragraph (6) must do so by telephone or in writing, as determined by HMRC in its discretion and notified to the employer.

(9) The employer must repay to HMRC the amount referred to in paragraph 6(b) within the period of 30 days beginning on the day on which the employer provides the information under paragraph (6) and the declaration under paragraph (7).

Correcting a claim when the amount has been mistakenly understated

10. Where an employer becomes aware that the employer mistakenly understated the amount in a claim (the "understated claim"), the employer may submit a claim in accordance with regulation 6 for the amount understated in respect of the same period, PAYE scheme and employees specified in the understated claim.

Recovery of overpayments

4.129   **11.**—(1) Where any sum has been overpaid to an employer under these Regulations (an "overpayment"), HMRC may recover it in accordance with this regulation.

(2) An officer of Revenue and Customs must decide the amount of the overpayment and must give notice in writing of the decision to the employer.

(3) The employer must repay the overpayment to HMRC within the period of 30 days beginning with the day on which the employer receives the notice of decision referred to in paragraph (2).

(4) Part 6 of the Taxes Management Act 1970 (collection and recovery) applies to the recovery of overpayments as if—
  (a) the amount of the overpayment were income tax charged on the employer named in the notice of decision referred to in paragraph (2);
  (b) that notice of decision were an assessment; and
  (c) that notice of decision were the matter complained of for the purposes of section 65(3) of that Act.

(5) In the application of section 101(4) of the Finance Act 2009 (late payment interest on sums due to HMRC) in relation to a repayment to HMRC of an overpayment under this regulation, the overpayment becomes due and payable on the date on which HMRC give the notice of decision referred to in paragraph (2).

PART 5

RECORDS AND INFORMATION REQUESTS

Preservation of records

4.130   **12.**—(1) An employer who makes a claim for a reimbursement amount must keep a record of the following in respect of the employee, or former employee, in relation to whom the amount was claimed—
  (a) the start date and end date of the period of incapacity for work related to coronavirus to which the reimbursement amount relates;
  (b) national insurance number;
  (c) the reason for incapacity for work provided by the employee or former employee; and
  (d) the days which were qualifying days in that period of incapacity for work.

(2) An employer who corrects the amount of a claim in accordance with regulation 9 or 10 must keep a record of the amount of the correction and the reason for the correction.

(3) The employer must keep the records specified in paragraphs (1) and (2) until the end of the period of 3 years beginning with the date on which payment under regulation 8 is received.

(4) An employer who makes a claim for a reimbursement amount must keep the confirmation of State aid letter until the end of the period of 4 years beginning on IP completion day.

(5) In paragraph (4), "the confirmation of State aid letter" means the letter containing confirmation of receipt of State aid under these Regulations sent by HMRC to the employer once a claim is made.

(SI 2020/5 reg.13)

Provision of information and records

13.—(1) HMRC may by notice require an employer who has made a claim for a reimbursement amount—
  (a) to provide to HMRC in the manner specified in the notice, or
  (b) to make available for inspection at a place within the United Kingdom by an officer of Revenue and Customs,
within the period specified in the notice, all documents, records and other information in the employer's possession or under the employer's control as HMRC may reasonably require, to ascertain whether the employer was entitled to receive a reimbursement amount under these Regulations, including whether it was unlawful State aid.

(2) Where records are maintained by computer, an employer required to make them available for inspection must provide the officer of Revenue and Customs making the inspection with all the facilities necessary for obtaining information from them.

The Statutory Sick Pay (General) (Coronavirus Amendment) Regulations 2022

(SI 2022/380)

The Secretary of State makes the following Regulations in exercise of the powers conferred by sections 151(4) and 175(1), (3), (4) and (5) of the Social Security Contributions and Benefits Act 1992.

In accordance with section 172(1) of the Social Security Administration Act 1992, the Secretary of State has referred the proposals in respect of these Regulations to the Social Security Advisory Committee.

Citation, commencement and extent

1.—(1) These Regulations may be cited as the Statutory Sick Pay (General) (Coronavirus Amendment) Regulations 2022 and come into force on 25th March 2022.

(2) These Regulations extend to England and Wales and Scotland.

Amendment of the Statutory Sick Pay (General) Regulations 1982

2.—(1) The Statutory Sick Pay (General) Regulations 1982 are amended as follows.

(2) In regulation 2(1)—
  (a) in sub-paragraph (a)(iii), after the words "contract of service,", insert "or";
  (b) omit sub-paragraphs (c) and (d).

The Statutory Sick Pay (General) (Coronavirus Amendment) Regulations 2022

(3) Regulation 2(4) is omitted.
(4) Schedules 1 and 2 are omitted.

GENERAL NOTE

4.134   Regulation 2(2), (3) and (4) of these Regulations revoke the provisions within the Statutory Sick Pay (General) Regulations 1982 which deem people to be incapable of work where they are unable to work either due to isolating themselves in such a manner as to prevent infection or contamination with coronavirus, or due to shielding themselves in such a manner as to prevent infection or contamination with coronavirus.

The Statutory Sick Pay (Coronavirus) (Suspension of Waiting Days) (Saving Provision) Regulations 2022

(SI 2022/381)

The Secretary of State makes the following Regulations in exercise of the power conferred by section 89(3) of the Coronavirus Act 2020.

Citation, commencement and extent

4.135   **1.**—(1) These Regulations may be cited as the Statutory Sick Pay (Coronavirus) (Suspension of Waiting Days) (Saving Provision) Regulations 2022 and come into force on 25th March 2022.
(2) These Regulations extend to England and Wales and Scotland.

Saving provision related to the suspension of waiting days

4.136   **2.**—(1) Despite the expiry of section 40 of the Coronavirus Act 2020, regulation 2 of the Statutory Sick Pay (Coronavirus) (Suspension of Waiting Days and General Amendment) Regulations 2020 ("the 2020 Regulations") shall continue to have effect, subject to the modifications specified in paragraph (3), as set out in this regulation.
(2) Regulation 2 of the 2020 Regulations shall continue to have effect, subject to the modifications specified in paragraph (3), in relation to a period of incapacity for work which is related to coronavirus where that period of incapacity for work begins on or before 24th March 2022.
(3) The modifications are that regulation 2 of the 2020 Regulations is treated as though the following were omitted—
  (a) the word "or" at the end of paragraph (3)(b)(i) of that regulation; and
  (b) paragraphs (3)(b)(ii) and (4) of that regulation.
(4) In this regulation—
  (a) "period of incapacity for work" has the meaning given by section 152 of the Social Security Contributions and Benefits Act 1992; and

(b) whether a period of incapacity for work is related to coronavirus is to be determined in accordance with regulation 2(3)(b) of the 2020 Regulations.

GENERAL NOTE

Section 155(1) of the SSCBA 1992 provides that SSP is not payable for the first three days of a period of incapacity for work. Section 40 of the Coronavirus Act 2020 allowed regulations to disapply SSCBA 1992 s.155(1) where a period of incapacity for work was related to coronavirus. Regulation 2 of the Statutory Sick Pay (Coronavirus) (Suspension of Waiting Days and General Amendment) Regulations 2020 (SI 2020/374), made under that power, enabled SSP to be payable from day one of a period of incapacity for work which was related to coronavirus, as opposed to day four as would otherwise be the case. However, s.40 of the Coronavirus Act 2020 expired at midnight on March 24, 2022, and as a result the 2020 Regulations also expired. Regulation 2(1) and (2) of SI 2022/381 make saving provision by providing that reg.2 of the 2020 Regulations continues to have effect where a period of incapacity for work commences on or before March 24, 2022. This is subject to the modifications in reg.2(3) which in turn reflect the revocation of the deeming provisions contained in reg.2(1)(c) and (d) and Schs 1 and 2 of the Statutory Sick Pay (General) Regulations 1982.

4.137

PART V

STATUTORY MATERNITY PAY

The Statutory Maternity Pay (General) Regulations 1986

(SI 1986/1960) (AS AMENDED)

The Secretary of State for Social Services, in exercise of the powers conferred by sections 46(4), (7) and (8), 47(1), (3), (6) and (7), 48(3) and (6), 50(1), (2), (4) and (5), 51(1)(g), (k), (n) and (r) and (4), 54(1), 83(1) and 84(1) of, and paragraphs 6, 8 and 12(3) of Schedule 4 to, the Social Security Act 1986(a), and of all other powers enabling him in that behalf, by this instrument, which contains only regulations made under the sections of the Social Security Act 1986 specified above and provisions consequential upon those sections and before the end of a period of 12 months from the commencement of those sections, makes the following regulations:

ARRANGEMENT OF REGULATIONS

PART I

INTRODUCTION

1. Citation, commencement and interpretation 5.1

PART II

ENTITLEMENT

2. The Maternity Pay Period
3. Contract of service ended for the purpose of avoiding liability for statutory maternity pay
4. Modification of entitlement provisions
5. Treatment of more than one contract of service as one
6. Prescribed rate of statutory maternity pay
7. Liability of Secretary of State to pay statutory maternity pay
8. Work after confinement
9. No liability to pay statutory maternity pay
9A. Working for not more than 10 days in the Maternity Pay Period
10. Death of woman

PART III

CONTINUOUS EMPLOYMENT AND NORMAL WORKING HOURS

11. Continuous employment
12. Continuous employment and unfair dismissal
13. Continuous employment and stoppages of work
14. Change of employer

15. Reinstatement after service with the armed forces
16. Normal working weeks
16A. Meaning of "week"

Part IV

General Provisions

17. Meaning of "employee"
18. Treatment of two or more employers as one
19. Payments to be treated as contractual remuneration
20. Meaning of "earnings"
21. Normal weekly earnings
21A. (*repealed*)
21B. Effect of maternity allowance on statutory maternity pay

Part V

Administration

22. Evidence of expected week of confinement
23. Notice of absence from work
24. Notification of employment after confinement
25. Provision of information in connection with determination of questions
25A. Provision of information relating to claims for certain other benefits
26. Records to be maintained by employers
26A. Production of employer's records

Part VI

Payment

27. Payment of statutory maternity pay
28. Rounding to avoid fractional amounts
29. Time when statutory maternity pay is to be paid
30. Payments by the Secretary of State
31. Persons unable to act

Part VII

Offences

32. (*repealed*)

(SI 1986/1960 reg.1) (as amended)

PART I

INTRODUCTION

Citation, commencement and interpretation

1.—(1) These regulations may be cited as the Statutory Maternity Pay (General) Regulations 1986 and shall come into operation in the case of regulations 1, 22 and 23 on 15th March, 1987, and in the case of the remainder of the regulations on 6th April, 1987.
(2) In these regulations, unless the context otherwise requires—
"the 1975 Act" means the Social Security Act 1975;
"the 1978 Act" means the Employment Protection (Consolidation) Act 1978;
"the 1986 Act" means the Social Security Act 1986.
[[1]"the Contributions and Benefits Act" means the Social Security Contributions and Benefits Act 1992.]
[[2]"statutory maternity leave" means ordinary maternity leave and any additional maternity leave under, respectively, sections 71 and 73 of the Employment Rights Act 1996.]
(3) Unless the context otherwise requires, any references in these regulations to—
  (a) a numbered regulation is a reference to the regulation bearing that number in these regulations and any reference in a regulation to a numbered paragraph is a reference to the paragraph of that regulation bearing that number;
  (b) any provision made by or contained in an enactment or instrument shall be construed as a reference to that provision as amended or extended by any enactment or instrument and as including a reference to any provision which it re-enacts or replaces, or which may reenact or replace it, with or without modifications.

AMENDMENTS

1. Social Security (Miscellaneous Provisions) Amendment (No.2) Regulations 1992 (SI 1992/2595) reg.12 (November 16, 1992).
2. Statutory Maternity Pay (General) (Amendment) Regulations 2005 (SI 2005/729) reg.2 (April 6, 2005).

GENERAL NOTE

The text of these Regulations pre-dates SSCBA 1992 and was not amended at the time of the SSCBA 1992 to reflect the provisions in the 1992 Act. The Regulations remain in force, of course, by virtue of s.17(2)(b) of the Interpretation Act 1978. As a result, regulations which survive unamended from the original text refer to the SSA 1975 and SSA 1986, whilst post-1992 amendments refer to the parallel provisions in SSCBA 1992. References to the 1975 Act should therefore be read as referring to SSCBA 1992, and those to Pt V of the SSA 1986 as referring to Pt XII of the SSCBA 1992.

The Statutory Maternity Pay (General) Regulations 1986

Part II

Entitlement

The Maternity Pay Period

5.4 [¹ **2.**—(1) Subject to paragraphs (3) to (5), where—
 (a) a woman gives notice to her employer of the date from which she expects his liability to pay her statutory maternity pay to begin; and
 (b) in conformity with that notice ceases to work for him in a week which is later than the 12th week before the expected week of confinement,
the first day of the maternity pay period shall be the day on which she expects his liability to pay her statutory maternity pay to begin in conformity with that notice provided that day is not later than the day immediately following the day on which she is confined.
 (2) The maternity pay period shall be a period of 39 consecutive weeks.
 (3) In a case where a woman is confined—
 (a) before the 11th week before the expected week of confinement; or
 (b) after the 12th week before the expected week of confinement and the confinement occurs on a day which precedes that mentioned in a notice given to her employer as being the day on which she expects his liability to pay her statutory maternity pay to begin,
section 165 of the Contributions and Benefits Act shall have effect so that the first day of the maternity pay period shall be the day following the day on which she is so confined.
 (4) In a case where a woman is absent from work wholly or partly because of pregnancy or confinement on any day—
 (a) which falls on or after the beginning of the 4th week before the expected week of confinement; but
 (b) not later than the day immediately following the day on which she is confined,
the first day of the maternity pay period shall be the day following the day on which she is so absent.
 (5) In a case where a woman leaves her employment—
 (a) at any time falling after the beginning of the 11th week before the expected week of confinement and before the start of the maternity pay period, but
 (b) not later than the day on which she is confined,
the first day of the maternity pay period shall be the day following the day on which she leaves her employment.]

Amendment

1. Statutory Maternity Pay, Social Security (Maternity Allowance) and Social Security (Overlapping Benefits) (Amendment) Regulations 2006 (SI 2006/2379) reg.3(2) (October 1, 2006).

General Note

5.5 This regulation was substantially recast with a new version substituted with effect from October 1, 2006 which applies in relation to women whose expected week of

(SI 1986/1960 reg.2) (as amended)

confinement falls on or after April 1, 2007. The new version of the regulation was prompted by the enactment of the Work and Families Act 2006, which improved the SMP scheme. There are two main differences between the current and previous versions of the regulation.

First, SMP is now payable for 39 weeks as opposed to the 26 weeks that applied before October 1, 2006 (para.(2)); note that before November 24, 2002, the previous maximum period had been 18 weeks.

Secondly, before October 1, 2006 the maternity pay period for SMP purposes started from the week following the week that the woman ceased work in accordance with the requisite notice given to her employer. In practice this meant the Sunday following the day she stopped work in accordance with the notice. The new rule enables the maternity pay period to start on any day of the week as specified by the woman in her notice to the employer. This allows the start of the maternity pay period to match the start of the woman's maternity leave. Accordingly the general rule for determining the start of the maternity pay period is set out in para.(1). There are then a number of further special cases detailed in paras (3)–(5). Paragraph (3) covers those situations where the woman gives birth early. Paragraph (4) makes special provision to deal with the situation where the woman stops working because of a pregnancy-related absence in the four weeks before the expected week of confinement. Finally, para.(5) covers women who leave their employment after the start of the 11th week before the expected week of confinement, but before the maternity pay period commences and not later than day of actual confinement.

Paragraph (1)
"in conformity with that notice cases to work"

This expression was considered by the Upper Tribunal (Tax and Chancery Chamber) in *Wade and North Yorkshire Police Authority v HMRC (FTC/35/2009, FTC/42/2009* and *FTC/43/2009)* [2011] I.R.L.R. 393, where Mrs Wade claimed SMP in relation to pregnancies in 2005 and 2007. It was held that a woman might cease to work "in conformity with that notice" for the purposes of para.(1) even if she had previously ceased to work on some other basis. An analogy with the statutory maternity leave regime provided support for that approach. A woman eligible for statutory maternity leave could claim it from a date of her choosing, regardless of the basis for her period of leave, provided only that the date was no earlier than the 11th week before the expected week of confinement and during the last four weeks before the expected week of confinement she was not absent from work because of pregnancy in advance of the specified date. It was held that it made sense that she should be able to claim SMP from a similar date, especially given the symmetries between the two regimes. This interpretation also produced clarity for both employer and employee. The result was that the claimant was entitled to SMP from the fourth week before each expected week of confinement. It did not matter whether, in respect of the second pregnancy, it was para.(1) or para.(4) that governed the position.

5.6

Contract of service ended for the purpose of avoiding liability for statutory maternity pay

3.—(1) A former employer shall be liable to make payments of statutory maternity pay to any woman who was employed by him for a continuous period of at least eight weeks and whose contract of service with him was brought to an end by the former employer solely or mainly for the purpose of avoiding liability for statutory maternity pay.

5.7

(2) In order to determine the amount payable by the former employer—
   (a) the woman shall be deemed for the purposes of Part V of the 1986 Act to have been employed by him from the date her employment with him ended until the end of the week immediately preceding the

The Statutory Maternity Pay (General) Regulations 1986

14th week before the expected week of confinement on the same terms and conditions of employment as those subsisting immediately before her employment ended; and

(b) her normal weekly earnings for the period of 8 weeks immediately preceding the 14th week before the expected week of confinement shall for those purposes be calculated by reference to her normal weekly earnings for the period of 8 weeks ending with the last day in respect of which she was paid under her former contract of service.

GENERAL NOTE

5.8 This regulation, made under SSCBA 1992 s.164(8), sets out the principles governing entitlement to statutory maternity pay where an employer dismisses a woman with a view to avoiding liability to pay statutory maternity pay. In order for this provision to apply, the woman must have been continuously employed for at least eight weeks (para.(1)). Such action will also constitute an automatically unfair dismissal under Employment Rights Act 1999 s.99 and an act of sex discrimination.

Modification of entitlement provisions

5.9 **4.**—(1) [¹...]

(2) In relation to a woman in employed earner's employment who was confined before the 14th week before the expected week of confinement [¹section 164(2)(a) and (b) of the Contributions and Benefits Act] shall have effect as if for the conditions there set out, there were substituted the conditions that—

(a) she would but for her confinement have been in employed earner's employment with an employer for a continuous period of at least 26 weeks ending with the week immediately preceding the 14th week before the expected week of confinement; and

(b) her normal weekly earnings for the period of 8 weeks ending with the week immediately preceding the week of her confinement are not less than the lower earnings limit in force [¹under section 5(1)(a) of the Contributions and Benefits Act] immediately before the commencement of the week of her confinement.

[¹(3) In relation to a woman to whom paragraph (2) applies, section 166 of the Contributions and Benefits Act shall be modified so that subsection (2) has effect as if the reference to the period of 8 weeks immediately preceding the 14th week before the expected week of confinement was a reference to the period of 8 weeks immediately preceding the week in which her confinement occurred.]

AMENDMENT

1. Social Security Maternity Benefits and Statutory Sick Pay (Amendment) Regulations 1994 (SI 1994/1367) reg.3 (June 11, 1994).

GENERAL NOTE

Paragraph (2)

5.10 If the baby is born either before or in the qualifying week, statutory maternity pay is still payable so long as the woman would have been employed for 26 weeks by the end of the qualifying week, on the assumption that the baby had not in fact been born early.

(SI 1986/1960 reg.5) (as amended)

Treatment of more than one contract of service as one

5.—Where 2 or more contracts of service exist concurrently between one employer and one employee, they shall be treated as one for the purposes of Part V of the 1986 Act, except where, by virtue of regulation 11 of the Social Security (Contributions) Regulations 1979 the earnings from those contracts of service are not aggregated for the purposes of earnings-related contributions.

[¹Prescribed rate of statutory maternity pay

6.—The rate of statutory maternity pay prescribed under section 166(1)(b) of the Contributions and Benefits Act is a weekly rate of [²£184.03.]

AMENDMENTS

1. Social Security, Statutory Maternity Pay and Statutory Sick Pay (Miscellaneous Amendments) Regulations 2002 (SI 2002/2690) reg.3 (April 6, 2003).
2. Social Security Benefits Up-rating Order 2024 (SI 2024/242) art.9 (April 7, 2024).

Liability of Secretary of State to pay Statutory Maternity Pay

7.—(1) Where—
(a) an adjudicating authority has determined that an employer is liable to make payments of statutory maternity pay to a woman; and
(b) the time for appealing against that determination has expired; and
(c) no appeal against the determination has been lodged or leave to appeal against the determination is required and has been refused,
then for any week in respect of which the employer was liable to make payments of statutory maternity pay but did not do so, and for any subsequent weeks in the maternity pay period the liability to make those payments shall, notwithstanding section 46(3) of the 1986 Act, be that of the Secretary of State and not the employer.

(2) In paragraph (1) adjudicating authority means, as the case may be, the Chief or any other adjudication officer, [² the First-tier Tribunal or the Upper Tribunal.]

(3) Liability to make payments of statutory maternity pay shall, notwithstanding section 46(3) of the 1986 Act, be a liability of the Secretary of State and not the employer as from the week in which the employer first becomes insolvent until the end of the maternity pay period.

(4) For the purposes of paragraph (3) an employer shall be taken to be insolvent if, and only if—
(a) in England and Wales—
  (i) he has been adjudged bankrupt or has made a composition or arrangement with his creditors;
  (ii) he has died and his estate falls to be administered in accordance with an order under section 421 of the Insolvency Act 1986; or
  (iii) where an employer is a company, a winding-up order [¹...] is made or a resolution for voluntary winding-up is passed with respect to it [¹or it enter administration], or a receiver or manager of its undertaking is duly appointed, or possession is taken by or on behalf of the holders of any debentures secured by a floating charge, of any property of the company comprised in or subject to the charge or a voluntary arrangement proposed

for the purposes of Part 1 of the Insolvency Act 1986 is approved under that Part;
(b) in Scotland—
  (i) an award of sequestration is made on his estate or he executes a trust deed for his creditors or enters into a composition contract;
  (ii) he has died and a judicial factor appointed under section 1A of the Judicial Factors (Scotland) Act 1889 is required by that section to divide his insolvent estate among his creditors; or
  (iii) where the employer is a company, a winding-up order [¹...] is made or a resolution for voluntary winding-up is passed with respect to it [¹or it enter administration] or a receiver of its undertaking is duly appointed or a voluntary arrangement proposed for the purposes of Part 1 of the Insolvency Act 1986 is approved under that Part.

AMENDMENTS

1. Enterprise Act 2002 (Insolvency) Order 2003 (SI 2003/2096) art.5 and Sch.2 para.44 (September 15, 2003).
2. Tribunals, Courts and Enforcement Act 2007 (Transitional and Consequential Provisions) Order 2008 (SI 2008/2683) art.6 and Sch.1 para.42 (November 3, 2008).

GENERAL NOTE

5.14 The functions under this regulation were transferred from the Secretary of State for Social Security to the Board of the Inland Revenue (now HMRC) under s.1(2) of and Sch.2 to the Social Security (Transfer of Functions, etc.) Act 1999. References in this regulation to SSA 1986 s.46(3) should now be read as referring to SSCBA 1992 s.164(3). The various references to insolvency law provisions include the special administration regime under the Investment Bank Special Administration Regulations 2011 (SI 2011/245) (see reg.27 and Sch.6 Pt 1 of those Regulations).

Work after confinement

5.15 **8.**—(1) Where in the week immediately preceding the 14th week before the expected week of confinement a woman had two or more employers but one or more of them were not liable to make payments to her of statutory maternity pay ("non-liable employer"), section 47(6) of the 1986 Act shall not apply in respect of any week after the week of confinement but within the maternity pay period in which she works only for a non-liable employer.
(2) Where after her confinement a woman—
(a) works for an employer who is not liable to pay her statutory maternity pay and is not a non-liable employer, but
(b) before the end of her maternity pay period ceases to work for that employer, the person who before she commenced work was liable to make payments of statutory maternity pay to her shall, notwithstanding section 46 of the 1986 Act, not be liable to make such payments to her for any weeks in the maternity pay period after she ceases work.

GENERAL NOTE

5.16 References in this regulation to SSA 1986 ss.46 and 47(6) should now be read as referring to SSCBA 1992 ss.164 and 165(6).

(SI 1986/1960 reg.9) (as amended)

No liability to pay statutory maternity pay

9.—Notwithstanding the provisions of section 46(1) of the 1986 Act, no liability to make payments of statutory maternity pay to a woman shall arise in respect of a week within the maternity pay period for any part of which she is detained in legal custody or sentenced to a term of imprisonment (except where the sentence is suspended), or of any subsequent week within that period.

GENERAL NOTE

The reference in this regulation to SSA 1986 s.46(1) should now be read as referring to SSCBA 1992 s.164(1).

[¹ Working for not more than 10 days in the Maternity Pay Period

9A.—In a case where a woman does any work under a contract of service with her employer on any day, but for not more than 10 days (whether consecutive or not), during her maternity pay period, statutory maternity pay shall continue to be payable to the employee by the employer.]

AMENDMENT

1. Statutory Maternity Pay, Social Security (Maternity Allowance) and Social Security (Overlapping Benefits) (Amendment) Regulations 2006 (SI 2006/2379) reg.3(3) (October 1, 2006).

GENERAL NOTE

This provision applies in relation to women whose expected week of confinement falls on or after April 1, 2007. It enables a woman to work for up to 10 days under her contract during the statutory maternity pay period for the employer paying her SMP and still retain her SMP for that week—previously a week's SMP was lost for any week in which such work was undertaken.

Death of woman

10.—An employer shall not be liable to make payments of statutory maternity pay in respect of a woman for any week within the maternity pay period which falls after the week in which she dies.

PART III

CONTINUOUS EMPLOYMENT AND NORMAL WORKING HOURS

Continuous employment

11.—(1) Subject to the following provisions of this regulation, where in any week a woman is, for the whole part of the week,—
  (a) incapable of work in consequence of sickness or injury; or
  (b) absent from work on account of a temporary cessation of work; or
  (c) absent from work in circumstances such that, by arrangement or custom, she is regarded as continuing in the employment of her employer for all or any purpose; or

(d) absent from work wholly or partly because of pregnancy or confinement, [²or
(e) absent from work in consequence of taking paternity leave, adoption leave [³, shared parental leave] [⁴, parental bereavement leave] or parental leave under Part 8 of the Employment Rights Act 1996,]

and returns to work for her employer after the incapacity for or absence from work, that week shall be treated for the purposes of Part V of the 1986 Act as part of a continuous period of employment with that employer, notwithstanding that no contract of service exists with that employer in respect of that week.

(2) Incapacity for work which lasts for more than 26 consecutive weeks shall not count for the purposes of paragraph (1)(a).

(3) Paragraph (1)(d) shall only apply to a woman who—
(a) has a contract of service with the same employer both before and after her confinement but not during any period of absence from work due to her confinement and the period between those contracts does not exceed 26 weeks; or
(b) returns to work in accordance with section 45(1) of the 1978 Act or in pursuance of an offer made in circumstances described in section 56A(2) of that Act after a period of absence from work wholly or partly occasioned by pregnancy or confinement.

[¹(3A) Where a woman who is pregnant—
(a) is an employee in an employed earner's employment in which the custom is for the employer—
  (i) to offer work for a fixed period of not more than 26 consecutive weeks;
  (ii) to offer work for such period on 2 or more occasions in a year for periods which do not overlap; and
  (iii) to offer the work available to those persons who had worked for him during the last or a recent such period, but
(b) is absent from work—
  (i) wholly or partly because of the pregnancy or her confinement; or
  (ii) because of incapacity arising from some specific disease or bodily or mental disablement,

then in her case paragraph (1) shall apply as if the words "and returns to work for an employer after the incapacity for or absence from work" were omitted and paragraph (4) shall not apply.]

(4) Where a woman is employed under a contract of service for part only of the week immediately preceding the 14th week before the expected week of confinement, the whole of that week shall count in computing any period of continuous employment for the purposes of Part V of the 1986 Act.

AMENDMENTS

1. Statutory Maternity Pay (General) Amendment Regulations 1990 (SI 1990/622) reg.2 (April 6, 1990).
2. Social Security, Statutory Maternity Pay and Statutory Sick Pay (Miscellaneous Amendments) Regulations 2002 (SI 2002/2690) reg.4 (April 6, 2003).
3. Shared Parental Leave and Statutory Shared Parental Pay (Consequential Amendments to Subordinate Legislation) Order 2014 (SI 2014/3255) art.4(2) (December 31, 2014).

(SI 1986/1960 reg.11) (as amended)

4. Parental Bereavement Leave and Pay (Consequential Amendments to Subordinate Legislation) Regulations 2020 (SI 2020/354) reg.4(2) (April 6, 2020).

DEFINITIONS

"the 1978 Act"—see reg.1(2).
"the 1986 Act"—see reg.1(2).

Continuous employment and unfair dismissal

12.—(1) This regulation applies to a woman in relation to whose dismissal an action is commenced which consists—
   (a) of the presentation by her of a complaint under section 67(1) of the 1978 Act; or
   (b) of her making a claim in accordance with a dismissals procedure agreement designated by an order under section 65 of that Act; or
   (c) of any action taken by a conciliation officer under section 134(3) of that Act; [¹or
   (d) of a decision arising out of the use of a statutory dispute resolution procedure contained in Schedule 2 to the Employment Act 2002 in a case where, in accordance with the Employment Act 2002 (Dispute Resolution) Regulations 2004, such a procedure applies.]
(2) If in consequence of an action of the kind specified in paragraph (1) a woman is reinstated or re-engaged by her employer or by a successor or associated employer of that employer the continuity of her employment shall be preserved for the purposes of Part V of the 1986 Act and any week which falls within the interval beginning with the effective date of termination and ending with the date of reinstatement or re-engagement, as the case may be, shall count in the computation of her period of continuous employment.
(3) In this regulation—
"successor" and "dismissals procedure agreement" have the same meanings as in section 30(3) and (4) of the Trade Union and Labour Relations Act 1974; and
"associated employer" shall be construed in accordance with section 153(4) of the 1978 Act.

AMENDMENT

1. Statutory Maternity Pay (General) and the Statutory Paternity Pay and Statutory Adoption Pay (General) (Amendment) Regulations 2005 (SI 2005/358) reg.3 (April 6, 2005).

DEFINITIONS

"the 1978 Act"—see reg.1(2).
"associated employer"—see para.(3).
"dismissals procedure agreement"—see para.(3).
"successor"—see para.(3).

Continuous employment and stoppages of work

13.—(1) Where for any week or part of a week a woman does no work because there is, within the meaning of section 19 of the 1975 Act a stoppage of work due to a trade dispute at her place of employment the continuity of her employment shall, subject to paragraph (2), be treated as continuing

5.23

5.24

throughout the stoppage but, subject to paragraph (3), no such week shall count in the computation of her period of employment.

(2) Subject to paragraph (3), where during the stoppage of work a woman is dismissed from her employment, the continuity of her employment shall not be treated in accordance with paragraph (1) as continuing beyond the commencement of the day she stopped work.

(3) The provisions of paragraph (1) to the extent that they provide that a week in which a stoppage of work occurred shall not count in the computation of a period of employment, and paragraph (2) shall not apply to a woman who proves that at no time did she have a direct interest in the trade dispute in question.

General Note

5.25   The reference in this regulation to SSA 1975 s.19 should now be read as referring to SSCBA 1992 s.27.

Change of employer

5.26   **14.**—A woman's employment shall, notwithstanding the change of employer, be treated as continuous employment with the second employer where—
- (a) the employer's trade or business or an undertaking (whether or not it is an undertaking established by or under an Act of Parliament) is transferred from one person to another;
- (b) by or under an Act of Parliament, whether public or local and whenever passed, a contract of employment between any body corporate and the woman is modified and some other body corporate is substituted as her employer;
- (c) on the death of her employer, the woman is taken into the employment of the personal representatives or trustees of the deceased;
- (d) the woman is employed by partners, personal representatives or trustees and there is a change in the partners, or, as the case may be, personal representatives or trustees;
- (e) the woman is taken into the employment of an employer who is, at the time she entered his employment, an associated employer of her previous employer, and for this purpose "associated employer" shall be construed in accordance with section 153(4) of the 1978 Act;
- (f) on the termination of her employment with an employer she is taken into the employment of another employer and [¹those employers are the governors of a school maintained by a [²local authority (written the meaning of the Education Act 1996) and that authority].

Amendments

1. Statutory Maternity Pay (General) Amendment Regulations 1990 (SI 1990/622) reg.3 (April 6, 1990).

2. Local Educational Authorities and Children's Services Authorities (Integration of Functions) (Local and Subordinate Legislation) Order 2010 (SI 2010/1172) art.4 and Sch.3 para.11 (May 5, 2010).

Definition

"the 1978 Act"—see reg.1(2).

(SI 1986/1960 reg.15) (as amended)

Reinstatement after service with the armed forces, etc.

15.—If a woman who is entitled to apply to her former employer under the Reserve Forces (Safeguard of Employment) Act 1985 enters the employment of that employer not later than the 6 month period mentioned in section 1(4)(b) of that Act, her previous period of employment with that employer (or if there was more than one such period, the last of those periods) and the period of employment beginning in the said period of 6 months shall be treated as continuous.

Normal working weeks

16.—(1) For the purposes of section 48(5) of the 1986 Act, a woman's contract of service shall be treated as not normally involving or having involved employment for less than 16 hours weekly where she is normally employed for 16 hours or more weekly.

(2) Where a woman's relations with her employer were governed for a continuous period of at least 2 years by a contract of service which normally involved employment for not less than 16 hours weekly and this period was followed by a further period, ending with the week immediately preceding the 14th week before the expected week of confinement, in which her relations with that employer were governed by a contract of service which normally involved employment for less than 16 hours, but not less than 8 hours weekly, then her contract of service shall be treated for the purpose of section 48(5) of the 1986 Act as not normally involving or having involved employment for less than 16 hours weekly.

(3) Where a woman's relations with her employer are or were governed for a continuous period of at least 2 years by a contract of service which involved—
  (a) for not more than 26 weeks in that period, employment for 8 hours or more but less than 16 hours weekly; and
  (b) for the whole of the remainder of that period employment for not less than 16 hours weekly, the contract of service shall be treated for the purposes of section 48(5) of the 1986 Act as not normally involving or having involved employment for less than 16 hours weekly.

GENERAL NOTE

The references in this regulation to SSA 1986 s.48(5) should now be read as referring to SSCBA 1992 s.166(5).

[¹Meaning of "week"

16A.—Where a woman has been in employed earner's employment with the same employer in each of 26 consecutive weeks (but no more than 26 weeks) ending with the week immediately preceding the 14th week before the expected week of confinement then for the purpose of determining whether that employment amounts to a continuous period of at least 26 weeks, the first of those 26 weeks shall be a period commencing on the first day of her employment with the employer and ending at midnight on the first Saturday thereafter or on that day where her first day is a Saturday.]

The Statutory Maternity Pay (General) Regulations 1986

AMENDMENT

1. Statutory Maternity Pay (General) Amendment Regulations 1990 (SI 1990/622) reg.4 (April 6, 1990).

PART IV

GENERAL PROVISIONS

Meaning of "employee"

5.31   **17.**—(1) [¹Subject to paragraph (1A),] in a case where, and in so far as, a woman [¹. . .] is treated as an employed earner by virtue of the Social Security (Categorisation of Earners) Regulations 1978 she shall be treated as an employee for the purposes of Part V of the 1986 Act and in a case where, and in so far as, such a woman is treated otherwise than as an employed earner by virtue of those regulations, she shall not be treated as an employee for the purposes of Part V.

[²(1A) Paragraph (1) shall have effect in relation to a woman who—
  (a) is under the age of 16; and
  (b) would or, as the case may be, would not have been treated as an employed earner by virtue of the Social Security (Categorisation of Earners) Regulations 1978 had she been over that age,
as it has effect in relation to a woman who is, or, as the case may be, is not so treated.]

(2) Any woman who is in employed earner's employment within the meaning of the 1975 Act under a contract of apprenticeship shall be treated as the employee for the purposes of Part V.

(3) A woman who is in employed earner's employment within the meaning of the 1975 Act but whose employer—
  (a) does not fulfil the conditions prescribed in regulation 119(1)(b) of the Social Security (Contributions) Regulations 1979 as to residence or presence in Great Britain, or
  (b) is a woman who, by reason of any international treaty to which the United Kingdom is a party of any international convention binding the United Kingdom—
      (i) is exempt from the provisions of the 1975 Act, or
      (ii) is a woman against whom the provisions of that Act are not enforceable, shall not be treated as an employee for the purposes of Part V of the 1986 Act.

AMENDMENTS

1. Employment Equality (Age) Regulations 2006 (SI 2006/1031) reg.49(1) and Sch.8 Pt 2 para.53 (October 1, 2006).

2. Employment Equality (Age) (Consequential Amendments) Regulations 2007 (SI 2007/825) reg.6 (April 6, 2007).

Treatment of two or more employers as one

5.32   **18.**—(1) In a case where the earnings paid to a woman in respect of 2 or more employments are aggregated and treated as a single payment of earnings under regulation 12(1) of the Social Security (Contributions)

(SI 1986/1960 reg.18) (as amended)

Regulations 1979, the employers of the woman in respect of those employments shall be treated as one for all purposes of Part V of the 1986 Act.

(2) Where two or more employers are treated as one under the provisions of paragraph (1), liability for statutory maternity pay payable by them to a woman shall be apportioned between them in such proportions as they may agree or, in default of agreement, in the proportions which the woman's earnings from each employment bear to the amount of the aggregated earnings.

GENERAL NOTE

Specific provision is also made in the Statutory Maternity Pay (National Health Service Employees) Regulations 1991 (SI 1991/590) for NHS workers with divided contracts.

Payments to be treated as contractual remuneration

19.—For the purposes of paragraph 12(1) and (2) of Schedule 4 to the 1986 Act, the payments which are to be treated as contractual remuneration are sums payable under the contract of service—
(a) by way of remuneration;
(b) for incapacity for work due to sickness or injury; and
(c) by reason of pregnancy or confinement.

DEFINITION

"the 1986 Act"—see reg.1(2).

Meaning of "earnings"

20.—(1) [¹...]
[²(2) For the purposes of section 171(4) of the Contributions and Benefits Act, the expression "earnings" refers to gross earnings and includes any remuneration or profit derived from a woman's employment except any payment or amount which is—
(a) excluded [⁶or disregarded in the calculation of a person's earnings under regulation 25, 27 or 123 of, or Schedule 3 to, the Social Security (Contributions) Regulations 2001] (payments to be disregarded and payments to directors to be disregarded respectively) [⁵(or would have been so excluded had she not been under the age of 16)];
(b) a chargeable emolument under section 10A of the Social Security Contributions and Benefits Act 1992, except where, in consequence of such a chargeable emolument being excluded from earnings, a woman would not be entitled to statutory maternity pay. [⁵(or where such a payment or amount would have been so excluded and in consequence she would not have been entitled to statutory maternity pay had she not been under the age of 16)]]
(3) [¹...]
(4) For the purposes of section [³section 171(4) of the Contributions and Benefits Act] the expression "earnings" includes also—
[⁶(za) any amount retrospectively treated as earnings by regulations made by virtue of section 4B(2) of the Contributions and Benefits Act;]
(a) any sum payable in respect of arrears of pay in pursuance of an order for reinstatement or re-engagement under the 1978 Act;

(b) any sum payable by way of pay in pursuance of an order under the 1978 Act for the continuation of a contract of employment;
(c) any sum payable by way of remuneration in pursuance of a protective award under the Employment Protection Act 1975;
(d) any sum payable by way of statutory sick pay, including sums payable in accordance with regulations made under section 1(5) of the Social Security and Housing Benefits Act 1982.
[4(e) any sum payable by way of statutory maternity pay, including sums payable in accordance with regulations made under section 164(9)(b) of the Contributions and Benefits Act;
(f) any sum payable by way of statutory paternity pay, including sums payable in accordance with regulations made under section 171ZD(3) of the Contributions and Benefits Act;
(g) any sum payable by way of statutory adoption pay, including sums payable in accordance with regulations made under section 171ZM(3) of the Contributions and Benefits Act;]
[7 (h) any sum payable by way of statutory shared parental pay, including any sums payable in accordance with regulations made under section 171ZX(3) of the Contributions and Benefits Act][8;
(i) any sum payable by way of statutory parental bereavement pay, including any sums payable in accordance with regulations made under section 171ZZ8(3) of the Contributions and Benefits Act].
(5) [1...]
(6) [1...]

AMENDMENTS

1. Social Security (Miscellaneous Provisions) Amendment (No.2) Regulations 1992 (SI 1992/2595) reg.13 (November 16, 1992).
2. Social Security Contributions, Statutory Maternity Pay and Statutory Sick Pay (Miscellaneous Amendments) Regulations 1999 (SI 1999/567) reg.12 (April 6, 1999).
3. Social Security, Statutory Maternity Pay and Statutory Sick Pay (Miscellaneous Amendments) Regulations 2002 (SI 2002/2690) reg.5(a) (November 24, 2002).
4. Social Security, Statutory Maternity Pay and Statutory Sick Pay (Miscellaneous Amendments) Regulations 2002 (SI 2002/2690) reg.5(b) (April 6, 2003).
5. Employment Equality (Age) Regulations 2006 (SI 2006/1031) reg.49(1) and Sch.8 Pt 2 para.53 (October 1, 2006, and in relation to any case where the expected week of confinement begins on or after January 14, 2007).
6. Social Security, Occupational Pension Schemes and Statutory Payments (Consequential Provisions) Regulations 2007 (SI 2007/1154) reg.4(2) and (3) (April 6, 2007).
7. Shared Parental Leave and Statutory Shared Parental Pay (Consequential Amendments to Subordinate Legislation) Order 2014 (SI 2014/3255) art.4(2) (December 31, 2014).
8. Parental Bereavement Leave and Pay (Consequential Amendments to Subordinate Legislation) Regulations 2020 (SI 2020/354) reg.4(3) (April 6, 2020).

GENERAL NOTE

5.36   Regulation 20 was considered by a First-tier Tribunal in the Finance and Tax Chamber in *Campus Living Villages UK Ltd v HMRC and Sexton* [2016] UKFTT 738 (TC). The tribunal found that "'Earnings' includes **any** remuneration or profit derived from a woman's employment with some immaterial exceptions. Irregular or one-off payments including bonuses therefore count as 'earnings' as long as they are derived from the woman's employment" (at [39], original emphasis). It should also be noted the bonus in that case was discretionary.

Normal weekly earnings

21.—(1) For the purposes of [¹Part XII of the Contributions and Benefits Act], a woman's normal weekly earnings shall be calculated in accordance with the following provisions of this regulation.

(2) In this regulation—

"the appropriate date" means the first day of the 14th week before the expected week of confinement, or the first day in the week in which the woman is confined, whichever is the earlier. [¹. . .]

"normal pay day" means a day on which the terms of a woman's contract of service require her to be paid, or the practice in her employment is for her to be paid, if any payment is due to her; and "day of payment" means a day on which the woman was paid.

(3) Subject to paragraph (4), the relevant period for the purposes of [¹section 171(4) of the Contributions and Benefits Act] is the period between—

(a) the last normal pay day to fall before the appropriate date; and
(b) the last normal pay day to fall at least eight weeks earlier than the normal pay day mentioned in sub-paragraph (a), including the normal pay day mentioned in sub-paragraph (a) but excluding that first mentioned in sub-paragraph (b).

(4) In a case where a woman has no identifiable normal pay day, paragraph (3) shall have effect as if the words "day of payment" were substituted for the words "normal pay day" in each place where they occur.

(5) In a case where a woman has normal pay days at intervals of or approximating to one or more calendar months (including intervals of or approximating to a year) her normal weekly earnings shall be calculated by dividing her earnings in the relevant period by the number of calendar months in that period (or, if it is not a whole number, the nearest whole number), multiplying the result by 12 and dividing by 52.

(6) In a case to which paragraph (5) does not apply and the relevant period is not an exact number of weeks, the woman's normal weekly earnings shall be calculated by dividing her earnings in the relevant period by the number of days in the relevant period and multiplying the result by 7.

[³(7) In any case where—
(a) a woman is awarded a pay increase (or would have been awarded such an increase had she not then been absent on statutory maternity leave); and
(b) that pay increase applies to the whole or any part of the period between the beginning of the relevant period and the end of her period of statutory maternity leave,

her normal weekly earnings shall be calculated as if such an increase applied in each week of the relevant period.]

[⁴(8) Paragraph (9) applies where for all or part of the relevant period—
(a) a woman is a furloughed employee;
(b) the woman's employer has claimed and is in receipt of financial support in respect of the woman's earnings under the Coronavirus Job Retention Scheme; and

(c) the woman's earnings are lower than they would otherwise have been as a result of that woman being a furloughed employee.

(9) Where this paragraph applies, the woman's normal weekly earnings are to be calculated as if, during the parts of the relevant period when the woman was a furloughed employee, she was paid the amount which she would have derived from her employment had she not been a furloughed employee.

(10) For the purposes of paragraphs (8) and (9)—

"Coronavirus Job Retention Scheme" ("the Scheme") means any scheme to provide for payments to be made to employers on a claim made in respect of them incurring costs of employment in respect of furloughed employees arising from the health, social and economic emergency in the United Kingdom resulting from coronavirus and coronavirus disease and contained in such Directions as may be issued from time to time pursuant to section 76 of the Coronavirus Act 2020;

"coronavirus" and "coronavirus disease" have the meanings given in section 1 of that Act;

"furloughed employee" has the meaning given for the purposes of the Scheme.]

AMENDMENTS

1. Social Security Maternity Benefits and Statutory Sick Pay (Amendment) Regulations 1994 (SI 1994/1367) reg.5 (June 11, 1994).
2. Statutory Maternity Pay (General) Amendment Regulations 1996 (SI 1996/1335) reg.2 (June 12, 1996).
3. Statutory Maternity Pay (General) (Amendment) Regulations 2005 (SI 2005/729) reg.3 (April 6, 2005).
4. Maternity Allowance, Statutory Maternity Pay, Statutory Paternity Pay, Statutory Adoption Pay, Statutory Shared Parental Pay and Statutory Parental Bereavement Pay (Normal Weekly Earnings etc.) (Coronavirus) (Amendment) Regulations 2020 (SI 2020/450) reg.3 (April 25, 2020).

GENERAL NOTE

5.38 Regulation 21 was considered by a First-tier Tribunal in the Finance and Tax Chamber in *Campus Living Villages UK Ltd v HMRC and Sexton* [2016] UKFTT 738 (TC). The tribunal held that under para.(5) the "computation is purely arithmetical. One takes the earnings in the relevant period (which in this case includes the bonus) and then calculates the weekly equivalent of that amount. There is no requirement that the pay during the relevant period must be 'normal' in the sense of the usual amount and Regulation 20(2) makes clear that all payments, whether usual or not are included in earnings for the purpose of the calculation" (at [41]).

Paragraph (7) is designed to give effect to the ECJ judgment in *Alabaster v Woolwich Plc and the Secretary of State for Social Security* (C-147/02) [2004] I.R.L.R. 486). It ensures that employers must recalculate a woman's entitlement (or potential entitlement) to statutory maternity pay to reflect any pay rise that the woman would have received, but for her maternity leave, and which is effective at any time between the start of the period used to calculate her entitlement and the end of her maternity leave. For the Court of Appeal judgment following the decision of the ECJ, see *Alabaster v Barclays Bank Plc and the Secretary of State for Social Security* [2005] EWCA Civ 508; [2005] I.C.R. 1246.

Paragraphs (8)-(10) were added as from April 25, 2020 with the intention of ensuring that an employee experienced no disadvantage in relation to their SMP entitlement as a result of their being placed on temporary leave under the Coronavirus Job Retention Scheme ("the CJRS"), set out in the Schedule to the

(SI 1986/1960 reg.21) (as amended)

Coronavirus Act 2020 Functions of Her Majesty's Revenue and Customs (Coronavirus Job Retention Scheme) Direction made on April 15, 2020. In short, the amendments are designed to ensure that an employee's eligibility for the earnings-related rate of SMP is the same as it would have been had they not been furloughed. Regulation 2 of the 2020 Regulations provides that these amendments are to apply where the first day of the period in respect of which payment of any of the benefits is to be made is on or after the day on which the 2020 Regulations come into force.

[¹Effect of statutory maternity pay on [²incapacity benefit]

21A.—[³. . .]

5.39

AMENDMENTS

1. Statutory Maternity Pay (General) Amendment Regulations 1988 (SI 1988/532) reg.3 (April 6, 1988).
2. Social Security (Incapacity Benefit) (Consequential and Transitional Amendments and Savings) Regulations 1995 (SI 1995/829) reg.18 (April 13, 1995).
3. Social Security, Statutory Maternity Pay and Statutory Sick Pay (Miscellaneous Amendments) Regulations 2002 (SI 2002/2690) reg.6 (November 24, 2002).

[¹Effect of maternity allowance on statutory maternity pay

21B.—Where a woman, in any week which falls within the maternity pay period, is—

5.40

(a) in receipt of maternity allowance pursuant to the provisions of sections 35 and 35A of the Contributions and Benefits Act; and
(b) entitled to receive statutory maternity pay in consequence of [²—
    (i) receiving a pay increase referred to in regulation 21(7), or
    (ii) being treated as having been paid retrospective earnings under regulation 20(4)(za),]

the employer shall not be liable to make payments of statutory maternity pay in respect of such a week unless, and to the extent by which, the rate of statutory maternity pay exceeds the rate of maternity allowance received by her in that week.]

AMENDMENTS

1. Statutory Maternity Pay (General) (Amendment) Regulations 2005 (SI 2005/729) reg.4 (April 6, 2005).
2. Social Security, Occupational Pension Schemes and Statutory Payments (Consequential Provisions) Regulations 2007 (SI 2007/1154) reg.4(4) (April 6, 2007).

PART V

ADMINISTRATION

Evidence of expected week of confinement

22.—(1) A woman shall in accordance with the following provisions of this regulation, provide the person who is liable to pay her statutory maternity pay with evidence as to—

5.41

(a) the week in which the expected date of confinement occurs, and
(b) where her entitlement to statutory maternity pay depends upon the fact of her confinement, the week in which she was confined.

The Statutory Maternity Pay (General) Regulations 1986

(2) For the purpose of paragraph (1)(b) a certificate of birth shall be sufficient evidence that the woman was confined in the week in which the birth occurred.

(3) The evidence shall be submitted to the person who will be liable to make payments of statutory maternity pay not later than the end of the third week of the maternity pay period so however that where the woman has good cause the evidence may be submitted later than that date but not later than the end of the 13th week of the maternity pay period.

(4) For the purposes of paragraph (3) evidence contained in an envelope which is properly addressed and sent by prepaid post shall be deemed to have been submitted on the day on which it was posted.

Notice of absence from work

23.—(1) Where a woman is confined before the beginning of the 14th week before the expected week of confinement, she shall be entitled to payments of statutory maternity pay only if—
- (a) she gives notice to the person who will be liable to pay it [²of the date on which she was confined], and
- (b) that notice is given within [²28 days] of the date she was confined or if in the particular circumstances that is not practicable, as soon as is reasonably practicable thereafter; and
- (c) where the person so requests, the notice in writing.

(2) Where a woman is confined before the date stated in a notice provided in accordance with [¹section 164(4) of the Contributions and Benefits Act] as being the date her absence from work is due to begin, she shall be entitled to payments of statutory maternity pay only if—
- (a) she gives a further notice to the person who will be liable to pay it specifying the date she was confined and the date her absence from work [². . .] began, and
- (b) that further notice is given within [²28 days] of the date she was confined or if in the particular circumstances that is not practicable, as soon as is reasonably practicable thereafter; and
- (c) where the person so requests, the notice is in writing.

(3) For the purposes of this regulation, a notice contained in an envelope which is properly addressed and sent by prepaid post shall be deemed to be given on the date on which it is posted.

[¹[²(4) Subject to paragraph (5), section 164(4) of the Contributions and Benefits Act (statutory maternity pay entitlement and liability to pay) shall not have effect in the case of a woman who leaves her employment with the person who will be liable to pay her statutory maternity pay after the beginning of the week immediately preceding the 14th week before the expected week of confinement.]

(5) A woman who is exempted from section 164(4) of the Contributions and Benefits Act by paragraph (4) but who is confined before the 11th week before the expected week of confinement shall only be entitled to statutory maternity pay if she gives the person who will be liable to pay it notice specifying the date she was confined.]

AMENDMENTS

1. Social Security Maternity Benefits and Statutory Sick Pay (Amendment) Regulations 1994 (SI 1994/1367) reg.6 (June 11, 1994).

2. Social Security, Statutory Maternity Pay and Statutory Sick Pay (Miscellaneous Amendments) Regulations 2002 (SI 2002/2690) reg.7 (November 24, 2002).

Notification of employment after confinement

24.—A woman who after the date of confinement but within the maternity pay period commences work in employed earner's employment with a person who is not liable to make payments of statutory maternity pay to her and is not a non-liable employer for the purposes of regulation 8(1), shall within seven days of the day she commenced work inform any person who is so liable of the date she commenced work.

Provision of information in connection with determination of questions

25.—Any woman claiming to be entitled to statutory maternity pay, or any other person who is a party to proceedings arising under the 1986 Act relating to statutory maternity pay, shall, if she receives notification from the Secretary of State that any information is required from her for the determination of any question arising in connection therewith, furnish that information to the Secretary of State within 10 days of receiving that notification.

DEFINITION

"the 1986 Act"—see reg.1(2).

GENERAL NOTE

The functions under this regulation were transferred from the Secretary of State for Social Security to the Board of the Inland Revenue (now HMRC) under s.1(2) of and Sch.2 to the Social Security (Transfer of Functions, etc.) Act 1999.

[1Provision of information relating to claims for certain other benefits

25A.—(1) Where an employer who has been given notice in accordance with [3section 164(4)(a) or (9)(ea) of the Contributions and Benefits Act] or regulation 23 by a woman who is or has been an employee—
(a) decides that he has no liability to make payments of statutory maternity pay to her; or
(b) has made one or more payments of statutory maternity pay to her but decides, before the end of the maternity pay period and for a reason specified in paragraph (3), that he has no liability to make further payments to her,
then, in connection with the making of a claim by the woman for a maternity allowance [4, incapacity benefit or an employment and support allowance], he shall furnish her with the information specified in the following provisions of this regulation.

(2) Where the employer decides he has no liability to make payments of statutory maternity pay to the woman, he shall furnish her with details of the decision and the reasons for it.

(3) Where the employer decides he has no liability to make further payments of statutory maternity pay to the woman because [3 . . .] she has within the maternity pay period been detained in legal custody or sentenced

to a term of imprisonment which was not suspended, [³ ...], he shall furnish her with—
(a) details of his decision and the reasons for it; and
(b) details of the last week in respect of which a liability to pay statutory maternity pay arose and the total number of weeks within the maternity pay period in which such a liability arose.
(4) The employer shall—
(a) return to the woman any maternity certificate provided by her in support of the notice referred to in paragraph (1); and
(b) comply with any requirements imposed by the preceding provisions of this regulation—
(i) in a case to which paragraph (2) applies, within 7 days of the decision being made, or, if earlier, within [³ 28 days] of the day the woman gave notice of her intended absence or of her confinement if that had occurred; or
(ii) in a case to which paragraph (3) refers, within 7 days of being notified of the woman's detention or sentence [³ ...].
(5) In this regulation, 'incapacity benefit' means [²incapacity benefit] or a severe disablement allowance.]

AMENDMENTS

1. Statutory Maternity Pay (General) Amendment Regulations 1990 (SI 1990/622) reg.7 (April 6, 1990).
2. Social Security (Incapacity Benefit) (Consequential and Transitional Amendments and Savings) Regulations 1995 (SI 1995/829) reg.18 (April 13, 1995).
3. Social Security, Statutory Maternity Pay and Statutory Sick Pay (Miscellaneous Amendments) Regulations 2002 (SI 2002/2690) reg.8 (November 24, 2002).
4. Employment and Support Allowance (Consequential Provisions) (No.2) Regulations 2008 (SI 2008/1554) reg.46 (October 27, 2008).

Records to be maintained by employers

26.—(1) Every employer shall maintain for 3 years after the end of the tax year in which the maternity pay period ends a record in relation to any woman who is or was an employee of his of—
(a) the date of the first day of absence from work wholly or partly because of pregnancy or confinement as notified by her and, if different, the date of the first day when such absence commenced;
(b) the weeks in that tax year in which statutory maternity pay was paid and the amount paid in each week; and
(c) any week in that tax year which was within her maternity pay period but for which no payment of statutory maternity pay was made to her and the reasons no payment was made.
(2) Except where he was not liable to make a payment of statutory maternity pay and subject to paragraphs (3) and (4), every employer shall retain for 3 years after the end of the tax year in which the maternity pay period ends any medical certificate or other evidence relating to the expected week of confinement, or as the case may be, the confinement which was provided to him by a woman who is or was an employee of his.
(3) Where an employer returns a medical certificate to an employee of his for the purpose of enabling her to make a claim for benefit under the 1975 Act, it shall be sufficient for the purposes of paragraph (2) if he retains a copy of that certificate.

(4) An employer shall not retain any certificate of birth provided to him as evidence of confinement by a woman who is or was an employee of his but shall retain a record of the date of birth.

DEFINITION

"the 1975 Act"—see reg.1(2).

[¹Production of employer's records

26A.—(1) An authorised officer of the Commissioners of Inland Revenue may by notice require an employer to produce to him at the place of keeping such records as are in the employer's possession or power and as (in the officer's reasonable opinion) contain, or may contain, information relevant to satisfy him that statutory maternity pay has been paid and is being paid in accordance with these regulations to employees or former employees who are entitled to it.

(2) A notice referred to in paragraph (1) shall be in writing and the employer shall produce the records referred to in that paragraph within 30 days after the date of such a notice.

(3) The production of records in pursuance of this regulation shall be without prejudice to any lien which a third party may have in respect of those records.

(4) References in this regulation to "records" means—
(a) any wage sheet or deductions working sheet; or
(b) any other document which relates to the calculation or payment of statutory maternity pay to his employees or former employees,
whether kept in written form, electronically, or otherwise.

(5) In paragraph (1), "place of keeping" means such place in Great Britain that an employer and an authorised officer may agree upon, or, in the absence of such agreement—
(a) any place in Great Britain where records referred to in paragraph (1) are normally kept; or
(b) if there is no such place, the employer's principal place of business in Great Britain.]

AMENDMENT

1. Statutory Maternity Pay (General) and Statutory Sick Pay (General) (Amendment) Regulations 2005 (SI 2005/989) reg.2(2) (April 6, 2005).

PART VI

PAYMENT

Payment of statutory maternity pay

27.—Payment of statutory maternity pay may be made in a like manner to payments of remuneration but shall not include payments in kind or by way of the provision of board or lodgings or of services or other facilities.

Rounding to avoid fractional amounts

[¹**28.**—Where any payment of statutory maternity pay is paid for any week or part of a week and the amount due includes a fraction of a penny, the payment shall be rounded up to the next whole number of pence.]

The Statutory Maternity Pay (General) Regulations 1986

AMENDMENT

1. Statutory Maternity Pay, Social Security (Maternity Allowance) and Social Security (Overlapping Benefits) (Amendment) Regulations 2006 (SI 2006/2379) reg.3(4) (October 1, 2006, and in relation to women whose expected week of confinement falls on or after April 1, 2007).

Time when statutory maternity pay is to be paid

29.—(1) In this regulation, "payday" means a day on which it has been agreed, or it is the normal practice between an employer or former employer and a woman who is or was an employee of his, that payments by way of remuneration are to be made, or, where there is no such agreement or normal practice, the last day of a calendar month.

(2) In any case where—

(a) a decision has been made by an adjudication officer, appeal tribunal or Commissioner in proceedings under [Social Security Administration Act 1992] as a result of which a woman is entitled to an amount of statutory maternity pay; and

(b) the time for bringing an appeal against the decision has expired and either—

  (i) no such appeal has been brought; or
  (ii) such an appeal has been brought and has been finally disposed of that amount of statutory maternity pay shall be paid within the time specified in paragraph (3).

(3) Subject to paragraphs (4) and (5), the employer or former employer shall pay the amount not later than the first pay day after—

(a) where an appeal has been brought, the day on which the employer or former employer receives notification that it has been finally disposed of,

(b) where leave to appeal has been refused and there remains no further opportunity to apply for leave, the day on which the employer or former employer receives notification of the refusal; and

(c) in any other case, the day on which the time for bringing an appeal expires.

(4) Subject to paragraph (5), where it is impracticable, in view of the employer's or former employer's methods of accounting for and paying remuneration, for the requirement of payment referred to in paragraph (3) to be met by the pay day referred to in that paragraph, it shall be met not later than the next following pay day.

(5) Where the employer or former employer would not have remunerated the woman for her work in the week in question as early as the pay day specified in paragraph (3) or (if it applies) paragraph (4), the requirement of payment shall be met on the first day on which the woman would have been remunerated for her work in that week.

Payments by the Secretary of State

30.—Where the Secretary of State becomes liable in accordance with regulation 7 to make payments of statutory maternity pay to a woman, the first payment shall be made as soon as reasonably practicable after he becomes so liable, and payments thereafter shall be made at weekly intervals, by means of an instrument of payment or by such other means as appears to the Secretary of State to be appropriate in the circumstances of any particular case.

(SI 1986/1960 reg.30) (as amended)

GENERAL NOTE

The functions under this regulation were transferred from the Secretary of State for Social Security to the Board of the Inland Revenue (now HMRC) under s.1(2) of and Sch.2 to the Social Security (Transfer of Functions, etc.) Act 1999.

Persons unable to act

31.—(1) Where in the case of any woman—
  (a) statutory maternity pay is payable to her or she is alleged to be entitled to it;
  (b) she is unable for the time being to act;
  (c) either—
    (i) no receiver has been appointed by the Court of Protection with power to receive statutory maternity pay on her behalf, or
    (ii) in Scotland, her estate is not being administered by any tutor, curator or other guardian acting or appointed in terms of law,
the Secretary of State may, upon written application to him by a person who, if a natural person, is over the age of 18, appoint that person to exercise, on behalf of the woman any right to which she may be entitled under Part V of the 1986 Act and to deal on her behalf with any sums payable to her.
(2) Where the Secretary of State has made an appointment under paragraph (1)—
  (a) he may at any time in his absolute discretion revoke it;
  (b) the person appointed may resign his office after having given one month's notice in writing to the Secretary of State of his intention to do so; and
  (c) the appointment shall terminate when the Secretary of State is notified that a receiver or other person to whom paragraph (1)(c) applies has been appointed.
(3) Anything required by Part V of the 1986 Act to be done by or to any woman who is unable to act may be done by or to the person appointed under this regulation to act on her behalf, and the receipt of the person so appointed shall be a good discharge to the woman's employer or former employer for any sum paid.

GENERAL NOTE

The functions under this regulation were transferred from the Secretary of State for Social Security to the Board of the Inland Revenue (now HMRC) under s.1(2) of and Sch.2 to the Social Security (Transfer of Functions, etc.) Act 1999.

PART VII

OFFENCES

[¹Offences

32.—[²...]

GENERAL NOTE

See now ss.113A and 113B of the Social Security Administration Act 1992.

The Statutory Maternity Pay (Medical Evidence) Regulations 1987

The Statutory Maternity Pay (Medical Evidence) Regulations 1987

(SI 1987/235) (AS AMENDED)

The Secretary of State for Social Services, in exercise of the powers conferred by sections 49 and 84(1) of and paragraph 6 of Schedule 4 to the Social Security Act 1986, and of all other powers enabling him in that behalf, by this instrument, which is made before the end of the period of 12 months from the commencement of the enactments contained in the 1986 Act under which it is made, makes the following regulations:

ARRANGEMENT OF REGULATIONS

1. Citation, commencement and interpretation
2. Evidence of pregnancy and confinement

SCHEDULE—Part I—Rules
   Part II—Form of certificate

Citation, commencement and interpretation

1.—(1) These regulations may be cited as the Statutory Maternity Pay (Medical Evidence) Regulations 1987 and shall come into force on 15th March 1987.
(2) In these regulations, unless the context otherwise requires—
"the Act" means the Social Security Act 1986;
[¹"registered midwife" means a midwife who is registered as a midwife with the Nursing and Midwifery Council under the Nursing and Midwifery Order 2001;]
"doctor" means a registered medical practitioner;
"signature" means, in relation to any statement or certificate given in accordance with these regulations, the name by which the person giving that statement or certificate, as the case may be, is usually known (any name other than the surname being either in full or otherwise indicated) written by that person in his own handwriting; and
"signed" shall be construed accordingly.
[²[³ . . .]]

AMENDMENTS

1. Nursing and Midwifery Order 2001 (Consequential Amendments) Order 2002 (SI 2002/881) art.2 and Sch. para.2 (April 17, 2002).
2. National Health Service Reform and Health Care Professions Act 2002 (Supplementary, Consequential etc. Provisions) Regulations 2002 (SI 2002/2469) reg.11 and Sch.8 (October 1, 2002).
3. National Treatment Agency (Abolition) and the Health and Social Care Act 2012 (Consequential, Transitional and Saving Provisions) Order 2013 (SI 2013/235) art.11 and Sch.2 para.9(2) (April 1, 2013).

(SI 1987/235 reg.2) (as amended)

Evidence of pregnancy and confinement

2.—The evidence as to pregnancy and the expected date of confinement which a woman is required to provide to a person who is liable to pay her statutory maternity pay shall be furnished in the form of a maternity certificate given by a doctor or by a registered midwife, not earlier than the beginning of the [¹20th week] before the expected week of confinement, in accordance with the rules set out in Part I of the Schedule to these regulations—
  (a) in the appropriate form as set out in Part II of that Schedule; or
  (b) in a form substantially to the like effect with such variations as the circumstances may require.

AMENDMENT

1. Social Security (Medical Evidence) and Statutory Maternity Pay (Medical Evidence) (Amendment) Regulations 2001 (SI 2001/2931) reg.3(2) (September 28, 2001).

DEFINITIONS

"doctor"—see reg.1(2).
"registered midwife"—see reg.1(2).

SCHEDULE   Regulation 2

PART I

RULES

1.—In these rules any reference to a woman is a reference to the woman in respect of whom a maternity certificate is given in accordance with these rules.
2.—A maternity certificate shall be given by a doctor or registered midwife attending the woman and shall not be given by the woman herself.
3.—The maternity certificate shall be on a form provided by the Secretary of State for the purpose and the wording shall be that set out in the appropriate part of the form specified in Part II of this Schedule.
4.—Every maternity certificate shall be completed in ink or other indelible substance and shall contain the following particulars—
  (a) the woman's name;
  (b) the week in which the woman is expected to be confined or, if the maternity certificate is given after confinement, the date of that confinement and the date the confinement was expected to take place [¹...];
  (c) the date of the examination on which the maternity certificate is based;
  (d) the date on which the maternity certificate is signed; and
  [⁴(e) the address of the doctor or where the maternity certificate is signed by a registered midwife the personal identification number given to her on her registration in [⁶...] the register maintained by the Nursing and Midwifery Council [⁶("NMC") under article 5 of] the Nursing and Midwifery Order 2001 and the expiry date of that registration,]
and shall bear opposite the word "Signature", the signature of the person giving the maternity certificate written after there has been entered on the maternity certificate the woman's name and the expected date or, as the case may be, the date of the confinement.
5.—After a maternity certificate has been given, no further maternity certificate based on the same examination shall be furnished other than a maternity certificate by way of replacement of an original which has been lost or mislaid, in which case it shall be clearly marked "duplicate".

The Statutory Maternity Pay (Medical Evidence) Regulations 1987

[² PART II

FORM OF CERTIFICATE

5.62 **MATERNITY CERTIFICATE**

Please fill in this form in ink

Name of patient

Fill in this part if you are giving the certificate before the confinement.

Do not fill this in more [³than 20 weeks] before the week the baby is expected.

I certify that I examined you on the date given below. In my opinion you can expect to have your baby in the week that includes

.... / .... / ....

Week means period of 7 days starting on a Sunday and ending on a Saturday. Fill in this part if you are giving the certificate after the confinement.

I certify that I attended you in connection with the birth which took place on .... / .... / .... when you were delivered of a child [ ] children.

In my opinion your baby was expected in the week that includes ..../ .... / ....

Date of examination ..... / ..... / ......

Date of signing .... / .... / ....

Signature

Registered midwives

Please give your [⁶NMC] Personal Identification Number and the expiry date of your registration with the [⁶NMC].

Doctors

Please stamp your name and address here [⁷ ...] [⁵ [⁷ unless the form has been stamped, in Wales, by the Local Health Board in whose medical performers list you are included or, in Scotland,] by the Health Board in whose primary medical services performers list you are included)].

AMENDMENTS

1. Social Security (Miscellaneous Provisions) Amendment Regulations 1991 (SI 1991/2284) reg.23 (November 1, 1991).
2. Social Security (Miscellaneous Provisions) Amendment Regulations 1991 (SI 1991/2284) reg.24 (November 1, 1991).

(SI 1987/235 Sch) (as amended)

3. Social Security (Medical Evidence) and Statutory Maternity Pay (Medical Evidence) (Amendment) Regulations 2001 (SI 2001/2931) reg.3(3) (September 28, 2001).
4. Nursing and Midwifery Order 2001 (Consequential Amendments) Order 2002 (SI 2002/881) art.2 and Sch. para.3 (April 17, 2002).
5. General Medical Services and Personal Medical Services Transitional and Consequential Provisions Order 2004 (SI 2004/865) art.119 and Sch.1 para.5 (April 1, 2004).
6. Health Act 1999 (Consequential Amendments) (Nursing and Midwifery) Order 2004 (SI 2004/1771) art.3 and Sch. para.51 (August 1, 2004).
7. National Treatment Agency (Abolition) and the Health and Social Care Act 2012 (Consequential, Transitional and Saving Provisions) Order 2013 (SI 2013/235) art.11 and Sch.2 para.9(3) (April 1, 2013).

DEFINITIONS

"doctor"—see reg.1(2).
"registered midwife"—see reg.1(2).
"signature"—see reg.1(2).
"signed"—see reg.1(2).

The Statutory Maternity Pay (Persons Abroad and Mariners) Regulations 1987

(SI 1987/418) (AS AMENDED)

The Secretary of State for Social Services, in exercise of the powers conferred upon him by sections 80 and 84(1) of the Social Security Act 1986 and of all other powers enabling him in that behalf, by this instrument, which is made before the end of the period of 12 months from the commencement of the enactments under which it is made, makes the following Regulations:

ARRANGEMENT OF REGULATIONS

1. Citation, commencement and interpretation
2. Persons in other member States—meaning of "employee"
2A. Persons absent from Great Britain—meaning of "employee"
3. Meaning of "employee"—general
4. *(repealed)*
5. Women who worked in the European Community
6. Time for compliance with Part V of the 1986 Act and Regulations
7. Mariners
8. Continental shelf
9. *(repealed)*

5.63

Citation, commencement and interpretation

1.—(1) These Regulations may be cited as the Statutory Maternity Pay (Persons Abroad and Mariners) Regulations 1987 and shall come into force on 6th April 1987.

5.64

(2) In these Regulations, the "1986 Act" means the Social Security Act 1986; [¹"the Contributions and Benefits Act" means the Social Security Contributions and Benefits Act 1992, "the Contributions Regulations" means the Social Security (Contributions) Regulations 1979"], and the "General Regulations" means the Statutory Maternity Pay (General) Regulations 1986.

(3) Unless the context otherwise requires, any reference in these Regulations to a numbered regulation is a reference to the regulation bearing that number in these Regulations and any reference in a regulation to a numbered paragraph is a reference to the paragraph of that regulation bearing that number.

AMENDMENT

1. Social Security Contributions, Statutory Maternity Pay and Statutory Sick Pay (Miscellaneous Amendments) Regulations 1996 (SI 1996/777) reg.4(2) (April 6, 1996).

GENERAL NOTE

These Regulations were made under the authority of what is now SSCBA 1992 s.170 and make special provision for statutory maternity pay as regards persons who are abroad or who are mariners. See also SMP (General) Regulations 1986 (SI 1986/1960) reg.17(3).

Persons in other member States—meaning of "employee"

2.—Subject to regulation 3, a woman who is—
  (a) gainfully employed in a member State other than the United Kingdom in such circumstances that if her employment were in Great Britain she would be an employee for the purposes of Part V of the 1986 Act or a woman treated as such an employee under regulation 17 of the General Regulations; and
  (b) subject to the legislation of the United Kingdom under Council Regulation (EEC) No.1408/71 [¹, as amended from time to time, or Regulation EC No.883/2004 of the European Parliament and of the Council of 29 April 2004, as amended from time to time, on the coordination of social security systems]; notwithstanding that she is not employed in Great Britain, shall be treated as an employee for the purposes of Part V of the 1986 Act.

AMENDMENT

1. Social Security (Updating of EU References) (Amendment) Regulations 2018 (SI 2018/1084) reg.4 and Sch. para.5 (November 15, 2018).

DEFINITIONS

"the 1986 Act"—see reg.1(2).
"the General Regulations"—see reg.1(2).

[¹Persons absent from Great Britain—meaning of "employee"

2A.—Subject to regulations 2, 3 and 7(3), where a woman, while absent from Great Britain for any purpose, is gainfully employed by an employer who is liable to pay in respect of her secondary Class 1 contributions under section 6 of the Contributions and Benefits Act or regulation 120 of the Contributions Regulations, she shall be treated as an employee for the purposes of Part XII of the Contributions and Benefits Act.]

(SI 1987/418 reg.2A) (as amended)

AMENDMENT

1. Social Security Contributions, Statutory Maternity Pay and Statutory Sick Pay (Miscellaneous Amendments) Regulations 1996 (SI 1996/777) reg.4(3) (April 6, 1996).

DEFINITIONS

"the Contributions and Benefits Act"—see reg.1(2).
"the Contributions Regulations"—see reg.1(2).

Meaning of "employee"—general

3.—No woman who, by virtue of regulation 17 of the General Regulations, would be treated as not being an employee for the purposes of Part V of the 1986 Act if her employment were in Great Britain, shall be treated as an employee by virtue of these Regulations.

5.68

DEFINITIONS

"the 1986 Act"—see reg.1(2).
"the General Regulations"—see reg.1(2).

Women outside the European Community

4.—[¹...]

5.69

AMENDMENT

1. Social Security Contributions, Statutory Maternity Pay and Statutory Sick Pay (Miscellaneous Amendments) Regulations 1996 (SI 1996/777) reg.4(4) (April 6, 1996).

Women who worked in the European Community

5.—(1) A woman who is an employee or treated as an employee under regulation 2 and who—
  (a) in the week immediately preceding the 14th week before the expected week of confinement was in employed earner's employment with an employer in Great Britain, and
  (b) had in any week within the period of [¹26 weeks] immediately preceding that week been employed by the same employer in another member State,
shall be treated for the purposes of sections 46(2) and 48 of the 1986 Act as having been employed in employed earner's employment in those weeks in which she was so employed in the other member State.
  (2) [¹...]

5.70

AMENDMENT

1. Social Security Contributions, Statutory Maternity Pay and Statutory Sick Pay (Miscellaneous Amendments) Regulations 1996 (SI 1996/777) reg.4(5) (April 6, 1996).

DEFINITION

"the 1986 Act"—see reg.1(2).

Statutory Maternity Pay (Persons Abroad and Mariners) Regulations 1987

Time for compliance with Part V of the 1986 Act and Regulations

5.71

6.—Where—
  (a) a woman is outside the United Kingdom;
  (b) Part V of the 1986 Act or Regulations made under that Act or under Part III of the Social Security Act 1975 require any act to be done forthwith or on the happening of a certain event or within a specified time; and
  (c) because the woman is outside the United Kingdom she or her employer cannot comply with the requirement;
the woman or the employer, as the case may be, shall be deemed to have complied with it if the act is performed as soon as reasonably practicable.

DEFINITION

"the 1986 Act"—see reg.1(2).

Mariners

5.72

7.—(1) In this regulation, "foreign-going ship", "home-trade ship" and "mariner" have the same meanings as in Case C of Part VIII of the Social Security (Contributions) Regulations 1979 and the expressions "ship" and "ship or vessel", except in paragraph (3), include hovercraft.

(2) Subject to regulation 3, a mariner engaged in employment on board a home-trade ship with an employer who has a place of business within the United Kingdom shall be treated as an employee for the purposes of Part V of the 1986 Act, notwithstanding that she may not be employed in Great Britain.

(3) A mariner who is engaged in employment—
  (a) on a foreign-going ship; or
  (b) on a home-trade ship with an employer who does not have a place of business within the United Kingdom, shall not be treated as an employee for the purposes of Part V of the 1986 Act, notwithstanding that she may have been employed in Great Britain.

DEFINITIONS

"foreign-going ship"—see para.(1).
"home-trade ship"—see para.(1).
"mariner"—see para.(1).
"ship"—see para.(1).
"ship or vessel"—see para.(1).

Continental shelf

5.73

8.—(1) In this regulation—
"designated area" means any area which may from time to time be designated by Order in Council under the Continental Shelf Act 1964 as an area within which the rights of the United Kingdom with respect to the seabed and subsoil and their natural resources may be exercised;
"prescribed area" means an area over which Norway or any member State (other than the United Kingdom) exercises sovereign rights for the purpose of exploring the seabed and subsoil and exploiting their natural resources, being an area outside the territorial seas of Norway or that member State or any other area which is from time to

time specified under section 22(5) of the Oil and Gas (Enterprise) Act 1982;

"prescribed employment" means employment in a designated area or prescribed area in connection with any activity mentioned in section 23(2) of the Oil and Gas (Enterprise) Act 1982 in any designated area or in any prescribed area.

(2) Subject to regulation 3, a woman in prescribed employment shall be treated as an employee for the purposes of Part V of the 1986 Act notwithstanding that she may not be employed in Great Britain.

DEFINITIONS

"the 1986 Act"—see reg.1(2).
"designated area"—see para.(2).
"prescribed area"—see para.(2).
"prescribed employment"—see para.(2).

Persons Abroad—maternity pay period not commencing or ending

9.—[1. . .]

AMENDMENT

1. Social Security Contributions, Statutory Maternity Pay and Statutory Sick Pay (Miscellaneous Amendments) Regulations 1996 (SI 1996/777) reg.4(6) (April 6, 1996).

The Statutory Maternity Pay (National Health Service Employees) Regulations 1991

(SI 1991/590)

The Secretary of State for Social Security, in exercise of the powers conferred by sections 49, 50(2A), 84(1) of, and paragraph 6 of Schedule 4 to the Social Security Act 1986 and of all other powers enabling him in that behalf, by this instrument, which contains only Regulations consequential upon paragraph 22 of Schedule 6 to the Social Security Act 1990, makes the following Regulations:

ARRANGEMENT OF REGULATIONS

1. Citation, commencement and interpretation
2. Treatment of more than one contract of employment as one contract
3. Notification of election
4. Provision of information
5. Treatment of two or more employers as one
6. Time for which an election is to have effect

Citation, commencement and interpretation

1.—(1) These Regulations may be cited as the Statutory, Maternity Pay (National Health Service Employees) Regulations 1991 and shall come into force on 1st April 1991.

(2) In these Regulations, a "health authority" [²shall in relation to Wales have the same meaning it has in section 8] of the National Health Service Act 1977, and in relation to Scotland mean the health board within the meaning of section 2 of the National Health Service (Scotland) Act 1978.

[¹(3) [⁴ . . .]]
[²(4)[⁴ . . .]]

[³(5) In these Regulations, a reference to "NHS trust" shall be construed to include a reference to an NHS foundation trust within the meaning of section 1(1) of the Health and Social Care (Community Health and Standards) Act 2003 where the application for authorisation to become an NHS foundation trust was made by an NHS trust.]

AMENDMENTS

1. Health Act 1999 (Supplementary, Consequential, etc. Provisions) (No.2) Order 2000 (SI 2000/694) art.3 and Sch. para.3(2) (April 1, 2000).
2. National Health Service Reform and Health Care Professions Act 2002 (Supplementary, Consequential etc. Provisions) Regulations 2002 (SI 2002/2469) reg.4 and Sch.1 Pt 2 para.51 (October 1, 2002).
3. Health and Social Care (Community Health and Standards) Act 2003 (Supplementary and Consequential Provision) (NHS Foundation Trusts) Order 2004 (SI 2004/696) art.3(17) and Sch.17 (April 1, 2004).
4. National Treatment Agency (Abolition) and the Health and Social Care Act 2012 (Consequential, Transitional and Saving Provisions) Order 2013 (SI 2013/235) art.11 and Sch.2 para.16(2) (April 1, 2013).

Treatment of more than one contract of employment as one contract

5.77 **2.**—Where, in consequence of the establishment of one or more National Health Service Trusts under Part I of the National Health Service and Community Care Act 1990, or the National Health Service (Scotland) Act 1978, a woman's contract of employment is treated by a scheme under that Part or Act as divided so as to constitute two or more contracts [¹ [² . . .]] she may elect for all those contracts to be treated as one contract for the purposes of Part V of the Social Security Act 1986.

AMENDMENTS

1. Health Act 1999 (Supplementary, Consequential etc. Provisions) (No.2) Order 2000 (SI 2000/694) art.3 and Sch. para.3(3) (April 1, 2000).
2. National Treatment Agency (Abolition) and the Health and Social Care Act 2012 (Consequential, Transitional and Saving Provisions) Order 2013 (SI 2013/235) art.11 and Sch.2 para.16(3) (April 1, 2013).

Notification of election

5.78 **3.**—A woman who makes an election under regulation 2 above shall give written notification of that election to each of her employers under the two or more contracts of service mentioned in that regulation at least [¹28 days] before the first day she is going to be absent from work with any of her employers, wholly or partly because of pregnancy, or if in the particular circumstances that is not practicable, as soon as is reasonably practicable.

(SI 1991/590 reg.3)

AMENDMENT

1. Social Security, Statutory Maternity Pay and Statutory Sick Pay (Miscellaneous Amendments) Regulations 2002 (SI 23002/2690) reg.11 (November 24, 2002).

Provision of information

4.—A woman who makes an election under regulation 2 above shall, within [¹28 days] of giving notice of that election or if in the particular circumstances that is not practicable, as soon as is reasonably practicable thereafter, provide each of her employers under the two or more contracts of service mentioned under that regulation with the following information—
   (a) the name and address of each of those employers; and
   (b) the date her employment with each of those employers commenced; and
   (c) details of her earnings during the relevant period from each employer and for this purpose the expressions "earnings" and "relevant period" have the same meanings as they have for the purposes of section 50(3) of the Social Security Act 1986.

5.79

AMENDMENT

1. Social Security, Statutory Maternity Pay and Statutory Sick Pay (Miscellaneous Amendments) Regulations 2002 (SI 2002/2690) reg.12 (November 24, 2002).

Treatment of two or more employers as one

5.—The employer to be regarded for the purposes of statutory maternity pay as the employer under the one contract where 2 or more contracts of service are treated as one in accordance with regulation 2 above shall be—
[¹(a) in the case of a woman whose contract of employment is treated by a scheme under Part I of the National Health Service and Community Care Act 1990 or the National Health Service (Scotland) Act 1978 as divided—
   (i) the Health Authority [² ...] from which the woman was transferred, in a case where any one of the contracts of service is with that Health Authority [² ...]; or
   (ii) the first NHS trust to which a contract of service was transferred in a case where none of the contracts of service are with the Health Authority [² ...] from which she was transferred.
[² ...]]

5.80

AMENDMENTS

1. Health Act 1999 (Supplementary, Consequential etc. Provisions) (No.2) Order 2000 (SI 2000/694) art.3 and Sch. para.3(4) (April 1, 2000).
2. National Treatment Agency (Abolition) and the Health and Social Care Act 2012 (Consequential, Transitional and Saving Provisions) Order 2013 (SI 2013/235) art.11 and Sch.2 para.15(3) (April 1, 2013).

Time for which an election is to have effect

6.—An election made under regulation 2 shall lapse at the end of the maternity pay period.

5.81

Statutory Maternity Pay and Miscellaneous Amendment Regulations 1994

The Statutory Maternity Pay (Compensation of Employers) and Miscellaneous Amendment Regulations 1994

(SI 1994/1882) (AS AMENDED)

The Secretary of State for Social Security, in exercise of powers conferred on him by sections 35(3), 167(1), (1A), (1B) and (4), 171(1) and 175(1) to (4) of the Social Security Contributions and Benefits Act 1992 and of all other powers enabling him in that behalf after agreement by the Social Security Advisory Committee that proposals in respect of regulation 9 should not be referred to it, hereby makes the following Regulations:

ARRANGEMENT OF REGULATIONS

1. Citation, commencement and interpretation
2. Meaning of "small employer"
3. Determination of the amount of additional payment to which a small employer shall be entitled
4. Right of employers to prescribed amount
5. Application for advance funding from the Board
6. Deductions from payments to the Board
6A. Payments to employers by the Board
7. Date when certain contributions are to be treated as paid
7A. Overpayments
8. Revocation
9. *Omitted*

Citation, commencement and interpretation

1.—(1) These Regulations may be cited as the Statutory Maternity Pay (Compensation of Employers) and Miscellaneous Amendment Regulations 1994 and regulations 2–7 shall have effect in relation to payments of statutory maternity pay due on or after 4th September 1994.

(2) This regulation and regulation 9 shall come into force on July 31, 1994.

(3) Regulations 2 to 8 shall come into force on 4th September 1994.

(4) In these Regulations—

[1"the Board" means the Commissioners of Inland Revenue;]

"the Contributions and Benefits Act" means the Social Security Contributions and Benefits Act 1992;

"the Maternity Allowance Regulations" means the Social Security (Maternity Allowance) Regulations 1987;

[1. . .];

[1"contributions payments" has the same meaning as in section 167(8) of the Contributions and Benefits Act;]

[1"the Contributions Regulations" means the Social Security (Contributions) Regulations 2001;]

"employer" shall include a person who was previously an employer of a woman to whom a payment of statutory maternity pay was made, whether or not that person remains her employer at the date any deduction from contributions payments is made by him in accordance

(SI 1994/1882 reg.3) (as amended)

AMENDMENTS

1. Statutory Maternity Pay (Compensation of Employers) Amendment Regulations 1995 (SI 1995/566) reg.2 (April 6, 1995).
2. Statutory Maternity Pay (Compensation of Employers) Amendment Regulations 2002 (SI 2002/225) reg.2 (April 6, 2002).
3. Statutory Maternity Pay (Compensation of Employers) Amendment Regulations 2003 (SI 2003/672) reg.3 (April 6, 2003).

DEFINITIONS

"employer"—see reg.1(4).
"payment of statutory maternity pay"—see reg.1(4).
"small employer"—see reg.2(1).

[¹Right of employers to prescribed amount

4.—An employer who has made, or is liable to make, any payment of statutory maternity pay shall be entitled to recover—
 (a) an amount equal to 92 per cent of such payment; or
 (b) if he is a small employer—
  (i) an amount equal to such payment; and
  (ii) an additional amount under regulation 3, in accordance with the provisions of these Regulations.]

5.87

AMENDMENT

1. Statutory Maternity Pay (Compensation of Employers) Amendment Regulations 2003 (SI 2003/672) reg.4 (April 6, 2003).

DEFINITIONS

"employer"—see reg.1(4).
"payment of statutory maternity pay"—see reg.1(4).
"small employer"—see reg.2(1).

[¹Application for advance funding from the Board

5.—(1) If an employer is entitled to recover an amount determined in accordance with regulation 4 in respect of statutory maternity pay which he is required to pay to an employee or employees in any income tax month or income tax quarter and the amount excceds the aggregate of—
 (a) the total amount of tax which the employer is required to pay to the collector of taxes in respect of deductions from the emoluments of his employees in accordance with the Income Tax (Employments) Regulations 1993 for that income tax month or income tax quarter;
 (b) the total amount of deductions made by the employer from the emoluments of his employees for that income tax month or income tax quarter in accordance with regulations made under section 22(5) of the Teaching and Higher Education Act 1998 or section 73B of the Education (Scotland) Act 1980 or in accordance with Article 3(5) of the Education (Student Support) (Northern Ireland) Order 1988;
 (c) the total amount of contributions payments which the employer is required to pay to the collector of taxes in respect of the emoluments of his employees (whether by means of deduction or otherwise) in accordance with the Contributions Regulations for that income tax month or income tax quarter;

5.88

Statutory Maternity Pay and Miscellaneous Amendment Regulations 1994

    (d) the total amount of payments which the employer is required to pay to the collector of taxes in respect of deductions made on account of tax from payments to sub-contractors in accordance with section 559 of the Income and Corporation Taxes Act 1988 for that income tax month or income tax quarter; and

    (e) the statutory paternity pay, statutory adoption pay and statutory maternity pay which the employer is required to pay to his employees in that income tax month or income tax quarter,

the employer may apply to the Board in accordance with paragraph (2) for funds ("advance funding") to pay that excess (or so much of it as remains outstanding) to the employee or employees.

(2) Where—

    (a) the conditions in paragraph (1) are satisfied; or

    (b) the employer considers that the conditions in paragraph (1) will be satisfied on the date of any subsequent payment of emoluments to one or more employees who are entitled to a payment of statutory maternity pay,

the employer may apply to the Board for advance funding on a form approved for that purpose by the Board.

(3) An application by an employer under paragraph (2) shall be for an amount not exceeding the amount of statutory maternity pay which the employer is entitled to recover in accordance with regulation 4 and which he is required to pay to an employee or employees for the income tax month or income tax quarter to which the payment of emoluments relates.]

AMENDMENT

1. Statutory Maternity Pay (Compensation of Employers) Amendment Regulations 2003 (SI 2003/672) reg.4 (April 6, 2003).

DEFINITIONS

    "advance funding"—see para.(1).
    "the Board"—see reg.1(4).
    "the Contributions Regulations"—see reg.1(4).
    "contributions payments"—see reg.1(4).
    "employer"—see reg.1(4).
    "income tax month"—see reg.1(4).
    "income tax quarter"—see reg.1(4).
    "statutory adoption pay"—see reg.1(4).
    "statutory paternity pay"—see reg.1(4).

[1Deductions from payments to the Board

6.—An employer who is entitled to recover an amount under regulation 4 may do so by making one or more deductions from the aggregate of the amounts specified in sub-paragraphs (a) to (e) of regulation 5(1), except where and insofar as—

    (a) those amounts relate to earnings paid before the beginning of the income tax month or income tax quarter in which the payment of statutory maternity pay was made;

    (b) those amounts are paid by him later than six years after the tax year in which the payment of statutory maternity pay was made;

    (c) the employer has received advance funding from the Board in accordance with an application under regulation 5; or

(SI 1994/1882 reg.6) (as amended)

    (d) the employer has made a request in writing under regulation 5 that the amount which he is entitled to recover under regulation 4 be paid to him and he has not received notification by the Board that such request is refused.]

AMENDMENT

1. Statutory Maternity Pay (Compensation of Employers) Amendment Regulations 2003 (SI 2003/672) reg.4 (April 6, 2003).

DEFINITIONS

"advance funding"—reg.5(1).
"the Board"—see reg.1(4).
"employer"—see reg.1(4).
"income tax month"—see reg.1(4).
"income tax quarter"—see reg.1(4).
"writing"—see reg.1(4).

[[1]Payments to employers by the Board

6A.—If, in an income tax month or an income tax quarter—
    (a) the total amount that the employer is entitled to deduct under regulation 6 is less than the amount which the employer is entitled to recover under regulation 4;
    (b) the Board is satisfied that this is so; and
    (c) the employer has so requested in writing, the Board shall pay to the employer the sum that the employer is unable to deduct under regulation 6.]

AMENDMENT

1. Statutory Maternity Pay (Compensation of Employers) Amendment Regulations 2003 (SI 2003/672) reg.4 (April 6, 2003).

DEFINITIONS

"the Board"—see reg.1(4).
"income tax month"—see reg.1(4).
"income tax quarter"—see reg.1(4).
"writing"—see reg.1(4).

Date when certain contributions are to be treated as paid

7.—Where an employer has made a deduction from a contributions payment under [[1]regulation 6], the date on which it is to be treated as having been paid for the purposes of [[1]section 167(6)] of the Contributions and Benefits Act (amount deducted to be treated as paid and received towards discharging liability in respect of Class 1 contributions) is—
    (a) in a case where the deduction did not extinguish the contributions payment, the date on which the remainder of the contributions payment or, as the case may be, the first date on which any part of the remainder of the contributions payment was paid; and
    (b) in a case where the deduction extinguished the contributions payment, the 14th day after the end of the income tax month during which there were paid the earnings in respect of which the contributions payment was payable.

Statutory Maternity Pay and Miscellaneous Amendment Regulations 1994

AMENDMENT

1. Statutory Maternity Pay (Compensation of Employers) Amendment Regulations 2003 (SI 2003/672) reg.5 (April 6, 2003).

DEFINITIONS

"the Contributions and Benefits Act"—see reg.1(4).
"contributions payments"—see *ibid.*
"employer"—see *ibid.*
"income tax month"—see *ibid.*

[¹Overpayments

5.92 **7A.**—(1) Where advance funding has been provided to an employer in accordance with an application under regulation 5, the Board may recover any part of it not used to pay statutory maternity pay ("the overpayment").

(2) An officer of the Board shall decide to the best of his judgement the amount of the overpayment and shall give notice in writing of his decision to the employer.

(3) A decision under paragraph (2) may be in respect of funding provided in accordance with regulation 5 for one or more income tax months or income tax quarters in a tax year—
   (a) in respect of one or more classes of employees specified in a decision notice (where a notice does not name any individual employee); or
   (b) in respect of one or more individual employees named in a decision notice.

(4) Subject to paragraphs (5), (6) or (7), Part 6 of the Taxes Management Act 1970 (collection and recovery) shall apply with any necessary modifications to a decision under this regulation as if the amount specified were an assessment and as if the amount set out in the notice were income tax charged on the employer.

(5) Where a decision under paragraph (2) relates to more than one employee, proceedings may be brought to recover the amount overpaid without distinguishing the sum to be repaid in respect of each employee and without specifying the employee in question.

(6) A decision to recover an amount made in accordance with this regulation shall give rise to one cause of action or matter of complaint for the purpose of proceedings under sections 65, 66 or 67 of the Taxes Management Act 1970.

(7) Nothing in paragraph (5) shall prevent separate proceedings being brought for the recovery of any amount which the employer is liable to repay in respect of each employee to whom the decision relates.]

DEFINITIONS

"the Board"—see reg.1(4).
"the overpayment"—see para.(1).
"advance funding"—see reg.5(1).
"employee"—see reg.1(5).
"employer"—see reg.1(4).
"income tax month"—see reg.1(4).

"income tax quarter"—see reg.1(4).
"tax year"—see reg.1(4).
"writing"—see reg.1(4).

Revocation

8.—The Statutory Maternity Pay (Compensation of Employers) Regulations 1987 are hereby revoked.

5.93

The Statutory Maternity Pay (General) (Modification and Amendment) Regulations 2000

(SI 2000/2883)

The Secretary of State for Social Security, in exercise of the powers conferred on him by sections 164(4), (9)(e) and (10), 165(1) and (3), 171(1) and 175(1) to (4) of the Social Security Contributions and Benefits Act 1992 and of all other powers enabling him in that behalf, after agreement by the Social Security Advisory Committee that proposals to make these Regulations should not be referred to it, hereby makes the following Regulations:

ARRANGEMENT OF REGULATIONS

1. Citation, commencement and interpretation
2. Modification of s.164(2)(a) of the Contributions and Benefits Act
3. Amendment of the Statutory Maternity Pay Regulations
4. Transitional provision

5.94

Citation, commencement and interpretation

1.—(1) These Regulations may be cited as the Statutory Maternity Pay (General) (Modification and Amendment) Regulations 2000 and shall come into force on 17th November 2000.
   (2) In these Regulations—
      "the Contributions and Benefits Act" means the Social Security Contributions and Benefits Act 1992;
      "the Statutory Maternity Pay Regulations" means the Statutory Maternity Pay (General) Regulations 1986.

5.95

Modification of s.164(2)(a) of the Contributions and Benefits Act

2.—Subject to regulation 4, in relation to a woman who is dismissed, or whose employment is otherwise terminated without her consent, after the beginning of the week immediately preceding the 14th week before the expected week of confinement, section 164(2)(a) of the Contributions and Benefits Act (conditions of entitlement to statutory maternity pay) shall be modified and have effect so that the words, "wholly or partly because of pregnancy or confinement" shall not apply.

5.96

1043

DEFINITION

"Contributions and Benefits Act"—see reg.1(2).

GENERAL NOTE

5.97   In order to qualify for statutory maternity pay, the general rule under SSCBA 1992 s.164(2)(a) is that the claimant must have been continuously employed in an employed earner's employment for 26 weeks up to the 15th week before the expected week of confinement but has then ceased to work for the employer "wholly or partly because of pregnancy or confinement". This latter requirement caused problems for women who were dismissed for some other reason (e.g. redundancy). These Regulations were therefore enacted in 2000 (but with effect from March 4, 2001: reg.4) so as to extend the right to statutory maternity pay to all women, unless they left their job voluntarily.

Amendment of the Statutory Maternity Pay Regulations

5.98   **3.**—[...]

GENERAL NOTE

5.99   The amendments made by reg.3 have been incorporated into the text of the Statutory Maternity Pay (General) Regulations 1986 (SI 1986/1960) in this volume.

Transitional provision

5.100   **4.**—In relation to a woman whose expected week of confinement begins before 4th March 2001, the Contributions and Benefits Act and the Statutory Maternity Pay Regulations shall have effect as if these Regulations were not in force.

DEFINITIONS

"Contributions and Benefits Act"—see reg.1(2).
"Statutory Maternity Pay Regulations"—see reg.1(2).

The Statutory Maternity Pay and Statutory Adoption Pay (Curtailment) Regulations 2014

(SI 2014/3054)

This instrument contains only regulations made by virtue of, or consequential upon, section 120(1), (4) and (6) of the Children and Families Act 2014 and is made before the end of the period of 6 months beginning with the coming into force of that enactment.

The Secretary of State for Work and Pensions, in exercise of the powers conferred by sections 165(3A), (3B), (3C) and (3D), 171ZN(2A), (2B), (2C) and (2D) and 175(1), (3) and (4) of the Social Security Contributions and Benefits Act 1992, makes the following Regulations:

(SI 2014/3054)

Arrangement Of Regulations

Part 1

General

5.101

1. Citation and commencement
2. Interpretation
3. Notices

Part 2

Curtailment Of Maternity Pay Period

4. Curtailment of maternity pay period (statutory shared parental pay: M)
5. Curtailment of maternity pay period (statutory shared parental pay: P)
6. Curtailment of maternity pay period (shared parental leave: P)
7. Maternity pay period curtailment notice
8. Revocation (maternity pay period curtailment notice)

Part 3

Curtailment Of Adoption Pay Period

9. Curtailment of adoption pay period (statutory shared parental pay: A)
10. Curtailment of adoption pay period (statutory shared parental pay: AP)
11. Curtailment of adoption pay period (shared parental leave: AP)
12. Adoption pay period curtailment notice
13. Revocation (adoption pay period curtailment notice)

General Note

These Regulations allow eligible women to curtail their statutory maternity pay in accordance with s.165(3A) of the SSCBA 1992 in order to enable them to take statutory shared parental pay (ShPP) in accordance with s.171ZU of the 1992 Act. The Regulations also allow eligible women to curtail their statutory maternity pay in accordance with SSCBA 1992 s.165(3A), in order to allow their partner to take ShPP in accordance with SSCBA 1992 s.171ZU, or shared parental leave in accordance with s.75E of the Employment Rights Act 1996.

5.102

Regulation 3 prescribes how notices may be given under these Regulations. Regulation 4 applies to a woman curtailing her statutory maternity pay in order to take ShPP. Regulation 5 applies to a woman curtailing her SMP so that her partner can take ShPP. Regulation 6 allows a woman who is not eligible for statutory maternity leave to curtail her SMP so that her partner can take shared parental leave. In these circumstances, an eligible partner will be entitled to 52 weeks of shared parental leave less the amount of SMP the child's mother has taken at the point of curtailing the maternity pay period. Regulation 7 prescribes the requirements with which a maternity pay period curtailment notice must comply. Regulation 8 allows a woman to revoke a notice to curtail her SMP in specified circumstances and subject to certain conditions being satisfied.

Statutory Maternity Pay and SAP (Curtailment) Regulations 2014

These Regulations also make equivalent provisions for adopters. The Regulations allow eligible adopters to curtail their adoption pay period in accordance with SSCBA 1992 s.171ZN(2A) so as to enable them to take ShPP in accordance with SSCBA 1992 s.171ZV. The Regulations also allow eligible adopters to curtail their adoption pay period in accordance with s.171ZN(2A) to allow their partner to take ShPP in accordance with s.171ZV, or shared parental leave in accordance with s.75G of the Employment Rights Act 1996.

PART 1

GENERAL

Citation and commencement

5.103   **1.**—These Regulations may be cited as the Statutory Maternity Pay and Statutory Adoption Pay (Curtailment) Regulations 2014 and come into force on 1st December 2014.

Interpretation

5.104   **2.**—In these Regulations—
"the 1992 Act" means the Social Security Contributions and Benefits Act 1992;
"the 1996 Act" means the Employment Rights Act 1996;
"A" means a person who is entitled to statutory adoption pay;
"adoption pay curtailment date" means, subject to regulation 12(4), the date specified in an adoption pay period curtailment notice;
"adoption pay period curtailment notice" means a notice given in accordance with regulation 12;
"AP" means the person who is married to, or the civil partner or the partner of, A;
"C" means the child in respect of whom an entitlement to—
(a) shared parental leave arises under section 75E (entitlement to shared parental leave: birth) or 75G (entitlement to shared parental leave: adoption) of the 1996 Act;
(b) statutory shared parental pay arises under section 171ZU (entitlement: birth) or 171ZV (entitlement: adoption) of the 1992 Act;
"calendar week" means a period of seven days beginning with a Sunday;
"M" means the mother (or expectant mother) of C;
"maternity pay period curtailment date" means, subject to regulation 7(5), the date specified in a maternity pay period curtailment notice;
"maternity pay period curtailment notice" means a notice given in accordance with regulation 7 and regulation 8(5);
"P" means the father of C, or the person who is married to, or the civil partner or the partner of, M;
"partner" in relation to M or A, means a person (whether of a different sex or the same sex) who lives with M or A and with C in an enduring family relationship but is not M's or A's child, parent, grandchild, grandparent, sibling, aunt, uncle, niece or nephew;
"SPL Regulations" means the Shared Parental Leave Regulations 2014;
"ShPP Regulations" means the Statutory Shared Parental Pay (General) Regulations 2014;

(SI 2014/3054 reg.2)

"statutory adoption pay" has the meaning given in section 171ZL (entitlement) of the 1992 Act;
"statutory maternity pay" has the meaning given in section 164(1) (statutory maternity pay—entitlement and liability to pay) of the 1992 Act.

Notices

3.—(1) Where a notice is to be given under these Regulations, it may be given—
   (a) where paragraph (2) applies, by electronic communication;
   (b) by post; or
   (c) by personal delivery.
(2) This paragraph applies where the person who is to receive the notice has agreed that the notice may be given to the person by being transmitted to an electronic address and in an electronic form specified by the person for the purpose.
(3) Where a notice is to be given under these Regulations it is to be taken to have been given—
   (a) if sent by electronic communication, on the day of transmission;
   (b) if sent by post in an envelope which is properly addressed and sent by prepaid post, on the day on which it is posted;
   (c) if delivered personally, on the day of delivery.

Part 2

Curtailment Of Maternity Pay Period

Curtailment of maternity pay period (statutory shared parental pay: M)

4.—M's maternity pay period shall end on the maternity pay period curtailment date if—
   (a) M gives a maternity pay period curtailment notice (unless the notice is revoked under regulation 8);
   (b) M satisfies the conditions in sub-paragraphs (a) and (d) of regulation 4(2) (entitlement of mother to statutory shared parental pay (birth)) of the ShPP Regulations; and
   (c) P satisfies the conditions in sub-paragraph (b) of regulation 4(3) of the ShPP Regulations.

Definitions

"maternity pay period curtailment date"—reg.2.
"maternity pay period curtailment notice"—reg.2.
"ShPP Regulations"—reg.2.

Curtailment of maternity pay period (statutory shared parental pay: P)

5.—M's maternity pay period shall end on the maternity pay period curtailment date if—

Statutory Maternity Pay and SAP (Curtailment) Regulations 2014

(a) M gives a maternity pay period curtailment notice (unless the notice is revoked under regulation 8);
(b) P satisfies the conditions in sub-paragraph (a) of regulation 5(2) (entitlement of father or partner to statutory shared parental pay (birth)) of the ShPP Regulations; and
(c) M satisfies the conditions in sub-paragraphs (b) and (c) of regulation 5(3) of the ShPP Regulations.

DEFINITIONS

"M"—reg.2.
"maternity pay period curtailment date"—reg.2.
"maternity pay period curtailment notice"—reg.2.
"P"—reg.2.
"partner"—reg.2.
"ShPP Regulations"—reg.2.

Curtailment of maternity pay period (shared parental leave: P)

5.108　　**6.**—M's maternity pay period shall end on the maternity pay period curtailment date if—
(a) M gives a maternity pay period curtailment notice (unless the notice is revoked under regulation 8);
(b) P satisfies the condition in sub-paragraph (a) of regulation 5(2) (father's or partner's entitlement to shared parental leave) of the SPL Regulations; and
(c) M satisfies the conditions in sub-paragraphs (a) and (c) of regulation 5(3) of the SPL Regulations.

DEFINITIONS

"M"—reg.2.
"P"—reg.2.
"maternity pay period curtailment date"—reg.2.
"maternity pay period curtailment notice"—reg.2.
"partner"—reg.2.
"ShPP Regulations"—reg.2.
"SPL Regulations"—reg.2.

Maternity pay period curtailment notice

5.109　　**7.**—(1) A maternity pay period curtailment notice must—
(a) be in writing;
(b) specify the date on which M's statutory maternity pay period is to end; and
(c) be given to the person who is liable to pay M's statutory maternity pay.
(2) The date specified in accordance with paragraph (1)(b) must be—
(a) the last day of a week;
(b) if M has the right to maternity leave under section 71 (ordinary maternity leave) of the 1996 Act, at least one day after the end of the compulsory maternity leave period, or, if M does not have that right, at least two weeks after the end of the pregnancy;
(c) at least eight weeks after the date on which M gave the maternity pay period curtailment notice; and

(d) at least one week before the last day of the maternity pay period.

(3) In paragraph (2) "the end of the compulsory maternity leave period" means whichever is the later of—
  (a) the last day of the compulsory maternity leave period provided for in regulations under section 72(2) (compulsory maternity leave) of the 1996 Act; or
  (b) where section 205 of the Public Health Act 1936 (women not to be employed in factories or workshops within four weeks after birth of a child) applies to M's employment, the last day of the period in which an occupier of a factory is prohibited from knowingly allowing M to be employed in that factory.

(4) If M has more than one entitlement to statutory maternity pay in relation to C, M must curtail the maternity pay period in relation to each (or none) of those entitlements, and in relation to each of those entitlements M must specify a maternity pay period curtailment date which falls in the same calendar week.

(5) Where M—
  (a) returns to work before giving a notice in accordance with paragraph (1); and
  (b) subsequently gives such a notice;
    the "maternity pay period curtailment date" shall be the last day of the week in which that notice is given (irrespective of the date given in that notice under paragraph (1)).

(6) For the purposes of paragraphs (2)(a) and (5), "week" has the meaning given in section 165(8) (the maternity pay period) of the 1992 Act.

(7) In this regulation, M is treated as returning to work where statutory maternity pay is not payable to her in accordance with section 165(4) or (6) of the 1992 Act.

DEFINITIONS

"the 1992 Act"—see reg.2.
"the 1996 Act"—see reg.2.
"calendar week"—reg.2.
"C"—reg.2.
"M"—reg.2.
"P"—reg.2.
"maternity pay period curtailment date"—reg.2.
"maternity pay period curtailment notice"—reg.2.
"partner"—reg.2.
"ShPP Regulations"—reg.2.
"SPL Regulations"—reg.2.
"statutory maternity pay"—reg.2.
"week"—subs.(6).

Revocation (maternity pay period curtailment notice)

8.—(1) Subject to paragraph (2), M may revoke a maternity pay period curtailment notice by giving a notice ("a revocation notice") before the maternity pay period curtailment date if—
  (a) she gave the maternity pay period curtailment notice before the birth of C; or
  (b) P dies.

5.110

Statutory Maternity Pay and SAP (Curtailment) Regulations 2014

(2) Revocation is effective under paragraph (1) where M gives a revocation notice to the person who is liable to pay M's statutory maternity pay that—
  (a) if given under paragraph (1)(a), is given within six weeks of the date of C's birth; or
  (b) if given under paragraph (1)(b), is given within a reasonable period from the date of P's death.

(3) A revocation notice must—
  (a) be in writing;
  (b) state that M revokes the maternity pay period curtailment notice; and
  (c) if given under paragraph (1)(b), state the date of P's death.

(4) Where in accordance with regulation 7(4) M has given a maternity pay period curtailment notice to more than one person, M must give a revocation notice to each of those persons.

(5) M may not give a maternity pay period curtailment notice in respect of the same maternity pay period subsequent to giving a revocation notice unless the revocation was made in accordance with paragraph (1)(a).

DEFINITIONS

"C"—reg.2.
"M"—reg.2.
"P"—reg.2.
"maternity pay period curtailment notice"—reg.2.
"revocation notice"—para.(1).
"statutory maternity pay"—reg.2.

PART 3

CURTAILMENT OF ADOPTION PAY PERIOD

Curtailment of adoption pay period (statutory shared parental pay: A)

5.111   9.—A's adoption pay period shall end on the adoption pay curtailment date if—
  (a) A gives an adoption pay period curtailment notice (unless the notice is revoked under regulation 13);
  (b) A satisfies the conditions in sub-paragraphs (a) and (d) of regulation 17(2) (entitlement of adopter to statutory shared parental pay (adoption)) of the ShPP Regulations; and
  (c) AP satisfies the condition in sub-paragraph (b) of regulation 17(3) of the ShPP Regulations.

DEFINITIONS

"A"—reg.2.
"adoption pay period curtailment date"—reg.2.
"adoption pay period curtailment notice"—reg.2.
"AP"—reg.2.
"ShPP Regulations"—reg.2.

(SI 2014/3054 reg.10)

Curtailment of adoption pay period (statutory shared parental pay: AP)

10.—A's adoption pay period shall end on the adoption pay curtailment date if—
  (a) A gives an adoption pay period curtailment notice (unless the notice is revoked under regulation 13);
  (b) AP satisfies the conditions in sub-paragraph (a) of regulation 18(2) (entitlement of adopter's partner to statutory shared parental pay (adoption)) of the ShPP Regulations; and
  (c) A satisfies the conditions in sub-paragraphs (b) and (c) of regulation 18(3) of the ShPP Regulations.

5.112

DEFINITIONS

"A"—reg.2.
"adoption pay period curtailment date"—reg.2.
"adoption pay period curtailment notice"—reg.2.
"AP"—reg.2.
"partner"—reg.2.
"ShPP Regulations"—reg.2.

Curtailment of adoption pay period (shared parental leave: AP)

11.—A's adoption pay period shall end on the adoption pay curtailment date if—
  (a) A gives an adoption pay period curtailment notice (unless the notice is revoked under regulation 13);
  (b) AP satisfies the condition in sub-paragraph (a) of regulation 21(2) (adopter's partner's entitlement to shared parental leave) of the SPL Regulations; and
  (c) A satisfies the conditions in sub-paragraphs (a) and (c) of regulation 21(3) of the SPL Regulations.

5.113

DEFINITIONS

"A"—reg.2.
"adoption pay period curtailment date"—reg.2.
"adoption pay period curtailment notice"—reg.2.
"AP"—reg.2.
"partner"—reg.2.
"SPL Regulations"—reg.2.

Adoption pay period curtailment notice

12.—(1) An adoption pay period curtailment notice must—
  (a) be in writing;
  (b) specify the date on which A's statutory adoption pay period is to end; and
  (c) be given to the person who is liable to pay A's statutory adoption pay.

5.114

(2) The date specified in accordance with paragraph (1)(b) must be—
  (a) the last day of a week;
  (b) at least eight weeks after the date on which A gave the adoption pay period curtailment notice;
  (c) at least two weeks after the first day of the adoption pay period; and

(d) at least one week before the last day of the adoption pay period.

(3) If A has more than one entitlement to statutory adoption pay in relation to C, A must curtail the adoption pay period in relation to each (or none) of those entitlements, and in relation to each of those entitlements A must specify an adoption pay curtailment date which falls in the same calendar week.

(4) Where A—
(a) returns to work before giving a notice in accordance with paragraph (1); and
(b) subsequently gives such a notice;
the adoption pay curtailment date shall be the last day of the week in which that notice is submitted (irrespective of the date given in that notice under paragraph (1)).

(5) For the purposes of paragraph (2)(a) and (4), "week" has the meaning given in section 171ZN(8) of the 1992 Act.

(6) In this regulation, A is treated as returning to work where statutory adoption pay is not payable to A in accordance with section 171ZN(3) or (5) of the 1992 Act.

DEFINITIONS

"the 1992 Act"—see reg.2.
"the 1996 Act"—see reg.2.
"A"—reg.2.
"adoption pay period curtailment date"—reg.2.
"adoption pay period curtailment notice"—reg.2.
"AP"—reg.2.
"calendar week"—reg.2.
"partner"—reg.2.
"SPL Regulations"—reg.2.
"statutory adoption pay"—reg.2.
"week"—para.(5).

Revocation (adoption pay period curtailment notice)

5.115   13.—(1) Where AP dies before the adoption pay curtailment date, A may revoke an adoption pay period curtailment notice by giving a notice ("a revocation notice") in accordance with paragraph (2).

(2) A revocation notice must be given to the person who is liable to pay A statutory adoption pay within a reasonable period from the date of AP's death and before the adoption pay curtailment date.

(3) A revocation notice must—
(a) be in writing;
(b) state that A revokes the adoption pay period curtailment notice; and
(c) state the date of AP's death.

(4) Where in accordance with regulation 12(3) A has given an adoption pay period curtailment notice to more than one person, A must give a revocation notice to each of those persons.

(5) A may not give an adoption pay period curtailment notice subsequent to giving a revocation notice.

DEFINITIONS

"A"—reg.2.
"adoption pay period curtailment date"—reg.2.

"adoption pay period curtailment notice"—reg.2.
"AP"—reg.2.
"revocation notice"—para.(1).

The Maternity Allowance, Statutory Maternity Pay, Statutory Paternity Pay, Statutory Adoption Pay, Statutory Shared Parental Pay and Statutory Parental Bereavement Pay (Normal Weekly Earnings etc.) (Coronavirus) (Amendment) Regulations 2020

(SI 2020/450)

The Secretary of State makes the following Regulations in exercise of the powers conferred by sections 35A(5)(a), 171(6), 171ZJ(8), 171ZS(8), 171ZZ4(8), 171ZZ14(8) and 175(3) and (4) of the Social Security Contributions and Benefits Act 1992.

Regulation 3 and regulations 5 to 7 are made with the concurrence of the Commissioners for Her Majesty's Revenue and Customs.

In accordance with section 173(1)(a) of the Social Security Administration Act 1992, it appears to the Secretary of State that by reason of the urgency of this matter it is inexpedient to refer the proposals in respect of these Regulations to the Social Security Advisory Committee.

Citation and commencement

1. These Regulations may be cited as the Maternity Allowance, Statutory Maternity Pay, Statutory Paternity Pay, Statutory Adoption Pay, Statutory Shared Parental Pay and Statutory Parental Bereavement Pay (Normal Weekly Earnings etc.) (Coronavirus) (Amendment) Regulations 2020 and come into force on 25th April 2020.

Application

2.—(1) The amendments made by regulation 3 and regulations 5 to 7 apply only in relation to the calculation of normal weekly earnings for the purpose of determining—
   (a) the entitlement of a person to any of the statutory payments; or
   (b) the rate at which any of the statutory payments are to be paid to that person,
in a case where the first day of the period in respect of which the statutory payment is to be made is on or after the day on which these Regulations come into force.

(2) In paragraph (1), "statutory payments" means the following payments under the Social Security Contributions and Benefits Act 1992 ("the 1992 Act")—
   (a) statutory maternity pay;
   (b) statutory paternity pay;
   (c) statutory adoption pay;
   (d) statutory shared parental pay; and
   (e) statutory parental bereavement pay.

(3) The amendments made by regulation 4 apply only in relation to the calculation of the average weekly amount of specified payments made to a woman for the purpose of determining—

(a) the entitlement of the woman to a maternity allowance under the 1992 Act; or
(b) the rate at which that allowance is to be paid to the woman,

in a case where the first day of the period in respect of which payment of that allowance is to be made is on or after the day on which these Regulations come into force.

Amendment of the Statutory Maternity Pay (General) Regulations 1986

5.118   **3.**— *[Amendments included in the Regulations above]*

Amendment of the Social Security (Maternity Allowance) (Earnings) Regulations 2000

5.119   **4.**— *[Amendments included in the Regulations in Vol. I]*

Amendment of the Statutory Paternity Pay and Statutory Adoption Pay (General) Regulations 2002

5.120   **5.**— *[Amendments included in the Regulations below in Part VI]*

Amendment of the Statutory Shared Parental Pay (General) Regulations 2014

5.121   **6.**— *[Amendments included in the Regulations below in Part VII]*

Amendment of the Statutory Parental Bereavement Pay (General) Regulations 2020

5.122   **7.**— *[Amendments included in the Regulations below in Part VIII]*

PART VI

STATUTORY PATERNITY PAY AND STATUTORY ADOPTION PAY

The Statutory Paternity Pay and Statutory Adoption Pay (Weekly Rates) Regulations 2002

(SI 2002/2818) (AS AMENDED)

Whereas a draft of the following Regulations was laid before Parliament in accordance with section 176(1)(a) of the Social Security Contributions and Benefits Act 1992 and approved by a resolution of each House of Parliament:

Now, therefore, the Secretary of State, in exercise of the powers conferred on her by sections 171ZE(1) and 171ZN(1) of the Social Security Contributions and Benefits Act 1992 and section 5(1)(l) of the Social Security Administration Act 1992, by this instrument, which contains only provision made by virtue of sections 2, 4 and 53 of and paragraphs 8 and 11 of Schedule 7 to the Employment Act 2002 and is made before the end of the period of 6 months from the coming into force of those enactments, hereby makes the following Regulations—

ARRANGEMENT OF REGULATIONS

1. Citation and commencement.
2. Weekly rate of payment of statutory paternity pay.
3. Weekly rate of payment of statutory adoption pay.
4. Rounding of fractional amounts.

Citation and commencement

1.—These Regulations may be cited as the Statutory Paternity Pay and Statutory Adoption Pay (Weekly Rates) Regulations and shall come into force on 8th December 2002.

GENERAL NOTE

These Regulations specify the weekly rate of statutory paternity pay and statutory adoption pay. In the current year, statutory paternity pay is the lower of £184.03 per week or 90 per cent of the employee's normal weekly earnings where the paternity pay period starts after that date (reg.2). Statutory adoption pay is set at the lower of £184.03 per week or 90 per cent of the employee's normal weekly earnings (reg.3). Fractional amounts are rounded in accordance with reg.4.

[¹Weekly rate of payment of statutory paternity pay

2.—The weekly rate of payment of statutory paternity pay shall be the smaller of the following two amounts—
  (a) [²£184.03];
  (b) 90 per cent. of the normal weekly earnings of the person claiming statutory paternity pay, determined in accordance with regulations 39 and 40 of the Statutory Paternity Pay and Statutory Adoption Pay (General) Regulations 2002.]

AMENDMENTS

1. Statutory Paternity Pay and Statutory Adoption Pay (Weekly Rates) (Amendment) Regulations 2004 (SI 2004/925) reg.2 (April 4, 2004).
2. Social Security Benefits Up-rating Order 2024 (SI 2024/242) art.10(1)(a) (April 7, 2024).

Weekly rate of payment of statutory adoption pay

3.—The weekly rate of payment of statutory adoption pay shall be the smaller of the following two amounts—
(a) [¹£184.03];
(b) 90 per cent of the normal weekly earnings of the person claiming statutory adoption pay, determined in accordance with regulations 39 and 40 of the Statutory Paternity Pay and Statutory Adoption Pay (General) Regulations 2002.

AMENDMENT

1. Social Security Benefits Up-rating Order 2024 (SI 2024/242) art.10(1)(b) (April 7, 2024).

Rounding of fractional amounts

[¹**4.**—Where any payment of—
(a) statutory paternity pay is made on the basis of a calculation at—
  (i) the weekly rate specified in regulation 2(b); or
  (ii) the daily rate of one-seventh of the weekly rate specified in regulation 2(a) or (b); or
(b) statutory adoption pay is made on the basis of a calculation at—
  (i) the weekly rate specified in regulation 3(b); or
  (ii) the daily rate of one-seventh of the weekly rate specified in regulation 3(a) or (b),
and that amount includes a fraction of a penny, the payment shall be rounded up to the next whole number of pence.]

AMENDMENT

1. Statutory Paternity Pay and Statutory Adoption Pay (General) and the Statutory Paternity Pay and Statutory Adoption Pay (Weekly Rates) (Amendment) Regulations 2006 (SI 2006/2236) reg.4 (October 1, 2006).

GENERAL NOTE

The amended version of reg.4 applies in relation to an entitlement to SPP (birth) in respect of children whose expected week of birth begins on or after April 1, 2007 and to SPP (adoption) and SAP in respect of children expected to be placed for adoption, where the placement is expected to occur on or after April 1, 2007 (see reg.2 of SI 2006/2236).

(SI 2002/2819) (as amended)

The Statutory Paternity Pay and Statutory Adoption Pay (National Health Service Employees) Regulations 2002

(SI 2002/2819) (AS AMENDED)

The Secretary of State, in exercise of the powers conferred on her by virtue of sections 171ZJ(9) and (10) and 171ZS(9) and (10) of the Social Security Contributions and Benefits Act 1992 and with the concurrence of the Commissioners of Inland Revenue by this instrument, which contains only provision made by virtue of sections 2 and 4 of the Employment Act 2002 and is made before the end of the period of 6 months from the coming into force of those enactments hereby makes the following Regulations—

ARRANGEMENT OF SECTIONS

1. Citation, commencement and interpretation.
2. Treatment of more than one contract of employment as one contract.
3. Notification of election.
4. Provision of information.
5. Treatment of two or more employers as one.
6. Time for which an election is to have effect.

Citation, commencement and interpretation

1.—(1) These Regulations may be cited as the Statutory Paternity Pay and Statutory Adoption Pay (National Health Service Employees) Regulations 2002 and shall come into force on 8th December 2002.

(2) In these Regulations—

"the Act" means the Social Security Contributions and Benefits Act 1992;

"the 1977 Act" means the National Health Service Act 1977;

"the 1978 Act" means the National Health Service (Scotland) Act 1978;

"the 1990 Act" means the National Health Service and Community Care Act 1990;

"the 2002 Act" means the National Health Service Reform and Health Care Professions Act 2002;

"Health Authority" means, in relation to Wales, a Health Authority established under section 8 of the 1977 Act and in relation to Scotland means a Health Board established under section 2 of the 1978 Act;

[1"NHS trust" shall be construed to include a reference to an NHS foundation trust within the meaning of section 1(1) of the Health and Social Care (Community Health and Standards) Act 2003 where the application for authorisation to become an NHS foundation trust was made by an NHS trust.]

[2 . . .]

"statutory adoption pay period" means the period prescribed under section 171ZN(2) of the Act as the period in respect of which statutory adoption pay is payable to a person;

"statutory paternity pay period" means the period determined in accordance with section 171ZE(2) of the Act as the period in respect of which statutory paternity pay is payable to a person;

Statutory Paternity Pay and Statutory Adoption Pay Regulations 2002

"Strategic Health Authority" means a Strategic Health Authority established under section 8 of the 1977 Act.

AMENDMENTS

1. Health and Social Care (Community Health and Standards) Act 2003 (Supplementary and Consequential Provision) (NHS Foundation Trusts) Order 2004 (SI 2004/696) art.3(1) and Sch.1 para.42 (April 1, 2004).
2. National Treatment Agency (Abolition) and the Health and Social Care Act 2012 (Consequential, Transitional and Saving Provisions) Order 2013 (SI 2013/235) art.11 and Sch.2 para.56(2) (April 1, 2013).

GENERAL NOTE

6.10   These Regulations, made under the authority of SSCBA 1992 ss.171ZJ(9) and (10) and 171ZS(9) and (10), make special provision for those NHS workers who are employed under two or more separate contracts of employment with different NHS Trusts. The regulations enable them to elect to have such contracts treated as one contract for the purposes of entitlement to statutory paternity pay and statutory adoption pay.

Treatment of more than one contract of employment as one contract

6.11   **2.**—Where, in consequence of the establishment of one or more National Health Service Trusts under section 5 of the 1990 Act or section 12A of the 1978 Act, a person's contract of employment is treated by a scheme under section 6 of the 1990 Act or section 12B of the 1978 Act as divided so as to constitute two or more contracts [¹. . .] he may elect for all those contracts to be treated as one contract for the purposes of Parts 12ZA and 12ZB of the Act.

AMENDMENT

1. National Treatment Agency (Abolition) and the Health and Social Care Act 2012 (Consequential, Transitional and Saving Provisions) Order 2013 (SI 2013/235) art.11 and Sch.2 para.56(3) (April 1, 2013).

DEFINITIONS

"the Act"—see reg.1(2).
"the 1977 Act"—see reg.1(2).
"the 1978 Act"—see reg.1(2).
"the 1990 Act"—see reg.1(2).

Notification of election

6.12   **3.**—A person who makes an election under regulation 2 above shall give written notification of that election to each of his employers under the two or more contracts of employment mentioned in that regulation at least 28 days before the beginning of the statutory paternity pay period or adoption pay period or, if in the particular circumstances that is not practicable, as soon as is reasonably practicable.

DEFINITIONS

"statutory adoption pay period"—see reg.1(2).
"statutory paternity pay period"—see reg.1(2).

(SI 2002/2819 reg.4) (as amended)

Provision of information

4.—A person who makes an election under regulation 2 above shall, within 28 days of giving notification of that election or, if in the particular circumstances that is not practicable, as soon as is reasonably practicable thereafter, provide each of his employers under the two or more contracts of employment mentioned in that regulation with the following information—
- (a) the name and address of each of those employers;
- (b) the date his employment with each of those employers commenced; and
- (c) details of his normal weekly earnings during the relevant period from each employer, and for this purpose the expressions "normal weekly earnings" and "relevant period" have the same meanings as they have for the purposes of Parts 12ZA and 12ZB of the Act.

DEFINITIONS

"normal weekly earnings"—para.(c) and SSCBA 1992 ss.171ZJ(6) and 171ZS(6) and Statutory Paternity Pay and Statutory Adoption Pay (General) Regulations 2002 (SI 2002/2822) reg.40.
"relevant period"—para.(c) and SSCBA 1992 ss.171ZJ(7) and 171ZS(7) and Statutory Paternity Pay and Statutory Adoption Pay (General) Regulations 2002 (SI 2002/2822) reg.40(3).

Treatment of two or more employers as one

5.—The employer to be regarded for the purposes of statutory paternity pay or statutory adoption pay as the employer under the one contract where two or more contracts are treated as one in accordance with regulation 2 above shall be—
- (a) in the case of a person whose contract of employment is treated by a scheme under section 6 of the 1990 Act or section 12B of the 1978 Act as divided—
  - (i) the Health Authority [1...] from which the person was transferred in a case where any one of the contracts of employment is with that Health Authority [1...]; or
  - (ii) the first NHS trust to which a contract of employment was transferred in a case where none of the contracts of employment is with the Health Authority [1...]; [1...]
  [1...]

AMENDMENT

1. National Treatment Agency (Abolition) and the Health and Social Care Act 2012 (Consequential, Transitional and Saving Provisions) Order 2013 (SI 2013/235) art.11 and Sch.2 para.56(4) (April 1, 2013).

DEFINITIONS

"the 1977 Act"—see reg.1(2).
"the 1978 Act"—see reg.1(2).
"Health Authority"—see reg.1(2).
"Primary Care Trust"—see reg.1(2).
"Strategic Health Authority"—see reg.1(2).

Time for which an election is to have effect

6.15 **6.**—An election made under regulation 2 shall lapse at the end of the statutory paternity pay period or, as the case may be, the adoption pay period.

DEFINITIONS

"statutory adoption pay period"—see reg.1(2).
"statutory paternity pay period"—see reg.1(2).

The Statutory Paternity Pay and Statutory Adoption Pay (Administration) Regulations 2002

(SI 2002/2820)

The Secretary of State, in exercise of the powers conferred on her by sections 7(1), (2)(a) and (b), (4)(a), (b) and (c) and (5), 8(1) and (2)(a), (b) and (c), 10(1) and (2) and 51(1) of the Employment Act 2002 and sections 8(1)(f) and (ga) and 25 of the Social Security Contributions (Transfer of Functions, etc.) Act 1999 and with the concurrence of the Commissioners of Inland Revenue, hereby makes the following Regulations—

ARRANGEMENT OF SECTIONS

6.16
1. Citation and commencement.
2. Interpretation.
3. Funding of employers' liabilities to make payments of statutory paternity or statutory adoption pay.
4. Application for funding from the Board.
5. Deductions from payments to the Board.
6. Payments to employers by the Board.
7. Date when certain contributions are to be treated as paid.
8. Overpayments.
9. Records to be maintained by employers.
10. Inspection of employers' records.
11. Provision of information relating to entitlement to statutory paternity pay or statutory adoption pay.
12. Application for the determination of any issue arising as to, or in connection with, entitlement to statutory paternity pay or statutory adoption pay.
13. Applications in connection with statutory paternity pay or statutory adoption pay.
14. Provision of information.

Citation and commencement

6.17 **1.**—These Regulations may be cited as the Statutory Paternity Pay and Statutory Adoption Pay (Administration) Regulations 2002 and shall come into force on 8th December 2002.

GENERAL NOTE

6.18 These Regulations provide for employers to be reimbursed for the cost of making payments of statutory paternity pay and statutory adoption pay. They are therefore modelled in part on the Statutory Maternity Pay (Compensation of Employers) and

(SI 2002/2820 reg.1)

Miscellaneous Amendment Regulations 1994 (SI 1994/1882). As with the regulations governing statutory maternity pay, they provide for employers to claim back 92 per cent of the total costs of their statutory paternity pay and statutory adoption pay payments, or 100 per cent in the case of small employers, with a small additional element in the latter instance (reg.3). Employers receive such monies by making deductions from income tax, National Insurance contributions and other payments that would otherwise be due to HMRC (reg.4). There is provision for HMRC to make a direct payment to an employer where such deductions would otherwise be insufficient (reg.6). HMRC also has the power to recover overpayments from employers (reg.8).

These Regulations also require employers to maintain relevant records (reg.9) and to permit HMRC officers to inspect such records (reg.10). Furthermore, employers who decide that they have no liability to pay statutory paternity pay or statutory adoption pay to an employee or ex-employee must give any such person details of that decision and the reasons for it (reg.11). Any question relating to entitlement to statutory paternity pay or statutory adoption pay may be submitted by the employee concerned to HMRC for decision (regs 12 and 13). HMRC has information-gathering powers as set out in reg.14.

Regulations 2 and 11 of these regulations are amended for the purposes of adoptions from overseas by the Statutory Paternity Pay (Adoption) and Statutory Adoption Pay (Adoptions from Overseas) (Administration) Regulations 2003 (SI 2003/1192).

Interpretation

2.—(1) In these Regulations—
"adopter", in relation to a child, means a person with whom the child is matched for adoption;
"adoption leave" means leave under section 75A of the Employment Rights Act 1996;
[¹...]
"the Board" means the Commissioners of Inland Revenue;
"the Contributions and Benefits Act" means the Social Security Contributions and Benefits Act 1992;
"contributions payments" has the same meaning as in section 7 of the Employment Act;
"the Contributions Regulations" means the Social Security (Contributions) Regulations 2001;
"the Employment Act" means the Employment Act 2002;
"income tax month" means the period beginning on the 6th day of any calendar month and ending on the 5th day of the following calendar month;
"income tax quarter" means the period beginning on the 6th day of April and ending on the 5th day of July, the period beginning on the 6th day of July and ending on the 5th day of October, the period beginning on the 6th day of October and ending on the 5th day of January or the period beginning on the sixth day of January and ending on the 5th day of April;
"paternity leave" means leave under section 80A or section 80B of the Employment Rights Act 1996;
[¹...]
["period of payment of adoption pay" means the period prescribed under section 171ZN(2) of the Contributions and Benefits Act as the period in respect of which statutory adoption pay is payable to a person;
"period of payment of paternity pay" means a period determined in accordance with section 171ZE(2) of the Contributions and Benefits Act as a period in respect of which statutory paternity pay is payable to a person;]

6.19

"statutory adoption pay" means any payment under section 171ZL of the Contributions and Benefits Act;
"statutory paternity pay" means any payment under section 171ZA or section 171ZB of the Contributions and Benefits Act;
"tax year" means the 12 months beginning with 6th April in any year;
"writing" includes writing delivered by means of electronic communications approved by directions issued by the Board pursuant to regulations under section 132 of the Finance Act 1999;

(2) Any reference in these Regulations to the employees of an employer includes former employees of his.

AMENDMENT

1. Statutory Paternity Pay (Amendment) Regulations 2024 (SI 2024/121) reg.29 (March 8, 2024).

Funding of employers' liabilities to make payments of statutory paternity or statutory adoption pay

3.—(1) An employer who has made any payment of statutory paternity pay or statutory adoption pay shall be entitled—
  (a) to an amount equal to 92 per cent of such payment; or
  (b) if the payment qualifies for small employer's relief by virtue of section 7(3) of the Employment Act—
    (i) to an amount equal to such payment; and
    (ii) to an additional payment equal to the amount to which the employer would have been entitled under section 167(2)(b) of the Contributions and Benefits Act had the payment been a payment of statutory maternity pay.

(2) The employer shall be entitled in either case (a) or case (b) to apply for advance funding in respect of such payment in accordance with regulation 4, or to deduct it in accordance with regulation 5 from amounts otherwise payable by him.

DEFINITIONS

"Contributions and Benefits Act"—see reg.2(1).
"Employment Act"—see reg.2(1).
"statutory adoption pay"—see reg.2(1).
"statutory paternity pay"—see reg.2(1).

Application for funding from the Board

4.—(1) If an employer is entitled to a payment determined in accordance with regulation 3 in respect of statutory paternity pay or statutory adoption pay which he is required to pay to an employee or employees for an income tax month or income tax quarter, and the payment exceeds the aggregate of—
  (a) the total amount of tax which the employer is required to pay to the collector of taxes in respect of the deductions from the emoluments of his employees in accordance with the Income Tax (Employments) Regulations 1993 for the same income tax month or income tax quarter;
  (b) the total amount of the deductions made by the employer from the emoluments of his employees for the same income tax month or

(SI 2002/2820 reg. 4)

income tax quarter in accordance with regulations under section 22(5) of the Teaching and Higher Education Act 1998 or section 73B of the Education (Scotland) Act 1980 or in accordance with article 3(5) of the Education (Student Support) (Northern Ireland) Order 1998;

(c) the total amount of contributions payments which the employer is required to pay to the collector of taxes in respect of the emoluments of his employees (whether by means of deduction or otherwise) in accordance with the Contributions Regulations for the same income tax month or income tax quarter; and

(d) the total amount of payments which the employer is required to pay to the collector of taxes in respect of the deductions made on account of tax from payments to sub-contractors in accordance with section 559 of the Income and Corporation Taxes Act 1988 for the same income tax month or income tax quarter,

the employer may apply to the Board in accordance with paragraph (2) for funds to pay the statutory paternity pay or statutory adoption pay (or so much of it as remains outstanding) to the employee or employees.

(2) Where—

(a) the condition in paragraph (1) is satisfied; or

(b) the employer considers that the condition in paragraph (1) will be satisfied on the date of any subsequent payment of emoluments to one or more employees who are entitled to payment of statutory paternity pay or statutory adoption pay,

the employer may apply to the Board for funding in a form approved for that purpose by the Board.

(3) An application by an employer under paragraph (2) shall be for an amount up to, but not exceeding, the amount of the payment to which the employer is entitled in accordance with regulation 3 in respect of statutory paternity pay and statutory adoption pay which he is required to pay to an employee or employees for the income tax month or income tax quarter to which the payment of emoluments relates.

DEFINITIONS

"the Board"—see reg.2(1).
"contributions payments"—see reg.2(1).
"the Contributions Regulations"—see reg.2(1).
"income tax month"—see reg.2(1).
"income tax quarter"—see reg.2(1).
"statutory adoption pay"—see reg.2(1).
"statutory paternity pay"—see reg.2(1).

Deductions from payments to the Board

5.—An employer who is entitled to a payment determined in accordance with regulation 3 may recover such payment by making one or more deductions from the aggregate of the amounts specified in subparagraphs (a) to (d) of regulation 4(1) except where and in so far as—

(a) those amounts relate to earnings paid before the beginning of the income tax month or income tax quarter in which the payment of statutory paternity pay or statutory adoption pay was made;

(b) those amounts are paid by him later than six years after the end of the tax year in which the payment of statutory paternity pay or statutory adoption pay was made;

6.22

Statutory Paternity Pay and Statutory Adoption Pay Regulations 2002

 (c) the employer has received payment from the Board under regulation 4; or
 (d) the employer has made a request in writing under regulation 4 that the payment to which he is entitled in accordance with regulation 3 be paid to him and he has not received notification by the Board that the request is refused.

DEFINITIONS

"the Board"—see reg.2(1).
"income tax month"—see reg.2(1).
"income tax quarter"—see reg.2(1).
"statutory adoption pay"—see reg.2(1).
"statutory paternity pay"—see reg.2(1).
"tax year"—see reg.2(1).
"writing"—see reg.2(1).

Payments to employers by the Board

6.23 **6.**—If the total amount which an employer is or would otherwise be entitled to deduct under regulation 5 is less than the payment to which the employer is entitled in accordance with regulation 3 in an income tax month or income tax quarter, and the Board are satisfied that this is so, then provided that the employer has in writing requested them to do so, the Board shall pay the employer such amount as the employer was unable to deduct.

DEFINITIONS

"the Board"—see reg.2(1).
"income tax month"—see reg.2(1).
"income tax quarter"—see reg.2(1).
"writing"—see reg.2(1).

Date when certain contributions are to be treated as paid

6.24 **7.**—Where an employer has made a deduction from a contributions payment under regulation 5, the date on which it is to be treated as having been paid for the purposes of section 7(5) of the Employment Act (when amount deducted from contributions payment to be treated as paid and received by the Board) is—
 (a) in a case where the deduction did not extinguish the contributions payment, the date on which the remainder of the contributions payment or, as the case may be, the first date on which any part of the remainder of the contributions payment was paid; and
 (b) in a case where the deduction extinguished the contributions payment, the 14th day after the end of the income tax month or income tax quarter during which there were paid the earnings in respect of which the contributions payment was payable.

DEFINITIONS

"the Board"—see reg.2(1).
"contributions payments"—see reg.2(1).
"Employment Act"—see reg.2(1).
"income tax month"—see reg.2(1).
"income tax quarter"—see reg.2(1).

Overpayments

8.—(1) This regulation applies where unds have been provided to the employer pursuant to regulation 4 in respect of one or more employees and it appears to an officer of the Board that the employer has not used the whole or part of those funds to pay statutory paternity pay or statutory adoption pay.

(2) An officer of the Board shall decide to the best of his judgement the amount of funds provided pursuant to regulation 4 and not used to pay statutory paternity pay or statutory adoption pay and shall serve notice in writing of his decision on the employer.

(3) A decision under this regulation may cover funds provided pursuant to regulation 4—
   (a) for any one income tax month or income tax quarter, or more than one income tax month or income tax quarter, in a tax year; and
   (b) in respect of a class or classes of employees specified in the decision notice (without naming the individual employees), or in respect of one or more employees named in the decision notice.

(4) Subject to the following provisions of this regulation, Part 6 of the Taxes Management Act 1970 (collection and recovery) shall apply with any necessary modifications to a decision under this regulation as if it were an assessment and as if the amount of funds determined were income tax charged on the employer.

(5) Where an amount of funds determined under this regulation relates to more than one employee, proceedings may be brought for the recovery of that amount without distinguishing the amounts making up that sum which the employer is liable to repay in respect of each employee and without specifying the employee in question, and the amount determined under this regulation shall be one cause of action or one matter of complaint for the purposes of proceedings under sections 65, 66 or 67 of the Taxes Management Act 1970.

(6) Nothing in paragraph (5) prevents the bringing of separate proceedings for the recovery of any amount which the employer is liable to repay in respect of each employee.

DEFINITIONS

"the Board"—see reg.2(1).
"income tax month"—see reg.2(1).
"income tax quarter"—see reg.2(1).
"statutory adoption pay"—see reg.2(1).
"statutory paternity pay"—see reg.2(1).
"tax year"—see reg.2(1).
"writing"—see reg.2(1).

Records to be maintained by employers

9.—Every employer shall maintain for three years after the end of a tax year in which he made payments of statutory paternity pay or statutory adoption pay to any employee of his a record of—
   (a) if [¹a period of payment of paternity pay or a period of payment of adoption pay] began in that year—

Statutory Paternity Pay and Statutory Adoption Pay Regulations 2002

(i) the date on which that period began; and
(ii) the evidence of entitlement to statutory paternity pay or statutory adoption pay provided by the employee pursuant to regulations made under section 171ZC(3)(c) or section 171ZL(8)(c) of the Contributions and Benefits Act;
(b) the weeks in that tax year in which statutory paternity pay or statutory adoption pay was paid to the employee and the amount paid in each week; and
(c) any week in that tax year which was within [¹a period of payment of paternity pay or a period of payment of adoption pay] but for which no payment of statutory paternity pay or statutory adoption pay was made to him and the reason no payment was made.

AMENDMENT

1. Statutory Paternity Pay (Amendment) Regulations 2024 (SI 2024/121) reg.30 (March 8, 2024).

DEFINITIONS

"adoption pay period"—see reg.2(1).
"the Contributions and Benefits Act"—see reg.2(1).
"paternity pay period"—see reg.2(1).
"statutory adoption pay"—see reg.2(1).
"statutory paternity pay"—see reg.2(1).
"tax year"—see reg.2(1).

Inspection of employers' records

10.—(1) Every employer, whenever called upon to do so by any authorised officer of the Board, shall produce the documents and records specified in paragraph (2) to that officer for inspection, at such time as that officer may reasonably require, at the prescribed place.
(2) The documents and records specified in this paragraph are—
(a) all wages sheets, deductions working sheets, records kept in accordance with regulation 9 and other documents and records whatsoever relating to the calculation or payment of statutory paternity pay or statutory adoption pay to his employees in respect of the years specified by such officer; or
(b) such of those wages sheets, deductions working sheets, or other documents and records as may be specified by the authorised officer.
(3) The "prescribed place" mentioned in paragraph (1) means—
(a) such place in Great Britain as the employer and the authorised officer may agree upon; or
(b) in default of such agreement, the place in Great Britain at which the documents and records referred to in paragraph (2)(a) are normally kept; or
(c) in default of such agreement and if there is no such place as is referred to in sub-paragraph (b) above, the employer's principal place of business in Great Britain.
(4) The authorised officer may—
(a) take copies of, or make extracts from, any document or record produced to him for inspection in accordance with paragraph (1);

(b) remove any document or record so produced if it appears to him to be necessary to do so, at a reasonable time and for a reasonable period.

(5) Where any document or record is removed in accordance with paragraph (4)(b), the authorised officer shall provide—
(a) a receipt for the document or record so removed; and
(b) a copy of the document or record, free of charge, within seven days, to the person by whom it was produced or caused to be produced where the document or record is reasonably required for the proper conduct of a business.

(6) Where a lien is claimed on a document produced in accordance with paragraph (1), the removal of the document under paragraph (4)(b) shall not be regarded as breaking the lien.

(7) Where records are maintained by computer, the person required to make them available for inspection shall provide the authorised officer with all facilities necessary for obtaining information from them.

DEFINITIONS

"the Board"—see reg.2(1).
"prescribed place"—see para.(3).
"statutory adoption pay"—see reg.2(1).
"statutory paternity pay"—see reg.2(1).

Provision of information relating to entitlement to statutory paternity pay or statutory adoption pay

11.—(1) Where an employer who has been given evidence of entitlement to statutory paternity pay or statutory adoption pay pursuant to regulations made under section 171ZC(3)(c) or section 171ZL(8)(c) of the Contributions and Benefits Act by a person who is or has been an employee decides that he has no liability to make payments of statutory paternity pay or statutory adoption pay to the employee, the employer shall furnish the employee with details of the decision and the reasons for it.

[³(2) An employer must provide to the employee the information specified in paragraph (2A) where the employer—
(a) has made one or more payments of statutory paternity pay or statutory adoption pay to the employee, but
(b) decides that it has no liability to make further payments to the employee because the employee has been detained in legal custody or sentenced to a term of imprisonment which was not suspended.

(2A) The information specified in this paragraph is—
(a) details of the employer's decision and the reasons for it;
(b) details of the week in respect of which a liability to pay statutory paternity pay or statutory adoption pay arose.]

(3) The employer shall—
(a) return to the employee any evidence provided by him as referred to in paragraph (1) [¹. . .]; [¹. . .]
(b) comply with the requirements imposed by paragraph (1) within 28 days of—
(i) in the case of entitlement to statutory paternity pay under section 171ZA(1) [¹or 171ZB(1)] of the Contributions and Benefits Act, the day the employee [³first gave notice under

6.28

Statutory Paternity Pay and Statutory Adoption Pay Regulations 2002

section 171ZC(1) of the week or weeks the employee expected there to be liability to pay statutory paternity pay] or the end of the fifteenth week before the expected week of birth, whichever is the later; or

(ii) in the case of entitlement to [¹. . .] statutory adoption pay under section 171ZL(1) of the Contributions and Benefits Act, the end of the seven-day period that starts on the date on which the adopter is notified of having been matched with the child;

(c) comply with the requirements imposed by paragraph (2) within seven days of being notified of the employee's detention or sentence.

(4) For the purposes of paragraph (3)(b)(ii), an adopter is notified of having been matched with a child on the date on which he receives notification, under regulation 11(2) of the Adoption Agencies Regulations 1983 or [¹ regulation 8(5) of the Adoption Agencies (Scotland) Regulations 2009] that an adoption agency has decided that he would be a suitable adoptive parent for the child.

[² *(4) For the purposes of paragraph (3)(b)(ii), an adopter is notified as having been matched with a child—*

(a) on the date that person receives notification of the adoption agency's decision under regulation 33(3)(a) of the Adoption Agencies Regulations 2005, regulation 28(3) of the Adoption Agencies (Wales) Regulations 2005 or regulation 8(5) of the Adoption Agencies (Scotland) Regulations 2009; or

(b) on the date on which that person receives notification in accordance with regulation 12B(2)(a) of the Adoption Agencies Regulations 2005.

(5) In this regulation "adoption agency" has the meaning given, in relation to England and Wales, by section 2 of the Adoption and Children Act 2002 and, in relation to Scotland, by section 119(1) of the Adoption and Children (Scotland) Act 2007.]

AMENDMENTS

1. Adoption and Children (Scotland) Act 2007 (Consequential Modifications) Order 2011 (SI 2011/1740) art.2 and Sch.1 para.31 (July 15, 2011).

2. Statutory Paternity Pay and Statutory Adoption Pay (Parental Orders and Prospective Adopters) Regulations 2014 (SI 2014/2934) reg.11 (December 1, 2014, but have effect only in relation to children matched with a person who is notified of having been matched on or after April 5, 2015).

3. Statutory Paternity Pay (Amendment) Regulations 2024 (SI 2024/121) reg.31 (March 8, 2024).

DEFINITIONS

"adopter"—see reg.2(1).
"adoption pay period"—see reg.2(1).
"the Contributions and Benefits Act"—see reg.2(1).
"statutory adoption pay"—see reg.2(1).
"statutory paternity pay"—see reg.2(1).

GENERAL NOTE

6.29 This regulation is modified for the purposes of adoptions from overseas by the Statutory Paternity Pay (Adoption) and Statutory Adoption Pay (Adoptions from Overseas) (Administration) Regulations 2003 (SI 2003/1192). The versions of paras (4) and (5) in italics have effect only in relation to children matched with a person who is notified of having been matched on or after April 5, 2015 (Statutory

Paternity Pay and Statutory Adoption Pay (Parental Orders and Prospective Adopters) Regulations 2014 (SI 2014/2934) reg.3).

Application for the determination of any issue arising as to, or in connection with, entitlement to statutory paternity pay or statutory adoption pay

12.—(1) An application for the determination of any issue arising as to, or in connection with, entitlement to statutory paternity pay or statutory adoption pay may be submitted to an officer of the Board by the employee concerned.

(2) Such an issue shall be decided by an officer of the Board only on the basis of such an application or on his own initiative.

DEFINITIONS

"the Board"—see reg.2(1).
"statutory adoption pay"—see reg.2(1).
"statutory paternity pay"—see reg.2(1).

Applications in connection with statutory paternity pay or statutory adoption pay

13.—(1) An application for the determination of any issue referred to in regulation 12 shall be made in a form approved for the purpose by the Board.
(2) Where such an application is made by an employee, it shall—
(a) be made to an officer of the Board within six months of the earliest day in respect of which entitlement to statutory paternity pay or statutory adoption pay is in issue;
(b) state the period in respect of which entitlement to statutory paternity pay or statutory adoption pay is in issue; and
(c) state the grounds (if any) on which the applicant's employer had denied liability for statutory paternity pay or statutory adoption pay in respect of the period specified in the application.

DEFINITIONS

"the Board"—see reg.2(1).
"statutory adoption pay"—see reg.2(1).
"statutory paternity pay"—see reg.2(1).

Provision of information

14.—(1) Any person specified in paragraph (2) shall, where information or documents are reasonably required from him to ascertain whether statutory paternity pay or statutory adoption pay is or was payable, furnish that information or those documents within 30 days of receiving a notification from an officer of the Board requesting such information or documents.

(2) The requirement to provide such information or documents applies to—
(a) any person claiming to be entitled to statutory paternity pay or statutory adoption pay;
(b) any person who is, or has been, the spouse [1, the civil partner] or partner of such a person as is specified in paragraph (a);

(c) any person who is, or has been, an employer of such a person as is specified in paragraph (a);
(d) any person carrying on an agency or other business for the introduction or supply to persons requiring them of persons available to do work or to perform services; and
(e) any person who is a servant or agent of any such person as is specified in paragraphs (a) to (d).

DEFINITIONS

"the Board"—see reg.2(1).
"statutory adoption pay"—see reg.2(1).
"statutory paternity pay"—see reg.2(1).

AMENDMENT

1. Civil Partnership Act 2004 (Amendments to Subordinate Legislation) Order 2005 (SI 2005/2114) art.2(17) and Sch.17 para.2 (December 5, 2005).

The Statutory Paternity Pay and Statutory Adoption Pay (Persons Abroad and Mariners) Regulations 2002

(SI 2002/2821) (AS AMENDED)

The Secretary of State, in exercise of the powers conferred upon her by virtue of sections 171ZI, 171ZJ(1), 171ZR and 171ZS(1) of the Social Security Contributions and Benefits Act 1992 and with the concurrence of the Treasury, by this instrument, which contains only provision made by virtue of sections 2 and 4 of the Employment Act 2002 and is made before the end of the period of 6 months from the coming into force of those enactments, hereby makes the following Regulations:

ARRANGEMENT OF REGULATIONS

1. Citation, commencement and interpretation.
2. Restriction on scope.
3. Treatment of persons in other EEA States as employees.
4. Treatment of certain persons absent from Great Britain as employees.
5. Entitlement to ordinary statutory paternity pay and additional statutory paternity pay where person has worked in an EEA State.
6. Entitlement to ordinary statutory adoption pay and additional statutory paternity paywhere person has worked in an EEA State.
7. Time for compliance with Parts XIIZA and XIIZB of the Act or regulations made under them.
8. Mariners.
9. Continental Shelf.
Schedule.

Citation, commencement and interpretation

1.—(1) These Regulations may be cited as the Statutory Paternity Pay and Statutory Adoption Pay (Persons Abroad and Mariners) Regulations 2002 and shall come into force on 8th December 2002.
(2) In these Regulations—

"the Act" means the Social Security Contributions and Benefits Act 1992;

[¹ [³...]]

[¹ [² "adopter", in relation to a child, means the person with whom a child is, or is expected to be, placed for adoption under the law of the United Kingdom;]]

"the Contributions Regulations" means the Social Security Contributions Regulations 2001;

"EEA" means European Economic Area;

"EEA Agreement" means the Agreement on the European Economic Area signed at Oporto on 2nd May 1992 as adjusted by Protocol signed at Brussels on 17th March 1993;

"EEA State" means a State which is a contracting party to the EEA Agreement;

[¹ "foreign-going ship" means any ship or vessel which is not a home-trade ship;]

"the General Regulations" means the Statutory Paternity Pay and Statutory Adoption Pay (General) Regulations 2002;

[¹ "home-trade ship" includes—
(a) every ship or vessel employed in trading or going within the following limits, that is to say, the United Kingdom (including for this purpose the Republic of Ireland), the Channel Islands, the Isle of Man, and the continent of Europe between the river Elbe and Brest inclusive;
(b) every fishing vessel not proceeding beyond the following limits—
on the South, Latitude 48°30'N,
on the West, Longitude 12°W, and
on the North, Latitude 61°N;

"mariner" means a person who is or has been in employment under a contract of service either as a master or member of the crew of any ship or vessel, or in any other capacity on board any ship or vessel where—
(a) the employment in that other capacity is for the purposes of that ship or vessel or her crew or any passengers or cargo or mails carried by the ship or vessel; and
(b) the contract is entered into in the United Kingdom with a view to its performance (in whole or in part) while the ship or vessel is on her voyage;

but does not include a person in so far as their employment is as a serving member of the forces;

"[³...] statutory paternity pay (adoption)" means statutory paternity pay payable in accordance with the provisions of Part 12ZA of the Act where the conditions specified in section 171ZB(2) of the Act are satisfied;

"[³...] statutory paternity pay (birth)" means statutory paternity pay payable in accordance with the provisions of Part 12ZA of the Act where the conditions specified in section 171ZA(2) of the Act are satisfied;

[² "placed for adoption" means—
(a) placed for adoption under the Adoption and Children Act 2002 or the Adoption and Children (Scotland) Act 2007; or
(b) placed in accordance with section 22C of the Children Act 1989 with a local authority foster parent who is also a prospective adopter;]

"serving member of the forces" means a person, other than one mentioned in Part 2 of the Schedule, who, being over the age of 16, is a member of any establishment or organisation specified in Part 1 of that Schedule (being a member who gives full pay service) but does not include any such person while absent on desertion;]

"week" means a period of 7 days beginning with Sunday.

[¹ [² (3) For the purposes of these Regulations—
(a) a person is matched with a child for adoption when an adoption agency decides that that person would be a suitable adoptive parent for the child;
(b) in a case where paragraph (a) applies, a person is notified as having been matched with a child on the date that person receives notification of the agency's decision, under regulation 33(3)(a) of the Adoption Agencies Regulations 2005, regulation 28(3) of the Adoption Agencies (Wales) Regulations 2005 or regulation 8(5) of the Adoption Agencies (Scotland) Regulations 2009;
(c) a person is also matched with a child for adoption when a decision has been made in accordance with regulation 22A of the Care Planning, Placement and Case Review (England) Regulations 2010 and an adoption agency has identified that person with whom the child is to be placed in accordance with regulation 12B of the Adoption Agencies Regulations 2005;
(d) in a case where paragraph (c) applies, a person is notified as having been matched with a child on the date on which that person receives notification in accordance with regulation 12B(2)(a) of the Adoption Agencies Regulations 2005.

(3A) The reference to "prospective adopter" in the definition of "placed for adoption" in paragraph (2) means a person who has been approved as suitable to adopt a child and has been notified of that decision in accordance with regulation 30B(4) of the Adoption Agencies Regulations 2005.

(3B) The reference to "adoption agency" in paragraph (3) has the meaning given, in relation to England and Wales, by section 2 of the Adoption and Children Act 2002 and in relation to Scotland, by section 119(1) of the Adoption and Children (Scotland) Act 2007.]

[¹ (4) For the purposes of these Regulations, the expressions "ship" and "ship or vessel" include hovercraft, except in regulation 8(3).]

AMENDMENTS

1. Statutory Paternity Pay and Statutory Adoption Pay (Persons Abroad and Mariners) Regulations 2002 (Amendment) Regulations 2010 (SI 2010/151) reg.3 (April 6, 2010).
2. Statutory Shared Parental Pay (Persons Abroad and Mariners) Regulations 2014 (SI 2014/3134) regs 12–14 (December 1, 2014).
3. Shared Parental Leave and Statutory Shared Parental Pay (Consequential Amendments to Subordinate Legislation) Order 2014 (SI 2014/3255) reg.13(2) (April 5, 2015).

GENERAL NOTE

6.35 These Regulations modify Pts XIIZA and XIIZB of the SSCBA 1992, which govern statutory paternity pay and statutory adoption pay respectively, in relation to persons abroad, those who work as mariners and persons who work on the Continental Shelf. They are modified in relation to adoptions from overseas by the

(SI 2002/2821 reg.1) (as amended)

Statutory Paternity Pay (Adoption) and Statutory Adoption Pay (Adoptions from Overseas) (Persons Abroad and Mariners) Regulations 2003 (SI 2003/1193).

Restriction on scope

2.—A person who would not be treated under regulation 32 of the General Regulations as an employee for the purposes of Parts 12ZA [1 ([3. . .] statutory paternity pay)] and 12ZB (statutory adoption pay) of the Act if his employment were in Great Britain shall not be treated as an employee under these Regulations.

AMENDMENTS

1. Statutory Paternity Pay and Statutory Adoption Pay (Persons Abroad and Mariners) Regulations 2002 (Amendment) Regulations 2010 (SI 2010/151) reg.4 (April 6, 2010).
2. Shared Parental Leave and Statutory Shared Parental Pay (Consequential Amendments to Subordinate Legislation) Order 2014 (SI 2014/3255) reg.13(3) (April 5, 2015).

DEFINITIONS

"the Act"—see reg.1(2).
"the General Regulations"—see reg.1(2).

Treatment of persons in other EEA States as employees

3.—A person who is—
(a) gainfully employed in an EEA State other than the United Kingdom in such circumstances that, if his employment were in Great Britain, he would be an employee for the purposes of Parts 12ZA and 12ZB of the Act, or a person treated as such an employee under regulation 32 of the General Regulations; and
(b) subject to the legislation of the United Kingdom under Council Regulation (EEC) No.1408/71 [1 as amended from time to time or Regulation (EC) 883/2004 of the European Parliament and of the Council of 29 April 2004 as amended from time to time on the coordination of social security systems],
notwithstanding that he is not employed in Great Britain, shall be treated as an employee for the purposes of Parts 12ZA and 12ZB of the Act.

AMENDMENT

1. Employment Rights (Amendment) (EU Exit) Regulations 2019 (SI 2019/535) reg.2(1) and Sch.1 para.16(c) Sch.1 para.11(c) (March 5, 2019).

DEFINITIONS

"the Act"—see reg.1(2).
"EEA"—see reg.1(2).
"EEA State"—see reg.1(2).
"the General Regulations"—see reg.1(2).

Treatment of certain persons absent from Great Britain as employees

4.—Subject to regulation 8(3), where a person, while absent from Great Britain for any purpose, is gainfully employed by an employer who is liable to pay secondary Class 1 contributions in respect of his employment under section 6 of the Act or regulation 146 of the Contributions Regulations, he shall be treated as an employee for the purposes of Parts 12ZA and 12ZB of the Act.

DEFINITIONS

"the Act"—see reg.1(2).
"the Contributions Regulations"—see *ibid.*

[¹ Entitlement to [² statutory paternity pay] where person has worked in an EEA State

5.—(1) A person who is an employee or treated as an employee under regulation 3 and who—
  (a) in the week immediately preceding the 14th week before the expected week of the child's birth was in employed earner's employment with an employer in Great Britain; and
  (b) had in any week within the period of 26 weeks immediately preceding that week been employed by the same employer in another EEA State,
shall be treated for the purposes of section 171ZA of the Act [² (entitlement to statutory paternity pay (birth))] [². . .] as having been employed in employed earner's employment in those weeks in which the person was so employed in the other EEA State.

(2) A person who is an employee or treated as an employee under regulation 3 and who—
  (a) in the week in which the adopter is notified of being matched with the child for purposes of adoption was in employed earner's employment with an employer in Great Britain; and
  (b) had in any week within the period of 26 weeks immediately preceding that week been employed by the same employer in another EEA State,
shall be treated for the purposes of section 171ZB of the Act [² (entitlement to statutory paternity pay (adoption))] [². . .] as having been employed in employed earner's employment in those weeks in which the person was so employed in the other EEA State.]

AMENDMENTS

1. Statutory Paternity Pay and Statutory Adoption Pay (Persons Abroad and Mariners) Regulations 2002 (Amendment) Regulations 2010 (SI 2010/151) reg.5 (April 6, 2010).
2. Shared Parental Leave and Statutory Shared Parental Pay (Consequential Amendments to Subordinate Legislation) Order 2014 (SI 2014/3255) reg.13(4) (April 5, 2015).

DEFINITIONS

"the Act"—see reg.1(2).
"adopter"—see reg.1(2).
"EEA"—see reg.1(2).
"EEA State"—see reg.1(2).
"statutory paternity pay (adoption)"—see reg.1(2).
"statutory paternity pay (birth)"—see reg.1(2).
"week"—see reg.1(2).

Entitlement to statutory adoption pay where person has worked in an EEA State

6.—A person who is an employee or treated as an employee under regulation 3 and who—
(a) in the week in which he is notified that he has been matched with the child for the purposes of adoption was in employed earner's employment with an employer in Great Britain; and
(b) had in any week within the period of 26 weeks immediately preceding that week been employed by the same employer in another EEA State,

shall be treated for the purposes of section 171ZL of the Act (entitlement to statutory adoption pay) as having been employed in employed earner's employment in those weeks in which he was so employed in the other EEA State.

DEFINITIONS

"the Act"—see reg.1(2).
"EEA"—see reg.1(2).
"EEA State"—see reg.1(2).
"week"—see reg.1(2).

Time for compliance with Parts 12ZA and 12ZB of the Act or regulations made under them

7.—Where—
(a) a person is outside the United Kingdom;
(b) Parts 12ZA or 12ZB of the Act or regulations made under them require any act to be done forthwith or on the happening of a certain event or within a specified time; and
(c) because the person is outside the United Kingdom he or his employer cannot comply with the requirement,

the person or the employer, as the case may be, shall be deemed to have complied with it if the act is performed as soon as reasonably practicable.

DEFINITION

"the Act"—see reg.1(2).

Mariners

8.—(1) [¹ . . .]
(2) A mariner engaged in employment on board a home-trade ship with an employer who has a place of business within the United Kingdom shall be treated as an employee for the purposes of Parts 12ZA and 12ZB of the Act, notwithstanding that he may not be employed in Great Britain.
(3) A mariner who is engaged in employment—
(a) on a foreign-going ship; or
(b) on a home-trade ship with an employer who does not have a place of business within the United Kingdom,

shall not be treated as an employee for the purposes of Parts 12ZA and 12ZB of the Act, notwithstanding that he may have been employed in Great Britain.

Statutory Paternity Pay and Statutory Adoption Pay Regulations 2002

AMENDMENT

1. Statutory Paternity Pay and Statutory Adoption Pay (Persons Abroad and Mariners) Regulations 2002 (Amendment) Regulations 2010 (SI 2010/151) reg.6 (April 6, 2010).

DEFINITIONS

"the Act"—see reg.1(2).
"the Contributions Regulations"—see reg.1(2).
"foreign-going ship"—see reg.1(2).
"home-trade ship"—see reg.1(2).
"mariner"—see reg.1(2).
"ship"—see reg.1(2).
"ship or vessel"—see reg.1(2).

Continental shelf

6.43

9.—(1) In this regulation—
"designated area" means any area which may from time to time be designated by Order in Council under section 1(7) of the Continental Shelf Act 1964 as an area within which the rights of the United Kingdom with respect to the seabed and subsoil and their natural resources may be exercised;
"prescribed employment" means any employment (whether under a contract of service or not) in a designated area in connection with continental shelf operations, as defined in section 120(2) of the Act.

(2) A person in prescribed employment shall be treated as an employee for the purposes of Parts 12ZA and 12ZB of the Act notwithstanding that he may not be employed in Great Britain.

DEFINITIONS

"the Act"—see reg.1(2).
"designated area"—see para.(1).
"prescribed employment"—see para.(1).

[¹ SCHEDULE

PART 1

Establishments and organisations

6.44

1. Any of the regular naval, military or air forces of the Crown.
2. Royal Fleet Reserve.
3. Royal Naval Reserve.
4. Royal Marines Reserve.
5. Army Reserve.
6. Territorial Army.
7. Royal Air Force Reserve.
8. Royal Auxiliary Air Force.
9. The Royal Irish Regiment, to the extent that its members are not members of any force falling within paragraph 1.

(SI 2002/2821 reg.10) (as amended)

PART 2

Establishments and organisations of which Her Majesty's Forces shall not consist

10.—Her Majesty's forces shall not be taken to consist of any of the establishments or organisations specified in Part 1 of this Schedule by virtue only of the employment in such establishment or organisation of the following persons—

(a) any person who is serving as a member of any naval force of Her Majesty's Forces and who (not having been an insured person under the National Insurance Act 1965 and not being a contributor under the Social Security Act 1975 or the Social Security Contributions and Benefits Act 1992) locally entered that force at an overseas base;

(b) any person who is serving as a member of any military force of Her Majesty's forces and who entered that force, or was recruited for that force outside the United Kingdom, and the depot of whose unit is situated outside the United Kingdom;

(c) any person who is serving as a member of any air force of Her Majesty's forces and who entered that force, or was recruited for that force, outside the United Kingdom, and is liable under the terms of his engagement to serve only in a specified part of the world outside the United Kingdom.]

6.45

AMENDMENT

1. Statutory Paternity Pay and Statutory Adoption Pay (Persons Abroad and Mariners) Regulations 2002 (Amendment) Regulations 2010 (SI 2010/151) reg.7 and Sch. (April 6, 2010).

The Statutory Paternity Pay and Statutory Adoption Pay (General) Regulations 2002

(SI 2002/2822) (AS AMENDED)

The Secretary of State, in exercise of the powers conferred on her by sections 171ZA(2)(a), 171ZB(2)(a), 171ZC(3)(a), (c), (d), (f) and (g), 171ZD(2) and (3), 171ZE(2)(a), (b)(i), (3), (7) and (8), 171ZG(3), 171ZJ(1), (3), (4), (7) and (8), 171ZL(8)(b) to (d), (f) and (g), 171ZM(2) and (3), 171ZN(2), (5) and (6), 171ZP(6), 171ZS(1), (3), (4), (7) and (8), and 175(4) of the Social Security Contributions and Benefits Act 1992 and section 5(1)(g), (i) and (p) of the Social Security Administration Act 1992 and with the concurrence of the Commissioners of Inland Revenue in so far as such concurrence is required, by this instrument, which contains only provision made by virtue of sections 2, 4 and 53 of and paragraphs 8 and 11 of Schedule 7 to the Employment Act 2002 and is made before the end of the period of 6 months from the coming into force of those enactments, hereby makes the following Regulations—

Statutory Paternity Pay and Statutory Adoption Pay (General) Regs 2002

ARRANGEMENT OF REGULATIONS

PART 1

Introduction

6.46
1. Citation and commencement.
2. Interpretation.
3. Application.

PART 2

Statutory paternity pay (birth)

4. Conditions of entitlement to statutory paternity pay (birth): relationship with newborn child and child's mother.
5. Modification of entitlement conditions: early birth.
6. Options in respect of periods of payment of statutory paternity pay (birth).
6A. Qualifying period for statutory paternity pay (birth).
6B. Notice and evidence requirements for statutory paternity pay (birth).
7. Additional notice requirements for statutory paternity pay (birth).
8. Repealed.
9. Repealed.
10. Entitlement to statutory paternity pay (birth) where there is more than one employer.

PART 3

Statutory paternity pay (adoption)

11. Conditions of entitlement to statutory paternity pay (adoption): relationship with child and with person with whom the child is placed for adoption.
12. Options in respect of periods of payment of statutory paternity pay (adoption).
12A. Qualifying period for statutory paternity pay (adoption).
12B. Notice and evidence requirements for statutory paternity pay (adoption).
13. Additional notice requirements for statutory paternity pay (adoption).
14. Repealed.
15. Repealed.
16. Entitlement to statutory paternity pay (adoption) where there is more than one employer.

PART 4

Statutory paternity pay: provisions applicable to both statutory paternity pay (birth) and statutory paternity pay (adoption)

16A. Change in circumstances.
17. Work during a period of payment of statutory paternity pay.
18. Cases where there is no liability to pay statutory paternity pay.
19. Statutory paternity pay and contractual remuneration.
20. Avoidance of liability for statutory paternity pay.

(SI 2002/2822) (as amended)

PART 5

Statutory adoption pay

21. Adoption pay period.
22. Adoption pay period in cases where adoption is disrupted.
23. Additional notice requirements for statutory adoption pay.
24. Evidence of entitlement to statutory adoption pay.
25. Entitlement to statutory adoption pay where there is more than one employer.
26. Work during an adoption pay period.
27. Cases where there is no liability to pay statutory adoption pay.
27A. Working for not more than 10 days during an adoption pay period.
28. Statutory adoption pay and contractual remuneration.
29. Termination of employment before start of adoption pay period.
30. Avoidance of liability for statutory adoption pay.

PART 6

Statutory paternity pay and statutory adoption pay: provisions applicable to both statutory paternity pay and statutory adoption pay

31. Introductory.
32. Treatment of persons as employees.
33. Continuous employment.
34. Continuous employment and unfair dismissal.
35. Continuous employment and stoppages of work.
36. Change of employer.
37. Reinstatement after service with the armed forces, etc.
38. Treatment of one or more employers or two or more contracts of service as one.
39. Meaning of "earnings".
40. Normal weekly earnings.
41. Payment of statutory paternity pay and statutory adoption pay.
42. Time when statutory paternity pay and statutory adoption pay are to be paid.
43. Liability of the Board to pay statutory paternity pay or statutory adoption pay.
44. Liability of the Board to pay statutory paternity or statutory adoption pay in cases of legal custody or imprisonment.
45. Payments by the Board.
46. Persons unable to act.
47. Service of notices by post.

PART 1

INTRODUCTION

Citation and commencement

1.—These Regulations may be cited as the Statutory Paternity Pay and Statutory Adoption Pay (General) Regulations 2002 and shall come into force on 8th December 2002.

6.47

Interpretation

2.—(1) In these Regulations—

"the Act" means the Social Security Contributions and Benefits Act 1992;

"adopter", in relation to a child, means a person who has been matched with the child for adoption;

"adoption agency" has the meaning given, in relation to England and Wales, by section 1(4) of the Adoption Act 1976 and in relation to Scotland, by [¹ section 119(1) of the Adoption and Children (Scotland) Act 2007];

"the Board" means the Commissioners of Inland Revenue;

"the Contributions Regulations" means the Social Security (Contributions) Regulations 2001;

"expected week", in relation to the birth of a child, means the week, beginning with midnight between Saturday and Sunday, in which it is expected that the child will be born;

[³"returned after being placed for adoption" means—

(a) returned under sections 31 to 35 of the Adoption and Children Act 2002;

(b) in Scotland, returned to the adoption agency, adoption society or nominated person in accordance with section 25(6) of the Adoption and Children (Scotland) Act 2007; or

(c) where the child is placed in accordance with section 22C of the Children Act 1989, returned to the adoption agency following a termination of the placement;]

"statutory paternity pay (adoption)" means statutory paternity pay payable in accordance with the provisions of Part 12ZA of the Act where the conditions specified in section 171ZB(2) of the Act are satisfied;

"statutory paternity pay (birth)" means statutory paternity pay payable in accordance with the provisions of Part 12ZA of the Act where the conditions specified in section 171ZA(2) of the Act are satisfied.

(2) For the purposes of these Regulations—

(a) a person is matched with a child for adoption when an adoption agency decides that that person would be a suitable adoptive parent for the child, either individually or jointly with another person; and

(b) a person is notified of having been matched with a child on the date on which he receives notification of the agency's decision, under regulation 11(2) of the Adoption Agencies Regulations 1983 or [¹ regulation 8(5) of the Adoption Agencies (Scotland) Regulations 2009].

[² *(2) For the purposes of these Regulations—*

(a) a person is matched with a child for adoption when an adoption agency decides that that person would be a suitable adoptive parent for the child;

(b) in a case where paragraph (a) applies, a person is notified as having been matched with a child on the date that person receives notification of the agency's decision, under regulation 33(3)(a) of the Adoption Agencies Regulations 2005, regulation 28(3) of the Adoption Agencies (Wales) Regulations 2005 or regulation 8(5) of the Adoption Agencies (Scotland) Regulations 2009;

(c) a person is also matched with a child for adoption when a decision is has been made in accordance with regulation 22A of the Care Planning, Placement

and Case Review (England) Regulations 2010 and an adoption agency has identified that person with whom the child is to be placed in accordance with regulation 12B of the Adoption Agencies Regulations 2005.
  (d) *in a case where paragraph (c) applies, a person is notified as having been matched with a child on the date on which that person receives notification in accordance with regulation 12B(2)(a) of the Adoption Agencies Regulations 2005.*
 (3) *A reference (however expressed) in these Regulations to "placed for adoption" means—*
  (a) *placed for adoption under the Adoption and Children Act 2002 or the Adoption and Children (Scotland) Act 2007; or*
  (b) *placed in accordance with section 22C of the Children Act 1989 with a local authority foster parent who is also a prospective adopter.*
 (4) *The reference to "prospective adopter" in paragraph (3) means a person who has been approved as suitable to adopt a child and has been notified of that decision in accordance with regulation 30B(4) of the Adoption Agencies Regulations 2005.]*

AMENDMENTS

1. Adoption and Children (Scotland) Act 2007 (Consequential Modifications) Order 2011 (SI 2011/1740) art.2 and Sch.1 para.32(2) (July 15, 2011).

2. *Statutory Paternity Pay and Statutory Adoption Pay (Parental Orders and Prospective Adopters) Regulations 2014 (SI 2014/2934) reg.4 (December 1, 2014, but have effect only in relation to children matched with a person who is notified of having been matched on or after April 5, 2015).*

3. Statutory Paternity Pay (Amendment) Regulations 2024 (SI 2024/121) reg.8 (March 8, 2024).

GENERAL NOTE

The versions of paras (2) to (4) in italics have effect only in relation to children matched with a person who is notified of having been matched on or after April 5, 2015 (Statutory Paternity Pay and Statutory Adoption Pay (Parental Orders and Prospective Adopters) Regulations 2014 (SI 2014/2934) reg.3).

6.49

Application

3.—(1) Subject to the provisions of Part 12ZA of the Act (statutory paternity pay) and of these Regulations, there is entitlement to—
  (a) statutory paternity pay (birth) in respect of children—
    (i) born on or after 6th April 2003; or
    (ii) whose expected week of birth begins on or after that date;
  (b) statutory paternity pay (adoption) in respect of children—
    (i) matched with a person who is notified of having been matched on or after 6th April 2003; or
    (ii) placed for adoption on or after that date.
 (2) Subject to the provisions of Part 12ZB of the Act (statutory adoption pay) and of these Regulations, there is entitlement to statutory adoption pay in respect of children—
  (a) matched with a person who is notified of having been matched on or after 6th April 2003; or
  (b) placed for adoption on or after that date.

6.50

DEFINITIONS
"the Act"—see reg.2(1).
"expected week"—see reg.2(1).
"statutory paternity pay (adoption)"—see reg.2(1).
"statutory paternity pay (birth)"—see reg.2(1).

PART 2

STATUTORY PATERNITY PAY (BIRTH)

Conditions of entitlement to statutory paternity pay (birth): relationship with newborn child and child's mother

6.51   **4.**—The conditions prescribed under section 171ZA(2)(a) of the Act are those prescribed in regulation 4(2)(b) and (c) of the Paternity and Adoption Leave Regulations 2002.

DEFINITION
"the Act"—see reg.2(1).

GENERAL NOTE

6.52   See the annotation to SSCBA 1992 s.171ZA.

Modification of entitlement conditions: early birth

6.53   **5.**—Where a person does not meet the conditions specified in section 171ZA(2)(b) to (d) of the Act because the child's birth occurred earlier than the 14th week before the expected week of the birth, it shall have effect as if, for the conditions there set out, there were substituted the conditions that—
    (a) the person would, but for the date on which the birth occurred, have been in employed earner's employment with an employer for a continuous period of at least 26 weeks ending with the week immediately preceding the 14th week before the expected week of the child's birth;
    (b) his normal weekly earnings for the period of 8 weeks ending with the week immediately preceding the week in which the child is born are not less than the lower earnings limit in force under section 5(1)(a) of the Act immediately before the commencement of the week in which the child is born.

DEFINITIONS
"the Act"—see reg.2(1).
"expected week"—see reg.2(1).

[¹Options in respect of periods of payment of statutory paternity pay (birth)

6.54   **6.**—(1) Within the qualifying period set out in regulation 6A, a person entitled to statutory paternity pay (birth) may choose a period of payment of statutory paternity pay to begin on—

(SI 2002/2822 reg.6) (as amended)

(a) the date on which the child is born or, where the person is at work on that day, the following day;
(b) the date falling such number of days after the date on which the child is born as the person may specify;
(c) a predetermined date, specified by the person, which is later than the first day of the expected week of the child's birth.

(2) A person may choose for statutory paternity pay (birth) to be paid in respect of—
(a) a single period of either one week or two weeks, or
(b) two non-consecutive periods of a week each.]

AMENDMENT

1. Statutory Paternity Pay (Amendment) Regulations 2024 (SI 2024/121) reg.9 (March 8, 2024).

[¹Qualifying period for statutory paternity pay (birth)

6A. Subject to regulation 16A, the qualifying period for the purposes of section 171ZE(3) of the Act (period within which a period of payment of statutory paternity pay must occur) is a period which begins on the date of the child's birth and ends—
(a) except in the case referred to in sub-paragraph (b), 52 weeks after that date, or
(b) in a case where the child is born before the first day of the expected week of its birth, 52 weeks after that day.]

AMENDMENT

1. Statutory Paternity Pay (Amendment) Regulations 2024 (SI 2024/121) reg.9 (March 8, 2024).

[¹Notice and evidence requirements for statutory paternity pay (birth)

6B.—(1) A person must provide evidence of entitlement to statutory paternity pay (birth) by providing in writing to whoever will be liable to pay it—
(a) the information specified in paragraph (2), and
(b) the declarations specified in paragraph (3).

(2) he information referred to in paragraph (1)(a) is as follows—
(a) the name of the person claiming statutory paternity pay (birth);
(b) the expected week of the child's birth.

(3) The declarations referred to in paragraph (1)(b) are—
(a) a declaration that the person satisfies the conditions prescribed in regulation 4, and
(b) a declaration that section 171ZE(4) of the Act does not apply.

(4) The information referred to in paragraph (2) and the declaration referred to in paragraph (3)(a) must be provided—
(a) in or before the 15th week before the expected week of the child's birth, or
(b) in a case where it was not reasonably practicable for the person to provide it in that period, as soon as is reasonably practicable.

Statutory Paternity Pay and Statutory Adoption Pay (General) Regs 2002

(5) The notice provided for in section 171ZC(1) of the Act (notice to be given stating the week or weeks in respect of which payments are to be made) must be given to whoever will be liable to pay statutory paternity pay (birth) at least 28 days before—
  (a) the first day of the expected week of the child's birth, where the option in regulation 6(1)(a) is chosen;
  (b) the date falling the specified number of days after the first day of the expected week of the child's birth, where the option in regulation 6(1)(b) is chosen;
  (c) the predetermined date, where the option in regulation 6(1)(c) is chosen;
or, if it is not reasonably practicable to do so, as soon as is reasonably practicable.

(6) On each occasion that a notice is given under paragraph (5), the declaration referred to in paragraph (3)(b) must be provided at the same time.

(7) Where a notice has previously been given under paragraph (5) or this paragraph, or under regulation 7(2), a notice of variation in writing may be given to the person who will be liable to pay statutory paternity pay which—
  (a) cancels the period of payment of statutory paternity pay specified in that notice, or
  (b) varies that period by choosing an option under regulation 6.

(8) Where the notice under paragraph (5) specifies a period of two weeks in respect of which statutory paternity pay is to be paid, notice of variation may be given in relation to either one or both of those weeks, regardless of whether those weeks are consecutive or non-consecutive.

(9) A notice of variation under paragraph (7) must be given by whichever is the earlier of at least 28 days before—
  (a) the original day or date referred to in paragraph (10)(a), or
  (b) the new day or date referred to in paragraph (10)(b),
or, if it is not reasonably practicable to do so, as soon as is reasonably practicable.

(10) For the purposes of—
  (a) paragraph (9)(a), where a notice has previously been given under either paragraph (5) or (7), the original day or date is—
    (i) the first day of the expected week of the child's birth, where the option in regulation 7(1)(a) was chosen in that notice;
    (ii) the specified number of days after the first day of the expected week of the child's birth, where the option in regulation 7(1)(b) was chosen in that notice;
    (iii) the predetermined date specified in that notice, where the option in regulation 7(1)(c) was chosen;
  (b) paragraph (9)(b), the new day or date is—
    (i) the first day of the expected week of the child's birth, where the option in regulation 7(1)(a) is chosen in the notice of variation;
    (ii) the date falling the specified number of days after the first day of the expected week of the child's birth, where the option in regulation 7(1)(b) is chosen in the notice of variation;
    (iii) the predetermined date specified in that notice, where the option in regulation 7(1)(c) is chosen in the notice of variation.

(11) The person who is entitled to statutory paternity pay (birth) must inform the person who is liable to pay it of the date of the child's birth if—

(SI 2002/2822 reg. 6B) (as amended)

(a) that person so requests, and
(b) that date has not previously been provided to that person,
within 28 days of the request, or as soon as is reasonably practicable thereafter.]

AMENDMENT

1. Statutory Paternity Pay (Amendment) Regulations 2024 (SI 2024/121) reg.9 (March 8, 2024).

[¹Additional notice requirements for statutory paternity pay (birth)

7.—(1) Where a person has given notice in accordance with regulation 6B(5)(a) or (b), the person must give further notice to the person liable to pay statutory paternity pay, as soon as is reasonably practicable after the child's birth, of the date the child was born.

(2) In a case where—
(a) a person has given notice in accordance with regulation 6B(5)(c), and
(b) the date of the child's birth is later than the date specified in that notice as the date on which a period of payment is to begin,
the person must vary the date on which the period of payment is to begin by giving notice to the person liable to pay statutory paternity pay (birth), as soon as is reasonably practicable, that the period in respect of which statutory paternity pay is to be paid will begin on a date different from that originally chosen.

(3) That date may be any date chosen in accordance with paragraph (1) of regulation 6.

(4) Where a notice is given under regulation 6B(7) or paragraph (2) above which varies the dates of a period of payment, a declaration under regulation 6B(3)(b) in relation to that period must be given at the same time as that notice.

(5) Paragraph (2) does not apply in circumstances where regulation 16A(5) applies.]

6.57

AMENDMENT

1. Statutory Paternity Pay (Amendment) Regulations 2024 (SI 2024/121) reg.9 (March 8, 2024).

Qualifying period for statutory paternity pay (birth)

8.—[¹...]

AMENDMENT

1. Statutory Paternity Pay (Amendment) Regulations 2024 (SI 2024/121) reg.9 (March 8, 2024).

Evidence of entitlement to statutory paternity pay (birth)

9.—[¹...]

AMENDMENT

1. Statutory Paternity Pay (Amendment) Regulations 2024 (SI 2024/121) reg.9 (March 8, 2024).

Entitlement to statutory paternity pay (birth) where there is more than one employer

6.58

10.—Statutory paternity pay (birth) shall be payable to a person in respect of a statutory pay week during any part of which he works only for an employer—
(a) who is not liable to pay him statutory paternity pay (birth); and
(b) for whom he has worked in the week immediately preceding the 14th week before the expected week of the child's birth.

DEFINITIONS

"expected week"—see reg.2(1).
"statutory paternity pay (birth)"—see reg.2(1).

PART 3

STATUTORY PATERNITY PAY (ADOPTION)

Conditions of entitlement to statutory paternity pay (adoption): relationship with child and with person with whom the child is placed for adoption

6.59

11.—(1) The conditions prescribed under section 171ZB(2)(a) of the Act are that a person—
(a) is married to [², the civil partner] or the partner of a child's adopter (or in a case where there are two adopters, married to [², the civil partner] or the partner of the other adopter); and
(b) has, or expects to have, the main responsibility (apart from the responsibility of the child's adopter, or in a case where there two adopters, together with the other adopter) for the upbringing of the child.

(2) For the purposes of paragraph (1), "partner" means a person (whether of a different sex or the same sex) who lives with the adopter and the child in an enduring family relationship but is not a relative of the adopter of a kind specified in paragraph [¹(2A)].

[¹(2A) The relatives of the adopter referred to in paragraph (2) are the adopter's parent, grandparent, sister, brother, aunt or uncle.]

(3) References to relationships in paragraph [¹(2A)]—
(a) are to relationships of the full blood or half blood, or, in the case of an adopted person, such of those relationships as would exist but for the adoption; and
(b) include the relationship of a child with his adoptive, or former adoptive parents but do not include any other adoptive relationships.

AMENDMENTS

1. Statutory Paternity Pay and Statutory Adoption Pay (Amendment) Regulations 2004 (SI 2004/488) reg.2 (April 6, 2004).
2. Civil Partnership Act 2004 (Amendments to Subordinate Legislation) Order 2005 (SI 2005/2114) art.2(17) and Sch.17 para.3 (December 5, 2005).

DEFINITIONS

"the Act"—see reg.2(1).
"adopter"—see reg.2(1).
"partner"—see para.(2).

(SI 2002/2822 reg.11) (as amended)

GENERAL NOTE

This regulation sets out the prescribed conditions for the purposes of SSCBA 1992 s.171ZB(2)(a), i.e. for the payment of statutory paternity pay in the case of adoption. The claimant must either be the adoptive parent's spouse or partner and expect to have the main responsibility (other than the adopter) for the child's upbringing. The definition of "partner" in para.(2) is innovative, in that it recognises that partners may be in a heterosexual or same sex relationship. The only qualifications are that the partner lives with the adopter and the child in "an enduring family relationship" and is not a relative of the adopter as defined in paras (2A) and (3). Guidance on the notion of "an enduring family relationship" in the context of a same-sex relationship might be sought in the decisions in *Fitzpatrick v Sterling Housing Association* [2001] A.C. 27 and *Ghaidan v Godin-Mendoza* [2004] UKHL 30; [2004] 3 W.L.R. 113. This explicit statutory recognition in English law of parity of treatment for heterosexual and same-sex couples pre-dated the Civil Partnership Act 2004.

6.60

[¹Options in respect of periods of payment of statutory paternity pay (adoption)

12.—(1) Within the qualifying period set out in regulation 12A, a person entitled to statutory paternity pay (adoption) may choose a period of payment of statutory paternity pay to begin on—
  (a) the date on which the child is placed with the adopter or, where the person is at work on that day, the following day;
  (b) the date falling such number of days after the date on which the child is placed with the adopter as the person may specify;
  (c) a predetermined date, specified by the person, which is later than the date on which the child is expected to be placed with the adopter.

(2) A person may choose for statutory paternity pay (adoption) to be paid in respect of—
  (a) a single period of either one week or two weeks, or
  (b) two non-consecutive periods of a week each.]

6.61

AMENDMENT

1. Statutory Paternity Pay (Amendment) Regulations 2024 (SI 2024/121) reg.10 (March 8, 2024).

Qualifying period for statutory paternity pay (adoption)

[¹**12A.** Subject to regulation 16A, the qualifying period for the purposes of section 171ZE(3) of the Act (period within which a period of payment of statutory paternity pay must occur) is a period of 52 weeks beginning with the date of the child's placement for adoption.]

6.62

AMENDMENT

1. Statutory Paternity Pay (Amendment) Regulations 2024 (SI 2024/121) reg.10 (March 8, 2024).

Notice and evidence requirements for statutory paternity pay (adoption)

[¹**12B.**—(1) A person must provide evidence of entitlement to statutory paternity pay (adoption) by providing in writing to whoever will be liable to pay it—
  (a) the information specified in paragraph (2), and

6.63

(b) the declarations specified in paragraph (3).

(2) The information referred to in paragraph (1)(a) is as follows—
   (a) the name of the person claiming statutory paternity pay (adoption);
   (b) the date the adopter was notified of having been matched with the child for the purposes of adoption;
   (c) the date on which the child is expected to be placed for adoption or, where the child has already been placed for adoption, the date of placement of the child.

(3) The declarations referred to in paragraph (1)(b) are—
   (a) a declaration that the person satisfies the conditions prescribed in regulation 11(1);
   (b) a declaration that the person has elected to receive statutory paternity pay (adoption), and not statutory adoption pay under Part 12ZB of the Act;
   (c) a declaration that section 171ZE(4) of the Act does not apply.

(4) The information referred to in paragraph (2) and the declarations referred to in sub-paragraphs (a) and (b) of paragraph (3) must be provided—
   (a) no more than seven days after the date on which the adopter is notified of having been matched with the child, or
   (b) in a case where it was not reasonably practicable for the person to provide it in that period, as soon as is reasonably practicable.

(5) The notice provided for in section 171ZC(1) of the Act (notice to be given stating the week or weeks in respect of which payments are to be made) must be given to whoever will be liable to pay statutory paternity pay (adoption)—
   (a) no more than seven days after the date on which the adopter is notified of having been matched with the child, or
   (b) in a case where it was not reasonably practicable for the person to provide it in that period, as soon as is reasonably practicable.

(6) The declaration referred to in paragraph (3)(c) must be provided at the same time that the notice is given under paragraph (5).

(7) Where notice has previously been given under paragraph (5) or this paragraph or under regulation 13(2), a notice of variation in writing may be given to the person who will be liable to pay statutory paternity pay which—
   (a) cancels the period of payment of statutory paternity pay specified in that notice, or
   (b) varies that period by choosing an option under regulation 12.

(8) Where the notice under paragraph (5) specifies a period of two weeks in respect of which statutory paternity pay is to be paid, notice of variation may be given in relation to either one or both of those weeks, regardless of whether those weeks are consecutive or non-consecutive.

(9) A notice of variation under paragraph (7) must be given by whichever is the earlier of at least 28 days before—
   (a) the original day or date referred to in paragraph (10)(a), or
   (b) the new day or date referred to in paragraph (10)(b),

or, if it is not reasonably practicable to do so, as soon as is reasonably practicable.

(10) For the purposes of—
   (a) paragraph (9)(a), where a notice has previously been given under either paragraph (5) or (7), the original day or date is—
      (i) the date provided under paragraph (2)(c) above as the date on which the child is expected to be placed for adoption, where the option in regulation 12(1)(a) was chosen in that notice;

(SI 2002/2822 reg.2B) (as amended)

  (ii) the date falling the specified number of days after the date provided under paragraph (2)(c) above as the date on which the child is expected to be placed for adoption, where the option in regulation 12(1)(b) was chosen in that notice;

  (iii) the predetermined date specified in that notice, where the option in regulation 12(1)(c) was chosen;

(b) paragraph (9)(b), the new day or date is—

  (i) the date provided under paragraph (2)(c) above as the date on which the child is expected to be placed for adoption, where the option in regulation 12(1)(a) is chosen in the notice of variation;

  (ii) the date falling the specified number of days after the date provided under paragraph (2)(c) above as the date on which the child is expected to be placed for adoption, where the option in regulation 12(1)(b) is chosen in the notice of variation;

  (iii) the predetermined date specified in the notice of variation, where the option in regulation 12(1)(c) is chosen;

(11) The person who is entitled to statutory paternity pay (adoption) must inform the person who is liable to pay it of the date of the child's placement if—

(a) that person so requests, and

(b) that date has not previously been provided to that person,

within 28 days of the request, or as soon as is reasonably practicable thereafter.]

AMENDMENT

1. Statutory Paternity Pay (Amendment) Regulations 2024 (SI 2024/121) reg.10 (March 8, 2024).

[¹Additional notice requirements for statutory paternity pay (adoption)

13.—(1) Where a person has chosen an option in regulation 12(1)(a) or (b) in a notice of a period of payment of statutory paternity pay, the person must give further notice to the person liable to pay statutory paternity pay, as soon as is reasonably practicable, of the date on which the placement occurred.

(2) In a case where—

(a) a person has chosen the option in regulation 12(1)(c) in a notice of a period of payment of statutory paternity pay, and

(b) the child is placed for adoption later than the date specified in that notice,

the person must vary the date on which the period of payment is to begin by giving notice to the person liable to pay statutory paternity pay (adoption), as soon as is reasonably practicable, that the period in respect of which statutory paternity pay is to be paid will begin on a date different from that originally chosen.

(3) That date may be any date chosen in accordance with paragraph (1) of regulation 12.

(4) Where a notice is given under regulation 12B(7) or paragraph (2) above which varies the dates of a period of payment, a declaration under regulation 12B(3)(c) in relation to that period must be given at the same time as that notice.

(5) Paragraph (2) does not apply in circumstances where regulation 16A(5) applies.]

6.64

Statutory Paternity Pay and Statutory Adoption Pay (General) Regs 2002

AMENDMENT

1. Statutory Paternity Pay (Amendment) Regulations 2024 (SI 2024/121) reg.10 (March 8, 2024).

Qualifying period for statutory paternity pay (adoption)

14.—[¹...]

AMENDMENT

1. Statutory Paternity Pay (Amendment) Regulations 2024 (SI 2024/121) reg.10 (March 8, 2024).

Evidence of entitlement to statutory paternity pay (adoption)

15.—[¹...]

AMENDMENT

1. Statutory Paternity Pay (Amendment) Regulations 2024 (SI 2024/121) reg.10 (March 8, 2024).

Entitlement to statutory paternity pay (adoption) where there is more than one employer

6.65

16.—Statutory paternity pay (adoption) shall be payable to a person in respect of a statutory pay week during any part of which he works only for an employer—
  (a) who is not liable to pay him statutory paternity pay (adoption); and
  (b) for whom he has worked in the week in which the adopter is notified of being matched with the child.

DEFINITIONS

"adopter"—see reg.2(1).
"statutory paternity pay (adoption)"—see reg.2(1).

PART 4

STATUTORY PATERNITY PAY: PROVISIONS APPLICABLE TO BOTH STATUTORY PATERNITY PAY (BIRTH) AND STATUTORY PATERNITY PAY (ADOPTION)

[¹Change in circumstances

6.66

16A.—(1) This regulation applies where a person is otherwise entitled to statutory paternity pay in respect of a child but a relevant event, as specified in paragraph (2), occurs.
  (2) A relevant event as referred to in paragraph (1) occurs when—
    (a) the person is notified that the child will no longer be placed with the person with whom the child was to be placed for adoption, or
    (b) the child—
      (i) dies, or
      (ii) is returned after being placed for adoption.
  (3) In a case where this regulation applies, the qualifying period for the purposes of section 171ZE(3) of the Act (period within which a period of payment of statutory paternity pay must occur) ends after the end of a

(SI 2002/2822 reg. 6A) (as amended)

period of eight weeks following the end of the relevant week specified in paragraph (4), except in the circumstances mentioned in paragraph (5).

(4) The relevant week referred to in paragraph (3) is—
(a) in a case falling within paragraph (2)(a), the week during which the person with whom the child was to be placed for adoption is notified that the placement will not be made;
(b) in a case falling within paragraph (2)(b)(i), the week during which the child dies;
(c) in a case falling within paragraph (2)(b)(ii), the week during which the child is returned.

(5) Where the person has complied with the requirements in regulation 6B (notice and evidential requirements for statutory paternity pay (birth)) or regulation 12B (notice and evidential requirements for statutory paternity pay (adoption)), as the case may be, the person will remain entitled to payment in respect of any period of payment which has been specified in a notice given, before the day on which the relevant event occurs, under whichever of those regulations is relevant.

(6) Where paragraph (5) applies, no further notices may be served under regulation 6B or 12B other than a notice to cancel a period of payment specified in a notice already given under regulations 6B, 7, 12B or 13.

(7) In this regulation—
(a) "week" means the period of seven days beginning with Sunday;
(b) references to the death of a child are to be read, in relation to a child stillborn after twenty-four weeks of pregnancy, as references to the birth of the child.]

AMENDMENT

1. Statutory Paternity Pay (Amendment) Regulations 2024 (SI 2024/121) reg.11 (March 8, 2024).

[¹Work during a period of payment of statutory paternity pay

17.—(1) Where a person (P) works for an employer falling within—
(a) paragraph (a) but not paragraph (b) of regulation 10, or
(b) paragraph (a) but not paragraph (b) of regulation 16
for any part of a period which is specified by P in a notice under regulation 6B, 7, 12B or 13, P must notify the person liable to pay statutory paternity pay of the fact of that work within seven days of the first day during which P does such work.

(2) The notification mentioned in paragraph (1) must be in writing, if the person who has been liable to pay statutory paternity pay so requests.]

6.67

AMENDMENT

1. Statutory Paternity Pay (Amendment) Regulations 2024 (SI 2024/121) reg.12 (March 8, 2024).

Cases where there is no liability to pay statutory paternity pay

18.— [¹(1)] There shall be no liability to pay statutory paternity pay in respect of any week—
(a) during any part of which the person entitled to it is entitled to statutory sick pay under Part 11 of the Act;
(b) following that in which the person claiming it has died; or

6.68

[¹(c) during any part of which the person entitled to it is detained in legal custody or sentenced to a term of imprisonment, except where that sentence is suspended (but see paragraph (2).]

[¹(2) There is liability to pay statutory paternity pay in respect of any week during any part of which the person who is entitled to that pay is detained in legal custody where that person—
   (a) is released subsequently without charge,
   (b) is subsequently found not guilty of any offence and is released, or
   (c) is convicted of an offence but does not receive a custodial sentence.]

AMENDMENT

1. Statutory Paternity Pay (Amendment) Regulations 2024 (SI 2024/121) reg.13 (March 8, 2024).

DEFINITION

"the Act"—see reg.2(1).

Statutory paternity pay and contractual remuneration

6.69   **19.**—For the purposes of section 171ZG(1) and (2) of the Act, the payments which are to be treated as contractual remuneration are sums payable under a contract of service—
   (a) by way of remuneration;
   (b) for incapacity for work due to sickness or injury;
   (c) by reason of the birth or adoption of a child.

DEFINITION

"the Act"—see reg.2(1).

Avoidance of liability for statutory paternity pay

6.70   **20.**—(1) A former employer shall be liable to make payments of statutory paternity pay to a former employee in any case where the employee had been employed for a continuous period of at least 8 weeks and his contract of service was brought to an end by the former employer solely, or mainly, for the purpose of avoiding liability for statutory paternity pay.

(2) In a case falling within paragraph (1)—
   (a) the employee shall be treated as if he had been employed for a continuous period ending with the child's birth or, as the case may be, the placement of the child for adoption;
   (b) his normal weekly earnings shall be calculated by reference to his normal weekly earnings for the period of 8 weeks ending with the last day in respect of which he was paid under his former contract of service.

PART 5

Statutory adoption pay

Adoption pay period

6.71   **21.**—(1) Subject to paragraph (2), a person entitled to statutory adoption pay may choose the adoption pay period to begin—

(SI 2002/2822 reg.21) (as amended)

(a) on the date on which the child is placed with him for adoption or, where he is at work on that day, on the following day;
(b) subject to paragraph (2), on a predetermined date, specified by him, which is no more than 14 days before the date on which the child is expected to be placed with him and no later than that date.

(2) In a case where statutory adoption pay is payable in respect of a child matched with an adopter who is notified of having been matched before 6th April 2003, the statutory adoption pay period shall begin on a predetermined date which is—
(a) on or after 6th April 2003; and
(b) no more than 14 days before the date on which the child is expected to be placed with the adopter.

(3) Subject to paragraph (4), where the choice made is that mentioned in sub-paragraph (b) of paragraph (1) or in a case where paragraph (2) applies, the adoption pay period shall, unless the employer agrees to the adoption pay period beginning earlier, begin no earlier than 28 days after notice under section 171ZL(6) of the Act has been given.

(4) Where the beginning of the adoption pay period determined in accordance with paragraph (3) is later than the date of placement, it shall be the date of placement.

(5) Subject to regulation 22, the duration of any adoption pay period shall be a continuous period of [¹39] weeks.

(6) A choice made under paragraph (1), or a date specified under paragraph (2), is not irrevocable, but where a person subsequently makes a different choice, section 171ZL(6) of the Act shall apply to it.

AMENDMENT

1. Statutory Paternity Pay and Statutory Adoption Pay (General) and the Statutory Paternity Pay and Statutory Adoption Pay (Weekly Rates) (Amendment) Regulations 2006 (SI 2006/2236) reg.4 (October 1, 2006).

DEFINITIONS

"the Act"—see reg.2(1).
"adopter"—see reg.2(1).

Adoption pay period in cases where adoption is disrupted

22.—(1) Where— 6.72
(a) after a child has been placed for adoption—
  (i) the child dies;
  (ii) the child is returned to the adoption agency under section 30(3) of the Adoption Act 1976 or [¹, in Scotland, the child is returned to the adoption agency, adoption society or nominated person in accordance with section 25(6) of the Adoption and Children (Scotland) Act 2007];
  [² *(ii) the child is returned after being placed, or*]
(b) the adoption pay period has begun prior to the date the child has been placed for adoption, but the placement does not take place, the adoption pay period shall terminate in accordance with the provisions of paragraph (2).

(2) The adoption pay period shall, in a case falling within paragraph (1), terminate 8 weeks after the end of the week specified in paragraph (3).

(3) The week referred to in paragraph (2) is—
(a) in a case falling within paragraph (1)(a)(i), the week during which the child dies;
(b) in a case falling within paragraph (1)(a)(ii), the week during which the child is returned;
(c) in a case falling within paragraph (1)(b), the week during which the person with whom the child was to be placed for adoption is notified that the placement will not be made.

(4) For the purposes of paragraph (3), "week" means a period of 7 days beginning with Sunday.
[² [³ . . .]]

AMENDMENTS

1. Adoption and Children (Scotland) Act 2007 (Consequential Modifications) Order 2011 (SI 2011/1740) art.2 and Sch.1 para.32(3) (July 15, 2011).
2. Statutory Paternity Pay and Statutory Adoption Pay (Parental Orders and Prospective Adopters) Regulations 2014 (SI 2014/2934) reg.5 (December 1, 2014, but have effect only in relation to children matched with a person who is notified of having been matched on or after April 5, 2015).
3. Statutory Paternity Pay (Amendment) Regulations 2024 (SI 2024/121) reg.14 (March 8, 2024).

DEFINITION

"week"—see para.(4).

Additional notice requirements for statutory adoption pay

6.73   23.—(1) Where a person gives notice under section 171ZL(6) of the Act he shall at the same time give notice of the date on which the child is expected to be placed for adoption.

(2) Where the choice made in accordance with paragraph (1) of regulation 21 and notified in accordance with section 171ZL(6) of the Act is that mentioned in sub-paragraph (a) of that paragraph, the person shall give further notice to the person liable to pay him statutory adoption pay as soon as is reasonably practicable of the date the child is placed for adoption.

DEFINITION

"the Act"—see reg.2(1).

Evidence of entitlement to statutory adoption pay

6.74   24.—(1) A person shall provide evidence of his entitlement to statutory adoption pay by providing to the person who will be liable to pay it—
(a) the information specified in paragraph (2), in the form of one or more documents provided to him by an adoption agency, containing that information;
(b) a declaration that he has elected to receive statutory adoption pay, and not statutory paternity pay (adoption) under Part 12ZA of the Act.

(2) The information referred to in paragraph (1) is—
(a) the name and address of the adoption agency and of the person claiming payment of statutory adoption pay;

(b) the date on which the child is expected to be placed for adoption or, where the child has already been placed for adoption, the date of placement; and
(c) the date on which the person claiming payment of statutory adoption pay was informed by the adoption agency that the child would be placed for adoption with him.

(3) The information and declaration referred to in paragraph (1) shall be provided to the person liable to pay statutory adoption pay at least 28 days before the date chosen as the beginning of the adoption pay period in accordance with paragraph (1) of regulation 21, or, if that is not reasonably practicable, as soon as is reasonably practicable thereafter.

DEFINITIONS

"the Act"—see reg.2(1).
"adoption agency"—see reg.2(1).
"statutory paternity pay (adoption)"—see reg.2(1).

Entitlement to statutory adoption pay where there is more than one employer

25.—Statutory adoption pay shall be payable to a person in respect of a week during any part of which he works only for an employer—
(a) who is not liable to pay him statutory adoption pay; and
(b) for whom he has worked in the week in which he is notified of being matched with the child.

Work during an adoption pay period

26.—(1) Where, in a case where statutory adoption pay is being paid to a person who works during the adoption pay period for an employer who is not liable to pay him statutory adoption pay and who does not fall within paragraph (b) of regulation 25, there shall be no liability to pay statutory adoption pay in respect of any remaining part of the adoption pay period.

(2) In a case falling within paragraph (1), the person shall notify the person liable to pay statutory adoption pay within 7 days of the first day during which he works during the adoption pay period.

(3) The notification contained in paragraph (2) shall be in writing if the person who has been liable to pay statutory adoption pay so requests.

Cases where there is no liability to pay statutory adoption pay

27.—(1) There shall be no liability to pay statutory adoption pay in respect of any week—
(a) during any part of which the person entitled to it is entitled to statutory sick pay under Part 9 of the Act;
(b) following that in which the person claiming it has died; or
(c) subject to paragraph (2), during any part of which the person entitled to it is detained in legal custody or sentenced to a term of imprisonment (except where the sentence is suspended).

(2) There shall be liability to pay statutory adoption pay in respect of any week during any part of which the person entitled to it is detained in legal custody where that person—
(a) is released subsequently without charge;
(b) is subsequently found not guilty of any offence and is released; or
(c) is convicted of an offence but does not receive a custodial sentence.

DEFINITION

"the Act"—see reg.2(1).

[¹ Working for not more than 10 days during an adoption pay period

6.78   **27A.**—In the case where an employee does any work under a contract of service with his employer on any day for not more than 10 such days during his adoption pay period, whether consecutive or not, statutory adoption pay shall continue to be payable to the employee by the employer.]

AMENDMENT

1. Statutory Paternity Pay and Statutory Adoption Pay (General) and the Statutory Paternity Pay and Statutory Adoption Pay (Weekly Rates) (Amendment) Regulations 2006 (SI 2006/2236) reg.5 (October 1, 2006).

Statutory adoption pay and contractual remuneration

6.79   **28.**—For the purposes of section 171ZP(4) and (5) of the Act, the payments which are to be treated as contractual remuneration are sums payable under a contract of service—
(a) by way of remuneration;
(b) for incapacity for work due to sickness or injury;
(c) by reason of the adoption of a child.

DEFINITION

"the Act"—see reg.2(1).

Termination of employment before start of adoption pay period

6.80   **29.**—(1) Where the employment of a person who satisfies the conditions of entitlement to statutory adoption pay terminates for whatever reason (including dismissal) before the adoption pay period chosen in accordance with regulation 21 has begun, the period shall begin 14 days before the expected date of placement or, where the termination occurs on, or within 14 days before, the expected date of placement, on the day immediately following the last day of his employment.

(2) In a case falling within paragraph (1), the notice requirements set out in section 171ZL(6) of the Act and these Regulations shall not apply.

DEFINITION

"the Act"—see reg.2(1).

Avoidance of liability for statutory adoption pay

6.81   **30.**—(1) A former employer shall be liable to make payments of statutory adoption pay to a former employee in any case where the employee had been employed for a continuous period of at least 8 weeks and his contract of service was brought to an end by the former employer solely, or mainly, for the purpose of avoiding liability for statutory adoption pay.

(2) In a case falling within paragraph (1)—
(a) the employee shall be treated as if he had been employed for a continuous period ending with the week in which he was notified of having been matched with the child for adoption; and

(b) his normal weekly earnings shall be calculated by reference to his normal weekly earnings for the period of 8 weeks ending with the last day in respect of which he was paid under his former contract of service.

PART 6

STATUTORY PATERNITY PAY AND STATUTORY ADOPTION PAY: PROVISIONS APPLICABLE TO BOTH STATUTORY PATERNITY PAY AND STATUTORY ADOPTION PAY

Introductory

31.—(1) Subject to paragraph (2), the provisions of regulations 32–47 below apply to statutory paternity pay payable under Part 12ZA of the Act and to statutory adoption pay payable under Part 12ZB of the Act.

(2) The provisions of regulation 44 only apply to statutory adoption pay.

DEFINITION

"the Act"—see reg.2(1).

Treatment of persons as employees

32.—(1) [¹Subject to paragraph (1A),] in a case where, and in so far as, a person [¹. . .] is treated as an employed earner by virtue of the Social Security (Categorisation of Earners) Regulations 1978 he shall be treated as an employee for the purposes of Parts 12ZA and 12ZB of the Act, and in a case where, and in so far as, such a person is treated otherwise than as an employed earner by virtue of those Regulations, he shall not be treated as an employee for the purposes of Parts 12ZA and 12ZB of the Act.

[²(1A) Paragraph (1) shall have effect in relation to a person who—
(a) is under the age of 16; and
(b) would or, as the case may be, would not have been treated as an employed earner by virtue of the Social Security (Categorisation of Earners) Regulations 1978 had he been over that age,
as it has effect in relation to a person who is or, as the case may be, is not so treated.]

(2) A person who is in employed earner's employment within the meaning of the Act under a contract of apprenticeship shall be treated as an employee for the purposes of Parts 12ZA and 12ZB of the Act.

(3) A person who is in employed earner's employment within the meaning of the Act but whose employer—
(a) does not fulfil the conditions prescribed in regulation 145(1) of the Contributions Regulations in so far as that provision relates to residence or presence in Great Britain; or
(b) is a person who, by reason of any international treaty to which the United Kingdom is a party or of any international convention binding the United Kingdom—
(i) is exempt from the provisions of the Act; or

(ii) is a person against whom the provisions of the Act are not enforceable,

shall not be treated as an employee for the purposes of Parts 12ZA and 12ZB of the Act.

AMENDMENTS

1. Employment Equality (Age) Regulations 2006 (SI 2006/1031) reg.49(1) and Sch.8 Pt 2 para.60 (October 1, 2006).
2. Employment Equality (Age) (Consequential Amendments) Regulations 2007 (SI 2007/825) reg.7 (April 6, 2007).

DEFINITIONS

"the Act"—see reg.2(1).
"Contributions Regulations"—see reg.2(1).

Continuous employment

33.—(1) Subject to the following provisions of this regulation, where in any week a person is, for the whole or part of the week—
  (a) incapable of work in consequence of sickness or injury;
  (b) absent from work on account of a temporary cessation of work;
  (c) absent from work in circumstances such that, by arrangement or custom, he is regarded as continuing in the employment of his employer for all or any purposes,

and returns to work for his employer after the incapacity for or absence from work, that week shall be treated for the purposes of sections 171ZA, 171ZB and 171ZL of the Act as part of a continuous period of employment with that employer, notwithstanding that no contract of service exists with that employer in respect of that week.

(2) Incapacity for work which lasts for more than 26 consecutive weeks shall not count for the purposes of paragraph (1)(a).

(3) Where a person—
  (a) is an employee in an employed earner's employment in which the custom is for the employer—
    (i) to offer work for a fixed period of not more than 26 consecutive weeks;
    (ii) to offer work for such period on two or more occasions in a year for periods which do not overlap; and
    (iii) to offer the work available to those persons who had worked for him during the last or a recent such period, but
  (b) is absent from work because of incapacity arising from some specific disease or bodily or mental disablement,

then in that case paragraph (1) shall apply as if the words "and returns to work for his employer after the incapacity for or absence from work," were omitted and paragraph (4) shall not apply.

(4) Where a person is employed under a contract of service for part only of the relevant week within the meaning of subsection (3) of section 171ZL of the Act (entitlement to statutory adoption pay), the whole of that week shall count in computing a period of continuous employment for the purposes of that section.

DEFINITION

"the Act"—see reg.2(1).

Continuous employment and unfair dismissal

34.—(1) This regulation applies to a person in relation to whose dismissal an action is commenced which consists—
   (a) of the presentation by him of a complaint under section 111(1) of the Employment Rights Act 1996;
   (b) of his making a claim in accordance with a dismissals procedure agreement designated by an order under section 110 of that Act; [¹...]
   (c) of any action taken by a conciliation officer under [² any of sections 18A to 18C] of the Employment Tribunals Act 1996; [¹or
   (d) of a decision arising out of the use of a statutory dispute resolution procedure contained in Schedule 2 to the Employment Act 2002 in a case where, in accordance with the Employment Act 2002 (Dispute Resolution) Regulations 2004, such a procedure applies.]

(2) If, in consequence of an action of the kind specified in paragraph (1), a person is reinstated or re-engaged by his employer or by a successor or associated employer of that employer, the continuity of his employment shall be preserved for the purposes of Part 12ZA or, as the case may be, Part 12ZB of the Act, and any week which falls within the interval beginning with the effective date of termination and ending with the date of reinstatement or re-engagement, as the case may be, shall count in the computation of his period of continuous employment.

(3) In this regulation—

"successor" and "dismissal procedures agreement" have the same meanings as in section 235 of the Employment Rights Act 1996; and

"associated employer" shall be construed in accordance with section 231 of the Employment Rights Act 1996.

AMENDMENTS

1. Statutory Maternity Pay (General) and the Statutory Paternity Pay and Statutory Adoption Pay (General) (Amendment) Regulations 2005 (SI 2005/358) reg.4 (April 56, 2005).
2. Enterprise and Regulatory Reform Act 2013 (Consequential Amendments) (Employment) Order 2014 (SI 2014/386) art.2 Sch. para.19.

DEFINITIONS

"the Act"—see reg.2(1).
"associated employer"—see para.(3).
"dismissal procedures agreement"—see para.(3).
"successor"—see para.(3).

Continuous employment and stoppages of work

35.—(1) Where, for any week or part of a week a person does not work because there is a stoppage of work due to a trade dispute within the meaning of section 35(1) of the Jobseekers Act 1995 at his place of employment, the continuity of his employment shall, subject to paragraph (2), be treated as continuing throughout the stoppage but, subject to paragraph (3), no such week shall count in the computation of his period of employment.

(2) Subject to paragraph (3), where during the stoppage of work a person is dismissed from his employment, the continuity of his employment shall not be treated in accordance with paragraph (1) as continuing beyond the commencement of the day he stopped work.

(3) The provisions of paragraph (1), to the extent that they provide that a week in which the stoppage of work occurred shall not count in the computation of a period of employment, and paragraph (2) shall not apply to a person who proves that at no time did he have a direct interest in the trade dispute in question.

[¹ Meaning of "week"

6.87 **35A.**—(1) This regulation applies where a person ("P") has been in employed earner's employment with the same employer in each of 26 consecutive weeks (but no more than 26 weeks), ending with—
 (a) in relation to P's entitlement to statutory paternity pay (birth), the week immediately preceding the 14th week before the expected week of the child's birth, or
 (b) in relation to P's entitlement to statutory paternity pay (adoption), the week in which P is notified that P has been matched with the child for the purposes of adoption.
(2) For the purpose of determining whether P's employment amounts to a continuous period of at least 26 weeks (see sections 171ZA(2)(b) and 171ZL(2)(b) of the Act), the first of those 26 weeks is a period commencing on the first day of P's employment with the employer ("the start date") and ending at midnight on—
 (a) the first Saturday after the start date, or
 (b) where the start date is a Saturday, that day.]

AMENDMENT

1. Statutory Paternity Pay, Statutory Adoption Pay and Statutory Shared Parental Pay (Amendment) Regulations 2015 (SI 2015/2065) reg.2(2) (February 1, 2016).

Change of employer

6.88 **36.**—A person's employment shall, notwithstanding a change of employer, be treated as continuous employment with the second employer where—
 (a) the employer's trade or business or an undertaking (whether or not it is an undertaking established by or under an Act of Parliament) is transferred from one person to another;
 (b) by or under an Act of Parliament, whether public or local and whenever passed, a contract of employment between any body corporate and the person is modified and some other body corporate is substituted as his employer;
 (c) on the death of his employer, the person is taken into employment of the personal representatives or trustees of the deceased;
 (d) the person is employed by partners, personal representatives or trustees and there is a change in the partners, or, as the case may be, personal representatives or trustees;
 (e) the person is taken into the employment of an employer who is, at the time he entered his employment, an associated employer of his previous employer, and for this purpose "associated employer" shall be construed in accordance with section 231 of the Employment Rights Act 1996;
 (f) on the termination of his employment with an employer he is taken into the employment of another employer and those employers are governors of a school maintained by a [¹local authority] and that authority.

AMENDMENT

1. Local Education Authorities and Children's Services Authorities (Integration of Functions) (Local Subordinate Legislation) Order 2010 (SI 2010/1172) art.4 and Sch.3 para.47 (May 5, 2010).

Reinstatement after service with the armed forces etc.

37.—If a person who is entitled to apply to his employer under the Reserve Forces (Safeguard of Employment) Act 1985 enters the employment of that employer within the 6-month period mentioned in section 1(4)(b) of that Act, his previous period of employment with that employer (or if there was more than one such period, the last of those periods) and the period of employment beginning in that 6-month period shall be treated as continuous.

6.89

DEFINITION

"the Act"—see reg.2(1).

Treatment of two or more employers or two or more contracts of service as one

38.—(1) In a case where the earnings paid to a person in respect of two or more employments are aggregated and treated as a single payment of earnings under regulation 15(1) of the Contributions Regulations, the employers of that person in respect of those employments shall be treated as one for the purposes of Part 12ZA or, as the case may be, Part 12ZB of the Act.

6.90

(2) Where two or more employers are treated as one under the provisions of paragraph (1), liability for statutory paternity pay or, as the case may be, statutory adoption pay, shall be apportioned between them in such proportions as they may agree or, in default of agreement, in the proportions which the person's earnings from each employment bear to the amount of the aggregated earnings.

(3) Where two or more contracts of service exist concurrently between one employer and one employee, they shall be treated as one for the purposes of Part 12ZA or, as the case may be, Part 12ZB of the Act, except where, by virtue of regulation 14 of the Contributions Regulations, the earnings from those contracts of service are not aggregated for the purposes of earnings-related contributions.

DEFINITIONS

"the Act"—see reg.2(1).
"Contributions Regulations"—see reg.2(1).

Meaning of "earnings"

39.—(1) For the purposes of section 171ZJ(6) (normal weekly earnings for the purposes of Part 12ZA of the Act) and of section 171ZS(6) of the Act (normal weekly earnings for the purposes of Part 12ZB of the Act), the expression "earnings" shall be construed in accordance with the following provisions of this regulation.

6.91

(2) The expression "earnings" refers to gross earnings and includes any remuneration or profit derived from a person's employment except any payment or amount which is—

(a) excluded from the computation of a person's earnings under regulation 25 of and Schedule 3 to, and regulation 123 of, the Contributions Regulations (payments to be disregarded) and regulation 27 of those Regulations (payments to directors to be disregarded) [¹(or would have been so excluded had he not been under the age of 16)];

(b) a chargeable emolument under section 10A of the Act, except where, in consequence of such a chargeable emolument being excluded from earnings, a person would not be entitled to statutory paternity pay or, as the case may be, statutory adoption pay [¹(or where such a payment or amount would have been so excluded and in consequence he would not have been entitled to statutory paternity pay and statutory adoption pay had he not been under the age of 16)].

(3) For the avoidance of doubt, "earnings" includes—

[²(za) any amount retrospectively treated as earnings by regulations made by virtue of section 4B(2) of the Act;]

(a) any sum payable in respect of arrears of pay in pursuance of an order for reinstatement or re-engagement under the Employment Rights Act 1996;

(b) any sum payable by way of pay in pursuance of an order made under the Employment Rights Act 1996 for the continuation of a contract of employment;

(c) any sum payable by way of remuneration in pursuance of a protective award under section 189 of the Trade Union and Labour Relations (Consolidation) Act 1992;

(d) any sum payable by way of statutory sick pay, including sums payable in accordance with regulations made under section 151(6) of the Act;

(e) any sum payable by way of statutory maternity pay;

(f) any sum payable by way of statutory paternity pay;

(g) any sum payable by way of statutory adoption pay.

AMENDMENTS

1. Employment Equality (Age) Regulations 2006 (SI 2006/1031) reg.49(1) and Sch.8 Pt 2 para.61 (October 1, 2006).

2. Social Security, Occupational Pension Schemes and Statutory Payments (Consequential Provisions) Regulations 2007 (SI 2007/1154) reg.6 (April 6, 2007).

DEFINITIONS

"the Act"—see reg.2(1).
"Contributions Regulations"—see reg.2(1).

Normal weekly earnings

6.92   40.—(1) For the purposes of Part 12ZA and Part 12ZB of the Act, a person's normal weekly earnings shall be calculated in accordance with the following provisions of this regulation.

(2) In this regulation—

"the appropriate date" means—

(a) in relation to statutory paternity pay (birth), the first day of the 14th week before the expected week of the child's birth or the first day in the week in which the child is born, whichever is the earlier;

(b) in relation to statutory paternity pay (adoption) and statutory adoption pay, the first day of the week after the week in which the adopter is notified of being matched with the child for the purposes of adoption;

"normal pay day" means a day on which the terms of a person's contract of service require him to be paid, or the practice in his employment is for him to be paid, if any payment is due to him; and

"day of payment" means a day on which the person was paid.

(3) Subject to paragraph (4), the relevant period for the purposes of sections 171ZJ(6) and 171ZS(6) is the period between—

(a) the last normal pay day to fall before the appropriate date; and
(b) the last normal pay day to fall at least 8 weeks earlier than the normal pay day mentioned in sub-paragraph (a),

including the normal pay day mentioned in sub-paragraph (a) but excluding that first mentioned in sub-paragraph (b).

(4) In a case where a person has no identifiable normal pay day, paragraph (3) shall have effect as if the words "day of payment" were substituted for the words "normal pay day" in each place where they occur.

(5) In a case where a person has normal pay days at intervals of or approximating to one or more calendar months (including intervals of or approximating to a year) his normal weekly earnings shall be calculated by dividing his earnings in the relevant period by the number of calendar months in that period (or, if it is not a whole number, the nearest whole number), multiplying the result by 12 and dividing by 52.

(6) In a case to which paragraph (5) does not apply and the relevant period is not an exact number of weeks, the person's normal weekly earnings shall be calculated by dividing his earnings in the relevant period by the number of days in the relevant period and multiplying the result by 7.

(7) In any case where a person receives a back-dated pay increase which includes a sum in respect of a relevant period, normal weekly earnings shall be calculated as if such a sum was paid in that relevant period even though received after that period.

[1(8) Paragraph (9) applies where for all or part of the relevant period—

(a) a woman is a furloughed employee;
(b) the woman's employer has claimed and is in receipt of financial support in respect of the woman's earnings under the Coronavirus Job Retention Scheme; and
(c) the woman's earnings are lower than they would otherwise have been as a result of that woman being a furloughed employee.

(9) Where this paragraph applies, the woman's normal weekly earnings are to be calculated as if, during the parts of the relevant period when the woman was a furloughed employee, she was paid the amount which she would have derived from her employment had she not been a furloughed employee.

(10) For the purposes of paragraphs (8) and (9)—

"Coronavirus Job Retention Scheme" ("the Scheme") means any scheme to provide for payments to be made to employers on a claim made in respect of them incurring costs of employment in respect of furloughed employees arising from the health, social and economic emergency in the United Kingdom resulting from coronavirus and coronavirus disease and contained in such Directions as may be issued from time to time pursuant to section 76 of the Coronavirus Act 2020;

"coronavirus" and "coronavirus disease" have the meanings given in section 1 of that Act;

"furloughed employee" has the meaning given for the purposes of the Scheme.]

AMENDMENT

1. Maternity Allowance, Statutory Maternity Pay, Statutory Paternity Pay, Statutory Adoption Pay, Statutory Shared Parental Pay and Statutory Parental Bereavement Pay (Normal Weekly Earnings etc.) (Coronavirus) (Amendment) Regulations 2020 (SI 2020/450) reg.5 (April 25, 2020).

DEFINITIONS

"the Act"—see reg.2(1).
"adopter"—see reg.2(1).
"the appropriate date"—see para.(2).
"day of payment"— see para.(2).
"expected week"—see reg.2(1).
"normal pay day"—see para.(2).
"statutory paternity pay (adoption)"—see reg.2(1).
"statutory paternity pay (birth)"—see reg.2(1).

GENERAL NOTE

6.93   Paragraphs (8)-(10) were added as from April 25, 2020 with the intention of ensuring that an employee experienced no disadvantage in relation to their SPP and SAP entitlement as a result of their being placed on temporary leave under the Coronavirus Job Retention Scheme ("the CJRS"), set out in the Schedule to the *Coronavirus Act 2020 Functions of Her Majesty's Revenue and Customs (Coronavirus Job Retention Scheme) Direction made on April 15, 2020*. In short, the amendments were designed to ensure that an employee's eligibility for the earnings-related rate of SPP/SAP is the same as it would have been had they not been furloughed. Regulation 2 of the 2020 Regulations (SI 2020/450) provides that these amendments are to apply where the first day of the period in respect of which payment of any of the benefits is to be made is on or after the day on which the 2020 Regulations come into force.

Payment of statutory paternity pay and statutory adoption pay

6.94   **41.**—Payments of statutory paternity pay and statutory adoption pay may be made in a like manner to payments of remuneration but shall not include payment in kind or by way of the provision of board or lodgings or of services or other facilities.

Time when statutory paternity pay and statutory adoption pay are to be paid

6.95   **42.**—(1) In this regulation, "pay day" means a day on which it has been agreed, or it is the normal practice between an employer or former employer and a person who is or was an employee of his, that payments by way of remuneration are to be made, or, where there is no such agreement or normal practice, the last day of a calendar month.

(2) In any case where—
(a) a decision has been made by an officer of the Board under section 8(1) of the Social Security Contributions (Transfer of Functions, etc.) Act 1999 as a result of which a person is entitled to an amount of statutory paternity pay or statutory adoption pay; and
(b) the time for bringing an appeal against the decision has expired and either—
   (i) no such appeal has been brought; or

(ii) such an appeal has been brought and has been finally disposed of,

that amount of statutory paternity pay or statutory adoption pay shall be paid within the time specified in paragraph (3).

(3) Subject to paragraphs (4) and (5), the employer or former employer shall pay the amount not later than the first pay day after—
- (a) where an appeal has been brought, the day on which the employer or former employer receives notification that it has been finally disposed of;
- (b) where leave to appeal has been refused and there remains no further opportunity to apply for leave, the day on which the employer or former employer receives notification of the refusal; and
- (c) in any other case, the day on which the time for bringing an appeal expires.

(4) Subject to paragraph (5), where it is impracticable, in view of the employer's or former employer's methods of accounting for and paying remuneration, for the requirement of payment referred to in paragraph (3) to be met by the pay day referred to in that paragraph, it shall be met not later than the next following pay day.

(5) Where the employer or former employer would not have remunerated the employee for his work in the week in question as early as the pay day specified in paragraph (3) or (if it applies) paragraph (4), the requirement of payment shall be met on the first day on which the employee would have been remunerated for his work in that week.

DEFINITIONS

"the Board"—see reg.2(1).
"pay day"—see para.(1).

Liability of the Board to pay statutory paternity pay or statutory adoption pay

43.—[²(1) Notwithstanding sections 171ZD and 171ZM of the Act, where the conditions in regulation 42(2)(a) and (b) are satisfied, liability to make payments of statutory paternity pay or statutory adoption pay, as the case may be, is to be that of the Board and not the employer for—
- (a) any week in respect of which the employer was liable to pay statutory paternity pay or statutory adoption pay to that person but did not do so, and
- (b) any subsequent week in respect of which that person is entitled to payments of statutory paternity pay or statutory adoption pay [²in respect of any week in which a person is entitled to such payments].]

(2) Liability to make payments of statutory paternity pay or, as the case may be, statutory adoption pay [² in respect of any week in which a person is entitled to such payments] shall, notwithstanding sections 171ZD and 171ZM of the Act, be a liability of the Board and not the employer as from the week in which the employer first becomes insolvent until the end of the [²adoption pay period or the qualifying period specified in regulations 6A or 12A, as the case may be].

(3) For the purposes of paragraph (2), an employer shall be taken to be insolvent if, and only if—
- (a) in England and Wales—

6.96

Statutory Paternity Pay and Statutory Adoption Pay (General) Regs 2002

   (i) he has been adjudged bankrupt or has made a composition or arrangement with his creditors;
   (ii) he has died and his estate falls to be administered in accordance with an order made under section 421 of the Insolvency Act 1986; or
   (iii) where an employer is a company or a limited liability partnership, a winding-up order [1. . .] is made or a resolution for a voluntary winding-up is passed (or, in the case of a limited liability partnership, a determination for a voluntary winding-up has been made) with respect to it [1or it enters administration], or a receiver or a manager of its undertaking is duly appointed, or possession is taken, by or on behalf of the holders of any debentures secured by a floating charge, of any property of the company or limited liability partnership comprised in or subject to the charge, or a voluntary arrangement proposed for the purposes of Part 1 of the Insolvency Act 1986 is approved under that Part of that Act;
 (b) in Scotland—
   (i) an award of sequestration is made on his estate or he executes a trust deed for his creditors or enters into a composition contract;
   (ii) he has died and a judicial factor appointed under section 11A of the Judicial Factors (Scotland) Act 1889 is required by that section to divide his insolvent estate among his creditors; or
   (iii) where the employer is a company or a limited liability partnership, a winding-up order [1. . .] is made or a resolution for voluntary winding-up is passed (or, in the case of a limited liability partnership, a determination for a voluntary winding-up is made) with respect to it [1or it enters administration], or a receiver of its undertaking is duly appointed, or a voluntary arrangement proposed for the purposes of Part 1 of the Insolvency Act 1986 is approved under that Part.

AMENDMENTS

1. Enterprise Act 2002 (Insolvency) Order 2003 (SI 2003/2096) art.5 and Sch.2 para.79 (September 15, 2003).
2. Statutory Paternity Pay (Amendment) Regulations 2024 (SI 2024/121) reg.15 (March 8, 2024).

DEFINITIONS

"the Act"—see reg.2(1).
"the Board"—see reg.2(1).

GENERAL NOTE

6.97   The various references to insolvency law provisions include the special administration regime under the Investment Bank Special Administration Regulations 2011 (SI 2011/245) (see reg.27 and Sch.6 Pt 1 of those Regulations).

[1Liability of the Board to pay statutory paternity or statutory adoption pay in cases of legal custody or imprisonment

6.98   **44.** Notwithstanding sections 171ZD and 171ZM of the Act, the liability to pay statutory paternity pay or statutory adoption pay, as the case may

(SI 2002/2822 reg.44) (as amended)

be, shall be that of the Board and not the employer where there is liability to pay—
(a) statutory adoption pay—
(i) in respect of a period which is subsequent to the last week falling within paragraph (1)(c) of regulation 27, or
(ii) during a period of detention in legal custody by virtue of the provisions of paragraph (2) of that regulation, or
(b) statutory paternity pay—
(i) in respect of a period which is subsequent to the period mentioned in sub-paragraph (1)(c) of regulation 18 (cases where there is no liability to pay statutory paternity pay), or
(ii) during a period of detention in legal custody by virtue of paragraph (2) of that regulation.]

AMENDMENT

1. Statutory Paternity Pay (Amendment) Regulations 2024 (SI 2024/121) reg.16 (March 8, 2024).

DEFINITIONS

"the Act"—see reg.2(1).
"the Board"—see reg.2(1).

Payments by the Board

45.—Where the Board become liable in accordance with regulation 43 or 44 to make payments of statutory paternity pay or, as the case may be, statutory adoption pay to a person, the first payment shall be made as soon as reasonably practicable after they become so liable, and payments thereafter shall be made at weekly intervals, by means of an instrument of payment or by such other means as appears to the Board to be appropriate in the circumstance of any particular case.

DEFINITION

"the Board"—see reg.2(1).

Persons unable to act

46.—(1) Where in the case of any person—
(a) statutory paternity pay or, as the case may be, statutory adoption pay is payable to him or he is alleged to be entitled to it;
(b) he is unable for the time being to act; and
(c) either—
(i) no receiver has been appointed by the Court of Protection with power to receive statutory paternity pay or, as the case may be, statutory adoption pay on his behalf; or
(ii) in Scotland, his estate is not being administered by any tutor, curator or other guardian acting or appointed in terms of law,
the Board may, upon written application to them by a person who, if a natural person, is over the age of 18, appoint that person to exercise, on behalf of the person unable to act, any right to which he may be entitled under Part 12ZA or, as the case may be, Part 12ZB of the Act and to deal on his behalf with any sums payable to him.

(2) Where the Board have made an appointment under paragraph (1)—
(a) they may at any time in their absolute discretion revoke it;
(b) the person appointed may resign his office after having given one month's notice in writing to the Board of his intention to do so; and
(c) the appointment shall terminate when the Board are notified that a receiver or other person to whom paragraph (1)(c) applies has been appointed.

(3) Anything required by Part 12ZA or 12ZB of the Act to be done by or to any person who is unable to act may be done by or to the person appointed under this regulation to act on his behalf, and the receipt of the person so appointed shall be a good discharge to the person's employer or former employer for any sum paid.

DEFINITIONS

"the Act"—see reg.2(1).
"the Board"—see reg.2(1).

Service of notices by post

47.—A notice given in accordance with the provisions of these Regulations in writing contained in an envelope which is properly addressed and sent by prepaid post shall be treated as having been given on the day on which it is posted.

The Social Security Contributions and Benefits Act 1992 (Application of Parts 12ZA [¹, 12ZB and 12ZC] to Adoptions from Overseas) Regulations 2003

(SI 2003/499) (AS AMENDED)

The Secretary of State, in exercise of the powers conferred on her by sections 171ZK and 171ZT of the Social Security Contributions and Benefits Act 1992 by this instrument, which contains only provision made by virtue of sections 2 and 4 of the Employment Act 2002 and is made before the end of the period of 6 months from the coming into force of those enactments, hereby makes the following Regulations—

ARRANGEMENT OF REGULATIONS

1. Citation, commencement and interpretation.
2. Application of Part 12ZA of the Act to adoptions from overseas.
3. Application of Part 12ZB of the Act to adoptions from overseas.
4. Application of Part 12ZC of the Act to adoptions from overseas

Schedule 1—Application of Part 12ZA of the Act to adoptions from overseas.
Schedule 2—Application of Part 12ZB of the Act to adoptions from overseas.

AMENDMENT

1. Social Security Contributions and Benefits Act 1992 (Application of Parts 12ZA and 12ZB to Adoptions from Overseas) (Amendment) Regulations 2014 (SI 2014/2857) regs 2 and 3 (November 19, 2014).

(SI 2003/499 reg.1) (as amended)

Citation, commencement and interpretation

1.—(1) These Regulations may be cited as the Social Security Contributions and Benefits Act 1992 (Application of Parts 12ZA [¹ , 12ZB and 12ZC] to Adoptions from Overseas) Regulations 2003 and shall come into force, in so far as they apply powers to make regulations, on 10th March 2003, and for all other purposes on 6th April 2003.

(2) In these Regulations—

"adoption from overseas" means the adoption of a child who enters Great Britain from outside the United Kingdom in connection with or for the purposes of adoption which does not involve the placement of the child for adoption under the law of any part of the United Kingdom;

"the Act" means the Social Security Contributions and Benefits Act 1992.

AMENDMENT

1. Social Security Contributions and Benefits Act 1992 (Application of Parts 12ZA and 12ZB to Adoptions from Overseas) (Amendment) Regulations 2014 (SI 2014/2857) regs 2 and 4 (November 19, 2014).

GENERAL NOTE

These Regulations, made under provisions inserted into the SSCBA 1992 by the Employment Act 2002, apply Pts XIIZA and XIIZB of the 1992 Act, as modified by these Regulations, to adoptions from overseas. These are adoptions of children who enter Great Britain from outside the UK in connection with or for the purposes of adoption which does not involve the placement of a child for adoption under the law of any part of the UK. The relevant adoption law requirements are set out in the Adoption (Bringing Children into the United Kingdom) Regulations 2003 (SI 2003/1173). The regulations relating to statutory paternity pay and statutory adoption pay in connection with such overseas adoptions are the Statutory Paternity Pay (Adoption) and Statutory Adoption Pay (Adoptions from Overseas) Regulations 2003 (SI 2003/500).

Application of Part 12ZA of the Act to adoptions from overseas

2.—Part 12ZA of the Act [¹ ([²...)] shall apply in relation to adoptions from overseas, with the modifications of sections 171ZB, 171ZE [¹, 171ZEB, 171ZEE] and 171ZJ of the Act specified in the second column of Schedule 1.

AMENDMENTS

1. Social Security Contributions and Benefits Act 1992 (Application of Parts 12ZA and 12ZB to Adoptions from Overseas) Regulations 2003 (Amendment) Regulations 2010 (SI 2010/153) reg.2(2) (April 6, 2010).
2. Shared Parental Leave and Statutory Shared Parental Pay (Consequential Amendments to Subordinate Legislation) Order 2014 (SI 2014/3255) reg.14(2) (April 5, 2015).

Application of Part 12ZB of the Act to adoptions from overseas

3.—Part 12ZB of the Act shall apply in relation to adoptions from overseas, with the modifications of sections 171ZL and 171ZS of the Act specified in the second column of Schedule 2.

[¹ Application of Part 12ZC of the Act to adoptions from overseas

6.107 **4.**—Part 12ZC of the Act shall apply in relation to adoptions from overseas, with the modifications of section 171ZV of the Act specified in the second column of Schedule 3.]

AMENDMENT

1. Social Security Contributions and Benefits Act 1992 (Application of Parts 12ZA and 12ZB to Adoptions from Overseas) (Amendment) Regulations 2014 (SI 2014/2857) regs 2 and 5 (November 19, 2014).

SCHEDULE 1   Regulation 2

APPLICATION OF PART 12ZA OF THE ACT TO ADOPTIONS FROM OVERSEAS

6.108

Provision	Modification
Section 171ZB(2)	[¹...] In paragraph (a)(i), for "who is placed for adoption under the law of any part of the United Kingdom" substitute "who is adopted from overseas".

Provision	Modification
	In paragraph (a)(ii), for "a person with whom the child is so placed for adoption" substitute "an adopter of the child". [¹In paragraph (b), omit "ending with the relevant week".] In paragraph (d), for "the day on which the child is placed for adoption" substitute "the day on which the child enters Great Britain". In paragraph (e), for "a person with whom the child is placed for adoption" substitute "an adopter of the child".

Section 171ZB(3)	[¹For subsection (3) substitute—
	"(3) The references in subsection (2)(c) and (d) to the relevant week are to—
	  (a) the week in which official notification is sent to the adopter, or
	  (b) the week at the end of which the person satisfies the condition in subsection (2)(b), whichever is the later."]

Section 171ZB(6)	For "the placement for adoption of more than one child as part of the same arrangement" substitute "the adoption from overseas of more than one child as part of the same arrangement".
Section 171ZB(7)	Omit subsection (7).
Section 171ZE(3)	In paragraph (b), for "with the date of the child's placement for adoption" substitute "with the date of the child's entry into Great Britain".
Section 171ZE(10)	For subsection (10) substitute— "(10) Where more than one child is the subject of adoption from overseas as part of the same arrangement, and the date of entry of each child is different, the reference in subsection (3)(b) to the date of the child's entry into Great Britain shall be interpreted as a reference to the date of the entry of the first child to enter Great Britain".
	[⁴...] [⁴...]

(SI 2003/499 Sch.1) (as amended)

Section 171ZJ(1)	In the appropriate places in the alphabetical order, insert— "adopter", in relation to a child, means a person by whom the child has been or is to be adopted;" "adoption from overseas" means the adoption of a child who enters Great Britain from outside the United Kingdom in connection with or for the purposes of adoption which does not involve the placement of the child for adoption under the law of any part of the United Kingdom, and the references to a child adopted from overseas shall be construed accordingly;" "official notification" means written notification, issued by or on behalf of the relevant domestic authority, that it is prepared to issue a certificate to the overseas authority concerned with the adoption of the child, or has issued a certificate and sent it to that authority, confirming, in either case, that the adopter is
Provision	Modification
	eligible to adopt and has been assessed and approved as being a suitable adoptive parent;" "relevant domestic authority" means— (a) in the case of an adopter to whom the Intercountry Adoption (Hague Convention) Regulations 2003 apply and who is habitually resident in Wales, the National Assembly of Wales; (b) in the case of an adopter to whom the [³Adoptions with a Foreign Element (Scotland) Regulations 2009] apply and who is habitually resident in Scotland, the Scottish Ministers; (c) in any other case, the Secretary of State".

AMENDMENTS

1. Statutory Paternity Pay and Statutory Adoption Pay (Amendment) Regulations 2004 (SI 2004/488) reg.3(2) (April 6, 2004).

2. Social Security Contributions and Benefits Act 1992 (Application of Parts 12ZA and 12ZB to Adoptions from Overseas) Regulations 2003 (Amendment) Regulations 2010 (SI 2010/153) reg.2(3) (April 6, 2010).

3. Adoptions with a Foreign Element (Scotland) Amendment Regulations 2011 (SSI 2011/159) reg.9(2) (March 21, 2011) (for Scotland) and Adoption and Children (Scotland) Act 2007 (Consequential Modifications) Order 2011 (SI 2011/1740) art.3 and Sch.2 para.7(2) (July 15, 2011) (for England, Wales and Northern Ireland).

4. Shared Parental Leave and Statutory Shared Parental Pay (Consequential Amendments to Subordinate Legislation) Order 2014 (SI 2014/3255) reg.14(3) (April 5, 2015).

SCHEDULE 2   **Regulation 3**

APPLICATION OF PART 12ZB OF THE ACT TO ADOPTIONS FROM OVERSEAS

6.109

Provision	Modification
Section 171ZL(2)	[¹. . .] In paragraph (a), for "with whom a child is, or is expected to be, placed for adoption under the law of any part of the United Kingdom" substitute "who is, or is expected to be, an adopter of a child from overseas". [¹In paragraph (b), omit "ending with the relevant week".]
Section 171ZL(3)	[¹For subsection (3) substitute— "(3) The reference in subsection (2)(d) to the relevant week is to— (a) the week in which official notification is sent to the adopter, or

Social Security Contributions and Benefits Act 1992 Regulations 2003

	(b) the week at the end of which the person satisfies the condition in subsection (2)(b), whichever is the later."] [¹...]
Section 171ZL(4)	In paragraph (b), for "placed for adoption with him" substitute "adopted by him".
Section 171ZL(5)	For "the placement, or expected placement, for adoption of more than one child" substitute "the adoption, or expected adoption, from overseas of more than one child".
Section 171ZS(1)	In the appropriate places in the alphabetical order, insert— ""adopter", in relation to a child, means a person by whom a child has been or is to be adopted;"

Provision	Modification
	"adoption from overseas" means the adoption of a child who enters Great Britain from outside the United Kingdom in connection with or for the purposes of adoption which does not involve the placement of the child for adoption under the law of any part of the United Kingdom, and the reference to an adopter from overseas shall be construed accordingly;" "official notification" means written notification, issued by or on behalf of the relevant domestic authority, that it is prepared to issue a certificate to the overseas authority concerned with the adoption of the child, or has issued a certificate and sent it to that authority, confirming, in either case, that the adopter is eligible to adopt and has been assessed and approved as being a suitable adoptive parent;" "relevant domestic authority" means— (a) in the case of an adopter to whom the Intercountry Adoption (Hague Convention) Regulations 2003 apply and who is habitually resident in Wales, the National Assembly of Wales; (b) in the case of an adopter to whom the [²Adoptions with a Foreign Element (Scotland) Regulations 2009] apply and who is habitually resident in Scotland, the Scottish Ministers; (c) in any other case, the Secretary of State".

AMENDMENTS

1. Statutory Paternity Pay and Statutory Adoption Pay (Amendment) Regulations 2004 (SI 2004/488) reg.3(3) (April 6, 2004).

2. Adoptions with a Foreign Element (Scotland) Amendment Regulations 2011 (SSI 2011/159) reg.9(3) (March 21, 2011) (for Scotland) and Adoption and Children (Scotland) Act 2007 (Consequential Modifications) Order 2011 (SI 2011/1740) art.3 and Sch.2 para.7(3) (July 15, 2011) (for England, Wales and Northern Ireland).

[¹ SCHEDULE 3   Regulation 4

APPLICATION OF PART 12ZC OF THE ACT TO ADOPTIONS FROM OVERSEAS

Provision	Modification
Section 171ZV	In subsection (1), for "with whom a child is, or is expected to be, placed for adoption under the law of any part of the United Kingdom" substitute "by whom a child is, or is expected to be, adopted from overseas".
	In paragraph (g) of subsection (2), for "placement for adoption of the child" substitute "adoption of the child from overseas".

	In paragraph (a) of subsection (4), for "with whom a child is, or is expected to be, placed for adoption under the law of any part of the United Kingdom" substitute "by whom a child is, or is expected to be, adopted from overseas".
	In paragraph (h) of subsection (4), for "placement for adoption of the child" substitute "adoption of the child from overseas".
	In subsection (16), for "placement for adoption" substitute "adoption from overseas".
	After subsection (16) insert—
	"(16A) For the purposes of this section, a person adopts a child from overseas if the person adopts a child who

Provision	Modification
	enters Great Britain from outside the United Kingdom in connection with or for the purposes of adoption which does not involve the placement of the child for adoption under the law of any part of the United Kingdom.".
	Omit subsection (17).
	Omit subsection (18).]

AMENDMENT

1. Social Security Contributions and Benefits Act 1992 (Application of Parts 12ZA and 12ZB to Adoptions from Overseas) (Amendment) Regulations 2014 (SI 2014/2857) regs 2 and 6 (November 19, 2014).

The Statutory Paternity Pay (Adoption) and Statutory Adoption Pay (Adoptions from Overseas) (Administration) Regulations 2003

(SI 2003/1192)

The Secretary of State, in exercise of the powers conferred on her by sections 7(1), 2(a) and (b), (4)(a), (b) and (c) and (5), 8(1) and (2)(a), (b) and (c), 10(1) and (2) and 51(1) of the Employment Act 2002 and sections 8(1)(f) and 25 of the Social Security Contributions (Transfer of Functions, etc.) Act 1999 and with the concurrence of the Commissioners of Inland Revenue, hereby makes the following Regulations:

ARRANGEMENT OF REGULATIONS

1. Citation and commencement.
2. Interpretation.
3. Application of the Statutory Paternity Pay and Statutory Adoption Pay (Administration) Regulations 2002 to adoptions from overseas.

Citation and commencement

1.—These Regulations may be cited as the Statutory Paternity Pay (Adoption) and Statutory Adoption Pay (Adoptions from Overseas) (Administration) Regulations 2003 and shall come into force on 23rd May 2003.

Statutory Paternity Pay and Statutory Adoption Pay Regulations 2003

GENERAL NOTE

6.113   These Regulations apply the Statutory Paternity Pay and Statutory Adoption Pay (Administration) Regulations 2002 (SI 2002/2820) to adoptions from overseas with the necessary modifications.

Interpretation

6.114   2.—In these Regulations, "adoption from overseas" means the adoption of a child who enters Great Britain from outside the United Kingdom in connection with or for the purposes of adoption which does not involve the placement of the child for adoption under the law of any part of the United Kingdom.

Application of the Statutory Paternity Pay and Statutory Adoption Pay (Administration) Regulations 2002 to adoptions from overseas

6.115   3.—(1) The Statutory Paternity Pay and Statutory Adoption Pay (Administration) Regulations 2002 shall apply in the case of adoptions from overseas with the modifications set out in the following paragraphs of this regulation.

(2) In regulation 2(1) (interpretation)—
(a) in the definition of "adopter", for the words "with whom the child is matched for adoption" substitute "by whom the child has been or is to be adopted";
(b) after the definition of "income tax quarter", insert—
"official notification" means written notification, issued by or on behalf of the relevant domestic authority, that it is prepared to issue a certificate to the overseas authority concerned with the adoption of the child, or has issued a certificate and sent it to that authority, confirming, in either case, that the adopter is eligible to adopt and has been assessed and approved as being a suitable adoptive parent";
(c) in the definition of "paternity leave", insert at the end "as modified in its application to adoptions from overseas by the Employment Rights Act 1996 (Application of Section 80B to Adoptions from Overseas) Regulations 2003"; and
(d) after the definition of "paternity pay period" insert—
"relevant domestic authority means:—
(a) in the case of an adopter to whom the Intercountry Adoption (Hague Convention) Regulations 2003 apply and who is habitually resident in Wales, the National Assembly for Wales;
(b) in the case of an adopter to whom the [¹Adoptions with a Foreign Element (Scotland) Regulations 2009] apply and who is habitually resident in Scotland, the Scottish Ministers; and
(c) in any other case, the Secretary of State;".
(3) After regulation 2(2), insert—
"(3) References in these Regulations to provisions of Parts 12ZA and 12ZB of the Contributions and Benefits Act are to be construed as references to those provisions as modified by the Social Security Contributions and Benefits Act 1992 (Application of Parts 12ZA and 12ZB to Adoptions from Overseas) Regulations 2003."
(4) In regulation 11(3)(b)(ii) (time within which an employer is required to give decision that he has no liability to make payments), for "the end of the seven-day period that starts on the date on which the adopter is notified

(SI 2003/1192 reg.3) (as amended)

of having been matched with the child" substitute "the date on which the employer's evidence was provided, or, where not all of the evidence referred to in paragraph (1) was provided on one date, the date on which the last of the evidence was provided".

(5) Omit regulation 11(4).

AMENDMENT

1. Adoptions with a Foreign Element (Scotland) Amendment Regulations 2011 (SSI 2011/159 reg.7 (March 21, 2011) (for Scotland) and Adoption and Children (Scotland) Act 2007 (Consequential Modifications) Order 2011 (SI 2011/1740) art.3 and Sch.2 para.9 (July 15, 2011) (for England, Wales and Northern Ireland).

The Statutory Paternity Pay (Adoption) and Statutory Adoption Pay (Adoptions from Overseas) (No.2) Regulations 2003

(SI 2003/1194) (AS AMENDED)

The Secretary of State, in exercise of the powers conferred on her by sections 171ZB(2)(a), 171ZC(3)(a) to (d), (f) and (g), 171ZD(2) and (3), 171ZE(2)(a) and (b)(i), (3)(b), (7) and (8), 171ZG(3), 171ZJ(1), (3), (4), (7) and (8), 171ZL(8)(b) to (d), (f) and (g), 171ZM(2) and (3), 171ZN(2), (5) and (6), 171ZP(6), 171ZS(1), (3), (4), (7) and (8), and 175(4) of the Social Security Contributions and Benefits Act 1992, section 5(1)(g), (i) and (p) of the Social Security Administration Act 1992 and with the concurrence of the Commissioners of Inland Revenue in so far as such concurrence is required, by this instrument, which contains only provision made by virtue of sections 2, 4 and 53 and paragraphs 8 and 11 of Schedule 7 to the Employment Act 2002 and is made before the end of the period of 6 months from the coming into force of these enactments, hereby makes the following Regulations:

ARRANGEMENT OF REGULATIONS

General

1. Citation and commencement.
2. Interpretation and scope.
3. Application of the General Regulations to these Regulations.
4. Application.

Statutory paternity pay (adoption)

5. Conditions of entitlement to statutory paternity pay (adoption) in respect of adoptions from overseas: relationship with child and with adopter.
6. Options in respect of periods of payment of statutory paternity pay (adoption) in respect of adoptions from overseas.
6A. Qualifying period for statutory paternity pay (adoption) in respect of adoptions from overseas.
6B. Notice and evidence requirements for statutory paternity pay (adoption) in respect of adoptions from overseas.
7. Additional notice requirements for statutory paternity pay (adoption) in respect of adoptions from overseas.
10. Entitlement to statutory paternity pay (adoption) where there is more than one employer in respect of adoptions from overseas.

6.116

11. Avoidance of liability for statutory paternity pay (adoption) in respect of adoptions from overseas.
11A. Change in circumstances.
11B. Work during a period of payment of statutory paternity pay (adoption).
12. Adoption pay period in respect of adoptions from overseas.

Statutory adoption pay

13. Adoption pay period in respect of adoptions from overseas where adoption is disrupted.
14. Additional notice requirements for statutory adoption pay in respect of adoptions from overseas.
15. Evidence of entitlement to statutory adoption pay in respect of adoptions from overseas.
16. Entitlement to statutory adoption pay in respect of adoptions from overseas where there is more than one employer.
17. Termination of employment and liability to pay statutory adoption pay in respect of adoptions from overseas.
18. Avoidance of liability for statutory adoption pay in respect of adoptions from overseas.
19. Revocation.

General

Citation and commencement

6.117   1.—These Regulations may be cited as the Statutory Paternity Pay (Adoption) and Statutory Adoption Pay (Adoptions from Overseas) (No.2) Regulations 2003 and shall come into force on 30th May 2003.

General Note

6.118   These Regulations, made under provisions inserted into the SSCBA 1992 by the Employment Act 2002, make provision relating to statutory paternity pay and statutory adoption pay in respect of adoptions from overseas. They should be read together with the Social Security Contributions and Benefits Act 1992 (Application of Pts XIIZA and XIIZB to Adoptions from Overseas) Regulations 2003 (SI 2003/499), which provide for Pts XIIZA and XIIZB of the 1992 Act to have effect, with the modification prescribed in those Regulations, in relation to cases which involve adoption, but not the placement of a child for adoption under the law of any part of the United Kingdom. Regulation 19 of these (No.2) Regulations revokes the Statutory Pay (Adoption) and Statutory Adoption Pay (Adoptions from Overseas) Regulations 2003 (SI 2003/500), which came into force on April 6, 2003 and originally made provision for paternity and adoption pay in the case of adoptions from overseas. The (No.2) Regulations are virtually in identical form to the original set. The main difference is the correction of "employee" to read "employer" in reg.11 where it first appears, but a number of other minor drafting amendments have also been made.

Interpretation and scope

6.119   2.—(1) In these Regulations—
"the Act" means the Social Security Contributions and Benefits Act 1992;
"adopter", in relation to a child, means a person by whom the child has been or is to be adopted;

"adoption from overseas" means the adoption of a child who enters Great Britain from outside the United Kingdom in connection with or for the purposes of adoption which does not involve the placement of the child for adoption under the law of any part of the United Kingdom;

"the Application Regulations" means the Social Security Contributions and Benefits Act 1992 (Application of Parts 12ZA and 12ZB to Adoptions from Overseas) Regulations 2003;

"the Board" means the Commissioners of Inland Revenue;

"enter Great Britain" means enter Great Britain from outside the United Kingdom in connection with or for the purposes of adoption, and cognate expressions shall be construed accordingly;

"the General Regulations" means the Statutory Paternity Pay and Statutory Adoption Pay (General) Regulations 2002;

"official notification" means written notification, issued by or on behalf of the relevant domestic authority, that it is prepared to issue a certificate to the overseas authority concerned with the adoption of the child, or has issued a certificate and sent it to that authority, confirming, in either case, that the adopter is eligible to adopt, and has been assessed and approved as being a suitable adoptive parent;

"relevant domestic authority" means—
(a) in the case of an adopter to whom the Intercountry Adoption (Hague Convention) Regulations 2003 apply and who is habitually resident in Wales, the National Assembly for Wales;
(b) in the case of an adopter to whom the [¹Adoptions with a Foreign Element (Scotland) Regulations 2009] apply and who is habitually resident in Scotland, the Scottish Ministers;
(c) in any other case, the Secretary of State;

"statutory paternity pay (adoption)" means statutory paternity pay payable in accordance with the provisions of Part 12ZA of the Act, as modified by the Application Regulations, where the conditions specified in section 171ZB(2) of the Act, as modified by the Application Regulations, are satisfied.

(2) References in these Regulations to the provisions of Parts 12ZA and 12ZB of the Act are to be construed as references to those provisions as modified by the Application Regulations.

(3) These Regulations apply to statutory paternity pay (adoption) and statutory adoption pay in respect of adoptions from overseas.

AMENDMENT

1. Adoptions with a Foreign Element (Scotland) Amendment Regulations 2011 (SSI 2011/159) reg. 6 (March 21, 2011) (for Scotland) and Adoption and Children (Scotland) Act 2007 (Consequential Modifications) Order 2011 (SI 2011/1740) art.3 and Sch.2 para.10 (July 15, 2011) (for England, Wales and Northern Ireland).

Application of the General Regulations to these Regulations

3.—(1) Subject to paragraph (2), the provisions of the General Regulations mentioned in paragraph (3) shall, in so far as they apply to statutory paternity pay (adoption) and statutory adoption pay, apply to adoptions from overseas.

(2) Any references to the provisions of Parts 12ZA or 12ZB of the Act in the regulations of the General Regulations mentioned in paragraph (3)

6.120

shall be construed as references to those provisions as modified by the Application Regulations.

(3) The provisions of the General Regulations referred to in paragraph (1) are regulations [²18, 19], 26 to 28, 31 to 39, 41 to 47 and, subject to paragraph (4), regulation 40.

(4) In the General Regulations, the provisions of regulation 40 shall apply as if—

[¹(a) in paragraph (2)(b), for "the week in which the adopter is notified of being matched with the child for the purposes of adoption" there were substituted—

"the week in which—
  (i) official notification is sent to the adopter or
  (ii) the person satisfies the condition in section 171ZB(2)(b) or 171ZL(2)(b) of the Act (26 weeks' continuous employment), whichever is the later;"]

(b) at the end of paragraph (2), there were added " 'official notification' has the same meaning in the Statutory Paternity Pay (Adoption) and Statutory Adoption Pay (Adoptions from Overseas) (No.2) Regulations 2003".

AMENDMENTS

1. Statutory Paternity Pay and Statutory Adoption Pay (Amendment) Regulations 2004 (SI 2004/488) reg.4 (April 6, 2004).
2. Statutory Paternity Pay (Amendment) Regulations 2024 (SI 2024/121) reg.18 (March 8, 2024).

DEFINITIONS

"the Act—see reg.2(1).
"adopter"—see reg.2(1).
"adoption from overseas"—see reg.2(1).
"the Application Regulation"—see reg.2(1).
"the General Regulations"—see reg.2(1).
"official notification"—see reg.2(1).
"statutory paternity pay (adoption)"—see reg.2(1).

Application

4.—(1) Subject to the provisions of Part 12ZA of the Act (statutory paternity pay), the provisions of the General Regulations mentioned in paragraph (3) of regulation 3 and these Regulations, there is entitlement to statutory paternity pay (adoption) in respect of children who enter Great Britain on or after 6th April 2003.

(2) Subject to the provisions of Part 12ZB of the Act (statutory adoption pay), the provisions of the General Regulations mentioned in paragraph (3) of regulation 3 and these Regulations, there is entitlement to statutory adoption pay in respect of children who enter Great Britain on or after 6th April, 2003.

DEFINITIONS

"the Act"—see reg.2(1).
"enter Great Britain"—see reg.2(1).
"the General Regulation"—see reg.2(1).

(SI 2003/1194 reg.4) (as amended)

"Part XIIZA"—see reg.(2).
"Pt XIIZB"—see reg.2(1).
"statutory paternity pay (adoption)"—see reg.2(1).

Statutory paternity pay (adoption)

Conditions of entitlement to statutory paternity pay (adoption) in respect of adoptions from overseas: relationship with child and with adopter

5.—(1) The conditions prescribed under section 171ZB(2)(a) of the Act are that a person—
 (a) is married to [¹, the civil partner] or the partner of a child's adopter (or in a case where there are two adopters, married to [¹, the civil partner] or the partner of the other adopter); and
 (b) has, or expects to have, the main responsibility (apart from the responsibility of the child's adopter or, in a case where there are two adopters, together with the other adopter) for the upbringing of the child.

(2) For the purpose of paragraph (1), "partner" means a person (whether of a different sex or the same sex) who lives with the adopter and the child in an enduring family relationship but is not a relative of the adopter of a kind specified in paragraph (3).

(3) The relatives of a child's adopter referred to in the definition of "partner" in paragraph (2) are the adopter's parent, grandparent, sister, brother, aunt or uncle.

(4) References to relationships in paragraph (3)—
 (a) are to relationships of the full blood or half blood or, in the case of an adopted person, such of those relationships as would exist but for the adoption; and
 (b) include the relationship of a child with his adoptive, or former adoptive parents but do not include any other adoptive relationships.

AMENDMENT

1. Civil Partnership Act 2004 (Amendments to Subordinate Legislation) Order 2005 (SI 2005/2114) art.2(17) and Sch.17 para.6 (December 5, 2005).

DEFINITIONS

"the Act"—see reg.2(1).
"adopter"—see reg.2(1).
"partner"—see para.(2).

[¹Options in respect of periods of payment of statutory paternity pay (adoption) in respect of adoptions from overseas

6.—(1) Within the qualifying period set out in regulation 6A, a person entitled to statutory paternity pay (adoption) may choose the statutory paternity pay period to begin on—
 (a) the date on which the child enters Great Britain or, where the person is at work on that day, the following day; or
 (b) a predetermined date, specified by the person, which is later than the date on which the child is expected to enter Great Britain.

(2) A person may choose for statutory paternity pay (adoption) to be paid in respect of—
  (a) a single period of either one week or two weeks, or
  (b) two non-consecutive periods of a week each.]

AMENDMENT

1. Statutory Paternity Pay (Amendment) Regulations 2024 (SI 2024/121) reg.19 (March 8, 2024).

[¹Qualifying period for statutory paternity pay (adoption) in respect of adoptions from overseas

6A. Subject to regulation 11A, the qualifying period for the purposes of section 171ZE(3) of the Act (period within which a period of payment of statutory paternity pay must occur) is a period of 52 weeks beginning with the date on which the child enters Great Britain.]

AMENDMENT

1. Statutory Paternity Pay (Amendment) Regulations 2024 (SI 2024/121) reg.19 (March 8, 2024).

[¹Notice and evidence requirements for statutory paternity pay (adoption) in respect of adoptions from overseas

6B.—(1) A person must provide evidence of entitlement to statutory paternity pay (adoption) by providing in writing to whoever will be liable to pay it—
  (a) the information specified in paragraph (2), and
  (b) the declarations specified in paragraph (3).
(2) The information referred to in paragraph (1)(a) is as follows—
  (a) the name of the person claiming statutory paternity pay (adoption);
  (b) the date on which the adopter of the child received an official notification;
  (c) the date on which the child is expected to enter Great Britain or, where the child has already entered Great Britain, the date of that entry.
(3) The declarations referred to in paragraph (1)(b) are declarations in writing that—
  (a) the person satisfies the conditions prescribed in regulation 5(1);
  (b) the adopter of the child has received an official notification in relation to the child;
  (c) the person has elected to receive statutory paternity pay (adoption), and not statutory adoption pay under Part 12ZB of the Act;
  (d) section 171ZE(4) of the Act does not apply.
(4) The information referred to in paragraph (2) and the declarations referred to in sub-paragraphs (a), (b) and (c) of paragraph (3) must be provided—
  (a) no more than 28 days after whichever is the later of—
    (i) the date on which the adopter of the child receives the official notification, or
    (ii) the date on which the person completes 26 weeks' continuous employment with the employer, or

(b) in a case where it was not reasonably practicable for the person to provide it in that period, as soon as is reasonably practicable.

(5) The notice provided for in section 171ZC(1) of the Act (notice to be given stating the week or weeks in respect of which payments are to be made) must be given to whoever will be liable to pay statutory paternity pay (adoption) at least 28 days before—
(a) the date provided under paragraph (2)(c) above as the date on which the child is expected to enter Great Britain, where the option in regulation 6(1)(a) is chosen;
(b) the predetermined date, where the option in regulation 6(1)(b) is chosen;
or, if it is not reasonably practicable to do so, as soon as is reasonably practicable.

(6) On each occasion that a notice is provided under paragraph (5), the declaration referred to in paragraph (3)(d) must be provided at the same time.

(7) Where notice has previously been given under paragraph (5) or this paragraph or under regulation 7(1), a notice of variation in writing may be given to the person who will be liable to pay statutory paternity pay which—
(a) cancels the period of statutory paternity pay specified in that notice, or
(b) varies that period by choosing an option under regulation 6.

(8) Where the notice under paragraph (5) specifies a period of two weeks in respect of which statutory paternity pay is to be paid, notice of variation may be given in relation to either one or both of those weeks, regardless of whether those weeks are consecutive or non-consecutive.

(9) A notice of variation under paragraph (7) must be given by whichever is the earlier of at least 28 days before—
(a) the original day or date referred to in paragraph (10)(a), or
(b) the new day or date referred to in paragraph (10)(b),
or, if it is not reasonably practicable to do so, as soon as is reasonably practicable.

(10) For the purposes of—
(a) paragraph (9)(a), where a notice has previously been given under either paragraph (5) or (7), the original day or date is—
  (i) the date referred to in paragraph (5)(a), where the option in regulation 6(1)(a) was chosen in that notice;
  (ii) the predetermined date specified in that notice where the option in regulation 6(1)(b) was chosen in that notice,
(b) paragraph (9)(b), the new day or date is—
  (i) the date referred to in paragraph (5)(a), where the option in regulation 6(1)(a) is chosen in the notice of variation;
  (ii) the predetermined date specified in the notice of variation, where the option in regulation 6(1)(b) is chosen.

(11) The person who is entitled to statutory paternity pay (adoption) must inform the person who is liable to pay it of the date on which the child enters Great Britain, as soon as reasonably practicable after that date, unless that information has already been provided.]

AMENDMENT

1. Statutory Paternity Pay (Amendment) Regulations 2024 (SI 2024/121) reg.19 (March 8, 2024).

[¹Additional notice requirements for statutory paternity pay (adoption) in relation to adoptions from overseas

7.—(1) In a case where—
  (a) a person has given notice in accordance with regulation 6B(5)(b), and
  (b) the child has not entered Great Britain on or before that date,
the person must vary the date on which the period of payment is to begin by giving notice to the person liable to pay statutory paternity pay (adoption), as soon as is reasonably practicable, that the period in respect of which statutory paternity pay is to be paid will begin on a date different from that originally chosen.

(2) That date may be any date chosen in accordance with paragraph (1) of regulation 6.

(3) Where a notice is given under regulation 6B(7) or paragraph (1) above which varies the dates of a period of payment, a declaration under regulation 6B(3)(d) in relation to that period must be given at the same time as that notice.

(4) Paragraph (1) does not apply in circumstances where regulation 11A(5) applies.]

AMENDMENT

1. Statutory Paternity Pay (Amendment) Regulations 2024 (SI 2024/121) reg.19 (March 8, 2024).

Entitlement to statutory paternity pay (adoption) where there is more than one employer in respect of adoptions from overseas

10.—Statutory paternity pay (adoption) shall be payable to a person in respect of a statutory pay week during any part of which he works only for an employer—
  (a) who is not liable to pay him statutory paternity pay (adoption); and
  (b) for whom he has worked in the week in which the adopter receives official notification.

DEFINITIONS

"adopter"—see reg.2(1).
"official notification"—see reg.2(1).
"statutory paternity pay (adoption)"—see reg.2(1).

Avoidance of liability for statutory paternity pay (adoption) in respect of adoptions from overseas

11.—(1) A former employer shall be liable to make payments of statutory paternity pay (adoption) to a former employee in any case where the employee has been employed for a continuous period of at least 8 weeks and his contract of service was brought to an end by the former employer solely, or mainly, for the purpose of avoiding liability for statutory paternity pay (adoption).

(2) In a case falling within paragraph (1)—
  (a) the employee shall be treated as if he had been employed for a continuous period ending with the day the child enters Great Britain;

(SI 2003/1194 reg.11) (as amended)

(b) his normal weekly earnings shall be calculated by reference to his normal weekly earnings for the period of 8 weeks ending with the last day in respect of which he was paid under his former contract of service.

DEFINITIONS

"enter Great Britain"—see reg.2(1).
"statutory paternity pay (adoption)"—see reg.2(1).

[¹**Change in circumstances**

11A.—(1) This regulation applies where a person is otherwise entitled to statutory paternity pay (adoption) in respect of a child but a relevant event, as specified in paragraph (2), occurs.
(2) A relevant event as referred to in paragraph (1) occurs when—
(a) the child ceases to live with the adopter, or
(b) the child dies.
(3) In a case where this regulation applies, the qualifying period for the purposes of section 171ZE(3) of the Act (period within which a period of payment of statutory paternity pay must occur) ends after the end of a period of eight weeks following the end of the relevant week specified in paragraph (4), except in the circumstances mentioned in paragraph (5).
(4) The relevant week referred to in paragraph (3) is—
(a) in a case falling within paragraph (2)(a), the week during which the child ceases to live with the adopter;
(b) in a case falling within paragraph (2)(b), the week during which the child dies.
(5) Where the person has complied with the requirements in regulation 6B (notice and evidential requirements for statutory paternity pay (adoption)), the person will remain entitled to payment in respect of any period of payment which has been specified in a notice given, before the day on which the relevant event occurs, under that regulation.
(6) Where paragraph (5) applies, no further notices may be served under regulation 6B other than a notice to cancel a period of payment specified in a notice already given under regulations 6B or 7.
(7) In paragraph (4), "week" means the period of seven days beginning with Sunday.]

6.129

AMENDMENT

1. Statutory Paternity Pay (Amendment) Regulations 2024 (SI 2024/121) reg.20 (March 8, 2024).

[¹**Work during a period of payment of statutory paternity pay**

11B.—(1) Where a person (P) works for an employer falling within paragraph (a), but not paragraph (b), of regulation 10, for any part of a period which has been specified by P in a notice under regulation 6B or 7, P must notify the person liable to pay statutory paternity pay of the fact of that work within seven days of the first day during which the person does such work.
(2) The notification mentioned in paragraph (1) must be in writing, if the person who has been liable to pay statutory paternity pay so requests.]

6.130

Statutory Paternity Pay and Statutory Adoption Pay (No.2) Regs 2003

AMENDMENT

1. Statutory Paternity Pay (Amendment) Regulations 2024 (SI 2024/121) reg.20 (March 8, 2024).

Statutory adoption pay

Adoption pay period in respect of adoptions from overseas

6.131
12.—(1) Subject to paragraph (2), a person entitled to statutory adoption pay may choose the adoption pay period to begin—
    (a) on the date on which the child enters Great Britain or, where the person is at work on that day, on the following day;
    (b) on the pre-determined date, specified by him, which is no later than 28 days after the date the child enters Great Britain.

(2) In a case where statutory adoption pay is payable in respect of a child where the adopter has received official notification before 6th April 2003, the statutory adoption pay period shall begin on a predetermined date, later than the date of entry, specified by the person entitled to such pay in a notice under section 171ZL(6) of the Act, which is at least 28 days after the date on which that notice was given, unless the person liable to pay statutory adoption pay agrees to the period commencing earlier.

(3) Where the choice made is that mentioned in sub-paragraph (b) of paragraph (1) or in a case where paragraph (2) applies, the adoption pay period shall, unless the employer agrees to the adoption pay period beginning earlier, begin no earlier than 28 days after notice under section 171ZL(6) of the Act has been given.

(4) Subject to regulation 13, the duration of any adoption pay period shall be a continuous period of 26 weeks.

(5) A choice made under paragraph (1), or a date specified under paragraph (2), is not irrevocable, but where a person subsequently makes a different choice or specifies a different date in relation to the beginning of the statutory adoption pay period, section 171ZL(6) of the Act shall apply to it.

DEFINITIONS

    "the Act"—see reg.2(1).
    "adopter"—see reg.2(1).
    "enter Great Britain"—see reg.2(1).
    "official notification"—see reg.2(1).

Adoption pay period in respect of adoptions from overseas where adoption is disrupted

6.132
13.—(1) Where after a child enters Great Britain the child—
    (a) dies; or
    (b) ceases to live with the adopter,
the adoption pay period shall terminate in accordance with the provisions of paragraph (2).

(2) The adoption pay period shall, in a case falling within paragraph (1), terminate 8 weeks after the end of the week specified in paragraph (3).

(SI 2003/1194 reg.17) (as amended)

virtue of that employment, the liability of the Board shall cease and section 171ZM(1) of the Act shall apply.

DEFINITIONS

"the Act"—see reg.2(1).
"adopter"—see reg.2(1).
"adoption from overseas"—see reg.2(1).
"the Board"—see reg.2(1).

Avoidance of liability for statutory adoption pay in respect of adoptions from overseas

18.—(1) A former employer shall be liable to make payments of statutory adoption pay to a former employee in any case where the employee had been employed for a continuous period of at least 8 weeks and his contract of service was brought to an end by the former employer solely, or mainly, for the purpose of avoiding liability for statutory adoption pay.

(2) In a case falling within paragraph (1)—
(a) the employee shall be treated as if he had been employed for a continuous period ending with the week in which he received official notification; and
(b) his normal weekly earnings shall be calculated by reference to his normal weekly earnings for the period of 8 weeks ending with the last day in respect of which he was paid under his former contract of service.

6.137

DEFINITION

"official notification"—see reg.2(1).

Revocation

19.—The Statutory Paternity Pay (Adoption) and Statutory Adoption Pay (Adoptions from Overseas) Regulations 2003 are hereby revoked.

6.138

The Ordinary Statutory Paternity Pay (Adoption), Additional Statutory Paternity Pay (Adoption) and Statutory Adoption Pay (Adoptions from Overseas) (Persons Abroad and Mariners) Regulations 2010

(SI 2010/150)

ARRANGEMENT OF REGULATIONS

1. Citation and commencement
2. Interpretation
3. Revocation
4. Application of the Statutory Paternity Pay and Statutory Adoption Pay (Persons Abroad and Mariners) Regulations 2002 to adoptions from overseas

6.139

Additional Statutory Paternity Pay (Adoptions from Overseas) Regs 2010

The Secretary of State makes the following Regulations in exercise of the powers conferred by sections 171ZI, 171ZJ(1), 171ZR and 171ZS(1) of the Social Security Contributions and Benefits Act 1992.

The Secretary of State makes these Regulations with the concurrence of the Treasury and after agreement by the Social Security Advisory Committee that the proposals in respect of these Regulations shall not be referred to it.

Citation and commencement

6.140   **1.**—(1) These Regulations may be cited as the Ordinary Statutory Paternity Pay (Adoption), Additional Statutory Paternity Pay (Adoption) and Statutory Adoption Pay (Adoptions from Overseas) (Persons Abroad and Mariners) Regulations 2010.

(2) These Regulations come into force immediately after the coming into force of the Statutory Paternity Pay and Statutory Adoption Pay (Persons Abroad and Mariners) Regulations 2002 (Amendment) Regulations 2010.

Interpretation

6.141   **2.**—In these Regulations, "adoption from overseas" means the adoption of a child who enters Great Britain from outside the United Kingdom in connection with or for the purposes of adoption which does not involve the placement of the child for adoption under the law of any part of the United Kingdom.

Revocation

6.142   **3.**—The Statutory Paternity Pay (Adoption) and Statutory Adoption Pay (Adoptions from Overseas) (Persons Abroad and Mariners) Regulations 2003 are revoked.

Application of the Statutory Paternity Pay and Statutory Adoption Pay (Persons Abroad and Mariners) Regulations 2002 to adoptions from overseas

6.143   **4.**—(1) The Statutory Paternity Pay and Statutory Adoption Pay (Persons Abroad and Mariners) Regulations 2002 shall have effect in relation to adoptions from overseas with the modifications set out in the following paragraphs of this regulation.

(2) In regulation 1(2) (interpretation)—
(a) omit the definitions of "additional statutory paternity pay (birth)" and "ordinary statutory paternity pay (birth);
(b) for the definition of "adopter", substitute—
""adopter", in relation to a child adopted from overseas, means—
 (a) a person by whom the child has been or is to be adopted, or
 (b) in a case where the child has been or is to be adopted by two people jointly, whichever of them has elected to take adoption leave under section 75A or 75B of the Employment Rights Act 1996 in respect of the child;";
(c) after the definition of "mariner", insert—
""official notification" means written notification, issued by or on behalf of the relevant

central authority, that it is prepared to issue a certificate to the overseas authority
concerned with the adoption of the child, or has issued a certificate and sent it to that
authority, confirming, in either case, that the adopter is eligible to adopt and has been
assessed and approved as being a suitable adoptive parent;";

(d) after the definition of "ordinary statutory paternity pay (adoption)", insert—

"relevant central authority" means—
(a) in the case of an adopter to whom Part 3 of the Adoptions with a Foreign Element Regulations 2005 apply and who is habitually resident in Wales, the Welsh Ministers;
(b) in the case of an adopter to whom [¹ ...] the Adoptions with a Foreign Element (Scotland) Regulations 2009 apply and who is habitually resident in Scotland, the Scottish Ministers; and
(c) in any other case, the Secretary of State;".

(3) For regulation 1(3), substitute—

"(3) References in these Regulations to provisions of Parts 12ZA and 12ZB of the Act are to be construed as references to those provisions as modified by the Social Security Contributions and Benefits Act 1992 (Application of Parts 12ZA and 12ZB to Adoptions from Overseas) Regulations 2003.".

(4) In regulation 5 (entitlement to ordinary statutory paternity pay and additional statutory paternity pay where person has worked in an EEA State)—
(a) omit paragraph (1);
(b) in the first line of paragraph (2), after "and who", insert ", in the week in which the person receives an official notification or completes 26 weeks' continuous employment with the person's employer, whichever is the later"; and
(c) in paragraph (2)(a) omit the words "in the week in which the adopter is notified of being matched with the child for the purposes of adoption".

(5) In regulation 6 (entitlement to statutory adoption pay where person has worked in an EEA State)—
(a) in the first line, after "and who", insert ", in the week in which the person receives an official notification or completes 26 weeks' continuous employment with the person's employer, whichever is the later";
(b) in paragraph (a), omit the words "in the week in which he is notified that he has been matched with the child for the purposes of adoption"; and
(c) in the full out, for the word "he", substitute "the person".

AMENDMENT

1. Adoptions with a Foreign Element (Scotland) Amendment Regulations 2011 (SSI 2011/159) reg.5 (March 21, 2011).

The Additional Statutory Paternity Pay (National Health Service Employees) Regulations 2010

(SI 2010/152)

6.144   These regulations are nominally still in force. However, the principal primary legislation governing additional statutory paternity pay (ss.171ZEA–171ZEE of the Social Security Contributions and Benefits Act 1992 was repealed by s.125(2) of the Children and Families Act 2014 with effect from April 5, 2015. As from that date statutory shared parental pay in effect replaced additional statutory paternity pay. However, the repeals made by s.125 of the 2014 Act did not have effect in relation to "(a) children whose expected week of birth ends on or before 4th April 2015; (b) children placed for adoption on or before 4th April 2015." See further art.14 of the Children and Families Act 2014 (Commencement No.3, Transitional Provisions and Savings) Order 2014 (SI 2014/1640). The regulations nominally still in force can be found in the 2016/17 edn of this book (at para.6.144).

The Additional Statutory Paternity Pay (General) Regulations 2010

(SI 2010/1056)

6.145   These regulations are nominally still in force. However, the principal primary legislation governing additional statutory paternity pay (ss.171ZEA–171ZEE of the Social Security Contributions and Benefits Act 1992 was repealed by s.125(2) of the Children and Families Act 2014 with effect from April 5, 2015. As from that date statutory shared parental pay in effect replaced additional statutory paternity pay. However, the repeals made by s.125 of the 2014 Act did not have effect in relation to "(a) children whose expected week of birth ends on or before 4th April 2015; (b) children placed for adoption on or before 4th April 2015." See further art.14 of the Children and Families Act 2014 (Commencement No.3, Transitional Provisions and Savings) Order 2014 (SI 2014/1640). The regulations nominally still in force can be found in the 2016/17 edn of this book (at para.6.151).

The Additional Statutory Paternity Pay (Adoptions from Overseas) Regulations 2010

(SI 2010/1057)

6.146   These regulations are nominally still in force. However, the principal primary legislation governing additional statutory paternity pay (ss.171ZEA–171ZEE of the Social Security Contributions and Benefits Act 1992 was repealed by s.125(2) of the Children and Families Act 2014 with effect from April 5, 2015. As from that date statutory shared parental pay in effect replaced additional statutory paternity pay. However, the repeals made by s.125 of the 2014 Act did not have effect in relation to "(a) children whose expected week of birth ends on or before 4th April 2015; (b) children placed for adoption on or before 4th April 2015." See further art.14 of the Children and Families Act 2014 (Commencement No.3, Transitional Provisions and Savings) Order 2014 (SI 2014/1640). The regulations nominally still in force can be found in the 2016/17 edn of this book (at para.6.192).

The Additional Statutory Paternity Pay (Weekly Rates) Regulations 2010

(SI 2010/1060)

6.147 These regulations are nominally still in force. However, the principal primary legislation governing additional statutory paternity pay (ss.171ZEA–171ZEE of the Social Security Contributions and Benefits Act 1992 was repealed by s.125(2) of the Children and Families Act 2014 with effect from April 5, 2015. As from that date statutory shared parental pay in effect replaced additional statutory paternity pay. However, the repeals made by s.125 of the 2014 Act did not have effect in relation to "(a) children whose expected week of birth ends on or before 4th April 2015; (b) children placed for adoption on or before 4th April 2015." See further art.14 of the Children and Families Act 2014 (Commencement No.3, Transitional Provisions and Savings) Order 2014 (SI 2014/1640). The regulations nominally still in force can be found in the 2016/17 edn of this book (at para.6.205).

The Social Security Contributions and Benefits Act 1992 (Application of Parts 12ZA, 12ZB and 12ZC to Parental Order Cases) Regulations 2014

(SI 2014/2866)

This instrument contains only regulations made by virtue of, or consequential upon, sections 119(1) and 122(5)(c) and (6)(c) of the Children and Families Act 2014 and is made before the end of the period of 6 months beginning with the coming into force of that enactment.

The Secretary of State, in exercise of the powers conferred by sections 171ZK(2), 171ZT(2) and 171ZZ5(2) of the Social Security Contributions and Benefits Act 1992, makes the following Regulations:

ARRANGEMENT OF REGULATIONS

6.148
1. Citation, commencement and application
2. Interpretation
3. Application of Part 12ZA of the Act to parental order parents
4. Application of Part 12ZB of the Act to parental order parents
5. Application of Part 12ZC of the Act to parental order parents

Sch.1. Application of Part 12ZA of the Act to parental order cases
Sch.2. Application of Part 12ZB of the Act to parental order cases
Sch.3 Application of Part 12ZC of the Act to parental order cases

Social Security Contributions and Benefits Act 1992 Regulations 2014

GENERAL NOTE

6.149 These Regulations apply Pts 12ZA, 12ZB and 12ZC of the SSCBA 1992, as modified by these Regulations, to parental order parents. A "parental order parent" is a person who has applied, or intends to apply, with another person, under s.54 of the Human Fertilisation and Embryology Act 2008 for a parental order in respect of a child or someone who has such an order. Part 12ZA provides for entitlement to statutory paternity pay. Part 12ZB provides for entitlement to statutory adoption pay. Part 12ZC (inserted into SSCBA 1992 by Pt 7 of the Children and Families Act 2014) provides for entitlement statutory shared parental pay. Official estimates are that the numbers of employees likely to be affected by these Regulations are very small; for example, in 2013 only 185 parental orders were granted. Of those who apply or intend to apply for a parental order (regardless of whether they subsequently obtain one), only a proportion will meet the eligibility requirements to be entitled to adoption leave and pay, paternity leave and pay or to be able to opt into shared parental leave and pay.

Citation, commencement and application

6.150 **1.**—(1) These Regulations may be cited as the Social Security Contributions and Benefits Act 1992 (Application of Parts 12ZA, 12ZB and 12ZC to Parental Order Cases) Regulations 2014.

(2) Subject to paragraphs (3) and (4), these Regulations come into force on 19th November 2014.

(3) The modification of section 171ZA of the Social Security Contributions and Benefits Act 1992 by the insertion of subsection (3C) as set out in Schedule 1 to these Regulations comes into force on the date that section 171ZA(2)(ba) comes into force.

(4) The modification of section 171ZL of the Social Security Contributions and Benefits Act 1992 by the insertion of subsection (3B) as set out in Schedule 2 to these Regulations comes into force on the date that section 171ZL(2)(ba) comes into force.

(5) Regulation 4 does not have effect in cases involving children whose expected week of birth ends on or before 4th April 2015.

Interpretation

6.151 **2.**—In these Regulations—

"the Act" means the Social Security Contributions and Benefits Act 1992;

[1 "intended parent", in relation to a child, means a person who, on the day of the child's birth—
  (a) applies, or intends to apply during the period of 6 months beginning with that day—
    (i) with another person for an order under section 54 of the Human Fertilisation and Embryology Act 2008 in respect of the child; or
    (ii) as the sole applicant for an order under section 54A of that Act in respect of the child; and
  (b) expects the court to make such an order in respect of the child;]

[1 . . .]
[1 . . .]
[1 "section 54 parental order parent" means a person—

(a) on whose application the court has made an order under section 54 of the Human Fertilisation and Embryology Act 2008 in respect of a child; or
(b) who is an intended parent of a child by reference to an application or intended application for such an order;
"section 54A parental order parent" means a person—
(a) on whose application the court has made an order under section 54A of the Human Fertilisation and Embryology Act 2008 in respect of a child; or
(b) who is an intended parent of a child by reference to an application or intended application for such an order.]

AMENDMENT

1. Human Fertilisation and Embryology Act 2008 (Remedial) Order 2018 (SI 2018/1413) Sch.2 para.6(2) (January 3, 2019).

Application of Part 12ZA of the Act to parental order parents

3.—Part 12ZA of the Act (statutory paternity pay) has effect in relation to [¹ section 54 parental order parents] with the modifications of sections 171ZA, 171ZB and 171ZE of the Act specified in the second column of Schedule 1 to these Regulations.

AMENDMENT

1. Human Fertilisation and Embryology Act 2008 (Remedial) Order 2018 (SI 2018/1413) Sch.2 para.6(3) (January 3, 2019).

Application of Part 12ZB of the Act to parental order parents

4.—Part 12ZB of the Act (statutory adoption pay) has effect in relation to [¹ section 54 parental order parents and section 54A parental order parents] with the modifications of sections 171ZL and 171ZN of the Act specified in the second column of Schedule 2 to these Regulations.

AMENDMENT

1. Human Fertilisation and Embryology Act 2008 (Remedial) Order 2018 (SI 2018/1413) Sch.2 para.6(4) (January 3, 2019).

Application of Part 12ZC of the Act to parental order parents

5.—Part 12ZC of the Act (statutory shared parental pay) has effect in relation to [¹ section 54 parental order parents] with the modifications of section 171ZV of the Act specified in the second column of Schedule 3 to these Regulations.

AMENDMENT

1. Human Fertilisation and Embryology Act 2008 (Remedial) Order 2018 (SI 2018/1413) Sch.2 para.6(5) (January 3, 2019).

Social Security Contributions and Benefits Act 1992 Regulations 2014

SCHEDULE 1   Regulation 3

6.155   Application of Part 12ZA of the Act to parental order cases

Provision	Modification
Section 171ZA	After subsection (4) insert— "(4A) A person who satisfies the conditions in section 171ZB(2)(a) to (d) in relation to a child is not entitled to statutory paternity pay under this section in respect of that child.".

Section 171ZB	For paragraph (a) of subsection (2) substitute—
	"(a) that he satisfies prescribed conditions as to being a person—
	   (i) on whose application the court has made a parental order in respect of a child, or
	   (ii) who is an intended parent of a child;
	(ab) that he satisfies prescribed conditions as to relationship with the other person on whose application the parental order was made or who is an intended parent of the child;".
	In paragraph (d) of subsection (2), for "placed for adoption" substitute "born".
	In paragraph (e) of subsection (2), omit "where he is a person with whom the child is placed for adoption,".
	For subsection (3) substitute—
	"(3) The references in this section to the relevant week are to

Provision	Modification
	the week immediately preceding the 14th week before the expected week of the child's birth.". After subsection (3) insert— "(3B) In a case where a child is born earlier than the 14th week before the expected week of the child's birth— (a) subsection (2)(b) shall be treated as satisfied in relation to a person if, had the birth occurred after the end of the relevant week, the person would have been in employed earner's employment with an employer for a continuous period of at least 26 weeks ending with the relevant week; (b) subsection (2)(c) shall be treated as satisfied in relation to a person if the person's normal weekly earnings for the period of 8 weeks ending with the week immediately preceding the week in which the child is born are not less than the lower earnings limit in force under section 5(1)(a) immediately before the commencement of the week in which the child is born; and (c) subsection (2)(d) shall not apply. (3C) In a case where a child is born before the end of the relevant week, subsection (2)(ba) shall be treated as satisfied in relation to a person if, had the birth occurred after the end of the relevant week, the person would have been entitled to be in the relevant employment at the end of the relevant week. In this subsection "the relevant employment" means the employment by reference to which the person satisfies the condition in subsection (2)(b).". In subsection (6), for "placement for adoption of more than one child as part of the same arrangement" substitute "birth, or expected birth, of more than one child as a result of the same pregnancy". For subsection (7) substitute— "(7) In this section— "intended parent", in relation to a child, means a person who, on the day of the child's birth—

	(a) applies, or intends to apply during the period of 6 months beginning with that day, with another person for a parental order in respect of the child, and
	(b) expects the court to make a parental order on that application in respect of the child; and
	"parental order" means an order under section 54(1) of the Human Fertilisation and Embryology Act 2008.".
	Omit subsection (8).
	Omit subsection (9).
Section 171ZE	In paragraph (b) of subsection (3), for "placement for adoption" substitute "birth".
	In subsection (4)—
	(a) in paragraph (a), for "sub-paragraph (i) of section 171ZA(2) (a)" substitute "section 171ZA(2)(a)(i)";
	(b) in paragraph (b), for "sub-paragraph (ii) of that provision" substitute "section 171ZA(2)(a)(ii) or 171ZB(2)(ab)".
	In subsection (9), for "the reference in subsection (3)(a) to the date of the child's birth shall be read as a reference" substitute "the references in subsection (3)(a) and (b) to the date of the child's birth shall be read as references".
	Omit subsection (10).
	Omit subsection (12).

SCHEDULE 2 — Regulation 4

Application of Part 12ZB of the Act to parental order cases

Provision	Modification
Section 171ZL	For paragraph (a) of subsection (2) substitute—
	"(a) that he is—
	(i) a person on whose application the court has made [¹ an order under section 54 or 54A of the Human Fertilisation and Embryology Act 2008] in respect of a child, or
	(ii) an intended parent of a child;".
	[¹ At the beginning of paragraph (e) of subsection (2) insert—
	"in the case of a person on whose application the court has made an order under section 54 of the Human Fertilisation and Embryology Act 2008 or who is an intended parent of a child by reference to an application or intended application for such an order,"]
	For subsection (3) substitute—
	"(3) The references in this section to the relevant week are to the week immediately preceding the 14th week before the expected week of the child's birth.".
	After subsection (3) insert—
	"(3A) In a case where a child is born earlier than the 14th week before the expected week of the child's birth—
	(a) subsection (2)(b) shall be treated as satisfied in relation to a person if, had the birth occurred after the end of the relevant week, the person would have been in employed earner's employment with an employer for a continuous period of at least 26 weeks ending with the relevant week; and
	(b) subsection (2)(d) shall be treated as satisfied in relation to a person if the person's normal weekly earnings for the period of 8 weeks ending with the week immediately preceding the week in which the child is born are not less than the lower earnings limit in force under section

Social Security Contributions and Benefits Act 1992 Regulations 2014

      5(1)(a) immediately before the commencement of the week in which the child is born.

  (3B) In a case where a child is born before the end of the relevant week, subsection (2)(ba) shall be treated as satisfied in relation to a person if, had the birth occurred after the end of the relevant week, the person would have been entitled to be in the relevant employment at the end of the relevant week.

In this subsection "the relevant employment" means the employment by reference to which the person satisfies the condition in subsection (2)(b).".

For paragraph (b) of subsection (4), substitute—

    "(b) the other person on whose application the court has made [¹ an order under section 54 of the Human Fertilisation and Embryology Act 2008] in respect of the child or who is an intended parent of the child—
      (i) is a person to whom the conditions in subsection (2) above apply, and
      (ii) has elected to receive statutory adoption pay.".

Omit subsection (4A).

Omit subsection (4B).

In subsection (5), for "placement, or expected placement, for adoption of more than one child as part of the same arrangement" substitute "birth, or expected birth, of more than one child as a result of the same pregnancy".

After subsection (8) insert—

[¹ "(8A) In this section "intended parent", in relation to a child, means a person who, on the day of the child's birth—

  (a) applies, or intends to apply during the period of 6 months beginning with that day—
    (i) with another person for an order under section 54 of the Human Fertilisation and Embryology Act 2008 in respect of the child; or
    (ii) as the sole applicant for an order under section 54A of that Act in respect of the child; and
  (b) expects the court to make such an order in respect of the child."]

Provision	Modification
	"parental order" means an order under section 54(1) of the Human Fertilisation and Embryology Act 2008.".
	Omit subsection (9).
	Omit subsection (10).
Section 171ZN	In subsection (2F) (5), for "in which the person is notified that the person has been matched with a child for the purposes of adoption" substitute "immediately preceding the 14th week before the expected week of the child's birth".
	Omit subsection (9).

AMENDMENT

1. Human Fertilisation and Embryology Act 2008 (Remedial) Order 2018 (SI 2018/1413) Sch.2 para.6(6) and (7) (January 3, 2019).

(SI 2014/2866 Sch.3)

SCHEDULE 3

Regulation 5

Application of Part 12ZC of the Act to parental order cases

Provision	Modification
Section 171ZV	In subsection (1), for "with whom a child is, or is expected to be, placed for adoption under the law of any part of the United Kingdom" substitute "on whose application the court has made a parental order in respect of a child or who is an intended parent of a child".
	In paragraph (a) of subsection (2), for "another person" substitute "the other person on whose application the court has made a parental order in respect of the child or who is an intended parent of the child".
	In paragraph (g) of subsection (2), for "the placement for adoption of the child" substitute "being a person on whose application the court has made a parental order in respect of the child or being an intended parent of the child".
	In paragraph (a) of subsection (4), for "with whom a child is, or is expected to be, placed for adoption under the law of any part of the United Kingdom" substitute "on whose application the court has made a parental order in respect of a child or who is an intended parent of a child".
	In paragraph (h) of subsection (4), for "the placement for adoption of the child" substitute "being a person on whose application the court has made a parental order in respect of the child or being an intended parent of the child".
	In subsection (16), for "the placement for adoption of more than one child as part of the same arrangement" substitute "the birth of more than one child as a result of the same pregnancy".
	After subsection (16) insert—
	"(16A) In this section—
	"intended parent", in relation to a child, means a person who, on the day of the child's birth—
	(a) applies, or intends to apply during the period of 6 months beginning with that day, with another person for a parental order in respect of the child, and
	(b) expects the court to make a parental order on that application in respect of the child; and
	"parental order" means an order under section 54(1) of the Human Fertilisation and Embryology Act 2008.".
	Omit subsection (17).
	Omit subsection (18).

The Statutory Paternity Pay and Statutory Adoption Pay (Parental Orders and Prospective Adopters) Regulations 2014

(SI 2014/2934)

This instrument contains only regulations made by virtue of, or consequential upon, section 119 of the Children and Families Act 2014 and is made before the end of the period of 6 months beginning with the coming into force of that enactment.

The Secretary of State in exercise of the powers conferred by sections 171ZB(2) (a), 171ZC(1A) and (3)(a), (c), (d), (f) and (g), 171ZD(2) and (3), 171ZE(2), (3), (7) and (8), 171ZG(3), 171ZJ(1), (3), (4), (7) and (8), 171ZL(8)(b) to (d), (f) and (g), 171ZM(2) and (3), 171ZN(2), (5) and (6), 171ZP(6), 171ZS(1), (3), (4), (7) and (8) and 175(4) of the Social Security Contributions and Benefits Act 1992, section 5(1)(g), (i) and (p) of the Social Security Administration Act 1992 and sections 8(1) and (2)(c) and 51(1) of the Employment Act 2002 and with the concurrence of the Commissioners for Her Majesty's Revenue and Customs, in so far as such concurrence is required, makes the following Regulations:

PART I

General

6.158

1. Citation and commencement
2.–3. Interpretation

PART 2

Amendment of the Pay Regulations

4.–5. Amendment of the Pay Regulations [*omitted*]

PART 3

Application and Modification of the Pay Regulations in Parental Order Cases

6.–24. Application of the Pay regulations to intended parents and parental order parents

PART 4

Amendment of the Administration Regulations

25. Amendment of the Administration Regulations [*omitted*]

PART 6

Modification of the Administration Regulations in Parental Order Cases

26. Modification of the Administration Regulations in parental order cases

GENERAL NOTE

6.159 Part 1 of these Regulations deals with citation, commencement and interpretation issues.

(SI 2014/2934)

Part 2 of these Regulations amends the Statutory Paternity Pay and Statutory Adoption Pay (General) Regulations (SI 2002/2822) to make provision for a new right to statutory adoption pay for local authority foster parents who are prospective adopters if they have been notified that a child is to be placed with them under s.22C of the Children Act 1989 (following consideration in accordance with s.22C(9B)(c)). The amendments made also make provision for new rights to statutory paternity pay to the spouses, civil partners and partners of these prospective adopters.

Part 3 of these Regulations make provision for an entitlement to statutory adoption pay and statutory paternity pay (adoption) in respect of cases which involve a person who has applied with another person for a parental order under s.54 of the Human Fertilisation and Embryology Act 2008. Under s.54 a court may make an order providing for a child of a surrogate mother to be treated as the child of the applicants if certain conditions are satisfied. Part 3 needs to be read in conjunction with the Social Security Contributions and Benefits Act 1992 (Application of Pts 12ZA, 12ZB and 12ZC to Parental Order Cases) Regulations 2014 (SI 2014/2866). This Part should also be read in conjunction with the Statutory Paternity Pay and Statutory Adoption Pay (General) Regulations (SI 2002/2822) which this Part applies with modifications.

Part 4 amends to Statutory Paternity Pay and Statutory Adoption Pay (Administration) Regulations 2002 (SI 2002/2820) to cover the situation where statutory paternity pay or statutory adoption pay is paid to local authority foster parents who are prospective adopters. Part 5 modifies those 2002 Regulations in a case where statutory paternity pay or statutory adoption pay is paid to a person who has applied with another person for a parental order.

PART 1

GENERAL

Citation and commencement

1.—These Regulations may be cited as the Statutory Paternity Pay and Statutory Adoption Pay (Parental Orders and Prospective Adopters) Regulations 2014 and come into force on 1st December 2014.

Interpretation

2.—In these Regulations—
"Administration Regulations" means the Statutory Paternity Pay and Statutory Adoption Pay (Administration) Regulations 2002;
[¹"intended parent", in relation to a child, means a person who, on the day of the child's birth—
(a) applies, or intends to apply during the period of 6 months beginning with that day—
   (i) with another person for an order under section 54 of the Human Fertilisation and Embryology Act 2008 in respect of the child; or
   (ii) as the sole applicant for an order under section 54A of that Act in respect of the child; and
(b) expects the court to make such an order in respect of the child;]
[¹...]

6.160

6.161

"Pay Regulations" means the Statutory Paternity Pay and Statutory Adoption Pay (General) Regulations 2002.

[¹"section 54 parental order parent" means a person—
(a) on whose application the court has made an order under section 54 of the Human Fertilisation and Embryology Act 2008 in respect of a child; or
(b) who is an intended parent of a child by reference to an application or intended application for such an order;

"section 54A parental order parent" means a person—
(a) on whose application the court has made an order under section 54A of the Human Fertilisation and Embryology Act 2008 in respect of a child; or
(b) who is an intended parent of a child by reference to an application or intended application for such an order.]

3.—(1) The amendments made in Part 2 and 4 of these Regulations have effect only in relation to children matched with a person who is notified of having been matched on or after 5th April 2015.

(2) For the purposes of paragraph (1)—
(a) a person is matched with a child for adoption when an adoption agency decides that that person would be a suitable adoptive parent for the child;
(b) in a case where paragraph (a) applies, a person is notified as having been matched with a child on the date that person receives notification of the agency's decision, under regulation 33(3)(a) of the Adoption Agencies Regulations 2005, regulation 28(3) of the Adoption Agencies (Wales) Regulations 2005 or regulation 8(5) of the Adoption Agencies (Scotland) Regulations 2009;
(c) a person is also matched with a child for adoption when a decision has been made in accordance with regulation 22A of the Care Planning, Placement and Case Review (England) Regulations 2010 and an adoption agency has identified that person with whom the child is to be placed in accordance with regulation 12B of the Adoption Agencies Regulations 2005;
(d) in a case where paragraph (c) applies, a person is notified as having been matched with a child on the date on which that person receives notification in accordance with regulation 12B(2)(a) of the Adoption Agencies Regulations 2005.

(3) In paragraph (2) "adoption agency" has the meaning given, in relation to England and Wales, by section 2 of the Adoption and Children Act 2002 and in relation to Scotland, by section 119(1) of the Adoption and Children (Scotland) Act 2007.

AMENDMENT

1. Human Fertilisation and Embryology Act 2008 (Remedial) Order 2018 (SI 2018/1413) Sch.2 para.7(1) and (2) (January 3, 2019).

(SI 2014/2934 reg.6)

PART 2

AMENDMENT OF THE PAY REGULATIONS

[*The amendments made by regs 4 and 5 are incorporated into the Statutory Paternity Pay and Statutory Adoption Pay (General) Regulations 2002 (SI 2002/2822)*].   6.163

PART 3

APPLICATION AND MODIFICATION OF THE PAY REGULATIONS IN PARENTAL ORDER CASES

Application of the Pay Regulations to intended parents and parental order parents

6.—[¹ (1) The provisions of the Pay Regulations, in so far as they apply to statutory paternity pay (adoption), shall apply to a section 54 parental order parent with the modifications set out in this Part of these Regulations.   6.164

(1A) The provisions of the Pay Regulations, in so far as they apply to statutory adoption pay, shall apply to—
(a) a section 54 parental order parent; and
(b) a section 54A parental order parent,
with the modifications set out in this Part of these Regulations.]

(2) In this regulation—
"statutory adoption pay" means statutory adoption pay payable in accordance with the provisions of Part 12ZB of the Social Security Contributions and Benefits Act 1992;
"statutory paternity pay (adoption)" means statutory paternity pay payable in accordance with the provisions of Part 12ZA of the Social Security Contributions and Benefits Act 1992 where the conditions specified in section 171ZB of that Act are satisfied.

AMENDMENT

1. Human Fertilisation and Embryology Act 2008 (Remedial) Order 2018 (SI 2018/1413) Sch.2 para.7(1) and (3) (January 3, 2019).

Application of the Pay Regulations to intended parents and parental order parents

7.—In regulation 2 (interpretation) of the Pay Regulations as they apply to an intended parent or a parental order parent—   6.165
(a) paragraph (1) shall read as if—
   (i) the definition of "adopter" were omitted;
   (ii) there were the following definitions—
[¹ ""intended parent", in relation to a child, means a person who, on the day of the child's birth—
(a) applies, or intends to apply during the period of 6 months beginning with that day—
   (i) with another person for an order under section 54 of the Human Fertilisation and Embryology Act 2008 in respect of the child; or

(ii) as the sole applicant for an order under section 54A of that Act in respect of the child; and
(b) expects the court to make such an order in respect of the child;]
"Parent A" in relation to a child means [¹ the section 54 parental order parent] who has elected to be Parent A;
[¹ "section 54 parental order parent" means a person—
(a) on whose application the court has made an order under section 54 of the Human Fertilisation and Embryology Act 2008 in respect of a child; or
(b) who is an intended parent of a child by reference to an application or intended application for such an order;
"section 54A parental order parent" means a person—
(a) on whose application the court has made an order under section 54A of the Human Fertilisation and Embryology Act 2008 in respect of a child; or
(b) who is an intended parent of a child by reference to an application or intended application for such an order;]
"statutory shared parental pay" means statutory shared parental pay payable in accordance with Part 12ZC of the Act;";
(b) paragraph (2) shall apply as if that paragraph read—
"(2) [¹ A section 54 parental order parent] elects to be Parent A in relation to a child if that person (A) agrees with [¹ the other section 54 parental order parent] of the child (B) that A and not B will be parent A.".

AMENDMENT

1. Human Fertilisation and Embryology Act 2008 (Remedial) Order 2018 (SI 2018/1413) Sch.2 para.7(1) and (4) (January 3, 2019).

Application of the Pay Regulations to intended parents and parental order parents

6.166
8.—In regulation 3 (application) of the Pay Regulations [¹ as they apply to a section 54 parental order parent]—
(a) paragraph (1)(b) shall read as if sub-paragraphs (i) and (ii) were omitted and replaced by—
"whose expected week of birth begins on or after 5th April 2015".
(b) paragraph (2) shall read as if sub-paragraphs (a) and (b) were omitted and replaced by—
"whose expected week of birth begins on or after 5th April 2015".

AMENDMENT

1. Human Fertilisation and Embryology Act 2008 (Remedial) Order 2018 (SI 2018/1413) Sch.2 para.7(1) and (5) (January 3, 2019).

6.167
[¹ 8A. Regulation 3 (application) of the Pay Regulations as they apply to a section 54A parental order parent shall read as if—
(a) paragraph (1) were omitted; and
(b) for paragraph (2) there were substituted—

"(2) Subject to the provisions of Part 12ZB of the Act (statutory adoption pay) and of these Regulations, there is entitlement to statutory adoption pay in respect of children whose expected week of birth begins on or after the day which follows the last day of the period of 120 days beginning with the day on which the

(SI 2014/2934 reg.8A)

Human Fertilisation and Embryology Act 2008 (Remedial) Order 2018 comes into force."]

AMENDMENT

1. Human Fertilisation and Embryology Act 2008 (Remedial) Order 2018 (SI 2018/1413) Sch.2 para.7(1) and (6) (January 3, 2019).

Application of the Pay Regulations to intended parents and parental order parents

9.—In regulation 11 (conditions of entitlement) of the Pay Regulations [¹ as they apply to a section 54 parental order parent]—
  (a) paragraph (1) shall apply as if sub-paragraphs (a) and (b) were omitted and replaced by—
  "(a) is [¹ a section 54] parental order parent in relation to the child; (b) is married to, the civil partner or the partner of Parent A; and (c) has or expects to have the main responsibility for the upbringing of the child (apart from the responsibility of Parent A)."
  (b) paragraph (2) shall read as if the words "the adopter" in both places where those words occur were "Parent A";
  (c) paragraph (2A) shall read as if the words "the adopter" in both places where those words occur were "Parent A".

6.168

AMENDMENT

1. Human Fertilisation and Embryology Act 2008 (Remedial) Order 2018 (SI 2018/1413) Sch.2 para.7(1) and (7) (January 3, 2019).

Application of the Pay Regulations to intended parents and parental order parents

10.—[¹. . .]

6.169

AMENDMENT

1. Statutory Paternity Pay (Amendment) Regulations 2024 (SI 2024/121) reg.22 (March 8, 2024).

Application of the Pay Regulations to intended parents and parental order parents

11.—In regulation 12 ([²options in respect of periods of payment] of statutory paternity pay (adoption)) of the Pay Regulations [¹ as they apply to a section 54 parental order parent]—
  (a) paragraph (1) shall apply as if that paragraph read—
  "(1) [²Within the qualifying period set out in regulation 12A], a person entitled to statutory paternity pay (adoption) may choose [²a period of payment of statutory paternity pay] to begin—
    (a) on the date on which the child is born or, where the person is at work on that day, the following day;
    (b) the date falling such number of days after the date on which the child is born as the person may specify; or
    (c) a predetermined date, specified by the person which is later than the expected week of the child's birth.";
  (b) paragraph (2) shall not apply;
  (c) [². . .].

6.170

1145

Social Security Contributions and Benefits Act 1992 Regulations 2014

AMENDMENTS

1. Human Fertilisation and Embryology Act 2008 (Remedial) Order 2018 (SI 2018/1413) Sch.2 para.7(1) and (9) (January 3, 2019).
2. Statutory Paternity Pay (Amendment) Regulations 2024 (SI 2024/121) reg.23 (March 8, 2024).

Application of the Pay Regulations to intended parents and parental order parents

6.171　　12.—In regulation 13 (additional notice requirements for statutory paternity pay (adoption)) of the Pay Regulations [¹ as they apply to a section 54 parental order parent]—
(a) paragraph (1) [²will not apply]
[²(b) paragraph (2)(b) shall read as if the words "is placed for adoption" to the end were "is born later than the date specified in that notice as the date on which a period of payment is to begin.]

AMENDMENTS

1. Human Fertilisation and Embryology Act 2008 (Remedial) Order 2018 (SI 2018/1413) Sch.2 para.7(1) and (10) (January 3, 2019).
2. Statutory Paternity Pay (Amendment) Regulations 2024 (SI 2024/121) reg.24 (March 8, 2024).

Application of the Pay Regulations to intended parents and parental order parents

6.172　　13.—[²Regulation 12A] (qualifying period for statutory paternity pay (adoption)) of the Pay Regulations [¹ as they apply to a section 54 parental order parent] shall read as if the words [²of 52 weeks] to the end were omitted and replaced by—
"which begins on the date of the child's birth and ends—
(a) except in the case referred to in paragraph (b), [²52 weeks] after that date;
(b) in a case where the child is born before the first day of the expected week of its birth, [²52 weeks] after that day.".

AMENDMENTS

1. Human Fertilisation and Embryology Act 2008 (Remedial) Order 2018 (SI 2018/1413) Sch.2 para.7(1) and (11) (January 3, 2019).
2. Statutory Paternity Pay (Amendment) Regulations 2024 (SI 2024/121) reg.25 (March 8, 2024).

Application of the Pay Regulations to intended parents and parental order parents

6.173　　14.—In [²regulation 12B (notice and evidence requirements for statutory paternity pay (adoption)] of the Pay Regulations [¹ as they apply to a section 54 parental order parent]—
(a) [²paragraph (2)] shall apply as if [²sub-paragraphs (b) and (c) were omitted and replaced by]—
"(b) the expected week of the child's birth;";

(b) [²...]
(c) [²paragraph (4)] shall apply as if sub-paragraphs (a) and (b) read—
"(a) in or before the 15th week before the expected week of the child's birth;
(b) in a case where it was not reasonably practicable for the employee to provide it in accordance with sub-paragraph (a), as soon as reasonably practicable.";
[²(ca) paragraph (5) shall apply as if, in sub-paragraphs (a) and (b), the words from "the date provided under" to "for adoption", in both places they occur, were omitted and replaced by "the first day of the expected week of the child's birth";]
[²(cb) paragraph (10) shall apply as if the words "the date referred to in paragraph (5)(a)", in each place they occur, were replaced by "the first day of the expected week of the child's birth";]
[²(d) paragraph (11) shall apply as if the words from "child's placement if" to the end were replaced by "birth as soon as is reasonably practicable thereafter".]

AMENDMENTS

1. Human Fertilisation and Embryology Act 2008 (Remedial) Order 2018 (SI 2018/1413) Sch.2 para.7(1) and (12) (January 3, 2019).
2. Statutory Paternity Pay (Amendment) Regulations 2024 (SI 2024/121) reg.26 (March 8, 2024).

[¹14A. In regulation 16A (change in circumstances)—

(a) paragraph (2) shall apply as if sub-paragraphs (a), (b) and (c) read—
"(a) the person does not apply for an order under section 54 of the Human Fertilisation and Embryology Act 2008 within the time limit set by subsection (3) of that section,
(b) the person's application for an order under that section for the child is refused, withdrawn or otherwise terminated without the order being granted and any time for an appeal or a new application has expired, or
(c) the child dies.";
(b) paragraph (4) shall apply as if sub-paragraphs (a), (b) and (c) read—
"(a) in a case falling within paragraph (2)(a), the week during which the time limit in section 54(3) of the Human Fertilisation and Embryology Act 2008 for an application for an order under that section for the child expires;
(b) in a case falling within paragraph (2)(b), the week during which the person's application for an order under that section is refused, withdrawn or otherwise terminated without the order being granted;
(c) in a case falling within paragraph (2)(c), the week during which the child dies.";
(c) paragraph (5) shall apply as if the words "regulation 6B (notice and evidential requirements for statutory paternity pay (birth)) or" and "as the case may be" were omitted;
(d) paragraph (6) shall apply as if the words "6B or" and "6B, 7," were omitted.]

6.174

Amendment

1. Statutory Paternity Pay (Amendment) Regulations 2024 (SI 2024/121) reg.27 (March 8, 2024).

Application of the Pay Regulations to intended parents and parental order parents

6.175   **15.**—In regulation 16 (entitlement to statutory paternity pay (adoption) where there is more than one employer) of the Pay Regulations [¹ as they apply to a section 54 parental order parent], paragraph (b) shall read as if the words "in which the adopter is notified of being matched with the child" were "immediately preceding the 14th week before the expected week of the child's birth".

Amendment

1. Human Fertilisation and Embryology Act 2008 (Remedial) Order 2018 (SI 2018/1413) Sch.2 para.7(1) and (13) (January 3, 2019).

Application of the Pay Regulations to intended parents and parental order parents

6.176   **16.**—In regulation 20 (avoidance of liability for statutory paternity pay) of the Pay Regulations [¹ as they apply to a section 54 parental order parent], paragraph (2)(a) shall read as if the words "or, as the case may be, the placement of the child for adoption" were omitted.

Amendment

1. Human Fertilisation and Embryology Act 2008 (Remedial) Order 2018 (SI 2018/1413) Sch.2 para.7(1) and (14) (January 3, 2019).

Application of the Pay Regulations to intended parents and parental order parents

6.177   **17.**—(1) In regulation 21 (adoption pay period) of the Pay Regulations [¹ as they apply to a section 54 parental order parent or a section 54A parental order parent], paragraph (1) shall read as if that paragraph read—

"(1) The adoption pay period in respect of a person entitled to statutory adoption pay shall begin on the day on which the child is born or, where the person is at work on that day, the following day."

(2) Paragraph (2), (3), (4) and (6) shall not apply.

Amendment

1. Human Fertilisation and Embryology Act 2008 (Remedial) Order 2018 (SI 2018/1413) Sch.2 para.7(1) and (15) (January 3, 2019).

Application of the Pay Regulations to intended parents and parental order parents

6.178   **18.**—In regulation 22 (adoption pay period in cases where adoption is disrupted) of the Pay Regulations [¹ as they apply to a section 54 parental order parent]—

(a) paragraph (1) shall apply as if that paragraph read—

(SI 2014/2934 reg.18)

"(1) The adoption pay period shall terminate in accordance with the provisions of paragraph (2) where—
(a) the child dies;
[¹ (b) the section 54 parental order parent who is entitled to statutory adoption pay does not apply for an order under section 54 of the Human Fertilisation and Embryology Act 2008 in respect of the child within the time limit set by subsection (3) of that section;] or
(c) the that person's application for [¹ an order under that section] in respect of the child is refused, withdrawn or otherwise terminated and any time limit for an appeal or a new application has expired;"
(b) in paragraph (3)—
  (i) sub-paragraph (a) shall apply as if the reference to paragraph (1)(a)(i) were a reference to paragraph (1)(a);
  (ii) sub-paragraph (b) shall apply as if that sub-paragraph read—
"(b) in a case falling within paragraph (1)(b) the week during which the time limit in section 54(3) of the Human Fertilisation and Embryology Act 2008 for an application for [¹ an order under that section] for the child expires;";
  (iii) sub-paragraph (c) shall apply as if that sub-paragraph read—
"(c) in a case falling within paragraph (1)(c) the week during which the person's application for [¹ an order under that section] is refused, withdrawn or otherwise terminated without the order being granted."

AMENDMENT

1. Human Fertilisation and Embryology Act 2008 (Remedial) Order 2018 (SI 2018/1413) Sch.2 para.7(1) and (16) (January 3, 2019).

[¹ **18A.** In regulation 22 (adoption pay period in cases where adoption is disrupted) of the Pay Regulations as they apply to a section 54A parental order parent— 6.179
(a) paragraph (1) shall apply as if that paragraph read—
"(1) The adoption pay period shall terminate in accordance with the provisions of paragraph (2) where—
(a) the child dies;
(b) the section 54A parental order parent does not apply for an order under section 54A of the Human Fertilisation and Embryology Act 2008 in respect of the child within the time limit set by subsection (2) of that section; or
(c) the section 54A parental order parent's application for an order under that section in respect of the child is refused, withdrawn or otherwise terminated and any time limit for an appeal or a new application has expired."; and
(b) in paragraph (3)—
  (i) sub-paragraph (a) shall apply as if the reference to paragraph (1)(a)(i) were a reference to paragraph (1)(a);
  (ii) sub-paragraph (b) shall apply as if that sub-paragraph read—
"(b) in a case falling within paragraph (1)(b) the week during which the time limit in section 54A(2) of the Human Fertilisation and Embryology Act 2008 for an application for an order under that section for the child expires;"; and
  (iii) sub-paragraph (c) shall apply as if that sub-paragraph read—

"(c) in a case falling within paragraph (1)(c) the week during which the section 54A parental order parent's application for an order under that section is refused, withdrawn or otherwise terminated without the order being granted."]

AMENDMENT

1. Human Fertilisation and Embryology Act 2008 (Remedial) Order 2018 (SI 2018/1413) Sch.2 para.7(1) and (17) (January 3, 2019).

Application of the Pay Regulations to intended parents and parental order parents

6.180   19.—In regulation 23 (additional notice requirements for statutory adoption pay) of the Pay Regulations [¹ as they apply to a section 54 parental order parent or a section 54A parental order parent]—
(a) paragraph (1) shall read as if the words "the date on which the child is expected to be placed for adoption" were "the expected week of the child's birth";
(b) paragraph (2) shall read as if—
 (i) the words from "Where the choice" to "sub-paragraph (a) of that paragraph," were omitted;
 (ii) the words "the date the child is placed for adoption" were "the date on which the child is born".

AMENDMENT

1. Human Fertilisation and Embryology Act 2008 (Remedial) Order 2018 (SI 2018/1413) Sch.2 para.7(1) and (18) (January 3, 2019).

Application of the Pay Regulations to intended parents and parental order parents

6.181   20.—In regulation 24 (evidence of entitlement to statutory adoption pay) of the Pay Regulations [¹ as they apply to a section 54 parental order parent]—
(a) in paragraph (1), sub-paragraph (a) shall apply as if that sub-paragraph read—
"(a) a statutory declaration specified in paragraph (2) where the person who will be liable to pay the statutory adoption pay requests it in accordance with paragraph (3)";
(b) paragraph (2) shall apply as if that paragraph read—
"(2) The statutory declaration referred to in paragraph (1)(a) is a statutory declaration stating that the person making the declaration—
(a) has applied, or intends to apply, under section 54 of the Human Fertilisation and Embryology Act 2008 with another person for [¹ an order under that section] in respect of the child within the time limit for making such an application; and
(b) expects the court to make [¹ an order under that section] on that application in respect of the child.";
(c) paragraph (3) shall apply as if that paragraph read—
"(3) The declaration in referred to—
(a) in paragraph (1)(a) shall be provided to the person liable to pay statutory adoption pay within 14 days of that person requesting that declaration where the person requests it within 14 days of receiving the notice under section 171ZL(6) of the Act;

(b) in paragraph (1)(b) shall be provided to the person liable to pay statutory adoption pay at least 28 days before the beginning of the adoption pay period, or if that is not reasonably practicable, as soon as reasonably practicable after that date."

AMENDMENT

1. Human Fertilisation and Embryology Act 2008 (Remedial) Order 2018 (SI 2018/1413) Sch.2 para.7(1) and (19) (January 3, 2019).

[¹ **20A.** In regulation 24 (evidence of entitlement to statutory adoption pay) of the Pay Regulations as they apply to a section 54A parental order parent—

"**24.**—(1) A section 54A parental order parent shall provide evidence of his or her entitlement to statutory adoption pay by providing to the person who will be liable to pay it ("E") a statutory declaration specified in paragraph (2) where E requests it in accordance with paragraph (3).
(2) The statutory declaration referred to in paragraph (1) is a statutory declaration stating that the person making the declaration—
  (a) has applied, or intends to apply, under section 54A of the Human Fertilisation and Embryology Act 2008 for an order under that section in respect of the child within the time limit for making such an application; and
  (b) expects the court to make an order under that section on that application in respect of the child.
(3) The declaration referred to in paragraph (1) shall be provided to E within 14 days of E requesting that declaration where E requests it within 14 days of receiving the notice under section 171ZL(6) of the Act."]

AMENDMENT

1. Human Fertilisation and Embryology Act 2008 (Remedial) Order 2018 (SI 2018/1413) Sch.2 para.7(1) and (20) (January 3, 2019).

Application of the Pay Regulations to intended parents and parental order parents

21.—In regulation 25 (entitlement to statutory adoption pay where there is more than one employer) of the Pay Regulations [¹ as they apply to a section 54 parental order parent or a section 54A parental order parent], paragraph (b) shall read as if the words "in which he is notified of being matched with the child" were "immediately preceding the 14th week before the expected week of the child's birth".

AMENDMENT

1. Human Fertilisation and Embryology Act 2008 (Remedial) Order 2018 (SI 2018/1413) Sch.2 para.7(1) and (21) (January 3, 2019).

Application of the Pay Regulations to intended parents and parental order parents

22.—In regulation 29 (termination of employment before start of adoption pay period) of the Pay Regulations [¹ as they apply to a section 54

parental order parent or a section 54A parental order parent], paragraph (1) shall apply as if—
(a) the words "chosen in accordance with regulation 21" were omitted;
(b) the words "14 days before the expected date of placement" to the end were "on the day on which the child is born".

AMENDMENT

1. Human Fertilisation and Embryology Act 2008 (Remedial) Order 2018 (SI 2018/1413) Sch.2 para.7(1) and (22) (January 3, 2019).

Application of the Pay Regulations to intended parents and parental order parents

6.185 23.—In regulation 30 (avoidance of liability for statutory adoption pay) of the Pay Regulations [¹ as they apply to a section 54 parental order parent or a section 54A parental order parent], in paragraph (2), sub-paragraph (a) shall read as if the words "in which he was notified of having been matched with the child for adoption" read "immediately preceding the 14th week before the expected week of the child's birth".

AMENDMENT

1. Human Fertilisation and Embryology Act 2008 (Remedial) Order 2018 (SI 2018/1413) Sch.2 para.7(1) and (23) (January 3, 2019).

Application of the Pay Regulations to intended parents and parental order parents

6.186 24.—In regulation 40 (normal weekly earnings) of the Pay Regulations [¹ as they apply to a section 54 parental order parent or a section 54A parental order parent], in paragraph (2), the definition of "the appropriate date" shall read—
""the appropriate date" means in relation to statutory paternity pay (adoption) and statutory adoption pay, the first day of the 14th week before the expected week of the child's birth or the first day in the week in which the child is born, whichever is earlier;".

AMENDMENT

1. Human Fertilisation and Embryology Act 2008 (Remedial) Order 2018 (SI 2018/1413) Sch.2 para.7(1) and (24) (January 3, 2019).

PART 4

AMENDMENT OF THE ADMINISTRATION REGULATIONS

[*The amendments made by reg.25 are incorporated into the Statutory Paternity Pay and Statutory Adoption Pay (Administration) Regulations 2002 (SI 2002/2820).*]

(SI 2014/2934 reg. 26)

PART 5

MODIFICATION OF THE ADMINISTRATION REGULATIONS IN PARENTAL ORDER CASES

26.—In the case of entitlement to statutory paternity pay or statutory adoption pay under section 171ZB or 171ZL of the Social Security Contributions and Benefits Act 1992 [¹ as those sections apply to a section 54 parental order parent or a section 54A parental order parent]—
  (a) paragraph (3)(b)(ii) of regulation 11 (provision of information) of the Administration Regulations shall read as if the words from "the end of the seven day period that starts on the date on which the adopter is notified of having been matched with the child" were—
"the day the employee gave notice of the employee's intended absence or the end of the fifteenth week before the expected week of birth, whichever is later;"
  (b) paragraph (4) and (5) of that regulation shall not apply.

AMENDMENT

1. Human Fertilisation and Embryology Act 2008 (Remedial) Order 2018 (SI 2018/1413) Sch.2 para.7(1) and (25) (January 3, 2019).

The Statutory Maternity Pay and Statutory Adoption Pay (Curtailment) Regulations 2014

(SI 2014/3054)

For the text of these Regulations, see Part V above.

PART VII

STATUTORY SHARED PARENTAL PAY

The Statutory Shared Parental Pay (Administration) Regulations 2014

(SI 2014/2929)

The Secretary of State makes these Regulations in exercise of powers conferred by sections 7, 8, 10 and 51(1) of the Employment Act 2002 and sections 8(1)(f) and (ga) and 25(3) and (6) of the Social Security Contributions (Transfer of Functions, etc.) Act 1999 with the concurrence of the Commissioners for Her Majesty's Revenue and Customs:

ARRANGEMENT OF REGULATIONS

1. Citation and commencement
2. Interpretation
3. Funding of employers' liabilities to make payments of statutory shared parental pay
4. Applications for funding from the Commissioners
5. Deductions from payments to the Commissioners
6. Payments to employers by the Commissioners
7. Date when certain contributions are to be treated as paid
8. Overpayments
9. Records to be maintained by employers
10. Inspection of employers' records
11. Provision of information relating to entitlement to statutory shared parental pay
12. Application for the determination of any issue arising as to, or in connection with, entitlement to statutory shared parental pay
13. Applications in connection with statutory shared parental pay
14. Provision of information

GENERAL NOTE

Part 7 of the Children and Families Act 2014 inserted a new Pt 12ZC into the SSCBA 1992 giving the Secretary of State the power to make regulations to create an entitlement to statutory shared parental pay (ShPP). These Regulations provide for the funding of employers' liabilities to make ShPP payments and also impose obligations on employers in connection with such payments and confer powers on the Commissioners for HMRC. Under reg.3, an employer is entitled to an amount equal to 92 per cent of ShPP payments made by the employer, or the whole of such payments if the employer is a small employer. Regulations 4 to 7 provide for employers to be reimbursed through deductions from income tax, national insurance and other payments that they would otherwise make to HMRC (and for HMRC to fund payments to the extent that employers cannot be fully reimbursed in this way). Regulation 8 enables HMRC to recover overpayments to employers. Regulation 9 requires employers to maintain records relevant to ShPP payments to employees or former employees, while reg.10 empowers HMRC officers to inspect, copy or remove employers' payment records. Regulation 11 requires an employer who decides not to make any (or any further) ShPP payments to an employee (or former employee) to give that person the details of the decision and the reasons for it. Regulations 12 and 13 provide for HMRC officers to determine issues relating to a person's ShPP entitlement. Regulation 14 provides for employers, employment agencies, ShPP claimants and others to furnish information or documents to HMRC officers on request.

The Statutory Shared Parental Pay (Administration) Regulations 2014

Citation and commencement

7.3 1.—These Regulations may be cited as the Statutory Shared Parental Pay (Administration) Regulations 2014 and come into force on 1st December 2014.

Interpretation

7.4 2.—(1) In these Regulations—
"the 1992 Act" means the Social Security Contributions and Benefits Act 1992;
"the Commissioners" means the Commissioners for Her Majesty's Revenue and Customs;
"contributions payments" has the same meaning as in section 7 of the Employment Act 2002;
"the Contributions Regulations" means the Social Security (Contributions) Regulations 2001;
"income tax month" means the period beginning on the 6th day of any calendar month and ending on the 5th day of the following calendar month;
"income tax quarter" means the period beginning on—
(a) the 6th day of April and ending on the 5th day of July;
(b) the 6th day of July and ending on the 5th day of October;
(c) the 6th day of October and ending on the 5th day of January;
(d) the 6th day of January and ending on the 5th day of April;
"period of payment of statutory shared parental pay" means each week during which statutory shared parental pay is payable to a person under section 171ZY(2) of the 1992 Act;
"statutory shared parental pay" means statutory shared parental pay payable in accordance with the provisions of Part 12ZC of the 1992 Act;
"tax year" means the 12 months beginning with 6th April in any year;
"writing" includes writing delivered by means of electronic communications to the extent that the electronic communications are approved by directions issued by the Commissioners pursuant to regulations under section 132 of the Finance Act 1999.

(2) Any reference in these Regulations to the employees of an employer includes the employer's former employees.

Funding of employers' liabilities to make payments of statutory shared parental pay

7.5 3.—(1) An employer who has made any payment of statutory shared parental pay shall be entitled—
(a) to an amount equal to 92% of such payment; or
(b) if the payment qualifies for small employer's relief by virtue of section 7(3) of the Employment Act 2002—
(i) to an amount equal to such payment; and
(ii) to an additional payment equal to the amount to which the employer would have been entitled under section 167(2)(b) of the 1992 Act had the payment been a payment of statutory maternity pay.

(2) The employer shall be entitled in either case (a) or case (b) to apply for advance funding in respect of such payment in accordance with regulation 4, or to deduct it in accordance with regulation 5 from amounts otherwise payable by the employer.

DEFINITION

"statutory shared parental pay"—reg.2(1).

Applications for funding from the Commissioners

4.—(1) An employer may apply to the Commissioners for funds to pay the statutory shared parental pay (or so much of it as remains outstanding) to the employee or employees in a form approved for that purpose by the Commissioners where—
 (a) the conditions in paragraph (2) are satisfied; or
 (b) the condition in paragraph (2)(a) is satisfied and the employer considers that the condition in paragraph (2)(b) will be satisfied on the date of any subsequent payment of emoluments to one or more employees who are entitled to payment of statutory shared parental pay.
(2) The conditions in this paragraph are—
(a) the employer is entitled to a payment determined in accordance with regulation 3 in respect of statutory shared parental pay which the employer is required to pay to an employee or employees for an income tax month or income tax quarter; and
(b) the payment exceeds the aggregate of—
 (i) the total amount of tax which the employer is required to pay to the collector of taxes in respect of the deduction from the emoluments of employees in accordance with the Income Tax (Pay as You Earn) Regulations 2003 for the same income tax month or income tax quarter;
 (ii) the total amount of the deductions made by the employer from the emoluments of employees for the same income tax month or income tax quarter in accordance with regulations under section 22(5) of the Teaching and Higher Education Act 1998 or under section 73B of the Education (Scotland) Act 1980 or in accordance with article 3(5) of the Education (Student Support) (Northern Ireland) Order 1998;
 (iii) the total amount of contributions payments which the employer is required to pay to the collector of taxes in respect of the emoluments of employees (whether by means of deduction or otherwise) in accordance with the Contributions Regulations for the same income tax month or income tax quarter; and
 (iv) the total amount of payments which the employer is required to pay to the collector of taxes in respect of the deductions made on account of tax from payments to sub-contractors in accordance with section 61 of the Finance Act 2004 for the same income tax month or income quarter.
(3) An application by an employer under paragraph (1) shall be for an amount up to, but not exceeding, the amount of the payment to which the employer is entitled in accordance with regulation 3 in respect of statutory shared parental pay which the employer is required to pay to an employee

or employees for the income tax month or income tax quarter to which the payment of emoluments relates.

DEFINITIONS

"the Commissioners"—reg.2(1).
"contributions payments"—reg.2(1).
"the Contributions Regulations"—reg.2(1).
"income tax month"—reg.2(1).
"income tax quarter"—reg.2(1).
"statutory shared parental pay"—reg.2(1).

Deductions from payments to the Commissioners

5.—An employer who is entitled to a payment determined in accordance with regulation 3 may recover such payment by making one or more deductions from the aggregate of the amounts specified in sub-paragraphs (i) to (iv) of regulation 4(2)(b) except where and in so far as—
  (a) those amounts relate to earnings paid before the beginning of the income tax month or income tax quarter in which the payment of statutory shared parental pay was made;
  (b) those amounts are paid by the employer later than six years after the end of the tax year in which the payment of statutory shared parental pay was made;
  (c) the employer has received payment from the Commissioners under regulation 4; or
  (d) the employer has made a request in writing under regulation 4 that the payment to which the employer is entitled in accordance with regulation 3 be paid and the employer has not received notification by the Commissioners that the request is refused.

DEFINITIONS

"the Commissioners"—reg.2(1).
"income tax month"—reg.2(1).
"income tax quarter"—reg.2(1).
"statutory shared parental pay"—reg.2(1).
"tax year"—reg.2(1).
"writing"—reg.2(1).

Payments to employers by the Commissioners

6.—The Commissioners shall pay the employer such amount as the employer was unable to deduct where—
  (a) the Commissioners are satisfied that the total amount which the employer is or would otherwise be entitled to deduct under regulation 5 is less than the payment to which the employer is entitled in accordance with regulation 3 in an income tax month or income tax quarter; and
  (b) the employer has in writing requested the Commissioners to do so.

DEFINITIONS

"the Commissioners"—reg.2(1).
"income tax month"—reg.2(1).
"income tax quarter"—reg.2(1).
"writing"—reg.2(1).

(SI 2014/2929 reg. 7)

Date when certain contributions are to be treated as paid

7.—Where an employee has made a deduction from a contributions payment under regulation 5, the date on which it is to be treated as having been paid for the purposes of subsection (5) of section 7 (funding of employers' liabilities) of the Employment 2002 is—
  (a) in a case where the deduction did not extinguish the contributions payment, the date on which the remainder of the contributions payment or, as the case may be, the first date on which any part of the remainder of the contributions payment was paid; and
  (b) in a case where deduction extinguished the contributions payment, the 14th day after the end of the income tax month or income tax quarter during which there were paid the earnings in respect of which the contributions payment was payable.

DEFINITIONS

"contributions payments"—reg.2(1).
"income tax month"—reg.2(1).
"income tax quarter"—reg.2(1).

Overpayments

8.—(1) This regulation applies where funds have been provided to the employer pursuant to regulation 4 in respect of one or more employees and it appears to an officer of Revenue and Customs that the employer has not used the whole or part of those funds to pay statutory shared parental pay.

(2) An officer of Revenue and Customs shall decide to the best of the officer's judgement the amount of funds provided pursuant to regulation 4 and not used to pay statutory shared parental pay and shall serve notice in writing of this decision on the employer.

(3) A decision under this regulation may cover funds provided pursuant to regulation 4—
  (a) for any one income tax month or income tax quarter, or more than one income tax month or income tax quarter, in a tax year; and
  (b) in respect of a class or classes of employees specified in the decision notice (without naming the individual employees), or in respect of one or more employees named in the decision notice.

(4) Subject to the following provisions of this regulation, Part 6 of the Taxes Management Act 1970 (collection and recovery) shall apply with any necessary modifications to a decision under this regulation as if it were an assessment and as if the amount of funds determined were income tax charged on the employer.

(5) Where an amount of funds determined under this regulation relates to more than one employee, proceedings may be brought for the recovery of that amount without distinguishing the amounts making up that sum which the employer is liable to repay in respect of each employee and without specifying the employee in question, and the amount determined under this regulation shall be one cause of action or one matter of complaint for the purposes of proceedings under section 65, 66 or 67 of the Taxes Management Act 1970.

(6) Nothing in paragraph (5) prevents the bringing of separate proceedings for the recovery of any amount which the employer is liable to repay in respect of each employee.

DEFINITIONS

"employee"—reg.2(2).
"income tax month"—reg.2(1).
"income tax quarter"—reg.2(1).
"statutory shared parental pay"—reg.2(1).

Records to be maintained by employers

7.11   **9.**—Every employer shall maintain for three years after the end of a tax year in which the employer made payments of statutory shared parental pay to any employee a record of—
    (a) if the employee's period of payment of statutory shared parental pay began in that year—
        (i) the date of which that period began; and
        (ii) the evidence of entitlement to statutory shared parental pay provided by the employee pursuant to regulations made under section 171ZW(1)(b) of the 1992 Act;
    (b) the weeks in that tax year in which statutory shared parental pay was paid to the employee and the amount paid in each week;
    (c) any week in that tax year which was within the employee's period of payment of statutory shared parental pay but for which no payment of statutory shared parental pay was made to the employee and the reason no payment was made.

DEFINITIONS

"employee"—reg.2(2).
"period of payment of statutory shared parental pay"—reg.2(1).
"statutory shared parental pay"—reg.2(1).
"tax year"—reg.2(1).
"writing"—reg.2(1).

Inspection of employers' records

7.12   **10.**—(1) Every employer, whenever called upon to do so by any authorised officer of Revenue and Customs, shall produce the documents and records specified in paragraph (2) to that officer for inspection, at such time as that officer may reasonably require, at the prescribed place.
(2) The documents and records specified in this paragraph are—
    (a) all wage sheets, deductions working sheets, records kept in accordance with regulation 9 and other documents relating to the calculation or payment of statutory shared parental pay to employees in respect of the years specified by such officer; or
    (b) such of those wages sheets, deductions working sheets, or other documents and records as may be specified by the authorised officer.
(3) The "prescribed place" mentioned in paragraph (1) means—
    (a) such place in Great Britain as the employer and the authorised officer may agree upon; or
    (b) in default of such agreement, the place in Great Britain at which the documents and records referred to in paragraph (2)(a) are normally kept; or
    (c) in default of such agreement and if there is no such place as it referred to in sub-paragraph (b), the employer's principal place of business in Great Britain.

(4) The authorised officer may—
(a) take copies of, or make extracts from, any document or record produced to the authorised officer for inspection in accordance with paragraph (1); and
(b) remove any document or record so produced if it appears to the authorised officer to be necessary to do so, at a reasonable time and for a reasonable period.

(5) Where any document or record is removed in accordance with paragraph (4)(b), the authorised officer shall provide—
(a) a receipt for the document or record so removed; and
(b) a copy of the document or record, free of charge, within seven days, to the person by whom it was produced or caused to be produced where the document or record is reasonably required for the proper conduct of business.

(6) Where a lien is claimed on a document produced in accordance with paragraph (1), the removal of the document under paragraph (4)(b) shall not be regarded as breaking the lien.

(7) Where records are maintained by computer, the person required to make them available for inspection shall provide the authorised officer with all facilities necessary for obtaining information from them.

DEFINITIONS

"employee"—reg.2(1).
"prescribed place"—para.(3).
"statutory shared parental pay"—reg.2(1).

Provision of information relating to entitlement to statutory shared parental pay

11.—(1) An employer shall furnish the employee with details of a decision that the employer has no liability to make payments of statutory shared parental pay to the employee and the reason for it where the employer—
(a) has been given evidence of entitlement to statutory shared parental pay pursuant to regulations made under section 171ZW(1)(b) of the 1992 Act; and
(b) decides that they have no liability to make payments of statutory shared parental pay to the employee.

(2) An employer who has been given such evidence of entitlement to statutory shared parental pay shall furnish the employee with the information specified in paragraph (3) where the employer—
(a) has made one or more payments of statutory shared parental pay to the employee but,
(b) decides, before the end of the period of payment of statutory shared parental pay, that they have no liability to make further payments to the employee because the employee has been detained in legal custody or sentenced to a term of imprisonment which was not suspended.

(3) The information specified in this paragraph is—
(a) details of the employer's decision and the reasons for it; and
(b) details of the last week in respect of which a liability to pay statutory shared parental pay arose and the total number of weeks within the period of payment of statutory shared parental pay in which such liability arose.

7.13

(4) The employer shall—
(a) return to the employee any evidence provided by the employee as referred to in paragraph (1) or (2);
(b) comply with the requirements imposed by paragraph (1) within 28 days of the day the employee gave evidence of entitlement to statutory shared parental pay pursuant to regulations made under section 171ZW(1)(b) of the 1992 Act; and
(c) comply with the requirements imposed by paragraph (2) within seven days of being notified of the employee's detention or sentence.

DEFINITIONS

"employee"—reg.2(2).
"period of payment of statutory shared parental pay"—reg.2(1).
"statutory shared parental pay"—reg.2(1).

Application for the determination of any issue arising as to, or in connection with, entitlement to statutory shared parental pay

7.14   **12.**—(1) An application for the determination of any issue arising as to, or in connection with, entitlement to statutory shared parental pay may be submitted to an officer of Revenue and Customs by the employee concerned.
(2) Such an issue shall be decided by an officer of Revenue and Customs only on the basis of such an application or on their own initiative.

DEFINITION

"statutory shared parental pay"—reg.2(1).

Applications in connection with statutory shared parental pay

7.15   **13.**—(1) An application for the determination of any issue referred to in regulation 12 shall be made in a form approved for the purpose by the Commissioners.
(2) Where such an application is made by an employee, it shall—
(a) be made to an officer of Revenue and Customs within six months of the earliest day in respect of which entitlement to statutory shared parental pay is an issue;
(b) state the period in respect of which entitlement to statutory shared parental pay is in issue; and
(c) state the grounds (if any) on which the applicant's employer had denied liability for statutory shared parental pay in respect of the period specified in the application.

DEFINITIONS

"Commissioners"—reg.2(1).
"employee"—reg.2(2).
"statutory shared parental pay"—reg.2(1).

Provision of information

7.16   **14.**—(1) Where an officer of Revenue and Customs—
(a) reasonably requires information or documents from a person specified in paragraph (2) to ascertain whether statutory shared parental pay is or was payable, and

(SI 2014/2929 reg.14)

(b) gives notification to that person requesting such information or documents, that person shall furnish that information within 30 days of receiving the notification.

(2) The requirement to provide such information or documents applies to—

(a) any person claiming to be entitled to statutory shared parental pay;
(b) any person who is, or has been, the spouse, civil partner or partner of such a person as is specified in sub-paragraph (a);
(c) any person who is, or has been, an employer of such a person as is specified in sub-paragraph (a);
(d) any person carrying on an agency or other business for the introduction or supply of persons available to do work or to perform services to persons requiring them; and
(e) any person who is a servant or agent of any such person as is specified in sub-paragraphs (a) to (d).

DEFINITION

"statutory shared parental pay"—reg.2(1).

The Statutory Shared Parental Pay (General) Regulations 2014

(SI 2014/3051)

A draft of these Regulations was laid before Parliament in accordance with section 176(1) of the Social Security Contributions and Benefits Act 1992 and approved by resolution of each House of Parliament.

This instrument contains only regulations made by virtue of, or consequential upon, section 119 of the Children and Families Act 2014 and is made before the end of the period of 6 months beginning with the coming into force of that enactment.

The Secretary of State, in exercise of the powers conferred by sections 171ZU(1), (2), (3), (4), (5), (12), (13), (14) and (15), 171ZV(1), (2), (3), (4), (5), (12), (13), (14), (15) and (17), 171ZW(1)(a) to (f), 171ZX(2) and (3), 171ZY(1), (3), (4) and (5), 171ZZ1(3), 171ZZ4(3), (4), (7) and (8) and 175(3) of the Social Security Contributions and Benefits Act 1992 and by section 5(1)(g), (i), (l) and (p) of the Social Security Administration Act 1992 and with the concurrence of the Commissioners for Her Majesty's Revenue and Customs in so far as such concurrence is required, makes the following Regulations:

ARRANGEMENT OF REGULATIONS

PART 1

1. Citation and commencement
2. Definitions
3. Application

7.17

The Statutory Shared Parental Pay (General) Regulations 2014

Part 2

4. Entitlement of mother to statutory shared parental pay (birth)
5. Entitlement of father or partner to statutory shared parental pay (birth)
6. Notification and evidential requirements relating to the mother
7. Notification and evidential requirements relating to the father or partner
8. Variation of number of weeks of pay to be claimed and of periods when pay is to be claimed
9. Modification of notice conditions in case of early birth
10. Extent of entitlement to statutory shared parental pay (birth)
11. When statutory shared parental pay (birth) is not to be paid
12. Work during period of payment of statutory shared parental pay (birth)
13. Care of child during period of payment of statutory shared parental pay
14. Other cases where there is no liability to pay statutory shared parental pay
15. Conditions of entitlement to statutory shared parental pay: absence from work
16. Entitlement to statutory shared parental pay (birth) in cases relating to death

Part 3

17. Entitlement of adopter to statutory shared parental pay (adoption)
18. Entitlement of partner to statutory shared parental pay (adoption)
19. Notification and evidential requirements relating to the adopter
20. Notification and evidential requirements relating to the partner
21. Variation of number of weeks of pay to be claimed and of periods when pay is to be claimed
22. Extent of entitlement to statutory shared parental pay (adoption)
23. When statutory shared parental pay (adoption) is not to be paid
24. Work during period of payment of statutory shared parental pay (adoption)
25. Care of child during period of payment of statutory shared parental pay
26. Other cases where there is no liability to pay statutory shared parental pay
27. Conditions of entitlement to statutory shared parental pay: absence from work
28. Entitlement to statutory shared parental pay (adoption) in cases relating to death

Part 4

29. Conditions relating to employment and earnings of a claimant's partner
30. Conditions as to continuity of employment and normal weekly earnings relating to a claimant for statutory shared parental pay (birth)
31. Conditions as to continuity of employment and normal weekly earnings in relation to a claimant for statutory shared parental pay (adoption)
32. Normal weekly earnings of a claimant for statutory shared parental pay
33. Treatment of persons as employees
34. Continuous employment
35. Continuous employment and unfair dismissal
36. Continuous employment and stoppages of work
37. Change of employer
38. Reinstatement after service with the armed forces etc
39. Treatment of two or more employers or two or more contracts of service as one

PART 5

40. Weekly rate of payment of statutory shared parental pay
41. Statutory shared parental pay and contractual remuneration
42. Avoidance of liability for statutory shared parental pay
43. Payment of statutory shared parental pay
44. Time when statutory shared parental pay is to be paid
45. Liability of the Commissioners to pay statutory shared parental pay
46. Liability of the Commissioners to pay statutory shared parental pay in case of legal custody or imprisonment
47. Payments by the Commissioners
48. Persons unable to act
49. Service of notices

Schedule   Statutory Shared Parental Pay in Special Circumstances

GENERAL NOTE

These Regulations introduce a new entitlement for mothers, fathers or the partners of mothers who are employed earners and for adopters and their partners who are employed earners to receive a statutory payment from their employers called statutory shared parental pay (ShPP). Part 7 of the Children and Families Act 2014 inserted a new Chapter 1B into Pt 8 of the Employment Rights Act 1996, giving the Secretary of State the power to make regulations to create an entitlement to shared parental leave. Part 7 of the 2014 Act also inserts a new Pt 12ZC into the SSCBA 1992 giving the Secretary of State the power to make regulations to create an entitlement to ShPP. Eligible employees will be able to share up to 50 weeks of shared parental leave and up to 37 weeks of ShPP. Shared parental leave and pay can be taken at any time between the birth of a child or the placement of a child for adoption or with prospective adopters. ShPP must be taken before the child's first birthday or the first anniversary of the placement.

7.18

Part 1 of the Regulations is introductory and in particular specifies for what children the new entitlement arises by reference to the time of their expected week of birth or placement for adoption.

Part 2 (regs 4–16) relates to entitlement to ShPP in connection with the birth of a child. Regulations 4 and 5 set out the conditions which a mother, mother's partner or father must satisfy in order to be entitled to this pay. Regulations 6 and 7 detail what notices and information the claimant mother, mother's partner or father must provide. Regulation 8 provides for the claimants to vary their entitlement once they have claimed it. Regulation 9 provides for the modification of the notice provisions in the case of an early birth. Regulation 10 details how many weeks of ShPP are available to claimants. Regulation 11 sets out when ShPP is not to be paid. Regulations 12 to 15 deal with further circumstances relating to such matters as work or absence from work which mean that pay may, or may not be, payable.

Part 3 (regs 17–28) concerns ShPP in connection with adoption. The provisions correspond to the provisions in Pt 2.

Part 4 (regs 29–39) sets out the conditions relating to employment and earnings that a claimant and the claimant's partner (or child's father) must satisfy in order for the claimant to be entitled to ShPP (regs 29–32). This Part also contains further provisions relating to employment (regs 33–39).

Part 5 (regs 40–48) contains provisions as to the rate of ShPP, how it is paid, when it is paid and who pays it.

The Schedule contains provisions modifying the regulations in various cases where a claimant, a claimant's partner or father of the child dies or where the child dies or, in the case of adoption, is returned after being placed.

Note also that these Regulations are modified for certain special purposes by two sets of other regulations. First, the Statutory Shared Parental Pay (Adoption from

Overseas) Regulations 2014 (SI 2014/3093) make provision relating to ShPP in respect of adoptions from overseas. Secondly, the Statutory Shared Parental Pay (Parental Order Cases) Regulations 2014 (SI 2014/3097) provide an entitlement to ShPP in cases which involve a person who has applied with another person for a parental order under s.54 of the Human Fertilisation and Embryology Act 2008.

PART 1

Citation and commencement

7.19   **1.**—These Regulations may be cited as the Statutory Shared Parental Pay (General) Regulations 2014 and come into force on 1st December 2014.

Definitions

7.20   **2.**—(1) In these Regulations—
"1992 Act" means the Social Security Contributions and Benefits Act 1992;
"A" means a person with whom C is, or is expected to be, placed for adoption under the law of any part of the United Kingdom;
"AP" means a person who at the date C is placed for adoption is married to, or is the civil partner of, or is the partner of A;
"C" means the child in relation to whom entitlement to statutory shared parental pay arises;
"M" means the mother (or expectant mother) of C;
"P" means the father of C or a person who at the date of C's birth is married to, or is the civil partner of, or is the partner of M;
"actual week of birth", in relation to a child, means the week beginning with midnight between Saturday and Sunday, in which the child was born;
"adoption agency" has the meaning given, in relation to England and Wales, by section 2 of the Adoption and Children Act 2002 and in relation to Scotland, by section 119(1) of the Adoption and Children (Scotland) Act 2007;
"child", in relation to A, means a person who is, or when placed with A for adoption was, under the age of 18;
"the Commissioners" means the Commissioners for Her Majesty's Revenue and Customs;
"expected week of birth", in relation to a child, means the week, beginning with midnight between Saturday and Sunday, in which, as appropriate, it is expected that the child will be born, or was expected that the child would be born;
"partner", in relation to M or A, means a person (whether of a different sex or the same sex) who lives with, as the case may be, M or A as well as C in an enduring family relationship but is not a relative of M or A of a kind specified in paragraph (2);
"placed for adoption" means—
(a) placed for adoption under the Adoption and Children Act 2002 or the Adoption and Children (Scotland) Act 2007; or

(b) placed in accordance with section 22C of the Children Act 1989 with a local authority foster parent who is also a prospective adopter;

"processing", in relation to information, has the meaning given by section 1(1) of the Data Protection Act 1998;

"shared parental leave" means leave under section 75E or 75G of the Employment Rights Act 1996;

"statutory shared parental pay" means statutory shared parental pay payable in accordance with Part 12ZC of the 1992 Act;

"statutory shared parental pay (adoption)" means statutory shared parental pay payable where entitlement to that pay arises under regulation 17 or 18;

"statutory shared parental pay (birth)" means statutory shared parental pay payable where entitlement to that pay arises under regulation 4 or 5;

"week" in Parts 2, 3 and 5 means a period of seven days.

(2) The relatives of M or A referred to in the definition of "partner" in paragraph (1) are M's, or, A's parent, grandparent, sister, brother, aunt, uncle, child, grandchild, niece or nephew.

(3) References to relationships in paragraph (2)—
(a) are to relationships of the full-blood or half-blood or, in the case of an adopted person, such of those relationships as would exist but for the adoption; and
(b) include the relationship of a child with his adoptive, or former adoptive parents, but do not include any other adoptive relationship.

(4) For the purpose of these Regulations—
(a) a person is matched with a child for adoption when an adoption agency decides that that person would be a suitable adoptive parent for the child;
(b) in a case where paragraph (a) applies, a person is notified as having been matched with a child on the date that person receives notification of the agency's decision, under regulation 33(3)(a) of the Adoption Agencies Regulations 2005, regulation 28(3) of the Adoption Agencies (Wales) Regulations 2005 or regulation 8(5) of the Adoption Agencies (Scotland) Regulations 2009;
(c) a person is also matched with a child for adoption when a decision has been made in accordance with regulation 22A of the Care Planning, Placement and Case Review (England) Regulations 2010 and an adoption agency has identified that person with whom the child is to be placed in accordance with regulation 12B of the Adoption Agencies Regulations 2005;
(d) in a case where paragraph (c) applies, a person is notified as having been matched with a child on the date on which that person receives notification in accordance with regulation 12B(2)(a) of the Adoption Agencies Regulations 2005.

(5) The reference to "local authority foster parent" in the definition of "placed for adoption" in paragraph (1) means a person approved as a local authority foster parent in accordance with regulations made by virtue of paragraph 12F of Schedule 2 to the Children Act 1989.

(6) The reference to "prospective adopter" in the definition of "placed for adoption" in paragraph (1) means a person who has been approved as suitable to adopt a child and has been notified of that decision in accordance with regulation 30B(4) of the Adoption Agencies Regulations 2005.

General Note

7.21   This regulation is modified for certain special cases by the Statutory Shared Parental Pay (Adoption from Overseas) Regulations 2014 (SI 2014/3093) and the Statutory Shared Parental Pay (Parental Order Cases) Regulations 2014 (SI 2014/3097).

Application

7.22   **3.**—These Regulations apply in relation to—
(a) statutory shared parental pay (birth) in respect of children whose expected week of birth begins on or after 5th April 2015;
(b) statutory shared parental pay (adoption) in respect of children placed for adoption on or after 5th April 2015.

Definitions

"child"—reg.2(1).
"expected week of birth"—reg.2(1).
"placed for adoption"—reg.2(1).
"statutory shared parental pay (adoption)"—reg.2(1).
"statutory shared parental pay (birth)"—reg.2(1).

General Note

7.23   This regulation is modified for certain special cases by the Statutory Shared Parental Pay (Adoption from Overseas) Regulations 2014 (SI 2014/3093) and the Statutory Shared Parental Pay (Parental Order Cases) Regulations 2014 (SI 2014/3097).

Part 2

Entitlement of mother to statutory shared parental pay (birth)

7.24   **4.**—(1) M is entitled to statutory shared parental pay (birth) if M satisfies the conditions specified in paragraph (2) and if P satisfies the conditions specified in paragraphs (3).
(2) The conditions referred to in paragraph (1) are that—
(a) M satisfies the conditions as to continuity of employment and normal weekly earnings specified in regulation 30;
(b) M has at the date of C's birth the main responsibility for the care of C (apart from the responsibility of P);
(c) M has complied with the requirements specified in regulation 6 (notification and evidential requirements of M);
(d) M became entitled by reference to the birth or expected birth of C to statutory maternity pay in respect of C;
(e) the maternity pay period that applies as a result of M's entitlement to statutory maternity pay is, and continues to be, reduced under section 165(3A) of the 1992 Act;
(f) it is M's intention to care for C during each week in respect of which statutory shared parental pay (birth) is paid to her;
(g) M is absent from work during each week in respect of which statutory shared parental pay (birth) is paid to her (except in the cases

referred to in regulation 15 (entitlement to shared parental pay: absence from work)); and
(h) where M is an employee (within the meaning of the Employment Rights Act 1996) M's absence from work as an employee during each week that statutory shared parental pay (birth) is paid to her is absence on shared parental leave in respect of C;
(3) The conditions referred to in paragraph (1) are that—
(a) P has at the date of C's birth the main responsibility for the care of C (apart from the responsibility of M); and
(b) P satisfies the conditions relating to employment and earnings in regulation 29 (conditions as to employment and earnings of claimant's partner).

DEFINITIONS

"1992 Act"—reg.2(1).
"C"—reg.2(1).
"expected week of birth"—reg.2(1).
"M"—reg.2(1).
"P"—reg.2(1).
"partner"—reg.2(1).
"statutory shared parental pay (birth)"—reg.2(1).
"week"—reg.2(1).

Entitlement of father or partner to statutory shared parental pay (birth)

5.—(1) P is entitled to statutory shared parental pay (birth) if P satisfies the conditions specified in paragraph (2) and M satisfies the conditions specified in paragraph (3).

7.25

(2) The conditions specified in paragraph (1) are that—
(a) P satisfies the conditions as to continuity of employment and normal weekly earnings specified in regulation 30;
(b) P has at the date of C's birth the main responsibility for the care of C (apart from the responsibility of M);
(c) P has complied with the requirements specified in regulation 7 (notification and evidential requirements of P);
(d) it is P's intention to care for C during each week in respect of which statutory shared parental pay (birth) is paid to P;
(e) P is absent from work during each week in respect of which statutory shared parental pay (birth) is paid to P (except in the cases referred to in regulation 15 (entitlement to statutory shared parental pay: absence from work)); and
(f) where P is an employee (within the meaning of the Employment Rights Act 1996 P's absence from work as an employee during each week that statutory shared parental pay (birth) is paid to P is absence on shared parental leave in respect of C.
(3) The conditions specified in paragraph (1) are—
(a) M has at the date of C's birth the main responsibility for the care of C (apart from the responsibility of P);
(b) M meets the conditions as to employment and earnings in regulation 29 (conditions as to employment and earnings of claimant's partner);

(c) M became entitled by reference to the birth, or expected birth, of C to statutory maternity pay or maternity allowance; and
(d) the maternity pay period or the maternity allowance period which applies to M as a result of her entitlement to statutory maternity pay or maternity allowance is, and continues to be, reduced under sections 35(3A) or 165(3A) of the 1992 Act.

DEFINITIONS

"1992 Act"—reg.2(1).
"C"—reg.2(1).
"expected week of birth"—reg.2(1).
"M"—reg.2(1).
"P"—reg.2(1).
"partner"—reg.2(1).
"statutory shared parental pay (birth)"—reg.2(1).
"week"—reg.2(1).

Notification and evidential requirements relating to the mother

7.26   **6.**—(1) The notice and evidential requirements referred to in regulation 4(2)(c) are that M gives the employer who will be liable to pay statutory shared parental pay (birth) to M the notice and information specified in—
(a) paragraphs (2) and (3)(a), (b), (d) and (e) at least 8 weeks before the beginning of the first period specified by M pursuant to paragraph (2)(d);
(b) paragraph (3)(c) at least 8 weeks before the beginning of the first period specified by M pursuant to paragraph (2)(d) or, where C is not born by that time, as soon as reasonably practicable after the birth of C but in any event before the beginning of that first period; and
(c) paragraph (4) within 14 days of that employer requesting that information where the employer requests it within 14 days of receiving the notice and information specified in paragraph (2) and (3)(a),(b),(d) and (e).
(2) The notice specified in this paragraph is notice of—
(a) the number of weeks in respect of which M would be entitled to claim statutory shared parental pay (birth) in respect of C if entitlement were fully exercised disregarding any intention of P to claim statutory shared parental pay in respect of C;
(b) the number of weeks out of those specified under sub-paragraph (a) in respect of which M intends to claim statutory shared parental pay (birth) in respect of C;
(c) the number of weeks out of those specified under sub-paragraph (a) in respect of which P intends to claim statutory shared parental pay (birth) in respect of C;
(d) the period or periods during which M intends to claim statutory shared parental pay (birth) in respect of C.
(3) The information specified in this paragraph is—
(a) a written declaration signed by P who in connection with M's claim is required to satisfy the conditions specified in regulation 4(3)—
    (i) that P consents to M's intended claim for statutory shared parental pay;

(ii) that P meets, or will meet, the conditions in regulation 4(3) (conditions to be satisfied by P);
(iii) specifying P's name, address and national insurance number or, if P has no national insurance number, stating that P has no such number; and
(iv) providing P's consent as regards the processing by the employer who will be liable to pay statutory shared parental pay (birth) to M of the information in the written declaration;
(b) C's expected week of birth;
(c) C's date of birth;
(d) M's name;
(e) a written declaration signed by M—
(i) that the information given by M under paragraphs (2) and (3) is correct;
(ii) that M meets, or will meet, the conditions in regulation 4(2);
(iii) that M will immediately inform the person who will be liable to pay statutory shared parental pay (birth) if M ceases to meet the condition in regulation 4(2)(e); and
(iv) specifying the date on which M's maternity pay period or maternity allowance period in respect of C began and the number of weeks by which it is, or will be, reduced.

(4) The information specified in this paragraph is—
(a) a copy of C's birth certificate or, if one has not been issued, a declaration signed by M which states that it has not been issued; and
(b) the name and address of P's employer or, if P has no employer, a written declaration signed by M that P has no employer.

Definitions

"C"—reg.2(1).
"expected week of birth"—reg.2(1).
"M"—reg.2(1).
"P"—reg.2(1).
"partner"—reg.2(1).
"processing"—reg.2(1).
"statutory shared parental pay (birth)"—reg.2(1).
"week"—reg.2(1).

Notification and evidential requirements relating to the father or partner

7.—(1) The notification and evidential requirements referred to in regulation 5(2)(c), are that P gives the employer who will be liable to pay statutory shared parental pay (birth) to P the notice and information specified in—

(a) paragraphs (2) and (3)(a), (b), (d) and (e) at least 8 weeks before the beginning of the first period specified by P pursuant to paragraph (2)(d);
(b) paragraph 3(c) at least 8 weeks before the beginning of the first period specified by P pursuant to paragraph (2)(d) or, where C is not born by that time, as soon as reasonably practicable after the birth of C but in any event before the beginning of that first period; and

7.27

(c) paragraph (4) within 14 days of that employer requesting that information where the employer requests it within 14 days of receiving all the notices and information specified in paragraphs (2) and (3)(a), (b), (d) and (e).

(2) The notice specified in this paragraph is notice of—
(a) the number of weeks in respect of which P would be entitled to claim statutory shared parental pay (birth) in respect of C if entitlement were fully exercised disregarding any intention of M to claim statutory shared parental pay in respect of C;
(b) the number of weeks out of those specified under sub-paragraph (a) in respect of which P intends to claim statutory shared parental pay (birth) in respect of C;
(c) the number of weeks out of those specified under sub-paragraph (a) in respect of which M intends to claim statutory shared parental pay (birth) in respect of C;
(d) the period or periods during which P intends to claim statutory shared parental pay (birth) in respect of C.

(3) The information specified in this paragraph is—
(a) a written declaration signed by M who in connection with P's claim is required to satisfy the conditions specified in regulation 5(3)—
   (i) that M consents to P's intended claim for statutory shared parental pay;
   (ii) that M meets, or will meet, the conditions in regulation 5(3) (conditions to be satisfied by M);
   (iii) that M will immediately inform P if M ceases to meet the condition in regulation 5(3)(d);
   (iv) specifying M's name, address and national insurance number or, if M has no national insurance number, stating that M has no such number;
   (v) specifying the date on which M's maternity pay period or maternity allowance period in respect of C began and the number of weeks by which it is, or will be, reduced; and
   (vi) providing M's consent as regards the processing by the person who is, or will be, liable to pay statutory shared parental pay (birth) to P under section 171ZX(1) of the 1992 Act of the information in the written declaration;
(b) C's expected week of birth;
(c) C's date of birth;
(d) P's name;
(e) a written declaration signed by P—
   (i) that the information given by P is correct;
   (ii) that P meets, or will meet, the conditions in regulation 5(2); and
   (iii) that P will immediately inform the person who will be liable to pay statutory shared parental pay (birth) if M ceases to meet the condition in regulation 5(3)(d).

(4) The information specified in this paragraph is—
(a) a copy of C's birth certificate or, if one has not been issued, a declaration signed by P which states that it has not been issued; and
(b) the name and address of M's employer (or, if M has no employer a written declaration signed by P that M has no employer.

DEFINITIONS

"C"—reg.2(1).
"expected week of birth"—reg.2(1).
"M"—reg.2(1).
"P"—reg.2(1).
"partner"—reg.2(1).
"statutory shared parental pay (birth)"—reg.2(1).
"week"—reg.2(1).

Variation of number of weeks of pay to be claimed and of periods when pay is to be claimed

8.—(1) M or, as the case may be, P may vary the period or periods during which they intend to claim statutory shared parental pay (birth) by notice in writing given to the employer who will be liable to pay that pay to M or P at least 8 weeks before the beginning of the first period specified in that notice.

(2) M may vary the number of weeks in respect of which M intends to claim statutory shared parental pay (birth) by notice in writing given to the employer who will be liable to pay statutory shared parental pay (birth) to M—
   (a) of the number of weeks during which M and P have exercised, or intend to exercise, an entitlement to statutory shared parental pay (birth) in respect of C; and
   (b) which is accompanied by a written declaration signed by P who in connection with M's claim is required to satisfy the conditions specified in regulation 4(3) that P consents to that variation.

(3) P may vary the number of weeks in respect of which P intends to claim statutory shared parental pay (birth) by notice in writing given to the employer who will be liable to pay statutory shared parental pay (birth) to P—
   (a) of the number of weeks during which P and M have exercised, or intend to exercise, an entitlement to statutory shared parental pay (birth) in respect of C; and
   (b) which is accompanied by a written declaration by M who in connection with P's claim is required to satisfy the conditions specified in regulation 5(3) that M consents to that variation.

DEFINITIONS

"C"—reg.2(1).
"M"—reg.2(1).
"P"—reg.2(1).
"statutory shared parental pay (birth)"—reg.2(1).
"week"—reg.2(1).

Modification of notice conditions in case of early birth

9.—(1) This paragraph applies where—
   (a) one or more of the periods specified in a notice given under regulation 6, 7, or 8 during which M or, as the case may be, P intends to claim statutory shared parental pay (birth) start in the 8 weeks following the first day of C's expected week of birth;
   (b) C's date of birth is before the first day of the expected week of birth; and

(c) M or, as the case may be, P varies by notice under regulation 8(1) the period or periods referred to in sub-paragraph (a) so that that period or those periods start the same length of time following C's date of birth as that period or those periods would have started after the first day of the expected week of birth.

(2) Where paragraph (1) applies the requirement in regulation 8(1) to give notice at least 8 weeks before the first period specified in the notice is satisfied if such notice is given as soon as reasonably practicable after C's date of birth.

(3) This paragraph applies where—

(a) C is born more than 8 weeks before the first day of the expected week of birth; and

(b) M or, as the case may be, P has not given the notice and information under regulations 6 or 7 before the date of C's birth.

(4) Where paragraph (3) applies and M, or as the case may be, P specifies in a notice under regulation 6 or 7 a period or periods of statutory shared parental pay (birth) which start in the 8 weeks following C's date of birth, then the following modifications apply—

(a) in regulation 6—

(i) paragraph (1)(a) shall apply as if it read—

"(a) paragraphs (2) and (3) as soon as reasonably practicable after the date of C's birth but in any event before the first period specified by M pursuant to paragraph (2)(d);";

(ii) paragraph (1)(b) and (c) shall not apply;

(iii) paragraph (4) shall not apply.

(b) in regulation 7—

(i) paragraph (1)(a) shall apply as if it read—

"(a) paragraphs (2) and (3) as soon as reasonably practicable after the date of C's birth but in any event before the first period specified by P pursuant to paragraph (2)(d). ";

(ii) paragraph (1)(b) and (c) shall not apply;

(iii) paragraph (4) shall not apply.

DEFINITIONS

"C"—reg.2(1).
"expected week of birth"—reg.2(1).
"M"—reg.2(1).
"P"—reg.2(1).
"statutory shared parental pay (birth)"—reg.2(1).
"week"—reg.2(1).

Extent of entitlement to statutory shared parental pay (birth)

10.—(1) The number of weeks in respect of which M or P is entitled to payments of statutory shared parental pay (birth) in respect of C is 39 weeks less—

(a) the number of weeks—

(i) in respect of which maternity allowance or statutory maternity pay is payable to M in respect of C up to the time M has returned to work (where M has returned to work without satisfying the condition in regulations 4(2)(e) or 5(3)(d) (condition as to reduction of the maternity pay period or the maternity allowance period)); or

(ii) in any other case, to which the maternity allowance period is reduced by virtue of section 35(3A) of the 1992 Act or, as the case may be, the maternity pay period is reduced by virtue of section 165(3A); and

(b) the number of weeks of statutory shared parental pay in respect of C which—

(i) in the case of M, P has notified P's intention to claim under regulation 7 or 8; or

(ii) in the case of P, M has notified M's intention to claim under regulation 6 or 8.

(2) In a case where—

(a) P was entitled to payments of statutory shared parental pay (birth) in respect of C; and

(b) P ceases to be so entitled because M ceases to satisfy the condition in regulation 5(3)(d); and

(c) P becomes entitled again to such payments as a result of M satisfying the condition in regulation 5(3)(d);

the number of weeks in which P claimed statutory shared parental pay (birth) up to the time P ceases to be so entitled is also to be deducted from the number of weeks specified in paragraph (1).

(3) Where paragraph (2) applies the number of weeks of statutory shared parental pay (birth) which P notified P's intention to claim under regulation 7(2)(b) (as varied under regulation 8(3)) before P ceases to be entitled to statutory shared parental pay (birth) is to be disregarded for the purposes of this regulation.

(4) In the case where M has more than one entitlement to statutory maternity pay in respect of C and in relation to all those entitlements she returns to work without satisfying the conditions in regulation 4(2)(e) or (5)(3)(d), paragraph (1)(a)(i) shall apply as though it read—

"(i) in respect of which statutory maternity pay is payable to M in respect of C up to the last day M returns to work;".

(5) In the case where M has more than one entitlement to statutory maternity pay in respect of C and the maternity pay periods which apply as a result of those entitlements are all reduced by virtue of section 165(3A) of the 1992 Act before she returns to work, paragraph (1)(a)(ii) shall apply as though it read—

"(ii) falling in the period beginning with the first day of the maternity pay period which is the earliest to begin and ending on the last day of the maternity pay period which is the last to end;".

(6) In the case where M has more than one entitlement to statutory maternity pay in respect of C and—

(a) M returns to work in relation to one or more of those entitlements without satisfying the condition regulation 4(2)(e) or 5(3)(d), and

(b) in relation to one or more of the maternity pay periods which apply as a result of those entitlements that period or those periods are reduced by virtue of section 165(3A) before M returns to work,

paragraph (1)(a) shall apply as though it read—

"(a) the number of weeks falling within the period beginning with the first day of the maternity pay period which is the earliest to begin and ending with the later of—

(i) the last day of the maternity pay period which is reduced by virtue of section 165(3A) before M returns to work (or, where

there is more than one such period, the last of those periods); and
(ii) the day on which M returned to work without satisfying the condition in regulation 4(2)(e) or 5(3)(d) in relation to that period (or, where there is more than one such period, the last of those periods);".

(7) In a case where P has more than one entitlement to statutory shared parental pay in respect of C, paragraph (1)(b)(i) shall apply as though it read—

"(i) in the case of M, P has notified P's intention to claim under regulation 7 or 8 falling within the period beginning with the first day of the earliest period so notified and ending with the last day of the latest period so notified;".

(8) In a case where M has more than one entitlement to statutory shared parental pay in respect of C, paragraph (1)(b)(ii) shall apply as though it read—

"(ii) in the case of P, M has notified M's intention to claim under regulations 6 or 8 falling within the period beginning with the first day of the earliest period so notified and ending with the last day of the latest period so notified;".

(9) In a case where P has more than one entitlement to statutory shared parental pay in respect of C, paragraph (2) shall apply as though the number of weeks referred to were the number of weeks which P claimed statutory shared parental pay in respect of C falling within the period beginning with the first day of the earliest period P claimed statutory shared parental pay and ending with the time P ceases to be so entitled.

(10) In this regulation a person is treated as returning to work if one of the following situations apply—
(a) in a case where the person is entitled to maternity allowance, the allowance is not payable to her by virtue of regulations made under section 35(3)(a)(i) of the 1992 Act;
(b) in a case where the person is entitled to statutory maternity pay, that payment is not payable to her in accordance with section 165(4) or (6) of the 1992 Act.

(11) In determining in paragraph (1)(a)(i) the number of weeks in respect of which maternity allowance is payable to M in respect of C up to the time M has returned to work, part of a week in respect of which maternity allowance is payable is to be treated as a whole week.

(12) In paragraph (1)(a)(ii), (6), (7), (8) and (9) part of a week is to be treated as a whole week.

(13) In paragraph (1)(a) "week" has the meaning given by section 122(1) of the 1992 Act, in relation to maternity allowance, or the meaning given by section 165(8) in relation to statutory maternity pay.

DEFINITIONS

"1992 Act"—reg.2(1).
"C"—reg.2(1).
"expected week of birth"—reg.2(1).
"M"—reg.2(1).
"P"—reg.2(1).
"statutory shared parental pay (birth)"—reg.2(1).
"week"—reg.2(1) and para.(13).

When statutory shared parental pay (birth) is not to be paid

11.—(1) Statutory shared parental pay (birth) is not payable after the day before C's first birthday (or where more than one child is born as a result of the same pregnancy the first birthday of the first child so born).

(2) Statutory shared parental pay (birth) is not payable to M before the end of M's maternity pay period.

DEFINITIONS

"C"—reg.2(1).
"child"—reg.2(1).
"M"—reg.2(1).
"statutory shared parental pay (birth)"—reg.2(1).

Work during period of payment of statutory shared parental pay (birth)

12.—(1) Despite section 171ZY(4) of the 1992 Act (statutory shared parental pay not payable to a person in respect of a week during any part of which the person works for any employer) statutory shared parental pay (birth) is payable to M or, as the case may be, P—
  (a) in respect of a statutory pay week during any part of which M or, as the case may be, P works only for an employer—
    (i) who is not liable to pay that person statutory shared parental pay; and
    (ii) for whom that person worked in the week immediately preceding the 14th week before the expected week of birth; or,
  (b) where M or, as the case may be, P does any work on any day under a contract of service with an employer during a statutory pay week during which that employer is liable to pay that person statutory shared parental pay (birth) in respect of C and where that day and any previous days so worked do not exceed 20.

(2) Where statutory shared parental pay (birth) is paid to M or P in respect of any week falling within a period specified in a notice under regulation 6, 7, and 8 during which M or P works for an employer falling within paragraph (1)(a)(i) but not paragraph (1)(a)(ii), M or, as the case may be, P shall notify the employer liable to pay statutory shared parental pay (birth) within seven days of the first day during which the former does such work.

(3) The notification mentioned in paragraph (2) shall be in writing, if the employer who has been liable to pay statutory shared parental pay (birth) so requests.

(4) In this regulation "statutory pay week" means a week in respect of which that person has chosen to exercise an entitlement to statutory shared parental pay (birth).

DEFINITIONS

"1992 Act"—reg.2(1).
"C"—reg.2(1).
"expected week of birth"—reg.2(1).
"M"—reg.2(1).
"P"—reg.2(1).
"statutory pay week"—para.(4).
"statutory shared parental pay (birth)"—reg.2(1).
"week"—reg.2(1).

Care of child during period of payment of statutory shared parental pay

7.33 13.—Despite section 171ZY(3) of the 1992 Act (statutory shared parental pay not payable to a person in respect of a week if it is not the person's intention at the beginning of the week to care for C) statutory shared parental pay (birth) is payable in the cases referred to in paragraph 6 of the Schedule (death of child).

DEFINITIONS

"1992 Act"—reg.2(1).
"C"—reg.2(1).
"expected week of birth"—reg.2(1).
"statutory shared parental pay (birth)"—reg.2(1).
"week"—reg.2(1).

Other cases where there is no liability to pay statutory shared parental pay

7.34 14.—(1) There is no liability to pay statutory shared parental pay (birth) to M or, as the case may be, P in respect of any week—
   (a) during any part of which the person who is entitled to that pay is entitled to statutory sick pay under Part 11 of the 1992 Act;
   (b) following that in which the person who is claiming that pay has died; or
   (c) during any part of which the person who is entitled to that pay is detained in legal custody or sentenced to a term of imprisonment except where the sentence is suspended (but see paragraph (2)).

(2) There is liability to pay statutory shared parental pay (birth) to M or, as the case may be, P in respect of any week during any part of which the person who is entitled to that pay is detained in legal custody where that person—
   (a) is released subsequently without charge;
   (b) is subsequently found not guilty of any offence and is released; or
   (c) is convicted of an offence but does not receive a custodial sentence.

DEFINITIONS

"1992 Act"—reg.2(1).
"M"—reg.2(1).
"P"—reg.2(1).
"statutory shared parental pay (birth)"—reg.2(1).
"week"—reg.2(1).

Conditions of entitlement to statutory shared parental pay: absence from work

7.35 15.—(1) The condition in regulation 4(2)(g) and 5(2)(e) does not apply where M or, as the case may be, P—
   (a) during any part of a statutory pay week works other than for an employer;
   (b) during any part of a statutory pay week works only for an employer who falls within paragraph (1)(a) of regulation 12 (work during period payment of statutory shared parental pay);
   (c) works in circumstances where paragraph (1)(b) of regulation 12 applies.

(2) In this regulation "statutory pay week" means a week in respect of which that person has chosen to exercise an entitlement to statutory shared parental pay (birth).

DEFINITIONS

"M"—reg.2(1).
"P"—reg.2(1).
"statutory pay week"—para.(2).
"statutory shared parental pay (birth)"—reg.2(1).
"week"—reg.2(1).

Entitlement to statutory shared parental pay (birth) in cases relating to death

16.—The Part 1 of the Schedule (statutory shared parental pay in special circumstances) has effect.

PART 3

Entitlement of adopter to statutory shared parental pay (adoption)

17.—(1) A is entitled to statutory shared parental pay (adoption) if A satisfies the conditions specified in paragraph (2) and AP satisfies the conditions specified in paragraph (3).
(2) The conditions referred to in paragraph (1) are that—
(a) A satisfies the conditions as to continuity of employment and normal weekly earnings specified in regulation 31 (conditions as to claimant's continuity of employment and normal weekly earnings);
(b) A has at the date of C's placement for adoption the main responsibility for the care of C (apart from the responsibility of AP);
(c) A has complied with the requirements specified in regulation 19 (notification and evidential requirements);
(d) A became entitled to statutory adoption pay by reference to the placement for adoption of C;
(e) the adoption pay period that applies as a result of A's entitlement to statutory adoption pay is, and continues to be, reduced under section 171ZN(2A) of the 1992 Act;
(f) it is A's intention to care for C during each week in respect of which statutory shared parental pay (adoption) is paid to A;
(g) A is absent from work during each week in respect of which statutory shared parental pay is paid to A (except in the cases referred to in regulation 27 (entitlement to statutory shared parental pay (adoption): absence from work); and
(h) where A is an employee (within the meaning of the Employment Rights Act 1996) A's absence from work as an employee during each week that statutory shared parental pay is paid to A is absence on shared parental leave in respect of C.
(3) The conditions referred to in paragraph (1) are that—
(a) AP has at the date of C's placement for adoption the main responsibility for the care of C (apart from the responsibility of A); and

(b) AP satisfies the employment and earnings conditions in regulation 29 (conditions relating to employment and earnings of claimant's partner).

DEFINITIONS

"1992 Act"—reg.2(1).
"A"—reg.2(1).
"AP"—reg.2(1).
"C"—reg.2(1).
"statutory shared parental pay (adoption)"—reg.2(1).
"week"—reg.2(1).

GENERAL NOTE

7.38   This regulation is modified for certain special cases by the Statutory Shared Parental Pay (Adoption from Overseas) Regulations 2014 (SI 2014/3093) and the Statutory Shared Parental Pay (Parental Order Cases) Regulations 2014 (SI 2014/3097).

Entitlement of partner to statutory shared parental pay (adoption)

7.39   **18.**—(1) AP is entitled to statutory shared parental pay (adoption) if AP satisfies the conditions specified in paragraph (2) and A satisfies the conditions specified in paragraph (3).
(2) The conditions specified in paragraph (1) are that—
(a) AP satisfies the conditions as to continuity of employment and normal weekly earnings specified in regulation 31 (conditions as to continuity of employment and normal weekly earnings);
(b) AP has at the date of C's placement for adoption the main responsibility for the care of C (apart from the responsibility of A);
(c) AP has complied with the requirements specified in regulation 20 (notification and evidential requirements);
(d) it is AP's intention to care for C during each week in respect of which statutory shared parental pay (adoption) is paid to AP;
(e) AP is absent from work during each week in respect of which statutory shared parental pay (adoption) is paid to AP (except in the cases referred to in regulation 27 (entitlement to statutory shared parental pay: absence from work)); and
(f) where AP is an employee (within the meaning of the Employment Rights Act 1996) AP's absence from work as an employee during each week that statutory shared parental pay is paid to AP is absence on shared parental leave in respect of C.
(3) The conditions specified in paragraph (1) are that—
(a) A has at the date of C's placement for adoption the main responsibility for the care of C (apart from any responsibility of AP);
(b) A satisfies the employment and earnings conditions in regulation 29;
(c) A became entitled to statutory adoption pay by reference to the placement for adoption of C; and
(d) the adoption pay period that applies as a result A's entitlement to statutory adoption pay is, and continues to be, reduced under section 171ZN(2A) of the 1992 Act.

DEFINITIONS

"1992 Act"—reg.2(1).

"A"—reg.2(1).
"AP"—reg.2(1).
"C"—reg.2(1).
"statutory shared parental pay (adoption)"—reg.2(1).
"week"—reg.2(1).

GENERAL NOTE

This regulation is modified for certain special cases by the Statutory Shared Parental Pay (Adoption from Overseas) Regulations 2014 (SI 2014/3093) and the Statutory Shared Parental Pay (Parental Order Cases) Regulations 2014 (SI 2014/3097).

7.40

Notification and evidential requirements relating to the adopter

19.—(1) The notification and evidential requirements referred to in regulation 17(2)(c) are that A gives the employer who will be liable to pay statutory shared parental pay (adoption) to A the notice and information specified in—

(a) paragraphs (2) and (3)(a), (b), (d) and (e) at least 8 weeks before the beginning of the first period specified by A pursuant to paragraph (2)(d);

(b) paragraph (3)(c) at least 8 weeks before the beginning of the first period specified by A pursuant to paragraph (2)(d) or, if C is not placed for adoption by that time, as soon as reasonably practicable after the placement of C but in any event before the beginning of that first period; and

(c) paragraph (4) within 14 days of that employer requesting that information where the employer requests it within 14 days of receiving the notice and information specified in paragraph (2) and (3)(a), (b), (d) and (e).

(2) The notice specified in this paragraph is notice of—

(a) the number of weeks in respect of which A would be entitled to claim statutory shared parental pay (adoption) in respect of C if entitlement were fully exercised disregarding any intention of AP to claim statutory shared parental pay (adoption) in respect of C;

(b) the number of weeks (out of those specified under paragraph (2)(a)) in respect of which A intends to claim statutory shared parental pay (adoption) in respect of C;

(c) the number of weeks (out of those specified under paragraph (2)(a)) in respect of which AP intends to claim statutory shared parental pay (adoption) in respect of C; and

(d) the period or periods during which A intends to claim statutory shared parental pay (adoption) in respect of C.

(3) The information specified in this paragraph is—

(a) a written declaration signed by AP who in connection with A's claim is required to satisfy the conditions specified in regulation 17(3)—

  (i) that AP consents to A's intended claim for statutory shared parental pay;

  (ii) that AP meets or will meet the conditions in regulation 17(3) (conditions to be satisfied by AP);

  (iii) specifying AP's name, address and national insurance number or, if AP has no national insurance number, stating that AP has no such number; and

7.41

(iv) providing AP's consent as regards the processing by the employer who will be liable to pay statutory shared parental pay (adoption) to A of the information in the written declaration;
(b) the date on which A was notified that A had been matched with C;
(c) the date of C's placement for adoption;
(d) A's name; and
(e) a written declaration signed by A—
   (i) that the information given by A under paragraph (2) and (3) is correct;
   (ii) that A meets or will meet the conditions in regulation 17(2); and
   (iii) that A will immediately inform the person who will be liable to pay statutory shared parental pay (adoption) if A ceases to meet the condition in regulation 17(2)(e); and
   (iv) specifying the date on which A's adoption pay period in respect of C began and the number of weeks by which it is, or will be, reduced.
(4) The information specified in this paragraph is—
(a) evidence, in the form of one or more documents issued by the adoption agency that matched A with C, of—
   (i) the name and address of the adoption agency;
   (ii) the date on which A was notified that A had been matched with C; and
   (iii) the date on which the adoption agency was expecting to place C with A; and
(b) the name and address of AP's employer or, if AP has no employer, a written declaration signed by A that AP has no employer.

DEFINITIONS

"A"—reg.2(1).
"AP"—reg.2(1).
"adoption agency"—reg.2(1).
"C"—reg.2(1).
"placed for adoption"—reg.2(1).
"processing"—reg.2(1).
"statutory shared parental pay (adoption)"—reg.2(1).
"week"—reg.2(1).

GENERAL NOTE

7.42   This regulation is modified for certain special cases by the Statutory Shared Parental Pay (Adoption from Overseas) Regulations 2014 (SI 2014/3093) and the Statutory Shared Parental Pay (Parental Order Cases) Regulations 2014 (SI 2014/3097).

Notification and evidential requirements relating to the partner

7.43   **20.**—(1) The notification and evidential conditions referred to in regulation 18(2)(c) are that AP gives the employer who will be liable to pay statutory shared parental pay (adoption) to AP the notice and information specified in—
(a) paragraphs (2) and (3)(a), (b), (d) and (e) at least 8 weeks before the beginning of the first period specified by AP pursuant to paragraph (2)(d);

(SI 2014/3051 reg.20)

(b) paragraph (3)(c) at least 8 weeks before the beginning of the first period specified by AP pursuant to paragraph (2)(d) or if C is not placed for adoption by that time, as soon as reasonably practicable after the placement of C but in any event before that first period; and

(c) paragraph (4) (where applicable) within 14 days of that employer requesting this information where the employer requests it within 14 days of receiving all the notice and information specified in paragraph (2) and (3)(a), (b), (d) and (e).

(2) The notice specified in this paragraph is notice of—

(a) the number of weeks in respect of which AP would be entitled to claim statutory shared parental pay (adoption) in respect of C if entitlement were fully exercised disregarding any intention of A to claim statutory shared parental pay (adoption) in respect of C;

(b) the number of weeks (out of those specified under paragraph (2)(a)) in respect of which AP intends to claim statutory shared parental pay (adoption) in respect of C;

(c) the number of weeks (out of those specified under paragraph (2)(a)) in respect of which A intends to claim statutory shared parental pay (adoption) in respect of C;

(d) the period or periods during which AP intends to claim statutory shared parental pay (adoption) in respect of C.

(3) The information specified in this paragraph is—

(a) a written declaration signed by A who in connection with AP's claim is required to satisfy the conditions in regulation 18(3)—
   (i) that A consents to AP's intended claim for statutory shared parental pay (adoption);
   (ii) that A meets, or will meet, the conditions in regulation 18(3) (conditions to be satisfied by A);
   (iii) that A will immediately inform AP if A ceases to meet the conditions in regulation 18(3)(d);
   (iv) specifying A's name, address and national insurance number or, if A has no national insurance number, stating that A has no such number;
   (v) specifying the date on which A's adoption pay period in respect of C began and the number of weeks by which it is, or will be, reduced; and
   (vi) providing A's consent as regards the processing by the employer who is, or will be, liable to pay statutory shared parental pay (adoption) to AP of the information in the written declaration;

(b) the date on which A was notified that A had been matched with C;

(c) the date of C's placement for adoption;

(d) AP's name;

(e) a written declaration signed by AP—
   (i) that the information given by AP is correct;
   (ii) that AP meets, or will meet, the conditions in regulation 18(2); and
   (iii) that AP will immediately inform the person who will be liable to pay statutory shared parental pay (adoption) if A ceases to meet the condition 18(3)(d).

(4) The information specified in this paragraph is—

(a) evidence, in the form of one or more documents issued by the adoption agency that matched A with C, of —
  (i) the name and address of the adoption agency;
  (ii) the date on which A was notified that A had been matched with C; and
  (iii) the date on which the adoption agency was expecting to place C for adoption with A; and
(b) the name and address of A's employer or, if A has no employer, a written declaration signed by AP that A has no employer.

DEFINITIONS

"A"—reg.2(1).
"AP"—reg.2(1).
"adoption agency"—reg.2(1).
"C"—reg.2(1).
"placed for adoption"—reg.2(1).
"processing"—reg.2(1).
"statutory shared parental pay (adoption)"—reg.2(1).
"week"—reg.2(1).

GENERAL NOTE

7.44 This regulation is modified for certain special cases by the Statutory Shared Parental Pay (Adoption from Overseas) Regulations 2014 (SI 2014/3093) and the Statutory Shared Parental Pay (Parental Order Cases) Regulations 2014 (SI 2014/3097).

Variation of number of weeks of pay to be claimed and of periods when pay is to be claimed

7.45 21.—(1) A or, as the case may be, AP may vary the period or periods during which they intend to claim statutory shared parental pay (adoption) by notice in writing given to the employer who will be liable to pay that pay to A or AP at least 8 weeks before the beginning of the first period specified in that notice.

(2) A may vary the number of weeks in respect of which A intends to claim statutory shared parental pay (adoption) by notice in writing given to the employer who will be liable to pay that pay to A—
(a) of the number of weeks during which A and AP have exercised, or intend to exercise, an entitlement to statutory shared parental pay in respect of C; and
(b) which contains a written declaration signed by AP who in connection with A's claim is required to satisfy the conditions in regulation 17(3) that AP consents to that variation.

(3) AP may vary the number of weeks in respect of which AP intends to claim statutory shared parental pay (adoption) by notice in writing given to the employer who will be liable to pay that pay to AP—
(a) of the number of weeks during which AP and A have exercised, or intend to exercise, an entitlement to statutory shared parental pay (adoption) in respect of C; and
(b) which is accompanied by a written declaration by A who in connection with AP's claim is requires to satisfy the conditions in regulation 18(3) that A consents to that variation.

(SI 2014/3051 reg.21)

DEFINITIONS

"A"—reg.2(1).
"AP"—reg.2(1).
"C"—reg.2(1).
"statutory shared parental pay (adoption)"—reg.2(1).
"week"—reg.2(1).

Extent of entitlement to statutory shared parental pay (adoption)

22.—(1) The number of weeks in respect of which A or, as the case may be, AP is entitled to payments of statutory shared parental pay (adoption) in respect of C is 39 weeks less—
(a) the number of weeks—
   (i) in respect of which statutory adoption pay is payable to A in respect of C up to the time that person has returned to work (where that person has returned to work without satisfying the conditions in regulations 17(2)(e) or 18(3)(d)) (condition as to reduction in adoption pay period); or
   (ii) in any other case, to which the adoption pay period is reduced by virtue of section 171ZN(2A) of the 1992 Act; and
(b) the number of weeks of statutory shared parental pay (adoption) in respect of C which—
   (i) in the case of A, AP has notified AP's intention to claim under regulation 20 or 21; or
   (ii) in the case of AP, A has notified A's intention to claim under regulation 19 or 21.

(2) In the case where A has more than one entitlement to statutory adoption pay in respect of C and in relation to all those entitlements A returns to work without satisfying the conditions in regulation 17(2)(e) or 18(3)(d), paragraph (1)(a)(i) shall apply as though it read—

"(i) in respect of which statutory adoption pay is payable to A in respect of C up to the last day A returns to work;".

(3) In the case where A has more than one entitlement to statutory adoption pay in respect of C and the adoption pay periods which apply as a result of those entitlements are all reduced by virtue of section 171ZN(2A) of the 1992 Act before A returns to work, paragraph (1)(a)(ii) shall apply as though it read—

"(ii) falling in the period beginning with the first day of the adoption pay period which is the earliest to begin and ending with the last day of the adoption pay period which is the last to end;".

(4) In a case where A has more than one entitlement to statutory adoption pay in respect of C and—
(a) A returns to work in relation to one or more of those entitlements without satisfying the conditions in regulation 17(2)(e) or 18(3)(d), and
(b) in relation to one or more of the adoption pay periods which apply as a result of those entitlements that period or those periods are reduced by virtue of section 171ZN(2A) of the 1992 Act before A returns to work,
paragraph (1)(a) shall apply as though it read—

"(a) the number of weeks falling within the period beginning with the first day of the adoption pay period which is the earliest to begin and ending with the later of—

7.46

(i) the last day of the adoption pay period which is reduced by virtue of section 171ZN(2A) of the 1992 Act before A returns to work (or, where there is more than one such period, the last of those periods); and

(ii) the day on which A returned to work without satisfying the conditions in regulation 17(2)(e) or 18(3)(d) in relation to that period (or, where there is more than one such period, the last of those periods);".

(5) In the case where AP has more than one entitlement to statutory shared parental pay in respect of C, paragraph (1)(b)(i) shall apply as though it read—

"(i) in the case of A, AP has notified AP's intention to claim under regulation 20 or 21 falling within the period beginning with the first day of the earliest period so notified and ending with the last day of the latest period so notified;".

(6) In the case where A has more than one entitlement to statutory shared parental pay in respect of C, paragraph (1)(b)(ii) shall apply as though it read—

"(ii) in the case of AP, A has notified A's intention to claim under regulation 19 or 21 falling within the period beginning with the first day of the earliest period so notified and ending with the last day of the latest period so notified;".

(7) In this regulation a person is treated as returning to work if statutory adoption pay is not payable to A in accordance with section 171ZN(3) or (5) of the 1992 Act.

(8) In paragraph (1)(a)(ii), (4), (5) and (6) part of a week is to be treated as a whole week.

(9) In paragraph (1)(a) "week" has the meaning given by section 171ZN(8) of the 1992 Act.

DEFINITIONS

"1992 Act"—reg.2(1).
"A"—reg.2(1).
"AP"—reg.2(1).
"C"—reg.2(1).
"statutory shared parental pay (adoption)"—reg.2(1).
"week"—reg.2(1) and para.(9).

When statutory shared parental pay (adoption) is not to be paid

23.—(1) Statutory shared parental pay (adoption) is not payable after the day before the first anniversary of the date on which C was placed for adoption (or where more than one child is placed for adoption through a single placement, the first anniversary of the date of placement of the first child).

(2) Statutory shared parental pay (adoption) is not payable to A before the end of A's adoption pay period.

DEFINITIONS

"A"—reg.2(1).
"C"—reg.2(1).
"child"—reg.2(1).
"placed for adoption"—reg.2(1).
"statutory shared parental pay (adoption)"—reg.2(1).

(SI 2014/3051 reg.23)

GENERAL NOTE

This regulation is modified for certain special cases by the Statutory Shared Parental Pay (Adoption from Overseas) Regulations 2014 (SI 2014/3093) and the Statutory Shared Parental Pay (Parental Order Cases) Regulations 2014 (SI 2014/3097).

7.48

Work during period of payment of statutory shared parental pay (adoption)

24.—(1) Despite section 171ZY(4) of the 1992 Act (statutory shared parental pay not payable to a person in respect of a week during any part of which person works for any employer) statutory shared parental pay (adoption) is payable to A or, as the case may be, AP—
  (a) in respect of a statutory pay week during any part of which A or, as the case may be, AP works only for an employer—
    (i) who is not liable to pay that person statutory shared parental pay; and
    (ii) for whom that person worked in the week immediately preceding the 14th week before the expected week of the placement for adoption; or
  (b) where A or, as the case may be, AP does any work on any day under a contract of service with an employer during a statutory pay week during which that employer is liable to pay that person statutory shared parental pay (adoption) in respect of C and where that day and any previous days so worked do not exceed 20.

(2) Where statutory shared parental pay (adoption) is paid to A or AP in respect of any week falling within a period specified in a notice under regulation 19, 20 or 21 during which A or AP works for an employer falling within paragraph (1)(a)(i) but not paragraph (1)(a)(ii) A or, as the case may be, AP shall notify the employer liable to pay statutory shared parental pay within seven days of the first day during which the former does such work.

(3) The notification mentioned in paragraph (2) shall be in writing, if the employer who has been liable to pay statutory shared parental pay so requests.

(4) In this regulation "statutory pay week" means a week in respect of which that person has chosen to exercise an entitlement to statutory shared parental pay (adoption).

7.49

DEFINITIONS

"1992 Act"—reg.2(1).
"A"—reg.2(1).
"AP"—reg.2(1).
"C"—reg.2(1).
"statutory pay week"—para.(4).
"statutory shared parental pay (adoption)"—reg.2(1).
"week"—reg.2(1).

GENERAL NOTE

This regulation is modified for certain special cases by the Statutory Shared Parental Pay (Adoption from Overseas) Regulations 2014 (SI 2014/3093) and the Statutory Shared Parental Pay (Parental Order Cases) Regulations 2014 (SI 2014/3097).

7.50

Care of child during period of payment of statutory shared parental pay

7.51   **25.**—Despite section 171ZY(3) of the 1992 Act (statutory shared parental pay not payable to a person in respect of a week if it is not the person's intention at the beginning of the week to care for C) statutory shared parental pay (adoption) is payable in the cases set out in paragraph 12 of the Schedule (disrupted placement or death of child).

DEFINITIONS

"1992 Act"—reg.2(1).
"C"—reg.2(1).
"child"—reg.2(1).
"statutory shared parental pay (adoption)"—reg.2(1).
"week"—reg.2(1).

Other cases where there is no liability to pay statutory shared parental pay

7.52   **26.**—(1) There is no liability to pay statutory shared parental pay (adoption) to A or, as the case may be, AP in respect of any week—
(a) during any part of which the person who is entitled to that pay is entitled to statutory sick pay under Part 11 of the 1992 Act;
(b) following that in which the person who is claiming that has died; or
(c) during any part of which the person who is entitled to it is detained in legal custody or sentenced to a term of imprisonment except where the sentence is suspended (but see paragraph (2)).

(2) There is liability to pay statutory shared parental pay to A or, as the case may be, AP in respect of any week during any part of which the person entitled to that pay is detained in legal custody where that person—
(a) is released subsequently without charge;
(b) is subsequently found not guilty of any offence and is released; or
(c) is convicted of an offence but does not receive a custodial sentence.

DEFINITIONS

"1992 Act"—reg.2(1).
"A"—reg.2(1).
"AP"—reg.2(1).
"statutory shared parental pay (adoption)"—reg.2(1).
"week"—reg.2(1).

Conditions of entitlement to statutory shared parental pay: absence from work

7.53   **27.**—(1) The condition in regulations 17(2)(g) and 18(2)(e) does not apply are where A or, as the case may be, AP—
(a) during any part of a statutory pay week works other than for an employer;
(b) during any part of a statutory pay week works only for an employer who falls within paragraph (1)(a) of regulation 24 (work during period payment of statutory shared parental pay);
(c) works in circumstances where paragraph (1)(b) of regulation 24 applies.

(2) In this regulation "statutory pay week" means a week in respect of which that person has chosen to exercise an entitlement to statutory shared parental pay (adoption).

DEFINITIONS

"A"—reg.2(1).
"AP"—reg.2(1).
"statutory pay week"—para.(2).
"statutory shared parental pay (adoption)"—reg.2(1).
"week"—reg.2(1).

Entitlement to statutory shared parental pay (adoption) in cases relating to death

28.—Part 2 of the Schedule (statutory shared parental pay in special circumstances) has effect.

PART 4

Conditions relating to employment and earnings of a claimant's partner

29.—(1) In relation to the entitlement of M, P, A or AP to statutory shared parental pay a person satisfies the conditions as to earnings and employment specified in regulations 4(3)(b), 5(3)(b), 17(3)(b) and 18(3)(b) if that person—
  (a) has been engaged in employment as an employed or self-employed earner for any part of the week in the case of at least 26 of the 66 weeks immediately preceding the calculation week; and
  (b) has average weekly earnings (determined in accordance with paragraph (2)) of not less than the amount set out in section 35A(6A) (state maternity allowance) of the 1992 Act in relation to the tax year before the tax year containing the calculation week.

(2) A person's average weekly earnings are determined by dividing by 13 the specified payments made, or treated as being made, to or for the benefit of that person in the 13 weeks (whether or not consecutive) in the period of 66 weeks immediately preceding the calculation week in which the payments are greatest.

(3) Where a person receives any pay after the end of the period in [¹ paragraph (2)] in respect of any week falling [¹ within] that period, the average weekly amount is to be determined as if such sum had been paid in that period.

(4) Where a person is not paid weekly, the payments made or treated as made for that person's benefit for the purposes of [¹ paragraph (2)], are to be determined by dividing the total sum paid to that individual by the nearest whole number of weeks in respect of which that sum is paid.

(5) In this regulation—
"calculation week" means in relation to—
  (a) statutory shared parental pay (birth) the expected week of birth of C; and
  (b) statutory shared parental pay (adoption), the week in which A was notified as having been matched for adoption with C;

"employed earner" has the meaning given by section 2 of the 1992 Act, subject for these purposes to the effect of regulations made under section 2(2)(b) of that Act;

"self-employed earner" has the meaning given by section 2 of the 1992 Act, subject for these purposes to the effect of regulations made under section 2(2)(b) of that Act;

"specified payments"—

(a) in relation to a self-employed earner who satisfies the conditions in paragraph (6), are to be treated as made to the self-employed earner at an amount per week equal to the amount set out in section 35(6A) of the 1992 Act that is in force at the end of the week;

(b) in relation to an employed earner, are all payments made to the employed earner or for that employed earner's benefit as an employed earner specified in regulation 2 (specified payments for employed earners) of the Social Security (Maternity Allowance) (Earnings) Regulations 2000;

"tax year" means the 12 months beginning with the 6th April in any year.

(6) The conditions referred to in paragraph (a) of the definition of "specified payments" are that, in respect of any week, the self-employed earner—

(a) does not hold a certificate of exception issued pursuant to regulation 44(1) of the Social Security (Contributions) Regulations 2001 and has paid a Class 2 contribution (within the meaning of section 1 of the 1992 Act), or

(b) holds such a certificate of exception.

AMENDMENT

1. Statutory Shared Parental Pay (General) (Amendment) Regulations 2015 (SI 2015/189) reg.2(2) (March 8, 2015).

DEFINITIONS

"1992 Act"—reg.2(1).
"A"—reg.2(1).
"AP"—reg.2(1).
"calculation week"—para.(5).
"employed earner"—para.(5).
"M"—reg.2(1).
"self-employed earner"—para.(5).
"specified payments"—para.(5).
"tax year"—para.(5).
"week"—reg.2(1).

GENERAL NOTE

7.56   This regulation is modified for certain special cases by the Statutory Shared Parental Pay (Adoption from Overseas) Regulations 2014 (SI 2014/3093) and the Statutory Shared Parental Pay (Parental Order Cases) Regulations 2014 (SI 2014/3097).

Conditions as to continuity of employment and normal weekly earnings relating to a claimant for statutory shared parental pay (birth)

7.57   **30.**—(1) The conditions as to continuity of employment and normal weekly earnings referred to in regulation 4(2)(a) and 5(2)(a) are—

(a) the person has been in employed earner's employment with an employer for a continuous period of at least 26 weeks ending with the relevant week;

(b) the person's normal weekly earnings (see regulation 32) with the employer by reference to which the condition in sub-paragraph (a) is satisfied for the period of eight weeks ending with the relevant week are not less than the lower earnings limit in force under subsection (1)(a) of section 5 (earnings limits and thresholds for class 1 contributions) of the 1992 Act at the end of the relevant week;

(c) the person continues in employed earner's employment with the employer by reference to which the condition in sub-paragraph (a) is satisfied for a continuous period beginning with the relevant week and ending with the week before the first week falling within the relevant period relating to that person under section 171ZY(2) of the 1992 Act.

[1 (1A) Paragraph (1B) applies where a person has been in employed earner's employment with the same employer in each of 26 consecutive weeks (but no more than 26 weeks), ending with the relevant week.

(1B) For the purpose of determining whether a person meets the condition in paragraph (1)(a), the first of those 26 weeks is a period commencing on the first day of the person's employment with the employer ("the start date") and ending at midnight on—

(a) the first Saturday after the start date, or

(b) where the start date is a Saturday, that day.]

(2) Where C's birth occurs earlier than the 14th week before C's expected week of birth paragraph (1) shall have effect as if, for the conditions set out there, there were substituted conditions that—

(a) the person would have been in employed earner's employment for a continuous period of at least 26 weeks ending with the relevant week had C been born after the relevant week;

(b) the person's normal weekly earnings for the period of eight weeks ending with the week immediately preceding C's actual week of birth are not less than the lower earnings limit in force under section 5(1)(a) of the 1992 Act immediately before the commencement of C's actual week of birth; and

(c) the person continues in employed earner's employment with the employer by reference to whom the condition in sub-paragraph (a) is satisfied for a continuous period beginning with the date of C's birth and ending with the week before the first week falling within the relevant period relating to that person under section 171ZY(2) of the 1992 Act.

(3) The references in this regulation to the relevant week are to the week immediately preceding the 14th week before C's expected week of birth.

(4) Where more than one child is born as a result of the same pregnancy the date the first child is born is to be used to determine C's actual week of birth or the date of C's birth.

AMENDMENT

1. Statutory Paternity Pay, Statutory Adoption Pay and Statutory Shared Parental Pay (Amendment) Regulations 2015 (SI 2015/2065) reg.3(2) (February 1, 2016).

The Statutory Shared Parental Pay (General) Regulations 2014

DEFINITIONS

"1992 Act"—reg.2(1).
"actual week of birth"—reg.2(1).
"C"—reg.2(1).
"expected week of birth"—reg.2(1).
"M"—reg.2(1).
"week"—reg.2(1).

Conditions as to continuity of employment and normal weekly earnings in relation to a claimant for statutory shared parental pay (adoption)

7.58 **31.**—(1) The conditions as to continuity of employment and normal weekly earnings referred to in regulations 17(2)(a) and 18(2)(a) relating to the entitlement of A and AP to statutory shared parental pay (adoption) are—

(a) the person has been in employed earner's employment with an employer for a continuous period of at least 26 weeks ending with the relevant week;

(b) the person's normal weekly earnings (see regulation 32) with the employer by reference to which the condition in sub-paragraph (a) is satisfied for the period of eight weeks ending with the relevant week are not less than the lower earnings limit in force under subsection (1)(a) of section 5 (earnings limits and thresholds for class 1 contributions) of the 1992 Act at the end of the [¹ relevant week];

(c) the person continues in employed earner's employment with the employer by reference to which the condition in sub-paragraph (a) is satisfied for a continuous period beginning with the relevant week and ending with the week before the first week falling within the relevant period relating to that person under section 171ZY(2) of the 1992 Act.

[² (1A) Paragraph (1B) applies where a person has been in employed earner's employment with the same employer in each of 26 consecutive weeks (but no more than 26 weeks), ending with the relevant week.

(1B) For the purpose of determining whether a person meets the condition in paragraph (1)(a), the first of those 26 weeks is a period commencing on the first day of the person's employment with the employer ("the start date") and ending at midnight on—

(a) the first Saturday after the start date, or
(b) where the start date is a Saturday, that day.]

(2) The references in paragraph (1) to the relevant week are to the week in which A was notified of having been matched with C.

AMENDMENTS

1. Statutory Shared Parental Pay (General) (Amendment) Regulations 2015 (SI 2015/189) reg.2(3) (March 8, 2015).
2. Statutory Paternity Pay, Statutory Adoption Pay and Statutory Shared Parental Pay (Amendment) Regulations 2015 (SI 2015/2065) reg.3(3) (February 1, 2016).

DEFINITIONS

"1992 Act"—reg.2(1).
"A"—reg.2(1).

"AP"—reg.2(1).
"statutory shared parental pay (adoption)"—reg.2(1).
"week"—reg.2(1).

GENERAL NOTE

This regulation is modified for certain special cases by the Statutory Shared Parental Pay (Adoption from Overseas) Regulations 2014 (SI 2014/3093) and the Statutory Shared Parental Pay (Parental Order Cases) Regulations 2014 (SI 2014/3097).

Normal weekly earnings of a claimant for statutory shared parental pay

32.—(1) For the purpose of section 171ZZ4(6) (which defines normal weekly earnings for the purposes of Part 12ZC of the 1992 Act) "earnings" and "relevant period" have the meanings given in this regulation.

(2) The relevant period is the period—
(a) ending on the last normal pay day to fall before the appropriate date; and
(b) beginning with the day following the last normal pay day to fall at least eight weeks earlier than the normal pay day mentioned in sub-paragraph (a).

(3) In a case where a person has no identifiable normal pay day, paragraph (2) shall have effect as if the words "day of payment" were substituted for the words "normal pay day" in each place where they occur.

(4) In a case where a person has normal pay days at intervals of or approximating to one or more calendar months (including intervals of or approximating to a year) that person's normal weekly earnings shall be calculated by dividing their earnings in the relevant period by the number of calendar months in that period (or, if it is not a whole number, the nearest whole number), multiplying the result by 12 and dividing by 52.

(5) In a case to which paragraph (4) does not apply and the relevant period is not an exact number of weeks, the person's normal weekly earnings shall be calculated by dividing their earnings in the relevant period by the number of days in the relevant period and multiplying the result by seven.

(6) In any case where a person receives a back-dated pay increase which includes a sum in respect of a relevant period, normal weekly earnings shall be calculated as if such a sum was paid in that relevant period even though received after that period.

[¹(6A) Paragraph (9) applies where for all or part of the relevant period—
(a) a woman is a furloughed employee;
(b) the woman's employer has claimed and is in receipt of financial support in respect of the woman's earnings under the Coronavirus Job Retention Scheme; and
(c) the woman's earnings are lower than they would otherwise have been as a result of that woman being a furloughed employee.

(6B) Where this paragraph applies, the woman's normal weekly earnings are to be calculated as if, during the parts of the relevant period when the woman was a furloughed employee, she was paid the amount which she would have derived from her employment had she not been a furloughed employee.

(6C) For the purposes of paragraphs (8) and (9)—
"Coronavirus Job Retention Scheme" ("the Scheme") means any scheme to provide for payments to be made to employers on a claim made in respect of them incurring costs of employment in respect of furloughed employees arising from the health, social and economic emergency in the United Kingdom resulting from coronavirus and coronavirus disease and contained in such Directions as may be issued from time to time pursuant to section 76 of the Coronavirus Act 2020;
"coronavirus" and "coronavirus disease" have the meanings given in section 1 of that Act;
"furloughed employee" has the meaning given for the purposes of the Scheme.]
(7) The expression "earnings" refers to gross earnings and includes any remuneration or profit derived from a person's employment except any amount which is—
  (a) excluded from the computation of a person's earnings under regulation 25 (payments to be disregarded) of, and Schedule 3 to, the Social Security (Contributions) Regulations 2001 and regulation 27 (payments to directors to be disregarded) of those Regulations (or would have been so excluded had they not been made under the age of 16);
  (b) a chargeable emolument under section 10A (class 1B contributions) of the 1992 Act except where, in consequence of such a chargeable emolument being excluded from earnings, a person would not be entitled to statutory shared parental pay (or where such a payment or amount would have been so excluded and in consequence the person would not have been entitled to statutory shared parental pay had they not been aged under the age of 16).
(8) The expression "earnings" includes—
  (a) any amount retrospectively treated as earnings by regulations made by virtue of section 4B(2) of the 1992 Act;
  (b) any sum payable in respect of arrears of pay in pursuance of an order for reinstatement or re-engagement under the Employment Rights Act 1996;
  (c) any sum payable by way of pay in pursuance of an order made under the Employment Rights Act 1996 for the continuation of a contract of employment;
  (d) any sum payable by way of remuneration in pursuance of a protective award under section 189 of the Trade Union and Labour Relations (Consolidation) Act 1992;
  (e) any sum payable by way of statutory sick pay, including sums payable in accordance with regulations made under section 151(6) of the 1992 Act;
  (f) any sum payable by way of statutory maternity pay;
  (g) any sum payable by way of statutory paternity pay;
  (h) any sum payable by way of statutory shared parental pay; and
  (i) any sum payable by way of statutory adoption pay.
(9) In paragraphs (2) to (4)—
  (a) "the appropriate date" means—
    (i) in relation to statutory shared parental pay (birth), the first day of the 14th week before the expected week of the child's birth or

(SI 2014/3051 reg.32)

the first day in the week in which the child is born, whichever is earlier (but see paragraph (10)),
(ii) in relation to statutory shared parental pay (adoption) the first day of the week after the week in which A is notified of being matched with the child for the purposes of adoption;
(b) "day of payment" means a day on which the person was paid; and
(c) "normal pay day" means a day on which the terms of a person's contract of service require the person to be paid, or the practice in that person's employment is for that person to be paid if any payment is due to them.

(10) Where more than one child is born as a result of the same pregnancy, the date the first child is born is to be used to determine the week in which the child is born.

AMENDMENT

1. Maternity Allowance, Statutory Maternity Pay, Statutory Paternity Pay, Statutory Adoption Pay, Statutory Shared Parental Pay and Statutory Parental Bereavement Pay (Normal Weekly Earnings etc.) (Coronavirus) (Amendment) Regulations 2020 (SI 2020/450) reg.6 (April 25, 2020).

DEFINITIONS

"1992 Act"—reg.2(1).
"A"—reg.2(1).
"the appropriate date"—para.(9).
"day of payment"—para.(9).
"earnings"—para.(1).
"normal pay day"—para.(9).
"relevant period"—para.(1).
"statutory shared parental pay"—reg.2(1).
"week"—reg.2(1).

GENERAL NOTE

This regulation is modified for certain special cases by the Statutory Shared Parental Pay (Adoption from Overseas) Regulations 2014 (SI 2014/3093) and the Statutory Shared Parental Pay (Parental Order Cases) Regulations 2014 (SI 2014/3097).

Paragraphs (6A)-(6C) were added as from April 25, 2020 with the intention of ensuring that an employee experienced no disadvantage in relation to their SPP and SAP entitlement as a result of their being placed on temporary leave under the Coronavirus Job Retention Scheme ("the CJRS"), set out in the Schedule to the *Coronavirus Act 2020 Functions of Her Majesty's Revenue and Customs (Coronavirus Job Retention Scheme) Direction* made on April 15, 2020. In short, the amendments were designed to ensure that an employee's eligibility for the earnings-related rate of SPP/SAP is the same as it would have been had they not been furloughed. Regulation 2 of the 2020 Regulations (SI 2020/450) provides that these amendments are to apply where the first day of the period in respect of which payment of any of the benefits is to be made is on or after the day on which the 2020 Regulations come into force.

7.61

Treatment of persons as employees

33.—(1) A person is treated as an employee for the purposes of Part 12ZC of the 1992 Act (even though not falling within the definition of 'employee' in section 171ZZ4(2) of that Act) where, and in so far as, that

7.62

person is treated as an employed earner by virtue of the Social Security (Categorisation of Earners) Regulations 1978 (but see paragraph (3)).

(2) A person shall not be treated as an employee for the purposes of Part 12ZC of the 1992 Act (even though falling within the definition of 'employee' in section 171ZZ4(2) of that Act) where, and in so far as, that person is not treated as an employed earner by virtue of those Regulations (but see paragraph (3)).

(3) Paragraphs (1) and (2) shall have effect in relation to a person who—
   (a) is under the age of 16; and
   (b) would, or as the case may be, would not have been treated as an employed earner by virtue of those Regulations had they been over that age;
as they have effect in relation to a person who is, or as the case may be, is not treated as an employed earner by virtue of those Regulations.

(4) A person is treated as an employee for the purpose of Part 12ZC of the 1992 Act (even though not falling within the definition of 'employee' in section 171ZZ4(2) of that Act) where that person is in employed earner's employment under a contract of apprenticeship.

(5) A person is not to be treated as an employee for the purposes of Part 12ZC of the 1992 Act (even though falling within the definition of 'employee' in section 171ZZ4(2) of that Act) where that person is in employed earner's employment but that person's employer—
   (a) does not fulfil the conditions prescribed in regulation 145(1) (conditions as to residence or presence) of the Social Security (Contributions) Regulations 2001 in so far as that provision relates to residence or presence in Great Britain; or
   (b) is a person who, by reason of any international treaty to which the United Kingdom is a party or of any international convention binding the United Kingdom—
      (i) is exempt from the provisions of the 1992 Act; or
      (ii) is a person against whom the provisions of the 1992 Act are not enforceable.

DEFINITION

"1992 Act"—reg.2(1).

Continuous employment

34.—(1) A week is to be treated for the purposes of sections 171ZU and 171ZV of the 1992 Act (see also regulations 30 and 31) as part of a period of continuous employment with the employer even though no contract of service exists with that employer in respect of that week in the circumstances mentioned in paragraph (2) and subject to paragraphs (3) and (4).

(2) The circumstances mentioned in paragraphs (1) are that in any week the person is, for the whole or part of the week—
   (a) incapable of work in consequence of sickness or injury;
   (b) absent from work on account of a temporary cessation of work; or
   (c) absent from work in circumstances such that, by arrangement or custom, that person is regarded as continuing in the employment of their employer for all or any purposes;

and returns to work for their employer after the incapacity for or absence from work.

(3) Incapacity for work which lasts for more than 26 consecutive weeks shall not count for the purposes of paragraph (2)(a).

(4) Where a person—
  (a) is an employee in employed earner's employment in which the custom is for the employer—
    (i) to offer work for a fixed period of not more than 26 consecutive weeks;
    (ii) to offer work for such period on two or more occasions in a year for periods which do not overlap; and
    (iii) to offer the work available to those persons who had worked for the employer during the last or a recent such period; but
  (b) is absent from work because of incapacity arising from some specific disease or bodily or mental disablement;
then in that case paragraph (2) shall apply as if the words "and returns to work for their employment for their employer after the incapacity for or absence from work" were omitted.

DEFINITION

"1992 Act"—reg.2(1).

Continuous employment and unfair dismissal

35.—(1) Where in consequence of specified action in relation to a person's dismissal, the person is reinstated or re-engaged by their employer or by a successor or associated employer of that employer then—

7.64

  (a) the continuity of their employment shall be preserved for the purposes of sections 171ZU and [¹ 171ZV] of the 1992 Act (see also regulations 30 and 31) for the period beginning with the effective date of termination and ending with the date of reinstatement or re-engagement; and
  (b) any week which falls within the interval beginning with the effective date of termination and ending with the date of reinstatement or re-engagement, as the case may be, shall count in the computation of their period of continuous employment.

(2) In this regulation—
  (a) "associated employer" shall be construed in accordance with section 231 of the Employment Rights Act 1996;
  (b) "dismissal procedures agreement" and "successor" have the same meanings as in section 235 of the Employment Rights Act 1996;
  (c) "specified action in relation to a person's dismissal" means action which consists of—
    (i) the presentation by that person of a complaint under section 111(1) (complaints to employment tribunal) of the Employment Rights Act 1996;
    (ii) that person making a claim in accordance with a dismissal procedure agreement designated by an order under section 110 of that Act; or
    (iii) any action taken by a conciliation officer under section 18 (conciliation) of the Employment Tribunals Act 1996.

AMENDMENT

1. Statutory Shared Parental Pay (General) (Amendment) Regulations 2015 (SI 2015/189) reg.2(4) (March 8, 2015).

DEFINITIONS

"1992 Act"—reg.2(1).
"associated employer"—para.(2)(a).
"dismissal procedures agreement"—para.(2)(b).
"specified action in relation to a person's dismissal"—para.(2)(c).
"successor"—para.(2)(b).
"week"—reg.2(1).

Continuous employment and stoppages of work

7.65   36.—(1) Where a person does not work for any week or part of a week because there is a stoppage of work at that person's place of employment due to a trade dispute within the meaning of section 35(1) of the Jobseekers Act 1995 then—
   (a) that person's continuity of employment shall be treated as continuing throughout the stoppage (but see paragraph (2)[¹)] for the purposes of sections 171ZU and [¹ 171ZV] of the 1992 Act (see also regulations 30 and 31); and
   (b) no such week shall count in the computation of their period of continuous employment (but see paragraph(3)).

(2) Where during the stoppage of work a person is dismissed from their employment, that person's continuity of employment shall not be treated under paragraph (1) as continuing beyond the commencement of the day that person stopped work (but see paragraph (3)).

(3) Paragraph (1)(b) and paragraph (2) do not apply to a person who proves that at no time did they have a direct interest in the trade dispute in question.

AMENDMENT

1. Statutory Shared Parental Pay (General) (Amendment) Regulations 2015 (SI 2015/189) reg.2(5) (March 8, 2015).

DEFINITIONS

"1992 Act"—reg.2(1).
"week"—reg.2(1).

Change of employer

7.66   37.—(1) Where a person's employer changes, a person's employment is to be treated for the purposes of sections 171ZU and 171ZV of the 1992 Act (see also regulations 30 and 31) as continuous employment with the second employer in the following circumstances—
   (a) the employer's trade or business or an undertaking (whether or not it is an undertaking established by or under an Act of Parliament) is transferred from one person to another;
   (b) a contract of employment between any body corporate and the person is modified by or under an Act of Parliament, whether public or local and whenever passed and some other body corporate is substituted as that person's employer;

(c) on the death of the employer, the person is taken into the employment of the personal representatives or trustees of the deceased;
(d) the person is employed by partners, personal representatives or trustees and there is a change in the partners, or as the case may be, personal representatives or trustees;
(e) the person is taken into the employment of an employer who is, at the time the person entered into to the employer's employment, an associated employer of the person's previous employer; or
(f) on the termination of the person's employment with an employer that person is taken into the employment of another employer and those employers are governors of a school maintained by a local education authority.

(2) In paragraph (1)(e) "associated employer" shall be construed in accordance with section 231 of the Employment Rights Act 1996.

DEFINITIONS

"1992 Act"—reg.2(1).
"associated employer"—para.(2).

Reinstatement after service with the armed forces etc

38.—Where a person—
(a) is entitled to apply to their employer under the Reserve Forces (Safeguard of Employment) Act 1985; and
(b) enters the employment of that employer within the six month period mentioned in section 1(4)(b) (obligation to reinstate) of that Act;

that person's previous period of employment with that employer (or if there was more than one such period, the last of those periods) and the period of employment beginning in that six month period shall be treated as continuous for the purposes of sections 171ZU and 171ZV of the 1992 Act (see also regulations 30 and 31).

DEFINITION

"1992 Act"—reg.2(1).

Treatment of two or more employers or two or more contracts of service as one

39.—(1) In a case where the earnings paid to a person in respect of two or more employments are aggregated and treated as a single payment of earnings under regulation 15(1) (aggregation of earnings paid in respect of different employed earner's employments by different persons) of the Social Security (Contributions) Regulations 2001, the employers of that person in respect of those employments shall be treated as one for the purposes of Part 12ZC of the 1992 Act (and these Regulations).

(2) Where two or more employers are treated as one under the provisions of paragraph (1), liability for statutory shared parental pay shall be apportioned between them in such proportions as they may agree, or in default of agreement, in the proportions which the person's normal weekly earnings from each employment bear to the amount of the aggregated normal weekly earnings over the relevant period as defined in regulation 32(2).

The Statutory Shared Parental Pay (General) Regulations 2014

(3) Where two or more contracts of service exist concurrently between one employer and one employee, they shall be treated as one for the purposes of Part 12ZC of the 1992 Act (and these Regulations) except where, by virtue of regulation 14 (aggregation of earnings paid in respect of separate employed earner's employments under the same employer) of the Social Security (Contributions) Regulations 2001, the earnings from those contracts of service are not aggregated for the purpose of earnings-related contributions.

DEFINITION

"1992 Act"—reg.2(1).

PART 5

Weekly rate of payment of statutory shared parental pay

7.69

40.—(1) The weekly rate of payment of statutory shared parental pay is the smaller of the following two amounts—
   (a) [¹ £184.03];
   (b) 90% of the normal weekly earnings of the individual claiming statutory shared parental pay determined in accordance with section 171ZZ4(6) of the 1992 Act and regulation 32).

(2) Where the amount of any payment of statutory shared parental pay is calculated by reference to—
   (a) the weekly rate specified in paragraph (1)(b), or
   (b) the daily rate of one-seventh of the weekly rate specified in paragraph (1)(a) or (b),

and that amount includes a fraction of a penny, the payment shall be rounded up to the nearest whole number of pence.

AMENDMENT

1. Social Security Benefits Up-rating Order 2024 (SI 2024/242) art.10(2) (April 7, 2024).

DEFINITIONS

"1992 Act"—reg.2(1).
"statutory shared parental pay"—reg.2(1).

Statutory shared parental pay and contractual remuneration

7.70

41.—For the purposes of section 171ZZ1(1) and (2) (payment of contractual remuneration to go towards discharging liability to pay statutory shared parental pay and payment of statutory shared parental pay to go towards discharging liability to pay contractual remuneration) the payments which are to be treated as contractual remuneration are sums payable under a contract of service—
   (a) by way of remuneration;
   (b) for incapacity for work due to sickness or injury; and
   (c) by reason of birth, adoption or care of a child.

(SI 2014/3051 reg.42)

Avoidance of liability for statutory shared parental pay

42.—(1) A former employer is liable to make payments of statutory shared parental pay to a former employee in any case where the employee has been employed for a continuous period of at least eight weeks and the employee's contract of service was brought to an end by the former employer solely, or mainly, for the purpose of avoiding liability for statutory shared parental pay.

(2) In a case falling within paragraph (1)—
(a) the employee shall be treated as if the employee had been employed for a continuous period ending with the period of seven days beginning with Sunday before the first week falling within the relevant period relating to that employee under section 171ZY(2) of the 1992 Act; and
(b) regulation 32(2) (relevant period for the purpose of the calculation of normal weekly earnings) shall apply as if it read—
"(2) The relevant period is the period—
(a) ending on the last day of payment under the former contract of employment; and
(b) beginning with the day following the day of payment under that contract to fall at least 8 weeks earlier than the day of payment mentioned in sub-paragraph (a).".

DEFINITIONS

"1992 Act"—reg.2(1).
"statutory shared parental pay"—reg.2(1).
"week"—reg.2(1).

Payment of statutory shared parental pay

43.—Payments of statutory shared parental pay may be made in like manner to payments of remuneration but shall not include payment in kind or by way of the provision of board and lodgings.

DEFINITION

"statutory shared parental pay"—reg.2(1).

Time when statutory shared parental pay is to be paid

44.—(1) In any case where—
(a) a decision has been made by an officer of Revenue and Customs under section 8(1) (decisions by officers) of the Social Security Contributions (Transfer of Functions, etc) Act 1999 as a result of which a person is entitled to an amount of statutory shared parental pay; and
(b) the time for bringing an appeal against the decision has expired and either—
  (i) no such appeal has been brought; or
  (ii) such appeal has been brought and has been finally disposed of;
that amount of statutory shared parental pay shall be paid within the time specified in paragraph (2).

(2) The employer or former employer shall pay the amount not later than the first pay day after the following days (but see paragraphs (3) and (4))—
   (a) where an appeal has been brought, the day on which the employer or former employer receives notification that it has been finally disposed of;
   (b) where leave to appeal has been refused, and there remains no further opportunity to apply for leave, the day on which the employer or former employer receives notification of the refusal; and
   (c) in any other case, the day on which the time for bringing an appeal expires.

(3) Where it is impracticable, in view of the employer's or former employer's methods of accounting for and paying remuneration, for the requirement of payment referred to in paragraph (2) to be met by the pay day referred to in that paragraph, it shall be met not later than the next following pay day (but see paragraph (4)).

(4) Where the employer or former employer would not have remunerated the employee for their work in the week in respect of which statutory shared parental pay is payable as early as the pay day specified in paragraph (2) or (if it applies) paragraph (3), the requirement of payment shall be met on the first day on which the employee would have been remunerated for his work in that week.

(5) In this regulation "pay day" means a day on which it has been agreed, or it is the normal practice between an employer or former employer to agree and a person who is or was an employee of theirs, that payments by way of remuneration are to be made, or, where there is no such agreement or normal practice, the last day of a calendar month.

DEFINITIONS

"statutory shared parental pay"—reg.2(1).
"pay day"—para.(5).

Liability of the Commissioners to pay statutory shared parental pay

7.74

45.—(1) Despite section 171ZX(1) of the 1992 Act (liability to make payments of statutory shared parental pay is liability of the employer) where the conditions in paragraph (2) are satisfied, liability to make payments of statutory shared parental pay to a person is to be liability of the Commissioners and not the employer for—
   (a) any week in respect of which the employer was liable to pay statutory shared parental pay to that person but did not do so; and
   (b) for any subsequent weeks that person is entitled to payments of statutory shared parental pay.

(2) The conditions in this paragraph are that—
   (a) an officer of the Revenue and Customs has decided under section 8(1) of the Social Security Contributions (Transfer of Functions, etc) Act 1999 that an employer is liable to make payments of statutory shared parental pay;
   (b) the time for appealing against the decision has expired; and
   (c) no appeal against the decision has been lodged or leave to appeal against the decision is required and has been refused.

(3) Despite section 171ZX(1) of the 1992 Act, liability to make payments of statutory shared parental pay to a person is to be a liability of the Commissioners and not the employer as from the week in which the employer first becomes insolvent (see paragraphs 4 and 5) until the last week that person is entitled to payment of statutory shared parental pay.

(4) For the purposes of paragraph (3) an employer shall be taken to be insolvent if, and only if, in England and Wales—
  (a) the employer has been adjudged bankrupt or has made a composition or arrangement with its creditors;
  (b) the employer has died and the employer's estate falls to be administered in accordance with an order made under section 421 Insolvency Act 1986; or
  (c) where an employer is a company or a limited liability partnership—
    (i) a winding-up order is made or a resolution for a voluntary winding-up is passed (or, in the case of a limited liability partnership, a determination for voluntary winding-up has been made) with respect to it,
    (ii) it enters administration,
    (iii) a receiver or manager of its undertaking is duly appointed,
    (iv) possession is taken, by or on behalf of the holders of any debentures secured by a floating charge, of any property of the company or limited liability partnership comprised in or subject to the charge, or
    (v) a voluntary arrangement proposed for the purposes of Part 1 of the Insolvency Act 1986 is approved under that Part.

(5) For the purposes of paragraph (3) an employer shall be taken to be insolvent if, and only if, in Scotland—
  (a) an award of sequestration is made on the employer's estate;
  (b) the employer executes a trust deed for its creditors;
  (c) the employer enters into a composition contract;
  (d) the employer has died and a judicial factor appointed under section 11A of the Judicial Factors (Scotland) Act 1889 is required by that section to divide the employer's insolvent estate among the employer's creditors; or
  (e) where the employer is a company or a limited liability partnership—
    (i) a winding-up order is made or a resolution for voluntary winding-up is passed (or in the case of a limited liability partnership, a determination for a voluntary winding-up is made) with respect to it,
    (ii) it enters administration,
    (iii) a receiver of its undertaking is duly appointed, or
    (iv) a voluntary arrangement proposed for the purposes of Part I of the Insolvency Act 1986 is approved under that Part.

DEFINITIONS

"1992 Act"—reg.2(1).
"Commissioners"—reg.2(1).
"statutory shared parental pay"—reg.2(1).
"week"—reg.2(1).

Liability of the Commissioners to pay statutory shared parental pay in case of legal custody or imprisonment

7.75 46.—Where there is liability to pay statutory shared parental pay—
 (a) in respect of a period which is subsequent to the last week falling within paragraph (1)(c) of regulations 14 and 26 (cases where there is no liability to pay statutory shared parental pay); or
 (b) during a period of detention in legal custody by virtue of paragraph (2) of those regulations;
that liability, despite section 171ZX(1) of the 1992 Act, shall be that of the Commissioners and not the employer.

DEFINITIONS

"1992 Act"—reg.2(1).
"Commissioners"—reg.2(1).
"statutory shared parental pay"—reg.2(1).

Payments by the Commissioners

7.76 47.—Where the Commissioners become liable in accordance with regulation 45 (liability of the Commissioners to pay statutory shared parental pay) or regulation 46 (liability of the Commissioners to pay statutory shared parental pay in case of legal custody or imprisonment) then—
 (a) the first payment is to be made as soon as reasonably practicable after they become so liable; and
 (b) subsequent payments are to be made at weekly intervals;
by means of an instrument of payment or by such other means as appear to the Commissioners to be appropriate in the circumstances of any particular case.

DEFINITIONS

"Commissioners"—reg.2(1).
"statutory shared parental pay"—reg.2(1).

Persons unable to act

7.77 48.—(1) This regulation applies where—
 (a) statutory shared parental pay is payable to a person or it is alleged that statutory shared parental pay is payable to a person;
 (b) that person is unable for the time being to act;
 (c) no deputy has been appointed by the Court of Protection with power to receive [¹ statutory shared parental pay] on their behalf or, in Scotland, their estate is not being administered by a guardian acting or appointed under the Adults with Incapacity (Scotland) Act 2000; and
 (d) a written application has been made to the Commissioners by a person, who, if a natural person, is over the age of 18 to exercise any right, or deal with any sums payable, under Part 12ZC of the 1992 Act on behalf of the person unable to act.
 (2) Where this regulation applies the Commissioners may appoint the person referred to in paragraph (1)(d)—

(a) to exercise, on behalf of the person unable to act, any right which the person unable to act may be entitled under Part 12ZC of the 1992 Act; and
(b) to deal, on behalf of the person unable to act, with any sums payable to the person unable to act under Part 12ZC of the 1992 Act.

(3) Where the Commissioners have made an appointment under paragraph (2)—
(a) they may at any time revoke it;
(b) the person appointed may resign their office after having given one month's notice in writing to the Commissioners of that person's intention to do so; and
(c) the appointment shall end when the Commissioners are notified that a deputy or other person to whom paragraph (1)(c) applies has been appointed.

(4) Anything required by Part 12ZC of the 1992 Act to be done by or to the person who is unable to act may be done by or to the person appointed under this regulation to act on behalf of the person unable to act, and the receipt of the person so appointed shall be a good discharge to the employer or former employer of the person unable to act for any sum paid.

AMENDMENT

1. Statutory Shared Parental Pay (General) (Amendment) Regulations 2015 (SI 2015/189) reg.2(6) (March 8, 2015).

DEFINITIONS

"1992 Act"—reg.2(1).
"Commissioners"—reg.2(1).
"statutory shared parental pay"—reg.2(1).

Service of notices

49.—(1) Where a notice is to be given under these Regulations, it may be given—
(a) where paragraph (2) applies, by electronic communication;
(b) by post; or
(c) by personal delivery.

(2) This paragraph applies where the person who is to receive the notice has agreed that the notice may be given to the person by being transmitted to an electronic address and in an electronic form specified by the person for that purpose.

(3) Where a notice is to be given under these Regulations it is to be taken to have been given—
(a) if sent by electronic communication, on the day of transmission;
(b) if sent by post in an envelope which is properly addressed and sent by prepaid post, on the day on which it is posted;
(c) if delivered personally, on the day of delivery.

The Statutory Shared Parental Pay (General) Regulations 2014

SCHEDULE   Regulations 16 and 28

STATUTORY SHARED PARENTAL PAY IN SPECIAL CIRCUMSTANCES

PART 1

STATUTORY SHARED PARENTAL PAY (BIRTH)

Entitlement of father or partner to statutory shared parental pay (birth) in the event of the death of M before curtailment

7.79

1.—(1) In a case where M dies—
 (a) before the end of her maternity allowance period in respect of C and without reducing that period under section 35(3A) of the 1992 Act, or
 (b) before the end of her maternity pay period in respect of C and without reducing that period under section 165(3A) of the 1992 Act,
then these Regulations shall apply, in respect of any period after M dies, subject to the modifications in the following provisions of this paragraph.
 (2) In regulation 2(1) a person is to be regarded as falling within the definition of P it that person would have done so but for the fact that M had died.
 (3) In regulation 5 (entitlement of father or partner)—
 (a) paragraph (3)(d) shall not apply;
 (b) in a case where M dies before her maternity allowance period or maternity pay period in respect of C starts then the condition in paragraph (3)(c) shall be taken to be satisfied if it would have been satisfied but for the fact that M had died.
 (4) In regulation 7 (notification and evidential requirements relating to father or mother's partner)—
 (a) paragraph (1)(a) shall apply as if it read—
"(a) paragraphs (2) and (3) at least 8 weeks before the beginning of the first period specified by P pursuant to paragraph (2)(d) or, where it is not reasonably practicable for P to satisfy this requirement, as soon as reasonably practicable after the death of M, but in any event before that period;";
 (b) paragraph (1)(b) and (c) shall not apply;
 (c) in paragraph (2)—
  (i) sub-paragraph (a) shall apply as if the words "disregarding any intention of M to claim statutory shared parental pay (birth) in respect of C" were omitted; and
  (ii) sub-paragraph (c) shall not apply;
 (d) in paragraph (3)—
  (i) sub-paragraph (a) shall not apply;
  (ii) sub-paragraph (d) shall apply as if it read—
"(d) the following information relating to P and M—
  (i) P's name, M's name and national insurance number (where this number is known to P), M's address immediately before she died and the date of M's death; and
  (ii) the start date of M's maternity pay period or maternity allowance period in respect of C or, where M's death occurred before her maternity allowance period or maternity pay period in respect of C started, the date that period would have started but for the fact that M had died;"; and
  (iii) sub-paragraph (e)(iii) shall not apply;
 (e) paragraph (4) shall not apply.
 (5) In regulation 8(3) (variation)—
 (a) sub-paragraph (a) shall apply as if the reference to M were omitted; and
 (b) sub-paragraph (b) shall not apply.
 (6) In regulation 10 (extent of entitlement), paragraph (1)(a) shall apply as if the number of weeks referred to is the number of weeks in which maternity allowance or statutory maternity pay was payable to M in respect of C up to the time of M's death.

Notification And Variation: Death Of Mother Or Partner After Curtailment

7.80

2.—(1) In the case where—
 (a) P, who in connection with a claim by M would be required to satisfy the conditions specified in regulation 4(3), dies after M has reduced her maternity allowance period in respect of C under section 35(3A) of the 1992 Act or her maternity pay period in respect of C under section 165(3A) of the 1992 Act; and
 (b) before P dies M has not given the notices and information specified in regulation 6 (notice and evidential requirements relation to the mother),

then these Regulations apply in respect of any period after P dies, subject to the modifications in the following provisions of this paragraph.

(2) In regulation 6 (notification and evidential requirements relating to the mother)—
   (a) paragraph (1)(a) shall apply as if it read—
   "(a) paragraphs (2) and (3) at least 8 weeks before the beginning of the first period specified by M pursuant to paragraph (2)(d) or where it is not reasonably practicable for M to satisfy this requirement as soon as reasonably practicable after the death of P, but in any event before that period;";
   (b) paragraph (1)(b) and (c) shall not apply;
   (c) in paragraph (2)—
      (i) sub-paragraph (a) shall apply as if the words "disregarding any intention of P to claim statutory shared parental pay in respect of C" were omitted;
      (ii) sub-paragraph (c) shall not apply;
   (d) in paragraph (3)—
      (i) sub-paragraph (a) shall not apply;
      (ii) sub-paragraph (d) shall apply as if it read—
   "(d) M's name, P's name and national insurance number (where this number is known to M), P's address immediately before P died and the date of P's death";
   (e) paragraph (4) shall not apply.
(3) In regulation 8 (variation)—
   (a) paragraph (2)(a) shall apply as if it read—
   "(a) of the number of weeks during which M and P have exercised, and the number of weeks M intends to exercise, an entitlement to statutory shared parental pay (birth) in respect of C";
   (b) paragraph (2)(b) shall not apply.
(4) In regulation 10 (extent of entitlement)—
   (a) paragraph (1)(b)(i) shall apply as if the words "P has notified P's intention to claim" to the end read "the number of weeks in which P claimed statutory shared parental pay (birth) in respect of C up to the time of P's death.";
   (b) paragraph (7) shall apply as if the words "the last day of the latest period so notified" were "the time of P's death".

3.—(1) In the case where—
   (a) P, who in connection with M's claim is required to satisfy the conditions specified in regulation 4(3), dies after M has reduced her maternity allowance period in respect of C under section 35(3A) of the 1992 Act or her maternity pay period in respect of C under section 165(3A) of the 1992 Act, and
   (b) before P dies M has given the notices and information specified in regulation 6 (notification and evidential requirements relating to the mother),
then these Regulations apply in respect of any period after P dies, subject to the modifications in the following provisions of this paragraph.

(2) In regulation 8 (variation)—
   (a) paragraph (1) shall apply in relation to the first notice made under that paragraph following P's death as if at the end of that paragraph there is added—
   "or, where it is not reasonably practicable for M to satisfy this requirement, by notice in writing given to that employer as soon as reasonably practicable after the death of P, but in any event before that period and which states the date of P's death";
   (b) paragraph (2)(a) shall apply as if it read—
   "(a) of the number of weeks during which M and P have exercised, and the number of weeks M intends to exercise, an entitlement to statutory shared parental pay (birth) in respect of C";
   (c) paragraph (2)(b) shall not apply.
(3) In regulation 10—
   (a) paragraph (1)(b)(i) shall apply as if the words "P has notified P's intention to claim" to the end read—
   "the number of weeks in which P claimed statutory shared parental pay (birth) in respect of C up to the time of P's death;";
   (b) paragraph (7) shall apply as if the words "the last day of the latest period so notified" were "the time of P's death".

4.—(1) In the case where—
   (a) M dies after she has reduced her maternity allowance period in respect of C under section 35(3A) of the 1992 Act or her maternity pay period in respect of C under section 165(3A) of the 1992 Act, and
   (b) before M dies P has not given the notices and information specified in regulation 7 (notification and evidential requirements relating to father or partner),

then these Regulations apply in respect of any period after M dies, subject to the modifications in the following provisions of this paragraph.

(2) In regulation 2(1) (definitions) a person is to be regarded as falling within the definition of P if that person would have done so but for the fact that M has died.

(3) In regulation 7 (notification and evidential requirements relating to P)—
  (a) in paragraph (1)—
    (i) sub-paragraph (a) shall apply as if it read—
      "(a) paragraphs (2) and (3) at least 8 weeks before the beginning of the first period specified by P pursuant to paragraph (2)(d) or where it is not reasonably practicable for P to satisfy this requirement as soon as reasonably practicable after the death of M, but in any event before that period;";
    (ii) sub-paragraphs (b) and (c) shall not apply;
  (b) in paragraph (2)—
    (i) sub-paragraph (a) shall apply as if the words "disregarding any intention of M to claim statutory shared parental pay in respect of C" were omitted;
    (ii) sub-paragraph (c) shall not apply;
  (c) in paragraph (3)—
    (i) sub-paragraph (a) shall not apply;
    (ii) sub-paragraph (d) shall apply as if it read—
      "(d) P's name, M's name and national insurance number (where this number is known to P), M's address immediately before she died and the date of M's death";
    (iii) sub-paragraph (e)(iii) shall not apply;
  (d) paragraph (4) shall not apply.

(4) In regulation 8(variation), in paragraph (3)—
  (a) sub-paragraph (a) shall apply as if it read—
  "(a) of the number of weeks during which P and M have exercised, and the number of weeks P intends to exercise, an entitlement to statutory shared parental pay (birth) in respect of C";
  (b) sub-paragraph (b) shall not apply.

(5) In regulation 10 (extent of entitlement)—
  (a) paragraph (1)(b)(ii) shall apply as if the words "M has notified M's intention to claim" to the end read—
  "the number of weeks in which M claimed statutory shared parental pay (birth) in respect of C up to the time of M's death;";
  (b) paragraph (8) shall apply as if the words "the last day of the latest period" were "the time of M's death".

5.—(1) In the case where—
  (a) M dies after she has reduced her maternity allowance period in respect of C under section 35(3A) of the 1992 Act or her maternity pay period in respect of C under section 165(3A) of the 1992 Act, and
  (b) before M dies P has given the notice and information specified in regulation 7 (notification and evidential requirements relating to father or mother's partner),

then these Regulations apply in in respect of any period after M dies subject to the modifications in the following provisions of this paragraph.

(2) In regulation 8 (variation)—
  (a) paragraph (1) shall apply in relation to the first notice made under that regulation following M's death as if at the end of that paragraph there is added—
  "or, where it is not reasonably practicable for P to satisfy this requirement, by notice in writing given to that employer as soon as reasonably practicable after the death of M, but in any event before that period and which states the date of M's death";
  (b) paragraph (3)(a) shall apply as if it read—
  "(a) of the number of weeks during which P and M have exercised, and the number of weeks P intends to exercise, an entitlement to statutory shared parental pay (birth) in respect of C";
  (c) paragraph (3)(b) shall not apply.

(3) In regulation 10 (extent of entitlement)—
  (a) paragraph (1)(b)(ii) shall apply as if the words "M has notified M's intention to claim" to the end read—
  "the number of weeks in which M claimed statutory shared parental pay (birth) in respect of C up to the time of M's death";
  (b) paragraph (8) shall apply as if the words "the last day of the latest period" were "the time of M's death".

Death Of Child

6.—(1) In the case where M has given the notice and information in accordance with regulation 6(1) and then C dies, then in respect of any period after C dies paragraph (2)(f) of regulation 4 (entitlement of mother to statutory shared parental pay), shall not apply, and regulation 8 shall apply in accordance with sub-paragraph (3).

(2) In the case where P has given the notices and information in accordance with regulation 7(1) and then C dies, then in respect of any period after C dies paragraph (2)(d) of regulation 5 (entitlement of father or partner to statutory shared parental pay) shall not apply and regulation 8 shall apply in accordance with sub-paragraph (3).

(3) Where paragraph (1) or (2) applies, regulation 8 (variation) shall apply as if it read—
"(1) M, or as the case may be, P may cancel the period or periods during which they intend to claim statutory shared parental pay (birth) by notice in writing which is given at least 8 weeks before the first period to be cancelled, or, if this is not reasonably practicable, as soon as reasonably practicable after the death of C, but in any event before that period to the employer who will be liable to pay statutory shared parental pay (birth) to M or P.
(2) M and P may each only give one notice under paragraph (1).".

(4) Where more than one child is born of the same pregnancy—
  (a) sub-paragraphs (2) and (3) only apply where all the children die; and
  (b) a reference in this paragraph relating to the death of C (however expressed) is to the death of the last of those children to die.

PART 2

STATUTORY SHARED PARENTAL PAY (ADOPTION)

Entitlement Of Adopter's Partner To Statutory Shared Parental Pay (Adoption) In The Event Of The Death Of Adopter Before Curtailment

7.—(1) In a case where A dies before the end of A's adoption pay period in respect of C and without reducing that period under section 171ZN(2A) of the 1992 Act then these Regulations apply in respect of any period after A dies, subject to the modifications in the following provisions of this paragraph.

(2) In regulation 2 a person is to be regarded as falling within the definition of AP if that person would have done so but for the fact that A had died.

(3) In regulation 18 (entitlement of partner to statutory shared parental pay (adoption))—
  (a) paragraph (3)(d) shall not apply;
  (b) in the case where A dies before A's adoption pay period in respect of C starts, then the condition in paragraph (3)(c) shall be taken to be satisfied if it would have been satisfied but for the fact that A had died.

(4) In regulation 20 (notification and evidential requirements relating to partner)—
  (a) paragraph (1)(a) shall apply as if it read—
"(a) paragraphs (2) and (3) at least 8 weeks before the beginning of the first period specified by AP pursuant to paragraph (2)(d) or, where it is not reasonably practicable for AP to satisfy this requirement, as soon as reasonably practicable after the death of A, but in any event before that week";
  (b) paragraph (1)(b) and (c) shall not apply;
  (c) in paragraph (2)—
    (i) sub-paragraph (a) shall apply as if the words "disregarding any intention of A to claim statutory shared parental pay (adoption) in respect of C" were omitted,
    (ii) sub-paragraph (c) shall not apply;
  (d) in paragraph (3)—
    (i) sub-paragraph (a) shall not apply,
    (ii) sub-paragraph (d) shall apply as if it read—
"(d) the following information about AP and A—
    (i) AP's name, A's name and national insurance number (where this number is known to AP), A's address immediately before she died and the date of A's death; and
    (ii) the start date of A's adoption pay period in respect of C;",
    (iii) sub-paragraph (e)(iii) shall not apply;
  (e) paragraph (4) shall not apply.

(5) In regulation 21 (variation), in paragraph (3)—
  (a) sub-paragraph (a) shall apply as if the reference to A were omitted;
  (b) sub-paragraph (b) shall not apply.

(6) In regulation 22 (extent of entitlement), paragraph (1)(a) shall apply as if the number of weeks referred to is the number of weeks in which statutory adoption pay was payable to A in respect of C up to the time of A's death.

Notification Or Variation: Death Of Adopter Or Adopter's Partner After Curtailment

7.86 8.—(1) In the case where—
(a) AP who in connection with a claim by A would be required to satisfy the conditions in regulation 17(3), dies after A has reduced A's adoption pay period in respect of C under section 171ZN(2A) of the 1992 Act, and
(b) before AP dies A has not given the notice and information specified in regulation 19 (notification and evidential requirements relating to the adopter),
then these Regulations apply in respect of any period after AP dies, subject to the modifications in the following provisions of this paragraph.

(2) In regulation 19 (notification and evidential requirements relating to the adopter)—
(a) paragraph (1)(a) shall apply as if it read—
"(a) paragraphs (2) and (3) at least 8 weeks before the beginning of the first period specified by A pursuant to paragraph (2)(d) or, where it is not reasonably practicable for A to satisfy this requirement, as soon as reasonably practicable after the death of AP but in any event before that period;";
(b) paragraph (1)(b) and (c) shall not apply;
(c) paragraph (2)(a) shall apply as if the words "disregarding any intention of AP to claim statutory shared parental pay (adoption) in respect of C" were omitted;
(d) paragraph (2)(c) shall not apply;
(e) paragraph (3)(a) shall not apply;
(f) paragraph (3)(d) shall apply as if it read—
"(d) A's name, AP's name and national insurance number (where this number is known to A), AP's address immediately before AP died and the date of AP's death";
(g) paragraph (4) shall not apply.

(3) In regulation 21 (variation), in paragraph (3) sub-paragraph (a) shall apply as if it read—
"(a) of the number of weeks during which A and AP have exercised, and the number of weeks A intends to exercise, an entitlement to statutory shared parental pay (adoption) in respect of C;";
(a) paragraph (b) shall not apply.

(4) In regulation 22 (extent of entitlement to statutory shared parental pay (adoption))—
(a) paragraph (1)(b)(i) shall apply as if the words "AP has notified AP's intention to claim" to the end read—
"the number of weeks in which AP claimed statutory shared parental pay (adoption) in respect of C up to the time of AP's death;";
(b) paragraph (5) shall apply as if the words "the last day of the latest period so notified" were "the time of AP's death".

7.87 9.—(1) In the case where—
(a) AP, who in connection with A's claim is required to satisfy the conditions specified in regulation 17(3), dies after A has reduced A's adoption pay period under section 171ZN(2A) of the 1992 Act, and
(b) before AP dies A has given the notices and information specified in regulation 19 (notification and evidential requirements relating to the adopter),
then these Regulations apply in respect of any period after AP dies, subject to the modifications in the following provisions of this paragraph.

(2) In regulation 21 (variation)—
(a) paragraph (1) shall apply in relation to the first notice made under that paragraph following AP's death as if at the end of that paragraph there is added—
"or, where it is not reasonably practicable for A to satisfy this requirement, by notice in writing given to that employer as soon as reasonably practicable after the death of AP, but in any event before that period and which states the date of AP's death";
(b) paragraph (2)(a) shall apply as if it read—
"(a) of the number of weeks during which A and AP have exercised, and the number of weeks A intends to exercise, an entitlement to statutory shared parental pay (adoption) in respect of C;";
(c) paragraph (2)(b) shall not apply.

(3) In regulation 22 (extent of entitlement)—
(a) paragraph (1)(b)(i) shall apply as if the words "AP has notified AP's intention to claim" to the end read "the number of weeks in which AP claimed statutory shared parental pay (adoption) in respect of C up to the time of AP's death;";

(b) paragraph (5) shall apply as if the words "the last day of the latest period so notified" were "the time of AP's death".

10.—(1) In the case where—

(a) A dies after A has reduced A's adoption pay period in respect of C under section 171ZN(2A) of the 1992 Act, and

(b) before A dies AP has not given the notice and information specified in regulation 20 (notification and evidential requirements relating to adopter's partner);

then the Regulations apply in respect of any period after A dies subject to the modifications in the following provisions of this paragraph.

(2) In regulation 2(1) (definitions) a person is to be regarded as falling within the definition of AP if that person would have done so but for the fact that A has died.

(3) In regulation 20 (notification and evidential requirements relating to partner)—

(a) paragraph (1)(a) shall apply as if it read—

"(a) paragraphs (2) and (3) at least 8 weeks before the beginning of the first period specified by AP pursuant to paragraph (2)(d) or if it is not reasonably practicable for AP to satisfy this requirement as soon as reasonably practicable after the death of A, but in any event before that period;";

(b) paragraph (1)(b) and (c) shall not apply;

(c) paragraph (2)(a) shall apply as if the words "disregarding any intention of A to claim statutory shared parental pay (adoption) in respect of C" were omitted;

(d) paragraph (2)(c) shall not apply;

(e) paragraph (3)(a) shall not apply;

(f) paragraph (3)(d) shall apply as if it read—

"(d) AP's name, A's name and national insurance number (where this number is known to AP), A's address immediately before A died and the date of A's death;";

(g) paragraph (4) shall not apply.

(4) In regulation 21 (variation), in paragraph (3)—

(a) sub-paragraph (a) shall apply as if it read—

"(a) of the number of weeks during which AP and A have exercised, and the number of weeks AP intends to exercise, an entitlement to statutory shared parental pay (adoption) in respect of C";

(b) sub-paragraph (b) shall not apply.

(5) In regulation 22 (extent of entitlement)—

(a) paragraph (1)(b)(ii) shall apply as if the words "A has notified A's intention to claim" to the end read—

"the number of weeks in which A claimed statutory shared parental pay (adoption) in respect of C up to the time of A's death;".

(b) paragraph (6) shall apply as if the words "the last day of the latest period so notified" were "the time of A's death".

11.—(1) In the case where—

(a) A dies after A has reduced A's adoption pay period in respect of C under section 171ZN(2A) of the 1992 Act; and

(b) before A dies AP has given the notice and information specified in regulation 20 (notification and evidential requirements relating to the partner);

then these Regulations apply in respect of any period after A dies subject to the modifications in the following provisions of this paragraph.

(2) In regulation 21 (variation)—

(a) paragraph (1) shall apply in relation to the first notice made under that regulation following A's death as if at the end of that paragraph there is added—

"or, where is it not reasonably practicable for AP to satisfy this requirement, by notice in writing given to that employer as soon as reasonably practicable after the death of A, but in any event before that period and which states the date of A's death;";

(b) paragraph (3)(a) shall apply as it is read—

"(a) of the number of weeks during which AP and A have exercised, and the number of weeks AP intends to exercise, an entitlement to statutory shared parental pay (adoption) in respect of C";

(c) paragraph (3)(b) shall not apply.

(3) In regulation 22 (extent of entitlement)—

(a) paragraph (1)(b)(ii) shall apply as if the words "A has notified A's intention to claim" to the end read—

"the number of weeks in which A claimed statutory shared parental pay (adoption) in respect of C up to the time of A's death.".

Death Of Child Or Disrupted Placement

7.90   12.—(1) In the case where A has given the notices and information specified in regulation 19(1) and then C dies or is returned after being placed then in respect of any period after C dies or is returned after being placed paragraph (2)(f) of regulation 17 (entitlement of adopter to statutory shared parental pay) shall not apply and regulation 21 shall apply in accordance with sub-paragraph (3).

(2) In the case where AP has given the notices and information specified in regulation 20(1) and then C dies or is returned after being placed then in respect of any period after C dies or is returned after being placed paragraph (2)(d) of regulation 18 (entitlement of adopter to statutory shared parental pay) shall not apply and regulation 21 shall apply in accordance with sub-paragraph (3).

(3) Where paragraph (1) or (2) applies, regulation 21 (variation) shall apply as if it read—

"(1) A or, as the case may be, AP may cancel the period or periods during which they intend to claim statutory shared parental pay (adoption) by notice in writing which is given at least 8 weeks before the first period to be cancelled or, if this is not reasonably practicable, as soon as reasonably practicable after the death of C or after C is returned after being placed, but in any event before that period to the employer who will be liable to pay statutory shared parental pay (adoption) to A or AP.

(2) A and AP may each only give one notice under paragraph (1).".

(4) Where more than one child is placed for adoption as a result of the same placement—
  (a) sub-paragraphs (1) and (2) only apply where all the children die or, as the case may be, all the children are returned after being placed;
  (b) a reference in this paragraph to the death of C or to the return of C after being placed (however expressed) is to the death of the last of those children to die or is to the last of those children to be returned after being placed.

(5) In this paragraph "returned after being placed" means—
  (a) returned to the adoption agency under sections 31 to 35 of the Adoption and Children Act 2002;
  (b) in Scotland, returned to the adoption agency, adoption society or nominated person in accordance with section 25(6) of the Adoption and Children (Scotland) Act 2007; or
  (c) where the child is placed in accordance with section 22C of the Children Act 1989, returned to the adoption agency following termination of the placement.

GENERAL NOTE

7.91   This Schedule is modified for certain special cases by the Statutory Shared Parental Pay (Adoption from Overseas) Regulations 2014 (SI 2014/3093) and the Statutory Shared Parental Pay (Parental Order Cases) Regulations 2014 (SI 2014/3097).

The Statutory Shared Parental Pay (Adoption From Overseas) Regulations 2014

(SI 2014/3093)

A draft of these Regulations was laid before Parliament in accordance with section 176(1) of the Social Security Contributions and Benefits Act 1992 and approved by resolution of each House of Parliament.

This instrument contains only regulations made by virtue of, or consequential upon, section 119(1) of the Children and Families Act 2014 and is made before the end of the period of 6 months beginning with the coming into force of that enactment.

The Secretary of State, in exercise of the powers conferred by sections 171ZV(1) to (5), and (12) to (15), 171ZW(1), 171ZX(2) and (3), 171ZY(1), and (3) to

(SI 2014/3093)

(5), 171ZZ1(3), 171ZZ4(3), (4), (7) and (8), and 175(3) of the Social Security Contributions and Benefits Act 1992 and by section 5(1)(g), (i), (l) and (p) of the Social Security Administration Act 1992 and with the concurrence of the Commissioners for Her Majesty's Revenue and Customs in so far as such concurrence is required, makes the following Regulations.

ARRANGEMENT OF REGULATIONS

1. Citation and commencement
2. Interpretation
3. Application of the General Regulations to adoptions from overseas
4.–16. Modifications to the General Regulations for the purposes of adoptions from overseas

Citation and commencement

1.—These Regulations may be cited as the Statutory Shared Parental Pay (Adoption from Overseas) Regulations 2014 and come into force on 5th April 2015.

Interpretation

2.—In these Regulations—
"1992 Act" means the Social Security Contributions and Benefits Act 1992;
"the Application Regulations" means the Social Security Contributions and Benefits Act 1992 (Application of Parts 12ZA, 12ZB and 12ZC to Adoptions from Overseas) Regulations 2003;
"the General Regulations" means the Statutory Shared Parental Pay (General) Regulations 2014; and
"statutory shared parental pay (adoption)" means any pay payable in accordance with the provisions of Part 12ZC of the 1992 Act where the conditions in section 171ZV of that Act are satisfied.

Application of the General Regulations to adoptions from overseas

3.—(1) The provisions of the General Regulations mentioned in paragraph (2), in so far as they apply to statutory shared parental pay (adoption), apply to adoptions from overseas, subject to paragraphs (3) and (4) and the modifications set out in regulations 4 to 16 below.
(2) The relevant provisions are—
(a) regulation 2;
(b) regulation 3(b);
(c) Parts 3 to 5;
(d) Part 2 of the Schedule.
(3) Any references in the provisions of the General Regulations mentioned in paragraph (2) to the provisions of Part 12ZC of the 1992 Act must be construed as references to the provisions of Part 12ZC as modified by the Application Regulations.
(4) Any references in the provisions of the General Regulations mentioned in paragraph (2) to other provisions of the General Regulations must be construed as references to those provisions as modified by these Regulations.

7.92

7.93

7.94

7.95

The Statutory Shared Parental Pay (Adoption From Overseas) Regulations 2014

Modifications to the General Regulations for the purposes of adoptions from overseas

7.96   **4.**—The General Regulations are modified as follows.

Modifications to the General Regulations for the purposes of adoptions from overseas

7.97   **5.**—(1) Regulation 2 (definitions) is modified as follows.
(2) In paragraph (1)—
(a) for the definition of "A" substitute—
""A", in relation to C, means the person by whom C has been or is to be adopted;" and
(b) insert the following definitions in the appropriate places alphabetically—
""enter Great Britain" means enter Great Britain from outside the United Kingdom in connection with or for the purposes of adoption;";
""official notification" means written notification, issued by or on behalf of the relevant central authority, that it is prepared to issue a certificate to the overseas authority concerned with the adoption of C, or that it has issued a certificate and sent it to that authority, confirming, in either case, that A is eligible to adopt, and has been assessed and approved as being a suitable adoptive parent;";
""relevant central authority" means—
(a) in the case of an adopter to whom Part 3 of the Adoptions with a Foreign Element Regulations 2005(1) applies and who is habitually resident in Wales, the Welsh Ministers;
(b) in the case of an adopter to whom the Adoptions with a Foreign Element (Scotland) Regulations 2009(2) apply and who is habitually resident in Scotland, the Scottish Ministers; and
(c) in any other case, the Secretary of State.".

Modifications to the General Regulations for the purposes of adoptions from overseas

7.98   **6.**—In regulation 3 (application), for paragraph (b) substitute—
"(b) statutory shared parental pay (adoption) in respect of children who enter Great Britain on or after 5th April 2015.".

Modifications to the General Regulations for the purposes of adoptions from overseas

7.99   **7.**—(1) Regulation 17 (entitlement of adopter to statutory shared parental pay (adoption)) is modified as follows.
(2) In paragraphs (2)(b) and (3)(a) for "date of C's placement for adoption" substitute "date C enters Great Britain".
(3) In paragraph (2)(d) for "the placement for adoption of C" substitute "the adoption of C".

Modifications to the General Regulations for the purposes of adoptions from overseas

7.100   **8.**—(1) Regulation 18 (entitlement of partner to statutory shared parental pay (adoption)) is modified as follows.

(SI 2014/3093 reg. 8)

(2) In paragraphs (2)(b) and (3)(a) for "date of C's placement for adoption" substitute "date C enters Great Britain".

(3) In paragraph 3(c) for "the placement for adoption of C" substitute "the adoption of C".

Modifications to the General Regulations for the purposes of adoptions from overseas

9.—(1) Regulation 19 (notification and evidential requirements relating to the adopter) is modified as follows.

(2) In paragraph (1)(b)—
(a) for "if C is not placed for adoption by that time" substitute "if C has not entered Great Britain by that time";
(b) for "placement of C" substitute "date of C's entry into Great Britain".

(3) In paragraph (3)(b) for "A was notified that A had been matched with C" substitute "A received the official notification".

(4) In paragraph (3)(c) for "date of C's placement for adoption" substitute "date of C's entry into Great Britain".

(5) For paragraph (4)(a) substitute—
"(a) the date on which A expects C to enter Great Britain; and".

7.101

Modifications to the General Regulations for the purposes of adoptions from overseas

10.—(1) Regulation 20 (notification and evidential requirements relating to the partner) is modified as follows.

(2) In paragraph (1)(b)—
(a) for "if C is not placed for adoption by that time" substitute "if C has not entered Great Britain by that time";
(b) for "placement of C" substitute "date of C's entry into Great Britain".

(3) In paragraph (3)(b) for "A was notified that A had been matched with C" substitute "A received the official notification".

(4) In paragraph (3)(c) for "date of C's placement for adoption" substitute "date of C's entry into Great Britain".

(5) For paragraph (4)(a) substitute—
"(a) the date on which A expects C to enter Great Britain; and".

7.102

Modifications to the General Regulations for the purposes of adoptions from overseas

11.—In regulation 23 (period of payment of statutory shared parental pay), in paragraph (1), for "C was placed for adoption (or where more than one child is placed for adoption as a result of the same arrangement, the date of placement of the first child to be placed as part of the arrangement)" substitute "C entered Great Britain (or where more than one child is adopted as a result of the same arrangement, the date on which the first child entered Great Britain)".

7.103

Modifications to the General Regulations for the purposes of adoptions from overseas

12.—In regulation 24 (work during a period of statutory shared parental pay), in paragraph (1)(a)(ii), for "immediately preceding the 14th week

7.104

Statutory Shared Parental Pay (Adoption From Overseas) Regulations 2014

before the expected week of the placement for adoption" substitute "in which A received the official notification".

Modifications to the General Regulations for the purposes of adoptions from overseas

7.105   **13.**—In regulation 29 (conditions relating to employment and earnings of claimant's partner), in paragraph (5), for the definition of "calculation week" substitute—
""calculation week" means the week in which A received the official notification;".

Modifications to the General Regulations for the purposes of adoptions from overseas

7.106   **14.**—In regulation 31 (conditions as to continuity of employment and earnings), in paragraph (2), for "A was notified of having been matched with C" substitute "A received the official notification".

Modifications to the General Regulations for the purposes of adoptions from overseas

7.107   **15.**—In regulation 32 (normal weekly earnings of a claimant), in paragraph (9), in the definition of "appropriate date" for "the week in which A is notified of being matched with the child for the purposes of adoption" substitute "the week in which the official notification is sent to A".

Modifications to the General Regulations for the purposes of adoptions from overseas

7.108   **16.**—(1) Paragraph 12 (death of child) of the Schedule is modified as follows.
(2) In sub-paragraphs (1) and (2) for "or is returned after being placed" substitute "or regulation 28 of the Adoptions with a Foreign Element Regulations 2005 or regulation 31 of the Adoptions with a Foreign Element (Scotland) Regulations 2009 applies,".
(3) In sub-paragraph (3) for "the death of C or after C is returned after being placed" substitute "the date on which C dies or regulation 28 of the Adoptions with a Foreign Element Regulations 2005 or regulation 31 of the Adoptions with a Foreign Element (Scotland) Regulations 2009 applies".
(4) In sub-paragraph (4)—
  (a) for "placed for adoption as a result of the same placement" substitute "adopted as a result of the same arrangement";
  (b) for "all the children are returned after being placed" substitute "regulation 28 of the Adoptions with a Foreign Element Regulations 2005 or regulation 31 of the Adoptions with a Foreign Element (Scotland) Regulations 2009 applies in relation to all of the children";
  (c) for paragraph (b) substitute—
"(b)a reference in this paragraph to the death of C or to the application of regulation 28 of the Adoptions with a Foreign Element Regulations 2005 or regulation 31 of the Adoptions with a Foreign Element

(Scotland) Regulations 2009 (however expressed) is to the death of the last of those children to die or is to the last of those children in relation to whom those regulations applied.".

(5) Omit sub-paragraph (5).

The Statutory Shared Parental Pay (Parental Order Cases) Regulations 2014

(SI 2014/3097)

A draft of these Regulations was laid before Parliament in accordance with section 176(1) of the Social Security Contributions and Benefits Act 1992 and approved by resolution of each House of Parliament.

This instrument contains only regulations made by virtue of, or consequential upon, section 119(1) of the Children and Families Act 2014 and is made before the end of the period 6 months beginning with the coming into force of that enactment.

The Secretary of State, in exercise of the powers conferred by sections 171ZV(1), (2), (3), (4), (5), (12), (13), (14) and (15), 171ZW(1)(a) to (f), 171ZX(2) and (3), 171ZY(1), (3), (4) and (5), 171ZZ1(3), 171ZZ4(3), (4), (7) and (8) and 175(3) of the Social Security Contributions and Benefits Act 1992 and by section 5(1)(g), (i), (l) and (p) of the Social Security Administration Act 1992 and with the concurrence of the Commissioners for Her Majesty's Revenue and Customs, in so far as such concurrence is required, makes the following Regulations:

ARRANGEMENT OF REGULATIONS

1. Commencement and Citation
2. Interpretation
3. Application of the Pay Regulations to an intended parent or a parental order parent
4.–16. Modifications of the Pay Regulations as they apply to an intended parent or a parental order parent

GENERAL NOTE

These Regulations provide an entitlement to statutory shared parental pay in respect of cases which involve a person who has applied, with another person, for a parental order under s.54 of the Human Fertilisation and Embryology Act 2008. Under s.54 a court may make an order providing for a child of a surrogate mother to be treated as the child of the applicants for the order if certain conditions are satisfied. These Regulations need to be read in conjunction with the Social Security Contributions and Benefits Act 1992 (Application of Parts 12ZA, 12ZB and 12ZC to Parental Order Cases) Regulations 2014 (SI 2014/2866). They should also be read in conjunction with the Statutory Shared Parental Pay (General) Regulations 2014 (SI 2014/3051) which they apply with modifications.

Statutory Shared Parental Pay (Parental Order Cases) Regulations 2014

Part 1

Introduction

Citation and commencement

7.111   **1.**—These Regulations may be cited as the Statutory Shared Parental Pay (Parental Order Cases) Regulations 2014 and come into force on 1st December 2014.

Interpretation

7.112   **2.**—In these Regulations—
"A" and "AP" have the same meanings as in the Pay Regulations as modified by these Regulations;
"C", "expected week of birth" and "statutory shared parental pay (adoption)" have the same meanings as under the Pay Regulations;
"parental order parent" means a person on whose application the court has made a parental order in respect of C;
"parental statutory declaration" means a statutory declaration stating that the person making the declaration—
(a) has applied, or intends to apply, under section 54 of the Human Fertilisation and Embryology Act 2008 with another person for a parental order in respect of C within the time limit for making such an application; and
(b) expects the court to make a parental order on that application in respect of C;
"Pay Regulations" means the Statutory Shared Parental Pay (General) Regulations 2014.

Application of the Pay Regulations to an intended parent or a parental order parent

7.113   **3.**—The provisions of the Pay Regulations in so far as they apply to statutory shared parental pay (adoption) shall apply to an intended parent or a parental order parent with the modifications set out in Part 2 of these Regulations.

Part 2

Modifications of the Pay Regulations as they apply to an intended parent or a parental order parent

7.114   **4.**—Regulation 2 (interpretation) of the Pay Regulations as they apply to an intended parent or a parental order parent shall read as if—
(a) in paragraph (1)—
(i) the definition of "A" read "means the intended parent or parental order parent in relation to C who has elected to receive statutory adoption pay under section 171ZL(2)(e) of the 1992 Act and to whom the conditions in that subsection apply;";

(SI 2014/3097 reg. 4)

  (ii) the definition of "AP" read "means the intended parent or parental order parent in relation to C who at the date of C's birth is married to, or is the civil partner of, or is the partner of A;";
  (iii) the definition of "child" were omitted;
  (iv) there was the following definition—
""parental order parent" means a person on whose application the court has made an order in respect of C under section 54(1) of the Human Fertilization and Embryology Act 2008;";
  (v) the definitions of "placed for adoption" and "adoption agency" were omitted;
 (b) paragraphs (4), (5) and (6) were omitted.

5.—In regulation 3 (application) of the Pay Regulations as they apply to an intended parent or a parental order parent paragraph (b) shall read as if the words in that paragraph were—   7.115
"statutory shared parental pay (adoption) in respect of children whose expected week of birth begins on or after 5th April 2015.".

6.—In regulation 17 (entitlement of adopter to statutory shared parental pay (adoption)) of the Pay Regulations as they apply to an intended parent or a parental order parent—   7.116
 (a) in paragraph (2)—
  (i) sub-paragraph (b) shall read as if the words in that sub-paragraph were—
"A has, or expects to have, at the date of C's birth the main responsibility for the care of C (apart from the responsibility of AP);";
  (ii) sub-paragraph (d) shall read as if the words "to the placement for adoption of C" read "to being the intended parent or parental order parent of C";
 (b) in paragraph (3), sub-paragraph (a) shall read as if the words in that sub-paragraph were—
"AP has, or expects to have, at the date of C's birth the main responsibility for the care of C (apart from the responsibility of A);".

7.—In regulation 18 (entitlement of partner to statutory shared parental pay (adoption)) of the Pay Regulations as they apply to an intended parent or a parental order parent—   7.117
 (a) in paragraph (2), sub-paragraph (b) shall read as if the words in that sub-paragraph were—
"AP has, or expects to have, at the date of C's birth the main responsibility for the care of C (apart from the responsibility of A)";
 (b) in paragraph (3)—
  (i) sub-paragraph (a) shall read as if the words in that sub-paragraph were—
"A has, or expects to have, at the date of C's birth the main responsibility for the care of C (apart from the responsibility of A);";
  (ii) sub-paragraph (c) shall read as if the words "to the placement for adoption of C" read "to being the intended parent or parental order parent of C".

8.—(1) In regulation 19 (notification and evidential requirements relating to the adopter) of the Pay Regulations as they apply to an intended parent or a parental order parent—   7.118
 (a) paragraph (1)(b) shall read as if the words "if C is not placed for adoption by that time as soon as reasonably practicable after the

placement of C " were "if C is not born by that time as soon as reasonably practicable after the birth of C";
  (b) in paragraph (3)—
    (i) sub-paragraph (b) shall read as if the words in that sub-paragraph were "the expected week of birth of C";
    (ii) sub-paragraph (c) shall read as if the words in that sub-paragraph were "C's date of birth";
    (iii) that paragraph shall apply as if there were also specified a parental statutory declaration by A unless the condition in paragraph (2)(a) or (b) of this regulation is satisfied;
  (c) paragraph (4) shall apply as if—
    (i) sub-paragraph (a) were omitted;
    (ii) there were also specified a copy of C's birth certificate or, if one has not been issued, a written declaration signed by A which states that it has not been issued;
    (iii) where A has not provided a parental statutory declaration as a result of the condition in paragraph (2)(a) of this regulation being satisfied, there were specified a parental statutory declaration.
(2) The conditions referred to in paragraph (1)(b)(iii) and (c)(iii) are—
  (a) that A has given the employer who will be liable to pay statutory shared parental pay (adoption) to A a statutory declaration as evidence of A's entitlement to statutory adoption pay in respect of C in accordance with regulation 24 of the Statutory Paternity Pay and Statutory Adoption Pay (General) Regulations 2002;
  (b) that A is a parental order parent and has given the employer a copy of the order in respect of C made under section 54(1) of the Human Fertilisation and Embryology Act 2008.

7.119 **9.**—In regulation 20 (notification and evidential requirements relating to the partner) of the Pay Regulations as they apply to an intended parent or a parental order parent—
  (a) paragraph (1)(b) shall read as if the words "if C is not placed for adoption by that time as soon as reasonably practicable after the placement of C " were "if C is not born by that time as soon as reasonably practicable after the birth of C";
  (b) in paragraph (3)—
    (i) sub-paragraph (b) shall read as if the words in that sub-paragraph were "the expected week of birth of C";
    (ii) sub-paragraph (c) shall read as if the words in that sub-paragraph were "C's date of birth";
    (iii) sub-paragraph (e) shall read as if the written declaration signed by AP was also required to contain the statement that A and AP are the intended parents or the parental order parents of C;
  (c) paragraph (4) shall apply as if—
    (i) sub-paragraph (a) were omitted; and
    (ii) there were specified a copy of C's birth certificate or, if one has not been issued, a written declaration signed by AP which states that it has not been issued.

7.120 **10.**—(1) The Pay Regulations apply to an intended parent or a parental order parent with the modification provided for in paragraph (2) where—
  (a) one or more of the periods specified in a notice under regulation 19, 20 or 21 of the Pay Regulations during which A or, as the case may

be, AP intends to claim statutory shared parental pay (adoption) start in the 8 weeks following the first day of C's expected week of birth;
(b) C's date of birth is before the first day of the expected week of birth; and
(c) A or, as the case may be, AP varies by notice under regulation 21(1) the period or periods referred to in sub-paragraph (a) so that that period or those periods start the same length of time following C's date of birth as that period or those periods would have started after the first day of the expected week of birth.

(2) The modification in this paragraph is that the requirement in regulation 21(1) to give notice at least 8 weeks before the first period specified in the notice is satisfied if such notice is given as soon as reasonably practicable after C's date of birth.

(3) The Pay Regulations apply to an intended parent or a parental order parent with the modifications provided for in paragraph (4) where—
(a) C is born more than 8 weeks before the first day of the expected week of birth;
(b) A or, as the case may be, AP has not given the notice and information under regulations 19 or 20 of the Pay Regulations before the date of C's birth; and
(c) A or, as the case may be, AP specifies in a notice under regulations 19 or 20 a period or periods of statutory shared parental pay (adoption) which start in the 8 weeks following C's date of birth.

(4) The modifications in this paragraph are—
(a) in regulation 19—
  (i) paragraph (1)(a) shall read as if the words in that sub-paragraph were—
"paragraphs (2) and (3) as soon as reasonably practicable after the date of C's birth but in any event before the first period specified by A pursuant to paragraph (2)(d) ";
  (ii) paragraph (1)(b) and (c) shall not apply;
  (iii) paragraph (4) shall not apply.
(b) in regulation 20—
  (i) paragraph (1)(a) shall read as if the words in that sub-paragraph were—
"paragraphs (2) and (3) as soon as reasonably practicable after the date of C's birth but in any event before the first period specified by AP pursuant to paragraph (2)(d)";
  (ii) paragraph (1)(b) and (c) shall not apply;
  (iii) paragraph (4) shall not apply.

11.—In regulation 23 (when statutory shared parental pay (adoption) is not to be paid) of the Pay Regulations as they apply to an intended parent or a parental order parent, paragraph (1) shall read—
"Statutory shared parental pay (adoption) is not payable after the day before the date of C's first birthday (or, where more than one child is born of the same pregnancy, the birthday of the first child so born).".

12.—In regulation 24 (work during period of payment of statutory shared parental pay) of the Pay Regulations as they apply to an intended parent or a parental order parent, paragraph (1)(a)(ii) shall read as if the words "the expected week of placement for adoption" read "the expected week of birth".

Statutory Shared Parental Pay (Parental Order Cases) Regulations 2014

7.123   **13.**—In regulation 29 (conditions relating to employment and earnings of a claimant's partner) of the Pay Regulations as they apply to an intended parent or a parental order parent, in paragraph (5), the definition of "calculation week" shall read—

""calculation week" means the expected week of birth of C;".

7.124   **14.**—Regulation 31 (conditions as to continuity of employment and normal weekly earnings in relation to a claimant) of the Pay Regulations as they apply to an intended parent or a parental order parent, shall read as if—

(a) the words in paragraph (2) were—

"Where C's birth occurs earlier than the 14th week before C's expected week of birth paragraph (1) shall have effect as if, for the conditions set out there, there were substituted conditions that—

(a) the person would have been in employer earner's employment for a continuous period of at least 26 weeks ending with the relevant week had C been born after the relevant week;

(b) the person's normal weekly earnings for the period of eight weeks ending with the week immediately preceding C's actual week of birth are not less than the lower earnings limit in force under section 5(1)(a) of the 1992 Act immediately before the commencement of C's actual week of birth; and

(c) the person continues in employed earner's employment with the employer by reference to whom the condition in sub-paragraph (a) is satisfied for a continuous period beginning with the date of C's birth and ending with the week before the first week falling within the relevant period relating to that person under section 171ZY(2) of the 1992 Act.".

(b) the following paragraphs were added—

"(3) The references in this regulation to the relevant week are to the week immediately preceding the 14th week before C's expected week of birth.

(4) Where more than one child is born as a result of the same pregnancy the date the first child is born is to be used to determine C's actual week of birth or the date of C's birth.".

7.125   **15.**—In regulation 32 (normal weekly earnings of a claimant for statutory shared parental pay) of the Pay Regulations as they apply to an intended parent or a parental order parent, in paragraph (9), sub-paragraph (a), the definition of "the appropriate date" shall read—

""the appropriate date" means the first day of the 14th week before the expected week of the child's birth or the first day in the week in which the child is born, whichever is earlier (but see paragraph (10)).".

7.126   **16.**—In the Schedule (statutory shared parental pay in special circumstances) to the Pay Regulations as they apply to an intended parent or a parental order parent, in paragraph 12—

(a) sub-paragraphs (1) and (2) shall read as if the words "is returned after being placed" (in each place where they occur) read "the parental order does not proceed";

(b) sub-paragraph (4) shall read as if the words in that sub-paragraph were—

"Where more than one child is born of the same pregnancy—

(a) sub-paragraphs (1) and (2) only apply where all the children die or the parental order does not proceed in respect of all the children; and

(b) a reference in this paragraph relating to the death of C (however expressed) is to the death of the last of those children to die.".
(c) sub-paragraph (5) shall read as if the words in that sub-paragraph were—
"For the purpose of this paragraph a parental order does not proceed if—
(a) A and AP have not made an application for an order in respect of C under section 54(1) of the Human Fertilisation and Embryology Act 2008 within the time limit for such an application under section 54(3) of that Act; or
(b) an application made for such an order in respect of C is refused, withdrawn or otherwise terminated and any time limit for an appeal or a new application has expired."

The Statutory Shared Parental Pay (Persons Abroad and Mariners) Regulations 2014

(SI 2014/3134)

The Secretary of State, in exercise of the powers conferred by sections 171ZZ3(1) and 171ZZ4(3)(b) of the Social Security Contributions and Benefits Act 1992, and with the concurrence of the Treasury, makes the following Regulations.

This instrument contains only regulations made by virtue of, or consequential upon, section 119 of the Children and Families Act 2014 and is made before the end of the period of 6 months beginning with the coming into force of that enactment.

ARRANGEMENT OF REGULATIONS

1. Citation and commencement
2. Interpretation
3. Application
4. Restriction on scope
5. Treatment of persons in other EEA states as employees
6. Treatment of certain persons absent from Great Britain as employees
7. Entitlement to statutory shared parental pay where person has worked in an EEA state
8. Time for compliance with Part 12ZC of the Act or regulations made under it
9. Mariners
10. Continental Shelf
11. Adoptions from overseas
12.–14. Statutory Paternity Pay and Statutory Adoption Pay
Sch.1. Establishments and organisations
Sch.2. Adoptions from Overseas

GENERAL NOTE

These Regulations relate to the treatment under Pt 12ZC of the SSCBA 1992 of persons abroad, persons who work as mariners and persons who work on the continental shelf. The effect is that persons who would

Statutory Shared Parental Pay (Persons Abroad and Mariners) Regulations 2014

otherwise not fulfil the qualifying conditions for entitlement to statutory shared parental pay (ShPP) because of the nature of their employment or the fact that they are outside the UK will have an entitlement to such pay.

PART 1

GENERAL

Citation and commencement

7.129   **1.**—These Regulations may be cited as the Statutory Shared Parental Pay (Persons Abroad and Mariners) Regulations 2014 and come into force on 1st December 2014.

PART 2

STATUTORY SHARED PARENTAL PAY

Interpretation

7.130   **2.**—(1) In these Regulations—
"the Act" means the Social Security Contributions and Benefits Act 1992;
"adopter", in relation to a child, means the person with whom a child is, or is expected to be, placed for adoption under the law of the United Kingdom;
"adoption from overseas" means the adoption of a child who enters Great Britain from outside the United Kingdom in connection with or for the purposes of adoption which does not involve the placement of the child for adoption under the law of any part of the United Kingdom;
"EEA" means European Economic Area;
"foreign-going ship" means any ship or vessel which is not a home-trade ship;
"General Regulations" means the Statutory Shared Parental Pay (General) Regulations 2014;
"home-trade ship" includes—
(a) every ship or vessel employed in trading or going within the following limits—
  (i) the United Kingdom (including for this purpose the Republic of Ireland),
  (ii) the Channel Islands,
  (iii) the Isle of Man, and
  (iv) the continent of Europe between the river Elbe and Brest inclusive;
(b) every fishing vessel not proceeding beyond the following limits—
  (i) on the South, Latitude 48°309N,
  (ii) on the West, Longitude 12°W, and
  (iii) on the North, Latitude 61°N;
"mariner" means a person who is or has been in employment under a contract of service either as a master or member of the crew of any

ship or vessel, or in any other capacity on board any ship or vessel where—
(a) the employment in that other capacity is for the purposes of that ship or vessel or her crew or any passengers or cargo or mails carried by the ship or vessel; and
(b) the contract is entered into in the United Kingdom with a view to its performance (in whole or in part) while the ship or vessel is on her voyage,
but does not include a person in so far as their employment is as a serving member of the forces;
"placed for adoption" means—
(a) placed for adoption under the Adoption and Children Act 2002 or the Adoption and Children (Scotland) Act 2007; or
(b) placed in accordance with section 22C of the Children Act 1989 with a local authority foster parent who is also a prospective adopter;
"serving member of the forces" means a person, other than one mentioned in Part 2 of Schedule 1, who, being over the age of 16, is a member of any establishment or organisation specified in Part 1 of that Schedule (being a member who gives full pay service) but does not include any such person while absent on desertion;
"statutory shared parental pay (adoption)" means statutory shared parental pay payable where entitlement to that pay arises under regulation 17 or 18 of the General Regulations;
"statutory shared parental pay (birth)" means statutory shared parental pay payable where entitlement to that pay arises under regulation 4 or 5 of the General Regulations.

(2) For the purposes of these regulations, the expressions "ship" and "ship or vessel" include hovercraft, except in regulation 9(2).

(3) For the purposes of these Regulations—
(a) a person is matched with a child for adoption when an adoption agency decides that that person would be a suitable adoptive parent for the child;
(b) in a case where paragraph (a) applies, a person is notified as having been matched with a child on the date that person receives notification of the agency's decision, under regulation 33(3)(a) of the Adoption Agencies Regulations 2005, regulation 28(3) of the Adoption Agencies (Wales) Regulations 2005 or regulation 8(5) of the Adoption Agencies (Scotland) Regulations 2009;
(c) a person is also matched with a child for adoption when a decision has been made in accordance with regulation 22A of the Care Planning, Placement and Case Review (England) Regulations 2010 and an adoption agency has identified that person with whom the child is to be placed in accordance with regulation 12B of the Adoption Agencies Regulations 2005;
(d) in a case where paragraph (c) applies, a person is notified as having been matched with a child on the date on which that person receives notification in accordance with regulation 12B(2)(a) of the Adoption Agencies Regulations 2005.

(4) The reference to "prospective adopter" in the definition of "placed for adoption" in paragraph (1) means a person who has been approved as suitable to adopt a child and has been notified of that decision in

accordance with regulation 30B(4) of the Adoption Agencies Regulations 2005.

(5) The reference to "adoption agency" in paragraph (3) has the meaning given, in relation to England and Wales, by section 2 of the Adoption and Children Act 2002 and in relation to Scotland, by section 119(1) of the Adoption and Children (Scotland) Act 2007.

Application

7.131 **3.**—These Regulations apply in relation to—
(a) statutory shared parental pay (birth) in respect of children whose expected week of birth begins on or after 5th April 2015;
(b) statutory shared parental pay (adoption) in respect of children placed for adoption on or after 5th April 2015.

DEFINITIONS

"statutory shared parental pay (adoption)"—reg.2(1).
"statutory shared parental pay (birth)"—reg.2(1).

Restriction on scope

7.132 **4.**—A person who would not be treated under regulation 33 (treatment of persons as employees) of the General Regulations as an employee for the purposes of Part 12ZC (statutory shared parental pay) of the Act if that person's employment were in Great Britain shall not be treated as an employee under these Regulations.

DEFINITION

"General Regulations"—reg.2(1).

Treatment of persons in other EEA states as employees

7.133 **5.**—A person who is—
(a) gainfully employed in an EEA state other than the United Kingdom in such circumstances that, if the employment were in Great Britain, the person would be an employee for the purposes of Part 12ZC of the Act, or a person treated as such an employee under regulation 33 of the General Regulations; and
(b) subject to the legislation of the United Kingdom under Council Regulation (EEC) No.1408/71 [[1]as amended from time to time or Regulation (EC) 883/2004 of the European Parliament and of the Council of 29 April 2004 as amended from time to time on the coordination of social security systems],

notwithstanding that person not being employed in Great Britain, shall be treated as an employee for the purposes of Parts 12ZC of the Act.

AMENDMENT

1. Employment Rights (Amendment) (EU Exit) Regulations 2019 (SI 2019/535) reg.2(1) and Sch.1 para.16(c) Sch.1 para.16(c) (March 5, 2019).

(SI 2014/3134 reg. 5)

DEFINITIONS
"EEA"—reg.2(1).
"General Regulations"—reg.2(1).

Treatment of certain persons absent from Great Britain as employees

6.—Subject to regulation 9(2), where a person, while absent from Great Britain for any purpose, is gainfully employed by an employer who is liable to pay secondary Class 1 contributions (within the meaning of section 1(2) of the Act) in respect of that person's employment under section 6 of the Act or regulation 146 of the Social Security Contributions Regulations 2001, that person shall be treated as an employee for the purposes of Part 12ZC of the Act.

7.134

Entitlement to statutory shared parental pay where person has worked in an EEA state

7.—(1) A person who—
(a) is an employee or treated as an employee under regulation 5;
(b) in the week immediately preceding the 14th week before the expected week of the child's birth was in employed earner's employment with an employer in Great Britain; and
(c) had in any week within the period of 26 weeks immediately preceding that week been employed by the same employer in another EEA state,
shall be treated for the purposes of section 171ZU of the Act (entitlement to shared parental pay: birth) as having been employed in employed earner's employment with an employer in those weeks in which the person was so employed in the other EEA state.

(2) A person who—
(a) is an employee or treated as an employee under regulation 5;
(b) in the week in which the adopter is notified of having been matched with the child for the purposes of adoption was in employed earner's employment with an employer in Great Britain; and
(c) had in any week within the period of 26 weeks immediately preceding that week been employed by the same employer in another EEA State,
shall be treated for the purposes of section 171ZV of the Act (entitlement to shared parental pay: adoption) as having been employed in employed earner's employment in those weeks in which the person was so employed in the other EEA State.

7.135

DEFINITIONS
"EEA"—reg.2(1).
"statutory shared parental pay (adoption)"—reg.2(1).
"statutory shared parental pay (birth)"—reg.2(1).

Time for compliance with Part 12ZC of the Act or regulations made under it

8.—Where—
(a) a person is outside the United Kingdom;

7.136

Statutory Shared Parental Pay (Persons Abroad and Mariners) Regulations 2014

    (b) Part 12ZC of the Act or regulations made under it require any act to be done forthwith or on the happening of a certain event or within a specified time; and
    (c) because the person is outside the United Kingdom that person or that person's employer cannot comply with the requirement,
the person or the employer, as the case may be, shall be deemed to have complied with the requirement if the act is performed as soon as reasonably practicable.

Mariners

7.137   **9.**—(1) A mariner engaged in employment on board a home-trade ship with an employer who has a place of business within the United Kingdom shall be treated as an employee for the purposes of Part 12ZC of the Act, notwithstanding that he may not be employed in Great Britain.
    (2) A mariner who is engaged in employment—
    (a) on a foreign-going ship; or
    (b) on a home-trade ship with an employer who does not have a place of business within the United Kingdom,
shall not be treated as an employee for the purposes of Part 12ZC of the Act, notwithstanding that the mariner may have been employed in Great Britain.

DEFINITIONS

    "foreign-going ship"—reg.2(1).
    "home-trade ship"—reg.2(1).
    "mariner"—reg.2(1).

Continental shelf

7.138   **10.**—(1) In this regulation—
    "designated area" means any area which may from time to time be designated by Order in Council under section 1(7) of the Continental Shelf Act 1964 as an area within which the rights of the United Kingdom with respect to the seabed and subsoil and their natural resources may be exercised;
    "prescribed employment" means any employment (whether under a contract of service or not) in a designated area in connection with continental shelf operations, as defined in section 120(2) of the Act.
    (2) A person in prescribed employment shall be treated as an employee for the purposes of Part 12ZC of the Act notwithstanding that that person may not be employed in Great Britain.

Adoptions from overseas

7.139   **11.**—Schedule 2 applies to adoptions from overseas.

(SI 2014/3134 reg.12)

PART 3

STATUTORY PATERNITY PAY AND STATUTORY ADOPTION PAY

12.—The Statutory Paternity Pay and Statutory Adoption Pay (Persons Abroad and Mariners) Regulations 2002 are amended as follows.

13.—(1) Paragraph (2) of regulation 1 is amended as follows
(2) For the definition "adopter" substitute—
""adopter", in relation to a child, means the person with whom a child is, or is expected to be, placed for adoption under the law of the United Kingdom;".
(3) Before the definition of "serving member of the forces" insert—
""placed for adoption" means—
(a) placed for adoption under the Adoption and Children Act 2002 or the Adoption and Children (Scotland) Act 2007; or
(b) placed in accordance with section 22C of the Children Act 1989 with a local authority foster parent who is also a prospective adopter;".

14.—For paragraph (3) of regulation 1 substitute—
"(3) For the purposes of these Regulations—
(a) a person is matched with a child for adoption when an adoption agency decides that that person would be a suitable adoptive parent for the child;
(b) in a case where paragraph (a) applies, a person is notified as having been matched with a child on the date that person receives notification of the agency's decision, under regulation 33(3)(a) of the Adoption Agencies Regulations 2005, regulation 28(3) of the Adoption Agencies (Wales) Regulations 2005 or regulation 8(5) of the Adoption Agencies (Scotland) Regulations 2009;
(c) a person is also matched with a child for adoption when a decision has been made in accordance with regulation 22A of the Care Planning, Placement and Case Review (England) Regulations 2010 and an adoption agency has identified that person with whom the child is to be placed in accordance with regulation 12B of the Adoption Agencies Regulations 2005;
(d) in a case where paragraph (c) applies, a person is notified as having been matched with a child on the date on which that person receives notification in accordance with regulation 12B(2)(a) of the Adoption Agencies Regulations 2005.
(3A) The reference to "prospective adopter" in the definition of "placed for adoption" in paragraph (2) means a person who has been approved as suitable to adopt a child and has been notified of that decision in accordance with regulation 30B(4) of the Adoption Agencies Regulations 2005.
(3B) The reference to "adoption agency" in paragraph (3) has the meaning given, in relation to England and Wales, by section 2 of the Adoption and Children Act 2002 and in relation to Scotland, by section 119(1) of the Adoption and Children (Scotland) Act 2007.".

Statutory Shared Parental Pay (Persons Abroad and Mariners) Regulations 2014

SCHEDULE 1　　　　　　　　　　　　　　　　Regulation 2(1)

Part 1

Establishments and organisations
1. Any of the regular, naval, military or air forces of the Crown.
2. Royal Fleet Reserve.
3. Royal Naval Reserve.
4. Royal Marines Reserve.
5. Army Reserve.
6. Territorial Army.
7. Royal Air Force Reserve.
8. Royal Auxiliary Air Force.
9. The Royal Irish Regiment, to the extent that its members are not members of any force falling within paragraph 1.

Part 2

Establishments And Organisations Of Which Her Majesty's Forces Shall Not Consist

7.143　　10.—Her Majesty's forces shall not be taken to consist of any of the establishments or organisations specified in Part 1 of this Schedule by virtue only of the employment in such establishment or organisation of the following persons –
   (a) any person who is serving as a member of any naval force of Her Majesty's forces and who (not having been an insured person under the National Insurance Act 1965 and not being a contributor under the Social Security Act 1975 or the Social Security Contributions and Benefits Act 1992) locally entered that force at an overseas base;
   (b) any person who is serving as a member of any military force of Her Majesty's forces and who entered that force, or was recruited for that force outside the United Kingdom, and the depot of whose unit is situated outside the United Kingdom;
   (c) any person who is serving as a member of any air force of Her Majesty's forces and who entered that force, or was recruited for that force, outside the United Kingdom, and is liable under the terms of his engagement to serve only in a specified part of the world outside the United Kingdom.

SCHEDULE 2　　　　　　　　　　　　　　　　Regulation 11

Adoptions from Overseas

Interpretation

7.144　　1.—In this Schedule "the Application Regulations" means the Social Security Contributions and Benefits Act 1992 (Application of Parts 12ZA, 12ZB and 12ZC to Adoptions from Overseas) Regulations 2003.

Application to adoptions from overseas

7.145　　2.—(1) The provisions of these Regulations, in so far as they apply to statutory shared parental pay (adoption) apply to adoptions from overseas with the modifications set out in paragraphs 3 to 6 and subject to sub-paragraphs (2) and (3).

(2) Any references in these Regulations to the provisions of Part 12ZC of the Act must be construed as references to the provisions of Part 12ZC as modified by the Application Regulations.

Modifications of the Regulations for the purposes of adoptions from overseas

3.—The Regulations are modified as follows. 7.146

4.—(1) Regulation 2 (interpretation) is modified as follows. 7.147

(2) In paragraph 1—
  (a) for the definition of "adopter" substitute—
""adopter", in relation to C, means the person by whom C has been or is to be adopted; ";
  (b) for the definition of "statutory shared parental pay (adoption)" substitute—
""statutory shared parental pay (adoption)" means statutory shared parental pay payable where entitlement to that pay arises under regulation 17 or 18 of the General Regulations as modified by the Statutory Shared Parental Pay (Adoption from Overseas) Regulations 2014;";
  (c) insert the following definitions in the appropriate places alphabetically—
""enter Great Britain" means enter Great Britain from outside the United Kingdom in connection with or for the purposes of adoption;";
""official notification" means written notification, issued by or on behalf of the relevant central authority, that it is prepared to issue a certificate to the overseas authority concerned with the adoption of the child, or that it has issued a certificate and sent it to that authority, confirming, in either case, that the adopter is eligible to adopt, and has been assessed and approved as being a suitable adoptive parent;";
""relevant central authority" means—
  (a) in the case of an adopter to whom Part 3 of the Adoptions with a Foreign Element Regulations 2005 apply and who is habitually resident in Wales, the Welsh Ministers;
  (b) in the case of an adopter to whom the Adoptions with a Foreign Element (Scotland) Regulations 2009 apply and who is habitually resident in Scotland, the Scottish Ministers; and
  (c) in any other case, the Secretary of State;".

5.—In Regulation 3 (application), for paragraph (1)(b) substitute— 7.148
"(b) statutory shared parental pay (adoption) in respect of children who enter Great Britain on or after 5th April 2015.".

6.—(1) In regulation 7 (entitlement to shared parental pay where person has worked in an EEA State), for paragraph (2) substitute— 7.149
"(2) A person who—
  (a) is an employee or treated as an employee under regulation 5;
  (b) in the week in which the adopter received the official notification was in employed earner's employment with an employer in Great Britain; and
  (c) had in any week within the period of 26 weeks immediately preceding that week been employed by the same employer in another EEA State,
shall be treated for the purposes of section 171ZV of the Act (entitlement to shared parental pay: adoption) as modified by the Application Regulations as having been employed in employed earner's employment in those weeks in which the person was so employed in the other EEA State.".

PART VIII

STATUTORY PARENTAL BEREAVEMENT PAY

The Statutory Parental Bereavement Pay (General) Regulations 2020

(SI 2020/233)

The Secretary of State, in exercise of the powers conferred by sections 171ZZ6(3) and (4), 171ZZ7(2) and (4)(a), (c) to (h), 171ZZ8(2) and (3), 171ZZ9(1) to (5), (8) and (9), 171ZZ11(3), 171ZZ14(3) to (5), (7) and (8), and 175(3) and (4) of the Social Security Contributions and Benefits Act 1992, and section 5(1)(g), (i), (l) and (p) of the Social Security Administration Act 1992 and with the concurrence of the Commissioners for Her Majesty's Revenue and Customs in so far as such concurrence is required, makes the following Regulations.

A draft of these Regulations was laid before Parliament in accordance with section 176(1) of the Social Security Contributions and Benefits Act 1992 and approved by resolution of each House of Parliament.

This instrument contains only regulations made by virtue of, or consequential upon, the Schedule to the Parental Bereavement (Leave and Pay) Act 2018 and is made before the end of the period of 6 months beginning with the coming into force of that enactment.

ARRANGEMENT OF REGULATIONS

PART 1

General

1. Citation and commencement
2. Application
3. Interpretation

PART 2

Entitlement

4. Conditions of entitlement to statutory parental bereavement pay
5. Number of weeks of pay
6. Options in respect of payment of statutory parental bereavement pay
7. Qualifying period
8. Notice and evidence requirements for statutory parental bereavement pay
9. Cases where there is no liability to pay statutory parental bereavement pay
10. Work during period of payment of statutory parental bereavement pay

PART 3

Conditions Of Entitlement Relating To Employment And Earnings

11. Treatment of persons as employees
12. Continuous employment

The Statutory Parental Bereavement Pay (General) Regulations 2020

13. Continuous employment and unfair dismissal
14. Continuous employment and stoppages of work
15. Modification for periods of employment between 25 and 26 weeks
16. Change of employer
17. Reinstatement after service with the armed forces
18. Treatment of two or more employers or two or more contracts of service as one
19. Normal weekly earnings

PART 4

Payment Of Statutory Parental Bereavement Pay

20. Weekly rate of payment
21. Statutory parental bereavement pay and contractual remuneration
22. Avoidance of liability for statutory parental bereavement pay
23. Payment of statutory parental bereavement pay
24. Time when statutory parental bereavement pay is to be paid
25. Liability of the Commissioners to pay statutory parental bereavement pay
26. Liability of the Commissioners to pay statutory parental bereavement pay in cases of legal custody or imprisonment
27. Payments by the Commissioners
28. Persons unable to act
29. Service of notices

PART 1

GENERAL

Citation and commencement

8.2   **1.** These Regulations may be cited as the Statutory Parental Bereavement Pay (General) Regulations 2020 and come into force on the day after the day on which they are made.

Application

8.3   **2.** These Regulations apply in respect of children who die on or after 6th April 2020.

Interpretation

8.4   **3.**—(1) In these Regulations—
"the 1992 Act" means the Social Security Contributions and Benefits Act 1992;
"adopter" means a person who intends to adopt C;
"C" means the child in relation to whom an entitlement to statutory parental bereavement pay arises;

"the Commissioners" means the Commissioners for Her Majesty's Revenue and Customs;

"intended parent" means a person who—
(a) has applied, or intended to apply during the period of 6 months beginning with the day of C's birth—
  (i) with another person for an order under section 54 (parental orders: two applicants) of the Human Fertilisation and Embryology Act 2008 in respect of C, or
  (ii) as the sole applicant for an order under section 54A (parental orders: one applicant) of that Act in respect of C, and
(b) expected the court to make such an order on that application in respect of C;

"official notification" means written notification, issued by or on behalf of the relevant domestic authority, that it is prepared to issue a certificate to the overseas authority concerned with the adoption of C, or has issued a certificate and sent it to that authority, confirming, in either case, that the adopter is eligible to adopt and has been assessed and approved as being a suitable adoptive parent;

"placed for adoption" means placed—
(a) for adoption under the Adoption and Children Act 2002 or the Adoption and Children (Scotland) Act 2007,
(b) in accordance with section 22C of the Children Act 1989 ways in which looked after children are to be accommodated and maintained) with a local authority foster parent who is also a prospective adopter, following consideration in accordance with subsection (9B)(c) of that section, or
(c) in accordance with section 81 of the Social Services and Well-being (Wales) Act 2014 with a prospective adopter, following consideration in accordance with subsection (10) of that section;

"prospective adopter" means a person who has been approved as suitable to adopt a child and has been notified of that decision in accordance with regulation 30B(4) of the Adoption Agencies Regulations 2005 or regulation 28(3) of the Adoption Agencies (Wales) Regulations 2005;

"relevant domestic authority" means—
(a) in the case of an adopter to whom Part 3 of the Adoptions with a Foreign Element Regulations 2005 apply and who is habitually resident in Wales, the National Assembly for Wales,
(b) in the case of an adopter to whom the Adoptions with a Foreign Element (Scotland) Regulations 2009 apply and who is habitually resident in Scotland, the Scottish Ministers, and
(c) in any other case, the Secretary of State;

"statutory parental bereavement pay" means statutory parental bereavement pay payable in accordance with Part 12ZD of the 1992 Act;

"week", except in Part 3, means a period of seven days;

"week of C's death" means the week, beginning with a Sunday, in which C dies.

(2) In these Regulations—
(a) references to a child include a child stillborn after twenty-four weeks of pregnancy, and
(b) references to the death of a child are to be read, in relation to a stillborn child, as references to the birth of the child.

The Statutory Parental Bereavement Pay (General) Regulations 2020

PART 2

ENTITLEMENT

Conditions of entitlement to statutory parental bereavement pay

8.5   **4.**—(1) The conditions prescribed under section 171ZZ6(3) of the 1992 Act (conditions as to relationship with a child who has died) are that, at the date of C's death, the person is—
(a) C's parent;
(b) C's natural parent and named in an order made pursuant to section 51A(2)(a) of the Adoption and Children Act 2002 or section 11(3)(aa) of the Children (Scotland) Act 1995, provided that such an order has not subsequently been revoked or discharged;
(c) a person with whom C has been placed for adoption, for so long as that placement has not been disrupted as mentioned in paragraph (2);
(d) an adopter—
  (i) with whom C was living, following C's entry into Great Britain from outside the United Kingdom in connection with or for the purposes of adoption which does not involve the placement of C for adoption under the law of any part of the United Kingdom, and
  (ii) who has received official notification in respect of C;
(e) an intended parent of C;
(f) C's parent in fact; or
(g) the partner of P.
(2) For the purposes of paragraph (1)(c), a placement has been disrupted—
(a) when C has been returned under sections 31 to 35 of the Adoption and Children Act 2002,
(b) in Scotland, when C has been returned to the adoption agency, adoption society or nominated person in accordance with section 25(6) of the Adoption and Children (Scotland) Act 2007, or
(c) when C's placement—
  (i) with a local authority foster parent who is also a prospective adopter in accordance with section 22C of the Children Act 1989 following consideration in accordance with subsection (9B)(c) of that section, or
  (ii) with a prospective adopter in accordance with section 81 of the Social Services and Well-being (Wales) Act 2014,
has been terminated.
(3) Subject to paragraph (5), a person is C's parent in fact if that person, for a continuous period of at least four weeks ending with the day on which C dies—
(a) lived with C in the person's own home, and
(b) had day to day responsibility for C's care.
(4) For the purposes of the continuous period mentioned in paragraph (3), no account is to be taken of any absences of a temporary or intermittent nature.
(5) A person is not to be regarded as C's parent in fact if—

(a) C is in the care of that person in premises in which any parent of C's, or any person who is not a parent of C's but who has responsibility for C, is living, or

(b) that person was or is entitled to receive remuneration, whether by way of wages or otherwise, in respect of the care of C.

(6) A person has responsibility for C, for the purposes of paragraph (5)(a), if the person—

(a) has parental responsibility, within the meaning of section 3 of the Children Act 1989, or

(b) in Scotland, has parental responsibilities or parental rights, within the meaning of sections 1 and 2 of the Children (Scotland) Act 1995.

(7) For the purposes of paragraph (5)(b), the following payments are not to be regarded as remuneration—

(a) any fee or allowance paid by a local authority to a foster parent;

(b) payments wholly or mainly intended to reimburse the person for expenses which arise from, or are expected to arise from, the person's care of C;

(c) amounts received pursuant to the terms of a will, trust or similar instrument which makes provision in respect of C's care.

(8) In this regulation—

(a) "P" means any person who satisfies one of the conditions in paragraphs (1)(a) to (f);

(b) "partner" means a person (whether of a different sex or the same sex) who lives with C and P in an enduring family relationship but is not a relative of P of a kind specified in sub-paragraph (c);

(c) the relatives of P referred to in sub-paragraph (b) are P's parent, grandparent, sister, brother, aunt or uncle;

(d) references to relationships in sub-paragraph (c)—

(i) are to relationships of the full blood or half blood or, in the case of an adopted person, such of those relationships as would exist but for the adoption, and

(ii) include the relationship of a child with his adoptive, or former adoptive, parents,

but do not include any other adoptive relationships.

DEFINITIONS

"C"—reg.3(1).
"intended parent"—reg.3(1)
"P"—para.(8)(a).
"official notification"—reg.3(1).
"partner"—para.(8)(b).
"placed for adoption"—reg.3(1).
"relative"—para.(8)(c).
"relationship"—para.(8)(d).

Number of weeks of pay

5. The number of weeks in respect of which a person is entitled to payments of statutory parental bereavement pay is two weeks.

DEFINITIONS

"statutory parental bereavement pay"—reg.3(1).
"week"—reg.3(1).

The Statutory Parental Bereavement Pay (General) Regulations 2020

Options in respect of payment of statutory parental bereavement pay

8.7   6. A person may choose for statutory parental bereavement pay to be paid in respect of—
   (a) a single period of either one week or two weeks, or
   (b) discontinuous periods of a week each.

DEFINITIONS

"statutory parental bereavement pay"—reg.3(1).
"week"—reg.3(1).

Qualifying period

8.8   7. The qualifying period for the purposes of section 171ZZ9(5) of the 1992 Act (period within which statutory parental bereavement pay is payable) is a period of 56 weeks beginning with the date of C's death.

DEFINITIONS

"statutory parental bereavement pay"—reg.3(1).
"week"—reg.3(1).

Notice and evidence requirements for statutory parental bereavement pay

8.9   8.—(1) The notice provided for in section 171ZZ7(1) of the 1992 Act (notice to be given stating the week or weeks in respect of which payments are to be made) must be given to whoever will be liable to pay statutory parental bereavement pay—
   (a) before the end of the period of 28 days beginning with the first day of the period in respect of which payment of statutory parental bereavement pay is to be made, or
   (b) in a case where it is not reasonably practicable for the person to give the notice in accordance with sub-paragraph (a), as soon as reasonably practicable.

(2)   A person must provide evidence of entitlement to statutory parental bereavement pay by providing in writing to whoever will be liable to pay statutory parental bereavement pay—
   (a) the information specified in paragraph (3), and
   (b) a declaration that the person meets one of the conditions prescribed in regulation 4(1).

(3) The information referred to in paragraph (2)(a) is as follows—
   (a) the name of the person claiming the statutory parental bereavement pay, and
   (b) the date of C's death.

(4) The information referred to in paragraph (3) must be provided at the same time as a notice is given under paragraph (1).

(5) The declaration referred to in paragraph (2)(b) must be provided at the same time as a notice is first given under paragraph (1) in respect of C's death.

(6) Where notice under paragraph (1) is given prior to the start of the week or weeks specified in that notice, the person may withdraw that notice by giving notice of withdrawal in writing to the person who will be liable

to pay statutory parental bereavement pay in the manner specified in paragraphs (7) and (8).

(7) Where the notice under paragraph (1) states two weeks in respect of which statutory parental bereavement pay is to be paid, notice of withdrawal may be given in relation to either one or both of those weeks, regardless of whether those weeks are consecutive or non-consecutive.

(8) Where the notice of withdrawal relates to a week which begins—
(a) in Period A, it must be given no later than on the first day of that week, and
(b) in Period B, it must be given no later than one week before the start of that week.

(9) In this regulation—
"Period A" means the period of 56 days beginning with the date of C's death;
"Period B" means the period beginning the day after the end of Period A and ending with the end of the period specified in regulation 7.

DEFINITIONS

"C"—reg.3(1).
"Period A"—para.(9).
"Period B"—para.(9).
"statutory parental bereavement pay"—reg.3(1).
"week"—reg.3(1).

Cases where there is no liability to pay statutory parental bereavement pay

9.—(1) There is no liability to pay statutory parental bereavement pay to a person in respect of any week—
(a) during any part of which the person who is entitled to that pay is entitled to statutory sick pay under Part 11 of the 1992 Act,
(b) following that in which the person entitled to it has died, or
(c) during any part of which the person who is entitled to that pay is detained in legal custody (unless one of the circumstances in paragraph (2) applies) or sentenced to a term of imprisonment (except where the sentence is suspended).

(2) There is liability to pay statutory parental bereavement pay in respect of any week during any part of which the person who is entitled to that pay is detained in legal custody where that person—
(a) is released subsequently without charge,
(b) is subsequently found not guilty of any offence and is released, or
(c) is convicted of an offence but does not receive a custodial sentence.

DEFINITIONS

"statutory parental bereavement pay"—reg.3(1).
"week"—reg.3(1).

Work during period of payment of statutory parental bereavement pay

10.—(1) Despite section 171ZZ9(8) of the 1992 Act (statutory parental bereavement pay not payable to a person in respect of a week during any part of which the person works for any employer who is not liable to pay

the person statutory parental bereavement pay), statutory parental bereavement pay is payable to a person in respect of a statutory pay week during any part of which the person works only for an employer—
  (a) who is not liable to pay the person statutory parental bereavement pay, and
  (b) for whom the person has worked in the week immediately preceding the week of C's death.

(2) Where a person works for an employer falling within paragraph (1)(a) but not paragraph (1)(b) for any part of a period which is specified by that person in a notice under regulation 8(1), the person must notify the employer liable to pay statutory parental bereavement pay of the fact of that work within seven days of the first day during which the person does such work.

(3) The notification mentioned in paragraph (2) must be in writing, if the employer who has been liable to pay statutory parental bereavement pay so requests.

DEFINITIONS

"statutory parental bereavement pay"—reg.3(1).
"week"—reg.3(1).

PART 3

CONDITIONS OF ENTITLEMENT RELATING TO EMPLOYMENT AND EARNINGS

Treatment of persons as employees

8.12 11.—(1) A person is treated as an employee for the purposes of Part 12ZD of the 1992 Act (even though not falling within the definition of 'employee' in section 171ZZ14(2) of that Act) where, and in so far as, that person is treated as an employed earner by virtue of the Social Security (Categorisation of Earners) Regulations 1978 (but see paragraph (3)).

(2) A person shall not be treated as an employee for the purposes of Part 12ZD of the 1992 Act (even though falling within the definition of 'employee' in section 171ZZ14(2) of that Act) where, and in so far as, that person is not treated as an employed earner by virtue of those Regulations (but see paragraph (3)).

(3) Paragraphs (1) and (2) shall have effect in relation to a person who—
  (a) is under the age of 16, and
  (b) would, or as the case may be, would not have been treated as an employed earner by virtue of those Regulations had they been over that age,
as they have effect in relation to a person who is, or as the case may be, is not treated as an employed earner by virtue of those Regulations.

(4) A person is treated as an employee for the purposes of Part 12ZD of the 1992 Act (even though not falling within the definition of 'employee' in section 171ZZ14(2) of that Act) where that person is in employed earner's employment under a contract of apprenticeship.

(5) A person is not to be treated as an employee for the purposes of Part 12ZD of the 1992 Act (even though falling within the definition of 'employee' in section 171ZZ14(2) of that Act) where that person is in employed earner's employment but that person's employer—
  (a) does not fulfil the conditions prescribed in regulation 145(1) (conditions as to residence or presence) of the Social Security (Contributions) Regulations 2001 in so far as that provision relates to residence or presence in Great Britain, or
  (b) is a person who, by reason of any international treaty to which the United Kingdom is a party or of any international convention binding the United Kingdom—
    (i) is exempt from the provisions of the 1992 Act, or
    (ii) is a person against whom the provisions of the 1992 Act are not enforceable.

Continuous employment

12.—(1) A week is to be treated for the purposes of section 171ZZ6 of the 1992 Act as part of a period of continuous employment with the employer even though no contract of service exists with that employer in respect of that week in the circumstances mentioned in paragraph (2) and subject to paragraphs (3) and (4).

(2) The circumstances mentioned in paragraph (1) are that in any week the person is, for the whole or part of the week—
  (a) incapable of work in consequence of sickness or injury,
  (b) absent from work on account of a temporary cessation of work, or
  (c) absent from work in circumstances such that, by arrangement or custom, that person is regarded as continuing in the employment of their employer for all or any purposes,
and returns to work for their employer after the incapacity for or absence from work.

(3) Incapacity for work which lasts for more than 26 consecutive weeks shall not count for the purposes of paragraph (2)(a).

(4) Where a person—
  (a) is an employee in employed earner's employment in which the custom is for the employer—
    (i) to offer work for a fixed period of not more than 26 consecutive weeks,
    (ii) to offer work for such period on two or more occasions in a year for periods which do not overlap, and
    (iii) to offer the work available to those persons who had worked for the employer during the last or a recent such period, but
  (b) is absent from work because of incapacity arising from some specific disease or bodily or mental disablement,
then in that case paragraph (2) shall apply as if the words "and returns to work for their employer after the incapacity for or absence from work" were omitted.

Continuous employment and unfair dismissal

13.—(1) Where in consequence of specified action in relation to a person's dismissal, the person is reinstated or re-engaged by their employer or by a successor or associated employer of that employer then—

(a) the continuity of their employment shall be preserved for the purposes of section 171ZZ6 of the 1992 Act for the period beginning with the effective date of termination and ending with the date of reinstatement or re-engagement, and

(b) any week which falls within the interval beginning with the effective date of termination and ending with the date of reinstatement or re-engagement, as the case may be, shall count in the computation of their period of continuous employment.

(2) In this regulation—

(a) "associated employer" shall be construed in accordance with section 231 of the Employment Rights Act 1996;

(b) "dismissal procedures agreement" and "successor" have the same meanings as in section 235 of the Employment Rights Act 1996;

(c) "specified action in relation to a person's dismissal" means action which consists of—

   (i) the presentation by that person of a complaint under section 111(1) (complaints to employment tribunal) of the Employment Rights Act 1996,

   (ii) that person making a claim in accordance with a dismissal procedures agreement designated by an order under section 110 of that Act, or

   (iii) any action taken by a conciliation officer under sections 18A to 18C (conciliation) of the Employment Tribunals Act 1996.

DEFINITIONS

"associated employer"—para.(2)(a).
"dismissal procedures agreement"—para.(2)(b).
"specified action in relation to a person's dismissal"—para.(2)(c).
"successor"—para.(2)(b).

Continuous employment and stoppages of work

14.—(1) Where a person does not work for any week or part of a week because there is a stoppage of work at that person's place of employment due to a trade dispute within the meaning of section 35(1) of the Jobseekers Act 1995 then—

(a) that person's continuity of employment shall be treated as continuing throughout the stoppage (but see paragraph (2)) for the purposes of section 171ZZ6 of the 1992 Act, and

(b) no such week shall count in the computation of their period of continuous employment (but see paragraph (3)).

(2) Where during the stoppage of work a person is dismissed from their employment, that person's continuity of employment shall not be treated under paragraph (1) as continuing beyond the commencement of the day that person stopped work (but see paragraph (3)).

(3) Paragraph (1)(b) and paragraph (2) do not apply to a person who proves that at no time did they have a direct interest in the trade dispute in question.

Modification for periods of employment between 25 and 26 weeks

15.—(1) This regulation applies where a person has been in employed earner's employment with the same employer in each of 26 consecutive weeks (but no more than 26 weeks), ending with the week immediately preceding the week of C's death.

(2) For the purpose of determining whether that person's employment amounts to a continuous period of at least 26 weeks (see section 171ZZ6 of the 1992 Act), the first of those 26 weeks is a period commencing on the first day of the person's employment with the employer ("the start date") and ending at midnight on—
   (a) the first Saturday after the start date, or
   (b) where the start date is a Saturday, that day.

DEFINITION

"C"—reg.3(1).

Change of employer

16.—(1) Where a person's employer changes, a person's employment is to be treated for the purposes of section 171ZZ6 of the 1992 Act as continuous employment with the second employer in the following circumstances— 8.17
   (a) the employer's trade or business or an undertaking (whether or not it is an undertaking established by or under an Act of Parliament) is transferred from one person to another;
   (b) a contract of employment between any body corporate and the person is modified by or under an Act of Parliament, whether public or local and whenever passed and some other body corporate is substituted as that person's employer;
   (c) on the death of the employer, the person is taken into the employment of the personal representatives or trustees of the deceased;
   (d) the person is employed by partners, personal representatives or trustees and there is a change in the partners, or as the case may be, personal representatives or trustees;
   (e) the person is taken into the employment of an employer who is, at the time the person entered into the employer's employment, an associated employer of the person's previous employer; or
   (f) on the termination of the person's employment with an employer that person is taken into the employment of another employer and those employers are governors of a school maintained by a local education authority.

(2) In paragraph (1)(e) "associated employer" must be construed in accordance with section 231 of the Employment Rights Act 1996.

DEFINITION

"associated employer"—para.(2).

Reinstatement after service with the armed forces

17. Where a person— 8.18
   (a) is entitled to apply to their employer under the Reserve Forces (Safeguard of Employment) Act 1985, and
   (b) enters the employment of that employer within the six month period mentioned in section 1(4)(b) (obligation to reinstate) of that Act,

that person's previous period of employment with that employer (or if there was more than one such period, the last of those periods) and the period of employment beginning in that six month period shall be treated as continuous for the purposes of section 171ZZ6 of the 1992 Act.

Treatment of two or more employers or two or more contracts of service as one

8.19   **18.**—(1) In a case where the earnings paid to a person in respect of two or more employments are aggregated and treated as a single payment of earnings under regulation 15(1) (aggregation of earnings paid in respect of different employed earner's employments by different persons) of the Social Security (Contributions) Regulations 2001, the employers of that person in respect of those employments shall be treated as one for the purposes of Part 12ZD of the 1992 Act (and these Regulations).

(2) Where two or more employers are treated as one under the provisions of paragraph (1), liability for statutory parental bereavement pay shall be apportioned between them in such proportions as they may agree or, in default of agreement, in the proportions which the person's normal weekly earnings from each employment bear to the amount of the aggregated normal weekly earnings over the relevant period as defined in regulation 19(4).

(3) Where two or more contracts of service exist concurrently between one employer and one employee, they shall be treated as one for the purposes of Part 12ZD of the 1992 Act (and these Regulations) except where, by virtue of regulation 14 (aggregation of earnings paid in respect of separate employed earner's employments under the same employer) of the Social Security (Contributions) Regulations 2001, the earnings from those contracts of service are not aggregated for the purpose of earnings-related contributions.

DEFINITION

"statutory parental bereavement pay"—reg.3(1).

Normal weekly earnings

8.20   **19.**—(1) For the purposes of section 171ZZ14(6) (which defines normal weekly earnings for the purposes of Part 12ZD of the 1992 Act) "earnings" and "relevant period" have the meanings given in this regulation.

(2) The expression "earnings" refers to gross earnings and includes any remuneration or profit derived from a person's employment except any amount which is—
   (a) excluded from the computation of a person's earnings under regulation 25 (payments to be disregarded) of, and Schedule 3 to, the Social Security (Contributions) Regulations 2001 or regulation 27 (payments to directors to be disregarded) of those Regulations (or would have been so excluded had they not been made under the age of 16), or
   (b) a chargeable emolument under section 10A (class 1B contributions) of the 1992 Act except where, in consequence of such a chargeable emolument being excluded from earnings, a person would not be entitled to statutory parental bereavement pay (or where such a payment or amount would have been so excluded and in consequence the person would not have been entitled to statutory parental bereavement pay had they not been aged under the age of 16).

(SI 2020/233 reg.19)

(3) The expression "earnings" includes—
(a) any amount retrospectively treated as earnings by regulations made by virtue of section 4B(2) of the 1992 Act;
(b) any sum payable in respect of arrears of pay in pursuance of an order for reinstatement or re-engagement under the Employment Rights Act 1996;
(c) any sum payable by way of pay in pursuance of an order made under the Employment Rights Act 1996 for the continuation of a contract of employment;
(d) any sum payable by way of remuneration in pursuance of a protective award under section 189 of the Trade Union and Labour Relations (Consolidation) Act 1992;
(e) any sum payable by way of statutory sick pay, including sums payable in accordance with regulations made under section 151(6) of the 1992 Act;
(f) any sum payable by way of statutory maternity pay;
(g) any sum payable by way of statutory paternity pay;
(h) any sum payable by way of statutory shared parental pay;
(i) any sum payable by way of statutory adoption pay;
(j) any sum payable by way of statutory parental bereavement pay.

(4) The relevant period is the period—
(a) ending on the last normal pay day to fall before the appropriate date, and
(b) beginning with the day following the last normal pay day to fall at least eight weeks earlier than the normal pay day mentioned in sub-paragraph (a).

(5) In a case where a person has no identifiable normal pay day, paragraph (4) shall have effect as if the words "day of payment" were substituted for the words "normal pay day" in each place where they occur.

(6) In a case where a person has normal pay days at intervals of or approximating to one or more calendar months (including intervals of or approximating to a year) that person's normal weekly earnings shall be calculated by dividing their earnings in the relevant period by the number of calendar months in that period (or, if it is not a whole number, the nearest whole number), multiplying the result by 12 and dividing by 52.

(7) In a case to which paragraph (6) does not apply and the relevant period is not an exact number of weeks, the person's normal weekly earnings shall be calculated by dividing their earnings in the relevant period by the number of days in the relevant period and multiplying the result by seven.

(8) In any case where a person receives a back-dated pay increase which includes a sum in respect of a relevant period, normal weekly earnings shall be calculated as if such a sum was paid in that relevant period even though received after that period.

[1(8A) Paragraph (9) applies where for all or part of the relevant period—
(a) a woman is a furloughed employee;
(b) the woman's employer has claimed and is in receipt of financial support in respect of the woman's earnings under the Coronavirus Job Retention Scheme; and
(c) the woman's earnings are lower than they would otherwise have been as a result of that woman being a furloughed employee.

(8B) Where this paragraph applies, the woman's normal weekly earnings are to be calculated as if, during the parts of the relevant period when the woman was a furloughed employee, she was paid the amount which she would have derived from her employment had she not been a furloughed employee.

(8C) For the purposes of paragraphs (8) and (9)—

"Coronavirus Job Retention Scheme" ("the Scheme") means any scheme to provide for payments to be made to employers on a claim made in respect of them incurring costs of employment in respect of furloughed employees arising from the health, social and economic emergency in the United Kingdom resulting from coronavirus and coronavirus disease and contained in such Directions as may be issued from time to time pursuant to section 76 of the Coronavirus Act 2020;

"coronavirus" and "coronavirus disease" have the meanings given in section 1 of that Act;

"furloughed employee" has the meaning given for the purposes of the Scheme.]

(9) In paragraphs (4) to (6)—
(a) "the appropriate date" means the first day of the week in which C dies;
(b) "day of payment" means a day on which a person is paid;
(c) "normal pay day" means a day on which the terms of a person's contract of service require the person to be paid, or the practice in that person's employment is for that person to be paid if any payment is due to them.

AMENDMENT

1. Maternity Allowance, Statutory Maternity Pay, Statutory Paternity Pay, Statutory Adoption Pay, Statutory Shared Parental Pay and Statutory Parental Bereavement Pay (Normal Weekly Earnings etc.) (Coronavirus) (Amendment) Regulations 2020 (SI 2020/450) reg.6 (April 25, 2020).

DEFINITIONS

"the appropriate date"—para.(9)(a).
"day of payment"—para.(9)(b).
"normal pay day"—para.(9)(c).
"statutory parental bereavement pay"—reg.3(1).

PART 4

PAYMENT OF STATUTORY PARENTAL BEREAVEMENT PAY

Weekly rate of payment

20.—(1) The weekly rate of payment of statutory parental bereavement pay is the smaller of the following two amounts—
(a) [¹ £184.03];
(b) 90% of the normal weekly earnings of the person claiming statutory parental bereavement pay determined in accordance with section 171ZZ14(6) of the 1992 Act and regulation 19.

(2) Where the amount of any payment of statutory parental bereavement pay is calculated by reference to—
(a) the weekly rate specified in paragraph (1)(b), or
(b) the daily rate of one-seventh of the weekly rate specified in paragraph (1)(a) or (b),
and that amount includes a fraction of a penny, the payment shall be rounded up to the nearest whole number of pence.

AMENDMENT

1. Social Security Benefits Up-rating Order 2024 (SI 2024/242) art.10(3) (April 7, 2024).

DEFINITION

"statutory parental bereavement pay"—reg.3(1).

Statutory parental bereavement pay and contractual remuneration

21. For the purposes of section 171ZZ11(1) and (2) of the 1992 Act (payment of contractual remuneration to go towards discharging liability to pay statutory parental bereavement pay and payment of statutory parental bereavement pay to go towards discharging liability to pay contractual remuneration), the payments which are to be treated as contractual remuneration are sums payable under a contract of service—
(a) by way of remuneration,
(b) for incapacity for work due to sickness or injury, or
(c) by reason of the birth, adoption, care or death of a child.

DEFINITION

"statutory parental bereavement pay"—reg.3(1).

Avoidance of liability for statutory parental bereavement pay

22.—(1) A former employer shall be liable to make payments of statutory parental bereavement pay to a former employee in any case where the employee had been employed for a continuous period of at least 8 weeks and the employee's contract of service was brought to an end by the former employer solely, or mainly, for the purpose of avoiding liability for statutory parental bereavement pay.
(2) In a case falling within paragraph (1)—
(a) the employee shall be treated as if the employee had been employed for a continuous period ending with C's death, and
(b) regulation 19(4) (relevant period for the purpose of the calculation of normal weekly earnings) shall apply as if it read—
"(4) The relevant period is the period—
(a) ending on the last day of payment under the former contract of employment, and
(b) beginning with the day following the day of payment under that contract to fall at least 8 weeks earlier than the day of payment mentioned in sub-paragraph (a)."

DEFINITIONS

"C"—reg.3(1).

The Statutory Parental Bereavement Pay (General) Regulations 2020

"statutory parental bereavement pay"—reg.3(1).
"week"—reg.3(1).

Payment of statutory parental bereavement pay

8.24   23. Payments of statutory parental bereavement pay may be made in like manner to payments of remuneration but shall not include payment in kind or by way of the provision of board and lodgings.

DEFINITION

"statutory parental bereavement pay"—reg.3(1).

Time when statutory parental bereavement pay is to be paid

8.25   24.—(1) In any case where—
   (a) a decision has been made by an officer of Revenue and Customs under section 8(1) (decisions by officers) of the Social Security Contributions (Transfer of Functions, etc) Act 1999 as a result of which a person is entitled to an amount of statutory parental bereavement pay, and
   (b) the time for bringing an appeal against the decision has expired and either—
      (i) no such appeal has been brought,
      (ii) leave to appeal against the decision is required and has been refused, or
      (iii) such appeal has been brought and has been finally disposed of,
that amount of statutory parental bereavement pay shall be paid within the time specified in paragraph (2).
   (2) The employer or former employer shall pay the amount not later than the first pay day after the following days (but see paragraphs (3) and (4))—
   (a) where an appeal has been brought, the day on which the employer or former employer receives notification that it has been finally disposed of,
   (b) where leave to appeal has been refused, and there remains no further opportunity to apply for leave, the day on which the employer or former employer receives notification of the refusal, and
   (c) in any other case, the day on which the time for bringing an appeal expires.
   (3) Where it is impracticable, in view of the employer's or former employer's methods of accounting for and paying remuneration, for the requirement of payment referred to in paragraph (2) to be met by the pay day referred to in that paragraph, it shall be met not later than the next following pay day (but see paragraph (4)).
   (4) Where the employer or former employer would not have remunerated the employee for their work in the week in respect of which statutory parental bereavement pay is payable as early as the pay day specified in paragraph (2) or (if it applies) paragraph (3), the requirement of payment shall be met on the first day on which the employee would have been remunerated for work in that week.
   (5) In this regulation "pay day" means a day on which it has been agreed, or it is the normal practice between an employer or former employer and a person who is or was an employee of theirs, that payments by way of

remuneration are to be made, or, where there is no such agreement or normal practice, the last day of a calendar month.

DEFINITIONS

"pay day"—para.(5).
"statutory parental bereavement pay"—reg.3(1).

Liability of the Commissioners to pay statutory parental bereavement pay

25.—(1) Despite section 171ZZ8(1) of the 1992 Act (liability to make payments of statutory parental bereavement pay is liability of the employer), where the conditions in regulation 24(1)(a) and (b) are satisfied, liability to make payments of statutory parental bereavement pay to a person is to be the liability of the Commissioners and not the employer for—
  (a) any week in respect of which the employer was liable to pay statutory parental bereavement pay to that person but did not do so, and
  (b) for any subsequent week that person is entitled to payments of statutory parental bereavement pay.

(2) Despite section 171ZZ8(1) of the 1992 Act, liability to make payments of statutory parental bereavement pay to a person is to be a liability of the Commissioners and not the employer as from the week in which the employer first becomes insolvent (see paragraphs (3) and (4)) until the last week that person is entitled to payment of statutory parental bereavement pay.

(3) For the purposes of paragraph (2) an employer shall be taken to be insolvent if, and only if, in England and Wales—
  (a) the employer has been adjudged bankrupt or has made a composition or arrangement with its creditors,
  (b) the employer has died and the employer's estate falls to be administered in accordance with an order made under section 421 of the Insolvency Act 1986, or
  (c) where an employer is a company or a limited liability partnership—
    (i) a winding-up order is made or a resolution for a voluntary winding-up is passed (or, in the case of a limited liability partnership, a determination for voluntary winding-up has been made) with respect to it,
    (ii) it enters administration,
    (iii) a receiver or manager of its undertaking is duly appointed,
    (iv) possession is taken, by or on behalf of the holders of any debentures secured by a floating charge, of any property of the company or limited liability partnership comprised in or subject to the charge, or
    (v) a voluntary arrangement proposed for the purposes of Part 1 of the Insolvency Act 1986 is approved under that Part.

(4) For the purposes of paragraph (2) an employer shall be taken to be insolvent if, and only if, in Scotland—
  (a) an award of sequestration is made on the employer's estate,
  (b) the employer executes a trust deed for its creditors,
  (c) the employer enters into a composition contract,
  (d) the employer has died and a judicial factor appointed under section 11A of the Judicial Factors (Scotland) Act 1889 is required by that

section to divide the employer's insolvent estate among the employer's creditors, or
(e) where the employer is a company or a limited liability partnership—
  (i) a winding-up order is made or a resolution for voluntary winding-up is passed (or in the case of a limited liability partnership, a determination for a voluntary winding-up is made) with respect to it,
  (ii) it enters administration,
  (iii) a receiver of its undertaking is duly appointed, or
  (iv) a voluntary arrangement proposed for the purposes of Part I of the Insolvency Act 1986 is approved under that Part.

DEFINITIONS

"the Commissioners"—reg.3(1).
"statutory parental bereavement pay"—reg.3(1).
"week"—reg.3(1).

Liability of the Commissioners to pay statutory parental bereavement pay in cases of legal custody or imprisonment

26. Where there is liability to pay statutory parental bereavement pay—
(a) in respect of a period which is subsequent to the period mentioned in paragraph (1)(c) of regulation 9 (cases where there is no liability to pay statutory parental bereavement pay), or
(b) during a period of detention in legal custody by virtue of paragraph (2) of that regulation,
that liability, despite section 171ZZ8(1) of the 1992 Act, shall be that of the Commissioners and not the employer.

DEFINITIONS

"the Commissioners"—reg.3(1).
"statutory parental bereavement pay"—reg.3(1).

Payments by the Commissioners

27. Where the Commissioners become liable in accordance with regulation 25 (liability of the Commissioners to pay statutory parental bereavement pay) or regulation 26 (liability of the Commissioners to pay statutory parental bereavement pay in case of legal custody or imprisonment) then payment is to be made as soon as reasonably practicable after they become so liable, by means of an instrument of payment or by such other means as appear to the Commissioners to be appropriate in the circumstances of any particular case.

DEFINITIONS

"the Commissioners"—reg.3(1).
"statutory parental bereavement pay"—reg.3(1).

Persons unable to act

28.—(1) This regulation applies where—
(a) statutory parental bereavement pay is payable to a person or it is alleged that statutory parental bereavement pay is payable to a person,

(b) that person is unable for the time being to act,
(c) no deputy has been appointed by the Court of Protection with power to receive statutory parental bereavement pay on their behalf or, in Scotland, their estate is not being administered by a guardian acting or appointed under the Adults with Incapacity (Scotland) Act 2000, and
(d) a written application has been made to the Commissioners by a person, who, if a natural person, is over the age of 18, to exercise any right, or deal with any sums payable, under Part 12ZD of the 1992 Act on behalf of the person unable to act.

(2) Where this regulation applies the Commissioners may appoint the person referred to in paragraph (1)(d)—
(a) to exercise, on behalf of the person unable to act, any right to which the person unable to act may be entitled under Part 12ZD of the 1992 Act, and
(b) to deal, on behalf of the person unable to act, with any sums payable to the person unable to act under Part 12ZD of the 1992 Act.

(3) Where the Commissioners have made an appointment under paragraph (2)—
(a) they may at any time revoke it,
(b) the person appointed may resign their office after having given one month's notice in writing to the Commissioners of that person's intention to do so, and
(c) the appointment shall end when the Commissioners are notified that a deputy or other person to whom paragraph (1)(c) refers has been appointed.

(4) Anything required by Part 12ZD of the 1992 Act to be done by or to the person who is unable to act may be done by or to the person appointed under this regulation to act on behalf of the person unable to act, and the receipt of the person so appointed shall be a good discharge to the employer or former employer of the person unable to act for any sum paid.

DEFINITIONS
"the Commissioners"—reg.3(1).
"statutory parental bereavement pay"—reg.3(1).

Service of notices

29.—(1) Where a notice is to be given under these Regulations, it may be given—
(a) where paragraph (2) applies, by electronic communication,
(b) by post, or
(c) by personal delivery.

(2) This paragraph applies where the person who is to receive the notice has agreed that the notice may be given to the person by being transmitted to an electronic address and in an electronic form specified by the person for that purpose.

(3) Where a notice is to be given under these Regulations it is to be taken to have been given—
(a) if sent by electronic communication, on the day of transmission;
(b) if sent by post in an envelope which is properly addressed and sent by prepaid post, on the day on which it is posted;
(c) if delivered personally, on the day of delivery.

Statutory Parental Bereavement Pay (Administration) Regulations 2020

The Statutory Parental Bereavement Pay (Administration) Regulations 2020

(SI 2020/246)

The Secretary of State makes the following Regulations in exercise of the powers conferred by sections 7, 8, 10 and 51(1) of the Employment Act 2002 and sections 8(1)(f) and (ga) and 25(3) and (6) of the Social Security Contributions (Transfer of Functions, etc.) Act 1999 with the concurrence of the Commissioners for Her Majesty's Revenue and Customs.

ARRANGEMENT OF REGULATIONS

1. Citation and commencement
2. Interpretation
3. Funding of employers' liabilities to make payments of statutory parental bereavement pay
4. Applications for funding from the Commissioners
5. Deductions from payments to the Commissioners
6. Payments to employers by the Commissioners
7. Date when certain contributions are to be treated as paid
8. Overpayments
9. Records to be maintained by employers
10. Inspection of employers' records
11. Provision of information relating to entitlement to statutory parental bereavement pay
12. Decision on any issue arising as to, or in connection with, entitlement to statutory parental bereavement pay
13. Applications in connection with statutory parental bereavement pay
14. Provision of information

Citation and commencement

1. These Regulations may be cited as the Statutory Parental Bereavement Pay (Administration) Regulations 2020 and come into force on 6th April 2020.

Interpretation

2.—(1) In these Regulations—
"the 1992 Act" means the Social Security Contributions and Benefits Act 1992;
"the Commissioners" means the Commissioners for HMRC;
"contributions payments" has the same meaning as in section 7 of the Employment Act 2002;
"HMRC" means Her Majesty's Revenue and Customs;
"income tax month" means the period beginning on the 6th day of any calendar month and ending on the 5th day of the following calendar month;
"income tax quarter" means the period beginning on—
(a) the 6th day of April and ending on the 5th day of July;
(b) the 6th day of July and ending on the 5th day of October;

(c) the 6th day of October and ending on the 5th day of January; or
(d) the 6th day of January and ending on the 5th day of April;

"statutory parental bereavement pay" means statutory parental bereavement pay payable in accordance with the provisions of Part 12ZD of the 1992 Act;

"tax year" means the 12 months beginning with 6th April in any year;

"writing" includes writing delivered by means of electronic communications to the extent that the electronic communications are approved by directions issued by the Commissioners pursuant to regulations under section 132 of the Finance Act 1999.

(2) Any reference in these Regulations to the employees of an employer includes the employer's former employees.

Funding of employers' liabilities to make payments of statutory parental bereavement pay

3.—(1) An employer who has made any payment of statutory parental bereavement pay is entitled—
 (a) to an amount equal to 92% of such payment, or
 (b) if the payment qualifies for small employer's relief by virtue of section 7(3) of the Employment Act 2002—
  (i) to an amount equal to such payment, and
  (ii) to an additional payment equal to the amount to which the employer would have been entitled under section 167(2)(b) of the 1992 Act had the payment been a payment of statutory maternity pay.

(2) The employer shall be entitled to apply for advance funding in respect of any such payment in accordance with regulation 4, or to deduct it in accordance with regulation 5 from amounts otherwise payable by the employer.

DEFINITION

"statutory parental bereavement pay"—reg.2(1).

Applications for funding from the Commissioners

4.—(1) An employer may apply to the Commissioners for funds to pay the statutory parental bereavement pay (or so much of it as remains outstanding) to the employee or employees in a form approved for that purpose by the Commissioners where—
 (a) the conditions in paragraph (2) are satisfied, or
 (b) the condition in paragraph (2)(a) is satisfied and the employer considers that the condition in paragraph (2)(b) will be satisfied on the date of any subsequent payment of emoluments to one or more employees who are entitled to payment of statutory parental bereavement pay.

(2) The conditions in this paragraph are—
 (a) the employer is entitled to a payment determined in accordance with regulation 3 in respect of statutory parental bereavement pay which the employer is required to pay to an employee or employees for an income tax month or income tax quarter, and
 (b) the payment exceeds the aggregate of—

(i) the total amount of tax which the employer is required to pay to HMRC in respect of the deduction from the emoluments of employees in accordance with the Income Tax (Pay as You Earn) Regulations 2003 for the same income tax month or income tax quarter,
(ii) the total amount of the deductions made by the employer from the emoluments of employees for the same income tax month or income tax quarter in accordance with regulations under section 22(5) of the Teaching and Higher Education Act 1998 or under section 73B of the Education (Scotland) Act 1980 or in accordance with article 3(5) of the Education (Student Support) (Northern Ireland) Order 1998,
(iii) the total amount of contributions payments which the employer is required to pay to HMRC in respect of the emoluments of employees (whether by means of deduction or otherwise) in accordance with the Social Security (Contributions) Regulations 2001 for the same income tax month or income tax quarter, and
(iv) the total amount of payments which the employer is required to pay to HMRC in respect of the deductions made on account of tax from payments to sub-contractors in accordance with section 61 of the Finance Act 2004 for the same income tax month or income quarter.

(3) An application by an employer under paragraph (1) may be for an amount up to, but not exceeding, the amount of the payment to which the employer is entitled in accordance with regulation 3 in respect of statutory parental bereavement pay which the employer is required to pay to an employee or employees for the income tax month or income tax quarter to which the payment of emoluments relates.

DEFINITIONS

"the Commissioners"—reg.2(1).
"contributions payments"—reg.2(1).
"HMRC"—reg.2(1).
"income tax month"—reg.2(1).
"income tax quarter"—reg.2(1).
"statutory parental bereavement pay"—reg.2(1).

Deductions from payments to the Commissioners

8.36   **5.** An employer who is entitled to a payment determined in accordance with regulation 3 may recover such payment by making one or more deductions from the aggregate of the amounts specified in sub-paragraphs (i) to (iv) of regulation 4(2)(b) except where and in so far as—
(a) those amounts relate to earnings paid before the beginning of the income tax month or income tax quarter in which the payment of statutory parental bereavement pay was made,
(b) those amounts are paid by the employer later than six years after the end of the tax year in which the payment of statutory parental bereavement pay was made,
(c) the employer has received payment from the Commissioners under regulation 4, or

(d) the employer has made a request in writing under regulation 4 that the payment to which the employer is entitled in accordance with regulation 3 be paid and the employer has not received notification by the Commissioners that the request is refused.

DEFINITIONS

"the Commissioners"—reg.2(1).
"income tax month"—reg.2(1).
"income tax quarter"—reg.2(1).
"statutory parental bereavement pay"—reg.2(1).
"tax year"—reg.2(1).

Payments to employers by the Commissioners

6. The Commissioners must pay the employer such amount as the employer was unable to deduct where—
(a) the Commissioners are satisfied that the total amount which the employer is or would otherwise be entitled to deduct under regulation 5 is less than the payment to which the employer is entitled in accordance with regulation 3 in an income tax month or income tax quarter, and
(b) the employer has in writing requested the Commissioners to do so.

DEFINITIONS

"the Commissioners"—reg.2(1).
"income tax month"—reg.2(1).
"income tax quarter"—reg.2(1).
"writing"—reg.2(1).

Date when certain contributions are to be treated as paid

7. Where an employer has made a deduction from a contributions payment under regulation 5, the date on which it is to be treated as having been paid for the purposes of subsection (5) of section 7 (funding of employers' liabilities) of the Employment Act 2002 is—
(a) in a case where the deduction did not extinguish the contributions payment, the date on which the remainder of the contributions payment or, as the case may be, the first date on which any part of the remainder of the contributions payment was paid, and
(b) in a case where deduction extinguished the contributions payment, the 14th day after the end of the income tax month or income tax quarter during which there were paid the earnings in respect of which the contributions payment was payable.

DEFINITIONS

"contributions payments"—reg.2(1).
"income tax month"—reg.2(1).
"income tax quarter"—reg.2(1).

Overpayments

8.—(1) This regulation applies where funds have been provided to the employer pursuant to regulation 4 in respect of one or more employees and it appears to an officer of Revenue and Customs that the employer has not used the whole or part of those funds to pay statutory parental bereavement pay.

(2) An officer of Revenue and Customs must decide to the best of the officer's judgement the amount of funds provided pursuant to regulation 4 and not used to pay statutory parental bereavement pay and must serve notice in writing of this decision on the employer.

(3) A decision under this regulation may cover funds provided pursuant to regulation 4—
  (a) for any one income tax month or income tax quarter, or more than one income tax month or income tax quarter, in a tax year, and
  (b) in respect of a class or classes of employees specified in the decision notice (without naming the individual employees), or in respect of one or more employees named in the decision notice.

(4) Subject to the following provisions of this regulation, Part 6 of the Taxes Management Act 1970 (collection and recovery) applies with any necessary modifications to a decision under this regulation as if it were an assessment and as if the amount of funds determined were income tax charged on the employer.

(5) Where an amount of funds determined under this regulation relates to more than one employee, proceedings may be brought for the recovery of that amount without distinguishing the amounts making up that sum which the employer is liable to repay in respect of each employee and without specifying the employee in question, and the amount determined under this regulation shall be one cause of action or one matter of complaint for the purposes of proceedings under sections 65, 66 or 67 of the Taxes Management Act 1970.

(6) Nothing in paragraph (5) prevents the bringing of separate proceedings for the recovery of any amount which the employer is liable to repay in respect of each employee.

DEFINITIONS

"contributions payments"—reg.2(1).
"income tax month"—reg.2(1).
"income tax quarter"—reg.2(1).
"statutory parental bereavement pay"—reg.2(1).
"tax year"—reg.2(1).
"writing"—reg.2(1).

Records to be maintained by employers

9.—(1) Subject to paragraphs (2) and (3), every employer must maintain a record of—
  (a) in relation to an employee's period of payment of statutory parental bereavement pay—
    (i) the date on which that period began,
    (ii) the evidence of entitlement to statutory parental bereavement pay provided by the employee pursuant to regulations made under section 171ZZ7(4)(d) of the 1992 Act, and
    (iii) any week which was within a period of payment of statutory parental bereavement pay but for which no payment of statutory parental bereavement pay was made to the employee and the reason no payment was made; and

(SI 2020/246 reg.9)

(b) the weeks in which such payments were made and the amount paid in each week.

(2) The records in paragraph (1)(a) must be maintained for a period of three years after the end of the tax year in which the employee's period of payment of statutory parental bereavement pay began.

(3) The records in paragraph (1)(b) must be maintained for a period of three years after the end of the tax year in which the employer made payments of statutory parental bereavement pay to the employee.

(4) In this regulation, "period of payment of statutory parental bereavement pay" means each week in respect of which statutory parental bereavement pay is payable to a person under section 171ZZ9(2) of the 1992 Act.

DEFINITIONS

"period of payment of statutory parental bereavement pay"—para.(4).
"statutory parental bereavement pay"—reg.2(1).
"tax year"—reg.2(1).

Inspection of employers' records

10.—(1) Every employer, whenever required to do so by any authorised officer of Revenue and Customs, must produce the documents and records specified in paragraph (2) to that officer for inspection, at such time as that officer may reasonably require, at the prescribed place.

(2) The documents and records specified in this paragraph are—
(a) all wage sheets, deductions working sheets, records kept in accordance with regulation 9 and other documents relating to the calculation or payment of statutory parental bereavement pay to employees in respect of the years specified by such officer, or
(b) such of those wages sheets, deductions working sheets, or other documents and records as may be specified by the authorised officer.

(3) The "prescribed place" mentioned in paragraph (1) means—
(a) such place in Great Britain as the employer and the authorised officer may agree upon, or
(b) in default of such agreement, the place in Great Britain at which the documents and records referred to in paragraph (2)(a) are normally kept, or
(c) in default of such agreement and if there is no such place as is referred to in sub-paragraph (b), the employer's principal place of business in Great Britain.

(4) The authorised officer may—
(a) take copies of, or make extracts from, any document or record produced to the authorised officer for inspection in accordance with paragraph (1), and
(b) remove any document or record so produced if it appears to the authorised officer to be necessary to do so, at a reasonable time and for a reasonable period.

(5) Where any document or record is removed in accordance with paragraph (4)(b), the authorised officer must provide—
(a) a receipt for the document or record so removed, and
(b) a copy of the document or record, free of charge, within seven days, to the person by whom it was produced or caused to be produced where the document or record is reasonably required for the proper conduct of business.

8.41

Statutory Parental Bereavement Pay (Administration) Regulations 2020

(6) Where a lien is claimed on a document produced in accordance with paragraph (1), the removal of the document under paragraph (4)(b) shall not be regarded as breaking the lien.

(7) Where records are maintained by computer, the person required to make them available for inspection must provide the authorised officer with all facilities necessary for obtaining information from them.

DEFINITIONS

"prescribed place" —para.(3).
"statutory parental bereavement pay"—reg.2(1).

Provision of information relating to entitlement to statutory parental bereavement pay

8.42

11.—(1) An employer must provide details to the employee of a decision that the employer has no liability to make payments of statutory parental bereavement pay to the employee and the reason for it where the employer—
  (a) has been given evidence of entitlement to statutory parental bereavement pay pursuant to regulations made under section 171ZZ7(4)(d) of the 1992 Act, and
  (b) decides that they have no liability to make payments of statutory parental bereavement pay to the employee.

(2) An employer must provide to the employee the information specified in paragraph (3) where the employer—
  (a) has made one or more payments of statutory parental bereavement pay to the employee, but
  (b) decides that they have no liability to make further payments to the employee because the employee has been detained in legal custody or sentenced to a term of imprisonment which was not suspended.

(3) The information specified in this paragraph is—
  (a) details of the employer's decision and the reasons for it, and
  (b) details of the week in respect of which a liability to pay statutory parental bereavement pay arose.

(4) The employer must—
  (a) return to the employee any evidence provided by the employee as referred to in paragraph (1) or (2),
  (b) comply with the requirements imposed by paragraph (1) within 28 days of the day the employee gave evidence of entitlement to statutory parental bereavement pay pursuant to regulations made under section 171ZZ7(4)(d) of the 1992 Act, and
  (c) comply with the requirements imposed by paragraph (2) within seven days of being notified of the employee's detention or sentence.

DEFINITION

"statutory parental bereavement pay"—reg.2(1).

Decision on any issue arising as to, or in connection with, entitlement to statutory parental bereavement pay

8.43

12. Any issue arising as to, or in connection with, entitlement to statutory parental bereavement pay may be decided by an officer of Revenue and Customs—

(a) on their own initiative, or
(b) on the basis of an application submitted by the employee concerned.

DEFINITION

"statutory parental bereavement pay"—reg.2(1).

Applications in connection with statutory parental bereavement pay

13.—(1) An application for the determination of any issue referred to in regulation 12 must be made in a form approved for the purpose by the Commissioners.

(2) Where such an application is made by an employee, it must—
(a) be submitted to an officer of Revenue and Customs within a period of six months beginning with the first day of the period in respect of which the determination of that issue is sought,
(b) state the period in respect of which entitlement to statutory parental bereavement pay is in issue, and
(c) state the grounds (if any) on which the applicant's employer had denied liability for statutory parental bereavement pay in respect of the period specified in the application.

8.44

DEFINITIONS

"the Commissioners"—reg.2(1).
"statutory parental bereavement pay"—reg.2(1).

Provision of information

14.—(1) Where an officer of Revenue and Customs—
(a) reasonably requires information or documents from a person specified in paragraph (2) to ascertain whether statutory parental bereavement pay is or was payable, and
(b) gives notification to that person requesting such information or documents,
that person must provide that information within 30 days of receiving the notification.

(2) The requirement to provide such information or documents applies to—
(a) any person claiming to be entitled to statutory parental bereavement pay;
(b) any person who is, or has been, the spouse, civil partner or partner of such a person as is specified in sub-paragraph (a);
(c) any person who is, or has been, an employer of such a person as is specified in sub-paragraph (a);
(d) any person carrying on an agency or other business for the introduction or supply of persons available to do work or to perform services to persons requiring them;
(e) any person who is a servant or agent of any such person as is specified in sub-paragraphs (a) to (d).

8.45

DEFINITION

"statutory parental bereavement pay"—reg.2(1).

The Statutory Parental Bereavement Pay Regulations 2020

The Statutory Parental Bereavement Pay (Persons Abroad and Mariners) Regulations 2020

(SI 2020/252)

The Secretary of State, with the concurrence of the Treasury, makes the following Regulations in exercise of the powers conferred by sections 171ZZ13 and 171ZZ14(3) of the Social Security Contributions and Benefits Act 1992.

This instrument only contains regulations made by virtue of, or consequential upon, the Schedule to the Parental Bereavement (Leave and Pay) Act 2018 and is made before the end of the period of 6 months beginning with the coming into force of that enactment.

8.46

ARRANGEMENT OF REGULATIONS

1. Citation and Commencement
2. Interpretation
3. Application
4. Restriction on scope
5. Treatment of persons in EEA states as employees
6. Treatment of certain persons absent from Great Britain as employees
7. Entitlement to statutory parental bereavement pay where person has worked in an EEA state in the 26 weeks preceding the death of a child
8. Time for compliance with Part 12ZD of the Act or regulations made under it
9. Mariners
10. Continental shelf

Citation and Commencement

8.47 **1.** These Regulations may be cited as the Statutory Parental Bereavement Pay (Persons Abroad and Mariners) Regulations 2020 and come into force on 6th April 2020.

Interpretation

8.48 **2.**—(1) In these Regulations—

"the Act" means the Social Security Contributions and Benefits Act 1992;

"foreign-going ship" means any ship or vessel which is not a home-trade ship;

"General Regulations" means the Statutory Parental Bereavement Pay (General) Regulations 2020;

"home-trade ship" includes—
  (a) every ship or vessel employed in trading or going within the following limits—
    (i) the United Kingdom (including for this purpose the Republic of Ireland),
    (ii) the Channel Islands,
    (iii) the Isle of Man, and
    (iv) the continent of Europe between the river Elbe and Brest inclusive;
  (b) every fishing vessel not proceeding beyond the following limits—

(SI 2020/252 reg.2)

    (i) on the South, Latitude 48°30—N,
    (ii) on the West, Longitude 12°W, and
    (iii) on the North, Latitude 61°N;

"mariner" means a person who is or has been in employment under a contract of service either as a master or member of the crew of any ship or vessel, or in any other capacity on board any ship or vessel where—

  (a) the employment in that other capacity is for the purposes of that ship or vessel or its crew or any passengers or cargo or mails carried by the ship or vessel, and

  (b) the contract is entered into in the United Kingdom with a view to its performance (in whole or in part) while the ship or vessel is on its voyage,

but does not include a person insofar as their employment is as a serving member of HM's forces;

"serving member of HM's forces" means a member of a regular force or reserve force ("M") as defined, in each case, by section 374 (definitions applying for purposes of the whole Act) of the Armed Forces Act 2006, unless—

  (a) M is under the age of 16,

  (b) M is committing an offence under section 8 of the Armed Forces Act 2006 (desertion),

  (c) the force concerned is one of Her Majesty's ("HM's") naval forces which M locally entered at an overseas base without previously being—
    (i) an insured person under the National Insurance Act 1965, or
    (ii) a contributor under the Act, or

  (d) the force concerned is one of HM's military forces or HM's air forces which M entered, or was recruited for, outside the United Kingdom and—
    (i) where that force is one of HM's military forces, the depot for M's unit is outside the United Kingdom, or
    (ii) where that force is one of HM's air forces, M is liable under the terms of M's engagement to serve only in a specified area outside the United Kingdom;

"statutory parental bereavement pay" means statutory parental bereavement pay payable in accordance with the provisions of Part 12ZD of the Act where the conditions specified in section 171ZZ6(2) of the Act are satisfied.

(2) For the purposes of these regulations, the expressions "ship" and "ship or vessel" include hovercraft, except in regulation 9(2).

Application

3. These Regulations apply in relation to children who die on or after 6th April 2020.

    8.49

Restriction on scope

4. A person who would not be treated under regulation 11 (treatment of persons as employees) of the General Regulations as an employee for the purposes of Part 12ZD (statutory parental bereavement pay) of the Act if that person's employment were in Great Britain shall not be treated as an employee under these Regulations.

    8.50

Treatment of persons in EEA states as employees

8.51 **5.** A person who is—
(a) gainfully employed in an EEA state in such circumstances that, if the employment were in Great Britain, the person would be an employee for the purposes of Part 12ZD of the Act, or a person treated as such an employee under regulation 11 (treatment of persons as employees) of the General Regulations, and
(b) subject to the legislation of the United Kingdom under Council Regulation (EEC) No 1408/71 of 14 June 1971 as amended from time to time or Regulation (EC) 883/2004 of the European Parliament and of the Council of 29 April 2004 as amended from time to time on the coordination of social security systems,

notwithstanding that person not being employed in Great Britain, shall be treated as an employee for the purposes of Part 12ZD of the Act.

DEFINITION

"General Regulations"—reg.2(1).

Treatment of certain persons absent from Great Britain as employees

8.52 **6.** Subject to regulation 9(2), where a person, while absent from Great Britain for any purpose, is gainfully employed by an employer who is liable to pay secondary Class 1 contributions (within the meaning of section 1(2) of the Act) in respect of that person's employment under section 6 of the Act or regulation 146 of the Social Security Contributions Regulations 2001, that person shall be treated as an employee for the purposes of Part 12ZD of the Act.

Entitlement to statutory parental bereavement pay where person has worked in an EEA state in the 26 weeks preceding the death of a child

8.53 **7.**—(1) A person who—
(a) is an employee or treated as an employee under regulation 5,
(b) in the relevant week, was in employed earner's employment with an employer in Great Britain, and
(c) had, in any week within the period of 26 weeks ending with the relevant week, been employed by the same employer in an EEA state,

shall be treated for the purposes of section 171ZZ6 of the Act (entitlement to statutory parental bereavement pay) as having been employed in employed earner's employment with an employer in those weeks in which the person was so employed in the EEA state.

(2) In paragraph (1), "relevant week" means the week immediately before the one in which the child dies.

DEFINITION

"relevant week" —para.(2)

(SI 2020/252 reg.8)

Time for compliance with Part 12ZD of the Act or regulations made under it

8. Where—
(a) a person is outside the United Kingdom,
(b) Part 12ZD of the Act or regulations made under it require any act to be done forthwith or on the happening of a certain event or within a specified time, and
(c) because the person is outside the United Kingdom that person or that person's employer cannot comply with the requirement,
the person or the employer, as the case may be, will be deemed to have complied with the requirement if the act is performed as soon as reasonably practicable.

8.54

Mariners

9.—(1) A mariner engaged in employment on board a home-trade ship with an employer who has a place of business within the United Kingdom shall be treated as an employee for the purposes of Part 12ZD of the Act, notwithstanding that the mariner may not be employed in Great Britain.

8.55

(2) A mariner who is engaged in employment—
(a) on a foreign-going ship, or
(b) on a home-trade ship with an employer who does not have a place of business within the United Kingdom,
shall not be treated as an employee for the purposes of Part 12ZD of the Act, notwithstanding that the mariner may have been employed in Great Britain.

DEFINITIONS

"foreign-going ship"—s.2(1).
"home-trade ship"—s.2(1).
"mariner"—s.2(1).

Continental shelf

10.—(1) In this regulation—
(a) "designated area" means any area which may from time to time be designated by Order in Council under section 1(7) of the Continental Shelf Act 1964 as an area within which the rights of the United Kingdom with respect to the seabed and subsoil and their natural resources may be exercised;
(b) "prescribed employment" means any employment (whether under a contract of service or not) in a designated area in connection with continental shelf operations, as defined in section 120(2) of the Act.

8.56

(2) A person in prescribed employment shall be treated as an employee for the purposes of Part 12ZD of the Act notwithstanding that that person may not be employed in Great Britain.

DEFINITIONS

"designated area"—para.(1)(a).
"prescribed employment"—para.(1)(b).

PART IX

CHILD TRUST FUNDS

The Child Trust Funds Act 2004 (Commencement No.1) Order 2004

(SI 2004/2422)

The Treasury, in exercise of the powers conferred upon them by section 27 of the Child Trust Funds Act 2004, make the following Order:

ARRANGEMENT OF ARTICLES

1. Citation and interpretation
2. Commencement of certain provisions of the Act

Citation and interpretation

1.—(1) This Order may be cited as the Child Trust Funds Act 2004 (Commencement No.1) Order 2004.

(2) In this Order—

"account" means an account which (from the appointed day) is capable of being a child trust fund (within the meaning in the Act);

"the Act" means the Child Trust Funds Act 2004;

"the appointed day" means the day appointed under section 27 of the Act for the purposes of sections 8 and 9 of the Act.

Commencement of certain provisions of the Act

2.—The following provisions of the Act shall come into force on 1st January 2005 for the purposes mentioned in relation to each provision:

Provision	*Purposes*
Section 1(3) of the Act	All purposes
Section 3(1) and (3) of the Act	All purposes (save that an account may only be a child trust fund from the appointed day)
Section 3(2), (4) to (9) and (12) of the Act	To allow accounts to be opened, and contracts with an account provider for their management to be signed, save that the account is only to be: (a) a child trust fund, or (b) subscribed to and operated, from the appointed day.
Section 5(1) and (2) of the Act	To ensure an orderly introduction of accounts, by issuing some vouchers before the appointed day.
Section 5(3) to (5) of the Act	Where a voucher has been issued before the appointed day under section 5(1) of the Act, to allow

The Child Trust Funds Act 2004 (Commencement No.1) Order 2004

Provision	Purposes
	accounts to be opened, save that the account is only to be: (a) a child trust fund, or (b) subscribed to and operated, from that day.
Section 15(1), (2)(a) and (3) of the Act	So far as those provisions relate to the persons referred to in section 15(2)(a) of the Act
Section 17 of the Act	All purposes
Section 18 of the Act	All purposes
Section 20(1) (except paragraphs (b) and (c)), (2) to (6), (7) (except paragraph (c)), (8) and (9) of the Act	All purposes (except for the purposes of sections 6, 7, 9, 10 or 13 of the Act)
Section 21 of the Act	For the purposes of the provisions of section 20 of the Act which are commenced by this Order
Section 22(1) and (6) of the Act	All purposes
Section 23(1) to (3) of the Act	For the purposes of section 22(1) and (6) of the Act
Section 24(1) (except paragraph (c)), (2) and (3) of the Act	For the purposes of section 22(1) and (6) of the Act
Section 24(5) to (7) of the Act	All purposes

The Child Trust Funds Act 2004 (Commencement No.2) Order 2004

(SI 2004/3369)

The Treasury, in exercise of the powers conferred upon them by section 27 of the Child Trust Funds Act 2004, make the following Order:

ARRANGEMENT OF ARTICLES

1. Citation and interpretation
2. Commencement of provisions of the Act

Citation and interpretation

1.—(1) This Order may be cited as the Child Trust Funds Act 2004 (Commencement No.2) Order 2004.
(2) In this Order—
"the Act" means the Child Trust Funds Act 2004;

(SI 2004/3369 reg.1)

"the earlier Order" means the Child Trust Funds Act 2004 (Commencement No.1) Order 2004.

Commencement of provisions of the Act

2.—(1) Sections 1 to 24 of the Act shall come into force on 6th April 2005, subject to the following paragraphs.

(2) Paragraph (1) does not apply to provisions brought into force for all purposes by the earlier Order.

(3) Section 23(1) of the Act shall come into force for all purposes on 1st January 2005.

(4) Where a provision of the Act (other than section 23(1)) was partially brought into force by the earlier Order, that provision shall come into force for all other purposes on 6th April 2005.

The Child Trust Funds Regulations 2004

(SI 2004/1450) (AS AMENDED)

ARRANGEMENT OF REGULATIONS

PART 1

Introductory

1. Citation and commencement
2. Interpretation
3. Vouchers
4. Descriptions of accounts
5. Opening of account by responsible person or the child
6. Opening of account by Inland Revenue—(Revenue allocated accounts)
7. Government contributions
7A. *(repealed)*
7B. Yearly disability payments

PART 2

Other requirements to be satisfied in relation to accounts

8. General requirements for accounts
9. Annual limit on subscriptions
10. Statements for an account
11. General investment rules
12. Qualifying investments for an account
13. Conditions for application by responsible person or the child to open an account (and changes to an account)
13A. Maturity of child trust fund – instructions
13B. Maturity of child trust fund – no instructions

13C. Matured CTF Account
14. Account provider—qualifications and Board's approval
15. Account provider—appointment of tax representative
16. Account provider—withdrawal by Board of approval
17. Account provider—appeal against non-approval or withdrawal of Board's approval
18. Permitted withdrawals from an account
18A. Permitted withdrawals from an account where the child is terminally ill
19. Account provider's intention to make a bulk transfer of accounts or to cease to act as an account provider
19A. Account provider ceasing to accept Revenue allocated accounts
20. Account provider ceasing to qualify
20A. Transfers to other accounts for children
21. Transfer of accounts to other account providers
22. Recoupment of Inland Revenue contributions to void accounts (and other accounts)
23. "Repair" of invalid accounts

PART 3

Tax and administration of accounts

24. Exemption from tax of account income and gains
25. Tax liabilities and reliefs—account provider to act on behalf of the named child
26. Repayments in respect of tax to account provider—interim tax claims
27. Repayments in respect of tax to account provider—annual tax claims
28. Account provider's tax claims—supplementary provisions
29. Assessments for withdrawing relief and recovering tax
30. Fortnightly claim and financial returns
31. Records to be kept by account provider
32. Returns of information by account provider
33. Information about "looked after children" from Local Authorities
33A. The person appointed by the Treasury or the Secretary of State by virtue of section 3(10) of the Act to be the person who has the authority to manage an account
34. *(repealed)*
35. *(repealed)*
36. Capital gains tax—adaptation of enactments
37. Administration of tax in relation to accounts—supplementary
38. Application of the provisions of Chapter 2 of Part 13 of the Taxes Act and of Chapter 9 of Part 4 of ITTOIA 2005 to policies

   Schedule — Stakeholder Accounts
    Description of stakeholder account
    Characteristics of stakeholder account etc
    Stakeholder accounts—charges etc

The Treasury, in exercise of the powers conferred upon them by sections 3(1) to (5) and (7), 5(1), (4) and (5), 6, 7, 8(1), 9(2) and (10)(b), 11(1), 12(2), 13, 15, 16, 23(1) and 28(1) to (4) of the Child Trust Funds Act 2004, hereby make the following Regulations:

(SI 2004/1450 reg.1) (as amended)

PART 1

INTRODUCTORY

Citation and commencement

1.—These Regulations may be cited as the Child Trust Funds Regulations 2004 and shall come into force for the purposes of—
(a) issuing vouchers (see regulation 3),
(b) completing account-opening formalities (see regulation 5),
(c) applications under regulation 13 to open an account with effect from the appointed day,
(d) applications under regulation 14 to be approved as an account provider to manage accounts from the appointed day,
(e) regulation 17, so far as it relates to applications referred to in paragraph (d), [¹ . . .]
(f) [¹ . . .]
on 1st January 2005, and for all other purposes on the appointed day.

AMENDMENT

1. Child Trust Funds (Amendment) Regulations 2013 (SI 2013/263) reg.2(4)(a) (March 16, 2013).

Interpretation

2.—(1) In these Regulations—
(a) the following expressions have the meanings given in the Child Trust Funds Act 2004 ("the Act")—
"child"
"child trust fund"
"eligible child"
[⁵ "the income threshold" (see section 9(6) of the Act)]
"Inland Revenue"
"Inland Revenue contributions" (see section 11(2) of the Act),
"parental responsibility" (see section 3(9) of the Act);
[⁵ "the relevant income" (see section 9(6) of the Act)]
"relevant person" (see section 15(2) of the Act),
[⁵ "relevant social security benefit" (see section 9(6) of the Act)]
"responsible person"[¹⁵ . . .] (see section 3(8) of the Act),
[⁵ "tax year" (see section 9(6) of the Act)]
"the person entitled to child benefit in respect of the child" (see section 2(1)(a), (4) and (6) of the Act);
(b) except where the context otherwise requires—
"account" means a scheme of investment which (except in regulation 22(1)) qualifies as a child trust fund, other than in the cases of—
(i) an account with a deposit-taker,
(ii) a share or deposit account with a building society, or
(iii) a deposit account with a person falling within [¹² section 991(2) of the Income Tax Act 2007], or a [⁶ credit union];

an "account investment" is an investment under the account which is a qualifying investment for an account within the meaning of regulation 12;

an "account provider" is a person who fulfils the conditions of these Regulations and is approved by the Board for the purpose of these Regulations as an account provider;

[6 "adoption order" has the meaning in section 46(1) of the Adoption and Children Act 2002 or section 28 of the Adoption and Children (Scotland) Act 2007 or of "Adoption Order" in Article 2(2) of the Adoption (Northern Ireland) Order 1987, as the case may be, and includes any corresponding order under the Adoption (Scotland) Act 1978, and any order of a court in the Isle of Man or any of the Channel Islands which, under section 108 of the Adoption and Children Act 2002, is declared to correspond to an adoption order made under that Act;]

"appointed day" means the day appointed, under section 27 of the Act, for the purposes of sections 8 and 9 of the Act;

"assurance undertaking" [16 means a direct life insurance undertaking within the meaning of Article 2 of Directive 2009/138/EC of the European Parliament and of the Council of 25 November 2009 on the taking-up and pursuit of the business of Insurance and Reinsurance (Solvency II)];

[1"Bank of England base rate" means the rate announced from time to time by the Monetary Policy Committee of the Bank of England as the official dealing rate, being the rate at which the Bank is willing to enter into transactions for providing short-term liquidity in the money markets;]

[3"the Board" means the Commissioners for Her Majesty's Revenue and Customs;]

"building society" means a building society within the meaning of the Building Societies Act 1986, or the Irish Building Societies Act 1989;

[4"building society bonus", except in regulation 24(a)(i), excludes any bonus, distribution of funds or the conferring of rights in relation to shares—
(a) in connection with an amalgamation, transfer of engagements or transfer of business of a building society, and
(b) mentioned in section 96 or 100 of the Building Societies Act 1986,

and "payment under a building society bonus scheme" shall be construed accordingly;]

"company", except in regulation 12(4)(a), means any body corporate having a share capital other than—
  (i) an open-ended investment company, within the meaning given by section 236 of the Financial Services and Markets Act 2000, [15 or]
  (ii) a UCITS [15 ;]
  (iii) [13[15 . . .]]
  (iv) [15 . . .];

[2"credit union" means a society registered as a credit union under the Industrial and Provident Societies Act 1965 or the Credit Unions (Northern Ireland) Order 1985;]

(SI 2004/1450 reg.2) (as amended)

"deposit-taker" has the meaning given by [⁶ section 853 (as extended under section 854) of ITA 2007];

"the Director of Savings" has the same meaning as in the National Debt Act 1972;

"the Distance Marketing Directive" means Directive 2002/65/EC of the European Parliament and of the Council of 23rd September 2002, and includes any provisions by which an EEA State or the United Kingdom has transposed the Directive or has corresponding obligations in its domestic law, and "distance contract" has the meaning in that Directive;

"electronic communications" includes any communications by means of a telecommunication system (within the meaning in the Telecommunications Act 1984);

[¹⁰ "EEA Agreement" means the agreement on the European Economic Area signed at Oporto on 2nd May 1992, together with the Protocol adjusting that Agreement signed at Brussels on 17th March 1993, as modified or supplemented from time to time;

"EEA State", in relation to any time, means a state which at that time is a member State, or any other state which at that time is a party to the EEA Agreement;]

"European institution" means an EEA firm of the kind mentioned in [¹² paragraph 5(a) to (d), (f) and (h)] of Schedule 3 to the Financial Services and Markets Act 2000 which is an authorised person for the purposes of that Act as a result of qualifying for authorisation under paragraph 12 [¹² (1) to (4) and (7)] of that Schedule;

"51 per cent. subsidiary" and "75 per cent. subsidiary" have the meanings given by section 838 of the Taxes Act;

[⁶ "FISMA 2000" means the Financial Services and Markets Act 2000";

"gains", except in regulations 22(1) to (3), 24(a)(ii), (iii) and (v), 37(5) and 38, means "chargeable gains" within the meaning in the 1992 Act;

"gilt-edged securities" has the meaning given by paragraphs 1 and 1A of Schedule 9 to the 1992 Act;

[⁶ "guardian" means a guardian of a child within the meaning in section 5 of the Children Act 1989, section 7 of the Children (Scotland) Act 1995 or Article 2(2) of the Children (Northern Ireland) Order 1995, as the case may be;]

"incorporated friendly society" means a society incorporated under the Friendly Societies Act 1992;

[¹³ . . .];

"investments under the account" has the same meaning as investments under a child trust fund in the Act;

[¹² [¹⁷ "investment trust" means an investment trust within the meaning of section 1158 of the Corporation Tax Act 2010;]]

[⁶ "ITA 2007" means the Income Tax Act 2007;]

[⁶ "ITTOIA 2005" means the Income Tax (Trading and Other Income) Act 2005;]

"the Management Act" means the Taxes Management Act 1970;

"market value" shall be construed in accordance with section 272 of the 1992 Act;

[²⁰ "matured CTF account" has the meaning given by regulation 13B(2)(a);]

[³[⁶. . .];
[⁹ "non-UCITS retail scheme"—
(a) has the meaning in COLL (that is, a scheme to which, or to whose authorised fund manager and depositary, sections 5.1, 5.4 and 5.6 of COLL apply),
(b) includes a "recognised scheme" by virtue of section [²²271A or] 270 or 272 of FISMA 2000, which would fall within paragraph (a) of this definition if it were an authorised fund, and
(c) includes a sub-fund of an umbrella which the terms of the scheme identify as a sub-fund which would fall within paragraph (a) or (b) of this definition if it were itself an authorised fund or a recognised scheme.
In this definition, expressions defined in the Glossary of the Financial Conduct Authority Handbook have those defined meanings;]
"the 1992 Act" means the Taxation of Chargeable Gains Act 1992;
"notice" except in regulations 12(12) and 37(6)(a), means notice in writing;
[³"qualifying units in or shares of a non-UCITS retail scheme" means that—
(a) the instrument constituting the scheme secures that redemption of the units or shares in question shall take place no less frequently than bi-monthly (see [⁹section] 6.2.16(6) of the [⁶. . .] [⁹ COLL] omitting the words "Except where (7) applies, and", read with [⁹section] 6.3.4(1), whether or not those [⁹sections] apply to the scheme), and
(b) a provision for suspension of dealings in exceptional conditions in accordance with [⁹section] 7.2 of [⁹ the COLL] (or any foreign procedure which is a direct foreign equivalent of that [⁹section]) shall not be treated as a provision contrary to paragraph (a) of this definition;]
"recognised stock exchange" has the same meaning as in [¹⁰ section 1005 of ITA 2007]
[¹⁵ "registered contact" means the person who has the authority to manage the child trust fund by virtue of section 3(6) of the Act;]
"registered friendly society" has the meaning given by the Friendly Societies Act 1992 and includes any society that by virtue of section 96(2) of that Act is to be treated as a registered friendly society;
[¹³ [¹⁵ . . .]]
[⁶ "relevant authorised person" means a firm mentioned in section 697(2)(b) of ITTOIA 2005];
[⁶. . .]
"security" means any loan stock or similar security of a company whether secured or unsecured;
[⁶ "special guardian" has the meaning in section 14A of the Children Act 1989;]
"subscriptions" has the meaning in section 12(1) of the Act (but excluding Inland Revenue contributions and income or gains arising from investments under the account);

"tax" where neither income tax nor capital gains tax is specified means either of those taxes;

"the Taxes Act" means the Income and Corporation Taxes Act 1988;

"year", except in the expression "subscription year" in regulations 9, 21(5)(b) and 32(2)(b)(iv), means a year of assessment (within the meaning in section 832(1) of the Taxes Act, or section 288(1) of the 1992 Act, as the case may be);

(c) "authorised fund" means—
  (i) an authorised unit trust, or
  (ii) an open-ended investment company [6. . .] in the case of which an authorisation order made [9. . .] under regulation 14 of the Open-Ended Investment Companies Regulations 2001 is in force;

"authorised unit trust" means a unit trust scheme in the case of which an authorisation order made [9. . .] under section 243 of the Financial Services and Markets Act 2000 is in force;

[9 "COLL" means the Collective Investment Schemes Sourcebook made by the Financial Conduct Authority under FISMA 2000;]

"depositary interest" means the rights of the person mentioned in paragraph (ii), under a certificate or other record (whether or not in the form of a document) acknowledging—
  (i) that a person holds relevant investments or evidence of the right to them, and
  (ii) that another person is entitled to rights in or in relation to those or identical relevant investments, including the right to receive such investments, or evidence of the right to them or the proceeds from such investments, from the person mentioned in paragraph (i),

where "relevant investments" means investments which are exclusively qualifying investments for an account falling within regulation 12(2)(a) to (i), and the rights mentioned in paragraph (ii) are exclusively rights in or in relation to relevant investments;

[7. . .]

[7 "insolvency event" means the procedures listed in the definition of "insolvency event" in [18 regulation 23(18) of the Payment Services Regulations 2017];]

"open-ended investment company" [7 means a company to which section 236 of FISMA 2000 applies], and "shares" in relation to an open-ended investment company, includes shares of any class and of any denomination of a given class and, in relation to a part of an umbrella company, means shares in the company which confer for the time being rights in that part;

[7[19 "recognised UCITS" means—
(a) [22. . .]
(b) an undertaking established in Gibraltar which is a UCITS under the law of Gibraltar which implemented Directive 2009/65/EC of the European Parliament and of the Council of 13 July 2009 on the coordination of laws, regulations and administrative provisions relating to undertakings for collective investment in transferable securities]] [21; or
[22(c) a recognised scheme by virtue of section 271A or 272 of FISMA 2000 that is a UCITS within the meaning given by section 236A of that Act;]]

[⁷. . .]
[⁷ "UK UCITS" means—
(a) a collective investment scheme [⁹ with Part 4A permission under FISMA 2000], which complies with the requirements to be a "UCITS scheme" for the purposes of [⁹ COLL], or
(b) a part of a UK UCITS mentioned in paragraph (a) of this definition which would be a sub-fund of an umbrella scheme which is a UK UCITS;]
"umbrella scheme" means an authorised fund which according to the terms of the scheme is an umbrella scheme belonging to the category under that name established by the [⁹ Financial Conduct Authority], and—
  (i) in the case of an authorised fund which is an authorised unit trust, references to a part of an umbrella scheme shall be construed in accordance with subsection (8) of section 468 of the Taxes Act, [⁷ and paragraphs (6) and (7) of regulation 7 of the Authorised Investment Funds (Tax) Regulations 2006 shall apply for the purposes of these Regulations as they apply for the purposes of those Regulations]
  (ii) in the case of an authorised fund which is an open-ended investment company, references to a part of an umbrella scheme shall be construed in accordance with [⁷ subsection (4) of section 468A of the Taxes Act, and paragraphs (2) and (3) of regulation 7 of the Authorised Investment Funds (Tax) Regulations 2006 shall apply for the purposes of these Regulations as they apply for the purposes of those Regulations];
[⁷. . .]
"units", in relation to an authorised unit trust, means the rights or interests (however described) of the unit holders in that unit trust and, in relation to a part of an umbrella scheme, means the rights or interests for the time being of the unit holders in that part;
[⁷ "units in, or shares of, a UK UCITS or recognised UCITS" means the rights (however described) of the holders of the units or shares in that UK UCITS or recognised UCITS;]
[⁷. . .]
[¹¹ (1A) In these Regulations-
(a) a "bulk transfer of accounts" occurs where two or more accounts are transferred, without a break in the management of the accounts, by an account provider ("the transferor") direct to another account provider ("the transferee")—
  (i) pursuant to an agreement made between the transferor and the transferee where the transfers are not made pursuant to requests made by the person who is the registered contact in relation to the accounts transferred; or
  (ii) pursuant to an insurance business transfer scheme or a banking business transfer scheme under Part 7 (Control of Business Transfers) of FISMA 2000;
(b) [¹⁴. . .]
(c) [¹⁴. . .]
(2) The table below indexes other definitions in these Regulations—

(SI 2004/1450 reg.2) (as amended)

Term defined	Regulation
"the applicant"	5
"the commencement date"	7(8)
"description" of an account	4
"the disqualifying circumstances"	16
[⁸...]	[⁸...]
[⁸...]	[⁸...]
"initial contribution"	7(1)
"interim tax claim"	26(2)
"local authority"	[¹⁷ 33A(6)]
"looked after child"	[¹⁷ 33A(6)]
"management agreement"	5
"the named child"	5 and 8(1)
"qualifying circumstances"	14
"qualifying investments for an account"	12
[¹⁵...]	[¹⁵...]
[⁸...]	[⁸...]
"special contribution"	7(1)
"subscription year"	9(2)
"supplementary contribution"	7(5)
"the termination event"	12(12)
"the transfer instructions"	8(2)(h)
"the internal transfer instructions"	8(2)(i)

AMENDMENTS

1. Child Trust Funds (Amendment) Regulations 2004 (SI 2004/2676) reg.3 (April 6, 2005).
2. Child Trust Funds (Amendment No.2) Regulations 2005 (SI 2005/909) reg.3 (April 6, 2005).
3. Child Trust Funds (Amendment No.3) Regulations 2005 (SI 2005/3349) reg.3 (December 27, 2005).
4. Child Trust Funds (Amendment No.3) Regulations 2006 (SI 2006/3195) reg.3 (January 1, 2007).
5. Child Trust Funds (Amendment) Regulations 2009 (SI 2009/475) reg.3 (April 6, 2009, but have effect where the Child Benefit commencement date for the child (first day for which child benefit was paid in respect of the child) is on or after April 6, 2008).
6. Child Trust Funds (Amendment) Regulations 2010 (SI 2010/582) reg.3(1) (April 6, 2010).
7. Child Trust Funds (Amendment) Regulations 2010 (SI 2010/582) reg.3(2) (April 6, 2010).
8. Child Trust Funds (Amendment) Regulations 2013 (SI 2013/263) reg.2(4)(b) (March 16, 2013).
9. Financial Services Act 2012 (Consequential Amendments and Transitional Provisions) Order 2013 (SI 2013/472) art.3 and Sch.2 para.93(a) and (b) (April 1, 2013).
10. Child Trust Funds (Amendment No.2) Regulations 2013 (SI 2013/1744) reg.3 (August 5, 2013).
11. Child Trust Funds (Amendment No.2) Regulations 2013 (SI 2013/1744) reg.4 (August 5, 2013).
12. Child Trust Funds (Amendment) Regulations 2014 (SI 2014/649) reg.3 (April 6, 2014).

13. Co-operative and Community Benefit Societies and Credit Unions Act 2010 (Consequential Amendments) Regulations 2014 (SI 2014/1815) reg.2 and Sch. para.13 (August 1, 2014).
14. Child Trust Funds (Amendment No.2) Regulations 2015 (SI 2015/876) regs 2 and 3 (April 6, 2015).
15. Child Trust Funds (Amendment No.3) Regulations 2015 (SI 2015/1371) regs 3 and 4 (July 1, 2015).
16. Solvency 2 Regulations 2015 (SI 2015/575) reg.60 and Sch.2 para.18 (January 1, 2016).
17. Child Trust Funds (Amendment) Regulations 2017 (SI 2017/185) reg.3 (April 6, 2017).
18. Payment Services Regulations 2017 (SI 2017/752) reg.156 and Sch.8 Pt.3 para.9 (January 13, 2018).
19. Child Trust Funds (Amendment) Regulations 2020 (SI 2020/29), reg.3(b) (January 31, 2020).
20. Child Trust Funds (Amendment) Regulations 2020 (SI 2020/29), reg.3(a) (April 6, 2020).
21. Child Trust Funds (Amendment) Regulations 2023 (SI 2023/269) reg.3 (April 6, 2023).
22. Child Trust Funds (Amendment) Regulations 2024 (SI 2024/349) reg.2 (April 6, 2024).

Vouchers

9.10

3.—(1) The voucher to be issued under section 5(1) of the Act shall contain the following particulars—
  (a) the full name of the child,
  (b) his date of birth,
  (c) his unique reference number,
  (d) the [² short expiry date] of the voucher, and
  (e) the amount of the initial contribution (see regulation 7(1)),
and a statement that the voucher cannot be exchanged for money.

(2) The voucher shall be sent to the person who is entitled to child benefit in respect of the child (or, in the case of a child who is an eligible child because of section 2(3) of the Act, to a responsible person in relation to the child) by post.

(3) The expiry date [¹. . .] shall be whichever is the earlier of—
  (a) the date 12 months from the date of issue of the voucher, or
  (b) where the child is over 17 years of age, the date on which he will attain the age of 18 years.

[² (4) But for references in these Regulations to the short expiry date of the voucher paragraph (3) applies with "60 days" instead of "12 months".]

AMENDMENTS

1. Child Trust Funds (Amendment) Regulations 2006 (SI 2006/199) reg.3 (February 7, 2006).
2. Child Trust Funds (Amendment No.3) Regulations 2011 (SI 2011/2447) reg.3 (November 1, 2011).

DEFINITIONS

  "child"—see reg.2(1)(a).
  "eligible child"—see reg.2(1)(a).
  "responsible person"—see reg.2(1)(a).

(SI 2004/1450 reg.4) (as amended)

Descriptions of accounts

4.—(1) An account may be of either of the following descriptions—

Stakeholder account

Where the account meets the characteristics and conditions in the Schedule to these Regulations.

Non-stakeholder account

Where any of those characteristics or conditions is not met.

(2) Accounts opened by the Inland Revenue (see regulation 6) must be stakeholder accounts.

DEFINITION

"account"—see reg.2(1)(b).

GENERAL NOTE

A child trust fund is not a "reportable account" for the purpose of the International Tax Compliance Regulations 2015 (SI 2015/878), which were introduced to give effect to Council Directive 2011/16/EU ("the DAC") and other international agreements designed to improve international tax compliance (see reg.2(2)(a) and Sch.2 para.5 of the 2015 Regulations).

Opening of account by responsible person or the child

5.—(1) For the purposes of these Regulations, subject to [¹paragraphs (1A) and (2)], an account is opened for a child ("the named child") with an account provider on the date the last of the following conditions is satisfied (in any order), where "the applicant" means—

(a) if the named child is 16 or over, the child; and
(b) in any other case, a responsible person in relation to the named child.

Condition 1

The applicant gives the voucher relating to the named child to the account provider [¹not later than 7 days after its [³ short expiry date] [² or, where the account provider has chosen to open accounts without sight of the relevant voucher, the applicant gives the following information to the account provider:

(a) the [³ short expiry date] of the voucher,
(b) the amount of the initial contribution as specified on the voucher, and
(c) where the date of birth shown on the voucher differs from the actual date of birth of the child (see regulation 13(5)(c)), the date of birth shown on the voucher]

Condition 2

The applicant enters into an agreement with the account provider (the "management agreement") for the management of the account (see regulation 8(1) and (2)), which includes the application and declaration required by regulation 13.

Condition 3

Where that application is not in writing the applicant has agreed, or is treated as having agreed, the contents of the copy of the declaration required by regulation 13(3).

Condition 4

(a) In any case where the management agreement is a distance contract, the agreement must be an initial service agreement for the purposes of the Distance Marketing Directive, and contain the instructions required by regulation 8(1)(f), and

(b) in every case where there is any right to cancel (or automatic cancellation of) the management agreement, the period during which it may be exercised or occur has expired without that right being exercised or cancellation occurring.

(2) An account must satisfy the requirements that—

(a) no subscription to the account is accepted by the account provider until the account has been opened in accordance with paragraph (1); and

(b) where the account is so opened before the appointed day, it shall not be treated as open for the purpose of accepting subscriptions until the appointed day.

[¹(1A) The application to open the account must be made, and Condition 2 satisfied, not later than the [³ short expiry date] of the voucher.]

AMENDMENTS

1. Child Trust Funds (Amendment) Regulations 2006 (SI 2006/199) reg.4 (February 7, 2006).

2. Child Trust Funds (Amendment No.2) Regulations 2009 (SI 2009/694) reg.3 (April 6, 2009).

3. Child Trust Funds (Amendment No.3) Regulations 2011 (SI 2011/2447) reg.4 (November 1, 2011).

DEFINITIONS

"account"—see reg.2(1)(b).
"account provider"—see reg.2(1)(b).
"appointed day"—see reg.2(1)(b).
"child"—see reg.2(1)(a).
"the Distance Marketing Directive"—see reg.2(1)(b).
"responsible person"—see reg.2(1)(a).
"subscriptions"—see reg.2(1)(b).

GENERAL NOTE

9.14 Note that the amendments made by SI 2011/2447 only have effect in relation to vouchers issued on or after January 1, 2012 (reg.1(2)).

Opening of account by Inland Revenue—(Revenue allocated accounts)

9.15 **6.**—(1) The Board shall apply to open an account for a child to whom section 6 of the Act applies, by forwarding to an account provider the particulars which would be required for a voucher (see regulation 3), but omitting paragraph (1)(d) of that regulation.

(SI 2004/1450 reg.6) (as amended)

(2) The account provider shall immediately open a stakeholder account in the name of the child, which shall have the same effect as if a responsible person for the child (or the child if aged 16 or over) had entered into the account provider's standard management agreement for the stakeholder account in question, including the terms mentioned in Condition 2 of regulation 5(1) (but treating the reference to the application and declaration required by regulation 13 as a reference to the authorisation required by regulation 13(4)) and regulation 8(1)(f).

(3) The Inland Revenue shall maintain (and update from time to time) a list of account providers who have agreed to accept Revenue allocated accounts under this regulation, in the order of the date of their agreement, and the account provider shall be selected in rotation from the current list.

(4) Where the account provider offers two or more types of stakeholder account [²—
- (a) the account provider shall select the type or types to be used for the purposes of this regulation (subject to sub-paragraph (b)),
- (b) any type selected must be offered to the general public at the time of opening a Revenue allocated account of that type, and
- (c) if more than one type has been selected, the account to be opened shall be chosen by the account provider in rotation between the selected types of accounts.]

[¹(5) The Inland Revenue shall write to the person who is entitled to child benefit in respect of the child (or, in the case of a child who is an eligible child because of section 2(3) of the Act, to a responsible person in relation to the child) to inform them of the opening of the account and particulars of it.]

AMENDMENTS

1. Child Trust Funds (Amendment) Regulations 2004 (SI 2004/2676) reg.4 (April 6, 2005).
2. Child Trust Funds (Amendment No.3) Regulations 2005 (SI 2005/3349) reg.4 (December 27, 2005).

DEFINITIONS

"account"—see reg.2(1)(b).
"account provider"—see reg.2(1)(b).
"child"—see reg.2(1)(a).
"eligible child"—see reg.2(1)(a).
"responsible person"—see reg.2(1)(a).

Government contributions

7.—(1) The amounts of the contribution for the purposes of section 8(1) of the Act are set out in paragraphs (2) to [⁴(4B)], (the amounts set out in paragraphs [⁴(2), (4)(a) and 4(A)] to be known as the "initial contribution", and the amounts set out in paragraphs [⁴(3), (4)(b) and 4(B)] as the "special contribution").

(2) Where the child is an eligible child on the appointed day by virtue of section 2(1)(a) of the Act (by reason of a child benefit award), and—
- (i) was born after 31st August 2002 but before 6th April 2003, the amount is £277,
- (ii) was born between 6th April 2003 and 5th April 2004, the amount is £268, and
- (iii) was born between 6th April 2004 and the day preceding the appointed day, the amount is £256.

(3) Where the child is an eligible child on the appointed day by virtue of section 2(1)(b) of the Act (by reason of being a child in the care of a local authority at that date) and—
    (i) was born after 31st August 2002 but before 6th April 2003, the amount is £554,
    (ii) was born between 6th April 2003 and 5th April 2004, the amount is £536, and
    (iii) was born between 6th April 2004 and the day preceding the appointed day, the amount is £512.

(4) [4Subject to paragraphs (4A) and (4B), where] the child [1becomes an eligible child] on or after the appointed day and—
    (a) is first an eligible child by virtue of section 2(1)(a) of the Act, the amount is £250, and
    (b) is first an eligible child by virtue of section 2(1)(b) of the Act, the amount is £500.

[4 (4A) Where a child—
    (a) is first an eligible child by virtue of section 2(1)(a) of the Act, and
    (b) the commencement date for the child (see paragraph (8)) is after the relevant 2010 date (see paragraph (10E)),
the amount is £50.

(4B) Where a child—
    (a) is first an eligible child by virtue of section 2(1)(b) of the Act, and
    (b) either—
        (i) is born on or after the relevant 2010 date, or
        (ii) is first in the United Kingdom (other than temporarily) on or after the relevant 2010 date, or
        (iii) becomes an eligible child on or after 3 months (less one day) after the relevant 2010 date,
the amount is £100.]

(5) The amounts of the supplementary contribution for the purposes of section 9(2) of the Act (to be known as the "supplementary contribution") are set out in paragraphs (6) and (7).

(6) Where the child is an eligible child on the appointed day (and is a child to whom section 9 of the Act applies), the amount—
    (a) if the commencement date was after 31st August 2002 but before 6th April 2003, is £266,
    (b) if the commencement date was between 6th April 2003 and 5th April 2004, is £258,
    (c) if the commencement date was between 6th April 2004 and the appointed day, is £250.

(7) [4Subject to pragraphs (7A), where] the child becomes an eligible child after the appointed day (and is a child to whom section 9 of the Act applies), the amount is £250.

[4 (7A) Where the child is one to whom section 9 of the Act applies, and the commencement date for the child is after the relevant 2010 date, the amount is £50.]

(8) The "commencement date", in relation to a child, means the first day for which child benefit was paid (under a decision mentioned in section 2(6) of the Act) in respect of the child, except that—
    (a) where entitlement to child benefit is wholly excluded by a directly applicable Community provision, it means the date on which that exclusion took effect, [4. . .]

(SI 2004/1450 reg. 7) (as amended)

(b) [⁴...]

[¹(9) The Inland Revenue shall, following final determination of entitlement to child tax credit, write to the person who is entitled to child benefit in respect of the child (or, in the case of a child who is an eligible child because of section 2(3) of the Act, to a responsible person in relation to the child) to inform them that the supplementary contribution is being paid into the child's account.]

[²(10) A further contribution under section 10 of the Act of [⁴£50] is due for any child where—
(a) the commencement date (for child benefit: see paragraph (8)) in relation to that child is after 5th April 2005, and
(b) income support or income-based jobseeker's allowance was paid for that commencement date to a person whose applicable amount included an amount in respect of the child.

[³ (10A) A further contribution under section 10 of the Act of [⁴£50] is due for any child if—
(a) an account is held by the child,
(b) the child was first an eligible child by virtue of section 2(1)(a) of the Act,
(c) section 9 of the Act does not apply to the child,
(d) a contribution is not, and has not been, due for the child under paragraph (10),
(e) the child is an eligible child on the day identified under the provisions of paragraph (10B) or (10C) as the case may be, and
(f) the condition in paragraph (10B) or (10C) is satisfied in relation to the child.

(10B) The condition in this paragraph is that it has been determined in accordance with the provision made by and by virtue of sections 18 to 21 of the Tax Credits Act 2002—
(a) that a person was, or persons were, entitled to child tax credit in respect of the child for any day falling—
  (i) after the commencement date, but
  (ii) not later than three months immediately preceding the expiry date of the voucher for the child (see regulation 3), and
(b) that either the relevant income of the person or persons for the tax year in which that day fell does not exceed the income threshold or the person, or either of those persons, was entitled to a relevant social security benefit for that day,
and that determination has not been overturned.

(10C) The condition in this paragraph is that income support, or income-based jobseeker's allowance, was paid for any day falling—
(a) after the commencement date, but
(b) not later than one month immediately preceding the expiry date of the voucher for the child (see regulation 3),
to a person whose applicable amount included an amount in respect of the child.]

[⁴ (10D) Her Majesty's Revenue and Customs must inform the account provider holding the child's account where an amount is payable to the account under paragraph (10) or (10A).

(10E) In this regulation, "the relevant 2010 date" means—
(a) 2nd August 2010; or
(b) if later, the day on which regulation 3 of the Child Trust Funds (Amendment No.3) Regulations 2010 came into force.]

(11) On receipt of the further contribution [³ mentioned in paragraph (10) or (10A)] from the Inland Revenue the account provider must credit the account held by the child with the amount of the payment.]

AMENDMENTS

1. Child Trust Funds (Amendment) Regulations 2004 (SI 2004/2676) reg.5 (April 6, 2005).
2. Child Trust Funds (Amendment) Regulations 2005 (SI 2005/383) reg.3 (April 6, 2005).
3. Child Trust Funds (Amendment) Regulations 2009 (SI 2009/475) reg.4 (April 6, 2009, but have effect where the Child Benefit commencement date for the child (first day for which child benefit was paid in respect of the child) is on or after April 6, 2008).
4. Child Trust Funds (Amendment No.3) Regulations 2010 (SI 2010/1894) reg.3 (August 2, 2010).

DEFINITIONS

"account"—see reg.2(1)(b).
"account provider"—see reg.2(1)(b).
"appointed day"—see reg.2(1)(b).
"child"—see reg.2(1)(a).
"eligible child"—see reg.2(1)(a).
"responsible person"—see reg.2(1)(a).

GENERAL NOTE

9.17 Note that the amended and reduced amount of £50 under para.(10) and (10A) has effect where the commencement date for the child (within the meaning of reg.7(8) of the Child Trust Funds Regulations 2004, as amended by reg.3(7) of the Child Trust Funds (Amendment No.3) Regulations 2010) is after the day on which reg.3 of those Regulations comes into force in accordance with reg.1(3) (see reg.1(4) of the 2010 Regulations).

[¹ **Age 7 payments**

9.18 **7A.**—[² . . .]

AMENDMENTS

1. Child Trust Funds Amendment Regulations 2009 (SI 2009/475) reg.5 (April 6, 2009).
2. Child Trust Funds (Amendment No.3) Regulations 2010 (SI 2010/1894) reg.4 (August 1, 2010).

[¹ **Yearly disability payments**

9.19 **7B.**—(1) A further contribution under section 10 of the Act is due for any eligible child who is entitled in [²the year 2009/10 or 2010/11] to a disability living allowance, in accordance with paragraphs (2) to (4).

(2) Where it has been determined that the child is entitled to the care component of a disability living allowance at the highest weekly rate (see section 72(4)(a) of either the Social Security Contributions and Benefits Act 1992 or the Social Security Contributions and Benefits (Northern Ireland) Act 1992), at any time in the year (whether it is paid or not), the contribution payable for the year shall be £200.

(3) In any other case where it has been determined that the child is entitled to a disability living allowance at any time in the year (whether it is paid or not), the contribution payable for the year shall be £100.

(SI 2004/1450 reg.7B) (as amended)

(4) [²...]

(5) Her Majesty's Revenue and Customs must inform the account provider holding the child's account where an amount is payable to that account under this regulation.

(6) On receipt of each further contribution from Her Majesty's Revenue and Customs, the account provider must credit the child's account with the amount of the payment.]

AMENDMENTS

1. Child Trust Funds (Amendment No.2) Regulations 2010 (SI 2010/836) reg.3 (April 1, 2010).
2. Child Trust Funds (Amendment No.3) Regulations 2010 (SI 2010/1894) reg.5 (August 1, 2010).

GENERAL NOTE

This regulation provides for *yearly* government contributions into the Child Trust Fund accounts of disabled and severely disabled children. It applies only to children who became entitled to disability living allowance (DLA) on or after April 6, 2009 (see Child Trust Funds (Amendment No.2) Regulations 2010 (SI 2010/836) reg.1(2)). It makes provision for the yearly disability payments into the fund of £200 where the child is entitled to the highest rate care component of DLA (para.(2)) and of £100 in other cases (para.(3)). The provision rests on "entitlement" to disability living allowance, rather than actual payment, in order to cover certain children in hospital in respect of whom payment is not made, but who would remain formally entitled to DLA.

9.20

PART 2

OTHER REQUIREMENTS TO BE SATISFIED IN RELATION TO ACCOUNTS

General requirements for accounts

8.—(1) An account must satisfy the requirements that—
(a) it is the account for a single child ("the named child");
(b) the named child is or has been an eligible child;
(c) no child may hold more than one account;
(d) [³...]
(e) the account must at all times be managed in accordance with these Regulations by an account provider and, subject to regulation 6(2), under terms agreed and recorded in a management agreement made between the account provider and the registered contact (on behalf of the named child where appropriate); and
(f) the management agreement must include instructions to the provider as to the manner in which Inland Revenue contributions and any subscriptions made are to be invested under the account.

(2) Apart from other requirements of these Regulations the terms so agreed shall include the conditions that—
(a) the account investments shall be in the beneficial ownership of the named child;
(b) the title to all account investments, except those falling within regulation 12(2)(k), (l) or (m), shall be vested in the account provider or his nominee, subject to sub-paragraph (f);

9.21

(c) where a share certificate or other document evidencing title to an account investment is issued, it shall be held by the account provider or as he may direct, subject to sub-paragraph (f);

(d) in relation to qualifying investments falling within regulation 12(2)(a), (b) and (f) to (j), the account provider shall, if the registered contact so elects (and subject to any charge for the arrangement), arrange for the registered contact to receive a copy of the annual report and accounts issued to investors by every company, unit trust, open-ended investment company or other entity in which account investments are held;

(e) in relation to qualifying investments falling within regulation 12(2)(a), (b) and (f) to (j), the account provider shall, if the registered contact so elects (subject to any charge for the arrangement, and to any provisions made under any enactment), be under an obligation to arrange for the registered contact to be able—
 (i) to attend any meetings of investors in companies, unit trusts, open-ended investment companies and other entities in which account investments are held,
 (ii) to vote, and
 (iii) to receive, in addition to the documents referred to in sub-paragraph (d), any other information issued to investors in such companies, unit trusts, open-ended investment companies and other entities;

(f) if and so long as a person falling within regulation 14(2)(d)(iv) acts as account provider of an account, and the account investments include a policy of life insurance—
 (i) the title to all such policies shall be vested in the registered contact, and
 (ii) where a policy document or other document evidencing title to such policies of life insurance is issued, it shall be held by the registered contact;

(g) the account provider shall satisfy himself that any person to whom he delegates any of his functions or responsibilities under the management agreement is competent to carry out those functions or responsibilities;

(h) on the instructions of the registered contact ("the transfer instructions") and within such time as is stipulated by the registered contact in the transfer instructions, the whole of an account, with all rights and obligations of the parties to it, shall be transferred free of expense (except any incidental expenses) to another account provider subject to and in accordance with regulation 21;

[^{1}(ha) where the account is or has been transferred to the account provider by a transfer under regulation 21, that no charges or expenses are due in respect of that transfer, except in accordance with sub-paragraph (h);]

[^{2}(hb) any transfer under regulation 20A shall be free of expense (except any incidental expenses);]

(i) where the account provider offers accounts of another description or type, on the instructions of the registered contact ("the internal transfer instructions") and within such time as is stipulated by the registered contact in the internal transfer instructions, the account shall become (free of expense, except any incidental expenses) an account of that other description or type (any necessary change in the investments being made accordingly); and

(j) the account provider shall notify the registered contact if by reason of any failure to satisfy the provisions of these Regulations an account is or will become no longer exempt from tax by virtue of regulation 24.

(3) Where the transfer instructions or internal transfer instructions, or any new management agreement entered into by the registered contact with the account provider (or a new account provider) under regulation 8(1)(e), is a distance contract, the transfer or internal transfer shall only take effect once those contracts satisfy Condition 4 in regulation 5(1).

(4) The time stipulated in transfer instructions or internal transfer instructions shall be subject to any reasonable business period (not exceeding 30 days) of the account provider required for the practical implementation of the instructions.

(5) In this regulation, "incidental expenses" means stamp duty and other dealing costs of disposing of or acquiring investments.

AMENDMENTS

1. Child Trust Funds (Amendment) Regulations 2004 (SI 2004/2676) reg.6 (April 6, 2005).
2. Child Trust Funds (Amendment No.2) Regulations 2015 (SI 2015/876) regs 2 and 4 (April 6, 2015).
3. Child Trust Funds (Amendment No.3) Regulations 2015 (SI 2015/1371) reg.5 (July 1, 2015).

DEFINITIONS

"account"—see reg.2(1)(b).
"account investment"—see reg.2(1)(b).
"account provider"—see reg.2(1)(b).
"child"—see reg.2(1)(a).
"company"—see reg.2(1)(b).
"incidental expenses"—see reg.8(5).
"open-ended investment company"—see reg.2(1)(c).
"responsible person"—see reg.2(1)(a).
"subscriptions"—see reg.2(1)(b).
"tax"—see reg.2(1)(b).

Annual limit on subscriptions

9.—(1) Any person (including the child) may make subscriptions to a child's account, subject to paragraphs (2) and (3).

(2) Subscriptions to an account made during any subscription year, that is—
(a) the period beginning with the day on which the account is opened (or if opened before the appointed day, opened for the purpose of accepting subscriptions under regulation 5(2)(b)), and ending immediately before the child's next birthday, and
(b) any succeeding period of twelve months,
shall not in aggregate exceed the sum of [1£9,000].

(3) Where the aggregate of subscriptions in any year falls short of [1£9,000] or is nil, there shall be no addition to the amount for any succeeding year.

AMENDMENT

1. Child Trust Funds (Amendment No.2) Regulations 2020 (SI 2020/269), reg.3 (April 6, 2020).

DEFINITIONS

"account"—see reg.2(1)(b).
"appointed day"—see reg.2(1)(b).
"child"—see reg.2(1)(a).
"subscriptions"—see reg.2(1)(b).

GENERAL NOTE

9.23   A child trust fund is tax-advantaged because no tax is paid on any interest or capital growth arising from investments in the account. In April 2019 the annual limit on subscriptions was raised slightly from £4,260 to £4,368. However, as from April 6, 2020 the annual subscription limit was increased from £4,368 to £9,000. This change in limit was intended to demonstrate the government's support for savings by younger people.

Statements for an account

9.24   **10.**—[² (1) The account provider must produce a statement for the account—
   (a) subject to paragraphs (6) and (7), annually ("an annual statement"), and
   (b) where an account is transferred [³ . . .] under regulation [³ 20A or] 21, as at the transfer date ("a transfer statement").
(2) References in paragraphs (2A)(b), (3), (4), (5), (6) and (8) to a statement (without more) shall be construed as references to any statement required to be produced in accordance with this regulation.
(2A) The account provider must produce an annual statement at a date (a "relevant date") not later than 12 months from the latest of—
   (a) the date of the opening of the account;
   (b) the date at which the most recent statement was produced; and
   (c) the last date at which, but for paragraph (6), a previous annual statement would have had to have been produced.]
(3) [² A statement required to be produced in accordance with this regulation] shall be sent—
   (a) where the named child is the registered contact, to the child,
   (b) where a responsible person is the registered contact, to the named child care of the registered contact,
[⁴ (c) where a person has been appointed by the Treasury or the Secretary of State by virtue of section 3(10) of the Act, to that person on behalf of the child, and]
   (d) in any other case, to the named child,
within 30 days of the [² date specified in paragraph (3A)].
[² (3A) The date specified in this paragraph is—
   (a) in relation to an annual statement, the relevant date;
   (b) in relation to a transfer statement, the transfer date; or
   (c) where paragraph (7) applies, the later of the relevant date in relation to the annual statement requested and the date that the request is received by the account provider.]
(4) Statements shall include the following information—
   (a) the full name of the child;
   (b) [⁶. . .];
   (c) [⁶. . .];
   (d) his unique reference number;

(e) the description of the account (see regulation 4);
(f) the name of the registered contact (if any);
(g) the [² relevant date];
[² (h) the total market value of the investments under the account at the date at which the most recent statement was produced (if any);]
   (i) the amount of any Government contributions [¹(see regulation 7) received by the account provider], during the period between—
      [² (i) the date at which the most recent statement was produced, or the opening of the account (whichever is the later), and]
      (ii) the [² relevant date];
(j) the aggregate amount of subscriptions (if any) received during the period in sub-paragraph (i);
(k) the total amount of deductions (including management charges) made during the period in sub-paragraph (i);
(l) the total market value of the investments under the account at the [² relevant date];
(m) the number or amount, description and market value of each of the investments under the account at the [² relevant date];
(n) the basis used in calculating the market value of each investment under the account (together with a statement of any change from a basis used in the previous statement); and
(o) the exchange rate used where any investment is, or is denominated in, a currency other than sterling.

[¹(5) As an alternative to the information in paragraph (4)(k), the statement may include, in relation to any management charges or other incidental expenses deducted from the account during the period in paragraph (4)(i)—
  (a) the rate, expressed as an annual percentage rate, at which, and the period in relation to which, such deductions were made, or
  (b) where such deductions were made in relation to different periods at different rates—
     (i) each rate, expressed as an annual percentage rate, at which those deductions were made; and
     (ii) the period in relation to which they were made at that rate.]

[² (6) Where, in relation to an annual statement, at a relevant date—
  (a) the aggregate market value of the account investments held under the account is less than £300, or
  (b) no subscriptions under regulation 9 have been made to the account during the relevant period,
then, subject to paragraph (7), the account provider need only produce the annual statement if it would be the first statement to be produced following the child's fourth, tenth [⁵, fifteenth or seventeenth] birthday.

(7) Paragraph (6) shall not apply where any potential recipient of an annual statement (see paragraph (3)) requests such a statement.

(8) "The relevant period" means the period—
  (a) beginning on the latest of—
     (i) the date of the opening of the account;
     (ii) the date at which the most recent statement was produced; and
     (iii) the last date as at which, but for paragraph (6), an annual statement would have had to have been produced; and
  (b) ending on the relevant date.]

AMENDMENTS

1. Child Trust Funds (Amendment) Regulations 2004 (SI 2004/2676) reg.7 (April 6, 2005).
2. Child Trust Funds (Amendment No.2) Regulations 2011 (SI 2011/992) reg.2 (April 20, 2011).
3. Child Trust Funds (Amendment No.2) Regulations 2015 (SI 2015/876) regs 2 and 5 (April 6, 2015).
4. Child Trust Funds (Amendment No.2) Regulations 2017 (SI 2017/748) reg.3 (October 1, 2017).
5. Child Trust Funds (Amendment) Regulations 2020 (SI 2020/29), reg.4 (April 6, 2020).
6. Child Trust Funds (Amendment) Regulations 2023 (SI 2023/269) reg.4 (April 6, 2023).

DEFINITIONS

"account"—see reg.2(1)(b).
"account provider"—see reg.2(1)(b).
"child"—see reg.2(1)(a).
"investments under the account"—see reg.2(1)(b).
"market value"—see reg.2(1)(b).
"responsible person"—see reg.2(1)(a).
"subscriptions"—see reg.2(1)(b).

General investment rules

9.25   11.—(1) All transactions by way of purchase by an account provider of investments under an account shall be made—
  (a) in the case of an authorised fund which is a dual priced unit trust, at the [³ maximum sale price of a unit of the relevant class at the relevant valuation point] within the meaning of, and complying with the requirements of, [³ [⁴ paragraphs] 6.3.5 and 6.3.5B] of the [⁴ COLL];
  (b) in the case of an authorised fund which is a single priced unit trust or an open-ended investment company, at the price of a unit [³ of the relevant class at the relevant valuation point] within the meaning of, and complying with the requirements of, [³ [⁴ paragraphs] 6.3.5 and 6.3.5A] of the [⁴ COLL]; and
  (c) in the case of all other account investments, at the price for which those investments might reasonably be expected to be purchased in the open market.
(2) In paragraph (1)—
"a dual priced unit trust" means an authorised unit trust in respect of which the manager gives different prices for buying and selling units at the same time;
"a single priced unit trust" means an authorised unit trust in respect of which the manager gives the same price for buying and selling units at the same time.
(3) All other transactions by way of sale or otherwise by an account provider in investments under an account shall be made at the price for which those investments might reasonably be expected to be sold or otherwise transacted, as the case may be, in the open market.
(4) Investments, or rights in respect of investments, may not at any time—
  (a) be purchased or made otherwise than out of cash which an account provider holds under an account at that time; or
  (b) be purchased from—

(SI 2004/1450 reg.11) (as amended)

    (i) the named child, or
    (ii) the spouse [³or civil partner] of the named child,
so as to become account investments under the account.

(5) Subject to paragraph (6), contributions, subscriptions and any other cash held by an account provider under an account shall be held only in sterling and be deposited in an account with a deposit-taker [¹(including for this purpose a credit union)], or a deposit account or a share account with a building society, which is designated as a CTF account for the purposes of these Regulations only.

(6) An account provider who is a European institution, a relevant authorised person or an assurance undertaking may hold an account investor's cash subscription and other cash held under an account in the currency of the EEA State in which he has his principal place of business and may deposit such cash in an account, which is designated as mentioned in paragraph (5), with any person authorised under the law of that State to accept deposits.

AMENDMENTS

1. Child Trust Funds (Amendment No.2) Regulations 2005 (SI 2005/909) reg.4 (April 6, 2005).
2. Civil Partnership Act 2004 (Tax Credits, etc.) (Consequential Amendments) Order 2005 (SI 2005/2919) art.15 (December 5, 2006).
3. Child Trust Funds (Amendment) Regulations 2010 (SI 2010/582) reg.4 (April 6, 2010).
4. Financial Services Act 2012 (Consequential Amendments and Transitional Provisions) Order 2013 (SI 2013/472) art.3 and Sch.2 para.93(c) (April 1, 2013).

DEFINITIONS

    "account"—see reg.2(1)(b).
    "account investment"—see reg.2(1)(b).
    "account provider"—see reg.2(1)(b).
    "assurance undertaking"—see reg.2(1)(b).
    "authorised fund"—see reg.2(1)(c).
    "building society"—see reg.2(1)(b).
    "child"—see reg.2(1)(a).
    "Collective Investment Schemes Sourcebook"—see reg.2(1)(c).
    "credit union"—see reg.2(1)(b).
    "deposit taker"—see reg.2(1)(b).
    "dual priced unit trust"—see reg.11(2).
    "EEA State"—see reg.2(1)(b).
    "European institution"—see reg.2(1)(b).
    "investments under the account"—see reg.2(1)(b).
    "open-ended investment company"—see reg.2(1)(c).
    "relevant authorised person"—see reg.2(1)(b).
    "single priced unit trust"—see reg.11(2).
    "subscriptions"—see reg.2(1)(b).
    "units"—see reg.2(1)(c).

Qualifying investments for an account

    12.—(1) This regulation specifies the kind of investments ("qualifying investments for an account") which may be purchased, made or held under an account.

9.26

(2) Qualifying investments for an account to which paragraph (1) refers are—
- (a) shares, not being shares in an investment trust, issued by a company wherever incorporated and [5either officially listed on a recognised stock exchange or, in the European Economic Area, admitted to trading on a recognised stock exchange (see paragraph (3))]
- (b) securities—
  - (i) issued by a company wherever incorporated, [3 and]
  - (ii) which satisfy at least one of the conditions specified in paragraph (5) [3...]
- (c) gilt-edged securities;
- (d) any securities issued by or on behalf of a government of any EEA State;
- (e) any securities which, in relation to a security mentioned in sub-paragraph (d), would be a strip of that security if "strip" had the same meaning as in section 47 of the Finance Act 1942, with the omission of the words "issued under the National Loans Act 1968";
- (f) shares in an investment trust [6...][3...][10 listed or admitted to trading on a recognised stock exchange in circumstances where the trust satisfies the condition specified in paragraph (3)];
- (g) [3...]
- (h) [3...]
- [3 (i) units in, or shares of, a UK UCITS or recognised UCITS;]
- (j) a depositary interest;
- (k) cash deposited in a deposit account with a building society, or a person falling within [3 section 991 of ITA 2007 (including for this purpose a credit union)], subject to paragraph (8);
- (l) cash deposited in a share account with a building society, subject to paragraph (8);
- (m) policies of life insurance which satisfy the conditions specified in paragraphs (9) and (10);
- (n) any securities issued under the National Loans Act 1968—
  - (i) for the purpose of or in connection with raising money under the auspices of the Director of Savings within the meaning of section 11(1)(a) of the National Debt Act 1972, and
  - (ii) other than national savings certificates, premium savings bonds, national savings stamps and national savings gift tokens,

  which, according to the terms and conditions subject to which they are issued and purchased, are expressly permitted to be held under an account.
- [2(o) arrangements falling within section 47 of the Finance Act 2005 (alternative finance arrangements) under which the person referred to in that section as Y is a financial institution;
- (p) arrangements falling within section 49 of that Act;
- (q) qualifying units in or shares of a non-UCITS retail scheme;]
- [7 (r) core capital deferred shares within the meaning of regulation 2 of the Building Societies (Core Capital Deferred Shares) Regulations 2013, provided that such shares are listed on the official list of a recognised stock exchange.]

[9(2A) Notwithstanding any provision of paragraph (2), investments which—
- (a) are held under an account on the coming into force of this paragraph; and

(b) immediately beforehand fell within paragraph (2)(i) by virtue of being units in, or shares of, a recognised UCITS,

are to be treated, for as long as they are so held, as qualifying investments for an account.]

(3) [⁶An investment in shares fulfils the conditions as to official listing and admission to trading in paragraph (2)(a)] [¹⁰or (f)][⁵,] if—
- (a) in pursuance of a public offer, the account provider applies for the allotment or allocation to him of shares in a company [⁶...] [¹⁰ or investment trust] which are due to be admitted to such listing [⁵or admitted to such trading] within 30 days of the allocation or allotment, and which, when admitted to such listing [⁵ or trading], would be qualifying investments for an account, and
- (b) the shares are not allotted or allocated to the account provider in the circumstances specified in paragraph (4).

(4) The circumstances specified in this paragraph are where—
- (a) the allotment or allocation of the shares was connected with the allotment or allocation of—
  - (i) shares in the company or investment trust of a different class, or
  - (ii) rights to shares in the company or investment trust of a different class, or
  - (iii) shares or rights to shares in another company or investment trust, or
  - (iv) units in or shares in, or rights to units in or shares in, an authorised fund or a part of an umbrella scheme, or
  - (v) securities or rights to securities of the company or investment trust, or of another company or investment trust,

to the account provider, the registered contact or any other person; and
- (b) the terms on which the first-mentioned shares in this paragraph were offered were significantly more favourable to the account provider or the named child than they would have been if their allotment or allocation had not been connected as described in sub-paragraph (a).

(5) The conditions specified in this paragraph are—
- (a) that the shares in the company issuing the securities are listed on the official list of a recognised stock exchange;
- (b) that the securities are so listed;
- (c) that the company issuing the securities is a 75 per cent subsidiary of a company whose shares are so listed;

[⁸ (d) that the shares in the company issuing the securities are admitted to trading on a recognised stock exchange in the European Economic Area;
- (e) that the securities are so admitted to trading;
- (f) that the company issuing the securities is a 75 per cent. subsidiary of a company whose shares are so admitted to trading.]

(6) [³...]

(7) In paragraph (4)(a), "company" means any body corporate having a share capital.

[⁴ (8) A deposit account or share account which is a qualifying investment for an account falling within paragraph (2)(k) or (l) must not be connected with any other investment, held by the named child or any other person.

(8A) For the purposes of paragraph (8), a deposit account or share account described in that paragraph, is connected with another investment if—

(a) either was opened or acquired with reference to the other, or with a view to enabling the other to be opened or acquired on particular terms, or with a view to facilitating the opening or acquisition of the other on particular terms,
(b) the terms on which the deposit account or share account was opened would have been significantly less favourable to the holder if the other investment had not been held, and
(c) the other investment is not a tax exempt investment.

(8B) The following are tax exempt investments for the purposes of paragraph (8A)—
(a) an account investment held under a child trust fund;
(b) an account investment within the meaning given in the Individual Savings Account Regulations 1998 held under an account opened (or treated as opened) in accordance with regulation 12 or 12A of those regulations.]

(9) The conditions specified in this paragraph are that—
(a) the insurance is on the life of the named child only;
(b) the terms and conditions of the policy provide—
  (i) that the policy may only be owned or held as a qualifying investment for an account which satisfies the provisions of these Regulations;
  (ii) that the policy shall automatically terminate if it comes to the notice of the account provider, in any manner, that the event specified in paragraph (11) has occurred in relation to the policy;
  (iii) for an express prohibition of any payment of the proceeds from the termination of the policy or a partial surrender of the rights conferred by the policy, to the named child (while he is still a child) [¹except in accordance with regulation 18A (terminal illness)]; and
  (iv) that the policy, the rights conferred by the policy and any share or interest in the policy or rights respectively, shall not be capable of assignment or (in Scotland) assignation, other than that they may be vested in the named child's personal representatives, and that the title to the policy may be transferred to a new account provider subject to and in accordance with regulations 8(2)(f) and 21;
(c) the policy evidences or secures a contract of insurance which—
  (i) falls within paragraph 1 or 3 of Part 2 of Schedule 1 to the Financial Services and Markets Act 2000 (Regulated Activities) Order 2001, or
  (ii) would fall within either of those paragraphs if the insurer were a company with permission under Part 4 of the Financial Services and Markets Act 2000 to effect or carry out contracts of insurance;
(d) the policy is not—
  (i) a contract to pay an annuity on human life,
  (ii) a personal portfolio bond within the meaning given by [³ section 516 of ITTOIA 2005], or
  (iii) a contract, the effecting and carrying out of which constitutes "pension business" within the meaning given by section 431B(1) of the Taxes Act; and
(e) after the first payment in respect of a premium in relation to the policy has been made, there is no contractual obligation on any person to make any other such payment.

(10) The condition specified in this paragraph is that no sum may at any time, at or after the making of the insurance, be lent to or at the direction of the named child or registered contact by or by arrangement with the insurer for the time being responsible for the obligations under the policy.

(11) The event specified in this paragraph is that—
  (a) there has been a breach of any of the conditions in paragraph (9) or (10), or any of those conditions was not satisfied at the date on which the insurance was made; and
  (b) the breach or non-compliance cannot be remedied in accordance with regulation 23, or (in any other case), has not been remedied within a reasonable time.

(12) Where the event specified in paragraph (11) occurs in relation to a policy, the policy shall nevertheless be treated, for the purposes of these Regulations, excepting paragraphs (9)(b)(ii) and (11), and regulations 37(6) and 38, as if it had satisfied the conditions in paragraphs (9) and (10) during the period—
  (a) commencing at the time when that specified event occurred, and
  (b) ending immediately before—
    [³ (i) the end of the final insurance year in relation to the policy, within the meaning given by section 499 of ITTOIA 2005,]
    (ii) the time at which that specified event came to the notice of the account provider,
whichever first occurs (the "termination event").

AMENDMENTS

1. Child Trust Funds (Amendment) Regulations 2004 (SI 2004/2676) reg.8 (April 6, 2005).
2. Child Trust Funds (Amendment No.3) Regulations 2005 (SI 2005/3349) reg.5 (December 27, 2005).
3. Child Trust Funds (Amendment) Regulations 2010 (SI 2010/582) reg.5 (April 6, 2010).
4. Child Trust Funds (Amendment) Regulations 2012 (SI 2012/1870) reg.2 (August 8, 2012).
5. Child Trust Funds (Amendment No.2) Regulations 2013 (SI 2013/1744) reg.5 (August 5, 2013).
6. Child Trust Funds (Amendment) Regulations 2014 (SI 2014/649) reg.5 (April 6, 2014).
7. Child Trust Funds (Amendment No.2) Regulations 2014 (SI 2014/1453) regs 2 and 4 (July 1, 2014).
8. Child Trust Funds (Amendment No.3) Regulations 2015 (SI 2015/1371) reg.6 (July 1, 2015).
9. Child Trust Funds (Amendment) Regulations 2020 (SI 2020/29), reg.5 (January 31, 2020).
10. Child Trust Funds (Amendment) Regulations 2023 (SI 2023/269) reg.5 (April 6, 2023).

DEFINITIONS

"account"—see reg.2(1)(b).
"account provider"—see reg.2(1)(b).
"authorised fund"—see reg.2(1)(c).
"building society"—see reg.2(1)(b).
"child"—see reg.2(1)(a).
"company"—see regs.2(1)(b) and 12(7).

"credit union"—see reg.2(1)(b).
"depositary interest"—see reg.2(1)(c).
"EEA State"—see reg.2(1)(b).
"European institution"—see reg.2(1)(b).
"fund of funds scheme"—see reg.2(1)(c).
"gilt-edged securities"—see reg.2(1)(b).
"investments under the account"—see reg.2(1)(b).
"investment trust"—see reg.2(1)(b).
"money market scheme"—see reg.2(1)(c).
"recognised stock exchange"—see reg.2(1)(b).
"relevant European institution"—see reg.2(1)(b).
"securities scheme"—see reg.2(1)(c).
"security"—see reg.2(1)(b).
"the Taxes Act"—see reg.2(1)(b).
"UCITS"—see reg.2(1)(c).
"umbrella scheme"—see reg.2(1)(c).
"units"—see reg.2(1)(c).
"warrant scheme"—see reg.2(1)(c).
"year"—see reg.2(1)(b).

Conditions for application by responsible person or the child to open an account (and changes to an account)

9.27

13.—(1) An application by a responsible person in relation to a child or the child if 16 or over, as the case may be, ("the applicant") to open an account for the child with an account provider must be made to the account provider in a statement which must satisfy the conditions specified in paragraphs (2) to (6).

(2) An application must specify the description of account applied for.

(3) An application must incorporate a declaration by the applicant that he—
   (a) is aged 16 years of age or over,
   (b) is—
      (i) (where the child is under 16) a responsible person in relation to the named child (that is, that he has parental responsibility [¹or, in Scotland, parental responsibilities] in relation to the child), or
      (ii) the child if 16 or over, and
   (c) is to be the registered contact for the account;
and where the application is not in writing, must authorise the account provider to record the terms of the declaration in a written declaration made on behalf of the applicant.

(4) The applicant must authorise the account provider (on behalf of the named child where appropriate)—
   (a) to hold the child's Inland Revenue contributions, subscriptions, account investments, interest, dividends and any other rights or proceeds in respect of those investments and cash, and
   (b) to make on his behalf any claims to relief from tax in respect of account investments,
and the authority must continue until a further application and declaration is made in accordance with paragraph (10).

(5) An application must contain—
   (a) the applicant's full name,
   (b) his address, including postcode,
   (c) the named child's full name [¹and date of birth],

(d) his address, including postcode, and
(e) the child's unique reference number on the voucher.

(6) There may be only one declaration and authorisation under paragraphs (3) to (5) in force for an account at any time.

(7) Except in the case—
(a) of the death or incapacity of the registered contact,
(b) where the registered contact cannot be contacted,
(c) of the bringing to an end of a Court order, under which he is a responsible person for the named child,
(d) of the named child attaining the age of 16 years,
[³ (da) where the new registered contact has been appointed to be a guardian or special guardian of the named child,
(db) where the new registered contact is the adopter of the named child under an adoption order,]
[⁵ (e) where a person is appointed by the Treasury or the Secretary of State by virtue of section 3(10) of the Act, or]
(f) where a Court so orders,

any change in the identity of the registered contact shall require confirmation by the current registered contact that his declaration and authorisation under paragraphs (3)(c) and (4) is cancelled [³, and in the cases in sub-paragraphs (a) to (f) it shall be treated as automatically cancelled].

(8) An account provider must decline to accept an application if he has reason to believe that—
(a) the voucher has expired, or is not or might not be genuine, or
(b) the applicant has given untrue information in his application.

(9) Where the application is not in writing, the account provider shall make the written declaration referred to in paragraph (3), and notify the applicant of its contents, and such declaration shall take effect from the date on which the applicant agrees the contents (subject to any corrections), and if he neither agrees or disagrees with the contents within 30 days, he shall be treated as having agreed them.

(10) Where—
(a) there is a change in the identity of the registered contact, the new registered contact, or
(b) an account has been opened by the Inland Revenue under regulation 6 (Revenue allocated accounts) [⁴ and—
  (i) a responsible person in relation to the child subsequently applies to the account provider to be the registered contact for the account, or
  (ii) the child, if the child is 16 or over and has elected to manage the account, subsequently applies to the account provider to be the registered contact for the account,

that individual must make the application or declaration required by paragraphs (3) to (5) but as if for regulation 13(3)(b) there were substituted—
"(b) is—
  (i) a responsible person in relation to the named child (that is, that he has parental responsibility or, in Scotland, parental responsibilities in relation to the child), or
  (ii) the child, where the child is 16 or over and has elected to manage the account."]

[¹(11) Where the new registered contact is [⁵the person appointed by the Treasury or the Secretary of State by virtue of section 3(10) of the

Act, that person.] shall make the declaration and authorisation required by paragraphs (3)(c) and (4) [²and shall be treated as a party to the existing management agreement for the account in question].]

AMENDMENTS

1. Child Trust Funds (Amendment) Regulations 2004 (SI 2004/2676) reg.9 (April 6, 2005).
2. Child Trust Funds (Amendment No.2) Regulations 2004 (SI 2004/3382) reg.3 (April 6, 2005).
3. Child Trust Funds (Amendment) Regulations 2010 (SI 2010/582) reg.6 (April 6, 2010).
4. Child Trust Funds (Amendment No.3) Regulations 2015 (SI 2015/1371) reg.7 (July 1, 2015).
5. Child Trust Funds (Amendment No.2) Regulations 2017 (SI 2017/748) reg.4 (October 1, 2017).

DEFINITIONS

"account"—see reg.2(1)(b).
"account investment"—see reg.2(1)(b).
"account provider"—see reg.2(1)(b).
"child"—see reg.2(1)(a).
"parental responsibility"—see reg.2(1)(a).
"responsible person"—see reg.2(1)(a).
"subscriptions"—see reg.2(1)(b).
"tax"—see reg.2(1)(b).

[¹ **Maturity of child trust fund – instructions**

9.28   **13A.**—(1) Instructions of a holder of a child trust fund to the account provider as to what is to be done with the investments under—
(a) the child trust fund on its maturity or,
(b) where regulation 13B(2)(a) applies, the matured CTF account,
are to be in accordance with paragraph (2).
(2) Those instructions may be—
(a) where the investments are held otherwise than in cash, to transfer them in specie or to realise them and to transfer the proceeds, or
(b) where they are held in cash, to transfer the cash amount.]

AMENDMENT

1. Child Trust Funds (Amendment) Regulations 2020 (SI 2020/29), reg.6 (April 6, 2020).

[¹ **Maturity of child trust fund – no instructions**

9.29   **13B.**—(1) On the 18th birthday of the holder of a child trust fund, where no instructions have been given under regulation 13A, all the investments under the child trust fund held immediately before that birthday are to be transferred by the account provider to a protected account held with the account provider.
(2) The protected account may be, at the option of the account provider, either—
(a) an account ("matured CTF account") which is to be treated as a continuing account of the person who held the child trust fund ("account holder") to be held subject to these regulations and

otherwise on the same terms and conditions which applied immediately before the account holder's 18th birthday as if the investments had remained in the account for the child trust fund; or
(b) an account, within the meaning of regulation 4 of the Individual Savings Account Regulations 1998, which is a cash account, in respect of investments which are held in cash, or a stocks and shares account, in respect of investments which are held as stocks or shares, to be held subject to those regulations and otherwise on the same terms and conditions which applied immediately before the account holder's 18th birthday as if the investments had remained in the account for the child trust fund.

(3) Investments which are held otherwise than in cash are to be transferred in specie.

(4) In the terms and conditions mentioned in paragraph (2) and in these regulations references to the following howsoever described—
(a) "account" and "child trust fund" are to be read as including the protected account,
(b) "named child", "eligible child" or "child" are to be read as the account holder of the protected account, and
(c) "registered contact" and "responsible person" are to be read as the account holder of the protected account where instructions, notifications, assessments, actions or decisions need to be made in relation to it.]

AMENDMENT

1. Child Trust Funds (Amendment) Regulations 2020 (SI 2020/29), reg.6 (April 6, 2020).

[¹ Matured CTF Account

13C.—(1) Where regulation 13B(2)(a) applies, then notwithstanding any other provision of these regulations, paragraphs (2) to (8) are to apply.

(2) No subscription is to be made to the matured CTF account.

(3) Amounts in respect of investments on the matured CTF account are to be credited to it.

(4) No transfer is to be made of any part of the matured CTF account otherwise than, in circumstances where the account provider intends to cease to act as an account provider, when regulation 19 (account provider's intention to make a bulk transfer of accounts or to cease to act as an account provider) or 21 (transfer of accounts) applies.

(5) In regulation 10 (statements for an account)—
(a) in paragraph (1)(a), the phrase "subject to paragraphs (6) and (7)" is to be treated as omitted,
(b) the words in paragraph (2A) are to be treated as replaced with—
"The account provider must produce a statement not later than 12 months beginning with the date the funds entered the matured account and annually thereafter", and
(c) paragraphs (4)[²...] (e), (f) and (m) to (o) are to be treated as omitted.

(6) Regulations 14(2)(b)(vi) (relating to publication of statements), 18A (permitted withdrawals from an account where the child is terminally ill) and 20A (transfers to other accounts for children) are to be treated as omitted.

(7) In regulation 32 (returns of information by account provider), paragraphs (2)(b)(i), (ii) and (iv) are to be treated as omitted.

(8) An account provider must, when all the investments have been transferred out of the matured CTF account in accordance with instructions under regulation 13A, close the account.]

AMENDMENTS

1. Child Trust Funds (Amendment) Regulations 2020 (SI 2020/29), reg.6 (April 6, 2020).

2. Child Trust Funds (Amendment) Regulations 2023 (SI 2023/269) reg.6 (April 6, 2023).

Account provider—qualifications and Board's approval

9.31 **14.**—(1) This regulation specifies the circumstances ("qualifying circumstances") in which a person may be approved by the Board as an account provider.

(2) The qualifying circumstances are the following—
(a) the person must make an application to the Board for approval in a form specified by the Board;
(b) the person must undertake with the Board—
   (i) to either offer stakeholder accounts to the general public (whether or not accounts of another description are offered), or to fulfil the requirements in paragraph (3),
   (ii) to accept vouchers from any responsible person or the child if 16 or over (subject to [²paragraph (iia) and] regulation 13(8)),
   [³(iia) in the case of a credit union, to accept vouchers from any responsible person or the child if 16 or over, if the child to which the voucher relates is a member, or fulfils or is treated as fulfilling a qualification for admission to membership, of the credit union (subject to regulation 13(8))]
   (iii) where the person accepts Revenue allocated accounts, to allow instructions for their management to be made or given by post (whether or not other methods are allowed),
   (iv) to publicise (and up-date where appropriate) statements of the minimum amount which may be subscribed to an account on a single occasion, and the permitted means of payment of subscriptions,
   (v) to inform persons proposing to make subscriptions to an account (other than the named child) that the subscription is a gift to the child,
   (vi) to publicise (and up-date where appropriate) statements of the extent to which social, environmental or ethical decisions are taken into account in selecting, retaining or realising investments,
   (vii) that a child's unique reference number shall only be used for the purposes of the child's account (and of fulfilling the requirements of these Regulations with regard to that account), and
   (viii) that whether there is an initial contribution or special contribution to an account, whether there is a supplementary contribution to the account, and whether the account is a Revenue allocated account is information held for the purposes mentioned in paragraph (vii) only, and shall not be used for other purposes (including marketing other products);
(c) [⁷...];

(SI 2004/1450 reg.14) (as amended)

- (d) an account provider must be—
  - (i) an authorised person within the meaning of [⁸ FISMA 2000], who has permission to carry on one or more of the activities specified in Articles 14, 21, 25, 37, 40, 45, [¹⁰ 51ZA, 51ZC, 51ZE], 53 and (in so far as it applies to any of those activities) 64 of the Financial Services and Markets Act 2000 (Regulated Activities) Order 2001, but excluding any person falling within paragraph (iv) below;
  - [⁴[⁵(iia) in the case of a credit union, an authorised person within the meaning of [⁹ FISMA 2000], who has permission to carry on one or more of the activities specified in Article 5 of the Financial Services and Markets Act 2000 (Regulated Activities) Order 2001;]
  - (ii) a European institution which carries on one or more of those activities;
  - (iii) a building society [⁶ or a person falling within section 991 of ITA 2007 (including for this purpose a credit union)]; or
  - (iv) an insurance company within the meaning given by section 431(2) of the Taxes Act, an incorporated friendly society or a registered friendly society, or any other assurance undertaking;
- [⁸ (e) an account provider must not be prevented from acting as such by any requirement imposed under Part 4A of FISMA 2000, or by any prohibition or prohibition order in or made under that Act; and]
- (f) an account provider who—
  - (i) [¹¹...]
  - (ii) falls within the expression "any other assurance undertaking" in sub-paragraph (d)(iv),

must fulfil one of the three requirements specified in regulation 15.

(3) The requirements in this paragraph are that the person provides to any potential applicant for a child trust fund ([¹before commencement of completion of] any application under regulation 13)—
- (a) a statement that a stakeholder account is available from a named alternative account provider who offers it on the terms in paragraph (2)(b)(i) (omitting the words from ", or to" to the end);
- (b) a detailed description of that stakeholder account; and
- (c) sufficient information (according to the method of communication used, and including documentation where appropriate) to put the potential applicant in the position to make an application to that alternative account provider, complying with regulation 13.

(4) The terms of the Board's approval may include conditions designed to ensure that the provisions of these Regulations are satisfied.

AMENDMENTS

1. Child Trust Funds (Amendment) Regulations 2004 (SI 2004/2676) reg.10 (April 6, 2005).

2. Child Trust Funds (Amendment No.2) Regulations 2005 (SI 2005/909) reg.6 (April 6, 2005).

3. Child Trust Funds (Amendment No.2) Regulations 2005 (SI 2005/909) reg.7 (April 6, 2005).

4. Child Trust Funds (Amendment No.2) Regulations 2005 (SI 2005/909) reg.8 (April 6, 2005).

5. Child Trust Funds (Amendment No.3) Regulations 2005 (SI 2005/3349) reg.6 (December 27, 2005).
6. Child Trust Funds (Amendment) Regulations 2010 (SI 2010/582) reg.7 (April 6, 2010).
7. Child Trust Funds (Amendment) Regulations 2013 (SI 2013/263) reg.2(4)(c) (March 16, 2013).
8. Financial Services Act 2012 (Consequential Amendments and Transitional Provisions) Order 2013 (SI 2013/472) art.3 and Sch.2 para.93(d) (April 1, 2013).
9. Financial Services Act 2012 (Consequential Amendments and Transitional Provisions) (No.3) Order 2013 (SI 2013/1765) reg.8 (September 1, 2013).
10. Child Trust Funds (Amendment) Regulations 2017 (SI 2017/185) reg.5 (April 6, 2017).
11. Child Trust Funds (Amendment) Regulations 2024 (SI 2024/349) reg.2 (April 6, 2024).

DEFINITIONS

"account"—see reg.2(1)(b).
"account provider"—see reg.2(1)(b).
"applicant"—see reg.5.
"assurance undertaking"—see reg.2(1)(b).
"building society"—see reg.2(1)(b).
"child"—see reg.2(1)(a).
"child trust fund"—see reg.2(1)(a).
"company"—see reg.2(1)(b).
"credit union"—see reg.2(1)(b).
"European institution"—see reg.2(1)(b).
"incorporated friendly society"—see reg.2(1)(b).
"registered friendly society"—see reg.2(1)(b).
"relevant authorised person"—see reg.2(1)(b).
"relevant European institution"—see reg.2(1)(b).
"responsible person"—see reg.2(1)(a).
"subscriptions"—see reg.2(1)(b).
"the Taxes Act"—see reg.2(1)(b).

Account provider—appointment of tax representative

9.32

15.—(1) This regulation specifies the requirements mentioned in regulation 14(2)(f).

(2) The first requirement specified in this regulation is that—
(a) a person who falls within [¹ section 698(2)(b) of ITTOIA 2005] is for the time being appointed by the account provider to be responsible for securing the discharge of the duties prescribed by paragraph (5) which fall to be discharged by the account provider, and
(b) his identity and the fact of his appointment have been notified to the Board by the account provider.

(3) The second requirement specified in this regulation is that there are for the time being other arrangements with the Board for a person other than the account provider to secure the discharge of such duties.

(4) The third requirement specified in this regulation is that there are for the time being other arrangements with the Board designed to secure the discharge of such duties.

(5) The duties prescribed by this paragraph are those that fall to be discharged by an account provider under these Regulations.

(SI 2004/1450 reg.15) (as amended)

(6) The appointment of a person in pursuance of the first requirement shall be treated as terminated in circumstances where—
  (a) the Board have reason to believe that the person concerned—
    (i) has failed to secure the discharge of any of the duties prescribed by paragraph (5), or
    (ii) does not have adequate resources to discharge those duties, and
  (b) the Board have notified the account provider and that person that they propose to treat his appointment as having terminated with effect from the date specified in the notice.

(7) Where, in accordance with the first requirement, a person is at any time responsible for securing the discharge of duties, the person concerned—
  (a) shall be entitled to act on the account provider's behalf for any of the purposes of the provisions relating to the duties;
  (b) shall secure (where appropriate by acting on the account provider's behalf) the account provider's compliance with and discharge of the duties; and
  (c) shall be personally liable in respect of any failure of the account provider to comply with or discharge any such duty as if the duties imposed on the account provider were imposed jointly and severally on the account provider and the person concerned.

AMENDMENT

1. Child Trust Funds (Amendment) Regulations 2010 (SI 2010/582) reg.8 (April 6, 2010).

DEFINITIONS

"account provider"—see reg.2(1)(b).
"notice"—see reg.2(1)(b).
"the Taxes Act"—see reg.2(1)(b).

Account provider—withdrawal by Board of approval

16.—(1) This regulation specifies the circumstances ("the disqualifying circumstances") in which the Board may by notice withdraw their approval of a person as an account provider in relation to an account.

(2) The disqualifying circumstances are that the Board have reason to believe—
  (a) that any provision of the Act or these Regulations, or any term of an undertaking given in accordance with regulation 14(2)(b) or condition under regulation 14(4), is not or at any time has not been satisfied, either in respect of an account managed by the account provider or otherwise; or
  (b) that a person to whom they have given approval to act as an account provider is not qualified so to act.

[² (2A) Where paragraph (2B) applies, a term of an undertaking given in accordance with regulation 14(2)(b) shall not be taken as not satisfied only by reason that the person to whom the Board's approval as an account provider has been given does not accept vouchers.

(2B) This paragraph applies where—
  (a) a person does not accept any voucher after a day specified by that person; and

9.33

(b) no less than 30 days before the specified day, notice in writing is given to the Board of the person's intention not to accept vouchers after that day.]

[³(3) The notice to which paragraph (1) refers must specify—
(a) the disqualifying circumstances;
(b) that the withdrawal shall only be effective from the date on which the last of the accounts has been transferred to another provider; and
(c) that from the date of the notice, the account provider must not accept subscriptions or open any new accounts.]

[¹ (4) On receiving the notice referred to in paragraph (1), subject to any appeal under section 22(1)(b) of the Act, the account provider shall notify the registered contact (or, if there is no registered contact, the named child) of the right to transfer the account under regulation 21, and of his or her rights under regulation 20(3).]

[³(5) From the date of the notice, the account provider must not accept subscriptions or open new accounts.]

AMENDMENTS

1. Child Trust Funds (Amendment) Regulations 2010 (SI 2010/582) reg.9 (April 6, 2010).
2. Child Trust Funds (Amendment No.4) Regulations 2010 (SI 2010/2599) reg.3(1) (November 16, 2010).
3. Child Trust Funds (Amendment) Regulations 2023 (SI 2023/269) reg.7 (April 6, 2023).

DEFINITIONS

"account"—see reg.2(1)(b).
"account provider"—see reg.2(1)(b).
"notice"—see reg.2(1)(b).

Account provider—appeal against non-approval or withdrawal of Board's approval

9.34   17.—A person who has been notified of a decision by the Board not to approve that person as an account provider, or an account provider to whom notice of withdrawal of approval has been given under regulation 16, may appeal against the decision by notice given to the Board within 30 days after the date of the notification or notice.

DEFINITIONS

"account provider"—see reg.2(1)(b).
"notice"—see reg.2(1)(b).

Permitted withdrawals from an account

9.35   18.—Withdrawals from an account before the date on which the named child attains the age of 18 years may only be made—
(a) by the account provider, to settle any management charges and other incidental expenses, which are due by or under the management agreement, or
[¹(ab) in accordance with regulation 18A, or]
(b) where the account provider is satisfied that the named child has died under that age.

(SI 2004/1450 reg.18) (as amended)

AMENDMENT

1. Child Trust Funds (Amendment) Regulations 2004 (SI 2004/2676) reg.11 (April 6, 2005).

DEFINITIONS

"account"—see reg.2(1)(b).
"account provider"—see reg.2(1)(b).
"child"—see reg.2(1)(a).

[¹Permitted withdrawals from an account where the child is terminally ill

18A.—(1) A person with parental responsibility (or, in Scotland, parental responsibilities) for the named child (including a local authority, but excluding a person under 16), or the named child if 16 or over, may make a claim to the Board, for withdrawals from an account to be permitted in accordance with this regulation.

9.36

(2) The claim shall be—
(a) made in a manner prescribed by the Board, which shall include the giving of any consent necessary for the verification or consideration of the claim, and
(b) accepted in either of the following cases:

[² Case 1

The child:
(i) in England and Wales [³ . . .] falls within either section 72(5) of the Social Security Contributions and Benefits Act 1992 (special rules for terminally ill person's entitlement to care component of disability living allowance) or section 82(4) of the Welfare Reform Act 2012 (terminal illness) [⁵ and, for this purpose, section 66(2)(a) of that Act (attendance allowance for the "terminally ill") is deemed to apply as if for "6 months" there were substituted "12 months"]; [³ . . .]
(ii) in Northern Ireland, falls within section 72(5) of the Social Security Contributions and Benefits (Northern Ireland) Act 1992 (the care component)[⁵ and, for this purpose, section 66(2)(a) of that Act (attendance allowance for the "terminally ill") is deemed to apply as if for "6 months" there were substituted "12 months"][³; or
(iii) in Scotland, falls within either of the provisions mentioned in paragraph (i), or is to be regarded as having a terminal illness, in accordance with regulations for disability assistance for children and young people [⁴, or regulations for disability assistance for working age people] made under section 31 of the Social Security (Scotland) Act 2018.]]

Case 2

Evidence that the named child is terminally ill has been supplied to the satisfaction of the Board.

(3) The Board shall issue a letter to the claimant authorising withdrawals from the account under this regulation [² . . .]

(4) Once a claim has been accepted, withdrawals may be made by the registered contact (on behalf of the named child, where he is not the child) at any time—

(a) provided that, immediately following any withdrawal, a balance sufficient to keep the account open is maintained in the account, and
(b) excepting any transfer of a policy of life insurance (as opposed to the proceeds from such a policy).

(5) Where account investments are withdrawn in a form other than sterling currency, regulation 36(1)(b) shall apply (with any necessary modifications) to any such investment immediately before it is withdrawn.

(6) In this regulation, "terminally ill" has the meaning

[²(a) for [³England and Wales] in section 66(2)(a) of the Social Security Contributions and Benefits Act 1992 [² or in section 82(4) of the Welfare Reform Act 2012 (terminal illness);
(b) for Northern Ireland, in section 72(5) of the Social Security Contributions and Benefits (Northern Ireland) Act 1992 (the care component)] [⁵ and, for this purpose, section 66(2)(a) of that Act (attendance allowance for the "terminally ill") is deemed to apply as if for "6 months" there were substituted "12 months"] [³; or
(c) for Scotland, as set out in regulations [⁴ for disability assistance for children and young people, or regulations for disability assistance for working age people,] made under section 31 of the Social Security (Scotland) Act 2018.]

AMENDMENTS

1. Child Trust Funds (Amendment) Regulations 2004 (SI 2004/2676) reg.12 (April 6, 2005).
2. Child Trust Funds (Amendment) Regulations 2014 (SI 2014/649) reg.6 (April 6, 2014).
3. Social Security (Scotland) Act 2018 (Disability Assistance, Young Carer Grants, Short-term Assistance and Winter Heating Assistance) (Consequential Provision and Modifications) Order 2021 (SI 2021/886) art.5(2) (July 26, 2021).
4. Social Security (Scotland) Act 2018 (Disability Assistance and Information-Sharing) (Consequential Provision and Modifications) Order 2022 (SI 2022/332) art.3(2) (March 21, 2022).
5. Child Trust Funds (Amendment) Regulations 2023 (SI 2023/269) reg.8 (April 6, 2023).

DEFINITIONS

"account"—see reg.2(1)(b).
"account investment"—see reg.2(1)(b).
"account provider"—see reg.2(1)(b).
"child"—see reg.2(1)(a).
"parental responsibility"—see reg.2(1)(a).

[¹ **Account provider's intention to make a bulk transfer of accounts or to cease to act as an account provider**

19.—(1) An account provider must give notice to the Board if the account provider—
(a) intends to cease to act as an account provider; or
(b) intends to make a bulk transfer of accounts.

(2) An account provider must give notice to the person who is the registered contact (or, if there is no registered contact, the named child) if the account provider—
(a) intends to cease to act as an account provider; or
(b) intends that the account will be one of the accounts transferred in a bulk transfer of accounts.

(3) The notices described in paragraphs (1) and (2) must—
(a) specify whether the account provider—
    (i) intends to cease to act as an account provider; or
    (ii) intends to make a bulk transfer of accounts;
(b) where the notice specifies an intention to cease to act as an account provider—
    (i) specify the day on or after which the account provider intends to cease to act as an account provider; and
    (ii) be given no less than 30 days before that day;
(c) where the notice specifies an intention to make a bulk transfer of accounts—
    (i) specify the day on or after which the account provider intends to make the first transfer in the bulk transfer of accounts;
    (ii) be given no less than 30 days before that day; and
    (iii) advise the name and address of the person to whom the account provider intends to transfer accounts.
(4) The notice described in paragraph (2) must also—
(a) identify the account to which it relates;
(b) in the case of a notice under paragraph (2)(a), advise the registered contact of the right to transfer the account under regulation 21 and of his rights under regulation 20(3);
(c) in the case of a notice under paragraph (2)(b) —
    (i) advise the registered contact that the account may be transferred otherwise than in a bulk transfer of accounts, such that regulation 21 applies, if sufficient instructions are provided to enable the account provider to do so; and
    (ii) advise the day by which the account provider must receive sufficient instructions for the account to be transferred otherwise than in a bulk transfer of accounts.
(5) Where an account provider intends to make a bulk transfer of accounts in consequence of an intention to cease to act as an account provider, such intention may be specified in a single notice to the Board or to a registered contact (or, if there is no registered contact, the named child) (as appropriate, respectively) provided the requirements of paragraphs (3), (4)(a) and (c) are met.
[²(6) An account provider must not cease to act in relation to an account until that account has been transferred to another provider.]

AMENDMENTS

1. Child Trust Funds (Amendment No.2) Regulations 2013 (SI 2013/1744) reg.6 (August 5, 2013).
2. Child Trust Funds (Amendment) Regulations 2023 (SI 2023/269) reg.9 (April 6, 2023).

[¹ Account provider ceasing to accept Revenue allocated accounts

19A.—A person shall give notice to the Board of his intention to cease to accept further Revenue allocated accounts under regulation 6, not less than 30 days before he so ceases.]

AMENDMENT

1. Child Trust Funds (Amendment No.2) Regulations 2013 (SI 2013/1744) reg.6 (August 5, 2013).

The Child Trust Funds Regulations 2004

Account provider ceasing to qualify

9.39   **20.**—(1) A person shall cease to qualify as an account provider and shall notify the Board within 30 days of the relevant event in sub-paragraphs (a) to (f), of that relevant event, where—
   (a) the person no longer fulfils the conditions of regulation 14;
[¹ (b) there is an insolvency event in relation to the account provider;
[² (ba) a debt relief order is made in respect of the person (under Part 7A of the Insolvency Act 1986);]
   (c) an application has been made for a bank insolvency order or a bank administration order;]
   (d) in the case of a building society, a person falling [¹ section 991 of ITA 2007 or a credit union]—
      (i) it ceases to be a building society or to fall within [¹ section 991 of ITA 2007 or to be a credit union], as the case may be;
      (ii) its directors have made a proposal under Part 1 of the Insolvency Act 1986 for a composition in satisfaction of its debts or a scheme of arrangement of its affairs; or
      (iii) a receiver or manager of its property has been appointed; or
   (f) in the case of a European institution, a relevant authorised person or an assurance undertaking which falls within regulation 14(2)(d)(iv), action corresponding to any described in sub-paragraph (b) to (e) has been taken by or in relation to the institution, person or undertaking under the law of an EEA State.
(2) On giving the notice referred to in paragraph (1), the person shall also notify the registered contact (or, if there is no registered contact, the named child) of the right to transfer the account under regulation 21, and the notice shall inform the recipient of the rights under paragraph (3).
(3) Where a registered contact—
   (a) receives a notice under paragraph (2), or regulation [¹ 16(4) or] [³ 19(2)(9)], and
   (b) within 30 days of the sending of the notice, transfers the account to another account provider pursuant to regulation 21,
the period between the transferor ceasing to act or qualify as an account provider, and the transfer to the transferee, shall be ignored in determining whether the account has at all times been managed by an account provider.

[⁴(4) An account provider must not cease to act in relation to an account until that account has been transferred to another account provider in accordance with these Regulations.]

AMENDMENTS

1. Child Trust Funds (Amendment) Regulations 2010 (SI 2010/582) reg.10 (April 6, 2010).
2. Tribunals, Courts and Enforcement Act 2007 (Consequential Amendments) Order 2012 (SI 2012/2404) art.3(3) and Sch.3 para.34 (October 1, 2012).
3. Child Trust Funds (Amendment No.2) Regulations 2013 (SI 2013/1744) reg.7 (August 5, 2013).
4. Child Trust Funds (Amendment) Regulations 2023 (SI 2023/269) reg.10 (April 6, 2023).

DEFINITIONS

"account"—see reg.2(1)(b).
"account provider"—see reg.2(1)(b).

"assurance undertaking"—see reg.2(1)(b).
"building society"—see reg.2(1)(b).
"child"—see reg.2(1)(a).
"company"—see reg.2(1)(b).
"EEA State"—see reg.2(1)(b).
"European institution"—see reg.2(1)(b).
"notice"—see reg.2(1)(b).
"relevant authorised person"—see reg.2(1)(b).
"relevant European institution"—see reg.2(1)(b).
"the Taxes Act"—see reg.2(1)(b).

[¹Transfers to other accounts for children

20A.—(1) An account provider must at the request of the registered contact—
 (a) transfer all the investments under the child trust fund, or an amount representing their value in cash, to a protected child account that is provided by a person chosen by the registered contact, and
 (b) when all the investments have been transferred, close the child trust fund.
(2) An account is only a protected child account for the purposes of section 7A(2) of the Act if it satisfies the condition of being a junior ISA account within regulation 2B of the Individual Savings Account Regulations 1998.]

9.40

AMENDMENT

1. Child Trust Funds (Amendment No.2) Regulations 2015 (SI 2015/876) regs 2 and 6 (April 6, 2015).

DEFINITIONS

"account"—see reg.2(1)(b).
"account provider"—see reg.2(1)(b).
"registered contact"—reg.8(1)(d).

GENERAL NOTE

The Individual Savings Account Regulations 1998 (SI 1998/1450) were amended by the Individual Savings Account (Amendment No.3) Regulations 2015 (SI 2015/941) so as to make them compatible with the transfer of child trust funds to junior ISAs under reg.20A.

9.41

Transfer of accounts [⁵ . . .]

21.—(1) Where—
 (a) arrangements are made by a registered contact to transfer the whole of the investments under an account from one account provider ("the transferor") to another account provider ("the transferee"), [⁴ . . .]
 (b) the whole of the investments under an account are so transferred in consequence of an account provider ("the transferor") ceasing to act or to qualify as an account provider, [⁴ [⁵ . . .]
[⁵ (ba) there is a transfer under regulation 20A to a protected child account, or]
[⁴(c) an account is transferred in a bulk transfer of accounts [⁵ . . .],]
the transfer shall be treated as a transfer of the account.
(2) The account and its description under regulation 4 shall not be affected for the purposes of these Regulations by reason of the transfer [⁵ in paragraph

9.42

(1)(a), (b) or (c)], save that, where the registered contact specifies in accordance with paragraph (3)(a) an account of a different description, the account shall, on the transfer, become an account of that other description.

(3) The registered contact shall make—
   (a) the application required by regulation 13(2) (modified as if the words "applied for" were replaced with [¹ following the transfer]), and
   (b) the application and declaration required by regulation 13(3) to (5), to the transferee [⁶ but (in the case mentioned in sub- paragraph (b)) as if for regulation 13(3)(b) there were substituted—
"(b) is—
   (i) a responsible person in relation to the named child (that is, that he has parental responsibility or, in Scotland, parental responsibilities in relation to the child, or
   (ii) the child, where the child is 16 or over and has elected to manage the account.]"

[⁴(3A) Paragraph (3) does not apply where an account is transferred [⁵ under regulation 20A or] in a bulk transfer of accounts.
   (3B) [⁵ . . .]
   (3C) [⁵ . . .]
   (3D) [⁵ . . .]
   (3E) [⁵ . . .]
   (3F) [⁵ . . .]
   (3G) An account transferred in accordance with this regulation in a bulk transfer of accounts is an account opened pursuant to an application in accordance with regulation 13 for the purposes of these Regulations [⁵ . . .].

[¹[⁴(3H) Where a registered contact applies in accordance with paragraph (3) to a potential transferee for a transfer under this regulation, specifying a stakeholder account offered by the transferee, the transferee shall not decline to accept that application (or the transfer in consequence of it) except where—
   (a) the transferee has reason to believe that the registered contact has given untrue information in his application;
   (b) the transferee demonstrates to the satisfaction of the Board that acceptance of transfers, or a class of transfers, during a particular period would jeopardise his ability to prevent any of the matters mentioned in regulation 16(2)(a); or
   (c) the transferor does not give the transferee the notice in accordance with paragraph (4).]

(4) The transferor shall on the date of the transfer give the transferee a notice containing the information specified in paragraph (5) [⁷ . . .].

[⁵ (4A) In relation to paragraph (1)(ba), the account provider shall on the date of the transfer give the person providing the protected child account a notice containing the information specified in paragraph (5)(a) and (b)(i), (ii) and (iv) [⁷ . . .].]

(5) The information specified in this paragraph is—
   (a) as regards the named child—
      (i) his full name,
      (ii) his date of birth,
      (iii) his unique reference number;
   (b) as regards the account—
      (i) the description of the account,
      (ii) the date of the transfer,

(SI 2004/1450 reg.21) (as amended)

      (iii) the total amount subscribed to the account during the period from the beginning of the subscription year in which the transfer takes place to the date of the transfer,

      (iv) any amount which has been claimed from the Board under regulations [3 26 or 27] and which has not been paid at the date of the transfer; [2, and

      (v) the total amount subscribed to the account during the previous subscription year, where that subscription year ended later than the 5th April preceding the date of the transfer.]

  (c) the full name and address, including postcode, of the registered contact who has made the transfer arrangements.

(6) [7 ...]

AMENDMENTS

1. Child Trust Funds (Amendment) Regulations 2004 (SI 2004/2676) reg.13 (April 6, 2005).
2. Child Trust Funds (Amendment) Regulations 2010 (SI 2010/582) reg.11 (April 6, 2010).
3. Child Trust Funds (Amendment) Regulations 2013 (SI 2013/263) reg.2(4)(d) (March 16, 2013).
4. Child Trust Funds (Amendment No.2) Regulations 2013 (SI 2013/1744) reg.8 (August 5, 2013).
5. Child Trust Funds (Amendment No.2) Regulations 2015 (SI 2015/876) regs 2, 7 and 8 (April 6, 2015).
6. Child Trust Funds (Amendment No.3) Regulations 2015 (SI 2015/1371) reg.8 (July 1, 2015).
7. Child Trust Funds (Amendment) Regulations 2017 (SI 2017/185) reg.6 (April 6, 2017).

DEFINITIONS

"account"—see reg.2(1)(b).
"account investment"—see reg.2(1)(b).
"account provider"—see reg.2(1)(b).
"child"—see reg.2(1)(a).
"eligible child"—see reg.2(1)(a).
"notice"—see reg.2(1)(b).

Recoupment of Inland Revenue contributions to void accounts (and other accounts)

22.—(1) Where—
(a) the named child has never been an eligible child (see regulation 8(1)(b)), or
(b) there is a breach of regulation 8(1)(c) in relation to an account,
the account is void, and the persons mentioned in paragraph (3) shall account to the Inland Revenue for Inland Revenue contributions paid in respect of the account, together with income and gains which have arisen in consequence of the crediting of any of those payments to the account.

(2) Where—
(a) the condition in section 9(5) of the Act [2 or regulation 7(10B) or 7A(4)] was satisfied in relation to a child, but the determination under sections 18 to 21 of the Tax Credits Act 2002 has been overturned, or
(b) the condition in section 9(8) of the Act was satisfied in relation to a child, but it has subsequently been determined that payment of the

relevant benefit or tax credit mentioned in that subsection should not have been made, or that the applicable amount or tax credit should not have included an amount or credit in respect of the child, [¹or

(c) the requirements of regulation 7(10) [², or the condition in regulation 7(10C) [³, 7A(5) or 7B(1)] was,] were satisfied in relation to a child, but it has subsequently been determined that payment of the relevant benefit mentioned in [² the relevant provision] should not have been made, or that the applicable amount should not have included an amount in respect of that child,]

the persons mentioned in paragraph (3) shall account to the Inland Revenue for any supplementary contribution [¹, or further contribution, as the case may be,] paid in respect of the account, together with income and gains which have arisen in consequence of the crediting of any such payment to the account.

(3) The persons mentioned in paragraphs (1) and (2) are—
(a) the account provider (to the extent that he has assets in his possession or control),
(b) the registered contact,
(c) the named child, and
(d) any person in whom the Inland Revenue contributions, income or gains, or any property directly or indirectly representing any of them, is vested (whether beneficially or otherwise)

and they shall be jointly and severally liable.

(4) Where a person accountable under this regulation is notified by the Inland Revenue that an amount is due from him under it, that amount shall be treated for the purposes of Part 6 of the Management Act (collection and recovery) as if it were tax charged in an assessment on that person, and due and payable.

AMENDMENTS

1. Child Trust Funds (Amendment) Regulations 2005 (SI 2005/383) reg.4 (April 6, 2005).
2. Child Trust Funds (Amendment) Regulations 2009 (SI 2009/475) reg.6 (April 6, 2009).
3. Child Trust Funds (Amendment No.2) Regulations 2010 (SI 2010/836) reg.4 (April 1, 2010).

DEFINITIONS

"account"—see reg.2(1)(b).
"account provider"—see reg.2(1)(b).
"child"—see reg.2(1)(a).
"eligible child"—see reg.2(1)(a).
"the Management Act"—see reg.2(1)(b).
"tax"—see reg.2(1)(b).

"Repair" of invalid accounts

9.44   23.—(1) Except in the case of a breach of regulation 8(1)(b) or (c) (where no repair of an account is possible), it is an overriding requirement to be satisfied in relation to an account that the account provider and registered contact, as the case may be, take any steps necessary to remedy any breach of these Regulations.

(2) Where a breach is remedied as mentioned in paragraph (1), the account shall, to the extent of that breach, be treated as having been a valid

account at all times, except for determining whether there has been a breach of these Regulations for the purposes of section 20 of the Act (penalties).

DEFINITIONS

"account"—see reg.2(1)(b).
"account provider"—see reg.2(1)(b).

PART 3

TAX AND ADMINISTRATION OF ACCOUNTS

Exemption from tax of account income and gains

24.—Subject to compliance with these Regulations (and in particular regulation 9)—
  (a) no tax shall be chargeable on the account provider or his nominee, or on the named child or registered contact (on his behalf)—
    (i) in respect of interest, dividends, distributions or gains in respect of account investments [²(excluding any building society bonus)],
    [¹(ia) in respect of alternative finance return or profit share return paid by a financial institution (within the meanings in Chapter 5 of Part 2 of the Finance Act 2005);]
    [²(ib) in respect of a payment under a building society bonus scheme, so far as the payment is calculated by reference to account investments (and if paid directly by the society into the account, the payment shall not count towards the subscription limit in regulation 9);]
    (ii) on any annual profits or gains treated [⁴ under Part 12 of ITA 2007] as having been received by any of them in respect of account investments,
    (iii) on an offshore income gain to which a disposal made by any of them of an account investment gives rise, which is treated by section 761(1) of the Taxes Act as constituting profits or gains,
    [⁴ (iv) on a profit on the disposal of a deeply discounted security within the meaning given by section 430 of ITTOIA 2005;] or
    (v) in respect of gains treated [⁴ under Chapter 9 of Part 4 of ITTOIA 2005] as arising in connection with a policy of life insurance which is an account investment;
  (b) losses accruing on any disposal of account investments shall be disregarded for the purposes of capital gains tax;
  [³(ba) any gain or loss accruing on and attributable to a payment within paragraph (ib) of sub-paragraph (a) shall not be a chargeable gain or allowable loss for capital gains tax purposes;]
  (c) [⁴ section 935 of ITA 2007] shall apply with the following modifications—
    (i) for references to a plan manager, substitute references to an account provider,
    (ii) for references to a plan, substitute references to an account, and
    (iii) for the reference to [¹Chapter 3 of Part 6 of ITTOIA 2005], substitute a reference to the Act;
  (d) [⁴ a deficiency arising in a tax year and falling within section 539(1) of ITTOIA 2005], so far as it relates to a policy of life insurance

which is an account investment, shall not be allowable as a deduction from the total income of the named child;
(e) relief in respect of tax shall be given in the manner and to the extent provided by these Regulations; and
(f) income arising from account investments shall not be regarded as income for any income tax purposes (including [¹section 629 of ITTOIA 2005]).

AMENDMENTS

1. Child Trust Funds (Amendment No.3) Regulations 2005 (SI 2005/3349) reg.7 (December 27, 2005).
2. Child Trust Funds (Amendment No.3) Regulations 2006 (SI 2006/3195) reg.4 (January 1, 2007).
3. Child Trust Funds (Amendment No.3) Regulations 2006 (SI 2006/3195) reg.5 (January 1, 2007).
4. Child Trust Funds (Amendment) Regulations 2010 (SI 2010/582) reg.12 (April 6, 2010).

DEFINITIONS

"account"—see reg.2(1)(b).
"account investment"—see reg.2(1)(b).
"account provider"—see reg.2(1)(b).
"child"—see reg.2(1)(a).
"gains"—see reg.2(1)(b).
"security"—see reg.2(1)(b).
"tax"—see reg.2(1)(b).
"the Taxes Act"—see reg.2(1)(b).
"year"—see reg.2(1)(b).

Tax liabilities and reliefs—account provider to act on behalf of the named child

25.—(1) An account provider may under these Regulations make tax claims, conduct appeals and agree on behalf of the named child (or of the registered contact in respect of the child) liabilities for and reliefs from tax in respect of an account.

(2) Tax claims shall be made to the Board in accordance with the provisions of regulations 26 and 27.

(3) Where any relief or exemption from tax previously given in respect of an account has by virtue of these Regulations become excessive, in computing the relief due on any claim there shall be deducted (so that amounts equal to that excess are set-off or repaid to the Board, as the case may be) notwithstanding that those amounts have been invested, any other amount of tax due to the Board by the account provider in respect of any tax liability in respect of account investments under an account including (but without prejudice to the making of an assessment under that Schedule) any amount falling due in respect of a liability under [¹ Chapter 9 of Part 15 of ITA 2007].

AMENDMENT

1. Child Trust Funds (Amendment) Regulations 2010 (SI 2010/582) reg.13 (April 6, 2010).

DEFINITIONS

"account"—see reg.2(1)(b).
"account investment"—see reg.2(1)(b).

"account provider"—see reg.2(1)(b).
"child"—see reg.2(1)(a).
"tax"—see reg.2(1)(a).
"the Taxes Act"—see reg.2(1)(a).

Repayments in respect of tax to account provider—interim tax claims

26.—(1) Notwithstanding the provisions of any other enactment, the Board shall not be under an obligation to make any repayment in respect of tax under these Regulations earlier than the end of the month following the month in which the claim for the repayment is received.

(2) A claim for repayment in respect of tax which is not an annual claim ("interim tax claim") may be made only for a period of a month (or a number of months not exceeding six) beginning on the 6th day of the month and ending on the 5th day of the relevant following month.

(3) No claim for repayment may be made for the month ending 5th October or any subsequent month in a year until the annual claim due under regulation 27(2) in respect of an account for the preceding year has been duly made by the account provider and received by the Board.

(4) Where, on the occasion of a claim, there is due to the Board an amount in respect of tax, that amount shall be recoverable by the Board in the same manner as tax charged by an assessment on the account provider which has become final and conclusive.

(5) This regulation and regulation 27 shall not apply to any repayment in respect of tax on account investments falling within regulation 12(2)(m) (life insurance), or on distributions and other rights or proceeds in respect of those investments.

9.47

DEFINITIONS

"account"—see reg.2(1)(b).
"account investment"—see reg.2(1)(b).
"account provider"—see reg.2(1)(b).
"tax"—see reg.2(1)(b).
"year"—see reg.2(1)(b).

Repayments in respect of tax to account provider—annual tax claims

27.—(1) An annual tax claim is a claim for repayment in respect of tax for a year and may not be made at any time more than six years after the end of the year.

(2) Where the account provider—
(a) has made at least one interim tax claim during a year, or
(b) wishes to reclaim tax, or there is due to the Board an amount in respect of tax, following the end of the year,
the account provider shall within six months after the end of the year make an annual tax claim to establish the total of tax repayments due under an account for that year.

(3) Where the aggregate of the repayments in respect of interim tax claims for the year shown by an annual tax claim exceeds the amount of tax repayable for the year shown on the claim, the account provider shall repay the amount of the excess to the Board with the claim.

9.48

(4) If an account provider fails to make the annual tax claim required under paragraph (2)(a) within the time limited, the Board may issue a notice to the account provider showing the aggregate of payments in respect of the interim tax claims for the year, and stating that the Board are not satisfied that the amount due to the account provider for that year exceeds the lower amount stated in the notice.

(5) If an annual tax claim is not delivered to the Board within 14 days after the issue of a notice under paragraph (4) the amount of the difference between the aggregate and the lower amount stated in the notice shall immediately become recoverable by the Board in the same manner as tax charged by an assessment on the account provider which has become final and conclusive.

(6) Where an annual tax claim has been made and the account provider subsequently discovers that an error or mistake has been made in the claim the account provider may make a supplementary annual claim within the time allowed in paragraph (1).

DEFINITIONS

"account"—see reg.2(1)(b).
"account provider"—see reg.2(1)(b).
"notice"—see reg.2(1)(b).
"tax"—see reg.2(1)(b).
"year"—see reg.2(1)(b).

Account provider's tax claims—supplementary provisions

28.—(1) Section 42 of the Management Act shall not apply to tax claims under these Regulations.

(2) No appeal shall lie from the Board's decision on an interim tax claim.

(3) An appeal [1 ...] from the Board's decision on an annual tax claim, [1...] shall be brought by giving notice to the Board within 30 days of receipt of notice of the decision.

(4) No payment or repayment made or other thing done on or in relation to an interim tax claim or a notice under regulation 27(4) shall prejudice the decision on an annual tax claim.

(5) The provisions contained in Part 5 of the Management Act (appeals and other proceedings) shall apply to an appeal under paragraph (3) above, [1 and, on an appeal that is notified to the tribunal, the tribunal] may vary the decision appealed against whether or not the variation is to the advantage of the appellant.

(6) All such assessments, payments and repayments shall be made as necessary to give effect to the Board's decision on an annual tax claim or to any variation of that decision on appeal.

(7) Claims under these Regulations shall be in such form and contain such particulars as the Board prescribe and, subject to regulation 32(1), shall be signed by the account provider, and forms prescribed for annual claims may require a report to be given by a person qualified for appointment as auditor of a company.

AMENDMENT

1. Transfer of Tribunal Functions and Revenue and Customs Appeals Order 2009 (SI 2009/56) art.3(2) and Sch.2 para.127 (April 1, 2009).

DEFINITIONS

"account provider"—see reg.2(1)(b).
"company"—see reg.2(1)(b).
"the Management Act"—see reg.2(1)(b).
"notice"—see reg.2(1)(b).
"tax"—see reg.2(1)(b).

Assessments for withdrawing relief and recovering tax

29.—(1) Where—
(a) any relief or exemption from tax given in respect of income or gains under an account is found not to be due or to be excessive, or
(b) the full amount of tax in respect of the income or gains under an account has not otherwise been fully accounted for and paid to the Board on behalf of the named child,

an assessment to tax may be made by the Board in the amount or further amount which in their opinion ought to be charged.

(2) An assessment to which paragraph (1) refers may be made on the account provider or on the registered contact (in respect of the child where the child is under the age of 16).

(3) If the assessment is made to recover tax in respect of income under an account it shall be made under Case VI of Schedule D.

(4) [1...].

AMENDMENT

1. Child Trust Funds, Registered Pension Schemes and Stamp Duty Reserve Tax (Consequential Amendments) Regulations 2012 (SI 2012/886) reg.2 (April 6, 2012).

DEFINITIONS

"account"—see reg.2(1)(b).
"account provider"—see reg.2(1)(b).
"child"—see reg.2(1)(a).
"gains"—see reg.2(1)(b).
"the Management Act"—see reg.2(1)(b).
"tax"—see reg.2(1)(b).

Fortnightly claim and financial returns

30.—[1...]

AMENDMENT

1. Child Trust Funds (Amendment) Regulations 2013 (SI 2013/263) reg.2(3) (March 16, 2013).

Records to be kept by account provider

31.—(1) An account provider shall at all times keep sufficient records in respect of an account to enable the requirements of these Regulations to be satisfied.

(2) In particular, an account provider shall produce (when required to do so by an officer of the Board) any—
(a) application made under regulation 13(1) or (10),
(b) voucher given to him,

(c) annual statement issued by him, and
(d) transfer notice given to him under regulation 21(4),
or electronic copies, within the period of 3 years from when it was made, issued or given (notwithstanding any transfer of the account under regulation [² 20A or] 21).

[¹ (3) [² ...]
(4) [² ...]]]

AMENDMENTS

1. Child Trust Funds (Amendment No.2) Regulations 2013 (SI 2013/1744) reg.9 (August 5, 2013).
2. Child Trust Funds (Amendment No.2) Regulations 2015 (SI 2015/876) regs 2 and 9 (April 6, 2015).

DEFINITIONS

"account"—see reg.2(1)(b).
"account provider"—see reg.2(1)(b).
"notice"—see reg.2(1)(b).
"year"—see reg.2(1)(b).

Returns of information by account provider

32.—(1) An account provider shall within 60 days after the end of each year in which he acts as an account provider, and after ceasing to act or to qualify as an account provider, deliver by means of electronic communications to the Board a return for that year, or for the part of that year in which he so acted or qualified, in a form specified by the Board, which contains the information specified in paragraph (2).

(2) The information specified in this paragraph is information relating to each account in respect of which he acted as account provider, in the year or the part of the year for which the return is made, other than accounts transferred [³ ...] under regulation [³ 20A or] 21 in that year or part of a year, as to—
 (a) as regards the named child—
  (i) [¹...]
  (ii) [¹...]
  (iii) his unique reference number;
 (b) as regards each such account—
  (i) whether or not the account is a stakeholder account,
  (ii) whether or not there is a registered contact for the account,
  (iii) the aggregate market value of the account investments held under the account, subject to paragraph (3), the value of each account investment being determined either as at 5th April in that year, or any other valuation date not falling earlier than 5th October in that year, and
  (iv) the total amount of cash subscribed to the account, in the subscription year ending during the year or the part of the year for which the return is made.

[² (2A) Where, during the year or part of the year, the named child reaches the age of 18 years or dies, there shall be substituted for paragraph (2)(b)(iii)—

("iii) the aggregate market value of the account investments held under the account immediately before the relevant event mentioned in paragraph (2A),"]

(SI 2004/1450 reg.32) (as amended)

(3) The reference in paragraph (2)(b)(iii) to market value shall be construed—
  (a) in the case of policies of life insurance, as a reference to their surrender value, and
  (b) as referring to separate values for—
    (i) cash falling within regulation 12(2)(k) or (l), and
    (ii) policies of life insurance and all other account investments.

(4) No claim for repayment, or repayment, may be made under regulations 26 and 27 until the returns which have become due under this regulation have been duly made by the account provider and received by the Board.

AMENDMENTS

1. Child Trust Funds (Amendment No.2) Regulations 2005 (SI 2005/909) reg.9 (April 6, 2005).
2. Child Trust Funds (Amendment) Regulations 2010 (SI 2010/582) reg.14 (April 6, 2010).
3. Child Trust Funds (Amendment No.2) Regulations 2015 (SI 2015/876) regs 2 and 10 (April 6, 2015).

DEFINITIONS

"account"—see reg.2(1)(b).
"account investment"—see reg.2(1)(b).
"account provider"—see reg.2(1)(b).
"child"—see reg.2(1)(a).
"electronic communications"—see reg.2(1)(b).
"market value"—see reg.2(1)(b).
"year"—see reg.2(1)(b).

Information about "looked after children" from Local Authorities

33.—[¹...]   9.54

AMENDMENT

1. Child Trust Funds (Amendment) Regulations 2011 (SI 2011/781) reg.3 (April 7, 2011).

[⁹ The person appointed by the Treasury or the Secretary of State by virtue of section 3(10) of the Act] to be the person who has the authority to manage an account

33A.—[⁴ [⁹ (1) The person appointed by the Treasury or the Secretary of State by virtue of section 3(10) of the Act is to be the person who has the authority to manage a child's account for the purposes of section 3(6)(b) of the Act where the circumstances specified in paragraph (2) apply.]]   9.55

(2) The circumstances specified are where—
[⁹(za) except in a case of a person who was a looked after child or a looked after and accommodated child on 30th September 2017, there is a continuous period of at least twelve months during which the circumstances under sub-paragraphs (a) and (b) apply,
 (zb) in a case of a person who was a looked after child or a looked after and accommodated child on 30th September 2017, the circumstances under sub-paragraphs (a) and (b) apply,]

(a) [⁹a child] is looked after (in Scotland, looked after and accommodated) by the local authority, and
(b) at least one of the following conditions is satisfied.

Condition 1

There is no person, or no person other than the local authority, who has parental responsibility (in Scotland, parental responsibilities) for the child.

Condition 2

It is part of the care plan for the child that—
  (a) the child will live indefinitely away from home (or his former home), and
  (b) the child will not have face to face contact with any parent having parental responsibility (in Scotland, parental responsibilities) for the child.

Condition 3

An order has been made under section 34(4) of the Children Act 1989 or Article 53(4) of the Children (Northern Ireland) Order 1995, authorising the local authority to refuse to allow contact between the child and any person with parental responsibility [⁶(or, in Scotland, a compulsory supervision order or an interim compulsory supervision order is in force and contains a direction regulating contact to the effect that the child has no contact with a person who has parental responsibilities in relation to that child)], and there is no other individual with parental responsibility (in Scotland, parental responsibilities) for the child to act as registered contact.
  [⁶ In this Condition—
  (a) "compulsory supervision order" has the meaning given by section 83 of the Children's Hearings (Scotland) Act 2011;
  (b) "interim compulsory supervision order" has the meaning given by section 86 of that Act; and
  (c) "contact direction" means a measure mentioned in section 83(2)(g) of that Act and contained within a compulsory supervision order or an interim compulsory supervision order.]

Condition 4

The Court of Protection has—
  (a) appointed a [³ deputy] for a person with parental responsibility for the child, or
[³ (b) determined that such a person lacks capacity within the meaning of the Mental Capacity Act 2005 (c.9) to manage the child's property and affairs]
and there is no other individual with parental responsibility for the child to act as registered contact.
In Scotland, in this Condition for—
  (a) "Court of Protection" substitute "Sheriff",
  (b) [³ "deputy"] substitute "guardian appointed under section 58 of the Adults with Incapacity (Scotland) Act 2000",
  (c) the reference to a [³ person lacking capacity], substitute "incapable for the purposes of the Adults with Incapacity (Scotland) Act 2000," and
  (d) "parental responsibility" substitute "parental responsibilities".

(SI 2004/1450 reg.33A) (as amended)

Condition 5

The child has been lost or abandoned, and there is no prospect for the foreseeable future of reunification of the child with a parent having parental responsibility (in Scotland, parental responsibilities) for the child.
In this Condition, "lost or abandoned"—
- (a) in England [⁸ ...], has the meaning in section 20(1)(b) of the Children Act 1989;
- [⁸ (ab) in Wales, has the meaning in section 76 of the Social Services and Well-being (Wales) Act 2014;]
- (b) in Northern Ireland, has the meaning in Article 21(1)(b) of the Children (Northern Ireland) Order 1995; and
- (c) in Scotland, has the meaning in section 25(1)(b) of the Children (Scotland) Act 1995.

[²Condition 6

In England and Wales, an adoption agency or local authority has been authorised to place the child for adoption under section 19, or by a placement order under section 21, of the Adoption and Children Act 2002, or in Northern Ireland, an Order has been made under Article 17 or 18 of the Adoption (Northern Ireland) Order 1987 to free the child for adoption.]
    [⁴ 2A [⁹ ...].]
    [⁵ (2B) [⁹ ...].]
    (3) [⁹ ...]
    (4) The [⁹person appointed by the Treasury or the Secretary of State by virtue of section 3(10) of the Act] shall cease to be the person who has the authority to manage the child's account (and shall be discharged from the duties of registered contact) where—
- (a) the child [⁷ is 16 or over and has elected to manage the account]
- (b) in any case where the child is [⁷ ...] looked after (in Scotland, looked after and accommodated) by a local authority—
  - (i) the local authority confirms to the [⁹person appointed by the Treasury or the Secretary of State by virtue of section 3(10) of the Act] that there is a named responsible person in relation to the child, who is able to be the registered contact for the child's account, and that none of the Conditions in paragraph (2) applies, and
  - (ii) the [⁹person appointed by the Treasury or the Secretary of State by virtue of section 3(10) of the Act] cancels his declaration and authorisation in accordance with regulation 13(7) and is replaced as registered contact by that responsible person, in accordance with regulation 13(10), or
- (c) in any case where the child [⁷ ...] is not looked after (in Scotland, looked after and accommodated) by a local authority—
  - (i) a responsible person for the child provides evidence to the satisfaction of the [⁹person appointed by the Treasury or the Secretary of State by virtue of section 3(10) of the Act], as the case may be, that he has parental responsibility for the child, and
  - (ii) the [⁹person appointed by the Treasury or the Secretary of State by virtue of section 3(10) of the Act] cancels his declaration and authorisation in accordance with regulation 13(7) and is replaced as registered contact by that responsible person, in accordance with regulation 13(10).

(5) [⁹ ...]

[⁴ (6) In this regulation—

"local authority" includes an authority within the meaning of the Children (Northern Ireland) Order 1995(3);

"looked after and accommodated child", in Scotland, means a child who is—
  (a) both looked after, and provided with or placed in accommodation, by a local authority within the meaning of those expressions in Part 2 of the Children (Scotland) Act 1995(4), or
  (b) accommodated by a local authority under section 22 of that Act,
and related expressions shall be construed accordingly;

"looked after child"—
  (a) in England [⁸ ...], has the meaning given in section 22(1) of the Children Act 1989(5), extended to include a child accommodated by a local authority under section 17 of that Act, [⁸ ...]
[⁸ (ab) in Wales means looked after by a local authority within the meaning of section 74 of the Social Services and Well-being (Wales) Act 2014;]
  (b) in Northern Ireland, means a child accommodated under Part 4 of the Children (Northern Ireland) Order 1995,
and related expressions shall be construed accordingly;
[⁹ ...]]

[⁹ (7) Where the appointment of a person ("original appointee") by the Treasury or the Secretary of State by virtue of section 3(10) of the Act ceases, the original appointee must provide any information held by that person in connection with the management of a child trust fund to the new person (if any) appointed instead.]

AMENDMENTS

1. Child Trust Funds (Amendment No.2) Regulations 2004 (SI 2004/3382) reg.5 (April 6, 2005).
2. Child Trust Funds (Amendment No.2) Regulations 2006 (SI 2006/2684) reg.5 (October 31, 2006).
3. Mental Capacity Act 2005 (Transitional and Consequential Provisions) Order 2007 (SI 2007/1898) art.6 and Sch.1 para.33 (October 1, 2007).
4. Child Trust Funds (Amendment) Regulations 2011 (SI 2011/781) reg.4 (April 7, 2011).
5. Child Trust Funds (Amendment No.3) Regulations 2011 (SI 2011/2447) reg.6 (November 1, 2011).
6. Children's Hearings (Scotland) Act 2011 (Consequential and Transitional Provisions and Savings) Order 2013 (SI 2013/1465) Sch.1 para.21 (June 24, 2013).
7. Child Trust Funds (Amendment No.3) Regulations 2015 (SI 2015/1371) reg.9 (July 1, 2015).
8. Child Trust Funds (Amendment) Regulations 2017 (SI 2017/185) reg.7 (April 6, 2017).
9. Child Trust Funds (Amendment No.2) Regulations 2017 (SI 2017/748) reg.5 (October 1, 2017).

DEFINITIONS

"account"—see reg.2(1)(b).
"child"—see reg.2(1)(a).
"parental responsibility"—see reg.2(1)(a).
"responsible person"—see reg.2(1)(a).

(SI 2004/1450 reg.34) (as amended)

Information to be provided to the Board

34.—[¹...]

AMENDMENT

1. Child Trust Funds (Amendment) Regulations 2010 (SI 2010/582) reg.16 (April 6, 2010).

Inspection of records by officer of the Board

35.—[¹...]

AMENDMENT

1. Child Trust Funds (Amendment) Regulations 2010 (SI 2010/582) reg.16 (April 6, 2010).

Capital gains tax—adaptation of enactments

36.—(1) For the purposes of capital gains tax—
  (a) any assets held by a named child as account investments shall be regarded as held by the child in a separate capacity from that in which he holds any other assets of the same description; and
  (b) the named child shall be treated as having sold all the account investments, and as having reacquired them in his personal capacity, for a consideration equal to their market value, immediately before he attains the age of 18 years (and ceases to be a child).

(2) Sections 127 to 131 of the 1992 Act shall not apply in relation to qualifying investments falling within any of sub-paragraphs (a), (b), and (f) to (i) of regulation 12(2) which are held under an account if there is by virtue of any allotment for payment as is mentioned in section 126(2) of that Act a reorganisation affecting those assets.

DEFINITIONS

  "account"—see reg.2(1)(b).
  "account investment"—see reg.2(1)(b).
  "child"—see reg.2(1)(a).
  "market value"—see reg.2(1)(b).
  "the 1992 Act"—see reg.2(1)(b).

Administration of tax in relation to accounts—supplementary

37.—(1) Nothing in these Regulations shall be taken to prejudice any powers conferred or duties imposed by or under any enactment in relation to the making of returns of income or gains, or for the recovery of tax, penalties or interest by means of an assessment or otherwise.

(2) Notwithstanding the provisions of these Regulations an account provider shall not be released from obligations under these Regulations in relation to an account except under conditions agreed in writing with and notified to that person by the Board.

(3) The provisions contained in the Management Act shall apply to any assessment under these Regulations as if it were an assessment to tax for the year in which, apart from these Regulations, the named child would have been liable (by reason of his ownership of the investments).

(4) No obligation as to secrecy imposed by statute or otherwise shall preclude the Board from disclosing to an account provider or registered contact that any provision of these Regulations has not been satisfied or that relief has been given or claimed in respect of investments under an account.

(5) If—
  (a) a chargeable event, within the meaning given by [¹ Chapter 9 of Part 4 of ITTOIA 2005], has happened in relation to a policy of life insurance which is an account investment, and
  (b) the body by whom the policy was issued is satisfied that no gain is to be treated as chargeable to tax on the happening of the event by virtue of regulation 24(a)(v),
the body shall not be obliged to deliver the certificates mentioned in section 552(1) of [¹ the Taxes Act].

This paragraph does not prevent the operation of section 552(1) in a case to which regulation 38(1) applies.

(6) Where—
  (a) it comes to the notice of the account provider, in any manner, that the event specified in regulation 12(11) has occurred in relation to a policy, and
  (b) the account provider is not the insurer for the time being responsible for the obligations under the policy or, where the policy is not still in existence, the person who was the last such insurer,
the account provider shall, within 30 days of the event coming to his notice give notice to that insurer, specifying the event mentioned in sub-paragraph (a) and the termination event.

AMENDMENT

1. Child Trust Funds (Amendment) Regulations 2010 (SI 2010/582) reg.17 (April 6, 2010).

DEFINITIONS

"account"—see reg.2(1)(b).
"account investment"—see reg.2(1)(b).
"account provider"—see reg.2(1)(b).
"child"—see reg.2(1)(a).
"gains"—see reg.2(1)(b).
"the Management Act"—see reg.2(1)(b).
"notice"—see reg.2(1)(b).
"tax"—see reg.2(1)(b).
"the Taxes Act"—see reg.2(1)(b).
"year"—see reg.2(1)(b).

Application of the provisions of Chapter 2 of Part 13 of the Taxes Act [¹ and of Chapter 9 of Part 4 of ITTOIA 2005] to policies

38.—(1) This paragraph applies to a case where—
  (a) the event specified in regulation 12(11) has occurred in relation to a policy of life insurance, and
  (b) a termination event within the meaning in regulation 12(12) occurs in relation to that policy.

(2) Where—
  (a) there is a case to which paragraph (1) applies, and

(SI 2004/1450 reg. 38) (as amended)

(b) a chargeable event in relation to the policy, within the meaning given by section 540 of the Taxes Act, has occurred prior to the time at which the termination event mentioned in paragraph (1)(b) occurs,

the named child shall cease to be, and shall be treated as not having been, entitled to relief from tax under regulation 24(a)(v), in respect of gains treated as arising on the occurrence of any chargeable event mentioned in sub-paragraph (b).

(3) The provisions of Chapter 2 of Part 13 of the Taxes Act shall apply, in a case to which paragraph (1) applies, to—
  (a) the termination event mentioned in paragraph (1)(b), and
  (b) any chargeable event mentioned in paragraph (2)(b),
with the modifications provided for in paragraphs (4) to (8) of this regulation, and the registered contact and the account provider shall account to the Board in accordance with this regulation for tax from which relief under regulation 24 has been given on the basis that the named child was so entitled, or in circumstances such that the named child was not so entitled.

(4) A termination of a policy of insurance pursuant to regulation 12(9)(b)(ii) shall be treated as the surrender [¹ of all rights under the policy for the purposes of section 484(1)(a)(i) of ITTOIA 2005].

[¹ (5) Section 530 of ITTOIA 2005 does not apply to a gain in a case to which paragraph (1) applies.]

(6) Relief under section 550 of the Taxes Act shall be computed as if paragraph (5) had not been enacted.

(7) In section 552 of the Taxes Act—
  (a) in subsection (1)(b) for "policy holder" substitute "named child";
  (b) in subsection (3)—
    (i) omit "(or, where the appropriate policy holder is a company, the corresponding financial year)";
    (ii) for "the name and address of the appropriate policy holder" substitute "the name and address of the named child";
    (iii) omit "and the corresponding financial year,";
  (c) in subsection (5)—
    (i) for "the appropriate policy holder" substitute "the named child";
    (ii) omit sub-paragraph (b)(ii);
    (iii) omit paragraph (c);
    (iv) in paragraph (d) omit "except where paragraph (c) above applies,";
    (v) omit paragraph (f);
  (d) in subsection (6)—
    (i) omit paragraph (b);
    (ii) for paragraph (c) substitute—
      "(c) if the event is a death, the period of three months beginning with the receipt of written notification of the death;";
    (iii) after paragraph (c) insert—
      "(d) if the event is—
        (i) a termination event, or
        (ii) a chargeable event preceding a termination event (as mentioned in regulation 38(2) of the Child Trust Funds Regulations 2004),
      the period of three months beginning with the date on which the insurer received notice under regulation 37(6) of

those Regulations or, if earlier, actual notice of the termination event.";
(e) in subsection (7)—
    (i) in paragraph (a) omit ", or, where the policy holder is a company, the financial year,";
    (ii) omit paragraph (b);
    (iii) for paragraph (c) substitute—
        "(c) if the event is a death, the period of three months beginning with the receipt of written notification of the death;";
    (iv) after paragraph (c) insert—
        "(ca) if the event is—
            (i) a termination event, or
            (ii) a chargeable event preceding such a termination event (as mentioned in regulation 38(2) of the Child Trust Funds Regulations 2004,
        the period of three months beginning with the date on which the insurer received notice under regulation 37(6) of those Regulations or, if earlier, actual notice of the termination event."; and
    (v) in paragraph (d) after "paragraph (c)" insert "or (ca)";
(f) in subsection (8)—
    (i) in paragraph (b) for "policy holder" substitute "named child in respect";
    (ii) in paragraph (c) omit the words from "or" to the end;
(g) in subsection (9) omit "or financial year" in each place where they occur;
(h) in subsection (10)—
    (i) before the definition of "amount" insert—
        "'named child' has the same meaning as in the Child Trust Funds Regulations 2004;";
    (ii) omit the definitions of "appropriate policy holder" and "financial year";
    (iii) for the definition of "the relevant year of assessment" substitute—
        "'the relevant year of assessment', in the case of any gain, means the year of assessment to which the gain is attributable;"; and
    (iv) after the definition of "section 546 excess" insert—
        "'termination event' has the same meaning as in the Child Trust Funds Regulations 2004;"; and
    (v) omit subsection (11).

(8) In section 552ZA of the Taxes Act—
(a) in subsection (2)(b) omit the words "or an assignment"; and
(b) omit subsections (3) and (4).

(9) The account provider shall account for and pay income tax at the [1 basic] rate in force for the year in which the termination event, or the chargeable event mentioned in paragraph (2)(b) occurred, as the case may be, and any amount so payable—
(a) may be set off against any repayment in respect of tax due under regulation 26 or 27 and subject thereto,
(b) shall be treated as an amount of tax due not later than 6 months after the end of the year in which the event specified in regulation 12(11) came to the notice of the account provider, and

(c) shall be payable without the making of an assessment.

(10) Where tax is charged in accordance with paragraph (3)(a) or (b)—
  (a) an assessment to income tax at the [¹ basic] rate in force for the relevant year may be made on the account provider or on the registered contact (on behalf of the named child), and
  (b) an assessment to income tax at the higher rate within the meaning of [¹ section 10(3) of ITA 2007], for that year, may be made on the registered contact (on behalf of the named child) within five years after the 31st January next following that year, and regulation 29 shall not apply.

AMENDMENT

1. Child Trust Funds (Amendment) Regulations 2010 (SI 2010/582) reg.18 (April 6, 2010).

DEFINITIONS

"account provider"—see reg.2(1)(b).
"child"—see reg.2(1)(a).
"company"—see reg.2(1)(b).
"notice"—see reg.2(1)(b).
"tax"—see reg.2(1)(b).
"the Taxes Act"—see reg.2(1)(b).
"year"—see reg.2(1)(b).

SCHEDULE

STAKEHOLDER ACCOUNTS

Description of stakeholder account

1.—An account is a stakeholder account where it has the characteristics and complies with the conditions set out in paragraph 2.

Characteristics of stakeholder account etc

2.—(1) A stakeholder account must have the characteristics set out in sub-paragraph (2) and must comply with the conditions set out in sub-paragraphs (3) to (5).
  (2) The characteristics of a stakeholder account are—
    (a) the account does not directly hold investments of any of the following kinds—
      (i) those referred to in regulation 12(2)(f) (shares in an investment trust);
      (ii) securities of an investment trust;
      (iii) rights in with-profits endowment policies;
      (iv) rights, under a contract of insurance, in a with-profits fund;
      (v) units or shares in a relevant collective investment scheme unless it is a requirement of that scheme that the purchase and sale price of those units or shares shall, at any given time, not differ from each other and that the price must be made available to the public on a daily basis;
      (vi) rights under a contract of insurance which are expressed as shares in funds held by the insurer unless it is a requirement of the contract of insurance that the purchase and sale price of those shares shall, at any given time, not differ from each other and that the price must be made available to the public on a daily basis;
      [¹(via) shares referred to in regulation 12(2)(a) (shares issued by a company wherever incorporated and officially listed on a recognised stock exchange [⁴ or, in the European Economic Area, admitted to trading on a recognised stock exchange])]
      (vii) depositary interests, where the investments concerned are investments of any of the kinds listed above in this paragraph;
    (b) [¹the requirement is fulfilled that] the account provider, and any relevant person, [¹. . .] ensure that, subject to the other provisions of this paragraph, the account has exposure to equities [¹. . .];

9.61

[¹(ba) interest accrues on investments referred to in regulation 12(2)(k) and (l) (cash deposited in a deposit account or in a share account) on a daily basis at a rate that is not less than the Bank of England base rate minus 1 per cent per annum [³, except where cash is held temporarily on deposit in the course of dealing in investments under the account];

[²(baa) when the Bank of England base rate increases, the interest rate on investments referred to in regulation 12(2)(k) and (l) (cash deposited in a deposit account or in a share account) must be raised within one month of the date of that increase;]

(bb) in relation to qualifying investments which are securities (other than in an investment trust) or a depositary interest where the relevant investments (within the meaning in that definition) are such securities, the requirement is fulfilled that—
    (i) the securities fall within regulation 12(2)(c) [², (d) or (e)], or
    (ii) where the securities fall within regulation 12(2)(b) [²...] or (n), the contract under which the securities are or have been acquired, or any other transaction entered into by the registered contact or any other person, has the effect that the named child is not exposed, or not exposed to a significant extent, to the risk of loss from fluctuations in the value of the securities exceeding 20% of the capital consideration paid or payable for the acquisition of those securities, during the period when the securities in question are held in the account.]

(c) [¹the requirement is fulfilled that] the account provider and any relevant person [¹...] have regard to—
    (i) the need for diversification of investments of the account, in so far as is appropriate to the circumstances of the account; and
    (ii) the suitability for the purposes of the account of any investment, investment strategy or investment option proposed; [⁶.]

(d) [⁶...]

(3) The account provider must permit payment of subscriptions to the account by—
(a) cheque;
(b) direct debit;
(c) standing order;
(d) direct credit (other than standing order).

[¹For the purposes of this sub-paragraph, those means of payment do not include payments by cash, credit card or debit card or any combination including a payment by cash, credit card or debit card.]

(4) The minimum amount which may be subscribed to the account on a single occasion is £10 except where the account provider permits a smaller amount.

(5) Deductions from the account may only be made in the circumstances, and to the extent, set out in paragraph 3.

(6) In this paragraph—

"equities" means shares issued by a company wherever incorporated and officially listed on a recognised stock exchange [⁴ or, in the European Economic Area, admitted to trading on a recognised stock exchange];

"insurer" means—
    (a) a person who has permission under Part 4 of the Financial Services and Markets Act 2000 to effect or carry out contracts of insurance, or
    (b) an EEA firm of the kind mentioned in paragraph 5(d) of Schedule 3 to that Act, which has permission under paragraph 15 of that Schedule (as a result of qualifying for authorisation under paragraph 12 of that Schedule) to effect or carry out contracts of insurance;

[⁶...]

"relevant collective investment scheme" means an authorised unit trust scheme, an authorised open-ended investment company or a recognised scheme, as the case may be, as defined in section 237(3) of the Financial Services and Markets Act 2000;

"relevant person" means any person to whom the account provider has delegated any of his functions or responsibilities under the management agreement; and

"with-profits fund" means a fund maintained by an insurer in respect of a particular part of its long-term business for which—
    (a) separate accounting records are maintained by the insurer in respect of all income and expenditure relating to that part of its business; and
    (b) the benefits payable in respect of policies allocated to that fund are determined partly by reference to a discretion exercisable by any person.

(7) In this paragraph, the definitions of "contract of insurance" and "insurer" must be read with—

(a) section 22 of the Financial Services and Markets Act 2000,
(b) any relevant order made under that section, and
(c) Schedule 2 to that Act.

Stakeholder accounts—charges etc

3.—(1) Deductions from a stakeholder account may only be made to the extent set out in this paragraph.

(2) Subject to sub-paragraph (5), charges for the management of, and other expenses in connection with, a stakeholder account may be recovered from the account to the extent that they do not exceed whichever is the greater of—
(a) 3/730 per cent of the value of the child's rights in the account for each day on which the account is held; or
(b) 3/730 per cent of the value of the investments under the account for each day on which the account is held.

(3) For the purposes of sub-paragraph (2)—
(a) the frequency, which must be daily, weekly or monthly, with which rights or investments are to be valued; and
(b) where valuation is to take place weekly or monthly, the day of the week or, as the case may be, the date in the month on which it is to take place,

must be specified in advance in writing by the account provider to the registered contact, and the specification may not be amended during the period of 12 months after the date on which it is made.

(4) When calculating the value of a child's rights or of investments for the purposes of sub-paragraph (2), where the account provider has specified under sub-paragraph (3) that they are to be valued weekly or monthly—
(a) where they are to be valued weekly, they are to be valued on such day of the week ("the specified day") as has been so specified by the account provider (except that, where that day is not a working day, the rights are to be valued on the next working day), and the value of the rights on each subsequent day prior to the next specified day is to be taken to be the value of the rights on the previous specified day; and
(b) where they are to be valued monthly, they are to be so valued on such date in each month ("the specified date") as has been so specified by the account provider (except that, where that date is not a working day, the rights are to be valued on the next working day), and the value of the rights on each subsequent day prior to the next specified date is to be taken to be the value of the rights on the previous specified date.

(5) The following charges and expenses may be deducted in full from the account and are not subject to and do not count towards the limit provided for in sub-paragraph (2)—
(a) any stamp duty, stamp duty reserve tax [¹, value added tax] or other charges [¹(including any dilution levy)] incurred by the account provider directly or indirectly in the sale or purchase of investments held under the account;
[¹(aa) where any amount of tax is paid or anticipated to be payable in respect of income received or capital gains realised by the account provider in respect of investments held for the purposes of the account, the amount so deducted or anticipated;]
(b) any charges or expenses incurred by the account provider directly or indirectly in complying with an order of the court or any other requirements imposed by law; and
(c) expenses incurred by the account provider in complying with its obligations under regulation 8(2)(d) and (e).

(6) Valuations for the purpose of sub-paragraph (2) shall be after the deduction of any charges or expenses properly deducted from the account under sub-paragraph (5).

AMENDMENTS

1. Child Trust Funds (Amendment) Regulations 2004 (SI 2004/2676) reg.15 (April 6, 2005).

2. Child Trust Funds (Amendment No.2) Regulations 2004 (SI 2004/3382) reg.6 (April 6, 2005).

3. Child Trust Funds (Amendment No.2) Regulations 2006 (SI 2006/2684) reg.6 (October 31, 2006).

4. Child Trust Funds (Amendment No.2) Regulations 2013 (SI 2013/1744) reg.10 (August 5, 2013).

5. Child Trust Funds (Amendment No.2) Regulations 2015 (SI 2015/876) regs 2 and 11 (April 6, 2015).
6. Child Trust Funds (Amendment) Regulations 2017 (SI 2017/185) reg.8 (April 6, 2017).

DEFINITIONS

"account"—see reg.2(1)(b).
"account provider"—see reg.2(1)(b).
"Bank of England base rate"—see reg.2(1)(b).
"child"—see reg.2(1)(a).
"company"—see reg.2(1)(b).
"contract of insurance"—see para.2(7).
"depositary interest"—see reg.2(1)(c).
"equities"—see para.2(6).
"insurer"—see para.2(6). and para.2(7).
"investments under the account"—see reg.2(1)(b).
"investment trust"—see reg.2(1)(b).
"lifestyling"—see para.2(6).
"open-ended investment company"—see reg.2(1)(c).
"recognised stock exchange"—see reg.2(1)(b).
"relevant collective investment scheme"—see para.2(6).
"relevant person"—see reg.2(1)(a) and para.2(6).
"subscriptions"—see reg.2(1)(b).
"tax"—see reg.2(1)(b).
"units"—see reg.2(1)(c).
"with-profits fund"—see para.2(6).

The Child Trust Funds (Insurance Companies) Regulations 2004

(SI 2004/2680)

The Treasury, in exercise of the powers conferred upon them by section 333B of the Income and Corporation Taxes Act 1988 as extended by section 14(1) of the Child Trust Funds Act 2004, hereby make the following Regulations:

ARRANGEMENT OF REGULATIONS

9.62

1. Citation and commencement
2. Interpretation
3. Child trust fund business
4.–17. Modifications of the Taxes Act
18.–19. Modification of the Taxation of Chargeable Gains Act 1992
20.–21. Modification of the Capital Allowances Act 2001
22. Amendments to the Insurance Companies Regulations

Citation and commencement

9.63

1.—These Regulations may be cited as the Child Trust Funds (Insurance Companies) Regulations 2004 and shall come into force on the day appointed under section 27 of the Child Trust Funds Act 2004, for the purposes of sections 8 and 9 of that Act.

Interpretation

2.—In these Regulations—
"child trust fund business" has the meaning given by regulation 3;
"individual savings account business" has the meaning given in the Insurance Companies Regulations;
"the Insurance Companies Regulations" means the Individual Savings Account (Insurance Companies) Regulations 1998;
"the principal Regulations" means the Child Trust Funds Regulations 2004;
"the Taxes Act" means the Income and Corporation Taxes Act 1988.

Child trust fund business

3.—For the purposes of these Regulations "child trust fund business", in relation to an insurance company, means so much of that company's life assurance business as is referable to any policy of life insurance, or to the reinsurance of liabilities under any such policy, where the policy is, on the date on which the insurance is made, a qualifying investment for an account within the meaning of regulation 12 of the principal Regulations.

Modifications of the Taxes Act

4.—Regulations 5 to 17 specify modifications of provisions of the Taxes Act so far as concerns the child trust fund business (and, in the case of regulations 11(b) and (c), 13 and 14, the individual savings account business) of insurance companies.

5.—In section 431(2) insert at the appropriate place the following definition—
"'child trust fund business' has the meaning given by regulation 3 of the Child Trust Funds (Insurance Companies) Regulations 2004;".

6.—In both of sections 431C(1) and 431D(1) after "pension business" insert ", child trust fund business".

7.—In section 431F after "pension business," insert "child trust fund business,".

8.—In section 432A(2) (as modified by the Insurance Companies Regulations) after paragraph (aa) insert—
"(ab) child trust fund business;".

9.—In section 432AA(4) (as modified by the Insurance Companies Regulations) after paragraph (aa) insert—
"(ab) child trust fund business;".

10.—In both of sections 432C(1) and 432D(1) after "pension business," insert "child trust fund business,".

11.—In section 436—
(a) after the words "pension business", in each place where they occur, insert "or child trust fund business";
(b) in subsection (1)(a) for "that business" substitute "the business of each such category".
(c) after subsection (3)(c) insert—
"(ca) there may be set off (so far as it has not been set off under paragraph (c)), against the profits of child trust fund business any loss, to be computed on the same basis as the profits, which has arisen from

individual savings account business, in the same or any previous accounting period;

(cb) there may be set off (so far as it has not been set off under paragraph (c)), against the profits of individual savings account business any loss, to be computed on the same basis as the profits, which has arisen from child trust fund business, in the same or any previous accounting period;".

9.72   12.—In section 438(1) add at the end "or child trust fund business".

9.73   13.—In section 440(4)(a) add at the end, "individual savings account business or child trust fund business, or assets linked to any of those categories but not to any other category of business".

9.74   14.—In section 440A(2)(a)(i) after "pension business" insert ", individual savings account business or child trust fund business or any of those categories of business".

9.75   15.—In section 466(2) insert at the appropriate place the following definition—

"'child trust fund business' shall be construed in accordance with section 431(2);".

9.76   16.—In section 755A (as modified by the Insurance Companies Regulations) after paragraph (aa) in each of subsections (4) and (13) insert—

"(ab) child trust fund business,".

9.77   17.—In paragraph 5(5) of Schedule 19AA after "pension business," insert "child trust fund business,".

Modification of the Taxation of Chargeable Gains Act 1992

9.78   18.—Regulation 19 specifies a modification of section 212 of the Taxation of Chargeable Gains Act 1992 so far as concerns child trust fund business of insurance companies.

9.79   19.—In section 212(2) after "pension business" insert, "child trust fund business".

Modification of the Capital Allowances Act 2001

9.80   20.—Regulation 21 specifies a modification of section 256 of the Capital Allowances Act 2001 so far as concerns child trust fund business of insurance companies.

9.81   21.—In section 256(3)(a) after "pension business" insert, "child trust fund business".

Amendments to the Insurance Companies Regulations

9.82   22.—Regulations 13(b), 15 and 16 of the Insurance Companies Regulations (which are superseded by regulations 11(b), 13 and 14 of these Regulations) shall cease to have effect.

GENERAL NOTE

9.83   These Regulations make various technical modifications to revenue law provisions. They provide for the exemption from corporation tax of income and gains made by an insurance company providing child trust funds, so far as they relate to the company's child trust fund business. They also provide for the profit from operating child trust fund business to be taxed in the same way as profits from the company's Individual Savings Account (ISA) business, and for losses arising one category to be set off against profits from the other.

(SI 2005/191)

The Child Trust Funds (Non-tax Appeals) Regulations 2005

(SI 2005/191)

Made 3 February 2005
Laid before Parliament 4 February 2005
Coming into force 25 February 2005

The Treasury, in exercise of the powers conferred upon them by sections 23(1), 24(5) and 28(1) to (4) of the Child Trust Funds Act 2004, make the following Regulations:

Citation, commencement and duration

1.—(1) These Regulations may be cited as the Child Trust Funds (Non-tax Appeals) Regulations 2005 and shall come into force on 25 February 2005.
(2) [¹ . . .]

AMENDMENT

1. Transfer of Tribunal Functions and Revenue and Customs Appeals Order 2009 (SI 2009/56) art.3(2) Sch.2 para.132 (April 1, 2009).

Interpretation

2.—*Omitted.*

Prescribed manner of notice of appeal

3.—(1) The prescribed manner of giving notice of appeal [¹, in respect of an appeal to an appeal tribunal,] to the Inland Revenue under section 23(1) of the Child Trust Funds Act 2004 is as follows.
(2) The notice must—
(a) be given in writing,
(b) contain sufficient information to identify the appellant and the decision against which the appeal is being made, and
(c) be signed by or on behalf of the appellant.
(3) In paragraph (2)(a) "writing" includes writing produced by electronic communications if those electronic communications are approved by the Commissioners of Inland Revenue.
(4) In paragraph (2)(c) "signed", where the notice is in writing produced by electronic communications, means authenticated in any manner approved by those Commissioners.

AMENDMENT

1. Tribunals, Courts and Enforcement Act 2007 (Transitional and Consequential Provisions) Order 2008 (SI 2008/2683) art.6(1) and Sch.1 para. 262 (November 3, 2008).

DEFINITIONS

"Inland Revenue"—see Child Trust Funds Act 2004 s.29, but see the note below.

The Child Trust Funds (Non-tax Appeals) Regulations 2005

"signed"—see para.(4).
"writing"—see para.(3).

GENERAL NOTE

9.88   For what amounts to a signature, see the annotation to reg.2 of the Tax Credits (Notice of Appeal) Regulations 2002. Also, see para.(4) for signatures on electronic documents.

The functions of the Commissioners of Inland Revenue have been transferred to the Commissioners for Her Majesty's Revenue and Customs (Commissioners for Revenue and Customs Act 2005 s.5(2)(a)).

9.89   **4.–15.**—*Omitted.*

The Child Trust Funds (Appeals) Regulations 2005

(SI 2005/990)

Made   24th March 2005
Coming into force in accordance with regulation 1(1)

9.90   Whereas a draft of this instrument was laid before Parliament in accordance with section 80(1) of the Social Security Act 1998 and approved by resolution of each House of Parliament.

Now therefore, the Secretary of State for Work and Pensions, in exercise of the powers conferred upon him by sections 7(6) and (7), 12(7), 14(10)(a) and (11), 16(1) and (3)(a), 28(1), 79(1) and (4) to (7) and 84 of, and paragraphs 7, 11 and 12 of Schedule 1 to, and paragraphs 1 to 6 of Schedule 5 to, the Social Security Act 1998, after consultation with the Council on Tribunals in accordance with section 8 of the Tribunals and Inquiries Act 1992, hereby makes the following Regulations:

Citation, commencement, duration and interpretation

9.91   **1.**—(1) These Regulations may be cited as the Child Trust Funds (Appeals) Regulations 2005 and shall come into force on the day after they are made.

(2) [² . . .]

(3) In these Regulations, unless the context otherwise requires—
"the Act" means the Social Security Act 1998;
"the 2004 Act" means the Child Trust Funds Act 2004;
"appeal" means an appeal under section 22 of the 2004 Act to [¹ the First-tier Tribunal];
"the Board" means the Commissioners of Inland Revenue;
[¹ . . .]
[¹ . . .]
[¹ . . .]
[¹ . . .]
"notification period" has the meaning given in regulation 3;
"party to the proceedings" means the Board and any person who brings an appeal;
[¹ . . .]

(SI 2005/990 reg.1)

(4) [¹ . . .]

AMENDMENTS

1. Tribunals, Courts and Enforcement Act 2007 (Transitional and Consequential Provisions) Order 2008 (SI 2008/2683) art.6(1) and Sch.1 para.291 (November 3, 2008).
2. Transfer of Tribunal Functions and Revenue and Customs Appeals Order 2009 (SI 2009/56) art.3(2) and Sch.2 para.136 (April 1, 2009).

GENERAL NOTE

Paragraph (3)—"the Board"

The functions of the Commissioners of Inland Revenue have been transferred to the Commissioners for Her Majesty's Revenue and Customs (Commissioners for Revenue and Customs Act 2005 s.5(2)(a)).

9.92

Service of notices or documents

2.—Where by any provision of these Regulations—
(a) any notice or other document is required to be given or sent to [¹ . . .] the Board, that notice or document shall be treated as having been so given or sent on the day that it is received by [¹ . . .] by the Board, and
(b) any notice or other document is required to be given or sent to any person other than [¹ . . .] the Board, that notice or document shall, if sent to that person's last known address, be treated as having been given or sent on the day that it was posted.

9.93

AMENDMENT

1. Tribunals, Courts and Enforcement Act 2007 (Transitional and Consequential Provisions) Order 2008 (SI 2008/2683) art.6(1) and Sch.1 para.292 (November 3, 2008).

DEFINITION

"the Board"—see reg.1(3), but see also the note below.

GENERAL NOTE

The functions of the Commissioners of Inland Revenue ("the Board") have been transferred to the Commissioners for Her Majesty's Revenue and Customs (Commissioners for Revenue and Customs Act 2005 s.5(2)(a)).

9.94

Disputes about notices of appeal

3.—Where a dispute arises as to whether notice of an appeal was given to the Board within the period of thirty days specified in section 23(1) of the 2004 Act ("the notification period") the dispute shall be referred to, and be determined by, [¹ the First-tier Tribunal].

9.95

AMENDMENT

1. Tribunals, Courts and Enforcement Act 2007 (Transitional and Consequential Provisions) Order 2008 (SI 2008/2683) art.6(1) and Sch.1 para.293 (November 3, 2008).

DEFINITIONS
"the 2004 Act"—see reg.1(3).
"the Board"—reg.1(3). but see also the note below.

GENERAL NOTE

9.96 The functions of the Commissioners of Inland Revenue ("the Board") have been transferred to the Commissioners for Her Majesty's Revenue and Customs (Commissioners for Revenue and Customs Act 2005 s.5(2)(a)).

Late appeals

9.97 **4.**—(1) Where the conditions specified in paragraphs [1 (4) to (8) are satisfied, the Board may treat an appeal as made in time where an appeal is] brought within a period of one year after the expiration of the notification period.

(2) [1 . . .]
(3) [1 . . .]

[1 (4) The Board must not treat the appeal as made in time unless the Board is satisfied that it is in the interests of justice.]

(5) For the purposes of paragraph (4) it is not in the interests of justice to [1 treat the appeal as made in time unless the Board are] satisfied that—
    (a) the special circumstances specified in paragraph (6) are relevant [1 . . .]; or
    (b) some other special circumstances exist which are wholly exceptional and relevant [1 . . .],
and as a result of those special circumstances, it was not practicable for the appeal to be brought within the notification period.

(6) For the purposes of paragraph (5)(a), the special circumstances are that—
    (a) the [1 appellant] or a partner or dependant of the [1 appellant] has died or suffered serious illness;
    (b) the [1 appellant] is not resident in the United Kingdom; or
    (c) normal postal services were disrupted.

(7) In determining whether it is in the interests of justice to [1 treat the appeal as made in time], regard shall be had to the principle that the greater the amount of time that has elapsed between the expiration of the notification period and the [1 submission of the notice of appeal, the more compelling should be the special circumstances.]

(8) In determining whether it is in the interests of justice to [1 treat the appeal as made in time] no account shall be taken of the following—
    (a) that the [1 appellant] or any person acting for him was unaware of or misunderstood the law applicable to his case (including ignorance or misunderstanding of the notification period); or
    (b) that [1 the Upper Tribunal] or a court has taken a different view of the law from that previously understood and applied.

(9) [1 . . .]
(10) [1 . . .]
(11) As soon as practicable after the decision is made a copy of the decision shall be sent or given to every party to the proceedings.

(SI 2005/990 reg.4)

AMENDMENT

1. Tribunals, Courts and Enforcement Act 2007 (Transitional and Consequential Provisions) Order 2008 (SI 2008/2683) art.6(1) and Sch.1 para.294 (November 3, 2008).

DEFINITIONS

"the 2004 Act"—see reg.1(3).
"appeal"—reg.1(3).
"the Board"—reg.1(3). but see also the note below.
"notification period"—reg.1(3).
"party to the proceedings"—reg.1(3).

GENERAL NOTE

See the note to reg.5 of the Tax Credit (Appeals) (No.2) Regulations 2002. **9.98**
The functions of the Commissioners of Inland Revenue ("the Board") have been transferred to the Commissioners for Her Majesty's Revenue and Customs (Commissioners for Revenue and Customs Act 2005 s.5(2)(a)).

Death of a party to an appeal

5.—In any proceedings relating to an appeal under section 22(2), (4), (5) **9.99**
or (6) of the 2004 Act, on the death of a party to the proceedings (other than the Board) the personal representative of the person who has died may represent him at any hearing.

DEFINITIONS

"the 2004 Act"—see reg.1(3).
"appeal"—reg.1(3).
"the Board"—reg.1(3). but see also the note below.
"party to the proceedings"—reg.1(3).

GENERAL NOTE

The functions of the Commissioners of Inland Revenue ("the Board") have **9.100**
been transferred to the Commissioners for Her Majesty's Revenue and Customs (Commissioners for Revenue and Customs Act 2005 s.5(2)(a)).

PART X

TAX-FREE CHILDCARE

The Childcare Payments (Eligibility) Regulations 2015

(SI 2015/448)

IN FORCE: MARCH 5, 2015

ARRANGEMENT OF REGULATIONS

1. Citation and commencement
2. Interpretation
3. Eligible persons: partners
4. When a person is regarded as responsible for a child
5. Meaning of qualifying child
6. Temporary absence from the United Kingdom
7. Persons treated as being, or not being, in the United Kingdom
8. The circumstances specified in this regulation are that a person. . .
9. The requirement to be in qualifying paid work
10. Calculation of expected income
11. Self-employed persons: start-up periods
12. Qualifying paid work: time off in connection with sickness or parenting
13. Qualifying paid work: caring, incapacity for work or limited capability for work
14. Qualifying childcare: work requirement
15. Income not to exceed a certain level
16. Application of section 11 to EEA residents
17. Application of sections 12 and 13 to EEA residents
18. Disqualifying tax credit and universal credit claimants from obtaining top-up payments: change of circumstances

The Treasury make the following Regulations, in exercise of the powers conferred by sections 2(3)(b) to (d), 3(4) and (5), 7(3), 8(2), 9(2) and (3), 10(2), (3) and (4), 14, 32(5), 33(5) and 69(2) and (4) of the Childcare Payments Act 2014(1).

In accordance with section 70(3) of that Act, a draft of this instrument was laid before Parliament and approved by resolution of each House of Parliament.

Citation and commencement

1.—These Regulations may be cited as the Childcare Payments (Eligibility) Regulations 2015 and come into force on the day after the day on which they are made.

Interpretation

2.—In these Regulations—
"the Act" means the Childcare Payments Act 2014, and a reference without more to a numbered section is a reference to the section of the Act bearing that number;
[4. . .]
"armed forces independence payment" means armed forces independence payment under the Armed Forces and Reserve Forces (Compensation Scheme) Order 2011;

[³"coronavirus" means severe acute respiratory syndrome coronavirus 2 (SARS-CoV-2);
"coronavirus support scheme" means—
(a) any scheme in relation to which HMRC have functions by virtue of a direction made under section 76 of the Coronavirus Act 2020 (HMRC functions)(HYPERLINK *"https://www.legislation.gov.uk/uksi/2020/1515/regulation/4/made#f00020"*2);
(b) the scheme known as the Small Business Grant Fund established in response to coronavirus;
(c) any scheme established in the tax year 2020-21 in response to coronavirus to support the fishing industry;
(d) the scheme known as the Retail, Hospitality and Leisure Grant Fund established in response to coronavirus;
(e) the scheme known as the Newly Self-Employed Hardship Fund established by the Scottish Ministers in the tax year 2020-2021 in response to coronavirus; and
(f) any other support scheme established in the tax year 2020–21 or 2021–2022 in response to coronavirus;]
[²"disability living allowance" means either—
(a) disability living allowance under sections 71 to 76 of the Social Security Contributions and Benefits Act 1992 or sections 71 to 76 of the Social Security Contributions and Benefits (Northern Ireland) Act 1992; or
[⁵(b) disability assistance given in accordance with regulations made under section 31 of the Social Security (Scotland) Act 2018.]
"employed", except in the expression "self-employed", [⁵ means—
(a) engaged] under a contract of service or in an office (including an elected office) or so engaged as a United Kingdom resident working overseas; [⁵ or
(b) an engagement in relation to which any of Chapters 7 to 10 of Part 2 of ITEPA 2003 applies (which relate to agency workers, workers under arrangements made by intermediaries and workers providing services through managed service companies);]
[¹ "minimum weekly income" means the amount a person would be paid for 16 hours of work a week at the hourly rate set out in regulations 4, 4A and 4B of the National Minimum Wage Regulations 2015;]
"paid work" means work done for payment or in expectation of payment and does not include being engaged by a charitable or voluntary organisation, or as a volunteer, in circumstances in which the payment received by or due to be paid to the person is in respect of expenses;
"partner" has the meaning given in regulation 3;
"personal independence payment" means a personal independence payment under Part 4 of the Welfare Reform Act 2012 [¹ or Part 5 of the Welfare Reform (Northern Ireland) Order 2015];
[⁴"prescribed state" means any EEA state or Switzerland;]
"prisoner" means—
(a) a person who is detained in custody pending trial or sentence upon conviction or under a sentence imposed by a court; or
(b) a person who is on temporary release in accordance with the provisions of the Prison Act 1952, the Prisons (Scotland) Act 1989 or the Prison Act (Northern Ireland) 1953,
other than a person who is detained in hospital under the provisions of the Mental Health Act 1983, in Scotland under the provisions of

the Mental Health (Care and Treatment) (Scotland) Act 2003 or the Criminal Procedure (Scotland) Act 1995 or, in Northern Ireland, under articles 12 to 17 of the Mental Health (Northern Ireland) Order 1986;

[³"Scottish Ministers" has the meaning given by section 44(2) of the Scotland Act 1998;]

"self-employed" means engaged in carrying on a trade, profession or vocation on a commercial basis and with a view to profit, either on one's own account or as a member of a business partnership;

"week" means a period of seven days starting with midnight between Saturday and Sunday.

AMENDMENTS

1. Childcare Payments (Eligibility) (Amendment) Regulations 2016 (SI 2016/793) reg.3 (September 5, 2016).

2. Tax Credits, Child Benefit, Guardian's Allowance and Childcare Payments (Miscellaneous Amendments) Regulations 2020 (SI 2020/297) reg.7 (April 6, 2020).

3. Tax Credits, Childcare Payments and Childcare (Extended Entitlement) (Coronavirus and Miscellaneous Amendments) Regulations 2020 (SI 2020/1515) reg.4(2) (January 14, 2021).

4. Childcare Payments (Miscellaneous Amendment) Regulations 2021 (SI 2021/781) reg.3(2) (July 22, 2021).

5. Childcare Payments (Miscellaneous Amendments) Regulations 2022 (SI 2022/1148) reg.2(2) (December 1, 2022).

Eligible persons: partners

3.—(1) For the purposes of the Act two people are regarded as partners at any time if they are both at least 16 years old at that time and either—
  (a) they are married to, or civil partners of, each other and are members of the same household; or
  (b) they are not married to, or civil partners of, each other but are living together as a married couple or as civil partners.

(2) Where two people are parties to a polygamous marriage, they are not regarded as partners for the purposes of the Act if—
  (a) one of them is party to an earlier marriage that still subsists; and
  (b) the other party to that earlier marriage is living in the same household.

(3) A person's partner who is temporarily absent from the person's household at the date of the declaration of eligibility is not to be regarded as the person's partner for the purposes of the Act if—
  (a) the absence exceeds, or is expected to exceed, 6 months; or
  (b) the absent person is a prisoner.

(4) In this regulation, "polygamous marriage" means a marriage during which a party to it is married to more than one person and which took place under the laws of a country which permits polygamy.

DEFINITIONS

"the Act"—see reg.2.
"partner"— see reg.2.
"polygamous marriage"—para.(4).
"prisoner"—see reg.2.

When a person is regarded as responsible for a child

4.—(1) For the purposes of the Act, a person is regarded as responsible for a child who normally lives with the person.

(2) A person is not regarded as responsible for a child during any period when the child is—
  (a) continuously absent from the person's household for a period which exceeds, or is expected to exceed, 6 months;
  (b) a prisoner;
  (c) looked after by a local authority; or
  (d) placed for adoption by an adoption agency in the home of a person proposing to adopt the child.
(3) A child is not looked after by a local authority for the purpose of paragraph (2)(c)—
  (a) during any period which is in the nature of a planned short term break, or is one of a series of such breaks, for the purpose of providing respite for the person with whom the child normally lives; or
  (b) during any period when the child is placed with, or continues to live with, the child's parent or a person who has parental responsibility for the child.
(4) For the purposes of paragraph (3), a person has parental responsibility if that person is not a foster parent and—
  (a) in England and Wales, has parental responsibility as defined by section 3 of the Children Act 1989;
  (b) in Scotland, has any or all of the legal responsibilities or rights described in section 1 or 2 of the Children (Scotland) Act 1995; or
  (c) in Northern Ireland, has parental responsibility as defined by article 6 of the Children (Northern Ireland) Order 1995.
(5) In this regulation—
"adoption agency" has the meaning given (for England and Wales) in section 2 of the Adoption and Children Act 2002, (for Scotland) in section 119 of the Adoption and Children (Scotland) Act 2007, and (for Northern Ireland) in article 3 of the Adoption (Northern Ireland) Order 1987;
"looked after by a local authority" has the meaning given in section 22 of the Children Act 1989, section 17(6) of the Children (Scotland) Act 1995 or article 25 of the Children (Northern Ireland) Order 1995 (with the modification that for the reference to a local authority there is substituted a reference to an authority within the meaning of article 2 of that Order);
"placed for adoption" means placed for adoption in accordance with—
  (a) the Adoption Agencies Regulations 2005;
  (b) the Adoption Agencies (Wales) Regulations 2005;
  (c) the Adoption Agencies (Scotland) Regulations 2009; or
  (d) the Adoption Agencies Regulations (Northern Ireland) 1989.

DEFINITIONS

"the Act"—see reg.2.
"adoption agency"—para.(5).
"looked after by a local authority"—para.(5).
"placed for adoption"—para.(5).
"prisoner"—see reg.2.

Meaning of qualifying child

5.—(1) A child is a qualifying child for the purposes of the Act until the last day of the week in which falls the 1st September following the child's eleventh birthday.

(2) A disabled child is a qualifying child for the purposes of the Act until the last day of the week in which falls the 1st September following the child's sixteenth birthday.

(3) If at any time any provisions of the Act are in force only in relation to children who have not reached a day earlier than the day referred to in paragraph (1) ("the relevant day"), paragraph (1) has effect for the purposes of the Act as if the reference in that paragraph to the relevant day were a reference to that earlier day.

(4) If at any time any provisions of the Act are in force only in relation to disabled children who have not reached a day earlier than the day referred to in paragraph (2) ("the relevant day"), paragraph (2) has effect for the purposes of the Act as if the reference in that paragraph to the relevant day were a reference to that earlier day.

(5) For the purposes of paragraphs (2) and (4), "disabled child" means—
- (a) a child in respect of whom any of the following is being paid—
  - (i) disability living allowance;
  - (ii) personal independence payment;
  - (iii) armed forces independence payment;
  - (iv) an allowance or payment made under the law of [¹ a prescribed] state which is substantially similar in character to an allowance or payment within paragraph (i), (ii) or (iii); or
- (b) a child who is certified as severely sight impaired or blind by a consultant ophthalmologist.

AMENDMENT

1. Childcare Payments (Miscellaneous Amendment) Regulations 2021 (SI 2021/781) reg.2(3) (July 22, 2021).

DEFINITIONS

"the Act"—see reg.2.
"armed forces independence payment"— see reg.2.
"disability living allowance"—see reg.2.
"disabled child"—para.(5)(a).
"personal independence payment"—see reg.2.
"the relevant day"—paras (3) and (4).

Temporary absence from the United Kingdom

6.—(1) A person's temporary absence from the United Kingdom is disregarded in determining whether the person meets the condition of eligibility in section 8 (the person must be in the UK) if—
- (a) the person is an eligible person, within the meaning of section 3, immediately before the beginning of the period of temporary absence; and
- (b) either—
  - (i) the absence is not expected to exceed, and does not exceed, 8 weeks; or
  - (ii) paragraph (2), (3) or (4) applies.

(2) This paragraph applies where the absence does not exceed 6 months and is solely in connection with—

(a) the person undergoing treatment for an illness or physical or mental impairment by, or under the supervision of, a qualified practitioner; or
(b) the person accompanying the person's partner or a child for whom the person is responsible for treatment as mentioned in sub-paragraph (a).

(3) This paragraph applies where the absence does not exceed 6 months and is solely in connection with the death of—
(a) the person's partner or a child for whom the person was responsible;
(b) a close relative of the person, or of the person's partner; or
(c) a close relative of a child for whom the person or the person's partner is responsible.

(4) This paragraph applies where the absence is not expected to exceed, and does not exceed, 6 months and the person is—
(a) a mariner; or
(b) a continental shelf worker who is in a designated area or a prescribed area.

(5) Regulation 4 applies for the purposes of this regulation.

(6) In this regulation—

"close relative" means—
(a) a parent, parent-in-law, son, son-in-law, daughter, daughter-in-law, step-parent, step-son, step-daughter, brother or sister; and
(b) if any of the above has a partner, that partner;

"continental shelf worker" means a person who is employed in a designated area or a prescribed area in connection with any activity mentioned in section 11(2) of the Petroleum Act 1998;

"designated area" means any area which may from time to time be designated by Order in Council under the Continental Shelf Act 1964 as an area within which the rights of the United Kingdom with respect to the seabed and subsoil and their natural resources may be exercised;

"mariner" means a person who is employed either as a master or member of the crew of any ship or vessel, or in any other capacity on board any ship or vessel where—
(a) the employment is entered into in the United Kingdom with a view to its performance (in whole or in part) while the ship or vessel is on its voyage; and
(b) the employment in that other capacity is for the purposes of that ship or vessel or its crew or any passengers or cargo or mails carried by the ship or vessel;

"prescribed area" means any area over which Norway or any member State [1of the EEA] [1. . .] exercises sovereign rights for the purpose of exploring the seabed and subsoil and exploiting their natural resources, being an area outside the territorial seas of Norway or such member State, or any other area which is from time to time specified under section 10(8) of the Petroleum Act 1998;

"qualified practitioner" means a person qualified to provide medical treatment, physiotherapy or a form of treatment which is similar to, or related to, either of those forms of treatment.

AMENDMENTS

1. Childcare Payments (Miscellaneous Amendment) Regulations 2021 (SI 2021/781) reg.2(4) (July 22, 2021).

(SI 2015/448 reg.6)

DEFINITIONS

"close relative"—para.(6).
"continental shelf worker"— para.(6).
"designated area"— para.(6).
"mariner"— para.(6).
"partner"—see reg.2.
"prescribed area"—para.(6).
"qualified practitioner"— para.(6).

Persons treated as being, or not being, in the United Kingdom

7.—(1) The following persons are treated for the purposes of the Act as being in the United Kingdom—
- (a) a person who is ordinarily resident in the United Kingdom;
- (b) a Crown servant or member of Her Majesty's forces posted overseas;
- (c) the partner of the person mentioned in sub-paragraph (b) when the partner is accompanying the person on that posting;
- (d) a resident of [¹ a prescribed] state [¹ who is not a person subject to immigration control and] who is in paid work in the United Kingdom.

(2) A person mentioned in paragraph (1)(b) is posted overseas if the person is performing overseas the duties of a Crown servant or member of Her Majesty's forces and was, immediately before their posting or the first of consecutive postings, ordinarily resident in the United Kingdom.

(3) The following persons are treated for the purposes of the Act as not being in the United Kingdom—
- (a) a person in the United Kingdom who—
  - (i) is not ordinarily resident in the United Kingdom; and
  - (ii) is not in the United Kingdom in one or more of the circumstances specified in regulation 8;
- (b) a person in the United Kingdom who—
  - (i) is resident in the United Kingdom but is taxed, by virtue of double taxation arrangements, as if they were not so resident; and
  - (ii) is not a resident of [¹ a prescribed] state who is in paid work in the United Kingdom;
- (c) a person who is subject to immigration control.

(4) In this regulation—
"Crown servant" means a person—
  - (i) holding an office or employment under the Crown;
  - (ii) whose duties of employment are of a public nature; and
  - (iii) whose salary is paid out of public funds of the United Kingdom;
"double taxation arrangements" means arrangements that have effect under section 2(1) of the Taxation (International and Other Provisions) Act 2010 (giving effect to arrangements made in relation to other territories);
"Her Majesty's forces" has the meaning in the Armed Forces Act 2006;
"person subject to immigration control" has the meaning in section 115(9) of the Immigration and Asylum Act 1999.

AMENDMENTS

1. Childcare Payments (Miscellaneous Amendment) Regulations 2021 (SI 2021/781) reg.2(5) (July 22, 2021).

DEFINITIONS

"the Act"—see reg.2.
"another EEA state"— see reg.2.
"Crown servant"—para.(4).
"double taxation arrangements"— para.(4).
"Her Majesty's forces"— para.(4).
"person subject to immigration control"— para.(4).

Persons treated as being, or not being, in the United Kingdom

10.9   **8.**—[¹(1)] The circumstances specified in this regulation are that a person is in the United Kingdom as—
  (a) a refugee within the definition in Article 1 of the Convention relating to the Status of Refugees done at Geneva on 28th July 1951, as extended by Article 1(2) of the Protocol relating to the Status of Refugees done at New York on 31st January 1967;
  (b) a person who has been granted, or who is deemed to have been granted, leave outside the rules (the "Immigration Rules") made under section 3(2) of the Immigration Act 1971 where that leave is—
    (i) discretionary leave to enter or remain in the United Kingdom;
    (ii) leave to remain under the Destitution Domestic Violence concession; or
    (iii) leave deemed to have been granted by virtue of regulation 3 of the Displaced Persons (Temporary Protection) Regulations 2005;
  (c) a person who has humanitarian protection granted under the Immigration Rules; [¹ . . .]
  (d) a person who has been deported, expelled or otherwise removed by compulsion of law from another country to the United Kingdom, but is not a person subject to immigration control as defined by section 115(9) of the Immigration and Asylum Act 1999. [¹; or
  (e) a person who has been granted section 67 leave.
(2) In this regulation "section 67 leave" means leave to remain in the United Kingdom granted by the Secretary of State to a person who has been relocated to the United Kingdom pursuant to arrangements made by the Secretary of State under section 67 of the Immigration Act 2016].

AMENDMENT

1. Child Benefit, Tax Credits and Childcare Payments (Section 67 Immigration Act 2016 Leave) (Amendment) Regulations 2018 (SI 2018/788) reg.6(2) (July 20, 2018).

DEFINITION

"Immigration Rules"—para.(b).

The requirement to be in qualifying paid work

10.10   **9.**—(1) For the purposes of the Act, a person is in qualifying paid work if [¹ the person or any partner [² holds] a National Insurance Number ("NINo") and]—
  (a) the person is in paid work as an employed person whose expected income from the work in the period specified in paragraph (4) is greater than or equal to the relevant threshold; or

(b) the person is in paid work as a self-employed person and either—
  (i) the person's expected income from the work in the period specified in paragraph (4) is greater than or equal to the [¹ threshold specified in paragraph (5A)]; or
  (ii) the person's expected income from the work in the period specified in paragraph (5) is greater than or equal to [² . . .] the relevant threshold [²; or
[⁴ (c) the person is in paid work as an employed person [⁵ and] as a self-employed person and the person's expected income from the work in the period specified in paragraph (4) is greater than or equal to the relevant threshold; or
(d) the person is in paid work as an employed person or as a self-employed person, the person's expected income does not meet the requirements of sub-paragraphs (a) or (b) due to coronavirus, and the person—
  (i) is receiving payments under a coronavirus support scheme; or
  (ii) has made a claim for and is reasonably expecting to receive payments under a coronavirus support scheme; or
  (iii) is intending to make a claim under a coronavirus support scheme, with the reasonable expectation of the claim being agreed; or
  (iv) is employed by an employer who is claiming a grant under a coronavirus support scheme to cover a proportion of the person's normal earnings.]

[¹ (1A) The requirement to hold a NINo in [² paragraph (1) does] not apply to a person's partner who is resident and in paid work in [⁴ a prescribed] state.]

(2) For the purposes of this regulation—
(a) a person is to be treated as in paid work as an employed person if the person—
  (i) has accepted an offer of work on or before the date of the declaration of eligibility; and
  (ii) expects the work to start within [²31] days of that day; and
(b) a person is to be treated as in paid work as an employed person if the person—
  (i) is absent from work on unpaid leave on the date of the declaration of eligibility; and
  (ii) expects to return to work within [²31] days of that day.

(3) A person's "expected income" is the income which the person has a reasonable expectation of receiving, calculated in accordance with regulation 10.

(4) The period specified in this paragraph is—
(a) the period of 3 months beginning with the date of the declaration of eligibility; or
(b) if paragraph (2)(a) or (2)(b) applies, the period of 3 months beginning with the day on which the work is expected to start or the person is expected to return to work.

(5) The period specified in this paragraph is, in relation to a declaration of eligibility, the tax year in which the date of the declaration falls.

[¹ (5A) The threshold specified in this paragraph is the product of the calculation—

$$M \times W$$

where

M is the minimum weekly income based on the person's age on the [²...] 6th April of the tax year in which the declaration of eligibility was made; and W is 52.]

(6) In this regulation, "the relevant threshold" is the product of the calculation—

$$M \times W$$

where—

[¹ M is the minimum weekly income based on the hourly rate applicable to the person at the date of the declaration of eligibility] and
W is the number of weeks in the period specified in paragraph (4).

AMENDMENTS

1. Childcare Payments (Eligibility) (Amendment No.2) Regulations 2016 (SI 2016/1021) reg.3 (November 14, 2016).
2. Childcare Payments (Eligibility) (Amendment) Regulations 2017 (SI 2017/1101) reg.3 (December 7, 2017).
3. Tax Credits, Childcare Payments and Childcare (Extended Entitlement) (Coronavirus and Miscellaneous Amendments) Regulations 2020 (SI 2020/1515) reg.4(3) (January 14, 2021).
4. Childcare Payments (Miscellaneous Amendment) Regulations 2021 (SI 2021/781) reg.2(6) (July 22, 2021).
5. Childcare Payments (Miscellaneous Amendments) Regulations 2022 (SI 2022/1148) reg.2(3) (December 1, 2022).

DEFINITIONS

"the Act"—see reg.2.
"employed"— see reg.2.
"expected income"—para.(3).
"minimum weekly income"—see reg.2.
"NINo"—para.(1).
"paid work"—see reg.2.
"the relevant threshold"—para.(6).
"self-employed"—see reg.2.
"week"— see reg.2.

Calculation of expected income

10.—(1) An employed person's expected income comprises the amount of earnings the person expects to receive from—
   (a) any employment under a contract of service;
   (b) any office, including an elected office [²;]
   [²(c) an engagement in relation to which any of Chapters 7 to 10 of Part 2 of ITEPA 2003 applies (which relate to agency workers, workers under arrangements made by intermediaries and workers providing services through managed service companies).]

(2) In paragraph (1), "earnings" has the meaning given by section 62 of ITEPA 2003 (general definition of earnings).

(3) A self-employed person's expected income comprises—
   (a) the amount of receipts the person expects to derive from a trade, profession or vocation less the amount of expenses the person expects to

incur wholly and exclusively for the purposes of the trade, profession or vocation; or
(b) if the person carries on a trade, profession or vocation in a business partnership, the share expected to be allocated to the person of the partnership's receipts less the share expected to be allocated to that person of the partnership's expenses incurred wholly and exclusively for the purposes of the trade, profession or vocation.

(4) In calculating a self-employed person's income, receipts and expenses of a capital nature are to be disregarded.

(5) [¹ . . .]

AMENDMENTS

1. Childcare Payments (Eligibility) (Amendment) Regulations 2017 (SI 2017/1101) reg.4 (December 7, 2017).
2. Childcare Payments (Miscellaneous Amendments) Regulations 2022 (SI 2022/1148) reg.2(4) (December 1, 2022).

DEFINITIONS

"earnings"—para.(2).
"employed"—see reg.2.
"self-employed"— see reg.2.

Self-employed persons: start-up periods

11.— [²(1) A self-employed person does not have to meet the condition in regulation 9(1)(b) or (c) in respect of—
(a) their first declaration of eligibility, if it is made within a start-up period; and
(b) declarations of eligibility in each of the three entitlement periods immediately following that start-up period.]
(2) A "start-up period" is the period of 12 months following the commencement by the self-employed person of any trade, profession or vocation.
(3) A self-employed person cannot rely on a second or subsequent start-up period (in relation to the commencement by that person of a new trade, profession or vocation) unless [¹ at least 48 months] have passed since the end of the previous start-up period.
(4) In paragraph (3) "the previous start-up period" is the period during which the person did not have to meet the condition in regulation 9(1)(b) [¹ or (c)].

10.12

AMENDMENTS

1. Childcare Payments (Eligibility) (Amendment) Regulations 2017 (SI 2017/1101) reg.5 (December 7, 2017).
2. Childcare Payments (Miscellaneous Amendments) Regulations 2022 (SI 2022/1148) reg.2(5) (December 1, 2022).

DEFINITIONS

"the previous start-up period"—para.(4).
"self-employed"—see reg.2.
"start-up period"—para.(2).

Qualifying paid work: time off in connection with sickness or parenting

10.13   **12.**—(1) This regulation applies for any period during which a person—
(a) is paid statutory sick pay under Part 11 of the Social Security Contributions and Benefits Act 1992 or Part 11 of the Social Security Contributions and Benefits (Northern Ireland) Act 1992;
(b) is paid maternity allowance under section 35 of the Social Security Contributions and Benefits Act 1992 or section 35 of the Social Security Contributions and Benefits (Northern Ireland) Act 1992;
(c) is paid statutory maternity pay under Part 12 of the Social Security Contributions and Benefits Act 1992 or Part 12 of the Social Security Contributions and Benefits (Northern Ireland) Act 1992;
(d) is absent from work during an ordinary maternity leave period under section 71 of the Employment Rights Act 1996 or article 103 of the Employment Rights (Northern Ireland) Order 1996;
(e) is absent from work during an additional maternity leave period under section 73 of the Employment Rights Act 1996 or article 105 of the Employment Rights (Northern Ireland) Order 1996;
(f) is paid [² . . .] statutory paternity pay under Part 12ZA of the Social Security Contributions and Benefits Act 1992 or Part 12ZA of the Social Security Contributions and Benefits (Northern Ireland) Act 1992;
(g) is absent from work during [² a] paternity leave period under section 80A or 80B of the Employment Rights Act 1996 or article 112A or 112B of the Employment Rights (Northern Ireland) Order 1996;
(h) [² . . .] [¹ . . .];
(i) is paid statutory adoption pay under Part 12ZB of the Social Security Contributions and Benefits Act 1992 or Part 12ZB of the Social Security Contributions and Benefits (Northern Ireland) Act 1992;
(j) is absent from work during an ordinary adoption leave period under section 75A of the Employment Rights Act 1996 or article 107A of the Employment Rights (Northern Ireland) Order 1996;
(k) is absent from work during an additional adoption leave period under section 75B of the Employment Rights Act 1996 or article 107B of the Employment Rights (Northern Ireland) Order 1996;
(l) is absent from work during a period of shared parental leave under section 75E or 75G of the Employment Rights Act 1996 [¹ or articles 107E or 107G of the Employment Rights (Northern Ireland) Order 1996]; [³ . . .]
(m) is absent from work during a statutory parental leave period under section 76 of the Employment Rights Act 1996 or Article 108 of the Employment Rights (Northern Ireland) Order 1996[³;
(n) [⁴ in relation to England, Wales and Scotland only,] is absent from work during a period of parental bereavement leave under section 80EA of the Employment Rights Act 1996; or
(o) [⁴ in relation to England, Wales and Scotland only,] is paid statutory parental bereavement pay under Part 12ZD of the Social Security Contributions and Benefits Act 1992].

(2) Subject to paragraphs (3), (4) and (5), that person is regarded for the purposes of the Act—
(a) as in paid work during the period in paragraph (1); and
(b) as having, for each week of that period, expected income from that work equal to the minimum weekly income.

(3) Paragraph (2) does not apply unless, immediately before the start of the period in any sub-paragraph of paragraph (1), either—
(a) the person was in qualifying paid work; or
(b) this regulation applied to the person by virtue of a different sub-paragraph of paragraph (1).

(4) For the purposes of the entitlement of a person, or of a person's partner, to receive top-up payments in respect of a child whose birth or adoption caused the period in paragraph (1)(b) to (m) to run, paragraph (2) applies only for the final [²31] days before the person returns to work.

(5) Paragraph (2) applies to a person by virtue of paragraph (1)(h) only for such period as that person would have been paid additional statutory paternity pay had the conditions of entitlement in Part 2 or 3 of the Additional Statutory Paternity Pay (General) Regulations 2010 or Part 2 or 3 of the Additional Statutory Paternity Pay (General) Regulations (Northern Ireland) 2010 been satisfied.

(6) This regulation applies to a self-employed person during any period for which paragraph (1) would have applied in that person's case but for the fact that the work performed in the week immediately before the period began, although done for payment or in expectation of payment, was not performed under a contract of service.

(7) This regulation applies to a resident of [⁴ a prescribed] state who is in paid work in the United Kingdom, or such a person's partner, who under the law of that state—
(a) receives payments which are substantially similar in character to the payments in paragraph (1)(a) to (c), (f) or (i); or
(b) is absent from work in circumstances which are substantially similar in character to a period of absence described in paragraph (1)(d), (e), (g), (h) or (j) to (m).

AMENDMENTS

1. Childcare Payments (Eligibility) (Amendment) Regulations 2016 (SI 2016/793) reg.4 (September 5, 2016).
2. Childcare Payments (Eligibility) (Amendment) Regulations 2017 (SI 2017/1101) reg.6 (December 7, 2017).
3. Parental Bereavement Leave and Pay (Consequential Amendments to Subordinate Legislation) Regulations 2020 (SI 2020/354) reg.36 (April 6, 2020).
4. Childcare Payments (Miscellaneous Amendment) Regulations 2021 (SI 2021/781) reg.2(7) (July 22, 2021).

DEFINITIONS

"minimum weekly income"— see reg.2.
"paid work"— see reg.2.
"partner"— see reg.2.
"self-employed"— see reg.2.
"week"— see reg.2.

Qualifying paid work: caring, incapacity for work or limited capability for work

13.—(1) This regulation applies for any period during which—
(a) a person ("P") has a partner who is in qualifying paid work; and
(b) P is paid or entitled to any of the following—
   (i) incapacity benefit under section 30A, 40 or 41 of the Social Security Contributions and Benefits Act 1992 or section 30A, 40 or 41 of the Social Security Contributions and Benefits (Northern Ireland) Act 1992;
   (ii) severe disablement allowance under section 68 of the Social Security Contributions and Benefits Act 1992 or section 68 of the Social Security Contributions and Benefits (Northern Ireland) Act 1992 (as they have effect by virtue of article 4 of the Welfare Reform and Pensions Act 1999 (Commencement No.9, and Transitional and Savings Provisions) Order 2000 and article 4 of the Welfare Reform and Pensions (1999 Order) (Commencement No.6 and Transitional and Savings Provisions) Order (Northern Ireland) 2000);
   (iii) long-term incapacity benefit under regulation 11(4) or 17(1) of the Social Security (Incapacity Benefit) (Transitional) Regulations 1995 or by regulation 11(4) or 17(1) of the Social Security (Incapacity Benefit) (Transitional) Regulations (Northern Ireland) 1995;
   (iv) carer's allowance under section 70 of the Social Security Contributions and Benefits Act 1992 or section 70 of the Social Security Contributions and Benefits (Northern Ireland) Act 1992;
   [^{1} (v) contributory employment and support allowance under section 1 of the Welfare Reform Act 2007 or section 1 of the Welfare Reform Act (Northern Ireland) 2007; [^{3}...]
   (vi) national insurance credits on the grounds of incapacity for work or limited capability for work under regulation 8B of the Social Security (Credits) Regulations 1975 or regulation 8B of the Social Security (Credits) Regulations (Northern Ireland) 1975 [^{3};]
   [^{3}(vii) carer's assistance given in accordance with regulations made under section 28 of the Social Security (Scotland) Act 2018, except young carer grants given under the Carer's Assistance (Young Carer Grants) (Scotland) Regulations 2019][^{4}, or]
[^{4}(c) in respect of England and Wales and Scotland only, P is absent from work during a period of carer's leave under section 80J of the Employment Rights Act 1996.]
(2) For the purposes of the Act, P is regarded—
(a) as in paid work during that period; and
(b) as having, for each week of that period, expected income from that work equal to the minimum weekly income.
(3) P's partner is not in qualifying paid work for the purposes of paragraph (1)(a) during any period when that partner is paid a benefit or an allowance, or is entitled to a credit, described in paragraph (1)(b).
(4) This regulation applies to a self-employed person, or that person's partner, during any period for which paragraph (1) would have applied in that person's (or partner's) case but for the fact that the work performed in the week immediately before the period began, although done for payment

or in expectation of payment, was not performed under a contract of service.

(5) This regulation applies to a resident of [² a prescribed] state who is in paid work in the United Kingdom, or such a person's partner, who under the law of that state is entitled to a benefit, allowance or credit which is substantially similar in character to a benefit, allowance or credit described in paragraph (1)(b).

AMENDMENTS

1. Childcare Payments (Eligibility) (Amendment) Regulations 2017 (SI 2017/1101) reg.7 (December 7, 2017).
2. Childcare Payments (Miscellaneous Amendment) Regulations 2021 (SI 2021/781) reg.2(8) (July 22, 2021).
3. Childcare Payments (Miscellaneous Amendments) Regulations 2022 (SI 2022/1148) reg.2(6) (December 1, 2022).
4. Carer's Leave (Consequential Amendments to Subordinate Legislation) Regulations 2024 (SI 2024/266) reg.8 (April 6, 2024).

DEFINITIONS

"minimum weekly income"— see reg.2.
"P"—para.(1)(a).
"paid work"—see reg.2.
"partner"— see reg.2.
"self-employed"— see reg.2.
"week"— see reg.2.

Qualifying childcare: work requirement

14.—(1) For the purposes of this regulation and section 2 (qualifying childcare) "work" means paid work.

(2) The condition in section 2(2)(b) is treated as being met in relation to a person to whom any of the cases in regulation 12(1)(a) to (m) or 13(1)(b) applies.

(3) The condition in section 2(2)(b) is treated as being met by a person who is on sick leave or paid annual leave.

(4) In this regulation—
"annual leave" means, in relation to a self-employed person, reasonable amounts of time off from work for the same purposes as the purposes for which annual leave is taken;
what are "reasonable amounts" is to be assessed having regard to the annual leave or sick leave to which an employee might reasonably expect to be entitled if doing similar work;
"sick leave" means, in relation to a self-employed person, reasonable amounts of time off from work due to sickness.

10.15

DEFINITIONS

"annual leave"—para.(4).
"reasonable amounts"—para.(4).
"sick leave"—para.(4).
"work"—para.(1).

Income not to exceed a certain level

15.—(1) A person is treated as meeting the condition of eligibility in section 10 (the income of the person and his or her partner must not exceed

10.16

limit) if the person does not expect [¹ their adjusted net income to exceed £100,000] for the relevant tax year.

[² (1A) [⁵. . .]]

[² (1B) [⁵. . .]]

(2) A resident of [⁴ a prescribed] state who is in paid work in the United Kingdom is treated as meeting the condition of eligibility in section 10 if that person would not expect [¹ their hypothetical adjusted net income to exceed £100,000] for the relevant tax year.

(3) A person is treated as not meeting the condition of eligibility in section 10 if—
- (a) the person has made, or expects to make, a claim under section 809B of the Income Tax Act 2007 (claim for remittance basis to apply) for the relevant tax year; or
- (b) the person expects section 809E of that Act (application of remittance basis in certain cases without claim) to apply to the person for the relevant tax year.

(4) In this regulation—

[¹ "adjusted net income" has the meaning given in section 58(1) of the Income Tax Act 2007;]

[² [³ . . .];

[² [⁵. . .]]

"hypothetical adjusted net income" is the amount that would be that individual's adjusted net income if that individual's income tax liability were calculated on the basis that the individual—
- (a) was UK resident for the tax year concerned (and the year was not a split year);
- (b) was domiciled in the United Kingdom for that tax year;
- (c) in that tax year, did not fall to be regarded as resident in a country outside the United Kingdom for the purposes of double taxation arrangements having effect at the time;
- (d) for that tax year, had made a claim for any available relief under section 6 of the Taxation (International and Other Provisions) Act 2010 (as required by subsection (6) of that section).]

An individual's adjusted hypothetical net income for a tax year is, to the extent that it is not sterling, to be calculated by reference to the average exchange rate for the year ending on 31 March in the tax year concerned.]

"the relevant tax year" has the meaning given in section 10(5).

AMENDMENTS

1. Childcare Payments (Eligibility) (Amendment) Regulations 2016 (SI 2016/793) reg.5 (September 5, 2016).

2. Childcare Payments (Coronavirus and Miscellaneous Amendments) Regulations 2020 (SI 2020/656) reg.3 (July 21, 2020).

3. Tax Credits, Childcare Payments and Childcare (Extended Entitlement) (Coronavirus and Miscellaneous Amendments) Regulations 2020 (SI 2020/1515) reg.4(4) (January 14, 2021).

4. Childcare Payments (Miscellaneous Amendment) Regulations 2021 (SI 2021/781) reg.2(9) (July 22, 2021).

5. Childcare Payments (Miscellaneous Amendments) Regulations 2022 (SI 2022/1148) reg.2(7) (December 1, 2022).

DEFINITIONS

"adjusted net income"—para.(4).
"hypothetical adjusted net income"—para.(4).
"partner"—see reg.2.
"the relevant tax year"—para.(4).

Application of section 11 to [¹ residents of prescribed states]

16.—(1) Section 11 (neither the person nor his or her partner may be claiming universal credit) applies with the modifications in paragraph (2) to a resident of [¹ a prescribed] state who is in paid work in the United Kingdom if, at the date of the declaration, that person or that person's partner either—
  (a) is, under the law of that state, being paid in respect of a relevant assessment period a credit (an "equivalent credit") which is substantially similar in character to universal credit; or
  (b) has made a claim that would result in an equivalent credit becoming payable to that person or that person's partner in respect of a relevant assessment period.
(2) The modifications in this paragraph are—
  (a) a reference to universal credit includes a reference to an equivalent credit; and
  (b) a reference to "the relevant legislation" includes a reference to the provisions governing the equivalent credit.

AMENDMENT

1. Childcare Payments (Miscellaneous Amendment) Regulations 2021 (SI 2021/781) reg.2(10) (July 22, 2021).

DEFINITIONS

"equivalent credit"—para.(1)(a).
"partner"—see reg.2.
"the relevant legislation"—para.(2)(b).

Application of sections 12 and 13 to [¹residents of prescribed states]

17.—(1) Sections 12 and 13 (neither the person nor his or her partner may be in a relevant childcare scheme or receiving other childcare support) apply to a resident of [¹a prescribed] state who is in paid work in the United Kingdom, and to such a person's partner, with the modifications in paragraph (2).
(2) The modifications in this paragraph are—
  (a) in section 12—
    (i) a reference to a "relevant childcare scheme" includes a scheme which, under the law of [¹ a prescribed] state, provides support of a substantially similar character to a scheme under section 270A (limited exemption for qualifying childcare vouchers) or 318 (childcare: exemption for employer-provided care) of ITEPA 2003; and
    (ii) "eligible employee" means a person who is eligible for such a scheme;
  (b) in section 13, a reference to "national authority" includes an authority of [¹a prescribed] state.

AMENDMENTS

1. Childcare Payments (Miscellaneous Amendment) Regulations 2021 (SI 2021/781) reg.2(11) (July 22, 2021).

DEFINITIONS

"eligible employee"—para.(2)(a)(ii).
"national authority"—para.(2)(b).
"partner"—see reg.2.
"relevant childcare scheme"—para.(2)(a)(i).

Disqualifying tax credit and universal credit claimants from obtaining top-up payments: change of circumstances

18.—(1) The following are to be regarded as changes of circumstances in relation to a person for the purposes of sections 32 and 33 (power to disqualify tax credit or universal credit claimants from obtaining top-up payments)—
  (a) a person no longer meets the conditions of eligibility in sections 7 to 9, or a person's partner no longer meets the condition in section 9;
  (b) the composition of a person's household changes, including where—
     (i) a person's partner joins the person's household or the person joins the partner's household;
     (ii) a person or a person's partner takes responsibility for another child or qualifying young person;
     (iii) a person's partner or a child leaves the household; or
     (iv) a person's partner or child dies;
  (c) a person or the person's partner is absent from the household for at least one month;
  (d) a person's child or the person's partner's child is awarded, or ceases to be entitled to, disability living allowance, personal independence payment or armed forces independence payment;
  (e) the principal employment of a person or a person's partner changes;
  (f) the employment status of a person or a person's partner changes;
  (g) a person becomes liable to pay HMRC an amount under section 35(2), 36(2), 37(2) or 38(3) (recovery of top-up payment where award of tax credit or universal credit made on review, revision or appeal); or
  (h) any other change entitles a person or a person's partner to make a claim that results in either—
     (i) a first award of a tax credit; or
     (ii) a first award of universal credit.
(2) For the purposes of paragraph (1)(b)(ii)—
  (a) in a case within section 32—
     (i) a person takes responsibility for a child or qualifying young person where the person takes such responsibility in accordance with the rules in regulation 3 of the Child Tax Credit Regulations 2002; and
     (ii) "qualifying young person" has the meaning given in regulations 2 and 5(3) and (4) of those Regulations;
  (b) in a case within section 33—
     (i) a person takes responsibility for a child or qualifying young person where the person takes such responsibility as determined by regulations 4 and 4A of the Universal Credit Regulations 2013; and

(SI 2015/448 reg.18)

(ii) "qualifying young person" has the meaning given in regulation 5 of those Regulations;
(c) "child" means a person under the age of 16.
(3) In paragraph (1)(b)(iii) and (iv) and (1)(d) "child" means a qualifying child for the purposes of the Act.
(4) In paragraph (1)(e), a person's "principal employment" is the employment in which the greater part of the person's working time is spent.

DEFINITIONS

"armed forces independence payment"— see reg.2.
"child"—para.(3).
"disability living allowance"—see reg.2.
"partner"— see reg.2.
"personal independence payment"—see reg.2.
"principal employment"—para.(4).

The Childcare Payments Regulations 2015

(SI 2015/522)

ARRANGEMENT OF REGULATIONS

10.20

1. Citation and commencement
2. Interpretation
3. Qualifying childcare: registered or approved childcare
4. Entitlement periods
5. Variation of entitlement periods
6. Declarations of eligibility
7. Late declarations of eligibility
8. Circumstances where eligible person unable to act— receivers etc.
9. Circumstances where eligible person unable to act—other appointed persons
10. Appointment by account-holder of person to manage childcare account
11. Opening a childcare account
12. Variation of relevant maximum: child ceasing to be qualifying child etc.
13. Variation of relevant maximum: appealable decisions
14. Variation of relevant maximum: delay in payment of allowances
15. Variation of relevant maximum: death of account-holder
16. Variation of relevant maximum: infrastructure failure
16A. Payments that may be made from childcare accounts
17. Compensatory payments
18. Account restriction orders
19. Closure of a childcare account
20. Power to obtain information or documents
21. Disqualification orders: meaning of "relevant benefit"
22. Use of electronic communications

The Commissioners for Her Majesty's Revenue and Customs make the following Regulations, in exercise of the powers conferred by sections 2(3)(a) and (4), 4(6), 5(3), 15(3), (4) and (5), 17(4), 19(6), 24(1), (3) and (4), 25, 26(1) and (3), 49(6), 62(1), (2), (3) and (5) and 69(3) and (4) of the Childcare Payments Act 2014.

Citation and commencement

10.21   **1.**—These Regulations may be cited as the Childcare Payments Regulations 2015 and come into force on 1st June 2015.

Interpretation

10.22   **2.**—In these Regulations—
"the Act" means the Childcare Payments Act 2014, and a reference without more to a numbered section is a reference to the section of the Act bearing that number;
[² . . .]
"armed forces independence payment" means an armed forces independence payment under the Armed Forces and Reserve Forces (Compensation Scheme) Order 2011;
"disability living allowance" means disability living allowance under sections 71 to 76 of the Social Security Contributions and Benefits Act 1992 or sections 71 to 76 of the Social Security Contributions and Benefits (Northern Ireland) Act 1992;
"disabled child" is to be read in accordance with regulations made under section 14 (qualifying child);
"personal independence payment" means a personal independence payment under Part 4 of the Welfare Reform Act 2012 [¹ or Part 5 of the Welfare Reform (Northern Ireland) Order 2015];
[²"prescribed state" means any EEA state or Switzerland;]
"relevant maximum" for an entitlement period is to be read in accordance with section 19 (payments into childcare accounts).

AMENDMENT

1. Childcare Payments (Amendment) Regulations 2016 (SI 2016/796) reg.3 (September 5, 2016).
2. Childcare Payments (Miscellaneous Amendment) Regulations 2021 (SI 2021/781) reg.3(2) (July 22, 2021).

Qualifying childcare: registered or approved childcare

10.23   **3.**—(1) For the purposes of section 2 (qualifying childcare), childcare described in paragraphs (2) to (6) is to be regarded as registered or approved childcare.
(2) Care provided in England for a child—
(a) by a person registered under Part 3 of the Childcare Act 2006;
(b) by or under the direction of the proprietor of a school as part of the school activities—
  (i) out of school hours, where a child has reached compulsory school age; or
  (ii) at any time, where a child has not yet reached compulsory school age; or
(c) by a domiciliary care provider registered with the Care Quality Commission in accordance with the requirements of the Health and Social Care Act 2008.
(3) Care provided in Wales for a child—
(a) by a person registered under Part 2 of the Children and Families (Wales) Measure 2010;

(SI 2015/522 reg.3)

   (b) by a person in circumstances where, but for article 11, 12 or 14 of the Child Minding and Day Care Exceptions (Wales) Order 2010, the care would be day care for the purposes of Part 2 of the Children and Families (Wales) Measure 2010;

   (c) out of school hours, by a school as part of the school activities or by a local authority;

[¹(d) by a person who is employed or engaged under a contract for services to provide care and support by the provider of a domiciliary support service within the meaning of Part 1 of the Regulation and Inspection of Social Care (Wales) Act 2016.]

   (e) by a foster parent in relation to a child (other than one whom the foster parent is fostering) in circumstances where the care would be child minding or day care for the purposes of Part 2 of the Children and Families (Wales) Measure 2010 but for the fact that the child is over the age of the children to whom that Measure applies; or

   (f) by a childcare provider approved in accordance with a scheme made by the National Assembly for Wales or the Welsh Ministers under [³either—
     (i) section 12(5) of the Tax Credit Act 2002; or
     (ii) section 60 of the Government of Wales Act 2006]

(4) Care provided in Scotland for a child—

   (a) by a person in circumstances where the care service provided by the person consists of child minding or of day care of children within the meaning of paragraph 12 or 13 of Schedule 12 to the Public Services Reform (Scotland) Act 2010(8) and is registered under Part 5 of that Act;

   (b) by a local authority in circumstances where the care service provided by the local authority consists of child minding or of day care of children within the meaning of paragraph 12 or 13 of Schedule 12 to the Public Services Reform (Scotland) Act 2010 and is registered under Part 5 of that Act; or

   (c) by a childcare agency where the care service consists of or includes supplying, or introducing to persons who use the service, childcarers within the meaning of paragraph 5 of Schedule 12 to the Public Services Reform (Scotland) Act 2010.

(5) Care provided in Northern Ireland for a child—

   (a) by a person registered under Part 11 of the Children (Northern Ireland) Order 1995;

   (b) out of school hours by a school as part of the school activities; or

   (c) by a childcare provider approved in accordance with a scheme under the Tax Credits (Approval of Home Child Care Providers) Scheme (Northern Ireland) 2006 [³; or]

[³(d) by a childcare provider approved by a Health and Social Care Trust in Northern Ireland for the purposes of providing approved home childcare.]

[² (6) Care provided for a child outside the United Kingdom—

   (a) where the care is provided by a Ministry of Defence approved childcare provider which is inspected by a person whose functions include regulating the provision of childcare in accordance with the statutory requirements of the Department for Education, or

   (b) in any other case, where care is provided within [²a prescribed] state by a childcare provider which is approved, regulated or accredited

under the legislation of the relevant state, by a person whose functions include regulating the provision of education or childcare.]
(7) The following are not registered or approved childcare—
(a) care provided for a child by the child's parent, step-parent or the parent's partner;
(b) care provided for a child by a relative of the child, wholly or mainly in the child's home;
(c) care provided by a person with parental responsibility for the child; and
(d) care provided by a person who is a foster parent of the child.

(8) Care is not within paragraph (2)(a) if it is provided in breach of a requirement to register under Part 3 of the Childcare Act 2006.

(9) Care is not within paragraph (5)(a) if it is provided in breach of a requirement to register under Part 11 of the Children (Northern Ireland) Order 1995.

(10) In this regulation—

"compulsory school age" is determined in accordance with section 8 of the Education Act 1996;

"foster parent" includes, in Scotland, a foster carer or kinship carer as defined by regulation 2 of the Looked After Children (Scotland) Regulations 2009;

"local authority" means—
(a) in relation to Wales, a county council, a county borough council or a community council;
(b) in relation to Scotland, a council constituted under section 2 of the Local Government etc. (Scotland) Act 1994;

[2 "Ministry of Defence approved childcare provider" means a childcare provider, outside the United Kingdom, approved by the Ministry of Defence for use by Her Majesty's forces, which has the same meaning as in the Armed Forces Act 2006, and their families, and civil servants employed by the Ministry of Defence and their families;]

"proprietor", in relation to a school, means—
(a) the governing body incorporated under section 19 of the Education Act 2002; or
(b) if there is no such body, the person or body of persons responsible for the management of the school;

"relative" means grandparent, aunt, uncle, brother or sister, whether of the full blood or half blood or by marriage or civil partnership;

"school"—
(a) in England and Wales, has the same meaning as in the Education Act 1996;
(b) in Northern Ireland, means a school as defined by article 2(2) of the Education and Libraries (Northern Ireland) Order 1986.

AMENDMENTS

1. Tax Credits and Childcare (Miscellaneous Amendments) Regulations 2018 (SI 2018/365) reg.5 (April 6, 2018).
2. Tax Credits, Child Benefit and Childcare Payments (Miscellaneous Amendments) Regulations 2019 (SI 2019/364) reg.12(2) (March 21, 2019).
3. Tax Credits, Child Benefit, Guardian's Allowance and Childcare Payments (Miscellaneous Amendments) Regulations 2020 (SI 2020/297) reg.8(2) (April 6, 2020).

(SI 2015/522 reg.3)

4. Childcare Payments (Miscellaneous Amendment) Regulations 2021 (SI 2021/781) reg.3(3) (July 22, 2021).

DEFINITIONS

"compulsory school age"—para.(1).
"foster parent"— para.(1).
"local authority"— para.(1).
"proprietor"— para.(1).
"relative"— para.(1).
"school"— para.(1).

Entitlement periods

4.—(1) A person's first entitlement period begins on the day on which HMRC confirm that the person is an eligible person for the entitlement period.

(2) Each subsequent entitlement period begins on the day after the previous entitlement period ends.

(3) Each entitlement period begins on the same day of a month except as follows—
  (a) if the first entitlement period begins or ends on the 31st day of a month, each subsequent entitlement period shall begin or end on the last day of the month; and
  (b) if the first entitlement period begins or ends on the 29th or 30th day of a month, each subsequent entitlement period shall begin or end on the 29th or 30th day of the month, except in February where it begins or ends on the 27th day or, in a leap year, the 28th day.

Variation of entitlement periods

5.—(1) HMRC may vary the length of an entitlement period—
  (a) on the opening of a childcare account in relation to a person's first entitlement period;
  (b) on the opening of a childcare account for a person's second or subsequent child; [1 . . .]
  (c) in order to align the entitlement periods of two account-holders [1; or
  (d) in order to align the entitlement period of an account holder ("A") with the declaration period of A's partner under [2 regulation 25 of the Childcare (Free of Charge for Working Parents) (England) Regulations 2022].]

[1 (1A) The length of the variation referred to in paragraph (1) shall not exceed two months.]

(2) The relevant maximum for the entitlement period varied under paragraph (1) is determined by the formula—

$$X \times A \div 91$$

where—
  X is, in the case of a disabled child, £4,000, or in the case of any other child, £2,000; and
  A is the number of days in the varied entitlement period.

AMENDMENTS

1. Childcare Payments (Amendment) Regulations 2017 (SI 2017/1096) reg.3 (December 7, 2017).
2. Childcare (Free of Charge for Working Parents) (England) Regulations 2022 (SI 2022/1134) reg.3 and Sch. para.3 (December 1, 2022).

Declarations of eligibility

10.26   **6.**—(1) A declaration of eligibility must—
(a) be in the form specified by HMRC;
(b) be made to HMRC in accordance with regulation 22; [4. . .]
(c) contain information specified by HMRC—
(i) to identify the person making the declaration, the person's partner (if any) and the child in respect of whom the childcare account is, or is to be, held; and
(ii) to determine whether the person is an eligible person [4;]
[4(d) be accompanied by a confirmation, if required by HMRC.]
(2) A declaration of eligibility made for the purposes of opening a childcare account must be made on the day the person applies to open the account.
(3) Subject to paragraph (4) and regulation 7, any other declaration of eligibility (a "reconfirming declaration") must be made during the period beginning 28 days before the beginning of the entitlement period for which the reconfirming declaration is made and ending when that entitlement period [2 begins].
(4) If a person makes a reconfirming declaration during the period of 7 days immediately preceding the beginning of the entitlement period for which that declaration is made, HMRC may not determine whether the declaration is valid for the purposes of the Act until—
(a) 7 days after the reconfirming declaration was made; or
(b) such earlier time as HMRC allow.
[1 (5) Where a declarant or their partner is self-employed and they make—
(a) the first declaration of the self-employment, the declarant must—
(i) provide any unique taxpayer's reference of the self-employment; or
(ii) confirm that the self-employed person has, for the tax year in which the reconfirmation is made, given notice to HMRC under section 7 of the Taxes Management Act 1970 in respect of the self-employment but has not yet received a unique taxpayer's reference;
(b) the second declaration of the self-employment, the declarant must provide any unique taxpayer's reference of the self-employed person.
(6) Any person whose partner is self-employed in [3a prescribed] state must in the course of reconfirming eligibility, provide information specified by HMRC to confirm that the partner is carrying out self-employed work in that [3prescribed] state.
[4(7) In this regulation—
"a confirmation" means a confirmation made to HMRC, orally or in writing, by a declarant or their partner that they have complied with the requirement in section 8(1)(a) of the Taxes Management Act 1970 within the period specified in section 8(1D), except where either section 8(1F) or 8(1G) applies where the time limit specified in that section applies;
"declarant" means a person who makes a declaration of eligibility for the purposes of either opening a childcare account or reconfirming eligibility.]]

(SI 2015/522 reg.6)

AMENDMENTS

1. Childcare Payments (Amendment) Regulations 2016 (SI 2016/796) reg.4 (September 5, 2016).
2. Childcare Payments (Amendment No.2) Regulations 2016 (SI 2016/1017) reg.2 (November 14, 2016).
3. Childcare Payments (Miscellaneous Amendment) Regulations 2021 (SI 2021/781) reg.3(4) (July 22, 2021).
4. Childcare Payments (Miscellaneous Amendments) Regulations 2022 (SI 2022/1148) reg.3(2) (December 1, 2022).

DEFINITIONS

"partner"— see reg.2.
"reconfirming declaration"—para.(3).

Late declarations of eligibility

[¹ 7.—(1) If a person makes a declaration of eligibility during the entitlement period for which it is made (a "late declaration of eligibility"), HMRC may not determine whether the declaration is valid for the purposes of the Act until—

(a) 7 days after the declaration was made; or
(b) such earlier time as HMRC allow.

(2) If a person ("P") makes a late declaration of eligibility P may make qualifying payments into the childcare account only for the remainder of the entitlement period after the day on which HMRC determine the declaration is valid.

(3) Where a late declaration of eligibility is made by P in circumstances where either—

(a) section 30(2) (termination of tax credit awards) applies; or
(b) P is subject to an assessment period under regulation 21 of the Universal Credit Regulations 2013 (assessment periods) and P's assessment period overlaps with the entitlement period;

the relevant maximum for the entitlement period is reduced to an amount determined by the formula—

$$X \times A \div B$$

where—

X is, in the case of a disabled child, £4,000, or in the case of any other child, £2,000;
A is the number of days remaining in the entitlement period after the day on which HMRC determine that the declaration is valid; and
B is the total number of days in the entitlement period.

(4) Paragraph (3) applies with the modification in subparagraph (5) to a resident of [² a prescribed] state who is in paid work in the United Kingdom if, at the date of the declaration, that person or that person's partner either—

(i) is, under the law of that state, being paid in respect of a relevant assessment period a credit (an "equivalent credit") which is substantially similar in character to universal credit; or
(ii) is, under the law of that state, in receipt of a credit ("an equivalent credit") which is substantially similar in character to an award of tax credit; or

10.27

(iii) has made a claim that would result in an equivalent credit becoming payable to that person or that person's partner.

(5) The modification in this paragraph is a reference to universal credit and tax credit includes a reference to an equivalent credit.]

AMENDMENTS

1. Childcare Payments (Amendment) Regulations 2016 (SI 2016/796) reg.5 (September 5, 2016).
2. Childcare Payments (Miscellaneous Amendment) Regulations 2021 (SI 2021/781) reg.3(5) (July 22, 2021).

DEFINITIONS

"disabled child"— see reg.2.
"equivalent credit"—para.(4)(i) and (ii).
"late declaration of eligibility"—para.(1).
"P"—para.(2).

Circumstances where eligible person unable to act—receivers etc.

10.28   8.—(1) In the circumstances specified in paragraph (2) a person mentioned in sub-paragraph (b) of that paragraph may act for the person mentioned in sub-paragraph (a) of that paragraph for the purposes of—
(a) making a declaration of eligibility;
(b) opening a childcare account;
(c) managing a childcare account.
(2) The circumstances specified in this paragraph are where—
(a) a person is, or is alleged to be, an eligible person but is unable for the time being to open and manage a childcare account; and
(b) there are any of the following—
  (i) a receiver appointed by the Court of Protection with power to open and manage a childcare account on behalf of the person;
  (ii) in Scotland, a tutor, curator or other guardian acting or appointed in terms of law who is administering the estate of the person; or
  (iii) in Northern Ireland, a controller appointed by the High Court, with power to open and manage a childcare account on behalf of the person.

Circumstances where eligible person unable to act—other appointed persons

10.29   9.—(1) In the circumstances specified in paragraph (2) a person mentioned in sub-paragraph (b) of that paragraph may act for the person mentioned in sub-paragraph (a) of that paragraph for the purposes of—
(a) making a declaration of eligibility;
(b) opening a childcare account;
(c) managing a childcare account.
(2) The circumstances specified in this paragraph are where—
(a) a person is, or is alleged to be, an eligible person but is unable for the time being to open and manage a childcare account; and
(b) in relation to that person, there is a person appointed under—

(i) regulation 33(1) of the Social Security (Claims and Payments) Regulations 1987;
(ii) regulation 33(1) of the Social Security (Claims and Payments) Regulations (Northern Ireland) 1987; or
(iii) paragraph (3).

(3) Where no person mentioned in regulation 8(2)(b) has been appointed in relation to the person who is unable to act, HMRC may appoint under this paragraph a person who—
(a) if a natural person, is aged 18 years or more; and
(b) has applied in writing to HMRC to be appointed to act on behalf of the person who is unable to act.

(4) A person's appointment under paragraph (3) ends—
(a) when HMRC terminate it;
(b) when the person appointed has resigned from the appointment having given one month's notice in writing to HMRC of that person's resignation; or
(c) when HMRC are notified that a receiver or other person mentioned in regulation 8(2)(b) has been appointed in relation to the person who is unable to open or manage a childcare account.

Appointment by account-holder of person to manage childcare account

10.—(1) An account-holder may appoint a person to manage a childcare account on behalf of the account-holder.

(2) The person appointed under paragraph (1) must be an individual whose name is notified to HMRC before any function is performed on behalf of the account-holder.

(3) Except where HMRC otherwise allow, an account-holder cannot appoint under paragraph (1)—
(a) an individual who is an account provider or is an owner of an account provider;
(b) an individual who provides services to an account provider in connection with the provision or management of a childcare account—
(i) as an employee of the account provider;
(ii) as an employee of a person providing such services to the account provider; or
(iii) as a self-employed person; or
(c) an individual who provides qualifying childcare for a child of the account-holder.

(4) A person may be appointed under paragraph (1) to manage not more than 5 childcare accounts at any time (whether or not on behalf of the same account-holder).

(5) A person appointed under paragraph (1) may not make a declaration of eligibility on behalf of the account-holder.

(6) Paragraphs (3), (4) and (5) do not apply to an account-holder's partner appointed under paragraph (1) to manage all the childcare accounts of that account-holder.

Opening a childcare account

11.—(1) An application to open a childcare account must—
(a) be in the form specified by HMRC;

(b) be made to HMRC in accordance with regulation 22;
(c) contain information specified by HMRC to identify the applicant, the applicant's partner (if any) and the child in respect of whom the account is to be held; and
(d) [¹ ...]
(2) [¹ ...]
(3) [¹ ...]

AMENDMENT

1. Childcare Payments (Amendment) Regulations 2016 (SI 2016/796) reg.6 (September 5, 2016).

DEFINITION

"partner"—see reg.2.

Variation of relevant maximum: child ceasing to be qualifying child etc.

12.—(1) If a child ceases to be a qualifying child during an entitlement period, the relevant maximum for that entitlement period is determined in accordance with paragraph (3).

(2) If an award of tax credit terminates in accordance with section 30(3) (termination of tax credit awards) in a case within section 30(1)(b), the relevant maximum for an entitlement period is determined in accordance with paragraph (3) for the entitlement period in which the relevant day falls.

(3) The relevant maximum is determined by the formula—

$$X \times A \div B$$

where—
(a) X is, in the case of a disabled child, £4,000, or in the case of any other child, £2,000;
(b) in a case within paragraph (1), A is the number of days beginning on the first day of the entitlement period and ending on the day after the day on which the child ceases to be a qualifying child; or
(c) in a case within paragraph (2), A is the number of days beginning on the relevant day and ending on the last day of the entitlement period; and
(d) B is the total number of days in the entitlement period.

(4) In this regulation, "relevant day" has the meaning given in section 30.

DEFINITIONS

"disabled child"—see reg.2.
"relevant day"—para.(4).
"relevant maximum"—see reg.2.

Variation of relevant maximum: appealable decisions

13.—(1) This regulation applies where an appealable decision under section 56(3)(a), (b), (c), (e) or (h) (appealable decisions) is either—
(a) varied or cancelled on a review under section 57 (review of decisions); or
(b) quashed (wholly or partly) under section 60 (powers of tribunal).

(SI 2015/522 reg.13)

(2) Where this regulation applies, the relevant maximum for an entitlement period beginning after the variation, cancellation or quashing of the appealable decision is increased by an amount equal to the relevant maximum that would (but for the decision) have been available to an active childcare account.

(3) Where a person has received compensation under section 62 (compensatory payments)—
- (a) no award of an increased relevant maximum may be made in respect of a variation or quashing of a decision for which the compensation was paid; and
- (b) any award of an increased relevant maximum that has been made in respect of such a variation or quashing is cancelled.

DEFINITION

"relevant maximum"—see reg.2.

Variation of relevant maximum: delay in payment of allowances

14.—(1) This regulation applies where—
- (a) a person has applied to open a childcare account but HMRC are unable to confirm eligibility solely because of a delay in the payment to the person, or to the person's partner, of—
  - (i) carer's allowance under section 70 of the Social Security Contributions and Benefits Act 1992 or section 70 of the Social Security Contributions and Benefits (Northern Ireland) Act 1992; [^{2}...]
  - [^{2}(ia) carer support payment under the Carer's Assistance (Carer Support Payment) (Scotland) Regulations 2023; or]
  - (ii) contributory employment and support allowance under section 1 of the Welfare Reform Act 2007 or section 1 of the Welfare Reform Act (Northern Ireland) 2007; or
- (b) in relation to a disabled child, a person has applied to open a childcare account but, solely because of a delay in the payment to the child of—
  - (i) disability living allowance;
  - (ii) personal independence payment; or
  - (iii) armed forces independence payment,

HMRC is unable to grant the application, or is able to grant it but subject to a relevant maximum less than the relevant maximum which applies in respect of a disabled child.

(2) Where this regulation applies, the relevant maximum for an entitlement period beginning after the delay is increased by an amount equal to the relevant maximum that would, but for the delay, have been available to an active childcare account held—
- (a) in a case within paragraph (1)(a), by that person; or
- (b) in a case within paragraph (1)(b), in respect of that child.

(3) Where a person has received compensation under section 62—
- (a) no award of an increased relevant maximum may be made in respect of a delay in payment for which the compensation was paid; and
- (b) any award of increased relevant maximum that has been made in respect of such a delay in payment is cancelled.

(4) In this regulation references to carer's allowance, [^{2}carer support payment,] contributory employment and support allowance, disability living allowance, personal independence payment and armed forces

10.34

independence payment include references to allowances and payments made under the law of [¹a prescribed] state which are substantially similar in character to those allowances and payments.

AMENDMENTS

1. Childcare Payments (Miscellaneous Amendment) Regulations 2021 (SI 2021/781) reg.3(6) (July 22, 2021).
2. Carer's Assistance (Carer Support Payment) (Scotland) Regulations 2023 (Consequential Modifications) Order 2023 (SI 2023/1214) reg.12(2) (November 16, 2023).

DEFINITIONS

"armed forces independence payment"— see reg.2.
"disability living allowance"—see reg.2.
"disabled child"— see reg.2.
"personal independence payment"— see reg.2.
"relevant maximum"—see reg.2.

Variation of relevant maximum: death of account-holder

10.35 15.—(1) This regulation applies where—
(a) an account-holder dies leaving funds in the childcare account ("account A");
(b) a person ("P") has an active childcare account ("account B") at the time account A is closed; and
(c) account A was, and account B is, held in respect of the same qualifying child.
(2) Where this regulation applies, the relevant maximum for P's next entitlement period beginning after the closure of account A is increased by an amount equal to the amount paid to the deceased account-holder's personal representatives under regulation 19(2)(b) and (3) (closure of a childcare account).

DEFINITIONS

"account A"—para.(1)(a).
"account B"—para.(1)(b).
"P"—para.(1)(b).

Variation of relevant maximum: infrastructure failure

10.36 16.—(1) This regulation applies where a payment is prevented from being made into a childcare account by a serious technical failure affecting—
(a) HMRC;
(b) the account provider; or
(c) a bank or provider of banking services.
(2) Where this regulation applies, the relevant maximum for the next entitlement period beginning after the failure is increased by—

$$X - Q$$

where—
X is, in the case of a disabled child, £4,000, or in the case of any other child, £2,000; and
Q is the sum of qualifying payments made into the childcare account during the entitlement period in which the failure occurred.

DEFINITION

"disabled child"—see reg.2.

[¹Payments that may be made from childcare accounts

16A.—(1) A payment is treated as a permitted payment where it includes a reasonable fee payable to an intermediary.

(2) For the purposes of paragraph (1), where there is more than one intermediary in the payment chain the total of all fees must be reasonable.

(3) In this regulation "intermediary" means a supplier of an electronic payment system which allows persons to make payments into that system for the ultimate purpose of making payments to qualifying childcare providers.]

AMENDMENT

1. Childcare Payments (Coronavirus and Miscellaneous Amendments) Regulations 2020 (SI 2020/656) regs. 4 and 5 (July 21, 2020).

Compensatory payments

17.—(1) Subject to paragraphs (5) and (6), the circumstances specified in [¹paragraphs (2), (3) [³, (3A) and (3B)]] are specified for the purposes of section 62.

(2) The circumstances specified in this paragraph are—
(a) an appealable decision under section 56(3)(a), (b), (c), (e) or (h) is—
   (i) varied or cancelled on a review under section 57; or
   (ii) quashed (wholly or partly) under section 60;
(b) a person has applied to open a childcare account but HMRC are unable to confirm eligibility solely because of a delay in the payment to the person, or to the person's partner, of—
   (i) carer's allowance under section 70 of the Social Security Contributions and Benefits Act 1992 or section 70 of the Social Security Contributions and Benefits (Northern Ireland) Act 1992; [⁵...]
   [⁵(ia) carer support payment under the Carer's Assistance (Carer Support Payment) (Scotland) Regulations 2023; or]
   (ii) contributory employment and support allowance under section 1 of the Welfare Reform Act 2007 or section 1 of the Welfare Reform Act (Northern Ireland) 2007; [⁴...]
(c) in relation to a disabled child, an application is made to open a childcare account but, solely because of a delay in the payment to the child of—
   (i) disability living allowance;
   (ii) personal independence payment; or
   (iii) armed forces independence payment,
   HMRC is unable to grant the application, or is able to grant it but subject to a relevant maximum less than the relevant maximum which applies in respect of a disabled child[⁴; or
(d) a person has applied for leave to enter or remain under the EU Settlement Scheme, and the application has not been determined or there is an outstanding appeal.]

(3) The circumstances specified in this paragraph are—
(a) the circumstances are as specified in paragraph (2)(b) but, at the time the payment is made, the person is no longer an eligible person for a reason unrelated to the delay in payment;

(b) the circumstances are as specified in paragraph (2)(b) but, at the time the payment is made, the child in relation to whom the application was made has died; or
(c) the circumstances are as specified in paragraph (2)(c) but the child dies during the period of delay in payment.

[¹ [² (3A) The circumstances specified in this paragraph are that—
(a) a person is unable to open a childcare account, or
(b) a person's childcare account fails to function effectively
for a continuous period of at least 14 days, due to a serious technical failure [³ or a design flaw] affecting HMRC or the account provider.]]

[³(3B) The circumstances specified in this paragraph are that a person's childcare account for a child ("C") is made subject to an account restriction order where—
(a) another person (B) wants to apply for, or make a declaration of eligibility for, 30 hours free childcare in respect of C under section 1 of the Childcare Act 2016; and
(b) B does not want to hold a childcare account for C in circumstances where holding that childcare account would prevent B from receiving tax credits in respect of C.]

(4) The amount paid to a person under section 62 in respect of a child for a period (the "compensation period") may not exceed the amount of top-up payments that person could have received if—
(a) the circumstances specified in [¹paragraphs (2), (3) [³, (3A) or (3B)]] had not arisen; and
(b) the person had held an active childcare account in respect of the child throughout the compensation period.

(5) Circumstances specified in paragraph (2)(b) or (c) or (3) are not specified for the purposes of section 62 for any period of delay in payment in respect of which an award of tax credits is or has been made to the person claiming a compensatory payment.

(6) Circumstances specified in paragraph (2) are not specified for the purposes of section 62 to the extent that a person has received, in respect of those circumstances, additional top-up payments by using an increased amount of relevant maximum awarded under regulation 13 or 14.

(7) A person claiming a compensatory payment must provide to HMRC evidence of payment of the costs incurred on qualifying childcare.

(8) In this regulation references to carer's allowance, [⁵carer support payment,] contributory employment and support allowance, disability living allowance, personal independence payment and armed forces independence payment include references to allowances and payments made under the law of [⁴a prescribed] state which are substantially similar in character to those allowances and payments.

[⁴(9) In this regulation —
"EU Settlement Scheme" means —
(i) the residence scheme immigration rules in Appendix EU to the immigration rules except those rules or changes to that appendix which are identified in the immigration rules as not having effect in the residence scheme that operates in connection with the withdrawal of the United Kingdom from the EU; and
(ii) any other rules which are identified in the immigration rules as having effect in connection with the withdrawal of the United Kingdom from the EU.]

(SI 2015/522 reg.17)

AMENDMENTS

1. Childcare Payments (Amendment) Regulations 2016 (SI 2016/796) reg.7 (September 5, 2016).
2. Childcare Payments (Amendment) Regulations 2017 (SI 2017/1096) reg.4 (December 7, 2017).
3. Tax Credits, Child Benefit, Guardian's Allowance and Childcare Payments (Miscellaneous Amendments) Regulations 2020 (SI 2020/297) reg.8(3) (April 6, 2020).
4. Childcare Payments (Miscellaneous Amendment) Regulations 2021 (SI 2021/781) reg.3(7) (July 22, 2021).
5. Carer's Assistance (Carer Support Payment) (Scotland) Regulations 2023 (Consequential Modifications) Order 2023 (SI 2023/1214) reg.12(3) (November 16, 2023).

DEFINITIONS

"armed forces independence payment"— see reg.2.
"compensation payment"—para.(4).
"disability living allowance"—see reg.2
"disabled child"— see reg.2.
"personal independence payment"— see reg.2.

Account restriction orders

18.—(1) HMRC may make an account restriction order— 10.38
(a) imposing a restriction under section 24(2)(a), if the condition specified in paragraph [¹ (1A), (1B),] (2), (3) [², (3A)] or (4) is met; or
(b) imposing a restriction under section 24(2)(b), if the condition specified in paragraph (5) is met.
[¹ (1A) The condition specified in this paragraph is that an amount has been assessed and notified to a person under section 41 (assessment and enforcement of recoverable amounts) in relation to any of sections 35 to 38 (recovery of top up payments).
(1B) The conditions specified in this paragraph are that—
  (i) an amount has been assessed and notified to a person under section 41 in relation to sections 39 or 40 (recovery of top up payments); and
  (ii) some or all of the amount assessed has not been paid to HMRC by the time specified in section 41(5).]
(2) The condition specified in this paragraph is—
(a) an amount has been assessed and notified to a person under section [¹ ...] 47 (assessment and enforcement of [¹ ...] penalties); and
(b) some or all of the amount assessed has not been paid to HMRC by the time specified in section [¹ ...] 47(4).
(3) The condition specified in this paragraph is—
(a) a person ("P") wishes—
  (i) to open a childcare account in respect of a child; or
  (ii) to make a declaration of eligibility in relation to a childcare account held in respect of a child; and
(b) P is prevented from so doing because another person holds an active childcare account in respect of the child.
[²(3A) The condition specified in this paragraph is that—
(a) a person (P) wants to apply for, or to make a declaration for, 30 hours free childcare in respect of a child ("C") under section 1 of the Childcare Act 2016; and

(b) P is prevented from receiving 30 hours free childcare because another person holds an active childcare account in respect of C.]

(4) The condition specified in this paragraph is that section 35(1), 36(1), 37(1) or 38(1) (recovery of top-up payments) applies in relation to an account-holder or the partner of an account-holder.

(5) The condition specified in this paragraph is—
  (a) HMRC have reasonable grounds to suspect that fraudulent payments are to be made from a childcare account; and
  (b) HMRC have reasonable grounds to believe that it will not be possible to recover top-up payments if the order is not made.

(6) In a case within paragraph (3), the person who wishes to open a childcare account may apply to HMRC for an account restriction order to be made in relation to the active childcare account.

(7) An account restriction order—
  (a) may impose a restriction on the account for the period specified in the order;
  (b) may provide that the restriction does not apply in circumstances specified in the order [¹;]
[¹ (c) may be imposed where the account holder agrees to this action;
  (d) must be revoked where the account holder, having previously agreed to the imposition under subparagraph (7)(c) above, requests a review of the decision to make the account restriction order.]

(8) HMRC may revoke an account restriction order if they consider it is no longer required, either on their own initiative or on an application by the account-holder.

(9) An account-holder may make such an application if—
  (a) the period for applying for a review of, or for bringing an appeal against, the order has elapsed; and
  (b) the circumstances of the account-holder have changed since that period elapsed.

AMENDMENT

1. Childcare Payments (Amendment) Regulations 2016 (SI 2016/796) reg.8 (September 5, 2016).
2. Tax Credits, Child Benefit, Guardian's Allowance and Childcare Payments (Miscellaneous Amendments) Regulations 2020 (SI 2020/297) reg.8(4) (April 6, 2020).

DEFINITION

"P"—para.(3)(a).

Closure of a childcare account

19.—(1) A childcare account must be closed if—
  (a) two years have elapsed since the end of the last entitlement period for which there was a valid declaration of eligibility; or
  (b) one year has elapsed since the end of the entitlement period during which the child ceased to be a qualifying child.

(2) At the time a childcare account is closed, whether under paragraph (1) or otherwise—
  (a) the top-up element of the funds remaining in the account at that time, calculated in accordance with section 21 (calculating the top-up element of payments etc), must be paid to HMRC; and

(b) the relevant percentage of the total funds in the account at that time, calculated in accordance with section 22 (withdrawals), must be returned to the account-holder.

(3) Where an account-holder has died, the relevant percentage to be returned under paragraph (2)(b) must be paid to the account-holder's personal representatives.

Power to obtain information or documents

20.—(1) A notice (an "information notice") under section 26(1) (power to obtain information or documents) may be addressed to, and may require information or documents from, any of the following persons—
  (a) an account-holder or a person who has applied to open a childcare account (the "applicant");
  (b) a person named in a declaration of eligibility or application as the partner of an account-holder or applicant;
  (c) an agent of a person specified in sub-paragraph (a) or (b);
  (d) a person who provides, or has provided, childcare to an account-holder or has received a payment from a childcare account;
  (e) an employer or former employer of an account-holder or applicant;
  (f) an employer who provides, or has provided, a relevant childcare scheme within the meaning of section 12(2) and any person who provides, or has provided, services to the employer in connection with the provision to employees of such a scheme;
  (g) a person or body of persons who HMRC reasonably expect can provide information or documents relevant to an allegation of, or an inquiry into, non-compliance with the Act.

(2) An information notice must—
  (a) specify the information or documents required and the form and manner in which they are to be provided;
  (b) set out the reason why HMRC are requesting the information or documents; and
  (c) specify the period within which the person must provide the information or documents.

(3) The period in paragraph (2)(c) must be at least 30 days beginning with the day on which the notice is issued.

DEFINITIONS

"applicant"—para.(1)(a).
"information notice"—para.(1).

Disqualification orders: meaning of "relevant benefit"

21.—For the purposes of section 49 (disqualification orders), a "relevant benefit" is—
  (a) any "disqualifying benefit" within the meaning given in section 6A(1) of the Social Security Fraud Act 2001; or
  (b) any benefit, payment, allowance, pension or credit made under the law of [¹a prescribed] state which is substantially similar in character to those specified in paragraph (a).

The Childcare Payments Regulations 2015

AMENDMENT

1. Childcare Payments (Miscellaneous Amendment) Regulations 2021 (SI 2021/781) reg.3(8) (July 22, 2021).

Use of electronic communications

10.42   **22.**—(1) Except as provided by paragraphs (3) and (4), an application to open a childcare account (an "application") or a declaration of eligibility (a "declaration") must be made to HMRC by electronic communications.

(2) Payments made from a childcare account by an account provider in respect of qualifying childcare must be made by electronic communications.

(3) Paragraph (1) does not apply if HMRC are satisfied that the person making the application or declaration—
  (a) is prevented, by a court order, from sending information by electronic communications;
  (b) holds beliefs which are incompatible with the use of electronic communications; [1 . . .]
  (c) is unable to send information by electronic communications by reason of—
    (i) age;
    (ii) disability;
    (iii) inability to operate a computer effectively in a manner that cannot be remedied by the use of assisted digital support; or
    (iv) living in a remote location so that it is not reasonably practicable to use electronic communications [1; or]
[1 (d) is prevented, for a continuous period of at least 7 days, by a technical failure affecting HMRC, from making a declaration or application.]

(4) An application or declaration made by a person to whom paragraph (3) applies must be made to HMRC in the manner specified by HMRC.

(5) If an application or declaration is made by electronic communications, it shall be treated for the purposes of the Act and these Regulations as having been made, and received by HMRC, on the date on which it is recorded on an official computer system.

(6) In this regulation—
  (a) "assisted digital support" includes advice and assistance on how to make an application or declaration by means of electronic communications and entering a person's information into the service on that person's behalf;
  (b) "electronic communications" includes any communications by means of an electronic communications service;
  (c) "electronic communications service" has the meaning given by section 32 of the Communications Act 2003;
  (d) "official computer system" means a computer system maintained by or on behalf of HMRC—
    (i) to send or store information; or
    (ii) to process or store information.

AMENDMENT

1. Childcare Payments (Amendment) Regulations 2016 (SI 2016/796) reg.9 (September 5, 2016).

(SI 2015/522 reg.22)

DEFINITIONS

"application"—para.(1).
"assisted digital support"—para.(6)(a).
"declaration" —para.(1).
"electronic communications"—para.(6)(b).
"electronic communications service"—para.(6)(c).
"official computer system"—para.(6)(d).

The Childcare Payments (Appeals) Regulations 2016

(SI 2016/1078)

IN FORCE: NOVEMBER 30, 2016

ARRANGEMENT OF REGULATIONS

1. Citation and commencement
2. Interpretation
3. Application of Chapter 2 of Part 1 of the Social Security Act 1998
4. Application of Chapter 2 of Part 2 of the Social Security (Northern Ireland) Order 1998 *[omitted]*
5. *[omitted as also relating solely to Northern Ireland]*
6. *[omitted as also relating solely to Northern Ireland]*
7. Application of section 54 of the Taxes Management Act 1970

10.43

The Commissioners for Her Majesty's Revenue and Customs, in exercise of the powers conferred on them by section 59(4)(a), (b) and (c) of the Childcare Payments Act 2014, make the following Regulations.

GENERAL NOTE

Section 56 of the Childcare Payments Act 2014 provides for a right of appeal against the various types of decision mentioned in that section. Section 59 further provides that regulations may make provision for existing appeals legislation to apply to appeals under the 2014 Act with such modifications as may be specified in regulations. These regulations make such modifications to the relevant social security legislation applying in Great Britain (reg.3) and Northern Ireland (regs 4–6) as well as to s.54 of the Taxes Management Act 1970 (reg.7), which applies in both jurisdictions.

10.44

These Regulations thus make modifications in reg.3 to the relevant social security legislation governing the position in Great Britain (a parallel change is made in Northern Ireland by reg.5). Section 17 of the Social Security Act 1998 (finality of decisions) is applied to childcare payments appeals with two modifications.

The first modification is potentially problematic (reg.3(2)). The existing s.17(1) of the 1998 Act essentially stipulates that any decision made in accordance with ss.8–16 of that Act is final, but subject to the provisions of Ch.2 of the 1998 Act and also to those in Ch.2 of Pt 1 of the Tribunals, Courts and Enforcement Act 2007 (i.e. the legislation which provides for an onward right of appeal from the First-tier Tribunal to the Upper Tribunal and thence to the Court of Appeal). Regulation 3(2) substitutes a new version of s.17(1) for childcare payments appeals. The modified s.17(1) for the purpose of childcare payment appeals makes no reference to the 2007 Act. In addition, at least as read literally, the modified s.17(1) would appear to suggest that the decision of a First-tier Tribunal in a childcare payments appeal "shall be final", i.e. that the right of appeal to the Upper Tribunal is excluded. However, it is questionable whether the right of appeal under s.11 of the 2007 Act can indeed be excluded in this way, not least as childcare payments appeals have not been designated as "excluded decisions" for the purposes of s.11(1).

The second modification is entirely unproblematic (reg.3(3)), as it simply omits s.17(2)(b) and (c) which have no relevance in the present context as they apply solely to child support and vaccine damage appeals respectively.

Citation and commencement

10.45 1.—These Regulations may be cited as the Childcare Payments (Appeals) Regulations 2016 and come into force on 30th November 2016.

Interpretation

10.46 2.—In these Regulations "childcare payments appeal" means an appeal under section 56 of the Childcare Payments Act 2014.

Application of Chapter 2 of Part 1 of the Social Security Act 1998

10.47 3.—(1) Section 17 of the Social Security Act 1998(1) (finality of decisions) shall apply to a decision of an appropriate tribunal on a childcare payments appeal with the modifications specified in paragraphs (2) and (3).

(2) For paragraph (1) of that section substitute the following paragraph—

"(1) Subject to the provisions of the Childcare Payments Act 2014 any decision made in accordance with those provisions in respect of an appeal which, by virtue of section 59 of the Childcare Payments Act 2014 (or of provisions of this Act applied by regulations made under that section), is to the First-tier Tribunal, shall be final.".

(3) Omit paragraphs (2)(b) and (c).

Application of Chapter 2 of Part 2 of the Social Security (Northern Ireland) Order 1998

10.48 4.–6.—[Omitted.]

Application of section 54 of the Taxes Management Act 1970

10.49 7.—(1) Section 54 of the Taxes Management Act 1970 (settling of appeals by agreement) shall apply to a childcare payments appeal to an appropriate tribunal with the modifications specified by paragraphs (2) to (6).

(2) In subsection (1) insert "appropriate" immediately before "tribunal" in both places where it occurs.

(3) In subsections (1), (2) and (4)(a) for "inspector or other proper officer of the Crown" substitute "HMRC".

(4) For subsection (3) substitute—

"(3) Where an agreement is not in writing—
  (a) the preceding provisions of this section shall not apply unless HMRC give notice, in such form and manner as they consider appropriate, to the appellant of the terms agreed between HMRC and the appellant; and
  (b) the references in those preceding provisions to the time when the agreement was come to shall be construed as references to the date of that notice.".

(5) In subsection (4)(b) and the fall out words after subsection (4)(b) for "inspector or other proper officer" substitute "HMRC".

PART XI

FREE CHILDCARE FOR WORKING PARENTS

The [¹Childcare Act 2016 (Consequential Amendments)] Regulations 2016

(SI 2016/1257)

Made   19th December 2016

Coming into force in accordance with regulation 1

The Secretary of State for Education makes the following Regulations in exercise of the powers conferred by sections 1(2), (3), (4) and (7), 2(1), (2), (4) and (5) and 4(2) of the Childcare Act 2016.

In accordance with section 4(4) of that Act, a draft of this instrument was laid before and approved by a resolution of each House of Parliament.

In accordance with section 2(3) of that Act, these Regulations are made with the consent of the Treasury.

AMENDMENT

1. Childcare (Free of Charge for Working Parents) (England) Regulations 2022 (SI 2022/1134) reg.3 and Sch. para.4(2) (December 1, 2022).

ARRANGEMENT OF REGULATIONS

PART 1

Preliminary

1. Citation and commencement
2. Interpretation

PARTS 2, 3 AND 4 (*repealed*)

PART 5 (*omitted*)

PART 1

PRELIMINARY

Citation and commencement

1.—(1) These Regulations may be cited as the [¹ Childcare Act 2016 (Consequential Amendments)] Regulations 2016.

The Childcare Regulations 2016

(2) Parts [¹1] and 5 of these Regulations come into force 21 days after the day on which these Regulations are made.

(3) [¹...]

AMENDMENT

1. Childcare (Free of Charge for Working Parents) (England) Regulations 2022 (SI 2022/1134) reg.3 and Sch. para.4(3)-(5)(a) (December 1, 2022).

GENERAL NOTE

11.2   On the jurisdictional issues raised by appeals relating to these Regulations, see the commentary above on the Childcare Act 2016 and the decision in *HMRC v JS, EL and LG* [2021] UKUT 264 (AAC).

Interpretation

11.3   2.—[¹...]

AMENDMENT

1. Childcare (Free of Charge for Working Parents) (England) Regulations 2022 (SI 2022/1134) reg.3 and Sch. para.4(5)(b) (December 1, 2022).

PARTS 2, 3 AND 4 (¹*repealed*)

AMENDMENT

1. Childcare (Free of Charge for Working Parents) (England) Regulations 2022 (SI 2022/1134) reg.3 and Sch. para.4(5)(c)–(e) (December 1, 2022).

PART 5

CONSEQUENTIAL AMENDMENTS

11.4   40.-43. [*Omitted*]

The Childcare (Free of Charge for Working Parents) (England) Regulations 2022

(SI 2022/1134)

The Secretary of State for Education makes these Regulations in exercise of the powers conferred by sections 1(2), (3), (4) and (7), 2(1), (2), (4) and (5) and 4(2) of the Childcare Act 2016.

In accordance with section 2(3) of the Childcare Act 2016, these Regulations are made with the consent of the Treasury.

(SI 2022/1134)

ARRANGEMENT OF REGULATIONS

PART 1

PRELIMINARY PROVISIONS

1. Citation and commencement
2. Extent and application
3. Consequential amendments and revocations

PART 2

INTERPRETATION

4. Definitions
5. Meaning of "care plan"
6. Meaning of "childcare provider"
7. Meaning of "employee"
8. Meaning of "foster parent"
9. Meaning of "looked after by a local authority"
10. Meaning of "partner"
11. Meaning of "person in the United Kingdom"
12. When periods begin and end

PART 3

DETERMINATIONS AS TO QUALIFYING CHILDREN OF WORKING PARENTS

Description of young child

13. Description of young child

Conditions relating to parent and partner of parent

14. Conditions relating to parent
15. Conditions relating to partner of parent
16. Qualifying paid work requirement: employee
17. Qualifying paid work requirement: self-employed person
18. Minimum income requirement

Declaration

19. How to make a declaration
20. When a declaration may be made
21. Form and manner of declaration

Determination

22. Determination of qualifying child of working parents: Commissioners
23. Power to decline to make a determination
24. Determination of qualifying child of working parents: responsible local authority

Effect of declaration

25. Period for which declaration has effect
26. When parallel declaration ceases to have effect

Eligibility for childcare

27. Period of eligibility for childcare

Disclosure of information

28. Information relating to immigration and social security
29. Information relating to qualifying child of working parents

PART 4

OFFENCES AND PENALTIES

Offences

30. Offence relating to onward disclosure of personal information

Penalties

31. Penalty for dishonest conduct
32. Penalty for false or misleading information
33. Penalty for material inaccuracy in declaration
34. Assessment of penalty
35. Enforcement of penalty

(SI 2022/1134)

PART 5

REVIEWS AND APPEALS

Reviews

36. Right to apply for review
37. Extension of right to apply for review
38. Review procedure

Appeals

39. Right to appeal following review
40. Appeal against decision to decline to make a determination
41. Appeal against determination as to qualifying child of working parents
42. Appeal against imposition of penalty or amount
43. Power to settle appeals by agreement

PART 6

DUTIES OF ENGLISH LOCAL AUTHORITIES

Childcare for qualifying children of working parents

44. Duty to secure childcare available free of charge

Arrangements for provision of childcare

45. Duty to make arrangements with childcare provider chosen by parent
46. Arrangements to provide for termination
47. Requirements permissible in arrangements
48. Requirements prohibited in arrangements

Guidance in discharging of functions

49. Duty of English local authority to have regard to guidance

SCHEDULE—Consequential amendments and revocations

The Childcare Regulations 2022

Part 1

Preliminary provisions

Citation and commencement

11.5   1. These Regulations—
   (a) may be cited as the Childcare (Free of Charge for Working Parents) (England) Regulations 2022, and
   (b) come into force on 1st December 2022.

Extent and application

11.6   2. These Regulations—
   (a) extend to England and Wales, and
   (b) apply in relation to England.

Consequential amendments and revocations

11.7   3. The Schedule makes consequential amendments and revocations.

Part 2

Interpretation

Definitions

11.8   4.—(1) In these Regulations—
"the Act" means the Childcare Act 2016;
"adjusted net income" has the meaning given in section 58 of the Income Tax Act 2007;
"care plan" has the meaning given in regulation 5;
"childcare provider" has the meaning given in regulation 6;
[1"childminder" means an early years childminder within the meaning given in section 96(4) of the Childcare Act 2006 but as if the definition in that subsection was not subject to subsection (5) of that section;]
"the Commissioners" means the Commissioners for His Majesty's Revenue and Customs;
"declaration" means a declaration under section 1(2)(e) of the Act;
"early years childminder agency" has the meaning given in section 98(1) of the Childcare Act 2006;
"employee" has the meaning given in regulation 7;
"the First-tier Tribunal" means the tribunal established under section 3(1) of the Tribunal, Courts and Enforcement Act 2007;
"foster parent" has the meaning given in regulation 8;
"inspection report" means—
   (a) in relation to an early years childminder agency, a report under section 51E of the Childcare Act 2006;

(b) in relation to a childcare provider, a report under any of the following—
  (i) section 5 of the Education Act 2005;
  (ii) section 50 of the Childcare Act 2006;
  (iii) section 109 of the Education and Skills Act 2008;
[¹"limited capability for work" means limited capability for work under—
(a) regulation 39 of the Universal Credit Regulations 2013, or
(b) regulation 40 of the Universal Credit Regulations (Northern Ireland) 2016;]
[¹limited capability for work and work-related activity" means limited capability for work and work-related activity under—
(a) regulation 40 of the Universal Credit Regulations 2013, or
(b) regulation 41 of the Universal Credit Regulations (Northern Ireland) 2016;]
"looked after by a local authority" has the meaning given in regulation 9;
"partner" has the meaning given in regulation 10;
"relevant tax year" means, in relation to a declaration, the tax year in which the declaration is made;
[²"responsible local authority" means—
(a) in relation to a child who meets the description in regulation 9(1)(a), the local authority who looks after the child, or
(b) in relation to a child who meets the description in regulation 9(1)(b), (c) or (d), the English local authority for the area in which the child may be a qualifying child of working parents;]
"review" means a review under regulation 36;
[¹...]
[¹"specified benefit" has the meaning given in regulation 11A;]
"tax year" has the meaning given in section 4(2) of the Income Tax Act 2007.

(2) The following table—
(a) sets out the expressions of the Act used in these Regulations, and
(b) shows where in that Act each of those expressions is defined.

Expression used in these Regulations	Location of definition in the Act
"childcare"	sections 1(9) and 2(8)
"English local authority"	section 2(8)
"parent"	section 1(9)
"qualifying child of working parents"	section 1(2)
"young child"	section 1(9)

AMENDMENTS

1. Childcare and Inspection of Education, Children's Services and Skills (Fees) (Amendments) Regulations 2023 (SI 2023/276) reg.11 (March 30, 2023).
2. Childcare (Free of Charge for Working Parents) (England) (Amendment and Transitional Provision) Regulations 2023 (SI 2023/1330) reg.2(2) (January 1, 2024).

Meaning of "care plan"

5. A "care plan" is any of the following—
(a) a care plan within the meaning given in regulation 2(1) of the Care Planning, Placement and Case Review (England) Regulations 2010;

(b) arrangements recorded in writing under regulation 3(5) of the Arrangements for Placement of Children (General) Regulations (Northern Ireland) 1996;
(c) a child's plan prepared under regulation 5 of the Looked After Children (Scotland) Regulations 2009;
(d) a care and support plan maintained under section 83 of the Social Services and Well-being (Wales) Act 2014.

Meaning of "childcare provider"

11.10   6.—(1) A "childcare provider" is an early years provider—
(a) who is not an excluded provider, and
(b) to whom section 40 of the Childcare Act 2006 (duty to implement Early Years Foundation Stage) applies.
(2) An excluded provider is any of the following—
(a) an independent school, other than an Academy school, that does not meet the standards prescribed under section 157(1)(b) of the Education Act 2002 (which relate to the spiritual, moral, social and cultural development of pupils at independent schools);
(b) an early years provider any English local authority has reasonable grounds to believe—
   (i) does not actively promote the fundamental British values of democracy, the rule of law, individual liberty and mutual respect and tolerance of those with different faiths and beliefs, or
   (ii) promotes as evidence-based views or theories those contrary to established scientific or historical evidence and explanations.
(3) In this regulation—
"Academy school" has the meaning given in section 1A of the Academies Act 2010;
"early years provider" has the meaning given in section 96(3) of the Childcare Act 2006.

Meaning of "employee"

11.11   7.—(1) An "employee" is any of the following—
(a) a person in employment under a contract of service who is not on unpaid leave;
(b) a person who is the holder of an office (including an elected office);
(c) a person in an engagement to which a relevant Chapter applies;
(d) a person who expects, in relation to a declaration, to be a person mentioned in any of paragraphs (a) to (c) within 31 days of the day on which the person makes the declaration.
(2) In this regulation—
"office" has the meaning given in section 5(3) of the Income Tax (Earnings and Pensions) Act 2003;
"relevant Chapter" means any of Chapters 7 to 10 of Part 2 of the Income Tax (Earnings and Pensions) Act 2003 (which relate to agency workers and workers' services provided through intermediaries or managed service companies).

Meaning of "foster parent"

11.12   8.—(1) A "foster parent" is any of the following—

(a) a person who—
  (i) is approved as a local authority foster parent in accordance with regulations made by virtue of paragraph 12F of Schedule 2 to the Children Act 1989, and
  (ii) has a child placed with the person under section 22C(5) of that Act;
(b) a person who—
  (i) is an authority foster parent within the meaning given in article 27(3) of the Children (Northern Ireland) Order 1995, and
  (ii) has a child placed with the person under article 27(2)(a) of that Order;
(c) a person who—
  (i) is a foster carer within the meaning given in regulation 2 of the Looked After Children (Scotland) Regulations 2009, and
  (ii) has a child placed with the person pursuant to a permanence order under section 80 of the Adoption and Children (Scotland) Act 2007;
(d) a person who—
  (i) is a local authority foster parent within the meaning given in section 197(1) of the Social Services and Well-being (Wales) Act 2014, and
  (ii) has a child placed with the person under section 81(5) of that Act.

Meaning of "looked after by a local authority"

9.—(1) A young child is "looked after by a local authority" if the child is any the following— 11.13
(a) a child who is looked after by a local authority within the meaning given in section 22(1) of the Children Act 1989;
(b) a child who is looked after by an authority within the meaning given in article 25(1) of the Children (Northern Ireland) Order 1995;
(c) a child who is looked after by a local authority within the meaning given in section 17(6) of the Children (Scotland) Act 1995;
(d) a child who is looked after by a local authority within the meaning given in section 74(1) of the Social Services and Well-being (Wales) Act 2014.

(2) Despite paragraph (1), a young child is not looked after by a local authority during any period the child is—
(a) being looked after by an English local authority for the purposes of providing a brief respite for the person with whom the child normally lives,
(b) placed with a foster parent (see regulation 8), or
(c) placed with any other person pursuant to arrangements made under—
  (i) section 22C(2) of the Children Act 1989,
  (ii) article 27(2)(a) of the Children (Northern Ireland) Order 1995,
  (iii) regulation 8(1) or 11 of the Looked After Children (Scotland) Regulations 2009, or
  (iv) section 81(2) of the Social Services and Well-being (Wales) Act 2014.

Meaning of "partner"

11.14 **10.**—(1) A person is a "partner" of another person if—
  (a) the person is—
    (i) married to, or the civil partner of, the other person, and
    (ii) a member of the same household as the other person, or
  (b) the person is living together with the other person as if they were a married couple or civil partners.

(2) Despite paragraph (1), a person is not a partner of another person if either person is—
  (a) under 16 years of age,
  (b) serving a sentence of imprisonment, or
  (c) remaining with a third person in a pre-existing relationship of a kind mentioned in paragraph (1).

[¹(3) A person is not a member of the same household as, or living together with, another person if—
  (a) the person is absent, and
  (b) the absence exceeds, or is expected to exceed, 6 months.]

AMENDMENT

1. Childcare and Inspection of Education, Children's Services and Skills (Fees) (Amendments) Regulations 2023 (SI 2023/276) reg.12 (March 30, 2023).

Meaning of "person in the United Kingdom"

11.15 **11.**—(1) A "person in the United Kingdom" is any of the following—
  (a) a person who is—
    (i) ordinarily resident in the United Kingdom, [¹...]
    (ii) not a person taxed as if they were not so resident by virtue of double taxation arrangements [¹, and]"
    [¹(iii) not a person subject to immigration control;]
  (b) a person who is—
    (i) a resident of an EEA State or Switzerland,
    (ii) in paid work in the United Kingdom, and
    (iii) not a person subject to immigration control;
  (c) a person who has been granted—
    (i) refugee permission to stay or temporary refugee permission to stay under rule 339QA of the Immigration Rules, or
    (ii) temporary humanitarian permission to stay under rule 339QB of the Immigration Rules;
  (d) a person who has been granted, or deemed to have been granted, outside the Immigration Rules—
    (i) discretionary leave to remain, or
    (ii) leave to remain under the destitution domestic violence concession;
  (e) a person who—
    (i) has been deported, expelled or otherwise removed by compulsion of law from another country to the United Kingdom, and
    (ii) is not a person subject to immigration control.

(2) In this regulation—

"a person subject to immigration control" has the meaning given in section 115(9) of the Immigration and Asylum Act 1999;

"double taxation arrangements" means arrangements that have effect under section 2(1) of the Taxation (International and Other Provisions) Act 2010;

"the Immigration Rules" means the rules laid before Parliament under section 3(2) of the Immigration Act 1971;

"paid work" means work done for payment or in expectation of payment and does not include being engaged by a charitable or voluntary organisation, or as a volunteer, in circumstances in which the payment received by or due to be paid to the person is in respect of expenses.

AMENDMENT

1. Childcare (Free of Charge for Working Parents) (England) (Amendment and Transitional Provision) Regulations 2023 (SI 2023/1330) reg.2(3) (January 1, 2024).

[¹Meaning of "specified benefit"

11A.—(1) A "specified benefit" is any of the following—
(a) carer's allowance under—
   (i) section 70 of the Social Security Contributions and Benefits Act 1992, or
   (ii) section 70 of the Social Security Contributions and Benefits (Northern Ireland) Act 1992;
(b) carer's assistance given in accordance with regulations made under section 28 of the Social Security (Scotland) Act 2018 except a young carer grant given under the Carer's Assistance (Young Carer Grants) (Scotland) Regulations 2019;
(c) the carer element under—
   (i) regulation 29 of the Universal Credit Regulations 2013, or
   (ii) regulation 30 of the Universal Credit Regulations (Northern Ireland) 2016;
(d) credits for incapacity for work or limited capability for work under—
   (i) regulation 8B of the Social Security (Credits) Regulations 1975, or
   (ii) regulation 8B of the Social Security (Credits) Regulations (Northern Ireland) 1975;
(e) employment and support allowance under—
   (i) section 1 of the Welfare Reform Act 2007, or
   (ii) section 1 of the Welfare Reform Act (Northern Ireland) 2007;
(f) long-term incapacity benefit under—
   (i) regulation 11(4) or 17(1) of the Social Security (Incapacity Benefit) (Transitional) Regulations 1995, or
   (ii) regulation 11(4) or 17(1) of the Social Security (Incapacity Benefit) (Transitional) Regulations (Northern Ireland) 1995;
(g) long-term or short-term incapacity benefit under—
   (i) section 30A, 40 or 41 of the Social Security Contributions and Benefits Act 1992, or
   (ii) section 30A, 40 or 41 of the Social Security Contributions and Benefits (Northern Ireland) Act 1992;
(h) severe disablement allowance under—

11.16

(i) section 68 of the Social Security Contributions and Benefits Act 1992, or
(ii) section 68 of the Social Security Contributions and Benefits (Northern Ireland) Act 1992.]

AMENDMENT

1. Childcare and Inspection of Education, Children's Services and Skills (Fees) (Amendments) Regulations 2023 (SI 2023/276) reg.13 (March 30, 2023).

When periods begin and end

11.17 12. A period of time described in these Regulations in a manner set out in the table is calculated in accordance with the corresponding rule.

If the period is described as—	then the period—
beginning [¹ or ending] with a specified day	includes that specified day.
being within a specified number of days of a specified day	does not include that specified day.
ending before a specified day	does not include that specified day.

AMENDMENT

1. Childcare (Free of Charge for Working Parents) (England) (Amendment and Transitional Provision) Regulations 2023 (SI 2023/1330) reg.2(4) (January 1, 2024).

PART 3

DETERMINATIONS AS TO QUALIFYING CHILDREN OF WORKING PARENTS

Description of young child

Description of young child

11.18 13.—(1) This regulation relates to section 1(2)(c) of the Act.
(2) A young child must be a child who—
(a) has attained the age of three, and
(b) is not looked after by a local authority (see regulation 9).

GENERAL NOTE

11.19 Note that in reg.13(2)(a) (description of young child), for the age of "three", amending regulations have initially substituted "two" (during the period beginning with April 1, 2024 and ending with August 31, 2024), and then "nine months" from September 1, 2024 (see the Childcare (Free of Charge for Working Parents) (England) (Amendment and Transitional Provision) Regulations 2023 (SI 2023/1330) reg.2(5) (January 1, 2024)).

(SI 2022/1134 reg.14)

Conditions relating to parent and partner of parent

Conditions relating to parent

14.—(1) This regulation relates to section 1(2)(d) of the Act.
(2) A parent of a young child must be a parent mentioned in paragraph (3) or (4).
(3) A parent who—
(a) meets the qualifying paid work requirement in regulation 16 or 17,
(b) seeks the childcare, which is available free of charge by virtue of the Act, to enable the parent, or the parent's partner (if any), to work,
(c) does not for the relevant tax year—
  (i) expect their adjusted net income to exceed £100,000,
  (ii) make a claim under section 809B of the Income Tax Act 2007 (which relates to certain residents not domiciled in the United Kingdom), or
  (iii) expect section 809E of Income Tax Act 2007 to apply (which relates to certain residents not domiciled in the United Kingdom), and
(d) if a foster parent of the young child, has confirmation from the responsible local authority that it is satisfied that engaging in paid work other than as a foster parent is consistent with the child's care plan (see regulation 5).
(4) A parent who—
(a) has a partner [¹mentioned in regulation 15(3),], and
(b) is any of the following—
  (i) a person with limited capability for work;
  (ii) a person with limited capability for work and work-related activity;
  (iii) a person entitled to a specified benefit;
  (iv) a resident of an EEA State or Switzerland who is, under the law of the EEA State or Switzerland, entitled to a benefit of a kind that is substantially similar to a specified benefit.
(5) [¹...]

11.20

AMENDMENT

1. Childcare and Inspection of Education, Children's Services and Skills (Fees) (Amendments) Regulations 2023 (SI 2023/276) reg.14 (March 30, 2023).

Conditions relating to partner of parent

15.—(1) This regulation relates to section 1(2)(d) of the Act.
[¹(2) If a parent of a young child has a partner, the partner must be a person mentioned in paragraph (3) or (4).]
[¹(3) A person who—
(a) meets the qualifying paid work requirement in regulation 16 or 17,
(b) does not for the relevant tax year—
  (i) expect their adjusted net income to exceed £100,000,
  (ii) make a claim under section 809B of the Income Tax Act 2007 (claim for remittance basis to apply), or
  (iii) expect section 809E of Income Tax Act 2007 to apply (application of remittance basis without claim: other cases), and

11.21

1397

(c) if a foster parent of the young child, has confirmation from the responsible local authority that it is satisfied that engaging in any paid work other than as a foster parent is consistent with the child's care plan.

(4) A person who is the partner of a parent mentioned in regulation 14(3) and who—
  (a) has limited capability for work;
  (b) has limited capability for work and work-related activity;
  (c) is entitled to a specified benefit; or
  (d) is a resident of an EEA State or Switzerland who is, under the law of the EEA State or Switzerland, entitled to a benefit of a kind that is substantially similar to a specified benefit.]

AMENDMENT

1. Childcare and Inspection of Education, Children's Services and Skills (Fees) (Amendments) Regulations 2023 (SI 2023/276) reg.15 (March 30, 2023).

Qualifying paid work requirement: employee

16.—(1) A person who is an employee is in qualifying paid work if the person—
  (a) holds a national insurance number (unless paragraph (2) applies), and
  (b) meets the minimum income requirement in regulation 18 (unless paragraph (3) applies).

(2) Despite paragraph (1)(a), a person is not required to hold a national insurance number if the person is—
  (a) a resident of an EEA State or Switzerland, and
  (b) not an employee in the United Kingdom.

(3) Despite paragraph (1)(b), a person is not required to meet the minimum income requirement during any of the following—
[¹(a) any period the person is—
    (i) a foster parent, [²...]
    [²(ii) absent from work during a period of parental bereavement leave under an employment rights enactment,
    (ii) in receipt of statutory parental bereavement pay under the Social Security Contributions and Benefits Act, or
    (iii) in receipt of statutory sick pay under the Social Security Contributions and Benefits Act;]]
[²(b) in the case of a person on specified leave relating to a young child in respect of whom a declaration is being made, other than where sub-paragraph (a)(ii), (iii) or (iv) applies, the period of 31 days ending before the day on which the person returns to work;]
  (c) in the case of a person in an EEA State or Switzerland, any period the person is, under the law of the EEA State or Switzerland, on leave of a kind substantially similar to specified leave.

(4) In this regulation—
[²...]
"employment rights enactment" means any of the following—
  (a) the Employment Rights Act 1996;
  (b) the Employment Rights (Northern Ireland) Order 1996;

"national insurance number" means a national insurance number allocated under any of the following—
  (a) the National Insurance Act 1965;
  (b) the National Insurance Act (Northern Ireland) 1966;
  (c) the Social Security Act 1975;
  (d) the Social Security (Northern Ireland) Act 1975;
[¹ "the Social Security Contributions and Benefits Act" means either of the following—
  (a) the Social Security Contributions and Benefits Act 1992;
  (b) the Social Security Contributions and Benefits (Northern Ireland) Act 1992;]
"specified leave" means, in relation to a person, any of the following—
  (a) a period the person is, under an employment rights enactment, absent from work during any of the following—
    [¹ (i) ordinary or additional maternity leave;
    (ii) ordinary or additional adoption leave;
    (iv) shared parental leave;
    (iv) parental leave;
    (v) paternity leave;
    (vi) parental bereavement leave;]
  (b) a period the person is, under [¹the Social Security Contributions and Benefits Act], receiving any of the following—
    (i) state maternity allowance;
    (ii) statutory adoption pay;
    (iii) statutory maternity pay;
    (iv) statutory parental bereavement pay;
    (v) statutory paternity pay;
    (vi) statutory shared parental pay;
    (vii) statutory sick pay.

AMENDMENTS

1. Childcare and Inspection of Education, Children's Services and Skills (Fees) (Amendments) Regulations 2023 (SI 2023/276) reg.16 (March 30, 2023).
2. Childcare (Free of Charge for Working Parents) (England) (Amendment and Transitional Provision) Regulations 2023 (SI 2023/1330) reg.2(6) (January 1, 2024).

Qualifying paid work requirement: self-employed person

17.—(1) A person who is a self-employed person is in qualifying paid work if the person—
  (a) holds a national insurance number (unless paragraph (2) applies), and
  (b) meets the minimum income requirement in regulation 18 (unless paragraph (3) applies).
(2) Despite paragraph (1)(a), a person is not required to hold a national insurance number if the person is—
  (a) a resident of an EEA State or Switzerland, and
  (b) not in self-employment in the United Kingdom.
(3) Despite paragraph (1)(b), a person is not required to meet the minimum income requirement during any of the following—

(a) any period the person would, if the person were an employee, not be required to meet the minimum income requirement (see regulation 16(3));

(b) if the person is in a start-up period, the period of 12 months beginning with the day on which the declaration relating to the person is made.

(4) In this regulation, "start-up period" means the period of 12 months—

(a) beginning with the day on which the person commences self-employment, but

(b) only if the person did not commence self-employment in any trade, profession or vocation in the period of five years ending before that day.

Minimum income requirement

11.24   18.—(1) A person meets the minimum income requirement if the amount of income the person expects to earn from qualifying paid work in the relevant period is an amount of income equal to or greater than the product of—

(a) the minimum weekly income, and

(b) the number of weeks in the relevant period.

(2) The person may include the amount of income the person expects to earn as—

(a) an employee,

(b) a self-employed person, or

(c) an employee and a self-employed person.

(3) In this regulation—

"income" means—

(a) in relation to an employee—

   (i) any earnings within the meaning given in section 62 of the Income Tax (Earnings and Pensions) Act 2003, and

   (ii) any amount treated as earnings under Chapters 7 to 10 of Part 2 of the Income Tax (Earnings and Pensions) Act 2003 (which relate to agency workers and workers' services provided through intermediaries or managed service companies);

(b) in relation to a self-employed person—

   (i) the amount of non-capital receipts the person expects to derive from a trade, profession or vocation less the amount of non-capital expenses the person expects to incur wholly and exclusively for the purposes of the trade, profession or vocation, or

   (ii) if the person carries on a trade, profession or vocation in a business partnership, the share expected to be allocated to the person of the partnership's non-capital receipts less the share expected to be allocated to that person of the partnership's non-capital expenses incurred wholly and exclusively for the purposes of the trade, profession or vocation;

"minimum weekly income" means, in relation to a person, the product of—

(a) 16, and

(b) the hourly rate of the national minimum wage to which the person is entitled to be paid under the National Minimum Wage Act 1998;

"non-capital" means not of a capital nature;
"relevant period" means one of the following—
(a) in the case of income as an employee, the period of three months [¹beginning with—
   (i) the day on which the declaration relating to the employee is made, or
   (ii) if regulation 7(1)(d) applies, the day on which the person expects to be a person mentioned in any of regulation 7(1)(a) to (c);]
(b) in the case of income as a self-employed person, any of the following—
   (i) the period [¹of three months beginning with the day on which the declaration relating to the employee is made];
   (ii) the relevant tax year;
(c) in the case of income as an employee and a self-employed person, the period mentioned in paragraph (a).

AMENDMENT

1. Childcare and Inspection of Education, Children's Services and Skills (Fees) (Amendments) Regulations 2023 (SI 2023/276) reg.17 (March 30, 2023).

Declaration

How to make a declaration

19.—(1) This regulation relates to section 1(2)(e) of the Act.
(2) A person who makes a declaration in respect of a young child must be—
(a) the parent, or the partner of the parent, with whom the child normally lives, and
(b) a person in the United Kingdom.
(3) The declaration must be made—
(a) to the relevant authority,
(b) in either of the periods mentioned in regulation 20, and
(c) in the form and manner specified under regulation 21 (if any).
(4) In this regulation—
"person in the United Kingdom" has the meaning given in regulation 11;
"relevant authority" means—
(a) in the case of a declaration in respect of a child who is placed with a foster parent, the responsible local authority, or
(b) in the case of any other declaration, the Commissioners.

When a declaration may be made

20. A declaration in respect of a young child may be made—
[¹(a) in the period of 16 weeks ending before the day on which the child will meet the description in regulation 13 (if known), except during the time—
   (i) beginning on 1st January 2024 and ending before the day on which the child will meet the description in regulation 13 (if known), where that day occurs on or before 31st March 2024, and

(ii) beginning on 1st June 2024 and ending before the day on which the child will meet the description in regulation 13 (if known), where that day occurs on or before 31st August 2024,

where the period referred to in this sub-paragraph is 13 weeks; or]

(b) in the period—
   (i) beginning with the day on which the child meets the description in regulation 13, and
   (ii) ending before the day on which the child ceases to satisfy the requirements of section 1(2)(a) or (b) of the Act.

AMENDMENT

1. Childcare (Free of Charge for Working Parents) (England) (Amendment and Transitional Provision) Regulations 2023 (SI 2023/1330) reg.2(7) (January 1, 2024).

Form and manner of declaration

11.27 21.—(1) The Commissioners or the responsible local authority (as the case may be) may specify the form of a declaration and the manner in which it is to be made.

(2) The specification may (amongst other things)—
(a) require a declaration to include information to—
   (i) identify the person making the declaration (and any partner of that person),
   (ii) identify the young child in respect of whom the declaration is being made, and
   (iii) determine whether the young child is a qualifying child of working parents;
(b) require a declaration to be made by electronic communications;
(c) if a declaration relates to a self-employed person, require a declaration to be accompanied by confirmation, orally or in writing, that the self-employed person has complied with any notice given under section 8(1) of the Taxes Management Act 1970 (which relates to personal returns).

Determination

Determination of qualifying child of working parents: Commissioners

11.28 22.—(1) This regulation applies if—
(a) a person makes a declaration to the Commissioners in respect of a young child, and
(b) the Commissioners have not declined to make a determination in respect of the declaration (see regulation 23).

(2) The Commissioners must—
(a) make a determination as to whether the child is a qualifying child of working parents,
(b) notify the person of the determination, and
(c) include in that notification a statement to the effect that the person has—
   (i) a right to apply to the Commissioners for a review of the determination (see regulation 36), and

(ii) a right to appeal to the First-tier Tribunal against the determination, but only after the Commissioners have considered an application for a review (see regulation 40).

Power to decline to make a determination

23.—(1) This regulation applies if—
(a) two or more persons each make a declaration to the Commissioners in respect of the same young child, and
(b) it appears to the Commissioners that two or more of those persons may meet the requirements in regulation 19(2) (which provides for who can make a declaration).

(2) The Commissioners may, in respect of one or more of the declarations, decline to make a determination as to whether the child is a qualifying child of working parents.

(3) If the Commissioners decline to make a determination, they must—
(a) notify the person who made the declaration, and
(b) include in the notification a statement to the effect that the person has—
   (i) a right to apply to the Commissioners for a review of the decision (see regulation 36), and
   (ii) a right to appeal to the First-tier Tribunal against the decision, but only after the Commissioners have considered an application for a review (see regulation 40).

Determination of qualifying child of working parents: responsible local authority

24.—(1) This regulation applies if a person makes a declaration to the responsible local authority in respect of a young child placed with a foster parent.

(2) The responsible local authority (on behalf of the Commissioners) must—
(a) make a determination as to whether the child is a qualifying child of working parents, and
(b) notify the person of the determination.

Effect of declaration

Period for which declaration has effect

25.—(1) A declaration in respect of a young child has effect for three months beginning with—
(a) the day on which the young child is determined to be a qualifying child of working parents, or
(b) if the declaration was made in accordance with regulation 20(a) (which provides for anticipatory declarations), the day on which the young child meets the description in regulation 13.

(2) Despite paragraph (1), the Commissioners may, if they consider it appropriate, vary the period for which a declaration has effect—
(a) by no more than two months to align the period with—
   (i) any entitlement period relating to the child in respect of whom the declaration was made,

(ii) the period for which any declaration relating to another child has effect, or

(iii) any entitlement period relating to another child, or

(b) by no more than one month for any other reason.

(3) This regulation is subject to regulation 26 (when parallel declaration ceases to have effect).

(4) In this regulation—

"another child" means—

(a) another child of the parent of the young child in respect of whom the declaration was made, or

(b) a child of the partner of that parent;

"entitlement period" means a period determined in accordance with section 5 of the Childcare Payments Act 2014 (which relates to the receipt of money towards childcare costs).

When a parallel declaration ceases to have effect

11.32   **26.**—(1) This regulation applies if—
(a) a person has made a declaration in respect of a young child ("Declaration A"),
(b) Declaration A has effect (see regulation 25),
(c) another person makes a declaration in respect of the same child ("Declaration B"), and
(d) the child is, in relation to Declaration B, determined to be a qualifying child of working parents.

(2) Declaration A ceases to have effect beginning with the day on which Declaration B has effect.

Eligibility for childcare

Period of eligibility for childcare

11.33   **27.**—(1) A child is eligible for childcare under section 1 of the Act for the period—
(a) beginning with whichever of 1st January, 1st April or 1st September is the first date on or after the day on which a declaration in respect of the child has effect, and
(b) ending before the day on which the child ceases to be a qualifying child of working parents.

(2) A year begins with the date calculated in accordance with paragraph (1) for the purposes of determining in relation to the child whether the duty in section 1(1) of the Act has been discharged.

Disclosure of information

Information relating to immigration and social security

11.34   **28.**—(1) The Secretary of State may disclose to the Commissioners any information held by the Secretary of State for the purposes of their functions relating to any of the following—
(a) immigration control;
(b) social security.

(2) The Commissioners may use the information only in connection with the making of a determination as to whether a child is a qualifying child of working parents.

Information relating to qualifying child of working parents

29. The Secretary of State, the Commissioners and an English local authority may disclose information to each other for the purpose of checking any of the following—
   (a) whether a declaration in respect of a child has been made;
   (b) if a declaration in respect of a child has been made, whether the child was determined to be a qualifying child of working parents (see regulations 22 and 24);
   (c) if a child was determined to be a qualifying child of working parents, whether the declaration in respect of the child has effect (see regulations 25 and 26).

PART 4

OFFENCES AND PENALTIES

Offences

Offence relating to onward disclosure of personal information

30.—(1) A person commits an offence if—
   (a) the person discloses information in contravention of regulation 28 or 29,
   (b) the disclosure relates to any person whose identity—
       (i) is specified in the disclosure, or
       (ii) can be deduced from it, and
   (c) the disclosure is made other than in accordance with—
       (i) an enactment,
       (ii) an order of a court, or
       (iii) the written consent of the person to whom the information relates.
(2) It is a defence for a person charged with an offence under this regulation to prove that the person reasonably believed—
   (a) that the disclosure was lawful, or
   (b) that the information had already and lawfully been made available to the public.
(3) A person guilty of an offence under this regulation is liable—
   (a) on conviction on indictment, to imprisonment for a term not exceeding two years, to a fine or to both, or
   (b) on summary conviction—
       (i) in England and Wales, to imprisonment for a term not exceeding 12 months, to a fine or to both;

(ii) in Northern Ireland, to imprisonment for a term not exceeding 6 months, to a fine not exceeding the statutory maximum or to both;
(iii) in Scotland, to imprisonment for a term not exceeding 12 months, to a fine not exceeding the statutory maximum or to both.

Penalties

Penalty for dishonest conduct

11.37   **31.**—(1) A person is liable to a penalty under this regulation if the person engages in dishonest conduct in connection with the process of making a determination of a child's eligibility for childcare under section 1 of the Act.
(2) The amount of the penalty must not exceed £3,000.

Penalty for false or misleading information

11.38   **32.**—(1) A person is liable to a penalty under this regulation if the person, by reason of a failure to take reasonable care, provides false or misleading information, or makes or provides a false or misleading statement, in connection with a determination of a child's eligibility for childcare under section 1 of the Act.
(2) Despite paragraph (1), the person is not liable to the penalty if the person—
 (a) becomes aware of the false or misleading information or statement, and
 (b) takes reasonable steps to inform the Commissioners or the responsible local authority (as the case may be).
(3) The amount of the penalty must not exceed £500.

Penalty for material inaccuracy in declaration

11.39   **33.**—(1) A person is liable to a penalty under this regulation if, by reason of a failure to take reasonable care, the person includes a material inaccuracy in a declaration.
(2) The amount of the penalty must not exceed £300.

Assessment of penalty

11.40   **34.**—(1) If a person becomes liable to a penalty under any of regulations 31, 32 or 33—
 (a) the Commissioners may, subject to paragraph (3), assess the penalty, and
 (b) if they do so, they must notify the person.
(2) The notification must include a statement to the effect that the person has—
 (a) a right to apply to the Commissioners for a review of the penalty or its amount (see regulation 36), and
 (b) a right to appeal to the First-tier Tribunal against the determination, but only after the Commissioners have considered an application for a review (see regulation 40).

(3) The Commissioners must not assess a penalty in relation to a person after the end of whichever of the following ends first—
  (a) the period of one year beginning with the day on which the Commissioners first believed, or had reasonable grounds for believing, the person was liable to the penalty;
  (b) in the case of a penalty under regulation 31, the period of 20 years beginning with the day on which the person became liable to the penalty;
  (c) in the case of a penalty under regulation 32, the period of four years beginning with the day on which the person became liable to the penalty.

Enforcement of penalty

35.—(1) This regulation applies if the Commissioners notify a person of a penalty (see regulation 34).
  (2) The person must pay the penalty—
  (a) if the person does not apply for a review (see regulation 36)—
    (i) within 30 days of the day on which the notification is made, or
    (ii) if the person is granted an extension to their right to apply for a review, on or before the date notified under regulation 37(5)(a)(ii);
  (b) if the person applies for a review, unless the penalty is set aside, within 30 days of the day on which the person is notified of the outcome of the review (see regulation 38(5));
  (c) if the person gives notice of appeal (see regulation 39), unless the penalty is set aside, on or before the day after the day on which—
    (i) the First-tier Tribunal gives a decision (see regulation 42), or
    (ii) if the person gives notice of the withdrawal of their case, the First-tier Tribunal consents to that withdrawal.
  (3) A penalty may be enforced as if it were income tax charged in an assessment and due and payable.

PART 5

REVIEWS AND APPEALS

Reviews

Right to apply for review

36.—(1) This regulation applies if the Commissioners notify a person of any of the following—
  (a) a decision to decline to make a determination as to whether a child is a qualifying child of working parents (see regulation 23);
  (b) a determination as to whether a child is a qualifying child of working parents (see regulation 22);
  (c) the assessment of a penalty (see regulation 34).

(2) The person may apply to the Commissioners for a review of (as the case may be)—
  (a) the decision,
  (b) the determination, or
  (c) the penalty or its amount.
(3) The application must—
  (a) be made—
    (i) within 30 days of the day on which the notification is made, or
    (ii) if the person is granted an extension of their right to apply for a review, on or before the date notified under regulation 37(5)(a)(ii),
  (b) be in the form and manner specified under paragraph (4) (if any), and
  (c) include the person's reasons for the application.
(4) The Commissioners may specify—
  (a) the form of an application, and
  (b) the manner in which it is to be made (which may require electronic communications).

Extension of right to apply for review

37.—(1) This regulation applies if the Commissioners notify a person of a matter mentioned in regulation 36(1).
(2) The person may apply to the Commissioners for an extension of their right to apply for a review.
(3) The application must—
  (a) be made within seven months of the day on which the notification is made,
  (b) be in the form and manner specified under paragraph (6) (if any), and
  (c) include the applicant's reasons why it is, or was, not practicable for the person to apply for the review within 30 days of the day on which the notification is made.
(4) The Commissioners may—
  (a) grant the application if they are satisfied—
    (i) it is (or was) not practicable due to special circumstances for the person to apply for the review within 30 days of the day on which the notification is made, and
    (ii) the granting of the application is reasonable in all the circumstances of the case, or
  (b) decline the application.
(5) If the Commissioners—
  (a) grant the application, they must—
    (i) specify a date on or before which the applicant must apply for the review, and
    (ii) notify the applicant of that date;
  (b) decline the application—
    (i) they must notify the applicant, and
    (ii) the applicant must not make any further application in respect of the matter.
(6) The Commissioners may specify—
  (a) the form of the application, and
  (b) the manner in which the application is made.

(SI 2022/1134 reg. 38)

Review procedure

38.—(1) This regulation applies if a person ("the applicant") makes an application for a review.

(2) The Commissioners must—
(a) review (as the case may be)—
    (i) the decision to decline to make a determination as to whether a child is a qualifying child of working parents,
    (ii) the determination as to whether a child is a qualifying child of working parents, or
    (iii) the imposition of the penalty or its amount, and
(b) complete the review—
    (i) if no request under paragraph (3) is made, within 30 days of the day on which the application is made,
    (ii) if a request under paragraph (3) is made, within 44 days of the day on which the application is made, or
    (iii) within any other period agreed between the Commissioners and the applicant.

(3) The Commissioners may ask the applicant to provide further information or evidence in support of their application.

(4) If the Commissioners ask for further information or evidence, the Commissioners—
(a) must consider any information or evidence the applicant provides to the Commissioners within 14 days of the day on which the request is made, and
(b) may disregard any information or evidence provided after that period.

(5) Following the review, the Commissioners must—
(a) confirm, revise or set aside (as the case may be)—
    (i) the decision,
    (ii) the determination, or
    (iii) the penalty or its amount, and
(b) notify the applicant of the result of the review.

(6) If the Commissioners revise a determination to determine that a child is a qualifying child of working parents, the date of the determination is the date on which the determination is revised.

11.44

Appeals

Right to appeal following review

39.—(1) This regulation applies if a person makes an application to the Commissioners for a review of—
(a) a decision to decline to make a determination as to whether a child is a qualifying child of working parents,
(b) a determination as to whether a child is a qualifying child of working parents, or
(c) a penalty or its amount.

(2) Following the review, the person may appeal to the First-tier Tribunal against (as the case may be)—
(a) the decision (see regulation 40),
(b) the determination (see regulation 41), or
(c) the penalty or its amount (see regulation 42).

11.45

Appeal against decision to decline to make a determination

40.—(1) This regulation applies if a person appeals to the First-tier Tribunal against a decision to decline to make a determination as to whether a child is a qualifying child of working parents.
(2) The Tribunal may—
(a) confirm the decision, or
(b) set aside the decision.
(3) If the Tribunal sets aside the decision, the Commissioners must comply with regulation 22(2) in respect of the declaration (which requires a determination as to whether a child is a qualifying child of working parents).

Appeal against determination as to qualifying child of working parents

41.—(1) This regulation applies if a person appeals to the First-tier Tribunal against a determination as to whether a child is a qualifying child of working parents.
(2) The Tribunal may—
(a) confirm the determination, or
(b) withdraw any part of the determination the Tribunal finds was—
  (i) based on an error in fact, or
  (ii) wrong in law.
(3) If the Tribunal withdraws a part of the determination—
(a) it must for that part substitute its own determination, and
(b) the substituted determination is to be treated as if it were a determination made by the Commissioners or the responsible local authority (as the case may be) on the date of the notice that states the Tribunal's decision.

Appeal against imposition of penalty or amount

42.—(1) This regulation applies if a person appeals to the First-tier Tribunal against the imposition of a penalty or its amount.
(2) The Tribunal may—
(a) uphold the imposition of the penalty,
(b) set aside the penalty, or
(c) substitute the amount of the penalty with an amount the Tribunal determines.

Power to settle appeals by agreement

43.—(1) This regulation applies if—
(a) a person has a right of appeal to the First-tier Tribunal (see regulation 39),
(b) the person starts proceedings in the Tribunal (by sending or delivering a notice of appeal to it), and
(c) the Tribunal has not finally disposed of all issues in the proceedings.
(2) The Commissioners may agree with the appellant, in writing or otherwise, that the Commissioners' decision, determination or penalty or its amount (as the case may be) is to be treated as—
(a) upheld without variation,
(b) as varied in a particular manner, or
(c) as discharged or cancelled.

(SI 2022/1134 reg.43)

(3) If the agreement is not in writing, the Commissioners must notify the appellant in writing of—
(a) the fact that an agreement was made,
(b) the terms agreed,
(c) the date of the agreement, and
(d) the appellant's right under paragraph (4) to repudiate or resile from the agreement.

(4) The appellant may, within 30 days of the day on which the agreement is made, give notice to the Commissioners that the appellant desires to repudiate or resile from the agreement.

(5) If the notice mentioned in paragraph (4) is not given—
(a) the Commissioners must send notice of the agreement to the First-tier Tribunal, and
(b) the Tribunal must treat the notice as if it were a request for a consent order.

(6) In this regulation—

"appellant" means the person mentioned in paragraph (1);

"consent order" means a consent order made by the First-tier Tribunal under rule 32 of the Tribunal Procedure (First-tier Tribunal) (Social Entitlement Chamber) Rules 2008;

PART 6

DUTIES OF ENGLISH LOCAL AUTHORITIES

Childcare for qualifying children of working parents

Duty to secure childcare available free of charge

44.—(1) An English local authority must secure that childcare is made available free of charge for every child in its area who is a qualifying child of working parents.

(2) The childcare must be—
(a) provided by a childcare provider, and
(b) made available for [²*1140*] hours during no fewer than 38 weeks in each year.

[¹(3) In determining, for the purposes of paragraph (1), the amount of childcare that is available to a child, account is to be taken of any childcare available under the duty imposed by section 7(1) of the Childcare Act 2006 (duty of English local authorities to secure early years provision free of charge in accordance with regulations)—
(a) during the period beginning with 1st April 2024 and ending with 31st August 2025, in respect of a young child who meets the condition in regulation 3(2), but who does not also meet the condition in regulation 3(3), of the Local Authority (Duty to Secure Early Years Provision Free of Charge) Regulations 2014 (prescribed description of a young child), and
(b) from 1st September 2025, in respect of a young child who meets the condition in regulation 3(2) or (3) of the Local Authority (Duty to Secure Early Years Provision Free of Charge) Regulations 2014.]

11.50

AMENDMENTS

1. Childcare (Free of Charge for Working Parents) (England) (Amendment and Transitional Provision) Regulations 2023 (SI 2023/1330) reg.2(8)(b) (January 1, 2024).

2. *Childcare (Free of Charge for Working Parents) (England) (Amendment and Transitional Provision) Regulations 2023 (SI 2023/1330) reg.2(8)(a) (January 1, 2025 for purposes connected only with regulations made under the School Standards and Framework Act 1998 s.47ZA and on September 1, 2025 for all other purposes).*

Arrangements for provision of childcare

Duty to make arrangements with childcare provider chosen by parent

45.—(1) The parent of a child in the area of an English local authority may choose a childcare provider to provide the childcare the local authority must secure for the child (see regulation 44).

(2) The local authority must make arrangements for the childcare if the provider is willing—
  (a) to provide the childcare to the child, and
  (b) to accept as part of the arrangements—
    (i) the local authority's terms as to payment for the childcare,
    (ii) the mandatory termination provision (see regulation 46), and
    (iii) any requirements the local authority seeks to impose (see regulation 47).

(3) Paragraph (2) does not apply if the provider is any of the following—
  (a) a childcare provider the local authority has grounds to believe would not be able to satisfy a requirement the authority would impose if arrangements were made;
  (b) a childminder registered with an early years childminder agency that—
    (i) fails in its most recent inspection report (if any) to achieve a grade of "effective" or better, or
    (ii) notifies the local authority that, in the agency's reasonable opinion, the childminder has ceased to provide childcare of satisfactory quality;
  (c) a childcare provider (other than a childminder registered with [¹an early years childminder agency]) that fails in its most recent inspection report (if any) to achieve Grade 3 ("requires improvement") or better for the overall effectiveness of its childcare.

(4) Paragraph (2)(b) does not apply if the provider is the governing body of a maintained school.

AMENDMENT

1. Childcare and Inspection of Education, Children's Services and Skills (Fees) (Amendments) Regulations 2023 (SI 2023/276) reg.18 (March 30, 2023).

Arrangements to provide for termination

46. An English local authority must, as part of arrangements with a childcare provider under regulation 45(2), include provision authorising the local authority to terminate the arrangements if the provider—
  (a) ceases to be a childcare provider (see regulation 6), or

(b) becomes a childcare provider mentioned in regulation 45(3)(b) or (c) (which relates to minimum standard of childcare).

Requirements permissible in arrangements

47.—(1) As part of any arrangements with a childcare provider under regulation 45(2), an English local authority may impose on the provider one or more of only the following requirements—
  (a) a requirement to enable the local authority to—
      (i) comply with its duty to make arrangements with a childcare provider chosen by the parent of a child (see regulation 45), and
      (ii) terminate the arrangements (see regulation 46);
  (b) a requirement for the purpose of satisfying one or more of the following objectives—
      (i) that the childcare is provided free of charge;
      (ii) that the childcare is provided in a pattern to suit the needs of the parents of the children for whom the childcare is provided;
      (iii) that any financial assistance provided by a local authority under the arrangements is used properly and in accordance with the arrangements;
  (c) a requirement for the purpose of meeting the needs of a child—
      (i) to whom the local authority owes a duty under regulation 45, and
      (ii) who has a disability or special educational needs;
  (d) a requirement that the provider actively promotes the fundamental British values of —
      (i) democracy,
      (ii) individual liberty,
      (iii) mutual respect and tolerance of those with different faiths and beliefs, and
      (iv) the rule of law;
  (e) a requirement that views or theories contrary to established scientific or historical evidence and explanations are not promoted as evidence-based views or theories;
  (f) a requirement that, if the childcare provider (being other than a childminder registered with [[1]an early years childminder agency]) achieves in its most recent inspection report (if any) the minimum grade mentioned in regulation 45(3)(c) or worse, the provider takes the measures specified in the report—
      (i) to improve the overall effectiveness of its childcare, and
      (ii) which may include the participation in any training or other quality improvement programme specified in the report;
  (g) a requirement necessary for the effective administration of the arrangements.

(2) In this regulation—

"disability" has the meaning given in section 6 of the Equality Act 2010;

"special educational needs" has the meaning given in section 20 of the Children and Families Act 2014.

AMENDMENT

1. Childcare and Inspection of Education, Children's Services and Skills (Fees) (Amendments) Regulations 2023 (SI 2023/276) reg.19 (March 30, 2023).

Requirements prohibited in arrangements

11.54　　48. An English local authority must not, as part of arrangements with a childcare provider under regulation 45(2), impose on the provider any of the following—
(a) a requirement that the provider attend a training or other quality improvement programme other than that specified in an inspection report;
(b) a requirement subjecting the provider to a quality assessment process conducted by the local authority relating to—
  (i) in the case of a childminder registered with an early years childminder agency, the quality of the agency's services, or
  (ii) in the case of any other childcare provider, the quality of the provider's childcare.

Guidance in discharging of functions

Duty of English local authority to have regard to guidance

11.55　　49. An English local authority must, when discharging its duties under these Regulations, have regard to any guidance given from time to time by the Secretary of State.

SCHEDULE　　　　　　　　　　　　　　　　　　Regulation 3

CONSEQUENTIAL AMENDMENTS AND REVOCATIONS

Consequential Amendments

Amendment of the Childcare Act 2006 (Provision of Information to Parents) (England) Regulations 2007

11.56　　1.—(1) The Childcare Act 2006 (Provision of Information to Parents) (England) Regulations 2007 are amended in accordance with paragraph (2).
(2) In regulation 1(2)—
(a) in the definition of "the extended entitlement", for "regulation 33 of the Childcare (Early Years Provision Free of Charge) (Extended Entitlement) Regulations 2016" substitute "regulation 44 of the Childcare (Free of Charge for Working Parents) (England) Regulations 2022";
(b) in the definition of "free early years provision", in paragraph (b), for "regulation 33 of the Childcare (Early Years Provision Free of Charge) (Extended Entitlement) Regulations 2016" substitute "regulation 44 of the Childcare (Free of Charge for Working Parents) (England) Regulations 2022".

Amendment of the First-tier Tribunal and Upper Tribunal (Chambers) Order 2010

11.57　　2.—(1) The First-tier Tribunal and Upper Tribunal (Chambers) Order 2010 is amended in accordance with sub-paragraph (2).

(2) In Article 6(eb), for "the Childcare (Early Years Provision Free of Charge) (Extended Entitlement) Regulations 2016" substitute "the Childcare (Free of Charge for Working Parents) (England) Regulations 2022".

Amendment of the Childcare Payments Regulations 2015

3.—(1) The Childcare Payments Regulations 2015 are amended on accordance with sub-paragraph (2).

(2) In regulation 5(1)(d), for "regulation 15 of the Childcare (Early Years Provision Free of Charge) (Extended Entitlement) Regulations 2016" substitute "regulation 25 of the Childcare (Free of Charge for Working Parents) (England) Regulations 2022".

Amendment of the Childcare (Early Years Provision Free of Charge) (Extended Entitlement) Regulations 2016

4.—(1) The Childcare (Early Years Provision Free of Charge) (Extended Entitlement) Regulations 2016 are amended in accordance with sub-paragraphs (2) to (5).

(2) In the title to the instrument, for "Childcare (Early Years Provision Free of Charge) (Extended Entitlement)" substitute "Childcare Act 2016 (Consequential Amendments)".

(3) In regulation 1(1), for "Childcare (Early Years Provision Free of Charge) (Extended Entitlement)" substitute "Childcare Act 2016 (Consequential Amendments)".

(4) In regulation 1(2), for "1, 2, 3" substitute "1";

(5) Omit—
(a) regulation 1(3) (which relates to the commencement of Part 4);
(b) regulation 2 (interpretation);
(c) Part 2 (a qualifying child of working parents);
(d) Part 3 (information, reviews, appeals and penalties);
(e) Part 4 (local authorities' duty to secure early years provision).

Amendment of the Childcare (Disqualification) and Childcare (Early Years Provision Free of Charge) (Extended Entitlement) (Amendment) Regulations 2018

5.—(1) The Childcare (Disqualification) and Childcare (Early Years Provision Free of Charge) (Extended Entitlement) (Amendment) Regulations 2018 are amended in accordance with sub-paragraph (2).

(2) Omit Part 3 (amendment of the Childcare (Early Years Provision Free of Charge) (Extended Entitlement) Regulations 2016).

Amendment of the Parental Bereavement Leave and Pay (Consequential Amendments to Subordinate Legislation) Regulations 2020

6.—(1) The Parental Bereavement Leave and Pay (Consequential Amendments to Subordinate Legislation) Regulations 2020 are amended in accordance with sub-paragraph (2).

(2) Omit regulation 40 (Childcare (Early Years Provision Free of Charge) (Extended Entitlement) Regulations 2016).

Amendment of the Tax Credits, Childcare Payments and Childcare (Extended Entitlement) (Coronavirus and Miscellaneous Amendments) Regulations 2020

11.62 7.—(1) The Tax Credits, Childcare Payments and Childcare (Extended Entitlement) (Coronavirus and Miscellaneous Amendments) Regulations 2020 are amended in accordance with sub-paragraph (2).

(2) Omit regulation 5 (Amendment of the Childcare (Early Years Provision Free of Charge) (Extended Entitlement) Regulations 2016).

Amendment of the Criminal Justice Act 2003 (Commencement No.33) and Sentencing Act 2020 (Commencement No.2) Regulations 2022

11.63 8.—(1) The Criminal Justice Act 2003 (Commencement No.33) and Sentencing Act 2020 (Commencement No.2) Regulations 2022 are amended in accordance with sub-paragraph (2).

(2) In the Schedule, in Part 2, in the table, in Column 1, omit the words "Regulation 19(5) of the Childcare (Early Years Provision Free of Charge) (Extended Entitlement) Regulations 2016 (S.I. 2016/1257)".

Revocations

Revocations

11.64 9. The enactments cited in the table are revoked.

Enactment	Citation
The Childcare (Early Years Provision Free of Charge) (Extended Entitlement) (Amendment) Regulations 2017	S.I. 2017/1160
The Childcare (Early Years Provision Free of Charge) (Extended Entitlement) (Coronavirus) (Amendment) Regulations 2020	S.I. 2020/712
The Childcare (Early Years Provision Free of Charge) (Extended Entitlement) (Amendment) Regulations 2021	S.I. 2021/674
The Childcare (Early Years Provision Free of Charge) (Extended Entitlement) (Amendment) (No.2) Regulations 2021	S.I. 2021/1168

PART XII

HMRC CHARTER, CODES OF PRACTICE AND GUIDANCE

NOTE

HMRC policy is to publish manuals, guides and forms dealing with all parts of the law under its management. As part of this policy, HMRC publishes a series of leaflets and factsheets about tax credits together with most of the relevant forms. These are now accessible through the GOV.UK lists of HMRC leaflets and forms. Hard copies are available through the helpline 0345 3003900. HMRC are also required by s.16A of the Commissioners for Revenue and Customs Act 2005 to publish a Charter, which must include "standards of behaviour and values to which Her Majesty's Revenue and Customs will aspire when dealing with people in the exercise of their functions".

All the guides are official publications. But none in this field carry the force of law. Nonetheless some of them are particularly important as they set out the terms on which HMRC exercises discretions (for example as to overpayments and penalties). They also detail the administrative procedures and standards that HMRC sets itself. The key guides to the way in which HMRC deals with overpayments and penalties are set out in this volume. They are marked in bold in the following list of leaflets:

How HMRC handle Tax Credit Overpayments	A leaflet available for advisers to download and print
Tax Credit Annual Review Help Sheets	(helpsheet for people who help and advise others on the tax credits renewals process—for download and print.)
WTC1	Child Tax Credit and Working Tax Credit An introduction
WTC2	A guide to Child Tax Credit and Working Tax Credit
WTC5	Working Tax Credit—Help with the costs of childcare
WTC5/CP	Working Tax Credit—The childcare element—Information for childcare providers
WTC7	Tax Credits penalties
WTC8	Child Tax Credit and Working Tax Credit—How do overpayments happen?
WTC/AP	Child Tax Credit and Working Tax Credit: how to appeal against a tax credit decision or award
WTC/FS1	Tax credits enquiry
WTC/FS2	Tax credits examinations
WTC/FS3	Tax credits formal request for information
WTC/FS4	Tax credits meetings
WTC/FS5	Tax credits—coming to the United Kingdom

Note

WTC/FS6	Tax credits—leaving the United Kingdom
WTC/FS9	Tax credits—suspension of payments
WTC/FS10	Tax credits checks
COP26	What happens if we have paid you too much tax credit?

The key standard forms are available to download from the site above. They are:

TC600	Tax Credits claim form
TC602	Checking a tax credits award
TC603R	Tax Credits renewal pack
TC603RD	Tax Credits renewal and annual declaration
TC689	Authority for intermediary to act
TC825	Working sheet for gift aid payments, pension contributions and trading losses
TC846	Form to dispute a tax credit overpayment
TC956	Disability working sheet

The standard manuals issued to staff are:

CCM	New Tax Credits Claimant Compliance Manual
NTC Manual	Clerical procedures
TCTM	Tax Credits Technical Manual

All are available on the site above (although some paragraphs are withheld under the Freedom of Information Act exemptions).

THE HMRC CHARTER ("YOUR CHARTER")

1. About the HMRC Charter

The HMRC Charter is a legal requirement under the Finance Act 2009. The legislation states that the Charter 'must include standards of behaviour and values to which Her Majesty's Revenue and Customs will aspire when dealing with people in the exercise of their functions'.

HMRC is committed to improving its customer experience and the HMRC Charter defines the service and standard of behaviour that customers should expect when interacting with us. The Charter is supported by further principles of support for customers who need extra help [see *https://www.gov.uk/government/publications/hmrc-charter/hmrcs-principles-of-support-for-customers-who-need-extra-help*].

12.1

2. The HMRC Charter

Working with you to get tax right

HMRC is here to collect the tax that pays for the UK's public services.

We'll help you meet your tax responsibilities and make sure you get any benefits, tax credits, refunds or other support you can claim. However, we will take firm action against the small minority who bend or break the law.

12.2

Our standards

Getting things right

We'll give you accurate, consistent and clear information. This will help you meet your obligations, and understand your rights and what you can claim. When we ask for information, we rely on you to give us full, accurate and timely answers. If you disagree with us, we'll tell you about options available to you and work with you to reach an appropriate outcome quickly and simply.

12.3

Making things easy

We'll provide services that are designed around what you need to do, and are accessible, easy and quick to use, minimising the cost to you.

12.4

Being responsive

When you get in touch with us, we'll make sure that the people you deal with have the right level of expertise. We'll answer your questions and resolve things first time, or as quickly as we can. Well also explain what happens next and when you can expect a response from us. If we make a mistake, we'll put it right as soon as possible. If you're not satisfied with the service you've received, we'll explain how you can make a complaint.

12.5

Treating you fairly

We'll work within the law to make sure everyone pays the right amount of tax and gets their benefits and other entitlements. We'll assume you're telling the truth, unless we've good reason to think you're not.

12.6

Being aware of your personal situation

12.7 We'll listen to your worries and answer any questions clearly and concisely. We'll be mindful of your wider personal situation, and will give you extra support if you need it.

Recognising that someone can represent you

12.8 We'll respect your wish to have someone else deal with us on your behalf, such as an accountant, friend or a relative. We'll only deal with them if you have authorised them to represent you. To protect you, HMRC works with professional bodies to set the standard expected of professional agents who support you to meet your tax obligations. We can refuse to work with professional agents who fail to adhere to this standard.

Keeping your data secure

12.9 We'll protect information we hold about you and treat it as private and confidential. We'll always use that information fairly and lawfully.

Mutual respect

12.10 We take any threats, intimidation or harassment very seriously and will take appropriate action against any behaviour of this type. We'll always treat you in line with our values of respect, professionalism and integrity. Our employees are people too and we expect you to treat them in the same way.

3. Feedback

12.11 HMRC undertakes to identify and keep under review how the Charter standards apply in all aspects of its work.

HMRC welcomes any feedback about your interactions with them and how they have performed against the Charter. You can email HMRC. Charter@hmrc.gov.uk. A summary of feedback received will be included in the regular reviews of performance conducted by HMRC's Customer Experience Committee.

4. If you are not happy with a decision or the service you have received

12.12 If you do not feel the service you've received has met the standards of the Charter you can make a complaint. HMRC will deal with it quickly and fairly. Please make sure you mention the Charter in your complaint and explain which aspects of the Charter you feel HMRC has not met.

If you disagree with a tax decision you can:

- ask for a statutory review of the decision
- appeal to the independent tax tribunal
- do both

A statutory review is undertaken by an impartial review officer in HMRC who was not involved in the original decision and acts as a fresh pair of eyes. A statutory review is quicker and more cost-effective than appealing directly to the tribunal. If you are still not satisfied following the review you can then

LEAFLET WTC7

appeal to the tribunal. Approximately three-quarters of disagreements are settled at review and do not need to go to tribunal.

Find out what to do if you disagree with a tax decision. If you received a decision letter from HMRC, that will also have instructions about what to do.

5. How we monitor and report on performance against the Charter

Performance against the Charter is monitored by specific service standards, customer surveys and other data, linked to wider HMRC performance measures. We have published the latest set of indicators and data.

HMRC's Customer Experience Committee oversees performance against the Charter - find out more about the Customer Experience Committee.

The committee provides a report each year, assessing HMRC's performance against the Charter, and includes progress and priorities for further improvement.

From December 2020 the committee will also conduct reviews of performance at its quarterly meeting. These quarterly reviews are also informed by feedback from the Adjudicator (who sits on the committee) and from a group of tax professionals, who will also meet quarterly with HMRC to provide their perspectives on HMRC's performance against the Charter.

12.13

6. More information about HMRC

Find out how to contact HMRC.
Learn more about our:

- role and responsibilities [see *https://www.gov.uk/government/organisations/hm-revenue-customs/about*]

- governance and how we're organised [*see https://www.gov.uk/government/organisations/hm-revenue-customs/about/our-governance*]

Read our:

- annual reports and accounts [see *https://www.gov.uk/government/collections/hmrcs-annual-report-and-accounts*]

- Personal Information Charter [*see https://www.gov.uk/government/organisations/hm-revenue-customs/about/personal-information-charter*]

- consultations [see *https://www.gov.uk/search/policy-papers-and-consultations?content_store_document_type%5B%5D=open_consultations&content_store_document_type%5B%5D=closed_consultations&organisations%5B%5D=hm-revenue-customs*]

12.14

General note

This is the charter of "standards and values" that HMRC are required to prepare under s.16A(1) of the Commissioners for Revenue and Customs Act 2005. Section 16A(2) provides "The Charter must include standards of behaviour and values to which Her Majesty's Revenue and Customs will aspire when dealing with people in the exercise of their functions".

The above version of the HMRC Charter has been in force since November 5, 2020. While the Charter itself commits HMRC to provide "accurate, consistent and

12.15

clear information", regrettably it provides inaccurate information about rights of appeal insofar as tax credits decisions are concerned. In tax credits cases, the right of appeal lies not to "the independent tax tribunal" but to the Social Entitlement Chamber of the First-tier Tribunal.

LEAFLET WTC7 (6 APRIL 2020)

TAX CREDITS PENALTIES

WHAT HAPPENS AT THE END OF A TAX CREDITS CHECK

This factsheet tells you about the penalties we may impose if you have failed to comply with requirements or acted fraudulently or negligently in connection with your claim. It also explains how to ask for a reconsideration if you disagree with those penalties.

Introduction

12.16   When you claim Child Tax Credit or Working Tax Credit you're responsible for making sure that the information on your claim is right.

Read this factsheet if we charged you a penalty after checking your tax credits claim. It tells you:
- what's likely to happen next
- what you can do if we charge you a penalty
- how to ask for a reconsideration if you disagree with the penalty.

Information about how and why we carry out tax credits checks is in factsheets WTC/FS1, 'Tax credits enquiry' and WTC/FS2, 'Tax credits examinations'. We normally give these to customers when we start a check.

Why we charge penalties

12.17   We charge penalties to:
- encourage people to be careful and make sure their claims are right in the future
- stop customers from giving us wrong information in the future
- penalise people who try to defraud the system.

Your penalty

12.18   We can charge you a penalty of up to £3,000 if you deliberately or negligently gave the wrong information:
- on your claim
- when telling us about a change of circumstances
- when providing information to us as part of our checks

We can also charge you a penalty of up to £300 if you've failed to give us information or tell us about certain changes of circumstances within one month of it happening.

LEAFLET WTC7

We'll explain why we believe you have failed to tell us of a change of circumstances within one month or why we believe you have deliberately declared the wrong information. If you don't accept our explanation, you can ask an independent tribunal to decide.

If we believe you may have committed a criminal offence, we may carry out an investigation and prosecute you. If this happens, we'll not charge you a penalty.

What is deliberate error

Deliberate error is where you gave the wrong information on purpose. This includes claiming for an element of tax credits you're not entitled to or to increase an element by making a false statement about your circumstances. This can include:

12.19

- claiming for children that do not exist or the wrong number of children
- claiming for childcare costs when none are paid for
- claiming for childcare costs above what is actually paid
- claiming for a young person as being in education/training that counts for tax credits when they aren't
- giving us wrong information about working hours, such as:
  - claiming to be working when you're not
  - claiming to be working over 16 or 30 hours when you do not
  - couples with children, who claim to be working a combined total of 24 hours when you do not work those hours, have not done so recently and have no intention of doing so
- claiming to be in prison, an inpatient in hospital or incapacitated when you're not
- claiming to be entitled to Carer's Allowance when you're not
- claiming to be entitled to the disability element when you're not
- telling us your income was less than it actually was
- failing to tell us about a source of income
- claiming as a single person when a partner is present and it's clear a joint claim should have been made
- making any other wrong declarations where the information concerns your own circumstances which you can be reasonably expected to know

Couples

If you have made a joint claim with your partner, you're both responsible for the information you provide in your claim.

12.20

We may charge you a penalty as a couple where either of you could have:

- told us about any change in circumstances
- given us new information

Tax Credits Penalties

If the information relates to one member of a couple and their partner couldn't reasonably have known it was wrong, we'll only charge a penalty to the partner who knew it wasn't right.

The maximum penalty for a joint claim is no more than the maximum penalty for an individual claim.

12.21 Penalty amounts

A maximum penalty of £300 may be charged if you do not:

- notify us of a change of circumstances within one month of it happening
- declare circumstances or income when requested during an annual review
- comply with a request for information - we have to ask an independent tribunal to impose this penalty

If any of these failures continue, we may charge a penalty of up to £60 a day.

For a deliberate and wrong declaration when reporting any other information, the penalty levels for a:

- first wrong declaration is 30% of the amount you've over-claimed (up to a maximum of £3,000)
- second wrong declaration is 50% of the amount you've over-claimed (up to a maximum of £3,000)
- third or subsequent wrong declaration is 100% of the amount you've over-claimed (up to a maximum of £3,000)

If you do not understand our explanation of the penalty, you can ask us to put it in writing so that you can get independent advice.

Interest

12.22

We may charge you interest if you pay a penalty late.

We'll contact you if we think that you have become liable to a penalty. We can do this:

- by phone
- in a meeting
- in writing

We'll tell you:

- the maximum amount that we can charge
- the penalty amount that we propose to charge and why

We're always willing to discuss with you the amount of the penalty and the reasons for it.

12.23 Payment arrangements

We'll discuss arrangements for paying:

- any overpaid tax credits
- the penalty
- any interest due

You can pay by debit card, credit card or Direct Debit using the internet and telephone banking.

For more information on how to pay, go to **www.gov.uk/dealing-with-hmrc/paying-hmrc**.

Co-operation

We may decide to reduce or stop your current tax credits payments based on the information we hold. The extent to which you co-operate and give us information is entirely up to you. If you're not sure whether to give us the information or if you're reluctant to co-operate, we suggest you get independent advice before deciding what to do. 12.24

A number of independent organisations offer help with tax credits, such as Citizens Advice. Go to **www.citizensadvice.org.uk** or you can find them in 'The Phone Book'.

About our decision

You have the right to ask us to reconsider our decision if we: 12.25

- ask you to pay penalties or interest on an overpayment
- change your award

We call this mandatory reconsideration. Our decision notice will tell you how to ask us to reconsider our decision.

Our leaflet WTC/AP, 'What to do if you think your Child Tax Credit or Working Tax Credit is wrong' gives more information about how to ask for a reconsideration.

Go to **GOV.UK** and search for WTC/AP. If we charge you a penalty, you'll get a copy of this leaflet with our decision notice.

We won't treat your request to reconsider as non-co-operation.

Independent tribunals

If we cannot change our decision, you can appeal to an independent tribunal. You'll find details about this in our Mandatory Reconsideration Notice. 12.26

Help with tax credits

For more information: 12.27

- go to www.gov.uk/taxcredits
- phone the Tax Credit Helpline on 0345 300 3900
- textphone the Tax Credit Helpline (for people with hearing or speech difficulties) on 0345 300 3909
- write to us at

    Tax Credit Office

HM Revenue and Customs
BX9 1ER

When you contact us, please tell us your:

- full name
- National Insurance number
- daytime phone number.

Yr Iaith Gymraeg

12.28   Ffoniwch 0300 200 1900 i dderbyn fersiynau Cymraeg o ffurflenni a chanllawiau.

The above version of WTC7 has been in force since April 6 2020.

CODE OF PRACTICE 26 (6 APRIL 2020)

WHAT HAPPENS IF WE'VE PAID YOU TOO MUCH TAX CREDITS

This leaflet explains why overpayments happen and how to pay them back. It also tells you when you don't have to pay them back and how to dispute an overpayment.

Introduction

Mandatory reconsideration

12.29   An overpayment means we've paid you more money than you're entitled to.

If you think the amount of tax credits is wrong, you can ask us to look at the decision again. This is called mandatory reconsideration and you must normally contact us within 30 days of the date shown on your decision notice. You can also ask us to look at any penalty we've imposed in connection with your tax credits claim or interest we decided to charge on your overpayment.

When we've looked at the decision again we'll send you a Mandatory Reconsideration Notice explaining what we've done. This will include all the information you need to appeal to HM Courts and Tribunals Service in England, Scotland and Wales or The Appeals Service in Northern Ireland, if you're still unhappy with our decision.

Appeals to the Tribunals or Appeals Service must be made in writing and within one month (30 days in Northern Ireland) of the date of the Mandatory Reconsideration Notice.

We'll put any recovery action on hold while we carry out the reconsideration or while your appeal is being considered.

CODE OF PRACTICE 26

For more information see our leaflet WTC/AP, 'What to do if you think your Child Tax Credit or Working Tax Credit is wrong'. Go to **GOV.UK** and search for WTC/AP or phone the Tax Credit Helpline on 0345 300 3900 for a copy. If you make a claim for Universal Credit (UC) and your mandatory reconsideration or appeal is successful, we will only be able to pay you tax credits up to the day before you made your claim for UC. This is because UC is replacing tax credits and if you make a claim to UC, tax credits must stop, even if you are not entitled to UC. For information go to www.gov.uk/how-tax-credits-affect

When you should dispute an overpayment

12.30 If you think our decision is right, but you don't agree that you should repay the overpayment, read pages 4 to 12 [see 11.38 to 11.60 below] of this leaflet for more information about whether you should dispute our decision to recover the overpayment.

Contact us (read page 17) [see 11.72 below] if:

- you do not agree that you've been overpaid

- you're unsure about disputing the decision to recover an overpayment

- you're unsure whether to ask for a mandatory reconsideration against the decision that caused the overpayment.

How we work out the amount of your tax credits

12.31 Tax credits depend on your income and your family circumstances. When your income or family circumstances change then your entitlement or the amount we pay you may change.

We pay you tax credits for a tax year – from 6 April one year to 5 April the next. When we first work out what to pay you, we look at your family's circumstances now and your income for the last tax year. If you think your income for the current tax year is going to be different than in the last year you can give us an estimate of what it will be. If we use this estimated figure it's important you tell us straightaway if you think your income is going to be lower or higher than the estimate you provided. If you don't, we may not be paying you enough tax credits or you may be overpaid.

After 5 April each year, we send you a renewal pack asking you to:

- check the information we hold about you is up to date

- tell us how much income you had in the last tax year

If your tax credits award is renewed automatically and you're in PAYE employment, we may have used income figures given to us by your employer. It's important that you check that these figures are correct for tax credits. Your renewal notes will help you to do this. Contact us if you think they're not and tell us why.

You should fill in and return your renewal form straightaway. We'll then work out the actual amount due to you for the year that has just ended and also the amount for the year that started on 6 April.

If you claim Universal Credit, we'll end your tax credits during the year rather than wait until the end of the year. We'll write to you to tell you what you need to do.

What happens if we've paid you too much tax credits

How an overpayment happens

12.32 An overpayment can happen if:

- you don't give us the right information either when you claim or when you renew your claim at the end of the year
- you're late telling us about a change in your circumstances
- your income in 2019 to 2020 is more than £2,500 higher than it was in 2018 to 2019
- you give us an estimated current year income which turns out to be too low
- you give us wrong information when you tell us about a change in your circumstances or income
- we make a mistake when we record the information you give us
- we don't act on information you give us.

Managing your tax credits

12.33 To understand how to manage your tax credits to get the money you're entitled to, watch our short YouTube video. Go to www.gov.uk/tax-credits-webinars-videos

Changes in your circumstances or income

12.34 You should keep us up to date with any changes in your income and your family circumstances. The law says that you must tell us about certain changes **within one month** of them happening.

Sometimes it might not be clear exactly when there has been a change so you must tell us **within one month** of the date when you realised a change has happened.

You should use the checklist TC602(SN) 'Check your tax credits award notice now' that we sent with your award notice to check what changes you need to tell us about. If you need to tell us about a change, you may find it helpful to keep a note of the date you contacted us, the name of the person you spoke to and details of the change.

After you tell us about a change we'll work out the new amount of tax credits payments you're due and send you a new award notice.

If a change of circumstances means you've already received more than we estimate for your full year award, your tax credits payments will normally stop. If this leaves you without enough to live on, tell us and we may consider making further payments.

Each case is assessed on an individual basis. If a change of circumstances means you have not received more than we estimated for your full year award, your tax credits payments will continue at a reduced rate (read page 15, 'Financial hardship' [see 11.67 below]).

If you start living with a partner, you separate from your partner or your partner dies

12.35 You must let us know **within one month** if:

- you marry or enter into a civil partnership or start living with someone as though you're married or in a civil partnership

- you're married, or in a civil partnership, and you separate legally or in circumstances likely to be permanent
- you stop living with someone as though you are married or in a civil partnership
- your partner dies

Your claim will legally end in these circumstances. If you can still claim tax credits, you'll need to make a new claim.

The longer you delay telling us about this type of change, the bigger any overpayment may be. If you've made a new tax credits claim we may consider reducing the amount that you have to pay back. We'll work out how much you would have been paid in your new claim if you'd told us about the change on time and take that amount off your overpayment.

Tax credits are being replaced for most people.

Go to *http://www.gov.uk/claim-tax-credits* for information on who can still claim.

You may be able to claim Universal Credit if you're of working age, or Pension Credit if you're of pension credit age.

For more information on claiming:
Universal Credit, go to *http://www.gov.uk/universal-credit*
Pension Credit, go to *http://www.gov.uk/pension-credit*

Our responsibilities and yours

To help get your award right and to help avoid building up an over-pay-ment, it's important that we meet our responsibilities and you meet yours.

12.36

Our responsibilities

When you contact us we should:

12.37

- give you correct advice based on the information you give us when you contact us for information
- accurately record and use the information you give us when you make or renew your claim, to work out your tax credits and pay you the correct amount
- include information you've given us about your family and your income when we send you an award notice – if you tell us that there's a mistake or something missing on your award notice, we should put it right and send you a corrected award notice
- accurately record what you've told us and send you a new award notice within 30 days when you tell us about a change of circumstance – the 30 days doesn't start until we get all of the information we need from you to make the change so it's important you give us all of the information about a change

Your responsibilities

You should:

12.38

- give us accurate, complete and up-to-date information

- tell us about any changes of circumstance throughout the year so we've accurate and up-to-date information, the law says you must tell us about certain changes within one month of them happening (you should use the checklist TC602(SN) we sent with your award notice to check what these changes are) – to reduce the chance of building up an overpayment, we recommend that you tell us about any changes in income as soon as possible
- let us know as soon as possible if you do not get an award notice within 30 days of telling us about a change in circumstance

- let us know as soon as possible if you do not get an award notice within 30 days of telling us about a change in circumstance"

You must tell us about some changes within one month of them happening – these are listed on the back of the checklist.

The main details we expect you to check are:

- if it's a joint award (for you and your partner) or a single award (based on your individual circumstances)
- the hours you work
- if you get Income Support, income-based Jobseeker's Allowance, income-related Employment and Support Allowance or Pension Credit
- that a disability element is shown if you, or anyone in the household, is entitled to it
- the number and age of any children in your household
- any childcare costs
- your total household income for the period shown on the award notice

We'll send you a corrected award notice if you tell us anything is wrong, missing or incomplete.

You should check that the payments you get match what we said they should be on your award notice. Tell us if you get any payments that don't match what is shown on your award notice.

If anything is wrong, missing or incomplete you must tell us straight away.

Make a note of when you got your award notice and when you told us about the mistake. We may ask you for this information to show that you acted **within 30 days**.

If you have difficult personal circumstances that mean you cannot check your award notice or bank payments, for example, a member of your family has been seriously ill, let us know if anything is missing or incomplete as soon as possible. Also tell is the reason why you're reporting this late.

If you don't understand your award notice, phone our helpline (read page 17).

If we fail to meet our responsibilities

12.39   If we fail to meet our responsibilities, but you meet **all** of yours, we won't ask you to pay back all of an overpayment caused by our failure.

CODE OF PRACTICE 26

However – you must tell us about any mistakes on your award notice within 30 days of the date on your award notice. If you do, then you won't be responsible for an overpayment caused by our mistake. If you tell us about a mistake **more than 30 days** after the date on your award notice we may ask you to pay back an overpayment up to the date you contacted us.

Example 1

12.40 On 1 September you tell us about a change in your circumstances but we don't change your award until 16 October. We won't collect back any overpayment that arises after 30 September.

Example 2

12.41 On 12 August you tell us about a change in your income. We send you a new award notice which you get on 19 August, but we haven't correctly recorded the information you gave us. If you spot this and tell us about the mistake by 18 September (30 days from 19 August) we won't collect any overpayment caused by our mistake.

Example 3

12.42 On 12 August you tell us about a change in your income. We send you a new award notice which you get on 19 August, but we haven't correctly recorded the information you gave us. If you spot this and don't tell us about the mistake until 27 September (39 days from 19 August) you may be responsible for the overpayment up to the date you contacted us.

Whenever you tell us about a mistake, we'll not collect an overpayment that may build up if we do not correct our mistake from this time.

If you fail to meet your responsibilities

12.43 If you fail to meet your responsibilities, but we meet **all** of ours, we'll normally ask you to pay back all of an overpayment. For example, if you tell us about a mistake on your award notice **more than 30 days** after the date on your award notice, then you may have to pay back an overpayment which has built up until the time you contacted us. But also read 'Exceptional circumstances' below.

If we both fail to meet our responsibilities

12.44 If we both fail to meet one or more of our responsibilities, we'll look at the circumstances of your case and may write off parts of an overpayment.

If we both meet our responsibilities

12.45 If we both meet our responsibilities, we'll usually ask you to pay back the overpayment.

Example 4

12.46 On 12 August you told us your income increased from 15 July. We updated your tax credit record on 11 September. We will still ask you to pay back any overpayments made during the period 15 July to 11 September.

What happens if we've paid you too much tax credits

If it takes you some time to tell us we didn't meet our responsibilities

12.47 We ask you to tell us about any mistakes we've made **within 30 days** of the date on your award notice. If you don't tell us **within 30 days**, we'll ask you to pay back an overpayment up to the date you told us. **We won't ask you to pay back an overpayment, which is caused by our mistake, after the date you told us.**

Exceptional circumstances

12.48 We understand that exceptional circumstances may prevent you from meeting your responsibilities on time. For example, you or a close family member may have been seriously ill so you couldn't report a change, check your award notice or tell us about our mistake **within 30 days** of the date on your award notice. Let us know, as soon as it becomes possible, if you think this applies to you, or if you're not sure whether we've made a mistake.

If you don't understand why there is an overpayment, contact us. We can give you an explanation over the phone or in writing. Our leaflet WTC8, 'Why overpayments happen' gives more information about things that can cause overpayments. You can get a copy:

- online, go to **GOV.UK** and search for WTC8
- by phoning our helpline (read page 17) if you don't have access to the internet

If you're not able to manage your own tax affairs, handle money or understand or complete forms, you can get another person to act on your behalf. We call these people appointees.

Appointees

12.49 Appointees can sometimes be appointed by:

- a court or government department, for example the Department for Work and Pensions
- you, if you need help in dealing with your tax affairs
- a carer, a voluntary sector organisation or a mental health or social care professional who would be able to act in all dealings with us

For more information, go to www.gov.uk/getting-help-with-yourtax-credits-claim/appointees

Challenging the recovery of an overpayment

How to dispute an overpayment

12.50 If you don't agree that we should ask you to pay back an overpayment you can ask us to look at this again. We call this **disputing** an overpayment. To do this, complete and return form TC846, 'Tax credits overpayment'. You can get a copy:

- online, go to **GOV.UK** and search for TC846
- by phoning our helpline (read page 17) [10.53 below] if you don't have access to the internet

You can write to us instead, but you must make sure you give us full details including:

- in what tax year the overpayment being disputed happened
- if and when you contacted us
- why you think the overpayment happened
- why you think you shouldn't have to pay back the overpayment

Usually you have to dispute recovery of an overpayment within 3 months from the date of:

- your final decision notice
- the decision on your Annual Review notice (if your award is renewed automatically)
- your Statement of Account
- the decision on your Award Review notice (if your award is ended automatically due to a claim for Universal Credit)
- the letter which gives you our decision on your mandatory reconsideration
- the letter from the Tribunals or Appeals Service which gives you their decision on your appeal

You can only dispute recovery of an overpayment that happened in the tax year the notice or letter relates to. You cannot dispute overpayments from previous awards where it's been more than 3 months since you received your final decision notice. We'll only accept a late dispute in exceptional circumstances, for example, if you were in hospital for that 3-month period. If you do send us a dispute, we'll continue to seek recovery of the overpayment while we're considering your dispute.

If we later change our decision and you receive another decision notice for the same year, you have 3 months from the date of that notice to dispute recovery of an overypayment.

Example 5

Mary and Alan have overpayments from 2012 to 2013 and 2013 to 2014 tax years. They're paying the overpayments back from their tax credits award in 2016 to 2017. They were late reporting a change of circumstances in 2016 to 2017 and there's a new overpayment shown on their final 2016 to 2017 award notice. Their final award notice also shows the overpayments from the earlier tax years.

Mary and Alan have 3 months from the date of their 2016 to 2017 decision notice to dispute the new overpayment only. But they'll not be able to dispute the overpayments from 2012 to 2013 and 2013 to 2014 tax years.

12.51

Historic debt

If you no longer get tax credits, you'll have been informed on past notices that, if you want to dispute an overpayment, you should do so as quickly as possible. You cannot dispute overpayments from previous awards where it's been more than 3 months since you received your final decision notice. However, if you can show there are exceptional circumstances why you haven't previously disputed the overpayment, such as being in hospital, we'll consider the dispute.

12.52

What happens if we've paid you too much tax credits

If you no longer get tax credits, but have received a final decision notice from us in the last 3 months you'll only be able to dispute the overpayment occurring in the tax year the notice relates to.

If you were able to reclaim tax credits and received payments, we'll tell you if we're recovering historic debts from your ongoing award. You'll only be able to dispute the overpayment in the 3 months after you received the final decision notice relating to your previous award. Read page 13 [10.43 below] "Paying back an overpayment".

Example 6

12.53 You receive your tax credits renewal pack on 21 May 2017 which requires you to confirm family details and income for the previous 12 months ending 5 April 2017. You check your household details and decide you have no changes to report. We then send out a final decision notice on 15 August 2017. This shows you have been overpaid tax credits because your eldest child left school in September 2016 though your award was only changed in January 2017.

You don't notice the information about the overpayment until December 2017 when you realise your monthly tax credits payments are being reduced to pay it back. You agree there's been an overpayment but believe you shouldn't have to pay it back because you told HMRC about your daughter leaving school in September 2016 and we didn't change your award until January 2017. You had 3 months to dispute the overpayment from 15 August 2017, when we sent the final decision notice. This means that you needed to dispute the overpayment by 15 November 2017.

As you're now out of time you can't dispute the overpayment unless you can show there are exceptional circumstances for missing the deadline, such as being in hospital.

Where we got a decision wrong

12.54 In some cases we may revise the decision which caused the overpayment. We can only do this where the decision is incorrect as a result of an error by us and we find that you didn't materially contribute to the error. We call this type of error an 'official error'. However, we will not revise a decision which is incorrect due to official error if more than 5 years have passed from the date of the decision, or if the revised decision wouldn't be in your favour.

If a dispute is found in your favour, we'll send you a revised award notice and refund any amount that has already been recovered.

Example 7

12.55 You have received Working Tax Credit since 2012. You became entitled to Disability Living Allowance in 2013 and asked us whether you were entitled to the disability element of Working Tax Credit.

We incorrectly told you that you were not entitled to the disability element and decided not to make the change you reported. In 2015 you visited Citizens Advice with a query about your tax credits award. The adviser noticed that you qualified for the disability element but it wasn't included on your award. You contacted us and asked about our original

CODE OF PRACTICE 26

decision in 2013. Since our decision was wrong, solely because of our error, your awards would be revised all the way back to 2013.

How we decide whether you should pay back some or all of an overpayment

When we're deciding if you should pay back an overpayment we'll check: 12.56

- that we accurately recorded and acted on any information you gave us **within 30 days** of you telling us about a change of circumstance
- that we accurately worked out and paid you your correct entitlement
- that the information we included on your award notice was accurate at the date of the notice
- what you told us if you contacted us, and whether the advice we gave you based on that information was correct
- whether you contacted us to discuss any queries on your award notice, and whether we answered them correctly
- that you gave us accurate and up-to-date information when you claimed tax credits
- that you told us about any changes of circumstance at the right time
- that you checked your award notice **within 30 days** of the date on your award notice and if and when you told us about any mistakes
- that you checked the payments you got matched the amounts on your award notice and if not, that you told us **within 30 days** of the date on your award notice
- whether you told us of any exceptional circumstances that meant you couldn't tell us about a change of circumstance or about our mistake **within 30 days**.

After we've checked that we've met our responsibilities and you've met yours, we'll decide if you must pay back:

- an overpayment
- all or only part of an overpayment"

We'll normally give you our decision, along with our reasons, in writing. However, we won't stop collecting an overpayment while we do this.

We may not ask you to pay back an overpayment if you contacted us to tell us that your exceptional personal circumstances meant you couldn't check your award notice or bank payments. For example, a member of your family may have been seriously ill. If this is the case please let us know as soon as possible.

If you still think you shouldn't pay back an overpayment

If you're still unhappy that we've decided to continue collecting an   12.57
overpayment you can ask us to look at the decision again if you give us

new and relevant information. You can only ask us to review the decision once and you'll have to do this **within 30 days** of receiving your dispute decision letter. Your overpayment will continue to be collected while we do this. We'll only accept a late request for a review in exceptional circumstances, for example, if you were in hospital for that 30 day period.

If you don't have any new information to give us, but you're still unhappy with our decision, you may wish to contact a professional adviser or organisation, for example, Citizens Advice. You can consider what options are open to you, including any through the courts.

If you're not happy with our service, please read 'Customer service' on page 17 [10.53 below].

Paying back an overpayment

12.58 We may collect back an overpayment from you in a number of ways including:

- reducing your payments from an ongoing tax credits award
- asking you to make direct payments to us
- adjusting your tax code

If you claim Universal Credit we may ask the Department for Work and Pensions or the Department for Communities (in Northern Ireland) to recover your tax credits overpayment.

In exceptional circumstances we may recover the overpayment directly from your bank account.

In some exceptional cases we may ask you to do more than one of the above.

From an ongoing tax credits award

12.59 If you're still getting tax credits payments we'll automatically reduce these payments to recover an overpayment from your ongoing tax credits. Overpayments we will recover may be from awards you:

- or your partner have had as single people
- and your partner have had together either now or previously

We won't recover from your ongoing tax credits, any overpayments from awards you or your partner have had with other partners.

We won't recover from your ongoing tax credits, any overpayments from awards you or your partner have had with other partners.

Recovery from an on-going tax credits award only takes place where an overpayment is established at the end of the year and that overpayment falls for cross year recovery.

If an overpayment still exists at the end of the year we'll recover from the award starting at 6 April of the following year.

How much we reduce your payments by will depend on how much you're getting. We reduce awards at different levels, read the table on page 14 to see the different rates used to recover overpayment.

If you want help understanding which recovery rate applies to you, contact us (read page 17) [11.70 below].

CODE OF PRACTICE 26

Type of award	The most we'll take back from your award
If you're entitled to the maximum tax credits with no reduction due to income	10%
If you're getting Child Tax Credit or Working Tax Credit below the maximum and your total household income is £20,000 or less	25%
If your total household income exceeds £20,000	50%
If you're only getting the family element of Child Tax Credit	100%

By direct payment

We'll ask you to make a direct payment to us, if: 12.60

- you're no longer entitled to tax credits

- your tax credits award ends - this can happen if there's a change in your household, for example, you were in a couple and now you're single

From an ongoing tax credits award and by direct payment

This may happen if you have an overpayment from an old award which ended and you have an overpayment from a current award. For example, you and your partner separated and you then made another claim as a single person or in a new couple. We could ask you to pay back an overpayment from your current award as well as a direct payment from your previous award. If this happens to you, you can ask for the direct payment to be put on hold until you have paid back the overpayment from your ongoing tax credits payments. 12.61

If you do have an outstanding overpayment from an old claim, in some circumstances we may recover this from your ongoing award, instead of asking you to pay this overpayment back directly.

Asking for more time to pay back a direct payment

If we've asked you to pay back an overpayment from a previous award directly, but you need more time to pay it back, please phone our Payment Helpline on **0345 302 1429** as soon as possible. We may be able to arrange for you to pay it back in equal instalments. If you'd like more details on different direct payment options, tell us when you phone. 12.62

By an adjustment to your tax code

If you're in PAYE employment or getting pension income and have a tax credits overpayment we may be able to adjust your tax code to collect your overpayment. We will write to you and let you know if we can collect your overpayment this way. If we do write to you and you would prefer not to 12.63

have your tax code adjusted, you can contact us to pay in full or to agree an instalment arrangement. The amount that is recovered depends on your income.

If you claim Universal Credit

12.64   If you claim Universal Credit we may transfer your tax credits debts to the DWP or the DfC so they can recover it from your Universal Credit payments unless they tell you otherwise. Where we've previously agreed a payment plan with you, this will stop and the method and/or rate of recovery made by DWP or DfC may differ from HMRC's. If this is going to happen we'll write to you with more details. For more information go to www.gov.uk/tax-credits-overpayments

12.65   *If you no longer claim tax credits and have an outstanding debt*

If you're no longer claiming tax credits and have an outstanding overpayment or penalty, we may transfer these to the DWP or the DfC for them to recover.

Financial hardship

12.66   If you need to discuss financial hardship with us, phone us to explain this.

When you phone we may ask you about any family circumstances that may lead to extra living costs. For example, if you're looking after someone who is chronically ill or disabled. In some exceptional circumstances, we may cancel an overpayment altogether.

If you can't pay for your essential living expenses

12.67   Phone the Payment Helpline on 0345 302 1429 if you cannot pay for your essential living expenses such as your rent, gas or electricity and:

- you're paying back an overpayment directly
- we've asked you to pay back an overpayment

We'll ask you about your circumstances in more detail to determine if we can adjust your payments. You'll be asked for more information regarding your income and living costs. Once we have this information we aim to make a decision within 2 working days.

If we've reduced your ongoing payments so you can pay back an overpayment you can find more information at www.gov.uk/taxcredits-overpayments or you can phone us on 0345 300 3900.

Whether you're repaying your overpayment through a reduction in your tax credits payments or through a direct payment, we may offer you an option for extending the period of time over which you pay back the overpayment. We can do this by reducing the amount we recover each month. However, this means it'll take you longer to pay off the overpayment.

If you can't pay for your essential living expenses and you're getting Universal Credit, you should contact the Department for Work and Pensions or the Department for Communities (in Northern Ireland).

CODE OF PRACTICE 26

If you and your partner separate

12.68 If you and your partner separate and your joint claim ends, we'll work out if you've been overpaid. If you have, we'll write to you both, usually at the end of the tax year to:

- tell you how much we've overpaid you by
- ask you to contact us to arrange to pay back the money

You and your ex-partner are both responsible for paying back an overpayment from your joint claim. The letter sent to each of you will show the total overpayment that you both owe.

You should try to agree with your ex-partner how much each of you should pay. The options are that:

- each of you pays half
- each of you pays a different amount
- one of you pays the full amount

When you've reached an agreement with your ex-partner, you should both phone the Payment Helpline on 0345 302 1429 to arrange repaying the overpayment. You'll then get a letter confirming what you have to pay back.

You might not be able to talk it over with your ex-partner, either because you don't want to contact them or you don't know where they are. Even if you do speak to them, you might not be able to agree on what each of you should pay back. If this happens, you should still speak to the Payment Helpline as quickly as possible. You'll then be asked to pay back half of the overpayment, with your partner being asked to pay back the rest. You won't be asked to pay back more than half of the overpayment.

You must tell us within one month if you and your partner separate. Your joint tax credits claim will end. To find out if you can make a new tax credits claim, go to www.gov.uk/claim-tax-credits

If you're able to make a new claim after a separation, we cannot reduce your payments from your new claim to collect back an overpayment that you had with your previous partner.

You must pay this overpayment back directly by ringing the Payment Helpline.

However, if you get back together with your ex-partner and are able to claim again, we may reduce your payments to recover the overpayment.

Contact us

12.69 When you contact us tell us:

- your full name
- your National Insurance number
- a daytime phone number

By phone

12.70
- Tax Credits Helpline **0345 300 3900**
- Payment Helpline **0345 302 1429**

- Next Generation Text (NGT) relay (if you cannot hear or speak on the phone) **18001-0345-300-3900**
- If you prefer to speak in Welsh, phone 0300 200 1900
- If you're abroad and can't get through on the helpline, phone **+44 2890 538 192**

In writing

12.71
- Tax Credits Office
- HM Revenue and Customs
- BX9 1ER

Help and support

12.72 To understand how to manage your tax credits to get the money you're entitled to, watch our short YouTube video. Go to www.gov.uk/tax-credits-webinars-videos

Customer service

12.73 For information about our complaints procedure, go to **www.gov.uk/complain-about-hmrc**

Your rights and obligations

12.74 Your Charter' explains what you can expect from us and what we expect from you. For more information, go to **www.gov.uk/hmrc/your-charter**.

General Note

12.75 The above version of Code of Practice 26 has been in force since April 6 2020.

PART XIII

SCOTTISH SOCIAL SECURITY LEGISLATION

Social Security (Scotland) Act 2018

(2018 asp 9)

CONTENTS

PART 1

TENETS AND OVERSIGHT

1 The Scottish social security principles
2 Effect of the principles
3 to 9 *Omitted*
10 Right to advocacy
11 Advocacy service standards
12 Restriction on private-sector involvement in assessments
13 Assessors to be suitably qualified
14 Assessments only to be required where necessary
15 The Scottish social security charter
16 to 18 *Omitted*
19 Effect of the charter
20 to 22 *Omitted*
23 Meaning of "Scottish social security system"

PART 2

GIVING OF ASSISTANCE BY SCOTTISH MINISTERS

CHAPTER 1

ASSISTANCE TO BE GIVEN ACCORDING TO DETERMINATION OF ENTITLEMENT

24 Duty to give assistance
25 Meaning of "determination of entitlement"
26 Individual's right to stop receiving assistance
27 Later determination supersedes earlier

CHAPTER 2

TYPES OF ASSISTANCE TO BE GIVEN

28 Carer's assistance
29 *Not yet in force*
30 Winter heating assistance

31 Disability assistance
32 Early years assistance
33 *Not yet in force*
34 Funeral expense assistance
35 *Not yet in force*
36 Short-term assistance

CHAPTER 3

DETERMINING ENTITLEMENT

Determination by the Scottish Ministers

37 Duty to make determination
38 Application for assistance
39 Withdrawal of application
40 Notice of determination

Re-determination by the Scottish Ministers

41 Right to request re-determination
42 Late request for re-determination
43 Duty to re-determine
44 Notice of re-determination
45 Notice where re-determination not made timeously

Appeal against the Scottish Ministers' determination

46 Right to appeal to First-tier Tribunal against determination
47 Initiating an appeal
48 Deadline for appealing
49 First-tier Tribunal's power to determine entitlement

The determination of entitlement

50 Decisions comprising determination
51 Determination on basis of ongoing entitlement
52 Determination without application
52A Re-determination and appeal deadlines
52B Applications for assistance

(2018 asp 9)

CHAPTER 4

FURTHER PROVISION ABOUT DETERMINING ENTITLEMENT

Identifying possible eligibility

53 *Renumbered as 84C*

Obtaining information to make determination

54 Obligation to provide information on request
55 Requirement to justify assessment requests
56 Duty to notify change of circumstances
57 Lifting of duty to notify change of circumstances

Appointees

58 *Repealed*

Support during discussions and assessments

59 Right to support

Access to reports

60 Right to reports used in determining entitlement

Right to appeal Scottish Ministers' process decisions

61 Appeal to First-tier Tribunal against process decisions

Presumption about when information is received

62 Presumption for purposes of sections 41, 48 and 61

Non-disclosure of health information

62A Non-disclosure of information about individual's health

CHAPTER 5

RECOVERY OF VALUE OF ASSISTANCE

Assistance given in error

63 Liability for assistance given in error
64 Exclusion from liability

65 Consideration for debtor's circumstances
66 *Omitted*
67 Exclusion of other rights of recovery
68 *Repealed*
69 Liability where assistance given for period after death

Funeral expense assistance

70 *Omitted*

CHAPTER 6

OFFENCES

71 to 74 *Omitted*
75 to 76 *Renumbered as 84A and 84B*

CHAPTER 7

UPRATING FOR INFLATION

Omitted

77 to 78 *Renumbered as 86A and 86B*

PART 3

SUPPLEMENTING ASSISTANCE UNDER OTHER ENACTMENTS

Top up of reserved benefits

79 Power to provide for top up
80 Restrictions on power
80A *Omitted.*

Carer's allowance: temporary provision

81 Carer's allowance supplement
82 Power to repeal temporary provision

PART 4

FURTHER PROVISION IN CONNECTION WITH PARTS 2 AND 3

83 to 84B *Omitted*

Identifying possible eligibility

84C   Duty to inform about possible eligibility

Information-sharing

85   Information-sharing

Appointees

85A   Appointment of person to act on behalf of a child
85B   Appointment of a person to act in other circumstances
85C   Guidelines for decisions about appointees
85D   *Not yet in force*
85E   Guidance for appointees
86   *Not yet in force*
86A to 87A *Omitted*

PART 5

DISCRETIONARY HOUSING PAYMENTS

88. Local authorities' power to make payments
89. Restrictions on power to make payments
90. Local authorities' duty to provide information about payments
91. Guidance
92. Local authorities need not make payments if not funded
93. Power to modify section 88

PART 6

UNIVERSAL CREDIT: PAYMENT TO JOINT CLAIMANTS

94   *Not yet in force*

PART 7

FINAL PROVISIONS

95   Ancillary provision
96   Regulation-making powers
97 to 98   *Omitted*
99   Commencement
100   Short title

Schedule 1   *Omitted*
Schedule 2   Carer's assistance regulations
Schedule 3   *Not yet in force*
Schedule 4   Winter heating assistance regulations
Schedule 5   Disability assistance regulations
Schedule 6   Early years assistance regulations

Social Security (Scotland) Act 2018

Schedule 7   *Not yet in force*
Schedule 8   Funeral expense assistance regulations
Schedule 9   *Not yet in force*
Schedule 10 Short-term assistance regulations

The Bill for this Act of the Scottish Parliament was passed by the Parliament on 25th April 2018 and received Royal Assent on 1st June 2018

An Act of the Scottish Parliament making provision about social security.

PART 1

TENETS AND OVERSIGHT

Principles

The Scottish social security principles

13.1

1. The Scottish social security principles are—
   (a) social security is an investment in the people of Scotland,
   (b) social security is itself a human right and essential to the realisation of other human rights,
   (c) the delivery of social security is a public service,
   (d) respect for the dignity of individuals is to be at the heart of the Scottish social security system,
   (e) the Scottish social security system is to contribute to reducing poverty in Scotland,
   (f) the Scottish social security system is to be designed with the people of Scotland on the basis of evidence,
   (g) opportunities are to be sought to continuously improve the Scottish social security system in ways which—
       (i) put the needs of those who require assistance first, and
       (ii) advance equality and non-discrimination,
   (h) the Scottish social security system is to be efficient and deliver value for money.

DEFINITION

"Scottish social security system"—see s.23.

GENERAL NOTE

13.2

Note, however, Lady Poole's observation in *NB v Social Security Scotland* [2023] UT 35 that "treating a claimant with dignity and respect does not entail making awards of social security assistance to which they are not entitled under the governing legislation" (para.30) and see further *CD v Social Security Scotland* [2024] UT 12 at [12]–[19].

Effect of the principles

13.3

2.—(1) The Scottish social security principles are set out in section 1 so that—
   (a) they can be reflected in the Scottish social security charter as required by section 15(3), and
   (b) the Scottish Commission on Social Security can have regard to them as required by section 97(6).

(2) A court or tribunal in civil or criminal proceedings may take the Scottish social security principles into account when determining any question arising in the proceedings to which the principles are relevant.

(3) Breach of the principles does not of itself give rise to grounds for any legal action.

3. to 9. *Omitted.*

Advocacy

Right to advocacy

10.—(1) Every individual to whom subsection (3) applies has a right of access to independent advocacy in connection with the determination of the individual's entitlement to be given assistance through the Scottish social security system.

(2) It is the duty of the Scottish Ministers to ensure that independent advocacy services are available to the extent necessary for that right to be exercised by the individuals who have it.

(3) This subsection applies to an individual if, owing to a disability, the individual requires an advocate's help to engage effectively with the process for determining entitlement to be given assistance through the Scottish social security system.

(4) For the purposes of this section—
 (a) "advocacy services" means services of support and representation that are made available for the purpose of enabling an individual to whom they are provided to have as much control of, or capacity to influence, the decisions that determine the individual's entitlement to be given assistance through the Scottish social security system as is, in the circumstances, appropriate,
 (b) advocacy services are independent if they are provided by a person other than the Scottish Ministers.

Advocacy service standards

11.—(1) It must be a term of any agreement that the Scottish Ministers enter into with a person for the provision of advocacy services in connection with their duty under section 10(2), that the person undertakes to comply with the advocacy service standards.

(2) The advocacy service standards are to be set by the Scottish Ministers in regulations and may, in particular, include provision in relation to—
 (a) the training and experience individuals providing advocacy services must have,
 (b) service quality,
 (c) quality assurance processes,
 (d) record keeping.

(3) The advocacy service standards, or a part of them, may be set by reference to another document (whether or not prepared by the Scottish Ministers).

Assessments

Restriction on private-sector involvement in assessments

12.—(1) An individual may not be required, in order to be given assistance through the Scottish social security system, to undergo an assessment of physical condition or mental health that is carried out by another individual who is not acting in the course of employment by a public body.

(2) In subsection (1), "public body" means any of the following—
   (a) a Minister of the Crown,
   (b) a person established by an enactment,
   (c) a body comprised solely of persons described by this subsection,
   (d) a body corporate that has no members other than (either or both)—
      (i) persons described by this subsection,
      (ii) persons acting on behalf of persons described by this subsection.

(3) For the purposes of this section, an individual may be regarded as carrying out an assessment in the course of employment by a body if the individual carries out the assessment pursuant to an agreement between the body and the individual; it is immaterial that the individual would not be regarded as an employee of the body for the purposes of any other enactment.

(4) Subsection (1) does not preclude its being made a requirement for being given assistance through the Scottish social security system that an individual be—
(a) in receipt of, or
(b) eligible or entitled to receive,
other assistance, despite entitlement to that other assistance depending on the fulfilment of a requirement that subsection (1) would preclude from being imposed in relation to the giving of assistance through the Scottish social security system.

(5) In subsection (4), "other assistance" means assistance other than assistance given through the Scottish social security system.

Assessors to be suitably qualified

13.7

13.—(1) The Scottish Ministers must ensure that any assessment to which subsection (2) applies is carried out by a suitably qualified person.

(2) This subsection applies to an assessment that—
   (a) is arranged—
      (i) by the Scottish Ministers,
      (ii) in connection with making a determination of what assistance an individual is eligible to be given through the Scottish social security system, and
   (b) is an assessment of physical condition or mental health.

(3) The Scottish Ministers may by regulations specify who is to be regarded as a suitably qualified person within the meaning of subsection (1) by reference to a person's—
   (a) training,
   (b) experience, or
   (c) holding a particular position.

(4) Regulations under subsection (3) must make different provision about who is suitably qualified to carry out an assessment depending on what the assessment is about.

Assessments only to be required where necessary

13.8

14.—It is implicit in the principle (expressed in section 1(d)) that respect for the dignity of individuals is to be at the heart of the Scottish social security system that—

1452

(a) an individual should not be required to undergo an assessment in order to be given assistance unless that is the only practicable way to obtain the information needed to determine what assistance the individual is eligible to be given, and

(b) the Scottish Ministers should take into consideration any preferences an individual has expressed to them about where and how any assessment is carried out.

Charter

The Scottish social security charter

15.—(1) A Scottish social security charter is to be prepared, published and from time to time reviewed in accordance with sections 16 to 18.

(2) The charter is to set out what should be expected—

(a) from the Scottish Ministers when—
   (i) developing social security policy, and
   (ii) exercising the functions conferred on them by this Part and Parts 2 and 3, and
(b) from the individuals who apply for, and receive, assistance through the Scottish social security system.

(3) The charter is to reflect the Scottish social security principles.

GENERAL NOTE

The charter is published at *https://www.socialsecurity.gov.scot/about-us/our-charter*.

16. to 18. *Omitted.*

Effect of the charter

19.—(1) A court or tribunal in civil or criminal proceedings may take the Scottish social security charter into account when determining any question arising in the proceedings to which the charter is relevant.

(2) Breach of the charter does not of itself give rise to grounds for any legal action.

20. to 22. *Omitted.*

Interpretation

Meaning of "Scottish social security system"

23. In this Part, "Scottish social security system" means the system for the Scottish Ministers giving assistance to individuals in accordance with any of the following—

(a) Part 2,
(b) regulations made under Part 3,
(c) a provision of any other Act of the Scottish Parliament if it is only by virtue of exception 10 of Section F1 of Part 2 of schedule 5 of the Scotland Act 1998 that the provision does not relate to reserved matters as defined in section 127 of that Act.

Social Security (Scotland) Act 2018

PART 2

GIVING OF ASSISTANCE BY SCOTTISH MINISTERS

CHAPTER 1

ASSISTANCE TO BE GIVEN ACCORDING TO DETERMINATION OF ENTITLEMENT

Duty to give assistance

13.13   24.—The Scottish Ministers must give an individual whatever assistance of a type described in Chapter 2 the individual is entitled to be given under a determination of the individual's entitlement to assistance.

Meaning of "determination of entitlement"

13.14   25.—(1) References in this Part to a determination of an individual's entitlement to assistance are to a determination made—
   (a) by the Scottish Ministers—
      (i) under section 37, or
      (ii) (following a request for a re-determination) under section 43,
   (b) by the First-tier Tribunal for Scotland—
      (i) under section 49 in an appeal against a determination made by the Scottish Ministers, or
      (ii) (subsequent to such an appeal) under its Tribunals Act powers,
   (c) by the Upper Tribunal for Scotland under its Tribunals Act powers (subsequent to an appeal against, or following a review of, a decision of the First-tier Tribunal),
   (d) by the Court of Session under its Tribunals Act powers (in an appeal against a decision of the Upper Tribunal), or
   (e) by the Supreme Court of the United Kingdom—
      (i) in an appeal under section 40 of the Court of Session Act 1988 against a decision of the Court of Session, or
      (ii) on a reference made by the Court of Session under schedule 6 of the Scotland Act 1998.
   (2) In this section, "Tribunals Act powers" means powers under Part 6 (review or appeal of decisions) of the Tribunals (Scotland) Act 2014.

Individual's right to stop receiving assistance

13.15   26.—(1) An individual may request that the Scottish Ministers cancel a determination of the individual's entitlement to assistance.
   (2) On being requested to do so under subsection (1), the Scottish Ministers must cancel a determination—
      (a) with immediate effect, or
      (b) with effect from a later date specified in the request.
   (3) An individual is not entitled, and is not to become entitled, to be given assistance by a determination after it has been cancelled.

(4) A request under subsection (1) must be made in such form as the Scottish Ministers require.

(5) The Scottish Ministers must publicise any requirements for the time being set under subsection (4).

Later determination supersedes earlier

27.—(1) The latest determination of an individual's entitlement to a particular type of assistance in respect of a given period or event supersedes any earlier determination insofar as it deals with the individual's entitlement to that type of assistance in respect of the same period or event.

(2) Accordingly the individual is not entitled, and is not to become entitled, to be given any assistance in respect of that period or event by the earlier determination insofar as it has been superseded.

GENERAL NOTE

Supersession in this legislation includes what would be revision under s.9 of the Social Security Act 1998. The grounds for redetermining entitlement are set out in regulations made under s.52 of this Act for each type of benefit.

CHAPTER 2

TYPES OF ASSISTANCE TO BE GIVEN

Carer's assistance

28.—(1) Carer's assistance is assistance (which may or may not take the form of money) given by the Scottish Ministers under section 24 to an individual who provides, or has provided, care to another individual who has a disability.

(2) The Scottish Ministers are to make regulations prescribing —
(a) the eligibility rules that are to be applied to determine whether an individual is entitled to carer's assistance, and
(b) what carer's assistance an individual who is entitled to it is to be given.

(3) Schedule 2 makes provision about the exercise of the power conferred by subsection (2).

29. *Not yet in force.*

Winter heating assistance

30.—(1) Winter heating assistance is assistance (which may or may not take the form of money) given by the Scottish Ministers under section 24 to an individual to meet, or help towards meeting, the individual's heating costs during the winter months.

(2) The Scottish Ministers are to make regulations prescribing —
(a) the eligibility rules that are to be applied to determine whether an individual is entitled to winter heating assistance, and
(b) what winter heating assistance an individual who is entitled to it is to be given.

(3) Schedule 4 makes provision about the exercise of the power conferred by subsection (2).

Disability assistance

13.20 **31.**—(1) Disability assistance is assistance (which may or may not take the form of money) given by the Scottish Ministers under section 24 to an individual on account of the individual having —
    (a) a disability arising from a physical or mental impairment, or
    (b) a terminal illness.
(2) The Scottish Ministers are to make regulations prescribing —
    (a) the eligibility rules that are to be applied to determine whether an individual is entitled to disability assistance, and
    (b) what disability assistance an individual who is entitled to it is to be given.
(3) Schedule 5 makes provision about the exercise of the power conferred by subsection (2).

Early years assistance

13.21 **32.**—(1) Early years assistance is assistance (which may or may not take the form of money) given by the Scottish Ministers under section 24 to help towards meeting some of the costs associated with having, or expecting to have, a child in the family.
(2) The Scottish Minsters are to make regulations prescribing —
    (a) the eligibility rules that are to be applied to determine whether an individual is entitled to early years assistance, and
    (b) what early years assistance an individual who is entitled to it is to be given.
(3) Schedule 6 makes provision about the exercise of the power conferred by subsection (2).

33. *Not yet in force.*

Funeral expense assistance

13.22 **34.**—(1) Funeral expense assistance is assistance (which may or may not take the form of money) given by the Scottish Ministers under section 24 to an individual to meet, or help towards meeting, funeral expenses.
(2) The Scottish Ministers are to make regulations prescribing —
    (a) the eligibility rules that are to be applied to determine whether an individual is entitled to funeral expense assistance, and
    (b) what funeral expense assistance an individual who is entitled to it is to be given.
(3) Schedule 8 makes provision about the exercise of the power conferred by subsection (2).

35. *Not yet in force.*

Short-term assistance

13.23 **36.**—(1) Short-term assistance is assistance (which may or may not take the form of money) given by the Scottish Ministers under section 24 to an individual on a short-term basis.
(2) The Scottish Ministers are to make regulations prescribing —
    (a) the eligibility rules that are to be applied to determine whether an individual is entitled to short-term assistance, and
    (b) what short-term assistance an individual who is entitled to it is to be given.

(2018 asp 9 s.36)

(3) Schedule 10 makes provision about the exercise of the power conferred by subsection (2).

CHAPTER 3

DETERMINING ENTITLEMENT

Determination by the Scottish Ministers

Duty to make determination

37.—The Scottish Ministers are to make a determination of an individual's entitlement to a type of assistance described in Chapter 2—
  (a) on receiving an application for that type of assistance from the individual, or
  (b) when required to do so by regulations under section 52.

GENERAL NOTE

The whole of this Chapter necessarily follows this section in applying only to "a type of assistance described in Chapter 2" and so it does not apply to either Scottish child payment or carer's allowance supplement. Separate, but similar, provision is made in respect of those benefits under the schedule of the Scottish Child Payment Regulations 2020 and Sch.2 of the Carer's Allowance Supplement and Young Carer Grants (Residence Requirements and Procedural Provisions) (EU Exit) (Scotland) Regulations 2020.

Application for assistance

38.—(1) An application for assistance must be—
  (a) made to the Scottish Ministers in such form, and
  (b) accompanied by such evidence,
as the Scottish Ministers require.
  (2) The Scottish Ministers must publicise any requirements for the time being set under subsection (1).
  (3) Once—
  (a) an individual has applied for a particular type of assistance in respect of a period or (as the case may be) event, and
  (b) the Scottish Minsters have made a determination of the individual's entitlement to that type of assistance in respect of the period or event,
the individual cannot make another application for that type of assistance in respect of the period or event.
  (4) Despite subsection (3), an individual may make another application for a particular type of assistance in respect of an event if the latest determination of the individual's entitlement to that type of assistance in respect of the event states that the individual may make another application.
  (5) If the Scottish Ministers reject something purporting to be an application for assistance, they must inform the individual concerned of—
  (a) the decision to do that,
  (b) the reasons for it, and
  (c) the individual's right to appeal under section 61.

Withdrawal of application

13.27   **39.**—(1) An individual who has made an application for assistance may request that the Scottish Ministers disregard it.
(2) If an individual requests that an application be disregarded—
(a) the Scottish Ministers are not to make a determination of the individual's entitlement to any type of assistance on the basis of the application, and
(b) accordingly, their duty to do so under section 37 ceases to apply.
(3) A request under subsection (1) must be made in such form as the Scottish Ministers require.
(4) The Scottish Ministers must publicise any requirements for the time being set under subsection (3).

Notice of determination

13.28   **40.**—(1) Having made a determination under section 37 of an individual's entitlement to assistance, the Scottish Ministers must inform the individual—
(a) of the determination,
(b) of the reasons for it,
(c) of the individual's right under section 41 to request that the Scottish Ministers re-determine the individual's entitlement to the assistance,
(d) that the individual will have the right under section 46 to appeal to the First-tier Tribunal against the determination should the Scottish Ministers fail to deal with a request for a re-determination within the period allowed for re-determination, and
(e) if relevant, that the individual has the right to request a copy of an assessment report under section 60.
(2) The Scottish Ministers must fulfil their duty under subsection (1) in a way that leaves the individual with a record of the information which the individual can show to, or otherwise share with, others.

Re-determination by the Scottish Ministers

Right to request re-determination

13.29   **41.**—(1) An individual may request that the Scottish Ministers re-determine the individual's entitlement to a particular type of assistance after being informed (in accordance with section 40) of a determination by the Ministers of the individual's entitlement to that type of assistance.
(2) A request for a re-determination is valid only if the conditions set out in the following subsections are satisfied—
(a) subsection (3), and
(b) subsection (4) [¹ (read with section 52A)].
(3) The condition referred to in subsection (2)(a) is satisfied if the request is made in such form as the Scottish Ministers require.
(4) The condition referred to in subsection (2)(b) is satisfied if—
(a) the request is made before the end of the period prescribed by the Scottish Ministers in regulations, or
(b) in a case where the request is made after that period has ended—

(i) the individual has a good reason for not requesting a re-determination sooner (see section 42), and
(ii) the request is made before the end of the day that falls one year after the day on which the individual is informed (in accordance with section 40) of the determination [¹ (but see section 52A)].

(5) The Scottish Ministers must publicise any requirements for the time being set under subsection (3).

(6) If the Scottish Ministers decide that something purporting to be a request for a re-determination does not satisfy the condition in subsection (3), they must inform the individual concerned of—
(a) the decision,
(b) the reasons for it, and
(c) the individual's right to appeal under section 61.

AMENDMENT

1. Coronavirus (Scotland) Act 2020 s.8 and Sch 7 paras 1 and 2 (April 7, 2020).

GENERAL NOTE

Subsection (4) 13.30

For most purposes, the period prescribed for requesting a re-determination of entitlement is 31 days beginning with the day that the claimant is informed of the right to make the request (para.1 of Sch.1 to the Early Years Assistance (Best Start Grants) (Scotland) Regulations 2018, reg.6(1) of the Funeral Expense (Scotland) Regulations 2019 and reg.9(1) of the Carer's Assistance (Young Carer Grants) (Scotland) Regulations 2019.

However, the period is 42 days where child winter heating assistance is concerned (reg.9(1) of the Winter Heating Assistance for Children and Young People (Scotland) Regulations 2020) and also where disability assistance is concerned (reg.37(1) of the Disability Assistance for Children and Young People (Scotland) Regulations 2021 and reg.54(1) of the Disability Assistance for Working Age People (Scotland) Regulations 2022).

This section does not apply to Scottish child payment or carer's allowance supplement, because they are not "a type of assistance described in Chapter 2" (see s.37), but similar provision is made and 31 days is the time for applying for reconsideration in both cases (para.14(2) of the schedule of the Scottish Child Payment Regulations 2020 and para.4(2) of sch.2 of the Carer's Allowance Supplement and Young Carer Grants (Residence Requirements and Procedural Provisions) (EU Exit) (Scotland) Regulations 2020), subject to provision made for late applications.

Late request for re-determination

42.—(1) It is for— 13.31
(a) the Scottish Ministers, or
(b) on appeal under section 61, the First-tier Tribunal for Scotland,
to decide whether, for the purpose of section 41(4)(b), an individual has a good reason for not requesting a re-determination sooner.

(2) Having made a decision under subsection (1), the Scottish Ministers must inform the individual concerned—
(a) of the decision, and
(b) if the decision is that the individual has no good reason for not requesting a re-determination sooner, of—
(i) the reasons for the decision, and
(ii) the individual's right to appeal under section 61.

Duty to re-determine

13.32 **43.**—(1) On being requested under section 41 to re-determine an individual's entitlement to a particular type of assistance, the Scottish Ministers are to make a determination of the individual's entitlement to that type of assistance.

(2) The Scottish Ministers must aim to make the determination within the period allowed for re-determination.

(3) If the Scottish Ministers fail to make the determination within the period allowed for re-determination—
  (a) their duty to make the determination ends (but they may still make it), and
  (b) section 45 applies.

(4) If the Scottish Ministers make the determination (whether or not within the period allowed for re-determination), section 44 applies.

(5) The period allowed for re-determination is to be prescribed by the Scottish Ministers in regulations.

(6) The reference in subsection (1) to a request under section 41 is to a request that is valid according to subsection (2) of that section.

General Note

13.33 *Subsection (2)*
For most forms of assistance, the period allowed for re-determination is 16 working days beginning with the day that the request for a re-determination is received by the Scottish Ministers or such further period as the Scottish Ministers or the First-tier Tribunal for Scotland may allow on the ground that the claimant had a "good reason" for the delay (para.2 of Sch.1 to the (Early Years Assistance (Best Start Grants) (Scotland) Regulations 2018, reg.6(2) of the Funeral Expense (Scotland) Regulations 2019, reg.9(2) of the Carer's Assistance (Young Carer Grants) (Scotland) Regulations 2019 and reg.9(2) of the Winter Heating Assistance for Children and Young People (Scotland) Regulations 2020.

However, for disability assistance, it is 56 days (reg.37(2) of the Disability Assistance for Children and Young People (Scotland) Regulations 2021 and reg.54(2) of the Disability Assistance for Working Age People (Scotland) Regulations 2022).

This section does not apply to Scottish child payment or carer's allowance supplement, because they are not "a type of assistance described in Chapter 2" (see s.37), but similar provision is made by para.16(2) of the schedule of the Scottish Child Payment Regulations 2020 and para.6(2) of sch.2 of the Carer's Allowance Supplement and Young Carer Grants (Residence Requirements and Procedural Provisions) (EU Exit) (Scotland) Regulations 2020.

Notice of re-determination

13.34 **44.**—(1) Having made a determination under section 43 of an individual's entitlement to a particular type of assistance, the Scottish Ministers must—
  (a) inform the individual—
    (i) of the determination,
    (ii) of the reasons for it,
    (iii) of the individual's right to appeal to the First-tier Tribunal under section 46 against the determination,
    (iv) if relevant, that the individual has the right to request a copy of an assessment report under section 60, and

(b) provide the individual with a form that the individual can complete and submit to the Scottish Ministers in order to bring an appeal against the determination.

(2) The Scottish Ministers must fulfil their duty under subsection (1)(a) in a way that leaves the individual with a record of the information which the individual can show to, or otherwise share with, others.

Notice where re-determination not made timeously

45.—(1) Having failed to make a determination under section 43 of an individual's entitlement to a particular type of assistance within the period allowed for re-determination, the Scottish Ministers must—
- (a) inform the individual—
  - (i) that the individual's request for a re-determination has not been dealt with within the period allowed, and
  - (ii) that the individual therefore has the right to appeal to the First-tier Tribunal against the determination under section 37 which prompted the request for a re-determination, and
- (b) provide the individual with a form that the individual can complete and submit to the Scottish Ministers in order to bring an appeal against the determination.

(2) The Scottish Ministers must fulfil their duty under subsection (1)(a) in a way that leaves the individual with a record of the information which the individual can show to, or otherwise share with, others.

13.35

Appeal against the Scottish Ministers' determination

Right to appeal to First-tier Tribunal against determination

46.—(1) An individual may appeal to the First-tier Tribunal for Scotland—
- (a) against a determination under section 43 of the individual's entitlement to assistance, or
- (b) in a case where subsection (2) applies, against the determination under section 37 referred to in that subsection.

(2) This subsection applies where—
- (a) having been informed of a determination under section 37 of the individual's entitlement to assistance, the individual has made a request for a re-determination under section 41, and
- (b) the Scottish Ministers have failed to make a determination under section 43 in consequence of that request within the period allowed for re-determination.

13.36

GENERAL NOTE

The First-tier Tribunal for Scotland is established under s.1 of the Tribunals (Scotland) Act 2014. See the annotation to that provision (below) and, for procedure in social security cases, see the First-tier Tribunal for Scotland Social Security Chamber (Procedure) Regulations 2018 (also below).

Note that separate, and more limited, provision is made by s.61 for appeals against process decisions.

Neither this section nor s.61 applies to Scottish child payment or carer's allowance supplement (see section 37), but similar rights of appeal are provided in respect of those benefits under Part 4 of the schedule of the Scottish Child Payment

13.37

Regulations 2020 and Part 3 of sch.2 of the Carer's Allowance Supplement and Young Carer Grants (Residence Requirements and Procedural Provisions) (EU Exit) (Scotland) Regulations 2020.

Initiating an appeal

13.38
47.—(1) In order to bring an appeal under section 46 against a determination, an individual must submit to the Scottish Ministers the form provided under section 44 or (as the case may be) 45 in relation to the determination.

(2) On receiving a form that they provided under section 44 or 45, the Scottish Ministers must send—
  (a) the form, and
  (b) the information held by them that they used to make the determination in question, to the First-tier Tribunal.

(3) Having complied with subsection (2), the Scottish Ministers must inform the individual to whom the determination in question relates that they have done so.

(4) In this section, references to a form include a copy of a form.

(5) For the avoidance of doubt, the form that the Scottish Ministers provide under section 44 or 45 need not be a physical form.

(6) Scottish Tribunal Rules providing for the form and manner in which an appeal under section 46 is to be brought may not displace the effect of subsection (1), but this section is otherwise without prejudice to what may be provided under any power to make Scottish Tribunal Rules.

Deadline for appealing

13.39
48.—(1) An appeal under section 46—
  (a) may be brought without the First-tier Tribunal's permission if an appeal application is made within the period of 31 days beginning with the day the relevant event occurred,
  (b) may be brought only with the First-tier Tribunal's permission if an appeal application is made after the period mentioned in paragraph (a),
  (c) may not be brought if an appeal application has not been made within the period of one year beginning with the day the relevant event occurred [¹ but see section 52A)].

(2) In subsection (1)—
  (a) "the relevant event" means—
    (i) in the case of an appeal against a determination under section 43, the individual to whom the determination relates being informed of it in accordance with section 44,
    (ii) in the case of an appeal against a determination under section 37, the individual to whom the determination relates being informed (in accordance with section 45) that the individual has the right to appeal against it,
  (b) an appeal application is made when a form, that relates to the determination in question and has been completed to the extent that Scottish Tribunal Rules require, is received by the Scottish Ministers having been submitted in accordance with section 47(1).

(3) The First-tier Tribunal may give permission under subsection (1)(b) for an appeal to be brought only if it is satisfied that there is a good reason for the application not having been made sooner.

(2018 asp 9 s.48)

AMENDMENT

1. Coronavirus (Scotland) Act 2020 s.8 and Sch.7 paras 1 and 3 (April 7, 2020).

First-tier Tribunal's power to determine entitlement

49.—In an appeal under section 46 against a determination of an individual's entitlement to a particular type of assistance, the First-tier Tribunal may—
  (a) uphold the determination, or
  (b) make its own determination of the individual's entitlement to the type of assistance in question.

13.40

The determination of entitlement

Decisions comprising determination

50.—(1) A determination of an individual's entitlement to a particular type of assistance consists of—
  (a) a decision about whether or not the eligibility rules prescribed in the applicable regulations are satisfied in the individual's case,
  (b) if those rules are satisfied, a decision (taken in accordance with the applicable regulations) about what assistance of the type in question the individual is entitled to be given,
  (c) if the determination is to be made on the basis that the individual has ongoing entitlement to the type of assistance in question (see section 51), a decision about what assistance of the type in question the determination is to entitle the individual to be given in the future, and
  (d) if the determination is of an individual's entitlement to assistance in respect of an event, a decision about whether the individual's application for assistance in respect of the event is possibly premature.

13.41

(2) If it is decided under subsection (1)(d) that an individual's application for assistance in respect of an event is possibly premature, the determination must include a statement that the individual may make another application for assistance in respect of the event.

(3) An individual's application for assistance in respect of an event is possibly premature for the purpose of subsection (1)(d) if—
  (a) the decision under subsection (1)(a) is that the eligibility rules prescribed in the applicable regulations are not satisfied in the individual's case, and
  (b) it is possible that circumstances may change so that, in relation to the event in question, those rules will be satisfied in the individual's case.

(4) In this section, "the applicable regulations" means the regulations made under the section in Chapter 2 that describes the type of assistance in question.

Determination on basis of ongoing entitlement

51.—(1) The Scottish Ministers may by regulations—

13.42

1463

(a) provide that a determination of an individual's entitlement to a specified type of assistance is to be made on the basis that the individual has ongoing entitlement to that type of assistance, and
(b) provide for exceptions to any provision made by virtue of paragraph (a).

(2) Regulations making provision by virtue of subsection (1)(a) are also to—
  (a) prescribe the time, or times, at which an individual is to become entitled to be given assistance under a determination made on the basis that the individual has ongoing entitlement, [¹ . . .].
[¹ (aa) make provision, in accordance with schedule 11, about—
    (i) the circumstances in which an individual who has an entitlement to assistance in respect of a period under such a determination is not to become entitled to be given some or all of that assistance at the time at which the individual otherwise would in accordance with provision under paragraph (a), and
    (ii) in that event, how and when the individual is to become entitled to be given that assistance, and]
  (b) provide that a decision about what assistance the individual is to become entitled to be given under such a determination in respect of any future period is to be taken in accordance with the applicable regulations on the strength of such assumptions as are specified.

(3) Without prejudice to the generality of subsection (2)(b), the assumptions that may be specified include an assumption that the eligibility rules prescribed in the applicable regulations will continue to be satisfied in an individual's case for a specified duration or indefinitely.

[¹ (3A) Schedule 11 makes provision about the exercise of the power conferred by subsection (2)(aa).]

(4) In this section—
"the applicable regulations" means the regulations made under the section in Chapter 2 that describes the type of assistance in question,
"specified" means specified by regulations under this section.

AMENDMENT

1. Social Security Administration and Tribunal Membership (Scotland) Act 2020 s.12 (1) and (2) (July 26, 2021).

Determination without application

13.43   52.—(1) The Scottish Ministers may by regulations provide that, in such circumstances as the regulations specify, the Scottish Ministers are to make a determination of an individual's entitlement to a particular type of assistance without receiving an application.

(2) The Scottish Ministers may by regulations make provision about the information that is to be used, and the assumptions that are to be made, in making a determination when required to do so by regulations under subsection (1).

GENERAL NOTE

13.44   For regulations made under this section, see para.2 of sch.1 to the Early Years Assistance (Best Start Grants) (Scotland) Regulations 2018, reg.4 of the Funeral

Expense (Scotland) Regulations 2019, reg.11 of the Carer's Assistance (Young Carer Grants) (Scotland) Regulations 2019 and regs 5 to 8 of the Winter Heating Assistance for Children and Young People (Scotland) Regulations 2020. Although this section does not apply to Scottish child payment or carer's allowance supplement (see section 37), separate provision is made in Part 2 of the Schedule of the Scottish Child Payment Regulations 2020 and regs 7 to 9 of the Carer's Allowance Supplement and Young Carer Grants (Residence Requirements and Procedural Provisions) (EU Exit) (Scotland) Regulations 2020.

It is apparent from s.37 that "application" in this section means an application for assistance. These powers to make regulations therefore to enable Scottish Ministers not only to make provision for assistance to be awarded without an application but also to provide for determinations that have the effect of superseding earlier determinations (see s.27).

[1 *Coronavirus: relaxation of deadlines*

Re-determination and appeal deadlines

52A.—(1) A request for a re-determination satisfies the condition in subsection (4) of section 41, despite being made after the expiry of the period described in paragraph (b) of that subsection, if the person deciding whether the individual has a good reason for not requesting a re-determination sooner decides that the individual has a good reason that is related to coronavirus.

(2) An appeal may be brought under section 46, despite the appeal application being made after the expiry of the period described in paragraph (c) of subsection (1) of section 48, if the First-tier Tribunal gives permission for the appeal to be brought under paragraph (b) of that section on the basis of being satisfied that the good reason for the application not being made sooner is related to coronavirus.

(3) Any provision of Scottish Tribunal Rules that would (but for this subsection) have the effect of precluding an appeal being brought by virtue of subsection (2) is to be disregarded to the extent that it would have that effect.

(4) In this section, "coronavirus" has the meaning given by section 1 of the Coronavirus (Scotland) Act 2020.]

13.45

AMENDMENT

1. Coronavirus (Scotland) Act 2020 s.8 and Sch 7 paras. 1 and 4 (April 7, 2020).

GENERAL NOTE

This section and s.52B were introduced by way of amendment rather than modification and so, although the provision introducing them expired on September 29, 2020, they remain effective. However, of course, they have effect only insofar as delay "is related to coronavirus". Section 1 of the Coronavirus (Scotland) Act 2020, which defines "coronavirus" as "severe acute respiratory syndrome coronavirus 2 (SARS-CoV-2)" and is applied for these purposes by ss. 52A(4) and 52B(4) of this Act, remains in force for these purposes, by virtue of reg.2 of the Coronavirus (Scotland) Acts (Saving Provision) Regulations 2022 (SSI 2022/261), notwithstanding that it has expired for most other purposes.

Although this section does not apply to Scottish child payment or carer's allowance supplement (see section 37), separate provision is made by para.19 of sch.2 of the Carer's Allowance Supplement and Young Carer Grants Regulations 2020 for cases where delay in a carer's allowance supplement case is for a good reason that is related to coronavirus.

13.46

[¹ Applications for assistance

52B.—(1) Subsection (2) applies where regulations under Chapter 2 make an individual's eligibility for assistance in respect of a period or event depend (in any way) on an application being made by a particular time.

(2) The person determining an individual's entitlement to the assistance may treat the individual's application as having been made by that time if satisfied that the reason for its not being made sooner is related to coronavirus.

(3) For the avoidance of doubt, regulations that make a person's age at the time of making an application material to the determination of an individual's entitlement to assistance are to be understood to make the individual's eligibility depend on the application being made by a particular time (namely the time at which the person ceases to be the specified age or fall within the specified age bracket).

(4) In this section, "coronavirus" has the meaning given by section 1 of the Coronavirus (Scotland) Act 2020.]

AMENDMENT

1. Coronavirus (Scotland) Act 2020 s.8 and Sch 7 paras. 1 and 4 (April 7, 2020).

GENERAL NOTE

See the note to s.52A and see further *CD v Social Security Scotland* [2024] UT 12.

CHAPTER 4

FURTHER PROVISION ABOUT DETERMINING ENTITLEMENT

Identifying possible eligibility

Duty to inform about possible eligibility

53. *Renumbered as 84C.*

Obtaining information to make determination

Obligation to provide information on request

54.—(1) When—
[¹ (a) the Scottish Ministers are either—
   (i) determining an individual's entitlement to assistance (whether under section 37 or 43), or
   (ii) considering whether regulations under section 52 require them to make a determination of an individual's entitlement to assistance without receiving an application, and
(b) they require further information in order to satisfy themselves about any matter material to the making of the determination of entitlement or (as the case may be) to their consideration of whether they are required to make a determination without receiving an application,]

they may request that the individual provide them with the information within such period as they specify.

[¹(1A) If—
(a) the Scottish Ministers are either—
  (i) determining the individual's entitlement to a type of assistance that the individual has ongoing entitlement to, or
  (ii) considering whether regulations under section 52 require them to make a determination of the individual's entitlement to assistance without receiving an application,
(b) the individual fails to provide the requested information by the end of the period specified under subsection (1), and
(c) it is the first time that the individual has failed to provide the Scottish Ministers with the requested information within a specified period since they began making the determination or considering the matter mentioned in paragraph (a)(ii),
the Scottish Ministers may issue a decision to suspend the assistance to the individual in accordance with regulations under section 51(2)(aa).

(1B) Where the Scottish Ministers issue such a decision, they must, at the same time, request that the individual provide them with the information within such further period as they specify.]

(2) If the individual fails to provide the requested information by the end of the [¹ the period specified under subsection (1) or (1B)] the Scottish Ministers may, without further consideration, proceed to make the determination on the basis that the eligibility rules prescribed in the applicable regulations are not satisfied in the individual's case (see section 50).

(3) For the avoidance of doubt, the information which the Scottish Ministers may request an individual to provide under subsection (1) includes the results of an assessment, including one which the individual has not undergone at the time the request is made.

[¹ (4) The reference in subsection (1A)(a) to an individual having ongoing entitlement to a type of assistance is to an individual being entitled to be given the type of assistance in question under section 24 under a determination made on the basis that the individual has ongoing entitlement to that type of assistance.]

AMENDMENT

1. Social Security Administration and Tribunal Membership (Scotland) Act 2020 s.12(1) and (3) (July 26, 2021).

Requirement to justify assessment requests

55.—(1) This section applies to a request for information from an individual under section 54(1) if fulfilling the request would require the individual to undergo an assessment.

(2) When making the request, the Scottish Ministers must inform the individual why they consider requiring the individual to undergo an assessment to be the only practicable way to obtain the information.

(3) If the individual would have to undergo a face-to-face assessment in order to fulfil the request, when making the request the Scottish Ministers must also inform the individual what consideration they have given to—
(a) any preference the individual has expressed to them concerning where and how assessments are carried out,

(b) whether the assessment could be carried out another way,
(c) what distance (if any) they expect the individual will have to travel in order to attend the assessment,
(d) the extent to which travelling to attend the assessment may—
  (i) cause the individual distress, or
  (ii) adversely affect the individual's health.

(4) In subsection (3), "face-to-face assessment" means an assessment involving—
(a) the individual, and
(b) the assessor,
being physically in the same place at the same time.

General Note

13.52 This section came into force on January 17, 2022, at the same time as ss. 12 to 14 and 60.

Duty to notify change of circumstances

13.53 **56.**—(1) The Scottish Ministers may place a duty to notify them about a change in circumstances on a person to whom subsection (3), (4) or (5) applies.

(2) The Scottish Ministers place a duty under subsection (1) on a person by informing the person—
(a) of the changes in circumstances which the person has a duty to notify them about,
(b) of the way in which the person is to notify them, and
(c) that failing to notify them about a change in any of those circumstances in that way may be an offence under section 72.

(3) This subsection applies to an individual who is to be given assistance under section 24 under a determination made on the basis that the individual has ongoing entitlement to the type of assistance in question.

(4) This subsection applies to a person acting on behalf of an individual to whom subsection (3) applies in relation to any application for the assistance or the determination of the individual's entitlement.

(5) This subsection applies to a person to whom payments are to be made under section 24 by way of assistance to another person under a determination made on the basis that that other person has ongoing entitlement to the type of assistance in question.

Lifting of duty to notify change of circumstances

13.54 **57.**—(1) A duty to notify the Scottish Ministers about a change of circumstances placed on a person under section 56 ceases to apply when—
(a) it is lifted under subsection (2), or
(b) it stops being the case that a change in any of the circumstances to which the duty relates can affect someone's entitlement to be given assistance under section 24.

(2) The Scottish Ministers may lift a duty placed on a person under section 56 by informing the person that the duty is lifted.

(2018 asp 9 s.57)

(3) Under subsection (2), the Scottish Ministers may lift a duty as it relates to some or all of the changes in circumstances which the person has a duty to notify them about.

Appointees

58. *Repealed.*

GENERAL NOTE

This section was repealed by s.2(2) of the Social Security Administration and Tribunal Membership (Scotland) Act 2020, with effect from January 24, 2022, when it was effectively replaced by the new s.85B of this Act.

Support during discussions and assessments

Right to support

59.—(1) The Scottish Ministers must comply with an individual's wish to have another person ("a supporter") present during any discussion or assessment relating to the individual's entitlement to a type of assistance described in Chapter 2, unless the wish is unreasonable.

(2) The Scottish Ministers' duty under subsection (1) includes ensuring that any person acting on their behalf complies with such a wish, unless the wish is unreasonable.

(3) The role of a supporter is to support the individual in question during the discussion or (as the case may be) assessment, and includes making representations on the individual's behalf.

(4) Nothing in this section is to be read as requiring the Scottish Ministers to provide or pay for a supporter.

Access to reports

Right to reports used in determining entitlement

60.—(1) If an individual requests it, the Scottish Ministers must give the individual a copy of any assessment report held by the Ministers that they took into account in making a determination of the individual's entitlement to assistance.

(2) Subsection (1) does not require the Scottish Ministers to provide an individual with information that they are exempt from the obligation to provide to the individual under Article 15 of the [1 UK GDPR] (whether by virtue of an enactment or otherwise).

[1 (3) In subsection (2), "the UK GDPR" has the meaning given in section 3(10) of the Data Protection Act 2018.]

AMENDMENT

1. Data Protection, Privacy and Electronic Communications (Amendments etc) (EU Exit) Regulations 2019 (S.I. 2019/419) Sch.3, para.26 (December 31, 2020).

General Note

13.59 Although amended in 2020, this section did not come into force until January 17, 2022, the same time as ss. 12 to 14 and 55.

Right to appeal Scottish Ministers' process decisions

Appeal to First-tier Tribunal against process decisions

13.60 **61.**—(1) An individual may appeal to the First-tier Tribunal for Scotland against a decision by the Scottish Ministers—
(a) to reject something purporting to be an application for assistance (see section 38),
(b) that something purporting to be a request for a re-determination does not satisfy the condition in section 41(3),
(c) that an individual has no good reason for not requesting a re-determination sooner (see section 42).
(2) An appeal under this section—
(a) may be brought without the First-tier Tribunal's permission within the period of 31 days beginning with the day the individual was informed of the decision in accordance with this Act,
(b) may be brought only with the First-tier Tribunal's permission after the period mentioned in paragraph (a),
(c) may not be brought after the end of the period of one year beginning with the day the individual was informed of the decision in accordance with this Act.
(3) The First-tier Tribunal may give permission under subsection (2)(b) for an appeal to be made only if it is satisfied that there is a good reason for the appeal not having been made sooner.
(4) A decision by the First-tier Tribunal about—
(a) the outcome of an appeal under this section, or
(b) whether to give permission under subsection (2)(b) for an appeal to be brought, is final.
(5) Accordingly (and without prejudice to the generality of subsection (4)), any such decision by the First-tier Tribunal may be neither—
(a) reviewed under section 43 of the Tribunals (Scotland) Act 2014, nor
(b) appealed against under section 46 of that Act.

General Note

13.61 Neither s.46 nor this section applies to Scottish child payment or carer's allowance supplement (see section 37), but similar rights of appeal are provided in respect of those benefits under Part 4 of the schedule of the Scottish Child Payment Regulations 2020 and Part 3 of Sch.2 of the Carer's Allowance Supplement and Young Carer Grants (Residence Requirements and Procedural Provisions) (EU Exit) (Scotland) Regulations 2020.

Presumption about when information is received

Presumption for purposes of sections 41, 48 and 61

13.62 **62.**—(1) Subsection (2) applies in relation to the references in sections 41, 48 and 61 to someone being informed of something by the Scottish Ministers in accordance with a provision of this Act.

(2) Where, in order to fulfil their duty to inform an individual of something, the Scottish Ministers send information—
  (a) through the postal service to the last known address the Scottish Ministers have for the individual, or
  (b) by email to the email address most recently provided to the Scottish Ministers by the individual for the purposes of this Act,
the individual is to be taken to have received the information 48 hours after it is sent by the Scottish Ministers unless the contrary is shown.

[1 *Non-disclosure of health information*

Non-disclosure of information about individual's health

62A.—(1) This section applies in relation to a duty of the Scottish Ministers arising from section 38(5), 40(1), 41(6), 42(2), 44(1) or 53(2) to inform a person ("the recipient") of certain things in connection with the determination of an individual's entitlement to assistance.
(2) Nothing in the duty is to be regarded as requiring the Scottish Ministers to disclose information if subsection (3) applies to it.
(3) This subsection applies to information if—
  (a) it relates to the physical or mental health of the individual, and
  (b) a registered medical practitioner or a registered nurse has informed the Scottish Ministers that disclosure of the information would be likely to cause serious harm to the physical or mental health of the recipient.]

AMENDMENT

1. Social Security Administration and Tribunal Membership (Scotland) Act 2020 s.3 (July 26, 2021).

CHAPTER 5

RECOVERY OF VALUE OF ASSISTANCE

Assistance given in error

Liability for assistance given in error

63.—(1) An individual is liable to pay the Scottish Ministers the value of any assistance that was given to the individual due to an error (but see section 64).
(2) For the avoidance of doubt, the individual's liability under subsection (1) is limited to the difference in value between—
  (a) the assistance that was given, and
  (b) the assistance (if any) that would have been given had the error not been made.
(3) If the assistance was given in a form other than money, its value for the purposes of this section is what giving it cost the Scottish Ministers (excluding any administration costs).
(4) In this section and section 64, references to an error are to—

(a) an error in the performance of a function conferred by virtue of this Part, including a decision under section 50(1) being made—
  (i) wrongly, or
  (ii) correctly but on the basis of—
    (A) incorrect information, or
    (B) an assumption which proves to be wrong,
(b) a new decision under section 50(1) not being made after an assumption on the basis of which an earlier decision was made has proved to be wrong.

Exclusion from liability

13.65   64.—(1) An individual has no liability under section 63(1) in respect of assistance given due to an error if the error is neither—
  (a) the individual's fault, nor
  (b) the kind of error that an individual could reasonably be expected to notice.
(2) For the purpose of this section, an error is an individual's fault if it is caused or contributed to by the individual—
  (a) providing false or misleading information,
  (b) failing to notify the Scottish Ministers about a change in circumstances in breach of a duty to do so under section 56, or
  (c) causing another person to do either of those things.
(3) In considering whether an error is of a kind that an individual could reasonably be expected to notice, the following are amongst the matters to which regard is to be had—
  (a) the extent to which the value of the assistance given in error exceeds the value of the assistance that would have been given (if any) had the error not been made,
  (b) whether any information given to the individual by the Scottish Ministers prior to, or immediately after, the assistance being given would have alerted a reasonable person to the fact that a decision had been, or was to be, made on the basis of incorrect information or a wrong assumption.
(4) In—
  (a) subsection (2)(a), the reference to providing information includes making a statement,
  (b) subsection (3)(b), the reference to information given to the individual by the Scottish Ministers does not include information explaining why the Ministers consider the assistance to have been given in error.

Consideration for debtor's circumstances

13.66   65.—(1) This section applies to decisions of the Scottish Ministers about—
  (a) whether to seek to recover money owed under section 63, and
  (b) the method by which money owed under that section is to be recovered.
(2) In making a decision to which this section applies, the Scottish Ministers must have regard to the financial circumstances of the individual who owes the money (so far as those circumstances are known to the Ministers).

66. *Omitted.*

Exclusion of other rights of recovery

67.—(1) An individual given assistance in error has no non-statutory obligation based on redress of unjustified enrichment to pay the value of that assistance to the Scottish Ministers.

(2) In subsection (1)—
(a) "non-statutory obligation" means an obligation that arises from a rule of law rather than an enactment,
(b) the reference to assistance being given in error is to be construed in accordance with section 63(4).

68. *Repealed*

GENERAL NOTE

This section was repealed by s.14 of the Social Security Administration and Tribunal Membership (Scotland) Act 2020 with effect from November 11, 2020. It was effectively replaced by the new s.87A of this Act, which similarly confers on Scottish Ministers a power to transfer to the First-tier Tribunal for Scotland some of the jurisdiction of sheriffs in relation to the recovery of assistance given in error.

Liability where assistance given for period after death

69.—(1) An individual's estate is liable to pay the Scottish Ministers the value of any assistance that was given to the individual under section 24 in respect of a period after the individual's death.

(2) For the avoidance of doubt, assistance may be regarded as having been given to an individual for the purposes of this section despite being given after the individual's death.

Funeral expense assistance

70. *Omitted*

CHAPTER 6

OFFENCES

71. to 74. *Omitted*
75. to 76. *Renumbered as 84A and 84B*

CHAPTER 7

UPRATING FOR INFLATION

77. to 78. *Renumbered as 86A and 86B*

Social Security (Scotland) Act 2018

PART 3

SUPPLEMENTING ASSISTANCE UNDER OTHER ENACTMENTS

Top up of reserved benefits

Power to provide for top up

13.73   **79.** —(1) The Scottish Ministers may by regulations provide for financial assistance to be given to an individual who —
   (a) is entitled to a reserved benefit, and
   (b) appears to the Scottish Ministers to require financial assistance (in addition to any amount the individual receives by way of reserved benefit) for the purpose, or one of the purposes, for which the benefit is being provided.
(2) The power conferred by subsection (1) includes the power to make provision about —
   (a) determining entitlement (including specifying further eligibility rules that are to be used to determine whether an individual is entitled to the assistance),
   (b) the amount of assistance,
   (c) applications for assistance,
   (d) obtaining information,
   (e) appeals,
   (f) assistance given in error,
[1 (g) offences.]
(3) In this section and section 80, "reserved benefit" means a benefit which is to any extent a reserved matter within the meaning of schedule 5 of the Scotland Act 1998.

AMENDMENT

1. Social Security Administration and Tribunal Membership (Scotland) Act 2020 s.4(2) (November 11, 2020).

GENERAL NOTE

13.74   The Scottish Child Payment Regulations are made under this section.

Restrictions on power

13.75   **80.** —(1) Regulations under section 79 may not provide for financial assistance to be given to meet or help to meet housing costs.
(2) Regulations under section 79 may not provide for financial assistance to be given where the need for the assistance arises solely from reduction, non-payability or suspension of a reserved benefit as a result of an individual's conduct (for example, non-compliance with work-related requirements relating to the benefit).
(3) But subsection (2) does not prevent assistance from being given where the need for the assistance in question —
   (a) also arises from some exceptional event or exceptional circumstances, and
   (b) is immediate.

[¹ (4) The maximum penalty that may be provided for in regulations under section 79 in respect of an offence under those regulations is —
(a) on summary conviction —
   (i) imprisonment for a term not exceeding 12 months,
   (ii) a fine not exceeding the statutory maximum, or
   (iii) both,
(b) on conviction on indictment —
   (i) imprisonment for a term not exceeding 5 years,
   (ii) a fine, or
   (iii) both.]

AMENDMENT

1. Social Security Administration and Tribunal Membership (Scotland) Act 2020 s.4(2) (November 11, 2020).

80A. *Omitted.*

Carer's allowance: temporary provision

Carer's Allowance Supplement

81.—(1) The Scottish Ministers must make a payment (a "carer's allowance supplement") to qualifying individuals in respect of each of the following periods of each financial year—
(a) 1 April to 30 September, and
(b) 1 October to 31 March.
[² (1A) A qualifying individual is an individual to whom subsection (2) or (2A) applies.]
(2) [²This subsection applies to] an individual who, on the qualifying date, was—
[⁴(a) in receipt of—
   (i) a carer's allowance under section 70 of the Social Security Contributions and Benefits Act 1992, or
   (ii) carer support payment under the Carer's Assistance (Carer Support Payment) (Scotland) Regulations 2023 (SSI 2023/302), and]
(b) resident in Scotland.
[² (2A) This subsection applies to an individual whom the Scottish Ministers have determined in accordance with Part 2 of the Carer's Allowance Supplement and Young Carers Grants (Residence Requirements and Procedural Provisions) (EU Exit) (Scotland) Regulations 2020 (SSI 2020/475)—
(a) met the eligibility conditions in subsection (9) on the qualifying date (where the qualifying date is before IP completion day),
(b) met the eligibility conditions in subsection (11) on the qualifying date (where the qualifying date is after IP completion day and the individual has rights arising from a relevant EU regulation), or
(c) met the eligibility conditions in subsection (13) on the qualifying date (where the qualifying date is after IP completion day and the individual has rights arising from the UK-Ireland convention mentioned in that subsection).]
(3) The qualifying date is a date determined by the Scottish Ministers falling within the period to which the payment relates.

(4) The amount of a carer's allowance supplement is to be calculated according to the following formula [¹ . .] [³ (but see also subsection (4B))]—

(JSA − CA) × 26

where—

JSA is whichever is the higher of—
- (a) the weekly amount specified in regulation 79(1)(c) of the Jobseeker's Allowance Regulations 1996 (SI 1996/207) as it has effect on the qualifying date, and
- (b) that amount as it would have effect on the qualifying date if it were adjusted for inflation in accordance with subsection (5), and

CA is the weekly rate of carer's allowance specified in Part 3 of schedule 4 of the Social Security Contributions and Benefits Act 1992 as it has effect in Scotland on the qualifying date.

[¹ (4A) . . .]

[³ (4B) The amount of a carer's allowance supplement in respect of the period of 1 October 2021 to 31 March 2022 is £231.40 greater than that calculated according to the formula in subsection (4).]

(5) The Scottish Ministers must, before the start of each new tax year, beginning with the first new tax year beginning after this section comes into force—
- (a) calculate what the weekly amount specified in regulation 79(1)(c) of the Jobseeker's Allowance Regulations 1996 ("the JSA Regulations") would be if it were adjusted for inflation,
- (b) publish a statement explaining how they have calculated inflation for this purpose.

(6) In calculating the amount for the purpose of subsection (5)(a), the Scottish Ministers may take account of any change in the weekly amount specified in regulation 79(1)(c) of the JSA Regulations since this section came into force.

(7) For the purposes of subsection (5), a tax year means a period beginning with 6 April in one year and ending with 5 April in the next.

(8) The Scottish Ministers may by regulations modify this section so as to modify who is a qualifying individual for the purposes of this section.

[² (9) An individual met the eligibility conditions referred to in subsection (2A)(a) on a given date if, on that date, the individual—

[⁴(a) in receipt of—
- (i) a carer's allowance under section 70 of the Social Security Contributions and Benefits Act 1992, or
- (ii) carer support payment under the Carer's Assistance (Carer Support Payment) (Scotland) Regulations 2023 (SSI 2023/302),]
- (b) was an individual—
  - (i) to whom a relevant EU Regulation applied, and
  - (ii) in respect of whom the United Kingdom was competent for payment of sickness benefits in cash for the purposes of Chapter 1 of Title III of the Regulation in question,
- (c) was resident in—
  - (i) Switzerland, or
  - (ii) an EEA State other than the United Kingdom, and
- (d) had a genuine and sufficient link to Scotland.

(10) The reference in subsection (9)(d) to an individual's link to Scotland being sufficient is to it being sufficiently close that if the individual were not entitled to the carer's allowance supplement this section—
  (a) would be incompatible with EU law, or
  (b) would have been incompatible with EU law immediately before IP completion day.
(11) An individual met the eligibility conditions referred to in subsection (2A)(b) on a given date if, on that date, the individual—
[⁴(a) in receipt of—
    (i) a carer's allowance under section 70 of the Social Security Contributions and Benefits Act 1992, or
    (ii) carer support payment under the Carer's Assistance (Carer Support Payment) (Scotland) Regulations 2023 (SSI 2023/302),]
  (b) was an individual—
    (i) to whom the rules set out in a relevant EU regulation applied by virtue of—
      (A) Title III of Part 2 of the EU withdrawal agreement,
      (B) Part 3 or Article 23(4) of the Swiss citizens' rights agreement (as defined in section 39(1) of the European Union (Withdrawal Agreement) Act 2020),
      (C) Title III of the EEA EFTA separation agreement (as defined in that section), or
      (D) the agreement constituted by the exchange of letters set out in the schedule of the Family Allowances, National Insurance and Industrial Injuries (Gibraltar) Order 1974 (SI 1974/555) between the United Kingdom and Gibraltar, and
    (ii) in respect of whom the United Kingdom is, as a result, competent for payment of sickness benefits in cash,
  (c) was resident in—
    (i) Switzerland,
    (ii) an EEA State, or
    (iii) Gibraltar, and
  (d) had a genuine and sufficient link to Scotland.
(12) The reference in paragraph (d) of subsection (11) to an individual's link to Scotland being sufficient is to it being sufficiently close that if the individual were not entitled to the carer's allowance supplement this section would be incompatible with the applicable agreement mentioned in paragraph (b)(i) of that subsection.
(13) An individual met the eligibility conditions referred to in subsection (2A)(c) on a given date if, on that date, the individual—
[⁴(a) in receipt of—
    (i) a carer's allowance under section 70 of the Social Security Contributions and Benefits Act 1992, or
    (ii) carer support payment under the Carer's Assistance (Carer Support Payment) (Scotland) Regulations 2023 (SSI 2023/302),]
  (b) was an individual—
    (i) to whom the convention on social security between the Government of the United Kingdom of Great Britain and Northern Ireland and the Government of Ireland signed at Dublin on 1 February 2019, as modified from time to time in accordance with any provision of it, applied, and
    (ii) in respect of whom the United Kingdom is, as a result, competent for payment of long term care benefits,

(c) was resident in Ireland, and
(d) had a genuine and sufficient link to Scotland.

(14) The reference in paragraph (d) of subsection (13) to an individual's link to Scotland being sufficient is to it being sufficiently close that if the individual were not entitled to the carer's allowance supplement, this section would be incompatible with the convention mentioned in paragraph (b) of that subsection.

(15) In this section—

"EEA State" means—
(a) a member State of the European Union, or
(b) any other State that is a party to the agreement on the European Economic Area signed at Oporto on 2 May 1992, together with the Protocol adjusting that Agreement signed at Brussels on 17 March 1993, as modified or supplemented from time to time,

"EU law" has the meaning given by subsection (9) of section 126 of the Scotland Act 1998, or if that subsection has been repealed, the meaning given by that subsection immediately before its repeal,

"relevant EU Regulation" means—
(a) one of the following Regulations—
   (i) Council Regulation (EC) No 1408/71 of 14 June 1971 on the application of social security schemes to employed persons, to self-employed persons and to members of their families moving within the Community,
   (ii) Regulation (EC) No 883/2004 of the European Parliament and of the Council of 29 April 2004 on the coordination of social security systems, or
(b) in relation to an individual to whom the exchange of letters mentioned in subsection (11)(b)(i)(D) applies, a Regulation mentioned in paragraph (a) as it forms part of domestic law by virtue of section 3 of the European Union (Withdrawal) Act 2018.]

AMENDMENTS

1. Coronavirus (Scotland) (No.2) Act 2020 s.16(1) sch.1 para.6(2) (May 27, 2020), adding words but expiring under the Coronavirus (Extension and Expiry) (Scotland) Act 2021 s.2(8)(b) at the end of September 30, 2021.

2. Carer's Allowance Supplement and Young Carer Grants (Residence Requirements and Procedural Provisions) (EU Exit) (Scotland) Regulations 2020 (SSI 2020/475) Sch.1 paras 1 to 5 (December 24, 2020).

3. Carer's Allowance Supplement (Scotland) Act 2021 s.1 (November 16, 2021)

4. Carer's Assistance (Carer Support Payment) (Scotland) Regulations 2023 (SSI 2023/302) Sch.1 para.9(2) (November 19, 2023).

GENERAL NOTE

The temporary modification made to subs.(4) and insertion of subs.(4A) had the effect of doubling the amount of the carer's allowance supplement for the period from April 1 to September 30, 2020. The amount of a carer's allowance supplement for the period 1 October 2020 to 30 September 2021 was only the sum calculated under the formula in subs.(4), but the effect of the new subs.(4B) was again to double that amount in respect of the period from 1 October 2021 to 30 March 2022, "in recognition of the pressures unpaid carers face because of the pandemic" (*https://www.mygov.scot/carers-allowance-supplement*). Section 2 of the Carer's Allowance Supplement (Scotland) Act 2021 will insert a subs.(4C) giving Scottish Ministers a permanent power, subject to the affirmative procedure in the Scottish

Parliament, to make regulations modifying this section "so as to provide that the amount of a carer's allowance supplement in respect of such period as may be specified in the regulations is an amount greater than the amount calculated according to the formula in subsection (4)", but it has not yet been brought into force.

Power to repeal temporary provision

82.—The Scottish Ministers may by regulations— 13.79
(a) repeal section 81 and revoke any regulations made under it, and
(b) repeal this section.

PART 4

FURTHER PROVISION IN CONNECTION WITH PARTS 2 AND 3

83. to 84B. *Omitted.* 13.80

[¹ *Identifying possible eligibility*

Duty to inform about possible eligibility

84C.—(1) Subsection (2) applies if, in the course of their making a determination of an individual's entitlement to assistance [under Part 2 or (as the case may be) regulations under section 79,], it appears to the Scottish Ministers that the individual may be eligible for other assistance. 13.81
(2) The Scottish Ministers must—
(a) inform the individual that the individual may be eligible for the other assistance, and
(b) either—
 (i) provide the individual with information about how to apply for it, or
 (ii) if regulations under section 52 [, or (as the case may be) section 79] so allow, ask the individual whether they should proceed with making a determination of the individual's entitlement to the other assistance without receiving an application.
(3) Subsection (2)(b)(ii) does not preclude the Scottish Ministers from requesting further information under section 54(1) [, or (as the case may be) regulations under section 79] for the purpose of determining the individual's entitlement to the other assistance.
(4) In this section, "other assistance" means—
(a) where the determination mentioned in subsection (1) relates to an individual's entitlement to assistance under Part 2—
 (i) a different type of assistance described in Chapter 2 of that Part from the type of assistance that the determination mentioned in subsection (1) relates to,
 (ii) the same type of assistance as that determination relates to, but in respect of a different period or (as the case may be) event, or
 (iii) assistance under regulations under section 79,
(b) where the determination mentioned in subsection (1) relates to an individual's entitlement to assistance under regulations under section 79—

(i) a different type of assistance described in regulations under section 79 from the type of assistance that the determination mentioned in subsection (1) relates to,
(ii) the same type of assistance as that determination relates to, but in respect of a different period or (as the case may be) event, or
(iii) a type of assistance described in Chapter 2 of Part 2.]

AMENDMENT

1. Social Security Administration and Tribunal Membership (Scotland) Act 2020 s.9 (July 26, 2021).

GENERAL NOTE

13.82   This section was formerly s.53. It was moved and renumbered by s.9 of the Social Security Administration and Tribunal Membership (Scotland) Act 2020, which also amended subs.(4). Section 10 of the 2020 Act provides that anything done under s.53 of the 2018 Act is to be treated as having been done under this section, and any reference to s.53 in any enactment or other document is to be read accordingly.

Information-sharing

Information-sharing

13.83   **85.**—(1) The Scottish Ministers may require a person mentioned in subsection (2) to supply information held by the person to the Ministers for the purpose of a social security function.
(2) The persons are—
 (a) a local authority,
 (b) a Health Board constituted under section 2(1)(a) of the National Health Service (Scotland) Act 1978 or a Special Health Board constituted under section 2(1)(b) of that Act,
 (c) an integration joint board established by order under section 9 of the Public Bodies (Joint Working) (Scotland) Act 2014,
 (d) the Registrar General for Scotland,
 (e) the Keeper of the Records of Scotland,
 (f) the Scottish Courts and Tribunals Service,
 (g) a person specified in regulations made by the Scottish Ministers.
(3) Where information is supplied to the Scottish Ministers under subsection (1) for use for any purpose, they may use it for any other purposes for which information held by them for that purpose may be used.
(4) In subsection (1), references to information held by a person include information held by another person providing services to the person.
(5) Information held by the Scottish Ministers for the purpose of a social security function may be supplied by the Ministers to a person mentioned in subsection (2) for use for the purposes of such function of the person as is specified in regulations made by the Ministers.
(6) Where information is supplied to a person under subsection (5) for use for any purpose, the person may use it for any other purposes for which information held by the person for that purpose may be used.
(7) In subsection (5), references to information held by the Scottish Ministers include information held by a person providing services to them.

(8) Information supplied under subsection (5) must not be supplied by the recipient of the information to any other person without the authority of the Scottish Ministers.

(9) This section does not permit or require the provision of information in breach of a prohibition or restriction on the disclosure of information arising by virtue of an enactment or rule of law.

(10) In this section, "social security function" means a function of the Scottish Ministers under or by virtue of this Act.

[¹ *Appointees*

Appointment of person to act on behalf of child

85A.—(1) The Scottish Ministers may appoint a person (an "appointee") to act on behalf of a child in connection with the determination of the child's entitlement to assistance under section 24 or regulations under section 79.

(2) An appointment under subsection (1) may, if the Scottish Ministers consider it appropriate, include an appointment of the person to receive such assistance on the child's behalf.

(3) The Scottish Ministers may only appoint an appointee if it appears to them that there is no person who—
   (a) has authority to act on behalf of the child,
   (b) resides with, and has care of, the child, and
   (c) is willing, and practically able, to act on the child's behalf in relation to the matter mentioned in subsection (1).

(4) An individual who is under 16 years may not be appointed as an appointee.

(5) Where an appointee is appointed under subsection (1) to act on behalf of a child—
   (a) the appointee can do anything that a person with authority (however arising) to act on behalf of the child in relation to the determination of the child's entitlement to assistance could do in connection with the determination of the child's entitlement to assistance (including making an application for assistance),
   (b) the Scottish Ministers may request that the appointee provide them with information that the Ministers may otherwise request under section 54 or (as the case may be) the regulations under section 79 (and in the case of section 54, subsections (2) and (3) of that section apply to that request as they apply to a request made to the child),
   (c) any information that would be given to the child under or by virtue of Part 2 or (as the case may be) the regulations, must be given to the appointee instead.

[² (5A) The Scottish Ministers must consider whether to make an appointment under subsection (1), or to terminate such an appointment, if requested to do so by—
   (a) the child, or
   (b) anyone else who appears to the Ministers to—
      (i) have authority to act on behalf of the child,
      (ii) reside with, and have care of, the child, or
      (iii) have an interest in the welfare or financial affairs of the child.

(5B) Subsection (5C) applies where the Scottish Ministers are deciding whether to make or terminate an appointment under subsection (1).

(5C) In making the decision the Scottish Ministers must, insofar as practicable, have regard to the views of—
  (a) the child,
  (b) anyone who is a relevant person in relation to the child within the meaning of section 200 of the Children's Hearings (Scotland) Act 2011, and
  (c) anyone else who appears to the Ministers to have an interest in the welfare or financial affairs of the child.]

(6) The Scottish Ministers may terminate an appointment under subsection (1) at any time.

(7) In this section, "child" means an individual who is under 16 years.]

AMENDMENTS

1. Social Security Administration and Tribunal Membership (Scotland) Act 2020 s.1 (November 11, 2020).
2. Social Security Administration and Tribunal Membership (Scotland) Act 2020 s.2(3) (January 24, 2022).

[¹ Appointment of person to act in other circumstances

85B.—(1) The Scottish Ministers may appoint a person (an "appointee") to act on behalf of an individual in connection with the determination of the individual's entitlement to assistance under section 24 or regulations under section 79.

(2) An appointment under subsection (1) may, if the Scottish Ministers consider it appropriate, include an appointment of the person to receive such assistance on the individual's behalf.

(3) The Scottish Ministers may only appoint an appointee if—
  (a) the individual is 16 years or over and the conditions in subsection (4) are met, or
  (b) it appears to them that subsection (6) or (7) applies.

(4) The conditions are—
  (a) the individual indicates (in such form as the Scottish Ministers require) that the individual agrees to the appointment, and
  (b) an appropriate person certifies (in such form as the Scottish Ministers require) that in the person's opinion—
    (i) the individual is not incapable within the meaning of the Adults with Incapacity (Scotland) Act 2000,
    (ii) the individual understands the effect of the appointment,
    (iii) the individual has not been subject to any undue influence in agreeing to the appointment, and
    (iv) the person proposed to be appointed is suitable to act as the individual's appointee.

(5) The Scottish Ministers are to make regulations defining "appropriate person" for the purposes of subsection (4)(b).

(6) This subsection applies if—
  (a) the individual is deceased, and
  (b) there is no executor appointed on the individual's estate.

(7) This subsection applies if, in relation to the matter mentioned in subsection (1)—

(a) the individual is incapable within the meaning of the Adults with Incapacity (Scotland) Act 2000,
(b) there is no guardian acting or appointed under that Act,
(c) the individual's estate is not being administered by a judicial factor, and
(d) there is no other person who has authority to act on behalf of the individual and is willing to do so.

(8) An individual who is under 16 years may not be appointed as an appointee.

(9) Where an appointee is appointed under subsection (1) to act on behalf of an individual—
(a) the appointee can do anything that a relevant individual could do in connection with the determination of the individual's entitlement to assistance (including making an application for assistance),
(b) the Scottish Ministers may request that the appointee provide them with information that the Ministers may otherwise request under section 54 or (as the case may be) the regulations under section 79 (and in the case of section 54, subsections (2) and (3) of that section apply to that request as they apply to a request made to the individual),
(c) any information that would be given to the individual under or by virtue of Part 2 or (as the case may be) the regulations, must be given to the appointee instead.

(10) In subsection (9)(a), "relevant individual" means—
(a) in the case of an appointment by virtue of subsection (3)(a), the individual in relation to whom the appointment is made,
(b) in the case of an appointment by virtue of subsection (6), an executor appointed on the individual's estate,
(c) in the case of an appointment by virtue of subsection (7), a person with authority (however arising) to act on behalf of the individual in relation to the determination of the individual's entitlement to assistance.

(11) The Scottish Ministers may terminate an appointment under subsection (1) at any time.

(12) The Scottish Ministers must—
(a) terminate an appointment made by virtue of subsection (3)(a) if the individual withdraws agreement to it,
(b) consider whether to terminate an appointment made by virtue of subsection (3)(a) if requested to do so by anyone who appears to the Ministers to have an interest in the welfare or financial affairs of the individual.

(13) The Scottish Ministers must consider whether to terminate an appointment made by virtue of subsection (6) if requested to do so by anyone who appears to the Ministers to have an interest in the financial affairs of the individual.

(14) The Scottish Ministers must consider whether to make an appointment by virtue of subsection (7), or to terminate such an appointment, if requested to do so by—
(a) the individual, or
(b) anyone else who appears to the Ministers to—
   (i) have authority to act on behalf of the individual, or
   (ii) have an interest in the welfare or financial affairs of the individual.

(15) Subsection (16) applies where the Scottish Ministers are deciding whether to make an appointment by virtue of subsection (7) or to terminate such an appointment.

(16) In making the decision, the Scottish Ministers must, insofar as practicable, have regard to—
  (a) the wishes and feelings of the individual, and
  (b) the views of anyone else who appears to the Ministers to have an interest in the welfare or financial affairs of the individual.]

AMENDMENT

1. Social Security Administration and Tribunal Membership (Scotland) Act 2020 s.2(4) (December 23, 2020, in part and for limited purposes, and January 24, 2022, fully but for limited purposes).

GENERAL NOTE

13.86 This section is only in force for the purpose of allowing appointments in the circumstances described in subs.(3)(b), rather than subs.(3)(a). Until January 24, 2022, only subs.(1) to (11) were in force and then only in relation to child payment under s.79.

This provision not only applies to assistance under Part 2 of this Act but is also applied for the purposes of carer's allowance supplement under s.81 (see para.18 of Sch.2 of the Carer's Allowance Supplement and Young Carer Grants (Residence Requirements and Procedural Provisions) (EU Exit) (Scotland) Regulations 2020.

[¹ **Guidelines for decisions about appointees**

13.87 85C.—(1) The Scottish Ministers—
  (a) must prepare guidelines governing their decisions in connection with appointments under sections 85A and 85B,
  (b) may revise the guidelines,
  (c) must make the latest version of the guidelines publicly available by such means as they consider appropriate.

(2) The guidelines must, in particular, set out—
  (a) the steps that the Scottish Ministers will take to determine that a person is suitable for appointment,
  (b) how a request that an appointment be made or terminated may be made and how it will be handled,
  (c) the process by which persons with an interest in the making or termination of an appointment will be involved in those decisions,
  (d) the steps that the Scottish Ministers will take to review appointments periodically (being in any case no more than 5 years) and the process by which that will occur,
  (e) how concerns about the acts, or omissions, of an appointee may be raised and how any concerns raised will be handled.

(3) In preparing or revising the guidelines, the Scottish Ministers must have regard (among other things) to the following considerations—
  (a) that an appointment in the case of a living individual should be made only if it appears to secure a benefit in respect of the individual that cannot reasonably be achieved without the appointment,
  (b) that such an appointment should last for only so long as it continues to secure that benefit,

(c) that, so far as reasonably practicable, before decisions are made—
  (i) persons who may be affected are consulted, and
  (ii) due account is taken of their views (or, if they are incapable within the meaning of the Adults with Incapacity (Scotland) Act 2000, their wishes and feelings),
(d) that decisions should be made on the basis of good information,
(e) that decision-making processes should, so far as reasonably practicable, take account of the circumstances of individual cases,
(f) that persons who may be affected by decisions are given adequate information and support in relation to their involvement in the decision-making process.
(4) In preparing or revising the guidelines, the Scottish Ministers must consult—
  (a) the Commissioner for Children and Young People in Scotland,
  (b) the Mental Welfare Commission for Scotland,
  (c) the Public Guardian (established by section 6 of the Adults with Incapacity (Scotland) Act 2000), and
  (d) local authorities.]

AMENDMENT

1. Social Security Administration and Tribunal Membership (Scotland) Act 2020 s.2(5) (July 26, 2021).

85D. *Not yet in force.*

[¹ **Guidance for appointees**

85E.—(1) A person appointed under section 85A or 85B must have regard to any guidance issued by the Scottish Ministers about the way in which the role of appointee should be carried out.
(2) The Scottish Ministers must make guidance issued for the purpose of subsection (1) publicly available.]

AMENDMENT

1. Social Security Administration and Tribunal Membership (Scotland) Act 2020 s.2(7) (January 24, 2022).

86. *Not yet in force.*
86A. to 87A. *Omitted.*

PART 5

DISCRETIONARY HOUSING PAYMENTS

Local authorities' power to make payments

88.—(1) A local authority has power to give financial assistance to a qualifying individual to meet, or help towards meeting, the individual's housing costs.

(2) In subsection (1), "qualifying individual" means an individual who—
(a) is entitled to—
  (i) housing benefit, or
  (ii) an award of universal credit which includes an amount for rent, and
(b) appears to the authority to need financial assistance under subsection (1) (in addition to any assistance of a kind mentioned in paragraph (a) which the individual receives) in order to meet housing costs.

(3) For the purposes of subsection (2)(a)—
(a) "housing benefit" means housing benefit provided by virtue of a scheme under section 123 of the Social Security Contributions and Benefits Act 1992,
(b) an award of universal credit includes an amount for rent if—
  (i) the calculation of the award includes an amount under section 11 of the Welfare Reform Act 2012, and
  (ii) that amount is included (wholly or partly) in respect of a liability to make payments within the meaning of paragraph 2 of schedule 1 of the Universal Credit Regulations 2013 (S.I. 2013/376).

(4) Financial assistance under this section may be given to an individual by way of—
(a) payment to the individual,
(b) payment to another person to meet, or contribute towards meeting, any liability the individual has to that person,
(c) deduction from any liability the individual has to the authority giving the assistance which is connected to housing costs,
(d) any combination of the ways mentioned in the preceding paragraphs.

Restrictions on power to make payments

89.—(1) Financial assistance may not be given under section 88 by way of a loan.

(2) Financial assistance may not be given under section 88 where the need for the assistance arises solely from reduction, non-payability or suspension of a reserved benefit as a result of an individual's conduct (for example, non-compliance with work-related requirements relating to the benefit).

(3) But subsection (2) does not prevent assistance from being given where the need for the assistance in question—
(a) also arises from some exceptional event or exceptional circumstances, and
(b) is immediate.

(4) In subsection (2), "reserved benefit" means a benefit which is to any extent a reserved matter within the meaning of schedule 5 of the Scotland Act 1998.

Local authorities' duty to provide information about payments

90.—Each local authority must make available to the public resident in its area information about—
(a) how to apply to the authority for financial assistance under section 88,
(b) which housing costs the authority gives assistance in relation to,

(c) the rules the authority applies in deciding—
   (i) whether to give someone assistance,
   (ii) the amount of assistance to give, and
   (iii) what period to give assistance for,
(d) how to apply for a review challenging a decision by the authority—
   (i) to refuse to give assistance,
   (ii) as to the amount of assistance it will give, or
   (iii) as to the period for which it will give assistance.

Guidance

91.—(1) Local authorities must have regard to any guidance issued by the Scottish Ministers in connection with the exercise of the power conferred by section 88.

(2) Guidance under subsection (1) may, in particular, deal with—
(a) the rules which authorities are to apply in deciding—
   (i) whether to give someone financial assistance,
   (ii) the amount of assistance to give, and
   (iii) what period to give assistance for,
(b) the form of applications for—
   (i) assistance, and
   (ii) review of authorities' decisions about the giving of assistance,
(c) the processes which authorities are to follow in—
   (i) determining applications for assistance and review, and
   (ii) deciding whether to stop giving someone assistance,
(d) the circumstances in which authorities should, and should not, seek to recover the value of assistance given in error or following a breach of any of the conditions under which it was given.

(3) Guidance under subsection (1) may be addressed to—
(a) an authority, or more than one authority, identified in the guidance, or
(b) all authorities.

(4) Before issuing guidance under subsection (1), the Scottish Ministers must consult such body representing authorities as the Ministers think fit.

(5) As soon as reasonably practicable after issuing guidance under subsection (1), the Scottish Ministers must lay a copy of the guidance before the Scottish Parliament.

(6) The Scottish Ministers must make guidance issued under subsection (1) publicly available.

(7) The power to issue guidance under subsection (1) includes the power to—
(a) issue guidance which varies guidance issued under that subsection, and
(b) revoke guidance issued under that subsection.

Local authorities need not make payments if not funded

92.—(1) The Scottish Ministers may make grants to local authorities to fund the giving of financial assistance under section 88.

(2) Monies granted to an authority under subsection (1) may be spent only on giving financial assistance under section 88.

(3) If an authority has spent all monies granted to it under subsection (1), the authority may refuse to consider any application for financial assistance under section 88.

(4) If, by virtue of subsection (3), an authority is refusing to consider applications, it need not comply with section 90.

(5) For the avoidance of doubt, subsection (3) does not prevent an authority from considering applications or giving financial assistance under section 88 should it choose to.

Power to modify section 88

93.—(1) The Scottish Ministers may by regulations make whatever amendment to section 88 they think appropriate in consequence of—
  (a) an enactment mentioned in that section being amended, repealed or revoked, or
  (b) the creation of a reserved benefit payable in respect of a liability to make rent payments.

(2) Expressions used in subsection (1)(b) have the same meaning as they have for the purposes of exception 6 in Section F1 of Part 2 of schedule 5 of the Scotland Act 1998.

PART 6

UNIVERSAL CREDIT: PAYMENT TO JOINT CLAIMANTS

13.91 94. *Not yet in force.*

PART 7

FINAL PROVISIONS

Ancillary provision

13.92 95.—The Scottish Ministers may by regulations make any incidental, supplementary, consequential, transitional, transitory or saving provision they consider appropriate for the purposes of, or in connection with, or for giving full effect to this Act or any provision made under it.

Regulation-making powers

13.93 96.—(1) A power to make regulations conferred by this Act includes the power to make different provision for different purposes and areas.

(2) Regulations under any of the following provisions are subject to the affirmative procedure: sections 11, 13, 22(1)(e), any section in Chapter 2 of Part 2 and sections 51, 52, [¹ ...] 79, 81(8), 82, [¹ 84A], 85(2)(g) and (5), 86, [¹ 87A] and 93 and paragraph 4(2)(c) of schedule 1.

(3) Regulations under any of the following provisions are subject to the negative procedure: sections 41(4)(a) and 43(5) and paragraph 13(2) of schedule 1.

(4) Regulations under section 95—
  (a) are subject to the affirmative procedure if they add to, replace or omit any part of the text of an Act (including this Act), but

(b) otherwise are subject to the negative procedure.

(5) Regulations under section 22(1)(e), which modify the functions of the Scottish Commission on Social Security, may not be made after the Commission is established unless the Scottish Ministers have consulted the Commission about the modification.

AMENDMENT

1. Social Security Administration and Tribunal Membership (Scotland) Act 2020 s.5(1) and (8) and 14(1) and (4) (November 11, 2020).

97. *Omitted.*

98. *Repealed.*

Commencement

99.—(1) The following provisions come into force on the day after Royal Assent: this section and sections 95, 96, 97, 98 and 100.

(2) The other provisions of this Act come into force on such day as the Scottish Ministers may by regulations appoint.

(3) The power conferred by subsection (2) includes the power to make transitional, transitory or saving provision.

Short title

100.—The short title of this Act is the Social Security (Scotland) Act 2018.

Schedule 1 *Omitted.*

SCHEDULE 2

(introduced by section 28)

CARER'S ASSISTANCE REGULATIONS

PART 1

ELIGIBILITY

CHAPTER 1

ELIGIBILITY IS TO DEPEND ON BEING OR HAVING BEEN A CARER

1. (1) The regulations must be framed so that (subject to any provision of the kind described in paragraph 2) an individual's eligibility in respect of a given period depends on the individual having provided regular and substantial care during that period to another individual to whom a disability benefit is normally payable.

(2) The regulations—
   (a) are to set out the circumstances in which an individual is to be regarded as having provided regular and substantial care to another individual during a period, and
   (b) may, in particular, do so by reference to whether or not the number of hours of care provided during the period exceeds (or is deemed to exceed) a threshold specified in the regulations.

(3) In sub-paragraph (1), "disability benefit" has the meaning given in the interpretation provision in Section F1 of Part 2 of schedule 5 of the Scotland Act 1998.

2. (1) The regulations may be framed so that, despite the criterion described in paragraph 1(1) not being fulfilled in relation to a given period, an individual may nevertheless be eligible in respect of that period.

(2) Where the regulations allow an individual to be eligible in respect of a period in relation to which the criterion described in paragraph 1(1) is not fulfilled, they must be framed so that the individual's eligibility depends on the individual—
  (a) having at some time provided care to another individual who has a disability, and
  (b) as a result of doing so, having received—
    (i) carer's assistance,
    (ii) carer's allowance, or
    (iii) invalid care allowance.

(3) In sub-paragraph (2)(b), "carer's allowance" and "invalid care allowance" both mean an allowance payable under section 70 of the Social Security Contributions and Benefits Act 1992.

Chapter 2

Further Criteria

Carer's other activities

13.99   3. The regulations may make an individual's eligibility depend on—
  (a) whether or not the individual is in—
    (i) employment, or
    (ii) education,
  (b) the length of time the individual spends over a given period in—
    (i) employment, or
    (ii) education.

Multiple carers

4. The regulations may make an individual's eligibility depend on being the individual (or one of the individuals) selected through a process set out in the regulations in a case where more than one individual would otherwise be eligible as a result of providing care to the same cared-for person during a given period.

Residence and presence

5. The regulations may make an individual's eligibility depend on either or both—
  (a) the individual, and
  (b) the cared-for person,
being resident and present in a particular place.

Age

13.100   6. The regulations may make an individual's eligibility depend on the age of either or both—
  (a) the individual, and
  (b) the cared-for person.

Financial circumstances

7. The regulations may make an individual's eligibility depend on the individual's financial circumstances.

Receipt of, or eligibility for, other types of State assistance

8. The regulations may make an individual's eligibility depend on the individual—
  (a) being, or not being, in receipt of another type of assistance (whether under this Act or another enactment),
  (b) being, or not being, eligible or entitled to receive such assistance.

Application within specified period

9. The regulations may provide that an individual ceases to be eligible in respect of a given period unless, by a deadline specified in the regulations—
  (a) the individual has applied for carer's assistance in respect of the period, or
  (b) the Scottish Ministers have become required to make a determination of the individual's entitlement to carer's assistance in respect of the period by regulations under section 52.

(2018 asp 9 Sch.2)

Part 2

Assistance to be Given

Meeting liabilities

10. The regulations may provide for the carer's assistance that is to be given to an individual to be given (in whole or in part) by way of—
    (a) payment to another person in order to meet, or contribute towards meeting, any liability the individual has to that person,
    (b) deduction from any liability the individual has to the Scottish Ministers under section 63.

Restriction on giving assistance in a form other than money

11.(1) The regulations may allow carer's assistance to be given to an individual in a form other than money only if the individual (or a person acting on the individual's behalf) has agreed to the assistance being given in that form.

(2) If the regulations include provision of the kind mentioned in sub-paragraph (1), they must allow an individual (or a person acting on the individual's behalf) to withdraw agreement to being given carer's assistance in a form other than money at any time.

(3) Despite sub-paragraph (1), the regulations may provide for carer's assistance to be given (in whole or in part) by way of deduction, at a reasonable level, from any liability the individual has to the Scottish Ministers under section 63 if the individual has unreasonably refused to agree to the assistance being given in that form.

(4) For the purpose of sub-paragraph (3), "reasonable level" means a level that is reasonable having regard to the financial circumstances of the individual.

[¹ *Power to set value of assistance as nil*

11A.—(1) Provision may be made in the regulations for the value of the carer's assistance that is to be given to an individual in respect of a period to be £0, but—
   (a) such provision must be framed so as to apply by reference to at least one of the following matters—
       (i) the individual being resident and present in a particular place during the period,
       (ii) the individual being in receipt of another type of assistance (whether under this Act or another enactment) during the period, and
   (b) the Scottish Ministers may only make such provision where they consider that it would be in the interests of the individuals to whom it applies to be entitled to carer's assistance with a value of £0 in respect of a period rather than not being entitled to carer's assistance at all.

(2) Nothing in sub-paragraph (1)(a) is to be taken to preclude provision being framed so as to apply by reference to further matters in addition to those mentioned there.]

Part 3

Final Provisions

Generality of enabling power unaffected

12. Nothing in this schedule, apart from the following provisions, is to be taken to limit what may be prescribed in the regulations—
    (a) Chapter 1 of Part 1,
    (b) [¹ paragraphs 11 and 11A] in Part 2.

Interpretation

13. In this schedule—

"cared-for person" means the individual by providing care to whom the individual whose eligibility is in question has fulfilled the criterion described in paragraph 1(1) or 2(2),

"eligibility" means eligibility for carer's assistance and "eligible" means eligible for carer's assistance,

"the regulations" means regulations under section 28(2).

Social Security (Scotland) Act 2018

AMENDMENT

1. Social Security Administration and Tribunal Membership (Scotland) Act 2020 s.13(1) and (2) (July 26, 2021)

13.103   **Schedule 3** *Not yet in force.*

SCHEDULE 4

(introduced by section 30)

WINTER HEATING ASSISTANCE REGULATIONS

PART 1

ELIGIBILITY

Residence and presence

13.104   1. The regulations may make an individual's eligibility depend on the individual being resident and present in a particular place.

Age

2. The regulations may make an individual's eligibility depend on the age of either or both—
  (a) the individual, and
  (b) anyone who lives with the individual.

Financial circumstances

3. Subject to paragraph 4, the regulations may not make an individual's eligibility depend on the financial circumstances of either or both—
  (a) the individual, and
  (b) anyone who lives with the individual.

Receipt of, or eligibility for, other types of State assistance

4. The regulations may make an individual's eligibility depend on either or both the individual and anyone who lives with the individual—
  (a) being, or not being, in receipt of another type of assistance (whether under this Act or another enactment),
  (b) being, or not being, eligible or entitled to receive such assistance.

Application within specified period

5. The regulations may provide that an individual ceases to be eligible in respect of a given period unless, by a deadline specified in the regulations—
  (a) the individual has applied for winter heating assistance in respect of the period, or
  (b) the Scottish Ministers have become required to make a determination of the individual's entitlement to winter heating assistance in respect of the period by regulations under section 52.

PART 2

ASSISTANCE TO BE GIVEN

Domestic circumstances and age

13.105   6. The regulations may make the value of the winter heating assistance that is to be given to an individual depend on—
  (a) whether or not other people live with the individual,
  (b) the age of either or both—
    (i) the individual, and
    (ii) anyone who lives with the individual.

Financial circumstances

7. Subject to paragraph 8, the regulations may not make the value of the winter heating assistance that is to be given to an individual depend on the financial circumstances of either or both—
   (a) the individual, and
   (b) anyone who lives with the individual.

Receipt of, or eligibility for, other types of State assistance

8. The regulations may make the value of assistance depend on either or both the individual and anyone who lives with the individual—
   (a) being, or not being, in receipt of another type of assistance (whether under this Act or another enactment),
   (b) being, or not being, eligible to receive such assistance.

Restriction on giving assistance in a form other than money

9.(1) The regulations may allow winter heating assistance to be given to an individual in a form other than money only if the individual (or a person acting on the individual's behalf) has agreed to the assistance being given in that form.
(2) If the regulations include provision of the kind mentioned in sub-paragraph (1), they must allow an individual (or a person acting on the individual's behalf) to withdraw agreement to being given winter heating assistance in a form other than money at any time.

PART 3

FINAL PROVISIONS

Generality of enabling power unaffected

10. Nothing in this schedule, apart from the following provisions, is to be taken to limit what may be prescribed in the regulations—
    (a) paragraph 3 in Part 1,
    (b) paragraphs 7 and 9 in Part 2.

Interpretation

11. In this schedule—
"eligibility" means eligibility for winter heating assistance and "eligible" means eligible for winter heating assistance,
"the regulations" means regulations under section 30(2).

SCHEDULE 5
(introduced by section 31)

DISABILITY ASSISTANCE REGULATIONS

PART 1

ELIGIBILITY

CHAPTER 1

ELIGIBILITY IS TO DEPEND ON HAVING, OR HAVING HAD, A DISABILITY

1. (1) The regulations must be framed so that (subject to any provision of the kind described in paragraph 2) an individual's eligibility in respect of a given period depends on the individual having, during that period—
   (a) a physical or mental impairment that—

(i) has a significant and not short-term adverse effect on the individual's ability to carry out normal day-to-day activities, or
(ii) otherwise gives rise to a significant and not short-term need, or
(b) a terminal illness.

(2) The regulations must provide that an individual is to be regarded as having a terminal illness for the purpose of determining entitlement to disability assistance if, having had regard to the guidance mentioned in sub-paragraph (3), it is the clinical judgement of [¹ an appropriate healthcare professional] that the individual has a progressive disease that can reasonably be expected to cause the individual's death.

[¹ (2A) The regulations may provide that, in the situation mentioned in sub-paragraph (2B), an individual who is not resident in the United Kingdom is to be regarded as having a terminal illness despite the clinical judgement described in sub-paragraph (2) not having been formed with regard to the guidance mentioned in sub-paragraph (3).

(2B) The situation referred to in sub-paragraph (2A) is that it would not be reasonable in the circumstances to insist on a clinical judgement being provided that has been formed with regard to the guidance.

(2C) The regulations are to define "appropriate healthcare professional" for the purpose of determining entitlement to disability assistance on the basis of an individual having a terminal illness.

(2D) In defining "appropriate healthcare professional" the regulations—
(a) must provide that being a registered medical practitioner or registered nurse is a requirement for being an appropriate healthcare professional,
(b) may provide that being a registered member of a healthcare profession otherwise than as mentioned in paragraph (a) is a requirement for being an appropriate healthcare professional,
(c) may include additional requirements that a person must satisfy in order to be an appropriate healthcare professional, including by reference to a person's—
(i) skills, training, qualifications and experience,
(ii) professional relationship to the individual in question,
(iii) being authorised to act as an appropriate healthcare professional in relation to the individual in question by—
(A) a Health Board constituted under section 2(1)(a) of the National Health Service (Scotland) Act 1978,
(B) a Special Health Board constituted under section 2(1)(b) of that Act,
(C) the Scottish Ministers.
(d) may make different provision about the requirements for being an appropriate healthcare professional for the purposes of determining the entitlement to disability assistance of individuals who are resident in the United Kingdom and those who are not.]

[¹ (3) The Chief Medical Officer of the Scottish Administration is—
(a) to prepare and from time to time revise, and
(b) to make publicly available by such means as the Chief Medical Officer considers appropriate,

guidance that sets out when a progressive disease can reasonably be expected to cause an individual's death for the purpose of determining entitlement to disability assistance.

(4) Before preparing or revising guidance under sub-paragraph (3), the Chief Medical Officer must consult appropriate healthcare professionals (as defined in sub-paragraph (2C)) who are registered in the United Kingdom as members of a healthcare profession.]

2.(1) The regulations may be framed so that, despite the criterion described in paragraph 1(1) not being fulfilled in respect of a given period, an individual may nevertheless be eligible in respect of that period.

(2) Where the regulations allow an individual to be eligible in respect of a period in relation to which the criterion described in paragraph 1(1) is not fulfilled, they must be framed so that the individual's eligibility depends on the individual having had, during some other period, a physical or mental impairment of the kind described in paragraph 1(1)(a).

CHAPTER 2

FURTHER CRITERIA

Nature and extent of disability and needs

3. The regulations may make an individual's eligibility depend on the nature and extent of—

(a) the individual's impairment,
(b) the needs of the individual in consequence of the impairment.

Residence and presence

4. The regulations may make an individual's eligibility depend on the individual being resident and present in a particular place.

Age

5. The regulations may make an individual's eligibility depend on the individual's age.

Financial circumstances

6. Subject to paragraph 7, the regulations may not make an individual's eligibility depend on the financial circumstances of either or both—
(a) the individual, and
(b) anyone who lives with the individual.

Receipt of, or eligibility for, other types of State assistance

7. The regulations may make an individual's eligibility depend on the individual—
(a) being, or not being, in receipt of another type of assistance (whether under this Act or another enactment),
(b) being, or not being, eligible or entitled to receive such assistance.

Application within specified period

8. The regulations may provide that an individual ceases to be eligible in respect of a given period unless, by a deadline specified in the regulations—
(a) the individual has applied for disability assistance in respect of the period, or
(b) the Scottish Ministers have become required to make a determination of the individual's entitlement to disability assistance in respect of the period by regulations under section 52.

CHAPTER 3

SPECIAL RULES FOR TERMINAL ILLNESS CASES

No minimum period

9. The regulations may not make the eligibility of an individual who has a terminal illness depend on the individual having had the illness for any length of time.

No requirement for assessment

10. The regulations may not make the eligibility of an individual who has a terminal illness depend on the individual producing any evidence of that fact beyond a diagnosis by [1 an appropriate healthcare professional (see paragraph 1(2C))].

Eligibility from date of application

11. The regulations must be framed so that an individual who applies for disability assistance on the basis of having a terminal illness, and does have a terminal illness, is eligible, at the latest, from the day the application is made.

Entitlement to maximum amount

12. The regulations must be framed so that an individual who is eligible by reason of having a terminal illness is entitled to the maximum amount of the assistance that the individual is eligible for.

Social Security (Scotland) Act 2018

Part 2

Assistance to be Given

Chapter 1

Value

Nature and extent of disability

13.110 13. The regulations may make the value of the disability assistance that is to be given to an individual depend on the nature and extent of—
 (a) the individual's impairment,
 (b) the needs of the individual in consequence of the impairment.

Age

14. The regulations may make the value of the disability assistance that is to be given to an individual depend on the individual's age.

[¹Power to set value of assistance as nil

14A.—(1) Provision may be made in the regulations for the value of the disability assistance that is to be given to an individual in respect of a period to be £0, but—
 (a) such provision must be framed so as to apply by reference to at least one of the following matters—
   (i) the individual being resident and present in a particular place during the period,
   (ii) the individual being in receipt of another type of assistance (whether under this Act or another enactment) during the period, and
 (b) the Scottish Ministers may only make such provision where they consider that it would be in the interests of the individuals to whom it applies to be entitled to disability assistance with a value of £0 in respect of a period rather than not being entitled to disability assistance at all.
(2) Nothing in sub-paragraph (1)(a) is to be taken to preclude provision being framed so as to apply by reference to further matters in addition to those mentioned there.]

Chapter 2

Form

Meeting liabilities

13.111 15. The regulations may provide for the disability assistance that is to be given to an individual to be given (in whole or in part) by way of—
 (a) payment to another person in order to meet, or contribute towards meeting, any liability the individual has to that person,
 (b) deduction from any liability the individual has to the Scottish Ministers under section 63.

Payment to someone else

16. The regulations may provide that, if the Scottish Ministers consider it appropriate in the circumstances, the disability assistance that is to be given to an individual may be given (in whole or in part) by way of payment to another person who is to use the payment to benefit the individual entitled to the assistance.

Restriction on giving assistance in a form other than money

17. (1) The regulations may allow disability assistance to be given to an individual in a form other than money only if the individual (or a person acting on the individual's behalf) has agreed to the assistance being given in that form.
(2) If the regulations include provision of the kind mentioned in sub-paragraph (1), they must allow an individual (or a person acting on the individual's behalf) to withdraw agreement to being given disability assistance in a form other than money at any time.
(3) Despite sub-paragraph (1), the regulations may provide for disability assistance to be given (in whole or in part) by way of deduction, at a reasonable level, from any liability the

Part 2

Assistance to be given

Restriction on giving assistance in a form other than money

7.(1) The regulations may allow early years assistance to be given to an individual in a form other than money only if the individual (or a person acting on the individual's behalf) has agreed to the assistance being given in that form.

(2) If the regulations include provision of the kind mentioned in sub-paragraph (1), they must allow an individual (or a person acting on the individual's behalf) to withdraw agreement to being given early years assistance in a form other than money at any time.

Part 3

Final Provisions

Generality of enabling power unaffected

8. Nothing in this schedule, apart from the following provisions, is to be taken to limit what may be prescribed in the regulations—
   (a) Chapter 1 of Part 1,
   (b) Part 2.

Interpretation

9. In this schedule—
"eligibility" means eligibility for early years assistance and "eligible" means eligible for early years assistance,
"the regulations" means regulations under section 32(2),
"specified" means specified in the regulations.

Schedule 7 *Not yet in force.*

SCHEDULE 8

(introduced by section 34)

Funeral Expense Assistance Regulations

Part 1

Eligibility

Chapter 1
Eligibility Is To Depend On Being Responsible For Funeral Expenses

1.(1) The regulations must be framed so that an individual's eligibility for funeral expense assistance depends on the individual having met, or being responsible for meeting, the expenses of a funeral.

(2) The regulations are to define "funeral" for the purpose of determining entitlement to funeral expense assistance.

Chapter 2
Further Criteria

Location of the funeral

2. The regulations may make an individual's eligibility depend on where the funeral takes place.

Relationship with the deceased

3. The regulations may make an individual's eligibility depend on the individual—
   (a) being related to the deceased person, or
   (b) having a relationship of a kind described in the regulations with the deceased person immediately before the death.

Value of deceased's estate

4. The regulations may make an individual's eligibility depend on the value of the deceased person's estate being below a level specified in the regulations.

Residence and presence

5. The regulations may make an individual's eligibility depend on either or both—
   (a) the individual being resident and present in a particular place,
   (b) the deceased person having been resident and present in a particular place at the date of death.

Financial circumstances

6. The regulations may make an individual's eligibility depend on the individual's financial circumstances.

Receipt of, or eligibility for, other types of State assistance

7. The regulations may make an individual's eligibility depend on either or both the individual and, immediately before dying, the deceased person—
   (a) being, or not being, in receipt of another type of assistance (whether under this Act or another enactment),
   (b) being, or not being, eligible or entitled to receive such assistance.

Application within specified period

8. The regulations may provide that an individual ceases to be eligible in respect of a funeral unless, by a deadline specified in the regulations—
   (a) the individual has applied for funeral expense assistance in respect of the funeral, or
   (b) the Scottish Ministers have become required to make a determination of the individual's entitlement to funeral expense assistance in respect of the funeral by regulations under section 52.

PART 2

ASSISTANCE TO BE GIVEN

9. The regulations may specify items of expense in relation to which funeral expense assistance will, or will not, be given.

10. The regulations may set a limit on the value of the funeral expense assistance that will be given in relation to items of expense.

11. The regulations may set a limit on the total value of the funeral expense assistance that will be given.

12. The regulations may provide for the amount of funeral expense assistance that will be given to be reduced to reflect the availability of other funds that may be used to meet, or help to meet, any of the expenses.

Restriction on giving assistance in a form other than money

13.(1) The regulations may allow funeral expense assistance to be given to an individual in a form other than money only if the individual (or a person acting on the individual's behalf) has agreed to the assistance being given in that form.

(2) If the regulations include provision of the kind mentioned in sub-paragraph (1), they must allow an individual (or a person acting on the individual's behalf) to withdraw agreement to being given funeral expense assistance in a form other than money at any time.

Part 3

Final Provisions

Generality of enabling power unaffected

14. Nothing in this schedule, apart from the following provisions, is to be taken to limit what may be prescribed in the regulations—
   (a) Chapter 1 of Part 1,
   (b) paragraph 13 in Part 2.

Interpretation

15. In this schedule—
"deceased person" means the person in respect of whose funeral assistance is sought,
"eligibility" means eligibility for funeral expense assistance and "eligible" means eligible for funeral expense assistance,
"the regulations" means regulations under section 34(2).

Schedule 9 *Not yet in force.*

SCHEDULE 10

(introduced by section 36)

Short-Term Assistance Regulations

Part 1

Eligibility

Entitlement to other assistance being reviewed

1.(1) The regulations must be framed so that an individual is eligible for short-term assistance if—
   (a) the individual is, or was, entitled to a particular type of assistance (other than short-term assistance) under a determination made on the basis that the individual has ongoing entitlement,
   (b) that determination has been superseded by a determination under section 37 with the result that the individual—
      (i) is no longer entitled to the type of assistance in question, or
      (ii) is entitled to less assistance of the type in question,
   (c) the individual's entitlement to the type of assistance in question is under review, and
   (d) any further eligibility rules prescribed in the regulations are satisfied in the individual's case.

(2) An individual's entitlement to a particular type of assistance is under review within the meaning of sub-paragraph (1)(c) if—
   (a) the individual has, under section 41, requested a re-determination of the individual's entitlement to the type of assistance in question and—
      (i) the Scottish Ministers have yet to make a determination of the individual's entitlement under section 43, and
      (ii) the individual has not, since requesting the re-determination, made an appeal to the First-tier Tribunal against a determination of the individual's entitlement, or
   (b) the individual has, under section 46, appealed to the First-tier Tribunal against a determination of the individual's entitlement to the type of assistance in question and the First-tier Tribunal has yet to make a decision under section 49, or
   (c) the First-tier Tribunal is considering, under section 48(1)(b), whether to give permission for the individual to bring an appeal against a determination of the individual's entitlement to the type of assistance in question.

Part 2

Assistance To Be Given

Value and form of assistance where entitlement to other assistance under review

2.—(1) This paragraph applies to any case in which an individual is eligible for short-term assistance by virtue of provision made in accordance with paragraph 1(1).

(2) In this paragraph, "the superseded determination" means the determination that has been superseded with one of the results mentioned in paragraph 1(1)(b), as a consequence of which the individual in question is eligible for short-term assistance.

(3) In relation to a case to which this paragraph applies, the regulations must provide for the value of the short-term assistance given to an individual in respect of any period to be equal to—

$$V1 - V2$$

where—

$V1$ is the value of the assistance that the individual would have been given in respect of the period under the superseded determination had it not been superseded, and

$V2$ is the value of the assistance that the individual is to be given in respect of the period under what is, at the time the individual becomes eligible for short-term assistance in respect of the period, the most recent determination of the individual's entitlement to the type of assistance to which the superseded determination relates.

(4) In relation to a case to which this paragraph applies, the regulations must provide for the rules regarding the form in which short-term assistance is given to an individual to be the same as the rules governing the form in which the type of assistance to which the superseded determination relates may be given.

Part 3

Final Provisions

Generality of enabling power unaffected

3. Nothing in this schedule is to be taken to preclude the regulations from providing for an individual to be eligible for short-term assistance in circumstances other than those described in paragraph 1.

Interpretation

4. In this schedule, "the regulations" means regulations under section 36(2).

[1 SCHEDULE 11

(introduced by section 51)

Suspension Of Assistance

Circumstances in which assistance may be suspended

1.—(1) The regulations may provide for an individual's assistance to be suspended in the following circumstances only—
  (a) under section 54(1A) the Scottish Ministers have issued a decision to suspend assistance to the individual due to a failure to provide information which the individual is yet to provide,
  (b) where the Scottish Ministers have made arrangements (whether under section 85A, 85B or otherwise) for a person to receive the assistance on the individual's behalf, and the Ministers consider that it is necessary to suspend the assistance—
    (i) in order to protect the individual from the risk of financial abuse,
    (ii) because the person with whom the Ministers have made arrangements is unable to continue to receive the assistance, or
    (iii) for any other reason specified in the regulations, or

(c) the individual has requested that the Scottish Ministers temporarily stop giving the assistance in question and is yet to request that they resume doing so.

(2) For the purpose of sub-sub-paragraph (1)(b), "financial abuse" includes—
(a) having money or other property stolen,
(b) being defrauded,
(c) being put under pressure in relation to money or other property,
(d) having money or other property misused.

Safeguards: requirement to consider financial circumstances before suspension

2. The regulations must require the Scottish Ministers, before suspending the assistance given to an individual, to have regard to the financial circumstances of the individual.

Safeguards: right to review suspension

3. The regulations must confer a right on an individual whose assistance has been suspended to require the Scottish Ministers to review their decision to suspend the individual's assistance.

Safeguards: information to be given following suspension

4.—(1) The regulations must require the Scottish Ministers to inform an individual whose assistance they have suspended—
(a) of their decision to suspend the individual's assistance,
(b) of the reasons for their decision,
(c) of any steps which might be taken by the individual in order for the Scottish Ministers to consider ending the suspension, and
(d) of the individual's right in accordance with the regulations to require the Scottish Ministers to review their decision to suspend the individual's assistance.

(2) The regulations must provide that the Scottish Ministers are to fulfil the duty described by sub-paragraph (1) in a way that leaves the individual with a record of the information which the individual can show to, or otherwise share with, others.

Safeguards: effect of suspension ending

5. The regulations must provide that when—
(a) the suspension of an individual's assistance ends, and
(b) under the latest determination of the individual's entitlement to the type of assistance in question, the individual would have become entitled to be given assistance during the period of the suspension,
the individual is immediately to be given under section 24 the assistance that the individual would have become entitled to be given under the determination during that period.

Generality of enabling power unaffected

6. Nothing in this schedule is to be taken to limit the provision that may be included in the regulations except to the extent stated.

Interpretation

7. In this schedule—
(a) references to an individual's assistance being suspended are to an individual, by virtue of the regulations, not becoming entitled to be given some or all of the assistance in respect of a period that the individual otherwise would at the time, or times, prescribed by regulations under section 51(2)(a),
(b) "the regulations" means regulations under section 51(1).]

AMENDMENT

1. Social Security Administration and Tribunal Membership (Scotland) Act 2020 s.12(1) and (4) (July 26, 2021).

Early Years Assistance (Best Start Grants) (Scotland) Regulations 2018

The Early Years Assistance (Best Start Grants) (Scotland) Regulations 2018

(SSI 2018/370)

Made   *9th December 2018*
Coming into force   *10th December 2018*

The Scottish Ministers make the following Regulations in exercise of the powers conferred by sections 32(2), 41(4)(a), 43(5) and 52 of the Social Security (Scotland) Act 2018 and all other powers enabling them to do so.

In accordance with section 96 of that Act, a draft of these Regulations has been laid before and approved by resolution of the Scottish Parliament.

ARRANGEMENT OF REGULATIONS

PART 1

Introduction

1. Citation
2. Commencement
3. Overview

PART 2

Interpretation

Expressions about time and timing

4. When an application is to be treated as made
5. Late application: nomination of date
6. Meaning of "birthday", for children born on 29th February
7. Calculations involving months

Expressions about inter-personal relationships

8. Meaning of "partner"
9. Meaning of being responsible for a child
10. Meaning of "dependant"

Expressions about social security assistance

11. Meaning of references to specified kinds of assistance
12. Meaning of references to assistance being awarded
13. Meaning of "assessment period" in relation to universal credit

Schedule 1   Procedural matters

(SSI 2018/370 reg.)

Schedule 2   Pregnancy and baby grant
Schedule 3   Early learning grant
Schedule 4   School-age grant

Part 1

Introduction

Citation

1. These Regulations may be cited as the Early Years Assistance (Best Start Grants) (Scotland) Regulations 2018.

13.128

Commencement

2. These Regulations come into force on the day after the day they are made.

13.129

Overview

3.—(1) Part 2 makes provision about the interpretation of these Regulations.

13.130

(2) Schedule 1 makes provision about matters of procedure for determining entitlement to early years assistance.

(3) Schedule 2 makes provision about the early years assistance that is to be given in connection with having, or expecting to have, a new baby in the family (referred to in these Regulations as "pregnancy and baby grant").

[¹ (4) Schedule 3 makes provision about the early years assistance that is to be given in connection with a child aged between 2 and 3½ years (referred to in these Regulations as "early learning grant").]

[² (5) Schedule 4 makes provision about the early years assistance that is to be given in connection with a child reaching the age at which children in Scotland usually start primary school (referred to in these Regulations as "school-age grant").]

Amendments

1. Early Years Assistance (Best Start Grants) (Scotland) Amendment (No.2) Regulations 2019 (S.S.I. 2019/157) reg.4 (April 29, 2019).
2. Early Years Assistance (Best Start Grants) (Scotland) Amendment (No.2) Regulations 2019 (S.S.I. 2019/157) reg.7 (June 3, 2019).

Early Years Assistance (Best Start Grants) (Scotland) Regulations 2018

Part 2

Interpretation

Expressions about time and timing

When an application is to be treated as made

13.131 4.—(1) An application is to be treated as made—
  (a) on the day it is received by the Scottish Ministers; or
  (b) if applicable, on—
    (i) the day chosen by the Scottish Ministers in accordance with paragraph (3); or
    (ii) the day the applicant nominates (or is deemed to have nominated) under regulation 5.
[¹ (2) In a case where, by virtue of a paragraph of Part 2 of schedule 1, a determination is to be, or has been, made without an application, references in these Regulations to the day the application is made are to be read in accordance with that paragraph.]
(3) If, before making a determination on the basis of an application, the Scottish Ministers consider that the applicant—
  (a) would not be eligible for the assistance applied for if the application were treated as made on the day they received it; and
  (b) would be eligible for the assistance if the application were treated as made on a day falling within the period of 10 days beginning with the day they received it,
the Scottish Ministers may choose the day within that 10 day period on which the application is to be treated as made.
(4) For the avoidance of doubt, a thing that purports to be an application is not an application unless it is—
  (a) made in the form; and
  (b) accompanied by the evidence,
required under section 38 of the Social Security (Scotland) Act 2018.

Amendment

1. Early Years Assistance (Best Start Grants) (Scotland) Amendment (No.1) Regulations 2019 (S.S.I. 2019/110), reg.4 (March 21, 2019).

Late application: nomination of date

13.132 5.—(1) An applicant may nominate the date on which an application will be treated as made by virtue of regulation 4(1)(b)(ii) if—
  (a) the award of universal credit or assistance of a kind specified in regulation 11 that the applicant is relying on to meet the relevant eligibility condition is a backdated award;
  (b) the backdated award is an award of assistance for—
    (i) a day that falls within the application window; or
    (ii) a period that includes at least 1 day that falls within the application window; and
  (c) the application is received by the Scottish Ministers—

(i) not more than 20 working days after the last day of the application window; and
(ii) within 3 months of the applicant being informed of the backdated award by or on behalf of the public authority who made it.

(2) If the backdated award is for—
(a) 1 day only; or
(b) a period and only 1 day of it falls within the application window,
the applicant may only nominate that day under this regulation.

(3) If—
(a) the backdated award is for a period; and
(b) more than 1 day of the period falls within the application window,
the applicant may nominate any of those days under this regulation.

(4) If the applicant is entitled to nominate a day under this regulation but has not done so, the applicant is to be deemed to have nominated—
(a) the only day the applicant could have nominated in accordance with paragraph (2); or
(b) the latest day the applicant could have nominated in accordance with paragraph (3).

(5) In this regulation—
"application window" means—
(a) in relation to an application for a pregnancy and baby grant, the period that—
   (i) [^{1} begins—
      (aa) on the first day of the 24th week of the pregnancy that resulted, or is to result, in the birth of the child in question, or
      (bb) in a case where the child is born before the 24th week of pregnancy is reached, on the day the child is born, and]
   (ii) ends with the deadline set by paragraph 2 of schedule 2;
(b) [^{2} in relation to an application for an early learning grant, the period described in paragraph 1(b) of schedule 3,]
(c) [^{3} in relation to an application for a school-age grant, the period described in paragraph 2 of schedule 4,]
"backdated award" means an award of assistance for a day, or a period that begins on a day, that falls before the day the decision to make the award was taken;
"the relevant eligibility condition" means—
(a) in relation to an application for a pregnancy and baby grant, the eligibility condition in paragraph 1(e) of schedule 2;
(b) [^{2} in relation to an application for an early learning grant, the eligibility condition in paragraph 1(f) of schedule 3,]
(c) [^{3} in relation to an application for a school-age grant, the eligibility condition in paragraph 1(f) of schedule 4,]
"working day" means a day other than—
(a) a Saturday;
(b) a Sunday; or
(c) a bank holiday in Scotland under the Banking and Financial Dealings Act 1971.

AMENDMENTS

1. Early Years Assistance (Best Start Grants) (Scotland) Amendment (No.1) Regulations 2019 (SSI 2019/110) reg.5 (March 21, 2019).

2. Early Years Assistance (Best Start Grants) (Scotland) Amendment (No.2) Regulations 2019 (SSI 2019/157) reg.5 (April 29, 2019).
3. Early Years Assistance (Best Start Grants) (Scotland) Amendment (No.2) Regulations 2019 (SSI 2019/157) reg.8 (June 3, 2019).

Meaning of "birthday", for children born on 29th February

13.133   6. In a non-leap year, the birthday of a child born on 29th February is to be taken to be 28th February.

Calculations involving months

13.134   7.—(1) Where a day ("day 1") is described as falling a specified number of months before or after another day ("day 2"), the date of day 1 is to be determined as follows.
(2) Count backwards or forwards (as the case may be) the specified number of months from the month in which day 2 falls.
(3) If the month arrived at in accordance with paragraph (2) has a day corresponding to day 2, day 1 is that day of the month arrived at.
(4) If the month arrived at in accordance with paragraph (2) has too few days to have a day corresponding to day 2, day 1 is the last day of the month arrived at.

GENERAL NOTE

13.135   In the Queen's Printer's copy of the Regulations, a footnote to reg.7(4) says—
"For example, if a child is born on 31st August, the day falling 6 months after the day the child is born is 28th February (or 29th February in a leap year)."

Expressions about inter-personal relationships

Meaning of "partner"

13.136   8. An individual is to be regarded as the partner of another individual on a day only if, on that day, the two individuals would be regarded as a couple for the purposes of Part 1 of the Welfare Reform Act 2012 (see section 39 of that Act).

Meaning of being responsible for a child

13.137   9.—(1) An individual is to be regarded as responsible for a child on a day only if at least one of the following statements is true:—
  (a) the child is a dependant of the individual on the day in question;
  (b) the individual is one of the child's parents and, on the day in question—
    (i) normally lives with the child;
    (ii) is under 20 years of age; and
    (iii) is a dependant of another individual;
  (c) the child is, on the day in question, treated in law as the child of the individual by virtue of an order under section 54 [1 or section 54A] of the Human Fertilisation and Embryology Act 2008;

(d) the child is, on the day in question, treated in law as the child of the individual by reason of an adoption either—
  (i) effected under the law of Scotland; or
  (ii) effected under the law of another country or jurisdiction and recognised by the law of Scotland;
(e) the child is, on the day in question, placed with the individual by an adoption agency;
(f) the individual is, on the day in question, a guardian of the child appointed by deed, will or by a court;
(g) the individual is, on the day in question, a kinship carer for the child.

(2) In paragraph (1)(e), "adoption agency" means—
(a) a local authority acting in its capacity as an adoption service provider under section 1 of the Adoption and Children (Scotland) Act 2007;
(b) an adoption service provided as mentioned in paragraph 8(1)(b) of schedule 12 of the Public Services Reform (Scotland) Act 2010 and registered under Part 5 of that Act;
(c) an adoption agency within the meaning of section 2(1) of the Adoption and Children Act 2002;
(d) an adoption agency within the meaning of article 3 of the Adoption (Northern Ireland) Order 1987.

[¹ (3) For the purpose of paragraph (1)(g), an individual is a kinship carer for a child on a day if—
(a) the individual is—
  (i) a person who is related to the child,
  (ii) a person who is known to the child and with whom the child has a pre-existing relationship, or
  (iii) a friend or acquaintance of a person related to the child, and
(b) on that day, the child lives with the individual (exclusively or predominantly) under the terms of—
  (i) a kinship care order as defined in section 72(1) of the Children and Young People (Scotland) Act 2014,
  (ii) any other order under section 11(1) of the Children (Scotland) Act 1995 ("the 1995 Act"), or
  (iii) an agreement between the individual, the individual's partner or both of them and—
    (aa) a local authority by which the child is looked after within the meaning of section 17(6) of the 1995 Act,
    (bb) a local authority in England or Wales by which the child is looked after within the meaning of section 105(4) of the Children Act 1989 ("the 1989 Act"), or
    (cc) an authority in Northern Ireland by which the child is looked after within the meaning of article 25 of the Children (Northern Ireland) Order 1995 ("the 1995 Order").

(4) A person described in paragraph (3)(a) must not be—
(a) the parent of the child within the meaning of section 15(1) of the 1995 Act,
(b) a foster carer within the meaning of regulation 2 of the Looked After Children (Scotland) Regulations 2009,
(c) a local authority foster parent in England and Wales within the meaning of section 105(1) of the 1989 Act, or

(d) an authority foster parent in Northern Ireland within the meaning of article 27(3) of the 1995 Order.

(5) In paragraph (3)(a) "related" means related either by blood, marriage or civil partnership.]

AMENDMENT

1. Social Security (Miscellaneous Amendment and Transitional Provision) (Scotland) Regulations 2022 (SSI 2022/336) reg.2(1) and (2) (November 14, 2022).

Meaning of "dependant"

10.—[¹ (1) An individual ("person A") is to be regarded as a dependant of another individual ("person B") on a day only if—
  (a) paragraph (1A) applies, or
  (b) on that day person B is a kinship carer for person A.
(1A) This paragraph applies if—
  (a) person B has been awarded—
    (i) child tax credit, child benefit or state pension credit for the day in question (or for a period that includes that day), or
    (ii) universal credit for—
      (aa) the assessment period that includes the day in question, or
      (bb) the assessment period that ended immediately before the assessment period mentioned in head (aa) started, and
  (b) person A is recognised to be a child or young person for whom person B has responsibility in terms of that award of assistance.]

(2) It is immaterial for the purpose of this regulation that the award of assistance to person B [¹ referred to in paragraph (1A)] does not include any amount in respect of person A due to a rule that restricts the number of dependants in respect of whom person B can be given that type of assistance.

[¹ (3) In this regulation, "kinship carer" has the meaning given in regulation 9(3).]

AMENDMENT

1. Early Years Assistance (Best Start Grants) (Scotland) Amendment (No.1) Regulations 2019 (SSI. 2019/110) reg.6 (March 21, 2019).

Expressions about social security assistance

Meaning of references to specified kinds of assistance

11. References in these Regulations to a kind of assistance specified in this regulation are to the following:—
  (a) child tax credit;
  (b) housing benefit;
  (c) income-based jobseeker's allowance;
  (d) income-related employment and support allowance;
  (e) income support;
  (f) state pension credit;
  (g) working tax credit.

Meaning of references to assistance being awarded

12.—(1) An individual is not to be regarded as having been awarded a kind of assistance for a day or a period if—
  (a) the award was made in error (whether or not induced by the individual); or
  (b) the sum awarded to the individual for the day or the period is £0.

(2) In sub-paragraph (1)(b), the reference to "the sum awarded" means, in a case where a deduction has been made—
  (a) in respect of any liability the individual has to another person; or
  (b) by way of a sanction,
the sum that would have been awarded had the deduction not been made.

(3) For the avoidance of doubt, in sub-paragraph (1) "kind of assistance" includes universal credit as well as the kinds of assistance specified in regulation 11.

Meaning of "assessment period" in relation to universal credit

13. "Assessment period" means a period in respect of which universal credit may be payable to the individual in question in accordance with section 7 of the Welfare Reform Act 2012

Regulation 3(2)

SCHEDULE 1

PROCEDURAL MATTERS

PART 1

RE-DETERMINATION TIMESCALES

Deadline for requesting re-determination

1. The period for requesting a re-determination of entitlement to early years assistance under section 41 of the Social Security (Scotland) Act 2018 is 31 days beginning with the day that the individual is informed, in accordance with section 40 of that Act, of the right to make the request.

Period allowed for re-determination

2.—(1) In relation to determining entitlement to early years assistance, the period allowed for re-determination (within the meaning of section 43 of the Social Security (Scotland) Act 2018) is 16 working days beginning with—
  [¹ (a) the day that the request for a re-determination is received by the Scottish Ministers, [³ ...]
  (b) in a case where the request for a re-determination is received by the Scottish Ministers outwith the period prescribed in paragraph 1, the day on which it is decided by the Scottish Ministers or (as the case may be) the First-tier Tribunal for Scotland that the individual in question has a good reason for not requesting a re-determination sooner.] [³ , or
  (c) in a case where the Scottish Ministers have informed the individual of their decision that the request for a re-determination was not made in such form as the Scottish Ministers require, the day on which it is subsequently decided by the First-Tier Tribunal for Scotland that the individual in question has made the request in such form as the Scottish Ministers require.]

(2) For the purpose of this paragraph, a "working day" is a day other than—
(a) a Saturday;
(b) a Sunday; or
(c) a bank holiday in Scotland under the Banking and Financial Dealings Act 1971.

PART 2

DETERMINATION WITHOUT APPLICATION

Determination following application in connection with another child

13.144   3.—(1) The Scottish Ministers are to make a determination of an individual's entitlement to early years assistance in connection with a child (without receiving an application) in the circumstance described in sub-paragraph (2).
(2) The circumstance referred to in sub-paragraph (1) is that—
(a) the individual has applied for early years assistance in respect of a child; and
(b) it appears to the Scottish Ministers from the available information that, unless circumstances change, the individual will become eligible for early years assistance in respect of another child within the period—
(i) beginning on the day the application is made; and
(ii) ending at the end of the day that falls 10 days later.
(3) The determination that sub-paragraph (1) requires to be made is to be made on, or as soon as reasonably practicable after, the day that the Scottish Ministers anticipate will be the day on which the individual first becomes eligible for early years assistance in respect of the child as mentioned in sub-paragraph (2)(b).
(4) The determination that sub-paragraph (1) requires to be made is to be made (subject to sub-paragraph (5)) on the basis that whatever can be discerned from the available information to have been the case on the day the application mentioned in sub-paragraph (2)(a) was made remains the case on the day the determination is made.
(5) A determination is not to be made on the basis of the assumption set out in sub-paragraph (4) if, and to the extent that, the Scottish Ministers have information suggesting the assumption is unsound.
[1 (5A) Where a determination is to be, or has been, made without an application by virtue of this paragraph, references in these Regulations to the day the application is made are to be read as references to the day the determination is made.]
(6) In this paragraph, "the available information" means—
(a) the information provided in the application referred to in sub-paragraph (2)(a); and
(b) any other information obtained by the Scottish Ministers in connection with that application.

[1 Determination following official error

13.145   4.—(1) The Scottish Ministers are to make a determination of an individual's entitlement to a best start grant in connection with a child (without receiving an application) where—
(a) they have previously made a determination of the individual's entitlement to the grant in connection with the child ("the original determination"),
(b) they establish that due to an official error the original determination was wrongly made resulting in the individual—
(i) not being given a grant for which the individual was eligible, or
(ii) being given a grant of lesser value than the grant to which the individual was entitled,
(c) the Scottish Ministers are not considering a request for a re-determination of the individual's entitlement to the grant, and
(d) the individual has not appealed to the First-tier Tribunal for Scotland against the Scottish Ministers' determination of the individual's entitlement to the grant.
(2) In making a determination required by sub-paragraph (1) the Scottish Ministers are to use—
(a) the information provided in the application that led to the original determination, and
(b) any other information they have obtained in connection with that application.

(3) Where a determination is to be, or has been, made without an application by virtue of this paragraph, references in these Regulations to the day the application is made are to be read as references to the day the application that led to the original determination was made.

(4) In this paragraph—

"best start grant" means one of the forms of early years assistance mentioned in regulation 3,

"official error" means an error made by someone acting on behalf of the Scottish Ministers or on behalf of a Minister of the Crown that was not materially contributed to by anyone not so acting.]

[¹ Determination following backdated award of assistance

5.—(1) The Scottish Ministers are to make a determination of an individual's entitlement to a best start grant in connection with a child (without receiving an application) where—
   (a) a determination has previously been made that the individual is not entitled to the grant in connection with the child ("the original determination"), and
   (b) the Scottish Ministers establish that—
      (i) following an appeal, an award of universal credit or assistance of a kind specified in regulation 11 is made that is a backdated award, and
      (ii) had that award been made before the original determination, a determination that the individual is entitled to the grant in connection with the child would have been made instead.

(2) In making a determination required by sub-paragraph (1) the Scottish Ministers are to use—
   (a) the information provided in the application that led to the original determination, and
   (b) any other information they have obtained in connection with that application.

(3) Where a determination is to be, or has been, made without an application by virtue of this paragraph, references in these Regulations to the day the application is made are to be read as references to the day the application that led to the original determination was made.

(4) In this paragraph, "best start grant" means one of the forms of early years assistance mentioned in regulation 3 and "backdated award" has the same meaning as in regulation 5.]

[⁴ Determination following award of Scottish child payment

5A.—(1) The Scottish Ministers are to make a determination of an individual's entitlement to an early learning grant or a school-age grant in connection with a child (without receiving an application) where the circumstances described in sub-paragraph (2) are met.

(2) The circumstances referred to in sub-paragraph (1) are that—
   (a) a determination has been made that the individual is entitled to a Scottish child payment in respect of the child and the individual has an ongoing entitlement to that payment by virtue of regulation 19 of the Scottish Child Payment Regulations,
   (b) the individual's Scottish child payment in respect of the child is not currently suspended within the meaning of regulation 19G(a) of the Scottish Child Payment Regulations, and
   (c) it appears to the Scottish Ministers from the available information that the individual is likely to be entitled to an early learning grant or a school-age grant in respect of the child.

(3) Where a determination is to be, or has been, made without an application by virtue of this paragraph, references in these Regulations to the day the application is made are to be read as references to the day the determination is made.

(4) Where an individual who is entitled to a Scottish child payment requests that the Scottish Ministers do not make a determination (without receiving an application) of the individual's entitlement to an early leaning grant or school-age grant—
   (a) the Scottish Ministers are not to make a determination (without receiving an application) under sub-paragraph (1), and
   (b) accordingly, their duty to do so under sub-paragraph (1) ceases to apply.

(5) In this paragraph—
   (a) "Scottish child payment" means Scottish child payment assistance given in accordance with the Scottish Child Payment Regulations,
   (b) "Scottish Child Payment Regulations" means the Scottish Child Payment Regulations 2020, and
   (c) "the available information" means—
      (i) the information provided in the individual's application for the Scottish child payment,

(ii) any other information obtained by the Scottish Ministers in connection with that application, and
(iii) any other information available to them that is relevant to their consideration of whether the individual is entitled to an early learning grant or a school-age grant.]

[² PART 3

COMPETING CLAIMS

Multiple applications in respect of the same child

6.—(1) Where two or more individuals have applied for early years assistance in respect of the same child, the Scottish Ministers are to make a determination of entitlement in accordance with sub-paragraphs (2) to (5).

(2) Where the Scottish Ministers decide that two or more individuals are eligible for early years assistance in respect of the child, they must apply the rules in sub-paragraphs (3) to (5) to determine which of the individuals is to be entitled to that assistance.

(3) The rules are that—
(a) where only one individual has been awarded child tax credit, state pension credit or universal credit for the day, or assessment period that includes the day, in question (and the child is recognised to be a child for whom the individual has responsibility in terms of that award of assistance), unless the Scottish Ministers decide otherwise in pursuance of the rule in sub-paragraph (5), that individual is entitled to early years assistance,
(b) where none of the individuals have been awarded assistance as described in sub-paragraph (3)(a), and only one individual has been awarded child benefit for the day in question (and the child is recognised to be a child for whom the individual has responsibility in terms of that award of assistance), that individual is entitled to early years assistance,
(c) where the individuals are kinship carers for the child, and none of them have been awarded any kind of assistance as described in sub-paragraph (3)(a) or (3)(b), the individual whose determination is to be made first is entitled to early years assistance,
(d) where one individual has been awarded child benefit for the day in question, and another individual is a kinship carer for the child, the individual who is the kinship carer for the child is entitled to early years assistance.

(4) For the purposes of sub-paragraph (3), the individual whose determination is to be made first is the individual whose application is to be treated as made first in accordance with regulation 4.

(5) Where—
(a) having applied the rules in sub-paragraph (3) in accordance with sub-paragraph (2) it appears to the Scottish Ministers from information available to them that none of the circumstances described in rules (a) to (d) are true in the case of the individuals in question, or
(b) the circumstances described in rule (a) of sub-paragraph (3) are true in the case of the individuals in question and one individual is a kinship carer for the child,

the Scottish Ministers must determine which of the individuals is entitled to the early years assistance having regard to the circumstances of the child.]

AMENDMENTS

1. Early Years Assistance (Best Start Grants) (Scotland) Amendment (No.1) Regulations 2019 (SSI. 2019/110) regs. 7 and 8 (March 21, 2019).
2. Best Start Grants and Scottish Child Payment (Miscellaneous Amendments) Regulations 2021 (SSI 2021/494) reg.2 (December 23, 2021).
3. Social Security (Period for Re-determination Requests) (Miscellaneous Amendments) (Scotland) Regulations 2021 (SSI 2021/469) reg.2 (February 9, 2022).
4. Social Security (Miscellaneous Amendment and Transitional Provision) (Scotland) Regulations 2022 (SSI 2022/336) reg.2(1) and (3) (November 28, 2022).

(SSI 2018/370 Sch. 1)

Regulation 3(3)

SCHEDULE 2

Pregnancy and baby grant

PART 1

Eligibility

Eligibility

1. An individual is eligible for a pregnancy and baby grant in respect of a child if—
   (a) the individual's application for the grant is made before the deadline set by paragraph 2 (see regulation 4 in relation to when an application is to be treated as made);
   [¹ (aa) the individual has not received, and is not due to receive, a sure start maternity grant in respect of the child,]
   (b) no-one else has received, or is due to receive, a pregnancy and baby grant or sure start maternity grant in respect of the child (but see paragraph 3);
   (c) on the day the application is made the individual satisfies the residence requirement set by paragraph 4;
   (d) at least one of these statements is true on the day the application is made—
      (i) the individual is the person who—
         (aa) is, or has been, more than 24 weeks pregnant with the child; or
         (bb) gave birth to the child before or during the 24th week of the pregnancy;
      (ii) the individual is the partner of the person described by head (i);
      (iii) the person described by head (i) is a dependant of the individual or the individual's partner (or both of them);
      (iv) either the individual or the individual's partner is (or both of them are) responsible for the child on the day the application is made;
   (e) at least one of these statements is true—
      (i) the individual or the individual's partner has (or both of them have) been awarded, for the day the application is made (or for a period which includes that day), assistance of a kind specified in regulation 11;
      (ii) the individual or the individual's partner has (or both of them have) been awarded universal credit for—
         (aa) the assessment period that includes the day the application is made; or
         (bb) the assessment period that ended immediately before the assessment period mentioned in sub-head (aa) started;
      (iii) on the day the application is made the individual is under 18 years of age;
      (iv) on the day the application is made the individual is—
         (aa) 18 or 19 years of age; and
         (bb) a dependant of another individual; [⁶. . .]
   (f) [⁶. . .]

13.149

Deadline for applying

2.—(1) The deadline for an individual to apply for a pregnancy and baby grant in respect of a child is—
   (a) the end of the day that falls 6 months after the day the child is born if sub-paragraph (2) applies to the individual;
   (b) the end of the day before the child's first birthday if sub-paragraph (2) does not apply to the individual.
(2) This sub-paragraph applies to—
   (a) the person who is, or has been, pregnant with the child; and
   (b) any individual who is, or has been during the period described by sub-paragraph (3)—
      (i) the partner of the person referred to in paragraph (a); or
      (ii) an individual, or the partner of an individual, for whom the person referred to in paragraph (a) is a dependant.
(3) The period referred to in sub-paragraph (2)(b)—

13.150

(i) begins on the first day of the 24th week of the pregnancy that resulted, or is to result, in the child's birth; and
(ii) ends at the end of the day that falls 6 months after the day the child is born.

Exception to paragraph 1(b)

3.—(1) For the purpose of determining the entitlement of the individual referred to in this paragraph as the applicant, the eligibility condition in paragraph 1(b) is to be ignored in the circumstance described by sub-paragraphs (2) to (5).

(2) An individual ("the first grant recipient") has been, or is due to be, given in respect of the child—
  (a) a pregnancy and baby grant; or
  (b) a sure start maternity grant.

(3) Another individual ("the applicant") [⁴ is] responsible for the child [⁴ . . .].

(4) [¹ Since the first grant recipient applied for a pregnancy and baby grant or a sure start maternity grant in respect of the child [⁴ . . .], the applicant has not been—
  (a) the partner of the first grant recipient;
  (b) a dependant of the first grant recipient; or
  (c) an individual, or the partner of an individual, for whom the first grant recipient is a dependant.

[¹ (4A) On the day the applicant's application for a pregnancy and baby grant in respect of the child is made, the child does not normally live with the first grant recipient.]

(5) On the day the applicant's application for a pregnancy and baby grant in respect of the child is made, no-one other than the first grant recipient has been, or is due to be, given a pregnancy and baby grant or a sure start maternity grant in respect of that child.

Residence requirement

4.—(1) The residence requirement referred to in paragraph 1(c) is satisfied by an individual on a day if, on that day—
  (a) the individual is ordinarily resident in Scotland; and
  (b) in a case where neither the individual nor the individual's partner has been awarded assistance as mentioned in paragraph 1(e)(i) or (ii), the condition set by sub-paragraph (2) is also met.

(2) The condition referred to in sub-paragraph (1)(b) is met on any day that the individual is—
  (a) habitually resident in the [¹ United Kingdom, the Channel Islands [² or the Isle of Man]
[² (aa) a person who, or has a partner who, is habitually resident in the European Economic Area or Switzerland and—
  (i) is a qualified person within the meaning of regulation 6(1)(a) (jobseeker), (b) (worker), (c) (self-employed person), (d) (self-sufficient person) or (e) (student) of the Immigration (European Economic Area) Regulations 2016 (the EEA Regulations);
  (ii) retains the status referred to in sub-head (i) pursuant to regulation 6(2) or (4) of the EEA Regulations;
  (iii) is a family member of a person referred to in sub-head (i) or (ii) within the meaning of regulation 7(1) of the EEA Regulations;
  (iv) has a right to reside permanently in the United Kingdom by virtue of regulation 15(1) of the EEA Regulations; or
  (v) has been granted indefinite or limited leave to enter, or remain in, the United Kingdom under the Immigration Act 1971 by virtue of Appendix EU to the immigration rules made under section 3(2) of that Act.]
[³ (ab) a person who—
  (i) [⁶ has] leave to enter or remain in the United Kingdom granted under the immigration rules made under section 3(2) of the Immigration Act 1971, by virtue of—
    (ia) the Afghan Relocations and Assistance Policy, or
    (ib) the previous scheme for locally-employed staff in Afghanistan (sometimes referred to as the ex-gratia scheme),
  (ii) has been granted discretionary leave outside the immigration rules as a dependant of a person referred to in sub-head (i), or
  (iii) has leave granted under the Afghan Citizens Resettlement Scheme.]

(SSI 2018/370 Sch.1)

[⁵ (ac) a person who was residing in Ukraine immediately before 1 January 2022, left Ukraine in connection with the Russian invasion which took place on 24 February 2022 and—
  (i) has been granted leave in accordance with immigration rules made under section 3(2) of the Immigration Act 1971, [⁶...]
  (ii) has a right of abode in the United Kingdom within the meaning given in section 2 of that Act,] [⁶ or
  (iii) does not require leave to enter or remain in the United Kingdom in accordance with section 3ZA of that Act,]
[⁷(ad) a person who was residing in Sudan before 15 April 2023, left Sudan in connection with the violence which rapidly escalated on 15 April 2023 in Khartoum and across Sudan and—
  (i) has been granted leave in accordance with immigration rules made under section 3(2) of the Immigration Act 1971,
  (ii) has a right of abode in the United Kingdom within the meaning given in section 2 of that Act, or
  (iii) does not require leave to enter or remain in the United Kingdom in accordance with section 3ZA of that Act,]
[⁸(ae) a person in Great Britain who was residing in Israel, the West Bank, the Gaza Strip, East Jerusalem, the Golan Heights or Lebanon immediately before 7 October 2023, left Israel, the West Bank, the Gaza Strip, East Jerusalem, the Golan Heights or Lebanon in connection with the Hamas terrorist attack in Israel on 7 October 2023 or the violence which rapidly escalated in the region following the attack and—
  (i) has been granted leave in accordance with immigration rules made under section 3(2) of the Immigration Act 1971,
  (ii) has a right of abode in the United Kingdom within the meaning given in section 2 of that Act, or
  (iii) does not require leave to enter or remain in the United Kingdom in accordance with section 3ZA of that Act,]
 (b) a refugee within the definition in Article 1 of the Convention relating to the status of refugees done at Geneva on 28th July 1951, as extended by article 1(2) of the Protocol relating to the status of refugees done at New York on 31st January 1967;
 (c) a person who has been granted, or who is deemed to have been granted, leave outside the rules made under section 3(2) of the Immigration Act 1971, [⁵ . . .]
 (d) a person who has humanitarian protection granted under the rules made under section 3(2) of the Immigration Act 1971; or
 (e) a person who—
  (i) is not subject to immigration control within the meaning of section 115(9) of the Immigration and Asylum Act 1999; and
  (ii) is in the United Kingdom as a result of deportation, expulsion or other removal by compulsion of law from another country to the United Kingdom.
[³ (3) In this paragraph, "the Afghan Citizens Resettlement Scheme" means the scheme announced by the United Kingdom Government on 18 August 2021.]

PART 2

ASSISTANCE TO BE GIVEN

Value of grant

5. The value of a pregnancy and baby grant is—
 (a) the basic amount determined in accordance with paragraph 6; and
 (b) any amount that falls to be added to the basic amount by way of a multiple pregnancy supplement (see paragraph 7).

The basic amount

6.—(1) The basic amount is—
 (a) [⁹ £754.65] if sub-paragraph (2) applies in relation to the child in respect of whom the grant is to be given; or
 (b) [⁹ £377.35] if it does not.
(2) This sub-paragraph applies in relation to the child (subject to sub-paragraph (3)) if, on the day the application for the grant is made—

(a) there is no-one under 16 years of age living in the same household as the individual to whom the grant is to be given; or
(b) if there is, that person is (or all of those persons are) one of the following:—
  (i) the child;
  (ii) a sibling of the child born as a result of the same pregnancy that resulted in the child's birth;
  (iii) a parent of the child;
  (iv) a sibling of a parent of the child;
  (v) [6 a child for whom neither the individual nor their partner is responsible,
  (vi) a child in any one of the circumstances described in sub-paragraph (4), (5) or (6).]

(3) Where more than one child is born, or is to be born, as a result of the same pregnancy—
(a) sub-paragraph (2) applies in relation to only one of the children; and
(b) it is for the Scottish Ministers to decide which.

[6 (4) The circumstance referred to in sub-paragraph (2)(b)(vi) is that—
(a) the child mentioned in sub-paragraph (2)(b)(vi) was, at the time of that child's birth, not a child of the—
  (i) individual to whom the grant is to be given, or
  (ii) individual's partner (where the individual has a partner on the day the application is made), and
(b) the individual first became responsible for the child mentioned in sub-paragraph (2)(b)(vi) when that child was aged 12 months or older.

(5) The circumstance referred to in sub-paragraph (2)(b)(vi) is that the individual to whom the grant is to be given has left their home with the child mentioned in sub-paragraph (2)(b)(vi) due to domestic abuse.

(6) The circumstance referred to in sub-paragraph (2)(b)(vi) is that—
(a) the child mentioned in sub-paragraph (2)(b)(vi) was born before the individual to whom the grant is to be given arrived in the United Kingdom, and
(b) the individual to whom the grant is to be given is one of the following—
  (i) a person who has leave to enter or remain in the United Kingdom granted under the immigration rules made under section 3(2) of the Immigration Act 1971 ("the 1971 Act") by virtue of—
    (aa) the Afghan Relocations and Assistance Policy, or
    (bb) the previous scheme for locally-employed staff in Afghanistan (sometimes referred to as the ex-gratia scheme),
  (ii) a person who has been granted discretionary leave outside the immigration rules as a dependant of a person referred to in sub-head (i),
  (iii) a person who has leave granted under the Afghan Citizens Resettlement Scheme,
  (iv) a person with leave to enter or remain in the United Kingdom granted under or outside the immigration rules made under section 3(2) of the 1971 Act, or with a right of abode in the United Kingdom within the meaning of section 2 of that Act or who does not require leave to enter or remain in the United Kingdom in accordance with section 3ZA of the Act, where the person—
    (aa) was residing in Ukraine immediately before 1 January 2022, and
    (bb) left Ukraine in connection with the Russian invasion which took place on 24 February 2022,
  (v) a refugee within the definition in Article 1 of the Convention relating to the status of refugees done at Geneva on 28 July 1951, as extended by article 1(2) of the Protocol relating to the status of refugees done at New York on 31 January 1967, or
  (vi) a person who has humanitarian protection granted under the rules made under section 3(2) of the 1971 Act.

(7) In paragraph (6) "the Afghan Citizens Resettlement Scheme" has the same meaning as in paragraph 4.]

Multiple pregnancy supplement

7.—(1) Subject to sub-paragraphs (2) and (3) a supplement of [9 £377.35] is to be added to the basic amount in respect of a child born, or to be born, as a result of a multiple pregnancy.

(2) The supplement is to be added to the grant in respect of only one of the children born, or to be born, as a result of the pregnancy, and it is for the Scottish Ministers to decide which child's grant to supplement.
(3) No supplement is to be added if the individual to whom the grant is to be given—
  (a) has not applied for a pregnancy and baby grant in respect of all of the children born, or to be born, as a result of the pregnancy; or
  (b) is not eligible for a pregnancy and baby grant in respect of any of those children.

Form in which grant is given

8.—(1) Subject to sub-paragraph (2), a pregnancy and baby grant is to be given as money.
(2) If—
  (a) the Scottish Ministers offer to give an individual some or all of the value of a pregnancy and baby grant in a form other than money; and
  (b) the individual agrees to be given the grant in that form,
the grant is to be given in that form, unless the individual withdraws agreement before the grant is given.

13.156

PART 3

INTERPRETATION

Meaning of "child", "birth" and "born"

9.—(1) In this schedule, except in paragraph 1(d)(i)(bb)—
"child" includes still-born child;
"birth" includes still-birth and "born" is to be construed accordingly;
"still-born child" and "still-birth" have the meanings given in section 56(1) of the Registration of Births, Deaths and Marriages (Scotland) Act 1965.
(2) Sub-paragraph (1) also applies for the purpose of interpreting—
  (a) the definition of "application window" in regulation 5(5) (which relates to the nomination of a date on which an application for assistance is to be treated as having been made); and
  (b) paragraph 3 of schedule 1 (which describes circumstances in which a determination of entitlement is to be made by the Scottish Ministers without an application).

13.157

Meaning of "sure start maternity grant"

10. In this schedule, "sure start maternity grant" means a payment under—
  (a) regulation 5(1) of the Social Fund Maternity and Funeral Expenses (General) Regulations 2005; or
  (b) regulation 5(1) of the Social Fund Maternity and Funeral Expenses (General) Regulations (Northern Ireland) 2005.

13.158

[6 Meaning of "domestic abuse"

11.—(1) Subject to sub-paragraph (3), in this schedule, "domestic abuse" means abusive behaviour within the meaning of sections 2 and 3 of the Domestic Abuse (Protection) (Scotland) Act 2021 ("the 2021 Act").
(2) For the purposes of this schedule, sections 2 and 3 of the 2021 Act apply as if—
  (a) references to "person A" were references to the partner or the ex-partner of the individual to whom the grant is to be given, and
  (b) references to "person B" were references to the individual to whom the grant is to be given.
(3) Sub-paragraphs (4) to (13) have effect until the day on which sections 2 and 3 of the 2021 Act come into force.
(4) "Abusive behaviour" means behaviour by the partner or ex-partner of the individual to whom the grant is to be given ("person A") which is abusive of the individual to whom the grant is to be given ("person B").
(5) Behaviour by person A is abusive of person B if a reasonable person would consider the behaviour to be likely to cause person B to suffer physical or psychological harm.

13.159

(6) Behaviour is behaviour of any kind, including (for example)—
  (a) saying or otherwise communicating as well as doing something,
  (b) intentionally failing—
    (i) to do something,
    (ii) to say or otherwise communicate something.
(7) Behaviour directed at a person is such behaviour however carried out, including (in particular)—
  (a) by way of conduct towards property,
  (b) through making use of a third party,
as well as behaviour in a personal or direct manner.
(8) In sub-paragraph (5), the reference to psychological harm includes fear, alarm and distress.
(9) Behaviour may consist of a single incident or a course of conduct.
(10) Behaviour which is abusive of person B includes (in particular)—
  (a) behaviour directed at person B that is violent, threatening or intimidating,
  (b) behaviour directed at person B, at a child of person B or at another person that either—
    (i) has its purpose (or among its purposes) one or more of the relevant effects set out in sub-paragraph (11), or
    (ii) would be considered by a reasonable person to be likely to have one or more of the relevant effects set out in sub-paragraph (11).
(11) The relevant effects are of—
  (a) making person B dependent on, or subordinate to, person A,
  (b) isolating person B from friends, relatives or other sources of support,
  (c) controlling, regulating or monitoring person B's day-to-day activities,
  (d) depriving person B of, or restricting person B's, freedom of action,
  (e) frightening, humiliating, degrading or punishing person B.
(12) In sub-paragraph (10)(a), the reference to violent behaviour includes sexual violence as well as physical violence.
(13) Person A and person B are partners (and "ex-partners" is to be construed accordingly) if they are—
  (a) spouses or civil partners of each other, or
  (b) in an intimate personal relationship with each other.]

AMENDMENTS

1. Early Years Assistance (Best Start Grants) (Scotland) Amendment (No.1) Regulations 2019 (SSI. 2019/110) reg.9 (March 21, 2019).
2. Social Security Co-ordination (EU Exit) (Scotland) (Amendment etc.) Regulations 2020 (SSI 2020/399) reg.3(1) and (2) (December 31, 2020).
3. Social Security (Residence Requirements) (Afghanistan) (Scotland) Regulations 2021 (SSI 2021/320) reg.3(1) and (2) (September 15, 2021).
4. Best Start Grants and Scottish Child Payment (Miscellaneous Amendments) Regulations 2021 (SSI 2021/494) reg.3 (December 23, 2021).
5. Social Security (Residence Requirements) (Ukraine) (Scotland) Regulations 2022 (SSI 2022/108) reg.4(1) and (2) (March 22, 2022).
6. Social Security (Miscellaneous Amendment and Transitional Provision) (Scotland) Regulations 2022 (SSI 2022/336) reg.2(1) and (4) (November 14, 2022).
7. Social Security (Residence Requirements) (Sudan) (Scotland) Regulations 2023 (SSI 2023/149) reg.4(2) (May 17, 2023).
8. Social Security (Residence and Presence Requirements) (Israel, the West Bank, the Gaza Strip, East Jerusalem, the Golan Heights and Lebanon) (Scotland) Regulations 2023 (SSI 2023/309) reg.4(2) (October 26, 2023).
9. Social Security (Up-rating) (Miscellaneous Amendments) (Scotland) Regulations 2024 (SSI 2024/105) reg.5(1) and (2) (April 1, 2024, subject to a saving under reg.14 and para.4 of Sch.).

(SSI 2018/370 Sch.3)

[¹ **SCHEDULE 3** Regulation 3(4)

EARLY LEARNING GRANT

PART 1

ELIGIBILITY

Eligibility

1. An individual is eligible for an early learning grant in respect of a child if—   13.160
    (a) the individual's application for the grant is made on or after the day that the Early Years Assistance (Best Start Grants) (Scotland) Amendment (No.2) Regulations 2019 are made (see regulation 4 in relation to when an application is to be treated as made),
    (b) the individual's application for the grant is made in the period that—
        (i) begins on the child's 2nd birthday, and
        (ii) ends at the end of the day that falls 6 months after the child's 3rd birthday,
    (c) no-one else has received, or is due to receive, an early learning grant in respect of the child (but see paragraph 2),
    (d) on the day the application is made the individual satisfies the residence requirement set by paragraph 3,
    (e) either the individual or the individual's partner is (or both of them are) responsible for the child on the day the application is made,
    (f) at least one of these statements is true—
        (i) the individual or the individual's partner has (or both of them have) been awarded, for the day the application is made (or for a period which includes that day), assistance of a kind specified in regulation 11,
        (ii) the individual or the individual's partner has (or both of them have) been awarded universal credit for—
            (aa) the assessment period that includes the day the application is made, or
            (bb) the assessment period that ended immediately before the assessment period mentioned in sub-head (aa) started,
        (iii) on the day the application is made the individual is under 18 years of age,
        (iv) on the day the application is made the individual is—
            (aa) 18 or 19 years of age, and
            (bb) a dependant of another individual, [⁶ . . .]
    (g) [⁶ . . .]

Exception to paragraph 1(c)

2.—(1) For the purpose of determining the entitlement of the individual referred to in this paragraph as the applicant, the eligibility condition in paragraph 1(c) is to be ignored in the circumstance described by sub-paragraphs (2) to (6).

(2) An individual ("the first grant recipient") has been, or is due to be, given an early learning grant in respect of the child.

(3) Another individual ("the applicant") [⁴ is] responsible for the child [⁴ . . .].

(4) The applicant has not been the partner of the first grant recipient at any time since the first grant recipient applied for an early learning grant in respect of the child.

(5) On the day the applicant applies, the child does not normally live with the first grant recipient.

(6) On the day the applicant applies, no-one other than the first grant recipient has been, or is due to be, given an early learning grant in respect of the child.

(7) In this paragraph, references to "the day the applicant applies" are to the day the applicant's application for an early learning grant in respect of the child is made.

Residence requirement

3.—(1) The residence requirement referred to in paragraph 1(d) is satisfied by an individual on a day if, on that day—
    (a) the individual is ordinarily resident in Scotland, and
    (b) in a case where neither the individual nor the individual's partner has been awarded assistance as mentioned in paragraph 1(f)(i) or (ii), the condition set by sub-paragraph (2) is also met.

(2) The condition referred to in sub-paragraph (1)(b) is met on any day that the individual is—

(a) habitually resident in the United Kingdom, the Channel Islands [² or the Isle of Man]

[² (aa) a person who, or has a partner who, is habitually resident in the European Economic Area or Switzerland and—
  (i) is a qualified person within the meaning of regulation 6(1)(a) (jobseeker), (b) (worker), (c) (self-employed person), (d) (self-sufficient person) or (e) (student) of the Immigration (European Economic Area) Regulations 2016 (the EEA Regulations);
  (ii) retains the status referred to in sub-head (i) pursuant to regulation 6(2) or (4) of the EEA Regulations;
  (iii) is a family member of a person referred to in sub-head (i) or (ii) within the meaning of regulation 7(1) of the EEA Regulations;
  (iv) has a right to reside permanently in the United Kingdom by virtue of regulation 15(1) of the EEA Regulations; or
  (v) has been granted indefinite or limited leave to enter, or remain in, the United Kingdom under the Immigration Act 1971 by virtue of Appendix EU to the immigration rules made under section 3(2) of that Act.]

[³ (ab) a person who—
  (i) has leave to enter or remain in the United Kingdom granted under the immigration rules made under section 3(2) of the Immigration Act 1971, by virtue of—
    (ia) the Afghan Relocations and Assistance Policy, or
    (ib) the previous scheme for locally-employed staff in Afghanistan (sometimes referred to as the ex-gratia scheme),
  (ii) has been granted discretionary leave outside the immigration rules as a dependant of a person referred to in sub-head (i), or
  (iii) has leave granted under the Afghan Citizens Resettlement Scheme.]

[⁵ (ac) a person who was residing in Ukraine immediately before 1 January 2022, left Ukraine in connection with the Russian invasion which took place on 24 February 2022 and—
  (i) has been granted leave in accordance with immigration rules made under section 3(2) of the Immigration Act 1971, or [⁶. . .]
  (ii) has a right of abode in the United Kingdom within the meaning given in section 2 of that Act,] [⁶ or
  (iii) does not require leave to enter or remain in the United Kingdom in accordance with section 3ZA of that Act,]

[⁷(ad) a person who was residing in Sudan before 15 April 2023, left Sudan in connection with the violence which rapidly escalated on 15 April 2023 in Khartoum and across Sudan and—
  (i) has been granted leave in accordance with immigration rules made under section 3(2) of the Immigration Act 1971,
  (ii) has a right of abode in the United Kingdom within the meaning given in section 2 of that Act, or
  (iii) does not require leave to enter or remain in the United Kingdom in accordance with section 3ZA of that Act,]

[⁸(ae) a person in Great Britain who was residing in Israel, the West Bank, the Gaza Strip, East Jerusalem, the Golan Heights or Lebanon immediately before 7 October 2023, left Israel, the West Bank, the Gaza Strip, East Jerusalem, the Golan Heights or Lebanon in connection with the Hamas terrorist attack in Israel on 7 October 2023 or the violence which rapidly escalated in the region following the attack and—
  (i) has been granted leave in accordance with immigration rules made under section 3(2) of the Immigration Act 1971,
  (ii) has a right of abode in the United Kingdom within the meaning given in section 2 of that Act, or
  (iii) does not require leave to enter or remain in the United Kingdom in accordance with section 3ZA of that Act,]

(b) a refugee within the definition in Article 1 of the Convention relating to the status of refugees done at Geneva on 28 July 1951, as extended by article 1(2) of the Protocol relating to the status of refugees done at New York on 31 January 1967,

(c) a person who has been granted, or who is deemed to have been granted, leave outside the rules made under section 3(2) of the Immigration Act 1971, [⁵ . . .],

(d) a person who has humanitarian protection granted under the rules made under section 3(2) of the Immigration Act 1971,

(e) a person who—

(i) is not subject to immigration control within the meaning of section 115(9) of the Immigration and Asylum Act 1999, and
(ii) is in the United Kingdom as a result of deportation, expulsion or other removal by compulsion of law from another country to the United Kingdom.
[³ (3) In this paragraph, "the Afghan Citizens Resettlement Scheme" means the scheme announced by the United Kingdom Government on 18 August 2021.]

PART 2

ASSISTANCE TO BE GIVEN

Value of grant

4. The value of an early learning grant is [⁹ £314.45].

Form in which grant is given

5.—(1) Subject to sub-paragraph (2), an early learning grant is to be given as money.
(2) If—
(a) the Scottish Ministers offer to give an individual some or all of the value of an early learning grant in a form other than money, and
(b) the individual agrees to be given the grant in that form,
the grant is to be given in that form, unless the individual withdraws agreement before the grant is given.]

AMENDMENTS

1. Early Years Assistance (Best Start Grants) (Scotland) Amendment (No.2) Regulations 2019 (S.S.I. 2019/157) sch.1 (April 29, 2019).
2. Social Security Co-ordination (EU Exit) (Scotland) (Amendment etc.) Regulations 2020 (SSI 2020/399) reg.3(1) and (3) (December 31, 2020).
3. Social Security (Residence Requirements) (Afghanistan) (Scotland) Regulations 2021 (SSI 2021/320) reg.3(1) and (3) (September 15, 2021).
4. Best Start Grants and Scottish Child Payment (Miscellaneous Amendments) Regulations 2021 (SSI 2021/494) reg.4 (December 23, 2021).
5. Social Security (Residence Requirements) (Ukraine) (Scotland) Regulations 2022 (SSI 2022/108) reg.4(1) and (3) (March 22, 2022).
6. Social Security (Miscellaneous Amendment and Transitional Provision) (Scotland) Regulations 2022 (SSI 2022/336) reg.2(1) and (5) (November 14, 2022).
7. Social Security (Residence Requirements) (Sudan) (Scotland) Regulations 2023 (SSI 2023/149) reg.4(3) (May 17, 2023).
8. Social Security (Residence and Presence Requirements) (Israel, the West Bank, the Gaza Strip, East Jerusalem, the Golan Heights and Lebanon) (Scotland) Regulations 2023 (SSI 2023/309) reg.4(3) (October 26, 2023).
9. Social Security (Up-rating) (Miscellaneous Amendments) (Scotland) Regulations 2024 (SSI 2024/105) reg.5(1) and (3) (April 1, 2024, subject to a saving under reg.14 and para.4 of Sch.).

[¹ **SCHEDULE 4**   Regulation 3(5)

SCHOOL-AGE GRANT

PART 1

ELIGIBILITY

Eligibility

1. An individual is eligible for a school-age grant in respect of a child if—
(a) the individual's application for the grant is made on or after 3 June 2019 (see regulation 4 in relation to when an application is to be treated as made),

(b) the individual's application for the grant is made within the period described in paragraph 2,
(c) no-one else has received, or is due to receive, a school-age grant in respect of the child (but see paragraph 3),
(d) on the day the application is made the individual satisfies the residence requirement set by paragraph 4,
(e) either the individual or the individual's partner is (or both of them are) responsible for the child on the day the application is made,
(f) at least one of these statements is true—
  (i) the individual or the individual's partner has (or both of them have) been awarded, for the day the application is made (or for a period which includes that day), assistance of a kind specified in regulation 11,
  (ii) the individual or the individual's partner has (or both of them have) been awarded universal credit for—
    (aa) the assessment period that includes the day the application is made, or
    (bb) the assessment period that ended immediately before the assessment period mentioned in sub-head (aa) started,
  (iii) on the day the application is made the individual is under 18 years of age,
  (iv) on the day the application is made the individual is—
    (aa) 18 or 19 years of age, and
    (bb) a dependant of another individual, [6 . . .]
(g) [6 . . .].

Period within which application must be made

2.—(1) The period referred to in paragraph 1(b)—
(a) begins on 1 June in the relevant year, and
(b) ends at the end of the last day of February in the following year.
(2) In sub-paragraph (1), "the relevant year" means—
(a) if the child's birthday is in January or February, the calendar year in which the child's 4th birthday falls,
(b) otherwise, the calendar year in which the child's 5th birthday falls.

Exception to paragraph 1(c)

3.—(1) For the purpose of determining the entitlement of the individual referred to in this paragraph as the applicant, the eligibility condition in paragraph 1(c) is to be ignored in the circumstance described by sub-paragraphs (2) to (6).
(2) An individual ("the first grant recipient") has been, or is due to be, given a school-age grant in respect of the child.
(3) Another individual ("the applicant") [4 is] responsible for the child [4 . . .].
(4) The applicant has not been the partner of the first grant recipient at any time since the first grant recipient applied for a school-age grant in respect of the child.
(5) On the day the applicant applies, the child does not normally live with the first grant recipient.
(6) On the day the applicant applies, no-one other than the first grant recipient has been, or is due to be, given a school-age grant in respect of the child.
(7) In this paragraph, references to "the day the applicant applies" are to the day the applicant's application for a school-age grant in respect of the child is made.

Residence requirement

4.—(1) The residence requirement referred to in paragraph 1(d) is satisfied by an individual on a day if, on that day—
(a) the individual is ordinarily resident in Scotland, and
(b) in a case where neither the individual nor the individual's partner has been awarded assistance as mentioned in paragraph 1(f)(i) or (ii), the condition set by sub-paragraph (2) is also met.
(2) The condition referred to in sub-paragraph (1)(b) is met on any day that the individual is—
(a) habitually resident in the United Kingdom, the Channel Islands [2 or the Isle of Man]
[2 (aa) a person who, or has a partner who, is habitually resident in the European Economic Area or Switzerland and—

(i) is a qualified person within the meaning of regulation 6(1)(a) (jobseeker), (b) (worker), (c) (self-employed person), (d) (self-sufficient person) or (e) (student) of the Immigration (European Economic Area) Regulations 2016 (the EEA Regulations);
(ii) retains the status referred to in sub-head (i) pursuant to regulation 6(2) or (4) of the EEA Regulations;
(iii) is a family member of a person referred to in sub-head (i) or (ii) within the meaning of regulation 7(1) of the EEA Regulations;
(iv) has a right to reside permanently in the United Kingdom by virtue of regulation 15(1) of the EEA Regulations; or
(v) has been granted indefinite or limited leave to enter, or remain in, the United Kingdom under the Immigration Act 1971 by virtue of Appendix EU to the immigration rules made under section 3(2) of that Act.]

[³ (ab) a person who—
(i) has leave to enter or remain in the United Kingdom granted under the immigration rules made under section 3(2) of the Immigration Act 1971, by virtue of—
(ia) the Afghan Relocations and Assistance Policy, or
(ib) the previous scheme for locally-employed staff in Afghanistan (sometimes referred to as the ex-gratia scheme),
(ii) has been granted discretionary leave outside the immigration rules as a dependant of a person referred to in sub-head (i), or
(iii) has leave granted under the Afghan Citizens Resettlement Scheme.]

[⁵ (ac) a person who was residing in Ukraine immediately before 1 January 2022, left Ukraine in connection with the Russian invasion which took place on 24 February 2022 and—
(i) has been granted leave in accordance with immigration rules made under section 3(2) of the Immigration Act 1971, [⁶ . . .]
(ii) has a right of abode in the United Kingdom within the meaning given in section 2 of that Act,] [⁶or
(iii) does not require leave to enter or remain in the United Kingdom in accordance with section 3ZA of that Act,]

[⁷(ad) a person who was residing in Sudan before 15 April 2023, left Sudan in connection with the violence which rapidly escalated on 15 April 2023 in Khartoum and across Sudan and—
(i) has been granted leave in accordance with immigration rules made under section 3(2) of the Immigration Act 1971,
(ii) has a right of abode in the United Kingdom within the meaning given in section 2 of that Act, or
(iii) does not require leave to enter or remain in the United Kingdom in accordance with section 3ZA of that Act,]

[⁸(ae) a person in Great Britain who was residing in Israel, the West Bank, the Gaza Strip, East Jerusalem, the Golan Heights or Lebanon immediately before 7 October 2023, left Israel, the West Bank, the Gaza Strip, East Jerusalem, the Golan Heights or Lebanon in connection with the Hamas terrorist attack in Israel on 7 October 2023 or the violence which rapidly escalated in the region following the attack and—
(i) has been granted leave in accordance with immigration rules made under section 3(2) of the Immigration Act 1971,
(ii) has a right of abode in the United Kingdom within the meaning given in section 2 of that Act, or
(iii) does not require leave to enter or remain in the United Kingdom in accordance with section 3ZA of that Act,]

(b) a refugee within the definition in Article 1 of the Convention relating to the status of refugees done at Geneva on 28 July 1951, as extended by article 1(2) of the Protocol relating to the status of refugees done at New York on 31 January 1967,
(c) a person who has been granted, or who is deemed to have been granted, leave outside the rules made under section 3(2) of the Immigration Act 1971 [⁵ . . .]
(d) a person who has humanitarian protection granted under the rules made under section 3(2) of the Immigration Act 1971,
(e) a person who—
(i) is not subject to immigration control within the meaning of section 115(9) of the Immigration and Asylum Act 1999, and
(ii) is in the United Kingdom as a result of deportation, expulsion or other removal by compulsion of law from another country to the United Kingdom.

[³ (3) In this paragraph, "the Afghan Citizens Resettlement Scheme" means the scheme announced by the United Kingdom Government on 18 August 2021.]

Early Years Assistance (Best Start Grants) (Scotland) Regulations 2018

PART 2

ASSISTANCE TO BE GIVEN

Value of grant

5. The value of a school-age grant is [⁹ £314.45].

Form in which grant is given

6.—(1) Subject to sub-paragraph (2), a school-age grant is to be given as money.
(2) If—
  (a) the Scottish Ministers offer to give an individual some or all of the value of a school-age grant in a form other than money, and
  (b) the individual agrees to be given the grant in that form,
the grant is to be given in that form, unless the individual withdraws agreement before the grant is given.]

AMENDMENTS

1. Early Years Assistance (Best Start Grants) (Scotland) Amendment (No.2) Regulations 2019 (SSI 2019/157) sch.2 (April 29, 2019).
2. Social Security Co-ordination (EU Exit) (Scotland) (Amendment etc.) Regulations 2020 (SSI 2020/399) reg.3(1) and (4) (December 31, 2020).
3. Social Security (Residence Requirements) (Afghanistan) (Scotland) Regulations 2021 (SSI 2021/320) reg.3(1) and (4) (September 15, 2021).
4. Best Start Grants and Scottish Child Payment (Miscellaneous Amendments) Regulations 2021 (SSI 2021/494) reg.5 (December 23, 2021).
5. Social Security (Residence Requirements) (Ukraine) (Scotland) Regulations 2022 (SSI 2022/108) reg.4(1) and (4) (March 22, 2022).
6. Social Security (Miscellaneous Amendment and Transitional Provision) (Scotland) Regulations 2022 (SSI 2022/336) reg.2(1) and (6) (November 14, 2022).
7. Social Security (Residence Requirements) (Sudan) (Scotland) Regulations 2023 (SSI 2023/149) reg.4(4) (May 17, 2023).
8. Social Security (Residence and Presence Requirements) (Israel, the West Bank, the Gaza Strip, East Jerusalem, the Golan Heights and Lebanon) (Scotland) Regulations 2023 (SSI 2023/309) reg.4(4) (October 26, 2023).
9. Social Security (Up-rating) (Miscellaneous Amendments) (Scotland) Regulations 2024 (SSI 2024/105) reg.5(1) and (4) (April 1, 2024, subject to a saving under reg.14 and para.4 of Sch.).

GENERAL NOTE

The effect of para.2 is that the child must be aged 5 at the time the claim is made, which must be between June 1st of one year and the end of February the next year. In *DR v Social Security Scotland* [2021] UT 16, the claimant's son was born in February 2014 and so was too old for a claim to be made when school-age grants were introduced in June 2019, even though he did not start school until August 2019, which is when the claim was made. The claimant argued that the legislation gave rise to discrimination contrary to the European Convention on Human Rights because a school-age grant was payable in respect of younger children starting school at the same time. The Upper Tribunal rejected the argument, largely because the child could have started school earlier and so before the new legislation came into force. Although the claimant had not been obliged to send him to school until August 2019, the education authority would have been obliged to make provision for him if she had wished to send him to school during the previous year, because his 5th birthday had been before the "appropriate latest date" in February. As the choice of a school starting date was therefore in the parent's hands, the Government was entitled to use the date of the child's birthday as the key criterion, rather than the date he actually started school.

(SSI 2019/292 reg.)

The Funeral Expense Assistance (Scotland) Regulations 2019

(SSI 2019/292)

Made   *12th September 2019*
Coming into force in accordance with regulation 1

The Scottish Ministers make the following Regulations in exercise of the powers conferred by sections 34, 41(4)(a), 43(5) and 52 of the Social Security (Scotland) Act 2018 and all other powers enabling them to do so.

In accordance with section 96(2) of that Act, a draft of this instrument has been laid before and approved by resolution of the Scottish Parliament.

In accordance with section 98 of that Act, no consultation with the Scottish Commission on Social Security was required.

ARRANGEMENT OF REGULATIONS

PART 1

INTRODUCTORY

1. Citation and commencement

PART 2

INTERPRETATION

2. Interpretation

PART 3

PROCEDURAL MATTERS

3. Applications
4. Determinations without application
5. Period for applications
6. Periods for redetermination requests

PART 4

ELIGIBILITY

7. Relationship to deceased person
8. Multiple applications
9. Residence conditions, place of funeral and status
10. Qualifying benefits
11. Estate of deceased person

The Funeral Expense Assistance (Scotland) Regulations 2019

PART 5

ASSISTANCE TO BE GIVEN

12. Calculation and form of funeral expense assistance
13. Amount of funeral expense assistance 2
14. Deductions from an award of funeral expense assistance

PART 1

INTRODUCTORY

Citation and commencement

13.165   **1.** These Regulations may be cited as the Funeral Expense Assistance (Scotland) Regulations 2019 and come into force on the first Monday after the day on which they are made.

PART 2

INTERPRETATION

Interpretation

13.166   **2.** In these Regulations—
"applicant" means a person who has applied for funeral expense assistance,
"backdated award" means an award of assistance for a day, or a period that begins on a day, that falls before the day the decision to make the award was taken,
"burial" does not include burial of ashes, where a person's remains have been cremated,
"determination" means a determination of an individual's entitlement under section 37 of the Social Security (Scotland) Act 2018,
"funeral" means a burial or a cremation of a deceased person or of a still-born child,
"partner" means—
  (i) where a person is living together with a spouse or civil partner, that other person,
  (ii) where a person is living together with a person as a married couple, that other person,
"still-born child" has the meaning given by section 56(1) of the Registration of Births, Deaths and Marriages (Scotland) Act 1965,
"working day" means a day other than a Saturday, a Sunday or a bank holiday in Scotland under the Banking and Financial Dealings Act 1971.

(SSI 2019/292 reg.2)

PART 3

PROCEDURAL MATTERS

Applications

3.—(1) A person who applies for funeral expense assistance is entitled to receive it if that person—
 (a) applies within the period described in regulation 5, and
 (b) meets the eligibility conditions prescribed in these Regulations.

(2) Regulation 4 sets out circumstances in which the Scottish Ministers are to determine an individual's entitlement to funeral expense assistance without receiving an application.

(3) Regulations 7 and 8 describe eligibility conditions relating to the applicant's relationship to the deceased person and multiple applications.

(4) Regulation 9 describes eligibility conditions relating to the applicant's residence, the last residence of the deceased person and the place where the funeral takes place.

(5) Regulations 10 and 11 describe eligibility conditions relating to the financial means of the applicant, based on receipt of income related benefits, and of the estate of the deceased person.

(6) An application is to be treated as made—
 (a) on the day it is received by the Scottish Ministers, or
 (b) if applicable, on the day nominated by the Scottish Ministers under regulation 5(5).

(7) For the avoidance of doubt, a thing that purports to be an application is not an application unless it is—
 (a) made to the Scottish Ministers in the form, and
 (b) accompanied by the evidence,
required by the Scottish Ministers under section 38(1) of the Social Security (Scotland) Act 2018.

Determinations without application

4.—(1) The Scottish Ministers are to make a determination of an individual's entitlement to funeral expense assistance without receiving an application where—
 (a) they have previously made a determination of the individual's entitlement to that assistance ("the original determination"),
 (b) they establish that due to an official error the original determination was wrongly made resulting in the individual—
  (i) not being given funeral expense assistance for which the individual was eligible, or
  (ii) being given less such assistance than that to which the individual was entitled,
 (c) the Scottish Ministers are not considering a request for re-determination of the individual's entitlement to such assistance, and
 (d) the individual has not appealed to the First-tier Tribunal for Scotland against the Scottish Ministers' determination of the individual's entitlement to such assistance.

The Funeral Expense Assistance (Scotland) Regulations 2019

(2) The Scottish Ministers are also to determine an individual's entitlement to funeral expense assistance without receiving an application where—
 (a) a determination has previously been made that the individual is not entitled to that assistance ("the original determination"), and
 (b) the Scottish Ministers establish that—
  (i) following an appeal, a backdated award of assistance described in regulation 10(1) has been made, and
  (ii) had that award been made before the original determination, a determination that the individual is entitled to funeral expense assistance would have been made instead.

(3) In making a determination required by paragraph (1) or (2) the Scottish Ministers are to use—
 (a) the information provided in the application that led to the original determination, and
 (b) any other information they obtained in connection with that application.

(4) Where a determination is to be, or has been, made without an application by virtue of this regulation, references in these Regulations to the day the application is made are to be read as references to the day the application that led to the original determination was made.

(5) In paragraph (1) "official error" means an error made by someone acting on behalf of the Scottish Ministers or on behalf of a Minister of the Crown that was not materially contributed to by anyone not so acting.

Period for applications

5.—(1) A person is not entitled to funeral expense assistance unless an application for that assistance is made within a period starting when the person whose funeral is being arranged dies and ending as calculated in paragraphs (3) and (4) ("the period for applications").

(2) No application for funeral expense assistance may be made while the person whose funeral is being arranged is alive.

(3) No application for funeral expense assistance may be made after the day falling six months after the day on which the funeral takes place, unless paragraph (5) applies.

(4) In calculating the end of the period for applications where the day of the month on which the funeral takes place is the 29th, 30th or 31st, and the month falling six months after that month does not have such a date, the period ends on the last day of the later month.

(5) The Scottish Ministers may nominate the date on which an application will be treated as made for the purposes of regulation 3(6)(b) if—
 (a) the award of assistance described in regulation 10(1) that the applicant is relying on to meet that eligibility condition is a backdated award,
 (b) the backdated award is an award of assistance for—
  (i) a day that falls within the period for applications, or
  (ii) a period that includes at least 1 day that falls within the period for applications, and
 (c) the application is received by the Scottish Ministers—
  (i) not more than 20 working days after the last day of the period for applications, and
  (ii) within 3 months of the applicant being informed of the backdated award by or on behalf of the public authority who made it.

(6) The date nominated by the Scottish Ministers under paragraph (5)—
(a) must be a day for which the backdated award is made, and
(b) must not be a day that falls outside the period for applications.

GENERAL NOTE

See further *CD v Social Security Scotland* [2024] UT 12.

Periods for redetermination requests

6.—(1) The period for requesting a re-determination of entitlement to funeral expense assistance, under section 41 of the Social Security (Scotland) Act 2018, is 31 days beginning with the day that the applicant is informed, in accordance with section 40 of that Act, of the right to make the request.

(2) Where such a request is validly made, the period allowed for re-determination (within the meaning of section 43 of that Act) is 16 working days beginning with—
(a) the day the request is received by the Scottish Ministers, [¹ ...]
(b) where the request is received by the Scottish Ministers later than the period prescribed by paragraph (1), the day on which the Scottish Ministers, or on appeal the First-tier Tribunal for Scotland, decide that the applicant has a good reason for not requesting the re-determination sooner [¹ , or
(c) in a case where the Scottish Ministers have informed the individual of their decision that the request for a re-determination was not made in such form as the Scottish Ministers require, the day on which it is subsequently decided by the First-Tier Tribunal for Scotland that the individual in question has made the request in such form as the Scottish Ministers require.]

AMENDMENT

1. Social Security (Period for Re-determination Requests) (Miscellaneous Amendments) (Scotland) Regulations 2021 (SSI 2021/469) reg.3 (February 9, 2022).

PART 4

ELIGIBILITY

Relationship to deceased person

7.—(1) To qualify for funeral expense assistance the applicant, or the partner of the applicant, must have accepted responsibility for the expenses of the funeral, and the Scottish Ministers must consider it to be reasonable for that responsibility to have been accepted.

(2) In determining whether it was reasonable to accept responsibility, the Scottish Ministers must consider—
(a) whether someone other than the applicant, or the partner of the applicant, would be the nearest relative of the deceased person in terms of section 65(3) to (6) (arrangements on death of adult) of the Burial and Cremation (Scotland) Act 2016, and

The Funeral Expense Assistance (Scotland) Regulations 2019

(b) any other relevant circumstances that the applicant brings to their attention.

(3) For the purposes of paragraph (2)(a), instead of section 65(3) to (6) of that Act regard is to be had to—

(a) section 66(3) to (5) (arrangements on death of a child) where the deceased person was under 16 years of age on the day of his or her death,

(b) section 74(3), (7) and (8) in relation to a still-born child.

Multiple applications

8.—(1) Where two or more persons accept responsibility for the expenses of the funeral, and each applies for funeral expense assistance, the Scottish Ministers must consider which of the persons is the nearer (or nearest) relative of the deceased person, applying the approach described in regulation 7(2)(a).

(2) The Scottish Ministers must determine the application by the nearer relative before they determine any other application for assistance.

(3) Where, in applying paragraph (1), two or more applicants for assistance rank equally as the nearer relative and are not in agreement as to which application is to be progressed, the Scottish Ministers must decide which application is to be progressed first.

(4) Where a determination is made to give a person funeral expense assistance in respect of a funeral, only that person is eligible for such assistance in respect of the expenses of a funeral of the deceased person.

(5) Where the Secretary of State decides to make a funeral payment within the meaning of the Social Fund Maternity and Funeral Expenses (General) Regulations 2005 or the Social Fund Maternity and Funeral Expenses (General) Regulations (Northern Ireland) 2005, no person is eligible for funeral expense assistance to meet, or help meet, expenses of a funeral in respect of the deceased person.

Residence conditions, place of funeral and status

9.—(1) To qualify for funeral expense assistance, the applicant must be ordinarily resident in Scotland at the date of their application for that assistance.

(2) The applicant is not entitled to that assistance unless—

(a) the deceased person was ordinarily resident in the United Kingdom at the date of his or her death, and

(b) the place of the funeral is in the United Kingdom, or in a case where paragraph (3) applies, in a member state of the EU, Iceland, Liechtenstein, Norway or Switzerland.

[1 (3) This paragraph applies where the applicant is, or has a partner who is—

(a) a qualified person within the meaning of regulation 6(1)(b) (worker) or (c) (self-employed person) of the Immigration (European Economic Area) Regulations 2016 (the EEA Regulations);

(b) a person who retains the status referred to in sub-paragraph (a) pursuant to regulation 6(2) or (4) of the EEA Regulations;

(c) a person who is a family member of a person referred to in sub-paragraph (a) or (b) within the meaning of regulation 7(1) of the EEA Regulations;

(SSI 2019/292 reg. 9)

(d) a person who has a right to reside permanently in the United Kingdom by virtue of regulation 15(1)(c), (d) or (e) of the EEA Regulations; or

(e) a person granted indefinite or limited leave to enter, or remain in, the United Kingdom under the Immigration Act 1971 by virtue of Appendix EU to the immigration rules made under section 3(2) of that Act.]

(4) [² . . .]

(5) A person is not entitled to funeral expense assistance if, at the time the application is made, the person is subject to immigration control within the meaning of section 115(9) of the Immigration and Asylum Act 1999, unless the person falls within a category or description of persons specified in Part 2 of the schedule of the Social Security (Immigration and Asylum) Consequential Amendments Regulations 2000 (persons not excluded under section 115 of that Act from entitlement to various social security benefits).

(6) Paragraph (2)(a) does not apply in respect of the funeral of a still-born child.

AMENDMENTS

1. Social Security Co-ordination (EU Exit) (Scotland) (Amendments etc.) Regulations 2020 SSI 2020/399) reg.5 (December 31, 2020).
2. Social Security (Up-rating) (Miscellaneous Amendment) (Scotland) Regulations 2021 (SSI 2021/170) reg.4(1) and (2) (April 1, 2021).

Qualifying benefits

10.—(1) To qualify for funeral expense assistance the applicant, or the partner of the applicant, must have been properly awarded in respect of the relevant day—

(a) income support under section 124 of the Social Security Contributions and Benefits Act 1992,
(b) state pension credit within the meaning given by section 1(1) of the State Pension Credit Act 2002,
(c) income-based jobseeker's allowance within the meaning of the Jobseekers Act 1995,
(d) working tax credit where the disability element or the severe disability element of working tax credit as specified in regulation 20(1)(b) and (f) of the Working Tax Credit (Entitlement and Maximum Rate) Regulations 2002 is included in the award,
(e) child tax credit within the meaning of the Tax Credits Act 2002,
(f) housing benefit within the meaning of section 123 of the Social Security Contributions and Benefits Act 1992,
(g) income-related employment and support allowance under Part 1 of the Welfare Reform Act 2007, or
(h) universal credit under Part 1 of the Welfare Reform Act 2012.

(2) An applicant, or the partner of the applicant, is not to be regarded as having been properly awarded assistance if—

(a) the award for the relevant day was made in error (whether or not induced by the individual),
(b) the award for the relevant day or the period that includes the relevant day is £0.

(3) In this paragraph "the relevant day" is—

13.175

(a) the day the application is received by the Scottish Ministers, or
(b) if applicable, the day nominated by the Scottish Ministers under regulation 5(5).

(4) For the purpose of paragraph (1)(h), the applicant, or the partner of the applicant, is awarded universal credit in respect of the relevant day if—
(a) the assessment period for their award includes the relevant day, or
(b) they had an award of universal credit for the assessment period that ended immediately before the start of the assessment period mentioned in sub-paragraph (a).

(5) In calculating the sum awarded for the purpose of paragraph (2)(b) where a deduction has been made from the award in respect of any liability to another person or by way of a sanction, the sum awarded is the sum that would have been awarded had the deduction not been made.

Estate of deceased person

11.—(1) A person is not entitled to funeral expense assistance if assets of the deceased person are available and sufficient to meet the costs of a funeral.

(2) No regard is to be had to the assets of a deceased person for the purpose of paragraph (1) if that person was under the age of 18 on the day of his or her death.

(3) For the purpose of paragraph (1) any lump sums due to the applicant or others by virtue of any insurance policy, occupational pension scheme, burial club, [¹ pre-paid funeral plan,] or similar scheme are to be considered an asset of the deceased person.

AMENDMENT

1. Funeral Expense Assistance and Young Carer Grants (Up-rating) (Miscellaneous Amendments) (Scotland) Regulations 2020 (S.S.I. 2020/99) reg.5(1) and (2) (April 1, 2020).

PART 5

ASSISTANCE TO BE GIVEN

Calculation and form of funeral expense assistance

12.—(1) The funeral expense assistance to be given is an amount calculated in accordance with regulation 13, less any applicable deductions provided for by regulation 14.

(2) Funeral expense assistance is to be given as money (subject to paragraph (3)).

(3) If—
(a) the Scottish Ministers offer to give an individual some or all of the value of funeral assistance in a form other than money, and
(b) the individual accepts the offer,
the assistance is to be given in the form offered.

Amount of funeral expense assistance

13.—(1) The amount of funeral expense assistance is—

(a) an amount calculated by reference to the costs which the person assisted incurs in arranging the funeral, so far as reasonable and of the types described in paragraphs (2) to (4),
(b) a payment of [² £1,257.75], except where paragraph (6) applies, and
(c) transport costs, so far as reasonable and of the types described in paragraph (7).

(2) The types of funeral costs for which assistance is given are the costs of—
(a) burial (see paragraph (3)) or cremation (see paragraph (4)),
(b) if required, any medical references and certificates from a registered medical practitioner, and
(c) obtaining any documents to release assets of the deceased person for the purposes of regulation 14 (deductions from an award).

(3) For a burial, the costs are—
(a) the cost of a new burial plot with a right of burial in it,
(b) fees levied by the local authority or person responsible for the operation of burials in the area where the burial takes place,
(c) the cost of grave-digging.

(4) For a cremation, the costs are—
(a) fees levied by the local authority or person responsible for the operation of crematoriums in the area where the cremation takes place,
(b) the fee for removal of any active implantable medical device, within the meaning of the Medical Devices Regulations 2002, subject to a limit of [² £25.35] where the removal is not carried out by a registered medical practitioner.

(5) Where a deceased person is not buried or cremated in the area in which they were ordinarily resident, and the costs of their burial or cremation (including transport costs) exceed those that would have applied had the burial or, as the case may be, cremation taken place in that area, no assistance is to be given for those additional costs.

(6) The payment in paragraph (1)(b) is [² £153.50] where the deceased person—
[¹ (a) has left in place a pre-paid funeral plan, and]
(b) was aged 18 or over on the day of his or her death.

(7) The types of transport costs for which assistance is given are the costs of—
(a) transport within the United Kingdom from the place where the body is situated to a funeral director's premises, to the deceased person's last residence, or to another place where it is appropriate for the body to lie prior to the funeral, plus a return journey, but not including the first 80 kilometres of travel,
(b) subject to paragraph (8), vehicular transport for the coffin and bearers, and one additional vehicle, from the funeral director's premises or place where the body is lying to the funeral, plus a return journey, but not including the first 80 kilometres of travel,
(c) one return journey by the person assisted either for the purpose of making arrangements for the funeral or for attendance at the funeral, but not exceeding the cost of a return journey from the person's home to the place of burial or cremation.

The Funeral Expense Assistance (Scotland) Regulations 2019

(8) Where assistance is given under paragraph (2)(a) for the costs of a burial or cremation, no assistance is to be given for transport costs under paragraph (7)(b) unless—
   (a) the distance travelled necessarily exceeds 80 kilometres, or
   (b) in the case of a burial, where no costs have been incurred for purchase of a burial plot, the distance travelled exceeds 80 kilometres.

AMENDMENTS

1. Funeral Expense Assistance and Young Carer Grants (Up-rating) (Miscellaneous Amendments) (Scotland) Regulations 2020 (SSI 2020/99) reg.5(1) and (3) (April 1, 2020, subject to a saving in reg.6).
2. Social Security (Up-rating) (Miscellaneous Amendments) (Scotland) Regulations 2024 (SSI 2024/105) reg.10 (April 1, 2024, subject to a saving under reg.14 and para.8 of Sch.).

Deductions from an award of funeral expense assistance

14.—(1) There is to be deducted from the amount of funeral expense assistance calculated in accordance with regulation 13 any funds or contributions which are available towards meeting the expense of the funeral from—
   (a) any assets of the deceased person which are available without confirmation having been granted, or (elsewhere in the United Kingdom) without probate or letters of administration, but ignoring any assets described in paragraph (3),
   (b) any [1 ...] insurance policy, burial club, occupational pension scheme, or any similar scheme or arrangement, unless the Scottish Ministers have made a contribution into that [1 ...] policy, club, scheme or arrangement,
   (c) a funeral grant, made out of public funds, in respect of the deceased person having been entitled to a war disablement pension within the meaning of section 17 of the State Pension Credit Act 2002.

(2) No deduction is to be made under paragraph (1) if the deceased person was under the age of 18 on the day of his or her death.

(3) For the purposes of paragraph (1)(a), the following sums payable to the estate of the deceased person are to be ignored—
   (a) arrears of any benefit under any enactment relating to social security in any part of the United Kingdom,
   (b) arrears of any assistance provided for by regulations under Parts 2 or 3 of the Social Security (Scotland) Act 2018, or under section 81 (carer's allowance supplement) of that Act.

AMENDMENT

1. Funeral Expense Assistance and Young Carer Grants (Up-rating) (Miscellaneous Amendments) (Scotland) Regulations 2020 (S.S.I. 2020/99) reg.5(1) and (4) (April 1, 2020).

(SSI 2019/324 reg.)

The Carer's Assistance (Young Carer Grants) (Scotland) Regulations 2019

(SSI 2019/324)

Made   *15th October 2019*
Coming into force in accordance with regulation 1

The Scottish Ministers make the following Regulations in exercise of the powers conferred by sections 28, 41(4)(a), 43(5) and 52 of the Social Security (Scotland) Act 2018 and all other powers enabling them to do so.

In accordance with section 96(2) of that Act, a draft of this instrument has been laid before and approved by resolution of the Scottish Parliament.

In accordance with section 97(2) of that Act, the Scottish Ministers have consulted the Scottish Commission on Social Security.

CONTENTS

1. Citation and Commencement
2. Interpretation
3. Overview
4. Making of applications
5. Conditions relating to the care being provided
6. Conditions relating to the person or persons being cared for
7. Further eligibility conditions
8. Conditions relating to residence
9. Periods for redetermination requests
10. Multiple applications involving care of the same person
11. Determination following backdated award of assistance
12. Amount and form of young carer grants

GENERAL NOTE

These regulations establish a scheme under s.28 of the Social Security (Scotland) Act 2018 for making grants to 16-18 year-olds who are acting as carers for disabled people.

PART 1

INTRODUCTORY AND INTERPRETATION

Citation and commencement

1. These Regulations may be cited as the Carer's Assistance (Young Carer Grants) (Scotland) Regulations 2019 and come into force on the first Monday after the day on which they are made.

Interpretation

2. In these Regulations—
"applicant" means a person who has applied for a young carer grant,

"determination" means a determination of an individual's entitlement under section 37 of the Social Security (Scotland) Act 2018,
"the qualifying period" means the period of 13 weeks described in regulation 5(1),
"young carer grant" means the grant provided for by these Regulations.

PART 2

ELIGIBILITY

Overview

3.—(1) A person who applies for a young carer grant is entitled to receive it if that person meets the conditions prescribed in these Regulations.

(2) Regulation 4 provides for the making of applications, including providing conditions related to the age of the applicant.

(3) Regulation 5 provides conditions relating to the care being provided and regulation 6 provides conditions relating to the person or persons being cared for.

(4) Regulation 7 provides further conditions relating to receipt of assistance and the status of the applicant.

(5) Regulation 8 provides conditions relating to the applicant's residence.

(6) Part 3 provides timescales for some procedural matters, including situations that involve multiple applications relating to care of the same person, and provides for when the Scottish Ministers must determine that an individual is entitled to a young carer grant without an application.

(7) Regulation 12 makes provision about the assistance that an applicant is entitled to receive.

Making of applications

4.—(1) A person is entitled to a young carer grant if, on the day their application for that assistance is made, they are aged at least 16 and are under the age of 19.

(2) In a non-leap year, the birthday of a person born on 29 February is to be taken to be 28 February.

[1(3) An application is to be treated as made—
(a) in a case where paragraph (7) applies, on the day after the end of the 13 week period to which the application relates,
(b) in any other case, on the day it is received by the Scottish Ministers.]

(4) In a case where, by virtue of a regulation 11, a determination is to be, or has been, made without an application, references in these Regulations to the day the application is made are to be read in accordance with paragraph (3) of that regulation.

(5) For the avoidance of doubt, a thing that purports to be an application is not an application unless it is—
(a) made in the form, and
(b) accompanied by the evidence,

required by the Scottish Ministers under section 38(1) of the Social Security (Scotland) Act 2018.

(6) For the purposes of determining assistance, the period of an application is the period of 13 weeks ending with the day before the day of the application for a grant and an application in respect of any other period of 13 weeks is to be regarded as an application for a different period, despite any overlap between the two periods.

[1(7) This paragraph applies where—
(a) an application for a young carer grant is made on or after the day on which the Carer's Allowance Supplement and Young Carer Grants (Residence Requirements and Procedural Provisions) (EU Exit) (Scotland) Regulations 2020 came into force,
(b) the application relates to a period of 13 weeks beginning after [2 22 July 2019] and ending before the day mentioned in sub-paragraph (a), and
(c) it appears to the Scottish Ministers that the applicant would be likely to have been entitled to a young carer grant on making an application on the day after the end of that 13 week period were it not for the requirement in regulation 8(3)(a) of these Regulations to have previously been properly paid a young carer grant, as it had effect immediately before the date on which the Carer's Allowance Supplement and Young Carer Grants (Residence Requirements and Procedural Provisions) (EU Exit) (Scotland) Regulations 2020 came into force.]

AMENDMENTS

1. Carer's Allowance Supplement and Young Carer Grants (Residence Requirements and Procedural Provisions) (EU Exit) (Scotland) Regulations 2020 (SI 2020/475) reg.11(2) (December 24, 2020).
2. Social Security (Up-rating) (Miscellaneous Amendment) (Scotland) Regulations 2021 (SSI 2021/170) reg.3(1) and (2) (April 1, 2021).

Conditions relating to the care being provided

5.—(1) To qualify for a young carer grant the applicant must have provided care, over the period of 13 weeks ending with the day before the day on which their application for a grant is made ("the qualifying period")—
(a) to a person or persons described in regulation 6,
(b) for the number of hours, and in the number of weeks, described in paragraph (2),
(c) as described in paragraph (3), and
(d) which was not provided in the manner described in paragraph (4).
(2) The care must have been provided—
(a) for at least 208 hours during the qualifying period, and
(b) in at least 10 weeks during that period.
(3) The care provided must involve activity that promotes the physical, mental or emotional well-being of the person being cared for.
(4) The care must not have been provided by the applicant—
(a) under or by virtue of a contract, unless the contract is of a kind specified by regulations under section 1(3)(a) of the Carers (Scotland) Act 2016 as not to be regarded as a contract for the purposes of that Act, or
(b) as voluntary work.

The Carer's Assistance (Young Carer Grants) (Scotland) Regulations 2019

Conditions relating to the person or persons being cared for

6.—(1) To qualify for a young carer grant the person or persons being cared for must, throughout the qualifying period and on the day the application for assistance is made, each be a person to whom a qualifying disability benefit is normally payable.

(2) An applicant may combine hours caring for up to three persons during the qualifying period.

(3) In paragraph (1), "qualifying disability benefit" means a disability benefit, or where applicable a component of a disability benefit, which is of a type, and being paid at a rate, that would entitle a person who cares for the recipient of that benefit and who meets the relevant qualifying conditions to—

(a) [¹Carer Support Payment payable under the Carer's Assistance (Carer Support Payment) (Scotland) Regulations 2023]
(b) carer's allowance, payable under section 70 of the Social Security Contributions and Benefits Act 1992) or section 70 of the Social Security Contributions and Benefits (Northern Ireland) Act 1992.

AMENDMENT

1. Carer's Assistance (Carer Support Payment) (Consequential and Miscellaneous Amendments and Transitional Provision) (Scotland) Regulations 2023 (SSI 2023/258) reg.7 (November 19, 2023).

Further eligibility conditions

7.—(1) An applicant is not entitled to a young carer grant if, [²at any point in the qualifying period or] on the day their application is made, the applicant is in receipt of a benefit named in regulation 6(3)(a) or (b) [². . .].

(2) An applicant is not entitled to a young carer grant if they have applied for a benefit named in regulation 6(3)(a) or (b) in respect of a period that includes the day their application is made, unless it has already been determined that the applicant is ineligible for that benefit in respect of that day.

[¹(3) An applicant is not entitled to a young carer grant if they have previously received a young carer grant, unless—

(a) the day their application is made is at least one year after the day of the application in respect of which that grant was paid, or
(b) in a case where regulation 4(7) applies, the day their application is made is at least one year either before or after the application in respect of which the grant was paid.]

[¹(4) Paragraph (5) applies if—

(a) any other person has been paid a young carer grant in respect of care of any of the persons being cared for in an application for a young carer grant, and
(b) either—
   (i) that grant was paid as a result of an application made during the year immediately preceding the day the applicant makes his or her application, or
   (ii) in a case where regulation 4(7) applies, that grant was paid as a result of an application made during the year immediately preceding or following the day the applicant makes his or her application.]

(5) The applicant is not entitled to a young carer grant unless—
(a) the other person who was paid a young carer grant has died, or
(b) the Scottish Ministers have concluded that a young carer grant should not have been paid to the other person.

(6) If an applicant has already received three young carer grants, they are not entitled to a further young carer grant.

[1(7) In paragraph (5)(a), in a case where regulation 4(7) applies, the reference to the other person who was paid a young carer grant having died is to be read as a reference to that other person having died before the day on which the applicant's application was made.]

AMENDMENTS

1. Funeral Expense Assistance and Young Carer Grants (Up-rating) (Miscellaneous Amendments) (Scotland) Regulations 2020 (SSI 2020/99) reg.3(1) and (2) (April 1, 2020) and Carer's Allowance Supplement and Young Carer Grants (Residence Requirements and Procedural Provisions) (EU Exit) (Scotland) Regulations 2020 (SI 2020/475) reg.11(3) (December 24, 2020).

2. Carer's Assistance (Carer Support Payment) (Scotland) Regulations 2023 (SSI 2023/302) Sch.1 para.11(2) (November 19, 2023).

Conditions relating to residence

8.—(1) Subject to paragraphs (2) and (3), to qualify for a young carer grant the applicant must, on the day their application is made for that assistance, be—
(a) habitually resident in the United Kingdom, the Channel Islands, the Isle of Man, the European Economic Area or Switzerland, and
(b) ordinarily resident in Scotland.

(2) Paragraph (1)(a) does not apply to the following persons (if they meet the condition in paragraph (1)(b) of being ordinarily resident in Scotland)—
(a) a refugee within the definition in Article 1 of the Convention relating to the status of refugees done at Geneva on 28 July 1951, as extended by article 1(2) of the Protocol relating to the status of refugees done at New York on 31 January 1967,
[2 (aa) a person who—
(i) has leave to enter or remain in the United Kingdom granted under the immigration rules made under section 3(2) of the Immigration Act 1971, by virtue of—
(ia) the Afghan Relocations and Assistance Policy, or
(ib) the previous scheme for locally-employed staff in Afghanistan (sometimes referred to as the ex-gratia scheme),
(ii) has been granted discretionary leave outside the immigration rules as a dependant of a person referred to in sub-head (i), or
(iii) has leave granted under the Afghan Citizens Resettlement Scheme.]
[3 (ab) a person who was residing in Ukraine immediately before 1 January 2022, left Ukraine in connection with the Russian invasion which took place on 24 February 2022 and—
(i) has been granted leave in accordance with immigration rules made under section 3(2) of the Immigration Act 1971, [4...]

(ii) has a right of abode in the United Kingdom within the meaning given in section 2 of that Act,] [⁶ or
(iii) does not require leave to enter or remain in the United Kingdom in accordance with section 3ZA of that Act,]
[⁵(ac) a person who was residing in Sudan before 15 April 2023, left Sudan in connection with the violence which rapidly escalated on 15 April 2023 in Khartoum and across Sudan and—
(i) has been granted leave in accordance with immigration rules made under section 3(2) of the Immigration Act 1971,
(ii) has a right of abode in the United Kingdom within the meaning given in section 2 of that Act, or
(iii) does not require leave to enter or remain in the United Kingdom in accordance with section 3ZA of that Act,]
[⁶(ad) a person in Great Britain who was residing in Israel, the West Bank, the Gaza Strip, East Jerusalem, the Golan Heights or Lebanon immediately before 7 October 2023, left Israel, the West Bank, the Gaza Strip, East Jerusalem, the Golan Heights or Lebanon in connection with the Hamas terrorist attack in Israel on 7 October 2023 or the violence which rapidly escalated in the region following the attack and—
(i) has been granted leave in accordance with immigration rules made under section 3(2) of the Immigration Act 1971,
(ii) has a right of abode in the United Kingdom within the meaning given in section 2 of that Act, or
(iii) does not require leave to enter or remain in the United Kingdom in accordance with section 3ZA of that Act,]
(b) a person who has been granted, or who is deemed to have been granted, leave outside the rules made under section 3(2) of the Immigration Act 1971[³ . . .]
(c) a person who has humanitarian protection granted under the rules made under section 3(2) of the Immigration Act 1971, or
(d) a person who—
(i) is not subject to immigration control within the meaning of section 115(9) of the Immigration and Asylum Act 1999, and
(ii) is in the United Kingdom as a result of deportation, expulsion or other removal by compulsion of law from another country to the United Kingdom.

[¹(3) An applicant who is not ordinarily resident in the United Kingdom does not have to meet the condition in paragraph (1)(b) (and therefore is entitled to a young carer grant) if—
(a) they satisfy the conditions in paragraph (4) on the day on which the application is made, if the application is made before IP completion day,
(b) they satisfy the conditions in paragraph (5) on the day the application is made, if the application is made after IP completion day and the individual has rights arising from a relevant EU regulation, or
(c) they satisfy the conditions in paragraph (6) on the day the application is made, if the application is made after IP completion day and the individual has rights arising from the UK-Ireland convention mentioned in that paragraph.

(4) The conditions referred to in paragraph (3)(a) are that the applicant must—

(a) be an individual—
  (i) to whom a relevant EU Regulation applies, and
  (ii) in respect of whom the United Kingdom is competent for payment of sickness benefits in cash for the purposes of Chapter 1 of Title III of the Regulation in question,
(b) be resident in—
  (i) Switzerland, or
  (ii) an EEA State other than the United Kingdom,
(c) have a genuine and sufficient link to Scotland, and
(d) meet the other conditions prescribed in these Regulations.

(5) The conditions referred to in paragraph (3)(b) are that the applicant must—
(a) be an individual—
  (i) to whom the rules set out in a relevant EU regulation apply by virtue of—
    (aa) Title III of Part 2 of the EU withdrawal agreement,
    (bb) Part 3 or Article 23(4) of the Swiss citizens' rights agreement (as defined in section 39(1) of the European Union (Withdrawal Agreement) Act 2020),
    (cc) Title III of the EEA EFTA separation agreement (as defined in that section), or
    (dd) the agreement constituted by the exchange of letters set out in the schedule of the Family Allowances, National Insurance and Industrial Injuries (Gibraltar) Order 1974, and
  (ii) in respect of whom the United Kingdom is, as a result, competent for payment of sickness benefits in cash,
(b) be resident in—
  (i) Switzerland,
  (ii) an EEA state, or
  (iii) Gibraltar,
(c) have a genuine and sufficient link to Scotland, and
(d) meet the other conditions prescribed in these Regulations.

(6) The conditions referred to in paragraph (3)(c) are that the applicant must—
(a) be an individual—
  (i) to whom the convention on Social Security between the Government of the United Kingdom of Great Britain and Northern Ireland and the Government of Ireland signed at Dublin on 1 February 2019, as modified from time to time in accordance with any provision of it, applies, and
  (ii) in respect of whom the United Kingdom is, as a result, competent for payment of long term care benefits,
(b) be resident in Ireland,
(c) have a genuine and sufficient link to Scotland, and
(d) meet the other conditions prescribed in these Regulations.

(7) The reference in paragraph (4)(c) to an individual's link to Scotland being sufficient is to it being sufficiently close that if the individual were not entitled to a young carer grant paragraph (4)—
(a) would be incompatible with EU law, or
(b) would have been incompatible with EU law immediately preceding IP completion day.

(8) The reference in paragraph (5)(c) to an individual's link to Scotland being sufficient is to it being sufficiently close that if the individual where not entitled to a young carer grant, paragraph (5) would be incompatible with the applicable agreement referred to in that paragraph.

(9) The reference in paragraph (6)(c) to an individual's link to Scotland being sufficient is to its being sufficiently close that if the individual were not entitled to a young carer grant, paragraph (6) would be incompatible with the convention mentioned in that paragraph.

(10) In this regulation—

[2 "the Afghan Citizens Resettlement Scheme" means the scheme announced by the United Kingdom Government on 18 August 2021.]

"EEA State" means—
(a) any member state of the European Union or
(b) any other state that is party to the agreement on the European Economic Area signed at Oporto on 2 May 1992, together with the Protocol adjusting that Agreement signed at Brussels on 17 March 1993, as modified or supplemented from time to time,

"EU law" has the meaning given by subsection (9) of section 126 of the Scotland Act 1998 or, if that subsection has been repealed, the meaning given by that subsection immediately before its repeal,

"relevant EU Regulation" means—
(a) one of the following Regulations—
  (i) Council Regulation (EC) No 1408/71 of 14 June 1971 on the application of social security schemes to employed persons, to self-employed persons and to members of their families moving within the Community,
  (ii) Regulation (EC) No 883/2004 of the European Parliament and of the Council of 29 April 2004 on the coordination of social security systems, or
(b) in relation to an individual to whom the exchange of letters mentioned in paragraph (5)(a)(i)(dd) applies, a Regulation mentioned in paragraph (a) as it forms part of domestic law by virtue of section 3 of the European Union (Withdrawal) Act 2018.

AMENDMENTS

1. Carer's Allowance Supplement and Young Carer Grants (Residence Requirements and Procedural Provisions) (EU Exit) (Scotland) Regulations 2020 (SI 2020/475) reg.11(4) (December 24, 2020).

2. Social Security (Residence Requirements) (Afghanistan) (Scotland) Regulations 2021 (SSI 2021/320) reg.5 (September 15, 2021).

3. Social Security (Residence Requirements) (Ukraine) (Scotland) Regulations 2022 (SSI 2022/108) reg.6 (March 22, 2022).

4. Social Security (Miscellaneous Amendment and Transitional Provision) (Scotland) Regulations 2022 (SSI 2022/336) reg.7 (November 14, 2022).

5. Social Security (Residence Requirements) (Sudan) (Scotland) Regulations 2023 (SSI 2023/149) reg.6(2) (May 17, 2023).

6. Social Security (Residence and Presence Requirements) (Israel, the West Bank, the Gaza Strip, East Jerusalem, the Golan Heights and Lebanon) (Scotland) Regulations 2023 (SSI 2023/309) reg.6(2) (October 26, 2023).

(SSI 2019/324 reg.9)

PART 3

PROCEDURAL MATTERS

Periods for redetermination requests

9.—(1) The period for requesting a re-determination of entitlement to a young carer grant, under section 41 of the Social Security (Scotland) Act 2018, is 31 days beginning with the day that the applicant is informed, in accordance with section 40 of that Act, of the right to make the request.

(2) The period allowed for re-determination (within the meaning of section 43 of that Act) is 16 working days beginning with—
  (a) the day that the request for a re-determination is received by the Scottish Ministers, [1 . . .]
  (b) where the request for a re-determination is received by the Scottish Ministers later than the period prescribed by paragraph (1), the day on which the Scottish Ministers, or on appeal the First-tier Tribunal for Scotland, decide that the applicant has a good reason for not requesting the re-determination sooner [1 , or
  (c) in a case where the Scottish Ministers have informed the individual of their decision that the request for a re-determination was not made in such form as the Scottish Ministers require, the day on which it is subsequently decided by the First-Tier Tribunal for Scotland that the individual in question has made the request in such form as the Scottish Ministers require.]

(3) For the purpose of paragraph (2), a "working day" is a day other than—
  (a) a Saturday,
  (b) a Sunday, or
  (c) a bank holiday in Scotland under the Banking and Financial Dealings Act 1971.

AMENDMENT

1. Social Security (Period for Re-determination Requests) (Miscellaneous Amendments) (Scotland) Regulations 2021 (SSI 2021/469) reg.4 (February 9, 2022).

Multiple applications involving care of the same person

10.—(1) Paragraphs (2) and (3) apply where two or more applicants state that they are caring for the same person.

(2) The Scottish Ministers must determine which (if any) of the applicants is to be entitled to receive a young carer grant.

(3) Where the applications were made at different times, the Scottish Ministers must determine the application made first before determining any other application.

Determination following backdated award of assistance

11.—(1) The Scottish Ministers are to make a determination of an individual's entitlement to a young carer grant without receiving an application where—

The Carer's Assistance (Young Carer Grants) (Scotland) Regulations 2019

(a) an application has previously been made for a young carer grant ("the application"),
(b) the determination made in respect of the application was that the applicant was not entitled to a young carer grant,
(c) the only reason for the applicant not being entitled to a young carer grant was that a person being cared for was not in receipt of a qualifying disability benefit as required by regulation 6 throughout the qualifying period for the application and on the day of the application,
(d) the Scottish Ministers establish that—
  (i) an award of a qualifying disability benefit has been made to the person being cared for that is a backdated award,
  (ii) had that award been made before the day of the application, a determination that the individual is entitled to a young carer grant would have been made instead, and
(e) no other person has received a young carer grant since the day of the application, in respect of care of the person being cared for.

(2) In making a determination required by paragraph (1) the Scottish Ministers are to use—
(a) the information provided in the application that led to the original determination, and
(b) any other information they have obtained in connection with that application.

(3) Where a determination is to be, or has been, made without an application by virtue of this regulation, references in these Regulations to the day the application is made are to be read as references to the day the application that led to the original determination was made.

(4) In this regulation a "backdated award" means an award of assistance for a day, or a period that begins on a day, that falls before the day the decision to make that award was taken.

PART 4

ASSISTANCE TO BE GIVEN

Amount and form of young carer grants

12.—(1) [¹Subject to paragraph (1A), a young carer grant] is to be given as a payment of [² £383.75].

[¹ (1A) Where the application for a young carer grant relates to a qualifying period which ended before the date on which the Carer's Allowance Supplement and Young Carer Grants (Residence Requirements and Procedural Provisions) (EU Exit) (Scotland) Regulations 2020 came into force, the amount of young carer grant to be given is the amount specified in paragraph (1) as it had effect on the day on which the application was made.]

(2) A young carer grant is to be given as money (subject to paragraph (3)).
(3) If—
(a) the Scottish Ministers offer to give an applicant some or all of the value of a young carer grant in a form other than money, and
(b) the applicant agrees to be given the grant in that form,
the grant is to be given in that form, unless the applicant withdraws agreement before the grant is given.

(SSI 2019/324 reg.12)

AMENDMENTS

1. Carer's Allowance Supplement and Young Carer Grants (Residence Requirements and Procedural Provisions) (EU Exit) (Scotland) Regulations 2020 (SI 2020/475) reg.11(5) (December 24, 2020).
2. Social Security (Up-rating) (Miscellaneous Amendments) (Scotland) Regulations 2024 (SSI 2024/105) reg.13 (April 1, 2024, subject to a saving under reg.14 and para.11 of Sch.).

GENERAL NOTE

Regulation 7(3) and (6) broadly has the effect that a young person may be entitled to one young carer's grant a year for up to three years, and so it is effectively an annual payment although a new application is required each year. The saving in the up-rating Regulations has the effect that the grant is paid at the rate in force on the day the application is made.

13.193

The Carer's Allowance (Coronavirus) (Breaks in Care) (Scotland) Regulations 2020

(SSI 2020/117)

Made   *1st April 2020*
Laid before the Scottish Parliament   *2nd April 2020*
Coming into force   *3rd April 2020*

The Scottish Ministers make the following Regulations in exercise of the powers conferred by sections 70(8) and 175(1) and (3) of the Social Security Contributions and Benefits Act 1992 and all other powers enabling them to do so.

Citation, commencement and interpretation

1.—(1) These Regulations may be cited as the Carer's Allowance (Coronavirus) (Breaks in Care) (Scotland) Regulations 2020 and come into force on 3 April 2020.

13.194

(2) In these Regulations—
"carer's allowance" means the allowance paid under section 70 of the Social Security Contributions and Benefits Act 1992 (invalid care allowance),
"coronavirus" means severe acute respiratory syndrome coronavirus 2 (SARS-CoV-2),
"isolation" in relation to a person means separation of that person from any other person in such manner as to prevent infection or contamination with coronavirus, and
"severely disabled person" has the meaning given in section 70(2) of the Social Security Contributions and Benefits Act 1992.

Entitlement to carer's allowance while unable to care as a result of coronavirus

2.—(1) This regulation applies where a person in receipt of carer's allowance ("A") is temporarily unable to care for the severely disabled person

13.195

("B") in respect of whom the carer's allowance is paid by reason of isolation due to, or infection with, coronavirus of either A or B.

(2) Regulation 4(2) of the Social Security (Invalid Care Allowance) Regulations 1976 (circumstances in which persons are or are not to be treated as engaged or regularly and substantially engaged in caring for severely disabled persons) is to be read as if the words from "and" at the end of sub-paragraph (a) to the end of sub-paragraph (b) were omitted.

Expiry

3. Regulation 2 ceases to have effect [^{1}on [^{2} 31 August] 2021 at 2359 hours].

AMENDMENTS

1. Carer's Allowance (Coronavirus) (Breaks in Care) (Scotland) Amendment Regulations 2020 (SSI 2020/350 reg.2(2) (December 3, 2020).
2. Carer's Allowance (Coronavirus) (Breaks in Care) (Scotland) Amendment Regulations 2021 (SSI 2021/140) reg.2(1) and (2) (May 12, 2021).

[^{1}Continued disregard of breaks in care related to coronavirus

4.—(1) This regulation applies where a person who is in receipt of carer's allowance ("A") on or after [^{2} 1 September] 2021 temporarily ceases to care for the severely disabled person ("B") in respect of whom the carer's allowance is paid.

(2) For the purposes of regulation 4(2)(b) of the Social Security (Invalid Care Allowance) Regulations 1976, there is to be disregarded any week in which A did not meet the requirements of regulation 4(1) of those Regulations in respect of care for B where—
   (a) the break in A's care for B occurred between 3 April 2020 and [^{2} 1 September] 2021, and
   (b) the break in care arose because of isolation due to, or infection with, coronavirus of either A or B.]

AMENDMENTS

1. Carer's Allowance (Coronavirus) (Breaks in Care) (Scotland) Amendment Regulations 2020 (SSI 2020/350 reg.2(3) (December 3, 2020).
2. Carer's Allowance (Coronavirus) (Breaks in Care) (Scotland) Amendment Regulations 2021 (SSI 2021/140) reg.2(1) and (3) (May 12, 2021).

The Scottish Child Payment Regulations 2020

(SSI 2020/351)

Made	*3rd November 2020*
Coming into force	*9th November 2020*

The Scottish Ministers make the following Regulations in exercise of the powers conferred by sections 79 and 95 of the Social Security (Scotland) Act 2018 and all other powers enabling them to do so.

In accordance with section 96(2) of that Act, a draft of these Regulations has been laid before and approved by resolution of the Scottish Parliament.

In accordance with section 97(2) of that Act, the Scottish Ministers have informed the Scottish Commission on Social Security of their proposals,

(SSI 2020/351 reg)

notified the Scottish Parliament that they have done so and made their proposals publicly available by such means as they consider appropriate.

ARRANGEMENT OF REGULATIONS

PART 1

INTRODUCTION

1. Citation
2. Commencement
3. Overview

PART 2

INTERPRETATION

General

4. Interpretation

Expressions about time and timing

5. When an application is to be treated as made
6. Meaning of "working day"
7. Calculation of the age of a child born on 29 February
8. Meaning of "week"

Expressions about inter-personal relationships

9. Meaning of being responsible for a child
10. Meaning of "partner"
11. Meaning of "kinship carer"
12. Meaning of "dependant"

Expressions about social security assistance

13. Meaning of determination of entitlement to a Scottish child payment
14. Meaning of references to specified kinds of assistance
15. Meaning of references to assistance being awarded
16. Meaning of "assessment period" in relation to universal credit

PART 3

ELIGIBILITY AND ASSISTANCE TO BE GIVEN

17. Duty to give assistance
18. Eligibility for a Scottish child payment
19. Ongoing entitlement
20. Value and form of a Scottish child payment

21. Time of payment
22. Individual's right to stop receiving assistance
23. Later determination supersedes earlier

PART 4

Transitory provision

24. Definitions – initial period
25. When an application is treated as made – initial period
26. Time of payment – initial period
27. Duty to notify – initial period

SCHEDULE   Procedural matters

PART 1

Introduction

Citation

13.198   **1.** These Regulations may be cited as the Scottish Child Payment Regulations 2020.

Commencement

13.199   **2.** These Regulations come into force on the first Monday after the day on which they are made.

Overview

13.200   **3.**—(1) Part 2 makes provision about the interpretation of these Regulations.

(2) Part 3 makes provision about eligibility and the assistance that is to be given to eligible individuals in connection with having responsibility for a child (referred to in these Regulations as a "Scottish child payment").

(3) Part 4 makes transitory provision.

(4) The schedule makes provision about matters of procedure for applying for, and determining entitlement to, a Scottish child payment.

PART 2

Interpretation

General

[¹ Interpretation

13.201   **4.** In these Regulations—
"the 2018 Act" means the Social Security (Scotland) Act 2018,

(SSI 2020/351 s.4)

"child" means a person under the age of 16, and
"coronavirus" means severe acute respiratory syndrome coronavirus 2 (SARS CoV-2).]

AMENDMENT

1. Social Security (Miscellaneous Amendment and Transitional Provision) (Scotland) Regulations 2022 (SSI 2022/336) reg.4(1) and (2) (November 14, 2022).

Expressions about time and timing

When an application is to be treated as made

5. A reference to the day on which an application is made means the day on which an application is received by the Scottish Ministers or, as the context may require, the day on which the application is treated as having been made by virtue of regulation 25 or the schedule.

13.202

Meaning of "working day"

6. A "working day" means a day other than—
   (a) a Saturday,
   (b) a Sunday, or
   (c) a day which is a bank holiday in Scotland under the Banking and Financial Dealings Act 1971.

13.203

Calculation of the age of a child born on 29 February

7. When calculating the age of a child born on 29 February for the purposes of these Regulations, in a non-leap year the birthday of the child is to be taken to be 28 February.

13.204

Meaning of "week"

8. A "week" means a period of 7 days.

13.205

Expressions about inter-personal relationships

Meaning of being responsible for a child

9. An individual is to be regarded as responsible for a child on a day only if at least one or more of the following statements is true—
   (a) the child is a dependant of the individual on that day,
   (b) the child is a dependant of the individual's partner on that day.

13.206

Meaning of "partner"

10. A person ("A") is the partner of another person ("B") on a day only if, on that day, A and B would be regarded as a couple for the purposes of Part 1 of the Welfare Reform Act 2012 (see section 39 of that Act).

13.207

Meaning of "kinship carer"

[¹11.—(1) An individual is a kinship carer for a child on a day if—

13.208

(a) the individual is—
   (i) a person who is related to the child,
   (ii) a person who is known to the child and with whom the child has a pre-existing relationship, or
   (iii) a friend or acquaintance of a person related to the child, and
(b) on that day, the child lives with the individual (exclusively or predominantly) under the terms of—
   (i) a kinship care order as defined in section 72(1) of the Children and Young People (Scotland) Act 2014,
   (ii) any other order under section 11(1) of the Children (Scotland) Act 1995 ("the 1995 Act"), or
   (iii) an agreement between the individual, the individual's partner or both of them and—
      (aa) a local authority by which the child is looked after within the meaning of section 17(6) of the 1995 Act,
      (bb) a local authority in England or Wales by which the child is looked after within the meaning of section 105(4) of the Children Act 1989 ("the 1989 Act"), or
      (cc) an authority in Northern Ireland by which the child is looked after within the meaning of article 25 of the Children (Northern Ireland) Order 1995 ("the 1995 Order").
(2) A person described in paragraph (1)(a) must not be—
(a) the parent of the child within the meaning of section 15(1) of the 1995 Act,
(b) a foster carer within the meaning of regulation 2 of the Looked After Children (Scotland) Regulations 2009,
(c) a local authority foster parent in England and Wales within the meaning of section 105(1) of the 1989 Act, or
(d) an authority foster parent in Northern Ireland within the meaning of article 27(3) of the 1995 Order.
(3) In paragraph (1)(a) "related" means related either by blood, marriage or civil partnership.]

AMENDMENT

1. Social Security (Miscellaneous Amendment and Transitional Provision) (Scotland) Regulations 2022 (SSI 2022/336) reg.4(1) and (3) (November 14, 2022).

Meaning of "dependant"

12.—(1) A child is to be regarded as a dependant of a person on a day only if—
   (a) paragraph (2) applies, or
   (b) on that day the person is a kinship carer for the child.
(2) This paragraph applies if—
(a) the person has been awarded—
   (i) child tax credit, child benefit or state pension credit for the day in question (or for a period that includes that day), or
   (ii) universal credit for an assessment period that includes the day in question, and
(b) the child is recognised to be a child for whom the person has responsibility in terms of that award of assistance.

(3) It is immaterial for the purpose of this regulation that the award of assistance to that person referred to in paragraph (2) does not include any amount in respect of the child due to a rule that restricts the number of dependants in respect of whom the person can be given that type of assistance.

Expressions about social security assistance

Meaning of determination of entitlement to a Scottish child payment

13.—(1) Unless the context otherwise requires, references in these Regulations to a determination of an individual's entitlement to a Scottish child payment are to a determination made—
(a) by the Scottish Ministers—
  (i) under paragraph 3 of the schedule, or
  (ii) (following a request for a re-determination) under paragraph 16 of the schedule,
(b) by the First-Tier Tribunal for Scotland—
  (i) under paragraph 22 of the schedule in an appeal against a determination made by the Scottish Ministers, or
  (ii) (subsequent to such an appeal) under its Tribunals Act powers,
(c) by the Upper Tribunal for Scotland under its Tribunals Act powers (subsequent to an appeal against, or following a review of, a decision of the First-tier Tribunal).

(2) In this regulation, "Tribunals Act powers" means powers under Part 6 (review or appeal of decisions) of the Tribunals (Scotland) Act 2014.

(3) A determination of an individual's entitlement to a Scottish child payment consists of—
(a) a decision about whether or not the eligibility rules specified in regulation 18 are satisfied in the individual's case,
(b) if those rules are satisfied, a decision (taken in accordance with these Regulations) about what assistance the individual is entitled to be given, and
(c) if the determination is to be made on the basis that the individual has ongoing entitlement to a Scottish child payment, a decision about what assistance the determination is to entitle the individual to be given in the future.

Meaning of references to specified kinds of assistance

14. For the purposes of these Regulations, references to a kind of assistance specified in this regulation are to—
(a) child tax credit under the Tax Credits Act 2002,
(b) income-based jobseeker's allowance under the Jobseekers Act 1995,
(c) income-related employment and support allowance under Part 1 of the Welfare Reform Act 2007,
(d) income support under Part VII of the Social Security Contributions and Benefits Act 1992,
(e) state pension credit under the State Pension Credit Act 2002,
(f) universal credit under Part 1 of the Welfare Reform Act 2012,
(g) working tax credit under the Tax Credits Act 2002.

Meaning of references to assistance being awarded

[¹ **15.**—(1) An individual is not to be regarded as having been awarded a kind of assistance specified in regulation 14 for a day or a period if—
   (a) the award was made in error (whether or not induced by the individual), or
   (b) the sum awarded to the individual for the day or the period is £0.

(2) In paragraph (1)(b), the reference to "the sum awarded" means, in a case where a deduction has been made—
   (a) in respect of any liability the individual has to another person, or
   (b) by way of a sanction,
the sum that would have been awarded had the deduction not been made.]

AMENDMENT

1. Scottish Child Payment Amendment Regulations 2021 (SSI 2021/16) reg. 3 (January 15, 2021).

Meaning of "assessment period" in relation to universal credit

16. "Assessment period" means a period in respect of which universal credit may be payable to the individual in question in accordance with section 7 of the Welfare Reform Act 2012.

PART 3

ELIGIBILITY AND ASSISTANCE TO BE GIVEN

Duty to give assistance

17. The Scottish Ministers must give an individual whatever assistance the individual is entitled to be given under a determination of the individual's entitlement to a Scottish child payment.

Eligibility for a Scottish child payment

18. An individual is eligible for a Scottish child payment in respect of a child if—
   (a) the individual has made an application for the payment (or an application is treated as having been made by the individual by virtue of a provision in the schedule requiring the Scottish Ministers to make a determination without application in the individual's case),
   (b) the child is under [¹ 16] years of age on the day the application is made,
   (c) no other individual has received, or is due to receive, a Scottish child payment in respect of the child and the period that the payment will cover (other than in circumstances where paragraph 10(1)(b) of the schedule applies),
   (d) the individual is ordinarily resident in Scotland on the day the application is made,
   (e) the individual is responsible for the child on the day the application is made, and

(f) the individual has been awarded, for the day the application is made (or for a period or universal credit assessment period which includes that day), assistance of a kind specified in regulation 14.

AMENDMENT

1. Social Security (Miscellaneous Amendment and Transitional Provision) (Scotland) Regulations 2022 (SSI 2022/336) reg.4(1) and (4) (November 14, 2022).

GENERAL NOTE

The amendments to reg.18(b) and 19 have the effect of extending the scope of child payments to those with children under 16, rather than only children under 6. Regulation 5 of the 2022 Regulations makes transitional provision—

"Transitional and consequential provision in connection with regulation 4

5.—(1) Any application for a Scottish child payment under the Scottish Child Payment Regulations in respect of a child who is aged 6 years old or older which is made before 14 November 2022 is to be treated for the purposes of those Regulations as having been made on 14 November 2022.

(2) Where the Scottish Ministers make a determination without receiving an application by virtue of Part 2 of the schedule of the Scottish Child Payment Regulations that an individual is entitled to a Scottish child payment in respect of—
   (a) a period that includes one or more days falling before 14 November 2022, and
   (b) a child who reached the age of 6 before that date, the individual's entitlement begins on 14 November 2022.

(3) In the case of any application to which paragraph (1) applies, regulation 18A of the Scottish Child Payment Regulations is to be read as though, for the words from "begins" to the end there were substituted "begins is 14 November 2022".

(4) In the case of any determination to which paragraph (2) applies, regulation 18A of the Scottish Child Payment Regulations does not apply.

(5) For the purposes of paragraph (1), an application is "made" on the date it is received by the Scottish Ministers."

See the annotation to reg.19 for further transitional provision in respect of those with ongoing entitlement in respect of children under 6.

[¹ Beginning of entitlement to assistance

18A. Where a determination is made that an individual is entitled to a Scottish child payment, the date on which entitlement begins is the date on which the application is made or treated as made in accordance with regulation 5.]

AMENDMENT

1. Social Security (Miscellaneous Amendment and Transitional Provision) (Scotland) Regulations 2022 (SSI 2022/336) reg.4(1) and (5) (November 14, 2022).

GENERAL NOTE

13.218   This provision is disapplied where transitional provision is made in the light of the extension of eligibility to cover children up to 16, rather than up to 6 (see the annotations to regs. 18 and 19, above and below respectively).

Ongoing entitlement

13.219   19.—(1) A determination of an individual's entitlement to a Scottish child payment in respect of a child and a week may be made on the basis that the individual has an ongoing entitlement to a Scottish child payment.

(2) A determination of ongoing entitlement is made on the basis that the individual will continue to be entitled to a Scottish child payment in respect of that child in each subsequent week until—
  (a) the week following any week in which the individual ceases to have responsibility for the child,
  (b) the week following that in which the child attains the age of [¹ 16] years,
  (c) the week following any week in which the individual ceases to be ordinarily resident in Scotland,
  (d) any week in which no award of assistance of a kind specified in regulation 14 is made to the individual for any day in that week.

AMENDMENT

1. Scottish Child Payment (Ancillary Provision) Regulations 2022 (SSI 2022/326) reg.2 (November 14, 2022).

GENERAL NOTE

13.220   The amendment to reg.19(2)(b) is consequential upon the similar amendment made to reg.18(b) (by different Regulations but from the same date, see above), which makes provision for child payments in respect of children up to the age of 16, rather than only for those aged up to 6. Regulation 4 of the amending Regulations makes transitional provision—

"**Transitional provision: determination to extend existing award of Scottish child payment**

4.—(1) The Scottish Ministers are to make a determination of an individual's entitlement to a Scottish child payment where paragraph (2) applies.

(2) On 14 November 2022, the individual has an ongoing entitlement to a Scottish child payment in accordance with regulation 19(1) of the 2020 Regulations (ongoing entitlement) by virtue of a determination that was made by the Scottish Ministers before that date.

(3) Subject to paragraph (4), a determination under paragraph (1) must be made—
  (a) on the assumption that the individual continues to meet the eligibility criteria set out in regulation 18 of the 2020 Regulations (eligibility for a Scottish child payment) on the date on which the determination is made, and
  (b) on the basis that the individual has an ongoing entitlement to a Scottish child payment on the basis described in regulation 19(2) of the 2020 Regulations.

(4) Where a determination is to be, or has been, made under this regulation—

(SSI 2020/351 s.19)

 (a) the individual's entitlement begins on 14 November 2022,
 (b) regulation 18A of the 2020 Regulations (beginning of entitlement to assistance) does not apply, and
 (c) the determination is to be treated for the purposes of the 2020 Regulations as a determination made by the Scottish Ministers under paragraph 3 of the schedule of those Regulations (duty to make a determination of entitlement)."

[¹ Circumstances in which assistance may be suspended

19A.—(1) The Scottish Ministers may decide that an individual who has an ongoing entitlement to Scottish child payment in respect of a period by virtue of regulation 19 is not to become entitled to be given some or all of that assistance at the time at which the individual otherwise would in accordance with that regulation, as read with regulation 21 (time of payment) (referred to in these Regulations as a decision to suspend the individual's Scottish child payment).

(2) Where such a decision is made in respect of an individual, payments of Scottish child payment to that individual are to be suspended until such time as the Scottish Ministers decide that the individual is once again to become entitled to be given Scottish child payment.

(3) The Scottish Ministers may decide to suspend an individual's Scottish child payment only in the circumstances where—
 (a) paragraph 25(2) of the schedule applies, or
 (b) the Scottish Ministers have made arrangements (whether under section 85A of the 2018 Act, section 85B of the 2018 Act or otherwise) for a person to receive the Scottish child payment on the individual's behalf, and the Scottish Ministers consider that it is necessary to suspend the Scottish child payment—
  (i) in order to protect the individual from the risk of financial abuse, or
  (ii) because the person with whom the Scottish Ministers have made arrangements is unable to continue to receive the Scottish child payment.

13.221

AMENDMENT

1. Scottish Child Payment Regulations 2020 and the Disability Assistance for Children and Young People (Scotland) Regulations 2021 (Miscellaneous Amendments) Regulations 2022 (SSI 2022/41) reg.2(1) and (2) (February 9, 2022).

[¹ Having regard to financial circumstances

19B. The Scottish Ministers must have regard to an individual's financial circumstances prior to making a decision to suspend payment to the individual of some or all of a Scottish child payment.]

13.222

AMENDMENT

1. Scottish Child Payment Regulations 2020 and the Disability Assistance for Children and Young People (Scotland) Regulations 2021 (Miscellaneous Amendments) Regulations 2022 (SSI 2022/41) reg.2(1) and (2) (February 9, 2022).

[¹ Information to be given following suspension

19C.—(1) Having made a decision to suspend an individual's Scottish child payment, the Scottish Ministers must inform the individual of—
  (a) their decision to suspend the individual's Scottish child payment,
  (b) the reasons for their decision,
  (c) any steps which might be taken by the individual in order for the Scottish Ministers to consider ending the suspension, and
  (d) the individual's right under regulation 19D to require the Scottish Ministers to review their decision.
(2) The Scottish Ministers must fulfil their duty under paragraph (1) in a way that leaves the individual with a record of the information which the individual can show to, or otherwise share with, others.]

AMENDMENT

1. Scottish Child Payment Regulations 2020 and the Disability Assistance for Children and Young People (Scotland) Regulations 2021 (Miscellaneous Amendments) Regulations 2022 (SSI 2022/41) reg.2(1) and (2) (February 9, 2022).

[¹ Right to review suspension

19D.—(1) An individual may require the Scottish Ministers to review a decision to suspend that individual's Scottish child payment.
(2) The Scottish Ministers must—
  (a) complete a review mentioned in paragraph (1) within 31 days beginning with the day on which they received notice from the individual requiring them to review their decision,
  (b) inform the individual of the outcome of the review including the reasons for it.
(3) The Scottish Ministers must fulfil their duty under paragraph (2)(b) in a way that leaves the individual with a record of the information which the individual can show to, or otherwise share with, others.]

AMENDMENT

1. Scottish Child Payment Regulations 2020 and the Disability Assistance for Children and Young People (Scotland) Regulations 2021 (Miscellaneous Amendments) Regulations 2022 (SSI 2022/41) reg.2(1) and (2) (February 9, 2022).

[¹ Ending a suspension

19E. The Scottish Ministers are to make a decision to end a suspension where—
  (a) the individual provides the information mentioned in paragraph 25(1) of the schedule and the Scottish Ministers consider that they do not require to make a determination without application,
  (b) regulation 19A(3)(a) applies and the Scottish Ministers make a determination without application under paragraph 6 (determination following official error resulting in underpayment), 7 (determination following error resulting in overpayment), 8 (determination following backdated award of assistance), 10 (determination following

(SSI 2020/351 s.19E)

change of circumstances, etc.), 11 (determination following award of a Scottish child payment in respect of another child), 12 (determination following cessation of award of a Scottish child payment) or 13 (determination to effect a deduction decision) of the schedule,
(c) the Scottish Ministers make a determination under paragraph 25(4) of the schedule,
(d) the circumstances mentioned in regulation 19A(3)(b) no longer apply, or
(e) the Scottish Ministers consider it appropriate in the circumstances, including having regard to the financial circumstances of the individual.]

AMENDMENT

1. Scottish Child Payment Regulations 2020 and the Disability Assistance for Children and Young People (Scotland) Regulations 2021 (Miscellaneous Amendments) Regulations 2022 (SSI 2022/41) reg.2(1) and (2) (February 9, 2022).

[¹ **Effect of suspension ending**

19F. When— 13.226
(a) the suspension of an individual's Scottish child payment ends, and
(b) under the latest determination of the individual's entitlement to Scottish child payment relating to the period of the suspension the individual would have become entitled to be given Scottish child payment during that period,

the individual is immediately to be given the Scottish child payment that the individual would have become entitled to be given under the determination during the period of suspension.]

AMENDMENT

1. Scottish Child Payment Regulations 2020 and the Disability Assistance for Children and Young People (Scotland) Regulations 2021 (Miscellaneous Amendments) Regulations 2022 (SSI 2022/41) reg.2(1) and (2) (February 9, 2022).

[¹ **Interpretation: regulations 19A to 19F**

19G. In regulations 19A to 19F— 13.227
(a) references to an individual's Scottish child payment being suspended are to an individual not becoming entitled to be given some or all of the Scottish child payment in respect of a period that the individual otherwise would at the time, or times, prescribed by regulation 19 (ongoing entitlement), and
(b) "financial abuse" includes—
    (i) having money or other property stolen,
    (ii) being defrauded,
    (iii) being put under pressure in relation to money or other property,
    (iv) having money or other property misused.]

AMENDMENT

1. Scottish Child Payment Regulations 2020 and the Disability Assistance for Children and Young People (Scotland) Regulations 2021 (Miscellaneous Amendments) Regulations 2022 (SSI 2022/41) reg.2(1) and (2) (February 9, 2022).

Value and form of a Scottish child payment

20.—(1) The value of a Scottish child payment in respect of a child is [² £26.70] per week.

(2) A Scottish child payment may only be given as money, except as provided for by paragraph (3).

(3) Where an individual has a liability to the Scottish Ministers under section 63 of the 2018 Act (liability for assistance given in error), or under paragraph 29 of the schedule of these Regulations, the individual's Scottish child payment may be given (in whole or in part) by way of deduction, at a reasonable level, from that liability either—
   (a) with the agreement of the individual, or
   (b) without the individual's agreement, where the individual has unreasonably refused to agree to the assistance being given in that form.

(4) For the purpose of sub-paragraph (3), "reasonable level" means a level that is reasonable having regard to the financial circumstances of the individual.

[¹ (5) For each week in the period of 12 weeks ending with the death of the child, the amount of Scottish child payment that is to be given to the individual is the weekly rate, multiplied by two.]

AMENDMENTS

1. Social Security (Miscellaneous Amendment and Transitional Provision) (Scotland) Regulations 2022 (SSI 2022/336) reg.4(1) and (6) (November 14, 2022, subject to a saving under reg.2 of the Scottish Child Payment (Saving Provisions) Regulations 2022 (SSI 2022/302)).

2. Social Security (Up-rating) (Miscellaneous Amendments) (Scotland) Regulations 2024 (SSI 2024/105) reg.11 (April 1, 2024, subject to a saving under reg.14 and para.9 of Sch.).

Time of payment

21.—(1) Following a determination that an individual is entitled to a Scottish child payment, the payment is to be given in accordance with [¹ paragraph (2) or, where paragraph (3) applies, paragraph (4)].

[² (2) Except where paragraph (3) applies, where a determination is made that an individual is entitled to a Scottish child payment, the Scottish Ministers are to make—
   (a) the first payment of a Scottish child payment on a date specified in the determination, and
   (b) subsequent payments in the last week of each successive period of 4 weeks in which the individual continues to be entitled to a Scottish child payment for at least one week by virtue of regulation 19.]

[¹ (3) This paragraph applies where the payment is to be made pursuant to a determination made in accordance with paragraph 11 of the schedule (determination following award of a Scottish child payment in respect of another child).

(4) Where paragraph (3) applies, payments are to be made so that—
   (a) the first payment is made on the same day as the next Scottish child payment that is due to be made to the individual in respect of their ongoing entitlement to that payment in respect of another child (see paragraph 11(1)(a) of the schedule),

(b) that first payment is made, in arrears, in respect of the period beginning with the day on which the application is made and ending with the day referred to in sub-paragraph (a), and

(c) subsequent payments are made in respect of periods of 4 weeks, in arrears, in the last week of each successive period of 4 weeks in which the individual continues to be entitled to a Scottish child payment for at least one week by virtue of regulation 19.

(5) Where the period mentioned in paragraph (4)(b) includes a part-week, for the purpose only of that first payment the part-week is to be treated as a full week.]

AMENDMENTS

1. Scottish Child Payment Amendment Regulations 2021 (SSI 2021/16) reg. 4 (January 15, 2021).

2. Social Security (Miscellaneous Amendment and Transitional Provision) (Scotland) Regulations 2022 (SSI 2022/336) reg.4(1) and (7) (November 14, 2022).

Individual's right to stop receiving assistance

22.—(1) An individual may request that the Scottish Ministers cancel a determination of the individual's entitlement to assistance.

(2) On being requested to do so under paragraph (1), the Scottish Ministers must cancel a determination—

(a) with immediate effect, or

(b) with effect from a later date specified in the request.

(3) An individual is not entitled, and is not to become entitled, to be given assistance by a determination after it has been cancelled.

(4) A request under paragraph (1) must be made in such form as the Scottish Ministers require.

(5) The Scottish Ministers must publicise any requirements for the time being set under paragraph (4).

Later determination supersedes earlier

23.—(1) The latest determination of an individual's entitlement to a Scottish child payment in respect of a given period or event supersedes any earlier determination insofar as it deals with the individual's entitlement to a Scottish child payment in respect of the same period or event.

(2) Accordingly the individual is not entitled, and is not to become entitled, to be given a Scottish child payment in respect of that period or event by the earlier determination insofar as it has been superseded.

PART 4

TRANSITORY PROVISION

Definitions – initial period

24.—(1) Regulations 25, 26, and 27 apply in respect of the initial application period and the initial payment period.

(2) For the purposes of this Part—
(a) the "initial application period" means the period beginning with the day on which these Regulations come into force and ending on the day which falls 14 weeks after that day, and
(b) the "initial payment period" means the period beginning with the day immediately after the end of the initial application period and ending on the day which falls 4 weeks after that day.

When an application is treated as made – initial period

13.233   **25.** Any application for a Scottish child payment which is received by the Scottish Ministers during the initial application period is to be treated for the purposes of these Regulations as having been made on the day immediately after the expiry of that period.

Time of payment – initial period

13.234   **26.** Where an individual's first payment period (see regulation 21(2)(a)) would fall wholly or partly in the initial payment period, regulation 21(2) does not apply and instead—
(a) the first payment to the individual is to be made in arrears on such date within the initial payment period as the Scottish Ministers consider appropriate,
(b) subsequent payments to the individual are to be made in the last week of each successive period of 4 weeks in which the individual continues to be entitled to a Scottish child payment for at least one week by virtue of regulation 19.

Duty to notify – initial period

13.235   **27.**—(1) The Scottish Ministers may place a duty to notify them about a change in circumstances on a person to whom sub-paragraph (3) or (4) applies.
(2) The Scottish Ministers place a duty under paragraph (1) by informing the person—
(a) of the changes in circumstances which the person has a duty to notify them about,
(b) of the way in which the person is to notify them, and
(c) that failing to notify them about a change in any of those circumstances in that way, so that an individual's entitlement to a Scottish child payment is determined on the basis of information that is false or misleading, may be an offence under section 72 of the 2018 Act.
(3) This sub-paragraph applies to an individual in respect of whom an application for a Scottish child payment is made during the initial application period.
(4) This sub-paragraph applies to a person acting on behalf of an individual to whom sub-paragraph (3) applies in relation to any application for a Scottish child payment during the initial period.

(SSI 2020/351 Sch)

SCHEDULE   Regulation 3(4)

PROCEDURAL MATTERS

PART 1

APPLICATIONS AND DETERMINATION OF APPLICATIONS

Requirement for applications

1.—(1) Except as provided for by Part 2 of this schedule, an individual is not entitled to a Scottish child payment unless an application is made to the Scottish Ministers.

(2) If, before making a determination on the basis of an application, the Scottish Ministers consider that the applicant—
  (a) would not be eligible for the Scottish child payment applied for if the application were treated as made on the day they received it, and
  (b) would be eligible for the Scottish child payment applied for if the application were treated as made on a day falling within the period of 14 days beginning with the day they received it,
the Scottish Ministers may choose the day within that 14 day period on which the application is to be treated as made.

(3) For the avoidance of doubt, an application for assistance must be—
  (a) made in such form, and
  (b) accompanied by such evidence,
as the Scottish Ministers require.

(4) If the Scottish Ministers reject something purporting to be an application for a Scottish child payment, they must inform the individual concerned of—
  (a) the decision to do that,
  (b) the reasons for it, and
  (c) the individual's right to appeal under paragraph 23(1).

Withdrawal of application

2.—(1) An individual who has made an application for a Scottish child payment may request that the Scottish Ministers disregard it.

(2) If an individual requests that an application be disregarded—
  (a) the Scottish Ministers are not to make a determination of the individual's entitlement to a Scottish child payment on the basis of the application, and
  (b) accordingly, their duty to do so under paragraph 3 ceases to apply.

(3) A request under sub-paragraph (1) must be made in such form as the Scottish Ministers require.

(4) The Scottish Ministers must publicise any requirements for the time being set under sub-paragraph (3).

Duty to make a determination of entitlement

3. The Scottish Ministers must make a determination of an individual's entitlement to a Scottish child payment—
  (a) on receiving an application for a Scottish child payment from the individual, or
  (b) when required to do so by Part 2 of this schedule.

Notice of determination

4.—(1) Having made a determination under paragraph 3 of an individual's entitlement to a Scottish child payment, the Scottish Ministers must inform the individual—
  (a) of the determination,
  (b) of the reasons for it,
  (c) of the individual's right under paragraph 14 to request that the Scottish Ministers re-determine the individual's entitlement to the payment, and
  (d) that the individual will have the right under paragraph 19 to appeal to the First-tier Tribunal against the determination should the Scottish Ministers fail to deal with a request for a re-determination in the period allowed for re-determination.

(2) The Scottish Ministers must fulfil their duty under sub-paragraph (1) in a way that leaves the individual with a record of the information which the individual can show to, or otherwise share with, others.

Multiple determinations involving the same child

5.—(1) Where the Scottish Ministers are required by paragraph 3 to make a determination of the entitlement of two or more individuals for a Scottish child payment in respect of the same child and the same period, the determination must be made in accordance with sub-paragraphs (2) to [¹ (6)].

(2) For the avoidance of doubt, the Scottish Ministers must—
   (a) make a determination of each individual's entitlement, notwithstanding that another individual may have previously been properly awarded a Scottish child payment in respect of the child (and continue to receive that payment), and
   (b) in so doing, determine which (if any) of the individuals is to be entitled to a Scottish child payment in respect of the child.

(3) Where the Scottish Ministers decide that two or more individuals are eligible for a Scottish child payment in respect of the child and the period (see regulations 18 and 19), they must apply the rules in [¹ sub-paragraphs (4) to (6)] to determine which of the individuals is to be entitled to the payment.

(4) The rules are that—
   (a) where only one individual has been awarded child tax credit, state pension credit or universal credit for the day, or assessment period that includes the day, in question (and the child is recognised to be a child for whom the individual has responsibility in terms of that award of assistance), [¹ unless the Scottish Ministers decide otherwise in pursuance of the rule in sub-paragraph (6),] that individual is entitled to the payment,
   (b) where none of the individuals have been awarded assistance as described in sub-paragraph (4)(a), and only one individual has been awarded child benefit for the day in question (and the child is recognised to be a child for whom the individual has responsibility in terms of that award of assistance), that individual is entitled to the payment,
   (c) where the individuals are kinship carers for the child, and none of them have been awarded any kind of assistance as described in sub-paragraph (4)(a) or (4)(b), the individual whose determination is to be made first is entitled to the payment,
   (d) where one individual has been awarded child benefit for the day in question, and another individual is a kinship carer for the child, the individual who is the kinship carer for the child is entitled to the payment.

(5) For the purposes of sub-paragraph (4), the Scottish Ministers must determine the entitlement of the individual whose entitlement first fell to be determined in accordance with paragraph 3 (whether on receipt of an application from the individual or by virtue of Part 2 of this schedule) before making any other determination.

[¹ (6) Where—
   (a) having applied the rules in sub-paragraph (4) in accordance with sub-paragraph (3) it appears to the Scottish Ministers from information available to them that none of the circumstances described in rules (a) to (d) are true in the case of the individuals in question, or
   (b) the circumstances described in rule (a) of subparagraph (4) are true in the case of the individuals in question and one individual is a kinship carer for the child,
the Scottish Ministers must determine which of the individuals is entitled to the payment having regard to the circumstances of the child.

AMENDMENT

1. Best Start Grants and Scottish Child Payment (Miscellaneous Amendments) Regulations 2021 (SSI 2021/494) reg.6 (December 23, 2021).

PART 2

DETERMINATION WITHOUT APPLICATION

Determination following official error resulting in underpayment

6.—(1) The Scottish Ministers are to make a determination of an individual's entitlement to a Scottish child payment (without receiving an application) where—

(a) they have previously made a determination of the individual's entitlement to the payment ("the original determination"),
(b) they establish that due to an official error the original determination was incorrect resulting in the individual—
   (i) not being given a Scottish child payment to which the individual was entitled, or
   (ii) being given a lower award than that to which the individual was entitled,
(c) the Scottish Ministers are not considering a request for a re-determination of the individual's entitlement to the Scottish child payment, and
(d) the individual has not appealed to the First-tier Tribunal for Scotland against the Scottish Ministers' determination of the individual's entitlement to the Scottish child payment.

(2) In making a determination required by sub-paragraph (1) the Scottish Ministers are to use—
(a) the information provided in the application that led to the original determination, and
(b) any other information they have obtained in connection with that application.

(3) Where a determination is to be, or has been, made without an application by virtue of this paragraph, references in these Regulations to the day the application is made are to be read as references to the day the application that led to the original determination was made.

(4) In this paragraph, "official error" means an error made by someone acting on behalf of the Scottish Ministers or on behalf of a Minister of the Crown that was not materially contributed to by anyone not so acting.

Determination following error resulting in overpayment

7.—(1) The Scottish Ministers are to make a determination of an individual's entitlement to a Scottish child payment (without receiving an application) where—
(a) they have previously made a determination of the individual's entitlement to the payment ("the original determination"),
(b) they establish that due to an error the original determination was incorrect resulting in the individual—
   (i) being given a Scottish child payment to which they were not entitled, or
   (ii) being given a higher award than that to which they were entitled,
(c) the Scottish Ministers are not considering a request for a re-determination of the individual's entitlement to the Scottish child payment, and
(d) the individual has not made an appeal (to the First-tier Tribunal for Scotland or Upper Tribunal) against the Scottish Ministers' determination of the individual's entitlement to the Scottish child payment, that has not yet been determined.

(2) In making a determination required by sub-paragraph (1) the Scottish Ministers are to use—
(a) the information provided in the application that led to the original determination,
(b) any other information they have obtained in connection with that application, and
(c) any other information available to them that is relevant to their consideration of whether the individual is entitled to a Scottish child payment.

(3) Where a determination is to be, or has been, made without an application by virtue of this paragraph, references in these Regulations to the day the application is made are to be read as references to the day the application that led to the original determination was made.

(4) In this paragraph, references to an "error" are to—
(a) an error in the performance of a function conferred by virtue of these Regulations, including a decision under regulation 13 being made—
   (i) wrongly, or
   (ii) correctly but on the basis of—
      (aa) incorrect information, or
      (bb) an assumption which proves to be wrong,
(b) a new decision under regulation 13 not being made after an assumption on the basis of which an earlier decision was made has proved to be wrong.

Determination following backdated award of assistance

8.—(1) The Scottish Ministers are to make a determination of an individual's entitlement to a Scottish child payment (without receiving an application) where the circumstances in sub-paragraphs (2) to (5) apply.

(2) A determination has previously been made that the individual is not entitled to the payment in connection with the child ("the original determination").

(3) The Scottish Ministers establish that a backdated award of assistance of a kind specified in—
(a) regulation 12(2)(a) is made in circumstances in which regulation 12(2)(b) applies, or
(b) regulation 14 is made.
(4) The award referred to in sub-paragraph (3) ("the backdated award") is backdated to a day, or a period that begins on a day, that falls no later than the day on which the original determination was made.
(5) Had the backdated award been made before the original determination, a determination that the individual is entitled to a Scottish child payment would have been made instead.
(6) For the purposes of this paragraph, an award is backdated if it relates to a day, or a period that begins on a day, that falls before the day the decision to make the award was taken.
9.—(1) In making a determination required by paragraph 8 the Scottish Ministers are to use—
(a) the information provided in the application that led to the original determination, and
(b) any other information they have obtained in connection with that application.
(2) Where a determination is to be, or has been, made without an application by virtue of paragraph 8, references in these Regulations to the day the application is made are to be read as references to the day the application that led to the original determination was made.

Determination following change of circumstances etc.

10.—(1) The Scottish Ministers are to make a determination of an individual's entitlement to a Scottish child payment in respect of a child (without receiving an application) where an individual has ongoing entitlement to a Scottish child payment (see regulation 19) and they—
(a) consider that a change in circumstances is likely to mean that an individual is no longer entitled to such a payment,
(b) wish to make an award of a Scottish child payment in relation to that child to a different individual following a determination that that other individual is to be entitled to the payment in respect of the child (see paragraph 5).
(2) Where—
(a) sub-paragraph (1)(a) applies, references in these Regulations to the day on which the application is made are to be read as references to the day on which the change in circumstances occurred or, if that is not known, the day on which the Scottish Ministers became aware of the change in circumstances,
(b) sub-paragraph (1)(b) applies, references in these Regulations to the day on which the application is made are to be read as references to the day on which the Scottish Ministers determine the entitlement of the other person referred to in that sub-paragraph.
(3) In sub-paragraph (1)(a), "a change in circumstances" means a change in the circumstances of the individual in relation to any of the matters listed in regulation 18.

Determination following award of a Scottish child payment in respect of another child

11.—(1) The Scottish Ministers are to make a determination of an individual's entitlement to a Scottish child payment in respect of a child (without receiving an application) where—
(a) the individual has been properly awarded a Scottish child payment in respect of another child and has an ongoing entitlement to that payment (see regulation 19),
(b) the individual notifies the Scottish Ministers that the individual has responsibility for the child (see regulation 9), and
(c) it appears to the Scottish Ministers that, unless there is a change in circumstances, the individual is likely to be entitled to a Scottish child payment in respect of the child.
(2) In making a determination required by sub-paragraph (1), the Scottish Ministers may use such of the information they have obtained in connection with the award referred to in sub-paragraph (1)(a) as appears to them to be relevant.
(3) Where a determination is to be made by virtue of this paragraph, references in these Regulations to the day the application is made are to be read as references to—
(a) the day on which notification is given under sub-paragraph (1)(b), or
(b) [1 where the child is under 6 years old] such earlier day not more than 4 weeks before that day on which the child was recognised to be a child for whom the individual has responsibility in terms of an award of assistance mentioned in regulation 12(2)(a) [2 or

(c) where the child is 6 years old or older, such earlier day which is—
   (i) not more than 4 weeks before that day on which the child was recognised to be a child for whom the individual has responsibility in terms of an award of assistance mentioned in regulation 12(2)(a), and
   (ii) on or after 14 November 2022.]

Determination following cessation of award of a Scottish child payment

12.—(1) The Scottish Ministers are to make a determination of an individual's entitlement to a Scottish child payment in respect of a child (without receiving an application) where the circumstances in sub-paragraphs (2) to (5) apply.

(2) The individual has previously been properly awarded a Scottish child payment in respect of a child.

(3) A determination has subsequently been made that the individual is no longer entitled to the Scottish child payment in respect of that child due to a change of circumstances relating to the matters listed in—
   (a) regulation 18(e) (where the individual ceased to have responsibility for the child), or
   (b) regulation 18(f) (where no award of assistance of a kind specified in regulation 14 was made to the individual for any day in a relevant week).

(4) It appears to the Scottish Ministers that, due to a change in the individual's circumstances in relation to the matters referred to in sub-paragraph (3), the individual is likely to once again be entitled to a Scottish child payment in respect of the child.

(5) Not more than 12 weeks have passed since the [² the day on which the change of circumstances] referred to in sub-paragraph (3) [² occurred].

(6) Where a determination is to be made by virtue of this paragraph, references in these Regulations to the day the application is made are to be read as references to the day on which the change in circumstances occurred or, if that is not known, the day on which the Scottish Ministers became aware of the change in circumstances.

Determination to effect a deduction decision

13.—(1) The Scottish Ministers are to make a determination of an individual's entitlement to a Scottish child payment (without receiving an application) where the circumstances in sub-paragraphs (2) and (3) apply.

(2) This sub-paragraph applies where—
   (a) regulation 20 allows a Scottish child payment to be given to the individual by way of deduction, or
   (b) a Scottish child payment is being given to the individual by way of deduction, and the Scottish Ministers consider that may no longer be appropriate.

(3) This sub-paragraph applies where the Scottish Ministers have decided to—
   (a) vary the amount of Scottish child payment to be given by way of deduction (including introducing a deduction, where the full amount of Scottish child payment was previously given as money),
   (b) vary any period for which the individual's Scottish child payment is to be given by way of deduction that may have been specified in a previous determination of the individual's entitlement, or
   (c) cease making deductions, and instead give the individual's Scottish child payment in the form of money.

(4) The Scottish Ministers are to make a determination (without receiving an application) where an individual who is receiving a Scottish child payment by way of deduction under a previous determination of entitlement notifies the Scottish Ministers that the individual—
   (a) withdraws their agreement to their Scottish child payment being given by way of deduction,
   (b) wishes the Scottish Ministers to increase the amount of their Scottish child payment that is given by way of deduction,
   (c) wishes the Scottish Ministers to decrease the amount of their Scottish child payment that is given by way of deduction (including ceasing the deduction), or
   (d) wishes the Scottish Ministers to amend the length of any period referred to in sub-paragraph (3)(b).

(5) Where a determination is made in pursuance of sub-paragraph (1) or (4), references in these Regulations to the day on which the application is made are to be read as references to the day on which the determination is made.

The Scottish Child Payment Regulations 2020

PART 3

Re-determination of entitlement

Right to request re-determination and periods allowed

14.—(1) An individual may request that the Scottish Ministers re-determine the individual's entitlement to a Scottish child payment, after being informed (in accordance with paragraph 4(1)) of a determination by the Ministers of the individual's entitlement to such a payment.

(2) Unless sub-paragraph (3) applies, a request for re-determination is valid only if it is made before the end of the period of 31 days beginning with the day that the individual is informed (in accordance with paragraph 4(1)) of the right to make the request.

(3) A request for re-determination is valid if it is made after that period has ended, but before the end of the day that falls one year after the day on which the individual is informed (in accordance with paragraph 4(1)) of the determination, if the individual has a good reason for not requesting a re-determination sooner (see paragraph 15).

(4) A request for re-determination is valid only if it is made in such form as the Scottish Ministers require.

(5) If the Scottish Ministers decide that something purporting to be a request for a re-determination does not satisfy the condition in sub-paragraph (4), they must inform the individual concerned of—
  (a) the decision,
  (b) the reasons for it, and
  (c) the individual's right to appeal under paragraph 23.

Late request for re-determination

15.—(1) It is for the Scottish Ministers, or on appeal under paragraph 23 the First-tier Tribunal for Scotland, to decide whether, for the purpose of paragraph 14(3), an individual has a good reason for not requesting a re-determination sooner.

(2) Where the Scottish Ministers have made a decision under sub-paragraph (1), they must inform the individual concerned—
  (a) of the decision, and
  (b) if the decision is that the individual has no good reason for not requesting a re-determination sooner, of—
    (i) the reasons for the decision, and
    (ii) the individual's right to appeal under paragraph 23.

Duty to re-determine and period allowed

16.—(1) On receiving a valid request under paragraph 14 to re-determine an individual's entitlement to a Scottish child payment, the Scottish Ministers are to make a determination of the individual's entitlement to that payment.

(2) The Scottish Ministers must aim to make that determination within the period of 16 working days beginning with—
  (a) the day that the request for a re-determination is received by the Scottish Ministers, [¹ . . .]
  (b) in the case of a request for a re-determination to which paragraph 14(3) applies (late requests), the day on which it is decided by the Scottish Ministers or (as the case may be) the First-tier Tribunal for Scotland that the individual has a good reason for not requesting a re-determination sooner [¹ , or
  (c) in a case where the Scottish Ministers have informed the individual of their decision that the request for a re-determination was not made in such form as the Scottish Ministers require, the day on which it is subsequently decided by the First-Tier Tribunal for Scotland that the individual in question has made the request in such form as the Scottish Ministers require.]

(3) If the Scottish Ministers fail to make the determination within that period—
  (a) their duty to make the determination ends (but they may still make it), and
  (b) paragraph 18 applies.

(SSI 2020/351 Sch)

AMENDMENT

1. Scottish Child Payment Regulations 2020 and the Disability Assistance for Children and Young People (Scotland) Regulations 2021 (Miscellaneous Amendments) Regulations 2022 (SSI 2022/41) reg.2(1) and (3) (February 9, 2022).

Notice of re-determination

17.—(1) Having made a determination under paragraph 16(1) of an individual's entitlement to a Scottish child payment, the Scottish Ministers must—
  (a) inform the individual—
    (i) of the determination,
    (ii) of the reasons for it,
    (iii) of the individual's right under paragraph 19 to appeal to the First-tier Tribunal against the determination, and
  (b) provide the individual with a form that the individual can complete and submit to the Scottish Ministers in order to bring an appeal against the determination.
(2) The Scottish Ministers must fulfil their duty under sub-paragraph (1)(a) in a way that leaves the individual with a record of the information which the individual can show to, or otherwise share with, others.

Notice where re-determination not made timeously

18.—(1) Where the Scottish Ministers fail to make a determination under paragraph 16 within the period allowed by paragraph 16(2), the Scottish Ministers must—
  (a) inform the individual—
    (i) that the individual's request for a re-determination has not been dealt with within the period allowed, and
    (ii) that the individual therefore has the right to appeal to the First-tier Tribunal against the determination under paragraph 3 which prompted the request for a re-determination, and
  (b) provide the individual with a form that the individual can complete and submit to the Scottish Ministers in order to bring an appeal against the determination.
(2) The Scottish Ministers must fulfil their duty under sub-paragraph (1)(a) in a way that leaves the individual with a record of the information which the individual can show to, or otherwise share with, others.

PART 4

APPEALS

Right to appeal to the First-tier Tribunal against determination

19.—(1) An individual may appeal to the First-tier Tribunal for Scotland—
  (a) against a determination under paragraph 16 of the individual's entitlement to a Scottish child payment, or
  (b) in a case where sub-paragraph (2) applies, against the determination under paragraph 3 referred to in that sub-paragraph.
(2) This sub-paragraph applies where—
  (a) having been informed of a determination under paragraph 3 of the individual's entitlement to a Scottish child payment, the individual has made a request for a re-determination under paragraph 14, and
  (b) the Scottish Ministers have failed to make a determination under paragraph 16 in consequence of that request within the period of 16 working days described in paragraph 16(2).

Initiating an appeal

20.—(1) To bring an appeal against a determination, an individual must submit to the Scottish Ministers the form provided under paragraph 17(1)(b) or (as the case may be) paragraph 18(1)(b) in relation to the determination.

(2) On receiving a form submitted under sub-paragraph (1), the Scottish Ministers must send—
 (a) the form, and
 (b) the information held by them that they used to make the determination in question,
to the First-tier Tribunal.
(3) Having complied with sub-paragraph (2), the Scottish Ministers must inform the individual to whom the determination in question relates that they have done so.
(4) In this paragraph, references to a form include a copy of a form.
(5) For the avoidance of doubt, the form that the Scottish Ministers provide under paragraph 17 and 18 need not be a physical form.

Deadline for appealing

21.—(1) An appeal under paragraph 19—
 (a) may be brought without the First-tier Tribunal's permission if an appeal application is made within the period of 31 days beginning with the day the relevant event occurred,
 (b) may be brought only with the First-tier Tribunal's permission if an appeal application is made after the period mentioned in sub-paragraph (1)(a),
 (c) may not be brought if an appeal application has not been made within the period of one year beginning with the day the relevant event occurred.
(2) In sub-paragraph (1)—
 (a) "the relevant event" means—
  (i) in the case of an appeal against a determination under paragraph 16(1), the individual to whom the determination relates being informed of it in accordance with paragraph 17(1),
  (ii) in the case of an appeal against a determination under paragraph 3 the individual to whom the determination relates being informed (in accordance with paragraph 18(1)) that the individual has the right to appeal against it,
 (b) an appeal application is made when a form, that relates to the determination in question and has been completed to the extent that Scottish Tribunal Rules require, is received by the Scottish Ministers having been submitted in accordance with paragraph 20(1).
(3) The First-tier Tribunal may give permission under sub-paragraph (1)(b) for an appeal to be brought only if it is satisfied that there is a good reason for the application not having been made sooner.

First-tier Tribunal's power to determine entitlement

22. In an appeal under paragraph 19 against a determination of an individual's entitlement to a Scottish child payment, the First-tier Tribunal may—
 (a) uphold the determination, or
 (b) make its own determination of the individual's entitlement to a Scottish child payment.

Appeal to First-tier Tribunal against process decisions

23.—(1) An individual may appeal to the First-tier Tribunal for Scotland against a decision by the Scottish Ministers—
 (a) to reject something purporting to be an application for assistance (see paragraph 1)),
 (b) that something purporting to be a request for a re-determination does not satisfy the condition in paragraph 14(4),
 (c) that an individual has no good reason for not requesting a re-determination sooner (see paragraph 15).
(2) An appeal under this paragraph—
 (a) may be brought without the First-tier Tribunal's permission within the period of 31 days beginning with the day the individual was informed of the decision in accordance with these Regulations,
 (b) may be brought only with the First-tier Tribunal's permission after the period mentioned in sub-paragraph (2)(a),
 (c) may not be brought after the end of the period of one year beginning with the day the individual was informed of the decision in accordance with these Regulations.

(3) The First-tier Tribunal may give permission under sub-paragraph (2)(b) for an appeal to be made only if it is satisfied that there is a good reason for the appeal not having been made sooner.

(4) A decision by the First-tier Tribunal about—
  (a) the outcome of an appeal under this paragraph, or
  (b) whether to give permission under sub-paragraph (2)(b) for an appeal to be brought,
is final.

(5) Accordingly (and without prejudice to the generality of sub-paragraph (4)), any such decision by the First-tier Tribunal may be neither—
  (a) reviewed under section 43 of the Tribunals (Scotland) Act 2014(19), nor
  (b) appealed against under section 46 of that Act.

Presumption for purposes of paragraphs 4, 14, 15, 17, 18 and 20

24.—(1) Sub-paragraph (2) applies in relation to the references in paragraphs 4, 14, 15, 17, 18, and 20 to an individual being informed of something by the Scottish Ministers in accordance with these Regulations.

(2) Where, in order to fulfil their duty to inform an individual of something, the Scottish Ministers send information—
  (a) through the postal service to the last known address the Scottish Ministers have for the individual, or
  (b) by email to the email address most recently provided to the Scottish Ministers by the individual for the purposes of these Regulations,
the individual is to be taken to have received the information 48 hours after it is sent by the Scottish Ministers unless the contrary is shown.

PART 5

FURTHER PROVISION ABOUT DETERMINING ENTITLEMENT

Obtaining information to make determination

[¹ **25.**—(1) Where—
  (a) the Scottish Ministers are either—
    (i) determining an individual's entitlement to a Scottish child payment, or
    (ii) considering whether paragraph 6, 7, 8, 10, 11, 12 or 13 requires them to make a determination of an individual's entitlement to a Scottish child payment (without receiving an application), and
  (b) they require further information in order to satisfy themselves about any matter material to the making of the determination of entitlement or (as the case may be) to their consideration of whether they are required to make a determination without receiving an application,
they may request that the individual provide them with the information within such period as they specify.

(2) If—
  (a) the Scottish Ministers are either—
    (i) determining the individual's entitlement to a Scottish child payment, or
    (ii) considering whether paragraph 6, 7, 8, 10, 11, 12 or 13 requires them to make a determination of an individual's entitlement to a Scottish child payment (without receiving an application),
  (b) the individual fails to provide the requested information within the period specified under sub-paragraph (1), and
  (c) it is the first time that the individual has failed to provide the Scottish Ministers with the requested information within a specified period since they began making the determination or considering the matter mentioned in head (a)(ii),
the Scottish Ministers may issue a decision to suspend the Scottish child payment to the individual in accordance with regulations 19A to 19G (suspension of entitlement).

(3) Where the Scottish Ministers issue such a decision, they must, at the same time, request that the individual provide them with the information within such further period as they specify.

(4) If the individual fails to provide information requested under sub-paragraph (1) within the period specified under sub-paragraph (1) or (3) the Scottish Ministers may, without

further consideration, proceed to make the determination on the basis that the individual does not satisfy the eligibility rules in regulation 18, or (as the case may be) that the individual has no ongoing entitlement under regulation 19.]

Duty to notify change of circumstances

26.—(1) The Scottish Ministers may place a duty to notify them about a change in circumstances on a person to whom sub-paragraph (3) or (4) applies.

(2) The Scottish Ministers place a duty under sub-paragraph (1) on a person by informing the person—
  (a) of the changes in circumstances which the person has a duty to notify them about,
  (b) of the way in which the person is to notify them, and
  (c) that failing to notify them about a change in any of those circumstances in that way may be an offence under section 72 of the 2018 Act.

(3) This sub-paragraph applies to an individual who is to be given a Scottish child payment under a determination made on the basis that the individual has ongoing entitlement to a Scottish child payment.

(4) This sub-paragraph applies to a person acting on behalf of an individual to whom sub-paragraph (3) applies in relation to any application for a Scottish child payment or the determination of the individual's entitlement.

Lifting of duty to notify change of circumstances

27.—(1) A duty to notify the Scottish Ministers about a change of circumstances placed on a person under regulation 27 or paragraph 26 ceases to apply when—
  (a) it is lifted under sub-paragraph (2), or
  (b) it stops being the case that a change in any of the circumstances to which the duty relates can affect someone's entitlement to be given a Scottish child payment.

(2) The Scottish Ministers may lift a duty placed on a person under regulation 27 or paragraph 26 by informing the person that the duty is lifted.

(3) Under sub-paragraph (2), the Scottish Ministers may lift a duty as it relates to some or all of the changes in circumstances which the person has a duty to notify them about.

Right to support

28.—(1) The Scottish Ministers must comply with an individual's wish to have another person ("a supporter") present during any discussion relating to the individual's entitlement to a Scottish child payment, unless the wish is unreasonable.

(2) The Scottish Ministers' duty under sub-paragraph (1) includes ensuring that any person acting on their behalf complies with such a wish, unless the wish is unreasonable.

(3) The role of a supporter is to support the individual in question during the discussion, and includes making representations on the individual's behalf.

(4) Nothing in this paragraph is to be read as requiring the Scottish Ministers to provide or pay for a supporter.

PART 6

RECOVERY OF VALUE OF ASSISTANCE

Liability for assistance given in error

29.—(1) An individual is liable to pay the Scottish Ministers the value of any assistance that was given to the individual due to an error (but see paragraph 30).

(2) For the avoidance of doubt, the individual's liability under sub-paragraph (1) is limited to the difference in value between—
  (a) the assistance that was given, and
  (b) the assistance (if any) that would have been given had the error not been made.

(3) If the assistance was given in a form other than money, its value for the purposes of this paragraph is what giving it cost the Scottish Ministers (excluding any administration costs).

(4) In this paragraph and paragraph 30, references to an error are to—
  (a) an error in the performance of a function conferred by virtue of these Regulations, including a decision under regulation 13 being made—

(i) wrongly, or
(ii) correctly but on the basis of—
(aa) incorrect information, or
(bb) an assumption which proves to be wrong.
(b) a new decision under regulation 13 not being made after an assumption on the basis of which an earlier decision was made has proved to be wrong.

Exclusion from liability

30.—(1) An individual has no liability under paragraph 29(1) in respect of assistance given due to an error if the error is neither—
(a) the individual's fault, nor
(b) the kind of error that an individual could reasonably be expected to notice.
(2) For the purpose of this paragraph, an error is an individual's fault if it is caused or contributed to by the individual—
(a) providing false or misleading information,
(b) failing to notify the Scottish Ministers about a change in circumstances in breach of a duty to do so under regulation 27 or paragraph 26, or
(c) causing another person to do either of those things.
(3) In considering whether an error is of a kind that an individual could reasonably be expected to notice, the following are amongst the matters to which regard is to be had—
(a) the extent to which the value of the assistance given in error exceeds the value of the assistance that would have been given (if any) had the error not been made,
(b) whether any information given to the individual by the Scottish Ministers prior to, or immediately after, the assistance being given would have alerted a reasonable person to the fact that a decision had been, or was to be, made on the basis of incorrect information or a wrong assumption.
(4) In—
(a) sub-paragraph (2)(a), the reference to providing information includes making a statement,
(b) sub-paragraph (3)(b), the reference to information given to the individual by the Scottish Ministers does not include information explaining why the Ministers consider the assistance to have been given in error.

Consideration for debtor's circumstances

31.—(1) This paragraph applies to decisions of the Scottish Ministers about—
(a) whether to seek to recover money owed under paragraph 29, and
(b) the method by which money owed under that paragraph is to be recovered.
(2) In making a decision to which this paragraph applies, the Scottish Ministers must have regard to the financial circumstances of the individual who owes the money (so far as those circumstances are known to the Ministers).

Exclusion of other rights of recovery

32.—(1) An individual given assistance in error has no non-statutory obligation based on redress or unjustified enrichment to pay the value of that assistance to the Scottish Ministers.
(2) In sub-paragraph (1)—
(a) "non-statutory obligation" means an obligation that arises from a rule of law rather than an enactment,
(b) the reference to assistance being given in error is to be construed in accordance with paragraph 29(4).

Liability where assistance given for period after death

33.—(1) An individual's estate is liable to pay the Scottish Ministers the value of any assistance that was given to the individual under regulation 17 in respect of a period after the individual's death.
(2) For the avoidance of doubt, assistance may be regarded as having been given to an individual for the purposes of this paragraph despite being given after the individual's death.

The Scottish Child Payment Regulations 2020

PART 7

CORONAVIRUS – RELAXATION OF DEADLINES

Re-determination and appeal deadlines

13.250

34.—(1) A request for a re-determination is valid, despite being made after the expiry of the period described in sub-paragraph (3) of paragraph 14, if the person deciding whether the individual has a good reason for not requesting a re-determination sooner decides that the individual has a good reason that is related to coronavirus.

(2) An appeal may be brought under paragraph 19, despite the appeal application being made after the expiry of the period described in sub-paragraph (1)(c) of paragraph 21, if the First-tier Tribunal gives permission for the appeal to be brought under sub-paragraph (1)(b) of that paragraph on the basis of being satisfied that the good reason for the application not being made sooner is related to coronavirus.

(3) Any provision of Scottish Tribunal Rules that would (but for this sub-paragraph) have the effect of precluding an appeal being brought by virtue of sub-paragraph (2) is to be disregarded to the extent that it would have that effect.

(4) [². . .].

Timing of applications for Scottish child payment

35.—(1) Sub-paragraph (2) applies where these Regulations make an individual's eligibility for a Scottish child payment depend (in any way) on an application being made by a particular time.

(2) The person determining an individual's entitlement to the assistance may treat the individual's application as having been made by that time if satisfied that the reason for its not being made sooner is related to coronavirus.

(3) For the avoidance of doubt, the provisions of these Regulations that make a child's age at the time an application is made material to the determination of an individual's entitlement to a Scottish child payment are to be understood to make the individual's eligibility depend on the application being made by a particular time (namely the time at which the child ceases to be the specified age or fall within the specified age bracket).

(4) [². . .].

AMENDMENTS

1. Scottish Child Payment Regulations 2020 and the Disability Assistance for Children and Young People (Scotland) Regulations 2021 (Miscellaneous Amendments) Regulations 2022 (SSI 2022/41) reg.2(1) and (4) (February 9, 2022).

2. Social Security (Miscellaneous Amendment and Transitional Provision) (Scotland) Regulations 2022 (SSI 2022/336) reg.4(1) and (8) (November 14, 2022, subject to a saving under reg.3 of the Scottish Child Payment (Ancillary Provision) Regulations 2022 (SSI 2022/326)).

The Winter Heating Assistance for Children and Young People (Scotland) Regulations 2020

(SSI 2020/352)

Made 3rd November 2020
Coming into force 9th November 2020

The Scottish Ministers make the following Regulations in exercise of the powers conferred by sections 30(2), 41(4)(a), 43(5) and 52 of the Social

(SSI 2020/352 reg.)

Security (Scotland) Act 2018 and all other powers enabling them to do so.

In accordance with section 96(2) of that Act, a draft of this instrument has been laid before and approved by resolution of the Scottish Parliament.

In accordance with section 97(2) of that Act, the Scottish Ministers have informed the Scottish Commission on Social Security of their proposals, notified the Scottish Parliament that they have done so and made their proposals publicly available by such means as they consider appropriate.

The powers to make these Regulations are exercised together by virtue of section 33(2) of the Interpretation and Legislative Reform (Scotland) Act 2010. These Regulations are subject to the affirmative procedure by virtue of section 33(3) of that Act.

ARRANGEMENT OF REGULATIONS

1. Citation and commencement
2. Interpretation
3. Overview
4. Eligibility rules for child winter heating assistance
5. Determination of entitlement to child winter heating assistance without application
6. Determination following official error – underpayments
7. Determination following official error – overpayments
8. Determination following backdated award of assistance
9. Periods for re-determination requests
10. Value and form of child winter heating assistance
11. Making payments

SCHEDULE

Citation and commencement

1. These Regulations may be cited as the Winter Heating Assistance for Children and Young People (Scotland) Regulations 2020 and they come into force on 9 November 2020.

Interpretation

2. In these Regulations—
   "the 2013 Regulations" means the Social Security (Personal Independence Payment) Regulations 2013,
   "the 2016 Regulations" means the Personal Independence Payment Regulations (Northern Ireland) 2016,
   "the 2018 Act" means the Social Security (Scotland) Act 2018,
   [1 "the 2021 Regulations" means the Disability Assistance for Children and Young People (Scotland) Regulations 2021,]
   [3 "the 2022 Regulations" means the Disability Assistance for Working Age People (Scotland) Regulations 2022,]
   [3 "Adult Disability Payment" means disability assistance for adults given in accordance with the 2022 Regulations,]
   "backdated award" means an award of assistance for a day, or period that begins on a day, that falls before the day the decision to make an award is taken,

"child" means a person who has not yet reached the age of 16 years,
[¹ "Child Disability Payment" means disability assistance for children and young people given in accordance with the 2021 Regulations,]
"child winter heating assistance" means winter heating assistance to which a child or young person is entitled,
"determination" means a determination of entitlement within the meaning of section 25 of the 2018 Act,
"Disability Living Allowance" means a disability living allowance under section 71 of the Social Security Contributions and Benefits Act 1992,
[² "first qualifying week" means the qualifying week in the same calendar year these Regulations came into force,]
[² "Personal Independence Payment" means personal independence payment under—
 (a) Part 4 of the Welfare Reform Act 2012, or
 (b) article 82 of the Welfare Reform (Northern Ireland) Order 2015,]
"qualifying week" means the week running from the third Monday in September in any year, and
"young person" means a person who is aged 16, 17 or 18.

AMENDMENTS

1. Disability Assistance for Children and Young People (Consequential Amendment and Transitional Provision) (Scotland) Regulations 2021 (SSI 2021/73) reg.18(1) and (2) (July 26, 2021).
2, Winter Heating Assistance for Children and Young People (Scotland) Amendment Regulations 2021 (SSI 2021/415) reg.2(1) and (2) (November 16, 2021).
3. Disability Assistance for Working Age People (Consequential and Miscellaneous Amendment and Transitional Provision) (Scotland) Regulations 2022 (2022/31) reg.18(1) and (2) (March 21, 2022).

Overview

3.—(1) Regulation 4 provides for eligibility rules for determining entitlement to child winter heating assistance.

(2) Regulations 5 to 9 make provision about matters of procedure for determining entitlement to child winter heating assistance.

(3) Regulations 10 and 11 make provision about the child winter heating assistance that is to be given to individuals who are eligible for assistance.

Eligibility rules for child winter heating assistance

4.—(1) An individual is entitled to be paid child winter heating assistance in respect of a qualifying week if, in respect of any day within the qualifying week the individual is—
 (a) a child or young person,
 [³ (b) entitled to receive payment of—
  (i) the highest rate of the care component of—
   (aa) Disability Living Allowance, or
   (bb) Child Disability Payment, or
  [⁴ (ii) the enhanced rate of the daily living component of—

(aa) Personal Independence Payment, or
(bb) Adult Disability Payment, and]]
(c) either—
(i) resident in Scotland, or
(ii) habitually resident in [¹ Switzerland or] an EEA state listed in the schedule and has a genuine and sufficient link to Scotland.

(2) For the purposes of the rule in [³ paragraph (1)(b)(i)(aa)], an individual is to be treated as being entitled to receive payment even if, throughout the qualifying week, [³ regulation 8 (Hospitalisation of persons aged 18 or over), or] regulation 9 (persons in care homes) of the Social Security (Disability Living Allowance) Regulations 1991 applies to the individual.

[² (3) For the purposes of the rule in [3 paragraph (1)(b)(i)(bb)], an individual is to be treated as being entitled to receive payment even if, throughout the qualifying week—
(a) regulation 17(2) (effect of admission to a care home on ongoing entitlement to care component) of the 2021 Regulations applies to the individual, or
(b) regulation 20 (entitlement beginning while in alternative accommodation) of the 2021 Regulations applies to the individual due to the individual being resident in a care home.

(4) In paragraph (3), "care home" has the meaning given in regulation 2 of the 2021 Regulations.]

[³ (5) For the purposes of the rule in [⁴ paragraph (1)(b)(ii)(aa)], an individual is to be treated as being entitled to receive payment even if, throughout the qualifying week—
(a) regulation 28 (care home residents) of either the 2013 Regulations or the 2016 Regulations applies to the individual due to the individual being resident in a care home, or
(b) regulation 29 (hospital in-patients aged 18 or over) of either the 2013 Regulations or the 2016 Regulations applies to the individual due to the individual being an in-patient in hospital.

(6) In paragraph (5)—
(a) "care home" has the meaning given in section 85(3) of the Welfare Reform Act 2012 or article 90(3) of the Welfare Reform Act (Northern Ireland) Order 2015, and
(b) "hospital" has the meaning given in regulation 29 of the 2013 Regulations or regulation 29 of the 2016 Regulations.

(7) An individual is entitled to be paid child winter heating assistance in respect of the first qualifying week if it appears to the Scottish Ministers from information available to them that the individual would have been entitled to be paid child winter heating assistance had the requirement in regulation 4(1)(b)(ii) had effect beginning with the day upon which these Regulations came into force.]

[⁴ (8) For the purposes of the rule in paragraph (1)(b)(ii)(bb), an individual is to be treated as being entitled to receive payment even if, throughout the qualifying week—
(a) regulation 27(2) (effect of admission to a care home on ongoing entitlement to daily living component) of the 2022 Regulations applies to the individual,
(b) regulation 28(2) (effect of admission to hospital on ongoing entitlement to Adult Disability Payment) of the 2022 Regulations applies to the individual,

(c) regulation 32 (entitlement beginning while in alternative accommodation) of the 2022 Regulations applies to the individual due to the individual being resident in a care home or being an in-patient in a hospital or similar institution.

(9) In paragraph (8), "care home" has the meaning given in regulation 2 of the 2022 Regulations.]

AMENDMENTS

1. Social Security (Up-rating) (Miscellaneous Amendment) (Scotland) Regulations 2021 (SSI 2021/170) reg.5(1) and (2) (April 1, 2021).
2. Disability Assistance for Children and Young People (Consequential Amendment and Transitional Provision) (Scotland) Regulations 2021 (SSI 2021/73) reg.18(1) and (3) (July 26, 2021).
3. Winter Heating Assistance for Children and Young People (Scotland) Amendment Regulations 2021 (SSI 2021/415) reg.2(1) and (3) (November 16, 2021).
4. Disability Assistance for Working Age People (Consequential and Miscellaneous Amendment and Transitional Provision) (Scotland) Regulations 2022 (SSI 2022/31) reg.18(1) and (3) (March 21, 2022).

Determination of entitlement to child winter heating assistance without application

5. The Scottish Ministers must, without receiving an application, make a determination of an individual's entitlement to child winter heating assistance under section 30 of the 2018 Act [¹ . . .] where it appears to the Scottish Ministers from information available to them that the individual is likely to meet the eligibility rules in regulation 4(1)(a), (b) and (c)(i).

AMENDMENT

1. Winter Heating Assistance for Children and Young People (Scotland) Amendment Regulations 2021 (SSI 2021/415) reg.2(1) and (4) (November 16, 2021).

Determination following official error – underpayments

6.—(1) The Scottish Ministers must make a determination of an individual's entitlement to child winter heating assistance without receiving an application where—
   (a) they have previously made a determination of the individual's entitlement to winter heating assistance, and
   (b) they establish that, due to official error, that determination was incorrect resulting in the individual not being given an award of winter heating assistance to which they were entitled.

(2) In this regulation, "official error" means an error made by the Scottish Ministers or a Minister of the Crown that was not materially contributed to by anyone else.

Determination following official error—overpayments

7.—(1) The Scottish Ministers must make a determination of an individual's entitlement to winter heating assistance without receiving an application where—
   (a) they have previously made a determination of the individual's entitlement to winter heating assistance, and

(b) they establish that, due to official error, that determination was incorrect resulting in the individual being given an award of winter heating assistance to which they were not entitled.

(2) In this regulation, "official error" means an error made by the Scottish Ministers or a Minister of the Crown that was—
  (a) not materially contributed to by anyone else, or
  (b) made on the basis of—
    (i) incorrect information, or
    (ii) an assumption which proves to be wrong.

Determination following backdated award of assistance

8. The Scottish Ministers must make a determination of an individual's entitlement to child winter heating assistance without receiving an application where—
  (a) a determination has previously been made that the individual is not entitled to child winter heating assistance, and
  (b) the Scottish Ministers establish that—
    [^{1} (i) following an appeal, an award of—
      (aa) the highest rate of the care component of Disability Living Allowance,
      (bb) the highest rate of the care component of Child Disability Payment, [^{2} ...]
      (cc) the enhanced rate of the daily living component of Personal Independence Payment, [^{2} or
      (dd) the enhanced rate of the daily living component of Adult Disability Payment,]
      is made that is a backdated award, and]
    (ii) had that award been made before the original determination, a determination that the individual is entitled to child winter heating assistance would have been made instead.

AMENDMENTS

1. Winter Heating Assistance for Children and Young People (Scotland) Amendment Regulations 2021 (SSI 2021/415) reg.2(1) and (5) (November 16, 2021).

2. Disability Assistance for Working Age People (Consequential and Miscellaneous Amendment and Transitional Provision) (Scotland) Regulations 2022 (SSI 2022/31) reg.18(1) and (4) (March 21, 2022).

Periods for re-determination requests

9.—(1) The period for requesting a re-determination of entitlement to child winter heating assistance under section 41 of the 2018 Act is 42 days beginning with the day that the individual is informed, in accordance with section 40 of that Act, of the right to make the request.

(2) In relation to determining entitlement to child winter heating assistance, the period allowed for re-determination (within the meaning of section 43 of that Act) is 16 working days beginning with—
  (a) the day that the request for a re-determination is received by the Scottish Ministers, [^{1} ...]
  (b) where the request for a re-determination is received by the Scottish Ministers later than the period prescribed by paragraph

(1), the day on which the Scottish Ministers, or, on appeal, the First-tier Tribunal for Scotland, decide that the individual has a good reason for not requesting the re-determination sooner [¹, or

(c) in a case where the Scottish Ministers have informed the individual of their decision that the request for a re-determination was not made in such form as the Scottish Ministers require, the day on which it is subsequently decided by the First-Tier Tribunal for Scotland that the individual in question has made the request in such form as the Scottish Ministers require.]

(3) For the purpose of paragraph (2), a "working day" is a day other than—
(a) a Saturday,
(b) a Sunday, or
(c) a bank holiday in Scotland under the Banking and Financial Dealings Act 1971.

AMENDMENT

1. Social Security (Period for Re-determination Requests) (Miscellaneous Amendments) (Scotland) Regulations 2021 (SSI 2021/469) reg.5 (February 9, 2022).

Value and form of child winter heating assistance

10.—(1) [¹ Subject to paragraph (1A), the value] of child winter heating assistance is [² £251.50].

[¹ (1A) Where an individual is entitled to be paid child winter heating assistance by virtue of regulation 4(7), the value of child winter heating assistance payable is the value specified in paragraph (1) as it had effect on the day these Regulations came into force.

(2) Child winter heating assistance is to be given in the form of money in a single payment.

AMENDMENTS

1. Winter Heating Assistance for Children and Young People (Scotland) Amendment Regulations 2021 (SSI 2021/415) reg.2(1) and (6) (November 16, 2021).
2. Social Security (Up-rating) (Miscellaneous Amendments) (Scotland) Regulations 2024 (SSI 2024/105) reg.9 (April 1, 2024, subject to a saving under reg.14 and para.7 of Sch.).

Making payments

11.—(1) Where child winter heating assistance is payable in respect of a [¹ child or young person], the Scottish Ministers may, where they consider it appropriate, make the payment to another person to be used for the benefit of the [¹ child or young person].

(2) Where the Scottish Ministers consider, for any reason, that it is no longer appropriate for a particular person who falls within paragraph (1) to continue to receive the payment, they may cease making payment to that person and pay it instead to the [¹ child or young person] or another person.

(SSI 2020/399 reg.)

AMENDMENT

1. Winter Heating Assistance for Children and Young People (Scotland) Amendment Regulations 2021 (SSI 2021/415) reg.2(1) and (7) (November 16, 2021).

SCHEDULE   Regulation 4   13.262

Republic of Austria
Kingdom of Belgium
Republic of Bulgaria
Republic of Croatia
Czech Republic
Kingdom of Denmark
Republic of Estonia
Republic of Finland
Federal Republic of Germany
Republic of Hungary
Republic of Iceland
Republic of Ireland
Republic of Italy
Republic of Latvia
Principality of Liechtenstein
Republic of Lithuania
Grand Duchy of Luxembourg
Kingdom of the Netherlands
Kingdom of Norway
Republic of Poland
Republic of Romania
Slovak Republic
Republic of Slovenia
Kingdom of Sweden
[1 . . .]

AMENDMENT

1. Social Security (Up-rating) (Miscellaneous Amendment) (Scotland) Regulations 2021 (SSI 2021/170) reg.5(1) and (4) (April 1, 2021).

The Social Security Co-ordination (EU Exit) (Scotland) (Amendments etc.) Regulations 2020

(SSI 2020/399)

Made   *at 10.45 a.m. on 26th November 2020*
Laid before the Scottish Parliament   *at 2.45 p.m. on 26th November 2020*
Coming into force   *in accordance with regulation 1*

The Scottish Ministers make the following Regulations in exercise of the powers conferred by paragraph 1(1) of schedule 2 of the European Union (Withdrawal) Act 2018(1) and all other powers enabling them to do so.

In accordance with paragraph 4(b) of schedule 2 of that Act(2), they have consulted the Secretary of State before making these Regulations.

The Social Security Co-ordination (EU Exit) Regulations 2020

Citation, commencement and interpretation

1. These Regulations may be cited as the Social Security Co-ordination (EU Exit) (Scotland) (Amendments etc.) Regulations 2020 and come into force on IP completion day.

2. In these Regulations, "devolved social security matters" means matters which are within the legislative competence of the Scottish Parliament by virtue of exceptions 1 to 10 in Section F1 of Part 2 of schedule 5 of the Scotland Act 1998(3).

Amendment of the Early Years Assistance (Best Start Grants) (Scotland) Regulations 2018

3. *Omitted (amendments incorporated into SSI 2018/370, above).*

Amendment of the Welfare Foods (Best Start Foods) (Scotland) Regulations 2019

4. *Omitted.*

Amendment of the Funeral Expense Assistance (Scotland) Regulations 2019

5. *Omitted (amendments incorporated into SSI 2019/292, above).*

Savings for Gibraltar

6.—(1) Notwithstanding regulation 7, the revoked RDEUL referred to in paragraph (2) forms part of domestic law by virtue of section 3 of the European Union (Withdrawal) Act 2018 to the extent specified in that paragraph.

(2) This paragraph applies to those parts of the revoked RDEUL which are necessary to give effect to the Exchange of Letters between the Governments of the United Kingdom and Gibraltar on the co-ordination of social security between the United Kingdom and Gibraltar in so far as it relates to devolved social security matters.

(3) The Exchange of Letters referred to in paragraph (2) is contained in the schedule of the Family Allowances, National Insurance and Industrial Injuries (Gibraltar) Order 1974.

(4) In this regulation, "the revoked RDEUL" means the retained direct EU legislation revoked by regulation 7.

Revocation of retained direct EU legislation

7. The following retained direct EU legislation is revoked in so far as it has effect in relation to devolved social security matters—
   (a) Regulation (EC) No 883/2004 of the European Parliament and of the Council of 29 April 2004 on the coordination of social security systems,
   (b) Regulation (EC) No 987/2009 of the European Parliament and of the Council of 16 September 2009 laying down the procedure for implementing Regulation (EC) No 883/2004,
   (c) Regulation (EEC) No 1408/71 of the Council of 14 June 1971 on the application of social security schemes to employed persons, to self-employed persons and to members of their families moving within the Community,

(d) Regulation (EEC) No 574/72 of 21 March 1972 fixing the procedure for implementing Regulation (EEC) No 1408/71 on the application of social security schemes to employed persons and their families moving with the community, and
(e) Council Regulation (EC) No 859/2003 of 14 May 2003 extending the provisions of Regulation (EEC) No 1408/71 to nationals of third countries who are not already covered by those provisions solely on the ground of their nationality.

General Note

The thinking behind regs. 7 and 8 was explained in the policy note issued with the draft Regulations, in which the policy objectives were stated to be to –

"... ensure that, aside from some specific savings provisions, the EU Social Security Co-ordination Regulations (SSC Regulations) which are retained on a unilateral basis under section 3 of the European Union (Withdrawal) Act 2018 (EUWA) will not take effect in domestic law from 31 December 2020 in areas of devolved competence. The regulations are drafted to preserve existing rights of eligible EU/EEA/Swiss nationals in accordance with the terms of the UK-EU Withdrawal Agreement."

It was further explained that –

"EU SSC Regulations 883/2004, 987/2009, 1408/1971, 574/1972 and 859/2003 will cease to have direct effect in domestic law from 31 December 2020 as specified in Article 126 of the Withdrawal Agreement. Section 3 of EUWA 2018 converts the EU SSC Regulations into "retained direct EU legislation" which will be incorporated into UK law at the end of the transition period. These rules form the basis of a reciprocal pan-European system of social security coordination of which the UK, including Scotland, will no longer be a member after 31 December 2020.
UK regulations were laid using powers in the Immigration and Social Security Co-ordination (EU Withdrawal) Act 2020 ("ISSC Act") on 17 November which make the same revocations and which have effect across the UK. However, to the extent that those regulations have effect in Scotland, the Scottish Government's view is that they only extend to forms of social security in Scotland which remain reserved to the UK Government, such as income replacement benefits. This is because the ISSC Act powers expressly cannot be used to make provision in relation to matters which are within the legislative competence of the Scottish Parliament. As such, the Scottish Government considers separate provision is required to implement the changes necessitated by the end of the EU Exit transition period."

Revocation of instruments

8. The following instruments are revoked in so far as they have effect in relation to devolved social security matters—
    (a) the Social Security Coordination (Council Regulation (EEC) No 574/72) (Amendment) (EU Exit) Regulations 2019,
    (b) the Social Security Coordination (Regulation (EC) No 883/2004, EEA Agreement and Swiss Agreement) (Amendment) (EU Exit) Regulations 2019,
    (c) the Social Security Coordination (Regulation (EC) No 987/2009) (Amendment) (EU Exit) Regulations 2019, and
    (d) the Social Security Coordination (Council Regulation (EEC) No 1408/71 and Council Regulation (EC) No 859/2003) (Amendment) (EU Exit) Regulations 2019.

The Social Security Co-ordination (EU Exit) Regulations 2020

GENERAL NOTE

13.271 See the note to reg.7, above.

The Carer's Allowance Supplement and Young Carer Grants (Residence Requirements and Procedural Provisions) (EU Exit) (Scotland) Regulations 2020

(SSI 2020/475)

Made   *23rd December 2020*
Coming into force   *24th December 2020*

The Scottish Ministers make the following Regulations in exercise of the powers conferred by sections 28(2), 81(8) and 95 of the Social Security (Scotland) Act 2018 ("the 2018 Act"), section 2(2) of the European Communities Act 1972, section 13 of the European Union (Withdrawal Agreement) Act 2020 and all other powers enabling them to do so.

In accordance with section 97(2) of the 2018 Act, the Scottish Ministers have informed the Scottish Commission on Social Security ("the Commission") of their proposals, notified the Scottish Parliament that they have done so and made their proposals publicly available by such means as they consider appropriate.

The Scottish Ministers have laid a response to the Commission's report on the proposals for the regulations in accordance with section 97(9)(a) of the 2018 Act.

In accordance with section 96(2) of the 2018 Act and paragraphs 2 and 2A of schedule 2 of the European Communities Act 1972, a draft of this instrument has been laid before and approved by resolution of the Scottish Parliament.

ARRANGEMENT OF REGULATIONS

PART 1

INTRODUCTORY

1. Citation and commencement
2. Interpretation

PART 2

CARER'S ALLOWANCE SUPPLEMENT FOR INDIVIDUALS RESIDENT OUTSIDE SCOTLAND

3. Amendment of the Social Security (Scotland) Act 2018
4. Meaning of determination of entitlement to a carer's allowance supplement
5. Determination of entitlement to a carer's allowance supplement for individuals resident outside Scotland

6. Timing of applications for a determination of entitlement to a carer's allowance supplement for individuals resident outside Scotland
7. Determination of entitlement to a carer's allowance supplement without application for individuals resident outside Scotland
8. Determination following official error - underpayments
9. Determination following error – overpayments
10. Procedure

PART 3

YOUNG CARER GRANTS

11. Amendment of eligibility conditions

SCHEDULE 1 Amendment of the Social Security (Scotland) Act 2018
SCHEDULE 2 Procedural Matters: Carer's Allowance Supplement

PART 1

INTRODUCTORY

Citation and commencement

1. These Regulations may be cited as the Carer's Allowance Supplement and Young Carer Grants (Residence Requirements and Procedural Provisions) (EU Exit) (Scotland) Regulations 2020 and come into force on the day after the day on which they are made.

Interpretation

2. In these Regulations—
"qualifying date" means a date determined by the Scottish Ministers in accordance with section 81(3) of the 2018 Act,
"the 2018 Act" means the Social Security (Scotland) Act 2018.

PART 2

CARER'S ALLOWANCE SUPPLEMENT FOR INDIVIDUALS RESIDENT OUTSIDE SCOTLAND

Amendment of the Social Security (Scotland) Act 2018

3. Section 81 of the 2018 Act is modified in accordance with schedule 1.

Meaning of determination of entitlement to a carer's allowance supplement

4.—(1) References in these Regulations to a determination of an individual's entitlement to a carer's allowance supplement for the purposes of section 81(2A) of the 2018 Act are references to a determination made—
(a) by the Scottish Ministers—

(i) under regulation 5, or
(ii) (following a request for a re-determination) under paragraph 6 of schedule 2 of these Regulations,
(b) by the First-tier Tribunal for Scotland—
(i) under paragraph 12 of schedule 2 of these Regulations in an appeal against a determination made by the Scottish Ministers, or
(ii) (subsequent to such an appeal) under its Tribunals Act powers,
(c) by the Upper Tribunal for Scotland under its Tribunals Act powers (subsequent to an appeal against, or a review of, a decision of the First-tier Tribunal),
(d) by the Court of Session under its Tribunals Act powers (in an appeal against a decision of the Upper Tribunal), or
(e) by the Supreme Court of the United Kingdom—
(i) in an appeal under section 40 of the Court of Session Act 1988 against a decision of the Court of Session, or
(ii) on a reference made by the Court of Session under schedule 6 of the Scotland Act 1998.

(2) In this regulation—
"determination" means—
(a) a decision about whether the individual meets the conditions in section 81(9), (11) or (13) of the 2018 Act,
(b) if those conditions are satisfied, a decision about what assistance by way of carer's allowance supplement the individual is entitled to be given,
(c) decision about whether the individual's application for a carer's allowance supplement is possibly premature,
"Tribunals Act powers" means the powers under Part 6 (review or appeal of decisions) of the Tribunals (Scotland) Act 2014.

Determination of entitlement to a carer's allowance supplement for individuals resident outside Scotland

5.—(1) The Scottish Ministers are to make a determination of an individual's entitlement to a carer's allowance supplement for the purposes of section 81(2A) of the 2018 Act—
(a) on receiving an application from the individual, or
(b) when required to do so by regulation 7, 8 or 9, without receiving an application.

(2) A determination may be made under paragraph (1) in respect of any qualifying date before or after the coming into force of these Regulations.

(3) Paragraph (4) applies where there is a subsequent determination of an individual's entitlement to a carer's allowance supplement in respect of a qualifying date.

(4) Where this paragraph applies—
(a) the latest determination supersedes any earlier determination insofar as it deals with the individual's entitlement to a carer's allowance supplement in respect of the same qualifying date, and
(b) the individual is not entitled, and is not to become entitled, to a carer's allowance supplement in respect of that qualifying date by the earlier determination.

(SSI 2020/475 reg.6)

Timing of applications for a determination of entitlement to a carer's allowance supplement for individuals resident outside Scotland

6. For the purposes of regulation 5, an individual may make an application on, or at any time after, the first qualifying date on which an individual considers themselves to have been a person to whom section 81(2A) of the 2018 Act applies.

Determination of entitlement to a carer's allowance supplement without application for individuals resident outside Scotland

7. The Scottish Ministers are to make a determination of an individual's entitlement to a carer's allowance supplement under regulation 5, without receiving an application, where—
 (a) it appears to the Scottish Ministers from information available to them that the individual is likely to meet the conditions in section 81(9) or (as the case may be) section 81(11) or (13) of the 2018 Act in respect of one or more qualifying dates,
 (b) the Scottish Ministers have previously made a determination that an individual does not meet the conditions in section 81(9) or (as the case may be) section 81(11) or (13) of the 2018 Act in respect of a qualifying date ("the original determination"), and—
  [¹(i) the Scottish Ministers establish that the individual has received an award of—
   (aa) carer's allowance under section 70 of the Social Security Contributions and Benefits Act 1992,
   (bb) carer support payment under the Carer's Assistance (Carer Support Payment) (Scotland) Regulations 2023 (S.S.I. 2023/302),]
  (ii) the award referred to in sub-paragraph (i) is backdated to include the relevant qualifying date, and
  (iii) it appears to the Scottish Ministers that, had the backdated award been made before the original determination, it is likely that a determination that the individual met the conditions in section 81(9) or (as the case may be) section 81(11) or (13) of the 2018 Act would have been made instead,
 (c) the individual received a payment of carer's allowance supplement in respect of the most recent qualifying date pursuant to a determination made by the Scottish Ministers under regulation 5.

AMENDMENT

1. Carer's Assistance (Carer Support Payment) (Scotland) Regulations 2023 (SSI 2023/302) Sch.1 para.10(2) (November 19, 2023).

Determination following official error - underpayments

8.—(1) The Scottish Ministers are to make a determination under regulation 5 without receiving an application where—
 (a) they have previously made a determination under regulation 5 of the individual's entitlement to a carer's allowance supplement, and

(b) they establish that due to an official error that determination was incorrect resulting in the individual not being paid a carer's allowance supplement to which they were entitled.

(2) In this regulation, "official error" means an error made by someone acting on behalf of the Scottish Ministers or on behalf of a Minister of the Crown that was not materially contributed to by anyone not so acting.

Determination following error – overpayments

9.—(1) The Scottish Ministers are to make a determination under regulation 5 without receiving an application where—
  (a) they have previously made a determination under regulation 5 of the individual's entitlement to a carer's allowance supplement, and
  (b) they establish that due to an error that determination was incorrect resulting in the individual being paid a carer's allowance supplement to which they were not entitled.

(2) In this regulation, "error" means an error in the performance of a function conferred by these Regulations which leads to a determination being made—
  (a) wrongly, or
  (b) correctly but on the basis of incorrect information.

Procedure

10. Schedule 2 makes further provision about matters of procedure for applying for, and determining entitlement to, a carer's allowance supplement for the purposes of section 81(2A) of the 2018 Act.

PART 3

YOUNG CARER GRANTS

AMENDMENT OF ELIGIBILITY CONDITIONS

11. *Omitted (amendments incorporated into SSI 2019/324, above).*

Schedule 1 *Omitted (amendments incorporated into the 2018 Act, above).*

SCHEDULE 2   Regulation 10

PROCEDURAL MATTERS: CARER'S ALLOWANCE SUPPLEMENT

PART 1

APPLICATION AND DETERMINATION OF APPLICATIONS

Form of application

1.—(1) An application under regulation 5 must be—
  (a) made in such form, and
  (b) accompanied by such evidence as the Scottish Ministers require.

(2) The Scottish Ministers must publicise any requirements for the time being set under sub-paragraph (1).
(3) Once—
   (a) an individual has applied for a carer's allowance supplement in respect of a particular qualifying date, and
   (b) the Scottish Ministers have made a determination of the individual's entitlement to a carer's allowance supplement in respect of that date,
the individual cannot make another application for carer's allowance supplement in respect of that qualifying date.
(4) Despite paragraph (3), an individual may make another application for a carer's allowance supplement in respect of that qualifying date if the latest determination of the individual's entitlement to assistance in respect of that date states that the individual may make another application.
(5) If the Scottish Ministers reject something purporting to be an application for a carer's allowance supplement they must inform the individual of—
   (a) the decision to do that,
   (b) the reasons for it, and
   (c) the individual's right to appeal under paragraph 13.

Withdrawal of application

2.—(1) An individual who has made an application for a carer's allowance supplement under regulation 5 may request that the Scottish Ministers disregard it.
(2) If an individual requests that an application be disregarded—
   (a) the Scottish Ministers are not to make a determination of entitlement on the basis of the application, and
   (b) accordingly, their duty to do so under regulation 5 ceases to apply.
(3) A request under sub-paragraph (1) must be made in such form as the Scottish Ministers require.
(4) The Scottish Ministers must publicise any requirements for the time being set under sub-paragraph (3).

Notice of determination

3.—(1) Having made a determination under regulation 5 of an individual's entitlement to a carer's allowance supplement the Scottish Ministers must inform the individual—
   (a) of the determination,
   (b) of the reasons for it,
   (c) of the individual's right under paragraph 4 to request that the Scottish Ministers re-determine the individual's entitlement to the payment, and
   (d) that the individual will have the right under paragraph 9 to appeal to the First-tier Tribunal against the determination should the Scottish Ministers fail to deal with a request for a re-determination in the period allowed for re-determination.
(2) The Scottish Ministers must fulfil their duty under sub-paragraph (1) in a way that leaves the individual with a record of the information which the individual can show to, or otherwise share with, others.

PART 2

RE-DETERMINATION OF ENTITLEMENT

Right to request re-determination and periods allowed

4.—(1) An individual may request that the Scottish Ministers re-determine the individual's entitlement to a carer's allowance supplement after being informed (in accordance with paragraph 3) of a determination by the Scottish Ministers of the individual's entitlement to such a payment.
(2) Unless sub-paragraph (3) applies, a request for re-determination is valid only if it is made before the end of the period of 31 days beginning with the day that the individual is informed (in accordance with paragraph 3) of the right to make the request.
(3) A request for re-determination is valid if it is made after that period has ended, but before the end of the day that falls one year after the day on which the individual is informed (in accordance with paragraph 3) of the determination, if the individual has a good reason for not requesting a re-determination sooner (see paragraph 5).

(4) A request for re-determination is valid only if it is made in such form as the Scottish Ministers require.
(5) The Scottish Ministers must publicise any requirement for the time being set under sub-paragraph (4).
(6) If the Scottish Ministers decide that something purporting to be a request for a re-determination does not satisfy the condition in sub-paragraph (4), they must inform the individual concerned of—
   (a) the decision,
   (b) the reasons for it, and
   (c) the individual's right to appeal under paragraph 13.

Late request for re-determination

5.—(1) It is for—
   (a) the Scottish Ministers, or
   (b) on appeal under paragraph 13 the First-tier Tribunal for Scotland,
to decide whether, for the purpose of paragraph 4(3), an individual has a good reason for not requesting a re-determination sooner.
(2) Where the Scottish Ministers have made a decision under sub-paragraph (1), they must inform the individual concerned—
   (a) of the decision, and
   (b) if the decision is that the individual has no good reason for not requesting a re-determination sooner, of—
      (i) the reasons for the decision, and
      (ii) the individual's right to appeal under paragraph 13.

Duty to re-determine and period allowed

6.—(1) On receiving a valid request under paragraph 4 to re-determine an individual's entitlement to a carer's allowance supplement the Scottish Ministers are to make a determination of the individual's entitlement to that payment.
(2) The Scottish Ministers must aim to make that determination within the period of 16 working days beginning with—
   (a) the day that the request for a re-determination is received by the Scottish Ministers, or
   (b) in the case of a request for a re-determination to which paragraph 4(3) applies (late requests), the day on which it is decided by the Scottish Ministers or (as the case may be) the First-tier Tribunal for Scotland that the individual has a good reason for not requesting a re-determination sooner.
(3) If the Scottish Ministers fail to make the determination within that period—
   (a) their duty to make the determination ends (but they may still make it), and
   (b) paragraph 8 applies.
(4) For the purpose of sub-paragraph (2), a "working day" is a day other than—
   (a) a Saturday
   (b) a Sunday, or
   (c) a bank holiday in Scotland under the Banking and Financial Dealings Act 1971.

Notice of re-determination

7.—(1) Having made a determination under paragraph 6 of an individual's entitlement to a carers allowance supplement, the Scottish Ministers must—
   (a) inform the individual—
      (i) of the determination,
      (ii) of the reasons for it,
      (iii) of the individual's right to appeal to the First-tier Tribunal under regulation 9 against the determination, and
   (b) provide the individual with a form that the individual can complete and submit to the Scottish Ministers in order to bring an appeal against the determination.
(2) The Scottish Ministers must fulfil their duty under sub-paragraph (1)(a) in a way that leaves the individual with a record of the information which the individual can show to, or otherwise share with, others.

Notice where re-determination not made timeously

8.—(1) Where the Scottish Ministers fail to make a determination under paragraph 6 within the period allowed by paragraph 6(2), the Scottish Ministers must—
 (a) inform the individual—
   (i) that the individual's request for a re-determination has not been dealt with within the period allowed, and
   (ii) that the individual therefore has the right to appeal to the First-tier Tribunal against the determination under regulation 5 which prompted the request for a re-determination, and
 (b) provide the individual with a form that the individual can complete and submit to the Scottish Ministers in order to bring an appeal against the determination.

(2) The Scottish Ministers must fulfil their duty under sub-paragraph (1)(a) in a way that leaves the individual with a record of the information which the individual can show to, or otherwise share with, others.

PART 3

APPEALS

Right to appeal to First-tier Tribunal against determination

9.—(1) An individual may appeal to the First-tier Tribunal for Scotland—
 (a) against a determination under paragraph 6 of the individual's entitlement to a carer's allowance supplement, or
 (b) in a case where sub-paragraph (2) applies, against the determination under regulation 5 referred to in that sub-paragraph.

(2) This sub-paragraph applies where—
 (a) having been informed of a determination under regulation 5 of the individual's entitlement to a carer's allowance supplement, the individual has made a request for a re-determination under paragraph 4, and
 (b) the Scottish Ministers have failed to make a determination under paragraph 6 in consequence of that request within the period described in paragraph 6(2).

Initiating an appeal

10.—(1) To bring an appeal against a determination, an individual must submit to the Scottish Ministers the form provided under paragraph 7(1)(b) or (as the case may be) paragraph 8(1)(b) in relation to the determination.

(2) On receiving a form submitted under sub-paragraph (1), the Scottish Ministers must send
 (a) the form, and
 (b) the information held by them that they used to make the determination in question,
to the First-tier Tribunal.

(3) Having complied with sub-paragraph (2), the Scottish Ministers must inform the individual to whom the determination in question relates that they have done so.

(4) In this paragraph, references to a form include a copy of a form.

(5) For the avoidance of doubt, the form that the Scottish Ministers provide under paragraph 7 or 8 need not be a physical form.

Deadline for appealing

11.—(1) An appeal under paragraph 9—
 (a) may be brought without the First-tier Tribunal's permission if an appeal application is made within the period of 31 days beginning with the day the relevant event occurred,
 (b) may be brought only with the First-tier Tribunal's permission if an appeal application is made after the period mentioned in sub-paragraph (1)(a),
 (c) may not be brought if an appeal application has not been made within the period of one year beginning with the day the relevant event occurred.

(2) In sub-paragraph (1)—
 (a) "the relevant event" means—
   (i) in the case of an appeal against a determination under paragraph 6, the individual to whom the determination relates being informed of it in accordance with paragraph 7(1),

(ii) in the case of an appeal against a determination under regulation 5, the individual to whom the determination relates being informed (in accordance with paragraph 8(1)) that the individual has the right to appeal against it,
 (b) an appeal application is made when a form, that relates to the determination in question and has been completed to the extent that Scottish Tribunal Rules require, is received by the Scottish Ministers having been submitted in accordance with paragraph 10(1).

(3) The First-tier Tribunal may give permission under sub-paragraph (1)(b) for an appeal to be brought only if it is satisfied that there is a good reason for the application not having been made sooner.

(4) In sub-paragraph (2)(b), "Scottish Tribunal Rules" has the meaning given by section 68(2) of the Tribunals (Scotland) Act 2014.

First-tier Tribunal's power to determine entitlement

12. In an appeal under paragraph 9 against a determination of an individual's entitlement to a carer's allowance supplement, the First-tier Tribunal may—
 (a) uphold the determination, or
 (b) make its own determination of the individual's entitlement to a carer's allowance supplement.

Appeal to First-tier Tribunal against process decisions

13.—(1) An individual may appeal to the First-tier Tribunal for Scotland against a decision by the Scottish Ministers—
 (a) to reject something purporting to be an application for a carer's allowance supplement (see paragraph 1)),
 (b) that something purporting to be a request for a re-determination does not satisfy the condition in paragraph 4(4),
 (c) that an individual has no good reason for not requesting a re-determination sooner (see paragraph 5).

(2) An appeal under this paragraph—
 (a) may be brought without the First-tier Tribunal's permission within the period of 31 days beginning with the day the individual was informed of the decision in accordance with these Regulations,
 (b) may be brought only with the First-tier Tribunal's permission after the period mentioned in sub-paragraph (2)(a),
 (c) may not be brought after the end of the period of one year beginning with the day the individual was informed of the decision in accordance with these Regulations.

(3) The First-tier Tribunal may give permission under sub-paragraph (2)(b) for an appeal to be made only if it is satisfied that there is a good reason for the appeal not having been made sooner.

(4) A decision by the First-tier Tribunal about—
 (a) the outcome of an appeal under this paragraph, or
 (b) whether to give permission under sub-paragraph (2)(b) for an appeal to be brought,
is final.

(5) Accordingly (and without prejudice to the generality of sub-paragraph (4)), any such decision by the First-tier Tribunal may be neither—
 (a) reviewed under section 43 of the Tribunals (Scotland) Act 2014, nor
 (b) appealed against under section 46 of that Act.

Presumption for purposes of paragraphs 1, 3, 4, 5, 7, 8 and 10

14.—(1) Sub-paragraph (2) applies in relation to the references in paragraphs 1, 3, 4, 5, 7, 8, and 10 to an individual being informed of something by the Scottish Ministers in accordance with a provision of these Regulations.

(2) Where, in order to fulfil their duty to inform an individual of something, the Scottish Ministers send information—
 (a) through the postal service to the last known address the Scottish Ministers have for the individual, or
 (b) by email to the email address most recently provided to the Scottish Ministers by the individual for the purposes of these Regulations,
the individual is to be taken to have received the information 48 hours after it is sent by the Scottish Ministers unless the contrary is shown.

The Carer's Allowance Supplement and Young Carer Regulations 2020

Amendment of the Social Security Appeals (Expenses and Allowances) (Scotland) Regulations 2018

15. *Omitted.*

PART 4

FURTHER PROVISION ABOUT DETERMINING ENTITLEMENT

Obtaining information to make a determination

16.—(1) When the Scottish Ministers are determining an individual's entitlement to a carer's allowance supplement for the purposes of section 81(2A) of the 2018 Act—
  (a) they require further information in order to satisfy themselves about any matter material to the making of the determination, and
  (b) they may request that the individual provide them with the information within such period as they specify.
(2) If the individual fails to provide the requested information by the end of the specified period, the Scottish Ministers may, without further consideration, proceed to make the determination on the basis that the individual does not satisfy the conditions in section 81(9) or (as the case may be) section 81(11) or (13) of the 2018 Act.

Duty to inform about possible eligibility

17.—(1) Paragraph (2) applies if, in the course of their making a determination of an individual's entitlement to a carer's allowance supplement under regulation 5, it appears to the Scottish Ministers that the individual may be entitled to a type of assistance described in Chapter 2 of Part 2 of the 2018 Act or to assistance provided for by regulations made under section 79 of that Act.
(2) The Scottish Ministers must—
  (a) inform the individual that the individual may be eligible for the assistance, and
  (b) either—
    (i) provide the individual with information about how to apply for it, or
    (ii) if regulations made under section 52 or 79 of the 2018 Act so allow, ask the individual whether they should proceed with making a determination of the individual's entitlement to the assistance without receiving an application.
(3) Paragraph (2)(b)(ii) does not preclude the Scottish Ministers from requesting further information under paragraph 16 for the purpose of determining the individual's entitlement to the assistance described in paragraph (1).

Appointment of a person to act on behalf of an individual

18. Section 58 or (as the case may be) section 85B of the 2018 Act applies in respect of the determination of an individual's entitlement to a carer's allowance supplement under regulation 5 as it does to a determination of entitlement to assistance under Part 2 or 3 of the 2018 Act.

PART 5

CORONAVIRUS – RELAXATION OF DEADLINES

Re-determination and appeal deadlines

19.—(1) A request for a re-determination is valid, despite being made after the expiry of the period described in paragraph 4(3), if the person deciding whether the individual has a good reason for not requesting a re-determination sooner decides that the individual has a good reason that is related to coronavirus.
(2) An appeal may be brought under paragraph 9 despite the appeal application being made after the expiry of the period described in paragraph 11(1)(c), if the First-tier Tribunal gives permission for the appeal to be brought under sub-paragraph (1)(b) of that paragraph on the basis of being satisfied that the good reason for the application not being made sooner is related to coronavirus.

(3) Any provision of Scottish Tribunal Rules that would (but for this sub-paragraph) have the effect of precluding an appeal being brought by virtue of sub-paragraph (2) is to be disregarded to the extent that it would have that effect.

(4) In this paragraph—

"coronavirus" has the meaning given by section 1 of the Coronavirus (Scotland) Act 2020,

"Scottish Tribunal Rules" has the meaning given by paragraph 11(4).

(SSI 2021/73)

The Disability Assistance for Children and Young People (Consequential Amendment and Transitional Provision) (Scotland) Regulations 2021

(SSI 2021/73)

Made	10th February 2021
Laid before the Scottish Parliament	12th February 2021
Coming into force	26th July 2021

The Scottish Ministers make the following Regulations in exercise of the powers conferred by section 95 of the Social Security (Scotland) Act 2018 and all other powers enabling them to do so.

1. to 18. *Omitted.*

Transitional provision–extinguishment of right to apply for Disability Living

19.—(1) No person may claim disability living allowance who is under the age of 16 years and—
  (a) during the initial period for applications for child disability payment, is resident in the local authority area of Perthshire and Kinross, City of Dundee or the Western Isles, or
  (b) after the expiry of that period—
    (i) is resident in Scotland, or
    (ii) is a person to whom regulation 5(4) or (6) (residence and presence conditions–individuals resident in Ireland, members of Her Majesty's forces and civil servants) or regulation 9 (persons residing outside the United Kingdom to whom a relevant EU regulation applies) of the Child Disability Payment Regulations applies.

(2) Paragraph (1) does not apply to a person who has an award of disability living allowance which is of—
  (a) both the mobility component and the care component and the award in respect of either or both is for a fixed term period, or
  (b) one of those components only and the award is for a fixed term period,
if the person has been notified by the Secretary of State for Work and Pensions that, because the fixed term period is due to come to an end, the person needs to claim disability living allowance again, or to apply for a supersession of the award, if the person wishes to continue to be entitled to disability living allowance in respect of the component or components subject to the fixed term period.

(3) In this regulation—
"child disability payment" means disability assistance for children and young people given in accordance with the Child Disability Payment Regulations,
"Child Disability Payment Regulations" means the Disability Assistance for Children and Young People (Scotland) Regulations 2021,

"disability living allowance" means a disability living allowance under section 71 of the Social Security Contributions and Benefits Act 1992,

"initial period for applications" means the period referred to in regulation 44 (transitory provision—initial period for applications) of the Child Disability Payment Regulations, beginning with 26 July 2021 and ending with 21 November 2021.

GENERAL NOTE

13.291 This regulation was made in anticipation of the making of the Disability Assistance for Children and Young People (Scotland) Regulations 2021. Its effect was that those entitled to make a claim for child disability payment under Scottish legislation were not entitled to claim disability living allowance under Great Britain legislation, unless a fixed term award of disability living allowance was coming to an end and they preferred to make a continuation claim for that allowance rather than claim child disability payment. Even that option was reduced as entitlement to disability living allowance was converted into entitlement to child disability payment.

It was originally intended that, for almost all those under the age of 16 and ordinarily resident in Scotland, conversion under Pt 3 of the schedule of the Disability Assistance for Children and Young People (Scotland) Regulations 2021 (see below) would have taken place by the end of 2022, but this slipped slightly to Spring 2023.

The Disability Assistance for Children and Young People (Scotland) Regulations 2021

(SSI 2021/174)

Made	24th March 2021
Coming into force	26th July 2021

The Scottish Ministers make the following Regulations in exercise of the powers conferred by sections 31(2), 36(2), 41(4)(a), 43(5), 51(1), 52 and 95 of the Social Security (Scotland) Act 2018 and all other powers enabling them to do so.

In accordance with section 96(2) of that Act, a draft of these Regulations has been laid before and approved by resolution of the Scottish Parliament.

In accordance with section 97(2) of that Act, the Scottish Ministers have informed the Scottish Commission on Social Security of their proposals, notified the Scottish Parliament that they have done so and made their proposals publicly available by such means as they consider appropriate.

Citation and commencement

13.292 1. These Regulations may be cited as the Disability Assistance for Children and Young People (Scotland) Regulations 2021 and come into force on 26 July 2021.

Interpretation—general

13.293 2. In these Regulations—

(SSI 2021/174 reg. 2)

"the 2018 Act" means the Social Security (Scotland) Act 2018,

[³ "Adult Disability Payment" means disability assistance for adults given in accordance with the Disability Assistance for Working Age People (Scotland) Regulations 2022,]

[⁴ "the ADP Regulations" means the Disability Assistance for Working Age People (Scotland) Regulations 2022,]

"armed forces independence payment" means the disability benefit paid in accordance with article 24A of the Armed Forces and Reserve Forces (Compensation Scheme) Order 2011,

"authorised provider of vehicles" means a supplier of vehicles for persons with disabilities approved under an accreditation scheme run by the Scottish Ministers,

"award" means that a determination has been made that an individual is entitled to be given assistance under section 24 of the 2018 Act in accordance with these Regulations, and cognate expressions are to be construed accordingly,

"bodily functions" means the normal actions of any organ of the body, including the brain, or of a number of organs acting together,

"care component" means the care component of Child Disability Payment within the meaning of regulation 11,

"care home" means an establishment which provides a care home service as defined in paragraph 2 of schedule 12 of the Public Services Reform (Scotland) Act 2010 and includes a residential educational establishment,

"Child Disability Payment" means disability assistance for children and young people given in accordance with section 31 of the 2018 Act,

"determination" or "determination of entitlement" has the meaning in section 25 of the 2018 Act,

"Disability Living Allowance" means a disability living allowance under—
(a) section 71 of the Social Security Contributions and Benefits Act 1992, or
(b) section 71 of the Social Security Contributions and Benefits (Northern Ireland) Act 1992,

"EEA State" means—
(a) any member state of the European Union, or
(b) any other state that is party to the agreement on the European Economic Area signed at Oporto on 2 May 1992, together with the Protocol adjusting that Agreement signed at Brussels on 17 March 1993, as modified or supplemented from time to time,

"hospice" means a hospital or other institution whose primary function is to provide palliative care for persons resident there who are suffering from a progressive disease in its final stages other than—
(a) a health service hospital (within the meaning of section 108(1) of the National Health Service (Scotland) Act 1978) in Scotland,
(b) a health service hospital (within the meaning of section 275(1) of the National Health Service Act 2006) in England,
(c) a hospital in Wales vested in—
   (i) an NHS trust,
   (ii) a Local Health Board, or
   (iii) the Welsh Ministers,
   for the purpose of functions under the National Health Service (Wales) Act 2006,

(d) a hospital maintained or administered by the Defence Council, or
(e) an institution similar to a hospital mentioned in any of the preceding paragraphs,

[¹ "legal detention" means detention in legal custody within the meaning of section 295 of the Criminal Procedure (Scotland) Act 1995,]

"mobility component" means the mobility component of Child Disability Payment within the meaning of regulations 12 and 13,

"personal independence payment" means personal independence payment under—
(a) Part 4 of the Welfare Reform Act 2012, or
(b) article 82 of the Welfare Reform (Northern Ireland) Order 2015,

"qualifying services" means accommodation, board and personal care,

"relevant EU Regulation" means—
(a) one of the following Regulations—
  (i) Council Regulation (EC) No 1408/71 of 14 June 1971 on the application of social security schemes to employed persons, to self-employed persons and to members of their families moving within the Community,
  (ii) Regulation (EC) No 883/2004 of the European Parliament and of the Council of 29 April 2004 on the coordination of social security systems, or
(b) in relation to an individual to whom the agreement constituted by the exchange of letters set out in the schedule of the Family Allowances, National Insurance and Industrial Injuries (Gibraltar) Order 1974 applies, a Regulation mentioned in paragraph (a) of this definition as it forms part of domestic law by virtue of section 3 of the European Union (Withdrawal) Act 2018,

"residential educational establishment" means a care home which provides education or training except for one where the costs of any qualifying services are borne wholly or partly out of public or local funds by virtue of—
(a) [¹ section 485 of the Education Act 1996 or section 14 of the Education Act 2002 (which relate to grants and financial assistance for education),]
(b) sections 49 or 73 of the Education (Scotland) Act 1980 (which relate respectively to the power of education authorities to assist persons to take advantage of educational facilities and the powers of the Secretary of State to make grants to education authorities and others),
(c) section 65 of the Further and Higher Education Act 1992, sections 39 or 40 of the Higher Education and Research Act 2017 or sections 4 or 11 of the Further and Higher Education (Scotland) Act 2005 (which relate respectively to the funding of further education and the administration of funds), or
(d) section 22 of the Teaching and Higher Education Act 1998,

[² "short-term assistance" means short-term assistance given in accordance with Part 1 of the schedule,]

"transferring individual" has the meaning set out in paragraph 7 of the schedule, and

"week" means a period of 7 days.

(SSI 2021/174 reg.2)

AMENDMENTS

1. Disability Assistance for Children and Young People (Scotland) Amendment Regulations 2021 (SSI 2021/416) regs 2 and 3 (November 22, 2021).
2. Scottish Child Payment Regulations 2020 and the Disability Assistance for Children and Young People (Scotland) Regulations 2021 (Miscellaneous Amendments) Regulations 2022 (SSI 2022/41) reg.3(1) and (2) (February 9, 2022).
3. Disability Assistance for Working Age People (Consequential and Miscellaneous Amendment and Transitional Provision) (Scotland) Regulations 2022 (SSI 2022/31) reg.19(1) and (2) (March 21, 2022).
4. Disability Assistance (Miscellaneous Amendment) (Scotland) Regulations 2023 (SSI 2023/346) reg.3(2) (November 20, 2023).

Overview

3.—(1) An individual is entitled to Child Disability Payment in accordance with these Regulations if they meet the eligibility rules in—
  (a) regulation 4 (age criteria),
  (b) regulations 5 to 9 (residence and presence conditions, etc.),
  (c) regulation 10 (entitlement to other benefits),
  (d) one or more of the following—
    (i) regulation 11 (care component criterion: lowest, middle and highest rate of care component),
    (ii) regulation 12 (mobility requirements: lower rate mobility component),
    (iii) regulation 13 (mobility requirements: higher rate mobility component),
    (iv) regulation 15 (entitlement under special rules for terminal illness),
    (v) regulation 16 (entitlement to care component when undergoing dialysis).
(2) Child Disability Payment is to consist of a care component and a mobility component.
(3) There are 3 weekly rates of the care component and 2 weekly rates of the mobility component and those rates are specified in regulation 23 (amount and form of Child Disability Payment).

Age criteria

4.—(1) Subject to [¹ paragraph (1A), (1B) [², (1C)] and (2)], Child Disability Payment may be paid in respect of an individual who is aged at least 3 months and is under the age of 18 years.
[¹ (1A) Where regulation 15 (entitlement under special rules for terminal illness) applies, the requirement in paragraph (1) to be aged at least 3 months does not apply.
[¹[²(1B) Child Disability Payment may continue to be paid in respect of an individual who is over the age of 17 years—
  (a) where they are an individual to whom regulation 15 (entitlement under special rules for terminal illness) applies,
  (b) until the age of 19 years where the individual is a transferring individual in terms of Part 3 of the schedule, and reaches the age of 18 on or before 31 December 2023, except where paragraph (1C) applies,
  (c) until the age of 19 years where they are an individual mentioned in regulation 35 (individuals in respect of whom Disability Living

Allowance is paid in another part of the United Kingdom immediately before moving to Scotland) who reaches the age of 18 on or before 31 December 2023, except where paragraph (1C) applies,
  (d) where the individual does not fall within sub-paragraph (a), (b) or (c) and—
    (i) they are awaiting a determination of their entitlement to Adult Disability Payment, or
    (ii) a determination has been made that the individual is entitled to Adult Disability Payment but payment has not begun,
until the age of 19 years, or the individual becomes entitled to Adult Disability Payment in accordance with regulation 58(2)(a) of the ADP Regulations, whichever is earlier.]]

[²(1C) Where an individual falls within paragraph (1B)(b) or (c) and—
  (a) a determination of their entitlement to Adult Disability Payment is made within the period of 4 weeks before the date on which the individual reaches the age of 19, and
  (b) that determination is that the individual is entitled to Adult Disability Payment,
Child Disability Payment may continue to be paid in respect of the individual after they reach the age of 19 until the day before the day on which the individual becomes entitled to Adult Disability Payment in accordance with regulation 58(2)(a) of the ADP Regulations.]

(2) [¹ Where an individual's entitlement to Child Disability Payment is first determined on the basis of an application made in accordance with section 38 of the 2018 Act,] Child Disability Payment may only be paid in respect of an individual who is under the age of 16 years on the day on which entitlement begins in accordance with regulation 24 (when an application is to be treated as made and beginning of entitlement to assistance).

(3) Where an individual was born on 29 February, the individual's birthday is to be taken to fall on 28 February in a year which is not a leap year.

AMENDMENTS

1. Disability Assistance for Children and Young People (Scotland) Amendment Regulations 2021 (SSI 2021/416) regs 2 and 4 (November 22, 2021).
2. Disability Assistance (Miscellaneous Amendment) (Scotland) Regulations 2023 (SSI 2023/346) reg.3(3) (November 20, 2023).

Residence and presence conditions

5.—(1) An individual satisfies the residence and presence conditions where on any day that individual—
  (a) is ordinarily resident in Scotland,
  (b) is habitually resident in the common travel area,
  [³ (c) is not a person subject to immigration control within the meaning of section 115(9) of the Immigration and Asylum Act 1999],
  (d) is present in the common travel area, and
  (e) has been present in the common travel area for a period of, or for periods amounting in the aggregate to, not less than 26 weeks in the 52 weeks immediately preceding that day.

(2) In the case of a child under the age of 6 months, paragraph (1) is to apply as if in sub-paragraph (e) for the reference to 26 weeks there was substituted a reference to 13 weeks.

(SSI 2021/174 reg. 5)

(3) Where in any particular case a child has by virtue of paragraph (2) entitlement to the care component immediately before the day the child attains the age of 6 months, then until the child attains the age of 12 months, paragraph (1)(e) shall continue to apply in that child's case as if for the reference to 26 weeks there was substituted a reference to 13 weeks.

(4) The residence condition set out in paragraph (1)(a) does not apply in relation to the care component where on any day the individual—
  (a) is habitually resident in Ireland,
  (b) has a genuine and sufficient link to Scotland, and
  (c) is an individual—
    (i) to whom the Convention on Social Security between the Government of the United Kingdom of Great Britain and Northern Ireland and the Government of Ireland signed at Dublin on 1 February 2019, as modified from time to time in accordance with any provision of it, applies, and
    (ii) in respect of whom the United Kingdom is, as a result, competent for payment of long term care benefits.

(5) The reference in paragraph (4)(b) to an individual's link to Scotland being sufficient is to it being sufficiently close that if the individual were not entitled to Child Disability Payment, paragraph (4) would be incompatible with Convention on Social Security between the Government of the United Kingdom of Great Britain and Northern Ireland and the Government of Ireland signed at Dublin on 1 February 2019.

[³ (5A) Paragraph (1)(c) does not apply to a person subject to immigration control within the meaning of section 115(9) of the Immigration and Asylum Act 1999 where they are a person who—
  (a) is lawfully working in the United Kingdom and is a national of a state with which the United Kingdom has concluded an agreement which replaces in whole or in part an agreement under Article 217 of the Treaty on the Functioning of the European Union which has ceased to apply to, and in, the United Kingdom, providing, in the field of social security, for the equal treatment of workers who are nationals of the signatory state and their families,
  (b) is a member of the family of, and living with, a person specified in sub-paragraph (a), or
  (c) has been given leave to enter, or remain in, the United Kingdom by the Secretary of State upon an undertaking by another person or persons pursuant to the immigration rules, to be responsible for their maintenance and accommodation.]

(6) A relevant individual is treated as satisfying the residence and presence conditions set out in paragraph (1)(a), [² (b) and (d)] where on any day that individual is outside the common travel area—
  (a) by reason of their capacity mentioned in paragraph (7)(b) provided that individual satisfied the residence and presence conditions set out in paragraph (1)(a), [² (b) and (d)] immediately prior to the start of their employment mentioned in paragraph (7)(b), or
  (b) by reason of being a person mentioned in paragraph (7)(a) living with an individual to whom sub-paragraph (a) applies.

(7) A "relevant individual" in paragraph (6) means an individual who is—
  (a) living with a person mentioned in sub-paragraph (b) and—

    (i) is the child, step-child or a child in care of that person, or
    (ii) is married to or in a civil partnership with that person, or is living together with that person as if they were married or in a civil partnership, or
  (b) outside the common travel area in their capacity as a—
    (i) serving member of Her Majesty's forces, or
    (ii) civil servant.
(8) An individual is to be treated as meeting the presence conditions set out in paragraphs (1)(d) and (e) for any period where that individual is—
  (a) outside the common travel area in their capacity as an aircraft worker or mariner, or
  (b) in employment prescribed for the purposes of section 120 (employment at sea (continental shelf operations)) of the Social Security Contributions and Benefits Act 1992 in connection with continental shelf operations.
(9) Where an individual—
  (a) does not meet the [² either or both of the presence conditions] set out in paragraph [² (1)(d) and (e)] on the date the application is received by the Scottish Ministers, and
  (b) appears to the Scottish Ministers likely to meet [² both of those conditions], unless there is a change of circumstances, on a date not later than 3 months after the application was received,
the Scottish Ministers may choose the date within that 3 month period on which the application is to be treated as being made.
[³ (10) The past presence condition in paragraph (1)(e) does not apply where an individual—
  (a) has a terminal illness within the meaning of regulation 15, or
  (b) is an individual described in paragraph (7).]
[¹ (10A) The habitual residence condition in paragraph (1)(b) and the past presence condition in paragraph (1)(e) do not apply where an individual—
  (a) has leave to enter or remain in the United Kingdom granted under the immigration rules by virtue of—
    (i) the Afghan Relocations and Assistance Policy, or
    (ii) the previous scheme for locally-employed staff in Afghanistan (sometimes referred to as the ex-gratia scheme),
  (b) has been granted discretionary leave outside the immigration rules as a dependant of a person referred to in sub-paragraph (a); [³ ...]
  (c) has leave granted under the Afghan Citizens Resettlement Scheme,]
[³ (d) has been granted refugee status or humanitarian protection under the immigration rules, [⁴ ...]
  (e) has leave to enter or remain in the United Kingdom as the dependant of a person granted refugee status or humanitarian protection under the immigration rules,] [⁴ [⁶...]
  (f) has leave to enter or remain in the United Kingdom granted under or outside the immigration rules, [⁵ has a right] of abode in the United Kingdom within the meaning given in section 2 of the Immigration Act 1971 [⁵ or does not require leave to enter or remain in the United Kingdom in accordance with section 3ZA of that Act], where the individual—
    (i) was residing in Ukraine immediately before 1 January 2022, and

(SSI 2021/174 reg.5)

    (ii) left Ukraine in connection with the Russian invasion which took place on 24 February 2022] [6, [7...]
- (g) has leave to enter or remain in the United Kingdom granted under or outside the immigration rules, has a right of abode in the United Kingdom within the meaning given in section 2 of the Immigration Act 1971 or does not require leave to enter or remain in the United Kingdom in accordance with section 3ZA of that Act, where the individual—
  - (i) was residing in Sudan before 15 April 2023, and
  - (ii) left Sudan in connection with the violence which rapidly escalated on 15 April 2023 in Khartoum and across Sudan] [7, or
- (h) has leave to enter or remain in the United Kingdom granted under or outside the immigration rules, has a right of abode in the United Kingdom within the meaning given in section 2 of the Immigration Act 1971 or does not require leave to enter or remain in the United Kingdom in accordance with section 3ZA of that Act, where the individual—
  - (i) was residing in Israel, the West Bank, the Gaza Strip, East Jerusalem, the Golan Heights or Lebanon immediately before 7 October 2023, and
  - (ii) left Israel, the West Bank, the Gaza Strip, East Jerusalem, the Golan Heights or Lebanon in connection with the Hamas terrorist attack in Israel on 7 October 2023 or the violence which rapidly escalated in the region following the attack.]

(11) [1 For the purposes of [3 paragraph (10A)]—
- (a) "immigration rules" means the rules laid before Parliament under section 3(2) of the Immigration Act 1971,
- (b) "the Afghan Citizens Resettlement Scheme" means the scheme announced by the United Kingdom Government on 18 August 2021.]

AMENDMENTS

    1. Social Security (Residence Requirements) (Afghanistan) (Scotland) Regulations 2021 (SSI 2021/320) reg.6 (September 15, 2021).
    2. Disability Assistance for Children and Young People (Scotland) Amendment Regulations 2021 (SSI 2021/416) regs 2 and 5 (November 22, 2021).
    3. Scottish Child Payment Regulations 2020 and the Disability Assistance for Children and Young People (Scotland) Regulations 2021 (Miscellaneous Amendments) Regulations 2022 (SSI 2022/41) reg.3(1) and (3) (February 9, 2022).
    4. Social Security (Residence Requirements) (Ukraine) (Scotland) Regulations 2022 (SSI 2022/108) reg.7 (March 22, 2022).
    5. Social Security (Miscellaneous Amendment and Transitional Provision) (Scotland) Regulations 2022 (SSI 2022/336) reg.8 (November 14, 2022).
    6. Social Security (Residence Requirements) (Sudan) (Scotland) Regulations 2023 (SSI 2023/149) reg.7(2) (May 17, 2023).
    7. Social Security (Residence and Presence Requirements) (Israel, the West Bank, the Gaza Strip, East Jerusalem, the Golan Heights and Lebanon) (Scotland) Regulations 2023 (SSI 2023/309) reg.7(2) (October 26, 2023).

Interpretation—residence and presence conditions

13.297

    6. In regulation 5—
"aircraft worker" means a person who is, or has been, employed under a contract of service either as a pilot, commander, navigator or other

member of the crew of any aircraft, or in any other capacity on board any aircraft where—
(a) the employment in that other capacity is for the purposes of the aircraft or its crew or of any passengers or cargo or mails carried on that aircraft, and
(b) the contract is entered into in the United Kingdom with a view to its performance (in whole or in part) while the aircraft is in flight,
but does not include a person in so far as that employment is as a serving member of Her Majesty's forces,

"child in care" means—
(a) under the law of Scotland, a child in respect of whom a relevant individual listed in regulation [² 5(7)(b)]—
  (i) Is a foster carer within the meaning of regulation 2 of the Looked After Children (Scotland) Regulations 2009,
  (ii) is a kinship carer within the meaning of regulation 2 of the Looked After Children (Scotland) Regulations 2009,
  (iii) has a kinship care order within the meaning of section 72 of the Children and Young People (Scotland) Act 2014, or
(b) under the law of England and Wales and Northern Ireland, a child in respect of whom a person listed in regulation [² 5(7)(b)] has a relationship equivalent to those listed in paragraph (a) under the law of Scotland,

[³...]
"civil servant" has the meaning given by section 1(4) of the Constitutional Reform and Governance Act 2010,
"common travel area" has the meaning given in section 1(3) of the Immigration Act 1971,
"mariner" means a person who is, or has been, in employment under a contract of service either as a master or member of the crew of any ship or vessel, or in any other capacity on board any ship or vessel where—
(a) the employment in that other capacity is for the purposes of that ship or vessel or its crew or any passengers or cargo or mails carried by the ship or vessel, and
(b) the contract is entered into in the United Kingdom with a view to its performance (in whole or in part) while the ship or vessel is on its voyage,
but does not include a person in so far as that employment is as a serving member of Her Majesty's forces,

[³...]
"serving member of Her Majesty's forces" means a member of a regular force or reserve force ("M") as defined, in each case, by section 374 (definitions applying for purposes of the whole Act) of the Armed Forces Act 2006, unless—
(a) M is under the age of 16,
(b) M is committing an offence under section 8 of the Armed Forces Act 2006 (desertion),
(c) the force concerned is one of Her Majesty's naval forces which M locally entered at an overseas base without [¹ ...]—
  (i) [¹ previously being] an insured person under the National Insurance Act 1965, or
  [(ii) paying or having previously paid one or more of the following classes of contributions under the Social Security Act

1975 or the Social Security Contributions and Benefits Act 1992—
- (aa) primary Class 1,
- (bb) Class 2, or
- (cc) Class 3, or]

(d) the force concerned is one of Her Majesty's military forces or Her Majesty's air forces which M entered, or was recruited for, outside the United Kingdom and—
  - (i) where that force is one of Her Majesty's military forces, the depot for M's unit is outside the United Kingdom, or
  - (ii) where that force is one of Her Majesty's air forces, M is liable under the terms of M's engagement to serve only in a specified area outside the United Kingdom.

AMENDMENTS

1. Disability Assistance for Children and Young People (Scotland) Amendment Regulations 2021 (SSI 2021/416) regs 2 and 6 (November 22, 2021).
2. Scottish Child Payment Regulations 2020 and the Disability Assistance for Children and Young People (Scotland) Regulations 2021 (Miscellaneous Amendments) Regulations 2022 (SSI 2022/41) reg.3(1) and (4) (February 9, 2022).
3. Disability Assistance for Working Age People (Transitional Provisions and Miscellaneous Amendment) (Scotland) Regulations 2022 (SSI 2022/217) reg.18(1) and (2) (August 29, 2022).

Temporary absence from the common travel area

7.—(1) Where an individual is temporarily absent from the common travel area, the individual is to be treated as present in the common travel area for—
- (a) the first 13 weeks of that absence for any reason, or
- (b) the first 26 weeks of that absence where—
  - (i) after the first 13 weeks, the absence is in connection with arrangements made for the medical treatment of the individual for a disease or bodily or mental disablement which commenced before leaving the common travel area, and
  - (ii) the arrangements relate to medical treatment—
    - (aa) outside the common travel area,
    - (bb) during the period when the individual is temporarily absent from the common travel area, and
    - (cc) by, or under the supervision of, a person appropriately qualified to carry out that treatment.

(2) For the purposes of paragraph (1)—
- (a) an individual is "temporarily absent" if, at the beginning of the period of absence, that absence is unlikely to exceed 52 weeks, and
- (b) "medical treatment" means medical, surgical, psychological or rehabilitative treatment (including any course, diet or regimen).

Persons residing in the United Kingdom to whom a relevant EU regulation applies

8. The past presence condition set out in regulation 5(1)(e) does not apply where on any day the individual is—

(a) ordinarily resident in Scotland,
(b) habitually resident in the United Kingdom,
(c) an individual—
  (i) to whom the rules set out in a relevant EU regulation applies by virtue of—
    (aa) Title III of Part 2 of the EU withdrawal agreement,
    (bb) Part 3 or Article 23(4) of the Swiss citizens' rights agreement (as defined in section 39(1) of the European Union (Withdrawal Agreement) Act 2020) ("the 2020 Act")),
    (cc) Title III of the EEA EFTA separation agreement (as defined in section 39(1) of the 2020 Act), or
    (dd) the agreement constituted by the exchange of letters set out in the schedule of the Family Allowances, National Insurance and Industrial Injuries (Gibraltar) Order 1974,
  (ii) in respect of whom the United Kingdom is, as a result, competent for payment of sickness benefits in cash.

Persons residing outside the United Kingdom to whom a relevant EU regulation applies

9.—(1) The residence and presence conditions set out in regulation 5(1) do not apply in relation to the care component where on any day the individual satisfies the conditions in paragraph (2).

(2) The conditions referred to in paragraph (1) are that the individual must—
(a) be an individual—
  (i) to whom the rules set out in a relevant EU regulation apply by virtue of—
    (aa) Title III of Part 2 of the EU withdrawal agreement,
    (bb) Part 3 or Article 23(4) of the Swiss citizens' rights agreement (as defined in section 39(1) of the European Union (Withdrawal Agreement) Act 2020 ("the 2020 Act")),
    (cc) Title III of the EEA EFTA separation agreement (as defined in section 39(1) of the 2020 Act), or
    (dd) the agreement constituted by the exchange of letters set out in the schedule of the Family Allowances, National Insurance and Industrial Injuries (Gibraltar) Order 1974, and
  (ii) in respect of whom the United Kingdom is, as a result, competent for payment of sickness benefits in cash,
(b) be habitually resident in—
  (i) Switzerland,
  (ii) an EEA state, or
  (iii) Gibraltar, and
(c) have a genuine and sufficient link to Scotland.

(3) The reference in paragraph (2)(c) to an individual's link to Scotland being sufficient is to it being sufficiently close that if the individual were not entitled to Child Disability Payment, paragraph (2) would be incompatible with the applicable agreement mentioned in sub-paragraph (a)(i) of that paragraph.

(SSI 2021/174 reg. 9)

[¹No entitlement to care component where UK is not competent state

9A. An individual to whom a relevant EU Regulation applies is not entitled to the care component for a period unless during that period the United Kingdom is competent for payment of sickness benefits in cash to the individual for the purposes of the relevant EU Regulation in question.]

13.301

AMENDMENT

1. Disability Assistance (Miscellaneous Amendment) (Scotland) Regulations 2023 (SSI 2023/346) reg.3(4) (November 20, 2023).

Entitlement to other benefits

10. An individual is not entitled to Child Disability Payment while they are entitled to—
   (a) Disability Living Allowance,
   (b) Personal Independence Payment, [¹ . . .]
   (c) armed forces independence payment [¹ , or
   (d) Adult Disability Payment.]

13.302

AMENDMENT

1. Disability Assistance for Working Age People (Consequential and Miscellaneous Amendment and Transitional Provision) (Scotland) Regulations 2022 (SSI 2022/31) reg.19(1) and (3) (March 21, 2022).

Care component criterion: lowest, middle or highest rate care component

11.—(1) An individual satisfies the care component criterion in respect of any period throughout which at least one of the following conditions is satisfied—
   (a) the individual is so severely disabled physically or mentally that they require in connection with their bodily functions attention from another person for a significant portion of the day (whether during a single period or a number of periods),
   (b) the individual is 16 years old or older and is so severely disabled physically or mentally that they cannot prepare a cooked main meal for themselves if they have the ingredients,
   (c) the individual is so severely disabled physically or mentally that they require from another person—
      (i) frequent attention throughout the day in connection with their bodily functions, or
      (ii) continual supervision throughout the day in order to avoid substantial danger to the individual or others, or
   (d) the individual is so severely disabled physically or mentally that they require—
      (i) prolonged or repeated attention from another person [¹ at] night in connection with their bodily functions, or
      (ii) another person to be awake for a prolonged period or at frequent intervals for the purpose of watching over the individual [¹ at] night in order to avoid substantial danger to the individual or others.

13.303

(2) No condition mentioned in paragraph (1) is to be taken to be satisfied unless—
- (a) the individual has requirements of a description mentioned in the condition substantially in excess of the normal requirements of a person of the same age, or
- (b) the individual has substantial requirements of such a description which younger persons in normal physical and mental health may also have but which persons of the individual's age and in normal physical and mental health would not have.

(3) An individual is not entitled to the care component unless—
- (a) throughout the period of 13 weeks immediately preceding the date on which the award of that component would begin, the individual has satisfied or is likely to satisfy at least one of the conditions mentioned in paragraph (1) as read with paragraph (2), and
- (b) the individual is likely to continue to satisfy at least one of those conditions throughout the period of 26 weeks beginning with that date.

(4) In the case of an individual who is under the age of 16 on the date on which the award of the care component would begin, paragraph (2) only applies in relation to so much of any period mentioned in that paragraph as falls before the day on which the individual reaches the age of 16.

(5) The amount of the care component that an individual is entitled to be given for each week in the period for which they are awarded that component is—
- (a) the highest rate (see regulation 23(1)(a)), if the individual falls within paragraph (3) by virtue of having satisfied or being likely to satisfy both the conditions mentioned in paragraph (1)(c) and (d) above throughout both the period mentioned in paragraph (3)(a) and that mentioned in paragraph (3)(b),
- (b) the middle rate (see regulation 23(1)(b)), if the individual falls within paragraph (3) by virtue of having satisfied or being likely to satisfy one of those conditions mentioned in paragraph (1)(c) or (d) throughout both those periods, and
- (c) the lowest rate (see regulation 23(1)(c)) in any other case.

(6) In paragraph (1)—
- (a) references to "day" and "night" are to be construed in relation to the ordinary domestic routine of the household in which the individual lives, and
- (b) "attention" means the provision of personal care, prompting or motivation in relation to bodily functions or assistance with communication needs.

(7) In paragraph (1) and regulation 12, "supervision" means the precautionary or anticipatory presence of another person to monitor an individual's physical, mental or emotional health including monitoring for obstacles or dangerous places or situations.

(8) In this regulation and regulations 12 and 13, "require" means reasonably require and cognate expressions are to be construed accordingly.

AMENDMENT

1. Disability Assistance for Children and Young People (Scotland) Amendment Regulations 2021 (SSI 2021/416) regs 2 and 7 (November 22, 2021).

GENERAL NOTE

This regulation substantially re-enacts s.72(1) to (4) of the Social Security Contributions and Benefits Act 1992, which provides for the care component of disability living allowance throughout Great Britain, but there are some differences apart from the use of gender-neutral language.

In particular, paras (6) to (8) make explicit in the legislation points that are only implicit in the 1992 Act and are made explicit for the purposes of that Act only in case law. In addition, the term "bodily functions" is defined in reg.2. Case law under the 1992 Act (see the annotations in Vol I) will nonetheless continue to be relevant.

The amendments to para.(1)(d) correct a drafting error that would have made the sub-paragraph disadvantageous to some claimants by comparison with s.72(1)(c) of the 1992 Act.

Mobility requirements: lower rate mobility component

12.—(1) An individual aged 5 years or more is entitled to be given the mobility component at the lower rate (see regulation 23(2)(b)) if the individual satisfies the condition set out in paragraph (2).

(2) The condition referred to in paragraph (1) is that the individual, though able to walk, cannot move around outdoors without requiring guidance or supervision from another person most of the time as a result of a physical or mental impairment.

(3) The guidance or supervision required must be—
(a) substantially in excess of the normal requirements of a person of the same age, or
(b) of such a description which younger persons in normal physical and mental health may also require but which persons of the individual's age and in normal physical and mental health would not require.

(4) In the case of an individual who is under the age of 16 on the date on which the award of the mobility component would begin, paragraph (3) only applies in relation to so much of any period mentioned in that paragraph as falls before the day on which the individual reaches the age of 16.

(5) Whether the individual satisfies the condition in paragraph (2), no account is to be taken of any ability which the individual has to use routes with which they are familiar, without guidance or supervision from another person.

(6) An individual is not entitled to the lower rate of the mobility component unless—
(a) throughout the period of 13 weeks immediately preceding the date on which the award of that component would begin, the individual has satisfied or is likely to satisfy the condition mentioned in paragraph (2), and
(b) the individual is likely to continue to satisfy the condition mentioned in paragraph (2) throughout the period of 26 weeks beginning with that date.

(7) In this regulation, "guidance" means direction or leading by physical means or verbal suggestion or persuasion.

GENERAL NOTE

This regulation substantially re-enacts s.73(1)(d), (1A)(b), (4A) and (9) of the Social Security Contributions and Benefits Act 1992, which provides for the mobility component of disability living allowance throughout Great Britain. Paragraph (7) makes explicit in the legislation the meaning of "guidance" suggested only in case law in relation to s.73. Note also that reg.11(7) and (8) define "supervision" and "require" for the purposes of reg.12 as well as reg.11. Case law under the 1992 Act will nonetheless continue to be relevant (see the annotations in Vol I).

Mobility requirements: higher rate mobility component

13.—(1) An individual aged 3 years or more is entitled to be given the mobility component at the higher rate (see regulation 23(2)(a)) if the individual satisfies at least one of the conditions mentioned in paragraph (2).

(2) The conditions referred to in paragraph (1) are—
(a) taking account of the individual's physical condition as a whole, the individual's condition is such that, without having regard to the nature of the location where the individual resides—
  (i) the individual is unable to walk,
  (ii) the individual's ability to walk out of doors is so limited, as regards the distance over which or the speed at which or the length of time for which or the manner in which the individual can make progress on foot without severe discomfort, that the individual is virtually unable to walk, or
  (iii) the exertion required to walk would constitute a danger to the individual's life, or would be likely to lead to a serious deterioration in the individual's health, from which there would no recovery, or from which recovery would take a significant period of time,
(b) the individual has no legs or no feet (regardless of the use of artificial limbs),
(c) the individual has a severe visual impairment,
(d) the individual is blind and deaf,
(e) the individual has a severe mental impairment and severe behavioural difficulties and satisfies both of the conditions mentioned in regulation 11(1)(c) and (d).

(3) Where paragraph (2)(a) applies in relation to an individual, the test of being unable or virtually unable to walk is not met where the individual—
(a) is not unable or virtually unable to walk with the use of an artificial limb or artificial aid which the individual normally wears or uses, or
(b) would not be unable or virtually unable to walk if the individual wore or used an artificial limb or artificial aid which is suitable to the individual's circumstances.

(4) Paragraph (3) is not relevant for the purpose of determining whether an individual is to be taken to satisfy the conditions set out in paragraphs (2)(b) to (e).

(5) An individual is to be taken to have a severe visual impairment, for the purpose of paragraph (2)(c), if the individual has a severe visual impairment fulfilling the definition given by the Visual Impairment Network for Children and Young People.

(6) An individual is taken to be blind and deaf, for the purpose of paragraph (2)(d), if the individual is—
(a) blind where the loss of vision amounts to an absolute loss of vision,
(b) deaf where loss of hearing when using any artificial aid which they habitually use or which is suitable in their case amounts to not less than 80% on a scale where 100% represents absolute deafness, and

(SSI 2021/174 reg.13)

   (c) unable, without the assistance of another person, to walk to any intended or required destination while out of doors.

  (7) An individual is to be taken to have a severe mental impairment, for the purpose of paragraph (2)(e), if the individual has a severe impairment of intelligence and social functioning resulting from—
   (a) a state of arrested development as a result of a failure of the individual's brain to grow or develop in the way normally expected, or
   (b) a deficiency in the functionality of the brain as a result of its incomplete physical development.

  (8) An individual is to be taken to have severe behavioural difficulties, for the purpose of paragraph (2)(e), if the individual exhibits disruptive behaviour which—
   (a) is extreme,
   (b) regularly requires another person to intervene in order to prevent or reduce the likelihood of physical injury to the individual or another person, and
   (c) is so unpredictable that another person requires to be awake and watching over the individual while the individual is awake.

  (9) In paragraph (8)(b), reference to another person intervening relates to the provision of care and support of, or treatment provided to, the individual.

  (10) An individual is not entitled to the [¹ higher rate of the] mobility component unless—
   (a) throughout the period of 13 weeks immediately preceding the date on which the award of that component would begin, the individual has satisfied or is likely to satisfy one of the conditions mentioned in paragraph (2), and
   (b) the individual is likely to continue to satisfy one of those conditions throughout the period of 26 weeks beginning with that date.

AMENDMENT

1. Disability Assistance for Children and Young People (Scotland) Amendment Regulations 2021 (SSI 2021/416) regs 2 and 8 (November 22, 2021).

GENERAL NOTE

13.308 This regulation substantially re-enacts the provisions of s.73 of the Social Security Contributions and Benefits Act 1992 relating to the higher rate of the mobility component of disability living allowance but, in place of the regulation-making powers in that section, it effectively re-enacts reg.12 of the Social Security (Disability Regulations 1991 which was made in the exercise of those powers. Although there are some differences of language, case law interpreting s.73 of the 1992 Act and reg.12 of the 1991 Regulations and their forerunners is likely to remain relevant (see the annotations to those provisions in Vol.I).

A footnote to reg.13(5) states that the Visual Impairment Network for Children and Young People is a "National Managed Clinical Network forming part of NHS Scotland" and provides a link to their definition of "visual impairment", which is to be found at *https://www.vincyp.scot.nhs.uk/vincyp-definition/* and is—

  Best corrected visual acuity (both eyes open) equal to or worse than 6/18/0.5 logmar
    Requires N18 print or larger to read comfortably
    Visual field loss with both eyes open which significantly affects function
    Any eye movement disorder which significantly affects visual function

The Disability Assistance for Children and Young People (Scot) Regs 2021

Any form of cognitive visual dysfunction due to disorders of the brain which can be demonstrated to significantly affect function

Note that reg.11(8) defines "require" for the purposes of regs.12 and 13 as well as reg.11.

Exclusion of entitlement to mobility component

13.309   **14.** An individual is not entitled to the mobility component of Child Disability Payment for a period unless, during most of that period, the individual's physical or mental condition is such that they are able, from time to time, to benefit from assistance for movement.

GENERAL NOTE

This regulation substantially re-enacts s.73(8) of the Social Security Contributions and Benefits Act 1992. See the annotations to that provision in Vol.I.

Entitlement under special rules for terminal illness

13.310   **15.**—(1) An individual who has a terminal illness is—
  (a) to be treated as satisfying the conditions for the highest rate of the care component of Child Disability Payment in regulation 11(5 (a), and
  (b) from the date on which the individual reaches the age of 3, to be treated as satisfying the conditions for the higher rate of the mobility component in regulation 13.
(2) Paragraph (1) applies regardless of—
  (a) the period of time for which the individual has had the terminal illness, and
  (b) any period of time spent by the individual in a hospital or hospice while in receipt of the assistance.
(3) Subject to paragraphs (4) and (5), the individual's entitlement to the rates referred to in paragraph (1) begins on the date on which—
  (a) the individual's application for Child Disability Payment was made, where the application included information about the individual's terminal illness,
  (b) the Scottish Ministers became aware of the individual's terminal illness (whether as a result of the individual notifying a change in circumstances or otherwise), where the individual was previously awarded, and has an ongoing entitlement to, Child Disability Payment, on the basis of a determination that the individual was entitled to the care component or the mobility component or both in relation to a condition other than terminal illness, or
  (c) the clinical judgement was made in accordance with paragraphs (6) and (7) ("the judgement"),
  whichever is the earlier.
(4) Where the judgement mentioned in paragraph (3)(c) is dated not more than 26 weeks earlier than whichever date in paragraph (3)(a) or (b) applies ("the relevant date"), the Scottish Ministers have the power, when making their determination, to specify that an individual's entitlement begins—
  (a) up to a maximum of 26 weeks prior to the relevant date, and
  (b) on or after the day these Regulations come into force.
(5) Where the judgement mentioned in paragraph (3)(c)—

(SSI 2021/174 reg.15)

(a) is dated more than 26 weeks earlier than whichever date in paragraph (3)(a) or (b) applies ("the relevant date"), and
(b) an appropriate healthcare professional confirms that the judgement is still accurate by making a judgement in accordance with paragraphs (6) and (7),

an individual's entitlement can only begin—

(c) up to a maximum of 26 weeks prior to the relevant date, and
(d) on or after the day these Regulations come into force.

(6) For the purpose of this regulation, an individual is to be regarded as having a terminal illness for the purpose of determining entitlement to Child Disability Payment if it is the judgement of an appropriate healthcare professional that the individual has a progressive disease that can reasonably be expected to cause the individual's death.

(7) Subject to paragraph (8), an appropriate healthcare professional exercising the judgement described in paragraph (6) must have regard to the guidance prepared and made publicly available by the Chief Medical Officer of the Scottish Administration in accordance with paragraph 1(3) of schedule 5 of the 2018 Act.

(8) Where regulation 9 (persons residing outside the United Kingdom to whom a relevant EU regulation applies) applies to the individual, an appropriate healthcare professional mentioned in paragraph (9)(b) need not have regard to the guidance mentioned in paragraph (7) where it would not be reasonable in the circumstances to insist on the judgement being formed with regard to that guidance.

(9) In this regulation, "an appropriate healthcare professional" means—

(a) a registered medical practitioner or a registered nurse who is—
  (i) involved in the diagnosis or care of the individual, and
  (ii) acting in their professional capacity, or
(b) where regulation 9 applies to the individual, a person who—
  (i) has equivalent qualifications to a registered medical practitioner or a registered nurse in an EEA state, Gibraltar or Switzerland,
  (ii) is a member of the professional body equivalent to the General Medical Council or Nursing and Midwifery Council in that EEA state, Gibraltar or Switzerland, and
  (iii) meets the requirements of sub-paragraph (a)(i) and (ii).

[¹ (10) Where an individual has previously received Child Disability Payment for a period and a determination is subsequently made that the same individual is entitled to Child Disability Payment at a higher rate for that period by virtue of this regulation, that individual will be entitled to the difference between the value of entitlement to Child Disability Payment under the subsequent determination and the value of Child Disability Payment to which that individual was previously entitled for that period.]

AMENDMENT

1. Disability Assistance for Children and Young People (Scotland) Amendment Regulations 2021 (SSI 2021/416) regs 2 and 9 (November 22, 2021).

Entitlement to care component when undergoing dialysis

16.—(1) Subject to paragraph (5), an individual who is at least 3 months old is to be treated as satisfying the conditions for the care component in regulation 11 (care component criterion: lowest, middle or highest rate of care component) where the individual undergoes renal dialysis—
  (a) where at least one of the conditions in paragraph (2) is met, and
  (b) at least twice a week,
as a consequence of a disability or physical impairment.
(2) The conditions are that—
  (a) the renal dialysis is of a type which normally requires the attendance or supervision of another person, or
  (b) due to particular circumstances, the individual requires another person to attend—
    (i) in connection with the individual's bodily functions, or
    (ii) to supervise the individual in order to avoid substantial danger to the individual,
  during the period of the dialysis.
(3) Where the renal dialysis mentioned in paragraph (2) takes place by day or at night, the individual is entitled to the middle rate care component.
(4) Where the renal dialysis mentioned in paragraph (2) takes place both by day and at night, the individual is entitled to the highest rate care component.
(5) An individual is not entitled to the care component unless—
  (a) throughout the period of 13 weeks immediately preceding the date on which the award of that component would begin, the individual has satisfied or is likely to satisfy the requirements in paragraph (1) as read with paragraph (2), and
  (b) the individual is likely to continue to satisfy those requirements throughout the period of 26 weeks beginning with that date.

Effect of admission to a care home on ongoing entitlement to care component

17.—(1) This regulation applies where an individual who has an ongoing entitlement to the care component of Child Disability Payment, becomes a resident of a care home.
(2) Subject to paragraphs (4) and (5), [¹ on the day after] the day on which the individual has been resident in a care home for 28 days, and for so long as the individual continues to reside in such a home, the value of the care component of Child Disability Payment that is to be given to the individual is £0 instead of the values set out in regulation 23 (amount and form of Child Disability Payment).
(3) The 28 days referred to in paragraph (2) may comprise two or more separate periods, provided that there is no more than 28 days between each period.
(4) Paragraph (2) does not apply to a resident in a care home, where the full costs of any qualifying services are met—
  (a) entirely out of the resources of the individual for whom the qualifying services are provided,
  (b) partly out of the resources of the individual for whom the qualifying services are provided and partly out of the resources of

another person (other than a local authority) or assistance from a charity, or

(c) entirely out of the resources of another person (other than a local authority) or assistance from a charity.

(5) For the purposes of this regulation, an individual is not resident in a care home during any period when the individual is being looked after by a local authority and—
- (a) has been placed temporarily in a private dwelling with a family, relative or some other suitable person while—
  - (i) under the age of 16, or
  - (ii) aged between 16 and 18 and receiving services under Part II of the Children (Scotland) Act 1995 by virtue of being a child in need within the meaning of section 93(4)(a)(ii) (impairment of health), or 93(4)(a)(iii) (disability) of that Act, or
- (b) is accommodated in a care home outside the United Kingdom, where the costs of any qualifying services are met [^{2} wholly or partly] by a local authority exercising its powers under section 25 of the Education (Additional Support for Learning) (Scotland) Act 2004.

(6) For the purposes of this regulation and regulation 20 (entitlement [^{1} to care component] beginning while in alternative accommodation), reference to an individual being "looked after by a local authority" is to be construed, as the case may be, in accordance with—
- (a) section 17(6) of the Children (Scotland) Act 1995,
- (b) section 105(4) of the Children Act 1989, or
- (c) article 25 of the Children (Northern Ireland) Order 1995.

AMENDMENTS

1. Disability Assistance for Children and Young People (Scotland) Amendment Regulations 2021 (SSI 2021/416) regs 2 and 10 (November 22, 2021).

2. Scottish Child Payment Regulations 2020 and the Disability Assistance for Children and Young People (Scotland) Regulations 2021 (Miscellaneous Amendments) Regulations 2022 (SSI 2022/41) reg.3(1) and (5) (February 9, 2022).

Effect of legal detention on ongoing entitlement to care component

18.—(1) This regulation applies where an individual who has an ongoing entitlement to the care component of Child Disability Payment is in legal detention.

[^{1} (1A) For the purposes of this regulation, an individual is to be treated as though they are not in legal detention on any day on which they are an in-patient in a hospital or hospice.]

(2) [^{1} On the day after] the day on which an individual has been in legal detention for 28 days, and for so long as the individual continues to be in legal detention, the value of the care component of Child Disability Payment that is to be given to the individual is to be £0, instead of the values set out in regulation 23 (amount and form of Child Disability Payment).

AMENDMENT

1. Disability Assistance for Children and Young People (Scotland) Amendment Regulations 2021 (SSI 2021/416) regs 2 and 11 (November 22, 2021).

Calculation of periods of time spent in a care home or in legal detention

19.—(1) Subject to paragraphs (2) and (3), a period during which an individual is resident in a care home for the purpose of regulation 17 or in legal detention for the purpose of regulation 18 is to be taken to—
  (a) begin on the day after the day on which the individual enters the care home or legal detention, and
  (b) end on the day before the day on which the individual leaves the care home or legal detention.
(2) Where an individual who is resident in a care home takes a period of leave from the home, the days on which the individual begins and returns from leave are not to be counted as days of residence in the home.
(3) Days constituting a period of leave are not to be counted as days of residence in a care home.
(4) Where an individual enters or returns to a care home as a result of a transfer from a hospital or a hospice, or from another care home, the day of transfer is to be counted as a day of residence in a care home.
(5) Where an individual enters legal detention as a result of a transfer from a hospital or a hospice, or from a care home, the day of transfer is to be counted as a day in legal detention.

[¹ Entitlement to care component beginning while in alternative accommodation]

20.—(1) This regulation applies where an individual is resident in a care home or in legal detention on the day on which entitlement to [¹ the care component of] Child Disability Payment begins.
(2) On and after that day, and for so long as the individual continues to reside in a care [¹home], or be in legal detention, the value of the care component of Child Disability Payment that is to be given to the individual is £0 instead of the values set out in regulation 23 (amount and form of Child Disability Payment).
(3) Paragraphs (1) and (2) do not apply where the costs of any qualifying services whilst resident in a care home are met—
  (a) entirely out of the resources of the individual for whom the qualifying services are provided,
  (b) partly out of the resources of the individual for whom the qualifying services are provided and partly out of the resources of another person (other than a local authority) or assistance from a charity, or
  (c) entirely out of the resources of another person (other than a local authority) or assistance from a charity.
(4) For the purposes of this regulation an individual is not resident in a care home during any period when the individual is being looked after by a local authority and—
  (a) has been placed temporarily in a private dwelling with a family, relative or some other suitable person while—
    (i) under the age of 16,
    (ii) aged between 16 and 18 and receiving services under Part II of the Children (Scotland) Act 1995 by virtue of being a child in need within the meaning of section 93(4)(a)(ii) (impairment of health), or 93(4)(a)(iii) (disability) of that Act, or

(b) is accommodated in a care home outside the United Kingdom, where the costs of any qualifying services are met [² wholly or partly] by a local authority exercising its powers under section 25 of the Education (Additional Support for Learning) (Scotland) Act 2004.

AMENDMENTS

1. Disability Assistance for Children and Young People (Scotland) Amendment Regulations 2021 (SSI 2021/416) regs 2 and 12 (November 22, 2021).
2. Scottish Child Payment Regulations 2020 and the Disability Assistance for Children and Young People (Scotland) Regulations 2021 (Miscellaneous Amendments) Regulations 2022 (SSI 2022/41) reg.3(1) and (6) (February 9, 2022).

Entitlement to care component of Child Disability Payment while an in-patient

21. For the avoidance of doubt, any period when an individual is an in-patient in a hospice or hospital, has no effect on the individual's entitlement to the care component of Child Disability Payment.

13.316

Making payments

22.—(1) Where Child Disability Payment is payable in respect of an individual, the Scottish Ministers may, where they consider it appropriate, make the payment to another person to be used for the benefit of the individual.

13.317

(2) Where the Scottish Ministers consider, for any reason, that it is no longer appropriate for a particular person who falls within paragraph (1) to continue to receive the payment, they may cease making payment to that person.

Amount and form of Child Disability Payment

23.—(1) The weekly rate of payment of the care component is where the individual is entitled to—
  (a) the highest rate, [² £108.55],
  (b) the middle rate, [² £72.65], or
  (c) the lowest rate, [² £28.70].

13.318

(2) The weekly rate of payment of the mobility component is where the individual is entitled to—
  (a) the higher rate, [² £75.75], or
  (b) the lower rate, [² £28.70].

(3) Where an individual is entitled to payment of the care component or the mobility component for a period shorter than one week, payment of that component is to be made at one-seventh of the relevant weekly rate, for each day of entitlement.

(4) For any week where an individual is entitled to—
  (a) the care component of Child Disability Payment, and
  (b) payment of an amount in respect of constant attendance under [¹ section 104 of the Social Security Contributions and Benefits Act 1992],
the amount of the care component of Child Disability Payment that is to be given to the individual is to be reduced by the amount paid under that section.

(5) For the purpose of calculating the amount of the care component that is to be given to the individual, in accordance with paragraph (4), where the amount in respect of constant attendance is equal to or greater than the amount of the care component of Child Disability Payment the value of Child Disability Payment that is to be given to the individual is to be £0.

(6) For any week where an individual is entitled to—
  (a) the mobility component of Child Disability Payment, and
  (b) payment of War Pensioners' Mobility Supplement within the meaning of—
    (i) the Naval, Military and Air Forces etc. (Disablement and Death) Service Pensions Order 1983 ("1983 Order"),
    (ii) the Personal Injuries (Civilians) Scheme 1983,
    (iii) the 1983 Order by virtue of the War Pensions (Naval Auxiliary Personnel) Scheme 1964,
    (iv) the Pensions (Polish Forces) Scheme 1964,
    (v) the War Pensions (Mercantile Marine) Scheme 1964, or
    (vi) an Order of Her Majesty in relation to the Home Guard dated 21 December 1964 or 22 December 1964, or in relation to the Ulster Defence Regiment dated 4 January 1971,
the amount of the mobility component of Child Disability Payment that is to be given to the individual is to be £0.

(7) For each week in the period of 8 weeks ending with the death of the individual—
  (a) the amount of Child Disability Payment that is to be given to that individual is the relevant weekly rate of each component to which the individual is entitled in that week, multiplied by two, and
  tlil(b)
    any provision in these Regulations reducing the amount to £0 has no effect.

(8) Child Disability Payment may only be given as money, except as provided for by regulation 27(1) (form of payment—giving Child Disability Payment by way of deduction).

AMENDMENTS

1. Scottish Child Payment Regulations 2020 and the Disability Assistance for Children and Young People (Scotland) Regulations 2021 (Miscellaneous Amendments) Regulations 2022 (SSI 2022/41) reg.3(1) and (7) (February 9, 2022).

2. Social Security (Up-rating) (Miscellaneous Amendments) (Scotland) Regulations 2024 (SSI 2024/105) reg.8 (April 8, 2024, subject to a saving under reg.14 and para.6 of Sch.).

When an application is to be treated as made and beginning of entitlement to assistance

24.—(1) An application for Child Disability Payment is to be treated as made—
  (a) on the day it is received by the Scottish Ministers, or
  (b) if applicable, on the day identified by the Scottish Ministers in accordance with paragraph (2).

(2) If, before making a determination on the basis of an application, the Scottish Ministers consider that the individual in respect of whom the application is made—

(a) would not satisfy the requirement in—
  (i) regulation 4 (age criteria),
  (ii) regulations 5 to 9 (residence and presence conditions etc.),
  (iii) [¹ . . .]
  (iv) regulation 11 (care component criterion: lowest, middle or highest rate of care component),
  (v) regulation 12 (mobility requirements: lower rate mobility component),
  (vi) regulation 13 (mobility requirements: higher rate mobility component), or
  (vii) regulation 16 (entitlement to care component when undergoing dialysis),
  if the application were treated as made on the day it was received, and
(b) would likely be entitled to receive Child Disability Payment if those requirements were satisfied within a 13-week period beginning on the day it was received,
the Scottish Ministers may choose the date within that 13 week period on which the application is to be treated as having been made.

(3) Where, on the basis of an application, a determination is made that an individual is entitled to Child Disability Payment, the date on which entitlement begins is to be identified in accordance with paragraphs (4) to (6).

(4) Where an application is made within 6 weeks of the day on which the full name and date of birth of an individual ("the required data") is submitted by, or on behalf of, the individual to the Scottish Ministers for the purpose of an application for Child Disability Payment, entitlement begins on whichever is the later of the day—
  (a) on which the required data was submitted, or
  (b) identified in accordance with paragraph (2).

(5) Subject to paragraph (6), where an application is made after the 6 week period described in paragraph (4), entitlement begins on the day on which the application is treated as having been made in accordance with paragraph (1).

(6) Where the Scottish Ministers are satisfied that there is good reason why an application was made after the 6 week period described in paragraph (4), they may treat the application as having been made within that period.

(7) For the purposes of section 38(3) (application for assistance) of the 2018 Act, the period covered by an application for Child Disability Payment—
  (a) under paragraph (1)(a)—
    (i) begins on the day on which the application is treated as having been made, and
    (ii) ends on the day on which the determination of entitlement is made, and
  (b) under paragraph (1)(b)—
    (i) is deemed to begin on the day before the determination is made provided that the requirements are satisfied, and
    (ii) ends on the day on which the determination is made.

AMENDMENT

1. Scottish Child Payment Regulations 2020 and the Disability Assistance for Children and Young People (Scotland) Regulations 2021 (Miscellaneous Amendments) Regulations 2022 (SSI 2022/41) reg.3(1) and (8) (February 9, 2022).

The Disability Assistance for Children and Young People (Scot) Regs 2021

Time of payment

25. Where an award of Child Disability Payment is made, the Scottish Ministers are to make—
   (a) the first payment of assistance on a date specified in the notice of determination, and
   (b) any subsequent payment—
      (i) 4 weekly in arrears, or
      (ii) where regulation 15 (entitlement under special rules for terminal illness) applies, weekly in advance.

Continuing eligibility

26.—(1) Subject to paragraphs (3) and (4), a determination that an individual is entitled to Child Disability Payment in respect of a period is to be made on the basis that the individual has an ongoing entitlement to Child Disability Payment after the end of that period, except where paragraph (2) applies.
   (2) This paragraph applies where, after the end of the period mentioned in paragraph (1), the individual no longer satisfies the eligibility rules.
   (3) A determination of ongoing entitlement is made on the basis that—
   (a) the individual will continue to be entitled to Child Disability Payment for a fixed or indefinite period as specified in the notice of determination, and
   (b) the decision that the individual is entitled to Child Disability Payment for each subsequent 4-week period is to be taken in accordance with these Regulations, on the strength of the assumptions set out in paragraph (4).
   (4) The assumptions are that—
   (a) the individual continues to satisfy the eligibility criteria which were satisfied to be entitled to Child Disability Payment under the determination mentioned in paragraph (1),
   (b) the information on which the determination mentioned in paragraph (1) was made still applies and is relevant in the individual's case, and
   (c) there is no change in circumstances of the individual which would require to be notified under section 56 (duty to notify change of circumstances) of the 2018 Act.

[¹ Circumstances in which assistance may be suspended

26A.—(1) The Scottish Ministers may decide that an individual who has an ongoing entitlement to Child Disability Payment in respect of a period by virtue of regulation 26 is not to become entitled to be given some or all of either component or both components of that assistance at the time at which the individual otherwise would in accordance with that regulation, as read with regulation 25 (time of payment) (referred to in these Regulations as a decision to suspend the individual's Child Disability Payment).
   (2) Where such a decision is made in respect of an individual, payments of Child Disability Payment to that individual are to be suspended until such time as the Scottish Ministers decide that the individual is once again to become entitled to be given Child Disability Payment.

(3) The Scottish Ministers may decide to suspend an individual's Child Disability Payment only in the circumstances where—
  (a) section 54(1A) of the 2018 Act applies,
  (b) the Scottish Ministers have made arrangements (whether under section 85A of the 2018 Act, section 85B of the 2018 Act or otherwise) for a person to receive the Child Disability Payment on the individual's behalf, and the Scottish Ministers consider that it is necessary to suspend the Child Disability Payment—
    (i) in order to protect the individual from the risk of financial abuse, or
    (ii) because the person with whom the Scottish Ministers have made arrangements is unable to continue to receive the Child Disability Payment, or
  (c) the individual has reached the age of 16 years and there is no arrangement to make that payment to—
    (i) the individual, or
    (ii) another person to be used for the benefit of the individual.
(4) In this regulation "financial abuse" includes—
  (a) having money or other property stolen,
  (b) being defrauded,
  (c) being put under pressure in relation to money or other property,
  (d) having money or other property misused.]

AMENDMENT

1. Scottish Child Payment Regulations 2020 and the Disability Assistance for Children and Young People (Scotland) Regulations 2021 (Miscellaneous Amendments) Regulations 2022 (SSI 2022/41) reg.3(1) and (9) (February 9, 2022).

[¹ **Having regard to financial circumstances**

26B. The Scottish Ministers must have regard to an individual's financial circumstances prior to making a decision to suspend payment to the individual of some or all of either component or both components of Child Disability Payment.]

AMENDMENT

1. Scottish Child Payment Regulations 2020 and the Disability Assistance for Children and Young People (Scotland) Regulations 2021 (Miscellaneous Amendments) Regulations 2022 (SSI 2022/41) reg.3(1) and (9) (February 9, 2022).

[¹ **Information to be given following suspension**

26C.—(1) Having made a decision to suspend an individual's Child Disability Payment, the Scottish Ministers must inform the individual of—
  (a) their decision to suspend the individual's Child Disability Payment,
  (b) the reasons for their decision,
  (c) any steps which might be taken by the individual in order for the Scottish Ministers to consider ending the suspension, and
  (d) the individual's right under regulation 26D to require the Scottish Ministers to review their decision.]

(2) The Scottish Ministers must fulfil their duty under paragraph (1) in a way that leaves the individual with a record of the information which the individual can show to, or otherwise share with, others.]

AMENDMENT

1. Scottish Child Payment Regulations 2020 and the Disability Assistance for Children and Young People (Scotland) Regulations 2021 (Miscellaneous Amendments) Regulations 2022 (SSI 2022/41) reg.3(1) and (9) (February 9, 2022).

[¹ Right to review suspension

26D.—(1) An individual may require the Scottish Ministers to review a decision to suspend that individual's Child Disability Payment.
(2) The Scottish Ministers must—
(a) complete a review mentioned in paragraph (1) within 31 days beginning with the day on which they received notice from the individual requiring them to review their decision,
(b) inform the individual of the outcome of the review including the reasons for it.
(3) The Scottish Ministers must fulfil their duty under paragraph (2)(b) in a way that leaves the individual with a record of the information which the individual can show to, or otherwise share with, others.]

AMENDMENT

1. Scottish Child Payment Regulations 2020 and the Disability Assistance for Children and Young People (Scotland) Regulations 2021 (Miscellaneous Amendments) Regulations 2022 (SSI 2022/41) reg.3(1) and (9) (February 9, 2022).

[¹ Ending a suspension

26E. The Scottish Ministers are to make a decision to end a suspension where—
(a) the individual provides the information requested under section 54(1) of the 2018 Act and the Scottish Ministers consider that they do not require to make a determination without application,
(b) regulation 26A(3)(a) applies and the Scottish Ministers make a determination without application under regulation 30 (consideration of entitlement after specified period), 31 (determination following change of circumstances, etc.), 32 (determination following official error – underpayments), 33 (determination following error – overpayments) or 34 (determination to effect a deduction decision),
(c) the Scottish Ministers make a determination under section 54(2) of the 2018 Act,
(d) the circumstances mentioned in regulation 26A(3)(b) or (c) no longer apply, or
(e) the Scottish Ministers consider it appropriate in the circumstances, including having regard to the financial circumstances of the individual.]

AMENDMENT

1. Scottish Child Payment Regulations 2020 and the Disability Assistance for Children and Young People (Scotland) Regulations 2021 (Miscellaneous Amendments) Regulations 2022 (SSI 2022/41) reg.3(1) and (9) (February 9, 2022).

(SSI 2021/174 reg.26F)

[¹ **Effect of suspension ending**

26F. When—
(a) the suspension of an individual's Child Disability Payment ends, and
(b) under the latest determination of the individual's entitlement to Child Disability Payment relating to the period of the suspension the individual would have become entitled to be given Child Disability Payment during that period,
the individual is immediately to be given the Child Disability Payment that the individual would have become entitled to be given under the determination during the period of suspension.]

AMENDMENT

1. Scottish Child Payment Regulations 2020 and the Disability Assistance for Children and Young People (Scotland) Regulations 2021 (Miscellaneous Amendments) Regulations 2022 (SSI 2022/41) reg.3(1) and (9) (February 9, 2022).

Form of payment—giving Child Disability Payment by way of deduction

27.—(1) Where an individual has a liability to the Scottish Ministers under section 63 of the 2018 Act (liability for assistance given in error), the individual's payment of Child Disability Payment may be given (in whole or in part) by way of deduction, at a reasonable level, from that liability either—
(a) with the agreement of the individual, or
(b) without the individual's agreement, where the individual has unreasonably refused to agree to the assistance being given in that form.
(2) For the purpose of paragraph (1), "reasonable level" means a level that is reasonable having regard to the financial circumstances of the individual.

When an increase in level of entitlement takes effect

28.—(1) Where, as a result of a determination without an application, the amount of Child Disability Payment payable in respect of an individual is increased or their entitlement to a component is awarded, the [¹ change takes effect]—
(a) in the case of an increase pursuant to a determination made under regulation [¹ 31(c) or (d)] (determination following change of circumstances etc.) on the day after the day on which Disability Living Allowance ceased to be paid in respect of the individual,
(b) in the case of an award of entitlement to a component or an increase pursuant to a determination made in accordance with regulation 31(a) [¹ ...] that affects their eligibility under regulation 11 (care component criterion: lowest, middle or highest rate of care component), 12 (mobility requirements: lower rate mobility component) or 13 (mobility requirements: higher rate mobility component), on the date when—
[¹(i) if as a result of the individual reporting the change—
(aa) if the individual reports the change within one month of the change occurring, the individual first satisfies the requirements for a higher rate of the care or mobility component,

(bb) if the individual reports the change more than one month but not more than 13 months of the change occurring, the individual first satisfies the requirements for a higher rate of the care or mobility component, but only if the Scottish Ministers consider that the individual had good reason for not notifying the change within one month,
(cc) in any other case, the individual reports the change,
(ii) if as a result of the Scottish Ministers becoming aware that an earlier determination of an individual's entitlement was made in ignorance of a material fact, on the date when the Scottish Ministers make the determination.]
(c) in the case of an earlier determination which was based on official error within the meaning of regulation 32 (determination following official error—underpayments) or on error within the meaning of regulation 33 (determination following error—overpayments), begins on the date when the earlier determination took effect, or
[² (ca) in the case of a determination made in accordance with regulation 31(a), where the period that an individual has been—
(i) for the purpose of regulation 17, resident in a care home,
(ii) for the purposes of regulation 18, in legal detention, or
(iii) for the purposes of regulation 20, resident in a care home or in legal detention, has come to an end, on the day on which the individual leaves that place, or]
(d) in any other case, on the date when Scottish Ministers make the determination.

(2) Where the Scottish Ministers consider that in all the circumstances it would be unjust not to do so, they may, when making their determination, set an earlier date for the purposes of paragraph 1(b), (c) or (d).

[¹ (2A) Where an individual has previously received Child Disability Payment for a period and a determination without application has been subsequently made that the same individual is entitled to Child Disability Payment at a higher rate for that period, that individual will be entitled to the difference between the value of entitlement to Child Disability Payment under the subsequent determination and the value of Child Disability Payment to which that individual was previously entitled for that period.]

(3) This regulation does not apply to an individual to whom regulation 15 (entitlement under special rules for terminal illness) applies.

AMENDMENTS

1. Disability Assistance for Children and Young People (Scotland) Amendment Regulations 2021 (SSI 2021/416) regs 2 and 13 (November 22, 2021).
2. Disability Assistance for Working Age People (Transitional Provisions and Miscellaneous Amendment) (Scotland) Regulations 2022 (SSI 2022/217) reg.18(1) and (3) (August 29, 2022).

When a decrease in level or cessation of entitlement takes effect

29.—(1) Where, as a result of a determination without an application, the amount of Child Disability Payment payable in respect of an individual is decreased or their entitlement to a component is ceased, the [¹ change takes effect]—

(a) in the case of a decrease pursuant to a determination made under regulation [¹ 31(c) or (d)] (determination following change of circumstances etc.) on the day after the day on which Disability Living Allowance ceased to be paid in respect of the individual,

[²(aa) in the case of a determination without application under regulation 31(b), on the date of the individual's death,]

(b) in the case of a determination without application under [¹ regulation 30 or] 31(a), on the date [¹ on which]—

[¹(i) where the individual was required to notify a change under section 56 of the 2018 Act, if the individual—
  (aa) knowingly fails to notify a change, or
  (bb) fails to notify the change as soon as reasonably practicable after it occurred,
  the individual should have notified the Scottish Ministers of the change,]

[²(ia) where the Scottish Ministers make a determination that the individual is entitled to Adult Disability Payment, on the day that the entitlement to Adult Disability Payment begins in terms of regulation 58 of the ADP Regulations,]

(ii) in any other case, the Scottish Ministers make the determination,

(c) in the case of an earlier determination which was based on official error within the meaning of regulation 32 (determination following official error—underpayments) or on error within the meaning of regulation 33 (determination following error—overpayments), begins on the date when the earlier determination took effect,

(d) in any other case, on the date when Scottish Ministers make the determination.

(2) Where the Scottish Ministers consider that in all the circumstances it would be unjust not to do so, they may, when making their determination, set a later date for the purposes of paragraph 1(b), (c) or (d).

AMENDMENTS

1. Disability Assistance for Children and Young People (Scotland) Amendment Regulations 2021 (SSI 2021/416) regs 2 and 14 (November 22, 2021).

2. Disability Assistance (Miscellaneous Amendment) (Scotland) Regulations 2023 (SSI 2023/346) reg.3(5) (November 20, 2023).

Consideration of entitlement after specified period

30. The Scottish Ministers must make a determination of an individual's entitlement to Child Disability Payment, without receiving an application, after the end of the period specified (if any) in—

(a) the individual's notice of determination under section 40 or notice of re-determination under section 44 (as the case may be), or

(b) a determination made by the First-tier Tribunal for Scotland under section 49, of the 2018 Act.

Determination following change of circumstances etc.

31. The Scottish Ministers must make a determination of an individual's entitlement to Child Disability Payment, without receiving an application, where the individual has an ongoing entitlement to Child Disability Payment and they become aware—

(a) of a change of circumstances, whether or not notified by the individual in accordance with section 56 of the 2018 Act, [¹ or where the Scottish Ministers become aware that a determination of an individual's entitlement was made in ignorance of a material fact,] which would possibly result in an alteration to the component or rate of Child Disability Payment payable to the individual or which is likely to mean that the individual is no longer entitled to Child Disability Payment,
(b) that the individual has died,
(c) of an alteration of the component or rate of award of Disability Living Allowance which the individual was entitled to immediately before the date of transfer to Child Disability Payment in accordance with Part 3 of the schedule (transitional provisions), as a result of a decision made pursuant to—
  (i) a revision under regulation 3 of the Social Security and Child Support (Decisions and Appeals) Regulations 1999 ("the 1999 Regulations"),
  (ii) a supersession under regulation 6of the 1999 Regulations,
  (iii) an appeal under section 12 of the Social Security Act 1998 ("the 1998 Act"),
  (iv) a re-consideration under section 13 of the 1998 Act, [¹ . . .]
  (v) an appeal to the Upper Tribunal under section 14 of the 1998 Act,
  [¹(vi) a revision under article 10 of the Social Security (Northern Ireland) Order 1998 ("the 1998 Order"),
  (vii) a supersession under article 11 of the 1998 Order,
  (viii) an appeal under article 13 of the 1998 Order, or
  (ix) an appeal to the Commissioner under article 15 of the 1998 Order,]
(d) of an alteration of the rate of award of Disability Living Allowance which the individual was entitled to immediately before moving to Scotland in circumstances in which regulation 35 (individuals in respect of whom Disability Living Allowance is paid in another part of the United Kingdom immediately before moving to Scotland) applies, as a result of a decision made pursuant to—
  (i) a revision under regulation 3 of the Social Security and Child Support (Decisions and Appeals) Regulations 1999,
  (ii) a supersession under regulation 6 of those Regulations,
  (iii) an appeal under section 12 of the Social Security Act 1998 ("the 1998 Act"),
  (iv) a re-consideration under section 13 of the 1998 Act,
  (v) an appeal to the Upper Tribunal under section 14 of the 1998 Act,
  (vi) a revision under article 10 of the Social Security (Northern Ireland) Order 1998 ("the 1998 Order"),
  (vii) a supersession under article 11 of the 1998 Order,
  (viii) an appeal under article 13 of the 1998 Order, or
  (ix) an appeal to the Commissioner under article 15 of the 1998 Order.

AMENDMENT

1. Disability Assistance for Children and Young People (Scotland) Amendment Regulations 2021 (SSI 2021/416) regs 2 and 15 (November 22, 2021).

(SSI 2021/174 reg.32)

Determination following official error—underpayments

32.—(1) The Scottish Ministers are to make a determination of an individual's entitlement to Child Disability Payment, without receiving an application, where—
  (a) they have previously made a determination of the individual's entitlement to Child Disability Payment ("the original determination"),
  (b) they establish that, due to an official error, the original determination was incorrect resulting in the individual—
    (i) not being given an award of Child Disability Payment, or
    (ii) being given a lower award than that,
    to which the individual was entitled,
  (c) the Scottish Ministers are not considering a request for a re-determination of the individual's entitlement to the Payment, and
  (d) the individual has not appealed to the First-tier Tribunal for Scotland against the Scottish Ministers' determination of the individual's entitlement to Child Disability Payment.

(2) In making a determination required by paragraph (1) the Scottish Ministers are to use—
  (a) the information—
    (i) provided in the application that led to the original determination,
    (ii) any other information they have obtained in connection with that application, [¹ and]
  (b) any other information they have obtained in connection with the individual's entitlement to Child Disability Payment.

(3) In this regulation "official error" means an error made by someone acting on behalf of the Scottish Ministers or on behalf of a Minister of the Crown that was not materially contributed to by anyone else.

AMENDMENT

1. Scottish Child Payment Regulations 2020 and the Disability Assistance for Children and Young People (Scotland) Regulations 2021 (Miscellaneous Amendments) Regulations 2022 (SSI 2022/41) reg.3(1) and (10) (February 9, 2022).

Determination following error—overpayments

33.—(1) The Scottish Ministers are to make a determination of an individual's entitlement to Child Disability Payment, without receiving an application, where—
  (a) they have previously made a determination of the individual's entitlement to Child Disability Payment ("the original determination"),
  (b) they establish that, due to an error, the original determination was incorrect resulting in the individual being given—
    (i) an award of Child Disability Payment to which the individual was not entitled, or
    (ii) a higher award than that to which the individual was entitled.
  (c) the Scottish Ministers are not considering a request for a re-determination of the individual's entitlement to the Payment, and
  (d) the individual has not made an appeal to the First-tier Tribunal for Scotland or Upper Tribunal against the Scottish Ministers' determination of the individual's entitlement to Child Disability Payment, that has not yet been determined.

(2) In making a determination required by paragraph (1) the Scottish Ministers are to use—
   (a) the information—
      (i) provided in the application that led to the original determination, and
      (ii) any other information they have obtained in connection with that application,
   (b) any other information they have obtained in connection with the individual's entitlement to Child Disability Payment, and
   (c) any other information available to them that is relevant to their consideration of whether the individual is entitled to Child Disability Payment.
(3) In this regulation references to an "error" are to—
   (a) an error in the performance of a function conferred by these Regulations or the 2018 Act, including a determination being made—
      (i) wrongly, or
      (ii) correctly but on the basis of—
         (aa) incorrect information, or
         (bb) an assumption which proves to be wrong, or
   (b) a new determination not being made after an assumption on the basis of which an earlier determination was made has proved to be wrong.

Determination to effect a deduction decision

34.—(1) The Scottish Ministers are to make a determination of an individual's entitlement to Child Disability Payment, without receiving an application, where the circumstances in paragraphs (2) and (3) apply.
(2) This paragraph applies where—
   (a) regulation 27 (form of payment—giving Child Disability Payment by way of deduction) allows Child Disability Payment to be given to the individual by way of deduction, or
   (b) Child Disability Payment is being given to the individual by way of deduction, and the Scottish Ministers consider that may no longer be appropriate.
(3) This paragraph applies where the Scottish Ministers have decided to—
   (a) vary the amount of Child Disability Payment to be given by way of deduction (including introducing a deduction, where the full amount of Child Disability Payment was previously given as money),
   (b) vary any period for which the individual's Child Disability [¹Payment] is to be given by way of deduction, that may have been specified in a previous determination of the individual's entitlement, or
   (c) cease making deductions, and instead give the individual's Child Disability Payment in the form of money.
(4) The Scottish Ministers are to make a determination, without receiving an application, where an individual who is receiving Child Disability Payment by way of deduction under a previous determination of entitlement notifies the Scottish Ministers that the individual—
   (a) withdraws their agreement to their Child Disability Payment being given by way of deduction,

(b) wishes the Scottish Ministers to increase the amount of their Child Disability Payment that is given by way of deduction,
(c) wishes the Scottish Ministers to decrease the amount of their Child Disability Payment that is given by way of deduction (including ceasing the deduction), or
(d) wishes the Scottish Ministers to amend the length of any period referred to in paragraph (3)(b).

AMENDMENT

1. Disability Assistance (Miscellaneous Amendment) (Scotland) Regulations 2023 (SSI 2023/346) reg.3(6) (November 20, 2023).

Individuals in respect of whom Disability Living Allowance is paid in another part of the United Kingdom immediately before moving to Scotland

35.—(1) Where an individual—
(a) is under 18 years of age,
(b) becomes resident in Scotland,
(c) was resident in another part of the United Kingdom, and
(d) was entitled to Disability Living Allowance immediately before the date of the move,
the Scottish Ministers are to make a determination without application of the individual's entitlement to Child Disability Payment.

(2) Entitlement to Child Disability Payment under paragraph (1) begins on the day after the day on which [¹ the individual's entitlement to Disability Living Allowance ends].

(3) In this regulation, "the date of the move" is the date when the individual becomes resident in Scotland as notified by the individual[¹ or otherwise communicated] to the Scottish Ministers (whether the notification takes place before or after the date of the move).

AMENDMENT

1. Disability Assistance for Children and Young People (Scotland) Amendment Regulations 2021 (SSI 2021/416) regs 2 and 16 (November 22, 2021).

Individuals in respect of whom Child Disability Payment is paid at the time of moving to another part of the United Kingdom

36.—(1) Where the Scottish Ministers [¹ become aware] that an individual who is entitled to Child Disability Payment has moved or is to move to become [¹ ...] resident in another part of the United Kingdom, the individual is to be treated as though the individual meets the condition [¹ under regulation 5(1)(a)] of being ordinarily resident in Scotland for a period of 13 weeks beginning [¹ in accordance with paragraph (4)].

(2) Subject to Part 5 (effect of time spent in care homes and in legal detention), where the Scottish Ministers [¹ become aware that an individual has moved or is to move to another part of the United Kingdom as] mentioned in paragraph (1), they are to make a determination without application at the end of the 13-week period mentioned in paragraph (1) that the individual's entitlement to Child Disability Payment is to terminate.

(3) Where before the end of the 13-week period, the Scottish Ministers [¹ become aware] that the individual is no longer to move to become [¹ . . .] resident in another part of the United Kingdom, [¹ . . .] the duty in paragraph (2) does not apply.

[¹ (4) The 13-week period mentioned in paragraph (1) begins—
(a) if the Scottish Ministers become aware that the individual is to become resident in another part of the United Kingdom, on the date the individual ceases to be ordinarily resident in Scotland,
(b) if the Scottish Ministers become aware after the date when the individual becomes resident in another part of the United Kingdom, but before they have been resident there for 13 weeks, on the date the individual notifies the Scottish Ministers of the move, or
(c) in any other case, on the date that the individual ceases to be ordinarily resident in Scotland.

(5) On the day after the 13-week period specified in paragraph (4) ends—
(a) entitlement to Child Disability Payment ends, and
(b) regulation 33 (determination following error—overpayments) applies to any Child Disability Payment paid to an individual in relation to a period after the end of that 13-week period.]

AMENDMENT

1. Disability Assistance for Children and Young People (Scotland) Amendment Regulations 2021 (SSI 2021/416) regs 2 and 17 (November 22, 2021).

Periods in respect of a re-determination request

37.—(1) The period for requesting a re-determination of entitlement to Child Disability Payment under section 41 (right to request re-determination) of the 2018 Act is 42 days beginning with the day that the individual is informed, in accordance with section 40 of the 2018 Act (notice of determination), of the right to make the request.

(2) In relation to determining entitlement to Child Disability Payment, the period allowed for re-determination (within the meaning of section 43 of the 2018 Act (duty to re-determine)) is 56 days beginning with—
(a) the day that the request for a re-determination is received by the Scottish Ministers, [¹ . . .]
(b) in a case where the request for a re-determination is received by the Scottish Ministers outwith the period prescribed in paragraph (1), the day on which it is decided by the Scottish Ministers or (as the case may be) the First-tier Tribunal for Scotland that the individual in question has a good reason for not requesting a re-determination sooner [¹ , or
(c) in a case where the Scottish Ministers have informed the individual of their decision that the request for a re-determination was not made in such form as the Scottish Ministers require, the day on which it is subsequently decided by the First-Tier Tribunal for Scotland that the individual in question has made the request in such form as the Scottish Ministers require.]

AMENDMENT

1. Disability Assistance for Children and Young People (Scotland) Amendment Regulations 2021 (SSI 2021/416) regs 2 and 18 (November 22, 2021).

Payment of mobility component to authorised providers of vehicles for individuals with disabilities

38.—(1) Where—
(a) an individual is entitled to the higher rate of the mobility component of Child Disability Payment, and
(b) the individual has entered into an agreement with an authorised provider of vehicles for persons with disabilities for the hire or hire-purchase of a vehicle,
the Scottish Ministers may, with the consent of the individual, pay that component (in whole or in part) to the provider to be used to meet, or contribute towards meeting, the individual's liability under the agreement.

(2) The Scottish Ministers must cease to make payments to the provider in accordance with paragraph (1) in the event that—
(a) the agreement is brought to an end in accordance with the terms of the agreement, or
(b) the individual withdraws their consent.

Vehicles for persons with disabilities—powers of appointees

39.—(1) Where a person (an "appointee") is appointed by the Scottish Ministers under the 2018 Act to act on an individual's behalf in connection with the determination of the individual's entitlement to assistance under section 24 of the 2018 Act (duty to give assistance), in addition to the powers conferred on the appointee by that Act the appointee can, on behalf of the individual—
(a) enter into an agreement with an authorised provider of vehicles for the hire or hire-purchase of a vehicle,
(b) terminate any such agreement,
(c) for the purpose of regulation 38(1), give consent to the Scottish Ministers to pay (in whole or in part) the mobility component to which the individual is entitled to the provider, and
(d) withdraw any such consent.

(2) An appointee may exercise the powers conferred by paragraph (1)(b) and (d) whether the agreement was entered into, or the consent given, by the appointee or by any other person.

Initial period for applications

40. Part 2 of the schedule makes provision about the initial period for applications.

Transfer to Child Disability Payment

41. Part 3 of the schedule makes provision about transferring from Disability Living Allowance to Child Disability Payment.

Entitlement to short-term assistance

42. Part 1 of the schedule makes provision about short-term assistance.

Consequential amendment

43. The amendment specified in Part 4 of the schedule has effect.

The Disability Assistance for Children and Young People (Scot) Regs 2021

Transitory provision—initial period for applications

44.—(1) During the initial period for applications, in addition to meeting the residence and presence conditions in regulation 5, an individual must be resident in one of the local authority areas specified in paragraph 6 of Part 2 of the schedule on the date their application is received by the Scottish Ministers.

(2) In this regulation and in Part 2 of the schedule, "initial period for applications" means the period beginning with 26 July 2021 and ending with 21 November 2021.

Exclusion to transitory provision

45.—(1) An individual who has made a claim for Disability Living Allowance prior to 26 July 2021 which has not yet been decided is not entitled to be paid Child Disability Payment during the initial period for applications.

(2) In paragraph (1) a claim for Disability Living Allowance is decided if it has—
   (a) been decided by the Secretary of State under section 8 (decisions by Secretary of State) of the Social Security Act 1998,
   (b) been withdrawn in accordance with regulation 5(2) of the Social Security (Claims and Payments) Regulations 1987, or
   (c) otherwise is no longer to be decided by the Secretary of State as mentioned in sub-paragraph (a).

SCHEDULE

Regulation 42

Part 1

Short-Term Assistance

Entitlement to short-term assistance

1.—(1) Subject to sub-paragraph (2), an individual who is, or was, entitled to Child Disability Payment under a determination made on the basis that the individual has ongoing entitlement is entitled to short-term assistance where—
   (a) a determination of the individual's entitlement to Child Disability Payment ("earlier determination") has been superseded by a subsequent determination ("subsequent determination") which has the effect that the individual is—
      (i) no longer entitled to Child Disability Payment, or
      (ii) entitled to a lower amount of Child Disability Payment,
   [¹ (b) the individual's entitlement to Child Disability Payment is under review within the meaning of—
      (i) paragraph 1(2) of schedule 10 of the 2018 Act, or
      (ii) sub-paragraph (1A), and]
   (c) the individual—
      (i) continues to meet the conditions as to residence and presence set out in regulations 5 to 9, or
      (ii) has transferred to become [¹ ...] resident in another part of the United Kingdom, and the matter under review is the determination of entitlement for the 13-week period beginning [¹ ...] in accordance with regulation 36[¹ (4)] (individuals in respect of whom Child Disability Payment is paid at the time of moving to another part of the United Kingdom).

[¹ (1A) An individual's entitlement to Child Disability Payment is under review in terms of sub-paragraph (1)(b)(ii) if—
  (a) a decision of the First-Tier Tribunal for Scotland under section 49 of the 2018 Act, in relation to the subsequent determination of the individual's entitlement to Child Disability Payment mentioned in paragraph 1(1)(a), is set aside after a review under section 43(2) of the Tribunals (Scotland) Act 2014 (review of decisions), and
  (b) the First-Tier Tribunal for Scotland decides not to uphold a determination of an individual's entitlement to Child Disability Payment in an appeal under section 46 of the 2018 Act and the First-Tier Tribunal for Scotland is to make a determination of the individual's entitlement to Child Disability Payment under section 49 of the 2018 Act.

(1B) Where [² a determination of] an individual's entitlement to Child Disability Payment is set aside after a review in terms of sub-paragraph (1A)(a) [² and the individual had previously been awarded short-term assistance on the basis that their entitlement to Child Disability Payment was under review by the First-tier Tribunal prior to it making the decision that has been set aside], the Scottish Ministers are to make a determination without application of the individual's entitlement to short-term assistance.]

[² (1C) Where the First-tier Tribunal for Scotland set aside a decision by the Scottish Ministers not to accept a request for a re-determination of the subsequent determination of the individual's entitlement to Child Disability Payment mentioned in sub-paragraph (1)(a), and the Scottish Ministers had previously determined, pursuant to an application made by the individual, that the individual was not entitled to short-term assistance on the basis that the subsequent determination was not under review, the Scottish Ministers are to make a determination without application of the individual's entitlement to short-term assistance.]

[³ (2) An individual is not entitled to short-term assistance where the individual is no longer entitled to Child Disability Payment as a result of a subsequent determination made under—
  (a) regulation 31(a) (determination following change of circumstances etc.) where the change of circumstances is that the individual—
    (i) no longer meets the requirements of regulation 4 (age criteria), or
    (ii) is entitled to Adult Disability Payment under a determination—
      (aa) made pursuant to an application made by the individual in accordance with regulation 58 (applications by individuals entitled to Child Disability Payment), or
      (bb) made without receiving an application in accordance with regulation 59 (determination without application – terminal illness),
  of the Disability Assistance for Working Age People (Scotland) Regulations 2022, or
  (b) regulation 31(b).

(3) An individual to whom regulation 17(2) (effect of admission to a care home on ongoing entitlement to care component) [¹ , 18(2)] (effect of legal detention on ongoing entitlement to care component) [¹ , or 20(2) (entitlement to care component beginning while in alternative accommodation)] applies is not entitled to short-term assistance in respect of the care component of Child Disability Payment.

(4) Where the Scottish Ministers have made a determination under section 37 of the 2018 Act (duty to make determination) that an individual is entitled to short-term assistance, entitlement to short-term assistance begins—
  (a) where a request is made under section 41 of the 2018 Act (right to request re-determination) for a re-determination [¹ ...] of the individual's entitlement to Child Disability Payment mentioned in paragraph 1(1)(a), on the day that request is made,
  (b) where a notice of appeal is submitted under section 47 of the 2018 Act (initiating an appeal) against the determination of the individual's entitlement to Child Disability Payment mentioned in paragraph 1(1)(a), on the day that request is made,
  (c) where a decision of the Scottish Ministers is made not to accept a request for a re-determination of the individual's entitlement to Child Disability Payment mentioned in paragraph 1(1)(a), on the day that decision is set aside by the First-tier Tribunal for Scotland, [¹ ...]
  (d) [¹ where] a request is made under section 48(1)(b) of the 2018 Act (deadline for appealing) for permission to appeal the determination of the individual's entitlement to Child Disability Payment mentioned in paragraph 1(1)(a), on the day that request is made [¹ , or
  (e) where a decision of the First-tier Tribunal for Scotland under section 49 of the 2018 Act, in relation to the subsequent determination of the individual's entitlement to Child Disability Payment mentioned in paragraph 1(1)(a), is set aside after review under section 43(2) of the Tribunals (Scotland) Act 2014 (review of decisions) and

the First-tier Tribunal for Scotland is to make a determination of the individual's entitlement to Child Disability Payment under section 49 of the 2018 Act, on the day that the decision is set aside.

(5) Regulation 37 (periods in respect of a re-determination request) applies to short-term assistance in the same way as it applies to Child Disability Payment.

Value and form

2.—(1) The value of short-term assistance payable is to be the difference between the amount of Child Disability Payment to which the individual was entitled under the earlier determination mentioned in paragraph 1(1)(a), and the amount of Child Disability Payment the individual is entitled to under the subsequent determination mentioned in paragraph 1(1)(a).

(2) The form in which the short term assistance is to be given is to be the same as the form in which Child Disability Payment was given under the earlier determination.

(3) Where the mobility component was being paid by the Scottish Ministers to an authorised provider of vehicles for persons with disabilities in accordance with regulation 38(1) (payment of mobility component to authorised provider of vehicles for individuals with disabilities) on the day before an individual's entitlement to the mobility component ended as a result of a subsequent determination mentioned in paragraph 1(1)(a)—
  (a) the amount of short-term assistance that is payable in respect of the mobility component may be paid by the Scottish Ministers to the authorised provider, and
  (b) paragraphs (1) and (2) of regulation 38 apply to the payment of short-term assistance as they had applied to the payment of mobility component prior to the individual's entitlement ending.

(4) Regulations [³ 25 (time of payment),] 27 (form of payment—giving Child Disability Payment by way of deduction), 32 (determination following official error—underpayments), 33 (determination following error—overpayments) and 34 (determination to effect a deduction decision) apply to short-term assistance in the same way as they apply to Child Disability Payment.

End of entitlement

3.—(1) Entitlement to short-term assistance ends on the day—
  (a) a determination of an individual's entitlement to short-term assistance is cancelled under section 26(2) of the 2018 Act (individual's right to stop receiving assistance),
  [¹ (b) a re-determination of an individual's entitlement to Child Disability Payment is made by the Scottish Ministers under section 43 of the 2018 Act (duty to re-determine),]
  (c) the First-tier Tribunal for Scotland makes a [¹ determination] under section 49 of the 2018 Act (First-tier Tribunal's power to determine entitlement) in relation to the subsequent determination of the individual's entitlement to Child Disability Payment mentioned in paragraph 1(1)(a), [¹ . . .]
  (d) that the First-tier Tribunal for Scotland makes a determination to refuse permission under section 48(1)(b) of the 2018 Act (deadline for appealing) to bring an appeal against the subsequent determination of the individual's entitlement to Child Disability Payment mentioned in paragraph 1(1)(a) [¹ , or
  (e) where the individual withdraws their application to bring an appeal against the subsequent determination of the individual's entitlement to Child Disability Payment mentioned in paragraph 1(1)(a), on that day.]

[¹ (2) Where an individual's entitlement to short-term assistance is to end under sub-paragraph (1), the Scottish Ministers are to make a determination without application.]

[⁴ **Reduction of payment of Child Disability Payment where short-term assistance is paid**

4. Where an individual has received short-term assistance for a period and a determination is subsequently made that the individual is entitled to Child Disability Payment for the same period, any payment of Child Disability Payment to be made as a result of the subsequent determination for that period—
  (a) where the individual is to be paid Child Disability Payment at the same rate as or a lower rate than any short-term assistance and any Child Disability Payment already paid to that individual for that period, is to be reduced to £0,
  (b) in any other case, is to be reduced by any short-term assistance and any Child Disability Payment already paid to that individual for that period.]

(SSI 2021/174 Sch)

Part 2

Initial Period For Applications

Initial period for applications

5.—(1) These Regulations apply to an individual who is resident in one of the local authority areas mentioned in paragraph 6 when they make an application for Child Disability Payment during the initial period for applications.

(2) An individual who is awarded Child Disability Payment pursuant to an application made during the initial period for applications will continue to be entitled if that person moves to another local authority area in Scotland.

Local authority areas for initial period for applications

6. The local authority areas are Perthshire and Kinross, City of Dundee and the Western Isles.

Regulation 41

Part 3

Transfer To Child Disability Payment

Interpretation

7. In this Part of the schedule—

"date of transfer" means the date when a transferring individual's entitlement to Child Disability Payment begins by virtue of a determination made under paragraph 9(1),

"relevant individual" means an individual—
  (a) who has an award of Disability Living Allowance who appears to the Scottish Ministers to be likely to be eligible for Child Disability Payment,
  (b) who is—
      (i) ordinarily resident in Scotland, or
      (ii) someone to whom regulation 5(4) (residence and presence conditions) or 9(2) (persons residing outside the United Kingdom to whom a relevant EU regulation applies) applies,

"sufficient" means a link to Scotland that is sufficiently close that regulations 5(4) or 9(2) would be incompatible with the applicable agreement mentioned in that regulation, if the relevant individual were not entitled to Child Disability Payment,

"transfer notice" means the notice required by paragraph 8, and

"transferring individual" means a relevant individual on whom the Scottish Ministers have served a notice of intention to transfer in accordance with paragraph 8.

Notice of intention to transfer to Child Disability Payment

8.—(1) The Scottish Ministers are to notify each relevant individual of their intention to transfer that individual's entitlement to disability assistance from an entitlement to Disability Living Allowance to an entitlement to Child Disability Payment.

(2) Notice under sub-paragraph (1) must—
  (a) be given in a way that leaves the relevant individual with a record of the information which they can show to, or otherwise share with, others,
  (b) inform the relevant individual that—
      (i) they have been identified as a relevant individual for the purposes of transfer to Child Disability Payment,
      (ii) the Scottish Ministers will make a determination without application to transfer the individual's entitlement to Disability Living Allowance to an entitlement to Child Disability Payment within [^{1} 17] weeks of the date of the notice (the individual will be notified when the determination is made and informed about their award and start date of Child Disability Payment), and
      (iii) the individual's award of Disability Living Allowance will cease immediately before the award of Child Disability Payment begins.

[^{5}(3) Where a notice under sub-paragraph (1) is given—
  (a) to a transferring individual who, before a determination is made under paragraph 9(1), ceases to be ordinarily resident in Scotland, or
  (b) in error where the individual is neither—

(i) ordinarily resident in Scotland, nor
(ii) an individual who is habitually resident in an EEA state, Gibraltar or Switzerland and has a genuine and sufficient link to Scotland,
the duty on the Scottish Ministers in paragraph 9(1) does not apply.]

(4) Where sub-paragraph (3) applies in respect of an individual and a determination under paragraph 9(1) has not been made, the Scottish Ministers are to notify the individual that the duty on the Scottish Ministers in paragraph 9(1) does not apply.

Determination without application of entitlement to Child Disability Payment

9.—(1) The Scottish Ministers are to make a determination without application in respect of a transferring individual of that individual's entitlement to Child Disability Payment.

(2) Entitlement to Child Disability Payment under a determination under sub-paragraph (1) begins on the date specified in the notice of determination given to the transferring individual in accordance with section 40 of the 2018 Act.

(3) The determination under sub-paragraph (1) is to be made on the basis of—
(a) such information as the Scottish Ministers have received from the Secretary of State for Work and Pensions in respect of the transferring individual's entitlement to Disability Living Allowance, and
(b) any other information available to the Scottish Ministers that appears to them to be relevant.

(4) Subject to paragraph 11, a determination under sub-paragraph (1) must be made on the basis that the transferring individual is entitled to the components and rates of Child Disability Payment that are equivalent to those components and rates of Disability Living Allowance to which the individual was entitled immediately before the date of transfer.

(5) A determination under sub-paragraph (1)—
(a) may be made on the assumption that whatever can be discerned about the transferring individual's circumstances from the information mentioned in sub-paragraph (3) remains accurate on the date on which the determination is made,
(b) notwithstanding the generality of head (a), is to be made on the assumption that the conditions relating to residence and presence set out in regulations 5 to 9 (residence and presence conditions etc.) are satisfied in the individual's case, and
(c) must be made not later than 13 weeks after the date of the notice under paragraph 8(1) unless the Scottish Ministers have—
(i) good reason to extend that period,
(ii) agreed the period for extension with the Secretary of State for Work and Pensions, and
(iii) notified the transferring individual of the extension and the reason for it.

Effect of determination on entitlement to Disability Living Allowance

[¹ **10.** Where a determination is made under paragraph 9 that the transferring individual is entitled to Child Disability Payment, the transferring individual's entitlement to Disability Living Allowance will end on—
(a) the date their entitlement to Child Disability Payment begins,
(b) where paragraph 11 applies, the date of the determination under paragraph 9(1), or
(c) where paragraph 12(1) applies, the date their entitlement to Child Disability Payment would have begun had paragraph 12(2) not applied to set an earlier date of entitlement.]

Exceptions to paragraph 9(4)

11.—(1) The following circumstances are exceptions to paragraph 9(4)—
[¹ (a) where the Scottish Ministers have—
(i) received information from the Secretary of State for Work and Pensions that the transferring individual is terminally ill in terms of section 82 of the Welfare Reform Act 2012 immediately before the date of transfer, or
(ii) not received information from the Secretary of State for Work and Pensions that the transferring individual is terminally ill in terms of section 82 of the Welfare Reform Act 2012, but become aware, before they have made a determination under paragraph 9(1), that the individual has a terminal illness in terms of regulation 15(6) (entitlement under special rules for terminal illness),
the determination made under paragraph 9(1) must be made on the basis that the transferring individual satisfies the conditions for the higher rate of the mobility component and highest rate of the care component of Child Disability Payment,]
(b) a transferring individual who is not awarded the care component of Disability Living Allowance and meets the condition in regulation 11(1)(b) (care component criterion:

lowest, middle or highest rate of care component) is entitled to the lowest rate of the care component of Child Disability Payment,
(c) a transferring individual whose entitlement to [¹ one or both components] of Disability Living Allowance was affected because they were under 16 and did not meet the [¹ requirements in either or both sections 72(1A)(b) or 73(4A)] of the Social Security Contributions and Benefits Act 1992, who is aged 16 or over is entitled to an increased rate of either component or both components [¹ as the case may be] of Child Disability Payment, and
(d) a transferring individual, whose entitlement to the mobility component of Disability Living Allowance was affected by not meeting the requirement of regulation 12(1A) of the Social Security (Disability Living Allowance) Regulations 1991, who meets the condition in regulation 13(5) (mobility requirements: higher rate mobility component), is entitled [to the higher rate of the mobility component of Child Disability Payment where the individual was either not entitled to the mobility component of Disability Living Allowance or entitled to the lower rate of that component.]

[¹ (2) Where sub-paragraph (1)(a) applies—
(a) paragraphs (7), (8) and (9) of regulation 15 (entitlement under special rules for terminal illness) are to be treated as satisfied for the individual, and
(b) the beginning of their entitlement is to be determined in terms of regulation 15(3), as modified by paragraph 13(zb).

(3) Where a transferring individual mentioned in sub-paragraph (1)(b), (c) or (d) whose entitlement to Child Disability Payment is determined under paragraph 9(1) to be at a higher value than their entitlement to Disability Living Allowance paid immediately before that determination, entitlement is to begin before the date of that determination but not before the later of—
(a) the date on which—
(i) sub-paragraph (1)(b) or (d) applies to a transferring individual by virtue of evidence supplied in relation to the transferring individual which is satisfactory to the Scottish Ministers, or
(ii) where sub-paragraph (1)(c) applies, when the transferring individual reaches the age of 16,
(b) 11 October 2021.

(4) Where an individual has previously received Disability Living Allowance for a period and a determination is subsequently made that the same individual is entitled to Child Disability Payment at a higher rate for that period by virtue of this paragraph, that individual will be entitled to the difference between the value of entitlement to Child Disability Payment under the subsequent determination and the value of Disability Living Allowance to which that individual was previously entitled for that period.]

Effect of legal custody on payment of the mobility component

12.—(1) Where a transferring individual is in legal detention immediately before the date of transfer and payment of the mobility component of Disability Living Allowance is suspended under regulation 3 of the Social Security (General Benefit) Regulations 1982, the mobility component of Child Disability Payment is to be paid at the rate equivalent to the rate of Disability Living Allowance paid to the transferring individual immediately prior to the suspension.

[¹ (2) Entitlement to the mobility component of Child Disability Payment of a transferring individual mentioned in sub-paragraph (1) is to begin before the date of the determination without application made under regulation 5(1) but not before the later of the date on which—
(a) the suspension of payment of the mobility component of Disability Living Allowance began,
(b) 11 October 2021.

(3) Where a transferring individual is in legal detention immediately before the date of transfer and entitlement to Child Disability Payment is determined under paragraph 9(1) to be at a higher rate than the Disability Living Allowance paid immediately before that determination, paragraph 11(4) does not apply for the purposes of determining the amount of the mobility component to be paid.]

Modification of these Regulations: transferring individuals

13. These Regulations apply to a transferring individual on and after the date of transfer with the following modifications—
[¹(za) where paragraph [⁴ 11(2), 11(3)] or 12(2) applies, for the period between the date when entitlement to Child Disability Payment begins and the date of the determination under paragraph 9(1), regulation 10 (entitlement to other benefits) is treated as omitted,

(zb) regulation 15 (entitlement under special rules for terminal illness) is to be read as if—
　(i) paragraph (3)(a) reads "the individual transferred by virtue of a determination under paragraph 9(1) ("the date of transfer")", where that determination is made in accordance with paragraph 11(1)(a) of the schedule",
　(ii) paragraph (3)(b) is omitted,
　(iii) in paragraphs (4) and (5) for "whichever date in paragraph (3)(a) or (b) applies" reads "the date in paragraph (3)(a),
　(iv) paragraph (10) reads "Where an individual has previously received Child Disability Payment or Disability Living Allowance for a period and a determination is subsequently made that the same individual is entitled to Child Disability Payment at a higher rate for that period by virtue of this regulation, that individual will be entitled to the difference between the value of entitlement to Child Disability Payment under the subsequent determination and the value of Child Disability Payment or Disability Living Allowance to which that individual was previously entitled for that period."]
(a) regulation 17 (effect of admission to a care home on ongoing entitlement to care component) and regulation 18 (effect of legal detention on ongoing entitlement to care component) are to be read as if the period of 28 days begins on the date of transfer, [⁴...]
[¹(aa) regulation 20 (entitlement to care component beginning while in alternative accommodation) is to be read as if—
　(i) in paragraph (1) after "begins" there are the words "in terms of part 3 of the schedule",
　(ii) in paragraph (2) "that day" reads "the day on which the individual has been entitled to Child Disability Payment for 28 days,]
(b) regulation 24 (when an application is to be treated as made and beginning of entitlement to assistance) is treated as omitted. [⁴, and
(c) regulation 25 (time of payment) is to be read as if for paragraph (b) there were substituted—
"(b) any subsequent payment—
　(i) 4 weekly in arrears,
　(ii) weekly in advance, or
　(iii) where the Scottish Ministers consider that it would be unjust not to do so, at such intervals as may be specified in the notice of determination."]

Appointees

14.—(1) A person appointed by the Secretary of State for Work and Pensions under regulation 33 or 43 of the Social Security (Claims and Payments) Regulations 1987(5) to receive Disability Living Allowance on behalf of a transferring individual is to be treated on and after the date of transfer as though appointed by the Scottish Ministers to act on behalf of that transferring individual under section 58 (or 85B(6)) or 85A of the 2018 Act.

(2) As soon as reasonably practicable after the date of transfer, the Scottish Ministers must—
(a) consider whether the conditions for making an appointment in respect of the transferring individual are met (having regard to whichever of section 58(4), 85A(3) or 85B(3) of the 2018 Act applies in the transferring individual's case),
(b) consider whether to terminate the appointment that is treated as having been made by virtue of sub-paragraph (1) and terminate it if they consider it appropriate, and
(c) if they have terminated an appointment in pursuance of head (b), appoint under section 58 (or 85B) or 85A of the 2018 Act another person to act on the transferring individual's behalf if they consider it appropriate to do so.

[⁵(3) The duty in sub-paragraph (2) does not apply where the Scottish Ministers have already appointed the person mentioned in sub-paragraph (1) to act on behalf of that transferring individual under section 85A or 85B of the 2018 Act.]

Regulation 43

PART 4

CONSEQUENTIAL AMENDMENT

15.—(1) The Social Security Contributions and Benefits Act 1992 is amended in accordance with paragraph (2).

(SSI 2021/174 Sch)

(2) In section 70(2) (invalid care allowance), after "enhanced rate" insert "or disability assistance by virtue of entitlement to the care component at the middle or highest rate under regulations made under section 31 of the Social Security (Scotland) Act 2018".

AMENDMENTS

1. Disability Assistance for Children and Young People (Scotland) Amendment Regulations 2021 (SSI 2021/416) regs 2, 19 and 20 (November 22, 2021).
2. Scottish Child Payment Regulations 2020 and the Disability Assistance for Children and Young People (Scotland) Regulations 2021 (Miscellaneous Amendments) Regulations 2022 (SSI 2022/41) reg.3(1) and (11) (February 9, 2022).
3. Disability Assistance for Working Age People (Consequential and Miscellaneous Amendment and Transitional Provision) (Scotland) Regulations 2022 (SSI 2022/31) reg.19(1) and (4) (March 21, 2022).
4. Disability Assistance for Working Age People (Transitional Provisions and Miscellaneous Amendment) (Scotland) Regulations 2022 (SSI 2022/217) reg.18(1), (4) and (5) (August 29, 2022).
5. Disability Assistance (Miscellaneous Amendment) (Scotland) Regulations 2023 (SSI 2023/346) reg.3(7) and (8) (November 20, 2023).

The Social Security Information-sharing (Scotland) Regulations 2021

(SSI 2021/178)

Made   *24th March 2021*
Coming into force   *26th July 2021*

The Scottish Ministers make the following Regulations in exercise of the powers conferred by sections 85(2)(g) and (5) and 95 of the Social Security (Scotland) Act 2018 and all other powers enabling them to do so.

In accordance with section 96(2) of that Act, a draft of this instrument has been laid before and approved by resolution of the Scottish Parliament.

Citation, commencement and interpretation

1.—(1) These Regulations may be cited as the Social Security Information-sharing (Scotland) Regulations 2021 and come into force on 26 July 2021.

(2) In these Regulations—
"the 1978 Act" means the National Health Service (Scotland) Act 1978,
"the 2018 Act" means the Social Security (Scotland) Act 2018,
"the Public Guardian" is to be construed in accordance with section 6 of the Adults with Incapacity (Scotland) Act 2000 (the Public Guardian and his functions).

Specification of persons who may be required to supply information

2.—(1) The persons described in paragraph (2) are specified for the purposes of section 85(2)(g) of the 2018 Act (persons who may be required to supply information).

(2) The persons are—
(a) any supplier of vehicles approved by the Scottish Ministers under an accreditation scheme run by Ministers to supply vehicles for the benefit of individuals who are entitled to the higher rate of the

13.351

13.352

mobility component of Child Disability Payment in accordance with regulation 13 of the Disability Assistance for Children and Young People (Scotland) Regulations 2021 (mobility requirements: higher rate mobility component),

[¹(aa) any supplier of vehicles approved by the Scottish Ministers under an accreditation scheme run by the Scottish Ministers to supply vehicles for the benefit of individuals who are entitled to the enhanced rate of the mobility component of Adult Disability Payment in accordance with regulation 6 of the Disability Assistance for Working Age People (Scotland) Regulations 2022 (mobility component),]

(b) the contractor under a general medical services contract within the meaning of section 17J of the 1978 Act (Health Boards' power to enter into general medical services contracts),

(c) the contractor under an arrangement under section 2C(2) of the 1978 Act (functions of Health Boards: primary medical services),

(d) the provider under an agreement under section 17C(1)(a) of the 1978 Act (agreement for provision of primary medical services), [¹ . . .]

(e) the Public Guardian [¹ and

(f) an integration authority as defined in section 59 of the Public Bodies (Joint Working) (Scotland) Act 2014.]

AMENDMENT

1. Social Security Information-sharing (Scotland) Amendment Regulations 2022 (SSI 2022/56) reg.2 (March 21, 2022).

Supplying information to receive information in return

3.—(1) Paragraph (2) applies where the Scottish Ministers require information to be supplied under section 85(1) of the 2018 Act (requirement to supply information) by—

(a) a Health Board constituted under section 2(1)(a) of the 1978 Act (Health Boards) or a Special Health Board constituted under section 2(1)(b) of the 1978 Act,

(b) a contractor or provider of primary medical services described in regulation 2(2)(b), (c) or (d), or

(c) a local authority,

for the purpose of determining an individual's entitlement to social security assistance in accordance with section 37 of the 2018 Act (duty to make determination).

(2) The Scottish Ministers may supply to the person such information relating to the individual as is necessary for the purpose of enabling the person to comply with the requirement under section 85(1) of the 2018 Act.

(3) Information may be supplied by the Scottish Ministers under paragraph (2) only with the authorisation of the individual to whom the information relates.

Use of information supplied by the Scottish Ministers

4.—(1) Information held by the Scottish Ministers for the purpose of a social security function may be supplied by Ministers under section 85(5) of the 2018 Act (specification of functions) to—

(a) a supplier of vehicles described in regulation 2(2)(a) for use for the purposes of the function of that person specified in paragraph (2),

(SSI 2021/178 reg.4)

(b) a local authority for use for the purposes of the functions of the local authority specified in paragraph (3),

[¹(c) where regulation 4A applies, a local authority for use for the purposes of the functions of the local authority specified in paragraph (3A),

(d) where regulation 4B applies, a local authority for use for the purposes of the functions of the local authority specified in paragraph (3B),

(e) where regulation 4C applies, the Public Guardian for use for the purposes of the function of the Public Guardian specified in paragraph (3C).]

(2) The specified function referred to in paragraph (1)(a) is the provision of a vehicle.

(3) The specified functions referred to in paragraph (1)(b) are—

(a) the assessment of liability to pay local taxes used to fund local authority expenditure,

(b) the administration under section 134(1) of the Social Security Administration Act 1992 (arrangements for housing benefit) of housing benefit provided by virtue of a scheme under section 123(1)(d) of the Social Security Contributions and Benefits Act 1992 (income-related benefit),

(c) the administration of the national travel concession scheme provided for by the National Bus Travel Concession Scheme for Older and Disabled Persons (Scotland) Order 2006,

(d) the administration of a travel concession scheme established under section 93 of the Transport Act 1985 (travel concession schemes),

(e) determining whether a person falls within the description of person prescribed for the purposes of section 21(2) of the Chronically Sick and Disabled Persons Act 1970 (issue of badges for display on motor vehicles to disabled persons falling within prescribed descriptions) by regulation 4(2)(ad) of the Disabled Persons (Badges for Motor Vehicles) (Scotland) Regulations 2000 (descriptions of disabled persons),

(f) determining whether to provide occasional financial or other assistance for the purpose described in section 2(1)(a) or (b) of the Welfare Funds (Scotland) Act 2015 (use of welfare funds: assistance for short term need and community care),

(g) determining—

  (i) whether to make discretionary housing payments under regulation 2(1) of the Discretionary Financial Assistance Regulations 2001 (provision of additional financial assistance towards meeting housing costs),

  (ii) the amount of any such payments.

[¹(3A) The specified functions referred to in paragraph (1)(c) are—

(a) the duty to promote social welfare under section 12 of the Social Work (Scotland) Act 1968 (general social welfare services of local authorities),

(b) the duty to children looked after by local authorities under section 17 of the Children (Scotland) Act 1995 (duty of local authority to child looked after by them),

(c) the duty to safeguard and promote the welfare of children who are in need under section 22 of the Children (Scotland) Act 1995 (promotion of welfare of children in need),

(d) the duty to make inquiries about a person's well-being, property or financial affairs under section 4 of the Adult Support and Protection (Scotland) Act 2007 (council's duty to make inquiries),
(e) the power to make an application for a child assessment order under section 35 of the Children's Hearings (Scotland) Act 2011 (child assessment orders),
(f) the duty to provide information to the Principal Reporter under section 60 of the Children's Hearings (Scotland) Act 2011 (local authority's duty to provide information to Principal Reporter).
(3B) The specified functions referred to in paragraph (1)(d) are—
(a) the duty to make inquiries about a person's property or financial affairs under section 4 of the Adult Support and Protection (Scotland) Act 2007 (council's duty to make inquiries),
(b) the duty to investigate any circumstances made known to the local authority in which the personal welfare of an adult seems to them to be at risk under section 10(1)(d) of the Adults with Incapacity (Scotland) Act 2000 (functions of local authorities).
(3C) The specified function referred to in paragraph (1)(e) is the duty to investigate circumstances where the property or financial affairs of an adult appear to be at risk under section 6(2)(d) of the Adults with Incapacity (Scotland) Act 2000 (the Public Guardian and his functions).]

AMENDMENT

1. Social Security Information-sharing (Scotland) Amendment Regulations 2024 (SSI 2024/8) reg.2 (January 16, 2024).

[¹Use of information supplied under regulation 4(1)(c)

4A.—(1) This regulation applies where—
(a) in the exercise of their social security functions, the Scottish Ministers know or believe that a person with whom they have come into contact ("person A") is—
  (i) at real risk of harm,
  (ii) has needs of care and support, and
  (iii) as a result of those needs, is unable to protect themselves against that risk, and
(b) the Scottish Ministers consider the supply of information is necessary to protect person A from harm.
(2) The information is to be supplied only with the explicit consent of person A unless paragraph (3) applies.
(3) This paragraph applies where—
(a) in the circumstances, person A's consent cannot be given,
(b) in the circumstances, the Scottish Ministers cannot reasonably be expected to obtain the consent of person A, or
(c) in the circumstances, the Scottish Ministers consider obtaining consent of person A would prejudice the protection mentioned in paragraph (1)(b).
(4) In this regulation—
(a) in paragraph (1)(a)(i)—
  (i) "real risk of harm" means being subjected to conduct causing or likely to cause a person to suffer significant—
    (aa) neglect, or

(bb) physical, mental or emotional harm,
and includes engaging in, or being likely to engage in, conduct which causes or is likely to cause self-harm, and
  (ii) "conduct" includes failures to act,
(b) in paragraph (1)(b) and in the definition of "real risk of harm", "harm" means neglect or physical, mental or emotional harm, and
(c) "person" means a natural person of any age.]

AMENDMENT

1. Social Security Information-sharing (Scotland) Amendment Regulations 2024 (SSI 2024/8) reg.3 (January 16, 2024).

[¹Use of information supplied under regulation 4(1)(d)

4B.—(1) This regulation applies where—
(a) in the exercise of their social security functions, the Scottish Ministers know or believe that—
  (i) the property or financial affairs of a person with whom they have come into contact ("person B") are at risk,
  (ii) person B has needs of care and support, and
  (iii) as a result of those needs, person B is unable to protect themselves against that risk, and
(b) the Scottish Ministers consider the supply of information is necessary to—
  (i) safeguard the property or financial affairs of person B, and
  (ii) protect person B from harm.
(2) The information is to be supplied only with the explicit consent of person B unless paragraph (3) applies.
(3) This paragraph applies where—
(a) in the circumstances, person B's consent cannot be given,
(b) in the circumstances, the Scottish Ministers cannot reasonably be expected to obtain the consent of person B, or
(c) in the circumstances, the Scottish Ministers consider obtaining consent of person B would prejudice the matters mentioned in paragraph (1)(b).
(4) In this regulation, "harm" means mental or emotional harm.]

AMENDMENT

1. Social Security Information-sharing (Scotland) Amendment Regulations 2024 (SSI 2024/8) reg.3 (January 16, 2024).

[¹Use of information supplied under regulation 4(1)(e)

4C.—(1) This regulation applies where—
(a) in the exercise of their social security functions, the Scottish Ministers know or believe that—
  (i) a person with whom they have come into contact ("person C") is incapable within the meaning of the Adults with Incapacity (Scotland) Act 2000, and
  (ii) the property or financial affairs of person C are at risk, and
(b) the Scottish Ministers consider the supply of information is necessary to—

The Social Security Information-sharing (Scotland) Regulations 2021

   (i) safeguard the property or financial affairs of person C, and
   (ii) protect person C from harm.
 (2) In this regulation, "harm" means mental or emotional harm.]

AMENDMENT

1. Social Security Information-sharing (Scotland) Amendment Regulations 2024 (SSI 2024/8) reg.3 (January 16, 2024).

[¹Supply of information to be no more than is necessary]

13.358   **5.** Where the Scottish Ministers supply information under these Regulations, which relates to an individual, the information supplied must be no more than is necessary for the purpose for which it is to be used by the recipient.

AMENDMENT

1. Social Security Information-sharing (Scotland) Amendment Regulations 2024 (SSI 2024/8) reg.4 (January 16, 2024).

The Disability Assistance for Working Age People (Consequential and Miscellaneous Amendment and Transitional Provision) (Scotland) Regulations 2022

(SSI 2022/31)

Made	*27th January 2022*
Laid before the Scottish Parliament	*31st January 2022*
Coming into force	*21st March 2022*

13.359   The Scottish Ministers make the following Regulations in exercise of the powers conferred by section 95 of the Social Security (Scotland) Act 2018 and all other powers enabling them to do so.

1. to 19. *Omitted.*

Transitional provision – extinguishment of right to apply for Personal Independence Payment

13.360   **20.**—(1) No person may claim personal independence payment who is aged 16 years or older and—
 (a) during the initial period for applications for adult disability payment—
  (i) in phase 1 is resident in the local authority area of Perthshire and Kinross, City of Dundee or Western Isles,
  (ii) in phase 2 is resident in the local authority area of Perthshire and Kinross, City of Dundee, Western Isles, Angus, North Lanarkshire or South,
  (iii) in phase 3 is resident in the local authority area of Perthshire and Kinross, City of Dundee, Western Isles, Angus, North

Lanarkshire, South Lanarkshire, Fife, City of Aberdeen, Aberdeenshire, Moray, North Ayrshire, East Ayrshire or South Ayrshire, or
(b) after the expiry of the initial period for applications—
  (i) is resident in Scotland, or
  (ii) is a person to whom regulation 15(3) (residence and presence conditions – individuals resident in Ireland), regulation 17 (serving members of Her Majesty's forces, civil servants and their family members) or regulation 20 (persons residing outside the United Kingdom to whom a relevant EU regulation applies) of the Adult Disability Payment Regulations applies.

(2) During the initial period for applications, paragraph (1) does not apply to a person—
(a) who was born after 8 April 1948,
(b) who has an award of disability living allowance, and
(c) to whom any of the following provisions of the PIP Transitional Regulations apply—
  (i) regulation 3(1) (invitations to persons entitled to disability living allowance to claim personal independence payment), where the person's award of disability living allowance is—
    (aa) subject to a scheduled review, or
    (bb) for a fixed term period which is due to come to an end,
  (ii) regulation 3(5), where the person has reported a change of circumstances,
  (iii) regulation 4 (claims by persons entitled to disability living allowance for personal independence payment other than by invitation), where the person voluntarily makes a claim for personal independence payment.

(3) During the initial period for applications, paragraph (1) does not apply to a person—
(a) who has an award of personal independence payment, and
(b) to whom regulation 33(2) (advance claim for and award of personal independence payment) of the PIP (Claims and Payments) Regulations applies, where the person makes a further claim for personal independence payment during the period of 6 months mentioned in that regulation.

(4) After the initial period for applications, paragraph (1) does not apply to a person—
(a) who was born after 8 April 1948,
(b) who has an award of disability living allowance, and
(c) to whom regulation 3(1) of the PIP Transitional Regulations applies, where the person received the invitation mentioned in that regulation prior to the end of the initial period for applications.

(5) In this regulation—
"adult disability payment" means disability assistance for adults given in accordance with the Adult Disability Payment Regulations,
"Adult Disability Payment Regulations" means the Disability Assistance for Working Age People (Scotland) Regulations 2022,
"disability living allowance" means a disability living allowance under section 71 of the Social Security Contributions and Benefits Act 1992
"initial period for applications" means the period referred to in regulation 64 (transitory provision– initial period for applications) of the Adult

Disability Payment Regulations, beginning with 21 March 2022 and ending with 29 August 2022 and references to phases of that period are to be construed in accordance with regulation 64(3) of those Regulations,

"personal independence payment" means personal independence payment under—

(a) Part 4 of the Welfare Reform Act 2012, or
(b) article 82 of the Welfare Reform (Northern Ireland) Order 2015,

"PIP (Claims and Payments) Regulations" means the Universal Credit, Personal Independence Payment, Jobseeker's Allowance and Employment and Support Allowance (Claims and Payments) Regulations 2013, and

"PIP Transitional Regulations" means the Personal Independence Payment (Transitional Provisions) Regulations 2013.

GENERAL NOTE

13.361 This regulation was made in anticipation of the making of the Disability Assistance for Working Age People (Scotland) Regulations 2022. Its effect is that those entitled to make a claim for disability assistance under those Regulations are not entitled to claim personal independence payment under Great Britain legislation, unless they already have an award of personal independence payment or disability living allowance and any of paras (2) to (4) applies.

Meanwhile, it is expected that for all those people who are entitled to personal independence payment and are ordinarily resident in Scotland, conversion of their awards to disability assistance under Pt 3 of Sch.2 of the Disability Assistance for Children and Young People (Scotland) Regulations 2021 (see below) will have taken place by the Summer of 2024.

The Disability Assistance for Working Age People (Scotland) Regulations 2022

(SSI 2022/54)

Made	9th February 2022
Coming into force	21st March 2022

CONTENTS

PART 1

INTRODUCTORY AND INTERPRETATION

1. Citation and commencement
2. Interpretation

PART 2

DISABILITY ASSISTANCE FOR WORKING AGE PEOPLE

3. Overview
4. Entitlement to other benefits

Part 3

Eligibility: Daily Living Component and Mobility Component

5. Daily Living Component
6. Mobility Component
7. Determination of ability to carry out activities
8. Scoring for daily living activities
9. Scoring for mobility activities
10. Scoring: further provision

Part 4

Required Period Condition

11. Required Period Condition: daily living component
12. Required Period Condition: mobility component
13. The relevant date
14. The relevant date: Adult Disability Payment after an interval

Part 5

Residence and Presence Conditions

15. Residence and presence conditions
16. Temporary absence from the common travel area
17. Serving members of Her Majesty's forces, civil servants and their family members
18. Aircraft workers, mariners and continental shelf operations
19. Persons residing in the United Kingdom to whom a relevant EU regulation applies
20. Persons residing outside the United Kingdom to whom a relevant EU regulation applies
20A. No entitlement to daily living component where UK is not competent state
21. Refugees

Part 6

Entitlement under Rules Relating to Age

22. Age Criteria
23. Exceptions: Adult Disability Payment after an interval and after reaching the relevant age
24. Persons who have reached the relevant age: other exceptions
25. Determination of an award after the person has reached the relevant age

Part 7

Entitlement under Special Rules for Terminal Illness

26. Entitlement under special rules for terminal illness

Part 8

Effect of Time Spent in Care Homes, Hospital and Legal Detention

27. Effect of admission to a care home on ongoing entitlement to daily living component
28. Effect of admission to hospital on ongoing entitlement to Adult Disability Payment

29. Exception: Hospices
30. Effect of legal detention on ongoing entitlement to Adult Disability Payment
31. Calculation of periods of time spent in a care home, hospital or legal detention
32. Entitlement beginning while in alternative accommodation

PART 9

MAKING OF APPLICATIONS AND PAYMENTS AND DURATION OF ELIGIBILITY

33. Making Payments
34. Amount and form of Adult Disability Payment
35. When an application is to be treated as made and beginning of entitlement to assistance
36. Time of Payment
37. Continuing Eligibility
38. Circumstances in which assistance may be suspended
39. Having regard to financial circumstances
40. Information to be given following suspension
41. Right to review suspension
42. Ending a suspension
43. Effect of suspension ending
44. Form of payment – giving Adult Disability Payment by way of deduction
45. When an increase in level of entitlement takes effect
46. When a decrease in level or cessation of entitlement takes effect

PART 10

DETERMINATION OF ENTITLEMENT TO ADULT DISABILITY PAYMENT WITHOUT APPLICATION

47. Consideration of entitlement after specified period
48. Determination following change of circumstances etc.
49. Determination following official error – underpayments
50. Determination following error – overpayments
51. Determination to effect a deduction decision

PART 11

MOVEMENT OF INDIVIDUALS BETWEEN SCOTLAND AND THE REST OF THE UNITED KINGDOM

52. Individuals in respect of whom Personal Independence Payment is paid in another part of the United Kingdom immediately before moving to Scotland
53. Individuals in respect of whom Adult Disability Payment is paid at the time of moving to another part of the United Kingdom

PART 12

PERIODS IN RESPECT OF A RE-DETERMINATION REQUEST

54. Periods in respect of a re-determination request

PART 13

PROVISION OF VEHICLES

55. Payment of mobility component to authorised providers of vehicles for individuals with disabilities

56. Vehicles for persons with disabilities – powers of appointees

PART 14

INITIAL PERIOD FOR APPLICATIONS

57. Initial period for applications

PART 15

APPLICATIONS FOR ADULT DISABILITY PAYMENT BY INDIVIDUALS ENTITLED TO CHILD DISABILITY PAYMENT

58. Applications by individuals entitled to Child Disability Payment
59. Determination without an application - terminal illness

PART 16

TRANSFER FROM PERSONAL INDEPENDENCE PAYMENT TO ADULT DISABILITY PAYMENT

60. Transfer from Personal Independence Payment to Adult Disability Payment

PART 17

QUALIFICATIONS AND EXPERIENCE NECESSARY TO CARRY OUT ASSESSMENTS

61. Qualifications and experience necessary to carry out assessments

PART 18

SHORT-TERM ASSISTANCE

62. Entitlement to short-term assistance

PART 19

CONSEQUENTIAL AMENDMENT

63. Consequential amendment

PART 20

TRANSITORY PROVISION

64. Transitory provision – initial period for applications
65. Exclusion to transitory provision

SCHEDULE 1 — ADULT DISABILITY PAYMENT DETERMINATION

PART 1 — Interpretation
PART 2 — Daily Living Activities
PART 3 — Mobility Activities

SCHEDULE 2

PART 1 — Short-term assistance
PART 2 — Initial period for applications

PART 3 — Transfer from Personal Independence Payment to Adult Disability Payment
PART 4 — Consequential amendments

The Scottish Ministers make the following Regulations in exercise of the powers conferred by sections 13(3), 31(2), 36(2), 41(4)(a), 43(5), 51(1), 52 and 95 of the Social Security (Scotland) Act 2018, and all other powers enabling them to do so.

In accordance with section 96(2) of that Act, a draft of these Regulations has been laid before and approved by resolution of the Scottish Parliament.

In accordance with section 97(2) of that Act, the Scottish Ministers have informed the Scottish Commission on Social Security of their proposals, notified the Scottish Parliament that they have done so and made their proposals publicly available by such means as they consider appropriate.

PART 1

INTRODUCTORY AND INTERPRETATION

Citation and commencement

13.362   1. These Regulations may be cited as the Disability Assistance for Working Age People (Scotland) Regulations 2022 and come into force on 21 March 2022.

Interpretation

13.363   2. In these Regulations—
"the 2018 Act" means the Social Security (Scotland) Act 2018,
"Adult Disability Payment" means disability assistance for adults given in accordance with these Regulations,
"aid or appliance"—
  (a) means any object or device which—
      (i) the individual needs to be able to perform an activity, and
      (ii) improves, provides or replaces the individual's impaired physical or mental function,
  (b) includes an object or device which a person without a disability might choose to use for the same function,
  (c) in relation to managing toilet needs includes the use of incontinence pads, and
  (d) includes a prosthesis,
"armed forces independence payment" means the disability benefit paid in accordance with article 24A of the Armed Forces and Reserve Forces (Compensation Scheme) Order 2011,
"assessment" means an assessment as described in section 13(2) of the 2018 Act,
"Attendance Allowance" means an attendance allowance under section 64 of the Social Security Contributions and Benefits Act 1992,
"authorised provider of vehicles" means a supplier of vehicles for persons with disabilities approved under an accreditation scheme run by the Scottish Ministers,
"award" means that a determination has been made that an individual is entitled to be given assistance under section 24 of the 2018 Act in accordance with these Regulations, and cognate expressions are to be construed accordingly,

"care home" means an establishment which provides a care home service as defined in paragraph 2 of schedule 12 of the Public Services Reform (Scotland) Act 2010 and includes a residential educational establishment,

"Child Disability Payment" means disability assistance for children and young people given in accordance with the Disability Assistance for Children and Young People (Scotland) Regulations 2021,

"daily living component" means the daily living component of Adult Disability Payment within the meaning of regulation 5,

"descriptor" means a descriptor in column 2 of the tables in Parts 2 and 3 of schedule 1,

"determination" and "determination of entitlement" have the meaning of "determination of entitlement" in section 25 of the 2018 Act,

"Disability Living Allowance" means a disability living allowance under—
(a) section 71 of the Social Security Contributions and Benefits Act 1992, or
(b) section 71 of the Social Security Contributions and Benefits (Northern Ireland) Act 1992,

[1...]

"immigration rules" means the rules laid before the United Kingdom Parliament under section 3(2) of the Immigration Act 1971,

"legal detention" means detention in legal custody within the meaning of section 295 of the Criminal Procedure (Scotland) Act 1995,

[1...]

"mobility component" means the mobility component of Adult Disability Payment within the meaning of regulation 6,

"needs" where used in relation to an aid or appliance, or supervision, prompting or assistance from another person, means that it is reasonably required, though it may not have been available or provided,

"Personal Independence Payment"—
(a) means personal independence payment under—
   (i) Part 4 of the Welfare Reform Act 2012, or
   (ii) article 82 of the Welfare Reform (Northern Ireland) Order 2015, and
(b) includes a concessionary payment made in lieu of personal independence payment under arrangements by the Secretary of State with the consent of the Treasury,

"previous award" means an award of either or both components of Adult Disability Payment to which an individual has ceased to be entitled,

[1 "qualifying services" means accommodation, board and personal care,]

"relevant date" means the date referred to in regulation 13 or, where applicable, regulation 14 or 23,

"relevant EU Regulation" means—
(a) one of the following Regulations—
   (i) Council Regulation (EC) No 1408/71 of 14 June 1971 on the application of social security schemes to employed persons, to self-employed persons and to members of their families moving within the Community,
   (ii) Regulation (EC) No 883/2004 of the European Parliament and of the Council of 29 April 2004 on the coordination of social security systems, or

(b) in relation to an individual to whom the agreement constituted by the exchange of letters set out in the schedule of the Family Allowances, National Insurance and Industrial Injuries (Gibraltar) Order 1974 applies, a Regulation mentioned in paragraph (a) of this definition as it forms part of domestic law by virtue of section 3 of the European Union (Withdrawal) Act 2018,

"residential educational establishment" means a care home which provides education or training except for one where the costs of any qualifying services are borne wholly or partly out of public or local funds by virtue of—

(a) section 485 of the Education Act 1996 or section 14 of the Education Act 2002 (which relate to grants in aid of educational services),
(b) sections 49 or 73 of the Education (Scotland) Act 1980 (which relate respectively to the power of education authorities to assist persons to take advantage of educational facilities and the powers of the Secretary of State to make grants to education authorities and others),
(c) section 65 of the Further and Higher Education Act 1992, sections 39 or 40 of the Higher Education and Research Act 2017 or sections 4 or 11 of the Further and Higher Education (Scotland) Act 2005 (which relate respectively to the funding of further education and the administration of funds), or
(d) section 22 of the Teaching and Higher Education Act 1998 (new arrangements for giving financial support to students),

"short-term assistance" means short-term assistance given in accordance with Part 1 of schedule 2 of these Regulations, and

"week" means a period of 7 days.

AMENDMENT

1. Disability Assistance for Working Age People (Transitional Provisions and Miscellaneous Amendment) (Scotland) Regulations 2022 (SSI 2022/217) reg.19(1) and (2) (August 29, 2022).

PART 2

DISABILITY ASSISTANCE FOR WORKING AGE PEOPLE

Overview

3.—(1) An individual is entitled to Adult Disability Payment in accordance with these Regulations if the individual meets the eligibility rules in—

(a) regulation 4 (entitlement to other benefits),
(b) regulations 15 to 21 (residence and presence conditions),
(c) regulation 22 (age criteria), and
(d) one or more of the following—
   (i) regulation 5 (daily living component),
   (ii) regulation 6 (mobility component),
   (iii) regulation 26 (entitlement under special rules for terminal illness).

(2) Adult Disability Payment is to consist of a daily living component and a mobility component.

(SSI 2022/54 reg.3)

(3) There are 2 weekly rates of the daily living component and 2 weekly rates of the mobility component and those rates are specified in regulation 34 (amount and form of Adult Disability Payment).

GENERAL NOTE

The general structure of adult disability payment is similar to that of the personal independence payment that it is replacing, which eases the transition. However, the structure of the legislation is not the same – not least because these regulations replace both Part 4 of the Welfare Reform Act 2012 and the Social Security (Personal Independence Payment) Regulations 2013 (see Vol.I) – and there are important differences in the wording. Therefore, while the case law of the United Kingdom Upper Tribunal and the Northern Ireland Social Security Commissioners in relation to personal independence payment (noted in the annotations in Vol.I) will often be relevant and of persuasive value (see *NB v Social Security Scotland* [2023] UT 35 at [34]), care must be taken because the schemes are not identical.

Entitlement to other benefits

4. An individual is not entitled to Adult Disability Payment while they are entitled to—
  (a) armed forces independence payment,
  (b) Attendance Allowance,
  (c) Child Disability Payment,
  (d) Disability Living Allowance, or
  (e) Personal Independence Payment.

13.365

PART 3

ELIGIBILITY: DAILY LIVING COMPONENT AND MOBILITY COMPONENT

Daily Living Component

4.—(1) An individual may be awarded the daily living component at either the standard rate or the enhanced rate.
(2) An individual is entitled to the daily living component at the standard rate if—
  (a) the individual's ability to carry out daily living activities is limited by the individual's physical or mental condition or conditions, and
  (b) the individual meets the required period condition in accordance with regulation 11.
(3) An individual is entitled to the daily living component at the enhanced rate if—
  (a) the individual's ability to carry out daily living activities is severely limited by the individual's physical or mental condition or conditions, and
  (b) the individual meets the required period condition in accordance with regulation 11.
(4) For the purpose of these Regulations—
  (a) "daily living activities" are the activities set out in column 1 of the table in Part 2 of schedule 1, and "a daily living activity" is to be construed accordingly,
  (b) "the standard rate" in relation to the daily living component means the weekly rate of the daily living component set in regulation 34(1 (a),

13.366

(c) "the enhanced rate" in relation to the daily living component means the weekly rate of the daily living component set in regulation 34(1) (b),

(5) Whether a person has limited or severely limited ability to carry out daily living activities is to be determined in accordance with regulation 8 (scoring for daily living activities).

Mobility Component

6.—(1) An individual may be awarded the mobility component at either the standard rate or the enhanced rate.

(2) An individual is entitled to the mobility component at the standard rate if—
   (a) the individual's ability to carry out mobility activities is limited by the individual's physical or mental condition or conditions, and
   (b) the individual meets the required period condition in accordance with regulation 12.

(3) A individual is entitled to the mobility component at the enhanced rate if—
   (a) the individual's ability to carry out mobility activities is severely limited by the individual's physical or mental condition or conditions, and
   (b) the individual meets the required period condition in accordance with regulation 12.

(4) For the purpose of these Regulations—
   (a) "mobility activities" are the activities set out in column 1 of the table in Part 3 of schedule 1, and "a mobility activity" is to be construed accordingly,
   (b) "the standard rate" in relation to the mobility component means the weekly rate of the mobility component set in regulation 34(2)(a),
   (c) "the enhanced rate" in relation to the mobility component means the weekly rate of the mobility component set in regulation 34(2)(b),

(5) Whether a person has limited or severely limited ability to carry out mobility activities is to be determined in accordance with regulation 9 (scoring for mobility activities).

Determination of ability to carry out activities

7.—(1) An individual's ability to carry out a daily living activity or mobility activity is to be determined—
   (a) on the basis of the individual's ability whilst wearing or using any aid or appliance which the individual normally wears or uses, or
   (b) as if the individual were wearing or using any aid or appliance which the individual could reasonably be expected to wear or use.

(2) An individual's ability to carry out an activity is to be determined—
   (a) by reference to the descriptors for the activity set out in column 2 of the table in Part 2 of schedule 1, [¹ or, as the case may be, column 2 of the table in Part 3 of schedule 1] and
   (b) on the basis of which descriptor applies for the individual to be able to carry out the activity—
      (i) safely,
      (ii) to an acceptable standard,
      (iii) repeatedly, and
      (iv) within a reasonable time period.

(3) In this regulation—
(a) "safely" means in a manner unlikely to cause harm to the individual or to another person, either during or after completion of the activity, with consideration given to—
  (i) the likelihood of harm, and
  (ii) the severity of the consequences of that harm,
(b) "to an acceptable standard" means to a reasonable standard for the activity, taking account of the impact on the individual of carrying out the activity to that standard,
(c) "repeatedly" means as often as the activity is reasonably required to be completed, and
(d) "reasonable time period" means no more than twice as long as the maximum period that an individual without a physical or mental condition or conditions which limits that individual's ability to carry out the activity in question would normally take to complete that activity.

AMENDMENT

1. Disability Assistance for Working Age People (Transitional Provisions and Miscellaneous Amendment) (Scotland) Regulations 2022 (SSI 2022/217) reg.19(1) and (3) (August 29, 2022).

GENERAL NOTE

This regulation is similar to reg.4 of the Social Security (Personal Independence Payment) Regulations 2013 (see Vol.I).

Scoring for daily living activities

8.—(1) The score an individual obtains in relation to daily living activities is determined by adding together the number of points (if any) awarded for each activity listed in column 1 of the table in Part 2 of schedule 1.

(2) For the purpose of paragraph (1), the number of points awarded to an individual for each activity listed in column 1 of the table is the number shown in column 3 of the table against whichever of the descriptors set out in column 2 of the table for the activity applies to the individual by virtue of regulation 10.

(3) For the purposes of regulation 5, an individual has—
(a) limited ability to carry out daily living activities where the individual obtains a score of at least 8 points and no more than 11 points in relation to daily living activities,
(b) severely limited ability to carry out daily living activities where the individual obtains a score of at least 12 points in relation to daily living activities.

Scoring for mobility activities

9.—(1) The score an individual obtains in relation to mobility activities is determined by adding together the number of points (if any) awarded for each activity listed in column 1 of the table in Part 3 of schedule 1.

(2) For the purpose of paragraph (1), the number of points awarded to an individual for each activity listed in column 1 of the table is the number shown in column 3 of the table against whichever of the descriptors set out

in column 2 of the table for the activity applies to the individual by virtue of regulation 10.

(3) For the purposes of regulation 6, an individual has—
  (a) limited ability to carry out mobility activities where the individual obtains a score of at least 8 points and no more than 11 points in relation to mobility activities,
  (b) severely limited ability to carry out mobility activities where the individual obtains a score of at least 12 points in relation to mobility activities.

Scoring: further provision

10.—(1) The descriptor which applies to an individual in relation to each activity in the tables referred to in regulations 8(2) and 9(2) is—
  (a) where one descriptor is satisfied on over 50% of the days of the required period, that descriptor,
  (b) where two or more descriptors are each satisfied on over 50% of the days of the required period, the descriptor which scores the higher or highest number of points, and
  (c) where no descriptor is satisfied on over 50% of the days of the required period but two or more descriptors (other than a descriptor which scores 0 points) are satisfied for periods which, when added together, amount to over 50% of the days of the required period—
    (i) the descriptor which is satisfied for the greater or greatest proportion of days of the required period, or
    (ii) where both or all descriptors are satisfied for the same proportion, the descriptor which scores the higher or highest number of points.

(2) For the purposes of paragraph (1), a descriptor is satisfied on a day in the required period if the descriptor has been satisfied for any part of the day which is not minimal or fleeting.

(3) In these Regulations, "required period" means—
  (a) where an individual's entitlement to Adult Disability Payment falls to be determined, the period of 13 weeks ending with the relevant date together with—
    (i) in relation to an application after an interval (see regulations 14 and 23), the period of 39 weeks beginning with the date on which that application is made,
    (ii) in relation to any other application, the period of 39 weeks beginning with the day after the relevant date.
  (b) where Adult Disability Payment has been awarded to an individual—
    (i) during the period of 13 weeks following a determination of entitlement in the circumstances where regulation 14 or 23 applies, the period of 13 weeks ending with the relevant date together with, for each day of the award, the period of 39 weeks beginning with the day after each day of the award,
    (ii) in any other case, for each day of the award, the period of 13 weeks ending with that day of the award together with the period of 39 weeks beginning with the day after that date.

(SSI 2022/54 reg.11)

Part 4

Required Period Condition

Required Period Condition: daily living component

11. An individual meets the required period condition for the purposes of regulation 5 where, if the individual's ability to carry out the daily living activities were determined every day in the required period, it is likely that the Scottish Ministers would determine on all of those days that the individual had limited or, as the case may be, severely limited ability to carry out the daily living activities.

GENERAL NOTE

See *Social Security Scotland v FK* [2024] UT 23.

Required Period Condition: mobility component

12. An individual meets the required period condition for the purposes of regulation 6 where, if the individual's ability to carry out the mobility activities were determined every day in the required period, it is likely that the Scottish Ministers would determine on all of those days that the individual had limited or, as the case may be, severely limited ability to carry out the mobility activities.

GENERAL NOTE

See *Social Security Scotland v FK* [2024] UT 23.

The relevant date

13. Except where regulation 14 or 23 applies, in these Regulations, the "relevant date" is—
    (a) where the individual has made an application for Adult Disability Payment which has not been determined—
        (i) the date of that application, or
        (ii) if later, the earliest date in relation to which, if the individual's ability to carry out daily living activities or, as the case may be, mobility activities, had been determined on every day in the previous 13 weeks, it is likely that the Scottish Ministers would have determined on all of those days that the individual has limited ability or, as the case may be, severely limited ability to carry out those activities, and
    (b) where the individual has an award of either or both components, each day of that award.

GENERAL NOTE

See *Social Security Scotland v FK* [2024] UT 23.

The relevant date: Adult Disability Payment after an interval

14.—(1) This regulation does not apply where regulation 23 (Adult Disability Payment after an interval and after reaching the relevant age) applies.

(2) Paragraphs (3) and (4) apply where—
(a) an individual makes an application for Adult Disability Payment ("the application"),
(b) that individual had a previous award of—
   (i) Adult Disability Payment,
   (ii) Child Disability Payment,
   (iii) Disability Living Allowance, or
   (iv) Personal Independence Payment,

which ended not more than two years before the date on which the application is made,
(c) the previous award referred to in sub-paragraph (b) consisted of the same component as the one to which the individual is entitled (or would be entitled if the individual met the required period condition) under the application, and
(d) the Scottish Ministers determine that the entitlement under the application results from—
   (i) substantially the same physical or mental condition or conditions for which the previous award was made, or
   (ii) a new physical or mental condition or conditions which developed as a result of a condition for which the previous award was made.

(3) In relation to determination of entitlement under the application, the relevant date for the purpose of regulation 10(3) is the date on which the previous award ended.

(4) Where an individual is awarded either or both components under the application, in relation to continued entitlement to that component or, as the case may be, those components, the relevant date for the purpose of regulation 10(3) is—
(a) during the period of 13 weeks following the date of the application, the date on which the previous award ended,
(b) in any other case, each day of the award.

(5) For the purposes of this regulation—
(a) an award of any of the following is to be treated as though it were an award of the daily living component of Adult Disability Payment—
   (i) the care component of Child Disability Payment,
   (ii) the care component of Disability Living Allowance, or
   (iii) the daily living component of Personal Independence Payment,
(b) an award of any of the following is to be treated as though it were an award of the mobility component of Adult Disability Payment—
   (i) the mobility component of Child Disability Payment,
   (ii) the mobility component of Disability Living Allowance, or
   (iii) the mobility component of Personal Independence Payment.

PART 5

RESIDENCE AND PRESENCE CONDITIONS

Residence and presence conditions

15.—(1) An individual satisfies the residence and presence conditions where on any day that individual—
(a) is ordinarily resident in Scotland,
(b) is habitually resident in the common travel area,

(c) is not a person subject to immigration control within the meaning of section 115(9) of the Immigration and Asylum Act 1999,
(d) is present in the common travel area, and
(e) has been present in the common travel area for a period of, or for periods amounting in the aggregate to, not less than 26 weeks out of the 52 weeks immediately preceding that day.

(2) In this Part, "common travel area" has the meaning given in section 1(3) of the Immigration Act 1971.

(3) The residence condition set out in paragraph (1)(a) does not apply in relation to the daily living component where on any day the individual—
(a) is habitually resident in Ireland,
(b) has a genuine and sufficient link to Scotland, and
(c) is an individual—
   (i) to whom the Convention on Social Security between the Government of the United Kingdom of Great Britain and Northern Ireland and the Government of Ireland signed at Dublin on 1 February 2019, as modified from time to time in accordance with any provision of it, applies, and
   (ii) in respect of whom the United Kingdom is, as a result, competent for payment of long term care benefits.

(4) The reference in paragraph (3)(b) to an individual's link to Scotland being sufficient is to it being sufficiently close that if the individual were not entitled to Adult Disability Payment, paragraph (3) would be incompatible with the Convention on Social Security between the Government of the United Kingdom of Great Britain and Northern Ireland and the Government of Ireland signed at Dublin on 1 February 2019.

(5) Paragraph (1)(c) does not apply to a person subject to immigration control within the meaning of section 115(9) of the Immigration and Asylum Act 1999 where the person—
(a) is lawfully working in United Kingdom and is a national of a state with which the United Kingdom has concluded an agreement which replaces in whole or in part an agreement under Article 217 of the Treaty on the Functioning of the European Union which has ceased to apply to, and in, the United Kingdom, providing, in the field of social security, for the equal treatment of workers who are nationals of the signatory state and their families,
(b) is a member of the family of, and living with, a person specified in sub-paragraph (a), or
(c) has been given leave to enter, or remain in, the United Kingdom by the Secretary of State upon an undertaking by another person or persons pursuant to the immigration rules, to be responsible for their maintenance and accommodation.

(6) The past presence condition in paragraph (1)(e) does not apply where an individual has a terminal illness within the meaning of regulation 26.

(7) The residence and presence conditions set out in paragraphs (1)(b) and (1)(e) do not apply where an individual is a person who—
(a) has leave to enter or remain in the United Kingdom granted under the immigration rules by virtue of—
   (i) the Afghan Relocations and Assistance Policy, or

(ii) the previous scheme for locally-employed staff in Afghanistan (sometimes referred to as the ex-gratia scheme),
(b) has been granted discretionary leave outside the immigration rules as a dependant of a person referred to in sub-paragraph (a), [1 . . .]
(c) has leave granted under the Afghan Citizens Resettlement Scheme, [1 [3 . . .]
(d) has leave to enter or remain in the United Kingdom granted under or outside the immigration rules, [2 has a right] of abode in the United Kingdom within the meaning given in section 2 of the Immigration Act 1971 [2 or does not require leave to enter or remain in the United Kingdom in accordance with section 3ZA of that Act], where the individual—
   (i) was residing in Ukraine immediately before 1 January 2022, and
   (ii) left Ukraine in connection with the Russian invasion which took place on 24 February 2022] [3, [4 . . .]
(e) has leave to enter or remain in the United Kingdom granted under or outside the immigration rules, has a right of abode in the United Kingdom within the meaning given in section 2 of the Immigration Act 1971 or does not require leave to enter or remain in the United Kingdom in accordance with section 3ZA of that Act, where the individual—
   (i) was residing in Sudan before 15 April 2023, and
   (ii) left Sudan in connection with the violence which rapidly escalated on 15 April 2023 in Khartoum and across Sudan [4, or
(f) has leave to enter or remain in the United Kingdom granted under or outside the immigration rules, has a right of abode in the United Kingdom within the meaning given in section 2 of the Immigration Act 1971 or does not require leave to enter or remain in the United Kingdom in accordance with section 3ZA of that Act, where the individual—
   (i) was residing in Israel, the West Bank, the Gaza Strip, East Jerusalem, the Golan Heights or Lebanon immediately before 7 October 2023, and
   (ii) left Israel, the West Bank, the Gaza Strip, East Jerusalem, the Golan Heights or Lebanon in connection with the Hamas terrorist attack in Israel on 7 October 2023 or the violence which rapidly escalated in the region following the attack.]

(8) For the purposes of paragraph (7), "the Afghan Citizens Resettlement Scheme" means the scheme announced by the United Kingdom Government on 18 August 2021.

AMENDMENTS

1. Social Security (Residence Requirements) (Ukraine) (Scotland) Regulations 2022 (SSI 2022/108), reg.8 (March 22, 2022).
2. Social Security (Miscellaneous Amendment and Transitional Provision) (Scotland) Regulations 2022 (SSI 2022/336) reg.9 (November 14, 2022).
3. Social Security (Residence Requirements) (Sudan) (Scotland) Regulations 2023 (SSI 2023/149) reg.8(2) (May 17, 2023).
4. Social Security (Residence and Presence Requirements) (Israel, the West Bank, the Gaza Strip, East Jerusalem, the Golan Heights and Lebanon) (Scotland) Regulations 2023 (SSI 2023/309) reg.8(2) (October 26, 2023).

(SSI 2022/54 reg.16)

Temporary absence from the common travel area

16.—(1) Where an individual is temporarily absent from the common travel area, the individual is to be treated as present in the common travel area for—
  (a) the first 13 weeks of that absence for any reason, or
  (b) the first 26 weeks of that absence where—
    (i) after the first 13 weeks, the absence is in connection with arrangements made for the medical treatment of the individual for a disease or bodily or mental disablement which commenced before leaving the common travel area, and
    (ii) the arrangements relate to medical treatment—
      (aa) outside the common travel area,
      (bb) during the period when the individual is temporarily absent from the common travel area, and
      (cc) by, or under the supervision of, a person appropriately qualified to carry out that treatment.
(2) For the purposes of paragraph (1)—
  (a) an individual is "temporarily absent" if, at the beginning of the period of absence, that absence is unlikely to exceed 52 weeks, and
  (b) "medical treatment" means medical, surgical, psychological or rehabilitative treatment (including any course or diet regimen).

Serving members of Her Majesty's forces, civil servants and their family members

17.—(1) A relevant individual is treated as meeting the residence and presence conditions set out in regulations 15(1)(a), (b) and (d) where on any day that individual is outside the common travel area—
  (a) by reason of their capacity mentioned in paragraph (3)(a) provided that the individual satisfied the residence and presence conditions set out in regulation 15(1)(a), (b) and (d) immediately prior to the start of their employment mentioned in paragraph (3)(a), or
  (b) by reason of being a person mentioned in paragraph (3)(b) living with an individual to whom paragraph (3)(a) applies.
(2) The past presence condition set out in regulation 15(1)(e) does not apply to a relevant individual.
(3) A "relevant individual" in paragraph (1) and (2) means an individual who is—
  (a) outside of the common travel area in their capacity as a—
    (i) serving member of Her Majesty's forces, or
    (ii) civil servant, or
  (b) living with a person mentioned in sub-paragraph (a) and—
    (i) is the child, step-child or child in care of that person,
    (ii) is the parent, step-parent or parent-in-law of that person, or
    (iii) is married to or in a civil partnership with that person, or is living together with that person as if they were married or in a civil partnership.
(4) In this regulation—
"child in care" means—
  (a) under the law of Scotland, a child in respect of whom a relevant individual listed in paragraph (3)(a)—

1661

(i) is a foster carer within the meaning of regulation 2 of the Looked After Children (Scotland) Regulations 2009,
(ii) is a kinship carer within the meaning of regulation 2 of the Looked After Children (Scotland) Regulations 2009,
(iii) has a kinship care order within the meaning of section 72 of the Children and Young People (Scotland) Act 2014, or
(b) under the law of England and Wales and Northern Ireland, a child in respect of whom a person listed in paragraph (3)(a) has a relationship equivalent to those listed under the law of Scotland,

[¹...]

"civil servant" has the meaning given by section 1(4) of the Constitutional Reform and Governance Act 2010,

[¹...]

"serving member of Her Majesty's forces" means a member of a regular force or a reserve force ("M") as defined, in each case, by section 374 (definitions applying for purposes of the whole Act) of the Armed Forces Act 2006, unless—
(a) M is under the age of 16,
(b) M is committing an offence under section 8 of the Armed Forces Act 2006 (desertion),
(c) the force concerned is one of Her Majesty's naval forces which M locally entered at an overseas base without—
(i) previously being an insured person under the National Insurance Act 1965, or
(ii) paying or having previously paid one or more of the following classes of contributions under the Social Security Act 1975 or the Social Security Contributions and Benefits Act 1992—
(aa) primary Class 1,
(bb) Class 2, or
(cc) Class 3, or
(d) the force concerned is one of Her Majesty's military forces or Her Majesty's air forces which M entered, or was recruited for, outside the United Kingdom and—
(i) where that force is one of Her Majesty's military forces, the depot for M's unit is outside the United Kingdom, or
(ii) where that force is one of Her Majesty's air forces, M is liable under the terms of M's engagement to serve only in a specified area outside the United Kingdom.

AMENDMENT

1. Disability Assistance for Working Age People (Transitional Provisions and Miscellaneous Amendment) (Scotland) Regulations 2022 (SSI 2022/217) reg.19(1) and (4) (August 29, 2022).

Aircraft workers, mariners and continental shelf operations

18.—(1) An individual is to be treated as meeting the presence conditions set out in regulation 15(1)(d) and (e) for any period where that individual is—
(a) outside the common travel area in their capacity as an aircraft worker or a mariner, or
(b) in employment prescribed for the purposes of section 120 (employment at sea (continental shelf operations)) of the Social Security

Contributions and Benefits Act 1992 in connection with continental shelf operations.

(2) In this regulation—

"aircraft worker" means a person who is, or has been, employed under a contract of service either as a pilot, commander, navigator or other member of the crew of any aircraft, or in any other capacity on board any aircraft where—
  (a) the employment in that other capacity is for the purposes of the aircraft or its crew or of any passengers or cargo or mail carried on that aircraft, and
  (b) the contract is entered into in the United Kingdom with a view to its performance (in whole or in part) while the aircraft is in flight,
but does not include a person so far as that employment is as a serving member of Her Majesty's forces, and

"mariner" means a person who is, or has been, in employment under a contract of service either as a master or member of the crew of any ship or vessel, or in any other capacity on board any ship or vessel where—
  (a) the employment in that other capacity is for the purposes of that ship or vessel or its crew or any passengers or cargo or mail carried by the ship or vessel, and
  (b) the contract is entered into in the United Kingdom with a view to its performance (in whole or in part) while the ship or vessel is on voyage,
but does not include a person in so far as that employment is as a serving member of Her Majesty's forces.

Persons residing in the United Kingdom to whom a relevant EU regulation applies

19.—(1) The past presence condition set out in regulation 15(1)(e) does not apply where on any day the individual is—
(a) ordinarily resident in Scotland,
(b) habitually resident in the United Kingdom,
(c) an individual—
  (i) to whom the rules set out in a relevant EU regulation apply by virtue of—
    (aa) Title III of Part 2 of the EU withdrawal agreement,
    (bb) Part 3 or Article 23(4) of the Swiss citizens' rights agreement (as defined in section 39(1) of the European Union (Withdrawal Agreement) Act 2020 ("the 2020 Act")),
    (cc) Title III of the EEA EFTA separation agreement (as defined in section 39(1) of the 2020 Act), or
    (dd) the agreement constituted by the exchange of letters set out in the schedule of the Family Allowances, National Insurance and Industrial Injuries (Gibraltar) Order 1974, and
  (ii) in respect of whom the United Kingdom is, as a result, competent for payment of sickness benefits in cash.

Persons residing outside the United Kingdom to whom a relevant EU regulation applies

20.—(1) The residence and presence conditions set out in regulation 15(1) do not apply in relation to the daily living component where on any day the individual satisfies the conditions in paragraph (2).

(2) The conditions referred to in paragraph (1) are that the individual must—
  (a) be an individual—
    (i) to whom the rules set out in a relevant EU regulation apply by virtue of—
      (aa) Title III of Part 2 of the EU withdrawal agreement,
      (bb) Part 3 or Article 23(4) of the Swiss citizens' rights agreement (as defined in section 39(1) of the European Union (Withdrawal Agreement) Act 2020 ("the 2020 Act")),
      (cc) Title III of the EEA EFTA separation agreement (as defined in section 39(1) of the 2020 Act), or
      (dd) the agreement constituted by the exchange of letters set out in the schedule of the Family Allowances, National Insurance and Industrial Injuries (Gibraltar) Order 1974, and
    (ii) in respect of whom the United Kingdom is, as a result, competent for payment of sickness benefits in cash,
  (b) be habitually resident in—
    (i) Switzerland,
    (ii) an EEA state, or
    (iii) Gibraltar, and
  (c) have a genuine and sufficient link to Scotland.
(3) The reference in paragraph (2)(c) to an individual's link to Scotland being sufficient is to it being sufficiently close that if the individual were not entitled to Adult Disability Payment, paragraph (2) would be incompatible with the applicable agreement mentioned in sub-paragraph (a)(i) of that paragraph.
(4) In this regulation, "EEA State" means—
  (a) any member state of the European Union, or
  (b) any other state that is party to the agreement on the European Economic Area signed at Oporto on 2 May 1992, together with the Protocol adjusting that Agreement signed at Brussels on 17 March 1993, as modified or supplemented from time to time.

[¹No entitlement to daily living component where UK is not competent state

20A. An individual to whom a relevant EU Regulation applies is not entitled to the daily living component for a period unless during that period the United Kingdom is competent for payment of sickness benefits in cash to the individual for the purposes of the relevant EU Regulation in question.]

AMENDMENT

1. Disability Assistance (Miscellaneous Amendment) (Scotland) Regulations 2023 (SSI 2023/346) reg.4(2) (November 20, 2023).

Refugees

21.—(1) The residence and presence conditions set out in regulations 15(1)(b) and (e) do not apply where an individual has—
  (a) been granted refugee status or humanitarian protection under the immigration rules, or

(b) leave to enter or remain in the United Kingdom as the dependant of a person granted refugee status or humanitarian protection under the immigration rules.

PART 6

ENTITLEMENT UNDER RULES RELATING TO AGE

Age Criteria

22.—(1) Adult Disability Payment may be paid in respect of an individual who—
(a) is at least 16 years of age, and
(b) has not reached the relevant age.
(2) In this Part, "the relevant age" means—
(a) pensionable age (within the meaning given by the rules in paragraph 1 of schedule 4 to the Pensions Act 1995), or
(b) if higher, 65.
(3) Where an individual was born on 29 February, their birthday is to be taken to fall on 28 February in a year which is not a leap year.
(4) Paragraph (1)(b) is subject to the exceptions provided in regulations 23 and 24.

Exceptions: Adult Disability Payment after an interval and after reaching the relevant age

23.—(1) This regulation applies where—
(a) an individual has reached the relevant age,
(b) the individual makes an application for Adult Disability Payment and—
   (i) they had a previous award of Adult Disability Payment which ended not more than one year before the day the new application is made, or
   (ii) they had a previous award of Personal Independence Payment or Disability Living Allowance which ended not more than one year before the day the new application is made,
(c) the previous award referred to in sub-paragraph (b) consisted of the same component as the one to which the individual is entitled (or would be entitled if they met the required period condition) under the new application, and
(d) the Scottish Ministers determine that the entitlement under the new application results from—
   (i) substantially the same physical or mental condition or conditions for which the previous award was made, or
   (ii) a new physical or mental condition or conditions which developed as a result of a condition for which the previous award was made.
(2) Where an application for Adult Disability Payment is made in terms of paragraph (1)—
(a) regulation 22(1)(b) does not apply, and
(b) paragraphs (5) and (6) apply to the determination of entitlement under the new application.

(3) In relation to determination of entitlement under the new application, the relevant date for the purpose of regulation 10(3) is the date on which the previous award ended.

(4) Where an individual is awarded either or both components under the new application, in relation to continued entitlement to that component or, as the case may be, those components, the relevant date for the purpose of regulation 10(3) is—
  (a) during the period of 13 weeks following the date of the new application, the date on which the previous award ended,
  (b) in any other case, each day of the award.

(5) Where the Scottish Ministers determine that the individual has severely limited ability to carry out mobility activities—
  (a) the individual is entitled to the enhanced rate of the mobility component only if they were entitled to that rate of that component under the previous award, and
  (b) where the individual is not entitled to the enhanced rate of that component because of sub-paragraph (a), they are entitled to the standard rate of that component provided that they were entitled to that rate of that component under the previous award.

(6) Where the Scottish Ministers determine that the individual has limited ability to carry out mobility activities, the individual is entitled to the standard rate of the mobility component only if they were entitled to that component, at either rate, under the previous award.

(7) For the purposes of this regulation—
  (a) an award of either of the following is to be treated as though it were an award of the daily living component of Adult Disability Payment—
    (i) the care component of Disability Living Allowance, or
    (ii) the daily living component of Personal Independence Payment, and
  (b) an award of either of the following is to be treated as though it were an award of the mobility component of Adult Disability Payment—
    (i) the mobility component of Daily Living Allowance, or
    (ii) the mobility component of Personal Independence Payment.

Persons who have reached the relevant age: other exceptions

24. Regulation 22(1)(b) does not apply where the individual has reached the relevant age, including for the purposes of any determination of their entitlement to Adult Disability Payment made after they have reached the relevant age, if they—
  (a) were entitled to an award of either or both components of Adult Disability Payment on the day preceding the day on which they reached the relevant age,
  (b) made an application for Adult Disability Payment before reaching the relevant age and that application was not determined before they reached that age, but an award of either or both components would be made in respect of the individual but for regulation 22(1)(b), [^{1}...]
  (c) are a transferring individual in terms of Part 3 of schedule 2 [^{1}, or
  (d) are a transferring individual in terms of the Disability Assistance for Working Age People (Transitional Provisions and Miscellaneous Amendment) (Scotland) Regulations 2022.]

(SSI 2022/54 reg.24)

AMENDMENT

1. Disability Assistance for Working Age People (Transitional Provisions and Miscellaneous Amendment) (Scotland) Regulations 2022 (SSI 2022/217) reg.19(1) and (5) (August 29, 2022).

Determination of an award after the person has reached the relevant age

25.—(1) This regulation applies where—
(a) the individual—
 (i) has reached the relevant age, and
 (ii) is entitled to an award ("the original award") [1. . .] of Adult Disability Payment, pursuant to an exception in regulation 23 or 24, and
(b) the Scottish Ministers are under a duty to make a subsequent determination of their entitlement by way of a determination without an application under regulation 48(a).

(2) The restrictions in paragraph (3) apply in relation to a determination referred to in paragraph (1)(b) where—
(a) [1. . .]
(b) the determination is being made under regulation 48(a) in relation to—
 (i) a change of circumstances which occurred after the person reached the relevant age, or
 (ii) a material fact which the Scottish Ministers were not previously aware of, or medical evidence received from a healthcare professional or other person approved by the Scottish Ministers, where the Scottish Ministers become aware of the material fact or medical evidence after the individual reached the relevant age.

(3) The restrictions referred to in paragraph (2) are—
(a) where the original mobility component award is for the standard rate then, regardless of whether the award would otherwise have been for the enhanced rate, the Scottish Ministers—
 (i) may only make an award for the standard rate of that component, and
 (ii) may only make such an award where entitlement results from substantially the same condition or conditions in respect of which the mobility component in the original award was given,
(b) where the original mobility component award is for the enhanced rate, the Scottish Ministers may only award that rate of that component where entitlement results from substantially the same condition or conditions in respect of which the mobility component in the original award was given,
[1 (c) where the original award did not include an award of the mobility component, the Scottish Ministers may not award that component at either the standard or enhanced rate.]

(4) Where the original award does not include an award of the mobility component but the individual had—
(a) a previous award of—
 (i) the mobility component of Adult Disability Payment,

(ii) the mobility component of Personal Independence Payment, or
(iii) the mobility component of Disability Living Allowance, and
(b) the previous award of the component under sub-paragraph (a) ceased no more than 1 year prior to the date on which the determination referred to in paragraph (1)(b) takes or would take effect,

for the purpose of this regulation, entitlement under that previous award is to be treated as if it were under the original award.

(5) Paragraph (2)(b)(ii) does not include medical evidence in the form of a clinical judgement which was made in accordance with regulation 26(7) and (8) before the individual reached the relevant age.

(6) In this regulation, "healthcare professional" means a—
(a) registered medical practitioner,
(b) registered nurse, or
(c) healthcare professional who is registered by the Health and Care Professions Council.

AMENDMENT

1. Disability Assistance for Working Age People (Transitional Provisions and Miscellaneous Amendment) (Scotland) Regulations 2022 (SSI 2022/217) reg.19(1) and (6) (August 29, 2022).

PART 7

ENTITLEMENT UNDER SPECIAL RULES FOR TERMINAL ILLNESS

Entitlement under special rules for terminal illness

26.—(1) An individual who has a terminal illness is to be treated as satisfying the conditions for the enhanced rate of both the daily living component and the mobility component of Adult Disability Payment.

(2) Paragraph (1) applies regardless of the period of time for which the individual has had the terminal illness.

[¹ (3) An individual to whom this regulation applies is to be treated as though—
(a) they have obtained the maximum points for each activity listed in column 1 of the tables in Part 2 and Part 3 of schedule 1, and
(b) they have satisfied regulations 5(3) and 6(3).]

(4) Subject to paragraphs (5) and (6), the individual's entitlement to the rates referred to in paragraph (1) begins on the date on which—
(a) the individual's application for Adult Disability Payment was made, where the application included information about the individual's terminal illness,
(b) the Scottish Ministers became aware of the individual's terminal illness (whether as a result of the individual notifying a change in circumstances or otherwise), where the individual was previously awarded, and has an ongoing entitlement to, Adult Disability Payment, on the basis of a determination that the individual was entitled to the daily living component or the mobility component or both in relation to a condition other than terminal illness, or
(c) the clinical judgement was made in accordance with paragraphs (7) and (8) ("the judgement"), whichever is the earlier.

(5) Where the judgement mentioned in paragraph (4)(c) is dated not more than 26 weeks earlier than whichever date in paragraph (4)(a) or (b) applies ("the applicable date"), the Scottish Ministers have the power, when making their determination, to specify that an individual's entitlement begins—
  (a) up to a maximum of 26 weeks prior to the applicable date, and
  (b) on or after the day these Regulations come into force.
(6) Where the judgement mentioned in paragraph (4)(c)—
  (a) is dated more than 26 weeks earlier than whichever date in paragraph (4)(a) or (b) applies ("the applicable date"), and
  (b) an appropriate healthcare professional confirms that the judgement is still accurate by making a judgement in accordance with paragraphs (7) and (8),
an individual's entitlement can only begin—
  (c) up to a maximum of 26 weeks prior to the applicable date, and
  (d) on or after the day these Regulations come into force.
(7) For the purposes of these Regulations an individual is to be regarded as having a terminal illness for the purpose of determining entitlement to Adult Disability Payment if it is the clinical judgement of an appropriate healthcare professional that the individual has a progressive disease that can reasonably be expected to cause the individual's death.
(8) Subject to paragraph (9), an appropriate healthcare professional exercising the judgement described in paragraph (7) must have regard to the guidance prepared and made publically available by the Chief Medical Officer of the Scottish Administration in accordance with paragraph 1(3) of schedule 5 of the 2018 Act.
(9) Where regulation 20 (persons residing outside the United Kingdom to whom a relevant EU regulation applies) applies to the individual, an appropriate healthcare professional mentioned in paragraph 10(b) need not have regard to the guidance mentioned in paragraph (8) where it would not be reasonable in the circumstances to insist on the judgement being formed with regard to that guidance.
(10) In this regulation, "an appropriate healthcare professional" means—
  (a) a registered medical practitioner or a registered nurse who is—
    (i) involved in the diagnosis or care of the individual, and
    (ii) acting in their professional capacity, or
  (b) where regulation 20 applies to the individual, a person who—
    (i) has equivalent qualifications to a registered medical practitioner or a registered nurse in an EEA state, Gibraltar or Switzerland,
    (ii) is a member of the professional body equivalent to the General Medical Council or Nursing and Midwifery Council in that EEA state, Gibraltar or Switzerland, and
    (iii) meets the requirements of sub-paragraph (a)(i) and (ii).
(11) Where an individual has previously received Adult Disability Payment or a benefit listed in paragraph 12(a) for a period and a determination is subsequently made that the individual is entitled to Adult Disability Payment at a higher rate for that period by virtue of this regulation, that individual will be entitled to the difference between the value of entitlement to Adult Disability Payment under the subsequent determination and the value of Adult Disability Payment or the benefit listed in paragraph 12(a) to which that individual was previously entitled for that period.

(12) For the purpose of paragraph 11—
 (a) the benefits are—
  (i) armed forces independence payment,
  (ii) Attendance Allowance,
  (iii) Child Disability Payment,
  (iv) Disability Living Allowance, or
  (v) Personal Independence Payment, and
 (b) regulation 4 (entitlement to other benefits) is treated as omitted.

AMENDMENT

1. Disability Assistance for Working Age People (Transitional Provisions and Miscellaneous Amendment) (Scotland) Regulations 2022 (SSI 2022/217) reg.19(1) and (7) (August 29, 2022).

PART 8

EFFECT OF TIME SPENT IN CARE HOMES, HOSPITAL AND LEGAL DETENTION

Effect of admission to a care home on ongoing entitlement to daily living component

27.—(1) This regulation applies where an individual who has an ongoing entitlement to the daily living component of Adult Disability Payment becomes a resident of a care home.

(2) Subject to paragraphs (4) and (5) and regulation 29, on the day after the day on which the individual has been resident in a care home for 28 days, and for so long as the individual continues to reside in such a home, the value of the daily living component of Adult Disability Payment that is to be given to the individual is to be £0 instead of the values set out in regulation 34 (amount and form of Adult Disability Payment).

(3) The 28 days referred to in paragraph (2) may comprise two or more separate periods, provided that there is no more than 28 days between each period.

(4) Paragraph (2) does not apply to a resident in a care home, where the full costs of any qualifying services are met—
 (a) entirely out of the resources of the individual for whom the qualifying services are provided,
 (b) partly out of the resources of the individual for whom the qualifying services are provided and partly out of the resources of another person (other than a local authority) or assistance from a charity, or
 (c) entirely out of the resources of another person (other than a local authority) or assistance from a charity.

(5) For the purposes of this regulation, an individual is not resident in a care home during any period when the individual is being looked after by a local authority and—
 (a) has been placed temporarily in a private dwelling with a family, relative or some other suitable person while aged between 16 and 18 and receiving services under Part II of the Children (Scotland) Act 1995 by virtue of being a child in need within the meaning of section 93(4)(a)(ii) (impairment of health), or 93(4)(a)(iii) (disability) of that Act, or
 (b) is accommodated in a care home outside the United Kingdom, where the costs of any qualifying services are met wholly or partly by a local authority exercising its powers under section 25 of the

Education (Additional Support for Learning) (Scotland) Act 2004 (attendance at establishments outwith the United Kingdom).

(6) For the purposes of this regulation and regulation 32 (entitlement beginning while in alternative accommodation), reference to an individual being "looked after by a local authority" is to be construed, as the case may be, in accordance with—
  (a) section 17(6) of the Children (Scotland) Act 1995,
  (b) section 105(4) of the Children Act 1989, or
  (c) article 25 of the Children (Northern Ireland) Order 1995.

Effect of admission to hospital on ongoing entitlement to Adult Disability Payment

28.—(1) This regulation applies where an individual who is aged 18 years or older and has an ongoing entitlement to either component of Adult Disability Payment—
  (a) is undergoing medical or other treatment as an in-patient at a hospital or similar institution, and
  (b) any of the costs of the treatment, accommodation and any related services provided for them are borne out of public funds.

(2) Subject to regulation 29, on the day after the day on which the individual has been an in-patient in a hospital or similar institution for 28 days, and for so long as the individual continues to be an in-patient in such an institution, the value of each component of Adult Disability Payment that is to be given to the individual is £0 instead of the values set out in regulation 34 (amount and form of Adult Disability Payment).

(3) The 28 days referred to in paragraph (2) may comprise two or more separate periods, provided that there is no more than 28 days between each period.

(4) For the purposes of paragraph (1), the costs of treatment, accommodation or any related services are borne out of public funds if the individual is undergoing medical or other treatment as an in-patient in—
  (a) a hospital or similar institution under—
    (i) the National Health Service Act 2006,
    (ii) the National Health Service (Wales) Act 2006, or
    (iii) the National Health Service (Scotland) Act 1978, or
  (b) a hospital or similar institution maintained or administered by the Defence Council.

(5) This regulation does not apply where an individual was under the age of 18 on the day on which they began their current period undergoing medical or other treatment as an in-patient at a hospital or similar institution.

Exception: Hospices

29.——(1) Regulations 27(2) and 28(2) do not apply where the individual is residing in a hospice and has a terminal illness.

(2) In this regulation, "hospice" means a hospital or other institution whose primary function is to provide palliative care for persons resident there who are suffering from a progressive disease in its final stages, other than—
  (a) a health service hospital (within the meaning of section 108(1) of the National Health Service (Scotland) Act 1978) in Scotland,

(b) a health service hospital (within the meaning of section 275(1) of the National Health Service Act 2006) in England,
(c) a hospital in Wales vested in—
  (i) an NHS trust,
  (ii) a Local Health Board, or
  (iii) the Welsh Ministers,
for the purpose of functions under the National Health Service (Wales) Act 2006,
(d) a hospital maintained or administered by the Defence Council, or
(e) an institution similar to a hospital mentioned in any of the preceding sub-paragraphs.
(3) In this regulation—
"NHS trust" means a body established under section 18 of the National Health Service (Wales) Act 2006, and
"Local Health Board" means a body established under section 11 of that Act.

Effect of legal detention on ongoing entitlement to Adult Disability Payment

30.—(1) This regulation applies where an individual who has an ongoing entitlement to Adult Disability Payment begins a period of legal detention.
(2) For the purposes of this regulation, an individual is to be treated as though they are not in legal detention on any day on which they are an in-patient in a hospital or in a hospice.
(3) On the day after the day on which the individual has been in legal detention for 28 days, and for so long as the individual continues to be in legal detention, instead of the values set out in regulation 34 (amount and form of Adult Disability Payment)—
 (a) where the individual is aged 18 or over, the value of each component of Adult Disability Payment that is to be given to the individual is to be £0, or
 (b) where the individual is aged 16 or 17, the value of the daily living component of Adult Disability Payment that is to be given to the individual is to be £0.
(4) The 28 days referred to in paragraph (3) may comprise two or more separate periods, provided there is no more than one year between each period.
(5) Paragraph (3) of this regulation does not apply to an individual where—
 (a) the individual is undergoing legal detention outside the United Kingdom, and
 (b) in similar circumstances in Scotland, the individual would have been excepted from the application of that paragraph by virtue of the operation of any provision of this regulation.

Calculation of periods of time spent in a care home, hospital or legal detention

31.—(1) Subject to paragraphs (3) to (6), a period during which an individual is—
 (a) resident in a care home for the purpose of regulation 27,

(b) an in-patient in hospital or similar institution for the purpose of regulation 28,
(c) in legal detention for the purpose of regulation 30, or
(d) resident in a care home, an in-patient in a hospital or similar institution, or in legal detention for the purposes of regulation 32, is to be determined in accordance with this regulation.

(2) Such a period is to be taken to—
(a) begin on the day after the day on which the individual enters the place, and
(b) end on the day before the day on which the individual leaves the place.

(3) Where an individual takes a period of leave from a place mentioned in paragraph (1), the days on which the individual begins and returns from leave are not to be counted as days of residence in that place.

(4) Days constituting a period of leave are not to be counted as days of residence in a place.

(5) Where an individual enters a place ("the second place") under paragraph (1) as a result of transfer from another place ("the first place") under that paragraph—
(a) the day of transfer is to be counted as a day of residence in the second place, and
(b) for the purposes of calculating when the individual has been in the second place for 28 days for the purposes of regulations 27(2), 28(2) and 30(3)—
　(i) the days that they were resident in the first place are to be treated as days of residence in the second place,
　(ii) if they were resident in the first place for more than 28 days, the individual is to be treated as though they have been resident in the second place for 28 days on the day before the day of transfer, and
(c) the period of residence in the first place is deemed to end on the day on which the period of residence in the second place ends.

(6) For the purposes of this regulation, 'days of residence' means—
(a) days resident in a care home in terms of regulation 27 or 32,
(b) days as an in-patient in hospital or similar institution in terms of regulation 28 or 32, and
(c) days in legal detention in terms of regulation 30 or 32.

Entitlement beginning while in alternative accommodation

32.—(1) This regulation applies where an individual is resident in a care home, an in-patient in a hospital or similar institution, or in legal detention on the day on which their entitlement to Adult Disability Payment begins.

(2) On and after that day, and for so long as the individual continues to reside in a place mentioned in paragraph (1), instead of the values set out in regulation 34 (amount and form of Adult Disability Payment), the individual is to be given the value of £0—
(a) where the individual is resident in a care home, in respect of the daily living component of Adult Disability Payment,
(b) where the individual is—
　(i) aged 18 or over,

13.397

(ii) undergoing medical or other treatment as an in-patient in a hospital or similar institution, and
(iii) any of the costs of the treatment, accommodation and any related services provided for them are borne out of public funds within the meaning of regulation 28(4), in respect of each component of Adult Disability Payment, or
(c) where the individual is in legal detention and—
(i) aged 18 or over, in respect of either component of Adult Disability Payment,
(ii) aged 16 or 17, in respect of the daily living component of Adult Disability Payment.

(3) Paragraphs (1) and (2) do not apply where the individual is a resident in a care home, and the full costs of any qualifying services are met—
(a) entirely out of the resources of the individual for whom the qualifying services are provided,
(b) partly out of the resources of the individual for whom the qualifying services are provided and partly out of the resources of another person (other than a local authority) or assistance from a charity, or
(c) entirely out of the resources of another person (other than a local authority) or assistance from a charity.

(4) For the purposes of this regulation, an individual is not resident in a care home during any period when the individual is being looked after by a local authority and—
(a) has been placed temporarily in a private dwelling with a family, relative or some other suitable person while aged between 16 and 18 and receiving services under Part II of the Children (Scotland) Act 1995 by virtue of being a child in need within the meaning of section 93(4)(a)(ii) (impairment of health), or 93(4)(a)(iii) (disability) of that Act, or
(b) is accommodated in a care home outside the United Kingdom, where the costs of any qualifying services are met wholly or partly by a local authority pursuant to their powers under section 25 of the Education (Additional Support for Learning) (Scotland) Act 2004 (attendance at establishments outwith the United Kingdom).

PART 9

MAKING OF APPLICATIONS AND PAYMENTS AND DURATION OF ELIGIBILITY

Making Payments

33.—(1) Where Adult Disability Payment is payable in respect of an individual, the Scottish Ministers may, where they consider it appropriate, make the payment to another person to be used for the benefit of the individual.

(2) Where the Scottish Ministers consider, for any reason, that it is no longer appropriate for a particular person who falls within paragraph (1) to continue to receive the payment, they may cease making payment to that person.

(SSI 2022/54 reg.34)

Amount and form of Adult Disability Payment

34.—(1) The weekly rate of payment of the daily living component is, where the individual is entitled to—
(a) the standard rate, [¹ £72.65], or
(b) the enhanced rate, [¹ £108.55].
(2) The weekly rate of the mobility component is, where the individual is entitled to—
(a) the standard rate, [¹ £28.70], or
(b) the enhanced rate, [¹ £75.75].
(3) Where an individual is entitled to payment of the daily living component or the mobility component for a period shorter than one week, payment of that component is to be made at one-seventh of the relevant weekly rate, for each day of entitlement.
(4) For any week where an individual is entitled to—
(a) the daily living component of Adult Disability Payment, and
(b) payment of an amount in respect of constant attendance under section 104 of the Social Security Contributions and Benefits Act 1992,
the amount of the daily living component of Adult Disability Payment that is to be given to the individual is to be reduced by the amount paid under that section.
(5) For the purpose of calculating the amount of the daily living component that is to be given to the individual, in accordance with paragraph (3), where the amount in respect of constant attendance is equal to or greater than the amount of the daily living component of Adult Disability Payment, the value of the daily living component of Adult Disability Payment that is to be given to the individual is to be £0.
(6) For any week where an individual is entitled to—
(a) the mobility component of Adult Disability Payment, and
(b) payment of War Pensioners' Mobility Supplement within the meaning of—
   (i) the Naval, Military and Air Forces etc. (Disablement and Death) Service Pensions Order 1983 ("1983 Order"),
   (ii) the Personal Injuries (Civilians) Scheme 1983,
   (iii) the 1983 Order by virtue of the War Pensions (Naval Auxiliary Personnel) Scheme 1964,
   (iv) the Pensions (Polish Forces) Scheme 1964,
   (v) the War Pensions (Mercantile Marine) Scheme 1964, or
   (vi) an Order of Her Majesty in relation to the Home Guard dated 21 December 1964 or 22 December 1964, or in relation to the Ulster Defence Regiment dated 4 January 1971,
the amount of the mobility component of Adult Disability Payment that is to be given to the individual is to be £0.
(7) Adult Disability Payment is only to be given in the form of money, except as provided for by regulation 44 (Form of payment – giving Adult Disability Payment by way of deduction).

AMENDMENT

1. Social Security (Up-rating) (Miscellaneous Amendments) (Scotland) Regulations 2024 (SSI 2024/105) reg.2 (April 8, 2024, subject to a saving under reg.14 and Sch. para.1).

When an application is to be treated as made and beginning of entitlement to assistance

35.—(1) An application for Adult Disability Payment is to be treated as made—
   (a) on the day it is received by the Scottish Ministers, or
   (b) if applicable, on the day identified by the Scottish Ministers in accordance with paragraph (2).

(2) If, before making a determination on the basis of an application, the Scottish Ministers consider that the individual in respect of whom the application is made—
   (a) would not satisfy a requirement in—
      (i) regulation 5 (daily living component),
      (ii) regulation 6 (mobility component),
      (iii) regulation 11 (required period condition: daily living component),
      (iv) regulation 12 (required period condition: mobility component),
      (v) Part 5 (residence and presence conditions), or
      (vi) regulation 22 (age criteria),
      if the application were treated as made on the day it was received, and
   (b) would likely be entitled to receive Adult Disability Payment if those requirements were satisfied within a 13-week period beginning on the day it was received, the Scottish Ministers may choose the date within that 13 week period on which the application is to be treated as made.

(3) Where, on the basis of an application (other than where regulation 58(1) applies), a determination is made that an individual is entitled to Adult Disability Payment, the date on which entitlement begins is to be identified in accordance with paragraphs (4) to (6).

(4) Where an application is made within 8 weeks of the day on which the full name and date of birth of an individual ("the required data") is submitted by, or on behalf of, the individual to the Scottish Ministers for the purpose of an application for Adult Disability Payment, entitlement begins on whichever is the later of the day—
   (a) on which the required data was submitted, or
   (b) identified in accordance with paragraph (2).

(5) Subject to paragraph (6), where an application is made after the 8 week period described in paragraph (4), entitlement begins on the day on which the application is treated as made in accordance with paragraph (1).

(6) Where the Scottish Ministers are satisfied that there is a good reason why an application was made after the 8 week period described in paragraph (4), they may treat the application as having been made within that period.

(7) For the purposes of section 38(3) of the 2018 Act, the period covered by an application for Adult Disability Payment—
   (a) under paragraph (1)(a)—
      (i) begins on the day on which the application is treated as having been made, and
      (ii) ends on the day on which the determination of entitlement is made, and

(b) under paragraph (1)(b)—
  (i) is deemed to begin on the day before the determination of entitlement is made provided that the requirements are satisfied, and
  (ii) ends on the day on which the determination of entitlement is made.

Time of Payment

36. Where an award of Adult Disability Payment is made, the Scottish Ministers are to make—
(a) the first payment of assistance on a date specified in the notice of determination, and
(b) any subsequent payment—
  (i) 4 weekly in arrears, or
  (ii) where regulation 26 (entitlement under special rules for terminal illness) applies, weekly in advance.

Continuing Eligibility

37.—(1) Subject to paragraphs (3) and (4), a determination that an individual is entitled to Adult Disability Payment in respect of a period is to be made on the basis that the individual has an ongoing entitlement to Adult Disability Payment after the end of that period, except where paragraph (2) applies.

(2) This paragraph applies where, after the end of the period mentioned in paragraph (1), the individual no longer satisfies the eligibility rules.

(3) A determination of ongoing entitlement is made on the basis that—
(a) the individual will continue to be entitled to Adult Disability Payment for a fixed or indefinite period as specified in the notice of determination, and
(b) the decision that the individual is entitled to Adult Disability Payment for each subsequent 4-week period is to be taken in accordance with these Regulations, on the strength of the assumptions set out in paragraph (4).

(4) The assumptions are that—
(a) the individual continues to satisfy the eligibility criteria which were satisfied to be entitled to Adult Disability Payment under the determination mentioned in paragraph (1),
(b) the information on which the determination mentioned in paragraph (1) was made still applies and is relevant in the individual's case, and
(c) there is no change in circumstances of the individual which would require to be notified under section 56 (duty to notify change of circumstances) of the 2018 Act.

Circumstances in which assistance may be suspended

38.—(1) The Scottish Ministers may decide that an individual who has an ongoing entitlement to Adult Disability Payment in respect of a period by virtue of regulation 37 (continuing eligibility) is not to become entitled to be given some or all of either component or both components of that assistance at the time at which the individual otherwise would in accordance with that regulation, as read with regulation 36 (time of payment) (referred to in these Regulations as a decision to suspend the individual's Adult Disability Payment).

(2) Where such a decision is made in respect of an individual, payments of Adult Disability Payment to that individual are to be suspended until such a time as the Scottish Ministers decide that the individual is once again to become entitled to be given Adult Disability Payment.

(3) The Scottish Ministers may decide to suspend an individual's Adult Disability Payment only in the circumstances where—
  (a) section 54(1A) of the 2018 Act applies, or
  (b) the Scottish Ministers have made arrangements (whether under section 85A of the 2018 Act, section 85B of the 2018 Act or otherwise) for a person to receive the Adult Disability Payment on the individual's behalf, and the Scottish Ministers consider that it is necessary to suspend the Adult Disability Payment—
    (i) in order to protect the individual from the risk of financial abuse, or
    (ii) because the person with whom the Scottish Ministers have made arrangements is unable to continue to receive the Adult Disability Payment.

(4) In this regulation, "financial abuse" includes—
  (a) having money or other property stolen,
  (b) being defrauded,
  (c) being put under pressure in relation to money or other property,
  (d) having money or other property misused.

Having regard to financial circumstances

39. The Scottish Ministers must have regard to an individual's financial circumstances prior to making a decision to suspend payment to the individual of some or all of either component or both components of Adult Disability Payment.

Information to be given following suspension

40.—(1) Having made a decision to suspend an individual's Adult Disability Payment, the Scottish Ministers must inform the individual of—
  (a) their decision to suspend the individual's Adult Disability Payment,
  (b) the reasons for their decision,
  (c) any steps which might be taken by the individual in order for the Scottish Ministers to consider ending the suspension, and
  (d) the individual's right under regulation 41 to require the Scottish Ministers to review their decision to suspend the individual's Adult Disability Payment.

(2) The Scottish Ministers must fulfil their duty under paragraph (1) in a way that leaves the individual with a record of the information which the individual can show to, or otherwise share with, others.

Right to review suspension

41.—(1) An individual may require the Scottish Ministers to review their decision to suspend that individual's Adult Disability Payment.

(2) The Scottish Ministers must—

(a) complete a review mentioned in paragraph (1) within 31 days beginning with the day when they received notice from the individual requiring them to review their decision,
(b) inform the individual of the outcome of the review including reasons for their decision.

(3) The Scottish Ministers must fulfil their duty under paragraph (2)(b) in a way that leaves the individual with a record of the information which the individual can show to, or otherwise share with, others.

Ending a suspension

42. The Scottish Ministers are to make a decision to end a suspension where—
(a) the individual provides the information requested under section 54(1) of the 2018 Act and the Scottish Ministers consider that they do not require to make a determination without application,
(b) regulation 38(3)(a) applies and the Scottish Ministers make a determination without application under regulation 47 (consideration of entitlement after specified period), 48 (determination following change of circumstances, etc.), 49 (determination following official error – underpayments), 50 (determination following error – overpayments) or 51 (determination to effect a deduction decision),
(c) the Scottish Ministers make a determination under section 54(2) of the 2018 Act,
(d) the circumstances mentioned in regulation 38(3)(b) no longer apply, or
(e) the Scottish Ministers consider it appropriate in the circumstances, including having regard to the financial circumstances of the individual.

Effect of suspension ending

43. When—
(a) the suspension of an individual's Adult Disability Payment ends, and
(b) under the latest determination of the individual's entitlement to Adult Disability Payment relating to the period of the suspension the individual would have become entitled to be given Adult Disability Payment during that period,
the individual is immediately to be given the Adult Disability Payment that the individual would have become entitled to be given under the determination during the period of suspension.

Form of payment – giving Adult Disability Payment by way of deduction

44.—(1) Where an individual has a liability to the Scottish Ministers under section 63 of the 2018 Act (liability for assistance given in error), the individual's payment of Adult Disability Payment may be given (in whole or in part) by way of deduction, at a reasonable level, from that liability either—
(a) with the agreement of the individual, or
(b) without the individual's agreement, where the individual has unreasonably refused to agree to the assistance being given in that form.

(2) For the purpose of paragraph (1), "reasonable level" means a level that is reasonable having regard to the financial circumstances of the individual.

When an increase in level of entitlement takes effect

45.—(1) Where, as a result of a determination without an application, the amount of Adult Disability Payment payable in respect of an individual is increased or their entitlement to a component is awarded, the change takes effect—
- (a) in the case of an increase pursuant to a determination made under regulation [¹ 48(c), 48(d) or 48(e)] (determination following change of circumstances etc.) on the day after the day on which Personal Independence Payment [¹ or Disability Living Allowance] ceased to be paid in respect of the individual,
- (b) in the case of an award of entitlement to a component or an increase pursuant to a determination made in accordance with regulation 48(a) that affects their eligibility under regulation 5 (daily living component) or regulation 6 (mobility component), on the date when—
    - (i) if as a result of the individual reporting the change—
        - (aa) if the individual reports the change within one month of the change occurring, the individual first satisfies the requirements for a higher rate of the daily living or mobility component,
        - (bb) if the individual reports the change within more than one month but not more than 13 months of the change occurring, the individual first satisfies the requirements for a higher rate of the care or mobility component, but only if the Scottish Ministers consider that the individual had good reason for not notifying the change within one month, or
        - (cc) in any other case, the individual reports the change.
    - (ii) if as a result of the Scottish Ministers becoming aware that a determination of an individual's entitlement was made in ignorance of a material fact, on the date when the Scottish Ministers make the determination.
- (c) in the case of an earlier determination which was based on official error [¹ . . .] within the meaning of regulation 49 (determination following official error – underpayments) or on error within the meaning of regulation 50 (determination following error – overpayments), [¹ . . .] on the date when the earlier determination took effect, [¹ . . .]
- [¹ (ca) in the case of a determination made in accordance with regulation 48(a), where the period that an individual has been—
    - (i) resident in a care home for the purpose of regulation 27,
    - (ii) an in-patient in hospital or similar institution for the purpose of regulation 28,
    - (iii) in legal detention for the purpose of regulation 30, or
    - (iv) resident in a care home, an in-patient in a hospital or similar institution, or in legal detention for the purposes of regulation 32,

has come to an end, on the day on which the individual leaves the place, or]
(d) in any other case, on the date when the Scottish Ministers make the determination.

(2) Where the Scottish Ministers consider that in all the circumstances it would be unjust not to do so, they may, when making their determination, set an earlier date for the purposes of paragraph (1)(b), (c) or (d).

(3) This regulation does not apply to an individual to whom regulation 26 (entitlement under special rules for terminal illness) applies.

(4) Where an individual has previously received Adult Disability Payment for a period and a determination without application has subsequently been made that the same individual is entitled to Adult Disability Payment at a higher rate for that period, that individual will be entitled to the difference between the value of entitlement to Adult Disability Payment under the subsequent determination and the value of Adult Disability Payment to which that individual was previously entitled for that period.

AMENDMENT

1. Disability Assistance for Working Age People (Transitional Provisions and Miscellaneous Amendment) (Scotland) Regulations 2022 (SSI 2022/217) reg.19(1) and (8) (August 29, 2022).

When a decrease in level or cessation of entitlement takes effect

46.—(1) Where, as a result of determination without an application, the amount of Adult Disability Payment payable in respect of an individual is decreased or their entitlement to a component is ceased, the change takes effect—
  (a) in the case of a decrease pursuant to a determination made under regulation [1 48(c), 48(d) or 48(e)] (determination following change of circumstances etc.) on the day after the day on which Personal Independence Payment [1 or Disability Living Allowance] ceased to be paid in respect of the individual,
[2(aa) in the case of a determination without application under regulation 48(b), on the date of the individual's death,]
  (b) in the case of a determination without application under regulation 47 or 48(a), on the date—
    (i) where the individual was required to notify a change under section 56 of the 2018 Act, if the individual—
      (aa) knowingly fails to notify a change, or
      (bb) fails to notify the change as soon as reasonably practicable after it occurred,
    the individual should have notified the Scottish Ministers of the change, or
    (ii) in any other case, the Scottish Ministers make the determination,
  (c) in the case of an earlier determination which was based on official error [1 ...] within the meaning of regulation 49 (determination following official error–underpayments) or on error within the meaning of regulation 50 (determination following error–overpayments), on the date when the earlier determination took effect,

(d) in any other case, on the date when the Scottish Ministers make the determination.

(2) Where the Scottish Ministers consider that in all the circumstances it would be unjust not to do so, they may, when making their determination, set a later date for the purposes of paragraph (1)(b), (c) or (d).

AMENDMENTS

1. Disability Assistance for Working Age People (Transitional Provisions and Miscellaneous Amendment) (Scotland) Regulations 2022 (SSI 2022/217) reg.19(1) and (9) (August 29, 2022).

2. Disability Assistance (Miscellaneous Amendment) (Scotland) Regulations 2023 (SSI 2023/346) reg.4(3) (November 20, 2023).

PART 10

DETERMINATION OF ENTITLEMENT TO ADULT DISABILITY PAYMENT WITHOUT APPLICATION

Consideration of entitlement after specified period

47. The Scottish Ministers must make a determination of an individual's entitlement to Adult Disability Payment, without receiving an application, after the end of the period specified (if any) in—
  (a) the individual's notice of determination under section 40 or notice of re-determination under section 44 (as the case may be), or
  (b) a determination made by the First-tier Tribunal for Scotland under section 49, of the 2018 Act.

Determination following change of circumstances etc.

48. The Scottish Ministers must make a determination of an individual's entitlement to Adult Disability Payment, without receiving an application, where the individual has an ongoing entitlement to Adult Disability Payment and they become aware—
  (a) of a change of circumstances, whether or not notified by the individual in accordance with section 56 of the 2018 Act, or where the Scottish Ministers become aware that a determination of an individual's entitlement was made in ignorance of a material fact, which would possibly result in an alteration to the component or rate of Adult Disability Payment payable to the individual or which is likely to mean that the individual is no longer entitled to Adult Disability Payment,
  (b) that the individual has died,
  (c) of an alteration of the component or rate of award of Personal Independence Payment which the individual was entitled to immediately before the date of transfer to Adult Disability Payment in accordance with Part 3 of schedule 2 (transitional provisions) as a result of a decision made pursuant to—
    (i) a revision under Part 2 of the Universal Credit, Personal Independence Payment, Jobseeker's Allowance and Employment and Support Allowance (Decisions and Appeals) Regulations 2013,
    (ii) a supersession under Part 3 of those Regulations,
    (iii) an appeal under section 12 of the Social Security Act 1998 ("the 1998 Act"),

(SSI 2022/54 reg.48)

- (iv) a re-consideration under section 13 of the 1998 Act, or
- (v) an appeal to the Upper Tribunal under section 14 of the 1998 Act,
- (vi) a revision under article 10 of the Social Security (Northern Ireland) Order 1998 ("the 1998 Order"),
- (vii) a supersession under article 11 of the 1998 Order,
- (viii) an appeal under article 13 of the 1998 Order, or
- (ix) an appeal to the Commissioner under article 15 of the 1998 Order,

(d) of an alteration of the component or rate of award of Personal Independence Payment which the individual was entitled to immediately before moving to Scotland in circumstances in which regulation 52 (individuals in respect of whom Personal Independence Payment is paid in another part of the United Kingdom immediately before moving to Scotland) applies, as a result of a decision made pursuant to—
  - (i) a revision under Part 2 of the Universal Credit, Personal Independence Payment, Jobseeker's Allowance and Employment and Support Allowance (Decisions and Appeals) Regulations 2013,
  - (ii) a supersession under Part 3 of those Regulations,
  - (iii) an appeal under section 12 of the Social Security Act 1998 ("the 1998 Act"),
  - (iv) a re-consideration under section 13 of the 1998 Act,
  - (v) an appeal to the Upper Tribunal under section 14 of the 1998 Act,
  - (vi) a revision under article 10 of the Social Security (Northern Ireland) Order 1998 ("the 1998 Order"),
  - (vii) a supersession under article 11 of the 1998 Order,
  - (viii) an appeal under article 13 of the 1998 Order, or
  - (ix) an appeal to the Commissioner under article 15 of the 1998 Order.

[1 (e) of an alteration of the component or rate of award of Disability Living Allowance which the individual was entitled to immediately before the date of transfer to Adult Disability Payment in accordance with regulation 4 (determination without application of entitlement to Adult Disability Payment) of the Disability Assistance for Working Age People (Transitional Provisions and Miscellaneous Amendment) (Scotland) Regulations 2022, as a result of a decision made pursuant to—
  - (i) revision under regulation 3 of the Social Security and Child Support (Decisions and Appeals) Regulations 1999 ("the 1999 Regulations"),
  - (ii) a supersession under regulation 6 of the 1999 Regulations,
  - (iii) an appeal under section 12 of the Social Security Act 1998 ("the 1998 Act"),
  - (iv) a re-consideration under section 13 of the 1998 Act,
  - (v) an appeal to the Upper Tribunal under section 14 of the 1998 Act,
  - (vi) a revision under article 10 of the Social Security (Northern Ireland) Order 1998 ("the 1998 Order"),
  - (vii) a supersession under article 11 of the 1998 Order,
  - (viii) an appeal under article 13 of the 1998 Order, or
  - (ix) an appeal to the Commissioner under article 15 of the 1998 Order.]

AMENDMENT

1. Disability Assistance for Working Age People (Transitional Provisions and Miscellaneous Amendment) (Scotland) Regulations 2022 (SSI 2022/217) reg.19(1) and (10) (August 29, 2022).

Determination following official error – underpayments

49.—(1) The Scottish Ministers are to make a determination of an individual's entitlement to Adult Disability Payment, without receiving an application, where—
  (a) they have previously made a determination of the individual's entitlement to Adult Disability Payment ("the original determination"),
  (b) they establish that, due to an official error, the original determination was incorrect resulting in the individual—
    (i) not being given an award of Adult Disability Payment, or
    (ii) being given a lower award than that, to which the individual was entitled,
  (c) the Scottish Ministers are not considering a request for a re-determination of the individual's entitlement to the Payment, and
  (d) the individual has not appealed to the First-tier Tribunal for Scotland against the Scottish Ministers' determination of the individual's entitlement to Adult Disability Payment.

(2) In making a determination required by paragraph (1) the Scottish Ministers are to use—
  (a) the information—
    (i) provided in the application that led to the original determination,
    (ii) any other information they have obtained in connection with that application, and
  (b) any other information they have obtained in connection with the individual's entitlement to Adult Disability Payment.

(3) In this regulation, "official error" means an error made by someone acting on behalf of the Scottish Ministers or on behalf of a Minister of the Crown that was not materially contributed to by anyone else.

Determination following error – overpayments

50.—(1) The Scottish Ministers are to make a determination of an individual's entitlement to Adult Disability Payment, without receiving an application, where—
  (a) they have previously made a determination of the individual's entitlement to Adult Disability Payment ("the original determination"),
  (b) they establish that, due to an error, the original determination was incorrect resulting in the individual being given—
    (i) an award of Adult Disability Payment to which the individual was not entitled, or
    (ii) a higher award than that to which the individual was entitled,
  (c) the Scottish Ministers are not considering a request for a re-determination of the individual's entitlement to the Payment, and
  (d) the individual has not made an appeal to the First-tier Tribunal for Scotland or Upper Tribunal against the Scottish Ministers' determination off the individual's entitlement to Adult Disability Payment, that has not yet been determined.

(2) In making a determination required by paragraph (1) the Scottish Ministers are to use—
- (a) the information—
  - (i) provided in the application that led to the original determination, and
  - (ii) any other information they have obtained in connection with that application,
- (b) any other information they have obtained in connection with the individual's entitlement to Adult Disability Payment, and
- (c) any other information available to them that is relevant to their consideration of whether the individual is entitled to Adult Disability Payment.

(3) In this regulation references to an "error" are to—
- (a) an error in the performance of a function conferred by these Regulations or the 2018 Act, including a determination being made—
  - (i) wrongly, or
  - (ii) correctly but on the basis of—
    - (aa) incorrect information, or
    - (bb) an assumption which proves to be wrong, or
- (b) a new determination having not been made after an assumption on the basis of which an earlier determination was made has proven to be wrong.

Determination to effect a deduction decision

51.—(1) The Scottish Ministers are to make a determination of an individual's entitlement to Adult Disability Payment, without receiving an application, where the circumstances in paragraphs (2) and (3) apply.

(2) This paragraph applies where—
- (a) regulation 44 (form of payment – giving Adult Disability Payment by way of deduction) allows Adult Disability Payment to be given to the individual by way of deduction, or
- (b) Adult Disability Payment is being given to the individual by way of deduction, and the Scottish Ministers consider that may no longer be appropriate.

(3) This paragraph applies where the Scottish Ministers have decided to—
- (a) vary the amount of Adult Disability Payment to be given by way of deduction (including introducing a deduction, where the full amount of Adult Disability Payment was previously given as money),
- (b) vary any period for which the individual's Adult Disability Payment is to be given by way of deduction, that may have been specified in a previous determination of the individual's entitlement, or
- (c) cease making deductions, and instead give the individual's Adult Disability Payment in the form of money.

(4) The Scottish Ministers are to make a determination, without receiving an application, where an individual who is receiving Adult Disability Payment by way of deduction under a previous determination of entitlement notifies the Scottish Ministers that the individual—

The Social Security Information-sharing (Scotland) Regulations 2021

   (a) withdraws their agreement to their Adult Disability Payment being given by way of deduction,
   (b) wishes the Scottish Ministers to increase the amount of their Adult Disability Payment that is given by way of deduction,
   (c) wishes the Scottish Ministers to decrease the amount of their Adult Disability Payment that is given by way of deduction (including ceasing the deduction), or
   (d) wishes the Scottish Ministers to amend the length of any period referred to in paragraph (3)(b).

PART 11

MOVEMENT OF INDIVIDUALS BETWEEN SCOTLAND AND THE REST OF THE UNITED KINGDOM

Individuals in respect of whom Personal Independence Payment is paid in another part of the United Kingdom immediately before moving to Scotland

52.—(1) Where an individual—
   (a) becomes resident in Scotland,
   (b) was resident in another part of the United Kingdom, and
   (c) was entitled to Personal Independence Payment immediately before the date of the move,
the Scottish Ministers are to make a determination without application of the individual's entitlement to Adult Disability Payment.

(2) Entitlement to Adult Disability Payment under paragraph (1) begins on the day after the day on which the individual's entitlement to Personal Independence Payment ends.

(3) In this regulation, "the date of the move" is the date when the individual becomes resident in Scotland, as notified by the individual or otherwise communicated to the Scottish Ministers (whether the notification takes place before or after the date of the move).

Individuals in respect of whom Adult Disability Payment is paid at the time of moving to another part of the United Kingdom

53.—(1) Where the Scottish Ministers become aware that an individual who is entitled to Adult Disability Payment has moved or is to move to become resident in another part of the United Kingdom, the individual is to be treated as though the individual meets the condition under regulation 15(1)(a) of being ordinarily resident in Scotland for a period of 13 weeks beginning in accordance with paragraph (4).

(2) Subject to Part 8 (effect of time spent in care homes, hospital and legal detention), where the Scottish Ministers become aware that an individual has moved or is to move to another part of the United Kingdom mentioned in paragraph (1), they are to make a determination without application at the end of the 13 week period mentioned in paragraph (1) that the individual's entitlement to Adult Disability Payment is to terminate.

(3) Where before the end of the 13-week period, the Scottish Ministers become aware that the individual is no longer to move to become resident in another part of the United Kingdom, the duty in paragraph (2) does not apply.

(4) The 13-week period mentioned in paragraph (1) begins on the date the individual ceases to be ordinarily resident in Scotland.

(5) On the day after the 13-week period specified in paragraph (4) ends—
  (a) entitlement to Adult Disability Payment ceases, and
  (b) regulation 50 (determination following error – overpayments) applies to any Adult Disability Payment paid to an individual in relation to a period after the end of that 13-week period.

PART 12

PERIODS IN RESPECT OF A RE-DETERMINATION REQUEST

Periods in respect of a re-determination request

54.—(1) The period for requesting a re-determination of entitlement to Adult Disability Payment under section 41 of the 2018 Act (right to request re-determination) is 42 days beginning with the day that the individual is informed, in accordance with section 40 of the 2018 Act (notice of determination), of the right to make the request.

(2) In relation to determining entitlement to Adult Disability Payment, the period allowed for re-determination (within the meaning of section 43 of the 2018 Act (duty to re-determine)) is 56 days beginning with—
  (a) the day that the request for a re-determination is received by the Scottish Ministers,
  (b) in a case where the request for a re-determination is received by the Scottish Ministers outwith the period prescribed in paragraph (1), the day on which it is decided by the Scottish Ministers or (as the case may be) the First-tier Tribunal for Scotland that the individual in question has a good reason for not requesting a re-determination sooner, or
  (c) in a case where the Scottish Ministers have informed the individual of their decision that the request for re-determination was not made in such form as the Scottish Ministers require, the day on which it is subsequently decided by the First-Tier Tribunal for Scotland that the individual in question has made the request in such form as the Scottish Ministers require.

PART 13

PROVISION OF VEHICLES

Payment of mobility component to authorised providers of vehicles for inividuals with disabilities

55.—(1) Where—
  (a) an individual is entitled to the enhanced rate of the mobility component of Adult Disability Payment, and
  (b) the individual has entered into an agreement with an authorised provider of vehicles for persons with disabilities for the hire or hire-purchase of a vehicle,

the Scottish Ministers may, with the consent of the individual, pay that component (in whole or in part) to the provider to be used to meet, or contribute towards meeting, the individual's liability under the agreement.

(2) The Scottish Ministers must cease to make payments in accordance with paragraph (1) in the event that—
  (a) the agreement is brought to an end in accordance with the terms of the agreement, or
  (b) the individual withdraws their consent.

Vehicles for persons with disabilities – powers of appointees

56.—(1) Where a person ("an appointee") is appointed by the Scottish Ministers under the 2018 Act to act on an individual's behalf in connection with the determination of the individual's entitlement to assistance under section 24 (duty to give assistance) of the 2018 Act, in addition to the powers conferred on the appointee by that Act the appointee can, on behalf of the individual—
  (a) enter into an agreement with an authorised provider of vehicles for the hire or hire-purchase of a vehicle,
  (b) terminate any such agreement,
  (c) for the purpose of regulation 55(1), give consent to the Scottish Ministers to pay (in whole or in part) the mobility component to which the individual is entitled to the provider, and
  (d) withdraw any such consent.

(2) An appointee may exercise the powers conferred by paragraphs (1)(b) and (d) whether the agreement was entered into, or the consent given, by the appointee or by any other person.

PART 14

INITIAL PERIOD FOR APPLICATIONS

Initial period for applications

57. Part 2 of schedule 2 makes provision about the initial period for applications.

PART 15

APPLICATIONS FOR ADULT DISABILITY PAYMENT BY INDIVIDUALS ENTITLED TO CHILD DISABILITY PAYMENT

Applications by individuals entitled to Child Disability Payment

58.—[²(1) This regulation applies where an individual who is entitled to Child Disability Payment submits the required data in terms of regulation 35(4) on a day on which the individual is still entitled to Child Disability Payment and makes an application for Adult Disability Payment—

(a) on a day on which the individual is still entitled to Child Disability Payment,
(b) on a day on which the individual is no longer entitled to Child Disability Payment, where that day falls within the period of 8 weeks starting on the day on which the individual submitted the required data, or
(c) on a day on which the individual is no longer entitled to Child Disability Payment, where that day is after the expiry of the 8 week period mentioned in sub-paragraph (b) and the Scottish Ministers are satisfied that there is good reason why the application was not made sooner.]

[²(2) Where, on the basis of that application, the Scottish Ministers make a determination of the individual's entitlement to Adult Disability Payment ("Adult Disability Payment determination"), and on the date of that determination—
(a) the individual is still entitled to Child Disability Payment, the date on which their entitlement to Adult Disability Payment begins is to be—
(i) the day after the first day on which the individual is to be paid Child Disability Payment after the date of the Adult Disability Payment determination in accordance with regulation 25(b)(i) of the Disability Assistance for Children and Young People (Scotland) Regulations 2021, or
(ii) 7 days after the first day on which the individual is to be paid Child Disability Payment after the date of the Adult Disability Payment determination in accordance with regulation 25(b)(ii) of the Disability Assistance for Children and Young People (Scotland) Regulations 2021,
(b) the individual is no longer entitled to Child Disability Payment, the date on which their entitlement to Adult Disability Payment begins is to be the date on which the Scottish Ministers make the Adult Disability Payment determination.]

[¹ (3) Where an individual receives a determination that they are entitled to a rate of Adult Disability Payment which is higher than the rate of Child Disability Payment they were entitled to immediately before their entitlement to Adult Disability Payment begins, paragraph (4) applies.

(4) The individual is to receive a payment equal to the value of Adult Disability Payment they would have received for the period specified in paragraph (5), reduced by the amount of Child Disability Payment that they were entitled to for the same period.

(5) The period specified for the purposes of paragraph (4) is the period between the date—
(a) their entitlement to Adult Disability Payment would have begun if this regulation did not apply to the individual, in terms of regulation 35(4) to (6), and
(b) their entitlement to Adult Disability Payment begins in terms of paragraph (2).]

AMENDMENTS

1. Disability Assistance for Working Age People (Transitional Provisions and Miscellaneous Amendment) (Scotland) Regulations 2022 (SSI 2022/217) reg.19(1) and (11) (August 29, 2022).

2. Disability Assistance (Miscellaneous Amendment) (Scotland) Regulations 2023 (SSI 2023/346) reg.4(4) (November 20, 2023).

Determination without an application - terminal illness

59.—(1) Where an individual is entitled to Child Disability Payment and has a terminal illness in terms of regulation 15 of the Disability Assistance for Children and Young People (Scotland) Regulations 2021, the Scottish Ministers are to make a determination of the individual's entitlement to Adult Disability Payment, without receiving an application, where—
   (a) the individual—
      (i) has reached the age of 16, and
      (ii) makes a request that the Scottish Ministers make a determination of their entitlement to Adult Disability Payment, or
   (b) the individual—
      (i) has reached the age of 18, and
      (ii) has not informed the Scottish Ministers that they do not want to receive Adult Disability Payment.

(2) Where the Scottish Ministers make a determination under paragraph (1)—
   (a) no judgement will be required in terms of regulation 26(7) and (8) (entitlement under special rules for terminal illness), and
   (b) regulation 26 applies with the following modifications—
      (i) for paragraph (4), read "The individual's entitlement to the rates referred to in paragraph (1) begins on the date on which the Scottish Ministers make the determination in terms of regulation 58(1).", and
      (ii) paragraph (5) and (6) are omitted.

Part 16

Transfer from Personal Independence Payment to Adult Disability Payment

Transfer from Personal Independence Payment to Adult Disability Payment

60. Part 3 of schedule 2 makes provision about transferring from Personal Independence Payment to Adult Disability Payment.

Part 17

Qualifications and experience necessary to carry out assessments

Qualifications and experience necessary to carry out assessments

61.—(1) A person is to be regarded as a suitably qualified person, within the meaning of section 13(1) of the 2018 Act, for the purpose of carrying out assessments if they satisfy the requirements specified in paragraph (2) or (4).

(2) A person is a suitably qualified person for the purpose of carrying out assessments under this paragraph if—
(a) the person meets one of the conditions under paragraph (3),
(b) the person has been employed in a capacity described in paragraph (3) in the provision to individuals of health care or social care services,
(c) where the assessment will involve consideration of the individual's mental condition or conditions, the person's employment in the provision of health care or social care services under paragraph (2)(b) included the provision of health care or social care services to individuals with mental conditions, and
(d) where the assessment will involve consideration of the individual's learning disability or disabilities, the person's employment in the provision of health care or social care services under paragraph (2)(b) included the provision of health care or social care services to individuals with learning disabilities.

(3) The conditions referred to in paragraph (2)(a) are that the person, at the time of carrying out the assessment—
(a) is an allied health professional with valid registration in the register maintained by the Health and Care Professions Council under article 5 of the Health Professions Order 2001,
(b) is an adult, learning disability, or mental health nurse with valid registration in the register maintained by the Nursing and Midwifery Council under article 5 of the Nursing and Midwifery Order 2001, or
(c) is a social worker with valid registration in the register maintained by the Scottish Social Services Council under section 44 of the Regulation of Care (Scotland) Act 2001.

(4) A person is a suitably qualified person for the purpose of carrying out assessments under this paragraph if—
(a) the person has achieved a social care qualification to a minimum of Level 9 of the Scottish Credit and Qualifications Framework,
(b) immediately prior to their employment for the purpose of carrying out assessments, the person was registered as a social service worker in the register maintained by the Scottish Social Services Council under section 44 of the Regulation of Care (Scotland) Act 2001,
(c) the person has been employed, in the provision to individuals of health care or social care services, as a social service worker with valid registration in the register maintained by the Scottish Social Services Council under section 44 of the Regulation of Care (Scotland) Act 2001,
(d) where the assessment will involve consideration of the individual's mental condition or conditions, the person's employment in the provision of health care or social care services under paragraph (4)(c) included the provision of health care or social care services to individuals with mental conditions, and
(e) where the assessment will involve consideration of the individual's learning disability or disabilities, the person's employment in the provision of health care or social care services under paragraph (4)(c) included the provision of health care or social care services to individuals with learning disabilities.

(5) In this regulation, "health and social care services" means services which require to be provided by an individual meeting the conditions under paragraph (3) or (4)(c).

PART 18

SHORT-TERM ASSISTANCE

Entitlement to short-term assistance

13.427   **62.** Part 1 of schedule 2 makes provision about short-term assistance.

PART 19

CONSEQUENTIAL AMENDMENT

Consequential amendment

13.428   **63.** The amendment specified in Part 4 of schedule 2 has effect.

PART 20

TRANSITORY PROVISION

Transitory provision – initial period for applications

13.429   **64.**—(1) During the initial period for applications, in addition to meeting the residence and presence conditions in Part 5, an individual must be resident in one of the local authority areas specified in relation to the relevant phase of that period in paragraph 6 of Part 2 of schedule 2 on the date their application is received by the Scottish Ministers.

(2) In this regulation and in Part 2 of schedule 2, "initial period for applications" means the period beginning with 21 March 2022 and ending with 29 August 2022.

(3) The initial period for applications comprises three phases—
  (a) phase 1, beginning with 21 March 2022 and ending with 19 June 2022,
  (b) phase 2, beginning with 20 June 2022 and ending with 24 July 2022, and
  (c) phase 3, beginning with 25 July 2022 and ending with 29 August 2022.

Exclusion to transitory provision

13.430   **65.**—(1) An individual who has made a claim for Personal Independence Payment prior to 21 March 2022 which has not yet been decided is not entitled to be paid Adult Disability Payment during the initial period for applications.

(2) In paragraph (1) a claim for Personal Independence Payment is decided if it has—

(SSI 2022/54 reg. 65)

(a) been decided by the Secretary of State under section 8 (decisions by Secretary of State) of the Social Security Act 1998,
(b) been withdrawn in accordance with regulation 31 (withdrawal of claim) of the Universal Credit, Personal Independence Payment, Jobseeker's Allowance and Employment and Support Allowance (Claims and Payments) Regulations 2013, or
(c) otherwise is no longer to be decided by the Secretary of State as mentioned in sub-paragraph (a).

SCHEDULE 1   Regulation 2

Part 1

Adult Disability Payment Determination

Interpretation
1. In this schedule—
"aided" means with—
  (a) the use of an aid or appliance, or
  (b) supervision, prompting or assistance,
"assistance" means physical intervention by another person and does not include speech,
"assistance dog" means a dog trained to guide or assist a person with a sensory impairment,
"basic verbal information" means information in the individual's native language conveyed verbally in a simple sentence and excludes information that is not communicated orally or received aurally,
"basic written information" means signs, symbols and dates written or printed in standard size text in the individual's native language,
"bathe" includes get into or out of an unadapted bath or shower,
"communication support" means support from a person trained or experienced in communicating with people in general, or the individual in particular, with specific communication needs, including interpreting verbal information into a non-verbal form and vice versa,
"complex budgeting decisions" means decisions involving—
  (a) calculating household and personal budgets,
  (b) managing and paying bills, and
  (c) planning future purchases,
"complex verbal information" means information in the individual's native language conveyed verbally in either more than one sentence or one complicated sentence and excludes information that is not communicated orally or received aurally,
"complex written information" means more than one sentence of written or printed standard size text in the individual's native language,
"cook" means heat food at or above waist height,
"dress" includes put on socks and shoes,
"engage socially" means—
  (a) interact with others in a contextually and socially appropriate manner,
  (b) understand body language, and
  (c) establish relationships,
"follow the route of a journey" means for an individual to navigate and make their way along a planned route to a planned destination,
"manage medication" means take medication which improves the individual's symptoms or health, or, take medication where failure to do so is likely to result in a deterioration in the individual's health,
"manage therapy" means undertake therapy which improves the individual's symptoms or health, or, undertake therapy where a failure to do so is likely to result in a deterioration in the individual's health,
"medication" means medication to be taken at home which is prescribed or recommended by a—
  (a) registered—

13.431

(i) medical practitioner,
(ii) nurse,
(iii) pharmacist, or
(b) health professional who is registered by the Health and Care Professions Council,

"monitor a health condition" means—
(a) detect significant changes in the individual's health condition which are likely to lead to a deterioration in the individual's health, and
(b) take action advised by a—
(i) registered medical practitioner,
(ii) registered nurse, or
(iii) health professional who is registered by the Health and Care Professions Council,
without which the individual's health is likely to deteriorate,

"orientation aid" means a specialist aid designed to assist disabled people to follow a route safely,

"prepare", in the context of food, means make food ready for cooking or eating,

"prompting" means reminding, encouraging or explaining by another person,

"psychological distress" means distress related to an enduring mental condition or an intellectual or cognitive impairment,

"read" includes read signs, symbols and words but does not include read Braille,

"simple budgeting decisions" means decisions involving—
(a) calculating the cost of goods, and
(b) calculating change required after a purchase,

"simple meal" means a cooked one-course meal for one using fresh ingredients,

"social support" means support from a person trained or experienced in assisting people in general, or the individual in particular, to engage in social situations,

"stand" means stand upright with at least one biological foot on the ground,

"supervision" means the continuous presence of another person for the purpose of ensuring an individual's safety,

"take nutrition" means—
(a) cut food into pieces, convey food and drink to one's mouth and chew and swallow food and drink, or
(b) ingest nutrition by using a therapeutic source,

"therapeutic source" means parenteral or enteral tube feeding, using a rate-limiting device such as a delivery system or feed pump,

"therapy" means therapy to be undertaken at home which is prescribed or recommended by a—
(a) registered—
(i) medical practitioner,
(ii) nurse, or
(iii) pharmacist, or
(b) health professional regulated by Health and Care Professions Council,
but does not include taking or applying, or otherwise receiving or administering, medication (whether orally, topically or by any other means), or any action which, in the individual's case, falls within the definition of "monitor a health condition",

"toilet needs" means—
(a) getting on and off an unadapted toilet,
(b) evacuating the bladder and bowel, and
(c) cleaning oneself afterwards,

"unaided" means without—
(a) the use or aid of an appliance, or
(b) supervision, prompting or assistance,

"undress" includes take off socks and shoes.

(SSI 2022/54 reg.65)

PART 2

DAILY LIVING ACTIVITIES

Activity	Descriptors	Points
1. Preparing food.	a. Can prepare and cook a simple meal unaided.	0
	b. Needs to use an aid or appliance to be able to either prepare or cook a simple meal.	2
	c. Cannot cook a simple meal using a conventional cooker but is able to do so using a microwave.	2
	d. Needs prompting to be able to either prepare or cook a simple meal.	2
	e. Needs supervision or assistance to either prepare or cook a simple meal.	4
	f. Cannot prepare and cook food.	8
2. Taking nutrition.	a. Can take nutrition unaided.	0
	b. Needs— (i) to use an aid or appliance to be able to take nutrition, or (ii) supervision to be able to take nutrition, or (iii) assistance to be able to cut up food.	2
	c. Needs a therapeutic source to be able to take nutrition.	2
	d. Needs prompting to be able to take nutrition.	4
	e. Needs assistance to be able to manage a therapeutic source to take nutrition.	6
	f. Cannot convey food and drink to their mouth and needs another person to do so.	10
3. Managing therapy or monitoring a health condition.	a. Either— (i) does not receive medication or therapy or need to monitor a health condition, or (ii) can manage medication or therapy or monitor a health condition unaided.	0
	b. Needs any one or more of the following— (i) to use an aid or appliance to be able to manage medication, (ii) supervision, prompting or assistance to be able to manage medication, (iii) supervision, prompting or assistance to be able to monitor a health condition.	1
	c. Needs supervision, prompting or assistance to be able to manage therapy that takes no more than 3.5 hours a week.	2
	d. Needs supervision, prompting or assistance to be able to manage therapy that takes more than 3.5 but no more than 7 hours a week.	4
	e. Needs supervision, prompting or assistance to be able to manage therapy that takes more than 7 but no more than 14 hours a week.	6
	f. Needs supervision, prompting or assistance to be able to manage therapy that takes more than 14 hours a week.	8
4. Washing and bathing.	a. Can wash and bathe unaided.	0
	b. Needs to use an aid or appliance to be able to wash or bathe.	2
	c. Needs supervision or prompting to be able to wash or bathe.	2
	d. Needs assistance to be able to wash either their hair or body below the waist.	2

Activity	Descriptors	Points
	e. Needs assistance to be able to get in or out of an unadapted bath or shower.	3
	f. Needs assistance to be able to wash their body between the shoulders and waist.	4
	g. Cannot wash and bathe at all and needs another person to wash their entire body.	8
5. Managing toilet needs or incontinence.	a. Can manage toilet needs or incontinence unaided.	0
	b. Needs to use an aid or appliance to be able to manage toilet needs or incontinence.	2
	c. Needs supervision or prompting to be able to manage toilet needs.	2
	d. Needs assistance to be able to manage toilet needs.	4
	e. Needs assistance to be able to manage incontinence of either bladder or bowel.	6
	f. Needs assistance to be able to manage incontinence of both bladder and bowel.	8
6. Dressing and undressing.	a. Can dress and undress unaided.	0
	b. Needs to use an aid or appliance to be able to dress or undress.	2
	c. Needs either— (i) prompting to be able to dress, undress or determine appropriate circumstances for remaining clothed, or (ii) prompting or assistance to be able to select appropriate clothing.	2
	d. Needs assistance to be able to dress or undress their lower body.	2
	e. Needs assistance to be able to dress or undress their upper body.	4
	f. Cannot dress or undress at all.	8
7. Communicating verbally.	a. Can express and understand basic and complex verbal information unaided.	0
	b. Needs to use an aid or appliance to be able to speak or hear.	2
	c. Needs communication support to be able to express or understand complex verbal information.	4
	d. Needs communication support to be able to express or understand basic verbal information.	8
	e. Cannot express or understand verbal information at all even with communication support.	12
8. Reading and understanding signs, symbols and words.	a. Can read and understand basic and complex written information either unaided or using spectacles or contact lenses.	0
	b. Needs to use an aid or appliance, other than spectacles or contact lenses, to be able to read or understand either basic or complex written information.	2
	c. Needs prompting to be able to read or understand complex written information.	2
	d. Needs prompting to be able to read or understand basic written information.	4
	e. Cannot read or understand signs, symbols or words at all.	8
9. Engaging socially with other people face to face.	a. Can engage socially with other people unaided.	0
	b. Needs prompting to be able to engage socially with other people.	2
	c. Needs social support to be able to engage socially with other people.	4

(SSI 2022/54 Sch.1)

Activity	Descriptors	Points
	d. Cannot engage socially with other people due to such engagement causing either— (i) overwhelming psychological distress to the individual, or (ii) the individual to exhibit behaviour which would result in substantial risk of harm to the individual or another person.	8
10. Making budgeting decisions.	a. Can manage complex budgeting decisions unaided.	0
	b. Needs prompting or assistance to be able to make complex budgeting decisions.	2
	c. Needs prompting or assistance to be able to make simple budgeting decisions.	4
	d. Cannot make any budgeting decisions at all.	6

PART 3

MOBILITY ACTIVITIES

13.433

Activity	Descriptors	Points
1. Planning and following journeys.	a. Can plan and follow the route of a journey unaided.	0
	b. Needs the prompting of another person to be able to undertake any journey to avoid overwhelming psychological distress to the individual.	4
	c. Cannot plan the route of a journey.	8
	d. Cannot follow the route of an unfamiliar journey without another person, assistance dog or orientation aid.	10
	e. Cannot undertake any journey because it would cause overwhelming psychological distress to the individual.	10
	f. Cannot follow the route of a familiar journey without another person, an assistance dog or an orientation aid.	12
2. Moving around.	a. Can stand and then move more than 200 metres, either aided or unaided.	0
	b. Can stand and then move more than 50 metres but no more than 200 metres, either aided or unaided.	4
	c. Can stand and then move unaided more than 20 metres but no more than 50 metres either aided or unaided.	8
	d. Can stand and then move using an aid or appliance more than 20 metres but no more than 50 metres, either aided or unaided.	10
	e. Can stand and then move more than 1 metre but no more than 20 metres, either aided or unaided.	12
	f. Cannot, either aided or unaided,— (i) stand, or (ii) move more than 1 metre.	12

The Social Security Information-sharing (Scotland) Regulations 2021

SCHEDULE 2   Regulation 2

PART 1

SHORT-TERM ASSISTANCE

Entitlement to short-term assistance

1.—(1) Subject to sub-paragraph (2), an individual who is, or was, entitled to Adult Disability Payment under a determination made on the
basis that the individual has ongoing entitlement is entitled to short-term assistance where—
  (a) a determination of the individual's entitlement to Adult Disability Payment ("earlier determination") has been superseded by a subsequent determination ("subsequent determination") which has the effect that the individual is—
    (i) no longer entitled to Adult Disability Payment, or
    (ii) entitled to a lower amount of Adult Disability Payment,
  (b) the individual's entitlement to Adult Disability Payment is under review within the meaning of—
    (i) paragraph 1(2) of schedule 10 of the 2018 Act, or
    (ii) sub-paragraph (2), and
  (c) the individual—
    (i) continues to meet the conditions as to residence and presence set out in Part 5, or
    (ii) has transferred to become resident in another part of the United Kingdom, and the matter under review is the determination of entitlement for the 13-week period beginning in accordance with regulation 53(4) (individuals in respect of whom Adult Disability Payment is paid at the time of moving to another part of the United Kingdom).

(2) An individual's entitlement to Adult Disability Payment is under review in terms of sub-paragraph (1)(b)(ii) if—
  (a) a decision of the First-tier Tribunal for Scotland under section 49 of the 2018 Act, in relation to the subsequent determination of the individual's entitlement to Adult Disability Payment mentioned in sub-paragraph (1)(a), is set aside after a review under section 43(2) of the Tribunals (Scotland) Act 2014 ("the 2014 Act"), and
  (b) the First-tier Tribunal for Scotland decide not to uphold a determination of an individual's entitlement to Adult Disability Payment in an appeal under section 46 of the 2018 Act and the First-tier Tribunal for Scotland are to make a determination of the individual's entitlement to Adult Disability Payment under section 49 of the 2018 Act.

(3) Where—
  (a) an individual's entitlement to Adult Disability Payment is set aside after a review in terms of sub-paragraph (2)(a), and
  (b) the individual had previously been awarded short-term assistance on the basis that their entitlement to Adult Disability Payment was under review by the First-tier Tribunal prior to it making the decision that has been set aside,
the Scottish Ministers are to make a determination without application of the individual's entitlement to short-term assistance.

(4) Where—
  (a) the First-tier Tribunal for Scotland set aside a decision by the Scottish Ministers not to accept a request for a re-determination of the individual's entitlement to Adult Disability Payment mentioned in sub-paragraph (1)(a), and
  (b) the Scottish Ministers had previously determined, pursuant to an application made by the individual, that the individual was not entitled to short-term assistance on the basis that the subsequent determination referred to in sub-paragraph (1)(a) was not under review,
the Scottish Ministers are to make a determination without application of the individual's entitlement to short-term assistance.

(5) An individual is not entitled to short-term assistance where the individual is no longer entitled to Adult Disability Payment as a result of a subsequent determination made under regulation 48(b) (determination following change of circumstances etc.).

(6) An individual to whom regulation 27(2) (effect of admission to a care home on ongoing entitlement to daily living component), regulation 28(2) (effect of admission to hospital on

ongoing entitlement to Adult Disability Payment), regulation 30(3) (effect of legal detention on ongoing entitlement to daily living component), or regulation 32(2) (entitlement beginning while in alternative accommodation) applies is not entitled to short-term assistance in respect of the component or components for which the value is to be £0 under those regulations.

(7) Where the Scottish Ministers have made a determination under section 37 of the 2018 Act (duty to make determination) that an individual is entitled to short-term assistance, entitlement to short-term assistance begins—
  (a) where a request is made under section 41 of the 2018 Act (right to request re-determination) for a re-determination of the individual's entitlement to Adult Disability Payment mentioned in sub-paragraph (1)(a), on the day that request is made,
  (b) where a notice of appeal is submitted under section 47 of the 2018 Act (initiating an appeal) against the determination of the individual's entitlement to Adult Disability Payment mentioned in sub-paragraph (1)(a), on the day that request is made,
  (c) where a decision of the Scottish Ministers is made not to accept a request for a re-determination of the individual's entitlement to Adult Disability Payment mentioned in sub-paragraph (1)(a), on the day that decision is set aside by the First-tier Tribunal for Scotland,
  (d) where a request is made under section 48(1)(b) of the 2018 Act (deadline for appealing) for permission to appeal the determination of the individual's entitlement to Adult Disability Payment mentioned in sub-paragraph (1)(a), on the day that request is made, or
  (e) where a decision of the First-tier Tribunal for Scotland under section 49 of the 2018 Act, in relation to the subsequent determination of the individual's entitlement to Adult Disability Payment mentioned in sub-paragraph (1)(a), is set aside after a review under section 43(2) of the 2014 Act (review of decisions) and the First-tier Tribunal for Scotland are to make a determination of the individual's entitlement to Adult Disability Payment under section 49 of the 2018 Act, on the day that the decision is set aside.

(8) Regulation 54 (periods in respect of a re-determination request) applies to short-term assistance in the same way as it applies to Adult Disability Payment.

Value and form

2.—(1) The value of short-term assistance payable is to be the difference between the amount of Adult Disability Payment to which the individual was entitled under the earlier determination mentioned in paragraph 1(1)(a), and the amount of Adult Disability Payment the individual is entitled to under the subsequent determination mentioned in paragraph 1(1)(a).

(2) The form in which the short-term assistance is to be given is to be the same as the form in which Adult Disability Payment was given under the earlier determination.

(3) Where the mobility component was being paid by the Scottish Ministers to an authorised provider of vehicles for persons with disabilities in accordance with regulation 55(1) (payment of mobility component to authorised provider of vehicles for individuals with disabilities) on the day before an individual's entitlement to the mobility component ended as a result of a subsequent determination mentioned in paragraph 1(1)(a)—
  (a) the amount of short-term assistance that is payable in respect of the mobility component may be paid by the Scottish Ministers to the authorised provider, and
  (b) paragraphs (1) and (2) of regulation 55 apply to the payment of short-term assistance as they had applied to the payment of mobility component prior to the individual's entitlement ending.

(4) Regulations 44 (form of payment - giving Adult Disability Payment by way of deduction), 49 (determination following official error – underpayments), 50 (determination following error – overpayments) and 51 (determination to effect a deduction decision) apply to short-term assistance in the same way as they apply to Adult Disability Payment.

End of entitlement

3.—(1) When an individual's entitlement to short-term assistance is to end under sub-paragraph (2), the Scottish Ministers are to make a determination without application.

(2) Entitlement to short-term assistance ends on the day—
  (a) a determination of an individual's entitlement to short-term assistance is cancelled under section 26(2) of the 2018 Act (individual's right to stop receiving assistance),
  (b) a re-determination of an individual's entitlement to Adult Disability Payment is made by the Scottish Ministers under section 43 of the 2018 Act (duty to re-determine),
  (c) the First-tier Tribunal for Scotland makes a determination under section 49 of the 2018 Act (First-tier Tribunal's power to determine entitlement) in relation to the

subsequent determination of the individual's entitlement to Adult Disability Payment mentioned in paragraph 1(1)(a),
   (d) that the First-tier Tribunal for Scotland makes a determination to refuse permission under section 48(1)(b) of the 2018 Act (deadline for appealing) to bring an appeal against the subsequent determination of the individual's entitlement to Adult Disability Payment mentioned in paragraph 1(1)(a), or
   (e) where the individual withdraws their application to bring an appeal against the subsequent determination of the individual's entitlement to Adult Disability Payment mentioned in paragraph 1(1)(a), on that day.

[1 **Reduction of Adult Disability Payment where short-term assistance is paid**
   4. Where an individual has received short-term assistance for a period and a determination is subsequently made that the individual is entitled to Adult Disability Payment for the same period, any payment of Adult Disability Payment to be made as a result of the subsequent determination for that period—
   (a) where the individual is to be paid Adult Disability Payment at the same rate as or a lower rate than any short-term assistance and any Adult Disability Payment already paid to that individual for that period, is to be reduced to £0, and
   (b) in any other case, is to be reduced by any short-term assistance and any Adult Disability Payment already paid to that individual for that period.]

Regulation 57

PART 2

INITIAL PERIOD FOR APPLICATIONS

Initial period for applications
5.—(1) These Regulations apply to an individual who is resident in one of the local authority areas mentioned in paragraph 6 when the individual makes an application for Adult Disability Payment during the initial period for applications.
(2) An individual who is awarded Adult Disability Payment pursuant to an application made during the initial period for applications will continue to be entitled if that person moves to another local authority area in Scotland.

Local authority areas for initial period for applications
6. The local authority areas specified for the purposes of regulation 64 are—
   (a) in phase 1, Perthshire and Kinross, City of Dundee and Western Isles,
   (b) in phase 2, Perthshire and Kinross, City of Dundee, Western Isles, Angus, North Lanarkshire and South Lanarkshire,
   (c) in phase 3, Perthshire and Kinross, City of Dundee, Western Isles, Angus, North Lanarkshire, South Lanarkshire, Fife, City of Aberdeen, Aberdeenshire, Moray, North Ayrshire, East Ayrshire and South Ayrshire.

Regulation 60

PART 3

TRANSFER FROM PERSONAL INDEPENDENCE PAYMENT TO ADULT DISABILITY PAYMENT

Interpretation
7. In this Part of the schedule—
"date of transfer" means the date when a transferring individual's entitlement to Adult Disability Payment begins by virtue of a determination made under paragraph 9(1),
"relevant individual" means an individual—
   (a) who has an award of Personal Independence Payment who appears to the Scottish Ministers to be likely to be eligible for Adult Disability Payment, and
   (b) who is—
      (i) ordinarily resident in Scotland, or

(ii) someone to whom regulation 15(3) (residence and presence conditions) or 20(2) (persons residing outside the United Kingdom to whom a relevant EU regulation applies) applies,

"sufficient" means a link to Scotland that is sufficiently close that regulations 15(3) or 20(2) would be incompatible with the applicable agreement mentioned in that regulation, if the relevant individual were not entitled to Adult Disability Payment,

"transfer notice" means the notice required by paragraph 8, and

"transferring individual" means [¹ an individual] on whom the Scottish Ministers have served a notice of intention to transfer in accordance with paragraph 8.

Notice of intention to transfer to Adult Disability Payment

8.—(1) The Scottish Ministers are to notify each relevant individual of their intention to transfer that individual's entitlement to disability assistance from an entitlement to Personal Independence Payment to an entitlement to Adult Disability Payment.

(2) Notice under sub-paragraph (1) must—
  (a) be given in a way that leaves the relevant individual with a record of the information which they can show to, or otherwise share with, others,
  (b) inform the relevant individual that—
    (i) they have been identified as a relevant individual for the purposes of transfer to Adult Disability Payment,
    (ii) the Scottish Ministers will make a determination, without receiving an application, to transfer the individual's entitlement to Personal Independence Payment to an entitlement to Adult Disability Payment within a period to be specified within the notice (the individual will be notified when the determination is made and informed about their award and start date of Adult Disability Payment), and
    (iii) the individual's award of Personal Independence Payment will cease immediately before the award of Adult Disability Payment begins.

[²(3) Where a notice under sub-paragraph (1) is given—
  (a) to a transferring individual who, before a determination is made under paragraph 9(1), ceases to be ordinarily resident in Scotland, or
  (b) in error where the individual is neither—
    (i) ordinarily resident in Scotland, nor
    (ii) an individual who is habitually resident in an EEA state, Gibraltar or Switzerland and has a genuine and sufficient link to Scotland,
the duty on the Scottish Ministers in paragraph 9(1) does not apply.]

(4) Where sub-paragraph (3) applies in respect of an individual and a determination under paragraph 9(1) has not been made, the Scottish Ministers are to notify the individual that the duty on the Scottish Ministers in paragraph 9(1) does not apply.

Determination without application of entitlement to Adult Disability Payment

9.—(1) The Scottish Ministers are to make a determination in respect of a transferring individual, without receiving an application, of that individual's entitlement to Adult Disability Payment.

(2) Entitlement to Adult Disability Payment under a determination under sub-paragraph (1) begins on the date specified in the notice of determination given to the transferring individual in accordance with section 40 of the 2018 Act.

(3) Subject to sub-paragraph (4), the determination under sub-paragraph (1) is to be made on the basis of—
  (a) such information as the Scottish Ministers have received from the Secretary of State for Work and Pensions in respect of the transferring individual's entitlement to Personal Independence Payment, and
  (b) any other information available to the Scottish Ministers that appears to them to be relevant.

(4) The determination under sub-paragraph (1) does not need to be made on the basis of the information mentioned in sub-paragraph (3)(b) where—
  (a) the individual—
    (i) before receiving a notice under paragraph 8(1), reported a change of circumstances to the Secretary of State for Work and Pensions, which has not been taken into account for the individual's entitlement to Personal Independence Payment, or
    (ii) has, since receiving a notice under paragraph 8(1), notified a change of circumstances to the Scottish Ministers, and
  (b) following the determination under sub-paragraph (1) a further determination is to be made under paragraph 12.

(5) Subject to paragraph 11, a determination under sub-paragraph (1) must be made on the basis that the transferring individual is entitled to the components and rates of Adult Disability Payment that are equivalent to those components and rates of Personal Independence Payment to which the individual was entitled immediately before the date of transfer.

(6) A determination under sub-paragraph (1)—
   (a) may be made on the assumption that whatever can be discerned about the transferring individual's circumstances from the information mentioned in sub-paragraph (3) remains accurate on the date on which the determination is made,
   (b) notwithstanding the generality of head (a), is to be made on the assumption that the conditions relating to residence and presence set out in regulations 15 to 21 (residence and presence conditions etc.) are satisfied in the individual's case, and
   (c) must be made not later than the end of the period specified within the notice under paragraph 8(1) unless the Scottish Ministers have—
      (i) good reason to extend that period,
      (ii) agreed the period for extension with the Secretary of State for Work and Pensions, and
      (iii) notified the transferring individual of the extension and the reason for it.

[¹ Effect of determination on entitlement to Personal Independence Payment

10.—(1) Where a determination is made under paragraph 9(1) that the transferring individual is entitled to Adult Disability Payment, the transferring individual's entitlement to Personal Independence Payment will cease on—
   (a) the date their entitlement to Adult Disability Payment begins,
   (b) where a transferring individual was paid Personal Independence Payment one week in advance and 3 weekly in arrears, the date one week after the date their entitlement to Adult Disability Payment begins, or
   (c) where paragraph 11 applies, the date their entitlement to Adult Disability Payment would have begun had paragraph 11(2) not applied to set an earlier date of entitlement.

(2) Where paragraph (1)(b) applies—
   (a) section 77(4) (personal independence payment) of the Welfare Reform Act 2012, and
   (b) regulation 4(e) of these Regulations (entitlement to other benefits),
do not apply in respect of the first week of entitlement to Adult Disability Payment.]

Exceptions to paragraph 9(5)

11.—(1) Where the Scottish Ministers have—
   (a) received information from the Secretary of State for Work and Pensions that the transferring individual is terminally ill in terms of section 82 of the Welfare Reform Act 2012 immediately before the date of transfer, or
   (b) not received information from the Secretary of State for Work and Pensions that the transferring individual is terminally ill in terms of section 82 of the Welfare Reform Act 2012, but become aware, before they have made a determination under paragraph 9(1), that a transferring individual has a terminal illness in terms of regulation 26(7),
[¹ except where sub-paragraph (1A) applies,] the determination made under paragraph 9(1) must be made on the basis that the transferring individual satisfies the conditions for the enhanced rate of both the daily living component and the mobility component of Adult Disability Payment.

[¹ (1A) Where the transferring individual reached the relevant age as defined in regulation 22(2) when they became terminally ill under section 82 of the Welfare Reform Act 2012 or in terms of regulation 26(7), the restrictions in sub-paragraph (1B) apply in relation to the determination under paragraph 9(1).

(1B) The restrictions referred to in sub-paragraph (1A) are—
   (a) where the transferring individual was entitled to the mobility component of Personal Independence Payment at the standard rate immediately before the date of transfer, then regardless of whether the award would otherwise have been for the enhanced rate, the Scottish Ministers—
      (i) may only make an award for the standard rate of that component, and
      (ii) may only make such an award where the entitlement results from substantially the same condition or conditions in respect of which the mobility component of Personal Independence payment was given,
   (b) where the transferring individual was entitled to the mobility component of Personal Independence Payment at the enhanced rate immediately before the date of transfer, the Scottish Ministers may only award that rate of that component where entitlement

results from substantially the same condition or conditions in respect of which the mobility component of Personal Independence Payment was given,

(c) where the transferring individual was not entitled to the mobility component of Personal Independence Payment immediately before the date of transfer, the Scottish Ministers may not award that component at either the standard or enhanced rate.]

(2) Where sub-paragraph (1) [¹ or (1A)] applies—
(a) paragraphs (4) to (6) of regulation 26 do not apply, and
(b) the transferring individual's entitlement to Adult Disability Payment will commence on whichever is the later of—
  (i) the date that these Regulations come into force,
  (ii) the day that the clinical judgement was made in accordance with regulation 26(7), or
  (iii) the day one year before the determination was made in accordance with paragraph 9(1).

Change of Circumstances

12.—[²(1) The Scottish Ministers must make a determination of an individual's entitlement to Adult Disability Payment (the "review determination"), without receiving an application, where—
(a) the individual, before a determination under paragraph 9(1) (the "transfer determination") is made, reported a change of circumstances to the Secretary of State for Work and Pensions, which had not been taken into account for the individual's entitlement to Personal Independence Payment,
(b) the Scottish Ministers have made a transfer determination, and
(c) the individual has not requested a re-determination under section 41 of the 2018 Act, or appealed under section 46 of the 2018 Act, in relation to the transfer determination.]

(2) The review determination is to be made as soon as reasonably practicable after the transfer determination.

(3) The change of circumstance notified under sub-paragraph (1)—
(a) is not to be regarded as relating to the individual's entitlement to Personal Independence Payment, and
(b) is to be taken into consideration by the Scottish Ministers in making the review determination.

(4) Where a transferring individual's entitlement to Adult Disability Payment is determined in the review determination to be at a higher rate than the transfer determination, entitlement will begin—
(a) if the individual notifies the change—
  (i) within one month of the change occurring, the date when the individual first satisfies the requirements for a higher rate of the [¹ daily living] or mobility component,
  (ii) within more than one month but not more than 13 months of the change occurring, the date when the individual first satisfies the requirements for a higher rate of the [¹ daily living] or mobility component, but only if the Scottish Ministers consider that the individual had good reason for not notifying the change within one month,
  (iii) in any other case, from the date of notification of the change, or
(b) if the date under sub-paragraph 4(a) is before these Regulations come into force, the date that these Regulations come into force.

(5) Where a transferring individual's entitlement to Adult Disability Payment is determined in the review determination to be at a lower rate than or at the same rate as awarded by the transfer determination, entitlement under the review determination will take effect on the day that the Scottish Ministers make the review determination.

(6) Where an individual has previously received Personal Independence Payment or Adult Disability Payment for a period and a review determination is subsequently made that the same individual is entitled to Adult Disability Payment at a higher rate for that period by virtue of this paragraph, that individual will be entitled to the difference between the value of entitlement to Adult Disability Payment under the review determination and the value of Personal Independence Payment or Adult Disability Payment to which that individual was previously entitled for that period.

[¹ (7) Where the change of circumstance notified under sub-paragraph (1) occurred after the person had reached the relevant age as defined in regulation 22(2), the restrictions in sub-paragraph (8) will apply in relation to the determination under sub-paragraph (1).

(8) The restrictions referred to in sub-paragraph (7) are—
  (a) where the transfer determination awarded the mobility component at the standard rate then, regardless of whether the award would have otherwise been for the enhanced rate, the Scottish Ministers—
    (i) may only make an award for the standard rate of that component, and
    (ii) may only make such an award where entitlement results from substantially the same condition or conditions in respect of which the mobility component in the transfer determination was given,
  (b) where the transfer determination awarded the mobility component at the enhanced rate, the Scottish Ministers may only award that rate of that component where entitlement results from substantially the same condition or conditions in respect of which the mobility component in the transfer determination was given,
  (c) where the transfer determination did not include an award of the mobility component, the Scottish Ministers may not award that component at either the standard or enhanced rate.]

Effect of legal detention on payment of the mobility component: 16 and 17 year olds
13.—(1) Sub-paragraph (2) and (3) apply where a transferring individual—
  (a) is aged 16 or 17 on the date of transfer,
  (b) was in legal detention immediately before the date of transfer, and
  (c) was entitled to the mobility component of Personal Independence Payment immediately before the date of transfer.
(2) Entitlement to the mobility component of Adult Disability Payment of a transferring individual mentioned in sub-paragraph (1) is to begin before the date of the determination under paragraph 9(1) but not before 13 June 2022.
(3) Where the transferring individual has received payment of the mobility component of Personal Independence Payment for any period after the date on which their entitlement to the mobility component of Adult Disability Payment commences under sub-paragraph (2), any payment of Adult Disability Payment to be made for that period is to be reduced by the amount already paid to the transferring individual for the mobility component of Personal Independence Payment for that period.

Modification of these Regulations: transferring individuals
14. These Regulations apply to a transferring individual on and after the date of transfer with the following modifications—
  (a) regulation 32 (entitlement beginning while in alternative accommodation) is to be read as if—
    (i) in paragraph (1) after "begins" there are the words "in terms of Part 3 of schedule 2", and
    (ii) in paragraph (2) for "that day" reads "the day on which the individual has been entitled to Adult Disability Payment for 28 days",
  (b) regulation 35 (when an application is to be treated as made and beginning of entitlement to assistance) is treated as omitted,
[¹ (ba) in regulation 36, for sub-paragraph (b), substitute—
  "(b) any subsequent payment—
    (i) 4 weekly in arrears,
    (ii) weekly in advance, or
    (iii) where the Scottish Ministers consider that it would be unjust not to do so, at such intervals as may be specified in the notice of determination.",]
  (c) in regulation 45—
    (i) for paragraph (4) substitute—
      "(4) Where an individual has previously received Adult Disability Payment or Personal Independence Payment for a period and a determination without application has subsequently been made that the individual is entitled to Adult Disability Payment at a higher rate for that period, the individual will be entitled to the difference between the value of entitlement to Adult Disability Payment under the subsequent determination and the value of Adult Disability Payment or Personal Independence Payment to which that individual was previously entitled for that period.",
    (ii) where regulation 45(4) as substituted by sub-paragraph (1) applies, for the period between the date when the individual's entitlement to a higher rate of Adult Disability Payment begins and the date of the determination under

(SSI 2022/54 Sch.2)

regulation 46, regulation 4 (entitlement to other benefits) is treated as omitted, and

(d) where paragraph 11, 12(6) or 13(3) applies, for the period between the date when entitlement to Adult Disability Payment begins and the date of the determination under paragraph 9(1), regulation 4 (entitlement to other benefits) is treated as omitted.

Appointees

15.—(1) A person appointed by the Secretary of State for Work and Pensions under regulation 57 of the Universal Credit, Personal Independence Payment, Jobseeker's Allowance and Employment and Support Allowance (Claims and Payments) Regulations 2013 to receive Personal Independence Payment on behalf of a transferring individual is to be treated on and after the date of transfer as though appointed by the Scottish Ministers to act on behalf of that transferring individual under section 85B of the 2018 Act .

(2) As soon as reasonably practicable after the date of transfer, the Scottish Ministers must—
  (a) consider whether the conditions for making an appointment in respect of the transferring individual are met (having regard to section 85B(3) of the 2018 Act),
  (b) consider whether to terminate the appointment that is treated as having been made by virtue of sub-paragraph (1) and terminate it if they consider it appropriate, and
  (c) if they have terminated an appointment in pursuance of head (b), appoint under section 85B of the 2018 Act another person to act on the transferring individual's behalf if they consider it appropriate to do so.

[²(3) The duty in sub-paragraph (2) does not apply where the Scottish Ministers have already appointed the person mentioned in sub-paragraph (1) to act on behalf of that transferring individual under section 85B of the 2018 Act.]

Regulation 63

PART 4

CONSEQUENTIAL AMENDMENTS

16. *Omitted.*

AMENDMENTS

1. Disability Assistance for Working Age People (Transitional Provisions and Miscellaneous Amendment) (Scotland) Regulations 2022 (SSI 2022/217) reg.19(1), (12) and (13) (August 29, 2022).

2. Disability Assistance (Miscellaneous Amendment) (Scotland) Regulations 2023 (SSI 2023/346) reg.4(5)–(7) (November 20, 2023).

The Disability Assistance for Working Age People (Transitional Provisions and Miscellaneous Amendment) (Scotland) Regulations 2022

(SSI 2022/217)

Made   *21st June 2022*
Coming into force   *29th August 2022*

The Scottish Ministers make the following Regulations in exercise of the powers conferred by sections 31(2), 36(2), 43(5), 52 and 95 of the Social Security (Scotland) Act 2018 and all other powers enabling them to do so.

The Social Security Information-sharing (Scotland) Regulations 2021

In accordance with section 96(2) of that Act, a draft of these Regulations has been laid before and approved by resolution of the Scottish Parliament.

In accordance with section 97(2) of that Act, the Scottish Ministers have informed the Scottish Commission on Social Security of their proposals, notified the Scottish Parliament that they have done so and made their proposals publicly available by such means as they consider appropriate.

PART 1

INTRODUCTORY AND INTERPRETATION

Citation, commencement and extent

1.—(1) These Regulations may be cited as the Disability Assistance for Working Age People (Transitional Provisions and Miscellaneous Amendment) (Scotland) Regulations 2022 and come into force on 29 August 2022.

(2) These Regulations extend to Scotland only.

Interpretation

2. In Parts 1, 2 and 3 of these Regulations—

"the 2018 Act" means the Social Security (Scotland) Act 2018,

"the ADP Regulations" means the Disability Assistance for Working Age People (Scotland) Regulations 2022,

"Adult Disability Payment" means disability assistance for adults given in accordance with the ADP Regulations,

"date of transfer" means the date when a transferring individual's entitlement to Adult Disability Payment begins by virtue of a transfer determination,

"daily living component of Adult Disability Payment" has the same meaning as "daily living component" in regulation 2 of the ADP Regulations,

"Disability Living Allowance" means a disability living allowance under section 71 of the Social Security Contributions and Benefits Act 1992,

"mobility component of Adult Disability Payment" has the same meaning as "mobility component" in regulation 2 of the ADP Regulations,

"notice of intention to transfer" means the notice required by regulation 3,

"relevant individual" means an individual who—

(a) has an award of Disability Living Allowance who appears to the Scottish Ministers to be likely to be eligible for Adult Disability Payment—

  (i) who has—

    (aa) notified a change of circumstances in terms of regulation 32 of the Social Security (Claims and Payments) Regulations 1987, or

    (bb) made a claim for personal independence payment in terms of regulation 4 of the Personal Independence Payment (Transitional Provisions) Regulations 2013,

  (ii) whose award is due to be renewed, or

(iii) who has requested to be transferred to Adult Disability Payment after 29 August 2022,
(b) was aged 16 years old or older but under 65 years old on 8 April 2013,
(c) is—
  (i) ordinarily resident in Scotland, or
  (ii) someone to whom regulation 15(3) (residence and presence conditions), regulation 17(1) (serving members of Her Majesty's forces, civil servants and their family members) or regulation 20(2) of the ADP Regulations (persons residing outside the United Kingdom to whom a relevant EU Regulation applies) applies,

"review determination" means the determination required by regulation 12(1),

"transfer determination" means the determination required by regulation 4(1),

"transferred individual" means an individual whose entitlement to Adult Disability Payment is given under a transfer determination, and

"transferring individual" means an individual on whom the Scottish Ministers have served a notice of intention to transfer in accordance with regulation 3.

PART 2

TRANSFER TO ADULT DISABILITY PAYMENT

Notice of intention to transfer to Adult Disability Payment

3.—(1) The Scottish Ministers are to notify each relevant individual of their intention to transfer that individual's entitlement to disability assistance from an entitlement to Disability Living Allowance to an entitlement to Adult Disability Payment.

(2) Notice under paragraph (1) must—
(a) be given in a way that leaves the relevant individual with a record of the information which they can show to, or otherwise share with, others, and
(b) inform the relevant individual that—
  (i) they have been identified as a relevant individual for the purposes of transfer to Adult Disability Payment,
  (ii) the Scottish Ministers will make a determination, without receiving an application, to transfer the individual's entitlement to Disability Living Allowance to an entitlement to Adult Disability Payment within a period to be specified within the notice (the individual will be notified when the transfer determination is made and informed about their award and start date of Adult Disability Payment),
  (iii) the individual's award of Disability Living Allowance will cease—
    (aa) immediately before the award of Adult Disability Payment begins, or

(bb) where a transferring individual was paid Disability Living Allowance one week in advance and 3 weekly in arrears, the date one week after the date their entitlement to Adult Disability Payment begins,

(iv) except where the individual is subject to the special rules for terminal illness in regulation 9, the Scottish Ministers will make a review determination of the individual's entitlement to Adult Disability Payment within 12 months of the date of the notice.

[[1](3) Where a notice under paragraph (1) is given—
(a) to a transferring individual who, before a transfer determination is made ceases to be ordinarily resident in Scotland, or
(b) in error where the individual is neither—
  (i) ordinarily resident in Scotland, nor
  (ii) an individual who is habitually resident in an EEA state, Gibraltar or Switzerland and has a genuine and sufficient link to Scotland,
the duty on the Scottish Ministers in regulation 4(1) does not apply.]

(4) Where paragraph (3) applies in respect of an individual and a transfer determination has not been made, the Scottish Ministers are to notify the individual that the duty on the Scottish Ministers in regulation 4(1) does not apply.

(5) In paragraph (3), "sufficient" means a link to Scotland that is sufficiently close that regulation 15(3) or 20(2) of the ADP Regulations would be incompatible with the applicable agreement mentioned in either of those regulations, if the relevant individual were not entitled to Adult Disability Payment.

AMENDMENT

1. Disability Assistance (Miscellaneous Amendment) (Scotland) Regulations 2023 (SSI 2023/346) reg.5(2) (November 20, 2023).

Transfer determination without application of entitlement to Adult Disability Payment

4.—(1) The Scottish Ministers are to make a determination in respect of a transferring individual, without receiving an application, of that individual's entitlement to Adult Disability Payment.

(2) A transfer determination must be made on the assumption that the transferring individual—
(a) other than Disability Living Allowance, is not entitled to any of the benefits set out in regulation 4, and
(b) meets the residence and presence conditions set out in regulations 15 to 21, of the ADP Regulations.

(3) Entitlement to Adult Disability Payment under a transfer determination begins on the date specified in the notice of determination given to the transferring individual in accordance with section 40 of the 2018 Act.

(4) The transfer determination is to be made on the basis of—
(a) such information as the Scottish Ministers have received from the Secretary of State for Work and Pensions in respect of the transferring individual's entitlement to Disability Living Allowance, and
(b) any other information available to the Scottish Ministers that appears to them to be relevant.

(5) Subject to regulation 9, a transfer determination must be made in accordance with regulation 5.

(6) The transfer determination does not need to be made on the basis of the information mentioned in paragraph (4)(b) where—
  (a) the individual—
    (i) before receiving notice under regulation 3(1), reported a change of circumstances to the Secretary of State for Work and Pensions, which has not been taken into account for the individual's entitlement to Disability Living Allowance, or
    (ii) has, since receiving a notice under regulation 3(1), notified a change of circumstances to the Scottish Ministers, and
  (b) following the transfer determination, a review determination is to be made.

(7) A determination under paragraph (1)—
  (a) may be made on the assumption that whatever can be discerned about the transferring individual's circumstances from the information mentioned in paragraph (4) remains accurate on the date on which the determination is made,
  (b) must be made no later than the end of the period specified within the notice of intention to transfer unless the Scottish Ministers have—
    (i) good reason to extend that period,
    (ii) agreed the period for extension with the Secretary of State for Work and Pensions, and
    (iii) notified the transferring individual of the extension and the reason for it.

Entitlement to Adult Disability Payment

5.—(1) For the purposes of a transfer determination, an individual may be awarded the daily living component of Adult Disability Payment at the transitional rate specified in regulation 6(1) instead of being awarded that component at the standard or the enhanced rate in accordance with regulation 5(2) or (3) of the ADP Regulations.

(2) A transfer determination is to be made on the basis that a transferring individual who had been entitled to the—
  (a) lowest rate of the care component of Disability Living Allowance immediately prior to the date of transfer is entitled to the transitional rate of the daily living component of Adult Disability Payment,
  (b) middle rate of the care component of Disability Living Allowance immediately prior to the date of transfer is entitled to the standard rate of the daily living component of Adult Disability Payment,
  (c) highest rate of the care component of Disability Living Allowance immediately prior to the date of transfer is entitled to the enhanced rate of the daily living component of Adult Disability Payment,
  (d) lower rate of the mobility component of Disability Living Allowance immediately prior to the date of transfer is entitled to the standard rate of the mobility component of Adult Disability Payment,
  (e) higher rate of the mobility component of Disability Living Allowance immediately prior to the date of transfer is entitled to the enhanced rate of the mobility component of Adult Disability Payment.

(3) A transferring individual mentioned in paragraph (2)(e) is to be treated as though they have obtained the maximum points for each

Amount and form and time of payment of Adult Disability Payment

13.443 6.—(1) The weekly rate of payment of the daily living component of Adult Disability Payment is, where the transferring individual is entitled to the transitional rate, [¹ 28.70].

(2) Where an award of Adult Disability Payment is made to a transferring individual, the Scottish Ministers are to make—
  (a) the first payment of assistance on a date specified in the notice of determination, and
  (b) any subsequent payment—
    (i) 4 weekly in arrears,
    (ii) weekly in advance, or
    (iii) where the Scottish Ministers consider that it would be unjust not to do so, at such intervals as may be specified in the notice of determination.

AMENDMENT

1. Social Security (Up-rating) (Miscellaneous Amendments) (Scotland) Regulations 2024 (SSI 2024/105) reg.3 (April 8, 2024).

Effect of determination on entitlement to Disability Living Allowance

13.444 7.—(1) Where a transfer determination is made that the transferring individual is entitled to Adult Disability Payment, the transferring individual's entitlement to Disability Living Allowance will cease on—
  (a) the date their entitlement to Adult Disability Payment begins,
  (b) where a transferring individual was paid Disability Living Allowance one week in advance and 3 weekly in arrears, the date one week after the date their entitlement to Adult Disability Payment begins, or
  (c) where regulation 9 applies, the date their entitlement to Adult Disability Payment would have begun had regulation 9(2) not applied to set an earlier date of entitlement.

(2) Where paragraph (1)(b) applies—
  (a) section 71(7) (disability living allowance) of the Social Security Contributions and Benefits Act 1992, and
  (b) regulation 4(d) of the ADP Regulations (entitlement to other benefits),

do not apply in respect of the first week of entitlement to Adult Disability Payment.

Periods in respect of a re-determination request in relation to a transfer determination

13.445 8.—(1) The period for requesting a re-determination of entitlement to Adult Disability Payment under section 41 of the 2018 Act (right to request re-determination) in relation to a transfer determination is 42 days beginning with the day that the individual is informed, in accordance with section 40 of the 2018 Act (notice of determination) of the right to make the request.

(SSI 2022/217 reg. 8)

(2) In relation to determining entitlement to Adult Disability Payment, the period allowed for re-determination in respect of a transfer determination (within the meaning of section 43 of the 2018 Act (duty to re-determine)) is as soon as reasonably practicable and not more than 182 days beginning with—
  (a) the day that the request for a re-determination is received by the Scottish Ministers,
  (b) in a case where the request for a re-determination is received by the Scottish Ministers outwith the period prescribed in paragraph (1), the day on which it is decided by the Scottish Ministers or (as the case may be) the First-tier Tribunal for Scotland that the individual in question has a good reason for not requesting a re-determination sooner, or
  (c) in a case where the Scottish Ministers have informed the individual of their decision that the request for re-determination was not made in such form as the Scottish Ministers require, the day on which it is subsequently decided by the First-tier Tribunal for Scotland that the individual in question has made the request in such form as the Scottish Ministers require.

Special rules for terminal illness - exception to regulation 4(5)

9.—(1) Where the Scottish Ministers have—
  (a) received information from the Secretary of State for Work and Pensions that the transferring individual is terminally ill in terms of section 72(5) of the Social Security Contributions and Benefits Act 1992 immediately before the date of transfer, or
  (b) not received information from the Secretary of State for Work and Pensions that the transferring individual is terminally ill in terms of section 72(5) of the Social Security Contributions and Benefits 1992, but become aware, before they have made a transfer determination, that a transferring individual has a terminal illness in terms of regulation 26(7) of the ADP Regulations,
the transfer determination must be made on the basis that the transferring individual satisfies the conditions for the enhanced rate of both the daily living component and the mobility component of Adult Disability Payment.
  (2) Where paragraph (1) applies—
  (a) paragraphs (4) to (6) of regulation 26 of the ADP Regulations do not apply, and
  (b) the transferring individual's entitlement to Adult Disability Payment will commence on whichever is the later of—
    (i) the date that the ADP Regulations came into force,
    (ii) the day that the clinical judgement was made in accordance with regulation 26(7) of the ADP Regulations, or
    (iii) the day one year before the date of the transfer determination.

Modification of the ADP Regulations: transferring individuals

10. The ADP Regulations apply to a transferring individual on and after the date of transfer with the following modifications—
  (a) regulation 3(3) (overview) is to be read as if—
    (i) for "2 weekly rates of the daily living component" there were substituted "3 weekly rates of the daily living component", and

(ii) after "(amount and form of Adult Disability Payment)" there were inserted "and regulation 6(1) of the Disability Assistance for Working Age People (Transitional Provisions and Miscellaneous Amendment) (Scotland) Regulations 2022",
(b) regulation 5 (daily living component) is to be read as if—
  (i) in paragraph (1) after "the enhanced rate" there were inserted "or, where the individual is a transferring individual as defined in regulation 2 of the Disability Assistance for Working Age People (Transitional Provisions and Miscellaneous Amendment) (Scotland) Regulations 2022, at the transitional rate,
  (ii) after paragraph (3) there were inserted—
    "(3A) An individual is entitled to the daily living component at the transitional rate where regulation 5(2)(a) of the Disability Assistance for Working Age People (Transitional Provisions and Miscellaneous Amendment) (Scotland) Regulations 2022 applies to the individual." and
  (iii) after paragraph (4)(c) there were inserted—
    "(d) "the transitional rate" in relation to the daily living component means the weekly rate of the daily living component set in regulation 6(1) of the Disability Assistance for Working Age People (Transitional Provisions and Miscellaneous Amendment) (Scotland) Regulations 2022",
(c) regulation 32 (entitlement beginning while in alternative accommodation) is to be read as if—
  (i) in paragraph (1) after "begins" there are the words "in terms of these Regulations", and
  (ii) in paragraph (2) for "that day" there were substituted "the day on which the individual has been entitled to Adult Disability Payment for 28 days",
(d) regulation 35 (when an application is to be treated as made and beginning of entitlement to assistance) is treated as omitted,
(e) regulation 36 (time of payment) is treated as omitted,
(f) [¹. . .]
(g) [¹. . .]
(h) regulation 54 (periods in respect of a re-determination request) is treated as omitted in relation to a request for a re-determination in respect of a transfer determination,
(i) where regulation 9 of these Regulations applies, for the period between the date when entitlement to Adult Disability Payment begins and the date of the transfer determination, regulation 4 (entitlement to other benefits) is treated as omitted.

AMENDMENT

1. Disability Assistance (Miscellaneous Amendment) (Scotland) Regulations 2023 (SSI 2023/346) reg.5(3) (November 20, 2023).

Appointees

11.—(1) A person appointed by the Secretary of State for Work and Pensions under regulation 33 of the Social Security (Claims and Payments) Regulations 1987 (persons unable to act) to receive Disability Living Allowance on behalf of a transferring individual is to be treated on and after the date of transfer as though appointed by the Scottish Ministers to act on behalf of that transferring individual under section 85B of the 2018 Act.

(2) As soon as reasonably practicable after the date of transfer, the Scottish Ministers must—
- (a) consider whether the conditions for making an appointment in respect of the transferring individual are met (having regard to section 85B(3) of the 2018 Act),
- (b) consider whether to terminate the appointment that is treated as having been made by virtue of sub-paragraph (1) and terminate it if they consider it appropriate, and
- (c) if they have terminated an appointment in pursuance of head (b), appoint under section 85B of the 2018 Act another person to act on the transferring individual's behalf if they consider it appropriate to do so.

[1(3) The duty in paragraph (2) does not apply where the Scottish Ministers have already appointed the person mentioned in paragraph (1) to act on behalf of that transferring individual under section 85B of the 2018 Act.]

AMENDMENT

1. Disability Assistance (Miscellaneous Amendment) (Scotland) Regulations 2023 (SSI 2023/346) reg.5(4) (November 20, 2023).

PART 3

REVIEW OF ENTITLEMENT TO ADULT DISABILITY PAYMENT

Review determination without application of entitlement to Adult Disability Payment

12.—(1) The Scottish Ministers are to make a determination in respect of a transferred individual, without receiving an application, of that individual's entitlement to Adult Disability Payment within the period of 12 months beginning with the date of that individual's notice of intention to transfer.

(2) Paragraph (1) does not apply—
- (a) to transferred individuals to whom regulation 9 applies, or
- (b) where a transferred individual has requested a re-determination under section 41 of the 2018 Act, or made an appeal under section 46 of the 2018 Act, in relation to the transfer determination.

(3) Subject to regulations 15 (when an increase in level of entitlement takes effect) and 16 (when a decrease in level or cessation of entitlement takes effect), entitlement to Adult Disability Payment under a determination under paragraph (1) begins on the date specified in the notice of determination given to the transferred individual in accordance with section 40 of the 2018 Act.

(4) The determination under paragraph (1) is to be made on the basis of any information that—
- (a) the Scottish Ministers have received from the Secretary of State for Work and Pensions in respect of the transferred individual's entitlement to Disability Living Allowance,

Time of payment

13. Where an award of Adult Disability Payment is made under a review determination, the Scottish Ministers are to make—
  (a) the first payment of assistance on a date specified in the notice of determination, and
  (b) any subsequent payment—
    (i) 4 weekly in arrears,
    (ii) weekly in advance, or
    (iii) where the Scottish Ministers consider that it would be unjust not to do so, at such intervals as may be specified in the notice of determination.

[¹Change of circumstances

14. Where the Scottish Ministers are making a review determination of an individual's entitlement to Adult Disability Payment, where the individual, before a transfer determination is made, reported a change of circumstances to the Secretary of State for Work and Pensions which had not been taken into account for the individual's entitlement to Disability Living Allowance, the change of circumstances—
  (a) is not to be regarded as relating to the individual's entitlement to Disability Living Allowance, and
  (b) is to be taken into consideration by the Scottish Minister in making the review determination.]

AMENDMENT

1. Disability Assistance (Miscellaneous Amendment) (Scotland) Regulations 2023 (SSI 2023/346) reg.5(5) (November 20, 2023).

When an increase in level of entitlement takes effect

15.—(1) Where, as a result of a review determination, the amount of Adult Disability Payment payable in respect of an individual is increased, or their entitlement to a component is awarded, the change takes effect on the date of transfer.

(2) Where an individual has previously received Adult Disability Payment for a period under a transfer determination and a review determination has subsequently been made that the same individual is entitled to Adult Disability Payment at a higher rate for that period, that individual is entitled to be paid the difference between the value of entitlement to Adult Disability Payment under the review determination and the value of Adult Disability Payment to which that individual was previously entitled under the transfer determination.

[¹(3) Where paragraph (1) applies, regulation 45 of the ADP Regulations does not apply.]

AMENDMENT

1. Disability Assistance (Miscellaneous Amendment) (Scotland) Regulations 2023 (SSI 2023/346) reg.5(6) (November 20, 2023).

(SSI 2022/217 reg.16)

[¹When a decrease in level or cessation of entitlement takes effect

16.—(1) Where an individual's entitlement to Adult Disability Payment is determined in the review determination to be at a lower rate than, or the same rate as awarded by, the transfer determination, entitlement under the review determination will take effect on the day that the Scottish Ministers make the review determination.

(2) Where paragraph (1) applies, regulation 46 of the ADP Regulations does not apply.]

AMENDMENT

1. Disability Assistance (Miscellaneous Amendment) (Scotland) Regulations 2023 (SSI 2023/346) reg.5(7) (November 20, 2023).

PART 4

MISCELLANEOUS AMENDMENTS

17. to 19. *Omitted.*

The Winter Heating Assistance (Low Income) (Scotland) Regulations 2023

(SSI 2023/16)

Made   *24th January 2023*
Coming into force   *25th January 2023*

The Scottish Ministers make the following Regulations in exercise of the powers conferred by sections 30(2), 41(4)(a), 43(5) and 52 of the Social Security (Scotland) Act 2018 and all other powers enabling them to do so.

In accordance with section 96(2) of that Act, a draft of these Regulations has been laid before and approved by resolution of the Scottish Parliament.

In accordance with section 97(2) of that Act, the Scottish Ministers have informed the Scottish Commission on Social Security of their proposals, notified the Scottish Parliament that they have done so and made their proposals publicly available by such means as they consider appropriate.

Citation and commencement

1. These Regulations may be cited as the Winter Heating Assistance (Low Income) (Scotland) Regulations 2023 and come into force on the day after the day on which they are made.

Interpretation

2. In these Regulations—
"the 2012 Act" means the Welfare Reform Act 2012,
"the 2018 Act" means the Social Security (Scotland) Act 2018,
"applicable amount" means—

The Winter Heating Assistance (Low Income) (Scotland) Regulations 2023

  (a) in the case of income-related employment and support allowance, the claimant's weekly applicable amount under regulations 67 to 70 of the Employment and Support Allowance Regulations 2008,
  (b) in the case of income support, the claimant's weekly applicable amount under regulations 17 to 21AA of the Income Support (General) Regulations 1987,
  (c) in the case of jobseeker's allowance, the claimant's weekly applicable amount under regulations 83 to 86C of the Jobseeker's Allowance Regulations 1996,

"determination" means a determination of entitlement within the meaning of section 25 of the 2018 Act,

"income-related employment and support allowance" means income-related employment and support allowance under Part 1 of the Welfare Reform Act 2007,

"income support" means income support under Part VII of the Social Security Contributions and Benefits Act 1992,

"qualifying week" means the week running from the first Monday in November in any year, and

"winter heating payment" means winter heating assistance given in accordance with these Regulations.

Overview

3.—(1) Regulation 4 makes provision in respect of eligibility rules for determining entitlement to winter heating payment.

(2) Regulations 5 to 8 make provision about matters of procedure for determining entitlement to winter heating payment.

(3) Regulations 9 and 10 make provision about the winter heating payment that is to be given to individuals who are eligible for assistance.

Eligibility rules for winter heating payment

4.—(1) An individual is entitled to be paid winter heating payment if the individual satisfies, in respect of a qualifying week, the conditions specified in paragraphs (2) to (4).

(2) The first condition is that, in respect of any day within the qualifying week, the individual—
  (a) has been awarded any of the following—
    (i) state pension credit,
    (ii) income support,
    (iii) an income-based jobseeker's allowance,
    (iv) an income-related employment and support allowance,
    (v) universal credit,
    (vi) owner-occupier loan payments and is treated as entitled to a benefit specified in heads (ii) to (iv),
    (vii) owner-occupier loan payments and is treated as entitled to state pension credit, and
  (b) is resident in Scotland.

(3) The second condition (which applies only if the individual falls within paragraph (2)(a)(ii), (iii), (iv), (v), or (vi)) is that, in respect of the day to which paragraph (2) relates—
  (a) the individual's family includes a member aged younger than 5 years old,

(SSI 2023/16 reg. 4)

(b) where the individual has been awarded income support, the individual's applicable amount includes one or more of the premiums specified in paragraphs 9 to 14 of Part 3 (premiums) of schedule 2 of the Income Support (General) Regulations 1987,

(c) where the individual has been awarded income-based jobseeker's allowance, the individual's applicable amount includes one or more of the premiums specified in paragraphs 10 to 16 of Part 3 (premiums) of schedule 1 of the Jobseeker's Allowance Regulations 1996,

(d) the individual's child tax credit includes a disability element within the meaning of section 9(3) (maximum rate) of the Tax Credits Act 2002,

(e) where the individual has been awarded income-related employment and support allowance—
  (i) the individual's applicable amount includes one or more of the premiums specified in paragraphs 5 to 7 of Part 2 (premiums) of schedule 4 of the Employment and Support Allowance Regulations 2008, or
  (ii) the individual is a member of the work-related activity group or is a member of the support group,

(f) where the individual has been awarded universal credit—
  (i) the individual's universal credit award includes an amount under section 10(2) of the 2012 Act (child or qualifying young person who is disabled), or
  (ii) the individual is determined as having limited capability for work or limited capability for work and work-related activity as construed in accordance with regulations 39 and 40 of the Universal Credit Regulations 2013, or

(g) where the individual has been awarded owner-occupier loan payments, the individual's applicable amount, if the individual were entitled to a benefit specified in paragraph (2)(a)(ii) to (iv), would include one or more of the premiums specified in—
  (i) where the individual is treated as entitled to income support, paragraphs 9 to 14 of Part 3 of schedule 2 of the Income Support (General) Regulations 1987,
  (ii) where the individual is treated as entitled to jobseeker's allowance, paragraphs 10 to 16 of Part 3 of schedule 1 of the Jobseeker's Allowance Regulations 1996,
  (iii) where the individual is treated as entitled to employment and support allowance, paragraphs 5 to 7 of Part 2 of schedule 4 of the Employment and Support Allowance Regulations 2008.

(4) The third condition, which applies only where the individual has been awarded universal credit and their award of universal credit does not include an amount under section 10(2) of the 2012 Act, is that the person is not in employment or gainful self-employment on any day during the qualifying week.

(5) In this regulation—
  (a) "employment" means employment under a contract of service, or in an office, including an elective office,
  (b) "family" has the meaning given to it in section 137 of the Social Security Contributions and Benefits Act 1992 and the Income Support (General) Regulations 1987,
  (c) a person is in "gainful self-employment" where—

(i) they are carrying on a trade, profession or vocation as their main employment,
(ii) their earnings from that trade, profession or vocation are treated as self-employed earnings for the purpose of regulations made under section 8(3) of the 2012 Act, and
(iii) the trade, profession or vocation is organised, developed, regular and carried on in expectation of profit,
(d) "income-based jobseeker's allowance" means income-based jobseeker's allowance under the Jobseekers Act 1995,
(e) "member of the support group" means a person who has or is treated as having limited capability for work-related activity under Part 6 of the Employment and Support Allowance Regulations 2008,
(f) "member of the work-related activity group" means a person who has or is treated as having limited capability for work under Part 5 of the Employment and Support Allowance Regulations 2008 other than by virtue of regulation 30 of those Regulations,
(g) "owner-occupier loan payments" means loan payments made under the Loans for Mortgage Interest Regulations 2017,
(h) "state pension credit" has the meaning given by section 1(1) of the State Pension Credit Act 2002,
(i) "treated as entitled to" a benefit, in respect of a person, has the meaning given in regulation 2(2)(aa) of the Loans for Mortgage Interest Regulations 2017,
(j) "universal credit" means universal credit under Part 1 of the 2012 Act.

Determination of entitlement to winter heating payment without application

5. The Scottish Ministers must, without receiving an application, make a determination of an individual's entitlement to winter heating payment under section 30 of the 2018 Act where it appears to the Scottish Ministers from information available to them that the individual is likely to meet the eligibility rules in regulation 4.

Determination following official error – underpayments

6.—(1) The Scottish Ministers must make a determination of an individual's entitlement to winter heating payment, without receiving an application, where—
(a) they have previously made a determination of the individual's entitlement to winter heating payment, and
(b) they establish that, due to an official error, that determination was incorrect resulting in the individual not being given an award of winter heating payment to which the individual was entitled.

(2) In this regulation, "official error" means an error made by someone acting on behalf of the Scottish Ministers or on behalf of a Minister of the Crown that was not materially contributed to by anyone else.

Determination following error – overpayments

7.—(1) The Scottish Ministers must make a determination of an individual's entitlement to winter heating payment, without receiving an application, where—

(a) they have previously made a determination of the individual's entitlement to winter heating payment, and
(b) they establish that, due to an error, that determination was incorrect resulting in the individual being given an award of winter heating payment to which the individual was not entitled.

(2) In this regulation, references to an "error" are to—
(a) an error in the performance of a function conferred by these Regulations or the 2018 Act, including a determination being made—
  (i) wrongly, or
  (ii) correctly but on the basis of—
    (aa) incorrect information, or
    (bb) an assumption which proves to be wrong, or
(b) a new determination not being made after an assumption on the basis of which an earlier determination was made has proved to be wrong.

Periods for re-determination requests

8.—(1) The period for requesting a re-determination of entitlement to winter heating payment under section 41 (right to request a re-determination) of the 2018 Act is 31 days beginning with the day that the individual is informed, in accordance with section 40 (notice of determination) of that Act, of the right to make the request.

(2) In relation to determining entitlement to winter heating payment, the period allowed for re-determination (within the meaning of section 43 (duty to re-determine) of that Act) is 16 working days beginning with—
(a) the day that the request for a re-determination is received by Scottish Ministers,
(b) where the request for a re-determination is received by the Scottish Ministers later than the period prescribed by paragraph (1), the day on which the Scottish Ministers, or, on appeal, the First-tier Tribunal for Scotland, decide that the individual in question has a good reason for not requesting the re-determination sooner, or
(c) in a case where the Scottish Ministers have informed the individual of their decision that the request for a re-determination was not made in such form as the Scottish Ministers require, the day on which it is subsequently decided by the First-tier Tribunal for Scotland that the individual in question has made the request in such form as the Scottish Ministers require.

(3) For the purpose of paragraph (2), a "working day" is a day other than—
(a) a Saturday,
(b) a Sunday, or
(c) a bank holiday in Scotland under the Banking and Financial Dealings Act 1971.

Value and form of winter heating payment

9.—(1) The value of winter heating payment is [¹ £58.75].
(2) Winter heating payment is to be given in the form of money in a single payment made in respect of the winter following the qualifying week.

The Winter Heating Assistance (Low Income) (Scotland) Regulations 2023

AMENDMENT

1. Social Security (Up-rating) (Miscellaneous Amendments) (Scotland) Regulations 2024 (SSI 2024/105) reg.12 (April 1, 2024, subject to a saving under reg.14 and para.10 of Sch.).

Making payments

10.—(1) Where winter heating payment is payable in respect of an individual, the Scottish Ministers may, where they consider it appropriate, make the payment to another person to be used for the benefit of the individual.

(2) Where the Scottish Ministers consider, for any reason, that it is no longer appropriate for a particular person who falls within paragraph (1) to continue to receive the payment, they may cease making payment to that person and pay it instead to the individual who is entitled to the payment or another person.

Carer's Assistance (Carer Support Payment) (Scotland) Regulations 2023

(SSI 2023/302)

Made   25th October 2023
Coming into force   *in accordance with regulation 1*

PART 1

INTRODUCTORY AND INTERPRETATION

1. Citation and commencement
2. Interpretation

PART 2

CARER SUPPORT PAYMENT

3. Overview

PART 3

ELIGIBILITY

4. Age criteria
5. Provision of care to a cared for person
6. Residence and presence conditions
7. Temporary absence from the common travel area
8. Serving members of His Majesty's forces, civil servants and their family members
9. Aircraft workers, mariners and continental shelf operations
10. Persons residing in the United Kingdom to whom a relevant EU regulation applies
11. Persons residing outside the United Kingdom to whom a relevant EU regulation applies

12. Entitlement to other benefits
13. Individuals in education
14. Earnings limit

PART 4

MAKING OF APPLICATIONS AND PAYMENTS AND DURATION OF ELIGIBILITY

15. Making payments
16. Amount and form of Carer Support Payment
17. Abatement in respect of a relevant benefit
18. When an application is to be treated as made and beginning of entitlement to assistance
19. Applications made within 13 weeks of a qualifying disability benefit decision
20. Entitlement beginning before the commencement of these Regulations
21. Amount and form of Carer Support Payment where payments are backdated
22. Time of payment
23. Temporary stop in entitlement
24. Multiple applications involving the same cared for person
25. Continuing eligibility
26. Form of payment—giving Carer Support Payment by way of deduction
27. When a decrease in amount or cessation of entitlement takes effect
28. When an increase in amount of entitlement takes effect

PART 5

SUSPENSIONS

29. Circumstances in which assistance may be suspended
30. Having regard to financial circumstances
31. Information to be given following suspension
32. Right to review suspension
33. Ending a suspension
34. Effect of suspension ending

PART 6

RE-CONSIDERATION OF ENTITLEMENT TO CARER SUPPORT PAYMENT: DETERMINATION WITHOUT APPLICATION

35. Consideration of entitlement after specified period
36. Determination following change of circumstances etc.
37. Determination following official error—underpayments
38. Determination following error—overpayments
39. Determination to effect a deduction decision

PART 7

BREAKS IN CARE

40. Temporary break in care

Carer's Assistance (Carer Support Payment) (Scotland) Regulations 2023

Part 8

Movement of individuals between Scotland and the rest of the United Kingdom

41. Individuals in respect of whom Carer's Allowance is paid in another part of the United Kingdom immediately before moving to Scotland
42. Individuals in respect of whom Carer Support Payment is paid at the time of moving to another part of the United Kingdom

Part 9

Periods in respect of a re-determination request

43. Periods in respect of a re-determination request

Part 10

Transfer from Carer's Allowance to Carer Support Payment

44. Transfer from Carer's Allowance to Carer Support Payment

Part 11

Initial period for applications

45. Initial period for applications

Part 12

Transitory provision

46. Transitory provision—initial period for applications
47. Exclusion to transitory provision

Part 13

Consequential amendments

48. Consequential amendments

Schedule 1

Schedule 2 CALCULATION OF EARNINGS

The Scottish Ministers make the following Regulations in exercise of the powers conferred by sections 28(2), 41(4)(a), 43(5), 51(1), 52, 81(8) and 95 of the Social Security (Scotland) Act 2018 and all other powers enabling them to do so.

In accordance with section 96(2) of that Act, a draft of these Regulations has been laid before and approved by resolution of the Scottish Parliament.

In accordance with section 97(2) of that Act, the Scottish Ministers have informed the Scottish Commission on Social Security of their proposals, notified the Scottish Parliament that they have done so and made their proposals publicly available by such means as they consider appropriate.

(SSI 2023/302 reg.1)

Part 1

Introductory and interpretation

Citation and commencement

1.—(1) These Regulations may be cited as the Carer's Assistance (Carer Support Payment) (Scotland) Regulations 2023.

(2) Subject to paragraph (3), these Regulations come into force on 19 November 2023.

(3) Regulation 13(2) and (3) come into force on 1 October 2024.

Interpretation

2. In these Regulations—
"the 2018 Act" means the Social Security (Scotland) Act 2018,
"the 1992 Act" means the Social Security Contributions and Benefits Act 1992,
"Adult Disability Payment" means disability assistance for adults given in accordance with the Disability Assistance for Working Age People (Scotland) Regulations 2022,
"Armed Forces Independence Payment" means a payment under the Armed Forces and Reserve Forces (Compensation Scheme) Order 2011,
"Attendance Allowance" means an attendance allowance under—
  (a) section 64 of the 1992 Act, or
  (b) the Social Security (Attendance Allowance) Regulations (Northern Ireland) 1992,
"award week" means a period of 7 days beginning on a Sunday and ending on a Saturday,
"cared for person" is a person described in regulation 5(1),
"carer element of Universal Credit" means the amount awarded by virtue of—
  (a) section 12(2)(c) of the Welfare Reform Act 2012, or
  (b) article 17(2)(c) of the Welfare Reform (Northern Ireland) Order 2015,
"Carer's Allowance" means a benefit for carers given under—
  (a) section 70 (carer's allowance) of the 1992 Act, or
  (b) section 70 (carer's allowance) of the Social Security Contributions and Benefits (Northern Ireland) Act 1992,
"Carer Support Payment" means carer's assistance given in accordance with these Regulations,
"Child Disability Payment" means disability assistance for children and young people given in accordance with the Disability Assistance for Children and Young People (Scotland) Regulations 2021,
"Constant Attendance Allowance" means an allowance under—
  (a) section 104 of the 1992 Act, or
  (b) article 8 of the Naval, Military and Air Forces Etc. (Disablement and Death) Service Pensions Order 2006,
"couple" has the meaning given by section 39 of the Welfare Reform Act 2012,
"determination" or "determination of entitlement" has the meaning in section 25 of the 2018 Act,
"Disability Living Allowance" means a disability living allowance under—

(a) section 71 of the 1992 Act, or
(b) section 71 of the Social Security Contributions and Benefits (Northern Ireland) Act 1992,

"EEA state" means—
(a) any member state of the European Union, or
(b) any other state that is party to the Agreement on the European Economic Area signed at Oporto on 2 May 1992, together with the Protocol adjusting that Agreement signed at Brussels on 17 March 1993, as modified or supplemented from time to time,

"Industrial Injuries Disablement Benefit" means a benefit payable under Part V and section 103 of the 1992 Act,

"legal detention" means detention in legal custody within the meaning of section 295 of the Criminal Procedure (Scotland) Act 1995,

"Personal Independence Payment" means personal independence payment under—
(a) Part 4 of the Welfare Reform Act 2012, or
(b) Article 82 of the Welfare Reform (Northern Ireland) Order 2015,

"qualifying disability benefit" means—
(a) the daily living component of Adult Disability Payment at the standard or enhanced rate,
(b) the daily living component of Personal Independence Payment,
(c) the care component of Child Disability Payment at the middle or highest rate,
(d) the care component of Disability Living Allowance at the middle or highest rate,
(e) Attendance Allowance,
(f) Armed Forces Independence Payment, or
(g) Constant Attendance Allowance—
   (i) at or above the normal maximum rate with Industrial Injuries Disablement Benefit, or
   (ii) at the basic (full day) rate with a War Disablement Pension,

"relevant EU Regulation" means—
(a) one of the following Regulations—
   (i) Council Regulation (EC) No 1408/71 of 14 June 1971 on the application of social security schemes to employed persons, to self-employed persons and to members of their families moving within the Community,
   (ii) Regulation (EC) No 883/2004 of the European Parliament and of the Council of 29 April 2004 on the coordination of social security systems, or
(b) in relation to an individual to whom the agreement constituted by the exchange of letters set out in the schedule of the Family Allowances, National Insurance and Industrial Injuries (Gibraltar) Order 1974 applies, a Regulation mentioned in paragraph (a) of this definition as it forms part of domestic law by virtue of section 3 of the European Union (Withdrawal) Act 2018,

"War Disablement Pension" means—
(a) any retired pay, pension or allowance granted in respect of disablement under powers conferred by or under the Air Force (Constitution) Act 1917, the Personal Injuries (Emergency Provisions) Act 1939, the Pensions (Navy, Army, Air Force and Mercantile Marine) Act 1939,

the Polish Resettlement Act 1947, or Part VII or section 151 of the Reserve Forces Act 1980,

(b) without prejudice to paragraph (a) of this definition, any retired pay or pension to which any of paragraphs (a) to (f) of section 641(1) of the Income Tax (Earnings and Pensions) Act 2003 applies, and

"Young Carer Grant" means a grant paid under the Carer's Assistance (Young Carer Grants) (Scotland) Regulations 2019.

PART 2

CARER SUPPORT PAYMENT

Overview

3. An individual is entitled to Carer Support Payment in accordance with these Regulations if they meet the eligibility rules in—
   (a) regulation 4 (age criteria),
   (b) regulation 5 (provision of care to a cared for person),
   (c) regulations 6 to 11 (residence and presence conditions),
   (d) regulation 12 (entitlement to other benefits),
   (e) regulation 13 (individuals in education),
   (f) regulation 14 (earnings limit).

PART 3

ELIGIBILITY

Age criteria

4.—(1) Carer Support Payment may only be paid in respect of an individual who is 16 years of age or older.

(2) Where an individual was born on 29 February, the individual's birthday is to be taken to fall on 28 February in a year which is not a leap year.

Provision of care to a cared for person

5.—(1) Carer Support Payment may only be paid to an individual in respect of a period during which that individual provides regular and substantial care to a person to whom a qualifying disability benefit is normally payable (a "cared for person").

(2) For the purposes of paragraph (1), an individual shall only be treated as being regularly and substantially engaged in caring for a cared for person on every day in a week if they are, or are likely to be, regularly engaged for at least 35 hours in an award week in caring for that cared for person.

(3) No individual can be entitled to Carer Support Payment in respect of a cared for person where another individual is entitled to—
   (a) Carer Support Payment,
   (b) Carer's Allowance, or
   (c) the carer element of Universal Credit,
in respect of that cared for person.

(4) The care must not be provided by an individual—
   (a) under or by virtue of a contract, unless the contract is of a kind specified by regulations made under section 1(3)(a) of the Carers (Scotland) Act 2016 as not to be regarded as a contract for the purposes of that Act, or

(b) as voluntary work done for a charity or other not-for-profit organisation for which no payment is received other than reasonable expenses.

(5) No individual can be entitled to more than one Carer Support Payment in respect of the same period.

(6) No individual can be entitled to Carer Support Payment in respect of a period during which they are in legal detention.

(7) For the avoidance of doubt, an individual may be entitled to Carer Support Payment in respect of a cared for person where another individual is entitled to Young Carer Grant for that cared for person.

Residence and presence conditions

6.—(1) An individual satisfies the residence and presence conditions where on any day that individual—
   (a) is ordinarily resident in Scotland,
   (b) is habitually resident in the common travel area,
   (c) is not a person subject to immigration control within the meaning of section 115(9) of the Immigration and Asylum Act 1999,
   (d) is present in the common travel area, and
   (e) has been present in the common travel area for a period of, or for periods amounting in the aggregate to, not less than 26 weeks of the 52 weeks immediately preceding that day.

(2) In this Part, "common travel area" has the meaning given in section 1(3) of the Immigration Act 1971.

(3) The residence condition set out in paragraph (1)(a) does not apply where on any day the individual—
   (a) is habitually resident in Ireland,
   (b) has a genuine and sufficient link to Scotland, and
   (c) is an individual—
      (i) to whom the Convention on Social Security between the Government of the United Kingdom of Great Britain and Northern Ireland and the Government of Ireland signed at Dublin on 1 February 2019, as modified from time to time in accordance with any provision of it, applies, and
      (ii) in respect of whom the United Kingdom is, as a result, competent for the payment of long term care benefits.

(4) The reference in paragraph (3)(b) to an individual's link to Scotland being sufficient is to it being sufficiently close that if the individual were not entitled to Carer Support Payment, paragraph (3) would be incompatible with the Convention on Social Security between the Government of the United Kingdom of Great Britain and Northern Ireland and the Government of Ireland signed at Dublin on 1 February 2019.

(5) Paragraph (1)(c) does not apply to a person subject to immigration control within the meaning of section 115(9) of the Immigration and Asylum Act 1999 where the person—
   (a) is lawfully working in the United Kingdom and is a national of a state with which the United Kingdom has concluded an agreement which replaces in whole or in part an agreement under Article 217 of the Treaty on the Functioning of the European Union which has ceased to apply to, and in, the United Kingdom, providing, in the field of social security, for the equal treatment of workers who are nationals of the signatory state and their families,

(b) is a member of the family of, and living with, a person specified in sub-paragraph (a), or

(c) has been given leave to enter, or remain in, the United Kingdom by the Secretary of State upon an undertaking by another person or persons pursuant to the immigration rules, to be responsible for their maintenance and accommodation.

(6) The past presence condition in paragraph (1)(e) does not apply where an individual—

(a) has a terminal illness, or
(b) cares for a cared for person who—
  (i) has a terminal illness,
  (ii) is in receipt of Armed Forces Independence Payment or Constant Attendance Allowance at or above the normal maximum rate with Industrial Injuries Disablement Benefit, or at the basic (full day) rate with a War Disablement Pension, or
  (iii) is not required to meet a past presence condition by virtue of an exception set out in—
    (aa) regulation 2A(1) or 2C(1) of the Social Security (Attendance Allowance) Regulations 1991,
    (bb) regulation 2A(1) or 2C(1) of the Social Security (Disability Living Allowance) Regulations 1991,
    (cc) regulation 2A(1), 2B, 2C(1) or paragraph 5 of Schedule 2 of the Social Security (Disability Living Allowance) Regulations (Northern Ireland) 1992,
    (dd) regulation 22 or 23A(1) of the Social Security (Personal Independence Payment) Regulations 2013,
    (ee) regulation 5(8), (10)(b), 5(10A) or 8 of the Disability Assistance for Children and Young People (Scotland) Regulations 2021, or
    (ff) regulation 15(7), 17(2), 18 or 19 of the Disability Assistance for Working Age People (Scotland) Regulations 2022.

(7) For the purposes of paragraph (6), an individual or a cared for person has a terminal illness where they are entitled to—

(a) Disability Living Allowance by virtue of regulation 2(4) of the Social Security (Disability Living Allowance) Regulations 1991,
(b) Disability Living Allowance by virtue of regulation 2(3) of the Social Security (Disability Living Allowance) Regulations (Northern Ireland) 1992,
(c) Attendance Allowance by virtue of section 66 of the 1992 Act,
(d) Attendance Allowance by virtue of regulation 2(3) of the Social Security (Attendance Allowance) Regulations (Northern Ireland) 1992,
(e) Personal Independence Payment by virtue of regulation 21 of the Social Security (Personal Independence Payment) Regulations 2013,
(f) Universal Credit by virtue of regulations 16(2), 28(5)(a) or 40(5) read with paragraph 1 of Schedule 9 of the Universal Credit Regulations 2013,
(g) Employment and Support Allowance by virtue of regulations 7(1)(a), 16(1)(a), 31(1)(a), 45(2) or 85(2)(b) of the Employment and Support Allowance Regulations 2013,
(h) Personal Independence Payment by virtue of regulation 21 of the Personal Independence Payment Regulations (Northern Ireland) 2016,

Carer's Assistance (Carer Support Payment) (Scotland) Regulations 2023

      (i) Child Disability Payment by virtue of regulation 15 of the Disability Assistance for Children and Young People (Scotland) Regulations 2021,

  (j) Adult Disability Payment by virtue of regulation 26 of the Disability Assistance for Working Age People (Scotland) Regulations 2022.

(8) The habitual residence condition in paragraph (1)(b) and the past presence condition in paragraph (1)(e) do not apply where an individual is a person who—

  (a) has leave to enter or remain in the United Kingdom granted under the immigration rules by virtue of—

      (i) the Afghan Relocations and Assistance Policy, or

      (ii) the previous scheme for locally-employed staff in Afghanistan (sometimes referred to as the ex-gratia scheme),

  (b) has been granted discretionary leave outside the immigration rules as a dependant of a person referred to in sub-paragraph (a),

  (c) has leave granted under the Afghan Citizens Resettlement Scheme,

  (d) has been granted refugee status or humanitarian protection under the immigration rules,

  (e) has leave to enter or remain in the United Kingdom as the dependant of a person referred to in sub-paragraph (d),

  (f) has leave to enter or remain in the United Kingdom granted under or outside the immigration rules, has a right of abode in the United Kingdom within the meaning given in section 2 of the Immigration Act 1971 or does not require leave to enter or remain in the United Kingdom in accordance with section 3ZA of that Act, where the individual—

      (i) was residing in Ukraine immediately before 1 January 2022, and

      (ii) left Ukraine in connection with the Russian invasion which took place on 24 February 2022, [¹ . . .]

  (g) has leave to enter or remain in the United Kingdom granted under or outside the immigration rules, has a right of abode in the United Kingdom within the meaning given in section 2 of the Immigration Act 1971 or does not require leave to enter or remain in the United Kingdom in accordance with section 3ZA of that Act, where the individual—

      (i) was residing in Sudan before 15 April 2023, and

      (ii) left Sudan in connection with the violence which rapidly escalated on 15 April 2023 in Khartoum and across Sudan[¹, or

  (h) has leave to enter or remain in the United Kingdom granted under or outside the immigration rules, a right of abode in the United Kingdom within the meaning given in section 2 of the Immigration Act 1971 or does not require leave to enter or remain in the United Kingdom in accordance with section 3ZA of that Act, where the individual—

      (i) was residing in Israel, the West Bank, the Gaza Strip, East Jerusalem, the Golan Heights or Lebanon immediately before 7 October 2023, and

      (ii) left Israel, the West Bank, the Gaza Strip, East Jerusalem, the Golan Heights or Lebanon in connection with the Hamas terrorist attack in Israel on 7 October 2023 or the violence which rapidly escalated in the region following the attack.]

(9) For the purposes of this regulation—
(a) "immigration rules" means the rules laid before Parliament under section 3(2) of the Immigration Act 1971,
(b) "the Afghan Citizens Resettlement Scheme" means the scheme announced by the United Kingdom Government on 18 August 2021.

AMENDMENT

1. Social Security (Residence and Presence Requirements) (Israel, the West Bank, the Gaza Strip, East Jerusalem, the Golan Heights and Lebanon) (Scotland) Regulations 2023 (SSI 2023/309) reg.11(2) (5.38 p.m. on October 26, 2023).

Temporary absence from the common travel area

7.—(1) Where an individual is temporarily absent from the common travel area, the individual is to be treated as present in the common travel area during the first—
(a) 4 weeks of any period of absence,
(b) 13 weeks of any period of absence where that period of absence, or any extension to that period of absence, is for the specific purpose of caring for a cared for person who is also absent from the common travel area and where that cared for person is paid a qualifying disability benefit during that period, or
(c) 26 weeks of any period of absence where—
  (i) that period of absence, or any extension to that period of absence, is for the specific purpose of caring for a cared for person and is in connection with arrangements made for the medical treatment of the cared for person for a disease or bodily or mental disablement which commenced before leaving the common travel area and where that cared for person is paid a qualifying disability benefit during that period, and
  (ii) the arrangements relate to medical treatment—
    (aa) outside the common travel area,
    (bb) during the period when the cared for person is temporarily absent from the common travel area, and
    (cc) by, or under the supervision of, a person appropriately qualified to carry out that treatment.
(2) For the purposes of paragraph (1)—
(a) an individual is "temporarily absent" if, at the beginning of the period of absence, that absence is unlikely to exceed 52 weeks, and
(b) "medical treatment" means medical, surgical, psychological or rehabilitative treatment (including any course or diet regimen).

Serving members of His Majesty's forces, civil servants and their family members

8.—(1) A relevant individual is to be treated as meeting the residence and presence conditions set out in regulations 6(1)(a), (b) and (d) where on any day that individual is outside the common travel area—
(a) by reason of their capacity mentioned in paragraph (3)(a) provided that the individual satisfied the residence and presence conditions set out in regulation 6(1)(a), (b) and (d) immediately prior to the start of their employment mentioned in paragraph (3)(a), or
(b) by reason of being a person mentioned in paragraph (3)(b) living with an individual to whom paragraph (3)(a) applies.

(2) The past presence condition set out in regulation 6(1)(e) does not apply to a relevant individual.

(3) A "relevant individual" in paragraph (1) and (2) means an individual who is—
   (a) outside of the common travel area in their capacity as a—
      (i) serving member of His Majesty's forces, or
      (ii) civil servant, or
   (b) living with a person mentioned in sub-paragraph (a) and—
      (i) is the child, step-child or child in care of that person,
      (ii) is the parent, step-parent or parent-in-law of that person, or
      (iii) is married to or in a civil partnership with that person, or is living together with that person as if they were married or in a civil partnership.

(4) In this regulation—

"child in care" means—
   (a) under the law of Scotland, a child in respect of whom a relevant individual listed in paragraph (3)(a)—
      (i) is a foster carer within the meaning of regulation 2 of the Looked After Children (Scotland) Regulations 2009,
      (ii) is a kinship carer within the meaning of regulation 2 of the Looked After Children (Scotland) Regulations 2009,
      (iii) has a kinship care order within the meaning of section 72 of the Children and Young People (Scotland) Act 2014, or
   (b) under the law of England and Wales and Northern Ireland, a child in respect of whom a person listed in paragraph (3)(a) has a relationship equivalent to those listed under the law of Scotland,

"civil servant" has the meaning given by section 1(4) of the Constitutional Reform and Governance Act 2010, and

"serving member of His Majesty's forces" means a member of a regular force or a reserve force ("M") as defined, in each case, by section 374 (definitions applying for purposes of the whole Act) of the Armed Forces Act 2006, unless—
   (a) M is under the age of 16,
   (b) M is committing an offence under section 8 of the Armed Forces Act 2006 (desertion),
   (c) the force concerned is one of His Majesty's naval forces which M locally entered at an overseas base without—
      (i) previously being an insured person under the National Insurance Act 1965, or
      (ii) paying or having previously paid one or more of the following classes of contributions under the Social Security Act 1975 or the 1992 Act—
         (aa) primary Class 1,
         (bb) Class 2, or
         (cc) Class 3, or
   (d) the force concerned is one of His Majesty's military forces or His Majesty's air forces which M entered, or was recruited for, outside the United Kingdom and—
      (i) where that force is one of His Majesty's military forces, the depot for M's unit is outside the United Kingdom, or
      (ii) where that force is one of His Majesty's air forces, M is liable under the terms of M's engagement to serve only in a specified area outside the United Kingdom.

(SSI 2023/302 reg. 9)

Aircraft workers, mariners and continental shelf operations

9.—(1) An individual is to be treated as meeting the presence conditions set out in regulation 6(1)(d) and (e) for any period where that individual is—
  (a) outside the common travel area in their capacity as an aircraft worker or a mariner, or
  (b) in employment prescribed for the purposes of section 120 (employment at sea (continental shelf operations)) of the 1992 Act in connection with continental shelf operations.

(2) In this regulation—
"aircraft worker" means a person who is, or has been, employed under a contract of service either as a pilot, commander, navigator or other member of the crew of any aircraft, or in any other capacity on board any aircraft where—
  (a) the employment in that other capacity is for the purposes of the aircraft or its crew or of any passengers or cargo or mail carried on that aircraft, and
  (b) the contract is entered into in the United Kingdom with a view to its performance (in whole or in part) while the aircraft is in flight,
but does not include a person so far as that employment is as a serving member His Majesty's forces, and

"mariner" means a person who is, or has been, in employment under a contract of service either as a master or member of the crew of any ship or vessel, or in any other capacity on board any ship or vessel where—
  (a) the employment in that other capacity is for the purposes of that ship or vessel or its crew or any passenger or cargo or mail carried by the ship or vessel, and
  (b) the contract is entered into in the United Kingdom with a view to its performance (in whole or in part) while the ship or vessel is on voyage,
but does not include a person in so far as that employment is as a serving member of His Majesty's forces.

Persons residing in the United Kingdom to whom a relevant EU regulation applies

10.—(1) The past presence condition set out in regulation 6(1)(e) (residence and presence conditions) does not apply where on any day the individual is—
  (a) ordinarily resident in Scotland,
  (b) habitually resident in the United Kingdom,
  (c) an individual—
    (i) to whom the rules set out in a relevant EU regulation apply by virtue of—
      (aa) Title III of Part 2 of the EU withdrawal agreement,
      (bb) Part 3 or Article 23(4) of the Swiss citizens' rights agreement (as defined in section 39(1) of the European Union (Withdrawal Agreement) Act 2020 ("the 2020 Act"),
      (cc) Title III of the EEA EFTA separation agreement (as defined in section 39(1) of the 2020 Act), or

(dd) the agreement constituted by the exchange of letters set out in the schedule of the Family Allowances, National Insurance and Industrial Injuries (Gibraltar) Order 1974,

(ii) in respect of whom the United Kingdom is, as a result, competent for payment of sickness benefits in cash.

(2) An individual to whom a relevant EU regulation applies is not entitled to Carer Support Payment for a period unless during that period the United Kingdom is competent for payment of sickness benefits in cash to the person for the purposes of the relevant EU regulation in question.

Persons residing outside the United Kingdom to whom a relevant EU regulation applies

11.—(1) The residence and presence conditions set out in regulation 6(1) (residence and presence conditions) do not apply in relation to Carer Support Payment where on any day the individual satisfies the conditions in paragraph (2).

(2) The conditions referred to in paragraph (1) are that the individual must—

(a) be an individual—
  (i) to whom the rules set out in a relevant EU regulation apply by virtue of—
    (aa) Title III of Part 2 of the EU withdrawal agreement,
    (bb) Part 3 or Article 23(4) of the Swiss citizens' rights agreement (as defined in section 39(1) of the European Union (Withdrawal Agreement) Act 2020 ("the 2020 Act")),
    (cc) Title III of the EEA EFTA separation agreement (as defined in section 39(1) of the 2020 Act), or
    (dd) the agreement constituted by the exchange of letters set out in the schedule of the Family Allowances, National Insurance and Industrial Injuries (Gibraltar) Order 1974, and
  (ii) in respect of whom the United Kingdom is, as a result, competent for payment of sickness benefits in cash,
(b) be habitually resident in—
  (i) Switzerland,
  (ii) an EEA state, or
  (iii) Gibraltar, and
(c) have a genuine and sufficient link to Scotland.

(3) The reference in paragraph (2)(c) to an individual's link to Scotland being sufficient is to it being sufficiently close that if the individual were not entitled to Carer Support Payment, paragraph (2) would be incompatible with the applicable agreement mentioned in sub-paragraph (a)(i) of that paragraph.

(4) An individual to whom a relevant EU regulation applies is not entitled to Carer Support Payment for a period unless during that period the United Kingdom is competent for payment of sickness benefits in cash to the person for the purposes of the relevant EU regulation in question.

Entitlement to other benefits

12.—(1) An individual is not entitled to Carer Support Payment in respect of a cared for person for any period that they are entitled to—

(a) Carer's Allowance,

(b) the carer element of Universal Credit in respect of a different cared for person, or
(c) Young Carer Grant.

(2) An individual may be entitled to Carer Support Payment in respect of a cared for person where they have previously been entitled to Young Carer Grant.

Individuals in education

13.—(1) An individual who has not reached the age of 20 will not be entitled to Carer Support Payment if they are—
  (a) undertaking a course of full-time education, which is not advanced education and which is not provided by virtue of their employment or any office held by them, or
  (b) being provided with "appropriate full-time education" in England within the meaning of section 4 (appropriate full-time education or training) of the Education and Skills Act 2008, which is not—
    (i) a course in preparation for a degree, a diploma of higher education, a higher national certificate, a higher national diploma, a teaching qualification, any other course which is of a standard above ordinary national diploma, a national diploma, or national certificate of Edexcel, a general certificate of education (advanced level), or Scottish national qualifications at higher or advanced higher level,
    (ii) provided by virtue of their employment of any office held by them,
  (c) undertaking approved training that is not provided by means of a contract of employment.

(2) This regulation does not apply to an individual if they are—
  (a) without parental support,
  (b) entitled to disability living allowance, child disability payment, adult disability payment or personal independence payment and, on a date before the date on which the individual starts receiving education—
    (i) it has been determined that they have limited capability for work or limited capability for work and work-related activity on the basis of an assessment under Part 5 of the Universal Credit Regulations 2013 or under Part 4 or 5 of the Employment and Support Allowance Regulations 2013, or
    (ii) they are treated as having limited capability for work under schedule 8 of the Universal Credit Regulations 2013 or limited capability for work and work-related activity under schedule 9 of the Universal Credit Regulations 2013,
  (c) responsible for a child or a qualifying young person,
  (d) single and is a foster parent with whom a child is placed,
  (e) a member of a couple—
    (i) and the other member of the couple is not undertaking a course of education, or
    (ii) both of whom are receiving education, and the other member of the couple falls within one of the exceptions set out in paragraph (2)(a) to (d).

(3) For the purposes of paragraph (2)(a), an individual is without parental support if they are not being looked after by a local authority and—

(a) has no parent,
(b) cannot live with their parents because—
    (i) the individual is estranged from them, or
    (ii) there is a serious risk to the individual's physical or mental health, or that individual would suffer significant harm if the individual lived with them,
(c) is living away from their parents, and neither parent is able to support the individual financially because that parent—
    (i) has a physical or mental impairment,
    (ii) is detained in custody pending trial or sentence upon conviction or under a sentence imposed by a court, or
    (iii) is prohibited from entering or re-entering Great Britain.

(4) For the purposes of this regulation—

"advanced education" means full-time education (which is not school education within the meaning of the Education (Scotland) Act 1980) for the purposes of—
(a) a course in preparation for a degree, a diploma of higher education, a higher national certificate, a higher national diploma, or a teaching qualification, or
(b) any other course which is of a standard above ordinary national diploma, a national diploma or national certificate of Edexcel, a general certificate of education (advanced level), or Scottish national qualifications at higher or advanced higher level,

"approved training" means arrangements made by the Government—
(a) in relation to Wales, known as "Traineeships" or "Foundation Apprenticeships",
(b) in relation to Scotland, known as "No One Left Behind", or
(c) in relation to Northern Ireland, known as "PEACE IV Children and Young People 2.1", "Training for Success", or "Skills for Life and Work",

"arrangements made by the Government" means arrangements—
(a) in relation to England and Wales, made by the Secretary of State under section 2 of the Employment and Training Act 1973,
(b) in relation to Scotland, made—
    (i) by the Scottish Ministers under section 2 of the Employment and Training Act 1973,
    (ii) by Scottish Enterprise or Highlands and Islands Enterprise under section 2 of the Enterprise and New Towns (Scotland) Act 1990, or
(c) in relation to Northern Ireland, made by the Department for Communities or the Department for the Economy under sections 1 and 3 of the Employment and Training Act (Northern Ireland) 1950,

"foster parent" means—
(a) under the law of Scotland, a foster carer or kinship carer with whom a child is placed under the Looked After Children (Scotland) Regulations 2009, or
(b) under the law of England and Wales and Northern Ireland, a person with whom a child is placed who has an equivalent relationship with the child to those listed under the law of Scotland,

"full-time education"—
(a) is education undertaken in pursuit of a course, where the average time spent during term time in receiving tuition, engaging in

practical work, or supervised study, or taking examinations exceeds 21 hours per week, and
(b) in calculating the time spent in pursuit of the course, no account is taken of time occupied by meal breaks or spent on unsupervised study, and

"qualifying young person" has the same meaning as regulation 5 of the Universal Credit Regulations 2013.

GENERAL NOTE

Note that reg.13(2) and (3) do not come into force until October 1, 2024.

Earnings limit

14.—(1) An individual is not entitled to Carer Support Payment in any award week in which their earnings in respect of that award week exceed [¹£151].

(2) Earnings are to be calculated in accordance with schedule 2.

AMENDMENT

1. Social Security (Up-rating) (Miscellaneous Amendments) (Scotland) Regulations 2024 (SSI 2024/105) reg.7(1) and (2) (April 7, 2024, subject to a saving under reg.14 and para.5 of Sch.).

PART 4

MAKING OF APPLICATIONS AND PAYMENTS AND DURATION OF ELIGIBILITY

Making payments

15.—(1) Where Carer Support Payment is payable in respect of an individual, the Scottish Ministers may, where they consider it appropriate, make the payment to another person to be used for the benefit of the individual.

(2) Where the Scottish Ministers consider, for any reason, that it is no longer appropriate for a particular person who falls within paragraph (1) to continue to receive the payment, they may cease making payment to that person.

Amount and form of Carer Support Payment

16.—(1) Subject to regulation 21 (amount and form of carer support payment where payments are backdated), the weekly rate of payment of Carer Support Payment is [¹£81.90].

(2) For any award week where an individual is entitled to one or more overlapping benefit, the amount of Carer Support Payment that is to be given to the individual is to be reduced—
(a) by the amount of the overlapping benefit paid, or
(b) where the amount of the overlapping benefit is equal to or greater than the amount of Carer Support Payment, the value of Carer Support Payment that is to be given to the individual is £0.

(3) In this regulation "overlapping benefit" means—
(a) State Pension or Retirement Pension,
(b) Incapacity Benefit,
(c) Severe Disablement Allowance,
(d) Unemployability Supplement that is paid with Industrial Injuries Disablement benefit or War Pension,

(e) Widow's Allowance or Widow's Benefit or Widowed Parent's Allowance or Widowed Mother's Allowance or Widow's Pension, excluding additional pension,
(f) Bereavement Allowance,
(g) War Widow's or Widower's Pension,
(h) Maternity Allowance,
(i) Industrial Death Benefit,
(j) Contribution-based Jobseeker's Allowance,
(k) Contributory Employment and Support Allowance,
(l) Training Allowance.

(4) When the cared for person dies and an individual was entitled to Carer Support Payment in respect of that cared for person immediately before their death, the individual's entitlement to Carer Support Payment will continue to be paid until whichever of the following comes first—
(a) until the first day of the award week following the award week in which the individual ceases to satisfy any of the eligibility requirements set out in regulations 6 to 14, or
(b) for a period of 8 award weeks after the first day of the award week following the award week in which the cared for person died.

(5) Carer Support Payment may only be given as money, except as provided for by—
(a) regulation 17 (abatement in respect of a relevant individual), or
(b) regulation 26 (form of payment—giving Carer Support Payment by way of deduction).

(6) For the purposes of this regulation—

"1914–1918 War Injuries Scheme" means any scheme made under the Injuries in War (Compensation) Act 1914 or under the Injuries in War Compensation Act 1914 (Session 2) or any Government scheme for compensation in respect of persons injured in any merchant ship or fishing vessel as the result of hostilities during the 1914-1918 War,

"Bereavement Allowance" means an allowance referred to in section 39B of the 1992 Act subject to the transitional provisions specified in article 4 of the Pensions Act 2014 (Commencement No.10) Order 2017,

"Contribution-based Jobseeker's Allowance" means an allowance under the Jobseekers Act 1995 as amended by the provisions of Part 1 of Schedule 14 to the Welfare Reform Act 2012 that remove references to an income-based allowance, and a contribution-based allowance under the Jobseekers Act as that Act has effect apart from those provisions,

"Contributory Employment and Support Allowance" means an allowance under Part 1 of the Welfare Reform Act 2007 as amended by the provisions of Schedule 3, and Part 1 of Schedule 14, to the Welfare Reform Act 2012 Act that remove references to an income-related allowance, and a contributory allowance under Part 1 of the Welfare Reform Act 2007 as that Part has effect apart from those provisions,

"Incapacity Benefit" means a benefit referred to in section 30A of the 1992 Act,

"Industrial Death Benefit" means a benefit referred to in Part VI of Schedule 7 to the 1992 Act,

"Maternity Allowance" means an allowance referred to in sections 35 and 35B of the 1992 Act,

(SSI 2023/302 reg.16)

"Personal Injuries Scheme" means any scheme made under the Personal Injuries (Emergency Provisions) Act 1939 or under the Pensions (Navy, Army, Air Force and Mercantile Marine) Act 1939,

"Retirement Pension" means a pension payable under Part II and Part III of the 1992 Act, excluding any additional pension or graduated retirement benefit,

"Service Pensions Instrument" means any instrument described in sub-paragraphs (a) or (b) below in so far, but only in so far, as the pensions or other benefits provided by that instrument are not calculated or determined by reference to length of service, namely:—
  (a) any instrument made in exercise of powers—
    (i) referred to in section 12(1) of the Social Security (Miscellaneous Provisions) Act 1977 (pensions or other benefits for disablement or death due to service in the armed forces of the Crown); or
    (ii) under section 1 of the Polish Resettlement Act 1947 (pensions and other benefits for disablement or death due to service in certain Polish forces); or
  (b) any instrument under which a pension or other benefit may be paid to a person (not being a member of the armed forces of the Crown) out of public funds in respect of death or disablement, wound, injury or disease due to service in any nursing service or other auxiliary service of any of the armed forces of the Crown, or in any other organisation established under the control of the Defence Council or formerly established under the control of the Admiralty, the Army Council or the Air Council,

"Severe Disablement Allowance" means an allowance referred to in sections 68 and 69 of the 1992 Act,

"State Pension" means a pension payable under Part 1 of the Pensions Act 2014,

"Training Allowance" means an allowance (whether by way of periodical grants or otherwise) payable out of public funds by a Government department or by or on behalf of Scottish Enterprise, Highlands and Islands Enterprise, the Secretary of State, the National Assembly for Wales to a person for their maintenance, or in respect of any dependant of theirs, for the period, or part of the period, during which they are following a course of training or instruction provided by, or in pursuance of arrangements made with, that department or approved by that department in relation to them or so provided or approved by or on behalf of the Scottish Enterprise, Highlands and Islands Enterprise, the National Assembly for Wales or the said Commission but it does not include—
  (a) an allowance paid by any Government department to or in respect of a person by reason of the fact that they are following a course of full-time education or is training as a teacher, or
  (b) a payment made by or on behalf of Scottish Enterprise, Highlands and Islands Enterprise or the Secretary of State to any person by way of training premium or training bonus in consequence of that person's use of facilities for training provided in pursuance of arrangements made under section 2 of the Employment and Training Act 1973 or section 2 of the Enterprise and New Towns (Scotland) Act 1990,

"Unemployability Supplement" includes an increase on account of unemployability under any Personal Injuries Scheme, Service Pensions Instrument or 1914–1918 War Injuries Scheme,

"War Widow's Pension" means any widow's or surviving civil partner's pension or allowance granted in respect of a death due to service or war injury and payable by virtue of any enactment mentioned in paragraph (a) of the definition of "War Disablement Pension" in regulation 2, or a pension or allowance for a widow or surviving civil partner granted under any scheme mentioned in section 641(1)(e) or (f) of the Income Tax (Earnings and Pensions) Act 2003,

"Widowed Mother's Allowance" means an allowance referred to in section 37 of the 1992 Act,

"Widowed Parent's Allowance" means an allowance referred to in section 39A of the 1992 Act,

"Widow's Pension" means a pension referred to in section 38 of the 1992 Act.

AMENDMENT

1. Social Security (Up-rating) (Miscellaneous Amendments) (Scotland) Regulations 2024 (SSI 2024/105) reg.7(1) and (3) (April 7, 2024, subject to a saving under reg.14 and para.5 of Sch.).

Abatement in respect of a relevant benefit

17.—(1) This regulation applies where an individual—
  (a) makes an application for Carer Support Payment, or
  (b) becomes entitled to an increased amount of Carer Support Payment following a determination without application, and
  (c) that individual is (or if they are a member of a couple, their partner is) in receipt of a relevant benefit at any time during the abatement period.

(2) Where this regulation applies, Carer Support Payment may be given (in whole or in part) to the Secretary of State in order to meet, or contribute towards meeting, any liability the individual has to the Secretary of State in connection with a relevant benefit, provided that the individual has—
  (a) agreed to the assistance being given in that form, or
  (b) unreasonably refused to agree to the assistance being given in that form.

(3) The amount of Carer Support Payment that is to be given by way of payment to the Secretary of State in accordance with paragraph (2) is to be the difference between—
  (a) the total amount of any relevant benefits the individual or their partner is paid during the abatement period, and
  (b) the total amount of any relevant benefits the individual or their partner would have been paid during the abatement period had their entitlement to those relevant benefits been adjusted as a result of their entitlement to Carer Support Payment (which, for the avoidance of doubt, includes any carer premia, carer additions, or carer elements that they would be entitled to receive).

(4) For the purposes of this regulation—
"abatement period" means—
  (a) where sub-paragraph (1)(a) applies, a period, as short as reasonably practicable, beginning with the first day of the award week in which

the individual's entitlement to Carer Support Payment begins and ending on the day before the first day of the award week in which the individual's first payment of Carer Support Payment is made, or
(b) where sub paragraph (1)(b) applies, a period, as short as reasonably practicable, beginning with the first day of the award week in which the individual's entitlement to Carer Support Payment increases and ending on the day before the first day of the award week in which the individual received the first payment of Carer Support Payment at that increased amount,

"Income Support" means a payment made under section 124 of the 1992 Act,

"Income-based Jobseeker's Allowance" means a jobseeker's allowance entitlement to which is based on the individual's satisfying conditions which include those set out in section 3 of the Jobseeker's Act 1995, or a joint-claim jobseeker's allowance,

"Income-related Employment and Support Allowance" means an income-related allowance under Part 1 of the Welfare Reform Act 2007,

"joint-claim jobseeker's allowance" means a jobseeker's allowance entitlement to which arises by virtue of section 1(2B) of the Jobseeker's Act 1995, and

"Pension Credit" means a pension credit under the State Pension Credit Act 2002, and

"relevant benefit" means—
(a) Income Support,
(b) Income-based Jobseeker's Allowance,
(c) Income-related Employment and Support Allowance, or
(d) Pension Credit.

When an application is to be treated as made and beginning of entitlement to assistance

18.—(1) An application for Carer Support Payment is to be treated as made on the day it is received by the Scottish Ministers.

(2) Where, on the basis of an application, a determination is made that an individual is entitled to Carer Support Payment, entitlement to assistance is to begin—
(a) on the first day of the award week in which the application is treated as made in accordance with paragraph (1),
(b) where the individual has notified the Scottish Ministers that they wish their entitlement to assistance to begin on a date prior to the day on which their application is treated as made, on the first day of the award week in which that chosen date falls, provided that—
 (i) the date chosen by the individual is no more than 13 weeks prior to the day on which their application is treated as made, and
 (ii) the individual satisfied the eligibility requirements set out in Part 3 of these Regulations on that chosen date, or
(c) where regulation 19 applies (applications made within 13 weeks of a qualifying disability benefit), a date to be chosen by the Scottish Ministers in accordance with that regulation.

(3) Where the individual does not satisfy the eligibility requirements set out in Part 3 of these Regulations on the chosen date mentioned in

paragraph (2)(b), the Scottish Ministers may choose that entitlement to assistance begins on a later date, provided the individual satisfied the eligibility requirements on that later date.

(4) For the purposes of section 38(3) of the 2018 Act, the period covered by an application for Carer Support Payment—
   (a) under paragraph (2)(a)—
      (i) begins on the day on which the application is treated as having been made, and
      (ii) ends on the day on which the determination of entitlement is made,
   (b) under paragraph (2)(b) or (c)—
      (i) begins on the date chosen or the later date in accordance with paragraph (3),
      (ii) ends on the day on which the determination of entitlement is made.

Applications made within 13 weeks of a qualifying disability benefit decision

19.—(1) Where an individual makes an application for Carer Support Payment in respect of a cared for person within 13 weeks of a relevant qualifying disability benefit decision, the Scottish Ministers may determine that entitlement to Carer Support Payment begins on the first day of the award week in which, as a result of that relevant qualifying disability benefit decision, entitlement to that benefit begins, provided the individual satisfied the eligibility requirements set out in Part 3 of these Regulations on that date.

(2) Where the individual does not satisfy the eligibility requirements set out in Part 3 of these Regulations on the date on which the relevant qualifying disability benefit decision falls, the Scottish Ministers may determine that entitlement to Carer Support Payment begins on a later date, provided the individual satisfies those eligibility requirements on that later date.

(3) For the purposes of this regulation, "relevant qualifying disability benefit decision" means a decision—
   (a) made by the Secretary of State, the Scottish Ministers, or the Department for Communities in Northern Ireland—
      (i) on a claim or an application, or
      (ii) on revision, determination of entitlement, or supersession, or
   (b) on appeal whether by the First-tier Tribunal, the First-tier Tribunal for Scotland, the Upper Tribunal, the court, the Northern Ireland Appeal Tribunal or the Northern Ireland Social Security and Child Support Commissioner,
awarding a qualifying disability benefit to the cared for person mentioned in paragraph (1).

Entitlement beginning before the commencement of these Regulations

20. Where the Scottish Ministers make a determination under regulation 19 (applications made within 13 weeks of a qualifying disability benefit decision) the effect of which is that an individual's entitlement to Carer Support Payment would begin on a date before the commencement of these Regulations—
   (a) the individual is treated as having made a claim for Carer's Allowance under section 70 of the 1992 Act for the period starting with that

date and ending on the day before the date of commencement of these Regulations,
(b) the determination is to be made on the assumption that the individual satisfied the eligibility requirements in section 70 of the 1992 Act, read with the Social Security (Invalid Care Allowance) Regulations 1976 for that period, and
(c) any payments of Carer Support Payment made in respect of that period are to be treated as though they were payments of Carer's Allowance.

Amount and form of Carer Support Payment where payments are backdated

21. Any payment of Carer Support Payment made in respect of a period—
(a) before the commencement of these Regulations is to be paid at the weekly rate specified in paragraph 4 of Part III of schedule 4 of the 1992 Act, or
(b) after the commencement of these Regulations is to be paid at the weekly rate specified in regulation 16(1) (amount and form of Carer Support Payment),
as it had effect during the period to which that payment relates.

Time of payment

22. Where an award of Carer Support Payment is made, the Scottish Ministers are to—
(a) make the first payment of assistance on a date specified in the notice of determination, and
(b) inform the individual that any subsequent payment will be made—
    (i) 4 weekly in arrears, or
    (ii) weekly in advance.

Temporary stop in entitlement

23.—(1) This paragraph applies where the Scottish Ministers have made a determination without application under regulation 36 (determination following a change of circumstances etc.) that an individual is no longer entitled to Carer Support Payment in respect of a cared for person because—
(a) the individual's earnings in respect of an award week exceeded the earnings limit set out in regulation 14,
(b) the cared for person has voluntarily relinquished their entitlement to their qualifying disability benefit and the individual therefore no longer satisfies the requirements of regulation 5(1) (provision of care to a cared for person) in respect of an award week, or
(c) subject to regulation 40 (temporary break in care), the individual failed to satisfy the requirements of regulation 5(1) (provision of care to a cared for person) in respect of an award week.
(2) Where paragraph (1) applies, the Scottish Ministers are to make a determination without application of the individual's entitlement to Carer Support Payment if, within 26 weeks of the determination mentioned in paragraph (1), the Scottish Ministers establish that the individual satisfies the eligibility requirements set out in Part 3 of these Regulations.

(3) The duty on the Scottish Ministers to make a determination without application mentioned in paragraph (2) does not apply where another individual has been awarded—
　(a) Carer Support Payment,
　(b) Carer's Allowance, or
　(c) the carer element of Universal Credit,
in respect of the cared for person mentioned in paragraph (1).

(4) This paragraph applies where an individual who has an ongoing entitlement to Carer Support Payment cares for a cared for person whose qualifying disability benefit has been—
　(a) reduced to £0,
　(b) ended as a result of the cared for person being—
　　(i) admitted to a hospital or care home, or
　　(ii) in legal detention,
　(c) suspended as a result of—
　　(i) the circumstances mentioned in—
　　　(aa) regulation 26A(3)(a) of the Disability Assistance for Children and Young People (Scotland) Regulations 2021, or
　　　(bb) regulation 38(3)(a) of the Disability Assistance for Working Age People (Scotland) Regulations 2022,
　　(ii) a failure to provide information in accordance with—
　　　(aa) regulation 17 of the Social Security and Child Support (Decisions and Appeals) Regulations 1999,
　　　(bb) regulation 17 of the Social Security and Child Support (Decisions and Appeals) Regulations (Northern Ireland) 1999,
　　　(cc) regulation 45 of the Universal Credit, Personal Independence Payment, Jobseeker's Allowance and Employment and Support Allowance (Decisions and Appeals) Regulations 2013, or
　　　(dd) regulation 44 of the Universal Credit, Personal Independence Payment, Jobseeker's Allowance and Employment and Support Allowance (Decisions and Appeals) Regulations (Northern Ireland) 2016, or
　　(iii) the circumstances mentioned in—
　　　(aa) regulation 16(3)(a)(i) or (ii) of the Social Security and Child Support (Decisions and Appeals) Regulations 1999,
　　　(bb) regulation 16(3)(a)(i) or (ii) of the Social Security and Child Support (Decisions and Appeals) Regulations (Northern Ireland) 1999,
　　　(cc) regulation 44(2)(a)(i) or (ii) of the Universal Credit, Personal Independence Payment, Jobseeker's Allowance and Employment and Support Allowance (Decisions and Appeals) Regulations 2013, or
　　　(dd) regulation 43(2)(a)(i) or (ii) of the Universal Credit, Personal Independence Payment, Jobseeker's Allowance and Employment and Support Allowance (Decisions and Appeals) Regulations (Northern Ireland) 2016.

(5) Where paragraph (4) applies, the Scottish Ministers are to make a determination without receiving an application that the individual is no longer entitled to Carer Support Payment.

(SSI 2023/302 reg.23)

(6) Where paragraph (4)(a) or (b) applies, the determination comes into effect on the first day of the award week following the award week in which the cared for person's qualifying disability benefit has been ended or reduced to £0.

(7) Where paragraph (4)(c) applies, the determination comes into effect on the first day of the award week following the day on which the cared for person's qualifying disability benefit has been suspended for 4 weeks.

(8) Where paragraph (5) applies, the Scottish Ministers are to make a determination without application of the individual's entitlement to Carer Support Payment if, within 26 weeks of the determination mentioned in paragraph (5), the Scottish Ministers establish that—
  (a) a determination is made that the value of the qualifying disability benefit that is to be given to the cared for person is an amount more than £0, or
  (b) the suspension of the cared for person's qualifying disability benefit mentioned in paragraph (4)(c) is ended and the cared for person would have been entitled to the qualifying disability benefit during the period of suspension.

(9) Where paragraph (2) applies, the individual's entitlement to assistance begins—
  (a) where the individual notifies the Scottish Ministers that they satisfy the eligibility requirements set out in Part 3 of these Regulations within 13 weeks of that change occurring, on the first day of the award week in which that change occurred,
  (b) where the individual notifies the Scottish Ministers that they satisfy the eligibility requirements set out in Part 3 of these Regulations later than 13 weeks of the change occurring, but where the Scottish Ministers consider that the individual has good reason for not notifying the change within 13 weeks, on the first day of the award week in which that change occurred,
  (c) where the individual notifies the Scottish Ministers that they satisfy the eligibility requirements set out in Part 3 of these Regulations later than 13 weeks of the change occurring and where the Scottish Ministers do not consider that the individual has good reason for not notifying that change within 13 weeks, on the first day of the award week in which the individual notified that change, or
  (d) in any other case, the first day of the award week in which the individual satisfies the eligibility requirements set out in Part 3 of these Regulations.

(10) Where paragraph (8)(a) applies, the individual's entitlement to assistance begins—
  (a) where the individual notifies the Scottish Ministers that the cared for person's qualifying disability benefit is paid at an amount more than £0 within 13 weeks of that change occurring, on the first day of the award week in which that change occurred,
  (b) where the individual notifies the Scottish Ministers that the cared for person's qualifying disability benefit is paid at an amount more than £0 later than 13 weeks of the change occurring, but where the Scottish Ministers consider that the individual has good reason for not notifying the change within 13 weeks, on the first day of the award week in which that change occurred,

(c) where the individual notifies the Scottish Ministers that the cared for person's qualifying disability benefit is paid at an amount more than £0 later than 13 weeks of the change occurring and where the Scottish Ministers do not consider that the individual has good reason for not notifying that change within 13 weeks, on the first day of the award week in which the individual notified that change, or

(d) in any other case, the first day of the award week in which the cared for person's qualifying disability benefit is paid at an amount more than £0.

(11) Where paragraph (8)(b) applies, the individual's entitlement to assistance begins—

(a) where it is determined that during the period of suspension, the cared for person would have been entitled to a qualifying disability benefit in respect of that period, on the first day of the award week in which the cared for person's entitlement to the qualifying disability benefit begins,

(b) in any other event, on the first day of the award week in which the suspension is ended.

Multiple applications involving the same cared for person

24.—(1) Where the Scottish Ministers receive two or more applications for Carer Support Payment from different individuals in respect of the same cared for person, the Scottish Ministers must determine the application made first before determining any other application.

(2) Where, but for regulation 5(3) (provision of care to a cared for person), two or more individuals would be entitled to Carer Support Payment in respect of the same cared for person for the same period, only one of them may be entitled, being either—

(a) one of them as they may jointly agree in accordance with paragraph (5), or

(b) in absence of such agreement, one of them as may be determined by the Scottish Ministers in accordance with paragraph (6).

(3) Where, but for regulation 5(3) (provision of care to a cared for person), a person ('carer A') would be entitled to Carer's Allowance payable by the Scottish Ministers and another person ('carer B') would be entitled to Carer Support Payment in respect of the same cared for person for the same period, carer B will only be entitled if—

(a) carer A and carer B jointly agree in accordance with paragraph (5) that carer A will not be entitled, or

(b) in absence of such agreement, the Scottish Ministers determine that carer B is or remains entitled to Carer Support Payment in respect of that period.

(4) Where, but for regulation 5(3) (provision of care to a cared for person), a person ('carer A') would have a relevant entitlement and another person ('carer B') would be entitled to Carer Support Payment in respect of the same cared for person for the same period, carer B will only be entitled to Carer Support Payment if—

(a) carer A and carer B jointly agree in accordance with paragraph (5) that carer A will not have a relevant entitlement, or

(b) in absence of such agreement, the Scottish Ministers determine that carer B is or remains entitled to Carer Support Payment in respect of that period, following—
   (i) in a case where the relevant entitlement is to—
      (aa) a Carer's Allowance payable by the Secretary of State under section 70 of the 1992 Act,
      (bb) the carer element of Universal Credit payable by the Secretary of State under section 12(2)(c) of the Welfare Reform Act 2012,
consultation with the Secretary of State,
   (ii) in a case where the relevant entitlement is to—
      (aa) a Carer's Allowance payable by the Department for Communities in Northern Ireland under section 70 of the Social Security Contributions and Benefits (Northern Ireland) Act 1992,
      (bb) the carer element of Universal Credit payable by the Department for Communities in Northern Ireland under Article 17(2)(c) of the Welfare Reform (Northern Ireland) Order 2015,
consultation with the Department for Communities in Northern Ireland.

(5) An agreement under paragraph (2)(a), (3)(a) or (4)(a) is to be made by giving the Scottish Ministers a notice in writing signed by the individuals mentioned in paragraph (2), (3) or (4) as the case may be, specifying one of them as the individual to be entitled to assistance.

(6) When making a determination under paragraph (2)(b), (3)(b) or (4)(b), the Scottish Ministers must have regard to factors including but not limited to—
   (a) the best interests of the cared for person,
   (b) whether any of the individuals mentioned in paragraph (2), (3) or (4)—
      (i) are family members of the cared for person,
      (ii) live with or near the cared for person,
      (iii) receive any benefits on behalf of, or as a result of their responsibility for, the cared for person.

(7) The Scottish Ministers may, having considered the factors set out in paragraph (6), make a determination without application that—
   (a) one of the individuals mentioned in paragraph (2) or (3), or
   (b) following consultation with the Secretary of State or, as the case may be, the Department for Communities in Northern Ireland, carer B mentioned in paragraph (4),
who has ongoing entitlement to Carer Support Payment, is no longer entitled to Carer Support Payment.

(8) For the purposes of this regulation, an individual has a "relevant entitlement" if the individual is entitled to—
   (a) a Carer's Allowance, or
   (b) the carer element of universal credit.

(9) Where paragraph (2) applies at the same time as paragraphs (3) or (4), the Scottish Ministers must make a determination under paragraph (2) before making a determination under paragraph (3) or (4).

Continuing eligibility

25.—(1) Subject to paragraphs (3) and (4), a determination that an individual is entitled to Carer Support Payment in respect of a period is to be made on the basis that the individual has an ongoing entitlement to Carer Support Payment after the end of that period, except where paragraph (2) applies.

(2) This paragraph applies where, after the end of the period mentioned in paragraph (1), the individual no longer satisfies the eligibility rules.

(3) A determination of ongoing entitlement is made on the basis that—
  (a) the individual will continue to be entitled to Carer Support Payment for a fixed or indefinite period as specified in the notice of determination, and
  (b) the decision that the individual is entitled to Carer Support Payment for each subsequent 4-week period is to be taken in accordance with these Regulations, on the strength of the assumptions set out in paragraph (4).

(4) The assumptions are that—
  (a) the individual continues to satisfy the eligibility criteria which were satisfied to be entitled to Carer Support Payment under the determination mentioned in paragraph (1),
  (b) the information on which the determination mentioned in paragraph (1) was made still applies and is relevant in the individual's case, and
  (c) there is no change in circumstances of the individual which would require to be notified under section 56 of the 2018 Act.

Form of payment—giving Carer Support Payment by way of deduction

26.—(1) Where an individual has a liability to the Scottish Ministers under section 63 of the 2018 Act, the individual's payment of Carer Support Payment may be given (in whole or in part) by way of deduction, at a reasonable level, from that liability either—
  (a) with the agreement of the individual, or
  (b) without the individual's agreement, where the individual has unreasonably refused to agree to the assistance being given in that form.

(2) For the purposes of paragraph (1), "reasonable level" means a level that is reasonable having regard to the financial circumstances of the individual.

When a decrease in amount or cessation of entitlement takes effect

27.—(1) Where, as a result of a determination without application, the amount of Carer Support Payment payable in respect of an individual is decreased or their entitlement to Carer Support Payment ceases, the change takes effect—
  (a) in the case of a determination without application under regulation 35 (consideration of entitlement after specified period) or 36(a) (determination following change of circumstances etc.), on the first day of the award week following the award week in which—
    (i) the individual should have notified the Scottish Ministers of the change, where the individual was required to notify a change under section 56 of the 2018 Act, if the individual—
      (aa) knowingly fails to notify a change, or

(bb) fails to notify the change as soon as reasonably practicable after it occurred, or
  (ii) in any other case, the Scottish Ministers make the determination,
(b) in the case of an earlier determination which was based on error within the meaning of—
  (i) regulation 37 (determination following official error—underpayments), on the first day of the award week in which the earlier determination took effect, or
  (ii) regulation 38 (determination following error—overpayments), on the first day of the award week following the award week in which the earlier determination took effect,
(c) in any other case, on the first day of the award week following the award week in which the Scottish Ministers make the determination.
(2) Where the Scottish Ministers consider that in all the circumstances it would be unjust not to do so, they may, when making their determination, set a later date for the purposes of paragraph (1).

When an increase in amount of entitlement takes effect

28.—(1) Where, as a result of a determination without application, the amount of Carer Support Payment payable in respect of an individual is increased, the change takes effect—
(a) in the case of an increase pursuant to a determination made under regulation 36(a) or (b) (determination following change of circumstances etc.), on the first day of the award week in which—
  (i) the individual first satisfies the requirements for an increased amount of Carer Support Payment—
    (aa) where the individual reports the change within 13 weeks of the change occurring, or
    (bb) where the individual reports the change more than 13 weeks after the change occurring, but only if the Scottish Ministers consider that the individual has good reason for not reporting the change within 13 weeks, or
  (ii) in any other case, the individual reports the change,
  (iii) where as a result of the Scottish Ministers becoming aware that a determination of an individual's entitlement was made in ignorance of a material fact, the Scottish Ministers make the determination.
(b) in the case of an earlier determination which was based on error within the meaning of—
  (i) regulation 37 (determination following official error—underpayments), on the first day of the award week in which the earlier determination took effect, or
  (ii) regulation 38 (determination following error—overpayments), on the first day of the award week following the award week in which the earlier determination took effect,
(c) in any other case, on the first day of the award week following the award week in which the Scottish Ministers make the determination.
(2) Where the Scottish Ministers consider that in all the circumstances it would be unjust not to do so, they may, when making their determination, set an earlier date for the purposes of paragraph (1).

Carer's Assistance (Carer Support Payment) (Scotland) Regulations 2023

Part 5

Suspensions

Circumstances in which assistance may be suspended

29.—(1) The Scottish Ministers may decide that an individual who has an ongoing entitlement to Carer Support Payment in respect of a period by virtue of regulation 25 (continuing eligibility) is not to become entitled to be given some or all of that assistance at the time at which the individual otherwise would in accordance with that regulation, as read with regulation 22 (time of payment) (referred to in these Regulations as a decision to suspend the individual's Carer Support Payment).

(2) Where such a decision is made in respect of an individual, payments of Carer Support Payment to that individual are to be suspended until such a time as the Scottish Ministers decide that the individual is once again to become entitled to be given Carer Support Payment.

(3) The Scottish Ministers may decide to suspend an individual's Carer Support Payment only in the circumstances where—
  (a) section 54(1A) of the 2018 Act applies, or
  (b) the Scottish Ministers have made arrangements (whether under section 85B of the 2018 Act or otherwise) for a person to receive Carer Support Payment on the individual's behalf, and the Scottish Ministers consider that it is necessary to suspend the Carer Support Payment—
    (i) in order to protect the individual from the risk of financial abuse, or
    (ii) because the person with whom the Scottish Ministers have made arrangements is unable to continue to receive the Carer Support Payment.
  (c) In this regulation "financial abuse" includes—
    (i) having money or other property stolen,
    (ii) being defrauded,
    (iii) being put under pressure in relation to money or other property,
    (iv) having money or other property misused.

Having regard to financial circumstances

30. The Scottish Ministers must have regard to an individual's financial circumstances prior to making a decision to suspend payment to the individual of some or all of Carer Support Payment.

Information to be given following suspension

31.—(1) Having made a decision to suspend an individual's Carer Support Payment, the Scottish Ministers must inform the individual of—
  (a) their decision to suspend the individual's Carer Support Payment,
  (b) the reasons for their decision,
  (c) any steps which might be taken by the individual in order for the Scottish Ministers to consider ending the suspension, and
  (d) the individual's right under regulation 32 (right to review suspension) to require the Scottish Ministers to review their decision.

(SSI 2023/302 reg.31)

(2) The Scottish Ministers must fulfil their duty under paragraph (1) in a way that leaves the individual with a record of the information which the individual can show to, or otherwise share with, others.

Right to review suspension

32.—(1) An individual may require the Scottish Ministers to review a decision to suspend that individual's Carer Support Payment.

(2) The Scottish Ministers must—
(a) complete a review mentioned in paragraph (1) within 31 days beginning with the day on which they received notice from the individual requiring them to review their decision,
(b) inform the individual of the outcome of the review including the reasons for it.

(3) The Scottish Ministers must fulfil their duty under paragraph (2)(b) in a way that leaves the individual with a record of the information which the individual can show to, or otherwise share with, others.

Ending a suspension

33. The Scottish Ministers are to make a decision to end a suspension where—
(a) the individual provides the information requested under section 54(1) of the 2018 Act and the Scottish Ministers consider that they do not require to make a determination without application,
(b) regulation 29(3)(a) (circumstances in which assistance may be suspended) applies and the Scottish Ministers make a determination without application under regulation 35 (consideration of entitlement after specified period), 36 (determination following change of circumstances, etc.), 37 (determination following official error—underpayments), 38 (determination following error—overpayments) or 39 (determination to effect a deduction decision),
(c) the Scottish Ministers make a determination under section 54(2) of the 2018 Act,
(d) the circumstances mentioned in regulation 29(3)(b) (circumstances in which assistance may be suspended) no longer apply, or
(e) the Scottish Ministers consider it appropriate in the circumstances, including having regard to the financial circumstances of the individual.

Effect of suspension ending

34. When—
(a) the suspension of an individual's Carer Support Payment ends, and
(b) under the latest determination of the individual's entitlement to Carer Support Payment relating to the period of the suspension the individual would have become entitled to be given Carer Support Payment during that period,

the individual is immediately to be given the Carer Support Payment that the individual would have become entitled to be given under the determination during the period of suspension.

PART 6

RE-CONSIDERATION OF ENTITLEMENT TO CARER SUPPORT PAYMENT: DETERMINATION WITHOUT APPLICATION

Consideration of entitlement after specified period

35. The Scottish Ministers must make a determination of an individual's entitlement to Carer Support Payment, without receiving an application, after the end of the period specified (if any) in—
  (a) the individual's notice of determination under section 40 or notice of re-determination under section 44 (as the case may be), or
  (b) a determination made by the First-tier Tribunal for Scotland under section 49,
of the 2018 Act.

Determination following change of circumstances etc.

36. The Scottish Ministers must make a determination of an individual's entitlement to Carer Support Payment, without receiving an application, where the individual has an ongoing entitlement to Carer Support Payment and they become aware—
  (a) of a change of circumstances whether or not notified by the individual in accordance with section 54 or 56 of the 2018 Act,
  (b) that a determination of an individual's entitlement was made in ignorance of a material fact which is likely to result in an alteration to the amount of Carer Support Payment payable to the individual or which is likely to mean that the individual is no longer entitled to Carer Support Payment,
  (c) that the individual has died,
  (d) that the cared for person has died,
  (e) that the individual has notified the Scottish Ministers that they wish for their entitlement to assistance to begin on a date prior to the day on which their application was treated as made, provided that—
    (i) the date chosen by the individual is no more than 13 weeks prior to the day on which their application was treated as made, and
    (ii) the individual satisfied the eligibility requirements set out in Part 3 of these Regulations on that chosen date,
  (f) of an alteration of the award of Carer's Allowance which the individual was entitled to immediately before the date of transfer to Carer Support Payment in accordance with Part 2 of schedule 1, as a result of a decision made pursuant to—
    (i) a revision under regulation 3 of the Social Security and Child Support (Decisions and Appeals) Regulations 1999 ("the 1999 Regulations"),
    (ii) a supersession under regulation 6 of the 1999 Regulations,
    (iii) an appeal under section 12 of the Social Security Act 1998 ("the 1998 Act"),
    (iv) a redetermination under section 13 of the 1998 Act,
    (v) an appeal to the Upper Tribunal under section 14 of the 1998 Act,
    (vi) a revision under article 10 of the Social Security (Northern Ireland) Order 1998 ("the 1998 Order"),

    (vii) a supersession under article 11 of the 1998 Order,
    (viii) an appeal under article 13 of the 1998 Order, or
    (ix) an appeal to the Commissioner under article 15 of the 1998 Order,
(g) of an alteration of the award of Carer's Allowance which the individual was entitled to immediately before moving to Scotland in circumstances in which regulation 41 (individuals in respect of whom Carer's Allowance is paid in another part of the United Kingdom immediately before moving to Scotland) applies, as a result of a decision made pursuant to—
    (i) a revision under regulation 3 of the Social Security and Child Support (Decisions and Appeals) Regulations 1999 ("the 1999 Regulations"),
    (ii) a supersession under regulation 6 of the 1999 Regulations,
    (iii) an appeal under section 12 of the Social Security Act 1998 ("the 1998 Act"),
    (iv) a re-consideration under section 13 of the 1998 Act,
    (v) an appeal to the Upper Tribunal under section 14 of the 1998 Act,
    (vi) a revision under article 10 of the Social Security (Northern Ireland) Order 1998 ("the 1998 Order"),
    (vii) a supersession under article 11 of the 1998 Order,
    (viii) an appeal under article 13 of the 1998 Order, or
    (ix) an appeal to the Commissioner under article 15 of the 1998 Order.

Determination following official error - underpayments

37.—(1) The Scottish Ministers are to make a determination of an individual's entitlement to Carer Support Payment, without receiving an application, where—
(a) they have previously made a determination of the individual's entitlement to Carer Support Payment ("the original determination"),
(b) they establish that, due to an official error, the original determination was incorrect resulting in the individual—
    (i) not being given an award of Carer Support Payment, or
    (ii) being given a lower award than that,
to which the individual was entitled,
(c) the Scottish Ministers are not considering a request for a re-determination of the individual's entitlement to Carer Support Payment, and
(d) the individual has not appealed to the First-tier Tribunal for Scotland against the Scottish Minister's determination of the individual's entitlement to Carer Support Payment.

(2) In making a determination required by paragraph (1) the Scottish Ministers are to use—
(a) any information—
    (i) provided in the application that led to the original determination,
    (ii) they have obtained in connection with that application, and
(b) any other information they have obtained in connection with the individual's entitlement to Carer Support Payment.

(3) In this regulation "official error" means an error made by someone acting on behalf of the Scottish Ministers or on behalf of a Minister of the Crown that was not materially contributed to by anyone else.

Determination following error—overpayments

38.—(1) The Scottish Ministers are to make a determination of an individual's entitlement to Carer Support Payment, without receiving an application, where—
  (a) they have previously made a determination of the individual's entitlement to Carer Support Payment ("the original determination"),
  (b) they establish that, due to an error, the original determination was incorrect resulting in the individual being given—
    (i) an award of Carer Support Payment to which the individual was not entitled, or
    (ii) a higher award than that to which the individual was entitled,
  (c) the Scottish Ministers are not considering a request for a re-determination of the individual's entitlement to Carer Support Payment, and
  (d) the individual has not made an appeal to the First-tier Tribunal for Scotland or Upper Tribunal against the Scottish Minister's determination of the individual's entitlement to Carer Support Payment, that has not yet been determined.
(2) In making a determination required by paragraph (1) the Scottish Ministers are to use—
  (a) any information—
    (i) provided in the application that led to the original determination, and
    (ii) they have obtained in connection with that application,
  (b) any other information they have obtained in connection with the individual's entitlement to Carer Support Payment, and
  (c) any other information available to them that is relevant to their consideration of whether the individual is entitled to Carer Support Payment.
(3) In this regulation references to an "error" are to—
  (a) an error in the performance of a function conferred by these Regulations or the 2018 Act, including a determination being made—
    (i) wrongly, or
    (ii) correctly but on the basis of—
      (aa) incorrect information, or
      (bb) an assumption which proves to be wrong, or
  (c) a new determination not being made after an assumption on the basis of which an earlier determination was made has proved to be wrong.

Determination to effect a deduction decision

39.—(1) The Scottish Ministers are to make a determination of an individual's entitlement to Carer Support Payment, without receiving an application, where the circumstances in paragraphs (2) and (3) apply.
(2) This paragraph applies where—

(a) regulation 26 (form of payment—giving Carer Support Payment by way of deduction) allows Carer Support Payment to be given to the individual by way of deduction, or

(b) Carer Support Payment is being given to the individual by way of deduction, and the Scottish Ministers consider that may no longer be appropriate.

(3) This paragraph applies where the Scottish Ministers have decided to—

(a) vary the amount of Carer Support Payment to be given by way of deduction (including introducing a deduction, where the full amount of Carer Support Payment was previously given as money),

(b) vary any period for which the individual's Carer Support Payment is to be given by way of deduction, that may have been specified in a previous determination of the individual's entitlement, or

(c) cease making deductions, and instead give the individual's Carer Support Payment in the form of money.

(4) The Scottish Ministers are to make a determination, without receiving an application, where an individual who is receiving Carer Support Payment by way of deduction under a previous determination of entitlement notifies the Scottish Ministers that the individual—

(a) withdraws their agreement to their Carer Support Payment being given by way of deduction,

(b) wishes the Scottish Ministers to increase the amount of their Carer Support Payment that is given by way of deduction,

(c) wishes the Scottish Ministers to decrease the amount of their Carer Support Payment that is given by way of deduction (including ceasing the deduction), or

(d) wishes the Scottish Ministers to amend the length of any period referred to in paragraph (3)(b).

PART 7

BREAKS IN CARE

Temporary break in care

40.—(1) An award week in respect of which an individual fails to satisfy the requirement of regulation 5(2) (provision of care to a cared for person) is to be treated as an award week in respect of which that individual satisfies that requirement if—

(a) that individual has only temporarily ceased to satisfy it, and

(b) that individual has satisfied it for at least 14 weeks in the period of 26 weeks ending with that award week and would have satisfied it for at least 22 weeks in that period but for the fact that—

(i) that individual was undergoing medical or other treatment as an in-patient in a hospital or similar institution, or

(ii) the cared for person was undergoing medical or other treatment as an in-patient in a hospital or similar institution.

(2) Regulation 14 (earnings limit) does not apply to an individual in respect of an award week mentioned in paragraph (1).

Carer's Assistance (Carer Support Payment) (Scotland) Regulations 2023

Part 8

Movement of individuals between Scotland and the rest of the United Kingdom

Individuals in respect of whom Carer's Allowance is paid in another part of the United Kingdom immediately before moving to Scotland

13.506   41.—(1) Where an individual—
(a) becomes resident in Scotland,
(b) was resident in another part of the United Kingdom, and
(c) was entitled to Carer's Allowance in respect of a cared for person immediately before the date of the move,
the Scottish Ministers are to make a determination without application of the individual's entitlement to Carer Support Payment.

(2) Entitlement to Carer Support Payment under paragraph (1) begins on the day after the day on which the individual's entitlement to Carer's Allowance ends.

(3) In this regulation, "the date of the move" is the date when the individual becomes resident in Scotland, as notified by the individual or otherwise communicated to the Scottish Ministers (whether the notification takes place before or after the date of the move).

Individuals in respect of whom Carer Support Payment is paid at the time of moving to another part of the United Kingdom

13.507   42.—(1) Where the Scottish Ministers become aware that an individual who is entitled to Carer Support Payment has moved or is to move to become resident in another part of the United Kingdom, the individual is to be treated as though the individual meets the condition under regulation 6(1)(a) (residence and presence conditions) of being ordinarily resident in Scotland for a period of 13 weeks beginning in accordance with paragraph (4).

(2) Where the Scottish Ministers become aware that an individual has moved or is to move to another part of the United Kingdom mentioned in paragraph (1), they are to make a determination without application at the end of the 13-week period mentioned in paragraph (1) that the individual's entitlement to Carer Support Payment is to terminate.

(3) Where before the end of the 13-week period, the Scottish Ministers become aware that the individual is no longer to move to become resident in another part of the United Kingdom, the duty in paragraph (2) does not apply.

(4) The 13-week period mentioned in paragraph (1) begins on the date the individual ceases to be ordinarily resident in Scotland.

(5) On the day after the 13-week period specified in paragraph (4) ends—
(a) entitlement to Carer Support Payment ceases, and
(b) regulation 38 (determination following error—overpayments) applies to any Carer Support Payment paid to an individual in relation to a period after the end of that 13-week period.

(SSI 2023/302 reg. 43)

PART 9

PERIODS IN RESPECT OF A RE-DETERMINATION REQUEST

Periods in respect of a re-determination request

43.—(1) The period for requesting a re-determination of entitlement to Carer Support Payment under section 41 of the 2018 Act is 42 days beginning with the day that the individual is informed, in accordance with section 40 of the 2018 Act, of the right to make the request.

(2) In relation to determining entitlement to Carer Support Payment, the period allowed for re-determination (within the meaning of section 43 of the 2018 Act) is 56 days beginning with—
  (a) the day that the request for a re-determination is received by the Scottish Ministers,
  (b) in a case where the request for a re-determination is received by the Scottish Ministers outwith the period prescribed in paragraph (1), the day on which it is decided by the Scottish Ministers or (as the case may be) the First-tier Tribunal for Scotland that the individual in question has a good reason for not requesting a re-determination sooner, or
  (c) in a case where the Scottish Ministers have informed the individual of their decision that the request for a re-determination was not made in such form as the Scottish Ministers require, the day on which it is subsequently decided by the First-tier Tribunal for Scotland that the individual in question has made the request in such form as the Scottish Ministers require.

PART 10

TRANSFER FROM CARER'S ALLOWANCE TO CARER SUPPORT PAYMENT

Transfer from Carer's Allowance to Carer Support Payment

44. Part 2 of schedule 1 makes provision about transferring from Carer's Allowance to Carer Support Payment.

PART 11

INITIAL PERIOD FOR APPLICATIONS

Initial period for applications

45. Part 1 of schedule 1 makes provision about the initial period for applications.

PART 12

TRANSITORY PROVISION

Transitory provision—initial period for applications

46.—(1) During the initial period for applications, in addition to satisfying the residence and presence conditions in regulations 6 to 11, an individual must be resident in one of the local authority areas specified in paragraph 2 of Part 1 of schedule 1 on the date their application is received by the Scottish Ministers.

(2) In this regulation and in Part 1 of schedule 1, "initial period for applications" means the period beginning with 19 November 2023 and ending with 30 September 2024.

Exclusion to transitory provision

47.—(1) An individual who has made a claim for Carer's Allowance prior to 19 November 2023 which has not yet been decided is not entitled to be paid Carer Support Payment during the initial period for applications.

(2) In paragraph (1) a claim for Carer's Allowance is decided if it has—
- (a) been decided by the Secretary of State under section 70 of the 1992 Act,
- (b) been withdrawn in accordance with regulation 5(2) of the Social Security (Claims and Payments) Regulations 1987, or
- (c) otherwise is no longer to be decided by the Secretary of State as mentioned in sub-paragraph (a).

PART 13

CONSEQUENTIAL AMENDMENTS

Consequential amendments

48. The amendments specified in Part 3 of schedule 1 have effect.

SCHEDULE 1   REGULATIONS 44, 45 AND 48

PART 1

INITIAL PERIOD FOR APPLICATIONS

Initial period for applications

1.—(1) These Regulations apply to an individual who is resident in one of the local authority areas mentioned in paragraph 2 when the individual makes an application for Carer Support Payment during the initial period for applications.

(2) An individual who is awarded Carer Support Payment pursuant to an application made during the initial period for applications will continue to be entitled if that individual moves to another local authority area in Scotland.

Local authority areas for initial period for applications

2. The local authority areas specified for the purposes of regulation 45 (initial period for applications) are—
- (a) Perthshire and Kinross,
- (b) City of Dundee, and
- (c) the Western Isles.

PART 2

TRANSFER TO CARER SUPPORT PAYMENT

Interpretation

3. In this Part of the schedule—

"date of transfer" means the date when a transferring individual's entitlement to Carer Support Payment begins by virtue of a determination made under paragraph 5(1),

"relevant individual" means an individual—
(a) who has an award of Carer's Allowance who appears to the Scottish Ministers to be likely to be eligible for Carer Support Payment, and
(b) who is—
  (i) ordinarily resident in Scotland, or
  (ii) someone to whom regulation 6(3) (residence and presence conditions) or 11(2) (persons residing outside the United Kingdom to whom a relevant EU regulation applies) applies,

"sufficient" means a link to Scotland that is sufficiently close that regulation 6(3) or 11(2) would be incompatible with the applicable agreement mentioned in that regulation, if the relevant individual were not entitled to Carer Support Payment,

"transfer notice" means the notice required by paragraph 4, and

"transferring individual" means an individual on whom the Scottish Ministers have served a notice of intention to transfer in accordance with paragraph 4.

NOTICE OF INTENTION TO TRANSFER TO CARER SUPPORT PAYMENT

4.—(1) The Scottish Ministers are to notify each relevant individual of their intention to transfer that individual's entitlement to carer's assistance from an entitlement to Carer's Allowance to an entitlement to Carer Support Payment.

(2) Notice under sub-paragraph (1) must—
(a) be given in a way that leaves the relevant individual with a record of the information which they can show to, or otherwise share with, others,
(b) inform the relevant individual that—
  (i) they have been identified as a relevant individual for the purpose of transfer to Carer Support Payment,
  (ii) the Scottish Ministers will make a determination without receiving an application to transfer the individual's entitlement to Carer's Allowance to an entitlement to Carer Support Payment within a period to be specified in the notice (the individual will be notified when the determination is made and informed about their award and start date of Carer Support Payment), and
  (iii) the individual's award of Carer's Allowance will cease immediately before the award of Carer Support Payment begins.

(3) Where a notice under sub-paragraph (1) is given—
(a) to a transferring individual who, before a determination is made under paragraph 5(1)—
  (i) ceases to be ordinarily resident in Scotland, or
  (ii) cares for a cared for person who dies, or
(b) in error where the individual is neither—
  (i) ordinarily resident in Scotland, nor
  (ii) an individual who is habitually resident in an EEA state, Gibraltar or Switzerland and has a genuine and sufficient link to Scotland,

the duty on the Scottish Ministers in paragraph 5(1) does not apply.

(4) Where sub-paragraph (3) applies in respect of an individual and a determination under paragraph 5(1) has not been made, the Scottish Ministers are to notify the individual that the duty on the Scottish Ministers in paragraph 5(1) does not apply.

Determination without application of entitlement to Carer Support Payment

5.—(1) The Scottish Ministers are to make a determination without receiving an application in respect of a transferring individual of that individual's entitlement to Carer Support Payment.

(2) Entitlement to Carer Support Payment under a determination under sub-paragraph (1) begins on the date specified in the notice of determination given to the transferring individual in accordance with section 40 of the 2018 Act.

(3) The determination under sub-paragraph (1) is to be made on the basis of—
  (a) such information as the Scottish Ministers have received from the Secretary of State in respect of the transferring individual's entitlement to Carer's Allowance, and
  (b) any other information available to the Scottish Ministers that appears to be relevant.

(4) A determination under sub-paragraph (1) must be made on the basis that the transferring individual is entitled to the amount of Carer Support Payment that is equivalent to the amount of Carer's Allowance to which the individual was entitled immediately before the date of transfer.

(5) A determination under sub-paragraph (1)—
  (a) may be made on the assumption that whatever can be discerned about the transferring individual's circumstances from the information mentioned in sub-paragraph (3) remains accurate on the date on which the determination is made,
  (b) notwithstanding the generality of head (a), is to be made on the assumption that the conditions relating to residence and presence set out in regulations 6 to 11 (residence and presence conditions etc.) are satisfied in the individual's case, and
  (c) must be made no later than the period specified in the notice under paragraph 4(1) (notice of intention to transfer to Carer Support Payment) unless the Scottish Ministers have—
    (i) good reason to extend that period,
    (ii) agreed the period for extension with the Secretary of State, and
    (iii) notified the transferring individual of the extension and reason for it.

(6) Where the Scottish Ministers make a determination under paragraph (1) that a transferring individual is entitled to Carer Support Payment, for the week in which that determination takes place, "award week" means—
  (a) where the individual cares for a cared for person who is in receipt of Constant Attendance Allowance, a period of 4 days, starting on the Wednesday of that week and ending on the following Saturday, or
  (b) in all other cases, a period of 6 days, starting on the Monday of that week and ending on the following Saturday.

(SSI 2023/302 Sch. 1)

Date of cessation of Carer's Allowance

6. Where a determination is made under paragraph 5(1) (determination without application of entitlement to Carer Support Payment) that the transferring individual is entitled to Carer Support Payment, the transferring individual's entitlement to Carer's Allowance will cease on the date their entitlement to Carer Support Payment begins.

Modification of these regulations: transferring individuals

7. These Regulations apply to a transferring individual on and after the date of transfer with the following modifications—

In regulation 22, for sub-paragraph (b), substitute—

"(b) inform the transferring individual that any subsequent payment will be made—
  (i) 4 weekly in arrears,
  (ii) weekly in advance,
  (iii) in respect of an individual who was paid Carer's Allowance one week in advance and 3 weekly in arrears—
    (aa) 4 weekly in arrears, or
    (bb) weekly in advance, provided that the individual has informed the Scottish Ministers that they wish to be paid weekly in advance before the date specified in the notice of intention to transfer given to the individual in accordance with paragraph 4(1) of schedule 1,
  (iv) where the Scottish Ministers consider that it would be unjust not to do so, at such intervals as may be specified in the notice of determination."

Appointees

8.—(1) A person appointed by the Secretary of State under regulation 33 (persons unable to act) of the Social Security (Claims and Payments) Regulations 1987 to receive Carer's Allowance on behalf of a transferring individual is to be treated on and after the date of transfer as though appointed by the Scottish Ministers to act on behalf of that transferring individual under section 85B of the 2018 Act.

(2) As soon as reasonably practicable after the date of transfer, the Scottish Ministers must—
  (a) consider whether the conditions for making an appointment in respect of the transferring individual are met (having regard to section 85B(3) of the 2018 Act),
  (b) consider whether to terminate the appointment that is treated as having been made by virtue of sub-paragraph (1) and terminate it if they consider it appropriate, and
  (c) if they have terminated an appointment in pursuance of head (b), appoint under section 85B of the 2018 Act another person to act on the transferring individual's behalf if they consider it appropriate to do so.

(3) The duty in paragraph (2) does not apply to a person in respect of whom the Scottish Ministers have already—
  (a) appointed to act on behalf of that transferring individual under section 85B of the 2018 Act, or

(b) considered whether the conditions for making an appointment are met in accordance with paragraph 15 (appointees) of Part 3 of schedule 2 of the Disability Assistance for Working Age People (Scotland) Regulations 2022 or paragraph 14 (appointees) of Part 3 of the schedule of the Disability Assistance for Children and Young People (Scotland) Regulations 2021.

PART 3

CONSEQUENTIAL AMENDMENTS

13.516 *These amendments have been noted above in relation to the substantive provisions concerned.*

SCHEDULE 2   Regulation 14

CALCULATION OF EARNINGS

Interpretation

13.517   1. In this schedule—

"basic rate" means the rate of income tax of that name determined in accordance with section 6(2) of the Income Tax Act 2007,

"board and lodging accommodation" means—
 (a) accommodation provided to a person or, if they are a member of a family, to them or any other member of their family, for a charge which includes the provision of that accommodation and at least some cooked or prepared meals (which are provided by a person other than the person to whom the accommodation is provided or a member of their family) and are consumed in that accommodation, or
 (b) accommodation provided to a person in a hotel, guest house, lodging house or some similar establishment,

except accommodation provided by a close relative of theirs or of any other member of their family, or other than on a commercial basis,

"close relative" means a parent, parent-in-law, son, son-in-law, daughter, daughter-in-law, step-parent, step-son, step-daughter, brother, sister, or if any of the preceding persons is one member of a couple, the other member of that couple,

"dwelling occupied as the home" means the dwelling together with any garage, garden and outbuildings, normally occupied by the individual as their home including any premises not so occupied which it is impracticable or unreasonable to sell separately, in particular, in Scotland, any croft land on which the dwelling is situated,

"employed earner" means a person who is in gainful employment in Great Britain under a contract of service, or in an office (including elective office) with emoluments chargeable to income tax under schedule E of the Income and Corporation Taxes Act 1988 and includes—
 (a) a person in any employment which would be such employment if it were in Great Britain, and
 (b) a person in any such employment which, in accordance with the provisions of the 1992 Act and of any regulations made under it, is to be disregarded in relation to liability for contributions,

"employment" includes any trade, business, profession, office or vocation,

"individual" means any person making an application for Carer Support Payment or transferring from Carer's Allowance to Carer Support Payment under these Regulations,

"maximum weekly amount" means the maximum weekly amount which, on the date on which the payment of compensation is made, is specified in section 227(1) of the Employment Rights Act 1996,

"occupational pension scheme" has the same meaning as in section 1 of the Pension Schemes Act 1993,

"pay period" means the period in respect of which an individual is, or expects to be, normally paid by their employer, being a week, a fortnight, 4 weeks, a calendar month, or such other period as the case may be, "personal pension scheme" has the same meaning as in section 1 of the Pension Schemes Act 1993 and, in the case of a self-employed earner, includes a scheme approved by the Inland Revenue under Chapter IV of Part XIV of the Income and Corporation Taxes Act 1988,

"relevant earnings limit" means the earnings limit set out in regulation 14 of these Regulations,

"retirement annuity contract" means a contract or trust scheme approved under Chapter III of Part XIV of the Income and Corporation Taxes Act 1988,

"Scottish basic rate" means the rate of income tax of that name calculated in accordance with section 6A of the Income Tax Act 2007,

"Scottish taxpayer" has the same meaning as in Chapter 2 of Part 4A of the Scotland Act 1998,

"self-employed earner" means a person who is in gainful employment in Great Britain otherwise than as an employed earner and includes a person in any—
  (a) employment which would be such employment if it were in Great Britain, and
  (b) such employment which, in accordance with the provisions of the 1992 Act and of any regulations made under it, is to be disregarded in relation to liability for contributions, and

"year of assessment" means, with reference to any income tax, the year for which such tax was granted by any enactment granting income tax.

Calculation of earnings

2.—(1) For the purposes of regulation 14 (earnings limit), the earnings of an individual are to be calculated by determining the weekly amount of their earnings in accordance with this schedule.

(2) The amount of an individual's earnings for any period are the whole of those earnings (including any earnings which they are treated as possessing under paragraph 3 (notional earnings)) except in so far as paragraphs 9 (calculation of net earnings of employed earners) and 12 (calculation of net profit of self-employed earners) provide that certain sums are to be disregarded or deducted.

Notional earnings

3.—(1) Where an individual's earnings are not ascertainable at the date on which the Scottish Ministers are determining the individual's entitlement to Carer Support Payment or considering whether they are required to make a determination of the individual's entitlement to Carer Support Payment without receiving an application, the individual is treated as possessing such earnings as is reasonable in the circumstances having regard to the number of hours worked and the earnings paid for comparable employment.

(2) Where an individual is treated as possessing any earnings under sub-paragraph (1), this schedule applies for the purposes of calculating the amount of those earnings as if a payment had actually been made and as if they were actual earnings which that individual does possess, except that paragraph 9(3) (calculation of net earnings of employed earners) does not apply and their net earnings are calculated by taking into account the earnings which they are treated as possessing, less—
  (a) an amount in respect of income tax equivalent to an amount calculated by applying to those earnings the basic rate, or in the case of a Scottish taxpayer, the Scottish basic rate, of tax in the year of assessment less only the personal reliefs to which the individual is entitled under Chapters 2, 3 and 3A of Part 3 of the Income Tax Act 2007 as are appropriate to their circumstances; but if the period over which those earnings are to be taken into account is less than a year, the earnings to which the basic rate, or Scottish basic rate, of tax is to be applied and the amount of the personal reliefs deductible under this paragraph are calculated on a pro rata basis,
  (b) where the weekly amount of those earnings equals or exceeds the lower earnings limit, an amount representing primary Class 1 contributions under the 1992 Act, calculated by applying to those earnings the initial and main primary percentages in accordance with section 8(1)(a) and (b) of that Act, and
  (c) one half of any sum payable by the individual in respect of a pay period by way of a contribution towards an occupational or personal pension scheme,
  (d) any care charges to which paragraph 15 (care charges to be deducted in the calculation of earnings) applies up to a maximum deduction, in respect of such care charges incurred by any individual, of 50% of their notional earnings.

Rounding of fractions

4. Where any calculation under this schedule results in a fraction of a penny that fraction is, if it would be to individual's advantage, treated as a penny, otherwise it is disregarded.

Calculation of earnings of employed earners

5.—(1) Earnings derived from employment as an employed earner are calculated or estimated over a period determined in accordance with the following paragraphs and at a weekly amount determined in accordance with paragraph 7 (calculation of weekly amount of earnings).

(2) Subject to sub-paragraphs (3) and (5) to (7), the period over which a payment is to be taken into account—
  (a) in a case where it is payable in respect of a period, is a period equal to the total number of award weeks in the period commencing on the date on which the earnings are treated as paid under paragraph 6 (date on which earnings are treated as paid) and ending on the day before the date on which earnings of the same kind (excluding earnings of the kind mentioned in paragraph 8(1)(a) to (j)) and from the same source would, or would if the employment was continuing, next be treated as paid under that paragraph, or
  (b) in any other case, and where it would cause the individual's earnings to exceed the relevant earnings limit if it were taken into account only in respect of the period in which it was received, is a period equal to such number of weeks as is equal to the number (less any fraction of a whole number) calculated in accordance with the formula—

$$\frac{P}{Q} + R$$

Where—
P is the net earnings,
Q is the amount of the relevant earnings limit plus one penny, and
R is the total of the sums which would fall to be disregarded or deducted as appropriate under paragraph 9(2) (calculation of net earnings of employed earners),
and that period begins on the date on which the payment is treated as paid under paragraph 6 (date on which earnings are treated as paid).

(3) Where earnings not of the same kind are derived from the same source and the periods in respect of which those earnings would, but for this sub-paragraph, fall to be taken into account overlap, wholly or partly, those earnings are taken into account over a period—
  (a) equal to the aggregate length of those periods, and
  (b) beginning with the earliest date on which any part of those earnings would otherwise be treated as paid under paragraph 6 (date on which earnings are treated as paid).

(4) In a case to which paragraph (3) applies, earnings under paragraph 8 (earnings of employed earners) are taken into account in the following order of priority—
  (a) earnings normally derived from the employment,
  (b) any payment to which paragraph 8(1)(b) or (c) applies,
  (c) any payment to which paragraph 8(1)(i) applies,
  (d) any payment to which paragraph 8(1)(d) applies.

(5) Where earnings to which paragraph 8(1)(b) to (d) (earnings of employed earners) applies are paid in respect of a part of a day, those earnings are taken into account over a period equal to a week.

(6) Where earnings to which paragraph 8(1)(i)(i) (earnings of employed earners) applies are paid in respect of or on the termination of any employment which is not part-time employment, the period over which they are taken into account is—
  (a) a period of weeks equal to the number of weeks (less any fraction of a whole number) obtained by dividing the net earnings by the maximum weekly amount which, on the date on which the payment of earnings is made, is specified in section 227(1) of the Employment Rights Act 1996, or
  (b) a period equal to the length of the specified period,
whichever is the shorter, and that period begins on the date on which the payment is treated as paid under paragraph 6 (date on which earnings are treated as paid).

(7) In this paragraph—
"part-time employment" means—
  (a) subject to the provisions of heads (b) to (d) of this definition, employment in which a person is engaged, or, where their hours of work fluctuate, they are engaged on average for less than 16 hours a week, being work for which payment is made or which is done in expectation of payment,
  (b) subject to head (c) of this definition, the number of hours for which an individual is engaged in work is determined—
    (i) where no recognisable cycle has been established in respect of an individual's work, by reference to the number of hours, or, where those hours are likely to fluctuate, the average of the hours, which they are expected to work in a week,

(ii) where the number of hours for which they are engaged fluctuates, by reference to the average of hours worked over—
   (aa) if there is a recognisable cycle of work, the period of one complete cycle (including, where the cycle involves periods in which the individual does not work, those periods but disregarding any other absences),
   (bb) in any other case, the period of 5 weeks immediately before the date on which an application for Carer Support Payment is treated as received, or the date on which a determination without application falls to be made, or such other length of time as may, in the particular case, enable the individual's average hours of work to be determined more accurately,
(c) where for the purpose of head (b)(ii)(aa) of this definition, an individual's recognisable cycle of work at a school, other education establishment or other place of employment is one year and includes periods of school holidays or similar vacations during which they do not work, those periods and any other periods not forming part of such holidays or vacations during which they are not required to work is disregarded in establishing the average hours for which they are engaged in work,
(d) for the purposes of heads (a) and (b) of this definition, in determining the number of hours for which an individual is engaged in work, that number includes any time allowed to that individual by their employer for a meal or for refreshment, but only where that individual is, or expects to be, paid earnings in respect of that time,

"specified period" means a period equal to—
   (a) a week or such number of weeks (less any fraction of a whole number) as comprise the period of notice which is applicable to an individual, or would have been applicable if it had not been waived, less
   (b) any part of that period during which the individual has continued to work in the employment in question or in respect of which they have received any payment in lieu of notice,

and for the purposes of this definition "period of notice" means the period of notice of termination of employment to which an individual is entitled by statute or by contract, whichever is the longer, or, if they are not entitled to such notice, the period of notice which is customary in the employment in question.

Date on which earnings are treated as paid

6. Earnings to which paragraph 5 (calculation of earnings of employed earners) or 10(2) (calculation of earnings of self-employed earners) applies are treated as paid on the first day of the award week in which the payment is received.

Calculation of weekly amount of earnings

7.—(1) For the purposes of paragraph 5 (calculation of earnings of employed earners), subject to sub-paragraphs (2) to (4), where the period in respect of which a payment is made—
   (a) does not exceed a week, the weekly amount is the amount of that payment,
   (b) exceeds a week, the weekly amount is determined—
      (i) where that period is a month, by multiplying the amount of that payment by 12 and dividing the product by 52,
      (ii) where that period is 3 months, by multiplying the amount of the payment by 4 and dividing the product by 52,
      (iii) where that period is a year, by dividing the amount of the payment by 52,
      (iv) for any other period, by multiplying the amount of the payment by 7 and dividing the product by the number equal to the number of days in the period in respect of which it is made.

(2) Where a payment of earnings from a particular source is or has been paid regularly and that payment falls to be taken into account in the same award week as a payment of the same kind from the same source, the amount of those earnings to be taken into account in any one award week will not exceed the weekly amount determined under sub-paragraph (1)(a) or (b), as the case may be, of the payment which under paragraph 6 (date on which earnings are treated as paid) is treated as paid first.

(3) Where the amount of the individual's net earnings fluctuates and has changed more than once, or an individual's regular pattern of work is such that they do not work every week, the application of sub-paragraphs (1) and (2) may be modified so that the weekly amount of their earnings is determined by reference to their average weekly earnings—
   (a) if there is a recognisable cycle of work, over the period of one complete cycle,
   (b) if the individual has provided the Scottish Ministers with payslips, over the period to which the payslips relate, up to a maximum period of 26 weeks, or
   (c) in any other case, over a period of 5 weeks or such other period as may, in the particular case, enable the individual's average weekly earnings to be determined more accurately.

Earnings of employed earners

8.—(1) Subject to sub-paragraphs (2) and (3), "earnings", in the case of employment as an employed earner means the remuneration or profit derived from the employment and includes—
- (a) any bonus or commission,
- (b) any payment in lieu of remuneration except any periodic sum paid to an individual on account of the termination of their employment by reason of redundancy,
- (c) any payment in lieu of notice,
- (d) any holiday pay except where it is payable more than 4 weeks after the termination or interruption of employment,
- (e) any payment by way of a retainer,
- (f) any payment made by the individual's employer in respect of expenses not wholly, exclusively and necessarily incurred in the performance of the duties of the employment, including any payment made by the employer in respect of—
  - (i) travelling expenses incurred by the individual between their home and place of employment,
  - (ii) expense incurred by the individual under arrangements made for the care of a member of their family owing to the individual's absence from home,
- (g) any award of compensation made under section 112(4) (the remedies: orders and compensation) or 117(3)(a) (enforcement of order and compensation) of the Employment Rights Act 1996 (remedies and compensation),
- (h) any such sum as is referred to in section 112(3) of the 1992 Act (certain sums to be earnings for social security purposes),
- (i) where—
  - (i) a payment of compensation is made in respect of employment which is not part-time employment and that payment is not less than the maximum weekly amount, the amount of the compensation less the deductible remainder, where that is applicable,
  - (ii) a payment of compensation is made in respect of employment which is part-time employment, the amount of the compensation,
- (j) any remuneration paid by or on behalf of an employer to the individual in respect of a period during which the individual is—
  - (i) on maternity leave or paternity leave,
  - (ii) on adoption leave, or
  - (iii) absent from work because they are ill.

(2) For the purposes of sub-paragraph (1)(i)(i), the "deductible remainder"—
- (a) applies in cases where dividing the amount of the compensation by the maximum weekly amount produces a whole number plus a fraction, and
- (b) is equal to the difference between—
  - (i) the amount of the compensation, and
  - (ii) the product of the maximum weekly amount multiplied by the whole number.

(3) "Earnings" do not include any payment in respect of expenses—
- (a) wholly, exclusively and necessarily incurred in the performance of the duties of the employment, or
- (b) arising out of the individual participating as a service user.

(4) The reference in sub-paragraph (3)(b) to the individual participating as a service user is to—
- (a) a person who is being consulted by or on behalf of—
  - (i) a body which has a statutory duty to provide services in the field of health, social care or social housing, or
  - (ii) a body which conducts research or undertakes monitoring for the purpose of planning or improving such services,

in their capacity as a user, potential user, carer of a user or person otherwise affected by the provision of those services,
- (b) a person who is being consulted by or on behalf of—
  - (i) the Secretary of State or the Scottish Ministers in relation to any of their functions in the field of social security or child support under section 2 of the Employment and Training Act 1973, or
  - (ii) a body which conducts research or undertakes monitoring for the purpose of planning or improving such functions,

in their capacity as a person affected or potentially affected by the exercise of those functions or the carer of such a person, or
- (c) the carer of a person consulted under sub-paragraphs (a) or (b).

(5) In this paragraph—
"adoption leave" means a period of absence from work on ordinary or additional adoption leave under section 75A or 75B of the Employment Rights Act 1996,
"compensation" means any payment made in respect of or on the termination of employment in a case where a person has not received or received only part of a payment in lieu of notice due or which would have been due to them had they not waived their right to receive it, other than—
  (a) any payment specified in sub-paragraph (1)(a) to (h),
  (b) any payment specified in sub-paragraph (3),
  (c) any redundancy payment within the meaning of section 135 of the Employment Rights Act 1996,
  (d) any refund of contributions to which that person was entitled under an occupational pension scheme,
"maternity leave" means a period during which a person is absent from work because they are pregnant or have given birth to a child, and at the end of which they have the right to return to work either under the terms of their contract or under Part 8 of the Employment Rights Act 1996,
"part-time employment" has the same meaning as in paragraph 5(7) (calculation of earnings of employed earners),
"paternity leave" means a period of absence from work on leave under section 80A (entitlement to paternity leave: birth) or 80B (entitlement to paternity leave: adoption) of the Employment Rights Act 1996.

Calculation of net earnings of employed earners

9.—(1) For the purposes of paragraphs 2 (calculation of earnings) and 5 (calculation of earnings of employed earners) the earnings of an individual derived from employment as an employed earner to be taken into account are, subject to sub-paragraphs (2) and (3), their net earnings.
(2) There is disregarded or deducted as appropriate from an individual's net earnings—
  (a) any sum, where applicable, specified in paragraph 14 (sums to be disregarded in the calculation of earnings), and
  (b) any care charges to which paragraph 15 (care charges to be deducted in the calculation of earnings) applies up to a maximum deduction, in respect of such care charges incurred by any individual, of 50% of their net earnings less those sums, if any, specified in paragraph 14 which are disregarded.
(3) For the purposes of sub-paragraph (1) net earnings are calculated by taking into account the gross earnings of the individual from that employment, less—
  (a) any amount deducted by way of—
    (i) income tax,
    (ii) primary Class 1 contributions under the 1992 Act, and
  (b) one half of any sum paid by the individual in respect of a pay period by way of a contribution towards an occupational or personal pension scheme.

Calculation of earnings of self-employed earners

10.—(1) Except where paragraph (2) applies, where an individual's earnings consist of earnings from employment as a self-employed earner the weekly amount of their earnings are determined by reference to their average weekly earnings from that employment—
  (a) over a period of one year, or
  (b) where the individual has been engaged in that employment for less than a year or there has been a change which is likely to affect their normal pattern of earnings, over such other period as may, in any particular case, enable the weekly amount of their earnings to be determined more accurately.
(2) Where the individual's earnings—
  (a) consist of royalties or other sums paid as a consideration for the use of, or the right to use, any copyright, design, patent or trade mark, and
  (b) the individual is the first owner of the copyright, design, patent or trade mark,
those earnings are taken into account over a period equal to such number of weeks as is equal to the number (less any fraction of a whole number) calculated in accordance with the formula—

$$\frac{S}{T} + U$$

where—
S is the earnings,

T is the relevant earnings limit plus one penny, and

U is the total of the sums which would fall to be disregarded or deducted as appropriate under paragraph 12(2) (calculation of net profit of self-employed earners).

(3) The period mentioned in sub-paragraph (2) begins on the date on which the payment is treated as paid under paragraph 6 (date on which earnings are treated as paid).

Earnings of self-employed earners

11. "Earnings", in the case of employment as a self-employed earner, means the net profits of the employment and includes any allowance paid under section 2 of the Employment and Training Act 1973 or section 2 of the Enterprise and New Towns (Scotland) Act 1990 to the individual for the purpose of assisting them in carrying on their business.

Calculation of net profit of self-employed earners

12.—(1) For the purposes of paragraphs 2 (calculation of earnings) and 10 (calculation of earnings of self-employed earners), the earnings of an individual to be taken into account are, in the case of a self-employed earner—
  (a) who is engaged in employment on their own account, the net profit derived from that employment,
  (b) whose employment is carried on in partnership or is that of a share fisherman, their share of the net profit derived from that employment less—
    (i) an amount in respect of income tax and social security contributions payable under the 1992 Act calculated in accordance with paragraph 13 (deduction of tax and contributions for self-employed earners), and
    (ii) one half of any premium paid in the period that is relevant under paragraph 10 in respect of a retirement annuity contract or a personal pension scheme,
  (c) in sub-paragraph (b), "share fisherman" means any person who—
    (i) is ordinarily employed in the fishing industry otherwise than under a contract of service, as a master or member of the crew of any fishing boat manned by more than one person, and is remunerated in respect of that employment in whole or in part by a share of profits or gross earnings of the fishing boat, or
    (ii) has ordinarily been so employed, but who by reason of age or infirmity permanently ceases to be so employed and becomes ordinarily engaged in employment ashore in Great Britain, otherwise than under a contract of service, performing any services ancillary to or in connection with a fishing boat and is remunerated in respect of that employment in whole or in part by a share of the profits or gross earnings of that boat and has not ceased to be ordinarily engaged in that employment.

(2) There is to be disregarded or deducted as appropriate from an individual's net profit—
  (a) any sum, where applicable, specified in paragraph 14 (sums to be disregarded in the calculation of earnings), and
  (b) any care charge to which paragraph 15 (care charges to be deducted in the calculation of earnings) applies up to a maximum deduction, in respect of such care charges incurred by any individual, of 50% of their net profit less those sums, if any, specified in paragraph 14 which are disregarded.

(3) For the purposes of sub-paragraph (1)(a), the net profit of the employment is, except where sub-paragraph (9) applies, calculated by taking into account the earnings of the employment over the period determined under paragraph 10 (calculation of earnings of self-employed earners), less—
  (a) subject to sub-paragraphs (5) to (7), any expenses wholly and exclusively paid in that period for the purposes of that employment,
  (b) an amount in respect of—
    (i) income tax, and
    (ii) social security contributions payable under the 1992 Act, calculated in accordance with paragraph 13 (deduction of tax and contributions for self-employed earners), and
  (c) one half of any premium paid in the period that is relevant under paragraph 10 (calculation of earnings of self-employed earners) in respect of a retirement annuity contract or a personal pension.

(4) For the purposes of sub-paragraph (1)(b), the net profit of the employment is calculated by taking into account the earnings of the employment over the period determined under paragraph 10 less, subject to sub-paragraphs (5) to (7), any expenses wholly and exclusively paid in that period for the purposes of that employment.

(5) Subject to paragraph (6), no deduction is to be made under paragraph (3)(a) or (4) in respect of—

(a) any capital expenditure,
(b) the depreciation of any capital asset,
(c) any sum employed or intended to be employed in the setting up or expansion of the employment,
(d) any loss incurred before the beginning of the period determined under paragraph 10 (calculation of earnings of self-employed earners),
(e) the repayment of capital on any loan taken out for the purposes of the employment,
(f) any expenses incurred in providing business entertainment,
(g) where the individual provides accommodation to another person in the dwelling the individual occupies as their home, any expenses paid by the individual in providing the accommodation to that person.

(6) A deduction is made under sub-paragraph (3)(a) or (4) in respect of the repayment of capital on any loan used for—
(a) the replacement in the course of business of equipment or machinery, and
(b) the repair of an existing business asset except to the extent that any sum is payable under an insurance policy for its repair.

(7) A deduction is not made in respect of any expenses under sub-paragraph (3)(a) or (4) where the Scottish Ministers are not satisfied that the expenses have been incurred or, having regard to the nature of the expense and its amount, that it has been reasonably incurred.

(8) For the avoidance of doubt—
(a) a deduction is not made under sub-paragraph (3)(a) or (4) in respect of any sum unless it has been expended for the purposes of the business,
(b) a deduction is made under sub-paragraph (3)(a) or (4) in respect of—
  (i) the excess of any VAT paid over VAT received in the period determined under paragraph 10 (calculation of earnings of self-employed earners),
  (ii) any income expended in the repair of an existing asset except to the extent that any sum is payable under an insurance policy for its repair,
  (iii) any payment of interest on a loan taken out for the purposes of the employment.

(9) Where an individual is engaged in employment as a child minder the net profit of the employment is one-third of the earnings of that employment, less—
(a) an amount in respect of—
  (i) income tax, and
  (ii) social security contributions payable under the 1992 Act, calculated in accordance with paragraph 13 (deduction of tax and contributions for self-employed earners), and
(b) one half of any premiums paid in respect of a retirement annuity or personal pension scheme.

(10) Notwithstanding paragraph 10 (calculation of earnings for self-employed earners) and sub-paragraphs (1) to (5) of this paragraph, the Scottish Ministers may assess any item of an individual's earnings or expenditure over a period other than that determined under paragraph 10 as may, in the particular case, enable the weekly amount of that item of earnings or expenditure to be determined more accurately.

Deduction of tax and contributions for self-employed earners

13.—(1) The amount to be deducted in respect of income tax under paragraph 12(1)(b)(i), (3)(b)(i) or (9)(a)(i) (calculation of net profit for self-employed earners) is calculated on the basis of the amount of chargeable income and as if that income were assessable to income tax at the basic rate, or in the case of a Scottish taxpayer, the Scottish basic rate, of tax less only the personal reliefs to which the individual is entitled under Chapters 2, 3 and 3A of Part 3 of the Income Tax Act 2007 and as are appropriate to their circumstances; but, if the period determined under paragraph 10 (calculation of earnings of self-employed earners) is less than a year, the earnings to which the basic rate, or the Scottish basic rate, of tax is to be applied and the amount of the personal reliefs deductible under this sub-paragraph is calculated on a pro rata basis.

(2) The amount to be deducted in respect of social security contributions under paragraph 12(1)(b)(i), (3)(b)(ii) or (9)(a)(ii) is the total of—
(a) the amount of Class 2 contributions payable under section 11(2) or, as the case may be, 11(8) of the 1992 Act at the rate applicable at the date on which a decision relating to the individual's entitlement to Carer Support Payment is made by the Scottish Ministers under these Regulations or, as the case may be, on appeal by the First-tier Tribunal for Scotland, except where the individual's chargeable income is equal to or less than the amount specified in section 11(4)(a) of that Act (lower profits threshold)

for the tax year in which that date falls; but if the assessment period is less than a year, the amount specified for that year is reduced pro rata, and
   (b) the amount of Class 4 contributions (if any) which would be payable under section 15 of the 1992 Act (Class 4 contributions recoverable under the Income Tax Acts) at the percentage rate applicable at the date on which a decision relating to the individual's entitlement to Carer Support Payment is made by the Scottish Ministers under these Regulations or, as the case may be, on appeal by the First-tier Tribunal for Scotland, on so much of the chargeable income as exceeds the lower limit but does not exceed the upper limit of profits and gains applicable for the tax year in which that date falls; but if the assessment period is less than a year, those limits are reduced pro rata.
(3) In this paragraph, "chargeable income" means—
   (a) in the case of employment as a child minder, one-third of the earnings of that employment, or
   (b) in all other cases, the earnings derived from the employment less any expenses deducted under paragraph 12(3)(a) or (4).

Sums to be disregarded in the calculation of earnings and profits

14. For the purposes of paragraphs 9(2) (calculation of net earnings of employed earners) and 12(2) (calculation of net profit of self-employed earners), the sums to be disregarded in the calculation of earnings and profits are—
   (a) any payment made to the individual by a person who normally resides with the individual, which is a contribution towards that person's living and accommodation costs, except where that person is residing with the individual in circumstances to which sub-paragraph (b) or (c) refers,
   (b) where the individual occupies a dwelling as their home and the dwelling is also occupied by another person and there is a contractual liability to make payments to the individual in respect of the occupation of the dwelling by that person or a member of their family—
      (i) where the aggregate of any payments made in respect of any one week in respect of that dwelling by that person or a member of their family, or by that person and a member of their family, is less than £20, the whole of that amount, or
      (ii) where the aggregate of those payments is £20 or more per week, £20,
   (c) where the individual occupies a dwelling as their home and they provide in that dwelling board and lodging accommodation, an amount, in respect of each person for whom that accommodation is provided for the whole or any part of a week, equal to—
      (i) where the aggregate of those payments made in respect of any one week does not exceed £20, 100% of those payments, or
      (ii) where the aggregate of those payments exceeds £20, £20 and 50% of the excess over £20,
   (d) except in the case of an individual who is absent from Great Britain and not disqualified for receiving any benefit, pension, allowance or supplement, by virtue of the Social Security Benefit (Persons Abroad) Regulations 1975—
      (i) any earnings derived from employment which are payable in a country outside the United Kingdom for such period during which there is a prohibition against the transfer to the United Kingdom of those earnings,
      (ii) where a payment of earnings is made in a currency other than sterling, any banking charge or commission payable in converting that payment into sterling,
   (e) any earnings which are due to be paid before the start of the award of Carer Support Payment and which would otherwise fall to be taken into account in the same award week as a payment of the same kind and from the same source,
   (f) any payment made by a local authority to the individual with whom a person is accommodated by virtue of arrangements made under section 22C (ways in which looked after children are to be accommodated and maintained) of the Children Act 1989 (provision of accommodation and maintenance for a child whom they are looking after), section 81 (ways in which looked after children are to be accommodated and maintained) of the Social Services and Well-being (Wales) Act 2014, or section 26 (manner of provision of accommodation to child looked after by local authority) of the Children (Scotland) Act 1995 or by a voluntary organisation under section 59(1)(a) (provision of accommodation by voluntary organisations) of the Children Act 1989.
   (g) any payment made by a health authority, an integrated care board, the National Health Service Commissioning Board, a local authority or a voluntary organisation to the individual in respect of a person who is not normally a member of the individual's household but is temporarily in their care,

(h) any payment paid at intervals of at least one year and derived from employments as—
  (i) a part-time fire fighter employed by a fire and rescue authority under the Fire and Rescue Services Act 2004 or by the Scottish Fire and Rescue Service established under section 1A of the Fire (Scotland) Act 2005,
  (ii) an auxiliary coastguard in respect of coast rescue activities,
  (iii) a person engaged part-time in the manning or launching of a lifeboat,
  (iv) a member of any territorial reserve force prescribed in Part I of schedule 1 of the Employment and Support Allowance Regulations 2013,
(i) any amount by way of refund of income tax deducted from profits or emoluments chargeable to income tax under schedule D or E of the Income and Corporation Taxes Act 1988,
(j) in the case of employment as an employed earner, any advance of earnings or any loan made by the individual's employer,
(k) any earnings, other than items to which sub-paragraph (l) applies, paid or due to be paid from the individual's employment as an employed earner which ended before the day in respect of which the individual first satisfied the eligibility criteria for Carer Support Payment set out in Part 3 of these Regulations,
(l) this sub-paragraph applies to—
  (i) any payment by way of occupational or personal pension, and
  (ii) except in a case where the individual's employment terminated by reason of retirement at a time when they had attained pensionable age (within the meaning given by the rules in paragraph 1 of schedule 4 of the Pensions Act 1995)—
    (aa) any payment or remuneration of the nature described in paragraph 8(1)(e) or (j), and
    (bb) any award or sum of the nature described in paragraph 8(1)(g) or (h) (including any payment made following the settlement of a complaint to an employment tribunal or of court proceedings).

Care charges to be deducted in the calculation of earnings

15.—(1) This paragraph applies where an individual is—
(a) entitled to Carer Support Payment in accordance with these Regulations, and
(b) incurring relevant care charges.

(2) In this paragraph—

"close relative" means a parent, son, daughter, brother, sister or partner,

"relevant care charges" means the charges paid by the individual for care which is provided by a person, who is not a close relative of either the cared for person or the individual, for—
(a) the cared for person, or
(b) any child under the age of 16 on the date on which the award week begins in respect of whom the individual or their partner is entitled to Child Benefit under section 141 of the 1992 Act because the individual is unable to care for any of those persons because they are carrying out duties in connection with their employment,

"cared for person" means the cared for person in respect of whom entitlement to Carer Support Payment arises.

PART XIV

SCOTTISH TRIBUNALS LEGISLATION

Tribunals (Scotland) Act 2014

(2014 asp 10)

CONTENTS

PART 1

THE SCOTTISH TRIBUNALS

CHAPTER 1

ESTABLISHMENT AND LEADERSHIP

Establishment and headship etc.

1   Establishment of the Tribunals   **14.1**
2 to 42 *Omitted*

PART 6

REVIEW OR APPEAL OF DECISIONS

CHAPTER 1

TRIBUNAL DECISIONS

Internal review

43   Review of decisions
44   Actions on review
45   Review once only

Appeal from First-tier Tribunal

46   Appeal from the Tribunal
47   Disposal of an appeal

Appeal from Upper Tribunal

48   Appeal from the Tribunal
49   Disposal of an appeal
50   Procedure on second appeal

Tribunals (Scotland) Act 2014

Excluded decisions

51 Excluded decisions
52 Decisions on review
53 Other appeal rights
54 *Omitted*

Miscellaneous procedure

55 Process for permission
56 Participation of non-parties

CHAPTER 2

SPECIAL JURISDICTION

57 to 60 *Omitted*

PART 7

POWERS, PROCEDURE AND ADMINISTRATION

CHAPTER 1

POWERS AND ENFORCEMENT

Cases and proceedings

61 Venue for hearings
62 Conduct of cases
63 Enforcement of decisions
64 Award of expenses

Supplementary provisions

65 Additional powers
66 Application of enactments
67 Offences in relation to proceedings

CHAPTER 2

PRACTICE AND PROCEDURE

Tribunal Rules

68 Tribunal Rules
69 Exercise of functions
70 Extent of rule-making

Particular matters

71 Proceedings and steps
72 Hearings in cases
73 Evidence and decisions

Issuing directions

74 Practice directions
75 Publication and effect

CHAPTER 3

FEES AND ADMINISTRATION

76 to 78 *Omitted*

PART 8

FINAL PROVISIONS

General and ancillary

79 Regulation-making
80 Ancillary regulations
81 *Omitted*

Interpretation, commencement and short title

82 Interpretation
83 Commencement
84 Short title

Schedules 1 to 9—*Omitted*
Schedule 10—Index of expressions

The Bill for this Act of the Scottish Parliament was passed by the Parliament on 11th March 2014 and received Royal Assent on 15th April 2014

An Act of the Scottish Parliament to establish the First-tier Tribunal for Scotland and the Upper Tribunal for Scotland; and for connected purposes.

Tribunals (Scotland) Act 2014

CHAPTER 1

ESTABLISHMENT AND LEADERSHIP

Establishment and headship etc.

Establishment of the Tribunals

14.2

1.—(1) There are established two tribunals to be known as—
  (a) the First-tier Tribunal for Scotland,
  (b) the Upper Tribunal for Scotland.
(2) The Tribunals mentioned in subsection (1) are referred to in this Act—
  (a) respectively as—
    (i) the First-tier Tribunal,
    (ii) the Upper Tribunal,
  (b) collectively as the Scottish Tribunals.
(3) The constitution, operation and administration of the Scottish Tribunals are as provided for by or under this Act or another Act.
(4) The jurisdiction, powers and other functions of the Scottish Tribunals are as conferred by or under this Act or another Act.

GENERAL NOTE

14.3

This section establishes the Scottish Tribunals which, despite their names being the same and their structure similar, are entirely separate from the First-tier Tribunal and Upper Tribunal constituted under s.3 of the Tribunals, Courts and Enforcement Act 2007. Indeed, Lord Ericht, sitting in the Upper Tribunal for Scotland in a tax case, *Barr Environmental limited v Revenue Scotland* [2022] UT 11, observed—

> "[38] This Tribunal is a Scottish Tribunal applying Scots tax legislation and Scots law and procedure. It is not bound by decisions of the English courts on English or UK tax legislation. Nor is it bound by the same rules of procedure or evidence which apply in the English courts or the UK tax Tribunals system. Having said that, this Tribunal and the First-tier Tribunal are entitled to consider tax law and decisions from other jurisdictions within the UK or further afield which have relevance to the matters before them. In particular, where there is equivalent UK or English tax law, the decisions of the English courts are persuasive but not binding."

The same approach is obviously required in social security cases.

The Lord President of the Court of Session is the Head of the Scottish Tribunals but there is also a President of Tribunals. The Lord President has assigned Lady Wise to that role from May 1, 2023.

The First-tier Tribunal for Scotland is divided into seven chambers (see the First-tier Tribunal for Scotland (Chambers) Regulations 2016 (SSI 2016/341, as amended by SSI 2018/349 and SSI 2021/448). As at the end of July 2023, only six of them had been brought into operation, with no firm date having been announced for the transfer of powers from the Mental Health Tribunal for Scotland to the remaining chamber.

The social security functions of the First-tier Tribunal, which are the functions conferred on it by the Social Security (Scotland) Act 2018 and by regulations made under that Act, are allocated to the Social Security Chamber (see reg.3 of the First-tier Tribunal for Scotland (Allocation of Functions to the Social Security Chamber) Regulations 2018 set out below). Currently, those functions are determining appeals under ss. 46 and 61 of the 2018 Act, paras 19 and 23 of the Sch. to the Scottish Child Payment Regulations 2020 and paras 9 and 13 of Sch.2 of the Carer's Allowance Supplement and Young Carer Grants (Residence Requirements and Procedural Provisions) (EU Exit) (Scotland) Regulations 2020. The Social Security Chamber's jurisdiction is expanding as new forms of assistance under the 2018 Act are introduced and, in due course, it is expected to take over the social security functions exercised in Scotland by the First-tier Tribunal constituted under the 2007 Act.

The Upper Tribunal for Scotland hears appeals from the First-tier Tribunal, but note that there is no right of appeal to the Upper Tribunal against a decision made by the First-tier Tribunal on an appeal against a process decision (see s.61(5)(b) of the 2018 Act, para.23(5)(b) of the sch. to the Scottish Child Payment Regulations 2020 and para.13(5)(b) of sch.2 of the Carer's Allowance Supplement and Young Carer Grants (Residence Requirements and Procedural Provisions) (EU Exit) (Scotland) Regulations 2020). The Court of Session may transfer judicial review proceedings to the Upper Tribunal under s.57 of the 2014 Act but, as under the 2007 Act in relation to judicial review proceedings brought under the law of Scotland, judicial review proceedings cannot be commenced in the Upper Tribunal.

2. to 42. *Omitted.*

PART 6

Review or appeal of decisions

CHAPTER 1

Tribunal decisions

Internal review

Review of decisions

43.—(1) Each of the First-tier Tribunal and the Upper Tribunal may review a decision made by it in any matter in a case before it.

(2) A decision is reviewable—
(a) at the Tribunal's own instance, or
(b) at the request of a party in the case.

(3) But—
(a) there can be no review under this section of an excluded decision,
(b) Tribunal Rules may make provision—
   (i) excluding other decisions from a review under this section,
   (ii) otherwise restricting the availability of a review under this section (including by specifying grounds for a review).

(4) The exercise of discretion whether a decision should be reviewed under this section cannot give rise to a review under this section or to an appeal under section 46 or 48.

(5) A right of appeal under section 46 or 48 is not affected by the availability or otherwise of a review under this section.

General Note

This power of review is excluded in the case of appeals to the First-tier Tribunal against process decisions regarding social security (see s.61(5)(a) of the Social

Security (Scotland) Act 2018, para.23(5)(a) of the sch. to the Scottish Child Payment Regulations 2020 and para.13(5)(a) of sch.2 of the Carer's Allowance Supplement and Young Carer Grants (Residence Requirements and Procedural Provisions) (EU Exit) (Scotland) Regulations 2020) and in the case of refusals of permission to appeal to the Upper Tribunal or the Court of Session (see s.55(2)(a) of this Act). Moreover, ss. 51 and 52 have the effect that a decision cannot be reviewed twice (see also s.45) and that most decisions in reviews are not themselves reviewable because they are "excluded decisions" for the purpose of s.43(3)(a).

In *Aberdeen CC v LS* [2021] UT 1, the Upper Tribunal was critical of the lengthy procedure adopted by the Health and Education Chamber of the First-tier Tribunal when considering applications for review and for permission to appeal brought on the same grounds. The judicial member, Lady Poole (a former judge of the UK Upper Tribunal), said that there was no reason why the same legal member could not have dealt with both applications at the same time and she also suggested that the approach taken in *R (RB) v First-tier Tribunal* [2010] UKUT 160 (AAC); [2010] AACR 41 in relation to reviews under s.9 of the Tribunals, Courts and Enforcement Act 2007 was equally applicable in Scottish tribunals, even though there are differences between the two systems. She said -

"Given the availability of an appeal on a point of law, in my opinion, a review is unlikely to be in the interests of justice within Rule 11 of the FtT Rules if what is being challenged is merely an arguable point of law. Set aside powers on a review under Section 44(1)(b) of the 2014 Act in my view cover situations in which there has been a clear error of law, which may encompass some material errors in fact. Review is primarily intended for cases where a decision is plainly wrong, so avoiding the need for an appeal that would inevitably succeed. This might happen, for example, if a binding legal authority or provision has been overlooked. It should be relatively obvious where this type of error exists, with the result that a review need not be an unduly time-consuming exercise. Review is not intended to usurp the function of the UTS to determine appeals on contentious points of law."

The approach taken in *RB* was approved by the Court of Appeal in *Point West GR Ltd v Bassi* [2020] EWCA Civ 765, to which the Upper Tribunal for Scotland referred in *South Lanarkshire Council v Boyd* [2021] UT 31 when assuming, but not deciding, that it should take the same approach.

Actions on review

14.7

44.—(1) In a review by the First-tier Tribunal or the Upper Tribunal under section 43, the Tribunal may—
 (a) take no action,
 (b) set the decision aside, or
 (c) correct a minor or accidental error contained in the decision.
(2) Where a decision is set aside by the First-tier Tribunal in a review, it may—
 (a) re-decide the matter concerned,
 (b) refer that matter to the Upper Tribunal, or
 (c) make such other order as the First-tier Tribunal considers appropriate.
(3) If a decision set aside by the First-tier Tribunal in a review is referred to the Upper Tribunal, the Upper Tribunal—
 (a) may re-decide the matter concerned or make such other order as it considers appropriate,
 (b) in re-deciding that matter, may do anything that the First-tier Tribunal could do if re-deciding it.

(4) Where a decision is set aside by the Upper Tribunal in a review, it may—
   (a) re-decide the matter concerned, or
   (b) make such other order as it considers appropriate.
(5) In re-deciding a matter under this section, the First-tier or Upper Tribunal may reach such findings in fact as it considers appropriate.

GENERAL NOTE

In *Skoll v Humanes* [2020] UT 36, the Upper Tribunal held that it was not competent to consider a reference under s.44(2)(b) because, in a housing and property case, the First-tier Tribunal had not set aside its decision under s.44(1)(b) before referring the case. The rules applicable in the Housing and Property Chamber do not limit the grounds of review to points of law (unlike r.35(1) of the rules applicable in the Social Security Chamber), but it was still necessary for the First-tier Tribunal to find that its decision had been wrong if it was to set it aside. Merely describing its consideration of a point of law as "incomplete and in places irrelevant" did not amount to a finding that the decision had been wrong. The Upper Tribunal remitted the case to the First-tier Tribunal and extended the claimant's time for applying to the First-tier Tribunal for permission to appeal. This appears to have been necessary because the Housing and Property Chamber rules do not provide for an application for review to be treated also as an application for permission to appeal (unlike r.36 of the rules applicable in the Social Security Chamber).

Review once only

45.—(1) A particular decision of the First-tier Tribunal or the Upper Tribunal may not be reviewed under section 43 more than once.
(2) These are to be regarded as different decisions for the purpose of subsection (1)—
   (a) a decision set aside under section 44(1)(b),
   (b) a decision made by virtue of section 44(2)(a), (3)(a) or (4).
(3) Nothing in this section prevents the taking, after a review in which the decision concerned is not set aside, of administrative steps by the First-tier or Upper Tribunal to correct a minor or accidental error made in disposing of the review.

Appeal from First-tier Tribunal

Appeal from the Tribunal

46.—(1) A decision of the First-tier Tribunal in any matter in a case before the Tribunal may be appealed to the Upper Tribunal.
(2) An appeal under this section is to be made—
   (a) by a party in the case,
   (b) on a point of law only.
(3) An appeal under this section requires the permission of—
   (a) the First-tier Tribunal, or
   (b) if the First-tier Tribunal refuses its permission, the Upper Tribunal.
(4) Such permission may be given in relation to an appeal under this section only if the First-tier Tribunal or (as the case may be) the Upper Tribunal is satisfied that there are arguable grounds for the appeal.
(5) This section—

(a) is subject to sections 43(4) and 55(2),
(b) does not apply in relation to an excluded decision.

GENERAL NOTE

14.11   This right of appeal is excluded in the case of appeals to the First-tier Tribunal against process decisions regarding social security (see s.61(5)(b) of the Social Security (Scotland) Act 2018, para.23(5)(b) of the sch. to the Scottish Child Payment Regulations 2020 and para.13(5)(b) of sch.2 of the Carer's Allowance Supplement and Young Carer Grants (Residence Requirements and Procedural Provisions) (EU Exit) (Scotland) Regulations 2020) and in the case of refusals by the First-tier Tribunal of permission to appeal to the Upper Tribunal (see s.55(2)(b) of this Act). In addition, ss. 51 and 52 have the effect that a decision that has been reviewed and most decisions in reviews are "excluded decisions" for the purpose of s.46(5)(b) and s.43(4) provides that the exercise of discretion whether a decision should be reviewed cannot give rise to an appeal.

The meaning of "a point of law" was considered in *Murray Group Holdings Ltd v Revenue and Customs Commissioners* [2015] CSIH 77; 2016 S.C. 201, an appeal against a decision of the United Kingdom Upper Tribunal, where the Inner House of the Court of Session said—

"[42] Although the concept of appeal on a point of law might seem simple, it has given rise to considerable controversy; indeed in the well-known case of *Edwards v Bairstow*, [1956] AC 14, an appeal was taken to the House of Lords to adjudicate upon differences of approach that had developed between the Scottish and English courts. We are of opinion that an appeal on a point of law covers four different categories of case. The first of these categories is appeals on the general law: the content of its rules. In tax appeals these are largely statutory, but the interpretation of a particular statutory provision may be a matter of general law, and tax law also includes a number of general non-statutory rules, such as the redirection principle and the *Ramsay* principle, both of which are relevant to this case. The second category comprises appeals on the application of the law to the facts as found by the First-tier Tribunal. This is in our opinion a clear example of an appeal on a point of law: it is the application of the general rules to particular factual situations that defines the frontiers of a legal rule and thus its practical scope. Furthermore, it is the application of the general rules to particular facts that brings about the development of those rules to meet new situations. For these reasons we consider that an appeal on the application of the general law to a particular factual situation must be regarded as being on a point of law. This is illustrated by the facts of *Edwards v Bairstow*. There the House of Lords, reversing the decisions of the General Commissioners and lower courts, held that a transaction involving the acquisition of spinning plant, dividing it into lots and selling those lots at a profit was an adventure in the nature of trade. In holding otherwise, the Commissioners and the lower courts had misdirected themselves as to the meaning and proper application of the expression "adventure ... in the nature of trade" found in the relevant taxing statute, the Income Tax Act 1918: see Lord Radcliffe at [1956] AC 36–37.

[43] The third category of appeal on a point of law is where the Tribunal has made a finding "for which there is no evidence or which is inconsistent with the evidence and contradictory of it": *IRC v Fraser*, 1942 SC 493, at 497–498, per LP Normand. This runs into a fourth category, comprising cases where the First-tier Tribunal has made a fundamental error in its approach to the case: for example, by asking the wrong question, or by taking account of manifestly irrelevant considerations, or by arriving at a decision that no reasonable tax tribunal could properly reach. In such cases we conceive that the Court of Session and the Upper Tribunal have power to interfere with the decision of the First-tier Tribunal as disclosing an error on a point of law: *Edwards v Bairstow*, per Lord Radcliffe at [1956] AC 36."

The Court (whose decision was upheld on appeal to the Supreme Court in *RFC 2012 Plc (formerly The Rangers Football Club Plc) v Advocate General for Scotland* [2017] UKSC 45; [2017] 1 W.L.R. 2767 without reference to these points) also observed that decisions of the First-tier Tribunal relating to tax frequently involve elements of evaluation and judgment and that: "In general, a court, or the Upper Tribunal, should be slow to interfere with the decision of the First- tier Tribunal in cases of this nature." Nonetheless: "It is a matter of degree: the higher the factual component in the evaluative exercise, the slower the court should be to interfere, but correspondingly if the factual component is relatively low and the legal component is high the court may properly interfere." Although the Court did not draw any distinction between the position of a court and the position of the Upper Tribunal, it is clear that, since one of the reasons why appellate bodies do not interfere is the specialist nature of the First-tier Tribunal, there may be some cases where the Upper Tribunal can properly interfere but an appellate court would not, because the Upper Tribunal may be able to claim as much relevant expertise as the First-tier Tribunal. However, this point did not arise for consideration in that case because the Upper Tribunal had dismissed the appeal from the First- tier Tribunal and the Court of Session decided that they were both wrong in law.

Where the First-tier Tribunal has had to consider what would be reasonable, the Upper Tribunal may substitute its own judgment only if the First-tier Tribunal's approach was flawed. Relevant authorities were summarised in *Boyle v Ford* [2023] UT 4, a housing case, where it was said—

"[46] Thus, reasonableness is not in itself a fact but instead a concept or conclusion determined by an exercise of judgment (*City of Edinburgh Council v Forbes* 2002 Hous. L. R. 61 at paragraph 7- 16, per Sheriff Principal Nicholson Q.C.).

[47] Accordingly, the UT may only interfere with the FtT's assessment of reasonableness if satisfied there are cogent and compelling reasons for suggesting that the FtT erred in the exercise of that judgment (*Glasgow West Housing Association v Harasimowicz* 2015 Hous. L. R. 77 at paragraph [11], per Sheriff Principal Scott Q.C).

[48] Matters of weight are normally for the FtT to decide; the UT will not interfere unless the FtT has misdirected itself or gone plainly wrong (*Bedfordshire Housing Association v Khan* 2007 EWCA Civ 1445 at paragraph [16], per Tuckey LJ). Infelicities in expression by the FtT are not sufficient in themselves to infer an error of law on the part of the FtT (*Barking and Dagenham LBC v Bakare* [2012] H.L.R 34 at paragraphs [32] to [36], per MacFarlane LJ).

[49] The FtT's task is to consider whether, in all the circumstances, granting an order for possession is reasonable, not the most reasonable course of action, nor one within a range of possible actions; if it so decides, it must grant the order (*East Lothian Council v Duffy* 2012 S.L.T. (Sh. Ct.) 113 at paragraphs [71] and [72], per Sheriff Braid)"

In that case, it was held that the First-tier Tribunal had erred because it had misdirected itself in law and had failed to demonstrate that it took into account, and properly weighed and balanced, all relevant considerations, in reaching that conclusion. See also *Ahmed v Russell* [2023] UT 7, where the issue was the level of sanction to be imposed under reg.10(1)(a) of the Tenancy Deposit Schemes (Scotland) Regulations 2011 (SSI 2011/176).

The most useful English authority on the meaning of "a point of law" is probably *R. (Iran) v Secretary of State for the Home Department* [2005] EWCA Civ 982, which is to much the same effect as the Court of Session's decision and is considered in detail in the annotation to s.11 of the Tribunals, Courts and Enforcement Act 2007 in Vol.III of this series. See also the detailed discussion in *Garrett v Your Place Property Management Limited* [2020] UT 34 at [20] to [23]. In an earlier determination in the latter case, it was held that the test of "arguability" in s.46(4) is "a relatively low hurdle" for an applicant to overcome (*Garrett v Your Place Property Management Limited* [2020] UT 32 at [4]). Permission to appeal will not generally be given unless the point of law is not only arguable but also material in the sense that it might have made a difference to the outcome (*Mansfield v Thomson* [2020] UT 14 at [7]; *Aberdeenshire Council v SS* [2020] UT 25 at [16] to [19]; *Alase v Iveson* [2022] UT 29).

In *Cowan v Somasundaram* [2021] UT 4, the Upper Tribunal applied the approach taken in *Advocate General for Scotland v Murray Group Holdings Limited* [2015] CSIH 77; 2016 SC 201 at [39] and held that it is competent for permission to appeal to be granted by the Upper Tribunal on grounds not argued before the First-tier Tribunal, although the Upper Tribunal should be slow to allow such an appeal, particularly where additional findings in fact are required, and should not do so if unfairness results. However, as the grounds advanced on behalf of Mr Cowan were not arguable, he was refused permission to appeal.

By way of contrast, in *Hughes v Glasgow City Council Private Sector* [2021] UT 12, the Appellant had raised a new argument when applying to the First-tier Tribunal for permission to appeal and the First-tier Tribunal had granted unlimited permission to appeal without giving reasons for considering the point to be arguable. The Upper Tribunal commented that that made it difficult for the Upper Tribunal to rule on the issue and it raised the question whether the First-tier Tribunal could err on an issue that it had not considered or ruled upon, and it also was concerned as to whether the First-tier Tribunal had made sufficient findings to enable the Upper Tribunal to deal with the issue but, in the end, it grasped the nettle and did in fact rule on the point of law, deciding it against the appellant. One consideration when the Upper Tribunal is deciding whether to allow a new argument of law, not advanced before the First-tier Tribunal, to be raised before it is whether the evidence and the findings in facts might have been different if the argument had been in play before the First-tier Tribunal (see *South Lanarkshire Council v Boyd* [2022] CSIH 41; 2022 G.W.D. 29–425 at [21]). However, if the First-tier Tribunal can be said to have erred in law in not raising the argument on its own initiative, the Upper Tribunal can remit the case to be reheard by the First-tier Tribunal if the First-tier Tribunal's failure to raise the point may have affected its findings. In this regard, it is important to note that the overriding objective in the Rules of Procedure in relation to the Social Security Chamber is different from the overriding objective in the Rules of Procedure in the Housing and Property Chamber, so that a more interventionist approach may be justified in social security cases (see the annotation to r.2 in Schedule of the First-tier Tribunal for Scotland Social Security Chamber (Procedure) Regulations 2018, below).

The fact that a respondent does not oppose an appeal does not relieve the Upper Tribunal of the obligation to identify an error of law before allowing the appeal (*Goodyear v Highland Council* [2022] UT 4; *Colraine v Bridges* [2023] UT 9), and so it is helpful if the respondent explains briefly why it is not opposing the appeal, even if only to make clear that it accepts the appellant's argument. In *Ostendorf v Rollos Solicitors & Estate Agents* [2021] UT 11, in which the appeal raised a not entirely straightforward point of law and both parties had legal representation, the Upper Tribunal commented –

> "Both parties supplied little by way of submission to this Tribunal. The failure of both parties to provide any serious analysis in support of their respective positions in this appeal is disappointing. . . . . It is important that professional representatives make substantive submissions to the Tribunal in appeals of this kind."

Breaches of procedural provisions, such as the duty to provide proper and adequate reasons, can amount to errors of law. For the standard of reasoning required from the First-tier Tribunal, see the note to r.29 of the procedural rules in the schedule of the First-tier Tribunal for Scotland Social Security Chamber (Procedure) Regulations 2018, below.

Disposal of an appeal

47.—(1) In an appeal under section 46, the Upper Tribunal may uphold or quash the decision on the point of law in question.

(2) If the Upper Tribunal quashes the decision, it may—
  (a) re-make the decision,
  (b) remit the case to the First-tier Tribunal, or
  (c) make such other order as the Upper Tribunal considers appropriate.

(3) In re-making the decision, the Upper Tribunal may—
  (a) do anything that the First-tier Tribunal could do if re-making the decision,
  (b) reach such findings in fact as the Upper Tribunal considers appropriate.

(4) In remitting the case, the Upper Tribunal may give directions for the First-tier Tribunal's reconsideration of the case.

(5) Such directions may relate to—
  (a) issues of law or fact (including the Upper Tribunal's opinion on any relevant point),
  (b) procedural issues (including as to the members to be chosen to reconsider the case).

GENERAL NOTE

In *New Lanark Hotels Limited v Office of the Scottish Charity Regulator* [2020] UT 9 and *New Lanark Trading Limited v Office of the Scottish Charity Regulator* [2020] UT 10, the Upper Tribunal held that when making its own decisions, having found the First-tier Tribunal to have erred in law, it must proceed on the basis of the findings of fact specifically made by the First-tier Tribunal, or obviously arising from its decision (the First-tier Tribunal decision not always clearly discriminating between what was properly stated as a finding of fact and what was a reason) insofar as they were not vitiated by the error of law, but that it was also appropriate, in the exercise of its power under s.47(3)(b) of the 2014 Act, to make additional findings based upon evidence led before the First-tier Tribunal, where such findings were not in any way inconsistent with other findings made, or to be attributed to, the First-tier Tribunal. It was not suggested by the parties that the Upper Tribunal should hear any additional evidence as the primary facts were not really in dispute. Appeals by the Regulator were subsequently dismissed by the Court of Session (*Office of the Scottish Charity Regulator v New Lanark Hotels Limited and New Lanark Trading Limited* [2021] CSIH 7), the Court emphasising that the Upper Tribunal was required to make a decision "of new" and was not merely exercising a supervisory jurisdiction.

Appeal from Upper Tribunal

Appeal from the Tribunal

48.—(1) A decision of the Upper Tribunal in any matter in a case before the Tribunal may be appealed to the Court of Session.

(2) An appeal under this section is to be made—
  (a) by a party in the case,
  (b) on a point of law only.

(3) An appeal under this section requires the permission of—
  (a) the Upper Tribunal, or

(b) if the Upper Tribunal refuses its permission, the Court of Session.

(4) Such permission may be given in relation to an appeal under this section only if the Upper Tribunal or (as the case may be) the Court of Session is satisfied that there are arguable grounds for the appeal.

(5) This section—
(a) is subject to sections 43(4) and 55(2),
(b) does not apply in relation to an excluded decision.

GENERAL NOTE

14.14   This right of appeal is excluded by s.55(2)(b) in the case of refusals by the Upper Tribunal of permission to appeal from the First-tier Tribunal to itself under s.46(3)(b) and, perhaps unnecessarily, of permission to appeal from itself to the Court of Session under s.48(3)(a). In addition, ss. 51 and 52 have the effect that a decision that has been reviewed and most decisions in reviews are "excluded decisions" for the purpose of s.48(5)(b) and s.43(4) provides that the exercise of discretion whether a decision should be reviewed cannot give rise to an appeal.

Where the Upper Tribunal's decision was given on an appeal from the First-tier Tribunal, permission to appeal may be given only if the further condition in s.50(4) is satisfied.

Disposal of an appeal

14.15   **49.**—(1) In an appeal under section 48, the Court of Session may uphold or quash the decision on the point of law in question.

(2) If the Court quashes the decision, it may—
(a) re-make the decision,
(b) remit the case to the Upper Tribunal, or
(c) make such other order as the Court considers appropriate.

(3) In re-making the decision, the Court may—
(a) do anything that the Upper Tribunal could do if re-making the decision,
(b) reach such findings in fact as the Court considers appropriate.

(4) In remitting the case, the Court may give directions for the Upper Tribunal's reconsideration of the case.

(5) Such directions may relate to—
(a) issues of law or fact (including the Court's opinion on any relevant point),
(b) procedural issues (including as to the members to be chosen to reconsider the case).

GENERAL NOTE

Where the Upper Tribunal's decision was given on appeal from the First-tier Tribunal, the Court of Session may choose to remit the case to the First-tier Tribunal, rather than to the Upper Tribunal (see s.50(6)). This will usually be the appropriate course where further findings of fact are required, although it might be appropriate for such a case to be remitted to the Upper Tribunal if it is particularly complicated but, nonetheless, any special expertise of the First-tier Tribunal is not required.

Procedure on second appeal

14.16   **50.**—(1) Section 48(4) is subject to subsections (3) and (4) as regards a second appeal.

(2) Section 49 is subject to subsections (5) and (6) as regards a second appeal.

(3) For the purpose of subsection (1), the Upper Tribunal or (as the case may be) the Court of Session may not give its permission to the making of a second appeal unless also satisfied that subsection (4) applies.

(4) This subsection applies where, in relation to the matter in question—
 (a) a second appeal would raise an important point of principle or practice, or
 (b) there is some other compelling reason for allowing a second appeal to proceed.

(5) For the purpose of subsection (2), subsections (2)(b) and (3)(a) of section 49 have effect in relation to a second appeal as if the references in them to the Upper Tribunal include (as alternatives) references to the First-tier Tribunal.

(6) Where, in exercising the choice arising by virtue of subsection (5) (and instead of re-making the decision in question), the Court of Session remits the case to the Upper Tribunal rather than the First-tier Tribunal—
 (a) the Upper Tribunal, instead of reconsidering the case itself, may remit the case to the First-tier Tribunal,
 (b) if the Upper Tribunal does so, it must send to the First-tier Tribunal any directions accompanying the Court's remittal of the case to the Upper Tribunal.

(7) In this section, "second appeal" means appeal under section 48 against a decision in an appeal under section 46.

GENERAL NOTE

The criteria in subs.(4) for giving permission for a second appeal were considered in *South Lanarkshire Council v Boyd* [2021] UT 31, where the Upper Tribunal decided that permission to appeal should be refused even though the would-be appellant had an arguable point of law as to whether the First-tier Tribunal's fact finding had been adequate, because the issue was specific to that particular case and had no wider implications. At [38], the Upper Tribunal held that –

"For an important point of principle or practice to be established it must be one that extends beyond the specific and limited interest of the appellant."

It appears that the Court of Session subsequently gave permission to appeal, but it ultimately dismissed the appeal (*South Lanarkshire Council v Boyd* [2022] CSIH 41; 2022 G.W.D. 49-425).

Excluded decisions

Excluded decisions

51.—A decision falling within any of sections 52 to 54 is an excluded decision for the purposes of—
 (a) a review under section 43,
 (b) an appeal under section 46 or 48.

14.17

Decisions on review

14.18   52.—(1) Falling within this section is—
(a) a decision set aside in a review under section 43 (see section 44(1)(b)),
(b) a decision in such a review, except a decision of the kind mentioned in subsection (2).
(2) That is, a decision made by virtue of section 44(2)(a), (3)(a) or (4) (and accordingly a decision so made is not an excluded decision).

Other appeal rights

14.19   53.—(1) Falling within this section is a decision against which there is a right of appeal under an enactment apart from this Act.
(2) The Scottish Ministers may by regulations make provision—
(a) to which subsection (1) is subject (for example, by specifying an exception to what falls within this section),
(b) for a right of appeal under an enactment apart from this Act to cease to be exercisable in relation to a decision no longer falling within this section.

14.20   54. *Omitted.*

Miscellaneous procedure

Process for permission

14.21   55.—(1) The Scottish Ministers may by regulations specify a time limit within which the permission required by section 46(3) or 48(3) must be sought.
(2) A refusal to give the permission required by section 46(3) or 48(3) is not—
(a) reviewable under section 43, or
(b) appealable under section 46 or 48.

GENERAL NOTE

14.22   For regulations made under subs.(1), see the Scottish Tribunals (Time Limits) Regulations 2016, below.

Subsection (2) does not prevent a person from effectively challenging a refusal by the First-tier Tribunal to give permission to appeal to the Upper Tribunal, because the obvious remedy is simply to make an application to the Upper Tribunal itself. Similarly, when the Upper Tribunal refuses permission to appeal to the Court of Session, the remedy is to make an application to the Court of Session itself. However, it does make it clear that there is no right of appeal to the Court of Session against a decision of the Upper Tribunal refusing permission to itself from a decision of the First-tier Tribunal and, equally, that there is no right of appeal to the Supreme Court against a decision of the Court of Session refusing permission to appeal against a decision of the Upper Tribunal. On the other hand, a decision of the Upper Tribunal to refuse permission to appeal from a decision of the First-tier Tribunal may in principle be challenged through an application to the Court of Session for judicial review, although the circumstances in which such an application might succeed will in practice be fairly limited (*Eba v Advocate General for Scotland* [2011] UKSC 29; 2012 S.C. (UKSC) 1, [2012] 1 AC 710).

Participation of non-parties

56.—(1) Subsection (2) applies for the purposes of—
(a) a review under section 43,
(b) an appeal under section 46 or 48.
(2) The Scottish Ministers may by regulations make provision extending any reference to a party in a case so that it also includes a person falling within a specified description.

CHAPTER 2

SPECIAL JURISDICTION

57. to 60. *Omitted.*

PART 7

POWERS, PROCEDURE AND ADMINISTRATION

CHAPTER 1

POWERS AND ENFORCEMENT

Cases and proceedings

Venue for hearings

61.—(1) Each of the First-tier Tribunal and the Upper Tribunal may be convened at any time and place in Scotland to hear or decide a case or for any other purpose relating to its functions.
(2) Subsection (1) is subject to any provision made by Tribunal Rules as to the question of when and where in Scotland the Scottish Tribunals are to be convened (and such Rules may allow the President of Tribunals to determine the question).

Conduct of cases

62.—(1) In relation to the things mentioned in subsection (3), each of the First-tier Tribunal and the Upper Tribunal has such powers, rights, privileges and other authority with respect to any case before it as are provided for in Tribunal Rules.
(2) Rules making provision for the purpose of subsection (1) may (in particular) do so in relation to any kind of authority by reference to any authority of a relevant description exercisable by the sheriff or the Court of Session.

(3) The things are—
(a) the citation, attendance or examination of witnesses,
(b) the recovery, production or inspection of relevant materials,
(c) the commissioning of reports of any relevant type,
(d) other procedural, evidential or similar measures.

(4) In subsection (3)(b), "materials" means documents and other items.

Enforcement of decisions

63.—(1) A decision made by the First-tier Tribunal or the Upper Tribunal in any matter in a case before it is enforceable by the means provided for in Tribunal Rules.

(2) Subsection (1) applies to a decision—
(a) on the merits of such a case,
(b) as to—
   (i) payment of a sum of money, or
   (ii) expenses by virtue of section 64, or
(c) otherwise affecting the rights, obligations or interests of a party in such a case.

(3) Subsection (1) is subject to section 58(3) as respects a determination to which that section relates.

(4) Rules making provision for the purpose of subsection (1) may (in particular) do so in relation to a relevant order by reference to the means of enforcing an order of the sheriff or the Court of Session.

(5) In subsection (4), "relevant order" means order of either of the Tribunals giving effect to a decision to which subsection (1) applies.

Award of expenses

64.—(1) In connection with proceedings in a case before the First-tier Tribunal or the Upper Tribunal, the Tribunal may award expenses so far as allowed in accordance with Tribunal Rules.

(2) Where such expenses are awarded, the awarding Tribunal is to specify by and to whom they are to be paid (and to what extent).

(3) Tribunal Rules may make provision—
(a) for scales or rates of awardable expenses,
(b) for—
   (i) such expenses to be set-off against any relevant sums,
   (ii) interest at the specified rate to be chargeable on such expenses where unpaid,
(c) stating the general or particular factors to be taken into account when exercising discretion as to such expenses,
(d) about such expenses in other respects.

(4) Tribunal Rules may make provision—
(a) for disallowing any wasted expenses,
(b) for requiring a person who has given rise to such expenses to meet them.

(5) Rules making provision as described in subsection (3) or (4) may also prescribe meanings for "relevant sums", "specified rate" and "wasted expenses" as used in this section.

Supplementary provisions

Additional powers

65.—(1) The Scottish Ministers may by regulations confer on the First-tier Tribunal and the Upper Tribunal such additional powers as are necessary or expedient for the proper exercise of their functions.

(2) Regulations under subsection (1) may include provision—
(a) relying on the effect of an act of sederunt made by the Court of Session,
(b) causing Part 1 of the Scottish Civil Justice Council and Criminal Legal Assistance Act 2013 to apply to the making of a relevant act of sederunt as it does to the making of Tribunal Rules.

(3) Before making regulations under subsection (1), the Scottish Ministers must obtain the Lord President's approval.

Application of enactments

66.—(1) The Scottish Ministers may by regulations modify the application of any enactment so far as they consider to be necessary or expedient for the purposes of or in connection with the matters to which this subsection applies.

(2) Regulations under subsection (1) may include provision—
(a) relying on the effect of an act of sederunt made by the Court of Session,
(b) causing Part 1 of the Scottish Civil Justice Council and Criminal Legal Assistance Act 2013 to apply to the making of a relevant act of sederunt as it does to the making of Tribunal Rules.

(3) Subsection (1) applies to—
(a) the making of Tribunal Rules,
(b) the effect of—
  (i) this Part, or
  (ii) Tribunal Rules.

(4) Before making regulations under subsection (1), the Scottish Ministers must obtain the Lord President's approval.

Offences in relation to proceedings

67.—(1) Scottish Ministers may by regulations make provision, in relation to proceedings before the First-tier Tribunal or the Upper Tribunal—
(a) for offences and penalties—
  (i) for making a false statement in an application in a case,
  (ii) for failure by a person to attend, or give evidence in, such proceedings when required to do so in accordance with Tribunal Rules,
  (iii) for alteration, concealment or destruction by a person of, or failure by a person to produce, something that is required to be produced in such proceedings in accordance with Tribunal Rules,
(b) about the circumstances in which a person need not give evidence or produce something (for example, where a person could not be

compelled to give evidence or produce something in proceedings in a case before the sheriff or in the Court of Session).

(2) The maximum penalties that may be provided for in regulations under subsection (1) are—
  (a) for an offence triable summarily only, imprisonment for a term not exceeding 12 months or a fine not exceeding level 5 on the standard scale (or both),
  (b) for an offence triable either summarily or on indictment—
    (i) on summary conviction, imprisonment for a term not exceeding 12 months or a fine not exceeding the statutory maximum (or both),
    (ii) on conviction on indictment, imprisonment for a term not exceeding 2 years or a fine (or both).

(3) Before making regulations under subsection (1), the Scottish Ministers must obtain the Lord President's approval.

CHAPTER 2

Practice and procedure

Tribunal Rules

Tribunal Rules

14.32

68.—(1) There are to be rules—
  (a) regulating the practice and procedure to be followed in proceedings at—
    (i) the First-tier Tribunal,
    (ii) the Upper Tribunal, and
  (b) containing provision of other sorts appropriate with respect to the Scottish Tribunals (including in relation to the exercise by them of their functions).

(2) Rules of the kind mentioned in subsection (1) are to be known as Scottish Tribunal Rules (and in this Act they are referred to as Tribunal Rules).

(3) Tribunal Rules are to be made by the Court of Session by act of sederunt.

(4) Part 1 of the Scottish Civil Justice Council and Criminal Legal Assistance Act 2013 includes further provision about the making of Tribunal Rules.

Exercise of functions

14.33

69.—(1) Tribunal Rules may confer functions on the persons mentioned in subsection (5) or the other members of the Scottish Tribunals.

(2) Tribunal Rules may, in relation to any functions exercisable by the persons mentioned in subsection (5) or the other members of the Scottish Tribunals—
  (a) state—

(i) how a function is to be exercised,
(ii) who is to exercise a function,
(b) cause something to require further authorisation,
(c) permit something to be done on a person's behalf,
(d) allow a specified person to make a decision about any of those matters.

(3) Tribunal Rules may make provision relying on the effect of directions issued, or to be issued, under section 74.

(4) Neither Tribunal Rules nor directions under section 74 may make provision altering the operation of section 37(1) or 39(1).

(5) For the purposes of subsections (1) and (2), the persons are—
(a) the Lord President,
(b) the President of Tribunals,
(c) in the First-tier Tribunal—
(i) a Chamber President,
(ii) a Deputy Chamber President,
(d) a Vice-President of the Upper Tribunal.

Extent of rule-making

70.—(1) Tribunal Rules may make—
(a) provision applying—
(i) equally to both of the First-tier Tribunal and the Upper Tribunal, or
(ii) specifically to one of them,
(b) particular provision for each of them about the same matter.

(2) Tribunal Rules may make particular provision for different—
(a) chambers or divisions,
(b) types of proceedings.

(3) Tribunal Rules may make different provision for different purposes in any other respects.

(4) The generality of section 68(1) is not limited by—
(a) sections 71 to 73, or
(b) any other provisions of this Act about the content of Tribunal Rules.

(5) As well as Chapter 1, see (for example) sections 28(5), 42(1), 43(3)(b) and 59(2).

Particular matters

Proceedings and steps

71.—(1) Tribunal Rules may make provision about proceedings in a case before the Scottish Tribunals.

(2) Rules making provision as described in subsection (1) may (in particular)—
(a) provide for the form and manner in which a case is to be brought,
(b) allow for the withdrawal of a case (with or without restrictions on subsequent proceedings as respects the same matter),
(c) set time limits for—
(i) making applications,
(ii) taking particular steps,

Tribunals (Scotland) Act 2014

(d) enable two or more applications to be conjoined in certain circumstances,
(e) specify circumstances in which the Tribunals may take particular steps of their own initiative.

Hearings in cases

14.36   **72.**—(1) Tribunal Rules may make provision about hearings in a case before the Scottish Tribunals.
(2) Rules making provision as described in subsection (1) may (in particular)—
  (a) provide for certain matters to be dealt with—
    (i) without a hearing,
    (ii) at a private hearing,
    (iii) at a public hearing,
  (b) require notice to be given of a hearing (and for the timing of such notice),
  (c) specify persons who may—
    (i) appear on behalf of a party in a case,
    (ii) attend a hearing in order to provide support to a party or witness in a case,
  (d) specify circumstances in which particular persons may appear or be represented at a hearing,
  (e) specify circumstances in which a hearing may go ahead—
    (i) at the request of a party in a case despite no notice of it having been given to another party in the case,
    (ii) in the absence of a particular member chosen to exercise the function of deciding any matter in a case,
  (f) enable two or more sets of proceedings to be taken concurrently at a hearing in certain circumstances,
  (g) allow for an adjournment of a hearing for the purpose of giving the parties in a case an opportunity to use a process of negotiation, mediation, arbitration or adjudication for resolving a dispute to which the case relates,
  (h) allow for the imposition of reporting restrictions for particular reasons arising in a case.

Evidence and decisions

14.37   **73.**—(1) Tribunal Rules may, in connection with proceedings before the Scottish Tribunals—
  (a) make provision about the giving of evidence and the administering of oaths,
  (b) modify the application of any other rules relating to either of those matters so far as they would otherwise apply to such proceedings.
(2) Tribunal Rules may, in connection with proceedings before the Scottish Tribunals, provide for the payment of expenses and allowances to a person who—
  (a) gives evidence,
  (b) a document, or
  (c) attends such proceedings (or is required to do so).

(3) Tribunal Rules may, in connection with proceedings before the Scottish Tribunals, make provision by way of presumption (for example, as to the serving of something on somebody).

(4) Tribunal Rules may make provision about decisions of the Scottish Tribunals, including as to—
  (a) the manner in which such decisions are to be made,
  (b) the incorporation in such decisions of findings in fact,
  (c) the recording, issuing and publication of such decisions.

Issuing directions

Practice directions

74.—(1) The President of Tribunals may issue directions as to the practice and procedure to be followed in proceedings at—
  (a) the First-tier Tribunal,
  (b) the Upper Tribunal.

(2) A Chamber President in the First-tier Tribunal may issue directions as to the practice and procedure to be followed in proceedings in the chamber over which the Chamber President presides.

(3) A Vice-President of the Upper Tribunal may issue directions as to the practice and procedure to be followed in proceedings in the division over which the Vice-President presides.

(4) Directions under subsection (2) or (3) may not be issued without the approval of the President of Tribunals.

14.38

Publication and effect

75.—(1) The President of Tribunals must arrange for directions under section 74(1), (2) or (3) to be published in such manner as the President of Tribunals considers appropriate.

(2) Directions under section 74(1), (2) or (3) may—
  (a) vary or revoke earlier such directions,
  (b) make different provision for different purposes (in the same respects as Tribunal Rules).

(3) If (and to the extent that) any conflict arises between—
  (a) directions issued under section 74(1), and
  (b) directions issued under section 74(2) or (3),
    those issued under section 74(1) are to prevail.

14.39

CHAPTER 3

FEES AND ADMINISTRATION

76. *Omitted.*
77. *Repealed.*
78. *Omitted.*

14.40

Tribunals (Scotland) Act 2014

PART 8

FINAL PROVISIONS

General and ancillary

Regulation-making

14.41   **79.**—(1) Regulations under the preceding Parts of this Act may—
(a) make different provision for different purposes,
(b) include supplemental, incidental, consequential, transitional, transitory or saving provision.
(2) Regulations under the following provisions of those Parts are subject to the affirmative procedure—
(a) section 20(2) or 23(2),
(b) section 27(2) or 28(2),
(c) section 38(1), 40(1) or 41(1),
(d) section 65(1), 66(1) or 67(1).
(3) Regulations under any other provisions of those Parts are subject to the negative procedure.

Ancillary regulations

14.42   **80.**—(1) The Scottish Ministers may by regulations make such supplemental, incidental, consequential, transitional, transitory or saving provision as they consider necessary or expedient for the purposes of or in connection with this Act.
(2) Regulations under this section—
(a) are subject to the affirmative procedure if they add to, replace or omit any part of the text of an Act (including this Act),
(b) otherwise, are subject to the negative procedure.

14.43   **81.** *Omitted.*

Interpretation, commencement and short title

Interpretation

14.44   **82.**—(1) In this Act, "Lord President" means Lord President of the Court of Session.
(2) Schedule 10 is an index of expressions used in this Act together with a note of some key provisions.

Commencement

14.45   **83.**—(1) Section 82, this section and section 84 come into force on the day after Royal Assent.
(2) The other provisions of this Act come into force on such day as the Scottish Ministers may by order appoint.
(3) An order under subsection (2) may include transitional, transitory or saving provision.

(2014 asp 10 s.84)

Short title

84.—The short title of this Act is the Tribunals (Scotland) Act 2014.

Schedules 1 to 9. *Omitted.*

SCHEDULE 10

(introduced by section 82)

INDEX OF EXPRESSIONS

Expressions used	Relevant provisions
Lord President	Section 82(1)
Head of the Scottish Tribunals	Section 2(1)
President of Tribunals	Section 5(3)
First-tier Tribunal and Upper Tribunal	Section 1(1)
the Scottish Tribunals	Section 1(2)
Chamber President of the First-tier Tribunal (including appointment to position)	Sections 21 and 22
Vice-President of the Upper Tribunal (including assignment or appointment to position)	Sections 24 to 26
chamber of a Tribunal (First-tier)	Section 20(1)
division of a Tribunal (Upper)	Section 23(1)
members of the Scottish Tribunals	Section 13(3)
ordinary member (First-tier)	Section 15(1)
ordinary member (Upper)	Section 16(1)
legal member (First-tier)	Section 15(2)
legal member (Upper)	Section 16(2)
judicial member (First-tier)	Section 19(1)
judicial member (Upper)	Section 19(2)
extra judge (Upper)	Section 19(4)
[¹ extra judge (First-tier)	Section 19(4)]
appointment and assignment (various positions)	Section 32(1) to (4)
transfer-in to membership (various positions)	Section 29(a) and (b)
listed tribunals	Section 27(1)
Tribunal rules	Section 68(2)

AMENDMENT

1. Social Security Administration and Tribunal Membership (Scotland) Act 2020 s.16(8) (May 13, 2022).

The Scottish Tribunals (Time Limits) Regulations 2016

(SSI 2016/231)

Made	*17th August 2016*
Laid before the Scottish Parliament	*19th August 2016*
Coming into force	*1st December 2016*

The Scottish Ministers make the following Regulations in exercise of the powers conferred by section 55(1), 79(1)(a) and paragraph 4(2) of schedule 9 of the Tribunals (Scotland) Act 2014 and all other powers enabling them to do so.

In accordance with paragraph 4(3) of schedule 9 of that Act, the Scottish Ministers have consulted with the President of Tribunals and such other persons as they considered appropriate.

Citation, commencement and interpretation

14.50   **1.**—(1) These Regulations may be cited as the Scottish Tribunals (Time Limits) Regulations 2016.
(2) These Regulations come into force on 1st December 2016.
(3) In these Regulations—
"the 2014 Act" means the Tribunals (Scotland) Act 2014;
"appellant" means a party applying for permission to appeal; and
"hearing" means an oral hearing and includes a hearing conducted in whole or in part by video link, telephone or other means of instantaneous two-way electronic communication.

Time limits for applying to the First-tier Tribunal or Upper Tribunal for permission to appeal against its own decision

14.51   **2.**—(1) An application for permission under sections 46(3)(a) or 48(3)(a) of the Act (application for permission to appeal the Tribunal's own decision) must be received by the Tribunal whose decision is being appealed against within the period of 30 days beginning with the relevant date.
(2) The First-tier Tribunal or the Upper Tribunal, as appropriate, may on cause shown extend the period beyond 30 days if it considers such an extension to be in the interests of justice.
(3) Subject to paragraph (4), the relevant date is the later of the date on which—
  (a) the decision appealed against was sent to the appellant;
  (b) the statement of reasons for the decision was sent to the appellant.
(4) But where a decision is given orally at a hearing, the relevant date is either—
  (a) the date on which written reasons were sent to the parties, if—
    (i) written reasons were requested at the hearing (or were requested in writing within 14 days beginning with the day after the last day of the hearing); or
    (ii) the First-tier Tribunal or the Upper Tribunal, as appropriate, undertook at the hearing to provide written reasons; or
  (b) the date of the oral decision, if—
    (i) written reasons were not requested at the hearing (or were not requested in writing within 14 days beginning with the day after the last day of the hearing); or
    (ii) the First-tier Tribunal or the Upper Tribunal, as appropriate, did not undertake at the hearing to provide written reasons.

GENERAL NOTE

14.52   Under para.(2), time may be extended by the Upper Tribunal if a late application for permission to appeal to the Upper Tribunal is made to the First-tier Tribunal and the First-tier Tribunal has refused to extend time.
In *Ramanathan v Patel* [2023] UT 8, the Upper Tribunal was concerned with whether an application to the First-tier Tribunal under reg.9 of the Tenancy Deposit Schemes (Scotland) Regulations 2011 (SSI 2011/176, as amended) had been

(SSI 2016/231 reg.2)

brought within time. This was therefore not a case concerned with an application for permission to appeal, but the approach taken would appear to be equally relevant to such applications. It was held that the application had been brought within time when an email was received by the First-tier Tribunal, because there had been no obligation to use the standard form and the applicant's typed name on the email had been sufficient to amount to a signature. The Upper Tribunal referred to *Hudson v Hathway* [2022] EWCA Civ 1648; [2023] H.L.R. 13, in which Lewison LJ, with whom Andrews and Nugee agreed, said at [67]—

"There is . . . a substantial body of authority to the effect that deliberately subscribing one's name to an email amounts to a signature. Given that so much correspondence takes place nowadays by email rather than by letters with a 'wet ink' signature, it is, in my judgment, entirely appropriate that the law should recognise that technological developments have extended what an ordinary person would understand by a signature."

Time limits for applying to the Upper Tribunal for permission to appeal against a decision of the First-tier Tribunal

3.—(1) An application for permission under section 46(3)(b) of the 2014 Act (application for permission to appeal to the Upper Tribunal against a decision of the First-tier Tribunal) must be received by the Upper Tribunal within the period of 30 days beginning with the relevant date.

(2) The relevant date is the date on which notice of the First-tier Tribunal's refusal of permission to appeal was sent to the appellant.

(3) The Upper Tribunal may on cause shown extend the period beyond 30 days if it considers such an extension to be in the interests of justice.

14.53

GENERAL NOTE

See the annotation to reg.2.

14.54

The First-tier Tribunal for Scotland Social Security Chamber (Procedure) Regulations 2018

(SSI 2018/273)

Made 11th September 2018
Laid before the Scottish Parliament 13th September 2018
Coming into force 22nd November 2018

The Scottish Ministers make the following Regulations in exercise of the powers conferred by section 43(3)(b) and paragraph 4(2) of schedule 9 of the Tribunals (Scotland) Act 2014 and all other powers enabling them to do so.

In accordance with paragraph 4(3) of schedule 9 of that Act, the Scottish Ministers have consulted the President of the Scottish Tribunals and such other persons as they considered appropriate.

14.55

Citation and commencement

14.56 **1.**—(1) These Regulations may be cited as the First-tier Tribunal for Scotland Social Security Chamber (Procedure) Regulations 2018 and the Rules contained in the schedule may be cited as the First-tier Tribunal for Scotland Social Security Chamber Rules of Procedure 2018.

(2) These Regulations come into force on 22nd November 2018.

Application of the Rules set out in the schedule

14.57 **2.** The Rules in the schedule apply to any proceedings before the First-tier Tribunal for Scotland Social Security Chamber when exercising functions conferred on the Tribunal by [1 —
- (a) the Social Security (Scotland) Act 2018;
- (b) regulations made under the Social Security (Scotland) Act 2018; or
- (c) the Carer's Allowance Supplement and Young Carer Grants (Residence Requirements and Procedural Provisions) (EU Exit) (Scotland) Regulations 2020.]

AMENDMENT

1. First-tier Tribunal for Scotland Social Security Chamber and Upper Tribunal for Scotland (Allocation of Functions, Procedure and Composition) (Miscellaneous Amendments) Regulations 2020 (SSI 2020/476) reg.5(1) and (2) (December 24, 2020).

Regulation 2

SCHEDULE

THE FIRST-TIER TRIBUNAL FOR SCOTLAND SOCIAL SECURITY CHAMBER RULES OF PROCEDURE 2018

CONTENTS

PART 1

INTRODUCTION

14.58
1. Interpretation
2. Overriding objective and parties' obligation to co-operate with the First-tier Tribunal
3. Delegation to staff

PART 2

GENERAL POWERS AND PROVISIONS

4. Case management powers
5. Procedure for applying for and giving orders
6. Failure to comply with rules etc
7. Dismissal of a party's case

8. Addition, substitution and removal of parties
9. Representatives
10. Supporters
11. Interpreters
12. Calculating time
13. Sending and delivery of documents
14. Disclosure of documents and information
15. Evidence and submissions
16. Citation of witnesses and orders to answer questions or produce documents
17. Withdrawal
18. Chairing member and voting
19. Recording of hearings

PART 3

PROCEDURE FOR CASES IN THE FIRST-TIER TRIBUNAL

20. Notice of appeal to the First-tier Tribunal against a determination of entitlement to assistance of a type provided for in Part 2 of the 2018 Act
21. Response of the decision maker to a notice of appeal against a determination of entitlement
22. Notice of appeal against a process decision
23. Decision with or without a hearing
24. Entitlement to attend a hearing
25. Notice of hearings
26. Public and private hearings
27. Hearings in a party's absence
28. Notice of decisions
29. Reasons for decisions
30. Publication of decisions

PART 4

CORRECTING, REVIEWING AND APPEALING DECISIONS OF THE FIRST-TIER TRIBUNAL

31. Interpretation
32. Correction of clerical mistakes or accidental slips or omissions
33. Application for permission to appeal against a decision of the First-tier Tribunal
34. First-tier Tribunal's consideration of application for permission to appeal against its decision
35. Review of a decision
36. Duty to treat a request for a review as an application for permission to appeal

F-tT for Scotland Social Security Chamber (Procedure) Regulations 2018

PART 1

INTRODUCTION

Interpretation

14.59   **1.**—(1) In these Rules—
"the 2014 Act" means the Tribunals (Scotland) Act 2014;
"the 2018 Act" means the Social Security (Scotland) Act 2018;
"the 2016 Regulations" means the Scottish Tribunals (Time Limits) Regulations 2016;
[2 "the 2020 Regulations" means the Scottish Child Payment Regulations 2020,]
[3 "the Carer's Allowance Supplement Regulations" means the Carer's Allowance Supplement and Young Carer Grants (Residence Requirements and Procedural Provisions) (EU Exit) (Scotland) Regulations 2020;]
"appellant" means the person who starts proceedings (whether by notifying an appeal, or applying for permission to appeal) or a person substituted as an appellant under rule 8 (addition, substitution and removal of parties);
"chairing member" means the chairing member of the First-tier Tribunal;
"Chamber President" means the President of the First-tier Tribunal;
"the [1 Convention rights]" has the meaning given to it in section 1 of the Human Rights Act 1998;
"decision maker" means the maker of a decision or determination against which an appeal to the First-tier Tribunal is brought;
"document" means anything in which information is recorded in any form, and an obligation under these Rules to provide or allow access to a document or a copy of a document for any purpose means, unless the First-tier Tribunal directs otherwise, an obligation to provide or allow access to such document or copy in a legible form or a form which can easily be made into a legible form;
"electronic communication" has the meaning given to it by section 15(1) of the Electronic Communications Act 2000;
"excluded decision" means a decision falling under section 51 of the 2014 Act;
"the First-tier Tribunal" means the First-tier Tribunal for Scotland Social Security Chamber;
"hearing" means an oral hearing and includes a hearing conducted in whole or in part by video link, telephone or other means of instantaneous two-way electronic communication;
"legal member" means an individual holding membership of the First-tier Tribunal for Scotland in accordance with section 15(2) of the 2014 Act;
"party" means a person who is (or was at the time that the First-tier Tribunal disposed of the proceedings) an appellant or a respondent in proceedings before the First-tier Tribunal;
"practice direction" means a direction given under section 74 of the 2014 Act;

[² "the prescribed time period" means—
(a) in relation to re-determination of entitlement to assistance under Chapter 2 of Part 2 of the 2018 Act, the period prescribed by the Scottish Ministers by virtue of section 43(5) of the 2018 Act;
(b) in relation to re-determination of entitlement to assistance under the 2020 Regulations, the period provided for in paragraph 14(2) of the schedule of the 2020 Regulations;
[³ (c) in relation to re-determination of entitlement to a carer's allowance supplement, the period provided for in paragraph 6(2) of schedule 2 of the Carer's Allowance Supplement Regulations.]]
[² "process decision" means—
(a) in relation to an appeal under section 61 of the 2018 Act, a decision made under section 38, 41(3) or 42 of that Act;
(b) in relation to an appeal under paragraph 23 of the schedule of the 2020 Regulations, a decision made under paragraph 1(4), 14(5) or 15(2)(b) of the schedule of those Regulations;
[³ (c) in relation to an appeal under paragraph 13 of schedule 2 of the Carer's Allowance Supplement Regulations, a decision made under paragraph 1(5), 4(6) or 5(2)(b) of schedule 2 of those Regulations.]]
"representative" means a lay representative or a legal representative;
"respondent" means—
(a) the decision maker in relation to a decision or determination against which an appeal to the First-tier Tribunal is brought; or
(b) a person substituted or added as a respondent under rule 8 (addition, substitution and removal of parties);
"review" means the internal review provided for by section 43(1) of the 2014 Act; and
"the Upper Tribunal" means the Upper Tribunal for Scotland.
(2) For the purposes of these Rules, where information is sent—
(a) via the postal service to the last known address held for an individual; or
(b) by email to the last known email address held for the individual, the individual is presumed to have received the information 48 hours after it is sent, unless the contrary is shown.

AMENDMENT

1. First-tier Tribunal for Scotland Social Security Chamber (Rules of Procedure) Amendment Regulations 2018 (SSI 2018/343) reg.2 (1) and (2) (December 21, 2018).

2. First-tier Tribunal for Scotland Social Security Chamber (Procedure and Composition) Amendment Regulations 2020 (SSI 2020/353) reg.3(1) and (2) (November 9, 2020).

3. First-tier Tribunal for Scotland Social Security Chamber and Upper Tribunal for Scotland (Allocation of Functions, Procedure and Composition) (Miscellaneous Amendments) Regulations 2020 (SSI 2020/476) reg.5(1) and (3)(a) (December 24, 2020).

Overriding objective and parties' obligation to co-operate with the First-tier Tribunal

2.—(1) The overriding objective of these Rules is to enable the First-tier Tribunal to deal with cases fairly and justly.

(2) Dealing with a case fairly and justly includes—
(a) dealing with the case in ways which are [¹ transparent and which are] proportionate to the importance of the case, the complexity of the issues, the anticipated expenses and the resources of the parties;
(b) avoiding unnecessary formality and seeking flexibility in the proceedings;
(c) ensuring, so far as practicable, that the parties are able to participate fully in the proceedings and are treated with dignity and respect;
(d) using any special expertise of the First-tier Tribunal effectively; and
(e) avoiding delay, so far as compatible with proper consideration of the issues.
(3) The First-tier Tribunal must seek to give effect to the overriding objective when it—
(a) exercises any power under these Rules; or
(b) interprets any rule or practice direction.
(4) Parties must, insofar as reasonably possible—
(a) help the First-tier Tribunal to further the overriding objective; and
(b) co-operate with the First-tier Tribunal generally.

AMENDMENT

1. First-tier Tribunal for Scotland Social Security Chamber (Rules of Procedure) Amendment Regulations 2018 (SSI 2018/343) reg.2(1) and (3) (December 21, 2018).

GENERAL NOTE

14.61   On the use of the First-tier Tribunal for Scotland (FTS)'s procedural powers see *NB v Social Security Scotland* [2023] UT 35, in which the Upper Tribunal for Scotland (Lady Poole) held that the FTS had erred in law by failing to consider exercising its inquisitorial powers to adduce further evidence and enable further participation by the appellant. Note, however, that the extent to which this is necessary is fact-specific: see further *AK v Social Security Scotland* [2024] UT 05 at para.6.

The Upper Tribunal considered in *Kindreich v Slater, Hogg & Howison* [2022] UT 16 (a case about letting agents) the extent to which the First-tier Tribunal is obliged, or is entitled, to assist an unrepresented party. Ultimately, the appellant failed because of the way he had argued the case before the First-tier Tribunal, but it is important to note that the overriding objective in the Rules of Procedure relating to the Housing and Property Chamber of the First-tier Tribunal is different from that in these Rules of Procedure. The Housing and Property Chamber equivalent of r.2(2)(c) requires the First-tier Tribunal to ensure "so far as practicable that parties are on an equal footing procedurally and are able to participate fully in the proceedings, including assisting any party in the presentation of the party's case without advocating the course they should take". In these Rules of Procedure, the reference to equality is omitted, leaving the emphasis on the enabling role of the Tribunal, provided there is no unfairness to the opposing party.

Similarly, in *Woro v Brown* (decided on October 13, 2022 but not numbered), the Upper Tribunal held in undefended housing proceedings that the First-tier Tribunal was required to rase any point as to competency but was not entitled to raise a point as to relevancy–in other words, it was bound to consider whether it had jurisdiction to determine the proceedings, but was not entitled to go into their merits. However, that conclusion was reached after considering the function of a sheriff in such proceedings before jurisdiction was transferred to the First-tier Tribunal. In contrast, it has long been held at the highest level that social security proceedings are not adversarial (see *Kerr v Department for Social Development* [2004] UKHL 23; [2004]

1 W.L.R 1372 (also reported as an appendix to *R1/04(SF)*), noted in the annotation to s.3 of the Tribunals, Courts and Enforcement Act 2007 in Vol.III).

In relation to proceeding in the absence of a party, see the annotation to r.27, below.

Delegation to staff

3.—(1) Staff of the Scottish Courts and Tribunals Service may, with the approval of the Chamber President, carry out functions of a judicial nature permitted or required to be undertaken by the First-tier Tribunal, provided the functions are of a preliminary or an incidental nature.

(2) The approval referred to in paragraph (1) may apply generally to the carrying out of specified functions by members of staff of a specified description in specified circumstances.

(3) Where the First-tier Tribunal sends notice of a decision made by a member of staff pursuant to an approval under paragraph (1) to a party, that party may, within the period of 14 days beginning with the day on which the party is presumed to have received the notice, make a written application to the First-tier Tribunal for that decision to be considered afresh by a member of the First-tier Tribunal.

14.62

PART 2

GENERAL POWERS AND PROVISIONS

Case management powers

4.—(1) Subject to the provisions of the 2014 Act and these Rules, the First-tier Tribunal may regulate its own procedure.

(2) The First-tier Tribunal may give an order in relation to the conduct and disposal of proceedings at any time, including an order amending, suspending or setting aside an earlier order.

(3) In particular, and without restricting the general powers in paragraphs (1) and (2), the First-tier Tribunal may—
  (a) extend or shorten the time for complying with any rule, practice direction or order;
  (b) conjoin or take concurrently two or more sets of proceedings or parts of proceedings raising common issues;
  (c) permit or require a party to amend a document;
  (d) permit or require a party or another person to provide documents, information, evidence or submissions to the First-tier Tribunal or a party;
  (e) deal with an issue in the proceedings as a preliminary issue;
  (f) hold a hearing to consider any matter, including a case management issue;
  (g) decide the form of any hearing;
  (h) adjourn or postpone a hearing;
  (i) require a party to produce a file of documents for a hearing;
  (j) sist proceedings;
  (k) transfer proceedings to another court or tribunal if that other court or tribunal has jurisdiction in relation to the proceedings and—

14.63

(i) because of a change of circumstances since the proceedings were started, the First-tier Tribunal no longer has jurisdiction in relation to the proceedings; or
(ii) the First-tier Tribunal considers that the other court or tribunal is a more appropriate forum for the determination of the case;
(l) suspend the effect of its own decision pending the determination by the First-tier Tribunal or the Upper Tribunal, as the case may be, of an application for permission to appeal against, and any appeal or review of, that decision.

General Note

14.64 The First-tier Tribunal should not deal with an issue as a preliminary issue at a separate hearing if that would cause undue delay (*Aberdeen CC v LS* [2021] UT 1 at [29.1]). Hearing all issues together may avoid the need for multiple hearings and be preferable even though a single hearing may be lengthy.

Procedure for applying for and giving orders

14.65 5.—(1) The First-tier Tribunal may give an order on the application of one or more of the parties or on its own initiative.
(2) An application for an order may be made—
(a) by sending or delivering a written application to the First-tier Tribunal; or
(b) orally during the course of a hearing.
(3) An application for an order must include the reasons for making that application.
(4) Unless the First-tier Tribunal considers that there is good reason not to do so, the Tribunal must send written notice of any order to each party to the case.
(5) If a party sent notice of the order under paragraph (4) wishes to challenge the order, the party may do so by applying for another order which amends, suspends or sets aside the first order.

General Note

14.66 Where a husband and wife are both appellants, it is wrong to send notice of case-management orders only to the husband (*Dymoke v Best* [2020] UT 18 at [20]).

Failure to comply with rules etc

14.67 6.—(1) An irregularity resulting from a failure to comply with any requirement in these Rules, a practice direction or an order does not of itself render void the proceedings or any step taken in the proceedings.
(2) If a party has failed to comply with a requirement in these Rules, a practice direction or an order, the First-tier Tribunal may take such action as it considers just, which may include—
(a) waiving the requirement;
(b) requiring the failure to be remedied; or
(c) exercising its power under rule 7 (dismissal of a party's case).

Dismissal of a party's case

14.68 7.—(1) The First-tier Tribunal must dismiss the whole or a part of the proceedings if the Tribunal—
(a) does not have jurisdiction in relation to the proceedings or that part of them; and

(b) does not exercise its power under rule 4(3)(k) (transfer to another court or tribunal) in relation to the proceedings or that part of them.

(2) The First-tier Tribunal may dismiss the whole or a part of the proceedings if—
 (a) the appellant has failed to comply with an order which stated that failure by the appellant to comply with the order could lead to the dismissal of the proceedings or part of them;
 (b) the appellant has failed to co-operate with the First-tier Tribunal to such an extent that the First-tier Tribunal considers that it cannot deal with the proceedings fairly and justly; or
 (c) where relevant, there is no possibility of the eligibility criteria being met for the particular form of assistance to which the proceedings relate.

(3) The First-tier Tribunal may not dismiss the whole or a part of the proceedings under paragraph (1) or (2)(b) without first giving the appellant an opportunity to make representations in relation to the proposed dismissal.

(4) If the proceedings, or part of them, have been dismissed under paragraph (2)(a), the appellant may apply for the proceedings, or part of them, to be reinstated, where the appellant can satisfy the Tribunal that the appellant has good reason to [¹ for the failure to comply].

(5) An application under paragraph (4) must be made in writing and received by the First-tier Tribunal within the period of 31 days beginning with the day on which notification of the dismissal sent to the appellant under paragraph (9) is presumed to have been received by the appellant.

(6) An application under paragraph (4) must set out the reasons on which the appellant relies in applying for reinstatement.

(7) This rule applies to a respondent as it applies to an appellant except that—
 (a) a reference to the dismissal of the proceedings is to be read as a reference to the barring of the respondent from taking further part in the proceedings; and
 (b) a reference to an application for the reinstatement of proceedings which have been dismissed is to be read as a reference to an application for the lifting of the bar on the respondent from taking further part in the proceedings.

(8) If the respondent has been barred from taking further part in proceedings under this rule and that bar has not been lifted, the First-tier Tribunal need not consider any response or other submission made by the respondent.

(9) The First-tier Tribunal must notify each party in writing that dismissal has taken place.

AMENDMENT

1. First-tier Tribunal for Scotland Social Security Chamber (Procedure and Allocation of Functions) Amendment Regulations 2020 (SSI 2020/100) reg.3(1) and (2) (March 26, 2020).

Addition, substitution and removal of parties

8.—(1) The First-tier Tribunal may give an order adding, substituting or removing a party if—
 (a) the wrong person has been named as a party; or
 (b) the addition, substitution or removal has become necessary because of a change in circumstances since the start of proceedings.

(2) If the First-tier Tribunal gives an order under paragraph (1) it may make such consequential orders as it considers appropriate.

(3) A person who is not a party may make a written application to the First-tier Tribunal to be added or substituted as a party under this rule.

(4) If the First-tier Tribunal refuses an application under paragraph (3) it must consider whether to permit the person who made the application to provide submissions or evidence to the First-tier Tribunal.

Representatives

14.70

9.—(1) A party may be represented in any proceedings by a representative whose details may be communicated to the First-tier Tribunal prior to any hearing.

(2) If the First-tier Tribunal receives notice that a party has appointed a representative under paragraph (1), it must send a copy of that notice to each party to the proceedings.

[1(3) Where the First-tier Tribunal receives notice of the appointment of a representative—
  (a) it must provide to the representative—
    (i) any document which it requires under these Rules to provide to the represented party on or after the day on which it receives the notice, in addition to providing the document to the represented party, and
    (ii) any document which it required under these Rules to provide to the represented party prior to the day on which it receives the notice; and
  (b) it may assume that the representative remains appointed unless it receives written notification that this is not so from the representative or represented party.]

(4) Notwithstanding paragraphs (1) to (3), a party may be represented at a hearing by a person other than any person whose details have been communicated to the First-tier Tribunal.

(5) A party may show any document or communicate any information about the proceedings to that party's representative without contravening any prohibition or restriction on disclosure of the document or information.

(6) Where a document or information is disclosed under paragraph (5), the representative is subject to any prohibition or disclosure in the same way that the party is.

AMENDMENT

1. First-tier Tribunal for Scotland Social Security Chamber (Rules of Procedure) Amendment Regulations 2018 (SSI 2018/343) reg.2(1) and (4) (December 21, 2018).

GENERAL NOTE

14.71

In *Roberts v Hacking and Paterson* [2020] UT 30, the Respondent had challenged the Applicant's mother's right to represent him before the First-tier Tribunal because no formal intimation had been made. The First-tier Tribunal had repelled that preliminary plea on the ground that, not only was it was evident from the Application and subsequent correspondence that the Applicant's mother was representing her son but also there was evidence that the Respondent had previously corresponded with her on behalf of the Applicant. Thus, the First-tier Tribunal, having regard to the overriding objective, had taken the view that the fact that the

Applicant's mother had been acting as her son's representative was evidence that he had appointed her to do so. However, when she applied to the First-tier Tribunal for permission to appeal, describing herself as the Applicant, the First-tier Tribunal rejected the Application on the ground that she was not a party. The Upper Tribunal considered that the First-tier Tribunal should have taken the same approach as it had taken in the substantive proceedings and, having regard to the requirement in the overriding objective to avoid unnecessary formality, should have treated her as making the application as agent for a disclosed principal who was a party.

Supporters

10. A party who is an individual may be accompanied by another person, who is not a representative, to act as a supporter.

14.72

Interpreters

11. Where an interpreter is appointed to assist the First-tier Tribunal, the interpreter must be independent of all parties to the case and of any representatives or supporters.

14.73

Calculating time

12.—(1) An act required by these Rules, a practice direction or an order to be done on or by a particular day must be done before 5pm on that day.

14.74

(2) If the time specified by these Rules, a practice direction or an order for doing any act ends on a day other than a working day, the act is done in time if it is done on the next working day.

(3) In this rule "working day" means any day except a Saturday or Sunday or a bank holiday in Scotland under section 1 of the Banking and Financial Dealings Act 1971.

Sending and delivery of documents

13.—(1) Any document to be provided to the First-tier Tribunal under these Rules, a practice direction or an order may be sent by pre-paid post, by fax or by electronic communication to the address specified for receipt by the First-tier Tribunal.

14.75

(2) Subject to paragraph (3), if a party or representative provides an email address or other details for the electronic transmission of documents to them, that party or representative must accept delivery of documents by that method.

(3) If a party informs the First-tier Tribunal that a particular form of communication (other than post) should not be used to provide documents to that party, that form of communication must not be so used by the Tribunal or any other party.

(4) If the First-tier Tribunal or a party sends a document to a party or the Tribunal by email or any other means of electronic communication, the recipient may request that the sender provides a hard copy of the document to the recipient, and the recipient must make any such a request as soon as reasonably practicable after receiving the document electronically.

(5) The First-tier Tribunal and each party may assume that the address provided by a party or its representative is and remains the address to which documents should be sent or delivered until receiving notification to the contrary.

Disclosure of documents and information

14. [¹ —(1)] The First-tier Tribunal may at any stage of the proceedings, on its own initiative or on application by one or more of the parties, make an order with a view to prohibiting or restricting the public disclosure of any aspect of those proceedings so far as it considers necessary in the interests of justice or in order to protect the Convention rights of any person.

[¹ (2) The First-tier Tribunal may at any stage of the proceedings, on its own initiative or on the request of one or more of the parties, give a direction prohibiting disclosure of a document or information to a person ("the recipient") if—
- (a) the document or information relates to the physical or mental health of a person,
- (b) a registered medical practitioner or a registered nurse has informed either the First-tier Tribunal, or one or more of the parties, that disclosure of the document or information would be likely to cause serious harm to the physical or mental health of the recipient or some other person,
- (c) the First-tier Tribunal is satisfied that such disclosure would be likely to cause serious harm to the physical or mental health of the recipient or some other person, and
- (d) the First-tier Tribunal is satisfied, having regard to the interests of justice, that it is proportionate to give such a direction.

(3) If a party considers that the First-tier Tribunal should give a direction under paragraph (2) prohibiting the disclosure of a document or information to a person ("the recipient"), the party must provide to the First-tier Tribunal the document or information, and the reason the party is requesting that it be withheld, so that the First-tier Tribunal may decide whether the document or information should be disclosed to the recipient or should be subject of a direction under paragraph (2).

(4) The First-tier Tribunal must conduct proceedings as appropriate in order to give effect to a direction given under paragraph (2).

(5) If the First-tier Tribunal gives a direction under paragraph (2) which prevents disclosure to a party who has a representative, or any other person acting on their behalf, the First-tier Tribunal may give a direction that the document or information be disclosed to that representative or person if the First-tier Tribunal is satisfied that—
- (a) disclosure to the representative or person would be in the interests of the party, and
- (b) the representative or person will act in accordance with paragraph (6).

(6) Documents or information disclosed to a representative or person in accordance with a direction under paragraph (5) must not be disclosed either directly or indirectly to any other person without the First-tier Tribunal's consent.]

AMENDMENT

1. First-tier Tribunal for Scotland Social Security Chamber and Upper Tribunal for Scotland (Rules of Procedure) (Miscellaneous Amendment) Regulations 2022 (SSI 2022/162) r.2 (June 21, 2022).

(SSI 2018/273 Sch - r.14)

GENERAL NOTE

This rule is in terms very similar to those of r.14 of the Tribunal Procedure (First-tier Tribunal) (Social Entitlement Chamber) Rules 2008 (see Vol.III), save that it is expressly provided in para.(2) that the relevant documents and the feared harm must both relate to a person's health.

14.77

Evidence and submissions

15.—(1) Without restriction on the general powers in rule 4 (case management powers), the First-tier Tribunal may give orders as to—
  (a) issues on which it requires evidence or submissions;
  (b) the nature of any such evidence or submissions;
  (c) whether the parties are permitted to provide expert evidence;
  (d) any limit on the number of witnesses whose evidence a party may put forward, whether in relation to a particular issue or generally;
  (e) the manner in which any evidence or submissions are to be provided, which may include an order for them to be given—
    (i) orally at a hearing; or
    (ii) by written submissions or witness statement; and
  (f) the time at which any evidence or submissions are to be provided.
(2) The First-tier Tribunal may exclude evidence that would otherwise be admissible where—
  (a) the evidence was not, without reasonable excuse, provided within the time allowed by an order or a practice direction;
  (b) the evidence was otherwise, without reasonable excuse, provided in a manner that did not comply with an order or practice direction; or
  (c) the Tribunal considers it would otherwise be unfair to admit the evidence.
(3) The First-tier Tribunal may admit evidence whether or not—
  (a) the evidence would be admissible in civil proceedings in Scotland; or
  (b) the evidence was available to a previous decision maker.
(4) The First-tier Tribunal may consent to a witness giving, or require any witness to give, evidence on oath, and may administer an oath for that purpose.

14.78

Citation of witnesses and orders to answer questions or produce documents

16.—(1) On the application of a party or on its own initiative, the First-tier Tribunal may—
  (a) by citation require any person to attend as a witness at a hearing at the time and place specified in the citation; or
  (b) order any person to answer any questions or produce any documents in that person's possession or control which relate to any issue in the proceedings.
(2) A citation under paragraph (1)(a) must—
  (a) give the person required to attend at least 14 days' notice of the hearing, or such other period as the First-tier Tribunal may order;

14.79

(b) where the person is not a party, make provision for the person's necessary expenses of attendance to be paid, and state who is to pay them;
(c) state that the person on whom the requirement is imposed may apply to the First-tier Tribunal to vary or set aside the citation or order, if the person did not have an opportunity to object to it before it was made or issued; and
(d) state the consequences of failure to comply with the citation or order.

(3) No person may be compelled to give any evidence or produce any document that the person could not be compelled to give or produce in civil proceedings in a Scottish court.

Withdrawal

14.80

17.—(1) Subject to paragraph (2), a party may give notice of the withdrawal of the party's case, or any part of that case—
(a) by sending or delivering to the First-tier Tribunal a written notice of withdrawal; or
(b) orally at a hearing.

(2) In the circumstances described in paragraph (3), a notice of withdrawal will not take effect unless the Tribunal consents to the withdrawal.

(3) The circumstances referred to in paragraph (2) are where a party gives notice of withdrawal—
(a) in a case in which the First-tier Tribunal has directed that any notice of withdrawal will take effect only with the consent of the Tribunal; or
(b) at a hearing.

(4) An application for a withdrawn case to be reinstated may be made by—
(a) the appellant; or
(b) a respondent,
where the appellant or respondent can satisfy the First-tier Tribunal that the appellant or respondent has good reason to apply for reinstatement.

(5) An application under paragraph (4) must be received by the First-tier Tribunal within 31 days of the earlier of—
(a) the day on which the applicant for reinstatement is presumed to have received the notification sent under paragraph (7) that the withdrawal has taken effect; or
(b) if the applicant for reinstatement was present at the hearing when the case was withdrawn orally under paragraph (1)(b), the day of that hearing.

(6) An application under paragraph (5) must set out the reasons on which the applicant relies in seeking reinstatement.

(7) The First-tier Tribunal must notify each party in writing that a withdrawal has taken effect under this rule.

Chairing member and voting

14.81

18. Where a matter is to be decided by two or more members of the First-tier Tribunal, the chairing member is to be the legal member, who is to have a casting vote.

Recording of hearings

19.—(1) Subject to paragraph (2), all hearings of the First-tier Tribunal must be recorded digitally.

(2) In the event of a failure of equipment, a written record of proceedings must be produced by the legal member.

PART 3

PROCEDURE FOR CASES IN THE FIRST-TIER TRIBUNAL

Notice of appeal to the First-tier Tribunal against a determination of entitlement to assistance of a type provided for in Part 2 of the 2018 Act

20.—(1) This rule applies where an individual brings an appeal under section 46 of the 2018 Act against a determination by the Scottish Ministers of the appellant's entitlement to social security assistance of a type described in Chapter 2 of Part 2 of the 2018 Act.

(2) Where in this rule, and in rule 21 (response of the decision maker to a notice of appeal against a determination of entitlement), reference is made to a "notice of appeal", this means the form provided by the Scottish Ministers under section 44 (or as the case may be section 45) of the 2018 Act, on notifying of the outcome of re-determination of entitlement, or of a failure to re-determine entitlement within the prescribed time period.

(3) An individual must start proceedings by submitting the notice of appeal to the Scottish Ministers along with any documents which have not so far been provided to Ministers that the appellant wishes them to submit to the First-tier Tribunal in support of the appeal.

(4) Except as provided for in paragraph (10), a notice of appeal must be received by the Scottish Ministers before the end of the period of 31 days beginning with whichever is the later of the day on which the appellant—
  (a) is informed of a determination made under section 43 of the 2018 Act, following a request for re-determination; or
  (b) is informed of the appellant's right to appeal against the original determination made under section 37 of the 2018 Act, as a result of the failure of the Scottish Ministers to re-determine entitlement within the prescribed time period.

(5) The notice of appeal must state—
  (a) the name and address of the appellant;
  (b) the name and address of the appellant's representative (if any);
  (c) a postal or email address where documents for the appellant may be sent or delivered;
  (d) the determination being challenged;
  (e) the reasons for bringing the appeal;
  (f) [¹ . . .]
  (g) [² where the notice of appeal is received after the end of the period of 31 days beginning with whichever is the later of —

(i) the day on which the appellant is informed of a determination made under section 43 of the 2018 Act; or
(ii) the day on which the appellant is informed of the right to appeal against the determination made under section 37 of the Act, the reasons why the notice of appeal was not submitted sooner.]

(6) A notice of appeal and any accompanying documents may be sent by pre-paid post, by fax, or by electronic communication to such address as may be specified for receipt by the Scottish Ministers.

(7) The Scottish Ministers must forward to the First-tier Tribunal any notice of appeal and accompanying documents submitted to them, regardless of whether the requirements set out in paragraph (5) are met, or the extent to which they are met, and inform the appellant when this has been done.

(8) At the same time as forwarding [¹ the notice of appeal] and any documents under paragraph (7), the Scottish Ministers must send—

[¹ (za) where the individual was first awarded assistance pursuant to an application for assistance in accordance with section 37(a) of the 2018 Act (duty to make determination), a copy of the application;]
(a) a copy of the determination issued under section 43 of the 2018 Act, following a request that entitlement be re-determined; or
(b) a copy of the determination issued under section 37 of the 2018 Act, where there has been a failure to re-determine entitlement within the prescribed time period; [² and the determination under section 37 is being appealed] and
(c) copy of any written record of the decision under challenge.

(9) [² Where [³ a] notice of appeal is received by the Scottish Ministers after the end of the period of 31 days beginning with the later of the days specified in paragraph (4) —
(a) if the notice of appeal is received before the end of the period of one year beginning with the day on which the appellant is informed of a determination made under section 43 of the 2018 Act or, as the case may be, of the right to appeal against the determination made under section 37 of the Act, the First-tier Tribunal may give permission for the appeal to proceed, but only if satisfied that there was a good reason for the notice of appeal not having been sent or delivered to the Scottish Ministers sooner; or
(b) if the notice of appeal is received after the end of the period of one year beginning with the day on which the appellant is informed of a determination made under section 43 of the 2018 Act or, as the case may be, of the right to appeal against the determination made under section 37 of the Act, the First-tier Tribunal must refuse to consider the notice of appeal.]

(10) [² The Scottish Ministers must forward a notice of appeal to the First-tier Tribunal even if one of the following situations applies—
(a) the notice of appeal is received after the end of the period of 31 days beginning with the later of the days specified in paragraph (4), but less than one year after that day; or
(b) the notice of appeal is received one year or more after the later of the days specified in paragraph (4).]

(SSI 2018/273 Sch - r.20)

AMENDMENTS

1. First-tier Tribunal for Scotland Social Security Chamber (Procedure and Allocation of Functions) Amendment Regulations 2020 (SSI 2020/100) reg.3(1) and (3) (March 26, 2020).
2. First-tier Tribunal for Scotland Social Security Chamber (Procedure and Composition) Amendment Regulations 2020 (SSI 2020/353) reg.3(1) and (3) (November 9, 2020).
3. First-tier Tribunal for Scotland Social Security Chamber and Upper Tribunal for Scotland (Allocation of Functions, Procedure and Composition) (Miscellaneous Amendments) Regulations 2020 (SSI 2020/476) reg.5(1) and (3)(b) (December 24, 2020).

[¹ Notice of appeal to the First-tier Tribunal against a determination of entitlement to a Scottish child payment

20A.—(1) This rule applies where an individual brings an appeal under paragraph 19 of the schedule of the 2020 Regulations against a determination by the Scottish Ministers of the appellant's entitlement to a Scottish child payment.

(2) Where in this rule, and in rule 21 (response of the decision maker to a notice of appeal against a determination of entitlement) in so far is it applies to the Scottish child payment, reference is made to a "notice of appeal", this means the form provided by the Scottish Ministers under paragraph 17(1)(b) (or as the case may be paragraph 18(1)(b)) of the schedule of the 2020 Regulations on notifying of the outcome of a re-determination of entitlement, or of a failure to re-determine entitlement within the prescribed time period.

(3) An individual must start proceedings by submitting the notice of appeal to the Scottish Ministers along with any documents which have not so far been provided to Ministers that the appellant wishes them to submit to the First-tier Tribunal in support of the appeal.

(4) Except as provided for in paragraph (10), a notice of appeal must be received by the Scottish Ministers before the end of the period of 31 days beginning with whichever is the later of the day on which the appellant—
  (a) is informed of a determination made under paragraph 16 of the schedule of the 2020 Regulations following a request for a re-determination; or
  (b) is informed of the appellant's right to appeal against the determination made under paragraph 3 of the schedule of the 2020 Regulations as a result of the failure of the Scottish Ministers to re-determine entitlement within the prescribed time period.

(5) The notice of appeal must state—
  (a) the name and address of the appellant;
  (b) the name and address of the appellant's representative (if any);
  (c) a postal or email address where documents for the appellant may be sent or delivered;
  (d) the determination being challenged;
  (e) the reasons for bringing the appeal; and
  (f) where the notice of appeal is received after the end of the period of 31 days beginning with whichever is the later of—
    (i) the day on which the appellant is informed of a determination made under paragraph 16; or

14.84

    (ii) the day on which the appellant is informed of the right to appeal against the determination made under paragraph 3, but less than one year after that day,
the reasons why the notice of appeal was not sent or delivered to the Scottish Ministers sooner.

(6) A notice of appeal and any accompanying documents may be sent by pre-paid post, by fax, or by electronic communication to such address as may be specified for receipt by the Scottish Ministers.

(7) The Scottish Ministers must forward to the First-tier Tribunal any notice of appeal and accompanying documents submitted to them, regardless of whether the requirements set out in paragraph (5) are met, or the extent to which they are met, and inform the appellant when this has been done.

(8) At the same time as forwarding the notice of appeal and any documents under paragraph (7), the Scottish Ministers must send—
  (a) a copy of any application for a Scottish child payment that has been made by the appellant under paragraph 1(1) of the schedule of the 2020 Regulations in respect of the child to whom the determination of entitlement which is being appealed relates;
  (b) a copy of—
    (i) the determination issued under paragraph 16 of the schedule of the 2020 Regulations following a request that entitlement be re-determined; or
    (ii) the determination issued under paragraph 3 of the schedule of the 2020 Regulations, where there has been a failure to re-determine entitlement within the prescribed time period and the determination under paragraph 3 is being appealed; and
  (c) a copy of any written record of the decision under challenge.

(9) Where [³ a] notice of appeal is received by the Scottish Ministers after the end of the period of 31 days beginning with the later of the days specified in paragraph (4)—
  (a) if the notice of appeal is received before the end of the period of one year beginning with the day on which the appellant is informed of a determination made under paragraph 16 of the schedule of the 2020 Regulations or, as the case may be, of the right to appeal against the determination made under paragraph 3, the First-tier Tribunal may give permission for the appeal to proceed, but only if satisfied that there was a good reason for the notice of appeal not having been sent or delivered to the Scottish Ministers sooner; or
  (b) if the notice of appeal is received after the end of the period of one year beginning with the day on which the appellant is informed of a determination made under paragraph 16 or, as the case may be, of the right to appeal against the determination made under paragraph 3, the First-tier Tribunal must refuse to consider the notice of appeal.

(10) The Scottish Ministers must forward a notice of appeal to the First-tier Tribunal even if one of the following situations applies—
  (a) the notice of appeal is received after the end of the period of 31 days beginning with the later of the days specified in paragraph (4) but less than one year after that day; or
  (b) the notice of appeal is received one year or more after the later of the days specified in paragraph (4).]

AMENDMENTS

1. First-tier Tribunal for Scotland Social Security Chamber (Procedure and Composition) Amendment Regulations 2020 (SSI 2020/353) reg.3(1) and (4) (November 9, 2020).
2. First-tier Tribunal for Scotland Social Security Chamber and Upper Tribunal for Scotland (Allocation of Functions, Procedure and Composition) (Miscellaneous Amendments) Regulations 2020 (SSI 2020/476) reg.5(1) and (3)(b) (December 24, 2020).

[1 Notice of appeal to the First-tier Tribunal against a determination of entitlement to a carer's allowance supplement

20B.—(1) This rule applies where an individual brings an appeal under paragraph 9 of schedule 2 of the Carer's Allowance Supplement Regulations against a determination by the Scottish Ministers of the appellant's entitlement to a carer's allowance supplement.

(2) Where in this rule, and in rule 21 (response of the decision maker to a notice of appeal against a determination of entitlement) in so far as it applies to carer's allowance supplement, reference is made to a "notice of appeal", this means the form provided by the Scottish Ministers under paragraph 7(1)(b) (or as the case may be paragraph 8(1)(b)) of schedule 2 of the Carer's Allowance Supplement Regulations on notifying of the outcome of a re-determination of entitlement, or of a failure to re-determine entitlement within the prescribed time period.

(3) An individual must start proceedings by submitting the notice of appeal to the Scottish Ministers along with any documents which have not so far been provided to Ministers that the appellant wishes them to submit to the First-tier Tribunal in support of the appeal.

(4) Except as provided for in paragraph (10), a notice of appeal must be received by the Scottish Ministers before the end of the period of 31 days beginning with whichever is the later of the day on which the appellant—
  (a) is informed of a determination made under paragraph 6 of schedule 2 of the Carer's Allowance Supplement Regulations following a request for a re-determination; or
  (b) is informed of the appellant's right to appeal against the determination made under regulation 5 (determination of EEA resident's entitlement to a carer's allowance supplement) of the Carer's Allowance Supplement Regulations as a result of the failure of the Scottish Ministers to re-determine entitlement within the prescribed time period.

(5) The notice of appeal must state—
  (a) the name and address of the appellant;
  (b) the name and address of the appellant's representative (if any);
  (c) a postal or email address where documents for the appellant may be sent or delivered;
  (d) the determination being challenged;
  (e) the reasons for bringing the appeal; and
  (f) where the notice of appeal is received after the end of the period of 31 days beginning with whichever is the later of—
    (i) the day on which the appellant is informed of a determination made under paragraph 6 of schedule 2 of the Carer's Allowance Supplement Regulations; or

(ii) the day on which the appellant is informed of the right to appeal against the determination made under regulation 5 of the Carer's Allowance Supplement Regulations, but less than one year after that day,

the reasons why the notice of appeal was not sent or delivered to the Scottish Ministers sooner.

(6) A notice of appeal and any accompanying documents may be sent by pre-paid post, by fax, or by electronic communication to such address as may be specified for receipt by the Scottish Ministers.

(7) The Scottish Ministers must forward to the First-tier Tribunal any notice of appeal and accompanying documents submitted to them, regardless of whether the requirements set out in paragraph (5) are met, or the extent to which they are met, and inform the appellant when this has been done.

(8) At the same time as forwarding the notice of appeal and any documents under paragraph (7), the Scottish Ministers must send—
  (a) a copy of any application for a carer's allowance supplement that has been made by the appellant under regulation 5 of the Carer's Allowance Supplement Regulations;
  (b) a copy of—
    (i) the determination issued under paragraph 6 of schedule 2 of the Carer's Allowance Supplement Regulations following a request that entitlement be re-determined; or
    (ii) the determination issued under regulation 5 of the Carer's Allowance Supplement Regulations, where there has been a failure to re-determine entitlement within the prescribed time period and the determination under regulation 5 is being appealed; and
  (c) a copy of any written record of the decision under challenge.

(9) Where a notice of appeal is received by the Scottish Ministers after the end of the period of 31 days beginning with the later of the days specified in paragraph (4)—
  (a) if the notice of appeal is received before the end of the period of one year beginning with the day on which the appellant is informed of a determination made under paragraph 6 of schedule 2 of the Carer's Allowance Supplement Regulations or, as the case may be, of the right to appeal against the determination made under regulation 5 of the Carer's Allowance Supplement Regulations, the First-tier Tribunal may give permission for the appeal to proceed, but only if satisfied that there was a good reason for the notice of appeal not having been sent or delivered to the Scottish Ministers sooner; or
  (b) if the notice of appeal is received after the end of the period of one year beginning with the day on which the appellant is informed of a determination made under paragraph 6 of schedule 2 or, as the case may be, of the right to appeal against the determination made under regulation 5, the First-tier Tribunal must refuse to consider the notice of appeal.

(10) The Scottish Ministers must forward a notice of appeal to the First-tier Tribunal even if one of the following situations applies—
  (a) the notice of appeal is received after the end of the period of 31 days beginning with the later of the days specified in paragraph (4) but less than one year after that day; or

(b) the notice of appeal is received one year or more after the later of the days specified in paragraph (4).]

AMENDMENT

1. First-tier Tribunal for Scotland Social Security Chamber and Upper Tribunal for Scotland (Allocation of Functions, Procedure and Composition) (Miscellaneous Amendments) Regulations 2020 (SSI 2020/476) reg.5(1) and (3)(c) (December 24, 2020).

Response of the decision maker to a notice of appeal against a determination of entitlement

21.— (1) [² The First-tier Tribunal must notify each party in writing when a notice of appeal submitted under any of the following provisions has been accepted as containing sufficient information to be valid—
  (a) rule 20 (notice of appeal to the First-tier Tribunal against a determination of entitlement to assistance of a type provided for in Part 2 of the 2018 Act);
  (b) rule 20A (notice of appeal to the First-tier Tribunal against a determination of entitlement to a Scottish child payment); or
  (c) rule 20B (notice of appeal to the First-tier Tribunal against a determination of entitlement to a carer's allowance supplement).]

(2) [² The decision maker must send or deliver to the First-tier Tribunal a response to any notice of appeal submitted under rule 20, 20A or 20B before the expiry of the period of 31 days beginning with the day on which the decision maker received notification from the First-tier Tribunal that the notice of appeal had been accepted as containing sufficient information to be valid.]

(3) The response must include—
  (a) the name and address of the decision maker;
  (b) the name and address of the decision maker's representative (if any);
  (c) a postal or email address where documents for the decision maker may be sent or delivered;
  (d) the position of the decision maker in relation to the appellant's case; and
  (e) any views of the decision maker as to whether the matter should be dealt with at a hearing or without a hearing.

(4) Unless a practice direction states otherwise, the decision maker must provide with the response copies of any documents relevant to the case which are in the decision-maker's possession and which have not already been provided to the First-tier Tribunal.

[¹(5) The First-tier Tribunal must provide the appellant with a copy of the decision-maker's response and any documents accompanying that response which have not already been supplied to the appellant.]

(6) The appellant may make written comments to the First-tier Tribunal and supply further documents to it in reply to the decision maker's response.

(7) Any comments or further documents referred to in paragraph (5) must be provided to the First-tier Tribunal within the period of 31 days beginning with the day on which the appellant is presumed to have received the response, as sent by the decision maker, and the First-tier Tribunal must send a copy to the decision maker.

14.86

AMENDMENTS

1. First-tier Tribunal for Scotland Social Security Chamber (Rules of Procedure) Amendment Regulations 2018 (SSI 2018/343) reg.2(1) and (5) (December 21, 2018).
2. First-tier Tribunal for Scotland Social Security Chamber and Upper Tribunal for Scotland (Allocation of Functions, Procedure and Composition) (Miscellaneous Amendments) Regulations 2020 (SSI 2020/476) reg.5(1) and (3)(d) (December 24, 2020).

GENERAL NOTE

14.87 The fact that a respondent does not oppose an appeal does not relieve the Upper Tribunal of the obligation to identify an error of law before allowing the appeal (*Goodyear v Highland Council* [2022] UT 4), and so it is helpful if the respondent explains briefly, when setting out its position as required by para.(3)(d), why it is not opposing the appeal, even if only to make clear that it accepts the appellant's argument.

Notice of appeal against a process decision

14.88 **22.**—(1) [³ This rule applies where an individual brings an appeal under any of the following provisions against a process decision—
  (a) section 61 of the 2018 Act;
  (b) paragraph 23 of the schedule of the 2020 Regulations; or
  (c) paragraph 13 of schedule 2 of the Carer's Allowance Supplement Regulations.]
(2) An individual must start proceedings by sending a notice of appeal and any accompanying documents to the First-tier Tribunal.
(3) Except as provided for in paragraph (5), a notice of appeal against a process decision must be received by the First-tier Tribunal before the end of the period of 31 days beginning with the day on which the individual is informed of the decision against which the individual wishes to appeal.
(4) The notice of appeal must state—
  (a) the name and address of the appellant;
  (b) the name and address of the appellant's representative (if any);
  (c) a postal or email address where documents for the appellant may be sent or delivered;
  (d) the decision being challenged;
  (e) the reasons for bringing the appeal;
  (f) [² . . .]; and
  (g) where the notice of appeal is received after the end of the period of 31 days beginning with the day on which the appellant is informed of the decision, but within less than one year of that day, reasons why the notice of appeal was not sent or delivered to the [¹ First-tier Tribunal] sooner.
(5) Where a notice of appeal is received after the end of the period of 31 days beginning with the day specified in paragraph (3)—
  (a) if the notice of appeal is received less than one year after that day, the First-tier Tribunal may give permission for the appeal to proceed, but only if satisfied that there was a good reason for the notice of appeal not having been sent or delivered sooner; or
  (b) if the notice of appeal is received one year or more after that day, the First-tier Tribunal must refuse to consider the notice [² of appeal].

AMENDMENTS

1. First-tier Tribunal for Scotland Social Security Chamber (Rules of Procedure) Amendment Regulations 2018 (SSI 2018/343) reg.2(1) and (6) (December 21, 2018).
2. First-tier Tribunal for Scotland Social Security Chamber (Procedure and Allocation of Functions) Amendment Regulations 2020 (SSI 2020/100) reg.3(1) and (4) March 26, 2020).
3. First-tier Tribunal for Scotland Social Security Chamber and Upper Tribunal for Scotland (Allocation of Functions, Procedure and Composition) (Miscellaneous Amendments) Regulations 2020 (SSI 2020/476) reg.5(1) and (3)(e) (December 24, 2020).

GENERAL NOTE

There appears to be no provision akin to r.21 that requires the respondent to provide a response of any kind to a notice of appeal given under this rule. There is not even any obligation on the respondent to provide any relevant documents. Presumably it is considered that that the decision being challenged and the grounds of appeal will be sufficient to enable the appeal to be determined.

14.89

Decision with or without a hearing

23.—(1) Subject to the following paragraphs of this rule, the First-tier Tribunal must hold a hearing before making a decision which disposes of proceedings unless—
  (a) the views of all parties have been sought and no party has objected to the matter being decided without a hearing; and
  (b) the First-tier Tribunal considers that it is able to decide the matter without a hearing.

(2) This rule does not apply to decisions under Part 4 of these Rules (correcting, reviewing and appealing decisions of the First-tier Tribunal).

(3) The First-tier Tribunal may dispose of proceedings, or a part of proceedings, under rule 7 (dismissal of a party's case) without a hearing.

(4) Where the First-tier Tribunal considers that the conditions set out in paragraph (1) are met, the Tribunal must proceed to determine the case without a hearing.

(5) A case determined in accordance with paragraph (4) is to be known as a "paper case."

14.90

Entitlement to attend a hearing

24. Subject to the power to exclude persons in rule 26(4) (public and private hearings), each party is entitled to attend any hearing together with any representative and supporter permitted by rules 9 (representatives) and 10 (supporters).

14.91

Notice of hearings

25.—(1) The First-tier Tribunal must give each party entitled to attend a hearing reasonable notice of the time and place of any hearing (including any adjourned or postponed hearing) and any changes to the time and place of any hearing.

(2) The period of notice under paragraph (1) must be at least 14 days except that the First-tier Tribunal may give shorter notice—

14.92

(a) with the parties' consent; or
(b) in urgent or exceptional circumstances.

General Note

14.93 In *Arshad v Khawaja* [2021] UT 33, a landlord applied for the postponement of a hearing scheduled to be heard on 20 February 2021. Both the landlord and the tenant were sent by the First-tier Tribunal a letter saying that the application had been refused for specified reasons but also that the hearing "will therefore go ahead as scheduled on Wednesday, 10 December 2021". The landlord did not attend the hearing, although the tenant did. The landlord subsequently appealed on the ground that he had not attended because he had been misled by the letter. The appeal was allowed, notwithstanding the internal inconsistency of the letter and the view of the First-tier Tribunal, when refusing permission to appeal, that the landlord should have realised that there had been an error. The Upper Tribunal held that the rule in the procedure regulations for the Housing and Property Chamber that is equivalent to this rule had not been complied with and that "[t]he appellant did not have proper intimation of the date of the hearing following his request to postpone".

Public and private hearings

14.94 **26.**—(1) Subject to the following paragraphs of this rule, all hearings of the First-tier Tribunal must be held in public.
(2) The First-tier Tribunal may give an order that a hearing, or part of it, is to be held in private if the First-tier Tribunal considers that restricting access to the hearing is justified—
(a) in the interests of public order;
(b) in order to protect a person's right to respect for their private and family life;
(c) in order to maintain the confidentiality of sensitive information;
(d) in order to avoid serious harm to the public interest; or
(e) because not to do so would prejudice the interests of justice.
(3) Where a hearing, or any part of it, is to be held in private, the First-tier Tribunal may determine who is permitted to attend the hearing or part of it.
(4) The First-tier Tribunal may give an order excluding from any hearing, or part of it—
(a) any person whose conduct the First-tier Tribunal considers is disrupting or is likely to disrupt the hearing;
(b) any person whose presence the First-tier Tribunal considers is likely to prevent another person from giving evidence or making submissions freely; or
(c) any person where the purpose of the hearing would be defeated by the attendance of that person.
(5) The First-tier Tribunal may give an order excluding a witness from a hearing until that witness gives evidence.
(6) When publishing a decision notice referred to in rule 28(2) (notice of decisions) resulting from a hearing which was held wholly or partly in private, the First-tier Tribunal must, so far as practicable, ensure that the decision notice does not disclose information which was referred to only in a part of the hearing that was held in private (including such information which enables the identification of any person whose affairs were dealt with in the part of the hearing that was held in private) if to do so would undermine the purpose of holding the hearing in private.

GENERAL NOTE

14.95 In *Hamilton v Glasgow Housing Association Limited* [2020] UT 37, the Appellant apparently had mental health difficulties and interrupted proceedings at a hearing before the Housing and Property Chamber of the First-tier Tribunal on numerous occasions. The First-tier Tribunal found that he "had endeavoured to control himself but was unable to do so." Rather than excluding him from the hearing under the provision equivalent to r.26(4) of these Rules, the First-tier Tribunal barred him from presenting submissions or presenting arguments or questioning witnesses in person, at that or any future hearings and then adjourned to allow him to obtain representation, which he was unable to do. The Upper Tribunal allowed his appeal against that decision, holding that it could not be assumed that a person could obtain representation and that the First-tier Tribunal had not had adequate regard either to the overriding objective or the possibility of taking other action. For instance, consideration had not been given to whether regular short breaks to enable the Appellant to recover his equilibrium might have been appropriate or whether a supporter (see r.10 of these Rules) might have been obtained.

In *Barr Environmental Limited v Revenue Scotland* [2022] UT 11 at [75], the Upper Tribunal pointed out that the putting of a case to witnesses is treated in Scotland as an aspect of fairness. It may well be unfair for the First-tier Tribunal to rely on a point without having given witnesses for the losing party an opportunity to comment on it at the hearing, but whether that is so in a particular case requires to be considered in the context of the particular circumstances of that case.

Hearings in a party's absence

27. If a party fails to attend a hearing the First-tier Tribunal may proceed with the hearing if the Tribunal— 14.96

(a) is satisfied that the party has been notified of the hearing or that reasonable steps have been taken to notify the party of the hearing; and

(b) considers that it is in the interests of justice to proceed with the hearing.

GENERAL NOTE

14.97 In *Devine v Bailo* [2022] UT 14, the Upper Tribunal set aside a decision of the First-tier Tribunal given in the absence of a party at a hearing by telephone conference, when the absent party had submitted an email setting out in detail why he considered a telephone hearing to be inadequate. In its reasons for decision, the First-tier Tribunal had explained why a telephone conference was permitted and referred to the overriding objective which, as in the present Rules, provides that dealing with cases justly includes "avoiding delay, so far as compatible with the proper consideration of the issues". However, while it had referred to the need to avoid delay, it had not addressed the absent party's arguments and had therefore failed to show that it had considered whether its decision was compatible with the proper consideration of the issues. The Upper Tribunal said—

"[13] In deciding whether to proceed in the face of an application to postpone it is likely that the FtT will have regard to the reason put forward by a party together with the nature of the dispute and whether that may be adjudicated upon fairly absent one of the parties. When delay is recognised as inevitable (in the event of acceding to the application to postpone) the FtT may have to assess what effect that will have upon the determination and what prejudice will be suffered by parties. If either or both parties are legally represented that may have a bearing on the assessment. Parties' ability to deal with the proposed means of convening the hearing (here at the telephone) will have to be weighed in the overall evaluation of whether to proceed or not. That will inevitably involve an assessment of what is said by parties about how they would react to telephone or video hearings. The scope of the hearing and how it is envisaged that the matter will be resolved–for example, with reference to oral testimony alone–may well be a relevant consideration. Documentary material including witness statements may well go some way to resolving, or assisting in the resolution of, disputed issues. The availability of alternative means of convening the hearing and informed estimates about when those may be accessed by the FtT may affect whether the application to postpone may be given effect to. These sorts of considerations may well have been relevant to the FtT's decision to postpone. The FtT decision is silent on what it made of these other factors, aside from delay, in the exercise of its discretion."

Notice of decisions

28.—(1) The First-tier Tribunal may give a decision orally at a hearing.

(2) The First-tier Tribunal must provide a decision notice to each party as soon as reasonably practicable after making a decision which finally disposes of all issues in the proceedings or of a preliminary issue dealt with following an order under rule 4(3)(e) (dealing with an issue as a preliminary issue).

(3) A decision notice must—
  (a) state the First-tier Tribunal's decision;
  (b) where appropriate, notify each party of the right to apply for a full written statement of reasons under rule 29(2) (reasons for decisions); and
  (c) once a written summary of a decision or a full statement of reasons has been issued, notify each party of the right to apply for permission to appeal to the Upper Tribunal against the decision, and the time within which, and the method by which, such an application must be made.

(4) This rule does not apply to a decision under Part 4 of these Rules (correcting, reviewing and appealing decisions of the First-tier Tribunal).

GENERAL NOTE

In *Barr Environmental Limited v Revenue Scotland* [2022] UT 11 at [76], the Upper Tribunal applied the approach taken in *Natwest Markets plc v Bilta (UK) Ltd (in liquidation)* [2021] EWCA Civ 680, where it was held at [43] that "delay may have so adversely affected the quality of the decision that it cannot be allowed to stand". That approach requires that regard be had to the particular circumstances in which delay has occurred and the likely effect of it on the making of the decision, given the issues in the case. Both those cases were very complicated and there was a delay in each case of about 18 months between the hearing and the giving of the decision. In *Natwest Markets*, the appeal was allowed but, in *Barr Environmental*, the delay in the giving of the decision was held not to vitiate it. There had been good reason for some of the delay and the First-tier Tribunal had not had to rely on its memory for the evidence and submissions because it had a full transcript of the hearing, as well as written submissions and 6,500 pages of documentary evidence.

Reasons for decisions

29.—(1) The First-tier Tribunal may give reasons for a decision which disposes of proceedings—
  (a) orally at a hearing; or
  (b) in a full written statement of reasons [¹ or a written summary of a decision, which is to be issued] to each party.

(SSI 2018/273 Sch - r.29)

(2) Unless the First-tier Tribunal has already provided a full written statement of reasons under paragraph (1)(b), a party may make a written application to the Tribunal for such statement following a decision which finally disposes of—
(a) all issues in the proceedings; or
(b) a preliminary issue dealt with following an order under rule 4(3)(e) (dealing with an issue as a preliminary issue).

(3) An application under paragraph (2) must be received within the period of 31 days beginning with the day on which the decision notice relating to the decision provided to the appellant by the First-tier Tribunal under rule 28 (notice of decisions) is presumed to have been received by the appellant.

(4) If a party makes an application in accordance with paragraphs (2) and (3), the First-tier Tribunal must, subject to rule 14 (disclosure of documents and information), send a full written statement of reasons to each party within the period of 31 days beginning with the day on which the Tribunal received the application or as soon as reasonably practicable after the end of that period.

(5) This rule does not apply to a decision under Part 4 of these Rules (correcting, reviewing and appealing decisions of the First-tier Tribunal).

AMENDMENT

1. First-tier Tribunal for Scotland Social Security Chamber (Rules of Procedure) Amendment Regulations 2018 (SSI 2018/343) reg.2(1) and (7) (December 21, 2018).

GENERAL NOTE

In *Wordie Property Co Ltd v Secretary of State for Scotland* 1984 SLT 345 at page 348, it was said that a decision maker was required to—

14.101

"... give proper and adequate reasons ... which deal with the substantial questions in issue in an intelligible way. The decision must, in short, leave the informed reader and the court in no real and substantial doubt as to what the reasons for it were and what were the material considerations which were taken into account in reaching it."

A failure by the First-tier Tribunal to give proper and adequate reasons is a breach of r.29 and therefore, if the breach is material, is an error of law. When considering whether the First-tier Tribunal had erred in law in *Midlothian Council v Barr* [2021] UT 17 at [25], the Upper Tribunal adopted the submissions of the appellant's representative, which it had summarised at [15]—

"[15] A decision must leave the informed reader in no real and substantial doubt as to what the reasons for it were and what were the material considerations which were taken into account in reaching it: *Wordie Property Co Ltd v Secretary of State for Scotland* 1984 SLT 345, at pages 347-348. A statement of reasons must identify what the decision maker decided to be the material considerations; must clearly and concisely set out his evaluation of them; and must set out the essence of the reasoning that has led him to his decision: *Ritchie v Aberdeen City Council* 2011 SC 579, Lord President (Gill) at paragraph 12; *JC v Midlothian Council* [2012] CSIH 77, Lord Menzies, paragraph 30, citing *Uprichard v Scottish Ministers* 2012 SC 172, Lord President (Gill) at paragraph 26. It was necessary to read the reasons as a whole: *City of Edinburgh Council v MDN* 2011 SC 513, paragraph 28."

Having found that the First-tier Tribunal's reasons were not adequate in that case, the Upper Tribunal made the following further observations—

"[57] I am conscious that tribunals need to provide reasonably concise and understandable decisions, and with that in mind, make the following additional observations in the context of this case.

[58] The FTT in this case wrote:

"It is not practical, appropriate or necessary to narrate every aspect of the evidence in this written decision. We note that many of the witnesses lodged written mini-CVs to assist the Tribunal. We also were provided with written statements which were entered into evidence."

and

"We do not seek to rehearse all the evidence before us. The Findings of Fact record the evidence we accepted."

[59] Fact-finding tribunals, such as the FTT is in a case of this sort, are under no obligation to narrate all of the evidence led before them, or to narrate in detail all of the evidence they rejected. There is no merit in a mechanistic recital of all of the evidence, and that sort of exercise should be avoided. The FTT does require to bear in mind, however, that the audience for a decision includes not only parties who were present at the hearing, but also, potentially, an appellate tribunal. The FTT's decision is the primary source of information for the appellate tribunal as to what the oral evidence was. It is also important more generally that a reader unconnected with the case should be able to understand why the decision was made. Anonymised decisions in cases of this type may be published. It is an aspect of open justice that members of the public should be able to see and understand the decisions of tribunals. The provision of comprehensible written reasons contributes to the maintenance of public confidence in the decision making process: *Chief Constable, Lothian and Borders Police v Lothian and Borders Police Board* 2005 SLT 315, paragraph 63.

[60] As I observed in the decision relating to permission to appeal in this case, findings in fact are expressions of a conclusion as to a matter of fact, formed on the basis of evidence. Some of the findings in fact in this case conform to that model. Some, however, include narrations of evidence. A number read "[name of witness] stated . . .". Some include discussions of the law. Finding in fact 25, for example, is in these terms:

"The burden of proof in this placing request rests with the Authority. The appeal hearing is a full reconsideration of the evidence and it is the current circumstances that apply at the date of the hearing that are relevant."

Others record findings in fact and law, rather than matters of fact, for example:

"The child has additional support needs in terms of section 1 of [the 2004 Act]"

The way in which the findings in fact in this case have been written means that they are less useful than the FTT must have intended in providing an indication as to the evidence that was accepted. In relation to an issue essential to the decision-making process of the tribunal, a decision should set out intelligibly the findings of fact relevant to that matter. Elsewhere in the decision a tribunal should make clear what evidence those findings were based on. Where there has been evidence to contrary effect, the decision should set out also what that evidence was, and why the competing bodies of evidence have, respectively, been accepted and rejected. The FTT should do so as concisely as is consistent with the nature and extent of the evidence in question.

[61] I have already referred to a finding in fact which expressed conclusions about mixed questions of fact and law. Another example is this:

"School A is suited to the ability and aptitude of the child".

I observe that the FTT should have been considering whether it was satisfied that the education normally provided at School A was not suited to the child's age, ability or aptitude. Ideally, findings in fact relevant to an issue of this sort would be factual findings as to the education normally provided at School A, and about the child's ability and his aptitude (and age, if that were a live issue). The reasons for the decision would then go on to explain what those factual findings demonstrated about the suitability or otherwise of that education for the child's age, ability and aptitude.

[62] The reader ought to be able to discern how the evidence related to the facts found, and how the facts found have been employed in considering whether the legal tests have been satisfied. A rigorous focus on the matters of fact relevant to each of the legal tests individually will be helpful in this regard."

14.102 In *South Lanarkshire Council v Boyd* [2021] UT 24, the Upper Tribunal followed the approach taken by Lord Hope of Craighead in *AH (Sudan) v Secretary of State for the Home Department* [2007] UKHL 49; [2008] AC 678 at [19], where he said—

"I agree also with what my noble and learned friend Baroness Hale of Richmond says about the caution with which the ordinary courts should approach the decision of an expert tribunal. A decision that is clearly based on a mistake of law must, of course, be corrected. Its reasoning must be explained, but it ought not to be subjected to an unduly critical analysis. As your Lordships have indicated, there are passages in the decision that is before us which might, when read in isolation, suggest that the tribunal misdirected itself. But I am quite satisfied that the decision as a whole was soundly based, and that a more accurate wording of the passages that have attracted criticism would have made no difference to the tribunal's conclusion on the facts that the Secretary of State's refusal of asylum in these cases should be upheld."

At [55] of its decision, the Upper Tribunal said—

"Where, as here, a challenge is based on a failure to give reasons, in some cases quite minimal explanation might suffice; reasons could be stated briefly, and the level of detail required would be dictated by the issues requiring determination. The informed reader should be left in no real or substantial doubt as to why the decision was taken: *Stefan v General Medical Council* [1999] UKPC 10 at [24]; [1999] 1 W.L.R. 1293 at p.1301F; *South Bucks District Council v Porter* (No 2) [2004] UKHL 33; [2004] 1 W.L.R. 1953, paragraph 36. In my view there is no doubt as to why the decision was taken. It also needs to be remembered that the tribunal decision is governed by the evidence and submissions which parties elect to place before it. The tribunal did not have the benefit of the comprehensive submissions made by Mr Upton. The tribunal is obliged to make its decision on the basis of the evidence and submissions which it has before it at the time of the hearing."

It is important to note that the Upper Tribunal referred to evidence as well as submissions. It therefore needs to be borne in mind that issues may arise on the evidence even if no party has explicitly raised them, so that, particularly when litigants are acting in person, a tribunal ought not to confine itself to issues raised in the parties' submissions but ought to address any other questions that are obviously raised by the evidence.

14.103 The Council's appeal was dismissed by the Court of Session, who observed that, when it permitted new argument, not advanced before the First-tier Tribunal, to be raised before it, the Upper Tribunal appeared not to have considered whether the evidence and the findings in facts might have been different if the argument had been in play before the First-tier Tribunal, and also that the evidence led by the Council before the First-tier Tribunal appeared to have been "somewhat scant and lacking in clarity". (*South Lanarkshire Council v Boyd* [2022] CSIH 41; 2022 G.W.D. 29 at [21]).

In *Midlothian Council v PD* [2019] UT 52, Lady Carmichael, sitting in the Upper Tribunal, gave the following general guidance about writing reasons—

"[24] Written decisions should (a) state clearly what facts the FTT has found, (b) the evidence on which those findings in fact are based, and, (c) where there has been a matter of controversy relevant to the resolution of an important issue in the appeal, an explanation of why the FTT has reached the conclusion that it has on the matter.

[25] The section headed findings in fact in this case contain many passages that are not findings in fact, but narrations of evidence, eg "Mr Chisholm stated that . . ..". A finding in fact is not a narration of evidence. It an expression of a conclusion, formed on the basis of evidence.

[26] Depending on the issues actually before a tribunal, and the extent to which particular matters have been contentious, it may be necessary to narrate what the evidence was that formed the basis for a particular conclusion. Where there are competing bodies of evidence on a crucial issue, the basis on which one has been accepted and another rejected should be stated clearly. This need not be a lengthy exercise. It should be as concise as is consistent with clarity in the context of the case and the issues for determination. The narration of any relevant evidence and the reasons for accepting or rejecting it should not be described as findings in fact, but included in a separate part of the decision.

[27] Where a tribunal is addressing legal tests it should structure its reasoning by reference to those tests and the language in those tests. The provision of written findings in fact and reasons is a requirement in terms of rule 48 of the FTT Procedure Rules [applicable in the Health and Education Chamber]. The purposes of written reasons are summarised by Lord Reed in *Chief Constable, Lothian and Borders Police v Lothian and Borders Police Board* 2005 SLT 315, particularly at 11 paragraphs 62–64, by reference to the authorities cited by him. Those purposes should be in the minds of those providing written reasons for tribunal decisions."

In relation to delay, see the note to r.28, above.

Publication of decisions

14.104　　30. [¹ . . .]

AMENDMENT

1. First-tier Tribunal for Scotland Social Security Chamber (Procedure and Allocation of Functions) Amendment Regulations 2020 (SSI 2020/100) reg.3(1) and (5) (March 26, 2020).

GENERAL NOTE

14.105　　The explanatory note to the amending Regulations says that the effect of revoking this rule "removes the option for a decision of the Social Security Chamber to be published" but it is arguable that it merely removes the *duty* on the Chamber President to make arrangements for the publication of such decisions. In any event, Chamber Presidents have adopted the practice of the Social Entitlement Chamber of the First-tier Tribunal in Great Britain, which does not publish its decisions. However, instead, they publish notes "on matters of interest and points of law arising in decisions" at *https://socialsecuritychamber.scot/home/about-us/decision-reports*. This is helpful because so few cases reach the Upper Tribunal for Scotland, although such notes obviously have no precedential status.

(SSI 2018/273 Sch - r.31)

PART 4

CORRECTING, REVIEWING AND APPEALING DECISIONS OF THE FIRST-TIER TRIBUNAL

Interpretation

31. In this Part—
"appeal" means the exercise of a right of appeal on a point of law under section 46(1) of the 2014 Act; and
"review" means the internal review provided for by section 43(1) of the 2014 Act.

Correction of clerical mistakes or accidental slips or omissions

[¹ **32.** The First-tier Tribunal may at any time correct any clerical mistake or other accidental slip or omission contained in a decision, order or any document produced by it by sending notification of the amended decision or order, or a copy of the amended document, to all parties.]

AMENDMENT

1. First-tier Tribunal for Scotland Social Security Chamber (Procedure and Allocation of Functions) Amendment Regulations 2020 (SSI 2020/100) reg.3(1) and (6) (March 26, 2020).

Application for permission to appeal against a decision of the First-tier Tribunal

33.—(1) A person seeking permission to appeal against a decision of the First-tier Tribunal must make a written application to the First-tier Tribunal for permission to appeal.
(2) An application under paragraph (1) must—
(a) identify the decision of the First-tier Tribunal to which it relates;
(b) identify the alleged point or points of law on which the person making the application wishes to appeal; and
(c) state the result that the [¹ person] making the application is seeking.
(3) Where an application under paragraph (1) has been submitted after the expiry of the 30 day period referred to in regulation 2(1) of the 2016 Regulations—
(a) the application must include a request for an extension of time and state the reasons why the application was not submitted in time; and
(b) unless the First-tier Tribunal extends the time period, the Tribunal must not admit the application.

AMENDMENT

1. First-tier Tribunal for Scotland Social Security Chamber (Rules of Procedure) Amendment Regulations 2018 (SSI 2018/343) reg.2(1) and (8) (December 21, 2018).

GENERAL NOTE

In the course of a 45-paragraph refusal of permission to appeal from a decision of the General Regulatory Chamber of the First-tier Tribunal, the Upper Tribunal held in *Doherty v City of Edinburgh Council* [2021] UT 10 that the First-tier Tribunal had been right to refuse permission to appeal on the ground that the applicant had failed to comply with the provision in the relevant procedure rules that was equivalent to r.33(2)(c) of these Rules, because he had not stated the result that he was seeking. The applicant argued that it was obvious what result he was seeking, but the Upper Tribunal held that it was not for the First-tier Tribunal to infer that from the surrounding circumstances. However, even if that is the correct approach in the General Regulatory Chamber under the procedure rules applicable in that case, it is difficult to see how it could be the correct approach in the Social Security Chamber, where there is an express power under r.6(2) to waive a requirement in these Rules.

Allegations of bias on the part of the First-tier Tribunal must be properly particularised and appropriately evidenced if permission to appeal is to be given on that ground (*Wilson v Fife Properties Ltd* [2021] UT 27, applying the approach taken in *Singh v Secretary of State for the Home Department* [2016] EWCA Civ 492).

14.110   In *Mahmood v Glasgow West Enterprises Ltd* [2021] UT 29, an important document was not sent to the applicant in advance of the hearing before the First-tier Tribunal but, when the applicant was offered an opportunity to apply for an adjournment so that he could consider the document, he declined to do so. The applicant accepted that the First-tier Tribunal's decision was not wrong in law on the evidence that was before it and the Upper Tribunal refused to give permission to appeal in order to allow the applicant to introduce new evidence to challenge the accuracy of the important document.

First-tier Tribunal's consideration of application for permission to appeal against its decision

14.111   **34.**—(1) On receiving an application for permission to appeal, the First-tier Tribunal must decide whether to give permission to appeal on any point of law.

(2) The First-tier Tribunal must provide a notice of its decision to the parties as soon as reasonably practicable.

(3) If the First-tier Tribunal refuses permission to appeal it must send with the notice of its decision—
   (a) a statement of its reasons for such a refusal; and
   (b) notification of the right to make an application to the Upper Tribunal for permission to appeal and the time within which, and the method by which, such an application must be made.

GENERAL NOTE

14.112   It was pointed out in *Aberdeen CC v LS* [2021] UT 1 that, like r.34, the equivalent provision in the rules applicable in the Housing and Education Chamber does not require reasons to be provided where permission to appeal is granted and it was suggested that it may not be necessary for the First-tier Tribunal to say much more than that grounds of appeal in respect of which permission has been granted are arguable (see s.46(4) of the Tribunals (Scotland) Act 2014), thus saving judicial time and avoiding both unnecessary delay and any impression of pre-judgement of issues to be decided in the substantive hearing of the appeal. However, it is good practice for the First-tier Tribunal to make clear that the issue of arguability has been addressed (*Zukowski v Charles White Limited* [2020] UT 26 at [19]).

Review of a decision

14.113   **35.**—(1) A party may request a review of a decision [¹ ...] of the First-tier Tribunal on the basis of a point of law [¹ (unless it is an excluded decision or a process decision)].

(2) An application for a review must—
(a) be made in writing;
(b) be made within the period of 14 days beginning with the day on which the decision was made or the day that the written reasons were sent to the parties (if later); and
(c) identify the alleged point or points of law on the basis of which a review is being sought.

(3) If the First-tier Tribunal considers that the application is without merit, the First-tier Tribunal must refuse the application and inform the parties of the reasons for the refusal.

(4) Except where the application is rejected under paragraph (3), the First-tier Tribunal must send a notice to the parties—
(a) setting a time limit for any response to the application by the other parties and seeking the views of the parties on whether the application can be determined without a hearing; and
(b) if the First-tier Tribunal considers it appropriate to do so, setting out its provisional views on the application.

(5) Except where the application is rejected under paragraph (3), the decision is to be reviewed at a hearing unless the First-tier Tribunal considers, having regard to all of the responses to the notice provided under paragraph [1 (4)], that a hearing is not necessary in the interests of justice.

(6) Where practicable, the review is to be undertaken by [2 the legal member] of the First-tier Tribunal who made the decision to which it relates.

(7) A notice of the decision on a review [1 carried out in accordance with paragraph (5)] must as soon as reasonably practicable be sent by the First-tier Tribunal to each party.

(8) [1 An application for a review] by the First-tier Tribunal in terms of paragraph (1) does not affect the time limit of 30 days in regulation 2(1) of the 2016 Regulations for making an application for permission to appeal.

AMENDMENTS

1. First-tier Tribunal for Scotland Social Security Chamber (Rules of Procedure) Amendment Regulations 2018 (SSI 2018/343) reg.2(1) and (9) (December 21, 2018).

2. First-tier Tribunal for Scotland Social Security Chamber (Procedure and Allocation of Functions) Amendment Regulations 2020 (SSI 2020/100) reg.3(1) and (7) (March 26, 2020).

Duty to treat a request for a review as an application for permission to appeal

36.—(1) The First-tier Tribunal must treat a request for a review under rule 35 (review of a decision) as also being an application for permission to appeal under rule 33 (application for permission to appeal against a decision of the First-tier Tribunal), unless the [1 party who requests the review] states expressly that they do not wish it to be so treated.

14.114

(2) Where [1 the party who requests the review] is given notice of the a review decision under rule 35(7) (notice of decision on a review to be sent as soon as reasonably practicable), [1 the party is] to be given the opportunity to state whether or not [1 the party wishes] to proceed with an appeal.

AMENDMENTS

1. First-tier Tribunal for Scotland Social Security Chamber (Procedure and Allocation of Functions) Amendment Regulations 2020 (SSI 2020/100) reg.3(1) and (8) (March 26, 2020).

The Upper Tribunal for Scotland (Social Security Rules of Procedure) Regulations 2018

(SSI 2018/274)

Made	*11th September 2018*
Laid before the Scottish Parliament	*13th September 2018*
Coming into force	*22nd November 2018*

14.115 The Scottish Ministers make the following Regulations in exercise of the powers conferred by paragraph 4(2) of schedule 9 of the Tribunals (Scotland) Act 2014 and all other powers enabling them to do so.

In accordance with paragraph 4(3) of schedule 9 of that Act, the Scottish Ministers have consulted the President of the Scottish Tribunals and such other persons as they considered appropriate.

Citation, commencement and interpretation

14.116 **1.**—(1) These Regulations may be cited as the Upper Tribunal for Scotland (Social Security Rules of Procedure) Regulations 2018 and the Rules contained in the schedule may be cited as the Upper Tribunal for Scotland Social Security Rules of Procedure 2018.

(2) These Regulations come into force on 22nd November 2018.

(3) In these Regulations, "the 2018 Act" means the Social Security (Scotland) Act 2018.

Disapplication of the Upper Tribunal for Scotland Rules 2016

14.117 **2.** The Upper Tribunal for Scotland Rules of Procedure 2016 do not apply to proceedings before the Upper Tribunal relating to the exercise by the Scottish Ministers of functions conferred on them by the 2018 Act or by regulations made under that Act.

Application of Rules in schedule

14.118 **3.** The Rules in the schedule of these Regulations apply to all proceedings before the Upper Tribunal relating to the exercise by the Scottish Ministers of functions conferred on them by [1 —
  (a) the 2018 Act;
  (b) regulations made under the 2018 Act; or
  (c) the Carer's Allowance Supplement and Young Carer Grants (Residence Requirements and Procedural Provisions) (EU Exit) (Scotland) Regulations 2020.]

(SSI 2018/274 Sch - r.3)

AMENDMENT

1. First-tier Tribunal for Scotland Social Security Chamber and Upper Tribunal for Scotland (Allocation of Functions, Procedure and Composition) (Miscellaneous Amendments) Regulations 2020 (SSI 2020/476) reg.3 (December 24, 2020).

Regulation 3

SCHEDULE

THE UPPER TRIBUNAL FOR SCOTLAND SOCIAL SECURITY RULES OF PROCEDURE 2018

PART 1

INTERPRETATION

1. Interpretation   14.119

PART 2

ROLE OF THE UPPER TRIBUNAL

2. Purpose of the Upper Tribunal and overriding objective

PART 3

PROCEDURE FOR CASES IN THE UPPER TRIBUNAL

3. Application for permission to appeal against a decision of the First-tier Tribunal
4. Notice of appeal against a decision of the First-tier Tribunal
5. Response to the notice of appeal
6. Appellant's reply

PART 4

GENERAL POWERS AND PROVISIONS

7. Delegation to staff
8. Case management
9. Procedure for applying for and giving orders
10. Failure to comply with rulesetc.
11. Dismissal of a party's case
12. Addition, substitution and removal of parties
13. Representatives
14. Supporters

The Upper Tribunal for Scotland (Social Security Rules of Procedure) Reg 2018

15. Calculating time
16. Sending and delivery of documents
17. Disclosure of documents and information
18. Evidence and submissions
19. Citation of witnesses and orders to answer questions or produce documents
20. Withdrawal
21. Chairing member

PART 5

Hearings

22. Decision with or without a hearing
23. Entitlement to attend a hearing
24. Notice of hearings
25. Public and private hearings
26. Hearings in a party's absence

PART 6

Decisions

27. Notice of decisions and reasons
28. Reviews

PART 7

Appealing Decisions of the Upper Tribunal

29. Interpretation
30. Application for permission to appeal a decision of the Upper Tribunal
31. Upper Tribunal's consideration of application for permission to appeal

PART 8

Legal Aid

32. Legal aid

PART 1

Interpretation

Interpretation

14.120

1.—(1) In these Rules—
"the 2014 Act" means the Tribunals (Scotland) Act 2014;
"the 2018 Act" means the Social Security (Scotland) Act 2018;

(SSI 2018/274 Sch - r.1)

"the 2016 Regulations" means the Scottish Tribunals (Time Limits) Regulations 2016;

"Appeal Appendix" means all the documents and authorities to be relied on for the purpose of the appeal along with an inventory of those documents and authorities;

"appellant" means—
(a) a person who makes an appeal to the Upper Tribunal; or
(b) a person substituted as an appellant under rule 12 (addition, substitution and removal of parties);

"the Convention rights" has the meaning given to it in section 1 of the Human Rights Act 1998;

"document" means anything in which information is recorded in any form;

"electronic communication" has the meaning given to it by section 15(1) of the Electronic Communications Act 2000;

"excluded decision" means a decision falling under section 51 of the 2014 Act;

"the First-tier Tribunal" means the First-tier Tribunal for Scotland Social Security Chamber;

"hearing" means an oral hearing and includes a hearing conducted in whole or in part by video link, telephone or other means of instantaneous two-way electronic communication;

"party" means a person who is (or was at the time that the Upper Tribunal disposed of the proceedings) an appellant or respondent in proceedings before the Upper Tribunal;

"practice direction" means a practice direction issued in terms of section 74 of the 2014 Act;

"President" means the President of the Scottish Tribunals;

"proceedings" includes a part of the proceedings;

"representative" means a lay representative or a legal representative;

"respondent" means—
(a) in an appeal against a decision of the First-tier Tribunal, that Tribunal and any person other than the appellant who was a party before the First-tier Tribunal; or
(b) a person substituted or added as a respondent under rule 12 (addition, substitution and removal of parties);

"review period" means the time period between the day of an application by a party for a review under rule 28(1) or, as the case may be, the Upper Tribunal's decision to review a decision under that rule, and the receipt by each party of a notice sent under rule 28(5);

"the Upper Tribunal" means the Upper Tribunal for Scotland; and

"witness statement" means a written statement of a witness ordered by the Upper Tribunal to stand for the evidence-in-chief of the witness.

(2) For the purposes of these Rules, where information is sent—
(a) via the postal service to the last known address held for an individual; or
(b) by email to the last known email address held for the individual, the individual is presumed to have received the information 48 hours after it is sent, unless the contrary is shown.

The Upper Tribunal for Scotland (Social Security Rules of Procedure) Reg 2018

PART 2

ROLE OF THE UPPER TRIBUNAL

Purpose of the Upper Tribunal and overriding objective

14.121 **2.**—(1) The Upper Tribunal hears and decides cases referred to it from the First-tier Tribunal for Scotland and hears and decides appeals from the First-tier Tribunal.

(2) The overriding objective of these Rules is to secure that proceedings before the Upper Tribunal to which the Rules apply are handled fairly and justly.

(3) Dealing with a case fairly and justly includes—
   (a) dealing with the case in ways which are transparent, proportionate to the importance of the case, the complexity of the issues, the anticipated expenses and the resources of the parties;
   (b) avoiding unnecessary formality and seeking flexibility in the proceedings;
   (c) ensuring, so far as practicable, that the parties are able to participate fully in the proceedings and are treated with dignity and respect;
   (d) using any special expertise of the Upper Tribunal effectively; and
   (e) avoiding delay, so far as compatible with proper consideration of the issues.

(4) The Upper Tribunal must seek to give effect to the overriding objective when it—
   (a) exercises any power under these Rules; or
   (b) interprets any rule or practice direction.

(5) Parties must, insofar as reasonably possible—
   (a) help the Upper Tribunal to further the overriding objective; and
   (b) co-operate with the Upper Tribunal generally.

PART 3

PROCEDURE FOR CASES IN THE UPPER TRIBUNAL

Application for permission to appeal against a decision of the First-tier Tribunal

14.122 **3.**—(1) A person may lodge with the Upper Tribunal an application for permission to appeal against a decision of the First-tier Tribunal, where the First-tier Tribunal has refused permission to appeal in whole or in part.

(2) An application for permission to appeal must—
   (a) identify the decision of the First-tier Tribunal to which it relates; and
   (b) identify the alleged point or points of law in relation to the decision.

(3) The appellant must provide with the application for permission a copy of—
   (a) any written record of the decision being challenged;
   (b) any separate written statement of reasons for that decision; and
   (c) the notice of refusal of permission to appeal from the First-tier Tribunal.

(4) If the appellant lodges the application for permission to appeal with the Upper Tribunal after the expiry of the 30 day period referred to in regulation 3(1) of the 2016 Regulations—
  (a) the application for permission to appeal must—
    (i) include a request for an extension of time;
    (ii) explain why the application for permission to appeal was not made in time; and
    (iii) state why it is said to be in the interests of justice that the time be extended.
  (b) unless the Upper Tribunal extends the time for lodging an application for permission to appeal the Upper Tribunal must not admit the application for permission to appeal.

(5) The Upper Tribunal may, where the First-tier Tribunal has refused permission to appeal—
  (a) refuse permission to appeal;
  (b) give permission to appeal; or
  (c) give permission to appeal on limited grounds or subject to conditions,
and must send a notice of its decision to each party including reasons for a refusal of permission or for limitations or conditions on any grant of permission.

(6) Where the Upper Tribunal, without a hearing—
  (a) refuses permission to appeal; or
  (b) gives permission to appeal on limited grounds or subject to conditions,
the appellant may make a written application (within the period of 14 days beginning with the day on which the appellant is presumed to have received notice of refusal of permission, sent under paragraph (5)) to the Upper Tribunal for the decision to be reconsidered at a hearing.

(7) An application under paragraph (6) must be heard and decided by a member or members of the Upper Tribunal different from the member or members who refused permission without a hearing.

(8) Where the Upper Tribunal gives permission to appeal against a decision of the First-tier Tribunal, a valid notice of appeal will be deemed to have been provided to the Upper Tribunal, for the purposes of rule 4 (notice of appeal against a decision of the First-tier Tribunal).

GENERAL NOTE

Considerations relevant when the First-tier Tribunal is considering an application for permission to appeal (see the note to r.33 of the First-tier Tribunal's procedural rules, above) are equally relevant in the Upper Tribunal.

The Upper Tribunal was content in *Malloch v Bernisdale Homes Ltd* [2021] UT 34 to consider a ground of appeal that had not been considered by the First-tier Tribunal. Reference was made to *Advocate General for Scotland v Murray Group Holdings Ltd* [2015] CSIH 77; 2016 S.C. 201, where the Court of Session said of its own practice—

> "[39] We are of opinion that in a statutory appeal of this nature it is competent for the court to entertain a ground of appeal that has not been argued in the First-tier or Upper Tribunals, although it should be slow to do so in any case where additional findings of fact are required, and should not do so if unfairness results."

In the event, the Upper Tribunal found the relevant ground of appeal to be unarguable and so permission was refused anyway.

14.123

The Upper Tribunal for Scotland (Social Security Rules of Procedure) Reg 2018

As the Upper Tribunal made clear in *PD v Midlothian Council* [2021] UT 19 at [10], when a judge is reconsidering under r.3(6) and (7) a refusal of permission to appeal, he or she is not reviewing the earlier decisions of the First-tier Tribunal and the Upper Tribunal to refuse permission; his or her task is simply to decide afresh whether the grounds of appeal disclose an arguable material error of law on the part of the First-tier Tribunal in its substantive decision.

In *Zahorowicz v Pawlowska* [2020] UT 19, the Upper Tribunal clearly doubted the value of the right to apply for reconsideration in r.3(7) of the rules applicable in cases other than social security cases, which is equivalent to para.(6) of this rule. The judicial member said—

"It may be desirable to review the function of rule 3(7), as the hearing amounted to no more than a further discussion of the explanation already set out in the original decision to refuse leave."

Notice of appeal against a decision of the First-tier Tribunal

14.124

4.—(1) Where the First-tier Tribunal sends a notice of permission to appeal to a party who has sought permission to appeal, that party, if intending to appeal, must provide a notice of appeal to the Upper Tribunal within the period of 30 days beginning with the day on which the party is presumed to have received the notice of permission.

(2) A notice of appeal must—
 (a) identify the decision of the First-tier Tribunal to which it relates;
 (b) identify the alleged point or points of law in relation to the decision; and
 (c) include any views of the appellant on whether the matter should be dealt with at a hearing or without a hearing.

(3) The appellant must provide with the notice of appeal a copy of—
 (a) any written record of the decision being challenged;
 (b) any separate written statement of reasons for that decision; and
 (c) the notice of permission to appeal.

(4) When the Upper Tribunal receives a notice of appeal it must send a copy of the notice and any accompanying documents to each respondent.

(5) If the appellant lodges the notice of appeal with the Upper Tribunal after the end of the period mentioned in paragraph (1)—
 (a) the notice of appeal must—
  (i) include a request for an extension of time;
  (ii) explain why the notice of appeal was not provided in time; and
  (iii) state why it is said to be in the interests of justice that the time be extended; and
 (b) unless the Upper Tribunal extends the time for lodging a notice of appeal the Upper Tribunal must not admit the notice of appeal.

Response to the notice of appeal

14.125

5.—(1) Subject to any order given by the Upper Tribunal, a respondent may provide a written response to a notice of appeal.

(2) Any response provided under paragraph (1) must be sent or delivered to the Upper Tribunal so that it is received before the end of the period of 30 days beginning with the day on which the respondent is presumed to have received the copy of the notice of appeal as sent by the Upper Tribunal.

(3) The response must state—
 (a) the name and address of the respondent;
 (b) the name and address of the representative (if any) of the respondent;

(c) an address where documents for the respondent may be sent or delivered;
(d) whether the respondent opposes the appeal;
(e) the grounds on which the respondent relies, including any grounds on which the respondent was unsuccessful in the proceedings which are the subject of the appeal, but intends to rely on in the appeal.

(4) The response may include a request that the case be dealt with at a hearing or without a hearing.

(5) If the respondent provides the response to the Upper Tribunal later than the time required by paragraph (2) or by an extension of time allowed under rule 8(3)(a) (power to extend time), the response must include a request for an extension of time and the reason why the response was not provided in time.

(6) When the Upper Tribunal receives the response it must send a copy of the response and any accompanying documents to the appellant.

Appellant's reply

6.—(1) Subject to any order given by the Upper Tribunal, the appellant may provide a written reply to any response provided under rule 5 (response to the notice of appeal).

(2) Any reply provided under paragraph (1) must be sent or delivered to the Upper Tribunal so that it is received within the period of 30 days beginning with the day on which the appellant is presumed to have received a copy of the response as sent by the Upper Tribunal.

(3) If the appellant provides the reply to the Upper Tribunal later than the time required by paragraph (2) or by an extension of time allowed under rule 8(3)(a) (power to extend time), the reply must include a request for an extension of time and the reason why the reply was not provided in time.

(4) When the Upper Tribunal receives the reply it must send a copy of the reply and any accompanying documents to each respondent.

PART 4

GENERAL POWERS AND PROVISIONS

Delegation to staff

7.—(1) Staff of the Scottish Courts and Tribunals Service may, with the approval of the President, carry out functions of a judicial nature permitted or required to be undertaken by the Upper Tribunal, provided that they are of a preliminary or an incidental nature.

(2) The approval referred to in paragraph (1) may apply generally to the carrying out of specified functions by members of staff of a specified description in specified circumstances.

(3) Where the Upper Tribunal sends notice of a decision made by a member of staff pursuant to an approval under paragraph (1) to a party, that party may, within the period of 14 days beginning with the day on which the party is presumed to have received the notice, make a written application to the Upper Tribunal for that decision to be considered afresh by a member of the Upper Tribunal.

The Upper Tribunal for Scotland (Social Security Rules of Procedure) Reg 2018

Case management

14.128
8.—(1) Subject to the provisions of the 2014 Act and these Rules, the Upper Tribunal may regulate its own procedure.

(2) The Upper Tribunal may give an order in relation to the conduct of proceedings before it at any time, including an order amending, suspending or setting aside an earlier order.

(3) In particular, and without restricting the general powers in paragraphs (1) and (2), the Upper Tribunal may—
  (a) extend or shorten the time for complying with any rule or order;
  (b) conjoin or take concurrently two or more sets of proceedings or parts of proceedings raising common issues;
  (c) specify one or more cases as a lead case or lead cases where—
     (i) two or more cases are before the Upper Tribunal;
     (ii) in each such case the proceedings have not been finally determined; and
     (iii) the cases give rise to common or related issues of fact or law, and sist the other cases until the common or related issues have been determined;
  (d) permit or require a party to amend a document;
  (e) permit or require a party or another person to provide documents, information, evidence or submissions to the Upper Tribunal or a party;
  (f) deal with an issue in the proceedings as a preliminary issue;
  (g) hold a hearing to consider any matter, including a case management issue;
  (h) decide the form of any hearing;
  (i) adjourn or postpone a hearing;
  (j) require a party to produce or lodge documents including but not confined to a note of argument and the Appeal Appendix;
  (k) sist proceedings;
  (l) transfer proceedings to another court or tribunal if that other court or tribunal has jurisdiction in relation to the proceedings and—
     (i) because of a change of circumstances since the proceedings were started, the Upper Tribunal no longer has jurisdiction in relation to the proceedings; or
     (ii) the Upper Tribunal considers that the other court or tribunal is a more appropriate forum for the determination of the case;
  (m) suspend the effect of its own decision pending an appeal of that decision;
  (n) in an appeal against the decision of the First-tier Tribunal, suspend the effect of that decision pending the determination of any permission to appeal or any appeal;
  (o) require the First-tier Tribunal to provide reasons for the decision, or other information or documents in relation to the decision or any proceedings before the First-tier Tribunal.

GENERAL NOTE

Grounds of appeal may be amended under r.8(3)(d) but, in considering whether to permit an amendment to a notice of appeal, the Upper Tribunal is not only entitled to have regard to the timing of the application for permission to amend but must also consider whether any new ground of appeal meets the test for permission to appeal (*Sharma, Petitioner* [2023] CSOH 40 at [43] to [46]).

Procedure for applying for and giving orders

9.—(1) The Upper Tribunal may give an order on the application of one or more of the parties or on its own initiative.

(2) An application for an order may be made—
 (a) by sending or delivering a written application to the Upper Tribunal; or
 (b) orally during the course of a hearing.

(3) An application for an order must include the reasons for making that application.

(4) The Tribunal must send written notice of any order to each party to the case.

(5) If a party sent a notice of the order under paragraph (4) wishes to challenge the order, the party may do so by applying for another order which amends, suspends or sets aside the first order.

Failure to comply with rules etc.

10.—(1) An irregularity resulting from a failure to comply with any requirement in these Rules, a practice direction or an order, does not of itself render void the proceedings or any step taken in the proceedings.

(2) If a party has failed to comply with a requirement in these Rules, a practice direction or an order, the Upper Tribunal may take such action as it considers just, which may include—
 (a) waiving the requirement;
 (b) requiring the failure to be remedied; or
 (c) exercising its power under rule 11 (dismissal of a party's case).

Dismissal of a party's case

11.—(1) The Upper Tribunal must dismiss the whole or a part of the proceedings if the Upper Tribunal—
 (a) does not have jurisdiction in relation to the proceedings or that part of them; and
 (b) does not exercise its power under rule 8(3)(l) (transfer to another court or tribunal) in relation to the proceedings or that part of them.

(2) The Upper Tribunal may dismiss the whole or a part of the proceedings if—
 (a) the appellant has failed to comply with an order which stated that failure by the appellant to comply with the order could lead to the dismissal of the proceedings or part of them; or
 (b) the appellant has failed to co-operate with the Upper Tribunal to such an extent that the Upper Tribunal considers that it cannot deal with the proceedings fairly.

(3) The Upper Tribunal may not dismiss the whole or a part of the proceedings under paragraph (1) or (2)(b) without first giving the appellant an opportunity to make representations in relation to the proposed dismissal.

(4) If the proceedings, or part of them, have been dismissed under paragraph (2)(a), the appellant may apply for the proceedings, or part of them, to be reinstated, where the appellant can satisfy the Upper Tribunal that the appellant has good reason to apply for reinstatement.

(5) An application under paragraph (4) must be made in writing and received by the Upper Tribunal within the period of 31 days beginning with

The Upper Tribunal for Scotland (Social Security Rules of Procedure) Reg 2018

the day on which the notification sent to the appellant under paragraph (8) is presumed to have been received.

(6) An application under paragraph (4) must set out the reasons on which the appellant relies in applying for reinstatement.

(7) This rule applies to a respondent as it does to an appellant except that—
  (a) a reference to the dismissal of the proceedings is to be read as a reference to the barring of the respondent from taking further part in the proceedings; and
  (b) a reference to an application for the reinstatement of proceedings which have been dismissed is to be read as a reference to an application for the lifting of the bar on the respondent taking further part in the proceedings.

(8) The Upper Tribunal must notify each party in writing that dismissal has taken place.

Addition, substitution and removal of parties

14.132   **12.**—(1) The Upper Tribunal may give an order adding, substituting or removing a party as an appellant or a respondent including where—
  (a) the wrong person has been named as a party; or
  (b) the addition, substitution or removal has become necessary because of a change in circumstances since the start of proceedings.

(2) If the Upper Tribunal gives an order under paragraph (1) it may give such consequential orders as it considers appropriate.

(3) A person who is not a party may make a written application to the Upper Tribunal to be added or substituted as a party under this rule.

(4) If the Upper Tribunal refuses an application under paragraph (3) it must consider whether to permit the person who made the application to provide submissions or evidence to the Upper Tribunal.

Representatives

14.133   **13.**—(1) A party may be represented in any proceedings by a representative whose details may be communicated to the Upper Tribunal prior to any hearing.

(2) A party may show any document or communicate any information about the proceedings to that party's representative without contravening any prohibition or restriction on disclosure of the document or information.

(3) Where a document or information is disclosed under paragraph (2), the representative is subject to any prohibition or restriction on disclosure in the same way that the party is.

(4) For the avoidance of doubt, a party may be represented at a hearing by a person other than any person whose details have been communicated to the Upper Tribunal under paragraph (1).

Supporters

14.134   **14.** A party who is an individual may be accompanied by another person, who is not a representative, to act as a supporter.

Calculating time

14.135   **15.**—(1) An act required by these Rules, a practice direction or an order to be done on or by a particular day must be done by 5 pm on that day.

(2) If the time specified by these Rules, a practice direction or an order for doing any act ends on a day other than a working day, the act is done in time if it is done on the next working day.

(3) In this rule and in rule 28 (reviews), "working day" means any day except a Saturday, a Sunday, or a bank holiday in Scotland under section 1 of the Banking and Financial Dealings Act 1971.

Sending and delivery of documents

16.—(1) Any document to be provided to the Upper Tribunal under these Rules, a practice direction or an order must be—
  (a) sent by pre-paid post or by document exchange, or delivered to, the address of the Upper Tribunal; or
  (b) sent or delivered by such other method as the Upper Tribunal may permit or direct.

(2) Subject to paragraph (3), if a party provides a fax number, email address or other details for the electronic transmission of documents to them, that party must accept delivery of documents by that method.

(3) If a party informs the Upper Tribunal and all other parties that a particular form of communication, other than post, should not be used to provide documents to that party, that form of communication must not be so used.

(4) If the Upper Tribunal or a party sends a document to a party or the Upper Tribunal by email or any other electronic means of communication, the recipient may request that the sender provides a hard copy of the document to the recipient, and the recipient must make any such a request as soon as reasonably practicable after receiving the document electronically.

(5) The Upper Tribunal and each party may assume that the address provided by a party or its representative is and remains the address to which documents should be sent or delivered until receiving written notification to the contrary.

Disclosure of documents and information

17. [¹ —(1)] The Upper Tribunal may at any stage of the proceedings, on its own initiative or on application by one or more of the parties, make an order with a view to preventing or restricting the public disclosure of any aspect of those proceedings so far as it considers necessary in the interests of justice or in order to protect the Convention rights of any person.

[¹ (2) The Upper Tribunal may at any stage of proceedings, on its own initiative or on the request of one or more of the parties, give a direction prohibiting disclosure of a document or information to a person ("the recipient") if—
  (a) the document or information relates to the physical or mental health of a person,
  (b) a registered medical practitioner or registered nurse has informed either the Upper Tribunal, or one or more of the parties, that disclosure of the information would be likely to cause serious harm to the physical or mental health of the recipient or some other person,

(c) the Upper Tribunal is satisfied that such disclosure would be likely to cause serious harm to the physical or mental health of the recipient or some other person, and

(d) the Upper Tribunal is satisfied, having regard to the interests of justice, that it is proportionate to give such a direction.

(3) If a party considers that the Upper Tribunal should give a direction under paragraph (2) prohibiting the disclosure of a document or information to a person ("the recipient"), the party must provide to the Upper Tribunal the document or information, and the reason the party is requesting that it be withheld, so that the Upper Tribunal may decide whether the document or information should be disclosed to the recipient or should be subject of a direction under paragraph (2).

(4) The Upper Tribunal must conduct proceedings as appropriate in order to give effect to a direction given under paragraph (2).

(5) If the Upper Tribunal gives a direction under paragraph (2) which prevents disclosure to a party who has a representative, or any other person acting on their behalf, the Upper Tribunal may give a direction that the document or information be disclosed to that representative or person if the Upper Tribunal is satisfied that—

(a) disclosure to the representative or person would be in the interests of the party, and

(b) the representative or person will act in accordance with paragraph (6).

(6) Documents or information disclosed to a representative or person in accordance with a direction under paragraph (5) must not be disclosed either directly or indirectly to any other person without the Upper Tribunal's consent.]

AMENDMENT

1. First-tier Tribunal for Scotland Social Security Chamber and Upper Tribunal for Scotland (Rules of Procedure) (Miscellaneous Amendment) Regulations 2022 (SSI 2022/162) r.3 (June 21, 2022).

GENERAL NOTE

14.138   Paragraphs (2) to (6) are in terms very similar to those of r.14(2) to (6) of the Tribunal Procedure (Upper Tribunal) Rules 2008 (see Vol.III), save that it is expressly provided that the relevant documents and the feared harm must both relate to a person's health.

Evidence and submissions

14.139   **18.**—(1) Without restriction on the general powers in rule 8(1) and (2) (case management powers), the Upper Tribunal may give orders as to—

(a) issues on which parties may lead fresh evidence or make submissions;

(b) the nature of any such evidence;

(c) whether the parties are permitted to provide expert evidence, and if so whether the parties must jointly appoint a single expert to provide such evidence;

(d) any limit on the number of witnesses whose evidence a party may put forward, whether in relation to a particular issue or generally;

(e) the manner in which any evidence or submissions are to be provided, which may include an order for them to be given—
  (i) orally at a hearing; or
  (ii) by written submissions or witness statement; and
(f) the time at which any evidence or submissions are to be provided.

(2) The Upper Tribunal may exclude evidence that would otherwise be admissible where—
  (a) the evidence was not, without reasonable excuse, provided within the time allowed by an order or a practice direction;
  (b) the evidence was otherwise, without reasonable excuse, provided in a manner that did not comply with an order or a practice direction; or
  (c) it would otherwise be unfair to admit the evidence.

(3) The Upper Tribunal may consent to a witness giving, or require any witness to give, evidence on oath or affirmation, and may administer an oath or affirmation for that purpose.

Citation of witnesses and orders to answer questions or produce documents

19.—(1) On the application of a party or on its own initiative, the Upper Tribunal may—
  (a) by citation require any person to attend as a witness at a hearing at the time and place specified in the citation; or
  (b) order any person to answer any questions or produce any documents in that person's possession or control which relate to any issue in the proceedings.

(2) A citation under paragraph (1)(a) must—
  (a) give the person required to attend 14 days' notice prior to the day of the hearing or such other period as the Upper Tribunal may order;
  (b) where the person is not a party, state how expenses of attendance necessarily incurred may be recovered;
  (c) state that the person on whom the requirement is imposed may apply to the Upper Tribunal to vary or set aside the citation or order, if the person did not have an opportunity to object to it before it was made or issued; and
  (d) state the consequences of failure to comply with the citation or order.

(3) A person making an application referred to in sub-paragraph (2)(c) must do so as soon as reasonably practicable after receiving notice of the citation or order.

(4) No person may be compelled to give any evidence or produce any document that the person could not be compelled to give or produce at a civil trial of an action in a court of law in Scotland.

Withdrawal

20.—(1) Subject to paragraph (2), a party may give notice to the Upper Tribunal of the withdrawal of the party's case, or any part of that case—
  (a) by sending or delivering to the Upper Tribunal a notice of withdrawal; or
  (b) orally at a hearing.

(2) Notice of withdrawal will not take effect unless the Upper Tribunal consents to the withdrawal except in relation to an application for permission to appeal.

(3) Unless satisfied that a party has already been notified, the Upper Tribunal must notify each party in writing that a withdrawal has taken effect under this rule.

(4) Where a case has been withdrawn in accordance with paragraphs (1) and (2), the party which has withdrawn its case may apply to the Upper Tribunal for the case to be reinstated, where the party can satisfy the Tribunal that the party has good reason to apply for reinstatement.

(5) An application under paragraph (4) must be made in writing and be received by the Upper Tribunal within the period of 31 days beginning with the earlier of—
   (a) the day on which the party which has withdrawn its case is presumed to have received the notification sent under paragraph (3) that the withdrawal has taken effect; or
   (b) if the party which has withdrawn its case was present at the hearing when the case was withdrawn orally under paragraph (1)(b), the day of that hearing.

(6) An application under paragraph (4) must set out the reasons on which the applicant relies in applying for reinstatement of the case.

Chairing member

14.142 21. Where a matter is to be decided by two or more members of the Upper Tribunal, the President must determine the chairing member.

PART 5

Hearings

Decision with or without a hearing

14.143 22.—(1) Subject to paragraph (2), the Upper Tribunal may make any decision without a hearing.

(2) The Upper Tribunal must have regard to any view expressed by any party when deciding whether to hold a hearing to consider any matter, and the form of any such hearing.

Entitlement to attend a hearing

14.144 23. Subject to the power to exclude persons in rule 25(4) (public and private hearings), each party is entitled to participate at a hearing together with any representatives and supporters permitted by rules 13 (representatives) and 14 (supporters).

Notice of hearings

14.145 24.—(1) The Upper Tribunal must give each party entitled to attend a hearing reasonable notice of the time and place of the hearing (including any adjourned or postponed hearing) and any change to the time and place of the hearing.

(2) The period of notice under paragraph (1) must be at least 14 days prior to the day of the hearing except that the Upper Tribunal may give shorter notice—
  (a) with the consent of the parties; or
  (b) in urgent or exceptional circumstances.

Public and private hearings

25.—(1) Subject to the following paragraphs, all hearings must be held in public.

(2) The Upper Tribunal may give an order that a hearing, or part of it, is to be held in private if the Upper Tribunal considers that restricting access to the hearing is justified—
  (a) in the interests of public order;
  (b) in order to protect a person's right to respect for their private and family life;
  (c) in order to maintain the confidentiality of sensitive information;
  (d) in order to avoid serious harm to the public interest; or
  (e) because to hold it in public would prejudice the interests of justice.

(3) Where a hearing, or any part of it, is to be held in private, the Upper Tribunal may determine who is entitled to attend the hearing or part of it.

(4) The Upper Tribunal may give an order excluding from any hearing, or part of it—
  (a) any person whose conduct the Upper Tribunal considers is disrupting or is likely to disrupt the hearing;
  (b) any person whose presence the Upper Tribunal considers is likely to prevent another person from giving evidence or making submissions freely; or
  (c) any person where the purpose of the hearing would be defeated by the attendance of that person.

(5) The Upper Tribunal may give a direction excluding a witness from a hearing until that witness gives evidence.

(6) When publishing a decision in terms of rule 27(4) (notice of decisions and reasons) following a hearing which was held wholly or partly in private, the Upper Tribunal must, so far as practicable, ensure that the decision does not disclose information which was referred to in a part of the hearing that was held in private.

Hearings in a party's absence

26. If a party fails to attend a hearing, the Upper Tribunal may proceed with the hearing if the Upper Tribunal—
  (a) is satisfied that the party has been notified of the hearing or that reasonable steps have been taken to notify the party of the hearing; and
  (b) considers that it is in the interests of justice to proceed with the hearing.

The Upper Tribunal for Scotland (Social Security Rules of Procedure) Reg 2018

PART 6

DECISIONS

Notice of decisions and reasons

14.148

27.—(1) Subject to the remainder of this rule, the Upper Tribunal may give a decision orally at a hearing.

(2) The Upper Tribunal must provide to each party as soon as reasonably practicable after making a decision (other than a decision under Part 7 (appealing decisions of the Upper Tribunal)) which finally disposes of all issues in the proceedings or on a preliminary issue dealt with following an order under rule 8(3)(f) (dealing with an issue as a preliminary issue)—
   (a) a decision notice stating the Upper Tribunal's decision; and
   (b) notification of any rights of appeal against the decision and the time and manner in which such rights of appeal may be exercised.

(3) If the Upper Tribunal does not provide written reasons for a decision, a party may request written reasons, within the period of 14 days beginning with the day of the decision.

(4) The Upper Tribunal may publish any of its decisions if it considers it in the public interest so to do, with the manner of publication also at the discretion of the Upper Tribunal.

Reviews

14.149

28.—(1) The Upper Tribunal may at its own instance or at the request of a party review a decision (except an excluded decision) made by it if it considers it necessary in the interests of justice to do so and on review it may confirm, set aside, or set aside and re-decide the decision.

(2) An application under paragraph (1) must be made in writing within the period of 14 days beginning with the day of the decision and must state the reasons for making the application.

(3) The Upper Tribunal must send a copy of the application to any other party involved in the proceedings within the period of 10 working days beginning with the day of receipt of the application.

(4) The review must be decided as soon as reasonably practicable by the Upper Tribunal, with insofar as practicable the same members that decided the case, or where this is not practicable with members selected by the President.

(5) A notice of the decision on a review under paragraph (1) must as soon as reasonably practicable be sent by the Upper Tribunal to each party.

(6) The 30 days referred to in regulation 3(1) of the 2016 Regulations in respect of an application to the Upper Tribunal is extended by any review period.

PART 7

APPEALING DECISIONS OF THE UPPER TRIBUNAL

Interpretation

14.150

29. In this Part, "appeal" means the exercise of a right of appeal under section 48(1) of the 2014 Act.

Application for permission to appeal a decision of the Upper Tribunal

30.—(1) A party seeking permission to appeal must make a written application to the Upper Tribunal.

(2) An application under paragraph (1) must—
(a) identify the decision of the Upper Tribunal to which it relates;
(b) identify the alleged point or points of law raised in relation to the decision; and
(c) state in terms of section 50(4) of the 2014 Act what important point of principle or practice would be raised by a second appeal or what other compelling reason there is that shows the appeal should be allowed to proceed.

Upper Tribunal's consideration of application for permission to appeal

31.—(1) The Upper Tribunal must consider whether to give permission to appeal in relation to the decision or part of it.

(2) The Upper Tribunal must provide a record of its decision to the parties as soon as practicable.

(3) If the Upper Tribunal refuses permission to appeal it must provide with the record of its decision—
(a) a statement of its reasons for such a refusal; and
(b) notification of the right to make an application to the Court of Session for permission to appeal and the time within which, and the method by which, such application must be made.

(4) The Upper Tribunal may give permission to appeal on limited grounds, but must comply with paragraph (3) in relation to any grounds on which it has refused permission.

PART 8

LEGAL AID

Legal aid

32. If a party is granted legal aid by the Scottish Legal Aid Board in respect of a case before the Upper Tribunal that party must as soon as practicable send a copy of the legal aid certificate to the Upper Tribunal.

The Social Security Appeals (Expenses and Allowances) (Scotland) Regulations 2018

(SSI 2018/275)

Made   *11th September 2018*
Laid before the Scottish Parliament   *13th September 2018*
Coming into force   *22nd November 2018*

The Social Security Appeals (Expenses and Allowances) Regulations 2018

The Scottish Ministers make the following Regulations in exercise of the powers conferred by section 95 of the Social Security (Scotland) Act 2018 and all other powers enabling them to do so.

Citation and commencement

14.154 **1.** These Regulations may be cited as the Social Security Appeals (Expenses and Allowances) (Scotland) Regulations 2018 and come into force on 22nd November 2018.

Interpretation

14.155 **2.** In these Regulations—
"electronic communication" has the meaning given to it by section 15(1) of the Electronic Communications Act 2001;
"hearing" means an oral hearing and includes a hearing conducted in whole or in part by video link, telephone or other means of instantaneous two-way electronic communication; and
"party" means a person who is an appellant or a respondent in proceedings described in regulation 3(1).

Payment of expenses

14.156 **3.**—(1) Paragraph (2) applies to proceedings relating to the exercise by the Scottish Ministers of functions conferred on them [¹ by the Social Security (Scotland) Act 2018, by regulations made under that Act or by the Carer's Allowance Supplement and Young Carer Grants (Residence Requirements and Procedural Provisions) (EU Exit) (Scotland) Regulations 2020, before]—
  (a) the First-tier Tribunal for Scotland Social Security Chamber; or
  (b) the Upper Tribunal for Scotland.
(2) The Scottish Courts and Tribunals Service may pay a party and any witness cited to attend a hearing—
  (a) expenses in respect of travel and subsistence;
  (b) allowances for loss of remunerative time,
reasonably incurred as a result of attending the hearing.
(3) Paragraph (2) does not apply to a representative of the Scottish Ministers.
(4) Expenses and allowances are to be paid at such level, and under such circumstances, as the Scottish Ministers may determine.

AMENDMENT

1. Carer's Allowance Supplement and Young Carer Grants (Residence Requirements and Procedural Provisions) (EU Exit) (Scotland) Regulations 2020 (SSI 2020/475) sch.2 para.15 (December 24, 2020).

The First-tier Tribunal for Scotland (Allocation of Functions to the Social Security Chamber) Regulations 2018

(SSI 2018/350)

Made *14th November 2018*
Coming into force *22nd November 2018*

(SSI 2018/350)

The Scottish Ministers make the following Regulations in exercise of the powers conferred by sections 20(2) and 79(1)(b) of the Tribunals (Scotland) Act 2014 and all other powers enabling them to do so.

In accordance with section 11(1) of that Act, they have obtained the approval of the Lord President for the making of these Regulations and have consulted such other persons as they considered appropriate.

In accordance with section 79(2)(a) of that Act, a draft of this instrument has been laid before and approved by resolution of the Scottish Parliament.

Citation and commencement

1.—(1) These Regulations may be cited as the First-tier Tribunal for Scotland (Allocation of Functions to the Social Security Chamber) Regulations 2018.

(2) These Regulations come into force on 22nd November 2018.

Interpretation

2. In these Regulations—
"the 2018 Act" means the Social Security (Scotland) Act 2018; and
"the First-tier Tribunal" means the First-tier Tribunal for Scotland.

Allocation of social security functions to the Social Security Chamber

3.—(1) The social security functions of the First-tier Tribunal are allocated to the Social Security Chamber.

(2) [¹ The social security functions of the First-tier Tribunal are the functions conferred on the Tribunal by—
(a) the 2018 Act;
(b) regulations made under the 2018 Act; and
(c) the Carer's Allowance Supplement and Young Carer Grants (Residence Requirements and Procedural Provisions) (EU Exit) (Scotland) Regulations 2020.]

AMENDMENT

1. First-tier Tribunal for Scotland Social Security Chamber and Upper Tribunal for Scotland (Allocation of Functions, Procedure and Composition) (Miscellaneous Amendments) Regulations 2020 (SSI 2020/476) reg.2 (December 24, 2020).

Scope of consideration by the Social Security Chamber

4. The First-tier Tribunal Social Security Chamber may consider all aspects of a determination or a decision which it is called upon to consider, in exercising the functions allocated to it by regulation 3, and not only the particular aspect challenged by the party appealing against the determination or decision.

GENERAL NOTE

This provision appears designed to have the same effect as s.12(8)(a) of the Social Security Act 1998 in Great Britain (see Vol.III).

Chamber president

5. *Omitted.*

INDEX

LEGAL TAXONOMY
FROM SWEET & MAXWELL

This index has been prepared using Sweet and Maxwell's Legal Taxonomy. Main index entries conform to keywords provided by the Legal Taxonomy except where references to specific documents or non-standard terms (denoted by quotation marks) have been included. These keywords provide a means of identifying similar concepts in other Sweet & Maxwell publications and online services to which keywords from the Legal Taxonomy have been applied. Readers may find some minor differences between terms used in the text and those which appear in the index. Suggestions to *sweetandmaxwell.taxonomy@thomson.com*.

(All references are to paragraph number)

Abatement
  carer support payments, 13.512
Additional payments
  tax credits
    disapplication of legislation, 2.568–2.569
Additional statutory paternity pay
  adoption, 1.128
  birth
    entitlement, 1.127
  contracting out, 1.132–1.133
  contractual remuneration, and, 1.134–1.135
  entitlement
    adoption, 1.128
    birth, 1.127
    statutory provision, 1.127–1.129
  liability of Commissioners, 1.130
  NHS employees, 6.144
  overseas adoptions
    application of other Regulations, 6.143
  pay period, 1.131
  payment, 1.130
  rate, 1.131
Additional Statutory Paternity Pay (Adoption), etc Regulations 2010
  arrangement, 6.139
  citation, 6.140
  commencement, 6.140
  definitions, 6.141
  general provision, 6.143
  revocation, 6.142
Administration of benefits
  See **Administrative requirements**
Administrative requirements (statutory adoption pay)
  adoption from overseas, 6.110–6.114
  determination of entitlement issues
    application, 6.30
    form of application, 6.31
  employers' records
    generally, 6.26
    inspection, 6.27

  funding of liabilities
    application to Revenue, 6.21
    date of payment of contributions, 6.24
    generally, 6.20
    method, 6.22–6.23
    overpayments, 6.25
    provision of information, 6.32
Administrative requirements (statutory maternity pay)
  employer's records
    maintenance, 5.47
    production, 5.48
  expected week of confinement, 5.41
  notice of absence from work, 5.42
  notification of employment after confinement, 5.43
  provision of information
    claims for other benefits, 5.46
    determination of questions, 5.44–5.45
Administrative requirements (statutory parental bereavement pay)
  applications, 8.44
  date when contributions treated as paid, 8.38
  decision on issues arising, 8.43
  definitions, 8.33
  entitlement, 8.42–8.43
  funding of employers' liabilities
    applications, 8.35
    deductions from payments to Commissioners, 8.36
    generally, 8.34
    payment to employers, 8.37
  overpayments, 8.39
  payment to employers, 8.37
  provision of information, 8.45
  records by employers
    generally, 8.40
    inspection, 8.41
  Regulations, 8.31–8.45

Index

Administrative requirements (statutory paternity pay)
adoption from overseas, 6.110–6.114
determination of entitlement issues
  application, 6.30
  form of application, 6.31
employers' records
  generally, 6.26
  inspection, 6.27
funding of liabilities
  application to Revenue, 6.21
  date of payment of contributions, 6.24
  generally, 6.20
  method, 6.22–6.23
  overpayments, 6.25
provision of information, 6.32

Administrative requirements (tax credits)
definitions, 2.441
general note, 2.439
forwarding of claims, 2.444
holding of claims, 2.444
provision of information
  by authorities, 2.443
  to authorities, 2.442
recording of claims, 2.444
statutory provision, 1.435–1.436

Adopted children
child benefit
  Regulations, 3.21
guardian's allowance
  Regulations, 3.71
  statutory provision, 1.46

Adoption
child tax credit
  continuation, 2.307–2.308
  generally, 2.301–2.302
statutory paternity pay
  common provisions, 6.66–6.70
  conditions of entitlement, 6.59–6.60
  evidence requirements, 6.56, 6.63
  notice requirements, 6.56–6.57, 6.63–6.64
  periods of payment, 6.54, 6.61
  qualifying period, 6.55, 6.62
  statutory provisions, 1.119–1.120
  treatment of more than one employer, 6.65
statutory shared parental pay
  conditions, 7.55–7.68
  definitions, 7.20–7.21
  entitlement, 7.37–7.54
  general note, 7.18
working tax credit, 2.135–2.138

Adoption from overseas
See **Intercountry adoption**

Adoption pay
See **Statutory adoption pay**

Adoptive parents
annual payments
  England and Wales, 1.812
  Scotland, 1.813
meaning, 6.34

Adult disability payments
See also **Child disability payments**
admission to care home
  calculation of periods of time spent, 13.396
  generally, 13.392
after an interval
  age criteria, 13.388
  relevant date, 13.378
age criteria
  after an interval, 13.388
  exceptions, 13.388–13.389
  further criteria, 13.108
  generally, 13.387
  persons reached relevant age, 13.389–13.390
aircraft workers, 13.382
alternative accommodation, 13.397
amount
  generally, 13.399
  transitional provision, 13.443
applications
  date, 13.400
  entitled individuals, by, 13.423
  initial period, 13.422
  terminal illness, where, 13.424
appointees, 13.448
assessments
  qualifications and experience of assessor, 13.426
authorised vehicle providers, 13.420
care homes
  calculation of periods of time spent, 13.396
  generally, 13.392
change of circumstances, 13.413
civil servants, 13.381
commencement date, 13.400
conditions
  presence, 13.379–13.386
  required period, 13.372–13.378
  residence, 13.379–13.386
consideration of entitlement after specified period, 13.412
continental shelf operations, 13.382
continuing eligibility, 13.402
daily living component
  daily living activities, 13.432
  determination of ability to carry out activity, 13.368
  generally, 13.366
  required period condition, 13.372–13.373
  scoring for activities, 13.369, 13.371
decrease in level of entitlement, 13.411
deduction, by
  determination to effect a decision, 13.416
  generally, 13.409
definitions, 13.363
detention under law
  calculation of periods of time spent, 13.396
  generally, 13.395

Index

determination of ability to carry out activity, 13.368
determination without application of entitlement, 13.441
Disability Living Allowance, and, 13.444
effecting a deduction decision, 13.416
eligibility
 age criteria, 13.387–13.390
 alternative accommodation, 13.397
 care home stays, 13.392
 continuation, 13.402
 daily living component, 13.366–13.371
 exclusions, 13.365
 hospices, 13.394
 hospital stays, 13.393–13.394
 legal detention, 13.395–13.396
 mobility component, 13.367–13.371
 presence condition, 13.379–13.386
 required period condition, 13.372–13.378
 residence condition, 13.379–13.386
 terminal illness, 13.391
entitlement
 date, 13.400
 determination without application, 13.441
 generally, 13.442
 other benefits, to, 13.365
errors
 overpayments, 13.415
 underpayments, 13.414
exclusions, 13.365
extent of disability and needs, 13.108
extinguishment of right to apply for PIP, 13.360–13.361
final provisions, 13.112
financial circumstances, 13.108
form
 generally, 13.399
 transitional provision, 13.443
further criteria, 13.108
generally, 13.20
HM Forces personnel, 13.381
hospices, 13.394
hospital stays
 calculation of periods of time spent, 13.396
 exceptions, 13.394
 generally, 13.393
imprisonment
 calculation of periods of time spent, 13.396
 generally, 13.395
increase in level of entitlement, 13.410
initial period for applications
 generally, 13.422
 miscellaneous provisions, 13.435
 transitory provision, 13.429
legal detention
 calculation of periods of time spent, 13.396
 generally, 13.395

level of entitlement
 decrease, 13.411
 increase, 13.410
mariners, 13.382
miscellaneous provisions, 13.107–13.112
mobility component
 determination of ability to carry out activity, 13.368
 generally, 13.367
 mobility activities, 13.433
 required period condition, 13.374–13.375
 scoring for activities, 13.370–13.371
moving to another part of UK, 13.417–13.418
nature of disability and needs, 13.108
notice of intention to transfer, 13.440
official errors
 overpayments, 13.415
 underpayments, 13.414
overpayments, 13.415
overview, 13.364
payments
 amount, 13.399
 authorised vehicle providers, 13.420
 commencement date, 13.400
 deduction, by, 13.409
 form, 13.399
 generally, 13.398
 overpayments, 13.415
 timing, 13.401
 underpayments, 13.414
period condition
 daily living component, 13.372–13.373
 mobility component, 13.374–13.375
 relevant date, 13.376–13.378
person to whom relevant EU regulation applies
 no entitlement to daily living component where UK is not competent state, 13.385
 residing in UK, 13.383
 residing outside UK, 13.384
personal independence payment
 extinguishment of right to apply for, 13.360–13.361
 paid in another part of UK before moving to Scotland, 13.417
persons reaching the relevant age
 determination of award, 13.390
 generally, 13.388
 other exceptions, 13.389
presence condition
 aircraft workers, 13.382
 civil servants, 13.381
 continental shelf operations, 13.382
 further criteria, 13.108
 generally, 13.379
 HM Forces personnel, 13.381
 mariners, 13.382
 person to whom relevant EU regulation applies, 13.383–13.385

1853

Index

refugees, 13.386
  temporary absence, 13.381
qualifications and experience of assessors, 13.426
rates, 13.399
receipt of other state assistance, 13.108
re-determination of entitlement
  generally, 13.412
  periods in respect of a request, 13.419
  transitional provision, 13.445
refugees, 13.386
Regulations (consequential and etc provisions)
  general provisions, 13.359–13.361
Regulations (general)
  citation, 13.362
  commencement, 13.362
  consequential amendments, 13.428
  definitions, 13.363
  overview, 13.364
  schedules, 13.431–13.437
  transitory provision, 13.429–13.430
Regulations (transitional provisions)
  citation, 13.438
  commencement, 13.438
  definitions, 13.439
  miscellaneous amendments, 13.454
  review of entitlement, 13.449–13.453
  transfer to ADP, 13.440–13.448
relevant date
  after an interval, 13.378
  generally, 13.376–13.377
required period condition
  daily living component, 13.372–13.373
  mobility component, 13.374–13.375
  relevant date, 13.376–13.378
residence condition
  aircraft workers, 13.382
  civil servants, 13.381
  continental shelf operations, 13.382
  further criteria, 13.108
  generally, 13.379
  HM Forces personnel, 13.381
  mariners, 13.382
  person to whom relevant EU regulation applies, 13.383–13.385
  refugees, 13.386
  temporary absence, 13.381
review of entitlement
  cessation date, 13.453
  change of circumstances, 13.451
  date of decrease, 13.453
  date of increase, 13.452
  determination without application, 13.449
  Regulations, 13.449–13.453
  time of payment, 13.450
scoring for activities
  daily living component, 13.369
  further provision, 13.371
  mobility component, 13.370

short-term assistance
  generally, 13.427
  miscellaneous provisions, 13.434
suspension
  effect of termination, 13.408
  generally, 13.127
  having regard to financial circumstances, 13.404
  information to be given after, 13.405
  relevant circumstances, 13.403
  right to review, 13.406
  termination, 13.407
temporary absence from Common Travel Area, 13.381
terminal illness cases
  determination of entitlement, 13.424
  generally, 13.109
  special rules, 13.391
  transitional provision, 13.446
time limit for applications, 13.108
time of payment
  generally, 13.401
  transitional provision, 13.443
transfer to
  amount of payment, 13.443
  appointees, 13.448
  determination without application of entitlement, 13.441
  effect on Disability Living Allowance, 13.444
  entitlement, 13.442
  form of payment, 13.443
  generally, 13.425
  miscellaneous provisions, 13.436
  modification of regulations, 14.430
  notice of intention, 13.440
  redetermination request period, 13.445
  Regulations, 13.440–13.448
  terminal illness, 13.446
  time of payment, 13.443
transitional provisions
  definitions, 13.439
  extinguishment of right to apply for PIP, 13.360–13.361
  miscellaneous amendments, 13.454
  Regulations, 13.438–13.454
  review of entitlement, 13.449–13.453
  transfer to ADP, 13.440–13.448
transitory provision
  exclusion, 13.430
  initial period for applications, 13.429
types, 13.110–13.111
underpayments, 13.414
vehicles for persons with disabilities
  payment to authorised providers, 13.420
  powers of appointees, 13.424
Advance claims
  generally, 2.362–2.363
  working tax credit, 2.364–2.365
"Advance funding"
  statutory maternity pay, 5.88

Index

Advance payments
universal credit, 2.66–2.68
Age
carer support payments, 13.498
statutory pay, 1.184
"Age 7 payments"
child trust funds, 9.18
Agency workers
employment income, 1.514
Air crew
carer support payments, 13.503
statutory adoption pay, 1.157–1.158
statutory maternity pay, 1.110
statutory paternity pay, 1.138–1.139
statutory sick pay
definitions, 4.52, 4.58–4.59, 4.65
general note, 4.49
statutory provision, 1.96
time for compliance, 4.67
Allocation (contributions)
child benefit, 3.5
Amendments
claims, 2.351
Amendments (tax returns)
Revenue, by
during enquiry, 1.11
generally, 1.8
taxpayer, by
during enquiry, 1.10
generally, 1.7
Amount treated as income of settlor
See **Settlement income**
Annual payments
adopters, to
England and Wales, 1.812
Scotland, 1.813
employment insurance payments, 1.810–1.811
foreign maintenance payments, 1.805
health insurance payments, 1.810–1.811
pension income, 2.221
periodical payments of personal injury damages
compensation awards, 1.807
generally, 1.806
persons entitled, 1.808
trusts, from, 1.809
Annual reports
tax credits, 1.416–1.417
"Annual review"
tax credits, 1.418–1.419
Annuities
life annuity payments
charge to tax, 1.788
income charged, 1.790
meaning, 1.789
person liable, 1.791
pension income, 2.221
Appeal notices
child trust funds
disputes concerning, 9.95–9.96
prescribed form, 9.87–9.88
service, 9.93–9.94

signature, 9.87–9.88
statutory provision, 1.705
Appeals
see also **Appeals (child trust funds)**,
Appeals (tax credits)
charge-free childcare
decision to decline to make determination, 11.46
determination as to qualifying child, 11.47
following review, 11.45–11.49
imposition of penalty, 11.48
settlement by agreement, 11.49
child trust funds
appealable decisions, 1.703–1.704
exercise of right, 1.705
general regulations, 9.90–9.100
notice of appeal, 9.84–9.89
penalties, 1.702
temporary modifications, 1.706
First-tier Tribunal, to, 1.226–1.227
late appeals
child trust fund appeals, 9.97–9.98
tax credit appeals, 2.455–2.456
settlement by agreement, 1.21–1.27
tax credits
appealable decisions, 1.402–1.409
exercise of right, 1.411–1.412
general regulations, 2.445–2.457
late appeals, 1.413–1.415
settlement, 1.21–1.27, 2.559–2.561
temporary modifications, 1.445–1.446
transition to universal credit, and, 1.410
tax-free childcare
definitions, 10.46
finality of decisions, 10.47
general note, 10.44
settlement by agreement, 10.49
tax returns
no questioning amounts of social security income, 1.28
notification of taxable amounts of social security income, 1.29–1.30
settlement by agreement, 1.21–1.27
universal credit
certain existing benefits, 2.59–2.60
generally, 2.61–2.62
tax credits, 1.410
verification of claims, 2.444
Appeals (child trust funds)
assessment of tax returns, 1.22–1.23
death of party, 9.99–9.100
decisions of Board, 1.236–1.237
definitions, 9.91–9.92
exercise of right
generally, 1.238–1.241, 1.705
regulations, 1.242–1.243
general regulations
citation, 9.91
commencement, 9.91
definitions, 9.91–9.92
duration, 9.91

1855

general provisions, 9.93–9.100
recitals, 9.90
late appeals, 9.97–9.98
notice of appeal
  disputes concerning, 9.95–9.96
  prescribed form, 9.87–9.88
  service, 9.93–9.94
  signature, 9.87–9.88
  statutory provision, 1.705
penalties, 1.702
Regulations
  general, 9.90–9.100
  notice of appeal, 9.84–9.89
service of notices or documents, 9.93–9.94
temporary modifications, 1.706
time limits, 9.97–9.98

Appeals (tax credits)
appealable decisions
  generally, 1.402–1.409
  transition to universal credit, and, 1.410
assessment of tax returns, 1.22–1.23
death of party, 2.457
decisions of Board, 1.238–1.241
definitions, 2.447–2.448
directions
  death of party, 2.457
exercise of right
  generally, 1.411–1.412
  other persons, 2.451–2.452
extensions of time, 2.455–2.456
general regulations
  general matters, 2.451–2.457
  service of notices, 2.449–2.450
late appeals
  generally, 1.413–1.415
  other persons, 2.455–2.456
'party to the proceedings', 2.448
Regulations
  general, 2.445–2.457
relevant decisions
  generally, 1.402–1.409
  transition to universal credit, and, 1.410
right of appeal
  decisions of Board, 1.238–1.241
  generally, 1.411–1.412
  other persons, 2.451–2.452
service of notices, 2.449–2.450
settlement, 2.559–2.561
temporary modifications, 1.445–1.446
time limits
  extension, 2.455–2.456
  generally, 2.453–2.454
transition to universal credit, and, 1.410

Approval of Child Care Providers Scheme
See **Childcare Approval Scheme**

Armed forces
carer support payments, 13.502

Aspect enquiries
amendment by taxpayer, 1.10
completion, 1.13
correction by Revenue, 1.11
notice, 1.9

Assault
HMRC officers, 1.870

Assignment
tax credits, 1.426–1.427

Asylum seekers
definitions, 2.466
exclusion from entitlement, 2.467–2.473
general note, 2.468
modifications of Act, 2.472–2.473
statutory provision, 1.420–1.421
transitional relief, 2.474–2.475

Attendance allowance
social security income, 2.233

"Avoidance of liability"
statutory adoption pay
  adoption from overseas, 6.137
  generally, 6.81
statutory maternity pay, 5.7–5.8
statutory paternity pay
  adoption from overseas, 6.128
  generally, 6.70
statutory sick pay, 4.11

Back payments
carer support payments, 13.516

Back to work bonus
social security income, 2.233

Backdating
See **Back payments**

Bad debts
trading income, 1.748

Bankruptcy
tax credits, 1.426–1.427

Basic element
See also **Working tax credit**
adoption, 2.135–2.138
alteration in hours worked due to coronavirus, 2.151
ceasing to undertake work, 2.149–2.150
childbirth, 2.135–2.138
gaps between jobs, 2.152–2.153
ill health, 2.139–2.140
parental bereavement, 2.135–2.138
pay in lieu of notice, 2.147–2.148
qualifying remunerative work, and
  excepted activities, 2.133
  generally, 2.127–2.129
  hours worked, 2.134
  minimum level of continuity, 2.131
  remunerative work, 2.132
  routes to entitlement, 2.130
seasonal work, 2.141–2.142
strike periods, 2.143–2.144
suspension from work, 2.145–2.146
term-time work, 2.141–2.142
working less than 16, 24 or 30 hours a week, 2.149–2.150

Benefit cap
generally, 1.896–1.897
universal credit, 2.50–2.52

Benefits Code
See also **Employment income, Taxable benefits**
definitions, 1.518

Index

meaning, 1.516
relationship with earnings, 1.517
Bereavement
See also **Statutory parental bereavement pay**
generally, 1.1073
working tax credit, 2.135–2.138
Bereavement support payments
social security income, 2.233
Best start grants
See also **Scotland**
application in connection with another child, 13.144
'assessment period', 13.141
assistance being awarded, 13.140
award of Scottish child payment, 13.147
backdated award of assistance, 13.146
being responsible for a child, 13.137
'birthday', 13.133
competing claims, 13.148
'dependant', 13.138
determination without application
application in connection with another child, 13.144
award of Scottish child payment, 13.147
backdated award of assistance, 13.146
official error, 13.145
early learning grant
eligibility, 13.160
types of assistance, 13.161
interpretation
personal relationships, 13.136–13.138
social security assistance, 13.139–13.20
timing, 13.131–13.135
late applications
nomination of date, 13.132
months, 13.134–13.135
nomination of date, 13.132
official error, 13.145
'partner', 13.136
personal relationships
being responsible for a child, 13.137
'dependant', 13.138
'partner', 13.136
pregnancy and baby grants
basic amount, 13.154
'birth', 13.157
'born', 13.157
'child', 13.157
definitions, 13.157–13.159
'domestic abuse', 13.159
eligibility, 13.149–13.152
form, 13.156
multiple pregnancy supplement, 13.155
residence requirement, 13.152
'sure start maternity grant', 13.158
time limit for application, 13.150–13.151
types of assistance, 13.153–13.156
value, 13.153
procedural matters
competing claims, 13.148

determination without application, 13.144–13.127
re-determination timescales, 13.142–13.143
re-determination timescales, 13.142–13.143
Regulations
citation, 13.128
commencement, 13.128
interpretation, 13.131–13.141
overview, 13.129
schedules, 13.142–13.164
school age grant
eligibility, 13.162
form, 13.163
value, 13.163
Scottish child payment award, 13.147
social security assistance
'assessment period', 13.141
assistance being awarded, 13.140
specified kinds, 13.139
timing of applications
'birthday', 13.133
late applications, 13.132
months, 13.134–13.135
when treated as made, 13.131
universal credit
'assessment period', 13.141
Betting
investment income, 2.243
Birth
evidence
statutory paternity pay, 6.56
tax credits, 2.402
statutory paternity pay
common provisions, 6.66–6.70
conditions of entitlement, 6.51–6.53
evidence requirements, 6.56
notice requirements, 6.56–6.57
periods of payment, 6.54
qualifying period, 6.55
statutory provisions, 1.113–1.118
treatment of more than one employer, 6.58
tax credits, 2.402
working tax credit, 2.135–2.138
Breach of regulations
See **Enforcement**
Brexit
carer's allowance supplement
appeals, 13.286
applications, 13.284
Coronavirus relaxations, 13.288
definitions, 13.273
determination of entitlement, 13.275–13.281
further provision, 13.287
overpayments, 13.280
procedural matters, 13.284–13.287
re-determination of entitlement, 13.285
Regulations, 13.272–13.288
underpayments, 13.279

Index

Scotland
  carer's allowance supplement, 13.272–13.288
  social security co-ordination amendments, 13.263–13.271
  young carer grants, 13.282
social security co-ordination amendments
  definitions, 13.263
  Gibraltar, 13.266
  Regulations, 13.263–13.271
  revocation of instruments, 13.270–13.271
  revocation of retained EU legislation, 13.268–13.269
young carer grants, 13.282

Building societies (dividends)
savings and investment income, 1.780

Business entertainment
trading income, 1.750

Capital
general rule, 2.202

Capital expenditure
trading income
  cash basis, 1.746
  generally, 1.745

Capital gains
child trust funds
  account provider to act on behalf of named child, 9.46
  account provider's tax claims, 9.47–9.48
  adaptation of enactments, 9.58
  administration, 9.59
  application of Taxes Act, 9.60
  assessment for withdrawal of relief, 9.50
  fortnightly claims, 9.51
  generally, 9.45
  information about looked after children, 9.54–9.55
  information to be provided to Board, 9.56
  inspection of records, 9.57
  records, 9.52
  repayments to account provider, 9.47–9.48
  returns of information, 9.53
  statutory provisions, 1.687–1.688
  tax returns, 9.51
generally, 2.202

Capital receipts
after leaving or under cash basis
  generally, 1.755
  supplementary, 1.756
generally, 1.754

Care (children)
child benefit
  Regulations, 3.21, 3.25
  statutory basis, 1.186

Care plans
charge-free childcare, 11.9

Careers services
generally, 3.2

Carer support payments
See also **Carer's assistance**
abatement, 13.512
age criteria, 13.498
aircraft workers, 13.503
amount
  backdating, 13.516
  decrease, 13.522
  generally, 13.511
  increase, 13.523
applications
  abatement, and, 13.512
  date on which treated as made, 13.513–13.515
  multiple, 13.519
  temporary stop in entitlement, 13.518
armed forces personnel, 13.502
backdating, 13.516
breaks in care, 13.535
calculation of earnings, 13.547
'cared for person', 13.496
cessation, 13.522
change of circumstances, 13.531
civil servants, 13.502
commencement of entitlement, 13.513
consequential amendments
  general provision, 13.543
  schedule provisions, 13.546
continental shelf operations, 13.503
continuing eligibility, 13.520
date on which treated as made, 13.513–13.515
decrease, 13.522
deduction, by
  determination to effect, 13.534
  generally, 13.521
definitions, 13.496
earnings limit, 13.509
education, 13.507–13.508
eligibility
  age criteria. 13.498
  aircraft workers, 13.503
  armed forces personnel, 13.502
  cessation, 13.522
  civil servants, 13.502
  continental shelf operations, 13.503
  continuation, 13.520
  earnings limit, 13.509
  education, 13.507–13.508
  entitlement to other benefits, 13.506
  mariners, 13.503
  persons to whom EU regulation applies, 13.504–13.505
  presence, 13.500
  provision of care, 13.499
  reconsideration, 13.530–13.534
  residence, 13.500
  temporary absence, 13.501
  temporary stop, 13.518
entitlement to other benefits, 13.506
errors
  overpayments, 13.533
  underpayments, 13.534
form
  backdating, 13.516
  generally, 13.511

Index

increase, 13.523
individuals in education, 13.507–13.508
initial period for applications
  general provision, 13.540
  schedule provisions, 13.544
  transitory provision, 13.541
mariners, 13.503
movement of individual between Scotland and rest of UK, 13.536–13.537
multiple applications, 13.519
official errors
  overpayments, 13.533
  underpayments, 13.534
overpayments, 13.533
overview, 13.497
payments
  abatement, 13.512
  amount, 13.511
  backdating, 13.516
  cessation, 13.522
  decrease, 13.522
  deduction, by, 13.521
  generally, 13.510
  timing, 13.517
periods in respect of redetermination request, 13.538
persons to whom an EU regulation applies
  residing in the UK, 13.504
  residing outside the UK, 13.505
presence, 13.500
provision of care to a cared for person, 13.499
reconsideration of entitlement
  change of circumstances, after, 13.531
  official error, after, 13.532–13.533
  specified period, after, 13.530
Regulations
  citation, 13.495
  commencement, 13.495
  definitions, 13.496
  general provisions, 13.497–13.543
  schedule, 13.544–13.547
residence
  general condition, 13.500
  persons to whom EU regulation applies, 13.504
serving members of armed forces, 13.502
suspensions
  cessation, 13.528–13.529
  criteria, 13.524
  effect of ending, 13.529
  financial circumstances, 13.525
  information to be given to individual, 13.526
  review, 13.527
  termination, 13.528–13.529
temporary absence from common travel area, 13.501
temporary breaks in care, 13.535
temporary stop in entitlement, 13.518
timing, 13.517
transfer from carer's allowance
  general provision, 13.539
  schedule provisions, 13.545
transitory provision
  exclusion, 13.542
  generally, 13.541
underpayments, 13.532
Carers
remunerative work, 2.133
Carer's allowance
social security income, 2.235
transfer to carer support payment
  general provision, 13.539
  schedule provisions, 13.545
Carer's allowance supplement
appeals
  Coronavirus, 13.288
  generally, 13.286
applications
  form, 13.284
  notice of determination, 13.284
  withdrawal, 13.284
Coronavirus relaxations, 13.288
definitions, 13.273
determination following official error
  overpayments, 13.280
  underpayments, 13.279
determination of entitlement
  following official error, 13.279–13.280
  further provision, 13.287
  generally, 13.276
  meaning, 13.275
  notice, 13.284
  procedure, 13.281
  timing of applications, 13.277
  without application, 13.278
EU Exit, and
  appeals, 13.286
  applications, 13.284
  Coronavirus relaxations, 13.288
  definitions, 13.273
  determination of entitlement, 13.275–13.281
  further provision, 13.287
  overpayments, 13.280
  procedural matters, 13.284–13.287
  re-determination of entitlement, 13.285
  Regulations, 13.272–13.288
  underpayments, 13.279
generally, 13.77–13.78
overpayments, 13.280
power to repeal temporary provision, 13.79
procedural matters
  appeals, 13.286
  determination of entitlement, 13.284
  form of application, 13.284
  further provision, 13.287
  introduction, 13.281
  re-determination, 13.285
re-determination of entitlement
  Coronavirus, 13.288
  generally, 13.285

Index

Regulations
  citation, 13.272
  commencement, 13.272
  definitions, 13.273
  general provisions, 13.274–13.283
  schedule, 13.284–13.288
temporary provision
  generally, 13.77–13.78
  repeal, 13.79
underpayments, 13.279

Carer's assistance
See also **Carer support payment;**
    Scotland; Young carer's grant
age, 13.100
carer's other activities, 13.99
Coronavirus
  breaks in care, 13.193–13.196
definitions, 13.102
eligibility, 13.98
final provisions, 13.102
financial circumstances, 13.100
further criteria, 13.99–13.100
generally, 13.18
meeting liabilities, 13.101
miscellaneous provisions, 13.98–13.102
multiple carers, 13.99
nil value, 13.101
presence, 13.99
receipt of other state assistance, 13.100
residence, 13.99
suspension, 13.127
time limit for applications, 13.100
types, 13.101
young carers
  amount, 13.192–13.192A
  citation, 13.181
  commencement, 13.181
  conditions, 13.185–13.188
  definitions, 13.182
  eligibility, 13.183–13.187
  form, 13.192–13.192A
  general note, 13.180
  general provisions, 13.183
  procedural matters, 13.189–13.191

Cash basis
See also **Trading income**
calculation of profits, 1.741
capital expenditures, 1.746
capital receipts
  generally, 1.755
  supplementary, 1.756
generally, 1.733
overview or rest of Part 2, 1.742
property income, and, 1.770
receipts, 1.753
rules restricting deductions, 1.744

Cash vouchers
See **Vouchers**

"Ceasing to undertake work"
working tax credit, 2.149–2.150

Change of circumstances
carer support payments,
    13.531

statutory adoption pay
  overseas adoptions, 6.129
statutory paternity pay, 6.66–6.70

Change of circumstances (tax credits)
advance, in, 2.397
amendment, 2.389
automatic, 1.293
childcare element (working tax credit),
    2.174–2.175
Coronavirus
  date of notification, 2.396.1
  decrease of rate, 2.386
date of notification
  Coronavirus, 2.396.1
  generally, 2.395–2.396
decrease of rate
  Coronavirus, 2.386
  generally, 2.383–2.385
definitions, 2.283
discretionary, 1.292
evidence of birth or adoption, 2.402
failure to report, 1.294
generally, 1.288–1.289
increase of maximum rate, 2.381–2.382
mandatory, 1.291
method of notification, 2.386–2.387
person acting on behalf of another, by,
    2.398–2.401
relevant changes, 1.290
relevant person, 2.388

Change of employer
see **Continuity of employment**

Charge-free childcare
appeals
  decision to decline to make
    determination, 11.46
  determination as to qualifying child,
    11.47
  following review, 11.45–11.49
  imposition of penalty, 11.48
  settlement by agreement, 11.49
arrangements for provision of childcare,
    11.51–11.54
'care plan', 11.9
childcare for qualifying children, 11.50
'childcare provider', 11.10
Commissioner determinations
  declining to make, 11.29
  generally, 11.28
conditions
  parent, 11.20
  partner of parent, 11.21
declarations
  duration, 11.31
  effect, 11.31–11.32
  form and manner, 11.27
  making, 11.25
  material inaccuracy, 11.39
  parallel, 11.32
  timing, 11.26
definitions
  'care plan', 11.9
  'childcare provider', 11.10

Index

'employee', 11.11
'foster parent', 11.12
general list, 11.8
'looked after by a local authority', 11.13
'partner', 11.14
'person in the UK', 11.15
'specified benefit', 11.16
determinations of qualifying child of working parent
  Commissioners, by, 11.28–11.29
  conditions, 11.20–11.21
  declarations, 11.25–11.27
  declining to make, 11.29
  disclosure of information, 11.34–11.35
  eligibility for childcare, 11.33
  minimum income, 11.24
  qualifying paid work, 11.22–11.23
  responsible local authority, by, 11.30
  young child, 11.18–11.19
disclosure of information
  immigration, 11.34
  social security, 11.35
dishonest conduct, 11.37
duration of declarations, 11.31
duties of local authorities
  arrangements for provision of childcare, 11.51–11.54
  childcare for qualifying children, 11.50
  guidance, 11.55
eligibility for childcare, 11.33
employees
  definition, 11.11
  qualifying paid work requirement, 11.22
false or misleading information, 11.38
'foster parent', 11.12
immigration-status information, 11.34
'looked after by a local authority', 11.13
material inaccuracy in declaration, 11.39
minimum income requirement, 11.24
misleading information, 11.38
offences, 11.36
'partner', 11.14
penalties
  assessment of, 11.40
  dishonest conduct, 11.37
  enforcement, 11.41
  false or misleading information, 11.38
  material inaccuracy in declaration, 11.39
period of eligibility for childcare, 11.33
'person in the UK', 11.15
qualifying paid work requirement
  employees, 11.22
  self-employed persons, 11.23
requirements
  minimum income, 11.24
  qualifying paid work, 11.22–11.23
responsible local authority, 11.30
reviews
  appeals, 11.45
  extension of right to apply, 11.43
  procedure, 11.44
  right to apply, 11.42

self-employed persons, 11.23
social security status information, 11.34
'specified benefit', 11.16
timing of declarations, 11.26
young child, 11.18–11.19

Charge to tax (income tax)
agency workers, 1.514
deductions from earnings, 1.548–1.559
dividend income
  non-resident UK companies, 1.785
  UK resident companies, 1.782
earnings, 1.515
emoluments (offices and employment)
  general note, 1.496–1.497
employment income
  agency workers, 1.514
  deductions from earnings, 1.548–1.559
  earnings, 1.515
  'employment', 1.503–1.504
  exemptions, 1.540–1.547
  general note, 1.496–1.497
  introductory provision, 1.501–1.502
  nature, 1.506–1.508
  office-holders, 1.505
  operation, 1.509–1.513
  taxable benefits, 1.516–1.539
foreign benefits, 1.611–1.614
general note
  ITA 2007, 1.875
  ITEPA 2003, under, 1.496–1.497
general rule
  ITA 2007, 1.878–1.880
  ITTOIA 2005, 1.716–1.718
  ITEPA 2003, under, 1.499
investments income
  dividends from non-resident UK companies, 1.785
  dividends from UK resident companies, 1.782
  interest, 1.776
  purchased life annuity payments, 1.788
miscellaneous income
  income not otherwise charged, 1.801
  settlements, 1.795–1.800
office-holders, 1.505
pension income
  amount charged, 1.563
  general note, 1.561
  general rules, 1.565–1.569
  introductory provision, 1.560
  nature of charge, 1.562
  person liable to tax, 1.564
  social security pensions, 1.570–1.573
property income
  generally, 1.766
  income charged, 1.768
  person liable, 1.769
  territorial scope, 1.767
purchased life annuity payments, 1.788
savings and investments income
  dividends from non-resident UK companies, 1.785

dividends from UK resident companies, 1.782
interest, 1.776
purchased life annuity payments, 1.788
Schedule E (offices and employment emoluments)
general note, 1.496–1.497
social security income
amount charged, 1.582
definitions, 1.615–1.616
exempt benefits, 1.591–1.606
foreign benefits, 1.611–1.614
general note, 1.575–1.576
introductory provision, 1.574
nature of charge, 1.577–1.579
person liable to tax, 1.583
taxable benefits, 1.584–1.590
wholly exempt benefits, 1.607–1.610
trading income
arrangements for avoiding tax, 1.726
generally, 1.724
income charged, 1.727
person liable, 1.728
territorial scope, 1.725
wholly exempt benefits, 1.607–1.610

Charitable work
See **Voluntary work**

Charters
HMRC
generally, 1.856–1.857
text, 12.1–12.15

Cheque vouchers
See **Vouchers**

Child benefit
adopted children, 3.21
advanced education, child in, 3.4–3.5
allocation of contributions, 3.5
care
Regulations, 3.21, 3.25
statutory basis, 1.186
'child', 1.49
child in care
Regulations, 3.21, 3.25
statutory basis, 1.186
child in detention
Regulations, 3.21–3.24
statutory basis, 1.186
child treated as being in GB, 3.28
child treated as being in Northern Ireland, 3.37
civil partnership, 3.18
continuation of entitlement, 3.6
Crown servants posted overseas
child, 3.46
generally, 3.43–3.44
partners, 3.45
days of absence, 3.4
death of child, after
Regulations, 3.27
statutory basis, 1.61
definitions, 1.65–1.66
detention, child in
Regulations, 3.21–3.24
statutory basis, 1.186
duplicate payments, 3.55–3.56
education and training condition, 3.4–3.5
election, 3.19
election not to receive, 1.210–1.211
electronic communications, use of, 3.57
employed trainees, 1.187
entitlement
child, 1.49
death of child, after, 1.61
exclusions, 1.58–1.59
generally, 1.47–1.48
person responsible for child, 1.50–1.57
persons subject to immigration control, 1.64
presence in GB, 1.62–1.63
priority, 1.58–1.59
qualifying young person, 1.49
exclusions
care, child in, 1.186
detention, child in, 1.186
employed trainees, 1.187
generally, 1.58–1.59
imprisoned child, 1.186
married child, 1.188
Regulations, 3.16–3.26
extension period, 3.7
full-time education, child in, 3.4–3.5
imprisoned child
Regulations, 3.24
statutory basis, 1.186
incapacity benefit, child receiving, 3.12
income support, child receiving, 3.12
increases for dependants, and
persons entitled treated as not entitled, 3.50–3.51
persons not entitled treated as entitled, 3.48–3.49
interruptions, 3.8–3.9
jobseeker's allowance, child receiving, 3.12
living with partner as spouse, 3.16–3.17
married child
Regulations, 3.18
statutory basis, 1.188
NI number, and, 3.54
overpayments, 1.214–1.215
person responsible for child
Regulations, 3.13–3.15
statutory basis, 1.50–1.57
person temporarily absent
from GB, 3.35–3.36
from Northern Ireland, 3.41
person treated as not being resident
in GB, 3.30–3.34
in Northern Ireland, 3.39–3.40
persons subject to immigration control, 1.64
polygamous marriages, 3.50–3.51
prescribed conditions
continuation of entitlement, 3.6
education and training condition, 3.4–3.5

Index

extension period, 3.7
interruptions, 3.8–3.9
introduction, 3.3
terminal dates, 3.10–3.11
presence in GB, 1.62–1.63
priority
  generally, 1.58–1.59
  miscellaneous provisions, 1.191–1.195
  Regulations, 3.20
qualifying young person
  continuation of entitlement, 3.6
  definition, 1.49
  education and training condition, 3.4–3.5
  extension period, 3.7
  interruptions, 3.8–3.9
  introduction, 3.3
  other financial support, 3.12
  person responsible for child, 3.13–3.15
  prescribed conditions, 3.3–3.12
  terminal dates, 3.10–3.11
rate
  generally, 1.60
  weekly rates, 3.60–3.65
residence
  child treated as being in GB, 3.28
  child treated as being in Northern Ireland, 3.37
  Crown servants posted overseas, 3.43–3.46
  overlap of entitlement, 3.42
  person temporarily absent from GB, 3.35–3.36
  person temporarily absent from Northern Ireland, 3.41
  person treated as not being in GB, 3.30–3.34
  person treated as not being in Northern Ireland, 3.39–3.40
  transitional provisions, 3.47
  residential accommodation, child in, 3.3
  residing together, persons treated as, 3.48–3.49
social security income, 2.233
temporary absence
  from GB, 3.35–3.36
  from Northern Ireland, 3.41
terminal dates, 3.10–3.11
training scheme, child in, 3.4–3.5
unmarried couples, 3.48–3.49
uprating
  Regulations 2024, 3.82–3.83
voluntary organisations, 3.52–3.53
'week', 1.66

Child Benefit (General) Regulations 2006
arrangement, 3.1
citation, 3.2
commencement, 3.2
definitions, 3.2
general provisions, 3.3–3.58

Child Benefit (Rates) Regulations 2006
arrangement, 3.60
citation, 3.61
commencement, 3.61
definitions, 3.61
general note, 3.65
general provisions, 3.62
saving, 3.63

Child Benefit (Residence and Persons Abroad) Regulations 1976
general note, 3.59

Child disability payments
See also **Adult disability payments**
admission to care home
  calculation of periods of time spent, 13.314
  generally, 13.312
age criteria, 13.295
alternative accommodation, 13.315
amount, 13.318
applications
  date, 13.319
  initial period, 13.341
authorised vehicle providers, 13.339
care component
  admission to care home, 13.312
  alternative accommodation, 13.315
  amount, 13.318
  calculation of periods of time spent, 13.314
  dialysis treatment, 13.311
  generally, 13.303–13.304
  in-patients, 13.316
  introduction, 13.294
  legal detention, 13.313
  rates, 13.318
change of circumstances, 13.332
conditions
  definitions, 13.297
  generally, 13.296
  person to whom relevant EU regulation applies, 13.299–13.301
  temporary absence, 13.298
consideration of entitlement after specified period, 13.331
continuing eligibility, 13.321
date of entitlement, 13.319
decrease in level of entitlement, 13.330
deduction, by
  determination to effect a decision, 13.335
  generally, 13.328
definitions, 13.293
detention under law
  calculation of periods of time spent, 13.314
  generally, 13.313
dialysis treatment, 13.311
disability living allowance paid in another part of UK before moving to Scotland, 13.336
effecting a deduction decision, 13.335

1863

Index

eligibility
  age criteria, 13.295
  care component, 13.303–13.304, 13.310–13.316
  continuation, 13.321
  entitlement to other benefits, 13.302
  generally, 13.107
  mobility requirement, 13.305–13.309
  presence, 13.296–13.297
  Regulations, 13.294–13.316
  residence, 13.296–13.297
entitlement date, 13.319
entitlement to other benefits, 13.302
errors
  overpayments, 13.334
  underpayments, 13.333
exclusions, 13.302
extent of disability and needs, 13.108
extinguishment of right to apply, 13.290–13.291
final provisions, 13.112
financial circumstances, 13.108
form, 13.318
further criteria, 13.108
generally, 13.20
imprisonment
  calculation of periods of time spent, 13.314
  generally, 13.313
increase in level of entitlement, 13.329
initial period for applications
  generally, 13.341
  miscellaneous provisions, 13.348
  transitory provision, 13.345
legal detention
  calculation of periods of time spent, 13.314
  generally, 13.313
level of entitlement
  decrease, 13.330
  increase, 13.329
miscellaneous provisions, 13.107–13.112
mobility requirement
  amount, 13.318
  exclusion of entitlement, 13.309
  higher rate component, 13.307–13.308
  introduction, 13.294
  lower rate component, 13.305–13.306
  payment to vehicle providers, 13.339
  rates, 13.318
  terminal illness, 13.310
moving to another part of UK, 13.336
nature of disability and needs, 13.108
official errors
  overpayments, 13.334
  underpayments, 13.333
overpayments, 13.334
payments
  amount, 13.318
  authorised vehicle providers, 13.339
  commencement date, 13.319
  deduction, by, 13.328
  form, 13.318
  generally, 13.317
  overpayments, 13.334
  timing, 13.320
  underpayments, 13.333
person to whom relevant EU regulation applies
  no entitlement to care component where UK not competent state, 13.301
  residing in UK, 13.299
  residing outside UK, 13.300
presence condition
  definitions, 13.297
  further provision, 13.108
  generally, 13.296
  person to whom relevant EU regulation applies, 13.299–13.301
  temporary absence, 13.298
rates, 13.318
receipt of other state assistance, 13.108
re-determination of entitlement
  generally, 13.331
  periods in respect of a request, 13.338
Regulations
  citation, 13.292
  commencement, 13.292
  consequential amendment, 13.344, 13.350
  general provisions, 13.295–13.343
  definitions, 13.293
  overview, 13.294
  schedules, 13.347–13.350
  transitory provision, 13.345
residence condition
  definitions, 13.297
  further provision, 13.108
  generally, 13.296
  person to whom relevant EU regulation applies, 13.299–13.301
  temporary absence, 13.298
short-term assistance
  generally, 13.343
  miscellaneous provisions, 13.347
suspension
  effect of termination, 13.327
  generally, 13.127
  having regard to financial circumstances, 13.323
  information to be given after, 13.324
  relevant circumstances, 13.322
  right to review, 13.325
  termination, 13.326
temporary absence from Common Travel Area, 13.298
terminal illness cases
  generally, 13.109
  special rules, 13.310
time limit for applications, 13.108
time of payment, 13.320
transfer to
  generally, 13.342
  miscellaneous provisions, 13.349
transitional provision, 13.289–13.291

Index

transitory provision
  exclusion, 13.346
  initial period for applications, 13.345
types, 13.110–13.111
underpayments, 13.333
vehicles for persons with disabilities
  payment to authorised providers, 13.339
  powers of appointees, 13.340

Child maintenance
See **Child support**

Child maintenance bonus
social security income
  income support, 1.594
  jobseeker's allowance, 1.599

Child support
disregards, 2.261

Child tax credit
See also **Appeals (tax credits)**
abolition, 1.890–1.891
administrative arrangements
  definitions, 2.441
  general note, 2.439
  provision of information, 2.442–2.443
  recording, etc. of claims, 2.444
  statutory provisions, 1.435–1.436
adoption, 2.301–2.302
age of child, 2.281–2.282
annual reports, 1.416–1.417
annual review, 1.418–1.419
appeals
  appealable decisions, 1.402–1.409
  exercise of right, 1.411–1.412
  general regulations, 2.445–2.457
  late appeals, 1.413–1.415
  temporary modifications, 1.445–1.446
  transition to universal credit, and, 1.410
assignment, 1.426–1.427
bankruptcy, 1.426–1.427
cases in which no rate of tax credit, 2.334–2.335
cases in which there is a reciprocal agreement, 2.332–2.333
changes of circumstances
  advance, in, 2.397
  amendment, 2.389
  automatic, 1.293
  date of, 2.390–2.396.1
  decrease of rate, 2.383–2.386
  definitions, 2.283
  discretionary, 1.292
  failure to report, 1.294
  generally, 1.288–1.289
  increase of maximum rate, 2.381–2.382
  mandatory, 1.291
  method, 2.386–2.387
  person acting on behalf of another, by, 2.398–2.401
  relevant changes, 1.290
  relevant person, 2.388
child care providers scheme, 2.537–2.542
claims
  definitions, 2.343–2.344
  evidence, 1.281–1.282
  generally, 2.345–2.379
  procedural issues, 1.281–1.282
  separation of spouses or civil partners, 1.279
  statutory provisions, 1.271–1.285
  unmarried couples, 1.280
Codes of Practice
  overpayments, 12.29–12.75
Crown employment, 1.424–1.425
cut-off provisions, 2.334–2.335
death of child, after, 2.285–2.286
decisions
  discovery, on, 1.347–1.349
  final decision, 1.341–1.343
  final notice, 1.339–1.340
  information requirements, 1.358–1.359
  initial decision, 1.323–1.329
  notice of, 1.360–1.362
  official error, 1.350–1.351
  other revised decisions, 1.332–1.338
  power to enquire, 1.344–1.346
  review, 1.352–1.357
  revision after notifications, 1.330–1.331
  subject to official error, 1.350–1.351
decisions on discovery
  generally, 1.347–1.348
  transition to universal credit, and, 1.349
definitions
  regulations, in, 2.270
  statute, in, 1.432–1.433
determination of rate
  cut-off provisions, 2.334–2.335
  full year periods, 2.330
  generally, 2.328–2.330
  introduction, 2.320–2.321
  reciprocal agreement cases, 2.332–2.333
  short periods, 2.331
development of system, 1.261
disabled child, 2.289–2.290
disclosure of information, 1.437–1.438
duration, 1.286–1.287
entitlement, 1.303–1.306
enquiry powers
  generally, 1.344–1.345
  transition to universal credit, and, 1.346
evidence of birth or adoption, 2.402
exceptions to restrictions on numbers
  adoption, 2.301–2.302
  ambit, 2.295
  classes, 2.293
  continuation, 2.307–2.308
  generally, 2.291–2.293
  justification, 2.297–2.298
  less favourable treatment, 2.296
  multiple births, 2.299–2.300
  non-consensual conception, 2.305–2.306
  non-parental caring arrangements, 2.303–2.304
  relevant status, 2.296
  SC & others decision, 2.294–2.298

1865

Index

failure to comply with requirements, 1.384–1.386
final decisions
  generally, 1.341–1.343
  transition to universal credit, and, 1.344
final notices
  generally, 1.339–1.340
  transition to universal credit, and, 1.340
forwarding of claims, 2.444
fraud, and
  generally, 1.388–1.389
  powers relating to documents, 1.390–1.391
functions of Commissioners, 1.269–1.270
general note, 1.259
holding of claims, 2.444
inalienability, 1.426–1.427
income test
  calculation, 2.210–2.211
  definitions, 2.208–2.209
  disregards, 2.261–2.267
  employment income, 2.212–2.220
  foreign income, 2.247–2.248
  general note, 2.200–2.206
  investment income, 2.243–2.244
  miscellaneous income, 2.259–2.260
  notional income, 2.249–2.258
  pension income, 2.221–2.228
  property income, 2.245–2.246
  social security income, 2.233–2.238
  statutory provision, 1.295–1.302
  transition to universal credit, and, 1.302
income thresholds, 2.313–2.315
incorrect statements
  conduct of penalty cases, 1.380–1.381
  fraudulently or negligently, 1.379
  generally, 1.376–1.378
  level of penalties, 1.382–1.383
individual element
  adoption, 2.301–2.302
  ambit, 2.295
  classes, 2.293
  continuation, 2.307–2.308
  generally, 2.291–2.293
  justification, 2.297–2.298
  less favourable treatment, 2.296
  multiple births, 2.299–2.300
  non-consensual conception, 2.305–2.306
  non-parental caring arrangements, 2.303–2.304
  relevant status, 2.296
  SC & others decision, 2.294–2.298
information requirements, 1.358–1.359
initial decisions, 1.323–1.329
interest
  definitions, 2.461
  general note, 2.460
  overpayments, on, 2.462
  prescribed rate, 2.463
  statutory provision, 1.400–1.401
  student income, 2.239–2.242
  trading income, 2.227–2.232

maximum rate
  generally, 2.287–2.288
  statutory provision, 1.307–1.310
means testing, 2.200
multiple births, 2.299–2.300
non-consensual conception, 2.305–2.306
non-parental caring arrangements, 2.303–2.304
Northern Ireland, 1.447–1.448
notice of decisions
  final notice, 1.339–1.340
  generally, 1.360–1.361
  initial decision, 1.323–1.329
  transition to universal credit, and, 1.362
notices by Board, 1.428–1.429
notices to provide information
  childcare provider, to, 2.404
  dates to be specified, 2.405
  definitions, 2.339
  electronic communications, 2.340–2.342
  employers, to, 2.403
  s.17 TCA 2002, under, 2.406–2.409
notification of change of circumstances
  advance, in, 2.397
  amendment, 2.389
  automatic, 1.293
  date of, 2.390–2.396.1
  decrease of rate, 2.383–2.386
  definitions, 2.283
  discretionary, 1.292
  evidence of birth or adoption, 2.402
  failure to report, 1.294
  generally, 1.288–1.289
  increase of maximum rate, 2.381–2.382
  mandatory, 1.291
  method, 2.386–2.387
  person acting on behalf of another, by, 2.398–2.401
  relevant changes, 1.290
  relevant person, 2.388
official errors
  definitions, 2.496–2.497
  general note, 2.499
  generally, 2.498
  statutory provisions, 1.350–1.351
notice of decisions
  final notice, 1.339–1.340
  generally, 1.360–1.361
  initial decision, 1.323–1.329
  transition to universal credit, and, 1.362
overpayments
  Code of Practice, 12.29–12.75
  generally, 1.367–1.369
  method of recovery, 2.433
  recovery, 1.370–1.372
payment
  employees' rights, 1.365–1.366
  generally, 1.363–1.364
payment by HMRC
  amount, 2.431–2.432
  bank account requirement, 2.436–2.437
  definitions, 2.413

Index

general note, 2.411
joint claims, for, 2.414–2.419
method, 2.434–2.435
person acting on behalf of another, for, 2.420–2.421
postponement, 2.429–2.430
recovery of overpayments, 2.433
renewal claims, 2.422–2.423
single payments, 2.427–2.428
timing, 2.424–2.426
penalties
  determination, 1.455
  failure to comply with requirements, 1.384–1.386
  general note, 1.460–1.463
  Guidance, 12.16–12.28
  incorrect statements, etc., 1.376–1.383
  mitigation, 1.457
  proceedings before Commissioners, 1.456
  recovery, 1.459
  supplementary, 1.387
  time limits, 1.458
period of award, 1.286–1.287
persons subject to immigration control
  amendments of Act, 2.472–2.473
  definitions, 2.466
  exclusion from entitlement, 2.467–2.473
  general note, 2.468
  statutory provision, 1.420–1.421
  transitional relief, 2.474–2.475
polygamous marriages
  amendment of Regulations, 2.511–2.517
  amendment of TCA 2002, 2.510
  definitions, 2.508–2.509
  general note, 2.506
  statutory provision, 1.422–1.423
provision of information
  authorities, by, 2.443
  authorities, to, 2.442
  functions relating to employment, 2.524, 2.536
  functions relating to health, 2.502–2.504, 2.521, 2.534
  functions relating to training, 2.524, 2.536
qualifying young person
  definition, 2.270
  maximum age, 2.283–2.284
rate, 1.321–1.322
reciprocal agreement cases, 2.332–2.333
recording of claims, 2.444
recovery of overpayments
  generally, 1.370–1.372
  method, 2.433
residence requirements
  Crown servants posted overseas, 2.489–2.491
  definitions, 2.478–2.479
  ordinary residence, 2.482–2.484
  person treated as not being in UK, 2.480–2.485

temporary absence from UK, 2.487–2.488
tests, 2.485
transitional provision, 2.492–2.493
responsibility for child
  competing claims, 2.274–2.276
  excepted cases, 2.276–2.280
  generally, 2.271–2.272
  normally living with test, 2.273
  special case, 2.280
review of decisions
  generally, 1.352–1.353
  late application, 1.354–1.357
revision after notifications, 1.330–1.331
severely disabled child, 2.289–2.290
statutory provisions
  appeals, 1.402–1.415
  child tax credit, 1.303–1.310
  decisions, 1.323–1.362
  fraud, 1.388–1.391
  generally, 1.267–1.302
  interest, 1.400–1.401
  payment, 1.363–1.375
  penalties, 1.376–1.388
  rate, 1.321–1.322
  supplementary, 1.416–1.433
  working tax credit, 1.311–1.320
subject to official error, 1.350–1.351
taper start point, 2.310
transition to universal credit, and
  appeals, 1.410
  decisions on discovery, 1.349
  enquiry powers, 1.346
  final decisions, 1.344
  final notices, 1.340
  generally, 2.73–2.78
  income test, 1.302
  notice of decisions, 1.362
  underpayments, 1.375
transitional provisions, 2.525–2.528
two child policy, 1.309
underpayments
  generally, 1.373–1.374
  transition to universal credit, 1.375
universal credit, and
  appeals, 1.410
  decisions on discovery, 1.349
  enquiry powers, 1.346
  final decisions, 1.344
  final notices, 1.340
  finalisation, 2.57–2.58
  generally, 1.266
  income test, 1.302
  modification of legislation, 2.55–2.58
  notice of decisions, 1.362
  ongoing awards, 2.53–2.54
  overpayments, 2.55–2.56
  penalties, 2.55–2.56
  underpayments, 1.375
use of information, 1.437–1.438
verification of claims, 2.444
Child Tax Credit Regulations 2002
  amendments to, 2.511
  arrangement, 2.268

citation, 2.269
commencement, 2.269
definitions, 2.270
effect, 2.269
general provisions, 2.271–2.290
Child trust funds
See also **Appeals (child trust funds)**
account providers
  appeal against non-approval or withdrawal of approval, 9.34
  appointment of tax representative, 9.32
  approval, 1.639–1.641
  ceasing to accept Revenue allocated accounts, 9.38
  ceasing to act, 9.37
  ceasing to qualify, 9.39
  definition, 1.712
  generally, 1.639
  intention to make bulk transfer of accounts, 9.37
  introduction, 1.618–1.619
  provision of information, 1.690–1.691
  qualifying circumstances, 9.31–9.34
  types of account, 1.638–1.642
  withdrawal of approval, 9.33
age 7 payments, 9.18
annual subscription limits
  generally, 9.22–9.23
  statutory provision, 1.685–1.686
appeals
  appealable decisions, 1.703–1.704
  exercise of right, 1.705
  general regulations, 9.90–9.100
  notice of appeal, 9.84–9.89
  penalties, 1.702
  temporary modifications, 1.706
approval of account providers
  appeals, 9.34
  appointment of tax representative, 9.32
  disqualifying circumstances, 9.33
  generally, 1.639–1.641
  qualifying circumstances, 9.31
  withdrawal, 9.33
assignment of investments, 1.647–1.648
background, 1.618
bankruptcy of child, 1.647–1.648
bulk transfer of accounts, 9.37
capital gains tax
  account provider to act on behalf of named child, 9.46
  account provider's tax claims, 9.47–9.48
  adaptation of enactments, 9.58
  administration, 9.59
  application of Taxes Act, 9.60
  assessment for withdrawal of relief, 9.50
  fortnightly claims, 9.51
  generally, 9.45
  information about looked after children, 9.54–9.55
  information to be provided to Board, 9.56
  inspection of records, 9.57

  records, 9.52
  repayments to account provider, 9.47–9.48
  returns of information, 9.53
  statutory provisions, 1.687–1.688
  tax returns, 9.51
characteristics
  eligible child, 1.627–1.636
  introduction, 1.622–1.626
  requirements to be satisfied, 1.637–1.646
charge over investments, 1.647–1.648
child benefit, 1.629
child in care, 1.630
'child trust fund business', 9.65
Commissioners of Inland Revenue, and
  General Commissioners, 9.67–9.85
  Special Commissioners, 9.86–9.89
contributions
  further, 1.678–1.682
  generally, 9.16–9.17
  initial, 1.668–1.669
  non-monetary subscriptions, 1.685–1.686
  recoupment, 1.683–1.684
  supplementary, 1.670–1.677
date of birth, 1.629
death of child, and
  payments to parent, 1.698–1.699
  withdrawal of fund, 1.642
definitions, 1.712
descriptions of accounts, 9.11–9.12
disclosure of information, 1.696–1.697
eligible child
  meaning, 1.627–1.636
  opening of fund, 1.649–1.655
further contributions, 1.678–1.682
future, 1.620
general note, 1.618–1.620
generally, 1.622–1.626
government contributions
  further, 1.678–1.682
  generally, 9.16–9.17
  initial, 1.668–1.669
  non-monetary subscriptions, 1.685–1.686
  recoupment, 1.683–1.684
  supplementary, 1.670–1.677
HMRC
  opening of fund, 1.656–1.662
  status and role, 1.626
inalienability, 1.647–1.648
income tax exemption
  account provider to act on behalf of named child, 9.46
  account provider's tax claims, 9.47–9.48
  adaptation of enactments, 9.58
  administration, 9.59
  application of Taxes Act, 9.60
  assessment for withdrawal of relief, 9.50
  fortnightly claims, 9.51
  generally, 9.45

Index

information about looked after children, 9.54–9.55
information to be provided to Board, 9.56
inspection of records, 9.57
records, 9.52
repayments to account provider, 9.47–9.48
returns of information, 9.53
statutory provisions, 1.687–1.688
tax returns, 9.51
information
  account providers, from, 1.690–1.691
  child in care of authority, about, 1.692–1.693
  disclosure of, 1.696–1.697
  use of, 1.694–1.695
initial contributions, 1.668–1.669
insurance companies
  'child trust fund business', 9.65
  general provision, 9.62–9.64
  modifications of Acts, 9.66
intention to make bulk transfer of accounts, 9.37
introduction, 1.618–1.619
invalid accounts
  'repair' of, 9.44
investment rules
  generally, 9.25
  qualifying investments, 9.26
jurisdiction of Commissioners
  General Commissioners, 9.67–9.85
  Special Commissioners, 9.86–9.89
looked after child
  authority to manage account, 9.55
  generally, 1.630
  information from local authorities, 9.54
management of, 1.644
matured account, 9.30
maturity
  instructions, 9.28
  no instructions, 9.29
  meaning, 1.622–1.626
migrant workers' children, 1.632
Northern Ireland, 1.707–1.706
objectives, 1.618
opening by eligible child
  conditions for application, 9.27
  generally, 9.13–9.14
  statutory provision, 1.649–1.655
opening by HMRC
  generally, 9.15
  statutory provision, 1.656–1.662
opening by responsible person
  conditions for application, 9.27
  generally, 9.13–9.14
  statutory provision, 1.649–1.655
parental responsibility, 1.637
payments to parent, 1.698–1.699
penalties
  appeals, 1.702
  decisions, 1.702
  generally, 1.700–1.701

mitigation, 1.702
recovery, 1.702
permitted withdrawals from account
  child is terminally ill, where, 9.36
  generally, 9.35
  statutory provision, 1.642
powers to safeguard interests of children, , 1.667
qualifying investments, 9.26
recoupment of IR contributions
  generally, 9.43
  statutory provision, 1.683–1.684
'repair' of invalid accounts, 9.44
repayments of tax to account provider
  annual claims, 9.48
  interim claims, 9.47
requirements to be satisfied
  generally, 9.21
  statutory provision, 1.637–1.646
residence, 1.632–1.631
responsible person
  meaning, 1.645–1.646
  opening of fund, 1.649–1.655
revenue allocated accounts
  account provider ceases to accept, where, 9.38
  generally, 9.15
  statutory provision, 1.656–1.662
safeguarding interests of children, 1.667
stakeholder accounts
  characteristics, 9.61
  charges, 9.61
  description, 9.61
  generally, 9.11–9.12
statements for an account, 9.24
subscription limits
  generally, 9.22–9.23
  statutory provision, 1.685–1.686
supplementary contributions, 1.670–1.677
tax exemption
  account provider to act on behalf of named child, 9.46
  account provider's tax claims, 9.47–9.48
  administration, 9.59
  application of Taxes Act, 9.60
  assessment for withdrawal of relief, 9.50
  capital gains tax, 1.687–1.688
  fortnightly claims, 9.51
  generally, 9.45
  income tax, 1.687–1.688
  information about looked after children, 9.54–9.55
  information to be provided to Board, 9.56
  inspection of records, 9.57
  records, 9.52
  repayments to account provider, 9.47–9.48
  returns of information, 9.53
  tax returns, 9.51

Index

transfers
  account provider ceases to act, where, 9.38
  account provider ceases to qualify, where, 9.39
  child reaching 18, on, 1.666
  generally, 1.663–1.664
  intention to make bulk transfer of accounts, 9.37
  other accounts for children, to, 1.665, 9.40–9.41
  procedure, 9.42
  statutory provision, 1.663–1.667
vouchers
  generally, 9.10
  statutory provision, 1.650–1.653
withdrawals from account
  child is terminally ill, where, 9.36
  generally, 9.35
  statutory provision, 1.642
yearly disability payments, 9.19–9.20

Child Trust Funds Act 2004
arrangement of sections, 1.617
commencement
  introduction, 1.621
  Order No.1, 9.1–9.3
  Order No.2, 9.4–9.6
definitions, 1.712
extent, 1.621
general note, 1.618–1.620
general provisions, 1.622–1.706
supplementary, 1.707–1.714

Child Trust Funds (Appeals) Regulations 2005
See also **Appeals (child trust funds)**
citation, 9.91
commencement, 9.91
definitions, 9.91–9.92
duration, 9.91
general provisions, 9.93–9.100
recitals, 9.90

Child Trust Funds (Insurance Companies) Regulations 2004
arrangement, 9.62
citation, 9.63
commencement, 9.63
definitions, 9.64
general note, 9.83
general provisions, 9.65–9.82

Child Trust Funds (Non-tax Appeals) Regulations 2005
citation, 9.85
commencement, 9.85
definitions, 9.86
general provisions, 9.87–9.89
recitals, 9.84

Child Trust Funds Regulations 2004
arrangement, 9.7
citation, 9.8
commencement, 9.8
definitions, 9.9
general provisions, 9.10–9.60
schedule, 9.61–9.61

Childbirth
See **Birth**

Childcare
See also **Charge-free childcare; Child Approval Scheme; Tax-free childcare; 30 hours scheme**
claims time limits, 2.354–2.359
employer-contracted and provided
  'care', 1.546
  'child', 1.546
  'eligible employee', 1.544
  employer-contracted, 1.542–1.543
  employer-provided, 1.540–1.541
  introductory note, 1.502
  'parental responsibility', 1.546
  'qualifying child care', 1.547
  'relevant earnings', 1.545
  regulations, 2.218
  'required time', 1.545
free of charge for working parents
  appeals, 11.45–11.49
  calculation of time, 11.17
  definitions, 11.8–11.16
  determinations as to qualifying children, 11.18–11.35
  duties of local authorities, 11.50–11.55
  offences, 11.36
  penalties, 11.37–11.41
  Regulations, 11.5–11.64
  reviews, 11.42–11.44
30 hours scheme
  availability, 1.1057–1.1060
  duty of Secretary of State, 1.1057–1.1060
  general note, 1.1056
  publication of information, 1.1061
  Regulations, 11.1–11.4

Childcare accounts
See also **Tax-free childcare**
appointment of person to manage, 10.30
closure of childcare accounts, 10.39
opening, 10.31
restriction orders, 10.38

Childcare Act 2016
See also **30 hours scheme**
citation, 1.1063
commencement, 1.1063
extent, 1.1062
general note, 1.1056
general provisions, 1.1057–1.1061

Childcare Act 2016 (Consequential Amendments) Regulations 2016
See also **Childcare**
citation, 11.1
commencement, 11.1
consequential amendments, 11.4
definitions, 11.3
general note, 11.2

Childcare Approval Scheme
revocation provisions, 2.537–2.542

Childcare element
See also **Working tax credit**
calculation of childcare charges, 2.172–2.173

1870

Index

change of circumstances, 2.174–2.175
'child', 2.169–2.171
'childcare', 2.169–2.171
generally, 2.166–2.168
incapacitation, 2.168
payment by HMRC, 2.414–2.415
qualifying young persons, 2.171
'relevant childcare charges', 2.169–2.171
statutory provision, 1.319–1.320
universal credit, 2.73–2.78

Childcare (Free of Charge for Working Parents) (England) Regulations 2022
See also **Charge-free childcare**
application, 11.6
calculation of time, 11.17
citation, 11.5
commencement, 11.5
consequential amendments
  generally, 11.7
  list, 11.54–11.63
definitions, 11.8–11.16
extent, 11.6
general provisions
  appeals, 11.45–11.49
  determinations as to qualifying children, 11.18–11.35
  duties of local authorities, 11.50–11.55
  offences, 11.36
  penalties, 11.37–11.41
  reviews, 11.42–11.44
revocations
  generally, 11.7
  list, 11.64
schedules, 11.54–11.64

Childcare payments
See **Tax-free childcare**

Childcare Payments Act 2014
See also **Tax-free childcare**
arrangement of sections, 1.910
citation, 1.1055
commencement
  general, 1.1055
  introduction, 1.912
consequential amendments, 1.1049–1.1050
definitions, 1.1047–1.1048
extent, 1.1053–1.1054
final provisions, 1.1043
financial provisions, 1.1051–1.1052
general note, 1.911
general provisions
  appeals, 1.1019–1.1030
  childcare accounts, 1.939–1.960
  compensatory payments, 1.1031–1.1032
  eligibility, 1.916–1.936
  information, 1.961–1.967
  miscellaneous, 1.1035–1.1042
  other enforcement, 1.1005–1.1018
  penalties, 1.991–1.1004
  qualifying children, 1.937–1.938
  recovery of payments, 1.978–1.990
  review of decisions, 1.1021–1.1024
  special rules, 1.968–1.977
  withdrawal of exemptions, 1.1033–1.1034
introductory provisions, 1.913–1.915
long title, 1.910
regulations
  general, 1.1043–1.1044
  Parliamentary control, 1.1045–1.1046
time limits for claims, 2.354–2.359

Childcare vouchers
meaning, 1.528

Children
childcare element (working tax credit), 2.169–2.171

Christmas bonus
social security income, 2.233

Civil partners
references in Income Tax Acts, 1.887

Civil partnerships
child benefit, 3.18

Civil penalties
See **Penalties**

Civil servants
carer support payments, 13.502

CJD
See **Creuzfeld-Jakob Disease**

Claims
administrative arrangements
  definitions, 2.441
  general note, 2.439
  provision of information, 2.442–2.443
  recording, etc. of claims, 2.444
advance, in
  generally, 2.362–2.363
  working tax credit, 2.364–2.365
amendment, 2.351
conditional, 2.372
dead applicants, on behalf of
  generally, 2.373–2.374
  joint claims, for, 2.375–2.376
deeming provision
  one member of couple on behalf of both, 2.370–2.371
  revenue final notices, in response to, 2.366–2.369
definitions
  generally, 2.339
  relevant date, 2.343–2.344
disability element of WTC, 2.360–2.361
electronic communications, 2.340–2.342
evidence, 1.281–1.282
forwarding of, 2.444
holding of, 2.444
method, 2.345–2.350
person acting on behalf of another, by
  generally, 2.377
  other appointed persons, 2.378–2.379
polygamous marriages, 2.514
procedural issues, 1.281–1.282
provision of information
  by authorities, 2.443
  to authorities, 2.442

recording, 2.444
separation of spouses or civil partners, 1.279
statutory provisions
  definitions, 2.343–2.344
  evidence, 1.281–1.282
  generally, 2.345–2.379
  procedural issues, 1.281–1.282
  separation of spouses or civil partners, 1.279
  statutory provisions, 1.271–1.285
  unmarried couples, 1.280
time limits
  Childcare Payments Act 2014, under, 2.354–2.359
  generally, 2.352–2.353
universal credit, 2.62–2.63
unmarried couples, 1.280
verification, 2.444

Clerical errors
carer support payments
  overpayments, 13.533
  underpayments, 13.534
tax returns
  during enquiry, 1.11
  generally, 1.8

Closure notices
tax return enquiries, 1.13

Codes of practice
overpayments, 12.29–12.75

Cohabitation
child benefit
  living with another, 3.16–3.17
  residing together, 3.48–3.49
references in Income Tax Acts, 1.117

Collective investment schemes
child trust funds, 9.9

Commissioners for Revenue and Customs
See **HMRC Commissioners**

Commissioners for Revenue and Customs Act 2005
arrangement of sections, 1.843
consequential amendments, 1.872
definitions, 1.873
general provisions, 1.845–1.871
introduction, 1.844
schedule, 1.874

Compensation of employers (statutory maternity pay)
additional payment to small employers, 5.86
advance funding, 5.88
date of payment of contributions, 5.91
definitions
  generally, 5.83
  'small employer', 5.85
general note, 5.84
method
  deduction from payments to Revenue, 5.89
  payments to employer by Revenue, 5.90

overpayments, 5.92
prescribed amount, 5.87

"Conditional claims"
generally, 2.372

"Connexions Service"
definition, 3.2

Continental shelf (employees)
carer support payments, 13.503
statutory adoption pay
  definitions, 6.34
  general note, 6.35
  generally, 6.43
statutory maternity pay
  definitions, 5.64
  general note, 5.65
  generally, 5.73
  statutory provisions, 1.110
statutory parental bereavement pay, 8.56
statutory paternity pay
  definitions, 6.34
  general note, 6.35
  generally, 6.43
  statutory provisions, 1.138–1.139
statutory shared parental pay, 7.138
statutory sick pay
  definitions, 4.53, 4.60, 4.66
  general note, 4.499
  statutory provision, 1.96
  time for compliance, 4.67

Continuity of employment
change of employer
  adoption pay, 6.88
  maternity pay, 5.26
  paternity pay, 6.88
  shared parental pay, 7.66
statutory adoption pay
  change of employer, 6.88
  generally, 6.84
  reinstatement after service with armed forces, 6.89
  stoppages of work, 6.86
  unfair dismissal, 6.85
  'week', 6.87
statutory maternity pay
  change of employer, 5.26
  generally, 5.22
  stoppages of work, 5.24–5.25
  unfair dismissal, 5.23
statutory parental bereavement pay
  generally, 8.13
  stoppages of work, 8.15
  unfair dismissal, 8.14
statutory paternity pay
  change of employer, 6.88
  generally, 6.84
  reinstatement after service with armed forces, 6.89
  stoppages of work, 6.86
  unfair dismissal, 6.85
  'week', 6.87
statutory shared parental pay
  adoption, 7.58–7.59
  birth, 7.57

Index

change of employer, 7.66
'continuous employment', 7.63
service with armed forces, 7.67
stoppages of work, 7.65
unfair dismissal, and, 7.64
stoppages of work
  adoption pay, 6.86
  maternity pay, 5.24–5.25
  paternity pay, 6.86
  shared parental pay, 7.65
unfair dismissal
  adoption pay, 6.85
  maternity pay, 5.23
  paternity pay, 6.85
  shared parental pay, 7.64

Contracting out
statutory adoption pay, 1.151–1.152
statutory paternity pay, 1.132–1.133

Contractual remuneration
See **Remuneration**

Contribution-based jobseekers' allowance
social security income, 2.233

Coronavirus
alteration in hours worked, 2.151
carer's assistance, 13.193–13.196
date of notification
  change of circumstances may increase the maximum rate, 2.392.1
  disability, 2.396.1
definition, 1.1075
function of HMRC, 1.1077
funding employers' liabilities (post-September 30, 2021)
  claims, 4.124–4.125
  corrections, 4.127–4.128
  definitions, 4.119
  eligibility, 4.121
  'eligible employer', 4.122
  general note, 4.118
  incapacity for work, 4.123
  making claims, 4.124
  mistaken statements, 4.128
  overpayments, 4.129
  overstated, 4.127
  payments, 4.126
  preservation of records, 4.130
  provision of information, 4.131
  records, 4.130–4.131
  recovery of payments, 4.129
  Regulations, 4.118–4.131
  statutory provisions, 1.92–1.93
  time limit for claims, 4.125
  understated, 4.128
funding employers' liabilities (pre-October 1, 2021)
  claims, 4.107–4.108
  corrections, 4.110–4.111
  definitions, 4.103
  eligibility, 4.104
  'eligible employer', 4.105
  general note, 4.101
  incapacity for work, 4.106
  making claims, 4.107
  mistaken statements, 4.110
  overpayments, 4.112
  overstated, 4.110
  payments, 4.109
  preservation of records, 4.113
  provision of information, 4.114
  records, 4.113–4.114
  recovery of payments, 4.112
  Regulations, 4.100–4.114
  statutory provisions, 1.92–1.93
  time limit for claims, 4.108
  understated, 4.111
normal weekly earnings, 5.116–5.122
Scotland
  applications for assistance, 13.47–13.48
  carer's allowance supplement, 13.288
  carer's assistance, 13.193–13.196
  child payments, 13.250
  re-determination and appeal deadlines, 13.45–13.46
statutory provisions
  funding employers' liabilities, 1.92–1.93
  generally, 1.1074–1.1079
statutory sick pay
  funding employers' liabilities, 4.100–4.114, 4.118–4.131
  general amendments, 4.132–4.134
  suspension of waiting days, 4.93–4.99, 4.135–4.137
suspension of waiting days
  amending Regulations, 4.93–4.99
  isolation, 4.45–4.45
  Regulations, 4.45–4.46.1
  saving provision, 4.135–4.137
  shielding, 4.46.1
  statutory provision, 1.1076
terminology, 1.1075
working tax credit
  alteration in hours worked, 2.151
  definition, 2.208
  uprating, 1.1078–1.1079

Coronavirus Act 2020
See also **Coronavirus**
arrangement of sections, 1.1074
definitions, 1.1075
general provisions, 1.1076–1.1079

Correction of errors
See **Clerical errors**

Council tax benefit
social security income, 2.233

Covid-19
See **Coronavirus**

Credit tokens
application of provisions, 1.530
benefit treated as earnings, 1.532
disregard for money, goods or services obtained, 1.533
meaning, 1.531

Creuzfeldt-Jakob disease
investment income, 2.243

Index

Crime prevention (fraud)
statutory adoption pay
generally, 1.478–1.479
procedure and appeals, 1.486–1.494
statutory paternity pay
generally, 1.478–1.479
procedure and appeals, 1.486–1.494
tax credits
generally, 1.388–1.389
powers relating to documents, 1.390–1.391
supply of information by tax authorities, 1.219

Crown servants
child benefit
child, 3.46
generally, 3.43–3.44
partners, 3.45
'Crown servant posted overseas', 3.2
overseas employees
generally, 2.489–2.490
partners, 2.491
statutory adoption pay, 1.155–1.156
statutory maternity pay, 1.109
statutory paternity pay, 1.136–1.137
statutory shared parental pay, 1.169
statutory sick pay, 1.95
tax credits, 1.424–1.425

"Curtailment of pay period"
statutory adoption pay
definitions, 5.104
general note, 5.102
notice, 5.114
revocation notice, 5.115
service of notices, 5.105
shared parental leave: AP, 5.113
statutory shared parental pay: A, 5.111
statutory shared parental pay: AP, 5.112
statutory maternity pay
definitions, 5.104
general note, 5.102
notice, 5.109
revocation notice, 5.110
service of notices, 5.105
shared parental leave: P, 5.108
statutory shared parental pay: M, 5.106
statutory shared parental pay: P, 5.107

Data protection
generally, 1.863

Data sharing
Scotland
definitions, 13.351
generally, 13.83
purpose, 13.353
Regulations, 13.351–13.358
specified persons, 13.352
supply of information, 13.358
use of information, 13.354–13.357

"Days of absence"
child benefit, 3.4

Death
child benefit
Regulations, 3.27
statutory basis, 1.61
child tax credit, 2.285–2.286
child trust fund appeals, 9.99–9.100
statutory maternity pay, 5.21
statutory parental bereavement pay, 8.10
statutory shared parental pay
entitlement (adoption), 7.54
entitlement (birth), 7.36
tax credit appeals, 2.457
tax credits
generally, 2.373–2.374
joint claims, for, 2.375–2.376
working tax credit, 2.179–2.180

Debts
trading income
debts incurred and later released, 1.757
doubtful debts, 1.748

Decisions (HMRC Commissioners)
amendment of existing legislation, 1.248–1.249
appeals
exercise of right, 1.238–1.241
generally, 1.236–1.237
regulations, 1.242–1.243
definitions, 1.250–1.252
generally, 1.230–1.231
matters arising, 1.244–1.245
regulations, 1.232–1.233
review of decisions
generally, 1.352–1.353
late application, 1.354–1.357
Secretary of State's delegated functions, 1.246–1.247
supersession of earlier decisions, 1.234–1.235
tax credits
discovery, on, 1.347–1.349
final decision, 1.341–1.343
final notice, 1.339–1.340
information requirements, 1.358–1.359
initial decision, 1.323–1.329
notice of decision, 1.360–1.362
official error, 1.350–1.351
other revised decisions, 1.332–1.338
power to enquire, 1.344–1.346
review, 1.352–1.357
revision after notifications, 1.330–1.331
subject to official error, 1.350–1.351
verification of claims, 2.444
variation of earlier decisions, 1.234–1.235

Deductions
application of provisions, 1.548
'deductibility provisions', 1.553
employment income, 2.218
expenses, 1.556
expenses paid by employee
effect of reimbursement, 1.555
generally, 1.554
general rules
double deductions, 1.551
income from which be made, 1.549
maximum amount, 1.550
order for making, 1.552

pension income, 2.224
regulations, 2.218
social security income, 2.236
trading income
  bad debts, 1.748
  business entertainment and gifts, 1.750
  capital expenditure, 1.745–1.746
  cash basis accounting, 1.744
  doubtful debts, 1.748
  generally, 2.230
  professions and vocations, 1.743
  relationship between rules, 1.740
  social security contributions, 1.751
  unconnected losses, 1.747
  unpaid remuneration, 1.749
  wholly and exclusively rules, 1.747
travel expenses
  necessary attendance, for, 1.558
  performance of duties, in, 1.557
  'workplace', 1.559
"Deemed income from capital"
generally, 2.202
"Depriving self of income to secure entitlement"
notional income, 2.253–2.254
Detention
child benefit
  Regulations, 3.21–3.24
  statutory basis, 1.186
statutory maternity pay, 5.17–5.18
statutory paternity pay, 6.98
statutory shared parental pay, 7.75
statutory sick pay, 4.9
"Determination of rate"
cases in which no rate of tax credit, 2.334–2.335
child tax credit
  full year periods, 2.330
  generally, 2.328–2.330
  short periods, 2.331
cut-off provisions, 2.334–2.335
generally, 2.320–2.321
reciprocal agreements, 2.332–2.333
working tax credit
  full year periods, 2.326
  generally, 2.322–2.325
  short periods, 2.327
Directions
tax credit appeals
  death of party, 2.457
Disability assistance
See **Adult disability payments; Child disability payments**
Disability Assistance for Working-Age People (Transitional Provisions and Miscellaneous Amendment) (Scotland) Regulations 2022
See also **Adult disability payments**
citation, 13.438
commencement, 13.438
definitions, 13.439
extent, 13.438

general provisions
  review of entitlement to ADP, 13.449–13.453
  transfer to ADP, 13.440–13.448
miscellaneous amendments, 13.454
Disability element (working tax credit)
Cases A to G, 2.155
first disability condition, 2.155
generally, 2.154–2.155
initial claims, 2.156–2.157
relevant disabilities, 2.183–2.196
second disability condition, 2.155
'training for work', 2.158–2.159
Disability living allowance
social security income, 2.233
Disability pension
See **Pension income**
"Disability periods"
working tax credit, 2.139–2.140
Disability working allowance
working tax credit, 2.155
Disabled persons
child tax credit, 2.289–2.290
Disabled persons tax credit
social security income, 2.233
Disabled persons' vehicles
maintenance grant, 1.817
Disclosure
information, of
  statutory maternity pay, 1.223
  statutory sick pay, 1.221
  tax credits, 1.437–1.438
prosecuting authority, to; 1.862
public interest disclosure, 1.861
wrongful disclosure, 1.860
Discretionary payments
disregards, 2.261
social security income, 2.233
Disregards
conditional exclusions, 2.266
employment income, 2.212
generally, 2.261–2.264
investment income, 2.243
partial disregard, 2.267
pension income, 2.221
social security income, 2.233
student income, 2.241–2.242
total disregard, 2.265
Divided contracts
employer's liability, 1.69–1.73
statutory adoption pay
  general note, 6.10
  generally, 6.11
  introduction, 1.141
  lapse of election, 6.15
  notification of election, 6.12
  provision of information, 6.13
  relevant employer, 6.14
statutory maternity pay
  generally, 5.11
  relevant employer, 5.32–5.33

statutory maternity pay (National Health Service)
  lapse of election, 5.81
  notification of election, 5.78
  provision of information, 5.79
  treatment of more than one contract as one, 5.77
  treatment of two or more employers as one, 5.80
statutory paternity pay
  general note, 6.10
  generally, 6.11
  introduction, 1.141
  lapse of election, 6.15
  notification of election, 6.12
  provision of information, 6.13
  relevant employer, 6.14
statutory sick pay
  generally, 4.41
  relevant employer, 4.39–4.40
statutory sick pay (National Health Service)
  lapse of election, 4.82
  notification of election, 4.79
  provision of information, 4.80
  treatment of more than one contract as one, 4.78
  treatment of two or more employers as one, 4.81

Dividends
non-resident UK companies, from
  charge to tax, 1.785
  income charged, 1.786
  person liable, 1.787
UK resident companies, from
  charge to tax, 1.782
  income charged, 1.783
  introduction, 1.781
  person liable, 1.784

Divorcees
guardian's allowance, 3.73

Duplication of payments
child benefit, 3.55–3.56

Early learning grants
See **Best start grants**

Early years assistance
See **Scotland**

Early Years Assistance (Best Start Grants) (Scotland) Regulations 2018
See also **Best start grants**
citation, 13.128
commencement, 13.128
interpretation, 13.131–13.141
overview, 13.129
schedules, 13.142–13.164

Earnings
carer support payments, 13.509
employment income, 1.515
statutory adoption pay
  generally, 6.91
  normal weekly earnings, 6.92–6.93
statutory maternity pay
  generally, 5.35–5.36
  normal weekly earnings, 5.37–5.38

statutory paternity pay
  generally, 6.91
  normal weekly earnings, 6.92–6.93
statutory shared parental pay
  generally, 7.60
  normal weekly earnings, 7.57–7.61
statutory sick pay
  excepted payments, 4.36
  generally, 4.35
  normal weekly earnings, 4.37–4.38

Education
carer support payments, 13.507–13.508
child benefit
  definition, 3.2
  generally, 3.4–3.5

Education maintenance allowance
disregards, 2.261

Eileen Trust
tax credits, 2.243

Election
child benefit
  generally, 3.19
  not to receive, 1.210–1.211
guardian's allowance, 3.79

Electronic communications
child benefit, 3.57
claims and notifications, 2.340–2.342

Employed earners
See **Employees**

Employees
statutory maternity pay, 5.31
statutory paternity pay, 6.83

Employer-contracted childcare
See **Childcare**

Employers
notice to provide information, 2.403
payment of WTC, 2.411
provision of information, and
  statutory maternity pay, 1.224
  statutory sick pay, 1.222

Employer's liabilities
See **Funding employers' liabilities**

Employment records
statutory adoption pay
  generally, 6.26
  inspection, 6.27
statutory maternity pay
  maintenance, 5.47
  production, 5.48
statutory paternity pay
  generally, 6.26
  inspection, 6.27
statutory sick pay
  maintenance, 4.27
  production, 4.28

Employment Act 2002
arrangement of sections, 1.465
general note, 1.466
general provisions
  maternity, 1.484–1.485
  paternity and adoption, 1.467–1.483
schedule, 1.486–1.494

Index

"Employment functions"
provision of information, and
general note, 2.522
generally, 2.524, 2.536
Employment income
agency workers, 1.514
amount of income charged, 1.509
benefits code
definitions, 1.518
meaning, 1.516
relationship with earnings, 1.517
cash vouchers
application of provisions, 1.522–1.523
benefit treated as earnings, 1.526
disregard for money, goods or services obtained, 1.533
meaning, 1.524
sickness-benefits related, 1.525
charge to tax
agency workers, 1.514
'employment', 1.503–1.504
exemptions, 1.502
introductory provision, 1.501–1.502
nature, 1.506–1.508
office-holders, 1.505
operation, 1.509–1.513
credit tokens
application of provisions, 1.530
benefit treated as earnings, 1.532
disregard for money, goods or services obtained, 1.533
meaning, 1.531
deductions from earnings
application of provisions, 1.548
'deductibility provisions', 1.553
expenses, 1.556
expenses paid by employee, 1.554–1.555
general rules, 1.549–1.552
regulations, 2.218
travel expenses, 1.557–1.559
definitions
'employment', 1.503–1.504
'employment income', 1.507
'exempt income', 1.508
'general earnings', 1.507
'net taxable earnings', 1.511
'net taxable specific income', 1.512
'paid', 1.520
'put at disposal', 1.520
'specific employment income', 1.507
'taxable earnings', 1.510
'taxable specific income', 1.510
differences from tax assessments, 2.217
disregarded payments, 2.212
earnings, 1.515
employer-contracted and provided childcare
'care', 1.546
'child', 1.546
definitions, 1.546–1.547
'eligible employee', 1.544
employer-contracted, 1.542–1.543
employer-provided, 1.540–1.541
introductory note, 1.502
'parental responsibility', 1.546
'qualifying child care', 1.547
'relevant earnings', 1.545
regulations, 2.218
'required time', 1.545
'employment', 1.503–1.504
employment-related benefits
cash equivalent treated as earnings, 1.536
cost of benefit, 1.537
excluded benefits, 1.535
meaning, 1.534
exemptions
'care', 1.546
'child', 1.546
definitions, 1.546–1.547
'eligible employee', 1.544
employer-contracted childcare, 1.542–1.543
employer-provided childcare, 1.540–1.541
introductory note, 1.502
'parental responsibility', 1.546
'qualifying child care', 1.547
'relevant earnings', 1.545
regulations, 2.218
'required time', 1.545
expenses payments
definitions, 1.520
relevant sums, 1.519
sums treated as earnings, 1.521
general note
regulations, 2.213
statutory provisions, 1.496–1.497
generally, 2.212
identity of taxpayer, 2.219
meaning, 1.507
minor benefits, 1.538–1.539
nature, 2.216
nature of charge to tax
definitions, 1.507–1.508
generally, 1.506
non-cash vouchers
application of provisions, 1.527
benefit treated as earnings, 1.529
disregard for money, goods or services obtained, 1.533
meaning, 1.528
office-holders, 1.505
operation of tax charge
amount of income charged, 1.509
definitions, 1.510–1.512
person liable to tax, 1.513
person liable to tax, 1.513
scope, 2.214
self-employment, 2.215
sickness-benefits related vouchers, 1.525
statutory provisions
charge to tax, 1.501–1.514
deductions from earnings, 1.548–1.559
earnings, 1.515

1877

Index

general note, 1.496–1.497
  taxable benefits, 1.516–1.539
taxable benefits
  benefits code, 1.516–1.518
  cash vouchers, 1.522–1.526
  credit tokens, 1.530–1.533
  expenses payments, 1.519–1.521
  minor benefits, 1.538–1.539
  non-cash vouchers, 1.527–1.529
  residual liability, 1.534–1.537
  vouchers, 1.522–1.529
time of calculation, 2.220
travel expenses
  necessary attendance, for, 1.558
  performance of duties, in, 1.557
  'workplace', 1.559
vouchers
  cash vouchers, 1.522–1.526
  non-cash vouchers, 1.527–1.529
"Employment insurance"
annual payments, 1.810–1.811
Employment records
statutory adoption pay
  generally, 6.26
  inspection, 6.27
statutory maternity pay
  maintenance, 5.47
  production, 5.48
statutory paternity pay
  generally, 6.26
  inspection, 6.27
statutory sick pay
  maintenance, 4.27
  production, 4.28
"Employment-related benefits"
cash equivalent treated as earnings, 1.536
cost of benefit, 1.537
excluded benefits, 1.535
meaning, 1.534
Employment zones
disregards, 2.261
remunerative work, 2.133
Enforcement
statutory maternity pay
  breach of regulations, 1.216–1.217
  fraud, 1.218
  negligence, 1.218
statutory sick pay
  breach of regulations, 1.216–1.217
  fraud, 1.218
  negligence, 1.218
Enquiries into tax returns
See **Tax enquiries**
Entitlement
statutory adoption pay
  determination of issues, 6.30–6.31
  evidence, 6.74
  provision of information, 6.28–6.29
  statutory provisions, 1.145–1.146
statutory maternity pay
  evidence, 5.60
  generally, 1.99–1.100

statutory paternity pay
  adoption of child, on, 6.59–6.65
  birth of child, on, 6.51–6.58
  common provisions, 6.66–6.70
  determination of issues, 6.30–6.31
  evidence, 6.56, 6.63
  provision of information, 6.28–6.29
  statutory provisions, 1.113–1.122
statutory sick pay
  employer's liability, 1.69–1.73
  evidence, 4.69–4.75
  general note, 1.67–1.68
  limitations, 1.85–1.87
  qualifying conditions, 1.74–1.84
Error by officials
See **Official errors**
Errors
See **Clerical errors**
"Evaluation studies"
generally, 2.530
Northern Ireland, 2.532
Evidence
See also **Medical evidence**
statutory adoption pay, 6.74
statutory maternity pay, 5.60
statutory parental bereavement pay, 8.9
statutory paternity pay
  adoption of child, on, 6.63
  birth of child, on, 6.56
statutory sick pay
  definitions, 4.69
  doctor's statement, 4.72–4.75
  general note, 4.70
  information required, 4.71
Ex gratia payments
social security income, 2.233
Exempt income
annual payments
  adopters, to, 1.812–1.813
  employment insurance payments, 1.810–1.811
  foreign maintenance payments, 1.805
  health insurance payments, 1.810–1.811
  periodical payments of personal injury damages, 1.806–1.809
employment income, 1.508
employment insurance payments, 1.810–1.811
foreign maintenance payments, 1.805
general disregard, 1.818
health insurance payments, 1.810–1.811
introduction, 1.716–1.717
overview, 1.804
payments to adopters
  England and Wales, 1.812
  Scotland, 1.813
periodical payments of personal injury damages
  compensation awards, 1.807
  generally, 1.806
  persons entitled, 1.808
  trusts, from, 1.809

Index

statutory overview, 1.719
tax credits
  employment income, 2.218
  pension income, 2.224
  social security income, 2.236
  trading income, 2.230
"Expected week of confinement"
statutory maternity pay, 5.41
Expenses
definitions, 1.520
relevant sums, 1.519
sums treated as earnings, 1.521
Extensions of time
child trust fund appeals, 9.97–9.98
tax credit appeals, 2.455–2.456
Failure to comply with requirements
See **Non-compliance**
Failure to disclose
overpayments, 1.214–1.215
Farming
trading income, 1.729
50-plus element
working tax credit, 2.178
First-tier Tribunal
appeals to, 1.226–1.227
allocation of functions to Social Security Chamber Regulations, 14.157–14.162
Foreign income
introduction, 1.716–1.717
social security income
  generally, 1.611–1.612
  person liable to tax, 1.614
  taxable income, 1.613
statutory overview, 1.719
tax credits, 2.247–2.248
"Foreign maintenance"
annual payments, 1.805
"Former Inland Revenue matters"
generally, 1.850
schedule, 1.874
"Forwarding claims"
administrative arrangements, 2.444
Foster care relief
amount per adult or child, 1.837
chargeable income, 1.840
definitions
  providing foster care, 1.830
  providing qualifying care, 1.829
  providing shared lives care, 1.831
  qualifying care receipts, 1.828
  residence, 1.832
  total qualifying care receipts, 1.833
full qualifying care relief
  chargeable income, 1.840
  introduction, 1.838
  trading income, 1.839
income period not a year, 1.836
individual's limit
  amount per adult or child, 1.837
  general, 1.834
  income period not a year, 1.836

residence used by more than one carer, 1.835
share of fixed amount, 1.835–1.836
overview, 1.825
providing foster care, 1.830
providing qualifying care, 1.829
providing shared lives care, 1.831
qualifying care receipts, 1.828
qualifying person, 1.826
residence
  generally, 1.832
  used by more than one carer, 1.835
share of fixed amount
  income period not a year, 1.836
  residence used by more than one carer, 1.835
total qualifying care receipts, 1.833
trading income, 1.839
Foster parents
charge-free childcare, 11.12
Fraud
loss of tax credits, and
  generally, 1.396–1.397
  introduction, 1.266
  Regulations, 2.546–2.549
  specified day, 2.543–2.545
  supplementary, 1.398–1.399
statutory adoption pay
  generally, 1.478–1.479
  procedure and appeals, 1.486–1.494
statutory maternity pay, 1.218
statutory paternity pay
  generally, 1.478–1.479
  procedure and appeals, 1.486–1.494
statutory sick pay, 1.218
tax credits
  generally, 1.388–1.389
  introduction, 1.266
  loss of tax credit, 1.392–1.399
  powers relating to documents, 1.390–1.391
  supply of information by tax authorities, 1.219
tax returns, 1.20
Fraud prevention
See **Crime prevention (fraud)**
Free childcare
See **Charge-free childcare; Tax-free childcare; 30 hours scheme**
Freedom of information
HMRC, 1.864
Full-time students
child benefit
  definition, 3.2
  generally, 3.4–3.5
"Funding employer's liabilities"
statutory adoption pay)
  application to Revenue, 6.21
  date of payment of contributions, 6.24
  generally, 6.20
  method, 6.22–6.23
  overpayments, 6.25
statutory maternity pay, 1.105–1.106

1879

statutory parental bereavement pay
  applications, 8.35
  deductions from payments to Commissioners, 8.36
  generally, 8.34
  payment to employers, 8.37
statutory paternity pay
  application to Revenue, 6.21
  date of payment of contributions, 6.24
  generally, 6.20
  method, 6.22–6.23
  overpayments, 6.25
statutory shared parental pay
  applications, 7.06
  date when contributions treated as paid, 7.09
  deductions from payments, 7.07
  generally, 7.05
  overpayments, 7.10
  payments to employers, 7.08
  records by employers, 7.11–7.12
statutory sick pay (post-September 30, 2021)
  claims, 4.124–4.125
  corrections, 4.127–4.128
  definitions, 4.119
  eligibility, 4.121
  'eligible employer', 4.122
  general note, 4.118
  incapacity for work, 4.123
  making claims, 4.124
  mistaken statements, 4.128
  overpayments, 4.129
  overstated, 4.127
  payments, 4.126
  preservation of records, 4.130
  provision of information, 4.131
  records, 4.130–4.131
  recovery of payments, 4.129
  Regulations, 4.118–4.131
  statutory provisions, 1.92–1.93
  time limit for claims, 4.125
  understated, 4.128
statutory sick pay (pre-October 1, 2021)
  claims, 4.107–4.108
  corrections, 4.110–4.111
  definitions, 4.103
  eligibility, 4.104
  'eligible employer', 4.105
  general note, 4.101
  incapacity for work, 4.106
  making claims, 4.107
  mistaken statements, 4.110
  overpayments, 4.112
  overstated, 4.110
  payments, 4.109
  preservation of records, 4.113
  provision of information, 4.114
  records, 4.113–4.114
  recovery of payments, 4.112
  Regulations, 4.100–4.114
  statutory provisions, 1.92–1.93
  time limit for claims, 4.108
  understated, 4.111

Funding of legal services
  See **Legal advice and funding**
Funeral expenses (Scotland)
  See also **Scotland**
  amount, 13.178
  applications, 13.167
  calculation, 13.177
  deductions from award, 13.179
  definitions, 13.122, 13.166
  determinations without application, 13.168
  eligibility
    estate of deceased person, 13.176
    general provision, 13.118
    multiple applications, 13.173
    place of funeral, 13.174
    qualifying benefits, 13.175
    relationship to deceased, 13.172
    residence conditions, 13.174
    status, 13.174
  estate of deceased person, 13.176
  final provisions, 13.122
  form, 13.177
  further criteria, 13.119–13.120
  generally, 13.22, 13.70
  miscellaneous provisions, 13.118–13.122
  multiple applications, 13.173
  period for applications, 13.169–13.170
  period for redetermination requests, 13.171
  place of funeral, 13.174
  procedural matters, 13.167–13.171
  qualifying benefits, 13.175
  redetermination requests, 13.171
  Regulations
    citation, 13.165
    commencement, 13.165
    definitions, 13.166
    general provisions, 13.167–13.179
  relationship to deceased, 13.172
  residence conditions, 13.174
  status, 13.174
  suspension of assistance, 13.127
  types, 13.121
Further education
  child benefit, 3.4–3.5
  definition, 3.2
Gambling
  investment income, 2.243
"Gaps between jobs"
  working tax credit, 2.152–2.153
"General earnings"
  employment income, 1.507
Generally accepted accounting practice
  trading income, 1.734
Gifts
  trading income, 1.750
Guardian's allowance
  See also **Non-contributory benefits**
  adopted child
    Regulations, 3.71
    statutory provision, 1.46
  divorced person's child, 3.73

Index

election, 3.79
entitlement
  conditions, 1.39–1.46
  generally, 1.37–1.38
illegitimate child, 3.72
imprisoned person's child, 3.74–3.75
overpayments, 1.214–1.215
prisoner's child, 3.74–3.75
residence, 3.78
social security income, 2.233
uprating
  Regulations 2024, 3.82–3.86
Guardian's Allowance (General) Regulations 2003
arrangement, 3.66
citation, 3.68
commencement, 3.68
definitions, 3.69
general provisions, 3.70–3.79
recitals, 3.67
revocations, 3.80
schedule, 3.81
Haemophilia
investment income, 2.243
Health
provision of information, and
  definitions, 2.503
  general note, 2.502
  generally, 2.504, 2.521
  Northern Ireland, 2.534
Health insurance
annual payments, 1.810–1.811
HMRC
ancillary powers, 1.851
appointments
  Commissioners, 1.845
  officers, 1.846
assault on officers, 1.870
Charter
  generally, 1.856–1.857
  text, 12.1–12.15
Commissioners
  appointment, 1.845
  Charter of standards and values, 1.856–1.857
  declaration of confidentiality, 1.847
  functions, 1.849–1.855
  staff appointments, 1.846
complaints, 1.867–1.868
conduct of proceedings, 1.852
confidentiality, 1.859
data protection, 1.863
declaration of confidentiality, 1.847
definitions, 1.873
delegation of functions, 1.854–1.855
disclosure
  prosecuting authority, to; 1.862
  public interest, 1.861
  wrongful, 1.860
evidence, 1.865–1.866
former Inland Revenue matters
  generally, 1.850
  schedule, 1.874

freedom of information, 1.864
functions
  ancillary powers, 1.851
  Charter of standards and values, 1.856–1.857
  conduct of proceedings, 1.852
  Coronavirus, 1.1077
  delegation, 1.854–1.855
  exercise by officers, 1.853
  former Inland Revenue matters, 1.850
  initial, 1.849
general note, 1.844
information
  confidentiality, 1.859
  disclosure to prosecuting authority, 1.862
  freedom of information, 1.864
  public interest disclosure, 1.861
  use, 1.858
  wrongful disclosure, 1.860
initial functions, 1.849
ITEPA 2003, 1.498
meaning, 1.848
misconduct, 1.867–1.868
obstruction, 1.869
offences
  assault, 1.870
  obstruction, 1.869
  power of arrest, 1.871
officers
  appointment, 1.846
  assault, 1.870
  declaration of confidentiality, 1.847
  definitions, 1.873
  exercise of functions, 1.853
  obstruction, 1.869
  power of arrest, 1.871
payments by
  general note, 2.411
  generally, 2.413–2.437
proceedings
  evidence, 1.865–1.866
public interest disclosure, 1.861
resignation, 1.845
staff appointments, 1.846
wrongful disclosure, 1.860
HMRC Commissioners
administration of taxes, 1.3
appointment, 1.845
assault, 1.870
Charter of standards and values, 1.856–1.857
child trust funds, and
  General Commissioners, 9.67–9.85
  Special Commissioners, 9.86–9.89
conduct of proceedings, 1.852
decisions
  amendment of existing legislation, 1.248–1.249
  appeals, 1.236–1.249
  definitions, 1.250–1.252
  generally, 1.230–1.231
  matters arising, 1.244–1.245

1881

Index

regulations, 1.232–1.233
Secretary of State's delegated functions, 1.246–1.247
supersession of earlier decisions, 1.234–1.235
tax credits, 1.323–1.362
verification of claims, 2.444
variation of earlier decisions, 1.234–1.235
declaration of confidentiality, 1.847
delegation of functions, 1.854–1.855
exercise of functions, 1.853
former Inland Revenue matters
  generally, 1.850
  schedule, 1.874
freedom of information, 1.864
functions
  ancillary powers, 1.851
  Charter of standards and values, 1.856–1.857
  conduct of proceedings, 1.852
  delegation, 1.854–1.855
  exercise by officers, 1.853
  former Inland Revenue matters, 1.850
  generally, 1.269–1.270
  initial functions, 1.849
general note, 1.844
information
  confidentiality, 1.859
  freedom of information, 1.864
  use, 1.858
initial functions, 1.849
ITEPA 2003, 1.498
notices
  tax credits, 1.428–1.429
obstruction, 1.869
offences
  assault, 1.870
  obstruction, 1.869
  power of arrest, 1.871
payments
  amount, 2.431–2.432
  bank account requirement, 2.436–2.437
  definitions, 2.413
  general note, 2.411
  joint claims, for, 2.414–2.419
  method, 2.434–2.435
  person acting on behalf of another, for, 2.420–2.421
  postponement, 2.429–2.430
  recovery of overpayments, 2.433
  renewal claims, 2.422–2.423
  single payments, 2.427–2.428
  timing, 2.424–2.426
resignation, 1.845
responsibility for certain taxes, 1.3
staff appointments, 1.846
statutory parental bereavement pay, 8.28
supply of information
  statutory adoption pay, 1.480
  statutory paternity pay, 1.480
tax credits
  functions, 1.269–1.270
  notices, 1.428–1.429

use of information
  statutory adoption pay, 1.482
HMRC officers
appointment, 1.846
assault, 1.870
declaration of confidentiality, 1.847
exercise of Commissioners functions, 1.853
generally, 1.846
obstruction, 1.869
power of arrest, 1.871
HMRC (payments)
amount, 2.431–2.432
bank account requirement, 2.436–2.437
child care element of WTC, 2.414–2.415
definitions, 2.413
general note, 2.411
joint claims, for
  child tax credit, 2.414–2.415
  child care element of WTC, 2.414–2.415
  death of one of couple, 2.418–2.419
  working tax credit, 2.416–2.417
method, 2.434–2.435
person acting on behalf of another, for, 2.420–2.421
postponement, 2.429–2.430
recovery of overpayments
  generally, 1.370–1.372
  method, 2.433
renewal, on, 2.422–2.423
single payments, 2.427–2.428
timing
  bank account, 2.424–2.425
  other than to bank account, 2.426
working tax credit, and
  generally, 2.416–2.417
  introduction, 2.411
"Holding claims"
administrative arrangements, 2.444
Hospitals
definition, 3.2
"Hours worked"
qualifying remunerative work, 2.134
Housing benefit
social security income, 2.233
Identity of taxpayer
See **Taxable persons**
Ill health
working tax credit, 2.139–2.140
Illegitimacy
guardian's allowance, 3.72
Immigrants
definitions, 2.466
exclusion from entitlement, 2.467–2.473
general note, 2.468
modifications of Act, 2.472–2.473
polygamous marriages, 2.517
statutory provision, 1.420–1.421
transitional relief, 2.474–2.475
Imprisonment
child benefit
  Regulations, 3.24
  statutory basis, 1.186

Index

guardian's allowance, 3.74–3.75
statutory maternity pay, 5.17–5.18
statutory parental bereavement pay, 8.10
statutory paternity pay, 6.98
statutory sick pay, 4.9
"Inalienability"
  tax credits, 1.426–1.427
"Incapacitation"
  childcare element (working tax credit), 2.168
Incapacity benefit
  child benefit, 3.12
  social security income
    long-term, 1.591
    short-term, 1.592
  statutory maternity pay
    generally, 5.39
    statutory provision, 1.206
  statutory sick pay, 1.202–1.203
  working tax credit, 2.233
Incapacity for work
  statutory sick pay
    notification, 4.16
    persons deemed incapable, 4.4–4.6
    persons unable to act, 4.23–4.24
  working tax credit, 2.139–2.140
Income
  calculation, 2.210–2.211
  capital, 2.202
  deemed income from capital, 2.202
  definitions, 2.208–2.209
  disregards
    conditional exclusions, 2.266
    generally, 2.261–2.264
    partial disregard, 2.267
    total disregard, 2.265
  employment income
    deductions, 2.218
    differences from tax assessments, 2.217
    disregarded payments, 2.212
    exemptions, 2.218
    general note, 2.213
    generally, 2.212
    identity of taxpayer, 2.219
    nature, 2.216
    scope, 2.214
    self-employment, 2.215
    time of calculation, 2.220
  foreign income, 2.247–2.248
  general note
    change in approach, 2.202
    cross-references, 2.205
    differences from tax assessments, 2.203
    introduction, 2.200
    modifications, 2.206
    questions to be decided, 2.204
    Tax Law Rewrite Project, 2.201
  investment income
    disregarded payments, 2.243
    general note, 2.244
    generally, 2.243
    very severe disablement payments, 2.243

  miscellaneous income, 2.259–2.260
  not otherwise charged
    charge to tax, 1.801
    income charged, 1.802
    person liable, 1.803
  notional income
    depriving self of income to secure entitlement, 2.253–2.254
    entitlement to sums, 2.255–2.256
    generally, 2.249–2.250
    provision of services for less than full earnings, 2.257–2.258
    sums treated as income under Taxes Acts, 2.251–2.252
  pension income
    deductions, 2.224
    disregarded payments, 2.221
    exemptions, 2.224
    general note, 2.222
    generally, 2.221
    identity of taxpayer, 2.225
    relevant income, 2.223
    time of calculation, 2.226
  polygamous marriages, 2.513
  property income, 2.245–2.246
  social security income
    deductions, 2.236
    disregarded payments, 2.233
    exemptions, 2.236
    general note, 2.234
    generally, 2.233
    identity of taxpayer, 2.237
    relevant income, 2.235
    time of calculation, 2.238
  statutory provision, 1.295–1.302
  student income
    disregarded payments, 2.241–2.242
    generally, 2.239–2.240
  taper start point, 2.310
  tax-exempt savings, 2.202
  thresholds
    definitions, 2.312
    generally, 2.313–2.315
  trading income
    deductions, 2.230
    exemptions, 2.230
    general note, 2.228
    generally, 2.227
    identity of taxpayer, 2.231
    relevant income, 2.230
    self-employment, 2.229
    time of calculation, 2.232
  transition to universal credit, and, 1.302
  voluntary work, 2.256–2.257
"Income not otherwise charged"
  charge to tax, 1.801
  income charged, 1.802
  person liable, 1.803
Income support
  child benefit, 3.12
  generally, 2.316–2.317
  income test, 2.205

Index

social security income
  amount in excess of taxable maximum, 1.595
  child maintenance bonus, 1.594
  definitions, 1.597–1.598
  general rule, 1.593
  generally, 2.233
  taxable maximum, 1.596
  trade disputes, 1.593

Income tax
  assessment, 2.203
  charge to tax, 1.878–1.880
  child trust funds
    account provider to act on behalf of named child, 9.46
    account provider's tax claims, 9.47–9.48
    adaptation of enactments, 9.58
    administration, 9.59
    application of Taxes Act, 9.60
    assessment for withdrawal of relief, 9.50
    fortnightly claims, 9.51
    generally, 9.45
    information about looked after children, 9.54–9.55
    information to be provided to Board, 9.56
    inspection of records, 9.57
    records, 9.52
    repayments to account provider, 9.47–9.48
    returns of information, 9.53
    statutory provisions, 1.687–1.688
    tax returns, 9.51
  definitions
    civil partners, 1.887
    'company', 1.886
    general list, 1.885
    living together, 1.887
    married persons, 1.887
    overview, 1.884
  employment income, 1.501–1.559
  exempt income, 1.804–1.818
  foster care relief
    amount per adult or child, 1.837
    chargeable income, 1.840
    definitions, 1.828–1.833
    full qualifying care relief, 1.838–1.840
    income period not a year, 1.836
    individual's limit, 1.834–1.837
    overview, 1.825
    providing foster care, 1.830
    providing qualifying care, 1.829
    providing shared lives care, 1.831
    qualifying care receipts, 1.828
    qualifying person, 1.826
    residence, 1.832
    share of fixed amount, 1.835–1.836
    total qualifying care receipts, 1.833
    trading income, 1.839
  general note
    ITA 2007, 1.875
    ITEPA 2003, 1.496–1.497
    ITTOIA 2005, 1.716–1.718

  general provisions, 1.841–1.842
  jointly held property
    declarations of unequal beneficial interests, 1.883
    generally, 1.881–1.882
  miscellaneous income, 1.792–1.803
  overview
    ITA 2007, 1.876–1.877
    ITEPA 2003, 1.499–1.500
    ITTOIA 2005, 1.719–1.720
  pension income, 1.560–1.573
  property income
    calculation of profits, 1.770
    cash basis, 1.770
    charge to tax, 1.766–1.769
    generating income from land, 1.765
    overseas property business, 1.764
    overview, 1.758–1.759
    priority rules, 1.760–1.761
    profits, 1.766–1.769
    property businesses, 1.762–1.770
    trading income rules, 1.770
    UK property business, 1.763
  qualifying care receipts, 1.828
  rent-a-room relief, 1.819–1.824
  returns, 1.4–1.35
  savings and investment income, 1.771–1.791
  shared lives care relief
    amount per adult or child, 1.837
    chargeable income, 1.840
    definitions, 1.828–1.833
    full qualifying care relief, 1.838–1.840
    income period not a year, 1.836
    individual's limit, 1.834–1.837
    overview, 1.825
    providing foster care, 1.830
    providing qualifying care, 1.829
    providing shared lives care, 1.831
    qualifying care receipts, 1.828
    qualifying person, 1.826
    residence, 1.832
    share of fixed amount, 1.835–1.836
    total qualifying care receipts, 1.833
    trading income, 1.839
  social security income, 1.574–1.614
  trading income, 1.721–1.757

Income Tax Act 2007
  See also **Income tax**
  arrangement of sections, 1.874
  definitions, 1.884–1.887
  general note, 1.875
  general provisions
    charge to tax, 1.878–1.880
    jointly held property, 1.881–1.883
    overview, 1.876–1.877

Income tax (charge to tax)
  emoluments (offices and employment)
    general note, 1.496–1.497
  employment income
    agency workers, 1.514
    deductions from earnings, 1.548–1.559
    earnings, 1.515

Index

'employment', 1.503–1.504
exemptions, 1.540–1.547
general note, 1.496–1.497
introductory provision, 1.501–1.502
nature, 1.506–1.508
office-holders, 1.505
operation, 1.509–1.513
taxable benefits, 1.516–1.539
general note
  ITA 2007, 1.875
  ITEPA 2003, under, 1.496–1.497
general rule
  ITA 2007, 1.878–1.880
  ITTOIA 2005, 1.716–1.718
  ITEPA 2003, under, 1.499
miscellaneous income
  income not otherwise charged, 1.801
  settlements, 1.795–1.800
pension income
  amount charged, 1.563
  general note, 1.561
  general rules, 1.565–1.569
  introductory provision, 1.560
  nature of charge, 1.562
  person liable to tax, 1.564
  social security pensions, 1.570–1.573
property income
  generally, 1.766
  income charged, 1.768
  person liable, 1.769
  territorial scope, 1.767
savings and investments income
  dividends from non-resident UK companies, 1.785
  dividends from UK resident companies, 1.782
  interest, 1.776
  purchased life annuity payments, 1.788
Schedule E (offices and employment emoluments)
  general note, 1.496–1.497
social security income
  amount charged, 1.582
  definitions, 1.615–1.616
  exempt benefits, 1.591–1.606
  foreign benefits, 1.611–1.614
  general note, 1.575–1.576
  introductory provision, 1.574
  nature of charge, 1.577–1.579
  person liable to tax, 1.583
  taxable benefits, 1.584–1.590
  wholly exempt benefits, 1.607–1.610
trading income
  arrangements for avoiding tax, 1.726
  generally, 1.724
  income charged, 1.727
  person liable, 1.728
  territorial scope, 1.725

Income Tax (Earnings and Pensions) Act 2003 (ITEPA)
See also **Income tax**
arrangement of sections, 1.495
definitions, 1.615–1.616

general note
  CRCA 2005, 1.498
  introduction, 1.496–1.497
general provisions
  employment income, 1.501–1.559
  overview, 1.499–1.500
  pension income, 1.560–1.573
  social security income, 1.574–1.614

Income tax (tax returns)
amendment by taxpayer
  during enquiry, 1.10
  generally, 1.7
appeals
  no questioning amounts of social security income, 1.28
  notification of taxable amounts of social security income, 1.29–1.30
  settlement by agreement, 1.21–1.27
assessment
  appeals, 1.21–1.32
  discovery of loss of tax, on, 1.14
  loss, destruction or damage, 1.33
  relief for excessive assessments, 1.15–1.16
  time limits, 1.17–1.20
  want of form, 1.34
closure notices, 1.13
correction by Revenue
  during enquiry, 1.11
  generally, 1.8
definitions, 1.35
destruction, etc., 1.25
enquiry
  amendment by taxpayer, 1.10
  completion, 1.13
  correction by Revenue, 1.11
  notice, 1.9
fraudulent conduct, 1.20
generally, 1.4
interpretation of section 8(4A), 1.5
loss, destruction or damage, 1.33
negligent conduct, 1.20
notice of enquiry, 1.9
ordinary time limits
  generally, 1.17
  self-assessments, 1.18
penalties, 1.32
records, 1.12
relief for excessive assessments
  double assessment, 1.15
  recovery of overpaid tax etc, 1.16
self-assessment, 1.6
time limits
  fraudulent conduct, 1.20
  income received after year for which assessable, 1.19
  negligent conduct, 1.20
  ordinary period, 1.17–1.18
  self-assessments, 1.18
want of form, 1.34

Income Tax (Trading and Other Income) Act 2005
See also **Income tax**

arrangement of sections, 1.715
general note, 1.716–1.718
general provisions
  exempt income, 1.804–1.818
  foster care relief, 1.825–1.840
  general rules, 1.841–1.842
  miscellaneous income, 1.792–1.803
  overview, 1.719–1.720
  property income, 1.758–1.770
  qualifying care relief, 1.825–1.840
  rent-a-room relief, 1.819–1.824
  savings and investment income, 1.771–1.791
  shared lives care relief, 1.825–1.840
  trading income, 1.721–1.757

Income test
See **Income**

Incorrect statements
See **Misstatements**

Individual savings accounts
income test, 2.202
investment income, 2.243

Industrial injuries benefits
social security income, 2.233

Information
administrative arrangements, and
  by authorities, 2.443
  to authorities, 2.442
employers, by
  statutory maternity pay, 1.224
  statutory sick pay, 1.222
functions relating to employment
  general note, 2.522
  generally, 2.524, 2.536
functions relating to health
  definitions, 2.503
  general note, 2.502
  generally, 2.504, 2.521
  Scotland, 2.534
functions relating to training
  general note, 2.522
  generally, 2.524, 2.536
Scotland
  definitions, 13.351
  generally, 13.83
  purpose, 13.353
  Regulations, 13.351–13.354
  specified persons, 13.352
  supply of information, 13.358
  use of information, 13.354–13.357
Secretary of State, by
  statutory maternity pay, 1.223
  statutory sick pay, 1.221
statutory adoption pay
  entitlement, as to, 6.28–6.29
  generally, 6.32
statutory maternity pay, 5.42
  claims for other benefits, 5.46
  determination of questions, 5.44–5.45
statutory parental bereavement pay
  entitlement, as to, 8.42
  generally, 8.45

statutory paternity pay
  entitlement, as to, 6.28–6.29
  generally, 6.32
statutory sick pay
  employee to Secretary of State, by, 4.29–4.30
  employer to employee, by, 4.31–4.32
tax authorities, by
  contributions purposes, for, 1.220
  fraud prevention, for, 1.219
tax credits
  generally, 2.530
  Northern Ireland, 2.532

Information sharing
See **Data sharing**

Inland Revenue
See **HMRC**

Insolvency (employers)
statutory sick pay, 4.21

Insurance companies
child trust funds
  'child trust fund business', 9.65
  general provision, 9.62–9.64
  modifications of Acts, 9.66

"Intensive Activity Period"
remunerative work, 2.133

Intercountry adoption
pay period, 6.131–6.132
statutory adoption pay
  administration, 6.110–6.114
  application of General Regulations 2002, 6.120
  application of SSCBA 1992, 6.102–6.109
  avoidance of liability, 6.137
  definitions, 6.119
  evidence of entitlement, 6.134
  general note, 6.118
  notice requirements, 6.133
  pay period, 6.131–6.132
  termination of employment, 6.136
  treatment of more than one employer, 6.135
statutory paternity pay
  administration, 6.110–6.114
  application of General Regulations 2002, 6.120
  application of SSCBA 1992, 6.102–6.109
  avoidance of liability, 6.128
  change of circumstances, 6.129
  conditions of entitlement, 6.122
  definitions, 6.119
  evidence requirements, 6.125
  general note, 6.118
  notice requirements, 6.125–6.126
  options as to periods of payment, 6.123
  qualifying period, 6.124
  treatment of more than one employer, 6.127
  work during a period of payment, 6.130
statutory shared parental pay
  application of General Regulations, 7.95

Index

definitions, 7.94
modification of General Regulations, 7.96–7.108
Interest
  charge to tax, 1.776
  income charged, 1.777
  person liable, 1.779
  tax credits
    definitions, 2.461
    general note, 2.460
    generally, 1.400–1.401
    overpayments, on, 2.462
    prescribed rate, 2.463
  territorial scope, 1.775
  trading income, 1.739
  valuation where not paid in cash, 1.778
"Interruption of employment"
  statutory sick pay, 4.26
Investment income
  building society dividends, 1.780
  dividends from non-resident UK companies
    charge to tax, 1.785
    income charged, 1.786
    person liable, 1.787
  dividends from UK resident companies
    charge to tax, 1.782
    income charged, 1.783
    introduction, 1.781
    person liable, 1.784
  general note, 1.772
  interest
    charge to tax, 1.776
    income charged, 1.777
    person liable, 1.779
    territorial scope, 1.775
    valuation of interest not paid in cash, 1.778
  introduction, 1.716–1.717
  overview, 1.771
  priority rules
    generally, 1.773–1.774
    introduction, 1.720
  purchased life annuity payments
    charge to tax, 1.788
    income charged, 1.790
    meaning, 1.789
    person liable, 1.791
  statutory overview
    introduction, 1.719
    priority rules, 1.720
  tax credits
    disregarded payments, 2.243
    general note, 2.244
    generally, 2.243
    very severe disablement payments, 2.243
  territorial scope of charge, 1.775
ISAs
  See **Individual investment accounts**
Jobseekers' allowance
  child benefit, 3.12
  child maintenance bonus, 1.599

generally, 2.316–2.317
income test, 2.205
Intensive Activity Period, 2.133
social security income
  amount in excess of taxable maximum, 1.600
  child maintenance bonus, 1.599
  definitions, 1.604
  generally, 2.233
  taxable maximum, 1.601–1.603
taxable maximum
  amount in excess of, 1.600
  contribution-based JSA, 1.603
  definitions, 1.604
  general, 1.601
  income-based JSA, 1.602
Joint property
  declarations of unequal beneficial interests, 1.883
  generally, 1.881–1.882
"Late appeals"
  child trust funds, 9.97–9.98
  tax credits
    generally, 1.413–1.415
    invalid regulation, 2.455–2.456
    Order, 2.550–2.552
Lifetime annuities
  charge to tax, 1.788
  income charged, 1.790
  meaning, 1.789
  person liable, 1.791
Linking periods
  statutory sick pay, 4.7–4.8
"Living away from home allowance"
  disregards, 2.261
"Living together"
  references in Income Tax Acts, 1.887
Lone-parent element
  working tax credit, 2.164–2.165
Lotteries
  investment income, 2.243
Macfarlane Trust
  tax credits, 2.243
Maintenance
  disregards, 2.261
"Managed migration"
  adjustment where other elements increase, 2.99–2.100
  appeal of award of existing benefit, 2.111–2.112
  capital disregard, 2.91–2.92
  cessation of transitional protection, 2.101
  definitions, 2.37
  determining application of transitional protection, 2.90
  effect of revision, 2.111–2.112
  ending of transitional protection
    application to subsequent awards, 2.102–2.103
    circumstances in which ceases, 2.101
  extension of deadline day, 2.81–2.82
  full-time students, 2.106–2.108
  general note, 2.35

indicative UC amount, 2.97–2.98
initial amount, 2.99–2.100
'migration day', 2.89
minimum income floor, 2.105
miscellaneous, 2.104–2.105
no claim before deadline, 2.83–2.84
notice, 2.79–2.80
notified persons who claim as different benefit unit, 2.85–2.85
process
  extension of deadline day, 2.81–2.82
  notice, 2.79–2.80
  persons who claim as different benefit unit, 2.85–2.85
  termination of existing benefits, 2.83–2.84
'qualifying claim'
  generally, 2.87–2.88
  setting later commencement day, 2.104
Regulations, 2.79–2.112
rounding, 2.109–2.110
students, 2.106–2.108
subsequent awards, 2.102–2.103
termination of existing benefits, 2.83–2.84
total legacy amount, 2.95–2.96
transitional capital disregard, 2.91–2.92
transitional element
  generally, 2.93–2.94
  indicative UC amount, 2.97–2.98
  initial amount, 2.99–2.100
  total legacy amount, 2.95–2.96
transitional protection
  capital disregard, 2.91–2.92
  determining application by Secretary of State, 2.90
  element, 2.93–2.100
  ending, 2.101
  'migration day', 2.89
  'qualifying claim', 2.87–2.88
Mariners
See **Seafarers**
Market gardening
trading income, 1.729
"Married child"
child benefit
  Regulations, 3.18
  statutory basis, 1.188
Married persons
See **Spouses**
Maternity allowance
normal weekly earnings
  Coronavirus, 5.116–5.122
statutory maternity pay, 5.40
working tax credit, 2.233
Maternity pay
See **Statutory maternity pay**
Means testing
capital, 2.202
general rule, 2.200
Medical evidence
maternity
  definitions, 5.59

evidence of pregnancy and confinement, 5.60
form of certificate, 5.61–5.62
sickness
  definitions, 4.69
  doctor's statement, 4.72–4.75
  general note, 4.70
  information required, 4.71
  modification of duration, 4.116–4.117
Migration
See **Managed migration**
Milk tokens
See **Welfare food**
"Miscellaneous income"
amount treated as income of settlor settlements, 1.795–1.800
income not otherwise charged
  charge to tax, 1.801
  income charged, 1.802
  person liable, 1.803
introduction, 1.716–1.717
overview, 1.792
priority rules
  generally, 1.793–1.794
  introduction, 1.720
settlements
  charge to tax, 1.795–1.796
  income charged, 1.799
  person liable, 1.800
  'settlement', 1.798
  'settlor', 1.798
  treatment as highest part of settlor's total income, 1.797
statutory overview
  introduction, 1.719
  priority rules, 1.720
tax credits
  general note, 2.260
  generally, 2.259
territorial scope, 1.795
Misrepresentation
overpayments, 1.214–1.215
Misstatements
statutory adoption pay, 1.478–1.479
statutory paternity pay, 1.478–1.479
tax credits
  conduct of penalty cases, 1.380–1.381
  fraudulently or negligently, 1.379
  generally, 1.376–1.378
  level of penalties, 1.382–1.383
Mistakes
See **Clerical errors**
Mobility supplement
See **War pensioner's mobility supplement**
National insurance contributions
trading income, 1.751
National insurance numbers
child benefit, 3.54
National Savings
income test, 2.202
Negligence
statutory maternity pay, 1.218

statutory sick pay, 1.218
tax returns, 1.20
"Net taxable earnings"
  employment income, 1.511
"Net taxable specific income"
  employment income, 1.512
New Deal
  disregards, 2.261
NHS employees (divided contracts)
  statutory maternity pay
    lapse of election, 5.81
    notification of election, 5.78
    provision of information, 5.79
    treatment of more than one contract as one, 5.11, 5.77
    treatment of two or more employers as one, 5.32–5.33, 5.80
  statutory paternity pay
    general note, 6.10
    lapse of election, 6.15
    notification of election, 6.12
    provision of information, 6.13
    relevant employer, 6.14
  statutory sick pay
    generally, 4.41
    lapse of election, 4.82
    notification of election, 4.79
    provision of information, 4.80
    relevant employer, 4.39–4.40
    treatment of more than one contract as one, 4.78
    treatment of two or more employers as one, 4.81
Non-cash vouchers
  See **Vouchers**
Non-compliance
  failure to comply with requirements
    statutory adoption pay, 1.476–1.477
    statutory paternity pay, 1.476–1.477
    tax credits, 1.384–1.386
Non-disclosure
  overpayments, 1.214–1.215
Non-residents
  person treated as not being resident
    in GB, 3.30–3.34
    in Northern Ireland, 3.39–3.40
Normal weekly income
  statutory adoption pay
    'earnings', 6.91
    generally, 6.92–6.93
  statutory maternity pay
    'earnings', 5.35–5.36
    generally, 5.37–5.38
  statutory parental bereavement pay, 8.20
  statutory paternity pay
    'earnings', 6.91
    generally, 6.92–6.93
  statutory shared parental pay
    adoption, 7.58–7.59
    'appropriate date', 7.60
    birth, 7.57
    'day of payment', 7.60
    'earnings', 7.60

meaning, 7.60–7.61
    'normal pay day', 7.60
    'relevant period', 7.60
"Normal working weeks"
  statutory maternity pay
    generally, 5.28–5.29
    'week', 5.30
"Normally living with test"
  child tax credit, 2.273
Northern Ireland
  tax credits
    evaluation and statistical studies, 2.531–2.532
    generally, 1.447–1.448
    tax-free childcare, 1.707–1.706
Notices
  absence from work
    statutory maternity pay, 5.42
  child trust fund appeals
    disputes concerning, 9.95–9.96
    prescribed form, 9.87–9.88
    service, 9.93–9.94
    signature, 9.87–9.88
    statutory provision, 1.705
  enquiries in returns, 1.9
  provision of information
    childcare provider, to, 2.404
    dates to be specified, 2.405
    definitions, 2.339
    electronic communications, 2.340–2.342
    employers, to, 2.403
    s.17 TCA 2002, under, 2.406–2.409
  statutory parental bereavement pay
    service, 8.30
  tax credits, 1.428–1.429
  tax returns, 1.9
Notification
  change of circumstances
    definitions, 2.339
    electronic communications, 2.340–2.342
    generally, 2.381–2.402
    polygamous marriages, 2.514
  employment after confinement, 5.43
  incapacity for work, 4.16
  statutory maternity pay, 5.43
  statutory sick pay, 4.16
Notification (change of circumstances)
  advance, in, 2.397
  amendment, 2.389
  Coronavirus
    cases where change may increase the maximum rate, 2.392
    decrease of rate, 2.386
    disability, 2.396.1
  date
    Coronavirus, 2.392
    disability element of CTC, 2.395–2.396.1
    disability element of WTC, 2.393–2.394
    increase of maximum rate, 2.390–2.392
  decrease of rate
    Coronavirus, 2.386
    generally, 2.383–2.385

definitions
  generally, 2.339
  notification date, 2.283
disability element of CTC
  Coronavirus, 2.396.1
  generally, 2.395–2.396
disability element of WTC,
  2.393–2.394
electronic communications,
  2.340–2.342
evidence of birth or adoption, 2.402
increase of maximum rate, and
  date of notification, 2.390–2.392
  general rule, 2.381–2.382
  method, 2.386–2.387
person acting on behalf of another, by
  generally, 2.398–2.399
  other appointed persons, 2.400–2.401
polygamous marriages, 2.514
relevant person, 2.388
Notional income
depriving self of income to secure
  entitlement, 2.253–2.254
entitlement to sums, 2.255–2.256
generally, 2.249–2.250
provision of services for less than full
  earnings, 2.257–2.258
sums treated as income under Taxes Acts,
  2.251–2.252
Obstruction
officers of HMRC, 1.869
Officeholders
employment income, 1.505
Officers of Revenue and Customs
See **HMRC officers**
"Official errors"
See also **Clerical errors**
carer support payments
  overpayments, 13.533
  underpayments, 13.534
definitions, 2.496–2.497
general note, 2.499
generally, 2.498
Offshore workers
statutory adoption pay
  definitions, 6.34
  general note, 6.35
  generally, 6.43
statutory maternity pay
  definitions, 5.64
  general note, 5.65
  generally, 5.73
  statutory provisions, 1.110
statutory paternity pay
  definitions, 6.34
  general note, 6.35
  generally, 6.43
  statutory provisions, 1.138–1.139
statutory sick pay
  definitions, 4.53, 4.60, 4.66
  general note, 4.49
  statutory provision, 1.96
  time for compliance, 4.67

Ordinary residence
Crown servants posted overseas
  generally, 2.489–2.490
  partners, 2.491
definitions, 2.478–2.479
HMRC code of practice, 2.483
meaning, 2.482–2.484
person treated as not being in UK,
  2.480–2.485
temporary absence from UK, 2.487–2.488
tests, 2.485
transitional provision, 2.492–2.493
**Ordinary Statutory Paternity Pay
  (Adoption), etc Regulations 2010**
arrangement, 6.139
citation, 6.140
commencement, 6.140
definitions, 6.141
general provision, 6.143
revocation, 6.142
Overpayments
carer support payments, 13.533
child benefit, 1.214–1.215
Code of Practice, 12.29–12.75
failure to disclose, 1.214–1.215
guardian's allowance, 1.214–1.215
interest, 2.462
misrepresentation, 1.214–1.215
statutory adoption pay, 6.25
statutory maternity pay, 5.92
statutory parental bereavement pay, 8.39
statutory paternity pay, 6.25
tax credits
  generally, 1.367–1.369
  method of recovery, 2.433
  modification of legislation, 2.55–2.56
  recovery, 1.370–1.372
  transition to universal credit, 2.55–2.56
Overseas adoption
See **Intercountry adoption**
Overseas employees
Crown servants
  generally, 2.489–2.490
  partners, 2.491
"Paid"
employment income, 1.520
**Parental Bereavement (Leave and Pay)
  Act 2018**
See also **Statutory parental
  bereavement pay**
arrangement of sections, 1.1070
citation, 1.1072
commencement, 1.1072
general note, 1.1073
general provision, 1.1071
Parental orders
application of Parts 12ZA, 12ZB and
  12ZC SSCBA 1992
  Regulations, 6.148–6.157
meaning, 6.151
statutory adoption pay, and
  application of Part 12ZB SSCBA 1992,
    6.153, 6.156

definitions, 6.151
Regulations, 6.158–6.187
statutory paternity pay, and
  application of Part 12ZA SSCBA 1992, 6.152, 6.155
  definitions, 6.151
  Regulations, 6.158–6.187
statutory shared parental pay, and
  application of Part 12ZC SSCBA 1992, 6.154, 6.157
  application of Pay Regulations, 7.113
  definitions, 6.151, 7.112
  general note, 7.110
  modification of Pay Regulations, 7.114–7.126

Parental responsibility
competing claims, 2.274–2.276
excepted cases, 2.276–2.280
generally, 2.271–2.272
normally living with test, 2.273
special case, 2.280

Partnership income
introduction, 1.716–1.717
statutory overview, 1.719

Paternity pay
see **Statutory paternity pay**

"Payment period"
overseas adoptions, 6.131–6.132
statutory adoption pay
  disrupted adoption, 6.72
  generally, 6.71
  statutory provision, 1.149–1.150
  treatment of more than one contract, 6.73
statutory maternity pay
  generally, 5.4–5.6
  statutory provision, 1.101–1.102
statutory paternity pay
  adoption of child, on, 6.61
  birth of child, on, 6.54
  statutory provision, 1.125–1.126
work during
  statutory adoption pay, 6.76
  statutory paternity pay, 6.67

Payments (employers) (statutory adoption pay)
funding
  application to Revenue, 6.21
  date of payment of contributions, 6.24
  generally, 6.20
  method, 6.22–6.23
  overpayments, 6.25
generally, 6.94
period
  adoption of child, on, 6.61
  birth of child, on, 6.54
  statutory provision, 1.125–1.126
persons acting on behalf of another, to, 6.100
timing, 6.95

Payments (employers) (statutory maternity pay)
funding

additional payment to small employers, 5.86
advance funding, 5.88
date of payment of contributions, 5.91
deduction from payments to Revenue, 5.89
definitions, 5.83
general note, 5.84
overpayments, 5.92
payments to employer by Revenue, 5.90
prescribed amount, 5.87
'small employer', 5.85
generally, 5.49
persons acting on behalf of another, to, 5.54–5.55
rounding, 5.50
Secretary of State, by, 5.52–5.53
timing, 5.51

Payments (employers) (statutory paternity pay)
funding
  application to Revenue, 6.21
  date of payment of contributions, 6.24
  generally, 6.20
  method, 6.22–6.23
  overpayments, 6.25
generally, 6.94
period
  adoption of child, on, 6.61
  birth of child, on, 6.54
persons acting on behalf of another, to, 6.100
timing, 6.95

Payments (employers) (statutory sick pay)
liability of Secretary of State, 4.19–4.20
method, 4.17
Secretary of State, by, 4.22
statements relating to, 4.33
time limits, 4.18

Payments (HMRC)
statutory adoption pay
  generally, 6.99
  liability, 6.96–6.98
statutory maternity pay, 5.90
statutory paternity pay
  generally, 6.99
  liability, 6.96–6.97

Payments (HMRC) (tax credits)
amount, 2.431–2.432
bank account requirement, 2.436–2.437
child care element of WTC, 2.414–2.415
definitions, 2.413
general note, 2.411
joint claims, for
  child tax credit, 2.414–2.415
  child care element of WTC, 2.414–2.415
  death of one of couple, 2.418–2.419
  working tax credit, 2.416–2.417
method, 2.434–2.435
person acting on behalf of another, for, 2.420–2.421
polygamous marriages, 2.515

1891

postponement, 2.429–2.430
recovery of overpayments
　generally, 1.370–1.372
　method, 2.433
renewal, on, 2.422–2.423
single payments, 2.427–2.428
timing
　bank account, 2.424–2.425
　other than to bank account, 2.426
working tax credit, and
　generally, 2.416–2.417
　introduction, 2.411
Payments in lieu of notice
working tax credit, 2.147–2.148
Penalties
charge-free childcare
　assessment of, 11.40
　dishonest conduct, 11.37
　enforcement, 11.41
　false or misleading information, 11.38
　material inaccuracy in declaration, 11.39
child trust funds
　appeals, 1.702
　decisions, 1.702
　generally, 1.700–1.701
　mitigation, 1.702
　recovery, 1.702
failure to comply with requirements
　statutory adoption pay, 1.476–1.477
　statutory paternity pay, 1.476–1.477
　tax credits, 1.384–1.386
incorrect statements
　statutory adoption pay, 1.478–1.479
　statutory paternity pay, 1.478–1.479
　tax credits, 1.376–1.383
incorrect statements (tax credits)
　conduct of penalty cases, 1.380–1.381
　fraudulently or negligently, 1.379
　generally, 1.376–1.378
　level of penalties, 1.382–1.383
statutory adoption pay
　appeals, 1.488
　definitions, 1.494
　determination, 1.486–1.487
　failure to comply, 1.476–1.477
　fraud, 1.478–1.479
　incorrect statements, 1.478–1.479
　interest, 1.493
　mitigation, 1.491
　proceedings before Commissioners, 1.489
　proceedings before court, 1.490
　time limits, 1.492
statutory maternity pay
　breach of regulations, 1.216–1.217
　fraud, 1.218
　negligence, 1.218
statutory paternity pay
　appeals, 1.488
　definitions, 1.494
　determination, 1.486–1.487
　failure to comply, 1.476–1.477

fraud, 1.478–1.479
incorrect statements, 1.478–1.479
interest, 1.493
mitigation, 1.491
proceedings before Commissioners, 1.489
proceedings before court, 1.490
time limits, 1.492
statutory sick pay
　breach of regulations, 1.216–1.217
　fraud, 1.218
　negligence, 1.218
tax credits
　determination, 1.455
　failure to comply with requirements, 1.384–1.386
　Guidance, 12.16–12.28
　incorrect statements, 1.376–1.383
　mitigation, 1.457
　proceedings before Commissioners, 1.456
　recovery, 1.459
　supplementary, 1.387–1.388
　time limits, 1.458
tax-free childcare
　assessment, 1.1001–1.1002
　dishonestly obtaining payments, 1.999–1.1000
　double jeopardy, 1.1003–1.1004
　enforcement, 1.1001–1.1002
　failure to comply with information notice, 1.993–1.994
　inaccurate declarations of eligibility, 1.991–1.992
　making prohibited payments, 1.997–1.998
　provision of inaccurate information, 1.995–1.996
tax returns, 1.24
Taxes Management Act 1970, 1.28
top-up payments
　assessment, 1.1001–1.1002
　dishonestly obtaining payments, 1.999–1.1000
　double jeopardy, 1.1003–1.1004
　enforcement, 1.1001–1.1002
　failure to comply with information notice, 1.993–1.994
　inaccurate declarations of eligibility, 1.991–1.992
　making prohibited payments, 1.997–1.998
　provision of inaccurate information, 1.995–1.996
Pension income
annual payments, 2.221
charge to tax
　amount charged, 1.563
　nature, 1.562
　person liable to tax, 1.564
deductions, 2.224
disregarded payments, 2.221
exemptions, 2.224

Index

general note
  regulations, 2.222
  statutory provisions, 1.561
general rules
  application of provisions, 1.565–1.566
  'pension', 1.567
  person liable to tax, 1.569
  taxable pension income, 1.568
generally, 2.221
identity of taxpayer, 2.225
relevant income, 2.223
state retirement pension
  application of provisions, 1.570–1.571
  person liable to tax, 1.573
  taxable pension income, 1.572
statutory provisions
  charge to tax, 1.562–1.564
  general note, 1.561
  general rules, 1.565–1.569
  introductory provision, 1.560
  social security pensions, 1.570–1.573
time of calculation, 2.226

"Period of payment"
overseas adoptions, 6.131–6.132
statutory adoption pay
  disrupted adoption, 6.72
  generally, 6.71
  statutory provision, 1.149–1.150
  treatment of more than one contract, 6.73
statutory maternity pay
  generally, 5.4–5.6
  statutory provision, 1.101–1.102
statutory paternity pay
  adoption of child, on, 6.61
  birth of child, on, 6.54
  statutory provision, 1.125–1.126
work during
  statutory adoption pay, 6.76
  statutory paternity pay, 6.67

Periodical payments (personal injury)
compensation awards, 1.807
generally, 1.806
persons entitled, 1.808
trusts, from, 1.809

"Person responsible for child"
best start grants, 13.137
child benefit, 3.13–3.15
Scottish child payments, 13.205

Person temporarily absent
See **Temporary absence**

Person treated as not being resident
See **Non-residents**

Personal allowances
income test, 2.203

Personal equity plans
investment income, 2.243

Personal injury (damages)
exempt income
  compensation awards, 1.807
  generally, 1.806
  persons entitled, 1.808
  trusts, from, 1.809
interest, 1.814

Persons abroad
statutory adoption pay
  absent from Great Britain, 6.38
  definitions, 6.34
  general note, 6.35
  has worked in other EEA States, 6.39
  in other EEA States, 6.37
  time for compliance, 6.41
statutory maternity pay
  absent from Great Britain, 5.67
  definitions, 5.64
  'employee', 5.68
  general note, 5.65
  in other Member States, 5.66
  time for compliance, 5.71
  women who worked in the EC, 5.70
statutory parental bereavement pay
  absent from GB as employees, 8.52
  continental shelf, 8.56
  definitions, 8.48
  EEA states as employees, 8.51
  mariners, 8.55
  Regulations, 8.46–8.56
  scope, 8.50
  time for compliance, 8.54
  worked in EEA state in 26 weeks preceding death of child, 8.53
statutory paternity pay
  absent from Great Britain, 6.38
  definitions, 6.34
  general note, 6.35
  has worked in other EEA States, 6.39
  in other EEA States, 6.37
  time for compliance, 6.41
statutory sick pay
  absent from Great Britain, 4.55–4.56
  definitions, 4.50–4.61
  employees, 4.62
  general note, 4.49
  persons abroad, 4.62–4.63
  in other Member States, 4.54
  time for compliance, 4.67

"Persons residing together"
child benefit, 3.16–3.17

Persons subject to immigration control
See **Immigrants**

Pilots
statutory adoption pay, 1.157–1.158
statutory maternity pay, 1.110
statutory paternity pay, 1.138–1.139
statutory sick pay
  definitions, 4.52, 4.58–4.59, 4.65
  general note, 4.49
  statutory provision, 1.96
  time for compliance, 4.67

Placement for adoption
generally, 6.34

Polygamy
child benefit, 3.50–3.51
tax credits
  amendment of Regulations, 2.511–2.517
  amendment of TCA 2002, 2.510

1893

definitions, 2.508–2.509
general note, 2.506
statutory provision, 1.422–1.423
Postponement
payments, 2.429–2.430
Pregnancy and baby grants
See **Best start grants**
Premium savings bonds
income test, 2.202
Presence
carer support payments, 13.500
"Presence in Great Britain"
guardian's allowance, 3.78
Priorities
child benefit
generally, 1.58–1.59
miscellaneous provisions, 1.191–1.195
Regulations, 3.20
Prisoners
See **Imprisonment**
Professions
basic rules, 1.732
receipts, 1.743
rules restricting deductions, 1.743
Property income
calculation of profits, 1.770
cash basis, 1.770
charge to tax
generally, 1.766
income charged, 1.768
person liable, 1.769
territorial scope, 1.767
generating income from land, 1.765
introduction, 1.716–1.717
overseas property business, 1.764
overview, 1.758–1.759
priority rules
generally, 1.760–1.761
introduction, 1.720
profits
generally, 1.766
income charged, 1.768
person liable, 1.769
territorial scope, 1.767
property businesses
introduction, 1.762–1.765
profits, 1.766–1.770
statutory overview
introduction, 1.719
priority rules, 1.720
tax credits
general note, 2.246
generally, 2.245
trading income rules, 1.770
UK property business, 1.763
Provision of information
administrative arrangements, and
by authorities, 2.443
to authorities, 2.442
employers, by
statutory maternity pay, 1.224
statutory sick pay, 1.222

functions relating to employment
general note, 2.522
generally, 2.524, 2.536
functions relating to health
definitions, 2.503
general note, 2.502
generally, 2.504, 2.521
Scotland, 2.534
functions relating to training
general note, 2.522
generally, 2.524, 2.536
Secretary of State, by
statutory maternity pay, 1.223
statutory sick pay, 1.221
statutory adoption pay
Board, by, 1.480
entitlement, as to, 6.28–6.29
generally, 6.32
Secretary of State, by, 1.481
statutory maternity pay, 5.42
claims for other benefits, 5.46
determination of questions, 5.44–5.45
statutory paternity pay
Board, by, 1.480
entitlement, as to, 6.28–6.29
generally, 6.32
Secretary of State, by, 1.481
statutory parental bereavement pay
entitlement, as to, 8.42
generally, 8.45
statutory sick pay
employee to Secretary of State, by, 4.29–4.30
employer to employee, by, 4.31–4.32
tax authorities, by
statutory adoption pay, 1.480–1.481
statutory paternity pay, 1.480–1.481
tax credits, 1.219–1.220
tax credits
contributions purposes, for, 1.220
fraud prevention, for, 1.219
generally, 2.530
Northern Ireland, 2.532
Public interest
disclosure, 1.861
"Purchased life annuity payments"
charge to tax, 1.788
income charged, 1.790
meaning, 1.789
person liable, 1.791
"Put at disposal"
employment income, 1.520
Qualifying care relief
See **Foster care relief; Shared lives care relief**
"Qualifying days"
statutory sick pay
generally, 4.12–4.14
statutory provision, 1.83–1.84
Qualifying periods
statutory parental bereavement pay, 8.8

Index

statutory paternity pay
  adoption of child, on, 6.62
  birth of child, on, 6.55
"Qualifying remunerative work"
  excepted activities, 2.133
  generally, 2.127–2.129
  hours worked, 2.134
  minimum level of continuity, 2.131
  remunerative work, 2.132
  routes to entitlement, 2.130
Qualifying young persons (child benefits)
  care, in
    generally, 3.25
    statutory basis, 1.188
  continuation of entitlement, 3.6
  definition, 1.49
  detention, in
    generally, 3.21–3.24
    statutory basis, 1.186
  education and training condition, 3.4–3.5
  extension period, 3.7
  interruptions, 3.8–3.9
  introduction, 3.3
  living with another as a couple, where, 3.16–3.17
  other financial support, 3.12
  person responsible for child, 3.13–3.15
  prescribed conditions, 3.3–3.12
  relevant relationship, in, 3.18
  terminal dates, 3.10–3.11
  youth training, in, 3.21–3.24
Qualifying young persons (tax credits)
  definition, 2.270
  maximum age, 2.283–2.284
  transition to universal credit, 2.69–2.70
  working tax credit, and
    childcare element, 2.171
    death, 2.179–2.180
Rate of payment
  child benefit
    generally, 1.60
    weekly rates, 3.60–3.65
Receipts
  basic rules, 1.736
  capital receipts
    generally, 1.755
    supplementary, 1.756
  debts incurred and later released, 1.757
  items treated as such under CAA 2001, 1.737
  professions and vocations, 1.752
Records
  administrative arrangements
    claims, 2.444
  statutory adoption pay
    generally, 6.26
    inspection, 6.27
  statutory maternity pay
    maintenance, 5.47
    production, 5.48

statutory parental bereavement pay
  generally, 8.40
  inspection, 8.41
statutory paternity pay
  generally, 6.26
  inspection, 6.27
statutory sick pay
  maintenance, 4.27
  production, 4.28
Taxes Management Act 1970, 1.12
Recovery of payments
  See **Repayments**
Reinstatement
  service with armed services
  statutory maternity pay, 5.27
Remuneration
  statutory adoption pay
    generally, 6.79
    statutory provision, 1.153–1.154
  statutory maternity pay
    generally, 5.34
    statutory provision, 1.207
  statutory paternity pay
    generally, 6.69
    statutory provision, 1.134–1.135
  statutory sick pay, 1.201
Rent-a-room relief
  definitions
    rent-a-room receipts, 1.821
    residence, 1.822
    total rent-a-room amount, 1.823
  individual's limit, 1.824
  introduction, 1.716–1.717
  overview, 1.819
  qualifying person, 1.820
  rent-a-room receipts, 1.821
  residence, 1.822
  statutory overview, 1.719
  total rent-a-room amount, 1.823
  trading income, 1.731
Repayments (statutory maternity pay)
  additional payment to small employers, 5.86
  advance funding, 5.88
  date of payment of contributions, 5.91
  definitions
    generally, 5.83
    'small employer', 5.85
  general note, 5.84
  method
    deduction from payments to Revenue, 5.89
    payments to employer by Revenue, 5.90
  overpayments, 5.92
  prescribed amount, 5.87
Repayments (statutory sick pay)
  generally, 4.88–4.92
  statutory provisions, 1.89–1.91
Repayments (tax credits)
  generally, 1.370–1.372
  method, 2.433
Representation
  See **Professional representation**

1895

Index

Residence
  carer support payments
    general condition, 13.500
    persons to whom EU regulation applies, 13.504
  child benefit
    child treated as being in GB, 3.28
    child treated as being in Northern Ireland, 3.37
    Crown servants posted overseas, 3.43–3.46
    overlap of entitlement, 3.42
    person temporarily absent from GB, 3.35–3.36
    person temporarily absent from Northern Ireland, 3.41
    person treated as not being in GB, 3.30–3.34
    person treated as not being in Northern Ireland, 3.39–3.40
    transitional provisions, 3.47
  Crown servants posted overseas
    generally, 2.489–2.490
    partners, 2.491
  definitions, 2.478–2.479
  guardian's allowance, 3.78
  ordinary residence
    Crown servants posted overseas, 2.489–2.491
    definitions, 2.478–2.479
    HMRC code of practice, 2.483
    meaning, 2.482–2.484
    person treated as not being in UK, 2.480–2.485
    temporary absence from UK, 2.487–2.488
    tests, 2.485
    transitional provision, 2.492–2.493
  person treated as not being in UK, 2.480–2.485
  polygamous marriages, 2.516
  rent-a-room relief, 1.822
  temporary absence from UK, 2.487–2.488
  tests, 2.485
  transitional provision, 2.492–2.493

Residential accommodation
  child benefit, 3.3

Respondent's observations
  See **Observations**

"Responsibility for child"
  competing claims, 2.274–2.276
  excepted cases, 2.276–2.280
  generally, 2.271–2.272
  normally living with test, 2.273
  special case, 2.280

Returns of income
  See **Tax returns**

Revenue and Customs
  See **HMRC**

Revenue and Customs officers
  See **HMRC officers**

Rounding
  statutory adoption pay, 6.6–6.7
  statutory maternity pay, 5.50
  statutory paternity pay, 6.6–6.7

Savings income
  building society dividends, 1.780
  dividends from non-resident UK companies
    charge to tax, 1.785
    income charged, 1.786
    person liable, 1.787
  dividends from UK resident companies
    charge to tax, 1.782
    income charged, 1.783
    introduction, 1.781
    person liable, 1.784
  general note, 1.772
  interest
    charge to tax, 1.776
    income charged, 1.777
    person liable, 1.779
    territorial scope, 1.775
    valuation of interest not paid in cash, 1.778
  introduction, 1.716–1.717
  overview, 1.771
  priority rules
    generally, 1.773–1.774
    introduction, 1.720
  purchased life annuity payments
    charge to tax, 1.788
    income charged, 1.790
    meaning, 1.789
    person liable, 1.791
  statutory overview
    introduction, 1.719
    priority rules, 1.720
  territorial scope of charge, 1.775

Schedules
  See also **Income tax**
  ITEPA 2003, 1.496–1.497
  ITTOIA 2005, 1.716–1.717

Scholarship income
  other income, 1.816
  tax credits, 2.241–2.242

School age grants
  See **Best start grants**

Scotland
  See also **Scottish Tribunals Service**
  adult disability payments
    general provisions, 13.107–13.112
    generally, 13.20
    Regulations, 13.362–13.454
  advocacy
    general right to, 13.4
    service standards, 13.5
  allocation of functions to Social Security Chamber
    Regulations, 14.157–14.162
  appeals against determination of entitlement
    general right, 13.36–13.37
    initiating, 13.38

Index

powers, 13.40
time limits, 13.39
appointees
  act in other circumstances, to, 13.85–13.86
  act on behalf of child, to, 13.84
  act on behalf of individual, to, 13.55–13.56
  guidance for, 13.89
  guidelines for decisions about, 13.87
assessments
  assessor qualifications, 13.7
  necessity, 13.8
  restriction on private-sector involvement, 13.6
assistance by Scottish Ministers
  'determination of entitlement', 13.14
  determining entitlement, 13.24–13.63
  duty to give, 13.13
  further provision, 13.80
  later determination, 13.16–13.17
  offences, 13.71
  recovery of value of assistance, 13.64–13.70
  right to stop receipt of assistance, 13.15
  superceding earlier determination, 13.16–13.17
  types of assistance, 13.18–13.23
  uprating for inflation, 13.72
assistance given in error
  recovery of value, 13.64–13.69
best start grants
  competing claims, 13.148
  determination without application, 13.144–13.147
  early learning grant, 13.160–13.161
  interpretation, 13.131–13.141
  months, 13.134–13.135
  personal relationships, 13.136–13.138
  pregnancy and baby payments, 13.149–13.159
  procedural matters, 13.142–13.148
  re-determination timescales, 13.142–13.143
  Regulations, 13.128–13.164
  school age grant, 13.162–13.163
  social security assistance, 13.139–13.141
  timing of applications, 13.131–13.135
carer's allowance supplement
  appeals, 13.286
  applications, 13.284
  Coronavirus relaxations, 13.288
  definitions, 13.273
  determination of entitlement, 13.275–13.281
  further provision, 13.287
  overpayments, 13.280
  procedural matters, 13.284–13.287
  re-determination of entitlement, 13.285
  Regulations, 13.272–13.288
  underpayments, 13.279
carer's assistance
  Coronavirus, 13.193–13.196
  eligibility, 13.98
  final provisions, 13.102
  further criteria, 13.99–13.100
  generally, 13.18
  Regulations, 13.98–13.102
  suspension, 13.127
  types, 13.101
  young carers, 13.180–13.192A
charter
  effect, 13.11
  general, 13.9–13.10
child disability payments
  admission to care home, 13.312
  age criteria, 13.295
  alternative accommodation, 13.315
  amount, 13.318
  application date, 13.319
  care component, 13.303–13.304, 13.311–13.318
  change of circumstances, 13.332
  conditions, 13.296–13.301
  consideration of entitlement after specified period, 13.331
  continuing eligibility, 13.321
  date of entitlement, 13.319
  decrease in level of entitlement, 13.330
  deduction, by, 13.328
  definitions, 13.293
  dialysis treatment, 13.311
  effecting a deduction decision, 13.335
  eligibility, 13.294–13.316
  entitlement date, 13.319
  entitlement to other benefits, 13.302
  errors, 13.333–13.334
  exclusions, 13.302
  extinguishment of right to apply, 13.290–13.291
  final provisions, 13.112
  form, 13.318
  further criteria, 13.108
  general provisions, 13.107–13.112
  generally, 13.20
  imprisonment, 13.313–13.314
  increase in level of entitlement, 13.329
  initial period for applications, 13.341
  level of entitlement, 13.329–13.330
  mobility requirement, 13.305–13.310
  moving to another part of UK, 13.335–13.336
  overpayments, 13.334
  payments, 13.317–13.320
  person to whom relevant EU regulation applies, 13.299–13.301
  rates, 13.318
  re-determination, 13.331
  Regulations, 13.292–13.350
  short-term assistance, 13.344
  suspension, 13.322–13.327
  temporary absence, 13.298
  terminal illness cases, 13.109
  time of payment, 13.320
  transfer to, 13.342
  transitional provision, 13.289–13.291

transitory provision, 13.345–13.346
underpayments, 13.333
vehicles, 13.339–13.340
child payments
   eligibility and assistance to be given, 13.213–13.231
   initial period, 13.232–13.235
   interpretation, 13.200
   overview, 13.199
   personal relationships, 13.205–13.208
   procedural matters, 13.236–13.250
   social security assistance, 13.209–13.212
   timing, 13.201–13.204
   transitory provision, 13.232–13.235
Coronavirus
   applications for assistance, 13.47–13.48
   carer's allowance supplement, 13.288
   carer's assistance, 13.193–13.196
   child payments, 13.250
   re-determination and appeal deadlines, 13.45–13.46
determination of entitlement by Scottish Ministers
   access to reports, 13.58–13.59
   appeals, 13.36–13.40
   appeals against process decisions, 13.60–13.61
   applications for assistance, 13.26
   appointees, 13.55–13.56
   change of circumstances, 13.53–13.54
   Coronavirus, 13.45–13.48
   decisions, 13.41–13.44
   duty, 13.24–13.25
   further provision, 13.49–13.63
   general provisions, 13.24–13.28
   identifying possible eligibility, 13.49
   meaning, 13.14
   non-disclosure of health information, 13.63
   notice, 13.28
   obtaining information, 13.50–13.54
   ongoing entitlement, of, 13.42
   presumption as to receipt of information, 13.62
   re-determination, 13.29–13.35
   support during assessments, 13.57
   without application, 13.43–13.44
   withdrawal of application, 13.27
disability assistance
   children, for, 13.292–13.350
   general provisions, 13.107–13.112
   generally, 13.20
   working age people, for, 13.362–13.454
discretionary housing payments, 13.90
early learning grant
   eligibility, 13.160
   types of assistance, 13.161
early years assistance
   Best Start Grants, 13.128–13.163
   eligibility, 13.113
   final provisions, 13.116
   further criteria, 13.114
   generally, 13.21

   Regulations, 13.113–13.116
   suspension, 13.127
   types, 13.115
eligibility
   identifying possibility of, 13.81–13.82
EU Exit
   carer's allowance supplement, 13.272–13.288
   social security co-ordination amendments, 13.263–13.271
   young carer grants, 13.282
First-tier Tribunal for Scotland
   allocation of functions to Social Security Chamber, 14.157–14.162
funeral expense assistance
   eligibility, 13.118
   final provisions, 13.122
   further criteria, 13.119–13.120
   generally, 13.22, 13.70
   miscellaneous provisions, 13.118–13.122
   Regulations, 13.165–13.179
   suspension of assistance, 13.127
   types, 13.121
further provision for Parts 2 and 3
   appointees, 13.84–13.89
   general, 13.80
   identifying possible eligibility, 13.81–13.82
   information sharing, 13.83
giving of assistance by Scottish Ministers
   'determination of entitlement', 13.14
   determining entitlement, 13.24–13.63
   duty, 13.13
   further provision, 13.80
   later determination, 13.16–13.17
   offences, 13.71
   recovery of value of assistance, 13.64–13.70
   right to stop receipt of assistance, 13.15
   superceding earlier determination, 13.16–13.17
   types of assistance, 13.18–13.23
   uprating for inflation, 13.72
identifying possible eligibility, 13.81–13.82
information sharing
   definitions, 13.351
   generally, 13.83
   purpose, 13.353
   Regulations, 13.351–13.354
   specified persons, 13.352
   supply of information, 13.358
   use of information, 13.354–13.357
possible eligibility, 13.81–13.82
pregnancy and baby grants
   basic amount, 13.154
   'birth', 13.157
   'born', 13.157
   'child', 13.157
   definitions, 13.157–13.159
   'domestic abuse', 13.159
   eligibility, 13.149–13.152
   form, 13.156

Index

multiple pregnancy supplement, 13.155
residence requirement, 13.152
'sure start maternity grant', 13.158
time limit for application, 13.150–13.151
types of assistance, 13.153–13.156
value, 13.153
principles
  effect, 13.3
  general, 13.1–13.2
recovery of value of assistance
  given in error, 13.64–13.69
re-determination by Scottish Ministers
  duty, 13.32–13.33
  late request, 13.31
  notice, 13.34
  notice where not made timeously, 13.35
  right to request, 13.29–13.30
regulation-making powers, 13.93
right to advocacy, 13.4
right to stop receipt of assistance, 13.15
school age grant
  eligibility, 13.162
  form, 13.163
  value, 13.163
Scottish child payments
  eligibility and assistance to be given, 13.213–13.231
  initial period, 13.232–13.235
  interpretation, 13.200
  overview, 13.199
  personal relationships, 13.205–13.208
  procedural matters, 13.236–13.250
  social security assistance, 13.209–13.212
  timing, 13.201–13.204
  transitory provision, 13.232–13.235
'Scottish social security system', 13.12
service standards
  advocacy, 13.5
sharing information
  definitions, 13.351
  generally, 13.83
  purpose, 13.353
  Regulations, 13.351–13.354
  specified persons, 13.352
  supply of information, 13.358
  use of information, 13.354–13.357
short-term assistance
  eligibility, 13.124
  final provisions, 13.126
  generally, 13.23
  Regulations, 13.124–13.126
  suspension, 13.127
  types, 13.125
social security charter
  effect, 13.11
  general, 13.9–13.10
social security co-ordination amendments
  definitions, 13.263
  Gibraltar, 13.266
  Regulations, 13.263–13.271
  revocation of instruments, 13.270–13.271
  revocation of retained EU legislation, 13.268–13.269

social security principles
  effect, 13.3
  general, 13.1–13.2
statutory provisions
  ancillary provision, 13.92
  definition, 13.12
  discretionary housing payments, 13.90
  further provision for Parts 2 and 3, 13.80
  giving of assistance, 13.13–13.72
  regulation-making powers, 13.93
  supplementing assistance, 13.73–13.79
  tenets and oversight, 13.1–13.11
  Universal Credit, 13.91
superceding earlier determination, 13.16–13.17
supplementing assistance
  carer's allowance supplement, 13.77–13.79
  top-up of reserved benefits, 13.73–13.75
supply of information, 13.358
tenets and oversight, 13.1–13.11
top-up of reserved benefits
  general power, 13.73–13.74
  restrictions on power, 13.75
tribunals
  decisions, 14.5–14.23
  definitions, 14.44
  establishment, 14.2–14.3
  powers and enforcement, 14.25–14.31
  practice and procedure, 14.32–14.39
  regulation-making provisions, 14.41
types of assistance, 13.18–13.23
Universal Credit
  'assessment period', 13.141
  generally, 13.91
uprating for inflation, 13.72
use of information, 13.354–13.357
winter heating assistance
  children, 13.251–13.262
  eligibility, 13.104
  final provisions, 13.106
  generally, 13.19
  low income, 13.455–13.464
  Regulations, 13.104–13.106
  suspension, 13.127
  types, 13.105
  young people, 13.251–13.262
young carers grant
  amount, 13.192–13.192A
  citation, 13.181
  commencement, 13.181
  conditions, 13.185–13.188
  definitions, 13.182
  eligibility, 13.183–13.187
  EU Exit, and, 13.282
  form, 13.192–13.192A
  general note, 13.180
  general provisions, 13.183
  procedural matters, 13.189–13.191
Scottish child payments
  amount, 13.227–13.228
  appeals, 13.244–13.245

applications
   Coronavirus relaxations, 13.250
   determination without, 13.238–13.240
   determinations, 13.238–13.237
   further provision, 13.246–13.247
   generally, 13.236–13.237
'assessment period', 13.212
assistance being awarded, 13.211
assistance to be given, 13.213
beginning of entitlement to assistance, 13.216–13.217
being responsible for a child, 13.205
child born on 29 February, 13.203
Coronavirus relaxations, 13.250
'dependant', 13.208
determination of entitlement
   generally, 13.209
   procedure, 13.236–13.237
   without application, 13.238–13.240
duty to give assistance, 13.213
eligibility
   beginning of, 13.216–13.217
   generally, 13.214–13.215
   ongoing, 13.218–13.219
form, 13.227–13.228
initial period
   definitions, 13.232
   duty to notify, 13.235
   time of payment, 13.234
   timing of application, 13.233
interpretation
   personal relationships, 13.205–13.208
   references to 2018 Act, 13.200
   social security assistance, 13.209–13.212
   timing, 13.201–13.204
'kinship carer', 13.207
later determination supersedes earlier, 13.231
ongoing entitlement, 13.218–13.219
overview, 13.199
'partner', 13.206
personal relationships
   being responsible for a child, 13.205
   'dependant', 13.208
   'kinship carer', 13.207
   'partner', 13.206
procedural matters
   appeals, 13.244–13.245
   applications, 13.236–13.237
   Coronavirus relaxations, 13.250
   determination without application, 13.238–13.240
   determinations, 13.238–13.237
   further provision, 13.246–13.247
   recovery of value of assistance, 13.248–13.249
   re-determination of entitlement, 13.241–13.243
recovery of value of assistance, 13.248–13.249
re-determination of entitlement, 13.241–13.243

Regulations
   citation, 13.197
   commencement, 13.198
   general provisions, 13.200–13.231
   overview, 13.199
   schedule, 13.236–13.250
   transitory provision, 13.232–13.235
right to stop receiving assistance, 13.230
social security assistance
   'assessment period', 13.212
   assistance being awarded, 13.211
   determination of entitlement, 13.209
   specified kinds, 13.210
suspension of assistance
   definitions, 13.226
   effect of termination, 13.225
   having regard to financial circumstances, 13.221
   information to be given after, 13.222
   relevant circumstances, 13.220
   right to review, 13.223
   termination, 13.224
time of payment
   generally, 13.229
   initial period, 13.234
timing of applications
   child born on 29 February, 13.203
   initial period, 13.233
   'week', 13.204
   when treated as made, 13.201
   'working day', 13.202
transitory provision
   definitions, 13.232
   duty to notify, 13.235
   time of payment, 13.234
   timing of application, 13.233
value
   generally, 13.227–13.228
   recovery, 13.248–13.249
'week', 13.204
'working day', 13.202

Scottish Child Payments Regulations 2020
See also **Scottish child payments**
citation, 13.197
commencement, 13.198
eligibility and assistance to be given, 13.213–13.231
initial period, 13.232–13.235
interpretation
   general, 13.200
   personal relationships, 13.205–13.208
   social security assistance, 13.209–13.212
   timing, 13.201–13.204
overview, 13.199
schedule, 13.236–13.250
transitory provision, 13.232–13.235

Scottish Tribunals Service
administration, 14.40
allowances, 14.154–14.156
ancillary regulations, 14.42

Index

appeals
  expenses and allowances, 14.154–14.156
  First-tier Tribunal, from, 14.10–14.12
  Upper Tribunal, from, 14.13–14.16
decisions
  appeals, 14.10–14.16
  excluded decisions, 14.17–14.20
  internal review, 14.5–14.9
  non-party participation, 14.23
  process for permission, 14.21–14.22
  rule-making, 14.37
definitions
  general, 14.44
  index, 14.48
directions, 14.38–14.39
establishment, 14.2–14.3
evidence, 14.37
exercise of functions, 14.33
expenses and allowances, 14.154–14.156
fees, 14.40
First-tier Tribunal
  appeals from, 14.10–14.12
  Procedure Regulations, 14.55–14.114
hearings, 14.36
index of expressions, 14.48
internal review of decisions, 14.5–14.9
powers and enforcement, 14.25–14.31
practice and procedure
  directions, 14.38–14.39
  First-tier Tribunal, 14.55–14.114
  particular matters, 14.35–14.37
  Rules, 14.32–14.34
  Upper Tribunal, 14.115–14.153
Practice Directions, 14.38–14.39
procedural rules (First-tier Tribunal)
  addition of parties, 14.69
  appeals, 14.108–14.112
  application for permission to appeal, 14.108
  attending hearings, 14.91
  calculation of time, 14.74
  case management, 14.63–14.64
  chairing member, 14.81
  citation of witnesses, 14.79
  correction of mistakes, 14.107
  decisions, 14.98–14.105
  decisions without hearings, 14.90
  definitions, 14.59
  delegation, 14.62
  delivery of documents, 14.75
  dismissal of case, 14.68
  disclosure, 14.76–14.77
  evidence, 14.78
  general powers, 14.63–14.82
  hearings, 14.90–14.97
  hearings in party's absence, 14.96–14.97
  interpreters, 14.73
  non-compliance with rules, 14.67
  notice of appeal against process decision, 14.88–14.89
  notice of decisions, 14.98–14.99
  notice of hearings, 14.92–14.93
  notices of appeal, 14.83–14.89
  order to answer questions or produce documents, 14.79
  orders, 14.65–14.66
  overriding objective, 14.60–14.61
  permission to appeal, 14.108–14.112
  private hearings, 14.94–14.95
  procedure, 14.83–14.105
  public hearings, 14.94–14.95
  publication of decisions, 14.104–14.105
  reasons for decisions, 14.100–14.103
  recording of hearings, 14.82
  removal of parties, 14.69
  representatives, 14.70–14.71
  response of decision maker to notice of appeal, 14.86–14.87
  review of decisions, 14.113–14.114
  service of documents, 14.75
  substitution of parties, 14.69
  submissions, 14.78
  supporters, 14.72
  time, 14.74
  withdrawal, 14.80
procedural rules (Upper Tribunal)
  absence of party, 14.147
  addition of parties, 14.132
  answering questions, 14.140
  appeals, 14.150–14.152
  appellant's reply, 14.126
  application, 14.118
  application for permission to appeal, 14.122–14.123
  arrangement, 14.119
  calculation of time, 14.135
  case management, 14.128
  Chairing member, 14.142
  citation of witnesses, 14.140
  decisions, 14.148
  definitions, 14.120
  delegation, 14.127
  delivery of documents, 14.136
  disapplication of 2016 rules, 14.117
  disclosure of documents, 14.137–14.138
  dismissal of a party's case, 14.131
  evidence, 14.139
  general powers, 14.127–14.142
  hearings, 14.143–14.147
  legal aid, 14.153
  non-compliance with rules, 14.130
  notice of appeal, 14.124–14.126
  orders, 14.129
  overriding objective, 14.121
  permission to appeal, 14.122–14.123
  procedure, 14.122–14.126
  production of documents, 14.140
  purpose of Tribunal, 14.121
  removal of parties, 14.132
  reply, 14.126
  representatives, 14.133
  response to notice of appeal, 14.125
  review of decisions, 14.149
  sending of documents, 14.136
  submissions, 14.139
  substitution of parties, 14.132

supporters, 14.134
    withdrawal of case, 14.141
    witnesses, 14.140
  proceedings, 14.35
  regulation-making provisions, 14.41
  review of decisions, 14.5–14.9
  Rules
    exercise of functions, 14.33
    extent of rule-making, 14.34
    general provision, 14.32
    special jurisdiction, 14.24
  time limits
    Regulations (2016), 14.49–14.54
  Upper Tribunal
    appeals from, 14.13–14.16
    Procedure Regulations, 14.115–14.153

Seafarers
  carer support payments, 13.503
  statutory adoption pay
    definitions, 6.34
    general note, 6.35
    generally, 6.42
  statutory maternity pay
    definitions, 5.64
    general note, 5.65
    generally, 5.72
    statutory provisions, 1.110
  statutory parental bereavement pay, 8.55
  statutory paternity pay
    definitions, 6.34
    general note, 6.35
    generally, 6.42
    statutory provisions, 1.138–1.139
  statutory shared parental pay
    definitions, 7.130
    general note, 7.128
    general provisions, 7.137–7.138
  statutory sick pay
    definitions, 4.50–4.51, 4.57, 4.64
    general note, 4.49
    statutory provision, 1.96
    time for compliance, 4.67

Seasonal workers
  working tax credit, 2.152–2.153

Second-adult element
  See **Working tax credit**

Self-assessment
  tax returns, 1.6

Self-employment
  employment income, 2.215
  trading income, 2.229

Service (notices)
  child trust fund appeals, 9.93–9.94
  statutory adoption pay, 6.101
  statutory parental bereavement pay, 8.30
  statutory paternity pay, 6.101
  tax credit appeals, 2.449–2.450

Settlement income
  charge to tax, 1.795–1.796
  income charged, 1.799
  person liable, 1.800
  'settlement', 1.798

  'settlor', 1.798
  treatment as highest part of settlor's total income, 1.797

Severe disability element
  working tax credit, 2.176–2.177

Severe disablement allowance
  investment income, 2.243
  social security income, 2.233

Severely disabled persons
  child tax credit, 2.289–2.290

Shared lives care relief
  amount per adult or child, 1.837
  chargeable income, 1.840
  definitions
    providing foster care, 1.830
    providing qualifying care, 1.829
    providing shared lives care, 1.831
    qualifying care receipts, 1.828
    residence, 1.832
    total qualifying care receipts, 1.833
  full qualifying care relief
    chargeable income, 1.840
    introduction, 1.838
    trading income, 1.839
  income period not a year, 1.836
  individual's limit
    amount per adult or child, 1.837
    general, 1.834
    income period not a year, 1.836
    residence used by more than one carer, 1.835
    share of fixed amount, 1.835–1.836
  overview, 1.825
  providing foster care, 1.830
  providing qualifying care, 1.829
  providing shared lives care, 1.831
  qualifying care receipts, 1.828
  qualifying person, 1.826
  residence
    generally, 1.832
    used by more than one carer, 1.835
  share of fixed amount
    income period not a year, 1.836
    residence used by more than one carer, 1.835
  total qualifying care receipts, 1.833
  trading income, 1.839

Shared parental leave
  curtailment of pay period
    statutory adoption pay: AP, 5.113
    statutory maternity pay: P, 5.108

Sharing information
  See **Data sharing**

Short-term assistance
  See **Scotland**

Sick pay
  See **Statutory sick pay**

Sickness benefits (vouchers)
  taxable benefits, 1.525

Sickness periods
  See **Working tax credit**

Social fund
  social security income, 2.233

Index

Social Security Act 1998
general provisions
appeals, 1.226–1.227
recitals, 1.225
Social Security Administration Act 1992
arrangement of sections, 1.209
general provisions
claims and payments, 1.210–1.213
enforcement, 1.216–1.218
information, 1.219–1.224
overpayments, 1.214–1.215
Social security administration (statutory adoption pay)
adoption from overseas, 6.110–6.114
determination of entitlement issues
application, 6.30
form of application, 6.31
employers' records
generally, 6.26
inspection, 6.27
funding of liabilities
application to Revenue, 6.21
date of payment of contributions, 6.24
generally, 6.20
method, 6.22–6.23
overpayments, 6.25
provision of information, 6.32
Social security administration (statutory maternity pay)
employer's records
maintenance, 5.47
production, 5.48
expected week of confinement, 5.41
notice of absence from work, 5.42
notification of employment after confinement, 5.43
provision of information
claims for other benefits, 5.46
determination of questions, 5.44–5.45
Social security administration (statutory paternity pay)
adoption from overseas, 6.110–6.114
determination of entitlement issues
application, 6.30
form of application, 6.31
employers' records
generally, 6.26
inspection, 6.27
funding of liabilities
application to Revenue, 6.21
date of payment of contributions, 6.24
generally, 6.20
method, 6.22–6.23
overpayments, 6.25
provision of information, 6.32
Social security contributions
See **National insurance contributions**
Social Security Contributions and Benefits Act 1992
application, 1.183
arrangement of sections, 1.36

definitions, 1.184–1.185
general provisions
child benefit, 1.47–1.66
guardian's allowance, 1.37–1.46
statutory adoption pay, 1.144–1.161
statutory maternity pay, 1.99–1.111
statutory parental bereavement pay, 1.173–1.182
statutory paternity pay, 1.112–1.143
statutory shared parental pay, 1.161–1.172
statutory sick pay, 1.67–1.98
modifications to
adoptions from overseas, 6.102–6.109
dismissal for reasons of pregnancy, 5.96–5.97
parental orders, 6.148–6.157
schedules, 1.186–1.208
Social Security Contributions (Transfer of Functions, etc.) Act 1999
arrangement of sections, 1.229
definitions, 1.252
general provisions, 1.230–1.250
long title, 1.228
miscellaneous provisions, 1.251–1.253
Social security income
charge to tax
amount charged, 1.582
definitions, 1.580–1.581
nature of charge, 1.577–1.579
person liable to tax, 1.583
child maintenance bonus
income support, 1.594
jobseeker's allowance, 1.599
deductions, 2.236
disregarded payments, 2.233
exemptions
generally, 2.236
incapacity benefit, 1.591–1.592
income support, 1.593–1.598
increases in respect of children, 1.599
jobseeker's allowance, 1.599–1.604
foreign benefits
generally, 1.611–1.612
person liable to tax, 1.614
taxable income, 1.613
general note
regulations, 2.234
statutory provisions, 1.575–1.576
generally, 2.233
identity of taxpayer, 2.237
incapacity benefit
long-term, 1.591
short-term, 1.592
income support
amount in excess of taxable maximum, 1.595
child maintenance bonus, 1.594
definitions, 1.597–1.598
general rule, 1.593
taxable maximum, 1.596
trade disputes, 1.593

1903

jobseeker's allowance
  amount in excess of taxable maximum, 1.600
  child maintenance bonus, 1.599
  definitions, 1.604
  taxable maximum, 1.601–1.603
relevant income, 2.235
statutory provisions
  charge to tax, 1.577–1.583
  exempt benefits, 1.591–1.606
  foreign benefits, 1.611–1.614
  general note, 1.575–1.576
  introductory provision, 1.574
  taxable benefits, 1.584–1.590
  wholly exempt benefits, 1.607–1.610
Table A benefits, 1.584–1.586
Table B benefits, 1.607–1.610
taxable benefits
  exemptions, 1.591–1.606
  person liable to tax, 1.589–1.590
  Table A, 1.584–1.586
  taxable income, 1.587–1.588
taxable foreign benefits
  generally, 1.611–1.612
  person liable to tax, 1.614
  taxable income, 1.613
time of calculation, 2.238
wholly exempt benefits, 1.607–1.610

Social security pensions
See **Pension income, State retirement pension**

Social Security (Scotland) Act 2018
ancillary provision, 13.92
citation, 13.96
commencement, 13.95
definition, 13.12
final provisions, 13.92–13.94
general provisions
  discretionary housing payments, 13.90
  further provision for Parts 2 and 3, 13.80
  giving of assistance, 13.13–13.72
  supplementing assistance, 13.73–13.79
  tenets and oversight, 13.1–13.11
  Universal Credit, 13.91
regulation-making powers, 13.93
schedules
  carer's assistance, 13.98–13.102
  disability assistance, 13.107–13.112
  early years assistance, 13.113–13.116
  funeral expense assistance, 13.118–13.122
  short-term assistance, 13.124–13.126
  suspension of assistance, 13.127
  winter heating assistance, 13.104–13.106

Specific employment income
See **Employment income**

"Sports awards"
remunerative work, 2.133

Spouses
references in Income Tax Acts, 1.887

State pension credit
generally, 2.317
income test, 2.205

State retirement pension
See also **Pension income**
application of provisions, 1.570–1.571
person liable to tax, 1.573
taxable pension income, 1.572

Statistical evidence
generally, 2.530
Northern Ireland, 2.532

Statutory adoption pay
administration
  determination of entitlement issues, 6.28–6.31
  employers' records, 6.26–6.27
  funding of liabilities, 6.20–6.25
  provision of information, 6.32
  statutory provision, 1.467–1.475
adoption without placement, 1.160–1.161
avoidance of liability, 6.81
benefits, 1.153–1.154
continental shelf employees
  definitions, 6.34
  general note, 6.35
  generally, 6.43
  statutory provision, 1.157–1.158
continuous employment
  change of employer, 6.88
  generally, 6.84
  reinstatement after service with armed forces, 6.89
  stoppages of work, 6.86
  unfair dismissal, 6.85
  'week', 6.87
contracting out restrictions, 1.151–1.152
contractual remuneration, and
  generally, 6.79
  statutory provision, 1.157–1.158
Coronavirus
  normal weekly earnings, 5.116–5.122
Crown employment, 1.155–1.156
curtailment of pay period
  definitions, 5.104
  general note, 5.102
  notice, 5.114
  revocation notice, 5.115
  service of notices, 5.105
  shared parental leave: AP, 5.113
  statutory shared parental pay: A, 5.111
  statutory shared parental pay: AP, 5.112
definitions, 1.159
determination of entitlement issues
  application, 6.30
  form of application, 6.31
divided contracts
  general note, 6.10
  lapse of election, 6.15
  notification of election, 6.12
  provision of information, 6.13
  relevant employer, 6.14

Index

earnings, 6.91
employed earners, 6.83
employer's liability
  funding, 1.469–1.470
  generally, 1.147–1.148
employers' records
  generally, 6.26
  inspection, 6.27
entitlement
  determination of issues, 6.30–6.31
  provision of information, 6.28–6.29
  statutory provisions, 1.145–1.146
evidence of entitlement, 6.74
excepted cases, 6.77
failure to comply, 1.476–1.477
fraud
  generally, 1.478–1.479
  procedure and appeals, 1.486–1.494
funding of liabilities
  application to Revenue, 6.21
  date of payment of contributions, 6.24
  generally, 6.20
  method, 6.22–6.23
  overpayments, 6.25
general note, 1.144
incorrect statements, 1.478–1.479
information
  power to require, 1.474–1.475
  supply, 1.480–1.481
  use by Board, 1.482
liability of Revenue, 6.96–6.98
mariners
  definitions, 6.34
  general note, 6.35
  generally, 6.42
  statutory provision, 1.157–1.158
NHS employees
  general note, 6.10
  lapse of election, 6.15
  notification of election, 6.12
  provision of information, 6.13
  relevant employer, 6.14
normal weekly earnings
  Coronavirus, 5.116–5.122
  earnings, 6.91
  generally, 6.92–6.93
notice requirements, 6.73
overseas adoptions
  administration, 6.110–6.114
  application of General Regulations 2002, 6.120
  application of SSCBA 1992, 6.102–6.109
  avoidance of liability, 6.137
  definitions, 6.119
  evidence of entitlement, 6.134
  general note, 6.118
  notice requirements, 6.133
  pay period, 6.131–6.132
  termination of employment, 6.136
  treatment of more than one employer, 6.135
parental orders, and
  application of Part 12ZB SSCBA 1992, 6.153, 6.156
  definitions, 6.151
  Regulations, 6.158–6.187
pay period
  disrupted adoption, 6.72
  generally, 6.71
  statutory provision, 1.149–1.150
  treatment of more than one contract, 6.73
payment
  generally, 6.94
  liability of Revenue, 6.96–6.98
  persons acting on behalf of another, to, 6.100
  Revenue, by, 6.99
  statutory provisions, 1.471–1.472
  timing, 6.95
penalties
  appeals, 1.488
  definitions, 1.494
  determination, 1.486–1.487
  failure to comply, 1.476–1.477
  fraud, 1.478–1.479
  incorrect statements, 1.478–1.479
  interest, 1.493
  mitigation, 1.491
  proceedings before Commissioners, 1.489
  proceedings before court, 1.490
  time limits, 1.492
persons abroad
  absent from Great Britain, 6.38
  definitions, 6.34
  general note, 6.35
  has worked in other EEA States, 6.40
  in other EEA States, 6.37
  time for compliance, 6.41
provision of information
  entitlement, as to, 6.28–6.29
  generally, 6.32
rate, 1.149–1.150
relationship with benefits, 1.153–1.154
rounding, 6.6–6.7
service of notices, 6.101
special classes of person, 1.157–1.158
statutory provisions
  administration, 1.467–1.475
  adoption without placement, 1.160–1.161
  contracting out restrictions, 1.1511–1.152
  Crown employment, 1.155–1.156
  definitions, 1.159
  employer's liability, 1.147–1.148
  entitlement, 1.145–1.146
  general note, 1.144
  information, 1.480–1.482
  pay period, 1.149–1.150
  penalties, 1.476–1.479
  rate, 1.149–1.150
  relationship with benefits, 1.153–1.154

1905

relationship with remuneration, 1.153–1.154
special classes of person, 1.157–1.158
supplementary, 1.159
supply of information
  Board, by, 1.480
  Secretary of State, by, 1.481
ten days or less working in pay period, 6.78
termination of employment before start of period, 6.80
treatment of more than one contract
  general note, 6.10
  generally, 6.75
  lapse of election, 6.15
  notification of election, 6.12
  provision of information, 6.13
  relevant employer, 6.14, 6.90
'week', 6.87
weekly rates
  general note, 6.3
  generally, 6.5
  rounding, 6.6–6.7
work during pay period, 6.76
working tax credits
  social security income, 2.233
working 10 days or less in pay period, 6.78
Statutory Adoption Pay (Administration) Regulations 2002
application
  Adoption from Overseas Regulations, to, 6.110–6.114
arrangement, 6.16
citation, 6.17
commencement, 6.17
definitions, 6.19
general note, 6.18
general provisions, 6.20–6.32
Statutory Adoption Pay (Adoptions from Overseas) (No.2) Regulations 2003
application, 6.121
arrangement, 6.115
citation, 6.117
commencement, 6.117
definitions, 6.119
general note, 6.118
general provisions, 6.131–6.137
revocation provision, 6.138
Statutory Adoption Pay (Adoptions from Overseas) (Persons Abroad and Mariners) Regulations 2010
arrangement, 6.139
citation, 6.140
commencement, 6.140
definitions, 6.141
general provision, 6.143
revocation, 6.142
Statutory Adoption Pay (Curtailment) Regulations 2014
arrangement, 5.101
citation, 5.103
commencement, 5.103
definitions, 5.104
general note, 5.102
general provisions, 5.105–5.114
revocation, 5.115
Statutory Adoption Pay (General) Regulations 2002
amendment
  Parental Orders and Prospective Adopters Regulations 2014, by, 6.158–6.187
application
  Adoption from Overseas (No.2) Regulations, to, 6.120
  generally, 6.50
arrangement, 6.46
citation, 6.47
commencement, 6.47
definitions, 6.48–6.49
general provisions, 6.71–6.101
Statutory Adoption Pay (NHS Employees) Regulations 2002
arrangement, 6.8
citation, 6.9
commencement, 6.9
definitions, 6.9
general note, 6.10
general provisions, 6.11–6.15
Statutory Adoption Pay (Parental Orders and Prospective Adopters) Regulations 2014
arrangement, 6.158
citation, 6.160
commencement, 6.160
definitions, 6.161
effective date of amendments, 6.162
general note, 6.159
general provisions, 6.164–6.187
Statutory Adoption Pay (Persons Abroad and Mariners) Regulations 2002
application to overseas adoptions, 6.143
arrangement, 6.33
citation, 6.34
commencement, 6.34
definitions, 6.34
general note, 6.35
general provisions, 6.36–6.43
schedules, 6.44–6.45
Statutory Adoption Pay (Weekly Rates) Regulations 2002
arrangement, 6.1
citation, 6.2
commencement, 6.2
general note, 6.3
general provisions, 6.4–6.7
Statutory maternity pay
administration
  employer's records, 5.47–5.48
  expected week of confinement, 5.41
  notice of absence from work, 5.42
  notification of employment after confinement, 5.43
  provision of information, 5.44–5.46

Index

avoidance of liability, 5.7–5.8
benefits, and
  generally, 1.107–1.108
  miscellaneous provision, 1.206–2.270
breach of regulations, 1.216–1.217
change of employer, 5.26
civil penalties
  breach of regulations, 1.216–1.217
  fraud, 1.218
  negligence, 1.218
compensation of employers
  additional payment to small employers, 5.86
  advance funding, 5.88
  date of payment of contributions, 5.91
  deduction from payments to Revenue, 5.89
  definitions, 5.83
  general note, 5.84
  overpayments, 5.92
  payments to employer by Revenue, 5.90
  prescribed amount, 5.87
  'small employer', 5.85
continental shelf employees
  definitions, 5.64
  general note, 5.65
  generally, 5.73
  statutory provisions, 1.110
continuous employment
  change of employer, 5.26
  generally, 5.22
  stoppages of work, 5.24–5.25
  unfair dismissal, 5.23
contractual remuneration, as
  generally, 5.34
  statutory provision, 1.207–1.208
Coronavirus
  normal weekly earnings, 5.116–5.122
Crown employment, 1.109
curtailment of pay period
  definitions, 5.104
  general note, 5.102
  notice, 5.109
  revocation notice, 5.110
  service of notices, 5.105
  shared parental leave: P, 5.108
  statutory shared parental pay: M, 5.106
  statutory shared parental pay: P, 5.107
death of woman, 5.21
definitions
  'earnings', 5.35–5.36
  'employee', 5.31
  generally, 5.2–5.3
  statutory provisions, 1.111
  'week', 5.30
detention in custody, 5.17–5.18
determination of entitlement
  application, 4.85
  definitions, 4.84
  procedure, 4.86
divided contracts (general Regulations)
  treatment of more than one contract as one, 5.11

  treatment of two or more employers as one, 5.32–5.33
divided contracts (NHS Regulations)
  lapse of election, 5.81
  notification of election, 5.78
  provision of information, 5.79
  treatment of more than one contract as one, 5.77
  treatment of two or more employers as one, 5.80
employee, 5.31
employee's duties, 1.213
employer's records
  maintenance, 5.47
  production, 5.48
employment contract terminated to avoid liability, 5.7–5.8
enforcement
  breach of regulations, 1.216–1.217
  fraud, 1.218
  negligence, 1.218
entitlement, 1.99–1.100
expected week of confinement, 5.41
fraud, 1.218
funding of employers' liabilities, 1.105–1.106
imprisonment, 5.17–5.18
incapacity benefit, and
  generally, 5.39
  statutory provision, 1.206
information
  disclosure by Secretary of State, 1.223
  employers, by, 1.224
liability of Secretary of State to pay
  generally, 5.13–5.14
  statutory provision, 1.99–1.100
mariners
  definitions, 5.64
  general note, 5.65
  generally, 5.72
  statutory provisions, 1.110
maternity allowance, 5.40
medical evidence
  definitions, 5.59
  evidence of pregnancy and confinement, 5.60
  form of certificate, 5.61–5.62
modification of provisions, 5.9–5.10
national health service employees
  lapse of election, 5.81
  notification of election, 5.78
  provision of information, 5.79
  treatment of more than one contract as one, 5.77
  treatment of two or more employers as one, 5.80
negligence, 1.218
normal working earnings
  Coronavirus, 5.116–5.122
  'earnings', 5.35–5.36
  generally, 5.37–5.38

normal working weeks
  generally, 5.28–5.29
  'week', 5.30
notice of absence from work, 5.42
notification of employment after confinement, 5.43
offences, 5.56–5.57
pay period
  generally, 5.4–5.6
  statutory provision, 1.101–1.102
payment
  generally, 5.49
  persons acting on behalf of another, to, 5.54–5.55
  rounding, 5.50
  Secretary of State, by, 5.52–5.53
  timing, 5.51
persons abroad
  absent from Great Britain, 5.67
  definitions, 5.64
  'employee', 5.68
  general note, 5.65
  in other Member States, 5.66
  time for compliance, 5.71
  women who worked in the EC, 5.70
persons acting on behalf of another, to, 5.54–5.55
provision of information
  claims for other benefits, 5.46
  determination of questions, 5.44–5.45
rate
  generally, 5.12
  statutory provision, 1.103–1.104
recovery of payments, 1.105–1.106
reinstatement after service with armed services, 5.27
relationship with benefits
  generally, 1.107–1.108
  miscellaneous provision, 1.206–2.270
rounding fractional amounts, 5.50
special classes of persons, 1.110
statutory provisions
  Crown employment, 1.109
  definitions, 1.111
  entitlement, 1.99–1.100
  pay period, 1.101–1.102
  rate, 1.103–1.104
  recovery of payments, 1.105–1.106
  relationship with benefits, 1.107–1.108
  special classes of persons, 1.110
stoppages of work, 5.24–5.25
ten days or less work in pay period, 5.19–5.20
treatment of more than one contract of service
  generally, 5.11
  NHS employees, 5.77
  relevant employer, 5.32–5.33
unfair dismissal, 5.23
work after confinement, 5.15–5.16

working tax credits
  social security income, 2.233
working 10 days or less in pay period, 5.19–5.20
Statutory Maternity Pay (Compensation of Employers) and Miscellaneous Amendment Regulations 1994
  arrangement, 5.82
  citation, 5.83
  commencement, 5.83
  definitions, 5.83
  general note, 5.84
  general provisions, 5.85–5.92
  revocations, 5.93
Statutory Maternity Pay (Curtailment) Regulations 2014
  arrangement, 5.101
  citation, 5.103
  commencement, 5.103
  definitions, 5.104
  general note, 5.102
  general provisions, 5.105–5.114
  revocation, 5.115
Statutory Maternity Pay (Decisions) Regulations 1999
  arrangement, 4.83
  citation, 4.84
  commencement, 4.84
  definitions, 4.84
  general provisions, 4.85–4.86
  revocations, 4.87
Statutory Maternity Pay (General) Regulations 1986
  amendments to 2000 Regulations, 5.94–5.100
  arrangement, 5.1
  citation, 5.2
  commencement, 5.2
  definitions, 5.2–5.3
  general provisions
    administration, 5.41–5.48
    employee, 5.31
    entitlement, 5.4–5.21
    miscellaneous, 5.31–5.40
    normal working weeks, 5.28–5.30
    offences, 5.56–5.57
    payment, 5.49–5.55
Statutory Maternity Pay (Medical Evidence) Regulations 1987
  arrangement, 5.58
  citation, 5.59
  commencement, 5.59
  definitions, 5.59
  general provisions, 5.60
  schedule, 5.61–5.62
Statutory Maternity Pay (National Health Service Employees) Regulations 1991
  arrangement, 5.75
  citation, 5.76
  commencement, 5.76
  definitions, 5.76
  general provisions, 5.77–5.81

Index

Statutory Maternity Pay (Persons Abroad and Mariners) Regulations 1987
arrangement, 5.63
citation, 5.64
commencement, 5.64
definitions, 5.64
general note, 5.65
general provisions, 5.66–5.74

Statutory parental bereavement pay
administration
  applications, 8.44
  date when contributions treated as paid, 8.38
  decision on issues arising, 8.43
  definitions, 8.33
  entitlement, 8.42–8.43
  funding of liabilities, 8.34–8.36
  overpayments, 8.39
  payment to employers, 8.37
  provision of information, 8.45
  records, 8.40–8.41
  Regulations, 8.31–8.45
applications, 8.44
avoidance of liability, 8.23
board and lodgings, and, 8.24
cases where no liability, 8.10
change of employer, 8.17
Commissioners, by, 8.28
conditions of entitlement
  change of employer, 8.17
  continuous employment, 8.13–8.15
  modification for periods between 25 and 26 weeks, 8.16
  multiple contracts of service, 8.19
  multiple employers, 8.19
  normal weekly earnings, 8.20
  prescribed, 8.5
  Regulations, 8.12–8.20
  reinstatement after service with armed forces, 8.18
  stoppages of work, 8.15
  treatment of person as employee, 8.12
  unfair dismissal, 8.14
continental shelf, 8.56
continuous employment
  generally, 8.13
  stoppages of work, 8.15
  unfair dismissal, 8.14
contracting out, and, 1.177
contractual remuneration, and
  generally, 8.22
  statutory provisions, 1.178
Coronavirus
  normal weekly earnings, 5.116–5.122
creation of entitlement, 1.1071–1.1073
Crown employment, 1.179
date when contributions treated as paid, 8.38
death, and, 8.10
decision on issues arising as to entitlement, 8.43
deductions from payments to Commissioners, 8.36
definitions, 1.181
duration, 1.176
entitlement
  cases where no liability, 8.10
  conditions, 8.12–8.20
  decision on issues arising, 8.43
  evidence, 8.9
  notice, 8.9
  number of weeks of pay, 8.6
  options as to payment, 8.7
  prescribed conditions, 8.5
  provision of information, 8.42
  qualifying period, 8.8
  Regulations, 8.5–8.11
  statutory provisions, 1.173–1.174
evidence, 8.9
exclusions, 8.10
funding of employers' liabilities
  applications, 8.35
  deductions from payments to Commissioners, 8.36
  generally, 8.34
  payment to employers, 8.37
imprisonment, and, 8.10
inspection of records, 8.41
liability of Commissioners
  generally, 8.26
  imprisonment, and, 8.27
liability to make payment, 1.175
mariners, 8.55
modification for periods between 25 and 26 weeks, 8.16
multiple contracts of service, 8.19
multiple employers, 8.19
normal weekly earnings
  Coronavirus, 5.116–5.122
  generally, 8.20
notice, 8.9
notices
  service, 8.30
number of weeks of pay, 8.6
options as to payment, 8.7
overpayments, 8.39
payment
  avoidance of liability, 8.23
  Commissioners, by, 8.28
  contractual remuneration, and, 8.22
  employers, to, 8.37
  liability of Commissioners, 8.26–8.27
  method, 8.24
  options, 8.7
  persons unable to act, 8.29
  Regulations, 8.21–8.30
  remuneration, as, 8.24
  timing, 8.25
  weekly rate, 8.21
payment in kind, and, 8.24
payment to employers, 8.37
period of pay, 1.176

Index

persons abroad
  absent from GB as employees, 8.52
  continental shelf, 8.56
  definitions, 8.48
  EEA states as employees, 8.51
  mariners, 8.55
  Regulations, 8.46–8.56
  scope, 8.50
  time for compliance, 8.54
  worked in EEA state in 26 weeks preceding death of child, 8.53
persons absent from GB as employees, 8.52
persons in EEA states as employees, 8.51
persons unable to act, 8.29
prescribed conditions, 8.5
prisoners, and, 8.10
provision of information
  entitlement, as to, 8.42
  generally, 8.45
qualifying period, 8.8
rate of pay, 1.176
records by employers
  generally, 8.40
  inspection, 8.41
Regulations
  administration, 8.31–8.45
  general provision, 8.1–8.30
  persons abroad, 8.46–8.56
reinstatement
  after service with armed forces, 8.18
remuneration, as, 8.24
service of notices, 8.30
special classes of person, 1.180
statutory provisions
  contracting out, and, 1.177
  contractual remuneration, and, 1.178
  creation of entitlement, 1.1071–1.1073
  Crown employment, 1.179
  definitions, 1.181
  duration of pay, 1.176
  entitlement, 1.173–1.174
  liability to make payment, 1.175
  period of pay, 1.176
  rate of pay, 1.176
  special classes of person, 1.180
  stillbirths, 1.182
  supplementary, 1.174
statutory sick pay, and, 8.10
stillbirths
  general note, 1.1073
  general provision, 1.182
stoppages of work, 8.15
timing, 8.25
treatment of person as employee, 8.12
unfair dismissal, 8.14
weekly rate, 8.21
work during period of payment, 8.11
Statutory Parental Bereavement Pay (Administration) Regulations 2020
arrangement, 8.31
citation, 8.32
commencement, 8.32
definitions, 8.33
general provisions, 8.34–8.45
Statutory Parental Bereavement Pay (General) Regulations 2020
application, 8.3
arrangement, 8.1
citation, 8.2
commencement, 8.2
definitions, 8.4
general provisions
  conditions of entitlement, 8.12–8.20
  entitlement, 8.5–8.11
  payment, 8.21–8.30
Statutory Parental Bereavement Pay (Persons Abroad and Mariners) Regulations 2020
arrangement, 8.46
citation, 8.47
commencement, 8.47
definitions, 8.48
general provisions, 8.49–8.56
Statutory paternity pay
additional pay
  entitlement (birth), 6.145
  overseas adoptions, 6.146
  statutory provision, 1.127–1.133
administration
  determination of entitlement issues, 6.28–6.31
  employers' records, 6.26–6.27
  funding of liabilities, 6.20–6.25
  provision of information, 6.32
  statutory provision, 1.467–1.475
adoption of child, on
  common provisions, 6.66–6.70
  conditions of entitlement, 6.59–6.60
  evidence requirements, 6.63
  notice requirements, 6.63–6.64
  periods of payment, 6.61
  qualifying period, 6.62
  statutory provisions, 1.119–1.120
  treatment of more than one employer, 6.65
adoption without placement, 1.142–1.143
avoidance of liability, 6.70
birth of child, on
  common provisions, 6.66–6.70
  conditions of entitlement, 6.51–6.53
  evidence requirements, 6.56
  notice requirements, 6.56–6.57
  periods of payment, 6.54
  qualifying period, 6.55
  statutory provisions, 1.113–1.118
  treatment of more than one employer, 6.58
change of circumstances, 6.66
common provisions, 6.66–6.70
conditions of entitlement
  adoption of child, on, 6.59–6.60
  birth of child, on, 6.51–6.53

Index

continental shelf employees
  definitions, 6.34
  general note, 6.35
  generally, 6.43
continuous employment
  change of employer, 6.88
  generally, 6.84
  reinstatement after service with armed forces, 6.89
  stoppages of work, 6.86
  unfair dismissal, 6.85
  'week', 6.87
contractual remuneration, and
  generally, 6.69
  statutory provision, 1.134–1.135
Coronavirus
  normal weekly earnings, 5.116–5.122
definitions, 1.140–1.141
detention in custody, 6.98
determination of entitlement issues
  application, 6.30
  form of application, 6.31
divided contracts
  general note, 6.10
  lapse of election, 6.15
  notification of election, 6.12
  provision of information, 6.13
  relevant employer, 6.14
earnings, 6.91
employed earners, 6.83
employer's liability, 1.123–1.124
employers' records
  generally, 6.26
  inspection, 6.27
entitlement
  adoption of child, on, 6.59–6.65
  birth of child, on, 6.51–6.58
  common provisions, 6.66–6.70
  determination of issues, 6.30–6.31
  provision of information, 6.28–6.29
  statutory provisions, 1.113–1.122
evidence of entitlement
  adoption of child, on, 6.59–6.60
  birth of child, on, 6.51–6.53
excepted cases, 6.68
failure to comply, 1.476–1.477
fraud
  generally, 1.478–1.479
  procedure and appeals, 1.486–1.494
funding of liabilities
  application to Revenue, 6.21
  date of payment of contributions, 6.24
  generally, 6.20
  method, 6.22–6.23
  overpayments, 6.25
imprisonment, 6.98
incorrect statements, 1.478–1.479
information
  power to require, 1.474–1.475
  supply, 1.480–1.481
  use by Board, 1.482

liability of Revenue to pay
  detention in custody, 6.98
  generally, 6.96–6.97
  imprisonment, 6.98
mariners
  definitions, 6.34
  general note, 6.35
  generally, 6.42
NHS employees
  general note, 6.10
  lapse of election, 6.15
  notification of election, 6.12
  provision of information, 6.13
  relevant employer, 6.14
normal weekly earnings
  Coronavirus, 5.116–5.122
  earnings, 6.91
  generally, 6.92–6.93
notice requirements
  adoption of child, on, 6.63–6.64
  birth of child, on, 6.56–6.57
  statutory provisions, 1.121–1.122
overseas adoptions
  administration, 6.110–6.114
  application of General Regulations 2002, 6.120
  application of SSCBA 1992, 6.102–6.109
  avoidance of liability, 6.128
  change of circumstances, 6.129
  conditions of entitlement, 6.122
  definitions, 6.119
  evidence requirements, 6.125
  general note, 6.118
  notice requirements, 6.125–6.126
  options as to periods of payment, 6.123
  qualifying period, 6.124
  treatment of more than one employer, 6.127
  work during a period of payment, 6.130
parental orders, and
  application of Part 12ZA SSCBA 1992, 6.152, 6.155
  definitions, 6.151
  Regulations, 6.158–6.187
payment
  generally, 6.94
  liability of Revenue, 6.96–6.98
  persons acting on behalf of another, to, 6.100
  Revenue, by, 6.99
  timing, 6.95
payment period
  adoption of child, on, 6.61
  birth of child, on, 6.54
  statutory provision, 1.125–1.126
penalties
  appeals, 1.488
  definitions, 1.494
  determination, 1.486–1.487
  failure to comply, 1.476–1.477
  fraud, 1.478–1.479
  incorrect statements, 1.478–1.479

interest, 1.493
mitigation, 1.491
proceedings before Commissioners, 1.489
proceedings before court, 1.490
time limits, 1.492
persons abroad
  absent from Great Britain, 6.38
  definitions, 6.34
  general note, 6.35
  has worked in other EEA States, 6.39
  in other EEA States, 6.37
  time for compliance, 6.41
provision of information
  entitlement, as to, 6.28–6.29
  generally, 6.32
qualifying period
  adoption of child, on, 6.62
  birth of child, on, 6.55
rate, 1.125–1.126
rounding, 6.6–6.7
service of notices, 6.101
special classes of persons, 1.138–1.139
statutory provisions
  additional pay, 1.127–1.131
  administration, 1.467–1.475
  adoption without placement, 1.142–1.143
  contracting out restrictions, 1.132–1.133
  Crown employment, 1.136–1.137
  definitions, 1.140–1.141
  employer's liability, 1.123–1.124
  entitlement, 1.113–1.122
  general note, 1.112–1.112A
  information, 1.480–1.482
  pay period, 1.125–1.126
  penalties, 1.476–1.479
  rate, 1.125–1.126
  relationship with contractual remuneration, 1.134–1.135
  special classes of persons, 1.138–1.139
  supplementary, 1.140
supply of information
  Board, by, 1.480
  Secretary of State, by, 1.481
treatment of more than one contract
  adoption of child, on, 6.65
  birth of child, on, 6.58
  general note, 6.10
  lapse of election, 6.15
  notification of election, 6.12
  provision of information, 6.13
  relevant employer, 6.14, 6.90
'week', 6.87
weekly rates
  general note, 6.3
  generally, 6.4
  rounding, 6.6–6.7
work during payment period, 6.67
working tax credits
  social security income, 2.233

Statutory Paternity Pay (Administration) Regulations 2002
application
  Adoption from Overseas Regulations, to, 6.110–6.114
arrangement, 6.16
citation, 6.17
commencement, 6.17
definitions, 6.19
general note, 6.18
general provisions, 6.20–6.32

Statutory Paternity Pay (Adoption from Overseas) (No.2) Regulations 2003
application, 6.121
arrangement, 6.115
citation, 6.117
commencement, 6.117
definitions, 6.119
general note, 6.118
general provisions, 6.122–6.130
revocation provision, 6.138

Statutory Paternity Pay (General) Regulations 2002
amendment
  Parental Orders and Prospective Adopters Regulations 2014, by, 6.158–6.187
application
  Adoption from Overseas (No.2) Regulations, to, 6.120
  generally, 6.50
arrangement, 6.46
citation, 6.47
commencement, 6.47
definitions, 6.48–6.49
general provisions
  adoption, 6.59–6.65
  birth, 6.51–6.58
  common provisions, 6.66–6.70
  miscellaneous, 6.82–6.101

Statutory Paternity Pay (NHS Employees) Regulations 2002
arrangement, 6.8
citation, 6.9
commencement, 6.9
definitions, 6.9
general note, 6.10

Statutory Paternity Pay (Parental Orders and Prospective Adopters) Regulations 2014
arrangement, 6.158
citation, 6.160
commencement, 6.160
definitions, 6.161
effective date of amendments, 6.162
general note, 6.159
general provisions, 6.164–6.187

Statutory Paternity Pay (Persons Abroad and Mariners) Regulations 2002
application to overseas adoptions, 6.143
arrangement, 6.33

Index

citation, 6.34
commencement, 6.34
definitions, 6.34
general note, 6.35
general provisions, 6.36–6.43
schedules, 6.44–6.45

Statutory Paternity Pay (Weekly Rates) Regulations 2002
arrangement, 6.1
citation, 6.2
commencement, 6.2
general note, 6.3
general provisions, 6.4–6.7

Statutory shared parental pay
absence from work
  entitlement (adoption), 7.53
  entitlement (birth), 7.35
administration
  applications, 7.14–7.15
  definitions, 7.04
  funding employers' liabilities, 7.05–7.10
  general note, 7.02
  provision of information as to entitlement, 7.13
  records by employers, 7.11–7.12
adoption
  conditions, 7.55–7.68
  definitions, 7.20–7.21
  entitlement, 7.37–7.54
  general note, 7.18
adoption (entitlement)
  absence from work, 7.53
  adopter, of, 7.37–7.38
  care of child during period of payment, 7.51
  death, and, 7.54
  evidential requirements, 7.41–7.44
  extent, 7.46
  notification requirements, 7.41–7.44
  number of weeks of pay to be claimed, 7.45
  other cases where no liability to pay, 7.52
  partner, of, 7.39–7.40
  periods when pay is to be claimed, 7.45
  statutory provision, 1.163
  variation of number of weeks of pay to be claimed, 7.45
  when not to be paid, 7.47
  work during period of payment, 7.49–7.50
adoption from overseas
  application of General Regulations, 7.95
  definitions, 7.94
  modification of General Regulations, 7.96–7.108
avoidance of liability, 7.71
birth
  conditions, 7.55–7.68
  definitions, 7.20–7.21
  entitlement, 7.24–7.36
  general note, 7.18
  special circumstances, in, 7.79–7.83
birth (entitlement)
  absence from work, 7.35
  care of child during period of payment, 7.33
  death, and, 7.36
  evidential requirements, 7.26–7.27
  extent, 7.30
  father, of, 7.25
  modification of notice conditions where early birth, 7.29
  mother, of, 7.24
  notification requirements, 7.26–7.27
  number of weeks of pay to be claimed, 7.28
  other cases where no liability to pay, 7.34
  partner, of, 7.25
  periods when pay is to be claimed, 7.28
  statutory provision, 1.162
  variation of number of weeks of pay to be claimed, 7.28
  when not to be paid, 7.31
  work during period of payment, 7.32
care of child during period of payment
  entitlement (adoption), 7.51
  entitlement (birth), 7.33
conditions of entitlement
  'continuous employment', 7.63–7.67
  continuity of employment of claimant, 7.57–7.59
  'employees', 7.62
  employment and earnings of claimant's partner, 7.55–7.56
  multiple employers, 7.68
  normal weekly earnings of claimant, 7.57–7.61
continental shelf, 7.138
continuity of employment of claimant
  adoption, 7.58–7.59
  birth, 7.57
  change of employer, 7.66
  'continuous employment', 7.63
  service with armed forces, 7.67
  stoppages of work, 7.65
  unfair dismissal, and, 7.64
contracting out, 1.167
contractual remuneration, and
  generally, 7.70
  statutory provision, 1.168
Coronavirus
  normal weekly earnings, 5.116–5.122
Crown employment, 1.169
curtailment of adoption pay period
  A, 5.111
  AP, 5.112
curtailment of maternity pay period
  M, 5.106
  P, 5.107
'day of payment', 7.60
date when contributions treated as paid, 7.09

death, and
  entitlement (adoption), 7.54
  entitlement (birth), 7.36
  special circumstances, in, 7.84
deductions from payments to
    Commissioners, 7.07
definitions
  administration regulations, 7.04
  general regulations, 7.20–7.21
  statutory provisions, 1.171
'earnings', 7.60
entitlement
  adoption, 1.163, 7.37–7.54
  application for determination of issues
      arising, 7.14–7.15
  birth, 1.162, 7.24–7.36
  conditions, 7.55–7.68
  definitions, 7.20–7.21
  general note, 7.18
  provision of information as to, 7.13
  statutory provisions, 1.162–1.164
entitlement (adoption)
  absence from work, 7.53
  adopter, of, 7.37–7.38
  care of child during period of payment,
      7.51
  death, and, 7.54
  evidential requirements, 7.41–7.44
  extent, 7.46
  notification requirements, 7.41–7.44
  number of weeks of pay to be claimed,
      7.45
  other cases where no liability to pay,
      7.52
  partner, of, 7.39–7.40
  periods when pay is to be claimed, 7.45
  statutory provision, 1.163
  variation of number of weeks of pay to
      be claimed, 7.45
  when not to be paid, 7.47
  work during period of payment,
      7.49–7.50
entitlement (birth)
  absence from work, 7.35
  care of child during period of payment,
      7.33
  death, and, 7.36
  evidential requirements, 7.26–7.27
  extent, 7.30
  father, of, 7.25
  modification of notice conditions where
      early birth, 7.29
  mother, of, 7.24
  notification requirements, 7.26–7.27
  number of weeks of pay to be claimed,
      7.28
  other cases where no liability to pay,
      7.34
  partner, of, 7.25
  periods when pay is to be claimed, 7.28
  statutory provision, 1.162
  variation of number of weeks of pay to
      be claimed, 7.28
  when not to be paid, 7.31
  work during period of payment, 7.32
evidential requirements
  entitlement (adoption), 7.41–7.44
  entitlement (birth), 7.26–7.27
fathers
  entitlement, 7.25
funding employers' liabilities
  applications, 7.06
  date when contributions treated as paid,
      7.09
  deductions from payments, 7.07
  generally, 7.05
  overpayments, 7.10
  payments to employers, 7.08
  records by employers, 7.11–7.12
imprisonment, in case of, 7.75
liability to pay, 1.165
mariners
  definitions, 7.130
  general note, 7.128
  general provisions, 7.137–7.138
mothers
  entitlement, 7.24
'normal pay day', 7.60
normal weekly earnings of claimant
  adoption, 7.58–7.59
  'appropriate date', 7.60
  birth, 7.57
  Coronavirus, 5.116–5.122
  'day of payment', 7.60
  'earnings', 7.60
  meaning, 7.60–7.61
  'normal pay day', 7.60
  'relevant period', 7.60
notification requirements
  entitlement (adoption), 7.41–7.44
  entitlement (birth), 7.26–7.27
number of weeks of pay to be claimed
  entitlement (adoption), 7.45
  entitlement (birth), 7.28
other cases where no liability to pay
  entitlement (adoption), 7.52
  entitlement (birth), 7.34
overpayments, 7.10
parental orders, and
  application of Part 12ZC SSCBA 1992,
      6.154, 6.157
  application of Pay Regulations, 7.113
  definitions, 6.151, 7.112
  general note, 7.110
  modification of Pay Regulations,
      7.114–7.126
partners
  entitlement (adoption), 7.39–7.40
  entitlement (birth), 7.25
pay period, 1.166
payment
  avoidance of liability, 7.71
  Commissioners, by, 7.74–7.76
  contractual remuneration, and, 7.70
  method, 7.72
  parental orders, and, 7.114–7.126

persons unable to act, where, 7.77
timing, 7.73
weekly rate, 7.69
payment by Commissioners
  custody or imprisonment, in case of, 7.75
  generally, 7.76
  liability, 7.74–7.75
payments to employers by Commissioners, 7.08
periods when pay is to be claimed
  entitlement (adoption), 7.45
  entitlement (birth), 7.28
persons abroad
  definitions, 7.130
  general note, 7.128
  general provisions, 7.131–7.136
persons unable to act, where, 7.77
power to apply Part 12ZC, 1.172
provision of information
  entitlement, as to, 7.13
  generally, 7.16
rate, 1.166
records by employers
  generally, 7.11
  inspection, 7.12
'relevant period', 7.60
remuneration, and, 1.168
service of notices, 7.78
service with armed forces, 7.67
special circumstances, in
  adoption, 7.85–7.91
  birth, 7.79–7.83
  death of child, 7.84
special classes of person, 1.170
stoppages of work, 7.65
unfair dismissal, and, 7.64
variation of number of weeks of pay to be claimed
  entitlement (adoption), 7.45
  entitlement (birth), 7.28
weekly rate, 7.69
when not to be paid
  entitlement (adoption), 7.47
  entitlement (birth), 7.31
work during period of payment
  entitlement (adoption), 7.49–7.50
  entitlement (birth), 7.32

Statutory Shared Parental Pay (Administration) Regulations 2014
arrangement, 7.01
citation, 7.03
commencement, 7.03
definitions, 7.04
general note, 7.02
general provisions, 7.05–7.16

Statutory Shared Parental Pay (Adoption from Overseas) Regulations 2014
arrangement, 7.92
citation, 7.93
commencement, 7.93
definitions, 7.94
general provisions, 7.94–7.108

Statutory Shared Parental Pay (General) Regulations 2014
application, 7.22–7.23
arrangement, 7.17
citation, 7.19
commencement, 7.19
definitions, 7.20–7.21
general note, 7.18
general provisions
  adoption, 7.37–7.54
  birth, 7.24–7.36
  conditions of entitlement, 7.55–7.68
  payment, 7.69–7.78
  schedule, 7.79–7.91

Statutory Shared Parental Pay (Parental Order Cases) Regulations 2014
arrangement, 7.109
citation, 7.111
commencement, 7.111
definitions, 7.112
general note, 7.110
general provisions, 7.113–7.126

Statutory Shared Parental Pay (Persons Abroad and Mariners) Regulations 2014
application, 7.131
arrangement, 7.127
citation, 7.129
commencement, 7.129
definitions, 7.130
general note, 7.128
general provisions, 7.132–7.142
schedule, 7.143–7.149

Statutory sick pay
air crew
  definitions, 4.52, 4.58–4.59, 4.65
  general note, 4.49
  statutory provision, 1.96
  time for compliance, 4.67
avoidance of liability, 4.11
benefits, and
  generally, 1.94
  miscellaneous provisions, 1.200–1.205
breach of regulations, 1.216–1.217
calculation of limit, 4.15
civil penalties
  breach of regulations, 1.216–1.217
  fraud, 1.218
  negligence, 1.218
continental shelf employees
  definitions, 4.53, 4.60, 4.66
  general note, 4.49
  statutory provision, 1.96
  time for compliance, 4.67
contractual remuneration, 1.201
Coronavirus
  funding employers' liabilities, 1.92–1.93, 4.100–4.114, 4.118–4.131
  general amendments, 4.132–4.134
  suspension of waiting days, 1.1076, 4.45–4.46.1, 4.93–4.99, 4.135–4.137

Index

Coronavirus (funding employers' liabilities post-September 30, 2021)
  claims, 4.124–4.125
  corrections, 4.127–4.128
  definitions, 4.119
  eligibility, 4.121
  'eligible employer', 4.122
  general note, 4.118
  incapacity for work, 4.123
  making claims, 4.124
  mistaken statements, 4.128
  overpayments, 4.129
  overstated, 4.127
  payments, 4.126
  preservation of records, 4.130
  provision of information, 4.131
  records, 4.130–4.131
  recovery of payments, 4.129
  Regulations, 4.118–4.131
  statutory provisions, 1.92–1.93
  time limit for claims, 4.125
  understated, 4.128
Coronavirus (funding employers' liabilities pre-October 1, 2021)
  claims, 4.107–4.108
  corrections, 4.110–4.111
  definitions, 4.103
  eligibility, 4.104
  'eligible employer', 4.105
  general note, 4.101
  incapacity for work, 4.106
  making claims, 4.107
  mistaken statements, 4.110
  overpayments, 4.112
  overstated, 4.110
  payments, 4.109
  preservation of records, 4.113
  provision of information, 4.114
  records, 4.113–4.114
  recovery of payments, 4.112
  Regulations, 4.100–4.114
  statutory provisions, 1.92–1.93
  time limit for claims, 4.108
  understated, 4.111
Coronavirus (suspension of waiting days)
  amending Regulations, 4.93–4.99
  isolation, 4.45–4.45
  saving provision, 4.135–4.137
  Regulations, 4.45–4.46.1
  shielding, 4.46.1
  statutory provision, 1.1076
Crown employment, 1.95
definitions
  earnings, 4.35
  employee, 4.34
  generally, 4.2–4.3
  statutory provisions, 1.97–1.98
detention in custody, 4.9
determination of entitlement
  application, 4.85
  definitions, 4.84
  procedure, 4.86

divided contracts (general Regulations)
  generally, 4.41
  relevant employer, 4.39–4.40
divided contracts (NHS Regulations)
  lapse of election, 4.82
  notification of election, 4.79
  provision of information, 4.80
  treatment of more than one contract as one, 4.78
  treatment of two or more employers as one, 4.81
earnings
  excepted payments, 4.36
  generally, 4.35
  normal weekly earnings, 4.37–4.38
employee's duties, 1.212
employer's liability
  Coronavirus funding 2020, 4.100–4.114
  Coronavirus funding 2020, 4.118–4.131
  generally, 1.69–1.73
employment contract terminated to avoid liability, 4.11
enforcement
  breach of regulations, 1.216–1.217
  fraud, 1.218
  negligence, 1.218
entitlement
  employer's liability, 1.69–1.73
  general note, 1.67–1.68
  limitations, 1.85–1.87
  qualifying conditions, 1.74–1.124
fraud, 1.218
funding employers' liabilities post-September 30, 2021
  claims, 4.124–4.125
  corrections, 4.127–4.128
  definitions, 4.119
  eligibility, 4.121
  'eligible employer', 4.122
  general note, 4.118
  incapacity for work, 4.123
  making claims, 4.124
  mistaken statements, 4.128
  overpayments, 4.129
  overstated, 4.127
  payments, 4.126
  preservation of records, 4.130
  provision of information, 4.131
  records, 4.130–4.131
  recovery of payments, 4.129
  Regulations, 4.118–4.131
  statutory provisions, 1.92–1.93
  time limit for claims, 4.125
  understated, 4.128
funding employers' liabilities pre-October 1, 2021
  claims, 4.107–4.108
  corrections, 4.110–4.111
  definitions, 4.103
  eligibility, 4.104
  'eligible employer', 4.105
  general note, 4.101
  incapacity for work, 4.106

Index

making claims, 4.107
mistaken statements, 4.110
overpayments, 4.112
overstated, 4.110
payments, 4.109
preservation of records, 4.113
provision of information, 4.114
records, 4.113–4.114
recovery of payments, 4.112
Regulations, 4.100–4.114
statutory provisions, 1.92–1.93
time limit for claims, 4.108
understated, 4.111
general note, 1.67–1.68
imprisonment, 4.9
incapacity benefit, 1.202–1.203
information
  disclosure by Secretary of State, 1.221
  employers, by, 1.222
insolvency of employer, 4.21
interruption of employment
  excepted days, 4.26
limitations on entitlement
  generally, 1.85–1.86
  notification of incapacity for work, 1.87
linking periods of incapacity. 4.7–4.8
mariners
  definitions, 4.50–4.51, 4.57, 4.64
  general note, 4.49
  statutory provision, 1.96
  time for compliance, 4.67
maximum entitlement, 4.10
medical evidence
  definitions, 4.69
  doctor's statement, 4.72–4.75
  general note, 4.70
  information required, 4.71
  modification of duration, 4.116–4.117
method of payment, 4.17
national health employees
  lapse of election, 4.82
  notification of election, 4.79
  provision of information, 4.80
  treatment of more than one contract as one, 4.78
  treatment of two or more employers as one, 4.81
negligence, 1.218
notification of incapacity for work
  generally, 4.16
  statutory provisions, 1.87
offences, 4.43–4.44
payment
  liability of Secretary of State, 4.19–4.20
  method, 4.17
  Secretary of State, by, 4.22
  statements relating to, 4.33
  time limits, 4.18
percentage threshold, 4.88–4.92
period of entitlement, 1.76–1.82, 1.196–1.199
period of incapacity for work, 1.74–1.75
persons abroad

  absent from Great Britain, 4.55–4.56
  definitions, 4.50–4.61
  employees, 4.62
  general note, 4.49
  persons abroad, 4.62–4.63
  in other Member States, 4.54
  time for compliance, 4.67
persons deemed incapable of work, 4.4–4.6
persons unable to act, 4.23–4.24
provision of information
  employee to Secretary of State, by, 4.29–4.30
  employer to employee, by, 4.31–4.32
qualifying conditions
  period of entitlement, 1.76–1.82, 1.196–1.199
  period of incapacity for work, 1.74–1.75
  qualifying days, 1.83–1.84
qualifying days
  generally, 4.12–4.14
  statutory provisions, 1.83–1.84
rate of payment, 1.88
records
  maintenance, 4.27
  production, 4.28
recovery of statutory sick pay
  generally, 4.88–4.92
  statutory provisions, 1.89–1.91
relationship with benefits
  generally, 1.94
  miscellaneous provisions, 1.200–1.205
'relevant infection or contamination', 4.4
rounding fractional amounts, 4.25
special classes of person, 1.96
statutory parental bereavement pay, 8.10
statutory provisions
  Crown employment, 1.95
  definitions, 1.97–1.98
  employer's liability, 1.69–1.73
  funding employers' liabilities, 1.92–1.93
  limitations on entitlement, 1.85–1.87
  qualifying conditions, 1.70–1.84
  rates of payment, 1.88
  recovery of payments, 1.89–1.91
  relationship with benefits, 1.94
  special classes of person, 1.96
suspension of waiting days
  amending Regulations, 4.93–4.99
  isolation, 4.45–4.45
  Regulations, 4.45–4.46.1
  saving provision, 4.135–4.137
  shielding, 4.46.1
  statutory provision, 1.1076
time limits for payment, 4.18
treatment of two or more contracts as one
  generally, 4.41
  NHS employees, 4.78
  relevant employer, 4.39–4.40
unemployability supplement, 1.203

Statutory Sick Pay (Decisions) Regulations 1999
arrangement, 4.83
citation, 4.84
commencement, 4.84
definitions, 4.84
general provisions, 4.85–4.86
revocation, 4.87
Statutory Sick Pay (General) Regulations 1982
arrangement, 4.1
citation, 4.2
commencement, 4.2
definitions, 4.2–4.3
general provisions, 4.4–4.44
schedules, 4.45–4.46.1
Statutory Sick Pay (Mariners, Air crew and Person Abroad) Regulations 1982
arrangement, 4.47
citation, 4.48
commencement, 4.48
definitions, 4.48
general note, 4.49
general provisions, 4.50–4.67
Statutory Sick Pay (Medical Evidence) Regulations 1985
arrangement, 4.68
citation, 4.69
commencement, 4.69
definitions, 4.69
general note, 4.70
general provisions, 4.71
schedules, 4.72–4.75
Statutory Sick Pay (Medical Evidence) Regulations 2021
citation, 4.115
commencement, 4.115
definitions, 4.115
extent, 4.115
general note, 4.117
general provisions, 4.116
Statutory Sick Pay (NHS Employees) Regulations 1985
arrangement, 4.76
citation, 4.77
commencement, 4.77
definitions, 4.77
general provisions, 4.78–4.82
Statutory Sick Pay Percentage Threshold (etc.) Order 2014
arrangement, 4.88
citation, 4.89
commencement, 4.89
revocations, 4.90
transitional and saving provisions, 4.91–4.92
Stillbirth
statutory parental bereavement pay
general note, 1.1073
general provision, 1.182
Strikes
statutory maternity pay, 5.24–5.25
working tax credit, 2.143–2.144

Student income
disregarded payments, 2.241–2.242
genverally, 2.239–2.240
Student loans
other income, 1.815
tax credits, 2.241–2.242
Supersession
decisions of Board, 1.234–1.235
Supply of information
See **Provision of income**
Suspension
carer support payments
cessation, 13.528–13.529
criteria, 13.524
effect of ending, 13.529
financial circumstances, 13.525
information to be given to individual, 13.526
review, 13.527
termination, 13.528–13.529
carer's assistance, 13.127
child disability payments
effect of termination, 13.327
generally, 13.127
having regard to financial circumstances, 13.323
information to be given after, 13.324
relevant circumstances, 13.322
right to review, 13.325
termination, 13.326
early years assistance, 13.113–13.116
funeral expense assistance, 13.127
Scottish child payments
definitions, 13.226
effect of termination, 13.225
having regard to financial circumstances, 13.221
information to be given after, 13.222
relevant circumstances, 13.220
right to review, 13.223
termination, 13.224
short-term assistance, 13.127
waiting days
amending Regulations, 4.93–4.99
isolation, 4.45–4.45
Regulations, 4.45–4.46.1
saving provision, 4.135–4.137
shielding, 4.46.1
statutory provision, 1.1076
winter heating assistance, 13.127
Suspension from work
working tax credit, 2.145–2.146
"Table A benefits"
social security income, 1.584–1.586
"Table B benefits"
social security income, 1.607–1.610
Tax
See also **Capital gains; Income tax**
child trust funds
account provider to act on behalf of named child, 9.46
account provider's tax claims, 9.47–9.48

Index

adaptation of enactments, 9.58
administration, 9.59
application of Taxes Act, 9.60
assessment for withdrawal of relief, 9.50
fortnightly claims, 9.51
generally, 9.45
information about looked after children, 9.54–9.55
information to be provided to Board, 9.56
inspection of records, 9.57
records, 9.52
repayments to account provider, 9.47–9.48
returns of information, 9.53
statutory provisions, 1.687–1.688
tax returns, 9.51

Tax credits
See also **Child tax credit; Working tax credit**
additional payments, 2.568–2.569
administrative arrangements, 1.435–1.436
annual reports, 1.416–1.417
annual review, 1.418–1.419
anti-fraud measures, 1.266
appeals
  appealable decisions, 1.402–1.409
  exercise of right, 1.411–1.412
  general regulations, 2.445–2.457
  late appeals, 1.413–1.415
  settlement, 1.21–1.27, 2.559–2.561
  temporary modifications, 1.445–1.446
  transition to universal credit, and, 1.410
assignment, 1.426–1.427
bankruptcy, 1.426–1.427
changes of circumstances
  automatic notification, 1.293
  discretionary notification, 1.292
  failure to report, 1.294
  generally, 1.288–1.289
  mandatory notification, 1.291
  relevant changes, 1.290
child tax credit
  abolition, 1.890–1.891
  entitlement, 1.303–1.306
  general note, 1.259
  maximum rate, 1.307–1.310
  two child policy, 1.309
claims
  generally, 1.271–1.283
  supplementary, 1.284–1.285
Codes of Practice
  overpayments, 12.29–12.75
Crown employment, 1.424–1.425
decisions
  discovery, on, 1.347–1.349
  final decision, 1.341–1.343
  final notice, 1.339–1.340
  information requirements, 1.358–1.359
  initial decision, 1.323–1.329
  notice of decision, 1.360–1.362
  official error, 1.350–1.351
  other revised decisions, 1.332–1.338
  power to enquire, 1.344–1.346
  review, 1.352–1.357
  revision after notifications, 1.330–1.331
  subject to official error, 1.350–1.351
decisions on discovery
  generally, 1.347–1.348
  transition to universal credit, and, 1.349
definitions, 1.432–1.433
development of system, 1.261
disapplication of legislation
  additional payments, 2.568–2.569
disclosure of information, 1.437–1.438
disqualification of claimants for top-up payments
  generally, 1.972–1.973
  notices, 1.976–1.977
duration, 1.286–1.287
enquiry powers
  generally, 1.344–1.345
  transition to universal credit, and, 1.346
evaluation studies
  generally, 2.530
  Northern Ireland, 2.532
exercise of functions
  definitions, 2.563
  Secretary of State, by, 2.564–2.567
failure to comply with requirements, 1.384–1.386
final decisions
  generally, 1.341–1.343
  transition to universal credit, and, 1.344
final notices
  generally, 1.339–1.340
  transition to universal credit, and, 1.340
finalisation, 2.57–2.58
fraud, and
  generally, 1.388–1.389
  introduction, 1.266
  loss of tax credit, 1.392–1.399
  powers relating to documents, 1.390–1.391
functions of Board, 1.269–1.270
general note
  anti-fraud measures, 1.266
  changes to Act, 1.264–1.265
  child tax credit, 1.259
  development of system, 1.261
  generally, 1.258
  problems with Act, 1.263
  repeal of Part 1 of Act, 1.255
  repeal of Act, 1.257
  scheme of Act, 1.256
  working tax credit, 1.260
generally, 1.267–1.268
inalienability, 1.426–1.427
income test, 1.295–1.302
incorrect statements
  conduct of penalty cases, 1.380–1.381
  fraudulently or negligently, 1.379
  generally, 1.376–1.378
  level of penalties, 1.382–1.383

information requirements, 1.358–1.359
initial decision, 1.323–1.329
interest, 1.400–1.401
loss of
   generally, 1.392–1.393
   Regulations, 2.546–2.549
   repeated benefit fraud, for, 1.396–1.399
   specified day, 2.543–2.545
   supplementary, 1.394–1.395
modification of legislation
   additional payments, 2.568–2.569
   finalisation, 2.57–2.58
   overpayments, 2.55–2.56
penalties, 2.55–2.56
Northern Ireland
   evaluation and statistical studies, 2.531–2.532
   generally, 1.447–1.448
notice of decisions
   final notice, 1.339–1.340
   generally, 1.360–1.361
   initial decision, 1.323–1.329
   transition to universal credit, and, 1.362
notices by Board, 1.428–1.429
official error, 1.350–1.351
ongoing awards, 2.53–2.54
overpayments
   Code of Practice, 12.29–12.75
   generally, 1.367–1.369
   method of recovery, 2.433
   recovery, 1.370–1.372
   transition to universal credit, and, 2.55–2.56
payment
   employees' rights, 1.365–1.366
   generally, 1.363–1.364
penalties
   determination, 1.455
   failure to comply with requirements, 1.384–1.386
   Guidance, 12.16–12.28
   incorrect statements, 1.376–1.383
   mitigation, 1.457
   proceedings before Commissioners, 1.456
   recovery, 1.459
   supplementary, 1.387–1.388
   time limits, 1.458
   transition to universal credit, and 2.55–2.56
period of award, 1.286–1.287
persons subject to immigration control, 1.420–1.421
polygamous marriages, 1.422–1.423
provision of information
   evaluation studies, 2.530
   statistical studies, 2.530
rate, 1.321–1.322
repeal of Act, 1.257
repeated benefit fraud, and
   generally, 1.396–1.397
   introduction, 1.266

Regulations, 2.546–2.549
specified day, 2.543–2.545
supplementary, 1.398–1.399
review of decisions
   generally, 1.352–1.353
   late application, 1.354–1.357
   revision after notifications, 1.330–1.331
settlement of appeals
   generally, 1.21–1.27
   Regulations, 2.560–2.561
statistical studies
   generally, 2.530
   Northern Ireland, 2.532
subject to official error, 1.350–1.351
tax-free childcare
   disqualification of claimants, 1.972–1.973, 1.976–1.977
   recovery of payments, 1.978–1.981
   termination of awards, 1.968–1.969
two child policy, 1.309
underpayments
   generally, 1.373–1.374
   transition to universal credit, 1.375
universal credit, and
   appeals, 1.410
   decisions on discovery, 1.349
   enquiry powers, 1.346
   final decisions, 1.344
   final notices, 1.340
   finalisation, 2.57–2.58
   generally, 1.266
   income test, 1.302
   modification of legislation, 2.55–2.58
   notice of decisions, 1.362
   ongoing awards, 2.53–2.54
   overpayments, 2.55–2.56
   penalties, 2.55–2.56
   underpayments, 1.375
uprating
   Regulations 2024, 3.82–3.83
use of information, 1.437–1.438
Welfare Reform Act 2012, and, 1.266
working tax credit
   abolition, 1.890–1.891
   childcare element, 1.319–1.320
   entitlement, 1.311–1.316
   general note, 1.260
   maximum rate, 1.317–1.318

Tax Credits Act 2002
arrangement of sections, 1.254
commencement
   generally, 1.441–1.442
   introduction, 1.262
consequential amendments, 1.430–1.431
definitions
   general, 1.451–1.452
   tax credits, 1.432–1.433
disapplication
   additional payments, 2.568–2.569
general note, 1.255–1.266
general provisions, 1.267–1.433

Index

modifications
  additional payments, 2.568–2.569
  finalisation, 2.57–2.58
  general, 2.55–2.58
  miscellaneous, 2.113
  overpayments, 2.55–2.56
  penalties, 2.55–2.56
  persons subject to immigration control, 2.472–2.473
  polygamous marriages, 2.510
Northern Ireland, 1.447–1.448
Parliamentary control, 1.450
regulations, orders and schemes, 1.449
repeal of provisions, 1.257
repeals, 1.439–1.440
savings, 1.443–1.444
schedules, 1.455–1.464
supplementary provisions, 1.435–1.438
tax credits
  appeals, 1.402–1.415
  child tax credit, 1.303–1.310
  decisions, 1.323–1.362
  fraud, 1.388–1.391
  generally, 1.267–1.302
  interest, 1.400–1.401
  loss of tax credit, 1.392–1.399
  payment, 1.363–1.375
  penalties, 1.376–1.388
  rate, 1.321–1.322
  supplementary, 1.416–1.433
  working tax credit, 1.311–1.320
temporary modifications, 1.445–1.446
transitional provisions
  child tax credit, 2.525–2.528
  generally, 1.443–1.444

Tax Credits (Additional Payments Modification and Disapplication) Regulations 2022
citation, 2.568
commencement, 2.568
definitions, 2.568
general provisions, 2.569

Tax Credits (Administrative Arrangements) Regulations 2002
arrangement, 2.438
citation, 2.440
commencement, 2.440
definitions, 2.441
general note, 2.439
general provisions, 2.442–2.444

Tax credits (appeals)
appealable decisions
  generally, 1.402–1.409
  transition to universal credit, and, 1.410
assessment of tax returns, 1.22–1.23
death of party, 2.457
decisions of Board, 1.238–1.241
definitions, 2.447–2.448
directions
  death of party, 2.457

exercise of right
  decisions of Board, 1.238–1.241
  generally, 1.411–1.412
  other persons, 2.451–2.452
extensions of time, 2.455–2.456
general regulations
  general matters, 2.451–2.457
  service of notices, 2.449–2.450
late appeals
  generally, 1.413–1.415
  invalid regulation, 2.455–2.456
  Order, 2.550–2.552
Orders
  late appeals, 2.550–2.552
'party to the proceedings', 2.448
Regulations
  general, 2.445–2.457
relevant decisions
  generally, 1.402–1.409
  transition to universal credit, and, 1.410
right of appeal
  decisions of Board, 1.238–1.241
  generally, 1.411–1.412
  other persons, 2.451–2.452
service of notices, 2.449–2.450
temporary modifications, 1.445–1.446
time limits
  extension, 2.455–2.456
  generally, 2.453–2.454
transition to universal credit, and, 1.410

Tax Credits (Appeals) (No. 2) Regulations 2002
arrangement, 2.445
citation, 2.447
commencement, 2.447
definitions, 2.447–2.448
duration, 2.447
general provisions
  general matters, 2.451–2.457
  service of notices, 2.449–2.450
recitals, 2.446

Tax Credits (Approval of Child Care Providers) Scheme 2005
revocation provisions, 2.537–2.542

Tax Credits, Child Benefit and Guardian's Allowance Reviews and Appeals Order 2014
citation, 2.553
commencement, 2.553
general provisions, 2.554–2.557

Tax Credits (Claims and Notifications) Regulations 2002
amendments to, 2.514
arrangement, 2.336
citation, 2.337
commencement, 2.337
definitions, 2.339
effect, 2.337
general provisions
  claims, 2.343–2.379
  electronic communications, 2.340–2.342
  final decisions, 2.406–2.409

1921

Index

  notice to provide information,
    2.403–2.405
  notifications, 2.380–2.402
  modification, 2.116, 2.338
**Tax Credits (Definition and
    Calculation of Income)
    Regulations 2002**
  amendment to, 2.513
  arrangement, 2.199
  citation, 2.207
  commencement, 2.207
  definitions, 2.208–2.209
  effect, 2.207
  general note
    change in approach, 2.202
    cross-references, 2.205
    differences between calculations and
      tax assessments, 2.203
    introduction, 2.200
    modifications, 2.206
    questions to be decided, 2.204
    Tax Law Rewrite Project, 2.201
  general provisions
    disregards, 2.261–2.267
    income, 2.210–2.260
  modification, 2.114, 2.206
**Tax Credits (Exercise of Functions)
    Order 2014**
  citation, 2.562
  commencement, 2.562
  definitions, 2.563
  general provisions, 2.564–2.567
**Tax Credits (Immigration) Regulations
    2003**
  amendments to, 2.517
  arrangement, 2.464
  citation, 2.465
  commencement, 2.465
  definitions, 2.466
  general provisions, 2.467–2.475
**Tax Credits (Income Thresholds and
    Determination of Rates)
    Regulations 2002**
  arrangement, 2.309
  citation, 2.311
  commencement, 2.311
  definitions, 2.312
  effect, 2.311
  general provisions, 2.313–2.335
  modification, 2.115, 2.310
**Tax Credits (Interest Rate) Regulations
    2003**
  arrangement, 2.458
  citation, 2.459
  commencement, 2.459
  definitions, 2.461
  general note, 2.460
  general provisions, 2.462–2.463
**Tax Credits (Late Appeals) Order
    2014**
  citation, 2.550
  commencement, 2.550
  general provisions, 2.551–2.552

**Tax Credits (Official Error) Regulations
    2003**
  arrangement, 2.494
  citation, 2.495
  commencement, 2.495
  definitions, 2.496–2.497
  general note, 2.499
  general provision, 2.498
**Tax Credits (Payments by the
    Commissioners) Regulations 2002**
  amendments to, 2.515
  arrangement, 2.410
  citation, 2.412
  commencement, 2.412
  definitions, 2.413
  effect, 2.412
  general note, 2.411
  general provisions, 2.414–2.437
  modification, 2.117
**Tax Credits (Polygamous Marriages)
    Regulations 2003**
  arrangement, 2.505
  citation, 2.507
  commencement, 2.507
  definitions, 2.508–2.509
  effect, 2.507
  general note, 2.506
  general provision, 2.510–2.517
**Tax Credits (Provision of Information)
    (Evaluation and Statistical
    Studies) Regulations 2003**
  citation, 2.529
  commencement, 2.529
  general provision, 2.530
**Tax Credits (Provision of Information)
    (Evaluation and Statistical
    Studies) (Northern Ireland)
    Regulations 2004**
  citation, 2.531
  commencement, 2.531
  general provision, 2.532
**Tax Credits (Provision of Information)
    (Functions Relating to
    Employment and Training)
    Regulations 2003**
  arrangement, 2.522
  citation, 2.523
  commencement, 2.523
  general note, 2.522
  general provision, 2.524
**Tax Credits (Provision of Information)
    (Functions Relating to
    Employment and Training)
    Regulations 2005**
  citation, 2.535
  commencement, 2.535
  general provision, 2.536
**Tax Credits (Provision of Information)
    (Functions Relating to Health)
    Regulations 2003**
  arrangement, 2.500
  citation, 2.501
  commencement, 2.501

Index

definitions, 2.503
general note, 2.502
general provision, 2.504
Tax Credits (Provision of Information) (Functions Relating to Health) (Scotland) Regulations 2004
citation, 2.533
commencement, 2.533
general provision, 2.534
Tax Credits (Provision of Information) (Functions Relating to Health) (No.2) Regulations 2003
arrangement, 2.518
citation, 2.520
commencement, 2.520
general note, 2.519
general provision, 2.521
Tax Credits (Residence) Regulations 2003
amendments to, 2.516
arrangement, 2.476
citation, 2.477
commencement, 2.477
definitions, 2.478–2.479
general provisions, 2.480–2.491
modification, 2.118
transitional provision, 2.492–2.493
Tax Credits (Settlement of Appeals) Regulations 2014
citation, 2.559
commencement, 2.559
definitions, 2.560
general provisions, 2.561
recitals, 2.558
Tax enquiries
amendment by taxpayer, 1.10
completion, 1.12
correction by Revenue, 1.11
notice, 1.9
"Tax-exempt savings"
income test, 2.202
investment income, 2.243
voluntary work, 2.256–2.257
Tax-free childcare
See also **30 hours scheme**
account providers, 1.941–1.942
account restriction orders
regulations, 10.38
statutory provisions, 1. 1.957–1.958
Appeal Regulations 2016
arrangement of, 10.43
citation, 10.45
commencement, 10.45
definitions, 10.46
general note, 10.44
general provisions, 10.47–10.49
appeals
appealable decisions, 10.33, 1.1019–1.1020
definitions, 10.46
exercise of right, 1.1025–1.1026
finality of decisions, 10.47
general note, 10.44

more than one eligible person, 1.1029–1.1030
powers of Tribunal, 1.1027–1.1028
settlement by agreement, 10.49
statutory provisions, 1.1019–1.1030
appealable decisions
regulations, 10.33
statutory provisions,1.1019–1.1020
appointment of person to manage childcare accounts, 10.30
approved childcare, 10.23
calculation of expected income
general, 10.11
not to exceed a certain level, 10.16
calculation of top-up element of payment, 1.951–1.952
caring
EEA residents, 10.17
generally, 10.14
change of circumstances, 10.19
child ceasing to be qualifying child, 10.32
'childcare', 1.914
childcare account restriction orders
regulations, 10.38
statutory provisions, 10.38
childcare accounts
account providers, 1.941–1.942
appointment of person to manage, 10.30
calculation of top-up element of payment, 1.951–1.952
closure, 10.39, 1.959–10.934
imposing restrictions, 1.957–1.958
more than one eligible person, 1.946–1.947
opening, 10.31, 1.943–1.944
payments from, 1.949–1.950
payments into, 1.948–1.948
refunds of payment made from, 1.955–1.956
Regulations, 10.36.1
restriction orders, 10.38
statutory provisions, 1.939–1.960
withdrawals, 1.953–1.954
circumstances where eligible persons unable to act
other appointed persons, 10.29
receivers, 10.28
civil partners, 10.04
claims
time limits, 2.354–2.359
closure of childcare accounts
regulations, 10.39
statutory provision, 1.959–10.934
compensatory payments
regulations, 10.37
statutory provisions, 1.1031–1.1032
conditions of eligibility
income of person must not exceed limit, 1.930–1.931
introduction, 1.911
neither person may be claiming universal credit, 1.932–1.933

1923

Index

neither person must be in childcare scheme, 1.935–1.936
person must be in qualifying paid work, 1.928–1.929
person must be in UK, 1.926–1.927
person must be responsible for child, 1.924–1.925
person must be 16 or over, 1.922–1.923
Crown servants, 10.08
death of account-holder, 10.35
declarations of eligibility
  inaccurate, 1.991–1.992
  regulations, 10.26–10.27
  statutory provision, 1.918–1.919
deduction of recoverable amounts from tax credit awards, 1.1011–1.1012
definitions
  appeal regulations, 10.46
  eligibility regulations, 10.03
  general regulations, 10.22
  statutory provision, 1.1047–1.1048
delay in payment of allowances, 10.34
dishonestly obtaining payments, 1.999–1.1000
disqualification of claimants
  notices, 1.976–1.977
  tax credit, 1.972–1.973
  universal credit, 1.974–1.975
disqualifying orders
  regulations, 10.41
  statutory provision, 1.1005–1.1006
disqualifying tax credit claimants
  regulations, 10.19
  statutory provision, 1.972–1.973, 1.976–1.977
disqualifying universal credit claimants
  regulations, 10.19
  statutory provision, 1.974–1.977
double jeopardy, 1.1003–1.1004
double taxation arrangements, 10.08
EEA residents
  qualifying paid work, 10.18
  self-employed persons, 10.17
electronic communications, 10.42
eligible persons
  regulations, 10.04
  statutory provisions, 1.916–1.917
eligible persons unable to act
  other appointed persons, 10.29
  receivers, 10.28
eligibility
  regulations, 10.01–10.19
  statutory provisions, 1.916–1.936
Eligibility Regulations 2015
  arrangement of, 10.01
  citation, 10.02
  commencement, 10.02
  definitions, 10.03
  general provisions, 10.04–10.19
enforcement
  compensatory payments, 1.1031–1.1032
  other, 1.1005–1.1018
  penalties, 1.991–1.1004

entitlement, 1.913
entitlement periods
  regulations, 10.24–10.25
  statutory provision, 1.920–1.921
expected income
  calculation, 10.11
  general, 10.10
  income not to exceed a certain level, 10.16
failure to comply with information notice, 1.993–1.994
general note, 1.911
inaccurate declarations of eligibility, 1.991–1.992
incapacity for work, 10.14
income of person must not exceed limit
  regulations, 10.16
  statutory provision, 1.930–1.931
information
  penalties for inaccurate provision, 1.995–1.996
  power to obtain, 1.961–1.962
  sharing between HMRC and others, 1.963–1.964
  supply to HMRC by childminder agencies, 1.967
  wrongful disclosure, 1.965–1.966
information notices
  failure to comply, 1.993–1.994
  regulations, 10.40
infrastructure failure, 10.36
interest
  power to charge, 1.1009
late declarations of eligibility
  regulations, 10.27
  statutory provision, 1.918–1.919
limited capability for work
  EEA residents, 10.17
  generally, 10.14
making prohibited payments, 1.997–1.998
more than one eligible person, 1.946–1.947
neither person may be claiming universal credit, 1.932–1.933
neither person may be receiving childcare support, 1.936
neither person must be in childcare scheme, 1.935
Northern Ireland, 1.1041–1.1042
opening childcare accounts
  regulations, 10.31
  statutory provision, 1.943–1.944
order in which payments taken to discharge debts, 1.1017–1.1018
parenting time off
  EEA residents, 10.17
  generally, 10.13
partners, and, 10.04
payments from childcare accounts, 1.949–1.950
payments into childcare accounts, 1.948–1.948
penalties
  assessment, 1.1001–1.1002

dishonestly obtaining payments, 1.999–1.1000
double jeopardy, 1.1003–1.1004
enforcement, 1.1001–1.1002
failure to comply with information notice, 1.993–1.994
inaccurate declarations of eligibility, 1.991–1.992
making prohibited payments, 1.997–1.998
provision of inaccurate information, 1.995–1.996
person must be in qualifying paid work
  regulations, 10.10–10.14
  statutory provision, 1.928–1.929
person must be in UK
  regulations, 10.08
  statutory provision, 1.926–1.927
person must be responsible for child
  regulations, 10.05
  statutory provision, 1.924–1.925
person must be 16 or over, 1.922–1.923
persons treated as being, or not being, in the UK
  regulations, 10.08
  statutory provision, 1.926–1.927
persons unable to act
  other appointed persons, 10.29
  receivers, 10.28
polygamous marriages, 10.04
power to obtain information or documents
  regulations, 10.40
  statutory provision, 1.961–1.962
provision of inaccurate information, 1.995–1.996
qualifying children
  regulations, 10.06
  statutory provision, 1.937–1.938
qualifying childcare
  approved childcare, 10.23
  general, 1.914–1.915
  power to exclude childcare, 1.1007–1.1008
  registered childcare, 10.23
  statutory provision, 1.1007–1.1008
  work requirement, 10.15
qualifying paid work
  calculation of expected income, 10.11
  caring, 10.14
  general requirement, 10.10
  incapacity for work, 10.14
  self-employed persons, 10.12
  statutory provision, 1.928–1.929
  time off, 10.13
receivers, 10.28
recovery of debts from childcare accounts, 1.1013–1.1014
recovery of payments
  assessment of amount, 1.989–1.990
  other cases, 1.987–1.988
  person fails to give childcare account notice, 1.986
  tax credits award made on appeal, 1.980–1.981
  tax credits award made on review, 1.978–1.979
  universal credit award made on appeal, 1.984–1.985
  universal credit award made on revision, 1.982–1.983
refugees, 10.09
refunds of payment made from childcare accounts, 1.955–1.956
registered childcare, 10.23
regulations
  appeals, 10.44–10.49
  eligibility, 10.01–10.19
  general, 1.1043–1.1044
  general provisions, 10.20–10.41
  Parliamentary control, 1.1045–1.1046
Regulations 2015
  arrangement of, 10.20
  citation, 10.21
  commencement, 10.21
  definitions, 10.22
  general provisions, 10.23–10.41
'relevant benefits', 10.40
responsible for a child, 10.05
restrictions on childcare accounts
  regulations, 10.38
  statutory provision, 1.957–1.958
review of decisions
  extension of time limit for applications, 1.1023–1.1024
  generally, 1.1021–1.1022
self-employed persons
  EEA residents, 10.17
  start-up periods, 10.12
set-off
  generally, 1.1015–1.1016
  tax liabilities, against; 1.1039–1.1040
sharing information between HMRC and others, 1.963–1.964
sick leave
  EEA residents, 10.17
  generally, 10.13
start-up periods, 10.12
supply of information to HMRC by childminder agencies, 1.967
tax credits
  deduction of recoverable amounts from awards, 1.1011–1.1012
  disqualification of claimants, 1.972–1.973, 1.976–1.977
  recovery of payments, 1.978–1.981
  termination of awards, 1.968–1.969
tax treatment, 1.1037–1.1038
temporary absence from the UK, 10.07
termination of tax credits, 1.968–1.969
termination of universal credit, 1.970–1.971
time limits for claims , 2.354–2.359
time off for sickness and parenting
  EEA residents, 10.17
  generally, 10.13

universal credit
  disqualification of claimants, 1.974–1.977
  recovery of payments, 1.982–1.985
  termination of awards, 1.970–1.971
  use of electronic communications, 10.42
  variation of entitlement period
    regulations, 10.25
    statutory provisions, 1.920–1.921
  variation of relevant maximum
    appealable decisions, 10.33
    child ceasing to be qualifying child, 10.32
    death of account-holder, 10.35
    delay in payment of allowances, 10.34
    infrastructure failure, 10.36
  withdrawals from childcare accounts, 1.953–1.954
  withdrawal of exemptions, 1.1033–1.1034
  work requirement, 10.15
  wrongful disclosure of information, 1.965–1.966

Tax reform
  Tax Law Rewrite Project
    calculation of income, 2.201

Tax returns
  amendment by taxpayer
    during enquiry, 1.10
    generally, 1.7
  appeals
    no questioning amounts of social security income, 1.28
    notification of taxable amounts of social security income, 1.29–1.30
    settlement by agreement, 1.21–1.27
  assessment
    appeals, 1.21–1.32
    discovery of loss of tax, on, 1.14
    loss, etc., 1.33
    relief for excessive assessments, 1.15–1.16
    time limits, 1.17–1.20
    want of form, 1.34
  closure notices, 1.13
  correction by Revenue
    during enquiry, 1.11
    generally, 1.8
  definitions, 1.35
  destruction, etc., 1.25
  enquiry
    amendment by taxpayer, 1.10
    completion, 1.13
    correction by Revenue, 1.11
    notice, 1.9
  fraudulent conduct, 1.20
  generally, 1.4
  loss, etc., 1.33
  negligent conduct, 1.20
  notice of enquiry, 1.9
  ordinary time limits
    generally, 1.17
    self-assessments, 1.18
  penalties, 1.32
  records, 1.12
  relief for excessive assessments
    double assessment, 1.15
    recovery of overpaid tax etc, 1.16
  self-assessment, 1.6
  settlement of appeals, 1.21–1.27
  time limits
    fraudulent conduct, 1.20
    income received after year for which assessable, 1.19
    negligent conduct, 1.20
    ordinary period, 1.17–1.18
    self-assessments, 1.18
  want of form, 1.34

Taxable benefits
  benefits code
    definitions, 1.518
    meaning, 1.516
    relationship with earnings, 1.517
  cash vouchers
    application of provisions, 1.522–1.523
    benefit treated as earnings, 1.526
    disregard for money, goods or services obtained, 1.533
    meaning, 1.524
    sickness-benefits related, 1.525
  credit tokens
    application of provisions, 1.530
    benefit treated as earnings, 1.532
    disregard for money, goods or services obtained, 1.533
    meaning, 1.531
  employment-related benefits
    cash equivalent treated as earnings, 1.536
    cost of benefit, 1.537
    excluded benefits, 1.535
    meaning, 1.534
  expenses payments
    definitions, 1.520
    relevant sums, 1.519
    sums treated as earnings, 1.521
  foreign benefits
    generally, 1.611–1.612
    person liable to tax, 1.614
    taxable income, 1.613
  general note
    regulations, 2.213
    statutory provisions, 1.496–1.497
  minor benefits, 1.538–1.539
  non-cash vouchers
    application of provisions, 1.527
    benefit treated as earnings, 1.529
    disregard for money, goods or services obtained, 1.533
    meaning, 1.528
  sickness-benefits related vouchers, 1.525
  social security income
    exemptions, 1.591–1.606
    person liable to tax, 1.589–1.590
    Table A, 1.584–1.586
    taxable income, 1.587–1.588

Index

vouchers
  cash vouchers, 1.522–1.526
  non-cash vouchers, 1.527–1.529
Taxable income
  employment income, 1.510
"Taxable maximum"
  income support
    amount in excess of, 1.595
    general, 1.596
  jobseeker's allowance, and
    amount in excess of, 1.600
    contribution-based JSA, 1.603
    definitions, 1.604
    general, 1.601
    income-based JSA, 1.602
Taxable persons
  See also **Income test**
  employment income, 2.219
  pension income, 2.225
  social security income, 2.237
  trading income, 2.231
"Taxable specific income"
  employment income, 1.510
Taxes Management Act 1970
  arrangement of sections, 1.1
  definitions, 1.35
  general note, 1.2
  general provisions
    administration, 1.3
    appeals, 1.21–1.32
    assessment and claims, 1.13–1.20
    penalties, 1.26
    records, 1.12
    returns of income and gains, 1.4–1.11
  miscellaneous provisions
    documents, 1.33–1.34
Temporary absence
  carer support payments, 13.501
  child benefit
    from GB, 3.35–3.36
    from Northern Ireland, 3.41
  residence requirements, 2.487–2.488
  tax-free childcare, 10.07
"Term-time work"
  working tax credit, 2.141–2.142
Territorial waters
  statutory pay, 1.183
TESSAs
  investment income, 2.243
30-hour element
  working tax credit, 2.160–2.161
30 hours scheme
  See also **Charge-free childcare; Tax-free childcare**
  availability
    consequential amendments, 1.1059
    discharge by regulations, 1.1058
    general note, 1.1056
    generally, 1.1057
    supplementary provision, 1.1060
  consequential amendments
    Regulations, 11.1–11.4

  duty of Secretary of State
    consequential amendments, 1.1059
    discharge by regulations, 1.1058
    generally, 1.1057
    supplementary provision, 1.1060
  general note, 1.1056
  notice to provide information by provider, 2.404
  publication of information, 1.1061
  Regulations
    consequential amendments, 11.1–11.4
  statutory provision
    consequential amendments, 1.1059
    discharge by regulations, 1.1058
    general note, 1.1056
    generally, 1.1057
    publication of information, 1.1061
    supplementary provision, 1.1060
Time
  See also **Time limits**
  calculation of income
    employment income, 2.220
    pension income, 2.226
    social security income, 2.238
    trading income, 2.232
Time limits
  child trust fund appeals, 9.97–9.98
  claims
    Childcare Payments Act 2014, under, 2.354–2.359
    generally, 2.352–2.353
  returns
    fraudulent conduct, 1.20
    income received after year for which assessable, 1.19
    negligent conduct, 1.20
    ordinary period, 1.17–1.18
    self-assessments, 1.18
  statutory sick pay, 4.18
  tax credit appeals
    extension, 2.455–2.456
    generally, 2.453–2.454
  tax credits, 2.352–2.353
Top-up payments
  account providers, 1.941–1.942
  account restriction orders
    regulations, 10.38
    statutory provisions, 1. 1.957–1.958
  Appeal Regulations 2016
    arrangement of, 10.43
    citation, 10.45
    commencement, 10.45
    definitions, 10.46
    general note, 10.44
    general provisions, 10.47–10.49
  appeals
    appealable decisions, 1.1019–1.1020, 10.33
    definitions, 10.46
    exercise of right, 1.1025–1.1026
    finality of decisions, 10.47
    general note, 10.44

more than one eligible person, 1.1029–1.1030
powers of Tribunal, 1.1027–1.1028
settlement by agreement, 10.49
statutory provisions, 1.1019–1.1030
appealable decisions
 regulations, 10.33
 statutory provisions,1.1019–1.1020
appointment of person to manage childcare accounts, 10.30
approved childcare, 10.23
calculation of expected income
 general, 10.11
 not to exceed a certain level, 10.16
calculation of top-up element of payment, 1.951–1.952
caring
 EEA residents, 10.17
 generally, 10.14
change of circumstances, 10.19
child ceasing to be qualifying child, 10.32
'childcare', 1.914
childcare account restriction orders
 regulations, 10.38
 statutory provisions, 10.38
childcare accounts
 account providers, 1.941–1.942
 appointment of person to manage, 10.30
 calculation of top-up element of payment, 1.951–1.952
 closure, 10.39, 1.959–10.934
 imposing restrictions, 1.957–1.958
 more than one eligible person, 1.946–1.947
 opening, 10.31, 1.943–1.944
 payments from, 1.949–1.950
 payments into, 1.948–1.948
 refunds of payment made from, 1.955–1.956
 restriction orders, 10.38
 statutory provisions, 1.939–1.960
 withdrawals, 1.953–1.954
circumstances where eligible persons unable to act
 other appointed persons, 10.29
 receivers, 10.28
civil partners, 10.04
claims
 time limits, 2.354–2.359
closure of childcare accounts
 regulations, 10.39
 statutory provision, 1.959–10.934
compensatory payments
 regulations, 10.37
 statutory provisions, 1.1031–1.1032
conditions of eligibility
 income of person must not exceed limit, 1.930–1.931
 introduction, 1.911
 neither person may be claiming universal credit, 1.932–1.933

neither person may be receiving childcare support, 1.936
neither person must be in childcare scheme, 1.935
person must be in qualifying paid work, 1.928–1.929
person must be in UK, 1.926–1.927
person must be responsible for child, 1.924–1.925
person must be 16 or over, 1.922–1.923
Crown servants, 10.08
death of account-holder, 10.35
declarations of eligibility
 inaccurate, 1.991–1.992
 regulations, 10.26–10.27
 statutory provision, 1.918–1.919
deduction of recoverable amounts from tax credit awards, 1.1011–1.1012
definitions
 appeal regulations, 10.46
 eligibility regulations, 10.03
 general regulations, 10.22
 statutory provision, 1.1047–1.1048
delay in payment of allowances, 10.34
dishonestly obtaining payments, 1.999–1.1000
disqualification of claimants
 notices, 1.976–1.977
 tax credit, 1.972–1.973
 universal credit, 1.974–1.975
disqualifying orders
 regulations, 10.41
 statutory provision, 1.1005–1.1006
disqualifying tax credit claimants
 regulations, 10.19
 statutory provision, 1.972–1.973, 1.976–1.977
disqualifying universal credit claimants
 regulations, 10.19
 statutory provision, 1.974–1.977
double jeopardy, 1.1003–1.1004
double taxation arrangements, 10.08
EEA residents
 qualifying paid work, 10.18
 self-employed persons, 10.17
electronic communications, 10.42
eligible persons
 regulations, 10.04
 statutory provisions, 1.916–1.917
eligible persons unable to act
 other appointed persons, 10.29
 receivers, 10.28
eligibility
 regulations, 10.01–10.19
 statutory provisions, 1.916–1.936
Eligibility Regulations 2015
 arrangement of, 10.01
 citation, 10.02
 commencement, 10.02
 definitions, 10.03
 general provisions, 10.04–10.19

Index

enforcement
  compensatory payments, 1.1031–1.1032
  other, 1.1005–1.1018
  penalties, 1.991–1.1004
entitlement, 1.913
entitlement periods
  regulations, 10.24–10.25
  statutory provision, 1.920–1.921
expected income
  calculation, 10.11
  general, 10.10
  income not to exceed a certain level, 10.16
failure to comply with information notice, 1.993–1.994
general note, 1.911
inaccurate declarations of eligibility, 1.991–1.992
incapacity for work, 10.14
income of person must not exceed limit
  regulations, 10.16
  statutory provision, 1.930–1.931
information
  penalties for inaccurate provision, 1.995–1.996
  power to obtain, 1.961–1.962
  sharing between HMRC and others, 1.963–1.964
  supply to HMRC by childminder agencies, 1.967
  wrongful disclosure, 1.965–1.966
information notices
  failure to comply, 1.993–1.994
  regulations, 10.40
infrastructure failure, 10.36
interest
  power to charge, 1.1009
late declarations of eligibility
  regulations, 10.27
  statutory provision, 1.918–1.919
limited capability for work
  EEA residents, 10.17
  generally, 10.14
making prohibited payments, 1.997–1.998
more than one eligible person, 1.946–1.947
neither person may be claiming universal credit, 1.932–1.933
neither person must be in childcare scheme, 1.935–1.936
Northern Ireland, 1.1041–1.1042
opening childcare accounts
  regulations, 10.31
  statutory provision, 1.943–1.944
order in which payments taken to discharge debts, 1.1017–1.1018
parenting time off
  EEA residents, 10.17
  generally, 10.13
partners, and, 10.04
payments from childcare accounts, 1.949–1.950

payments into childcare accounts, 1.948–1.948
penalties
  assessment, 1.1001–1.1002
  dishonestly obtaining payments, 1.999–1.1000
  double jeopardy, 1.1003–1.1004
  enforcement, 1.1001–1.1002
  failure to comply with information notice, 1.993–1.994
  inaccurate declarations of eligibility, 1.991–1.992
  making prohibited payments, 1.997–1.998
  provision of inaccurate information, 1.995–1.996
person must be in qualifying paid work
  regulations, 10.10–10.14
  statutory provision, 1.928–1.929
person must be in UK
  regulations, 10.08
  statutory provision, 1.926–1.927
person must be responsible for child
  regulations, 10.05
  statutory provision, 1.924–1.925
person must be 16 or over, 1.922–1.923
persons treated as being, or not being, in the UK
  regulations, 10.08
  statutory provision, 1.926–1.927
persons unable to act
  other appointed persons, 10.29
  receivers, 10.28
polygamous marriages, 10.04
power to obtain information or documents
  regulations, 10.40
  statutory provision, 1.961–1.962
provision of inaccurate information, 1.995–1.996
qualifying children
  regulations, 10.06
  statutory provision, 1.937–1.938
qualifying childcare
  approved childcare, 10.23
  general, 1.914–1.915
  power to exclude childcare, 1.1007–1.1008
  registered childcare, 10.23
  statutory provision, 1.1007–1.1008
  work requirement, 10.15
qualifying paid work
  calculation of expected income, 10.11
  caring, 10.14
  general requirement, 10.10
  incapacity for work, 10.14
  self-employed persons, 10.12
  statutory provision, 1.928–1.929
  time off, 10.13
receivers, 10.28
recovery of debts from childcare accounts, 1.1013–1.1014

Index

recovery of payments
  assessment of amount, 1.989–1.990
  other cases, 1.987–1.988
  person fails to give childcare account notice, 1.986
  tax credits award made on appeal, 1.980–1.981
  tax credits award made on review, 1.978–1.979
  universal credit award made on appeal, 1.984–1.985
  universal credit award made on revision, 1.982–1.983
refugees, 10.09
refunds of payment made from childcare accounts, 1.955–1.956
registered childcare, 10.23
regulations
  appeals, 10.44–10.49
  eligibility, 10.01–10.19
  general, 1.1043–1.1044
  general provisions, 10.20–10.41
  Parliamentary control, 1.1045–1.1046
Regulations 2015
  arrangement of, 10.20
  citation, 10.21
  commencement, 10.21
  definitions, 10.22
  general provisions, 10.23–10.41
  'relevant benefits', 10.40
responsible for a child, 10.05
restrictions on childcare accounts
  regulations, 10.38
  statutory provision, 1.957–1.958
review of decisions
  extension of time limit for applications, 1.1023–1.1024
  generally, 1.1021–1.1022
self-employed persons
  EEA residents, 10.17
  start-up periods, 10.12
set-off
  generally, 1.1015–1.1016
  tax liabilities, against; 1.1039–1.1040
sharing information between HMRC and others, 1.963–1.964
sick leave
  EEA residents, 10.17
  generally, 10.13
start-up periods, 10.12
supply of information to HMRC by childminder agencies, 1.967
tax credits
  deduction of recoverable amounts from awards, 1.1011–1.1012
  disqualification of claimants, 1.972–1.973, 1.976–1.977
  recovery of payments, 1.978–1.981
  termination of awards, 1.968–1.969
tax treatment, 1.1037–1.1038
temporary absence from the UK, 10.07
termination of tax credits, 1.968–1.969
termination of universal credit, 1.970–1.971

time limits for claims , 2.354–2.359
time off for sickness and parenting
  EEA residents, 10.17
  generally, 10.13
universal credit
  disqualification of claimants, 1.974–1.977
  recovery of payments, 1.982–1.985
  termination of awards, 1.970–1.971
use of electronic communications, 10.42
variation of entitlement period
  regulations, 10.25
  statutory provisions, 1.920–1.921
variation of relevant maximum
  appealable decisions, 10.33
  child ceasing to be qualifying child, 10.32
  death of account-holder, 10.35
  delay in payment of allowances, 10.34
  infrastructure failure, 10.36
  withdrawals from childcare accounts, 1.953–1.954
withdrawal of exemptions, 1.1033–1.1034
work requirement, 10.15
wrongful disclosure of information, 1.965–1.966

Trading income
arrangements for avoiding tax, 1.726
bad debts, 1.748
basic rules
  calculation of losses, 1.735
  cash basis of accounting, 1.733
  deductions, 1.740
  GAAP, 1.734
  interest, 1.739
  money's worth, 1.738
  professions and vocations, 1.732
  receipts and expenses, 1.736–1.737
business entertainment and gifts, 1.750
calculation of losses, 1.735
capital expenditure
  cash basis, 1.746
  generally, 1.745
capital receipts
  generally, 1.755
  supplementary, 1.756
care relief, 1.731
cash basis
  calculation of profits, 1.741
  capital expenditures, 1.746
  capital receipts, 1.754–1.756
  generally, 1.733
  overview or rest of Part 2, 1.742
  property income, and, 1.770
  receipts, 1.753
  rules restricting deductions, 1.744
charge to tax
  arrangements for avoiding tax, 1.726
  generally, 1.724
  income charged, 1.727
  person liable, 1.728
  territorial scope, 1.725
debts incurred and later released, 1.757

deductions
    relationship between rules, 1.740
    rules restricting, 1.743–1.751
doubtful debts, 1.748
farming, 1.729
foster care relief, 1.731
generally accepted accounting practice, 1.734
income treated as trade profits
    charge to tax, 1.724–1.728
    starting and cessation, 1.730
interest, 1.739
introduction, 1.716–1.717
market gardening, 1.729
money's worth, 1.738
overview, 1.721–1.722
priority rules
    generally, 1.723
    introduction, 1.720
professions and vocations
    basic rules, 1.732
    receipts, 1.743
    rules restricting deductions, 1.743
property income, and, 1.770
qualifying care relief, 1.731
receipts
    basic rules, 1.736
    capital receipts, 1.754–1.756
    cash basis accounting, 1.753
    debts incurred and later released, 1.757
    items treated as such under CAA 2001, 1.737
    professions and vocations, 1.752
rent-a-room relief, 1.731
rules restricting deductions
    bad debts, 1.748
    business entertainment and gifts, 1.750
    capital expenditure, 1.745–1.746
    cash basis accounting, 1.744
    doubtful debts, 1.748
    professions and vocations, 1.743
    social security contributions, 1.751
    unconnected losses, 1.747
    unpaid remuneration, 1.749
    wholly and exclusively rules, 1.747
social security contributions, 1.751
statutory overview
    introduction, 1.719
    priority rules, 1.720
tax credits
    deductions, 2.230
    exemptions, 2.230
    general note, 2.228
    generally, 2.227
    identity of taxpayer, 2.231
    relevant income, 2.230
    self-employment, 2.229
    time of calculation, 2.232
trade profits
    basic rules, 1.732–1.740
    cash basis, 1.741–1.742

income treated as, 1.724–1.730
receipts, 1.752–1.757
rules restricting deductions, 1.743–1.751
unconnected losses, 1.747
unpaid remuneration, 1.749
wholly and exclusively rules, 1.747
Training
child benefit, 3.4–3.5
disability element (working tax credit), 2.158–2.159
disregards
    grants, 2.262
    provision of information, and
        general note, 2.522
        generally, 2.524, 2.536
remunerative work, 2.133
working tax credit, 2.158–2.159
Transport vouchers
see **Vouchers**
Travelling expenses
disregards, 2.261–2.262
necessary attendance, for, 1.558
performance of duties, in, 1.557
'workplace', 1.559
Treatment of more than one contract as one
see **Divided contracts**
"Treatment of one or more employers as one"
statutory adoption pay, 6.90
statutory maternity pay
    generally, 5.32–5.33
    NHS employees, 5.80
statutory paternity pay, 6.90
statutory shared parental pay, 7.68
statutory sick pay
    generally, 4.39–4.40
    NHS employees, 4.81
Tribunal (Scotland) Act 2014
see also **Scottish Tribunals Service**
ancillary regulations, 14.42
arrangement of sections, 14.1
citation, 14.46
commencement, 14.45
definitions, 14.44
general provisions
    decisions, 14.5–14.23
    establishment, 14.2–14.3
    powers and enforcement, 14.25–14.31
    practice and procedure, 14.32–14.39
index of expressions, 14.48
regulation-making provisions, 14.41
schedules, 14.47–14.48
Unconnected losses
see **Trading income**
Underpayments
carer support payments, 13.532
tax credits, 1.373–1.374
universal credit, 1.375
Unemployability supplement
statutory sick pay, 1.203

1931

Index

Universal credit
advance payments, 2.66–2.68
appeals
  certain existing benefits, 2.59–2.60
  universal credit, 2.61–2.62
benefit cap, 2.50–2.52
child element, and, 2.73–2.78
claims and payments, 2.62–2.63
disqualification of claimants from top-up payments
  generally, 1.974–1.975
  notices, 1.976–1.977
effect of transition
  advance payments, 2.66–2.68
  claims and payments, 2.62–2.63
  loss of benefit penalties, 2.71–2.72
  persons unable to act, 2.64–2.65
  'qualifying young person', 2.69–2.70
exclusions
  certain existing benefits, 2.41–2.49
  entitlement to other benefits, 2.39–2.40
existing benefits
  appeals, 2.59–2.60
  restriction on claims, 2.41–2.43
  termination of awards, 2.44–2.49
finalisation of tax credits, 2.57–2.58
housing benefit claims, and, 2.41–2.43
income support claims, and, 2.41–2.43
loss of benefit penalties
  transition from working tax credit, 2.71–2.72
managed migration
  adjustment where other elements increase, 2.99–2.100
  appeal of award of existing benefit, 2.111–2.112
  capital disregard, 2.91–2.92
  cessation of transitional protection, 2.101
  definitions, 2.37
  determining application of transitional protection, 2.90
  effect of revision, 2.111–2.112
  ending of transitional protection, 2.101
  extension of deadline day, 2.81–2.82
  full-time students, 2.106–2.108
  general note, 2.35
  indicative UC amount, 2.97–2.98
  initial amount, 2.99–2.100
  'migration day', 2.89
  minimum income floor, 2.105
  miscellaneous, 2.104–2.105
  no claim before deadline, 2.83–2.84
  notice, 2.79–2.80
  notified persons who claim as different benefit unit, 2.85–2.85
  process, 2.79–2.85
  'qualifying claim', 2.87–2.88, 2.104
  Regulations, 2.79–2.112
  rounding, 2.109–2.110
  students, 2.106–2.108
  subsequent awards, 2.102–2.103
  termination of existing benefits, 2.83–2.84
  total legacy amount, 2.95–2.96
  transitional capital disregard, 2.91–2.92
  transitional element, 2.93–2.100
  transitional protection, 2.87–2.101
migration
  definitions, 2.37
  general note, 2.35
  general provisions, 1.898–1.905
  introduction, 1.892–1.893
  managed migration, 2.79–2.112
  Regulations, 2.33–2.119
modification of tax credits legislation
  finalisation, 2.57–2.58
  general, 2.55–2.58
  miscellaneous, 2.113–2.119
  overpayments, 2.55–2.56
  penalties, 2.55–2.56
natural migration, 2.35
ongoing awards
  tax credits, 2.53–2.54
ongoing entitlement to certain benefits
  benefit cap, 2.50–2.52
overpayments of tax credits, 2.55–2.56
persons unable to act, 2.64–2.65
'qualifying young person', 2.69–2.70
Regulations
  transitional provisions, 2.33–2.119
recovery of childcare payments, 1.982–1.985
Scotland
  'assessment period', 13.141
  generally, 13.91
tax credits
  appeals, 1.410
  decisions on discovery, 1.349
  enquiry powers, 1.346
  finalisation, 2.57–2.58
  generally, 1.266
  income test, 1.302
  modification of legislation, 2.55–2.58
  notice of decisions, 1.362
  ongoing awards, 2.53–2.54
  overpayments, 2.55–2.56
  penalties, 2.55–2.56
  restriction on claims, 2.41–2.43
  underpayments, 1.375
tax-free childcare
  disqualification of claimants, 1.974–1.977
  recovery of payments, 1.982–1.985
  termination of awards, 1.970–1.971
termination of awards for existing benefits
  new claimant partners, 2.44
  other claimants, 2.45–2.49
transitional provisions
  changes to child element, 2.73–2.78
  definitions, 2.37
  general note, 2.34–2.35
  managed migration, 2.79–2.112

Index

Regulations, 2.33–2.119
 transition to universal credit,
   2.39–2.72
 working tax credit, and, 2.71–2.72
Universal Credit (Transitional Provisions) Regulations 2014
 arrangement, 2.33
 citation, 2.36
 commencement, 2.36
 definitions, 2.37
 general note, 2.34–2.35
 general provisions
   changes to child element, 2.73–2.78
   managed migration, 2.79–2.112
   transition to universal credit,
     2.39–2.72
 operation, 2.38
 schedules
   modification of legislation,
     2.113–2.119
Unfair dismissal
 statutory maternity pay, 5.23
 statutory parental bereavement pay,
   8.14
Unmarried couples
 child benefit
   general provision, 3.48–3.49
   young persons, 3.16–3.17
 child tax credit claims, 1.280
"Unpaid remuneration"
 trading income, 1.749
Uprating
 freezing for four years, 1.1066–1.1069
 generally, 1.907
 Regulations 2024, 3.82–3.86
 'relevant amounts', 1.908–1.909
Variation
 decisions of Board, 1.234–1.235
Vehicle maintenance grant
 See **Disabled persons' vehicles**
Verification
 claims, 2.444
Vocations
 See **Professions**
Voluntary organisations
 child benefit, 3.52–3.53
Voluntary work
 income test, 2.256–2.257
 remunerative work, 2.133
Vouchers
 cash
   application of provisions,
     1.522–1.523
   benefit treated as earnings, 1.526
   disregard for money, goods or services
     obtained, 1.533
   meaning, 1.524
   sickness-benefits related, 1.525
 cheque vouchers, 1.528
 child trust funds
   generally, 9.10
   statutory provision, 1.650–1.653
 childcare vouchers, 1.528

non-cash
   application of provisions, 1.527
   benefit treated as earnings, 1.529
   disregard for money, goods or services
     obtained, 1.533
   meaning, 1.528
   sickness benefits related, 1.525
 transport vouchers, 1.528
War pensioner's mobility supplement
 pension income, 2.221
"Week"
 continuity of employment
   statutory adoption pay, 6.87
   statutory paternity pay, 6.87
"Weekly rates"
 statutory adoption pay
   general note, 6.3
   generally, 6.4
   rounding, 6.6–6.7
 statutory parental bereavement pay,
   8.21
 statutory paternity pay
   general note, 6.3
   generally, 6.4
   rounding, 6.6–6.7
Welfare Benefits Up-rating Act 2013
 arrangement of sections, 1.906
 general provisions, 1.907
 schedule, 1.908–1.909
Welfare food
 milk tokens, 2.233
Welfare Reform Act 2012
 arrangement of sections, 1.888
 commencement
   Order No. 9, 2.1–2.10
   Order No. 23, 2.11–2.17
   Order No. 29, 2.18–2.22
   Order No. 32, 2.23–2.32
 general note, 1.889
 general provisions
   other benefit changes, 1.894–1.897
   universal credit, 1.890–1.893
 savings
   Order 2013, 2.1–2.10
   Order 2019, 2.23–2.32
 schedule
   universal credit, 1.898–1.905
 transitional provisions
   Order 2013, 2.1–2.10
   Order 2015, 2.11–2.17
   Order 2017, 2.18–2.22
   Order 2019, 2.23–2.32
Welfare Reform and Work Act 2016
 arrangement of sections, 1.1065
 general provisions, 1.1066–1.1068
 schedule, 1.1069
Wholly and exclusively
 see **Trading income**
Wholly exempt benefits
 see **Social security income**
Widowed mother's allowance
 social security income, 2.235

1933

Index

Widowed parent's allowance
social security income, 2.235
Winter heating assistance
See also **Scotland**
age
  assistance to be given, 13.105
  eligibility, 13.104
amount of payment, 13.463
children, 13.251–13.262
determination of entitlement, 13.459
domestic circumstances, 13.105
eligibility
  generally, 13.104
  low income, 13.458
final provisions, 13.106
financial circumstances
  assistance to be given, 13.105
  eligibility, 13.104
generally, 13.19
low income
  amount of payment, 13.463
  definitions, 13.456
  determination of entitlement, 13.459
  eligibility, 13.458
  form, 13.463
  official errors, 13.460–13.461
  overpayments, 13.461
  overview, 13.457
  payment method, 13.464
  re-determination request period, 13.462
  Regulations, 13.455–13.464
  underpayments, 13.460
  value, 13.463
official errors
  overpayments, 13.461
  underpayments, 13.460
overpayments, 13.461
payment method, 13.464
presence, 13.104
receipt of other state assistance, 13.104
re-determination request period, 13.462
Regulations
  general, 13.104–13.106
  low income, 13.455–13.464
residence, 13.104
suspension, 13.127
time limit for applications, 13.104
types, 13.105
underpayments, 13.460
value, 13.463
young people, 13.251–13.262
"Work after confinement"
statutory maternity pay, 5.15–5.16
"Work during payment period"
statutory adoption pay, 6.76
statutory paternity pay, 6.67
Working less than 16 hours a week
see **Working tax credit**
Working tax credit
50-plus element, 2.178
abolition, 1.890–1.891

administrative arrangements
  definitions, 2.441
  general note, 2.439
  provision of information, 2.442–2.443
  recording, etc. of claims, 2.444
  statutory provision, 1.435–1.436
adoption, 2.135–2.138
alteration in hours worked due to coronavirus, 2.151
annual reports, 1.416–1.417
annual review, 1.418–1.419
anti-fraud measures, 1.266
appeals
  appealable decisions, 1.402–1.409
  exercise of right, 1.411–1.412
  general regulations, 2.445–2.457
  late appeals, 1.413–1.415
  temporary modifications, 1.445–1.446
  transition to universal credit, and, 1.410
assignment, 1.426–1.427
bankruptcy, 1.426–1.427
basic element
  adoption, 2.135–2.138
  alteration in hours worked due to coronavirus, 2.151
  ceasing to undertake work, 2.149–2.150
  childbirth, 2.135–2.138
  gaps between jobs, 2.152–2.153
  ill health, 2.139–2.140
  parental bereavement, 2.135–2.138
  pay in lieu of notice, 2.147–2.148
  qualifying remunerative work, 2.127–2.134
  seasonal work, 2.141–2.142
  strike periods, 2.143–2.144
  suspension from work, 2.145–2.146
  term-time work, 2.141–2.142
  working less than 16, 24 or 30 hours a week, 2.149–2.150
benefit offences, and
  generally, 1.392–1.393
  introduction, 1.266
  Regulations, 2.546–2.549
  specified day, 2.543–2.545
  supplementary, 1.394–1.395
benefit cap, 1.896–1.897
calculation, 1.894–1.895
capital rule, 2.202
carers, 2.133
cases in which no rate of tax credit, 2.334–2.335
cases in which there is a reciprocal agreement, 2.332–2.333
ceasing to undertake work, 2.149–2.150
change of circumstances
  advance, in, 2.397
  amendment, 2.389
  automatic, 1.293
  date of, 2.390–2.396.1
  decrease of rate, 2.383–2.386
  definitions, 2.380
  discretionary, 1.292
  evidence of birth or adoption, 2.402

1934

Index

failure to report, 1.294
generally, 1.288–1.289
increase of maximum rate, 2.381–2.382
mandatory, 1.291
method, 2.386–2.387
person acting on behalf of another, by, 2.398–2.401
relevant changes, 1.290
relevant person, 2.388
charitable work, 2.133
child care providers, 2.537–2.542
childbirth, 2.135–2.138
childcare element
  calculation of childcare charges, 2.172–2.173
  change of circumstances, 2.174–2.175
  'child', 2.169–2.171
  'childcare', 2.169–2.171
  generally, 2.166–2.168
  incapacitation, 2.168
  qualifying young persons, 2.171
  'relevant childcare charges', 2.169–2.171
  statutory provisions, 1.319–1.320
claims
  definitions, 2.343–2.344
  generally, 2.345–2.379
  statutory provision, 1.271–1.285
Codes of Practice
  overpayments, 12.29–12.75
conditions of entitlement
  basic element, 2.127–2.159
  childcare element, 2.166–2.175
  death of child, after, 2.179–2.180
  disability element, 2.154–2.159
  50-plus element, 2.178
  lone-parent element, 2.164–2.165
  second-adult element, 2.162–2.163
  severe disablement, 2.176–2.177
  30-hour element, 2.160–2.161
Coronavirus
  alteration in hours worked, 2.151
  definition, 2.208
  uprating, 1.1078–1.1079
Crown employment, 1.424–1.425
cut-off provisions, 2.334–2.335
death of child, after, 2.179–2.180
decisions
  discovery, on, 1.347–1.349
  final decision, 1.341–1.343
  final notice, 1.339–1.340
  information requirements, 1.358–1.359
  initial decision, 1.323–1.329
  notice of decision, 1.360–1.362
  official error, 1.350–1.351
  other revised decisions, 1.332–1.338
  power to enquire, 1.344–1.346
  review, 1.352–1.357
  revision after notifications, 1.330–1.331
  subject to official error, 1.350–1.351
decisions on discovery
  generally, 1.347–1.348
  transition to universal credit, and, 1.349

definitions
  regulations, in, 2.123–2.124
  statute, in, 1.432–1.433
determination of rate
  cut-off provisions, 2.334–2.335
  full year periods, 2.326
  generally, 2.322–2.325
  introduction, 2.320–2.321
  reciprocal agreement cases, 2.332–2.333
  short periods, 2.327
development of system, 1.261
disability element
  Cases A to G, 2.155
  first disability condition, 2.155
  generally, 2.154–2.155
  initial claims, 2.156–2.157
  relevant disabilities, 2.183–2.196
  second disability condition, 2.155
  'training for work', 2.158–2.159
disability periods, 2.139–2.140
disability work allowance, 2.155
disclosure of information, 1.437–1.438
duration, 1.286–1.287
elements of credit
  basic element, 2.127–2.159
  childcare element, 2.166–2.175
  death of child, after, 2.179–2.180
  disability element, 2.154–2.159
  50-plus element, 2.178
  generally, 2.125–2.126
  lone-parent element, 2.164–2.165
  second-adult element, 2.162–2.163
  severe disability element, 2.176–2.177
  30-hour element, 2.160–2.161
employment zone programme, 2.133
enquiry powers
  generally, 1.344–1.345
  transition to universal credit, and, 1.346
entitlement, 1.311–1.316
excepted activities, 2.133
failure to comply with requirements, 1.384–1.386
final decisions
  generally, 1.341–1.343
  transition to universal credit, and, 1.344
final notices
  generally, 1.339–1.340
  transition to universal credit, and, 1.340
50-plus element, 2.178
fraud, and
  generally, 1.388–1.389
  introduction, 1.266
  loss of tax credit, 1.392–1.399
  powers relating to documents, 1.390–1.391
forwarding of claims, 2.444
functions of Board, 1.269–1.270
gaps between jobs, 2.152–2.153
general note, 1.260
holding of claims, 2.444
hours worked, 2.134
ill health, 2.139–2.140

1935

Index

inalienability, 1.426–1.427
incapacity for work, 2.139–2.140
income test
  calculation, 2.210–2.211
  definitions, 2.208–2.209
  disregards, 2.261–2.267
  employment income, 2.212–2.220
  foreign income, 2.247–2.248
  general note, 2.200–2.206
  investment income, 2.243–2.244
  miscellaneous income, 2.259–2.260
  notional income, 2.249–2.258
  pension income, 2.221–2.228
  property income, 2.245–2.246
  social security income, 2.233–2.238
  statutory provision, 1.295–1.302
  student income, 2.239–2.242
  trading income, 2.227–2.232
  transition to universal credit, and, 1.302
income thresholds, 2.313–2.315
incorrect statements
  conduct of penalty cases, 1.380–1.381
  fraudulently or negligently, 1.379
  generally, 1.376–1.378
  level of penalties, 1.382–1.383
information requirements, 1.358–1.359
initial decision, 1.323–1.329
Intensive Activity Period, 2.133
interest
  definitions, 2.461
  general note, 2.460
  overpayments, on, 2.462
  prescribed rate, 2.463
  statutory provision, 1.400–1.401
late application for review
  award of relevant disability benefits, 1.356–1.357
  generally, 1.354–1.355
lone-parent element, 2.164–2.165
loss of tax credits, and
  benefit offences, for, 1.392–1.395
  Regulations, 2.546–2.549
  repeated benefit fraud, for, 1.396–1.399
  specified day, 2.543–2.545
maximum rate
  amount, 2.197–2.198
  generally, 2.181–2.182
  statutory provision, 1.317–1.318
means testing, 2.200
minimum level of continuity, 2.131
Northern Ireland, 1.447–1.448
notice of decisions
  final notice, 1.339–1.340
  generally, 1.360–1.361
  initial decision, 1.323–1.329
  transition to universal credit, and, 1.362
notices by Board, 1.428–1.429
notices to provide information, and
  childcare provider, to, 2.404
  dates to be specified, 2.405
  definitions, 2.339
  electronic communications, 2.340–2.342
  employers, to, 2.403
  s.17 TCA 2002, under, 2.406–2.409
notification of change of circumstances
  advance, in, 2.397
  amendment, 2.389
  automatic, 1.293
  date of, 2.390–2.396.1
  decrease of rate, 2.383–2.386
  definitions, 2.283
  discretionary, 1.292
  evidence of birth or adoption, 2.402
  failure to report, 1.294
  generally, 1.288–1.289
  increase of maximum rate, 2.381–2.382
  mandatory, 1.291
  method, 2.386–2.387
  person acting on behalf of another, by, 2.398–2.401
  relevant changes, 1.290
  relevant person, 2.388
official errors
  definitions, 2.496–2.497
  general note, 2.499
  generally, 2.498
overpayments
  Code of Practice, 12.29–12.75
  generally, 1.367–1.369
  method of recovery, 2.433
  recovery, 1.370–1.372
parental bereavement, 2.135–2.138
pay in lieu of notice, 2.147–2.148
payment
  employees' rights, 1.365–1.366
  generally, 1.363–1.364
payment by HMRC
  child care element, 2.414–2.415
  generally, 2.416–2.417
  introduction, 2.411
penalties
  determination, 1.455
  failure to comply with requirements, 1.384–1.386
  Guidance, 12.16–12.28
  incorrect statements, 1.376–1.383
  mitigation, 1.457
  proceedings before Commissioners, 1.456
  recovery, 1.459
  supplementary, 1.387–1.388
  time limits, 1.458
period of award, 1.286–1.287
persons subject to immigration control
  amendment of Act, 2.472–2.473
  definitions, 2.466
  exclusion from entitlement, 2.467–2.473
  general note, 2.468
  statutory provision, 1.420–1.421
  transitional relief, 2.474–2.475
polygamous marriages
  amendment of Regulations, 2.511–2.517
  amendment of TCA 2002, 2.510

definitions, 2.508–2.509
general note, 2.506
statutory provision, 1.422–1.423
provision of information
  authorities, by, 2.443
  authorities, to, 2.442
  functions relating to employment, 2.524, 2.536
  functions relating to health, 2.502–2.504, 2.521, 2.534
  functions relating to training, 2.524, 2.536
qualifying remunerative work
  excepted activities, 2.133
  generally, 2.127–2.129
  hours worked, 2.134
  minimum level of continuity, 2.131
  remunerative work, 2.132
  routes to entitlement, 2.130
qualifying young persons
  childcare element, 2.171
  death, 2.179–2.180
rate, 1.321–1.322
reciprocal agreement cases, 2.332–2.333
recording of claims, 2.444
remunerative work, 2.132
repeated benefit fraud, and
  generally, 1.396–1.397
  introduction, 1.266
  Regulations, 2.546–2.549
  specified day, 2.543–2.545
  supplementary, 1.398–1.399
residence requirements
  Crown servants posted overseas, 2.489–2.491
  definitions, 2.478–2.479
  ordinary residence, 2.482–2.484
  person treated as not being in UK, 2.480–2.485
  tests, 2.485
  temporary absence from UK, 2.487–2.488
review of decisions
  award of relevant disability benefits, 1.356–1.357
  generally, 1.352–1.353
  late application, 1.354–1.357
revision after notifications, 1.330–1.331
routes to entitlement, 2.130
seasonal work, 2.141–2.142
second-adult element, 2.162–2.163
severe disability element, 2.176–2.177
sickness, 2.139–2.140
sports award, 2.133
statutory provisions
  appeals, 1.402–1.415
  child tax credit, 1.303–1.310
  decisions, 1.323–1.362
  fraud, 1.388–1.391
  generally, 1.267–1.302
  interest, 1.400–1.401
  loss of tax credit, 1.392–1.399
  payment, 1.363–1.375

  penalties, 1.376–1.388
  rate, 1.321–1.322
  supplementary, 1.416–1.433
  transition to universal credit, and, 1.302
  working tax credit, 1.311–1.320
strike periods, 2.143–2.144
subject to official error, 1.350–1.351
suspension from work, 2.145–2.146
taper start point, 2.310
term-time work, 2.141–2.142
30-hour element, 2.160–2.161
training allowance, 2.155
transition from universal credit, and
  appeals, 1.410
  decisions on discovery, 1.349
  enquiry powers, 1.346
  final decisions, 1.344
  final notices, 1.340
  generally, 2.71–2.72
  income test, 1.302
  notice of decisions, 1.362
  underpayments, 1.375
underpayments
  generally, 1.373–1.374
  transition to universal credit, 1.375
universal credit, and
  appeals, 1.410
  decisions on discovery, 1.349
  enquiry powers, 1.346
  final decisions, 1.344
  final notices, 1.340
  finalisation, 2.57–2.58
  generally, 1.266
  income test, 1.302
  modification of legislation, 2.55–2.58
  notice of decisions, 1.362
  ongoing awards, 2.53–2.54
  overpayments, 2.55–2.56
  penalties, 2.55–2.56
  underpayments, 1.375
uprating
  Coronavirus, 1.1078–1.1079
use of information, 1.437–1.438
verification of claims, 2.444
voluntary work, 2.133
working less than 16, 24 or 30 hours a week, 2.149–2.150

Working Tax Credit (Entitlement and Maximum Rate) Regulations 2002
amendments to, 2.512
arrangement, 2.120
citation, 2.121
commencement, 2.121
definitions, 2.123–2.124
effect, 2.121–2.122
general note, 2.122
general provisions
  conditions of entitlement, 2.127–2.180
  elements of credit, 2.125–2.126
  maximum rate, 2.181–2.182
schedules
  disabilities, 2.183–2.196
  maximum rates, 2.197–2.198

Working Tax Credit (Payment by Employers) Regulations 2002
general note, 2.411
Wounds pension
see **Pension income**
Wrongful disclosure
generally, 1.860
Yearly disability payments
See **Child trust funds**
Young carers grant
See also **Scotland**
amount, 13.192–13.192A
applications, 13.184
backdated award of assistance, 13.191
breaks in care, 13.193–13.196
care being provided, 13.185
conditions
  care being provided, 13.185
  further eligibility, 13.187
  person(s) being cared for, 13.186
  residence, 13.188
Coronavirus, 13.193–13.196
definitions, 13.182
determination after backdated award, 13.191
eligibility
  amendment of conditions, 13.282–13.283
  applications, 13.184
  conditions, 13.185–13.187
  EU Exit, and, 13.282
  overview, 13.183
form, 13.192–13.192A
general note, 13.180
multiple applications, 13.190
periods for re-determination requests, 13.189
person(s) being cared for, 13.186
procedural matters
  backdated award, 13.191
  multiple applications, 13.190
  re-determination requests, 13.189
re-determination requests, 13.189
Regulations
  citation, 13.181
  commencement, 13.181
  definitions, 13.182
  general note, 13.180
  general provisions, 13.183–13.192A
  residence conditions, 13.188
Young persons (child benefit)
care, in
  generally, 3.25
  statutory basis, 1.186
continuation of entitlement, 3.6
definition, 1.49
detention, in
  generally, 3.21–3.24
  statutory basis, 1.186
education and training condition, 3.4–3.5
extension period, 3.7
interruptions, 3.8–3.9
introduction, 3.3
living with another as a couple, where, 3.16–3.17
other financial support, 3.12
person responsible for child, 3.13–3.15
prescribed conditions, 3.3–3.12
relevant relationship, in, 3.18
terminal dates, 3.10–3.11
youth training, in, 3.21–3.24

JOURNAL OF SOCIAL SECURITY LAW

General Editors

Neville Harris Emeritus Professor of Law, University of Manchester

Gráinne McKeever Professor of Law and Social Justice, University of Ulster

The *Journal of Social Security Law* provides expert coverage and analysis of the latest developments in law, policy and practice across the field of social security law, covering the wide range of welfare benefits and tax credits in the UK and internationally.

To mark - and celebrate - the Journal's 30th anniversary the first two issues in 2024 have been designated as special issues. The articles in issue 2, comprise:

- Philip Larkin: Universal Credit: Route To "Virtuous" Citizenship or Engine of Continued Welfare Dependency?

- Lisa Scullion, Katherine Curchin, David Young, Philip Martin, Celia Hynes and Joe Pardoe: Towards a Trauma-Informed Social Security System in the United Kingdom

- Mark Simpson: "Precarious and Somewhat Battered"? 75 Years of "Citizenship and Social Class", 30 Years of the JSSL and Marshall's Social Citizenship

- Nick Wikeley: Tribunals and Judicial Independence in the Post-War Welfare State: G.L. Haggen and the "Practical Man's" Approach to "Good Cause"

Available in print, as an eBook on ProView and online on Westlaw UK

CALL 0345 600 9355
EMAIL TRLUKI.orders@thomsonreuters.co
VISIT sweetandmaxwell.co.uk

Sweet & Maxwell

Thomson Reuters

Thomson Reuters™

5 reasons to choose ProView eBooks

1. Always Have Your Publications On Hand
Never worry about an internet connection again. With ProView's offline access, your essential titles are always available, wherever your work takes you.

2. The Feel of a Real Book
ProView's book-like features, including page numbers and bookmarks, offer a seamless transition to digital without losing the touch of tradition.

3. Effortless Library Management
Access previous editions, transfer annotations to new releases, and automatically update your looseleaf materials—all in one place.

4. Tailor Your Reading Experience
With ProView, customize your reading with adjustable display settings, font sizes, and colour schemes. Read your way, effortlessly.

5. Find Information in a Flash
Cut through the clutter with ProView's advanced search. Pinpoint the information you need across your entire library with speed and precision.

Scan the QR code to find out more or contact us at proviewtrial@tr.com for a free trial

Sweet & Maxwell